KT-435-018

COLLINS CONCISE THESAURUS

COLLINS CONCISE THESAURUS

HarperCollins*Publishers*

HarperCollins Publishers
PO Box, Glasgow G4 0NB

First Edition 1997
Reprinted 1997, 1998, 1999
Latest reprint 2000

ISBN 0 00 472110-1

10 9 8 7 6 5

The HarperCollins website address is
www.**fire**and**water**.com

Corpus Acknowledgements
We would like to thank those authors and publishers who kindly gave permission for copyright material to be used in the *Bank of English*. We would also like to thank *Times Newspapers Ltd* and the BBC World Service for providing valuable data.

A catalogue record for this book
is available from the british Library.

Typeset by Morton Word Processing Ltd.
Scarborough, England

Printed and bound in Great Britian by
Caledonian International Book Manufacturing Ltd, Glasgow, G64

FOREWORD

When Collins A-Z Thesaurus was first published in 1984, it revolutionized the whole concept of thesauruses. It represented a new idea, a thesaurus in which the material was arranged in a single A-Z listing of main-entry words, with all the alternatives for any word found at the one place where you would be most likely to look it up. The simplicity of this approach made the book an instant success and it has been a consistent best-seller ever since.

The **Collins Concise Thesaurus** retains all the virtues of this A-Z arrangement, while its massively-expanded new text provides over 350,000 synonyms and antonyms. The English language today is changing more rapidly than at any time in the past. New words and new ways of expressing old ideas are continually coming into existence, and these are recorded and monitored by the Collins English Dictionaries language-monitoring programme and the *Bank of English*, a unique computer-based collection of more than 323 million words of written and spoken English created and continuously updated by Collins Dictionaries and the University of Birmingham. The **Collins Concise Thesaurus** has drawn on these resources to ensure that the very latest new synonyms and antonyms have been included. So, for instance, the entry *daredevil* has gained a new synonym *adrenalin junky*; *exciting* has gained *high-octane*; *desirable* the synonym *to-die-for*; *brush off*, *blank*; *concur*, *buy into*; *stalemate*, *gridlock*; and so on.

A wide range of main-entry words – nearly 16,000 – is included, the criterion for selection being that the word or term in question is likely to be looked up as an entry in its own right. If the word which you have in mind does not feature as a main entry (for instance, *intransigence*) you can still find synonyms for this concept by trying a more familiar word with the same general meaning (for instance, *inflexibility* or *obstinacy*). Having looked up the word which you have in mind, you will find at one place in the book alternatives for all the possible meanings of it. These are numbered to enable you to find the particular meaning which fits the context you have in mind. All the synonyms given have been chosen as being fully substitutable for the headword in at least one context. Because of this, and because of the range of alternatives given, you can always find the better or more appropriate word that you are searching for.

The **Collins Concise Thesaurus** also includes antonym lists at many of the main-entry words. These lists give a range of opposites which provide you with another way of expressing yourself. For instance, if you wish to say that something is difficult, it can sometimes be effective to use a negative construction and, taking a word from the antonym list, you may think of a phrase such as "by no means straightforward".

The whole range of language from taboo and slang to formal and technical is represented, with helpful labels to identify areas of usage. Vocabulary is also included from all the regions of the world where English is spoken, while the wide coverage of idiomatic English will help you to add colour to your language.

The name Thesaurus came to us from Greek, where it meant, "treasure, treasury or storehouse", and our thesaurus is so named because it is a treasury or storehouse of words. The **Collins Concise Thesaurus** is a wordfinder for anyone who wants to increase their command of English, or simply enjoy its enormous variety and scope.

FEATURES OF THE THESAURUS

Synonyms
words, listed in alphabetical order, that can be used in place of the headword

Labels
show context of use

Sense numbers
synonyms divided according to meaning to help you find the sense you want

Parts of speech

Antonyms
words, listed in alphabetical order, that mean the opposite of the headword

abortive *adjective* **1.** bootless, failed, fail~ ing, fruitless, futile, idle, ineffectual, miscarried, unavailing, unsuccessful, useless, vain **2.** *Biology* imperfectly de~ veloped, incomplete, rudimentary, stunted *~noun* **3.** *Medical* abortifacient

abound be jammed with, be packed with, be plentiful, crowd, flourish, increase, infest, luxuriate, overflow, proliferate, superabound, swarm, swell, teem, thrive

abounding abundant, bountiful, copious, filled, flourishing, flowing, flush, full, lavish, luxuriant, overflowing, plen~ teous, plentiful, profuse, prolific, rank, replete, rich, superabundant, teeming, thick on the ground, two a penny

about *preposition* **1.** anent *(Scot.)*, as re~ gards, concerned with, concerning, con~ nected with, dealing with, on, re, refer~ ring to, regarding, relating to, relative to, respecting, touching, with respect to **2.** adjacent, beside, circa *(used with dates)*, close to, near, nearby **3.** around, encircling, on all sides, round, sur~ rounding **4.** all over, over, through, throughout *~adverb* **5.** almost, ap~ proaching, approximately, around, close to, more or less, nearing, nearly, rough~ ly **6.** from place to place, here and there, hither and thither, to and fro *~adjective* **7.** active, around, astir, in motion, pres~ ent, stirring

about to intending to, on the point of, on the verge *or* brink of, ready to

above *preposition* **1.** atop, beyond, ex~ ceeding, higher than, on top of, over, upon **2.** before, beyond, exceeding, prior to, superior to, surpassing *~adverb* **3.** aloft, atop, in heaven, on high, overhead *~adjective* **4.** aforementioned, aforesaid, earlier, foregoing, preceding, previous, prior

▷ **Antonyms** *~preposition* (*sense 1*) below, beneath, under, underneath (*sense 2*) inferior, lesser, less than, lower than, subordinate

aboveboard **1.** *adverb* candidly, forth~ rightly, frankly, honestly, honourably, openly, overtly, straightforwardly, truly, truthfully, uprightly, veraciously, with~ out guile **2.** *~adjective* candid, fair and square, forthright, frank, guileless, honest, honourable, kosher (*informal*), legitimate, on the up and up, open, overt, square, straight, straightforward, true, trustworthy, truthful, upfront (*in~ formal*), upright, veracious

▷ **Antonyms** *~adjective* clandestine, crooked, deceitful, deceptive, devious, dishonest, fraudulent, furtive, secret, secretive, shady, sly, sneaky, underhand

abracadabra **1.** chant, charm, conjuration, hocus-pocus, incantation, invocation, magic, mumbo jumbo, sorcery, spell, voodoo, witchcraft **2.** babble, balderdash, blather, drivel, gibberish, gobbledegook,

Greek (*informal*), jabber, jargon, non~sense, pap, twaddle

abrade erase, erode, file, grind, rub off, scour, scrape away, scrape out, wear away, wear down, wear off

abrasion **1**. *Medical* chafe, graze, scrape, scratch, scuff, surface injury, trauma (*Pathology*) **2**. abrading, chafing, ero~sion, friction, grating, rubbing, scouring, scraping, scratching, scuffing, wearing away, wearing down

abrasive *adjective* **1**. chafing, erosive, frictional, grating, rough, scraping, scratching, scratchy, scuffing **2**. annoy~ing, biting, caustic, cutting, galling, grating, hurtful, irritating, nasty, rough, sharp, unpleasant, vitriolic *~noun* **3**. abradant, burnisher, grinder, scarifier, scourer

abreast **1**. alongside, beside, level, neck and neck, shoulder to shoulder, side by side **2**. acquainted, *au courant*, au fait, conversant, familiar, informed, in the picture, in touch, keeping one's finger on the pulse, knowledgeable, up to date, up to speed

abridge abbreviate, abstract, clip, com~press, concentrate, condense, contract, curtail, cut, cut down, decrease, digest, diminish, downsize, epitomize, lessen, précis, reduce, shorten, summarize, synopsize (*U.S.*), trim

▷ **Antonyms** amplify, augment, enlarge, expand, extend, go into detail, lengthen, prolong, protract, spin out, stretch out

abridgment abbreviation, abstract, com~pendium, condensation, conspectus, contraction, curtailment, cutting, de~crease, digest, diminishing, diminution, epitome, lessening, limitation, outline, précis, reduction, restraint, restriction, résumé, shortening, summary, synopsis

abroad **1**. beyond the sea, in foreign lands, out of the country, overseas **2**. about, at large, away, circulating, cur~rent, elsewhere, extensively, far, far and wide, forth, in circulation, out, out-of-doors, outside, publicly, widely, without

abrogate abolish, annul, cancel, counter~mand, end, invalidate, nullify, obviate, override, quash, repeal, repudiate, re~scind, retract, reverse, revoke, scrap (*informal*), set aside, void, withdraw

abrogation abolition, annulment, cancel~lation, countermanding, ending, invali~dation, nullification, overriding, quash~ing, repeal, repudiation, rescission, re~traction, reversal, revocation, scrapping (*informal*), setting aside, voiding, with~drawal

abrupt **1**. blunt, brisk, brusque, clipped, curt, direct, discourteous, gruff, impa~tient, impolite, monosyllabic, rough, rude, short, snappish, snappy, terse, unceremonious, uncivil, ungracious **2**. precipitous, sharp, sheer, steep, sudden **3**. hasty, headlong, hurried, precipitate,

Labels
a label in brackets applies only to the word preceding it

a label which is not in brackets relates to the whole of that particular sense

Foreign words and phrases

Antonyms

Hyphens
used to distinguish a word or phrase which is always written with a hyphen

Swung dashes
used to show that a word has been broken only because it happens to fall at the end of a line

EDITORIAL STAFF

Publishing Manager
Diana Treffry

Managing Editor
Lorna Gilmour

Lexicographers
Andrew Holmes Mary O'Neill
Ian Brookes Elspeth Summers

Computing Staff
Ray Carrick Paul J Hassett

A, a

abaft *Nautical* aft, astern, behind

abandon *verb* **1.** desert, forsake, jilt, leave, leave behind, leave in the lurch, let (someone) stew in their own juice, strand **2.** evacuate, quit, vacate, withdraw from **3.** abdicate, cede, give up, relinquish, renounce, resign, surrender, waive, yield **4.** desist, discontinue, drop, forgo, kick (*informal*) *~noun* **5.** careless freedom, dash, recklessness, unrestraint, wantonness, wild impulse, wildness

▷ **Antonyms** *~verb* claim, continue, defend, hold, keep, maintain, take, uphold *~noun* control, moderation, restraint

abandoned 1. cast aside, cast away, cast out, derelict, deserted, discarded, ditched, dropped, forlorn, forsaken, jilted, left, neglected, outcast, out of the window, rejected, relinquished, stranded, unoccupied, vacant **2.** corrupt, debauched, depraved, dissipated, dissolute, profligate, reprobate, sinful, wanton, wicked **3.** uncontrolled, uninhibited, unrestrained, wild

▷ **Antonyms** (*sense 1*) claimed, kept, maintained, occupied (*sense 2*) good, high-principled, honest, moral, pure, reputable, righteous, upright, virtuous, worthy (*sense 3*) conscious, restrained

abandonment 1. dereliction, desertion, forsaking, jilting, leaving **2.** evacuation, quitting, withdrawal from **3.** abdication, cession, giving up, relinquishment, renunciation, resignation, surrender, waiver **4.** desistance, discontinuation, dropping

abase belittle, bring low, cast down, debase, degrade, demean, demote, denigrate, depress, disgrace, dishonour, downgrade, humble, humiliate, lower, mortify, put in one's place, reduce

▷ **Antonyms** advance, aggrandize, dignify, elevate, exalt, glorify, honour, prefer, promote, raise, upgrade

abasement belittlement, debasement, degradation, demotion, depression, disgrace, dishonour, downgrading, humbling, humiliation, lowering, mortification, reduction, shame

abash affront, astound, bewilder, chagrin, confound, confuse, discomfit, discompose, disconcert, discountenance, embarrass, faze, humble, humiliate, mortify, perturb, shame, take the wind out of someone's sails

abashed affronted, ashamed, astounded, bewildered, chagrined, confounded, confused, discomfited, discomposed, disconcerted, discountenanced, dismayed, embarrassed, humbled, humiliated, mortified, perturbed, shamefaced, taken aback

▷ **Antonyms** at ease, blatant, bold, brazen, composed, confident, unashamed, undaunted, undismayed, unperturbed

abashment astonishment, bewilderment, chagrin, confusion, consternation, discomfiture, discomposure, disconcertion, dismay, embarrassment, humiliation, mortification, perturbation, shame

abate 1. alleviate, appease, attenuate, decline, decrease, diminish, dull, dwindle, ease, ebb, fade, lessen, let up, mitigate, moderate, quell, reduce, relax, relieve, sink, slacken, slake, slow, subside, taper off, wane, weaken **2.** deduct, discount, subtract

▷ **Antonyms** add to, amplify, augment, boost, enhance, escalate, increase, intensify, magnify, multiply, strengthen

abatement 1. alleviation, allowance, attenuation, cessation, decline, decrease, diminution, dulling, dwindling, easing, extenuation, fading, lessening, let-up (*informal*), mitigation, moderation, quelling, reduction, relief, remission, slackening, slaking, slowing, tapering off, waning, weakening **2.** deduction, discount, subtraction

abbey cloister, convent, friary, monastery, nunnery, priory

abbreviate abridge, abstract, clip, compress, condense, contract, curtail, cut, digest, epitomize, précis, reduce, shorten, summarize, trim, truncate

▷ **Antonyms** amplify, draw out, elongate, expand, extend, increase, lengthen, prolong, protract, spin out, stretch out

abbreviation abridgment, abstract, clipping, compendium, compression, condensation, conspectus, contraction, curtailment, digest, epitome, précis, reduction, résumé, shortening, summary, synopsis, trimming, truncation

abdicate abandon, abjure, abnegate, cede, forgo, give up, quit, relinquish, re~

nounce, resign, retire, step down (*informal*), surrender, vacate, waive, yield

abdication abandonment, abjuration, abnegation, cession, giving up, quitting, relinquishment, renunciation, resignation, retiral (*especially Scot.*), retirement, surrender, waiver, yielding

abdomen belly, breadbasket (*slang*), corporation (*informal*), guts (*slang*), midriff, midsection, paunch, pot, stomach, tummy (*informal*)

abdominal gastric, intestinal, stomachic, stomachical, visceral

abduct carry off, kidnap, make off with, run away with, run off with, seize, snatch (*slang*)

abduction carrying off, kidnapping, seizure

aberrant 1. abnormal, anomalous, defective, deviant, divergent, eccentric, irregular, odd, oddball (*informal*), off-the-wall (*slang*), outré, peculiar, queer, rambling, straying, untypical, wacko (*slang*), wandering **2.** delusive, delusory, disordered, hallucinatory, illusive, illusory, unstable **3.** corrupt, corrupted, degenerate, depraved, deviant, erroneous, perverse, perverted, wrong

aberration 1. aberrancy, abnormality, anomaly, defect, deviation, divergence, eccentricity, irregularity, lapse, oddity, peculiarity, quirk, rambling, straying, wandering **2.** delusion, hallucination, illusion, instability, mental disorder, vagary

abet 1. aid, assist, back, condone, connive at, help, promote, sanction, second, succour, support, sustain, uphold **2.** egg on, encourage, incite, prompt, spur, urge

abettor 1. accessory, accomplice, assistant, associate, backer, confederate, conniver, cooperator, helper, henchman, second **2.** encourager, fomenter, inciter, instigator, prompter

abeyance 1. adjournment, deferral, discontinuation, inactivity, intermission, postponement, recess, reservation, suspense, suspension, waiting **2. in abeyance** hanging fire, in cold storage (*informal*), on ice (*informal*), pending, shelved, suspended

abeyant adjourned, deferred, discontinued, dormant, inactive, intermitted, latent, postponed, put off, quiescent, reserved, shelved, suspended, waiting

abhor abominate, detest, execrate, hate, loathe, recoil from, regard with repugnance *or* horror, shrink from, shudder at

▷ **Antonyms** admire, adore, cherish, covet, delight in, desire, enjoy, like, love, relish

abhorrence abomination, animosity, aversion, detestation, disgust, distaste, enmity, execration, hate, hatred, horror, loathing, odium, repugnance, revulsion

abhorrent abominable, detestable, disgusting, distasteful, execrable, hated, hateful, heinous, horrible, horrid, loathsome, obnoxious, obscene, odious, offensive, repellent, repugnant, repulsive, revolting, yucky *or* yukky (*slang*)

abide 1. accept, bear, brook, endure, hack (*slang*), put up with, stand, stomach, submit to, suffer, tolerate **2.** dwell, linger, live, lodge, reside, rest, sojourn, stay, stop, tarry, wait **3.** continue, endure, last, persist, remain, survive

abide by 1. acknowledge, agree to, comply with, conform to, follow, obey, observe, submit to, toe the line **2.** adhere to, carry out, discharge, fulfil, hold to, keep to, persist in, stand by

abiding constant, continuing, durable, enduring, eternal, everlasting, fast, firm, immortal, immutable, indissoluble, lasting, permanent, persistent, persisting, steadfast, surviving, tenacious, unchanging, unending

▷ **Antonyms** brief, ephemeral, evanescent, fleeting, momentary, passing, short, short-lived, temporary, transient, transitory

ability adeptness, aptitude, capability, capacity, competence, competency, craft, dexterity, endowment, energy, expertise, expertness, facility, faculty, flair, force, gift, knack, know-how (*informal*), potentiality, power, proficiency, qualification, skill, talent

▷ **Antonyms** inability, incapability, incapacity, incompetence, powerlessness, weakness

abject 1. base, contemptible, cringing, debased, degraded, despicable, dishonourable, fawning, grovelling, humiliating, ignoble, ignominious, low, mean, servile, slavish, sordid, submissive, vile, worthless **2.** deplorable, forlorn, hopeless, miserable, outcast, pitiable, wretched

▷ **Antonyms** august, dignified, distinguished, elevated, eminent, exalted, grand, great, high, lofty, noble, patrician, worthy

abjectness 1. abjection, baseness, contemptibleness, debasement, degradation, dishonour, humbleness, humiliation, ignominy, lowness, meanness, servility, slavishness, sordidness, submissiveness, vileness, worthlessness **2.** destitution, forlornness, hopelessness, misery, pitiableness, pitifulness, squalor, wretchedness

abjuration 1. denial, disavowal, disclaiming, disclamation, forswearing, recantation, renunciation, retraction **2.** abnegation, abstention, eschewal, rejection, relinquishment, self-denial

abjure 1. deny, disavow, disclaim, forswear, recant, renege on, renounce, retract **2.** abandon, abnegate, abstain from, eschew, forsake, give up, kick (*informal*), refrain from, reject, relinquish

ablaze 1. afire, aflame, alight, blazing, burning, fiery, flaming, ignited, lighted, on fire **2.** aglow, brilliant, flashing, gleaming, glowing, illuminated, incandescent, luminous, radiant, sparkling **3.** angry, aroused, enthusiastic, excited, fervent, foaming at the mouth, frenzied, fuming, furious, impassioned, incensed, on the warpath, passionate, raging, stimulated

able accomplished, adept, adequate, adroit, capable, clever, competent, effective, efficient, experienced, expert, fit, fitted, gifted, highly endowed, masterful, masterly, powerful, practised, proficient, qualified, skilful, skilled, strong, talented

▷ **Antonyms** amateurish, inadequate, incapable, incompetent, ineffective, inefficient, inept, mediocre, no great shakes (*informal*), unfit, unskilful, weak

able-bodied firm, fit, hale, hardy, healthy, hearty, lusty, powerful, right as rain (*Brit. informal*), robust, sound, staunch, stout, strapping, strong, sturdy, vigorous

▷ **Antonyms** ailing, debilitated, feeble, fragile, frail, sickly, tender, weak

ablution bath, bathing, cleansing, lavation, purification, shower, wash, washing

abnegate abandon, abdicate, abjure, abstain from, concede, decline, deny, disallow, eschew, forbear, forgo, forsake, give up, kick (*informal*), refrain from, refuse, reject, relinquish, renounce, sacrifice, surrender, yield

abnegation abandonment, abjuration, abstinence, continence, disallowance, eschewal, forbearance, giving up, refusal, rejection, relinquishment, renunciation, sacrifice, self-denial, surrender, temperance

abnormal aberrant, anomalous, atypical, curious, deviant, eccentric, erratic, exceptional, extraordinary, irregular, monstrous, odd, oddball (*informal*), off-the-wall (*slang*), outré, peculiar, queer, singular, strange, uncommon, unexpected, unnatural, untypical, unusual, wacko (*slang*), weird

▷ **Antonyms** common, conventional, customary, familiar, natural, normal, ordinary, regular, unexceptional, usual

abnormality aberration, anomaly, atypicalness, bizarreness, deformity, deviation, eccentricity, exception, extraordinariness, flaw, irregularity, monstrosity, oddity, peculiarity, queerness, singularity, strangeness, uncommonness, unexpectedness, unnaturalness, untypicalness, unusualness, weirdness

abode domicile, dwelling, dwelling-place, habitat, habitation, home, house, lodging, pad (*slang*), quarters, residence

abolish abrogate, annihilate, annul, axe (*informal*), blot out, cancel, destroy, do away with, eliminate, end, eradicate, expunge, exterminate, extinguish, extirpate, invalidate, nullify, obliterate, overthrow, overturn, put an end to, quash, repeal, repudiate, rescind, revoke, stamp out, subvert, suppress, terminate, vitiate, void, wipe out

▷ **Antonyms** authorize, continue, create, establish, found, institute, introduce, legalize, promote, reinstate, reintroduce, restore, revive, sustain

abolition abrogation, annihilation, annulment, blotting out, cancellation, destruction, elimination, end, ending, eradication, expunction, extermination, extinction, extirpation, invalidation, nullification, obliteration, overthrow, overturning, quashing, repeal, repudiation, rescission, revocation, stamping out, subversion, suppression, termination, vitiation, voiding, wiping out, withdrawal

abominable abhorrent, accursed, atrocious, base, contemptible, despicable, detestable, disgusting, execrable, foul, godawful (*slang*), hateful, heinous, hellish, horrible, horrid, loathsome, nauseous, obnoxious, obscene, odious, repellent, reprehensible, repugnant, repulsive, revolting, terrible, vile, villainous, wretched, yucky *or* yukky (*slang*)

▷ **Antonyms** admirable, agreeable, charming, commendable, delightful, desirable, good, laudable, likable *or* likeable, lovable, pleasant, pleasing, wonderful

abominate abhor, detest, execrate, hate, loathe, recoil from, regard with repugnance, shudder at

▷ **Antonyms** admire, adore, cherish, dote on, esteem, idolize, love, revere, treasure, worship

abomination 1. abhorrence, antipathy, aversion, detestation, disgust, distaste, execration, hate, hatred, horror, loathing, odium, repugnance, revulsion **2.** anathema, bête noire, bugbear, curse, disgrace, evil, horror, plague, shame, torment

aboriginal ancient, autochthonous, earliest, first, indigenous, native, original, primary, primeval, primitive, primordial, pristine

aborigine aboriginal, autochthon, indigene, native, original inhabitant

abort 1. miscarry, terminate (*a pregnancy*) **2.** arrest, axe (*informal*), call off, check, end, fail, halt, stop, terminate

abortion 1. aborticide, deliberate miscarriage, feticide, miscarriage, termination **2.** disappointment, failure, fiasco, misadventure, monstrosity, vain effort

abortive *adjective* **1.** bootless, failed, failing, fruitless, futile, idle, ineffectual, miscarried, unavailing, unsuccessful, useless, vain **2.** *Biology* imperfectly developed, incomplete, rudimentary, stunted *~noun* **3.** *Medical* abortifacient

abound be jammed with, be packed with, be plentiful, crowd, flourish, increase, infest, luxuriate, overflow, proliferate, superabound, swarm, swell, teem, thrive

abounding abundant, bountiful, copious, filled, flourishing, flowing, flush, full, lavish, luxuriant, overflowing, plenteous, plentiful, profuse, prolific, rank, replete, rich, superabundant, teeming, thick on the ground, two a penny

about *preposition* **1.** anent (*Scot.*), as regards, concerned with, concerning, connected with, dealing with, on, re, referring to, regarding, relating to, relative to, respecting, touching, with respect to **2.** adjacent, beside, circa (*used with dates*), close to, near, nearby **3.** around, encircling, on all sides, round, surrounding **4.** all over, over, through, throughout *~adverb* **5.** almost, approaching, approximately, around, close to, more or less, nearing, nearly, roughly **6.** from place to place, here and there, hither and thither, to and fro *~adjective* **7.** active, around, astir, in motion, present, stirring

about to intending to, on the point of, on the verge *or* brink of, ready to

above *preposition* **1.** atop, beyond, exceeding, higher than, on top of, over, upon **2.** before, beyond, exceeding, prior to, superior to, surpassing *~adverb* **3.** aloft, atop, in heaven, on high, overhead *~adjective* **4.** aforementioned, aforesaid, earlier, foregoing, preceding, previous, prior

▷ **Antonyms** *~preposition* (*sense 1*) below, beneath, under, underneath (*sense 2*) inferior, lesser, less than, lower than, subordinate

aboveboard **1.** *adverb* candidly, forthrightly, frankly, honestly, honourably, openly, overtly, straightforwardly, truly, truthfully, uprightly, veraciously, without guile **2.** *~adjective* candid, fair and square, forthright, frank, guileless, honest, honourable, kosher (*informal*), legitimate, on the up and up, open, overt, square, straight, straightforward, true, trustworthy, truthful, upfront (*informal*), upright, veracious

▷ **Antonyms** *~adjective* clandestine, crooked, deceitful, deceptive, devious, dishonest, fraudulent, furtive, secret, secretive, shady, sly, sneaky, underhand

abracadabra **1.** chant, charm, conjuration, hocus-pocus, incantation, invocation, magic, mumbo jumbo, sorcery, spell, voodoo, witchcraft **2.** babble, balderdash, blather, drivel, gibberish, gobbledegook, Greek (*informal*), jabber, jargon, nonsense, pap, twaddle

abrade erase, erode, file, grind, rub off, scour, scrape away, scrape out, wear away, wear down, wear off

abrasion **1.** *Medical* chafe, graze, scrape, scratch, scuff, surface injury, trauma (*Pathology*) **2.** abrading, chafing, erosion, friction, grating, rubbing, scouring, scraping, scratching, scuffing, wearing away, wearing down

abrasive *adjective* **1.** chafing, erosive, frictional, grating, rough, scraping, scratching, scratchy, scuffing **2.** annoying, biting, caustic, cutting, galling, grating, hurtful, irritating, nasty, rough, sharp, unpleasant, vitriolic *~noun* **3.** abradant, burnisher, grinder, scarifier, scourer

abreast **1.** alongside, beside, level, neck and neck, shoulder to shoulder, side by side **2.** acquainted, *au courant,* au fait, conversant, familiar, informed, in the picture, in touch, keeping one's finger on the pulse, knowledgeable, up to date, up to speed

abridge abbreviate, abstract, clip, compress, concentrate, condense, contract, curtail, cut, cut down, decrease, digest, diminish, downsize, epitomize, lessen, précis, reduce, shorten, summarize, synopsize (*U.S.*), trim

▷ **Antonyms** amplify, augment, enlarge, expand, extend, go into detail, lengthen, prolong, protract, spin out, stretch out

abridgment abbreviation, abstract, compendium, condensation, conspectus, contraction, curtailment, cutting, decrease, digest, diminishing, diminution, epitome, lessening, limitation, outline, précis, reduction, restraint, restriction, résumé, shortening, summary, synopsis

abroad **1.** beyond the sea, in foreign lands, out of the country, overseas **2.** about, at large, away, circulating, current, elsewhere, extensively, far, far and wide, forth, in circulation, out, out-of-doors, outside, publicly, widely, without

abrogate abolish, annul, cancel, countermand, end, invalidate, nullify, obviate, override, quash, repeal, repudiate, rescind, retract, reverse, revoke, scrap (*informal*), set aside, void, withdraw

abrogation abolition, annulment, cancellation, countermanding, ending, invalidation, nullification, overriding, quashing, repeal, repudiation, rescission, retraction, reversal, revocation, scrapping (*informal*), setting aside, voiding, withdrawal

abrupt **1.** blunt, brisk, brusque, clipped, curt, direct, discourteous, gruff, impatient, impolite, monosyllabic, rough, rude, short, snappish, snappy, terse, unceremonious, uncivil, ungracious **2.** precipitous, sharp, sheer, steep, sudden **3.** hasty, headlong, hurried, precipitate, quick, sudden, surprising, swift, unanticipated, unexpected, unforeseen **4.** broken, disconnected, discontinuous, irregular, jerky, uneven

▷ **Antonyms** (*sense 1*) civil, courteous, gracious, polite (*sense 2*) gradual (*sense 3*) easy, leisurely, slow, thoughtful, unhurried

abscond bolt, clear out, decamp, disappear, do a bunk (*Brit. slang*), do a runner (*slang*), escape, flee, flit (*informal*), fly, fly the coop (*U.S. & Canad. informal*), make off, run off, skedaddle (*informal*), slip away, sneak away, steal away, take a powder (*U.S. & Canad. slang*), take it on the lam (*U.S. & Canad. slang*)

absence 1. absenteeism, nonappearance, nonattendance, truancy **2.** default, defect, deficiency, lack, need, nonexistence, omission, privation, unavailability, want **3.** absent-mindedness, abstraction, distraction, inattention, preoccupation, reverie

absent *adjective* **1.** away, elsewhere, gone, lacking, missing, nonattendant, nonexistent, not present, out, truant, unavailable, wanting **2.** absent-minded, absorbed, abstracted, bemused, blank, daydreaming, distracted, dreamy, empty, faraway, heedless, inattentive, musing, oblivious, preoccupied, unaware, unconscious, unheeding, unthinking, vacant, vague *~verb* **3. absent oneself** abscond, bunk off (*slang*), depart, keep away, play truant, remove, slope off (*informal*), stay away, truant, withdraw

▷ **Antonyms** *~adjective* (*sense 1*) attendant, in attendance, present (*sense 2*) alert, attentive, aware, conscious, thoughtful *~verb* attend, show up (*informal*)

absently absent-mindedly, abstractedly, bemusedly, blankly, distractedly, dreamily, emptily, heedlessly, inattentively, obliviously, on automatic pilot, unconsciously, unheedingly, vacantly, vaguely

absent-minded absent, absorbed, abstracted, bemused, distracted, dreaming, dreamy, engrossed, faraway, forgetful, heedless, in a brown study, inattentive, musing, oblivious, preoccupied, unaware, unconscious, unheeding, unthinking, vague

▷ **Antonyms** alert, awake, observant, on one's toes, on the ball, perceptive, quick, vigilant, wary, wide-awake

absolute 1. arrant, complete, consummate, deep-dyed (*usually derogatory*), downright, entire, full-on (*informal*), out-and-out, outright, perfect, pure, sheer, thorough, total, unadulterated, unalloyed, unmitigated, unmixed, unqualified, utter **2.** actual, categorical, certain, conclusive, decided, decisive, definite, exact, genuine, infallible, positive, precise, sure, unambiguous, unequivocal, unquestionable **3.** absolutist, arbitrary, autarchical, autocratic, autonomous, despotic, dictatorial, full, peremptory, sovereign, supreme, tyrannical, unbounded, unconditional, unlimited, unqualified, unquestionable, unrestrained, unrestricted

absolutely 1. completely, consummately, entirely, every inch, fully, lock, stock and barrel, one hundred per cent, perfectly, purely, thoroughly, totally, to the hilt, unmitigatedly, utterly, wholly **2.** actually, categorically, certainly, conclusively, decidedly, decisively, definitely, exactly, genuinely, infallibly, positively, precisely, surely, truly, unambiguously, unequivocally, unquestionably **3.** arbitrarily, autocratically, autonomously, despotically, dictatorially, fully, peremptorily, sovereignly, supremely, tyrannically, unconditionally, unquestionably, unrestrainedly, without qualification

▷ **Antonyms** conditionally, fairly, probably, reasonably, somewhat

absoluteness 1. consummateness, entirety, perfection, purity, thoroughness, totality, unmitigatedness, wholeness **2.** assuredness, certainty, certitude, conclusiveness, correctness, decidedness, decisiveness, definiteness, exactitude, genuineness, infallibility, positiveness, precision, sureness, surety, truth, unambiguousness, unequivocalness **3.** arbitrariness, autonomy, despotism, dictatorialness, fullness, peremptoriness, supremacy, tyranny, unboundedness, unquestionability, unrestrainedness, unrestrictedness

absolution acquittal, amnesty, deliverance, discharge, dispensation, exculpation, exemption, exoneration, forgiveness, freeing, indulgence, liberation, mercy, pardon, release, remission, setting free, shriving, vindication

absolutism absoluteness, arbitrariness, autarchy, authoritarianism, autocracy, despotism, dictatorship, totalitarianism, tyranny

absolutist arbiter, authoritarian, autocrat, despot, dictator, totalitarian, tyrant

absolve acquit, clear, deliver, discharge, exculpate, excuse, exempt, exonerate, forgive, free, let off, liberate, loose, pardon, release, remit, set free, shrive, vindicate

▷ **Antonyms** blame, censure, charge, condemn, convict, damn, denounce, excoriate, pass sentence on, reprehend, reproach, reprove, sentence, upbraid

absorb 1. assimilate, consume, devour, digest, drink in, exhaust, imbibe, incorporate, ingest, osmose, receive, soak up, suck up, take in **2.** captivate, engage, engross, enwrap, fascinate, fill, fill up, fix, hold, immerse, monopolize, occupy, preoccupy, rivet

absorbed **1.** captivated, concentrating, engaged, engrossed, fascinated, fixed, held, immersed, involved, lost, occupied, preoccupied, rapt, riveted, up to one's ears, wrapped up **2.** assimilated, consumed, devoured, digested, exhausted, imbibed, incorporated, received

absorbent absorptive, assimilative, blotting, imbibing, penetrable, permeable, pervious, porous, receptive, spongy

absorbing arresting, captivating, engrossing, fascinating, gripping, interesting, intriguing, preoccupying, riveting, spellbinding
▷ **Antonyms** boring, dreary, dull, humdrum, mind-numbing, monotonous, tedious, tiresome, unexciting

absorption **1.** assimilation, consumption, digestion, exhaustion, incorporation, osmosis, soaking up, sucking up **2.** captivation, concentration, engagement, fascination, holding, immersion, intentness, involvement, occupation, preoccupation, raptness

abstain avoid, cease, decline, deny (oneself), desist, fast, forbear, forgo, give up, keep from, kick (*informal*), refrain, refuse, renounce, shun, stop, withhold
▷ **Antonyms** abandon oneself, give in, indulge, partake, yield

abstemious abstinent, ascetic, austere, continent, frugal, moderate, self-denying, sober, sparing, temperate
▷ **Antonyms** gluttonous, greedy, immoderate, incontinent, intemperate, self-indulgent

abstention abstaining, abstinence, avoidance, desistance, eschewal, forbearance, nonindulgence, refraining, refusal, self-control, self-denial, self-restraint

abstinence abstemiousness, asceticism, avoidance, continence, forbearance, moderation, refraining, self-denial, self-restraint, soberness, sobriety, teetotalism, temperance
▷ **Antonyms** abandon, acquisitiveness, covetousness, excess, gluttony, greediness, indulgence, self-indulgence, wantonness

abstinent abstaining, abstemious, continent, forbearing, moderate, self-controlled, self-restraining, sober, temperate

abstract *adjective* **1.** abstruse, arcane, complex, conceptual, deep, general, generalized, hypothetical, indefinite, intellectual, nonconcrete, notional, occult, philosophical, profound, recondite, separate, subtle, theoretic, theoretical, unpractical, unrealistic *~noun* **2.** abridgment, compendium, condensation, digest, epitome, essence, outline, précis, recapitulation, résumé, summary, synopsis *~verb* **3.** abbreviate, abridge, condense, digest, epitomize, outline, précis, shorten, summarize, synopsize (*U.S.*) **4.** detach, dissociate, extract, isolate, remove, separate, steal, take away, take out, withdraw
▷ **Antonyms** *~adjective* actual, concrete, definite, factual, material, real, specific *~noun* enlargement, expansion *~verb* (*sense 4*) add, combine, inject

abstracted **1.** absent, absent-minded, bemused, daydreaming, dreamy, faraway, inattentive, preoccupied, remote, withdrawn, woolgathering **2.** abbreviated, abridged, condensed, digested, epitomized, shortened, summarized, synopsized (*U.S.*)

abstraction **1.** absence, absent-mindedness, bemusedness, dreaminess, inattention, pensiveness, preoccupation, remoteness, woolgathering **2.** concept, formula, generality, generalization, hypothesis, idea, notion, theorem, theory, thought

abstruse abstract, arcane, complex, dark, deep, Delphic, enigmatic, esoteric, hidden, incomprehensible, mysterious, mystical, obscure, occult, perplexing, profound, puzzling, recondite, subtle, unfathomable, vague
▷ **Antonyms** apparent, bold, clear, conspicuous, evident, manifest, open, overt, patent, perceptible, plain, self-evident, transparent, unsubtle

abstruseness arcaneness, complexity, deepness, depth, esotericism, incomprehensibility, mysteriousness, obscurity, occultness, perplexity, profundity, reconditeness, subtlety, vagueness

absurd crazy (*informal*), daft (*informal*), farcical, foolish, idiotic, illogical, inane, incongruous, irrational, laughable, ludicrous, meaningless, nonsensical, preposterous, ridiculous, senseless, silly, stupid, unreasonable
▷ **Antonyms** intelligent, logical, prudent, rational, reasonable, sagacious, sensible, smart, wise

absurdity bêtise (*rare*), craziness (*informal*), daftness (*informal*), farce, farcicality, farcicalness, folly, foolishness, idiocy, illogicality, illogicalness, incongruity, irrationality, joke, ludicrousness, meaninglessness, nonsense, preposterousness, ridiculousness, senselessness, silliness, stupidity, unreasonableness

abundance **1.** affluence, ampleness, bounty, copiousness, exuberance, fullness, heap (*informal*), plenitude, plenteousness, plenty, profusion **2.** affluence, big bucks (*informal, chiefly U.S.*), big money, fortune, megabucks (*U.S. & Canad. slang*), opulence, pretty penny (*informal*), riches, tidy sum (*informal*), wad (*U.S. & Canad. slang*), wealth
▷ **Antonyms** dearth, deficiency, lack, need, paucity, scantiness, scarcity, sparseness

abundant ample, bounteous, bountiful, copious, exuberant, filled, full, lavish, luxuriant, overflowing, plenteous, plentiful, profuse, rank, rich, teeming, thick on the ground, two a penny, well-provided, well-supplied

▷ **Antonyms** deficient, few, few and far between, inadequate, in short supply, insufficient, lacking, rare, scant, scanty, scarce, short, sparse, thin on the ground

abuse *verb* **1.** damage, dump on (*slang, chiefly U.S.*), exploit, harm, hurt, ill-treat, impose upon, injure, maltreat, manhandle, mar, misapply, misuse, oppress, shit on (*taboo slang*), spoil, take advantage of, wrong **2.** calumniate, castigate, curse, defame, disparage, insult, inveigh against, libel, malign, revile, scold, slander, slate (*informal, chiefly Brit.*), smear, swear at, traduce, upbraid, vilify, vituperate *~noun* **3.** damage, exploitation, harm, hurt, ill-treatment, imposition, injury, maltreatment, manhandling, misapplication, misuse, oppression, spoiling, wrong **4.** blame, calumniation, castigation, censure, character assassination, contumely, curses, cursing, defamation, derision, disparagement, insults, invective, libel, opprobrium, reproach, revilement, scolding, slander, swearing, tirade, traducement, upbraiding, vilification, vituperation **5.** corruption, crime, delinquency, fault, injustice, misconduct, misdeed, offence, sin, wrong, wrongdoing

▷ **Antonyms** *~verb* (*sense 1*) care for, protect (*sense 2*) acclaim, commend, compliment, extol, flatter, praise, respect

abusive **1.** calumniating, castigating, censorious, contumelious, defamatory, derisive, disparaging, insulting, invective, libellous, maligning, offensive, opprobrious, reproachful, reviling, rude, scathing, scolding, slanderous, traducing, upbraiding, vilifying, vituperative **2.** brutal, cruel, destructive, harmful, hurtful, injurious, rough

▷ **Antonyms** (*sense 1*) approving, complimentary, eulogistic, flattering, laudatory, panegyrical, praising

abut adjoin, border, impinge, join, meet, touch, verge

abutment brace, bulwark, buttress, pier, prop, strut, support

abutting adjacent, adjoining, bordering, contiguous, joining, meeting, next to, touching, verging

abysmal bottomless, boundless, complete, deep, endless, extreme, immeasurable, incalculable, infinite, profound, thorough, unending, unfathomable, vast

abyss abysm, bottomless depth, chasm, crevasse, fissure, gorge, gulf, pit, void

academic *adjective* **1.** bookish, campus, college, collegiate, erudite, highbrow, learned, lettered, literary, scholarly, scholastic, school, studious, university **2.** abstract, conjectural, hypothetical, impractical, notional, speculative, theoretical *~noun* **3.** academician, don, fellow, lecturer, master, professor, pupil, scholar, scholastic, schoolman, student, tutor

accede **1.** accept, acquiesce, admit, agree, assent, comply, concede, concur, consent, endorse, grant, own, yield **2.** assume, attain, come to, enter upon, inherit, succeed, succeed to (*as heir*)

accelerate advance, expedite, forward, further, hasten, hurry, pick up speed, precipitate, quicken, speed, speed up, spur, step up (*informal*), stimulate

▷ **Antonyms** decelerate, delay, hinder, impede, obstruct, slow down

acceleration expedition, hastening, hurrying, quickening, speeding up, spurring, stepping up (*informal*), stimulation

accent *noun* **1.** beat, cadence, emphasis, force, ictus, pitch, rhythm, stress, timbre, tonality **2.** articulation, brogue, enunciation, inflection, intonation, modulation, pronunciation, tone *~verb* **3.** accentuate, emphasize, stress, underline, underscore

accentuate accent, draw attention to, emphasize, foreground, highlight, stress, underline, underscore

▷ **Antonyms** gloss over, make light of, make little of, minimize, play down, soft-pedal (*informal*), underplay

accept **1.** acquire, gain, get, have, obtain, receive, secure, take **2.** accede, acknowledge, acquiesce, admit, adopt, affirm, agree to, approve, believe, buy (*slang*), buy into (*slang*), concur with, consent to, cooperate with, recognize, swallow (*informal*), take on board **3.** bear, bow to, brook, defer to, like it or lump it (*informal*), put up with, stand, submit to, suffer, take, yield to **4.** acknowledge, admit, assume, avow, bear, take on, undertake

▷ **Antonyms** decline, deny, disown, rebut, refuse, reject, repudiate, spurn

acceptable **1.** agreeable, delightful, grateful, gratifying, pleasant, pleasing, welcome **2.** adequate, admissible, all right, fair, moderate, passable, satisfactory, so-so (*informal*), standard, tolerable, up to scratch (*informal*)

▷ **Antonyms** unacceptable, unsatisfactory, unsuitable

acceptance **1.** accepting, acquiring, gaining, getting, having, obtaining, receipt, securing, taking **2.** accedence, accession, acknowledgment, acquiescence, admission, adoption, affirmation, agreement, approbation, approval, assent, belief, compliance, concession, concurrence, consensus, consent, cooperation, credence, O.K. *or* okay (*informal*), permission, recognition, stamp *or* seal of approval **3.** deference, standing, submission, taking, yielding **4.** acknowledgment, admission, assumption, avowal, taking on, undertaking

accepted acceptable, acknowledged, admitted, agreed, agreed upon, approved, authorized, common, confirmed, conventional, customary, established, normal, received, recognized, regular, sanctioned, standard, time-honoured, traditional, universal, usual

▷ **Antonyms** abnormal, irregular, unconventional, uncustomary, unorthodox, unusual, unwonted

access 1. admission, admittance, approach, avenue, course, door, entering, entrance, entrée, entry, gateway, key, passage, passageway, path, road **2.** *Medical* attack, fit, onset, outburst, paroxysm

accessibility 1. approachability, attainability, availability, handiness, nearness, obtainability, possibility, readiness **2.** affability, approachability, conversableness, cordiality, friendliness, informality **3.** exposedness, openness, susceptibility

accessible 1. achievable, a hop, skip and a jump away, at hand, at one's fingertips, attainable, available, get-at-able (*informal*), handy, near, nearby, obtainable, on hand, possible, reachable, ready **2.** affable, approachable, available, conversable, cordial, friendly, informal **3.** exposed, liable, open, subject, susceptible, vulnerable, wide-open

▷ **Antonyms** far-off, hidden, inaccessible, secreted, unapproachable, unavailable, unobtainable, unreachable

accession 1. addition, augmentation, enlargement, extension, increase **2.** assumption, attaining to, attainment of, entering upon, succession (*to a throne, dignity, or office*), taking on, taking over **3.** accedence, acceptance, acquiescence, agreement, assent, concurrence, consent

accessory *noun* **1.** abettor, accomplice, assistant, associate (*in crime*), colleague, confederate, helper, partner **2.** accent, accompaniment, addition, add-on, adjunct, adornment, aid, appendage, attachment, component, convenience, decoration, extension, extra, frill, help, supplement, trim, trimming *~adjective* **3.** abetting, additional, aiding, ancillary, assisting in, auxiliary, contributory, extra, secondary, subordinate, supplemental, supplementary

accident 1. blow, calamity, casualty, chance, collision, crash, disaster, misadventure, mischance, misfortune, mishap, pile-up (*informal*) **2.** chance, fate, fluke, fortuity, fortune, hazard, luck

accidental adventitious, casual, chance, contingent, fortuitous, haphazard, inadvertent, incidental, inessential, nonessential, random, uncalculated, uncertain, unessential, unexpected, unforeseen, unintended, unintentional, unlooked-for, unplanned, unpremeditated, unwitting

▷ **Antonyms** calculated, designed, expected, foreseen, intended, intentional, planned, prepared

accidentally adventitiously, by accident, by chance, by mistake, casually, fortuitously, haphazardly, inadvertently, incidentally, randomly, unconsciously, undesignedly, unexpectedly, unintentionally, unwittingly

▷ **Antonyms** by design, consciously, deliberately, designedly, on purpose, wilfully

acclaim 1. *verb* applaud, approve, celebrate, cheer, clap, commend, crack up (*informal*), eulogize, exalt, extol, hail, honour, laud, praise, salute, welcome **2.** *~noun* acclamation, applause, approbation, approval, celebration, cheering, clapping, commendation, eulogizing, exaltation, honour, kudos, laudation, plaudits, praise, welcome

▷ **Antonyms** *~noun* bad press, brickbats, censure, criticism, denigration, disparagement, fault-finding, flak (*informal*), panning (*informal*), stick (*slang*), vituperation

acclamation acclaim, adulation, approbation, cheer, cheering, cheers, enthusiasm, kudos, laudation, loud homage, ovation, plaudit, praise, salutation, shouting, tribute

acclimatization acclimation, accommodation, acculturation, adaptation, adjustment, habituation, inurement, naturalization

acclimatize accommodate, acculturate, acculture, accustom, adapt, adjust, become seasoned to, get used to, habituate, inure, naturalize

acclivity ascent, hill, rise, rising ground, steep upward slope

accommodate 1. billet, board, cater for, entertain, harbour, house, lodge, put up, quarter, shelter **2.** afford, aid, assist, furnish, help, oblige, provide, purvey, serve, supply **3.** accustom, adapt, adjust, comply, compose, conform, fit, harmonize, modify, reconcile, settle

accommodating complaisant, considerate, cooperative, friendly, helpful, hospitable, kind, obliging, polite, unselfish, willing

▷ **Antonyms** disobliging, inconsiderate, rude, uncooperative, unhelpful

accommodation 1. adaptation, adjustment, compliance, composition, compromise, conformity, fitting, harmony, modification, reconciliation, settlement **2.** board, digs (*Brit. informal*), harbouring, house, housing, lodging(s), quartering, quarters, shelter, sheltering **3.** aid, assistance, help, provision, service, supply

accompany 1. attend, chaperon, conduct, convoy, escort, go with, hold (someone's) hand, squire, usher 2. belong to, coexist with, coincide with, come with, follow, go cheek by jowl, go together with, join with, occur with, supplement

accompanying accessory, added, additional, appended, associate, associated, attached, attendant, complementary, concomitant, concurrent, connected, fellow, joint, related, supplemental, supplementary

accomplice abettor, accessory, ally, assistant, associate, coadjutor, collaborator, colleague, confederate, helper, henchman, partner

accomplish achieve, attain, bring about, bring off (*informal*), carry out, complete, conclude, consummate, do, effect, effectuate, execute, finish, fulfil, manage, perform, produce, put the tin lid on, realize

▷ **Antonyms** fail, fall short, forsake, give up

accomplished 1. achieved, attained, brought about, carried out, completed, concluded, consummated, done, effected, executed, finished, fulfilled, in the can (*informal*), managed, performed, produced, realized 2. adept, consummate, cultivated, expert, gifted, masterly, polished, practised, proficient, skilful, skilled, talented

▷ **Antonyms** (*sense 2*) amateurish, incapable, incompetent, inexpert, unestablished, unproven, unrealized, unskilled, untalented

accomplishment 1. achievement, attainment, bringing about, carrying out, completion, conclusion, consummation, doing, effecting, execution, finishing, fulfilment, management, performance, production, realization 2. achievement, act, attainment, coup, deed, exploit, feat, stroke, triumph 3. ability, achievement, art, attainment, capability, craft, gift, proficiency, skill, talent

accord *verb* 1. agree, assent, be in tune (*informal*), concur, conform, correspond, fit, harmonize, match, suit, tally 2. allow, bestow, concede, confer, endow, give, grant, present, render, tender, vouchsafe *~noun* 3. accordance, agreement, assent, concert, concurrence, conformity, congruence, correspondence, harmony, rapport, sympathy, unanimity, unison

▷ **Antonyms** *~verb* (*sense 1*) conflict, contrast, differ, disagree, discord (*sense 2*) hold back, refuse, withhold *~noun* conflict, contention, disagreement, discord

accordance 1. accord, agreement, assent, concert, concurrence, conformity, congruence, correspondence, harmony, rapport, sympathy, unanimity 2. according, allowance, bestowal, concession, conferment, conferral, endowment, gift, giving, granting, presentation, rendering, tendering

accordingly 1. appropriately, correspondingly, fitly, properly, suitably 2. as a result, consequently, ergo, hence, in consequence, so, therefore, thus

according to 1. commensurate with, in proportion, in relation 2. as believed by, as maintained by, as stated by, in the light of, on the authority of, on the report of 3. after, after the manner of, consistent with, in accordance with, in compliance with, in conformity with, in harmony with, in keeping with, in line with, in obedience to, in step with, in the manner of, obedient to

accost address, approach, buttonhole, confront, greet, hail, halt, salute, solicit (*as a prostitute*), stop

account *noun* 1. chronicle, description, detail, explanation, history, narration, narrative, recital, record, relation, report, statement, story, tale, version 2. *Commerce* balance, bill, book, books, charge, computation, inventory, invoice, ledger, reckoning, register, score, statement, tally 3. advantage, benefit, consequence, distinction, esteem, honour, import, importance, merit, note, profit, rank, repute, significance, standing, use, value, worth 4. basis, cause, consideration, ground, grounds, interest, motive, reason, regard, sake, score *~verb* 5. appraise, assess, believe, calculate, compute, consider, count, deem, esteem, estimate, explain, gauge, hold, judge, rate, reckon, regard, think, value, weigh

accountability 1. answerability, chargeability, culpability, liability, responsibility 2. comprehensibility, explainability, explicability, intelligibility, understandability

accountable 1. amenable, answerable, charged with, liable, obligated, obliged, responsible 2. comprehensible, explainable, explicable, intelligible, understandable

account for 1. answer for, clarify, clear up, elucidate, explain, illuminate, justify, rationalize 2. destroy, incapacitate, kill, put out of action, put paid to

accoutre adorn, appoint, array, bedeck, deck, decorate, equip, fit out, furnish, kit out, outfit, provide, supply

accoutrements adornments, appurtenances, array, bells and whistles, clothing, decorations, dress, equipage, equipment, fittings, fixtures, furnishings, garb, gear, kit, ornamentation, outfit, paraphernalia, tackle, trappings, trimmings

accredit 1. appoint, authorize, certify, commission, depute, empower, endorse, entrust, guarantee, license, recognize, sanction, vouch for 2. ascribe, assign, attribute, credit

accredited appointed, authorized, certified, commissioned, deputed, deputized, empowered, endorsed, guaranteed, licensed, official, recognized, sanctioned, vouched for

accretion accumulation, addition, augmentation, enlargement, growth, increase, increment, supplement

accrue accumulate, amass, arise, be added, build up, collect, enlarge, ensue, flow, follow, grow, increase, issue, spring up

accumulate accrue, amass, build up, collect, cumulate, gather, grow, hoard, increase, pile up, stockpile, store
▷ **Antonyms** diffuse, disperse, disseminate, dissipate, distribute, propagate, scatter

accumulation aggregation, augmentation, build-up, collection, conglomeration, gathering, growth, heap, hoard, increase, mass, pile, rick, stack, stock, stockpile, store

accuracy accurateness, authenticity, carefulness, closeness, correctness, exactitude, exactness, faithfulness, faultlessness, fidelity, meticulousness, niceness, nicety, precision, strictness, truth, truthfulness, veracity, verity
▷ **Antonyms** carelessness, erroneousness, imprecision, inaccuracy, incorrectness, inexactitude, laxity, laxness

accurate authentic, careful, close, correct, exact, faithful, faultless, just, meticulous, nice, precise, proper, regular, right, scrupulous, spot-on (*Brit. informal*), strict, true, truthful, unerring, veracious
▷ **Antonyms** careless, defective, faulty, imperfect, imprecise, inaccurate, incorrect, inexact, slovenly, wrong

accurately authentically, carefully, closely, correctly, exactly, faithfully, faultlessly, justly, meticulously, nicely, precisely, properly, regularly, rightly, scrupulously, strictly, to the letter, truly, truthfully, unerringly, veraciously

accursed **1.** bedevilled, bewitched, condemned, cursed, damned, doomed, hopeless, ill-fated, ill-omened, jinxed, luckless, ruined, undone, unfortunate, unlucky, wretched **2.** abominable, despicable, detestable, execrable, hateful, hellish, horrible
▷ **Antonyms** (*sense 1*) blessed, charmed, favoured, fortunate, lucky

accusation allegation, arraignment, attribution, charge, citation, complaint, denunciation, impeachment, imputation, incrimination, indictment, recrimination

accuse allege, arraign, attribute, blame, censure, charge, cite, denounce, impeach, impute, incriminate, indict, point a *or* the finger at, recriminate, tax
▷ **Antonyms** absolve, answer, defend, deny, exonerate, plea, reply, vindicate

accustom acclimatize, acquaint, adapt, discipline, exercise, familiarize, habituate, inure, season, train

accustomed **1.** acclimatized, acquainted, adapted, disciplined, exercised, familiar, familiarized, given to, habituated, in the habit of, inured, seasoned, trained, used **2.** common, conventional, customary, established, everyday, expected, fixed, general, habitual, normal, ordinary, regular, routine, set, traditional, usual, wonted
▷ **Antonyms** (*sense 1*) unaccustomed, unfamiliar, unused (*sense 2*) abnormal, infrequent, occasional, odd, peculiar, rare, strange, unaccustomed, uncommon, unfamiliar, unusual

ace *noun* **1.** *Cards, dice, etc.* one, single point **2.** *informal* adept, buff (*informal*), champion, dab hand (*Brit. informal*), expert, genius, hotshot (*informal*), master, maven (*U.S.*), star, virtuoso, whizz (*informal*), winner, wizard (*informal*) *~adjective* **3.** *informal* awesome (*slang*), brilliant, champion, excellent, expert, fine, great, masterly, outstanding, superb, virtuoso

acerbic **1.** acid, acrid, acrimonious, bitter, brusque, churlish, harsh, nasty, rancorous, rude, severe, sharp, stern, unfriendly, unkind **2.** acerb, acetic, acid, acidulous, acrid, astringent, bitter, harsh, sharp, sour, tart, vinegary

acerbity **1.** acrimony, asperity, bitterness, brusqueness, churlishness, harshness, nastiness, pungency, rancour, rudeness, severity, sharpness, sternness, unfriendliness, unkindness **2.** acidity, acidulousness, acridity, acridness, astringency, bitterness, sourness, tartness

ache *verb* **1.** hurt, pain, pound, smart, suffer, throb, twinge **2.** agonize, eat one's heart out, grieve, mourn, sorrow, suffer **3.** covet, crave, desire, eat one's heart out over, hanker, hope, hunger, long, need, pine, set one's heart on, thirst, yearn *~noun* **4.** hurt, pain, pang, pounding, smart, smarting, soreness, suffering, throb, throbbing **5.** anguish, grief, mourning, sorrow, suffering **6.** craving, desire, hankering, hope, hunger, longing, need, pining, thirst, yearning

achievable accessible, accomplishable, acquirable, attainable, feasible, obtainable, possible, practicable, reachable, realizable, winnable, within one's grasp

achieve accomplish, acquire, attain, bring about, carry out, complete, consummate, do, earn, effect, execute, finish, fulfil, gain, get, obtain, perform, procure, put the tin lid on, reach, realize, win

achievement **1.** accomplishment, acquirement, attainment, completion, execution, fulfilment, performance, production, realization **2.** accomplishment, act, deed, effort, exploit, feat, feather in one's cap, stroke

acid **1.** acerb, acerbic, acetic, acidulous, acrid, biting, pungent, sharp, sour, tart, vinegarish, vinegary **2.** acerbic, biting, bitter, caustic, cutting, harsh, hurtful, mordacious, mordant, pungent, sharp, stinging, trenchant, vitriolic

▷ **Antonyms** (*sense 1*) alkaline, bland, mild, pleasant, sweet (*sense 2*) benign, bland, gentle, kindly, mild, pleasant, sweet

acidity **1.** acerbity, acidulousness, acridity, acridness, bitterness, pungency, sharpness, sourness, tartness, vinegariness, vinegarishness **2.** acerbity, acridity, acridness, bitterness, causticity, causticness, harshness, hurtfulness, mordancy, pungency, sharpness, trenchancy

acidulous **1.** acerb, acerbic, acetic, acid, bitter, harsh, sharp, sour, tart, vinegarish, vinegary **2.** acid, biting, bitter, caustic, cutting, harsh, pungent, sharp, sour, vitriolic

acknowledge **1.** accede, accept, acquiesce, admit, allow, concede, confess, declare, grant, own, profess, recognize, yield **2.** address, greet, hail, notice, recognize, salute **3.** answer, notice, react to, recognize, reply to, respond to, return

▷ **Antonyms** (*sense 1*) contradict, deny, disclaim, discount, reject, renounce, repudiate (*senses 2 & 3*) deny, disavow, disdain, disregard, ignore, rebut, reject, snub, spurn

acknowledged accepted, accredited, admitted, answered, approved, conceded, confessed, declared, professed, recognized, returned

acknowledgment **1.** acceptance, accession, acquiescence, admission, allowing, confession, declaration, profession, realization, yielding **2.** addressing, greeting, hail, hailing, notice, recognition, salutation, salute **3.** answer, appreciation, Brownie points, credit, gratitude, reaction, recognition, reply, response, return, thanks

acme apex, climax, crest, crown, culmination, height, high point, optimum, peak, pinnacle, summit, top, vertex, zenith

▷ **Antonyms** bottom, depths, low point, minimum, nadir, rock bottom, zero

acolyte adherent, admirer, altar boy, assistant, attendant, follower, helper

acquaint advise, announce, apprise, disclose, divulge, enlighten, familiarize, inform, let (someone) know, notify, reveal, tell

acquaintance **1.** associate, colleague, contact **2.** association, awareness, cognizance, companionship, conversance, conversancy, experience, familiarity, fellowship, intimacy, knowledge, relationship, social contact, understanding

▷ **Antonyms** (*sense 1*) buddy, good friend, intimate, stranger (*sense 2*) ignorance, unfamiliarity

acquainted alive to, apprised of, *au fait,* aware of, cognizant of, conscious of, conversant with, experienced in, familiar with, informed of, in on, knowledgeable about, privy to, up to speed with, versed in

acquiesce accede, accept, agree, allow, approve, assent, bow to, comply, concur, conform, consent, give in, go along with, play ball (*informal*), submit, yield

▷ **Antonyms** balk at, contest, demur, disagree, dissent, fight, object, protest, refuse, resist, veto

acquiescence acceptance, accession, agreement, approval, assent, compliance, concurrence, conformity, consent, giving in, obedience, submission, yielding

acquiescent acceding, accepting, agreeable, agreeing, approving, assenting, compliant, concurrent, conforming, consenting, obedient, submissive, yielding

acquire achieve, amass, attain, buy, collect, earn, gain, gather, get, land, obtain, pick up, procure, realize, receive, score (*slang*), secure, win

▷ **Antonyms** be deprived of, forfeit, forgo, give up, lose, relinquish, renounce, surrender, waive

acquirement accomplishment, achievement, acquisition, attainment, gathering, grip, knowledge, learning, mastery, qualification, skill

acquisition **1.** buy, gain, possession, prize, property, purchase **2.** achievement, acquirement, attainment, gaining, learning, obtainment, procurement, pursuit

acquisitive avaricious, avid, covetous, grabbing, grasping, greedy, predatory, rapacious

▷ **Antonyms** bounteous, bountiful, generous, lavish, liberal, munificent, open-handed, unselfish, unstinting

acquisitiveness avarice, avidity, avidness, covetousness, graspingness, greed, predatoriness, rapaciousness, rapacity

acquit **1.** absolve, clear, deliver, discharge, exculpate, exonerate, free, fulfil, liberate, release, relieve, vindicate **2.** discharge, pay, pay off, repay, satisfy, settle **3.** bear, behave, comport, conduct, perform

▷ **Antonyms** (*sense 1*) blame, charge, condemn, convict, damn, find guilty, sentence

acquittal absolution, clearance, deliverance, discharge, exculpation, exoneration, freeing, liberation, release, relief, vindication

acquittance acknowledgment, discharge, payment, receipt, release, settlement, settling

acrid 1. acerb, acid, astringent, biting, bitter, burning, caustic, harsh, irritating, pungent, sharp, stinging, vitriolic **2.** acrimonious, biting, bitter, caustic, cutting, harsh, mordacious, mordant, nasty, sarcastic, sharp, trenchant, vitriolic

acrimonious acerbic, astringent, biting, bitter, caustic, censorious, churlish, crabbed, cutting, irascible, mordacious, mordant, peevish, petulant, pungent, rancorous, sarcastic, severe, sharp, spiteful, splenetic, tart, testy, trenchant, vitriolic

▷ **Antonyms** affable, benign, forgiving, good-tempered

acrimony acerbity, asperity, astringency, bitterness, churlishness, harshness, ill will, irascibility, mordancy, peevishness, pungency, rancour, sarcasm, spleen, tartness, trenchancy, virulence

▷ **Antonyms** amity, friendliness, friendship, good feelings, goodwill, liking, warmth

act *noun* **1.** accomplishment, achievement, action, blow, deed, doing, execution, exertion, exploit, feat, move, operation, performance, step, stroke, undertaking **2.** bill, decree, edict, enactment, law, measure, ordinance, resolution, statute **3.** affectation, attitude, counterfeit, dissimulation, fake, feigning, front, performance, pose, posture, pretence, sham, show, stance **4.** performance, routine, show, sketch, turn *~verb* **5.** acquit, bear, behave, carry, carry out, comport, conduct, do, enact, execute, exert, function, go about, make, move, operate, perform, react, serve, strike, take effect, undertake, work **6.** affect, assume, counterfeit, dissimulate, feign, imitate, perform, pose, posture, pretend, put on, seem, sham **7.** act out, characterize, enact, impersonate, mime, mimic, perform, personate, personify, play, play *or* take the part of, portray, represent

act for cover for, deputize for, fill in for, function in place of, replace, represent, serve, stand in for, substitute for, take the place of

acting *adjective* **1.** interim, *pro tem,* provisional, substitute, surrogate, temporary *~noun* **2.** characterization, dramatics, enacting, impersonation, performance, performing, playing, portrayal, portraying, stagecraft, theatre **3.** assuming, counterfeiting, dissimulation, feigning, imitating, imitation, imposture, play-acting, posing, posturing, pretence, pretending, putting on, seeming, shamming

action 1. accomplishment, achievement, act, blow, deed, exercise, exertion, exploit, feat, move, operation, performance, step, stroke, undertaking **2.** activity, energy, force, liveliness, spirit, vigour, vim, vitality **3.** activity, effect, effort, exertion, force, functioning, influence, motion, movement, operation, power, process, work, working **4.** battle, combat, conflict, fighting, warfare **5.** affray, battle, clash, combat, contest, encounter, engagement, fight, fray, skirmish, sortie **6.** case, cause, lawsuit, litigation, proceeding, prosecution, suit

actions bearing, behaviour, comportment, conduct, demeanour, deportment, manners, ways

activate actuate, animate, arouse, energize, galvanize, get going, impel, initiate, kick-start (*informal*), mobilize, motivate, move, prod, prompt, propel, rouse, set going, set in motion, set off, start, stimulate, stir, switch on, trigger (off), turn on

▷ **Antonyms** arrest, check, deactivate, halt, impede, stall, stop, terminate, turn off

active 1. acting, astir, at work, doing, effectual, functioning, in action, in business, in force, in operation, live, moving, operative, running, stirring, working **2.** bustling, busy, engaged, full, hard-working, involved, occupied, on the go (*informal*), on the move, strenuous **3.** alert, alive and kicking, animated, diligent, energetic, industrious, lively, nimble, on the go (*informal*), quick, spirited, sprightly, spry, vibrant, vigorous, vital, vivacious **4.** activist, aggressive, ambitious, assertive, committed, devoted, energetic, engaged, enterprising, enthusiastic, forceful, forward, hard-working, industrious, militant, zealous

▷ **Antonyms** dormant, dull, idle, inactive, inoperative, lazy, sedentary, slow, sluggish, torpid, unimaginative, unoccupied

activity 1. action, activeness, animation, bustle, enterprise, exercise, exertion, hurly-burly, hustle, labour, life, liveliness, motion, movement, stir, work **2.** act, avocation, deed, endeavour, enterprise, hobby, interest, job, labour, occupation, pastime, project, pursuit, scheme, task, undertaking, venture, work

▷ **Antonyms** (*sense 1*) dullness, idleness, immobility, inaction, inactivity, indolence, inertia, lethargy, passivity, sluggishness, torpor

act on, act upon 1. act in accordance with, carry out, comply with, conform to, follow, heed, obey, yield to **2.** affect, alter, change, impact, influence, modify, sway, transform

actor 1. actress, dramatic artist, leading man, luvvie (*informal*), performer, play-actor, player, thesp (*informal*), Thespian, tragedian, trouper **2.** agent, doer, executor, factor, functionary, operative, operator, participant, partici~

pator, performer, perpetrator, practitioner, worker

actress actor, dramatic artist, leading lady, performer, play-actor, player, starlet, Thespian, tragedienne, trouper

actual 1. absolute, categorical, certain, concrete, corporeal, definite, factual, indisputable, indubitable, physical, positive, real, substantial, tangible, undeniable, unquestionable 2. authentic, confirmed, genuine, real, realistic, true, truthful, verified 3. current, existent, extant, live, living, present, present-day, prevailing

▷ **Antonyms** (*senses 1 & 2*) fictitious, hypothetical, made-up, probable, supposed, theoretical, unreal, untrue

actuality 1. corporeality, factuality, materiality, reality, realness, substance, substantiality, truth, verity 2. fact, reality, truth, verity

actually absolutely, as a matter of fact, de facto, essentially, indeed, in fact, in point of fact, in reality, in truth, literally, really, truly, veritably

actuate animate, arouse, cause, dispose, drive, excite, get going, impel, incite, induce, influence, inspire, instigate, motivate, move, prompt, quicken, rouse, set off, spur, stimulate, stir, urge

act up be naughty, carry on, cause trouble, give bother, give trouble, horse around (*informal*), malfunction, mess about, misbehave, piss about (*taboo slang*), piss around (*taboo slang*), play up (*Brit. informal*), raise Cain

act upon *see* ACT ON

acumen acuteness, astuteness, cleverness, discernment, ingenuity, insight, intelligence, judgment, keenness, penetration, perception, perspicacity, perspicuity, sagacity, sharpness, shrewdness, smartness, smarts (*slang, chiefly U.S.*), wisdom, wit

acute 1. astute, canny, clever, discerning, discriminating, incisive, ingenious, insightful, intuitive, keen, observant, on the ball (*informal*), penetrating, perceptive, perspicacious, piercing, sensitive, sharp, smart, subtle 2. critical, crucial, dangerous, decisive, essential, grave, important, serious, severe, sudden, urgent, vital 3. cutting, distressing, excruciating, exquisite, fierce, harrowing, intense, overpowering, overwhelming, piercing, poignant, powerful, racking, severe, sharp, shooting, shrill, stabbing, sudden, violent 4. cuspate, needle-shaped, peaked, pointed, sharp, sharpened

▷ **Antonyms** (*sense 1*) dense, dim, dim-witted, dull, obtuse, slow, stupid, unintelligent (*sense 4*) blunt, blunted, dull, obtuse, unsharpened

acuteness 1. acuity, astuteness, canniness, cleverness, discernment, discrimination, ingenuity, insight, intuition, intuitiveness, keenness, perception, perceptiveness, perspicacity, sensitivity, sharpness, smartness, subtleness, subtlety, wit 2. criticality, criticalness, cruciality, danger, dangerousness, decisiveness, essentiality, gravity, importance, seriousness, severity, suddenness, urgency, vitalness 3. distressingness, exquisiteness, fierceness, intenseness, intensity, poignancy, powerfulness, severity, sharpness, shrillness, suddenness, violence 4. pointedness, sharpness

adage aphorism, apophthegm, axiom, by-word, dictum, maxim, motto, precept, proverb, saw, saying

adamant 1. determined, firm, fixed, immovable, inexorable, inflexible, insistent, intransigent, obdurate, relentless, resolute, rigid, set, stiff, stubborn, unbending, uncompromising, unrelenting, unshakable, unyielding 2. adamantine, flinty, hard, impenetrable, indestructible, rock-hard, rocky, steely, stony, tough, unbreakable

▷ **Antonyms** (*sense 1*) compliant, compromising, easy-going, flexible, lax, pliant, receptive, responsive, susceptible, tensile, tractable, yielding (*sense 2*) bendy, ductile, flexible, pliable, pliant, yielding

adapt acclimatize, accommodate, adjust, alter, apply, change, comply, conform, convert, customize, familiarize, fashion, fit, habituate, harmonize, make, match, modify, prepare, qualify, remodel, shape, suit, tailor, tweak (*informal*)

adaptability adaptableness, adjustability, alterability, changeability, compliancy, convertibility, flexibility, malleability, modifiability, plasticity, pliability, pliancy, resilience, variability, versatility

adaptable adjustable, alterable, changeable, compliant, conformable, convertible, easy-going, easy-oasy (*slang*), flexible, malleable, modifiable, plastic, pliant, resilient, variable, versatile

adaptation 1. adjustment, alteration, change, conversion, modification, refitting, remodelling, reworking, shift, transformation, variation, version 2. acclimatization, accustomedness, familiarization, habituation, naturalization

add 1. adjoin, affix, amplify, annex, append, attach, augment, enlarge by, include, increase by, supplement 2. add up, compute, count up, reckon, sum up, total, tot up

▷ **Antonyms** deduct, diminish, lessen, reduce, remove, subtract, take away, take from

addendum addition, adjunct, affix, appendage, appendix, attachment, augmentation, codicil, extension, extra, postscript, supplement

addict 1. dope-fiend (*slang*), fiend (*informal*), freak (*informal*), head (*slang*), junkie (*informal*), pill-popper (*informal*), user (*informal*) **2**. adherent, buff (*informal*), devotee, enthusiast, fan, follower, freak (*informal*), nut (*slang*)

addicted absorbed, accustomed, dedicated, dependent, devoted, disposed, fond, habituated, hooked (*slang*), inclined, obsessed, prone

addiction craving, dependence, enslavement, habit, obsession

addition 1. accession, adding, adjoining, affixing, amplification, annexation, attachment, augmentation, enlargement, extension, inclusion, increasing **2**. addendum, additive, adjunct, affix, appendage, appendix, extension, extra, gain, increase, increment, supplement **3**. adding up, computation, counting up, reckoning, summation, summing up, totalling, totting up **4**. **in addition (to)** additionally, also, as well (as), besides, into the bargain, moreover, over and above, to boot, too, withal

▷ **Antonyms** (*senses 1, 2 & 3*) deduction, detachment, diminution, lessening, reduction, removal, subtraction

additional added, add-on, affixed, appended, extra, fresh, further, increased, more, new, other, over-and-above, spare, supplementary

addle-brained *or* **addle-pated** befuddled, bewildered, confused, daft (*informal*), dead from the neck up (*informal*), dim-witted, dopey (*informal*), dozy (*Brit. informal*), flustered, foolish, goofy (*informal*), halfwitted, mixed-up, muddled, muddleheaded, nonsensical, perplexed, silly, simple, simple-minded, stupid, thick, thickheaded, witless, woolly-minded

addled 1. at sea, befuddled, bewildered, confused, flustered, foolish, mixed-up, muddled, perplexed, silly **2**. bad, gone bad, off, rancid, rotten, turned

address *noun* **1**. abode, domicile, dwelling, home, house, location, lodging, pad (*slang*), place, residence, situation, whereabouts **2**. direction, inscription, superscription **3**. discourse, disquisition, dissertation, harangue, lecture, oration, sermon, speech, talk **4**. adroitness, art, dexterity, discretion, expertness, ingenuity, skilfulness, skill, tact *~verb* **5**. accost, apostrophize, approach, greet, hail, invoke, salute, speak to, talk to **6**. discourse, give a speech, give a talk, harangue, lecture, orate, sermonize, speak, spout, talk **7**. **address (oneself) to** apply (oneself) to, attend to, concentrate on, devote (oneself) to, engage in, focus on, knuckle down to, look to, take care of, take up, turn to, undertake

adduce advance, allege, cite, designate, mention, name, offer, present, quote

add up 1. add, compute, count, count up, reckon, sum up, total, tot up **2**. amount, come to, imply, indicate, mean, reveal, signify **3**. be plausible, be reasonable, hold water, make sense, ring true, stand to reason

adept 1. *adjective* able, accomplished, adroit, dexterous, expert, masterful, masterly, practised, proficient, skilful, skilled, versed **2**. *~noun* buff (*informal*), dab hand (*Brit. informal*), expert, genius, hotshot (*informal*), master, maven (*U.S.*), whizz (*informal*)

▷ **Antonyms** *~adjective* amateurish, awkward, clumsy, inept, unskilled

adequacy capability, commensurateness, competence, fairness, requisiteness, satisfactoriness, sufficiency, suitability, tolerability

adequate capable, commensurate, competent, enough, fair, passable, requisite, satisfactory, sufficient, suitable, tolerable, up to scratch (*informal*)

▷ **Antonyms** deficient, inadequate, insufficient, lacking, meagre, scant, short, unsatisfactory, unsuitable

adhere 1. attach, cement, cleave, cling, cohere, fasten, fix, glue, glue on, hold fast, paste, stick, stick fast, unite **2**. abide by, be attached, be constant, be devoted, be faithful, be loyal, be true, cleave to, cling, follow, fulfil, heed, keep, keep to, maintain, mind, obey, observe, respect, stand by, support

adherent 1. *noun* admirer, advocate, devotee, disciple, fan, follower, hanger-on, henchman, partisan, protagonist, sectary, supporter, upholder, votary **2**. *~adjective* adhering, adhesive, clinging, gluey, glutinous, gummy, holding, mucilaginous, sticking, sticky, tacky, tenacious

▷ **Antonyms** *~noun* adversary, antagonist, disputant, dissentient, enemy, foe, opponent, opposer, opposition, rival

adhesion 1. adherence, adhesiveness, attachment, coherence, cohesion, grip, holding fast, sticking, union **2**. allegiance, attachment, constancy, devotion, faithfulness, fidelity, fulfilment, heed, loyalty, obedience, observation, respect, support, troth (*archaic*)

adhesive 1. *adjective* adhering, attaching, clinging, cohesive, gluey, glutinous, gummy, holding, mucilaginous, sticking, sticky, tacky, tenacious **2**. *~noun* cement, glue, gum, mucilage, paste

adieu congé, farewell, goodbye, leave-taking, parting, valediction

adipose fat, fatty, greasy, obese, oily, oleaginous, sebaceous

adjacent abutting, adjoining, alongside, beside, bordering, cheek by jowl, close, contiguous, near, neighbouring, next door, proximate, touching, within sniffing distance (*informal*)

▷ **Antonyms** distant, far away, remote, separated

adjoin abut, add, affix, annex, append, approximate, attach, border, combine, communicate with, connect, couple, impinge, interconnect, join, link, neighbour, touch, unite, verge

adjoining abutting, adjacent, bordering, connecting, contiguous, impinging, interconnecting, joined, joining, near, neighbouring, next door, touching, verging

adjourn defer, delay, discontinue, interrupt, postpone, prorogue, put off, put on the back burner (*informal*), recess, stay, suspend, take a rain check on (*U.S. & Canad. informal*)
▷ **Antonyms** assemble, continue, convene, gather, open, remain, reopen, stay

adjournment deferment, deferral, delay, discontinuation, interruption, postponement, prorogation, putting off, recess, stay, suspension

adjudge adjudicate, allot, apportion, assign, award, decide, declare, decree, determine, distribute, judge, order, pronounce

adjudicate adjudge, arbitrate, decide, determine, judge, mediate, referee, settle, umpire

adjudication adjudgment, arbitration, conclusion, decision, determination, finding, judgment, pronouncement, ruling, settlement, verdict

adjunct accessory, addendum, addition, add-on, appendage, appurtenance, auxiliary, complement, supplement

adjure **1.** appeal to, beg, beseech, entreat, implore, invoke, pray, supplicate **2.** charge, command, direct, enjoin, order

adjust acclimatize, accommodate, accustom, adapt, alter, arrange, compose, convert, customize, dispose, fit, fix, harmonize, make conform, measure, modify, order, reconcile, rectify, redress, regulate, remodel, set, settle, suit, tune (up), tweak (*informal*)

adjustable adaptable, alterable, flexible, malleable, modifiable, mouldable, movable, tractable

adjustment **1.** adaptation, alteration, arrangement, arranging, fitting, fixing, modification, ordering, rectification, redress, regulation, remodelling, setting, tuning **2.** acclimatization, harmonization, orientation, reconciliation, settlement, settling in

ad-lib **1.** *verb* busk, extemporize, improvise, make up, speak extemporaneously, speak impromptu, speak off the cuff, vamp, wing it (*informal*) **2.** *~adjective* extemporaneous, extempore, extemporized, impromptu, improvised, made up, off-the-cuff (*informal*), off the top of one's head, unprepared, unrehearsed **3.** *~adverb* extemporaneously, extempore, impromptu, off the cuff, off the top of one's head (*informal*), without preparation, without rehearsal

administer **1.** conduct, control, direct, govern, handle, manage, oversee, run, superintend, supervise **2.** apply, contribute, dispense, distribute, execute, give, impose, mete out, perform, provide

administration **1.** administering, application, conduct, control, direction, dispensation, distribution, execution, governing, government, management, overseeing, performance, provision, running, superintendence, supervision **2.** executive, governing body, government, management, ministry, term of office

administrative directorial, executive, governmental, gubernatorial (*chiefly U.S.*), management, managerial, organizational, regulatory, supervisory

admirable choice, commendable, estimable, excellent, exquisite, fine, laudable, meritorious, praiseworthy, rare, sterling, superior, valuable, wonderful, worthy
▷ **Antonyms** bad, commonplace, deplorable, disappointing, displeasing, mediocre, no great shakes (*informal*), worthless

admiration adoration, affection, amazement, appreciation, approbation, approval, astonishment, delight, esteem, pleasure, praise, regard, respect, surprise, veneration, wonder, wonderment

admire **1.** adore, appreciate, approve, esteem, idolize, look up to, praise, prize, respect, take one's hat off to, think highly of, value, venerate, worship **2.** appreciate, delight in, marvel at, take pleasure in, wonder at
▷ **Antonyms** contemn, deride, despise, look down on, look down one's nose at (*informal*), misprize, scorn, sneer at, spurn, undervalue

admirer **1.** beau, boyfriend, lover, suitor, sweetheart, wooer **2.** adherent, buff (*informal*), devotee, disciple, enthusiast, fan, follower, partisan, protagonist, supporter, votary, worshipper

admissible acceptable, allowable, allowed, passable, permissible, permitted, tolerable, tolerated
▷ **Antonyms** disallowed, inadmissible, intolerable, unacceptable

admission **1.** acceptance, access, admittance, entrance, entrée, entry, ingress, initiation, introduction **2.** acknowledgment, admitting, affirmation, allowance, avowal, concession, confession, declaration, disclosure, divulgence, profession, revelation

admit **1.** accept, allow, allow to enter, give access, initiate, introduce, let in, receive, take in **2.** acknowledge, affirm, avow, concede, confess, cough (*slang*), declare, disclose, divulge, own, profess, reveal **3.** agree, allow, grant, let, permit, recognize

▷ **Antonyms** (*sense 1*) exclude, keep out (*senses 2 & 3*) deny, dismiss, forbid, negate, prohibit, reject

admittance acceptance, access, admitting, allowing, entrance, entry, letting in, passage, reception

admix add, alloy, amalgamate, blend, combine, commingle, commix, include, incorporate, intermingle, meld, merge, mingle, mix, put in

admixture 1. alloy, amalgamation, blend, combination, compound, fusion, intermixture, medley, meld **2.** component, constituent, element, ingredient

admonish advise, bawl out (*informal*), berate, carpet (*informal*), caution, censure, check, chew out (*U.S. & Canad. informal*), chide, counsel, enjoin, exhort, forewarn, give a rocket (*Brit. & N.Z. informal*), rap over the knuckles, read the riot act, rebuke, reprimand, reprove, scold, slap on the wrist, tear into (*informal*), tear (someone) off a strip (*Brit. informal*), tell off (*informal*), upbraid, warn

▷ **Antonyms** applaud, commend, compliment, congratulate, praise

admonition advice, berating, caution, chiding, counsel, rebuke, remonstrance, reprimand, reproach, reproof, scolding, telling off (*informal*), upbraiding, warning

admonitory admonishing, advisory, cautionary, rebuking, reprimanding, reproachful, reproving, scolding, warning

ado agitation, bother, bustle, commotion, confusion, delay, disturbance, excitement, flurry, fuss, pother, stir, to-do, trouble

adolescence 1. boyhood, girlhood, juvenescence, minority, teens, youth **2.** boyishness, childishness, girlishness, immaturity, juvenility, puerility, youthfulness

adolescent 1. *adjective* boyish, girlish, growing, immature, juvenile, puerile, teenage, young, youthful **2.** *~noun* juvenile, minor, teenager, youngster, youth

adopt 1. accept, appropriate, approve, assume, choose, embrace, endorse, espouse, follow, maintain, ratify, select, support, take on, take over, take up **2.** foster, take in

▷ **Antonyms** (*sense 1*) abandon, abnegate, cast aside, cast off, disavow, disclaim, disown, forswear, give up, reject, renounce, repudiate, spurn, wash one's hands of

adoption 1. acceptance, approbation, appropriation, approval, assumption, choice, embracing, endorsement, espousal, following, maintenance, ratification, selection, support, taking on, taking over, taking up **2.** adopting, fosterage, fostering, taking in

adorable appealing, attractive, captivating, charming, cute, darling, dear, delightful, fetching, lovable, pleasing, precious

▷ **Antonyms** despicable, displeasing, hateful, unlikable *or* unlikeable, unlovable

adoration admiration, esteem, estimation, exaltation, glorification, honour, idolatry, idolization, love, reverence, veneration, worship, worshipping

adore admire, bow to, cherish, dote on, esteem, exalt, glorify, honour, idolize, love, revere, reverence, venerate, worship

▷ **Antonyms** abhor, abominate, despise, detest, execrate, hate, loathe

adorn array, beautify, bedeck, deck, decorate, embellish, emblazon, enhance, enrich, festoon, garnish, gild the lily, grace, ornament, trim

adornment 1. accessory, decoration, embellishment, festoon, frill, frippery, ornament, trimming **2.** beautification, decorating, decoration, embellishment, ornamentation, trimming

adrift 1. afloat, drifting, unanchored, unmoored **2.** aimless, directionless, goalless, purposeless **3.** amiss, astray, off course, wrong

adroit able, adept, apt, artful, bright (*informal*), clever, cunning, deft, dexterous, expert, ingenious, masterful, neat, nimble, proficient, quick-witted, skilful, skilled

▷ **Antonyms** awkward, blundering, bungling, cack-handed (*informal*), clumsy, ham-fisted *or* ham-handed (*informal*), inept, inexpert, maladroit, uncoordinated, unhandy, unskilful

adroitness ability, ableness, address, adeptness, aptness, artfulness, cleverness, craft, cunning, deftness, dexterity, expertise, ingeniousness, ingenuity, knack, masterfulness, mastery, nimbleness, proficiency, quick-wittedness, skilfulness, skill

adulation blandishment, bootlicking (*informal*), extravagant flattery, fawning, fulsome praise, servile flattery, sycophancy, worship

▷ **Antonyms** abuse, calumniation, censure, condemnation, disparagement, revilement, ridicule, vilification, vituperation

adulatory blandishing, bootlicking (*informal*), fawning, flattering, obsequious, praising, servile, slavish, sycophantic, worshipping

adult 1. *adjective* full grown, fully developed, fully grown, grown-up, mature, of age, ripe **2.** *~noun* grown *or* grown-up person (man *or* woman), grown-up, person of mature age

adulterate 1. *verb* attenuate, bastardize, contaminate, corrupt, debase, depreci~

ate, deteriorate, devalue, make impure, mix with, thin, vitiate, water down, weaken **2.** *~adjective* adulterated, attenuated, bastardized, contaminated, corrupt, debased, depreciated, deteriorated, devalued, mixed, thinned, vitiated, watered down, weakened

adumbrate 1. delineate, indicate, outline, silhouette, sketch, suggest **2.** augur, forecast, foreshadow, foretell, portend, predict, prefigure, presage, prognosticate, prophesy **3.** bedim, darken, eclipse, obfuscate, obscure, overshadow

adumbration 1. delineation, draft, indication, outline, rough, silhouette, sketch, suggestion **2.** augury, forecast, foreshadowing, foretelling, omen, portent, prediction, prefiguration, prefigurement, presage, prognostication, prophecy, sign **3.** bedimming, cloud, darkening, darkness, eclipse, eclipsing, obfuscation, obscuring, overshadowing, shadow

advance *verb* **1.** accelerate, bring forward, bring up, come forward, elevate, go ahead, go forward, go on, hasten, make inroads, move onward, move up, press on, proceed, progress, promote, send forward, send up, speed, upgrade **2.** benefit, further, grow, improve, multiply, prosper, thrive **3.** adduce, allege, cite, offer, present, proffer, put forward, submit, suggest **4.** lend, pay beforehand, supply on credit *~noun* **5.** advancement, development, forward movement, headway, inroad, onward movement, progress **6.** advancement, amelioration, betterment, breakthrough, furtherance, gain, growth, improvement, progress, promotion, step **7.** appreciation, credit, deposit, down payment, increase (*in price*), loan, prepayment, retainer, rise (*in price*) **8. advances** approach, approaches, moves, overtures, proposals, proposition *~adjective* **9.** beforehand, early, foremost, forward, in front, leading, prior **10. in advance** ahead, beforehand, earlier, in the forefront, in the lead, in the van, on the barrelhead, previously

▷ **Antonyms** *~verb* (*sense 1*) demote, hold back, impede, move back, regress, retard, retreat, set back, withdraw (*sense 2*) decrease, diminish, lessen, weaken (*sense 3*) hide, hold back, suppress, withhold (*sense 4*) defer payment, withhold payment

advanced ahead, avant-garde, extreme, foremost, forward, higher, late, leading, precocious, progressive

▷ **Antonyms** backward, behind, retarded, underdeveloped, undeveloped

advancement 1. advance, forward movement, headway, onward movement, progress **2.** advance, amelioration, betterment, gain, growth, improvement, preferment, progress, promotion, rise

advantage ace in the hole, ace up one's sleeve, aid, ascendancy, asset, assistance, avail, benefit, blessing, boon, convenience, dominance, edge, gain, good, help, inside track, interest, lead, mileage (*informal*), precedence, pre-eminence, profit, service, start, superiority, sway, upper hand, use, utility, welfare

▷ **Antonyms** curse, difficulty, disadvantage, downside, drawback, handicap, hindrance, inconvenience, snag

advantageous 1. dominant, dominating, favourable, superior **2.** beneficial, convenient, expedient, helpful, of service, profitable, useful, valuable, worthwhile

▷ **Antonyms** detrimental, unfavourable, unfortunate, unhelpful, useless

advent appearance, approach, arrival, coming, entrance, occurrence, onset, visitation

adventitious accidental, casual, chance, extraneous, foreign, fortuitous, incidental, nonessential, unexpected

adventure 1. *noun* chance, contingency, enterprise, escapade, experience, exploit, hazard, incident, occurrence, risk, speculation, undertaking, venture **2.** *~verb* dare, endanger, hazard, imperil, jeopardize, risk, venture

adventurer 1. daredevil, hero, heroine, knight-errant, soldier of fortune, swashbuckler, traveller, venturer, voyager, wanderer **2.** charlatan, fortune-hunter, gambler, mercenary, opportunist, rogue, speculator

adventurous adventuresome, audacious, bold, dangerous, daredevil, daring, enterprising, foolhardy, have-a-go (*informal*), hazardous, headstrong, intrepid, rash, reckless, risky, temerarious (*rare*), venturesome

▷ **Antonyms** careful, cautious, chary, circumspect, hesitant, prudent, safe, tentative, timid, timorous, unadventurous, wary

adversary antagonist, competitor, contestant, enemy, foe, opponent, opposer, rival

▷ **Antonyms** accomplice, ally, associate, collaborator, colleague, confederate, co-worker, friend, helper, partner, supporter

adverse antagonistic, conflicting, contrary, detrimental, disadvantageous, hostile, inexpedient, inimical, injurious, inopportune, negative, opposing, opposite, reluctant, repugnant, unfavourable, unfortunate, unfriendly, unlucky, unpropitious, unwilling

▷ **Antonyms** advantageous, auspicious, beneficial, favourable, fortunate, helpful, lucky, opportune, promising, propitious, suitable

adversity affliction, bad luck, calamity, catastrophe, deep water, disaster, distress, hardship, hard times, ill-fortune, ill-luck, misery, misfortune, mishap, reverse, sorrow, suffering, trial, trouble, woe, wretchedness

advert *verb* allude, draw attention (to), mention, notice, observe, refer, regard, remark

advertise advise, announce, apprise, blazon, crack up (*informal*), declare, display, flaunt, inform, make known, notify, plug (*informal*), praise, proclaim, promote, promulgate, publicize, publish, puff, push (*informal*), tout

advertisement ad (*informal*), advert (*Brit. informal*), announcement, bill, blurb, circular, commercial, display, notice, placard, plug (*informal*), poster, promotion, publicity, puff

advice **1.** admonition, caution, counsel, guidance, help, injunction, opinion, recommendation, suggestion, view **2.** information, instruction, intelligence, notice, notification, warning, word

advisability appropriateness, aptness, desirability, expediency, fitness, judiciousness, profitability, propriety, prudence, seemliness, soundness, suitability, wisdom

advisable appropriate, apt, desirable, expedient, fit, fitting, judicious, politic, profitable, proper, prudent, recommended, seemly, sensible, sound, suggested, suitable, wise

▷ **Antonyms** ill-advised, impolitic, improper, imprudent, inappropriate, inexpedient, injudicious, silly, stupid, undesirable, unfitting, unprofitable, unseemly, unsound, unsuitable, unwise

advise **1.** admonish, caution, commend, counsel, enjoin, prescribe, recommend, suggest, urge **2.** acquaint, apprise, inform, make known, notify, report, tell, warn

adviser aide, authority, coach, confidant, consultant, counsel, counsellor, guide, helper, lawyer, mentor, right-hand man, solicitor, teacher, tutor

advisory advising, consultative, counselling, helping, recommending

advocacy advancement, argument for, backing, campaigning for, championing, defence, encouragement, espousal, justification, pleading for, promotion, promulgation, propagation, proposal, recommendation, spokesmanship, support, upholding, urging

advocate *verb* **1.** advise, argue for, campaign for, champion, commend, countenance, defend, encourage, espouse, favour, hold a brief for (*informal*), justify, plead for, prescribe, press for, promote, propose, recommend, speak for, support, uphold, urge ~*noun* **2.** apologist, apostle, backer, campaigner, champion, counsellor, defender, pleader, promoter, proponent, proposer, speaker, spokesman, supporter, upholder **3.** *Law* attorney, barrister, counsel, lawyer, solicitor

▷ **Antonyms** ~*verb* contradict, oppose, resist, speak against, take a stand against, take issue with

aegis advocacy, auspices, backing, favour, guardianship, patronage, protection, shelter, sponsorship, support, wing

affability amiability, amicability, approachability, benevolence, benignity, civility, congeniality, cordiality, courtesy, friendliness, geniality, good humour, good nature, graciousness, kindliness, mildness, obligingness, pleasantness, sociability, urbanity, warmth

affable amiable, amicable, approachable, benevolent, benign, civil, congenial, cordial, courteous, friendly, genial, good-humoured, good-natured, gracious, kindly, mild, obliging, pleasant, sociable, urbane, warm

▷ **Antonyms** brusque, cold, discourteous, distant, haughty, rude, stand-offish, surly, unapproachable, uncivil, unfriendly, ungracious, unpleasant, unsociable

affair **1.** activity, business, circumstance, concern, episode, event, happening, incident, interest, matter, occurrence, proceeding, project, question, subject, transaction, undertaking **2.** amour, intrigue, liaison, relationship, romance

affect **1.** act on, alter, bear upon, change, concern, impact, impinge upon, influence, interest, involve, modify, prevail over, regard, relate to, sway, transform **2.** disturb, impress, move, overcome, perturb, stir, touch, tug at (someone's) heartstrings (*often facetious*), upset **3.** adopt, aspire to, assume, contrive, counterfeit, feign, imitate, pretend, put on, sham, simulate

affectation act, affectedness, appearance, artificiality, assumed manners, façade, fakery, false display, insincerity, mannerism, pose, pretence, pretension, pretentiousness, sham, show, simulation, unnatural imitation

affected **1.** afflicted, altered, changed, concerned, damaged, deeply moved, distressed, hurt, impaired, impressed, influenced, injured, melted, stimulated, stirred, touched, troubled, upset **2.** artificial, assumed, camp (*informal*), conceited, contrived, counterfeit, feigned, insincere, la-di-da (*informal*), mannered, mincing, phoney *or* phony (*informal*), pompous, precious, pretended, pretentious, put-on, sham, simulated, spurious, stiff, studied, unnatural

▷ **Antonyms** (*sense 1*) cured, unaffected, unconcerned, unharmed, uninjured, unmoved, untouched (*sense 2*) genuine, natural, real, unaffected

affecting moving, pathetic, piteous, pitiable, pitiful, poignant, sad, saddening, touching

affection amity, attachment, care, desire, feeling, fondness, friendliness, goodwill, inclination, kindness, liking, love, passion, propensity, tenderness, warmth

affectionate attached, caring, devoted, doting, fond, friendly, kind, loving, tender, warm, warm-hearted
▷ **Antonyms** cold, cool, glacial, indifferent, stony, uncaring, undemonstrative, unfeeling, unresponsive

affiance betroth, bind, engage, pledge, promise

affiliate ally, amalgamate, annex, associate, band together, combine, confederate, connect, incorporate, join, unite

affiliation alliance, amalgamation, association, banding together, coalition, combination, confederation, connection, incorporation, joining, league, merging, relationship, union

affinity 1. alliance, analogy, closeness, compatibility, connection, correspondence, kinship, likeness, relation, relationship, resemblance, similarity **2.** attraction, fondness, inclination, leaning, liking, partiality, rapport, sympathy
▷ **Antonyms** (*sense 1*) difference, disparity, dissimilarity (*sense 2*) abhorrence, animosity, antipathy, aversion, dislike, hatred, hostility, loathing, repugnance, revulsion

affirm assert, asseverate, attest, aver, avouch, avow, certify, confirm, declare, maintain, pronounce, ratify, state, swear, testify
▷ **Antonyms** deny, disallow, rebut, refute, reject, renounce, repudiate, rescind, retract

affirmation assertion, asseveration, attestation, averment, avouchment, avowal, certification, confirmation, declaration, oath, pronouncement, ratification, statement, testimony

affirmative agreeing, approving, assenting, concurring, confirming, consenting, corroborative, favourable, positive
▷ **Antonyms** denying, disagreeing, disapproving, dissenting, negating, negative

affix add, annex, append, attach, bind, fasten, glue, join, paste, put on, stick, subjoin, tack, tag
▷ **Antonyms** detach, disconnect, remove, take off, unfasten, unglue

afflict ail, beset, burden, distress, grieve, harass, hurt, oppress, pain, plague, rack, smite, torment, trouble, try, wound

affliction adversity, calamity, cross, curse, depression, disease, distress, grief, hardship, misery, misfortune, ordeal, pain, plague, scourge, sickness, sorrow, suffering, torment, trial, tribulation, trouble, woe, wretchedness

affluence abundance, big bucks (*informal, chiefly U.S.*), big money, exuberance, fortune, megabucks (*U.S. & Canad. slang*), opulence, plenty, pretty penny (*informal*), profusion, prosperity, riches, tidy sum (*informal*), wad (*U.S. & Canad. slang*), wealth

affluent 1. loaded (*slang*), moneyed, opulent, prosperous, rich, rolling in money (*slang*), wealthy, well-heeled (*informal*), well-off, well-to-do **2.** abundant, copious, exuberant, plenteous, plentiful
▷ **Antonyms** (*sense 1*) broke (*informal*), destitute, down at heel, hard-up (*informal*), impecunious, impoverished, indigent, on the breadline, penniless, penurious, poor, poverty-stricken, skint (*Brit. slang*), stony-broke (*Brit. slang*)

afford 1. bear, spare, stand, sustain **2.** bestow, furnish, give, grant, impart, offer, produce, provide, render, supply, yield

affray *bagarre,* brawl, contest, disturbance, dogfight, encounter, feud, fight, fracas, free-for-all (*informal*), mêlée, outbreak, quarrel, scrap, scrimmage, scuffle, set-to (*informal*), shindig (*informal*), shindy (*informal*), skirmish, tumult

affront 1. *verb* abuse, anger, annoy, displease, insult, offend, outrage, pique, provoke, put *or* get one's back up, slight, vex **2.** *~noun* abuse, indignity, injury, insult, offence, outrage, provocation, slap in the face (*informal*), slight, slur, vexation, wrong

afire 1. ablaze, aflame, alight, blazing, burning, fiery, flaming, ignited, lighted, lit, on fire **2.** aglow, aroused, excited, fervent, impassioned, passionate, stimulated

aflame 1. ablaze, afire, alight, blazing, burning, fiery, flaming, ignited, lighted, lit, on fire **2.** afire, aroused, excited, fervent, impassioned, passionate, stimulated **3.** aglow, flushed, inflamed, red, ruddy

afoot about, abroad, afloat, astir, brewing, circulating, current, going on, hatching, in preparation, in progress, in the wind, on the go (*informal*), operating, up (*informal*)

afraid 1. alarmed, anxious, apprehensive, cowardly, faint-hearted, fearful, frightened, intimidated, nervous, reluctant, scared, suspicious, timid, timorous **2.** regretful, sorry, unhappy
▷ **Antonyms** (*sense 1*) audacious, bold, fearless, happy, inapprehensive, indifferent, pleased, unafraid

afresh again, anew, newly, once again, once more, over again

after afterwards, behind, below, following, later, subsequently, succeeding, thereafter
▷ **Antonyms** before, earlier, in advance, in front, previously, prior to, sooner

aftermath after-effects, consequences, ef~

fects, end, end result, outcome, results, sequel, upshot, wake

again 1. afresh, anew, another time, once more 2. also, besides, furthermore, in addition, moreover, on the contrary, on the other hand

against 1. anti (*informal*), averse to, contra (*informal*), counter, hostile to, in contrast to, in defiance of, in opposition to, in the face of, opposed to, opposing, resisting, versus 2. abutting, close up to, facing, fronting, in contact with, on, opposite to, touching, upon 3. in anticipation of, in expectation of, in preparation for, in provision for

agape 1. gaping, wide, wide open, yawning 2. agog, amazed, astonished, astounded, awestricken, dumbfounded, eager, expectant, flabbergasted, gobsmacked (*Brit. slang*), spellbound, surprised, thunderstruck

age *noun* 1. date, day(s), duration, epoch, era, generation, lifetime, period, span, time 2. advancing years, decline (*of life*), majority, maturity, old age, senescence, senility, seniority *~verb* 3. decline, deteriorate, grow old, mature, mellow, ripen

▷ **Antonyms** *~noun* (*sense 2*) adolescence, boyhood, childhood, girlhood, immaturity, juvenescence, salad days, young days, youth

aged age-old, ancient, antiquated, antique, elderly, getting on, grey, hoary, old, past it (*informal*), senescent, superannuated

▷ **Antonyms** adolescent, boyish, childish, girlish, immature, juvenile, young, youthful

agency 1. action, activity, auspices, efficiency, force, influence, instrumentality, intercession, intervention, means, mechanism, mediation, medium, operation, power, work 2. bureau, business, department, office, organization

agenda calendar, diary, list, plan, programme, schedule, timetable

agent 1. advocate, deputy, emissary, envoy, factor, go-between, negotiator, rep (*informal*), representative, substitute, surrogate 2. actor, author, doer, executor, mover, officer, operative, operator, performer, worker 3. agency, cause, force, instrument, means, power, vehicle

agglomeration accumulation, clump, cluster, collection, heap, lump, mass, pile, rick, stack

agglutinate adhere, attach, bond, cement, fasten, glue, gum, join, solder, stick, unite

aggrandize advance, amplify, augment, dignify, elevate, enlarge, ennoble, enrich, exaggerate, exalt, inflate, intensify, magnify, promote, widen

aggravate 1. add insult to injury, exacerbate, exaggerate, fan the flames of, heighten, increase, inflame, intensify, magnify, make worse, worsen 2. *informal* annoy, be on one's back (*slang*), bother, exasperate, gall, get in one's hair (*informal*), get on one's nerves (*informal*), get on one's wick (*Brit. slang*), get under one's skin (*informal*), get up one's nose (*informal*), hassle (*informal*), irk, irritate, nark (*Brit., Austral., & N.Z. slang*), needle (*informal*), nettle, pester, piss one off (*taboo slang*), provoke, rub (someone) up the wrong way (*informal*), tease, vex

▷ **Antonyms** (*sense 1*) alleviate, assuage, calm, diminish, ease, improve, lessen, mitigate, smooth (*sense 2*) assuage, calm, pacify, please

aggravation 1. exacerbation, exaggeration, heightening, increase, inflaming, intensification, magnification, worsening 2. *informal* annoyance, exasperation, gall, grief (*informal*), hassle (*informal*), irksomeness, irritation, provocation, teasing, vexation

aggregate 1. *verb* accumulate, amass, assemble, collect, combine, heap, mix, pile 2. *~noun* accumulation, agglomeration, amount, assemblage, body, bulk, collection, combination, heap, lump, mass, mixture, pile, sum, total, whole 3. *~adjective* accumulated, added, assembled, collected, collective, combined, composite, corporate, cumulative, mixed, total

aggression 1. assault, attack, encroachment, injury, invasion, offence, offensive, onslaught, raid 2. aggressiveness, antagonism, belligerence, destructiveness, hostility, pugnacity

aggressive 1. belligerent, destructive, hostile, offensive, pugnacious, quarrelsome 2. assertive, bold, dynamic, energetic, enterprising, forceful, in-your-face (*slang*), militant, pushing, pushy (*informal*), vigorous, zealous

▷ **Antonyms** friendly, mild, peaceful, quiet, retiring, submissive

aggressor assailant, assaulter, attacker, invader

aggrieved afflicted, distressed, disturbed, harmed, hurt, ill-used, injured, peeved (*informal*), saddened, unhappy, woeful, wronged

aghast afraid, amazed, appalled, astonished, astounded, awestruck, confounded, frightened, horrified, horror-struck, shocked, startled, stunned, thunderstruck

agile active, acute, alert, bright (*informal*), brisk, clever, limber, lissom(e), lithe, lively, nimble, prompt, quick, quick-witted, sharp, sprightly, spry, supple, swift

▷ **Antonyms** awkward, clumsy, heavy, lumbering, ponderous, slow, slow-moving, stiff, ungainly, unsupple

agility activity, acuteness, alertness, briskness, cleverness, litheness, liveliness, nimbleness, promptitude, promptness, quickness, quick-wittedness, sharpness, sprightliness, spryness, suppleness, swiftness

agitate 1. beat, churn, convulse, disturb, rock, rouse, shake, stir, toss 2. alarm, arouse, confuse, disconcert, disquiet, distract, disturb, excite, faze, ferment, fluster, incite, inflame, perturb, rouse, ruffle, stimulate, trouble, unnerve, upset, work up, worry 3. argue, debate, discuss, dispute, examine, ventilate
▷ **Antonyms** (*sense 2*) appease, assuage, calm, calm down, mollify, pacify, placate, quiet, quieten, soothe, still, tranquillize

agitation 1. churning, convulsion, disturbance, rocking, shake, shaking, stir, stirring, tossing, turbulence, upheaval 2. alarm, arousal, clamour, commotion, confusion, discomposure, disquiet, distraction, disturbance, excitement, ferment, flurry, fluster, incitement, lather (*informal*), outcry, stimulation, tizzy, tizz *or* tiz-woz (*informal*), trouble, tumult, turmoil, upheaval, upset, worry 3. argument, controversy, debate, discussion, disputation, dispute, ventilation

agitator agent provocateur, demagogue, firebrand, inciter, instigator, rabble-rouser, revolutionary, stirrer (*informal*), troublemaker

agog avid, curious, eager, enthralled, enthusiastic, excited, expectant, impatient, in suspense, keen
▷ **Antonyms** apathetic, incurious, indifferent, unconcerned, uninterested

agonize afflict, be in agony, be in anguish, distress, go through the mill, harrow, labour, pain, rack, strain, strive, struggle, suffer, torment, torture, worry, writhe

agony affliction, anguish, distress, misery, pain, pangs, suffering, throes, torment, torture, woe

agree 1. accede, acquiesce, admit, allow, assent, be of the same mind, comply, concede, concur, consent, engage, grant, permit, see eye to eye, settle, shake hands 2. accord, answer, chime, coincide, conform, correspond, fit, get on (together), harmonize, match, square, suit, tally
▷ **Antonyms** contradict, deny, differ, disagree, dispute, dissent, rebut, refute, retract

agreeable 1. acceptable, congenial, delightful, enjoyable, gratifying, likable *or* likeable, pleasant, pleasing, pleasurable, satisfying, to one's liking, to one's taste 2. appropriate, befitting, compatible, consistent, fitting, in keeping, proper, suitable 3. acquiescent, amenable, approving, complying, concurring, consenting, in accord, responsive, sympathetic, well-disposed, willing
▷ **Antonyms** (*sense 1*) disagreeable, displeasing, horrid, offensive, unlikable *or* unlikeable, unpleasant (*sense 2*) inappropriate, unacceptable, unfitting, unsuitable

agreement 1. accord, accordance, affinity, analogy, assent, compatibility, compliance, concert, concord, concurrence, conformity, congruity, consistency, correspondence, harmony, similarity, suitableness, union, unison 2. arrangement, bargain, compact, contract, covenant, deal (*informal*), pact, settlement, treaty, understanding
▷ **Antonyms** (*sense 1*) altercation, argument, clash, conflict, difference, discord, discrepancy, disparity, dispute, dissent, dissimilarity, diversity, division, falling-out, incompatibility, incongruity, quarrel, row, squabble, strife, tiff, wrangle

agriculture agronomics, agronomy, cultivation, culture, farming, husbandry, tillage

aground ashore, beached, foundered, grounded, high and dry, on the rocks, stranded, stuck

ahead along, at an advantage, at the head, before, forwards, in advance, in front, in the foreground, in the lead, in the vanguard, leading, on, onwards, to the fore, winning

aid *verb* 1. abet, assist, befriend, encourage, favour, give a leg up (*informal*), help, promote, relieve, second, serve, subsidize, succour, support, sustain *~noun* 2. assistance, benefit, encouragement, favour, help, promotion, relief, service, succour, support 3. abettor, adjutant, aide, aide-de-camp, assistant, helper, second, supporter
▷ **Antonyms** *~verb* detract from, harm, hinder, hurt, impede, obstruct, oppose, thwart *~noun* hindrance

ail 1. afflict, annoy, be the matter with, bother, distress, irritate, pain, sicken, trouble, upset, worry 2. be ill, be indisposed, be *or* feel off colour, be sick, be unwell, feel unwell

ailing debilitated, diseased, feeble, ill, indisposed, infirm, invalid, off colour, poorly, sick, sickly, suffering, under the weather (*informal*), unsound, unwell, weak

ailment affliction, complaint, disease, disorder, illness, infirmity, lurgi (*informal*), malady, sickness

aim 1. *verb* aspire, attempt, design, direct, draw a bead (on), endeavour, intend, level, mean, plan, point, propose, purpose, resolve, seek, set one's sights on, sight, strive, take aim (at), train, try, want, wish 2. *~noun* ambition, aspiration, course, design, desire, direction, end, goal, Holy Grail (*informal*), intent, intention, mark, object, objective, plan, purpose, scheme, target, wish

aimless chance, directionless, erratic, frivolous, goalless, haphazard, pointless, purposeless, random, stray, undirected, unguided, unpredictable, vagrant, way~ward

▷ **Antonyms** decided, deliberate, deter~mined, firm, fixed, positive, purposeful, resolute, resolved, settled, single-minded

air *noun* **1.** atmosphere, heavens, sky **2.** blast, breath, breeze, draught, puff, waft, whiff, wind, zephyr **3.** ambience, appearance, atmosphere, aura, bearing, character, demeanour, effect, feeling, flavour, impression, look, manner, mood, quality, style, tone, vibes (*slang*) **4.** circulation, display, dissemination, exposure, expression, publicity, ut~terance, vent, ventilation **5.** aria, lay, melody, song, tune *~verb* **6.** aerate, ex~pose, freshen, ventilate **7.** circulate, communicate, declare, disclose, display, disseminate, divulge, exhibit, expose, express, give vent to, make known, make public, proclaim, publicize, reveal, take the wraps off, tell, utter, ventilate, voice

airily 1. animatedly, blithely, breezily, buoyantly, gaily, happily, high-spiritedly, jauntily, light-heartedly **2.** daintily, delicately, ethereally, grace~fully, lightly

airiness 1. breeziness, draughtiness, freshness, gustiness, lightness, open~ness, windiness **2.** ethereality, imma~teriality, incorporeality, insubstantial~ity, lightness, weightlessness **3.** anima~tion, blitheness, breeziness, buoyancy, gaiety, happiness, high spirits, jaunti~ness, light-heartedness, lightness of heart

airing 1. aeration, drying, freshening, ventilation **2.** excursion, jaunt, outing, promenade, stroll, walk **3.** circulation, display, dissemination, exposure, ex~pression, publicity, utterance, vent, ventilation

airless breathless, close, heavy, muggy, oppressive, stale, stifling, stuffy, suffo~cating, sultry, unventilated

▷ **Antonyms** airy, blowy, breezy, draughty, fresh, gusty, light, open, spa~cious, well-ventilated

airs affectation, affectedness, arrogance, haughtiness, hauteur, pomposity, pre~tensions, superciliousness, swank (*in~formal*)

airy 1. blowy, breezy, draughty, fresh, gusty, light, lofty, open, spacious, un~cluttered, well-ventilated, windy **2.** aer~ial, delicate, ethereal, fanciful, flimsy, illusory, imaginary, immaterial, incor~poreal, insubstantial, light, vaporous, visionary, weightless, wispy **3.** animat~ed, blithe, buoyant, cheerful, cheery, chirpy (*informal*), debonair, frolicsome, gay, genial, graceful, happy, high-spirited, jaunty, light, light-hearted, lively, merry, nonchalant, sprightly, upbeat (*informal*)

▷ **Antonyms** (*sense 1*) airless, close, heavy, muggy, oppressive, stale, stifling, stuffy, suffocating, unventilated (*sense 2*) concrete, corporeal, material, real, realistic, substantial, tangible (*sense 3*) cheerless, dismal, gloomy, glum, melan~choly, miserable, morose, sad

aisle alley, corridor, gangway, lane, pas~sage, passageway, path

ajar agape, gaping, open, partly open, unclosed

akin affiliated, alike, allied, analogous, cognate, comparable, congenial, con~nected, consanguineous, corresponding, kin, kindred, like, of a piece, parallel, related, similar

alacrity alertness, avidity, briskness, cheerfulness, dispatch, eagerness, en~thusiasm, gaiety, hilarity, joyousness, liveliness, promptness, quickness, readiness, speed, sprightliness, willing~ness, zeal

▷ **Antonyms** apathy, dullness, inertia, lethargy, reluctance, slowness, slug~gishness, unconcern, unwillingness

à la mode all the go (*informal*), all the rage (*informal*), chic, fashionable, in (*informal*), in fashion, in vogue, latest, modish, popular, stylish, the latest rage (*informal*), with it (*informal*)

alarm *verb* **1.** daunt, dismay, distress, frighten, give (someone) a turn (*infor~mal*), make (someone's) hair stand on end, panic, put the wind up (someone) (*informal*), scare, startle, terrify, un~nerve **2.** alert, arouse, signal, warn *~noun* **3.** anxiety, apprehension, con~sternation, dismay, distress, fear, fright, nervousness, panic, scare, terror, trepi~dation, unease, uneasiness **4.** alarm-bell, alert, bell, danger signal, distress signal, hooter, siren, tocsin, warning **5.** *archaic* call to arms, summons to arms

▷ **Antonyms** *~verb* (*sense 1*) assure, calm, comfort, reassure, relieve, soothe *~noun* (*sense 3*) calm, calmness, composure, sang-froid, serenity

alarming daunting, dismaying, distress~ing, disturbing, dreadful, frightening, scaring, shocking, startling, terrifying, unnerving

albeit although, even if, even though, notwithstanding that, tho' (*U.S. or po~etic*), though

alcoholic 1. *adjective* brewed, distilled, fermented, hard, inebriant, inebriating, intoxicating, spirituous, strong, vinous **2.** *~noun* bibber, boozer (*informal*), dip~somaniac, drunk, drunkard, hard drinker, inebriate, soak (*slang*), sot, sponge (*informal*), tippler, toper, tosspot (*informal*), wino (*informal*)

alcove bay, bower, compartment, corner, cubbyhole, cubicle, niche, nook, recess

alert 1. *adjective* active, agile, attentive, awake, bright-eyed and bushy-tailed (*informal*), brisk, careful, circumspect, heedful, keeping a weather eye on, lively, nimble, observant, on guard, on one's toes, on the ball (*informal*), on the lookout, on the watch, perceptive, quick, ready, spirited, sprightly, vigilant, wary, watchful, wide-awake **2.** *~noun* alarm, signal, siren, warning **3.** *~verb* alarm, forewarn, inform, notify, signal, warn

▷ **Antonyms** *~adjective* careless, heedless, inactive, languid, lethargic, listless, oblivious, slow, unaware, unconcerned, unwary *~noun* all clear *~verb* lull

alertness activeness, agility, attentiveness, briskness, carefulness, circumspection, heedfulness, liveliness, nimbleness, perceptiveness, promptitude, quickness, readiness, spiritedness, sprightliness, vigilance, wariness, watchfulness

alias 1. *adverb* also called, also known as, otherwise, otherwise known as **2.** *~noun* assumed name, *nom de guerre,* nom de plume, pen name, pseudonym, stage name

alibi defence, excuse, explanation, justification, plea, pretext, reason

alien 1. *adjective* adverse, beyond one's ken, conflicting, contrary, estranged, exotic, foreign, inappropriate, incompatible, incongruous, not native, not naturalized, opposed, outlandish, remote, repugnant, separated, strange, unfamiliar **2.** *~noun* foreigner, newcomer, outsider, stranger

▷ **Antonyms** *~adjective* affiliated, akin, alike, allied, analogous, cognate, connected, corresponding, kindred, like, parallel, related, similar *~noun* citizen, countryman, dweller, inhabitant, national, resident

alienate 1. break off, disaffect, divert, divorce, estrange, make unfriendly, separate, set against, turn away, withdraw **2.** *Law* abalienate, convey, transfer

alienation 1. breaking off, disaffection, diversion, divorce, estrangement, indifference, remoteness, rupture, separation, setting against, turning away, withdrawal **2.** *Law* abalienation, conveyance, transfer

alight[1] *verb* come down, come to rest, descend, disembark, dismount, get down, get off, land, light, perch, settle, touch down

▷ **Antonyms** ascend, climb, float up, fly up, go up, lift off, mount, move up, rise, scale, soar, take off

alight[2] *adjective* **1.** ablaze, aflame, blazing, burning, fiery, flaming, flaring, ignited, lighted, lit, on fire **2.** bright, brilliant, illuminated, lit up, shining

align 1. arrange in line, coordinate, even, even up, line up, make parallel, order, range, regulate, sequence, straighten **2.** affiliate, agree, ally, associate, cooperate, join, side, sympathize

alignment 1. adjustment, arrangement, coordination, evening, evening up, line, lining up, order, ranging, regulating, sequence, straightening up **2.** affiliation, agreement, alliance, association, cooperation, sympathy, union

alike 1. *adjective* akin, analogous, corresponding, cut from the same cloth, duplicate, equal, equivalent, even, identical, like two peas in a pod, of a piece, parallel, resembling, similar, the same, uniform **2.** *~adverb* analogously, correspondingly, equally, evenly, identically, similarly, uniformly

▷ **Antonyms** *~adjective* different, dissimilar, diverse, separate, unlike *~adverb* differently, distinctly, unequally

aliment fare, feed, fodder, food, meat, nourishment, nutriment, nutrition, provender, sustenance, tack (*informal*), vittles (*obsolete or dialect*)

alimentary beneficial, nourishing, nutritional, nutritious, nutritive, sustaining, wholesome

alive 1. animate, breathing, having life, in the land of the living (*informal*), living, subsisting **2.** active, existent, existing, extant, functioning, in existence, in force, operative, unquenched **3.** active, alert, animated, awake, brisk, cheerful, chirpy (*informal*), eager, energetic, full of beans (*informal*), full of life, lively, quick, spirited, sprightly, spry, vigorous, vital, vivacious, zestful

▷ **Antonyms** (*sense 1*) dead, deceased, departed, expired, extinct, gone, inanimate, lifeless (*sense 2*) extinct, inactive, inoperative, lost (*sense 3*) apathetic, dull, inactive, lifeless, spiritless

alive to alert to, awake to, aware of, cognizant of, eager for, sensible of, sensitive to, susceptible to

alive with abounding in, bristling with, bustling with, buzzing with, crawling with, hopping with, infested with, jumping with, lousy with (*slang*), overrun by, packed with, swarming with, teeming with, thronged with

all *adjective* **1.** every bit of, the complete, the entire, the sum of, the totality of, the total of, the whole of **2.** each, each and every, every, every one of, every single **3.** complete, entire, full, greatest, perfect, total, utter *~noun* **4.** aggregate, entirety, everything, sum, sum total, total, total amount, totality, utmost, whole, whole amount *~adverb* **5.** altogether, completely, entirely, fully, totally, utterly, wholly

allay alleviate, appease, assuage, blunt, calm, check, compose, diminish, dull, ease, lessen, mitigate, moderate, mollify, pacify, pour oil on troubled waters, quell, quiet, reduce, relax, relieve, smooth, soften, soothe, subdue

allegation accusation, affirmation, assertion, asseveration, averment, avowal, charge, claim, declaration, deposition, plea, profession, statement

allege advance, affirm, assert, asseverate, aver, avow, charge, claim, declare, depose, maintain, plead, profess, put forward, state

▷ **Antonyms** abjure, contradict, deny, disagree with, disavow, disclaim, gainsay (*archaic or literary*), oppose, refute, renounce, repudiate

alleged **1.** affirmed, asserted, averred, declared, described, designated, stated **2.** doubtful, dubious, ostensible, professed, purported, so-called, supposed, suspect, suspicious

allegiance adherence, constancy, devotion, duty, faithfulness, fealty, fidelity, homage, loyalty, obedience, obligation, troth (*archaic*)

▷ **Antonyms** disloyalty, faithlessness, falseness, inconstancy, infidelity, perfidy, treachery, treason, unfaithfulness

allegorical emblematic, figurative, parabolic, symbolic, symbolizing

allegory apologue, emblem, fable, myth, parable, story, symbol, symbolism, tale

allergic **1.** affected by, hypersensitive, sensitive, sensitized, susceptible **2.** *informal* antipathetic, averse, disinclined, hostile, loath, opposed

allergy **1.** antipathy, hypersensitivity, sensitivity, susceptibility **2.** *informal* antipathy, aversion, disinclination, dislike, hostility, loathing, opposition

alleviate abate, allay, assuage, blunt, check, diminish, dull, ease, lessen, lighten, mitigate, moderate, mollify, palliate, quell, quench, quiet, reduce, relieve, slacken, slake, smooth, soften, soothe, subdue

alleviation diminution, dulling, easing, lessening, lightening, mitigation, moderation, palliation, quelling, quenching, reduction, relief, slackening, slaking

alley alleyway, backstreet, lane, passage, passageway, pathway, walk

alliance affiliation, affinity, agreement, association, coalition, combination, compact, concordat, confederacy, confederation, connection, federation, league, marriage, pact, partnership, treaty, union

▷ **Antonyms** alienation, breach, break, disaffection, dissociation, disunion, disunity, division, rupture, separation, severance, split, split-up

allied affiliated, amalgamated, associated, bound, combined, confederate, connected, hand in glove (*informal*), in cahoots (*U.S. informal*), in league, joined, joint, kindred, leagued, linked, married, related, unified, united, wed

allocate allot, apportion, appropriate, assign, budget, designate, earmark, mete, set aside, share out

allocation allotment, allowance, apportionment, appropriation, grant, lot, measure, portion, quota, ration, share, stint, stipend

allot allocate, apportion, appropriate, assign, budget, designate, earmark, mete, set aside, share out

allotment **1.** allocation, allowance, apportionment, appropriation, grant, lot, measure, portion, quota, ration, share, stint, stipend **2.** kitchen garden, patch, plot, tract

all-out complete, determined, exhaustive, full, full-on (*informal*), full-scale, maximum, optimum, outright, resolute, supreme, thorough, thoroughgoing, total, undivided, unlimited, unremitting, unrestrained, unstinted, utmost

▷ **Antonyms** careless, cursory, half-hearted, negligent, off-hand, perfunctory, unenthusiastic

allow **1.** acknowledge, acquiesce, admit, concede, confess, grant, own **2.** approve, authorize, bear, brook, enable, endure, give leave, let, permit, put up with (*informal*), sanction, stand, suffer, tolerate **3.** allocate, allot, assign, deduct, give, grant, provide, remit, spare

▷ **Antonyms** (*sense 1*) contradict, deny, disagree with, gainsay (*archaic or literary*), oppose (*sense 2*) ban, disallow, forbid, prohibit, proscribe, refuse (*sense 3*) deny, forbid, refuse

allowable acceptable, admissible, all right, appropriate, approved, permissible, sanctionable, sufferable, suitable, tolerable

allowance **1.** allocation, allotment, amount, annuity, apportionment, grant, lot, measure, pension, portion, quota, ration, remittance, share, stint, stipend, subsidy **2.** admission, concession, sanction, sufferance, toleration **3.** concession, deduction, discount, rebate, reduction

allow for arrange for, consider, foresee, keep in mind, make allowances for, make concessions for, make provision for, plan for, provide for, set (something) aside for, take into account, take into consideration

alloy *noun* **1.** admixture, amalgam, blend, combination, composite, compound, hybrid, meld, mixture *~verb* **2.** admix, amalgamate, blend, combine, compound, fuse, meld, mix **3.** adulterate, debase, devalue, diminish, impair

all right *adjective* **1.** acceptable, adequate, average, fair, O.K. *or* okay (*informal*), passable, satisfactory, so-so (*informal*), standard, unobjectionable, up to scratch (*informal*) **2.** hale, healthy, out of the woods, safe, sound, unharmed, unimpaired, uninjured, well, whole *~adverb* **3.** acceptably, adequately, O.K. *or* okay (*informal*), passably, satisfactorily, unobjectionably, well enough

▷ **Antonyms** *~adjective* (*sense 1*) bad, inadequate, not good enough, not up to scratch (*informal*), objectionable, poor, unacceptable, unsatisfactory (*sense 2*) ailing, bad, ill, injured, off colour, out of sorts, poorly, sick, sickly, unhealthy, unwell

allude advert, glance, hint, imply, insinuate, intimate, mention, refer, remark, speak of, suggest, tip the wink, touch upon

allure 1. *verb* attract, beguile, cajole, captivate, charm, coax, decoy, enchant, entice, inveigle, lead on, lure, persuade, seduce, tempt, win over **2.** *~noun* appeal, attraction, charm, enchantment, enticement, glamour, lure, persuasion, seductiveness, temptation

alluring attractive, beguiling, bewitching, captivating, come-hither, enchanting, fascinating, fetching, glamorous, intriguing, seductive, sexy, tempting

▷ **Antonyms** abhorrent, off-putting (*Brit. informal*), repellent, repugnant, repulsive, unattractive

allusion casual remark, glance, hint, implication, indirect reference, innuendo, insinuation, intimation, mention, suggestion

ally 1. *noun* abettor, accessory, accomplice, associate, coadjutor, collaborator, colleague, confederate, co-worker, friend, helper, partner **2.** *~verb* affiliate, associate, band together, collaborate, combine, confederate, connect, join, join battle with, join forces, league, marry, unify, unite

▷ **Antonyms** *~noun* adversary, antagonist, competitor, enemy, foe, opponent, rival *~verb* alienate, disaffect, disunite, divide, drive apart, separate, set at odds

almighty 1. absolute, all-powerful, invincible, omnipotent, supreme, unlimited **2.** *informal* awful, desperate, enormous, excessive, great, intense, loud, severe, terrible

▷ **Antonyms** (*sense 1*) helpless, impotent, powerless, weak (*sense 2*) feeble, insignificant, paltry, poor, slight, tame, weak

almost about, all but, approximately, as good as, close to, just about, nearly, not far from, not quite, on the brink of, practically, so near (and) yet so far, virtually, well-nigh

alms benefaction, bounty, charity, donation, gift, relief

aloft above, heavenward, higher, high up, in the air, in the sky, on high, overhead, skyward, up, up above, upward

alone 1. abandoned, apart, by itself, by oneself, deserted, desolate, detached, forlorn, forsaken, isolated, lonely, lonesome, only, on one's tod (*slang*), out on a limb, separate, single, single-handed, sole, solitary, unaccompanied, unaided, unassisted, unattended, uncombined, unconnected, under one's own steam, unescorted **2.** incomparable, matchless, peerless, singular, unequalled, unique, unparalleled, unsurpassed

▷ **Antonyms** (*sense 1*) accompanied, aided, among others, assisted, escorted, helped, jointly, together (*sense 2*) equalled, surpassed

aloof 1. chilly, cold, cool, detached, distant, forbidding, formal, haughty, indifferent, remote, reserved, standoffish, supercilious, unapproachable, unfriendly, uninterested, unresponsive, unsociable, unsympathetic **2.** above, apart, at a distance, at arm's length, away, distanced, distant

▷ **Antonyms** (*sense 1*) friendly, gregarious, neighbourly, open, sociable, sympathetic, warm

aloud 1. audibly, clearly, distinctly, intelligibly, out loud, plainly **2.** clamorously, loudly, noisily, vociferously

already as of now, at present, before now, by now, by that time, by then, by this time, even now, heretofore, just now, previously

also additionally, along with, and, as well, as well as, besides, further, furthermore, in addition, including, into the bargain, moreover, on top of that, plus, to boot, too

alter adapt, adjust, amend, change, convert, diversify, metamorphose, modify, recast, reform, remodel, reshape, revise, shift, transform, transmute, turn, tweak (*informal*), vary

alteration adaptation, adjustment, amendment, change, conversion, difference, diversification, metamorphosis, modification, reformation, remodelling, reshaping, revision, shift, transformation, transmutation, variance, variation

altercate argue, be at sixes and sevens, bicker, clash, contend, controvert, cross swords, disagree, dispute, dissent, fall out (*informal*), quarrel, row, squabble, wrangle

altercation argument, bickering, clash, contention, controversy, disagreement, discord, dispute, dissension, quarrel, row, squabble, wrangle

alternate *verb* **1.** act reciprocally, alter, change, fluctuate, follow in turn, follow one another, interchange, intersperse, oscillate, rotate, substitute, take turns, vary *~adjective* **2.** alternating, every other, every second, interchanging, rotating **3.** alternative, another, different, second, substitute

alternative 1. *noun* choice, option, other (*of two*), preference, recourse, selection, substitute **2.** *~adjective* alternate, an~

other, different, other, second, substitute

alternatively as an alternative, by way of alternative, if not, instead, on the other hand, or, otherwise

although albeit, despite the fact that, even if, even supposing, even though, notwithstanding, tho' (*U.S. or poetic*), though, while

altitude elevation, height, loftiness, peak, summit

altogether **1.** absolutely, completely, every inch, fully, lock, stock and barrel, perfectly, quite, thoroughly, totally, utterly, wholly **2.** all in all, all things considered, as a whole, collectively, generally, in general, *in toto,* on the whole **3.** all told, everything included, in all, in sum, *in toto,* taken together

▷ **Antonyms** (*sense 1*) halfway, incompletely, in part, in some measure, not fully, partially, relatively, slightly, somewhat, to a certain degree *or* extent, up to a certain point

altruistic benevolent, charitable, considerate, generous, humanitarian, philanthropic, public-spirited, self-sacrificing, unselfish

▷ **Antonyms** egoistic, egoistical, egotistic, egotistical, greedy, looking out for number one (*informal*), mean, self-centred, self-interested, selfish, self-seeking, ungenerous

always aye (*Scot.*), consistently, constantly, continually, eternally, ever, everlastingly, evermore, every time, forever, *in perpetuum,* invariably, perpetually, repeatedly, unceasingly, without exception

▷ **Antonyms** hardly, hardly ever, infrequently, once in a blue moon, once in a while, only now and then, on rare occasions, rarely, scarcely ever, seldom

amalgam admixture, alloy, amalgamation, blend, combination, composite, compound, fusion, meld, mixture, union

amalgamate alloy, ally, blend, coalesce, combine, commingle, compound, fuse, incorporate, integrate, intermix, meld, merge, mingle, unite

▷ **Antonyms** disunite, divide, part, separate, split, split up

amalgamation admixture, alliance, alloy, amalgam, amalgamating, blend, coalition, combination, commingling, composite, compound, fusion, incorporation, integration, joining, meld, merger, mingling, mixing, mixture, union

amass accumulate, aggregate, assemble, collect, compile, garner, gather, heap up, hoard, pile up, rake up, scrape together

amateur dabbler, dilettante, layman, nonprofessional

amateurish amateur, bungling, clumsy, crude, inexpert, unaccomplished, unprofessional, unskilful

▷ **Antonyms** experienced, expert, practised, professional, skilled

amatory amorous, aphrodisiac, erotic, lascivious, libidinous, passionate, romantic, sensual, sexual, sexy, steamy (*informal*)

amaze alarm, astonish, astound, bewilder, boggle the mind, bowl over (*informal*), confound, daze, dumbfound, electrify, flabbergast, shock, stagger, startle, stun, stupefy, surprise

amazement admiration, astonishment, bewilderment, confusion, marvel, perplexity, shock, stupefaction, surprise, wonder

ambassador agent, consul, deputy, diplomat, emissary, envoy, legate, minister, plenipotentiary, representative

ambience air, atmosphere, aura, character, complexion, feel, flavour, impression, milieu, mood, quality, setting, spirit, surroundings, temper, tenor, tone, vibes (*slang*), vibrations (*slang*)

ambiguity doubt, doubtfulness, dubiety, dubiousness, enigma, equivocacy, equivocality, equivocation, inconclusiveness, indefiniteness, indeterminateness, obscurity, puzzle, tergiversation, uncertainty, unclearness, vagueness

ambiguous clear as mud (*informal*), cryptic, Delphic, doubtful, dubious, enigmatic, enigmatical, equivocal, inconclusive, indefinite, indeterminate, obscure, oracular, puzzling, uncertain, unclear, vague

▷ **Antonyms** clear, definite, explicit, obvious, plain, simple, specific, unequivocal, unmistakable, unquestionable

ambition **1.** aspiration, avidity, desire, drive, eagerness, enterprise, get-up-and-go (*informal*), hankering, longing, striving, yearning, zeal **2.** aim, aspiration, desire, dream, end, goal, Holy Grail (*informal*), hope, intent, objective, purpose, wish

ambitious **1.** aspiring, avid, desirous, driving, eager, enterprising, hopeful, intent, purposeful, striving, zealous **2.** arduous, bold, challenging, demanding, difficult, elaborate, energetic, exacting, formidable, grandiose, hard, impressive, industrious, pretentious, severe, strenuous

▷ **Antonyms** (*sense 1*) apathetic, good-for-nothing, lazy, unambitious, unaspiring (*sense 2*) easy, modest, simple, unambitious

ambivalence clash, conflict, contradiction, doubt, equivocation, fluctuation, hesitancy, indecision, irresolution, opposition, uncertainty, vacillation, wavering

ambivalent clashing, conflicting, contradictory, debatable, doubtful, equivocal, fluctuating, hesitant, inconclusive, in two minds, irresolute, mixed, opposed,

uncertain, undecided, unresolved, unsure, vacillating, warring, wavering
▷ **Antonyms** certain, clear, conclusive, convinced, decided, definite, free from doubt, positive, sure, unwavering

amble dawdle, meander, mosey (*informal*), ramble, saunter, stroll, walk, wander

ambush **1.** *noun* ambuscade, concealment, cover, hiding, hiding place, lying in wait, retreat, shelter, trap, waylaying **2.** *~verb* ambuscade, bushwhack (*U.S.*), ensnare, surprise, trap, waylay

ameliorate advance, allay, alleviate, amend, assuage, benefit, better, ease, elevate, improve, meliorate, mend, mitigate, promote, raise, reform, relieve

amenable **1.** able to be influenced, acquiescent, agreeable, open, persuadable, responsive, susceptible, tractable **2.** accountable, answerable, chargeable, liable, responsible
▷ **Antonyms** (*sense 1*) inflexible, intractable, mulish, obdurate, obstinate, pigheaded, recalcitrant, stiff-necked, stubborn, unbending, unyielding

amend alter, ameliorate, better, change, correct, enhance, fix, improve, mend, modify, rectify, reform, remedy, repair, revise, tweak (*informal*)

amendment **1.** alteration, amelioration, betterment, change, correction, emendation, enhancement, improvement, mending, modification, rectification, reform, remedy, repair, revision **2.** addendum, addition, adjunct, alteration, attachment, clarification

amends apology, atonement, compensation, expiation, indemnity, recompense, redress, reparation, requital, restitution, restoration, satisfaction

amenity **1.** advantage, comfort, convenience, facility, service **2.** affability, agreeableness, amiability, complaisance, courtesy, mildness, pleasantness (*of situation*), politeness, refinement, suavity
▷ **Antonyms** (*sense 2*) bad manners, discourtesy, impoliteness, incivility, rudeness, ungraciousness

amiability affability, agreeableness, amiableness, attractiveness, benignity, charm, cheerfulness, delightfulness, engagingness, friendliness, friendship, geniality, good humour, good nature, kindliness, kindness, lovableness, pleasantness, pleasingness, sociability, sweetness, sweetness and light (*informal*), sweet temper, winsomeness

amiable affable, agreeable, attractive, benign, charming, cheerful, congenial, delightful, engaging, friendly, genial, good-humoured, good-natured, kind, kindly, likable *or* likeable, lovable, obliging, pleasant, pleasing, sociable, sweet-tempered, winning, winsome
▷ **Antonyms** disagreeable, displeasing, hostile, ill-natured, loathsome, repellent, sour, unfriendly, unpleasant

amicability amiability, amicableness, amity, brotherliness, civility, cordiality, courtesy, fraternity, friendliness, friendship, goodwill, harmony, kindliness, kindness, neighbourliness, peace, peaceableness, peacefulness, politeness, sociability

amicable amiable, brotherly, civil, cordial, courteous, fraternal, friendly, good-humoured, harmonious, kind, kindly, neighbourly, peaceable, peaceful, polite, sociable
▷ **Antonyms** antagonistic, bellicose, belligerent, disagreeable, hostile, ill-disposed, impolite, inimical, pugnacious, quarrelsome, uncivil, unfriendly, unkind, unsociable

amid amidst, among, amongst, in the middle of, in the midst of, in the thick of, surrounded by

amiss **1.** *adjective* awry, confused, defective, erroneous, fallacious, false, faulty, improper, inaccurate, inappropriate, incorrect, mistaken, out of order, unsuitable, untoward, wrong **2.** *~adverb* as an insult, as offensive, erroneously, faultily, improperly, inappropriately, incorrectly, mistakenly, out of turn, unsuitably, wrongly
▷ **Antonyms** *~adjective* accurate, appropriate, correct, in order, O.K. *or* okay (*informal*), perfect, proper, right, suitable, true *~adverb* appropriately, correctly, properly, rightly, suitably, well

amity accord, amicability, brotherhood, comity, comradeship, concord, cordiality, fellowship, fraternity, friendliness, friendship, goodwill, harmony, kindliness, peace, peacefulness, tranquillity, understanding

ammunition armaments, cartridges, explosives, materiel, munitions, powder, rounds, shells, shot, shot and shell

amnesty absolution, condonation, dispensation, forgiveness, general pardon, immunity, oblivion, remission (*of penalty*), reprieve

amok *see* AMUCK

among, amongst **1.** amid, amidst, in association with, in the middle of, in the midst of, in the thick of, midst, surrounded by, together with, with **2.** between, to each of **3.** in the class of, in the company of, in the group of, in the number of, out of **4.** by all of, by the joint action of, by the whole of, mutually, with one another

amorous affectionate, amatory, ardent, attached, doting, enamoured, erotic, fond, impassioned, in love, lovesick, loving, lustful, passionate, tender
▷ **Antonyms** aloof, cold, distant, frigid, frosty, indifferent, passionless, stand-offish, undemonstrative, unfeeling, unloving

amorphous characterless, formless, inchoate, indeterminate, irregular, nebulous, nondescript, shapeless, unformed, unshaped, unshapen, unstructured, vague
▷ **Antonyms** definite, distinct, regular, shaped, structured

amount **1.** bulk, expanse, extent, lot, magnitude, mass, measure, number, quantity, supply, volume **2.** addition, aggregate, entirety, extent, lot, sum, sum total, total, whole **3.** full effect, full value, import, result, significance

amount to add up to, aggregate, become, come to, develop into, equal, grow, mean, purport, total

amour affair, *affaire de coeur,* intrigue, liaison, love affair, relationship, romance

ample abounding, abundant, big, bountiful, broad, capacious, commodious, copious, enough and to spare, expansive, extensive, full, generous, great, large, lavish, liberal, plenteous, plentiful, plenty, profuse, rich, roomy, spacious, substantial, two a penny, unrestricted, voluminous, wide
▷ **Antonyms** inadequate, insufficient, little, meagre, restricted, scant, skimpy, small, sparse, unsatisfactory

amplification augmentation, boosting, deepening, development, dilation, elaboration, enlargement, expansion, expatiation, extension, fleshing out, heightening, increase, intensification, lengthening, magnification, raising, rounding out, strengthening, stretching, supplementing, widening

amplify augment, boost, deepen, develop, dilate, elaborate, enlarge, expand, expatiate, extend, flesh out, go into detail, heighten, increase, intensify, lengthen, magnify, raise, round out, strengthen, stretch, supplement, widen
▷ **Antonyms** abbreviate, abridge, boil down, condense, curtail, cut down, decrease, reduce, simplify

amplitude **1.** bigness, breadth, bulk, capaciousness, compass, dimension, expanse, extent, greatness, hugeness, largeness, magnitude, mass, range, reach, scope, size, spaciousness, sweep, vastness, width **2.** abundance, ampleness, completeness, copiousness, fullness, plenitude, plethora, profusion, richness

amply abundantly, bountifully, capaciously, completely, copiously, extensively, fully, generously, greatly, lavishly, liberally, plenteously, plentifully, profusely, richly, substantially, thoroughly, unstintingly, well, with a blank cheque, with a free hand, without stinting
▷ **Antonyms** inadequately, insufficiently, meagrely, poorly, scantily, skimpily, sparsely, thinly

amputate curtail, cut off, lop, remove, separate, sever, truncate

amuck, amok berserk, destructively, ferociously, frenziedly, in a frenzy, insanely, madly, maniacally, murderously, savagely, uncontrollably, violently, wildly

amulet charm, fetish, juju, periapt (*rare*), talisman

amuse beguile, charm, cheer, delight, divert, enliven, entertain, gladden, gratify, interest, occupy, please, recreate, regale, tickle
▷ **Antonyms** be tedious, bore, jade, pall on, send to sleep, tire, weary

amusement **1.** beguilement, cheer, delight, diversion, enjoyment, entertainment, fun, gladdening, gratification, hilarity, interest, jollies (*slang*), laughter, merriment, mirth, pleasing, pleasure, recreation, regalement, sport **2.** distraction, diversion, entertainment, game, hobby, joke, lark, pastime, prank, recreation, sport
▷ **Antonyms** boredom, displeasure, monotony, sadness, tedium

amusing charming, cheerful, cheering, comical, delightful, diverting, droll, enjoyable, entertaining, facetious, funny, gladdening, gratifying, humorous, interesting, jocular, laughable, lively, merry, pleasant, pleasing, rib-tickling, waggish, witty
▷ **Antonyms** boring, dead, dull, flat, humdrum, monotonous, stale, tedious, tiresome, unamusing, unexciting, unfunny, uninteresting, wearisome

anaemic ashen, bloodless, characterless, colourless, dull, enervated, feeble, frail, infirm, like death warmed up (*informal*), pale, pallid, sickly, wan, weak
▷ **Antonyms** blooming, florid, full-blooded, glowing, hearty, radiant, rosy, rosy-cheeked, rubicund, ruddy, sanguine

anaesthetic **1.** *noun* analgesic, anodyne, narcotic, opiate, painkiller, sedative, soporific, stupefacient, stupefactive **2.** *~adjective* analgesic, anodyne, deadening, dulling, narcotic, numbing, opiate, pain-killing, sedative, sleep-inducing, soporific, stupefacient, stupefactive

analogous agreeing, akin, alike, comparable, corresponding, equivalent, homologous, like, of a piece, parallel, related, resembling, similar
▷ **Antonyms** contrasting, different, discrepant, disparate, dissimilar, diverse, unlike

analogy agreement, comparison, correlation, correspondence, equivalence, homology, likeness, parallel, relation, resemblance, similarity, similitude

analyse **1.** assay, estimate, evaluate, examine, interpret, investigate, judge, research, test, work over **2.** anatomize, break down, consider, dissect, dissolve, divide, resolve, separate, study, think through

analysis 1. anatomization, anatomy, assay, breakdown, dissection, dissolution, division, enquiry, examination, investigation, perusal, resolution, scrutiny, separation, sifting, test **2.** estimation, evaluation, finding, interpretation, judgment, opinion, reasoning, study

analytic, analytical detailed, diagnostic, discrete, dissecting, explanatory, expository, inquiring, inquisitive, interpretative, interpretive, investigative, logical, organized, problem-solving, questioning, rational, searching, studious, systematic, testing

anarchic chaotic, confused, disordered, disorganized, lawless, misgoverned, misruled, off the rails, rebellious, revolutionary, rioting, riotous, ungoverned

▷ **Antonyms** controlled, decorous, disciplined, law-abiding, ordered, peaceable, peaceful, quiet, restrained, well-behaved

anarchist insurgent, nihilist, rebel, revolutionary, terrorist

anarchy chaos, confusion, disorder, disorganization, lawlessness, misgovernment, misrule, rebellion, revolution, riot

▷ **Antonyms** control, discipline, government, law, law and order, order, peace, rule

anathema 1. ban, condemnation, curse, damnation, denunciation, excommunication, execration, imprecation, malediction, proscription, taboo **2.** abomination, bane, bête noire, bugbear, enemy, pariah

anathematize abominate, ban, condemn, curse, damn, denounce, excommunicate, execrate, imprecate, proscribe

anatomize analyse, break down, dissect, dissolve, divide, examine, resolve, scrutinize, separate, study

anatomy 1. analysis, dismemberment, dissection, division, enquiry, examination, investigation, study **2.** build, composition, frame, framework, make-up, structure

ancestor forebear, forefather, forerunner, precursor, predecessor, progenitor

▷ **Antonyms** descendant, inheritor, issue, offspring, progeny, successor

ancestry ancestors, antecedents, blood, derivation, descent, extraction, family, forebears, forefathers, genealogy, house, line, lineage, origin, parentage, pedigree, progenitors, race, stock

anchorite eremite, hermit, recluse

ancient aged, age-old, antediluvian, antiquated, antique, archaic, bygone, early, hoary, obsolete, old, old as the hills, olden, old-fashioned, outmoded, out-of-date, primeval, primordial, superannuated, timeworn

▷ **Antonyms** current, fresh, in vogue, late, modern, modish, new, newfangled, new-fashioned, novel, recent, state-of-the-art, up-to-date, with it (*informal*), young

ancillary accessory, additional, auxiliary, contributory, extra, secondary, subordinate, subsidiary, supplementary

▷ **Antonyms** cardinal, chief, main, major, premier, primary, prime, principal

and along with, also, as well as, furthermore, in addition to, including, moreover, plus, together with

androgynous androgyne, bisexual, epicene, hermaphrodite, hermaphroditic

anecdote reminiscence, short story, sketch, story, tale, urban legend, yarn

anew afresh, again, another time, from scratch, from the beginning, once again, once more, over again

angel 1. archangel, cherub, divine messenger, guardian spirit, seraph, spiritual being **2.** *informal* beauty, darling, dear, dream, gem, ideal, jewel, paragon, saint, treasure

angelic 1. celestial, cherubic, ethereal, heavenly, seraphic **2.** adorable, beatific, beautiful, entrancing, innocent, lovely, pure, saintly, virtuous

▷ **Antonyms** (*sense 1*) demonic, devilish, diabolic, diabolical, fiendish, hellish, infernal, satanic

anger 1. *noun* annoyance, antagonism, choler, displeasure, exasperation, fury, ill humour, ill temper, indignation, ire, irritability, irritation, outrage, passion, pique, rage, resentment, seeing red, spleen, temper, vexation, wrath **2.** *~verb* affront, aggravate (*informal*), annoy, antagonize, be on one's back (*slang*), displease, enrage, exasperate, excite, fret, gall, get in one's hair (*informal*), get one's back up, get one's dander up (*informal*), get on one's nerves (*informal*), hassle (*informal*), incense, infuriate, irritate, madden, make one's blood boil, nark (*Brit., Austral., & N.Z. slang*), nettle, offend, outrage, pique, piss one off (*taboo slang*), provoke, put one's back up, rile, vex

▷ **Antonyms** *~noun* acceptance, amiability, approval, calmness, forgiveness, goodwill, gratification, liking, patience, peace, pleasure *~verb* appease, calm, pacify, placate, please, soothe

angle *noun* **1.** bend, corner, crook, crotch, cusp, edge, elbow, intersection, knee, nook, point **2.** approach, aspect, outlook, perspective, point of view, position, side, slant, standpoint, viewpoint *~verb* **3.** cast, fish

angle for aim for, be after (*informal*), cast about *or* around for, contrive, fish for, hunt, invite, look for, scheme, seek, set one's sights on, solicit, try for

angry annoyed, antagonized, as black as thunder, at daggers drawn, choked,

choleric, cross, displeased, enraged, exasperated, foaming at the mouth, furious, hacked (off) (*U.S. slang*), heated, hot, hot under the collar (*informal*), ill-tempered, incensed, indignant, infuriated, in high dudgeon, irascible, irate, ireful, irritable, irritated, mad (*informal*), nettled, on the warpath, outraged, passionate, piqued, pissed off (*taboo slang*), provoked, raging, resentful, riled, splenetic, tumultuous, up in arms, uptight (*informal*), wrathful
▷ **Antonyms** agreeable, amiable, calm, congenial, friendly, gratified, happy, loving, mild, peaceful, pleasant, pleased

anguish agony, distress, grief, heartache, heartbreak, misery, pain, pang, sorrow, suffering, throe, torment, torture, woe

anguished afflicted, agonized, brokenhearted, distressed, grief-stricken, suffering, tormented, tortured, wounded, wretched

angular bony, gaunt, lank, lanky, lean, macilent (*rare*), rangy, rawboned, scrawny, skinny, spare

animadversion blame, censure, comment, condemnation, criticism, knocking (*informal*), rebuke, reprehension, reproach, reproof, stick (*slang*), strictures

animal *noun* **1.** beast, brute, creature **2.** *applied to a person* barbarian, beast, brute, monster, savage, wild man *~adjective* **3.** bestial, bodily, brutish, carnal, fleshly, gross, physical, sensual

animate *verb* **1.** activate, breathe life into, embolden, encourage, energize, enliven, excite, fire, gladden, impel, incite, inspire, inspirit, instigate, invigorate, kick-start (*informal*), kindle, move, prod, quicken, revive, rouse, spark, spur, stimulate, stir, urge, vitalize, vivify *~adjective* **2.** alive, alive and kicking, breathing, live, living, moving **3.** gay, lively, spirited, vivacious
▷ **Antonyms** *~verb* check, curb, deaden, deter, devitalize, discourage, dull, inhibit, kill, make lifeless, put a damper on, restrain

animated active, airy, alive and kicking, ardent, brisk, buoyant, dynamic, ebullient, elated, energetic, enthusiastic, excited, fervent, full of beans (*informal*), gay, lively, passionate, quick, sparky, spirited, sprightly, vibrant, vigorous, vital, vivacious, vivid, zealous, zestful
▷ **Antonyms** apathetic, boring, dejected, depressed, dull, inactive, lethargic, lifeless, listless, monotonous, passive

animation action, activity, airiness, ardour, brio, briskness, buoyancy, dynamism, ebullience, elation, energy, enthusiasm, excitement, exhilaration, fervour, gaiety, high spirits, life, liveliness, passion, pep, pizzazz *or* pizazz (*informal*), sparkle, spirit, sprightliness, verve, vibrancy, vigour, vitality, vivacity, zeal, zest, zing (*informal*)

animosity acrimony, animus, antagonism, antipathy, bad blood, bitterness, enmity, hate, hatred, hostility, ill will, malevolence, malice, malignity, rancour, resentment, virulence
▷ **Antonyms** amity, benevolence, congeniality, friendliness, friendship, goodwill, harmony, kindness, love, rapport, sympathy

animus 1. acrimony, animosity, antagonism, antipathy, bad blood, bitterness, enmity, hate, hatred, hostility, ill will, malevolence, malice, malignity, rancour, resentment, virulence **2.** animating force, intention, motive, purpose, will

annals accounts, archives, chronicles, history, journals, memorials, records, registers

anneal case-harden, harden, indurate, steel, strengthen, temper, toughen

annex 1. add, adjoin, affix, append, attach, connect, fasten, join, subjoin, tack, unite **2.** acquire, appropriate, arrogate, conquer, expropriate, occupy, seize, take over
▷ **Antonyms** (*sense 1*) detach, disconnect, disengage, disjoin, disunite, remove, separate, unfasten

annexation annexing, appropriation, arrogation, conquest, expropriation, occupation, seizure, takeover

annexe 1. ell, extension, supplementary building, wing **2.** addendum, addition, adjunct, affix, appendix, attachment, supplement

annihilate abolish, destroy, eradicate, erase, exterminate, extinguish, extirpate, liquidate, nullify, obliterate, root out, wipe from the face of the earth, wipe out

annihilation abolition, destruction, eradication, erasure, extermination, extinction, extinguishing, extirpation, liquidation, nullification, obliteration, rooting out, wiping out

annotate commentate, comment on, elucidate, explain, footnote, gloss, illustrate, interpret, make observations, note

annotation comment, commentary, elucidation, exegesis, explanation, explication, footnote, gloss, illustration, interpretation, note, observation

announce 1. advertise, blow wide open (*slang*), broadcast, declare, disclose, divulge, give out, intimate, make known, proclaim, promulgate, propound, publish, report, reveal, shout from the rooftops (*informal*), tell **2.** augur, betoken, foretell, harbinger, herald, portend, presage, signal, signify
▷ **Antonyms** (*sense 1*) bury, conceal, cover up, hide, hold back, hush, hush up, keep back, keep quiet, keep secret, suppress, withhold

announcement advertisement, broadcast, bulletin, communiqué, declaration, disclosure, divulgence, intimation, proclamation, promulgation, publication, report, revelation, statement

announcer anchor man, broadcaster, commentator, master of ceremonies, newscaster, news reader, reporter

annoy aggravate (*informal*), anger, badger, bedevil, be on one's back (*slang*), bore, bother, bug (*informal*), displease, disturb, exasperate, gall, get (*informal*), get in one's hair (*informal*), get one's back up, get one's dander up (*informal*), get one's goat (*slang*), get on one's nerves (*informal*), get on one's wick (*Brit. slang*), get under one's skin (*informal*), get up one's nose (*informal*), harass, harry, hassle (*informal*), incommode, irk, irritate, madden, make one's blood boil, molest, nark (*Brit., Austral., & N.Z. slang*), needle (*informal*), nettle, peeve, pester, piss one off (*taboo slang*), plague, provoke, put one's back up, rile, rub (someone) up the wrong way (*informal*), ruffle, tease, trouble, vex
▷ **Antonyms** appease, calm, comfort, console, mollify, solace, soothe

annoyance **1**. aggravation, anger, bedevilment, bother, displeasure, disturbance, exasperation, grief (*informal*), harassment, hassle (*informal*), irritation, nuisance, provocation, trouble, vexation **2**. bind (*informal*), bore, bother, drag (*informal*), gall, nuisance, pain (*informal*), pain in the arse (*taboo informal*), pain in the neck (*informal*), pest, plague, tease

annoying aggravating, bedevilling, boring, bothersome, displeasing, disturbing, exasperating, galling, harassing, irksome, irritating, maddening, peeving (*informal*), provoking, teasing, troublesome, vexatious
▷ **Antonyms** agreeable, amusing, charming, delightful, diverting, enjoyable, entertaining, gratifying, pleasant

annual once a year, yearlong, yearly

annually by the year, each year, every year, once a year, per annum, per year, year after year, yearly

annul abolish, abrogate, cancel, countermand, declare *or* render null and void, invalidate, negate, nullify, obviate, recall, repeal, rescind, retract, reverse, revoke, void
▷ **Antonyms** bring back, re-enforce, re-establish, reimpose, reinstate, reintroduce, restore

annulment abolition, abrogation, cancellation, countermanding, invalidation, negation, nullification, recall, repeal, rescindment, rescission, retraction, reversal, revocation, voiding

anodyne **1**. *noun* analgesic, narcotic, painkiller, painreliever, palliative **2**. *~adjective* analgesic, deadening, dulling, narcotic, numbing, pain-killing, pain-relieving, palliative

anoint **1**. daub, embrocate, grease, oil, rub, smear, spread over **2**. anele (*archaic*), bless, consecrate, hallow, sanctify

anomalous aberrant, abnormal, atypical, bizarre, deviating, eccentric, exceptional, incongruous, inconsistent, irregular, odd, oddball (*informal*), off-the-wall (*slang*), outré, peculiar, rare, unusual
▷ **Antonyms** common, customary, familiar, natural, normal, ordinary, regular, typical, usual

anomaly aberration, abnormality, departure, deviation, eccentricity, exception, incongruity, inconsistency, irregularity, oddity, peculiarity, rarity

anon before long, betimes (*archaic*), erelong (*archaic or poetic*), forthwith, in a couple of shakes (*informal*), presently, promptly, shortly, soon

anonymous **1**. incognito, innominate, nameless, unacknowledged, unattested, unauthenticated, uncredited, unidentified, unknown, unnamed, unsigned **2**. characterless, nondescript, unexceptional
▷ **Antonyms** (*sense 1*) accredited, acknowledged, attested, authenticated, credited, identified, known, named, signed

answer *noun* **1**. acknowledgment, comeback, counterattack, defence, explanation, plea, reaction, refutation, rejoinder, reply, report, resolution, response, retort, return, riposte, solution, vindication *~verb* **2**. acknowledge, explain, react, refute, rejoin, reply, resolve, respond, retort, return, solve **3**. conform, correlate, correspond, do, fill, fit, fulfil, measure up, meet, pass, qualify, satisfy, serve, suffice, suit, work
▷ **Antonyms** *~noun* inquiry, interrogation, query, question *~verb* (*sense 2*) ask, inquire, interrogate, query, question

answerable **1**. accountable, amenable, chargeable, liable, responsible, subject, to blame **2**. explainable, refutable, resolvable, solvable

answer back argue, be cheeky, be impertinent, cheek (*informal*), contradict, disagree, dispute, rebut, retort, talk back

answer for **1**. be accountable for, be answerable for, be chargeable for, be liable for, be responsible for, be to blame for, take the rap for (*slang*) **2**. atone for, make amends for, pay for, suffer for

answer to **1**. be accountable to, be answerable to, be responsible to, be ruled by, obey **2**. agree, confirm, correspond, fit, match, meet

antagonism antipathy, competition, conflict, contention, discord, dissension, friction, hostility, opposition, rivalry
▷ **Antonyms** accord, agreement, amity,

friendship, harmony, love, peacefulness, sympathy

antagonist adversary, competitor, con~ tender, enemy, foe, opponent, opposer, rival

antagonistic adverse, antipathetic, at odds, at variance, averse, conflicting, contentious, hostile, ill-disposed, incom~ patible, in dispute, inimical, opposed, unfriendly

antagonize 1. aggravate (*informal*), al~ ienate, anger, annoy, be on one's back (*slang*), disaffect, estrange, gall, get in one's hair (*informal*), get on one's nerves (*informal*), get on one's wick (*Brit. slang*), get under one's skin (*informal*), get up one's nose (*informal*), hassle (*in~ formal*), insult, irritate, nark (*Brit., Austral., & N.Z. slang*), offend, piss one off (*taboo slang*), repel, rub (someone) up the wrong way (*informal*) **2.** contend with, counteract, neutralize, oppose, struggle with, work against

▷ **Antonyms** (*sense 1*) appease, calm, conciliate, disarm, mollify, pacify, pla~ cate, propitiate, soothe, win over

antecedent anterior, earlier, foregoing, former, preceding, precursory, prelimi~ nary, previous, prior

▷ **Antonyms** after, coming, consequent, ensuing, following, later, posterior, sub~ sequent, succeeding, successive

antecedents 1. ancestors, ancestry, blood, descent, extraction, family, forebears, forefathers, genealogy, line, progenitors, stock **2.** background, history, past

antedate anticipate, come first *or* before, forego, go before, precede, predate

antediluvian 1. prehistoric, primeval, primitive, primordial **2.** ancient, anti~ quated, antique, archaic, obsolete, old as the hills, old-fashioned, out-of-date, out of the ark (*informal*), passé

anterior 1. fore, forward, front, frontward **2.** antecedent, earlier, foregoing, former, introductory, preceding, previous, prior

anteroom antechamber, foyer, lobby, outer room, reception room, vestibule, waiting room

anthem 1. canticle, carol, chant, chorale, hymn, psalm **2.** paean, song of praise

anthology analects, choice, collection, compendium, compilation, digest, gar~ land, miscellany, selection, treasury

anticipate 1. apprehend, await, count upon, expect, forecast, foresee, foretell, hope for, look for, look forward to, pre~ dict, prepare for **2.** antedate, beat (someone) to it (*informal*), forestall, intercept, prevent

anticipation apprehension, awaiting, ex~ pectancy, expectation, foresight, fore~ taste, forethought, hope, preconception, premonition, prescience, presentiment

anticlimax bathos, comedown (*informal*), disappointment, letdown

▷ **Antonyms** climax, culmination, height, highlight, high point, peak, summit, top, zenith

antics buffoonery, capers, clowning, es~ capades, foolishness, frolics, horseplay, larks, mischief, monkey tricks, playful~ ness, pranks, silliness, skylarking, stunts, tomfoolery, tricks

antidote antitoxin, antivenin, corrective, counteragent, countermeasure, cure, neutralizer, nostrum, preventive, rem~ edy, specific

antipathetic abhorrent, antagonistic, averse, disgusting, distasteful, hateful, hostile, incompatible, invidious, loath~ some, obnoxious, odious, offensive, re~ pellent, repugnant, repulsive, revolting, yucky *or* yukky (*slang*)

antipathy abhorrence, animosity, animus, antagonism, aversion, bad blood, contrariety, disgust, dislike, distaste, enmity, hatred, hostility, ill will, incom~ patibility, loathing, odium, opposition, rancour, repugnance, repulsion

▷ **Antonyms** affection, affinity, attrac~ tion, bond, empathy, fellow-feeling, goodwill, harmony, partiality, rapport, sympathy, tie

antiquated 1. antediluvian, antique, ar~ chaic, dated, obsolete, old-fashioned, old hat, outmoded, out-of-date, outworn, passé **2.** aged, ancient, elderly, hoary, old, old as the hills, past it (*informal*), superannuated

▷ **Antonyms** all-singing, all-dancing, current, fashionable, fresh, modern, modish, new, state-of-the-art, stylish, up-to-date, young

antique *adjective* **1.** aged, ancient, elderly, old, superannuated **2.** archaic, obsolete, old-fashioned, outdated **3.** antiquarian, classic, olden, vintage *~noun* **4.** bygone, heirloom, object of virtu, relic

antiquity 1. age, ancientness, elderliness, old age, oldness **2.** ancient times, distant past, olden days, time immemorial **3.** antique, relic, ruin

antiseptic 1. *adjective* aseptic, clean, germ-free, hygienic, pure, sanitary, sterile, uncontaminated, unpolluted **2.** *~noun* bactericide, disinfectant, germi~ cide, purifier

▷ **Antonyms** *~adjective* contaminated, dirty, impure, infected, insanitary, pol~ luted, septic, unhygienic

antisocial 1. alienated, asocial, misan~ thropic, reserved, retiring, uncommuni~ cative, unfriendly, unsociable, with~ drawn **2.** antagonistic, belligerent, dis~ orderly, disruptive, hostile, menacing, rebellious

▷ **Antonyms** (*sense 1*) companionable, friendly, gregarious, philanthropic, so~ ciable, social

antithesis 1. antipode, contrary, contrast, converse, inverse, opposite, reverse **2.** contradiction, contraposition, contrari~

ety, contrast, inversion, opposition, re~ versal

antithetical, antithetic antipodal, contra~ dictory, contrary, contrasted, contrast~ ing, converse, counter, inverse, opposed, opposite, poles apart, reverse

anxiety angst, apprehension, care, con~ cern, disquiet, disquietude, distress, foreboding, fretfulness, misgiving, nerv~ ousness, restlessness, solicitude, sus~ pense, tension, trepidation, unease, un~ easiness, watchfulness, worry

▷ **Antonyms** assurance, calmness, confi~ dence, contentment, relief, security, se~ renity

anxious 1. angsty, apprehensive, careful, concerned, disquieted, distressed, dis~ turbed, fearful, fretful, hot and both~ ered, in suspense, nervous, neurotic, on pins and needles, on tenterhooks, over~ wrought, restless, solicitous, taut, tense, troubled, twitchy (*informal*), uneasy, unquiet (*chiefly literary*), watchful, wired (*slang*), worried **2.** ardent, avid, desirous, eager, expectant, impatient, intent, itching, keen, yearning

▷ **Antonyms** (*sense 1*) assured, calm, certain, collected, composed, confident, cool, nonchalant, unfazed (*informal*), unperturbed (*sense 2*) disinclined, hesi~ tant, loath, nonchalant, reluctant

apace at full speed, expeditiously, post~ haste, quickly, rapidly, speedily, swiftly, with dispatch, without delay

apart 1. afar, alone, aloof, aside, away, by itself, by oneself, cut off, distant, dis~ tinct, divorced, excluded, independent, independently, isolated, out on a limb, piecemeal, separate, separated, sepa~ rately, singly, to itself, to oneself, to one side **2.** asunder, in bits, in pieces, into parts, to bits, to pieces **3. apart from** aside from, besides, but, except for, ex~ cluding, not counting, other than, save

apartment accommodation, chambers, compartment, flat, living quarters, penthouse, quarters, room, rooms, suite

apathetic cold, cool, emotionless, impas~ sive, indifferent, insensible, listless, passive, phlegmatic, sluggish, stoic, stoical, torpid, unconcerned, unemo~ tional, unfeeling, uninterested, un~ moved, unresponsive

▷ **Antonyms** active, anxious, aroused, bothered, caring, committed, concerned, emotional, enthusiastic, excited, inter~ ested, moved, passionate, responsive, troubled, worried, zealous

apathy coldness, coolness, emotion~ lessness, impassibility, impassivity, indifference, inertia, insensibility, listlessness, nonchalance, passiveness, passivity, phlegm, sluggishness, stoicism, torpor, unconcern, unfeeling~ ness, uninterestedness, unrespons~ iveness

▷ **Antonyms** anxiety, attention, concern, emotion, enthusiasm, feeling, interest, zeal

ape affect, caricature, copy, counterfeit, echo, imitate, mimic, mirror, mock, parody, parrot

aperture breach, chink, cleft, crack, eye, eyelet, fissure, gap, hole, interstice, opening, orifice, passage, perforation, rent, rift, slit, slot, space, vent

apex acme, apogee, climax, crest, crown, culmination, height, high point, peak, pinnacle, point, summit, tip, top, vertex, zenith

▷ **Antonyms** base, bottom, depths, low~ est point, nadir, perigee, rock bottom

aphorism adage, apothegm, axiom, dic~ tum, gnome, maxim, precept, proverb, saw, saying

apiece each, for each, from each, individ~ ually, respectively, separately, several~ ly, to each

▷ **Antonyms** all together, as a group, collectively, en masse, overall, together

apish 1. affected, foolish, foppish, silly, stupid, trifling **2.** imitative, mimicking

aplomb balance, calmness, composure, confidence, coolness, equanimity, level-headedness, poise, sang-froid, self-assurance, self-confidence, self-possession, stability

▷ **Antonyms** awkwardness, chagrin, confusion, discomfiture, discomposure, embarrassment, self-consciousness

apocalyptic ominous, oracular, porten~ tous, prophetic, revelational, vatic

apocryphal doubtful, dubious, equivocal, fictitious, legendary, mythical, ques~ tionable, spurious, unauthenticated, uncanonical, unsubstantiated, unveri~ fied

▷ **Antonyms** attested, authentic, authenticated, authorized, canonical, credible, factual, substantiated, true, undisputed, unquestionable, verified

apogee acme, apex, climax, crest, crown, culmination, height, high point, peak, pinnacle, summit, tip, top, vertex, zen~ ith

apologetic contrite, penitent, regretful, remorseful, rueful, sorry

apologist advocate, arguer, champion, defender, justifier, maintainer, pleader, spokesman, supporter, vindicator

apologize ask forgiveness, beg pardon, express regret, say one is sorry, say sor~ ry

apologue allegory, fable, parable, story, tale

apology 1. acknowledgment, confession, defence, excuse, explanation, extenu~ ation, justification, plea, vindication **2.** caricature, excuse, imitation, makeshift, mockery, stopgap, substitute, travesty

apostasy backsliding, defection, deser~ tion, disloyalty, faithlessness, falseness, heresy, perfidy, recreance *or* recreancy (*archaic*), treachery, unfaithfulness

apostate 1. *noun* backslider, defector, deserter, heretic, recreant (*archaic*), renegade, traitor, turncoat **2.** *~adjective* backsliding, disloyal, faithless, false, heretical, perfidious, recreant, traitorous, treacherous, unfaithful, untrue

apostatize backslide, defect, desert, renege, turn traitor

apostle 1. evangelist, herald, messenger, missionary, preacher, proselytizer **2.** advocate, champion, pioneer, propagandist, propagator, proponent

apothegm adage, aphorism, axiom, dictum, gnome, maxim, precept, proverb, saw, saying

apotheosis deification, elevation, exaltation, glorification, idealization, idolization

apotheosize deify, elevate, exalt, glorify, idealize, idolize

appal alarm, astound, daunt, dishearten, dismay, frighten, harrow, horrify, intimidate, make one's hair stand on end (*informal*), outrage, petrify, scare, shock, terrify, unnerve

appalling alarming, astounding, awful, daunting, dire, disheartening, dismaying, dreadful, fearful, frightening, frightful, from hell (*informal*), ghastly, godawful (*slang*), grim, harrowing, hellacious (*U.S. slang*), hideous, horrible, horrid, horrific, horrifying, intimidating, petrifying, scaring, shocking, terrible, terrifying, unnerving
▷ **Antonyms** comforting, consolatory, consoling, encouraging, heartening, reassuring

apparatus 1. appliance, contraption (*informal*), device, equipment, gear, implements, machine, machinery, materials, means, mechanism, outfit, tackle, tools, utensils **2.** bureaucracy, chain of command, hierarchy, network, organization, setup (*informal*), structure, system

apparel accoutrements, array (*poetic*), attire, clothes, clothing, costume, dress, equipment, garb, garments, gear (*informal*), habiliments, habit, outfit, raiment (*archaic or poetic*), robes, threads (*slang*), trappings, vestments

apparent 1. blatant, bold, clear, conspicuous, discernible, distinct, evident, indubitable, manifest, marked, obvious, open, overt, patent, plain, plain as the nose on your face, salient, understandable, unmistakable, visible **2.** ostensible, outward, seeming, specious, superficial
▷ **Antonyms** (*sense 1*) ambiguous, doubtful, dubious, hazy, indefinite, indistinct, obscure, uncertain, unclear, vague (*sense 2*) actual, authentic, bona fide, genuine, honest, intrinsic, real, sincere, true

apparently it appears that, it seems that, on the face of it, ostensibly, outwardly, seemingly, speciously, superficially

apparition 1. appearance, manifestation, materialization, presence, vision, visitation **2.** chimera, eidolon, ghost, phantom, revenant, shade (*literary*), spectre, spirit, spook (*informal*), visitant, wraith

appeal *noun* **1.** adjuration, application, entreaty, invocation, petition, plea, prayer, request, solicitation, suit, supplication **2.** allure, attraction, attractiveness, beauty, charm, engagingness, fascination, interestingness, pleasingness *~verb* **3.** adjure, apply, ask, beg, beseech, call, call upon, entreat, implore, petition, plead, pray, refer, request, resort to, solicit, sue, supplicate **4.** allure, attract, charm, engage, entice, fascinate, interest, invite, please, tempt
▷ **Antonyms** *~noun* (*sense 1*) denial, refusal, rejection, repudiation (*sense 2*) repulsiveness *~verb* (*sense 3*) deny, refuse, reject, repudiate, repulse (*sense 4*) alienate, bore, repulse, revolt

appear 1. arise, arrive, attend, be present, come forth, come into sight, come into view, come out, come to light, crop up (*informal*), develop, emerge, issue, loom, materialize, occur, show (*informal*), show one's face, show up (*informal*), surface, turn out, turn up **2.** look (like *or* as if), occur, seem, strike one as **3.** be apparent, be clear, be evident, be manifest, be obvious, be patent, be plain **4.** become available, be created, be developed, be invented, be published, come into being, come into existence, come out **5.** act, be exhibited, come on, come onstage, enter, perform, play, play a part, take part
▷ **Antonyms** (*senses 1 & 4*) disappear, vanish (*senses 2 & 3*) be doubtful, be unclear

appearance 1. advent, appearing, arrival, coming, debut, emergence, introduction, presence, showing up (*informal*), turning up **2.** air, aspect, bearing, demeanour, expression, face, figure, form, image, look, looks, manner, mien (*literary*) **3.** front, guise, illusion, image, impression, outward show, pretence, semblance

appease allay, alleviate, assuage, blunt, calm, compose, conciliate, diminish, ease, lessen, lull, mitigate, mollify, pacify, placate, pour oil on troubled waters, quell, quench, quiet, satisfy, soften, soothe, subdue, tranquillize
▷ **Antonyms** aggravate (*informal*), anger, annoy, antagonize, arouse, be on one's back (*slang*), disturb, enrage, get in one's hair (*informal*), get on one's nerves (*informal*), hassle (*informal*), incense, inflame, infuriate, irritate, madden, nark (*Brit., Austral., & N.Z. slang*),

piss one off (*taboo slang*), provoke, rile, upset

appeasement **1.** acceding, accommodation, compromise, concession, conciliation, placation, propitiation **2.** abatement, alleviation, assuagement, blunting, easing, lessening, lulling, mitigation, mollification, pacification, quelling, quenching, quieting, satisfaction, softening, solace, soothing, tranquillization

appellation address, description, designation, epithet, name, sobriquet, style, term, title

append add, adjoin, affix, annex, attach, fasten, hang, join, subjoin, tack on, tag on

▷ **Antonyms** detach, disconnect, disengage, remove, separate, take off

appendage **1.** accessory, addendum, addition, adjunct, affix, ancillary, annexe, appendix, appurtenance, attachment, auxiliary, supplement **2.** *Zoology* extremity, limb, member, projection, protuberance

appendant *adjective* **1.** added, additional, adjoined, affixed, annexed, appended, attached, auxiliary, fastened, joined, subjoined, supplementary, tacked on, tagged on **2.** accompanying, associated, attendant, concomitant, connected, consequential, following, related, resulting *~noun* **3.** addition, adjunct, affix, annexe, appendage, appendix, attachment, supplement

appendix addendum, addition, add-on, adjunct, appendage, codicil, postscript, supplement

appertain (*usually with* **to**) apply, bear upon, be characteristic of, be connected, belong, be part of, be pertinent, be proper, be relevant, have to do with, inhere in, pertain, refer, relate, touch upon

appetence, appetency **1.** ache, appetite, craving, desire, hankering, hunger, longing, need, yearning **2.** bent, drive, inclination, instinct, leaning, penchant, propensity **3.** affection, affinity, allurement, attraction, fondness, liking, partiality

appetite appetence, appetency, craving, demand, desire, hankering, hunger, inclination, liking, longing, passion, proclivity, propensity, relish, stomach, taste, willingness, yearning, zeal, zest

▷ **Antonyms** abhorrence, aversion, disgust, disinclination, dislike, distaste, loathing, repugnance, repulsion, revulsion

appetizer **1.** antipasto, canapé, cocktail, hors d'oeuvre, titbit **2.** apéritif, cocktail **3.** foretaste, sample, taste

appetizing appealing, delicious, inviting, mouthwatering, palatable, savoury, scrumptious (*informal*), succulent, tasty, tempting

▷ **Antonyms** distasteful, nauseating, unappetizing, unpalatable, unsavoury

applaud acclaim, approve, cheer, clap, commend, compliment, crack up (*informal*), encourage, eulogize, extol, give (someone) a big hand, laud, magnify (*archaic*), praise

▷ **Antonyms** blast, boo, censure, condemn, criticize, decry, deprecate, deride, disparage, excoriate, hiss, lambast(e), pan (*informal*), put down, ridicule, run down, slag (off) (*slang*), tear into (*informal*), vilify

applause acclaim, acclamation, accolade, approbation, approval, big hand, cheering, cheers, commendation, eulogizing, hand, hand-clapping, laudation, ovation, plaudit, praise

appliance apparatus, device, gadget, implement, instrument, machine, mechanism, tool

applicable apposite, appropriate, apropos, apt, befitting, fit, fitting, germane, pertinent, relevant, suitable, suited, to the point, to the purpose, useful

▷ **Antonyms** inapplicable, inappropriate, irrelevant, unsuitable, wrong

applicant aspirant, candidate, claimant, inquirer, petitioner, postulant, suitor, suppliant

application **1.** appositeness, exercise, function, germaneness, pertinence, practice, purpose, relevance, use, value **2.** appeal, claim, inquiry, petition, request, requisition, solicitation, suit **3.** assiduity, attention, attentiveness, commitment, dedication, diligence, effort, hard work, industry, perseverance, study **4.** balm, cream, dressing, emollient, lotion, ointment, poultice, salve, unguent

apply **1.** administer, assign, bring into play, bring to bear, carry out, employ, engage, execute, exercise, exert, implement, practise, put to use, use, utilize **2.** appertain, be applicable, be appropriate, bear upon, be fitting, be relevant, fit, pertain, refer, relate, suit **3.** anoint, bring into contact with, cover with, lay on, paint, place, put on, smear, spread on, touch to **4.** appeal, claim, inquire, make application, petition, put in, request, requisition, solicit, sue **5.** address, be assiduous, be diligent, be industrious, buckle down (*informal*), commit, concentrate, dedicate, devote, direct, give, make an effort, pay attention, persevere, study, try, work hard

appoint **1.** allot, arrange, assign, choose, decide, designate, determine, establish, fix, set, settle **2.** assign, choose, commission, delegate, elect, install, name, nominate, select **3.** command, decree, direct, enjoin, ordain **4.** equip, fit out, furnish, provide, supply

▷ **Antonyms** (*sense 1*) cancel (*sense 2*) discharge, dismiss, fire, give the sack (*informal*), sack (*informal*) (*sense 4*) dismantle, divest, strip

appointed 1. allotted, arranged, assigned, chosen, decided, designated, determined, established, fixed, set, settled **2.** assigned, chosen, commissioned, delegated, elected, installed, named, nominated, selected **3.** commanded, decreed, directed, enjoined, ordained **4.** equipped, fitted out, furnished, provided, supplied

appointment 1. arrangement, assignation, consultation, date, engagement, interview, meeting, rendezvous, session, tryst (*archaic*) **2.** allotment, assignment, choice, choosing, commissioning, delegation, designation, election, installation, naming, nomination, selection **3.** assignment, berth (*informal*), job, office, place, position, post, situation, station **4.** appointee, candidate, delegate, nominee, office-holder, representative **5.** (*usually plural*) accoutrements, appurtenances, equipage, fittings, fixtures, furnishings, gear, outfit, paraphernalia, trappings

apportion allocate, allot, assign, deal, dispense, distribute, divide, dole out, measure out, mete out, parcel out, ration out, share

apportionment allocation, allotment, assignment, dealing out, dispensing, distribution, division, doling out, measuring out, meting out, parcelling out, rationing out, sharing

apposite appertaining, applicable, appropriate, apropos, apt, befitting, fitting, germane, pertinent, proper, relevant, suitable, suited, to the point, to the purpose

▷ **Antonyms** inapplicable, inappropriate, inapt, irrelevant, unsuitable, unsuited

appraisal 1. assessment, estimate, estimation, evaluation, judgment, opinion, recce (*slang*), sizing up (*informal*) **2.** assay, pricing, rating, reckoning, survey, valuation

appraise assay, assess, estimate, evaluate, eye up, gauge, inspect, judge, price, rate, recce (*slang*), review, size up (*informal*), survey, value

appreciable ascertainable, clear-cut, considerable, definite, detectable, discernible, distinguishable, evident, marked, material, measurable, noticeable, obvious, perceivable, perceptible, pronounced, recognizable, significant, substantial, visible

▷ **Antonyms** immaterial, imperceptible, inappreciable, indiscernible, indistinguishable, insignificant, invisible, minor, minute, negligible, small, trivial, undetectable, unnoticeable, unsubstantial

appreciate 1. be appreciative, be grateful for, be indebted, be obliged, be thankful for, give thanks for **2.** acknowledge, be alive to, be aware of, be cognizant of, be conscious of, comprehend, estimate, know, perceive, realize, recognize, sympathize with, take account of, understand **3.** admire, cherish, enjoy, esteem, like, prize, rate highly, regard, relish, respect, savour, treasure, value **4.** enhance, gain, grow, improve, increase, inflate, raise the value of, rise

▷ **Antonyms** (*sense 1*) be ungrateful (*sense 2*) be unaware, misunderstand, underrate (*sense 3*) belittle, denigrate, disdain, disparage, scorn (*sense 4*) deflate, depreciate, devaluate, fall

appreciation 1. acknowledgment, gratefulness, gratitude, indebtedness, obligation, thankfulness, thanks **2.** admiration, appraisal, assessment, awareness, cognizance, comprehension, enjoyment, esteem, estimation, knowledge, liking, perception, realization, recognition, regard, relish, respect, responsiveness, sensitivity, sympathy, understanding, valuation **3.** enhancement, gain, growth, improvement, increase, inflation, rise **4.** acclamation, criticism, critique, notice, praise, review, tribute

▷ **Antonyms** (*sense 1*) ingratitude (*sense 2*) antipathy, dislike, ignorance, incomprehension (*sense 3*) decline, depreciation, devaluation, fall

appreciative 1. beholden, grateful, indebted, obliged, thankful **2.** admiring, aware, cognizant, conscious, enthusiastic, in the know (*informal*), knowledgeable, mindful, perceptive, pleased, regardful, respectful, responsive, sensitive, supportive, sympathetic, understanding

apprehend 1. arrest, bust (*informal*), capture, catch, collar (*informal*), feel one's collar (*slang*), lift (*slang*), nab (*informal*), nail (*informal*), nick (*slang, chiefly Brit.*), pinch (*informal*), run in (*slang*), seize, take, take prisoner **2.** appreciate, believe, comprehend, conceive, get the message, get the picture, grasp, imagine, know, perceive, realize, recognize, think, understand **3.** be afraid of, dread, fear

▷ **Antonyms** (*sense 1*) discharge, free, let go, liberate, release (*sense 2*) be at cross-purposes, be unaware of, be unconscious of, get one's lines crossed, misapprehend, misconceive, miss, misunderstand

apprehension 1. alarm, anxiety, apprehensiveness, concern, disquiet, doubt, dread, fear, foreboding, misgiving, mistrust, on pins and needles, premonition, suspicion, trepidation, unease, uneasiness, worry **2.** arrest, capture, catching, seizure, taking **3.** awareness, comprehension, grasp, intellect, intelligence, ken, knowledge, perception, understanding **4.** belief, concept, conception, conjecture, idea, impression, notion, opinion, sentiment, thought, view

▷ **Antonyms** (*sense 1*) assurance, composure, confidence, nonchalance, serenity, unconcern (*sense 2*) discharge, liberation, release (*sense 3*) incomprehension

apprehensive afraid, alarmed, anxious, concerned, disquieted, doubtful, fearful, foreboding, mistrustful, nervous, neurotic, suspicious, twitchy (*informal*), uneasy, worried

▷ **Antonyms** assured, at ease, composed, confident, nonchalant, unafraid

apprentice beginner, learner, neophyte, novice, probationer, pupil, student, trainee, tyro

▷ **Antonyms** ace (*informal*), adept, dab hand (*Brit. informal*), expert, master, past master, pro

apprise acquaint, advise, communicate, enlighten, give notice, inform, make aware, make cognizant, notify, tell, warn

approach *verb* **1.** advance, catch up, come close, come near, come to, draw near, gain on, meet, move towards, near, push forward, reach **2.** appeal to, apply to, broach the matter with, make advances to, make a proposal to, make overtures to, sound out **3.** begin, begin work on, commence, embark on, enter upon, make a start, set about, undertake **4.** approximate, be comparable to, be like, come close to, come near to, compare with, resemble *~noun* **5.** access, advance, advent, arrival, avenue, coming, drawing near, entrance, nearing, passage, road, way **6.** approximation, likeness, semblance **7.** (*often plural*) advance, appeal, application, invitation, offer, overture, proposal, proposition **8.** attitude, course, manner, means, method, mode, modus operandi, procedure, style, technique, way

approachable 1. accessible, attainable, come-at-able (*informal*), get-at-able (*informal*), reachable **2.** affable, congenial, cordial, friendly, open, sociable

▷ **Antonyms** (*sense 1*) inaccessible, out of reach, out-of-the-way, remote, un-get-at-able (*informal*), unreachable (*sense 2*) aloof, chilly, cold as ice, cool, distant, frigid, remote, reserved, standoffish, unfriendly, unsociable, withdrawn

approbation acceptance, acclaim, applause, approval, assent, commendation, congratulation, encouragement, endorsement, favour, laudation, praise, ratification, recognition, sanction, support

▷ **Antonyms** blame, censure, condemnation, disapprobation, disapproval, disfavour, dislike, displeasure, dissatisfaction, reproof, stricture

appropriate *adjective* **1.** adapted, applicable, apposite, appurtenant, apropos, apt, becoming, befitting, belonging, congruous, correct, felicitous, fit, fitting, germane, meet (*archaic*), opportune, pertinent, proper, relevant, right, seemly, suitable, to the point, to the purpose, well-suited, well-timed *~verb* **2.** allocate, allot, apportion, assign, devote, earmark, set apart **3.** annex, arrogate, assume, commandeer, confiscate, expropriate, impound, pre-empt, seize, take, take over, take possession of, usurp **4.** embezzle, filch, misappropriate, pilfer, pocket, steal

▷ **Antonyms** *~adjective* improper, inappropriate, incompatible, incorrect, inopportune, irrelevant, unfitting, unsuitable, untimely *~verb* (*sense 2*) withhold (*senses 3 & 4*) cede, donate, give, relinquish

appropriateness applicability, appositeness, aptness, becomingness, congruousness, correctness, felicitousness, felicity, fitness, fittingness, germaneness, opportuneness, pertinence, properness, relevance, rightness, seemliness, suitability, timeliness, well-suitedness

appropriation 1. allocation, allotment, apportionment, assignment, earmarking, setting apart **2.** annexation, arrogation, assumption, commandeering, confiscation, expropriation, impoundment, pre-emption, seizure, takeover, taking, usurpation

approval 1. acquiescence, agreement, assent, authorization, blessing, compliance, concurrence, confirmation, consent, countenance, endorsement, imprimatur, leave, licence, mandate, O.K. *or* okay (*informal*), permission, ratification, recommendation, sanction, the go-ahead (*informal*), the green light, validation **2.** acclaim, admiration, applause, appreciation, approbation, Brownie points, commendation, esteem, favour, good opinion, liking, praise, regard, respect

▷ **Antonyms** denigration, disapproval, dislike, disparagement, displeasure, dissatisfaction, objection

approve 1. acclaim, admire, applaud, appreciate, be pleased with, commend, esteem, favour, have a good opinion of, like, praise, regard highly, respect, think highly of **2.** accede to, accept, advocate, agree to, allow, assent to, authorize, bless, buy into (*informal*), concur in, confirm, consent to, countenance, endorse, give the go-ahead (*informal*), give the green light, go along with, mandate, O.K. *or* okay (*informal*), pass, permit, ratify, recommend, sanction, second, subscribe to, uphold, validate

▷ **Antonyms** (*sense 1*) blame, censure, condemn, deplore, deprecate, disapprove, dislike, find unacceptable, frown on, look down one's nose at (*informal*), object to, take exception to (*sense 2*) disallow, discountenance, veto

approximate *adjective* **1.** almost accurate, almost exact, close, near **2.** estimated, inexact, loose, rough **3.** analogous, close, comparable, like, near, relative, similar, verging on **4.** adjacent, bordering, close together, contiguous, near, nearby, neighbouring *~verb* **5.** approach, border on, come close, come near, reach, resemble, touch, verge on

▷ **Antonyms** *~adjective* (*senses 1 & 2*) accurate, correct, definite, exact, precise, specific

approximately about, almost, around, circa (*used with dates*), close to, generally, in the neighbourhood of, in the region of, in the vicinity of, just about, loosely, more or less, nearly, not far off, relatively, roughly

approximation **1.** ballpark estimate (*informal*), ballpark figure (*informal*), conjecture, estimate, estimation, guess, guesswork, rough calculation, rough idea **2.** approach, correspondence, likeness, resemblance, semblance

appurtenance **1.** accessory, accompaniment, adjunct, annexe, appendage, appurtenant, attachment, auxiliary, concomitant, incidental, piece of equipment, subordinate, subsidiary, supplement **2.** *plural* accessories, accompaniments, accoutrements, appendages, equipment, impedimenta, paraphernalia, trappings

appurtenant accessory, appertaining, applicable, appropriate, belonging, concerned, connected, germane, incidental, pertaining, pertinent, proper, related, relating, relevant

a priori **1.** deduced, deductive, from cause to effect, inferential **2.** conjectural, postulated, postulational, presumptive, self-evident, suppositional, theoretical

apron pinafore, pinny (*informal*)

apropos *adjective* **1.** applicable, apposite, appropriate, apt, befitting, belonging, correct, fit, fitting, germane, meet (*archaic*), opportune, pertinent, proper, related, relevant, right, seemly, suitable, to the point, to the purpose *~adverb* **2.** appropriately, aptly, opportunely, pertinently, relevantly, suitably, timely, to the point, to the purpose **3.** by the bye, by the way, incidentally, in passing, parenthetically, while on the subject

apropos of *preposition* in respect of, on the subject of, re, regarding, respecting, with reference to, with regard to, with respect to

apt **1.** applicable, apposite, appropriate, apropos, befitting, correct, fit, fitting, germane, meet (*archaic*), pertinent, proper, relevant, seemly, suitable, timely, to the point, to the purpose **2.** disposed, given, inclined, liable, likely, of a mind, prone, ready **3.** astute, bright, clever, expert, gifted, ingenious, intelligent, prompt, quick, sharp, skilful, smart, talented, teachable

▷ **Antonyms** (*sense 1*) ill-fitted, ill-suited, ill-timed, improper, inapplicable, inapposite, inappropriate, infelicitous, inopportune, irrelevant, unsuitable, untimely (*sense 3*) awkward, clumsy, dull, gauche, incompetent, inept, inexpert, maladroit, slow, stupid

aptitude **1.** bent, disposition, inclination, leaning, predilection, proclivity, proneness, propensity, tendency **2.** ability, aptness, capability, capacity, cleverness, faculty, flair, gift, giftedness, intelligence, knack, proficiency, quickness, talent **3.** applicability, appositeness, appropriateness, fitness, relevance, suitability, suitableness

aptness **1.** applicability, appositeness, appropriateness, becomingness, congruousness, correctness, felicitousness, felicity, fitness, fittingness, germaneness, opportuneness, pertinence, properness, relevance, rightness, seemliness, suitability, timeliness, well-suitedness **2.** aptitude, bent, disposition, inclination, leaning, liability, likelihood, likeliness, predilection, proclivity, proneness, propensity, readiness, tendency **3.** ability, capability, capacity, cleverness, faculty, fitness, flair, gift, giftedness, intelligence, knack, proficiency, quickness, suitability, talent

arable cultivable, farmable, fecund, fertile, fruitful, ploughable, productive, tillable

arbiter **1.** adjudicator, arbitrator, judge, referee, umpire **2.** authority, controller, dictator, expert, governor, lord, master, pundit, ruler

arbitrariness **1.** capriciousness, fancifulness, inconsistency, randomness, subjectivity, unreasonableness, whimsicality, wilfulness **2.** absoluteness, despotism, dictatorialness, dogmatism, domineeringness, high-handedness, imperiousness, magisterialness, overbearingness, peremptoriness, summariness, tyrannicalness, tyrannousness, tyranny, uncontrolledness, unlimitedness, unrestrainedness

arbitrary **1.** capricious, chance, discretionary, erratic, fanciful, inconsistent, optional, personal, random, subjective, unreasonable, whimsical, wilful **2.** absolute, autocratic, despotic, dictatorial, dogmatic, domineering, high-handed, imperious, magisterial, overbearing, peremptory, summary, tyrannical, tyrannous, uncontrolled, unlimited, unrestrained

▷ **Antonyms** (*sense 1*) consistent, judicious, logical, objective, rational, reasonable, reasoned, sensible, sound

arbitrate adjudge, adjudicate, decide, determine, judge, mediate, pass judgment, referee, settle, sit in judgment, umpire

arbitration adjudication, arbitrament, decision, determination, judgment, settlement

arbitrator adjudicator, arbiter, judge, referee, umpire

arc arch, bend, bow, crescent, curve, half-moon

arcane cabbalistic, esoteric, hidden, mysterious, occult, recondite, secret

arch[1] *noun* **1.** archway, curve, dome, span, vault **2.** arc, bend, bow, curvature, curve, hump, semicircle *~verb* **3.** arc, bend, bow, bridge, curve, embow, span

arch[2] *adjective* **1.** accomplished, chief, consummate, expert, finished, first, foremost, greatest, head, highest, lead, leading, main, major, master, pre-eminent, primary, principal, top **2.** artful, frolicsome, knowing, mischievous, pert, playful, roguish, saucy, sly, waggish, wily

archaic ancient, antiquated, antique, behind the times, bygone, obsolete, old, olden (*archaic*), old-fashioned, old hat, outmoded, out of date, passé, primitive, superannuated

▷ **Antonyms** contemporary, current, fresh, latest, modern, modish, new, newfangled, novel, present, recent, state-of-the-art, up-to-date, up-to-the-minute, with it (*informal*)

arched curved, domed, embowed, vaulted

archer bowman (*archaic*), toxophilite (*formal*)

archetype classic, exemplar, form, ideal, model, norm, original, paradigm, pattern, prime example, prototype, standard

architect **1.** designer, master builder, planner **2.** author, contriver, creator, deviser, engineer, founder, instigator, inventor, maker, originator, planner, prime mover, shaper

architecture **1.** architectonics, building, construction, design, planning **2.** construction, design, framework, make-up, structure, style

archives **1.** annals, chronicles, documents, papers, records, registers, rolls **2.** museum, record office, registry, repository

arctic **1.** far-northern, hyperborean, polar **2.** *informal* chilly, cold, cold as ice, freezing, frigid, frost-bound, frosty, frozen, gelid, glacial, icy

ardent ablaze, amorous, avid, eager, enthusiastic, fervent, fervid, fierce, fiery, flaming, hot, hot-blooded, impassioned, intense, keen, keen as mustard, lusty, passionate, spirited, vehement, warm, warm-blooded, zealous

▷ **Antonyms** apathetic, cold, cool, frigid, impassive, indifferent, lukewarm, unenthusiastic, unloving

ardour avidity, devotion, eagerness, earnestness, enthusiasm, feeling, fervour, fierceness, fire, heat, intensity, keenness, passion, spirit, vehemence, warmth, zeal

arduous backbreaking, burdensome, difficult, exhausting, fatiguing, formidable, gruelling, hard, harsh, heavy, laborious, onerous, painful, punishing, rigorous, severe, steep, strenuous, taxing, tiring, toilsome, tough, troublesome, trying

▷ **Antonyms** child's play (*informal*), easy, easy-peasy (*slang*), effortless, facile, light, no bother, no trouble, painless, simple, undemanding

area **1.** district, domain, locality, neck of the woods (*informal*), neighbourhood, patch, plot, realm, region, sector, sphere, stretch, territory, tract, turf (*U.S. slang*), zone **2.** ambit, breadth, compass, expanse, extent, range, scope, size, width **3.** arena, department, domain, field, province, realm, sphere, territory **4.** part, portion, section, sector **5.** sunken space, yard

arena **1.** amphitheatre, bowl, coliseum, field, ground, park (*U.S. & Canad.*), ring, stadium, stage **2.** area, battlefield, battleground, domain, field, field of conflict, lists, province, realm, scene, scope, sector, sphere, territory, theatre

argot cant, dialect, idiom, jargon, lingo (*informal*), parlance, patois, patter, slang, vernacular

argue **1.** altercate, bandy words, be at sixes and sevens, bicker, cross swords, disagree, dispute, fall out (*informal*), feud, fight, fight like cat and dog, go at it hammer and tongs, have an argument, quarrel, squabble, wrangle **2.** assert, claim, contend, controvert, debate, discuss, dispute, expostulate, hold, maintain, plead, question, reason, remonstrate **3.** convince, persuade, prevail upon, talk into, talk round **4.** demonstrate, denote, display, evince, exhibit, imply, indicate, manifest, point to, show, suggest

argument **1.** altercation, barney (*informal*), bickering, clash, controversy, difference of opinion, disagreement, dispute, falling out (*informal*), feud, fight, quarrel, row, squabble, wrangle **2.** assertion, claim, contention, debate, discussion, dispute, expostulation, plea, pleading, questioning, remonstrance, remonstration **3.** argumentation, case, defence, dialectic, ground(s), line of reasoning, logic, polemic, reason, reasoning **4.** abstract, gist, outline, plot, story, story line, subject, summary, synopsis, theme

▷ **Antonyms** (*senses 1 & 2*) accord, agreement, concurrence

argumentative **1.** belligerent, combative, contentious, contrary, disputatious, litigious, opinionated, quarrelsome **2.** contentious, controversial, disputed, polemic

▷ **Antonyms** (*sense 1*) accommodating,

amenable, complaisant, compliant, con~ciliatory, easy-going, obliging

arid **1.** barren, desert, dried up, dry, moistureless, parched, sterile, torrid, waterless **2.** as dry as dust, boring, col~ourless, dreary, dry, dull, flat, jejune, lifeless, spiritless, tedious, tiresome, uninspired, uninteresting, vapid

▷ **Antonyms** (*sense 1*) fertile, fruitful, lush, rich, verdant (*sense 2*) exciting, in~teresting, lively, sexy (*informal*), spirit~ed, stimulating, vivacious

aridity, aridness **1.** barrenness, dryness, moisturelessness, parchedness, sterility, waterlessness **2.** boredom, colourless~ness, dreariness, dryness, dullness, flatness, jejuneness, jejunity, lifeless~ness, spiritlessness, tediousness, te~dium, uninspiredness, uninterest~ingness, vapidity, vapidness

aright accurately, appropriately, aptly, correctly, duly, exactly, fitly, in due or~der, justly, properly, rightly, suitably, truly, without error

arise **1.** appear, begin, come into being, come to light, commence, crop up (*infor~mal*), emanate, emerge, ensue, follow, happen, issue, occur, originate, proceed, result, set in, spring, start, stem **2.** get to one's feet, get up, go up, rise, stand up, wake up **3.** ascend, climb, lift, mount, move upward, rise, soar, tower

aristocracy body of nobles, elite, gentry, *haut monde,* nobility, noblesse (*literary*), patricians, patriciate, peerage, ruling class, upper class, upper crust (*infor~mal*)

▷ **Antonyms** commoners, common peo~ple, hoi polloi, lower classes, masses, plebeians, plebs, proles (*derogatory slang, chiefly Brit.*), proletariat, working classes

aristocrat aristo (*informal*), grandee, lady, lord, noble, nobleman, noble~woman, patrician, peer, peeress

aristocratic **1.** blue-blooded, elite, gentle (*archaic*), gentlemanly, highborn, lordly, noble, patrician, titled, upper-class, well-born **2.** courtly, dignified, elegant, fine, haughty, polished, refined, snob~bish, stylish, well-bred

▷ **Antonyms** (*sense 1*) common, lower-class, plebeian, proletarian, working-class (*sense 2*) boorish, coarse, common, crass, crude, ill-bred, uncouth, unre~fined, vulgar

arm[1] *noun* **1.** appendage, limb, upper limb **2.** bough, branch, department, de~tachment, division, extension, offshoot, projection, section, sector **3.** branch, channel, estuary, firth, inlet, sound, strait, tributary **4.** authority, command, force, might, potency, power, strength, sway

arm[2] *verb* **1.** *especially with weapons* ac~coutre, array, deck out, equip, furnish, issue with, outfit, provide, rig, supply **2.** mobilize, muster forces, prepare for war, take up arms **3.** brace, equip, forearm, fortify, gird one's loins, guard, make ready, outfit, prepare, prime, protect, strengthen

armada fleet, flotilla, navy, squadron

armaments ammunition, arms, guns, materiel, munitions, ordnance, weapon~ry, weapons

armed accoutred, arrayed, carrying weapons, equipped, fitted out, fore~armed, fortified, furnished, girded, guarded, in arms, prepared, primed, protected, provided, ready, rigged out, strengthened, supplied, under arms

armistice ceasefire, peace, suspension of hostilities, truce

armour armour plate, covering, protec~tion, sheathing, shield

armoured armour-plated, bombproof, bulletproof, ironclad, mailed, protected, steel-plated

armoury ammunition dump, arms depot, arsenal, magazine, ordnance depot

arms **1.** armaments, firearms, guns, in~struments of war, ordnance, weaponry, weapons **2.** blazonry, crest, escutcheon, heraldry, insignia

army **1.** armed force, host (*archaic*), land forces, legions, military, military force, soldiers, soldiery, troops **2.** *figurative* array, horde, host, multitude, pack, swarm, throng, vast number

aroma bouquet, fragrance, odour, per~fume, redolence, savour, scent, smell

aromatic balmy, fragrant, odoriferous, perfumed, pungent, redolent, savoury, spicy, sweet-scented, sweet-smelling

▷ **Antonyms** acrid, bad-smelling, fetid, foul, foul-smelling, malodorous, niffy (*Brit. slang*), noisome, offensive, olid, rank, reeking, smelly, stinking, whiffy (*Brit. slang*)

around *preposition* **1.** about, encircling, enclosing, encompassing, environing, on all sides of, on every side of, surround~ing **2.** about, approximately, circa (*used with dates*), roughly ~*adverb* **3.** about, all over, everywhere, here and there, in all directions, on all sides, throughout, to and fro **4.** at hand, close, close at hand, close by, near, nearby, nigh (*archaic or dialect*)

arouse agitate, animate, awaken, call forth, enliven, excite, foment, foster, goad, incite, inflame, instigate, kindle, move, prod, provoke, quicken, rouse, sharpen, spark, spur, stimulate, stir up, summon up, waken, wake up, warm, whet, whip up

▷ **Antonyms** allay, alleviate, assuage, calm, dampen, dull, end, lull, pacify, quell, quench, still

arraign accuse, call to account, charge, complain about, denounce, impeach, in~criminate, indict, prosecute, take to task

arraignment accusation, charge, complaint, denunciation, impeachment, incrimination, indictment, prosecution

arrange 1. align, array, class, classify, dispose, file, form, group, line up, marshal, order, organize, position, put in order, range, rank, sequence, set out, sort, sort out (*informal*), systematize, tidy **2.** adjust, agree to, come to terms, compromise, construct, contrive, determine, devise, fix up, organize, plan, prepare, project, schedule, settle **3.** adapt, instrument, orchestrate, score

▷ **Antonyms** (*senses 1 & 2*) disarrange, disorganize, disturb, mess up, scatter

arrangement 1. alignment, array, classification, design, display, disposition, form, grouping, line-up, marshalling, order, ordering, organization, ranging, rank, setup (*informal*), structure, system **2.** (*often plural*) adjustment, agreement, compact, compromise, construction, deal, devising, organization, plan, planning, preparation, provision, schedule, settlement, terms **3.** adaptation, instrumentation, interpretation, orchestration, score, version

arrant absolute, atrocious, blatant, complete, deep-dyed (*usually derogatory*), downright, egregious, extreme, flagrant, gross, infamous, monstrous, notorious, out-and-out, outright, rank, thorough, thoroughgoing, undisguised, unmitigated, utter, vile

array *noun* **1.** arrangement, collection, display, disposition, exhibition, formation, line-up, marshalling, muster, order, parade, show, supply **2.** *poetic* apparel, attire, clothes, dress, finery, garb, garments, raiment (*archaic or poetic*), regalia, threads (*slang*) *~verb* **3.** align, arrange, display, dispose, draw up, exhibit, form up, group, line up, marshal, muster, order, parade, place in order, range, sequence, set in line (*Military*), show **4.** accoutre, adorn, apparel (*archaic*), attire, bedeck, caparison, clothe, deck, decorate, dress, equip, festoon, fit out, garb, get ready, outfit, robe, supply, wrap

arrest *verb* **1.** apprehend, bust (*informal*), capture, catch, collar (*informal*), detain, feel one's collar (*slang*), lay hold of, lift (*slang*), nab (*informal*), nail (*informal*), nick (*slang, chiefly Brit.*), pinch (*informal*), run in (*slang*), seize, take, take into custody, take prisoner **2.** block, check, delay, end, halt, hinder, hold, inhibit, interrupt, obstruct, restrain, retard, slow, stall, stay, stop, suppress **3.** absorb, catch, engage, engross, fascinate, grip, hold, intrigue, occupy *~noun* **4.** apprehension, bust (*informal*), capture, cop (*slang*), detention, seizure **5.** blockage, check, delay, end, halt, hindrance, inhibition, interruption, obstruction, restraint, stalling, stay, stoppage, suppression

▷ **Antonyms** *~verb* (*sense 1*) free, let go, release, set free (*sense 2*) accelerate, encourage, precipitate, promote, quicken, speed up *~noun* (*sense 4*) freeing, release (*sense 5*) acceleration, encouragement, precipitation, promotion, quickening

arresting conspicuous, dramatic, engaging, extraordinary, impressive, noticeable, outstanding, remarkable, salient, striking, stunning, surprising

▷ **Antonyms** inconspicuous, unimpressive, unnoticeable, unremarkable

arrival 1. advent, appearance, arriving, coming, entrance, happening, occurrence, taking place **2.** arriver, caller, comer, entrant, incomer, newcomer, visitant, visitor

arrive 1. appear, attain, befall, come, enter, get to, happen, occur, reach, show up (*informal*), take place, turn up **2.** *informal* achieve recognition, become famous, make good, make it (*informal*), make one's mark (*informal*), make the grade (*informal*), reach the top, succeed

▷ **Antonyms** (*sense 1*) depart, disappear, exit, go, go away, leave, pack one's bags (*informal*), retire, take (one's) leave, vanish, withdraw

arrogance bluster, conceit, conceitedness, contemptuousness, disdainfulness, haughtiness, hauteur, high-handedness, hubris, imperiousness, insolence, loftiness, lordliness, overweeningness, pomposity, pompousness, presumption, pretension, pretentiousness, pride, scornfulness, superciliousness, swagger, uppishness (*Brit. informal*)

▷ **Antonyms** bashfulness, diffidence, humility, meekness, modesty, politeness, shyness

arrogant assuming, blustering, conceited, contemptuous, disdainful, haughty, high and mighty (*informal*), high-handed, imperious, insolent, looking down one's nose at, lordly, overbearing, overweening, pompous, presumptuous, pretentious, proud, scornful, supercilious, swaggering, too big for one's boots *or* breeches, turning up one's nose at, uppish (*Brit. informal*)

▷ **Antonyms** bashful, deferential, diffident, humble, modest, polite, servile, shy, unassuming

arrogate appropriate, assume, claim unduly, commandeer, demand, expropriate, presume, seize, usurp

arrogation appropriation, assumption, commandeering, demand, expropriation, presumption, seizure, usurpation

arrow 1. bolt, dart, flight, quarrel, reed (*archaic*), shaft (*archaic*) **2.** indicator, pointer

arsenal ammunition dump, armoury, arms depot, magazine, ordnance depot, stock, stockpile, store, storehouse, supply

art 1. adroitness, aptitude, artifice (*archaic*), artistry, craft, craftsmanship, dexterity, expertise, facility, ingenuity, knack, knowledge, mastery, method, profession, skill, trade, virtuosity **2.** artfulness, artifice, astuteness, craftiness, cunning, deceit, duplicity, guile, trickery, wiliness

artful adept, adroit, clever, crafty, cunning, deceitful, designing, dexterous, foxy, ingenious, intriguing, masterly, politic, proficient, resourceful, scheming, sharp, shrewd, skilful, sly, smart, subtle, tricky, wily
▷ **Antonyms** artless, clumsy, frank, ingenuous, open, simple, straightforward, unadept, unskilled, untalented

article 1. commodity, item, object, piece, substance, thing, unit **2.** composition, discourse, essay, feature, item, paper, piece, story, treatise **3.** branch, clause, count, detail, division, head, heading, item, matter, paragraph, part, particular, passage, piece, point, portion, section

articulate *adjective* **1.** clear, coherent, comprehensible, eloquent, expressive, fluent, intelligible, lucid, meaningful, understandable, vocal, well-spoken *~verb* **2.** enounce, enunciate, express, pronounce, say, speak, state, talk, utter, verbalize, vocalize, voice **3.** connect, couple, fit together, hinge, join, joint
▷ **Antonyms** *~adjective* dumb, faltering, halting, hesitant, incoherent, incomprehensible, indistinct, mumbled, mute, poorly-spoken, silent, speechless, stammering, stuttering, tongue-tied, unclear, unintelligible, voiceless

articulation 1. delivery, diction, enunciation, expression, pronunciation, saying, speaking, statement, talking, utterance, verbalization, vocalization, voicing **2.** connection, coupling, hinge, joint, jointing, juncture

artifice 1. contrivance, device, dodge, expedient, hoax, machination, manoeuvre, ruse, stratagem, subterfuge, tactic, trick, wile **2.** artfulness, chicanery, craft, craftiness, cunning, deception, duplicity, guile, scheming, slyness, trickery **3.** adroitness, cleverness, deftness, facility, finesse, ingenuity, invention, inventiveness, skill

artificer 1. artisan, craftsman, mechanic **2.** architect, builder, contriver, creator, designer, deviser, inventor, maker, originator

artificial 1. man-made, manufactured, non-natural, plastic, synthetic **2.** bogus, counterfeit, ersatz, fake, imitation, mock, phoney *or* phony (*informal*), pseudo (*informal*), sham, simulated, specious, spurious **3.** affected, assumed, contrived, false, feigned, forced, hollow, insincere, meretricious, phoney *or* phony (*informal*), pretended, spurious, unnatural
▷ **Antonyms** authentic, frank, genuine, honest, natural, sincere, true, unaffected

artillery battery, big guns, cannon, cannonry, gunnery, ordnance

artisan artificer, craftsman, handicraftsman, journeyman, mechanic, skilled workman, technician

artistic aesthetic, beautiful, creative, cultivated, cultured, decorative, elegant, exquisite, graceful, imaginative, ornamental, refined, sensitive, sophisticated, stylish, tasteful
▷ **Antonyms** inartistic, inelegant, tasteless, unattractive, untalented

artistry accomplishment, art, artistic ability, brilliance, craft, craftsmanship, creativity, finesse, flair, genius, mastery, proficiency, sensibility, skill, style, talent, taste, touch, virtuosity, workmanship

artless 1. candid, direct, fair, frank, genuine, guileless, honest, open, plain, round, sincere, straightforward, true, undesigning, upfront (*informal*) **2.** humble, natural, plain, pure, simple, unadorned, unaffected, uncontrived, unpretentious **3.** awkward, bungling, clumsy, crude, incompetent, inept, maladroit, primitive, rude, unskilled, untalented **4.** childlike, ingenuous, innocent, jejune, naive, trustful, trusting, unsophisticated
▷ **Antonyms** (*sense 1*) artful, crafty, cunning, designing, dishonest, false, insincere (*sense 2*) affected, artificial, unnatural (*sense 3*) aesthetic, artful, artistic, crafty, cunning, sophisticated (*sense 4*) sophisticated, suspicious

as *conjunction* **1.** at the time that, during the time that, just as, when, while **2.** in the manner that, in the way that, like **3.** that which, what **4.** because, considering that, seeing that, since **5.** in the same manner with, in the same way that, like **6.** for instance, like, such as *~preposition* **7.** being, in the character of, in the role of, under the name of **8. as for** as regards, in reference to, on the subject of, with reference to, with regard to, with respect to **9. as it were** in a manner of speaking, in a way, so to say, so to speak

ascend climb, float up, fly up, go up, lift off, mount, move up, rise, scale, slope upwards, soar, take off, tower
▷ **Antonyms** alight, descend, dip, drop, fall, go down, incline, move down, plummet, plunge, sink, slant, slope, subside, tumble

ascendancy, ascendency authority, command, control, dominance, domination, dominion, hegemony, influence, mastery, power, predominance, pre-eminence, prevalence, reign, rule, sov~

ereignty, superiority, supremacy, sway, upper hand
▷ **Antonyms** inferiority, servility, sub~jection, subordination, weakness

ascendant, ascendent *adjective* **1.** ascend~ing, climbing, going upwards, mounting, rising **2.** authoritative, commanding, controlling, dominant, influential, pow~erful, predominant, pre-eminent, pre~vailing, ruling, superior, supreme, uppermost *~noun* **3. in the ascendant** ascending, climbing, commanding, dominant, dominating, flourishing, growing, increasing, mounting, on the rise, on the way up, prevailing, rising, supreme, up-and-coming, uppermost, winning

ascension ascent, climb, mounting, mov~ing upwards, rise, rising

ascent 1. ascending, ascension, clamber~ing, climb, climbing, mounting, rise, rising, scaling, upward movement **2.** ac~clivity, gradient, incline, ramp, rise, ris~ing ground, upward slope

ascertain confirm, determine, discover, establish, ferret out, find out, fix, iden~tify, learn, make certain, settle, suss (out) (*slang*), verify

ascetic 1. *noun* abstainer, anchorite, her~mit, monk, nun, recluse, self-denier **2.** *~adjective* abstemious, abstinent, aus~tere, celibate, frugal, harsh, plain, puri~tanical, rigorous, self-denying, self-disciplined, severe, Spartan, stern
▷ **Antonyms** *~noun* hedonist, sensualist, voluptuary *~adjective* abandoned, com~fortable, luxurious, self-indulgent, sen~suous, voluptuous

asceticism abstemiousness, abstinence, austerity, celibacy, frugality, harshness, mortification of the flesh, plainness, pu~ritanism, rigorousness, rigour, self-abnegation, self-denial, self-discipline, self-mortification

ascribe assign, attribute, charge, credit, impute, put down, refer, set down

ashamed abashed, bashful, blushing, chagrined, conscience-stricken, crest~fallen, discomfited, distressed, embar~rassed, guilty, humbled, humiliated, mortified, prudish, reluctant, remorse~ful, shamefaced, sheepish, shy, sorry
▷ **Antonyms** gratified, honoured, pleased, proud, satisfied, unashamed, vain

ashen anaemic, ashy, colourless, grey, leaden, like death warmed up (*infor~mal*), livid, pale, pallid, pasty, wan, white
▷ **Antonyms** blooming, blushing, florid, flushed, glowing, radiant, red, reddish, rosy, rosy-cheeked, rubicund, ruddy

ashore aground, landwards, on dry land, on land, on the beach, on the shore, shorewards, to the shore

aside 1. *adverb* alone, alongside, apart, away, beside, in isolation, in reserve, on one side, out of mind, out of the way, privately, separately, to one side, to the side **2.** *~noun* departure, digression, ex~cursion, excursus, interpolation, inter~position, parenthesis, tangent

asinine braindead (*informal*), brainless, daft (*informal*), dead from the neck up (*informal*), dunderheaded, fatuous, fool~ish, goofy (*informal*), gormless (*Brit. in~formal*), halfwitted, idiotic, imbecile, imbecilic, inane, moronic, obstinate, senseless, silly, stupid, thickheaded, thick-witted
▷ **Antonyms** brainy (*informal*), bright, clever, intelligent, quick-witted, sage, sane, sensible, sharp, smart, wise

ask 1. inquire, interrogate, query, ques~tion, quiz **2.** appeal, apply, beg, beseech, claim, crave, demand, entreat, implore, petition, plead, pray, request, seek, so~licit, sue, supplicate **3.** bid, invite, sum~mon
▷ **Antonyms** (*sense 1*) answer, reply, re~spond

askance 1. awry, indirectly, obliquely, out of the corner of one's eye, sideways, with a side glance **2.** disapprovingly, dis~trustfully, doubtfully, dubiously, mis~trustfully, sceptically, suspiciously

askew *adverb/adjective* aslant, awry, cockeyed (*informal*), crooked, crookedly, lopsided, oblique, obliquely, off-centre, skewwhiff (*Brit. informal*), to one side
▷ **Antonyms** aligned, even, in line, level, right, square, straight, true

asleep crashed out (*slang*), dead to the world (*informal*), dormant, dozing, fast asleep, napping, out for the count, sleeping, slumbering, snoozing (*infor~mal*), sound asleep

aspect 1. air, appearance, attitude, bear~ing, condition, countenance, demeanour, expression, look, manner, mien (*liter~ary*) **2.** bearing, direction, exposure, out~look, point of view, position, prospect, scene, situation, view **3.** angle, facet, feature, side

asperity acerbity, acrimony, bitterness, churlishness, crabbedness, crossness, harshness, irascibility, irritability, mo~roseness, peevishness, roughness, rug~gedness, severity, sharpness, sourness, sullenness

asperse abuse, calumniate, cast asper~sions (on), defame, detract, disparage, reproach, slander, slur, smear, traduce, vilify, vituperate

aspersion abuse, calumny, censure, char~acter assassination, defamation, deni~gration, detraction, disparagement, ob~loquy, reproach, slander, slur, smear, traducement, vilification, vituperation

asphyxiate choke, smother, stifle, stran~gle, strangulate, suffocate, throttle

aspirant 1. *noun* applicant, aspirer, candidate, hopeful, postulant, seeker, suitor **2.** *~adjective* ambitious, aspiring, eager, endeavouring, hopeful, longing, striving, wishful

aspiration aim, ambition, craving, desire, dream, eagerness, endeavour, goal, hankering, Holy Grail (*informal*), hope, longing, object, objective, wish, yearning

aspire aim, be ambitious, be eager, crave, desire, dream, hanker, hope, long, pursue, seek, set one's heart on, wish, yearn

aspiring *adjective* ambitious, aspirant, eager, endeavouring, hopeful, longing, striving, wishful, would-be

ass 1. donkey, jennet, moke (*slang*) **2.** airhead (*slang*), berk (*Brit. slang*), blockhead, bonehead (*slang*), charlie (*Brit. informal*), coot, daftie (*informal*), dickhead (*slang*), dipstick (*Brit. slang*), divvy (*Brit. slang*), dolt, dope (*informal*), dork (*slang*), dunce, dweeb (*U.S. slang*), fathead (*informal*), fool, fuckwit (*taboo slang*), geek (*slang*), gobshite (*Irish taboo slang*), gonzo (*slang*), halfwit, idiot, jackass, jerk (*slang, chiefly U.S. & Canad.*), nerd *or* nurd (*slang*), nincompoop, ninny, nitwit (*informal*), numbskull *or* numskull, numpty (*Scot. informal*), oaf, pillock (*Brit. slang*), plank (*Brit. slang*), plonker (*slang*), prat (*slang*), prick (*slang*), schmuck (*U.S. slang*), simpleton, twerp *or* twirp (*informal*), twit (*informal, chiefly Brit.*), wally (*slang*)

assail 1. assault, attack, belabour, beset, charge, encounter, fall upon, invade, lay into (*informal*), maltreat, set about, set upon **2.** abuse, berate, blast, criticize, go for the jugular, impugn, lambast(e), malign, put down, revile, tear into (*informal*), vilify

assailant aggressor, assailer, assaulter, attacker, invader

assassin eliminator (*slang*), executioner, hatchet man (*slang*), hit man (*slang*), killer, liquidator, murderer, slayer

assassinate blow away (*slang, chiefly U.S.*), eliminate (*slang*), hit (*slang*), kill, liquidate, murder, slay, take out (*slang*)

assault 1. *noun* aggression, attack, campaign, charge, incursion, inroad, invasion, offensive, onset, onslaught, storm, storming, strike **2.** *~verb* assail, attack, belabour, beset, charge, fall upon, invade, lay into (*informal*), set about, set upon, storm, strike at

▷ **Antonyms** *~noun* defence, protection, resistance *~verb* defend, protect, resist

assay *verb* **1.** analyse, appraise, assess, evaluate, examine, inspect, investigate, prove, test, try, weigh *~noun* **2.** *archaic* attempt, endeavour, essay, stab (*informal*), try, venture **3.** analysis, examination, inspection, investigation, test, trial

assemblage accumulation, aggregation, assembly, body, collection, company, conclave, congregation, convocation, crowd, flock, gathering, group, mass, meeting, multitude, rally, throng

assemble 1. accumulate, amass, bring together, call together, collect, come together, congregate, convene, convoke, flock, foregather, gather, marshal, meet, muster, rally, round up, summon **2.** build up, connect, construct, erect, fabricate, fit together, join, make, manufacture, piece together, put together, set up

▷ **Antonyms** adjourn, break up (*informal*), disassemble, disband, dismiss, disperse, distribute, divide, scatter, take apart

assembly 1. accumulation, aggregation, assemblage, body, collection, company, conclave, conference, congregation, congress, convention, convocation, council, crowd, diet, flock, gathering, group, house, mass, meeting, multitude, rally, synod, throng **2.** building up, connecting, construction, erection, fabrication, fitting together, joining, manufacture, piecing together, putting together, setting up

assent 1. *verb* accede, accept, acquiesce, agree, allow, approve, comply, concur, consent, fall in with, go along with, grant, permit, sanction, subscribe **2.** *~noun* acceptance, accession, accord, acquiescence, agreement, approval, compliance, concurrence, consent, permission, sanction

▷ **Antonyms** *~verb* deny, differ, disagree, dissent, object, protest, rebut, reject, retract *~noun* denial, disagreement, disapproval, dissension, dissent, objection, refusal

assert 1. affirm, allege, asseverate, attest, aver, avouch (*archaic*), avow, contend, declare, maintain, predicate, profess, pronounce, state, swear **2.** claim, defend, insist upon, press, put forward, stand up for, stress, uphold, vindicate **3. assert oneself** exert one's influence, make one's presence felt, put oneself forward, put one's foot down (*informal*)

▷ **Antonyms** (*senses 1 & 2*) deny, disavow, disclaim, rebut, refute, retract

assertion 1. affirmation, allegation, asseveration, attestation, avowal, claim, contention, declaration, predication, profession, pronouncement, statement **2.** defence, insistence, maintenance, stressing, vindication

assertive aggressive, confident, decided, decisive, demanding, dogmatic, domineering, emphatic, feisty (*informal, chiefly U.S. & Canad.*), firm, forceful, forward, insistent, in-your-face (*Brit. slang*), overbearing, positive, pushy (*informal*), self-assured, strong-willed

▷ **Antonyms** backward, bashful, diffident, hesitant, insecure, meek, modest, reserved, retiring, self-conscious, self-effacing, sheepish, shrinking, shy, timid, timorous, unassertive, unobtrusive

assess **1**. appraise, compute, determine, estimate, evaluate, eye up, fix, gauge, judge, rate, size up (*informal*), value, weigh **2**. demand, evaluate, fix, impose, levy, rate, tax, value

assessment **1**. appraisal, computation, determination, estimate, estimation, evaluation, judgment, rating, valuation **2**. charge, demand, duty, evaluation, fee, impost, levy, rate, rating, tariff, tax, taxation, toll, valuation

asset **1**. ace in the hole, ace up one's sleeve, advantage, aid, benefit, blessing, boon, feather in one's cap, help, resource, service **2**. *plural* capital, estate, funds, goods, holdings, means, money, possessions, property, reserves, resources, valuables, wealth

▷ **Antonyms** (*sense 1*) albatross, burden, disadvantage, drag, drawback, encumbrance, handicap, hindrance, impediment, liability, millstone, minus (*informal*), nuisance

asseverate affirm, assert, attest, aver, avouch (*archaic*), avow, declare, maintain, predicate, profess, pronounce, protest, state, swear

asseveration affirmation, assertion, attestation, averment, avowal, declaration, predication, profession, pronouncement, protestation, statement, vow

assiduity application, assiduousness, attentiveness, constancy, diligence, indefatigability, industriousness, industry, laboriousness, perseverance, persistence, sedulity, sedulousness, steadiness, studiousness, tirelessness

assiduous attentive, constant, diligent, hard-working, indefatigable, industrious, laborious, persevering, persistent, sedulous, steady, studious, unflagging, untiring, unwearied

▷ **Antonyms** careless, idle, inattentive, indolent, lax, lazy, negligent, slack

assign **1**. appoint, choose, delegate, designate, name, nominate, select **2**. allocate, allot, apportion, consign, distribute, give, give out, grant, make over **3**. appoint, appropriate, determine, fix, set apart, stipulate **4**. accredit, ascribe, attribute, put down

assignation **1**. clandestine meeting, illicit meeting, rendezvous, secret meeting, tryst (*archaic*) **2**. allocation, allotment, appointment, apportionment, appropriation, ascription, assignment, attribution, choice, consignment, delegation, designation, determination, distribution, giving, grant, nomination, selection, specification, stipulation

assignment **1**. appointment, charge, commission, duty, job, mission, position, post, responsibility, task **2**. allocation, allotment, appointment, apportionment, appropriation, ascription, assignation (*Law, chiefly Scot.*), attribution, choice, consignment, delegation, designation, determination, distribution, giving, grant, nomination, selection, specification, stipulation

assimilate **1**. absorb, digest, imbibe (*literary*), incorporate, ingest, learn, take in **2**. acclimatize, accommodate, acculturate, accustom, adapt, adjust, become like, become similar, blend in, conform, fit, homogenize, intermix, mingle

assist abet, aid, back, benefit, boost, collaborate, cooperate, encourage, expedite, facilitate, further, give a leg up (*informal*), help, lend a helping hand, promote, reinforce, relieve, second, serve, succour, support, sustain, work for, work with

▷ **Antonyms** frustrate, hamper, handicap, hinder, hold back, hold up, impede, obstruct, resist, thwart, work against

assistance abetment, aid, backing, benefit, boost, collaboration, cooperation, encouragement, furtherance, help, helping hand, promotion, reinforcement, relief, service, succour, support, sustenance

▷ **Antonyms** hindrance, obstruction, opposition, resistance

assistant abettor, accessory, accomplice, aide, aider, ally, associate, auxiliary, backer, coadjutor (*rare*), collaborator, colleague, confederate, cooperator, helper, helpmate, henchman, partner, protagonist, right-hand man, second, supporter

associate *verb* **1**. affiliate, ally, combine, confederate, conjoin, connect, correlate, couple, identify, join, league, link, lump together, mention in the same breath, mix, pair, relate, think of together, unite, yoke **2**. accompany, befriend, be friends, consort, fraternize, hang about, hang out (*informal*), hobnob, mingle, mix, run around (*informal*) ~*noun* **3**. ally, collaborator, colleague, companion, compeer, comrade, confederate, confrère, co-worker, follower, friend, mate, partner

▷ **Antonyms** (*sense 1*) detach, disconnect, dissociate, distance, distinguish, divorce, isolate, segregate, separate, set apart (*sense 2*) avoid, be alienated, be estranged, break off, part company

association **1**. affiliation, alliance, band, clique, club, coalition, combine, company, confederacy, confederation, cooperative, corporation, federation, fraternity, group, league, order, organization, partnership, society, syndicate, union **2**. affinity, companionship, comradeship, familiarity, fellowship, fraternization, friendship, intimacy, liaison, partnership, relations, relationship **3**. blend, bond, combination, concomitance, connection, correlation, identification, joining, juxtaposition, linkage, linking, lumping together, mixing, mixture, pairing, relation, tie, union, yoking

assort arrange, array, categorize, classify, dispose, distribute, file, grade, group, range, rank, sort, type

assorted 1. different, diverse, diversified, heterogeneous, manifold, miscellaneous, mixed, motley, sundry, varied, variegated, various **2.** arranged, arrayed, categorized, classified, disposed, filed, graded, grouped, ranged, ranked, sorted, typed
▷ **Antonyms** (*sense 1*) alike, homogeneous, identical, like, same, similar, uniform, unvaried

assortment 1. array, choice, collection, diversity, farrago, hotchpotch, jumble, medley, *mélange,* miscellany, mishmash, mixed bag (*informal*), mixture, pick 'n' mix, potpourri, salmagundi, selection, variety **2.** arrangement, categorizing, classification, disposition, distribution, filing, grading, grouping, ranging, ranking, sorting, typing

assuage 1. allay, alleviate, calm, ease, lessen, lighten, mitigate, moderate, palliate, quench, relieve, soothe, temper **2.** appease, calm, lull, mollify, pacify, pour oil on troubled waters, quiet, relax, satisfy, soften, soothe, still, tranquillize
▷ **Antonyms** (*sense 1*) aggravate, exacerbate, heighten, increase, intensify, worsen (*sense 2*) aggravate, embitter, enrage, infuriate, madden, provoke

assume 1. accept, believe, expect, fancy, guess (*informal, chiefly U.S. & Canad.*), imagine, infer, presume, presuppose, suppose, surmise, suspect, take for granted, think **2.** adopt, affect, counterfeit, feign, imitate, impersonate, mimic, pretend to, put on, sham, simulate **3.** accept, acquire, attend to, begin, don, embark upon, embrace, enter upon, put on, set about, shoulder, take on, take over, take responsibility for, take up, undertake **4.** acquire, appropriate, arrogate, commandeer, expropriate, pre-empt, seize, take, take over, usurp
▷ **Antonyms** (*sense 1*) know, prove (*senses 3 & 4*) give up, hand over, leave, put aside, relinquish

assumed 1. affected, bogus, counterfeit, fake, false, feigned, fictitious, imitation, made-up, make-believe, phoney *or* phony (*informal*), pretended, pseudonymous, sham, simulated, spurious **2.** accepted, expected, hypothetical, presumed, presupposed, supposed, surmised, taken for granted **3.** appropriated, arrogated, pre-empted, seized, usurped
▷ **Antonyms** (*senses 1 & 2*) actual, authentic, known, natural, positive, real, stated, true

assuming *adjective* arrogant, bold, conceited, disdainful, domineering, egotistic, forward, haughty, imperious, overbearing, presumptuous, pushy (*informal*), rude

assumption 1. acceptance, belief, conjecture, expectation, fancy, guess, hypothesis, inference, postulate, postulation, premise, premiss, presumption, presupposition, supposition, surmise, suspicion, theory **2.** acceptance, acquisition, adoption, embracing, entering upon, putting on, shouldering, takeover, taking on, taking up, undertaking **3.** acquisition, appropriation, arrogation, expropriation, pre-empting, seizure, takeover, taking, usurpation **4.** arrogance, conceit, imperiousness, presumption, pride, self-importance

assurance 1. affirmation, assertion, declaration, guarantee, oath, pledge, profession, promise, protestation, vow, word, word of honour **2.** assertiveness, assuredness, boldness, certainty, certitude, confidence, conviction, coolness, courage, faith, firmness, nerve, poise, positiveness, security, self-confidence, self-reliance, sureness **3.** arrogance, brass neck (*Brit. informal*), chutzpah (*U.S. & Canad. informal*), effrontery, gall (*informal*), impudence, neck (*informal*), nerve (*informal*), presumption, sassiness (*U.S. informal*)
▷ **Antonyms** (*sense 1*) falsehood, lie (*senses 2 & 3*) apprehension, diffidence, distrust, doubt, self-doubt, self-effacement, shyness, timidity, uncertainty

assure 1. comfort, convince, embolden, encourage, hearten, persuade, reassure, soothe **2.** affirm, attest, certify, confirm, declare confidently, give one's word to, guarantee, pledge, promise, swear, vow **3.** clinch, complete, confirm, ensure, guarantee, make certain, make sure, seal, secure

assured 1. beyond doubt, clinched, confirmed, dependable, ensured, fixed, guaranteed, indubitable, in the bag (*slang*), irrefutable, made certain, sealed, secure, settled, sure, unquestionable **2.** assertive, audacious, bold, brazen, certain, complacent, confident, overconfident, poised, positive, pushy (*informal*), resting on one's laurels, self-assured, self-confident, self-possessed, sure of oneself
▷ **Antonyms** (*sense 1*) ambiguous, doubtful, indefinite, questionable, uncertain, unconfirmed, unsettled, unsure (*sense 2*) bashful, diffident, hesitant, retiring, self-conscious, self-effacing, timid

astir active, afoot, awake, in motion, on the go (*informal*), on the move (*informal*), out of bed, roused, up and about, up and around

astonish amaze, astound, bewilder, boggle the mind, confound, daze, dumbfound, flabbergast (*informal*), stagger, stun, stupefy, surprise

astonishing amazing, astounding, bewildering, breathtaking, brilliant, impressive, sensational (*informal*), staggering, striking, stunning, stupefying, surprising, wondrous (*archaic or literary*)
▷ **Antonyms** anticipated, expected, foreseen

astonishment amazement, awe, bewilderment, confusion, consternation, stupefaction, surprise, wonder, wonderment

astound amaze, astonish, bewilder, boggle the mind, confound, daze, dumbfound, flabbergast (*informal*), overwhelm, stagger, stun, stupefy, surprise, take one's breath away

astounding amazing, astonishing, bewildering, breathtaking, brilliant, impressive, sensational (*informal*), staggering, striking, stunning, stupefying, surprising, wondrous (*archaic or literary*)

astray *adjective/adverb* **1.** adrift, afield, amiss, lost, off, off course, off the mark, off the right track, off the subject **2.** into error, into sin, to the bad, wrong

astringent 1. acerbic, austere, caustic, exacting, grim, hard, harsh, rigid, rigorous, severe, stern, strict, stringent **2.** contractile, contractive, styptic

astronaut cosmonaut, spaceman, space pilot, space traveller, spacewoman

astute adroit, artful, bright, calculating, canny, clever, crafty, cunning, discerning, foxy, insightful, intelligent, keen, knowing, on the ball (*informal*), penetrating, perceptive, politic, sagacious, sharp, shrewd, sly, subtle, wily
▷ **Antonyms** dull, ingenuous, naive, slow, straightforward, stupid, unintelligent, unknowing

astuteness acumen, adroitness, artfulness, brightness, canniness, cleverness, craftiness, cunning, discernment, foxiness, insight, intelligence, keenness, knowledge, penetration, perceptiveness, sagacity, sharpness, shrewdness, slyness, smarts (*slang, chiefly U.S.*), subtlety, suss (*slang*), wiliness

asunder *adverb/adjective* apart, in pieces, into pieces, rent, to bits, to pieces, torn, to shreds

asylum 1. harbour, haven, preserve, refuge, retreat, safety, sanctuary, shelter **2.** *old-fashioned* funny farm (*facetious*), hospital, institution, laughing academy (*U.S. slang*), loony bin (*slang*), madhouse (*informal*), mental hospital, nuthouse (*slang*), psychiatric hospital, rubber room (*U.S. slang*)

atheism disbelief, freethinking, godlessness, heathenism, infidelity, irreligion, nonbelief, paganism, scepticism, unbelief

atheist disbeliever, freethinker, heathen, infidel, irreligionist, nonbeliever, pagan, sceptic, unbeliever

athlete competitor, contender, contestant, games player, gymnast, player, runner, sportsman, sportswoman

athletic 1. *adjective* able-bodied, active, brawny, energetic, fit, herculean, husky (*informal*), lusty, muscular, powerful, robust, sinewy, strapping, strong, sturdy, vigorous, well-proportioned **2.** *~plural noun* contests, exercises, games of strength, gymnastics, races, sports, track and field events
▷ **Antonyms** (*sense 1*) delicate, feeble, frail, puny, sickly, weedy (*informal*)

atmosphere 1. aerosphere, air, heavens, sky **2.** air, ambience, aura, character, climate, environment, feel, feeling, flavour, mood, quality, spirit, surroundings, tone, vibes (*slang*)

atom bit, crumb, dot, fragment, grain, iota, jot, mite, molecule, morsel, mote, particle, scintilla (*rare*), scrap, shred, speck, spot, tittle, trace, whit

atone 1. (*with* **for**) answer for, compensate, do penance for, make amends for, make redress, make reparation for, make up for, pay for, recompense, redress **2.** appease, expiate, make expiation for, propitiate, reconcile, redeem

atonement amends, compensation, expiation, payment, penance, propitiation, recompense, redress, reparation, restitution, satisfaction

atrocious 1. barbaric, brutal, cruel, diabolical, fiendish, flagrant, godawful (*slang*), heinous, hellacious (*U.S. slang*), infamous, infernal, inhuman, monstrous, nefarious, ruthless, savage, vicious, villainous, wicked **2.** appalling, detestable, execrable, grievous, horrible, horrifying, shocking, terrible
▷ **Antonyms** admirable, civilized, fine, generous, gentle, good, honourable, humane, kind, merciful, tasteful

atrocity 1. abomination, act of savagery, barbarity, brutality, crime, cruelty, enormity, evil, horror, monstrosity, outrage, villainy **2.** atrociousness, barbarity, barbarousness, brutality, cruelty, enormity, fiendishness, grievousness, heinousness, horror, infamy, inhumanity, monstrousness, nefariousness, ruthlessness, savagery, shockingness, viciousness, villainousness, wickedness

atrophy 1. *noun* decay, decaying, decline, degeneration, deterioration, diminution, meltdown (*informal*), shrivelling, wasting, wasting away, withering **2.** *~verb* decay, decline, degenerate, deteriorate, diminish, dwindle, fade, shrink, shrivel, waste, waste away, wilt, wither

attach 1. add, adhere, affix, annex, ap~ pend, bind, connect, couple, fasten, fix, join, link, make fast, secure, stick, sub~ join, tie, unite **2.** accompany, affiliate, associate, become associated with, com~ bine, enlist, join, join forces with, latch on to, sign on with, sign up with, unite with **3.** ascribe, assign, associate, attrib~ ute, connect, impute, invest with, lay, place, put **4.** allocate, allot, appoint, as~ sign, consign, designate, detail, ear~ mark, second, send

▷ **Antonyms** detach, disconnect, dissoci~ ate, loosen, remove, retire, separate, untie, withdraw

attached 1. affectionate towards, devoted, fond of, full of regard for, possessive **2.** accompanied, engaged, married, part~ nered, spoken for

attachment 1. adaptor *or* adapter, bond, clamp, connection, connector, coupling, fastener, fastening, joint, junction, link, tie **2.** affection, affinity, attraction, bond, devotion, fidelity, fondness, friendship, liking, love, loyalty, partiality, posses~ siveness, predilection, regard, tender~ ness **3.** accessory, accoutrement, adaptor *or* adapter, addition, add-on, adjunct, appendage, appurtenance, auxiliary, extension, extra, fitting, fixture, sup~ plement, supplementary part

▷ **Antonyms** (*sense 2*) animosity, antipa~ thy, aversion, disinclination, distaste, hatred, hostility, loathing

attack *noun* 1. aggression, assault, cam~ paign, charge, foray, incursion, inroad, invasion, offensive, onset, onslaught, raid, rush, strike **2.** abuse, blame, cal~ umny, censure, character assassination, criticism, denigration, impugnment, stick (*slang*), vilification **3.** access, bout, convulsion, fit, paroxysm, seizure, spasm, spell, stroke *~verb* **4.** assail, as~ sault, charge, fall upon, invade, lay into (*informal*), raid, rush, set about, set upon, storm, strike (at) **5.** abuse, berate, bite someone's head off, blame, blast, censure, criticize, excoriate, go for the jugular, have a go (at) (*informal*), im~ pugn, lambast(e), malign, put down, re~ vile, snap someone's head off, tear into (*informal*), vilify

▷ **Antonyms** *~noun* (*senses 1 & 2*) de~ fence, retreat, support, vindication, withdrawal *~verb* defend, guard, protect, retreat, support, sustain, vindicate, withdraw

attacker aggressor, assailant, assaulter, intruder, invader, raider

attain accomplish, achieve, acquire, ar~ rive at, bring off, complete, earn, effect, fulfil, gain, get, grasp, land, obtain, pro~ cure, reach, realize, reap, score (*slang*), secure, win

attainable accessible, accomplishable, achievable, at hand, feasible, gettable, graspable, likely, obtainable, possible, potential, practicable, probable, procur~ able, reachable, realizable, within reach

▷ **Antonyms** impossible, impracticable, improbable, inaccessible, out of reach, unattainable, unfeasible, unlikely, un~ obtainable, unprocurable, unreachable

attainment 1. accomplishment, achieve~ ment, acquirement, acquisition, arrival at, completion, feat, fulfilment, gaining, getting, obtaining, procurement, reach~ ing, realization, reaping, winning **2.** ability, accomplishment, achievement, art, capability, competence, gift, mas~ tery, proficiency, skill, talent

attempt 1. *noun* assault, attack, bid, crack (*informal*), effort, endeavour, es~ say, experiment, go (*informal*), shot (*in~ formal*), stab (*informal*), trial, try, undertaking, venture **2.** *~verb* endeav~ our, essay, experiment, have a crack, have a go (*informal*), have a shot (*infor~ mal*), have a stab (*informal*), jump through hoops (*informal*), seek, strive, tackle, take on, take the bit between one's teeth, try, try one's hand at, undertake, venture

attend 1. appear, be at, be here, be pres~ ent, be there, frequent, go to, haunt, make one (*archaic*), put in an appear~ ance, show oneself, show up (*informal*), turn up, visit **2.** care for, look after, mind, minister to, nurse, take care of, tend **3.** follow, hear, hearken (*archaic*), heed, listen, look on, mark, mind, note, notice, observe, pay attention, pay heed, regard, take to heart, watch **4.** accom~ pany, arise from, be associated with, be connected with, be consequent on, fol~ low, go hand in hand with, issue from, occur with, result from **5.** (*with* **to**) apply oneself to, concentrate on, devote one~ self to, get to work on, look after, occupy oneself with, see to, take care of **6.** ac~ company, chaperon, companion, convoy, escort, guard, squire, usher **7.** be in the service of, serve, wait upon, work for

▷ **Antonyms** (*sense 1*) be absent, miss, play truant (*sense 2*) neglect (*senses 3 & 5*) discount, disregard, ignore, neglect (*sense 4*) dissociate

attendance 1. appearance, attending, be~ ing there, presence **2.** audience, crowd, gate, house, number present, turnout

attendant 1. *noun* aide, assistant, aux~ iliary, chaperon, companion, custodian, escort, flunky, follower, guard, guide, helper, lackey, menial, page, servant, steward, underling, usher, waiter **2.** *~adjective* accessory, accompanying, as~ sociated, concomitant, consequent, re~ lated

attention 1. concentration, consideration, contemplation, deliberation, heed, heedfulness, intentness, mind, scrutiny, thinking, thought, thoughtfulness **2.** awareness, consciousness, considera~ tion, notice, observation, recognition,

regard **3.** care, concern, looking after, ministration, treatment **4.** (*often plural*) assiduities, care, civility, compliment, consideration, courtesy, deference, gallantry, mindfulness, politeness, regard, respect, service
▷ **Antonyms** carelessness, discourtesy, disregard, disrespect, distraction, impoliteness, inattention, laxity, laxness, negligence, thoughtlessness, unconcern

attentive 1. alert, awake, careful, concentrating, heedful, intent, listening, mindful, observant, on one's toes, regardful, studious, watchful **2.** accommodating, civil, conscientious, considerate, courteous, devoted, gallant, gracious, kind, obliging, polite, respectful, thoughtful
▷ **Antonyms** absent-minded, careless, distracted, dreamy, heedless, inattentive, neglectful, negligent, preoccupied, remiss, thoughtless, unheeding, unmindful

attenuate *verb* **1.** adulterate, contract, decrease, devaluate, dilute, diminish, enervate, enfeeble, lessen, lower, reduce, sap, water down, weaken **2.** draw out, elongate, extend, lengthen, make fine, make slender, rarefy, refine, slim, spin out, stretch out, thin *~adjective also* **attenuated 3.** adulterated, contracted, decreased, devalued, dilute, diluted, diminished, enervated, enfeebled, lessened, lowered, reduced, sapped, watered down, weakened **4.** drawn out, elongated, extended, lengthened, rarefied, refined, slender, slimmed, spun out, stretched out, thinned

attest adjure, affirm, assert, authenticate, aver, bear out, bear witness, certify, confirm, corroborate, declare, demonstrate, display, evince, exhibit, give evidence, invoke, manifest, prove, ratify, seal, show, substantiate, swear, testify, verify, vouch for, warrant, witness
▷ **Antonyms** contradict, controvert, deny, disprove, gainsay (*archaic or literary*), give the lie to, make a nonsense of, prove false, rebut, refute

attic[1] *adjective* chaste, classical, correct, elegant, graceful, polished, pure, refined, simple, tasteful

attic[2] *noun* garret, loft

attire 1. *noun* accoutrements, apparel, array (*poetic*), clothes, clothing, costume, dress, garb, garments, gear (*informal*), habiliments, habit, outfit, raiment (*archaic or poetic*), robes, threads (*slang*), uniform, vestment, wear **2.** *~verb* accoutre, apparel (*archaic*), array, clothe, costume, deck out, dress, equip, fit out, garb, get ready, rig out, robe, turn out

attitude 1. approach, disposition, frame of mind, mood, opinion, outlook, perspective, point of view, position, posture, stance, standing, view **2.** air, aspect, bearing, carriage, condition, demeanour, manner, mien (*literary*), pose, position, posture, stance

attract allure, appeal to, bewitch, captivate, catch (someone's) eye, charm, decoy, draw, enchant, endear, engage, entice, fascinate, incline, induce, interest, invite, lure, pull (*informal*), tempt
▷ **Antonyms** disgust, give one the creeps (*informal*), put one off, repel, repulse, revolt, turn one off (*informal*)

attraction allure, appeal, attractiveness, bait, captivation, charm, come-on (*informal*), draw, enchantment, endearment, enticement, fascination, incentive, inducement, interest, invitation, lure, magnetism, pull (*informal*), temptation, temptingness

attractive agreeable, alluring, appealing, beautiful, bonny, captivating, charming, comely, cute, engaging, enticing, fair, fascinating, fetching, glamorous, good-looking, gorgeous, handsome, interesting, inviting, likable *or* likeable, lovely, magnetic, pleasant, pleasing, prepossessing, pretty, seductive, tempting, winning, winsome
▷ **Antonyms** disagreeable, displeasing, distasteful, offensive, repulsive, ugly, unappealing, unbecoming, uninviting, unlikable *or* unlikeable, unpleasant, unsightly

attribute 1. *verb* apply, ascribe, assign, blame, charge, credit, impute, lay at the door of, put down to, refer, set down to, trace to **2.** *~noun* aspect, character, characteristic, facet, feature, idiosyncrasy, indication, mark, note, peculiarity, point, property, quality, quirk, sign, symbol, trait, virtue

attrition 1. abrasion, chafing, erosion, friction, grinding, rubbing, scraping, wear, wearing away, wearing down **2.** attenuation, debilitation, harassment, harrying, thinning out, weakening, wearing down

attune acclimatize, accord, accustom, adapt, adjust, coordinate, familiarize, harmonize, modulate, regulate, set, tune

auburn chestnut-coloured, copper-coloured, henna, nutbrown, reddish-brown, russet, rust-coloured, tawny, Titian red

au courant abreast of, acquainted, *au fait,* conversant, enlightened, in the know, in the swim, knowledgeable, up-to-date, up to speed, well-informed, well up

audacious 1. adventurous, bold, brave, courageous, daredevil, daring, dauntless, death-defying, enterprising, fearless, intrepid, rash, reckless, risky, valiant, venturesome **2.** assuming, brazen, cheeky, defiant, disrespectful, forward, fresh (*informal*), impertinent, impudent, insolent, in-your-face (*Brit. slang*), pert, presumptuous, rude, sassy (*U.S. informal*), shameless

▷ **Antonyms** (*sense 1*) careful, cautious, cowardly, frightened, guarded, prudent, timid, unadventurous, unenterprising (*sense 2*) deferential, gracious, tactful, unassuming

audacity **1.** adventurousness, audaciousness, boldness, bravery, courage, daring, dauntlessness, enterprise, face (*informal*), fearlessness, front, guts (*informal*), intrepidity, nerve, rashness, recklessness, valour, venturesomeness **2.** audaciousness, brass neck (*Brit. informal*), cheek, chutzpah (*U.S. & Canad. informal*), defiance, disrespectfulness, effrontery, forwardness, gall (*informal*), impertinence, impudence, insolence, neck (*informal*), nerve, pertness, presumption, rudeness, sassiness (*U.S. informal*), shamelessness

audible clear, detectable, discernible, distinct, hearable, perceptible

▷ **Antonyms** faint, imperceptible, inaudible, indistinct, low, out of earshot

audience **1.** assemblage, assembly, congregation, crowd, gallery, gathering, house, listeners, onlookers, spectators, turnout, viewers **2.** devotees, fans, following, market, public **3.** consultation, hearing, interview, meeting, reception

audit *Accounting* **1.** *noun* balancing, check, checking, examination, inspection, investigation, review, scrutiny, verification **2.** *~verb* balance, check, examine, go over, go through, inspect, investigate, review, scrutinize, verify

au fait abreast of, *au courant,* clued-up (*informal*), conversant, expert, familiar, fully informed, in the know, in touch, knowledgeable, on the ball (*informal*), up to speed, well-acquainted, well up

augment add to, amplify, boost, build up, dilate, enhance, enlarge, expand, extend, grow, heighten, increase, inflate, intensify, magnify, multiply, raise, reinforce, strengthen, swell

▷ **Antonyms** contract, curtail, cut down, decrease, diminish, lessen, lower, reduce, shrink

augmentation accession, addition, amplification, boost, build-up, dilation, enhancement, enlargement, expansion, extension, growth, heightening, increase, inflation, intensification, magnification, multiplication, reinforcement, rise, strengthening, swelling

augur **1.** *noun* auspex, diviner, haruspex, oracle, prophet, seer, soothsayer **2.** *~verb* be an omen of, bespeak (*archaic*), betoken, bode, foreshadow, harbinger, herald, portend, predict, prefigure, presage, promise, prophesy, signify

augury **1.** divination, prediction, prophecy, soothsaying, sortilege **2.** auspice, forerunner, forewarning, harbinger, herald, omen, portent, precursor, presage, prognostication, promise, prophecy, sign, token, warning

august dignified, exalted, glorious, grand, high-ranking, imposing, impressive, kingly, lofty, magnificent, majestic, monumental, noble, regal, solemn, stately, superb

aura air, ambience, aroma, atmosphere, emanation, feel, feeling, mood, odour, quality, scent, suggestion, tone, vibes (*slang*), vibrations (*slang*)

auspice *noun* **1.** (*usually plural*) advocacy, aegis, authority, backing, care, championship, charge, control, countenance, guidance, influence, patronage, protection, sponsorship, supervision, support **2.** augury, indication, omen, portent, prognostication, prophecy, sign, token, warning

auspicious bright, encouraging, favourable, felicitous, fortunate, happy, hopeful, lucky, opportune, promising, propitious, prosperous, rosy, timely

▷ **Antonyms** bad, black, discouraging, ill-omened, inauspicious, infelicitous, ominous, unfavourable, unfortunate, unlucky, unpromising, unpropitious

austere **1.** cold, exacting, forbidding, formal, grave, grim, hard, harsh, inflexible, rigorous, serious, severe, solemn, stern, stiff, strict, stringent, unfeeling, unrelenting **2.** abstemious, abstinent, ascetic, chaste, continent, economical, exacting, puritanical, rigid, self-denying, self-disciplined, sober, solemn, Spartan, strait-laced, strict, unrelenting **3.** bleak, economical, harsh, plain, severe, simple, spare, Spartan, stark, subdued, unadorned, unornamented

▷ **Antonyms** (*sense 1*) affable, cheerful, convivial, flexible, free-and-easy, genial, indulgent, jovial, kindly, permissive, sweet (*sense 2*) abandoned, free-and-easy, immoral, indulgent, loose, permissive (*sense 3*) comfortable, indulgent, luxurious

austerity **1.** coldness, exactingness, forbiddingness, formality, gravity, grimness, hardness, harshness, inflexibility, rigour, seriousness, severity, solemnity, sternness, stiffness, strictness **2.** abstemiousness, abstinence, asceticism, chasteness, chastity, continence, economy, exactingness, puritanism, rigidity, self-denial, self-discipline, sobriety, solemnity, Spartanism, strictness **3.** economy, plainness, severity, simplicity, spareness, Spartanism, starkness

authentic accurate, actual, authoritative, bona fide, certain, dependable, factual, faithful, genuine, legitimate, on the level (*informal*), original, pure, real, reliable, simon-pure (*rare*), the real McCoy, true, true-to-life, trustworthy, valid, veritable

▷ **Antonyms** counterfeit, fake, false, fictitious, fraudulent, hypothetical, imita~

tion, misleading, mock, pseudo (*informal*), spurious, supposed, synthetic, unfaithful, unreal, untrue

authenticate attest, authorize, avouch, certify, confirm, endorse, guarantee, validate, verify, vouch for, warrant

▷ **Antonyms** annul, invalidate, render null and void

authenticity accuracy, actuality, authoritativeness, certainty, dependability, factualness, faithfulness, genuineness, legitimacy, purity, realness, reliability, trustworthiness, truth, truthfulness, validity, veritableness, verity

author architect, composer, creator, designer, doer, fabricator, father, founder, framer, initiator, inventor, maker, mover, originator, parent, planner, prime mover, producer, writer

authoritarian 1. *adjective* absolute, autocratic, despotic, dictatorial, disciplinarian, doctrinaire, dogmatic, domineering, harsh, imperious, rigid, severe, strict, tyrannical, unyielding **2.** *~noun* absolutist, autocrat, despot, dictator, disciplinarian, tyrant

▷ **Antonyms** *~adjective* broad-minded, democratic, flexible, indulgent, lenient, liberal, permissive, tolerant

authoritative 1. accurate, authentic, definitive, dependable, factual, faithful, learned, reliable, scholarly, sound, true, trustworthy, truthful, valid, veritable **2.** assertive, autocratic, commanding, confident, decisive, dictatorial, dogmatic, dominating, imperative, imperious, imposing, lordly, masterly, peremptory, self-assured **3.** approved, authorized, commanding, legitimate, official, sanctioned, sovereign

▷ **Antonyms** (*sense 1*) deceptive, undependable, unreliable (*sense 2*) humble, subservient, timid, weak (*sense 3*) unauthorized, unofficial, unsanctioned

authority 1. ascendancy, charge, command, control, direction, domination, dominion, force, government, influence, jurisdiction, might, power, prerogative, right, rule, say-so, strength, supremacy, sway, weight **2. the authorities** administration, government, management, officialdom, police, powers that be, the establishment **3.** a blank cheque, authorization, justification, licence, permission, permit, sanction, say-so, warrant **4.** arbiter, bible, connoisseur, expert, judge, master, professional, scholar, specialist, textbook **5.** attestation, avowal, declaration, evidence, profession, say-so, statement, testimony, word

authorization 1. ability, a blank cheque, authority, power, right, say-so, strength **2.** approval, credentials, leave, licence, permission, permit, sanction, say-so, warrant

authorize 1. accredit, commission, empower, enable, entitle, give authority **2.** accredit, allow, approve, confirm, countenance, give a blank cheque to, give authority for, give leave, give the green light for, license, permit, ratify, sanction, vouch for, warrant

▷ **Antonyms** ban, debar, disallow, exclude, forbid, outlaw, preclude, prohibit, proscribe, rule out, veto

autocracy absolutism, despotism, dictatorship, tyranny

autocrat absolutist, despot, dictator, tyrant

autocratic absolute, all-powerful, despotic, dictatorial, domineering, imperious, tyrannical, tyrannous, unlimited

automatic 1. automated, mechanical, mechanized, push-button, robot, self-acting, self-activating, self-moving, self-propelling, self-regulating **2.** habitual, kneejerk, mechanical, perfunctory, routine, unconscious **3.** instinctive, instinctual, involuntary, mechanical, natural, reflex, spontaneous, unconscious, unwilled **4.** assured, certain, inescapable, inevitable, necessary, routine, unavoidable

▷ **Antonyms** (*sense 1*) done by hand, hand-operated, human, manual, physical (*senses 2 & 3*) conscious, deliberate, intentional, voluntary

autonomous free, independent, self-determining, self-governing, self-ruling, sovereign

autonomy freedom, home rule, independence, self-determination, self-government, self-rule, sovereignty

▷ **Antonyms** dependency, foreign rule, subjection

autopsy dissection, necropsy, postmortem, postmortem examination

auxiliary 1. *adjective* accessory, aiding, ancillary, assisting, back-up, emergency, fall-back, helping, reserve, secondary, subsidiary, substitute, supplementary, supporting **2.** *~noun* accessory, accomplice, ally, assistant, associate, companion, confederate, helper, henchman, partner, protagonist, reserve, subordinate, supporter

▷ **Antonyms** *~adjective* cardinal, chief, essential, first, leading, main, primary, prime, principal

avail *verb* **1.** aid, assist, be effective, benefit, be of advantage, be of use, be useful, help, profit, serve, work **2. avail oneself of** employ, exploit, have recourse to, make the most of, make use of, profit from, take advantage of, turn to account, use, utilize *~noun* **3.** advantage, aid, assistance, benefit, effectiveness, efficacy, good, help, mileage (*informal*), profit, purpose, service, use, usefulness, utility

available accessible, applicable, at hand, at one's disposal, at one's fingertips, attainable, convenient, free, handy, ob~

tainable, on hand, on tap, ready, ready for use, to hand, vacant

▷ **Antonyms** busy, engaged, inaccessible, in use, occupied, spoken for, taken, unattainable, unavailable, unobtainable

avalanche 1. landslide, landslip, snow-slide, snow-slip **2.** barrage, deluge, flood, inundation, torrent

avant-garde *adjective* experimental, far-out (*slang*), ground-breaking, innovative, innovatory, pioneering, progressive, unconventional, way-out (*informal*)

▷ **Antonyms** conservative, conventional, hidebound, reactionary, traditional

avarice acquisitiveness, close-fistedness, covetousness, cupidity, graspingness, greed, greediness, meanness, miserliness, niggardliness, parsimony, penny-pinching, penuriousness, rapacity, stinginess

▷ **Antonyms** benevolence, bountifulness, extravagance, generosity, largesse *or* largess, liberality, unselfishness

avaricious acquisitive, close-fisted, covetous, grasping, greedy, mean, miserable, miserly, niggardly, parsimonious, penny-pinching, penurious, rapacious, snoep (*S. Afr. informal*), stingy, tight-arsed (*taboo slang*), tight as a duck's arse (*taboo slang*), tight-assed (*U.S. taboo slang*)

avenge even the score for, get even for (*informal*), get one's own back, hit back, pay (someone) back in his *or* her own coin, punish, repay, requite, retaliate, revenge, take satisfaction for, take vengeance

avenue access, alley, approach, boulevard, channel, course, drive, driveway, entrance, entry, pass, passage, path, pathway, road, route, street, thoroughfare, way

aver affirm, allege, assert, asseverate, avouch, avow, declare, maintain, proclaim, profess, pronounce, protest, say, state, swear

average *noun* **1.** common run, mean, medium, midpoint, norm, normal, par, rule, run, run of the mill, standard **2. on average** as a rule, for the most part, generally, normally, typically, usually *~adjective* **3.** banal, bog-standard (*Brit. & Irish slang*), common, commonplace, fair, general, indifferent, mediocre, middle-of-the-road, middling, moderate, no great shakes (*informal*), normal, not bad, ordinary, passable, regular, run-of-the-mill, so-so (*informal*), standard, tolerable, typical, undistinguished, unexceptional, usual, vanilla (*slang*) **4.** intermediate, mean, median, medium, middle *~verb* **5.** balance out to, be on average, do on average, even out to, make on average

▷ **Antonyms** *~adjective* (*sense 3*) abnormal, awful, bad, different, exceptional, great, memorable, notable, outstanding, remarkable, special, terrible, unusual (*sense 4*) maximum, minimum

averse antipathetic, backward, disinclined, hostile, ill-disposed, indisposed, inimical, loath, opposed, reluctant, unfavourable, unwilling

▷ **Antonyms** agreeable, amenable, disposed, eager, favourable, inclined, keen, sympathetic, willing

aversion abhorrence, animosity, antipathy, detestation, disgust, disinclination, dislike, distaste, hate, hatred, horror, hostility, indisposition, loathing, odium, opposition, reluctance, repugnance, repulsion, revulsion, unwillingness

▷ **Antonyms** desire, inclination, liking, love, willingness

avert 1. turn, turn aside, turn away **2.** avoid, fend off, forestall, frustrate, preclude, prevent, stave off, ward off

aviation aeronautics, flight, flying, powered flight

aviator aeronaut, airman, flyer, pilot

avid 1. ardent, devoted, eager, enthusiastic, fanatical, fervent, intense, keen, keen as mustard, passionate, zealous **2.** acquisitive, athirst, avaricious, covetous, grasping, greedy, hungry, insatiable, rapacious, ravenous, thirsty, voracious

▷ **Antonyms** (*sense 1*) apathetic, impassive, indifferent, lukewarm, unenthusiastic

avidity 1. ardour, devotion, eagerness, enthusiasm, fervour, keenness, zeal **2.** acquisitiveness, avarice, covetousness, cupidity, desire, graspingness, greediness, hankering, hunger, insatiability, longing, rapacity, ravenousness, thirst, voracity

avocation 1. diversion, hobby, occupation, pastime, recreation **2.** business, calling, employment, job, occupation, profession, pursuit, trade, vocation, work

avoid avert, body-swerve (*Scot.*), bypass, circumvent, dodge, duck (out of) (*informal*), elude, escape, eschew, evade, fight shy of, give a wide berth to, keep aloof from, keep away from, prevent, refrain from, shirk, shun, sidestep, slip through the net, steer clear of

▷ **Antonyms** approach, confront, contact, face, find, invite, pursue, seek out, solicit

avoidance body swerve (*Scot.*), circumvention, dodging, eluding, escape, eschewal, evasion, keeping away from, prevention, refraining, shirking, shunning, steering clear of

avouch acknowledge, affirm, allege, assert, asseverate, aver, avow, declare, guarantee, maintain, proclaim, profess, pronounce, state, swear, vouch for

avow acknowledge, admit, affirm, allege, assert, asseverate, aver, confess, de~

clare, maintain, own, proclaim, profess, recognize, state, swear

avowal acknowledgment, admission, affirmation, allegation, assertion, asseveration, averment, confession, declaration, maintenance, oath, owning, proclamation, profession, recognition, statement

avowed acknowledged, admitted, confessed, declared, open, professed, self-proclaimed, sworn

await 1. abide, anticipate, expect, look for, look forward to, stay for, wait for **2.** attend, be in readiness for, be in store for, be prepared for, be ready for, wait for

awake *verb* **1.** awaken, rouse, wake, wake up **2.** activate, alert, animate, arouse, awaken, breathe life into, call forth, enliven, excite, fan, incite, kick-start (*informal*), kindle, provoke, revive, stimulate, stir up, vivify *~adjective* **3.** alert, alive, aroused, attentive, awakened, aware, bright-eyed and bushy-tailed, conscious, heedful, not sleeping, observant, on guard, on one's toes, on the alert, on the lookout, vigilant, wakeful, waking, watchful, wide-awake

▷ **Antonyms** *~adjective* asleep, crashed out (*slang*), dead to the world (*informal*), dormant, dozing, inattentive, napping, sleeping, unaware, unconscious

awaken activate, alert, animate, arouse, awake, breathe life into, call forth, enliven, excite, fan, incite, kick-start (*informal*), kindle, provoke, revive, rouse, stimulate, stir up, vivify, wake

awakening *noun* activation, animating, arousal, awaking, birth, enlivening, incitement, kindling, provocation, revival, rousing, stimulation, stirring up, vivification, waking, waking up

award *verb* **1.** accord, adjudge, allot, apportion, assign, bestow, confer, decree, distribute, endow, gift, give, grant, hand out, present, render *~noun* **2.** adjudication, allotment, bestowal, conferment, conferral, decision, decree, endowment, gift, hand-out, order, presentation, stipend **3.** bonsela (*S. Afr.*), decoration, gift, grant, prize, trophy, verdict

aware acquainted, alive to, appreciative, apprised, attentive, *au courant,* clued-up (*informal*), cognizant, conscious, conversant, enlightened, familiar, hip (*slang*), informed, in the picture, keeping one's finger on the pulse, knowing, knowledgeable, mindful, sensible, sentient, wise (*slang*)

▷ **Antonyms** ignorant, insensible, oblivious, unaware, unfamiliar with, unknowledgeable

awareness acquaintance, appreciation, attention, cognizance, consciousness, enlightenment, familiarity, knowledge, mindfulness, perception, realization, recognition, sensibility, sentience, understanding

away *adverb* **1.** abroad, elsewhere, from here, from home, hence, off **2.** apart, at a distance, far, remote **3.** aside, out of the way, to one side **4.** continuously, incessantly, interminably, relentlessly, repeatedly, uninterruptedly, unremittingly *~adjective* **5.** abroad, absent, elsewhere, gone, not at home, not here, not present, not there, out *~interjection* **6.** beat it (*slang*), begone, be off, bugger off (*taboo slang*), fuck off (*offensive taboo slang*), get lost (*informal*), get out, go, go away, on your bike (*slang*), on your way

awe 1. *noun* admiration, amazement, astonishment, dread, fear, horror, respect, reverence, terror, veneration, wonder **2.** *~verb* amaze, astonish, cow, daunt, frighten, horrify, impress, intimidate, put the wind up (*informal*), stun, terrify

▷ **Antonyms** *~noun* arrogance, boldness, contempt, disrespect, fearlessness, irreverence, scorn

awe-inspiring amazing, astonishing, awesome, breathtaking, daunting, fearsome, impressive, intimidating, magnificent, striking, stunning (*informal*), wonderful, wondrous (*archaic or literary*)

▷ **Antonyms** bland, boring, dull, flat, humdrum, insipid, prosaic, tame, tedious, unimpressive, uninspiring, vapid

awesome alarming, amazing, astonishing, awe-inspiring, awful, breathtaking, daunting, dreadful, fearful, fearsome, formidable, frightening, horrible, horrifying, imposing, impressive, intimidating, magnificent, majestic, overwhelming, redoubtable, shocking, solemn, striking, stunning, stupefying, terrible, terrifying, wonderful, wondrous (*archaic or literary*)

awestruck *or* **awe-stricken** afraid, amazed, astonished, awed, awe-inspired, cowed, daunted, dumbfounded, fearful, frightened, horrified, impressed, intimidated, shocked, struck dumb, stunned, terrified, wonder-stricken, wonder-struck

awful 1. abysmal, alarming, appalling, deplorable, dire, distressing, dreadful, fearful, frightful, from hell (*informal*), ghastly, godawful (*slang*), gruesome, harrowing, hellacious (*U.S. slang*), hideous, horrendous, horrible, horrid, horrific, horrifying, nasty, shocking, terrible, tremendous, ugly, unpleasant, unsightly **2.** *archaic* amazing, awe-inspiring, awesome, dread, fearsome, majestic, portentous, solemn

▷ **Antonyms** (*sense 1*) amazing, brilliant, excellent, fabulous (*informal*), fantastic, great (*informal*), magnificent, marvellous, miraculous, sensational (*informal*), smashing (*informal*), super (*informal*), superb, terrific, tremendous, wonderful

awfully 1. badly, disgracefully, disreputably, dreadfully, inadequately, reprehensibly, shoddily, unforgivably, unpleasantly, wickedly, woefully, wretchedly **2.** *informal* badly, dreadfully, exceedingly, exceptionally, excessively, extremely, greatly, immensely, quite, seriously (*informal*), terribly, very, very much

awhile briefly, for a little while, for a moment, for a short time, for a while

awkward 1. all thumbs, artless, blundering, bungling, clownish, clumsy, coarse, gauche, gawky, graceless, ham-fisted *or* ham-handed (*informal*), ill-bred, inelegant, inept, inexpert, lumbering, maladroit, oafish, rude, skill-less, stiff, uncoordinated, uncouth, ungainly, ungraceful, unpolished, unrefined, unskilful, unskilled **2.** clunky (*informal*), cumbersome, difficult, inconvenient, troublesome, unhandy, unmanageable, unwieldy **3.** compromising, cringe-making (*Brit. informal*), cringeworthy (*Brit. informal*), delicate, difficult, embarrassed, embarrassing, ill at ease, inconvenient, inopportune, painful, perplexing, sticky (*informal*), thorny, ticklish, troublesome, trying, uncomfortable, unpleasant, untimely **4.** annoying, bloody-minded (*Brit. informal*), difficult, disobliging, exasperating, hard to handle, intractable, irritable, perverse, prickly, stubborn, touchy, troublesome, trying, uncooperative, unhelpful, unpredictable, vexatious, vexing **5.** chancy (*informal*), dangerous, difficult, hazardous, perilous, risky

▷ **Antonyms** (*sense 1*) adept, adroit, dexterous, graceful, skilful (*sense 2*) convenient, easy, handy (*sense 3*) comfortable, pleasant

awkwardness 1. artlessness, clownishness, clumsiness, coarseness, gaucheness, gaucherie, gawkiness, gracelessness, ill-breeding, inelegance, ineptness, inexpertness, maladroitness, oafishness, rudeness, stiffness, uncoordination, uncouthness, ungainliness, unskilfulness, unskilledness **2.** cumbersomeness, difficulty, inconvenience, troublesomeness, unhandiness, unmanageability, unwieldiness **3.** delicacy, difficulty, discomfort, embarrassment, inconvenience, inopportuneness, painfulness, perplexingness, stickiness (*informal*), thorniness, ticklishness, unpleasantness, untimeliness **4.** bloody-mindedness (*Brit. informal*), difficulty, disobligingness, intractability, irritability, perversity, prickliness, stubbornness, touchiness, uncooperativeness, unhelpfulness, unpredictability **5.** chanciness (*informal*), danger, difficulty, hazardousness, peril, perilousness, risk, riskiness

awry *adverb/adjective* amiss, askew, asymmetrical, cockeyed (*informal*), crooked, crookedly, misaligned, obliquely, off-centre, off course, out of line, out of true, skew-whiff (*informal*), to one side, twisted, uneven, unevenly, wrong

axe *noun* **1.** adze, chopper, hatchet **2. an axe to grind** grievance, personal consideration, pet subject, private ends, private purpose, ulterior motive **3. the axe** *informal* cancellation, cutback, discharge, dismissal, termination, the boot (*slang*), the chop (*slang*), the (old) heave-ho (*informal*), the order of the boot (*slang*), the sack (*informal*), wind-up *~verb* **4.** chop, cut down, fell, hew **5.** *informal* cancel, cut back, discharge, dismiss, dispense with, eliminate, fire (*informal*), get rid of, give (someone) their marching orders, give the boot to (*slang*), give the bullet to (*Brit. slang*), give the push, oust, pull, pull the plug on, relegate, remove, sack (*informal*), terminate, throw out, turn off (*informal*), wind up

axiom adage, aphorism, apophthegm, dictum, fundamental, gnome, maxim, postulate, precept, principle, truism

axiomatic 1. absolute, accepted, apodictic *or* apodeictic, assumed, certain, fundamental, given, granted, indubitable, manifest, presupposed, self-evident, understood, unquestioned **2.** aphoristic, apophthegmatic, epigrammatic, gnomic, pithy, terse

axis 1. axle, centre line, pivot, shaft, spindle **2.** alliance, bloc, coalition, compact, entente, league, pact

axle arbor, axis, mandrel, pin, pivot, rod, shaft, spindle

azure blue, cerulean, clear blue, sky-blue, sky-coloured, ultramarine

B, b

babble 1. *verb* blab, burble, cackle, chatter, gabble, gibber, gurgle, jabber, mumble, murmur, mutter, prate, prattle, rabbit (on) (*Brit. informal*), run off at the mouth (*slang*), waffle (*informal, chiefly Brit.*) 2. *~noun* burble, clamour, drivel, gabble, gibberish, murmur, waffle (*informal, chiefly Brit.*)

babe 1. ankle-biter (*Austral. slang*), baby, bairn (*Scot.*), child, infant, nursling, rug rat (*slang*), sprog (*slang*), suckling 2. babe in arms, ingénue *or (masc.)* ingénu, innocent

babel bedlam, clamour, confusion, din, disorder, hubbub, hullabaloo, hurly-burly, pandemonium, tumult, turmoil, uproar

baby 1. *noun* ankle-biter (*Austral. slang*), babe, babe in arms, bairn (*Scot.*), child, infant, newborn child, rug rat (*slang*), sprog (*slang*) 2. *~adjective* diminutive, dwarf, little, midget, mini, miniature, minute, pygmy *or* pigmy, small, teensy-weensy, teeny-weeny, tiny, wee 3. *~verb* coddle, cosset, humour, indulge, mollycoddle, overindulge, pamper, pet, spoil, spoon-feed

babyish baby, childish, foolish, immature, infantile, juvenile, namby-pamby, puerile, silly, sissy, soft (*informal*), spoiled

▷ **Antonyms** adult, grown-up, mature, of age

bacchanal 1. carouser, debauchee, drunkard, reveller, roisterer, winebibber 2. debauch, debauchery, orgy, revel, revelry

back *verb* 1. abet, advocate, assist, champion, countenance, encourage, endorse, espouse, favour, finance, promote, sanction, second, side with, sponsor, subsidize, support, sustain, underwrite 2. back off, backtrack, go back, move back, regress, retire, retreat, reverse, turn tail, withdraw *~noun* 3. backside, end, far end, hind part, hindquarters, posterior, rear, reverse, stern, tail end *~adjective* 4. end, hind, hindmost, posterior, rear, tail 5. *From an earlier time* delayed, earlier, elapsed, former, overdue, past, previous 6. **behind one's back** covertly, deceitfully, secretly, sneakily, surreptitiously

▷ **Antonyms** *~verb* (*sense 1*) attack, combat, hinder, thwart, undermine, weaken (*sense 2*) advance, approach, move forward, progress *~noun* face, fore, front, head *~adjective* (*sense 4*) advance, fore, front (*sense 5*) future, late

backbite abuse, bad-mouth (*slang, chiefly U.S. & Canad.*), calumniate, defame, denigrate, detract, knock (*informal*), libel, malign, revile, rubbish (*informal*), slag (off) (*slang*), slander, traduce, vilify, vituperate

backbiting abuse, aspersion, bitchiness (*slang*), calumniation, calumny, cattiness (*informal*), defamation, denigration, detraction, disparagement, gossip, malice, scandalmongering, slander, spite, spitefulness, vilification, vituperation

backbone 1. *Medical* spinal column, spine, vertebrae, vertebral column 2. bottle (*Brit. slang*), character, courage, determination, firmness, fortitude, grit, hardihood, mettle, moral fibre, nerve, pluck, resolution, resolve, stamina, steadfastness, strength of character, tenacity, toughness, will, willpower 3. basis, foundation, mainstay, support

backbreaking arduous, crushing, exhausting, gruelling, hard, killing, laborious, punishing, strenuous, toilsome, wearing, wearying

back down accede, admit defeat, back-pedal, concede, give in, surrender, withdraw, yield

backer advocate, angel (*informal*), benefactor, patron, promoter, second, sponsor, subscriber, supporter, underwriter, well-wisher

backfire boomerang, disappoint, fail, flop (*informal*), miscarry, rebound, recoil

background breeding, circumstances, credentials, culture, education, environment, experience, grounding, history, milieu, preparation, qualifications, tradition, upbringing

backhanded ambiguous, double-edged, equivocal, indirect, ironic, oblique, sarcastic, sardonic, two-edged, with tongue in cheek

backing abetment, accompaniment, advocacy, aid, assistance, championing, encouragement, endorsement, espousal, funds, grant, moral support, patronage, promotion, sanction, seconding, spon~ sorship, subsidy, support

backlash backfire, boomerang, counter~ action, counterblast, kickback, reaction, recoil, repercussion, resentment, resist~ ance, response, retaliation, retroaction

backlog accumulation, build-up, excess, hoard, reserve, reserves, resources, stock, supply

back out abandon, cancel, chicken out (*informal*), cop out (*slang*), give up, go back on, recant, renege, resign, retreat, withdraw

backslide fall from grace, go astray, go wrong, lapse, regress, relapse, renege, retrogress, revert, sin, slip, stray, weaken

backslider apostate, deserter, recidivist, recreant, renegade, reneger, turncoat

back up aid, assist, bolster, confirm, cor~ roborate, reinforce, second, stand by, substantiate, support

backward *adjective* **1.** bashful, diffident, hesitating, late, reluctant, shy, sluggish, tardy, unwilling, wavering **2.** behind, behindhand, braindead (*informal*), dead from the neck up (*informal*), dense, dozy (*Brit. informal*), dull, obtuse, retarded, slow, stupid, subnormal, underdevel~ oped, undeveloped *~adverb* **3.** aback, be~ hind, in reverse, rearward

▷ **Antonyms** *~adjective* (*sense 1*) bold, brash, eager, forward, pushy (*informal*), willing (*sense 2*) advanced, ahead *~adverb* correctly, forward, frontward, properly

backwoods 1. *adjective* agrestic, hick (*in~ formal, chiefly U.S. & Canad.*), isolated, remote, rustic, uncouth **2.** *~noun* back country (*U.S.*), backlands (*U.S.*), back of beyond, middle of nowhere, outback, sticks (*informal*)

bacteria bacilli, bugs (*slang*), germs, mi~ crobes, microorganisms, pathogens, vi~ ruses

bad 1. chickenshit (*U.S. slang*), defective, deficient, duff (*Brit. informal*), erro~ neous, fallacious, faulty, imperfect, in~ adequate, incorrect, inferior, low-rent (*informal, chiefly U.S.*), of a sort *or* of sorts, pathetic, poor, poxy (*slang*), sub~ standard, unsatisfactory **2.** damaging, dangerous, deleterious, detrimental, harmful, hurtful, injurious, ruinous, unhealthy **3.** base, corrupt, criminal, delinquent, evil, immoral, mean, sinful, vile, villainous, wicked, wrong **4.** dis~ obedient, mischievous, naughty, unruly **5.** decayed, mouldy, off, putrid, rancid, rotten, sour, spoiled **6.** disastrous, dis~ tressing, grave, harsh, painful, serious, severe, terrible **7.** ailing, diseased, ill, sick, unwell **8.** apologetic, conscience-stricken, contrite, guilty, regretful, re~ morseful, sad, sorry, upset **9.** adverse, discouraged, discouraging, distressed, distressing, gloomy, grim, low, melan~ choly, troubled, troubling, unfortunate, unpleasant **10. not bad** all right, aver~ age, fair, fair to middling (*informal*), moderate, O.K. *or* okay (*informal*), passable, respectable, so-so (*informal*), tolerable

▷ **Antonyms** (*sense 1*) adequate, fair, satisfactory (*sense 2*) agreeable, benefi~ cial, good, healthful, safe, sound, whole~ some (*sense 3*) ethical, fine, first-rate, good, moral, righteous, virtuous (*sense 4*) biddable, docile, good, obedient, well-behaved

bad blood acrimony, anger, animosity, antagonism, dislike, enmity, feud, ha~ tred, ill feeling, ill will, malevolence, malice, rancour, resentment, seeing red

badge brand, device, emblem, identifica~ tion, insignia, mark, sign, stamp, token

badger bend someone's ear (*informal*), bully, chivvy, goad, harass, harry, hound, importune, nag, pester, plague, torment

badinage banter, chaff, drollery, mock~ ery, persiflage, pleasantry, raillery, rep~ artee, teasing, waggery, wordplay

badly 1. carelessly, defectively, erro~ neously, faultily, imperfectly, inad~ equately, incorrectly, ineptly, poorly, shoddily, wrong, wrongly **2.** unfavour~ ably, unfortunately, unsuccessfully **3.** criminally, evilly, immorally, improper~ ly, naughtily, shamefully, unethically, wickedly **4.** acutely, deeply, desperately, exceedingly, extremely, gravely, greatly, intensely, painfully, seriously, severely

▷ **Antonyms** (*senses 1 & 2*) ably, compe~ tently, correctly, properly, rightly, sat~ isfactorily, splendidly, well (*sense 3*) ethically, morally, righteously, rightly

bad manners boorishness, churlishness, coarseness, discourtesy, disrespect, im~ politeness, incivility, inconsideration, indelicacy, rudeness, unmannerliness

▷ **Antonyms** civility, cordiality, cour~ teousness, courtesy, good manners, gra~ ciousness, politeness, urbanity

baffle 1. amaze, astound, bewilder, boggle the mind, confound, confuse, daze, dis~ concert, dumbfound, elude, flummox, mystify, nonplus, perplex, puzzle, stump, stun **2.** balk, check, defeat, foil, frustrate, hinder, thwart, upset

▷ **Antonyms** (*sense 1*) clarify, clear up, elucidate, explain, explicate, interpret, make plain, shed *or* throw light upon, spell out

bag *verb* **1.** balloon, bulge, droop, sag, swell **2.** acquire, capture, catch, gain, get, kill, land, shoot, take, trap

baggage accoutrements, bags, belong~ ings, equipment, gear, impedimenta, luggage, paraphernalia, suitcases, things

baggy billowing, bulging, droopy, floppy, ill-fitting, loose, oversize, roomy, sag~ ging, seated, slack

▷ **Antonyms** close, close-fitting, con~stricted, cramped, narrow, snug, stretched, taut, tight, tight-fitting

bail[1] *noun* bond, guarantee, guaranty, pledge, security, surety, warranty

bail[2], **bale** *verb* dip, drain off, ladle, scoop

bail out, bale out 1. aid, help, relieve, res~cue, save (someone's) bacon (*informal, chiefly Brit.*) **2.** escape, quit, retreat, withdraw

bait *noun* **1.** allurement, attraction, bribe, carrot and stick, decoy, enticement, in~centive, inducement, lure, snare, temp~tation *~verb* **2.** aggravate (*informal*), an~noy, be on one's back (*slang*), bother, gall, get *or* take a rise out of, get in one's hair (*informal*), get one's back up, get on one's nerves (*informal*), harass, hassle (*informal*), hound, irk, irritate, nark (*Brit., Austral. & N.Z. slang*), needle (*informal*), persecute, piss one off (*taboo slang*), provoke, put one's back up, tease, torment, wind up (*Brit. slang*) **3.** allure, beguile, entice, lure, seduce, tempt

baked arid, desiccated, dry, parched, scorched, seared, sun-baked, torrid

balance *verb* **1.** level, match, parallel, poise, stabilize, steady **2.** adjust, com~pensate for, counteract, counterbalance, counterpoise, equalize, equate, make up for, neutralize, offset **3.** assess, compare, consider, deliberate, estimate, evaluate, weigh **4.** calculate, compute, settle, square, tally, total *~noun* **5.** correspond~ence, equilibrium, equipoise, equity, equivalence, evenness, parity, symme~try **6.** composure, equanimity, poise, self-control, self-possession, stability, steadiness **7.** difference, remainder, residue, rest, surplus

▷ **Antonyms** *~verb* (*senses 1 & 2*) out~weigh, overbalance, upset *~noun* (*senses 5 & 6*) disproportion, instability, shaki~ness, unbalance, uncertainty

balanced disinterested, equitable, even-handed, fair, impartial, just, unbiased, unprejudiced

▷ **Antonyms** biased, distorted, jaundiced, lopsided, one-sided, partial, predis~posed, prejudiced, slanted, unfair, warped, weighted

balance sheet account, budget, credits and debits, ledger, report, statement

balcony 1. terrace, veranda **2.** gallery, gods, upper circle

bald 1. baldheaded, baldpated, depilated, glabrous (*Biology*), hairless **2.** barren, bleak, exposed, naked, stark, treeless, uncovered **3.** bare, blunt, direct, down~right, forthright, outright, plain, severe, simple, straight, straightforward, un~adorned, unvarnished, upfront (*infor~mal*)

balderdash balls (*taboo slang*), bilge (*in~formal*), bosh (*informal*), bull (*slang*), bullshit (*taboo slang*), bunk (*informal*), bunkum *or* buncombe (*chiefly U.S.*), claptrap (*informal*), cobblers (*Brit. taboo slang*), crap (*slang*), drivel, eyewash (*informal*), garbage (*informal*), gibber~ish, guff (*slang*), hogwash, hokum (*slang, chiefly U.S. & Canad.*), horsefeathers (*U.S. slang*), hot air (*in~formal*), kak (*S. Afr. slang*), moonshine, nonsense, pap, piffle (*informal*), poppy~cock (*informal*), rot, rubbish, shit (*taboo slang*), tommyrot, tosh (*slang, chiefly Brit.*), trash, tripe (*informal*), twaddle, waffle

baldness 1. alopecia (*Pathology*), baldheadedness, baldpatedness, gla~brousness (*Biology*), hairlessness **2.** bar~renness, bleakness, nakedness, sparse~ness, starkness, treelessness **3.** auster~ity, bluntness, plainness, severity, sim~plicity, spareness

bale *see* BAIL[2]

baleful calamitous, deadly, evil, harmful, hurtful, injurious, maleficent, malevo~lent, malignant, menacing, mournful, noxious, ominous, pernicious, ruinous, sad, sinister, venomous, woeful

▷ **Antonyms** beneficial, benevolent, be~nign, friendly, good, healthy, salubrious

bale out *see* BAIL OUT

balk 1. demur, dodge, evade, flinch, hesi~tate, jib, recoil, refuse, resist, shirk, shrink from **2.** baffle, bar, check, counteract, defeat, disconcert, foil, fore~stall, frustrate, hinder, obstruct, pre~vent, thwart

▷ **Antonyms** (*sense 1*) accede, accept, ac~quiesce, comply, relent, submit, yield (*sense 2*) abet, advance, aid, assist, fur~ther, help, promote, support, sustain

balky intractable, obstinate, stubborn, uncooperative, unmanageable, unpre~dictable, unruly

ball 1. drop, globe, globule, orb, pellet, sphere, spheroid **2.** ammunition, bullet, grapeshot, pellet, shot, slug

ballast balance, counterbalance, counter~weight, equilibrium, sandbag, stability, stabilizer, weight

balloon *verb* belly, billow, bloat, blow up, dilate, distend, enlarge, expand, grow rapidly, inflate, puff out, swell

ballot election, poll, polling, vote, voting

ballyhoo 1. babble, commotion, fuss, hub~bub, hue and cry, hullabaloo, noise, racket, to-do **2.** advertising, build-up, hype, PR, promotion, propaganda, publi~city

balm 1. balsam, cream, embrocation, emollient, lotion, ointment, salve, un~guent **2.** anodyne, comfort, consolation, curative, palliative, restorative, solace

balmy 1. clement, mild, pleasant, sum~mery, temperate **2.** *also* **barmy** crackpot (*informal*), crazy, daft (*informal*), dool~ally (*slang*), foolish, gonzo (*slang*), goofy

(*informal*), idiotic, insane, loony (*slang*), loopy (*informal*), nuts (*slang*), nutty (*slang*), odd, off one's rocker (*slang*), off one's trolley (*slang*), out of one's mind, out to lunch (*informal*), round the twist (*Brit. slang*), silly, stupid, up the pole (*informal*), wacko *or* whacko (*informal*)
▷ **Antonyms** (*sense 1*) annoying, discomforting, harsh, inclement, intense, irksome, rough, stormy

bamboozle 1. cheat, con (*informal*), deceive, defraud, delude, dupe, fool, hoax, hoodwink, pull a fast one on (*informal*), skin (*slang*), swindle, trick **2.** baffle, befuddle, confound, confuse, mystify, perplex, puzzle, stump

ban 1. *verb* banish, bar, black, blackball, block, boycott, debar, disallow, disqualify, exclude, forbid, interdict, outlaw, prohibit, proscribe, restrict, suppress **2.** *~noun* block, boycott, censorship, disqualification, embargo, interdict, interdiction, prohibition, proscription, restriction, stoppage, suppression, taboo
▷ **Antonyms** *~verb* allow, approve, authorize, enable, let, permit, sanction *~noun* allowance, approval, permission, sanction

banal clichéd, cliché-ridden, commonplace, everyday, hackneyed, humdrum, mundane, old hat, ordinary, pedestrian, platitudinous, stale, stereotyped, stock, threadbare, tired, trite, unimaginative, unoriginal, vanilla (*slang*), vapid
▷ **Antonyms** challenging, distinctive, fresh, ground-breaking, imaginative, interesting, new, novel, original, stimulating, unique, unusual

banality bromide (*informal*), cliché, commonplace, platitude, triteness, trite phrase, triviality, truism, vapidity

band[1] *noun* bandage, belt, binding, bond, chain, cord, fetter, fillet, ligature, manacle, ribbon, shackle, strap, strip, tie

band[2] *noun* **1.** assembly, association, bevy, body, camp, clique, club, company, coterie, crew (*informal*), gang, horde, party, posse (*informal*), society, troop **2.** combo, ensemble, group, orchestra *~verb* **3.** affiliate, ally, consolidate, federate, gather, group, join, merge, unite
▷ **Antonyms** *~verb* cleave, disperse, disunite, divide, part, segregate, separate, split, sunder

bandage 1. *noun* compress, dressing, gauze, plaster **2.** *~verb* bind, cover, dress, swathe

bandit brigand, crook, desperado, footpad, freebooter, gangster, gunman, highwayman, hijacker, marauder, outlaw, pirate, racketeer, robber, thief

bandy 1. *verb* barter, exchange, interchange, pass, shuffle, swap, throw, toss, trade **2.** *~adjective* bandy-legged, bent, bowed, bow-legged, crooked, curved

bane affliction, bête noire, blight, burden, calamity, curse, despair, destruction, disaster, downfall, misery, nuisance, pest, plague, ruin, scourge, torment, trial, trouble, woe
▷ **Antonyms** blessing, comfort, consolation, joy, pleasure, relief, solace, support

baneful baleful, calamitous, deadly, deleterious, destructive, disastrous, fatal, harmful, hurtful, injurious, maleficent, noxious, pernicious, pestilential, ruinous, venomous

bang *noun* **1.** boom, burst, clang, clap, clash, detonation, explosion, peal, pop, report, shot, slam, thud, thump **2.** belt (*informal*), blow, box, bump, cuff, hit, knock, punch, smack, stroke, wallop (*informal*), whack *~verb* **3.** bash (*informal*), beat, belt (*informal*), bump, clatter, crash, hammer, knock, pound, pummel, rap, slam, strike, thump, tonk (*informal*) **4.** boom, burst, clang, detonate, drum, echo, explode, peal, resound, thump, thunder *~adverb* **5.** abruptly, hard, headlong, noisily, precisely, slap, smack, straight, suddenly

banish 1. deport, drive away, eject, evict, exclude, excommunicate, exile, expatriate, expel, ostracize, outlaw, shut out, transport **2.** ban, cast out, discard, dislodge, dismiss, dispel, eliminate, eradicate, get rid of, oust, remove, shake off
▷ **Antonyms** accept, admit, embrace, hail, invite, offer hospitality to, receive, welcome

banishment deportation, exile, expatriation, expulsion, proscription, transportation

banisters balusters, balustrade, handrail, rail, railing

bank[1] 1. *noun* accumulation, depository, fund, hoard, repository, reserve, reservoir, savings, stock, stockpile, store, storehouse **2.** *~verb* deal with, deposit, keep, save, transact business with

bank[2] *noun* **1.** banking, embankment, heap, mass, mound, pile, ridge **2.** brink, edge, margin, shore, side *~verb* **3.** amass, heap, mass, mound, pile, stack **4.** camber, cant, heel, incline, pitch, slant, slope, tilt, tip

bank[3] *noun* array, file, group, line, rank, row, sequence, series, succession, tier, train

bank on assume, believe in, count on, depend on, lean on, look to, rely on, trust

bankrupt beggared, broke (*informal*), depleted, destitute, exhausted, failed, impoverished, in queer street, insolvent, in the red, lacking, on one's uppers, on the rocks, ruined, spent, wiped out (*informal*)
▷ **Antonyms** in the money (*informal*), on the up and up, prosperous, solvent, sound, wealthy

bankruptcy crash, disaster, exhaustion, failure, indebtedness, insolvency, lack, liquidation, ruin

banner banderole, burgee, colours, en~sign, fanion, flag, gonfalon, pennant, pennon, standard, streamer

banquet dinner, feast, meal, repast, rev~el, treat

banter 1. *verb* chaff, deride, jeer, jest, joke, josh (*slang, chiefly U.S. & Canad.*), kid (*informal*), make fun of, rib (*infor~mal*), ridicule, take the mickey (*infor~mal*), taunt, tease, twit **2.** *~noun* badi~nage, chaff, chaffing, derision, jeering, jesting, joking, kidding (*informal*), mockery, persiflage, pleasantry, raillery, repartee, ribbing (*informal*), ridicule, wordplay

baptism 1. christening, immersion, puri~fication, sprinkling **2.** beginning, debut, dedication, initiation, introduction, launching, rite of passage

baptize 1. besprinkle, cleanse, immerse, purify **2.** admit, enrol, initiate, recruit **3.** call, christen, dub, name, title

bar *noun* **1.** batten, crosspiece, paling, palisade, pole, rail, rod, shaft, stake, stick **2.** barricade, barrier, block, deter~rent, hindrance, impediment, interdict, obstacle, obstruction, rail, railing, stop **3.** boozer (*Brit., Austral. & N.Z. infor~mal*), canteen, counter, hostelry (*archaic or facetious*), inn, lounge, pub (*informal, chiefly Brit.*), public house, saloon, tap~room, tavern, watering hole (*facetious slang*) **4.** bench, court, courtroom, dock, law court **5.** *Law* barristers, body of lawyers, counsel, court, judgment, tri~bunal *~verb* **6.** barricade, bolt, fasten, latch, lock, secure **7.** ban, black, black~ball, exclude, forbid, hinder, keep out, obstruct, prevent, prohibit, restrain
▷ **Antonyms** *~noun* (*sense 2*) aid, benefit, help *~verb* (*sense 7*) accept, admit, allow, clear, let, open, permit, receive

barb 1. bristle, point, prickle, prong, quill, spike, spur, thorn **2.** affront, cut, dig, gibe, insult, rebuff, sarcasm, scoff, sneer

barbarian *noun* **1.** brute, hooligan, lout, lowbrow, ned (*slang*), ruffian, savage, vandal, yahoo **2.** bigot, boor, ignoramus, illiterate, lowbrow, philistine *~adjective* **3.** boorish, crude, lowbrow, philistine, primitive, rough, uncouth, uncultivated, uncultured, unsophisticated, vulgar, wild
▷ **Antonyms** *~adjective* civil, civilized, cultured, genteel, highbrow, refined, so~phisticated, urbane, well-mannered

barbaric 1. primitive, rude, uncivilized, wild **2.** barbarous, boorish, brutal, coarse, crude, cruel, fierce, inhuman, savage, uncouth, vulgar
▷ **Antonyms** civilized, cultivated, cul~tured, gentlemanly, gracious, humane, refined, sophisticated, urbane

barbarism 1. coarseness, crudity, savage~ry, uncivilizedness **2.** atrocity, barbarity, enormity, outrage **3.** corruption, misus~age, misuse, solecism, vulgarism

barbarity brutality, cruelty, inhumanity, ruthlessness, savagery, viciousness

barbarous 1. barbarian, brutish, primi~tive, rough, rude, savage, uncivilized, uncouth, wild **2.** barbaric, brutal, cruel, ferocious, heartless, inhuman, mon~strous, ruthless, vicious **3.** coarse, crude, ignorant, uncultured, unlettered, unre~fined, vulgar

barbed 1. hooked, jagged, prickly, pronged, spiked, spiny, thorny, toothed **2.** acid, acrid, catty (*informal*), critical, cutting, hostile, hurtful, nasty, pointed, scathing, unkind

bare 1. buck naked (*slang*), denuded, ex~posed, in the bare scud (*slang*), in the raw (*informal*), naked, naked as the day one was born (*informal*), nude, peeled, scuddy (*slang*), shorn, stripped, unclad, unclothed, uncovered, undressed, with~out a stitch on (*informal*) **2.** barren, blank, empty, lacking, mean, open, poor, scanty, scarce, unfurnished, vacant, void, wanting **3.** austere, bald, basic, cold, essential, hard, literal, plain, se~vere, sheer, simple, spare, spartan, stark, unadorned, unembellished, unfussy, unvarnished
▷ **Antonyms** (*sense 1*) attired, clad, clothed, concealed, covered, dressed, hidden (*sense 2*) abundant, full, plenti~ful, profuse, well-stocked (*sense 3*) adorned

barefaced 1. audacious, bold, brash, bra~zen, impudent, insolent, shameless **2.** bald, blatant, flagrant, glaring, mani~fest, naked, obvious, open, palpable, pa~tent, transparent, unconcealed
▷ **Antonyms** (*sense 2*) concealed, covered, hidden, inconspicuous, masked, ob~scured, secret, tucked away, unseen

barely almost, at a push, by the skin of one's teeth, hardly, just, only just, scarcely
▷ **Antonyms** amply, completely, fully, profusely

bargain *noun* **1.** agreement, arrangement, business, compact, contract, convention, engagement, negotiation, pact, pledge, promise, stipulation, transaction, trea~ty, understanding **2.** (cheap) purchase, discount, giveaway, good buy, good deal, good value, reduction, snip (*informal*), steal (*informal*) *~verb* **3.** agree, contract, covenant, negotiate, promise, stipulate, transact **4.** barter, buy, deal, haggle, sell, trade, traffic

bargain for anticipate, contemplate, ex~pect, foresee, imagine, look for, plan for

bargain on assume, bank on, count on, depend on, plan on, rely on

barge canal boat, flatboat, lighter, nar~row boat, scow

barge in break in, burst in, butt in, infringe, interrupt, intrude, muscle in (*informal*)

barge into bump into, cannon into, collide with, hit, push, shove

bark[1] **1.** *noun* casing, cortex (*Anatomy, botany*), covering, crust, husk, rind, skin **2.** *~verb* abrade, flay, rub, scrape, shave, skin, strip

bark[2] **1.** *noun/verb* bay, growl, howl, snarl, woof, yap, yelp **2.** *~verb figurative* bawl, bawl at, berate, bluster, growl, shout, snap, snarl, yell

barmy 1. *also* **balmy** crackpot (*informal*), crazy, daft (*informal*), dippy, doolally (*slang*), foolish, gonzo (*slang*), goofy (*informal*), idiotic, insane, loony (*slang*), loopy (*informal*), nuts (*slang*), nutty (*slang*), odd, off one's rocker (*slang*), off one's trolley (*slang*), out of one's mind, out to lunch (*informal*), round the twist (*Brit. slang*), silly, stupid, up the pole (*informal*), wacko *or* whacko (*informal*) **2.** fermenting, foamy, frothy, spumy, yeasty

▷ **Antonyms** (*sense 1*) all there (*informal*), in one's right mind, of sound mind, rational, reasonable, sane, sensible

baroque bizarre, convoluted, elaborate, extravagant, flamboyant, florid, grotesque, ornate, overdecorated, rococo

barracks billet, camp, cantonment, casern, encampment, garrison, quarters

barrage 1. battery, bombardment, cannonade, curtain of fire, fusillade, gunfire, salvo, shelling, volley **2.** assault, attack, burst, deluge, hail, mass, onslaught, plethora, profusion, rain, storm, stream, torrent

barred 1. banded, crosshatched, lined, marked, ribbed, ridged, streaked, striped, veined **2.** banned, excluded, forbidden, off limits, outlawed, prohibited, proscribed, taboo

barren 1. childless, infecund, infertile, sterile, unprolific **2.** arid, desert, desolate, dry, empty, unfruitful, unproductive, waste **3.** boring, dull, flat, fruitless, lacklustre, stale, uninformative, uninspiring, uninstructive, uninteresting, unrewarding, useless, vapid

▷ **Antonyms** (*senses 1 & 2*) fecund, fertile, fruitful, lush, productive, profitable, rich, useful (*sense 3*) instructive, interesting, productive, profitable, useful

barricade 1. *noun* barrier, blockade, bulwark, fence, obstruction, palisade, rampart, stockade **2.** *~verb* bar, block, blockade, defend, fortify, obstruct, protect, shut in

barrier 1. bar, barricade, block, blockade, boundary, ditch, fence, fortification, obstacle, obstruction, pale, railing, rampart, stop, wall **2.** *figurative* check, difficulty, drawback, handicap, hazard, hindrance, hurdle, impediment, limitation, obstacle, restriction, stumbling block

barter bargain, drive a hard bargain, exchange, haggle, sell, swap, trade, traffic

base[1] *noun* **1.** bed, bottom, foot, foundation, groundwork, pedestal, rest, stand, support **2.** basis, core, essence, essential, fundamental, heart, key, origin, principle, root, source **3.** camp, centre, headquarters, home, post, settlement, starting point, station *~verb* **4.** build, construct, depend, derive, establish, found, ground, hinge, locate, station

▷ **Antonyms** (*sense 1*) apex, crest, crown, peak, summit, top, vertex

base[2] *adjective* **1.** abject, contemptible, corrupt, depraved, despicable, dishonourable, disreputable, evil, ignoble, immoral, infamous, scandalous, shameful, sordid, vile, villainous, vulgar, wicked **2.** downtrodden, grovelling, low, lowly, mean, menial, miserable, paltry, pitiful, poor, servile, slavish, sorry, subservient, worthless, wretched **3.** adulterated, alloyed, counterfeit, debased, fake, forged, fraudulent, impure, inferior, pinchbeck, spurious

▷ **Antonyms** (*sense 1*) admirable, good, honest, honourable, just, moral, noble, pure, rare, righteous, upright, valuable, virtuous (*sense 2*) lofty, noble (*sense 3*) pure, unalloyed

baseless groundless, unconfirmed, uncorroborated, unfounded, ungrounded, unjustifiable, unjustified, unsubstantiated, unsupported

▷ **Antonyms** authenticated, confirmed, corroborated, proven, substantiated, supported, validated, verified, well-founded

baseness 1. contemptibility, degradation, depravation, depravity, despicability, disgrace, ignominy, infamy, notoriety, obloquy, turpitude **2.** lowliness, meanness, misery, poverty, servility, slavishness, subservience, vileness, worthlessness, wretchedness **3.** adulteration, debasement, fraudulence, phoneyness *or* phoniness (*informal*), pretence, speciousness, spuriousness

bash 1. *verb* belt (*informal*), biff (*slang*), break, chin (*slang*), crash, crush, deck (*slang*), hit, lay one on (*slang*), punch, slosh (*Brit. slang*), smash, sock (*slang*), strike, tonk (*informal*), wallop (*informal*) **2.** *~noun* attempt, crack (*informal*), go (*informal*), shot (*informal*), stab (*informal*), try

bashful abashed, blushing, confused, constrained, coy, diffident, easily embarrassed, nervous, overmodest, reserved, reticent, retiring, self-conscious, self-effacing, shamefaced, sheepish, shrinking, shy, timid, timorous

▷ **Antonyms** aggressive, arrogant, bold, brash, conceited, confident, egoistic, fearless, forward, immodest, impudent, intrepid, pushy (*informal*), self-assured

bashfulness constraint, coyness, diffidence, embarrassment, hesitation, modesty, reserve, self-consciousness, sheepishness, shyness, timidity, timorousness

basic bog-standard (*informal*), central, elementary, essential, fundamental, immanent, indispensable, inherent, intrinsic, key, necessary, primary, radical, underlying, vital

▷ **Antonyms** complementary, minor, peripheral, secondary, supplementary, supporting, trivial, unessential

basically at bottom, at heart, *au fond*, essentially, firstly, fundamentally, inherently, in substance, intrinsically, mostly, primarily, radically

basics brass tacks (*informal*), core, essentials, facts, fundamentals, hard facts, necessaries, nitty-gritty (*informal*), nuts and bolts (*informal*), practicalities, principles, rudiments

basis 1. base, bottom, footing, foundation, ground, groundwork, support **2.** chief ingredient, core, essential, fundamental, heart, premise, principal element, principle, theory

bask 1. laze, lie in, loll, lounge, relax, sunbathe, swim in, toast oneself, warm oneself **2.** delight in, enjoy, indulge oneself, luxuriate, relish, revel, savour, take pleasure, wallow

bass deep, deep-toned, grave, low, low-pitched, resonant, sonorous

bastard 1. *noun* illegitimate (child), love child, natural child, whoreson (*archaic*) **2.** *~adjective* adulterated, baseborn, counterfeit, false, illegitimate, imperfect, impure, inferior, irregular, misbegotten, sham, spurious

bastardize adulterate, cheapen, corrupt, debase, defile, degrade, demean, devalue, distort, pervert

bastion bulwark, citadel, defence, fastness, fortress, mainstay, prop, rock, stronghold, support, tower of strength

bat bang, hit, punch, rap, smack, strike, swat, thump, wallop (*informal*), whack

batch accumulation, aggregation, amount, assemblage, bunch, collection, crowd, group, lot, pack, quantity, set

bath 1. *noun* ablution, cleansing, douche, douse, scrubbing, shower, soak, soaping, sponging, tub, wash, washing **2.** *~verb* bathe, clean, douse, lave (*archaic*), scrub down, shower, soak, soap, sponge, tub, wash

bathe 1. *verb* cleanse, cover, dunk, flood, immerse, moisten, rinse, soak, steep, suffuse, wash, wet **2.** *~noun* dip, dook (*Scot.*), swim, wash

bathetic anticlimactic, mawkish, sentimental

bathing costume bathing suit, bikini, swimming costume, swimsuit, trunks

bathos anticlimax, false pathos, letdown, mawkishness, sentimentality

baton club, crook, mace, rod, sceptre, staff, stick, truncheon, wand

battalion army, brigade, company, contingent, division, force, horde, host, legion, multitude, regiment, squadron, throng

batten[1] *verb* board up, clamp down, cover up, fasten, fasten down, fix, nail down, secure, tighten

batten[2] *verb* fatten, flourish, gain, grow, increase, prosper, thrive, wax

batter 1. assault, bash (*informal*), beat, beat the living daylights out of, belabour, break, buffet, clobber (*slang*), dash against, lambast(e), lash, pelt, pound, pummel, smash, smite, thrash, wallop (*informal*) **2.** bruise, crush, deface, demolish, destroy, disfigure, hurt, injure, mangle, mar, maul, ruin, shatter, shiver, total (*slang*), trash (*slang*)

battered beaten, beat-up (*informal*), black-and-blue, broken-down, bruised, crushed, damaged, dilapidated, injured, ramshackle, squashed, weather-beaten

battery 1. chain, ring, sequence, series, set, suite **2.** assault, attack, beating, mayhem, onslaught, physical violence, thumping **3.** artillery, cannon, cannonry, gun emplacements, guns

battle *noun* **1.** action, attack, combat, encounter, engagement, fight, fray, hostilities, skirmish, war, warfare **2.** agitation, campaign, clash, conflict, contest, controversy, crusade, debate, disagreement, dispute, head-to-head, strife, struggle *~verb* **3.** agitate, argue, clamour, combat, contend, contest, dispute, feud, fight, lock horns, strive, struggle, war

▷ **Antonyms** *~noun* accord, agreement, armistice, ceasefire, concord, entente, peace, suspension of hostilities, truce

battle-axe ballbreaker (*slang*), disciplinarian, fury, harridan, scold, shrew, tartar, termagant, virago, vixen

battle cry catchword, motto, slogan, war cry, war whoop, watchword

battlefield battleground, combat zone, field, field of battle, front

battlement barbican, bartizan, bastion, breastwork, bulwark, crenellation, fortification, parapet, rampart

battleship capital ship, gunboat, man-of-war, ship of the line, warship

batty as daft as a brush (*informal, chiefly Brit.*), barking (*slang*), barking mad (*slang*), barmy (*slang*), bats (*slang*), bonkers (*slang, chiefly Brit.*), cracked (*slang*), crackers (*Brit. slang*), crackpot (*informal*), cranky (*informal*), crazy, daft (*informal*), doolally (*slang*), dotty (*slang, chiefly Brit.*), eccentric, gonzo (*slang*), insane, loony (*slang*), loopy (*informal*), lunatic, mad, not the full shilling (*informal*), nuts (*slang*), nutty (*slang*), odd, oddball (*informal*), off one's rocker (*slang*), off one's trolley (*slang*), off the rails, off-the-wall (*slang*), out of one's mind, outré, out to lunch (*informal*), peculiar, potty (*Brit. informal*), queer (*informal*), round the twist (*Brit. slang*), screwy (*informal*), touched, up the pole (*informal*), wacko *or* whacko (*slang*)

bauble bagatelle, gewgaw, gimcrack, kickshaw, knick-knack, plaything, toy, trifle, trinket

baulk *see* BALK

bawd brothel-keeper, madam, pimp, procuress, prostitute, whore, working girl (*facetious slang*)

bawdy blue, coarse, dirty, erotic, gross, indecent, indecorous, indelicate, lascivious, lecherous, lewd, libidinous, licentious, lustful, near the knuckle (*informal*), obscene, prurient, ribald, risqué, rude, salacious, smutty, steamy (*informal*), suggestive, vulgar, X-rated (*informal*)

▷ **Antonyms** chaste, clean, decent, good, modest, moral, respectable, seemly, undefiled, upright, virtuous

bawl **1.** bellow, call, clamour, halloo, howl, roar, shout, vociferate, yell **2.** blubber, cry, sob, squall, wail, weep

bay[1] *noun* bight, cove, gulf, inlet, natural harbour, sound

bay[2] *noun* alcove, compartment, embrasure, niche, nook, opening, recess

bay[3] **1.** *verb/noun* bark, bell, clamour, cry, growl, howl, yelp **2.** *~noun* **at bay** caught, cornered, trapped

bayonet *verb* impale, knife, run through, spear, stab, stick, transfix

bays chaplet, garland, glory, laurel crown, praise, prize, renown, trophy

bazaar **1.** exchange, market, marketplace, mart **2.** bring-and-buy, fair, fête, sale of work

be **1.** be alive, breathe, exist, inhabit, live **2.** befall, come about, come to pass, happen, occur, take place, transpire (*informal*) **3.** abide, continue, endure, last, obtain, persist, prevail, remain, stand, stay, survive

beach coast, lido, littoral, margin, plage, sands, seaboard (*chiefly U.S.*), seashore, seaside, shingle, shore, strand, water's edge

beachcomber forager, loafer, scavenger, scrounger, tramp, vagabond, vagrant, wanderer

beached abandoned, aground, ashore, deserted, grounded, high and dry, marooned, stranded, wrecked

beacon beam, bonfire, flare, lighthouse, pharos, rocket, sign, signal, signal fire, smoke signal, watchtower

bead blob, bubble, dot, drop, droplet, globule, pellet, pill, spherule

beads chaplet, choker, necklace, necklet, pearls, pendant, rosary

beak **1.** bill, mandible, neb (*archaic or dialect*), nib **2.** nose, proboscis, snout **3.** *Nautical* bow, prow, ram, rostrum, stem

beaked curved, hooked, pointed, sharp

beam *noun* **1.** girder, joist, plank, rafter, spar, support, timber **2.** bar, emission, gleam, glimmer, glint, glow, radiation, ray, shaft, streak, stream *~verb* **3.** broadcast, emit, glare, gleam, glitter, glow, radiate, shine, transmit **4.** grin, laugh, smile

beaming **1.** beautiful, bright, brilliant, flashing, gleaming, glistening, glittering, radiant, scintillating, shining, sparkling **2.** cheerful, grinning, happy, joyful, smiling, sunny

bear **1.** bring, carry, convey, hump (*Brit. slang*), move, take, tote (*informal*), transport **2.** cherish, entertain, exhibit, harbour, have, hold, maintain, possess, shoulder, support, sustain, uphold, weigh upon **3.** abide, admit, allow, brook, endure, hack (*slang*), permit, put up with (*informal*), stomach, suffer, tolerate, undergo **4.** beget, breed, bring forth, develop, engender, generate, give birth to, produce, yield

▷ **Antonyms** (*sense 1*) drop, put down, shed (*senses 2 & 3*) abandon, cease, desert, discontinue, drop, give up, leave, quit, relinquish

bearable admissible, endurable, manageable, passable, sufferable, supportable, sustainable, tolerable

▷ **Antonyms** insufferable, insupportable, intolerable, oppressive, too much (*informal*), unacceptable, unbearable, unendurable

beard **1.** *noun* bristles, five-o'clock shadow, stubble, whiskers **2.** *~verb* brave, confront, dare, defy, face, oppose, tackle

bearded bewhiskered, bristly, bushy, hairy, hirsute, shaggy, stubbly, unshaven, whiskered

beardless **1.** barefaced, clean-shaven, hairless, smooth, smooth-faced **2.** callow, fresh, green, immature, inexperienced

bear down **1.** burden, compress, encumber, press down, push, strain, weigh down **2.** advance on, approach, attack, close in, converge on, move in

bearer **1.** agent, carrier, conveyor, messenger, porter, runner, servant **2.** beneficiary, consignee, payee

bearing **1.** air, aspect, attitude, behaviour, carriage, demeanour, deportment, manner, mien, posture **2.** *Nautical* course, direction, point of compass **3.** application, connection, import, pertinence, reference, relation, relevance, significance

▷ **Antonyms** (*sense 3*) inappositeness,

inappropriateness, inaptness, inconsequence, irrelevance, irrelevancy, non sequitur

bearings aim, course, direction, location, orientation, position, situation, track, way, whereabouts

bearish **1.** churlish, clumsy, gruff, rough, sullen, surly **2.** *Stock Exchange* declining, falling, slumping

bear on affect, appertain to, belong to, concern, involve, pertain to, refer to, relate to, touch upon

bear out confirm, corroborate, endorse, justify, prove, substantiate, support, uphold, vindicate

bear up bear the brunt, carry on, endure, go through the mill, grin and bear it (*informal*), keep one's chin up, persevere, suffer, take it on the chin (*informal*), withstand

bear with be patient, forbear, make allowances, put up with (*informal*), suffer, tolerate, wait

beast **1.** animal, brute, creature **2.** barbarian, brute, fiend, ghoul, monster, ogre, sadist, savage, swine

beastly **1.** animal, barbarous, bestial, brutal, brutish, coarse, cruel, depraved, inhuman, monstrous, repulsive, sadistic, savage **2.** awful, disagreeable, foul, horrid, mean, nasty, rotten, shitty (*taboo slang*), terrible, unpleasant

▷ **Antonyms** (*sense 1*) humane, sensitive (*sense 2*) agreeable, fine, good, pleasant

beat *verb* **1.** bang, batter, belt (*informal*), break, bruise, buffet, cane, chin (*slang*), clobber (*slang*), cudgel, deck (*slang*), drub, flog, hit, knock, lambast(e), lash, lay one on (*slang*), lick (*informal*), maul, pelt, pound, punch, strike, thrash, thwack, tonk (*informal*), whip **2.** best, blow out of the water (*slang*), bring to their knees, clobber (*slang*), conquer, defeat, excel, knock spots off (*informal*), lick (*informal*), make mincemeat of (*informal*), master, outdo, outrun, outstrip, overcome, overwhelm, pip at the post, put in the shade (*informal*), run rings around (*informal*), stuff (*slang*), subdue, surpass, tank (*slang*), undo, vanquish, wipe the floor with (*informal*) **3.** fashion, forge, form, hammer, model, shape, work **4.** flap, flutter, palpitate, pound, pulsate, pulse, quake, quiver, shake, throb, thump, tremble, vibrate **5. beat it** bugger off (*taboo slang*), depart, exit, fuck off (*offensive taboo slang*), get lost (*informal*), get on one's bike (*Brit. slang*), go away, go to hell (*informal*), hook it (*slang*), hop it (*slang*), leave, make tracks, pack one's bags (*informal*), piss off (*taboo slang*), scarper (*Brit. slang*), scram (*informal*), shoo, skedaddle (*informal*), sling one's hook (*Brit. slang*), vamoose (*slang, chiefly U.S.*) *~noun* **6.** belt (*informal*), blow, hit, lash, punch, shake, slap, strike, swing, thump **7.** flutter, palpitation, pulsation, pulse, throb **8.** accent, cadence, ictus, measure (*Prosody*), metre, rhythm, stress, time **9.** circuit, course, path, rounds, route, way *~adjective* **10.** *slang* clapped out (*Austral. & N.Z. informal*), exhausted, fatigued, on one's last legs, shagged out (*Brit. slang*), tired, wearied, wiped out (*informal*), worn out, zonked (*slang*)

beaten **1.** baffled, cowed, defeated, disappointed, disheartened, frustrated, overcome, overwhelmed, thwarted, vanquished **2.** forged, formed, hammered, shaped, stamped, worked **3.** much travelled, trampled, trodden, well-trodden, well-used, worn **4.** blended, foamy, frothy, mixed, stirred, whipped, whisked

beatific blessed, blissed out, blissful, divine, ecstatic, enraptured, exalted, glorious, heavenly, joyful, rapt, rapturous, sent, serene, sublime

beating **1.** belting (*informal*), caning, chastisement, corporal punishment, flogging, pasting (*slang*), slapping, smacking, thrashing, whipping **2.** conquest, defeat, downfall, overthrow, pasting (*slang*), rout, ruin

beatitude beatification, blessedness, bliss, ecstasy, exaltation, felicity, happiness, holy joy, saintliness

beat up assault, attack, batter, beat the living daylights out of (*informal*), clobber (*slang*), do over (*Brit., Austral. & N.Z. slang*), duff up (*Brit. slang*), fill in (*Brit. slang*), knock about *or* around, lambast(e), put the boot in (*slang*), thrash, work over (*slang*)

beau **1.** admirer, boyfriend, escort, fancy man (*slang*), fiancé, guy (*informal*), leman (*archaic*), lover, suitor, swain, sweetheart **2.** cavalier, coxcomb, dandy, fop, gallant, ladies' man, popinjay, swell (*informal*)

beautiful alluring, appealing, attractive, charming, comely, delightful, drop-dead (*slang*), exquisite, fair, fine, glamorous, good-looking, gorgeous, graceful, handsome, lovely, pleasing, radiant, ravishing, stunning (*informal*)

▷ **Antonyms** awful, bad, hideous, repulsive, terrible, ugly, unattractive, unpleasant, unsightly

beautify adorn, array, bedeck, deck, decorate, embellish, enhance, festoon, garnish, gild, glamorize, grace, ornament

beauty **1.** allure, attractiveness, bloom, charm, comeliness, elegance, exquisiteness, fairness, glamour, grace, handsomeness, loveliness, pulchritude, seemliness, symmetry **2.** belle, charmer, cracker (*slang*), goddess, good-looker, humdinger (*slang*), lovely (*slang*), stunner (*informal*), Venus **3.** advantage, as~

set, attraction, benefit, blessing, boon, excellence, feature, good thing
▷ **Antonyms** (*sense 1*) repulsiveness, ugliness, unpleasantness, unseemliness (*sense 3*) detraction, disadvantage, flaw

beaver away exert oneself, graft (*informal*), hammer away, keep one's nose to the grindstone, peg away, persevere, persist, plug away (*informal*), slog, work

becalmed motionless, settled, still, stranded, stuck

because as, by reason of, in that, on account of, owing to, since, thanks to

beck gesture, nod, signal, summons, wave

beckon 1. bid, gesticulate, gesture, motion, nod, signal, summon, wave at **2.** allure, attract, call, coax, draw, entice, invite, lure, pull, tempt

becloud bedim, befog, complicate, confuse, darken, muddle, muddy the waters, obfuscate, obscure, overcast, screen, veil

become 1. alter to, be transformed into, change into, develop into, evolve into, grow into, mature into, metamorphose into, ripen into **2.** embellish, enhance, fit, flatter, grace, harmonize, ornament, set off, suit

becoming 1. attractive, comely, enhancing, flattering, graceful, neat, pretty, tasteful **2.** appropriate, befitting, *comme il faut,* compatible, congruous, decent, decorous, fit, fitting, in keeping, meet (*archaic*), proper, seemly, suitable, worthy
▷ **Antonyms** (*sense 1*) ugly, unattractive, unbecoming (*sense 2*) improper, unfit, unsuitable, unworthy

bed *noun* **1.** bedstead, berth, bunk, cot, couch, divan, pallet **2.** area, border, garden, patch, plot, row, strip **3.** base, bottom, foundation, groundwork, substratum ~*verb* **4.** base, embed, establish, fix, found, implant, insert, plant, settle, set up

bedaub besmear, smear, smirch, soil, spatter, splash, stain

bedazzle amaze, astound, bewilder, blind, captivate, confuse, daze, dazzle, dumbfound, enchant, overwhelm, stagger, stun, sweep off one's feet

bedclothes bedding, bed linen, blankets, coverlets, covers, duvets, eiderdowns, pillowcases, pillows, quilts, sheets

bed down hit the hay (*slang*), lie, retire, settle down, sleep, turn in (*informal*)

bedeck adorn, array, bedight (*archaic*), bedizen (*archaic*), decorate, embellish, festoon, garnish, ornament, trim

bedevil afflict, aggravate (*informal*), annoy, be on one's back (*slang*), breathe down someone's neck, confound, distress, fret, frustrate, get in one's hair (*informal*), get on one's nerves (*informal*), get on one's wick (*Brit. slang*), get under one's skin (*informal*), get up one's nose (*informal*), harass, hassle (*informal*), irk, irritate, pester, plague, torment, torture, trouble, vex, worry

bedew besprinkle, dampen, drench, moisten, shower, soak, spray, sprinkle, water, wet

bedim becloud, bedarken, cloak, cloud, darken, dim, obscure, overcast, shade, shadow

bedlam chaos, clamour, commotion, confusion, furore, hubbub, hullabaloo, madhouse (*informal*), noise, pandemonium, tumult, turmoil, uproar

bedraggled dirty, dishevelled, disordered, drenched, dripping, messy, muddied, muddy, sodden, soiled, stained, sullied, unkempt, untidy

bedridden confined, confined to bed, flat on one's back, incapacitated, laid up (*informal*)

bedrock 1. bed, bottom, foundation, nadir, rock bottom, substratum, substructure **2.** basics, basis, core, essentials, fundamentals, nuts and bolts (*informal*), roots

beef 1. *informal* brawn, flesh, heftiness, muscle, physique, robustness, sinew, strength **2.** *slang* complaint, criticism, dispute, grievance, gripe (*informal*), grouch (*informal*), grouse, grumble, objection, protest, protestation

beefy *informal* **1.** brawny, bulky, burly, hulking, muscular, stalwart, stocky, strapping, sturdy, thickset **2.** chubby, corpulent, fat, fleshy, heavy, obese, overweight, paunchy, plump, podgy, portly, pudgy, rotund
▷ **Antonyms** feeble, frail, puny, scrawny, skinny, weak

beetle, beetling *adjective* hanging over, jutting, leaning over, overhanging, pendent, projecting, prominent, protruding, sticking out, swelling over

befall bechance, betide, chance, come to pass, ensue, fall, follow, happen, materialize, occur, supervene, take place, transpire (*informal*)

befitting apposite, appropriate, becoming, fit, fitting, meet (*archaic*), proper, right, seemly, suitable
▷ **Antonyms** improper, inappropriate, irrelevant, unbecoming, unfit, unsuitable, wrong

befog becloud, blur, confuse, darken, fuzz, make hazy, make indistinct, make vague, muddle, muddy the waters, obfuscate, obscure

befool bamboozle (*informal*), beguile, cheat, con, cozen, delude, dupe, fool, hoax, hoodwink, humbug, impose on, mislead, outwit, trick

before 1. *adverb* ahead, earlier, formerly, in advance, in front, previously, sooner **2.** ~*preposition* earlier than, in advance of, in front of, in the presence of, prior to

▷ **Antonyms** *~adverb* after, afterwards, behind, later, subsequently, thereafter *~preposition* after, behind, following, succeeding

beforehand ahead of time, already, before, before now, earlier, in advance, in anticipation, previously, sooner

befriend advise, aid, assist, back, benefit, encourage, favour, help, patronize, side with, stand by, succour, support, sustain, uphold, welcome

befuddle baffle, bewilder, confuse, daze, disorient, intoxicate, muddle, puzzle, stupefy

▷ **Antonyms** clarify, clear up, elucidate, explicate, illuminate, interpret, make clear, make plain, resolve, simplify, throw *or* shed light on

befuddled at sea, confused, dazed, fuddled, groggy (*informal*), inebriated, intoxicated, muddled, woozy (*informal*)

beg **1.** beseech, crave, desire, entreat, implore, importune, petition, plead, pray, request, solicit, supplicate **2.** blag (*slang*), cadge, call for alms, mooch (*slang*), scrounge, seek charity, solicit charity, sponge on, touch (someone) for (*slang*) **3.** *as in* **beg the question** avoid, dodge, duck (*informal*), equivocate, eschew, evade, fend off, flannel (*Brit. informal*), hedge, parry, shirk, shun, sidestep

▷ **Antonyms** (*sense 1*) apportion, award, bestow, commit, confer, contribute, donate, give, grant, impart, present (*sense 2*) claim, demand, exact, extort, insist on

beget **1.** breed, father, generate, get, procreate, propagate, sire **2.** bring, bring about, cause, create, effect, engender, give rise to, occasion, produce, result in

beggar *noun* **1.** bag lady (*chiefly U.S.*), bum (*informal*), cadger, mendicant, scrounger (*informal*), sponger (*informal*), supplicant, tramp, vagrant **2.** bankrupt, down-and-out, pauper, starveling *~verb* **3.** *as in* **beggar description** baffle, challenge, defy, surpass

beggarly abject, base, contemptible, despicable, destitute, impoverished, inadequate, indigent, low, meagre, mean, miserly, needy, niggardly, pathetic, pitiful, poor, poverty-stricken, stingy, vile, wretched

beggary bankruptcy, destitution, indigence, need, pauperism, poverty, vagrancy, want, wretchedness

begin **1.** commence, embark on, get the show on the road (*informal*), inaugurate, initiate, instigate, institute, prepare, set about, set on foot, start **2.** appear, arise, be born, come into being, come into existence, commence, crop up (*informal*), dawn, emerge, happen, originate, spring, start

▷ **Antonyms** cease, complete, end, finish, stop, terminate

beginner amateur, apprentice, cub, fledgling, freshman, greenhorn (*informal*), initiate, learner, neophyte, novice, recruit, starter, student, tenderfoot, trainee, tyro

▷ **Antonyms** authority, expert, master, old hand, old stager, old-timer, past master, past mistress, pro (*informal*), professional, trouper, veteran

beginning **1.** birth, commencement, inauguration, inception, initiation, onset, opening, opening move, origin, outset, overture, preface, prelude, rise, rudiments, source, start, starting point **2.** embryo, fount, fountainhead, germ, root, seed

▷ **Antonyms** (*sense 1*) closing, completion, conclusion, end, ending, finish, termination

begrime besmirch, blacken, dirty, muddy, smear, smirch, soil, spatter, stain, sully, tarnish

begrudge be jealous, be reluctant, be stingy, envy, grudge, resent

beguile **1.** befool, cheat, deceive, delude, dupe, fool, hoodwink, impose on, mislead, take for a ride (*informal*), trick **2.** amuse, charm, cheer, delight, distract, divert, engross, entertain, occupy, solace, tickle the fancy of

▷ **Antonyms** (*sense 1*) alarm, alert, enlighten, put right

beguiling alluring, attractive, bewitching, captivating, charming, diverting, enchanting, entertaining, enthralling, interesting, intriguing

behalf account, advantage, benefit, defence, good, interest, part, profit, sake, side, support

behave **1.** act, function, operate, perform, run, work **2.** act correctly, conduct oneself properly, keep one's nose clean, mind one's manners

▷ **Antonyms** (*sense 2*) act up (*informal*), be bad, be insubordinate, be naughty, carry on (*informal*), get up to mischief (*informal*), misbehave, muck about (*Brit. slang*)

behaviour **1.** actions, bearing, carriage, comportment, conduct, demeanour, deportment, manner, manners, ways **2.** action, functioning, operation, performance

behest bidding, canon, charge, command, commandment, decree, dictate, direction, expressed desire, injunction, instruction, mandate, order, precept, wish

behind *preposition* **1.** after, at the back of, at the heels of, at the rear of, following, later than **2.** at the bottom of, causing, initiating, instigating, responsible for **3.** backing, for, in agreement, on the side of, supporting *~adverb* **4.** after, afterwards, following, in the wake (of), next, subsequently **5.** behindhand, in arrears, in debt, overdue *~noun* **6.** arse (*taboo slang*), ass (*U.S. & Canad. taboo slang*),

bottom, bum (*Brit. slang*), buns (*U.S. slang*), butt (*U.S. & Canad. informal*), buttocks, derrière (*euphemistic*), jacksy (*Brit. slang*), posterior, rump, seat, tail (*informal*), tush (*U.S. slang*)
▷ **Antonyms** (*sense 1*) earlier than, in advance of, in front of, in the presence of, prior to (*sense 4*) ahead, earlier, formerly, in advance, previously, sooner

behindhand backward, behind time, dilatory, late, remiss, slow, tardy

behind the times antiquated, dated, *démodé,* obsolete, old-fashioned, old hat, outmoded, out of date, out of the ark (*informal*), passé
▷ **Antonyms** advanced, avant-garde, experimental, far-out (*slang*), groundbreaking, innovative, pioneering, progressive, trendy (*Brit. informal*), unconventional, way-out (*informal*)

behold 1. *verb* check, check out (*informal*), clock (*Brit. slang*), consider, contemplate, discern, eye, eyeball (*U.S. slang*), get a load of (*informal*), look at, observe, perceive, recce (*slang*), regard, scan, survey, take a dekko at (*Brit. slang*), view, watch, witness **2.** ~*interjection* lo, look, mark, observe, see, watch

beholden bound, grateful, indebted, obligated, obliged, owing, under obligation

behove be advisable, befit, be fitting, be incumbent upon, be necessary, benefit, be obligatory, beseem, be wise

beige biscuit, buff, *café au lait,* camel, cinnamon, coffee, cream, ecru, fawn, khaki, mushroom, neutral, oatmeal, sand, tan

being 1. actuality, animation, existence, life, living, reality **2.** entity, essence, nature, soul, spirit, substance **3.** animal, beast, body, creature, human being, individual, living thing, mortal, thing
▷ **Antonyms** (*senses 1 & 2*) nihility, nonbeing, nonexistence, nothingness, nullity, oblivion

belabour 1. batter, beat, clobber (*slang*), flog, lambast(e), thrash, whip **2.** attack, berate, blast, castigate, censure, criticize, excoriate, flay, go for the jugular, lambast(e), lay into (*informal*), put down, tear into (*informal*)

belated behindhand, behind time, delayed, late, late in the day, overdue, tardy

belch 1. burp (*informal*), eruct, eructate, hiccup **2.** discharge, disgorge, emit, erupt, give off, gush, spew forth, vent, vomit

beleaguer 1. assail, beset, besiege, blockade, encompass, environ, hem in, surround **2.** aggravate (*informal*), annoy, badger, be on one's back (*slang*), bother, breathe down someone's neck, get in one's hair (*informal*), get on one's nerves (*informal*), get on one's wick (*Brit. slang*), harass, hassle (*informal*), pester, vex

beleaguered badgered, beset, besieged, bothered, harassed, nagged, persecuted, plagued, put upon, set upon, vexed

belie 1. confute, contradict, deny, disprove, gainsay (*archaic or literary*), give the lie to, make a nonsense of, negate, rebut, repudiate **2.** conceal, deceive, disguise, falsify, gloss over, mislead, misrepresent

belief 1. admission, assent, assurance, confidence, conviction, credit, feeling, impression, judgment, notion, opinion, persuasion, presumption, reliance, theory, trust, view **2.** credence, credo, creed, doctrine, dogma, faith, ideology, principles, tenet
▷ **Antonyms** disbelief, distrust, doubt, dubiety, incredulity, mistrust, scepticism

believable acceptable, authentic, credible, creditable, imaginable, likely, plausible, possible, probable, reliable, trustworthy, verisimilar
▷ **Antonyms** cock-and-bull (*informal*), doubtful, dubious, fabulous, implausible, incredible, questionable, unacceptable, unbelievable

believe 1. accept, be certain of, be convinced of, buy (*slang*), count on, credit, depend on, have faith in, hold, place confidence in, presume true, rely on, swallow (*informal*), swear by, take as gospel, take on board, trust **2.** assume, conjecture, consider, gather, guess (*informal, chiefly U.S. & Canad.*), imagine, judge, maintain, postulate, presume, reckon, speculate, suppose, think
▷ **Antonyms** disbelieve, distrust, doubt, know, question

believer adherent, convert, devotee, disciple, follower, proselyte, protagonist, supporter, upholder, zealot
▷ **Antonyms** agnostic, atheist, disbeliever, doubting Thomas, infidel, sceptic, unbeliever

belittle decry, denigrate, deprecate, depreciate, deride, derogate, detract, diminish, disparage, downgrade, minimize, scoff at, scorn, sneer at, underestimate, underrate, undervalue
▷ **Antonyms** boast about, elevate, exalt, magnify, praise, vaunt

bellicose aggressive, antagonistic, belligerent, combative, defiant, hawkish, hostile, jingoistic, militaristic, provocative, pugnacious, quarrelsome, sabre-rattling, warlike, warloving, warmongering

belligerence aggressiveness, animosity, antagonism, combativeness, hostility, pugnacity, unfriendliness

belligerent 1. *adjective* aggressive, antagonistic, argumentative, bellicose, combative, contentious, hostile, litigious, pugnacious, quarrelsome, un~

friendly, warlike, warring **2.** *~noun* combatant, fighter, warring nation
▷ **Antonyms** *~adjective* amicable, benign, conciliatory, friendly, harmonious, nonviolent, without hostility

bellow *noun/verb* bawl, bell, call, clamour, cry, howl, roar, scream, shout, shriek, yell

belly 1. *noun* abdomen, breadbasket (*slang*), corporation (*informal*), gut, insides (*informal*), paunch, potbelly, stomach, tummy, vitals **2.** *~verb* billow, bulge, fill, spread, swell, swell out

belong 1. (*with* **to**) be at the disposal of, be held by, be owned by, be the property of **2.** (*with* **to**) be affiliated to, be allied to, be a member of, be associated with, be included in **3.** attach to, be connected with, be fitting, be part of, fit, go with, have as a proper place, pertain to, relate to

belonging acceptance, affiliation, affinity, association, attachment, fellowship, inclusion, kinship, loyalty, rapport, relationship

belongings accoutrements, chattels, effects, gear, goods, paraphernalia, personal property, possessions, stuff, things

beloved admired, adored, cherished, darling, dear, dearest, loved, pet, precious, prized, revered, sweet, treasured, worshipped

below *adverb* **1.** beneath, down, lower, under, underneath *~preposition* **2.** inferior, lesser, lesser than, subject, subordinate, unworthy of **3. below par** below average, imperfect, inferior, off colour, off form, poor, second-rate, unfit

belt 1. band, cincture, cummerbund, girdle, girth, sash, waistband **2.** *Geography* area, district, layer, region, stretch, strip, tract, zone **3. below the belt** cowardly, foul, not playing the game (*informal*), unfair, unjust, unscrupulous, unsporting, unsportsmanlike

bemoan bewail, cry over spilt milk, deplore, express sorrow, grieve for, lament, moan over, mourn, regret, rue, weep for

bemuse amaze, bewilder, confuse, daze, flummox, muddle, nonplus, overwhelm, perplex, puzzle, stun

bemused absent-minded, at sea, bewildered, confused, dazed, engrossed, flummoxed, fuddled, half-drunk, muddled, nonplussed, perplexed, preoccupied, stunned, stupefied, tipsy

bench 1. form, pew, seat, settle, stall **2.** board, counter, table, trestle table, workbench, worktable **3.** court, courtroom, judge, judges, judiciary, magistrate, magistrates, tribunal

benchmark criterion, example, gauge, level, measure, model, norm, par, reference, reference point, standard, touchstone, yardstick

bend *verb* **1.** arc, arch, bow, buckle, contort, crouch, curve, deflect, diverge, flex, incline, incurvate, lean, stoop, swerve, turn, twist, veer, warp **2.** compel, direct, influence, mould, persuade, shape, subdue, submit, sway, yield *~noun* **3.** angle, arc, arch, bow, corner, crook, curve, hook, loop, turn, twist, zigzag

beneath 1. *adverb* below, in a lower place, underneath **2.** *~preposition* below, inferior to, less than, lower than, unbefitting, underneath, unworthy of
▷ **Antonyms** *~preposition* above, atop, beyond, exceeding, higher than, on top of, over, upon

benediction beatitude, *benedictus,* benison, blessing, consecration, favour, grace, gratitude, invocation, orison, prayer, thankfulness, thanksgiving

benefaction 1. beneficence, benevolence, charity, generosity, largesse *or* largess, liberality, munificence, philanthropy **2.** alms, bequest, boon, charity, contribution, donation, endowment, gift, grant, gratuity, hand-out, largesse *or* largess, legacy, offering, present, stipend

benefactor angel (*informal*), backer, contributor, donor, helper, patron, philanthropist, promoter, sponsor, subscriber, subsidizer, supporter, well-wisher

benefice Church living, emolument, incumbency, office, prebend, preferment, sinecure, stipend

beneficence 1. altruism, benevolence, compassion, generosity, goodness, goodwill, helpfulness, kindness, largesse *or* largess, liberality, love, unselfishness, virtue **2.** aid, benefaction, bestowal, donation, gift, hand-out, largesse *or* largess, present, relief, succour

beneficent benevolent, benign, bounteous, bountiful, charitable, generous, helpful, kind, liberal, munificent, princely

beneficial advantageous, benign, expedient, favourable, gainful, healthful, helpful, profitable, salubrious, salutary, serviceable, useful, valuable, wholesome
▷ **Antonyms** detrimental, disadvantageous, harmful, pernicious, useless

beneficiary assignee, heir, inheritor, legatee, payee, receiver, recipient, successor

benefit 1. *noun* advantage, aid, asset, assistance, avail, betterment, blessing, boon, favour, gain, good, help, inside track (*informal*), interest, mileage (*informal*), profit, use, utility **2.** *~verb* advance, advantage, aid, ameliorate, assist, avail, better, enhance, further, improve, profit, promote, serve
▷ **Antonyms** *~noun* damage, detriment, disadvantage, downside, harm, impairment, injury, loss *~verb* damage, deprive, detract from, harm, impair, injure, worsen

benevolence altruism, charity, compassion, fellow feeling, generosity, goodness, goodwill, humanity, kind-heartedness, kindness, sympathy
▷ **Antonyms** ill will, malevolence, selfishness, stinginess, unkindness

benevolent affable, altruistic, beneficent, benign, bounteous, bountiful, caring, charitable, compassionate, considerate, generous, humane, humanitarian, kind, kind-hearted, liberal, philanthropic, tender-hearted, warm-hearted, well-disposed

benighted backward, crude, ignorant, illiterate, primitive, uncivilized, uncultivated, unenlightened

benign **1.** affable, amiable, complaisant, friendly, generous, genial, gracious, kind, kindly, liberal, obliging, sympathetic **2.** balmy, gentle, healthful, mild, refreshing, temperate, warm, wholesome **3.** advantageous, auspicious, beneficial, encouraging, favourable, good, lucky, propitious, salutary **4.** *Medical* curable, harmless, limited, remediable, slight, superficial
▷ **Antonyms** (*sense 1*) bad, disobliging, harsh, hateful, inhumane, malicious, malign, severe, stern, unfavourable, unkind, unpleasant, unsympathetic (*sense 2*) bad, harsh, severe, unfavourable, unpleasant (*sense 3*) bad, unfavourable, unlucky (*sense 4*) malignant

bent *adjective* **1.** angled, arched, bowed, crooked, curved, hunched, stooped, twisted **2.** (*with* **on**) determined, disposed, fixed, inclined, insistent, predisposed, resolved, set ~*noun* **3.** ability, aptitude, bag (*slang*), cup of tea (*informal*), facility, faculty, flair, forte, inclination, knack, leaning, penchant, preference, proclivity, propensity, talent, tendency
▷ **Antonyms** (*sense 1*) aligned, erect, even, horizontal, in line, level, perpendicular, plumb, smooth, square, straight, true, upright, vertical

benumb anaesthetize, chill, deaden, freeze, numb, paralyse, shock, stun, stupefy

benumbed anaesthetized, dazed, deadened, frozen, immobilized, insensible, insensitive, numb, paralysed, stunned, stupefied, unfeeling, unresponsive

bequeath bestow, commit, endow, entrust, give, grant, hand down, impart, leave to by will, pass on, transmit, will

bequest bequeathal, bestowal, dower, endowment, estate, gift, heritage, inheritance, legacy, settlement, trust

berate bawl out (*informal*), blast, carpet (*informal*), castigate, censure, chew out (*U.S. & Canad. informal*), chide, criticize, excoriate, give a rocket (*Brit. & N.Z. informal*), harangue, lambast(e), put down, rail at, rap over the knuckles, read the riot act, rebuke, reprimand, reproach, reprove, revile, scold, slap on the wrist, slate (*informal, chiefly Brit.*), tear into (*informal*), tear (someone) off a strip (*Brit. informal*), tell off (*informal*), upbraid, vituperate
▷ **Antonyms** acclaim, admire, applaud, approve, cheer, commend, compliment, congratulate, extol, laud, praise, take one's hat off to

bereave afflict, deprive of kindred, dispossess, divest, make destitute, strip, take away from, widow

bereavement affliction, death, deprivation, loss, misfortune, tribulation

bereft cut off, deprived, destitute, devoid, lacking, minus, parted from, robbed of, shorn, wanting

berserk amok, ape (*slang*), apeshit (*slang*), crazy, enraged, frantic, frenzied, insane, mad, maniacal, manic, rabid, raging, uncontrollable, violent, wild

berth *noun* **1.** bed, billet, bunk, cot (*Nautical*), hammock **2.** anchorage, dock, harbour, haven, pier, port, quay, slip, wharf **3.** appointment, employment, job, living, position, post, situation ~*verb* **4.** *Nautical* anchor, dock, drop anchor, land, moor, tie up

beseech adjure, ask, beg, call upon, crave, entreat, implore, importune, petition, plead, pray, solicit, sue, supplicate

beset **1.** assail, attack, besiege, encircle, enclose, encompass, environ, hem in, surround **2.** *figurative* badger, bedevil, embarrass, entangle, harass, perplex, pester, plague

besetting habitual, harassing, inveterate, persistent, prevalent, troublesome

beside **1.** abreast of, adjacent to, alongside, at the side of, cheek by jowl, close to, near, nearby, neighbouring, next door to, next to, overlooking **2.** **beside oneself** apoplectic, at the end of one's tether, berserk, crazed, delirious, demented, deranged, desperate, distraught, frantic, frenzied, insane, mad, out of one's mind, unbalanced, uncontrolled, unhinged

besides **1.** *adverb* also, as well, further, furthermore, in addition, into the bargain, moreover, otherwise, too, what's more **2.** ~*preposition* apart from, barring, excepting, excluding, in addition to, other than, over and above, without

beside the point extraneous, immaterial, inapplicable, inapposite, inappropriate, inconsequent, irrelevant, neither here nor there, unconnected
▷ **Antonyms** admissible, applicable, apposite, appropriate, appurtenant, apt, fitting, germane, pertinent, relevant, significant, to the point

besiege **1.** beleaguer, beset, blockade, confine, encircle, encompass, environ, hedge in, hem in, invest (*rare*), lay siege to, shut in, surround **2.** badger, bend someone's ear (*informal*), bother, harass, harry, hassle (*informal*), hound, importune, nag, pester, plague, trouble

besmirch daub, defame, dishonour, slander, smear, smirch, soil, stain, sully, tarnish

besotted **1.** befuddled, bevvied (*dialect*), bladdered (*slang*), blitzed (*slang*), blotto (*slang*), bombed (*slang*), Brahms and Liszt (*slang*), drunk, intoxicated, legless (*informal*), lit up (*slang*), out of it (*slang*), out to it (*Austral. & N.Z. slang*), paralytic (*informal*), pissed (*taboo slang*), rat-arsed (*taboo slang*), smashed (*slang*), steamboats (*Scot. slang*), steaming (*slang*), stupefied, wasted (*slang*), wrecked (*slang*), zonked (*slang*) **2.** doting, hypnotized, infatuated, smitten, spellbound **3.** confused, foolish, muddled, witless

bespatter bedaub, befoul, begrime, besmirch, besprinkle, muddy, smear, spatter, splatter, sully

bespeak **1.** engage, order beforehand, prearrange, solicit **2.** betoken, denote, display, evidence, evince, exhibit, foretell, imply, indicate, predict, proclaim, reveal, show, signify, suggest, testify to

best *adjective* **1.** chief, finest, first, first-class, first-rate, foremost, highest, leading, most excellent, outstanding, perfect, pre-eminent, principal, superlative, supreme, unsurpassed **2.** advantageous, apt, correct, golden, most desirable, most fitting, right **3.** greatest, largest, most *~adverb* **4.** advantageously, attractively, excellently, most fortunately **5.** extremely, greatly, most deeply, most fully, most highly *~noun* **6.** choice, cream, *crème de la crème,* elite, favourite, finest, first, flower, pick, prime, top **7.** hardest, highest endeavour, utmost *~verb* **8.** beat, blow out of the water (*slang*), conquer, defeat, get the better of, lick (*informal*), master, outclass, outdo, put in the shade (*informal*), run rings around (*informal*), stuff (*slang*), surpass, tank (*slang*), thrash, triumph over, trounce, undo, wipe the floor with (*informal*)

bestial animal, barbaric, barbarous, beastlike, beastly, brutal, brutish, carnal, degraded, depraved, gross, inhuman, low, savage, sensual, sordid, vile

bestir activate, actuate, animate, awaken, exert, get going, incite, motivate, rouse, set off, stimulate, stir up, trouble

bestow accord, allot, apportion, award, commit, confer, donate, endow, entrust, give, grant, hand out, honour with, impart, lavish, present, render to

▷ **Antonyms** acquire, attain, come by, earn, gain, get, land, make, net, obtain, procure, secure

bestride bestraddle, bridge, dominate, extend, mount, span, step over, straddle, tower over

bet **1.** *noun* ante, gamble, hazard, long shot, pledge, risk, speculation, stake, venture, wager **2.** *~verb* chance, gamble, hazard, pledge, punt (*chiefly Brit.*), put money on, put one's shirt on, risk, speculate, stake, venture, wager

bethink cogitate, consider, ponder, recall, recollect, reconsider, reflect, remember, review, take thought

betide bechance, befall, chance, come to pass, crop up (*informal*), ensue, happen, occur, overtake, supervene, take place, transpire (*informal*)

betimes anon, beforehand, before long, early, erelong (*archaic or poetic*), first thing, in good time, punctually, seasonably, soon

betoken augur, bespeak, bode, declare, denote, evidence, indicate, manifest, mark, portend, presage, prognosticate, promise, represent, signify, suggest, typify

betray **1.** be disloyal, be treacherous, be unfaithful, break one's promise, break with, double-cross (*informal*), grass (*Brit. slang*), grass up (*slang*), inform on *or* against, put the finger on (*informal*), sell down the river (*informal*), sell out (*informal*), sell the pass (*informal*), shop (*slang, chiefly Brit.*), stab in the back **2.** blurt out, disclose, divulge, evince, expose, give away, lay bare, let slip, manifest, reveal, show, tell, tell on, uncover, unmask **3.** beguile, corrupt, deceive, delude, dupe, ensnare, entrap, lead astray, mislead, take for a ride (*informal*), undo **4.** abandon, desert, forsake, jilt, walk out on

betrayal **1.** deception, disloyalty, double-cross (*informal*), double-dealing, duplicity, falseness, perfidy, sell-out (*informal*), treachery, treason, trickery, unfaithfulness **2.** blurting out, disclosure, divulgence, giving away, revelation, telling

▷ **Antonyms** (*sense 1*) allegiance, constancy, devotion, faithfulness, fealty, fidelity, loyalty, steadfastness, trustiness, trustworthiness (*sense 2*) guarding, keeping, keeping secret, preserving, safeguarding

betrayer apostate, conspirator, deceiver, renegade, snake in the grass, traitor

betroth affiance, contract, engage to marry, pledge in marriage, plight, plight one's troth (*old-fashioned*), promise, take the plunge (*informal*), tie the knot (*informal*)

betrothal affiancing, betrothing, engagement, espousal (*archaic*), marriage compact, plight, promise, troth, vow

better *adjective* **1.** bigger, excelling, finer, fitter, greater, higher-quality, larger, more appropriate, more desirable, more expert, more fitting, more suitable, more useful, more valuable, preferable, streets ahead, superior, surpassing, worthier **2.** cured, fitter, fully recovered, healthier, improving, less ill, mending, more healthy, on the mend (*informal*), progressing, recovering, stronger, well **3.** bigger, greater, larger, longer *~adverb* **4.** in a more excellent manner, in a superior way, more advantageously, more attractively, more competently, more completely, more effectively, more thoroughly, to a greater degree *~verb* **5.** advance, ameliorate, amend, correct, enhance, forward, further, improve, meliorate, mend, promote, raise, rectify, reform **6.** beat, cap (*informal*), clobber (*slang*), exceed, excel, improve on *or* upon, knock spots off (*informal*), lick (*informal*), outdo, outstrip, put in the shade (*informal*), run rings around (*informal*), surpass, top *~noun* **7. get the better of** beat, best, defeat, get the upper hand, outdo, outsmart (*informal*), outwit, prevail over, score off, surpass, triumph over, worst

▷ **Antonyms** *~adjective* (*senses 1 & 3*) inferior, lesser, smaller, substandard, worse (*sense 2*) worse *~adverb* worse *~verb* (*sense 5*) depress, devaluate, go downhill, impoverish, lessen, lower, weaken, worsen

betterment amelioration, edification, improvement, melioration

between amidst, among, betwixt, halfway, in the middle of, mid

bevel 1. *noun* angle, bezel, cant, chamfer, diagonal, mitre, oblique, slant, slope **2.** *~verb* cant, chamfer, cut at an angle, mitre

beverage bevvy (*dialect*), draught, drink, libation (*facetious*), liquid, liquor, potable, potation, refreshment

bevy 1. band, bunch (*informal*), collection, company, crowd, gathering, group, pack, troupe **2.** covey, flight, flock

bewail bemoan, cry over, deplore, express sorrow, grieve for, keen, lament, moan, mourn, regret, repent, rue, wail, weep over

beware avoid, be careful, be cautious, be wary, guard against, heed, look out, mind, refrain from, shun, steer clear of, take heed, watch out

bewilder baffle, befuddle, bemuse, confound, confuse, daze, flummox, mix up, mystify, nonplus, perplex, puzzle, stun, stupefy

bewildered at a loss, at sea, awed, baffled, bamboozled (*informal*), confused, disconcerted, dizzy, flummoxed, giddy, mystified, nonplussed, perplexed, puzzled, speechless, startled, stunned, surprised, taken aback, uncertain

bewitch absorb, allure, attract, beguile, captivate, charm, enchant, enrapture, entrance, fascinate, hypnotize, ravish, spellbind

▷ **Antonyms** disgust, give one the creeps (*informal*), make one sick, offend, repel, repulse, sicken, turn off (*informal*)

bewitched charmed, enchanted, entranced, mesmerized, possessed, spellbound, transformed, under a spell, unrecognizable

beyond above, apart from, at a distance, away from, before, farther, out of range, out of reach, outwith (*Scot.*), over, past, remote, superior to, yonder

bias *noun* **1.** bent, bigotry, favouritism, inclination, jobs for the boys (*informal*), leaning, nepotism, one-sidedness, partiality, penchant, predilection, predisposition, prejudice, proclivity, proneness, propensity, tendency, turn, unfairness **2.** angle, cross, diagonal line, slant *~verb* **3.** distort, influence, predispose, prejudice, slant, sway, twist, warp, weight

▷ **Antonyms** (*sense 1*) equality, equity, fairness, impartiality, neutrality, objectivity, open-mindedness

biased distorted, embittered, jaundiced, one-sided, partial, predisposed, prejudiced, slanted, swayed, twisted, warped, weighted

bicker argue, cross swords, disagree, dispute, fight, fight like cat and dog, go at it hammer and tongs, quarrel, row (*informal*), scrap (*informal*), spar, squabble, wrangle

▷ **Antonyms** accord, acquiesce, agree, assent, concur, cooperate, get on, harmonize

bid *verb* **1.** offer, proffer, propose, submit, tender **2.** call, greet, say, tell, wish **3.** ask, call, charge, command, desire, direct, enjoin, instruct, invite, require, solicit, summon, tell *~noun* **4.** advance, amount, offer, price, proposal, proposition, submission, sum, tender **5.** attempt, crack (*informal*), effort, endeavour, go (*informal*), stab (*informal*), try, venture

biddable amenable, complaisant, cooperative, docile, obedient, teachable, tractable

▷ **Antonyms** awkward, difficult, disobedient, intractable, petulant, querulous, refractory, unruly

bidding 1. beck, beck and call, behest, call, canon, charge, command, demand, direction, injunction, instruction, invitation, order, request, summons **2.** auction, offer, offers, proposal, tender

big 1. bulky, burly, colossal, considerable, elephantine, enormous, extensive, gigantic, great, huge, hulking, humongous *or* humungous (*U.S. slang*), immense, large, mammoth, massive, ponderous, prodigious, sizable *or* sizeable, spacious, stellar (*informal*), substantial, vast, voluminous **2.** big-time (*informal*), eminent, important, influential, leading, main, major league (*informal*), momentous, paramount, powerful, prime, prin~

cipal, prominent, serious, significant, valuable, weighty **3.** adult, elder, grown, grown-up, mature **4.** altruistic, benevolent, generous, gracious, heroic, magnanimous, noble, princely, unselfish **5.** arrogant, boastful, bragging, conceited, haughty, inflated, pompous, pretentious, proud

▷ **Antonyms** (*senses 1 & 3*) diminutive, immature, insignificant, little, mini, miniature, petite, pint-sized (*informal*), pocket-sized, pygmy *or* pigmy, small, tiny, wee, young (*sense 2*) humble, ignoble, insignificant, minor, modest, ordinary, unimportant, unknown

bigot dogmatist, fanatic, persecutor, sectarian, zealot

bigoted biased, dogmatic, illiberal, intolerant, narrow-minded, obstinate, opinionated, prejudiced, sectarian, twisted, warped

▷ **Antonyms** broad-minded, equitable, open-minded, tolerant, unbiased, unbigoted, unprejudiced

bigotry bias, discrimination, dogmatism, fanaticism, ignorance, injustice, intolerance, mindlessness, narrow-mindedness, pig-ignorance (*slang*), prejudice, provincialism, racialism, racism, sectarianism, sexism, unfairness

▷ **Antonyms** broad-mindedness, forbearance, open-mindedness, permissiveness, tolerance

bigwig big cheese (*slang, old-fashioned*), big gun (*informal*), big name, big noise (*informal*), big shot (*informal*), celeb (*informal*), celebrity, dignitary, heavyweight (*informal*), mogul, nob (*slang*), notability, notable, panjandrum, personage, somebody, V.I.P.

▷ **Antonyms** cipher, lightweight (*informal*), nobody, nonentity, nothing, zero

bile anger, bitterness, churlishness, ill humour, irascibility, irritability, nastiness, peevishness, rancour, spleen

bilious 1. liverish, nauseated, out of sorts, queasy, sick **2.** bad-tempered, cantankerous, crabby, cross, crotchety, edgy, grouchy (*informal*), grumpy, ill-humoured, ill-tempered, irritable, like a bear with a sore head, nasty, peevish, ratty (*Brit. & N.Z. informal*), short-tempered, testy, tetchy, touchy

bilk bamboozle (*informal*), cheat, con (*informal*), cozen, deceive, defraud, do (*slang*), fleece, pull a fast one on (*informal*), rook (*slang*), sell a pup, skin (*slang*), stiff (*slang*), swindle, trick

bill[1] *noun* **1.** account, charges, invoice, note of charge, reckoning, score, statement, tally **2.** advertisement, broadsheet, bulletin, circular, handbill, handout, leaflet, notice, placard, playbill, poster **3.** agenda, card, catalogue, inventory, list, listing, programme, roster, schedule, syllabus **4.** measure, piece of legislation, projected law, proposal *~verb* **5.** charge, debit, figure, invoice, reckon, record **6.** advertise, announce, give advance notice of, post

bill[2] *noun* beak, mandible, neb (*archaic or dialect*), nib

billet 1. *noun* accommodation, barracks, lodging, quarters **2.** *~verb* accommodate, berth, quarter, station

billow *noun* **1.** breaker, crest, roller, surge, swell, tide, wave **2.** cloud, deluge, flood, outpouring, rush, surge, wave *~verb* **3.** balloon, belly, puff up, rise up, roll, surge, swell

billowy heaving, rippling, rolling, surging, swelling, swirling, undulating, waving, wavy

bind *verb* **1.** attach, fasten, glue, hitch, lash, paste, rope, secure, stick, strap, tie, tie up, truss, wrap **2.** compel, constrain, engage, force, necessitate, obligate, oblige, prescribe, require **3.** confine, detain, hamper, hinder, restrain, restrict **4.** bandage, cover, dress, encase, swathe, wrap **5.** border, edge, finish, hem, trim *~noun* **6.** *informal* bore, difficulty, dilemma, drag (*informal*), hot water (*informal*), nuisance, pain in the arse (*taboo informal*), pain in the neck (*informal*), predicament, quandary, spot (*informal*), tight spot

▷ **Antonyms** (*senses 1 & 3*) free, loosen, release, unbind, undo, unfasten, untie

binding *adjective* compulsory, conclusive, imperative, indissoluble, irrevocable, mandatory, necessary, obligatory, unalterable

▷ **Antonyms** discretionary, free, noncompulsory, optional, uncompelled, unconstrained, unforced, voluntary

binge beano (*Brit. slang*), bender (*informal*), blind (*slang*), bout, feast, fling, jag (*slang*), orgy, spree

biography account, curriculum vitae, CV, life, life history, life story, memoir, memoirs, profile, record

birth 1. childbirth, delivery, nativity, parturition **2.** beginning, emergence, fountainhead, genesis, origin, rise, source **3.** ancestry, background, blood, breeding, derivation, descent, extraction, forebears, genealogy, line, lineage, nobility, noble extraction, parentage, pedigree, race, stock, strain

▷ **Antonyms** (*senses 1 & 2*) death, demise, end, extinction, passing, passing away *or* on

bisect bifurcate, cross, cut across, cut in half, cut in two, divide in two, halve, intersect, separate, split, split down the middle

bisexual AC/DC (*slang*), ambidextrous (*slang*), androgyne, androgynous, bi (*slang*), epicene, gynandromorphic *or* gynandromorphous (*Entomology*), gynandrous, hermaphrodite, hermaphro~

ditic, monoclinous (*Botany*), swinging both ways (*slang*)

bishopric diocese, episcopacy, episcopate, primacy, see

bit[1] *noun* **1.** atom, chip, crumb, fragment, grain, iota, jot, mite, morsel, mouthful, part, piece, remnant, scrap, segment, slice, small piece, speck, tittle, whit **2.** instant, jiffy (*informal*), little while, minute, moment, period, second, spell, tick (*Brit. informal*), time

bit[2] *noun* **1.** brake, check, curb, restraint, snaffle **2. take the bit in** *or* **between one's teeth** defy, disobey, get stuck into (*informal*), get to grips with, rebel, resist, revolt, run amok, rush into, set about

bitchy backbiting, catty (*informal*), cruel, malicious, mean, nasty, rancorous, shrewish, snide, spiteful, venomous, vicious, vindictive, vixenish

▷ **Antonyms** charitable, generous, gracious, kindly, magnanimous, nice

bite *verb* **1.** champ, chew, clamp, crunch, crush, cut, gnaw, grip, hold, masticate, nibble, nip, pierce, pinch, rend, seize, snap, tear, wound **2.** burn, corrode, eat away, eat into, erode, smart, sting, tingle, wear away *~noun* **3.** itch, nip, pinch, prick, smarting, sting, tooth marks, wound **4.** food, light meal, morsel, mouthful, piece, refreshment, snack, taste **5.** edge, kick (*informal*), piquancy, punch (*informal*), pungency, spice

biting 1. bitter, blighting, cold, cold as ice, cutting, freezing, harsh, nipping, penetrating, piercing, sharp **2.** caustic, cutting, incisive, mordacious, mordant, sarcastic, scathing, severe, sharp, stinging, trenchant, vitriolic, withering

bitter 1. acerb, acid, acrid, astringent, sharp, sour, tart, unsweetened, vinegary **2.** acrimonious, begrudging, crabbed, embittered, hostile, morose, rancorous, resentful, sore, sour, sullen, with a chip on one's shoulder **3.** calamitous, cruel, dire, distressing, galling, grievous, harsh, heartbreaking, merciless, painful, poignant, ruthless, savage, vexatious **4.** biting, fierce, freezing, intense, severe, stinging

▷ **Antonyms** (*sense 1*) bland, mellow, mild, pleasant, sugary, sweet (*sense 2*) appreciative, friendly, gentle, grateful, happy, mellow, mild, pleasant, sweet, thankful (*sense 3*) fortunate, happy, pleasant (*sense 4*) balmy, gentle, mild, pleasant

bitterness 1. acerbity, acidity, sharpness, sourness, tartness, vinegariness **2.** animosity, chip on one's shoulder (*informal*), grudge, hostility, pique, rancour, resentment **3.** acrimoniousness, asperity, pungency, sarcasm, venom, virulence

bizarre abnormal, comical, curious, eccentric, extraordinary, fantastic, freakish, grotesque, left-field (*informal*), ludicrous, odd, oddball (*informal*), offbeat, off the rails, off-the-wall (*slang*), outlandish, outré, peculiar, queer, ridiculous, rum (*Brit. slang*), strange, unusual, wacko (*slang*), way-out (*informal*), weird, zany

▷ **Antonyms** common, customary, normal, ordinary, regular, routine, standard, typical

blab blow the gaff (*Brit. slang*), blow wide open (*slang*), blurt out, disclose, divulge, gossip, let slip, let the cat out of the bag, reveal, shop (*slang, chiefly Brit.*), sing (*slang, chiefly U.S.*), spill one's guts (*slang*), spill the beans (*informal*), tattle, tell, tell all, tell on

blabber 1. *noun* busybody, gossip, informer, rumour-monger, scandalmonger, talebearer, tattler, telltale **2.** *~verb* blather, blether (*Scot.*), chatter, gab (*informal*), jabber, prattle, run off at the mouth

blabbermouth bigmouth (*slang*), blatherskite, flibbertigibbet, gossip, loudmouth (*informal*), motormouth (*slang*), windbag (*slang*)

black *adjective* **1.** coal-black, dark, dusky, ebony, inky, jet, murky, pitchy, raven, sable, starless, stygian, swarthy **2.** *figurative* atrocious, depressing, dismal, distressing, doleful, foreboding, funereal, gloomy, hopeless, horrible, lugubrious, mournful, ominous, sad, sombre **3.** dingy, dirty, filthy, grimy, grubby, soiled, sooty, stained **4.** angry, furious, hostile, menacing, resentful, sullen, threatening **5.** bad, evil, iniquitous, nefarious, villainous, wicked *~verb* **6.** ban, bar, blacklist, boycott *~noun* **7. in the black** in credit, in funds, solvent, without debt

▷ **Antonyms** (*sense 1*) bright, illuminated, light, lighted, lit, moonlit, sunny (*sense 2*) cheerful, happy, warm (*sense 3*) clean, pure, white, whitish (*sense 4*) amicable, cheerful, friendly, happy, pleased, warm (*sense 5*) good, honourable, moral, pure

blackball *verb* ban, bar, blacklist, debar, drum out, exclude, expel, ostracize, oust, repudiate, snub, vote against

blacken 1. befoul, begrime, cloud, darken, grow black, make black, smudge, soil **2.** bad-mouth (*slang, chiefly U.S. & Canad.*), calumniate, decry, defame, defile, denigrate, dishonour, knock (*informal*), malign, rubbish (*informal*), slag (off) (*slang*), slander, smear, smirch, stain, sully, taint, tarnish, traduce, vilify

blackguard bad egg (*old-fashioned informal*), bastard (*offensive*), blighter (*Brit. informal*), bounder (*old-fashioned Brit. slang*), bugger (*taboo slang*), miscreant, rascal, rogue, scoundrel, scumbag (*slang*), shit (*taboo slang*), skelm (*S.

Afr.), son-of-a-bitch (*slang, chiefly U.S. & Canad.*), swine, villain, wretch

blacklist *verb* ban, bar, blackball, boycott, debar, exclude, expel, ostracize, preclude, proscribe, reject, repudiate, snub, vote against

black magic black art, diabolism, necromancy, sorcery, voodoo, witchcraft, wizardry

blackmail 1. *noun* bribe, exaction, extortion, hush money (*slang*), intimidation, milking, pay-off (*informal*), protection (*informal*), ransom, shakedown (*U.S. slang*), slush fund **2.** *~verb* bleed (*informal*), bribe, coerce, compel, demand, exact, extort, force, hold to ransom, milk, squeeze, threaten

blackness darkness, duskiness, gloom, inkiness, melanism, murkiness, nigrescence, nigritude (*rare*), swarthiness

▷ **Antonyms** brightness, brilliance, effulgence, incandescence, lambency, light, lightness, luminescence, luminosity, phosphorescence, radiance

blackout *noun* **1.** coma, faint, loss of consciousness, oblivion, swoon, syncope (*Pathology*), unconsciousness **2.** power cut, power failure **3.** censorship, noncommunication, radio silence, secrecy, suppression, withholding news

black out *verb* **1.** conceal, cover, darken, eclipse, obfuscate, shade **2.** collapse, faint, flake out (*informal*), lose consciousness, pass out, swoon

black sheep bad egg (*old-fashioned informal*), disgrace, dropout, ne'er-do-well, outcast, prodigal, renegade, reprobate, wastrel

blamable answerable, blameworthy, culpable, deserving of censure, faulty, guilty, in the wrong, liable, reprehensible, reproachable, reprovable, responsible

blame *noun* **1.** accountability, culpability, fault, guilt, incrimination, liability, onus, rap (*slang*), responsibility **2.** accusation, castigation, censure, charge, complaint, condemnation, criticism, recrimination, reproach, reproof, stick (*slang*) *~verb* **3.** accuse, admonish, blast, censure, charge, chide, condemn, criticize, disapprove, express disapprobation, find fault with, hold responsible, lambast(e), point a *or* the finger at, put down, reprehend, reproach, reprove, tax, tear into (*informal*), upbraid

▷ **Antonyms** *~noun* absolution, acclaim, alibi, Brownie points, commendation, credit, excuse, exoneration, honour, praise, tribute, vindication *~verb* absolve, acclaim, acquit, approve of, clear, commend, compliment, excuse, exonerate, forgive, praise, vindicate

blameless above suspicion, clean, faultless, guiltless, immaculate, impeccable, innocent, in the clear, irreproachable, perfect, squeaky-clean, stainless, unblemished, unimpeachable, unoffending, unspotted, unsullied, untarnished, upright, virtuous

▷ **Antonyms** at fault, censurable, culpable, guilty, reprovable, responsible, to blame

blameworthy discreditable, disreputable, indefensible, inexcusable, iniquitous, reprehensible, reproachable, shameful

blanch become *or* grow white, become pallid, bleach, blench, drain, fade, pale, turn pale, wan, whiten

bland 1. boring, dull, flat, humdrum, insipid, monotonous, tasteless, tedious, tiresome, undistinctive, unexciting, uninspiring, uninteresting, unstimulating, vanilla (*informal*), vapid, weak **2.** affable, amiable, congenial, courteous, debonair, friendly, gentle, gracious, smooth, suave, unemotional, urbane **3.** balmy, calm, mild, mollifying, nonirritant *or* nonirritating (*Medical*), soft, soothing, temperate

▷ **Antonyms** (*sense 1*) distinctive, exciting, inspiring, interesting, rousing, stimulating, turbulent, volatile (*sense 3*) annoying, harsh, irritating, rough, severe

blandishments blarney, cajolery, coaxing, compliments, fawning, flattery, ingratiation, inveiglement, soft soap (*informal*), soft words, sweet talk (*informal*), wheedling, winning caresses

blank *adjective* **1.** bare, clean, clear, empty, plain, spotless, uncompleted, unfilled, unmarked, void, white **2.** deadpan, dull, empty, expressionless, hollow, impassive, inane, lifeless, poker-faced (*informal*), vacant, vacuous, vague **3.** at a loss, at sea, bewildered, confounded, confused, disconcerted, dumbfounded, flummoxed, muddled, nonplussed, uncomprehending **4.** absolute, complete, out and out, outright, thorough, unqualified, utter *~noun* **5.** emptiness, empty space, gap, nothingness, space, tabula rasa, vacancy, vacuity, vacuum, void

▷ **Antonyms** *~adjective* (*sense 1*) busy, completed, filled in, full, marked (*sense 2*) expressive, interested, lively (*sense 3*) alert, intelligent, thoughtful

blanket *noun* **1.** afghan, cover, coverlet, rug **2.** carpet, cloak, coat, coating, covering, envelope, film, layer, mantle, sheet, wrapper, wrapping *~adjective* **3.** across-the-board, all-inclusive, comprehensive, overall, sweeping, wide-ranging *~verb* **4.** cloak, cloud, coat, conceal, cover, eclipse, hide, mask, obscure, suppress, surround

blankness abstraction, fatuity, inanity, indifference, no recollection, obliviousness, vacancy, vacuity

blare blast, boom, clamour, clang, honk, hoot, peal, resound, roar, scream, sound out, toot, trumpet

blarney blandishment, cajolery, coaxing, exaggeration, flattery, honeyed words, overpraise, soft soap (*informal*), spiel, sweet talk (*informal*), wheedling

blasé apathetic, bored, cloyed, glutted, indifferent, jaded, lukewarm, nonchalant, offhand, satiated, surfeited, unconcerned, unexcited, uninterested, unmoved, weary, world-weary

▷ **Antonyms** affected, caring, enthusiastic, excited, interested, responsive, stimulated

blaspheme abuse, anathematize, curse, damn, desecrate, execrate, profane, revile, swear

blasphemous godless, impious, irreligious, irreverent, profane, sacrilegious, ungodly

▷ **Antonyms** devout, God-fearing, godly, pious, religious, respectful, reverent, reverential

blasphemy cursing, desecration, execration, impiety, impiousness, indignity (*to God*), irreverence, profanation, profaneness, profanity, sacrilege, swearing

blast *noun/verb* **1.** blare, blow, clang, honk, peal, scream, toot, wail *~noun* **2.** bang, blow-up, burst, crash, detonation, discharge, eruption, explosion, outburst, salvo, volley **3.** gale, gust, squall, storm, strong breeze, tempest *~verb* **4.** blow sky-high, blow up, break up, burst, demolish, destroy, explode, put paid to, ruin, shatter **5.** blight, kill, shrivel, wither **6.** attack, castigate, criticize, flay, lambast(e), put down, rail at, tear into (*informal*)

blasted blighted, desolated, destroyed, devastated, ravaged, ruined, shattered, spoiled, wasted, withered

blastoff *noun* discharge, expulsion, firing, launch, launching, liftoff, projection, shot

blatant 1. bald, brazen, conspicuous, flagrant, flaunting, glaring, naked, obtrusive, obvious, ostentatious, outright, overt, prominent, pronounced, sheer, unmitigated **2.** clamorous, deafening, ear-splitting, harsh, loud, noisy, piercing, strident

▷ **Antonyms** agreeable, cultured, dignified, hidden, inconspicuous, quiet, refined, soft, subtle, tasteful, unnoticeable, unobtrusive, well-mannered

blather claptrap (*informal*), drivel, gibberish, gobbledegook, jabber, jabbering, moonshine, pap, twaddle

blaze *noun* **1.** bonfire, conflagration, fire, flame, flames **2.** beam, brilliance, flare, flash, glare, gleam, glitter, glow, light, radiance **3.** blast, burst, eruption, flare-up, fury, outbreak, outburst, rush, storm, torrent *~verb* **4.** beam, burn, fire, flame, flare, flash, glare, gleam, glow, shine **5.** boil, explode, flare up, fume, seethe

blazon broadcast, celebrate, flourish, make known, proclaim, renown, trumpet

bleach blanch, etiolate, fade, grow pale, lighten, peroxide, wash out, whiten

bleached achromatic, etiolated, faded, lightened, peroxided, stone-washed, washed-out

bleak 1. bare, barren, chilly, cold, desolate, exposed, gaunt, open, raw, stark, unsheltered, weather-beaten, windswept, windy **2.** cheerless, comfortless, depressing, discouraging, disheartening, dismal, dreary, gloomy, grim, hopeless, joyless, sombre, unpromising

▷ **Antonyms** (*sense 1*) protected, sheltered, shielded (*sense 2*) cheerful, cosy, encouraging, promising

bleary blurred, blurry, dim, fogged, foggy, fuzzy, hazy, indistinct, misty, murky, rheumy, watery

bleed 1. exude, flow, gush, lose blood, ooze, run, seep, shed blood, spurt, trickle, weep **2.** deplete, drain, draw *or* take blood, exhaust, extort, extract, fleece, leech, milk, phlebotomize (*Medical*), reduce, sap, squeeze **3.** ache, agonize, feel for, grieve, pity, suffer, sympathize

blemish 1. *noun* blot, blotch, blot on one's escutcheon, blur, defect, demerit, disfigurement, disgrace, dishonour, fault, flaw, imperfection, mark, scar, smirch, smudge, speck, spot, stain, taint **2.** *~verb* blot, blotch, blur, damage, deface, disfigure, flaw, impair, injure, mar, mark, smirch, smudge, spoil, spot, stain, sully, taint, tarnish

▷ **Antonyms** *~noun* enhancement, improvement, ornament, perfection, purity, refinement *~verb* correct, enhance, improve, perfect, purify, refine, restore

blench cower, cringe, falter, flinch, hesitate, quail, quake, quiver, recoil, shrink, shudder, shy, start, wince

blend *verb* **1.** amalgamate, coalesce, combine, compound, fuse, intermix, meld, merge, mingle, mix, synthesize, unite **2.** complement, fit, go well, go with, harmonize, suit *~noun* **3.** alloy, amalgam, amalgamation, combination, composite, compound, concoction, fusion, meld, mix, mixture, synthesis, union

bless 1. anoint, consecrate, dedicate, exalt, extol, give thanks to, glorify, hallow, invoke happiness on, magnify, ordain, praise, sanctify, thank **2.** bestow, endow, favour, give, grace, grant, provide

▷ **Antonyms** (*sense 1*) accuse, anathematize, curse, damn, excommunicate, execrate, fulminate, imprecate (*sense 2*) afflict, blight, burden, curse, destroy, doom, plague, scourge, torment, trouble, vex

blessed 1. adored, beatified, divine, hallowed, holy, revered, sacred, sanctified **2.** endowed, favoured, fortunate, grant~

ed, jammy (*Brit. slang*), lucky **3.** blissful, contented, glad, happy, joyful, joyous

blessedness beatitude, bliss, blissfulness, content, felicity, happiness, heavenly joy, pleasure, sanctity, state of grace, *summum bonum*

blessing 1. benediction, benison, commendation, consecration, dedication, grace, invocation, thanksgiving **2.** approbation, approval, backing, concurrence, consent, favour, good wishes, leave, permission, regard, sanction, support **3.** advantage, benefit, boon, bounty, favour, gain, gift, godsend, good fortune, help, kindness, manna from heaven, profit, service, windfall

▷ **Antonyms** (*senses 1 & 2*) condemnation, curse, disapproval, disfavour, malediction, objection, reproof (*sense 3*) damage, deprivation, disadvantage, drawback, harm, misfortune

blight *noun* **1.** canker, decay, disease, fungus, infestation, mildew, pest, pestilence, rot **2.** affliction, bane, contamination, corruption, curse, evil, plague, pollution, scourge, woe *~verb* **3.** blast, destroy, injure, nip in the bud, ruin, shrivel, taint with mildew, wither **4.** *figurative* annihilate, crush, dash, disappoint, frustrate, mar, nullify, put a damper on, ruin, spoil, undo, wreck

▷ **Antonyms** (*sense 2*) benefaction, blessing, boon, bounty, favour, godsend, help, service

blind *adjective* **1.** destitute of vision, eyeless, sightless, stone-blind, unseeing, unsighted, visionless **2.** *figurative* careless, heedless, ignorant, inattentive, inconsiderate, indifferent, indiscriminate, injudicious, insensitive, morally darkened, neglectful, oblivious, prejudiced, thoughtless, unaware of, unconscious of, uncritical, undiscerning, unmindful of, unobservant, unreasoning **3.** hasty, impetuous, irrational, mindless, rash, reckless, senseless, uncontrollable, uncontrolled, unthinking, violent, wild **4.** closed, concealed, dark, dead-end, dim, hidden, leading nowhere, obscured, obstructed, without exit *~noun* **5.** camouflage, cloak, cover, façade, feint, front, mask, masquerade, screen, smoke screen

▷ **Antonyms** *~adjective* (*sense 1*) seeing, sighted (*senses 2 & 3*) alive to, attentive, aware, concerned, conscious, discerning, heedful, knowledgeable, noticeable, observant (*sense 4*) obvious, open

blindly 1. aimlessly, at random, confusedly, frantically, indiscriminately, instinctively, madly, purposelessly, wildly **2.** carelessly, heedlessly, impulsively, inconsiderately, passionately, recklessly, regardlessly, senselessly, thoughtlessly, unreasonably, wilfully

blink 1. bat, flutter, glimpse, nictate, nictitate, peer, squint, wink **2.** flash, flicker, gleam, glimmer, scintillate, shine, sparkle, twinkle, wink **3.** *figurative* condone, connive at, disregard, ignore, overlook, pass by, turn a blind eye to **4.** **on the blink** *slang* faulty, malfunctioning, not working (properly), on the fritz (*U.S. slang*), out of action, out of order, playing up

bliss beatitude, blessedness, blissfulness, ecstasy, euphoria, felicity, gladness, happiness, heaven, joy, nirvana, paradise, rapture

▷ **Antonyms** affliction, anguish, distress, grief, heartbreak, misery, mourning, regret, sadness, sorrow, unhappiness, woe, wretchedness

blissful cock-a-hoop, delighted, ecstatic, elated, enchanted, enraptured, euphoric, happy, heavenly (*informal*), in ecstasies, joyful, joyous, over the moon (*informal*), rapt, rapturous

blister abscess, blain, bleb, boil, bubble, canker, carbuncle, cyst, furuncle (*Pathology*), pimple, pustule, sore, swelling, ulcer, welt, wen

blithe 1. animated, buoyant, carefree, cheerful, cheery, chirpy (*informal*), debonair, gay, genial, gladsome (*archaic*), happy, jaunty, light-hearted, merry, mirthful, sprightly, sunny, upbeat (*informal*), vivacious **2.** careless, casual, heedless, indifferent, nonchalant, thoughtless, unconcerned, untroubled

▷ **Antonyms** concerned, dejected, depressed, gloomy, kind-hearted, melancholy, morose, preoccupied, sad, thoughtful, unhappy

blitz assault, attack, blitzkrieg, bombardment, campaign, offensive, onslaught, raid, strike

blizzard blast, gale, snowstorm, squall, storm, tempest

bloat balloon, blow up, dilate, distend, enlarge, expand, inflate, puff up, swell

▷ **Antonyms** contract, deflate, shrink, shrivel, wither, wrinkle

blob ball, bead, bubble, dab, dewdrop, drop, droplet, glob, globule, lump, mass, pearl, pellet, pill

bloc alliance, axis, cabal, clique, coalition, combine, entente, faction, group, league, ring, schism, union, wing

block *noun* **1.** bar, brick, cake, chunk, cube, hunk, ingot, lump, mass, nugget, piece, square **2.** bar, barrier, blockage, hindrance, impediment, jam, obstacle, obstruction, occlusion, stoppage *~verb* **3.** bung up (*informal*), choke, clog, close, obstruct, plug, stem the flow, stop up **4.** arrest, bar, check, deter, halt, hinder, hobble, impede, obstruct, put a spoke in someone's wheel, stop, throw a spanner in the works, thwart

▷ **Antonyms** *~verb* (*sense 3*) clear, open, unblock, unclog (*sense 4*) advance, aid, expedite, facilitate, foster, further, lend support to, promote, push, support

blockade barricade, barrier, block, closure, encirclement, hindrance, impediment, obstacle, obstruction, restriction, siege, stoppage

blockage block, blocking, impediment, obstruction, occlusion, stoppage, stopping up

blockhead berk (*Brit. slang*), bimbo (*slang*), bonehead (*slang*), charlie (*Brit. informal*), chump (*informal*), coot, dickhead (*slang*), dimwit (*informal*), dipstick (*Brit. slang*), divvy (*Brit. slang*), dolt, dork (*slang*), dullard, dunce, dweeb (*U.S. slang*), fathead (*informal*), fool, fuckwit (*taboo slang*), geek (*slang*), gobshite (*Irish taboo slang*), gonzo (*slang*), idiot, ignoramus, jerk (*slang, chiefly U.S. & Canad.*), nerd *or* nurd (*slang*), nitwit, noodle, numbskull *or* numskull, numpty (*Scot. informal*), pillock (*Brit. slang*), plank (*Brit. slang*), plonker (*slang*), prat (*slang*), prick (*slang*), schmuck (*U.S. slang*), thickhead, twit (*informal, chiefly Brit.*), wally (*slang*)

block out chart, map out, outline, plan, sketch

bloke bastard (*informal*), bod (*informal*), body, boy, bugger (*slang*), chap, character (*informal*), customer (*informal*), fellow, guy (*informal*), individual, man, person, punter (*informal*)

blond, blonde fair, fair-haired, fair-skinned, flaxen, golden-haired, light, light-coloured, light-complexioned, tow-headed

blood 1. gore, lifeblood, vital fluid **2.** ancestry, birth, consanguinity, descendants, descent, extraction, family, kindred, kinship, lineage, noble extraction, relations **3.** *figurative* anger, disposition, feeling, passion, spirit, temper

bloodcurdling appalling, chilling, dreadful, fearful, frightening, hair-raising, horrendous, horrifying, scaring, spine-chilling, terrifying

bloodless 1. cold, languid, lifeless, listless, passionless, spiritless, torpid, unemotional, unfeeling **2.** anaemic, ashen, chalky, colourless, like death warmed up (*informal*), pale, pallid, pasty, sallow, sickly, wan

bloodshed blood bath, bloodletting, butchery, carnage, gore, killing, massacre, murder, slaughter, slaying

bloodthirsty barbarous, brutal, cruel, cut-throat, ferocious, gory, inhuman, murderous, ruthless, savage, vicious, warlike

bloody 1. bleeding, blood-soaked, blood-spattered, bloodstained, gaping, raw, unstaunched **2.** cruel, ferocious, fierce, sanguinary, savage

bloom *noun* **1.** blossom, blossoming, bud, efflorescence, flower, opening (*of flowers*) **2.** *figurative* beauty, blush, flourishing, flush, freshness, glow, health, heyday, lustre, perfection, prime, radiance, rosiness, vigour *~verb* **3.** blossom, blow, bud, burgeon, open, sprout **4.** develop, fare well, flourish, grow, prosper, succeed, thrive, wax

▷ **Antonyms** *~noun* (*sense 2*) bloodlessness, paleness, pallor, wanness, whiteness *~verb* decay, decline, die, droop, fade, fail, languish, perish, shrink, shrivel, wane, waste, wilt, wither

blossom *noun* **1.** bloom, bud, floret, flower, flowers *~verb* **2.** bloom, burgeon, flower **3.** *figurative* bloom, develop, flourish, grow, mature, progress, prosper, thrive

blot *noun* **1.** blotch, mark, patch, smear, smudge, speck, splodge, spot **2.** blemish, blot on one's escutcheon, blur, defect, demerit, disgrace, fault, flaw, scar, smirch, spot, stain, taint *~verb* **3.** bespatter, disfigure, disgrace, mark, smirch, smudge, spoil, spot, stain, sully, tarnish **4.** absorb, dry, soak up, take up **5. blot out** cancel, darken, destroy, eclipse, efface, erase, expunge, obliterate, obscure, shadow

blotch blemish, blot, mark, patch, scar, smirch, smudge, smutch, splash, splodge, spot, stain

blotchy blemished, macular, patchy, reddened, scurvy, spotty, uneven

blow[1] *verb* **1.** blast, breathe, exhale, fan, pant, puff, waft **2.** flow, rush, stream, whirl **3.** bear, buffet, drive, fling, flutter, sweep, waft, whirl, whisk **4.** blare, mouth, pipe, play, sound, toot, trumpet, vibrate *~noun* **5.** blast, draught, flurry, gale, gust, puff, strong breeze, tempest, wind

blow[2] *noun* **1.** bang, bash (*informal*), belt (*informal*), buffet, clomp (*slang*), clout (*informal*), clump (*slang*), knock, punch, rap, slosh (*Brit. slang*), smack, sock (*slang*), stroke, thump, tonk (*informal*), wallop (*informal*), whack **2.** *figurative* affliction, bolt from the blue, bombshell, bummer (*slang*), calamity, catastrophe, choker (*informal*), comedown (*informal*), disappointment, disaster, jolt, misfortune, reverse, setback, shock, sucker punch, upset, whammy (*informal, chiefly U.S.*)

blowout 1. blast, detonation, eruption, explosion **2.** break, burst, escape, flat, flat tyre, fuse, leak, puncture, rupture, tear **3.** beano (*Brit. slang*), binge (*informal*), carousal, carouse, feast, hooley *or* hoolie (*chiefly Irish & N.Z.*), party, rave (*Brit. slang*), rave-up (*Brit. slang*), spree

blow out 1. extinguish, put out, snuff **2.** burst, erupt, explode, rupture, shatter

blow over be forgotten, cease, die down, disappear, end, finish, pass, pass away, subside, vanish

blow up 1. bloat, distend, enlarge, expand, fill, inflate, puff up, pump up, swell **2.** blast, blow sky-high, bomb, burst, detonate, dynamite, explode, go off, rupture, shatter **3.** blow out of (all) proportion, enlarge, enlarge on, exaggerate, heighten, magnify, make a mountain out of a molehill, make a production out of, overstate **4.** *informal* become angry, become enraged, blow a fuse (*slang, chiefly U.S.*), crack up (*informal*), erupt, flip one's lid (*slang*), fly off the handle (*informal*), go ballistic (*slang, chiefly U.S.*), go off the deep end (*informal*), go up the wall (*slang*), hit the roof (*informal*), lose one's temper, rage, see red (*informal*)

blowy blustery, breezy, draughty, exposed, fresh, stormy, well-ventilated, windy

blowsy, blowzy 1. bedraggled, dishevelled, frowzy, slatternly, slipshod, sloppy, slovenly, sluttish, tousled, unkempt, untidy **2.** florid, red-faced, ruddy

bludgeon *noun* **1.** club, cosh (*Brit.*), cudgel, shillelagh, truncheon *~verb* **2.** beat, beat up, club, cosh (*Brit.*), cudgel, knock down, strike **3.** browbeat, bulldoze (*informal*), bully, coerce, dragoon, force, hector, put the screws on, railroad (*informal*), steamroller

blue 1. azure, cerulean, cobalt, cyan, navy, sapphire, sky-coloured, ultramarine **2.** *figurative* dejected, depressed, despondent, dismal, downcast, down-hearted, down in the dumps (*informal*), down in the mouth, fed up, gloomy, glum, low, melancholy, sad, unhappy **3.** *informal* bawdy, dirty, indecent, lewd, naughty, near the knuckle (*informal*), obscene, risqué, smutty, vulgar, X-rated (*informal*)

▷ **Antonyms** (*sense 2*) blithe, cheerful, cheery, chirpy (*informal*), elated, genial, happy, jolly, merry, optimistic, sunny (*sense 3*) decent, respectable

blueprint design, draft, layout, norm, outline, pattern, pilot scheme, plan, project, prototype, scheme, sketch

blues dejection, depression, despondency, doldrums, dumps (*informal*), gloom, gloominess, glumness, low spirits, melancholy, moodiness, the hump (*Brit. informal*)

bluff[1] 1. *verb* con, deceive, defraud, delude, fake, feign, humbug, lie, mislead, pretend, pull the wool over someone's eyes, sham **2.** *~noun* bluster, boast, braggadocio, bragging, bravado, deceit, deception, fake, feint, fraud, humbug, idle boast, lie, mere show, pretence, sham, show, subterfuge

bluff[2] *noun* **1.** bank, cliff, crag, escarpment, headland, peak, precipice, promontory, ridge, scarp *~adjective* **2.** abrupt, blunt, blustering, downright, frank, genial, good-natured, hearty, open, outspoken, plain-spoken **3.** abrupt, perpendicular, precipitous, sheer, steep, towering

▷ **Antonyms** (*sense 2*) delicate, diplomatic, discreet, judicious, sensitive, tactful, thoughtful

blunder *noun* **1.** error, fault, inaccuracy, mistake, oversight, slip, slip-up (*informal*) **2.** bloomer (*Brit. informal*), boob (*Brit. slang*), boo-boo (*informal*), clanger (*informal*), faux pas, gaffe, gaucherie, howler (*informal*), impropriety, indiscretion, mistake *~verb* **3.** bodge (*informal*), botch, bungle, drop a brick (*Brit. informal*), drop a clanger (*informal*), err, flub (*U.S. slang*), put one's foot in it (*informal*), slip up (*informal*) **4.** bumble, confuse, flounder, misjudge, stumble

▷ **Antonyms** *~noun* accuracy, achievement, correctness, success *~verb* be correct, be exact, get it right, go alertly

blunt *adjective* **1.** dull, dulled, edgeless, pointless, rounded, unsharpened **2.** *figurative* bluff, brusque, discourteous, downright, explicit, forthright, frank, impolite, outspoken, plain-spoken, rude, straightforward, straight from the shoulder, tactless, trenchant, uncivil, unpolished, upfront (*informal*) *~verb* **3.** dampen, deaden, dull, numb, soften, take the edge off, water down, weaken

▷ **Antonyms** *~adjective* (*sense 1*) keen, pointed, sharp (*sense 2*) acute, courteous, diplomatic, keen, pointed, sensitive, sharp, subtle, tactful *~verb* animate, put an edge on, sharpen, stimulate, vitalize

blur *verb* **1.** becloud, bedim, befog, blear, cloud, darken, dim, fog, make hazy, make indistinct, make vague, mask, obscure, soften **2.** blot, smear, smudge, spot, stain *~noun* **3.** blear, blurredness, cloudiness, confusion, dimness, fog, haze, indistinctness, obscurity **4.** blot, smear, smudge, spot, stain

blurred bleary, blurry, faint, foggy, fuzzy, hazy, ill-defined, indistinct, lacking definition, misty, nebulous, out of focus, unclear, vague

blurt out babble, blab, blow the gaff (*Brit. slang*), cry, disclose, exclaim, gush, let the cat out of the bag, reveal, run off at the mouth (*slang*), spill, spill one's guts (*slang*), spill the beans (*informal*), spout (*informal*), sputter, tattle, tell all, utter suddenly

blush 1. *verb* colour, crimson, flush, go red as a beetroot, redden, turn red, turn scarlet **2.** *~noun* colour, flush, glow, pink tinge, reddening, rosiness, rosy tint, ruddiness

▷ **Antonyms** *~verb* blanch, blench, drain, fade, pale, turn pale, whiten

bluster 1. *verb* blow one's own horn (*U.S. & Canad.*), blow one's own trumpet, boast, brag, bulldoze, bully, domineer, hector, rant, roar, roister, storm, swagger, swell, vaunt **2.** *~noun* bluff, boasting, boisterousness, bombast, bragging, bravado, crowing, hot air (*informal*), swagger, swaggering

blustery blusterous, boisterous, gusty, inclement, squally, stormy, tempestuous, violent, wild

board *noun* **1**. panel, piece of timber, plank, slat, timber **2**. daily meals, food, meals, provisions, victuals **3**. advisers, advisory group, committee, conclave, council, directorate, directors, panel, quango, trustees *~verb* **4**. embark, embus, enplane, enter, entrain, mount **5**. accommodate, feed, house, lodge, put up, quarter, room

▷ **Antonyms** (*sense 4*) alight, arrive, disembark, dismount, get off, go ashore, land

boast *verb* **1**. blow one's own trumpet, bluster, brag, crow, exaggerate, puff, strut, swagger, talk big (*slang*), vaunt **2**. be proud of, congratulate oneself on, exhibit, flatter oneself, possess, pride oneself on, show off *~noun* **3**. avowal, brag, gasconade (*rare*), rodomontade (*literary*), swank (*informal*), vaunt **4**. gem, joy, pride, pride and joy, source of pride, treasure

▷ **Antonyms** *~verb* cover up, depreciate, disavow, disclaim *~noun* disavowal, disclaimer

boastful bragging, cocky, conceited, crowing, egotistical, full of oneself, puffed-up, swaggering, swanky (*informal*), swollen-headed, vainglorious, vaunting

▷ **Antonyms** deprecating, humble, modest, self-belittling, self-effacing, unassuming

bob bounce, duck, hop, jerk, leap, nod, oscillate, quiver, skip, waggle, weave, wobble

bob up appear, arise, emerge, materialize, pop up, rise, spring up, surface, turn up

bode augur, betoken, forebode, foreshadow, foretell, forewarn, impart, omen, portend, predict, presage, prophesy, signify, threaten

bodiless disembodied, ghostly, immaterial, incorporeal, insubstantial, spectral, spiritual, supernatural

bodily 1. *adjective* actual, carnal, corporal, corporeal, fleshly, material, physical, substantial, tangible **2**. *~adverb* altogether, as a body, as a group, collectively, completely, en masse, entirely, fully, totally, wholly

body 1. build, figure, form, frame, physique, shape, torso, trunk **2**. cadaver, carcass, corpse, dead body, relics, remains, stiff (*slang*) **3**. being, creature, human, human being, individual, mortal, person **4**. bulk, essence, main part, mass, material, matter, substance **5**. association, band, bloc, collection, company, confederation, congress, corporation, society **6**. crowd, horde, majority, mass, mob, multitude, throng **7**. consistency, density, firmness, richness, solidity, substance

boffin authority, bluestocking (*usually disparaging*), brain(s) (*informal*), brainbox, egghead, genius, intellect, intellectual, inventor, mastermind, maven (*U.S.*), planner, thinker, virtuoso, wizard

bog fen, marsh, marshland, mire, morass, moss (*Scot. & Northern English dialect*), peat bog, quagmire, slough, swamp, wetlands

bog down delay, halt, impede, sink, slow down, slow up, stall, stick

bogey 1. apparition, bogeyman, goblin, hobgoblin, imp, spectre, spirit, spook (*informal*), sprite **2**. bête noire, bugaboo, bugbear, nightmare

boggle 1. be alarmed, be confused, be surprised, be taken aback, shy, stagger, startle, take fright **2**. demur, dither (*chiefly Brit.*), doubt, equivocate, falter, hang back, hesitate, hover, jib, shilly-shally (*informal*), shrink from, vacillate, waver

boggy fenny, marshy, miry, muddy, oozy, quaggy, soft, spongy, swampy, waterlogged, yielding

bogus artificial, counterfeit, dummy, ersatz, fake, false, forged, fraudulent, imitation, phoney *or* phony (*informal*), pseudo (*informal*), sham, spurious

▷ **Antonyms** actual, authentic, genuine, real, true

bohemian 1. *adjective* alternative, artistic, arty (*informal*), avant-garde, eccentric, exotic, left bank, nonconformist, oddball (*informal*), offbeat, off-the-wall (*slang*), outré, unconventional, unorthodox, way-out (*informal*) **2**. *~noun* beatnik, dropout, hippy, iconoclast, nonconformist

▷ **Antonyms** *~adjective* bourgeois, conservative, conventional, Pooterish, square (*informal*), straight (*slang*), straight-laced, stuffy

boil[1] *verb* **1**. agitate, bubble, churn, effervesce, fizz, foam, froth, seethe **2**. be angry, be indignant, blow a fuse (*slang, chiefly U.S.*), crack up (*informal*), fly off the handle (*informal*), foam at the mouth (*informal*), fulminate, fume, go ballistic (*slang, chiefly U.S.*), go off the deep end (*informal*), go up the wall (*slang*), rage, rave, see red (*informal*), storm

boil[2] *noun* blain, blister, carbuncle, furuncle (*Pathology*), gathering, pustule, tumour, ulcer

boil down come down, condense, decrease, reduce, summarize

boiling 1. baking, blistering, hot, roasting, scorching, tropical, very hot **2**. angry, choked, cross, enraged, foaming at the mouth, fuming, furious, incensed, indignant, infuriated, on the warpath

boisterous 1. bouncy, clamorous, disorderly, impetuous, loud, noisy, obstreperous, riotous, rollicking, rowdy, rumbustious, unrestrained, unruly, uproarious, vociferous, wild **2.** blustery, gusty, raging, rough, squally, stormy, tempestuous, tumultuous, turbulent

▷ **Antonyms** (*sense 1*) calm, controlled, peaceful, quiet, restrained, self-controlled, subdued (*sense 2*) calm, peaceful, quiet

bold 1. adventurous, audacious, brave, courageous, daring, dauntless, enterprising, fearless, gallant, gritty, heroic, intrepid, lion-hearted, valiant, valorous **2.** barefaced, brash, brazen, cheeky, confident, feisty (*informal, chiefly U.S. & Canad.*), forward, fresh (*informal*), impudent, insolent, in-your-face (*Brit. slang*), pert, pushy (*informal*), rude, sassy (*U.S. informal*), saucy, shameless **3.** bright, colourful, conspicuous, eye-catching, flashy, forceful, lively, loud, prominent, pronounced, salient, showy, spirited, striking, strong, vivid

▷ **Antonyms** (*senses 1 & 2*) conservative, cool, courteous, cowardly, faint-hearted, fearful, meek, modest, polite, retiring, shy, tactful, timid, timorous (*sense 3*) dull, ordinary, pale, soft, unimaginative

bolster aid, assist, augment, boost, brace, buoy up, buttress, cushion, give a leg up (*informal*), help, hold up, maintain, pillow, prop, reinforce, shore up, stay, strengthen, support

bolt *noun* **1.** bar, catch, fastener, latch, lock, sliding bar **2.** peg, pin, rivet, rod **3.** bound, dart, dash, escape, flight, rush, spring, sprint **4.** arrow, dart, missile, projectile, shaft, thunderbolt *~verb* **5.** bar, fasten, latch, lock, secure **6.** cram, devour, gobble, gorge, gulp, guzzle, stuff, swallow whole, wolf **7.** abscond, bound, dash, decamp, do a runner (*slang*), escape, flee, fly, fly the coop (*U.S. & Canad. informal*), hurtle, jump, leap, make a break (for it), run, run for it, rush, skedaddle (*informal*), spring, sprint, take a powder (*U.S. & Canad. slang*), take it on the lam (*U.S. & Canad. slang*)

bomb 1. *noun* bombshell, charge, device, explosive, grenade, mine, missile, projectile, rocket, shell, torpedo **2.** *~verb* attack, blow sky-high, blow up, bombard, destroy, shell, strafe, torpedo

bombard 1. assault, blast, blitz, bomb, cannonade, fire upon, open fire, pound, shell, strafe **2.** assail, attack, barrage, batter, beset, besiege, harass, hound, pester

bombardment assault, attack, barrage, blitz, bombing, cannonade, fire, flak, fusillade, shelling, strafe

bombast bluster, brag, braggadocio, extravagant boasting, fustian, gasconade (*rare*), grandiloquence, grandiosity, hot air (*informal*), magniloquence, pomposity, rant, rodomontade (*literary*)

bombastic declamatory, fustian, grandiloquent, grandiose, high-flown, histrionic, inflated, magniloquent, pompous, ranting, turgid, verbose, windy, wordy

bona fide actual, authentic, genuine, honest, kosher (*informal*), lawful, legal, legitimate, on the level (*informal*), real, the real McCoy, true

▷ **Antonyms** bogus, counterfeit, ersatz, fake, false, imitation, phoney *or* phony (*informal*), sham

bond *noun* **1.** band, binding, chain, cord, fastening, fetter, ligature, link, manacle, shackle, tie **2.** affiliation, affinity, attachment, connection, link, relation, tie, union **3.** agreement, compact, contract, covenant, guarantee, obligation, pledge, promise, word *~verb* **4.** bind, connect, fasten, fix together, fuse, glue, gum, paste

bondage captivity, confinement, duress, enslavement, enthralment, imprisonment, serfdom, servitude, slavery, subjection, subjugation, thraldom, vassalage, yoke

bonny 1. beautiful, comely, fair, handsome, lovely, pretty, sweet **2.** bouncing, buxom, chubby, fine, plump, rounded, shapely **3.** blithe, cheerful, cheery, gay, joyful, merry, sunny, winsome

bonus benefit, bounty, commission, dividend, extra, gift, gratuity, hand-out, honorarium, icing on the cake, perk (*Brit. informal*), plus, premium, prize, reward

bon viveur *bon vivant,* epicure, epicurean, foodie, gastronome, gourmet, hedonist, luxurist, pleasure-seeker, voluptuary

▷ **Antonyms** abstainer, ascetic, celibate, self-denier

bony angular, emaciated, gangling, gaunt, lanky, lean, macilent (*rare*), rawboned, scrawny, skin and bone, skinny, thin

booby berk (*Brit. slang*), blockhead, charlie (*Brit. informal*), coot, dickhead (*slang*), dimwit (*informal*), dipstick (*Brit. slang*), divvy (*Brit. slang*), dork (*slang*), duffer (*informal*), dunce, dweeb (*U.S. slang*), fathead (*informal*), fool, fuckwit (*taboo slang*), geek (*slang*), gobshite (*Irish taboo slang*), gonzo (*slang*), goof (*informal*), idiot, jerk (*slang, chiefly U.S. & Canad.*), lamebrain (*informal*), muggins (*Brit. slang*), nerd *or* nurd (*slang*), nitwit, numbskull *or* numskull, numpty (*Scot. informal*), oaf, pillock (*Brit. slang*), plank (*Brit. slang*), plonker (*slang*), prat (*slang*), prick (*slang*), schmuck (*U.S. slang*), simpleton, twit (*informal, chiefly Brit.*), wally (*slang*)

book *noun* **1.** hardback, manual, paperback, publication, roll, scroll, textbook, title, tome, tract, volume, work **2.** album, diary, exercise book, jotter, notebook, pad *~verb* **3.** arrange for, bill, charter, engage, line up, make reservations, organize, procure, programme, reserve, schedule **4.** enrol, enter, insert, list, log, mark down, note, post, put down, record, register, write down

bookish academic, donnish, erudite, intellectual, learned, literary, pedantic, scholarly, studious, well-read

boom *verb* **1.** bang, blast, crash, explode, resound, reverberate, roar, roll, rumble, thunder **2.** develop, expand, flourish, gain, grow, increase, intensify, prosper, spurt, strengthen, succeed, swell, thrive *~noun* **3.** bang, blast, burst, clap, crash, explosion, roar, rumble, thunder **4.** advance, boost, development, expansion, gain, growth, improvement, increase, jump, push, spurt, upsurge, upswing, upturn

▷ **Antonyms** *~verb* (*sense 2*) crash, fail, fall, slump *~noun* (*sense 4*) bust (*informal*), collapse, crash, decline, depression, downturn, failure, hard times, recession, slump

boomerang backfire, come back, come home to roost, rebound, recoil, return, reverse, ricochet

boon[1] *noun* advantage, benefaction, benefit, blessing, donation, favour, gift, godsend, grant, gratuity, hand-out, manna from heaven, present, windfall

boon[2] *adjective* close, intimate, special

boor barbarian, brute, bumpkin, churl, clodhopper (*informal*), clodpole, hayseed (*U.S. & Canad. informal*), hick (*informal, chiefly U.S. & Canad.*), lout, oaf, peasant, philistine, redneck (*U.S. slang*), vulgarian

boorish awkward, barbaric, bearish, churlish, clownish, coarse, crude, gross, gruff, hick (*informal, chiefly U.S. & Canad.*), ill-bred, loutish, lubberly, oafish, rude, rustic, uncivilized, uncouth, uneducated, unrefined, vulgar

▷ **Antonyms** cultured, gallant, genteel, polite, refined, sophisticated, urbane

boost *noun* **1.** encouragement, help, hype, improvement, praise, promotion **2.** heave, hoist, lift, push, raise, shove, thrust **3.** addition, expansion, improvement, increase, increment, jump, rise *~verb* **4.** advance, advertise, assist, crack up (*informal*), encourage, foster, further, hype, improve, inspire, plug (*informal*), praise, promote, support, sustain **5.** elevate, heave, hoist, lift, push, raise, shove, thrust **6.** add to, amplify, develop, enlarge, expand, heighten, hoick, increase, jack up, magnify, raise

▷ **Antonyms** *~noun* (*senses 1 & 3*) condemnation, criticism, cut-back, decline, decrease, deterioration, fall, knock (*informal*), reduction *~verb* (*senses 4 & 6*) condemn, criticize, cut, decrease, diminish, drop, hinder, hold back, knock (*informal*), lessen, let down, lower, moderate, pare, reduce, scale down (*sense 5*) drop, let down, lower

boot *verb* **1.** drive, drop-kick, kick, knock, punt, put the boot in(to) (*slang*), shove **2.** *informal* dismiss, eject, expel, give (someone) their marching orders, give the boot (*slang*), give the bullet (*Brit. slang*), give the bum's rush (*slang*), give the heave *or* push (*informal*), kick out, kiss off (*slang, chiefly U.S. & Canad.*), oust, relegate, sack (*informal*), show one the door, throw out, throw out on one's ear (*informal*)

bootless fruitless, futile, ineffective, profitless, unavailing, unsuccessful, useless, vain

bootlicker ass-kisser (*U.S. & Canad. taboo slang*), brown-noser (*taboo slang*), fawner, flatterer, flunky, lackey, spaniel, sycophant, toady, yes man

booty boodle (*slang, chiefly U.S.*), gains, haul, loot, pillage, plunder, prey, spoil, spoils, swag (*slang*), takings, winnings

border *noun* **1.** bound, boundary, bounds, brim, brink, confine, confines, edge, flange, hem, limit, limits, lip, margin, pale, rim, skirt, verge **2.** borderline, boundary, frontier, line, march *~verb* **3.** bind, decorate, edge, fringe, hem, rim, trim

borderline *adjective* ambivalent, doubtful, equivocal, indecisive, indefinite, indeterminate, inexact, marginal, unclassifiable

border on **1.** abut, adjoin, connect, contact, impinge, join, march, neighbour, touch, verge on **2.** approach, approximate, be like, be similar to, come close to, come near, echo, match, parallel, resemble

bore[1] **1.** *verb* burrow, drill, gouge out, mine, penetrate, perforate, pierce, sink, tunnel **2.** *~noun* borehole, calibre, drill hole, hole, shaft, tunnel

bore[2] **1.** *verb* annoy, be tedious, bother, exhaust, fatigue, jade, pall on, pester, send to sleep, tire, trouble, vex, wear out, weary, worry **2.** *~noun* anorak (*informal*), bother, drag (*informal*), dullard, dull person, headache (*informal*), nuisance, pain (*informal*), pain in the arse (*taboo informal*), pain in the neck (*informal*), pest, tiresome person, wearisome talker, yawn (*informal*)

▷ **Antonyms** *~verb* amuse, divert, engross, excite, fascinate, hold the attention of, interest, stimulate

boredom apathy, doldrums, dullness, ennui, flatness, irksomeness, monotony, sameness, tediousness, tedium, weariness, world-weariness

▷ **Antonyms** amusement, entertainment, excitement, interest, stimulation

boring dead, dull, flat, ho-hum (*informal*), humdrum, insipid, mind-numbing, monotonous, old, repetitious, routine, stale, tedious, tiresome, tiring, unexciting, uninteresting, unvaried, wearisome

borrow **1.** blag (*slang*), cadge, mooch (*slang*), scrounge (*informal*), take and return, take on loan, touch (someone) for (*slang*), use temporarily **2.** acquire, adopt, appropriate, copy, filch, imitate, obtain, pilfer, pirate, plagiarize, simulate, steal, take, use, usurp

▷ **Antonyms** advance, give, lend, loan, provide, return, supply

bosom *noun* **1.** breast, bust, chest **2.** affections, emotions, feelings, heart, sentiments, soul, spirit, sympathies **3.** centre, circle, core, midst, protection, shelter *~adjective* **4.** boon, cherished, close, confidential, intimate, very dear

boss[1] **1.** *noun* administrator, big cheese (*slang, old-fashioned*), chief, director, employer, executive, foreman, gaffer (*informal, chiefly Brit.*), governor (*informal*), head, kingpin, leader, manager, master, Mister Big (*slang, chiefly U.S.*), numero uno (*informal*), overseer, owner, superintendent, supervisor, torchbearer **2.** *~verb* administrate, call the shots, call the tune, command, control, direct, employ, manage, oversee, run, superintend, supervise, take charge

boss[2] *noun* knob, nub, nubble, point, protuberance, stud, tip

boss around bully, dominate, domineer, oppress, order, overbear, push around (*slang*), put upon, ride roughshod over, tyrannize

bossy arrogant, authoritarian, autocratic, despotic, dictatorial, domineering, hectoring, high-handed, imperious, lordly, overbearing, tyrannical

botch **1.** *verb* balls up (*taboo slang*), blunder, bodge (*informal*), bungle, butcher, cobble, cock up (*Brit. slang*), flub (*U.S. slang*), fuck up (*offensive taboo slang*), fumble, make a nonsense of (*informal*), make a pig's ear of (*informal*), mar, mend, mess, mismanage, muff, patch, screw up (*informal*), spoil **2.** *~noun* balls-up (*taboo slang*), blunder, bungle, bungling, cock-up (*Brit. slang*), failure, fuck-up (*offensive taboo slang*), fumble, hash, mess, miscarriage, pig's breakfast (*informal*), pig's ear (*informal*)

bother **1.** *verb* alarm, annoy, bend someone's ear (*informal*), breathe down someone's neck, concern, dismay, distress, disturb, gall, get on one's nerves (*informal*), get on one's wick (*Brit. slang*), harass, hassle (*informal*), inconvenience, irritate, molest, nag, nark (*Brit., Austral. & N.Z. slang*), pester, plague, put out, trouble, upset, vex, worry **2.** *~noun* aggravation, annoyance, bustle, difficulty, flurry, fuss, gall, grief (*informal*), hassle (*informal*), inconvenience, irritation, molestation, nuisance, perplexity, pest, problem, strain, trouble, vexation, worry

▷ **Antonyms** *~verb* aid, assist, facilitate, further, help, relieve, succour, support *~noun* advantage, aid, benefit, comfort, convenience, help, service, use

bothersome aggravating, annoying, distressing, exasperating, inconvenient, irritating, tiresome, troublesome, vexatious, vexing

▷ **Antonyms** appropriate, beneficial, commodious, convenient, handy, helpful, serviceable, useful

bottleneck block, blockage, congestion, hold-up, impediment, jam, obstacle, obstruction, snarl-up (*informal, chiefly Brit.*)

bottle up check, contain, curb, keep back, restrict, shut in, suppress, trap

bottom *noun* **1.** base, basis, bed, deepest part, depths, floor, foot, foundation, groundwork, lowest part, pedestal, support **2.** lower side, sole, underneath, underside **3.** arse (*taboo slang*), ass (*U.S. & Canad. taboo slang*), backside, behind (*informal*), bum (*Brit. slang*), buns (*U.S. slang*), butt (*U.S. & Canad. informal*), buttocks, derrière (*euphemistic*), fundament, jacksy (*Brit. slang*), posterior, rear, rear end, rump, seat, tail (*informal*), tush (*U.S. slang*) **4.** base, basis, cause, core, essence, ground, heart, mainspring, origin, principle, root, source, substance *~adjective* **5.** base, basement, basic, fundamental, ground, last, lowest, undermost

▷ **Antonyms** *~noun* (*senses 1 & 2*) cover, crown, height, lid, peak, summit, surface, top *~adjective* higher, highest, top, upper

bottomless boundless, deep, fathomless, immeasurable, inexhaustible, infinite, unfathomable, unlimited

bounce *verb* **1.** bob, bound, bump, jounce, jump, leap, rebound, recoil, resile, ricochet, spring, thump **2.** *slang* boot out (*informal*), eject, fire (*informal*), kick out (*informal*), oust, relegate, throw out *~noun* **3.** bound, elasticity, give, rebound, recoil, resilience, spring, springiness **4.** animation, brio, dynamism, energy, go (*informal*), life, liveliness, pep, vigour, vitality, vivacity, zip (*informal*)

bouncing alive and kicking, blooming, bonny, fighting fit, fit as a fiddle (*informal*), healthy, robust, thriving, vigorous, full of beans (*informal*)

bound[1] *adjective* **1.** cased, fastened, fixed, pinioned, secured, tied, tied up **2.** certain, destined, doomed, fated, sure **3.** beholden, committed, compelled, constrained, duty-bound, forced, obligated, obliged, pledged, required

bound[2] *verb/noun* bob, bounce, caper, frisk, gambol, hurdle, jump, leap, lope, pounce, prance, skip, spring, vault

bound[3] *noun* **1.** (*usually plural*) border, boundary, confine, edge, extremity, fringe, limit, line, march, margin, pale, periphery, rim, termination, verge **2. out of bounds** banned, barred, forbidden, off-limits (*chiefly U.S. military*), prohibited, taboo *~verb* **3.** circumscribe, confine, define, delimit, demarcate, encircle, enclose, hem in, limit, restrain, restrict, surround, terminate

boundary barrier, border, borderline, bounds, brink, confines, edge, extremity, fringe, frontier, limits, march, margin, pale, precinct, termination, verge

boundless endless, illimitable, immeasurable, immense, incalculable, inexhaustible, infinite, limitless, measureless, the sky's the limit, unbounded, unconfined, unending, unlimited, untold, vast

▷ **Antonyms** bounded, confined, limited, little, restricted, small

bountiful 1. abundant, ample, bounteous, copious, exuberant, lavish, luxuriant, plenteous, plentiful, prolific **2.** beneficent, bounteous, generous, liberal, magnanimous, munificent, open-handed, princely, prodigal, unstinting

bounty 1. almsgiving, assistance, beneficence, benevolence, charity, generosity, kindness, largesse *or* largess, liberality, open-handedness, philanthropy **2.** bonus, donation, gift, grant, gratuity, largesse *or* largess, meed (*archaic*), premium, present, recompense, reward

bouquet 1. boutonniere, bunch of flowers, buttonhole, corsage, garland, nosegay, posy, spray, wreath **2.** aroma, fragrance, perfume, redolence, savour, scent

bourgeois conventional, hidebound, materialistic, middle-class, Pooterish, traditional

bourn[1] *noun archaic* border, boundary, confine, destination, goal, limit

bourn[2] *noun* **1.** *chiefly southern Brit.* brook, burn, rill, rivulet, stream, torrent **2.** *figurative* death

bout 1. course, fit, period, round, run, session, spell, spree, stint, stretch, term, time, turn **2.** battle, boxing match, competition, contest, encounter, engagement, fight, head-to-head, match, set-to, struggle

bovine dense, dozy (*Brit. informal*), dull, slow, sluggish, stolid, stupid, thick

bow[1] *verb* **1.** bend, bob, droop, genuflect, incline, make obeisance, nod, stoop **2.** accept, acquiesce, comply, concede, defer, give in, kowtow, relent, submit, succumb, surrender, yield **3.** cast down, conquer, crush, depress, overpower, subdue, subjugate, vanquish, weigh down *~noun* **4.** bending, bob, genuflexion, inclination, kowtow, nod, obeisance, salaam

bow[2] *noun Nautical* beak, fore, head, prow, stem

bowdlerize blue-pencil, censor, clean up, expurgate, mutilate, sanitize

bowels 1. entrails, guts, innards (*informal*), insides (*informal*), intestines, viscera, vitals **2.** belly, core, deep, depths, hold, inside, interior **3.** *archaic* compassion, mercifulness, mercy, pity, sympathy, tenderness

bower alcove, arbour, grotto, leafy shelter, shady recess, summerhouse

bowl[1] *noun* basin, deep dish, vessel

bowl[2] *verb* fling, hurl, pitch, revolve, roll, rotate, spin, throw, trundle, whirl

bowl over 1. amaze, astonish, astound, dumbfound, stagger, startle, stun, surprise, sweep off one's feet **2.** bring down, deck (*slang*), fell, floor, knock down, overthrow, overturn

bow out abandon, back out, call it a day *or* night, cop out (*slang*), get out, give up, pull out, quit, resign, retire, step down (*informal*), throw in the sponge, throw in the towel, withdraw

box[1] **1.** *noun* ark (*dialect*), carton, case, casket, chest, coffret, container, kist (*Scot. & Northern English dialect*), pack, package, portmanteau, receptacle, trunk **2.** *~verb* pack, package, wrap

box[2] *verb* **1.** exchange blows, fight, spar **2.** belt (*informal*), buffet, butt, chin (*slang*), clout (*informal*), cuff, deck (*slang*), hit, lay one on (*slang*), punch, slap, sock (*slang*), strike, thwack, tonk (*informal*), wallop (*informal*), whack *~noun* **3.** belt (*informal*), blow, buffet, clout (*informal*), cuff, punch, slap, stroke, thumping, wallop (*informal*)

boxer fighter, prizefighter, pugilist, sparrer, sparring partner

box in cage, confine, contain, coop up, enclose, hem in, isolate, shut in, surround, trap

boxing fisticuffs, prizefighting, pugilism, sparring, the fight game (*informal*), the ring

boy fellow, junior, lad, schoolboy, stripling, youngster, youth

boycott ban, bar, black, blackball, blacklist, embargo, exclude, ostracize, outlaw, prohibit, proscribe, refrain from, refuse, reject, spurn

▷ **Antonyms** accept, advocate, back, champion, defend, espouse, help, patronize, promote, support, welcome

boyfriend admirer, beau, date, follower, leman (*archaic*), lover, man, steady, suitor, swain, sweetheart, toy boy, young man

boyish adolescent, childish, immature, innocent, juvenile, puerile, young, youthful

brace 1. *noun* bolster, bracer, bracket, buttress, prop, reinforcement, stanchion, stay, strut, support, truss 2. *~verb* bandage, bind, bolster, buttress, fasten, fortify, hold up, prop, reinforce, shove, shove up, steady, strap, strengthen, support, tie, tighten

bracing brisk, chilly, cool, crisp, energizing, exhilarating, fortifying, fresh, invigorating, lively, refreshing, restorative, reviving, rousing, stimulating, tonic, vigorous

▷ **Antonyms** debilitating, draining, enervating, exhausting, fatiguing, sapping, soporific, taxing, tiring, weakening

brackish bitter, brak (*S. Afr.*), briny, saline, salt, salty, undrinkable

▷ **Antonyms** clean, clear, fresh, pure, sweet, unpolluted

brag blow one's own horn (*U.S. & Canad.*), blow one's own trumpet, bluster, boast, crow, swagger, talk big (*slang*), vaunt

braggart bigmouth (*slang*), bluffer, blusterer, boaster, brag, braggadocio, bragger, hot dog (*chiefly U.S.*), show-off (*informal*), swaggerer, swashbuckler

braid entwine, interlace, intertwine, interweave, lace, plait, ravel, twine, weave

brain bluestocking (*usually disparaging*), brainbox, egghead (*informal*), genius, highbrow, intellect, intellectual, mastermind, prodigy, pundit, sage, scholar

brainless braindead (*informal*), dead from the neck up (*informal*), foolish, idiotic, inane, inept, mindless, senseless, stupid, thoughtless, unintelligent, witless

brains capacity, intellect, intelligence, mind, nous (*Brit. slang*), reason, sagacity, savvy (*slang*), sense, shrewdness, smarts (*slang, chiefly U.S.*), suss (*slang*), understanding, wit

brainwashing alteration, conditioning, indoctrination, persuasion, re-education

brainy bright, brilliant, clever, intelligent, smart

brake 1. *noun* check, constraint, control, curb, rein, restraint 2. *~verb* check, decelerate, halt, moderate, reduce speed, slacken, slow, stop

branch 1. arm, bough, limb, offshoot, prong, ramification, shoot, spray, sprig 2. chapter, department, division, local office, office, part, section, subdivision, subsection, wing

branch out add to, develop, diversify, enlarge, expand, extend, have a finger in every pie, increase, multiply, proliferate, ramify, spread out

brand *noun* 1. cast, class, grade, kind, make, quality, sort, species, type, variety 2. emblem, hallmark, label, mark, marker, sign, stamp, symbol, trademark 3. blot, disgrace, infamy, mark, reproach, slur, smirch, stain, stigma, taint *~verb* 4. burn, burn in, label, mark, scar, stamp 5. censure, denounce, discredit, disgrace, expose, mark, stigmatize

brandish display, exhibit, flaunt, flourish, parade, raise, shake, swing, wield

brash 1. audacious, foolhardy, hasty, impetuous, impulsive, indiscreet, precipitate, rash, reckless 2. bold, brazen, cocky, forward, heedless, impertinent, impudent, insolent, pushy (*informal*), rude

▷ **Antonyms** careful, cautious, polite, prudent, reserved, respectful, thoughtful, timid, uncertain

brass audacity, brass neck (*Brit. informal*), cheek, chutzpah (*U.S. & Canad. informal*), effrontery, face (*informal*), front, gall, impertinence, impudence, insolence, neck (*informal*), nerve (*informal*), presumption, rudeness, sassiness (*U.S. informal*)

brassy 1. barefaced, bold, brash, brazen, forward, impudent, insolent, loud-mouthed, pert, pushy (*informal*), saucy 2. blatant, flashy, garish, gaudy, hard, jazzy (*informal*), loud, obtrusive, showy, vulgar 3. blaring, cacophonous, dissonant, grating, harsh, jangling, jarring, loud, noisy, piercing, raucous, shrill, strident

▷ **Antonyms** discreet, low-key, modest, played down, quiet, restrained, subdued, toned down, understated

brat cub, guttersnipe, jackanapes, kid (*informal*), puppy (*informal*), rascal, spoilt child, urchin, whippersnapper, youngster

bravado bluster, boast, boastfulness, boasting, bombast, brag, braggadocio, fanfaronade (*rare*), swagger, swaggering, swashbuckling, vaunting

brave 1. *adjective* ballsy (*taboo slang*), bold, courageous, daring, dauntless, fearless, gallant, gritty, heroic, intrepid, plucky, resolute, undaunted, valiant, valorous 2. *~verb* bear, beard, challenge, confront, dare, defy, endure, face, face the music, go through the mill, stand up to, suffer, tackle, walk into the lion's den, withstand

▷ **Antonyms** *~adjective* afraid, boneless, chickenshit (*U.S. slang*), cowardly, craven, faint-hearted, fearful, frightened, scared, shrinking, timid *~verb* give in to, retreat from, surrender to

bravery balls (*taboo slang*), ballsiness (*taboo slang*), boldness, bravura, courage, daring, dauntlessness, doughtiness, fearlessness, fortitude, gallantry, grit, guts (*informal*), hardihood, hardiness, heroism, indomitability, intrepidity, mettle, pluck, pluckiness, spirit, spunk (*informal*), valour

▷ **Antonyms** cowardice, faint-heartedness, fearfulness, fright, timidity

bravo assassin, bandit, brigand, cutthroat, desperado, hired killer, murderer, villain

bravura animation, audacity, boldness, brilliance, brio, daring, dash, display, élan, energy, exhibitionism, ostentation, panache, punch (*informal*), spirit, verve, vigour, virtuosity

brawl 1. *noun* affray (*Law*), altercation, argument, *bagarre,* battle, broil, clash, disorder, dispute, donnybrook, fight, fracas, fray, free-for-all (*informal*), melee *or* mêlée, punch-up (*Brit. informal*), quarrel, row (*informal*), ruckus (*informal*), rumpus, scrap (*informal*), scrimmage, scuffle, shindig (*informal*), shindy (*informal*), skirmish, squabble, tumult, uproar, wrangle **2.** *~verb* altercate, argue, battle, dispute, fight, fight like Kilkenny cats, go at it hammer and tongs, quarrel, row (*informal*), scrap (*informal*), scuffle, tussle, wrangle, wrestle

brawn beef (*informal*), beefiness (*informal*), brawniness, flesh, might, muscle, muscles, muscularity, power, robustness, strength, vigour

brawny athletic, beefy (*informal*), bulky, burly, fleshy, hardy, hefty (*informal*), herculean, husky (*informal*), lusty, muscular, powerful, robust, sinewy, stalwart, strapping, strong, sturdy, thewy, thickset, vigorous, well-built, well-knit

▷ **Antonyms** frail, scrawny, skinny, thin, undeveloped, weak, weakly, weedy (*informal*), wimpish *or* wimpy (*informal*)

bray 1. *verb* bell, bellow, blare, heehaw, hoot, roar, screech, trumpet **2.** *~noun* bawl, bell, bellow, blare, cry, harsh sound, heehaw, hoot, roar, screech, shout

brazen *adjective* **1.** audacious, barefaced, bold, brash, brassy (*informal*), defiant, forward, immodest, impudent, insolent, pert, pushy (*informal*), saucy, shameless, unabashed, unashamed **2.** brass, brassy, bronze, metallic *~verb* **3.** (*with* **out**) be impenitent, be unashamed, confront, defy, outface, outstare, persevere, stare out

▷ **Antonyms** (*sense 1*) cautious, decorous, diffident, mannerly, modest, reserved, respectful, reticent, secret, shy, stealthy, timid

breach 1. aperture, break, chasm, cleft, crack, fissure, gap, hole, opening, rent, rift, rupture, split **2.** contravention, disobedience, infraction, infringement, noncompliance, nonobservance, offence, transgression, trespass, violation **3.** alienation, difference, disaffection, disagreement, dissension, division, estrangement, falling-out (*informal*), parting of the ways, quarrel, schism, separation, severance, variance

▷ **Antonyms** (*sense 2*) adherence to, attention, compliance, discharge, fulfilment, heeding, honouring, observation, performance

bread 1. aliment, diet, fare, food, necessities, nourishment, nutriment, provisions, subsistence, sustenance, viands, victuals **2.** *slang* ackers (*slang*), brass (*Northern English dialect*), cash, dibs (*slang*), dosh (*Brit. & Austral. slang*), dough (*slang*), finance, funds, money, necessary (*informal*), needful (*informal*), rhino (*Brit. slang*), shekels (*informal*), silver, spondulicks (*slang*), tin (*slang*)

breadth 1. beam (*of a ship*), broadness, latitude, span, spread, wideness, width **2.** amplitude, area, compass, comprehensiveness, dimension, expanse, extensiveness, extent, magnitude, measure, range, reach, scale, scope, size, space, spread, sweep, vastness **3.** broad-mindedness, freedom, latitude, liberality, open-mindedness, openness, permissiveness

break *verb* **1.** batter, burst, crack, crash, demolish, destroy, disintegrate, divide, fracture, fragment, part, rend, separate, sever, shatter, shiver, smash, snap, splinter, split, tear, total (*slang*), trash (*slang*) **2.** breach, contravene, disobey, disregard, infract (*Law*), infringe, renege on, transgress, violate **3.** cow, cripple, demoralize, dispirit, enervate, enfeeble, impair, incapacitate, subdue, tame, undermine, weaken **4.** abandon, cut, discontinue, give up, interrupt, pause, rest, stop, suspend **5.** bust (*informal*), degrade, demote, discharge, dismiss, humiliate, impoverish, make bankrupt, reduce, ruin **6.** announce, come out, come out in the wash, disclose, divulge, impart, inform, let out, make public, proclaim, reveal, tell **7.** *of a record, etc.* beat, better, cap (*informal*), exceed, excel, go beyond, outdo, outstrip, surpass, top **8.** appear, burst out, come forth suddenly, emerge, erupt, happen, occur **9.** cut and run (*informal*), dash, escape, flee, fly, get away, hook it (*slang*), run away **10.** cushion, diminish, lessen, lighten, moderate, reduce, soften, weaken *~noun* **11.** breach, cleft, crack, division, fissure, fracture, gap, gash, hole, opening, rent, rift, rupture, split, tear **12.** breather (*informal*), breathing space, entr'acte, halt, hiatus, interlude, intermission, interruption, interval, let-up (*informal*), lull, pause, recess, respite, rest, suspension **13.** alienation, breach, disaffection, dispute, divergence, estrangement, rift, rupture, schism, separation, split **14.** *informal* advantage, chance, fortune, opening, opportunity, stroke of luck

▷ **Antonyms** (*sense 1*) attach, bind, connect, fasten, join, repair, unite (*sense 2*) abide by, adhere to, conform, discharge, follow, obey, observe

breakable brittle, crumbly, delicate, flimsy, fragile, frail, frangible, friable
▷ **Antonyms** durable, indestructible, infrangible, lasting, nonbreakable, resistant, rugged, shatterproof, solid, strong, toughened, unbreakable

breakaway *adjective* dissenting, heretical, rebel, schismatic, seceding, secessionist

break away 1. decamp, escape, flee, fly, hook it (*slang*), make a break for it, make a run for it (*informal*), make off, run away **2.** break with, detach, part company, secede, separate

breakdown 1. collapse, crackup (*informal*), disintegration, disruption, failure, mishap, stoppage **2.** analysis, categorization, classification, detailed list, diagnosis, dissection, itemization

break down be overcome, collapse, come unstuck, conk out (*informal*), crack up (*informal*), fail, fall apart at the seams, give way, go kaput (*informal*), go phut, go to pieces, seize up, stop, stop working

breaker billow, comber, roller, wave, whitecap, white horse

break-in breaking and entering, burglary, invasion, robbery

break in 1. barge in, burst in, butt in, interfere, interject, interpose, interrupt, intervene, intrude, put one's oar in, put one's two cents in (*U.S. slang*) **2.** break and enter, burgle, invade, rob **3.** accustom, condition, get used to, habituate, initiate, prepare, tame, train

break into begin, burst into, burst out, commence, dissolve into, give way to, launch into

break off 1. detach, divide, part, pull off, separate, sever, snap off, splinter **2.** cease, desist, discontinue, end, finish, halt, pause, pull the plug on, stop, suspend, terminate

break out 1. appear, arise, begin, commence, emerge, happen, occur, set in, spring up, start **2.** abscond, bolt, break loose, burst out, escape, flee, get free **3.** burst out, erupt

breakthrough advance, development, discovery, find, finding, gain, improvement, invention, leap, progress, quantum leap, step forward

break through achieve, burst through, crack it (*informal*), cut it (*informal*), emerge, get past, pass, penetrate, shine forth, succeed

break-up breakdown, breaking, crackup (*informal*), disintegration, dispersal, dissolution, divorce, ending, parting, rift, separation, split, splitting, termination, wind-up

break up adjourn, disband, dismantle, disperse, disrupt, dissolve, divide, divorce, end, part, scatter, separate, sever, split, stop, suspend, terminate

breakwater groyne, jetty, mole, sea wall, spur

break with break away from, depart from, ditch (*slang*), drop (*informal*), jilt, part company, reject, renounce, repudiate, separate from

breast 1. boob (*slang*), bosom, bust, chest, front, teat, thorax, tit (*slang*), udder **2.** being, conscience, core, emotions, feelings, heart, seat of the affections, sentiments, soul, thoughts

breath 1. air, animation, breathing, exhalation, gasp, gulp, inhalation, pant, respiration, wheeze **2.** aroma, niff (*Brit. slang*), odour, smell, vapour, whiff **3.** break, breather, breathing-space, instant, moment, pause, respite, rest, second **4.** faint breeze, flutter, gust, puff, sigh, slight movement, waft, zephyr **5.** hint, murmur, suggestion, suspicion, undertone, whisper **6.** animation, energy, existence, life, lifeblood, life force, vitality

breathe 1. draw in, gasp, gulp, inhale and exhale, pant, puff, respire, wheeze **2.** imbue, impart, infuse, inject, inspire, instil, transfuse **3.** articulate, express, murmur, say, sigh, utter, voice, whisper

breather break, breathing space, breath of air, halt, pause, recess, respite, rest

breathless 1. choking, exhausted, gasping, gulping, out of breath, out of whack (*informal*), panting, short-winded, spent, wheezing, winded **2.** agog, anxious, astounded, avid, eager, excited, flabbergasted (*informal*), gobsmacked (*Brit. slang*), on tenterhooks, open-mouthed, thunderstruck, with bated breath

breathtaking amazing, astonishing, awe-inspiring, awesome, brilliant, dramatic, exciting, heart-stirring, impressive, magnificent, moving, overwhelming, sensational, striking, stunning (*informal*), thrilling, wondrous (*archaic or literary*)

breech arse (*taboo slang*), ass (*U.S. & Canad. taboo slang*), backside (*informal*), behind (*informal*), bum (*Brit. slang*), buns (*U.S. slang*), butt (*U.S. & Canad. informal*), buttocks, derrière (*euphemistic*), fundament, jacksy (*Brit. slang*), posterior, rump, seat, tail (*informal*), tush (*U.S. slang*)

breed *verb* **1.** bear, beget, bring forth, engender, generate, hatch, multiply, originate, procreate, produce, propagate, reproduce **2.** bring up, cultivate, develop, discipline, educate, foster, instruct, nourish, nurture, raise, rear **3.** arouse, bring about, cause, create, generate, give rise to, induce, make, occasion, originate, produce, stir up ~*noun* **4.** brand, class, extraction, family, ilk, kind, line, lineage, pedigree, progeny, race, sort, species, stamp, stock, strain, type, variety

breeding **1.** ancestry, cultivation, development, lineage, nurture, raising, rearing, reproduction, training, upbringing **2.** civility, conduct, courtesy, cultivation, culture, gentility, manners, polish, refinement, sophistication, urbanity

breeze **1.** *noun* air, breath of wind, capful of wind, current of air, draught, flurry, gust, light wind, puff of air, waft, whiff, zephyr **2.** *~verb* flit, glide, hurry, move briskly, pass, sail, sally, sweep, trip

breezy **1.** airy, blowing, blowy, blusterous, blustery, fresh, gusty, squally, windy **2.** airy, animated, blithe, buoyant, carefree, casual, cheerful, chirpy (*informal*), debonair, easy-going, free and easy, full of beans (*informal*), genial, informal, jaunty, light, light-hearted, lively, sparkling, sparky, spirited, sprightly, sunny, upbeat (*informal*), vivacious

▷ **Antonyms** (*sense 1*) calm, heavy, oppressive, windless (*sense 2*) calm, depressed, dull, heavy, lifeless, mournful, sad, serious

brevity **1.** conciseness, concision, condensation, crispness, curtness, economy, pithiness, succinctness, terseness **2.** briefness, ephemerality, impermanence, shortness, transience, transitoriness

▷ **Antonyms** (*sense 1*) circuity, diffuseness, discursiveness, long-windedness, prolixity, rambling, redundancy, tautology, tediousness, verbiage, verboseness, verbosity, wordiness

brew *verb* **1.** boil, ferment, infuse (*tea*), make (*beer*), prepare by fermentation, seethe, soak, steep, stew **2.** breed, concoct, contrive, develop, devise, excite, foment, form, gather, hatch, plan, plot, project, scheme, start, stir up *~noun* **3.** beverage, blend, concoction, distillation, drink, fermentation, infusion, liquor, mixture, preparation

bribe **1.** *noun* allurement, backhander (*slang*), boodle (*slang, chiefly U.S.*), corrupting gift, enticement, graft (*informal*), hush money (*slang*), incentive, inducement, kickback (*U.S.*), pay-off (*informal*), payola (*informal*), reward for treachery, sop, sweetener (*slang*) **2.** *~verb* buy off, corrupt, get at, grease the palm *or* hand of (*slang*), influence by gifts, lure, oil the palm of (*informal*), pay off (*informal*), reward, square, suborn

bribery buying off, corruption, graft (*informal*), inducement, palm-greasing (*slang*), payola (*informal*), protection, subornation

bric-a-brac baubles, bibelots, curios, gewgaws, kickshaws, knick-knacks, objects of virtu, *objets d'art,* ornaments, trinkets

bridal bride's, conjugal, connubial, hymeneal, marital, marriage, matrimonial, nuptial, spousal, wedding

bridge *noun* **1.** arch, flyover, overpass, span, viaduct **2.** band, bond, connection, link, tie *~verb* **3.** arch over, attach, bind, connect, couple, cross, cross over, extend across, go over, join, link, reach across, span, traverse, unite

▷ **Antonyms** *~verb* cleave, come apart, disjoin, divide, keep apart, separate, sever, split, sunder, widen

bridle *verb* **1.** check, constrain, control, curb, govern, have in one's pocket, keep a tight rein on, keep in check, keep on a string, master, moderate, rein, repress, restrain, subdue **2.** be indignant, bristle, draw (oneself) up, get angry, get one's back up, raise one's hackles, rear up *~noun* **3.** check, control, curb, rein, restraint, trammels

brief *adjective* **1.** clipped, compendious, compressed, concise, crisp, curt, laconic, limited, monosyllabic, pithy, short, succinct, terse, thumbnail, to the point **2.** ephemeral, fast, fleeting, hasty, little, momentary, quick, quickie (*informal*), short, short-lived, swift, temporary, transitory **3.** abrupt, blunt, brusque, curt, sharp, short, surly *~noun* **4.** abridgment, abstract, digest, epitome, outline, précis, sketch, summary, synopsis **5.** argument, case, contention, data, defence, demonstration *~verb* **6.** advise, clue in (*informal*), explain, fill in (*informal*), gen up (*Brit. informal*), give (someone) a rundown, give (someone) the gen (*Brit. informal*), inform, instruct, keep posted, prepare, prime, put (someone) in the picture (*informal*)

▷ **Antonyms** *~adjective* circuitous, detailed, diffuse, extensive, lengthy, long, long-drawn-out, long-winded, protracted

briefing conference, directions, guidance, information, instruction, instructions, meeting, preamble, preparation, priming, rundown

briefly abruptly, briskly, casually, concisely, cursorily, curtly, fleetingly, hastily, hurriedly, in a few words, in a nutshell, in brief, in outline, in passing, momentarily, precisely, quickly, shortly, temporarily

brigade band, body, camp, company, contingent, corps, crew, force, group, organization, outfit, party, squad, team, troop, unit

brigand bandit, desperado, footpad (*archaic*), freebooter, gangster, highwayman, marauder, outlaw, plunderer, robber, ruffian

bright **1.** beaming, blazing, brilliant, dazzling, effulgent, flashing, gleaming, glistening, glittering, glowing, illuminated, intense, lambent, luminous, lustrous, radiant, resplendent, scintillating, shimmering, shining, sparkling, twinkling, vivid **2.** clear, clement, cloudless, fair, limpid, lucid, pellucid, pleasant, sunny, translucent, transparent, unclouded **3.** acute, astute, aware, brainy, brilliant, clear-headed, clever, ingenious, intelligent, inventive, keen, quick, quick-witted, sharp, smart, wide-awake **4.** auspicious, encouraging, excellent, favourable, golden, good, hopeful, optimistic, palmy, promising, propitious, prosperous, rosy **5.** cheerful, chirpy (*informal*), full of beans (*informal*), gay, genial, glad, happy, jolly, joyful, joyous, light-hearted, lively, merry, sparky, upbeat (*informal*), vivacious **6.** distinguished, famous, glorious, illustrious, magnificent, outstanding, remarkable, splendid

▷ **Antonyms** (*senses 1 & 2*) cloudy, dark, dim, dusky, gloomy, grey, overcast, poorly lit (*sense 3*) dense, dim, dim-witted (*informal*), dull, dumb (*informal*), foolish, idiotic, ignorant, retarded, simple, slow, stupid, thick, unintelligent, witless

brighten 1. clear up, enliven, gleam, glow, illuminate, lighten, light up, make brighter, shine **2.** become cheerful, buck up (*informal*), buoy up, cheer, encourage, enliven, gladden, hearten, make happy, perk up

▷ **Antonyms** (*sense 1*) becloud, blacken, cloud over *or* up, dim, dull, obscure, overshadow, shade, shadow (*sense 2*) become angry, become gloomy, blacken, cloud, deject, depress, dispirit, look black, sadden

brilliance, brilliancy 1. blaze, brightness, dazzle, effulgence, gleam, glitter, intensity, luminosity, lustre, radiance, refulgence, resplendence, sheen, sparkle, vividness **2.** acuity, aptitude, braininess, cleverness, distinction, excellence, genius, giftedness, greatness, inventiveness, talent, wisdom **3.** éclat, gilt, glamour, gorgeousness, grandeur, illustriousness, magnificence, pizzazz *or* pizazz (*informal*), splendour

▷ **Antonyms** (*sense 1*) darkness, dimness, dullness, obscurity, paleness, thickness (*sense 3*) folly, idiocy, inanity, incompetence, ineptitude, silliness, simple-mindedness, stupidity

brilliant 1. ablaze, bright, coruscating, dazzling, glittering, glossy, intense, luminous, lustrous, radiant, refulgent, resplendent, scintillating, shining, sparkling, vivid **2.** celebrated, eminent, exceptional, famous, glorious, illustrious, magnificent, notable, outstanding, splendid, superb **3.** accomplished, acute, astute, brainy, clever, discerning, expert, gifted, intellectual, intelligent, inventive, masterly, penetrating, profound, quick, talented

▷ **Antonyms** (*sense 1*) dark, dim, dull, gloomy, obscure (*sense 2*) dull, ordinary, run-of-the-mill, unaccomplished, unexceptional, untalented (*sense 3*) dim, simple, slow, stupid

brim 1. *noun* border, brink, circumference, edge, flange, lip, margin, rim, skirt, verge **2.** *~verb* fill, fill up, hold no more, overflow, run over, spill, well over

brimful brimming, filled, flush, full, level with, overflowing, overfull, packed, running over

brindled mottled, patched, speckled, spotted, streaked, tabby

brine pickling solution, saline solution, salt water, sea water, the sea

bring 1. accompany, bear, carry, conduct, convey, deliver, escort, fetch, gather, guide, import, lead, take, transfer, transport, usher **2.** cause, contribute to, create, effect, engender, inflict, occasion, produce, result in, wreak **3.** compel, convince, dispose, force, induce, influence, make, move, persuade, prevail on *or* upon, prompt, sway **4.** command, earn, fetch, gross, net, produce, return, sell for, yield

bring about accomplish, achieve, bring to pass, cause, compass, create, effect, effectuate, generate, give rise to, make happen, manage, occasion, produce, realize

bring down abase, cut down, drop, fell, floor, lay low, level, lower, overthrow, overturn, pull down, reduce, shoot down, undermine, upset

bring in accrue, bear, be worth, fetch, gross, produce, profit, realize, return, yield

bring off accomplish, achieve, bring home the bacon (*informal*), bring to pass, carry off, carry out, crack it (*informal*), cut it (*informal*), discharge, execute, perform, pull off, succeed

bring up 1. breed, develop, educate, form, nurture, raise, rear, support, teach, train **2.** advance, allude to, broach, introduce, mention, move, propose, put forward, submit

brink border, boundary, brim, edge, fringe, frontier, limit, lip, margin, point, rim, skirt, threshold, verge

brisk 1. active, agile, alert, animated, bustling, busy, energetic, lively, nimble, no-nonsense, quick, sparky, speedy, sprightly, spry, vigorous, vivacious **2.** biting, bracing, crisp, exhilarating, fresh, invigorating, keen, nippy, refreshing, sharp, snappy, stimulating

▷ **Antonyms** boring, dull, enervating, heavy, lazy, lethargic, slow, sluggish, tiring, unenergetic, wearisome

briskly actively, apace, brusquely, coolly, decisively, efficiently, energetically, firmly, incisively, nimbly, pdq (*slang*), posthaste, promptly, pronto (*informal*), quickly, rapidly, readily, smartly, vigorously

bristle *noun* **1.** barb, hair, prickle, spine, stubble, thorn, whisker *~verb* **2.** horripilate, prickle, rise, stand on end, stand up **3.** be angry, be infuriated, be maddened, bridle, flare up, get one's dander up (*slang*), go ballistic (*slang, chiefly U.S.*), rage, see red, seethe, spit (*informal*) **4.** (*with* **with**) abound, be alive, be thick, crawl, hum, swarm, teem

bristly bearded, bewhiskered, hairy, prickly, rough, stubbly, unshaven, whiskered

brittle 1. breakable, crisp, crumbling, crumbly, delicate, fragile, frail, frangible, friable, shatterable, shivery **2.** curt, edgy, irritable, nervous, prim, stiff, stilted, tense, wired (*slang*)
▷ **Antonyms** (*sense 1*) durable, elastic, flexible, infrangible, nonbreakable, resistant, rugged, shatterproof, strong, sturdy, toughened

broach 1. approach, bring up, hint at, introduce, mention, open up, propose, raise the subject, speak of, suggest, talk of, touch on **2.** crack, draw off, open, pierce, puncture, start, tap, uncork

broad 1. ample, beamy (*of a ship*), capacious, expansive, extensive, generous, large, roomy, spacious, vast, voluminous, wide, widespread **2.** all-embracing, catholic, comprehensive, encyclopedic, far-reaching, general, global, inclusive, nonspecific, sweeping, undetailed, universal, unlimited, wide, wide-ranging **3.** *as in* **broad daylight** clear, full, obvious, open, plain, straightforward, undisguised **4.** broad-minded, liberal, open, permissive, progressive, tolerant, unbiased **5.** blue, coarse, gross, improper, indecent, indelicate, near the knuckle (*informal*), unrefined, vulgar
▷ **Antonyms** (*senses 1 & 2*) close, confined, constricted, cramped, limited, meagre, narrow, restricted, tight

broadcast *verb* **1.** air, beam, cable, put on the air, radio, relay, show, televise, transmit **2.** advertise, announce, circulate, disseminate, make public, proclaim, promulgate, publish, report, shout from the rooftops (*informal*), spread *~noun* **3.** programme, show, telecast, transmission

broaden augment, develop, enlarge, expand, extend, fatten, increase, open up, spread, stretch, supplement, swell, widen
▷ **Antonyms** circumscribe, constrain, diminish, narrow, reduce, restrict, simplify, tighten

broad-minded catholic, cosmopolitan, dispassionate, flexible, free-thinking, indulgent, liberal, open-minded, permissive, responsive, tolerant, unbiased, unbigoted, undogmatic, unprejudiced
▷ **Antonyms** biased, bigoted, closed-minded, dogmatic, inflexible, intolerant, narrow-minded, prejudiced, uncharitable

broadside abuse, assault, attack, battering, bombardment, censure, criticism, denunciation, diatribe, philippic, stick (*slang*)

brochure advertisement, booklet, circular, folder, handbill, hand-out, leaflet, mailshot, pamphlet

broil 1. *noun* affray, altercation, *bagarre*, brawl, brouhaha, dispute, feud, fracas, fray, quarrel, scrimmage, shindig (*informal*), shindy (*informal*), skirmish, strife, wrangle **2.** *~verb* brawl, dispute, quarrel, scrimmage, wrangle

broke bankrupt, bust (*informal*), cleaned out (*slang*), dirt-poor (*informal*), down and out, flat broke (*informal*), impoverished, in queer street, insolvent, in the red, not have a penny to one's name, on one's uppers, penniless, penurious, ruined, short, skint (*Brit. slang*), stony-broke (*Brit. slang*), strapped for cash (*informal*), without two pennies to rub together (*informal*)
▷ **Antonyms** affluent, comfortable, flush (*informal*), in the money (*informal*), prosperous, rich, solvent, wealthy, well-to-do

broken 1. burst, demolished, destroyed, fractured, fragmented, rent, ruptured, separated, severed, shattered, shivered **2.** buggered (*slang, chiefly Brit.*), defective, exhausted, feeble, imperfect, kaput (*informal*), not functioning, on one's last legs, on the blink (*slang*), out of order, ruined, run-down, spent, weak **3.** disconnected, discontinuous, disturbed, erratic, fragmentary, incomplete, intermittent, interrupted, spasmodic **4.** beaten, browbeaten, crippled, crushed, defeated, demoralized, humbled, oppressed, overpowered, subdued, tamed, vanquished **5.** dishonoured, disobeyed, disregarded, forgotten, ignored, infringed, isolated, retracted, traduced, transgressed **6.** disjointed, halting, hesitating, imperfect, stammering

broken-down collapsed, dilapidated, in disrepair, inoperative, kaput (*informal*), not functioning, not in working order, old, on the blink (*slang*), on the fritz (*U.S. slang*), out of commission, out of order, worn out

brokenhearted choked, crestfallen, desolate, despairing, devastated, disappointed, disconsolate, down in the dumps (*informal*), grief-stricken, heartbroken, heart-sick, inconsolable, miserable, mournful, prostrated, sorrowful, wretched

broker agent, dealer, factor, go-between, intermediary, middleman, negotiator

bromide banality, cliché, commonplace, hackneyed saying, platitude, stereotype, trite remark, truism

bronze brownish, chestnut, copper, copper-coloured, metallic brown, rust, tan

brood *verb* **1.** agonize, dwell upon, eat one's heart out, fret, have a long face, meditate, mope, mull over, muse, ponder, repine, ruminate, think upon **2.** cover, hatch, incubate, set, sit upon *~noun* **3.** breed, chicks, children, clutch, family, hatch, infants, issue, litter, offspring, progeny, young

brook[1] *noun* beck, burn, gill (*dialect*), rill, rivulet, runnel (*literary*), stream, streamlet, watercourse

brook[2] *verb* abide, accept, allow, bear, countenance, endure, hack (*slang*), put up with (*informal*), stand, stomach, suffer, support, swallow, thole (*dialect*), tolerate, withstand

brothel bagnio, bawdy house (*archaic*), bordello, cathouse (*U.S. slang*), house of ill fame, house of ill repute, house of prostitution, knocking shop (*slang*), red-light district, stews (*archaic*), whorehouse

brother 1. blood brother, kin, kinsman, relation, relative, sibling **2.** associate, chum (*informal*), cock (*Brit. informal*), colleague, companion, compeer, comrade, confrère, fellow member, mate, pal (*informal*), partner **3.** cleric, friar, monk, regular, religious

brotherhood 1. brotherliness, camaraderie, companionship, comradeship, fellowship, friendliness, kinship **2.** alliance, association, clan, clique, community, coterie, fraternity, guild, league, order, society, union

brotherly affectionate, altruistic, amicable, benevolent, cordial, fraternal, friendly, kind, neighbourly, philanthropic, sympathetic

brow 1. air, appearance, aspect, bearing, countenance, eyebrow, face, forehead, front, mien, temple **2.** brim, brink, crest, crown, edge, peak, rim, summit, tip, top, verge

browbeat badger, bulldoze (*informal*), bully, coerce, cow, domineer, dragoon, hector, intimidate, lord it over, oppress, overawe, overbear, ride roughshod over, threaten, tyrannize

▷ **Antonyms** beguile, cajole, coax, entice, flatter, inveigle, lure, manoeuvre, seduce, sweet-talk (*informal*), tempt, wheedle

brown 1. *adjective* auburn, bay, brick, bronze, bronzed, browned, brunette, chestnut, chocolate, coffee, dark, donkey brown, dun, dusky, fuscous, ginger, hazel, rust, sunburnt, tan, tanned, tawny, toasted, umber **2.** *~verb* cook, fry, grill, sauté, seal, sear

browned off cheesed off (*Brit. slang*), discontented, discouraged, disgruntled, disheartened, fed up, pissed off (*taboo slang*), sick as a parrot (*informal*), weary

brown study absorption, abstractedness, abstraction, contemplation, meditation, musing, preoccupation, reflection, reverie, rumination

browse 1. dip into, examine cursorily, flip through, glance at, leaf through, look round, look through, peruse, scan, skim, survey **2.** crop, eat, feed, graze, nibble, pasture

bruise *verb* **1.** blacken, blemish, contuse, crush, damage, deface, discolour, injure, mar, mark, pound, pulverize **2.** displease, grieve, hurt, injure, insult, offend, pain, sting, wound *~noun* **3.** black-and-blue mark, black mark, blemish, contusion, discoloration, injury, mark, swelling, trauma (*Pathology*)

brunt burden, force, full force, impact, pressure, shock, strain, stress, thrust, violence

brush[1] *noun* **1.** besom, broom, sweeper **2.** clash, conflict, confrontation, encounter, fight, fracas, scrap (*informal*), set-to (*informal*), skirmish, slight engagement, spot of bother (*informal*), tussle *~verb* **3.** buff, clean, paint, polish, sweep, wash **4.** caress, contact, flick, glance, graze, kiss, scrape, stroke, sweep, touch

brush[2] *noun* brushwood, bushes, copse, scrub, shrubs, thicket, undergrowth, underwood

brush aside discount, dismiss, disregard, have no time for, ignore, kiss off (*slang, chiefly U.S. & Canad.*), override, sweep aside

brush-off *noun* bum's rush (*slang*), cold shoulder, cut, dismissal, go-by (*slang*), kick in the teeth (*slang*), kiss-off (*slang, chiefly U.S. & Canad.*), knock-back (*slang*), rebuff, refusal, rejection, repudiation, repulse, slight, snub, the (old) heave-ho (*informal*)

brush off *verb* blank (*slang*), cold-shoulder, cut, deny, disdain, dismiss, disown, disregard, ignore, kiss off (*slang, chiefly U.S. & Canad.*), put down, rebuff, refuse, reject, repudiate, scorn, send to Coventry, slight, snub, spurn

brush up bone up on (*informal*), cram, go over, polish up, read up, refresh one's memory, relearn, revise, study

brusque abrupt, blunt, curt, discourteous, gruff, hasty, impolite, monosyllabic, sharp, short, surly, tart, terse, unmannerly

▷ **Antonyms** accommodating, civil, courteous, gentle, patient, polite, well-mannered

brutal 1. barbarous, bloodthirsty, cruel, ferocious, heartless, inhuman, merciless, pitiless, remorseless, ruthless, savage, uncivilized, vicious **2.** animal, beastly, bestial, brute, brutish, carnal, coarse, crude, sensual **3.** bearish, callous, gruff, harsh, impolite, insensitive, rough, rude, severe, uncivil, unfeeling, unmannerly

▷ **Antonyms** civilized, gentle, humane, kind, merciful, polite, refined, sensitive, soft-hearted

brutality atrocity, barbarism, barbarity, bloodthirstiness, brutishness, cruelty, ferocity, inhumanity, ruthlessness, sav~ ageness, savagery, viciousness

brutally barbarically, barbarously, brut~ ishly, callously, cruelly, ferociously, fiercely, hardheartedly, heartlessly, in cold blood, inhumanly, meanly, merci~ lessly, murderously, pitilessly, remorse~ lessly, ruthlessly, savagely, unkindly, viciously

brute *noun* **1.** animal, beast, creature, wild animal **2.** barbarian, beast, devil, fiend, ghoul, monster, ogre, sadist, sav~ age, swine *~adjective* **3.** bodily, carnal, fleshly, instinctive, mindless, physical, senseless, unthinking **4.** bestial, coarse, depraved, gross, sensual

brutish barbarian, boorish, coarse, crass, crude, cruel, gross, loutish, savage, stu~ pid, subhuman, swinish, uncouth, vul~ gar

bubble *noun* **1.** air ball, bead, blister, blob, drop, droplet, globule, vesicle **2.** bagatelle, delusion, fantasy, illusion, toy, trifle, vanity *~verb* **3.** boil, effer~ vesce, fizz, foam, froth, percolate, seethe, sparkle **4.** babble, burble, gurgle, murmur, purl, ripple, trickle, trill

bubbles effervescence, fizz, foam, froth, head, lather, spume, suds

bubbly **1.** carbonated, curly, effervescent, fizzy, foamy, frothy, lathery, sparkling, sudsy **2.** alive and kicking, animated, bouncy, elated, excited, full of beans (*informal*), happy, lively, merry, sparky

buccaneer corsair, freebooter, pirate, pri~ vateer, sea-rover

buck *noun* **1.** *archaic* beau, blade, blood, coxcomb, dandy, fop, gallant, popinjay, spark *~verb* **2.** bound, jerk, jump, leap, prance, spring, start, vault **3.** dislodge, throw, unseat **4.** *informal* cheer, en~ courage, gladden, gratify, hearten, in~ spirit, please

buckle *noun* **1.** catch, clasp, clip, fastener, hasp **2.** bulge, contortion, distortion, kink, warp *~verb* **3.** catch, clasp, close, fasten, hook, secure **4.** bend, bulge, cave in, collapse, contort, crumple, distort, fold, twist, warp

buckle down apply oneself, exert oneself, launch into, pitch in, put one's shoulder to the wheel, set to

buck up **1.** get a move on, hasten, hurry up, shake a leg, speed up **2.** brighten, cheer up, encourage, hearten, inspirit, perk up, rally, take heart

bucolic agrarian, agrestic, agricultural, country, pastoral, rural, rustic

bud **1.** *noun* embryo, germ, shoot, sprout **2.** *~verb* burgeon, burst forth, develop, grow, pullulate, shoot, sprout

budding beginning, burgeoning, develop~ ing, embryonic, fledgling, flowering, germinal, growing, incipient, nascent, potential, promising

budge **1.** dislodge, give way, inch, move, propel, push, remove, roll, shift, slide, stir **2.** bend, change, convince, give way, influence, persuade, sway, yield

budget **1.** *noun* allocation, allowance, cost, finances, financial statement, fiscal estimate, funds, means, resources **2.** *~verb* allocate, apportion, cost, cost out, estimate, plan, ration

buff[1] **1.** *adjective* sandy, straw, tan, yel~ lowish, yellowish-brown **2.** *~noun* **in the buff** bare, buck naked (*slang*), in one's birthday suit (*informal*), in the alto~ gether (*informal*), in the bare scud (*slang*), in the raw (*informal*), naked, nude, scuddy (*slang*), unclad, unclothed, with bare skin, without a stitch on (*in~ formal*) **3.** *~verb* brush, burnish, polish, rub, shine, smooth

buff[2] *noun informal* addict, admirer, afi~ cionado, connoisseur, devotee, enthusi~ ast, expert, fan, fiend (*informal*), freak (*informal*), grandmaster, hotshot (*infor~ mal*), maven (*U.S.*), whizz (*informal*)

buffer bulwark, bumper, cushion, fender, intermediary, safeguard, screen, shield, shock absorber

buffet[1] *noun* brasserie, café, cafeteria, cold table, counter, refreshment counter, salad bar, sideboard, smorgas~ bord, snack bar

buffet[2] **1.** *verb* bang, batter, beat, box, bump, clobber (*slang*), cuff, flail, knock, lambast(e), pound, pummel, punch, push, rap, shove, slap, strike, thump, wallop (*informal*) **2.** *~noun* bang, blow, box, bump, cuff, jolt, knock, push, rap, shove, slap, smack, thump, wallop (*in~ formal*)

buffoon clown, comedian, comic, droll, fool, harlequin, jester, joker, merry-andrew, silly billy (*informal*), wag

buffoonery clowning, drollery, jesting, nonsense, silliness, tomfoolery, wag~ gishness

bug *noun* **1.** *informal* bacterium, disease, germ, infection, lurgi (*informal*), micro~ organism, virus **2.** craze, fad, mania, ob~ session, rage **3.** blemish, catch, defect, error, failing, fault, flaw, glitch, grem~ lin, imperfection, snarl-up (*informal, chiefly Brit.*), virus *~verb* **4.** *informal* ag~ gravate (*informal*), annoy, badger, be on one's back (*slang*), bother, disturb, gall, get in one's hair (*informal*), get on one's nerves (*informal*), get on one's wick (*Brit. slang*), get under one's skin (*in~ formal*), get up one's nose (*informal*), harass, hassle (*informal*), irk, irritate, nark (*Brit., Austral. & N.Z. slang*), needle (*informal*), nettle, pester, piss one off (*taboo slang*), plague, vex **5.** eavesdrop, listen in, spy, tap, wiretap

bugbear anathema, bane, bête noire, bogey, bogeyman, bugaboo, devil, dread, fiend, horror, nightmare, pet hate

build *verb* **1.** assemble, construct, erect, fabricate, form, make, put up, raise **2.** base, begin, constitute, establish, formulate, found, inaugurate, initiate, institute, originate, set up, start **3.** accelerate, amplify, augment, develop, enlarge, escalate, extend, improve, increase, intensify, strengthen *~noun* **4.** body, figure, form, frame, physique, shape, structure

▷ **Antonyms** *~verb* (*sense 1*) demolish, dismantle, tear down (*sense 2*) end, finish, relinquish, suspend (*sense 3*) contract, debilitate, decline, decrease, dilute, harm, impair, lower, reduce, sap, weaken

building **1.** domicile, dwelling, edifice, fabric, house, pile, structure **2.** architecture, construction, erection, fabricating, raising

build-up **1.** accumulation, development, enlargement, escalation, expansion, gain, growth, increase **2.** ballyhoo (*informal*), hype, plug (*informal*), promotion, publicity, puff **3.** accretion, accumulation, heap, load, mass, rick, stack, stockpile, store

build up **1.** add to, amplify, augment, develop, enhance, expand, extend, fortify, heighten, improve, increase, intensify, reinforce, strengthen **2.** advertise, boost, plug (*informal*), promote, publicize, spotlight

built-in essential, immanent, implicit, in-built, included, incorporated, inherent, inseparable, integral, part and parcel of

bulbous bloated, bulging, convex, rounded, swelling, swollen

bulge *noun* **1.** bump, hump, lump, projection, protrusion, protuberance, swelling **2.** boost, increase, intensification, rise, surge *~verb* **3.** bag, dilate, distend, enlarge, expand, project, protrude, puff out, sag, stand out, stick out, swell, swell out

▷ **Antonyms** (*sense 1*) bowl, cave, cavity, concavity, crater, dent, depression, hole, hollow, indentation, pit, trough

bulk *noun* **1.** amplitude, bigness, dimensions, immensity, largeness, magnitude, massiveness, size, substance, volume, weight **2.** better part, body, generality, lion's share, main part, majority, major part, mass, most, nearly all, plurality, preponderance *~verb* **3.** **bulk large** be important, carry weight, dominate, loom, loom large, preponderate, stand out, threaten

bulky big, colossal, cumbersome, elephantine, enormous, ginormous (*informal*), heavy, huge, hulking, humongous *or* humungous (*U.S. slang*), immense, mammoth, massive, massy, mega (*slang*), ponderous, substantial, unmanageable, unwieldy, very large, voluminous, weighty

▷ **Antonyms** convenient, handy, manageable, neat, slim, small, wieldy

bulldoze **1.** demolish, flatten, level, raze **2.** drive, force, propel, push, shove, thrust **3.** browbeat, bully, coerce, cow, dragoon, hector, intimidate, put the screws on, railroad (*informal*)

bullet ball, missile, pellet, projectile, shot, slug

bulletin account, announcement, communication, communiqué, dispatch, message, news flash, notification, report, statement

bull-headed headstrong, inflexible, mulish, obstinate, pig-headed, stiff-necked, stubborn, stupid, tenacious, uncompromising, unyielding, wilful

bullish assured, bold, confident, expectant, improving, positive, rising

bully **1.** *noun* big bully, browbeater, bully boy, coercer, intimidator, oppressor, persecutor, ruffian, tormentor, tough **2.** *~verb* bluster, browbeat, bulldoze (*informal*), bullyrag, coerce, cow, domineer, hector, intimidate, oppress, overbear, persecute, push around (*slang*), ride roughshod over, swagger, terrorize, tyrannize **3.** *~adjective* admirable, excellent, fine, nifty (*informal*), radical (*informal*), very good **4.** *~interjection* bravo, capital, good, grand, great, well done

bulwark **1.** bastion, buttress, defence, embankment, fortification, outwork, partition, rampart, redoubt **2.** buffer, guard, mainstay, safeguard, security, support

bumbling awkward, blundering, botching, bungling, clumsy, incompetent, inefficient, inept, lumbering, maladroit, muddled, stumbling

▷ **Antonyms** able, brisk, capable, competent, efficient, equal, fit

bump *verb* **1.** bang, collide (with), crash, hit, knock, slam, smash into, strike **2.** bounce, jar, jerk, jolt, jostle, jounce, rattle, shake **3.** budge, dislodge, displace, move, remove, shift *~noun* **4.** bang, blow, collision, crash, hit, impact, jar, jolt, knock, rap, shock, smash, thud, thump **5.** bulge, contusion, hump, knob, knot, lump, node, nodule, protuberance, swelling

bumper *adjective* abundant, bountiful, excellent, exceptional, jumbo (*informal*), massive, mega (*slang*), prodigal, spanking (*informal*), teeming, unusual, whacking (*informal, chiefly Brit.*), whopping (*informal*)

bump into chance upon, come across, encounter, happen upon, light upon, meet, meet up with, run across, run into

bumpkin boor, clodhopper, clown, country bumpkin, hayseed (*U.S. & Canad. informal*), hick (*informal, chiefly U.S. & Canad.*), hillbilly, lout, lubber, oaf, peasant, rustic, yokel

bump off assassinate, blow away (*slang, chiefly U.S.*), dispatch, do away with, do in (*slang*), eliminate, finish off, kill, knock off (*slang*), liquidate, murder, remove, rub out (*U.S. slang*), take out (*slang*), wipe out (*informal*)

bumptious arrogant, boastful, brash, cocky, conceited, egotistic, forward, full of oneself, impudent, overbearing, overconfident, presumptuous, pushy (*informal*), self-assertive, showy, swaggering, vainglorious, vaunting

bumpy bone-breaking, bouncy, choppy, irregular, jarring, jerky, jolting, jolty, knobby, lumpy, pitted, potholed, rough, rutted, uneven

bunch *noun* **1.** assortment, batch, bouquet, bundle, clump, cluster, collection, heap, lot, mass, number, parcel, pile, quantity, rick, sheaf, spray, stack, tuft **2.** band, bevy, crew (*informal*), crowd, flock, gang, gathering, group, knot, mob, multitude, party, posse (*informal*), swarm, team, troop *~verb* **3.** assemble, bundle, cluster, collect, congregate, cram together, crowd, flock, group, herd, huddle, mass, pack

bundle *noun* **1.** accumulation, assortment, batch, bunch, collection, group, heap, mass, pile, quantity, rick, stack **2.** bag, bale, box, carton, crate, pack, package, packet, pallet, parcel, roll *~verb* **3.** bale, bind, fasten, pack, package, palletize, tie, tie together, tie up, truss, wrap **4.** (*with* **out, off, into,** *etc.*) hurry, hustle, push, rush, shove, throw, thrust **5.** (*with* **up**) clothe warmly, muffle up, swathe, wrap up

bungle blow (*slang*), blunder, bodge (*informal*), botch, butcher, cock up (*Brit. slang*), drop a brick *or* clanger (*informal*), flub (*U.S. slang*), foul up, fuck up (*offensive taboo slang*), fudge, louse up (*slang*), make a mess of, make a nonsense of (*informal*), make a pig's ear of (*informal*), mar, mess up, miscalculate, mismanage, muff, ruin, screw up (*informal*), spoil

▷ **Antonyms** accomplish, achieve, carry off, effect, fulfil, succeed, triumph

bungler blunderer, botcher, butcher, butterfingers (*informal*), duffer (*informal*), fumbler, incompetent, lubber, muddler, muff

bungling awkward, blundering, botching, cack-handed (*informal*), clumsy, ham-fisted (*informal*), ham-handed (*informal*), incompetent, inept, maladroit, unskilful

bunk[1] *verb* abscond, beat it (*slang*), bolt, clear out (*informal*), cut and run (*informal*), decamp, do a bunk (*Brit. slang*), do a runner (*slang*), flee, fly the coop (*U.S. & Canad. informal*), run for it (*informal*), scram (*informal*), skedaddle (*informal*), take a powder (*U.S. & Canad. slang*), take it on the lam (*U.S. & Canad. slang*)

bunk[2], **bunkum** *noun* balderdash, balls (*taboo slang*), baloney (*informal*), bilge (*informal*), bosh (*informal*), bullshit (*taboo slang*), cobblers (*Brit. taboo slang*), crap (*slang*), eyewash (*informal*), garbage (*informal*), guff (*slang*), havers (*Scot.*), hogwash, hokum (*slang, chiefly U.S. & Canad.*), hooey (*slang*), horsefeathers (*U.S. slang*), hot air (*informal*), kak (*S. Afr. slang*), moonshine, nonsense, piffle (*informal*), poppycock (*informal*), rot, rubbish, shit (*taboo slang*), stuff and nonsense, tarradiddle, tomfoolery, tommyrot, tosh (*slang, chiefly Brit.*), trash, tripe (*informal*), truck (*informal*), twaddle

buoy **1.** *noun* beacon, float, guide, marker, signal **2.** *~verb* (*with* **up**) boost, cheer, cheer up, encourage, hearten, keep afloat, lift, raise, support, sustain

buoyancy **1.** floatability, lightness, weightlessness **2.** animation, bounce (*informal*), cheerfulness, cheeriness, good humour, high spirits, liveliness, pep, spiritedness, sunniness, zing (*informal*)

buoyant **1.** afloat, floatable, floating, light, weightless **2.** animated, blithe, bouncy, breezy, bright, carefree, cheerful, chirpy (*informal*), debonair, full of beans (*informal*), genial, happy, jaunty, joyful, light-hearted, lively, peppy (*informal*), sparky, sunny, upbeat (*informal*), vivacious

▷ **Antonyms** (*sense 2*) cheerless, depressed, despairing, dull, forlorn, gloomy, glum, hopeless, melancholy, moody, morose, pessimistic, sad, sullen, unhappy

burden *noun* **1.** affliction, albatross, anxiety, care, clog, encumbrance, grievance, load, millstone, obstruction, onus, pigeon (*informal*), responsibility, sorrow, strain, stress, trial, trouble, weight, worry **2.** *Nautical* cargo, freight, lading, tonnage *~verb* **3.** bother, encumber, handicap, load, oppress, overload, overwhelm, saddle with, strain, tax, weigh down, worry

burdensome crushing, difficult, exacting, heavy, irksome, onerous, oppressive, taxing, troublesome, trying, weighty

bureau **1.** desk, writing desk **2.** agency, branch, department, division, office, service

bureaucracy **1.** administration, authorities, civil service, corridors of power, directorate, government, ministry, offi~

cialdom, officials, the system **2.** bumble~dom, officialdom, officialese, red tape, regulations

bureaucrat administrator, apparatchik, civil servant, functionary, mandarin, minister, office-holder, officer, official, public servant

burglar cat burglar, filcher, housebreak~er, picklock, pilferer, robber, sneak thief, thief

burglary break-in, breaking and entering, filching, housebreaking, larceny, pilfer~age, robbery, stealing, theft, thieving

burial burying, entombment, exequies, funeral, inhumation, interment, obse~quies, sepulture

burial ground cemetery, churchyard, God's acre, golgotha (*rare*), graveyard, necropolis

buried 1. coffined, consigned to the grave, entombed, interred, laid to rest **2.** dead and buried, dead and gone, in the grave, long gone, pushing up the daisies, six feet under **3.** covered, forgotten, hidden, repressed, sunk in oblivion, suppressed **4.** cloistered, concealed, hidden, private, sequestered, tucked away **5.** caught up, committed, concentrating, devoted, en~grossed, immersed, intent, lost, occu~pied, preoccupied, rapt

burlesque 1. *noun* caricature, mock, mockery, parody, satire, send-up (*Brit. informal*), spoof (*informal*), takeoff (*in~formal*), travesty **2.** *~adjective* caricatur~al, comic, farcical, hudibrastic, ironical, ludicrous, mock, mock-heroic, mocking, parodic, satirical, travestying **3.** *~verb* ape, caricature, exaggerate, imitate, lampoon, make a monkey out of, make fun of, mock, parody, ridicule, satirize, send up (*Brit. informal*), spoof (*infor~mal*), take off (*informal*), take the piss out of (*taboo slang*), travesty

burly beefy (*informal*), big, brawny, bulky, hefty, hulking, muscular, power~ful, stocky, stout, strapping, strong, sturdy, thickset, well-built

▷ **Antonyms** lean, puny, scraggy, scrawny, slight, spare, thin, weak, weedy (*informal*), wimpish *or* wimpy (*informal*)

burn 1. be ablaze, be on fire, blaze, flame, flare, flash, flicker, glow, go up in flames, smoke **2.** brand, calcine, char, ignite, incinerate, kindle, light, parch, reduce to ashes, scorch, sear, set on fire, shrivel, singe, toast, wither **3.** bite, hurt, pain, smart, sting, tingle **4.** be angry, be aroused, be excited, be inflamed, be passionate, blaze, desire, fume, seethe, simmer, smoulder, yearn **5.** consume, eat up, expend, use

burning 1. blazing, fiery, flaming, flash~ing, gleaming, glowing, hot, illuminated, scorching, smouldering **2.** ablaze, afire, all-consuming, ardent, eager, earnest, fervent, fervid, flaming, frantic, fren~zied, impassioned, intense, passionate, vehement, zealous **3.** acrid, biting, caus~tic, irritating, painful, piercing, prick~ling, pungent, reeking, smarting, sting~ing, tingling **4.** acute, compelling, criti~cal, crucial, essential, important, now or never, pressing, significant, urgent, vi~tal

▷ **Antonyms** (*sense 2*) apathetic, calm, cool, faint, indifferent, mild, passive (*sense 3*) cooling, mild, numbing, sooth~ing

burnish 1. *verb* brighten, buff, furbish, glaze, polish, rub up, shine, smooth **2.** *~noun* gloss, lustre, patina, polish, sheen, shine

▷ **Antonyms** *~verb* abrade, graze, scratch, scuff

burrow 1. *noun* den, hole, lair, retreat, shelter, tunnel **2.** *~verb* delve, dig, exca~vate, hollow out, scoop out, tunnel

burst *verb* **1.** blow up, break, crack, disin~tegrate, explode, fly open, fragment, puncture, rend asunder, rupture, shat~ter, shiver, split, tear apart **2.** barge, break, break out, erupt, gush forth, run, rush, spout *~noun* **3.** bang, blast, blast~ing, blowout, blow-up, breach, break, crack, discharge, explosion, rupture, split **4.** eruption, fit, gush, gust, out~break, outburst, outpouring, rush, spate, spurt, surge, torrent *~adjective* **5.** flat, punctured, rent, ruptured, split

bury 1. consign to the grave, entomb, in~earth, inhume, inter, lay to rest, sepul~chre **2.** conceal, cover, cover up, draw a veil over, enshroud, hide, secrete, shroud, stash (*informal*), stow away **3.** drive in, embed, engulf, implant, sink, submerge **4.** absorb, engage, engross, immerse, interest, occupy

▷ **Antonyms** (*senses 1 & 2*) bring to light, dig up, discover, disinter, dredge up, exhume, expose, find, reveal, turn up, uncover, unearth

bush 1. hedge, plant, shrub, shrubbery, thicket **2.** back country (*U.S.*), backlands (*U.S.*), backwoods, brush, scrub, scrub~land, the wild, woodland

bushy bristling, bristly, fluffy, fuzzy, luxuriant, rough, shaggy, spreading, stiff, thick, unruly, wiry

busily actively, assiduously, briskly, carefully, diligently, earnestly, ener~getically, industriously, intently, pur~posefully, speedily, strenuously

business 1. calling, career, craft, employ~ment, function, job, line, métier, occu~pation, profession, pursuit, trade, voca~tion, work **2.** company, concern, corpo~ration, enterprise, establishment, firm, organization, venture **3.** bargaining, commerce, dealings, industry, manufac~turing, merchandising, selling, trade, trading, transaction **4.** affair, assign~ment, concern, duty, function, issue, matter, pigeon (*informal*), point, prob~

lem, question, responsibility, subject, task, topic

businesslike correct, efficient, matter-of-fact, methodical, orderly, organized, practical, professional, regular, routine, systematic, thorough, well-ordered, workaday
▷ **Antonyms** careless, disorderly, disorganized, frivolous, impractical, inefficient, irregular, sloppy, unprofessional, unsystematic, untidy

businessman, businesswoman capitalist, employer, entrepreneur, executive, financier, *homme d'affaires,* industrialist, merchant, tradesman, tycoon

bust¹ *noun* bosom, breast, chest, torso

bust² *verb* **1.** break, burst, fracture, rupture **2.** bankrupt, break, crash, fail, impoverish, ruin **3.** arrest, catch, collar (*informal*), cop (*slang*), feel one's collar (*slang*), lift (*slang*), nab (*informal*), nail (*informal*), raid, search ~*adjective* **4. go bust** become insolvent, be ruined, break, fail, go bankrupt ~*noun* **5.** arrest, capture, cop (*slang*), raid, search, seizure

bustle 1. *verb* beetle, bestir, dash, flutter, fuss, hasten, hurry, rush, scamper, scramble, scurry, scuttle, stir, tear **2.** ~*noun* activity, ado, agitation, commotion, excitement, flurry, fuss, haste, hurly-burly, hurry, pother, stir, to-do, tumult
▷ **Antonyms** ~*verb* be indolent, idle, laze, lie around, loaf, loiter, loll, relax, rest, take it easy ~*noun* inaction, inactivity, quiet, quietness, stillness, tranquillity

bustling active, astir, busy, buzzing, crowded, energetic, eventful, full, humming, hustling, lively, rushing, stirring, swarming, teeming, thronged

busy *adjective* **1.** active, assiduous, brisk, diligent, employed, engaged, engrossed, hard at work, industrious, in harness, occupied, on active service, on duty, persevering, rushed off one's feet, slaving, working **2.** active, energetic, exacting, full, hectic, hustling, lively, on the go (*informal*), restless, strenuous, tireless, tiring **3.** fussy, inquisitive, interfering, meddlesome, meddling, nosy, officious, prying, snoopy, stirring, troublesome ~*verb* **4.** absorb, employ, engage, engross, immerse, interest, occupy
▷ **Antonyms** (*senses 1 & 2*) idle, inactive, indolent, lackadaisical, lazy, off duty, relaxed, shiftless, slothful, unoccupied

busybody eavesdropper, gossip, intriguer, intruder, meddler, nosy parker (*informal*), pry, scandalmonger, snoop, snooper, stirrer (*informal*), troublemaker

but *conjunction* **1.** further, however, moreover, nevertheless, on the contrary, on the other hand, still, yet **2.** bar, barring, except, excepting, excluding, notwithstanding, save, with the exception of ~*adverb* **3.** just, merely, only, simply, singly, solely

butcher *noun* **1.** destroyer, killer, murderer, slaughterer, slayer ~*verb* **2.** carve, clean, cut, cut up, dress, joint, prepare, slaughter **3.** assassinate, cut down, destroy, exterminate, kill, liquidate, massacre, put to the sword, slaughter, slay **4.** bodge (*informal*), botch, destroy, mess up, mutilate, ruin, spoil, wreck

butchery blood bath, blood-letting, bloodshed, carnage, killing, massacre, mass murder, murder, slaughter

butt¹ *noun* **1.** haft, handle, hilt, shaft, shank, stock **2.** base, end, fag end (*informal*), foot, leftover, stub, tail, tip

butt² *noun* Aunt Sally, dupe, laughing stock, mark, object, point, subject, target, victim

butt³ *verb/noun* **1.** *With or of the head or horns* buck, buffet, bump, bunt, jab, knock, poke, prod, punch, push, ram, shove, thrust ~*verb* **2.** abut, join, jut, meet, project, protrude **3.** (*with* **in** *or* **into**) chip in (*informal*), cut in, interfere, interrupt, intrude, meddle, put one's oar in, put one's two cents in (*U.S. slang*), stick one's nose in

butt⁴ *noun* barrel, cask, pipe

butter up blarney, brown-nose (*taboo slang*), cajole, coax, fawn on *or* upon, flatter, honey up, kiss (someone's) ass (*U.S. slang*), oil one's tongue, pander to, soft-soap, suck up to (*informal*), wheedle

buttocks arse (*taboo slang*), ass (*U.S. & Canad. taboo slang*), backside (*informal*), behind (*informal*), bottom, bum (*Brit. slang*), buns (*U.S. slang*), butt (*U.S. & Canad. informal*), derrière (*euphemistic*), fundament, gluteus maximus (*Anatomy*), haunches, hindquarters, jacksy (*Brit. slang*), nates (*technical name*), posterior, rear, rump, seat, tail (*informal*), tush (*U.S. slang*)

buttonhole *verb figurative* accost, bore, catch, detain in talk, grab, importune, persuade importunately, take aside, waylay

buttress 1. *noun* abutment, brace, mainstay, pier, prop, reinforcement, shore, stanchion, stay, strut, support **2.** ~*verb* augment, back up, bolster, brace, prop, prop up, reinforce, shore, shore up, strengthen, support, sustain, uphold

buxom ample, bosomy, busty, comely, curvaceous, debonair, fresh-looking, full-bosomed, healthy, hearty, jocund, jolly, lively, lusty, merry, plump, robust, sprightly, voluptuous, well-rounded, winsome
▷ **Antonyms** delicate, frail, slender, slight, slim, svelte, sylphlike, thin, trim

buy *verb* **1.** acquire, get, invest in, obtain, pay for, procure, purchase, score (*slang*), shop for **2.** (*often with* **off**) bribe, corrupt, fix (*informal*), grease someone's palm

(*slang*), square, suborn *~noun* **3.** acquisition, bargain, deal, purchase
▷ **Antonyms** *~verb* (*sense 1*) auction, barter, retail, sell, vend

buzz *noun* **1.** bombilation *or* bombination (*literary*), buzzing, drone, hiss, hum, murmur, purr, ring, ringing, sibilation, susurration *or* susurrus (*literary*), whir, whisper **2.** dirt (*U.S. slang*), gen (*Brit. informal*), gossip, hearsay, latest (*informal*), news, report, rumour, scandal, scuttlebutt (*U.S. slang*), whisper *~verb* **3.** bombilate *or* bombinate (*literary*), drone, fizzle, hum, murmur, reverberate, ring, sibilate, susurrate (*literary*), whir, whisper, whizz **4.** chatter, gossip, natter, rumour, tattle

by *preposition* **1.** along, beside, by way of, close to, near, next to, over, past, via **2.** through, through the agency of, under the aegis of *~adverb* **3.** aside, at hand, away, beyond, close, handy, in reach, near, past, to one side

by and by anon, before long, erelong (*archaic or poetic*), eventually, in a while, in the course of time, one day, presently, shortly, soon

bygone ancient, antiquated, departed, erstwhile, extinct, forgotten, former, gone by, lost, of old, of yore, olden, one-time, past, past recall, previous, sunk in oblivion
▷ **Antonyms** coming, forthcoming, future, prospective, to be, to come

bypass avoid, body-swerve (*Scot.*), circumvent, depart from, detour round, deviate from, get round, give a wide berth to, go round, ignore, neglect, outflank, pass round
▷ **Antonyms** abut, adjoin, come together, connect, converge, cross, intersect, join, link, meet, touch, unite

bystander eyewitness, looker-on, observer, onlooker, passer-by, spectator, viewer, watcher, witness
▷ **Antonyms** contributor, partaker, participant, party

byword adage, aphorism, apophthegm, dictum, epithet, gnome, maxim, motto, precept, proverb, saw, saying, slogan

C, c

cab hackney, hackney carriage, minicab, taxi, taxicab

cabal camp, caucus, clique, coalition, combination, conclave, confederacy, conspiracy, coterie, faction, intrigue, junta, league, machination, party, plot, scheme, schism, set

cabbalistic cryptic, dark, esoteric, fanciful, mysterious, mystic, mystical, obscure, occult, secret

cabin 1. berth, bothy, chalet, cot, cottage, crib, hovel, hut, lodge, shack, shanty, shed **2.** berth, compartment, deckhouse, quarters, room

cabinet 1. case, chiffonier, closet, commode, cupboard, dresser, escritoire, locker **2.** administration, assembly, council, counsellors, ministry **3.** *archaic* apartment, boudoir, chamber (*archaic*)

cache 1. *noun* accumulation, fund, garner (*archaic*), hiding place, hoard, nest egg, repository, reserve, stash (*informal*), stockpile, store, storehouse, supply, treasury **2.** *~verb* bury, conceal, hide, put away, secrete, stash (*informal*), store

cackle babble, blather, chatter, chuckle, cluck, crow, gabble, gibber, giggle, jabber, prattle, snicker, snigger, titter

cacophonous discordant, dissonant, grating, harsh, inharmonious, jarring, raucous, strident

cacophony caterwauling, discord, disharmony, dissonance, stridency

cad bounder (*old-fashioned Brit. slang*), churl, cur, dastard (*archaic*), heel (*slang*), knave, rat (*informal*), rotter (*slang, chiefly Brit.*), scoundrel, scumbag (*slang*)

cadaverous ashen, blanched, bloodless, corpselike, deathlike, deathly, emaciated, exsanguinous, gaunt, ghastly, haggard, hollow-eyed, like death warmed up (*informal*), pale, pallid, wan

caddish despicable, ill-bred, low, ungentlemanly, unmannerly

▷ **Antonyms** gentlemanly, honourable, laudable, mannerly, pleasant, praiseworthy

cadence 1. beat, lilt, measure (*Prosody*), metre, pulse, rhythm, swing, tempo, throb **2.** accent, inflection, intonation, modulation

cadre core, framework, hard core, infrastructure, key group, nucleus

café brasserie, cafeteria, coffee bar, coffee shop, lunchroom, restaurant, snack bar, tearoom

cage 1. *verb* confine, coop up, fence in, immure, impound, imprison, incarcerate, lock up, mew, pound, restrain, shut up **2.** *~noun* corral (*U.S.*), enclosure, pen, pound

cagey, cagy careful, cautious, chary, discreet, guarded, noncommittal, shrewd, wary, wily

▷ **Antonyms** careless, dull, imprudent, indiscreet, reckless, stolid, unthinking, unwary

caitiff 1. *noun* coward, knave, miscreant, rascal, rogue, scoundrel, traitor, vagabond, villain, wretch **2.** *~adjective* base, cowardly, craven, dastardly, ignoble

cajole beguile, coax, decoy, dupe, entice, entrap, flatter, inveigle, lure, manoeuvre, mislead, seduce, sweet-talk (*informal*), tempt, wheedle

cajolery beguilement, blandishments, blarney, coaxing, enticement, flattery, inducement(s), inveigling, persuasion, soft soap (*informal*), sweet talk (*informal*), wheedling

cake 1. *verb* bake, cement, coagulate, congeal, consolidate, dry, encrust, harden, inspissate (*archaic*), ossify, solidify, thicken **2.** *~noun* bar, block, cube, loaf, lump, mass, slab

calamitous blighting, cataclysmic, catastrophic, deadly, devastating, dire, disastrous, fatal, pernicious, ruinous, tragic, woeful

▷ **Antonyms** advantageous, beneficial, favourable, fortunate, good, helpful

calamity adversity, affliction, cataclysm, catastrophe, disaster, distress, downfall, hardship, misadventure, mischance, misfortune, mishap, reverse, ruin, scourge, tragedy, trial, tribulation, woe, wretchedness

▷ **Antonyms** advantage, benefit, blessing, boon, good fortune, good luck, help

calculate 1. adjust, compute, consider, count, determine, enumerate, estimate, figure, gauge, judge, rate, reckon, value, weigh, work out **2.** aim, design, intend, plan

calculated considered, deliberate, intended, intentional, planned, premeditated, purposeful

▷ **Antonyms** haphazard, hasty, heedless, hurried, impetuous, impulsive, rash, spontaneous, unintentional, unplanned, unpremeditated

calculating canny, cautious, contriving, crafty, cunning, designing, devious, Machiavellian, manipulative, politic, scheming, sharp, shrewd, sly

▷ **Antonyms** blunt, direct, downright, frank, guileless, honest, open, outspoken, sincere, undesigning

calculation 1. answer, computation, estimate, estimation, figuring, forecast, judgment, reckoning, result **2.** caution, circumspection, contrivance, deliberation, discretion, foresight, forethought, planning, precaution

calibre 1. bore, diameter, gauge, measure **2.** *figurative* ability, capacity, distinction, endowment, faculty, force, gifts, merit, parts, quality, scope, stature, strength, talent, worth

call *verb* **1.** announce, arouse, awaken, cry, cry out, hail, halloo, proclaim, rouse, shout, waken, yell **2.** assemble, bid, collect, contact, convene, convoke, gather, invite, muster, rally, summon **3.** give (someone) a bell (*Brit. slang*), phone, ring up (*informal, chiefly Brit.*), telephone **4.** christen, denominate, describe as, designate, dub, entitle, label, name, style, term **5.** announce, appoint, declare, decree, elect, ordain, order, proclaim, set apart **6.** consider, estimate, judge, regard, think *~noun* **7.** cry, hail, scream, shout, signal, whoop, yell **8.** announcement, appeal, command, demand, invitation, notice, order, plea, request, ring (*informal, chiefly Brit.*), summons, supplication, visit **9.** cause, claim, excuse, grounds, justification, need, occasion, reason, right, urge

▷ **Antonyms** *~verb* (*sense 1*) be quiet, be silent, murmur, mutter, speak softly, whisper (*senses 2 & 5*) call off, cancel, dismiss, disperse, excuse, release *~noun* (*sense 7*) murmur, mutter, whisper (*sense 8*) dismissal, release

call for 1. demand, entail, involve, necessitate, need, occasion, require, suggest **2.** collect, fetch, pick up, uplift (*Scot.*)

calling business, career, employment, life's work, line, métier, mission, occupation, profession, province, pursuit, trade, vocation, walk of life, work

▷ **Antonyms** affliction, avocation, curse, dislike, hobby

call on 1. drop in on, look in on, look up, see, visit **2.** appeal to, ask, bid, call upon, entreat, invite, invoke, request, summon, supplicate

callous affectless, apathetic, case-hardened, cold, hard-bitten, hard-boiled (*informal*), hardened, hardhearted, harsh, heartless, indifferent, indurated (*rare*), insensate, insensible, insensitive, inured, obdurate, soulless, thick-skinned, torpid, uncaring, unfeeling, unresponsive, unsusceptible, unsympathetic

▷ **Antonyms** caring, compassionate, considerate, gentle, sensitive, soft, sympathetic, tender, understanding

callow green, guileless, immature, inexperienced, jejune, juvenile, naive, puerile, raw, unfledged, unsophisticated, untried

calm *adjective* **1.** balmy, halcyon, mild, pacific, peaceful, placid, quiet, restful, serene, smooth, still, tranquil, windless **2.** as cool as a cucumber, collected, composed, cool, dispassionate, equable, impassive, imperturbable, keeping one's cool, relaxed, sedate, self-possessed, undisturbed, unemotional, unexcitable, unexcited, unfazed (*informal*), unflappable (*informal*), unmoved, unruffled *~verb* **3.** hush, mollify, placate, quieten, relax, soothe *~noun* **4.** calmness, hush, peace, peacefulness, quiet, repose, serenity, stillness

▷ **Antonyms** *~adjective* agitated, aroused, discomposed, disturbed, emotional, excited, fierce, frantic, heated, perturbed, rough, shaken, stormy, troubled, wild, worried *~verb* aggravate, agitate, arouse, disturb, excite, irritate, stir *~noun* agitation, disturbance, wildness

calmness 1. calm, composure, equability, hush, motionlessness, peace, peacefulness, placidity, quiet, repose, restfulness, serenity, smoothness, stillness, tranquillity **2.** composure, cool (*slang*), coolness, dispassion, equanimity, impassivity, imperturbability, poise, sang-froid, self-possession

calumniate asperse, backbite, bad-mouth (*slang, chiefly U.S. & Canad.*), blacken, defame, denigrate, detract, knock (*informal*), lampoon, libel, malign, misrepresent, revile, rubbish (*informal*), slag (off) (*slang*), slander, stigmatize, traduce, vilify, vilipend (*rare*)

calumnious abusive, aspersive, backbiting, defamatory, derogatory, detractive, insulting, libellous, lying, slanderous, vituperative

calumny abuse, aspersion, backbiting, calumniation, defamation, denigration, derogation, detraction, evil-speaking, insult, libel, lying, misrepresentation, obloquy, revilement, slander, smear, stigma, vilification, vituperation

camaraderie brotherhood, brotherliness, companionability, companionship, comradeship, esprit de corps, fellowship, fraternization, good-fellowship, togetherness

camouflage 1. *noun* blind, cloak, concealment, cover, deceptive markings, disguise, false appearance, front, guise,

mask, masquerade, mimicry, protective colouring, screen, subterfuge **2.** *~verb* cloak, conceal, cover, disguise, hide, mask, obfuscate, obscure, screen, veil
▷ **Antonyms** *~verb* bare, display, exhibit, expose, reveal, show, uncover, unmask, unveil

camp[1] *noun* bivouac, camping ground, camp site, cantonment (*Military*), encampment, tents

camp[2] *adjective* affected, artificial, camped up (*informal*), campy (*informal*), effeminate, mannered, ostentatious, poncy (*slang*), posturing

campaign attack, crusade, drive, expedition, jihad (*rare*), movement, offensive, operation, push

canaille hoi polloi, masses, mob, plebs, populace, proletariat, rabble, ragtag, riffraff, scum, vulgar herd

cancel **1.** abolish, abort, abrogate, annul, blot out, call off, countermand, cross out, delete, do away with, efface, eliminate, erase, expunge, obliterate, obviate, quash, repeal, repudiate, rescind, revoke **2.** balance out, compensate for, counterbalance, make up for, neutralize, nullify, obviate, offset, redeem

cancellation abandoning, abandonment, abolition, annulment, deletion, elimination, quashing, repeal, revocation

cancer blight, canker, carcinoma (*Pathology*), corruption, evil, growth, malignancy, pestilence, rot, sickness, tumour

candid **1.** blunt, downright, fair, forthright, frank, free, guileless, honest, impartial, ingenuous, just, open, outspoken, plain, round, sincere, straightforward, truthful, unbiased, unequivocal, unprejudiced, upfront (*informal*) **2.** impromptu, informal, uncontrived, unposed
▷ **Antonyms** biased, complimentary, diplomatic, flattering, kind, subtle

candidate applicant, aspirant, claimant, competitor, contender, contestant, entrant, nominee, possibility, runner, solicitant, suitor

candour artlessness, directness, fairness, forthrightness, frankness, guilelessness, honesty, impartiality, ingenuousness, naïveté, openness, outspokenness, simplicity, sincerity, straightforwardness, truthfulness, unequivocalness
▷ **Antonyms** bias, cunning, deceit, diplomacy, dishonesty, flattery, insincerity, prejudice, subtlety

canker **1.** *verb* blight, consume, corrode, corrupt, embitter, envenom, inflict, poison, pollute, rot, rust, waste away **2.** *~noun* bane, blight, blister, cancer, corrosion, corruption, infection, lesion, rot, scourge, sore, ulcer

cannon **1.** artillery piece, big gun, field gun, gun, mortar **2.** *plural* artillery, battery, big guns, cannonry, field guns, guns, ordnance

cannonade barrage, battery, bombardment, broadside, pounding, salvo, shelling, volley

canny acute, artful, astute, careful, cautious, circumspect, clever, judicious, knowing, on the ball (*informal*), perspicacious, prudent, sagacious, sharp, shrewd, subtle, wise, worldly-wise
▷ **Antonyms** bumbling, inept, lumpen (*informal*), obtuse, unskilled

canon **1.** criterion, dictate, formula, precept, principle, regulation, rule, standard, statute, yardstick **2.** catalogue, list, roll

canonical accepted, approved, authoritative, authorized, orthodox, recognized, sanctioned

canopy awning, baldachin, covering, shade, sunshade, tester

cant *noun* **1.** affected piety, humbug, hypocrisy, insincerity, lip service, pious platitudes, pretence, pretentiousness, sanctimoniousness, sham holiness **2.** argot, jargon, lingo, patter, slang, vernacular *~verb* **3.** angle, bevel, incline, rise, slant, slope, tilt

cantankerous bad-tempered, captious, choleric, contrary, crabby, cranky (*U.S., Canad., & Irish informal*), crotchety (*informal*), crusty, difficult, disagreeable, grouchy (*informal*), grumpy, ill-humoured, irascible, irritable, liverish, peevish, perverse, quarrelsome, ratty (*Brit. & N.Z. informal*), testy, tetchy, waspish
▷ **Antonyms** agreeable, amiable, breezy, cheerful, complaisant, congenial, genial, good-natured, happy, kindly, merry, placid, pleasant, vivacious

canter *noun* amble, dogtrot, easy gait, jog, lope

canting hypocritical, insincere, Janus-faced, sanctimonious, two-faced

canvass *verb* **1.** analyse, campaign, electioneer, examine, fly a kite, inspect, investigate, poll, scan, scrutinize, sift, solicit, solicit votes, study, ventilate **2.** agitate, debate, discuss, dispute *~noun* **3.** examination, investigation, poll, scrutiny, survey, tally

canyon coulee (*U.S.*), gorge, gulch (*U.S.*), gulf, gully, ravine

cap *verb* beat, better, clobber (*slang*), complete, cover, crown, eclipse, exceed, excel, finish, lick (*informal*), outdo, outstrip, overtop, put in the shade, run rings around (*informal*), surpass, top, transcend

capability ability, capacity, competence, facility, faculty, means, potential, potentiality, power, proficiency, qualification(s), wherewithal
▷ **Antonyms** inability, incompetence, inefficiency, ineptitude, powerlessness

capable able, accomplished, adapted, adept, adequate, apt, clever, competent, efficient, experienced, fitted, gifted, intelligent, masterly, proficient, qualified, skilful, suited, susceptible, talented
▷ **Antonyms** incapable, incompetent, ineffective, inept, inexpert, unqualified, unskilled

capacious ample, broad, comfortable, commodious, comprehensive, expansive, extended, extensive, generous, liberal, roomy, sizable *or* sizeable, spacious, substantial, vast, voluminous, wide
▷ **Antonyms** confined, constricted, cramped, enclosed, incommodious, insubstantial, limited, narrow, poky, restricted, small, tight, tiny, uncomfortable, ungenerous

capacity **1.** amplitude, compass, dimensions, extent, magnitude, range, room, scope, size, space, volume **2.** ability, aptitude, aptness, brains, capability, cleverness, competence, competency, efficiency, facility, faculty, forte, genius, gift, intelligence, power, readiness, strength **3.** appointment, function, office, position, post, province, role, service, sphere

cape chersonese (*poetic*), head, headland, ness (*archaic*), peninsula, point, promontory

caper **1.** *verb* bounce, bound, cavort, cut a rug (*informal*), dance, frisk, frolic, gambol, hop, jump, leap, romp, skip, spring, trip **2.** *~noun* antic, dido (*informal*), escapade, gambol, high jinks, hop, jape, jest, jump, lark (*informal*), leap, mischief, practical joke, prank, revel, shenanigan (*informal*), sport, stunt

capital *adjective* **1.** cardinal, central, chief, controlling, essential, foremost, important, leading, main, major, overruling, paramount, pre-eminent, primary, prime, principal, prominent, vital **2.** excellent, fine, first, first-rate, prime, splendid, sterling, superb, world-class *~noun* **3.** assets, cash, finance, finances, financing, funds, investment(s), means, money, principal, property, resources, stock, wealth, wherewithal

capitalism free enterprise, *laissez faire or* laisser faire, private enterprise, private ownership

capitulate come to terms, give in, give up, relent, submit, succumb, surrender, yield
▷ **Antonyms** beat, conquer, crush, defeat, get the better of, lick (*informal*), overcome, overpower, subdue, subjugate, vanquish

capitulation accedence, submission, surrender, yielding

caprice changeableness, fad, fancy, fickleness, fitfulness, freak, humour, impulse, inconstancy, notion, quirk, vagary, whim, whimsy

capricious changeful, crotchety (*informal*), erratic, fanciful, fickle, fitful, freakish, impulsive, inconsistent, inconstant, mercurial, odd, queer, quirky, unpredictable, variable, wayward, whimsical
▷ **Antonyms** certain, consistent, constant, decisive, determined, firm, resolute, responsible, stable, unchangeable, unmoveable, unwavering

capsize invert, keel over, overturn, tip over, turn over, turn turtle, upset

capsule **1.** bolus, lozenge, pill, tablet, troche (*Medical*) **2.** case, pericarp (*Botany*), pod, receptacle, seed vessel, sheath, shell, vessel

captain boss, chief, chieftain, commander, head, leader, master, number one (*informal*), officer, (senior) pilot, skipper, torchbearer

captious **1.** carping, cavilling, censorious, critical, deprecating, disparaging, fault-finding, hypercritical, nagging, nit-picking (*informal*) **2.** acrimonious, cantankerous, crabbed, cross, irritable, peevish, ratty (*Brit. & N.Z. informal*), testy, tetchy, touchy

captivate absorb, allure, attract, beguile, bewitch, charm, dazzle, enamour, enchant, enrapture, enslave, ensnare, enthral, entrance, fascinate, hypnotize, infatuate, lure, mesmerize, ravish, seduce, sweep off one's feet, win
▷ **Antonyms** alienate, disenchant, disgust, repel, repulse

captive **1.** *noun* bondservant, convict, detainee, hostage, internee, prisoner, prisoner of war, slave **2.** *~adjective* caged, confined, enslaved, ensnared, imprisoned, incarcerated, locked up, penned, restricted, subjugated

captivity bondage, confinement, custody, detention, durance (*archaic*), duress, enthralment, imprisonment, incarceration, internment, restraint, servitude, slavery, thraldom, vassalage

capture **1.** *verb* apprehend, arrest, bag, catch, collar (*informal*), feel one's collar (*slang*), lift (*slang*), nab (*informal*), nail (*informal*), secure, seize, take, take into custody, take prisoner **2.** *~noun* apprehension, arrest, catch, imprisonment, seizure, taking, taking captive, trapping
▷ **Antonyms** *~verb* free, let go, let out, liberate, release, set free, turn loose

car **1.** auto (*U.S.*), automobile, jalopy (*informal*), machine, motor, motorcar, vehicle, wheels (*informal*) **2.** buffet car, cable car, coach, dining car, (railway) carriage, sleeping car, van

carafe decanter, flagon, flask, jug, pitcher

carcass body, cadaver (*Medical*), corpse, corse (*archaic*), dead body, framework, hulk, remains, shell, skeleton

cardinal capital, central, chief, essential, first, foremost, fundamental, greatest,

highest, important, key, leading, main, paramount, pre-eminent, primary, prime, principal
▷ **Antonyms** dispensable, inessential, least important, lowest, secondary, subordinate

care 1. affliction, anxiety, burden, concern, disquiet, hardship, interest, perplexity, pressure, responsibility, solicitude, stress, tribulation, trouble, vexation, woe, worry **2.** attention, carefulness, caution, circumspection, consideration, direction, forethought, heed, management, meticulousness, pains, prudence, regard, vigilance, watchfulness **3.** charge, control, custody, guardianship, keeping, management, ministration, protection, supervision, ward
▷ **Antonyms** (*sense 1*) pleasure, relaxation (*sense 2*) abandon, carelessness, heedlessness, inattention, indifference, laxity, laxness, neglect, negligence, unconcern

career *noun* **1.** calling, employment, life's work, livelihood, occupation, pursuit, vocation **2.** course, passage, path, procedure, progress, race, walk *~verb* **3.** barrel (along) (*informal, chiefly U.S. & Canad.*), bolt, burn rubber (*informal*), dash, hurtle, race, rush, speed, tear

care for 1. attend, foster, look after, mind, minister to, nurse, protect, provide for, tend, watch over **2.** be fond of, desire, enjoy, find congenial, like, love, prize, take to, want

carefree airy, blithe, breezy, buoyant, careless, cheerful, cheery, chirpy (*informal*), easy-going, halcyon, happy, happy-go-lucky, insouciant, jaunty, light-hearted, lightsome (*archaic*), radiant, sunny, untroubled
▷ **Antonyms** blue, careworn, cheerless, dejected, depressed, desolate, despondent, down, down in the dumps (*informal*), gloomy, low, melancholy, miserable, sad, unhappy, worried

careful 1. accurate, attentive, cautious, chary, circumspect, conscientious, discreet, fastidious, heedful, painstaking, precise, prudent, punctilious, scrupulous, thoughtful, thrifty **2.** alert, concerned, judicious, mindful, particular, protective, solicitous, vigilant, wary, watchful
▷ **Antonyms** abandoned, careless, casual, inaccurate, inattentive, inexact, neglectful, negligent, reckless, remiss, slovenly, thoughtless, unconcerned, untroubled

careless 1. absent-minded, cursory, forgetful, hasty, heedless, incautious, inconsiderate, indiscreet, negligent, perfunctory, regardless, remiss, thoughtless, unconcerned, unguarded, unmindful, unthinking **2.** cavalier, inaccurate, irresponsible, lackadaisical, neglectful, offhand, slapdash, slipshod, sloppy (*informal*) **3.** artless, casual, nonchalant, unstudied
▷ **Antonyms** accurate, alert, anxious, attentive, careful, cautious, concerned, correct, neat, on the ball (*informal*), orderly, painstaking, tidy, wary, watchful

carelessness inaccuracy, inattention, inconsiderateness, indiscretion, irresponsibility, laxity, laxness, neglect, negligence, omission, remissness, slackness, sloppiness (*informal*), thoughtlessness

caress 1. *verb* cuddle, embrace, fondle, hug, kiss, neck (*informal*), nuzzle, pet, stroke **2.** *~noun* cuddle, embrace, fondling, hug, kiss, pat, stroke

caretaker 1. *noun* concierge, curator, custodian, janitor, keeper, porter, superintendent, warden, watchman **2.** *~adjective* holding, interim, short-term, temporary

cargo baggage, consignment, contents, freight, goods, lading, load, merchandise, shipment, tonnage, ware

caricature 1. *noun* burlesque, cartoon, distortion, farce, lampoon, mimicry, parody, pasquinade, satire, send-up (*Brit. informal*), takeoff (*informal*), travesty **2.** *~verb* burlesque, distort, lampoon, mimic, mock, parody, ridicule, satirize, send up (*Brit. informal*), take off (*informal*)

carnage blood bath, bloodshed, butchery, havoc, holocaust, massacre, mass murder, murder, shambles, slaughter

carnal 1. amorous, animal, erotic, fleshly, impure, lascivious, lecherous, lewd, libidinous, licentious, lustful, prurient, randy (*informal, chiefly Brit.*), raunchy (*slang*), salacious, sensual, sensuous, sexual, sexy (*informal*), steamy (*informal*), unchaste, voluptuous, wanton **2.** bodily, corporeal, earthly, human, mundane, natural, physical, profane, secular, sublunary, temporal, unregenerate, unspiritual, worldly

carnality bestiality, corporeality, fleshliness, lechery, lust, lustfulness, prurience, salaciousness, sensuality, voluptuousness, worldliness

carnival celebration, fair, festival, fête, fiesta, gala, holiday, jamboree, jubilee, Mardi Gras, merrymaking, revelry

carol canticle, canzonet, chorus, ditty, hymn, lay, noel, song, strain

carouse bend the elbow (*informal*), bevvy (*dialect*), booze (*informal*), drink, imbibe, make merry, quaff, roister, wassail

carp beef (*slang*), cavil, censure, complain, criticize, find fault, hypercriticize, knock (*informal*), kvetch (*U.S. slang*), nag, pick holes, quibble, reproach
▷ **Antonyms** admire, applaud, approve, commend, compliment, extol, laud (*literary*), pay tribute to, praise, sing the praises of, speak highly of

carpenter cabinet-maker, joiner, woodworker

carping captious, cavilling, critical, fault-finding, grouchy (*informal*), hard to please, hypercritical, nagging, nit-picking (*informal*), on someone's back (*informal*), picky (*informal*), reproachful

carriage **1.** carrying, conveyance, convey~ ing, delivery, freight, transport, trans~ portation **2.** cab, coach, conveyance, ve~ hicle **3.** *figurative* air, bearing, behav~ iour, comportment, conduct, demeanour, deportment, gait, manner, mien, pos~ ture, presence

carry **1.** bear, bring, conduct, convey, fetch, haul, hump (*Brit. slang*), lift, lug, move, relay, take, tote (*informal*), transfer, transmit, transport **2.** accom~ plish, capture, effect, gain, secure, win **3.** drive, impel, influence, motivate, spur, urge **4.** bear, bolster, hold up, maintain, shoulder, stand, suffer, sup~ port, sustain, underpin, uphold **5.** broadcast, communicate, display, dis~ seminate, give, offer, publish, release, stock

carry on **1.** continue, endure, keep going, last, maintain, perpetuate, persevere, persist **2.** administer, manage, operate, run **3.** *informal* create (*slang*), make a fuss, misbehave, raise Cain

carry out accomplish, achieve, carry through, consummate, discharge, effect, execute, fulfil, implement, perform, re~ alize

carton box, case, container, pack, pack~ age, packet

cartoon animated cartoon, animated film, animation, caricature, comic strip, lam~ poon, parody, satire, sketch, takeoff (*in~ formal*)

cartridge **1.** capsule, case, cassette, con~ tainer, cylinder, magazine **2.** charge, round, shell

carve chip, chisel, cut, divide, engrave, etch, fashion, form, grave (*archaic*), hack, hew, incise, indent, inscribe, mould, sculpt, sculpture, slash, slice, whittle

cascade **1.** *noun* avalanche, cataract, del~ uge, downpour, falls, flood, fountain, outpouring, shower, torrent, waterfall **2.** *~verb* descend, flood, gush, overflow, pitch, plunge, pour, spill, surge, teem, tumble

case **1.** box, cabinet, canister, capsule, carton, cartridge, casket, chest, coffret, compact, container, crate, holder, re~ ceptacle, suitcase, tray, trunk **2.** capsule, casing, cover, covering, envelope, folder, integument, jacket, sheath, shell, wrap~ per, wrapping **3.** circumstance(s), condi~ tion, context, contingency, dilemma, event, plight, position, predicament, situation, state **4.** example, illustration, instance, occasion, occurrence, specimen **5.** *Law* action, cause, dispute, lawsuit, proceedings, process, suit, trial

cash ackers (*slang*), banknotes, brass (*Northern English dialect*), bread (*slang*), bullion, change, coin, coinage, currency, dibs (*slang*), dosh (*Brit. & Austral. slang*), dough (*slang*), funds, money, necessary (*informal*), needful (*informal*), notes, payment, ready (*in~ formal*), ready money, resources, rhino (*Brit. slang*), shekels (*informal*), silver, specie, spondulicks (*slang*), tin (*slang*), wherewithal

cashier **1.** *noun* accountant, bank clerk, banker, bursar, clerk, purser, teller, treasurer **2.** *~verb* break, cast off, dis~ card, discharge, dismiss, drum out, ex~ pel, give the boot to (*slang*)

casket ark (*dialect*), box, case, chest, cof~ fer, coffret, jewel box, kist (*Scot. & Northern English dialect*)

cast *verb* **1.** chuck (*informal*), drive, drop, fling, hurl, impel, launch, lob, pitch, project, shed, shy, sling, throw, thrust, toss **2.** bestow, deposit, diffuse, distrib~ ute, emit, give, radiate, scatter, shed, spread **3.** allot, appoint, assign, choose, name, pick, select **4.** add, calculate, compute, figure, forecast, reckon, total **5.** form, found, model, mould, set, shape *~noun* **6.** fling, lob, throw, thrust, toss **7.** air, appearance, complexion, demean~ our, look, manner, mien, semblance, shade, stamp, style, tinge, tone, turn **8.** actors, characters, company, dramatis personae, players, troupe

cast down deject, depress, desolate, dis~ courage, dishearten, dispirit

caste class, estate, grade, lineage, order, race, rank, social order, species, station, status, stratum

castigate bawl out (*informal*), beat, be~ rate, blast, cane, carpet (*informal*), cen~ sure, chasten, chastise, chew out (*U.S. & Canad. informal*), correct, criticize, discipline, dress down (*informal*), exco~ riate, flail, flay, flog, give a rocket (*Brit. & N.Z. informal*), haul over the coals (*informal*), lambast(e), lash, put down, rap over the knuckles, read the riot act, rebuke, reprimand, scold, scourge, slap on the wrist, slate (*informal, chiefly Brit.*), tear into (*informal*), tear (some~ one) off a strip (*Brit. informal*), whip

castle chateau, citadel, donjon, fastness, fortress, keep, mansion, palace, peel, stronghold, tower

castrate emasculate, geld, neuter, unman

casual **1.** accidental, chance, contingent, fortuitous, hit-and-miss *or* hit-or-miss (*informal*), incidental, irregular, occa~ sional, random, serendipitous, uncer~ tain, unexpected, unforeseen, uninten~ tional, unpremeditated **2.** apathetic, blasé, careless, cursory, indifferent, in~ formal, insouciant, lackadaisical, non~ chalant, offhand, perfunctory, relaxed, unconcerned **3.** informal, non-dressy, sporty

▷ **Antonyms** (*sense 1*) arranged, deliberate, expected, fixed, foreseen, intentional, planned, premeditated (*sense 2*) committed, concerned, direct, enthusiastic, passionate, serious, systematic (*sense 3*) ceremonial, dressy, formal

casualties dead, fatalities, losses, missing, wounded

casualty **1.** loss, sufferer, victim **2.** accident, calamity, catastrophe, chance, contingency, disaster, misadventure, misfortune, mishap

casuistry chicanery, equivocation, oversubtleness, sophism, sophistry, speciousness

cat feline, gib, grimalkin, kitty, malkin (*archaic*), moggy (*slang*), mouser, puss (*informal*), pussy (*informal*), tabby

cataclysm calamity, catastrophe, collapse, convulsion, debacle, disaster, upheaval

catacomb crypt, ossuary, tomb, vault

catalogue **1.** *noun* directory, gazetteer, index, inventory, list, record, register, roll, roster, schedule **2.** *~verb* accession, alphabetize, classify, file, index, inventory, list, register, tabulate

catapult **1.** *noun* ballista, sling, slingshot (*U.S.*), trebuchet **2.** *~verb* heave, hurl, hurtle, pitch, plunge, propel, shoot, toss

cataract **1.** cascade, deluge, downpour, falls, Niagara, rapids, torrent, waterfall **2.** *Medical* opacity (*of the eye*)

catastrophe **1.** adversity, affliction, blow, bummer (*slang*), calamity, cataclysm, deep water, devastation, disaster, failure, fiasco, ill, meltdown (*informal*), mischance, misfortune, mishap, reverse, tragedy, trial, trouble, whammy (*informal, chiefly U.S.*) **2.** conclusion, culmination, curtain, debacle, dénouement, end, finale, termination, upshot, winding-up

catcall **1.** *verb* boo, deride, gibe, give the bird to (*informal*), hiss, jeer, whistle **2.** *~noun* boo, gibe, hiss, jeer, raspberry, whistle

catch *verb* **1.** apprehend, arrest, capture, clutch, ensnare, entangle, entrap, feel one's collar (*slang*), get, grab, grasp, grip, lay hold of, lift (*slang*), nab (*informal*), nail (*informal*), seize, snare, snatch, take **2.** catch in the act, detect, discover, expose, find out, surprise, take unawares, unmask **3.** bewitch, captivate, charm, delight, enchant, enrapture, fascinate **4.** contract, develop, get, go down with, incur, succumb to, suffer from **5.** apprehend, discern, feel, follow, get, grasp, hear, perceive, recognize, sense, take in, twig (*Brit. informal*) *~noun* **6.** bolt, clasp, clip, fastener, hasp, hook, hook and eye, latch, sneck (*dialect, chiefly Scot. & N. English*), snib (*Scot.*) **7.** disadvantage, drawback, fly in the ointment, hitch, snag, stumbling block, trap, trick

▷ **Antonyms** *~verb* (*sense 1*) drop, free, give up, liberate, loose, release (*sense 3*) alienate, bore, disenchant, disgust, fail to interest, repel (*sense 4*) avert, avoid, escape, ward off *~noun* (*sense 7*) advantage, benefit, bonus, boon, reward

catching **1.** communicable, contagious, infectious, infective, transferable, transmittable **2.** attractive, captivating, charming, enchanting, fascinating, fetching, taking, winning

▷ **Antonyms** (*sense 1*) incommunicable, non-catching, non-contagious, non-infectious, non-transmittable

catch on comprehend, find out, get the picture, grasp, see, see the light of day, see through, twig (*Brit. informal*), understand

catchword byword, motto, password, refrain, slogan, watchword

catchy captivating, haunting, memorable, popular

catechize cross-examine, drill, examine, grill (*informal*), interrogate, question

catechumen convert, disciple, initiate, learner, neophyte, novice, probationer, tyro

categorical absolute, direct, downright, emphatic, explicit, express, positive, unambiguous, unconditional, unequivocal, unqualified, unreserved

▷ **Antonyms** conditional, hesitant, indefinite, qualified, questionable, uncertain, vague

category class, classification, department, division, grade, grouping, head, heading, list, order, rank, section, sort, type

cater furnish, outfit, provide, provision, purvey, supply, victual

cater to coddle, fawn on, feed, gratify, humour, indulge, minister to, mollycoddle, pamper, pander to, spoil

caterwaul bawl, howl, scream, screech, shriek, squall, wail, yowl

catharsis abreaction, cleansing, lustration, purgation, purging, purification, release

catholic all-embracing, all-inclusive, broad-minded, charitable, comprehensive, eclectic, ecumenical, general, global, liberal, tolerant, unbigoted, universal, unsectarian, whole, wide, world-wide

▷ **Antonyms** bigoted, exclusive, illiberal, limited, narrow-minded, parochial, sectarian

cattle beasts, bovines, cows, kine (*archaic*), livestock, neat (*archaic*), stock

catty backbiting, bitchy (*informal*), ill-natured, malevolent, malicious, mean, rancorous, shrewish, snide, spiteful, venomous

▷ **Antonyms** benevolent, charitable,

compassionate, considerate, generous, kind, pleasant

caucus assembly, conclave, congress, convention, get-together (*informal*), meeting, parley, session

cause *noun* **1.** agent, beginning, creator, genesis, mainspring, maker, origin, originator, prime mover, producer, root, source, spring **2.** account, agency, aim, basis, consideration, end, grounds, incentive, inducement, motivation, motive, object, purpose, reason, the why and wherefore **3.** attempt, belief, conviction, enterprise, ideal, movement, purpose, undertaking *~verb* **4.** begin, bring about, compel, create, effect, engender, generate, give rise to, incite, induce, lead to, motivate, occasion, precipitate, produce, provoke, result in

▷ **Antonyms** *~noun* consequence, effect, end, outcome, result *~verb* deter, foil, inhibit, prevent, stop

caustic 1. acrid, astringent, biting, burning, corroding, corrosive, keen, mordant, vitriolic **2.** acrimonious, cutting, mordacious, pungent, sarcastic, scathing, severe, stinging, trenchant, virulent, vitriolic

▷ **Antonyms** agreeable, bland, gentle, healing, kind, loving, mild, pleasant, pleasing, soft, soothing, sweet, temperate

caution *noun* **1.** alertness, belt and braces, care, carefulness, circumspection, deliberation, discretion, forethought, heed, heedfulness, prudence, vigilance, watchfulness **2.** admonition, advice, counsel, injunction, warning *~verb* **3.** admonish, advise, tip off, urge, warn

▷ **Antonyms** *~noun* carelessness, daring, imprudence, rashness, recklessness *~verb* dare

cautious alert, belt-and-braces, cagey (*informal*), careful, chary, circumspect, discreet, guarded, heedful, judicious, keeping a weather eye on, on one's toes, prudent, tentative, vigilant, wary, watchful

▷ **Antonyms** adventurous, bold, careless, daring, foolhardy, heedless, impetuous, inattentive, incautious, indiscreet, madcap, rash, reckless, unguarded, unheedful, venturesome, venturous

cavalcade array, march-past, parade, procession, spectacle, train

cavalier *noun* **1.** chevalier, equestrian, horseman, knight, royalist **2.** beau, blade (*archaic*), escort, gallant, gentleman *~adjective* **3.** arrogant, condescending, curt, disdainful, haughty, insolent, lofty, lordly, offhand, scornful, supercilious

cavalry horse, horsemen, mounted troops

▷ **Antonyms** foot soldiers, infantrymen

cave cavern, cavity, den, grotto, hollow

caveat admonition, caution, warning

cavern cave, hollow, pothole

cavernous 1. concave, deep-set, hollow, sunken, yawning **2.** echoing, resonant, reverberant, sepulchral

cavil beef (*slang*), carp, censure, complain, find fault, hypercriticize, kvetch (*U.S. slang*), object, quibble

cavilling captious, carping, censorious, critical, fault-finding, hypercritical, nit-picking (*informal*), quibbling

cavity crater, dent, gap, hole, hollow, pit

cavort caper, caracole, frisk, frolic, gambol, prance, romp, sport

cease break off, bring *or* come to an end, conclude, culminate, desist, die away, discontinue, end, fail, finish, halt, leave off, refrain, stay, stop, terminate

▷ **Antonyms** begin, commence, continue, initiate, start

ceaseless constant, continual, continuous, endless, eternal, everlasting, incessant, indefatigable, interminable, never-ending, nonstop, perennial, perpetual, unending, unremitting, untiring

▷ **Antonyms** broken, erratic, intermittent, irregular, occasional, periodic, spasmodic, sporadic

cede abandon, abdicate, allow, concede, convey, grant, hand over, make over, relinquish, renounce, resign, step down (*informal*), surrender, transfer, yield

celebrate bless, commemorate, commend, crack up (*informal*), drink to, eulogize, exalt, extol, glorify, honour, keep, kill the fatted calf, laud, observe, perform, praise, proclaim, publicize, put the flags out, rejoice, reverence, solemnize, toast

celebrated acclaimed, distinguished, eminent, famed, famous, glorious, illustrious, lionized, notable, outstanding, popular, pre-eminent, prominent, renowned, revered, well-known

▷ **Antonyms** dishonoured, forgotten, insignificant, obscure, trivial, unacclaimed, undistinguished, unknown, unnotable, unpopular

celebration 1. beano (*Brit. slang*), carousal, -fest (*in combination*), festival, festivity, gala, hooley *or* hoolie (*chiefly Irish & N.Z.*), jollification, jubilee, junketing, merrymaking, party, rave (*Brit. slang*), rave-up (*Brit. slang*), red-letter day, revelry **2.** anniversary, commemoration, honouring, observance, performance, remembrance, solemnization

celebrity 1. big name, big shot (*informal*), bigwig (*informal*), celeb (*informal*), dignitary, face (*informal*), lion, luminary, megastar (*informal*), name, personage, personality, star, superstar, V.I.P. **2.** distinction, éclat, eminence, fame, glory, honour, notability, popularity, pre-eminence, prestige, prominence, renown, reputation, repute, stardom

▷ **Antonyms** has-been, nobody, obscurity, unknown

celerity dispatch, expedition, fleetness, haste, promptness, quickness, rapidity, speed, swiftness, velocity, vivacity

celestial angelic, astral, divine, elysian, empyrean (*poetic*), eternal, ethereal, godlike, heavenly, immortal, seraphic, spiritual, sublime, supernatural

celibacy chastity, continence, purity, singleness, virginity

cell 1. cavity, chamber, compartment, cubicle, dungeon, stall **2.** caucus, coterie, group, nucleus, unit

cement 1. *verb* attach, bind, bond, cohere, combine, glue, gum, join, plaster, seal, solder, stick together, unite, weld **2.** *~noun* adhesive, binder, glue, gum, paste, plaster, sealant

cemetery burial ground, churchyard, God's acre, graveyard, necropolis

censor blue-pencil, bowdlerize, cut, expurgate

censorious captious, carping, cavilling, condemnatory, disapproving, disparaging, fault-finding, hypercritical, scathing, severe

censurable at fault, blamable, blameworthy, chargeable, contemptible, culpable, faulty, guilty, reprehensible, scandalous

censure 1. *verb* abuse, bawl out (*informal*), berate, blame, blast, carpet (*informal*), castigate, chew out (*U.S. & Canad. informal*), chide, condemn, criticize, denounce, excoriate, give (someone) a rocket (*Brit. & N.Z. informal*), lambast(e), put down, rap over the knuckles, read the riot act, rebuke, reprehend, reprimand, reproach, reprove, scold, slap on the wrist, slate (*informal, chiefly U.S.*), tear into (*informal*), tear (someone) off a strip (*Brit. informal*), upbraid **2.** *~noun* blame, castigation, condemnation, criticism, disapproval, dressing down (*informal*), obloquy, rebuke, remonstrance, reprehension, reprimand, reproach, reproof, stick (*slang*), stricture

▷ **Antonyms** *~verb* applaud, commend, compliment, laud (*literary*) *~noun* approval, commendation, compliment, encouragement

central chief, essential, focal, fundamental, inner, interior, key, main, mean, median, mid, middle, primary, principal

▷ **Antonyms** exterior, minor, outer, outermost, secondary, subordinate, subsidiary

centralize amalgamate, compact, concentrate, concentre, condense, converge, incorporate, rationalize, streamline, unify

centre 1. *noun* bull's-eye, core, crux, focus, heart, hub, kernel, mid (*archaic*), middle, midpoint, nucleus, pivot **2.** *~verb* cluster, concentrate, converge, focus, revolve

▷ **Antonyms** *~noun* border, boundary, brim, circumference, edge, fringe, limit, lip, margin, perimeter, periphery, rim *~verb* bestrew, diffuse, disseminate, fling, scatter, spread, sprinkle, strew, toss

centrepiece cynosure, epergne, focus, highlight, hub, star

centrifugal diffusive, divergent, diverging, efferent, radial, radiating

ceremonial 1. *adjective* formal, liturgical, ritual, ritualistic, solemn, stately **2.** *~noun* ceremony, formality, rite, ritual, solemnity

▷ **Antonyms** casual, informal, relaxed, simple

ceremonious civil, courteous, courtly, deferential, dignified, exact, formal, precise, punctilious, ritual, solemn, starchy (*informal*), stately, stiff

ceremony 1. commemoration, function, observance, parade, rite, ritual, service, show, solemnities **2.** ceremonial, decorum, etiquette, form, formal courtesy, formality, niceties, pomp, propriety, protocol

certain 1. assured, confident, convinced, positive, satisfied, sure **2.** ascertained, conclusive, incontrovertible, indubitable, irrefutable, known, plain, true, undeniable, undoubted, unequivocal, unmistakable, valid **3.** bound, definite, destined, fated, ineluctable, inescapable, inevitable, inexorable, sure **4.** decided, definite, established, fixed, settled **5.** assured, constant, dependable, reliable, stable, staunch, steady, trustworthy, unfailing, unquestionable **6.** express, individual, particular, precise, special, specific

▷ **Antonyms** disputable, doubtful, dubious, equivocal, fallible, indefinite, questionable, uncertain, unconvinced, undecided, unlikely, unreliable, unsettled, unsure

certainty 1. assurance, authoritativeness, certitude, confidence, conviction, faith, indubitableness, inevitability, positiveness, sureness, trust, validity **2.** fact, reality, sure thing (*informal*), surety, truth

▷ **Antonyms** disbelief, doubt, indecision, qualm, scepticism, uncertainty, unsureness

certificate authorization, credential(s), diploma, document, licence, testimonial, voucher, warrant

certify ascertain, assure, attest, authenticate, aver, avow, confirm, corroborate, declare, endorse, guarantee, notify, show, testify, validate, verify, vouch, witness

certitude assurance, certainty, confidence, conviction

cessation abeyance, arrest, break, ceasing, discontinuance, ending, entr'acte, halt, halting, hiatus, intermission, in~terruption, interval, let-up (*informal*), pause, recess, remission, respite, rest, standstill, stay, stoppage, suspension, termination, time off

cession abandonment, abnegation, ca~pitulation, ceding, conceding, conces~sion, conveyance, grant, relinquish~ment, renunciation, surrender, yielding

chafe abrade, anger, annoy, exasperate, fret, fume, gall, get *or* take a rise out of, get on someone's nerves, get on someone's wick (*Brit. slang*), grate, in~cense, inflame, irritate, nark (*Brit., Austral., & N.Z. slang*), offend, provoke, rage, rasp, rub, rub (someone) up the wrong way (*informal*), ruffle, scrape, scratch, vex, worry

▷ **Antonyms** allay, alleviate, appease, assuage, calm, conciliate, mollify, paci~fy, placate, please, soothe

chaff *noun* **1.** dregs, glumes, hulls, husks, refuse, remains, rubbish, trash, waste **2.** badinage, banter, joking, josh (*slang, chiefly U.S. & Canad.*), persiflage, rail~lery, teasing *~verb* **3.** banter, deride, jeer, josh (*slang, chiefly U.S. & Canad.*), mock, rib (*informal*), ridicule, scoff, take the piss out of (*taboo slang*), taunt, tease

chagrin 1. *noun* annoyance, discomfiture, discomposure, displeasure, disquiet, dissatisfaction, embarrassment, fretful~ness, humiliation, ill-humour, irritation, mortification, peevishness, spleen, vexation **2.** *~verb* annoy, discomfit, dis~compose, displease, disquiet, dissatisfy, embarrass, humiliate, irk, irritate, mortify, peeve, vex

chain *verb* **1.** bind, confine, enslave, fet~ter, gyve (*archaic*), handcuff, manacle, restrain, shackle, tether, trammel, unite *~noun* **2.** bond, coupling, fetter, link, manacle, shackle, union **3.** concatena~tion, progression, sequence, series, set, string, succession, train

chairman chairperson, chairwoman, di~rector, master of ceremonies, president, presider, speaker, spokesman, toast~master

chalk up accumulate, achieve, attain, credit, enter, gain, log, mark, record, register, score, tally, win

challenge 1. *verb* accost, arouse, beard, brave, call out, call (someone's) bluff, claim, confront, dare, defy, demand, dispute, face off (*slang*), impugn, inves~tigate, object to, provoke, question, re~quire, stimulate, summon, tackle, tax, test, throw down the gauntlet, try **2.** *~noun* confrontation, dare, defiance, face-off (*slang*), interrogation, provoca~tion, question, summons to contest, test, trial, ultimatum

chamber 1. apartment, bedroom, cavity, compartment, cubicle, enclosure, hall, hollow, room **2.** assembly, council, legis~lative body, legislature

champion 1. *noun* backer, challenger, conqueror, defender, guardian, hero, nonpareil, patron, protector, title hold~er, upholder, victor, vindicator, warrior, winner **2.** *~verb* advocate, back, com~mend, defend, encourage, espouse, fight for, promote, stick up for (*informal*), support, uphold

chance *noun* **1.** liability, likelihood, occa~sion, odds, opening, opportunity, pos~sibility, probability, prospect, scope, time, window **2.** accident, casualty, co~incidence, contingency, destiny, fate, fortuity, fortune, luck, misfortune, peril, providence **3.** gamble, hazard, jeopardy, risk, speculation, uncertainty *~verb* **4.** befall, betide, come about, come to pass, fall out, happen, occur **5.** endanger, gamble, go out on a limb, hazard, jeop~ardize, risk, skate on thin ice, stake, try, venture, wager *~adjective* **6.** accidental, casual, contingent, fortuitous, inadvert~ent, incidental, random, serendipitous, unforeseeable, unforeseen, unintention~al, unlooked-for

▷ **Antonyms** *~noun* certainty, design, impossibility, improbability, intention, surety, unlikelihood *~adjective* ar~ranged, deliberate, designed, expected, foreseen, intentional, planned

chancy dangerous, dicey (*informal, chiefly Brit.*), dodgy (*Brit., Austral., & N.Z. slang*), hazardous, perilous, prob~lematical, risky, speculative, uncertain

▷ **Antonyms** certain, reliable, safe, se~cure, sound, stable, sure

change *verb* **1.** alter, convert, diversify, fluctuate, metamorphose, moderate, modify, mutate, reform, remodel, reor~ganize, restyle, shift, transform, trans~mute, vacillate, vary, veer **2.** alternate, barter, convert, displace, exchange, interchange, remove, replace, substi~tute, swap (*informal*), trade, transmit *~noun* **3.** alteration, difference, innova~tion, metamorphosis, modification, mu~tation, permutation, revolution, trans~formation, transition, transmutation, vicissitude **4.** conversion, exchange, interchange, substitution, trade **5.** break (*informal*), departure, diversion, novel~ty, variation, variety, whole new ball game (*informal*)

▷ **Antonyms** *~verb* hold, keep, remain, stay *~noun* constancy, invariability, mo~notony, permanence, stability, uniform~ity

changeable capricious, changeful, cheq~uered, erratic, fickle, fitful, fluid, incon~stant, irregular, kaleidoscopic, labile (*Chemistry*), mercurial, mobile, mu~table, protean, shifting, temperamental, uncertain, uneven, unpredictable, unre~liable, unsettled, unstable, unsteady, vacillating, variable, versatile, volatile,

wavering, whimsical
▷ **Antonyms** constant, invariable, irreversible, regular, reliable, stable, steady, unchangeable

changeless abiding, consistent, constant, eternal, everlasting, fixed, immovable, immutable, permanent, perpetual, regular, reliable, resolute, settled, stationary, steadfast, steady, unalterable, unchanging, uniform, unvarying

channel *noun* **1.** canal, chamber, conduit, duct, fluting, furrow, groove, gutter, main, passage, route, strait **2.** *figurative* approach, artery, avenue, course, means, medium, path, route, way *~verb* **3.** conduct, convey, direct, guide, transmit

chant 1. *noun* carol, chorus, melody, psalm, song **2.** *~verb* carol, chorus, croon, descant, intone, recite, sing, warble

chaos anarchy, bedlam, confusion, disorder, disorganization, entropy, lawlessness, mayhem, pandemonium, tumult
▷ **Antonyms** neatness, orderliness, organization, tidiness

chaotic anarchic, confused, deranged, disordered, disorganized, lawless, purposeless, rampageous, riotous, topsy-turvy, tumultuous, uncontrolled

chap bloke (*Brit. informal*), character, cove (*slang*), customer (*informal*), dude (*U.S. & Canad. informal*), fellow, guy (*informal*), individual, person, sort, type

chaperon 1. *noun* companion, duenna, escort, governess **2.** *~verb* accompany, attend, escort, protect, safeguard, shepherd, watch over

chaplet bouquet, coronal, garland, wreath

chapter clause, division, episode, part, period, phase, section, stage, topic

char carbonize, cauterize, scorch, sear, singe

character 1. attributes, bent, calibre, cast, complexion, constitution, disposition, individuality, kidney, make-up, marked traits, nature, personality, quality, reputation, temper, temperament, type **2.** honour, integrity, rectitude, strength, uprightness **3.** card (*informal*), eccentric, nut (*slang*), oddball (*informal*), odd bod (*informal*), oddity, original, queer fish (*Brit. informal*), wacko *or* whacko (*informal*) **4.** cipher, device, emblem, figure, hieroglyph, letter, logo, mark, rune, sign, symbol, type **5.** part, persona, portrayal, role **6.** fellow, guy (*informal*), individual, person, sort, type

characteristic 1. *adjective* distinctive, distinguishing, idiosyncratic, individual, peculiar, representative, singular, special, specific, symbolic, symptomatic, typical **2.** *~noun* attribute, faculty, feature, idiosyncrasy, mark, peculiarity, property, quality, quirk, trait
▷ **Antonyms** *~adjective* rare, uncharacteristic, unrepresentative, unusual

characterize brand, distinguish, identify, indicate, inform, mark, represent, stamp, typify

charade fake, farce, pantomime, parody, pretence, travesty

charge *verb* **1.** accuse, arraign, blame, impeach, incriminate, indict, involve *~noun* **2.** accusation, allegation, imputation, indictment *~verb* **3.** assail, assault, attack, rush, stampede, storm *~noun* **4.** assault, attack, onset, onslaught, rush, sortie, stampede *~verb* **5.** afflict, burden, commit, entrust, tax *~noun* **6.** burden, care, concern, custody, duty, office, responsibility, safekeeping, trust, ward **7.** amount, cost, damage (*informal*), expenditure, expense, outlay, payment, price, rate, toll *~verb* **8.** fill, instil, lade, load, suffuse **9.** bid, command, demand, enjoin, exhort, instruct, order, require *~noun* **10.** canon, command, demand, dictate, direction, exhortation, injunction, instruction, mandate, order, precept
▷ **Antonyms** *~verb* (*sense 1*) absolve, acquit, clear, exonerate, pardon *~noun* (*sense 2*) absolution, acquittal, clearance, exoneration, pardon, reprieve *~verb* (*sense 3*) back off, retreat, withdraw *~noun* (*sense 4*) retreat, withdrawal

charitable 1. beneficent, benevolent, bountiful, eleemosynary, generous, kind, lavish, liberal, philanthropic **2.** broad-minded, considerate, favourable, forgiving, gracious, humane, indulgent, kindly, lenient, magnanimous, sympathetic, tolerant, understanding
▷ **Antonyms** inconsiderate, mean, stingy, strict, uncharitable, unforgiving, ungenerous, unkind, unsympathetic

charity 1. alms-giving, assistance, benefaction, contributions, donations, endowment, fund, gift, hand-out, largesse *or* largess, philanthropy, relief **2.** affection, Agape, altruism, benevolence, benignity, bountifulness, bounty, compassion, fellow feeling, generosity, goodness, goodwill, humanity, indulgence, love, pity, tenderheartedness
▷ **Antonyms** (*sense 1*) meanness, miserliness, selfishness, stinginess, uncharitableness (*sense 2*) hatred, ill will, intolerance, malice

charlatan cheat, con man (*informal*), fake, fraud, fraudster, grifter (*slang, chiefly U.S. & Canad.*), impostor, mountebank, phoney *or* phony (*informal*), pretender, quack, sham, swindler

charm *verb* **1.** absorb, allure, attract, beguile, bewitch, cajole, captivate, delight, enamour, enchant, enrapture, entrance, fascinate, mesmerize, please, ravish, win, win over *~noun* **2.** allure, allurement, appeal, attraction, desirability,

enchantment, fascination, magic, magnetism, sorcery, spell **3.** amulet, fetish, good-luck piece, lucky piece, periapt (*rare*), talisman, trinket
▷ **Antonyms** ~*verb* alienate, repel, repulse ~*noun* (*sense 2*) repulsiveness, unattractiveness

charming appealing, attractive, bewitching, captivating, cute, delectable, delightful, engaging, eye-catching, fetching, irresistible, likable *or* likeable, lovely, pleasant, pleasing, seductive, winning, winsome
▷ **Antonyms** disgusting, horrid, repulsive, unappealing, unattractive, unlikable *or* unlikeable, unpleasant, unpleasing

chart 1. *noun* blueprint, diagram, graph, map, plan, table, tabulation **2.** ~*verb* delineate, draft, graph, map out, outline, plot, shape, sketch

charter 1. *noun* bond, concession, contract, deed, document, franchise, indenture, licence, permit, prerogative, privilege, right **2.** ~*verb* authorize, commission, employ, hire, lease, rent, sanction

chary 1. careful, cautious, circumspect, guarded, heedful, leery (*slang*), prudent, reluctant, scrupulous, slow, suspicious, uneasy, wary **2.** careful (*Brit.*), frugal, niggardly, parsimonious, thrifty

chase 1. *verb* course, drive, drive away, expel, follow, hound, hunt, pursue, put to flight, run after, track **2.** ~*noun* hunt, hunting, pursuit, race, venery (*archaic*)

chasm abyss, alienation, breach, cavity, cleft, crater, crevasse, fissure, gap, gorge, gulf, hiatus, hollow, opening, ravine, rent, rift, split, void

chassis anatomy, bodywork, frame, framework, fuselage, skeleton, substructure

chaste austere, decent, decorous, elegant, immaculate, incorrupt, innocent, modest, moral, neat, pure, quiet, refined, restrained, simple, unaffected, uncontaminated, undefiled, unsullied, vestal, virginal, virtuous, wholesome
▷ **Antonyms** blemished, corrupt, dirty, dishonourable, gaudy, immoral, impure, married, ornate, promiscuous, self-indulgent, tainted, unchaste, unclean, unrestrained, wanton

chasten afflict, castigate, chastise, correct, cow, curb, discipline, humble, humiliate, put in one's place, repress, soften, subdue, tame

chastise beat, berate, castigate, censure, correct, discipline, flog, lash, lick (*informal*), punish, scold, scourge, upbraid, whip
▷ **Antonyms** caress, commend, compliment, congratulate, cuddle, embrace, fondle, hug, praise, reward

chastity celibacy, continence, innocence, maidenhood, modesty, purity, virginity, virtue
▷ **Antonyms** debauchery, immorality, lewdness, licentiousness, profligacy, promiscuity, wantonness

chat 1. *noun* chatter, chinwag (*Brit. informal*), confab (*informal*), gossip, heart-to-heart, natter, schmooze (*slang*), talk, tête-à-tête **2.** ~*verb* chatter, chew the rag *or* fat (*slang*), gossip, jaw (*slang*), natter, rabbit (on) (*Brit. informal*), run off at the mouth (*U.S. slang*), schmooze *slang* shoot the breeze (*U.S. slang*), talk

chatter *noun/verb* babble, blather, chat, gab (*informal*), gossip, jabber, natter, prate, prattle, rabbit (on) (*Brit. informal*), run off at the mouth (*U.S. slang*), schmooze (*slang*), tattle, twaddle

chatty colloquial, familiar, friendly, gossipy, informal, newsy (*informal*), talkative
▷ **Antonyms** aloof, cold, distant, formal, hostile, quiet, reserved, shy, silent, standoffish, taciturn, timid, unfriendly, unsociable

cheap 1. bargain, cheapo (*informal*), cut-price, economical, economy, inexpensive, keen, low-cost, low-priced, reasonable, reduced, sale **2.** bush-league (*Austral. & N.Z. informal*), chickenshit (*U.S. slang*), common, crappy (*slang*), dime-a-dozen (*informal*), inferior, low-rent (*informal, chiefly U.S.*), paltry, piss-poor (*U.S. taboo slang*), poor, poxy (*slang*), second-rate, shoddy, tatty, tawdry, tinhorn (*U.S. slang*), two a penny, two-bit (*U.S. & Canad. slang*), worthless **3.** base, contemptible, despicable, low, mean, scurvy, sordid, vulgar
▷ **Antonyms** (*sense 1*) costly, dear, expensive, pricey (*informal*), steep (*senses 2 & 3*) admirable, charitable, decent, elegant, generous, good, high-class, honourable, superior, tasteful, valuable

cheapen belittle, debase, degrade, demean, denigrate, depreciate, derogate, devalue, discredit, disparage, lower

cheat *verb* **1.** bamboozle (*informal*), beguile, bilk, con (*informal*), cozen, deceive, defraud, diddle (*informal*), do (*informal*), do the dirty on (*Brit. informal*), double-cross (*informal*), dupe, finagle (*informal*), fleece, fool, gull (*archaic*), hoax, hoodwink, kid (*informal*), mislead, pull a fast one on (*informal*), rip off (*slang*), skin (*slang*), stiff (*slang*), sting (*informal*), stitch up (*slang*), swindle, take for a ride (*informal*), take in (*informal*), thwart, trick, victimize **2.** baffle, check, defeat, deprive, foil, frustrate, prevent, thwart ~*noun* **3.** artifice, deceit, deception, fraud, imposture, rip-off (*slang*), scam (*slang*), sting (*informal*), swindle, trickery **4.** charlatan, cheater, chiseller (*informal*), con man (*informal*), deceiver, dodger, double-crosser (*informal*), fraudster, grifter (*slang, chiefly*

U.S. & Canad.), impostor, knave (*archaic*), rogue, shark, sharper, swindler, trickster

check *verb* **1.** check out (*informal*), compare, confirm, enquire into, examine, inspect, investigate, look at, look over, make sure, monitor, note, probe, research, scrutinize, study, take a dekko at (*Brit. slang*), test, tick, verify, vet, work over **2.** arrest, bar, bridle, control, curb, delay, halt, hinder, hobble, impede, inhibit, limit, nip in the bud, obstruct, pause, put a spoke in someone's wheel, rein, repress, restrain, retard, stem the flow, stop, thwart **3.** admonish, bawl out (*informal*), blame, carpet (*informal*), chew out (*U.S. & Canad. informal*), chide, give (someone) a rocket (*Brit. & N.Z. informal*), give (someone) a row (*informal*), rap over the knuckles, rate, read the riot act, rebuff, rebuke, reprimand, reprove, scold, slap on the wrist, tear into (*informal*), tear (someone) off a strip (*Brit. informal*), tell off (*informal*) *~noun* **4.** examination, inspection, investigation, once-over (*informal*), research, scrutiny, test **5.** constraint, control, curb, damper, hindrance, impediment, inhibition, limitation, obstacle, obstruction, rein, restraint, stoppage **6.** blow, disappointment, frustration, rejection, reverse, setback, whammy (*informal, chiefly U.S.*)

▷ **Antonyms** *~verb* (*sense 1*) disregard, ignore, neglect, overlook, pass over, pay no attention to (*sense 2*) accelerate, advance, begin, encourage, further, give free rein, help, release, start

cheek audacity, brass neck (*Brit. informal*), brazenness, chutzpah (*U.S. & Canad. informal*), disrespect, effrontery, face (*informal*), front, gall (*informal*), impertinence, impudence, insolence, lip (*slang*), neck (*informal*), nerve, sassiness (*U.S. informal*), sauce (*informal*), temerity

cheeky audacious, disrespectful, forward, fresh (*informal*), impertinent, impudent, insolent, insulting, lippy (*U.S. & Canad. slang*), pert, sassy (*U.S. informal*), saucy

▷ **Antonyms** civil, complaisant, courteous, decorous, deferential, mannerly, polite, respectful, well-behaved, well-mannered

cheer *verb* **1.** animate, brighten, buoy up, cheer up, comfort, console, elate, elevate, encourage, enliven, exhilarate, gladden, hearten, incite, inspirit, solace, uplift, warm **2.** acclaim, applaud, clap, hail, hurrah *~noun* **3.** animation, buoyancy, cheerfulness, comfort, gaiety, gladness, glee, hopefulness, joy, liveliness, merriment, merry-making, mirth, optimism, solace **4.** acclamation, applause, ovation, plaudits

▷ **Antonyms** *~verb* (*sense 1*) darken, depress, discourage, dishearten, sadden (*sense 2*) blow a raspberry, boo, hiss, jeer, ridicule

cheerful animated, blithe, bright, bucked (*informal*), buoyant, cheery, chirpy (*informal*), contented, enlivening, enthusiastic, gay, genial, glad, gladsome (*archaic*), happy, hearty, jaunty, jolly, joyful, light-hearted, lightsome (*archaic*), merry, optimistic, pleasant, sparkling, sprightly, sunny, upbeat (*informal*)

▷ **Antonyms** cheerless, dejected, depressed, depressing, despondent, dismal, down, downcast, down in the dumps (*informal*), dull, gloomy, lifeless, low, melancholy, miserable, morose, pensive, sad, unhappy, unpleasant

cheerfulness buoyancy, exuberance, gaiety, geniality, gladness, good cheer, good humour, high spirits, jauntiness, joyousness, light-heartedness

cheering auspicious, bright, comforting, encouraging, heartening, promising, propitious

cheerless austere, bleak, comfortless, dark, dejected, depressed, desolate, despondent, disconsolate, dismal, dolorous, drab, dreary, dull, forlorn, funereal, gloomy, grim, joyless, melancholy, miserable, mournful, sad, sombre, sorrowful, sullen, unhappy, woebegone, woeful

▷ **Antonyms** cheerful, cheery, elated, happy, jolly, joyful, light-hearted, merry

cheer up brighten, buck up (*informal*), comfort, encourage, enliven, gladden, hearten, jolly along (*informal*), perk up, rally, take heart

cheery breezy, carefree, cheerful, chirpy (*informal*), full of beans (*informal*), genial, good-humoured, happy, jovial, lively, pleasant, sunny, upbeat (*informal*)

chef d'oeuvre brainchild, *magnum opus*, masterpiece, masterwork, *tour de force*

chemical compound, drug, potion, synthetic

cherish care for, cleave to, cling to, comfort, cosset, encourage, entertain, foster, harbour, hold dear, love, nourish, nurse, nurture, prize, shelter, support, sustain, treasure

▷ **Antonyms** abandon, desert, despise, disdain, dislike, forsake, hate, neglect

cherubic adorable, angelic, heavenly, innocent, lovable, seraphic, sweet

chest ark (*dialect*), box, case, casket, coffer, crate, kist (*Scot. & Northern English dialect*), strongbox, trunk

chew **1.** bite, champ, chomp, crunch, gnaw, grind, masticate, munch **2.** *figurative* (*usually with* **over**) consider, deliberate upon, meditate, mull (over), muse on, ponder, reflect upon, ruminate, weigh

chic elegant, fashionable, modish, sexy (*informal*), smart, stylish, trendy (*Brit. informal*), up-to-date, urbane
▷ **Antonyms** dinosaur, inelegant, naff (*Brit. slang*), old-fashioned, outmoded, out-of-date, passé, shabby, unfashion~able

chicanery artifice, cheating, chicane, de~ception, deviousness, dodge, double-dealing, duplicity, intrigue, sharp prac~tice, skulduggery (*informal*), sophistry, stratagems, subterfuge, trickery, underhandedness, wiles, wire-pulling (*chiefly U.S.*)

chide admonish, bawl out (*informal*), be~rate, blame, blast, carpet (*informal*), censure, check, chew out (*U.S. & Canad. informal*), criticize, find fault, give (someone) a rocket (*Brit. & N.Z. informal*), give (someone) a row (*infor~mal*), lambast(e), lecture, put down, rap over the knuckles, read the riot act, re~buke, reprehend, reprimand, reproach, reprove, scold, slap on the wrist, slate (*informal, chiefly Brit.*), tear into (*infor~mal*), tear (someone) off a strip (*Brit. informal*), tell off (*informal*), upbraid

chief **1.** *adjective* big-time (*informal*), capital, cardinal, central, especial, es~sential, foremost, grand, highest, key, leading, main, major league (*informal*), most important, outstanding, para~mount, predominant, pre-eminent, premier, prevailing, primary, prime, principal, superior, supreme, upper~most, vital **2.** *~noun* boss (*informal*), captain, chieftain, commander, director, governor, head, leader, lord, manager, master, principal, ringleader, ruler, superintendent, superior, suzerain, torchbearer
▷ **Antonyms** *~adjective* least, minor, subordinate, subsidiary *~noun* follower, subject, subordinate

chiefly above all, especially, essentially, in general, in the main, largely, mainly, mostly, on the whole, predominantly, primarily, principally, usually

child ankle-biter (*Austral. slang*), babe, babe in arms (*informal*), baby, bairn (*Scot.*), brat, chit, descendant, infant, issue, juvenile, kid (*informal*), little one, minor, nipper (*informal*), nursling, off~spring, progeny, rug rat (*slang*), sprog (*slang*), suckling, toddler, tot, wean (*Scot.*), youngster

childbirth accouchement, child-bearing, confinement, delivery, labour, lying-in, parturition, travail

childhood boyhood, girlhood, immaturity, infancy, minority, schooldays, youth

childish boyish, foolish, frivolous, girlish, immature, infantile, juvenile, puerile, silly, simple, trifling, weak, young
▷ **Antonyms** adult, grown-up, manly, mature, sensible, sophisticated, wom~anly

childlike artless, credulous, guileless, in~genuous, innocent, naive, simple, trust~ful, trusting, unfeigned

chill *adjective* **1.** biting, bleak, chilly, cold, freezing, frigid, parky (*Brit. informal*), raw, sharp, wintry **2.** *figurative* aloof, cool, depressing, distant, frigid, hostile, stony, unfriendly, ungenial, unrespon~sive, unwelcoming *~verb* **3.** congeal, cool, freeze, refrigerate **4.** *figurative* dampen, deject, depress, discourage, dishearten, dismay *~noun* **5.** bite, cold, coldness, coolness, crispness, frigidity, nip, raw~ness, sharpness

chilly **1.** blowy, breezy, brisk, cool, crisp, draughty, fresh, nippy, parky (*Brit. in~formal*), penetrating, sharp **2.** cold as ice, frigid, hostile, unfriendly, unre~sponsive, unsympathetic, unwelcoming
▷ **Antonyms** (*sense 1*) balmy, hot, mild, scorching, sunny, sweltering, warm (*sense 2*) affable, chummy (*informal*), congenial, cordial, friendly, responsive, sociable, sympathetic, warm, welcoming

chime boom, clang, dong, jingle, peal, ring, sound, strike, tinkle, tintin~nabulate, toll

chimera bogy, delusion, dream, fantasy, figment, hallucination, ignis fatuus, il~lusion, monster, monstrosity, snare, spectre, will-o'-the-wisp

chimerical delusive, fabulous, fanciful, fantastic, hallucinatory, illusive, illuso~ry, imaginary, quixotic, unfounded, un~real, vain, visionary, wild

china ceramics, crockery, porcelain, pot~tery, service, tableware, ware

chink aperture, cleft, crack, cranny, crev~ice, cut, fissure, flaw, gap, opening, rift

chip **1.** *noun* dent, flake, flaw, fragment, nick, notch, paring, scrap, scratch, shard, shaving, sliver, wafer **2.** *~verb* chisel, damage, gash, nick, whittle

chip in contribute, donate, go Dutch (*in~formal*), interpose, interrupt, pay, sub~scribe

chirp cheep, chirrup, peep, pipe, tweet, twitter, warble

chivalrous bold, brave, courageous, cour~teous, courtly, gallant, gentlemanly, he~roic, high-minded, honourable, intrepid, knightly, magnanimous, true, valiant
▷ **Antonyms** boorish, cowardly, cruel, dishonourable, disloyal, rude, uncourtly, ungallant, unmannerly

chivalry courage, courtesy, courtliness, gallantry, gentlemanliness, knight-errantry, knighthood, politeness

chivvy annoy, badger, bend someone's ear (*informal*), breathe down someone's neck (*informal*), bug (*informal*), harass, hassle (*informal*), hound, nag, pester, plague, pressure (*informal*), prod, tor~ment

choice **1.** *noun* alternative, discrimina~tion, election, option, pick, preference, say, selection, variety **2.** *~adjective* bad (*slang*), best, crucial (*slang*), dainty, def (*slang*), elect, elite, excellent, exclusive, exquisite, hand-picked, nice, precious, prime, prize, rare, select, special, superior, uncommon, unusual, valuable

choke asphyxiate, bar, block, bung, clog, close, congest, constrict, dam, gag, obstruct, occlude, overpower, smother, stifle, stop, strangle, suffocate, suppress, throttle

choleric angry, bad-tempered, cross, fiery, hasty, hot, hot-tempered, ill-tempered, irascible, irritable, passionate, petulant, quick-tempered, ratty (*Brit. & N.Z. informal*), testy, tetchy, touchy

choose adopt, cherry-pick, cull, designate, desire, elect, espouse, fix on, opt for, pick, predestine, prefer, see fit, select, settle upon, single out, take, wish
▷ **Antonyms** decline, dismiss, exclude, forgo, leave, refuse, reject, throw aside

choosy discriminating, exacting, faddy, fastidious, finicky, fussy, particular, picky (*informal*), selective
▷ **Antonyms** easy (*informal*), easy to please, indiscriminate, undemanding, unselective

chop 1. *verb* axe, cleave, cut, fell, hack, hew, lop, sever, shear, slash, truncate **2.** *~noun* **the chop** *slang* dismissal, one's cards, sacking (*informal*), termination, the axe (*informal*), the boot (*slang*), the (old) heave-ho (*informal*), the order of the boot (*slang*), the sack (*informal*)

choppy blustery, broken, rough, ruffled, squally, tempestuous
▷ **Antonyms** calm, smooth, windless

chop up cube, dice, divide, fragment, mince

chore burden, duty, errand, fag (*informal*), job, no picnic, task

chortle cackle, chuckle, crow, guffaw

chorus 1. choir, choristers, ensemble, singers, vocalists **2.** burden, refrain, response, strain **3.** accord, concert, harmony, unison

christen baptize, call, designate, dub, name, style, term, title

chronic 1. confirmed, deep-rooted, deep-seated, habitual, incessant, incurable, ineradicable, ingrained, inveterate, persistent **2.** *informal* abysmal, appalling, atrocious, awful, dreadful
▷ **Antonyms** infrequent, occasional, temporary

chronicle 1. *noun* account, annals, diary, history, journal, narrative, record, register, story **2.** *~verb* enter, narrate, put on record, record, recount, register, relate, report, set down, tell

chronicler annalist, diarist, historian, historiographer, narrator, recorder, reporter, scribe

chronological consecutive, historical, in sequence, ordered, progressive, sequential
▷ **Antonyms** haphazard, intermittent, irregular, out-of-order, random

chubby buxom, flabby, fleshy, plump, podgy, portly, rotund, round, stout, tubby
▷ **Antonyms** lean, skinny, slender, slight, slim, sylphlike, thin

chuck cast, discard, fling, heave, hurl, pitch, shy, sling, throw, toss

chuckle chortle, crow, exult, giggle, laugh, snigger, titter

chum cock (*Brit. informal*), companion, comrade, crony, friend, mate (*informal*), pal (*informal*)

chummy affectionate, buddy-buddy (*slang, chiefly U.S. & Canad.*), close, friendly, intimate, matey *or* maty (*Brit. informal*), pally (*informal*), palsy-walsy (*informal*), thick (*informal*)

chunk block, dollop (*informal*), hunk, lump, mass, nugget, piece, portion, slab, wad, wodge (*Brit. informal*)

chunky beefy (*informal*), dumpy, stocky, stubby, thickset

church basilica, cathedral, chapel, house of God, kirk (*Scot.*), minster, place of worship, procathedral, tabernacle, temple

churl 1. boor, lout, oaf **2.** bumpkin, clodhopper (*informal*), clown, hayseed (*U.S. & Canad. informal*), hick (*informal, chiefly U.S. & Canad.*), hillbilly, peasant, rustic, yokel **3.** curmudgeon, miser, niggard, skinflint

churlish 1. boorish, brusque, crabbed, harsh, ill-tempered, impolite, loutish, morose, oafish, rude, sullen, surly, uncivil, uncouth, unmannerly, vulgar **2.** close-fisted, illiberal, inhospitable, mean, miserly, niggardly, unneighbourly, unsociable
▷ **Antonyms** admirable, agreeable, amiable, civil, courteous, cultivated, generous, good-tempered, mannerly, noble, pleasant, polite, well-bred

churlishness boorishness, crassness, crudeness, loutishness, oafishness, rudeness, surliness, uncouthness

churn agitate, beat, boil, convulse, foam, froth, seethe, stir up, swirl, toss

chute channel, gutter, incline, ramp, runway, slide, slope, trough

cicerone courier, dragoman, escort, guide, mentor, pilot

cigarette cancer stick (*slang*), ciggy (*informal*), coffin nail (*slang*), fag (*Brit. slang*), gasper (*slang*), smoke

cinema big screen (*informal*), films, flicks (*slang*), motion pictures, movies, pictures

cipher 1. nil, nothing, nought, zero **2.** nobody, nonentity **3.** character, digit, figure, number, numeral, symbol **4.** code, cryptograph **5.** device, logo, mark, monogram

circa about, approximately, around, in the region of, roughly

circle *noun* **1.** band, circumference, coil, cordon, cycle, disc, globe, lap, loop, orb, perimeter, periphery, revolution, ring, round, sphere, turn **2.** area, bounds, circuit, compass, domain, enclosure, field, orbit, province, range, realm, region, scene, sphere **3.** assembly, class, clique, club, company, coterie, crowd, fellowship, fraternity, group, order, school, set, society *~verb* **4.** belt, circumnavigate, circumscribe, coil, compass, curve, encircle, enclose, encompass, envelop, gird, hem in, pivot, revolve, ring, rotate, surround, tour, whirl

circuit 1. area, compass, course, journey, lap, orbit, perambulation, revolution, round, route, tour, track **2.** boundary, bounding line, bounds, circumference, compass, district, limit, pale, range, region, tract

circuitous ambagious (*archaic*), devious, indirect, labyrinthine, meandering, oblique, rambling, roundabout, tortuous, winding

▷ **Antonyms** as the crow flies, direct, straight, undeviating, unswerving

circuitousness deviousness, indirectness, obliqueness, rambling, roundaboutness, tortuousness

circulate 1. broadcast, diffuse, disseminate, distribute, issue, make known, promulgate, propagate, publicize, publish, spread **2.** flow, gyrate, radiate, revolve, rotate

circulation 1. currency, dissemination, distribution, spread, transmission, vogue **2.** circling, flow, motion, rotation **3.** bloodstream

circumference ambit, border, boundary, bounds, circuit, edge, extremity, fringe, limits, outline, pale, perimeter, periphery, rim, verge

circumlocution beating about the bush (*informal*), diffuseness, discursiveness, euphemism, indirectness, periphrasis, prolixity, redundancy, wordiness

circumscribe bound, confine, define, delimit, delineate, demarcate, encircle, enclose, encompass, environ, hem in, limit, mark off, restrain, restrict, straiten, surround

circumspect attentive, canny, careful, cautious, deliberate, discreet, discriminating, guarded, heedful, judicious, observant, politic, prudent, sagacious, sage, vigilant, wary, watchful

▷ **Antonyms** bold, careless, daring, foolhardy, heedless, imprudent, rash, venturous

circumspection canniness, care, caution, chariness, deliberation, discretion, keeping one's head down, prudence, wariness

circumstance accident, condition, contingency, detail, element, event, fact, factor, happening, incident, item, occurrence, particular, position, respect, situation

circumstances lie of the land, lifestyle, means, position, resources, situation, state, state of affairs, station, status, times

circumstantial conjectural, contingent, detailed, founded on circumstances, hearsay, incidental, indirect, inferential, particular, presumptive, provisional, specific

circumvent beguile, bypass, deceive, dupe, elude, ensnare, entrap, evade, hoodwink, mislead, outflank, outgeneral, outwit, overreach, sidestep, steer clear of, thwart, trick

circumvention chicanery, deceit, deception, dodge, duplicity, evasion, fraud, guile, imposition, imposture, trickery, wiles

cistern basin, reservoir, sink, tank, vat

citadel bastion, fastness, fortification, fortress, keep, stronghold, tower

citation 1. commendation, excerpt, illustration, passage, quotation, quote, reference, source **2.** award, commendation, mention

cite 1. adduce, advance, allude to, enumerate, evidence, extract, mention, name, quote, specify **2.** *Law* call, subpoena, summon

citizen burgess, burgher, denizen, dweller, freeman, inhabitant, ratepayer, resident, subject, townsman

city 1. *noun* conurbation, megalopolis, metropolis, municipality **2.** *~adjective* civic, metropolitan, municipal, urban

civic borough, communal, community, local, municipal, public

civil 1. civic, domestic, home, interior, municipal, political **2.** accommodating, affable, civilized, complaisant, courteous, courtly, obliging, polished, polite, refined, urbane, well-bred, well-mannered

▷ **Antonyms** (*sense 1*) military, religious, state (*sense 2*) discourteous, ill-mannered, impolite, rude, uncivil, unfriendly, ungracious, unpleasant

civility affability, amiability, breeding, complaisance, cordiality, courteousness, courtesy, good manners, graciousness, politeness, politesse, tact, urbanity

civilization 1. advancement, cultivation, culture, development, education, enlightenment, progress, refinement, sophistication **2.** community, nation, people, polity, society **3.** customs, mores, way of life

civilize cultivate, educate, enlighten, hu~

manize, improve, polish, refine, sophisticate, tame

civilized cultured, educated, enlightened, humane, polite, sophisticated, tolerant, urbane

▷ **Antonyms** barbarous, green, ignorant, naive, primitive, simple, uncivilized, uncultivated, uncultured, undeveloped, uneducated, unenlightened, unsophisticated, untutored, wild

claim 1. *verb* allege, ask, assert, call for, challenge, collect, demand, exact, hold, insist, maintain, need, pick up, profess, require, take, uphold **2.** *~noun* affirmation, allegation, application, assertion, call, demand, petition, pretension, privilege, protestation, request, requirement, right, title

claimant applicant, petitioner, pretender, suppliant, supplicant

clairvoyant 1. *adjective* extrasensory, fey, oracular, prescient, prophetic, psychic, second-sighted, sibylline, telepathic, vatic, visionary **2.** *~noun* augur, diviner, fortune-teller, haruspex, oracle, prophet, prophetess, seer, sibyl, soothsayer, telepath, telepathist, visionary

clamber claw, climb, scale, scrabble, scramble, shin

clammy close, damp, dank, drizzly, moist, pasty, slimy, sticky, sweating, sweaty

clamorous blaring, deafening, insistent, lusty, noisy, riotous, strident, tumultuous, uproarious, vehement, vociferous

clamour agitation, babel, blare, brouhaha, commotion, din, exclamation, hubbub, hullabaloo, noise, outcry, racket, shout, shouting, uproar, vociferation

clamp 1. *noun* bracket, fastener, grip, press, vice **2.** *~verb* brace, clinch, fasten, fix, impose, make fast, secure

clan band, brotherhood, clique, coterie, faction, family, fraternity, gens, group, house, order, race, schism, sect, sept, set, society, sodality, tribe

clandestine cloak-and-dagger, closet, concealed, covert, fraudulent, furtive, hidden, private, secret, sly, stealthy, surreptitious, underground, underhand, under-the-counter

clang 1. *verb* bong, chime, clank, clash, jangle, resound, reverberate, ring, toll **2.** *~noun* clangour, ding-dong, knell, reverberation

clannish cliquish, exclusive, insular, narrow, sectarian, select, unfriendly

clap 1. acclaim, applaud, cheer, give (someone) a big hand **2.** bang, pat, punch, slap, strike gently, thrust, thwack, wallop (*informal*), whack

▷ **Antonyms** (*sense 1*) blow a raspberry, boo, catcall, hiss, jeer

claptrap affectation, balls (*taboo slang*), bilge (*informal*), blarney, bombast, bosh (*informal*), bull (*slang*), bullshit (*taboo slang*), bunk (*informal*), bunkum *or* buncombe (*chiefly U.S.*), cobblers (*Brit. taboo slang*), crap (*slang*), drivel, eyewash (*informal*), flannel (*Brit. informal*), garbage (*informal*), guff (*slang*), hogwash, hokum (*slang, chiefly U.S. & Canad.*), horsefeathers (*U.S. slang*), hot air (*informal*), humbug, insincerity, moonshine, nonsense, pap, piffle (*informal*), poppycock (*informal*), rodomontade (*literary*), rot, rubbish, shit (*taboo slang*), tommyrot, tosh (*slang, chiefly Brit.*), trash, tripe (*informal*), twaddle

clarification elucidation, explanation, exposition, illumination, interpretation, simplification

clarify 1. clear the air, clear up, elucidate, explain, explicate, illuminate, interpret, make plain, resolve, simplify, throw *or* shed light on **2.** cleanse, purify, refine

clarion *adjective* blaring, clear, inspiring, loud, ringing, stirring, strident

clarity clearness, comprehensibility, definition, explicitness, intelligibility, limpidity, lucidity, obviousness, precision, simplicity, transparency

▷ **Antonyms** cloudiness, complexity, complication, dullness, haziness, imprecision, intricacy, murkiness, obscurity

clash *verb* **1.** bang, clang, clank, clatter, crash, jangle, jar, rattle **2.** conflict, cross swords, feud, grapple, lock horns, quarrel, war, wrangle *~noun* **3.** brush, collision, conflict, confrontation, difference of opinion, disagreement, fight, showdown (*informal*)

clasp *verb* **1.** concatenate, connect, fasten **2.** attack, clutch, embrace, enfold, grapple, grasp, grip, hold, hug, press, seize, squeeze *~noun* **3.** brooch, buckle, catch, clip, fastener, fastening, grip, hasp, hook, pin, press stud, snap **4.** embrace, grasp, grip, hold, hug

class 1. *noun* caste, category, classification, collection, denomination, department, division, genre, genus, grade, group, grouping, kind, league, order, rank, set, sort, species, sphere, stamp, status, type, value **2.** *~verb* brand, categorize, classify, codify, designate, grade, group, label, rank, rate

classic *adjective* **1.** best, consummate, finest, first-rate, masterly, world-class **2.** archetypal, definitive, exemplary, ideal, master, model, paradigmatic, quintessential, standard **3.** characteristic, regular, standard, time-honoured, typical, usual **4.** abiding, ageless, deathless, enduring, immortal, lasting, undying *~noun* **5.** exemplar, masterpiece, masterwork, model, paradigm, prototype, standard

▷ **Antonyms** *~adjective* inferior, modern, poor, second-rate, terrible, unrefined, unrepresentative *~noun* trash

classical 1. chaste, elegant, harmonious, pure, refined, restrained, symmetrical, understated, well-proportioned **2.** Attic, Augustan, Grecian, Greek, Hellenic, Latin, Roman

classification analysis, arrangement, cataloguing, categorization, codification, grading, sorting, taxonomy

classify arrange, catalogue, categorize, codify, dispose, distribute, file, grade, pigeonhole, rank, sort, systematize, tabulate

classy elegant, exclusive, high-class, high-toned, posh (*informal, chiefly Brit.*), ritzy (*slang*), select, stylish, superior, swanky (*informal*), swish (*informal, chiefly Brit.*), top-drawer, up-market, urbane

clause 1. article, chapter, condition, paragraph, part, passage, section **2.** heading, item, point, provision, proviso, rider, specification, stipulation

claw 1. *noun* nail, nipper, pincer, talon, tentacle, unguis **2.** *~verb* dig, graze, lacerate, mangle, maul, rip, scrabble, scrape, scratch, tear

clean *adjective* **1.** faultless, flawless, fresh, hygienic, immaculate, impeccable, laundered, pure, sanitary, spotless, squeaky-clean, unblemished, unsoiled, unspotted, unstained, unsullied, washed **2.** antiseptic, clarified, decontaminated, natural, purified, sterile, sterilized, unadulterated, uncontaminated, unpolluted **3.** chaste, decent, exemplary, good, honourable, impeccable, innocent, moral, pure, respectable, undefiled, upright, virtuous **4.** delicate, elegant, graceful, neat, simple, tidy, trim, uncluttered **5.** complete, conclusive, decisive, entire, final, perfect, thorough, total, unimpaired, whole *~verb* **6.** bath, cleanse, deodorize, disinfect, do up, dust, launder, lave, mop, purge, purify, rinse, sanitize, scour, scrub, sponge, swab, sweep, vacuum, wash, wipe

▷ **Antonyms** *~adjective* (*sense 1*) dirty, filthy, mucky, scuzzy (*slang, chiefly U.S.*), soiled, sullied, unwashed (*sense 2*) adulterated, contaminated, infected, polluted (*sense 3*) dishonourable, immoral, impure, indecent, unchaste (*sense 4*) chaotic, disorderly, disorganized, higgledy-piggledy (*informal*), shambolic (*informal*), untidy *~verb* adulterate, defile, dirty, disorder, disorganize, infect, mess up, pollute, soil, stain

clean-cut chiselled, clear, definite, etched, neat, outlined, sharp, trim, well-defined

cleanse absolve, clean, clear, lustrate, purge, purify, rinse, scour, scrub, wash

cleanser detergent, disinfectant, purifier, scourer, soap, soap powder, solvent

clear[1] *adjective* **1.** bright, cloudless, fair, fine, halcyon, light, luminous, shining, sunny, unclouded, undimmed **2.** apparent, articulate, audible, blatant, bold, coherent, comprehensible, conspicuous, cut-and-dried (*informal*), definite, distinct, evident, explicit, express, incontrovertible, intelligible, lucid, manifest, obvious, palpable, patent, perceptible, plain, pronounced, recognizable, unambiguous, unequivocal, unmistakable, unquestionable **3.** empty, free, open, smooth, unhampered, unhindered, unimpeded, unlimited, unobstructed **4.** crystalline, glassy, limpid, pellucid, see-through, translucent, transparent **5.** certain, convinced, decided, definite, positive, resolved, satisfied, sure **6.** clean, guiltless, immaculate, innocent, pure, sinless, stainless, unblemished, undefiled, untarnished, untroubled

▷ **Antonyms** (*sense 1*) cloudy, dark, dull, foggy, hazy, misty, murky, overcast, stormy (*sense 2*) ambiguous, confused, doubtful, equivocal, hidden, inarticulate, inaudible, incoherent, indistinct, inexplicit, obscured, unrecognizable (*sense 3*) barricaded, blocked, closed, engaged, hampered, impeded, obstructed (*sense 4*) cloudy, muddy, non-translucent, non-transparent, opaque, turbid

clear[2] *verb* **1.** clean, cleanse, erase, purify, refine, sweep away, tidy (up), wipe **2.** break up, brighten, clarify, lighten **3.** absolve, acquit, excuse, exonerate, justify, vindicate **4.** emancipate, free, liberate, set free **5.** disengage, disentangle, extricate, free, loosen, open, rid, unblock, unclog, unload, unpack **6.** jump, leap, miss, pass over, vault **7.** acquire, earn, gain, make, reap, secure

▷ **Antonyms** (*sense 3*) accuse, blame, charge, condemn, convict, find guilty

clearance 1. authorization, blank cheque, consent, endorsement, go-ahead (*informal*), green light, leave, O.K. *or* okay (*informal*), permission, sanction **2.** allowance, gap, headroom, margin **3.** depopulation, emptying, evacuation, eviction, removal, unpeopling, withdrawal

clear-cut black-and-white, cut-and-dried (*informal*), definite, explicit, plain, precise, specific, straightforward, unambiguous, unequivocal

clearing dell, glade

clearly beyond doubt, distinctly, evidently, incontestably, incontrovertibly, markedly, obviously, openly, overtly, undeniably, undoubtedly

clearness audibility, brightness, clarity, coherence, distinctness, glassiness, intelligibility, lucidity, luminosity, transparency

clear out 1. empty, exhaust, get rid of, sort, tidy up **2.** beat it (*slang*), decamp, depart, hook it (*slang*), leave, make oneself scarce, make tracks, pack one's bags (*informal*), retire, slope off, take oneself off, withdraw

clear up 1. answer, clarify, elucidate, ex~

plain, resolve, solve, straighten out, unravel **2.** order, rearrange, tidy (up)

cleave[1] *verb* abide by, adhere, agree, attach, be devoted to, be true, cling, cohere, hold, remain, stand by, stick

cleave[2] *verb* crack, dissever, disunite, divide, hew, open, part, rend, rive, sever, slice, split, sunder, tear asunder

cleft 1. *noun* breach, break, chasm, chink, crack, cranny, crevice, fissure, fracture, gap, opening, rent, rift **2.** *~adjective* cloven, parted, rent, riven, ruptured, separated, split, sundered, torn

clemency compassion, forbearance, forgiveness, humanity, indulgence, kindness, leniency, mercifulness, mercy, mildness, moderation, pity, quarter, soft-heartedness, tenderness

clement 1. compassionate, forbearing, forgiving, gentle, humane, indulgent, kind, kind-hearted, lenient, merciful, mild, soft-hearted, tender **2.** balmy, calm, fair, fine, mild, temperate

clergy churchmen, clergymen, clerics, ecclesiastics, first estate, holy orders, ministry, priesthood, the cloth

clergyman chaplain, cleric, curate, divine, father, man of God, man of the cloth, minister, padre, parson, pastor, priest, rabbi, rector, reverend (*informal*), vicar

clerical 1. ecclesiastical, pastoral, priestly, sacerdotal **2.** book-keeping, clerkish, clerkly, office, secretarial, stenographic

clever able, adroit, apt, astute, brainy (*informal*), bright, canny, capable, cunning, deep, dexterous, discerning, expert, gifted, ingenious, intelligent, inventive, keen, knowing, knowledgeable, quick, quick-witted, rational, resourceful, sagacious, sensible, shrewd, skilful, smart, talented, witty

▷ **Antonyms** awkward, boring, clumsy, dense, dull, ham-fisted (*informal*), inept, inexpert, maladroit, slow, stupid, thick, unaccomplished, unimaginative, witless

cleverness ability, adroitness, astuteness, brains, brightness, canniness, dexterity, flair, gift, gumption (*Brit. informal*), ingenuity, intelligence, nous (*Brit. slang*), quickness, quick wits, resourcefulness, sagacity, sense, sharpness, shrewdness, smartness, smarts (*slang, chiefly U.S.*), suss (*slang*), talent, wit

cliché banality, bromide, chestnut (*informal*), commonplace, hackneyed phrase, old saw, platitude, stereotype, truism

click *noun/verb* **1.** beat, clack, snap, tick *~verb* **2.** *informal* become clear, come home (to), fall into place, make sense **3.** *slang* be compatible, be on the same wavelength, feel a rapport, get on, get on like a house on fire (*informal*), go over, hit it off (*informal*), make a hit, succeed, take to each other

client applicant, buyer, consumer, customer, dependant, habitué, patient, patron, protégé, shopper

clientele business, clients, customers, following, market, patronage, regulars, trade

cliff bluff, crag, escarpment, face, overhang, precipice, rock face, scar, scarp

climactic climactical, critical, crucial, decisive, paramount, peak

climate 1. clime, country, region, temperature, weather **2.** ambience, disposition, feeling, mood, temper, tendency, trend

climax 1. *noun* acme, apogee, crest, culmination, head, height, highlight, high spot (*informal*), *ne plus ultra,* pay-off (*informal*), peak, summit, top, zenith **2.** *~verb* come to a head, culminate, peak

climb ascend, clamber, mount, rise, scale, shin up, soar, top

climb down 1. descend, dismount **2.** back down, eat crow (*U.S. informal*), eat one's words, retract, retreat

clinch 1. assure, cap, conclude, confirm, decide, determine, seal, secure, set the seal on, settle, sew up (*informal*), tip the balance, verify **2.** bolt, clamp, fasten, fix, make fast, nail, rivet, secure **3.** clutch, cuddle, embrace, grasp, hug, squeeze

cling adhere, attach to, be true to, clasp, cleave to, clutch, embrace, fasten, grasp, grip, hug, stick, twine round

clinical analytic, antiseptic, cold, detached, disinterested, dispassionate, emotionless, impersonal, objective, scientific, unemotional

clip[1] **1.** *verb* crop, curtail, cut, cut short, dock, pare, prune, shear, shorten, snip, trim **2.** *~noun/verb informal* belt (*informal*), blow, box, clout (*informal*), cuff, knock, punch, skelp (*dialect*), smack, thump, wallop (*informal*), whack **3.** *~noun informal* gallop, lick (*informal*), rate, speed, velocity

clip[2] *verb* attach, fasten, fix, hold, pin, staple

clipping cutting, excerpt, extract, piece

clique cabal, circle, clan, coterie, crew (*informal*), crowd, faction, gang, group, mob, pack, posse (*informal*), schism, set

cloak 1. *verb* camouflage, conceal, cover, disguise, hide, mask, obscure, screen, veil **2.** *~noun* blind, cape, coat, cover, front, mantle, mask, pretext, shield, wrap

clodhopper booby, boor, bumpkin, clown, galoot (*slang, chiefly U.S.*), loon (*informal*), lout, oaf, yokel

clog 1. *verb* block, bung, burden, congest, dam up, hamper, hinder, impede, jam, obstruct, occlude, shackle, stop up **2.** *~noun* burden, dead weight, drag, encumbrance, hindrance, impediment, obstruction

cloistered cloistral, confined, hermitic, insulated, reclusive, restricted, seclud~

ed, sequestered, sheltered, shielded, shut off, withdrawn
▷ **Antonyms** extrovert, genial, gregarious, outgoing, public, sociable, social

close[1] *verb* **1.** bar, block, bung, choke, clog, confine, cork, fill, lock, obstruct, plug, seal, secure, shut, shut up, stop up **2.** axe (*informal*), cease, complete, conclude, culminate, discontinue, end, finish, mothball, shut down, terminate, wind up **3.** come together, connect, couple, fuse, grapple, join, unite
▷ **Antonyms** (*sense 1*) clear, free, open, release, unblock, unclog, uncork, unstop, widen (*sense 2*) begin, commence, initiate, open, start (*sense 3*) disconnect, disjoin, disunite, divide, part, separate, split, uncouple

close[2] *adjective* **1.** adjacent, adjoining, a hop, skip and a jump away, approaching, at hand, cheek by jowl, handy, hard by, imminent, impending, just round the corner, near, nearby, neighbouring, nigh, proximate, upcoming, within sniffing distance, within spitting distance (*informal*), within striking distance (*informal*) **2.** compact, congested, cramped, cropped, crowded, dense, impenetrable, jam-packed, packed, short, solid, thick, tight **3.** accurate, conscientious, exact, faithful, literal, precise, strict **4.** alert, assiduous, attentive, careful, concentrated, detailed, dogged, earnest, fixed, intense, intent, keen, minute, painstaking, rigorous, searching, thorough **5.** attached, confidential, dear, devoted, familiar, inseparable, intimate, loving **6.** airless, confined, frowsty, fuggy, heavy, humid, muggy, oppressive, stale, stifling, stuffy, suffocating, sweltering, thick, unventilated **7.** hidden, private, reticent, retired, secluded, secret, secretive, taciturn, uncommunicative, unforthcoming **8.** illiberal, mean, mingy (*Brit. informal*), miserly, near, niggardly, parsimonious, penurious, stingy, tight as a duck's arse (*taboo slang*), tight-fisted, ungenerous
▷ **Antonyms** (*sense 1*) distant, far, far away, far off, future, outlying, remote (*sense 2*) dispersed, empty, free, loose, penetrable, porous, uncongested, uncrowded (*sense 5*) alienated, aloof, chilly, cold, cool, distant, indifferent, standoffish, unfriendly (*sense 6*) airy, fresh, refreshing, roomy, spacious (*sense 8*) charitable, extravagant, generous, lavish, liberal, magnanimous, unstinting

close[3] *noun* cessation, completion, conclusion, culmination, denouement, end, ending, finale, finish, run-in, termination

closed 1. fastened, locked, out of business, out of service, sealed, shut **2.** concluded, decided, ended, finished, over, resolved, settled, terminated **3.** exclusive, restricted
▷ **Antonyms** (*sense 1*) ajar, open, unclosed, unfastened, unlocked, unsealed

closure 1. cessation, closing, conclusion, end, finish, stoppage **2.** bung, cap, lid, plug, seal, stopper **3.** *in a deliberative assembly* cloture, guillotine

clot *noun* **1.** clotting, coagulation, curdling, embolism, embolus, gob, lump, mass, occlusion, thrombus **2.** ass, berk (*Brit. slang*), buffoon, charlie (*Brit. informal*), coot, dickhead (*slang*), dipstick (*Brit. slang*), divvy (*Brit. slang*), dolt, dope (*informal*), dork (*slang*), dunderhead, dweeb (*U.S. slang*), fathead (*informal*), fool, fuckwit (*taboo slang*), geek (*slang*), gobshite (*Irish taboo slang*), gonzo (*slang*), idiot, jerk (*slang, chiefly U.S. & Canad.*), nerd *or* nurd (*slang*), nincompoop, nit (*informal*), nitwit (*informal*), numbskull *or* numskull, numpty (*Scot. informal*), pillock (*Brit. slang*), plank (*Brit. slang*), plonker (*slang*), prat (*slang*), prick (*slang*), schmuck (*U.S. slang*), twerp *or* twirp (*informal*), twit (*informal, chiefly Brit.*), wally (*slang*) ~*verb* **3.** coagulate, coalesce, congeal, curdle, jell, thicken

cloth dry goods, fabric, material, stuff, textiles

clothe accoutre, apparel, array, attire, bedizen (*archaic*), caparison, cover, deck, doll up (*slang*), drape, dress, endow, enwrap, equip, fit out, garb, get ready, habit, invest, outfit, rig, robe, swathe
▷ **Antonyms** disrobe, divest, expose, strip, strip off, unclothe, uncover, undress

clothes, clothing apparel, attire, clobber (*Brit. slang*), costume, dress, duds (*informal*), ensemble, garb, garments, gear (*informal*), get-up (*informal*), glad rags (*informal*), habits, outfit, raiment (*archaic or poetic*), rigout (*informal*), threads (*slang*), togs (*informal*), vestments, vesture, wardrobe, wear

cloud *noun* **1.** billow, darkness, fog, gloom, haze, mist, murk, nebula, nebulosity, obscurity, vapour **2.** crowd, dense mass, flock, horde, host, multitude, shower, swarm, throng ~*verb* **3.** becloud, darken, dim, eclipse, obfuscate, obscure, overcast, overshadow, shade, shadow, veil **4.** confuse, disorient, distort, impair, muddle, muddy the waters

cloudy blurred, confused, dark, dim, dismal, dull, dusky, emulsified, gloomy, hazy, indistinct, leaden, louring *or* lowering, muddy, murky, nebulous, obscure, opaque, overcast, sombre, sullen, sunless
▷ **Antonyms** bright, clear, distinct, fair, obvious, plain, sunny, uncloudy

clout 1. *verb* box, chin (*slang*), clobber (*slang*), cuff, deck (*slang*), hit, lay one on (*slang*), punch, skelp (*dialect*), sock (*slang*), strike, thump, tonk (*informal*), wallop (*informal*), wham **2.** *~noun* authority, bottom, influence, power, prestige, pull, standing, weight

cloven bisected, cleft, divided, split

clown *noun* **1.** buffoon, comedian, dolt, fool, harlequin, jester, joker, merry-andrew, mountebank, pierrot, prankster, punchinello **2.** boor, clodhopper (*informal*), hind (*obsolete*), peasant, swain (*archaic*), yahoo, yokel *~verb* **3.** act the fool, act the goat, jest, mess about, piss about *or* around (*taboo slang*), play the fool, play the goat

clownish **1.** comic, foolish, galumphing (*informal*), nonsensical, slapstick, zany **2.** awkward, boorish, churlish, clumsy, ill-bred, rough, rude, rustic, uncivil, ungainly, vulgar

cloy disgust, glut, gorge, nauseate, sate, satiate, sicken, surfeit, weary

cloying excessive, icky (*informal*), nauseating, oversweet, sickly, treacly

club **1.** *noun* bat, bludgeon, cosh (*Brit.*), cudgel, stick, truncheon **2.** *~verb* bash, baste, batter, beat, bludgeon, clobber (*slang*), clout (*informal*), cosh (*Brit.*), hammer, pommel (*rare*), pummel, strike **3.** *~noun* association, circle, clique, company, fraternity, group, guild, lodge, order, set, society, sodality, union

clue evidence, hint, indication, inkling, intimation, lead, pointer, sign, suggestion, suspicion, tip, tip-off, trace

clump **1.** *noun* bunch, bundle, cluster, mass, shock **2.** *~verb* bumble, clomp, lumber, plod, stamp, stomp, stump, thud, thump, tramp

clumsy accident-prone, awkward, blundering, bumbling, bungling, butter-fingered (*informal*), cack-handed (*informal*), gauche, gawky, ham-fisted (*informal*), ham-handed (*informal*), heavy, ill-shaped, inept, inexpert, klutzy (*U.S. & Canad. slang*), like a bull in a china shop, lumbering, maladroit, ponderous, uncoordinated, uncouth, ungainly, unhandy, unskilful, unwieldy

▷ **Antonyms** adept, adroit, competent, deft, dexterous, expert, graceful, handy, proficient, skilful

cluster **1.** *noun* assemblage, batch, bunch, clump, collection, gathering, group, knot **2.** *~verb* assemble, bunch, collect, flock, gather, group

clutch catch (up), clasp, cling to, embrace, fasten, grab, grapple, grasp, grip, seize, snatch

clutches claws, control, custody, grasp, grip, hands, keeping, possession, power, sway

clutter **1.** *noun* confusion, disarray, disorder, hotchpotch, jumble, litter, mess, muddle, untidiness **2.** *~verb* litter, scatter, strew

▷ **Antonyms** *~noun* neatness, order, organization, tidiness *~verb* arrange, order, organize, straighten, tidy

coach *noun* **1.** bus, car, carriage, charabanc, vehicle **2.** handler, instructor, teacher, trainer, tutor *~verb* **3.** cram, drill, exercise, instruct, prepare, train, tutor

coagulate clot, congeal, curdle, jell, thicken

coalesce amalgamate, blend, cohere, combine, come together, commingle, commix, consolidate, fraternize, fuse, incorporate, integrate, meld, merge, mix, unite

coalition affiliation, alliance, amalgam, amalgamation, association, bloc, combination, compact, confederacy, confederation, conjunction, fusion, integration, league, merger, union

coarse **1.** boorish, brutish, coarse-grained, foul-mouthed, gruff, loutish, rough, rude, uncivil **2.** bawdy, earthy, immodest, impolite, improper, impure, indelicate, inelegant, mean, offensive, raunchy (*slang*), ribald, rude, smutty, vulgar **3.** coarse-grained, crude, homespun, impure, rough-hewn, unfinished, unpolished, unprocessed, unpurified, unrefined

▷ **Antonyms** (*senses 1 & 2*) civilized, cultured, elegant, fine, genteel, inoffensive, pleasant, polished, polite, proper, refined, sophisticated, urbane, well-bred, well-mannered (*sense 3*) fine-grained, polished, purified, refined, smooth, soft

coarsen anaesthetize, blunt, callous, deaden, desensitize, dull, harden, indurate, roughen

coarseness bawdiness, boorishness, crudity, earthiness, indelicacy, offensiveness, poor taste, ribaldry, roughness, smut, smuttiness, uncouthness, unevenness

coast **1.** *noun* beach, border, coastline, littoral, seaboard, seaside, shore, strand **2.** *~verb* cruise, drift, freewheel, get by, glide, sail, taxi

coat *noun* **1.** fleece, fur, hair, hide, pelt, skin, wool **2.** coating, covering, layer, overlay *~verb* **3.** apply, Artex (*Trademark*), cover, plaster, smear, spread

coating blanket, coat, covering, dusting, film, finish, glaze, lamination, layer, membrane, patina, sheet, skin, varnish, veneer

coax allure, beguile, cajole, decoy, entice, flatter, inveigle, persuade, prevail upon, soft-soap (*informal*), soothe, sweet-talk (*informal*), talk into, twist (someone's) arm, wheedle

▷ **Antonyms** browbeat, bully, coerce, force, harass, intimidate, pressurize, threaten

cobble botch, bungle, clout, mend, patch, tinker

cock **1.** *noun* chanticleer, cockerel, rooster **2.** *~verb* perk up, prick, raise, stand up

cockeyed absurd, askew, asymmetrical, awry, crazy, crooked, lopsided, ludicrous, nonsensical, preposterous, skewwhiff (*Brit. informal*), squint (*informal*)

cocksure arrogant, brash, bumptious, cocky, full of oneself, hubristic, overconfident, presumptuous

cocky arrogant, brash, cocksure, conceited, egotistical, full of oneself, lordly, swaggering, swollen-headed, vain
▷ **Antonyms** hesitant, lacking confidence, modest, self-effacing, uncertain, unsure

cocoon cushion, envelop, insulate, pad, protect, swaddle, swathe, wrap

coddle baby, cosset, humour, indulge, mollycoddle, nurse, pamper, pet, spoil, wet-nurse (*informal*)

code **1.** cipher, cryptograph **2.** canon, convention, custom, ethics, etiquette, manners, maxim, regulations, rules, system

codify catalogue, classify, collect, condense, digest, organize, summarize, systematize, tabulate

coerce browbeat, bulldoze (*informal*), bully, compel, constrain, dragoon, drive, force, intimidate, press-gang, pressurize, railroad (*informal*), twist (someone's) arm (*informal*)

coercion browbeating, bullying, compulsion, constraint, duress, force, intimidation, pressure, strong-arm tactics (*informal*), threats

coeval coetaneous (*rare*), coexistent, contemporaneous, contemporary, synchronous

coffer ark (*dialect*), case, casket, chest, kist (*Scot. & Northern English dialect*), repository, strongbox, treasure chest, treasury

coffers assets, capital, finances, funds, means, reserves, treasury, vaults

cogency conviction, force, potency, power, strength

cogent compelling, compulsive, conclusive, convincing, effective, forceful, forcible, influential, irresistible, potent, powerful, strong, urgent, weighty

cogitate consider, contemplate, deliberate, meditate, mull over, muse, ponder, reflect, ruminate, think

cogitation consideration, contemplation, deliberation, meditation, reflection, rumination, thought

cognate affiliated, akin, alike, allied, analogous, associated, connected, kindred, related, similar

cognition apprehension, awareness, comprehension, discernment, insight, intelligence, perception, reasoning, understanding

cognizance acknowledgment, apprehension, cognition, knowledge, notice, perception, percipience, recognition, regard

cognizant acquainted, aware, clued-up (*informal*), conscious, conversant, familiar, informed, knowledgeable, versed

cohere **1.** adhere, bind, cling, coalesce, combine, consolidate, fuse, glue, hold, stick, unite **2.** agree, be connected, be consistent, correspond, hang together, harmonize, hold good, hold water, square

coherence agreement, comprehensibility, concordance, congruity, connection, consistency, consonance, correspondence, intelligibility, rationality, union, unity

coherent articulate, comprehensible, consistent, intelligible, logical, lucid, meaningful, orderly, organized, rational, reasoned, systematic
▷ **Antonyms** confusing, disjointed, illogical, incomprehensible, inconsistent, meaningless, rambling, unintelligible, vague

cohort **1.** band, company, contingent, legion, regiment, squadron, troop **2.** *chiefly U.S.* accomplice, assistant, comrade, follower, henchman, mate, myrmidon, partner, protagonist, sidekick (*slang*), supporter

coil convolute, curl, entwine, loop, snake, spiral, twine, twist, wind, wreathe, writhe

coin **1.** *verb* conceive, create, fabricate, forge, formulate, frame, invent, make up, mint, mould, originate, think up **2.** *~noun* cash, change, copper, dosh (*Brit. & Austral. slang*), money, silver, specie

coincide **1.** be concurrent, coexist, occur simultaneously, synchronize **2.** accord, harmonize, match, quadrate, square, tally **3.** acquiesce, agree, concur, correspond
▷ **Antonyms** be inconsistent, be unlike, contradict, differ, disagree, diverge, divide, part, separate

coincidence **1.** accident, chance, eventuality, fluke, fortuity, happy accident, luck, stroke of luck **2.** concomitance, concurrence, conjunction, correlation, correspondence, synchronism

coincident coinciding, concomitant, concurring, consonant, contemporaneous, coordinate, correspondent, synchronous

coincidental **1.** accidental, casual, chance, fluky (*informal*), fortuitous, unintentional, unplanned **2.** coincident, concomitant, concurrent, simultaneous, synchronous
▷ **Antonyms** (*sense 1*) calculated, deliberate, done on purpose, intentional, planned, prearranged

coitus coition, congress, copulation, coupling, mating, nookie (*slang*), rumpy-pumpy (*slang*), sexual intercourse, the other (*informal*), union

cold *adjective* **1.** arctic, biting, bitter, bleak, brumal, chill, chilly, cool, freezing, frigid, frosty, frozen, gelid, harsh, icy, inclement, parky (*Brit. informal*), raw, wintry **2.** benumbed, chilled, chilly, freezing, frozen to the marrow, numbed, shivery **3.** affectless, aloof, apathetic, cold-blooded, dead, distant, frigid, glacial, indifferent, inhospitable, lukewarm, passionless, phlegmatic, reserved, spiritless, standoffish, stony, undemonstrative, unfeeling, unmoved, unresponsive, unsympathetic *~noun* **4.** chill, chilliness, coldness, frigidity, frostiness, iciness, inclemency

▷ **Antonyms** (*sense 1*) balmy, heated, hot, mild, sunny, warm (*sense 3*) alive, animated, caring, compassionate, conscious, demonstrative, emotional, friendly, loving, open, passionate, responsive, spirited, sympathetic, warm

cold-blooded barbarous, brutal, callous, cruel, dispassionate, heartless, inhuman, merciless, pitiless, ruthless, savage, steely, stony-hearted, unemotional, unfeeling, unmoved

▷ **Antonyms** caring, charitable, civilized, concerned, emotional, feeling, friendly, humane, involved, kind, kind-hearted, merciful, open, passionate, sensitive, warm

cold-hearted callous, detached, frigid, hardhearted, harsh, heartless, indifferent, inhuman, insensitive, stony-hearted, uncaring, unfeeling, unkind, unsympathetic

collaborate **1.** cooperate, coproduce, join forces, participate, play ball (*informal*), team up, work together **2.** collude, conspire, cooperate, fraternize

collaboration alliance, association, concert, cooperation, partnership, teamwork

collaborator **1.** associate, colleague, confederate, co-worker, partner, team-mate **2.** collaborationist, fraternizer, quisling, traitor, turncoat

collapse **1.** *verb* break down, cave in, come to nothing, crack up (*informal*), crumple, fail, faint, fall, fall apart at the seams, fold, founder, give way, go belly-up (*informal*), subside **2.** *~noun* breakdown, cave-in, disintegration, downfall, exhaustion, failure, faint, flop, prostration, ruin, slump, subsidence

collar *verb* apprehend, appropriate, capture, catch, catch in the act, grab, lay hands on, nab (*informal*), nail (*informal*), seize

collate adduce, analogize, collect, compare, compose, gather (*Printing*)

collateral *noun* **1.** assurance, deposit, guarantee, pledge, security, surety *~adjective* **2.** concurrent, confirmatory, corroborative, indirect, not lineal, parallel, related, supporting **3.** ancillary, auxiliary, secondary, subordinate

colleague aider, ally, assistant, associate, auxiliary, coadjutor (*rare*), collaborator, companion, comrade, confederate, confrère, fellow worker, helper, partner, team-mate, workmate

collect **1.** accumulate, aggregate, amass, assemble, gather, heap, hoard, save, stockpile **2.** assemble, cluster, congregate, convene, converge, flock together, rally **3.** acquire, muster, obtain, raise, secure, solicit

▷ **Antonyms** disperse, distribute, scatter, spread, strew

collected as cool as a cucumber, calm, composed, confident, cool, keeping one's cool, placid, poised, sedate, self-possessed, serene, together (*slang*), unfazed (*informal*), unperturbable, unperturbed, unruffled

▷ **Antonyms** agitated, distressed, emotional, excitable, irritable, nervous, perturbed, ruffled, shaky, troubled, twitchy (*informal*), unpoised, unsteady

collection **1.** accumulation, anthology, compilation, congeries, heap, hoard, mass, pile, set, stockpile, store **2.** assemblage, assembly, assortment, cluster, company, congregation, convocation, crowd, gathering, group **3.** alms, contribution, offering, offertory

collective aggregate, combined, common, composite, concerted, cooperative, corporate, cumulative, joint, shared, unified, united

▷ **Antonyms** divided, individual, piecemeal, split, uncombined, uncooperative

collide clash, come into collision, conflict, crash, meet head-on

collision **1.** accident, bump, crash, impact, pile-up (*informal*), prang (*informal*), smash **2.** clash, clashing, conflict, confrontation, encounter, opposition, skirmish

colloquial conversational, demotic, everyday, familiar, idiomatic, informal, vernacular

colloquy confabulation, conference, conversation, debate, dialogue, discourse, discussion, talk

collude abet, be in cahoots (*informal*), collaborate, complot, connive, conspire, contrive, intrigue, machinate, plot, scheme

collusion cahoots (*informal*), complicity, connivance, conspiracy, craft, deceit, fraudulent artifice, intrigue, secret understanding

colonist colonial, colonizer, frontiersman, homesteader (*U.S.*), immigrant, pioneer, planter, settler

colonize open up, people, pioneer, populate, put down roots, settle

colonnade arcade, cloisters, covered walk, peristyle, portico

colony community, dependency, domin~

ion, outpost, possession, province, satellite state, settlement, territory

colossal Brobdingnagian, elephantine, enormous, gargantuan, gigantic, ginormous (*informal*), herculean, huge, humongous *or* humungous (*U.S. slang*), immense, mammoth, massive, monstrous, monumental, mountainous, prodigious, stellar (*informal*), titanic, vast
▷ **Antonyms** average, diminutive, little, miniature, minute, ordinary, pygmy *or* pigmy, slight, small, tiny, weak, wee

colour *noun* **1.** colorant, coloration, complexion, dye, hue, paint, pigment, pigmentation, shade, tincture, tinge, tint **2.** animation, bloom, blush, brilliance, flush, glow, liveliness, rosiness, ruddiness, vividness **3.** *figurative* appearance, disguise, excuse, façade, false show, guise, plea, pretence, pretext, semblance *~verb* **4.** colourwash, dye, paint, stain, tinge, tint **5.** *figurative* disguise, distort, embroider, exaggerate, falsify, garble, gloss over, misrepresent, pervert, prejudice, slant, taint **6.** blush, burn, crimson, flush, go as red as a beetroot, go crimson, redden

colourful **1.** bright, brilliant, Day-glo (*Trademark*), intense, jazzy (*informal*), kaleidoscopic, motley, multicoloured, psychedelic, rich, variegated, vibrant, vivid **2.** characterful, distinctive, graphic, interesting, lively, picturesque, rich, stimulating, unusual, vivid
▷ **Antonyms** (*sense 1*) colourless, dark, drab, dreary, dull, faded, pale, washed out (*sense 2*) boring, characterless, dull, flat, lifeless, monotonous, unexciting, uninteresting, unvaried

colourless **1.** achromatic, achromic, anaemic, ashen, bleached, drab, faded, neutral, sickly, wan, washed out **2.** characterless, dreary, insipid, lacklustre, tame, uninteresting, unmemorable, vacuous, vapid
▷ **Antonyms** (*sense 1*) blooming, flushed, glowing, healthy, radiant, robust, ruddy (*sense 2*) animated, bright, colourful, compelling, distinctive, exciting, interesting, unusual

colours **1.** banner, emblem, ensign, flag, standard **2.** *figurative* aspect, breed, character, identity, nature, stamp, strain

coltish frisky, frolicsome, lively, playful, romping, skittish, sportive, unruly

column **1.** cavalcade, file, line, list, procession, queue, rank, row, string, train **2.** caryatid, obelisk, pilaster, pillar, post, shaft, support, upright

columnist correspondent, critic, editor, gossip columnist, journalist, journo (*slang*), reporter, reviewer

coma insensibility, lethargy, oblivion, somnolence, stupor, torpor, trance, unconsciousness

comatose drugged, insensible, lethargic, somnolent, soporose (*Medical*), stupefied, torpid, unconscious

comb *verb* **1.** arrange, curry, dress, groom, untangle **2.** *of flax, wool, etc.* card, hackle, hatchel, heckle, tease, teasel, teazle **3.** *figurative* forage, go through with a fine-tooth comb, hunt, rake, ransack, rummage, scour, screen, search, sift, sweep

combat **1.** *noun* action, battle, conflict, contest, encounter, engagement, fight, skirmish, struggle, war, warfare **2.** *~verb* battle, contend, contest, cope, defy, do battle with, engage, fight, oppose, resist, strive, struggle, withstand
▷ **Antonyms** *~noun* agreement, armistice, peace, surrender, truce *~verb* accept, acquiesce, declare a truce, give up, make peace, support, surrender

combatant **1.** *noun* adversary, antagonist, belligerent, contender, enemy, fighter, fighting man, gladiator, opponent, serviceman, soldier, warrior **2.** *~adjective* battling, belligerent, combative, conflicting, contending, fighting, opposing, warring

combative aggressive, antagonistic, bellicose, belligerent, contentious, militant, pugnacious, quarrelsome, truculent, warlike
▷ **Antonyms** nonaggressive, nonbelligerent, nonviolent, pacific, pacifist, peaceable, peaceful, peace-loving

combination **1.** amalgam, amalgamation, blend, coalescence, composite, connection, meld, mix, mixture **2.** alliance, association, cabal, cartel, coalition, combine, compound, confederacy, confederation, consortium, conspiracy, federation, merger, syndicate, unification, union

combine amalgamate, associate, bind, blend, bond, compound, connect, cooperate, fuse, incorporate, integrate, join (together), link, marry, meld, merge, mix, pool, put together, synthesize, unify, unite
▷ **Antonyms** detach, dissociate, dissolve, disunite, divide, part, separate, sever

combustible explosive, flammable, incendiary, inflammable

come **1.** advance, appear, approach, arrive, become, draw near, enter, happen, materialize, move, move towards, near, occur, originate, show up (*informal*), turn out, turn up (*informal*) **2.** appear, arrive, attain, enter, materialize, reach, show up (*informal*), turn up (*informal*) **3.** fall, happen, occur, take place **4.** arise, emanate, emerge, end up, flow, issue, originate, result, turn out **5.** extend, reach **6.** be available, be made, be offered, be on offer, be produced

come about arise, befall, come to pass, happen, occur, result, take place, transpire (*informal*)

come across bump into (*informal*), chance upon, discover, encounter, find, happen upon, hit upon, light upon, meet, notice, stumble upon, unearth

come along develop, improve, mend, perk up, pick up, progress, rally, recover, recuperate

come apart break, come unstuck, crumble, disintegrate, fall to pieces, give way, separate, split, tear

come at **1**. attain, discover, find, grasp, reach **2**. assail, assault, attack, charge, fall upon, fly at, go for, light into, rush, rush at

comeback **1**. rally, rebound, recovery, resurgence, return, revival, triumph **2**. rejoinder, reply, response, retaliation, retort, riposte

come back reappear, recur, re-enter, return

come between alienate, divide, estrange, interfere, meddle, part, separate, set at odds

come by acquire, get, land, lay hold of, obtain, procure, score (*slang*), secure, take possession of, win

come clean acknowledge, admit, come out of the closet, confess, cough up (*slang*), get (something) off one's chest (*informal*), make a clean breast of, own up, reveal, sing (*slang, chiefly U.S.*), spill one's guts (*slang*)

comedian card (*informal*), clown, comic, funny man, humorist, jester, joker, laugh (*informal*), wag, wit

comedown anticlimax, blow, decline, deflation, demotion, disappointment, humiliation, letdown, reverse, whammy (*informal, chiefly U.S.*)

come down **1**. decline, degenerate, descend, deteriorate, fall, go downhill, go to pot (*informal*), reduce, worsen **2**. choose, decide, favour, recommend

come down on bawl out (*informal*), blast, carpet (*informal*), chew out (*U.S. & Canad. informal*), criticize, dress down (*informal*), give (someone) a rocket (*Brit. & N.Z. informal*), jump on (*informal*), lambast(e), put down, rap over the knuckles, read the riot act, rebuke, reprimand, tear into (*informal*), tear (someone) off a strip (*Brit. informal*)

come down to amount to, boil down to, end up as, result in

come down with ail, be stricken with, catch, contract, fall ill, fall victim to, get, sicken, take, take sick

comedy chaffing, drollery, facetiousness, farce, fun, hilarity, humour, jesting, joking, light entertainment, sitcom (*informal*), slapstick, wisecracking, witticisms

▷ **Antonyms** high drama, melancholy, melodrama, opera, sadness, seriousness, serious play, soap opera, solemnity, tragedy

come forward offer one's services, present *or* proffer oneself, volunteer

come in appear, arrive, cross the threshold, enter, finish, reach, show up (*informal*)

come in for acquire, bear the brunt of, endure, get, receive, suffer

comely **1**. attractive, beautiful, becoming, blooming, bonny, buxom, cute, fair, good-looking, graceful, handsome, lovely, pleasing, pretty, wholesome, winsome **2**. *archaic* decent, decorous, fit, fitting, proper, seemly, suitable

▷ **Antonyms** affected, disagreeable, distasteful, faded, homely, improper, indecorous, mumsy, plain, repulsive, ugly, unattractive, unbecoming, unfitting, unnatural, unpleasant, unseemly

come off go off, happen, occur, succeed, take place, transpire (*informal*)

come on **1**. advance, develop, improve, make headway, proceed, progress **2**. appear, begin, take place

come out **1**. appear, be announced, be divulged, be issued, be published, be released, be reported, be revealed **2**. conclude, end, result, terminate

come out with acknowledge, come clean, declare, disclose, divulge, lay open, own, own up, say

come round **1**. accede, acquiesce, allow, concede, grant, mellow, relent, yield **2**. come to, rally, recover, regain consciousness, revive **3**. call, drop in, pop in, stop by, visit

come through **1**. accomplish, achieve, make the grade (*informal*), prevail, succeed, triumph **2**. endure, survive, weather the storm, withstand

come up arise, crop up, happen, occur, rise, spring up, turn up

comeuppance chastening, deserts, due reward, dues, merit, punishment, recompense, requital, retribution

come up to admit of comparison with, approach, compare with, equal, match, measure up to, meet, resemble, rival, stand *or* bear comparison with

come up with advance, create, discover, furnish, offer, present, produce, propose, provide, submit, suggest

comfort *verb* **1**. alleviate, assuage, cheer, commiserate with, compassionate (*archaic*), console, ease, encourage, enliven, gladden, hearten, inspirit, invigorate, reassure, refresh, relieve, solace, soothe, strengthen *~noun* **2**. aid, alleviation, cheer, compensation, consolation, ease, encouragement, enjoyment, help, relief, satisfaction, succour, support **3**. cosiness, creature comforts, ease, luxury, opulence, snugness, wellbeing

▷ **Antonyms** *~verb* aggravate (*informal*), agitate, annoy, bother, depress, discomfort, distress, excite, hassle (*informal*), irk, irritate, rile, ruffle, sadden, trouble

~*noun* aggravation, annoyance, discouragement, displeasure, hassle (*informal*), inconvenience, irritation

comfortable 1. adequate, agreeable, ample, commodious, convenient, cosy, delightful, easy, enjoyable, homely, loose, loose-fitting, pleasant, relaxing, restful, roomy, snug **2.** at ease, at home, contented, gratified, happy, relaxed, serene **3.** affluent, in clover (*informal*), prosperous, well-off, well-to-do
▷ **Antonyms** (*sense 1*) disagreeable, inadequate, skin-tight, tight, tight-fitting, uncomfortable, unpleasant (*sense 2*) distressed, disturbed, ill at ease, like a fish out of water, miserable, nervous, on tenterhooks, tense, troubled, uncomfortable, uneasy

comforting cheering, consolatory, consoling, encouraging, heart-warming, inspiriting, reassuring, soothing
▷ **Antonyms** alarming, dismaying, disturbing, perplexing, upsetting, worrying

comfortless 1. bleak, cheerless, cold, desolate, dismal, dreary **2.** disconsolate, forlorn, inconsolable, miserable, sick at heart, woebegone, wretched

comic 1. *adjective* amusing, comical, droll, facetious, farcical, funny, humorous, jocular, joking, light, rich, waggish, witty **2.** ~*noun* buffoon, clown, comedian, funny man, humorist, jester, wag, wit
▷ **Antonyms** depressing, melancholy, pathetic, sad, serious, solemn, touching, tragic

comical absurd, amusing, comic, diverting, droll, entertaining, farcical, funny, hilarious, humorous, laughable, ludicrous, priceless, ridiculous, risible, side-splitting, silly, whimsical, zany

coming *adjective* **1.** approaching, at hand, due, en route, forthcoming, future, imminent, impending, in store, in the wind, just round the corner, near, next, nigh, on the cards, upcoming **2.** aspiring, future, promising, up-and-coming ~*noun* **3.** accession, advent, approach, arrival

command *verb* **1.** bid, charge, compel, demand, direct, enjoin, order, require **2.** administer, call the shots, call the tune, control, dominate, govern, handle, head, lead, manage, reign over, rule, supervise, sway ~*noun* **3.** behest, bidding, canon, commandment, decree, demand, direction, directive, edict, fiat, injunction, instruction, mandate, order, precept, requirement, ultimatum **4.** authority, charge, control, direction, domination, dominion, government, grasp, management, mastery, power, rule, supervision, sway, upper hand
▷ **Antonyms** (*sense 1*) appeal (to), ask, beg, beseech, plead, request, supplicate (*sense 2*) be inferior, be subordinate, follow

commandeer appropriate, confiscate, expropriate, hijack, requisition, seize, sequester, sequestrate, usurp

commander boss, captain, chief, C in C, C.O., commander-in-chief, commanding officer, director, head, leader, officer, ruler

commanding 1. advantageous, controlling, decisive, dominant, dominating, superior **2.** assertive, authoritative, autocratic, compelling, forceful, imposing, impressive, peremptory
▷ **Antonyms** retiring, shrinking, shy, submissive, timid, unassertive, unimposing, weak

commemorate celebrate, honour, immortalize, keep, memorialize, observe, pay tribute to, remember, salute, solemnize
▷ **Antonyms** disregard, forget, ignore, omit, overlook, pass over, take no notice of

commemoration ceremony, honouring, memorial service, observance, remembrance, tribute

commemorative celebratory, dedicatory, in honour, in memory, in remembrance, memorial

commence begin, embark on, enter upon, get the show on the road (*informal*), inaugurate, initiate, open, originate, start
▷ **Antonyms** bring *or* come to an end, cease, complete, conclude, desist, end, finish, halt, stop, terminate, wind up

commend 1. acclaim, applaud, approve, compliment, crack up (*informal*), eulogize, extol, praise, recommend, speak highly of **2.** commit, confide, consign, deliver, entrust, hand over, yield
▷ **Antonyms** (*sense 1*) attack, blast, censure, condemn, criticize, denounce, disapprove, knock (*informal*), lambast(e), put down, slam, tear into (*informal*) (*sense 2*) hold back, keep, keep back, retain, withdraw, withhold

commendable admirable, creditable, deserving, estimable, exemplary, laudable, meritorious, praiseworthy, worthy

commendation acclaim, acclamation, approbation, approval, Brownie points, credit, encomium, encouragement, good opinion, panegyric, praise, recommendation

commensurate adequate, appropriate, coextensive, comparable, compatible, consistent, corresponding, due, equivalent, fit, fitting, in accord, proportionate, sufficient

comment *verb* **1.** animadvert, interpose, mention, note, observe, opine, point out, remark, say, utter **2.** annotate, criticize, elucidate, explain, interpret ~*noun* **3.** animadversion, observation, remark, statement **4.** annotation, commentary, criticism, elucidation, explanation, exposition, illustration, note

commentary analysis, critique, descrip~

tion, exegesis, explanation, narration, notes, review, treatise, voice-over

commentator **1.** commenter, reporter, special correspondent, sportscaster **2.** annotator, critic, expositor, interpreter, scholiast

commerce **1.** business, dealing, exchange, merchandising, trade, traffic **2.** communication, dealings, intercourse, relations, socializing

commercial **1.** business, mercantile, profit-making, sales, trade, trading **2.** in demand, marketable, popular, profitable, saleable **3.** exploited, materialistic, mercenary, monetary, pecuniary, profit-making, venal

commingle amalgamate, blend, combine, commix, intermingle, intermix, join, meld, mingle, unite

commiserate compassionate (*archaic*), condole, console, feel for, pity, sympathize

commiseration compassion, condolence, consolation, fellow feeling, pity, sympathy

commission *noun* **1.** appointment, authority, charge, duty, employment, errand, function, mandate, mission, task, trust, warrant **2.** allowance, brokerage, compensation, cut, fee, percentage, rake-off (*slang*), royalties **3.** board, body of commissioners, commissioners, committee, delegation, deputation, representative *~verb* **4.** appoint, authorize, contract, delegate, depute, empower, engage, nominate, order, select, send

commit **1.** carry out, do, enact, execute, perform, perpetrate **2.** commend, confide, consign, deliver, deposit, engage, entrust, give, hand over **3.** align, bind, compromise, endanger, make liable, obligate, pledge, rank **4.** confine, imprison, put in custody

▷ **Antonyms** (*sense 1*) omit (*sense 2*) receive, withhold (*sense 3*) disavow, vacillate, waver (*sense 4*) free, let out, release, set free

commitment **1.** duty, engagement, liability, obligation, responsibility, tie **2.** adherence, dedication, devotion, involvement, loyalty **3.** assurance, guarantee, pledge, promise, undertaking, vow, word

▷ **Antonyms** disavowal, indecisiveness, negation, vacillation, wavering

commodious ample, capacious, comfortable, convenient, expansive, extensive, large, loose, roomy, spacious

commodities goods, merchandise, produce, products, stock, wares

common **1.** a dime a dozen, average, bog-standard (*Brit. & Irish slang*), commonplace, conventional, customary, daily, everyday, familiar, frequent, general, habitual, humdrum, obscure, ordinary, plain, regular, routine, run-of-the-mill, simple, standard, stock, usual, vanilla (*slang*), workaday **2.** accepted, general, popular, prevailing, prevalent, universal, widespread **3.** collective, communal, community, popular, public, social **4.** coarse, hackneyed, inferior, low, pedestrian, plebeian, stale, trite, undistinguished, vulgar

▷ **Antonyms** (*sense 1*) abnormal, distinguished, famous, formal, important, infrequent, noble, outstanding, rare, scarce, sophisticated, strange, superior, uncommon, unknown, unpopular, unusual (*sense 3*) personal, private (*sense 4*) cultured, gentle, refined, sensitive

commonplace **1.** *adjective* banal, common, customary, dime-a-dozen (*informal*), everyday, humdrum, mundane, obvious, ordinary, pedestrian, run-of-the-mill, stale, threadbare, trite, uninteresting, vanilla (*slang*), widespread, worn out **2.** *~noun* banality, cliché, platitude, truism

▷ **Antonyms** *~adjective* exciting, extraordinary, ground-breaking, infrequent, interesting, left-field (*informal*), new, novel, original, rare, strange, uncommon, unfamiliar, unique, unusual

common-sense, common-sensical *adjective* astute, down-to-earth, hard-headed, judicious, level-headed, matter-of-fact, practical, realistic, reasonable, sane, sensible, shrewd, sound

▷ **Antonyms** airy-fairy (*informal*), daft (*informal*), foolish, impractical, irrational, unrealistic, unreasonable, unthinking, unwise

common sense good sense, gumption (*Brit. informal*), horse sense, level-headedness, mother wit, native intelligence, nous (*Brit. slang*), practicality, prudence, reasonableness, smarts (*slang, chiefly U.S.*), sound judgment, soundness, wit

commotion ado, agitation, brouhaha, bustle, disorder, disturbance, excitement, ferment, furore, fuss, hubbub, hue and cry, hullabaloo, hurly-burly, perturbation, racket, riot, rumpus, to-do, tumult, turmoil, upheaval, uproar

communal collective, communistic, community, general, joint, neighbourhood, public, shared

▷ **Antonyms** exclusive, individual, personal, private, single, unshared

commune[1] *verb* **1.** communicate, confer, confide in, converse, discourse, discuss, parley **2.** contemplate, meditate, muse, ponder, reflect

commune[2] *noun* collective, community, cooperative, kibbutz

communicable catching, contagious, infectious, taking, transferable, transmittable

communicate acquaint, announce, be in contact, be in touch, connect, convey, correspond, declare, disclose, disseminate, divulge, impart, inform, make

known, pass on, phone, proclaim, pub~ lish, report, reveal, ring up (*informal, chiefly Brit.*), signify, spread, transmit, unfold
▷ **Antonyms** conceal, cover up, hold back, hush up, keep back, keep secret, keep under wraps, repress, sit on (*in~ formal*), suppress, whitewash (*infor~ mal*), withhold

communication 1. connection, contact, conversation, correspondence, dissemi~ nation, intercourse, link, transmission **2.** announcement, disclosure, dispatch, information, intelligence, message, news, report, statement, word

communications 1. routes, transport, travel **2.** information technology, media, publicity, public relations, telecommu~ nications

communicative candid, chatty, convers~ able, expansive, forthcoming, frank, in~ formative, loquacious, open, outgoing, talkative, unreserved, voluble
▷ **Antonyms** quiet, reserved, reticent, secretive, taciturn, uncommunicative, uninformative, untalkative

communion 1. accord, affinity, agree~ ment, closeness, communing, concord, consensus, converse, fellowship, harmo~ ny, intercourse, participation, rapport, sympathy, togetherness, unity **2.** *Church* Eucharist, Lord's Supper, Mass, Sacrament

communiqué announcement, bulletin, dispatch, news flash, official communi~ cation, report

communism Bolshevism, collectivism, Eurocommunism, Maoism, Marxism, Marxism-Leninism, socialism, Stalin~ ism, state socialism, Titoism, Trotsky~ ism

communist Bolshevik, collectivist, Marx~ ist, Red (*informal*), socialist

community 1. association, body politic, brotherhood, commonwealth, company, district, general public, locality, people, populace, population, public, residents, society, state **2.** affinity, agreement, identity, likeness, sameness, similarity

commute 1. barter, exchange, inter~ change, substitute, switch, trade **2.** *Law: of penalties, etc.* alleviate, curtail, miti~ gate, modify, reduce, remit, shorten, soften

commuter 1. *noun* daily traveller, strap~ hanger (*informal*), suburbanite **2.** *~adjective* suburban

compact[1] *adjective* **1.** close, compressed, condensed, dense, firm, impenetrable, impermeable, pressed together, solid, thick **2.** brief, compendious, concise, epi~ grammatic, laconic, pithy, pointed, suc~ cinct, terse, to the point *~verb* **3.** com~ press, condense, cram, pack down, stuff, tamp
▷ **Antonyms** *~adjective* (*sense 1*) dis~ persed, large, loose, roomy, scattered, spacious, sprawling (*sense 2*) circum~ locutory, garrulous, lengthy, long-winded, prolix, rambling, verbose, wordy *~verb* disperse, loosen, separate

compact[2] *noun* agreement, alliance, ar~ rangement, bargain, bond, concordat, contract, covenant, deal, entente, pact, stipulation, treaty, understanding

companion 1. accomplice, ally, associate, buddy (*informal*), colleague, comrade, confederate, consort, crony, friend, gos~ sip (*archaic*), homeboy (*slang, chiefly U.S.*), mate (*informal*), partner **2.** aide, assistant, attendant, chaperon, duenna, escort, squire **3.** complement, counter~ part, fellow, match, mate, twin

companionable affable, congenial, con~ versable, convivial, cordial, familiar, friendly, genial, gregarious, neighbour~ ly, outgoing, sociable

companionship amity, camaraderie, com~ pany, comradeship, conviviality, esprit de corps, fellowship, fraternity, friend~ ship, rapport, togetherness

company 1. assemblage, assembly, band, bevy, body, camp, circle, collection, community, concourse, convention, co~ terie, crew, crowd, ensemble, gathering, group, league, party, set, throng, troop, troupe, turnout **2.** association, business, concern, corporation, establishment, firm, house, partnership, syndicate **3.** callers, companionship, fellowship, guests, party, presence, society, visitors

comparable 1. a match for, as good as, commensurate, equal, equivalent, in a class with, on a par, proportionate, tan~ tamount **2.** akin, alike, analogous, cog~ nate, corresponding, cut from the same cloth, of a piece, related, similar
▷ **Antonyms** different, dissimilar, in~ commensurable, incomparable, unequal

comparative approximate, by compari~ son, qualified, relative

compare 1. (*with* **with**) balance, collate, contrast, juxtapose, set against, weigh **2.** (*with* **to**) correlate, equate, identify with, liken, mention in the same breath, parallel, resemble **3.** *be the equal of* ap~ proach, approximate to, bear compari~ son, be in the same class as, be on a par with, come up to, compete with, equal, hold a candle to, match, vie

comparison 1. collation, contrast, distinc~ tion, juxtaposition **2.** analogy, compa~ rability, correlation, likeness, resem~ blance, similarity

compartment 1. alcove, bay, berth, booth, carrel, carriage, cell, chamber, cubby~ hole, cubicle, locker, niche, pigeonhole, section **2.** area, category, department, division, section, subdivision

compass *noun* **1.** area, bound, boundary, circle, circuit, circumference, enclosure, extent, field, limit, range, reach, realm, round, scope, sphere, stretch, zone *~verb* **2.** beset, besiege, blockade, circumscribe, encircle, enclose, encompass, environ, hem in, invest (*rare*), surround **3.** accomplish, achieve, attain, bring about, effect, execute, fulfil, perform, procure, realize

compassion charity, clemency, commiseration, compunction, condolence, fellow feeling, heart, humanity, kindness, mercy, pity, quarter, ruth (*archaic*), soft-heartedness, sorrow, sympathy, tender-heartedness, tenderness
▷ **Antonyms** apathy, cold-heartedness, indifference, mercilessness, unconcern

compassionate benevolent, charitable, humane, humanitarian, indulgent, kind-hearted, kindly, lenient, merciful, pitying, sympathetic, tender, tender-hearted, understanding
▷ **Antonyms** callous, harsh, heartless, inhumane, pitiless, uncaring, unfeeling, unmerciful, unsympathetic

compatibility affinity, agreement, amity, concord, congeniality, empathy, harmony, like-mindedness, rapport, single-mindedness, sympathy

compatible accordant, adaptable, agreeable, congenial, congruent, congruous, consistent, consonant, harmonious, in harmony, in keeping, like-minded, reconcilable, suitable
▷ **Antonyms** contradictory, inappropriate, inapt, incompatible, unfitting, unharmonious, unsuitable

compatriot countryman, fellow citizen, fellow countryman

compel bulldoze (*informal*), coerce, constrain, dragoon, drive, enforce, exact, force, hustle (*slang*), impel, make, necessitate, oblige, railroad (*informal*), restrain, squeeze, urge

compelling 1. cogent, conclusive, convincing, forceful, irrefutable, powerful, telling, weighty **2.** enchanting, enthralling, gripping, hypnotic, irresistible, mesmeric, spellbinding **3.** binding, coercive, imperative, overriding, peremptory, pressing, unavoidable, urgent
▷ **Antonyms** (*sense 1*) boring, dull, humdrum, monotonous, ordinary, repetitious, tiresome, uneventful, uninteresting, wearisome

compendious abbreviated, abridged, brief, comprehensive, concise, condensed, contracted, short, succinct, summarized, summary, synoptic

compensate 1. atone, indemnify, make good, make restitution, recompense, refund, reimburse, remunerate, repay, requite, reward, satisfy **2.** balance, cancel (out), counteract, counterbalance, countervail, make amends, make up for, offset, redress

compensation amends, atonement, damages, indemnification, indemnity, meed (*archaic*), offset, payment, recompense, reimbursement, remuneration, reparation, requital, restitution, reward, satisfaction

compete be in the running, challenge, contend, contest, emulate, fight, pit oneself against, rival, strive, struggle, vie

competence ability, adequacy, appropriateness, capability, capacity, competency, craft, expertise, fitness, proficiency, skill, suitability
▷ **Antonyms** inability, inadequacy, incompetence

competent able, adapted, adequate, appropriate, capable, clever, endowed, equal, fit, pertinent, proficient, qualified, sufficient, suitable
▷ **Antonyms** cowboy (*informal*), inadequate, incapable, incompetent, inexperienced, inexpert, undependable, unqualified, unskilled

competition 1. contention, contest, emulation, one-upmanship (*informal*), opposition, rivalry, strife, struggle **2.** championship, contest, event, head-to-head, puzzle, quiz, tournament **3.** challengers, field, opposition, rivals

competitive aggressive, ambitious, antagonistic, at odds, combative, cut-throat, dog-eat-dog, emulous, opposing, rival, vying

competitor adversary, antagonist, challenger, competition, contestant, emulator, opponent, opposition, rival

compilation accumulation, anthology, assemblage, assortment, collection, treasury

compile accumulate, amass, anthologize, collect, cull, garner, gather, marshal, organize, put together

complacency contentment, gratification, pleasure, satisfaction, self-satisfaction, smugness

complacent contented, gratified, pleased, pleased with oneself, resting on one's laurels, satisfied, self-assured, self-contented, self-righteous, self-satisfied, serene, smug, unconcerned
▷ **Antonyms** discontent, dissatisfied, insecure, rude, troubled, uneasy, unsatisfied

complain beef (*slang*), bellyache (*slang*), bemoan, bewail, bitch (*slang*), bleat, carp, deplore, find fault, fuss, grieve, gripe (*informal*), groan, grouch (*informal*), grouse, growl, grumble, kick up a fuss (*informal*), kvetch (*U.S. slang*), lament, moan, put the boot in (*slang*), whine, whinge (*informal*)

complaint 1. accusation, annoyance, beef (*slang*), bitch (*slang*), charge, criticism, dissatisfaction, fault-finding, grievance, gripe (*informal*), grouch (*informal*), grouse, grumble, lament, moan, plaint, protest, remonstrance, trouble, wail **2.** affliction, ailment, disease, disorder, ill~

ness, indisposition, malady, sickness, upset

complaisance accommodativeness, acquiescence, agreeableness, compliance, deference, obligingness

complaisant accommodating, amiable, compliant, conciliatory, deferential, obliging, polite, solicitous

complement *noun* **1.** companion, completion, consummation, correlative, counterpart, finishing touch, rounding-off, supplement **2.** aggregate, capacity, entirety, quota, total, totality, wholeness *~verb* **3.** cap (*informal*), complete, crown, round off, set off

complementary companion, completing, correlative, corresponding, fellow, interdependent, interrelating, matched, reciprocal

▷ **Antonyms** contradictory, different, incompatible, incongruous, uncomplementary

complete *adjective* **1.** all, entire, faultless, full, intact, integral, plenary, unabridged, unbroken, undivided, unimpaired, whole **2.** accomplished, achieved, concluded, ended, finished **3.** absolute, consummate, deep-dyed (*usually derogatory*), dyed-in-the-wool, outright, perfect, thorough, thoroughgoing, total, utter *~verb* **4.** accomplish, achieve, cap, close, conclude, crown, discharge, do, end, execute, fill in, finalize, finish, fulfil, perfect, perform, put the tin lid on, realize, round off, settle, terminate, wrap up (*informal*)

▷ **Antonyms** *~adjective* deficient, imperfect, incomplete, inconclusive, partial, spoilt, unaccomplished, unfinished, unsettled *~verb* begin, commence, initiate, mar, spoil, start

completely absolutely, a hundred per cent, altogether, down to the ground, en masse, entirely, every inch, from A to Z, from beginning to end, fully, heart and soul, hook, line and sinker, in full, *in toto,* lock, stock and barrel, one hundred per cent, perfectly, quite, root and branch, solidly, thoroughly, totally, utterly, wholly

completion accomplishment, attainment, bitter end, close, conclusion, consummation, culmination, end, expiration, finalization, fruition, fulfilment, realization

complex *adjective* **1.** circuitous, complicated, convoluted, Daedalian (*literary*), elaborate, intricate, involved, knotty, labyrinthine, mingled, mixed, tangled, tortuous **2.** composite, compound, compounded, heterogeneous, manifold, multifarious, multiple *~noun* **3.** aggregate, composite, network, organization, scheme, structure, synthesis, system **4.** fixation, fixed idea, *idée fixe,* obsession, phobia, preoccupation

▷ **Antonyms** (*sense 1*) clear, easy, easy-peasy (*slang*), elementary, obvious, simple, straightforward, uncomplicated

complexion 1. colour, colouring, hue, pigmentation, skin, skin tone **2.** appearance, aspect, cast, character, countenance, disposition, guise, light, look, make-up, nature, stamp

complexity complication, convolution, elaboration, entanglement, intricacy, involvement, multiplicity, ramification

compliance acquiescence, agreement, assent, complaisance, concession, concurrence, conformity, consent, deference, obedience, observance, passivity, submission, submissiveness, yielding

▷ **Antonyms** defiance, disobedience, non-compliance, nonconformity, opposition, refusal, resistance, revolt

complicate confuse, embroil, entangle, interweave, involve, make intricate, muddle, ravel, snarl up

▷ **Antonyms** clarify, clear up, disentangle, elucidate, explain, facilitate, simplify, spell out, unsnarl

complicated 1. Byzantine (*of attitudes, etc.*), complex, convoluted, elaborate, interlaced, intricate, involved, labyrinthine **2.** difficult, involved, perplexing, problematic, puzzling, troublesome

▷ **Antonyms** clear, easy, easy-peasy (*slang*), simple, straightforward, uncomplicated, undemanding, understandable, uninvolved, user-friendly

complication 1. combination, complexity, confusion, entanglement, intricacy, mixture, web **2.** aggravation, difficulty, drawback, embarrassment, factor, obstacle, problem, snag

complicity abetment, collaboration, collusion, concurrence, connivance

compliment 1. *noun* admiration, bouquet, commendation, congratulations, courtesy, eulogy, favour, flattery, honour, praise, tribute **2.** *~verb* commend, congratulate, crack up (*informal*), extol, felicitate, flatter, laud, pat on the back, pay tribute to, praise, salute, sing the praises of, speak highly of, wish joy to

▷ **Antonyms** *~noun* complaint, condemnation, criticism, disparagement, insult, reproach *~verb* blast, condemn, criticize, decry, disparage, insult, lambast(e), put down, reprehend, reproach, tear into (*informal*)

complimentary 1. appreciative, approving, commendatory, congratulatory, eulogistic, flattering, laudatory, panegyrical **2.** courtesy, donated, free, free of charge, gratis, gratuitous, honorary, on the house

▷ **Antonyms** (*sense 1*) abusive, critical, disparaging, fault-finding, insulting, scathing, uncomplimentary, unflattering

compliments good wishes, greetings, regards, remembrances, respects, salutation

comply abide by, accede, accord, acquiesce, adhere to, agree to, conform to, consent to, defer, discharge, follow, fulfil, obey, observe, perform, play ball (*informal*), respect, satisfy, submit, toe the line, yield
▷ **Antonyms** break, defy, disobey, disregard, fight, ignore, oppose, refuse to obey, reject, repudiate, resist, spurn, violate

component 1. *noun* constituent, element, ingredient, item, part, piece, unit **2.** *~adjective* composing, constituent, inherent, intrinsic

comport 1. accord, agree, coincide, correspond, fit, harmonize, square, suit, tally **2.** acquit, act, bear, behave, carry, conduct, demean

compose 1. build, compound, comprise, constitute, construct, fashion, form, make, make up, put together **2.** contrive, create, devise, frame, imagine, indite, invent, produce, write **3.** adjust, arrange, reconcile, regulate, resolve, settle **4.** appease, assuage, calm, collect, control, pacify, placate, quell, quiet, soothe, still, tranquillize
▷ **Antonyms** (*sense 1*) bulldoze, demolish, destroy, dismantle, obliterate, raze (*sense 4*) agitate, disturb, excite, perturb, trouble, unsettle, upset

composed as cool as a cucumber, at ease, calm, collected, confident, cool, imperturbable, keeping one's cool, laid-back (*informal*), level-headed, poised, relaxed, sedate, self-possessed, serene, together (*slang*), tranquil, unfazed (*informal*), unflappable, unruffled, unworried
▷ **Antonyms** agitated, anxious, disturbed, excited, hot and bothered (*informal*), nervous, ruffled, twitchy (*informal*), uncontrolled, uneasy, unpoised, upset

composite 1. *adjective* blended, combined, complex, compound, conglomerate, mixed, synthesized **2.** *~noun* amalgam, blend, compound, conglomerate, fusion, meld, synthesis

composition 1. arrangement, configuration, constitution, design, form, formation, layout, make-up, organization, structure **2.** compilation, creation, fashioning, formation, formulation, invention, making, mixture, production **3.** creation, essay, exercise, literary work, opus, piece, study, treatise, work, writing **4.** arrangement, balance, concord, consonance, harmony, placing, proportion, symmetry

compost humus, mulch, organic fertilizer

composure aplomb, calm, calmness, collectedness, cool (*slang*), coolness, dignity, ease, equanimity, imperturbability, placidity, poise, sang-froid, sedateness, self-assurance, self-possession, serenity, tranquillity
▷ **Antonyms** agitation, discomposure, excitability, impatience, nervousness, perturbation, uneasiness

compound *verb* **1.** amalgamate, blend, coalesce, combine, concoct, fuse, intermingle, meld, mingle, mix, synthesize, unite **2.** add insult to injury, add to, aggravate, augment, complicate, exacerbate, heighten, intensify, magnify, worsen **3.** *used of a dispute, difference, etc.* adjust, arrange, compose, settle *~noun* **4.** alloy, amalgam, blend, combination, composite, composition, conglomerate, fusion, medley, meld, mixture, synthesis *~adjective* **5.** complex, composite, conglomerate, intricate, multiple, not simple
▷ **Antonyms** *~verb* decrease, divide, lessen, minimize, moderate, modify, part, segregate *~noun* element *~adjective* pure, simple, single, unmixed

comprehend 1. apprehend, assimilate, conceive, discern, fathom, get the hang of (*informal*), get the picture, grasp, know, make out, perceive, see, see the light of day, take in, understand **2.** comprise, contain, embody, embrace, enclose, encompass, include, involve, take in
▷ **Antonyms** (*sense 1*) be at cross-purposes, get (it) wrong, get one's lines crossed, get the wrong end of the stick, misapprehend, misconceive, misconstrue, misinterpret, miss the point of, mistake, misunderstand, pervert

comprehensible clear, coherent, conceivable, explicit, graspable, intelligible, plain, understandable, user-friendly

comprehension 1. conception, discernment, grasp, intelligence, judgment, knowledge, perception, realization, sense, understanding **2.** compass, domain, field, limits, province, range, reach, scope
▷ **Antonyms** (*sense 1*) incomprehension, misapprehension, misunderstanding, unawareness

comprehensive all-embracing, all-inclusive, blanket, broad, catholic, complete, encyclopedic, exhaustive, extensive, full, inclusive, sweeping, thorough, umbrella, wide
▷ **Antonyms** incomplete, limited, narrow, restricted, specialized, specific

compress abbreviate, compact, concentrate, condense, constrict, contract, cram, crowd, crush, knit, press, pucker, shorten, squash, squeeze, summarize, wedge

compressed abridged, compact, compacted, concentrated, concise, consolidated, constricted, flattened, reduced, shortened, squashed, squeezed

compression condensation, consolidation, constriction, crushing, pressure, squeezing, wedging

comprise 1. be composed of, comprehend, consist of, contain, embrace, encompass, include, take in **2**. compose, constitute, form, make up

compromise **1**. *verb* adjust, agree, arbitrate, compose, compound, concede, give and take, go fifty-fifty (*informal*), meet halfway, settle, strike a balance **2**. *~noun* accommodation, accord, adjustment, agreement, concession, give-and-take, half measures, middle ground, settlement, trade-off **3**. *~verb* discredit, dishonour, embarrass, endanger, expose, hazard, imperil, implicate, jeopardize, prejudice, weaken

▷ **Antonyms** *~verb* argue, assure, boost, contest, differ, disagree, enhance, support *~noun* contention, controversy, difference, disagreement, dispute, quarrel

compulsion **1**. coercion, constraint, demand, duress, force, obligation, pressure, urgency **2**. drive, necessity, need, obsession, preoccupation, urge

compulsive besetting, compelling, driving, irresistible, neurotic, obsessive, overwhelming, uncontrollable, urgent

compulsory binding, *de rigueur,* forced, imperative, mandatory, obligatory, required, requisite

▷ **Antonyms** discretionary, elective, non-obligatory, non-requisite, optional, unimperative, unnecessary, voluntary

compunction contrition, misgiving, penitence, qualm, regret, reluctance, remorse, repentance, sorrow, stab *or* sting of conscience

compute add up, calculate, cast up, cipher, count, enumerate, estimate, figure, figure out, measure, rate, reckon, sum, tally, total

comrade ally, associate, buddy (*informal*), cock (*Brit. informal*), colleague, companion, compatriot, compeer, confederate, co-worker, crony, fellow, friend, homeboy (*slang, chiefly U.S.*), mate (*informal*), pal (*informal*), partner

con **1**. *verb* bamboozle (*informal*), bilk, cheat, cozen, deceive, defraud, diddle (*informal*), do the dirty on (*Brit. informal*), double-cross (*informal*), dupe, gull (*archaic*), hoax, hoodwink, humbug, inveigle, kid (*informal*), mislead, pull a fast one on (*informal*), rip off (*slang*), rook (*slang*), sell a pup, skin (*slang*), stiff (*slang*), sting (*informal*), swindle, take for a ride (*informal*), trick **2**. *~noun* bluff, canard, deception, fraud, scam (*slang*), sting (*informal*), swindle, trick

concatenation chain, connection, interlocking, linking, nexus, sequence, series, succession

concave cupped, depressed, excavated, hollow, hollowed, incurved, indented, scooped, sunken

▷ **Antonyms** bulging, convex, curving, protuberant, rounded

conceal bury, camouflage, cover, disguise, dissemble, draw a veil over, hide, keep dark, keep secret, keep under one's hat, mask, obscure, screen, secrete, shelter, stash (*informal*)

▷ **Antonyms** disclose, display, divulge, expose, lay bare, reveal, show, uncover, unmask, unveil

concealed covered, covert, hidden, inconspicuous, masked, obscured, screened, secret, secreted, tucked away, under wraps, unseen

concealment camouflage, cover, disguise, hideaway, hide-out, hiding, secrecy

▷ **Antonyms** disclosure, display, exposure, give-away, leak, revelation, showing, uncovering

concede **1**. accept, acknowledge, admit, allow, confess, grant, own **2**. cede, give up, hand over, relinquish, surrender, yield

▷ **Antonyms** (*sense 1*) contest, deny, disclaim, dispute, protest, refute, reject (*sense 2*) beat, conquer, defeat, fight to the bitter end, make a stand

conceit **1**. amour-propre, arrogance, complacency, egotism, narcissism, pride, self-importance, self-love, swagger, vainglory, vanity **2**. *archaic* belief, fancy, fantasy, idea, image, imagination, judgment, notion, opinion, quip, thought, vagary, whim, whimsy

conceited arrogant, bigheaded (*informal*), cocky, egotistical, full of oneself, immodest, narcissistic, overweening, puffed up, self-important, stuck up (*informal*), swollen-headed, too big for one's boots *or* breeches, vain, vainglorious

▷ **Antonyms** humble, modest, self-effacing, unassuming

conceivable believable, credible, imaginable, possible, thinkable

▷ **Antonyms** inconceivable, incredible, unbelievable, unimaginable, unthinkable

conceive **1**. appreciate, apprehend, believe, comprehend, envisage, fancy, get the picture, grasp, imagine, realize, suppose, understand **2**. contrive, create, design, develop, devise, form, formulate, produce, project, purpose, think up **3**. become impregnated, become pregnant

concentrate **1**. be engrossed in, consider closely, focus attention on, give all one's attention to, put one's mind to, rack one's brains **2**. bring to bear, centre, cluster, converge, focus **3**. accumulate, cluster, collect, congregate, gather, huddle

▷ **Antonyms** (*sense 1*) disregard, let one's mind wander, lose concentration, pay no attention to, pay no heed to (*senses 2 & 3*) deploy, diffuse, disperse, dissipate, scatter, spread out

concentrated **1**. all-out (*informal*), deep, hard, intense, intensive **2**. boiled down, condensed, evaporated, reduced, rich, thickened, undiluted

concentration 1. absorption, application, heed, single-mindedness **2.** bringing to bear, centralization, centring, combination, compression, consolidation, convergence, focusing, intensification **3.** accumulation, aggregation, cluster, collection, convergence, horde, mass
▷ **Antonyms** (*sense 1*) absent-mindedness, disregard, distraction, inattention (*senses 2 & 3*) diffusion, dispersal, scattering, spreading-out

concept abstraction, conception, conceptualization, hypothesis, idea, image, impression, notion, theory, view

conception 1. concept, design, idea, image, notion, plan **2.** beginning, birth, formation, inception, initiation, invention, launching, origin, outset **3.** appreciation, clue, comprehension, impression, inkling, perception, picture, understanding **4.** fertilization, germination, impregnation, insemination

concern *verb* **1.** affect, apply to, bear on, be relevant to, interest, involve, pertain to, regard, touch *~noun* **2.** affair, business, charge, department, field, interest, involvement, job, matter, mission, occupation, pigeon (*informal*), responsibility, task, transaction **3.** bearing, importance, interest, reference, relation, relevance *~verb* **4.** bother, disquiet, distress, disturb, make anxious, make uneasy, perturb, trouble, worry *~noun* **5.** anxiety, apprehension, attention, burden, care, consideration, disquiet, disquietude, distress, heed, responsibility, solicitude, worry **6.** business, company, corporation, enterprise, establishment, firm, house, organization

concerned 1. active, implicated, interested, involved, mixed up, privy to **2.** anxious, bothered, distressed, disturbed, exercised, troubled, uneasy, upset, worried **3.** attentive, caring, interested, solicitous
▷ **Antonyms** aloof, carefree, detached, indifferent, neglectful, unconcerned, uninterested, untroubled, without a care

concerning about, anent (*Scot.*), apropos of, as regards, as to, in the matter of, on the subject of, re, regarding, relating to, respecting, touching, with reference to

concert *noun* **1.** accord, agreement, concord, concordance, harmony, unanimity, union, unison **2. in concert** concertedly, in collaboration, in league, in unison, jointly, shoulder to shoulder, together, unanimously

concerted agreed upon, collaborative, combined, coordinated, joint, planned, prearranged, united
▷ **Antonyms** disunited, separate, uncontrived, uncooperative, unplanned

concession 1. acknowledgment, admission, assent, confession, surrender, yielding **2.** adjustment, allowance, boon, compromise, grant, indulgence, permit, privilege, sop

conciliate appease, clear the air, disarm, mediate, mollify, pacify, placate, pour oil on troubled waters, propitiate, reconcile, restore harmony, soothe, win over

conciliation appeasement, disarming, mollification, pacification, placation, propitiation, reconciliation, soothing

conciliatory appeasing, disarming, irenic, mollifying, pacific, peaceable, placatory, propitiative

concise brief, compact, compendious, compressed, condensed, epigrammatic, in a nutshell, laconic, pithy, short, succinct, summary, synoptic, terse, to the point
▷ **Antonyms** diffuse, discursive, garrulous, lengthy, long-winded, prolix, rambling, verbose, wordy

conclave assembly, cabinet, conference, congress, council, parley, secret *or* private meeting, session

conclude 1. bring down the curtain, cease, close, come to an end, complete, draw to a close, end, finish, round off, terminate, wind up **2.** assume, decide, deduce, gather, infer, judge, reckon (*informal*), sum up, suppose, surmise **3.** accomplish, bring about, carry out, clinch, decide, determine, effect, establish, fix, pull off, resolve, settle, work out
▷ **Antonyms** (*sense 1*) begin, commence, extend, initiate, open, protract, start

conclusion 1. bitter end, close, completion, end, finale, finish, result, termination **2.** consequence, culmination, end result, issue, outcome, result, sequel, upshot **3.** agreement, conviction, decision, deduction, inference, judgment, opinion, resolution, settlement, verdict **4. in conclusion** finally, in closing, lastly, to sum up

conclusive clinching, convincing, decisive, definite, definitive, final, irrefutable, ultimate, unanswerable, unarguable
▷ **Antonyms** contestable, disputable, doubtful, dubious, impeachable, inconclusive, indecisive, indefinite, questionable, refutable, unconvincing, vague

concoct brew, contrive, cook up (*informal*), design, devise, fabricate, formulate, hatch, invent, make up, manufacture, mature, plot, prepare, project, think up, trump up

concoction blend, brew, combination, compound, contrivance, creation, mixture, preparation

concomitant accompanying, associative, attendant, coexistent, coincidental, collateral, complementary, concurrent, contemporaneous, contributing, coterminous, synchronous

concord 1. accord, agreement, amity, concert, consensus, consonance, friendship, good understanding, goodwill, harmony, peace, rapport, unanimity, unison 2. agreement, compact, concordat, convention, entente, protocol, treaty

concourse 1. assemblage, assembly, collection, confluence, convergence, crowd, crush, gathering, meeting, multitude, rout (*archaic*), throng 2. entrance, foyer, gathering *or* meeting place, hall, lounge, rallying point

concrete *adjective* 1. actual, definite, explicit, factual, material, real, sensible, specific, substantial, tangible 2. calcified, compact, compressed, conglomerated, consolidated, firm, petrified, solid, solidified *~noun* 3. cement (*not in technical usage*), concretion

▷ **Antonyms** (*sense 1*) abstract, immaterial, indefinite, insubstantial, intangible, notional, theoretical, unspecified, vague

concubine courtesan, kept woman, leman (*archaic*), mistress, odalisque, paramour

concupiscence appetite, desire, horniness (*slang*), lasciviousness, lechery, libidinousness, libido, lickerishness (*archaic*), lust, lustfulness, randiness (*informal, chiefly Brit.*)

concupiscent horny (*slang*), lascivious, lecherous, lewd, libidinous, lickerish (*archaic*), lustful, randy (*informal, chiefly Brit.*)

concur accede, accord, acquiesce, agree, approve, assent, buy into (*informal*), coincide, combine, consent, cooperate, harmonize, join

concurrent 1. coexisting, coincident, concerted, concomitant, contemporaneous, simultaneous, synchronous 2. confluent, convergent, converging, uniting 3. agreeing, at one, compatible, consentient, consistent, cooperating, harmonious, in agreement, in rapport, like-minded, of the same mind

concussion clash, collision, crash, impact, jarring, jolt, jolting, shaking, shock

condemn 1. blame, censure, damn, denounce, disapprove, excoriate, reprehend, reproach, reprobate, reprove, upbraid 2. convict, damn, doom, pass sentence on, proscribe, sentence

▷ **Antonyms** (*sense 1*) acclaim, applaud, approve, commend, compliment, condone, praise (*sense 2*) acquit, free, liberate

condemnation 1. blame, censure, denouncement, denunciation, disapproval, reproach, reprobation, reproof, stricture 2. conviction, damnation, doom, judgment, proscription, sentence

condemnatory accusatory, accusing, censorious, critical, damnatory, denunciatory, disapproving, proscriptive, reprobative, scathing

condensation 1. abridgment, contraction, digest, précis, synopsis 2. condensate, deliquescence, distillation, liquefaction, precipitate, precipitation 3. compression, concentration, consolidation, crystallization, curtailment, reduction

condense 1. abbreviate, abridge, compact, compress, concentrate, contract, curtail, encapsulate, epitomize, précis, shorten, summarize 2. boil down, coagulate, concentrate, decoct, precipitate (*Chemistry*), reduce, solidify, thicken

▷ **Antonyms** (*sense 1*) elaborate, enlarge, expand, expatiate, increase, lengthen, pad out, spin out (*sense 2*) dilute, make thinner, thin (out), water down, weaken

condensed 1. abridged, compressed, concentrated, curtailed, shortened, shrunken, slimmed down, summarized 2. boiled down, clotted, coagulated, concentrated, precipitated (*Chemistry*), reduced, thickened

condescend 1. be courteous, bend, come down off one's high horse (*informal*), deign, humble *or* demean oneself, lower oneself, see fit, stoop, submit, unbend (*informal*), vouchsafe 2. patronize, talk down to

condescending disdainful, lofty, lordly, on one's high horse (*informal*), patronizing, snobbish, snooty (*informal*), supercilious, superior, toffee-nosed (*slang, chiefly Brit.*)

condescension 1. airs, disdain, haughtiness, loftiness, lordliness, patronizing attitude, superciliousness, superiority 2. affability, civility, courtesy, deference, favour, graciousness, humiliation, obeisance

condign *used especially of a punishment* adequate, appropriate, deserved, fitting, just, meet (*archaic*), merited, richly-deserved, suitable

condition *noun* 1. case, circumstances, lie of the land, plight, position, predicament, shape, situation, state, state of affairs, *status quo* 2. arrangement, article, demand, limitation, modification, prerequisite, provision, proviso, qualification, requirement, requisite, restriction, rider, rule, stipulation, terms 3. fettle, fitness, health, kilter, order, shape, state of health, trim 4. ailment, complaint, infirmity, malady, problem, weakness 5. caste, class, estate, grade, order, position, rank, status, stratum *~verb* 6. accustom, adapt, educate, equip, habituate, inure, make ready, prepare, ready, tone up, train, work out

conditional contingent, dependent, limited, provisional, qualified, subject to, with reservations

▷ **Antonyms** absolute, categorical, unconditional, unrestricted

conditioned acclimatized, accustomed, adapted, adjusted, familiarized, habituated, inured, made ready, prepared, seasoned, trained, used

conditioning *noun* **1.** grooming, preparation, readying, training **2.** accustoming, familiarization, hardening, inurement, reorientation, seasoning *~adjective* **3.** astringent, toning

conditions circumstances, environment, milieu, situation, surroundings, way of life

condole commiserate, compassionate (*archaic*), console, feel for, sympathize

condolence commiseration, compassion, consolation, fellow feeling, pity, sympathy

condom flunky (*slang*), Frenchie (*slang*), French letter (*slang*), French tickler (*slang*), rubber (*U.S. slang*), rubber johnny (*Brit. slang*), safe (*U.S. & Canad. slang*), scumbag (*U.S. slang*), sheath

condone disregard, excuse, forgive, let pass, look the other way, make allowance for, overlook, pardon, turn a blind eye to, wink at

▷ **Antonyms** censure, condemn, denounce, disapprove, punish

conduce advance, aid, avail, contribute, lead, promote, tend

conducive calculated to produce, contributive, contributory, favourable, helpful, leading, productive of, promotive, tending

conduct *noun* **1.** administration, control, direction, guidance, leadership, management, organization, running, supervision *~verb* **2.** administer, carry on, control, direct, govern, handle, lead, manage, organize, preside over, regulate, run, supervise **3.** accompany, attend, chair, convey, escort, guide, pilot, preside over, steer, usher *~noun* **4.** attitude, bearing, behaviour, carriage, comportment, demeanour, deportment, manners, mien (*literary*), ways *~verb* **5.** acquit, act, behave, carry, comport, deport

conduit canal, channel, duct, main, passage, pipe, tube

confab, confabulation chat, chinwag (*Brit. informal*), conversation, discussion, gossip, natter, powwow, session, talk

confabulate chat, chew the rag *or* fat (*slang*), converse, discuss, gossip, natter, shoot the breeze (*slang, chiefly U.S.*), talk

confederacy alliance, bund, coalition, compact, confederation, conspiracy, covenant, federation, league, union

confederate 1. *adjective* allied, associated, combined, federal, federated, in alliance **2.** *~noun* abettor, accessory, accomplice, ally, associate, colleague, partner **3.** *~verb* ally, amalgamate, associate, band together, combine, federate, merge, unite

confer 1. accord, award, bestow, give, grant, hand out, present, vouchsafe **2.** consult, converse, deliberate, discourse, parley, talk

conference colloquium, congress, consultation, convention, convocation, discussion, forum, meeting, seminar, symposium, teach-in

confess 1. acknowledge, admit, allow, blurt out, come clean (*informal*), come out of the closet, concede, confide, disclose, divulge, get (something) off one's chest (*informal*), grant, make a clean breast of, own, own up, recognize, sing (*slang, chiefly U.S.*), spill one's guts (*slang*) **2.** affirm, assert, attest, aver, confirm, declare, evince, manifest, profess, prove, reveal

▷ **Antonyms** button one's lips, conceal, cover, deny, hide, hush up, keep mum, keep secret, keep under wraps, repudiate, suppress, withhold

confession acknowledgment, admission, avowal, disclosure, divulgence, exposure, revelation, unbosoming

confidant, confidante alter ego, bosom friend, close friend, crony, familiar, intimate

confide 1. admit, breathe, confess, disclose, divulge, impart, reveal, whisper **2.** commend, commit, consign, entrust

confidence 1. belief, credence, dependence, faith, reliance, trust **2.** aplomb, assurance, boldness, courage, firmness, nerve, self-possession, self-reliance **3. in confidence** between you and me (and the gatepost), confidentially, in secrecy, privately

▷ **Antonyms** (*sense 1*) disbelief, distrust, doubt, misgiving, mistrust (*sense 2*) apprehension, fear, self-doubt, shyness, uncertainty

confident 1. certain, convinced, counting on, positive, satisfied, secure, sure **2.** assured, bold, dauntless, fearless, self-assured, self-reliant

▷ **Antonyms** (*sense 1*) doubtful, dubious, not sure, tentative, uncertain, unconvinced, unsure (*sense 2*) afraid, hesitant, insecure, jittery, lacking confidence, mousy, nervous, scared, self-doubting, unsure

confidential 1. classified, hush-hush (*informal*), intimate, off the record, private, privy, secret **2.** faithful, familiar, trusted, trustworthy, trusty

confidentially behind closed doors, between ourselves, in camera, in confidence, in secret, personally, privately, sub rosa

configuration arrangement, cast, conformation, contour, figure, form, outline, shape

confine 1. *verb* bind, bound, cage, circumscribe, clip someone's wings, enclose, hem in, hold back, immure, imprison, incarcerate, intern, keep, limit, repress, restrain, restrict, shut up, straiten 2. *~noun* border, boundary, frontier, limit, precinct

confined 1. enclosed, limited, restricted 2. in childbed, in childbirth, lying-in

confinement 1. custody, detention, imprisonment, incarceration, internment, porridge (*slang*) 2. *accouchement,* childbed, childbirth, labour, lying-in, parturition, time, travail

confines boundaries, bounds, circumference, edge, limits, pale, precincts

confirm 1. assure, buttress, clinch, establish, fix, fortify, reinforce, settle, strengthen 2. approve, authenticate, bear out, corroborate, endorse, ratify, sanction, substantiate, validate, verify

confirmation 1. authentication, corroboration, evidence, proof, substantiation, testimony, validation, verification 2. acceptance, agreement, approval, assent, endorsement, ratification, sanction

▷ **Antonyms** (*sense 1*) contradiction, denial, disavowal, repudiation (*sense 2*) annulment, cancellation, disapproval, refusal, rejection

confirmed chronic, dyed-in-the-wool, habitual, hardened, ingrained, inured, inveterate, long-established, rooted, seasoned

confiscate appropriate, commandeer, expropriate, impound, seize, sequester, sequestrate

▷ **Antonyms** free, give, give back, hand back, release, restore, return

confiscation appropriation, expropriation, forfeiture, impounding, seizure, sequestration, takeover

conflagration blaze, fire, holocaust, inferno, wildfire

conflict *noun* 1. battle, clash, collision, combat, contention, contest, encounter, engagement, fight, fracas, head-to-head, set-to (*informal*), strife, war, warfare 2. antagonism, bad blood, difference, disagreement, discord, dissension, divided loyalties, friction, hostility, interference, opposition, strife, variance *~verb* 3. be at variance, clash, collide, combat, contend, contest, differ, disagree, fight, interfere, strive, struggle

▷ **Antonyms** *~noun* accord, agreement, harmony, peace, treaty, truce *~verb* agree, coincide, harmonize, reconcile

conflicting antagonistic, clashing, contradictory, contrary, discordant, inconsistent, opposed, opposing, paradoxical

▷ **Antonyms** accordant, agreeing, compatible, congruous, consistent, harmonious, similar, unopposing

confluence 1. concurrence, conflux, convergence, junction 2. assemblage, assembly, concourse, concurrence, crowd, host, meeting, multitude, union

conform 1. adapt, adjust, comply, fall in with, follow, follow the crowd, obey, run with the pack, toe the line, yield 2. accord, agree, assimilate, correspond, harmonize, match, square, suit, tally

conformation anatomy, arrangement, build, configuration, form, framework, outline, shape, structure

conformist *noun* Babbitt (*U.S.*), conventionalist, stick-in-the-mud (*informal*), traditionalist, yes man

conformity 1. allegiance, Babbittry (*U.S.*), compliance, conventionality, observance, orthodoxy 2. affinity, agreement, conformance, congruity, consonance, correspondence, harmony, likeness, resemblance, similarity

confound 1. amaze, astonish, astound, baffle, be all Greek to (*informal*), bewilder, boggle the mind, confuse, dumbfound, flabbergast (*informal*), flummox, mix up, mystify, nonplus, perplex, startle, surprise 2. annihilate, contradict, demolish, destroy, explode, make a nonsense of, overthrow, overwhelm, refute, ruin

confront accost, beard, brave, bring face to face with, call out, challenge, defy, encounter, face, face off (*slang*), face the music, face up to, oppose, stand up to, tackle, walk into the lion's den

▷ **Antonyms** avoid, body-swerve (*Scot.*), circumvent, dodge, evade, flee, give a wide berth to, keep clear of, sidestep, steer clear of

confrontation conflict, contest, crisis, encounter, face-off (*slang*), head-to-head, set-to (*informal*), showdown (*informal*)

confuse 1. baffle, be all Greek to (*informal*), bemuse, bewilder, darken, faze, flummox, muddy the waters, mystify, nonplus, obscure, perplex, puzzle 2. blend, confound, disarrange, disorder, intermingle, involve, jumble, mingle, mistake, mix up, muddle, ravel, snarl up (*informal*), tangle 3. abash, addle, demoralize, discomfit, discompose, disconcert, discountenance, disorient, embarrass, fluster, mortify, nonplus, rattle (*informal*), shame, throw off balance, unnerve, upset

confused 1. at a loss, at sea, at sixes and sevens, baffled, bewildered, dazed, discombobulated (*informal, chiefly U.S. & Canad.*), disorganized, disorientated, flummoxed, muddled, muzzy (*U.S. informal*), nonplussed, not knowing if one is coming or going, not with it (*informal*), perplexed, puzzled, taken aback, thrown off balance, upset 2. at sixes and sevens, chaotic, disarranged, disarrayed, disordered, disorderly, disorganized, higgledy-piggledy (*informal*), hugger-mugger (*archaic*), in disarray, jumbled, mistaken, misunderstood, mixed up, out of order, topsy-turvy, untidy

▷ **Antonyms** arranged, aware, enlightened, informed, in order, on the ball (*informal*), ordered, orderly, organized, tidy, with it (*informal*)

confusing ambiguous, baffling, clear as mud (*informal*), complicated, contradictory, disconcerting, inconsistent, misleading, muddling, perplexing, puzzling, unclear

▷ **Antonyms** clear, definite, explicit, plain, simple, straightforward, uncomplicated, understandable

confusion **1.** befuddlement, bemusement, bewilderment, disorientation, mystification, perplexity, puzzlement **2.** bustle, chaos, clutter, commotion, disarrangement, disarray, disorder, disorganization, hodgepodge (*U.S.*), hotchpotch, jumble, mess, muddle, pig's breakfast (*informal*), shambles, state, tangle, turmoil, untidiness, upheaval **3.** abashment, chagrin, demoralization, discomfiture, distraction, embarrassment, fluster, perturbation

▷ **Antonyms** (*sense 1*) clarification, composure, enlightenment, explanation, solution (*sense 2*) arrangement, neatness, order, organization, tidiness

confute blow out of the water (*slang*), controvert, disprove, invalidate, oppugn, overthrow, prove false, rebut, refute, set aside

congeal benumb, clot, coagulate, condense, curdle, freeze, gelatinize, harden, jell, set, solidify, stiffen, thicken

congenial adapted, affable, agreeable, companionable, compatible, complaisant, favourable, fit, friendly, genial, kindly, kindred, like-minded, pleasant, pleasing, suitable, sympathetic, well-suited

congenital **1.** constitutional, immanent, inborn, inbred, inherent, innate, natural **2.** *informal* complete, deep-dyed (*usually derogatory*), inveterate, thorough, utter

congested blocked-up, clogged, crammed, crowded, jammed, overcrowded, overfilled, overflowing, packed, stuffed, stuffed-up, teeming

▷ **Antonyms** clear, empty, free, half-full, uncongested, uncrowded, unhampered, unhindered, unimpeded, unobstructed

congestion bottleneck, clogging, crowding, jam, mass, overcrowding, snarl-up (*informal, chiefly Brit.*), surfeit

conglomerate **1.** *adjective* amassed, clustered, composite, heterogeneous, massed **2.** *~verb* accumulate, agglomerate, aggregate, cluster, coalesce, snowball **3.** *~noun* agglomerate, aggregate, multinational

conglomeration accumulation, aggregation, assortment, combination, composite, hotchpotch, mass, medley, miscellany, mishmash, potpourri

congratulate compliment, felicitate, pat on the back, wish joy to

congratulations best wishes, compliments, felicitations, good wishes, greetings, pat on the back

congregate assemble, collect, come together, concentrate, convene, converge, convoke, flock, forgather, gather, mass, meet, muster, rally, rendezvous, throng

▷ **Antonyms** break up, dispel, disperse, dissipate, part, scatter, separate, split up

congregation assembly, brethren, crowd, fellowship, flock, host, laity, multitude, parish, parishioners, throng

congress assembly, chamber of deputies, conclave, conference, convention, convocation, council, delegates, diet, house, legislative assembly, legislature, meeting, parliament, quango, representatives

congruence accord, agreement, coincidence, compatibility, concurrence, conformity, congruity, consistency, correspondence, harmony, identity

congruous appropriate, apt, becoming, compatible, concordant, congruent, consistent, consonant, correspondent, corresponding, fit, meet, seemly, suitable

conic, conical cone-shaped, conoid, funnel-shaped, pointed, pyramidal, tapered, tapering

conjectural academic, hypothetical, speculative, supposed, suppositional, surmised, tentative, theoretical

conjecture **1.** *verb* assume, fancy, guess, hypothesize, imagine, infer, suppose, surmise, suspect, theorize **2.** *~noun* assumption, conclusion, fancy, guess, guesstimate (*informal*), guesswork, hypothesis, inference, notion, presumption, shot in the dark, speculation, supposition, surmise, theorizing, theory

conjugal bridal, connubial, hymeneal, marital, married, matrimonial, nuptial, spousal, wedded

conjunction association, coincidence, combination, concurrence, juxtaposition, union

conjuncture combination, concurrence, connection, crisis, crossroads, crucial point, emergency, exigency, juncture, pass, predicament, stage, turning point

conjure **1.** juggle, play tricks **2.** bewitch, call upon, cast a spell, charm, enchant, fascinate, invoke, raise, rouse, summon up **3.** adjure, appeal to, beg, beseech, crave, entreat, implore, importune, pray, supplicate

conjuror, conjurer illusionist, magician, miracle-worker, sorcerer, thaumaturge (*rare*), wizard

conjure up bring to mind, contrive, create, evoke, produce as by magic, recall, recollect

connect affix, ally, associate, attach, cohere, combine, couple, fasten, join, link, relate, unite
▷ **Antonyms** detach, disconnect, dissociate, divide, part, separate, sever, unfasten

connected 1. affiliated, akin, allied, associated, banded together, bracketed, combined, coupled, joined, linked, related, united **2.** *of speech* coherent, comprehensible, consecutive, intelligible

connection 1. alliance, association, attachment, coupling, fastening, junction, link, tie, union **2.** affiliation, affinity, association, bond, commerce, communication, correlation, correspondence, intercourse, interrelation, liaison, link, marriage, nexus, relation, relationship, relevance, tie-in **3.** context, frame of reference, reference **4.** acquaintance, ally, associate, contact, friend, sponsor **5.** kin, kindred, kinsman, kith, relation, relative

connivance abetment, abetting, collusion, complicity, conspiring, tacit consent

connive 1. cabal, collude, conspire, cook up (*informal*), intrigue, plot, scheme **2.** (*with* **at**) abet, aid, be an accessory to, be a party to, be in collusion with, blink at, disregard, lend oneself to, let pass, look the other way, overlook, pass by, shut one's eyes to, turn a blind eye to, wink at

connoisseur aficionado, appreciator, arbiter, authority, buff (*informal*), cognoscente, devotee, expert, judge, maven (*U.S.*), savant, specialist, whiz (*informal*)

connotation association, colouring, implication, nuance, significance, suggestion, undertone

connote betoken, hint at, imply, indicate, intimate, involve, signify, suggest

connubial conjugal, marital, married, matrimonial, nuptial, wedded

conquer 1. beat, blow out of the water (*slang*), bring to their knees, checkmate, clobber (*slang*), crush, defeat, discomfit, get the better of, humble, lick (*informal*), make mincemeat of (*informal*), master, overcome, overpower, overthrow, prevail, put in their place, quell, rout, run rings around (*informal*), stuff (*slang*), subdue, subjugate, succeed, surmount, tank (*slang*), triumph, undo, vanquish, wipe the floor with (*informal*) **2.** acquire, annex, obtain, occupy, overrun, seize, win
▷ **Antonyms** (*sense 1*) be defeated, capitulate, give in, give up, lose, quit, submit, surrender, throw in the towel, yield

conqueror champion, conquistador, defeater, hero, lord, master, subjugator, vanquisher, victor, winner

conquest 1. defeat, discomfiture, mastery, overthrow, pasting (*slang*), rout, triumph, vanquishment, victory **2.** acquisition, annexation, appropriation, coup, invasion, occupation, subjection, subjugation, takeover **3.** captivation, enchantment, enthralment, enticement, seduction **4.** acquisition, adherent, admirer, catch, fan, feather in one's cap, follower, prize, supporter, worshipper

consanguinity affinity, blood-relationship, family tie, kin, kindred, kinship

conscience 1. moral sense, principles, scruples, sense of right and wrong, still small voice **2. in all conscience** assuredly, certainly, fairly, honestly, in truth, rightly, truly

conscience-stricken ashamed, compunctious, contrite, disturbed, guilty, penitent, remorseful, repentant, sorry, troubled

conscientious 1. careful, diligent, exact, faithful, having one's nose to the grindstone, meticulous, painstaking, particular, punctilious, thorough **2.** high-minded, high-principled, honest, honourable, incorruptible, just, moral, responsible, scrupulous, straightforward, strict, upright
▷ **Antonyms** careless, irresponsible, negligent, remiss, slack, thoughtless, unconscientious, unprincipled, unreliable, unscrupulous, untrustworthy

conscious 1. alert, alive to, awake, aware, clued-up (*informal*), cognizant, percipient, responsive, sensible, sentient, wise to (*slang*) **2.** calculated, deliberate, intentional, knowing, premeditated, rational, reasoning, reflective, responsible, self-conscious, studied, wilful
▷ **Antonyms** (*sense 1*) ignorant, insensible, oblivious, unaware, unconscious (*sense 2*) accidental, uncalculated, unintended, unintentional, unplanned, unpremeditated, unwitting

consciousness apprehension, awareness, knowledge, realization, recognition, sensibility

consecrate dedicate, devote, exalt, hallow, ordain, sanctify, set apart, venerate

consecutive chronological, following, in sequence, in turn, running, sequential, seriatim, succeeding, successive, uninterrupted

consensus agreement, assent, common consent, concord, concurrence, general agreement, harmony, unanimity, unity

consent 1. *verb* accede, acquiesce, agree, allow, approve, assent, comply, concede, concur, permit, play ball (*informal*), yield **2.** *~noun* acquiescence, agreement, approval, assent, compliance, concession, concurrence, go-ahead (*informal*), green light, O.K. *or* okay (*informal*), permission, sanction
▷ **Antonyms** *~verb* decline, demur, disagree, disapprove, dissent, refuse, resist

~noun disagreement, disapproval, dissent, refusal, unwillingness

consequence 1. effect, end, end result, event, issue, outcome, repercussion, result, sequel, upshot 2. account, concern, import, importance, interest, moment, note, portent, significance, value, weight 3. bottom, distinction, eminence, notability, rank, repute, standing, status 4. **in consequence** as a result, because, following

consequent ensuing, following, resultant, resulting, sequential, subsequent, successive

consequential 1. eventful, far-reaching, grave, important, momentous, serious, significant, weighty 2. arrogant, bumptious, conceited, inflated, pompous, pretentious, self-important, supercilious, vainglorious 3. consequent, indirect, resultant

consequently accordingly, ergo, hence, necessarily, subsequently, therefore, thus

conservation custody, economy, guardianship, husbandry, maintenance, preservation, protection, safeguarding, safekeeping, saving, upkeep

conservative 1. *adjective* cautious, conventional, die-hard, guarded, hidebound, middle-of-the-road, moderate, quiet, reactionary, right-wing, sober, tory, traditional 2. *~noun* middle-of-the-roader, moderate, reactionary, right-winger, stick-in-the-mud (*informal*), tory, traditionalist

▷ **Antonyms** *~adjective* imaginative, innovative, liberal, progressive, radical *~noun* changer, innovator, progressive, radical

conservatory glasshouse, greenhouse, hothouse

conserve go easy on, hoard, husband, keep, nurse, preserve, protect, save, store up, take care of, use sparingly

▷ **Antonyms** be extravagant, blow (*slang*), dissipate, fritter away, misspend, misuse, spend, spend like water, squander, use up, waste

consider 1. chew over, cogitate, consult, contemplate, deliberate, discuss, examine, eye up, meditate, mull over, muse, ponder, reflect, revolve, ruminate, study, think about, turn over in one's mind, weigh, work over 2. believe, deem, hold to be, judge, rate, regard as, think 3. bear in mind, care for, keep in view, make allowance for, reckon with, regard, remember, respect, take into account

considerable 1. abundant, ample, appreciable, comfortable, goodly, great, large, lavish, marked, much, noticeable, plentiful, reasonable, sizable *or* sizeable, substantial, tidy, tolerable 2. distinguished, important, influential, notable, noteworthy, renowned, significant, venerable

▷ **Antonyms** insignificant, insubstantial, meagre, ordinary, paltry, small, unimportant, unremarkable

considerably appreciably, greatly, markedly, noticeably, remarkably, seriously (*informal*), significantly, substantially, very much

considerate attentive, charitable, circumspect, concerned, discreet, forbearing, kind, kindly, mindful, obliging, patient, tactful, thoughtful, unselfish

▷ **Antonyms** heedless, inconsiderate, selfish, thoughtless

consideration 1. analysis, attention, cogitation, contemplation, deliberation, discussion, examination, perusal, reflection, regard, review, scrutiny, study, thought 2. concern, factor, issue, point 3. concern, considerateness, friendliness, kindliness, kindness, respect, solicitude, tact, thoughtfulness 4. fee, payment, perquisite, recompense, remuneration, reward, tip 5. **take into consideration** bear in mind, make allowance for, take into account, weigh

considering all in all, all things considered, insomuch as, in the light of, in view of

consign commend to, commit, convey, deliver, deposit with, entrust, hand over, relegate, ship (*cargo*), transfer, transmit

consignment 1. *act of consigning* assignment, committal, dispatch, distribution, entrusting, handing over, relegation, sending, shipment, transmittal 2. *something consigned* batch, delivery, goods, shipment

consist 1. (*with* **of**) amount to, be composed of, be made up of, comprise, contain, embody, include, incorporate, involve 2. (*with* **in**) be expressed by, be found *or* contained in, inhere, lie, reside

consistency 1. compactness, density, firmness, thickness, viscosity 2. accordance, agreement, coherence, compatibility, congruity, correspondence, harmony 3. constancy, evenness, regularity, steadfastness, steadiness, uniformity

consistent 1. constant, dependable, persistent, regular, steady, true to type, unchanging, undeviating 2. accordant, agreeing, all of a piece, coherent, compatible, congruous, consonant, harmonious, logical

▷ **Antonyms** (*sense 1*) changing, deviating, erratic, inconsistent, irregular (*sense 2*) contradictory, contrary, discordant, incompatible, incongruous, inconsistent, inharmonious

consolation alleviation, assuagement, cheer, comfort, ease, easement, encouragement, help, relief, solace, succour, support

console assuage, calm, cheer, comfort, encourage, express sympathy for, re~lieve, solace, soothe
▷ **Antonyms** aggravate (*informal*), agi~tate, annoy, discomfort, distress, hassle (*informal*), hurt, sadden, torment, trou~ble, upset

consolidate 1. amalgamate, cement, com~bine, compact, condense, conjoin, feder~ate, fuse, harden, join, solidify, thicken, unite **2.** fortify, reinforce, secure, stabi~lize, strengthen

consolidation alliance, amalgamation, association, compression, condensation, federation, fortification, fusion, re~inforcement, strengthening

consonance accord, agreement, concord, conformity, congruence, congruity, con~sistency, correspondence, harmony, suitableness, unison

consonant accordant, according, compat~ible, concordant, congruous, consistent, correspondent, harmonious, in agree~ment, suitable

consort *noun* **1.** associate, companion, fellow, husband, partner, significant other (*U.S. informal*), spouse, wife *~verb* **2.** associate, fraternize, go around with, hang about, around *or* out with, keep company, mingle, mix **3.** accord, agree, correspond, harmonize, square, tally

conspectus abstract, compendium, di~gest, epitome, outline, précis, résumé, summary, survey, syllabus, synopsis

conspicuous 1. apparent, blatant, clear, discernible, easily seen, evident, mani~fest, noticeable, obvious, patent, per~ceptible, salient, visible **2.** celebrated, distinguished, eminent, famous, illus~trious, notable, outstanding, prominent, remarkable, salient, signal, striking **3.** blatant, flagrant, flashy, garish, glaring, showy
▷ **Antonyms** (*sense 1*) concealed, hidden, imperceptible, inconspicuous, indis~cernible, invisible, obscure, unnoticeable (*sense 2*) humble, inconspicuous, insig~nificant, ordinary, unacclaimed, undis~tinguished, unmemorable, unnotable

conspiracy cabal, collusion, confederacy, frame-up (*slang*), intrigue, league, machination, plot, scheme, treason

conspirator cabalist, conspirer, intriguer, plotter, schemer, traitor

conspire 1. cabal, confederate, contrive, devise, hatch treason, intrigue, machi~nate, manoeuvre, plot, scheme **2.** com~bine, concur, conduce, contribute, co~operate, tend, work together

constancy decision, determination, devo~tion, fidelity, firmness, fixedness, per~manence, perseverance, regularity, resolution, stability, steadfastness, steadiness, tenacity, uniformity

constant 1. continual, even, firm, fixed, habitual, immovable, immutable, in~variable, permanent, perpetual, regular, stable, steadfast, steady, unalterable, unbroken, uniform, unvarying **2.** cease~less, continual, continuous, endless, eternal, everlasting, incessant, intermi~nable, never-ending, nonstop, perpetual, persistent, relentless, sustained, unin~terrupted, unrelenting, unremitting **3.** determined, dogged, persevering, reso~lute, unflagging, unshaken, unwavering **4.** attached, dependable, devoted, faith~ful, loyal, stalwart, staunch, tried-and-true, true, trustworthy, trusty, unfailing
▷ **Antonyms** (*senses 1 & 2*) changeable, changing, deviating, erratic, inconstant, intermittent, irregular, occasional, ran~dom, uneven, unstable, unsustained, variable (*sense 4*) disloyal, fickle, irreso~lute, undependable

constantly all the time, always, aye (*Scot.*), continually, continuously, end~lessly, everlastingly, incessantly, inter~minably, invariably, morning, noon and night, night and day, nonstop, perpet~ually, persistently, relentlessly
▷ **Antonyms** (every) now and then, every so often, from time to time, intermit~tently, irregularly, now and again, oc~casionally, off and on, periodically, sometimes

consternation alarm, amazement, anxi~ety, awe, bewilderment, confusion, dis~may, distress, dread, fear, fright, horror, panic, shock, terror, trepidation

constituent *adjective* **1.** basic, component, elemental, essential, integral *~noun* **2.** component, element, essential, factor, ingredient, part, principle, unit **3.** elec~tor, voter

constitute 1. compose, comprise, create, enact, establish, fix, form, found, make, make up, set up **2.** appoint, authorize, commission, delegate, depute, empower, name, nominate, ordain

constitution 1. composition, establish~ment, formation, organization **2.** build, character, composition, disposition, form, habit, health, make-up, nature, physique, structure, temper, tempera~ment

constitutional *adjective* **1.** congenital, im~manent, inborn, inherent, intrinsic, or~ganic **2.** chartered, statutory, vested *~noun* **3.** airing, stroll, turn, walk

constrain 1. bind, coerce, compel, drive, force, impel, necessitate, oblige, pres~sure, pressurize, urge **2.** chain, check, confine, constrict, curb, hem in, rein, restrain, straiten

constrained embarrassed, forced, guard~ed, inhibited, reserved, reticent, sub~dued, unnatural

constraint 1. coercion, compulsion, force, necessity, pressure, restraint **2.** bash~fulness, diffidence, embarrassment, in~hibition, repression, reservation, re~straint, timidity **3.** check, curb, damper, deterrent, hindrance, limitation, rein, restriction

constrict choke, compress, contract, cramp, inhibit, limit, narrow, pinch, re~ strict, shrink, squeeze, strangle, stran~ gulate, tighten

constriction blockage, compression, con~ straint, cramp, impediment, limitation, narrowing, pressure, reduction, restric~ tion, squeezing, stenosis (*Pathology*), stricture, tightness

construct assemble, build, compose, cre~ ate, design, elevate, engineer, erect, es~ tablish, fabricate, fashion, form, formu~ late, found, frame, make, manufacture, organize, put up, raise, set up, shape
▷ **Antonyms** bulldoze, demolish, destroy, devastate, dismantle, flatten, knock down, level, pull down, raze, tear down

construction **1.** assembly, building, com~ position, creation, edifice, erection, fab~ ric, fabrication, figure, form, formation, shape, structure **2.** explanation, infer~ ence, interpretation, reading, rendering, take (*informal, chiefly U.S.*)

constructive helpful, positive, practical, productive, useful, valuable
▷ **Antonyms** destructive, futile, ineffec~ tive, limp-wristed, negative, unhelpful, unproductive, useless, vain, worthless

construe analyse, deduce, explain, ex~ pound, interpret, parse, read, read be~ tween the lines, render, take, translate

consult **1.** ask, ask advice of, commune, compare notes, confer, consider, debate, deliberate, interrogate, pick (someone's) brains, question, refer to, take counsel, turn to **2.** consider, have regard for, re~ gard, respect, take account of, take into consideration

consultant adviser, authority, specialist

consultation appointment, conference, council, deliberation, dialogue, discus~ sion, examination, hearing, interview, meeting, seminar, session

consume **1.** absorb, deplete, dissipate, drain, eat up, employ, exhaust, expend, finish up, fritter away, lavish, lessen, spend, squander, use, use up, utilize, vanish, waste, wear out **2.** devour, eat, eat up, gobble (up), guzzle, polish off (*informal*), put away, swallow **3.** annihi~ late, decay, demolish, destroy, devas~ tate, lay waste, ravage **4.** (*often passive*) absorb, devour, dominate, eat up, en~ gross, monopolize, obsess, preoccupy

consumer buyer, customer, purchaser, shopper, user

consuming absorbing, compelling, de~ vouring, engrossing, excruciating, grip~ ping, immoderate, overwhelming, tor~ menting

consummate **1.** *verb* accomplish, achieve, carry out, compass, complete, conclude, crown, effectuate, end, finish, perfect, perform, put the tin lid on **2.** *~adjective* absolute, accomplished, complete, con~ spicuous, deep-dyed (*usually deroga~ tory*), finished, matchless, perfect, pol~ ished, practised, skilled, superb, su~ preme, total, transcendent, ultimate, unqualified, utter
▷ **Antonyms** *~verb* begin, commence, conceive, get under way, inaugurate, initiate, originate, start

consummation achievement, completion, culmination, end, fulfilment, perfection, realization

consumption **1.** consuming, decay, de~ crease, depletion, destruction, diminu~ tion, dissipation, drain, exhaustion, ex~ penditure, loss, use, using up, utilization, waste **2.** *Medical* atrophy, emaciation, phthisis, T.B., tuberculosis

contact *noun* **1.** association, communica~ tion, connection **2.** approximation, con~ tiguity, junction, juxtaposition, touch, union **3.** acquaintance, connection *~verb* **4.** approach, call, communicate with, get hold of, get *or* be in touch with, phone, reach, ring (up) (*informal, chiefly Brit.*), speak to, touch base with (*U.S. & Canad. informal*), write to

contagion **1.** contamination, corruption, infection, pestilence, plague, pollution, taint **2.** communication, passage, spread, transference, transmittal

contagious catching, communicable, epi~ demic, epizootic (*Veterinary medicine*), infectious, pestiferous, pestilential, spreading, taking (*informal*), transmis~ sible

contain **1.** accommodate, enclose, have capacity for, hold, incorporate, seat **2.** comprehend, comprise, embody, em~ brace, include, involve **3.** control, curb, hold back, hold in, keep a tight rein on, repress, restrain, stifle

container holder, receptacle, repository, vessel

contaminate adulterate, befoul, corrupt, defile, deprave, infect, pollute, radioac~ tivate, smirch, soil, stain, sully, taint, tarnish, vitiate
▷ **Antonyms** clean, cleanse, decontami~ nate, deodorize, disinfect, fumigate, pu~ rify, sanitize, sterilize

contamination adulteration, contagion, corruption, decay, defilement, dirtying, filth, foulness, impurity, infection, poi~ soning, pollution, radioactivation, rot~ tenness, taint

contemn despise, disdain, disregard, hold cheap, neglect, scorn, slight, spurn, treat with contempt

contemplate **1.** brood over, consider, de~ liberate, meditate, meditate on, mull over, muse over, observe, ponder, reflect upon, revolve *or* turn over in one's mind, ruminate (upon), study **2.** behold, check out (*informal*), examine, eye, eye up, gaze at, inspect, recce (*slang*), regard, scrutinize, stare at, survey, view, weigh **3.** aspire to, consider, design, envisage, expect, foresee, have in view *or* in mind, intend, mean, plan, propose, think of

contemplation 1. cogitation, consideration, deliberation, meditation, musing, pondering, reflection, reverie, rumination, thought **2.** examination, gazing at, inspection, looking at, observation, recce (*slang*), scrutiny, survey, viewing

contemplative deep *or* lost in thought, in a brown study, intent, introspective, meditative, musing, pensive, rapt, reflective, ruminative, thoughtful

contemporary *adjective* **1.** coetaneous (*rare*), coeval, coexistent, coexisting, concurrent, contemporaneous, synchronous **2.** à la mode, current, happening (*informal*), in fashion, latest, modern, newfangled, present, present-day, recent, trendy (*Brit. informal*), ultramodern, up-to-date, up-to-the-minute, with it (*informal*) *~noun* **3.** compeer, fellow, peer

▷ **Antonyms** *~adjective* antecedent, antique, early, obsolete, old, old-fashioned, out-of-date, passé, succeeding

contempt 1. condescension, contumely, derision, despite (*archaic*), disdain, disregard, disrespect, mockery, neglect, scorn, slight **2.** *a state of contempt* disgrace, dishonour, humiliation, shame

▷ **Antonyms** admiration, esteem, honour, liking, regard, respect

contemptible abject, base, cheap, degenerate, despicable, detestable, ignominious, low, low-down (*informal*), mean, measly, paltry, pitiful, scurvy, shabby, shameful, vile, worthless

▷ **Antonyms** admirable, attractive, honourable, laudable, pleasant, praiseworthy

contemptuous arrogant, cavalier, condescending, contumelious, derisive, disdainful, haughty, high and mighty, insolent, insulting, on one's high horse (*informal*), scornful, sneering, supercilious, withering

▷ **Antonyms** civil, courteous, deferential, gracious, humble, mannerly, obsequious, polite, respectful

contend 1. clash, compete, contest, cope, emulate, grapple, jostle, litigate, skirmish, strive, struggle, vie **2.** affirm, allege, argue, assert, aver, avow, debate, dispute, hold, maintain

content[1] **1.** *verb* appease, delight, gladden, gratify, humour, indulge, mollify, placate, please, reconcile, sate, satisfy, suffice **2.** *~noun* comfort, contentment, ease, gratification, peace, peace of mind, pleasure, satisfaction **3.** *~adjective* agreeable, at ease, comfortable, contented, fulfilled, satisfied, willing to accept

content[2] *noun* **1.** burden, essence, gist, ideas, matter, meaning, significance, substance, text, thoughts **2.** capacity, load, measure, size, volume

contented at ease, at peace, cheerful, comfortable, complacent, content, glad, gratified, happy, pleased, satisfied, serene, thankful

▷ **Antonyms** annoyed, discontented, displeased, dissatisfied, pissed off (*taboo slang*), troubled, uncomfortable, uneasy

contention 1. bone of contention, competition, contest, discord, dispute, dissension, enmity, feuding, hostility, rivalry, row, strife, struggle, wrangling **2.** affirmation, allegation, argument, assertion, asseveration, belief, claim, declaration, ground, idea, maintaining, opinion, position, profession, stand, thesis, view

contentious argumentative, bickering, cantankerous, captious, cavilling, combative, controversial, cross, disputatious, factious, litigious, peevish, perverse, pugnacious, quarrelsome, querulous, wrangling

contentment comfort, complacency, content, contentedness, ease, equanimity, fulfilment, gladness, gratification, happiness, peace, pleasure, repletion, satisfaction, serenity

▷ **Antonyms** discomfort, discontent, discontentment, displeasure, dissatisfaction, uneasiness, unhappiness

contents 1. constituents, elements, ingredients, load **2.** chapters, divisions, subject matter, subjects, themes, topics

contest *noun* **1.** competition, game, head-to-head, match, tournament, trial **2.** affray, altercation, battle, combat, conflict, controversy, debate, discord, dispute, encounter, fight, shock, struggle *~verb* **3.** compete, contend, fight, fight over, strive, vie **4.** argue, call in *or* into question, challenge, debate, dispute, doubt, litigate, object to, oppose, question

contestant aspirant, candidate, competitor, contender, entrant, participant, player

context 1. background, connection, frame of reference, framework, relation **2.** ambience, circumstances, conditions, situation

contiguous abutting, adjacent, adjoining, beside, bordering, conterminous, in contact, juxtaposed, juxtapositional, near, neighbouring, next, next door to, touching

continence abstinence, asceticism, celibacy, chastity, moderation, self-control, self-restraint, temperance

continent *adjective* abstemious, abstinent, ascetic, austere, celibate, chaste, self-restrained, sober

contingency accident, chance, emergency, event, eventuality, fortuity, happening, incident, juncture, possibility, uncertainty

contingent *adjective* **1.** (*with* **on** *or* **upon**) conditional, controlled by, dependent, subject to **2.** accidental, casual, fortuitous, haphazard, random, uncertain *~noun* **3.** batch, body, bunch (*informal*), deputation, detachment, group, mission, quota, section, set

continual constant, continuous, endless, eternal, everlasting, frequent, incessant, interminable, oft-repeated, perpetual, recurrent, regular, repeated, repetitive, unceasing, uninterrupted, unremitting
▷ **Antonyms** broken, ceasing, erratic, fluctuating, fragmentary, infrequent, intermittent, interrupted, irregular, occasional, periodic, spasmodic, sporadic, terminable

continually all the time, always, aye (*Scot.*), constantly, endlessly, eternally, everlastingly, forever, incessantly, interminably, nonstop, persistently, repeatedly

continuance continuation, duration, period, protraction, term

continuation 1. addition, extension, furtherance, postscript, sequel, supplement **2.** maintenance, perpetuation, prolongation, resumption

continue 1. abide, carry on, endure, last, live on, persist, remain, rest, stay, stay on, survive **2.** go on, keep at, keep on, keep one's hand in, keep the ball rolling, keep up, maintain, persevere, persist in, prolong, pursue, stick at, stick to, sustain **3.** draw out, extend, lengthen, project, prolong, reach **4.** carry on, pick up where one left off, proceed, recommence, resume, return to, take up
▷ **Antonyms** (*sense 1*) abdicate, leave, quit, resign, retire, step down (*senses 2 & 4*) break off, call it a day, cease, discontinue, give up, leave off, pack in (*Brit. informal*), quit, stop

continuing enduring, in progress, lasting, ongoing, sustained

continuity cohesion, connection, flow, interrelationship, progression, sequence, succession, whole

continuous connected, constant, continued, extended, prolonged, unbroken, unceasing, undivided, uninterrupted
▷ **Antonyms** broken, disconnected, ending, inconstant, intermittent, interrupted, occasional, passing, severed, spasmodic

contort convolute, deform, distort, gnarl, knot, misshape, twist, warp, wrench, writhe

contour curve, figure, form, lines, outline, profile, relief, shape, silhouette

contraband 1. *noun* black-marketing, bootlegging, moonshine (*U.S.*), rum-running, smuggling, trafficking **2.** *~adjective* banned, black-market, bootleg, bootlegged, forbidden, hot (*informal*), illegal, illicit, interdicted, prohibited, smuggled, unlawful

contract *verb* **1.** abbreviate, abridge, compress, condense, confine, constrict, curtail, diminish, dwindle, epitomize, knit, lessen, narrow, pucker, purse, reduce, shrink, shrivel, tighten, wither, wrinkle **2.** agree, arrange, bargain, clinch, close, come to terms, commit oneself, covenant, engage, enter into, negotiate, pledge, shake hands, stipulate **3.** acquire, be afflicted with, catch, develop, get, go down with, incur *~noun* **4.** agreement, arrangement, bargain, bond, commission, commitment, compact, concordat, convention, covenant, deal (*informal*), engagement, pact, settlement, stipulation, treaty, understanding
▷ **Antonyms** (*sense 1*) broaden, develop, distend, enlarge, expand, grow, increase, inflate, multiply, spread, stretch, swell, widen (*sense 2*) decline, disagree, refuse, turn down (*sense 3*) avert, avoid, escape, ward off

contraction abbreviation, compression, constriction, diminution, drawing in, elision, narrowing, reduction, shortening, shrinkage, shrivelling, tensing, tightening

contradict be at variance with, belie, challenge, contravene, controvert, counter, counteract, deny, dispute, fly in the face of, gainsay (*archaic or literary*), impugn, make a nonsense of, negate, oppose, rebut
▷ **Antonyms** affirm, agree, authenticate, confirm, defend, endorse, support, verify

contradiction conflict, confutation, contravention, denial, incongruity, inconsistency, negation, opposite

contradictory antagonistic, antithetical, conflicting, contrary, discrepant, incompatible, inconsistent, irreconcilable, opposed, opposite, paradoxical, repugnant

contraption apparatus, contrivance, device, gadget, instrument, mechanism, rig

contrary *adjective* **1.** adverse, antagonistic, clashing, contradictory, counter, discordant, hostile, inconsistent, inimical, opposed, opposite, paradoxical **2.** awkward, balky, cantankerous, cussed (*informal*), difficult, disobliging, froward (*archaic*), intractable, obstinate, perverse, stroppy (*Brit. slang*), thrawn (*Northern English dialect*), unaccommodating, wayward, wilful *~noun* **3.** antithesis, converse, opposite, reverse **4. on the contrary** conversely, in contrast, not at all, on the other hand, quite the opposite *or* reverse
▷ **Antonyms** (*sense 1*) accordant, congruous, consistent, harmonious, in agreement, parallel, unopposed (*sense 2*) accommodating, agreeable, amiable, co-operative, eager to please, helpful, obliging, tractable, willing

contrast 1. *noun* comparison, contrariety, difference, differentiation, disparity, dissimilarity, distinction, divergence, foil, opposition **2.** *~verb* compare, differ, differentiate, distinguish, oppose, set in opposition, set off

contravene 1. break, disobey, go against, infringe, transgress, violate **2.** conflict with, contradict, counteract, cross, go against, hinder, interfere, oppose, refute, thwart

contretemps accident, calamity, difficulty, misfortune, mishap, mistake, predicament

contribute 1. add, afford, bestow, chip in (*informal*), donate, furnish, give, provide, subscribe, supply **2.** be conducive, be instrumental, be partly responsible for, conduce, help, lead, tend

contribution addition, bestowal, donation, gift, grant, input, offering, stipend, subscription

contributor 1. backer, bestower, conferrer, donor, giver, patron, subscriber, supporter **2.** correspondent, freelance, freelancer, journalist, journo (*slang*), reporter

contrite chastened, conscience-stricken, humble, in sackcloth and ashes, penitent, regretful, remorseful, repentant, sorrowful, sorry

contrition compunction, humiliation, penitence, remorse, repentance, self-reproach, sorrow

contrivance 1. artifice, design, dodge, expedient, fabrication, formation, intrigue, inventiveness, machination, measure, plan, plot, project, ruse, scheme, stratagem, trick **2.** apparatus, appliance, contraption, device, equipment, gadget, gear, implement, instrument, invention, machine, mechanism

contrive 1. concoct, construct, create, design, devise, engineer, fabricate, frame, improvise, invent, manufacture, wangle (*informal*) **2.** arrange, bring about, effect, hit upon, manage, manoeuvre, plan, plot, scheme, succeed

contrived artificial, elaborate, forced, laboured, overdone, planned, recherché, strained, unnatural

▷ **Antonyms** genuine, natural, relaxed, spontaneous, unaffected, unconstrained, unfeigned, unforced, unpretentious

control *verb* **1.** administer, boss (*informal*), call the shots, call the tune, command, conduct, direct, dominate, govern, handle, have charge of, have (someone) in one's pocket, hold the purse strings, keep a tight rein on, keep on a string, lead, manage, manipulate, oversee, pilot, reign over, rule, steer, superintend, supervise **2.** bridle, check, constrain, contain, curb, hold back, limit, master, rein in, repress, restrain, subdue **3.** *used of a machine, an experiment, etc.* counteract, determine, monitor, regulate, verify *~noun* **4.** authority, charge, command, direction, discipline, government, guidance, jurisdiction, management, mastery, oversight, rule, superintendence, supervision, supremacy **5.** brake, check, curb, limitation, regulation, restraint

controls console, control panel, dash, dashboard, dials, instruments

controversial at issue, contended, contentious, controvertible, debatable, disputable, disputed, open to question, polemic, under discussion

controversy altercation, argument, contention, debate, discussion, dispute, dissension, polemic, quarrel, row, squabble, strife, wrangle, wrangling

controvert 1. challenge, contradict, counter, deny, fly in the face of, make a nonsense of, oppose, refute **2.** argue, contest, debate, discuss, dispute, wrangle

contumacious haughty, headstrong, insubordinate, intractable, intransigent, obdurate, obstinate, perverse, pig-headed, rebellious, recalcitrant, refractory, stiff-necked, stubborn

contumacy contempt, contrariety, delinquency, disobedience, haughtiness, insubordination, intransigence, obstinacy, perverseness, pig-headedness, rebelliousness, recalcitrance, refractoriness, stubbornness

contumelious contemptuous, disdainful, insolent, insulting, scornful, sneering, sniffy (*informal*), supercilious, withering

contumely abuse, affront, arrogance, contempt, derision, disdain, humiliation, indignity, insolence, insult, obloquy, opprobrium, rudeness, scorn, superciliousness

contusion bruise, discoloration, injury, knock, swelling, trauma (*Pathology*)

conundrum brain-teaser (*informal*), enigma, poser, problem, puzzle, riddle, teaser

convalescence improvement, recovery, recuperation, rehabilitation, return to health

convalescent *adjective* getting better, improving, mending, on the mend, recovering, recuperating

convene assemble, bring together, call, come together, congregate, convoke, gather, meet, muster, rally, summon

convenience 1. accessibility, appropriateness, availability, fitness, handiness, opportuneness, serviceability, suitability, usefulness, utility **2.** *a convenient time or situation* chance, leisure, opportunity, spare moment, spare time **3.** accommodation, advantage, benefit, comfort, ease, enjoyment, satisfaction, service, use **4.** *a useful device* amenity, appliance, comfort, facility, help, labour-saving device

▷ **Antonyms** discomfort, hardship, inconvenience, uselessness

convenient **1.** adapted, appropriate, beneficial, commodious, fit, fitted, handy, helpful, labour-saving, opportune, seasonable, serviceable, suitable, suited, timely, useful, well-timed **2.** accessible, at hand, available, close at hand, handy, just round the corner, nearby, within reach

▷ **Antonyms** awkward, distant, inaccessible, inconvenient, out-of-the-way, unsuitable, useless

convent convent school, nunnery, religious community

convention **1.** assembly, conference, congress, convocation, council, delegates, meeting, representatives **2.** code, custom, etiquette, formality, practice, propriety, protocol, tradition, usage **3.** agreement, bargain, compact, concordat, contract, pact, protocol, stipulation, treaty

conventional **1.** accepted, bog-standard (*Brit. & Irish slang*), common, correct, customary, decorous, expected, formal, habitual, normal, ordinary, orthodox, prevailing, prevalent, proper, regular, ritual, standard, traditional, usual, wonted **2.** banal, bourgeois, commonplace, hackneyed, hidebound, pedestrian, Pooterish, prosaic, routine, run-of-the-mill, stereotyped, unoriginal, vanilla (*slang*)

▷ **Antonyms** abnormal, left-field (*informal*), off-the-wall (*slang*), uncommon, unconventional, unorthodox

converge coincide, combine, come together, concentrate, focus, gather, join, meet, merge, mingle

convergence approach, blending, coincidence, concentration, concurrence, confluence, conflux, conjunction, junction, meeting, merging, mingling

conversant (*usually with* **with**) acquainted, *au fait,* experienced, familiar, knowledgeable, practised, proficient, skilled, versed, well-informed, well up in (*informal*)

conversation chat, chinwag (*Brit. informal*), colloquy, communication, communion, confab (*informal*), confabulation, conference, converse, dialogue, discourse, discussion, exchange, gossip, intercourse, powwow, talk, tête-à-tête

conversational chatty, colloquial, communicative, informal

converse[1] *verb* **1.** chat, commune, confer, discourse, exchange views, shoot the breeze (*slang, chiefly U.S. & Canad.*) **2.** *obsolete* associate, consort *~noun* **3.** chat, communication, conference, conversation, dialogue, talk

converse[2] **1.** *noun* antithesis, contrary, obverse, opposite, other side of the coin, reverse **2.** *~adjective* contrary, counter, opposite, reverse, reversed, transposed

conversion **1.** change, metamorphosis, transfiguration, transformation, transmogrification (*jocular*), transmutation **2.** adaptation, alteration, modification, reconstruction, remodelling, reorganization **3.** change of heart, proselytization, rebirth, reformation, regeneration

convert[1] *verb* **1.** alter, change, interchange, metamorphose, transform, transmogrify (*jocular*), transmute, transpose, turn **2.** adapt, apply, appropriate, customize, modify, remodel, reorganize, restyle, revise **3.** baptize, bring to God, convince, proselytize, reform, regenerate, save

convert[2] *noun* catechumen, disciple, neophyte, proselyte

convertible adaptable, adjustable, exchangeable, interchangeable

convex bulging, gibbous, outcurved, protuberant, rounded

▷ **Antonyms** concave, cupped, depressed, excavated, hollowed, indented, sunken

convey **1.** bear, bring, carry, conduct, fetch, forward, grant, guide, move, send, support, transmit, transport **2.** communicate, disclose, impart, make known, relate, reveal, tell **3.** *Law* bequeath, cede, deliver, demise, devolve, grant, lease, transfer, will

conveyance **1.** carriage, movement, transfer, transference, transmission, transport, transportation **2.** transport, vehicle

convict **1.** *verb* condemn, find guilty, imprison, pronounce guilty, sentence **2.** *~noun* con (*slang*), criminal, culprit, felon, jailbird, lag (*slang*), malefactor, prisoner, villain

conviction **1.** assurance, certainty, certitude, confidence, earnestness, fervour, firmness, reliance **2.** belief, creed, faith, opinion, persuasion, principle, tenet, view

convince assure, bring round, gain the confidence of, persuade, prevail upon, prove to, satisfy, sway, win over

convincing cogent, conclusive, credible, impressive, incontrovertible, likely, persuasive, plausible, powerful, probable, telling, verisimilar

▷ **Antonyms** beyond belief, cock-and-bull (*informal*), dubious, far-fetched, implausible, improbable, inconclusive, incredible, unconvincing, unlikely

convivial back-slapping, cheerful, festive, friendly, fun-loving, gay, genial, hearty, hilarious, jolly, jovial, lively, merry, mirthful, partyish (*informal*), sociable

conviviality bonhomie, cheer, cordiality, festivity, gaiety, geniality, good fellowship, jollification, jollity, joviality, liveliness, merrymaking, mirth, sociability

convocation assemblage, assembly, conclave, concourse, congregation, congress, convention, council, diet, meeting, synod

convoke assemble, call together, collect, convene, gather, muster, summon

convolution coil, coiling, complexity, contortion, curlicue, helix, intricacy, involution, loop, sinuosity, sinuousness, spiral, tortuousness, twist, undulation, winding

convoy 1. *noun* armed guard, attendance, attendant, escort, guard, protection **2.** *~verb* accompany, attend, escort, guard, pilot, protect, shepherd, usher

convulse agitate, churn up, derange, disorder, disturb, shake, shatter, twist, work

convulsion 1. agitation, commotion, disturbance, furore, shaking, tumult, turbulence, upheaval **2.** contortion, contraction, cramp, fit, paroxysm, seizure, spasm, throe (*rare*), tremor

convulsive churning, fitful, jerky, paroxysmal, spasmodic, sporadic, violent

cook up concoct, contrive, devise, dream up, fabricate, improvise, invent, manufacture, plot, prepare, scheme, trump up

cool *adjective* **1.** chilled, chilling, chilly, coldish, nippy, refreshing **2.** calm, collected, composed, deliberate, dispassionate, imperturbable, laid-back (*informal*), level-headed, placid, quiet, relaxed, sedate, self-controlled, self-possessed, serene, together (*slang*), unemotional, unexcited, unfazed (*informal*), unruffled **3.** aloof, apathetic, distant, frigid, incurious, indifferent, lukewarm, offhand, reserved, standoffish, uncommunicative, unconcerned, unenthusiastic, unfriendly, uninterested, unresponsive, unwelcoming **4.** audacious, bold, brazen, cheeky, impertinent, impudent, presumptuous, shameless **5.** *informal* cosmopolitan, elegant, sophisticated, urbane *~verb* **6.** chill, cool off, freeze, lose heat, refrigerate **7.** abate, allay, assuage, calm (down), dampen, lessen, moderate, quiet, temper *~noun* **8.** *slang* calmness, composure, control, poise, self-control, self-discipline, self-possession, temper

▷ **Antonyms** *~adjective* (*sense 1*) lukewarm, moderately hot, sunny, tepid, warm (*sense 2*) agitated, delirious, excited, impassioned, nervous, overwrought, perturbed, tense, troubled, twitchy (*informal*) (*sense 3*) amiable, chummy (*informal*), cordial, friendly, outgoing, receptive, responsive, sociable, warm *~verb* (*sense 6*) heat, reheat, take the chill off, thaw, warm, warm up

coop 1. *noun* box, cage, corral (*chiefly U.S. & Canad.*), enclosure, hutch, pen, pound **2.** *~verb* cage, confine, immure, impound, imprison, pen, pound, shut up

cooperate abet, aid, assist, collaborate, combine, concur, conduce, conspire, contribute, coordinate, go along with, help, join forces, lend a helping hand, pitch in, play ball (*informal*), pool resources, pull together, work together

▷ **Antonyms** conflict, contend with, fight, hamper, hamstring, hinder, impede, obstruct, oppose, prevent, put the mockers on (*informal*), resist, struggle against, stymie, thwart

cooperation assistance, collaboration, combined effort, concert, concurrence, esprit de corps, give-and-take, helpfulness, participation, responsiveness, teamwork, unity

▷ **Antonyms** discord, dissension, hindrance, opposition, rivalry

cooperative 1. accommodating, helpful, obliging, responsive, supportive **2.** coactive, collective, combined, concerted, coordinated, joint, shared, unified, united

coordinate 1. *verb* correlate, harmonize, integrate, match, mesh, organize, relate, synchronize, systematize **2.** *~adjective* coequal, correlative, correspondent, equal, equivalent, parallel, tantamount

cope 1. carry on, get by (*informal*), hold one's own, make out (*informal*), make the grade, manage, rise to the occasion, struggle through, survive **2. cope with** contend, deal, dispatch, encounter, grapple, handle, struggle, tangle, tussle, weather, wrestle

copious abundant, ample, bounteous, bountiful, extensive, exuberant, full, generous, lavish, liberal, luxuriant, overflowing, plenteous, plentiful, profuse, rich, superabundant

copiousness abundance, amplitude, bountifulness, bounty, cornucopia, exuberance, fullness, horn of plenty, lavishness, luxuriance, plentifulness, plenty, richness, superabundance

cop-out alibi, dodge, fraud, pretence, pretext

cop out abandon, desert, dodge, quit, renege, renounce, revoke, skip, skive (*Brit. slang*), withdraw

copulate ball (*taboo slang, chiefly U.S.*), bonk (*informal*), fuck (*taboo slang*), have intercourse, have sex, hump (*taboo slang*), screw (*taboo slang*), shag (*taboo slang, chiefly Brit.*)

copulation carnal knowledge, coition, coitus, congress, coupling, intimacy, legover (*slang*), love, lovemaking, mating, nookie (*slang*), rumpy-pumpy (*slang*), sex, sex act, sexual intercourse, the other (*informal*), venery (*archaic*)

copy *noun* **1.** archetype, carbon copy, counterfeit, duplicate, facsimile, fake, fax, forgery, image, imitation, likeness, model, pattern, photocopy, Photostat (*Trademark*), print, replica, replication, representation, reproduction, transcription, Xerox (*Trademark*) *~verb* **2.**

counterfeit, duplicate, photocopy, Photostat (*Trademark*), replicate, reproduce, transcribe, Xerox (*Trademark*) **3.** ape, echo, emulate, follow, follow suit, follow the example of, imitate, mimic, mirror, parrot, repeat, simulate
▷ **Antonyms** *~noun* model, original, pattern, prototype, the real thing *~verb* create, originate

coquet dally, flirt, lead on, make eyes at, philander, tease, toy, trifle, vamp (*informal*)

coquettish amorous, arch, come-hither (*informal*), coy, dallying, flighty, flirtatious, flirty, inviting, teasing

cord 1. line, rope, string, twine **2.** bond, connection, link, tie

cordial affable, affectionate, agreeable, cheerful, congenial, earnest, friendly, genial, heartfelt, hearty, invigorating, sociable, warm, warm-hearted, welcoming, wholehearted
▷ **Antonyms** aloof, cold, distant, formal, frigid, reserved, unfriendly, ungracious

cordiality affability, amiability, friendliness, geniality, heartiness, sincerity, warmth, wholeheartedness

cordon 1. *noun* barrier, chain, line, ring **2.** *~verb* **cordon off** close off, encircle, enclose, fence off, isolate, picket, separate, surround

core centre, crux, essence, gist, heart, kernel, nub, nucleus, pith

corner *noun* **1.** angle, bend, crook, joint **2.** cavity, cranny, hideaway, hide-out, hidey-hole (*informal*), hole, niche, nook, recess, retreat **3.** hole (*informal*), hot water (*informal*), pickle (*informal*), predicament, spot (*informal*), tight spot *~verb* **4.** bring to bay, run to earth, trap **5.** *as in* **corner the market** dominate, engross, hog (*slang*), monopolize

cornerstone 1. quoin **2.** basis, bedrock, key, premise, starting point

corny banal, commonplace, dull, feeble, hackneyed, maudlin, mawkish, old-fashioned, old hat, sentimental, stale, stereotyped, trite

corollary conclusion, consequence, deduction, induction, inference, result, sequel, upshot

corporal anatomical, bodily, carnal, corporeal (*archaic*), fleshly, material, physical, somatic

corporate allied, collaborative, collective, combined, communal, joint, merged, pooled, shared, united

corporation 1. association, corporate body, society **2.** civic authorities, council, municipal authorities, town council **3.** *informal* beer belly (*informal*), middle-age spread (*informal*), paunch, pod, pot, potbelly, spare tyre (*Brit. slang*), spread (*informal*)

corporeal bodily, fleshy, human, material, mortal, physical, substantial

corps band, body, company, contingent, crew, detachment, division, regiment, squad, squadron, team, troop, unit

corpse body, cadaver, carcass, remains, stiff (*slang*)

corpulence beef (*informal*), blubber, burliness, *embonpoint,* fatness, fleshiness, obesity, plumpness, portliness, rotundity, stoutness, tubbiness

corpulent beefy (*informal*), bulky, burly, fat, fattish, fleshy, large, lusty, obese, overweight, plump, portly, roly-poly, rotund, stout, tubby, well-padded
▷ **Antonyms** anorexic, bony, emaciated, gaunt, scrawny, skin and bones (*informal*), skinny, slim, thin, thin as a rake, underweight

corpus body, collection, compilation, complete works, entirety, *oeuvre,* whole

correct *verb* **1.** adjust, amend, cure, emend, improve, rectify, redress, reform, regulate, remedy, right, set the record straight **2.** admonish, chasten, chastise, chide, discipline, punish, reprimand, reprove *~adjective* **3.** accurate, equitable, exact, faultless, flawless, just, O.K. *or* okay (*informal*), on the right lines, precise, regular, right, strict, true **4.** acceptable, appropriate, diplomatic, fitting, kosher (*informal*), O.K. *or* okay (*informal*), proper, seemly, standard
▷ **Antonyms** *~verb* (*sense 1*) damage, harm, impair, ruin, spoil (*sense 2*) compliment, excuse, praise *~adjective* (*sense 3*) false, inaccurate, incorrect, untrue, wrong (*sense 4*) improper, inappropriate, unacceptable, unfitting, unsuitable

correction 1. adjustment, alteration, amendment, emendation, improvement, modification, rectification, righting **2.** admonition, castigation, chastisement, discipline, punishment, reformation, reproof

corrective *adjective* **1.** palliative, rehabilitative, remedial, restorative, therapeutic **2.** disciplinary, penal, punitive, reformatory

correctly accurately, aright, perfectly, precisely, properly, right, rightly

correctness 1. accuracy, exactitude, exactness, faultlessness, fidelity, preciseness, precision, regularity, truth **2.** *bon ton,* civility, decorum, good breeding, propriety, seemliness

correlate associate, compare, connect, coordinate, correspond, equate, interact, parallel, tie in

correlation alternation, correspondence, equivalence, interaction, interchange, interdependence, interrelationship, reciprocity

correspond 1. accord, agree, be consistent, coincide, complement, conform, correlate, dovetail, fit, harmonize, match, square, tally **2.** communicate, exchange letters, keep in touch, write

▷ **Antonyms** be at variance, be dissimilar, be inconsistent, belie, be unlike, differ, disagree, diverge, vary

correspondence 1. agreement, analogy, coincidence, comparability, comparison, concurrence, conformity, congruity, correlation, fitness, harmony, match, relation, similarity **2.** communication, letters, mail, post, writing

correspondent *noun* **1.** letter writer, pen friend *or* pal **2.** contributor, gazetteer (*archaic*), journalist, journo (*slang*), reporter, special correspondent *~adjective* **3.** analogous, comparable, like, of a piece, parallel, reciprocal, similar

corresponding analogous, answering, complementary, correlative, correspondent, equivalent, identical, interrelated, matching, reciprocal, similar, synonymous

corridor aisle, alley, hallway, passage, passageway

corroborate authenticate, back up, bear out, confirm, document, endorse, establish, ratify, substantiate, support, sustain, validate

▷ **Antonyms** contradict, disprove, invalidate, negate, rebut, refute

corrode canker, consume, corrupt, deteriorate, eat away, erode, gnaw, impair, oxidize, rust, waste, wear away

corrosive 1. acrid, biting, caustic, consuming, corroding, erosive, virulent, vitriolic, wasting, wearing **2.** caustic, cutting, incisive, mordant, sarcastic, trenchant, venomous, vitriolic

corrugated channelled, creased, crinkled, fluted, furrowed, grooved, puckered, ridged, rumpled, wrinkled

corrupt *adjective* **1.** bent (*slang*), bribable, crooked (*informal*), dishonest, fraudulent, rotten, shady (*informal*), unethical, unprincipled, unscrupulous, venal **2.** abandoned, debased, defiled, degenerate, demoralized, depraved, dishonoured, dissolute, profligate, vicious *~verb* **3.** bribe, buy off, debauch, demoralize, deprave, entice, fix (*informal*), grease (someone's) palm (*slang*), lure, pervert, square, suborn, subvert *~adjective* **4.** adulterated, altered, contaminated, decayed, defiled, distorted, doctored, falsified, infected, polluted, putrescent, putrid, rotten, tainted *~verb* **5.** adulterate, contaminate, debase, defile, doctor, infect, putrefy, spoil, taint, tamper with, vitiate

▷ **Antonyms** *~adjective* (*senses 1 & 2*) ethical, honest, honourable, moral, noble, principled, righteous, scrupulous, straight, undefiled, upright, virtuous *~verb* (*sense 3*) correct, purify, reform

corruption 1. breach of trust, bribery, bribing, crookedness (*informal*), demoralization, dishonesty, extortion, fiddling (*informal*), fraud, fraudulency, graft (*informal*), jobbery, profiteering, shadiness, shady dealings (*informal*), unscrupulousness, venality **2.** baseness, decadence, degeneration, degradation, depravity, evil, immorality, impurity, iniquity, perversion, profligacy, sinfulness, turpitude, vice, viciousness, wickedness **3.** adulteration, debasement, decay, defilement, distortion, doctoring, falsification, foulness, infection, pollution, putrefaction, putrescence, rot, rottenness

corsair buccaneer, freebooter, picaroon (*archaic*), pirate, rover, sea rover

corset 1. belt, bodice, corselet, foundation garment, girdle, panty girdle, stays (*rare*) **2.** *figurative* check, curb, limitation, restriction

cortege cavalcade, entourage, procession, retinue, suite, train

cosmetic *adjective* beautifying, nonessential, superficial, surface, touching-up

cosmic grandiose, huge, immense, infinite, limitless, measureless, stellar (*informal*), universal, vast

cosmonaut astronaut, spaceman, space pilot

cosmopolitan 1. *adjective* broad-minded, catholic, open-minded, sophisticated, universal, urbane, well-travelled, worldly, worldly-wise **2.** *~noun* cosmopolite, jetsetter, man *or* woman of the world, sophisticate

▷ **Antonyms** *~adjective* hidebound, illiberal, insular, limited, narrow-minded, parochial, provincial, restricted, rustic, unsophisticated

cosmos 1. creation, macrocosm, universe, world **2.** harmony, order, structure

cosset baby, coddle, cosher (*Irish*), mollycoddle, pamper, pet, wrap up in cotton wool (*informal*)

cost *noun* **1.** amount, charge, damage (*informal*), expenditure, expense, figure, outlay, payment, price, rate, worth **2.** damage, deprivation, detriment, expense, harm, hurt, injury, loss, penalty, sacrifice, suffering *~verb* **3.** come to, command a price of, sell at, set (someone) back (*informal*) **4.** *figurative* do disservice to, harm, hurt, injure, lose, necessitate

costly 1. dear, excessive, exorbitant, expensive, extortionate, highly-priced, steep (*informal*), stiff, valuable **2.** gorgeous, lavish, luxurious, opulent, precious, priceless, rich, splendid, sumptuous **3.** *entailing loss or sacrifice* catastrophic, damaging, deleterious, disastrous, harmful, loss-making, ruinous, sacrificial

▷ **Antonyms** (*sense 1*) cheap, cheapo (*informal*), dirt-cheap, economical, fair, inexpensive, low-priced, reasonable, reduced

costs 1. budget, expenses, outgoings,

overheads **2. at all costs** at any price, no matter what, regardless, without fail

costume apparel, attire, clothing, dress, ensemble, garb, get-up (*informal*), livery, national dress, outfit, robes, uniform

cosy comfortable, comfy (*informal*), cuddled up, homely, intimate, secure, sheltered, snug, snuggled down, tucked up, warm

coterie cabal, camp, circle, clique, gang, group, outfit (*informal*), posse (*informal*), set

cottage but-and-ben (*Scot.*), cabin, chalet, cot, hut, lodge, shack

couch 1. *verb* express, frame, phrase, set forth, utter, word **2.** *~noun* bed, chaise longue, chesterfield, daybed, divan, ottoman, settee, sofa

cough 1. *noun* bark, frog *or* tickle in one's throat, hack **2.** *~verb* bark, clear one's throat, hack, hawk, hem

cough up ante up (*informal, chiefly U.S.*), come across, deliver, fork out (*slang*), give up, hand over, shell out (*informal*), surrender

council assembly, board, cabinet, chamber, committee, conclave, conference, congress, convention, convocation, diet, governing body, house, ministry, panel, parliament, quango, synod

counsel *noun* **1.** admonition, advice, caution, consideration, consultation, deliberation, direction, forethought, guidance, information, recommendation, suggestion, warning **2.** advocate, attorney, barrister, lawyer, legal adviser, solicitor *~verb* **3.** admonish, advise, advocate, caution, exhort, instruct, prescribe, recommend, urge, warn

count *verb* **1.** add (up), calculate, cast up, check, compute, enumerate, estimate, number, reckon, score, tally, tot up **2.** consider, deem, esteem, impute, judge, look upon, rate, regard, think **3.** carry weight, cut any ice (*informal*), enter into consideration, matter, rate, signify, tell, weigh **4.** include, number among, take into account *or* consideration *~noun* **5.** calculation, computation, enumeration, numbering, poll, reckoning, sum, tally

countenance *noun* **1.** appearance, aspect, expression, face, features, look, mien, physiognomy, visage **2.** aid, approval, assistance, backing, endorsement, favour, sanction, support *~verb* **3.** abet, aid, approve, back, champion, commend, condone, encourage, endorse, help, sanction, support **4.** brook, endure, hack (*slang*), put up with (*informal*), stand for (*informal*), tolerate

counter 1. *adverb* against, at variance with, contrarily, contrariwise, conversely, in defiance of, versus **2.** *~adjective* adverse, against, conflicting, contradictory, contrary, contrasting, obverse, opposed, opposing, opposite **3.** *~verb* answer, hit back, meet, obviate, offset, parry, resist, respond, retaliate, return, ward off

▷ **Antonyms** *~adverb/adjective* accordant, in agreement, parallel, similar *~verb* accept, give in, surrender, take, yield

counteract annul, check, contravene, counterbalance, countervail, cross, defeat, foil, frustrate, hinder, invalidate, negate, neutralize, obviate, offset, oppose, resist, thwart

counterbalance balance, compensate, counterpoise, countervail, make up for, offset, set off

counterfeit 1. *verb* copy, fabricate, fake, feign, forge, imitate, impersonate, pretend, sham, simulate **2.** *~adjective* bogus, copied, ersatz, faked, false, feigned, forged, fraudulent, imitation, phoney *or* phony (*informal*), pseud *or* pseudo (*informal*), sham, simulated, spurious, suppositious **3.** *~noun* copy, fake, forgery, fraud, imitation, phoney *or* phony (*informal*), reproduction, sham

▷ **Antonyms** authentic, genuine, good, original, real, the real thing

countermand annul, cancel, override, repeal, rescind, retract, reverse, revoke

counterpane bedcover, bedspread, cover, coverlet, doona (*Austral.*), quilt

counterpart complement, copy, correlative, duplicate, equal, fellow, match, mate, opposite number, supplement, tally, twin

countless endless, immeasurable, incalculable, infinite, innumerable, legion, limitless, measureless, multitudinous, myriad, numberless, uncounted, untold

▷ **Antonyms** finite, limited, restricted

count on *or* **upon** bank on, believe (in), depend on, lean on, pin one's faith on, reckon on, rely on, take for granted, take on trust, trust

count out disregard, except, exclude, leave out, leave out of account, pass over

countrified agrestic, Arcadian, bucolic, cracker-barrel (*U.S.*), homespun, idyllic, pastoral, picturesque, provincial, rural, rustic

country *noun* **1.** commonwealth, kingdom, nation, people, realm, sovereign state, state **2.** fatherland, homeland, motherland, nationality, native land, *patria* **3.** land, part, region, terrain, territory **4.** citizenry, citizens, community, electors, grass roots, inhabitants, nation, people, populace, public, society, voters **5.** back country (*U.S.*), backlands (*U.S.*), backwoods, boondocks (*U.S. slang*), countryside, farmland, green belt, outback (*Austral. & N.Z.*), outdoors, provinces, rural areas, sticks (*informal*), the back of beyond, the middle of nowhere, wide open spaces (*informal*)

~adjective **6.** agrarian, agrestic, Arcadian, bucolic, georgic (*literary*), landed, pastoral, provincial, rural, rustic
▷ **Antonyms** *~noun* (*sense 5*) city, metropolis, town *~adjective* city, cosmopolitan, sophisticated, urban, urbane

countryman 1. bumpkin, cockie (*N.Z.*), country dweller, farmer, hayseed (*U.S. & Canad. informal*), hick (*informal, chiefly U.S. & Canad.*), hind (*obsolete*), husbandman, peasant, provincial, rustic, swain, yokel **2.** compatriot, fellow citizen

countryside country, farmland, green belt, outback (*Austral. & N.Z.*), outdoors, panorama, sticks (*informal*), view, wide open spaces (*informal*)

count up add, reckon up, sum, tally, total

county 1. *noun* province, shire **2.** *~adjective* green-wellie, huntin', shootin', and fishin' (*informal*), plummy (*informal*), tweedy, upper-class, upper-crust (*informal*)

coup accomplishment, action, deed, exploit, feat, manoeuvre, masterstroke, stratagem, stroke, stroke of genius, stunt, *tour de force*

coup de grâce clincher (*informal*), comeuppance (*slang*), deathblow, final blow, kill, knockout blow, mercy stroke, mortal blow, quietus

coup d'état coup, overthrow, palace revolution, putsch, rebellion, seizure of power, takeover

couple 1. *noun* brace, duo, item, pair, span (*of horses or oxen*), twain (*archaic*), two, twosome **2.** *~verb* buckle, clasp, conjoin, connect, hitch, join, link, marry, pair, unite, wed, yoke

coupon card, certificate, detachable portion, slip, ticket, token, voucher

courage balls (*taboo slang*), ballsiness (*taboo slang*), boldness, bottle (*Brit. slang*), bravery, daring, dauntlessness, fearlessness, firmness, fortitude, gallantry, grit, guts (*informal*), hardihood, heroism, intrepidity, lion-heartedness, mettle, nerve, pluck, resolution, spunk (*informal*), valour
▷ **Antonyms** cowardice, cravenness, faint-heartedness, fear, timidity

courageous audacious, ballsy (*taboo slang*), bold, brave, daring, dauntless, fearless, gallant, gritty, hardy, heroic, indomitable, intrepid, lion-hearted, plucky, resolute, stalwart, stouthearted, valiant, valorous
▷ **Antonyms** chicken (*slang*), chicken-hearted, chickenshit (*U.S. slang*), cowardly, craven, dastardly, faint-hearted, gutless (*informal*), lily-livered, pusillanimous, scared, spineless, timid, timorous, yellow (*informal*)

courier 1. bearer, carrier, emissary, envoy, herald, messenger, pursuivant (*Historical*), runner **2.** guide, representative

course *noun* **1.** advance, advancement, continuity, development, flow, furtherance, march, movement, order, progress, progression, sequence, succession, tenor, unfolding **2.** channel, direction, line, orbit, passage, path, road, route, tack, track, trail, trajectory, way **3.** duration, lapse, passage, passing, sweep, term, time **4.** behaviour, conduct, manner, method, mode, plan, policy, procedure, programme, regimen **5.** cinder track, circuit, lap, race, racecourse, round **6.** classes, course of study, curriculum, lectures, programme, schedule, studies *~verb* **7.** dash, flow, gush, move apace, race, run, scud, scurry, speed, stream, surge, tumble **8.** chase, follow, hunt, pursue **9. in due course** eventually, finally, in the course of time, in the end, in time, sooner or later **10. of course** certainly, definitely, indubitably, naturally, needless to say, obviously, undoubtedly, without a doubt

court *noun* **1.** cloister, courtyard, piazza, plaza, quad (*informal*), quadrangle, square, yard **2.** hall, manor, palace **3.** attendants, cortege, entourage, retinue, royal household, suite, train **4.** bar, bench, court of justice, lawcourt, seat of judgment, tribunal **5.** addresses, attention, homage, respects, suit *~verb* **6.** chase, date, go (out) with, go steady with (*informal*), keep company with, make love to, pay court to, pay one's addresses to, pursue, run after, serenade, set one's cap at, sue (*archaic*), take out, walk out with, woo **7.** cultivate, curry favour with, fawn upon, flatter, pander to, seek, solicit **8.** attract, bring about, incite, invite, prompt, provoke, seek

courteous affable, attentive, ceremonious, civil, courtly, elegant, gallant, gracious, mannerly, polished, polite, refined, respectful, urbane, well-bred, well-mannered
▷ **Antonyms** discourteous, disrespectful, ill-mannered, impolite, insolent, rude, uncivil, ungracious, unkind

courtesan call girl, demimondaine, *fille de joie,* harlot, hetaera, kept woman, mistress, paramour, prostitute, scarlet woman, whore, working girl (*facetious slang*)

courtesy 1. affability, civility, courteousness, courtliness, elegance, gallantness, gallantry, good breeding, good manners, grace, graciousness, polish, politeness, urbanity **2.** benevolence, consent, consideration, favour, generosity, indulgence, kindness

courtier attendant, follower, henchman, liegeman, pursuivant (*Historical*), squire, train-bearer

courtliness affability, breeding, ceremony, chivalrousness, correctness, cour~

tesy, decorum, elegance, formality, gallantry, gentility, graciousness, politeness, politesse, propriety, refinement, stateliness, urbanity

courtly affable, aristocratic, ceremonious, chivalrous, civil, decorous, dignified, elegant, flattering, formal, gallant, highbred, lordly, obliging, polished, refined, stately, urbane

courtship courting, engagement, keeping company, pursuit, romance, suit, wooing

courtyard area, enclosure, peristyle, playground, quad, quadrangle, yard

cove[1] *noun* anchorage, bay, bayou, creek, firth *or* frith (*Scot.*), inlet, sound

cove[2] *noun* bloke (*Brit. informal*), chap, character, customer, fellow, type

covenant *noun* **1**. arrangement, bargain, commitment, compact, concordat, contract, convention, pact, promise, stipulation, treaty, trust **2**. bond, deed *~verb* **3**. agree, bargain, contract, engage, pledge, shake hands, stipulate, undertake

cover *verb* **1**. camouflage, cloak, conceal, cover up, curtain, disguise, eclipse, enshroud, hide, hood, house, mask, obscure, screen, secrete, shade, shroud, veil *~noun* **2**. cloak, cover-up, disguise, façade, front, mask, pretence, screen, smoke screen, veil, window-dressing *~verb* **3**. defend, guard, protect, reinforce, shelter, shield, watch over *~noun* **4**. camouflage, concealment, defence, guard, hiding place, protection, refuge, sanctuary, shelter, shield, undergrowth, woods *~verb* **5**. canopy, clothe, coat, daub, dress, encase, envelop, invest, layer, mantle, overlay, overspread, put on, wrap *~noun* **6**. awning, binding, canopy, cap, case, clothing, coating, covering, dress, envelope, jacket, lid, sheath, top, wrapper *~verb* **7**. comprehend, comprise, consider, contain, deal with, embody, embrace, encompass, examine, include, incorporate, involve, provide for, refer to, survey, take account of **8**. double for, fill in for, hold the fort (*informal*), relieve, stand in for, substitute, take over, take the rap for (*slang*) **9**. describe, detail, investigate, narrate, recount, relate, report, tell of, write up **10**. balance, compensate, counterbalance, insure, make good, make up for, offset *~noun* **11**. compensation, indemnity, insurance, payment, protection, reimbursement *~verb* **12**. cross, pass through *or* over, range, travel over, traverse **13**. engulf, flood, overrun, submerge, wash over

▷ **Antonyms** *~verb* exclude, exhibit, expose, omit, reveal, show, unclothe, uncover, unmask, unwrap *~noun* base, bottom

coverage analysis, description, reportage, reporting, treatment

covering 1. *noun* blanket, casing, clothing, coating, cover, housing, layer, overlay, protection, shelter, top, wrap, wrapper, wrapping **2**. *~adjective* accompanying, descriptive, explanatory, introductory

covert 1. *adjective* clandestine, concealed, disguised, dissembled, hidden, private, secret, sly, stealthy, surreptitious, underhand, unsuspected, veiled **2**. *~noun* brush (*archaic*), bushes, coppice, shrubbery, thicket, undergrowth, underwood

cover-up complicity, concealment, conspiracy, front, smoke screen, whitewash (*informal*)

cover up 1. conceal, cover one's tracks, draw a veil over, feign ignorance, hide, hush up, keep dark, keep secret, keep silent about, keep under one's hat (*informal*), repress, stonewall, suppress, sweep under the carpet, whitewash (*informal*) **2**. Artex (*Trademark*), coat, cover, encrust, envelop, hide, plaster, slather (*U.S. slang*), swathe

covet aspire to, begrudge, crave, desire, envy, fancy (*informal*), hanker after, have one's eye on, long for, lust after, set one's heart on, thirst for, would give one's eyeteeth for, yearn for

covetous acquisitive, avaricious, close-fisted, envious, grasping, greedy, jealous, mercenary, rapacious, yearning

covey bevy, brood, cluster, flight, flock, group, nye *or* nide (*of pheasants*)

cow awe, browbeat, bully, daunt, dishearten, dismay, frighten, intimidate, overawe, psych out (*informal*), scare, subdue, terrorize, unnerve

coward caitiff (*archaic*), chicken (*slang*), craven, dastard (*archaic*), faint-heart, funk (*informal*), poltroon, recreant (*archaic*), renegade, scaredy-cat (*informal*), skulker, sneak, wimp (*informal*), yellow-belly (*slang*)

cowardly abject, base, caitiff (*archaic*), chicken (*slang*), chicken-hearted, chickenshit (*U.S. slang*), craven, dastardly, faint-hearted, fearful, gutless (*informal*), lily-livered, pusillanimous, recreant (*archaic*), scared, shrinking, soft, spineless, timorous, weak, weak-kneed (*informal*), white-livered, yellow (*informal*)

▷ **Antonyms** audacious, bold, brave, courageous, daring, dauntless, doughty, intrepid, plucky, valiant

cowboy broncobuster (*U.S.*), buckaroo (*U.S.*), cattleman, cowhand, cowpuncher (*U.S. informal*), drover, gaucho (*S. American*), herder, herdsman, rancher, ranchero (*U.S.*), stockman, wrangler (*U.S.*)

cower cringe, crouch, draw back, fawn, flinch, grovel, quail, shrink, skulk, sneak, tremble, truckle

coxcomb beau, Beau Brummell, dandy, dude (*U.S. & Canad. informal*), exquisite, fop, macaroni (*obsolete*), peacock, popinjay, poser (*informal*), prig, puppy, spark (*rare*), swell (*informal*)

coy arch, backward, bashful, coquettish, demure, evasive, flirtatious, kittenish, modest, overmodest, prudish, reserved, retiring, self-effacing, shrinking, shy, skittish, timid
▷ **Antonyms** bold, brash, brass-necked (*Brit. informal*), brassy (*informal*), brazen, flip (*informal*), forward, impertinent, impudent, pert, pushy (*informal*), saucy, shameless

coyness affectation, archness, backwardness, bashfulness, coquettishness, demureness, diffidence, evasiveness, modesty, primness, prissiness (*informal*), prudery, prudishness, reserve, shrinking, shyness, skittishness, timidity

cozen bilk, cheat, circumvent, con (*informal*), deceive, diddle (*informal*), double-cross (*informal*), dupe, gull (*archaic*), hoodwink, impose on, inveigle, stiff (*slang*), stitch up (*slang*), swindle, take advantage of, take for a ride (*informal*), victimize

crabbed **1.** acrid, acrimonious, captious, churlish, cross, cynical, difficult, fretful, harsh, ill-tempered, irritable, morose, perverse, petulant, prickly, ratty (*Brit. & N.Z. informal*), sour, splenetic, surly, tart, testy, tetchy, tough, trying **2.** *of handwriting* awkward, cramped, hieroglyphical, illegible, indecipherable, laboured, squeezed, unreadable

crabby acid, awkward, bad-tempered, cross, crotchety (*informal*), grouchy (*informal*), ill-humoured, irritable, mardy (*dialect*), misanthropic, nasty-tempered, prickly, ratty (*Brit. & N.Z. informal*), snappish, snappy, sour, surly, testy, tetchy, unsociable

crack *verb* **1.** break, burst, chip, chop, cleave, crackle, craze, fracture, rive, snap, splinter, split *~noun* **2.** breach, break, chink, chip, cleft, cranny, crevice, fissure, fracture, gap, interstice, rift *~verb* **3.** burst, crash, detonate, explode, pop, ring, snap *~noun* **4.** burst, clap, crash, explosion, pop, report, snap *~verb* **5.** break down, collapse, give way, go to pieces, lose control, succumb, yield *~verb/noun* **6.** *informal* buffet, clip (*informal*), clout (*informal*), cuff, slap, thump, wallop (*informal*), whack *~verb* **7.** decipher, fathom, get the answer to, solve, work out *~noun* **8.** *informal* attempt, go (*informal*), opportunity, shot, stab (*informal*), try **9.** *slang* dig, funny remark, gag (*informal*), insult, jibe, joke, quip, smart-alecky remark, wisecrack, witticism *~adjective* **10.** *slang* ace, choice, elite, excellent, first-class, first-rate, hand-picked, superior, world-class

crackbrained cracked (*slang*), crackers (*Brit. slang*), crackpot (*informal*), crazy (*informal*), gonzo (*slang*), idiotic, insane, loopy (*informal*), lunatic, off one's rocker (*slang*), off one's trolley (*slang*), out of one's mind, out to lunch (*informal*), round the twist (*Brit. slang*), up the pole (*informal*), wacko *or* whacko (*informal*)

crackdown clampdown, crushing, repression, suppression

cracked **1.** broken, chipped, crazed, damaged, defective, faulty, fissured, flawed, imperfect, split **2.** *slang* bats (*slang*), batty (*slang*), crackbrained, crackpot (*informal*), crazy (*informal*), daft (*informal*), doolally (*slang*), eccentric, gonzo (*slang*), insane, loony (*slang*), loopy (*informal*), nuts (*slang*), nutty (*slang*), oddball (*informal*), off one's head *or* nut (*slang*), off one's rocker (*slang*), off one's trolley (*slang*), off-the-wall (*slang*), out of one's mind, outré, out to lunch (*informal*), round the bend (*slang*), round the twist (*Brit. slang*), touched, up the pole (*informal*), wacko *or* whacko (*informal*)

cracked up blown up, exaggerated, hyped (up), overpraised, overrated, puffed up

crack up break down, collapse, come apart at the seams (*informal*), flip one's lid (*slang*), fly off the handle (*informal*), freak out (*informal*), go ape (*slang*), go apeshit (*slang*), go berserk, go crazy (*informal*), go off one's head (*slang*), go off one's rocker (*slang*), go off the deep end (*informal*), go out of one's mind, go to pieces, have a breakdown, throw a wobbly (*slang*)

cradle *noun* **1.** bassinet, cot, crib, Moses basket **2.** *figurative* beginning, birthplace, fount, fountainhead, origin, source, spring, wellspring *~verb* **3.** hold, lull, nestle, nurse, rock, support **4.** nourish, nurture, tend, watch over

craft **1.** ability, aptitude, art, artistry, cleverness, dexterity, expertise, expertness, ingenuity, knack, know-how (*informal*), skill, technique, workmanship **2.** artfulness, artifice, contrivance, craftiness, cunning, deceit, duplicity, guile, ruse, scheme, shrewdness, stratagem, subterfuge, subtlety, trickery, wiles **3.** business, calling, employment, handicraft, handiwork, line, occupation, pursuit, trade, vocation, work **4.** aircraft, barque, boat, plane, ship, spacecraft, vessel

craftiness artfulness, astuteness, canniness, cunning, deviousness, duplicity, foxiness, guile, shrewdness, slyness, subtlety, trickiness, wiliness

craftsman artificer, artisan, maker, master, skilled worker, smith, technician, wright

craftsmanship artistry, expertise, mastery, technique, workmanship

crafty artful, astute, calculating, canny, cunning, deceitful, designing, devious,

duplicitous, foxy, fraudulent, guileful, insidious, knowing, scheming, sharp, shrewd, sly, subtle, tricksy, tricky, wily
▷ **Antonyms** as green as grass, candid, ethical, frank, honest, ingenuous, innocent, naive, open, simple, wet behind the ears

crag aiguille, bluff, peak, pinnacle, rock, tor

craggy broken, cragged, jagged, jaggy (*Scot.*), precipitous, rock-bound, rocky, rough, rugged, stony, uneven

cram 1. compact, compress, crowd, crush, fill to overflowing, force, jam, overcrowd, overfill, pack, pack in, press, ram, shove, squeeze, stuff **2.** glut, gorge, gormandize, guzzle, overeat, overfeed, pig out (*slang*), put *or* pack away, satiate, stuff **3.** *informal* bone up on (*informal*), con, grind, mug up (*slang*), revise, study, swot, swot up

cramp[1] *verb* check, circumscribe, clip someone's wings, clog, confine, constrain, encumber, hamper, hamstring, handicap, hinder, impede, inhibit, obstruct, restrict, shackle, stymie, thwart

cramp[2] *noun* ache, contraction, convulsion, crick, pain, pang, shooting pain, spasm, stiffness, stitch, twinge

cramped 1. awkward, circumscribed, closed in, confined, congested, crowded, hemmed in, jammed in, narrow, overcrowded, packed, restricted, squeezed, uncomfortable **2.** *especially of handwriting* crabbed, indecipherable, irregular, small
▷ **Antonyms** (*sense 1*) capacious, commodious, large, open, roomy, sizable *or* sizeable, spacious, uncongested, uncrowded

crank case (*informal*), character (*informal*), freak (*informal*), kook (*U.S. & Canad. informal*), nut (*slang*), oddball (*informal*), odd fish (*informal*), queer fish (*Brit. informal*), rum customer (*Brit. slang*), screwball (*slang, chiefly U.S. & Canad.*), wacko *or* whacko (*informal*), weirdo *or* weirdie (*informal*)

cranky bizarre, capricious, eccentric, erratic, freakish, freaky (*slang*), funny (*informal*), idiosyncratic, odd, oddball (*informal*), off-the-wall (*slang*), outré, peculiar, queer, quirky, rum (*Brit. slang*), strange, wacko *or* whacko (*informal*), wacky (*slang*)

cranny breach, chink, cleft, crack, crevice, fissure, gap, hole, interstice, nook, opening, rift

crash *noun* **1.** bang, boom, clang, clash, clatter, clattering, din, racket, smash, smashing, thunder *~verb* **2.** break, break up, dash to pieces, disintegrate, fracture, fragment, shatter, shiver, smash, splinter **3.** come a cropper (*informal*), dash, fall, fall headlong, give way, hurtle, lurch, overbalance, pitch, plunge, precipitate oneself, sprawl, topple **4.** bang, bump (into), collide, crash-land (*an aircraft*), drive into, have an accident, hit, hurtle into, plough into, run together, wreck *~noun* **5.** accident, bump, collision, jar, jolt, pile-up (*informal*), prang (*informal*), smash, smash-up, thud, thump, wreck **6.** bankruptcy, collapse, debacle, depression, downfall, failure, ruin, smash *~verb* **7.** be ruined, collapse, fail, fold, fold up, go belly up (*informal*), go broke (*informal*), go bust (*informal*), go to the wall, go under, smash *~adjective* **8.** *of a course of studies, etc.* emergency, immediate, intensive, round-the-clock, speeded-up, telescoped, urgent

crass asinine, blundering, boorish, bovine, coarse, dense, doltish, gross, indelicate, insensitive, lumpish, oafish, obtuse, stupid, unrefined, witless
▷ **Antonyms** brainy (*informal*), bright, clever, elegant, intelligent, polished, refined, sensitive, sharp, smart

crassness asininity, boorishness, coarseness, denseness, doltishness, grossness, indelicacy, insensitivity, oafishness, stupidity, tactlessness, vulgarity

crate 1. *noun* box, case, container, packing case, tea chest **2.** *~verb* box, case, encase, enclose, pack, pack up

crater depression, dip, hollow, shell hole

crave 1. be dying for, cry out for (*informal*), desire, eat one's heart out over, fancy (*informal*), hanker after, hope for, hunger after, long for, lust after, need, pant for, pine for, require, set one's heart on, sigh for, thirst for, want, would give one's eyeteeth for, yearn for **2.** ask, beg, beseech, entreat, implore, petition, plead for, pray for, seek, solicit, supplicate

craven 1. *adjective* abject, caitiff (*archaic*), chicken-hearted, chickenshit (*U.S. slang*), cowardly, dastardly, fearful, lily-livered, mean-spirited, niddering (*archaic*), pusillanimous, scared, timorous, weak, yellow (*informal*) **2.** *~noun* base fellow (*archaic*), caitiff (*archaic*), coward, dastard (*archaic*), niddering (*archaic*), poltroon, recreant (*archaic*), renegade, wheyface, yellow-belly (*slang*)

craving ache, appetite, cacoethes, desire, hankering, hope, hunger, longing, lust, thirst, urge, yearning, yen (*informal*)

craw crop, gizzard, gullet, maw, stomach, throat

crawl 1. advance slowly, creep, drag, go on all fours, inch, move at a snail's pace, move on hands and knees, pull *or* drag oneself along, slither, worm one's way, wriggle, writhe **2.** be alive, be full of, be lousy, be overrun (*slang*), swarm, teem **3.** abase oneself, brown-nose (*taboo slang*), cringe, fawn, grovel, humble oneself, kiss ass (*U.S. & Canad. taboo slang*), lick someone's arse (*taboo slang*),

lick someone's boots (*slang*), pander to, toady, truckle
▷ **Antonyms** (*sense 1*) dart, dash, fly, hasten, hurry, race, run, rush, sprint, step on it (*informal*), walk

craze 1. *noun* enthusiasm, fad, fashion, infatuation, mania, mode, novelty, passion, preoccupation, rage, the latest (*informal*), thing, trend, vogue 2. *~verb* bewilder, confuse, dement, derange, distemper, drive mad, enrage, infatuate, inflame, madden, make insane, send crazy *or* berserk, unbalance, unhinge, unsettle

crazy 1. *informal* a bit lacking upstairs (*informal*), as daft as a brush (*informal, chiefly Brit.*), barking (*slang*), barking mad (*slang*), barmy (*slang*), batty (*slang*), berserk, bonkers (*slang, chiefly Brit.*), cracked (*slang*), crackpot (*informal*), crazed, cuckoo (*informal*), daft (*informal*), delirious, demented, deranged, doolally (*slang*), idiotic, insane, loopy (*informal*), lunatic, mad, mad as a hatter, mad as a March hare, maniacal, mental (*slang*), not all there (*informal*), not right in the head, not the full shilling (*informal*), nuts (*slang*), nutty (*slang*), nutty as a fruitcake (*slang*), off one's head (*slang*), off one's rocker (*slang*), off one's trolley (*slang*), off-the-wall (*slang*), of unsound mind, out of one's mind, out to lunch (*informal*), potty (*Brit. informal*), round the bend (*slang*), round the twist (*Brit. slang*), touched, unbalanced, unhinged, up the pole (*informal*) 2. bizarre, eccentric, fantastic, odd, oddball (*informal*), outrageous, peculiar, ridiculous, rum (*Brit. slang*), silly, strange, wacko *or* whacko (*informal*), weird 3. absurd, bird-brained (*informal*), cockeyed (*informal*), derisory, fatuous, foolhardy, foolish, half-baked (*informal*), idiotic, ill-conceived, impracticable, imprudent, inane, inappropriate, irresponsible, ludicrous, nonsensical, potty (*Brit. informal*), preposterous, puerile, quixotic, senseless, short-sighted, unrealistic, unwise, unworkable, wild 4. *informal* ablaze, ardent, beside oneself, devoted, eager, enamoured, enthusiastic, fanatical, hysterical, infatuated, into (*informal*), mad, passionate, smitten, very keen, wild (*informal*), zealous
▷ **Antonyms** (*sense 1*) all there (*informal*), *compos mentis,* down-to-earth, in one's right mind, intelligent, mentally sound, practical, prudent, rational, reasonable, sane, sensible, smart, wise (*sense 2*) common, conventional, normal, ordinary, orthodox, regular, usual (*sense 3*) appropriate, brilliant, feasible, possible, practicable, prudent, realistic, responsible, sensible, wise, workable (*sense 4*) cool, indifferent, uncaring, unenthusiastic, uninterested

creak *verb* grate, grind, groan, rasp, scrape, scratch, screech, squeak, squeal

creaky creaking, grating, rasping, raspy, rusty, squeaking, squeaky, unoiled

cream *noun* 1. cosmetic, emulsion, essence, liniment, lotion, oil, ointment, paste, salve, unguent 2. best, *crème de la crème,* elite, flower, pick, prime *~adjective* 3. off-white, yellowish-white

creamy buttery, creamed, lush, milky, oily, rich, smooth, soft, velvety

crease 1. *verb* corrugate, crimp, crinkle, crumple, double up, fold, pucker, ridge, ruck up, rumple, screw up, wrinkle 2. *~noun* bulge, corrugation, fold, groove, line, overlap, pucker, ridge, ruck, tuck, wrinkle

create 1. beget, bring into being *or* existence, coin, compose, concoct, design, develop, devise, dream up (*informal*), form, formulate, generate, give birth to, give life to, hatch, initiate, invent, make, originate, produce, spawn 2. appoint, constitute, establish, found, install, invest, make, set up 3. bring about, cause, lead to, occasion
▷ **Antonyms** annihilate, close, demolish, destroy

creation 1. conception, formation, generation, genesis, making, procreation, siring 2. constitution, development, establishment, formation, foundation, inception, institution, laying down, origination, production, setting up 3. achievement, brainchild (*informal*), *chef-d'oeuvre,* concept, concoction, handiwork, invention, *magnum opus, pièce de résistance,* production 4. all living things, cosmos, life, living world, natural world, nature, universe, world

creative artistic, clever, fertile, gifted, imaginative, ingenious, inspired, inventive, original, productive, stimulating, visionary

creativity cleverness, fecundity, fertility, imagination, imaginativeness, ingenuity, inspiration, inventiveness, originality, productivity, talent

creator architect, author, begetter, designer, father, framer, God, initiator, inventor, maker, originator, prime mover

creature 1. animal, beast, being, brute, critter (*U.S. dialect*), dumb animal, living thing, lower animal, quadruped 2. body, character, fellow, human being, individual, man, mortal, person, soul, wight (*archaic*), woman 3. cohort (*chiefly U.S.*), dependant, hanger-on, hireling, instrument (*informal*), lackey, minion, puppet, retainer, tool, wretch

credence acceptance, assurance, belief, certainty, confidence, credit, dependence, faith, reliance, trust

credentials attestation, authorization, card, certificate, deed, diploma, docket, letter of recommendation *or* introduction, letters of credence, licence, missive, passport, recommendation, reference(s), testament, testimonial, title, voucher, warrant

credibility believability, believableness, integrity, plausibility, reliability, tenability, trustworthiness

credible 1. believable, conceivable, imaginable, likely, plausible, possible, probable, reasonable, supposable, tenable, thinkable, verisimilar **2.** dependable, honest, reliable, sincere, trustworthy, trusty

▷ **Antonyms** (*sense 1*) doubtful, implausible, inconceivable, incredible, questionable, unbelievable, unlikely (*sense 2*) dishonest, insincere, not dependable, unreliable, untrustworthy

credit *noun* **1.** acclaim, acknowledgment, approval, Brownie points, commendation, fame, glory, honour, kudos, merit, praise, recognition, thanks, tribute **2.** character, clout (*informal*), esteem, estimation, good name, influence, position, prestige, regard, reputation, repute, standing, status **3.** belief, confidence, credence, faith, reliance, trust **4.** *as in* **be a credit to** feather in one's cap, honour, source of satisfaction *or* pride **5. on credit** by deferred payment, by instalments, on account, on hire-purchase, on (the) H.P., on the slate (*informal*), on tick (*informal*) ~*verb* **6.** (*with* **with**) accredit, ascribe to, assign to, attribute to, chalk up to (*informal*), impute to, refer to **7.** accept, bank on, believe, buy (*slang*), depend on, fall for, have faith in, rely on, swallow (*informal*), trust

creditable admirable, commendable, deserving, estimable, exemplary, honourable, laudable, meritorious, praiseworthy, reputable, respectable, worthy

credulity blind faith, credulousness, gullibility, naïveté, silliness, simplicity, stupidity

credulous as green as grass, born yesterday (*informal*), dupable, green, gullible, naive, overtrusting, trustful, uncritical, unsuspecting, unsuspicious, wet behind the ears (*informal*)

▷ **Antonyms** cynical, incredulous, sceptical, suspecting, unbelieving, wary

creed articles of faith, belief, canon, catechism, confession, credo, doctrine, dogma, persuasion, principles, profession (*of faith*), tenet

creek 1. bay, bight, cove, firth *or* frith (*Scot.*), inlet **2.** *U.S., Canad., & Austral.* bayou, brook, rivulet, runnel, stream, streamlet, tributary, watercourse

creep *verb* **1.** crawl, crawl on all fours, glide, insinuate, slither, squirm, worm, wriggle, writhe **2.** approach unnoticed, skulk, slink, sneak, steal, tiptoe **3.** crawl, dawdle, drag, edge, inch, proceed at a snail's pace **4.** bootlick (*informal*), brown-nose (*taboo slang*), cower, cringe, fawn, grovel, kiss (someone's) ass (*U.S. & Canad. taboo slang*), kowtow, pander to, scrape, suck up to (*informal*), toady, truckle ~*noun* **5.** *slang* ass-kisser (*U.S. & Canad. taboo slang*), bootlicker (*informal*), brown-noser (*taboo slang*), sneak, sycophant, toady **6. give one the creeps** *or* **make one's flesh creep** disgust, frighten, horrify, make one flinch, make one quail, make one shrink, make one squirm, make one's hair stand on end, make one wince (*informal*), repel, repulse, scare, terrify, terrorize

creeper climber, climbing plant, rambler, runner, trailing plant, vine (*chiefly U.S.*)

creepy awful, direful, disgusting, disturbing, eerie, forbidding, frightening, ghoulish, goose-pimply (*informal*), gruesome, hair-raising, horrible, macabre, menacing, nightmarish, ominous, scary (*informal*), sinister, terrifying, threatening, unpleasant, weird

crepitate crack, crackle, rattle, snap

crescent *noun* **1.** half-moon, meniscus, new moon, old moon, sickle, sickle-shape ~*adjective* **2.** arched, bow-shaped, curved, falcate, semicircular, sickle-shaped **3.** *archaic* growing, increasing, waxing

Crescent, the Islam, Mohammedanism, Muslim Empire, Turkey

crest 1. apex, crown, head, height, highest point, peak, pinnacle, ridge, summit, top **2.** aigrette, caruncle (*Zoology*), cockscomb, comb, crown, mane, panache, plume, tassel, topknot, tuft **3.** *Heraldry* badge, bearings, charge, device, emblem, insignia, symbol

crestfallen chapfallen, choked, dejected, depressed, despondent, disappointed, disconsolate, discouraged, disheartened, downcast, downhearted, sick as a parrot (*informal*)

▷ **Antonyms** cock-a-hoop, elated, encouraged, exuberant, happy, in seventh heaven, joyful, on cloud nine (*informal*), over the moon (*informal*)

crevasse abyss, bergschrund, chasm, cleft, crack, fissure

crevice chink, cleft, crack, cranny, fissure, fracture, gap, hole, interstice, opening, rent, rift, slit, split

crew 1. hands, (ship's) company, (ship's) complement **2.** company, corps, gang, party, posse, squad, team, working party **3.** *informal* assemblage, band, bunch (*informal*), camp, company, crowd, gang, herd, horde, lot, mob, pack, posse (*informal*), set, swarm, troop

crib *noun* **1.** bassinet, bed, cot, cradle **2.** bin, box, bunker, manger, rack, stall **3.** *informal* key, translation, trot (*U.S. slang*) ~*verb* **4.** *informal* cheat, pass off as one's own work, pilfer, pirate, plagiarize, purloin, steal **5.** box up, cage, con~

fine, coop, coop up, enclose, fence, imprison, limit, pen, rail, restrict, shut in

crick **1.** *noun* convulsion, cramp, spasm, twinge **2.** *~verb* jar, rick, wrench

crime **1.** atrocity, fault, felony, job (*informal*), malfeasance, misdeed, misdemeanour, offence, outrage, transgression, trespass, unlawful act, violation, wrong **2.** corruption, delinquency, guilt, illegality, iniquity, lawbreaking, malefaction, misconduct, sin, unrighteousness, vice, villainy, wickedness, wrong, wrongdoing

criminal *noun* **1.** con (*slang*), con man (*informal*), convict, crook (*informal*), culprit, delinquent, evildoer, felon, jailbird, lag (*slang*), lawbreaker, malefactor, offender, sinner, skelm (*S. Afr.*), transgressor, villain *~adjective* **2.** bent (*slang*), corrupt, crooked (*informal*), culpable, felonious, illegal, illicit, immoral, indictable, iniquitous, lawless, nefarious, peccant (*rare*), under-the-table, unlawful, unrighteous, vicious, villainous, wicked, wrong **3.** *informal* deplorable, foolish, preposterous, ridiculous, scandalous, senseless

▷ **Antonyms** commendable, honest, honourable, innocent, law-abiding, lawful, legal, right

criminality corruption, culpability, delinquency, depravity, guiltiness, illegality, sinfulness, turpitude, villainy, wickedness

cringe **1.** blench, cower, dodge, draw back, duck, flinch, quail, quiver, recoil, shrink, shy, start, tremble, wince **2.** bend, bootlick (*informal*), bow, brown-nose (*taboo slang*), crawl, creep, crouch, fawn, grovel, kiss ass (*U.S. & Canad. taboo slang*), kneel, kowtow, pander to, sneak, stoop, toady, truckle

crinkle *noun/verb* **1.** cockle, crimp, crimple, crumple, curl, fold, pucker, ruffle, rumple, scallop, twist, wrinkle **2.** crackle, hiss, rustle, swish, whisper

crinkly buckled, cockled, curly, fluted, frizzy, furrowed, gathered, kinky, knit, puckered, ruffled, scalloped, wrinkled

cripple *verb* **1.** debilitate, disable, enfeeble, hamstring, incapacitate, lame, maim, mutilate, paralyse, weaken **2.** bring to a standstill, cramp, damage, destroy, halt, impair, put out of action, put paid to, ruin, spoil, vitiate

▷ **Antonyms** advance, aid, assist, assist the progress of, ease, expedite, facilitate, further, help, promote

crippled bedridden, deformed, disabled, enfeebled, handicapped, housebound, incapacitated, laid up (*informal*), lame, paralysed

crisis **1.** climacteric, climax, confrontation, critical point, crunch (*informal*), crux, culmination, height, moment of truth, point of no return, turning point **2.** catastrophe, critical situation, deep water, dilemma, dire straits, disaster, emergency, exigency, extremity, meltdown (*informal*), mess, panic stations (*informal*), pass, plight, predicament, quandary, strait, trouble

crisp **1.** brittle, crispy, crumbly, crunchy, firm, fresh, unwilted **2.** bracing, brisk, fresh, invigorating, refreshing **3.** brief, brusque, clear, incisive, pithy, short, succinct, tart, terse **4.** clean-cut, neat, orderly, smart, snappy, spruce, tidy, trig (*archaic or dialect*), well-groomed, well-pressed

▷ **Antonyms** (*sense 1*) drooping, droopy, flaccid, floppy, limp, soft, wilted, withered (*sense 2*) balmy, clement, mild, pleasant, warm

criterion bench mark, canon, gauge, measure, norm, par, principle, proof, rule, standard, test, touchstone, yardstick

critic **1.** analyst, arbiter, authority, commentator, connoisseur, expert, expositor, judge, pundit, reviewer **2.** attacker, carper, caviller, censor, censurer, detractor, fault-finder, knocker (*informal*), Momus, reviler, vilifier

critical **1.** captious, carping, cavilling, censorious, derogatory, disapproving, disparaging, fault-finding, nagging, niggling, nit-picking (*informal*), on someone's back (*informal*), scathing **2.** accurate, analytical, diagnostic, discerning, discriminating, fastidious, judicious, penetrating, perceptive, precise **3.** all-important, crucial, dangerous, deciding, decisive, grave, hairy (*slang*), high-priority, momentous, now or never, perilous, pivotal, precarious, pressing, psychological, risky, serious, urgent, vital

▷ **Antonyms** appreciative, approving, complimentary, permissive, safe, secure, settled, uncritical, undiscriminating, unimportant

criticism **1.** animadversion, bad press, brickbats (*informal*), censure, character assassination, critical remarks, denigration, disapproval, disparagement, fault-finding, flak (*informal*), knocking (*informal*), panning (*informal*), slam (*slang*), slating (*informal*), stick (*slang*), stricture **2.** analysis, appraisal, appreciation, assessment, comment, commentary, critique, elucidation, evaluation, judgment, notice, review

criticize **1.** animadvert on *or* upon, blast, carp, censure, condemn, disapprove of, disparage, excoriate, find fault with, give (someone *or* something) a bad press, have a go (at) (*informal*), knock (*informal*), lambast(e), nag at, pan (*informal*), pass strictures upon, pick holes in, pick to pieces, put down, slam (*slang*), slate (*informal*), tear into (*informal*) **2.** analyse, appraise, assess,

comment upon, evaluate, give an opinion, judge, pass judgment on, review
▷ **Antonyms** commend, compliment, extol, laud (*literary*), praise

critique analysis, appraisal, assessment, commentary, essay, examination, review, treatise

croak *verb* **1.** caw, gasp, grunt, squawk, utter *or* speak harshly, utter *or* speak huskily, utter *or* speak throatily, wheeze **2.** *informal* complain, groan, grouse, grumble, moan, murmur, mutter, repine **3.** *slang* buy it (*U.S. slang*), buy the farm (*U.S. slang*), check out (*U.S. slang*), die, expire, go belly-up (*slang*), hop the twig (*informal*), kick it (*slang*), kick the bucket (*informal*), pass away, peg it (*informal*), peg out (*informal*), perish, pop one's clogs (*informal*)

crone beldam (*archaic*), gammer (*dialect*), hag, old bag (*derogatory slang*), old bat (*slang*), witch

crony accomplice, ally, associate, buddy (*informal*), china (*Brit. slang*), chum (*informal*), cock (*Brit. informal*), colleague, companion, comrade, friend, gossip (*archaic*), homeboy (*slang, chiefly U.S.*), mate (*informal*), pal (*informal*), sidekick (*slang*)

crook 1. *noun informal* cheat, chiseller (*informal*), criminal, fraudster, grifter (*slang, chiefly U.S. & Canad.*), knave (*archaic*), lag (*slang*), racketeer, robber, rogue, shark, skelm (*S. Afr.*), swindler, thief, villain **2.** *~verb* angle, bend, bow, curve, flex, hook

crooked 1. anfractuous, bent, bowed, crippled, curved, deformed, deviating, disfigured, distorted, hooked, irregular, meandering, misshapen, out of shape, tortuous, twisted, twisting, warped, winding, zigzag **2.** angled, askew, asymmetric, at an angle, awry, lopsided, off-centre, skewwhiff (*Brit. informal*), slanted, slanting, squint, tilted, to one side, uneven, unsymmetrical **3.** *informal* bent (*slang*), corrupt, crafty, criminal, deceitful, dishonest, dishonourable, dubious, fraudulent, illegal, knavish, nefarious, questionable, shady (*informal*), shifty, treacherous, underhand, under-the-table, unlawful, unprincipled, unscrupulous
▷ **Antonyms** (*sense 1*) flat, straight (*sense 3*) ethical, fair, honest, honourable, lawful, legal, straight, upright

croon breathe, hum, purr, sing, warble

crop *noun* **1.** fruits, gathering, harvest, produce, reaping, season's growth, vintage, yield *~verb* **2.** clip, curtail, cut, dock, lop, mow, pare, prune, reduce, shear, shorten, snip, top, trim **3.** bring home, bring in, collect, garner, gather, harvest, mow, pick, reap **4.** browse, graze, nibble

crop up appear, arise, emerge, happen, occur, spring up, turn up

cross *adjective* **1.** angry, annoyed, cantankerous, captious, choked, churlish, crotchety (*informal*), crusty, disagreeable, fractious, fretful, grouchy (*informal*), grumpy, hacked (off) (*U.S. slang*), ill-humoured, ill-tempered, impatient, in a bad mood, irascible, irritable, liverish, out of humour, peeved (*informal*), peevish, pettish, petulant, pissed off (*taboo slang*), put out, querulous, ratty (*Brit. & N.Z. informal*), shirty (*slang, chiefly Brit.*), short, snappish, snappy, splenetic, sullen, surly, testy, tetchy, vexed, waspish *~verb* **2.** bridge, cut across, extend over, ford, meet, pass over, ply, span, traverse, zigzag **3.** crisscross, intersect, intertwine, lace, lie athwart of **4.** blend, crossbreed, cross-fertilize, cross-pollinate, hybridize, interbreed, intercross, mix, mongrelize **5.** block, deny, foil, frustrate, hinder, impede, interfere, obstruct, oppose, resist, thwart *~noun* **6.** affliction, burden, grief, load, misery, misfortune, trial, tribulation, trouble, woe, worry **7.** crucifix, rood **8.** crossing, crossroads, intersection, junction **9.** amalgam, blend, combination, crossbreed, cur, hybrid, hybridization, mixture, mongrel, mutt (*slang*) *~adjective* **10.** crosswise, intersecting, oblique, transverse **11.** adverse, contrary, opposed, opposing, unfavourable **12.** *involving an interchange* opposite, reciprocal
▷ **Antonyms** (*sense 1*) affable, agreeable, calm, cheerful, civil, congenial, even-tempered, genial, good-humoured, good-natured, nice, placid, pleasant, sweet

cross-examine catechize, grill (*informal*), interrogate, pump, question, quiz

cross-grained awkward, cantankerous, crabby, difficult, disobliging, ill-natured, morose, peevish, perverse, refractory, shrewish, stubborn, truculent, wayward

cross out *or* **off** blue-pencil, cancel, delete, eliminate, strike off *or* out

crosspatch bear, crank (*U.S., Canad., & Irish informal*), curmudgeon, grump (*informal*), killjoy, scold, shrew, sorehead (*informal, chiefly U.S.*), sourpuss (*informal*)

crosswise, crossways across, aslant, at an angle, athwart, at right angles, awry, crisscross, diagonally, from side to side, on the bias, over, sideways, transversely

crotch crutch, groin

crotchet caprice, fad, fancy, quirk, vagary, whim, whimsy

crotchety awkward, bad-tempered, cantankerous, contrary, crabby, cross, crusty, curmudgeonly, difficult, disagreeable, fractious, grumpy, irritable, liverish, obstreperous, peevish, ratty (*Brit. & N.Z. informal*), surly, testy, tetchy

crouch 1. bend down, bow, duck, hunch, kneel, squat, stoop 2. abase oneself, cower, cringe, fawn, grovel, pander to, truckle

crow blow one's own trumpet, bluster, boast, brag, drool, exult, flourish, gloat, glory in, strut, swagger, triumph, vaunt

crowd *noun* 1. army, assembly, bevy, company, concourse, flock, herd, horde, host, mass, mob, multitude, pack, press, rabble, swarm, throng, troupe 2. bunch (*informal*), circle, clique, group, lot, set 3. attendance, audience, gate, house, spectators *~verb* 4. cluster, congregate, cram, flock, foregather, gather, huddle, mass, muster, press, push, stream, surge, swarm, throng 5. bundle, congest, cram, pack, pile, squeeze 6. batter, butt, elbow, jostle, shove 7. **the crowd** hoi polloi, masses, mob, people, populace, proletariat, public, rabble, rank and file, riffraff, vulgar herd

crowded busy, congested, cramped, crushed, full, huddled, jam-packed, mobbed, overflowing, packed, populous, swarming, teeming, thronged

crown *noun* 1. chaplet, circlet, coronal (*poetic*), coronet, diadem, tiara 2. bays, distinction, garland, honour, kudos, laurels, laurel wreath, prize, trophy 3. emperor, empress, king, monarch, monarchy, queen, *rex,* royalty, ruler, sovereign, sovereignty 4. acme, apex, crest, head, perfection, pinnacle, summit, tip, top, ultimate, zenith *~verb* 5. adorn, dignify, festoon, honour, invest, reward 6. be the climax *or* culmination of, cap, complete, consummate, finish, fulfil, perfect, put the finishing touch to, put the tin lid on, round off, surmount, terminate, top 7. *slang* belt (*informal*), biff (*slang*), box, cuff, hit over the head, punch

crowning *adjective* climactic, consummate, culminating, final, mother (of all), paramount, sovereign, supreme, ultimate

crucial 1. central, critical, decisive, pivotal, psychological, searching, testing, trying 2. *informal* essential, high-priority, important, momentous, now or never, pressing, urgent, vital

crucify 1. execute, harrow, persecute, rack, torment, torture 2. *slang* lampoon, pan (*informal*), ridicule, tear to pieces, wipe the floor with (*informal*)

crude 1. boorish, coarse, crass, dirty, gross, indecent, lewd, obscene, smutty, tactless, tasteless, uncouth, vulgar, X-rated (*informal*) 2. natural, raw, unmilled, unpolished, unprepared, unprocessed, unrefined 3. clumsy, makeshift, outline, primitive, rough, rough-and-ready, rough-hewn, rude, rudimentary, sketchy, undeveloped, unfinished, unformed, unpolished
▷ **Antonyms** (*sense 1*) genteel, polished, refined, subtle, tasteful (*sense 2*) fine, fine-grained, polished, prepared, processed, refined

crudely bluntly, clumsily, coarsely, impolitely, indecently, pulling no punches (*informal*), roughly, rudely, sketchily, tastelessly, vulgarly

crudity 1. coarseness, crudeness, impropriety, indecency, indelicacy, lewdness, loudness, lowness, obscenity, obtrusiveness, smuttiness, vulgarity 2. clumsiness, crudeness, primitiveness, roughness, rudeness

cruel 1. atrocious, barbarous, bitter, bloodthirsty, brutal, brutish, callous, cold-blooded, depraved, excruciating, fell (*archaic*), ferocious, fierce, flinty, grim, hard, hard-hearted, harsh, heartless, hellish, implacable, inclement, inexorable, inhuman, inhumane, malevolent, murderous, painful, poignant, ravening, raw, relentless, remorseless, sadistic, sanguinary, savage, severe, spiteful, stony-hearted, unfeeling, unkind, unnatural, vengeful, vicious 2. merciless, pitiless, ruthless, unrelenting
▷ **Antonyms** benevolent, caring, compassionate, gentle, humane, kind, merciful, sympathetic, warm-hearted

cruelly 1. barbarously, brutally, brutishly, callously, ferociously, fiercely, heartlessly, in cold blood, mercilessly, pitilessly, sadistically, savagely, spitefully, unmercifully, viciously 2. bitterly, deeply, fearfully, grievously, monstrously, mortally, severely

cruelty barbarity, bestiality, bloodthirstiness, brutality, brutishness, callousness, depravity, ferocity, fiendishness, hardheartedness, harshness, heartlessness, inhumanity, mercilessness, murderousness, ruthlessness, sadism, savagery, severity, spite, spitefulness, venom, viciousness

cruise *verb* 1. coast, sail, voyage 2. coast, drift, keep a steady pace, travel along *~noun* 3. boat trip, sail, sea trip, voyage

crumb atom, bit, grain, mite, morsel, particle, scrap, shred, sliver, snippet, *soupçon,* speck

crumble 1. bruise, crumb, crush, fragment, granulate, grind, pound, powder, pulverize, triturate 2. break down, break up, collapse, come to dust, decay, decompose, degenerate, deteriorate, disintegrate, fall apart, go to pieces, go to wrack and ruin, moulder, perish, tumble down

crumbly brashy, brittle, friable, powdery, rotted, short (*of pastry*)

crummy bush-league (*Austral. & N.Z. informal*), cheap, chickenshit (*U.S. slang*), contemptible, crappy (*slang*), dime-a-dozen (*informal*), duff (*Brit. informal*), for the birds (*informal*), half-baked (*informal*), inferior, lousy (*slang*), low-rent (*informal, chiefly U.S.*), miser~

able, of a sort *or* of sorts, piss-poor (*taboo slang*), poor, poxy (*slang*), rotten (*informal*), rubbishy, second-rate, shitty (*taboo slang*), shoddy, strictly for the birds (*informal*), third-rate, tinhorn (*U.S. slang*), trashy, two-bit (*U.S. & Canad. slang*), useless, weak, worthless

crumple 1. crease, crush, pucker, rumple, screw up, scrumple, wrinkle **2.** break down, cave in, collapse, fall, give way, go to pieces

crunch 1. *verb* champ, chew noisily, chomp, grind, masticate, munch **2.** *~noun informal* crisis, critical point, crux, emergency, hour of decision, moment of truth, test

crusade campaign, cause, drive, holy war, jihad, movement, push

crusader advocate, campaigner, champion, reformer

crush *verb* **1.** bray, break, bruise, comminute, compress, contuse, crease, crumble, crumple, crunch, mash, pound, pulverize, rumple, scrumple, smash, squash, squeeze, wrinkle **2.** conquer, extinguish, overcome, overpower, overwhelm, put down, quell, stamp out, subdue, vanquish **3.** abash, browbeat, chagrin, dispose of, humiliate, mortify, put down (*slang*), quash, shame **4.** embrace, enfold, hug, press, squeeze *~noun* **5.** crowd, huddle, jam, party

crust caking, coat, coating, concretion, covering, film, incrustation, layer, outside, scab, shell, skin, surface

crusty 1. brittle, crisp, crispy, friable, hard, short, well-baked, well-done **2.** brusque, cantankerous, captious, choleric, crabby, cross, curt, gruff, ill-humoured, irritable, peevish, prickly, ratty (*Brit. & N.Z. informal*), short, short-tempered, snappish, snarling, splenetic, surly, testy, tetchy, touchy

crux core, decisive point, essence, heart, nub

cry 1. *verb* bawl, bewail, blubber, boohoo, greet (*Scot. or archaic*), howl one's eyes out, keen, lament, mewl, pule, shed tears, snivel, sob, wail, weep, whimper, whine, whinge (*informal*), yowl **2.** *~noun* bawling, blubbering, crying, greet (*Scot. or archaic*), howl, keening, lament, lamentation, plaint (*archaic*), snivel, snivelling, sob, sobbing, sorrowing, wailing, weep, weeping **3.** *~verb* bawl, bell, bellow, call, call out, ejaculate, exclaim, hail, halloo, holler (*informal*), howl, roar, scream, screech, shout, shriek, sing out, vociferate, whoop, yell **4.** *~noun* bawl, bell, bellow, call, ejaculation, exclamation, holler (*informal*), hoot, howl, outcry, roar, scream, screech, shriek, squawk, whoop, yell, yelp, yoo-hoo **5.** *~verb* advertise, announce, bark (*informal*), broadcast, bruit, hawk, noise, proclaim, promulgate, publish, shout from the rooftops (*informal*), trumpet **6.** *~noun* announcement, barking (*informal*), noising, proclamation, publication **7.** *~verb* beg, beseech, clamour, entreat, implore, plead, pray **8.** *~noun* appeal, entreaty, petition, plea, prayer, supplication

▷ **Antonyms** *~verb* (*sense 1*) chortle, chuckle, giggle, laugh, snicker, snigger, twitter (*sense 3*) drone, mumble, murmur, mutter, speak in hushed tones, speak softly, utter indistinctly, whisper

cry down asperse, bad-mouth (*slang, chiefly U.S. & Canad.*), belittle, decry, denigrate, disparage, knock (*informal*), rubbish (*informal*), run down, slag (off) (*slang*)

cry off back out, beg off, cop out (*slang*), excuse oneself, quit, withdraw, withdraw from

crypt catacomb, ossuary, tomb, undercroft, vault

cryptic abstruse, ambiguous, apocryphal, arcane, cabbalistic, coded, dark, Delphic, enigmatic, equivocal, esoteric, hidden, mysterious, obscure, occult, oracular, perplexing, puzzling, recondite, secret, vague, veiled

crystallize appear, coalesce, form, harden, materialize, take shape

cub 1. offspring, whelp, young **2.** babe (*informal*), beginner, fledgling, greenhorn (*informal*), lad, learner, puppy, recruit, tenderfoot, trainee, whippersnapper, youngster

cubbyhole 1. den, hideaway, hole, snug **2.** compartment, niche, pigeonhole, recess, slot

cuddle bill and coo, canoodle (*slang*), clasp, cosset, embrace, fondle, hug, nestle, pet, snuggle

cuddly buxom, cuddlesome, curvaceous, huggable, lovable, plump, soft, warm

cudgel 1. *noun* bastinado, baton, bludgeon, club, cosh (*Brit.*), shillelagh, stick, truncheon **2.** *~verb* bang, baste, batter, beat, bludgeon, cane, cosh (*Brit.*), drub, maul, pound, pummel, thrash, thump, thwack

cue catchword, hint, key, nod, prompting, reminder, sign, signal, suggestion

cuff[1] 1. *verb* bat (*informal*), beat, belt (*informal*), biff (*slang*), box, buffet, clap, clobber (*slang*), clout (*informal*), knock, lambast(e), pummel, punch, slap, smack, thump, whack **2.** *~noun* belt (*informal*), biff (*slang*), box, buffet, clout (*informal*), knock, punch, rap, slap, smack, thump, whack

cuff[2] *noun* **off the cuff** ad lib, extempore, impromptu, improvised, offhand, off the top of one's head, on the spur of the moment, spontaneous, spontaneously, unrehearsed

cul-de-sac blind alley, dead end

cull 1. cherry-pick, choose, pick, pluck,

select, sift, thin, thin out, winnow **2.** amass, collect, gather, glean, pick up

culminate climax, close, come to a climax, come to a head, conclude, end, end up, finish, rise to a crescendo, terminate, wind up

culmination acme, apex, apogee, climax, completion, conclusion, consummation, crown, crowning touch, finale, height, *ne plus ultra,* peak, perfection, pinnacle, punch line, summit, top, zenith

culpability answerability, blame, blameworthiness, fault, guilt, liability, responsibility

culpable answerable, at fault, blamable, blameworthy, censurable, found wanting, guilty, in the wrong, liable, reprehensible, sinful, to blame, wrong
▷ **Antonyms** blameless, clean (*slang*), guiltless, innocent, in the clear, not guilty, squeaky-clean

culprit criminal, delinquent, evildoer, felon, guilty party, malefactor, miscreant, offender, person responsible, rascal, sinner, transgressor, villain, wrongdoer

cult 1. body, church, clique, denomination, faction, faith, following, party, religion, school, sect **2.** admiration, craze, devotion, idolization, reverence, veneration, worship

cultivate 1. bring under cultivation, farm, fertilize, harvest, plant, plough, prepare, tend, till, work **2.** ameliorate, better, bring on, cherish, civilize, develop, discipline, elevate, enrich, foster, improve, polish, promote, refine, train **3.** aid, devote oneself to, encourage, forward, foster, further, help, patronize, promote, pursue, support **4.** associate with, butter up, consort with, court, dance attendance upon, run after, seek out, seek someone's company *or* friendship, take trouble *or* pains with

cultivation 1. agronomy, farming, gardening, husbandry, planting, ploughing, tillage, tilling, working **2.** breeding, civility, civilization, culture, discernment, discrimination, education, enlightenment, gentility, good taste, learning, letters, manners, polish, refinement, sophistication, taste **3.** advancement, advocacy, development, encouragement, enhancement, fostering, furtherance, help, nurture, patronage, promotion, support **4.** devotion to, pursuit, study

cultural artistic, broadening, civilizing, developmental, edifying, educational, educative, elevating, enlightening, enriching, humane, humanizing, liberal, liberalizing

culture 1. civilization, customs, lifestyle, mores, society, stage of development, the arts, way of life **2.** accomplishment, breeding, education, elevation, enlightenment, erudition, gentility, good taste, improvement, polish, politeness, refinement, sophistication, urbanity **3.** agriculture, agronomy, cultivation, farming, husbandry

cultured accomplished, advanced, educated, enlightened, erudite, genteel, highbrow, knowledgeable, polished, refined, scholarly, sophisticated, urbane, versed, well-bred, well-informed, well-read
▷ **Antonyms** coarse, common, inelegant, uncultivated, uneducated, unpolished, unrefined, vulgar

culvert channel, conduit, drain, gutter, watercourse

cumbersome awkward, bulky, burdensome, clumsy, clunky (*informal*), cumbrous, embarrassing, heavy, hefty (*informal*), incommodious, inconvenient, oppressive, unmanageable, unwieldy, weighty
▷ **Antonyms** compact, convenient, easy to use, handy, manageable, practical, serviceable, wieldy

cumulative accruing, accumulative, aggregate, amassed, collective, heaped, increasing, snowballing

cunning 1. *adjective* artful, astute, canny, crafty, devious, foxy, guileful, knowing, Machiavellian, sharp, shifty, shrewd, subtle, tricky, wily **2.** *~noun* artfulness, astuteness, craftiness, deceitfulness, deviousness, foxiness, guile, shrewdness, slyness, trickery, wiliness **3.** *~adjective* adroit, deft, dexterous, imaginative, ingenious, skilful **4.** *~noun* ability, adroitness, art, artifice, cleverness, craft, deftness, dexterity, finesse, ingenuity, skill, subtlety
▷ **Antonyms** *~adjective* artless, dull, ethical, frank, honest, ingenuous, maladroit *~noun* candour, clumsiness, ingenuousness, sincerity

cup 1. beaker, cannikin, chalice, demitasse, goblet, mug, teacup **2.** trophy

cupboard ambry (*obsolete*), cabinet, closet, locker, press

Cupid amoretto, Eros, god of love, love

cupidity acquisitiveness, avarice, avidity, covetousness, graspingness, greed, greediness, hunger, itching, longing, rapaciousness, rapacity, voracity, yearning

cupola dome, onion dome

cur 1. canine, hound, mongrel, mutt (*slang*), stray **2.** bad egg (*old-fashioned informal*), bastard (*offensive*), blackguard, bugger (*taboo slang*), cocksucker (*taboo slang*), coward, good-for-nothing, heel (*slang*), rat (*informal*), rotter (*slang, chiefly Brit.*), scoundrel, scumbag (*slang*), shit (*taboo slang*), son-of-a-bitch (*slang, chiefly U.S. & Canad.*), villain, wretch

curative alleviative, corrective, healing, healthful, health-giving, medicinal, remedial, restorative, salutary, therapeutic, tonic

curb **1.** *verb* bite back, bridle, check, constrain, contain, control, hinder, impede, inhibit, keep a tight rein on, moderate, muzzle, repress, restrain, restrict, retard, stem the flow, subdue, suppress **2.** *~noun* brake, bridle, check, control, deterrent, limitation, rein, restraint

curdle clot, coagulate, condense, congeal, curd, solidify, thicken, turn sour
▷ **Antonyms** deliquesce, dissolve, liquefy, melt, soften, thaw

cure **1.** *verb* alleviate, correct, ease, heal, help, make better, mend, rehabilitate, relieve, remedy, restore, restore to health **2.** *~noun* alleviation, antidote, corrective, healing, medicine, nostrum, panacea, recovery, remedy, restorative, specific, treatment **3.** *~verb* dry, kipper, pickle, preserve, salt, smoke

cure-all catholicon, elixir, *elixir vitae,* nostrum, panacea

curio antique, bibelot, bygone, collector's item, knick-knack, trinket

curiosity **1.** inquisitiveness, interest, nosiness (*informal*), prying, snooping (*informal*) **2.** celebrity, freak, marvel, novelty, oddity, phenomenon, rarity, sight, spectacle, wonder **3.** bibelot, bygone, collector's item, curio, knickknack, *objet d'art,* trinket

curious **1.** inquiring, inquisitive, interested, puzzled, questioning, searching **2.** inquisitive, meddling, nosy (*informal*), peeping, peering, prying, snoopy (*informal*) **3.** bizarre, exotic, extraordinary, marvellous, mysterious, novel, odd, peculiar, puzzling, quaint, queer, rare, rum (*Brit. slang*), singular, strange, unconventional, unexpected, unique, unorthodox, unusual, wonderful
▷ **Antonyms** (*senses 1 & 2*) incurious, indifferent, uninquisitive, uninterested (*sense 3*) common, everyday, familiar, ordinary

curl **1.** *verb* bend, coil, convolute, corkscrew, crimp, crinkle, crisp, curve, entwine, frizz, loop, meander, ripple, spiral, turn, twine, twirl, twist, wind, wreathe, writhe **2.** *~noun* coil, curlicue, kink, ringlet, spiral, twist, whorl

curly corkscrew, crimped, crimpy, crinkly, crisp, curled, curling, frizzy, fuzzy, kinky, permed, spiralled, waved, wavy, winding

curmudgeon bear, bellyacher (*slang*), churl, crosspatch (*informal*), grouch (*informal*), grouser, grumbler, grump (*informal*), malcontent, sourpuss (*informal*)

currency **1.** bills, coinage, coins, dosh (*Brit. & Austral. slang*), medium of exchange, money, notes **2.** acceptance, circulation, exposure, popularity, prevalence, publicity, transmission, vogue

current *adjective* **1.** accepted, circulating, common, common knowledge, customary, general, going around, in circulation, in progress, in the air, in the news, ongoing, popular, present, prevailing, prevalent, rife, topical, widespread **2.** contemporary, fashionable, happening (*informal*), in, in fashion, in vogue, now (*informal*), present-day, sexy (*informal*), trendy (*Brit. informal*), up-to-date, up-to-the-minute *~noun* **3.** course, draught, flow, jet, progression, river, stream, tide, tideway, undertow **4.** atmosphere, drift, feeling, inclination, mood, tendency, trend, undercurrent, vibes (*slang*)
▷ **Antonyms** (*sense 2*) archaic, obsolete, old-fashioned, outmoded, out-of-date, passé, past

curse *noun* **1.** blasphemy, expletive, oath, obscenity, swearing, swearword **2.** anathema, ban, denunciation, evil eye, excommunication, execration, hoodoo (*informal*), imprecation, jinx, malediction, malison (*archaic*) **3.** affliction, bane, burden, calamity, cross, disaster, evil, hardship, misfortune, ordeal, plague, scourge, torment, tribulation, trouble, vexation *~verb* **4.** be foul-mouthed, blaspheme, cuss (*informal*), swear, take the Lord's name in vain, turn the air blue (*informal*), use bad language **5.** accurse, anathematize, damn, excommunicate, execrate, fulminate, imprecate **6.** afflict, blight, burden, destroy, doom, plague, scourge, torment, trouble, vex

cursed **1.** accursed, bedevilled, blighted, cast out, confounded, damned, doomed, excommunicate, execrable, fey (*Scot.*), foredoomed, ill-fated, star-crossed, unholy, unsanctified, villainous **2.** abominable, damnable, detestable, devilish, fell (*archaic*), fiendish, hateful, infamous, infernal, loathsome, odious, pernicious, pestilential, vile

cursory brief, careless, casual, desultory, hasty, hurried, offhand, passing, perfunctory, rapid, slapdash, slight, summary, superficial

curt abrupt, blunt, brief, brusque, concise, gruff, monosyllabic, offhand, pithy, rude, sharp, short, snappish, succinct, summary, tart, terse, unceremonious, uncivil, ungracious

curtail abbreviate, abridge, contract, cut, cut back, cut short, decrease, diminish, dock, lessen, lop, pare down, reduce, retrench, shorten, trim, truncate

curtailment abbreviation, abridgment, contraction, cutback, cutting, cutting short, docking, retrenchment, truncation

curtain **1.** *noun* drape (*chiefly U.S.*), hanging **2.** *~verb* conceal, drape, hide, screen, shroud, shut off, shutter, veil

curvaceous bosomy, buxom, comely, curvy, shapely, voluptuous, well-rounded, well-stacked (*Brit. slang*)

curvature arching, bend, curve, curving, curvity, deflection, flexure, incurvation

curve 1. *verb* arc, arch, bend, bow, coil, hook, inflect, spiral, swerve, turn, twist, wind **2.** *~noun* arc, bend, camber, curvature, half-moon, loop, trajectory, turn

curved arced, arched, bent, bowed, crooked, humped, rounded, serpentine, sinuous, sweeping, turned, twisted, twisty

cushion 1. *noun* beanbag, bolster, hassock, headrest, pad, pillow, scatter cushion, squab **2.** *~verb* bolster, buttress, cradle, dampen, deaden, muffle, pillow, protect, soften, stifle, support, suppress

cushy comfortable, easy, jammy (*Brit. slang*), soft, undemanding

custodian caretaker, curator, guardian, keeper, overseer, protector, superintendent, warden, warder, watchdog, watchman

custody 1. aegis, auspices, care, charge, custodianship, guardianship, keeping, observation, preservation, protection, safekeeping, supervision, trusteeship, tutelage, ward, watch **2.** arrest, confinement, detention, durance (*archaic*), duress, imprisonment, incarceration

custom 1. habit, habitude (*rare*), manner, mode, procedure, routine, way, wont **2.** convention, etiquette, fashion, form, formality, matter of course, observance, observation, policy, practice, praxis, ritual, rule, style, tradition, unwritten law, usage, use **3.** customers, patronage, trade

customarily as a rule, commonly, generally, habitually, in the ordinary way, normally, ordinarily, regularly, traditionally, usually

customary accepted, accustomed, acknowledged, bog-standard (*Brit. & Irish slang*), common, confirmed, conventional, established, everyday, familiar, fashionable, general, habitual, normal, ordinary, popular, regular, routine, traditional, usual, wonted

▷ **Antonyms** exceptional, infrequent, irregular, occasional, rare, uncommon, unusual

customer buyer, client, consumer, habitué, patron, prospect, purchaser, regular (*informal*), shopper

customs duty, import charges, tariff, taxes, toll

cut *verb* **1.** chop, cleave, divide, gash, incise, lacerate, lance, nick, notch, penetrate, pierce, score, sever, slash, slice, slit, wound **2.** carve, chip, chisel, chop, engrave, fashion, form, inscribe, saw, sculpt, sculpture, shape, whittle **3.** clip, dock, fell, gather, hack, harvest, hew, lop, mow, pare, prune, reap, saw down, shave, snip, trim **4.** contract, cut back, decrease, diminish, downsize, ease up on, lower, rationalize, reduce, slash, slim (down) **5.** abbreviate, abridge, condense, curtail, delete, edit out, excise, precis, shorten **6.** (*often with* **through, off,** *or* **across**) bisect, carve, cleave, cross, dissect, divide, interrupt, intersect, part, segment, sever, slice, split, sunder **7.** avoid, cold-shoulder, freeze (someone) out (*informal*), grieve, hurt, ignore, insult, look straight through (someone), pain, put down, send to Coventry, slight, snub, spurn, sting, turn one's back on, wound *~noun* **8.** gash, graze, groove, incision, laceration, nick, rent, rip, slash, slit, snip, stroke, wound **9.** cutback, decrease, decrement, diminution, economy, fall, lowering, reduction, saving **10.** *informal* chop (*slang*), division, kickback (*chiefly U.S.*), percentage, piece, portion, rake-off (*slang*), section, share, slice **11.** configuration, fashion, form, look, mode, shape, style **12. a cut above** *informal* better than, higher than, more capable than, more competent than, more efficient than, more reliable than, more trustworthy than, more useful than, superior to **13. cut and dried** *informal* automatic, fixed, organized, prearranged, predetermined, settled, sorted out (*informal*)

▷ **Antonyms** (*sense 5*) add to, augment, enlarge, expand, extend, fill out, increase (*sense 7*) accept gladly, embrace, greet, hail, receive, welcome with open arms

cut along dash (off), fly, go, hurry (away), leave, press on

cutback cut, decrease, economy, lessening, reduction, retrenchment

cut back check, curb, decrease, downsize, draw *or* pull in one's horns (*informal*), economize, lessen, lower, prune, reduce, retrench, slash, trim

cut down 1. fell, hew, level, lop, raze **2.** (*sometimes with* **on**) decrease, lessen, lower, reduce **3.** blow away (*slang, chiefly U.S.*), dispatch, kill, massacre, mow down, slaughter, slay (*archaic*), take out (*slang*) **4. cut (someone) down to size** abash, humiliate, make (someone) look small, take the wind out of (someone's) sails

cute appealing, attractive, charming, delightful, engaging, lovable, sweet, winning, winsome

cut in break in, butt in, interpose, interrupt, intervene, intrude, move in (*informal*)

cut off 1. disconnect, intercept, interrupt, intersect **2.** bring to an end, discontinue, halt, obstruct, suspend **3.** isolate, separate, sever **4.** disinherit, disown, renounce

cut out 1. cease, delete, extract, give up, kick (*informal*), refrain from, remove, sever, stop **2.** *informal* displace, eliminate, exclude, oust, supersede, supplant

cut out for adapted, adequate, competent, designed, eligible, equipped, fitted, qualified, suitable, suited

cut-price bargain, cheap, cheapo (*informal*), cut-rate (*chiefly U.S.*), reduced, sale

cutpurse footpad (*archaic*), mugger (*informal*), pickpocket, robber, thief

cut short abort, break off, bring to an end, check, dock, halt, interrupt, leave unfinished, postpone, pull the plug on, stop, terminate, truncate

cut-throat *noun* **1.** assassin, bravo, butcher, executioner, heavy (*slang*), hit man (*slang*), homicide, killer, liquidator, murderer, slayer (*archaic*), thug ~*adjective* **2.** barbarous, bloodthirsty, bloody, cruel, death-dealing, ferocious, homicidal, murderous, savage, thuggish, violent **3.** competitive, dog-eat-dog, fierce, relentless, ruthless, unprincipled

cutting *adjective* **1.** biting, bitter, chill, keen, numbing, penetrating, piercing, raw, sharp, stinging **2.** acid, acrimonious, barbed, bitter, caustic, hurtful, malicious, mordacious, pointed, sarcastic, sardonic, scathing, severe, trenchant, vitriolic, wounding

▷ **Antonyms** (*sense 1*) balmy, pleasant, soothing (*sense 2*) consoling, flattering, kind, mild

cut up *verb* **1.** carve, chop, dice, divide, mince, slice **2.** injure, knife, lacerate, slash, wound **3.** *informal* blast, criticize, crucify (*slang*), give (someone *or* something) a rough ride, lambast(e), pan (*informal*), put down, ridicule, slate (*informal*), tear into (*informal*), vilify ~*adjective* **4.** *informal* agitated, dejected, desolated, distressed, disturbed, heartbroken, stricken, upset, wretched

cycle aeon, age, circle, era, period, phase, revolution, rotation, round (*of years*)

cyclone hurricane, tempest, tornado, twister (*U.S. informal*), typhoon, whirlwind

cynic doubter, misanthrope, misanthropist, pessimist, sceptic, scoffer

cynical contemptuous, derisive, distrustful, ironic, misanthropic, misanthropical, mocking, mordacious, pessimistic, sarcastic, sardonic, sceptical, scoffing, scornful, sneering, unbelieving

▷ **Antonyms** credulous, green, gullible, hopeful, optimistic, trustful, trusting, unsceptical, unsuspecting

cynicism disbelief, doubt, misanthropy, pessimism, sarcasm, sardonicism, scepticism

cynosure attraction, centre, centre of attention, focus, focus of attention, leading light (*informal*), point (of attraction), shining example

cyst bleb, blister, growth, sac, vesicle, wen

D, d

dab *verb* **1.** blot, daub, pat, stipple, swab, tap, touch, wipe *~noun* **2.** bit, dollop (*informal*), drop, fleck, pat, smidgen *or* smidgin (*informal, chiefly U.S. & Canad.*), smudge, speck, spot **3.** flick, pat, peck, smudge, stroke, tap, touch

dabble 1. dip, guddle (*Scot.*), moisten, paddle, spatter, splash, sprinkle, wet **2.** dally, dip into, play at, potter, tinker, trifle (with)

dabbler amateur, dilettante, potterer, tinkerer, trifler

dab hand ace (*informal*), adept, buff (*informal*), dabster (*dialect*), expert, hotshot (*informal*), maven (*U.S.*), past master, whizz (*informal*), wizard

daft 1. absurd, asinine, crackpot (*informal*), crazy, doolally (*slang*), dopey (*informal*), foolish, giddy, gonzo (*slang*), goofy (*informal*), idiotic, inane, loopy (*informal*), off one's head (*informal*), off one's trolley (*slang*), out to lunch (*informal*), scatty (*Brit. informal*), silly, simple, stupid, up the pole (*informal*), wacko *or* whacko (*slang*), witless **2.** barking (*slang*), barking mad (*slang*), crackers (*Brit. slang*), crazy, demented, deranged, insane, lunatic, mental (*slang*), not right in the head, not the full shilling (*informal*), nuts (*slang*), nutty (*slang*), round the bend (*Brit. slang*), touched, unhinged **3.** (*with* **about**) besotted by, crazy (*informal*), doting, dotty (*slang, chiefly Brit.*), infatuated by, mad, nuts (*slang*), nutty (*informal*), potty (*Brit. informal*), sweet on

dagger 1. bayonet, dirk, poniard, skean, stiletto **2. at daggers drawn** at enmity, at loggerheads, at odds, at war, on bad terms, up in arms **3. look daggers** frown, glare, glower, look black, lour *or* lower, scowl

daily *adjective* **1.** circadian, diurnal, everyday, quotidian **2.** common, commonplace, day-to-day, everyday, ordinary, quotidian, regular, routine *~adverb* **3.** constantly, day after day, day by day, every day, often, once a day, per diem, regularly

dainty *adjective* **1.** charming, delicate, elegant, exquisite, fine, graceful, neat, petite, pretty **2.** choice, delectable, delicious, palatable, savoury, tasty, tender, toothsome **3.** choosy, fastidious, finical, finicky, fussy, mincing, nice, particular, picky (*informal*), refined, scrupulous *~noun* **4.** *bonne bouche,* delicacy, fancy, sweetmeat, titbit

▷ **Antonyms** (*sense 1*) awkward, clumsy, coarse, gauche, inelegant, maladroit, uncouth, ungainly

dale bottom, coomb, dell, dingle, glen, strath (*Scot.*), vale, valley

dalliance *noun* **1.** dabbling, dawdling, delay, dilly-dallying (*informal*), frittering, frivolling (*informal*), idling, loafing, loitering, playing, pottering, procrastination, toying, trifling **2.** *archaic* amorous play, coquetry, flirtation

dally 1. dawdle, delay, dilly-dally (*informal*), drag one's feet *or* heels, fool (about *or* around), fritter away, hang about, linger, loiter, procrastinate, tarry, waste time, while away **2.** (*often with* **with**) caress, flirt, fondle, fool (about *or* around), frivol (*informal*), lead on, play, play fast and loose (*informal*), tamper, tease, toy, trifle

▷ **Antonyms** (*sense 1*) hasten, hurry (up), make haste, push forward *or* on, run, step on it (*informal*)

dam 1. *noun* barrage, barrier, embankment, hindrance, obstruction, wall **2.** *~verb* barricade, block, block up, check, choke, confine, hold back, hold in, obstruct, restrict

damage *noun* **1.** destruction, detriment, devastation, harm, hurt, impairment, injury, loss, mischief, mutilation, suffering **2.** *informal* bill, charge, cost, expense, total **3.** *plural* compensation, fine, indemnity, reimbursement, reparation, satisfaction *~verb* **4.** deface, harm, hurt, impair, incapacitate, injure, mar, mutilate, play (merry) hell with (*informal*), ruin, spoil, tamper with, undo, weaken, wreck

▷ **Antonyms** *~noun* (*sense 1*) gain, improvement, reparation *~verb* better, fix, improve, mend, repair

damaging deleterious, detrimental, disadvantageous, harmful, hurtful, injurious, prejudicial, ruinous

▷ **Antonyms** advantageous, favourable, healthful, helpful, profitable, salutary, useful, valuable, wholesome

dame baroness, dowager, *grande dame,* lady, matron (*archaic*), noblewoman, peeress

damn *verb* **1.** blast, castigate, censure, condemn, criticize, denounce, denunciate, excoriate, inveigh against, lambast(e), pan (*informal*), put down, slam (*slang*), slate (*informal*), tear into (*informal*) **2.** abuse, anathematize, blaspheme, curse, execrate, imprecate, revile, swear **3.** condemn, doom, sentence *~noun* **4.** brass farthing, hoot, iota, jot, tinker's curse *or* damn (*slang*), two hoots, whit **5. not give a damn** be indifferent, not care, not mind

▷ **Antonyms** (*sense 1*) acclaim, admire, applaud, approve, cheer, compliment, congratulate, extol, honour, laud, praise, take one's hat off to (*sense 2*) adore, bless, exalt, glorify, magnify (*archaic*), pay homage to

damnable abominable, accursed, atrocious, culpable, cursed, despicable, detestable, execrable, hateful, horrible, offensive, wicked

▷ **Antonyms** admirable, commendable, creditable, excellent, exemplary, fine, honourable, laudable, meritorious, praiseworthy, worthy

damnation anathema, ban, condemnation, consigning to perdition, damning, denunciation, doom, excommunication, objurgation, proscription, sending to hell

damned 1. accursed, anathematized, condemned, doomed, infernal, lost, reprobate, unhappy **2.** *slang* confounded, despicable, detestable, hateful, infamous, infernal, loathsome, revolting

damning accusatorial, condemnatory, damnatory, dooming, implicating, implicative, incriminating

damp *noun* **1.** clamminess, dampness, dankness, dew, drizzle, fog, humidity, mist, moisture, mugginess, vapour *~adjective* **2.** clammy, dank, dewy, dripping, drizzly, humid, misty, moist, muggy, sodden, soggy, sopping, vaporous, wet *~verb* **3.** dampen, moisten, wet **4.** *figurative* allay, check, chill, cool, curb, dash, deaden, deject, depress, diminish, discourage, dispirit, dull, inhibit, moderate, pour cold water on, restrain, stifle *~noun* **5.** *figurative* check, chill, cold water (*informal*), curb, damper, discouragement, gloom, restraint, wet blanket (*informal*)

▷ **Antonyms** *~noun* (*sense 1*) aridity, dryness *~adjective* arid, dry, watertight *~verb* (*sense 4*) encourage, hearten, inspire

dampen 1. bedew, besprinkle, make damp, moisten, spray, wet **2.** *figurative* check, dash, deaden, depress, deter, dishearten, dismay, dull, lessen, moderate, muffle, reduce, restrain, smother, stifle

damper chill, cloud, cold water (*informal*), curb, discouragement, gloom, hindrance, kill-joy, pall, restraint, wet blanket (*informal*)

dance 1. *verb* bob up and down, caper, cut a rug (*informal*), frolic, gambol, hop, jig, prance, rock, skip, spin, sway, swing, trip, whirl **2.** *~noun* ball, dancing party, disco, discotheque, hop (*informal*), knees-up (*Brit. informal*), social

dandle amuse, caress, cradle, cuddle, dance, fondle, give a knee ride, pet, rock, toss, toy (with)

dandy 1. *noun* beau, blade (*archaic*), blood (*rare*), buck (*archaic*), coxcomb, dude (*U.S. & Canad. informal*), exquisite (*obsolete*), fop, macaroni (*obsolete*), man about town, peacock, popinjay, swell (*informal*), toff (*Brit. slang*) **2.** *~adjective informal* capital, excellent, fine, first-rate, great, splendid

danger endangerment, hazard, insecurity, jeopardy, menace, peril, pitfall, precariousness, risk, threat, venture, vulnerability

dangerous alarming, breakneck, chancy (*informal*), exposed, hairy (*slang*), hazardous, insecure, menacing, nasty, parlous (*archaic*), perilous, precarious, risky, threatening, treacherous, ugly, unchancy (*Scot.*), unsafe, vulnerable

▷ **Antonyms** harmless, innocuous, O.K. *or* okay (*informal*), out of danger, out of harm's way, protected, safe, safe and sound, secure

dangerously 1. alarmingly, carelessly, daringly, desperately, harmfully, hazardously, perilously, precariously, recklessly, riskily, unsafely, unsecurely **2.** critically, gravely, seriously, severely

dangle *verb* **1.** depend, flap, hang, hang down, sway, swing, trail **2.** brandish, entice, flaunt, flourish, lure, tantalize, tempt, wave

dangling disconnected, drooping, hanging, loose, swaying, swinging, trailing, unconnected

dank chilly, clammy, damp, dewy, dripping, moist, slimy, soggy

dapper active, brisk, chic, dainty, natty (*informal*), neat, nice, nimble, smart, soigné *or* soignée, spruce, spry, stylish, trig (*archaic or dialect*), trim, well-groomed, well turned out

▷ **Antonyms** blowsy, disarrayed, dishevelled, dowdy, frowzy, ill-groomed, rumpled, slobby (*informal*), sloppy (*informal*), slovenly, unkempt, untidy

dapple *verb* bespeckle, dot, fleck, freckle, mottle, speckle, spot, stipple

dappled brindled, checkered, flecked, freckled, mottled, piebald, pied, speckled, spotted, stippled, variegated

dare *verb* **1.** challenge, defy, goad, provoke, taunt, throw down the gauntlet **2.** adventure, brave, endanger, gamble, hazard, make bold, presume, risk, skate on thin ice, stake, venture *~noun* **3.** challenge, defiance, provocation, taunt

daredevil 1. *noun* adrenalin junky (*slang*), adventurer, desperado, exhibitionist, hot dog (*chiefly U.S.*), madcap, show-off (*informal*), stunt man **2.** *~adjective* adventurous, audacious, bold, daring, death-defying, madcap, reckless

daring 1. *adjective* adventurous, audacious, ballsy (*taboo slang*), bold, brave, daredevil, fearless, game (*informal*), have-a-go (*informal*), impulsive, intrepid, plucky, rash, reckless, valiant, venturesome **2.** *~noun* audacity, balls (*taboo slang*), ballsiness (*taboo slang*), boldness, bottle (*Brit. slang*), bravery, courage, derring-do (*archaic*), face (*informal*), fearlessness, grit, guts (*informal*), intrepidity, nerve (*informal*), pluck, rashness, spirit, spunk (*informal*), temerity

▷ **Antonyms** *~adjective* anxious, careful, cautious, cowardly, faint-hearted, fearful, timid, uncourageous, wary *~noun* anxiety, caution, cowardice, fear, timidity

dark *adjective* **1.** black, brunette, dark-skinned, dusky, ebony, sable, swarthy **2.** cloudy, darksome (*literary*), dim, dingy, indistinct, murky, overcast, pitch-black, pitchy, shadowy, shady, sunless, unlit **3.** abstruse, arcane, concealed, cryptic, deep, Delphic, enigmatic, hidden, mysterious, mystic, obscure, occult, puzzling, recondite, secret **4.** bleak, cheerless, dismal, doleful, drab, gloomy, grim, joyless, morbid, morose, mournful, sombre **5.** benighted, ignorant, uncultivated, unenlightened, unlettered **6.** atrocious, damnable, evil, foul, hellish, horrible, infamous, infernal, nefarious, satanic, sinful, sinister, vile, wicked **7.** angry, dour, forbidding, frowning, glowering, glum, ominous, scowling, sulky, sullen, threatening *~noun* **8.** darkness, dimness, dusk, gloom, murk, murkiness, obscurity, semi-darkness **9.** evening, night, nightfall, night-time, twilight **10.** *figurative* concealment, ignorance, secrecy

▷ **Antonyms** (*sense 1*) blond, blonde, fair, fair-haired, flaxen-haired, light, light-complexioned, towheaded (*senses 2 & 4*) bright, cheerful, clear, genial, glad, hopeful, pleasant, sunny

darken 1. becloud, blacken, cloud up *or* over, deepen, dim, eclipse, make dark, make darker, make dim, obscure, overshadow, shade, shadow **2.** become angry, become gloomy, blacken, cast a pall over, cloud, deject, depress, dispirit, grow troubled, look black, sadden

▷ **Antonyms** (*sense 1*) brighten, clear up, enliven, gleam, glow, illuminate, lighten, light up, make bright, shine (*sense 2*) become cheerful, cheer, encourage, gladden, hearten, make happy, perk up

darkling 1. *adjective* black, dark, darksome (*literary*), dim, dusky, gloomy, pitchy, shadowy, tenebrous **2.** *~adverb* at *or* by night, in the dark, in the dead of night, in the night

darkness 1. blackness, dark, dimness, dusk, duskiness, gloom, murk, murkiness, nightfall, obscurity, shade, shadiness, shadows **2.** *figurative* blindness, concealment, ignorance, mystery, privacy, secrecy, unawareness

darling *noun* **1.** beloved, dear, dearest, love, sweetheart, truelove **2.** apple of one's eye, blue-eyed boy, fair-haired boy (*U.S.*), favourite, pet, spoilt child *~adjective* **3.** adored, beloved, cherished, dear, precious, treasured **4.** adorable, attractive, captivating, charming, cute, enchanting, lovely, sweet

darn 1. *verb* cobble up, mend, patch, repair, sew up, stitch **2.** *~noun* invisible repair, mend, patch, reinforcement

dart 1. bound, dash, flash, flit, fly, race, run, rush, scoot, shoot, spring, sprint, start, tear, whistle, whizz **2.** cast, fling, hurl, launch, propel, send, shoot, sling, throw

dash *verb* **1.** break, crash, destroy, shatter, shiver, smash, splinter **2.** cast, fling, hurl, slam, sling, throw **3.** barrel (along) (*informal, chiefly U.S. & Canad.*), bolt, bound, burn rubber (*informal*), dart, fly, haste, hasten, hurry, race, run, rush, speed, spring, sprint, tear **4.** abash, chagrin, confound, dampen, disappoint, discomfort, discourage **5.** blight, foil, frustrate, ruin, spoil, thwart, undo *~noun* **6.** bolt, dart, haste, onset, race, run, rush, sortie, sprint, spurt **7.** brio, élan, flair, flourish, panache, spirit, style, verve, vigour, vivacity **8.** bit, drop, flavour, hint, little, pinch, smack, *soupçon,* sprinkling, suggestion, tinge, touch

▷ **Antonyms** *~verb* (*sense 3*) crawl, dawdle, walk (*sense 5*) enhance, improve *~noun* (*sense 8*) lot, much

dashing 1. bold, daring, debonair, exuberant, gallant, lively, plucky, spirited, swashbuckling **2.** dapper, dazzling, elegant, flamboyant, jaunty, showy, smart, sporty, stylish, swish (*informal, chiefly Brit.*), urbane

▷ **Antonyms** boring, dreary, dull, lacklustre, stolid, unexciting, uninteresting

dastard *noun* caitiff (*archaic*), coward, craven, niddering (*archaic*), poltroon, recreant (*archaic*), renegade, sneak, traitor, worm

dastardly *adjective* abject, base, caitiff (*archaic*), contemptible, cowardly, craven, despicable, faint-hearted, low, mean, niddering (*archaic*), recreant (*archaic*), sneaking, sneaky, spiritless, underhand, vile, weak-kneed (*informal*)

data details, documents, dope (*informal*), facts, figures, info (*informal*), information, input, materials, statistics

date *noun* **1.** age, epoch, era, period, stage, time **2.** appointment, assignation, engagement, meeting, rendezvous, tryst **3.** escort, friend, partner, steady (*informal*) **4. out of date** antiquated, archaic, dated, obsolete, old, old-fashioned, passé **5. to date** now, so far, up to now, up to the present, up to this point, yet **6. up-to-date** à la mode, contemporary, current, fashionable, modern, trendy (*Brit. informal*), up-to-the-minute *~verb* **7.** assign a date to, determine the date of, fix the period of, put a date on **8.** bear a date, belong to, come from, exist from, originate in **9.** become obsolete, be dated, obsolesce, show one's age

dated antiquated, archaic, *démodé*, obsolete, old-fashioned, old hat, out, outdated, outmoded, out of date, out of the ark (*informal*), passé, unfashionable, untrendy (*Brit. informal*)

▷ **Antonyms** à la mode, all the rage, chic, cool (*informal*), current, hip (*slang*), in vogue, latest, modern, modish, popular, stylish, trendy (*Brit. informal*), up-to-date

daub *verb* **1.** coat, cover, paint, plaster, slap on (*informal*), smear **2.** bedaub, begrime, besmear, blur, deface, dirty, grime, smirch, smudge, spatter, splatter, stain, sully *~noun* **3.** blot, blotch, smear, smirch, splodge, splotch, spot, stain

daunt 1. alarm, appal, cow, dismay, frighten, frighten off, intimidate, overawe, scare, subdue, terrify **2.** deter, discourage, dishearten, dispirit, put off, shake

▷ **Antonyms** cheer, comfort, encourage, hearten, inspire, inspirit, reassure, spur, support

daunted *adjective* alarmed, cowed, demoralized, deterred, discouraged, disillusioned, dismayed, dispirited, downcast, frightened, hesitant, intimidated, overcome, put off, unnerved

dauntless bold, brave, courageous, daring, doughty, fearless, gallant, gritty, heroic, indomitable, intrepid, lion-hearted, resolute, stouthearted, undaunted, unflinching, valiant, valorous

dawdle dally, delay, dilly-dally (*informal*), drag one's feet *or* heels, fritter away, hang about, idle, lag, loaf, loiter, potter, trail, waste time

▷ **Antonyms** fly, get a move on (*informal*), hasten, hurry, lose no time, make haste, rush, scoot, step on it (*informal*)

dawdler laggard, lingerer, loiterer, slowcoach (*Brit. informal*), slowpoke (*U.S. & Canad. informal*), snail, tortoise

dawn *noun* **1.** aurora (*poetic*), cockcrow, crack of dawn, dawning, daybreak, daylight, dayspring (*poetic*), morning, sunrise, sunup *~verb* **2.** break, brighten, gleam, glimmer, grow light, lighten *~noun* **3.** advent, beginning, birth, dawning, emergence, genesis, inception, onset, origin, outset, rise, start, unfolding *~verb* **4.** appear, begin, develop, emerge, initiate, open, originate, rise, unfold **5.** come into one's head, come to mind, cross one's mind, flash across one's mind, hit, occur, register (*informal*), strike

day 1. daylight, daylight hours, daytime, twenty-four hours, working day **2.** age, ascendancy, cycle, epoch, era, generation, height, heyday, period, prime, time, zenith **3.** date, particular day, point in time, set time, time **4. call it a day** *informal* end, finish, knock off (*informal*), leave off, pack it in (*slang*), pack up (*informal*), shut up shop, stop **5. day after day** continually, monotonously, persistently, regularly, relentlessly **6. day by day** daily, gradually, progressively, steadily

daybreak break of day, cockcrow, crack of dawn, dawn, dayspring (*poetic*), first light, morning, sunrise, sunup

daydream *noun* **1.** dream, imagining, musing, reverie, stargazing, vision, woolgathering **2.** castle in the air *or* in Spain, dream, fancy, fantasy, figment of the imagination, fond hope, pipe dream, wish *~verb* **3.** dream, envision, fancy, fantasize, hallucinate, imagine, muse, stargaze

daydreamer castle-builder, dreamer, fantast, pipe dreamer, visionary, Walter Mitty, wishful thinker, woolgatherer

daylight 1. light of day, sunlight, sunshine **2.** broad day, daylight hours, daytime **3.** full view, light of day, openness, public attention

daze *verb* **1.** benumb, numb, paralyse, shock, stun, stupefy **2.** amaze, astonish, astound, befog, bewilder, blind, confuse, dazzle, dumbfound, flabbergast (*informal*), flummox, nonplus, perplex, stagger, startle, surprise *~noun* **3.** bewilderment, confusion, distraction, shock, stupor, trance, trancelike state

dazed at sea, baffled, bemused, bewildered, confused, disorientated, dizzy, dopey (*slang*), flabbergasted (*informal*), flummoxed, fuddled, groggy (*informal*), light-headed, muddled, nonplussed, numbed, perplexed, punch-drunk, shocked, staggered, stunned, stupefied, woozy (*informal*)

dazzle *verb* **1.** bedazzle, blind, blur, confuse, daze **2.** amaze, astonish, awe, bowl over (*informal*), fascinate, hypnotize, impress, overawe, overpower, overwhelm, strike dumb, stupefy, take one's breath away *~noun* **3.** brilliance, éclat, flash, glitter, magnificence, razzle-dazzle (*slang*), razzmatazz (*slang*), sparkle, splendour

dazzling brilliant, divine, drop-dead (*slang*), glittering, glorious, radiant, ravishing, scintillating, sensational (*in~*

formal), shining, sparkling, splendid, stunning, sublime, superb, virtuoso
▷ **Antonyms** dull, ordinary, tedious, unexceptional, unexciting, uninspiring, uninteresting, unmemorable, unremarkable, vanilla (*slang*)

dead *adjective* **1.** deceased, defunct, departed, extinct, gone, inanimate, late, lifeless, passed away, perished, pushing up (the) daisies **2.** apathetic, callous, cold, dull, frigid, glassy, glazed, indifferent, inert, lukewarm, numb, paralysed, spiritless, torpid, unresponsive, wooden **3.** barren, inactive, inoperative, not working, obsolete, stagnant, sterile, still, unemployed, unprofitable, useless **4.** boring, dead-and-alive, dull, flat, ho-hum (*informal*), insipid, stale, tasteless, uninteresting, vapid **5.** *figurative* absolute, complete, downright, entire, outright, thorough, total, unqualified, utter **6.** *informal* dead beat (*informal*), exhausted, spent, tired, worn out *~noun* **7.** depth, middle, midst *~adverb* **8.** absolutely, completely, directly, entirely, exactly, totally
▷ **Antonyms** *~adjective* (*sense 1*) alive, alive and kicking, animate, existing, living (*sense 2*) animated, lively, responsive (*sense 3*) active, alive, effective, in use, operative, productive, working (*sense 4*) active, alive, alive and kicking, animated, full of beans (*informal*), lively, vivacious

deaden abate, alleviate, anaesthetize, benumb, blunt, check, cushion, damp, dampen, diminish, dull, hush, impair, lessen, muffle, mute, numb, paralyse, quieten, reduce, smother, stifle, suppress, weaken

deadlock cessation, dead heat, draw, full stop, gridlock, halt, impasse, stalemate, standoff, standstill, tie

deadly 1. baleful, baneful, dangerous, death-dealing, deathly, destructive, fatal, lethal, malignant, mortal, noxious, pernicious, poisonous, venomous **2.** cruel, grim, implacable, mortal, ruthless, savage, unrelenting **3.** ashen, deathlike, deathly, ghastly, ghostly, pallid, wan, white **4.** accurate, effective, exact, on target, precise, sure, true, unerring, unfailing **5.** *informal* as dry as dust, boring, dull, ho-hum (*informal*), mind-numbing, monotonous, tedious, tiresome, uninteresting, wearisome

deadpan *adjective* blank, empty, expressionless, impassive, inexpressive, inscrutable, poker-faced, straight-faced

deaf *adjective* **1.** hard of hearing, stone deaf, without hearing **2.** indifferent, oblivious, unconcerned, unhearing, unmoved

deafen din, drown out, make deaf, split *or* burst the eardrums

deafening booming, dinning, ear-piercing, ear-splitting, intense, overpowering, piercing, resounding, ringing, thunderous

deal *verb* **1.** (*with* **with**) attend to, come to grips with, cope with, get to grips with, handle, manage, oversee, see to, take care of, treat **2.** (*with* **with**) concern, consider, treat (of) **3.** (*with* **with**) act, behave, conduct oneself **4.** bargain, buy and sell, do business, negotiate, sell, stock, trade, traffic, treat (with) *~noun* **5.** *informal* agreement, arrangement, bargain, contract, pact, transaction, understanding *~verb* **6.** allot, apportion, assign, bestow, dispense, distribute, divide, dole out, give, mete out, reward, share *~noun* **7.** amount, degree, distribution, extent, portion, quantity, share, transaction **8.** cut and shuffle, distribution, hand, round, single game

dealer chandler, marketer, merchandiser, merchant, purveyor, supplier, trader, tradesman, wholesaler

dealings business, business relations, commerce, trade, traffic, transactions, truck

dear *adjective* **1.** beloved, cherished, close, darling, esteemed, familiar, favourite, intimate, precious, prized, respected, treasured **2.** at a premium, costly, expensive, high-priced, overpriced, pricey (*informal*) *~noun* **3.** angel, beloved, darling, loved one, precious, treasure *~adverb* **4.** at a heavy cost, at a high price, at great cost, dearly
▷ **Antonyms** (*sense 1*) disliked, hated (*sense 2*) cheap, common, inexpensive, worthless

dearly 1. extremely, greatly, profoundly, very much **2.** affectionately, devotedly, fondly, lovingly, tenderly **3.** at a heavy cost, at a high price, at great cost, dear

dearth absence, deficiency, exiguousness, famine, inadequacy, insufficiency, lack, need, paucity, poverty, scantiness, scarcity, shortage, sparsity, want

death 1. bereavement, cessation, curtains (*informal*), decease, demise, departure, dissolution, dying, end, exit, expiration, loss, passing, quietus, release **2.** annihilation, destruction, downfall, eradication, extermination, extinction, finish, grave, obliteration, ruin, ruination, undoing
▷ **Antonyms** (*senses 1 & 2*) beginning, birth, emergence, genesis, growth, origin, rise, source

deathless eternal, everlasting, immortal, imperishable, incorruptible, timeless, undying
▷ **Antonyms** corporeal, earthly, ephemeral, human, mortal, passing, temporal, transient, transitory

deathly 1. cadaverous, deathlike, gaunt, ghastly, grim, haggard, like death warmed up (*informal*), pale, pallid, wan **2.** deadly, extreme, fatal, intense, mortal, terrible

debacle catastrophe, collapse, defeat, devastation, disaster, downfall, fiasco, havoc, overthrow, reversal, rout, ruin, ruination

debar bar, black, blackball, deny, exclude, hinder, interdict, keep out, obstruct, preclude, prevent, prohibit, refuse admission to, restrain, segregate, shut out, stop

debase 1. abase, cheapen, degrade, demean, devalue, disgrace, dishonour, drag down, humble, humiliate, lower, reduce, shame **2.** adulterate, bastardize, contaminate, corrupt, defile, depreciate, impair, pollute, taint, vitiate
▷ **Antonyms** (*sense 1*) elevate, enhance, exalt, improve, uplift (*sense 2*) purify

debased 1. adulterated, depreciated, devalued, impure, lowered, mixed, polluted, reduced **2.** abandoned, base, corrupt, debauched, degraded, depraved, fallen, low, perverted, sordid, vile
▷ **Antonyms** (*sense 1*) pure (*sense 2*) chaste, decent, ethical, good, honourable, incorruptible, innocent, moral, pure, upright, virtuous

debasement 1. adulteration, contamination, depreciation, devaluation, pollution, reduction **2.** abasement, baseness, corruption, degradation, depravation, perversion

debatable arguable, borderline, controversial, disputable, doubtful, dubious, iffy (*informal*), in dispute, moot, open to question, problematical, questionable, uncertain, undecided, unsettled

debate 1. *verb* argue, contend, contest, controvert, discuss, dispute, question, wrangle **2.** *~noun* altercation, argument, contention, controversy, discussion, disputation, dispute, polemic, row **3.** *~verb* cogitate, consider, deliberate, meditate upon, mull over, ponder, reflect, revolve, ruminate, weigh **4.** *~noun* cogitation, consideration, deliberation, meditation, reflection

debauch *verb* **1.** corrupt, demoralize, deprave, lead astray, pervert, pollute, seduce, subvert, vitiate **2.** deflower, ravish, ruin, seduce, violate *~noun* **3.** bacchanalia, bender (*informal*), binge (*informal*), bout, carousal, carouse, fling, orgy, saturnalia, spree

debauched *adjective* abandoned, corrupt, debased, degenerate, degraded, depraved, dissipated, dissolute, immoral, licentious, perverted, pervy (*slang*), profligate, sleazy, wanton

debauchee libertine, Lothario, playboy, profligate, rake, roué, sensualist, wanton

debauchery carousal, depravity, dissipation, dissoluteness, excess, gluttony, incontinence, indulgence, intemperance, lewdness, licentiousness, lust, orgy, overindulgence, revel

debilitate devitalize, enervate, enfeeble, exhaust, incapacitate, prostrate, relax, sap, undermine, weaken, wear out
▷ **Antonyms** animate, brighten, energize, enliven, excite, fire, invigorate, pep up, perk up, rouse, stimulate, vitalize, wake up

debility decrepitude, enervation, enfeeblement, exhaustion, faintness, feebleness, frailty, incapacity, infirmity, languor, malaise, sickliness, weakness

debonair affable, buoyant, charming, cheerful, courteous, dashing, elegant, jaunty, light-hearted, refined, smooth, sprightly, suave, urbane, well-bred

debouch come forth, come out, come out in the open, disembogue, emerge, issue, sally, sortie

debrief 1. cross-examine, examine, interrogate, probe, question, quiz **2.** describe, detail, report

debris bits, brash, detritus, dross, fragments, litter, pieces, remains, rubbish, rubble, ruins, waste, wreck, wreckage

debt 1. arrears, bill, claim, commitment, debit, due, duty, liability, obligation, score **2. in debt** accountable, beholden, in arrears, in hock (*informal, chiefly U.S.*), in the red (*informal*), liable, owing, responsible

debtor borrower, defaulter, insolvent, mortgagor

debunk cut down to size, deflate, disparage, expose, lampoon, mock, puncture, ridicule, show up

debut beginning, bow, coming out, entrance, first appearance, inauguration, initiation, introduction, launching, presentation

decadence corruption, debasement, decay, decline, degeneration, deterioration, dissipation, dissolution, fall, perversion, retrogression

decadent corrupt, debased, debauched, decaying, declining, degenerate, degraded, depraved, dissolute, immoral, self-indulgent
▷ **Antonyms** decent, ethical, good, high-minded, honourable, incorruptible, moral, principled, proper, upright, upstanding, virtuous

decamp 1. abscond, bolt, desert, do a bunk (*Brit. slang*), do a runner (*slang*), escape, flee, flit (*informal*), fly, fly the coop (*U.S. & Canad. informal*), hightail (*informal, chiefly U.S.*), hook it (*slang*), make off, run away, scarper (*Brit. slang*), skedaddle (*informal*), sneak off, steal away, take a powder (*U.S. & Canad. slang*), take it on the lam (*U.S. & Canad. slang*) **2.** break up camp, evacuate, march off, move off, strike camp, vacate

decant drain, draw off, pour out, tap

decapitate behead, execute, guillotine

decay *verb* **1.** atrophy, break down, crumble, decline, degenerate, deteriorate, disintegrate, dissolve, dwindle, moulder, shrivel, sink, spoil, wane, waste away, wear away, wither **2.** corrode, decompose, mortify, perish, putrefy, rot *~noun* **3.** atrophy, collapse, decadence, decline, degeneracy, degeneration, deterioration, dying, fading, failing, wasting, withering **4.** caries, cariosity, decomposition, gangrene, mortification, perishing, putrefaction, putrescence, putridity, rot, rotting
▷ **Antonyms** *~verb* expand, flourish, flower, grow, increase *~noun* growth

decayed bad, carious, carrion, corroded, decomposed, perished, putrefied, putrid, rank, rotten, spoiled, wasted, withered

decaying crumbling, deteriorating, disintegrating, gangrenous, perishing, putrefacient, rotting, wasting away, wearing away

decease 1. *noun* death, demise, departure, dissolution, dying, release **2.** *~verb* buy it (*U.S. slang*), cease, check out (*U.S. slang*), croak (*slang*), die, expire, go belly-up (*slang*), kick it (*slang*), kick the bucket (*slang*), pass away *or* on *or* over, peg it (*informal*), peg out (*informal*), perish, pop one's clogs (*informal*)

deceased *adjective* dead, defunct, departed, expired, finished, former, gone, late, lifeless, lost, pushing up daisies

deceit 1. artifice, cheating, chicanery, craftiness, cunning, deceitfulness, deception, dissimulation, double-dealing, duplicity, fraud, fraudulence, guile, hypocrisy, imposition, pretence, slyness, treachery, trickery, underhandedness **2.** artifice, blind, cheat, chicanery, deception, duplicity, fake, feint, fraud, imposture, misrepresentation, pretence, ruse, scam (*slang*), sham, shift, sting (*informal*), stratagem, subterfuge, swindle, trick, wile
▷ **Antonyms** candour, frankness, honesty, openness, sincerity, truthfulness

deceitful counterfeit, crafty, deceiving, deceptive, designing, dishonest, disingenuous, double-dealing, duplicitous, fallacious, false, fraudulent, guileful, hypocritical, illusory, insincere, knavish (*archaic*), sneaky, treacherous, tricky, two-faced, underhand, untrustworthy

deceive 1. bamboozle (*informal*), beguile, betray, cheat, con (*informal*), cozen, delude, disappoint, double-cross (*informal*), dupe, ensnare, entrap, fool, hoax, hoodwink, impose upon, kid (*informal*), lead (someone) on (*informal*), mislead, outwit, pull a fast one (*slang*), pull the wool over (someone's) eyes, stiff (*slang*), sting (*informal*), swindle, take for a ride (*informal*), take in (*informal*), trick **2. be deceived by** be made a fool of, be taken in (by), be the dupe of, bite, fall for, fall into a trap, swallow (*informal*), swallow hook, line, and sinker (*informal*), take the bait

deceiver betrayer, charlatan, cheat, chiseller (*informal*), con man (*informal*), cozener, crook (*informal*), deluder, dissembler, double-dealer, fake, fraud, fraudster, grifter (*slang, chiefly U.S. & Canad.*), hypocrite, impostor, inveigler, mountebank, pretender, sharper, snake in the grass, swindler, trickster

decency appropriateness, civility, correctness, courtesy, decorum, etiquette, fitness, good form, good manners, modesty, propriety, respectability, seemliness

decent 1. appropriate, becoming, befitting, chaste, comely, *comme il faut,* decorous, delicate, fit, fitting, modest, nice, polite, presentable, proper, pure, respectable, seemly, suitable **2.** acceptable, adequate, ample, average, competent, fair, passable, reasonable, satisfactory, sufficient, tolerable **3.** accommodating, courteous, friendly, generous, gracious, helpful, kind, obliging, thoughtful
▷ **Antonyms** (*sense 1*) awkward, immodest, improper, incorrect, indecent, unseemly, unsuitable (*sense 2*) clumsy, inept, unsatisfactory (*sense 3*) awkward, discourteous

deception 1. craftiness, cunning, deceit, deceitfulness, deceptiveness, dissimulation, duplicity, fraud, fraudulence, guile, hypocrisy, imposition, insincerity, legerdemain, treachery, trickery **2.** artifice, bluff, canard, cheat, decoy, feint, fraud, hoax, hokum (*slang, chiefly U.S. & Canad.*), illusion, imposture, leg-pull (*Brit. informal*), lie, pork pie (*Brit. slang*), porky (*Brit. slang*), ruse, sham, snare, snow job (*slang, chiefly U.S. & Canad.*), stratagem, subterfuge, trick, wile
▷ **Antonyms** artlessness, candour, fidelity, frankness, honesty, openness, scrupulousness, straightforwardness, trustworthiness, truthfulness

deceptive ambiguous, deceitful, delusive, dishonest, fake, fallacious, false, fraudulent, illusory, misleading, mock, specious, spurious, unreliable

decide adjudge, adjudicate, choose, come to a conclusion, commit oneself, conclude, decree, determine, elect, end, make a decision, make up one's mind, purpose, reach *or* come to a decision, resolve, settle, tip the balance
▷ **Antonyms** be indecisive, be unable to decide, blow hot and cold (*informal*), dither (*chiefly Brit.*), falter, fluctuate, hesitate, hum and haw, seesaw, shilly-shally (*informal*), swither (*Scot.*), vacillate

decided 1. absolute, categorical, certain, clear-cut, definite, distinct, express, indisputable, positive, pronounced, un~

ambiguous, undeniable, undisputed, unequivocal, unquestionable **2.** assertive, decisive, deliberate, determined, emphatic, firm, resolute, strong-willed, unfaltering, unhesitating

▷ **Antonyms** (*sense 1*) doubtful, dubious, questionable, undetermined (*sense 2*) hesitant, indecisive, irresolute, undetermined, weak

decidedly absolutely, certainly, clearly, decisively, distinctly, downright, positively, unequivocally, unmistakably

deciding chief, conclusive, critical, crucial, decisive, determining, influential, prime, principal, significant

decipher construe, crack, decode, deduce, explain, figure out (*informal*), interpret, make out, read, reveal, solve, suss (out) (*slang*), understand, unfold, unravel

decision 1. arbitration, conclusion, finding, judgment, outcome, resolution, result, ruling, sentence, settlement, verdict **2.** decisiveness, determination, firmness, purpose, purposefulness, resoluteness, resolution, resolve, strength of mind *or* will

decisive 1. absolute, conclusive, critical, crucial, definite, definitive, fateful, final, influential, momentous, positive, significant **2.** decided, determined, firm, forceful, incisive, resolute, strong-minded, trenchant

▷ **Antonyms** (*sense 1*) doubtful, indecisive, uncertain, undecided (*sense 2*) hesitant, hesitating, indecisive, in two minds (*informal*), irresolute, pussyfooting (*informal*), uncertain, undecided, vacillating

deck *verb* **1.** adorn, apparel (*archaic*), array, attire, beautify, bedeck, bedight (*archaic*), bedizen (*archaic*), clothe, decorate, dress, embellish, festoon, garland, grace, ornament, trim **2. deck up** *or* **out** doll up (*slang*), get ready, prettify, pretty up, prink, rig out, tog up *or* out, trick out

declaim 1. harangue, hold forth, lecture, orate, perorate, proclaim, rant, recite, speak, spiel (*informal*) **2. declaim against** attack, decry, denounce, inveigh, rail

declamation address, harangue, lecture, oration, rant, recitation, speech, tirade

declamatory bombastic, discursive, fustian, grandiloquent, high-flown, inflated, magniloquent, orotund, pompous, rhetorical, stagy, stilted, theatrical, turgid

declaration 1. acknowledgment, affirmation, assertion, attestation, averment, avowal, deposition, disclosure, protestation, revelation, statement, testimony **2.** announcement, edict, manifesto, notification, proclamation, profession, promulgation, pronouncement, pronunciamento

declarative, declaratory affirmative, definite, demonstrative, enunciatory, explanatory, expository, expressive, positive

declare 1. affirm, announce, assert, asseverate, attest, aver, avow, certify, claim, confirm, maintain, notify, proclaim, profess, pronounce, state, swear, testify, utter, validate **2.** confess, convey, disclose, make known, manifest, reveal, show

declension 1. decadence, decay, decline, degeneracy, descent, deterioration, diminution, fall **2.** inflection, variation

declination decline, declivity, descent, deviation, dip, divergence, inclination, obliquity, slope

decline *verb* **1.** abstain, avoid, deny, forgo, refuse, reject, say 'no', send one's regrets, turn down **2.** decrease, diminish, drop, dwindle, ebb, fade, fail, fall, fall off, flag, lessen, shrink, sink, wane *~noun* **3.** abatement, diminution, downturn, drop, dwindling, falling off, lessening, recession, slump *~verb* **4.** decay, degenerate, deteriorate, droop, languish, pine, weaken, worsen *~noun* **5.** decay, decrepitude, degeneration, deterioration, enfeeblement, failing, senility, weakening, worsening **6.** *archaic* consumption, phthisis, tuberculosis *~verb* **7.** descend, dip, sink, slant, slope *~noun* **8.** declivity, hill, incline, slope

▷ **Antonyms** *~verb* (*sense 1*) accept, agree, consent (*sense 2*) improve, increase, rise *~noun* (*sense 3*) improvement, rise, upswing

declivity brae (*Scot.*), declination, descent, incline, slant, slope

decompose 1. break up, crumble, decay, fall apart, fester, putrefy, rot, spoil **2.** analyse, atomize, break down, break up, decompound, disintegrate, dissect, dissolve, distil, separate

decomposition atomization, breakdown, corruption, decay, disintegration, dissolution, division, putrefaction, putrescence, putridity, rot

décor colour scheme, decoration, furnishing style, ornamentation

decorate 1. adorn, beautify, bedeck, deck, embellish, enrich, festoon, grace, ornament, trim **2.** colour, do up (*informal*), furbish, paint, paper, renovate, wallpaper **3.** cite, honour, pin a medal on

decoration 1. adornment, beautification, elaboration, embellishment, enrichment, garnishing, ornamentation, trimming **2.** arabesque, bauble, cartouch(e), curlicue, falderal, festoon, flounce, flourish, frill, furbelow, garnish, ornament, scroll, spangle, trimmings, trinket **3.** award, badge, colours, emblem, garter, medal, order, ribbon, star

decorative adorning, arty-crafty, beauti~

fying, enhancing, fancy, nonfunctional, ornamental, pretty

decorous appropriate, becoming, befitting, comely, *comme il faut,* correct, decent, dignified, fit, fitting, mannerly, polite, proper, refined, sedate, seemly, staid, suitable, well-behaved

▷ **Antonyms** inapposite, inappropriate, malapropos, out of keeping, unbefitting, undignified, unseemly

decorum behaviour, breeding, courtliness, decency, deportment, dignity, etiquette, gentility, good grace, good manners, gravity, politeness, politesse, propriety, protocol, punctilio, respectability, seemliness

▷ **Antonyms** bad manners, churlishness, impoliteness, impropriety, indecorum, rudeness, unseemliness

decoy 1. *noun* attraction, bait, ensnarement, enticement, inducement, lure, pretence, trap **2.** *~verb* allure, bait, deceive, ensnare, entice, entrap, inveigle, lure, seduce, tempt

decrease 1. *verb* abate, contract, curtail, cut down, decline, diminish, drop, dwindle, ease, fall off, lessen, lower, peter out, reduce, shrink, slacken, subside, wane **2.** *~noun* abatement, contraction, cutback, decline, diminution, downturn, dwindling, ebb, falling off, lessening, loss, reduction, shrinkage, subsidence

▷ **Antonyms** *~verb* enlarge, expand, extend, increase *~noun* expansion, extension, growth

decree 1. *noun* act, canon, command, demand, dictum, edict, enactment, law, mandate, order, ordinance, precept, proclamation, regulation, ruling, statute **2.** *~verb* command, decide, demand, determine, dictate, enact, establish, lay down, ordain, order, prescribe, proclaim, pronounce, rule

decrepit 1. aged, crippled, debilitated, doddering, effete, feeble, frail, incapacitated, infirm, past it, superannuated, wasted, weak **2.** antiquated, battered, beat-up (*informal*), broken-down, deteriorated, dilapidated, ramshackle, rickety, run-down, tumble-down, weather-beaten, worn-out

decrepitude 1. debility, dotage, feebleness, incapacity, infirmity, invalidity, old age, senility, wasting, weakness **2.** decay, degeneration, deterioration, dilapidation

decry abuse, asperse, belittle, blame, blast, censure, condemn, criticize, cry down, denigrate, denounce, depreciate, derogate, detract, devalue, discredit, disparage, excoriate, lambast(e), put down, rail against, run down, tear into (*informal*), traduce, underestimate, underrate, undervalue

dedicate 1. commit, devote, give over to, pledge, surrender **2.** address, assign, inscribe, offer **3.** bless, consecrate, hallow, sanctify, set apart

dedicated committed, devoted, enthusiastic, given over to, purposeful, single-minded, sworn, wholehearted, zealous

▷ **Antonyms** indifferent, uncaring, uncommitted, unconcerned, uninterested, unresponsive

dedication 1. adherence, allegiance, commitment, devotedness, devotion, faithfulness, loyalty, single-mindedness, wholeheartedness **2.** address, inscription, message **3.** consecration, hallowing, sanctification

▷ **Antonyms** (*sense 1*) apathy, coolness, indifference, insensibility, torpor, unconcern, uninterestedness

deduce conclude, derive, draw, gather, glean, infer, put two and two together, read between the lines, reason, take to mean, understand

deducible derivable, inferable, to be inferred, traceable

deduct decrease by, knock off (*informal*), reduce by, remove, subtract, take away, take from, take off, take out, withdraw

▷ **Antonyms** add, add to, enlarge

deduction 1. assumption, conclusion, consequence, corollary, finding, inference, reasoning, result **2.** abatement, allowance, decrease, diminution, discount, reduction, subtraction, withdrawal

deed 1. achievement, act, action, exploit, fact, feat, performance, reality, truth **2.** *Law* contract, document, indenture, instrument, title, title deed, transaction

deem account, believe, conceive, consider, esteem, estimate, hold, imagine, judge, reckon, regard, suppose, think

deep *adjective* **1.** abyssal, bottomless, broad, far, profound, unfathomable, wide, yawning **2.** abstract, abstruse, arcane, esoteric, hidden, mysterious, obscure, recondite, secret **3.** acute, discerning, learned, penetrating, sagacious, wise **4.** artful, astute, canny, cunning, designing, devious, insidious, knowing, scheming, shrewd **5.** extreme, grave, great, intense, profound, serious (*informal*), unqualified **6.** absorbed, engrossed, immersed, lost, preoccupied, rapt **7.** *of a colour* dark, intense, rich, strong, vivid **8.** *of a sound* bass, booming, full-toned, low, low-pitched, resonant, sonorous *~noun* **9.** (*usually preceded by* **the**) briny (*informal*), high seas, main, ocean, sea **10.** culmination, dead, middle, mid point *~adverb* **11.** deeply, far down, far into, late

▷ **Antonyms** *~adjective* (*senses 1 & 2*) shallow (*sense 3*) simple (*sense 4*) shallow, simple (*sense 5*) shallow, superficial (*sense 7*) light, pale (*sense 8*) high, sharp

deepen 1. dig out, dredge, excavate, hollow, scoop out, scrape out **2.** grow, increase, intensify, magnify, reinforce, strengthen

deeply 1. completely, gravely, profoundly, seriously, severely, thoroughly, to the core, to the heart, to the quick **2.** acutely, affectingly, distressingly, feelingly, intensely, mournfully, movingly, passionately, sadly

deep-rooted *or* **deep-seated** confirmed, dyed-in-the-wool, entrenched, fixed, ineradicable, ingrained, inveterate, rooted, settled, subconscious, unconscious
▷ **Antonyms** eradicable, exterior, external, on the surface, peripheral, shallow, skin-deep, slight, superficial, surface

deface blemish, deform, destroy, disfigure, impair, injure, mar, mutilate, obliterate, spoil, sully, tarnish, total (*slang*), trash (*slang*), vandalize

defacement blemish, damage, destruction, disfigurement, distortion, impairment, injury, mutilation, vandalism

de facto 1. *adverb* actually, in effect, in fact, in reality, really **2.** *~adjective* actual, existing, real

defalcation default, deficiency, deficit, embezzlement, fraud, misappropriation, shortage

defamation aspersion, calumny, character assassination, denigration, disparagement, libel, obloquy, opprobrium, scandal, slander, slur, smear, traducement, vilification

defamatory abusive, calumnious, contumelious, denigrating, derogatory, disparaging, injurious, insulting, libellous, slanderous, vilifying, vituperative

defame asperse, bad-mouth (*slang, chiefly U.S. & Canad.*), belie, besmirch, blacken, calumniate, cast a slur on, cast aspersions on, denigrate, detract, discredit, disgrace, dishonour, disparage, knock (*informal*), libel, malign, rubbish (*informal*), slag (off) (*slang*), slander, smear, speak evil of, stigmatize, traduce, vilify, vituperate

default 1. *noun* absence, defect, deficiency, dereliction, failure, fault, lack, lapse, neglect, nonpayment, omission, want **2.** *~verb* bilk, defraud, dodge, evade, fail, levant (*Brit.*), neglect, rat (*informal*), swindle, welsh (*slang*)

defaulter delinquent, embezzler, levanter (*Brit.*), nonpayer, offender, peculator, welsher (*slang*)

defeat *verb* **1.** beat, blow out of the water (*slang*), clobber (*slang*), conquer, crush, lick (*informal*), make mincemeat of (*informal*), master, outplay, overpower, overthrow, overwhelm, pip at the post, quell, repulse, rout, run rings around (*informal*), stuff (*slang*), subdue, subjugate, tank (*slang*), trounce, undo, vanquish, wipe the floor with (*informal*), worst **2.** baffle, balk, confound, disappoint, discomfit, foil, frustrate, get the better of, ruin, thwart *~noun* **3.** beating, conquest, debacle, overthrow, pasting (*slang*), repulse, rout, trouncing, vanquishment **4.** disappointment, discomfiture, failure, frustration, rebuff, repulse, reverse, setback, thwarting
▷ **Antonyms** *~verb* bow, lose, submit, succumb, surrender, yield *~noun* success, triumph, victory

defeated balked, beaten, bested, checkmated, conquered, crushed, licked (*informal*), overcome, overpowered, overwhelmed, routed, thrashed, thwarted, trounced, vanquished, worsted
▷ **Antonyms** conquering, dominant, glorious, successful, triumphal, triumphant, undefeated, victorious, winning

defeatist 1. *noun* pessimist, prophet of doom, quitter, submitter, yielder **2.** *~adjective* pessimistic

defecate crap (*taboo slang*), egest, empty, evacuate (*Physiology*), excrete, move, open the bowels, pass a motion, shit (*taboo slang*), void excrement

defecation egestion, elimination, emptying *or* opening of the bowels, evacuation (*Physiology*), excrement, excretion, motion, movement, voiding excrement

defect *noun* **1.** blemish, blotch, error, failing, fault, flaw, foible, imperfection, mistake, spot, taint, want **2.** absence, default, deficiency, frailty, inadequacy, lack, shortcoming, weakness *~verb* **3.** abandon, apostatize, break faith, change sides, desert, go over, rebel, revolt, tergiversate, walk out on (*informal*)

defection abandonment, apostasy, backsliding, dereliction, desertion, rebellion, revolt

defective 1. broken, deficient, faulty, flawed, imperfect, inadequate, incomplete, insufficient, not working, on the blink (*slang*), out of order, scant, short **2.** abnormal, mentally deficient, retarded, subnormal
▷ **Antonyms** (*sense 1*) adequate, intact, perfect, whole, working (*sense 2*) normal

defector apostate, deserter, rat (*informal*), recreant (*archaic*), renegade, runagate (*archaic*), tergiversator, turncoat

defence 1. armament, cover, deterrence, guard, immunity, protection, resistance, safeguard, security, shelter **2.** barricade, bastion, buckler, bulwark, buttress, fastness, fortification, rampart, shield **3.** apologia, apology, argument, excuse, exoneration, explanation, extenuation, justification, plea, vindication **4.** *Law* alibi, case, declaration, denial, plea, pleading, rebuttal, testimony

defenceless endangered, exposed, helpless, naked, powerless, unarmed, unguarded, unprotected, vulnerable, wide open
▷ **Antonyms** free from harm, guarded, out of harm's way, protected, safe, safe and sound, secure

defend 1. cover, fortify, guard, keep safe, preserve, protect, safeguard, screen, secure, shelter, shield, ward off, watch over **2.** assert, champion, endorse, espouse, justify, maintain, plead, speak up for, stand by, stand up for, stick up for (*informal*), support, sustain, uphold, vindicate

defendant appellant, defence, litigant, offender, prisoner at the bar, respondent, the accused

defender 1. bodyguard, escort, guard, protector **2.** advocate, champion, patron, sponsor, supporter, vindicator

defensible 1. holdable, impregnable, safe, secure, unassailable **2.** justifiable, pardonable, permissible, plausible, tenable, valid, vindicable

▷ **Antonyms** (*sense 2*) faulty, inexcusable, insupportable, unforgivable, unjustifiable, unpardonable, untenable, wrong

defensive averting, defending, on the defensive, opposing, protective, safeguarding, uptight (*informal*), watchful, withstanding

defensively at bay, in defence, in self-defence, on guard, on the defensive, suspiciously

defer[1] *verb* adjourn, delay, hold over, postpone, procrastinate, prorogue, protract, put off, put on ice, put on the back burner (*informal*), set aside, shelve, suspend, table, take a rain check on (*U.S. & Canad. informal*)

defer[2] *verb* accede, bow, capitulate, comply, give in, give way to, respect, submit, yield

deference 1. acquiescence, capitulation, complaisance, compliance, obedience, obeisance, submission, yielding **2.** attention, civility, consideration, courtesy, esteem, homage, honour, obeisance, politeness, regard, respect, reverence, thoughtfulness, veneration

▷ **Antonyms** (*sense 1*) disobedience, insubordination, noncompliance, nonobservance, revolt (*sense 2*) contempt, discourtesy, dishonour, disregard, disrespect, impertinence, impoliteness, impudence, incivility, insolence, irreverence, lack of respect, rudeness

deferential civil, complaisant, considerate, courteous, dutiful, ingratiating, obedient, obeisant, obsequious, polite, regardful, respectful, reverential, submissive

deferment, deferral adjournment, delay, moratorium, postponement, putting off, stay, suspension

defiance challenge, confrontation, contempt, contumacy, disobedience, disregard, insolence, insubordination, opposition, provocation, rebelliousness, recalcitrance, spite

▷ **Antonyms** accordance, acquiescence, compliance, deference, obedience, observance, regard, respect, subservience

defiant aggressive, audacious, bold, challenging, contumacious, daring, disobedient, insolent, insubordinate, mutinous, provocative, rebellious, recalcitrant, refractory, truculent

▷ **Antonyms** cowardly, meek, obedient, respectful, submissive

deficiency 1. defect, demerit, failing, fault, flaw, frailty, imperfection, shortcoming, weakness **2.** absence, dearth, deficit, inadequacy, insufficiency, lack, scantiness, scarcity, shortage

▷ **Antonyms** (*sense 2*) abundance, adequacy, sufficiency, superfluity, surfeit

deficient 1. defective, faulty, flawed, impaired, imperfect, incomplete, inferior, unsatisfactory, weak **2.** exiguous, inadequate, insufficient, lacking, meagre, pathetic, scant, scanty, scarce, short, skimpy, wanting

deficit arrears, default, deficiency, loss, shortage, shortfall

defile[1] *verb* **1.** befoul, contaminate, corrupt, dirty, make foul, pollute, smear, smirch, soil, taint, tarnish, vitiate **2.** besmirch, debase, degrade, disgrace, dishonour, smirch, stain, sully **3.** desecrate, profane, treat sacrilegiously **4.** abuse, deflower, molest, rape, ravish, seduce, violate

defile[2] *noun* gorge, gully, pass, passage, ravine, way through

defiled besmirched, desecrated, dishonoured, impure, polluted, profaned, ravished, spoilt, tainted, unclean

▷ **Antonyms** chaste, clean, immaculate, innocent, spotless, uncontaminated, uncorrupted, undefiled, unstained, unsullied, untainted

defilement contamination, corruption, debasement, degradation, depravity, desecration, disgrace, pollution, sullying, violation

definable apparent, definite, describable, determinable, explicable, perceptible, specific

define 1. characterize, describe, designate, detail, determine, explain, expound, interpret, specify, spell out **2.** bound, circumscribe, delimit, delineate, demarcate, limit, mark out, outline

definite 1. black-and-white, clear, clear-cut, clearly defined, cut-and-dried (*informal*), determined, exact, explicit, express, fixed, marked, obvious, particular, precise, specific **2.** assured, certain, decided, guaranteed, positive, settled, sure

▷ **Antonyms** confused, fuzzy, general, hazy, ill-defined, imprecise, indefinite, indeterminate, indistinct, inexact, loose, obscure, uncertain, unclear, undetermined, vague

definitely absolutely, beyond any doubt, categorically, certainly, clearly, come hell or high water (*informal*), decidedly, easily, far and away, finally, indubitably, needless to say, obviously, plainly, positively, surely, undeniably, unequivocally, unmistakably, unquestionably, without doubt, without fail, without question

definition 1. clarification, description, elucidation, explanation, exposition, statement of meaning **2.** delimitation, delineation, demarcation, determination, fixing, outlining, settling **3.** clarity, contrast, distinctness, focus, precision, sharpness

definitive absolute, authoritative, complete, conclusive, decisive, exhaustive, final, mother (of all) (*informal*), perfect, reliable, ultimate

deflate 1. collapse, contract, empty, exhaust, flatten, puncture, shrink, void **2.** chasten, dash, debunk (*informal*), disconcert, dispirit, humble, humiliate, mortify, put down (*slang*), squash, take the wind out of (someone's) sails **3.** *Economics* decrease, depreciate, depress, devalue, diminish, reduce
▷ **Antonyms** (*sense 1*) aerate, balloon, bloat, blow up, dilate, distend, enlarge, expand, increase, inflate, puff up *or* out, pump up, swell (*sense 3*) boost, expand, increase, inflate

deflect bend, deviate, diverge, glance off, ricochet, shy, sidetrack, slew, swerve, turn, turn aside, twist, veer, wind

deflection aberration, bend, declination, deviation, divergence, drift, refraction, swerve, veer

deflower 1. assault, force, molest, rape, ravish, ruin, seduce, violate **2.** defile, desecrate, despoil, harm, mar, spoil, violate

deform 1. buckle, contort, distort, gnarl, malform, mangle, misshape, twist, warp **2.** cripple, deface, disfigure, injure, maim, mar, mutilate, ruin, spoil

deformed 1. bent, blemished, crippled, crooked, disfigured, distorted, maimed, malformed, mangled, marred, misbegotten, misshapen **2.** depraved, gross, offensive, perverted, twisted, warped

deformity 1. abnormality, defect, disfigurement, distortion, irregularity, malformation, misproportion, misshapenness, ugliness **2.** corruption, depravity, grossness, hatefulness, vileness

defraud beguile, bilk, cheat, con (*informal*), cozen, delude, diddle (*informal*), do (*slang*), dupe, embezzle, fleece, gull (*archaic*), gyp (*slang*), outwit, pilfer, pull a fast one on (*informal*), rip off (*slang*), rob, rook (*slang*), skin (*slang*), stiff (*slang*), stitch up (*slang*), swindle, trick

defray clear, cover, discharge, foot the bill, liquidate, meet, pay, settle

defrayal, defrayment clearance, discharge, liquidation, payment, settlement

deft able, adept, adroit, agile, clever, dexterous, expert, handy, neat, nimble, proficient, skilful
▷ **Antonyms** awkward, bumbling, cack-handed (*informal*), clumsy, gauche, inept, maladroit, unskilful

defunct 1. dead, deceased, departed, extinct, gone **2.** a dead letter, bygone, expired, inoperative, invalid, nonexistent, not functioning, obsolete, out of commission

defy 1. beard, brave, challenge, confront, contemn, dare, despise, disregard, face, flout, hurl defiance at, provoke, scorn, slight, spurn **2.** baffle, call (someone's) bluff, defeat, elude, foil, frustrate, repel, repulse, resist, thwart, withstand

degeneracy 1. corruption, decadence, degradation, depravity, dissoluteness, immorality, inferiority, meanness, poorness, turpitude **2.** debasement, decay, decline, decrease, depravation, deterioration

degenerate 1. *adjective* base, corrupt, debased, debauched, decadent, degenerated, degraded, depraved, deteriorated, dissolute, fallen, immoral, low, mean, perverted, pervy (*slang*) **2.** *~verb* decay, decline, decrease, deteriorate, fall off, go to pot, lapse, regress, retrogress, rot, sink, slip, worsen

degeneration debasement, decline, degeneracy, descent, deterioration, dissipation, dissolution, regression

degradation 1. abasement, debasement, decadence, decline, degeneracy, degeneration, demotion, derogation, deterioration, downgrading, perversion **2.** discredit, disgrace, dishonour, humiliation, ignominy, mortification, shame

degrade 1. cheapen, corrupt, debase, demean, deteriorate, discredit, disgrace, dishonour, humble, humiliate, impair, injure, pervert, shame, vitiate **2.** break, cashier, demote, depose, downgrade, lower, reduce to inferior rank **3.** adulterate, dilute, doctor, mix, thin, water, water down, weaken
▷ **Antonyms** (*senses 1 & 2*) dignify, elevate, enhance, ennoble, honour, improve, promote, raise

degraded abandoned, base, corrupt, debased, debauched, decadent, depraved, despicable, disgraced, disreputable, dissolute, low, mean, profligate, sordid, vicious, vile

degrading cheapening, contemptible, debasing, demeaning, disgraceful, dishonourable, humiliating, infra dig (*informal*), lowering, shameful, undignified, unworthy

degree 1. class, grade, level, order, position, rank, standing, station, status **2.**

division, extent, gradation, grade, interval, limit, mark, measure, notch, point, rung, scale, stage, step, unit **3.** ambit, calibre, extent, intensity, level, measure, proportion, quality, quantity, range, rate, ratio, scale, scope, severity, standard **4. by degrees** bit by bit, gently, gradually, imperceptibly, inch by inch, little by little, slowly, step by step

dehydrate desiccate, drain, dry out, dry up, evaporate, exsiccate, parch

deification apotheosis, elevation, ennoblement, exaltation, glorification, idolization

deify apotheosize, elevate, ennoble, enthrone, exalt, extol, glorify, idealize, idolize, immortalize, venerate, worship

deign condescend, consent, deem worthy, lower oneself, see fit, stoop, think fit

deity celestial being, divine being, divinity, god, goddess, godhead, idol, immortal, supreme being

deject cast down, dampen, daunt, demoralize, depress, discourage, dishearten, dismay, dispirit

dejected blue, cast down, crestfallen, depressed, despondent, disconsolate, disheartened, dismal, doleful, down, downcast, downhearted, down in the dumps (*informal*), gloomy, glum, low, low-spirited, melancholy, miserable, morose, sad, sick as a parrot (*informal*), woebegone, wretched

▷ **Antonyms** blithe, cheerful, chirpy (*informal*), encouraged, genial, happy, joyous, light-hearted, upbeat (*informal*)

dejection blues, depression, despair, despondency, doldrums, downheartedness, dumps (*informal*), gloom, gloominess, heavy-heartedness, low spirits, melancholy, sadness, sorrow, the hump (*Brit. informal*), unhappiness

de jure according to the law, by right, legally, rightfully

delay 1. *verb* beat about the bush, defer, hold over, play for time, postpone, procrastinate, prolong, protract, put off, put on the back burner (*informal*), shelve, stall, suspend, table, take a rain check on (*U.S. & Canad. informal*), temporize **2.** *~noun* deferment, postponement, procrastination, stay, suspension **3.** *~verb* arrest, bog down, check, detain, halt, hinder, hold back, hold up, impede, obstruct, retard, set back, slow up, stop, throw a spanner in the words **4.** *~noun* check, detention, hindrance, hold-up, impediment, interruption, interval, obstruction, setback, stoppage, wait **5.** *~verb* dawdle, dilly-dally (*informal*), drag, drag one's feet *or* heels (*informal*), lag, linger, loiter, tarry **6.** *~noun* dawdling, dilly-dallying (*informal*), lingering, loitering, tarrying

▷ **Antonyms** *~verb* accelerate, advance, dispatch, expedite, facilitate, forward, hasten, hurry, precipitate, press, promote, quicken, rush, speed (up), urge

delectable adorable, agreeable, appetizing, charming, dainty, delicious, delightful, enjoyable, enticing, gratifying, inviting, luscious, lush, pleasant, pleasurable, satisfying, scrumptious (*informal*), tasty, toothsome, yummy (*slang*)

▷ **Antonyms** awful, disagreeable, disgusting, distasteful, dreadful, horrible, horrid, nasty, offensive, terrible, unappetizing, unpleasant, yucky *or* yukky (*slang*)

delectation amusement, delight, diversion, enjoyment, entertainment, gratification, happiness, jollies (*slang*), pleasure, refreshment, relish, satisfaction

delegate *noun* **1.** agent, ambassador, commissioner, deputy, envoy, legate, representative, vicar *~verb* **2.** accredit, appoint, authorize, commission, depute, designate, empower, mandate **3.** assign, consign, devolve, entrust, give, hand over, pass on, relegate, transfer

delegation 1. commission, contingent, deputation, embassy, envoys, legation, mission **2.** assignment, commissioning, committal, deputizing, devolution, entrustment, relegation

delete blot out, blue-pencil, cancel, cross out, cut out, dele, edit, edit out, efface, erase, excise, expunge, obliterate, remove, rub out, strike out

deleterious bad, damaging, destructive, detrimental, harmful, hurtful, injurious, pernicious, prejudicial, ruinous

deliberate *verb* **1.** cogitate, consider, consult, debate, discuss, meditate, mull over, ponder, reflect, think, weigh *~adjective* **2.** calculated, conscious, considered, designed, intentional, planned, prearranged, premeditated, purposeful, studied, thoughtful, wilful **3.** careful, cautious, circumspect, heedful, measured, methodical, ponderous, prudent, slow, thoughtful, unhurried, wary

▷ **Antonyms** (*sense 2*) accidental, inadvertent, unconscious, unintended, unpremeditated, unthinking (*sense 3*) fast, haphazard, hasty, heedless, hurried, impetuous, impulsive, rash

deliberately by design, calculatingly, consciously, determinedly, emphatically, in cold blood, intentionally, knowingly, on purpose, pointedly, resolutely, studiously, wilfully, wittingly

deliberation 1. calculation, care, carefulness, caution, circumspection, cogitation, consideration, coolness, forethought, meditation, prudence, purpose, reflection, speculation, study, thought, wariness **2.** conference, consultation, debate, discussion

delicacy 1. accuracy, daintiness, elegance, exquisiteness, fineness, lightness, nicety, precision, subtlety **2.** debility, flimsiness, fragility, frailness, frailty, infir~

mity, slenderness, tenderness, weak~ness **3**. discrimination, fastidiousness, finesse, purity, refinement, sensibility, sensitiveness, sensitivity, tact, taste **4**. *bonne bouche,* dainty, luxury, relish, sa~voury, titbit, treat

delicate 1. ailing, debilitated, flimsy, fragile, frail, sickly, slender, slight, ten~der, weak **2**. choice, dainty, delicious, el~egant, exquisite, fine, graceful, savoury, tender **3**. faint, muted, pastel, soft, sub~dued, subtle **4**. accurate, deft, detailed, minute, precise, skilled **5**. considerate, diplomatic, discreet, sensitive, tactful **6**. built on sand, critical, difficult, precari~ous, sensitive, sticky (*informal*), tick~lish, touchy **7**. careful, critical, discrimi~nating, fastidious, nice, prudish, pure, refined, scrupulous, squeamish

▷ **Antonyms** (*sense 1*) healthy, strong (*sense 2*) harsh, strong (*sense 3*) bright, harsh, rough (*sense 4*) careless, crude, rough (*sense 5*) harsh, inconsiderate, in~delicate, insensitive, rough (*sense 7*) coarse, crude, indelicate, unrefined

delicately carefully, daintily, deftly, el~egantly, exquisitely, fastidiously, finely, gracefully, lightly, precisely, sensitively, skilfully, softly, subtly, tactfully

delicious 1. ambrosial, appetizing, choice, dainty, delectable, luscious, mouth~watering, nectareous, palatable, sa~voury, scrumptious (*informal*), tasty, toothsome, yummy (*slang*) **2**. agreeable, charming, delightful, enjoyable, enter~taining, exquisite, pleasant, pleasing

▷ **Antonyms** disagreeable, distasteful, unpleasant

delight *noun* **1**. ecstasy, enjoyment, felic~ity, gladness, glee, gratification, happi~ness, jollies (*slang*), joy, pleasure, rap~ture, transport *~verb* **2**. amuse, charm, cheer, divert, enchant, gratify, please, ravish, rejoice, satisfy, thrill **3**. (*with* **in**) appreciate, enjoy, feast on, glory in, in~dulge in, like, love, luxuriate in, relish, revel in, savour

▷ **Antonyms** *~noun* disapprobation, dis~favour, dislike, displeasure, dissatisfac~tion, distaste *~verb* (*sense 2*) disgust, displease, dissatisfy, gall, irk, offend, upset, vex

delighted blissed out, captivated, charmed, cock-a-hoop, ecstatic, elated, enchanted, gladdened, happy, in sev~enth heaven, joyous, jubilant, overjoyed, over the moon (*informal*), pleased, rapt, sent, thrilled

delightful agreeable, amusing, captivat~ing, charming, congenial, delectable, enchanting, engaging, enjoyable, enter~taining, fascinating, gratifying, heaven~ly, pleasant, pleasing, pleasurable, rap~turous, ravishing, thrilling

▷ **Antonyms** disagreeable, displeasing, distasteful, horrid, nasty, unpleasant

delimit bound, define, demarcate, deter~mine, fix, mark (out)

delineate characterize, chart, contour, depict, describe, design, draw, figure, map out, outline, paint, picture, portray, render, sketch, trace

delineation account, chart, depiction, de~scription, design, diagram, drawing, outline, picture, portrait, portrayal, representation, tracing

delinquency crime, fault, misbehaviour, misconduct, misdeed, misdemeanour, offence, wrongdoing

delinquent criminal, culprit, defaulter, juvenile delinquent, lawbreaker, mal~efactor, miscreant, offender, villain, wrongdoer, young offender

delirious 1. crazy, demented, deranged, gonzo (*slang*), incoherent, insane, light-headed, mad, raving, unhinged **2**. beside oneself, blissed out, carried away, corybantic, ecstatic, excited, frantic, frenzied, hysterical, sent, wild

▷ **Antonyms** calm, clear-headed, coher~ent, *compos mentis,* in one's right mind, lucid, rational, sane, sensible

delirium 1. aberration, derangement, hal~lucination, insanity, lunacy, madness, raving **2**. ecstasy, fever, frenzy, fury, hysteria, passion, rage

deliver 1. bear, bring, carry, cart, convey, distribute, transport **2**. cede, commit, give up, grant, hand over, make over, relinquish, resign, surrender, transfer, turn over, yield **3**. acquit, discharge, emancipate, free, liberate, loose, ran~som, redeem, release, rescue, save **4**. announce, declare, give, give forth, pre~sent, proclaim, pronounce, publish, read, utter **5**. administer, aim, deal, di~rect, give, inflict, launch, strike, throw **6**. discharge, dispense, feed, give forth, provide, purvey, release, supply

deliverance emancipation, escape, libera~tion, ransom, redemption, release, res~cue, salvation

delivery 1. consignment, conveyance, dis~patch, distribution, handing over, sur~render, transfer, transmission, trans~mittal **2**. articulation, elocution, enun~ciation, intonation, speech, utterance **3**. *Medical* childbirth, confinement, labour, parturition **4**. deliverance, escape, lib~eration, release, rescue

delude bamboozle (*informal*), beguile, cheat, con (*informal*), cozen, deceive, dupe, fool, gull (*archaic*), hoax, hood~wink, impose on, kid (*informal*), lead up the garden path (*informal*), misguide, mislead, pull the wool over someone's eyes, take for a ride (*informal*), take in (*informal*), trick

deluge *noun* **1**. cataclysm, downpour, flood, inundation, overflowing, spate, torrent **2**. *figurative* avalanche, barrage, flood, rush, spate, torrent *~verb* **3**. douse, drench, drown, flood, inundate, soak, submerge, swamp **4.** *figurative* engulf, inundate, overload, overrun, overwhelm, swamp

delusion deception, error, fallacy, false impression, fancy, hallucination, illusion, misapprehension, misbelief, misconception, mistake, phantasm, self-deception

delusive chimerical, deceptive, fallacious, illusive, illusory, misleading, specious, spurious

de luxe choice, costly, elegant, exclusive, expensive, gorgeous, grand, luxurious, opulent, palatial, plush (*informal*), rich, select, special, splendid, splendiferous (*facetious*), sumptuous, superior

delve burrow, dig into, examine, explore, ferret out, forage, investigate, look into, probe, ransack, research, rummage, search, unearth

demagogue agitator, firebrand, haranguer, rabble-rouser, soapbox orator

demand *verb* **1.** ask, challenge, inquire, interrogate, question, request **2.** call for, cry out for, entail, involve, necessitate, need, require, take, want **3.** claim, exact, expect, insist on, order *~noun* **4.** bidding, charge, inquiry, interrogation, order, question, request, requisition **5.** call, claim, market, necessity, need, requirement, want **6. in demand** fashionable, in vogue, like gold dust, needed, popular, requested, sought after

▷ **Antonyms** *~verb* come up with, contribute, furnish, give, grant, produce, provide, supply, yield

demanding 1. challenging, difficult, exacting, exhausting, exigent, hard, taxing, tough, trying, wearing **2.** clamorous, imperious, importunate, insistent, nagging, pressing, urgent

▷ **Antonyms** (*sense 1*) a piece of cake (*informal*), child's play (*informal*), easy, easy-peasy (*slang*), effortless, facile, no bother, painless, simple, straightforward, uncomplicated, undemanding

demarcate define, delimit, determine, differentiate, distinguish between, fix, mark, separate

demarcation 1. bound, boundary, confine, enclosure, limit, margin, pale **2.** delimitation, differentiation, distinction, division, separation

demean abase, debase, degrade, descend, humble, lower, stoop

demeanour air, bearing, behaviour, carriage, comportment, conduct, deportment, manner, mien

demented barking (*slang*), barking mad (*slang*), crackbrained, crackpot (*informal*), crazed, crazy, daft (*informal*), deranged, distraught, doolally (*slang*), dotty (*slang, chiefly Brit.*), foolish, frenzied, gonzo (*slang*), idiotic, insane, loopy (*informal*), lunatic, mad, maniacal, manic, *non compos mentis,* not the full shilling (*informal*), off one's trolley (*slang*), out to lunch (*informal*), unbalanced, unhinged, up the pole (*informal*), wacko *or* whacko (*slang*)

▷ **Antonyms** all there (*informal*), *compos mentis,* in one's right mind, lucid, mentally sound, normal, of sound mind, rational, reasonable, sensible, sound

demise *noun* **1.** death, decease, departure, expiration **2.** collapse, dissolution, downfall, end, failure, fall, ruin, termination **3.** *Law* alienation, conveyance, transfer, transmission *~verb* **4.** *Law* bequeath, convey, grant, leave, transfer, will

democracy commonwealth, government by the people, representative government, republic

democratic autonomous, egalitarian, popular, populist, representative, republican, self-governing

demolish 1. bulldoze, destroy, dismantle, flatten, knock down, level, overthrow, pulverize, raze, ruin, tear down, total (*slang*), trash (*slang*) **2.** *figurative* annihilate, blow out of the water (*slang*), defeat, destroy, lick (*informal*), master, overthrow, overturn, stuff (*slang*), tank (*slang*), undo, wipe the floor with (*informal*), wreck **3.** consume, devour, eat, gobble up, put away

▷ **Antonyms** (*senses 1 & 2*) build, construct, create, repair, restore, strengthen

demolition bulldozing, destruction, explosion, knocking down, levelling, razing, wrecking

demon 1. devil, evil spirit, fiend, ghoul, goblin, malignant spirit **2.** *figurative* devil, fiend, ghoul, monster, rogue, villain **3.** ace (*informal*), addict, fanatic, fiend, go-getter (*informal*), master, wizard **4.** daemon, daimon, genius, guardian spirit, ministering angel, numen

demonic, demoniac, demoniacal 1. devilish, diabolic, diabolical, fiendish, hellish, infernal, satanic **2.** crazed, frantic, frenetic, frenzied, furious, hectic, like one possessed, mad, maniacal, manic

demonstrable attestable, axiomatic, certain, evident, evincible, incontrovertible, indubitable, irrefutable, obvious, palpable, positive, provable, self-evident, undeniable, unmistakable, verifiable

demonstrate 1. display, establish, evidence, evince, exhibit, indicate, manifest, prove, show, testify to **2.** describe, explain, illustrate, make clear, show how, teach **3.** march, parade, picket, protest, rally

demonstration 1. affirmation, confirmation, display, evidence, exhibition, expression, illustration, manifestation, proof, substantiation, testimony, validation **2.** description, explanation, exposition, presentation, test, trial **3.** march, mass lobby, parade, picket, protest, rally, sit-in

demonstrative **1.** affectionate, effusive, emotional, expansive, expressive, gushing, loving, open, unreserved, unrestrained **2.** evincive, explanatory, expository, illustrative, indicative, symptomatic

▷ **Antonyms** (*sense 1*) aloof, cold, contained, distant, formal, impassive, reserved, restrained, stiff, unaffectionate, undemonstrative, unemotional, unresponsive

demoralization **1.** agitation, crushing, devitalization, discomfiture, enervation, lowering *or* loss of morale, panic, perturbation, trepidation, unmanning, weakening **2.** corruption, debasement, depravation, lowering, perversion, vitiation

demoralize **1.** cripple, daunt, deject, depress, disconcert, discourage, dishearten, dispirit, enfeeble, psych out (*informal*), rattle (*informal*), sap, shake, undermine, unnerve, weaken **2.** corrupt, debase, debauch, deprave, lower, pervert, vitiate

▷ **Antonyms** (*sense 1*) boost, cheer, egg on, encourage, hearten, spur

demoralized **1.** broken, crushed, depressed, discouraged, disheartened, dispirited, downcast, sick as a parrot (*informal*), subdued, unmanned, unnerved, weakened **2.** bad, base, corrupt, degenerate, depraved, dissolute, immoral, low, reprobate, sinful, wicked

demote declass, degrade, disrate (*Naval*), downgrade, kick downstairs (*slang*), lower in rank, relegate

▷ **Antonyms** advance, elevate, kick upstairs (*informal*), prefer, raise, upgrade

demulcent calming, easing, emollient, lenitive, mild, mollifying, relieving, sedative, softening, soothing

demur **1.** *verb* balk, cavil, disagree, dispute, doubt, hesitate, object, pause, protest, refuse, take exception, waver **2.** *~noun* compunction, demurral, demurrer, dissent, hesitation, misgiving, objection, protest, qualm, scruple

demure **1.** decorous, diffident, grave, modest, reserved, reticent, retiring, sedate, shy, sober, staid, unassuming **2.** affected, bashful, coy, niminy-piminy, priggish, prim, prissy (*informal*), prudish, strait-laced

▷ **Antonyms** brash, brazen, forward, immodest, impudent, shameless

den **1.** cave, cavern, haunt, hide-out, hole, lair, shelter **2.** cloister, cubbyhole, hideaway, retreat, sanctuary, sanctum, snuggery, study

denial adjuration, contradiction, disavowal, disclaimer, dismissal, dissent, negation, prohibition, rebuff, refusal, rejection, renunciation, repudiation, repulse, retraction, veto

▷ **Antonyms** acknowledgment, admission, affirmation, avowal, confession, declaration, disclosure, divulgence, profession, revelation

denigrate asperse, bad-mouth (*slang, chiefly U.S. & Canad.*), belittle, besmirch, blacken, calumniate, decry, defame, disparage, impugn, knock (*informal*), malign, revile, rubbish (*informal*), run down, slag (off) (*slang*), slander, vilify

▷ **Antonyms** acclaim, admire, approve, cheer, compliment, eulogize, extol, honour, laud, praise, take one's hat off to

denigration aspersion, backbiting, defamation, detraction, disparagement, obloquy, scandal, scurrility, slander, vilification

denizen citizen, dweller, inhabitant, occupant, resident

denominate call, christen, designate, dub, entitle, name, phrase, style, term

denomination **1.** belief, communion, creed, persuasion, religious group, school, sect **2.** grade, size, unit, value **3.** body, category, class, classification, group **4.** appellation, designation, label, name, style, term, title

denotation designation, indication, meaning, signification, specification

denote betoken, designate, express, imply, import, indicate, mark, mean, show, signify, typify

dénouement climax, conclusion, culmination, finale, outcome, resolution, solution, termination, upshot

denounce accuse, arraign, attack, brand, castigate, censure, condemn, declaim against, decry, denunciate, excoriate, impugn, point a *or* the finger at, proscribe, revile, stigmatize, vilify

dense **1.** close, close-knit, compact, compressed, condensed, heavy, impenetrable, opaque, solid, substantial, thick, thickset **2.** blockish, braindead (*informal*), crass, dead from the neck up (*informal*), dozy (*Brit. informal*), dull, obtuse, slow, slow-witted, stolid, stupid, thick, thick-witted

▷ **Antonyms** (*sense 1*) light, scattered, sparse, thin, transparent (*sense 2*) alert, bright, clever, intelligent, quick

density **1.** body, bulk, closeness, compactness, consistency, crowdedness, denseness, impenetrability, mass, solidity, thickness, tightness **2.** crassness, dullness, obtuseness, slowness, stolidity, stupidity, thickness

dent **1.** *noun* chip, concavity, crater, depression, dimple, dip, hollow, impression, indentation, pit **2.** *~verb* depress, dint, gouge, hollow, imprint, make a dent in, make concave, press in, push in

denude bare, divest, expose, lay bare, strip, uncover

denunciate castigate, condemn, curse, damn, denounce, stigmatize, vituperate

denunciation accusation, castigation, censure, character assassination, condemnation, criticism, denouncement, fulmination, incrimination, invective, obloquy, stick (*slang*), stigmatization

denunciatory accusatory, censorious, comminatory, condemnatory, fulminatory, incriminatory, recriminatory, reproachful

deny 1. contradict, disagree with, disprove, gainsay (*archaic or literary*), oppose, rebuff, rebut, refute **2.** abjure, disavow, discard, disclaim, disown, recant, renege, renounce, repudiate, retract, revoke **3.** begrudge, decline, disallow, forbid, negative, refuse, reject, turn down, veto, withhold
▷ **Antonyms** accept, acknowledge, admit, affirm, agree, allow, concede, confirm, grant, let, permit, receive, recognize, take on board

deodorant air freshener, antiperspirant, deodorizer, disinfectant, fumigant

deodorize aerate, disinfect, freshen, fumigate, purify, refresh, ventilate

depart 1. absent (oneself), decamp, disappear, escape, exit, go, go away, hook it (*slang*), leave, make tracks, migrate, pack one's bags (*informal*), quit, remove, retire, retreat, set forth, slope off, start out, take (one's) leave, vanish, withdraw **2.** deviate, differ, digress, diverge, stray, swerve, turn aside, vary, veer
▷ **Antonyms** (*sense 1*) arrive, remain, show up (*informal*), stay, turn up

departed dead, deceased, expired, late

department 1. district, division, province, region, sector **2.** branch, bureau, division, office, section, station, subdivision, unit **3.** area, domain, function, line, province, realm, responsibility, speciality, sphere

departure 1. exit, exodus, going, going away, leave-taking, leaving, removal, retirement, withdrawal **2.** abandonment, branching off, deviation, digression, divergence, variation, veering **3.** branching out, change, difference, innovation, novelty, shift, whole new ball game (*informal*)
▷ **Antonyms** (*sense 1*) advent, appearance, arrival, coming, entrance, return

depend 1. bank on, build upon, calculate on, confide in, count on, lean on, reckon on, rely upon, trust in, turn to **2.** be based on, be contingent on, be determined by, be subject to, be subordinate to, hang on, hinge on, rest on, revolve around

dependable faithful, reliable, reputable, responsible, staunch, steady, sure, trustworthy, trusty, unfailing
▷ **Antonyms** irresponsible, undependable, unreliable, unstable, untrustworthy

dependant *noun* child, client, cohort (*chiefly U.S.*), hanger-on, henchman, minion, minor, protégé, relative, retainer, subordinate, vassal

dependence, dependency 1. assurance, belief, confidence, expectation, faith, hope, reliance, trust **2.** addiction, attachment, helplessness, need, subordination, subservience, vulnerability, weakness

dependent *adjective* **1.** counting on, defenceless, helpless, immature, reliant, relying on, vulnerable, weak **2.** conditional, contingent, depending, determined by, liable to, relative, subject to **3.** feudal, subject, subordinate, tributary
▷ **Antonyms** (*senses 1 & 3*) autarkic, autonomous, independent, self-determining, self-governing, self-reliant

depict 1. delineate, draw, illustrate, limn, outline, paint, picture, portray, render, reproduce, sculpt, sketch **2.** characterize, describe, detail, narrate, outline, sketch

depiction delineation, description, drawing, illustration, image, likeness, outline, picture, portrayal, representation, sketch

deplete bankrupt, consume, decrease, drain, empty, evacuate, exhaust, expend, impoverish, lessen, milk, reduce, use up
▷ **Antonyms** add to, augment, enhance, expand, increase, raise, step up (*informal*), swell

depleted consumed, decreased, depreciated, devoid of, drained, effete, emptied, exhausted, lessened, out of, reduced, short of, spent, used (up), wasted, weakened, worn out

depletion attenuation, consumption, decrease, deficiency, diminution, drain, dwindling, exhaustion, expenditure, lessening, lowering, reduction, using up

deplorable 1. calamitous, dire, disastrous, distressing, grievous, heartbreaking, lamentable, melancholy, miserable, pitiable, regrettable, sad, unfortunate, wretched **2.** blameworthy, disgraceful, dishonourable, disreputable, execrable, opprobrious, reprehensible, scandalous, shameful
▷ **Antonyms** A1 *or* A-one (*informal*), admirable, bad (*slang*), bodacious (*slang, chiefly U.S.*), brilliant, excellent, fantastic, great (*informal*), laudable, marvellous, notable, outstanding, praiseworthy, super (*informal*), superb

deplore 1. bemoan, bewail, grieve for, lament, mourn, regret, rue, sorrow over **2.** abhor, censure, condemn, denounce, deprecate, disapprove of, excoriate, object to, take a dim view of

deploy arrange, dispose, extend, position, redistribute, set out, set up, spread out, station, use, utilize

deport 1. banish, exile, expatriate, expel, extradite, oust **2.** (*used reflexively*) acquit, act, bear, behave, carry, comport, conduct, hold

deportation banishment, eviction, exile, expatriation, expulsion, extradition, transportation

deportment air, appearance, aspect, bearing, behaviour, carriage, cast, comportment, conduct, demeanour, manner, mien, posture, stance

depose 1. break, cashier, degrade, demote, dethrone, dismiss, displace, downgrade, oust, remove from office **2.** *Law* avouch, declare, make a deposition, testify

deposit *verb* **1.** drop, lay, locate, place, precipitate, put, settle, sit down **2.** amass, bank, consign, entrust, hoard, lodge, save, store ~*noun* **3.** down payment, instalment, money (*in bank*), part payment, pledge, retainer, security, stake, warranty **4.** accumulation, alluvium, deposition, dregs, lees, precipitate, sediment, silt

depositary fiduciary (*Law*), guardian, steward, trustee

deposition 1. dethronement, dismissal, displacement, ousting, removal **2.** *Law* affidavit, declaration, evidence, sworn statement, testimony

depository depot, repository, safe-deposit box, store, storehouse, warehouse

depot 1. depository, repository, storehouse, warehouse **2.** *Military* arsenal, dump **3.** bus station, garage, terminus

deprave brutalize, corrupt, debase, debauch, degrade, demoralize, lead astray, pervert, seduce, subvert, vitiate

depraved abandoned, corrupt, debased, debauched, degenerate, degraded, dissolute, evil, immoral, lascivious, lewd, licentious, perverted, pervy (*slang*), profligate, shameless, sinful, sink, vicious, vile, wicked

▷ **Antonyms** chaste, decent, ethical, good, honourable, innocent, moral, principled, proper, pure, upright, virtuous, wholesome

depravity baseness, contamination, corruption, criminality, debasement, debauchery, degeneracy, depravation, evil, immorality, iniquity, profligacy, sinfulness, turpitude, vice, viciousness, vitiation, wickedness

deprecate 1. condemn, deplore, disapprove of, frown on, object to, protest against, take exception to **2.** belittle, denigrate, depreciate, detract, disparage

deprecatory 1. censuring, condemnatory, disapproving, opprobrious, reproachful **2.** apologetic, contrite, penitent, regretful, remorseful, rueful

depreciate 1. decrease, deflate, devaluate, devalue, lessen, lose value, lower, reduce **2.** belittle, decry, denigrate, deride, detract, disparage, look down on, ridicule, run down, scorn, sneer at, traduce, underestimate, underrate, undervalue

▷ **Antonyms** (*sense 1*) add to, appreciate, augment, enhance, enlarge, expand, grow, increase, rise (*sense 2*) admire, appreciate, cherish, esteem, like, prize, rate highly, regard, respect, value

depreciation 1. deflation, depression, devaluation, drop, fall, slump **2.** belittlement, denigration, deprecation, derogation, detraction, disparagement, pejoration

depredation desolation, despoiling, destruction, devastation, harrying, laying waste, marauding, pillage, plunder, ransacking, rapine, ravaging, robbery, spoliation, theft

depredator despoiler, destroyer, looter, marauder, pillager, plunderer, raider, ransacker, ravager, rifler, sacker

depress 1. cast down, chill, damp, daunt, deject, desolate, discourage, dishearten, dispirit, make despondent, oppress, sadden, weigh down **2.** debilitate, devitalize, drain, enervate, exhaust, lower, sap, slow up, weaken **3.** cheapen, depreciate, devaluate, devalue, diminish, downgrade, impair, lessen, lower, reduce **4.** flatten, level, lower, press down, push down

▷ **Antonyms** (*senses 1 & 2*) cheer, elate, hearten, heighten, increase, lift, raise, strengthen, uplift (*sense 3*) heighten, increase, raise, strengthen (*sense 4*) heighten, lift, raise

depressed 1. blue, crestfallen, dejected, despondent, discouraged, dispirited, down, downcast, downhearted, down in the dumps (*informal*), fed up, glum, low, low-spirited, melancholy, moody, morose, pessimistic, sad, unhappy **2.** concave, hollow, indented, recessed, set back, sunken **3.** *of an area, circumstances* deprived, destitute, disadvantaged, distressed, grey, needy, poor, poverty-stricken, run-down **4.** cheapened, depreciated, devalued, impaired, weakened

depressing black, bleak, daunting, dejecting, depressive, discouraging, disheartening, dismal, dispiriting, distressing, dreary, funereal, gloomy, harrowing, heartbreaking, hopeless, melancholy, sad, saddening, sombre

depression 1. dejection, despair, despondency, dolefulness, downheartedness, dumps (*informal*), gloominess, hopelessness, low spirits, melancholia, melancholy, sadness, the blues, the hump (*Brit. informal*) **2.** *Commerce* dullness, economic decline, hard *or* bad times, inactivity, lowness, recession, slump, stagnation **3.** bowl, cavity, con~

cavity, dent, dimple, dip, excavation, hollow, impression, indentation, pit, sag, sink, valley

deprivation **1.** denial, deprival, dispossession, divestment, expropriation, removal, withdrawal, withholding **2.** destitution, detriment, disadvantage, distress, hardship, need, privation, want

deprive bereave, despoil, dispossess, divest, expropriate, rob, strip, wrest

deprived bereft, denuded, destitute, disadvantaged, down at heel, forlorn, in need, in want, lacking, necessitous, needy, poor

▷ **Antonyms** born with a silver spoon in one's mouth, favoured, fortunate, golden, happy, having a charmed life, lucky, prosperous, sitting pretty (*informal*), successful, well-off

depth **1.** abyss, deepness, drop, extent, measure, profoundness, profundity **2.** *figurative* astuteness, discernment, insight, penetration, profoundness, profundity, sagacity, wisdom **3.** abstruseness, complexity, obscurity, reconditeness **4.** intensity, richness, strength **5.** (*often plural*) abyss, bowels of the earth, deepest part, furthest part, innermost part, middle, midst, most intense part, nadir, remotest part, slough of despond **6. in depth** comprehensively, extensively, intensively, thoroughly

▷ **Antonyms** (*sense 1*) apex, apogee, crest, crown, height, peak, pinnacle, summit, top, vertex, zenith (*sense 2*) *figurative* emptiness, lack of depth *or* substance, superficiality, triviality

deputation **1.** commission, delegates, delegation, deputies, embassy, envoys, legation **2.** appointment, assignment, commission, designation, nomination

depute *verb* accredit, appoint, authorize, charge, commission, delegate, empower, entrust, mandate

deputize **1.** commission, delegate, depute **2.** act for, stand in for, take the place of, understudy

deputy **1.** *noun* agent, ambassador, commissioner, delegate, legate, lieutenant, nuncio, proxy, representative, second-in-command, substitute, surrogate, vicegerent **2.** *~adjective* assistant, depute (*Scot.*), subordinate

derange **1.** confound, confuse, disarrange, disarray, discompose, disconcert, disorder, displace, disturb, ruffle, unsettle, upset **2.** craze, dement (*rare*), drive mad, madden, make insane, unbalance, unhinge

deranged barking (*slang*), barking mad (*slang*), berserk, crackpot (*informal*), crazed, crazy, delirious, demented, distracted, doolally (*slang*), frantic, frenzied, gonzo (*slang*), insane, irrational, loopy (*informal*), lunatic, mad, maddened, not the full shilling (*informal*), off one's trolley (*slang*), out to lunch (*informal*), unbalanced, unhinged, up the pole (*informal*), wacko *or* whacko (*slang*)

▷ **Antonyms** all there (*informal*), calm, *compos mentis,* in one's right mind, lucid, mentally sound, normal, of sound mind

derangement **1.** confusion, disarrangement, disarray, disorder, disturbance, irregularity, jumble, muddle **2.** aberration, alienation, delirium, dementia, hallucination, insanity, loss of reason, lunacy, madness, mania

derelict *adjective* **1.** abandoned, deserted, dilapidated, discarded, forsaken, neglected, ruined **2.** careless, irresponsible, lax, negligent, remiss, slack *~noun* **3.** bag lady (*chiefly U.S.*), bum (*informal*), down-and-out, good-for-nothing, ne'er-do-well, outcast, tramp, vagrant, wastrel

dereliction **1.** delinquency, evasion, failure, faithlessness, fault, neglect, negligence, nonperformance, remissness **2.** abandonment, abdication, desertion, forsaking, relinquishment, renunciation

deride chaff, contemn, detract, disdain, disparage, flout, gibe, insult, jeer, knock (*informal*), mock, pooh-pooh, ridicule, scoff, scorn, sneer, take the piss out of (*taboo slang*), taunt

de rigueur *comme il faut,* conventional, correct, decent, decorous, done, fitting, necessary, proper, required, right, the done thing

derision contempt, contumely, denigration, disdain, disparagement, disrespect, insult, laughter, mockery, raillery, ridicule, satire, scoffing, scorn, sneering

derisive contemptuous, jeering, mocking, ridiculing, scoffing, scornful, taunting

derisory contemptible, insulting, laughable, ludicrous, outrageous, preposterous, ridiculous

derivable attributable, deducible, determinable, extractable, inferable, obtainable, traceable

derivation **1.** acquiring, deriving, extraction, getting, obtaining **2.** ancestry, basis, beginning, descent, etymology, foundation, genealogy, origin, root, source

derivative *adjective* **1.** acquired, borrowed, derived, inferred, obtained, procured, transmitted **2.** copied, imitative, plagiaristic, plagiarized, rehashed, secondary, second-hand, uninventive, unoriginal *~noun* **3.** by-product, derivation, descendant, offshoot, outgrowth, spin-off

▷ **Antonyms** *~adjective* archetypal, authentic, first-hand, genuine, master, original, prototypical, seminal

derive **1.** collect, deduce, draw, elicit, extract, follow, gain, gather, get, glean, infer, obtain, procure, receive, trace **2.** (*with* **from**) arise, descend, emanate, flow, issue, originate, proceed, spring from, stem from

derogate **1.** cheapen, compromise, depreciate, detract, devaluate, diminish, disparage, lessen, run down **2.** *of oneself* decline, degenerate, degrade, descend, deteriorate, deviate from, retrogress, stoop

derogatory belittling, damaging, defamatory, depreciative, detracting, discreditable, dishonouring, disparaging, injurious, offensive, slighting, uncomplimentary, unfavourable, unflattering

▷ **Antonyms** appreciative, complimentary, flattering, fulsome, laudatory

descant *verb* **1.** amplify, animadvert, comment on, dilate, discourse, discuss, enlarge, expatiate *~noun* **2.** animadversion, commentary, criticism, discourse, discussion, dissertation **3.** counterpoint, decoration, melody, song, tune

descend **1.** alight, dismount, drop, fall, go down, move down, plummet, plunge, sink, subside, tumble **2.** dip, gravitate, incline, slant, slope **3.** be handed down, be passed down, derive, issue, originate, proceed, spring **4.** abase oneself, condescend, degenerate, deteriorate, lower oneself, stoop **5.** (*often with* **on**) arrive, assail, assault, attack, come in force, invade, pounce, raid, swoop

▷ **Antonyms** (*senses 1 & 2*) ascend, climb, go up, mount, rise, scale, soar

descent **1.** coming down, drop, fall, plunge, swoop **2.** declination, declivity, dip, drop, incline, slant, slope **3.** ancestry, extraction, family tree, genealogy, heredity, lineage, origin, parentage **4.** debasement, decadence, decline, degradation, deterioration **5.** assault, attack, foray, incursion, invasion, pounce, raid, swoop

describe **1.** characterize, define, depict, detail, explain, express, illustrate, narrate, portray, recount, relate, report, specify, tell **2.** delineate, draw, mark out, outline, trace

description **1.** account, characterization, delineation, depiction, detail, explanation, narration, narrative, portrayal, report, representation, sketch **2.** brand, breed, category, class, genre, genus, ilk, kidney, kind, order, sort, species, type, variety

descriptive circumstantial, depictive, detailed, explanatory, expressive, graphic, illustrative, pictorial, picturesque, vivid

descry behold, detect, discern, discover, distinguish, espy, make out, mark, notice, observe, perceive, recognize, see, sight, spy out

desecrate abuse, blaspheme, commit sacrilege, contaminate, defile, despoil, dishonour, pervert, pollute, profane, violate

▷ **Antonyms** esteem, exalt, glorify, hallow, prize, respect, revere, value, venerate, worship

desecration blasphemy, debasement, defilement, impiety, profanation, sacrilege, violation

desert[1] **1.** *noun* solitude, waste, wasteland, wilderness, wilds **2.** *~adjective* arid, bare, barren, desolate, infertile, lonely, solitary, uncultivated, uninhabited, unproductive, untilled, waste, wild

desert[2] *verb* abandon, abscond, betray, decamp, defect, forsake, give up, go over the hill (*Military slang*), jilt, leave, leave high and dry, leave (someone) in the lurch, leave stranded, maroon, quit, rat (on) (*informal*), relinquish, renounce, resign, run out on (*informal*), strand, throw over, vacate, walk out on (*informal*)

▷ **Antonyms** be a source of strength to, look after, maintain, provide for, succour, sustain, take care of

desert[3] *noun* **1.** (*often plural*) comeuppance (*slang*), due, guerdon (*poetic*), meed (*archaic*), payment, recompense, requital, retribution, return, reward, right **2.** excellence, merit (*or* demerit), virtue, worth

deserted abandoned, bereft, cast off, derelict, desolate, empty, forlorn, forsaken, godforsaken, isolated, left in the lurch, left stranded, lonely, neglected, solitary, unfriended, unoccupied, vacant

deserter absconder, apostate, defector, escapee, fugitive, rat (*informal*), renegade, runaway, traitor, truant

desertion abandonment, absconding, apostasy, betrayal, defection, departure, dereliction, escape, evasion, flight, forsaking, relinquishment, truancy

deserve be entitled to, be worthy of, earn, gain, justify, merit, procure, rate, warrant, win

deserved appropriate, condign, due, earned, fair, fitting, just, justifiable, justified, meet (*archaic*), merited, proper, right, rightful, suitable, warranted, well-earned

deserving commendable, estimable, laudable, meritorious, praiseworthy, righteous, worthy

▷ **Antonyms** not deserving of, not good enough, not worth, undeserving, unworthy

desiccate dehydrate, drain, dry, evaporate, exsiccate, parch

desiccated **1.** dehydrated, dried, dry, powdered **2.** cold, dead, dry, dry-as-dust, dull, empty, inanimate, inert, lifeless, passionless, spiritless

desideratum aim, aspiration, dream, essential, goal, heart's desire, hope, ideal, lack, need, objective, *sine qua non,* want, wish

design *verb* **1.** delineate, describe, draft, draw, outline, plan, sketch, trace *~noun* **2.** blueprint, delineation, draft, drawing, model, outline, plan, scheme, sketch

~verb **3.** conceive, create, fabricate, fashion, invent, originate, think up *~noun* **4.** arrangement, configuration, construction, figure, form, motif, organization, pattern, shape, style *~verb* **5.** aim, contrive, destine, devise, intend, make, mean, plan, project, propose, purpose, scheme, tailor *~noun* **6.** enterprise, plan, project, schema, scheme, undertaking **7.** aim, end, goal, intent, intention, meaning, object, objective, point, purport, purpose, target, view **8.** (*often plural*) conspiracy, evil intentions, intrigue, machination, plot, scheme

designate **1.** call, christen, dub, entitle, label, name, nominate, style, term **2.** allot, appoint, assign, choose, delegate, depute, nominate, select **3.** characterize, define, denote, describe, earmark, indicate, pinpoint, show, specify, stipulate

designation **1.** denomination, description, epithet, label, mark, name, title **2.** appointment, classification, delegation, indication, selection, specification

designedly by design, calculatedly, deliberately, intentionally, knowingly, on purpose, purposely, studiously, wilfully, wittingly

designer **1.** architect, artificer, couturier, creator, deviser, inventor, originator, planner, stylist **2.** conniver, conspirator, intriguer, plotter, schemer

designing artful, astute, conniving, conspiring, crafty, crooked (*informal*), cunning, deceitful, devious, intriguing, Machiavellian, plotting, scheming, sharp, shrewd, sly, treacherous, tricky, unscrupulous, wily

desirability advantage, benefit, merit, profit, usefulness, value, worth

desirable **1.** advantageous, advisable, agreeable, beneficial, covetable, eligible, enviable, good, pleasing, preferable, profitable, to die for (*informal*), worthwhile **2.** adorable, alluring, attractive, fascinating, fetching, glamorous, seductive, sexy (*informal*), to-die-for (*informal*)

▷ **Antonyms** (*sense 1*) disagreeable, distasteful, unacceptable, unappealing, unattractive, undesirable, unpleasant, unpopular (*sense 2*) unappealing, unattractive, undesirable, unsexy (*informal*)

desire *verb* **1.** aspire to, covet, crave, desiderate, fancy, hanker after, hope for, long for, set one's heart on, thirst for, want, wish for, yearn for *~noun* **2.** ache, appetite, aspiration, craving, hankering, hope, longing, need, thirst, want, wish, yearning, yen (*informal*) *~verb* **3.** ask, entreat, importune, petition, request, solicit *~noun* **4.** appeal, entreaty, importunity, petition, request, solicitation, supplication **5.** appetite, concupiscence, lasciviousness, lechery, libido, lust, lustfulness, passion

desired accurate, appropriate, correct, exact, expected, express, fitting, necessary, particular, proper, required, right

desirous ambitious, anxious, aspiring, avid, craving, desiring, eager, hopeful, hoping, keen, longing, ready, willing, wishing, yearning

▷ **Antonyms** averse, disinclined, grudging, indisposed, loath, opposed, reluctant, unenthusiastic, unwilling

desist abstain, break off, cease, discontinue, end, forbear, give over (*informal*), give up, have done with, kick (*informal*), leave off, pause, refrain from, remit, stop, suspend

desolate *adjective* **1.** bare, barren, bleak, desert, dreary, godforsaken, ruined, solitary, unfrequented, uninhabited, waste, wild *~verb* **2.** depopulate, despoil, destroy, devastate, lay low, lay waste, pillage, plunder, ravage, ruin *~adjective* **3.** abandoned, bereft, cheerless, comfortless, companionless, dejected, depressing, despondent, disconsolate, dismal, downcast, down in the dumps (*informal*), forlorn, forsaken, gloomy, lonely, melancholy, miserable, wretched *~verb* **4.** daunt, deject, depress, discourage, dishearten, dismay, distress, grieve

▷ **Antonyms** *~adjective* (*sense 1*) inhabited, populous (*sense 3*) cheerful, happy, joyous, light-hearted *~verb* (*sense 2*) develop (*sense 4*) cheer, encourage, hearten, nourish

desolation **1.** destruction, devastation, havoc, ravages, ruin, ruination **2.** barrenness, bleakness, desolateness, forlornness, isolation, loneliness, solitariness, solitude, wildness **3.** anguish, dejection, despair, distress, gloom, gloominess, melancholy, misery, sadness, unhappiness, woe, wretchedness

despair *verb* **1.** despond, give up, lose heart, lose hope *~noun* **2.** anguish, dejection, depression, desperation, despondency, disheartenment, gloom, hopelessness, melancholy, misery, wretchedness **3.** burden, cross, hardship, ordeal, pain, trial, tribulation

despairing anxious, at the end of one's tether, broken-hearted, dejected, depressed, desperate, despondent, disconsolate, dismal, downcast, down in the dumps (*informal*), frantic, grief-stricken, hopeless, inconsolable, melancholy, miserable, suicidal, wretched

despatch *see* DISPATCH

desperado bandit, criminal, cut-throat, gangster, gunman, heavy (*slang*), hoodlum (*chiefly U.S.*), lawbreaker, mugger (*informal*), outlaw, ruffian, skelm (*S. African*), thug, villain

desperate **1.** audacious, dangerous, daring, death-defying, determined, foolhardy, frantic, furious, hasty, hazardous, headstrong, impetuous, madcap, precipitate, rash, reckless, risky, vio~

lent, wild **2.** acute, critical, dire, drastic, extreme, great, urgent, very grave **3.** at the end of one's tether, despairing, despondent, forlorn, hopeless, inconsolable, irrecoverable, irremediable, irretrievable, wretched

desperately 1. badly, dangerously, gravely, perilously, seriously, severely **2.** appallingly, fearfully, frightfully, hopelessly, shockingly

desperation 1. defiance, foolhardiness, frenzy, heedlessness, impetuosity, madness, rashness, recklessness **2.** agony, anguish, anxiety, despair, despondency, distraction, heartache, hopelessness, misery, pain, sorrow, torture, trouble, unhappiness, worry

despicable abject, base, beyond contempt, cheap, contemptible, degrading, detestable, disgraceful, disreputable, hateful, ignominious, infamous, low, mean, pitiful, reprehensible, scurvy, shameful, sordid, vile, worthless, wretched

▷ **Antonyms** admirable, estimable, ethical, exemplary, good, honest, honourable, moral, noble, praiseworthy, righteous, upright, virtuous, worthy

despise abhor, contemn, deride, detest, disdain, disregard, flout, have a down on (*informal*), loathe, look down on, neglect, revile, scorn, slight, spurn, undervalue

▷ **Antonyms** admire, adore, be fond of, be keen on, cherish, dig (*slang*), esteem, fancy (*informal*), love, relish, revel in, take to

despite against, even with, in contempt of, in defiance of, in spite of, in the face of, in the teeth of, notwithstanding, regardless of, undeterred by

despoil denude, deprive, destroy, devastate, dispossess, divest, loot, pillage, plunder, ravage, rifle, rob, strip, total (*slang*), trash (*slang*), vandalize, wreak havoc upon, wreck

despoliation depredation, despoilment, destruction, devastation, havoc, looting, pillage, plunder, ruin, vandalism, wreckage

despond be cast down, be depressed, despair, give up, lose heart, lose hope, mourn, sorrow

despondency dejection, depression, despair, desperation, disconsolateness, discouragement, dispiritedness, downheartedness, gloom, hopelessness, low spirits, melancholy, misery, sadness, the hump (*Brit. informal*), wretchedness

despondent blue, dejected, depressed, despairing, disconsolate, discouraged, disheartened, dismal, dispirited, doleful, down, downcast, downhearted, down in the dumps (*informal*), gloomy, glum, hopeless, in despair, low, low-spirited, melancholy, miserable, morose, sad, sick as a parrot (*informal*), sorrowful, woebegone, wretched

▷ **Antonyms** buoyant, cheerful, cheery, chirpy (*informal*), genial, glad, happy, hopeful, joyful, light-hearted, optimistic, upbeat (*informal*)

despot autocrat, dictator, monocrat, oppressor, tyrant

despotic absolute, arbitrary, arrogant, authoritarian, autocratic, dictatorial, domineering, imperious, monocratic, oppressive, tyrannical, unconstitutional

despotism absolutism, autarchy, autocracy, dictatorship, monocracy, oppression, totalitarianism, tyranny

destination 1. harbour, haven, journey's end, landing-place, resting-place, station, stop, terminus **2.** aim, ambition, design, end, goal, intention, object, objective, purpose, target

destine allot, appoint, assign, consecrate, decree, design, devote, doom, earmark, fate, intend, mark out, ordain, predetermine, preordain, purpose, reserve

destined 1. bound, certain, designed, doomed, fated, foreordained, ineluctable, inescapable, inevitable, intended, meant, ordained, predestined, unavoidable **2.** assigned, booked, bound for, directed, en route, heading, on the road to, routed, scheduled

destiny cup, divine decree, doom, fate, fortune, karma, kismet, lot, portion

destitute 1. dirt-poor (*informal*), distressed, down and out, flat broke (*informal*), impecunious, impoverished, indigent, in queer street (*informal*), insolvent, moneyless, necessitous, needy, on one's uppers, on the breadline (*informal*), on the rocks, penniless, penurious, poor, poverty-stricken, short, without two pennies to rub together (*informal*) **2.** bereft of, deficient in, depleted, deprived of, devoid of, drained, empty of, in need of, lacking, wanting, without

destitution beggary, dire straits, distress, impecuniousness, indigence, neediness, pauperism, pennilessness, penury, privation, utter poverty, want

▷ **Antonyms** affluence, fortune, good fortune, life of luxury, luxury, plenty, prosperity, riches, wealth

destroy annihilate, blow sky-high, blow to bits, break down, crush, demolish, desolate, devastate, dismantle, dispatch, eradicate, extinguish, extirpate, gut, kill, put paid to, ravage, raze, ruin, shatter, slay, smash, torpedo, total (*slang*), trash (*slang*), waste, wipe out, wreck

destruction annihilation, crushing, demolition, devastation, downfall, end, eradication, extermination, extinction, havoc, liquidation, massacre, overthrow, overwhelming, ruin, ruination, shattering, slaughter, undoing, wreckage, wrecking

destructive 1. baleful, baneful, calamitous, cataclysmic, catastrophic, damaging, deadly, deleterious, detrimental, devastating, fatal, harmful, hurtful, injurious, lethal, maleficent, noxious, pernicious, ruinous 2. adverse, antagonistic, contrary, derogatory, discouraging, discrediting, disparaging, hostile, invalidating, negative, opposed, undermining, vicious

desultory aimless, capricious, cursory, disconnected, discursive, disorderly, erratic, fitful, haphazard, inconsistent, inconstant, inexact, irregular, loose, maundering, off and on, rambling, random, roving, spasmodic, unmethodical, unsettled, unsystematic, vague

detach cut off, disconnect, disengage, disentangle, disjoin, disunite, divide, free, isolate, loosen, remove, segregate, separate, sever, tear off, unbridle, uncouple, unfasten, unhitch

▷ **Antonyms** attach, bind, connect, fasten

detached 1. disconnected, discrete, disjoined, divided, free, loosened, separate, severed, unconnected 2. aloof, disinterested, dispassionate, impartial, impersonal, neutral, objective, reserved, unbiased, uncommitted, uninvolved, unprejudiced

▷ **Antonyms** biased, concerned, interested, involved, partisan, prejudiced

detachment 1. aloofness, coolness, indifference, nonchalance, remoteness, unconcern 2. disinterestedness, fairness, impartiality, neutrality, nonpartisanship, objectivity 3. disconnection, disengagement, disjoining, separation, severing 4. *Military* body, detail, force, party, patrol, squad, task force, unit

detail *noun* 1. aspect, component, count, element, fact, factor, feature, item, particular, point, respect, specific, technicality 2. *plural* fine points, ins and outs, minutiae, niceties, particulars, parts, trivia, trivialities 3. **in detail** comprehensively, exhaustively, inside out, item by item, point by point, thoroughly 4. *Military* assignment, body, detachment, duty, fatigue, force, party, squad *~verb* 5. catalogue, delineate, depict, describe, enumerate, individualize, itemize, narrate, particularize, portray, recite, recount, rehearse, relate, specify, tabulate 6. allocate, appoint, assign, charge, commission, delegate, detach, send

detailed blow-by-blow, circumstantial, comprehensive, elaborate, exact, exhaustive, full, intricate, itemized, meticulous, minute, particular, particularized, specific, thorough

▷ **Antonyms** brief, compact, concise, condensed, limited, pithy, short, slight, succinct, summary, superficial, terse

detain 1. check, delay, hinder, hold up, impede, keep, keep back, retard, slow up (*or* down), stay, stop 2. arrest, confine, hold, intern, restrain

detect 1. ascertain, catch, descry, distinguish, identify, note, notice, observe, recognize, scent, spot 2. catch, disclose, discover, expose, find, reveal, track down, uncover, unmask

detection discovery, exposé, exposure, ferreting out, revelation, tracking down, uncovering, unearthing, unmasking

detective bizzy (*slang*), C.I.D. man, constable, cop (*slang*), copper (*slang*), dick (*slang, chiefly U.S.*), gumshoe (*U.S. slang*), investigator, private eye, private investigator, sleuth (*informal*), tec (*slang*)

detention confinement, custody, delay, hindrance, holding back, imprisonment, incarceration, keeping in, porridge (*slang*), quarantine, restraint, withholding

▷ **Antonyms** acquittal, discharge, emancipation, freedom, liberation, liberty, release

deter caution, check, damp, daunt, debar, discourage, dissuade, frighten, hinder, inhibit from, intimidate, prevent, prohibit, put off, restrain, stop, talk out of

detergent 1. *noun* cleaner, cleanser 2. *~adjective* abstergent, cleaning, cleansing, detersive, purifying

deteriorate 1. corrupt, debase, decline, degenerate, degrade, deprave, depreciate, go downhill (*informal*), go to pot, go to the dogs (*informal*), impair, injure, lower, slump, spoil, worsen 2. be the worse for wear (*informal*), break down, crumble, decay, decline, decompose, disintegrate, ebb, fade, fall apart, lapse, retrogress, weaken, wear away

▷ **Antonyms** advance, ameliorate, get better, improve, upgrade

deterioration atrophy, corrosion, debasement, decline, degeneration, degradation, *dégringolade,* depreciation, descent, dilapidation, disintegration, downturn, drop, fall, lapse, meltdown (*informal*), retrogression, slump, vitiation, worsening

determinable answerable, ascertainable, assessable, definable, describable, discoverable

determinate absolute, certain, conclusive, decided, decisive, defined, definite, definitive, determined, distinct, established, explicit, express, fixed, limited, positive, precise, quantified, settled, specified

determination 1. backbone, constancy, conviction, dedication, doggedness, drive, firmness, fortitude, indomitability, perseverance, persistence, resoluteness, resolution, resolve, single-mindedness, steadfastness, tenacity, willpower 2. conclusion, decision, judgment, purpose, resolve, result, settle~

ment, solution, verdict
▷ **Antonyms** (*sense 1*) doubt, hesitancy, hesitation, indecision, instability, ir~resolution, vacillation

determine 1. arbitrate, conclude, decide, end, finish, fix upon, ordain, regulate, settle, terminate **2**. ascertain, certify, check, detect, discover, find out, learn, verify, work out **3**. choose, decide, elect, establish, fix, make up one's mind, pur~pose, resolve **4**. affect, condition, control, decide, dictate, direct, govern, impel, impose, incline, induce, influence, lead, modify, regulate, rule, shape

determined bent on, constant, dogged, firm, fixed, immovable, intent, per~severing, persistent, purposeful, reso~lute, set on, single-minded, stalwart, steadfast, strong-minded, strong-willed, tenacious, unflinching, unwavering

determining conclusive, critical, crucial, deciding, decisive, definitive, essential, final, important, settling

deterrent *noun* check, curb, defensive measures, determent, discouragement, disincentive, hindrance, impediment, obstacle, restraint
▷ **Antonyms** bait, carrot (*informal*), en~ticement, incentive, inducement, lure, motivation, spur, stimulus

detest abhor, abominate, despise, dislike intensely, execrate, feel aversion to~wards, feel disgust towards, feel hostil~ity towards, feel repugnance towards, hate, loathe, recoil from
▷ **Antonyms** adore, cherish, dig (*slang*), dote on, love, relish

detestable abhorred, abominable, ac~cursed, despicable, disgusting, ex~ecrable, hateful, heinous, loathsome, obnoxious, obscene, odious, offensive, repugnant, repulsive, revolting, shock~ing, vile, yucky *or* yukky (*slang*)

detestation 1. abhorrence, abomination, animosity, animus, antipathy, aversion, disgust, dislike, execration, hatred, hos~tility, loathing, odium, repugnance, re~vulsion **2**. abomination, anathema, bête noire, hate

dethrone depose, oust, uncrown, unseat

detonate blast, blow up, discharge, ex~plode, fulminate, set off, touch off, trig~ger

detonation bang, blast, blow-up, boom, discharge, explosion, fulmination, report

detour bypass, byway, circuitous route, deviation, diversion, indirect course, roundabout way

detract 1. derogate, devaluate, diminish, lessen, lower, reduce, take away from **2**. deflect, distract, divert, shift
▷ **Antonyms** add to, augment, boost, complement, enhance, improve, re~inforce, strengthen

detraction abuse, aspersion, belittlement, calumny, defamation, denigration, dep~recation, disparagement, innuendo, in~sinuation, misrepresentation, muckrak~ing, running down, scandalmongering, scurrility, slander, traducement, vitu~peration

detractor backbiter, belittler, defamer, denigrator, derogator (*rare*), disparager, muckraker, scandalmonger, slanderer, traducer

detriment damage, disadvantage, disser~vice, harm, hurt, impairment, injury, loss, mischief, prejudice

detrimental adverse, baleful, damaging, deleterious, destructive, disadvanta~geous, harmful, inimical, injurious, mischievous, pernicious, prejudicial, unfavourable
▷ **Antonyms** advantageous, beneficial, efficacious, favourable, good, helpful, salutary

detritus debris, fragments, litter, re~mains, rubbish, waste

de trop in the way, redundant, superflu~ous, surplus, unnecessary, unwanted, unwelcome

devastate 1. demolish, desolate, despoil, destroy, lay waste, level, pillage, plun~der, ravage, raze, ruin, sack, spoil, total (*slang*), trash (*slang*), waste, wreck **2**. *informal* chagrin, confound, discomfit, discompose, disconcert, floor (*informal*), nonplus, overpower, overwhelm, take aback

devastating caustic, cutting, deadly, de~structive, effective, incisive, keen, mor~dant, overpowering, overwhelming, rav~ishing, sardonic, satirical, savage, stun~ning, trenchant, vitriolic, withering

devastation demolition, depredation, desolation, destruction, havoc, pillage, plunder, ravages, ruin, ruination, spo~liation

develop 1. advance, blossom, cultivate, evolve, flourish, foster, grow, mature, progress, promote, prosper, ripen **2**. am~plify, augment, broaden, dilate upon, elaborate, enlarge, expand, unfold, work out **3**. acquire, begin, breed, commence, contract, establish, form, generate, in~vent, originate, pick up, start **4**. be a di~rect result of, break out, come about, ensue, follow, happen, result

development 1. advance, advancement, evolution, expansion, growth, improve~ment, increase, maturity, progress, pro~gression, spread, unfolding, unravelling **2**. change, circumstance, event, happen~ing, incident, issue, occurrence, out~come, phenomenon, result, situation, turn of events, upshot

deviant 1. *adjective* aberrant, abnormal, bent (*slang*), deviate, devious, freaky (*slang*), heretical, kinky (*slang*), per~verse, perverted, pervy (*slang*), queer (*informal, derogatory*), sick (*informal*), sicko (*informal*), twisted, warped, way~

ward **2.** *~noun* deviate, freak, misfit, odd type, pervert, queer (*informal, derogatory*), sicko (*informal*)

▷ **Antonyms** *~adjective* conventional, normal, orthodox, straight, straightforward

deviate avert, bend, deflect, depart, differ, digress, diverge, drift, err, meander, part, stray, swerve, turn, turn aside, vary, veer, wander

deviation aberration, alteration, change, deflection, departure, digression, discrepancy, disparity, divergence, fluctuation, inconsistency, irregularity, shift, variance, variation

device 1. apparatus, appliance, contraption, contrivance, gadget, gimmick, gizmo *or* gismo (*slang, chiefly U.S. & Canad.*), implement, instrument, invention, tool, utensil **2.** artifice, design, dodge, expedient, gambit, improvisation, manoeuvre, plan, ploy, project, purpose, ruse, scheme, shift, stratagem, strategy, stunt, trick, wile **3.** badge, colophon, crest, design, emblem, figure, insignia, logo, motif, motto, symbol, token

devil 1. (*sometimes capital*) Abbadon, Apollyon, archfiend, Beelzebub, Belial, Clootie (*Scot.*), deil (*Scot.*), demon, Deuce, Evil One, fiend, Foul Fiend, Lord of the Flies, Lucifer, Mephisto, Mephistopheles, Old Gentleman (*informal*), Old Harry (*informal*), Old Hornie (*informal*), Old Nick (*informal*), Old One, Old Scratch (*informal*), Prince of Darkness, Satan, Tempter, Wicked One **2.** beast, brute, demon, fiend, ghoul, monster, ogre, rogue, savage, terror, villain **3.** imp, monkey (*informal*), pickle (*Brit. informal*), rascal, rogue, scamp, scoundrel **4.** beggar, creature, thing, unfortunate, wretch **5.** demon, enthusiast, fiend, go-getter (*informal*)

devilish accursed, atrocious, damnable, detestable, diabolic, diabolical, execrable, fiendish, hellish, infernal, satanic, wicked

devil-may-care careless, casual, easy-going, flippant, happy-go-lucky, heedless, insouciant, nonchalant, reckless, swaggering, swashbuckling, unconcerned

devilment devilry, knavery, mischief, mischievousness, naughtiness, rascality, roguery, roguishness

devilry, deviltry 1. devilment, jiggery-pokery (*informal, chiefly Brit.*), knavery, mischief, mischievousness, monkey-business (*informal*), rascality, roguery **2.** cruelty, evil, malevolence, malice, vice, viciousness, villainy, wickedness **3.** black magic, diablerie, diabolism, sorcery

devious 1. calculating, crooked (*informal*), deceitful, dishonest, double-dealing, evasive, indirect, insidious, insincere, not straightforward, scheming, sly, surreptitious, treacherous, tricky, underhand, wily **2.** circuitous, confusing, crooked, deviating, erratic, excursive, indirect, misleading, rambling, roundabout, tortuous, wandering

▷ **Antonyms** (*sense 1*) blunt, candid, direct, downright, forthright, frank, honest, straight, straightforward (*sense 2*) blunt, direct, downright, forthright, straight, straightforward, undeviating, unswerving

devise arrange, conceive, concoct, construct, contrive, design, dream up, form, formulate, frame, imagine, invent, plan, plot, prepare, project, scheme, think up, work out

devitalize cripple, debilitate, enervate, enfeeble, exhaust, reduce, sap, undermine, weaken

devoid barren, bereft, deficient, denuded, destitute, empty, free from, lacking, sans (*archaic*), vacant, void, wanting, without

devolution decentralization, delegation

devolve 1. be transferred, commission, consign, delegate, depute, entrust, fall upon *or* to, rest with, transfer **2.** *Law* alienate, be handed down, convey

devote allot, apply, appropriate, assign, commit, concern oneself, consecrate, dedicate, enshrine, give, occupy oneself, pledge, reserve, set apart

devoted ardent, caring, committed, concerned, constant, dedicated, devout, faithful, fond, loving, loyal, staunch, steadfast, true

▷ **Antonyms** disloyal, inconstant, indifferent, uncommitted, undedicated, unfaithful

devotee addict, adherent, admirer, aficionado, buff (*informal*), disciple, enthusiast, fan, fanatic, follower, supporter, votary

devotion 1. adherence, allegiance, commitment, consecration, constancy, dedication, faithfulness, fidelity, loyalty **2.** adoration, devoutness, godliness, holiness, piety, prayer, religiousness, reverence, sanctity, spirituality, worship **3.** affection, ardour, attachment, earnestness, fervour, fondness, intensity, love, passion, zeal **4.** *plural* church service, divine office, prayers, religious observance

▷ **Antonyms** (*sense 1*) carelessness, disregard, inattention, indifference, laxity, laxness, neglect, thoughtlessness (*sense 2*) derision, disrespect, impiety, irreverence

devotional devout, holy, pious, religious, reverential, sacred, solemn, spiritual

devour 1. bolt, consume, cram, dispatch, eat, gobble, gorge, gulp, guzzle, pig out on (*slang*), polish off (*informal*), stuff, swallow, wolf **2.** annihilate, consume, destroy, ravage, spend, waste, wipe out **3.** absorb, appreciate, be engrossed by, be preoccupied, delight in, drink in, enjoy, feast on, go through, read compulsively *or* voraciously, relish, revel in, take in

devouring consuming, excessive, flaming, insatiable, intense, overwhelming, passionate, powerful

devout 1. godly, holy, orthodox, pious, prayerful, pure, religious, reverent, saintly **2.** ardent, deep, devoted, earnest, fervent, genuine, heartfelt, intense, passionate, profound, serious, sincere, zealous

▷ **Antonyms** (*sense 1*) impious, irreligious, irreverent, sacrilegious (*sense 2*) indifferent, passive

devoutly fervently, heart and soul, profoundly, sincerely, with all one's heart

dexterity 1. adroitness, artistry, craft, deftness, effortlessness, expertise, facility, finesse, handiness, knack, mastery, neatness, nimbleness, proficiency, skill, smoothness, touch **2.** ability, address, adroitness, aptitude, aptness, art, cleverness, expertness, ingenuity, readiness, skilfulness, tact

▷ **Antonyms** clumsiness, gaucheness, inability, incapacity, incompetence, ineptitude, uselessness

dexterous able, active, acute, adept, adroit, agile, apt, clever, deft, expert, handy, ingenious, masterly, neat, nimble, nimble-fingered, proficient, prompt, quick, skilful

diabolic 1. demoniac, demonic, devilish, fiendish, hellish, infernal, satanic **2.** atrocious, cruel, evil, fiendish, monstrous, nefarious, vicious, villainous, wicked

diabolical abysmal, appalling, atrocious, damnable, difficult, disastrous, dreadful, excruciating, fiendish, from hell (*informal*), hellacious (*U.S. slang*), hellish, nasty, outrageous, shocking, tricky, unpleasant, vile

diadem circlet, coronet, crown, tiara

diagnose analyse, determine, distinguish, identify, interpret, investigate, pinpoint, pronounce, put one's finger on, recognize

diagnosis 1. analysis, examination, investigation, scrutiny **2.** conclusion, interpretation, opinion, pronouncement

diagnostic demonstrative, distinctive, distinguishing, idiosyncratic, indicative, particular, peculiar, recognizable, symptomatic

diagonal *adjective* angled, cater-cornered (*U.S. informal*), cornerways, cross, crossways, crosswise, oblique, slanting

diagonally aslant, at an angle, cornerwise, crosswise, obliquely, on the bias, on the cross

diagram chart, drawing, figure, graph, layout, outline, plan, representation, sketch

dialect accent, brogue, idiom, jargon, language, lingo (*informal*), localism, patois, pronunciation, provincialism, speech, tongue, vernacular

dialectal dialect, idiomatic, local, nonstandard, regional, restricted, vernacular

dialectic 1. *adjective* analytic, argumentative, dialectical, logical, polemical, rational, rationalistic **2.** ~*noun* (*often plural*) argumentation, contention, discussion, disputation, logic, polemics, ratiocination, reasoning

dialogue 1. colloquy, communication, confabulation, conference, conversation, converse, discourse, discussion, duologue, interlocution **2.** conversation, lines, script, spoken part

diametric, diametrical antipodal, antithetical, conflicting, contrary, contrasting, counter, opposed, opposite, poles apart

diametrically absolutely, completely, entirely, utterly

diaphanous chiffon, clear, cobwebby, delicate, filmy, fine, gauzy, gossamer, light, pellucid, see-through, sheer, thin, translucent, transparent

diarrhoea *noun* dysentery, gippy tummy, holiday tummy, looseness, Montezuma's revenge (*informal*), Spanish tummy, the runs, the skits (*informal*), the skitters (*informal*), the trots (*informal*)

diary appointment book, chronicle, daily record, day-to-day account, engagement book, Filofax (*Trademark*), journal

diatribe abuse, castigation, criticism, denunciation, disputation, harangue, invective, philippic, reviling, stream of abuse, stricture, tirade, verbal onslaught, vituperation

dicey chancy (*informal*), dangerous, difficult, hairy (*slang*), risky, ticklish, tricky

dicky *adjective* fluttery, queer, shaky, unreliable, unsound, unsteady, weak

dictate *verb* **1.** read out, say, speak, transmit, utter **2.** command, decree, demand, direct, enjoin, establish, impose, lay down, lay down the law, ordain, order, prescribe, pronounce ~*noun* **3.** behest, bidding, command, decree, demand, direction, edict, fiat, injunction, mandate, order, ordinance, requirement, statute, ultimatum, word **4.** canon, code, dictum, law, precept, principle, rule

dictator absolute ruler, autocrat, despot, oppressor, tyrant

dictatorial 1. absolute, arbitrary, autocratic, despotic, totalitarian, tyrannical, unlimited, unrestricted **2.** authoritarian, bossy (*informal*), dogmatical, domineering, imperious, iron-handed, magiste~

rial, oppressive, overbearing
▷ **Antonyms** constitutional, democratic, egalitarian, humble, restricted, servile, suppliant, tolerant

dictatorship absolute rule, absolutism, authoritarianism, autocracy, despotism, reign of terror, totalitarianism, tyranny

diction **1.** expression, language, phraseology, phrasing, style, usage, vocabulary, wording **2.** articulation, delivery, elocution, enunciation, fluency, inflection, intonation, pronunciation, speech

dictionary concordance, encyclopedia, glossary, lexicon, vocabulary, wordbook

dictum **1.** canon, command, decree, demand, dictate, edict, fiat, order, pronouncement **2.** adage, axiom, gnome, maxim, precept, proverb, saw, saying

didactic edifying, educational, enlightening, homiletic, instructive, moral, moralizing, pedagogic, pedantic, preceptive

die **1.** breathe one's last, buy it (*U.S. slang*), buy the farm (*U.S. slang*), check out (*U.S. slang*), croak (*slang*), decease, depart, expire, finish, give up the ghost, go belly-up (*slang*), hop the twig (*slang*), kick it (*slang*), kick the bucket (*slang*), pass away, peg it (*informal*), peg out (*informal*), perish, pop one's clogs (*informal*), snuff it (*slang*) **2.** decay, decline, disappear, dwindle, ebb, end, fade, lapse, pass, sink, subside, vanish, wane, wilt, wither **3.** break down, fade out *or* away, fail, fizzle out, halt, lose power, peter out, run down, stop **4.** ache, be eager, desire, hunger, languish, long, pine for, set one's heart on, swoon, yearn **5.** (*usually with* **of**) be overcome, collapse, succumb to
▷ **Antonyms** be born, begin, build, come to life, exist, flourish, grow, increase, live, survive

die-hard **1.** *noun* fanatic, intransigent, old fogey, reactionary, stick-in-the-mud (*informal*), ultraconservative, zealot **2.** *~adjective* dyed-in-the-wool, immovable, inflexible, intransigent, reactionary, ultraconservative, uncompromising, unreconstructed (*chiefly U.S.*)

diet[1] *noun* **1.** abstinence, dietary, fast, regime, regimen **2.** aliment, comestibles, commons, edibles, fare, food, nourishment, nutriment, provisions, rations, subsistence, sustenance, viands, victuals *~verb* **3.** abstain, eat sparingly, fast, lose weight, reduce, slim
▷ **Antonyms** *~verb* get fat, glut, gobble, gormandize, guzzle, indulge, overindulge, pig out (*slang*), stuff oneself

diet[2] *noun* chamber, congress, convention, council, legislative assembly, legislature, meeting, parliament, sitting

dieter calorie counter, faster, reducer, slimmer, weight watcher

differ **1.** be dissimilar, be distinct, contradict, contrast, depart from, diverge, run counter to, stand apart, vary **2.** clash, contend, debate, demur, disagree, dispute, dissent, oppose, take issue
▷ **Antonyms** accord, acquiesce, agree, assent, coincide, concur, cooperate, harmonize

difference **1.** alteration, change, contrast, deviation, differentiation, discrepancy, disparity, dissimilarity, distinction, distinctness, divergence, diversity, unlikeness, variation, variety **2.** distinction, exception, idiosyncrasy, particularity, peculiarity, singularity **3.** argument, clash, conflict, contention, contrariety, contretemps, controversy, debate, disagreement, discordance, dispute, quarrel, row, set-to (*informal*), strife, tiff, wrangle **4.** balance, remainder, rest, result
▷ **Antonyms** (*senses 1, 2 & 3*) affinity, agreement, comparability, concordance, conformity, congruence, likeness, relation, resemblance, sameness, similarity, similitude

different **1.** altered, at odds, at variance, changed, clashing, contrasting, deviating, discrepant, disparate, dissimilar, divergent, diverse, inconsistent, opposed, streets apart, unlike **2.** another, discrete, distinct, individual, other, separate **3.** assorted, divers (*archaic*), diverse, manifold, many, miscellaneous, multifarious, numerous, several, some, sundry, varied, various **4.** another story, atypical, bizarre, distinctive, extraordinary, left-field (*informal*), out of the ordinary, peculiar, rare, singular, something else, special, strange, uncommon, unconventional, unique, unusual

differential **1.** *adjective* diacritical, discriminative, distinctive, distinguishing **2.** *~noun* amount of difference, difference, discrepancy, disparity

differentiate **1.** contrast, discern, discriminate, distinguish, make a distinction, mark off, separate, set off *or* apart, tell apart **2.** adapt, alter, change, convert, make different, modify, transform

difficult **1.** arduous, burdensome, demanding, formidable, hard, laborious, like getting blood out of a stone, no picnic (*informal*), onerous, painful, strenuous, toilsome, uphill, wearisome **2.** abstract, abstruse, baffling, complex, complicated, delicate, enigmatical, intricate, involved, knotty, obscure, perplexing, problematical, thorny, ticklish **3.** demanding, fastidious, fractious, fussy, hard to please, intractable, obstreperous, perverse, refractory, rigid, tiresome, troublesome, trying, unaccommodating, unamenable, unmanageable **4.** dark, full of hardship, grim, hard, straitened, tough, trying
▷ **Antonyms** (*senses 1 & 2*) easy, easy-peasy (*slang*), light, manageable, obvious, plain, simple, straightforward, un-

complicated (*sense 3*) accommodating, amenable, co-operative, pleasant (*sense 4*) easy, pleasant

difficulty 1. arduousness, awkwardness, hardship, laboriousness, labour, pain, painfulness, strain, strenuousness, tribulation **2.** deep water, dilemma, distress, embarrassment, fix (*informal*), hot water (*informal*), jam (*informal*), mess, perplexity, pickle (*informal*), plight, predicament, quandary, spot (*informal*), straits, tight spot, trial, trouble **3.** (*often plural*) complication, hassle (*informal*), hazard, hindrance, hurdle, impediment, objection, obstacle, opposition, pitfall, problem, protest, snag, stumbling block

diffidence backwardness, bashfulness, constraint, doubt, fear, hesitancy, hesitation, humility, insecurity, lack of self-confidence, meekness, modesty, reluctance, reserve, self-consciousness, sheepishness, shyness, timidity, timidness, timorousness, unassertiveness

▷ **Antonyms** assurance, boldness, confidence, courage, firmness, self-confidence, self-possession

diffident backward, bashful, constrained, distrustful, doubtful, hesitant, insecure, meek, modest, reluctant, reserved, self-conscious, self-effacing, sheepish, shrinking, shy, suspicious, timid, timorous, unassertive, unassuming, unobtrusive, unsure, withdrawn

diffuse *adjective* **1.** circumlocutory, copious, diffusive, digressive, discursive, long-winded, loose, maundering, meandering, prolix, rambling, vague, verbose, waffling (*informal*), wordy **2.** dispersed, scattered, spread out, unconcentrated *~verb* **3.** circulate, dispel, dispense, disperse, disseminate, dissipate, distribute, propagate, scatter, spread

▷ **Antonyms** *~adjective* (*sense 1*) apposite, brief, compendious, concise, succinct, terse, to the point (*sense 2*) concentrated

diffusion 1. circulation, dispersal, dispersion, dissemination, dissipation, distribution, expansion, propaganda, propagation, scattering, spread **2.** circuitousness, diffuseness, digressiveness, discursiveness, long-windedness, prolixity, rambling, verbiage, verbosity, wandering, wordiness

dig *verb* **1.** break up, burrow, delve, excavate, gouge, grub, hoe, hollow out, mine, penetrate, pierce, quarry, scoop, till, tunnel, turn over **2.** drive, jab, poke, prod, punch, thrust **3.** delve, dig down, go into, investigate, probe, research, search **4.** (*with* **out** *or* **up**) bring to light, come across, come up with, discover, expose, extricate, find, retrieve, root (*informal*), rootle, uncover, unearth, uproot **5.** *informal* appreciate, enjoy, follow, groove (*dated slang*), like, understand *~noun* **6.** jab, poke, prod, punch, thrust **7.** barb, crack (*slang*), cutting remark, gibe, insult, jeer, quip, sneer, taunt, wisecrack (*informal*)

digest *verb* **1.** absorb, assimilate, concoct, dissolve, incorporate, macerate **2.** absorb, assimilate, con, consider, contemplate, grasp, master, meditate, ponder, study, take in, understand **3.** arrange, classify, codify, dispose, methodize, systematize, tabulate **4.** abridge, compress, condense, reduce, shorten, summarize *~noun* **5.** abridgment, abstract, compendium, condensation, epitome, précis, résumé, summary, synopsis

digestion absorption, assimilation, conversion, incorporation, ingestion, transformation

dig in 1. defend, entrench, establish, fortify, maintain **2.** *informal* begin, fall to, set about, start eating, tuck in (*informal*)

dignified august, decorous, distinguished, exalted, formal, grave, honourable, imposing, lofty, lordly, noble, reserved, solemn, stately, upright

▷ **Antonyms** crass, inelegant, unbecoming, undignified, unseemly, vulgar

dignify adorn, advance, aggrandize, distinguish, elevate, ennoble, exalt, glorify, grace, honour, promote, raise

dignitary *noun* bigwig (*informal*), celeb (*informal*), high-up (*informal*), notability, notable, personage, pillar of society, pillar of the church, pillar of the state, public figure, V.I.P., worthy

dignity 1. courtliness, decorum, grandeur, gravity, hauteur, loftiness, majesty, nobility, propriety, solemnity, stateliness **2.** elevation, eminence, excellence, glory, greatness, honour, importance, nobleness, rank, respectability, standing, station, status **3.** *amour-propre,* pride, self-esteem, self-importance, self-possession, self-regard, self-respect

digress be diffuse, depart, deviate, diverge, drift, expatiate, get off the point *or* subject, go off at a tangent, meander, ramble, stray, turn aside, wander

digression apostrophe, aside, departure, detour, deviation, divergence, diversion, footnote, obiter dictum, parenthesis, straying, wandering

digressive anecdotal, circuitous, circumlocutory, diffuse, discursive, divergent, drifting, episodic, excursive, meandering, rambling

dilapidated battered, beat-up (*informal*), broken-down, crumbling, decayed, decaying, decrepit, fallen in, falling apart, gone to rack and ruin, in ruins, neglected, ramshackle, rickety, ruined, ruinous, run-down, shabby, shaky, tumbledown, uncared for, worn-out

dilapidation collapse, decay, demolition, destruction, deterioration, disintegration, disrepair, dissolution, downfall, ruin, waste, wear and tear

dilate **1.** broaden, distend, enlarge, expand, extend, puff out, stretch, swell, widen **2.** amplify, be profuse, be prolix, descant, detail, develop, dwell on, enlarge, expand, expatiate, expound, spin out

▷ **Antonyms** (*sense 1*) compress, constrict, contract, narrow, shrink

dilation broadening, dilatation, distension, enlargement, expansion, extension, increase, spread

dilatory backward, behindhand, dallying, delaying, laggard, lingering, loitering, procrastinating, putting off, slack, slow, sluggish, snail-like, tardy, tarrying, time-wasting

▷ **Antonyms** on-the-ball (*informal*), prompt, punctual, sharp (*informal*)

dilemma **1.** difficulty, embarrassment, fix (*informal*), how-do-you-do (*informal*), jam (*informal*), mess, perplexity, pickle (*informal*), plight, predicament, problem, puzzle, quandary, spot (*informal*), strait, tight corner *or* spot **2. on the horns of a dilemma** between a rock and a hard place (*informal*), between Scylla and Charybdis, between the devil and the deep blue sea

dilettante aesthete, amateur, dabbler, nonprofessional, trifler

diligence activity, application, assiduity, assiduousness, attention, attentiveness, care, constancy, earnestness, heedfulness, industry, intentness, laboriousness, perseverance, sedulousness

diligent active, assiduous, attentive, busy, careful, conscientious, constant, earnest, hard-working, indefatigable, industrious, laborious, painstaking, persevering, persistent, sedulous, studious, tireless

▷ **Antonyms** careless, dilatory, good-for-nothing, inconstant, indifferent, lazy

dilly-dally dally, dawdle, delay, dither (*chiefly Brit.*), falter, fluctuate, hesitate, hover, hum and haw, linger, loiter, potter, procrastinate, shillyshally (*informal*), trifle, vacillate, waver

dilute *verb* **1.** adulterate, cut, make thinner, thin (out), water down, weaken **2.** *figurative* attenuate, decrease, diffuse, diminish, lessen, mitigate, reduce, temper, weaken

▷ **Antonyms** concentrate, condense, intensify, strengthen, thicken

diluted adulterated, cut, dilute, thinned, watered down, watery, weak, weakened, wishy-washy (*informal*)

dim *adjective* **1.** caliginous (*archaic*), cloudy, dark, darkish, dusky, grey, overcast, poorly lit, shadowy, tenebrous, unilluminated **2.** bleary, blurred, faint, fuzzy, ill-defined, indistinct, obscured, shadowy, unclear **3.** braindead (*informal*), dense, doltish, dozy (*Brit. informal*), dull, dumb (*informal*), obtuse, slow, slow on the uptake (*informal*), stupid, thick **4.** confused, hazy, imperfect, indistinct, intangible, obscure, remote, shadowy, vague **5.** dingy, dull, feeble, lacklustre, muted, opaque, pale, sullied, tarnished, weak **6.** dashing, depressing, discouraging, gloomy, sombre, unfavourable, unpromising **7. take a dim view** be displeased, be sceptical, disapprove, look askance, reject, suspect, take exception, view with disfavour *~verb* **8.** bedim, blur, cloud, darken, dull, fade, lower, obscure, tarnish, turn down

▷ **Antonyms** (*sense 1*) bright, clear, cloudless, fair, limpid, pleasant, sunny, unclouded (*sense 2*) bright, brilliant, clear, distinct, limpid, palpable (*sense 3*) acute, astute, aware, brainy, bright, clever, intelligent, keen, quick-witted, sharp, smart

dimension (*often plural*) **1.** amplitude, bulk, capacity, extent, measurement, proportions, size, volume **2.** bigness, extent, greatness, importance, largeness, magnitude, measure, range, scale, scope

diminish **1.** abate, contract, curtail, cut, decrease, downsize, lessen, lower, reduce, retrench, shrink, taper, weaken **2.** decline, die out, dwindle, ebb, fade away, peter out, recede, shrivel, slacken, subside, wane **3.** belittle, cheapen, demean, depreciate, devalue

▷ **Antonyms** (*senses 1 & 2*) amplify, augment, enhance, enlarge, expand, grow, heighten, increase

diminution abatement, contraction, curtailment, cut, cutback, decay, decline, decrease, deduction, lessening, reduction, retrenchment, weakening

diminutive *adjective* bantam, Lilliputian, little, midget, mini, miniature, minute, petite, pocket(-sized), pygmy *or* pigmy, small, teensy-weensy, teeny-weeny, tiny, undersized, wee

▷ **Antonyms** big, colossal, enormous, giant, gigantic, great, immense, jumbo (*informal*), king-size, massive (*informal*)

dimwit blockhead, bonehead (*slang*), booby, dullard, dunce, dunderhead, fathead (*informal*), gobshite (*Irish taboo slang*), ignoramus, lamebrain (*informal*), nitwit (*informal*), numbskull *or* numskull, numpty (*Scot. informal*)

din **1.** *noun* babel, clamour, clangour, clash, clatter, commotion, crash, hubbub, hullabaloo, noise, outcry, pandemonium, racket, row, shout, uproar **2.** *~verb* (*usually with* **into**) drum into, go on at, hammer into, inculcate, instil, instruct, teach

▷ **Antonyms** *~noun* calm, calmness,

hush, peace, quiet, quietness, silence, tranquillity

dine 1. banquet, chow down (*slang*), eat, feast, lunch, sup **2.** (*often with* **on, off** *or* **upon**) consume, eat, feed on

dingle dale, dell, glen, hollow, vale, valley

dingy bedimmed, colourless, dark, dim, dirty, discoloured, drab, dreary, dull, dusky, faded, gloomy, grimy, murky, obscure, seedy, shabby, soiled, sombre, tacky (*informal*)

dinky cute, dainty, mini, miniature, natty (*informal*), neat, petite, small, trim

dinner banquet, beanfeast (*Brit. informal*), blowout (*slang*), collation, feast, main meal, meal, refection, repast, spread (*informal*)

dint 1. *as in* **by dint of** force, means, power, use, virtue **2.** blow, dent, depression, indentation, stroke

dip *verb* **1.** bathe, douse, duck, dunk, immerse, plunge, rinse, souse **2.** decline, descend, disappear, droop, drop (down), fade, fall, lower, sag, set, sink, slope, slump, subside, tilt **3.** ladle, scoop, spoon **4.** (*with* **in** *or* **into**) browse, dabble, glance at, peruse, play at, run over, sample, skim, try **5.** (*with* **in** *or* **into**) draw upon, reach into ~*noun* **6.** douche, drenching, ducking, immersion, plunge, soaking **7.** bathe, dive, plunge, swim **8.** concoction, dilution, infusion, mixture, preparation, solution, suspension **9.** basin, concavity, depression, hole, hollow, incline, slope **10.** decline, drop, fall, lowering, sag, slip, slump

diplomacy 1. international negotiation, statecraft, statesmanship **2.** artfulness, craft, delicacy, discretion, finesse, savoir-faire, skill, subtlety, tact

▷ **Antonyms** (*sense 2*) awkwardness, clumsiness, ineptness, tactlessness, thoughtlessness

diplomat conciliator, go-between, mediator, moderator, negotiator, politician, public relations expert, tactician

diplomatic adept, discreet, polite, politic, prudent, sensitive, subtle, tactful

▷ **Antonyms** impolitic, insensitive, rude, tactless, thoughtless, undiplomatic, unsubtle

dire 1. alarming, appalling, awful, calamitous, cataclysmic, catastrophic, cruel, disastrous, godawful (*slang*), horrible, horrid, ruinous, terrible, woeful **2.** dismal, dreadful, fearful, gloomy, grim, ominous, portentous **3.** critical, crucial, crying, desperate, drastic, exigent, extreme, now or never, pressing, urgent

direct[1] *verb* **1.** administer, advise, call the shots, call the tune, conduct, control, dispose, govern, guide, handle, lead, manage, mastermind, oversee, preside over, regulate, rule, run, superintend, supervise **2.** bid, charge, command, demand, dictate, enjoin, instruct, order **3.** guide, indicate, lead, point in the direction of, point the way, show **4.** address, aim, cast, fix, focus, intend, level, mean, point, train, turn **5.** address, label, mail, route, send, superscribe

direct[2] *adjective* **1.** candid, downright, frank, honest, man-to-man, matter-of-fact, open, outspoken, plain-spoken, round, sincere, straight, straightforward, upfront (*informal*) **2.** absolute, blunt, categorical, downright, explicit, express, plain, point-blank, unambiguous, unequivocal **3.** nonstop, not crooked, shortest, straight, through, unbroken, undeviating, uninterrupted **4.** face-to-face, first-hand, head-on, immediate, personal

▷ **Antonyms** (*sense 1*) circuitous, crooked, devious, indirect, sly, subtle (*sense 2*) ambiguous, circuitous, indirect (*sense 3*) circuitous, crooked, indirect (*sense 4*) indirect, mediated

direction 1. administration, charge, command, control, government, guidance, leadership, management, order, oversight, superintendence, supervision **2.** aim, bearing, course, line, path, road, route, track, way **3.** bent, bias, current, drift, end, leaning, orientation, proclivity, tack, tendency, tenor, trend **4.** address, label, mark, superscription

directions briefing, guidance, guidelines, indication, instructions, plan, recommendation, regulations

directive *noun* canon, charge, command, decree, dictate, edict, fiat, imperative, injunction, instruction, mandate, notice, order, ordinance, regulation, ruling

directly 1. by the shortest route, exactly, in a beeline, precisely, straight, unswervingly, without deviation **2.** as soon as possible, at once, dead, due, forthwith, immediately, in a second, instantaneously, instantly, pdq (*slang*), posthaste, presently, promptly, pronto (*informal*), quickly, right away, soon, speedily, straightaway **3.** candidly, face-to-face, honestly, in person, openly, overtly, personally, plainly, point-blank, straightforwardly, truthfully, unequivocally, without prevarication

directness bluntness, candour, forthrightness, frankness, honesty, outspokenness, plain speaking, sincerity, straightforwardness

director administrator, boss (*informal*), chairman, chief, controller, executive, governor, head, leader, manager, organizer, principal, producer, supervisor

direful appalling, awful, calamitous, dire, dreadful, fearful, ghastly, gloomy, godawful (*slang*), horrible, horrid, shocking, terrible

dirge coronach (*Scot. & Irish*), dead march, elegy, funeral song, lament, requiem, threnody

dirt **1.** crap (*slang*), crud (*slang*), dust, excrement, filth, grime, grot (*slang*), impurity, kak (*S. African slang*), mire, muck, mud, shit (*taboo slang*), slime, slob (*Irish*), smudge, stain, tarnish **2.** clay, earth, loam, soil **3.** indecency, obscenity, pornography, sleaze, smut

dirty *adjective* **1.** begrimed, filthy, foul, grimy, grotty (*slang*), grubby, grungy (*slang, chiefly U.S.*), messy, mucky, muddy, nasty, polluted, scuzzy (*slang, chiefly U.S.*), soiled, sullied, unclean **2.** blue, indecent, obscene, off-colour, pornographic, risqué, salacious, sleazy, smutty, vulgar, X-rated (*informal*) **3.** clouded, dark, dull, miry, muddy, not clear **4.** corrupt, crooked, dishonest, fraudulent, illegal, treacherous, unfair, unscrupulous, unsporting **5.** base, beggarly, contemptible, cowardly, despicable, ignominious, low, low-down (*informal*), mean, nasty, scurvy, shabby, sordid, squalid, vile **6.** angry, annoyed, bitter, choked, indignant, offended, resentful, scorching **7.** *of weather* gusty, louring *or* lowering, rainy, squally, stormy *~verb* **8.** begrime, blacken, defile, foul, mess up, muddy, pollute, smear, smirch, smudge, soil, spoil, stain, sully

▷ **Antonyms** *~adjective* (*sense 1*) clean, pure (*sense 2*) clean, decent (*sense 4*) decent, honest, moral, reputable, respectable, upright (*sense 7*) pleasant *~verb* clean, tidy up

disability **1.** affliction, ailment, complaint, defect, disablement, disorder, handicap, impairment, infirmity, malady **2.** disqualification, impotency, inability, incapacity, incompetency, unfitness, weakness

disable **1.** cripple, damage, debilitate, enfeeble, hamstring, handicap, immobilize, impair, incapacitate, paralyse, prostrate, put out of action, render *hors de combat*, render inoperative, unfit, unman, weaken **2.** disenable, disqualify, invalidate, render *or* declare incapable

disabled bedridden, crippled, handicapped, incapacitated, infirm, lame, maimed, mangled, mutilated, paralysed, weak, weakened, wrecked

▷ **Antonyms** able-bodied, fit, hale, healthy, hearty, robust, sound, strong, sturdy

disabuse correct, enlighten, free from error, open the eyes of, set right, set straight, shatter (someone's) illusions, undeceive

disadvantage **1.** damage, detriment, disservice, harm, hurt, injury, loss, prejudice **2.** (*often plural*) burden, downside, drawback, flaw, fly in the ointment (*informal*), handicap, hardship, hindrance, impediment, inconvenience, liability, minus (*informal*), nuisance, privation, snag, trouble, weakness, weak point **3.** **at a disadvantage** boxed in, cornered, handicapped, in a corner, vulnerable, with one's hands tied behind one's back

▷ **Antonyms** (*senses 1 & 2*) advantage, aid, benefit, convenience, gain, help, merit, profit

disadvantaged deprived, discriminated against, handicapped, impoverished, struggling, underprivileged

disadvantageous adverse, damaging, deleterious, detrimental, harmful, hurtful, ill-timed, inconvenient, inexpedient, injurious, inopportune, prejudicial, unfavourable

disaffect alienate, antagonize, disunite, divide, estrange, repel

disaffected alienated, antagonistic, discontented, disloyal, dissatisfied, estranged, hostile, mutinous, rebellious, seditious, uncompliant, unsubmissive

disaffection alienation, animosity, antagonism, antipathy, aversion, breach, disagreement, discontent, dislike, disloyalty, dissatisfaction, estrangement, hostility, ill will, repugnance, resentment, unfriendliness

disagree **1.** be discordant, be dissimilar, conflict, contradict, counter, depart, deviate, differ, diverge, run counter to, vary **2.** argue, be at sixes and sevens, bicker, clash, contend, contest, cross swords, debate, differ (in opinion), dispute, dissent, fall out (*informal*), have words (*informal*), object, oppose, quarrel, take issue with, wrangle **3.** be injurious, bother, discomfort, distress, hurt, make ill, nauseate, sicken, trouble, upset

▷ **Antonyms** accord, agree, coincide, concur, get on (together), harmonize

disagreeable **1.** bad-tempered, brusque, churlish, contrary, cross, difficult, disobliging, ill-natured, irritable, nasty, peevish, ratty (*Brit. & N.Z. informal*), rude, surly, tetchy, unfriendly, ungracious, unlikable *or* unlikeable, unpleasant **2.** disgusting, displeasing, distasteful, horrid, nasty, objectionable, obnoxious, offensive, repellent, repugnant, repulsive, uninviting, unpalatable, unpleasant, unsavoury, yucky *or* yukky (*slang*)

▷ **Antonyms** (*sense 1*) agreeable, congenial, delightful, friendly, good-natured, lovely, nice, pleasant (*sense 2*) agreeable, delightful, enjoyable, lovely, nice, pleasant

disagreement **1.** difference, discrepancy, disparity, dissimilarity, dissimilitude, divergence, diversity, incompatibility, incongruity, unlikeness, variance **2.** altercation, argument, clash, conflict, debate, difference, discord, dispute, dissent, division, falling out, misunderstanding, quarrel, row, squabble, strife, tiff, wrangle **3.** **in disagreement** at daggers drawn, at loggerheads, at odds, at

variance, disunited, in conflict, in disharmony
▷ **Antonyms** (*senses 1 & 2*) accord, agreement, assent, consensus, correspondence, harmony, similarity, unison, unity

disallow 1. abjure, disavow, disclaim, dismiss, disown, rebuff, refuse, reject, repudiate 2. ban, boycott, cancel, embargo, forbid, prohibit, proscribe, veto

disappear 1. abscond, be lost to view, depart, drop out of sight, ebb, escape, evanesce, fade away, flee, fly, go, pass, recede, retire, vanish from sight, vanish off the face of the earth, wane, withdraw 2. cease, cease to be known, die out, dissolve, end, evaporate, expire, fade, leave no trace, melt away, pass away, perish, vanish
▷ **Antonyms** appear, arrive, materialize, reappear

disappearance departure, desertion, disappearing, disappearing trick, eclipse, evanescence, evaporation, fading, flight, going, loss, melting, passing, vanishing, vanishing point

disappoint 1. chagrin, dash, deceive, delude, disenchant, disgruntle, dishearten, disillusion, dismay, dissatisfy, fail, let down, sadden, vex 2. baffle, balk, defeat, disconcert, foil, f ıstrate, hamper, hinder, thwart

disappointed balked, cast down, choked, depressed, despondent, discontented, discouraged, disenchanted, disgruntled, disillusioned, dissatisfied, distressed, downhearted, foiled, frustrated, let down, saddened, thwarted, upset
▷ **Antonyms** content, contented, fulfilled, happy, pleased, satisfied

disappointing depressing, disagreeable, disconcerting, discouraging, failing, inadequate, inferior, insufficient, lame, not much cop (*Brit. slang*), pathetic, sad, second-rate, sorry, unexpected, unhappy, unsatisfactory, unworthy, upsetting

disappointment 1. chagrin, discontent, discouragement, disenchantment, disillusionment, displeasure, dissatisfaction, distress, failure, frustration, ill-success, mortification, regret, unfulfilment 2. blow, calamity, choker (*informal*), disaster, failure, fiasco, letdown, miscarriage, misfortune, setback, washout (*informal*), whammy (*informal, chiefly U.S.*)

disapprobation blame, censure, condemnation, disapproval, disfavour, dislike, displeasure, dissatisfaction, reproof, stricture

disapproval censure, condemnation, criticism, denunciation, deprecation, disapprobation, displeasure, dissatisfaction, objection, reproach, stick (*slang*)

disapprove 1. (*often with* **of**) blame, censure, condemn, deplore, deprecate, discountenance, dislike, find unacceptable, frown on, have a down on (*informal*), look down one's nose at (*informal*), object to, raise an *or* one's eyebrow, reject, take a dim view of, take exception to 2. disallow, set aside, spurn, turn down, veto
▷ **Antonyms** applaud, approve, commend, compliment, endorse, give the go-ahead (to) (*informal*), like, O.K. *or* okay (*informal*)

disarm 1. disable, render defenceless, unarm 2. deactivate, demilitarize, demobilize, disband 3. persuade, set at ease, win over

disarmament arms limitation, arms reduction, de-escalation, demilitarization, demobilization

disarming charming, irresistible, likable *or* likeable, persuasive, winning

disarrange confuse, derange, discompose, disorder, disorganize, disturb, jumble (up), mess (up), scatter, shake (up), shuffle, unsettle, untidy

disarray 1. confusion, discomposure, disharmony, dismay, disorder, disorderliness, disorganization, disunity, indiscipline, unruliness, upset 2. chaos, clutter, dishevelment, hodgepodge (*U.S.*), hotchpotch, jumble, mess, mix-up, muddle, pig's breakfast (*informal*), shambles, state, tangle, untidiness
▷ **Antonyms** arrangement, harmony, method, neatness, order, orderliness, organization, pattern, plan, regularity, symmetry, system, tidiness

disassemble deconstruct, dismantle, dismount, knock down, strike, take apart, take down

disaster accident, act of God, adversity, blow, bummer (*slang*), calamity, cataclysm, catastrophe, misadventure, mischance, misfortune, mishap, reverse, ruin, ruination, stroke, tragedy, trouble, whammy (*informal, chiefly U.S.*)

disastrous adverse, calamitous, cataclysmal, cataclysmic, catastrophic, destructive, detrimental, devastating, dire, dreadful, fatal, hapless, harmful, ill-fated, ill-starred, ruinous, terrible, tragic, unfortunate, unlucky, unpropitious, untoward

disavow abjure, contradict, deny, disclaim, disown, forswear, gainsay (*archaic or literary*), rebut, reject, repudiate, retract

disavowal abjuration, contradiction, denial, disclaimer, gainsaying (*archaic or literary*), recantation, rejection, renunciation, repudiation, retraction

disband break up, demobilize, dismiss, disperse, dissolve, go (their) separate ways, let go, part company, scatter, send home, separate

disbelief distrust, doubt, dubiety, incredulity, mistrust, scepticism, unbelief

▷ **Antonyms** belief, credence, credulity, faith, trust

disbelieve discount, discredit, give no credence to, mistrust, not accept, not buy (*slang*), not credit, not swallow (*informal*), reject, repudiate, scoff at, suspect

disbeliever agnostic, atheist, doubter, doubting Thomas, questioner, sceptic, scoffer

▷ **Antonyms** adherent, believer, devotee, disciple, follower, proselyte, supporter, upholder, zealot

disbelievingly askance, cynically, doubtingly, incredulously, mistrustfully, quizzically, sceptically, suspiciously, with a pinch of salt

disburden alleviate, diminish, discharge, disencumber, ease, free, lighten, relieve, take a load off one's mind, unburden, unload

disburse expend, fork out (*slang*), lay out, pay out, shell out (*informal*), spend

disbursement disposal, expenditure, outlay, payment, spending

discard abandon, axe (*informal*), cast aside, chuck (*informal*), dispense with, dispose of, ditch (*slang*), drop, dump (*informal*), get rid of, jettison, junk (*informal*), reject, relinquish, remove, repudiate, scrap, shed, throw away *or* out

▷ **Antonyms** hang *or* hold on to, hold back, keep, reserve, retain, save

discern **1.** behold, catch sight of, descry, discover, espy, make out, notice, observe, perceive, recognize, see, suss (out) (*slang*) **2.** detect, determine, differentiate, discriminate, distinguish, judge, make a distinction, pick out

discernible apparent, appreciable, clear, detectable, discoverable, distinct, distinguishable, noticeable, observable, obvious, perceptible, plain, recognizable, visible

discerning acute, astute, clear-sighted, critical, discriminating, ingenious, intelligent, judicious, knowing, penetrating, perceptive, percipient, perspicacious, piercing, sagacious, sensitive, sharp, shrewd, subtle, wise

discernment acumen, acuteness, astuteness, awareness, clear-sightedness, cleverness, discrimination, ingenuity, insight, intelligence, judgment, keenness, penetration, perception, perceptiveness, percipience, perspicacity, sagacity, sharpness, shrewdness, understanding

discharge *verb* **1.** absolve, acquit, allow to go, clear, exonerate, free, liberate, pardon, release, set free *~noun* **2.** acquittal, clearance, exoneration, liberation, pardon, release, remittance *~verb* **3.** cashier, discard, dismiss, eject, expel, fire (*informal*), give (someone) the boot (*slang*), give (someone) the sack (*informal*), oust, remove, sack (*informal*) *~noun* **4.** congé, demobilization, dismissal, ejection, the boot (*slang*), the (old) heave-ho (*informal*), the order of the boot (*slang*), the sack (*informal*) *~verb* **5.** detonate, explode, fire, let loose (*informal*), let off, set off, shoot *~noun* **6.** blast, burst, detonation, discharging, explosion, firing, fusillade, report, salvo, shot, volley *~verb* **7.** disembogue, dispense, emit, empty, excrete, exude, give off, gush, leak, ooze, pour forth, release, void *~noun* **8.** emission, emptying, excretion, flow, ooze, pus, secretion, seepage, suppuration, vent, voiding *~verb* **9.** disburden, lighten, off-load, remove, unburden, unload *~noun* **10.** disburdening, emptying, unburdening, unloading *~verb* **11.** accomplish, carry out, do, execute, fulfil, observe, perform *~noun* **12.** accomplishment, achievement, execution, fulfilment, observance, performance *~verb* **13.** clear, honour, meet, pay, relieve, satisfy, settle, square up *~noun* **14.** payment, satisfaction, settlement

disciple adherent, apostle, believer, catechumen, convert, devotee, follower, learner, partisan, proselyte, pupil, student, supporter, votary

▷ **Antonyms** guru, leader, master, swami, teacher

disciplinarian authoritarian, despot, drill sergeant, hard master, martinet, stickler, strict teacher, taskmaster, tyrant

discipline *noun* **1.** drill, exercise, method, practice, regimen, regulation, training **2.** conduct, control, orderliness, regulation, restraint, self-control, strictness **3.** castigation, chastisement, correction, punishment **4.** area, branch of knowledge, course, curriculum, field of study, speciality, subject *~verb* **5.** break in, bring up, check, control, drill, educate, exercise, form, govern, instruct, inure, prepare, regulate, restrain, train **6.** bring to book, castigate, chasten, chastise, correct, penalize, punish, reprimand, reprove

disclaim abandon, abjure, abnegate, decline, deny, disaffirm, disallow, disavow, disown, forswear, rebut, reject, renege, renounce, repudiate, retract

disclaimer abjuration, contradiction, denial, disavowal, rejection, renunciation, repudiation, retraction

disclose **1.** blow wide open (*slang*), broadcast, communicate, confess, divulge, get off one's chest (*informal*), impart, leak, let slip, make known, make public, out (*informal*), publish, relate, reveal, spill one's guts about (*slang*), spill the beans about (*informal*), tell, unveil, utter **2.** bring to light, discover, exhibit, expose, lay bare, reveal, show, take the wraps off, uncover, unveil

▷ **Antonyms** conceal, cover, dissemble,

hide, keep dark, keep secret, mask, obscure, secrete, veil

disclosure acknowledgment, admission, announcement, broadcast, confession, declaration, discovery, divulgence, exposé, exposure, leak, publication, revelation, uncovering

discoloration blemish, blot, blotch, mark, patch, smirch, splotch, spot, stain

discolour fade, mar, mark, rust, soil, stain, streak, tarnish, tinge

discomfit 1. abash, confound, confuse, demoralize, discompose, disconcert, embarrass, faze, flurry, fluster, perplex, perturb, rattle (*informal*), ruffle, take aback, take the wind out of someone's sails, unnerve, unsettle, worry 2. baffle, balk, beat, checkmate, defeat, foil, frustrate, outwit, overcome, thwart, trump, worst

discomfiture 1. abashment, chagrin, confusion, demoralization, discomposure, embarrassment, humiliation, shame, unease 2. beating, defeat, disappointment, failure, frustration, overthrow, rout, ruin, undoing

discomfort 1. *noun* ache, annoyance, disquiet, distress, gall, hardship, hurt, inquietude, irritation, malaise, nuisance, pain, soreness, trouble, uneasiness, unpleasantness, vexation 2. *~verb* discomfit, discompose, disquiet, distress, disturb, embarrass, make uncomfortable

▷ **Antonyms** *~noun* comfort, ease, reassurance, solace *~verb* alleviate, assuage, comfort, ease, reassure, solace, soothe

discommode annoy, bother, burden, disquiet, disturb, harass, hassle (*informal*), incommode, inconvenience, molest, put out, trouble

discompose agitate, annoy, bewilder, confuse, discomfit, disconcert, displease, disturb, embarrass, faze, flurry, fluster, fret, hassle (*informal*), irritate, nettle, perplex, perturb, provoke, rattle (*informal*), ruffle, unnerve, unsettle, upset, vex, worry

discomposure agitation, anxiety, confusion, discomfiture, disquiet, disquietude, distraction, disturbance, embarrassment, fluster, inquietude, malaise, nervousness, perturbation, trepidation, uneasiness

disconcert 1. abash, agitate, bewilder, discompose, disturb, faze, flummox, flurry, fluster, nonplus, perplex, perturb, put out of countenance, rattle (*informal*), ruffle, shake up (*informal*), take aback, throw off balance, trouble, unbalance, unnerve, unsettle, upset, worry 2. baffle, balk, confuse, defeat, disarrange, frustrate, hinder, put off, thwart, undo

disconcerted annoyed, at sea, bewildered, caught off balance, confused, distracted, disturbed, embarrassed, fazed, flummoxed, flurried, flustered, mixed-up, nonplussed, out of countenance, perturbed, rattled (*informal*), ruffled, shook up (*informal*), taken aback, thrown (*informal*), troubled, unsettled, upset

disconcerting alarming, awkward, baffling, bewildering, bothersome, confusing, dismaying, distracting, disturbing, embarrassing, off-putting (*Brit. informal*), perplexing, upsetting

disconnect cut off, detach, disengage, divide, part, separate, sever, take apart, uncouple

disconnected confused, disjointed, garbled, illogical, incoherent, irrational, jumbled, mixed-up, rambling, uncoordinated, unintelligible, wandering

disconnection cessation, cut-off, cutting off, discontinuation, discontinuity, interruption, separation, severance, stoppage, suspension

disconsolate crushed, dejected, desolate, despairing, dismal, down in the dumps (*informal*), forlorn, gloomy, grief-stricken, heartbroken, hopeless, inconsolable, low, melancholy, miserable, sad, unhappy, woeful, wretched

discontent *noun* discontentment, displeasure, dissatisfaction, envy, fretfulness, regret, restlessness, uneasiness, unhappiness, vexation

discontented brassed off (*Brit. slang*), cheesed off (*Brit. slang*), complaining, disaffected, disgruntled, displeased, dissatisfied, exasperated, fed up, fretful, miserable, pissed off (*taboo slang*), unhappy, vexed, with a chip on one's shoulder (*informal*)

▷ **Antonyms** cheerful, content, contented, happy, pleased, satisfied

discontinuance adjournment, cessation, discontinuation, disjunction, intermission, interruption, separation, stop, stoppage, stopping, suspension, termination

discontinue abandon, axe (*informal*), break off, cease, drop, end, finish, give up, halt, interrupt, kick (*informal*), leave off, pause, pull the plug on, put an end to, quit, refrain from, stop, suspend, terminate, throw in the sponge, throw in the towel

discontinued abandoned, ended, finished, given up *or* over, halted, no longer made, terminated

discontinuity disconnectedness, disconnection, disjointedness, disruption, disunion, incoherence, interruption, lack of coherence, lack of unity

discontinuous broken, disconnected, fitful, intermittent, interrupted, irregular, spasmodic

discord 1. clashing, conflict, contention, difference, disagreement, discordance, dispute, dissension, disunity, division,

friction, incompatibility, lack of concord, opposition, row, rupture, strife, variance, wrangling **2.** cacophony, din, disharmony, dissonance, harshness, jangle, jarring, racket, tumult
▷ **Antonyms** (*sense 1*) accord, agreement, concord, friendship, harmony, peace, understanding, unison, unity (*sense 2*) concord, euphony, harmony, melody, tunefulness, unison

discordant 1. at odds, clashing, conflicting, contradictory, contrary, different, disagreeing, divergent, incompatible, incongruous, inconsistent, opposite **2.** cacophonous, dissonant, grating, harsh, inharmonious, jangling, jarring, shrill, strident, unmelodious

discount *verb* **1.** brush off (*slang*), disbelieve, disregard, ignore, leave out of account, overlook, pass over **2.** deduct, lower, mark down, rebate, reduce, take off ~*noun* **3.** abatement, allowance, concession, cut, cut price, deduction, drawback, percentage (*informal*), rebate, reduction

discountenance *verb* **1.** abash, chagrin, confuse, discompose, disconcert, embarrass, humiliate, put down (*slang*), shame **2.** condemn, disapprove, discourage, disfavour, frown on, object to, oppose, resist, take exception to, veto

discourage 1. abash, awe, cast down, cow, damp, dampen, dash, daunt, deject, demoralize, depress, dishearten, dismay, dispirit, frighten, intimidate, overawe, psych out (*informal*), put a damper on, scare, unman, unnerve **2.** check, curb, deprecate, deter, discountenance, disfavour, dissuade, divert from, hinder, inhibit, prevent, put off, restrain, talk out of, throw cold water on (*informal*)
▷ **Antonyms** bid, countenance, embolden, encourage, hearten, inspire, urge, welcome

discouraged crestfallen, dashed, daunted, deterred, disheartened, dismayed, dispirited, downcast, down in the mouth, glum, pessimistic, put off, sick as a parrot (*informal*)

discouragement 1. cold feet (*informal*), dejection, depression, despair, despondency, disappointment, discomfiture, dismay, downheartedness, hopelessness, loss of confidence, low spirits, pessimism **2.** constraint, curb, damper, deterrent, disincentive, hindrance, impediment, obstacle, opposition, rebuff, restraint, setback

discouraging dampening, daunting, depressing, disappointing, disheartening, dispiriting, off-putting (*Brit. informal*), unfavourable, unpropitious

discourse *noun* **1.** chat, communication, conversation, converse, dialogue, discussion, seminar, speech, talk **2.** address, disquisition, dissertation, essay, homily, lecture, oration, sermon, speech, talk, treatise ~*verb* **3.** confer, converse, debate, declaim, discuss, expatiate, hold forth, speak, talk

discourteous abrupt, bad-mannered, boorish, brusque, curt, disrespectful, ill-bred, ill-mannered, impolite, insolent, offhand, rude, uncivil, uncourteous, ungentlemanly, ungracious, unmannerly
▷ **Antonyms** civil, courteous, courtly, gracious, mannerly, polite, respectful, well-mannered

discourtesy 1. bad manners, disrespectfulness, ill-breeding, impertinence, impoliteness, incivility, insolence, rudeness, ungraciousness, unmannerliness **2.** affront, cold shoulder, insult, kick in the teeth (*slang*), rebuff, slight, snub

discover 1. bring to light, come across, come upon, dig up, find, light upon, locate, turn up, uncover, unearth **2.** ascertain, descry, detect, determine, discern, disclose, espy, find out, get wise to (*informal*), learn, notice, perceive, realize, recognize, reveal, see, spot, suss (out) (*slang*), turn up, uncover **3.** conceive, contrive, design, devise, invent, originate, pioneer

discoverer author, explorer, founder, initiator, inventor, originator, pioneer

discovery 1. ascertainment, detection, disclosure, espial, exploration, finding, introduction, locating, location, origination, revelation, uncovering **2.** bonanza, breakthrough, coup, find, findings, godsend, innovation, invention, secret

discredit *verb* **1.** blame, bring into disrepute, censure, defame, degrade, detract from, disgrace, dishonour, disparage, reproach, slander, slur, smear, vilify ~*noun* **2.** aspersion, censure, disgrace, dishonour, disrepute, ignominy, ill-repute, imputation, odium, reproach, scandal, shame, slur, smear, stigma ~*verb* **3.** challenge, deny, disbelieve, discount, dispute, distrust, doubt, mistrust, question ~*noun* **4.** distrust, doubt, mistrust, question, scepticism, suspicion
▷ **Antonyms** ~*verb* acclaim, applaud, commend, honour, laud, pay tribute to, praise ~*noun* acclaim, acknowledgment, approval, commendation, credit, honour, merit, praise

discreditable blameworthy, degrading, disgraceful, dishonourable, humiliating, ignominious, improper, infamous, reprehensible, scandalous, shameful, unprincipled, unworthy

discredited brought into disrepute, debunked, discarded, exploded, exposed, obsolete, outworn, refuted, rejected

discreet careful, cautious, circumspect, considerate, diplomatic, discerning, guarded, judicious, politic, prudent, reserved, sagacious, sensible, tactful, wary
▷ **Antonyms** incautious, indiscreet, inju~

dicious, rash, tactless, undiplomatic, unthinking, unwise

discrepancy conflict, contrariety, difference, disagreement, discordance, disparity, dissimilarity, dissonance, divergence, incongruity, inconsistency, variance, variation

discrepant at variance, conflicting, contradictory, contrary, differing, disagreeing, discordant, incompatible, incongruous, inconsistent

discrete detached, disconnected, discontinuous, distinct, individual, separate, unattached

discretion 1. acumen, care, carefulness, caution, circumspection, consideration, diplomacy, discernment, good sense, heedfulness, judgment, judiciousness, maturity, prudence, sagacity, tact, wariness **2.** choice, disposition, inclination, liking, mind, option, pleasure, predilection, preference, responsibility, volition, will, wish

▷ **Antonyms** (*sense 1*) carelessness, indiscretion, insensitivity, rashness, tactlessness, thoughtlessness

discretionary arbitrary (*Law*), elective, nonmandatory, open, open to choice, optional, unrestricted

discriminate 1. disfavour, favour, show bias, show prejudice, single out, treat as inferior, treat differently, victimize **2.** assess, differentiate, discern, distinguish, draw a distinction, evaluate, segregate, separate, separate the wheat from the chaff, sift, tell the difference

discriminating acute, astute, critical, cultivated, discerning, fastidious, keen, particular, refined, selective, sensitive, tasteful

▷ **Antonyms** careless, desultory, general, hit or miss (*informal*), indiscriminate, random, undiscriminating, unselective, unsystematic

discrimination 1. bias, bigotry, favouritism, inequity, intolerance, prejudice, unfairness **2.** acumen, acuteness, clearness, discernment, insight, judgment, keenness, penetration, perception, refinement, sagacity, subtlety, taste

discriminatory, discriminative 1. biased, favouring, inequitable, one-sided, partial, partisan, preferential, prejudiced, prejudicial, unjust, weighted **2.** analytical, astute, differentiating, discerning, discriminating, perceptive, perspicacious

discursive circuitous, desultory, diffuse, digressive, erratic, long-winded, loose, meandering, prolix, rambling, roundabout, roving

discuss argue, confer, consider, consult with, converse, debate, deliberate, examine, exchange views on, get together, go into, reason about, review, sift, talk about, thrash out, ventilate, weigh up the pros and cons

discussion analysis, argument, colloquy, confabulation, conference, consideration, consultation, conversation, debate, deliberation, dialogue, discourse, examination, exchange, review, scrutiny, seminar, symposium

disdain 1. *verb* belittle, contemn, deride, despise, disregard, look down on, look down one's nose at (*informal*), misprize, pooh-pooh, reject, scorn, slight, sneer at, spurn, undervalue **2.** *~noun* arrogance, contempt, contumely, derision, dislike, haughtiness, hauteur, indifference, scorn, sneering, snobbishness, superciliousness

disdainful aloof, arrogant, contemptuous, derisive, haughty, high and mighty (*informal*), hoity-toity (*informal*), insolent, looking down one's nose (at), on one's high horse (*informal*), proud, scornful, sneering, supercilious, superior, turning up one's nose (at)

disease 1. affliction, ailment, complaint, condition, disorder, ill health, illness, indisposition, infection, infirmity, lurgi (*informal*), malady, sickness, upset **2.** *figurative* blight, cancer, canker, contagion, contamination, disorder, malady, plague

diseased ailing, infected, rotten, sick, sickly, tainted, unhealthy, unsound, unwell, unwholesome

disembark alight, arrive, get off, go ashore, land, step out of

disembodied bodiless, ghostly, immaterial, incorporeal, intangible, phantom, spectral, spiritual, unbodied

disembowel draw, eviscerate, gut, paunch

disenchant break the spell, bring (someone) down to earth, destroy (someone's) illusions, disabuse, disillusion, open (someone's) eyes, undeceive

disenchanted blasé, cynical, disappointed, disillusioned, indifferent, jaundiced, let down, out of love, sick of, soured, undeceived

disenchantment disappointment, disillusion, disillusionment, revulsion, rude awakening

disencumber disburden, discharge, disembarrass, disembroil, extricate, lighten, unburden, unhamper, unload

disengage 1. disentangle, ease, extricate, free, liberate, loosen, release, set free, unbridle, unloose, untie **2.** detach, disconnect, disjoin, disunite, divide, separate, undo, withdraw

disengaged 1. apart, detached, free, loose, out of gear, released, separate, unattached, unconnected, uncoupled **2.** at ease, at leisure, free, not busy, uncommitted, unoccupied, vacant

disengagement detachment, disconnection, disentanglement, division, separation, withdrawal

disentangle 1. detach, disconnect, disengage, extricate, free, loose, separate, sever, unfold, unravel, unsnarl, untangle, untwist **2.** clarify, clear (up), resolve, simplify, sort out, work out

disfavour 1. disapprobation, disapproval, dislike, displeasure **2.** *as in* **fall into disfavour** bad books (*informal*), discredit, disesteem, disgrace, doghouse (*informal*), shame, unpopularity **3.** bad turn, discourtesy, disservice

disfigure blemish, damage, deface, deform, disfeature, distort, injure, maim, make ugly, mar, mutilate, scar

disfigurement blemish, defacement, defect, deformity, distortion, impairment, injury, mutilation, scar, spot, stain, trauma (*Pathology*)

disgorge 1. barf (*U.S. slang*), belch, blow lunch (*U.S. slang*), chuck (up) (*slang, chiefly U.S.*), chunder (*slang, chiefly Austral.*), discharge, do a technicolour yawn (*slang*), eject, empty, expel, lose one's lunch (*U.S. slang*), regurgitate, spew, spit up, spout, throw up, toss one's cookies (*U.S. slang*), upchuck (*U.S. slang*), vomit **2.** cede, give up, relinquish, renounce, resign, surrender, yield

disgrace *noun* **1.** baseness, degradation, dishonour, disrepute, ignominy, infamy, odium, opprobrium, shame **2.** aspersion, blemish, blot, blot on one's escutcheon, defamation, reproach, scandal, slur, stain, stigma **3.** contempt, discredit, disesteem, disfavour, obloquy *~verb* **4.** abase, bring shame upon, defame, degrade, discredit, disfavour, dishonour, disparage, humiliate, reproach, shame, slur, stain, stigmatize, sully, taint

▷ **Antonyms** *~noun* credit, esteem, favour, grace, honour, repute *~verb* credit, grace, honour

disgraced branded, degraded, discredited, dishonoured, humiliated, in disgrace, in the doghouse (*informal*), mortified, shamed, stigmatized, under a cloud

disgraceful blameworthy, contemptible, degrading, detestable, discreditable, dishonourable, disreputable, ignominious, infamous, low, mean, opprobrious, scandalous, shameful, shocking, unworthy

disgruntled annoyed, cheesed off (*Brit. slang*), discontented, displeased, dissatisfied, grumpy, hacked (off) (*U.S. slang*), huffy, irritated, malcontent, peeved, peevish, petulant, pissed off (*taboo slang*), put out, sulky, sullen, testy, vexed

disguise *verb* **1.** camouflage, cloak, conceal, cover, hide, mask, screen, secrete, shroud, veil **2.** deceive, dissemble, dissimulate, fake, falsify, fudge, gloss over, misrepresent *~noun* **3.** camouflage, cloak, costume, cover, get-up (*informal*), mask, screen, veil **4.** deception, dissimulation, façade, front, pretence, semblance, trickery, veneer

disguised camouflaged, cloaked, covert, fake, false, feigned, incognito, in disguise, masked, pretend, undercover, unrecognizable

disgust 1. *verb* cause aversion, displease, fill with loathing, gross out (*U.S. slang*), nauseate, offend, outrage, put off, repel, revolt, sicken, turn one's stomach **2.** *~noun* abhorrence, abomination, antipathy, aversion, detestation, dislike, distaste, hatefulness, hatred, loathing, nausea, odium, repugnance, repulsion, revulsion

▷ **Antonyms** *~verb* delight, impress, please *~noun* liking, love, pleasure, satisfaction, taste

disgusted appalled, nauseated, offended, outraged, repelled, repulsed, scandalized, sick and tired of (*informal*), sickened, sick of (*informal*)

disgusting abominable, cringe-making (*Brit. informal*), detestable, distasteful, foul, gross, grotty (*slang*), hateful, loathsome, nasty, nauseating, nauseous, noisome, objectionable, obnoxious, odious, offensive, repellent, repugnant, revolting, shameless, sickening, stinking, vile, vulgar, yucky *or* yukky (*slang*)

dish *noun* **1.** bowl, plate, platter, salver **2.** fare, food, recipe *~verb* **3.** *slang* finish, muck up (*slang*), ruin, spoil, torpedo, wreck

disharmony clash, conflict, disaccord, discord, discordance, dissonance, friction, inharmoniousness

dishearten cast down, crush, damp, dampen, dash, daunt, deject, depress, deter, discourage, dismay, dispirit, put a damper on

▷ **Antonyms** buck up (*informal*), cheer up, encourage, hearten, lift, perk up, rally

disheartened choked, crestfallen, crushed, daunted, dejected, depressed, disappointed, discouraged, dismayed, dispirited, downcast, downhearted, sick as a parrot (*informal*)

dishevelled bedraggled, blowsy, disarranged, disarrayed, disordered, frowzy, hanging loose, messy, ruffled, rumpled, tousled, uncombed, unkempt, untidy

▷ **Antonyms** chic, dapper, neat, smart, soigné *or* soignée, spick-and-span, spruce, tidy, trim, well-groomed

dishonest bent (*slang*), cheating, corrupt, crafty, crooked (*informal*), deceitful, deceiving, deceptive, designing, disreputable, double-dealing, false, fraudulent, guileful, knavish (*archaic*), lying, mendacious, perfidious, shady (*informal*), swindling, treacherous, unfair, unprincipled, unscrupulous, untrustworthy, untruthful

▷ **Antonyms** honest, honourable, law-abiding, lawful, principled, true, trustworthy, upright

dishonesty cheating, chicanery, corruption, craft, criminality, crookedness, deceit, duplicity, falsehood, falsity, fraud, fraudulence, graft (*informal*), improbity, mendacity, perfidy, sharp practice, stealing, treachery, trickery, unscrupulousness, wiliness

dishonour *verb* **1.** abase, blacken, corrupt, debase, debauch, defame, degrade, discredit, disgrace, shame, sully **2.** defile, deflower, pollute, rape, ravish, seduce *~noun* **3.** abasement, degradation, discredit, disfavour, disgrace, disrepute, ignominy, infamy, obloquy, odium, opprobrium, reproach, scandal, shame **4.** abuse, affront, discourtesy, indignity, insult, offence, outrage, sacrilege, slight

▷ **Antonyms** *~verb* esteem, exalt, respect, revere, worship *~noun* decency, goodness, honour, integrity, morality, principles, rectitude

dishonourable 1. base, contemptible, despicable, discreditable, disgraceful, ignoble, ignominious, infamous, not cricket (*informal*), scandalous, shameful **2.** blackguardly, corrupt, disreputable, shameless, treacherous, unprincipled, unscrupulous, untrustworthy

dish out allocate, distribute, dole out, hand out, inflict, mete out

dish-shaped concave, cupped, cup-shaped, depressed, hollow, hollowed out, incurvate, incurved, pushed in, scooped, scooped out, scyphiform, sunken

dish up hand out, ladle, prepare, present, produce, scoop, serve, spoon

disillusion *verb* break the spell, bring down to earth, disabuse, disenchant, open the eyes of, shatter one's illusions, undeceive

disillusioned disabused, disappointed, disenchanted, enlightened, indifferent, out of love, sadder and wiser, undeceived

disincentive damper, determent, deterrent, discouragement, dissuasion, impediment

disinclination alienation, antipathy, aversion, demur, dislike, hesitance, lack of desire, lack of enthusiasm, loathness, objection, opposition, reluctance, repugnance, resistance, unwillingness

disinclined antipathetic, averse, balking, hesitating, indisposed, loath, not in the mood, opposed, reluctant, resistant, unwilling

disinfect clean, cleanse, decontaminate, deodorize, fumigate, purify, sanitize, sterilize

▷ **Antonyms** contaminate, defile, infect, poison, pollute, taint, vitiate

disinfectant antiseptic, germicide, sanitizer, sterilizer

disingenuous artful, cunning, deceitful, designing, dishonest, duplicitous, feigned, guileful, insidious, insincere, shifty, sly, two-faced, uncandid, underhanded, unfair, wily

disinherit cut off, cut off without a penny, disown, dispossess, oust, repudiate

disintegrate break apart, break up, crumble, disunite, fall apart, fall to pieces, go to pieces, go to seed, reduce to fragments, separate, shatter, splinter

disinter 1. dig up, disentomb, exhume, unearth **2.** bring to light, disclose, discover, expose, uncover, unearth

disinterest candidness, detachment, disinterestedness, dispassionateness, equity, fairness, impartiality, justice, neutrality, unbiasedness

disinterested candid, detached, dispassionate, equitable, even-handed, free from self-interest, impartial, impersonal, neutral, outside, unbiased, uninvolved, unprejudiced, unselfish

▷ **Antonyms** biased, involved, partial, prejudiced, selfish

disjointed 1. aimless, confused, disconnected, disordered, fitful, incoherent, loose, rambling, spasmodic, unconnected **2.** disconnected, dislocated, displaced, disunited, divided, separated, split

dislikable, dislikeable detestable, displeasing, distasteful, hatable, nasty, objectionable, odious, unattractive, unlikable *or* unlikeable, unpleasant

dislike 1. *noun* animosity, animus, antagonism, antipathy, aversion, detestation, disapprobation, disapproval, disgust, disinclination, displeasure, distaste, enmity, hatred, hostility, loathing, odium, repugnance **2.** *~verb* abhor, abominate, be averse to, despise, detest, disapprove, disfavour, disrelish, hate, have a down on (*informal*), have no taste *or* stomach for, loathe, not be able to bear *or* abide, object to, scorn, shun, take a dim view of

▷ **Antonyms** *~noun* admiration, attraction, delight, esteem, inclination, liking *~verb* esteem, favour, like

dislocate 1. disorder, displace, disrupt, disturb, misplace, shift **2.** disarticulate, disconnect, disengage, disjoint, disunite, luxate (*Medical*), put out of joint, unhinge

dislocation 1. disarray, disorder, disorganization, disruption, disturbance, misplacement **2.** disarticulation, disconnection, disengagement, luxation (*Medical*), unhinging

dislodge dig out, disentangle, displace, disturb, eject, extricate, force out, knock loose, oust, remove, uproot

disloyal apostate, disaffected, faithless, false, perfidious, seditious, subversive, traitorous, treacherous, treasonable, two-faced, unfaithful, unpatriotic, un~

trustworthy
▷ **Antonyms** constant, dependable, dutiful, faithful, loyal, steadfast, true, trustworthy, trusty

disloyalty betrayal of trust, breach of trust, breaking of faith, deceitfulness, double-dealing, falseness, falsity, inconstancy, infidelity, perfidy, Punic faith, treachery, treason, unfaithfulness

dismal black, bleak, cheerless, dark, depressing, despondent, discouraging, dolorous, dreary, forlorn, funereal, gloomy, gruesome, lonesome, louring *or* lowering, lugubrious, melancholy, sad, sombre, sorrowful, wretched
▷ **Antonyms** bright, cheerful, cheery, glad, happy, joyful, light-hearted, sunny

dismantle demolish, disassemble, dismount, raze, strike, strip, take apart, take to pieces, unrig

dismay *verb* **1.** affright, alarm, appal, distress, fill with consternation, frighten, horrify, paralyse, scare, terrify, unnerve **2.** daunt, disappoint, discourage, dishearten, disillusion, dispirit, put off *~noun* **3.** agitation, alarm, anxiety, apprehension, consternation, distress, dread, fear, fright, horror, panic, terror, trepidation **4.** chagrin, disappointment, discouragement, disillusionment, upset

dismember amputate, anatomize, cut into pieces, disjoint, dislimb, dislocate, dissect, divide, mutilate, rend, sever

dismiss 1. axe (*informal*), cashier, discharge, fire (*informal*), give notice to, give (someone) their marching orders, give the boot to (*slang*), give the bullet to (*Brit. slang*), kiss off (*slang, chiefly U.S. & Canad.*), lay off, oust, remove, sack (*informal*), send packing (*informal*) **2.** disband, disperse, dissolve, free, let go, release, send away **3.** banish, discard, dispel, disregard, drop, lay aside, pooh-pooh, put out of one's mind, reject, relegate, repudiate, set aside, shelve, spurn

dismissal 1. adjournment, congé, end, freedom to depart, permission to go, release **2.** discharge, expulsion, kiss-off (*slang, chiefly U.S. & Canad.*), marching orders (*informal*), notice, one's books *or* cards (*informal*), removal, the boot (*slang*), the bum's rush (*slang*), the (old) heave-ho (*informal*), the order of the boot (*slang*), the push (*slang*), the sack (*informal*)

dismount alight, descend, get down, get off, light

disobedience indiscipline, infraction, insubordination, mutiny, noncompliance, nonobservance, recalcitrance, revolt, unruliness, waywardness

disobedient contrary, contumacious, defiant, disorderly, froward (*archaic*), insubordinate, intractable, mischievous, naughty, noncompliant, nonobservant, obstreperous, refractory, undisciplined, unruly, wayward, wilful
▷ **Antonyms** biddable, compliant, dutiful, manageable, obedient, submissive, well-behaved

disobey contravene, defy, dig one's heels in (*informal*), disregard, flout, go counter to, ignore, infringe, overstep, rebel, refuse to obey, resist, transgress, violate

disoblige 1. annoy, bother, discommode, disturb, inconvenience, put out, trouble, upset **2.** affront, displease, insult, offend, slight

disobliging awkward, bloody-minded (*Brit. informal*), cussed (*informal*), disagreeable, discourteous, ill-disposed, rude, unaccommodating, uncivil, uncooperative, unhelpful, unobliging, unpleasant

disorder *noun* **1.** chaos, clutter, confusion, derangement, disarray, disorderliness, disorganization, hodgepodge (*U.S.*), hotchpotch, irregularity, jumble, mess, muddle, pig's breakfast (*informal*), shambles, state, untidiness **2.** *bagarre,* brawl, clamour, commotion, disturbance, fight, fracas, hubbub, hullabaloo, quarrel, riot, rumpus, scrimmage, shindig (*informal*), shindy (*informal*), tumult, turbulence, turmoil, unrest, unruliness, upheaval, uproar **3.** *Medical* affliction, ailment, complaint, disease, illness, indisposition, malady, sickness *~verb* **4.** clutter, confound, confuse, derange, disarrange, discompose, disorganize, disturb, jumble, make hay of, mess up, mix up, muddle, scatter, unsettle, upset

disordered all over the place, confused, deranged, disarranged, disarrayed, dislocated, disorganized, displaced, higgledy-piggledy (*informal*), in a mess, in confusion, jumbled, misplaced, muddled, out of kilter, out of place, untidy

disorderly 1. chaotic, confused, disorganized, higgledy-piggledy (*informal*), indiscriminate, irregular, jumbled, messy, shambolic (*informal*), unsystematic, untidy **2.** boisterous, disruptive, indisciplined, lawless, obstreperous, rebellious, refractory, riotous, rowdy, stormy, tumultuous, turbulent, ungovernable, unlawful, unmanageable, unruly
▷ **Antonyms** (*sense 1*) arranged, neat, orderly, organized, tidy

disorganization chaos, confusion, derangement, disarray, disjointedness, disorder, disruption, incoherence, unconnectedness

disorganize break up, confuse, convulse, derange, destroy, disarrange, discompose, disorder, disrupt, disturb, jumble, make a shambles of, muddle, turn topsy-turvy, unsettle, upset

disorganized chaotic, confused, disordered, haphazard, jumbled, muddled, off the rails, shuffled, unmethodical, unorganized, unsystematic

disorientate, disorient cause to lose one's bearings, confuse, dislocate, mislead, perplex, upset

disorientated, disoriented adrift, all at sea, astray, bewildered, confused, lost, mixed up, not adjusted, off-beam, off-course, out of joint, perplexed, unbalanced, unhinged, unsettled, unstable

disown abandon, abnegate, cast off, deny, disallow, disavow, disclaim, rebut, refuse to acknowledge *or* recognize, reject, renounce, repudiate, retract

disparage asperse, bad-mouth (*slang, chiefly U.S. & Canad.*), belittle, blast, criticize, decry, defame, degrade, denigrate, deprecate, depreciate, deride, derogate, detract from, discredit, disdain, dismiss, knock (*informal*), lambast(e), malign, minimize, put down, ridicule, rubbish (*informal*), run down, scorn, slag (off) (*slang*), slander, tear into (*informal*), traduce, underestimate, underrate, undervalue, vilify

disparagement aspersion, belittlement, condemnation, contempt, contumely, criticism, debasement, degradation, denigration, denunciation, depreciation, derision, derogation, detraction, discredit, disdain, impairment, lessening, prejudice, reproach, ridicule, scorn, slander, underestimation

disparate at odds, at variance, contrary, contrasting, different, discordant, discrepant, dissimilar, distinct, diverse, unlike

disparity difference, discrepancy, disproportion, dissimilarity, dissimilitude, distinction, gap, imbalance, incongruity, inequality, unevenness, unlikeness

dispassion candidness, detachment, disinterestedness, impartiality, neutrality, objectivity

dispassionate 1. calm, collected, composed, cool, imperturbable, moderate, quiet, serene, sober, temperate, unemotional, unexcitable, unexcited, unfazed (*informal*), unmoved, unruffled **2.** candid, detached, disinterested, fair, impartial, impersonal, indifferent, neutral, objective, unbiased, uninvolved, unprejudiced

▷ **Antonyms** (*sense 1*) ablaze, ardent, emotional, excited, fervent, impassioned, intense, passionate (*sense 2*) biased, concerned, interested, involved, partial, prejudiced

dispatch, despatch *verb* **1.** accelerate, consign, dismiss, express, forward, hasten, hurry, quicken, remit, send, transmit **2.** conclude, discharge, dispose of, expedite, finish, make short work of (*informal*), perform, settle **3.** assassinate, blow away (*slang, chiefly U.S.*), bump off (*slang*), butcher, eliminate (*slang*), execute, finish off, kill, murder, put an end to, slaughter, slay, take out (*slang*) ~*noun* **4.** alacrity, celerity, expedition, haste, precipitateness, promptitude, promptness, quickness, rapidity, speed, swiftness **5.** account, bulletin, communication, communiqué, document, instruction, item, letter, message, missive, news, piece, report, story

dispel allay, banish, chase away, dismiss, disperse, dissipate, drive away, eliminate, expel, resolve, rout, scatter

dispensable disposable, expendable, inessential, needless, nonessential, superfluous, unnecessary, unrequired, useless

▷ **Antonyms** crucial, essential, important, indispensable, necessary, requisite, vital

dispensation 1. allotment, appointment, apportionment, bestowal, conferment, consignment, dealing out, disbursement, distribution, endowment, supplying **2.** award, dole, part, portion, quota, share **3.** administration, direction, economy, management, plan, regulation, scheme, stewardship, system **4.** exception, exemption, immunity, indulgence, licence, permission, privilege, relaxation, relief, remission, reprieve

dispense 1. allocate, allot, apportion, assign, deal out, disburse, distribute, dole out, mete out, share **2.** measure, mix, prepare, supply **3.** administer, apply, carry out, direct, discharge, enforce, execute, implement, operate, undertake **4.** except, excuse, exempt, exonerate, let off (*informal*), release, relieve, reprieve **5.** (*with* **with**) abstain from, do without, forgo, give up, omit, relinquish, waive **6.** (*with* **with**) abolish, brush aside, cancel, dispose of, disregard, do away with, get rid of, ignore, pass over, render needless, shake off

disperse 1. broadcast, circulate, diffuse, disseminate, dissipate, distribute, scatter, spread, strew **2.** break up, disappear, disband, dismiss, dispel, dissolve, rout, scatter, send off, separate, vanish

▷ **Antonyms** amass, assemble, collect, concentrate, congregate, convene, gather, muster, pool

dispersal broadcast, circulation, diffusion, dispersion, dissemination, dissipation, distribution, scattering, spread

dispirit cast down, damp, dampen, dash, deject, depress, deter, discourage, dishearten, disincline, sadden

dispirited crestfallen, dejected, depressed, despondent, discouraged, disheartened, down, downcast, gloomy, glum, in the doldrums, low, morose, sad, sick as a parrot (*informal*)

displace 1. derange, disarrange, disturb, misplace, move, shift, transpose **2.** cashier, depose, discard, discharge, dismiss, fire (*informal*), remove, sack (*informal*) **3.** crowd out, oust, replace, succeed, supersede, supplant, take the place of **4.** dislocate, dislodge, dispossess, eject, evict, force out, unsettle

display *verb* **1.** betray, demonstrate, disclose, evidence, evince, exhibit, expose, manifest, open, open to view, present, reveal, show, take the wraps off, unveil **2.** expand, extend, model, open out, spread out, stretch out, unfold, unfurl **3.** boast, flash (*informal*), flaunt, flourish, parade, show off, vaunt *~noun* **4.** array, demonstration, exhibition, exposition, exposure, manifestation, presentation, revelation, show **5.** flourish, ostentation, pageant, parade, pomp, show, spectacle

▷ **Antonyms** *~verb* conceal, cover, hide, keep dark, keep secret, mask, secrete, veil

displease aggravate (*informal*), anger, annoy, disgust, dissatisfy, exasperate, gall, hassle (*informal*), incense, irk, irritate, nark (*Brit., Austral., & N.Z. slang*), nettle, offend, pique, piss one off (*taboo slang*), provoke, put one's back up, put out, rile, upset, vex

displeasure anger, annoyance, disapprobation, disapproval, disfavour, disgruntlement, dislike, dissatisfaction, distaste, indignation, irritation, offence, pique, resentment, vexation, wrath

▷ **Antonyms** approval, endorsement, pleasure, satisfaction

disport 1. amuse, beguile, cheer, delight, divert, entertain, make merry **2.** caper, frisk, frolic, gambol, play, revel, romp, sport

disposable 1. biodegradable, compostable, decomposable, nonreturnable, paper, throwaway **2.** at one's service, available, consumable, expendable, free for use, spendable

disposal 1. clearance, discarding, dumping (*informal*), ejection, jettisoning, parting with, relinquishment, removal, riddance, scrapping, throwing away **2.** arrangement, array, dispensation, disposition, distribution, grouping, placing, position **3.** assignment, bequest, bestowal, consignment, conveyance, dispensation, gift, settlement, transfer **4.** *as in* **at one's disposal** authority, conduct, control, determination, direction, discretion, government, management, ordering, regulation, responsibility

dispose 1. adjust, arrange, array, determine, distribute, fix, group, marshal, order, place, put, range, rank, regulate, set, settle, stand **2.** actuate, adapt, bias, condition, incline, induce, influence, lead, motivate, move, predispose, prompt, tempt

disposed apt, given, inclined, liable, likely, of a mind to, predisposed, prone, ready, subject, tending towards

dispose of 1. deal with, decide, determine, end, finish with, settle **2.** bestow, give, make over, part with, sell, transfer **3.** bin (*informal*), chuck (*informal*), destroy, discard, dump (*informal*), get rid of, get shot of, jettison, junk (*informal*), scrap, throw out *or* away, unload

disposition 1. character, constitution, make-up, nature, spirit, temper, temperament **2.** bent, bias, habit, inclination, leaning, predisposition, proclivity, proneness, propensity, readiness, tendency **3.** adjustment, arrangement, classification, disposal, distribution, grouping, ordering, organization, placement **4.** control, direction, disposal, management, regulation

dispossess deprive, dislodge, divest, drive out, eject, evict, expel, oust, strip, take away, turn out

dispraise 1. *verb* animadvert on *or* upon, blame, blast, censure, condemn, criticize, disapprove, disparage, lambast(e), put down, reproach, reprove, tear into (*informal*) **2.** *~noun* blame, censure, depreciation, discredit, disgrace, dishonour, disparagement, opprobrium, reproach, shame

disproof confutation, counterargument, denial, disproval, invalidation, negation, rebuttal, refutation

disproportion asymmetry, discrepancy, disparity, imbalance, inadequacy, inequality, insufficiency, lopsidedness, unevenness, unsuitableness

▷ **Antonyms** balance, congruity, harmony, proportion, symmetry

disproportionate excessive, incommensurate, inordinate, out of proportion, too much, unbalanced, unequal, uneven, unreasonable

disprove blow out of the water (*slang*), confute, contradict, controvert, discredit, expose, give the lie to, invalidate, make a nonsense of, negate, prove false, rebut, refute

▷ **Antonyms** ascertain, bear out, confirm, evince, prove, show, substantiate, verify

disputable arguable, controversial, debatable, doubtful, dubious, iffy (*informal*), moot, open to discussion, questionable, uncertain

disputant adversary, antagonist, arguer, contender, contestant, debater, opponent

disputation argumentation, controversy, debate, dispute, dissension, polemics

disputatious argumentative, cantankerous, captious, cavilling, contentious, dissentious, litigious, polemical, pugnacious, quarrelsome

dispute *verb* **1.** altercate, argue, brawl, clash, contend, cross swords, debate, discuss, quarrel, row, spar, squabble, wrangle **2.** challenge, contest, contradict, controvert, deny, doubt, impugn, question, rebut *~noun* **3.** altercation, argument, *bagarre,* brawl, conflict, disagreement, discord, disturbance, feud, friction, quarrel, shindig (*informal*), shindy (*informal*), strife, wrangle **4.** argument, contention, controversy, debate, discussion, dissension

disqualification 1. disability, disablement, incapacitation, incapacity, unfitness **2.** ban, debarment, disenablement, disentitlement, elimination, exclusion, incompetence, ineligibility, rejection

disqualified debarred, eliminated, ineligible, knocked out, out of the running

disqualify 1. disable, incapacitate, invalidate, unfit (*rare*) **2.** ban, debar, declare ineligible, disentitle, preclude, prohibit, rule out

disquiet 1. *noun* alarm, angst, anxiety, concern, disquietude, distress, disturbance, fear, foreboding, fretfulness, nervousness, restlessness, trepidation, trouble, uneasiness, unrest, worry **2.** *~verb* agitate, annoy, bother, concern, discompose, distress, disturb, fret, harass, hassle (*informal*), incommode, make uneasy, perturb, pester, plague, trouble, unsettle, upset, vex, worry

disquieting annoying, bothersome, disconcerting, distressing, disturbing, harrowing, irritating, perturbing, troubling, unnerving, unsettling, upsetting, vexing, worrying

disquisition discourse, dissertation, essay, exposition, lecture, paper, thesis, treatise

disregard *verb* **1.** brush aside *or* away, discount, disobey, ignore, laugh off, leave out of account, make light of, neglect, overlook, pass over, pay no attention to, pay no heed to, take no notice of, turn a blind eye to **2.** brush off (*slang*), cold-shoulder, contemn, despise, disdain, disparage, send to Coventry, slight, snub *~noun* **3.** brushoff (*slang*), contempt, disdain, disrespect, heedlessness, ignoring, inattention, indifference, neglect, negligence, oversight, slight, the cold shoulder

▷ **Antonyms** *~verb* attend, heed, listen to, mind, note, pay attention to, regard, respect, take into consideration, take notice of

disrelish 1. *verb* be averse to, be turned off by (*informal*), disfavour, dislike, loathe, regard with distaste **2.** *~noun* antipathy, aversion, disfavour, disgust, disinclination, dislike, distaste, loathing, repugnance

disrepair 1. collapse, decay, deterioration, dilapidation, ruination **2. in disrepair** broken, bust (*informal*), decayed, decrepit, kaput (*informal*), not functioning, on the blink (*slang*), out of commission, out of order, worn-out

disreputable 1. base, contemptible, derogatory, discreditable, disgraceful, dishonourable, disorderly, ignominious, infamous, louche, low, mean, notorious, opprobrious, scandalous, shady (*informal*), shameful, shocking, unprincipled, vicious, vile **2.** bedraggled, dilapidated, dingy, dishevelled, down at heel, scruffy, seedy, shabby, threadbare, worn

▷ **Antonyms** (*sense 1*) decent, reputable, respectable, respected, upright, worthy

disrepute discredit, disesteem, disfavour, disgrace, dishonour, ignominy, ill favour, ill repute, infamy, obloquy, shame, unpopularity

disrespect cheek, contempt, discourtesy, dishonour, disregard, impertinence, impoliteness, impudence, incivility, insolence, irreverence, lack of respect, lese-majesty, rudeness, sauce, unmannerliness

▷ **Antonyms** esteem, regard, respect

disrespectful bad-mannered, cheeky, contemptuous, discourteous, ill-bred, impertinent, impolite, impudent, insolent, insulting, irreverent, misbehaved, rude, uncivil

disrobe bare, denude, divest, doff, remove, shed, strip, take off, unclothe, uncover, undress

disrupt 1. agitate, confuse, convulse, disorder, disorganize, disturb, spoil, throw into disorder, upset **2.** break up *or* into, interfere with, interrupt, intrude, obstruct, unsettle, upset

disruption confusion, disarray, disorder, disorderliness, disturbance, interference, interruption, stoppage

disruptive confusing, disorderly, distracting, disturbing, obstreperous, troublemaking, troublesome, unruly, unsettling, upsetting

▷ **Antonyms** biddable, cooperative, docile, obedient, well-behaved

dissatisfaction annoyance, chagrin, disappointment, discomfort, discontent, dislike, dismay, displeasure, distress, exasperation, frustration, irritation, regret, resentment, unhappiness

dissatisfied disappointed, discontented, disgruntled, displeased, fed up, frustrated, not satisfied, unfulfilled, ungratified, unhappy, unsatisfied

▷ **Antonyms** content, contented, pleased, satisfied

dissatisfy annoy, disappoint, discontent, disgruntle, displease, give cause for complaint, irritate, leave dissatisfied, not pass muster, not suffice, put out, vex

dissect 1. anatomize, cut up *or* apart, dismember, lay open **2.** analyse, break down, explore, inspect, investigate, research, scrutinize, study

dissection 1. anatomization, anatomy, autopsy, dismemberment, necropsy, postmortem (examination) **2.** analysis, breakdown, examination, inspection, investigation, research, scrutiny

dissemble 1. camouflage, cloak, conceal, cover up, disguise, dissimulate, hide, mask 2. affect, counterfeit, falsify, feign, pretend, sham, simulate

dissembler charlatan, con man (*informal*), deceiver, dissimulator, feigner, fraud, hypocrite, impostor, pretender, trickster, whited sepulchre

disseminate broadcast, circulate, diffuse, disperse, dissipate, distribute, proclaim, promulgate, propagate, publicize, publish, scatter, sow, spread

dissemination broadcasting, circulation, diffusion, distribution, promulgation, propagation, publication, publishing, spread

dissension conflict, conflict of opinion, contention, difference, disagreement, discord, discordance, dispute, dissent, friction, quarrel, row, strife, variance

dissent **1.** *verb* decline, differ, disagree, object, protest, refuse, withhold assent *or* approval **2.** *~noun* difference, disagreement, discord, dissension, dissidence, nonconformity, objection, opposition, refusal, resistance

▷ **Antonyms** *~verb* agree, assent, concur *~noun* accord, agreement, assent, concurrence, consensus

dissenter disputant, dissident, nonconformist, objector, protestant

dissenting *adjective* conflicting, differing, disagreeing, dissenting, dissident, opposing, protesting

dissertation critique, discourse, disquisition, essay, exposition, thesis, treatise

disservice bad turn, disfavour, harm, ill turn, injury, injustice, unkindness, wrong

▷ **Antonyms** courtesy, good turn, indulgence, kindness, obligement (*Scot. or archaic*), service

dissever cleave, disunite, divorce, part, rend, rift, separate, sever, sunder

dissidence difference of opinion, disagreement, discordance, dispute, dissent, feud, rupture, schism

dissident **1.** *adjective* differing, disagreeing, discordant, dissentient, dissenting, heterodox, nonconformist, schismatic **2.** *~noun* agitator, dissenter, protester, rebel, recusant

dissimilar different, disparate, divergent, diverse, heterogeneous, manifold, mismatched, not alike, not capable of comparison, not similar, unlike, unrelated, various

▷ **Antonyms** alike, comparable, congruous, corresponding, in agreement, much the same, resembling, uniform

dissimilarity difference, discrepancy, disparity, dissimilitude, distinction, divergence, heterogeneity, incomparability, nonuniformity, unlikeness, unrelatedness

dissimilitude difference, discrepancy, disparity, dissimilarity, diversity, heterogeneity, incomparability, nonuniformity, unlikeness, unrelatedness

dissimulate camouflage, cloak, conceal, disguise, dissemble, feign, hide, mask, pretend

dissimulation concealment, deceit, deception, dissembling, double-dealing, duplicity, feigning, hypocrisy, play-acting, pretence, sham, wile

dissipate **1.** burn up, consume, deplete, expend, fritter away, indulge oneself, lavish, misspend, run through, spend, squander, waste **2.** disappear, dispel, disperse, dissolve, drive away, evaporate, scatter, vanish

dissipated **1.** abandoned, debauched, dissolute, intemperate, profligate, rakish, self-indulgent **2.** consumed, destroyed, exhausted, scattered, squandered, wasted

dissipation **1.** abandonment, debauchery, dissoluteness, drunkenness, excess, extravagance, indulgence, intemperance, lavishness, prodigality, profligacy, squandering, wantonness, waste **2.** amusement, distraction, diversion, entertainment, gratification **3.** disappearance, disintegration, dispersal, dissemination, dissolution, scattering, vanishing

dissociate **1.** break off, disband, disrupt, part company, quit **2.** detach, disconnect, distance, divorce, isolate, segregate, separate, set apart

dissociation break, detachment, disconnection, disengagement, distancing, disunion, division, divorce, isolation, segregation, separation, severance

dissolute abandoned, corrupt, debauched, degenerate, depraved, dissipated, immoral, lax, lewd, libertine, licentious, loose, profligate, rakish, unrestrained, vicious, wanton, wild

▷ **Antonyms** chaste, clean-living, good, moral, squeaky-clean, upright, virtuous, worthy

dissolution **1.** breaking up, disintegration, division, divorce, parting, resolution, separation **2.** death, decay, decomposition, demise, destruction, dispersal, extinction, overthrow, ruin **3.** adjournment, conclusion, disbandment, discontinuation, dismissal, end, ending, finish, suspension, termination **4.** corruption, debauchery, dissipation, intemperance, wantonness **5.** disappearance, evaporation, liquefaction, melting, solution

▷ **Antonyms** (*sense 1*) alliance, amalgamation, coalition, combination, unification, union

dissolve **1.** deliquesce, flux, fuse, liquefy, melt, soften, thaw **2.** break down, crumble, decompose, diffuse, disappear, disintegrate, disperse, dissipate, dwindle, evanesce, evaporate, fade, melt away, perish, vanish, waste away **3.** axe (*informal*), break up, destroy, discontinue, dismiss, end, overthrow, ruin, suspend, terminate, wind up **4**. break into *or* up, collapse, disorganize, disunite, divorce, loose, resolve into, separate, sever

dissonance **1**. cacophony, discord, discordance, harshness, jangle, jarring, unmelodiousness, want of harmony **2**. difference, disagreement, discord, discrepancy, disparity, dissension, incongruity, inconsistency, variance

dissonant **1**. cacophonous, discordant, grating, harsh, inharmonious, jangling, jarring, out of tune, raucous, strident, tuneless, unmelodious **2**. anomalous, at variance, different, differing, disagreeing, discrepant, dissentient, incompatible, incongruous, inconsistent, irreconcilable, irregular

dissuade advise against, deter, discourage, disincline, divert, expostulate, persuade not to, put off, remonstrate, talk out of, urge not to, warn
▷ **Antonyms** bring round (*informal*), coax, convince, persuade, sway, talk into

dissuasion caution, damper, determent, deterrence, deterrent, discouragement, disincentive, expostulation, hindrance, remonstrance, setback

dissuasive admonitory, cautionary, discouraging, disincentive, dissuading, monitory, off-putting (*Brit. informal*), remonstrative, warning

distance *noun* **1**. absence, extent, gap, interval, lapse, length, range, reach, remoteness, remove, separation, space, span, stretch, width **2**. aloofness, coldness, coolness, frigidity, reserve, restraint, stiffness **3**. **go the distance** bring to an end, complete, finish, see through, stay the course **4**. **keep one's distance** avoid, be aloof, be indifferent, be reserved, keep (someone) at arm's length, shun **5**. **in the distance** afar, far away, far off, on the horizon, yonder *~verb* **6**. dissociate oneself, put in proportion, separate oneself **7**. leave behind, outdistance, outdo, outrun, outstrip, pass

distant **1**. abroad, afar, far, faraway, far-flung, far-off, outlying, out-of-the-way, remote, removed **2**. apart, disparate, dispersed, distinct, scattered, separate **3**. aloof, at arm's length, ceremonious, cold, cool, formal, haughty, reserved, restrained, reticent, standoffish, stiff, unapproachable, unfriendly, withdrawn **4**. faint, indirect, indistinct, obscure, slight, uncertain
▷ **Antonyms** (*senses 1 & 2*) adjacent, adjoining, at hand, close, handy, imminent, just round the corner, near, nearby, neighbouring, nigh, proximate, within sniffing distance (*informal*) (*sense 3*) close, friendly, intimate, warm

distaste abhorrence, antipathy, aversion, detestation, disfavour, disgust, disinclination, dislike, displeasure, disrelish, dissatisfaction, horror, loathing, odium, repugnance, revulsion

distasteful abhorrent, disagreeable, displeasing, loathsome, nauseous, objectionable, obnoxious, obscene, offensive, repugnant, repulsive, undesirable, uninviting, unpalatable, unpleasant, unsavoury
▷ **Antonyms** agreeable, charming, enjoyable, pleasing, pleasurable

distend balloon, bloat, bulge, dilate, enlarge, expand, increase, inflate, puff, stretch, swell, widen

distended bloated, dilated, enlarged, expanded, inflated, puffy, stretched, swollen, tumescent

distension dilatation, dilation, enlargement, expansion, extension, inflation, intumescence, spread

distil condense, draw out, evaporate, express, extract, press out, purify, rectify, refine, sublimate, vaporize

distillation elixir, essence, extract, quintessence, spirit

distinct **1**. apparent, black-and-white, blatant, bold, clear, clear-cut, decided, definite, evident, lucid, manifest, marked, noticeable, obvious, palpable, patent, plain, recognizable, sharp, unambiguous, unmistakable, well-defined **2**. detached, different, discrete, dissimilar, individual, separate, unconnected
▷ **Antonyms** (*sense 1*) fuzzy, indefinite, indistinct, obscure, unclear, vague (*sense 2*) common, connected, identical, indistinct, similar

distinction **1**. differentiation, discernment, discrimination, penetration, perception, separation **2**. contrast, difference, differential, division, fine line, separation **3**. characteristic, distinctiveness, feature, individuality, mark, particularity, peculiarity, quality **4**. account, celebrity, consequence, credit, eminence, excellence, fame, greatness, honour, importance, merit, name, note, prominence, quality, rank, renown, reputation, repute, superiority, worth

distinctive characteristic, different, distinguishing, extraordinary, idiosyncratic, individual, original, peculiar, singular, special, typical, uncommon, unique
▷ **Antonyms** common, ordinary, run-of-the-mill, typical

distinctly clearly, decidedly, definitely, evidently, manifestly, markedly, noticeably, obviously, palpably, patently, plainly, precisely, sharply

distinctness **1**. clarity, lucidity, obviousness, plainness, sharpness, vividness **2**. detachment, difference, discreteness, disparateness, dissimilarity, dissociation, distinctiveness, individuality, separation

distinguish **1**. ascertain, decide, determine, differentiate, discriminate, judge, tell apart, tell between, tell the difference **2.** categorize, characterize, classify, individualize, make distinctive, mark, separate, set apart, single out **3.** discern, know, make out, perceive, pick out, recognize, see, tell **4.** celebrate, dignify, honour, immortalize, make famous, signalize

distinguishable bold, clear, conspicuous, discernible, evident, manifest, noticeable, obvious, perceptible, plain, recognizable, well-marked

distinguished **1.** acclaimed, celebrated, conspicuous, eminent, famed, famous, illustrious, notable, noted, renowned, well-known **2.** conspicuous, extraordinary, marked, outstanding, signal, striking

▷ **Antonyms** common, inelegant, inferior, undistinguished, unknown

distinguishing characteristic, different, differentiating, distinctive, individualistic, marked, peculiar, typical

distort **1.** bend, buckle, contort, deform, disfigure, misshape, twist, warp, wrench, wrest **2.** bias, colour, falsify, garble, misrepresent, pervert, slant, twist

distortion **1.** bend, buckle, contortion, crookedness, deformity, malformation, twist, twistedness, warp **2.** bias, colouring, falsification, misrepresentation, perversion, slant

distract **1.** divert, draw away, sidetrack, turn aside **2.** amuse, beguile, engross, entertain, occupy **3.** agitate, bewilder, confound, confuse, derange, discompose, disconcert, disturb, harass, madden, perplex, puzzle, torment, trouble

distracted **1.** agitated, at sea, bemused, bewildered, confounded, confused, flustered, harassed, in a flap (*informal*), perplexed, puzzled, troubled **2.** at the end of one's tether, crazy, deranged, desperate, distraught, frantic, frenzied, gonzo (*slang*), grief-stricken, insane, mad, overwrought, raving, wild

distracting bewildering, bothering, confusing, disconcerting, dismaying, disturbing, off-putting (*Brit. informal*), perturbing

distraction **1.** abstraction, agitation, bewilderment, commotion, confusion, discord, disorder, disturbance **2.** amusement, beguilement, diversion, divertissement, entertainment, pastime, recreation **3.** disturbance, diversion, interference, interruption **4.** aberration, alienation, delirium, derangement, desperation, frenzy, hallucination, incoherence, insanity, mania

distrait absent, absent-minded, abstracted, distracted, forgetful, inattentive, oblivious, preoccupied, unaware

distraught agitated, anxious, at the end of one's tether, beside oneself, crazed, desperate, distracted, distressed, frantic, hysterical, mad, out of one's mind, overwrought, raving, wild, worked-up, wrought-up

distress *noun* **1.** affliction, agony, anguish, anxiety, desolation, discomfort, grief, heartache, misery, pain, sadness, sorrow, suffering, torment, torture, woe, worry, wretchedness **2.** adversity, calamity, destitution, difficulties, hardship, indigence, misfortune, need, poverty, privation, straits, trial, trouble *~verb* **3.** afflict, agonize, bother, disturb, grieve, harass, harrow, pain, perplex, sadden, torment, trouble, upset, worry, wound

distressed **1.** afflicted, agitated, anxious, distracted, distraught, saddened, tormented, troubled, upset, worried, wretched **2.** destitute, down at heel, indigent, needy, poor, poverty-stricken, straitened

distressing affecting, afflicting, distressful, disturbing, grievous, harrowing, heart-breaking, hurtful, lamentable, nerve-racking, painful, sad, upsetting, worrying

distribute **1.** administer, allocate, allot, apportion, assign, deal, dispense, dispose, divide, dole out, give, measure out, mete, share **2.** circulate, convey, deliver, hand out, pass round **3.** diffuse, disperse, disseminate, scatter, spread, strew **4.** arrange, assort, categorize, class, classify, file, group

distribution **1.** allocation, allotment, apportionment, dispensation, division, dole, partition, sharing **2.** circulation, diffusion, dispersal, dispersion, dissemination, propagation, scattering, spreading **3.** arrangement, assortment, classification, disposition, grouping, location, organization, placement **4.** *Commerce* dealing, delivery, handling, mailing, marketing, trading, transport, transportation

district area, community, locale, locality, neck of the woods (*informal*), neighbourhood, parish, quarter, region, sector, vicinity, ward

distrust **1.** *verb* be sceptical of, be suspicious of, be wary of, disbelieve, discredit, doubt, misbelieve, mistrust, question, smell a rat (*informal*), suspect, wonder about **2.** *~noun* disbelief, doubt, dubiety, lack of faith, misgiving, mistrust, qualm, question, scepticism, suspicion, wariness

▷ **Antonyms** *~verb* believe, depend, have confidence, have faith, trust *~noun* confidence, faith, reliance, trust

distrustful chary, cynical, disbelieving, distrusting, doubtful, doubting, dubious, leery (*slang*), mistrustful, sceptical, suspicious, uneasy, wary

disturb **1.** bother, butt in on, disrupt, interfere with, interrupt, intrude on,

pester, rouse, startle **2.** confuse, derange, disarrange, disorder, disorganize, muddle, unsettle **3.** agitate, alarm, annoy, confound, discompose, distract, distress, excite, fluster, harass, hassle (*informal*), perturb, ruffle, shake, trouble, unnerve, unsettle, upset, worry
▷ **Antonyms** (*senses 1 & 3*) calm, compose, lull, pacify, quiet, quieten, reassure, relax, relieve, settle, soothe

disturbance 1. agitation, annoyance, bother, confusion, derangement, disorder, distraction, hindrance, interruption, intrusion, molestation, perturbation, upset **2.** bother (*informal*), brawl, commotion, disorder, fracas, fray, hubbub, riot, ruckus (*informal*), ruction (*informal*), rumpus, shindig (*informal*), shindy (*informal*), tumult, turmoil, upheaval, uproar

disturbed 1. *Psychiatry* disordered, maladjusted, neurotic, troubled, unbalanced, upset **2.** agitated, angsty (*informal*), anxious, apprehensive, bothered, concerned, disquieted, nervous, troubled, uneasy, upset, worried
▷ **Antonyms** (*sense 1*) balanced, untroubled (*sense 2*) balanced, calm, collected, self-possessed, unfazed (*informal*), untroubled

disturbing agitating, alarming, disconcerting, discouraging, dismaying, disquieting, distressing, frightening, harrowing, perturbing, startling, threatening, troubling, unsettling, upsetting, worrying

disunion 1. abstraction, detachment, disconnection, disjunction, division, partition, separation, severance **2.** alienation, breach, disagreement, discord, dissension, dissidence, estrangement, feud, rupture, schism, split

disunite 1. detach, disband, disconnect, disengage, disjoin, disrupt, divide, part, segregate, separate, sever, split, sunder **2.** alienate, embroil, estrange, set at odds, set at variance

disunity alienation, breach, disagreement, discord, discordance, dissension, dissent, estrangement, rupture, schism, split, variance

disuse abandonment, decay, desuetude, discontinuance, idleness, neglect, non-employment, nonuse
▷ **Antonyms** application, employment, practice, service, usage, use

ditch *noun* **1.** channel, drain, dyke, furrow, gully, moat, trench, watercourse *~verb* **2.** dig, drain, excavate, gouge, trench **3.** *slang* abandon, axe (*informal*), bin (*informal*), chuck (*informal*), discard, dispose of, drop, dump (*informal*), get rid of, jettison, junk (*informal*), scrap, throw out *or* overboard

dither 1. *verb* faff about (*Brit. informal*), falter, haver, hesitate, hum and haw, oscillate, shillyshally (*informal*), swither (*Scot.*), teeter, vacillate, waver **2.** *~noun* bother, flap (*informal*), fluster, flutter, pother, stew (*informal*), tiz-woz (*informal*), tizzy (*informal*), twitter (*informal*)
▷ **Antonyms** *~verb* come to a conclusion, conclude, decide, make a decision, make up one's mind, reach *or* come to a decision, resolve, settle

diurnal circadian, daily, daytime, everyday, quotidian, regular

dive *verb* **1.** descend, dip, disappear, drop, duck, fall, go underwater, jump, leap, nose-dive, pitch, plummet, plunge, submerge, swoop *~noun* **2.** dash, header (*informal*), jump, leap, lunge, nose dive, plunge, spring **3.** *slang* honky-tonk (*U.S. slang*), joint (*slang*), sleazy bar

diverge 1. bifurcate, branch, divaricate, divide, fork, part, radiate, separate, split, spread **2.** be at odds, be at variance, conflict, differ, disagree, dissent **3.** depart, deviate, digress, meander, stray, turn aside, wander

divergence branching out, deflection, departure, deviation, difference, digression, disparity, divagation, ramification, separation, varying

divergent conflicting, deviating, different, differing, disagreeing, dissimilar, diverging, diverse, separate, variant

divers different, manifold, many, multifarious, numerous, several, some, sundry, varied, various

diverse 1. assorted, diversified, manifold, miscellaneous, of every description, several, sundry, varied, various **2.** different, differing, discrete, disparate, dissimilar, distinct, divergent, separate, unlike, varying

diversify alter, assort, branch out, change, expand, have a finger in every pie, mix, modify, spread out, transform, variegate, vary

diversion 1. alteration, change, deflection, departure, detour, deviation, digression, variation **2.** amusement, beguilement, delight, distraction, divertissement, enjoyment, entertainment, game, gratification, jollies (*slang*), pastime, play, pleasure, recreation, relaxation, sport

diversity assortment, difference, dissimilarity, distinctiveness, divergence, diverseness, diversification, heterogeneity, medley, multiplicity, range, unlikeness, variance, variegation, variety

divert 1. avert, deflect, redirect, switch, turn aside **2.** amuse, beguile, delight, entertain, gratify, recreate, regale **3.** detract, distract, draw *or* lead away from, lead astray, sidetrack

diverted 1. changed, deflected, made use of, rebudgeted, rechannelled, reclassified, redirected, taken over, turned aside **2.** amused, entertained, taken out of oneself, tickled

diverting amusing, beguiling, enjoyable, entertaining, fun, humorous, pleasant

divest 1. denude, disrobe, doff, remove, strip, take off, unclothe, undress **2.** deprive, despoil, dispossess, strip

divide 1. bisect, cleave, cut (up), detach, disconnect, part, partition, segregate, separate, sever, shear, split, subdivide, sunder **2.** allocate, allot, apportion, deal out, dispense, distribute, divvy (up) (*informal*), dole out, measure out, portion, share **3.** alienate, break up, cause to disagree, come between, disunite, estrange, set at variance *or* odds, set *or* pit against one another, sow dissension, split **4.** arrange, categorize, classify, grade, group, put in order, separate, sort

▷ **Antonyms** (*sense 1*) combine, come together, connect, join, knit, marry, splice, unite

dividend bonus, cut (*informal*), divvy (*informal*), extra, gain, plus, portion, share, surplus

divination augury, clairvoyance, divining, foretelling, fortune-telling, prediction, presage, prognostication, prophecy, soothsaying, sortilege

divine *adjective* **1.** angelic, celestial, godlike, heavenly, holy, spiritual, superhuman, supernatural **2.** consecrated, holy, religious, sacred, sanctified, spiritual **3.** beatific, blissful, exalted, mystical, rapturous, supreme, transcendent, transcendental, transmundane **4.** *informal* beautiful, excellent, glorious, marvellous, perfect, splendid, superlative, wonderful *~noun* **5.** churchman, clergyman, cleric, ecclesiastic, minister, pastor, priest, reverend *~verb* **6.** apprehend, conjecture, deduce, discern, foretell, guess, infer, intuit, perceive, prognosticate, suppose, surmise, suspect, understand **7.** *of water or minerals* dowse

diviner 1. astrologer, augur, oracle, prophet, seer, sibyl, soothsayer **2.** *of water or minerals* dowser

divinity 1. deity, divine nature, godhead, godhood, godliness, holiness, sanctity **2.** daemon, deity, genius, god, goddess, guardian spirit, spirit **3.** religion, religious studies, theology

divisible dividable, fractional, separable, splittable

division 1. bisection, cutting up, detaching, dividing, partition, separation, splitting up **2.** allotment, apportionment, distribution, sharing **3.** border, boundary, demarcation, divide, divider, dividing line, partition **4.** branch, category, class, compartment, department, group, head, part, portion, section, sector, segment **5.** breach, difference of opinion, disagreement, discord, disunion, estrangement, feud, rupture, split, variance

▷ **Antonyms** (*sense 5*) accord, agreement, concord, harmony, peace, union, unity

divisive alienating, damaging, detrimental, discordant, disruptive, estranging, inharmonious, pernicious, troublesome, unsettling

divorce 1. *noun* annulment, breach, break, decree nisi, dissolution, disunion, rupture, separation, severance, split-up **2.** *~verb* annul, disconnect, dissociate, dissolve (*marriage*), disunite, divide, part, separate, sever, split up, sunder

divulge betray, blow wide open (*slang*), communicate, confess, cough (*slang*), declare, disclose, exhibit, expose, get off one's chest (*informal*), impart, leak, let slip, make known, out (*informal*), proclaim, promulgate, publish, reveal, spill (*informal*), spill one's guts about (*slang*), tell, uncover

▷ **Antonyms** conceal, hide, keep secret

divvy 1. *noun* cut (*informal*), dividend, percentage, portion, quota, share, whack (*informal*) **2.** *~verb* (*sometimes with* **up**) apportion, cut, distribute, divide, parcel out, share (out), split

dizzy 1. faint, giddy, light-headed, off balance, reeling, shaky, staggering, swimming, vertiginous, weak at the knees, wobbly, woozy (*informal*) **2.** at sea, befuddled, bemused, bewildered, confused, dazed, dazzled, muddled **3.** lofty, steep, vertiginous **4.** *informal* capricious, fickle, flighty, foolish, frivolous, giddy, light-headed, scatterbrained, silly

do *verb* **1.** accomplish, achieve, act, carry out, complete, conclude, discharge, end, execute, perform, produce, transact, undertake, work **2.** answer, be adequate, be enough, be of use, be sufficient, cut the mustard, pass muster, satisfy, serve, suffice, suit **3.** arrange, be responsible for, fix, get ready, look after, make, make ready, organize, prepare, see to, take on **4.** decipher, decode, figure out, puzzle out, resolve, solve, work out **5.** adapt, render, translate, transpose **6.** bear oneself, behave, carry oneself, comport oneself, conduct oneself **7.** fare, get along, get on, make out, manage, proceed **8.** bring about, cause, create, effect, produce **9.** *of a play, etc.* act, give, perform, present, produce, put on **10.** *informal* cover, explore, journey through *or* around, look at, stop in, tour, travel, visit **11.** *informal* cheat, con (*informal*), cozen, deceive, defraud, diddle (*informal*), dupe, fleece, hoax, pull a fast one on (*informal*), skin (*slang*), stiff (*slang*), swindle, take (someone) for a ride (*informal*), trick *~noun* **12.** *informal* affair, event, function, gathering, occasion, party **13. do's and don'ts** *informal* code, customs, etiquette, instructions, regulations, rules, standards

do away with 1. blow away (*slang, chiefly U.S.*), bump off (*slang*), destroy, do in (*slang*), exterminate, kill, liquidate, murder, slay, take out (*slang*) **2.** abolish, axe (*informal*), chuck (*informal*), discard, discontinue, eliminate, get rid of, junk (*informal*), pull, put an end to, put paid to, remove

docile amenable, biddable, compliant, ductile, manageable, obedient, pliant, submissive, teachable (*rare*), tractable

▷ **Antonyms** difficult, intractable, obstreperous, troublesome, trying, uncooperative, unmanageable

docility amenability, biddableness, compliance, ductility, manageability, meekness, obedience, pliancy, submissiveness, tractability

dock[1] *noun* **1.** harbour, pier, quay, waterfront, wharf *~verb* **2.** anchor, berth, drop anchor, land, moor, put in, tie up **3.** *of spacecraft* couple, hook up, join, link up, rendezvous, unite

dock[2] *verb* **1.** clip, crop, curtail, cut off, cut short, diminish, lessen, shorten **2.** decrease, deduct, diminish, lessen, reduce, subtract, withhold

▷ **Antonyms** (*sense 2*) augment, boost, increase, raise

docket 1. *noun* bill, certificate, chit, chitty, counterfoil, label, receipt, tab, tag, tally, ticket, voucher **2.** *~verb* catalogue, file, index, label, mark, register, tab, tag, ticket

doctor *noun* **1.** general practitioner, G.P., medic (*informal*), medical practitioner, physician *~verb* **2.** apply medication to, give medical treatment to, treat **3.** botch, cobble, do up (*informal*), fix, mend, patch up, repair **4.** alter, change, disguise, falsify, fudge, misrepresent, pervert, tamper with **5.** add to, adulterate, cut, dilute, mix with, spike, water down

doctrinaire *adjective* **1.** biased, dogmatic, fanatical, inflexible, insistent, opinionated, rigid **2.** hypothetical, ideological, impractical, speculative, theoretical, unpragmatic, unrealistic

doctrine article, article of faith, belief, canon, concept, conviction, creed, dogma, opinion, precept, principle, teaching, tenet

document 1. *noun* certificate, instrument, legal form, paper, record, report **2.** *~verb* authenticate, back up, certify, cite, corroborate, detail, give weight to, instance, particularize, substantiate, support, validate, verify

dodder quake, quaver, quiver, shake, shamble, shiver, shuffle, stagger, sway, teeter, totter, tremble

doddering aged, decrepit, doddery, faltering, feeble, floundering, infirm, senile, shaky, shambling, tottery, trembly, unsteady, weak

doddle cakewalk (*informal*), child's play (*informal*), cinch (*slang*), easy-peasy (*slang*), money for (jam and) old rope, no sweat (*slang*), picnic (*informal*), piece of cake (*informal*), pushover (*slang*)

dodge *verb* **1.** body-swerve (*Scot.*), dart, duck, shift, sidestep, swerve, turn aside **2.** avoid, body-swerve (*Scot.*), deceive, elude, equivocate, evade, fend off, flannel (*Brit. informal*), fudge, get out of, hedge, parry, shirk, shuffle, trick *~noun* **3.** contrivance, device, feint, flannel (*Brit. informal*), machination, ploy, ruse, scheme, stratagem, subterfuge, trick, wheeze (*Brit. slang*), wile

dodger evader, shifty so-and-so, shirker, skiver, slacker, slippery one, slyboots, trickster

dodgy chancy (*informal*), dangerous, delicate, dicey (*informal, chiefly Brit.*), dicky (*Brit. informal*), difficult, problematic(al), risky, ticklish, tricky, uncertain, unreliable

doer achiever, active person, activist, bustler, dynamo, go-getter (*informal*), live wire (*slang*), organizer, powerhouse (*slang*), wheeler-dealer (*informal*)

doff 1. *of a hat* lift, raise, remove, take off, tip, touch **2.** *of clothing* cast off, discard, remove, shed, slip off, slip out of, take off, throw off, undress

do for defeat, destroy, finish (off), kill, ruin, shatter, slay, undo

dog *noun* **1.** bitch, canine, cur, hound, kuri *or* goorie (*N.Z.*), man's best friend, mongrel, mutt (*slang*), pooch (*slang*), pup, puppy, tyke **2.** *informal* beast, blackguard, cur, heel (*slang*), knave (*archaic*), scoundrel, villain **3. dog-eat-dog** cut-throat, ferocious, fierce, ruthless, vicious, with no holds barred **4. go to the dogs** *informal* degenerate, deteriorate, go down the drain, go to pot, go to ruin *~verb* **5.** haunt, hound, plague, pursue, shadow, tail (*informal*), track, trail, trouble

dogged determined, firm, immovable, indefatigable, obstinate, persevering, persistent, pertinacious, resolute, single-minded, staunch, steadfast, steady, stiff-necked, stubborn, tenacious, unflagging, unshakable, unyielding

▷ **Antonyms** doubtful, half-hearted, hesitant, irresolute, undetermined, unsteady

doggedness bulldog tenacity, determination, endurance, obstinacy, perseverance, persistence, pertinacity, relentlessness, resolution, single-mindedness, steadfastness, steadiness, stubbornness, tenaciousness, tenacity

doggo lie doggo be in hiding, go to earth, keep a low profile, keep one's head down, keep out of the public eye, stay out of sight

dogma article, article of faith, belief, credo, creed, doctrine, opinion, precept, principle, teachings, tenet

dogmatic 1. arbitrary, arrogant, assertive, categorical, dictatorial, doctrinaire, downright, emphatic, imperious, magisterial, obdurate, opinionated, overbearing, peremptory **2.** authoritative, canonical, categorical, doctrinal, ex cathedra, oracular, positive

dogmatism arbitrariness, arrogance, dictatorialness, imperiousness, opinionatedness, peremptoriness, positiveness, presumption

dogsbody drudge, general factotum, maid *or* man of all work, menial, skivvy (*chiefly Brit.*), slave

do in 1. blow away (*slang, chiefly U.S.*), butcher, dispatch, eliminate (*slang*), execute, kill, liquidate, murder, slaughter, slay, take out (*slang*) **2.** exhaust, fag (*informal*), fatigue, knacker (*slang*), shatter (*informal*), tire, wear out, weary

doing achievement, act, action, carrying out *or* through, deed, execution, exploit, handiwork, implementation, performance

doings actions, affairs, concerns, dealings, deeds, events, exploits, goings-on (*informal*), handiwork, happenings, proceedings, transactions

doldrums apathy, blues, boredom, depression, dullness, dumps (*informal*), ennui, gloom, inertia, lassitude, listlessness, malaise, stagnation, tedium, the hump (*Brit. informal*), torpor

dole *noun* **1.** allowance, alms, benefit, donation, gift, grant, gratuity, modicum, parcel, pittance, portion, quota, share **2.** allocation, allotment, apportionment, dispensation, distribution, division ~*verb* **3.** (*usually with* **out**) administer, allocate, allot, apportion, assign, deal, dispense, distribute, divide, give, hand out, mete, share

doleful cheerless, depressing, dismal, distressing, dolorous, down in the mouth, dreary, forlorn, funereal, gloomy, low, lugubrious, melancholy, mournful, painful, pitiful, rueful, sad, sombre, sorrowful, woebegone, woeful, wretched

doll up deck out, dress up (like a dog's dinner), get ready, gussy up (*slang*), preen, primp, prink, tart up (*slang*), titivate, trick out

dolorous anguished, dismal, distressing, doleful, grievous, harrowing, heart-rending, melancholy, miserable, mournful, painful, rueful, sad, sorrowful, woebegone, woeful, wretched

dolour anguish, distress, grief, heartache, heartbreak, heaviness of heart, misery, ruth (*archaic*), sadness, sorrow, suffering

dolt ass, berk (*Brit. slang*), blockhead, booby, charlie (*Brit. informal*), chump (*informal*), clot (*Brit. informal*), coot, dimwit (*informal*), dipstick (*Brit. slang*), dope (*informal*), dork (*slang*), dullard, dunce, dweeb (*U.S. slang*), fathead (*informal*), fool, fuckwit (*taboo slang*), geek (*slang*), gobshite (*Irish taboo slang*), gonzo (*slang*), idiot, ignoramus, jerk (*slang, chiefly U.S. & Canad.*), lamebrain (*informal*), nerd *or* nurd (*slang*), nitwit (*informal*), numbskull *or* numskull, numpty (*Scot. informal*), oaf, plank (*Brit. slang*), plonker (*slang*), prat (*slang*), prick (*slang*), schmuck (*U.S. slang*), simpleton, thickhead, twit (*informal, chiefly Brit.*), wally (*slang*)

doltish asinine, boneheaded (*slang*), brainless, clottish (*Brit. informal*), dense, dim-witted (*informal*), dopey (*informal*), dumb (*informal*), foolish, goofy (*informal*), halfwitted, idiotic, inane, mindless, silly, stupid

domain 1. demesne, dominion, empire, estate, kingdom, lands, policies (*Scot.*), province, realm, region, territory **2.** area, authority, bailiwick, concern, department, discipline, field, jurisdiction, orbit, power, realm, scope, speciality, sphere, sway

domestic *adjective* **1.** domiciliary, family, home, household, private **2.** domesticated, home-loving, homely, housewifely, stay-at-home **3.** domesticated, house, house-trained, pet, tame, trained **4.** indigenous, internal, native, not foreign ~*noun* **5.** char (*informal*), charwoman, daily, daily help, help, maid, servant, woman (*informal*)

domesticate 1. break, gentle, house-train, tame, train **2.** acclimatize, accustom, familiarize, habituate, naturalize

domesticated 1. *of plants or animals* broken (in), naturalized, tame, tamed **2.** *of people* domestic, home-loving, homely, house-trained (*jocular*), housewifely

▷ **Antonyms** (*sense 1*) feral, ferocious, savage, unbroken, undomesticated, untamed, wild

domesticity domestication, home life, home-lovingness, homemaking, housekeeping, housewifery

domicile abode, dwelling, habitation, home, house, legal residence, mansion, pad (*slang*), residence, residency, settlement

dominance ascendancy, authority, command, control, domination, government, mastery, paramountcy, power, rule, supremacy, sway

dominant 1. ascendant, assertive, authoritative, commanding, controlling, governing, leading, presiding, ruling, superior, supreme **2.** chief, influential, main, outstanding, paramount, predominant, pre-eminent, prevailing, prevalent, primary, principal, prominent

▷ **Antonyms** ancillary, auxiliary, inferior, junior, lesser, lower, minor, secondary, subservient, subsidiary

dominate **1.** control, direct, domineer, govern, have the upper hand over, have the whip hand over, keep under one's thumb, lead, lead by the nose (*informal*), master, monopolize, overbear, rule, rule the roost, tyrannize **2.** bestride, loom over, overlook, stand head and shoulders above, stand over, survey, tower above **3.** detract from, eclipse, outshine, overrule, overshadow, predominate, prevail over

domination **1.** ascendancy, authority, command, control, influence, mastery, power, rule, superiority, supremacy, sway **2.** despotism, dictatorship, oppression, repression, subjection, subordination, suppression, tyranny

domineer bluster, boss around *or* about (*informal*), browbeat, bully, hector, intimidate, lord (it) over, menace, overbear, ride roughshod over, swagger, threaten, tyrannize

domineering arrogant, authoritarian, autocratic, bossy (*informal*), coercive, despotic, dictatorial, high-handed, imperious, iron-handed, magisterial, masterful, oppressive, overbearing, tyrannical

▷ **Antonyms** meek, obsequious, servile, shy, submissive, subservient

dominion **1.** ascendancy, authority, command, control, domination, government, jurisdiction, mastery, power, rule, sovereignty, supremacy, sway **2.** country, domain, empire, kingdom, patch, province, realm, region, territory, turf (*U.S. slang*)

don clothe oneself in, dress in, get into, pull on, put on, slip on *or* into

donate bequeath, bestow, chip in (*informal*), contribute, gift, give, hand out, make a gift of, present, subscribe

donation alms, benefaction, boon, contribution, gift, grant, gratuity, hand-out, largesse *or* largess, offering, present, stipend, subscription

done *adjective* **1.** accomplished, completed, concluded, consummated, ended, executed, finished, in the can (*informal*), over, perfected, realized, terminated, through **2.** cooked, cooked enough, cooked sufficiently, cooked to a turn, ready **3.** depleted, exhausted, finished, spent, used up **4.** acceptable, conventional, *de rigueur,* proper **5.** *informal* cheated, conned (*informal*), duped, taken for a ride (*informal*), tricked *~interjection* **6.** agreed, it's a bargain, O.K. *or* okay (*informal*), settled, you're on (*informal*) **7. done for** *informal* beaten, broken, dashed, defeated, destroyed, doomed, finished, foiled, lost, ruined, undone, wrecked **8. done in** *or* **up** *informal* all in (*slang*), bushed (*informal*), clapped out (*Austral. & N.Z. informal*), creamcrackered (*Brit. slang*), dead (*informal*), dead beat (*informal*), dog-tired (*informal*), exhausted, fagged out (*informal*), knackered (*slang*), on one's last legs, ready to drop, tired out, worn out, worn to a frazzle (*informal*), zonked (*slang*) **9. have done with** be through with, desist, end relations with, finish with, give up, throw over, wash one's hands of

donnish bookish, erudite, formalistic, pedagogic, pedantic, precise, scholarly, scholastic

donor almsgiver, benefactor, contributor, donator, giver, grantor (*Law*), philanthropist

▷ **Antonyms** assignee, beneficiary, inheritor, legatee, payee, receiver, recipient

doom *noun* **1.** catastrophe, death, destiny, destruction, downfall, fate, fortune, lot, portion, ruin **2.** condemnation, decision, decree, judgment, sentence, verdict **3.** Armageddon, Doomsday, end of the world, Judgment Day, the Last Day, the Last Judgment, the last trump *~verb* **4.** condemn, consign, damn, decree, destine, foreordain, judge, predestine, preordain, sentence, sound the death knell, threaten

doomed bedevilled, bewitched, condemned, cursed, fated, hopeless, ill-fated, ill-omened, luckless, star-crossed

door **1.** doorway, egress, entrance, entry, exit, ingress, opening **2. lay at the door of** blame, censure, charge, hold responsible, impute to **3. out of doors** alfresco, in the air, out, outdoors, outside **4. show someone the door** ask to leave, boot out (*informal*), bounce (*slang*), eject, oust, show out

do out of balk, bilk, cheat, con (*informal*), cozen, deprive, diddle (*informal*), swindle, trick

dope *noun* **1.** drugs, narcotic, opiate **2.** berk (*Brit. slang*), blockhead, charlie (*Brit. informal*), coot, dickhead (*slang*), dimwit (*informal*), dipstick (*Brit. slang*), divvy (*Brit. slang*), dolt, dork (*slang*), dunce, dweeb (*U.S. slang*), fathead (*informal*), fool, fuckwit (*taboo slang*), geek (*slang*), gobshite (*Irish taboo slang*), gonzo (*slang*), idiot, jerk (*slang, chiefly U.S. & Canad.*), lamebrain (*informal*), nerd *or* nurd (*slang*), nitwit (*informal*), numbskull *or* numskull, numpty (*Scot. informal*), oaf, pillock (*Brit. slang*), plank (*Brit. slang*), plonker (*slang*), prat (*slang*), prick (*slang*), schmuck (*U.S. slang*), simpleton, twit (*informal, chiefly Brit.*), wally (*slang*) **3.** details, facts, gen (*Brit. informal*), info (*informal*), information, inside information, lowdown (*informal*), news, tip *~verb* **4.** anaesthetize, doctor, drug, inject, knock out, narcotize, sedate, stupefy

dopey, dopy **1.** asinine, dense, dozy (*Brit. informal*), dumb (*informal*), foolish, goofy (*informal*), idiotic, senseless, silly, simple, slow, stupid, thick **2.** dazed, drowsy, drugged, groggy (*informal*), muzzy, stupefied, woozy (*informal*)

dormant asleep, comatose, fallow, hibernating, inactive, inert, inoperative, latent, quiescent, sleeping, sluggish, slumbering, suspended, torpid
▷ **Antonyms** active, alert, alive and kicking, aroused, awake, awakened, conscious, wakeful, wide-awake

dose dosage, draught, drench, measure, portion, potion, prescription, quantity

dot *noun* **1.** atom, circle, dab, fleck, full stop, iota, jot, mark, mite, mote, point, speck, speckle, spot **2. on the dot** exactly, on the button (*informal*), on time, precisely, promptly, punctually, to the minute *~verb* **3.** dab, dabble, fleck, speckle, spot, sprinkle, stipple, stud

dotage 1. decrepitude, feebleness, imbecility, old age, second childhood, senility, weakness **2.** doting, foolish fondness, infatuation

dote on *or* **upon** admire, adore, hold dear, idolize, lavish affection on, prize, treasure

doting adoring, devoted, fond, foolish, indulgent, lovesick

dotty 1. batty (*slang*), crackpot (*informal*), crazy, doolally (*slang*), eccentric, feeble-minded, loopy (*informal*), oddball (*informal*), off one's trolley (*slang*), off-the-wall (*slang*), outré, out to lunch (*informal*), peculiar, potty (*Brit. informal*), touched, up the pole (*informal*), wacko *or* whacko (*slang*) **2.** (*with* **about**) crazy (*informal*), daft (*informal*), fond of, keen on

double *adjective* **1.** binate (*Botany*), coupled, doubled, dual, duplicate, in pairs, paired, twice, twin, twofold **2.** deceitful, dishonest, false, hypocritical, insincere, Janus-faced, knavish (*archaic*), perfidious, treacherous, two-faced, vacillating *~verb* **3.** duplicate, enlarge, fold, grow, increase, magnify, multiply, plait, repeat *~noun* **4.** clone, copy, counterpart, dead ringer (*slang*), Doppelgänger, duplicate, fellow, impersonator, lookalike, mate, replica, ringer (*slang*), spitting image (*informal*), twin **5. at** *or* **on the double** at full speed, briskly, immediately, in double-quick time, pdq (*slang*), posthaste, quickly, without delay

double back backtrack, circle, dodge, loop, retrace one's steps, return, reverse

double-cross betray, cheat, cozen, defraud, hoodwink, mislead, sell down the river (*informal*), swindle, trick, two-time (*informal*)

double-dealer betrayer, cheat, con man (*informal*), cozener, deceiver, dissembler, double-crosser (*informal*), fraud, fraudster, grifter (*slang, chiefly U.S. & Canad.*), hypocrite, rogue, snake in the grass (*informal*), swindler, traitor, two-timer (*informal*)

double-dealing 1. *noun* bad faith, betrayal, cheating, deceit, deception, dishonesty, duplicity, foul play, hypocrisy, mendacity, perfidy, treachery, trickery, two-timing (*informal*) **2.** *~adjective* cheating, crooked (*informal*), deceitful, dishonest, duplicitous, fraudulent, hypocritical, lying, perfidious, sneaky, swindling, treacherous, tricky, two-faced, two-timing (*informal*), underhanded, untrustworthy, wily

double entendre ambiguity, double meaning, innuendo, play on words, pun

doublet 1. jacket, jerkin, vest, waistcoat **2.** couple, pair, set, two

doubly again, as much again, even more, in double measure, once more, over again, twice, twofold

doubt *verb* **1.** discredit, distrust, fear, lack confidence in, misgive, mistrust, query, question, suspect *~noun* **2.** apprehension, disquiet, distrust, fear, incredulity, lack of faith, misgiving, mistrust, qualm, scepticism, suspicion *~verb* **3.** be dubious, be uncertain, demur, fluctuate, hesitate, scruple, vacillate, waver *~noun* **4.** dubiety, hesitancy, hesitation, indecision, irresolution, lack of conviction, suspense, uncertainty, vacillation **5.** ambiguity, can of worms (*informal*), confusion, difficulty, dilemma, perplexity, problem, quandary **6. no doubt** admittedly, assuredly, certainly, doubtless, doubtlessly, probably, surely
▷ **Antonyms** (*senses 1 & 3*) accept, believe, buy (*slang*), have faith in, swallow (*informal*), take on board, trust (*senses 2, 4 & 6*) belief, certainty, confidence, conviction, trust

doubter agnostic, disbeliever, doubting Thomas, questioner, sceptic, unbeliever

doubtful 1. ambiguous, debatable, dodgy (*Brit., Austral., & N.Z. informal*), dubious, equivocal, hazardous, iffy (*informal*), inconclusive, indefinite, indeterminate, inexact, obscure, precarious, problematic(al), questionable, unclear, unconfirmed, unsettled, vague **2.** distrustful, hesitating, in two minds (*informal*), irresolute, leery (*slang*), perplexed, sceptical, suspicious, tentative, uncertain, unconvinced, undecided, unresolved, unsettled, unsure, vacillating, wavering **3.** disreputable, dodgy (*Brit., Austral., & N.Z. informal*), dubious, questionable, shady (*informal*), suspect, suspicious
▷ **Antonyms** (*senses 1 & 2*) certain, decided, definite, indubitable, positive, resolute

doubtless 1. assuredly, certainly, clearly, indisputably, of course, precisely, surely, truly, undoubtedly, unquestionably, without doubt **2.** apparently, most like~

ly, ostensibly, presumably, probably, seemingly, supposedly

doughty bold, brave, courageous, daring, dauntless, fearless, gallant, gritty, hardy, heroic, intrepid, redoubtable, resolute, stouthearted, valiant, valorous

dour **1.** dismal, dreary, forbidding, gloomy, grim, morose, sour, sullen, unfriendly **2.** austere, hard, inflexible, obstinate, rigid, rigorous, severe, strict, uncompromising, unyielding

▷ **Antonyms** carefree, cheerful, cheery, chirpy (*informal*), genial, good-humoured, happy, jovial, pleasant, sunny

douse, dowse **1.** drench, duck, dunk, immerse, plunge into water, saturate, soak, souse, steep, submerge **2.** blow out, extinguish, put out, smother, snuff (out)

dovetail *verb* **1.** fit, fit together, interlock, join, link, mortise, tenon, unite **2.** accord, agree, coincide, conform, correspond, harmonize, match, tally

dowdy dingy, drab, frowzy, frumpish, frumpy, ill-dressed, old-fashioned, scrubby (*Brit. informal*), shabby, slovenly, tacky (*U.S. informal*), unfashionable

▷ **Antonyms** chic, dressy, fashionable, neat, smart, spruce, trim, well-dressed

dower **1.** dowry, inheritance, legacy, portion, provision, share **2.** endowment, faculty, gift, talent

do without abstain from, dispense with, forgo, get along without, give up, kick (*informal*), manage without

down *adjective* **1.** blue, dejected, depressed, disheartened, dismal, downcast, down in the dumps (*informal*), low, miserable, sad, sick as a parrot (*informal*), unhappy *~verb* **2.** bring down, deck (*slang*), fell, floor, knock down, overthrow, prostrate, subdue, tackle, throw, trip **3.** *informal* drain, drink (down), gulp, put away, swallow, toss off *~noun* **4.** decline, descent, drop, dropping, fall, falling, reverse **5. have a down on** *informal* be antagonistic *or* hostile to, be anti (*informal*), bear a grudge towards, be contra (*informal*), be prejudiced against, be set against, feel ill will towards, have it in for (*slang*) **6. down with** away with, get rid of, kick out (*informal*), oust, push out

down and out **1.** *adjective* derelict, destitute, dirt-poor (*informal*), flat broke (*informal*), impoverished, on one's uppers (*informal*), penniless, ruined, short, without two pennies to rub together (*informal*) **2. down-and-out** *~noun* bag lady (*chiefly U.S.*), beggar, bum (*informal*), derelict, dosser (*Brit. slang*), loser, outcast, pauper, tramp, vagabond, vagrant

downcast cheerless, choked, crestfallen, daunted, dejected, depressed, despondent, disappointed, disconsolate, discouraged, disheartened, dismal, dismayed, dispirited, down in the dumps (*informal*), miserable, sad, sick as a parrot (*informal*), unhappy

▷ **Antonyms** cheerful, cheery, chirpy (*informal*), contented, elated, genial, happy, joyful, light-hearted, optimistic

downfall **1.** breakdown, collapse, comedown, comeuppance (*slang*), debacle, descent, destruction, disgrace, fall, overthrow, ruin, undoing **2.** cloudburst, deluge, downpour, rainstorm

downgrade **1.** degrade, demote, humble, lower *or* reduce in rank, take down a peg (*informal*) **2.** decry, denigrate, detract from, disparage, run down

▷ **Antonyms** (*sense 1*) advance, ameliorate, better, elevate, enhance, improve, promote, raise, upgrade

downhearted blue, chapfallen, crestfallen, dejected, depressed, despondent, discouraged, disheartened, dismayed, dispirited, downcast, low-spirited, sad, sick as a parrot (*informal*), sorrowful, unhappy

downpour cloudburst, deluge, flood, inundation, rainstorm, torrential rain

downright **1.** absolute, arrant, blatant, categorical, clear, complete, deep-dyed (*usually derogatory*), explicit, out-and-out, outright, plain, positive, simple, thoroughgoing, total, undisguised, unequivocal, unqualified, utter **2.** blunt, candid, forthright, frank, honest, open, outspoken, plain, sincere, straightforward, straight-from-the-shoulder, upfront (*informal*)

down-to-earth common-sense, hard-headed, matter-of-fact, mundane, no-nonsense, plain-spoken, practical, realistic, sane, sensible, unsentimental

downtrodden abused, afflicted, distressed, exploited, helpless, oppressed, subjugated, subservient, tyrannized

downward *adjective* declining, descending, earthward, heading down, sliding, slipping

downy feathery, fleecy, fluffy, plumate (*Zoology, Botany*), silky, soft, velvety, woolly

dowse *see* DOUSE

doze **1.** *verb* catnap, drop off (*informal*), drowse, kip (*Brit. slang*), nap, nod, nod off (*informal*), sleep, sleep lightly, slumber, snooze (*informal*), zizz (*Brit. informal*) **2.** *~noun* catnap, forty winks (*informal*), kip (*Brit. slang*), little sleep, nap, shuteye (*slang*), siesta, snooze (*informal*), zizz (*Brit. informal*)

dozy **1.** dozing, drowsy, half asleep, nodding, sleepy **2.** *informal* daft (*informal*), goofy (*informal*), not all there, senseless, silly, simple, slow, slow-witted, stupid, witless

drab cheerless, colourless, dingy, dismal, dreary, dull, flat, gloomy, grey, lack~lustre, shabby, sombre, uninspired, vapid
▷ **Antonyms** bright, cheerful, colourful, jazzy (*informal*), vibrant, vivid

draft *verb* **1.** compose, delineate, design, draw, draw up, formulate, outline, plan, sketch *~noun* **2.** abstract, delineation, outline, plan, preliminary form, rough, sketch, version **3.** bill (*of exchange*), cheque, order, postal order

drag *verb* **1.** draw, hale, haul, lug, pull, tow, trail, tug, yank **2.** crawl, creep, go slowly, inch, limp along, shamble, shuf~fle **3.** dawdle, draggle, lag behind, linger, loiter, straggle, trail behind **4.** (*with* **on** *or* **out**) draw out, extend, keep going, lengthen, persist, prolong, protract, spin out, stretch out **5. drag one's feet** *infor~mal* block, hold back, obstruct, procras~tinate, stall *~noun* **6.** *slang* annoyance, bore, bother, nuisance, pain (*informal*), pain in the arse (*taboo informal*), pest

dragging boring, dull, going slowly, hum~drum, mind-numbing, monotonous, te~dious, tiresome, wearisome

draggle 1. befoul, bemire, besmirch, drabble, trail **2.** dally, dawdle, dilly-dally (*informal*), lag, straggle, trail be~hind

dragoon *verb* browbeat, bully, coerce, compel, constrain, drive, force, impel, intimidate, railroad (*informal*), strong-arm (*informal*)

drain *verb* **1.** bleed, draw off, dry, empty, evacuate, milk, pump off *or* out, remove, tap, withdraw **2.** consume, deplete, dis~sipate, empty, exhaust, sap, strain, tax, use up, weary **3.** discharge, effuse, ex~ude, flow out, leak, ooze, seep, trickle, well out **4.** drink up, finish, gulp down, quaff, swallow *~noun* **5.** channel, con~duit, culvert, ditch, duct, outlet, pipe, sewer, sink, trench, watercourse **6.** de~pletion, drag, exhaustion, expenditure, reduction, sap, strain, withdrawal **7. down the drain** gone, gone for good, lost, ruined, wasted

drainage bilge (water), seepage, sewage, sewerage, waste

dram drop, glass, measure, shot (*infor~mal*), slug, snifter (*informal*), snort (*slang*), tot

drama 1. dramatization, play, show, stage play, stage show, theatrical piece **2.** acting, dramatic art, dramaturgy, stagecraft, theatre, Thespian art **3.** cri~sis, dramatics, excitement, histrionics, scene, spectacle, theatrics, turmoil

dramatic 1. dramaturgic, dramaturgical, theatrical, Thespian **2.** breathtaking, climactic, electrifying, emotional, excit~ing, high-octane (*informal*), melodra~matic, sensational, shock-horror (*fa~cetious*), startling, sudden, suspenseful, tense, thrilling **3.** affecting, effective, expressive, impressive, moving, power~ful, striking, vivid
▷ **Antonyms** (*senses 2 & 3*) ordinary, run-of-the-mill, undramatic, unexcep~tional, unmemorable

dramatist dramaturge, playwright, screen-writer, scriptwriter

dramatize act, exaggerate, lay it on (thick) (*slang*), make a performance of, overdo, overstate, play-act, play to the gallery

drape 1. adorn, array, cloak, cover, fold, swathe, wrap **2.** dangle, droop, drop, hang, lean over, let fall, suspend

drastic desperate, dire, extreme, forceful, harsh, radical, severe, strong

draught 1. *of air* current, flow, influx, movement, puff **2.** dragging, drawing, haulage, pulling, traction **3.** cup, dose, drench, drink, potion, quantity

draw *verb* **1.** drag, haul, pull, tow, tug **2.** delineate, depict, design, map out, mark out, outline, paint, portray, sketch, trace **3.** deduce, derive, get, infer, make, take **4.** allure, attract, bring forth, call forth, elicit, engage, entice, evoke, in~duce, influence, invite, persuade **5.** ex~tort, extract, pull out, take out **6.** at~tenuate, elongate, extend, lengthen, stretch **7.** breathe in, drain, inhale, in~spire, puff, pull, respire, suck **8.** com~pose, draft, formulate, frame, prepare, write **9.** choose, pick, select, single out, take *~noun* **10.** *informal* attraction, en~ticement, lure, pull (*informal*) **11.** dead heat, deadlock, impasse, stalemate, tie

drawback defect, deficiency, detriment, difficulty, disadvantage, downside, fault, flaw, fly in the ointment (*infor~mal*), handicap, hazard, hindrance, hitch, impediment, imperfection, nui~sance, obstacle, snag, stumbling block, trouble
▷ **Antonyms** advantage, asset, benefit, gain, help, service, use

draw back back off, recoil, retract, re~treat, shrink, start back, withdraw

drawing cartoon, delineation, depiction, illustration, outline, picture, portrayal, representation, sketch, study

drawl *verb of speech sounds* drag out, draw out, extend, lengthen, prolong, protract

drawling dragging, drawly, droning, dull, twanging, twangy

drawn fatigued, fraught, haggard, har~assed, harrowed, pinched, sapped, strained, stressed, taut, tense, tired, worn

draw on employ, exploit, extract, fall back on, have recourse to, make use of, rely on, take from, use

draw out drag out, extend, lengthen, make longer, prolong, prolongate, pro~tract, spin out, stretch, string out
▷ **Antonyms** curtail, cut, cut short, dock,

pare down, reduce, shorten, trim, truncate

draw up 1. bring to a stop, halt, pull up, run in, stop, stop short **2.** compose, draft, formulate, frame, prepare, write out

dread 1. *verb* anticipate with horror, cringe at, fear, have cold feet (*informal*), quail, shrink from, shudder, tremble **2.** *~noun* affright, alarm, apprehension, aversion, awe, dismay, fear, fright, funk (*informal*), heebie-jeebies (*slang*), horror, terror, trepidation **3.** *~adjective* alarming, awe-inspiring, awful, dire, dreaded, dreadful, frightening, frightful, horrible, terrible, terrifying

dreadful abysmal, alarming, appalling, atrocious, awful, dire, distressing, fearful, formidable, frightful, from hell (*informal*), ghastly, godawful (*slang*), grievous, hellacious (*U.S. slang*), hideous, horrendous, horrible, monstrous, shocking, terrible, tragic, tremendous

dream *noun* **1.** daydream, delusion, fantasy, hallucination, illusion, imagination, pipe dream, reverie, speculation, trance, vagary, vision **2.** ambition, aspiration, design, desire, goal, Holy Grail (*informal*), hope, notion, thirst, wish **3.** beauty, delight, gem, joy, marvel, pleasure, treasure *~verb* **4.** build castles in the air *or* in Spain, conjure up, daydream, envisage, fancy, fantasize, hallucinate, have dreams, imagine, stargaze, think, visualize

dreamer daydreamer, Don Quixote, fantasist, fantasizer, fantast, idealist, romancer, theorizer, utopian, visionary, Walter Mitty

dreamland cloud-cuckoo-land, cloudland, dream world, fairyland, fantasy, illusion, land of dreams, land of make-believe, land of Nod, never-never land (*informal*), sleep

dreamlike chimerical, hallucinatory, illusory, phantasmagoric, phantasmagorical, surreal, trancelike, unreal, unsubstantial, visionary

dream up concoct, contrive, cook up (*informal*), create, devise, hatch, imagine, invent, spin, think up

dreamy 1. airy-fairy, dreamlike, fanciful, imaginary, impractical, quixotic, speculative, surreal, vague, visionary **2.** chimerical, dreamlike, fantastic, intangible, misty, phantasmagoric, phantasmagorical, shadowy, unreal **3.** absent, abstracted, daydreaming, faraway, in a reverie, musing, pensive, preoccupied, vague, with one's head in the clouds **4.** calming, gentle, lulling, relaxing, romantic, soothing

▷ **Antonyms** common-sense, down-to-earth, feet-on-the-ground, practical, pragmatic, realistic, unromantic

dreary 1. bleak, cheerless, comfortless, depressing, dismal, doleful, downcast, drear, forlorn, funereal, gloomy, glum, joyless, lonely, lonesome, melancholy, mournful, sad, solitary, sombre, sorrowful, wretched **2.** as dry as dust, boring, colourless, drab, dull, ho-hum (*informal*), humdrum, lifeless, mind-numbing, monotonous, routine, tedious, tiresome, uneventful, uninteresting, wearisome

▷ **Antonyms** bright, cheerful, happy, interesting, joyful

dredge up dig up, discover, drag up, draw up, fish up, raise, rake up, uncover, unearth

dreg bit, drop, mite, particle, piece, remnant, scrap

dregs 1. deposit, draff, dross, grounds, lees, residue, residuum, scourings, scum, sediment, trash, waste **2.** *slang canaille,* down-and-outs, good-for-nothings, outcasts, rabble, ragtag and bobtail, riffraff, scum

drench 1. *verb* drown, duck, flood, imbrue, inundate, saturate, soak, souse, steep, wet **2.** *~noun Veterinary* dose, physic, purge

dress *noun* **1.** costume, ensemble, frock, garment, get-up (*informal*), gown, outfit, rigout (*informal*), robe, suit **2.** apparel, attire, clothes, clothing, costume, garb, garments, gear (*informal*), guise, habiliment, raiment (*archaic or poetic*), threads (*slang*), togs, vestment *~verb* **3.** attire, change, clothe, don, garb, put on, robe, slip on *or* into **4.** adorn, apparel (*archaic*), array, bedeck, deck, decorate, drape, embellish, festoon, furbish, ornament, rig, trim **5.** adjust, align, arrange, comb (out), dispose, do (up), fit, get ready, groom, prepare, set, straighten **6.** bandage, bind up, plaster, treat

▷ **Antonyms** (*sense 3*) disrobe, divest oneself of, peel off (*slang*), shed, strip, take off one's clothes

dress down bawl out (*informal*), berate, carpet (*informal*), castigate, chew out (*U.S. & Canad. informal*), give a rocket (*Brit. & N.Z. informal*), haul over the coals, rap over the knuckles, read the riot act, rebuke, reprimand, reprove, scold, slap on the wrist, tear into (*informal*), tear (someone) off a strip (*Brit. informal*), tell off (*informal*), upbraid

dressmaker couturier, modiste, seamstress, sewing woman, tailor

dress up 1. doll up (*slang*), dress for dinner, dress formally, put on one's best bib and tucker (*informal*), put on one's glad rags (*informal*) **2.** disguise, play-act, put on fancy dress, wear a costume **3.** beautify, do oneself up, embellish, gild, improve, titivate, trick out *or* up

dressy classy (*slang*), elaborate, elegant, formal, ornate, ritzy (*slang*), smart, stylish, swish (*informal, chiefly Brit.*)

dribble 1. drip, drop, fall in drops, leak,

ooze, run, seep, trickle **2.** drip saliva, drivel, drool, slaver, slobber

driblet bit, dash, drop, droplet, fragment, gobbet, morsel, piece, scrap, speck, sprinkling

drift *verb* **1.** be carried along, coast, float, go (aimlessly), meander, stray, waft, wander **2.** accumulate, amass, bank up, drive, gather, pile up *~noun* **3.** accumulation, bank, heap, mass, mound, pile **4.** course, current, direction, flow, impulse, movement, rush, sweep, trend **5.** *figurative* aim, design, direction, gist, implication, import, intention, meaning, object, purport, scope, significance, tendency, tenor, thrust

drifter bag lady (*chiefly U.S.*), beachcomber, bum (*informal*), hobo (*U.S.*), itinerant, rolling stone, tramp, vagabond, vagrant, wanderer

drill *verb* **1.** coach, discipline, exercise, instruct, practise, rehearse, teach, train *~noun* **2.** discipline, exercise, instruction, practice, preparation, repetition, training *~verb* **3.** bore, penetrate, perforate, pierce, puncture, sink in *~noun* **4.** bit, borer, boring-tool, gimlet, rotary tool

drink *verb* **1.** absorb, drain, gulp, guzzle, imbibe, partake of, quaff, sip, suck, sup, swallow, swig (*informal*), swill, toss off, wash down, wet one's whistle (*informal*) **2.** bend the elbow (*informal*), bevvy (*dialect*), booze (*informal*), carouse, go on a binge *or* bender (*informal*), hit the bottle (*informal*), indulge, pub-crawl (*informal, chiefly Brit.*), revel, tipple, tope, wassail *~noun* **3.** beverage, liquid, potion, refreshment, thirst quencher **4.** alcohol, booze (*informal*), Dutch courage, hooch *or* hootch (*informal, chiefly U.S. & Canad.*), liquor, spirits, the bottle (*informal*) **5.** cup, draught, glass, gulp, noggin, sip, snifter (*informal*), swallow, swig (*informal*), taste, tipple **6. the drink** *informal* the briny (*informal*), the deep, the main, the ocean, the sea

drinkable drinking, fit to drink, potable, quaffable

drinker alcoholic, bibber, boozer (*informal*), dipsomaniac, drunk, drunkard, guzzler, inebriate, lush (*slang*), soak (*slang*), sot, sponge (*informal*), tippler, toper, wino (*informal*)

drink in absorb, assimilate, be all ears (*informal*), be fascinated by, be rapt, hang on (someone's) words, hang on the lips of, pay attention

drinking bout bacchanalia, bender (*informal*), bevvy (*dialect*), binge (*informal*), celebration, debauch, orgy, pub-crawl (*informal, chiefly Brit.*), spree, wassail

drink to pledge, pledge the health of, salute, toast

drip *verb* **1.** dribble, drizzle, drop, exude, filter, plop, splash, sprinkle, trickle *~noun* **2.** dribble, dripping, drop, leak, trickle **3.** *informal* milksop, mummy's boy (*informal*), namby-pamby, ninny, softie (*informal*), weakling, weed (*informal*), wet (*Brit. informal*)

drive *verb* **1.** herd, hurl, impel, propel, push, send, urge **2.** direct, go, guide, handle, manage, motor, operate, ride, steer, travel **3.** actuate, coerce, compel, constrain, dragoon, force, goad, harass, impel, motivate, oblige, overburden, overwork, press, prick, prod, prompt, railroad (*informal*), rush, spur **4.** dash, dig, hammer, plunge, ram, sink, stab, thrust *~noun* **5.** excursion, hurl (*Scot.*), jaunt, journey, outing, ride, run, spin (*informal*), trip, turn **6.** action, advance, appeal, campaign, crusade, effort, push (*informal*), surge **7.** ambition, effort, energy, enterprise, get-up-and-go (*informal*), initiative, motivation, pep, pressure, push (*informal*), vigour, zip (*informal*)

drive at aim, allude to, get at, have in mind, hint at, imply, indicate, insinuate, intend, intimate, mean, refer to, signify, suggest

drivel *verb* **1.** dribble, drool, slaver, slobber **2.** babble, blether, gab (*informal*), gas (*informal*), maunder, prate, ramble, waffle (*informal, chiefly Brit.*) *~noun* **3.** balderdash, balls (*taboo slang*), bilge (*informal*), blah (*slang*), bosh (*informal*), bull (*slang*), bullshit (*taboo slang*), bunk (*informal*), bunkum *or* buncombe (*chiefly U.S.*), cobblers (*Brit. taboo slang*), crap (*slang*), dross, eyewash (*informal*), fatuity, garbage (*informal*), gibberish, guff (*slang*), hogwash, hokum (*slang, chiefly U.S. & Canad.*), horsefeathers (*U.S. slang*), hot air (*informal*), moonshine, nonsense, pap, piffle (*informal*), poppycock (*informal*), prating, rot, rubbish, shit (*taboo slang*), stuff, tommyrot, tosh (*slang, chiefly Brit.*), trash, tripe (*informal*), twaddle, waffle (*informal, chiefly Brit.*) **4.** saliva, slaver, slobber

driveller **1.** drooler, slaverer, slobberer, splutterer, sputterer **2.** babbler, blatherskite, prater, prattler, rambler, twaddler, waffler (*informal, chiefly Brit.*), windbag (*slang*)

driving compelling, dynamic, energetic, forceful, galvanic, sweeping, vigorous, violent

drizzle **1.** *noun* fine rain, Scotch mist, smir (*Scot.*) **2.** *~verb* mizzle (*dialect*), rain, shower, spot *or* spit with rain, spray, sprinkle

droll amusing, clownish, comic, comical, diverting, eccentric, entertaining, farcical, funny, humorous, jocular, laughable, ludicrous, odd, oddball (*informal*), off-the-wall (*slang*), quaint, ridiculous, risible, waggish, whimsical

drollery absurdity, archness, buffoonery, comicality, farce, fun, humour, jocular~

ity, pleasantry, waggishness, whimsicality, wit

drone[1] *noun* couch potato (*slang*), idler, leech, loafer, lounger, parasite, scrounger (*informal*), skiver (*Brit. slang*), sluggard, sponger (*informal*)

drone[2] *verb* **1.** buzz, hum, purr, thrum, vibrate, whirr **2.** (*often with* **on**) be boring, chant, drawl, intone, prose about, speak monotonously, spout, talk interminably *~noun* **3.** buzz, hum, murmuring, purr, thrum, vibration, whirr, whirring

drool 1. (*often with* **over**) dote on, fondle, gloat over, gush, make much of, pet, rave (*informal*), slobber over, spoil **2.** dribble, drivel, salivate, slaver, slobber, water at the mouth

droop 1. bend, dangle, drop, fall down, hang (down), sag, sink **2.** decline, diminish, fade, faint, flag, languish, slump, wilt, wither **3.** despond, falter, give in, give up, give way, lose heart *or* hope

droopy 1. drooping, flabby, floppy, languid, languorous, lassitudinous, limp, pendulous, sagging, stooped, wilting **2.** blue, dejected, disheartened, dispirited, doleful, downcast, down (in the dumps) (*informal*), sick as a parrot (*informal*)

drop *noun* **1.** bead, bubble, driblet, drip, droplet, globule, pearl, tear **2.** dab, dash, mouthful, nip, pinch, shot (*informal*), sip, spot, taste, tot, trace, trickle **3.** abyss, chasm, declivity, descent, fall, plunge, precipice, slope **4.** cut, decline, decrease, deterioration, downturn, fall-off, lowering, reduction, slump *~verb* **5.** dribble, drip, fall in drops, trickle **6.** decline, depress, descend, diminish, dive, droop, fall, lower, plummet, plunge, sink, tumble **7.** abandon, axe (*informal*), cease, desert, discontinue, forsake, give up, kick (*informal*), leave, quit, relinquish, remit, terminate **8.** *informal* disown, ignore, jilt, reject, renounce, repudiate, throw over **9.** (*sometimes with* **off**) deposit, leave, let off, set down, unload

drop in (on) blow in (*informal*), call, call in, go and see, look in (on), look up, pop in (*informal*), roll up (*informal*), stop, turn up, visit

drop off 1. decline, decrease, diminish, dwindle, fall off, lessen, slacken **2.** allow to alight, deliver, leave, let off, set down **3.** *informal* catnap, doze (off), drowse, fall asleep, have forty winks (*informal*), nod (off), snooze (*informal*)

drop out abandon, back out, cop out (*slang*), fall by the wayside, forsake, give up, leave, quit, renege, stop, withdraw

dross crust, debris, dregs, impurity, lees, recrement, refuse, remains, scoria, scum, waste

drought 1. aridity, dehydration, drouth (*Scot.*), dryness, dry spell, dry weather, parchedness **2.** dearth, deficiency, insufficiency, lack, need, scarcity, shortage, want

▷ **Antonyms** (*sense 1*) deluge, downpour, flood, flow, inundation, outpouring, rush, stream, torrent (*sense 2*) abundance, profusion

drove collection, company, crowd, flock, gathering, herd, horde, mob, multitude, press, swarm, throng

drown 1. deluge, drench, engulf, flood, go down, go under, immerse, inundate, sink, submerge, swamp **2.** *figurative* deaden, engulf, muffle, obliterate, overcome, overpower, overwhelm, stifle, swallow up, wipe out

drowse 1. *verb* be drowsy, be lethargic, be sleepy, doze, drop off (*informal*), kip (*Brit. slang*), nap, nod, sleep, slumber, snooze (*informal*), zizz (*Brit. informal*) **2.** *~noun* doze, forty winks (*informal*), kip (*Brit. slang*), nap, sleep, slumber, zizz (*Brit. informal*)

drowsy 1. comatose, dazed, dopey (*slang*), dozy, drugged, half asleep, heavy, lethargic, nodding, sleepy, somnolent, tired, torpid **2.** dreamy, lulling, restful, sleepy, soothing, soporific

▷ **Antonyms** (*sense 1*) alert, awake, bright-eyed and bushy-tailed, full of beans (*informal*), lively, perky

drub 1. bang, beat, birch, cane, clobber (*slang*), club, cudgel, flog, hit, knock, lambast(e), pound, pummel, punch, strike, thrash, thump, tonk (*informal*), whack **2.** beat, best, blow out of the water (*slang*), defeat, hammer (*informal*), lick (*informal*), master, outclass, overcome, rout, run rings around (*informal*), stuff (*slang*), tank (*slang*), trounce, undo, vanquish, wipe the floor with (*informal*), worst

drubbing beating, clobbering (*slang*), defeat, flogging, hammering (*informal*), licking (*informal*), pasting (*slang*), pounding, pummelling, thrashing, trouncing, walloping (*informal*), whipping

drudge 1. *noun* dogsbody (*informal*), factotum, hack, maid *or* man of all work, menial, plodder, scullion (*archaic*), servant, skivvy (*chiefly Brit.*), slave, toiler, worker **2.** *~verb* grind (*informal*), keep one's nose to the grindstone, labour, moil (*archaic or dialect*), plod, plug away (*informal*), slave, toil, work

drudgery chore, donkey-work, fag (*informal*), grind (*informal*), hack work, hard work, labour, menial labour, skivvying (*Brit.*), slavery, slog, sweat (*informal*), sweated labour, toil

drug *noun* **1.** medicament, medication, medicine, physic, poison, remedy **2.** dope (*slang*), narcotic, opiate, stimulant *~verb* **3.** administer a drug, dope (*slang*), dose, medicate, treat **4.** anaesthetize, deaden, knock out, numb, poison, stupefy

drug addict *noun* acid head (*informal*), crack-head (*informal*), dope-fiend (*slang*), head (*informal*), hop-head (*informal*), junkie (*informal*), tripper (*informal*)

drugged bombed (*slang*), comatose, doped (*slang*), dopey (*slang*), flying (*slang*), high (*informal*), on a trip (*informal*), out of it (*slang*), out of one's mind (*slang*), out to it (*Austral. & N.Z. slang*), smashed (*slang*), spaced out (*slang*), stoned (*slang*), stupefied, turned on (*slang*), under the influence (*informal*), wasted (*slang*), wrecked (*slang*), zonked (*slang*)

drum *verb* **1.** beat, pulsate, rap, reverberate, tap, tattoo, throb **2.** (*with* **into**) din into, drive home, hammer away, harp on, instil, reiterate

drum out cashier, discharge, dismiss, disown, drive out, expel, oust, outlaw

drum up attract, bid for, canvass, obtain, petition, round up, solicit

drunk 1. *adjective* babalas (*S. African*), bacchic, bevvied (*dialect*), bladdered (*slang*), blitzed (*slang*), blotto (*slang*), bombed (*slang*), Brahms and Liszt (*slang*), canned (*slang*), drunken, flying (*slang*), fu' (*Scot.*), fuddled, half seas over (*informal*), inebriated, intoxicated, legless (*informal*), lit up (*slang*), loaded (*slang, chiefly U.S. & Canad.*), maudlin, merry (*Brit. informal*), muddled, out of it (*slang*), out to it (*Austral. & N.Z. slang*), paralytic (*informal*), pickled (*informal*), pie-eyed (*slang*), pissed (*taboo slang*), plastered (*slang*), rat-arsed (*taboo slang*), sloshed (*slang*), smashed (*slang*), soaked (*informal*), steamboats (*Scot. slang*), steaming (*slang*), stewed (*slang*), stoned (*slang*), tanked up (*slang*), tiddly (*slang, chiefly Brit.*), tight (*informal*), tipsy, tired and emotional (*euphemistic*), under the influence (*informal*), wasted (*slang*), well-oiled (*slang*), wrecked (*slang*), zonked (*slang*) **2.** *~noun* boozer (*informal*), drunkard, inebriate, lush (*slang*), soak (*slang*), sot, toper, wino (*informal*)

drunkard alcoholic, carouser, dipsomaniac, drinker, drunk, lush (*slang*), soak (*slang*), sot, tippler, toper, wino (*informal*)

drunken 1. bevvied (*dialect*), bibulous, bladdered (*slang*), blitzed (*slang*), blotto (*slang*), bombed (*slang*), boozing (*informal*), Brahms and Liszt (*slang*), drunk, flying (*slang*), (gin-)sodden, inebriate, intoxicated, legless (*informal*), lit up (*slang*), out of it (*slang*), out to it (*Austral. & N.Z. slang*), paralytic (*informal*), pissed (*taboo slang*), rat-arsed (*taboo slang*), red-nosed, smashed (*slang*), sottish, steamboats (*Scot. slang*), steaming (*slang*), tippling, toping, under the influence (*informal*), wasted (*slang*), wrecked (*slang*), zonked (*slang*) **2.** bacchanalian, bacchic, boozy (*informal*), debauched, dionysian, dissipated, orgiastic, riotous, saturnalian

drunkenness alcoholism, bibulousness, dipsomania, inebriety, insobriety, intemperance, intoxication, sottishness, tipsiness

dry *adjective* **1.** arid, barren, dehydrated, desiccated, dried up, juiceless, moistureless, parched, sapless, thirsty, torrid, waterless **2.** *figurative* boring, dreary, dull, ho-hum (*informal*), monotonous, plain, tedious, tiresome, uninteresting **3.** *figurative* cutting, deadpan, droll, keen, low-key, quietly humorous, sarcastic, sharp, sly *~verb* **4.** dehumidify, dehydrate, desiccate, drain, make dry, parch, sear **5.** (*with* **out** *or* **up**) become dry, become unproductive, harden, mummify, shrivel up, wilt, wither, wizen

▷ **Antonyms** *~adjective* (*sense 1*) damp, humid, moist, wet (*sense 2*) entertaining, interesting, lively *~verb* (*sense 4*) moisten, wet

dryness aridity, aridness, dehumidification, dehydration, drought, thirst, thirstiness

dual binary, coupled, double, duplex, duplicate, matched, paired, twin, twofold

duality biformity, dichotomy, doubleness, dualism, duplexity, polarity

dub 1. bestow, confer, confer knighthood upon, entitle, knight **2.** call, christen, denominate, designate, label, name, nickname, style, term

dubiety doubt, doubtfulness, dubiosity, incertitude, indecision, misgiving, mistrust, qualm, scepticism, uncertainty

dubious 1. doubtful, hesitant, iffy (*informal*), leery (*slang*), sceptical, uncertain, unconvinced, undecided, unsure, wavering **2.** ambiguous, debatable, dodgy (*Brit., Austral., & N.Z. informal*), doubtful, equivocal, indefinite, indeterminate, obscure, problematical, unclear, unsettled **3.** dodgy (*Brit., Austral., & N.Z. informal*), fishy (*informal*), questionable, shady (*informal*), suspect, suspicious, undependable, unreliable, untrustworthy

▷ **Antonyms** certain, definite, dependable, obvious, positive, reliable, sure, trustworthy

dubitable debatable, doubtable, doubtful, dubious, iffy (*informal*), in doubt, more than doubtful, open to doubt, problematic(al), questionable, unconvincing

duck 1. bend, bob, bow, crouch, dodge, drop, lower, stoop **2.** dip, dive, douse, dunk, immerse, plunge, souse, submerge, wet **3.** *informal* avoid, body-swerve (*Scot.*), dodge, escape, evade, shirk, shun, sidestep

duct blood vessel, canal, channel, conduit, funnel, passage, pipe, tube

ductile 1. extensible, flexible, malleable, plastic, pliable, pliant, tensile **2.** amenable, biddable, compliant, docile, manageable, tractable, yielding

dud 1. *noun* clinker (*slang, chiefly U.S.*), failure, flop (*informal*), washout (*informal*) **2.** *~adjective* broken, bust (*informal*), duff (*Brit. informal*), failed, inoperative, kaput (*informal*), not functioning, valueless, worthless

dudgeon 1. *archaic* indignation, ire, resentment, umbrage, wrath **2. in high dudgeon** angry, choked, fuming, indignant, offended, resentful, vexed

due *adjective* **1.** in arrears, outstanding, owed, owing, payable, unpaid **2.** appropriate, becoming, bounden, deserved, fit, fitting, just, justified, merited, obligatory, proper, requisite, right, rightful, suitable, well-earned **3.** adequate, ample, enough, plenty of, sufficient **4.** expected, expected to arrive, scheduled *~noun* **5.** comeuppance (*slang*), deserts, merits, prerogative, privilege, right(s) *~adverb* **6.** dead, direct, directly, exactly, straight, undeviatingly

duel *noun* **1.** affair of honour, single combat **2.** clash, competition, contest, encounter, engagement, fight, head-to-head, rivalry *~verb* **3.** clash, compete, contend, contest, fight, lock horns, rival, struggle, vie with

dues charge, charges, contribution, fee, levy, membership fee

duff bad, counterfeit, dud (*informal*), fake, false, not working, useless, worthless

duffer blunderer, booby, bungler, clod, clot (*Brit. informal*), galoot (*slang, chiefly U.S.*), lubber, lummox (*informal*), oaf

dulcet agreeable, charming, delightful, euphonious, harmonious, honeyed, mellifluent, mellifluous, melodious, musical, pleasant, pleasing, soothing, sweet

dull *adjective* **1.** braindead (*informal*), daft, dense, dim, dim-witted (*informal*), doltish, dozy (*Brit. informal*), obtuse, slow, stolid, stupid, thick, unintelligent **2.** apathetic, blank, callous, dead, empty, heavy, indifferent, insensible, insensitive, lifeless, listless, passionless, slow, sluggish, unresponsive, unsympathetic, vacuous **3.** as dry as dust, boring, commonplace, dozy, dreary, dry, flat, ho-hum (*informal*), humdrum, mind-numbing, monotonous, plain, prosaic, run-of-the-mill, tedious, tiresome, unimaginative, uninteresting, vapid **4.** blunt, blunted, dulled, edgeless, not keen, not sharp, unsharpened **5.** cloudy, dim, dismal, gloomy, leaden, opaque, overcast, turbid **6.** depressed, inactive, slack, slow, sluggish, torpid, uneventful **7.** drab, faded, feeble, indistinct, lacklustre, muffled, murky, muted, sombre, subdued, subfusc, toned-down *~verb* **8.** dampen, deject, depress, discourage, dishearten, dispirit, sadden **9.** allay, alleviate, assuage, blunt, lessen, mitigate, moderate, palliate, paralyse, relieve, soften, stupefy, take the edge off **10.** cloud, darken, dim, fade, obscure, stain, sully, tarnish

▷ **Antonyms** *~adjective* (*sense 1*) bright, clever, intelligent, sharp (*sense 2*) active, full of beans (*informal*), lively (*sense 3*) exciting, interesting (*sense 4*) sharp (*sense 5*) bright

dullard blockhead, clod, dimwit (*informal*), dolt, dope (*informal*), dunce, fathead (*informal*), gobshite (*Irish taboo slang*), lamebrain (*informal*), nitwit (*informal*), numbskull *or* numskull, numpty (*Scot. informal*), oaf

duly 1. accordingly, appropriately, befittingly, correctly, decorously, deservedly, fittingly, properly, rightfully, suitably **2.** at the proper time, on time, punctually

dumb 1. at a loss for words, inarticulate, mum, mute, silent, soundless, speechless, tongue-tied, voiceless, wordless **2.** *informal* asinine, braindead (*informal*), dense, dim-witted (*informal*), dozy (*Brit. informal*), dull, foolish, obtuse, stupid, thick, unintelligent

▷ **Antonyms** (*sense 1*) articulate (*sense 2*) bright, clever, intelligent, quick-witted, smart

dumbfound, dumfound amaze, astonish, astound, bewilder, bowl over (*informal*), confound, confuse, flabbergast (*informal*), flummox, nonplus, overwhelm, stagger, startle, stun, take aback

dumbfounded, dumfounded amazed, astonished, astounded, at sea, bewildered, bowled over (*informal*), breathless, confounded, confused, dumb, flabbergasted (*informal*), flummoxed, gobsmacked (*Brit. slang*), knocked for six (*informal*), knocked sideways (*informal*), lost for words, nonplussed, overcome, overwhelmed, speechless, staggered, startled, stunned, taken aback, thrown, thunderstruck

dummy *noun* **1.** figure, form, lay figure, manikin, mannequin, model **2.** copy, counterfeit, duplicate, imitation, sham, substitute **3.** *slang* berk (*Brit. slang*), blockhead, charlie (*Brit. informal*), coot, dickhead (*slang*), dimwit (*informal*), dipstick (*Brit. slang*), divvy (*Brit. slang*), dolt, dork (*slang*), dullard, dunce, dweeb (*U.S. slang*), fathead (*informal*), fool, fuckwit (*taboo slang*), geek (*slang*), gobshite (*Irish taboo slang*), gonzo (*slang*), jerk (*slang, chiefly U.S. & Canad.*), lamebrain (*informal*), nerd *or* nurd (*slang*), nitwit (*informal*), numbskull *or* numskull, numpty (*Scot. informal*), oaf, pillock (*Brit. slang*), plank (*Brit. slang*), plonker (*slang*), prat (*slang*), prick (*slang*), schmuck (*U.S. slang*), simpleton, wally (*slang*) ~*adjective* **4**. artificial, bogus, fake, false, imitation, mock, phoney *or* phony (*informal*), sham, simulated **5**. mock, practice, simulated, trial

dump *verb* **1**. deposit, drop, fling down, let fall, throw down **2**. coup (*Scot.*), discharge, dispose of, ditch (*slang*), empty out, get rid of, jettison, scrap, throw away *or* out, tip, unload ~*noun* **3**. junkyard, refuse heap, rubbish heap, rubbish tip, tip **4**. *informal* hole (*informal*), hovel, joint (*slang*), mess, pigsty, shack, shanty, slum

dumps blues, dejection, depression, despondency, dolour, gloom, gloominess, low spirits, melancholy, mopes, sadness, the hump (*Brit. informal*), unhappiness, woe

dumpy chubby, chunky, fubsy (*archaic or dialect*), homely, plump, podgy, pudgy, roly-poly, short, squab, squat, stout, tubby

dun *verb* beset, importune, pester, plague, press, urge

dunce ass, blockhead, bonehead (*slang*), dimwit (*informal*), dolt, donkey, duffer (*informal*), dullard, dunderhead, fathead (*informal*), goose (*informal*), halfwit, ignoramus, lamebrain (*informal*), loon (*informal*), moron, nincompoop, nitwit (*informal*), numbskull *or* numskull, oaf, simpleton, thickhead

dungeon cage, calaboose (*U.S. informal*), cell, donjon, lockup, oubliette, prison, vault

dupe *noun* **1**. fall guy (*informal*), gull, mug (*Brit. slang*), pigeon (*slang*), pushover (*slang*), sap (*slang*), simpleton, sucker (*slang*), victim **2**. cat's-paw, instrument, pawn, puppet, stooge (*slang*), tool ~*verb* **3**. bamboozle (*informal*), beguile, cheat, con (*informal*), cozen, deceive, defraud, delude, gull (*archaic*), hoax, hoodwink, humbug, kid (*informal*), outwit, overreach, pull a fast one on (*informal*), rip off (*slang*), swindle, take for a ride (*informal*), trick

duplicate **1**. *adjective* corresponding, identical, matched, matching, twin, twofold **2**. ~*noun* carbon copy, clone, copy, dead ringer (*slang*), double, facsimile, fax, likeness, lookalike, match, mate, photocopy, Photostat (*Trademark*), replica, reproduction, ringer (*slang*), twin, Xerox (*Trademark*) **3**. ~*verb* clone, copy, double, echo, fax, photocopy, Photostat (*Trademark*), reinvent the wheel, repeat, replicate, reproduce, Xerox (*Trademark*)

duplicity artifice, chicanery, deceit, deception, dishonesty, dissimulation, double-dealing, falsehood, fraud, guile, hypocrisy, perfidy

▷ **Antonyms** candour, honesty, straightforwardness

durability constancy, durableness, endurance, imperishability, lastingness, permanence, persistence

durable abiding, constant, dependable, enduring, fast, firm, fixed, hard-wearing, lasting, long-lasting, permanent, persistent, reliable, resistant, sound, stable, strong, sturdy, substantial, tough

▷ **Antonyms** breakable, brittle, delicate, fragile, impermanent, perishable, weak

duration continuance, continuation, extent, length, period, perpetuation, prolongation, span, spell, stretch, term, time

duress **1**. coercion, compulsion, constraint, pressure, threat **2**. captivity, confinement, constraint, hardship, imprisonment, incarceration, restraint

dusk **1**. dark, evening, eventide, gloaming (*Scot. or poetic*), nightfall, sundown, sunset, twilight **2**. *poetic* darkness, gloom, murk, obscurity, shade, shadowiness

▷ **Antonyms** (*sense 1*) aurora (*poetic*), cockcrow, dawn, dawning, daybreak, daylight, morning, sunlight, sunup

dusky **1**. dark, dark-complexioned, dark-hued, sable, swarthy **2**. caliginous (*archaic*), cloudy, crepuscular, darkish, dim, gloomy, murky, obscure, overcast, shadowy, shady, tenebrous, twilight, twilit, veiled

dust *noun* **1**. fine fragments, grime, grit, particles, powder, powdery dirt **2**. dirt, earth, ground, soil **3**. *informal* commotion, disturbance, fuss, racket, row **4**. **bite the dust** *informal* die, drop dead, expire, fall in battle, pass away, perish **5**. **lick the dust** *informal* be servile, bootlick (*informal*), demean oneself, grovel, kowtow, toady **6**. **throw dust in the eyes of** con (*slang*), confuse, deceive, fool, have (someone) on, hoodwink, mislead, take in (*informal*) ~*verb* **7**. cover, dredge, powder, scatter, sift, spray, spread, sprinkle

dust-up argument, brush, conflict, encounter, fight, fracas, punch-up (*Brit. informal*), quarrel, scrap (*informal*), set-to (*informal*), shindig (*informal*), skirmish, tussle

dusty **1**. dirty, grubby, sooty, unclean, undusted, unswept **2**. chalky, crumbly, friable, granular, powdery, sandy

dutiful compliant, conscientious, deferential, devoted, docile, duteous (*archaic*), filial, obedient, punctilious, respectful, reverential, submissive

▷ **Antonyms** disobedient, disrespectful, insubordinate, remiss, uncaring

duty **1**. assignment, business, calling, charge, engagement, function, mission, obligation, office, onus, pigeon (*informal*), province, responsibility, role, service, task, work **2**. allegiance, deference, loyalty, obedience, respect, reverence **3**.

customs, due, excise, impost, levy, tariff, tax, toll **4. do duty for** stand in, substitute, take the place of **5. be the duty of** behove (*archaic*), be incumbent upon, belong to, be (someone's) pigeon (*Brit. informal*), be up to (*informal*), devolve upon, pertain to, rest with **6. off duty** at leisure, free, off, off work, on holiday **7. on duty** at work, busy, engaged, on active service

dwarf *noun* **1.** bantam, homunculus, hop-o'-my-thumb, Lilliputian, manikin, midget, munchkin (*informal, chiefly U.S.*), pygmy *or* pigmy, Tom Thumb **2.** gnome, goblin *~adjective* **3.** baby, bonsai, diminutive, dwarfed, Lilliputian, miniature, petite, pint-sized, pocket, small, teensy-weensy, teeny-weeny, tiny, undersized *~verb* **4.** dim, diminish, dominate, minimize, overshadow, tower above *or* over **5.** check, cultivate by bonsai, lower, retard, stunt

dwarfish diminutive, dwarfed, knee high to a grasshopper (*informal*), low, miniature, minute, pint-size (*informal*), pygmaean, pygmy *or* pigmy, runtish, runty, short, small, stunted, teensy-weensy, teeny-weeny, tiny, undersized

dwell abide, establish oneself, hang out (*informal*), inhabit, live, lodge, quarter, remain, reside, rest, settle, sojourn, stay, stop

dwelling abode, domicile, dwelling house, establishment, habitation, home, house, lodging, pad (*slang*), quarters, residence

dwell on *or* **upon** be engrossed in, continue, elaborate, emphasize, expatiate, harp on, linger over, tarry over

dwindle abate, contract, decay, decline, decrease, die away, die down, die out, diminish, ebb, fade, fall, grow less, lessen, peter out, pine, shrink, shrivel, sink, subside, taper off, wane, waste away, weaken, wither

▷ **Antonyms** advance, amplify, develop, dilate, enlarge, escalate, expand, grow, heighten, increase, magnify, multiply, swell, wax

dye 1. *noun* colorant, colour, colouring, pigment, stain, tinge, tint **2.** *~verb* colour, pigment, stain, tincture, tinge, tint

dyed-in-the-wool complete, confirmed, deep-dyed (*usually derogatory*), deep-rooted, die-hard, entrenched, established, inveterate, through-and-through

dying at death's door, ebbing, expiring, fading, failing, final, going, *in extremis,* moribund, mortal, not long for this world, passing, perishing, sinking

dynamic active, alive and kicking, driving, electric, energetic, forceful, full of beans (*informal*), go-ahead, go-getting (*informal*), high-octane (*informal*), high-powered, lively, magnetic, powerful, vigorous, vital, zippy (*informal*)

▷ **Antonyms** apathetic, couldn't-care-less (*informal*), impassive, inactive, listless, sluggish, torpid, undynamic, unenergetic

dynamism brio, drive, energy, enterprise, forcefulness, get-up-and-go (*informal*), go (*informal*), initiative, liveliness, pep, push (*informal*), vigour, zap (*slang*), zip (*informal*)

dynasty ascendancy, dominion, empire, government, house, regime, rule, sovereignty, sway

E, e

each 1. *adjective* every 2. *~pronoun* each and every one, each one, every one, one and all 3. *~adverb* apiece, for each, from each, individually, per capita, per head, per person, respectively, singly, to each

eager agog, anxious, ardent, athirst, avid, bright-eyed and bushy-tailed (*informal*), earnest, enthusiastic, fervent, fervid, greedy, hot, hungry, impatient, intent, keen, keen as mustard, longing, raring, up for it (*informal*), vehement, yearning, zealous

▷ **Antonyms** apathetic, blasé, impassive, indifferent, lazy, nonchalant, opposed, unambitious, unconcerned, unenthusiastic, unimpressed, uninterested

eagerness ardour, avidity, earnestness, enthusiasm, fervour, greediness, heartiness, hunger, impatience, impetuosity, intentness, keenness, longing, thirst, vehemence, yearning, zeal

ear *figurative* 1. attention, consideration, hearing, heed, notice, regard 2. appreciation, discrimination, musical perception, sensitivity, taste

early *adjective* 1. advanced, forward, premature, untimely 2. primeval, primitive, primordial, undeveloped, young *~adverb* 3. ahead of time, beforehand, betimes (*archaic*), in advance, in good time, prematurely, too soon

▷ **Antonyms** (*sense 2*) developed, mature, ripe, seasoned (*sense 3*) behind, belated, late, overdue, tardy

earmark 1. *verb* allocate, designate, flag, keep back, label, mark out, reserve, set aside, tag 2. *~noun* attribute, characteristic, feature, hallmark, label, quality, signature, stamp, tag, token, trademark, trait

earn 1. bring in, collect, draw, gain, get, gross, make, net, obtain, procure, realize, reap, receive 2. acquire, attain, be entitled to, be worthy of, deserve, merit, rate, warrant, win

earnest *adjective* 1. close, constant, determined, firm, fixed, grave, intent, resolute, resolved, serious, sincere, solemn, stable, staid, steady, thoughtful 2. ablaze, ardent, devoted, eager, enthusiastic, fervent, fervid, heartfelt, impassioned, keen, keen as mustard, passionate, purposeful, urgent, vehement, warm, zealous *~noun* 3. determination, reality, resolution, seriousness, sincerity, truth 4. assurance, deposit, down payment, earnest money (*Law*), foretaste, guarantee, pledge, promise, security, token

▷ **Antonyms** *~adjective* apathetic, couldn't-care-less, flippant, frivolous, half-hearted, indifferent, insincere, light, slack, trifling, unconcerned, unenthusiastic, uninterested, unstable *~noun* (*sense 3*) apathy, indifference, unconcern

earnestness ardour, determination, devotion, eagerness, enthusiasm, fervour, gravity, intentness, keenness, passion, purposefulness, resolution, seriousness, sincerity, urgency, vehemence, warmth, zeal

earnings emolument, gain, income, pay, proceeds, profits, receipts, remuneration, return, reward, salary, stipend, takings, wages

earth 1. globe, orb, planet, sphere, terrestrial sphere, world 2. clay, clod, dirt, ground, land, loam, mould, sod, soil, topsoil, turf

earthenware ceramics, crockery, crocks, pots, pottery, terracotta

earthiness bawdiness, coarseness, crudeness, crudity, lustiness, naturalness, ribaldry, robustness, uninhibitedness

earthly 1. mundane, sublunary, tellurian, telluric, terrene, terrestrial, worldly 2. human, material, mortal, non-spiritual, profane, secular, temporal, worldly 3. base, carnal, fleshly, gross, low, materialistic, physical, sensual, sordid, vile 4. *informal* conceivable, feasible, imaginable, likely, possible, practical

▷ **Antonyms** (*senses 1, 2 & 3*) ethereal, heavenly, immaterial, immortal, otherworldly, spiritual, supernatural, unearthly

earthy bawdy, coarse, crude, down-to-earth, homely, lusty, natural, raunchy (*slang*), ribald, robust, rough, simple, uninhibited, unrefined, unsophisticated

ease *noun* 1. affluence, calmness, comfort, content, contentment, enjoyment, happiness, leisure, peace, peace of mind, quiet, quietude, relaxation, repose, rest, restfulness, serenity, tranquillity 2. easiness, effortlessness, facility, readiness, simplicity 3. flexibility, freedom, informality, liberty, naturalness, unaffectedness, unconstraint, unreservedness **4.** aplomb, composure, insouciance, nonchalance, poise, relaxedness *~verb* **5.** abate, allay, alleviate, appease, assuage, calm, comfort, disburden, lessen, lighten, mitigate, moderate, mollify, pacify, palliate, quiet, relax, relent, relieve, slacken, soothe, still, tranquillize **6.** aid, assist, expedite, facilitate, forward, further, give a leg up (*informal*), lessen the labour of, make easier, simplify, smooth, speed up **7.** edge, guide, inch, manoeuvre, move carefully, slide, slip, squeeze, steer

▷ **Antonyms** *~noun* (*sense 1*) concern, difficulty, discomfort, hardship, irritation, pain, poverty, tribulation (*sense 2*) arduousness, awkwardness, clumsiness, difficulty, effort, exertion, toil (*sense 3*) awkwardness, clumsiness, constraint, formality (*sense 4*) agitation, awkwardness, clumsiness, discomfort, disturbance, tension *~verb* (*senses 5 & 6*) aggravate, discomfort, exacerbate, hinder, irritate, make nervous, make uneasy, retard, worsen

easeful calm, comfortable, easy, peaceful, quiet, reposeful, restful, soothing, tranquil

easily 1. comfortably, effortlessly, facilely, like a knife through butter, readily, simply, smoothly, standing on one's head, with ease, with one hand tied behind one's back, with one's eyes closed *or* shut, without difficulty, without trouble **2.** absolutely, beyond question, by far, certainly, clearly, definitely, doubtlessly, far and away, indisputably, indubitably, plainly, surely, undeniably, undoubtedly, unequivocally, unquestionably, without a doubt **3.** almost certainly, probably, well

easy 1. a bed of roses, a piece of cake (*informal*), a piece of piss (*taboo slang*), a pushover (*slang*), child's play (*informal*), clear, easy-peasy (*slang*), effortless, facile, light, no bother, not difficult, no trouble, painless, plain sailing, simple, smooth, straightforward, uncomplicated, undemanding **2.** calm, carefree, comfortable, contented, cushy (*informal*), easeful, leisurely, peaceful, pleasant, quiet, relaxed, satisfied, serene, tranquil, undisturbed, untroubled, unworried, well-to-do **3.** flexible, indulgent, lenient, liberal, light, mild, permissive, tolerant, unburdensome, unoppressive **4.** affable, casual, easy-going, friendly, gentle, graceful, gracious, informal, laid-back (*informal*), mild, natural, open, pleasant, relaxed, smooth, tolerant, unaffected, unceremonious, unconstrained, undemanding, unforced, unpretentious **5.** accommodating, amenable, biddable, compliant, docile, gullible, manageable, pliant, soft, submissive, suggestible, susceptible, tractable, trusting, yielding **6.** comfortable, gentle, leisurely, light, mild, moderate, temperate, undemanding, unexacting, unhurried

▷ **Antonyms** (*sense 1*) arduous, complex, demanding, difficult, exacting, exhausting, formidable, hard, impossible, onerous, stiff (*sense 2*) difficult, insecure, stressful, uncomfortable, worried (*sense 3*) demanding, dictatorial, difficult, exacting, hard, harsh, inflexible, intolerant, rigid, stern, strict, unyielding (*sense 4*) affected, anxious, forced, formal, self-conscious, stiff, uncomfortable, unnatural, worried (*sense 5*) difficult, impossible, unyielding (*sense 6*) arduous, demanding, difficult, exacting

easy-going amenable, calm, carefree, casual, complacent, easy, easy-oasy (*slang*), even-tempered, flexible, happy-go-lucky, indulgent, insouciant, laid-back (*informal*), lenient, liberal, mild, moderate, nonchalant, permissive, placid, relaxed, serene, tolerant, unconcerned, uncritical, undemanding, unhurried

▷ **Antonyms** anxious, edgy, fussy, hung-up (*slang*), intolerant, irritated, nervy (*Brit. informal*), neurotic, on edge, strict, tense, uptight (*informal*)

eat 1. chew, consume, devour, gobble, ingest, munch, scoff (*slang*), swallow **2.** break bread, chow down (*slang*), dine, feed, have a meal, take food, take nourishment **3.** corrode, crumble, decay, dissolve, erode, rot, waste away, wear away **4. eat one's words** abjure, recant, rescind, retract, take (statement) back

eatable comestible (*rare*), digestible, edible, esculent, fit to eat, good, harmless, palatable, wholesome

eavesdrop bug (*informal*), earwig (*informal*), listen in, monitor, overhear, snoop (*informal*), spy, tap

eavesdropper listener, monitor, snooper (*informal*), spy

ebb *verb* **1.** abate, fall away, fall back, flow back, go out, recede, retire, retreat, retrocede, sink, subside, wane, withdraw *~noun* **2.** ebb tide, going out, low tide, low water, reflux, regression, retreat, retrocession, subsidence, wane, waning, withdrawal *~verb* **3.** decay, decline, decrease, degenerate, deteriorate, diminish, drop, dwindle, fade away, fall away, flag, lessen, peter out, shrink, sink, slacken, weaken *~noun* **4.** decay, decline, decrease, degeneration, deterioration, diminution, drop, dwindling, fading away, flagging, lessening, petering out, shrinkage, sinking, slackening, weakening

ebullience 1. brio, buoyancy, effervescence, effusiveness, elation, enthusiasm, excitement, exhilaration, exuberance, high spirits, vivacity, zest **2.** boiling, bubbling, ebullition, effervescence, ferment, fermentation, foam, froth, frothing, seething

ebullient **1.** buoyant, effervescent, effusive, elated, enthusiastic, excited, exhilarated, exuberant, frothy, gushing, in high spirits, irrepressible, vivacious, zestful **2.** boiling, bubbling, effervescent, foaming, frothing, seething

ebullition **1.** boiling, bubbling, effervescence, fermentation, frothing, outburst, overflow, seething **2.** access, fit, outbreak, outburst, overflow, paroxysm, spasm, storm, throe (*rare*)

eccentric **1.** *adjective* aberrant, abnormal, anomalous, bizarre, capricious, erratic, freakish, idiosyncratic, irregular, odd, oddball (*informal*), off the rails, off-the-wall (*slang*), outlandish, outré, peculiar, queer (*informal*), quirky, rum (*Brit. slang*), singular, strange, uncommon, unconventional, wacko (*slang*), weird, whimsical **2.** *~noun* card (*informal*), case (*informal*), character (*informal*), crank (*informal*), freak (*informal*), kook (*U.S. & Canad. informal*), loose cannon, nonconformist, nut (*slang*), oddball (*informal*), odd fish (*informal*), oddity, queer fish (*Brit. informal*), rum customer (*Brit. slang*), screwball (*slang, chiefly U.S. & Canad.*), wacko (*slang*), weirdo *or* weirdie (*informal*)

▷ **Antonyms** *~adjective* average, conventional, normal, ordinary, regular, run-of-the-mill, straightforward, typical

eccentricity aberration, abnormality, anomaly, bizarreness, caprice, capriciousness, foible, freakishness, idiosyncrasy, irregularity, nonconformity, oddity, oddness, outlandishness, peculiarity, queerness (*informal*), quirk, singularity, strangeness, unconventionality, waywardness, weirdness, whimsicality, whimsicalness

ecclesiastic **1.** *noun* churchman, clergyman, cleric, divine, holy man, man of the cloth, minister, parson, pastor, priest **2.** *~adjective also* **ecclesiastical** church, churchly, clerical, divine, holy, pastoral, priestly, religious, spiritual

echelon degree, grade, level, office, place, position, rank, tier

echo *verb* **1.** repeat, resound, reverberate **2.** ape, copy, imitate, mirror, parallel, parrot, recall, reflect, reiterate, reproduce, resemble, ring, second *~noun* **3.** answer, repetition, reverberation **4.** copy, imitation, mirror image, parallel, reflection, reiteration, reproduction, ringing **5.** allusion, evocation, hint, intimation, memory, reminder, suggestion, trace **6.** (*often plural*) aftereffect, aftermath, consequence, repercussion

echoic imitative, onomatopoeic

éclat **1.** brilliance, effect, success **2.** display, lustre, ostentation, pomp, show, showmanship, splendour **3.** celebrity, distinction, fame, glory, renown **4.** acclaim, acclamation, applause, approval, plaudits

eclectic all-embracing, broad, catholic, comprehensive, dilettantish, diverse, diversified, general, heterogeneous, liberal, manifold, many-sided, multifarious, selective, varied, wide-ranging

eclipse *verb* **1.** blot out, cloud, darken, dim, extinguish, obscure, overshadow, shroud, veil **2.** exceed, excel, outdo, outshine, put in the shade (*informal*), surpass, transcend *~noun* **3.** darkening, dimming, extinction, obscuration, occultation, shading **4.** decline, diminution, failure, fall, loss

eclogue bucolic, georgic, idyll, pastoral

economic **1.** business, commercial, financial, industrial, mercantile, trade **2.** money-making, productive, profitable, profit-making, remunerative, solvent, viable **3.** bread-and-butter (*informal*), budgetary, financial, fiscal, material, monetary, pecuniary **4.** *informal also* **economical** cheap, fair, inexpensive, low, low-priced, modest, reasonable

economical **1.** cost-effective, efficient, money-saving, neat, sparing, time-saving, unwasteful, work-saving **2.** careful, economizing, frugal, prudent, saving, scrimping, sparing, thrifty **3.** *also* **economic** cheap, fair, inexpensive, low, low-priced, modest, reasonable

▷ **Antonyms** (*sense 1*) loss-making, uneconomical, unprofitable, wasteful (*sense 2*) extravagant, generous, imprudent, lavish, profligate, spendthrift, uneconomical, unthrifty, wasteful (*sense 3*) exorbitant, expensive, unprofitable

economize be economical, be frugal, be on a shoestring, be sparing, cut back, draw in one's horns, husband, pull in one's horns, retrench, save, scrimp, tighten one's belt

▷ **Antonyms** be extravagant, push the boat out (*informal*), spend, splurge, squander

economy frugality, husbandry, parsimony, providence, prudence, restraint, retrenchment, saving, sparingness, thrift, thriftiness

ecstasy bliss, delight, elation, enthusiasm, euphoria, exaltation, fervour, frenzy, joy, rapture, ravishment, rhapsody, seventh heaven, trance, transport

▷ **Antonyms** affliction, agony, anguish, distress, hell, misery, pain, suffering, torment, torture

ecstatic blissed out, blissful, cock-a-hoop, delirious, elated, enraptured, enthusiastic, entranced, euphoric, fervent, floating on air, frenzied, in exaltation, in seventh heaven, in transports of delight, joyful, joyous, on cloud nine (*informal*), overjoyed, over the moon (*informal*), rapturous, rhapsodic, sent, transported, walking on air

ecumenical catholic, general, unifying, universal, worldwide

eddy 1. *noun* counter-current, counterflow, swirl, tideway, undertow, vortex, whirlpool 2. *~verb* swirl, whirl

edge *noun* 1. border, bound, boundary, brim, brink, contour, flange, fringe, limit, line, lip, margin, outline, perimeter, periphery, rim, side, threshold, verge 2. acuteness, animation, bite, effectiveness, force, incisiveness, interest, keenness, point, pungency, sharpness, sting, urgency, zest 3. advantage, ascendancy, dominance, lead, superiority, upper hand 4. **on edge** apprehensive, eager, edgy, excited, ill at ease, impatient, irritable, keyed up, nervous, on tenterhooks, tense, tetchy, twitchy (*informal*), uptight (*informal*), wired (*slang*) *~verb* 5. bind, border, fringe, hem, rim, shape, trim 6. creep, ease, inch, sidle, steal, work, worm 7. hone, sharpen, strop, whet

edgy anxious, ill at ease, irascible, irritable, keyed up, nervous, nervy (*Brit. informal*), neurotic, on edge, on pins and needles, on tenterhooks, restive, tense, tetchy, touchy, twitchy (*informal*), uptight (*informal*), wired (*slang*)

edible comestible (*rare*), digestible, eatable, esculent, fit to eat, good, harmless, palatable, wholesome

▷ **Antonyms** baneful, harmful, indigestible, inedible, noxious, pernicious, poisonous, uneatable

edict act, canon, command, decree, demand, dictate, dictum, enactment, fiat, injunction, law, mandate, manifesto, order, ordinance, proclamation, pronouncement, pronunciamento, regulation, ruling, statute, ukase (*rare*)

edification education, elevation, enlightenment, guidance, improvement, information, instruction, nurture, schooling, teaching, tuition, uplifting

edifice building, construction, erection, fabric (*rare*), habitation, house, pile, structure

edify educate, elevate, enlighten, guide, improve, inform, instruct, nurture, school, teach, uplift

edit 1. adapt, annotate, censor, check, condense, correct, emend, polish, redact, rephrase, revise, rewrite 2. assemble, compose, put together, rearrange, reorder, select

edition copy, impression, issue, number, printing, programme (*TV, Radio*), version, volume

educate civilize, coach, cultivate, develop, discipline, drill, edify, enlighten, exercise, foster, improve, indoctrinate, inform, instruct, mature, rear, school, teach, train, tutor

educated 1. coached, informed, instructed, nurtured, schooled, taught, tutored 2. civilized, cultivated, cultured, enlightened, experienced, informed, knowledgeable, learned, lettered, literary, polished, refined, sophisticated, tasteful

▷ **Antonyms** (*sense 1*) ignorant, illiterate, uneducated, unlettered, unread, unschooled, untaught (*sense 2*) benighted, lowbrow, philistine, uncultivated, uncultured, uneducated

education breeding, civilization, coaching, cultivation, culture, development, discipline, drilling, edification, enlightenment, erudition, improvement, indoctrination, instruction, knowledge, nurture, scholarship, schooling, teaching, training, tuition, tutoring

educational cultural, didactic, edifying, educative, enlightening, heuristic, improving, informative, instructive

educative didactic, edifying, educational, enlightening, heuristic, improving, informative, instructive

educator coach, edifier, educationalist *or* educationist, instructor, pedagogue, schoolmaster, schoolmistress, schoolteacher, teacher, trainer, tutor

educe 1. come out, develop, evolve 2. bring forth, bring out, derive, draw out, elicit, evoke, extract 3. *Logic* conclude, deduce, infer

eerie awesome, creepy (*informal*), eldritch (*poetic*), fearful, frightening, ghostly, mysterious, scary (*informal*), spectral, spooky (*informal*), strange, uncanny, unearthly, uneasy, weird

efface 1. annihilate, blot out, cancel, cross out, delete, destroy, dim, eradicate, erase, excise, expunge, extirpate, obliterate, raze, rub out, wipe out 2. *of oneself* be bashful, be diffident, be modest, be retiring, be timid, be unassertive, humble, lower, make inconspicuous, withdraw

effect *noun* 1. aftermath, conclusion, consequence, end result, event, fruit, issue, outcome, result, upshot 2. clout (*informal*), effectiveness, efficacy, efficiency, fact, force, influence, power, reality, strength, use, validity, vigour, weight 3. drift, essence, impact, import, impression, meaning, purport, purpose, sense, significance, tenor 4. action, enforcement, execution, force, implementation, operation 5. **in effect** actually, effectively, essentially, for practical purposes, in actuality, in fact, in reality, in truth, really, to all intents and purposes, virtually 6. **take effect** become operative, begin, come into force, produce results, work *~verb* 7. accomplish, achieve, actuate, bring about, carry out, cause, complete, consummate, create, effectuate, execute, fulfil, give rise to, initiate, make, perform, produce

effective 1. able, active, adequate, capable, competent, effectual, efficacious, efficient, energetic, operative, productive, serviceable, useful **2.** cogent, compelling, convincing, emphatic, forceful, forcible, impressive, moving, persuasive, potent, powerful, striking, telling **3.** active, actual, current, in effect, in execution, in force, in operation, operative, real

▷ **Antonyms** feeble, futile, inactive, inadequate, incompetent, ineffective, ineffectual, inefficient, inoperative, insufficient, otiose, pathetic, powerless, tame, unimpressive, unproductive, useless, vain, weak, worthless

effectiveness bottom, capability, clout (*informal*), cogency, effect, efficacy, efficiency, force, influence, potency, power, strength, success, use, validity, vigour, weight

effects belongings, chattels, furniture, gear, goods, movables, paraphernalia, possessions, property, things, trappings

effectual 1. capable, effective, efficacious, efficient, forcible, influential, potent, powerful, productive, serviceable, successful, telling, useful **2.** authoritative, binding, in force, lawful, legal, licit (*rare*), sound, valid

effectuate accomplish, achieve, bring about, carry out *or* through, cause, complete, create, do, effect, execute, fulfil, make, perform, procure, produce

effeminacy delicacy, femininity, softness, tenderness, unmanliness, weakness, womanishness, womanliness

effeminate camp (*informal*), delicate, feminine, poofy (*slang*), sissy, soft, tender, unmanly, weak, wimpish *or* wimpy (*informal*), womanish, womanlike, womanly

▷ **Antonyms** butch (*slang*), he-man (*informal*), macho, manly, virile

effervesce bubble, ferment, fizz, foam, froth, sparkle

effervescence 1. bubbling, ferment, fermentation, fizz, foam, foaming, froth, frothing, sparkle **2.** animation, brio, buoyancy, ebullience, enthusiasm, excitedness, excitement, exhilaration, exuberance, gaiety, high spirits, liveliness, pizzazz *or* pizazz (*informal*), vim (*slang*), vitality, vivacity, zing (*informal*)

effervescent 1. bubbling, bubbly, carbonated, fermenting, fizzing, fizzy, foaming, foamy, frothing, frothy, sparkling **2.** animated, bubbly, buoyant, ebullient, enthusiastic, excited, exhilarated, exuberant, gay, in high spirits, irrepressible, lively, merry, vital, vivacious, zingy (*informal*)

▷ **Antonyms** (*sense 1*) flat, flavourless, insipid, stale, watery, weak (*sense 2*) boring, dull, flat, insipid, jejune, lacklustre, lifeless, spiritless, stale, unexciting, vapid

effete 1. corrupt, debased, decadent, decayed, decrepit, degenerate, dissipated, enervated, enfeebled, feeble, ineffectual, overrefined, spoiled, weak **2.** burnt out, drained, enervated, exhausted, played out, spent, used up, wasted, worn out **3.** barren, fruitless, infecund, infertile, sterile, unfruitful, unproductive, unprolific

efficacious active, adequate, capable, competent, effective, effectual, efficient, energetic, operative, potent, powerful, productive, serviceable, successful, useful

▷ **Antonyms** abortive, futile, ineffective, ineffectual, inefficacious, unavailing, unproductive, unsuccessful, useless

efficacy ability, capability, competence, effect, effectiveness, efficaciousness, efficiency, energy, force, influence, potency, power, strength, success, use, vigour, virtue, weight

efficiency ability, adeptness, capability, competence, economy, effectiveness, efficacy, power, productivity, proficiency, readiness, skilfulness, skill

efficient able, adept, businesslike, capable, competent, economic, effective, effectual, organized, powerful, productive, proficient, ready, skilful, well-organized, workmanlike

▷ **Antonyms** cowboy (*informal*), disorganized, incompetent, ineffectual, inefficient, inept, slipshod, sloppy, unbusinesslike, unproductive, wasteful

effigy dummy, figure, guy, icon, idol, image, likeness, picture, portrait, representation, statue

effluence discharge, effluent, effluvium, efflux, emanation, emission, exhalation, flow, issue, outflow, outpouring, secretion

effluent *noun* **1.** effluvium, pollutant, sewage, waste **2.** discharge, effluence, efflux, emanation, emission, exhalation, flow, issue, outflow, outpouring *~adjective* **3.** discharged, emanating, emitted, outflowing

effluvium exhalation, exhaust, fumes, malodour, mephitis, miasma, niff (*Brit. slang*), odour, pong (*Brit. informal*), reek, smell, stench, stink

effort 1. application, blood, sweat, and tears (*informal*), elbow grease (*facetious*), endeavour, energy, exertion, force, labour, pains, power, strain, stress, stretch, striving, struggle, toil, travail (*literary*), trouble, work **2.** attempt, endeavour, essay, go (*informal*), shot (*informal*), stab (*informal*), try **3.** accomplishment, achievement, act, creation, deed, feat, job, product, production

effortless easy, easy-peasy (*slang*), facile, painless, plain sailing, simple, smooth, uncomplicated, undemanding, untroublesome

▷ **Antonyms** demanding, difficult, formidable, hard, onerous, uphill

effrontery arrogance, assurance, audacity, boldness, brashness, brass (*informal*), brass neck (*Brit. informal*), brazenness, cheek (*informal*), cheekiness, chutzpah (*U.S. & Canad. informal*), disrespect, face (*informal*), front, gall (*informal*), impertinence, impudence, incivility, insolence, neck (*informal*), nerve, presumption, rudeness, shamelessness, temerity

effulgence blaze, brightness, brilliance, dazzle, fire, flame, fluorescence, glow, incandescence, luminosity, lustre, radiance, refulgence (*literary*), resplendence, shine, splendour, vividness

effulgent beaming, blazing, bright, brilliant, Day-Glo, dazzling, flaming, fluorescent, fulgent (*poetic*), glowing, incandescent, lucent, luminous, lustrous, radiant, refulgent (*literary*), resplendent, shining, splendid, vivid

effusion 1. discharge, effluence, efflux, emission, gush, issue, outflow, outpouring, shedding, stream **2.** address, outpouring, speech, talk, utterance, writing

effusive demonstrative, ebullient, enthusiastic, expansive, extravagant, exuberant, free-flowing, fulsome, gushing, lavish, overflowing, profuse, talkative, unreserved, unrestrained, wordy

egg on encourage, exhort, goad, incite, prod, prompt, push, spur, urge

▷ **Antonyms** deter, discourage, dissuade, hold back, put off, talk out of

egocentric egoistic, egoistical, egotistic, egotistical, self-centred, selfish

egoism egocentricity, egomania, egotism, narcissism, self-absorption, self-centredness, self-interest, selfishness, self-love, self-regard, self-seeking, vanity

egoist egomaniac, egotist, narcissist, self-seeker

egoistic, egoistical egocentric, egomaniacal, egotistic, egotistical, full of oneself, narcissistic, self-absorbed, self-centred, self-important, self-seeking

egotism conceitedness, egocentricity, egoism, egomania, narcissism, self-admiration, self-centredness, self-conceit, self-esteem, self-importance, self-love, self-praise, superiority, vainglory, vanity

egotist bighead (*informal*), blowhard (*informal*), boaster, braggadocio, braggart, egoist, egomaniac, self-admirer, swaggerer

egotistic, egotistical boasting, bragging, conceited, egocentric, egoistic, egoistical, egomaniacal, full of oneself, narcissistic, opinionated, self-admiring, self-centred, self-important, superior, vain, vainglorious

egregious arrant, enormous, flagrant, glaring, grievous, gross, heinous, infamous, insufferable, intolerable, monstrous, notorious, outrageous, rank, scandalous, shocking

egress departure, emergence, escape, exit, exodus, issue, outlet, passage out, vent, way out, withdrawal

ejaculate 1. discharge, eject, emit, spurt **2.** blurt out, burst out, cry out, exclaim, shout

ejaculation 1. cry, exclamation, shout **2.** discharge, ejection, emission, spurt

eject 1. cast out, discharge, disgorge, emit, expel, spew, spout, throw out, vomit **2.** banish, boot out (*informal*), bounce (*slang*), deport, dispossess, drive out, evacuate, evict, exile, expel, give the bum's rush (*slang*), oust, relegate, remove, show one the door, throw out, throw out on one's ear (*informal*), turn out **3.** discharge, dislodge, dismiss, fire (*informal*), get rid of, kick out (*informal*), oust, sack (*informal*), throw out

ejection 1. casting out, disgorgement, expulsion, spouting, throwing out **2.** banishment, deportation, dispossession, evacuation, eviction, exile, expulsion, ouster (*Law*), removal, the bum's rush (*slang*) **3.** discharge, dislodgement, dismissal, firing (*informal*), sacking (*informal*), the boot (*slang*), the sack (*informal*)

eke out 1. be economical with, be frugal with, be sparing with, economize on, husband, stretch out **2.** add to, enlarge, increase, make up (with), supplement

elaborate *adjective* **1.** careful, detailed, exact, intricate, laboured, minute, painstaking, perfected, precise, skilful, studied, thorough **2.** complex, complicated, decorated, detailed, extravagant, fancy, fussy, involved, ornamented, ornate, ostentatious, showy *~verb* **3.** add detail, amplify, complicate, decorate, develop, devise, embellish, enhance, enlarge, expand (upon), flesh out, garnish, improve, ornament, polish, produce, refine, work out

▷ **Antonyms** *~adjective* (*sense 2*) basic, minimal, modest, plain, severe, simple, unadorned, unembellished, unfussy *~verb* abbreviate, condense, put in a nutshell, reduce to essentials, simplify, streamline, summarize, truncate

élan animation, brio, dash, esprit, flair, impetuosity, panache, spirit, style, verve, vigour, vivacity, zest

elapse glide by, go, go by, lapse, pass, pass by, roll by, roll on, slip away, slip by

elastic 1. ductile, flexible, plastic, pliable, pliant, resilient, rubbery, springy, stretchable, stretchy, supple, tensile, yielding **2.** accommodating, adaptable, adjustable, complaisant, compliant, flexible, supple, tolerant, variable, yielding **3.** bouncy, buoyant, irrepressible, resilient

▷ **Antonyms** (*sense 1*) firm, immovable,

inflexible, rigid, set, stiff, unyielding (*sense 2*) firm, immovable, inflexible, intractable, obdurate, resolute, rigid, set, stiff, strict, stringent, unyielding

elasticity 1. ductileness, ductility, flexibility, give (*informal*), plasticity, pliability, pliancy, pliantness, resilience, rubberiness, springiness, stretch, stretchiness, suppleness **2.** adaptability, adjustability, complaisance, compliantness, flexibility, suppleness, tolerance, variability **3.** bounce (*informal*), buoyancy, irrepressibility, resilience

elated animated, blissed out, blissful, cheered, cock-a-hoop, delighted, ecstatic, elevated, euphoric, excited, exhilarated, exultant, floating *or* walking on air, gleeful, in high spirits, in seventh heaven, joyful, joyous, jubilant, overjoyed, over the moon (*informal*), proud, puffed up, rapt, roused, sent

▷ **Antonyms** dejected, depressed, discouraged, dispirited, downcast, down in the dumps (*informal*), miserable, sad, unhappy, woebegone

elation bliss, delight, ecstasy, euphoria, exaltation, exhilaration, exultation, glee, high spirits, joy, joyfulness, joyousness, jubilation, rapture

elbow *noun* **1.** angle, bend, corner, joint, turn **2. at one's elbow** at hand, close by, handy, near, to hand, within reach **3. out at elbow(s)** beggarly, down at heel, impoverished, in rags, ragged, seedy, shabby, tattered **4. rub elbows with** associate, fraternize, hang out (*informal*), hobnob, mingle, mix, socialize **5. up to the elbows** absorbed, busy, engaged, engrossed, immersed, occupied, tied up, up to the ears, wrapped up *~verb* **6.** bump, crowd, hustle, jostle, knock, nudge, push, shoulder, shove

elbowroom freedom, latitude, leeway, play, room, scope, space

elder *adjective* **1.** ancient, earlier born, first-born, older, senior *~noun* **2.** older person, senior **3.** *Presbyterianism* church official, office bearer, presbyter

elect 1. *verb* appoint, choose, decide upon, designate, determine, opt for, pick, pick out, prefer, select, settle on, vote **2.** *~adjective* choice, chosen, elite, hand-picked, picked, preferred, select, selected

election appointment, choice, choosing, decision, determination, judgment, preference, selection, vote, voting

elector chooser, constituent, selector, voter

electric *figurative* charged, dynamic, exciting, high-octane (*informal*), rousing, stimulating, stirring, tense, thrilling

electrify *figurative* amaze, animate, astonish, astound, excite, fire, galvanize, invigorate, jolt, rouse, shock, startle, stimulate, stir, take one's breath away, thrill

▷ **Antonyms** be tedious, bore, fatigue, jade, send to sleep, weary

eleemosynary almsgiving, altruistic, benevolent, charitable, philanthropic

elegance, elegancy 1. beauty, courtliness, dignity, exquisiteness, gentility, grace, gracefulness, grandeur, luxury, polish, politeness, refinement, sumptuousness **2.** discernment, distinction, propriety, style, taste

elegant 1. à la mode, artistic, beautiful, chic, choice, comely, courtly, cultivated, delicate, exquisite, fashionable, fine, genteel, graceful, handsome, luxurious, modish, nice, polished, refined, stylish, sumptuous, tasteful, urbane **2.** appropriate, apt, clever, effective, ingenious, neat, simple

▷ **Antonyms** (*sense 1*) awkward, clumsy, coarse, gauche, graceless, inelegant, misshapen, plain, tasteless, tawdry, ugly, uncouth, undignified, ungraceful, unrefined

elegiac dirgeful, funereal, keening, lamenting, melancholy, mournful, nostalgic, plaintive, sad, threnodial, threnodic, valedictory

elegy coronach (*Scot. & Irish*), dirge, keen, lament, plaint (*archaic*), requiem, threnody

element 1. basis, component, constituent, essential factor, factor, feature, hint, ingredient, member, part, section, subdivision, trace, unit **2.** domain, environment, field, habitat, medium, milieu, sphere

elemental 1. basic, elementary, essential, fundamental, original, primal, primitive, primordial **2.** atmospheric, meteorological, natural

elementary 1. clear, easy, facile, plain, rudimentary, simple, straightforward, uncomplicated **2.** basic, bog-standard (*informal*), elemental, fundamental, initial, introductory, original, primary, rudimentary

▷ **Antonyms** advanced, complex, complicated, higher, highly-developed, progressive, secondary, sophisticated

elements 1. basics, essentials, foundations, fundamentals, nuts and bolts (*informal*), principles, rudiments **2.** atmospheric conditions, atmospheric forces, powers of nature, weather

elephantine bulky, clumsy, enormous, heavy, huge, hulking, humongous *or* humungous (*U.S. slang*), immense, laborious, lumbering, massive, monstrous, ponderous, weighty

elevate 1. heighten, hoist, lift, lift up, raise, uplift, upraise **2.** advance, aggrandize, exalt, prefer, promote, upgrade **3.** animate, boost, brighten, buoy up, cheer, elate, excite, exhilarate, hearten, lift up, perk up, raise, rouse, uplift **4.** augment, boost, heighten, increase, intensify, magnify, swell

elevated 1. dignified, exalted, grand, high, high-flown, high-minded, inflated, lofty, noble, sublime **2.** animated, bright, cheerful, cheery, elated, excited, exhilarated, gleeful, in high spirits, overjoyed
▷ **Antonyms** (*sense 1*) humble, lowly, modest, simple

elevation 1. altitude, height **2.** acclivity, eminence, height, hill, hillock, mountain, rise, rising ground **3.** exaltedness, grandeur, loftiness, nobility, nobleness, sublimity **4.** advancement, aggrandizement, exaltation, preferment, promotion, upgrading

elfin arch, charming, elfish, elflike, elvish, frolicsome, impish, mischievous, playful, prankish, puckish, sprightly

elicit bring forth, bring out, bring to light, call forth, cause, derive, draw out, educe, evoke, evolve, exact, extort, extract, give rise to, obtain, wrest

eligible acceptable, appropriate, desirable, fit, preferable, proper, qualified, suitable, suited, worthy
▷ **Antonyms** inappropriate, ineligible, unacceptable, unqualified, unsuitable, unsuited

eliminate 1. cut out, dispose of, do away with, eradicate, exterminate, get rid of, get shot of, remove, stamp out, take out, wipe from the face of the earth **2.** axe (*informal*), dispense with, disregard, drop, eject, exclude, expel, ignore, knock out, leave out, omit, put out, reject, throw out **3.** *slang* annihilate, blow away (*slang, chiefly U.S.*), bump off (*slang*), kill, liquidate, murder, rub out (*U.S. slang*), slay, take out (*slang*), terminate, waste (*informal*)

elite 1. *noun* aristocracy, best, cream, *crème de la crème,* elect, flower, gentry, high society, nobility, pick, upper class **2.** *~adjective* aristocratic, best, choice, crack (*slang*), elect, exclusive, first-class, noble, pick, selected, upper-class
▷ **Antonyms** *~noun* dregs, hoi polloi, rabble, riffraff

elixir 1. cure-all, nostrum, panacea, sovereign remedy **2.** concentrate, essence, extract, pith, principle, quintessence **3.** mixture, potion, solution, syrup, tincture

elliptical 1. oval **2.** abstruse, ambiguous, concentrated, concise, condensed, cryptic, laconic, obscure, recondite, terse

elocution articulation, declamation, delivery, diction, enunciation, oratory, pronunciation, public speaking, rhetoric, speech, speechmaking, utterance, voice production

elongate draw out, extend, lengthen, make longer, prolong, protract, stretch

elope abscond, bolt, decamp, disappear, escape, leave, run away, run off, slip away, steal away

eloquence expression, expressiveness, fluency, forcefulness, oratory, persuasiveness, rhetoric, way with words

eloquent 1. articulate, fluent, forceful, graceful, moving, persuasive, silver-tongued, stirring, well-expressed **2.** expressive, meaningful, pregnant, revealing, suggestive, telling, vivid
▷ **Antonyms** (*sense 1*) faltering, halting, hesitant, inarticulate, speechless, stumbling, tongue-tied, wordless

elsewhere abroad, absent, away, hence (*archaic*), in *or* to another place, not here, not present, somewhere else

elucidate annotate, clarify, clear the air, clear up, explain, explicate, expound, gloss, illuminate, illustrate, interpret, make plain, shed *or* throw light upon, spell out, unfold

elucidation annotation, clarification, comment, commentary, explanation, explication, exposition, gloss, illumination, illustration, interpretation

elude 1. avoid, body-swerve (*Scot.*), circumvent, dodge, duck (*informal*), escape, evade, flee, get away from, outrun, shirk, shun, slip through one's fingers, slip through the net **2.** baffle, be beyond (someone), confound, escape, foil, frustrate, puzzle, stump, thwart

elusive 1. difficult to catch, shifty, slippery, tricky **2.** baffling, fleeting, indefinable, intangible, puzzling, subtle, transient, transitory **3.** ambiguous, deceitful, deceptive, elusory, equivocal, evasive, fallacious, fraudulent, illusory, misleading, oracular, unspecific

Elysian blessed, blissful, celestial, charming, delightful, enchanting, glorious, happy, heavenly, paradisiac, paradisiacal, ravishing, seraphic

emaciated atrophied, attenuate, attenuated, cadaverous, gaunt, haggard, lank, lean, macilent (*rare*), meagre, pinched, scrawny, skeletal, skin and bone, thin, undernourished, wasted

emaciation atrophy, attenuation, gauntness, haggardness, leanness, meagreness, scrawniness, thinness, wasting away

emanate 1. arise, come forth, derive, emerge, flow, issue, originate, proceed, spring, stem **2.** discharge, emit, exhale, give off, give out, issue, radiate, send forth

emanation 1. arising, derivation, emergence, flow, origination, proceeding **2.** discharge, effluent, efflux, effusion, emission, exhalation, radiation

emancipate deliver, discharge, disencumber, disenthral, enfranchise, free, liberate, manumit, release, set free, unbridle, unchain, unfetter, unshackle
▷ **Antonyms** bind, capture, enchain, en~

slave, enthral, fetter, shackle, subju~ gate, yoke

emancipation deliverance, discharge, en~ franchisement, freedom, liberation, lib~ erty, manumission, release
▷ **Antonyms** bondage, captivity, confine~ ment, detention, enthralment, impris~ onment, servitude, slavery, thraldom, vassalage

emasculate **1.** castrate, geld **2.** cripple, debilitate, deprive of force, enervate, impoverish, soften, weaken

embalm **1.** mummify, preserve **2.** *of memories* cherish, consecrate, conserve, enshrine, immortalize, store, treasure **3.** *poetic* make fragrant, perfume, scent

embargo **1.** *noun* ban, bar, barrier, block, blockage, boycott, check, hindrance, im~ pediment, interdict, interdiction, prohi~ bition, proscription, restraint, restric~ tion, stoppage **2.** *~verb* ban, bar, block, boycott, check, impede, interdict, pro~ hibit, proscribe, restrict, stop

embark **1.** board ship, go aboard, put on board, take on board, take ship **2.** (*with* **on** *or* **upon**) begin, broach, commence, engage, enter, get the show on the road (*informal*), initiate, launch, plunge into, set about, set out, start, take up, under~ take
▷ **Antonyms** (*sense 1*) alight, arrive, get off, go ashore, land, step out of

embarrass abash, chagrin, confuse, dis~ comfit, discompose, disconcert, discoun~ tenance, distress, faze, fluster, mortify, put out of countenance, shame, show up (*informal*)

embarrassing awkward, blush-making, compromising, cringe-making (*Brit. in~ formal*), cringeworthy (*Brit. informal*), discomfiting, disconcerting, distressing, humiliating, mortifying, sensitive, shameful, shaming, touchy, tricky, un~ comfortable

embarrassment **1.** awkwardness, bash~ fulness, chagrin, confusion, discomfi~ ture, discomposure, distress, humilia~ tion, mortification, self-consciousness, shame, showing up (*informal*) **2.** bind (*informal*), difficulty, mess, pickle (*in~ formal*), predicament, scrape (*informal*) **3.** excess, overabundance, superabun~ dance, superfluity, surfeit, surplus

embed dig in, drive in, fix, hammer in, implant, plant, ram in, root, set, sink

embellish adorn, beautify, bedeck, deck, decorate, dress up, elaborate, embroi~ der, enhance, enrich, exaggerate, fes~ toon, garnish, gild, gild the lily, grace, ornament, tart up (*slang*), varnish

embellishment adornment, decoration, elaboration, embroidery, enhancement, enrichment, exaggeration, gilding, or~ nament, ornamentation, trimming

embers ashes, cinders, live coals

embezzle abstract, appropriate, defalcate (*Law*), filch, have one's hand in the till (*informal*), misapply, misappropriate, misuse, peculate, pilfer, purloin, rip off (*slang*), steal

embezzlement abstraction, appropria~ tion, defalcation (*Law*), filching, fraud, larceny, misapplication, misappropria~ tion, misuse, peculation, pilferage, pil~ fering, purloining, stealing, theft, thiev~ ing

embitter **1.** alienate, anger, disaffect, dis~ illusion, envenom, make bitter *or* re~ sentful, poison, sour **2.** aggravate, exac~ erbate, exasperate, worsen

emblazon **1.** adorn, blazon, colour, deco~ rate, embellish, illuminate, ornament, paint **2.** crack up (*informal*), extol, glori~ fy, laud (*literary*), praise, proclaim, publicize, publish, trumpet

emblem badge, crest, device, figure, im~ age, insignia, mark, representation, sigil (*rare*), sign, symbol, token, type

emblematic, emblematical figurative, representative, symbolic

embodiment **1.** bodying forth, epitome, example, exemplar, exemplification, ex~ pression, incarnation, incorporation, manifestation, personification, realiza~ tion, reification, representation, symbol, type **2.** bringing together, codification, collection, combination, comprehension, concentration, consolidation, inclusion, incorporation, integration, organization, systematization

embody **1.** body forth, concretize, exem~ plify, express, incarnate, incorporate, manifest, personify, realize, reify, rep~ resent, stand for, symbolize, typify **2.** bring together, codify, collect, combine, comprehend, comprise, concentrate, consolidate, contain, include, incorpo~ rate, integrate, organize, systematize

embolden animate, cheer, encourage, fire, hearten, inflame, inspirit, invigor~ ate, nerve, reassure, rouse, stimulate, stir, strengthen, vitalize

embrace *verb* **1.** clasp, cuddle, encircle, enfold, envelop, grasp, hold, hug, neck (*informal*), seize, squeeze, take *or* hold in one's arms **2.** accept, adopt, avail oneself of, espouse, grab, make use of, receive, seize, take on board, take up, welcome **3.** comprehend, comprise, con~ tain, cover, deal with, embody, enclose, encompass, include, involve, provide for, subsume, take in, take into account *~noun* **4.** canoodle (*slang*), clasp, clinch (*slang*), cuddle, hug, squeeze

embroil complicate, compromise, con~ found, confuse, disorder, disturb, en~ cumber, enmesh, ensnare, entangle, implicate, incriminate, involve, mire, mix up, muddle, perplex, stitch up (*slang*), trouble

embryo beginning, germ, nucleus, root, rudiment

embryonic beginning, early, germinal, immature, inchoate, incipient, primary, rudimentary, seminal, undeveloped
▷ **Antonyms** advanced, developed, progressive

emend amend, correct, edit, improve, rectify, redact, revise

emendation amendment, correction, editing, improvement, rectification, redaction, revision

emerge 1. appear, arise, become visible, come forth, come into view, come out, come up, emanate, issue, proceed, rise, spring up, surface 2. become apparent, become known, come out, come out in the wash, come to light, crop up, develop, materialize, transpire, turn up
▷ **Antonyms** depart, disappear, enter, fade, fall, recede, retreat, sink, submerge, vanish from sight, wane, withdraw

emergence advent, apparition, appearance, arrival, coming, dawn, development, disclosure, emanation, issue, materialization, rise

emergency crisis, danger, difficulty, exigency, extremity, necessity, panic stations (*informal*), pass, pinch, plight, predicament, quandary, scrape (*informal*), strait

emergent appearing, budding, coming, developing, rising

emetic vomitive, vomitory

emigrate migrate, move, move abroad, remove

emigration departure, exodus, migration, removal

eminence 1. celebrity, dignity, distinction, esteem, fame, greatness, illustriousness, importance, notability, note, pre-eminence, prestige, prominence, rank, renown, reputation, repute, superiority 2. elevation, height, high ground, hill, hillock, knoll, rise, summit

eminent big-time (*informal*), celebrated, conspicuous, distinguished, elevated, esteemed, exalted, famous, grand, great, high, high-ranking, illustrious, important, major league (*informal*), notable, noted, noteworthy, outstanding, paramount, pre-eminent, prestigious, prominent, renowned, signal, superior, well-known
▷ **Antonyms** anonymous, commonplace, infamous, lowly, ordinary, undistinguished, unheard-of, unimportant, unknown, unremarkable, unsung

eminently conspicuously, exceedingly, exceptionally, extremely, greatly, highly, notably, outstandingly, prominently, remarkably, seriously (*informal*), signally, strikingly, surpassingly, well

emissary agent, ambassador, courier, delegate, deputy, envoy, go-between, herald, legate, messenger, representative, scout, secret agent, spy

emission diffusion, discharge, ejaculation, ejection, emanation, exhalation, exudation, issuance, issue, radiation, shedding, transmission, utterance, venting

emit breathe forth, cast out, diffuse, discharge, eject, emanate, exhale, exude, give off, give out, give vent to, issue, radiate, send forth, send out, shed, throw out, transmit, utter, vent
▷ **Antonyms** absorb, assimilate, consume, devour, digest, drink in, incorporate, ingest, receive, soak up, suck up, take in

emollient 1. *adjective* assuaging, assuasive, balsamic, demulcent, lenitive, mollifying, softening, soothing 2. *~noun* balm, lenitive, liniment, lotion, moisturizer, oil, ointment, salve

emolument benefit, compensation, earnings, fee, gain, hire, pay, payment, profits, recompense, remuneration, return, reward, salary, stipend, wages

emotion agitation, ardour, excitement, feeling, fervour, passion, perturbation, sensation, sentiment, vehemence, warmth

emotional 1. demonstrative, excitable, feeling, hot-blooded, passionate, responsive, sensitive, sentimental, susceptible, temperamental, tender, touchy-feely (*informal*), warm 2. affecting, emotive, exciting, heart-warming, moving, pathetic, poignant, sentimental, stirring, tear-jerking (*informal*), thrilling, touching 3. ablaze, ardent, enthusiastic, fervent, fervid, fiery, flaming, heated, impassioned, passionate, roused, stirred, zealous
▷ **Antonyms** apathetic, cold, detached, dispassionate, insensitive, phlegmatic, undemonstrative, unemotional, unenthusiastic, unexcitable, unfeeling, unmoved, unruffled, unsentimental

emotionless affectless, blank, cold, cold-blooded, cool, detached, distant, frigid, glacial, impassive, indifferent, remote, toneless, undemonstrative, unemotional, unfeeling

emotive 1. argumentative, controversial, delicate, sensitive, touchy 2. affecting, emotional, exciting, heart-warming, moving, pathetic, poignant, sentimental, stirring, tear-jerking (*informal*), three-hankie (*informal*), thrilling, touching 3. ardent, emotional, enthusiastic, fervent, fervid, fiery, heated, impassioned, passionate, roused, stirred, zealous

emphasis accent, accentuation, attention, decidedness, force, importance, impressiveness, insistence, intensity, moment, positiveness, power, pre-eminence, priority, prominence, significance, strength, stress, underscoring, weight

emphasize accent, accentuate, dwell on, foreground, give priority to, highlight, insist on, lay stress on, play up, press home, put the accent on, stress, underline, underscore, weight
▷ **Antonyms** gloss over, make light of, make little of, minimize, play down, soft-pedal (*informal*), underplay

emphatic absolute, categorical, certain, decided, definite, direct, distinct, earnest, energetic, forceful, forcible, important, impressive, insistent, in spades, marked, momentous, positive, powerful, pronounced, resounding, significant, striking, strong, telling, unequivocal, unmistakable, vigorous
▷ **Antonyms** commonplace, equivocal, hesitant, insignificant, tame, tentative, uncertain, undecided, unremarkable, unsure, weak

empire 1. commonwealth, domain, imperium (*rare*), kingdom, realm **2.** authority, command, control, dominion, government, power, rule, sovereignty, supremacy, sway

empirical, empiric experiential, experimental, first-hand, observed, practical, pragmatic
▷ **Antonyms** academic, assumed, conjectural, hypothetical, putative, speculative, theoretic, theoretical

emplace insert, place, position, put, put in place, set up, station

emplacement 1. location, lodgment, platform, position, site, situation, station **2.** placement, placing, positioning, putting in place, setting up, stationing

employ *verb* **1.** commission, engage, enlist, hire, retain, take on **2.** engage, fill, keep busy, make use of, occupy, spend, take up, use up **3.** apply, bring to bear, exercise, exert, make use of, ply, put to use, use, utilize *~noun* **4.** employment, engagement, hire, service

employed active, busy, engaged, in a job, in employment, in work, occupied, working
▷ **Antonyms** idle, jobless, laid off, on the dole (*Brit. informal*), out of a job, out of work, redundant, unoccupied

employee hand, job-holder, staff member, wage-earner, worker, workman

employer boss (*informal*), business, company, establishment, firm, gaffer (*informal, chiefly Brit.*), organization, outfit (*informal*), owner, patron, proprietor

employment 1. engagement, enlistment, hire, retaining, taking on **2.** application, exercise, exertion, use, utilization **3.** avocation (*archaic*), business, calling, craft, employ, job, line, métier, occupation, profession, pursuit, service, trade, vocation, work

emporium bazaar, market, mart, shop, store, warehouse

empower allow, authorize, commission, delegate, enable, entitle, license, permit, qualify, sanction, warrant

emptiness 1. bareness, blankness, desertedness, desolation, destitution, vacancy, vacuum, void, waste **2.** aimlessness, banality, barrenness, frivolity, futility, hollowness, inanity, ineffectiveness, meaninglessness, purposelessness, senselessness, silliness, unreality, unsatisfactoriness, unsubstantiality, vainness, valuelessness, vanity, worthlessness **3.** cheapness, hollowness, idleness, insincerity, triviality, trivialness **4.** absentness, blankness, expressionlessness, unintelligence, vacancy, vacantness, vacuity, vacuousness **5.** *informal* desire, hunger, ravening

empty *adjective* **1.** bare, blank, clear, deserted, desolate, destitute, hollow, unfurnished, uninhabited, unoccupied, untenanted, vacant, void, waste **2.** aimless, banal, bootless, frivolous, fruitless, futile, hollow, inane, ineffective, meaningless, otiose, purposeless, senseless, silly, unreal, unsatisfactory, unsubstantial, vain, valueless, worthless **3.** cheap, hollow, idle, insincere, trivial **4.** absent, blank, expressionless, unintelligent, vacant, vacuous **5.** *informal* esurient, famished, hungry, ravenous, starving (*informal*), unfed, unfilled *~verb* **6.** clear, consume, deplete, discharge, drain, dump, evacuate, exhaust, gut, pour out, unburden, unload, use up, vacate, void
▷ **Antonyms** *~adjective* (*sense 1*) full, inhabited, occupied, packed, stuffed *2 & 3* busy, fulfilled, full, interesting, meaningful, occupied, purposeful, satisfying, serious, significant, useful, valuable, worthwhile *~verb* cram, fill, pack, replenish, stock, stuff

empty-headed brainless, ditsy (*U.S. informal*), dizzy (*informal*), featherbrained, flighty, frivolous, giddy, goofy (*informal*), harebrained, inane, scatterbrained, silly, skittish, vacuous

empyrean, empyreal aerial, airy, celestial, ethereal, heavenly, refined, skylike, sublime

emulate challenge, compete with, contend with, copy, echo, follow, follow in the footsteps of, follow suit, follow the example of, imitate, mimic, rival, take after, take a leaf out of someone's book, vie with

emulation challenge, competition, contention, contest, copying, envy, following, imitation, jealousy, mimicry, rivalry, strife

emulous aspiring, competitive, contending, imitative, vying

enable allow, authorize, capacitate, commission, empower, entitle, facilitate, fit, license, permit, prepare, qualify, sanction, warrant

▷ **Antonyms** bar, block, hinder, impede, obstruct, prevent, stop, thwart

enact 1. authorize, command, decree, establish, legislate, ordain, order, pass, proclaim, ratify, sanction **2.** act, act out, appear as, depict, perform, personate, play, play the part of, portray, represent

enactment 1. authorization, canon, command, commandment, decree, dictate, edict, law, legislation, order, ordinance, proclamation, ratification, regulation, statute **2.** acting, depiction, performance, personation, play-acting, playing, portrayal, representation

enamour absorb, bewitch, captivate, charm, enchant, endear, enrapture, entrance, fascinate, infatuate, sweep off one's feet

enamoured bewitched, captivated, charmed, crazy about (*informal*), enchanted, enraptured, entranced, fascinated, fond, infatuated, in love, nuts on *or* about (*slang*), smitten, swept off one's feet, taken, wild about (*informal*)

encampment base, bivouac, camp, camping ground, campsite, cantonment, quarters, tents

encapsulate, incapsulate abridge, compress, condense, digest, epitomize, précis, summarize, sum up

enchain bind, enslave, fetter, hold, hold fast, manacle, pinion, put in irons, shackle

enchant beguile, bewitch, captivate, cast a spell on, charm, delight, enamour, enrapture, enthral, fascinate, hypnotize, mesmerize, ravish, spellbind

enchanter conjuror, magician, magus, necromancer, sorcerer, spellbinder, warlock, witch, wizard

enchanting alluring, appealing, attractive, bewitching, captivating, charming, delightful, endearing, entrancing, fascinating, lovely, pleasant, ravishing, winsome

enchantment 1. allure, allurement, beguilement, bliss, charm, delight, fascination, hypnotism, mesmerism, rapture, ravishment, transport **2.** charm, conjuration, incantation, magic, necromancy, sorcery, spell, witchcraft, wizardry

enchantress 1. conjuror, lamia, magician, necromancer, sorceress, spellbinder, witch **2.** charmer, *femme fatale,* seductress, siren, vamp (*informal*)

encircle begird (*poetic*), circle, circumscribe, compass, enclose, encompass, enfold, envelop, environ, enwreath, gird in, girdle, hem in, ring, surround

enclose, inclose 1. bound, circumscribe, cover, encase, encircle, encompass, environ, fence, hedge, hem in, impound, pen, pound, shut in, wall in, wrap **2.** include, insert, put in, send with **3.** comprehend, contain, embrace, hold, include, incorporate

encomium acclaim, acclamation, applause, compliment, eulogy, homage, laudation, panegyric, praise, tribute

encompass 1. circle, circumscribe, encircle, enclose, envelop, environ, enwreath, girdle, hem in, ring, surround **2.** bring about, cause, contrive, devise, effect, manage **3.** admit, comprehend, comprise, contain, cover, embody, embrace, hold, include, incorporate, involve, subsume, take in

encounter *verb* **1.** bump into (*informal*), chance upon, come upon, confront, experience, face, happen on *or* upon, meet, run across, run into (*informal*) **2.** attack, clash with, combat, come into conflict with, contend, cross swords with, do battle with, engage, face off (*slang*), fight, grapple with, join battle with, strive, struggle *~noun* **3.** brush, confrontation, meeting, rendezvous **4.** action, battle, clash, collision, combat, conflict, contest, dispute, engagement, face-off (*slang*), fight, head-to-head, run-in (*informal*), set to (*informal*), skirmish

encourage 1. animate, buoy up, cheer, comfort, console, embolden, hearten, incite, inspire, inspirit, rally, reassure, rouse, stimulate **2.** abet, advance, advocate, aid, boost, commend, egg on, favour, forward, foster, further, help, promote, prompt, spur, strengthen, succour, support, urge

▷ **Antonyms** daunt, depress, deter, discourage, dishearten, dispirit, dissuade, hinder, inhibit, intimidate, prevent, retard, scare, throw cold water on (*informal*)

encouragement advocacy, aid, boost, cheer, clarion call, consolation, favour, help, incitement, inspiration, inspiritment, promotion, reassurance, security blanket (*informal*), stimulation, stimulus, succour, support, urging

encouraging bright, cheerful, cheering, comforting, good, heartening, hopeful, promising, reassuring, rosy, satisfactory, stimulating

▷ **Antonyms** daunting, depressing, disappointing, discouraging, disheartening, dispiriting, offputting (*informal*), unfavourable, unpropitious

encroach appropriate, arrogate, impinge, infringe, intrude, invade, make inroads, overstep, trench, trespass, usurp

encroachment appropriation, arrogation, impingement, incursion, infringement, inroad, intrusion, invasion, trespass, usurpation, violation

encumber burden, clog, cramp, embarrass, hamper, handicap, hinder, impede, incommode, inconvenience, make difficult, obstruct, oppress, overload, retard, saddle, slow down, trammel, weigh down

encumbrance albatross, burden, clog, difficulty, drag, embarrassment, handicap, hindrance, impediment, inconvenience, liability, load, millstone, obstacle, obstruction

encyclopedic all-embracing, all-encompassing, all-inclusive, complete, comprehensive, exhaustive, thorough, universal, vast, wide-ranging

end *noun* **1.** bound, boundary, edge, extent, extreme, extremity, limit, point, terminus, tip **2.** attainment, cessation, close, closure, completion, conclusion, consequence, consummation, culmination, denouement, ending, end result, expiration, expiry, finale, finish, issue, outcome, resolution, result, sequel, stop, termination, upshot, wind-up **3.** aim, aspiration, design, drift, goal, intent, intention, object, objective, point, purpose, reason **4.** part, piece, portion, responsibility, share, side **5.** bit, butt, fragment, leftover, oddment, remainder, remnant, scrap, stub, tag end, tail end **6.** annihilation, death, demise, destruction, dissolution, doom, extermination, extinction, ruin, ruination **7. the end** *slang* beyond endurance, insufferable, intolerable, the final blow, the last straw, the limit (*informal*), the worst, too much (*informal*), unbearable, unendurable *~verb* **8.** axe (*informal*), bring to an end, cease, close, complete, conclude, culminate, dissolve, expire, finish, nip in the bud, pull the plug on, put paid to, resolve, stop, terminate, wind up **9.** abolish, annihilate, destroy, exterminate, extinguish, kill, put to death, ruin

▷ **Antonyms** *~noun* (*senses 1, 2 & 6*) beginning, birth, commencement, inception, launch, opening, origin, outset, prelude, source, start *~verb* begin, come into being, commence, initiate, launch, originate, start

endanger compromise, hazard, imperil, jeopardize, put at risk, put in danger, risk, threaten

▷ **Antonyms** defend, guard, preserve, protect, safeguard, save, secure

endear attach, attract, bind, captivate, charm, engage, win

endearing adorable, attractive, captivating, charming, cute, engaging, lovable, sweet, winning, winsome

endearment **1.** affectionate utterance, loving word, sweet nothing **2.** affection, attachment, fondness, love

endeavour **1.** *noun* aim, attempt, crack (*informal*), effort, enterprise, essay, go (*informal*), shot (*informal*), stab (*informal*), trial, try, undertaking, venture **2.** *~verb* aim, aspire, attempt, bend over backwards (*informal*), break one's neck (*informal*), bust a gut (*informal*), do one's best, do one's damnedest (*informal*), essay, give it one's all (*informal*), give it one's best shot (*informal*), go for broke (*slang*), go for it (*informal*), have a crack (*informal*), have a go, have a shot (*informal*), have a stab (*informal*), jump through hoops (*informal*), knock oneself out (*informal*), labour, make an all-out effort (*informal*), make an effort, rupture oneself (*informal*), strive, struggle, take pains, try, undertake

ending catastrophe, cessation, close, completion, conclusion, consummation, culmination, denouement, end, finale, finish, resolution, termination, wind-up

▷ **Antonyms** birth, commencement, inauguration, inception, onset, opening, origin, preface, source, start, starting point

endless **1.** boundless, ceaseless, constant, continual, eternal, everlasting, immortal, incessant, infinite, interminable, limitless, measureless, perpetual, unbounded, unbroken, undying, unending, uninterrupted, unlimited **2.** interminable, monotonous, overlong **3.** continuous, unbroken, undivided, whole

▷ **Antonyms** (*senses 1 & 2*) bounded, brief, circumscribed, finite, limited, passing, restricted, temporary, terminable, transient, transitory

endorse, indorse **1.** advocate, affirm, approve, authorize, back, champion, confirm, espouse, favour, prescribe, promote, ratify, recommend, sanction, subscribe to, support, sustain, vouch for, warrant **2.** countersign, sign, superscribe, undersign

endorsement, indorsement **1.** comment, countersignature, qualification, signature, superscription **2.** advocacy, affirmation, approbation, approval, authorization, backing, championship, confirmation, espousal, favour, fiat, O.K. *or* okay (*informal*), promotion, ratification, recommendation, sanction, seal of approval, subscription to, support, warrant

endow award, bequeath, bestow, confer, donate, endue, enrich, favour, finance, fund, furnish, give, grant, invest, leave, make over, provide, purvey, settle on, supply, will

endowment **1.** award, benefaction, bequest, bestowal, boon, donation, fund, gift, grant, hand-out, income, largesse *or* largess, legacy, presentation, property, provision, revenue, stipend **2.** (*often plural*) ability, aptitude, attribute, capability, capacity, faculty, flair, genius, gift, power, qualification, quality, talent

endue, indue endow, fill, furnish, invest, provide, supply

end up **1.** become eventually, finish as, finish up, pan out (*informal*), turn out to be **2.** arrive finally, come to a halt, fetch up (*informal*), finish up, stop, wind up

endurable acceptable, bearable, sufferable, supportable, sustainable, tolerable

▷ **Antonyms** insufferable, insupportable, intolerable, too much (*informal*), unbearable, unendurable

endurance 1. bearing, fortitude, patience, perseverance, persistence, pertinacity, resignation, resolution, stamina, staying power, strength, submission, sufferance, tenacity, toleration **2.** continuation, continuity, durability, duration, immutability, lastingness, longevity, permanence, stability

endure 1. bear, brave, cope with, experience, go through, stand, stick it out (*informal*), suffer, support, sustain, take it (*informal*), thole (*Scot.*), undergo, weather, withstand **2.** abide, allow, bear, brook, countenance, hack (*slang*), permit, put up with, stand, stick (*slang*), stomach, submit to, suffer, swallow, take patiently, tolerate **3.** abide, be durable, continue, have a good innings, hold, last, live, live on, persist, prevail, remain, stand, stay, survive, wear well

enduring abiding, continuing, durable, eternal, firm, immortal, immovable, imperishable, lasting, living, long-lasting, perennial, permanent, persistent, persisting, prevailing, remaining, steadfast, steady, surviving, unfaltering, unwavering

▷ **Antonyms** brief, ephemeral, fleeting, momentary, passing, short, short-lived, temporary, transient, transitory

enemy adversary, antagonist, competitor, foe, opponent, rival, the opposition, the other side

▷ **Antonyms** ally, confederate, friend, supporter

energetic active, alive and kicking, animated, bright-eyed and bushy-tailed (*informal*), brisk, dynamic, forceful, forcible, full of beans (*informal*), high-octane (*informal*), high-powered, indefatigable, lively, potent, powerful, spirited, strenuous, strong, tireless, vigorous, zippy (*informal*)

▷ **Antonyms** debilitated, dull, enervated, inactive, lazy, lethargic, lifeless, listless, slow, sluggish, torpid, weak

energize 1. activate, animate, enliven, inspirit, invigorate, liven up, motivate, pep up, quicken, stimulate, vitalize **2.** activate, electrify, kick-start, start up, switch on, turn on

energy activity, animation, ardour, brio, drive, efficiency, élan, elbow grease (*facetious*), exertion, fire, force, forcefulness, get-up-and-go (*informal*), go (*informal*), intensity, life, liveliness, pep, pluck, power, spirit, stamina, strength, strenuousness, verve, vigour, vim (*slang*), vitality, vivacity, zeal, zest, zip (*informal*)

enervate 1. *verb* debilitate, devitalize, enfeeble, exhaust, fatigue, incapacitate, paralyse, prostrate, sap, tire, unnerve, wash out, weaken, wear out **2.** *~adjective* debilitated, devitalized, done in (*informal*), enervated, enfeebled, exhausted, fatigued, feeble, incapacitated, limp, paralysed, prostrate, prostrated, rundown, sapped, spent, tired, undermined, unnerved, washed out, weak, weakened, worn out

enervation debilitation, debility, enfeeblement, exhaustedness, exhaustion, fatigue, feebleness, impotence, incapacity, infirmity, lassitude, paralysis, powerlessness, prostration, tiredness, weakening, weakness

enfeeble debilitate, deplete, devitalize, diminish, exhaust, fatigue, render feeble, sap, undermine, unhinge, unnerve, weaken, wear out

enfold, infold clasp, embrace, enclose, encompass, envelop, enwrap, fold, hold, hug, shroud, swathe, wrap, wrap up

enforce administer, apply, carry out, coerce, compel, constrain, exact, execute, implement, impose, insist on, oblige, prosecute, put in force, put into effect, reinforce, require, urge

enforced compelled, compulsory, constrained, dictated, imposed, involuntary, necessary, ordained, prescribed, required, unavoidable, unwilling

enforcement 1. administration, application, carrying out, exaction, execution, implementation, imposition, prosecution, reinforcement **2.** coercion, compulsion, constraint, insistence, obligation, pressure, requirement

enfranchise 1. give the vote to, grant suffrage to, grant the franchise to, grant voting rights to **2.** emancipate, free, liberate, manumit, release, set free

enfranchisement 1. giving the vote, granting suffrage *or* the franchise, granting voting rights **2.** emancipation, freedom, freeing, liberating, liberation, manumission, release, setting free

engage 1. appoint, commission, employ, enlist, enrol, hire, retain, take on **2.** bespeak, book, charter, hire, lease, prearrange, rent, reserve, secure **3.** absorb, busy, engross, grip, involve, occupy, preoccupy, tie up **4.** allure, arrest, attach, attract, captivate, catch, charm, draw, enamour, enchant, fascinate, fix, gain, win **5.** embark on, enter into, join, partake, participate, practise, set about, take part, undertake **6.** affiance, agree, betroth (*archaic*), bind, commit, contract, covenant, guarantee, obligate, oblige, pledge, promise, undertake, vouch, vow **7.** *Military* assail, attack, combat, come to close quarters with, encounter, face off (*slang*), fall on, fight with, give battle to, join battle with, meet, take on **8.** activate, apply, bring into operation, energize, set going, switch on **9.** dovetail, interact, interconnect, interlock, join, mesh

▷ **Antonyms** (*sense 1*) axe (*informal*), discharge, dismiss, fire (*informal*), give notice to, lay off, oust, remove, sack (*informal*)

engaged 1. affianced, betrothed (*archaic*), pledged, promised, spoken for **2.** ab~ sorbed, busy, committed, employed, en~ grossed, in use, involved, occupied, pre~ occupied, tied up, unavailable

▷ **Antonyms** (*sense 1*) available, fancy-free, free, unattached, uncommitted, unengaged (*sense 2*) available, free, un~ committed, unengaged

engagement 1. assurance, betrothal, bond, compact, contract, oath, obliga~ tion, pact, pledge, promise, troth (*ar~ chaic*), undertaking, vow, word **2.** ap~ pointment, arrangement, commitment, date, meeting **3.** commission, employ~ ment, gig (*informal*), job, post, situation, stint, work **4.** action, battle, combat, conflict, confrontation, contest, encoun~ ter, face-off (*slang*), fight

engaging agreeable, appealing, attrac~ tive, captivating, charming, cute, en~ chanting, fascinating, fetching (*infor~ mal*), likable *or* likeable, lovable, pleas~ ant, pleasing, winning, winsome

▷ **Antonyms** disagreeable, objectionable, obnoxious, offensive, repulsive, unat~ tractive, unlikable *or* unlikeable, un~ lovely, unpleasant

engender 1. beget, breed, bring about, cause, create, excite, foment, generate, give rise to, hatch, incite, induce, insti~ gate, lead to, make, occasion, precipi~ tate, produce, provoke **2.** beget, breed, bring forth, father, generate, give birth to, procreate, propagate, sire, spawn

engine 1. machine, mechanism, motor **2.** agency, agent, apparatus, appliance, contrivance, device, implement, instru~ ment, means, tool, weapon

engineer 1. *noun* architect, contriver, de~ signer, deviser, director, inventor, man~ ager, manipulator, originator, planner, schemer **2.** *~verb* bring about, cause, concoct, contrive, control, create, devise, effect, encompass, finagle (*informal*), manage, manoeuvre, mastermind, originate, plan, plot, scheme, wangle (*informal*)

engorge bolt, cram, devour, eat, fill, glut, gobble, gorge, gulp, guzzle, pig out (*slang*), satiate, stuff, wolf

engraft, ingraft graft, implant, incorpo~ rate, inculcate, infix, infuse, ingrain, in~ stil

engrain *see* INGRAIN

engrave 1. carve, chase, chisel, cut, en~ chase (*rare*), etch, grave (*archaic*), in~ scribe **2.** impress, imprint, print **3.** em~ bed, fix, impress, imprint, infix, ingrain, lodge

engraving 1. carving, chasing, chiselling, cutting, dry point, enchasing (*rare*), etching, inscribing, inscription **2.** block, carving, etching, inscription, plate, woodcut **3.** etching, impression, print

engross 1. absorb, arrest, engage, engulf, hold, immerse, involve, occupy, preoc~ cupy **2.** corner, monopolize, sew up (*U.S.*)

engrossed absorbed, captivated, caught up, deep, enthralled, fascinated, gripped, immersed, intent, intrigued, lost, preoccupied, rapt, riveted

engrossing absorbing, captivating, com~ pelling, enthralling, fascinating, grip~ ping, interesting, intriguing, riveting

engulf, ingulf absorb, bury, consume, del~ uge, drown, encompass, engross, envel~ op, flood (out), immerse, inundate, over~ run, overwhelm, plunge, submerge, swallow up, swamp

enhance add to, augment, boost, comple~ ment, elevate, embellish, exalt, height~ en, improve, increase, intensify, lift, magnify, raise, reinforce, strengthen, swell

▷ **Antonyms** debase, decrease, depreci~ ate, devalue, diminish, lower, minimize, reduce, spoil

enigma conundrum, mystery, problem, puzzle, riddle, teaser

enigmatic, enigmatical ambiguous, cryp~ tic, Delphic, doubtful, equivocal, incom~ prehensible, indecipherable, inexpli~ cable, inscrutable, mysterious, obscure, oracular, perplexing, puzzling, recon~ dite, sphinxlike, uncertain, unfathom~ able, unintelligible

▷ **Antonyms** clear, comprehensible, sim~ ple, straightforward, uncomplicated

enjoin 1. advise, bid, call upon, charge, command, counsel, demand, direct, in~ struct, order, prescribe, require, urge, warn **2.** *Law* ban, bar, disallow, forbid, interdict, place an injunction on, pre~ clude, prohibit, proscribe, restrain

enjoy 1. appreciate, be entertained by, be pleased with, delight in, like, rejoice in, relish, revel in, take joy in, take pleas~ ure in *or* from **2.** be blessed *or* favoured with, experience, have, have the benefit of, have the use of, own, possess, reap the benefits of, use **3. enjoy oneself** have a ball (*informal*), have a field day (*in~ formal*), have a good time, have fun, let one's hair down, make merry

▷ **Antonyms** (*sense 1*) abhor, despise, detest, dislike, hate, have no taste *or* stomach for, loathe

enjoyable agreeable, amusing, delectable, delicious, delightful, entertaining, gratifying, pleasant, pleasing, pleasur~ able, satisfying, to one's liking

▷ **Antonyms** despicable, disagreeable, displeasing, hateful, loathsome, obnox~ ious, offensive, repugnant, unenjoyable, unpleasant, unsatisfying, unsavoury

enjoyment 1. amusement, beer and skit~ tles (*informal*), delectation, delight, di~ version, entertainment, fun, gladness, gratification, gusto, happiness, indul~ gence, joy, pleasure, recreation, relish, satisfaction, zest **2**. advantage, benefit, exercise, ownership, possession, use

enkindle 1. fire, ignite, kindle, light, put a match to, put to the torch, set ablaze, set alight, set fire to, set on fire, torch **2**. arouse, awake, excite, foment, incite, inflame, inspire, provoke, stir

enlarge 1. add to, amplify, augment, blow up (*informal*), broaden, diffuse, dilate, distend, elongate, expand, extend, grow, heighten, increase, inflate, lengthen, magnify, make *or* grow larger, multiply, stretch, swell, wax, widen **2**. amplify, descant, develop, dilate, elaborate, expand, expatiate, give details

▷ **Antonyms** (*sense 1*) compress, condense, curtail, decrease, diminish, lessen, narrow, reduce, shorten, shrink, trim, truncate (*sense 2*) abbreviate, abridge, condense, shorten

enlighten advise, apprise, cause to understand, civilize, counsel, edify, educate, inform, instruct, make aware, teach

enlightened aware, broad-minded, civilized, cultivated, educated, informed, knowledgeable, liberal, literate, open-minded, reasonable, refined, sophisticated

▷ **Antonyms** ignorant, narrow-minded, short-sighted, small-minded, unaware, uneducated, unenlightened

enlightenment awareness, broad-mindedness, civilization, comprehension, cultivation, edification, education, information, insight, instruction, knowledge, learning, literacy, open-mindedness, refinement, sophistication, teaching, understanding, wisdom

enlist engage, enrol, enter (into), gather, join, join up, muster, obtain, procure, recruit, register, secure, sign up, volunteer

enliven animate, brighten, buoy up, cheer, cheer up, excite, exhilarate, fire, gladden, hearten, inspire, inspirit, invigorate, pep up, perk up, quicken, rouse, spark, stimulate, vitalize, vivify, wake up

▷ **Antonyms** chill, dampen, deaden, depress, put a damper on, repress, subdue

en masse all at once, all together, as a group, as a whole, as one, ensemble, in a body, in a group, in a mass, together

enmesh catch, embroil, ensnare, entangle, implicate, incriminate, involve, net, snare, snarl, tangle, trammel, trap

enmity acrimony, animosity, animus, antagonism, antipathy, aversion, bad blood, bitterness, hate, hatred, hostility, ill will, malevolence, malice, malignity, rancour, spite, venom

▷ **Antonyms** affection, amity, cordiality, friendliness, friendship, geniality, goodwill, harmony, love, warmth

ennoble aggrandize, dignify, elevate, enhance, exalt, glorify, honour, magnify, raise

ennui boredom, dissatisfaction, lassitude, listlessness, tedium, the doldrums

enormity 1. atrociousness, atrocity, depravity, disgrace, evilness, heinousness, monstrousness, nefariousness, outrageousness, turpitude, viciousness, vileness, villainy, wickedness **2**. abomination, atrocity, crime, disgrace, evil, horror, monstrosity, outrage, villainy **3**. *informal* enormousness, greatness, hugeness, immensity, magnitude, massiveness, vastness

enormous 1. astronomic, Brobdingnagian, colossal, elephantine, excessive, gargantuan, gigantic, ginormous (*informal*), gross, huge, humongous *or* humungous (*U.S. slang*), immense, jumbo (*informal*), mammoth, massive, monstrous, mountainous, prodigious, stellar (*informal*), titanic, tremendous, vast **2**. *archaic* abominable, atrocious, depraved, disgraceful, evil, heinous, monstrous, nefarious, odious, outrageous, vicious, vile, villainous, wicked

▷ **Antonyms** (*sense 1*) diminutive, dwarf, infinitesimal, insignificant, Lilliputian, little, meagre, microscopic, midget, minute, petite, pint-sized (*informal*), small, tiny, trivial, wee

enough 1. *adjective* abundant, adequate, ample, plenty, sufficient **2**. *~noun* abundance, adequacy, ample supply, plenty, right amount, sufficiency **3**. *~adverb* abundantly, adequately, amply, fairly, moderately, passably, reasonably, satisfactorily, sufficiently, tolerably

enquire 1. ask, query, question, request information, seek information **2**. *also* **inquire** conduct an inquiry, examine, explore, inspect, investigate, look into, make inquiry, probe, research, scrutinize, search

enquiry 1. query, question **2**. *also* **inquiry** examination, exploration, inquest, inspection, investigation, probe, research, scrutiny, search, study, survey

enrage aggravate (*informal*), anger, exasperate, gall, get one's back up, incense, incite, inflame, infuriate, irritate, madden, make one's blood boil, make one see red (*informal*), nark (*Brit., Austral., & N.Z. slang*), provoke, put one's back up

▷ **Antonyms** appease, assuage, calm, conciliate, mollify, pacify, placate, soothe

enraged aggravated (*informal*), angered, angry, boiling mad, choked, cross, exasperated, fuming, furious, incensed, inflamed, infuriated, irate, irritated, livid (*informal*), mad (*informal*), on the warpath, raging, raging mad, wild

enrapture absorb, beguile, bewitch, captivate, charm, delight, enamour, en~

chant, enthral, entrance, fascinate, rav~ ish, spellbind, transport

enrich 1. make rich, make wealthy **2.** ag~ grandize, ameliorate, augment, culti~ vate, develop, endow, enhance, improve, refine, supplement **3.** adorn, decorate, embellish, grace, ornament

enrol 1. chronicle, inscribe, list, note, rec~ ord **2.** accept, admit, engage, enlist, join up, matriculate, recruit, register, sign up *or* on, take on

enrolment acceptance, admission, en~ gagement, enlistment, matriculation, recruitment, registration

en route in transit, on *or* along the way, on the road

ensconce 1. curl up, establish, install, nestle, settle, snuggle up **2.** conceal, cover, hide, protect, screen, shelter, shield

ensemble *noun* **1.** aggregate, assemblage, collection, entirety, set, sum, total, to~ tality, whole, whole thing **2.** costume, get-up (*informal*), outfit, suit **3.** band, cast, chorus, company, group, support~ ing cast, troupe *~adverb* **4.** all at once, all together, as a group, as a whole, at once, at the same time, en masse, in concert

enshrine apotheosize, cherish, consecrate, dedicate, embalm, exalt, hallow, pre~ serve, revere, sanctify, treasure

enshroud cloak, cloud, conceal, cover, en~ close, enfold, envelop, enwrap, hide, ob~ scure, pall, shroud, veil, wrap

ensign badge, banner, colours, flag, jack, pennant, pennon, standard, streamer

enslave bind, dominate, enchain, enthral, reduce to slavery, subjugate, yoke

ensnare catch, embroil, enmesh, entan~ gle, entrap, net, snare, snarl, trap

ensue arise, attend, be consequent on, befall, come after, come next, come to pass (*archaic*), derive, flow, follow, is~ sue, proceed, result, stem, succeed, supervene, turn out *or* up

▷ **Antonyms** antecede, come first, fore~ run, go ahead of, go before, introduce, lead, pave the way, precede, usher

ensure, insure 1. certify, confirm, effect, guarantee, make certain, make sure, secure, warrant **2.** guard, make safe, protect, safeguard, secure

entail bring about, call for, cause, de~ mand, encompass, give rise to, impose, involve, lead to, necessitate, occasion, require, result in

entangle 1. catch, compromise, embroil, enmesh, ensnare, entrap, foul, impli~ cate, involve, knot, mat, mix up, ravel, snag, snare, tangle, trammel, trap **2.** bewilder, complicate, confuse, jumble, mix up, muddle, perplex, puzzle, snarl, twist

▷ **Antonyms** (*sense 1*) detach, disconnect, disengage, disentangle, extricate, free, loose, separate, sever, unfold, unravel, unsnarl, untangle, untwist (*sense 2*) clarify, clear (up), resolve, simplify, work out

entanglement 1. complication, confusion, ensnarement, entrapment, imbroglio (*obsolete*), involvement, jumble, knot, mesh, mess, mix-up, muddle, snare, snarl-up (*informal, chiefly Brit.*), tangle, toils, trap **2.** difficulty, embarrassment, imbroglio, involvement, liaison, pre~ dicament, tie

entente *also* **entente cordiale** agreement, arrangement, compact, deal, friendship, pact, treaty, understanding

enter 1. arrive, come *or* go in *or* into, in~ sert, introduce, make an entrance, pass into, penetrate, pierce **2.** become a member of, begin, commence, commit oneself to, embark upon, enlist, enrol, join, participate in, set about, set out on, sign up, start, take part in, take up **3.** inscribe, list, log, note, record, register, set down, take down **4.** offer, present, proffer, put forward, register, submit, tender

▷ **Antonyms** (*sense 1*) depart, exit, go, issue from, leave, take one's leave, withdraw (*senses 2 & 4*) drop out, go, leave, pull out, resign, retire, withdraw

enterprise 1. adventure, effort, endeav~ our, essay, operation, plan, programme, project, undertaking, venture **2.** activity, adventurousness, alertness, audacity, boldness, daring, dash, drive, eagerness, energy, enthusiasm, get-up-and-go (*in~ formal*), gumption (*informal*), initiative, pep, push (*informal*), readiness, re~ source, resourcefulness, spirit, vigour, zeal **3.** business, company, concern, es~ tablishment, firm, operation

enterprising active, adventurous, alert, audacious, bold, daring, dashing, eager, energetic, enthusiastic, go-ahead, in~ trepid, keen, ready, resourceful, spirit~ ed, stirring, up-and-coming, venture~ some, vigorous, zealous

entertain 1. amuse, charm, cheer, delight, divert, occupy, please, recreate (*rare*), regale **2.** accommodate, be host to, har~ bour, have company, have guests *or* visitors, lodge, put up, show hospitality to, treat **3.** cherish, cogitate on, conceive, consider, contemplate, foster, harbour, hold, imagine, keep in mind, maintain, muse over, ponder, support, think about, think over

entertaining amusing, charming, cheer~ ing, delightful, diverting, funny, hu~ morous, interesting, pleasant, pleasing, pleasurable, recreative (*rare*), witty

entertainment amusement, beer and skittles (*informal*), cheer, distraction, diversion, enjoyment, fun, good time, leisure activity, pastime, play, pleasure, recreation, satisfaction, sport, treat

enthral absorb, beguile, captivate, charm, enchant, enrapture, entrance, fascinate, grip, hold spellbound, hypnotize, in~ trigue, mesmerize, ravish, rivet, spell~ bind

enthralling beguiling, captivating, charming, compelling, compulsive, en~ chanting, entrancing, fascinating, grip~ ping, hypnotizing, intriguing, mesmer~ izing, riveting, spellbinding

enthusiasm **1.** ardour, avidity, devotion, eagerness, earnestness, excitement, fer~ vour, frenzy, interest, keenness, pas~ sion, relish, vehemence, warmth, zeal, zest, zing (*informal*) **2.** craze, fad (*infor~ mal*), hobby, hobbyhorse, interest, ma~ nia, passion, rage

enthusiast admirer, aficionado, buff (*in~ formal*), devotee, fan, fanatic, fiend (*in~ formal*), follower, freak (*informal*), lover, supporter, zealot

enthusiastic ablaze, ardent, avid, bright-eyed and bushy-tailed (*informal*), devoted, eager, earnest, ebullient, excit~ ed, exuberant, fervent, fervid, forceful, full of beans (*informal*), hearty, keen, keen as mustard, lively, passionate, spirited, unqualified, unstinting, vehe~ ment, vigorous, warm, wholehearted, zealous

▷ **Antonyms** apathetic, blasé, bored, cool, dispassionate, half-hearted, indifferent, nonchalant, unconcerned, unenthusias~ tic, uninterested

entice allure, attract, beguile, cajole, coax, dangle a carrot in front of (someone's) nose, decoy, draw, inveigle, lead on, lure, persuade, prevail on, se~ duce, tempt, wheedle

enticement allurement, attraction, bait, blandishments, cajolery, coaxing, come-on (*informal*), decoy, incentive, in~ ducement, inveiglement, lure, persua~ sion, seduction, temptation

entire **1.** complete, full, gross, total, whole **2.** absolute, full, outright, thorough, to~ tal, undiminished, unmitigated, unre~ served, unrestricted **3.** intact, perfect, sound, unbroken, undamaged, un~ marked, unmarred, whole, without a scratch **4.** continuous, integrated, un~ broken, undivided, unified

entirely **1.** absolutely, altogether, com~ pletely, every inch, fully, in every re~ spect, lock, stock and barrel, perfectly, thoroughly, totally, unreservedly, utterly, wholly, without exception, without reservation **2.** exclusively, only, solely

▷ **Antonyms** incompletely, moderately, partially, partly, piecemeal, slightly, somewhat, to a certain extent *or* degree

entirety **1.** absoluteness, completeness, fullness, totality, undividedness, unity, wholeness **2.** aggregate, sum, total, unity, whole

entitle **1.** accredit, allow, authorize, em~ power, enable, enfranchise, fit for, li~ cense, make eligible, permit, qualify for, warrant **2.** call, characterize, christen, denominate, designate, dub, label, name, style, term, title

entity **1.** being, body, creature, existence, individual, object, organism, presence, quantity, substance, thing **2.** essence, essential nature, quiddity (*Philosophy*), quintessence, real nature

entomb bury, inhume, inter, inurn, lay to rest, sepulchre

entombment burial, inhumation, inter~ ment, inurnment, sepulture

entourage **1.** associates, attendants, com~ panions, company, cortege, court, escort, followers, following, retainers, retinue, staff, suite, train **2.** ambience, environ~ ment, environs, milieu, surroundings

entrails bowels, guts, innards (*informal*), insides (*informal*), intestines, offal, vis~ cera

entrance[1] *noun* **1.** access, avenue, door, doorway, entry, gate, ingress, inlet, opening, passage, portal, way in **2.** ap~ pearance, arrival, coming in, entry, in~ gress, introduction **3.** access, admission, admittance, entrée, entry, ingress, per~ mission to enter **4.** beginning, com~ mencement, debut, initiation, introduc~ tion, outset, start

▷ **Antonyms** (*sense 1*) exit, outlet, way out (*sense 2*) departure, egress, exit, exodus, leave-taking

entrance[2] *verb* **1.** absorb, bewitch, capti~ vate, charm, delight, enchant, enrap~ ture, enthral, fascinate, gladden, ravish, spellbind, transport **2.** hypnotize, mes~ merize, put in a trance

▷ **Antonyms** bore, disenchant, irritate, offend, put off, turn off (*informal*)

entrant **1.** beginner, convert, initiate, neophyte, newcomer, new member, novice, probationer, tyro **2.** candidate, competitor, contestant, entry, partici~ pant, player

entrap **1.** capture, catch, ensnare, net, snare, trap **2.** allure, beguile, decoy, em~ broil, enmesh, ensnare, entangle, entice, implicate, inveigle, involve, lead on, lure, seduce, trick

entreat appeal to, ask, ask earnestly, beg, beseech, conjure, crave, enjoin, exhort, implore, importune, petition, plead with, pray, request, supplicate

entreaty appeal, earnest request, exhor~ tation, importunity, petition, plea, prayer, request, solicitation, suit, sup~ plication

entrench, intrench **1.** construct defences, dig in, dig trenches, fortify **2.** anchor, dig in, embed, ensconce, establish, fix, im~ plant, ingrain, install, lodge, plant, root, seat, set, settle **3.** encroach, impinge, in~

fringe, interlope, intrude, make inroads, trespass

entrenched, intrenched deep-rooted, deep-seated, firm, fixed, indelible, in~eradicable, ingrained, rooted, set, un~shakable, well-established

entre nous between ourselves, between the two of us, between you and me, con~fidentially, in confidence, off the record, privately

entrepreneur businessman, business~woman, contractor, director, financier, impresario, industrialist, magnate, ty~coon

entrust, intrust assign, authorize, charge, commend, commit, confide, consign, delegate, deliver, give custody of, hand over, invest, trust, turn over

entry 1. appearance, coming in, entering, entrance, initiation, introduction **2.** ac~cess, avenue, door, doorway, entrance, gate, ingress, inlet, opening, passage, passageway, portal, way in **3.** access, admission, entrance, entrée, free pas~sage, permission to enter **4.** account, item, jotting, listing, memo, memoran~dum, minute, note, record, registration **5.** attempt, candidate, competitor, con~testant, effort, entrant, participant, player, submission

▷ **Antonyms** (*sense 1*) departure, egress, exit, leave, leave-taking, withdrawal (*sense 2*) exit, way out

entwine, intwine braid, embrace, encircle, entwist (*archaic*), interlace, intertwine, interweave, knit, plait, ravel, surround, twine, twist, weave, wind

▷ **Antonyms** disentangle, extricate, free, separate, straighten out, undo, unravel, untangle, unwind

enumerate 1. cite, detail, itemize, list, mention, name, quote, recapitulate, re~cite, recount, rehearse, relate, specify, spell out, tell **2.** add up, calculate, com~pute, count, number, reckon, sum up, tally, total

enunciate 1. articulate, enounce, pro~nounce, say, sound, speak, utter, vocal~ize, voice **2.** declare, proclaim, promul~gate, pronounce, propound, publish, state

envelop blanket, cloak, conceal, cover, embrace, encase, encircle, enclose, en~compass, enfold, engulf, enwrap, hide, obscure, sheathe, shroud, surround, swaddle, swathe, veil, wrap

envelope case, casing, coating, cover, covering, jacket, sheath, shell, skin, wrapper, wrapping

envenom 1. contaminate, infect, poison, taint **2.** acerbate, aggravate (*informal*), embitter, enrage, exacerbate, exasper~ate, incense, inflame, irritate, madden, provoke, sour

enviable advantageous, blessed, covet~able, desirable, favoured, fortunate, lucky, much to be desired, privileged, to die for (*informal*)

▷ **Antonyms** disagreeable, painful, thankless, uncomfortable, undesirable, unenviable, unpleasant

envious begrudging, covetous, green-eyed, green with envy, grudging, jaun~diced, jealous, malicious, resentful, spiteful

environ beset, besiege, encircle, enclose, encompass, engird, envelop, gird, hem, invest (*rare*), ring, surround

environment atmosphere, background, conditions, context, domain, element, habitat, locale, medium, milieu, scene, setting, situation, surroundings, terri~tory

environmentalist conservationist, ecolo~gist, friend of the earth, green

environs district, locality, neighbourhood, outskirts, precincts, purlieus, suburbs, surrounding area, vicinity

envisage 1. conceive (of), conceptualize, contemplate, fancy, imagine, picture, think up, visualize **2.** anticipate, envi~sion, foresee, predict, see

envision anticipate, conceive of, contem~plate, envisage, foresee, predict, see, visualize

envoy agent, ambassador, courier, del~egate, deputy, diplomat, emissary, intermediary, legate, messenger, minis~ter, plenipotentiary, representative

envy 1. *noun* covetousness, enviousness, grudge, hatred, ill will, jealousy, malice, malignity, resentfulness, resentment, spite, the green-eyed monster (*informal*) **2.** *~verb* be envious (of), begrudge, be jealous (of), covet, grudge, resent

ephemeral brief, evanescent, fleeting, flitting, fugacious, fugitive, imperma~nent, momentary, passing, short, short-lived, temporary, transient, tran~sitory

▷ **Antonyms** abiding, durable, enduring, eternal, immortal, lasting, long-lasting, persisting, steadfast

epicene *adjective* **1.** androgyne, androgy~nous, bisexual, gynandrous, hermaph~rodite, hermaphroditic **2.** asexual, neu~ter, sexless **3.** camp (*informal*), effemi~nate, unmanly, weak, womanish *~noun* **4.** androgyne, bisexual, gynandromorph, hermaphrodite

epicure 1. *bon vivant,* epicurean, foodie, gastronome, gourmet **2.** glutton, gour~mand, hedonist, sensualist, sybarite, voluptuary

epicurean 1. *adjective* bacchanalian, glut~tonous, gourmandizing, hedonistic, lib~ertine, luscious, lush, luxurious, pleasure-seeking, self-indulgent, sen~sual, sybaritic, voluptuous **2.** *~noun bon vivant,* epicure, foodie, gastronome, gourmet

epidemic 1. *adjective* general, pandemic, prevailing, prevalent, rampant, rife, sweeping, wide-ranging, widespread 2. *~noun* contagion, growth, outbreak, plague, rash, spread, upsurge, wave

epigram aphorism, *bon mot,* quip, witticism

epigrammatic concise, laconic, piquant, pithy, pointed, pungent, sharp, short, succinct, terse, witty

epilogue afterword, coda, concluding speech, conclusion, postscript

▷ **Antonyms** exordium, foreword, introduction, preamble, preface, prelude, prologue

episode 1. adventure, affair, business, circumstance, escapade, event, experience, happening, incident, matter, occurrence 2. chapter, instalment, part, passage, scene, section

episodic anecdotal, digressive, disconnected, discursive, disjointed, intermittent, irregular, occasional, picaresque, rambling, sporadic, wandering

epistle communication, letter, message, missive, note

epithet appellation, description, designation, moniker *or* monicker (*slang*), name, nickname, sobriquet, tag, title

epitome 1. archetype, embodiment, essence, exemplar, norm, personification, quintessence, representation, type, typical example 2. abbreviation, abridgment, abstract, compendium, condensation, conspectus, contraction, digest, précis, résumé, summary, syllabus, synopsis

epitomize 1. embody, exemplify, illustrate, incarnate, personify, represent, symbolize, typify 2. abbreviate, abridge, abstract, condense, contract, curtail, cut, encapsulate, précis, reduce, shorten, summarize, synopsize

epoch age, date, era, period, time

equable 1. agreeable, calm, composed, easy-going, even-tempered, imperturbable, level-headed, placid, serene, temperate, unexcitable, unfazed (*informal*), unflappable (*informal*), unruffled 2. consistent, constant, even, on an even keel, regular, smooth, stable, steady, temperate, tranquil, unchanging, uniform, unvarying

▷ **Antonyms** (*sense 1*) excitable, nervous, temperamental (*sense 2*) changeable, fitful, inconsistent, irregular, temperamental, uneven, unstable, volatile

equal *adjective* 1. alike, commensurate, equivalent, identical, like, one and the same, proportionate, tantamount, the same, uniform 2. balanced, corresponding, egalitarian, even, evenly balanced, evenly matched, evenly proportioned, fifty-fifty (*informal*), level pegging (*Brit. informal*), matched, regular, symmetrical, uniform, unvarying 3. able, adequate, capable, competent, fit, good enough, ready, strong enough, suitable, up to 4. egalitarian, equable, even-handed, fair, impartial, just, unbiased *~noun* 5. brother, compeer, counterpart, equivalent, fellow, match, mate, parallel, peer, rival, twin *~verb* 6. agree with, amount to, balance, be equal to, be even with, be level with, be tantamount to, come up to, correspond to, equalize, equate, even, level, match, parallel, rival, square with, tally with, tie with

▷ **Antonyms** *~adjective* (*sense 1*) different, disproportionate, dissimilar, diverse, unequal, unlike (*sense 2*) irregular, unbalanced, unequal, uneven, unmatched (*sense 3*) inadequate, incapable, incompetent, not good enough, not up to, unequal, unfit (*sense 4*) biased, inequitable, partial, unequal, unfair, unjust *~verb* be different, be unequal, disagree

equality balance, coequality, correspondence, egalitarianism, equal opportunity, equatability, equivalence, evenness, fairness, identity, likeness, parity, sameness, similarity, uniformity

▷ **Antonyms** bias, discrimination, disparity, imparity, inequality, lack of balance, prejudice, unevenness, unfairness

equalize balance, equal, equate, even up, level, make equal, match, regularize, smooth, square, standardize

equanimity aplomb, calm, calmness, composure, coolness, imperturbability, level-headedness, peace, phlegm, placidity, poise, presence of mind, sang-froid, self-possession, serenity, steadiness, tranquillity

equate agree, balance, be commensurate, compare, correspond with *or* to, equalize, liken, make *or* be equal, match, mention in the same breath, offset, pair, parallel, square, tally, think of together

equation agreement, balancing, comparison, correspondence, equality, equalization, equating, equivalence, likeness, match, pairing, parallel

equestrian 1. *adjective* in the saddle, mounted, on horseback 2. *~noun* cavalier (*archaic*), horseman, knight, rider

equilibrate balance, ballast, compensate (for), counterbalance, counterpoise, countervail, equipoise, even up, neutralize, offset

equilibrium 1. balance, counterpoise, equipoise, evenness, rest, stability, steadiness, symmetry 2. calm, calmness, collectedness, composure, coolness, equanimity, poise, self-possession, serenity, stability, steadiness

equip accoutre, arm, array, attire, deck out, dress, endow, fit out, fit up, furnish, kit out, outfit, prepare, provide, rig, stock, supply

equipage 1. carriage, coach 2. accoutre~

ments, apparatus, baggage, equipment, gear, materiel, munitions, stores

equipment accoutrements, apparatus, appurtenances, baggage, equipage, fur~nishings, furniture, gear, materiel, out~fit, paraphernalia, rig, stuff, supplies, tackle, tools

equipoise *noun* **1.** balance, equilibrium, even balance, evenness, stability, steadiness, symmetry **2.** ballast, counterbalance, counterpoise, counter~weight, offset *~verb* **3.** balance, ballast, compensate (for), counterbalance, counterpoise, countervail, equilibrate, neutralize, offset

equitable candid, disinterested, dispas~sionate, due, even-handed, fair, honest, impartial, just, nondiscriminatory, proper, proportionate, reasonable, right, rightful, unbiased, unprejudiced

equity disinterestedness, equitableness, even-handedness, fair-mindedness, fair~ness, fair play, honesty, impartiality, integrity, justice, reasonableness, recti~tude, righteousness, uprightness

▷ **Antonyms** bias, discrimination, injus~tice, partiality, preference, prejudice, unfairness

equivalence agreement, alikeness, con~formity, correspondence, equality, even~ness, identity, interchangeableness, likeness, match, parallel, parity, same~ness, similarity, synonymy

equivalent 1. *adjective* alike, commensu~rate, comparable, correspondent, corre~sponding, equal, even, homologous, interchangeable, of a kind, of a piece, same, similar, synonymous, tantamount **2.** *~noun* correspondent, counterpart, equal, match, opposite number, parallel, peer, twin

▷ **Antonyms** *~adjective* different, dis~similar, incomparable, unequal, unlike

equivocal ambiguous, ambivalent, doubt~ful, dubious, evasive, indefinite, inde~terminate, misleading, oblique, obscure, oracular, prevaricating, questionable, suspicious, uncertain, vague

▷ **Antonyms** absolute, certain, clear, clear-cut, cut-and-dried (*informal*), de~cisive, definite, evident, explicit, incon~trovertible, indubitable, manifest, plain, positive, straight, unambiguous, un~equivocal

equivocate avoid the issue, beat about the bush (*informal*), dodge, evade, fence, flannel (*Brit. informal*), fudge, hedge, parry, prevaricate, pussyfoot (*informal*), quibble, shuffle, sidestep, tergiversate, waffle (*informal, chiefly Brit.*)

equivocation ambiguity, double talk, doubtfulness, evasion, hedging, pre~varication, quibbling, shuffling, tergi~versation, waffle (*informal, chiefly Brit.*), weasel words (*informal, chiefly U.S.*)

era aeon, age, cycle, date, day *or* days, epoch, generation, period, stage, time

eradicate abolish, annihilate, deracinate, destroy, efface, eliminate, erase, excise, expunge, exterminate, extinguish, ex~tirpate, obliterate, put paid to, remove, root out, stamp out, uproot, weed out, wipe from the face of the earth, wipe out

eradication abolition, annihilation, de~racination, destruction, effacement, elimination, erasure, expunction, exter~mination, extinction, extirpation, oblit~eration, removal

erase blot, cancel, delete, efface, excise, expunge, obliterate, remove, rub out, scratch out, wipe out

erect *adjective* **1.** elevated, firm, perpen~dicular, pricked-up, raised, rigid, stand~ing, stiff, straight, upright, vertical *~verb* **2.** build, construct, elevate, lift, mount, pitch, put up, raise, rear, set up, stand up **3.** create, establish, form, found, initiate, institute, organize, set up

▷ **Antonyms** *~adjective* bent, flaccid, horizontal, leaning, limp, prone, recum~bent, relaxed, supine *~verb* demolish, destroy, dismantle, raze, tear down

erection 1. assembly, building, construc~tion, creation, elevation, establishment, fabrication, manufacture **2.** building, construction, edifice, pile, structure

erelong *archaic or poetic* before long, early, quickly, shortly, soon, speedily

eremite anchorite, hermit, recluse, soli~tary

ergo accordingly, consequently, for that reason, hence, in consequence, so, then, therefore, thus

erode abrade, consume, corrode, destroy, deteriorate, disintegrate, eat away, grind down, spoil, wear down *or* away

erosion abrasion, attrition, consumption, corrasion, corrosion, destruction, de~terioration, disintegration, eating away, grinding down, spoiling, wear, wearing down *or* away

erotic amatory, aphrodisiac, carnal, erogenous, lustful, rousing, seductive, sensual, sexy (*informal*), steamy (*infor~mal*), stimulating, suggestive, titillat~ing, voluptuous

err 1. be inaccurate, be incorrect, be in error, blot one's copybook (*informal*), blunder, drop a brick *or* clanger (*infor~mal*), go astray, go wrong, make a mis~take, misapprehend, miscalculate, mis~judge, mistake, put one's foot in it (*in~formal*), slip up (*informal*) **2.** be out of order, blot one's copybook (*informal*), deviate, do wrong, fall, go astray, lapse, misbehave, offend, sin, transgress, tres~pass

errand charge, commission, job, message, mission, task

errant **1**. *archaic* itinerant, journeying, nomadic, peripatetic, rambling, roam~ ing, roving, wandering **2**. aberrant, de~ viant, erring, offending, sinning, stray~ ing, wayward, wrong

erratic **1**. aberrant, abnormal, capricious, changeable, desultory, eccentric, fitful, inconsistent, inconstant, irregular, shifting, uneven, unpredictable, unreli~ able, unstable, variable, wayward **2**. directionless, meandering, planetary, wandering
▷ **Antonyms** certain, consistent, con~ stant, dependable, invariable, natural, normal, predictable, regular, reliable, stable, steady, straight, unchanging, undeviating

erroneous amiss, fallacious, false, faulty, flawed, inaccurate, incorrect, inexact, invalid, mistaken, spurious, unfounded, unsound, untrue, wide of the mark, wrong
▷ **Antonyms** accurate, correct, factual, faultless, flawless, precise, right, true, veracious

error **1**. bloomer (*Brit. informal*), blunder, boner (*slang*), boob (*Brit. slang*), delu~ sion, erratum, fallacy, fault, flaw, howl~ er (*informal*), inaccuracy, misapprehen~ sion, miscalculation, misconception, mistake, oversight, slip, solecism **2**. de~ linquency, deviation, fault, lapse, mis~ deed, offence, sin, transgression, tres~ pass, wrong, wrongdoing

ersatz artificial, bogus, counterfeit, fake, imitation, phoney *or* phony (*informal*), pretended, sham, simulated, spurious, substitute, synthetic

erstwhile bygone, ex (*informal*), former, late, old, once, one-time, past, previous, quondam, sometime

erudite cultivated, cultured, educated, knowledgeable, learned, lettered, liter~ ate, scholarly, well-educated, well-read
▷ **Antonyms** ignorant, illiterate, shallow, uneducated, uninformed, unlettered, unschooled, untaught, unthinking

erudition education, knowledge, learning, letters, lore, scholarship

erupt **1**. be ejected, belch forth, blow up, break out, burst forth, burst into, burst out, discharge, explode, flare up, gush, pour forth, spew forth *or* out, spit out, spout, throw off, vent, vomit **2**. *Medical* appear, break out

eruption **1**. discharge, ejection, explosion, flare-up, outbreak, outburst, sally, venting **2**. *Medical* inflammation, out~ break, rash

escalate amplify, ascend, be increased, enlarge, expand, extend, grow, height~ en, increase, intensify, magnify, mount, raise, rise, step up
▷ **Antonyms** abate, contract, decrease, descend, diminish, fall, lessen, limit, lower, shrink, wane, wind down

escapade adventure, antic, caper, fling, lark (*informal*), mischief, prank, romp, scrape (*informal*), spree, stunt, trick

escape **1**. *verb* abscond, bolt, break free *or* out, decamp, do a bunk (*Brit. slang*), do a runner (*slang*), flee, fly, fly the coop (*U.S. & Canad. informal*), get away, hook it (*slang*), make *or* effect one's es~ cape, make one's getaway, run away *or* off, skedaddle (*informal*), skip, slip away, slip through one's fingers, take a powder (*U.S. & Canad. slang*), take it on the lam (*U.S. & Canad. slang*) **2**. *~noun* bolt, break, break-out, decamp~ ment, flight, getaway **3**. *~verb* avoid, body-swerve (*Scot.*), circumvent, dodge, duck, elude, evade, pass, shun, slip **4**. *~noun* avoidance, circumvention, elu~ sion, evasion **5**. *~verb* discharge, drain, emanate, exude, flow, gush, issue, leak, pour forth, seep, spurt **6**. *~noun* dis~ charge, drain, effluence, efflux, emana~ tion, emission, gush, leak, leakage, out~ flow, outpour, seepage, spurt **7**. *~verb* baffle, be beyond (someone), be forgotten by, elude, puzzle, stump **8**. *~noun* dis~ traction, diversion, pastime, recreation, relief

eschew abandon, abjure, abstain from, avoid, elude, fight shy of, forgo, for~ swear, give a wide berth to, give up, have nothing to do with, keep *or* steer clear of, kick (*informal*), refrain from, renounce, shun, swear off

escort *noun* **1**. bodyguard, company, con~ voy, cortege, entourage, guard, protec~ tion, retinue, safeguard, train **2**. attend~ ant, beau, chaperon, companion, guide, partner, protector, squire (*rare*) *~verb* **3**. accompany, chaperon, conduct, convoy, guard, guide, hold (someone's) hand, lead, partner, protect, shepherd, squire, usher

esculent eatable, edible, fit to eat, palat~ able, wholesome

esoteric abstruse, arcane, cabbalistic, cryptic, hidden, inner, inscrutable, mysterious, mystic, mystical, obscure, occult, private, recondite, secret

especial **1**. chief, distinguished, excep~ tional, extraordinary, marked, notable, noteworthy, outstanding, principal, sig~ nal, special, uncommon, unusual **2**. ex~ clusive, express, individual, particular, peculiar, personal, private, singular, special, specific, unique

especially **1**. chiefly, conspicuously, ex~ ceptionally, extraordinarily, largely, mainly, markedly, notably, outstand~ ingly, principally, remarkably, seriously (*informal*), signally, specially, striking~ ly, supremely, uncommonly, unusually **2**. exclusively, expressly, particularly, peculiarly, singularly, specifically, uniquely

espionage counter-intelligence, intelli~

gence, spying, surveillance, undercover work

espousal 1. adoption, advocacy, backing, championing, championship, defence, embracing, maintenance, promotion, support, taking up 2. *archaic* affiancing, betrothal, betrothing (*archaic*), engagement, espousing (*archaic*), marriage, nuptials, plighting, wedding

espouse 1. adopt, advocate, back, champion, defend, embrace, maintain, promote, stand up for, support, take up 2. *archaic* betroth (*archaic*), marry, plight one's troth (*old-fashioned*), take as spouse, take to wife, wed

esprit animation, brio, élan, liveliness, quickness, sparkle, spirit, sprightliness, verve, vitality, vivacity, wit, zest

espy behold, catch a glimpse of, catch sight of, descry, detect, discern, discover, glimpse, make out, notice, observe, perceive, sight, spot, spy

essay[1] *noun* article, composition, discourse, disquisition, dissertation, paper, piece, tract, treatise

essay[2] 1. *noun* aim, attempt, bid, crack (*informal*), effort, endeavour, exertion, experiment, go (*informal*), shot (*informal*), stab (*informal*), struggle, test, trial, try, undertaking, venture 2. *~verb* aim, attempt, endeavour, have a bash (*informal*), have a crack (*informal*), have a go, have a shot (*informal*), put to the test, strive, take on, test, try, try out, undertake

essence 1. being, bottom line, core, crux, entity, heart, kernel, life, lifeblood, meaning, nature, pith, principle, quiddity, quintessence, significance, soul, spirit, substance 2. concentrate, distillate, elixir, extract, spirits, tincture 3. *rare* cologne, fragrance, perfume, scent 4. **in essence** basically, essentially, fundamentally, in effect, in substance, in the main, materially, substantially, to all intents and purposes, virtually 5. **of the essence** crucial, essential, indispensable, of the utmost importance, vital, vitally important

essential *adjective* 1. crucial, important, indispensable, necessary, needed, requisite, vital 2. basic, cardinal, constitutional, elemental, elementary, fundamental, immanent, inherent, innate, intrinsic, key, main, principal, radical 3. absolute, complete, ideal, perfect, quintessential 4. concentrated, distilled, extracted, rectified, refined, volatile *~noun* 5. basic, fundamental, must, necessity, prerequisite, principle, requisite, rudiment, *sine qua non,* vital part
▷ **Antonyms** (*senses 1 & 2*) accessory, dispensable, expendable, extra, extraneous, incidental, inessential, lesser, minor, nonessential, optional, secondary, superfluous, surplus, trivial, unimportant, unnecessary

establish 1. base, constitute, create, decree, enact, ensconce, entrench, fix, form, found, ground, implant, inaugurate, install, institute, organize, plant, put down roots, root, secure, settle, set up, sow the seeds, start 2. authenticate, certify, confirm, corroborate, demonstrate, prove, ratify, show, substantiate, validate, verify

establishment 1. creation, enactment, formation, foundation, founding, inauguration, installation, institution, organization, setting up 2. business, company, concern, corporation, enterprise, firm, house, institute, institution, organization, outfit (*informal*), setup (*informal*), structure, system 3. building, factory, house, office, plant, quarters 4. abode, domicile, dwelling, home, house, household, pad (*slang*), residence 5. **the Establishment** established order, institutionalized authority, ruling class, the powers that be, the system

estate 1. area, demesne, domain, holdings, lands, manor, property 2. *Property law* assets, belongings, effects, fortune, goods, possessions, property, wealth 3. caste, class, order, rank 4. condition, lot, period, place, position, quality, rank, situation, standing, state, station, status

esteem *verb* 1. admire, be fond of, cherish, honour, like, love, prize, regard highly, respect, revere, reverence, take off one's hat to, think highly of, treasure, value, venerate 2. *formal* account, believe, calculate, consider, deem, estimate, hold, judge, rate, reckon, regard, think, view *~noun* 3. admiration, Brownie points, consideration, credit, estimation, good opinion, honour, regard, respect, reverence, veneration

estimable admirable, esteemed, excellent, good, honourable, honoured, meritorious, reputable, respectable, respected, valuable, valued, worthy

estimate *verb* 1. appraise, assess, calculate roughly, evaluate, gauge, guess, judge, number, reckon, value 2. assess, believe, conjecture, consider, form an opinion, guess, judge, rank, rate, reckon, surmise, think *~noun* 3. appraisal, appraisement, approximate calculation, assessment, ballpark estimate (*informal*), ballpark figure (*informal*), evaluation, guess, guesstimate (*informal*), judgment, reckoning, valuation 4. appraisal, appraisement, assessment, belief, conjecture, educated guess, estimation, judgment, opinion, surmise, thought(s)

estimation 1. appraisal, appreciation, assessment, belief, consideration, considered opinion, estimate, evaluation, judgment, opinion, view 2. admiration, Brownie points, credit, esteem, good opinion, honour, regard, respect, reverence, veneration

estrange alienate, antagonize, disaffect, disunite, divide, drive apart, lose *or* destroy the affection of, make hostile, part, separate, set at odds, withdraw, withhold

▷ **Antonyms** ally, associate, coalesce, couple, fuse, join, link, marry, unite

estrangement alienation, antagonization, breach, break-up, disaffection, dissociation, disunity, division, hostility, parting, separation, split, withdrawal, withholding

estuary creek, firth, fjord, inlet, mouth

et cetera and others, and so forth, and so on, and the like, and the rest, et al.

etch carve, corrode, cut, eat into, engrave, furrow, impress, imprint, incise, ingrain, inscribe, stamp

etching carving, engraving, impression, imprint, inscription, print

eternal **1.** abiding, ceaseless, constant, deathless, endless, everlasting, immortal, infinite, interminable, never-ending, perennial, perpetual, sempiternal (*literary*), timeless, unceasing, undying, unending, unremitting, without end **2.** deathless, enduring, everlasting, immortal, immutable, imperishable, indestructible, lasting, permanent

▷ **Antonyms** changing, ephemeral, evanescent, finite, fleeting, infrequent, irregular, mortal, occasional, perishable, random, rare, temporal, transient, transitory

eternity **1.** age, ages, endlessness, for ever, immortality, infinitude, infinity, perpetuity, timelessness, time without end **2.** *Theology* heaven, paradise, the afterlife, the hereafter, the next world

ethereal **1.** dainty, delicate, exquisite, fine, insubstantial, light, rarefied, refined, subtle, tenuous **2.** aerial, airy, fairy, impalpable, intangible, light, rarefied **3.** celestial, empyreal, heavenly, spiritual, sublime, unearthly, unworldly

ethical conscientious, correct, decent, fair, fitting, good, honest, honourable, just, moral, principled, proper, right, righteous, upright, virtuous

▷ **Antonyms** dishonourable, disreputable, immoral, improper, indecent, low-down (*informal*), not cricket (*informal*), underhand, unethical, unfair, unscrupulous, unseemly

ethics conscience, moral code, morality, moral philosophy, moral values, principles, rules of conduct, standards

ethnic cultural, folk, indigenous, national, native, racial, traditional

ethos attitude, beliefs, character, disposition, ethic, spirit, tenor

etiolated achromatic, blanched, bleached, colourless, faded, pale, wan, washed out, white, whitened

etiquette civility, code, convention, courtesy, customs, decorum, formalities, good *or* proper behaviour, manners, politeness, politesse, propriety, protocol, p's and q's, rules, usage

eulogize acclaim, applaud, commend, compliment, crack up (*informal*), cry up, exalt, extol, glorify, laud, magnify (*archaic*), panegyrize, pay tribute to, praise, sing *or* sound the praises of

eulogy acclaim, acclamation, accolade, applause, commendation, compliment, encomium, exaltation, glorification, laudation, paean, panegyric, plaudit, praise, tribute

euphonic, euphonious canorous (*rare*), clear, consonant, dulcet, harmonious, mellifluous, mellow, melodic, melodious, musical, pleasing to the ear, silvery, sweet-toned, tuneful

euphony consonance, harmony, mellifluousness, mellowness, melodiousness, melody, music, musicality, tunefulness, unison

euphoria bliss, ecstasy, elation, exaltation, exhilaration, exultation, glee, high spirits, intoxication, joy, joyousness, jubilation, rapture, transport

▷ **Antonyms** depression, despair, despondency, dolefulness, downheartedness, dumps (*informal*), gloominess, hopelessness, low spirits, melancholia, melancholy, sadness, the blues

evacuate **1.** abandon, clear, decamp, depart, desert, forsake, leave, move out, pull out, quit, relinquish, remove, vacate, withdraw **2.** crap (*taboo slang*), defecate, discharge, eject, eliminate, empty, excrete, expel, shit (*taboo slang*), void

evade **1.** avoid, body-swerve (*Scot.*), circumvent, decline, dodge, duck, elude, escape, escape the clutches of, eschew, get away from, shirk, shun, sidestep, slip through one's fingers, slip through the net, steer clear of **2.** balk, beat about the bush, circumvent, cop out (*slang*), equivocate, fence, fend off, flannel (*Brit. informal*), fudge, hedge, parry, prevaricate, quibble, waffle (*informal, chiefly Brit.*)

▷ **Antonyms** (*sense 1*) brave, confront, encounter, face, meet, meet face to face

evaluate appraise, assay, assess, calculate, estimate, gauge, judge, rank, rate, reckon, size up (*informal*), value, weigh

evaluation appraisal, assessment, calculation, estimate, estimation, judgment, opinion, rating, valuation

evanesce clear, disappear, disperse, dissolve, evaporate, fade, melt, vanish, vanish off the face of the earth

evanescence brevity, briefness, ephemerality, ephemeralness, fleetingness, fugaciousness, fugacity, impermanence, momentariness, transience, transitori~ness

evanescent brief, ephemeral, fading, fleeting, fugacious, fugitive, imperma~nent, momentary, passing, short-lived, transient, transitory, vanishing

evangelical, evangelistic crusading, mis~sionary, propagandizing, proselytizing, zealous

evaporate 1. dehydrate, desiccate, dry, dry up, vaporize **2.** dematerialize, dis~appear, dispel, disperse, dissipate, dis~solve, evanesce, fade, fade away, melt, melt away, vanish

evaporation 1. dehydration, desiccation, drying, drying up, vaporization **2.** de~materialization, disappearance, dispel~ling, dispersal, dissipation, dissolution, evanescence, fading, fading away, melt~ing, melting away, vanishing

evasion artifice, avoidance, circumven~tion, cop-out (*slang*), cunning, dodge, elusion, equivocation, escape, evasive~ness, excuse, fudging, obliqueness, pre~text, prevarication, ruse, shift, shirking, shuffling, sophism, sophistry, subter~fuge, trickery, waffle (*informal, chiefly Brit.*)

evasive cagey (*informal*), casuistic, casu~istical, cunning, deceitful, deceptive, devious, dissembling, elusive, elusory, equivocating, indirect, misleading, oblique, prevaricating, shifty, shuffling, slippery, sophistical, tricky

▷ **Antonyms** candid, direct, frank, guile~less, honest, open, straight, straight~forward, truthful, unequivocating

eve 1. day before, night before, vigil **2.** brink, edge, point, threshold, verge

even *adjective* **1.** flat, flush, horizontal, level, parallel, plane, plumb, smooth, steady, straight, true, uniform **2.** con~stant, metrical, regular, smooth, steady, unbroken, uniform, uninterrupted, un~varying, unwavering **3.** calm, composed, cool, equable, equanimous, even-tempered, imperturbable, peaceful, placid, serene, stable, steady, tranquil, undisturbed, unexcitable, unruffled, well-balanced **4.** coequal, commensu~rate, comparable, drawn, equal, equal~ized, equally balanced, fifty-fifty (*infor~mal*), identical, level, level pegging (*Brit. informal*), like, matching, neck and neck, on a par, parallel, similar, square, the same, tied, uniform **5.** bal~anced, disinterested, dispassionate, equitable, fair, fair and square, impar~tial, just, unbiased, unprejudiced **6. get even (with)** *informal* be revenged *or* re~venge oneself, even the score, get one's own back, give tit for tat, pay back, pay (someone) back in his *or* her own coin, reciprocate, repay, requite, return like for like, settle the score, take an eye for an eye, take vengeance *~adverb* **7.** all the more, much, still, yet **8.** despite, dis~regarding, in spite of, notwithstanding **9. even as** at the same time as, at the time that, during the time that, exactly as, just as, while, whilst **10. even so** all the same, be that as it may, despite (that), however, in spite of (that), nevertheless, nonetheless, notwith~standing (that), still, yet *~verb* **11.** (*often followed by* **out** *or* **up**) align, balance, become level, equal, equalize, flatten, level, match, regularize, smooth, square, stabilize, steady **12. even the score** be revenged *or* revenge oneself, equalize, get even (*informal*), get one's own back, give tit for tat, pay (someone) back, reciprocate, repay, requite, return like for like, settle the score, take an eye for an eye, take vengeance

▷ **Antonyms** (*senses 1 & 2*) asymmetri~cal, awry, broken, bumpy, changeable, changing, curving, different, fluctuat~ing, irregular, odd, rough, twisting, un~dulating, uneven, variable, wavy (*sense 3*) agitated, changeable, emotional, ex~citable, quick-tempered, unpredictable (*sense 4*) disproportionate, ill-matched, imbalanced, irregular, unequal, uneven (*sense 5*) biased, partial, prejudiced, un~balanced, unequal, unfair

even-handed balanced, disinterested, equitable, fair, fair and square, impar~tial, just, unbiased, unprejudiced

evening crepuscule, dusk, e'en (*archaic or poetic*), eve, even (*archaic*), eventide (*archaic or poetic*), gloaming (*Scot. or poetic*), twilight, vesper (*archaic*)

event 1. adventure, affair, business, cir~cumstance, episode, escapade, experi~ence, fact, happening, incident, matter, milestone, occasion, occurrence **2.** con~clusion, consequence, effect, end, issue, outcome, result, termination, upshot **3.** bout, competition, contest, game, tour~nament **4. at all events** at any rate, come what may, in any case, in any event, re~gardless, whatever happens

even-tempered calm, composed, cool, cool-headed, equable, imperturbable, level-headed, peaceful, placid, serene, steady, tranquil, unexcitable, unruffled

▷ **Antonyms** emotional, excitable, hasty, highly-strung, hot-headed, hot-tempered, irascible, quick-tempered, temperamental, touchy, volatile

eventful active, busy, consequential, critical, crucial, decisive, dramatic, ex~citing, fateful, full, historic, important, lively, memorable, momentous, notable, noteworthy, remarkable, significant

▷ **Antonyms** commonplace, dull, hum~drum, insignificant, ordinary, trivial, uneventful, unexceptional, unexciting, unimportant, uninteresting, unremark~able

eventual concluding, consequent, ensu~ing, final, future, later, overall, prospec~tive, resulting, ultimate

eventuality case, chance, contingency, event, likelihood, possibility, probability

eventually after all, at the end of the day, finally, in the course of time, in the end, in the fullness of time, in the long run, one day, some day, some time, sooner or later, ultimately, when all is said and done

eventuate be a consequence, be consequent, come about, come to pass (*archaic*), ensue, follow, issue, result

ever 1. at all, at any period, at any point, at any time, by any chance, in any case, on any occasion **2.** always, at all times, aye (*Scot.*), constantly, continually, endlessly, eternally, everlastingly, evermore, for ever, incessantly, perpetually, relentlessly, to the end of time, unceasingly, unendingly

everlasting 1. abiding, deathless, endless, eternal, immortal, imperishable, indestructible, infinite, interminable, never-ending, perpetual, timeless, undying **2.** ceaseless, constant, continual, continuous, endless, incessant, interminable, never-ending, unceasing, uninterrupted, unremitting
▷ **Antonyms** brief, ephemeral, fleeting, impermanent, passing, short-lived, temporary, transient, transitory

evermore always, eternally, ever, for ever, *in perpetuum,* to the end of time

every all, each, each one, the whole number

everybody all and sundry, each one, each person, everyone, every person, one and all, the whole world

everyday 1. daily, quotidian **2.** accustomed, banal, bog-standard (*Brit. & Irish slang*), common, common or garden (*informal*), commonplace, conventional, customary, dime-a-dozen (*informal*), dull, familiar, frequent, habitual, informal, mundane, ordinary, routine, run-of-the-mill, stock, unexceptional, unimaginative, usual, vanilla (*slang*), wonted, workaday
▷ **Antonyms** (*sense 1*) infrequent, irregular, now and then, occasional, periodic (*sense 2*) best, exceptional, exciting, extraordinary, incidental, individual, infrequent, interesting, irregular, now and then, occasional, original, outlandish, periodic, special, uncommon, unusual

everyone all and sundry, each one, each person, everybody, every person, one and all, the whole world

everything all, each thing, the aggregate, the entirety, the lot, the sum, the total, the whole caboodle (*informal*), the whole kit and caboodle (*informal*), the whole lot

everywhere all around, all over, far and wide *or* near, high and low, in each place, in every nook and cranny, in every place, omnipresent, the world over, to *or* in all places, ubiquitous, ubiquitously

evict boot out (*informal*), chuck out (*informal*), dislodge, dispossess, eject, expel, kick out (*informal*), oust, put out, remove, show the door (to), throw on to the streets, throw out, turf out (*informal*), turn out

eviction clearance, dislodgement, dispossession, ejection, expulsion, ouster (*Law*), removal

evidence 1. *noun* affirmation, attestation, averment, confirmation, corroboration, data, declaration, demonstration, deposition, grounds, indication, manifestation, mark, proof, sign, substantiation, testimony, token, witness **2.** *~verb* demonstrate, denote, display, evince, exhibit, indicate, manifest, prove, reveal, show, signify, testify to, witness

evident apparent, blatant, bold, clear, conspicuous, incontestable, incontrovertible, indisputable, manifest, noticeable, obvious, palpable, patent, perceptible, plain, plain as the nose on your face, salient, tangible, unmistakable, visible
▷ **Antonyms** ambiguous, concealed, doubtful, dubious, hidden, imperceptible, obscure, questionable, secret, uncertain, unclear, unknown, vague

evidently 1. clearly, doubtless, doubtlessly, incontestably, incontrovertibly, indisputably, manifestly, obviously, patently, plainly, undoubtedly, unmistakably, without question **2.** apparently, it seems, it would seem, ostensibly, outwardly, seemingly, to all appearances

evil *adjective* **1.** bad, base, corrupt, depraved, heinous, immoral, iniquitous, maleficent, malevolent, malicious, malignant, nefarious, reprobate, sinful, unholy, vicious, vile, villainous, wicked, wrong *~noun* **2.** badness, baseness, corruption, curse, depravity, heinousness, immorality, iniquity, maleficence, malignity, sin, sinfulness, turpitude, vice, viciousness, villainy, wickedness, wrong, wrongdoing *~adjective* **3.** baneful (*archaic*), calamitous, catastrophic, deleterious, destructive, detrimental, dire, disastrous, harmful, hurtful, inauspicious, injurious, mischievous, painful, pernicious, ruinous, sorrowful, unfortunate, unlucky, woeful *~noun* **4.** affliction, calamity, catastrophe, disaster, harm, hurt, ill, injury, mischief, misery, misfortune, pain, ruin, sorrow, suffering, woe *~adjective* **5.** foul, mephitic, noxious, offensive, pestilential, putrid, unpleasant, vile

evince attest, bespeak, betoken, demonstrate, display, establish, evidence, exhibit, express, indicate, make clear, make evident, manifest, reveal, show, signify

evoke 1. arouse, awaken, call, excite, give rise to, induce, recall, rekindle, stimulate, stir up, summon up 2. call forth, educe (*rare*), elicit, produce, provoke 3. arouse, call, call forth, conjure up, invoke, raise, summon

▷ **Antonyms** contain, hold in check, inhibit, muffle, repress, restrain, smother, stifle, suppress

evolution development, enlargement, evolvement, expansion, growth, increase, maturation, progress, progression, unfolding, unrolling, working out

evolve develop, disclose, educe, elaborate, enlarge, expand, grow, increase, mature, open, progress, unfold, unroll, work out

exacerbate add insult to injury, aggravate (*informal*), embitter, enrage, envenom, exasperate, excite, fan the flames of, inflame, infuriate, intensify, irritate, madden, provoke, vex, worsen

exact *adjective* 1. accurate, careful, correct, definite, explicit, express, faithful, faultless, identical, literal, methodical, orderly, particular, precise, right, specific, true, unequivocal, unerring, veracious, very 2. careful, exacting, meticulous, painstaking, punctilious, rigorous, scrupulous, severe, strict *~verb* 3. call for, claim, command, compel, demand, extort, extract, force, impose, insist upon, require, squeeze, wrest, wring

▷ **Antonyms** *~adjective* approximate, careless, imprecise, inaccurate, incorrect, indefinite, inexact, loose, rough, slovenly

exacting demanding, difficult, hard, harsh, imperious, oppressive, painstaking, rigid, rigorous, severe, stern, strict, stringent, taxing, tough, unsparing

▷ **Antonyms** easy, easy-peasy (*slang*), effortless, no bother, simple, undemanding

exaction compulsion, contribution, demand, extortion, imposition, oppression, rapacity, requirement, requisition, shakedown (*U.S. slang*), squeeze (*informal*), tribute

exactitude accuracy, carefulness, correctness, exactness, faithfulness, faultlessness, nicety, orderliness, painstakingness, preciseness, precision, promptitude, regularity, rigorousness, rigour, scrupulousness, strictness, truth, unequivocalness, veracity

exactly *adverb* 1. accurately, carefully, correctly, definitely, explicitly, faithfully, faultlessly, literally, methodically, precisely, rigorously, scrupulously, severely, strictly, truly, truthfully, unequivocally, unerringly, veraciously 2. absolutely, bang, explicitly, expressly, indeed, in every respect, just, on the button (*informal*), particularly, precisely, prompt (*informal*), quite, specifically, to the letter 3. **not exactly** *ironical* by no means, certainly not, hardly, in no manner, in no way, not at all, not by any means, not quite, not really *~interjection* 4. absolutely, assuredly, as you say, certainly, indeed, just so, of course, precisely, quite, quite so, spot-on (*Brit. informal*), truly

exactness accuracy, carefulness, correctness, exactitude, faithfulness, faultlessness, nicety, orderliness, painstakingness, preciseness, precision, promptitude, regularity, rigorousness, rigour, scrupulousness, strictness, truth, unequivocalness, veracity

▷ **Antonyms** imprecision, inaccuracy, incorrectness, inexactness, unfaithfulness

exaggerate amplify, blow out of all proportion, embellish, embroider, emphasize, enlarge, exalt, hyperbolize, inflate, lay it on thick (*informal*), magnify, make a federal case of (*U.S. informal*), make a mountain out of a molehill (*informal*), make a production (out) of (*informal*), overdo, overemphasize, overestimate, overstate

exaggerated amplified, exalted, excessive, extravagant, fulsome, highly coloured, hyped, hyperbolic, inflated, overblown, overdone, overestimated, overstated, over the top (*informal*), pretentious, tall (*informal*)

exaggeration amplification, embellishment, emphasis, enlargement, exaltation, excess, extravagance, hyperbole, inflation, magnification, overemphasis, overestimation, overstatement, pretension, pretentiousness

▷ **Antonyms** litotes, meiosis, restraint, underplaying, understatement

exalt 1. advance, aggrandize, dignify, elevate, ennoble, honour, promote, raise, upgrade 2. acclaim, apotheosize, applaud, bless, crack up (*informal*), extol, glorify, idolize, laud, magnify (*archaic*), pay homage to, pay tribute to, praise, reverence, set on a pedestal, worship 3. animate, arouse, electrify, elevate, excite, fire the imagination (of), heighten, inspire, inspirit, stimulate, uplift 4. delight, elate, exhilarate, fill with joy, thrill

exaltation 1. advancement, aggrandizement, dignity, elevation, eminence, ennoblement, grandeur, high rank, honour, loftiness, prestige, promotion, rise, upgrading 2. acclaim, acclamation, apotheosis, applause, blessing, extolment, glorification, glory, homage, idolization, laudation, lionization, magnification, panegyric, plaudits, praise, reverence, tribute, worship 3. animation, elevation, excitement, inspiration, stimulation, uplift 4. bliss, delight, ecstasy, elation, exhilaration, exultation, joy, joyousness, jubilation, rapture, transport

exalted 1. august, dignified, elevated, eminent, grand, high, high-ranking, honoured, lofty, prestigious 2. elevated, high-minded, ideal, intellectual, lofty, noble, sublime, superior, uplifting 3. *informal* elevated, exaggerated, excessive, inflated, overblown, pretentious 4. animated, blissful, cock-a-hoop, ecstatic, elated, elevated, excited, exhilarated, exultant, in high spirits, in seventh heaven, inspired, inspirited, joyous, jubilant, on cloud nine (*informal*), over the moon (*informal*), rapturous, stimulated, transported, uplifted

examination analysis, assay, catechism, checkup, exploration, inquiry, inquisition, inspection, interrogation, investigation, observation, once-over (*informal*), perusal, probe, questioning, quiz, recce (*slang*), research, review, scrutiny, search, study, survey, test, trial

examine 1. analyse, appraise, assay, check, check out, consider, explore, go over *or* through, inspect, investigate, look over, peruse, ponder, pore over, probe, recce (*slang*), research, review, scan, scrutinize, sift, study, survey, take stock of, test, vet, weigh, work over 2. catechize, cross-examine, grill (*informal*), inquire, interrogate, question, quiz

example 1. case, case in point, exemplification, illustration, instance, sample, specimen 2. archetype, exemplar, ideal, illustration, model, norm, paradigm, paragon, pattern, precedent, prototype, standard 3. admonition, caution, lesson, warning 4. **for example** as an illustration, by way of illustration, e.g., *exempli gratia,* for instance, to cite an instance, to illustrate

exasperate aggravate (*informal*), anger, annoy, bug (*informal*), embitter, enrage, exacerbate, excite, gall, get (*informal*), get in one's hair (*informal*), get on one's nerves (*informal*), get on one's wick (*Brit. slang*), hassle (*informal*), incense, inflame, infuriate, irk, irritate, madden, nark (*Brit., Austral., & N.Z. slang*), needle (*informal*), nettle, peeve (*informal*), pique, piss one off (*taboo slang*), provoke, rankle, rile (*informal*), rouse, try the patience of, vex

▷ **Antonyms** appease, assuage, calm, conciliate, mollify, pacify, placate, soothe

exasperation aggravation (*informal*), anger, annoyance, exacerbation, fury, ire (*literary*), irritation, passion, pique, provocation, rage, vexation, wrath

excavate burrow, cut, delve, dig, dig out, dig up, gouge, hollow, mine, quarry, scoop, trench, tunnel, uncover, unearth

excavation burrow, cavity, cut, cutting, dig, diggings, ditch, dugout, hole, hollow, mine, pit, quarry, shaft, trench, trough

exceed 1. beat, be superior to, better, cap (*informal*), eclipse, excel, go beyond, knock spots off (*informal*), outdistance, outdo, outreach, outrun, outshine, outstrip, overtake, pass, put in the shade (*informal*), run rings around (*informal*), surmount, surpass, top, transcend 2. go beyond the bounds of, go over the limit of, go over the top, overstep

exceeding enormous, exceptional, excessive, extraordinary, great, huge, pre-eminent, streets ahead, superior, superlative, surpassing, vast

exceedingly enormously, especially, exceptionally, excessively, extraordinarily, extremely, greatly, highly, hugely, inordinately, seriously (*informal*), superlatively, surpassingly, to a fault, to the nth degree, unusually, vastly, very

excel 1. beat, be superior, better, cap (*informal*), eclipse, exceed, go beyond, outdo, outrival, outshine, pass, put in the shade (*informal*), run rings around (*informal*), steal the show (*informal*), surmount, surpass, top, transcend 2. be good, be master of, be proficient, be skilful, be talented, have (something) down to a fine art, predominate, shine, show talent, take precedence

excellence distinction, eminence, fineness, goodness, greatness, high quality, merit, perfection, pre-eminence, purity, superiority, supremacy, transcendence, virtue, worth

excellent A1 *or* A-one (*informal*), admirable, bitchin' (*U.S. slang*), bodacious (*slang, chiefly U.S.*), boffo (*slang*), brill (*informal*), brilliant, capital, champion, chillin' (*U.S. slang*), choice, cracking (*Brit. informal*), crucial (*slang*), def (*slang*), distinguished, dope (*slang*), estimable, exemplary, exquisite, fine, first-class, first-rate, good, great, jim-dandy (*slang*), mean (*slang*), mega (*slang*), meritorious, notable, noted, outstanding, prime, select, sovereign, sterling, superb, superior, superlative, the dog's bollocks (*taboo slang*), tiptop, top-notch (*informal*), topping (*Brit. slang*), world-class, worthy

▷ **Antonyms** abysmal, bad, dreadful, faulty, imperfect, incompetent, inexpert, inferior, lousy (*slang*), mediocre, no great shakes (*informal*), piss-poor (*taboo slang*), poor, rotten (*informal*), second-class, second-rate, substandard, terrible, unskilled

except 1. *preposition also* **except for** apart from, bar, barring, besides, but, excepting, excluding, exclusive of, omitting, other than, save (*archaic*), saving, with the exception of 2. *~verb* ban, bar, disallow, exclude, leave out, omit, pass over, reject, rule out

exception **1**. debarment, disallowment, excepting, exclusion, leaving out, omission, passing over, rejection **2**. anomaly, departure, deviation, freak, inconsistency, irregularity, oddity, peculiarity, quirk, special case **3**. **take exception** be offended, be resentful, demur, disagree, object, quibble, take offence, take umbrage

exceptionable disagreeable, inappropriate, objectionable, unacceptable, unbearable, undesirable, unsatisfactory, unwelcome

exceptional **1**. aberrant, abnormal, anomalous, atypical, deviant, extraordinary, inconsistent, irregular, odd, peculiar, rare, singular, special, strange, uncommon, unusual **2**. bodacious (*slang, chiefly U.S.*), excellent, extraordinary, marvellous, notable, one in a million, outstanding, phenomenal, prodigious, remarkable, special, superior

▷ **Antonyms** (*sense 1*) average, common, customary, familiar, normal, ordinary, regular, straightforward, typical, unexceptional, unremarkable, usual (*sense 2*) average, awful, bad, lousy (*slang*), mediocre, no great shakes (*informal*), second-rate

excerpt **1**. *noun* citation, extract, fragment, part, passage, pericope, piece, portion, quotation, quote (*informal*), section, selection **2**. *~verb* cite, cull, extract, pick out, quote, select, take

excess *noun* **1**. glut, leftover, overabundance, overdose, overflow, overload, plethora, remainder, superabundance, superfluity, surfeit, surplus, too much **2**. debauchery, dissipation, dissoluteness, exorbitance, extravagance, immoderation, intemperance, overindulgence, prodigality, unrestraint *~adjective* **3**. extra, leftover, redundant, remaining, residual, spare, superfluous, surplus

▷ **Antonyms** (*sense 1*) dearth, deficiency, insufficiency, lack, shortage, want (*sense 2*) moderation, restraint, self-control, self-discipline, self-restraint, temperance

excessive disproportionate, enormous, exaggerated, exorbitant, extravagant, extreme, fulsome, immoderate, inordinate, intemperate, needless, O.T.T. (*slang*), overdone, overmuch, over the odds, over the top (*slang*), prodigal, profligate, superfluous, too much, unconscionable, undue, unreasonable

exchange *verb* **1**. bandy, barter, change, commute, convert into, interchange, reciprocate, swap (*informal*), switch, trade, truck *~noun* **2**. barter, dealing, interchange, quid pro quo, reciprocity, substitution, swap (*informal*), switch, tit for tat, trade, traffic, truck **3**. Bourse, market

excise[1] *noun* customs, duty, impost, levy, surcharge, tariff, tax, toll

excise[2] *verb* **1**. cross out, cut, delete, destroy, eradicate, erase, expunge, exterminate, extirpate, strike out, wipe from the face of the earth **2**. cut off *or* out, extract, remove

excision deletion, destruction, eradication, extermination, extirpation, removal

excitable edgy, emotional, hasty, highly strung, hot-headed, hot-tempered, irascible, mercurial, nervous, passionate, quick-tempered, sensitive, susceptible, temperamental, testy, touchy, uptight (*informal*), violent, volatile

▷ **Antonyms** calm, cool, cool-headed, even-tempered, imperturbable, laid-back (*informal*), placid, unexcitable, unruffled

excite agitate, animate, arouse, awaken, discompose, disturb, electrify, elicit, evoke, fire, foment, galvanize, incite, inflame, inspire, instigate, kindle, move, provoke, quicken, rouse, stimulate, stir up, thrill, titillate, waken, whet

excited aflame, agitated, animated, aroused, awakened, discomposed, disturbed, enthusiastic, feverish, flurried, high (*informal*), hot and bothered (*informal*), moved, nervous, overwrought, roused, stimulated, stirred, thrilled, tumultuous, wild, worked up

excitement **1**. action, activity, ado, adventure, agitation, animation, commotion, discomposure, elation, enthusiasm, ferment, fever, flurry, furore, heat, kicks (*informal*), passion, perturbation, thrill, tumult, warmth **2**. impulse, incitement, instigation, motivation, motive, provocation, stimulation, stimulus, urge

exciting dramatic, electrifying, exhilarating, inspiring, intoxicating, moving, provocative, rip-roaring (*informal*), rousing, sensational, sexy (*informal*), stimulating, stirring, thrilling, titillating

▷ **Antonyms** boring, dreary, dull, flat, humdrum, mind-numbing, monotonous, unexciting, uninspiring, uninteresting

exclaim call, call out, cry, cry out, declare, ejaculate, proclaim, shout, utter, vociferate, yell

exclamation call, cry, ejaculation, expletive, interjection, outcry, shout, utterance, vociferation, yell

exclude **1**. ban, bar, black, blackball, boycott, debar, disallow, embargo, forbid, interdict, keep out, ostracize, prohibit, proscribe, refuse, shut out, veto **2**. count out, eliminate, except, ignore, leave out, omit, pass over, preclude, reject, repudiate, rule out, set aside **3**. bounce (*slang*), drive out, eject, evict, expel, force out, get rid of, oust, remove, throw out

▷ **Antonyms** accept, admit, allow, count, include, let in, permit, receive, welcome

exclusion 1. ban, bar, boycott, debarment, disqualification, embargo, forbiddance, interdict, nonadmission, preclusion, prohibition, proscription, refusal, veto 2. elimination, exception, omission, rejection, repudiation 3. eviction, expulsion, removal

exclusive 1. absolute, complete, entire, full, only, private, single, sole, total, undivided, unique, unshared, whole 2. aristocratic, chic, choice, clannish, classy (*slang*), cliquish, closed, discriminative, elegant, fashionable, high-toned, limited, narrow, posh (*informal, chiefly Brit.*), private, restricted, restrictive, ritzy (*slang*), select, selfish, snobbish, swish (*informal, chiefly Brit.*), top-drawer, up-market 3. confined, limited, peculiar, restricted, unique 4. debarring, except for, excepting, excluding, leaving aside, not counting, omitting, restricting, ruling out
▷ **Antonyms** common, communal, inclusive, nonexclusive, open, partial, popular, public, shared, sociable, unrestricted

excogitate conceive, contemplate, contrive, deliberate, devise, evolve, frame, invent, mull over, ponder, ruminate, think out *or* up, weigh, work out

excommunicate anathematize, ban, banish, cast out, denounce, eject, exclude, expel, proscribe, remove, repudiate, unchurch

excoriate 1. abrade, flay, gall, peel, scarify, scrape, scratch, skin, strip 2. attack, bawl out (*informal*), berate, blast, carpet (*informal*), castigate, censure, chastise, chew out (*U.S. & Canad. informal*), condemn, criticize, denounce, flay, give a rocket (*Brit. & N.Z. informal*), lambast(e), put down, read the riot act, rebuke, reproach, reprove, revile, scold, slam (*slang*), slate (*informal, chiefly Brit.*), tear into (*informal*), tear (someone) off a strip (*Brit. informal*), upbraid, vilify

excrescence 1. *Medical* growth, lump, swelling, tumour, wart 2. knob, lump, outgrowth, process, projection, prominence, protrusion, protuberance

excrete crap (*taboo slang*), defecate, discharge, egest, eject, eliminate, evacuate, expel, exude, shit (*taboo slang*), void

excruciate afflict, agonize, harrow, rack, torment, torture

excruciating acute, agonizing, burning, exquisite, extreme, harrowing, insufferable, intense, piercing, racking, searing, severe, tormenting, torturous, unbearable, unendurable, violent

exculpate absolve, acquit, clear, discharge, dismiss, excuse, exonerate, free, justify, pardon, release, vindicate

excursion 1. airing, day trip, expedition, jaunt, journey, outing, pleasure trip, ramble, tour, trip 2. detour, deviation, digression, episode, excursus, wandering

excursive devious, diffusive, digressive, discursive, episodic, errant, rambling, roaming, roving, wandering

excusable allowable, defensible, forgivable, justifiable, minor, pardonable, permissible, slight, understandable, venial, warrantable

excuse *verb* 1. absolve, acquit, bear with, exculpate, exonerate, extenuate, forgive, indulge, make allowances for, overlook, pardon, pass over, tolerate, turn a blind eye to, wink at 2. apologize for, condone, defend, explain, justify, mitigate, vindicate 3. absolve, discharge, exempt, free, let off, liberate, release, relieve, spare *~noun* 4. apology, defence, explanation, grounds, justification, mitigation, plea, pretext, reason, vindication 5. cop-out (*slang*), disguise, evasion, expedient, makeshift, pretence, pretext, semblance, shift, subterfuge 6. *informal* apology, makeshift, mockery, substitute, travesty
▷ **Antonyms** *~verb* accuse, arraign, blame, censure, charge, chasten, chastise, compel, condemn, convict, correct, criticize, hold responsible, indict, oblige, point a *or* the finger at, punish, sentence *~noun (sense 4)* accusation, charge, imputation, indictment

execrable abhorrent, abominable, accursed, atrocious, cringe-making (*Brit. informal*), damnable, deplorable, despicable, detestable, disgusting, foul, hateful, heinous, horrible, loathsome, nauseous, obnoxious, obscene, odious, offensive, repulsive, revolting, sickening, vile, yucky *or* yukky (*slang*)

execrate abhor, abominate, anathematize, condemn, curse, damn, denounce, deplore, despise, detest, excoriate, hate, imprecate, loathe, revile, slam (*slang*), vilify

execration abhorrence, abomination, anathema, condemnation, contempt, curse, damnation, detestation, excoriation, hate, hatred, imprecation, loathing, malediction, odium, vilification

execute 1. behead, electrocute, guillotine, hang, kill, put to death, shoot 2. accomplish, achieve, administer, bring off, carry out, complete, consummate, discharge, do, effect, enact, enforce, finish, fulfil, implement, perform, prosecute, put into effect, realize, render 3. *Law* deliver, seal, serve, sign, validate

execution 1. accomplishment, achievement, administration, carrying out, completion, consummation, discharge, effect, enactment, enforcement, implementation, operation, performance, prosecution, realization, rendering 2. capital punishment, hanging, killing 3. delivery, manner, mode, performance, rendition, style, technique 4. *Law* warrant, writ

executioner 1. hangman, headsman **2.** assassin, exterminator, hit man (*slang*), killer, liquidator, murderer, slayer

executive *noun* **1.** administrator, director, manager, official **2.** administration, directorate, directors, government, hierarchy, leadership, management *~adjective* **3.** administrative, controlling, decision-making, directing, governing, managerial

exemplar 1. criterion, epitome, example, ideal, model, paradigm, paragon, pattern, standard **2.** example, exemplification, illustration, instance, prototype, specimen, type

exemplary 1. admirable, commendable, correct, estimable, excellent, fine, good, honourable, ideal, laudable, meritorious, model, praiseworthy, punctilious, sterling **2.** admonitory, cautionary, monitory, warning **3.** characteristic, illustrative, representative, typical

exemplify demonstrate, depict, display, embody, evidence, exhibit, illustrate, instance, manifest, represent, serve as an example of, show

exempt 1. *verb* absolve, discharge, except, excuse, exonerate, free, grant immunity, let off, liberate, release, relieve, spare **2.** *~adjective* absolved, clear, discharged, excepted, excused, favoured, free, immune, liberated, not liable, not subject, privileged, released, spared

▷ **Antonyms** *~adjective* accountable, answerable, chargeable, liable, obligated, responsible, subject

exemption absolution, discharge, dispensation, exception, exoneration, freedom, immunity, privilege, release

exercise *verb* **1.** apply, bring to bear, employ, enjoy, exert, practise, put to use, use, utilize, wield **2.** discipline, drill, habituate, inure, practise, train, work out **3.** afflict, agitate, annoy, burden, distress, disturb, occupy, pain, perturb, preoccupy, trouble, try, vex, worry *~noun* **4.** action, activity, discipline, drill, drilling, effort, labour, toil, training, work, work-out **5.** accomplishment, application, discharge, employment, enjoyment, exertion, fulfilment, implementation, practice, use, utilization **6.** drill, lesson, practice, problem, schooling, schoolwork, task, work

exert 1. apply, bring into play, bring to bear, employ, exercise, expend, make use of, put forth, use, utilize, wield **2.** **exert oneself** apply oneself, bend over backwards (*informal*), break one's neck (*informal*), bust a gut (*informal*), do one's best, do one's damnedest (*informal*), endeavour, get one's finger out (*Brit. informal*), give it one's all (*informal*), give it one's best shot (*informal*), go for broke (*slang*), go for it (*informal*), knock oneself out (*informal*), labour, make an all-out effort (*informal*), make an effort, pull one's finger out (*Brit. informal*), rupture oneself (*informal*), spare no effort, strain, strive, struggle, toil, try hard, work

exertion action, application, attempt, effort, elbow grease (*facetious*), employment, endeavour, exercise, industry, labour, pains, strain, stretch, struggle, toil, travail (*literary*), trial, use, utilization

exhalation breath, breathing out, discharge, effluvium, emanation, emission, evaporation, exhaust, expiration, fog, fume, mist, smoke, steam, vapour

exhale breathe, breathe out, discharge, eject, emanate, emit, evaporate, expel, give off, issue, respire, steam

exhaust 1. bankrupt, cripple, debilitate, disable, drain, enervate, enfeeble, fatigue, impoverish, prostrate, sap, tire, tire out, weaken, wear out **2.** consume, deplete, dissipate, expend, finish, run through, spend, squander, use up, waste **3.** drain, dry, empty, strain, void **4.** be emitted, discharge, emanate, escape, issue

exhausted 1. all in (*slang*), beat (*slang*), buggered (*slang*), clapped out (*Austral. & N.Z. informal*), creamcrackered (*Brit. slang*), crippled, dead (*informal*), dead beat (*informal*), dead tired, debilitated, disabled, dog-tired (*informal*), done in (*informal*), drained, effete, enervated, enfeebled, fatigued, jaded, knackered (*slang*), on one's last legs (*informal*), out on one's feet (*informal*), prostrated, ready to drop, sapped, shagged out (*Brit. slang*), spent, tired out, wasted, weak, wiped out (*informal*), worn out, worn to a frazzle (*informal*), zonked (*slang*) **2.** at an end, consumed, depleted, dissipated, done, expended, finished, gone, spent, squandered, used up, wasted **3.** bare, drained, dry, empty, void

▷ **Antonyms** (*sense 1*) active, alive and kicking, animated, enlivened, invigorated, refreshed, rejuvenated, restored, revived, stimulated (*sense 2*) conserved, kept, preserved, replenished, restored

exhausting arduous, backbreaking, crippling, debilitating, difficult, draining, enervating, fatiguing, gruelling, hard, laborious, punishing, sapping, strenuous, taxing, testing, tiring

exhaustion 1. debilitation, enervation, fatigue, feebleness, lassitude, prostration, tiredness, weariness **2.** consumption, depletion, emptying

exhaustive all-embracing, all-inclusive, all-out (*informal*), complete, comprehensive, detailed, encyclopedic, extensive, far-reaching, full, full-scale, in-depth, intensive, sweeping, thorough, thoroughgoing, total

▷ **Antonyms** casual, cursory, desultory, incomplete, perfunctory, sketchy, superficial

exhibit 1. *verb* air, demonstrate, disclose, display, evidence, evince, expose, express, flaunt, indicate, make clear *or* plain, manifest, offer, parade, present, put on view, reveal, show **2.** *~noun* display, exhibition, illustration, model, show

exhibition airing, demonstration, display, exhibit, expo (*informal*), exposition, fair, manifestation, performance, presentation, representation, show, showing, spectacle

exhilarate animate, cheer, delight, elate, enliven, exalt, gladden, inspirit, invigorate, lift, pep *or* perk up, rejoice, stimulate, thrill

exhilarating breathtaking, cheering, enlivening, exalting, exciting, exhilarant, exhilarative, exhilaratory, gladdening, invigorating, stimulating, thrilling, vitalizing

exhilaration animation, cheerfulness, delight, elation, exaltation, excitement, gaiety, gladness, gleefulness, high spirits, hilarity, joy, joyfulness, liveliness, mirth, sprightliness, vivacity

▷ **Antonyms** dejection, depression, despondency, gloom, low spirits, melancholy, misery, sadness

exhort admonish, advise, beseech, bid, call upon, caution, counsel, encourage, enjoin, entreat, goad, incite, persuade, press, prompt, spur, urge, warn

exhortation admonition, advice, beseeching, bidding, caution, clarion call, counsel, encouragement, enjoinder (*rare*), entreaty, goading, incitement, lecture, persuasion, sermon, urging, warning

exhume dig up, disentomb, disinter, unbury, unearth

▷ **Antonyms** bury, entomb, inearth, inhume, inter

exigency, exigence 1. acuteness, constraint, criticalness, demandingness, difficulty, distress, emergency, imperativeness, necessity, needfulness, pressingness, pressure, stress, urgency **2.** constraint, demand, necessity, need, requirement, wont **3.** crisis, difficulty, emergency, extremity, fix (*informal*), hardship, jam (*informal*), juncture, panic stations (*informal*), pass, pickle (*informal*), pinch, plight, predicament, quandary, scrape (*informal*), strait

exigent 1. acute, constraining, critical, crucial, imperative, importunate, insistent, necessary, needful, pressing, urgent **2.** arduous, demanding, difficult, exacting, hard, harsh, rigorous, severe, stiff, strict, stringent, taxing, tough

exiguous bare, meagre, negligible, paltry, scanty, skimpy, slender, spare, sparse

exile *noun* **1.** banishment, deportation, expatriation, expulsion, ostracism, proscription, separation **2.** deportee, émigré, expatriate, outcast, refugee *~verb* **3.** banish, deport, drive out, eject, expatriate, expel, ostracize, oust, proscribe

exist 1. abide, be, be extant, be living, be present, breathe, continue, endure, happen, last, live, obtain, occur, prevail, remain, stand, survive **2.** eke out a living, get along *or* by, keep one's head above water, stay alive, subsist, survive

existence 1. actuality, animation, being, breath, continuance, continuation, duration, endurance, life, subsistence, survival **2.** being, creature, entity, thing **3.** creation, life, reality, the world

existent abiding, alive, around, current, enduring, existing, extant, in existence, living, obtaining, present, prevailing, remaining, standing, surviving, to the fore (*Scot.*)

exit *noun* **1.** door, egress, gate, outlet, passage out, vent, way out **2.** adieu, departure, evacuation, exodus, farewell, going, goodbye, leave-taking, retirement, retreat, withdrawal **3.** death, decease, demise, expiry, passing away *~verb* **4.** bid farewell, depart, go away, go offstage (*Theatre*), go out, issue, leave, make tracks, retire, retreat, say goodbye, take one's leave, withdraw

▷ **Antonyms** (*sense 1*) entrance, entry, ingress, inlet, opening, way in (*sense 4*) arrive, come *or* go in *or* into, enter, make an entrance

exodus departure, evacuation, exit, flight, going out, leaving, migration, retirement, retreat, withdrawal

exonerate 1. absolve, acquit, clear, discharge, dismiss, exculpate, excuse, justify, pardon, vindicate **2.** discharge, dismiss, except, excuse, exempt, free, let off, liberate, release, relieve

exoneration 1. absolution, acquittal, amnesty, discharge, dismissal, exculpation, justification, pardon, vindication **2.** deliverance, discharge, dismissal, exception, exemption, freeing, liberation, release, relief

exorbitance excess, excessiveness, extravagance, extremeness, immoderateness, immoderation, inordinateness, preposterousness, unreasonableness

exorbitant enormous, excessive, extortionate, extravagant, extreme, immoderate, inordinate, outrageous, preposterous, ridiculous, unconscionable, undue, unreasonable, unwarranted

▷ **Antonyms** cheap, fair, moderate, reasonable

exorcise adjure, cast out, deliver (from), drive out, expel, purify

exorcism adjuration, casting out, deliverance, driving out, expulsion, purification

exordium beginning, foreword, introduction, opening, opening remarks, preamble, preface, prelude, proem, prolegomenon, prologue

exotic **1.** alien, external, extraneous, extrinsic, foreign, imported, introduced, naturalized, not native **2.** beyond one's ken, bizarre, colourful, curious, different, extraordinary, fascinating, glamorous, mysterious, outlandish, peculiar, strange, striking, unfamiliar, unusual
▷ **Antonyms** (*sense 2*) conventional, familiar, ordinary, pedestrian, plain, run-of-the-mill, unmemorable, unremarkable

expand **1.** amplify, augment, bloat, blow up, broaden, develop, dilate, distend, enlarge, extend, fatten, fill out, grow, heighten, increase, inflate, lengthen, magnify, multiply, prolong, protract, swell, thicken, wax, widen **2.** diffuse, open (out), outspread, spread (out), stretch (out), unfold, unfurl, unravel, unroll **3.** amplify, develop, dilate, elaborate, embellish, enlarge, expatiate, expound, flesh out, go into detail
▷ **Antonyms** (*senses 1 & 2*) close, condense, contract, decrease, reduce, shorten, shrink (*sense 3*) abbreviate, condense, shorten

expanse area, breadth, extent, field, plain, range, space, stretch, sweep, tract

expansion amplification, augmentation, development, diffusion, dilatation, distension, enlargement, expanse, growth, increase, inflation, magnification, multiplication, opening out, spread, swelling, unfolding, unfurling

expansive **1.** dilating, distending, elastic, enlargeable, expanding, extendable, inflatable, stretching, stretchy, swelling **2.** all-embracing, broad, comprehensive, extensive, far-reaching, inclusive, thorough, voluminous, wide, wide-ranging, widespread **3.** affable, communicative, easy, effusive, free, friendly, garrulous, genial, loquacious, open, outgoing, sociable, talkative, unreserved, warm

expatiate amplify, descant, develop, dilate, dwell on, elaborate, embellish, enlarge, expound, go into detail

expatriate **1.** *adjective* banished, emigrant, émigré, exiled, refugee **2.** *~noun* emigrant, émigré, exile **3.** *~verb* banish, exile, expel, ostracize, proscribe

expect **1.** assume, believe, calculate, conjecture, forecast, foresee, imagine, presume, reckon, suppose, surmise, think, trust **2.** anticipate, await, bargain for, contemplate, envisage, hope for, look ahead to, look for, look forward to, predict, watch for **3.** call for, count on, demand, insist on, look for, rely upon, require, want, wish

expectancy **1.** anticipation, assumption, belief, conjecture, expectation, hope, looking forward, prediction, presumption, probability, supposition, surmise, suspense, waiting **2.** likelihood, outlook, prospect

expectant **1.** anticipating, anxious, apprehensive, awaiting, eager, expecting, hopeful, in suspense, ready, watchful **2.** enceinte, expecting (*informal*), gravid, pregnant

expectation **1.** assumption, assurance, belief, calculation, confidence, conjecture, forecast, likelihood, presumption, probability, supposition, surmise, trust **2.** anticipation, apprehension, chance, expectancy, fear, hope, looking forward, outlook, possibility, prediction, promise, prospect, suspense **3.** demand, insistence, reliance, requirement, trust, want, wish

expecting enceinte, expectant, gravid, in the club (*Brit. slang*), in the family way (*informal*), pregnant, with child

expediency, expedience **1.** advantageousness, advisability, appropriateness, aptness, benefit, convenience, desirability, effectiveness, fitness, helpfulness, judiciousness, meetness, practicality, pragmatism, profitability, properness, propriety, prudence, suitability, usefulness, utilitarianism, utility **2.** contrivance, device, expedient, makeshift, manoeuvre, means, measure, method, resort, resource, scheme, shift, stopgap, stratagem, substitute

expedient **1.** *adjective* advantageous, advisable, appropriate, beneficial, convenient, desirable, effective, fit, helpful, judicious, meet, opportune, politic, practical, pragmatic, profitable, proper, prudent, suitable, useful, utilitarian, worthwhile **2.** *~noun* contrivance, device, expediency, makeshift, manoeuvre, means, measure, method, resort, resource, scheme, shift, stopgap, stratagem, substitute
▷ **Antonyms** *~adjective* detrimental, disadvantageous, futile, harmful, ill-advised, impractical, imprudent, inadvisable, inappropriate, ineffective, inexpedient, unwise, wrong

expedite accelerate, advance, assist, dispatch, facilitate, forward, hasten, hurry, precipitate, press, promote, quicken, rush, speed (up), urge
▷ **Antonyms** block, curb, decelerate, delay, handicap, hold up, obstruct, restrict, slow up *or* down

expedition **1.** enterprise, excursion, exploration, journey, mission, quest, safari, tour, trek, trip, undertaking, voyage **2.** company, crew, explorers, team, travellers, voyagers, wayfarers **3.** alacrity, celerity, dispatch, expeditiousness, haste, hurry, promptness, quickness, rapidity, readiness, speed, swiftness

expeditious active, alert, brisk, diligent, efficient, fast, hasty, immediate, instant, nimble, prompt, quick, rapid, ready, speedy, swift

expel **1.** belch, cast out, discharge, dislodge, drive out, eject, remove, spew, throw out **2.** ban, banish, bar, black, blackball, discharge, dismiss, drum out, evict, exclude, exile, expatriate, give the bum's rush (*slang*), oust, proscribe, relegate, send packing, show one the door, throw out, throw out on one's ear (*informal*), turf out (*informal*)

▷ **Antonyms** (*sense 2*) admit, allow to enter, give access, let in, receive, take in, welcome

expend consume, disburse, dissipate, employ, exhaust, fork out (*slang*), go through, lay out (*informal*), pay out, shell out (*informal*), spend, use (up)

expendable dispensable, inessential, nonessential, replaceable, unimportant, unnecessary

▷ **Antonyms** crucial, essential, indispensable, key, necessary, vital

expenditure application, charge, consumption, cost, disbursement, expense, outgoings, outlay, output, payment, spending, use

expense charge, consumption, cost, disbursement, expenditure, loss, outlay, output, payment, sacrifice, spending, toll, use

expensive costly, dear, excessive, exorbitant, extravagant, high-priced, inordinate, lavish, overpriced, rich, steep (*informal*), stiff

▷ **Antonyms** bargain, budget, cheap, cut-price, economical, inexpensive, low-cost, low-priced, reasonable

experience *noun* **1.** contact, doing, evidence, exposure, familiarity, involvement, know-how (*informal*), knowledge, observation, participation, practice, proof, training, trial, understanding **2.** adventure, affair, encounter, episode, event, happening, incident, occurrence, ordeal, test, trial *~verb* **3.** apprehend, become familiar with, behold, encounter, endure, face, feel, go through, have, know, live through, meet, observe, participate in, perceive, sample, sense, suffer, sustain, taste, try, undergo

experienced 1. accomplished, adept, capable, competent, expert, familiar, knowledgeable, master, practised, professional, qualified, seasoned, skilful, tested, trained, tried, veteran, well-versed **2.** knowing, mature, sophisticated, wise, worldly, worldly-wise

▷ **Antonyms** apprentice, green, incompetent, inexperienced, new, unqualified, unskilled, untrained, untried

experiment 1. *noun* assay, attempt, examination, experimentation, investigation, procedure, proof, research, test, trial, trial and error, trial run, venture **2.** *~verb* assay, examine, investigate, put to the test, research, sample, test, try, verify

experimental empirical, exploratory, pilot, preliminary, probationary, provisional, speculative, tentative, test, trial, trial-and-error

expert 1. *noun* ace (*informal*), adept, authority, buff (*informal*), connoisseur, dab hand (*Brit. informal*), hotshot (*informal*), master, maven (*U.S.*), past master, pro (*informal*), professional, specialist, virtuoso, whizz (*informal*), wizard **2.** *~adjective* able, adept, adroit, apt, clever, deft, dexterous, experienced, facile, handy, knowledgeable, master, masterly, practised, professional, proficient, qualified, skilful, skilled, trained, virtuoso

▷ **Antonyms** *~noun* amateur, dabbler, ham, layman, nonprofessional, novice *~adjective* amateurish, cack-handed (*informal*), clumsy, incompetent, inexperienced, unpractised, unqualified, unskilled, untrained

expertise ableness, adroitness, aptness, cleverness, command, craft, deftness, dexterity, expertness, facility, grasp, grip, judgment, knack, know-how (*informal*), knowing inside out, knowledge, masterliness, mastery, proficiency, skilfulness, skill

expertness ableness, adroitness, aptness, command, craft, deftness, dexterity, expertise, facility, grasp, grip, judgment, know-how (*informal*), knowing inside out, knowledge, masterliness, mastery, proficiency, skilfulness, skill

expiate atone for, do penance for, make amends for, redeem, redress

expiation amends, atonement, penance, redemption, redress, shrift (*archaic*)

expiration 1. cessation, close, conclusion, end, expiry, finis, finish, termination **2.** death, decease, demise, departure

expire 1. cease, close, come to an end, conclude, end, finish, lapse, run out, stop, terminate **2.** breathe out, emit, exhale, expel **3.** buy it (*U.S. slang*), check out (*U.S. slang*), croak (*slang*), decease, depart, die, go belly-up (*slang*), kick it (*slang*), kick the bucket (*informal*), pass away *or* on, peg it (*informal*), peg out (*informal*), perish, pop one's clogs (*informal*), snuff it (*informal*)

explain 1. clarify, clear up, define, demonstrate, describe, disclose, elucidate, explicate (*formal*), expound, illustrate, interpret, make clear *or* plain, resolve, solve, teach, unfold **2.** account for, excuse, give an explanation for, give a reason for, justify

explanation 1. clarification, definition, demonstration, description, elucidation, explication, exposition, illustration, interpretation, resolution **2.** account, answer, cause, excuse, justification, meaning, mitigation, motive, reason, sense, significance, the why and wherefore, vindication

explanatory demonstrative, descriptive, elucidatory, explicative, expository, illuminative, illustrative, interpretive, justifying

explicable accountable, definable, explainable, intelligible, interpretable, justifiable, resolvable, understandable

explicate **1.** clarify, clear up, elucidate, explain, expound, interpret, make clear *or* explicit, make plain, unfold, untangle **2.** construct, develop, devise, evolve, formulate, work out

explicit absolute, categorical, certain, clear, definite, direct, distinct, exact, express, frank, open, outspoken, patent, plain, positive, precise, round, specific, stated, straightforward, unambiguous, unequivocal, unqualified, unreserved, upfront (*informal*)

▷ **Antonyms** ambiguous, cryptic, general, implicit, implied, indefinite, indirect, inexact, obscure, oracular, suggested, uncertain, vague

explode **1.** blow up, burst, detonate, discharge, erupt, go off, set off, shatter, shiver **2.** belie, blow out of the water (*slang*), debunk, discredit, disprove, give the lie to, invalidate, refute, repudiate

exploit *noun* **1.** accomplishment, achievement, adventure, attainment, deed, escapade, feat, stunt ~*verb* **2.** abuse, dump on (*slang, chiefly U.S.*), impose upon, manipulate, milk, misuse, play on *or* upon, shit on (*taboo slang*), take advantage of **3.** capitalize on, cash in on (*informal*), live off the backs of, make capital out of, make use of, profit by *or* from, put to use, turn to account, use, use to advantage, utilize

exploration **1.** analysis, examination, inquiry, inspection, investigation, once-over (*informal*), probe, research, scrutiny, search, study **2.** expedition, recce (*slang*), reconnaissance, survey, tour, travel, trip

exploratory analytic, experimental, fact-finding, investigative, probing, searching, trial

explore **1.** analyse, examine, inquire into, inspect, investigate, look into, probe, prospect, research, scrutinize, search, work over **2.** case (*slang*), have *or* take a look around, range over, recce (*slang*), reconnoitre, scout, survey, tour, travel, traverse

explosion **1.** bang, blast, burst, clap, crack, detonation, discharge, outburst, report **2.** eruption, fit, outbreak, outburst, paroxysm

explosive **1.** unstable, volatile **2.** fiery, stormy, touchy, vehement, violent **3.** charged, dangerous, hazardous, overwrought, perilous, tense, ugly

exponent **1.** advocate, backer, champion, defender, promoter, propagandist, proponent, spokesman, spokeswoman, supporter, upholder **2.** commentator, demonstrator, elucidator, expositor, expounder, illustrator, interpreter **3.** example, exemplar, illustration, indication, model, norm, sample, specimen, type **4.** executant, interpreter, performer, player, presenter

expose **1.** display, exhibit, manifest, present, put on view, reveal, show, take the wraps off, uncover, unveil **2.** air, betray, blow wide open (*slang*), bring to light, denounce, detect, disclose, divulge, lay bare, let out, make known, out (*informal*), reveal, show up, smoke out, uncover, unearth, unmask **3.** endanger, hazard, imperil, jeopardize, lay open, leave open, make vulnerable, risk, subject **4.** (*with* **to**) acquaint with, bring into contact with, familiarize with, introduce to, make conversant with

▷ **Antonyms** (*senses 1, 2 & 3*) conceal, cover, hide, keep secret, mask, protect, screen, shelter, shield

exposé disclosure, divulgence, exposure, revelation, uncovering

exposed **1.** bare, exhibited, laid bare, made manifest, made public, on display, on show, on view, revealed, shown, unconcealed, uncovered, unveiled **2.** open, open to the elements, unprotected, unsheltered **3.** in danger, in peril, laid bare, laid open, left open, liable, open, susceptible, vulnerable, wide open

exposition **1.** account, commentary, critique, description, elucidation, exegesis, explanation, explication, illustration, interpretation, presentation **2.** demonstration, display, exhibition, expo (*informal*), fair, presentation, show

expository descriptive, elucidative, exegetic, explanatory, explicative, explicatory, hermeneutic, illustrative, interpretive

expostulate argue (with), dissuade, protest, reason (with), remonstrate (with)

exposure **1.** baring, display, exhibition, manifestation, presentation, publicity, revelation, showing, uncovering, unveiling **2.** airing, betrayal, denunciation, detection, disclosure, divulgence, divulging, exposé, revelation, unmasking **3.** danger, hazard, jeopardy, risk, vulnerability **4.** acquaintance, contact, conversancy, experience, familiarity, introduction, knowledge **5.** aspect, frontage, location, outlook, position, setting, view

expound describe, elucidate, explain, explicate (*formal*), illustrate, interpret, set forth, spell out, unfold

express *verb* **1.** articulate, assert, asseverate, communicate, couch, declare, enunciate, phrase, pronounce, put, put across, put into words, say, speak, state, tell, utter, verbalize, voice, word **2.** bespeak, convey, denote, depict, designate, disclose, divulge, embody, evince, exhibit, indicate, intimate, make known, manifest, represent, reveal, show, signify, stand for, symbolize, testify **3.** ex~

tract, force out, press out, squeeze out ~*adjective* **4.** accurate, categorical, certain, clear, definite, direct, distinct, exact, explicit, outright, plain, pointed, precise, unambiguous **5.** clear-cut, especial, particular, singular, special **6.** direct, fast, high-speed, nonstop, quick, quickie (*informal*), rapid, speedy, swift

expression 1. announcement, assertion, asseveration, communication, declaration, enunciation, mention, pronouncement, speaking, statement, utterance, verbalization, voicing **2.** demonstration, embodiment, exhibition, indication, manifestation, representation, show, sign, symbol, token **3.** air, appearance, aspect, countenance, face, look, mien (*literary*) **4.** choice of words, delivery, diction, emphasis, execution, intonation, language, phraseology, phrasing, speech, style, wording **5.** idiom, locution, phrase, remark, set phrase, term, turn of phrase, word

expressionless blank, deadpan, dull, empty, inscrutable, poker-faced (*informal*), straight-faced, vacuous, wooden

expressive 1. eloquent, emphatic, energetic, forcible, lively, mobile, moving, poignant, striking, strong, sympathetic, telling, vivid **2.** allusive, demonstrative, indicative, meaningful, pointed, pregnant, revealing, significant, suggestive, thoughtful

▷ **Antonyms** (*sense 1*) blank, dead-pan, dull, empty, impassive, inscrutable, poker-faced (*informal*), straight-faced, vacuous, wooden

expressly 1. especially, exactly, intentionally, on purpose, particularly, precisely, purposely, specially, specifically **2.** absolutely, categorically, clearly, decidedly, definitely, distinctly, explicitly, in no uncertain terms, manifestly, outright, plainly, pointedly, positively, unambiguously, unequivocally, unmistakably

expropriate appropriate, arrogate, assume, commandeer, confiscate, impound, requisition, seize, take, take over

expulsion banishment, debarment, discharge, dislodgment, dismissal, ejection, eviction, exclusion, exile, expatriation, extrusion, proscription, removal

expunge abolish, annihilate, annul, blot out, cancel, delete, destroy, efface, eradicate, erase, excise, exterminate, extinguish, extirpate, obliterate, raze, remove, strike out, wipe from the face of the earth, wipe out

expurgate blue-pencil, bowdlerize, censor, clean up (*informal*), cut, purge, purify, sanitize

exquisite 1. beautiful, dainty, delicate, elegant, fine, lovely, precious **2.** attractive, beautiful, charming, comely, lovely, pleasing, striking **3.** admirable, choice, consummate, delicious, divine, excellent, fine, flawless, incomparable, matchless, outstanding, peerless, perfect, rare, select, splendid, superb, superlative **4.** appreciative, consummate, cultivated, discerning, discriminating, fastidious, impeccable, meticulous, polished, refined, selective, sensitive **5.** acute, excruciating, intense, keen, piercing, poignant, sharp

▷ **Antonyms** (*senses 1 & 2*) ill-favoured, ugly, unattractive, unlovely, unsightly (*sense 3*) flawed, imperfect

extant existent, existing, in existence, living, remaining, subsisting, surviving, undestroyed

extemporaneous, extemporary 1. ad-lib, extempore, free, impromptu, improv (*informal*), improvisatory, improvised, made-up, offhand, off-the-cuff, off the top of one's head, spontaneous, unplanned, unpremeditated, unprepared, unrehearsed **2.** expedient, improvised, makeshift, on-the-spot, temporary

extempore *adverb/adjective* ad lib, extemporaneous, extemporary, freely, impromptu, improvised, offhand, off the cuff (*informal*), off the top of one's head, on the spot, spontaneously, unplanned, unpremeditated, unprepared

extemporize ad-lib, busk, improvise, make up, play (it) by ear, vamp, wing it (*informal*)

extend 1. carry on, continue, drag out, draw out, elongate, lengthen, make longer, prolong, protract, spin out, spread out, stretch, unfurl, unroll **2.** carry on, continue, go on, last, take **3.** amount to, attain, go as far as, reach, spread **4.** add to, amplify, augment, broaden, develop, dilate, enhance, enlarge, expand, increase, spread, supplement, widen **5.** advance, bestow, confer, give, grant, hold out, impart, offer, present, proffer, put forth, reach out, stretch out, yield

▷ **Antonyms** (*sense 1*) condense, contract, curtail, cut, decrease, limit, reduce, restrict, shorten, take back (*sense 4*) abbreviate, abridge, condense, contract, cut, decrease, reduce, restrict, shorten (*sense 5*) take back, withdraw

extended 1. continued, drawn-out, elongated, enlarged, lengthened, long, prolonged, protracted, spread (out), stretched out, unfolded, unfurled, unrolled **2.** broad, comprehensive, enlarged, expanded, extensive, far-reaching, large-scale, sweeping, thorough, wide, widespread **3.** conferred, outstretched, proffered, stretched out

extension 1. amplification, augmentation, broadening, continuation, delay, development, dilatation, distension, elongation, enlargement, expansion, extent, increase, lengthening, postponement, prolongation, protraction, spread, stretching, widening **2.** addendum, ad~

dition, add-on, adjunct, annexe, appendage, appendix, branch, ell, supplement, wing

extensive all-inclusive, broad, capacious, commodious, comprehensive, expanded, extended, far-flung, far-reaching, general, great, huge, humongous *or* humungous (*U.S. slang*), large, large-scale, lengthy, long, pervasive, prevalent, protracted, spacious, sweeping, thorough, universal, vast, voluminous, wholesale, wide, widespread

▷ **Antonyms** circumscribed, confined, constricted, limited, narrow, restricted, tight

extent **1.** ambit, bounds, compass, play, range, reach, scope, sphere, sweep **2.** amount, amplitude, area, breadth, bulk, degree, duration, expanse, expansion, length, magnitude, measure, quantity, size, stretch, term, time, volume, width

extenuate **1.** decrease, diminish, excuse, lessen, make allowances for, minimize, mitigate, moderate, palliate, play down, qualify, reduce, soften, temper, weaken **2.** discount, make light of, underestimate, underrate, undervalue

extenuating justifying, mitigating, moderating, qualifying, serving as an excuse

exterior *noun* **1.** appearance, aspect, coating, covering, façade, face, finish, outside, shell, skin, surface *~adjective* **2.** external, outer, outermost, outside, outward, superficial, surface **3.** alien, exotic, external, extraneous, extrinsic, foreign, outside

▷ **Antonyms** *~noun* inner, inside, interior *~adjective* (*sense 2*) immanent, inherent, inside, interior, internal, intrinsic (*sense 3*) domestic, internal, intrinsic

exterminate abolish, annihilate, destroy, eliminate, eradicate, extirpate

external **1.** apparent, exterior, outer, outermost, outside, outward, superficial, surface, visible **2.** alien, exotic, exterior, extramural, extraneous, extrinsic, foreign, independent, outside

▷ **Antonyms** (*sense 1*) immanent, inherent, inner, inside, interior, internal, intrinsic (*sense 2*) inside, interior, intrinsic

extinct **1.** dead, defunct, gone, lost, vanished **2.** doused, extinguished, inactive, out, quenched, snuffed out **3.** abolished, defunct, ended, obsolete, terminated, void

▷ **Antonyms** active, alive and kicking, existing, extant, flourishing, living, surviving, thriving

extinction abolition, annihilation, death, destruction, dying out, eradication, excision, extermination, extirpation, obliteration, oblivion

extinguish **1.** blow out, douse, put out, quench, smother, snuff out, stifle **2.** abolish, annihilate, destroy, eliminate, end, eradicate, erase, expunge, exterminate, extirpate, kill, obscure, put paid to, remove, suppress, wipe out

extirpate abolish, annihilate, deracinate, destroy, eliminate, eradicate, erase, excise, expunge, exterminate, extinguish, pull up by the roots, remove, root out, uproot, wipe from the face of the earth, wipe out

extol acclaim, applaud, celebrate, commend, crack up (*informal*), cry up, eulogize, exalt, glorify, laud, magnify (*archaic*), panegyrize, pay tribute to, praise, sing the praises of

extort blackmail, bleed (*informal*), bully, coerce, exact, extract, force, squeeze, wrest, wring

extortion **1.** blackmail, coercion, compulsion, demand, exaction, force, oppression, rapacity, shakedown (*U.S. slang*) **2.** enormity, exorbitance, expensiveness, overcharging

extortionate **1.** excessive, exorbitant, extravagant, immoderate, inflated, inordinate, outrageous, preposterous, sky-high, unreasonable **2.** blood-sucking (*informal*), exacting, grasping, hard, harsh, oppressive, rapacious, rigorous, severe, usurious

▷ **Antonyms** (*sense 1*) fair, inexpensive, moderate, modest, reasonable

extra *adjective* **1.** accessory, added, additional, add-on, ancillary, auxiliary, fresh, further, more, new, other, supplemental, supplementary **2.** excess, extraneous, inessential, leftover, needless, redundant, reserve, spare, supererogatory, superfluous, supernumerary, surplus, unnecessary, unneeded, unused *~noun* **3.** accessory, addendum, addition, add-on, adjunct, affix, appendage, appurtenance, attachment, bonus, complement, extension, supernumerary, supplement *~adverb* **4.** especially, exceptionally, extraordinarily, extremely, particularly, remarkably, uncommonly, unusually

▷ **Antonyms** *~adjective* (*sense 2*) compulsory, essential, mandatory, necessary, needed, obligatory, required, requisite, vital *~noun* essential, must, necessity, precondition, prerequisite, requirement, requisite

extract *verb* **1.** draw, extirpate, pluck out, pull, pull out, remove, take out, uproot, withdraw **2.** bring out, derive, draw, elicit, evoke, exact, gather, get, glean, obtain, reap, wrest, wring **3.** deduce, derive, develop, educe, elicit, evolve **4.** distil, draw out, express, obtain, press out, separate out, squeeze, take out **5.** abstract, choose, cite, copy out, cull, cut out, quote, select *~noun* **6.** concentrate, decoction, distillate, distillation, essence, juice **7.** abstract, citation, clipping, cutting, excerpt, passage, quotation, selection

extraction 1. drawing, extirpation, pulling, removal, taking out, uprooting, withdrawal 2. derivation, distillation, separation 3. ancestry, birth, blood, derivation, descent, family, lineage, origin, parentage, pedigree, race, stock

extraneous 1. accidental, additional, adventitious, extra, incidental, inessential, needless, nonessential, peripheral, redundant, superfluous, supplementary, unessential, unnecessary, unneeded 2. beside the point, immaterial, impertinent, inadmissible, inapplicable, inapposite, inappropriate, inapt, irrelevant, off the subject, unconnected, unrelated 3. adventitious, alien, exotic, external, extrinsic, foreign, out of place, strange

extraordinary amazing, beyond one's ken, bizarre, curious, exceptional, fantastic, marvellous, notable, odd, out of this world (*informal*), outstanding, particular, peculiar, phenomenal, rare, remarkable, serious (*informal*), singular, special, strange, surprising, uncommon, unfamiliar, unheard-of, unique, unprecedented, unusual, unwonted, weird, wonderful, wondrous (*archaic or literary*)

▷ **Antonyms** banal, common, commonplace, customary, everyday, ordinary, unexceptional, unremarkable, usual

extravagance 1. improvidence, lavishness, overspending, prodigality, profligacy, profusion, squandering, waste, wastefulness 2. absurdity, dissipation, exaggeration, excess, exorbitance, folly, immoderation, outrageousness, preposterousness, recklessness, unreasonableness, unrestraint, wildness

extravagant 1. excessive, having money to burn, improvident, imprudent, lavish, prodigal, profligate, spendthrift, wasteful 2. absurd, exaggerated, excessive, exorbitant, fanciful, fantastic, foolish, immoderate, inordinate, O.T.T. (*slang*), outrageous, outré, over the top (*slang*), preposterous, reckless, unreasonable, unrestrained, wild 3. fancy, flamboyant, flashy, garish, gaudy, grandiose, ornate, ostentatious, pretentious, showy 4. costly, excessive, exorbitant, expensive, extortionate, inordinate, overpriced, steep (*informal*), unreasonable

▷ **Antonyms** (*sense 1*) careful, close, economical, frugal, miserly, moderate, prudent, sensible, sparing, thrifty, tight-fisted (*informal*) (*sense 2*) conservative, down-to-earth, moderate, prudent, realistic, reasonable, restrained, sensible, sober (*sense 3*) conservative, moderate, restrained, sober (*sense 4*) economical, moderate, reasonable

extravaganza display, flight of fancy, pageant, show, spectacle, spectacular

extreme *adjective* 1. acute, great, greatest, high, highest, intense, maximum, mother (of all) (*informal*), severe, supreme, ultimate, utmost, uttermost, worst 2. downright, egregious, exaggerated, exceptional, excessive, extraordinary, extravagant, fanatical, immoderate, inordinate, intemperate, O.T.T. (*slang*), out-and-out, outrageous, over the top (*slang*), radical, remarkable, sheer, uncommon, unconventional, unreasonable, unusual, utter, zealous 3. dire, Draconian, drastic, harsh, radical, rigid, severe, stern, strict, unbending, uncompromising 4. faraway, far-off, farthest, final, last, most distant, outermost, remotest, terminal, ultimate, utmost, uttermost *~noun* 5. acme, apex, apogee, boundary, climax, consummation, depth, edge, end, excess, extremity, height, limit, maximum, minimum, nadir, pinnacle, pole, termination, top, ultimate, zenith

▷ **Antonyms** *~adjective* (*senses 1, 2 & 3*) average, common, mild, moderate, modest, ordinary, reasonable, traditional, unremarkable (*sense 4*) nearest

extremely acutely, awfully (*informal*), exceedingly, exceptionally, excessively, extraordinarily, greatly, highly, inordinately, intensely, markedly, quite, severely, terribly, to a fault, to *or* in the extreme, to the nth degree, ultra, uncommonly, unusually, utterly, very

extremist die-hard, fanatic, radical, ultra, zealot

extremity 1. acme, apex, apogee, border, bound, boundary, brim, brink, edge, end, extreme, frontier, limit, margin, maximum, minimum, nadir, pinnacle, pole, rim, terminal, termination, terminus, tip, top, ultimate, verge, zenith 2. acuteness, climax, consummation, depth, excess, height 3. adversity, crisis, dire straits, disaster, emergency, exigency, hardship, pass, pinch, plight, setback, trouble 4. *plural* fingers and toes, hands and feet, limbs

extricate clear, deliver, disembarrass, disengage, disentangle, free, get out, get (someone) off the hook (*slang*), liberate, release, relieve, remove, rescue, withdraw, wriggle out of

extrinsic alien, exotic, exterior, external, extraneous, foreign, imported, outside, superficial

extrovert amiable, exuberant, gregarious, hearty, out-going, sociable, social

▷ **Antonyms** introspective, introverted, inward-looking, self-contained, withdrawn

extrude eject, expel, force out, press out, squeeze out, thrust out

exuberance 1. animation, brio, buoyancy, cheerfulness, eagerness, ebullience, effervescence, energy, enthusiasm, excitement, exhilaration, high spirits, life, liveliness, pep, spirit, sprightliness, vigour, vitality, vivacity, zest 2. effusiveness, exaggeration, excessiveness, ful~

someness, lavishness, prodigality, superfluity **3.** abundance, copiousness, lavishness, lushness, luxuriance, plenitude, profusion, rankness, richness, superabundance, teemingness

exuberant 1. animated, buoyant, cheerful, chirpy (*informal*), eager, ebullient, effervescent, elated, energetic, enthusiastic, excited, exhilarated, full of beans (*informal*), full of life, high-spirited, in high spirits, lively, sparkling, spirited, sprightly, upbeat (*informal*), vigorous, vivacious, zestful **2.** effusive, exaggerated, excessive, fulsome, lavish, overdone, prodigal, superfluous **3.** abundant, copious, lavish, lush, luxuriant, overflowing, plenteous, plentiful, profuse, rank, rich, superabundant, teeming

▷ **Antonyms** (*sense 1*) apathetic, dull, lifeless, subdued, unenthusiastic

exude 1. bleed, discharge, emanate, emit, excrete, filter through, issue, leak, ooze, secrete, seep, sweat, trickle, weep, well forth **2.** display, emanate, exhibit, manifest, radiate, show

exult 1. be delighted, be elated, be in high spirits, be joyful, be jubilant, be overjoyed, celebrate, jubilate, jump for joy, make merry, rejoice **2.** boast, brag, crow, drool, gloat, glory (in), revel, take delight in, taunt, triumph, vaunt

exultant cock-a-hoop, delighted, elated, exulting, flushed, gleeful, joyful, joyous, jubilant, overjoyed, over the moon (*informal*), rapt, rejoicing, revelling, transported, triumphant

exultation 1. celebration, delight, elation, glee, high spirits, joy, joyousness, jubilation, merriness, rejoicing, transport **2.** boasting, bragging, crowing, gloating, glory, glorying, revelling, triumph

eye *noun* **1.** eyeball, optic (*informal*), orb (*poetic*), peeper (*slang*) **2.** appreciation, discernment, discrimination, judgment, perception, recognition, taste **3.** (*often plural*) belief, judgment, mind, opinion, point of view, viewpoint **4. keep an** *or* **one's eye on** guard, keep in view, keep tabs on (*informal*), keep under surveillance, look after, look out for, monitor, observe, pay attention to, regard, scrutinize, supervise, survey, watch, watch like a hawk, watch over **5. an eye for an eye** justice, reprisal, requital, retaliation, retribution, revenge, vengeance **6. lay, clap** *or* **set eyes on** behold, come across, encounter, meet, notice, observe, run into, see **7. see eye to eye** accord, agree, back, be in unison, coincide, concur, fall in, get on, go along, harmonize, jibe (*informal*), subscribe to **8. up to one's eyes** busy, caught up, engaged, flooded out, fully occupied, inundated, overwhelmed, up to here, up to one's elbows, wrapped up in *~verb* **9.** behold (*archaic or literary*), check, check out (*informal*), clock (*Brit. slang*), contemplate, eyeball (*U.S. slang*), gaze at, get a load of (*informal*), glance at, have *or* take a look at, inspect, look at, peruse, recce (*slang*), regard, scan, scrutinize, stare at, study, survey, take a dekko at (*Brit. slang*), view, watch **10.** eye up, give (someone) the (glad) eye, leer at, make eyes at, ogle

eye-catching arresting, attractive, captivating, dramatic, showy, spectacular, striking

eyeful 1. butcher's (*Brit. slang*), gander (*informal*), gaze, glance, look, shufti (*Brit. slang*), sight, view **2.** beauty, dazzler, humdinger (*slang*), knockout (*informal*), show, sight, sight for sore eyes (*informal*), spectacle, stunner (*informal*), vision

eyesight observation, perception, range of vision, sight, vision

eyesore atrocity, blemish, blight, blot, disfigurement, disgrace, horror, mess, monstrosity, sight (*informal*), ugliness

eyewitness bystander, looker-on, observer, onlooker, passer-by, spectator, viewer, watcher, witness

F, f

Fabian attritional, cautious, circumspect, cunctative *or* cunctatory (*rare*), delaying, procrastinating

fable 1. allegory, apologue, legend, myth, parable, story, tale **2.** fabrication, fairy story (*informal*), falsehood, fantasy, fib, fiction, figment, invention, lie, romance, tall story (*informal*), untruth, urban legend, white lie, yarn (*informal*)

▷ **Antonyms** actuality, certainty, fact, reality, truth, verity

fabled fabulous, famed, famous, fictional, legendary, mythical, storied

fabric 1. cloth, material, stuff, textile, web **2.** constitution, construction, foundations, framework, infrastructure, make-up, organization, structure

fabricate 1. assemble, build, construct, erect, fashion, form, frame, make, manufacture, shape **2.** coin, concoct, devise, fake, falsify, feign, forge, form, invent, make up, trump up

fabrication 1. assemblage, assembly, building, construction, erection, manufacture, production **2.** cock-and-bull story (*informal*), concoction, fable, fairy story (*informal*), fake, falsehood, fiction, figment, forgery, invention, lie, myth, pork pie (*Brit. slang*), porky (*Brit. slang*), untruth

fabulous 1. amazing, astounding, breathtaking, fictitious, immense, inconceivable, incredible, legendary, phenomenal, unbelievable **2.** *informal* brilliant, fantastic (*informal*), magic (*informal*), marvellous, out-of-this-world (*informal*), sensational (*informal*), spectacular, superb, wonderful **3.** apocryphal, fantastic, fictitious, imaginary, invented, legendary, made-up, mythical, unreal

▷ **Antonyms** actual, common, commonplace, credible, genuine, natural, ordinary, real

façade appearance, exterior, face, front, frontage, guise, mask, pretence, semblance, show, veneer

face *noun* **1.** clock (*Brit. slang*), countenance, dial (*Brit. slang*), features, kisser (*slang*), lineaments, mug (*slang*), phiz *or* phizog (*slang*), physiognomy, visage **2.** appearance, aspect, expression, frown, grimace, look, *moue,* pout, scowl, smirk **3.** air, appearance, disguise, display, exterior, façade, front, mask, pretence, semblance, show **4.** authority, dignity, honour, image, prestige, reputation, self-respect, standing, status **5.** *informal* assurance, audacity, boldness, brass neck (*Brit. informal*), cheek (*informal*), chutzpah (*U.S. & Canad. informal*), confidence, effrontery, front, gall (*informal*), impudence, neck (*informal*), nerve, presumption, sauce (*informal*) **6.** aspect, cover, exterior, facet, front, outside, right side, side, surface **7. face to face** *à deux,* confronting, eyeball to eyeball, in confrontation, opposite, tête-à-tête, vis-à-vis **8. fly in the face of** act in defiance of, defy, disobey, go against, oppose, rebel against, snap one's fingers at (*informal*) **9. on the face of it** apparently, at first sight, seemingly, to all appearances, to the eye **10. pull** (*or* **make**) **a long face** frown, grimace, knit one's brows, look black, look disapproving, look displeased, look put out, look stern, lour *or* lower, pout, scowl, sulk **11. show one's face** approach, be seen, come, put in *or* make an appearance, show up (*informal*), turn up **12. to one's face** directly, in one's presence, openly, straight *~verb* **13.** be confronted by, brave, come up against, confront, cope with, deal with, defy, encounter, experience, face off (*slang*), meet, oppose, tackle **14.** be opposite, front onto, give towards *or* onto, look onto, overlook **15.** clad, coat, cover, dress, finish, level, line, overlay, sheathe, surface, veneer

face-lift 1. cosmetic surgery, plastic surgery **2.** renovation, restoration

facer difficulty, dilemma, how-do-you-do (*informal*), poser, problem, puzzle, teaser

facet angle, aspect, face, part, phase, plane, side, slant, surface

facetious amusing, comical, droll, flippant, frivolous, funny, humorous, jesting, jocose, jocular, merry, playful, pleasant, tongue in cheek, unserious, waggish, witty

▷ **Antonyms** earnest, genuine, grave, lugubrious, pensive, sedate, serious, sincere, sober, thoughtful

face up to accept, acknowledge, come to terms with, confront, cope with, deal with, face the music, meet head-on, tackle

facile 1. adept, adroit, dexterous, easy, effortless, fluent, light, proficient, quick, ready, simple, skilful, smooth, uncomplicated 2. cursory, glib, hasty, shallow, slick, superficial
▷ **Antonyms** (*sense 1*) awkward, careful, clumsy, difficult, intractable, maladroit, slow, thoughtful, unskilful

facilitate assist the progress of, ease, expedite, forward, further, help, make easy, oil the wheels, pave the way for, promote, smooth the path of, speed up
▷ **Antonyms** delay, encumber, frustrate, hamper, handicap, hinder, hold up *or* back, impede, obstruct, prevent, restrain, thwart

facility 1. ability, adroitness, craft, dexterity, ease, efficiency, effortlessness, expertness, fluency, gift, knack, proficiency, quickness, readiness, skilfulness, skill, smoothness, talent 2. (*often plural*) advantage, aid, amenity, appliance, convenience, equipment, means, opportunity, resource
▷ **Antonyms** (*sense 1*) awkwardness, clumsiness, difficulty, hardship, ineptness, maladroitness, pains

facing 1. *adjective* fronting, opposite, partnering 2. *~noun* cladding, coating, façade, false front, front, overlay, plaster, reinforcement, revetment, stucco, surface, trimming, veneer

facsimile carbon, carbon copy, copy, duplicate, fax (*Trademark*), photocopy, Photostat (*Trademark*), print, replica, reproduction, transcript, Xerox (*Trademark*)

fact 1. act, deed, event, *fait accompli*, happening, incident, occurrence, performance 2. actuality, certainty, gospel (truth), naked truth, reality, truth 3. circumstance, detail, feature, item, particular, point, specific 4. **in fact** actually, indeed, in point of fact, in reality, in truth, really, truly
▷ **Antonyms** (*sense 2*) delusion, fable, fabrication, falsehood, fiction, invention, lie, tall story, untruth, yarn (*informal*)

faction 1. bloc, cabal, camp, caucus, clique, coalition, combination, confederacy, contingent, coterie, division, gang, ginger group, group, junta, lobby, minority, party, pressure group, schism, section, sector, set, splinter group 2. conflict, disagreement, discord, disharmony, dissension, disunity, division, divisiveness, friction, infighting, rebellion, sedition, strife, tumult, turbulence
▷ **Antonyms** (*sense 2*) accord, agreement, amity, assent, concord, consensus, friendship, goodwill, harmony, peace, rapport, unanimity, unity

factious conflicting, contentious, disputatious, dissident, divisive, insurrectionary, litigious, malcontent, mutinous, partisan, rebellious, refractory, rival, sectarian, seditious, troublemaking, tumultuous, turbulent, warring

factitious affected, artificial, assumed, counterfeited, engineered, fabricated, fake, false, imitation, insincere, made-up, manufactured, mock, phoney *or* phony (*informal*), pinchbeck, pseudo (*informal*), put-on, sham, simulated, spurious, synthetic, unnatural, unreal

factor 1. aspect, cause, circumstance, component, consideration, determinant, element, influence, item, part, point, thing 2. *Scot.* agent, deputy, estate manager, middleman, reeve, steward

factory manufactory (*obsolete*), mill, plant, works

factotum Girl Friday, handyman, jack of all trades, Man Friday, man of all work, odd job man

facts data, details, gen (*Brit. informal*), info (*informal*), information, ins and outs, the lowdown (*informal*), the score (*informal*), the whole story

factual accurate, authentic, circumstantial, close, correct, credible, exact, faithful, genuine, literal, matter-of-fact, objective, precise, real, sure, true, true-to-life, unadorned, unbiased, veritable
▷ **Antonyms** embellished, fanciful, fictitious, fictive, figurative, imaginary, unreal

faculties capabilities, intelligence, powers, reason, senses, wits

faculty 1. ability, adroitness, aptitude, bent, capability, capacity, cleverness, dexterity, facility, gift, knack, power, propensity, readiness, skill, talent, turn 2. branch of learning, department, discipline, profession, school, teaching staff (*chiefly U.S.*) 3. authorization, licence, prerogative, privilege, right
▷ **Antonyms** (*sense 1*) failing, inability, shortcoming, unskilfulness, weakness, weak point

fad affectation, craze, fancy, fashion, mania, mode, rage, trend, vogue, whim

fade 1. blanch, bleach, blench, dim, discolour, dull, grow dim, lose colour, lose lustre, pale, wash out 2. decline, die away, die out, dim, disappear, disperse, dissolve, droop, dwindle, ebb, etiolate, evanesce, fail, fall, flag, languish, melt away, perish, shrivel, vanish, vanish into thin air, wane, waste away, wilt, wither

faded bleached, dim, discoloured, dull, etiolated, indistinct, lustreless, pale, washed out

fading declining, decreasing, disappearing, dying, on the decline, vanishing

faeces bodily waste, droppings, dung, excrement, excreta, ordure, stools

fag[1] *noun* bind (*informal*), bore, bother, chore, drag (*informal*), inconvenience, irritation, nuisance, pain in the arse (*taboo informal*)

fag[2] *noun* bender (*slang*), catamite, fairy (*slang*), gay, homo (*informal*), homosexual, nancy boy (*slang*), poof (*slang*), poofter (*slang*), queen (*slang*), queer (*informal, derogatory*), woofter (*slang*)

fagged out all in (*slang*), beat (*slang*), clapped out (*Austral. & N.Z. informal*), creamcrackered (*Brit. informal*), exhausted, fatigued, jaded, jiggered (*informal*), knackered (*slang*), on one's last legs (*informal*), shagged out (*Brit. slang*), wasted, weary, wiped out (*informal*), worn out, zonked (*slang*)

fail 1. be defeated, be found lacking *or* wanting, be in vain, be unsuccessful, bite the dust, break down, come a cropper (*informal*), come to grief, come to naught, come to nothing, come unstuck, fall, fall by the wayside, fall flat, fall flat on one's face, fall short, fall short of, fall through, fizzle out (*informal*), flop (*informal*), founder, go astray, go belly-up (*slang*), go by the board, go down, go down like a lead balloon (*informal*), go up in smoke, lay an egg (*slang, chiefly U.S. & Canad.*), meet with disaster, miscarry, misfire, miss, not make the grade (*informal*), run aground, turn out badly **2.** abandon, break one's word, desert, disappoint, forget, forsake, let down, neglect, omit, turn one's back on **3.** be on one's last legs (*informal*), cease, conk out (*informal*), cut out, decline, die, disappear, droop, dwindle, fade, fall apart at the seams, give out, give up, go phut, gutter, languish, peter out, sicken, sink, stop working, wane, weaken **4.** become insolvent, close down, crash, fold (*informal*), go bankrupt, go broke (*informal*), go bust (*informal*), go into receivership, go out of business, go to the wall, go under, smash **5. without fail** conscientiously, constantly, dependably, like clockwork, punctually, regularly, religiously, without exception

▷ **Antonyms** bloom, flourish, grow, pass, prosper, strengthen, succeed, thrive, triumph

failing 1. *noun* blemish, blind spot, defect, deficiency, drawback, error, failure, fault, flaw, foible, frailty, imperfection, lapse, miscarriage, misfortune, shortcoming, weakness **2.** *~preposition* in default of, in the absence of, lacking

▷ **Antonyms** (*sense 1*) advantage, asset, forte, metier, speciality, strength, strong suit

failure 1. abortion, breakdown, collapse, defeat, downfall, fiasco, frustration, lack of success, miscarriage, overthrow, wreck **2.** black sheep, clinker (*slang, chiefly U.S.*), dead duck (*slang*), disappointment, dud (*informal*), flop (*informal*), incompetent, loser, ne'er-do-well, no-good, no-hoper (*chiefly Austral.*), nonstarter, washout (*informal*) **3.** default, deficiency, dereliction, neglect, negligence, nonobservance, nonperformance, nonsuccess, omission, remissness, shortcoming, stoppage **4.** breakdown, decay, decline, deterioration, failing, loss **5.** bankruptcy, crash, downfall, folding (*informal*), insolvency, liquidation, ruin

▷ **Antonyms** adequacy, care, effectiveness, fortune, observance, prosperity, strengthening, success, triumph

fain *adverb* **1.** as lief (*rare*), as soon, cheerfully, eagerly, gladly, willingly *~adjective* **2.** anxious, eager, glad, well-pleased **3.** compelled, constrained, with no alternative but

faint *adjective* **1.** bleached, delicate, dim, distant, dull, faded, faltering, feeble, hazy, hushed, ill-defined, indistinct, light, low, muffled, muted, soft, subdued, thin, vague, whispered **2.** feeble, remote, slight, unenthusiastic, weak **3.** dizzy, drooping, enervated, exhausted, faltering, fatigued, giddy, languid, lethargic, light-headed, muzzy, vertiginous, weak, woozy (*informal*) **4.** faint-hearted, lily-livered, spiritless, timid, timorous *~verb* **5.** black out, collapse, fade, fail, flake out (*informal*), keel over (*informal*), languish, lose consciousness, pass out, swoon (*literary*), weaken *~noun* **6.** blackout, collapse, swoon (*literary*), syncope (*Pathology*), unconsciousness

▷ **Antonyms** *~adjective* bold, brave, bright, clear, conspicuous, courageous, distinct, energetic, fresh, hearty, loud, powerful, strong, vigorous

faint-hearted chickenshit (*U.S. slang*), cowardly, diffident, half-arsed (*Brit. slang*), half-assed (*U.S. & Canad. slang*), half-hearted, irresolute, spineless, timid, timorous, weak, yellow

▷ **Antonyms** audacious, bold, brave, courageous, daring, dauntless, fearless, game (*informal*), intrepid, plucky, stouthearted

faintly 1. feebly, in a whisper, indistinctly, softly, weakly **2.** a little, dimly, slightly, somewhat

faintness dimness, dizziness, feebleness, giddiness, indistinctness, languor, loss of strength, shakiness, weakness

fair[1] *adjective* **1.** above board, according to the rules, clean, disinterested, dispassionate, equal, equitable, even-handed, honest, honourable, impartial, just, lawful, legitimate, objective, on the level (*informal*), proper, square, trustworthy, unbiased, unprejudiced, upright **2.** blond, blonde, fair-haired, flaxen-haired, light, light-complexioned, tow-haired, towheaded **3.** adequate, all right, average, decent, mediocre, middling, moderate, not bad, O.K. *or* okay (*informal*), passable, reasonable, respectable, satisfactory, so-so (*informal*), tolerable **4.** beauteous, beautiful, bonny, comely, handsome, lovely, pretty, well-favoured **5.** bright, clear, clement, cloudless, dry, favourable, fine, sunny, sunshiny, unclouded

▷ **Antonyms** (*sense 1*) bad, biased, bigoted, discriminatory, dishonest, inequitable, one-sided, partial, partisan, prejudiced, unfair, unjust (*sense 4*) homely, plain, ugly

fair[2] *noun* bazaar, carnival, expo (*informal*), exposition, festival, fête, gala, market, show

fair-and-square above board, correct, honest, just, kosher (*informal*), on the level (*informal*), straight

fairly 1. adequately, moderately, pretty well, quite, rather, reasonably, somewhat, tolerably **2.** deservedly, equitably, honestly, impartially, justly, objectively, properly, without fear or favour **3.** absolutely, in a manner of speaking, positively, really, veritably

fair-minded disinterested, even-handed, impartial, just, open-minded, unbiased, unprejudiced

fairness decency, disinterestedness, equitableness, equity, impartiality, justice, legitimacy, rightfulness, uprightness

fairy brownie, elf, hob, leprechaun, peri, pixie, Robin Goodfellow, sprite

fairy tale *or* **fairy story 1.** folk tale, romance **2.** cock-and-bull story (*informal*), fabrication, fantasy, fiction, invention, lie, pork pie (*Brit. slang*), porky (*Brit. slang*), tall story, untruth

faith 1. assurance, confidence, conviction, credence, credit, dependence, reliance, trust **2.** belief, church, communion, creed, denomination, dogma, persuasion, religion **3.** allegiance, constancy, faithfulness, fealty, fidelity, loyalty, troth (*archaic*), truth, truthfulness **4.** *as in* **keep faith, in good faith** honour, pledge, promise, sincerity, vow, word, word of honour

▷ **Antonyms** agnosticism, apprehension, denial, disbelief, distrust, doubt, incredulity, infidelity, misgiving, mistrust, rejection, scepticism, suspicion, uncertainty

faithful 1. attached, constant, dependable, devoted, immovable, loyal, reliable, staunch, steadfast, true, true-blue, trusty, truthful, unswerving, unwavering **2.** accurate, close, exact, just, precise, strict, true **3. the faithful** adherents, believers, brethren, communicants, congregation, followers, the elect

▷ **Antonyms** (*sense 1*) disloyal, doubting, faithless, false, false-hearted, fickle, inconstant, perfidious, recreant (*archaic*), traitorous, treacherous, unbelieving, unfaithful, unreliable, untrue, untrustworthy, untruthful

faithfulness 1. adherence, constancy, dependability, devotion, fealty, fidelity, loyalty, trustworthiness **2.** accuracy, closeness, exactness, justice, strictness, truth

faithless disloyal, doubting, false, false-hearted, fickle, inconstant, perfidious, recreant (*archaic*), traitorous, treacherous, unbelieving, unfaithful, unreliable, untrue, untrustworthy, untruthful

faithlessness betrayal, disloyalty, fickleness, inconstancy, infidelity, perfidy, treachery, unfaithfulness

fake 1. *verb* affect, assume, copy, counterfeit, fabricate, feign, forge, pretend, put on, sham, simulate **2.** *~noun* charlatan, copy, forgery, fraud, hoax, imitation, impostor, mountebank, phoney *or* phony (*informal*), reproduction, sham **3.** *~adjective* affected, artificial, assumed, counterfeit, false, forged, imitation, mock, phoney *or* phony (*informal*), pinchbeck, pseudo (*informal*), reproduction, sham

▷ **Antonyms** *~adjective* actual, authentic, bona fide, faithful, genuine, honest, legitimate, real, true, veritable

faker fake, fraud, humbug, impostor, phoney *or* phony (*informal*), pretender, sham

fall *verb* **1.** be precipitated, cascade, collapse, come a cropper (*informal*), crash, descend, dive, drop, drop down, go head over heels, keel over, nose-dive, pitch, plummet, plunge, settle, sink, stumble, subside, topple, trip, trip over, tumble **2.** abate, become lower, decline, decrease, depreciate, diminish, drop, dwindle, ebb, fall off, flag, go down, lessen, slump, subside **3.** be overthrown, be taken, capitulate, give in *or* up, give way, go out of office, pass into enemy hands, resign, succumb, surrender, yield **4.** be a casualty, be killed, be lost, be slain, die, meet one's end, perish **5.** become, befall, chance, come about, come to pass, fall out, happen, occur, take place **6. fall foul of** brush with, come into conflict with, cross swords with, have trouble with, make an enemy of **7. fall in love (with)** become attached to, become enamoured of, become fond of, become infatuated (with), be smitten by, conceive an affection for, fall (for), lose one's heart (to), take a fancy to **8.** fall away, incline, incline downwards, slope **9.** backslide, err, go astray, lapse, offend, sin, transgress, trespass, yield to temptation *~noun* **10.** descent, dive, drop, nose dive, plummet, plunge, slip, spill, tumble **11.** cut, decline, decrease, diminution, dip, drop, dwindling, falling off, lessening, lowering, reduction, slump **12.** capitulation, collapse, death, defeat, destruction, downfall, failure, overthrow, resignation, ruin, surrender **13.** declivity, descent, downgrade, incline, slant, slope **14.** degradation, failure, lapse, sin, slip, transgression

▷ **Antonyms** (*sense 1*) ascend, climb, go

up, increase, mount, rise, scale, soar, wax (*sense 2*) advance, appreciate, climb, escalate, extend, heighten, in~crease (*senses 3 & 4*) endure, hold out, prevail, survive, triumph

fallacious deceptive, delusive, delusory, erroneous, false, fictitious, illogical, il~lusory, incorrect, misleading, mistaken, sophistic, sophistical, spurious, untrue, wrong

fallacy casuistry, deceit, deception, delu~sion, error, falsehood, faultiness, flaw, illusion, inconsistency, misapprehen~sion, misconception, mistake, sophism, sophistry, untruth

fall apart break up, come apart at the seams, crumble, disband, disintegrate, disperse, dissolve, fall to bits, go *or* come to pieces, go to seed, lose cohesion, shatter

fall asleep doze off, drop off (*informal*), go out like a light, go to sleep, nod off (*in~formal*)

fall back back off, draw back, recede, re~coil, retire, retreat, withdraw

fall back on call upon, employ, have re~course to, make use of, press into ser~vice, resort to

fall behind be in arrears, drop back, get left behind, lag, lose one's place, trail

fall down disappoint, fail, fail to make the grade, fall short, go wrong, prove unsuccessful

fallen *adjective* **1.** collapsed, decayed, flat, on the ground, ruinous, sunken **2.** dis~graced, dishonoured, immoral, loose, lost, ruined, shamed, sinful, unchaste **3.** dead, killed, lost, perished, slain, slaughtered

fall for 1. become infatuated with, desire, fall in love with, lose one's head over, succumb to the charms of **2.** accept, be deceived by, be duped by, be fooled by, be taken in by, buy (*slang*), give cre~dence to, swallow (*informal*), take on board

fallible erring, frail, ignorant, imperfect, mortal, prone to error, uncertain, weak

▷ **Antonyms** divine, faultless, impec~cable, infallible, omniscient, perfect, superhuman, unerring, unimpeachable

fall in cave in, collapse, come down about one's ears, fall apart at the seams, sink

falling off *noun* deceleration, decline, de~crease, deterioration, downward trend, drop, slackening, slowing down, slump, waning, worsening

fall in with accept, agree with, assent, buy into (*informal*), concur with, co~operate with, go along with, support, take on board

fall on *or* **fall upon** assail, assault, attack, belabour, descend upon, lay into, pitch into (*informal*), set upon *or* about, snatch, tear into (*informal*)

fall out 1. altercate, argue, clash, come to blows, differ, disagree, fight, quarrel, squabble **2.** chance, come to pass, hap~pen, occur, pan out (*informal*), result, take place, turn out

fallow dormant, idle, inactive, inert, resting, uncultivated, undeveloped, un~planted, untilled, unused

falls cascade, cataract, force (*Northern English dialect*), linn (*Scot.*), rapids, waterfall

fall short be deficient, be lacking, be wanting, fail, miss, prove inadequate

fall through come to nothing, fail, fizzle out (*informal*), go by the board, miscar~ry

fall to 1. apply oneself to, begin, com~mence, set about, start **2.** be up to, come down to, devolve upon

false 1. concocted, erroneous, faulty, ficti~tious, improper, inaccurate, incorrect, inexact, invalid, mistaken, unfounded, unreal, wrong **2.** lying, mendacious, truthless, unreliable, unsound, untrue, untrustworthy, untruthful **3.** artificial, bogus, counterfeit, ersatz, fake, feigned, forged, imitation, mock, pretended, pseudo (*informal*), sham, simulated, spurious, synthetic **4.** deceitful, deceiv~ing, deceptive, delusive, fallacious, fraudulent, hypocritical, misleading, trumped up **5.** dishonest, dishonourable, disloyal, double-dealing, duplicitous, faithless, false-hearted, hypocritical, perfidious, treacherous, treasonable, two-faced, unfaithful, untrustworthy **6. play (someone) false** betray, cheat, de~ceive, double-cross, give the Judas kiss to, sell down the river (*informal*), stab in the back

▷ **Antonyms** authentic, bona fide, cor~rect, exact, faithful, genuine, honest, kosher (*informal*), loyal, real, right, sin~cere, sound, true, trustworthy, valid

falsehood 1. deceit, deception, dishonesty, dissimulation, inveracity (*rare*), men~dacity, perjury, prevarication, untruth~fulness **2.** fabrication, fib, fiction, lie, misstatement, pork pie (*Brit. slang*), porky (*Brit. slang*), story, untruth

falsification adulteration, deceit, dis~simulation, distortion, forgery, misrep~resentation, perversion, tampering with

falsify alter, belie, cook (*slang*), counter~feit, distort, doctor, fake, forge, garble, misrepresent, misstate, pervert, tamper with

falsity 1. deceit, deceptiveness, dishones~ty, double-dealing, duplicity, fraudu~lence, hypocrisy, inaccuracy, mendacity, perfidy, treachery, unreality, untruth **2.** cheating, deception, fraud, lie, pork pie (*Brit. slang*), porky (*Brit. slang*)

falter break, hesitate, shake, speak halt~ingly, stammer, stumble, stutter, totter, tremble, vacillate, waver

▷ **Antonyms** continue, endure, keep going, last, persevere, persist, proceed, stand firm, stick at, survive

faltering broken, hesitant, irresolute, stammering, tentative, timid, uncertain, weak

fame celebrity, credit, eminence, glory, honour, illustriousness, name, prominence, public esteem, renown, reputation, repute, stardom

▷ **Antonyms** disgrace, dishonour, disrepute, ignominy, infamy, oblivion, obscurity, shame

famed acclaimed, celebrated, recognized, renowned, widely-known

familiar 1. accustomed, common, common or garden (*informal*), conventional, customary, domestic, everyday, frequent, household, mundane, ordinary, recognizable, repeated, routine, stock, well-known **2. familiar with** abreast of, acquainted with, at home with, *au courant, au fait,* aware of, conscious of, conversant with, introduced, knowledgeable, no stranger to, on speaking terms with, versed in, well up in **3.** amicable, buddy-buddy (*slang, chiefly U.S. & Canad.*), chummy (*informal*), close, confidential, cordial, easy, free, free-and-easy, friendly, hail-fellow-well-met, informal, intimate, near, open, palsy-walsy (*informal*), relaxed, unceremonious, unconstrained, unreserved **4.** bold, disrespectful, forward, impudent, intrusive, overfree, presuming, presumptuous

▷ **Antonyms** (*sense 1*) infrequent, unaccustomed, uncommon, unfamiliar, unknown, unusual (*sense 2*) ignorant, unaccustomed, unacquainted, unfamiliar, uninformed, unskilled (*sense 3*) aloof, cold, detached, distant, formal, unfriendly

familiarity 1. acquaintance, acquaintanceship, awareness, experience, grasp, understanding **2.** absence of reserve, closeness, ease, fellowship, freedom, friendliness, friendship, informality, intimacy, naturalness, openness, sociability, unceremoniousness **3.** boldness, disrespect, forwardness, liberties, liberty, presumption

▷ **Antonyms** constraint, decorum, distance, formality, ignorance, inexperience, propriety, reserve, respect, unfamiliarity

familiarize accustom, bring into common use, coach, get to know (about), habituate, instruct, inure, make conversant, make used to, prime, school, season, train

family 1. brood, children, descendants, folk (*informal*), household, issue, kin, kindred, kinsfolk, kinsmen, kith and kin, ménage, offspring, one's nearest and dearest, one's own flesh and blood, people, progeny, relations, relatives **2.** ancestors, ancestry, birth, blood, clan, descent, dynasty, extraction, forebears, forefathers, genealogy, house, line, lineage, parentage, pedigree, race, sept, stemma, stirps, strain, tribe **3.** class, classification, genre, group, kind, network, subdivision, system

family tree ancestry, extraction, genealogy, line, lineage, line of descent, pedigree, stemma, stirps

famine dearth, destitution, hunger, scarcity, starvation

famished ravening, ravenous, ready to eat a horse (*informal*), starved, starving, voracious

famous acclaimed, celebrated, conspicuous, distinguished, eminent, excellent, far-famed, glorious, honoured, illustrious, legendary, lionized, much-publicized, notable, noted, prominent, remarkable, renowned, signal, well-known

▷ **Antonyms** forgotten, mediocre, obscure, uncelebrated, undistinguished, unexceptional, unknown, unremarkable

fan[1] *verb* **1.** *Often fig.* add fuel to the flames, agitate, arouse, enkindle, excite, impassion, increase, provoke, rouse, stimulate, stir up, whip up, work up **2.** air-condition, air-cool, blow, cool, refresh, ventilate, winnow (*rare*) *~noun* **3.** air conditioner, blade, blower, propeller, punkah (*in India*), vane, ventilator

fan[2] *noun* addict, adherent, admirer, aficionado, buff (*informal*), devotee, enthusiast, fiend (*informal*), follower, freak (*informal*), groupie (*slang*), lover, rooter (*U.S.*), supporter, zealot

fanatic *noun* activist, addict, bigot, buff (*informal*), devotee, energumen, enthusiast, extremist, militant, visionary, zealot

fanatical bigoted, burning, enthusiastic, extreme, fervent, frenzied, immoderate, mad, obsessive, overenthusiastic, passionate, rabid, visionary, wild, zealous

fanaticism bigotry, dedication, devotion, enthusiasm, extremism, immoderation, infatuation, madness, monomania, obsessiveness, overenthusiasm, single-mindedness, zeal, zealotry

fancier aficionado, amateur, breeder, connoisseur, expert

fanciful capricious, chimerical, curious, extravagant, fabulous, fairy-tale, fantastic, ideal, imaginary, imaginative, mythical, poetic, romantic, unreal, visionary, whimsical, wild

▷ **Antonyms** conventional, down-to-earth, dry, dull, literal, matter of fact, ordinary, pedestrian, predictable, routine, sensible, sober, unimaginative, uninspired

fancy *verb* **1.** be inclined to think, believe, conceive, conjecture, guess (*informal, chiefly U.S. & Canad.*), imagine, infer, reckon, suppose, surmise, think, think likely **2.** be attracted to, crave, desire, dream of, hanker after, have a yen for, hope for, long for, relish, thirst for, wish for, would like, yearn for **3.** *informal* be attracted to, be captivated by, desire, favour, go for, have an eye for, like, lust after, prefer, take a liking to, take to ~*noun* **4.** caprice, desire, humour, idea, impulse, inclination, notion, thought, urge, whim **5.** fondness, hankering, inclination, liking, partiality, predilection, preference, relish, thirst **6.** conception, image, imagination, impression **7.** chimera, daydream, delusion, dream, fantasy, nightmare, phantasm, vision ~*adjective* **8.** baroque, decorated, decorative, elaborate, elegant, embellished, extravagant, fanciful, intricate, ornamental, ornamented, ornate **9.** capricious, chimerical, delusive, fanciful, fantastic, far-fetched, illusory, whimsical

▷ **Antonyms** (*sense 5*) aversion, disinclination, dislike (*sense 8*) basic, cheap, common, inferior, ordinary, plain, simple, unadorned, undecorated, unfussy

fanfare ballyhoo, fanfaronade, flourish, trump (*archaic*), trumpet call, tucket (*archaic*)

fang tooth, tusk

fan out disperse, lay out, open out, space out, spread, spread out, unfurl

fantasize build castles in the air, daydream, dream, envision, give free rein to the imagination, hallucinate, imagine, invent, live in a dream world, romance, see visions

fantastic 1. comical, eccentric, exotic, fanciful, freakish, grotesque, imaginative, odd, oddball (*informal*), off-the-wall (*slang*), outlandish, outré, peculiar, phantasmagorical, quaint, queer, rococo, strange, unreal, weird, whimsical, zany **2.** ambitious, chimerical, extravagant, far-fetched, grandiose, illusory, ludicrous, ridiculous, unrealistic, visionary, wild **3.** absurd, capricious, cock-and-bull (*informal*), implausible, incredible, irrational, mad, preposterous, unlikely **4.** *informal* enormous, extreme, great, overwhelming, severe, tremendous **5.** *informal* awesome (*slang*), bitchin' (*U.S. slang*), boffo (*slang*), brill (*informal*), chillin' (*U.S. slang*), cracking (*Brit. informal*), crucial (*slang*), def (*slang*), dope (*slang*), excellent, first-rate, jim-dandy (*slang*), marvellous, mean (*slang*), mega (*slang*), out of this world (*informal*), sensational (*informal*), sovereign, superb, the dog's bollocks (*taboo slang*), topping (*Brit. slang*), wonderful, world-class

▷ **Antonyms** common, credible, everyday, moderate, normal, ordinary, poor, rational, realistic, sensible, typical

fantasy, phantasy 1. creativity, fancy, imagination, invention, originality **2.** apparition, daydream, delusion, dream, fancy, figment of the imagination, flight of fancy, hallucination, illusion, mirage, nightmare, pipe dream, reverie, vision

far *adverb* **1.** afar, a good way, a great distance, a long way, deep, miles **2.** considerably, decidedly, extremely, greatly, incomparably, much, very much **3. by far** by a long chalk (*informal*), by a long shot, by a long way, easily, far and away, immeasurably, incomparably, to a great degree, very much **4. far and wide** broadly, everywhere, extensively, far and near, here, there and everywhere, in every nook and cranny, widely, worldwide **5. so far** thus far, to date, until now, up to now, up to the present ~*adjective* **6.** distant, faraway, far-flung, far-off, far-removed, long, outlying, out-of-the-way, remote, removed

▷ **Antonyms** adjacent, adjoining, alongside, at close quarters, beside, bordering, close, contiguous, just round the corner, near, nearby, neighbouring, proximate, within sniffing distance (*informal*)

faraway 1. beyond the horizon, distant, far, far-flung, far-off, far-removed, outlying, remote **2.** absent, abstracted, distant, dreamy, lost, vague

farce 1. broad comedy, buffoonery, burlesque, comedy, satire, slapstick **2.** absurdity, joke, mockery, nonsense, parody, ridiculousness, sham, travesty

farcical absurd, amusing, comic, custard-pie, derisory, diverting, droll, funny, laughable, ludicrous, nonsensical, preposterous, ridiculous, risible, slapstick

fare *noun* **1.** charge, passage money, price, ticket money, transport cost **2.** passenger, pick-up (*informal*), traveller **3.** commons, diet, eatables, feed, food, meals, menu, nosebag (*slang*), provisions, rations, sustenance, table, tack (*informal*), victuals, vittles (*obsolete or dialect*) ~*verb* **4.** do, get along, get on, make out, manage, prosper **5.** (*used impersonally*) go, happen, pan out (*informal*), proceed, turn out

farewell adieu, adieux *or* adieus, departure, goodbye, leave-taking, parting, sendoff (*informal*), valediction

far-fetched cock-and-bull (*informal*), doubtful, dubious, fantastic, hard to swallow (*informal*), implausible, improbable, incredible, preposterous, strained, unbelievable, unconvincing, unlikely, unnatural, unrealistic

▷ **Antonyms** acceptable, authentic, believable, credible, feasible, imaginable, likely, plausible, possible, probable, realistic, reasonable

farm 1. *noun* acreage, acres, croft (*Scot.*), farmstead, grange, holding, homestead, land, plantation, ranch (*chiefly North American*), smallholding, station (*Austral. & N.Z.*) **2.** *~verb* bring under cultivation, cultivate, operate, plant, practise husbandry, till the soil, work

farmer agriculturist, agronomist, cockie (*N.Z.*), husbandman, smallholder, yeoman

farming agriculture, agronomy, husbandry

far-out advanced, avant-garde, bizarre, off-the-wall (*slang*), outlandish, outré, unconventional, weird, wild

farrago gallimaufry, hash, hodgepodge, hotchpotch, jumble, medley, *mélange,* miscellany, mishmash, mixed bag, mixture, potpourri, salmagundi

far-reaching broad, extensive, important, momentous, pervasive, significant, sweeping, widespread

far-sighted acute, canny, cautious, discerning, far-seeing, judicious, politic, prescient, provident, prudent, sage, shrewd, wise

fascinate absorb, allure, beguile, bewitch, captivate, charm, delight, enamour, enchant, engross, enrapture, enravish, enthral, entrance, hold spellbound, hypnotize, infatuate, intrigue, mesmerize, ravish, rivet, spellbind, transfix
▷ **Antonyms** alienate, bore, disenchant, disgust, irritate, jade, put one off, sicken, turn one off (*informal*)

fascinated absorbed, beguiled, bewitched, captivated, charmed, engrossed, enthralled, entranced, hooked on, hypnotized, infatuated, smitten, spellbound, under a spell

fascinating alluring, bewitching, captivating, compelling, enchanting, engaging, engrossing, enticing, gripping, intriguing, irresistible, ravishing, riveting, seductive
▷ **Antonyms** boring, dull, mind-numbing, unexciting, uninteresting

fascination allure, attraction, charm, enchantment, glamour, lure, magic, magnetism, pull, sorcery, spell

fascism *noun* absolutism, authoritarianism, autocracy, dictatorship, Hitlerism, totalitarianism

fashion *noun* **1.** convention, craze, custom, fad, latest, latest style, look, mode, prevailing taste, rage, style, trend, usage, vogue **2.** attitude, demeanour, manner, method, mode, style, way **3.** appearance, configuration, cut, figure, form, guise (*archaic*), line, make, model, mould, pattern, shape, stamp **4.** description, kind, sort, stamp, type **5.** beau monde, fashionable society, high society, jet set **6. after a fashion** in a manner of speaking, in a way, moderately, somehow, somehow or other, to a degree, to some extent *~verb* **7. construct, contrive,** create, design, forge, **form, make,** manufacture, mould, shape, work **8.** accommodate, adapt, adjust, fit, suit, tailor

fashionable à la mode, all the go (*informal*), all the rage, chic, cool (*slang*), current, customary, genteel, happening (*informal*), hip (*slang*), in (*informal*), in vogue, latest, modern, modish, popular, prevailing, smart, stylish, trendsetting, trendy (*Brit. informal*), up-to-date, up-to-the-minute, usual, voguish (*informal*), with it (*informal*)
▷ **Antonyms** behind the times, dated, frumpy, obsolete, old-fashioned, old-hat, outmoded, out of date, out of the ark (*informal*), uncool (*slang*), unfashionable, unpopular, unstylish, untrendy (*Brit. informal*)

fast[1] *adjective* **1.** accelerated, brisk, fleet, flying, hasty, hurried, mercurial, nippy (*Brit. informal*), quick, quickie (*informal*), rapid, speedy, swift, winged *~adverb* **2.** apace, at a rate of knots, hastily, hell for leather (*informal*), hotfoot, hurriedly, in haste, like a bat out of hell (*slang*), like a flash, like a shot (*informal*), like greased lightning (*informal*), like lightning, like nobody's business (*informal*), like the clappers (*Brit. informal*), pdq (*slang*), posthaste, presto, quickly, rapidly, speedily, swiftly, with all haste *~adjective* **3.** close, constant, fastened, firm, fixed, fortified, immovable, impregnable, lasting, loyal, permanent, secure, sound, stalwart, staunch, steadfast, tight, unwavering *~adverb* **4.** deeply, firmly, fixedly, securely, soundly, tightly *~adjective* **5.** dissipated, dissolute, extravagant, gadabout (*informal*), giddy, immoral, intemperate, licentious, loose, profligate, promiscuous, rakish, reckless, self-indulgent, wanton, wild *~adverb* **6.** extravagantly, intemperately, loosely, promiscuously, rakishly, recklessly, wildly **7. pull a fast one** bamboozle (*informal*), cheat, con (*informal*), deceive, defraud, hoodwink, put one over on (*informal*), swindle, take advantage of, take for a ride (*informal*), trick
▷ **Antonyms** (*sense 1*) leisurely, plodding, slow, slow moving, unhurried (*sense 2*) at a snail's pace, at one's leisure, gradually, leisurely, slowly, steadily, unhurriedly (*sense 3*) inconstant, irresolute, unfaithful, unreliable, unstable, wavering, weak

fast[2] **1.** *verb* abstain, deny oneself, go hungry, go without food, practise abstention, refrain from food *or* eating **2.** *~noun* abstinence, fasting

fasten **1.** affix, anchor, attach, bind, bolt, chain, connect, fix, grip, join, lace, link, lock, make fast, make firm, seal, secure, tie, unite **2.** *figurative* aim, bend, concentrate, direct, fix, focus, rivet

fastidious choosy, critical, dainty, difficult, discriminating, finicky, fussy, hard to please, hypercritical, meticulous, nice, overdelicate, overnice, particular, pernickety, picky (*informal*), punctilious, squeamish
▷ **Antonyms** careless, casual, disorderly, easygoing, lenient, slack, slipshod, sloppy, slovenly, unsystematic

fat *adjective* **1.** beefy (*informal*), broad in the beam (*informal*), corpulent, elephantine, fleshy, gross, heavy, obese, overweight, plump, podgy, portly, roly-poly, rotund, solid, stout, tubby **2.** adipose, fatty, greasy, lipid, oily, oleaginous, suety **3.** affluent, cushy (*slang*), fertile, flourishing, fruitful, jammy (*Brit. slang*), lucrative, lush, productive, profitable, prosperous, remunerative, rich, thriving *~noun* **4.** adipose tissue, beef (*informal*), blubber, bulk, cellulite, corpulence, fatness, flab, flesh, obesity, overweight, paunch, weight problem
▷ **Antonyms** (*sense 1*) angular, bony, empty, gaunt, lank, lean, scrawny, skinny, slender, slight, slim, spare, thin (*sense 2*) lean (*sense 3*) barren, poor, scanty, scarce, unproductive, unprofitable, unrewarding

fatal 1. deadly, destructive, final, incurable, killing, lethal, malignant, mortal, pernicious, terminal **2.** baleful, baneful, calamitous, catastrophic, disastrous, lethal, ruinous **3.** critical, crucial, decisive, destined, determining, doomed, fateful, final, foreordained, inevitable, predestined
▷ **Antonyms** (*senses 1 & 2*) beneficial, benign, harmless, inconsequential, innocuous, inoffensive, minor, non-lethal, non-toxic, salutary, vitalizing, wholesome

fatalism acceptance, determinism, necessitarianism, passivity, predestinarianism, resignation, stoicism

fatality casualty, deadliness, death, disaster, fatal accident, lethalness, loss, mortality

fate 1. chance, destiny, divine will, fortune, kismet, nemesis, predestination, providence, weird (*archaic*) **2.** cup, fortune, horoscope, lot, portion, stars **3.** end, future, issue, outcome, upshot **4.** death, destruction, doom, downfall, end, ruin

fated destined, doomed, foreordained, ineluctable, inescapable, inevitable, marked down, predestined, pre-elected, preordained, sure, written

fateful 1. critical, crucial, decisive, important, portentous, significant **2.** deadly, destructive, disastrous, fatal, lethal, ominous, ruinous
▷ **Antonyms** inconsequential, insignificant, nugatory, ordinary, unimportant

Fates, the *Greek myth* Providence, the Moirai, the Norns (*Norse myth*), the Parcae (*Roman Myth*), the Three Sisters, the Weird Sisters

fathead ass, berk (*Brit. slang*), booby, charlie (*Brit. informal*), coot, dickhead (*slang*), dimwit (*informal*), dipstick (*Brit. slang*), divvy (*Brit. slang*), dope (*informal*), dork (*slang*), dunderhead, dweeb (*U.S. slang*), fool, fuckwit (*taboo slang*), geek (*slang*), gobshite (*Irish taboo slang*), gonzo (*slang*), goose, idiot, imbecile, jackass, jerk (*slang, chiefly U.S. & Canad.*), lamebrain (*informal*), nerd *or* nurd (*slang*), nincompoop, nitwit (*informal*), numbskull *or* numskull, numpty (*Scot. informal*), pillock (*Brit. slang*), plank (*Brit. slang*), plonker (*slang*), prat (*slang*), prick (*derogatory slang*), schmuck (*U.S. slang*), twerp *or* twirp (*informal*), twit (*informal, chiefly Brit.*), wally (*slang*)

father *noun* **1.** begetter, dad (*informal*), daddy (*informal*), governor (*informal*), old boy (*informal*), old man (*informal*), pa (*informal*), papa (*old-fashioned informal*), pater, paterfamilias, patriarch, pop (*informal*), sire **2.** ancestor, forebear, forefather, predecessor, progenitor **3.** architect, author, creator, founder, inventor, maker, originator, prime mover **4.** city father, elder, leader, patriarch, patron, senator **5.** abbé, confessor, curé, padre (*informal*), pastor, priest *~verb* **6.** beget, get, procreate, sire **7.** create, engender, establish, found, institute, invent, originate

fatherland homeland, land of one's birth, land of one's fathers, motherland, native land, old country

fatherly affectionate, benevolent, benign, forbearing, indulgent, kind, kindly, paternal, patriarchal, protective, supportive, tender

fathom 1. divine, estimate, gauge, measure, penetrate, plumb, probe, sound **2.** comprehend, get to the bottom of, grasp, interpret, understand

fathomless abysmal, bottomless, deep, immeasurable, impenetrable, incomprehensible, profound, unfathomable, unplumbed

fatigue 1. *verb* drain, drain of energy, exhaust, fag (out) (*informal*), jade, knacker (*slang*), overtire, poop (*informal*), take it out of (*informal*), tire, weaken, wear out, weary, whack (*Brit. informal*) **2.** *~noun* debility, ennui, heaviness, languor, lethargy, listlessness, overtiredness, tiredness
▷ **Antonyms** *~verb* refresh, rejuvenate, relieve, rest, revive, stimulate *~noun* alertness, animation, energy, freshness, get-up-and-go (*informal*), go, indefatigability, life, vigour, zest

fatigued all in (*slang*), bushed (*informal*), clapped out (*Austral. & N.Z. informal*), creamcrakered (*Brit. informal*), dead beat (*informal*), exhausted, fagged (out) (*informal*), jaded, jiggered (*informal*), knackered (*slang*), on one's last legs, overtired, tired, tired out, wasted, weary, whacked (*Brit. informal*), zonked (*slang*)

fatness beef (*informal*), bulkiness, corpulence, *embonpoint,* flab, flesh, fleshiness, girth, grossness, heaviness, obesity, overweight, podginess, rotundity, size, stoutness, weight, weight problem

fatten 1. broaden, coarsen, expand, gain weight, grow fat, put on weight, spread, swell, thicken, thrive **2.** (*often with* **up**) bloat, build up, cram, distend, feed, feed up, nourish, overfeed, stuff

fatty adipose, fat, greasy, oily, oleaginous, rich

fatuity absurdity, bêtise (*rare*), brainlessness, daftness (*informal*), denseness, fatuousness, folly, foolishness, idiocy, imbecility, insanity, ludicrousness, lunacy, mindlessness, stupidity

fatuous absurd, asinine, brainless, dense, dull, foolish, idiotic, inane, ludicrous, lunatic, mindless, moronic, puerile, silly, stupid, vacuous, weak-minded, witless

fault *noun* **1.** blemish, defect, deficiency, demerit, drawback, failing, flaw, imperfection, infirmity, lack, shortcoming, snag, weakness, weak point **2.** blunder, boob (*Brit. slang*), error, error of judgment, inaccuracy, indiscretion, lapse, mistake, negligence, offence, omission, oversight, slip, slip-up **3.** accountability, culpability, liability, responsibility **4.** delinquency, frailty, lapse, misconduct, misdeed, misdemeanour, offence, peccadillo, sin, transgression, trespass, wrong **5. at fault** answerable, blamable, culpable, guilty, in the wrong, responsible, to blame **6. find fault with** carp at, complain, criticize, pick holes in, pull to pieces, quibble, take to task **7. to a fault** excessively, immoderately, in the extreme, needlessly, out of all proportion, overly (*U.S.*), overmuch, preposterously, ridiculously, unduly *~verb* **8.** blame, call to account, censure, criticize, find fault with, find lacking, hold (someone) accountable, hold (someone) responsible, hold (someone) to blame, impugn

▷ **Antonyms** (*sense 1*) asset, attribute, credit, goodness, merit, perfection, strength, virtue

fault-finding 1. *noun* carping, hair-splitting, nagging, niggling, nit-picking (*informal*) **2.** *~adjective* captious, carping, censorious, critical, hypercritical, on (someone's) back (*informal*), pettifogging

▷ **Antonyms** complimentary, easily pleased, indiscriminate, uncritical, undiscerning, unexacting, unfussy, unperceptive

faultless 1. accurate, classic, correct, exemplary, faithful, flawless, foolproof, impeccable, model, perfect, unblemished **2.** above reproach, blameless, guiltless, immaculate, impeccable, innocent, irreproachable, pure, sinless, spotless, stainless, unblemished, unspotted, unsullied

faulty bad, blemished, broken, damaged, defective, erroneous, fallacious, flawed, impaired, imperfect, imprecise, inaccurate, incorrect, invalid, malfunctioning, not working, on the blink, out of order, unsound, weak, wrong

faux pas bloomer (*Brit. informal*), blunder, boob (*Brit. slang*), breach of etiquette, clanger (*informal*), gaffe, gaucherie, impropriety, indiscretion, solecism

favour *noun* **1.** approbation, approval, backing, bias, championship, espousal, esteem, favouritism, friendliness, good opinion, goodwill, grace, kindness, kind regard, partiality, patronage, promotion, support **2.** benefit, boon, courtesy, good turn, indulgence, kindness, obligement (*Scot. or archaic*), service **3. in favour of** all for (*informal*), backing, for, on the side of, pro, supporting, to the benefit of **4.** gift, keepsake, love-token, memento, present, souvenir, token **5.** badge, decoration, knot, ribbons, rosette *~verb* **6.** be partial to, esteem, have in one's good books, indulge, pamper, pull strings for (*informal*), reward, side with, smile upon, spoil, treat with partiality, value **7.** advocate, approve, back, be in favour of, champion, choose, commend, countenance, encourage, espouse, fancy, incline towards, like, opt for, patronize, prefer, single out, support **8.** abet, accommodate, advance, aid, assist, befriend, do a kindness to, facilitate, help, oblige, promote, succour **9.** *informal* be the image *or* picture of, look like, resemble, take after **10.** ease, extenuate, spare

▷ **Antonyms** *~noun* (*sense 1*) animosity, antipathy, disapproval, disfavour, ill will, malevolence (*sense 2*) disservice, harm, injury, wrong *~verb* disapprove, disdain, dislike, inconvenience, object to, oppose, thwart

favourable 1. advantageous, appropriate, auspicious, beneficial, convenient, encouraging, fair, fit, good, helpful, hopeful, opportune, promising, propitious, suitable, timely **2.** affirmative, agreeable, amicable, approving, benign, encouraging, enthusiastic, friendly, kind, positive, reassuring, sympathetic, understanding, welcoming, well-disposed

▷ **Antonyms** disadvantageous, disapproving, ill-disposed, inauspicious, unfavourable, unfriendly, unhelpful, unpromising, unsympathetic, useless

favourably 1. advantageously, auspiciously, conveniently, fortunately, op~

portunely, profitably, to one's advantage, well **2.** agreeably, approvingly, enthusiastically, genially, graciously, helpfully, in a kindly manner, positively, with approbation, with approval, with cordiality, without prejudice

favoured 1. best-liked, chosen, favourite, pet, preferred, recommended, selected, singled out **2.** advantaged, blessed, elite, jammy (*Brit. slang*), lucky, privileged

favourite 1. *adjective* best-loved, choice, dearest, esteemed, favoured, preferred **2.** *~noun* beloved, blue-eyed boy (*informal*), choice, darling, dear, idol, pet, pick, preference, teacher's pet, the apple of one's eye

favouritism bias, jobs for the boys (*informal*), nepotism, one-sidedness, partiality, partisanship, preference, preferential treatment

▷ **Antonyms** equality, equity, evenhandedness, fairness, impartiality, neutrality, objectivity, open-mindedness

fawn[1] *adjective* beige, buff, greyish-brown, neutral

fawn[2] *verb* (*often with* **on** *or* **upon**) be obsequious, be servile, bow and scrape, brown-nose (*taboo slang*), court, crawl, creep, cringe, curry favour, dance attendance, flatter, grovel, ingratiate oneself, kiss ass (*U.S. & Canad. taboo slang*), kneel, kowtow, lick (someone's) arse (*taboo slang*), lick (someone's) boots, pander to, pay court, toady, truckle

fawning abject, bootlicking (*informal*), bowing and scraping, crawling, cringing, deferential, flattering, grovelling, obsequious, prostrate, servile, slavish, sycophantic

fealty allegiance, devotion, faith, faithfulness, fidelity, homage, loyalty, obeisance, submission, troth (*archaic*)

fear *noun* **1.** alarm, apprehensiveness, awe, blue funk (*informal*), consternation, cravenness, dismay, dread, fright, horror, panic, qualms, terror, timidity, tremors, trepidation **2.** bête noire, bogey, bugbear, horror, nightmare, phobia, spectre **3.** agitation, anxiety, apprehension, concern, disquietude, distress, doubt, foreboding(s), misgiving(s), solicitude, suspicion, unease, uneasiness, worry **4.** awe, reverence, veneration, wonder *~verb* **5.** apprehend, be afraid, be apprehensive, be frightened, be in a blue funk (*informal*), be scared, dare not, dread, have a horror of, have a phobia about, have butterflies in one's stomach (*informal*), have qualms, live in dread of, shake in one's shoes, shudder at, take fright, tremble at **6.** anticipate, apprehend, be afraid, expect, foresee, suspect **7.** (*with* **for**) be anxious about, be concerned, be disquieted over, be distressed, feel concern for, tremble for, worry about **8.** respect, revere, reverence, stand in awe of, venerate

fearful 1. afraid, alarmed, anxious, apprehensive, diffident, faint-hearted, frightened, hellacious (*U.S. slang*), hesitant, intimidated, jittery (*informal*), jumpy, nervous, nervy (*Brit. informal*), neurotic, panicky, pusillanimous, scared, shrinking, tense, timid, timorous, uneasy, wired (*slang*) **2.** appalling, atrocious, awful, dire, distressing, dreadful, frightful, ghastly, grievous, grim, gruesome, hair-raising, harrowing, hideous, horrendous, horrible, horrific, monstrous, shocking, terrible, unspeakable

▷ **Antonyms** (*sense 1*) ballsy (*taboo slang*), bold, brave, confident, courageous, daring, dauntless, doughty, gallant, game (*informal*), gutsy (*slang*), heroic, indomitable, intrepid, lion-hearted, plucky, unabashed, unafraid, undaunted, unflinching, valiant, valorous

fearfully 1. apprehensively, diffidently, in fear and trembling, nervously, timidly, timorously, uneasily, with bated breath, with many misgivings *or* forebodings, with one's heart in one's mouth **2.** awfully, exceedingly, excessively, frightfully, terribly, tremendously, very

fearless ballsy (*taboo slang*), bold, brave, confident, courageous, daring, dauntless, doughty, gallant, game (*informal*), gutsy (*slang*), heroic, indomitable, intrepid, lion-hearted, plucky, unabashed, unafraid, undaunted, unflinching, valiant, valorous

fearlessness balls (*taboo slang*), ballsiness (*taboo slang*), boldness, bravery, confidence, courage, dauntlessness, guts (*informal*), indomitability, intrepidity, lion-heartedness, nerve, pluckiness

fearsome alarming, appalling, awe-inspiring, awesome, awful, baleful, daunting, dismaying, formidable, frightening, hair-raising, hellacious (*U.S. slang*), horrendous, horrifying, menacing, unnerving

feasibility expediency, practicability, usefulness, viability, workability

feasible achievable, attainable, likely, possible, practicable, realizable, reasonable, viable, workable

▷ **Antonyms** impossible, impracticable, inconceivable, unreasonable, untenable, unviable, unworkable

feast *noun* **1.** banquet, barbecue, beanfeast (*Brit. informal*), beano (*Brit. slang*), blowout (*slang*), carousal, carouse, dinner, entertainment, festive board, jollification, junket, repast, revels, slap-up meal (*Brit. informal*), spread (*informal*), treat **2.** celebration, **-fest**, festival, fête, gala day, holiday, **holy day**, red-letter day, saint's day **3.** **delight**, enjoyment, gratification, pleas~

ure, treat *~verb* **4.** eat one's fill, eat to one's heart's content, fare sumptuously, gorge, gormandize, indulge, overindulge, pig out (*slang*), stuff, stuff one's face (*slang*), wine and dine **5.** entertain, hold a reception for, kill the fatted calf for, regale, treat, wine and dine **6.** delight, gladden, gratify, rejoice, thrill

feat accomplishment, achievement, act, attainment, deed, exploit, feather in one's cap, performance

feathers down, plumage, plumes

feathery downy, feathered, fluffy, plumate *or* plumose (*Botany & Zoology*), plumed, plumy, wispy

feature *noun* **1.** aspect, attribute, characteristic, facet, factor, hallmark, mark, peculiarity, point, property, quality, trait **2.** attraction, crowd puller (*informal*), draw, highlight, innovation, main item, special, special attraction, speciality, specialty **3.** article, column, comment, item, piece, report, story *~verb* **4.** accentuate, call attention to, emphasize, foreground, give prominence to, give the full works (*slang*), headline, play up, present, promote, set off, spotlight, star

featured given prominence, headlined, highlighted, in the public eye, presented, promoted, recommended, specially presented, starred

features countenance, face, lineaments, physiognomy

featuring calling attention to, displaying, drawing attention to, giving a star role, giving prominence to, giving the full works (*slang*), highlighting, making the main attraction, presenting, promoting, pushing, recommending, showing, showing off, starring, turning the spotlight on

febrile delirious, fevered, feverish, fiery, flushed, hot, inflamed, pyretic (*Medical*)

feckless aimless, feeble, futile, good-for-nothing, hopeless, incompetent, ineffectual, irresponsible, shiftless, useless, weak, worthless

fecund fertile, fructiferous, fruitful, productive, prolific, teeming

fecundity fertility, fructiferousness, fruitfulness, productiveness

federate *verb* amalgamate, associate, combine, confederate, integrate, syndicate, unify, unite

federation alliance, amalgamation, association, *Bund,* coalition, combination, confederacy, copartnership, entente, federacy, league, syndicate, union

fed up (with) annoyed, blue, bored, brassed off (*Brit. slang*), browned-off (*informal*), depressed, discontented, dismal, dissatisfied, down, down in the mouth, gloomy, glum, hacked (off) (*U.S. slang*), pissed off (*taboo slang*), sick and tired of (*informal*), tired of, weary of

fee account, bill, charge, compensation, emolument, hire, honorarium, meed (*archaic*), pay, payment, recompense, remuneration, reward, toll

feeble 1. debilitated, delicate, doddering, effete, enervated, enfeebled, etiolated, exhausted, failing, faint, frail, infirm, languid, powerless, puny, shilpit (*Scot.*), sickly, weak, weakened, weedy (*informal*) **2.** flat, flimsy, inadequate, incompetent, indecisive, ineffective, ineffectual, inefficient, insignificant, insufficient, lame, paltry, pathetic, poor, slight, tame, thin, unconvincing, weak

▷ **Antonyms** ardent, effective, energetic, forceful, hale, healthy, hearty, lusty, robust, stalwart, strong, sturdy, successful, vigorous

feeble-minded addle-pated, bone-headed (*slang*), braindead (*informal*), deficient, dim-witted (*informal*), dozy (*Brit. informal*), dull, dumb (*informal*), half-witted, idiotic, imbecilic, lacking, moronic, obtuse, retarded, simple, slow on the uptake, slow-witted, soft in the head (*informal*), stupid, vacant, weak-minded

▷ **Antonyms** astute, aware, bright, clear-headed, clever, intelligent, keen, quick-witted, smart

feebleness 1. debility, delicacy, effeteness, enervation, etiolation, exhaustion, frailness, frailty, incapacity, infirmity, lack of strength, languor, lassitude, sickliness, weakness **2.** flimsiness, inadequacy, incompetence, indecisiveness, ineffectualness, insignificance, insufficiency, lameness, weakness

feed *verb* **1.** cater for, nourish, provide for, provision, supply, sustain, victual, wine and dine **2.** (*sometimes with* **on**) devour, eat, exist on, fare, graze, live on, nurture, partake of, pasture, subsist, take nourishment **3.** augment, bolster, encourage, foster, fuel, minister to, strengthen, supply *~noun* **4.** fodder, food, forage, pasturage, provender, silage **5.** *informal* feast, meal, nosh (*slang*), nosh-up (*Brit. slang*), repast, spread (*informal*), tuck-in (*informal*)

feel *verb* **1.** caress, finger, fondle, handle, manipulate, maul, paw, run one's hands over, stroke, touch **2.** be aware of, be sensible of, endure, enjoy, experience, go through, have, have a sensation of, know, notice, observe, perceive, suffer, take to heart, undergo **3.** explore, fumble, grope, sound, test, try **4.** be convinced, feel in one's bones, have a hunch, have the impression, intuit, sense **5.** believe, be of the opinion that, consider, deem, hold, judge, think **6.** appear, resemble, seem, strike one as **7.** (*with* **for**) be moved by, be sorry for, bleed for, commiserate, compassionate, condole with, empathize, feel compassion for, pity, sympathize with **8. feel like** could do with, desire, fancy, feel in~

clined, feel the need for, feel up to, have the inclination, want *~noun* **9.** finish, surface, texture, touch **10.** air, ambience, atmosphere, feeling, impression, quality, sense, vibes (*slang*)

feeler 1. antenna, tentacle, whisker **2.** advance, approach, probe, trial balloon

feeling 1. feel, perception, sensation, sense, sense of touch, touch **2.** apprehension, consciousness, hunch, idea, impression, inkling, notion, presentiment, sense, suspicion **3.** affection, ardour, emotion, fervour, fondness, heat, intensity, passion, sentiment, sentimentality, warmth **4.** appreciation, compassion, concern, empathy, pity, sensibility, sensitivity, sympathy, understanding **5.** inclination, instinct, opinion, point of view, view **6.** air, ambience, atmosphere, aura, feel, mood, quality, vibes (*slang*) **7. bad feeling** anger, dislike, distrust, enmity, hostility, upset

feelings ego, emotions, self-esteem, sensitivities, susceptibilities

feign act, affect, assume, counterfeit, devise, dissemble, fabricate, fake, forge, give the appearance of, imitate, make a show of, pretend, put on, sham, simulate

feigned affected, artificial, assumed, counterfeit, ersatz, fabricated, fake, false, imitation, insincere, pretended, pseudo (*informal*), sham, simulated, spurious

feint *noun* artifice, blind, bluff, distraction, dodge, expedient, gambit, manoeuvre, mock attack, play, pretence, ruse, stratagem, subterfuge, wile

felicitate compliment, congratulate, wish joy to

felicitous apposite, appropriate, apropos, apt, fitting, happy, inspired, neat, opportune, pat, propitious, suitable, timely, well-chosen, well-timed

felicity 1. blessedness, bliss, blissfulness, delectation, ecstasy, happiness, joy **2.** applicability, appropriateness, aptness, becomingness, effectiveness, grace, propriety, suitability, suitableness

feline 1. catlike, leonine **2.** graceful, sinuous, sleek, slinky, smooth, stealthy

fell[1] *verb* cut, cut down, deck (*slang*), demolish, flatten, floor, hew, knock down, level, prostrate, raze, strike down

fell[2] *adjective* **1.** barbarous, bloody, cruel, ferocious, fierce, grim, implacable, inhuman, malicious, malignant, merciless, murderous, pitiless, relentless, ruthless, sanguinary, savage, vicious **2.** baneful, deadly, destructive, fatal, malign, mortal, noxious, pernicious, pestilential, ruinous

fellow *noun* **1.** bloke (*Brit. informal*), boy, chap (*informal*), character, customer (*informal*), guy (*informal*), individual, man, person, punter (*informal*) **2.** associate, colleague, companion, compeer, comrade, co-worker, equal, friend, member, partner, peer **3.** brother, counterpart, double, duplicate, match, mate, twin *~adjective* **4.** affiliated, akin, allied, associate, associated, co-, like, related, similar

fellow feeling compassion, empathy, pity, sympathy, understanding

fellowship 1. amity, brotherhood, camaraderie, communion, companionability, companionship, familiarity, fraternization, intercourse, intimacy, kindliness, sociability **2.** association, brotherhood, club, fraternity, guild, league, order, sisterhood, society, sodality

feminine 1. delicate, gentle, girlish, graceful, ladylike, modest, soft, tender, womanly **2.** camp (*informal*), effeminate, effete, unmanly, unmasculine, weak, womanish

▷ **Antonyms** Amazonian, butch, indelicate, manly, mannish, masculine, rough, unfeminine, unladylike, unwomanly, virile

femininity delicacy, feminineness, gentleness, girlishness, muliebrity, softness, womanhood, womanliness

femme fatale charmer, Circe, enchantress, seductress, siren, vamp (*informal*)

fen bog, holm (*dialect*), marsh, morass, moss (*Scot.*), quagmire, slough, swamp

fence *noun* **1.** barbed wire, barricade, barrier, defence, guard, hedge, paling, palisade, railings, rampart, shield, stockade, wall **2. on the fence** between two stools, irresolute, uncertain, uncommitted, undecided, vacillating *~verb* **3.** (*often with* **in** *or* **off**) bound, circumscribe, confine, coop, defend, encircle, enclose, fortify, guard, hedge, impound, pen, pound, protect, restrict, secure, separate, surround **4.** beat about the bush, cavil, dodge, equivocate, evade, flannel (*Brit. informal*), hedge, parry, prevaricate, quibble, shift, stonewall, tergiversate

fencing *figurative* beating about the bush, double talk, equivocation, evasiveness, hedging, parrying, prevarication, quibbling, stonewalling, tergiversation, weasel words (*informal, chiefly U.S.*)

fend for look after, make do, make provision for, provide for, shift for, support, sustain, take care of

fend off avert, beat off, deflect, drive back, hold *or* keep at bay, keep off, parry, repel, repulse, resist, stave off, turn aside, ward off

feral 1. unbroken, uncultivated, undomesticated, untamed, wild **2.** bestial, brutal, fell, ferocious, fierce, savage, vicious

ferment *verb* **1.** boil, brew, bubble, concoct, effervesce, foam, froth, heat, leaven, rise, seethe, work *~noun* **2.** bacteria, barm, fermentation agent, leaven, leavening, mother, mother-of-vinegar, yeast *~verb* **3.** *figurative* agitate, boil, excite, fester, foment, heat, incite, inflame, provoke, rouse, seethe, smoulder, stir up *~noun* **4.** *figurative* agitation, brouhaha, commotion, disruption, excitement, fever, frenzy, furore, glow, heat, hubbub, imbroglio, state of unrest, stew, stir, tumult, turbulence, turmoil, unrest, uproar
▷ **Antonyms** *~noun* calmness, hush, peacefulness, quiet, restfulness, stillness, tranquillity

ferocious 1. feral, fierce, predatory, rapacious, ravening, savage, violent, wild **2.** barbaric, barbarous, bloodthirsty, brutal, brutish, cruel, merciless, pitiless, relentless, ruthless, tigerish, vicious
▷ **Antonyms** calm, docile, gentle, mild, subdued, submissive, tame

ferocity barbarity, bloodthirstiness, brutality, cruelty, ferociousness, fierceness, inhumanity, rapacity, ruthlessness, savageness, savagery, viciousness, wildness

ferret out bring to light, dig up, disclose, discover, drive out, elicit, get at, nose out, root out, run to earth, search out, smell out, trace, track down, unearth

ferry 1. *noun* ferryboat, packet, packet boat **2.** *~verb* carry, chauffeur, convey, run, ship, shuttle, transport

fertile abundant, fat, fecund, flowering, flowing with milk and honey, fruit-bearing, fruitful, generative, luxuriant, plenteous, plentiful, productive, prolific, rich, teeming, yielding
▷ **Antonyms** barren, dry, impotent, infecund, infertile, poor, sterile, unfruitful, unimaginative, uninventive, unproductive

fertility abundance, fecundity, fruitfulness, luxuriance, productiveness, richness

fertilization 1. implantation, impregnation, insemination, pollination, procreation, propagation **2.** dressing, manuring, mulching, top dressing

fertilize 1. fecundate, fructify, impregnate, inseminate, make fruitful, make pregnant, pollinate **2.** compost, dress, enrich, feed, manure, mulch, top-dress

fertilizer compost, dressing, dung, guano, manure, marl

fervent, fervid animated, ardent, devout, eager, earnest, ecstatic, emotional, enthusiastic, excited, fiery, flaming, heartfelt, impassioned, intense, perfervid (*literary*), vehement, warm, zealous
▷ **Antonyms** apathetic, cold, cool, detached, dispassionate, frigid, impassive, unfeeling, unimpassioned

fervour animation, ardour, eagerness, earnestness, enthusiasm, excitement, fervency, intensity, passion, vehemence, warmth, zeal

fester 1. become inflamed, decay, gather, maturate, putrefy, suppurate, ulcerate **2.** *figurative* aggravate, chafe, gall, intensify, irk, rankle, smoulder

festering 1. gathering, inflamed, maturating, poisonous, purulent, pussy, septic, suppurating, ulcerated **2.** black-hearted, smouldering, venomous, vicious, virulent

festival 1. anniversary, commemoration, feast, fête, fiesta, holiday, holy day, red-letter day, saint's day **2.** carnival, celebration, entertainment, -fest, festivities, fête, field day, gala, jubilee, treat

festive back-slapping, carnival, celebratory, cheery, Christmassy, convivial, festal, gala, gay, gleeful, happy, hearty, holiday, jolly, jovial, joyful, joyous, jubilant, light-hearted, merry, mirthful, sportive
▷ **Antonyms** depressing, drab, dreary, funereal, gloomy, lugubrious, mournful, sad

festivity 1. amusement, conviviality, fun, gaiety, jollification, joviality, joyfulness, merriment, merrymaking, mirth, pleasure, revelry, sport **2.** (*often plural*) beano (*Brit. slang*), carousal, celebration, entertainment, festival, festive event, festive proceedings, fun and games, hooley *or* hoolie (*chiefly Irish & N.Z.*), jollification, party, rave (*Brit. slang*), rave-up (*Brit. slang*)

festoon 1. *noun* chaplet, garland, lei, swag, swathe, wreath **2.** *~verb* array, bedeck, beribbon, deck, decorate, drape, garland, hang, swathe, wreathe

fetch 1. bring, carry, conduct, convey, deliver, escort, get, go for, lead, obtain, retrieve, transport **2.** draw forth, elicit, give rise to, produce **3.** bring in, earn, go for, make, realize, sell for, yield

fetching alluring, attractive, captivating, charming, cute, enchanting, enticing, fascinating, intriguing, sweet, taking, winsome

fetch up arrive, come, end up, finish up, halt, land, reach, stop, turn up

fête, fete 1. *noun* bazaar, fair, festival, gala, garden party, sale of work **2.** *~verb* bring out the red carpet for (someone), entertain regally, hold a reception for (someone), honour, kill the fatted calf for (someone), lionize, make much of, treat, wine and dine

fetid corrupt, foul, malodorous, mephitic, noisome, noxious, offensive, olid, rancid, rank, reeking, stinking

fetish 1. amulet, cult object, talisman **2.** fixation, *idée fixe,* mania, obsession, thing (*informal*)

fetter *verb* bind, chain, clip someone's wings, confine, curb, encumber, gyve (*archaic*), hamper, hamstring, hobble, hold captive, manacle, put a straitjacket on, restrain, restrict, shackle, straiten, tie, tie up, trammel

fetters *noun* **1.** bilboes, bonds, chains, gyves (*archaic*), irons, leg irons, mana~ cles, shackles **2.** bondage, captivity, check, curb, hindrance, obstruction, re~ straint

feud 1. *noun* argument, bad blood, bick~ ering, broil, conflict, contention, dis~ agreement, discord, dissension, enmity, estrangement, faction, falling out, grudge, hostility, quarrel, rivalry, row, strife, vendetta **2.** *~verb* be at daggers drawn, be at odds, bicker, brawl, clash, contend, dispute, duel, fall out, quarrel, row, squabble, war

fever 1. *figurative* agitation, delirium, ec~ stasy, excitement, ferment, fervour, flush, frenzy, heat, intensity, passion, restlessness, turmoil, unrest **2.** ague, pyrexia (*Medical*)

fevered burning, feverish, flushed, hectic, hot, on fire, pyretic (*Medical*)

feverish 1. burning, febrile, fevered, flaming, flushed, hectic, hot, inflamed, pyretic (*Medical*) **2.** agitated, desperate, distracted, excited, frantic, frenetic, frenzied, impatient, obsessive, over~ wrought, restless

▷ **Antonyms** (*sense 2*) calm, collected, composed, cool, dispassionate, noncha~ lant, offhand, serene, tranquil, unemo~ tional, unexcitable, unfazed (*informal*), unruffled

few *adjective* **1.** hardly any, inconsider~ able, infrequent, insufficient, meagre, negligible, not many, rare, scant, scanty, scarce, scarcely any, scattered, sparse, sporadic, thin **2. few and far be~ tween** at great intervals, hard to come by, infrequent, in short supply, irregu~ lar, rare, scarce, scattered, seldom met with, thin on the ground, uncommon, unusual, widely spaced *~pronoun* **3.** handful, scarcely any, scattering, small number, some

▷ **Antonyms** *~adjective* (*senses 1 & 2*) abundant, bounteous, divers (*archaic*), inexhaustible, manifold, many, multi~ farious, plentiful, sundry

fiancé, fiancée betrothed, intended, pro~ spective spouse, wife- *or* husband-to-be

fiasco balls-up (*taboo slang*), catastrophe, cock-up (*Brit. slang*), debacle, disaster, failure, flap (*informal*), fuck-up (*offen~ sive taboo slang*), mess, rout, ruin, washout (*informal*)

fiat 1. authorization, permission, sanc~ tion, warrant **2.** canon, command, de~ cree, demand, dictate, dictum, edict, mandate, order, ordinance, precept, proclamation, ukase

fib *noun* fiction, lie, pork pie (*Brit. slang*), porky (*Brit. slang*), prevarication, story, untruth, white lie, whopper (*informal*)

fibre 1. fibril, filament, pile, staple, strand, texture, thread, wisp **2.** *figura~ tive* essence, nature, quality, spirit, substance **3.** *figurative as in* **moral fibre** resolution, stamina, strength, strength of character, toughness

fickle blowing hot and cold, capricious, changeable, faithless, fitful, flighty, in~ constant, irresolute, mercurial, mutable, quicksilver, temperamental, unfaithful, unpredictable, unstable, unsteady, vac~ illating, variable, volatile

▷ **Antonyms** changeless, constant, faith~ ful, firm, invariable, loyal, reliable, resolute, settled, stable, staunch, stead~ fast, true, trustworthy

fickleness capriciousness, fitfulness, flightiness, inconstancy, mutability, un~ faithfulness, unpredictability, unsteadi~ ness, volatility

fiction 1. fable, fantasy, legend, myth, novel, romance, story, storytelling, tale, urban legend, work of imagination, yarn (*informal*) **2.** cock and bull story (*infor~ mal*), concoction, fabrication, falsehood, fancy, fantasy, figment of the imagina~ tion, imagination, improvisation, inven~ tion, lie, pork pie (*Brit. slang*), porky (*Brit. slang*), tall story, untruth

fictional imaginary, invented, legendary, made-up, nonexistent, unreal

fictitious apocryphal, artificial, assumed, bogus, counterfeit, fabricated, false, fanciful, feigned, imaginary, imagined, improvised, invented, made-up, make-believe, mythical, spurious, unreal, un~ true

▷ **Antonyms** actual, authentic, genuine, legitimate, real, true, truthful, vera~ cious, veritable

fiddle *verb* **1.** (*often with* **with**) fidget, fin~ ger, interfere with, mess about *or* around, play, tamper with, tinker, toy, trifle **2.** *informal* cheat, cook the books (*informal*), diddle (*informal*), finagle (*informal*), fix, gerrymander, graft (*in~ formal*), manoeuvre, racketeer, sting (*informal*), swindle, wangle (*informal*) *~noun* **3.** violin **4. fit as a fiddle** bloom~ ing, hale and hearty, healthy, in fine fettle, in good form, in good shape, in rude health, in the pink, sound, strong **5.** *informal* fix, fraud, graft (*informal*), piece of sharp practice, racket, scam (*slang*), sting (*informal*), swindle, wan~ gle (*informal*)

fiddling futile, insignificant, nickel-and-dime (*U.S. slang*), pettifogging, petty, trifling, trivial

fidelity 1. allegiance, constancy, depend~ ability, devotedness, devotion, faith, faithfulness, fealty, integrity, lealty (*ar~ chaic or Scot.*), loyalty, staunchness, troth (*archaic*), true-heartedness, trust~

worthiness **2.** accuracy, adherence, closeness, correspondence, exactitude, exactness, faithfulness, preciseness, precision, scrupulousness

▷ **Antonyms** (*sense 1*) disloyalty, faithlessness, falseness, infidelity, perfidiousness, treachery, unfaithfulness, untruthfulness (*sense 2*) inaccuracy, inexactness

fidget 1. *verb* be like a cat on hot bricks (*informal*), bustle, chafe, fiddle (*informal*), fret, jiggle, jitter (*informal*), move restlessly, squirm, twitch, worry **2.** *~noun* (*usually* **the fidgets**) fidgetiness, jitters (*informal*), nervousness, restlessness, unease, uneasiness

fidgety impatient, jerky, jittery (*informal*), jumpy, nervous, on edge, restive, restless, twitchy (*informal*), uneasy

field *noun* **1.** grassland, green, greensward (*archaic or literary*), lea (*poetic*), mead (*archaic*), meadow, pasture **2.** applicants, candidates, competition, competitors, contestants, entrants, possibilities, runners **3.** area, bailiwick, bounds, confines, department, discipline, domain, environment, limits, line, metier, pale, province, purview, range, scope, speciality, specialty, sphere of activity, sphere of influence, sphere of interest, sphere of study, territory *~verb* **4.** catch, pick up, retrieve, return, stop **5.** *figurative* deal with, deflect, handle, turn aside

fiend 1. demon, devil, evil spirit, hellhound **2.** barbarian, beast, brute, degenerate, ghoul, monster, ogre, savage **3.** *informal* addict, energumen, enthusiast, fanatic, freak (*informal*), maniac

fiendish accursed, atrocious, black-hearted, cruel, demoniac, devilish, diabolical, hellish, implacable, infernal, inhuman, malevolent, malicious, malignant, monstrous, satanic, savage, ungodly, unspeakable, wicked

fierce 1. baleful, barbarous, brutal, cruel, dangerous, fell (*archaic*), feral, ferocious, fiery, menacing, murderous, passionate, savage, threatening, tigerish, truculent, uncontrollable, untamed, vicious, wild **2.** blustery, boisterous, furious, howling, inclement, powerful, raging, stormy, strong, tempestuous, tumultuous, uncontrollable, violent **3.** cut-throat, intense, keen, relentless, strong

▷ **Antonyms** affectionate, calm, civilized, cool, docile, domesticated, gentle, harmless, kind, mild, peaceful, submissive, tame, temperate, tranquil

fiercely ferociously, frenziedly, furiously, in a frenzy, like cat and dog, menacingly, passionately, savagely, tempestuously, tigerishly, tooth and nail, uncontrolledly, viciously, with bared teeth, with no holds barred

fierceness 1. ferocity, fieriness, mercilessness, ruthlessness, savageness, viciousness, wildness **2.** bluster, destructiveness, roughness, storminess, tempestuousness, turbulence, violence **3.** avidity, fervidness, fervour, intensity, passion, relentlessness, strength

fiery 1. ablaze, afire, aflame, blazing, burning, flaming, glowing, in flames, on fire, red-hot **2.** choleric, excitable, fierce, hot-headed, impetuous, irascible, irritable, passionate, peppery, violent **3.** burning, febrile, fevered, feverish, flushed, heated, hot, inflamed

fight *verb* **1.** assault, battle, bear arms against, box, brawl, carry on war, clash, close, combat, come to blows, conflict, contend, cross swords, do battle, engage, engage in hostilities, exchange blows, feud, fight like Kilkenny cats, go to war, grapple, joust, lock horns, row, scrap (*informal*), spar, struggle, take the field, take up arms against, tilt, tussle, wage war, war, wrestle **2.** contest, defy, dispute, make a stand against, oppose, resist, stand up to, strive, struggle, withstand **3.** argue, bicker, dispute, fall out (*informal*), squabble, wrangle **4.** carry on, conduct, engage in, prosecute, wage **5. fight shy of** avoid, duck out of (*informal*), keep aloof from, keep at arm's length, shun, steer clear of *~noun* **6.** action, affray (*Law*), altercation, *bagarre,* battle, bout, brawl, brush, clash, combat, conflict, contest, dispute, dissension, dogfight, duel, encounter, engagement, exchange of blows, fracas, fray, free-for-all (*informal*), head-to-head, hostilities, joust, melee *or* mêlée, passage of arms, riot, row, rumble (*U.S. & N.Z. slang*), scrap (*informal*), scrimmage, scuffle, set-to (*informal*), shindig (*informal*), shindy (*informal*), skirmish, sparring match, struggle, tussle, war **7.** *figurative* belligerence, gameness, mettle, militancy, pluck, resistance, spirit, will to resist

fight back 1. defend oneself, give tit for tat, hit back, put up a fight, reply, resist, retaliate **2.** bottle up, contain, control, curb, hold back, hold in check, restrain

fight down bottle up, control, curb, hold back, repress, restrain, suppress

fighter 1. fighting man, man-at-arms, soldier, warrior **2.** boxer, bruiser (*informal*), prize fighter, pugilist **3.** antagonist, battler, belligerent, combatant, contender, contestant, disputant, militant

fighting 1. *adjective* aggressive, argumentative, bellicose, belligerent, combative, contentious, disputatious, hawkish, martial, militant, pugnacious, sabre-rattling, truculent, warlike **2.** *~noun* battle, bloodshed, blows struck, combat, conflict, hostilities, warfare

fight off beat off, keep *or* hold at bay, repel, repress, repulse, resist, stave off, ward off

figment creation, fable, fabrication, falsehood, fancy, fiction, improvisation, invention, production

figurative **1.** allegorical, emblematical, metaphorical, representative, symbolical, typical **2.** descriptive, fanciful, florid, flowery, ornate, pictorial, poetical, tropical (*Rhetoric*)

▷ **Antonyms** accurate, exact, factual, faithful, literal, prosaic, simple, true, unpoetical, unvarnished

figure *noun* **1.** character, cipher, digit, number, numeral, symbol **2.** amount, cost, price, sum, total, value **3.** form, outline, shadow, shape, silhouette **4.** body, build, chassis (*slang*), frame, physique, proportions, shape, torso **5.** depiction, design, device, diagram, drawing, emblem, illustration, motif, pattern, representation, sketch **6.** big name, celebrity, character, dignitary, face (*informal*), force, leader, notability, notable, personage, personality, presence, somebody, worthy *~verb* **7.** (*often with* **up**) add, calculate, compute, count, reckon, sum, tally, tot up, work out **8.** (*usually with* **in**) act, appear, be conspicuous, be featured, be included, be mentioned, contribute to, feature, have a place in, play a part **9. it figures** it follows, it goes without saying, it is to be expected

figured adorned, decorated, embellished, marked, ornamented, patterned, variegated

figurehead cipher, dummy, front man (*informal*), leader in name only, man of straw, mouthpiece, name, nonentity, puppet, straw man (*chiefly U.S.*), titular *or* nominal head, token

figure of speech conceit, image, trope, turn of phrase

figure out **1.** calculate, compute, reckon, work out **2.** comprehend, decipher, fathom, make head or tail of (*informal*), make out, resolve, see, suss (out) (*slang*), understand

filament cilium (*Biology & Zoology*), fibre, fibril, pile, staple, strand, string, thread, wire, wisp

filch abstract, cabbage (*Brit. slang*), crib (*informal*), embezzle, half-inch (*old-fashioned slang*), lift (*informal*), misappropriate, nick (*slang, chiefly Brit.*), pilfer, pinch (*informal*), purloin, rip off (*slang*), snaffle (*Brit. informal*), steal, swipe (*slang*), take, thieve, walk off with

file[1] *verb* abrade, burnish, furbish, polish, rasp, refine, rub, rub down, scrape, shape, smooth

file[2] *noun* **1.** case, data, documents, dossier, folder, information, portfolio *~verb* **2.** document, enter, pigeonhole, put in place, record, register, slot in (*informal*) *~noun* **3.** column, line, list, queue, row, string *~verb* **4.** march, parade, troop

filibuster *noun* **1.** *chiefly U.S., with reference to legislation* delay, hindrance, obstruction, postponement, procrastination *~verb* **2.** *chiefly U.S., with reference to legislation* delay, hinder, obstruct, play for time, prevent, procrastinate, put off *~noun* **3.** adventurer, buccaneer, corsair, freebooter, pirate, sea robber, sea rover, soldier of fortune

filigree lace, lacework, lattice, tracery, wirework

fill **1.** brim over, cram, crowd, furnish, glut, gorge, inflate, pack, pervade, replenish, sate, satiate, satisfy, stock, store, stuff, supply, swell **2.** charge, imbue, impregnate, overspread, pervade, saturate, suffuse **3.** block, bung, close, cork, plug, seal, stop **4.** assign, carry out, discharge, engage, execute, fulfil, hold, occupy, officiate, perform, take up **5. one's fill** all one wants, ample, a sufficiency, enough, plenty, sufficient

▷ **Antonyms** diminish, drain, empty, exhaust, shrink, subside, vacate, void

fill in **1.** answer, complete, fill out (*U.S.*), fill up **2.** *informal* acquaint, apprise, bring up to date, give the facts *or* background, inform, put wise (*slang*) **3.** deputize, replace, represent, stand in, sub, substitute, take the place of

filling **1.** *noun* contents, filler, innards (*informal*), inside, insides, padding, stuffing, wadding **2.** *~adjective* ample, heavy, satisfying, square, substantial

fillip *noun* goad, incentive, prod, push, spice, spur, stimulus, zest

film *noun* **1.** coat, coating, covering, dusting, gauze, integument, layer, membrane, pellicle, scum, skin, tissue **2.** blur, cloud, haze, haziness, mist, mistiness, opacity, veil **3.** flick (*slang*), motion picture, movie (*U.S. informal*) *~verb* **4.** photograph, shoot, take, video, videotape **5.** (*often with* **over**) blear, blur, cloud, dull, haze, mist, veil

filmy **1.** chiffon, cobwebby, delicate, diaphanous, fine, finespun, flimsy, floaty, fragile, gauzy, gossamer, insubstantial, see-through, sheer, transparent **2.** bleared, bleary, blurred, blurry, cloudy, dim, hazy, membranous, milky, misty, opalescent, opaque, pearly

filter *verb* **1.** clarify, filtrate, purify, refine, screen, sieve, sift, strain, winnow **2.** (*often with* **through** *or* **out**) dribble, escape, exude, leach, leak, ooze, penetrate, percolate, seep, trickle, well *~noun* **3.** gauze, membrane, mesh, riddle, sieve, strainer

filth **1.** carrion, contamination, crap (*slang*), crud (*slang*), defilement, dirt, dung, excrement, excreta, faeces, filthiness, foul matter, foulness, garbage, grime, grot (*slang*), kak (*S. African slang*), muck, nastiness, ordure, pollution, putrefaction, putrescence, refuse, sewage, shit (*taboo slang*), slime, sludge, squalor, uncleanness **2.** corruption, dirty-mindedness, impurity, indecency, obscenity, pornography, smut, vileness, vulgarity

filthy 1. dirty, faecal, feculent, foul, nasty, polluted, putrid, scummy, scuzzy (*slang, chiefly U.S.*), slimy, squalid, unclean, vile **2.** begrimed, black, blackened, grimy, grubby, miry, mucky, muddy, mud-encrusted, scuzzy (*slang, chiefly U.S.*), smoky, sooty, unwashed **3.** bawdy, coarse, corrupt, depraved, dirty-minded, foul, foul-mouthed, impure, indecent, lewd, licentious, obscene, pornographic, smutty, suggestive, X-rated (*informal*) **4.** base, contemptible, despicable, low, mean, offensive, scurvy, vicious, vile

final 1. closing, concluding, end, eventual, last, last-minute, latest, terminal, terminating, ultimate **2.** absolute, conclusive, decided, decisive, definite, definitive, determinate, finished, incontrovertible, irrevocable, settled

▷ **Antonyms** earliest, first, initial, introductory, maiden, opening, original, precursory, prefatory, premier, preparatory

finale climax, close, conclusion, crowning glory, culmination, dénouement, ending, epilogue, finis, last act

▷ **Antonyms** commencement, exordium, foreword, intro (*informal*), lead-in, opening, overture, preamble, preface, preliminaries, prelude, proem, prolegomenon, prologue

finality certitude, conclusiveness, decidedness, decisiveness, definiteness, inevitableness, irrevocability, resolution, unavoidability

finalize agree, clinch, complete, conclude, decide, settle, sew up (*informal*), shake hands, tie up, work out, wrap up (*informal*)

finally 1. at last, at length, at long last, at the end of the day, at the last, at the last moment, eventually, in the end, in the fullness of time, in the long run, lastly, ultimately, when all is said and done **2.** in conclusion, in summary, to conclude **3.** beyond the shadow of a doubt, completely, conclusively, convincingly, decisively, for all time, for ever, for good, inescapably, inexorably, irrevocably, once and for all, permanently

finance 1. *noun* accounts, banking, business, commerce, economics, financial affairs, investment, money, money management **2.** *~verb* back, bankroll (*U.S.*), float, fund, guarantee, pay for, provide security for, set up in business, subsidize, support, underwrite

finances affairs, assets, capital, cash, financial condition, funds, money, resources, wherewithal

financial budgeting, economic, fiscal, monetary, money, pecuniary

financing *noun* costs, expenditure, expense(s), funding, operating expenses, outlay

find *verb* **1.** catch sight of, chance upon, come across, come up with, descry, discover, encounter, espy, expose, ferret out, hit upon, lay one's hand on, light upon, locate, meet, recognize, run to earth, run to ground, spot, stumble upon, track down, turn up, uncover, unearth **2.** achieve, acquire, attain, earn, gain, get, obtain, procure, win **3.** get back, recover, regain, repossess, retrieve **4.** arrive at, ascertain, become aware, detect, discover, experience, learn, note, notice, observe, perceive, realise, remark **5.** be responsible for, bring, contribute, cough up (*informal*), furnish, provide, purvey, supply *~noun* **6.** acquisition, asset, bargain, catch, discovery, good buy

▷ **Antonyms** (*sense 1*) lose, mislay, misplace, miss, overlook

finding award, conclusion, decision, decree, judgment, pronouncement, recommendation, verdict

find out 1. detect, discover, learn, note, observe, perceive, realize **2.** bring to light, catch, detect, disclose, expose, reveal, rumble (*Brit. informal*), suss (out) (*slang*), uncover, unmask

fine[1] *adjective* **1.** accomplished, admirable, beautiful, choice, divine, excellent, exceptional, exquisite, first-class, first-rate, great, magnificent, masterly, ornate, outstanding, rare, select, showy, skilful, splendid, sterling, superior, supreme, world-class **2.** balmy, bright, clear, clement, cloudless, dry, fair, pleasant, sunny **3.** dainty, delicate, elegant, expensive, exquisite, fragile, quality **4.** abstruse, acute, critical, discriminating, fastidious, hairsplitting, intelligent, keen, minute, nice, precise, quick, refined, sensitive, sharp, subtle, tasteful, tenuous **5.** delicate, diaphanous, fine-grained, flimsy, gauzy, gossamer, light, lightweight, powdered, powdery, pulverized, sheer, slender, small, thin **6.** clear, pure, refined, solid, sterling, unadulterated, unalloyed, unpolluted **7.** attractive, bonny, good-looking, handsome, lovely, smart, striking, stylish, well-favoured **8.** acceptable, agreeable, all right, convenient, good, hunky-dory (*informal*), O.K. *or* okay (*informal*), satisfactory, suitable **9.** brilliant, cutting, honed, keen, polished, razor-sharp, sharp

▷ **Antonyms** (*sense 1*) indifferent, inferior, poor, second rate, substandard (*sense 2*) cloudy, dull, overcast, unpleasant (*senses 3 & 4*) blunt, coarse, crude, dull, heavy, rough, uncultured, unfinished, unrefined

fine[2] **1.** *verb* amerce (*archaic*), mulct, penalize, punish **2.** *~noun* amercement (*obsolete*), damages, forfeit, penalty, punishment

finery best bib and tucker (*informal*), decorations, frippery, gear (*informal*), gewgaws, glad rags (*informal*), ornaments, showiness, splendour, Sunday best, trappings, trinkets

finesse *noun* **1.** adeptness, adroitness, artfulness, cleverness, craft, delicacy, diplomacy, discretion, know-how (*informal*), polish, quickness, savoir-faire, skill, sophistication, subtlety, tact **2.** artifice, bluff, feint, manoeuvre, ruse, stratagem, trick, wile *~verb* **3.** bluff, manipulate, manoeuvre

finger *verb* **1.** feel, fiddle with (*informal*), handle, manipulate, maul, meddle with, paw (*informal*), play about with, touch, toy with **2. put one's finger on** bring to mind, discover, find out, hit the nail on the head, hit upon, identify, indicate, locate, pin down, place, recall, remember

finicky choosy (*informal*), critical, dainty, difficult, fastidious, finicking, fussy, hard to please, nit-picking (*informal*), overnice, overparticular, particular, picky (*informal*), scrupulous, squeamish

finish *verb* **1.** accomplish, achieve, bring to a close *or* conclusion, carry through, cease, close, complete, conclude, culminate, deal with, discharge, do, end, execute, finalize, fulfil, get done, get out of the way, make short work of, put the finishing touch(es) to, put the tin lid on, round off, settle, stop, terminate, wind up, wrap up (*informal*) **2.** (*sometimes with* **up** *or* **off**) consume, deplete, devour, dispatch, dispose of, drain, drink, eat, empty, exhaust, expend, spend, use, use up **3.** (*often with* **off**) administer *or* give the coup de grâce, annihilate, best, bring down, defeat, destroy, dispose of, drive to the wall, exterminate, get rid of, kill, move in for the kill, overcome, overpower, put an end to, put paid to, rout, ruin, worst *~noun* **4.** cessation, close, closing, completion, conclusion, culmination, dénouement, end, ending, finale, last stage(s), run-in, termination, winding up (*informal*), wind-up **5.** annihilation, bankruptcy, curtains (*informal*), death, defeat, end, end of the road, liquidation, ruin *~verb* **6.** elaborate, perfect, polish, refine *~noun* **7.** cultivation, culture, elaboration, perfection, polish, refinement, sophistication *~verb* **8.** coat, face, gild, lacquer, polish, smooth off, stain, texture, veneer, wax *~noun* **9.** appearance, grain, lustre, patina, polish, shine, smoothness, surface, texture

▷ **Antonyms** *~verb* (*senses 1 & 2*) begin, commence, create, embark on, instigate, start, undertake *~noun* (*sense 4*) beginning, birth, commencement, conception, genesis, inauguration, inception, instigation, preamble, preface, prologue

finished **1.** accomplished, classic, consummate, cultivated, elegant, expert, flawless, impeccable, masterly, perfected, polished, professional, proficient, refined, skilled, smooth, urbane **2.** accomplished, achieved, closed, complete, completed, concluded, done, ended, entire, final, finalized, full, in the past, over, over and done with, sewed up (*informal*), shut, terminated, through, tied up, wrapped up (*informal*) **3.** done, drained, empty, exhausted, gone, played out (*informal*), spent, used up **4.** bankrupt, defeated, devastated, done for (*informal*), doomed, gone, liquidated, lost, ruined, through, undone, washed up (*informal, chiefly U.S.*), wiped out, wound up, wrecked

▷ **Antonyms** basic, begun, coarse, crude, imperfect, inartistic, incomplete, inelegant, inexperienced, raw, rough, unfinished, unrefined, unskilled, unsophisticated

finite bounded, circumscribed, conditioned, delimited, demarcated, limited, restricted, subject to limitations, terminable

▷ **Antonyms** boundless, endless, eternal, everlasting, immeasurable, infinite, interminable, limitless, perpetual, unbounded

fire *noun* **1.** blaze, combustion, conflagration, flames, inferno **2.** barrage, bombardment, cannonade, flak, fusillade, hail, salvo, shelling, sniping, volley **3.** *figurative* animation, ardour, brio, burning passion, dash, eagerness, élan, enthusiasm, excitement, fervency, fervour, force, heat, impetuosity, intensity, life, light, lustre, passion, pizzazz *or* pizazz (*informal*), radiance, scintillation, sparkle, spirit, splendour, verve, vigour, virtuosity, vivacity **4. hanging fire** delayed, in abeyance, in cold storage, on ice, pending, postponed, put back, put off, shelved, suspended, undecided **5. on fire: a.** ablaze, aflame, alight, blazing, burning, fiery, flaming, in flames **b.** ardent, eager, enthusiastic, excited, inspired, passionate *~verb* **6.** enkindle, ignite, kindle, light, put a match to, set ablaze, set aflame, set alight, set fire to, set on fire, torch **7.** detonate, discharge, eject, explode, hurl, launch, let loose (*informal*), let off, loose, pull the trigger, set off, shell, shoot, touch off **8.** *figurative* animate, arouse, electrify, enliven, excite, galvanize, impassion, incite, inflame, inspire, inspirit, irritate, quicken, rouse, stir **9.** *informal* cashier, discharge, dismiss, give marching orders, give the boot (*slang*), give the bullet (*Brit. slang*), give the push, kiss off (*slang, chiefly U.S. & Canad.*), make redundant, sack (*informal*), show the door

firebrand *figurative* agitator, demagogue, fomenter, incendiary, instigator, rabble-rouser, soapbox orator, tub-thumper (*informal*)

fireworks 1. illuminations, pyrotechnics **2.** *figurative* fit of rage, hysterics, paroxysms, rage, rows, storm, temper, trouble, uproar, wax (*informal, chiefly Brit.*)

firm[1] *adjective* **1.** close-grained, compact, compressed, concentrated, congealed, dense, hard, inelastic, inflexible, jelled, jellified, rigid, set, solid, solidified, stiff, unyielding **2.** anchored, braced, cemented, embedded, fast, fastened, fixed, immovable, motionless, riveted, robust, rooted, secure, secured, stable, stationary, steady, strong, sturdy, taut, tight, unfluctuating, unmoving, unshakable **3.** adamant, constant, definite, fixed, immovable, inflexible, obdurate, resolute, resolved, set on, settled, stalwart, staunch, steadfast, strict, true, unalterable, unbending, unfaltering, unflinching, unshakable, unshaken, unswerving, unwavering, unyielding

▷ **Antonyms** flabby, flaccid, flimsy, inconstant, insecure, irresolute, limp, loose, shaky, soft, unreliable, unstable, unsteady, wavering

firm[2] *noun* association, business, company, concern, conglomerate, corporation, enterprise, house, organization, outfit (*informal*), partnership

firmament empyrean (*poetic*), heaven, heavens, sky, the blue, the skies, vault, vault of heaven, welkin (*archaic*)

firmly 1. enduringly, immovably, like a rock, motionlessly, securely, steadily, tightly, unflinchingly, unshakably **2.** determinedly, resolutely, staunchly, steadfastly, strictly, through thick and thin, unchangeably, unwaveringly, with a rod of iron, with decision

firmness 1. compactness, density, fixedness, hardness, inelasticity, inflexibility, resistance, rigidity, solidity, stiffness **2.** immovability, soundness, stability, steadiness, strength, tautness, tensile strength, tension, tightness **3.** constancy, fixedness, fixity of purpose, inflexibility, obduracy, resolution, resolve, staunchness, steadfastness, strength of will, strictness

first *adjective* **1.** chief, foremost, head, highest, leading, pre-eminent, prime, principal, ruling **2.** earliest, initial, introductory, maiden, opening, original, premier, primeval, primitive, primordial, pristine **3.** basic, cardinal, elementary, fundamental, key, primary, rudimentary *~adverb* **4.** at the beginning, at the outset, before all else, beforehand, firstly, initially, in the first place, to begin with, to start with *~noun* **5.** *as in* **from the first** beginning, commencement, inception, introduction, outset, start, starting point, word "go" (*informal*)

first-hand direct, straight from the horse's mouth

first-rate admirable, A1 *or* A-one (*informal*), bitchin' (*U.S. slang*), bodacious (*slang, chiefly U.S.*), boffo (*slang*), brill (*informal*), chillin' (*U.S. slang*), crack (*slang*), cracking (*Brit. informal*), crucial (*slang*), def (*slang*), dope (*slang*), elite, excellent, exceptional, exclusive, first class, jim-dandy (*slang*), mean (*slang*), mega (*slang*), outstanding, prime, second to none, sovereign, superb, superlative, the dog's bollocks (*taboo slang*), tiptop, top, top-notch (*informal*), topping (*Brit. slang*), tops (*slang*), world-class

fiscal budgetary, economic, financial, monetary, money, pecuniary

fish for angle for, elicit, hint at, hope for, hunt for, invite, look for, search for, seek, solicit

fish out extract, extricate, find, haul out, produce, pull out

fishy 1. *informal* cock-and-bull (*informal*), dodgy (*Brit., Austral., & N.Z. informal*), doubtful, dubious, funny (*informal*), implausible, improbable, odd, queer, questionable, rum (*Brit. slang*), suspect, suspicious, unlikely **2.** blank, deadpan, dull, expressionless, glassy, glassy-eyed, inexpressive, lacklustre, lifeless, vacant, wooden **3.** fishlike, piscatorial, piscatory, piscine

fission breaking, cleavage, division, parting, rending, rupture, schism, scission, splitting

fissure breach, break, chink, cleavage, cleft, crack, cranny, crevice, fault, fracture, gap, hole, interstice, opening, rent, rift, rupture, slit, split

fit[1] *adjective* **1.** able, adapted, adequate, apposite, appropriate, apt, becoming, capable, competent, convenient, correct, deserving, equipped, expedient, fitted, fitting, good enough, meet (*archaic*), prepared, proper, qualified, ready, right, seemly, suitable, trained, well-suited, worthy **2.** able-bodied, as right as rain, hale, healthy, in good condition, in good shape, in good trim, robust, strapping, toned up, trim, well *~verb* **3.** accord, agree, be consonant, belong, concur, conform, correspond, dovetail, go, interlock, join, match, meet, suit, tally **4.** (*often with* **out** *or* **up**) accommodate, accoutre, arm, equip, fit out, kit out, outfit, prepare, provide, rig out **5.** adapt, adjust, alter, arrange, customize, dispose, fashion, modify, place, position, shape, tweak (*informal*)

▷ **Antonyms** (*sense 1*) amiss, ill-fitted, ill-suited, improper, inadequate, inappropriate, unfit, unprepared, unseemly, unsuitable, untimely (*sense 2*) flabby, in poor condition, out of shape, out of trim, unfit, unhealthy

fit² *noun* **1.** attack, bout, convulsion, paroxysm, seizure, spasm **2.** caprice, fancy, humour, mood, whim **3.** bout, burst, outbreak, outburst, spell **4. by fits and starts** erratically, fitfully, intermittently, irregularly, on and off, spasmodically, sporadically, unsystematically

fitful broken, desultory, disturbed, erratic, flickering, fluctuating, haphazard, impulsive, inconstant, intermittent, irregular, spasmodic, sporadic, uneven, unstable, variable
▷ **Antonyms** constant, equable, even, orderly, predictable, regular, steady, systematic, unchanging, uniform

fitfully by fits and starts, desultorily, erratically, in fits and starts, in snatches, intermittently, interruptedly, irregularly, off and on, spasmodically, sporadically

fitness 1. adaptation, applicability, appropriateness, aptness, competence, eligibility, pertinence, preparedness, propriety, qualifications, readiness, seemliness, suitability **2.** good condition, good health, health, robustness, strength, vigour

fitted 1. adapted, cut out for, equipped, fit, qualified, right, suitable, tailor-made **2.** (*often with* **with**) accoutred, appointed, armed, equipped, furnished, outfitted, provided, rigged out, set up, supplied **3.** built-in, permanent

fitting 1. *adjective* apposite, appropriate, becoming, *comme il faut,* correct, decent, decorous, desirable, meet (*archaic*), proper, right, seemly, suitable **2.** *~noun* accessory, attachment, component, connection, part, piece, unit
▷ **Antonyms** ill-suited, improper, unfitting, unseemly, unsuitable

fittings accessories, accoutrements, appointments, appurtenances, bells and whistles, conveniences, equipment, extras, furnishings, furniture, trimmings

fix *verb* **1.** anchor, embed, establish, implant, install, locate, place, plant, position, root, set, settle **2.** attach, bind, cement, connect, couple, fasten, glue, link, make fast, pin, secure, stick, tie **3.** agree on, appoint, arrange, arrive at, conclude, decide, define, determine, establish, limit, name, resolve, set, settle, specify **4.** adjust, correct, mend, patch up, put to rights, regulate, repair, see to, sort **5.** congeal, consolidate, harden, rigidify, set, solidify, stiffen, thicken **6.** direct, focus, level at, rivet **7.** *informal* bribe, fiddle (*informal*), influence, manipulate, manoeuvre, pull strings (*informal*), rig **8.** *slang* cook (someone's) goose (*informal*), get even with (*informal*), get revenge on, pay back, settle (someone's) hash (*informal*), sort (someone) out (*informal*), take retribution on, wreak vengeance on *~noun* **9.** *informal* difficult situation, difficulty, dilemma, embarrassment, hole (*slang*), hot water (*informal*), jam (*informal*), mess, pickle (*informal*), plight, predicament, quandary, spot (*informal*), ticklish situation, tight spot

fixation addiction, complex, hang-up (*informal*), *idée fixe,* infatuation, mania, obsession, preoccupation, thing (*informal*)

fixed 1. anchored, attached, established, immovable, made fast, permanent, rigid, rooted, secure, set **2.** intent, level, resolute, steady, unbending, unblinking, undeviating, unflinching, unwavering **3.** agreed, arranged, decided, definite, established, planned, resolved, settled **4.** going, in working order, mended, put right, repaired, sorted **5.** *informal* framed, manipulated, packed, put-up, rigged
▷ **Antonyms** bending, inconstant, mobile, motile, moving, pliant, unfixed, varying, wavering

fixity doggedness, intentness, perseverance, persistence, stability, steadiness

fix up 1. agree on, arrange, fix, organize, plan, settle, sort out **2.** (*often with* **with**) accommodate, arrange for, bring about, furnish, lay on, provide

fizz bubble, effervesce, fizzle, froth, hiss, sparkle, sputter

fizzle out abort, collapse, come to nothing, die away, end in disappointment, fail, fall through, fold (*informal*), miss the mark, peter out

fizzy bubbling, bubbly, carbonated, effervescent, gassy, sparkling

flab beef (*informal*), fat, flabbiness, flesh, fleshiness, heaviness, overweight, plumpness, slackness, weight

flabbergasted abashed, amazed, astonished, astounded, bowled over (*informal*), confounded, dazed, disconcerted, dumbfounded, gobsmacked (*Brit. slang*), lost for words, nonplussed, overcome, overwhelmed, rendered speechless, speechless, staggered, struck dumb, stunned

flabbiness bloatedness, flaccidity, limpness, looseness, pendulousness, slackness

flabby 1. baggy, drooping, flaccid, floppy, hanging, lax, limp, loose, pendulous, sagging, slack, sloppy, toneless, unfit, yielding **2.** effete, enervated, feeble, impotent, ineffective, ineffectual, nerveless, spineless, weak, wimpish *or* wimpy (*informal*)
▷ **Antonyms** firm, hard, solid, strong, taut, tense, tight, tough

flaccid drooping, flabby, lax, limp, loose, nerveless, slack, soft, weak

flaccidity flabbiness, limpness, looseness, nervelessness, slackness, softness

flag¹ *verb* abate, decline, die, droop, ebb, fade, fail, faint, fall, fall off, feel the pace, languish, peter out, pine, sag, sink, slump, succumb, taper off, wane, weaken, weary, wilt

flag[2] *noun* **1.** banderole, banner, colours, ensign, gonfalon, jack, pennant, pennon, standard, streamer *~verb* **2.** (*sometimes with* **down**) hail, salute, signal, warn, wave **3.** docket, indicate, label, mark, note, tab

flagellate beat, castigate, chastise, flay, flog, lambast(e), lash, scourge, thrash, whip

flagellation beating, flogging, lashing, thrashing, whipping

flagging declining, decreasing, deterio~rating, ebbing, fading, failing, faltering, giving up, sinking, slowing down, tiring, waning, weakening, wilting

flagrancy blatancy, enormity, heinous~ness, infamy, insolence, ostentation, outrageousness, public display, shame~lessness

flagrant arrant, atrocious, awful, bare~faced, blatant, bold, brazen, crying, dreadful, egregious, enormous, flagi~tious, flaunting, glaring, heinous, im~modest, infamous, notorious, open, os~tentatious, out-and-out, outrageous, scandalous, shameless, undisguised

▷ **Antonyms** delicate, faint, implied, in~direct, insinuated, slight, subtle, under~stated

flagstone block, flag, paving stone, slab

flail *verb* beat, thrash, thresh, windmill

flair **1.** ability, accomplishment, aptitude, faculty, feel, genius, gift, knack, mas~tery, talent **2.** chic, dash, discernment, elegance, panache, style, stylishness, taste

flak *figurative* abuse, bad press, brickbats (*informal*), censure, complaints, con~demnation, criticism, denigration, dis~approbation, disapproval, disparage~ment, fault-finding, hostility, opposition, stick (*slang*)

flake **1.** *noun* disk, lamina, layer, peeling, scale, shaving, sliver, squama (*Biology*), wafer **2.** *~verb* blister, chip, desquamate, peel (off), scale (off)

flake out collapse, faint, keel over, lose consciousness, pass out, swoon (*literary*)

flamboyant **1.** actorly, baroque, camp (*in~formal*), elaborate, extravagant, florid, ornate, ostentatious, over the top (*in~formal*), rich, rococo, showy, theatrical **2.** brilliant, colourful, dashing, dazzling, exciting, glamorous, glitzy (*slang*), swashbuckling

flame *verb* **1.** blaze, burn, flare, flash, glare, glow, shine *~noun* **2.** blaze, brightness, fire, light **3.** *figurative* affec~tion, ardour, enthusiasm, fervency, fer~vour, fire, intensity, keenness, passion, warmth **4.** *informal* beau, beloved, boy~friend, girlfriend, heart-throb (*Brit.*), ladylove, lover, sweetheart

flameproof fire-resistant, incombustible, nonflammable, non-inflammable

flaming **1.** ablaze, afire, blazing, brilliant, burning, fiery, glowing, ignited, in flames, raging, red, red-hot **2.** angry, ar~dent, aroused, frenzied, hot, impas~sioned, intense, raging, scintillating, vehement, vivid

flammable combustible, ignitable, incen~diary, inflammable

flank *noun* **1.** ham, haunch, hip, loin, quarter, side, thigh **2.** side, wing *~verb* **3.** border, bound, edge, fringe, line, screen, skirt, wall

flannel *figurative* **1.** *noun* baloney (*infor~mal*), blarney, equivocation, flattery, hedging, prevarication, soft soap (*infor~mal*), sweet talk (*U.S. informal*), waffle (*informal, chiefly Brit.*), weasel words (*informal, chiefly U.S.*) **2.** *~verb* blarney, butter up, equivocate, flatter, hedge, prevaricate, pull the wool over (someone's) eyes, soft-soap (*informal*), sweet-talk (*informal*), waffle (*informal, chiefly Brit.*)

flap *verb* **1.** agitate, beat, flail, flutter, shake, swing, swish, thrash, thresh, vi~brate, wag, wave *~noun* **2.** bang, bang~ing, beating, flutter, shaking, swinging, swish, waving *~verb* **3.** *informal* dither (*chiefly Brit.*), fuss, panic *~noun* **4.** *infor~mal* agitation, commotion, fluster, pan~ic, state (*informal*), stew (*informal*), sweat (*informal*), tizzy (*informal*), twit~ter (*informal*) **5.** apron, cover, fly, fold, lapel, lappet, overlap, skirt, tab, tail

flare *verb* **1.** blaze, burn up, dazzle, flick~er, flutter, glare, waver **2.** (*often with* **out**) broaden, spread out, widen *~noun* **3.** blaze, burst, dazzle, flame, flash, flicker, glare

flare up blaze, blow one's top (*informal*), boil over, break out, explode, fire up, fly off the handle (*informal*), lose control, lose one's cool (*informal*), lose one's temper, throw a tantrum

flash *verb* **1.** blaze, coruscate, flare, flick~er, glare, gleam, glint, glisten, glitter, light, scintillate, shimmer, sparkle, twinkle *~noun* **2.** blaze, burst, corusca~tion, dazzle, flare, flicker, gleam, ray, scintillation, shaft, shimmer, spark, sparkle, streak, twinkle *~verb* **3.** barrel (along) (*informal, chiefly U.S. & Canad.*), bolt, burn rubber (*informal*), dart, dash, fly, race, shoot, speed, sprint, streak, sweep, whistle, zoom *~noun* **4.** bat of an eye (*informal*), in~stant, jiffy (*informal*), moment, second, shake, split second, trice, twinkling, twinkling of an eye, two shakes of a lamb's tail (*informal*) *~verb* **5.** display, exhibit, expose, flaunt, flourish, show *~noun* **6.** burst, demonstration, display, manifestation, outburst, show, sign, touch *~adjective* **7.** *informal* cheap, glamorous, naff (*Brit. slang*), ostentatious, tacky (*informal*), tasteless, vulgar

flashy brash, cheap, cheap and nasty, flamboyant, flaunting, garish, gaudy, glittery, glitzy (*slang*), in poor taste, jazzy (*informal*), loud, meretricious, naff (*Brit. slang*), ostentatious, over the top (*informal*), showy, snazzy (*informal*), tacky (*informal*), tasteless, tawdry, tinselly
▷ **Antonyms** downbeat, low-key, modest, natural, plain, unaffected, understated

flat[1] *adjective* **1.** even, horizontal, level, levelled, low, planar, plane, smooth, unbroken **2.** laid low, lying full length, outstretched, prone, prostrate, reclining, recumbent, supine **3.** boring, dead, dull, flavourless, ho-hum (*informal*), insipid, jejune, lacklustre, lifeless, monotonous, pointless, prosaic, spiritless, stale, tedious, tiresome, uninteresting, vapid, watery, weak **4.** absolute, categorical, direct, downright, explicit, final, fixed, out-and-out, peremptory, plain, positive, straight, unconditional, unequivocal, unmistakable, unqualified **5.** blown out, burst, collapsed, deflated, empty, punctured *~noun* **6.** (*often plural*) lowland, marsh, mud flat, plain, shallow, shoal, strand, swamp *~adverb* **7.** absolutely, categorically, completely, exactly, point blank, precisely, utterly **8.** **flat out** all out, at full gallop, at full speed, at full tilt, for all one is worth, hell for leather (*informal*), posthaste, under full steam
▷ **Antonyms** (*sense 1*) broken, hilly, irregular, rolling, rough, rugged, slanting, sloping, uneven, up and down (*sense 2*) on end, perpendicular, straight, upright, vertical (*sense 3*) bubbly, effervescent, exciting, fizzy, palatable, sparkling, tasty, zestful

flat[2] *noun* apartment, rooms

flatly absolutely, categorically, completely, positively, unhesitatingly

flatness **1.** evenness, horizontality, levelness, smoothness, uniformity **2.** dullness, emptiness, insipidity, monotony, staleness, tedium, vapidity

flatten **1.** compress, even out, iron out, level, plaster, raze, roll, smooth off, squash, trample **2.** bowl over, crush, deck (*slang*), fell, floor, knock down, knock off one's feet, prostrate, subdue

flatter **1.** blandish, butter up, cajole, compliment, court, fawn, flannel (*Brit. informal*), humour, inveigle, lay it on (thick) (*slang*), pander to, praise, puff, soft-soap (*informal*), sweet-talk (*informal*), wheedle **2.** become, do something for, enhance, set off, show to advantage, suit

flattering **1.** becoming, effective, enhancing, kind, well-chosen **2.** adulatory, complimentary, fawning, fulsome, gratifying, honeyed, honey-tongued, ingratiating, laudatory, sugary
▷ **Antonyms** (*sense 1*) not shown in the best light, not shown to advantage, plain, unattractive, unbecoming, unflattering (*sense 2*) blunt, candid, honest, straight, uncomplimentary, warts and all

flattery adulation, blandishment, blarney, cajolery, false praise, fawning, flannel (*Brit. informal*), fulsomeness, honeyed words, obsequiousness, servility, soft-soap (*informal*), sweet-talk (*informal*), sycophancy, toadyism

flatulence **1.** borborygmus (*Medical*), eructation, wind **2.** *figurative* boasting, bombast, claptrap, empty words, fanfaronade (*rare*), fustian, hot air (*informal*), pomposity, prolixity, rodomontade, twaddle

flatulent *figurative* bombastic, inflated, long-winded, pompous, pretentious, prolix, swollen, tedious, tiresome, turgid, wordy

flaunt boast, brandish, display, disport, exhibit, flash about, flourish, make an exhibition of, make a (great) show of, parade, show off, sport (*informal*), vaunt

flaunting brazen, flamboyant, gaudy, ostentatious, pretentious

flavour *noun* **1.** aroma, essence, extract, flavouring, odour, piquancy, relish, savour, seasoning, smack, tang, taste, zest, zing (*informal*) **2.** aspect, character, essence, feel, feeling, property, quality, soupçon, stamp, style, suggestion, tinge, tone, touch *~verb* **3.** ginger up, imbue, infuse, lace, leaven, season, spice
▷ **Antonyms** (*sense 1*) blandness, flatness, insipidity, odourlessness, tastelessness, vapidity

flavouring essence, extract, spirit, tincture, zest

flaw **1.** blemish, chink in one's armour, defect, disfigurement, failing, fault, imperfection, scar, speck, spot, weakness, weak spot **2.** breach, break, cleft, crack, crevice, fissure, fracture, rent, rift, scission, split, tear

flawed blemished, broken, chipped, cracked, damaged, defective, erroneous, faulty, imperfect, unsound

flawless **1.** faultless, impeccable, perfect, spotless, unblemished, unsullied **2.** intact, sound, unbroken, undamaged, whole

flay **1.** excoriate, skin **2.** *figurative* castigate, excoriate, execrate, give a tongue-lashing, pull to pieces (*informal*), revile, slam (*slang*), tear a strip off, tear into (*informal*), upbraid

fleabite drop in the ocean, nothing, piddling amount, pinprick, trifle

flea-bitten crawling, decrepit, fetid, flea-ridden, frowsty, grotty (*slang*), grubby, infested, insalubrious, lousy, mean, mucky, pediculous (*Medical*), run-down, scabby, scruffy, scurfy, sleazy, slummy, sordid, squalid, tatty, unhygienic

fleck **1.** *verb* bespeckle, besprinkle, dapple, dot, dust, mark, mottle, speckle, spot, stipple, streak, variegate **2.** *~noun* dot, mark, pinpoint, speck, speckle, spot, streak

fledgling **1.** chick, nestling **2.** apprentice, beginner, learner, neophyte, newcomer, novice, rookie (*informal*), trainee, tyro

flee abscond, avoid, beat a hasty retreat, bolt, cut and run (*informal*), decamp, depart, do a runner (*slang*), escape, fly, fly the coop (*U.S. & Canad. informal*), get away, hook it (*slang*), leave, make a quick exit, make off, make oneself scarce (*informal*), make one's escape, make one's getaway, run away, scarper (*Brit. slang*), shun, skedaddle (*informal*), slope off, split (*slang*), take a powder (*U.S. & Canad. slang*), take flight, take it on the lam (*U.S. & Canad. slang*), take off (*informal*), take to one's heels, turn tail, vanish

fleece *verb* **1.** *figurative* bleed (*informal*), cheat, con (*informal*), cozen, defraud, despoil, diddle (*informal*), mulct, overcharge, plunder, rifle, rip off (*slang*), rob, rook (*slang*), sell a pup, skin (*slang*), soak (*U.S. & Canad. slang*), steal, stiff (*slang*), swindle, take for a ride (*informal*), take to the cleaners (*slang*) **2.** clip, shear *~noun* **3.** wool

fleecy downy, fluffy, shaggy, soft, woolly

fleet[1] *noun* argosy, armada, flotilla, naval force, navy, sea power, squadron, task force, vessels, warships

fleet[2] *adjective* fast, flying, mercurial, meteoric, nimble, nimble-footed, quick, rapid, speedy, swift, winged

fleeting brief, ephemeral, evanescent, flitting, flying, fugacious, fugitive, here today, gone tomorrow, momentary, passing, short, short-lived, temporary, transient, transitory

▷ **Antonyms** abiding, continuing, durable, enduring, eternal, imperishable, lasting, long-lasting, long-lived, permanent

fleetness celerity, lightning speed, nimble-footedness, nimbleness, quickness, rapidity, speed, speediness, swiftness, velocity

flesh **1.** beef (*informal*), body, brawn, fat, fatness, food, meat, tissue, weight **2.** animality, body, carnality, flesh and blood, human nature, physicality, physical nature, sensuality **3.** homo sapiens, humankind, human race, living creatures, man, mankind, mortality, people, race, stock, world **4.** **one's own flesh and blood** blood, family, kin, kindred, kinsfolk, kith and kin, relations, relatives

fleshiness chubbiness, corpulence, flabbiness, heaviness, obesity, plumpness, stoutness

fleshly **1.** animal, bodily, carnal, erotic, lascivious, lecherous, lustful, sensual **2.** corporal, corporeal, earthly, human, material, mundane, of this world, physical, secular, terrestrial, worldly

fleshy ample, beefy (*informal*), brawny, chubby, chunky, corpulent, fat, hefty, meaty, obese, overweight, plump, podgy, stout, tubby, well-padded

flex *verb* angle, bend, contract, crook, curve, tighten

flexibility adaptability, adjustability, complaisance, elasticity, give (*informal*), pliability, pliancy, resilience, springiness, tensility

flexible **1.** bendable, ductile, elastic, limber, lissom(e), lithe, mouldable, plastic, pliable, pliant, springy, stretchy, supple, tensile, whippy, willowy, yielding **2.** adaptable, adjustable, discretionary, open, variable **3.** amenable, biddable, complaisant, compliant, docile, gentle, manageable, responsive, tractable

▷ **Antonyms** absolute, determined, fixed, immovable, inexorable, inflexible, intractable, obdurate, rigid, staunch, stiff, tough, unyielding

flick *verb* **1.** dab, fillip, flip, hit, jab, peck, rap, strike, tap, touch **2.** (*with* **through**) browse, flip, glance, skim, skip, thumb *~noun* **3.** fillip, flip, jab, peck, rap, tap, touch

flicker *verb* **1.** flare, flash, glimmer, gutter, shimmer, sparkle, twinkle **2.** flutter, quiver, vibrate, waver *~noun* **3.** flare, flash, gleam, glimmer, spark **4.** atom, breath, drop, glimmer, iota, spark, trace, vestige

flickering fitful, guttering, twinkling, unsteady, wavering

flight[1] *noun* **1.** flying, mounting, soaring, winging **2.** *of air travel* journey, trip, voyage **3.** aerial navigation, aeronautics, air transport, aviation, flying **4.** cloud, flock, formation, squadron, swarm, unit, wing

flight[2] *noun* **1.** departure, escape, exit, exodus, fleeing, getaway, retreat, running away **2.** **put to flight** chase off, disperse, drive off, rout, scare off, scatter, send packing, stampede **3.** **take (to) flight** abscond, beat a retreat, bolt, decamp, do a bunk (*Brit. slang*), do a runner (*slang*), flee, fly the coop (*U.S. & Canad. informal*), light out (*informal*), make a hasty retreat, run away *or* off, skedaddle (*informal*), take a powder (*U.S. & Canad. slang*), take it on the lam (*U.S. & Canad. slang*), turn tail, withdraw hastily

flightiness capriciousness, fickleness, flippancy, frivolity, giddiness, irresponsibility, levity, lightness, mercurialness, volatility

flighty capricious, changeable, ditsy (*U.S. informal*), dizzy, fickle, frivolous, giddy, harebrained, impetuous, impulsive, irresponsible, light-headed, mercurial, scatterbrained, skittish, thoughtless, unbalanced, unstable, unsteady, volatile, wild

flimsy 1. delicate, fragile, frail, gimcrack, insubstantial, makeshift, rickety, shaky, shallow, slight, superficial, unsubstantial **2.** chiffon, gauzy, gossamer, light, sheer, thin, transparent **3.** feeble, frivolous, implausible, inadequate, pathetic, poor, tenuous, thin, transparent, trivial, unconvincing, unsatisfactory, weak
▷ **Antonyms** durable, heavy, robust, serious, solid, sound, stout, strong, sturdy, substantial

flinch back off, baulk, blench, cower, cringe, draw back, duck, flee, quail, recoil, retreat, shirk, shrink, shy away, start, swerve, wince, withdraw

fling *verb* **1.** cast, catapult, chuck (*informal*), heave, hurl, jerk, let fly, lob (*informal*), pitch, precipitate, propel, send, shy, sling, throw, toss *~noun* **2.** cast, lob, pitch, shot, throw, toss **3.** bash, beano (*Brit. slang*), binge (*informal*), bit of fun, good time, hooley *or* hoolie (*chiefly Irish & N.Z.*), indulgence, party, rave (*Brit. slang*), rave-up (*Brit. slang*), spree **4.** attempt, bash (*informal*), crack (*informal*), gamble, go (*informal*), shot (*informal*), stab (*informal*), trial, try, venture, whirl (*informal*)

flinty adamant, cruel, hard, hard-hearted, harsh, heartless, inflexible, obdurate, pitiless, steely, stern, stony, unfeeling, unmerciful, unyielding

flip *verb/noun* cast, flick, jerk, pitch, snap, spin, throw, toss, twist

flippancy cheek (*informal*), cheekiness, disrespectfulness, frivolity, impertinence, irreverence, levity, pertness, sauciness

flippant cheeky, disrespectful, flip (*informal*), frivolous, glib, impertinent, impudent, irreverent, offhand, pert, rude, saucy, superficial
▷ **Antonyms** gracious, mannerly, polite, respectful, serious, sincere, solicitous, well-mannered

flirt *verb* **1.** chat up (*informal*), coquet, dally, lead on, make advances, make eyes at, make sheep's eyes at, philander **2.** (*usually with* **with**) consider, dabble in, entertain, expose oneself to, give a thought to, play with, toy with, trifle with *~noun* **3.** coquette, heart-breaker, philanderer, tease, trifler, wanton

flirtation coquetry, dalliance, intrigue, philandering, teasing, toying, trifling

flirtatious amorous, arch, come-hither, come-on (*informal*), coquettish, coy, enticing, flirty, provocative, sportive, teasing

flirting amorous play, chatting up (*informal*), coquetry, dalliance, sport

flit dart, flash, fleet, flutter, fly, pass, skim, speed, whisk, wing

float *verb* **1.** be buoyant, be *or* lie on the surface, displace water, hang, hover, poise, rest on water, stay afloat **2.** bob, drift, glide, move gently, sail, slide, slip along **3.** get going, launch, promote, push off, set up
▷ **Antonyms** (*senses 1 & 2*) dip, drown, founder, go down, settle, sink, submerge (*sense 3*) abolish, annul, cancel, dissolve, terminate

floating 1. afloat, buoyant, buoyed up, nonsubmersible, ocean-going, sailing, swimming, unsinkable **2.** fluctuating, free, migratory, movable, unattached, uncommitted, unfixed, variable, wandering

flock *verb* **1.** collect, congregate, converge, crowd, gather, group, herd, huddle, mass, throng, troop *~noun* **2.** colony, drove, flight, gaggle, herd, skein **3.** assembly, bevy, collection, company, congregation, convoy, crowd, gathering, group, herd, host, mass, multitude, throng

flog 1. beat, castigate, chastise, flagellate, flay, lambast(e), lash, scourge, thrash, trounce, whack, whip **2.** drive, oppress, overexert, overtax, overwork, punish, push, strain, tax

flogging beating, caning, flagellation, hiding (*informal*), horsewhipping, lashing, scourging, thrashing, trouncing, whipping

flood *verb* **1.** brim over, deluge, drown, immerse, inundate, overflow, pour over, submerge, swamp, teem **2.** engulf, flow, gush, overwhelm, rush, surge, swarm, sweep **3.** choke, fill, glut, oversupply, saturate *~noun* **4.** deluge, downpour, flash flood, freshet, inundation, overflow, spate, tide, torrent **5.** abundance, flow, glut, multitude, outpouring, profusion, rush, stream, torrent

floor 1. *noun* level, stage, storey, tier **2.** *~verb figurative* baffle, beat, bewilder, bowl over (*informal*), bring up short, confound, conquer, deck (*slang*), defeat, discomfit, disconcert, dumbfound, faze, knock down, nonplus, overthrow, perplex, prostrate, puzzle, stump, throw (*informal*)

flop *verb* **1.** collapse, dangle, droop, drop, fall, hang limply, sag, slump, topple, tumble **2.** *informal* bomb (*U.S. & Canad. slang*), close, come to nothing, come unstuck, fail, fall flat, fall short, fold (*informal*), founder, go belly-up (*slang*), go down like a lead balloon (*informal*), misfire *~noun* **3.** *informal* cock-up (*Brit. slang*), debacle, disaster, failure, fiasco, loser, nonstarter, washout (*informal*)
▷ **Antonyms** *~verb* (*sense 2*) flourish,

make a hit, make it (*informal*), prosper, succeed, triumph, work ~*noun* hit, success, triumph

floppy baggy, droopy, flaccid, flapping, flip-flop, hanging, limp, loose, pendulous, sagging, soft

floral flower-patterned, flowery

florescence blooming, blossoming, development, flourishing, flowering, fruition, maturity

florid 1. blowsy, flushed, high-coloured, high-complexioned, rubicund, ruddy **2.** baroque, busy, embellished, euphuistic, figurative, flamboyant, flowery, fussy, grandiloquent, high-flown, ornate, overelaborate

▷ **Antonyms** (*sense 1*) anaemic, bloodless, pale, pallid, pasty, wan, washed out (*sense 2*) bare, dull, plain, unadorned

flossy downy, feathery, fluffy, satiny, silky, soft

flotsam debris, detritus, jetsam, junk, odds and ends, sweepings, wreckage

flounce *verb* bounce, fling, jerk, spring, stamp, storm, throw, toss

flounder *verb* be in the dark, blunder, fumble, grope, muddle, plunge, struggle, stumble, thrash, toss, tumble, wallow

flourish *verb* **1.** bear fruit, be in one's prime, be successful, be vigorous, bloom, blossom, boom, burgeon, develop, do well, flower, get ahead, get on, go great guns (*slang*), go up in the world, grow, grow fat, increase, prosper, succeed, thrive **2.** brandish, display, flaunt, flutter, shake, sweep, swing, swish, twirl, vaunt, wag, wave, wield ~*noun* **3.** brandishing, dash, display, fanfare, parade, shaking, show, showy gesture, twirling, wave **4.** curlicue, decoration, embellishment, ornamentation, plume, sweep

▷ **Antonyms** (*sense 1*) decline, diminish, dwindle, fade, fail, grow less, pine, shrink, wane

flourishing blooming, burgeoning, doing well, going places, going strong, in the pink, in top form, lush, luxuriant, mushrooming, on a roll, on the up and up (*informal*), prospering, rampant, successful, thriving

flout defy, deride, gibe at, insult, jeer at, laugh in the face of, mock, outrage, ridicule, scoff at, scorn, scout (*archaic*), show contempt for, sneer at, spurn, take the piss out of (*taboo slang*), taunt, treat with disdain

▷ **Antonyms** attend, esteem, heed, honour, mind, note, pay attention to, regard, respect, revere, value

flow *verb* **1.** circulate, course, glide, gush, move, pour, purl, ripple, roll, run, rush, slide, surge, sweep, swirl, whirl **2.** cascade, deluge, flood, inundate, issue, overflow, pour, run, run out, spew, spill, spurt, squirt, stream, teem, well forth **3.** arise, emanate, emerge, issue, pour, proceed, result, spring ~*noun* **4.** course, current, drift, flood, flux, gush, issue, outflow, outpouring, spate, stream, tide, tideway, undertow **5.** abundance, deluge, effusion, emanation, outflow, outpouring, plenty, plethora, succession, train

flower *noun* **1.** bloom, blossom, efflorescence **2.** *figurative* best, choicest part, cream, *crème de la crème,* elite, freshness, greatest *or* finest point, height, pick, vigour ~*verb* **3.** bloom, blossom, blow, burgeon, effloresce, flourish, mature, open, unfold

flowering *adjective* abloom, blooming, blossoming, florescent, in bloom, in blossom, in flower, open, out, ready

flowery baroque, embellished, euphuistic, fancy, figurative, florid, high-flown, ornate, overwrought, rhetorical

▷ **Antonyms** austere, bare, basic, modest, muted, plain, restrained, simple, spartan, unadorned, unembellished

flowing 1. falling, gushing, rolling, rushing, smooth, streaming, sweeping **2.** continuous, cursive, easy, fluent, smooth, unbroken, uninterrupted **3.** abounding, brimming over, flooded, full, overrun, prolific, rich, teeming

fluctuate alter, alternate, change, ebb and flow, go up and down, hesitate, oscillate, rise and fall, seesaw, shift, swing, undulate, vacillate, vary, veer, waver

fluctuation alternation, change, fickleness, inconstancy, instability, oscillation, shift, swing, unsteadiness, vacillation, variation, wavering

fluency articulateness, assurance, command, control, ease, facility, glibness, readiness, slickness, smoothness, volubility

fluent articulate, easy, effortless, facile, flowing, glib, natural, ready, smooth, smooth-spoken, voluble, well-versed

▷ **Antonyms** faltering, halting, hesitant, hesitating, inarticulate, stammering, stumbling, terse, tongue-tied

fluff 1. *noun* down, dust, dustball, fuzz, lint, nap, oose (*Scot.*), pile **2.** ~*verb informal* bungle, cock up (*Brit. slang*), foul up (*informal*), fuck up (*offensive taboo slang*), make a mess off, make a nonsense of, mess up (*informal*), muddle, screw up (*informal*), spoil

fluffy downy, feathery, fleecy, flossy, fuzzy, gossamer, silky, soft

fluid *adjective* **1.** aqueous, flowing, in solution, liquefied, liquid, melted, molten, running, runny, watery **2.** adaptable, adjustable, changeable, flexible, floating, fluctuating, indefinite, mercurial, mobile, mutable, protean, shifting **3.** easy, elegant, feline, flowing, graceful, sinuous, smooth ~*noun* **4.** liquid, liquor,

solution
▷ **Antonyms** *~adjective* definite, firm, fixed, hard, immobile, immutable, rigid, set, solid

fluke accident, blessing, break, chance, chance occurrence, coincidence, fortuity, freak, lucky break, quirk, quirk of fate, serendipity, stroke, stroke of luck, windfall

fluky 1. accidental, coincidental, fortuitous, lucky **2.** at the mercy of events, chancy, incalculable, uncertain, variable

flummox baffle, bamboozle (*informal*), bewilder, bring up short, defeat, fox, mystify, nonplus, perplex, stump, stymie

flummoxed at a loss, at sea, baffled, bewildered, foxed, mystified, nonplussed, stumped, stymied

flunky 1. assistant, cohort (*chiefly U.S.*), drudge, hanger-on, menial, minion, slave, toady, tool, underling, yes man **2.** footman, lackey, manservant, valet

flurry *noun* **1.** *figurative* ado, agitation, bustle, commotion, disturbance, excitement, ferment, flap, fluster, flutter, furore, fuss, hurry, stir, to-do, tumult, whirl **2.** flaw, gust, squall **3.** burst, outbreak, spell, spurt *~verb* **4.** agitate, bewilder, bother, bustle, confuse, disconcert, disturb, faze, fluster, flutter, fuss, hassle (*informal*), hurry, hustle, rattle (*informal*), ruffle, unnerve, unsettle, upset

flush[1] *verb* **1.** blush, burn, colour, colour up, crimson, flame, glow, go as red as a beetroot, go red, redden, suffuse *~noun* **2.** bloom, blush, colour, freshness, glow, redness, rosiness *~verb* **3.** cleanse, douche, drench, eject, expel, flood, hose down, rinse out, swab, syringe, wash out

flush[2] *adjective* **1.** even, flat, level, plane, square, true **2.** abundant, affluent, full, generous, lavish, liberal, overflowing, prodigal **3.** *informal* in funds, in the money (*informal*), moneyed, rich, rolling (*slang*), wealthy, well-heeled (*informal*), well-off, well-supplied *~adverb* **4.** even with, hard against, in contact with, level with, squarely, touching

flush[3] *verb* discover, disturb, drive out, put to flight, rouse, start, uncover

flushed 1. blushing, burning, crimson, embarrassed, feverish, glowing, hot, red, rosy, rubicund, ruddy **2.** (*often with* **with**) ablaze, animated, aroused, elated, enthused, excited, exhilarated, high (*informal*), inspired, intoxicated, thrilled

fluster 1. *verb* agitate, bother, bustle, confound, confuse, disturb, excite, flurry, hassle (*informal*), heat, hurry, make nervous, perturb, rattle (*informal*), ruffle, throw off balance, unnerve, upset **2.** *~noun* agitation, bustle, commotion, disturbance, dither (*chiefly Brit.*), flap (*informal*), flurry, flutter, furore, perturbation, ruffle, state (*informal*), turmoil

fluted channelled, corrugated, furrowed, grooved

flutter *verb* **1.** agitate, bat, beat, flap, flicker, flit, flitter, fluctuate, hover, palpitate, quiver, ripple, ruffle, shiver, tremble, vibrate, waver *~noun* **2.** palpitation, quiver, quivering, shiver, shudder, tremble, tremor, twitching, vibration **3.** agitation, commotion, confusion, dither (*chiefly Brit.*), excitement, flurry, fluster, perturbation, state (*informal*), state of nervous excitement, tremble, tumult

flux alteration, change, flow, fluctuation, fluidity, instability, modification, motion, mutability, mutation, transition, unrest

fly[1] *verb* **1.** flit, flutter, hover, mount, sail, soar, take to the air, take wing, wing **2.** aviate, be at the controls, control, manoeuvre, operate, pilot **3.** display, flap, float, flutter, show, wave **4.** elapse, flit, glide, pass, pass swiftly, roll on, run its course, slip away **5.** barrel (along) (*informal, chiefly U.S. & Canad.*), be off like a shot (*informal*), bolt, burn rubber (*informal*), career, dart, dash, hare (*Brit. informal*), hasten, hurry, race, rush, scamper, scoot, shoot, speed, sprint, tear, whizz (*informal*), zoom **6.** abscond, avoid, beat a retreat, clear out (*informal*), cut and run (*informal*), decamp, disappear, do a runner (*slang*), escape, flee, fly the coop (*U.S. & Canad. informal*), get away, hasten away, hightail (*informal, chiefly U.S.*), light out (*informal*), make a getaway, make a quick exit, make one's escape, run, run for it, run from, show a clean pair of heels, shun, skedaddle (*informal*), take a powder (*U.S. & Canad. slang*), take flight, take it on the lam (*U.S. & Canad. slang*), take off, take to one's heels **7. fly off the handle** blow one's top, explode, flip one's lid (*slang*), fly into a rage, go ballistic (*slang, chiefly U.S.*), have a tantrum, hit *or* go through the roof (*informal*), let fly (*informal*), lose one's cool (*slang*), lose one's temper **8. let fly: a.** burst forth, give free reign, keep nothing back, lash out, let (someone) have it, lose one's temper, tear into (*informal*), vent **b.** cast, chuck (*informal*), fire, fling, heave, hurl, hurtle, launch, let off, lob (*informal*), shoot, sling, throw *~noun* **9. fly in the ointment** difficulty, drawback, flaw, hitch, problem, rub, small problem, snag

fly[2] *adjective* astute, canny, careful, knowing, nobody's fool, not born yesterday, on the ball (*informal*), sharp, shrewd, smart, wide-awake

fly at assail, assault, attack, belabour, fall upon, get stuck into (*informal*), go for, go for the jugular, have a go at (*informal*), lay about, pitch into (*informal*), rush at

fly-by-night *adjective* **1.** cowboy (*informal*), dubious, questionable, shady, undependable, unreliable, untrustworthy **2.** brief, here today, gone tomorrow, impermanent, short-lived

flying *adjective* **1.** brief, fleeting, fugacious, hasty, hurried, rushed, short-lived, transitory **2.** express, fast, fleet, mercurial, mobile, rapid, speedy, winged **3.** airborne, flapping, floating, fluttering, gliding, hovering, in the air, soaring, streaming, volitant, waving, wind-borne, winging

foam 1. *noun* bubbles, froth, head, lather, spray, spume, suds **2.** *~verb* boil, bubble, effervesce, fizz, froth, lather

foamy bubbly, foaming, frothy, lathery, spumescent, sudsy

fob off 1. appease, deceive, equivocate with, flannel (*Brit. informal*), give (someone) the run-around (*informal*), put off, stall **2.** dump, foist, get rid of, inflict, palm off, pass off, unload

focus *noun* **1.** bull's eye, centre, centre of activity, centre of attraction, core, cynosure, focal point, headquarters, heart, hub, meeting place, target **2. in focus** clear, distinct, sharp-edged, sharply defined **3. out of focus** blurred, fuzzy, ill-defined, indistinct, muzzy, unclear *~verb* **4.** aim, bring to bear, centre, concentrate, converge, direct, fix, join, meet, pinpoint, rivet, spotlight, zero in (*informal*), zoom in

fodder feed, food, foodstuff, forage, provender, rations, tack (*informal*), victuals, vittles (*obsolete or dialect*)

foe adversary, antagonist, enemy, foeman (*archaic*), opponent, rival
▷ **Antonyms** ally, companion, comrade, confederate, friend, partner

fog *noun* **1.** gloom, miasma, mist, murk, murkiness, peasouper (*informal*), smog **2.** *figurative* blindness, confusion, daze, haze, mist, obscurity, perplexity, stupor, trance *~verb* **3.** becloud, bedim, befuddle, bewilder, blear, blind, cloud, confuse, darken, daze, dim, muddle, muddy the waters, obfuscate, obscure, perplex, stupefy **4.** cloud, mist over *or* up, steam up

foggy 1. blurred, brumous (*rare*), cloudy, dim, grey, hazy, indistinct, misty, murky, nebulous, obscure, smoggy, soupy, vaporous **2.** *figurative* befuddled, bewildered, clouded, cloudy, confused, dark, dazed, dim, indistinct, muddled, obscure, stupefied, stupid, unclear, vague
▷ **Antonyms** accurate, alert, awake, bright, clear, decisive, distinct, lucid, palpable, sharp, shrewd, undimmed

fogey, fogy anachronism, antique (*informal*), back number (*informal*), dinosaur, dodo (*informal*), fossil (*informal*), fuddy-duddy (*informal*), relic, square (*informal*), stick-in-the-mud (*informal*)

foible defect, failing, fault, idiosyncrasy, imperfection, infirmity, peculiarity, quirk, weakness, weak point

foil[1] *verb* baffle, balk, check, checkmate, circumvent, cook (someone's) goose (*informal*), counter, defeat, disappoint, elude, frustrate, nip in the bud, nullify, outwit, put a spoke in (someone's) wheel (*Brit.*), stop, thwart

foil[2] *noun* antithesis, background, complement, contrast, setting

foist fob off, get rid of, impose, insert, insinuate, interpolate, introduce, palm off, pass off, put over, sneak in, unload

fold *verb* **1.** bend, crease, crumple, dog-ear, double, double over, gather, intertwine, overlap, pleat, tuck, turn under *~noun* **2.** bend, crease, double thickness, folded portion, furrow, knife-edge, layer, overlap, pleat, turn, wrinkle *~verb* **3.** do up, enclose, enfold, entwine, envelop, wrap, wrap up **4.** *informal* be ruined, close, collapse, crash, fail, go bankrupt, go belly-up (*slang*), go bust (*informal*), go by the board, go down like a lead balloon (*informal*), go to the wall, go under, shut down

folder binder, envelope, file, portfolio

folk clan, ethnic group, family, kin, kindred, people, race, tribe

follow 1. come after, come next, step into the shoes of, succeed, supersede, supplant, take the place of **2.** chase, dog, hound, hunt, pursue, run after, shadow, stalk, tail (*informal*), track, trail **3.** accompany, attend, bring up the rear, come after, come *or* go with, escort, tag along, tread on the heels of **4.** act in accordance with, be guided by, comply, conform, give allegiance to, heed, mind, note, obey, observe, regard, toe the line, watch **5.** appreciate, catch, catch on (*informal*), comprehend, fathom, get, get the hang of (*informal*), get the picture, grasp, keep up with, realize, see, take in, understand **6.** arise, be consequent, develop, emanate, ensue, flow, issue, proceed, result, spring, supervene **7.** adopt, copy, emulate, imitate, live up to, pattern oneself upon, take a leaf out of someone's book, take as example **8.** be a devotee *or* supporter of, be devoted to, be interested in, cultivate, keep abreast of, support
▷ **Antonyms** abandon, avoid, desert, disobey, elude, escape, flout, forsake, give up, guide, ignore, lead, precede, reject, renounce, shun, steer

follower 1. adherent, admirer, apostle, backer, believer, cohort (*chiefly U.S.*), convert, devotee, disciple, fan, fancier, habitué, henchman, partisan, protago~

nist, pupil, representative, supporter, votary, worshipper **2.** attendant, companion, hanger-on, helper, henchman, lackey, minion, retainer (*History*), sidekick (*slang*)
▷ **Antonyms** (*sense 1*) guru, leader, mentor, svengali, swami, teacher, tutor (*sense 2*) antagonist, contender, enemy, foe, opponent, rival

following 1. *adjective* coming, consequent, consequential, ensuing, later, next, specified, subsequent, succeeding, successive **2.** *~noun* audience, circle, clientele, coterie, entourage, fans, patronage, public, retinue, suite, support, supporters, train

follow through bring to a conclusion, complete, conclude, consummate, pursue, see through

follow up 1. check out, find out about, investigate, look into, make inquiries, pursue, research **2.** consolidate, continue, make sure, reinforce

folly absurdity, bêtise (*rare*), daftness (*informal*), desipience, fatuity, foolishness, idiocy, imbecility, imprudence, indiscretion, irrationality, lunacy, madness, nonsense, preposterousness, rashness, recklessness, silliness, stupidity
▷ **Antonyms** judgment, level-headedness, moderation, prudence, rationality, reason, sanity, sense, wisdom

foment abet, agitate, arouse, brew, encourage, excite, fan the flames, foster, goad, incite, instigate, promote, provoke, quicken, raise, rouse, sow the seeds of, spur, stimulate, stir up, whip up

fomenter agitator, demagogue, firebrand, incendiary, inciter, instigator, rabble-rouser, stirrer (*informal*), troublemaker

fond 1. (*with* **of**) addicted to, attached to, enamoured of, have a fancy for, have a liking for, have a taste for, have a soft spot for, hooked on, into (*informal*), keen on, partial to, predisposed towards **2.** adoring, affectionate, amorous, caring, devoted, doting, indulgent, loving, tender, warm **3.** absurd, credulous, deluded, delusive, delusory, empty, foolish, indiscreet, naive, overoptimistic, vain
▷ **Antonyms** (*senses 1 & 2*) aloof, austere, averse, disinterested, indifferent, rational, sensible, unaffectionate, unconcerned, undemonstrative

fondle caress, cuddle, dandle, pat, pet, stroke

fondly 1. affectionately, dearly, indulgently, lovingly, possessively, tenderly, with affection **2.** credulously, foolishly, naively, stupidly, vainly

fondness 1. attachment, fancy, liking, love, partiality, penchant, predilection, preference, soft spot, susceptibility, taste, weakness **2.** affection, attachment, devotion, kindness, love, tenderness, warmth
▷ **Antonyms** abhorence, animosity, animus, antagonism, antipathy, aversion, bad blood, coldness, contempt, detestation, dislike, enmity, harshness, hatred, hostility, ill will, loathing, malevolence, malice, opposition, repugnance, resentment, unfriendliness

food 1. aliment, board, bread, chow (*informal*), comestibles, commons, cooking, cuisine, diet, eatables (*slang*), eats (*slang*), edibles, fare, feed, foodstuffs, grub (*slang*), larder, meat, menu, nosebag (*slang*), nosh (*slang*), nourishment, nutriment, nutrition, pabulum (*rare*), provender, provisions, rations, refreshment, scoff (*slang*), stores, subsistence, survival rations, sustenance, table, tack (*informal*), tuck (*informal*), tucker (*Austral. & N.Z. informal*), viands, victuals, vittles (*obsolete or dialect*) **2.** *Cattle, etc.* feed, fodder, forage, provender

foodie *bon vivant, bon viveur,* connoisseur, epicure, gastronome, gourmand, gourmet

fool *noun* **1.** ass, berk (*Brit. slang*), birdbrain (*informal*), blockhead, bonehead (*slang*), charlie (*Brit. informal*), chump (*informal*), clodpate (*archaic*), clot (*Brit. informal*), coot, dickhead (*slang*), dimwit (*informal*), dipstick (*Brit. slang*), divvy (*Brit. slang*), dolt, dope (*informal*), dork (*slang*), dunce, dunderhead, dweeb (*U.S. slang*), fathead (*informal*), fuckwit (*taboo slang*), geek (*slang*), gobshite (*Irish taboo slang*), gonzo (*slang*), goose (*informal*), halfwit, idiot, ignoramus, illiterate, imbecile (*informal*), jackass, jerk (*slang, chiefly U.S. & Canad.*), lamebrain (*informal*), loon, mooncalf, moron, nerd *or* nurd (*slang*), nincompoop, ninny, nit (*informal*), nitwit (*informal*), numbskull *or* numskull, numpty (*Scot. informal*), oaf, pillock (*Brit. slang*), plank (*Brit. slang*), plonker (*slang*), prat (*slang*), prick (*derogatory slang*), sap (*slang*), schmuck (*U.S. slang*), silly, simpleton, twerp *or* twirp (*informal*), twit (*informal, chiefly Brit.*), wally (*slang*) **2.** butt, chump (*informal*), dupe, easy mark (*informal*), fall guy (*informal*), greenhorn (*informal*), gull (*archaic*), laughing stock, mug (*Brit. slang*), stooge (*slang*), sucker (*slang*) **3.** buffoon, clown, comic, harlequin, jester, merry-andrew, motley, pierrot, punchinello **4. act** *or* **play the fool** act the goat, act up, be silly, cavort, clown, cut capers, frolic, lark about (*informal*), mess about, piss about (*taboo slang*), piss around (*taboo slang*), play (silly) games, play the goat, show off (*informal*) *~verb* **5.** bamboozle, beguile, bluff, cheat, con (*informal*), deceive, delude, dupe, gull (*archaic*), have (someone) on, hoax, hoodwink, kid (*informal*), make a fool of, mislead, play a trick on, pull a fast one on (*informal*), put one over on (*informal*), stiff (*slang*), take for a ride (*informal*), take in, trick **6**. act the fool, cut capers, feign, jest, joke, kid (*informal*), make believe, piss about (*taboo slang*), piss around (*taboo slang*), pretend, tease **7**. (*with* **with, around with,** *or* **about with**) fiddle (*informal*), meddle, mess, monkey, piss about (*taboo slang*), piss around (*taboo slang*), play, tamper, toy, trifle

▷ **Antonyms** (*senses 1 & 2*) expert, genius, master, sage, savant, scholar, wise man

fool around *or* **about** act the fool, dawdle, footle (*informal*), hang around, idle, kill time, lark, mess about, play about, play the fool, waste time

foolery antics, capers, carry-on (*informal, chiefly Brit.*), childishness, clowning, desipience, folly, fooling, horseplay, larks, mischief, monkey tricks (*informal*), nonsense, practical jokes, pranks, shenanigans (*informal*), silliness, tomfoolery

foolhardy adventurous, bold, hot-headed, impetuous, imprudent, incautious, irresponsible, madcap, precipitate, rash, reckless, temerarious, venturesome, venturous

▷ **Antonyms** alert, careful, cautious, chary, circumspect, heedful, judicious, prudent, shrewd, solicitous, thoughtful, wary, watchful

fooling *noun* bluffing, buffoonery, clownishness, farce, joking, kidding (*informal*), mockery, nonsense, pretence, shamming, skylarking (*informal*), teasing, tricks, trifling

foolish 1. absurd, asinine, ill-advised, ill-considered, ill-judged, imprudent, inane, incautious, indiscreet, injudicious, nonsensical, senseless, short-sighted, silly, unintelligent, unreasonable, unwise **2**. as daft as a brush (*informal, chiefly Brit.*), braindead (*informal*), brainless, crackpot (*informal*), crazy, daft (*informal*), doltish, fatuous, goofy (*informal*), half-baked (*informal*), half-witted, harebrained, idiotic, imbecilic, inane, loopy (*informal*), ludicrous, mad, moronic, off one's head (*informal*), potty (*Brit. informal*), ridiculous, senseless, silly, simple, stupid, weak, witless

▷ **Antonyms** bright, cautious, clever, commonsensical, intelligent, judicious, prudent, rational, sagacious, sane, sensible, sharp, smart, sound, thoughtful, wise

foolishly absurdly, idiotically, ill-advisedly, imprudently, incautiously, indiscreetly, injudiciously, like a fool, mistakenly, short-sightedly, stupidly, unwisely, without due consideration

foolishness 1. absurdity, bêtise (*rare*), folly, idiocy, imprudence, inanity, indiscretion, irresponsibility, silliness, stupidity, weakness **2**. bunk (*informal*), bunkum *or* buncombe (*chiefly U.S.*), carrying-on (*informal, chiefly Brit.*), claptrap (*informal*), foolery, nonsense, rigmarole, rubbish, trash

foolproof certain, guaranteed, infallible, never-failing, safe, sure-fire (*informal*), unassailable, unbreakable

footing 1. basis, establishment, foot-hold, foundation, ground, groundwork, installation, settlement **2**. condition, grade, position, rank, relations, relationship, standing, state, status, terms

footling fiddling, fussy, hairsplitting, immaterial, insignificant, irrelevant, minor, nickel-and-dime (*U.S. slang*), niggly, petty, pointless, silly, time-wasting, trifling, trivial, unimportant

footslog hike, hoof it (*slang*), march, plod, tramp, trudge, yomp (*slang*)

footstep 1. footfall, step, tread **2**. footmark, footprint, trace, track

fop beau, Beau Brummel, clotheshorse, coxcomb (*archaic*), dandy, exquisite (*obsolete*), fashion plate, macaroni (*obsolete*), peacock, popinjay, smoothie *or* smoothy (*slang*), swell

foppish coxcombical, dandified, dandyish, dapper, dressy (*informal*), finical, natty (*informal*), preening, prinking, spruce, vain

forage 1. *noun Cattle, etc.* feed, fodder, food, foodstuffs, provender **2**. *~verb* cast about, explore, hunt, look round, plunder, raid, ransack, rummage, scavenge, scour, scrounge (*informal*), search, seek

foray depredation, descent, incursion, inroad, invasion, irruption, raid, reconnaissance, sally, sortie, swoop

forbear abstain, avoid, cease, decline, desist, eschew, hold back, keep from, omit, pause, refrain, resist the temptation to, restrain oneself, stop, withhold

forbearance 1. indulgence, leniency, lenity, longanimity (*rare*), long-suffering, mildness, moderation, patience, resignation, restraint, self-control, temperance, tolerance **2**. abstinence, avoidance, refraining

▷ **Antonyms** (*sense 1*) anger, impatience, impetuosity, intolerance, irritability, shortness

forbearing clement, easy, forgiving, indulgent, lenient, long-suffering, merciful, mild, moderate, patient, tolerant

forbid ban, debar, disallow, exclude, hinder, inhibit, interdict, outlaw, preclude, prohibit, proscribe, rule out, veto

▷ **Antonyms** allow, approve, authorize, bid, enable, endorse, grant, let, license, O.K. *or* okay (*informal*), order, permit, sanction

forbidden banned, outlawed, out of bounds, prohibited, proscribed, taboo, *verboten,* vetoed

forbidding 1. abhorrent, disagreeable, odious, offensive, off-putting (*Brit. informal*

formal), repellent, repulsive **2.** baleful, daunting, foreboding, frightening, grim, hostile, menacing, ominous, sinister, threatening, unfriendly
▷ **Antonyms** (*sense 1*) alluring, attractive, beguiling, enticing, inviting, magnetic, tempting, welcoming, winning

force *noun* **1.** dynamism, energy, impact, impulse, life, might, momentum, muscle, potency, power, pressure, stimulus, strength, stress, vigour **2.** arm-twisting (*informal*), coercion, compulsion, constraint, duress, enforcement, pressure, violence **3.** bite, cogency, effect, effectiveness, efficacy, influence, persuasiveness, power, punch (*informal*), strength, validity, weight **4.** drive, emphasis, fierceness, intensity, persistence, vehemence, vigour **5.** army, battalion, body, corps, detachment, division, host, legion, patrol, regiment, squad, squadron, troop, unit **6. in force: a.** binding, current, effective, in operation, on the statute book, operative, valid, working **b.** all together, in full strength, in great numbers *~verb* **7.** bring pressure to bear upon, coerce, compel, constrain, dragoon, drive, impel, impose, make, necessitate, obligate, oblige, overcome, press, press-gang, pressure, pressurize, put the screws on (*informal*), put the squeeze on (*informal*), railroad (*informal*), strong-arm (*informal*), twist (someone's) arm, urge **8.** blast, break open, prise, propel, push, thrust, use violence on, wrench, wrest **9.** drag, exact, extort, wring
▷ **Antonyms** *~noun* debility, enervation, feebleness, fragility, frailty, impotence, ineffectiveness, irresolution, powerlessness, weakness *~verb* (*sense 8*) coax, convince, induce, persuade, prevail, talk into

forced 1. compulsory, conscripted, enforced, involuntary, mandatory, obligatory, slave, unwilling **2.** affected, artificial, contrived, false, insincere, laboured, stiff, strained, unnatural, wooden
▷ **Antonyms** easy, natural, simple, sincere, spontaneous, unforced, unpretending, voluntary

forceful cogent, compelling, convincing, dynamic, effective, persuasive, pithy, potent, powerful, telling, vigorous, weighty
▷ **Antonyms** enervated, exhausted, faint, feeble, frail, powerless, spent, weak

forcible 1. active, cogent, compelling, effective, efficient, energetic, forceful, impressive, mighty, potent, powerful, strong, telling, valid, weighty **2.** aggressive, armed, coercive, compulsory, drastic, violent

forcibly against one's will, by force, by main force, compulsorily, under compulsion, under protest, willy-nilly

forebear ancestor, father, forefather, forerunner, predecessor, progenitor

forebode augur, betoken, foreshadow, foreshow, foretell, foretoken, forewarn, indicate, portend, predict, presage, prognosticate, promise, vaticinate (*rare*), warn of

foreboding 1. anxiety, apprehension, apprehensiveness, chill, dread, fear, misgiving, premonition, presentiment **2.** augury, foreshadowing, foretoken, omen, portent, prediction, presage, prognostication, sign, token, warning

forecast 1. *verb* anticipate, augur, calculate, divine, estimate, foresee, foretell, plan, predict, prognosticate, prophesy, vaticinate (*rare*) **2.** *~noun* anticipation, conjecture, foresight, forethought, guess, outlook, planning, prediction, prognosis, projection, prophecy

forefather ancestor, father, forebear, forerunner, predecessor, primogenitor, procreator, progenitor

forefront centre, fore, foreground, front, lead, prominence, spearhead, van, vanguard

forego *see* FORGO

foregoing above, antecedent, anterior, former, preceding, previous, prior

foreground centre, forefront, front, limelight, prominence

foreign 1. alien, beyond one's ken, borrowed, distant, exotic, external, imported, outlandish, outside, overseas, remote, strange, unfamiliar, unknown **2.** extraneous, extrinsic, incongruous, irrelevant, unassimilable, uncharacteristic, unrelated
▷ **Antonyms** applicable, characteristic, customary, domestic, familiar, intrinsic, native, pertinent, relevant, suited, well-known

foreigner alien, immigrant, incomer, newcomer, outlander, stranger

foreknowledge clairvoyance, foresight, forewarning, precognition, prescience, prevision, prior knowledge

foremost chief, first, front, headmost, highest, inaugural, initial, leading, paramount, pre-eminent, primary, prime, principal, supreme

foreordain doom, fate, foredoom, prearrange, predestine, predetermine, preordain, reserve

forerunner 1. ancestor, announcer, envoy, forebear, foregoer, harbinger, herald, precursor, predecessor, progenitor, prototype **2.** augury, foretoken, indication, omen, portent, premonition, prognostic, sign, token

foresee anticipate, divine, envisage, forebode, forecast, foretell, predict, prophesy, vaticinate (*rare*)

foreshadow adumbrate, augur, betoken, bode, forebode, imply, indicate, portend, predict, prefigure, presage, promise, prophesy, signal

foresight anticipation, care, caution, circumspection, far-sightedness, forethought, precaution, premeditation, preparedness, prescience, prevision (*rare*), provision, prudence
▷ **Antonyms** carelessness, hindsight, imprudence, inconsideration, lack of foresight, neglect, retrospection, thoughtlessness, unpreparedness

forestall anticipate, balk, circumvent, frustrate, head off, hinder, intercept, nip in the bud, obviate, parry, preclude, prevent, provide against, thwart

forestry arboriculture, dendrology (*Botany*), silviculture, woodcraft, woodmanship

foretaste *noun* example, foretoken, indication, prelude, preview, sample, trailer, warning, whiff

foretell adumbrate, augur, bode, forebode, forecast, foreshadow, foreshow, forewarn, portend, predict, presage, prognosticate, prophesy, signify, soothsay, vaticinate (*rare*)

forethought anticipation, far-sightedness, foresight, precaution, providence, provision, prudence
▷ **Antonyms** carelessness, imprudence, impulsiveness, inconsideration, neglect, unpreparedness

foretoken *verb* augur, forebode, foreshadow, foreshow, give notice of, give warning of, portend, presage, signify, warn of

forever **1.** always, evermore, for all time, for good and all (*informal*), for keeps, in perpetuity, till Doomsday, till the cows come home (*informal*), till the end of time, world without end **2.** all the time, constantly, continually, endlessly, eternally, everlastingly, incessantly, interminably, perpetually, unremittingly

forewarn admonish, advise, alert, apprise, caution, dissuade, give fair warning, put on guard, put on the qui vive, tip off

foreword introduction, preamble, preface, preliminary, prolegomenon, prologue

forfeit **1.** *noun* amercement (*obsolete*), damages, fine, forfeiture, loss, mulct, penalty **2.** *~verb* be deprived of, be stripped of, give up, lose, relinquish, renounce, say goodbye to, surrender

forfeiture confiscation, giving up, loss, relinquishment, sequestration (*Law*), surrender

forge *verb* **1.** construct, contrive, create, devise, fabricate, fashion, form, frame, hammer out, invent, make, mould, shape, work **2.** coin, copy, counterfeit, fake, falsify, feign, imitate

forger coiner, counterfeiter, falsifier

forgery **1.** coining, counterfeiting, falsification, fraudulence, fraudulent imitation **2.** counterfeit, fake, falsification, imitation, phoney *or* phony (*informal*), sham

forget **1.** consign to oblivion, dismiss from one's mind, let bygones be bygones, let slip from the memory **2.** leave behind, lose sight of, omit, overlook
▷ **Antonyms** bring to mind, mind, recall, recollect, remember, retain

forgetful absent-minded, apt to forget, careless, dreamy, having a memory like a sieve, heedless, inattentive, lax, neglectful, negligent, oblivious, slapdash, slipshod, unmindful, vague
▷ **Antonyms** attentive, careful, mindful, retentive, unforgetful, unforgetting

forgetfulness absent-mindedness, abstraction, carelessness, dreaminess, heedlessness, inattention, lapse of memory, laxity, laxness, oblivion, obliviousness, woolgathering

forgive absolve, accept (someone's) apology, acquit, bear no malice, condone, excuse, exonerate, let bygones be bygones, let off (*informal*), pardon, remit
▷ **Antonyms** blame, censure, charge, condemn, find fault with, reproach, reprove

forgiveness absolution, acquittal, amnesty, condonation, exoneration, mercy, overlooking, pardon, remission

forgiving clement, compassionate, forbearing, humane, lenient, magnanimous, merciful, mild, soft-hearted, tolerant

forgo, forego abandon, abjure, cede, do without, give up, kick (*informal*), leave alone *or* out, relinquish, renounce, resign, sacrifice, say goodbye to, surrender, waive, yield

forgotten blotted out, buried, bygone, consigned to oblivion, gone (clean) out of one's mind, left behind *or* out, lost, obliterated, omitted, past, past recall, unremembered

fork *verb* bifurcate, branch, branch off, diverge, divide, go separate ways, part, split

forked angled, bifurcate(d), branched, branching, divided, pronged, split, tined, zigzag

forlorn abandoned, bereft, cheerless, comfortless, deserted, desolate, destitute, disconsolate, down in the dumps (*informal*), forgotten, forsaken, friendless, helpless, homeless, hopeless, lonely, lost, miserable, pathetic, pitiable, pitiful, unhappy, woebegone, wretched
▷ **Antonyms** busy, cheerful, happy, hopeful, optimistic, thriving

form[1] *verb* **1.** assemble, bring about, build, concoct, construct, contrive, create, devise, establish, fabricate, fashion, forge, found, invent, make, manufac~

ture, model, mould, produce, put together, set up, shape, stamp **2.** arrange, combine, design, dispose, draw up, frame, organize, pattern, plan, think up **3.** accumulate, appear, become visible, come into being, crystallize, grow, materialize, rise, settle, show up (*informal*), take shape **4.** acquire, contract, cultivate, develop, get into (*informal*), pick up **5.** compose, comprise, constitute, make, make up, serve as **6.** bring up, discipline, educate, instruct, rear, school, teach, train

form[2] *noun* **1.** appearance, cast, configuration, construction, cut, fashion, formation, model, mould, pattern, shape, stamp, structure **2.** anatomy, being, body, build, figure, frame, outline, person, physique, shape, silhouette **3.** arrangement, character, description, design, guise, kind, manifestation, manner, method, mode, order, practice, semblance, sort, species, stamp, style, system, type, variety, way **4.** format, framework, harmony, order, orderliness, organization, plan, proportion, structure, symmetry **5.** condition, fettle, fitness, good condition, good spirits, health, shape, trim **6. off form** below par, not in the pink (*informal*), not up to the mark, out of condition, stale, under the weather (*informal*), unfit **7.** behaviour, ceremony, conduct, convention, custom, done thing, etiquette, formality, manners, procedure, protocol, ritual, rule **8.** application, document, paper, sheet **9.** class, grade, rank

formal 1. approved, ceremonial, explicit, express, fixed, lawful, legal, methodical, official, prescribed, *pro forma,* regular, rigid, ritualistic, set, solemn, strict **2.** affected, aloof, ceremonious, conventional, correct, exact, precise, prim, punctilious, reserved, starched, stiff, unbending

▷ **Antonyms** casual, easy-going, informal, laid-back (*informal*), relaxed, unceremonious, unofficial

formality 1. ceremony, convention, conventionality, custom, form, gesture, matter of form, procedure, red tape, rite, ritual **2.** ceremoniousness, correctness, decorum, etiquette, politesse, protocol, p's and q's, punctilio

format appearance, arrangement, construction, form, layout, look, make-up, plan, style, type

formation 1. accumulation, compilation, composition, constitution, crystallization, development, establishment, evolution, forming, generation, genesis, manufacture, organization, production **2.** arrangement, configuration, design, disposition, figure, grouping, pattern, rank, structure

formative 1. impressionable, malleable, mouldable, pliant, sensitive, susceptible **2.** determinative, developmental, influential, moulding, shaping

former 1. antecedent, anterior, *ci-devant,* earlier, erstwhile, ex-, late, one-time, previous, prior, quondam, whilom (*archaic*) **2.** ancient, bygone, departed, long ago, long gone, of yore, old, old-time, past **3.** above, aforementioned, aforesaid, first mentioned, foregoing, preceding

▷ **Antonyms** coming, current, ensuing, following, future, latter, modern, present, present-day, subsequent, succeeding

formerly aforetime (*archaic*), already, at one time, before, heretofore, lately, once, previously

formidable 1. appalling, baleful, dangerous, daunting, dismaying, dreadful, fearful, frightful, horrible, intimidating, menacing, shocking, terrifying, threatening **2.** arduous, challenging, colossal, difficult, mammoth, onerous, overwhelming, staggering, toilsome **3.** awesome, great, impressive, indomitable, mighty, powerful, puissant, redoubtable, terrific, tremendous

▷ **Antonyms** cheering, comforting, easy, encouraging, genial, heartening, pleasant, reassuring

formless amorphous, disorganized, inchoate, incoherent, indefinite, nebulous, shapeless, unformed, vague

formula 1. form of words, formulary, rite, ritual, rubric **2.** blueprint, method, modus operandi, precept, prescription, principle, procedure, recipe, rule, way

formulate 1. codify, define, detail, express, frame, give form to, particularize, set down, specify, systematize **2.** coin, develop, devise, evolve, forge, invent, map out, originate, plan, work out

forsake 1. abandon, cast off, desert, disown, jettison, jilt, leave, leave in the lurch, quit, repudiate, strand, throw over **2.** abdicate, forgo, forswear, give up, have done with, kick (*informal*), relinquish, renounce, set aside, surrender, turn one's back on, yield

forsaken abandoned, cast off, deserted, destitute, disowned, ditched, forlorn, friendless, ignored, isolated, jilted, left behind, left in the lurch, lonely, marooned, outcast, solitary, stranded

forswear 1. abandon, abjure, drop (*informal*), forgo, forsake, give up, renounce, swear off **2.** deny, disavow, disclaim, disown, recant, reject, repudiate, retract **3.** lie, perjure oneself, renege, swear falsely

fort 1. blockhouse, camp, castle, citadel, fastness, fortification, fortress, garrison, redoubt, station, stronghold **2. hold the fort** carry on, keep things moving, keep things on an even keel, maintain the status quo, stand in, take over the reins

forte gift, long suit (*informal*), métier, speciality, strength, strong point, talent
▷ **Antonyms** Achilles heel, chink in one's armour, defect, failing, imperfection, shortcoming, weak point

forth ahead, away, forward, into the open, onward, out, out of concealment, outward

forthcoming **1.** approaching, coming, expected, future, imminent, impending, prospective, upcoming **2.** accessible, at hand, available, in evidence, obtainable, on tap (*informal*), ready **3.** chatty, communicative, expansive, free, informative, open, sociable, talkative, unreserved

forthright above-board, blunt, candid, direct, downright, frank, open, outspoken, plain-spoken, straightforward, straight from the shoulder (*informal*), upfront (*informal*)
▷ **Antonyms** dishonest, furtive, secret, secretive, sneaky, underhand, untruthful

forthwith at once, directly, immediately, instantly, quickly, right away, straightaway, *tout de suite,* without delay

fortification **1.** bastion, bulwark, castle, citadel, defence, fastness, fort, fortress, keep, protection, stronghold **2.** embattlement, reinforcement, strengthening

fortify **1.** augment, brace, buttress, embattle, garrison, protect, reinforce, secure, shore up, strengthen, support **2.** brace, cheer, confirm, embolden, encourage, hearten, invigorate, reassure, stiffen, strengthen, sustain
▷ **Antonyms** debilitate, demoralize, dilute, dishearten, impair, reduce, sap the strength of, weaken

fortitude backbone, braveness, courage, dauntlessness, determination, endurance, fearlessness, firmness, grit, guts (*informal*), hardihood, intrepidity, patience, perseverance, pluck, resolution, staying power, stoutheartedness, strength, strength of mind, valour

fortress castle, citadel, fastness, fort, redoubt, stronghold

fortuitous **1.** accidental, arbitrary, casual, chance, contingent, incidental, random, unforeseen, unplanned **2.** fluky (*informal*), fortunate, happy, lucky, providential, serendipitous

fortunate **1.** born with a silver spoon in one's mouth, bright, favoured, golden, happy, having a charmed life, in luck, jammy (*Brit. slang*), lucky, on a roll, prosperous, rosy, sitting pretty (*informal*), successful, well-off **2.** advantageous, auspicious, convenient, encouraging, expedient, favourable, felicitous, fortuitous, helpful, opportune, profitable, promising, propitious, providential, timely
▷ **Antonyms** disastrous, hapless, ill-fated, ill-starred, miserable, poor, unfortunate, unhappy, unlucky, unsuccessful, wretched

fortunately by a happy chance, by good luck, happily, luckily, providentially

fortune **1.** affluence, an arm and a leg (*informal*), big bucks (*informal, chiefly U.S.*), big money, gold mine, megabucks (*U.S. & Canad. slang*), opulence, possessions, pretty penny (*informal*), property, prosperity, riches, tidy sum (*informal*), treasure, wad (*U.S. & Canad. slang*), wealth **2.** accident, chance, contingency, destiny, fate, fortuity, hap (*archaic*), hazard, kismet, luck, providence **3.** (*often plural*) adventures, circumstances, destiny, doom, expectation, experience(s), history, life, lot, portion, star, success **4.** bomb (*Brit. slang*), bundle (*slang*), king's ransom, mint, packet (*slang*), pile (*informal*), wealth
▷ **Antonyms** (*sense 1*) destitution, hardship, indigence, penury, poverty, privation

forward *adjective* **1.** advanced, advancing, early, forward-looking, onward, precocious, premature, progressive, well-developed **2.** advance, first, fore, foremost, front, head, leading **3.** assuming, bare-faced, bold, brash, brass-necked (*Brit. informal*), brazen, brazen-faced, cheeky, confident, familiar, fresh (*informal*), impertinent, impudent, overassertive, overweening, pert, presuming, presumptuous, pushy (*informal*), sassy (*U.S. informal*) *~adverb* **4.** *also* **forwards** ahead, forth, on, onward **5.** into consideration, into prominence, into the open, into view, out, to light, to the fore, to the surface *~verb* **6.** advance, aid, assist, back, encourage, expedite, favour, foster, further, hasten, help, hurry, promote, speed, support **7.** *Commerce* dispatch, freight, post, route, send, send on, ship, transmit
▷ **Antonyms** *~adjective* backward, diffident, modest, regressive, retiring, shy *~adverb* backward(s) *~verb* bar, block, hinder, hold up, impede, obstruct, retard, thwart

forward-looking dynamic, enlightened, enterprising, go-ahead, go-getting (*informal*), liberal, modern, progressive, reforming

forwardness boldness, brashness, brazenness, cheek (*informal*), cheekiness, chutzpah (*U.S. & Canad. informal*), impertinence, impudence, overconfidence, pertness, presumption

fossilized **1.** dead, dead as a dodo, extinct, inflexible, ossified, petrified, prehistoric **2.** anachronistic, antediluvian, antiquated, archaistic, behind the times, *démodé,* obsolete, out of the ark (*informal*), passé, superannuated

foster **1.** cultivate, encourage, feed, foment, nurture, promote, stimulate, sup~

port, uphold **2.** bring up, mother, nurse, raise, rear, take care of **3.** accommodate, cherish, entertain, harbour, nourish, sustain

▷ **Antonyms** combat, curb, curtail, hold out against, inhibit, oppose, resist, re~strain, subdue, suppress, withstand

foul *adjective* **1.** contaminated, dirty, dis~gusting, fetid, filthy, grotty (*slang*), grungy (*slang, chiefly U.S.*), impure, loathsome, malodorous, mephitic, nasty, nauseating, noisome, offensive, olid, polluted, putrid, rank, repulsive, revolt~ing, rotten, scuzzy (*slang, chiefly U.S.*), squalid, stinking, sullied, tainted, un~clean, yucky *or* yukky (*slang*) **2.** abusive, blasphemous, blue, coarse, dirty, filthy, foul-mouthed, gross, indecent, lewd, low, obscene, profane, scatological, scurrilous, smutty, vulgar **3.** abhorrent, abominable, base, despicable, detest~able, disgraceful, dishonourable, egre~gious, hateful, heinous, infamous, in~iquitous, nefarious, notorious, offensive, scandalous, shameful, shitty (*taboo slang*), vicious, vile, wicked **4.** crooked, dirty, dishonest, fraudulent, inequi~table, shady (*informal*), underhand, un~fair, unjust, unscrupulous, un~sportsmanlike **5.** bad, blustery, dis~agreeable, foggy, murky, rainy, rough, stormy, wet, wild *~verb* **6.** begrime, be~smear, besmirch, contaminate, defile, dirty, pollute, smear, smirch, soil, stain, sully, taint **7.** block, catch, choke, clog, ensnare, entangle, jam, snarl, twist

▷ **Antonyms** *~adjective* admirable, at~tractive, clean, clear, decent, fair, fra~grant, fresh, pleasant, pure, respectable, spotless, undefiled *~verb* clean, cleanse, clear, honour, purge, purify, sanitize

foul-mouthed abusive, blasphemous, coarse, Fescennine (*rare*), obscene, of~fensive, profane

foul play chicanery, corruption, crime, deception, dirty work, double-dealing, duplicity, fraud, perfidy, roguery, sharp practice, skulduggery, treachery, vil~lainy

foul up bodge (*informal*), botch, bungle, cock up (*Brit. slang*), flub (*U.S. slang*), fuck up (*offensive taboo slang*), make a mess of, make a nonsense of, make a pig's ear of (*informal*), mismanage, muck up (*slang*), put a spanner in the works (*Brit. informal*), spoil

found **1.** bring into being, constitute, con~struct, create, endow, erect, establish, fix, inaugurate, institute, organize, originate, plant, raise, settle, set up, start **2.** base, bottom, build, ground, rest, root, sustain

foundation **1.** base, basis, bedrock, bot~tom, footing, groundwork, substructure, underpinning **2.** endowment, establish~ment, inauguration, institution, organi~zation, setting up, settlement

founder[1] *noun* architect, author, begin~ner, benefactor, builder, constructor, designer, establisher, father, framer, generator, initiator, institutor, inventor, maker, organizer, originator, patriarch

founder[2] *verb* **1.** be lost, go down, go to the bottom, sink, submerge **2.** *figurative* abort, bite the dust, break down, col~lapse, come to grief, come to nothing, come unstuck, fail, fall by the wayside, fall through, go belly-up (*slang*), go down like a lead balloon (*informal*), miscarry, misfire **3.** collapse, fall, go lame, lurch, sprawl, stagger, stumble, trip

foundling orphan, outcast, stray, waif

fountain **1.** font, fount, jet, reservoir, spout, spray, spring, well **2.** *figurative* beginning, cause, commencement, deri~vation, fount, fountainhead, genesis, origin, rise, source, wellhead, wellspring

fountainhead *fons et origo,* fount, inspi~ration, mainspring, origin, source, spring, well, wellspring

foursquare **1.** *adverb* firmly, resolutely, squarely **2.** *~adjective* firm, firmly-based, immovable, resolute, solid, steady, strong, unyielding

foxy artful, astute, canny, crafty, cun~ning, devious, guileful, knowing, sharp, shrewd, sly, tricky, wily

foyer antechamber, anteroom, entrance hall, lobby, reception area, vestibule

fracas affray (*Law*), aggro (*slang*), *bagarre,* brawl, disturbance, donny~brook, fight, free-for-all (*informal*), me~lee *or* mêlée, quarrel, riot, row, rumpus, scrimmage, scuffle, shindig (*informal*), shindy (*informal*), skirmish, trouble, uproar

fractious awkward, captious, crabby, cross, fretful, froward (*archaic*), grouchy (*informal*), irritable, peevish, pettish, petulant, querulous, ratty (*Brit. & N.Z. informal*), recalcitrant, refractory, testy, tetchy, touchy, unruly

▷ **Antonyms** affable, agreeable, amiable, biddable, complaisant, genial, good-natured, good-tempered, tractable

fracture **1.** *noun* breach, break, cleft, crack, fissure, gap, opening, rent, rift, rupture, schism, split **2.** *~verb* break, crack, rupture, splinter, split

fragile breakable, brittle, dainty, delicate, feeble, fine, flimsy, frail, frangible, in~firm, slight, weak

▷ **Antonyms** durable, elastic, flexible, hardy, lasting, reliable, resilient, robust, strong, sturdy, tough

fragility brittleness, delicacy, feebleness, frailty, frangibility, infirmity, weakness

fragment **1.** *noun* bit, chip, fraction, mor~sel, oddment, part, particle, piece, por~tion, remnant, scrap, shiver, shred, sliver **2.** *~verb* break, break up, come apart, come to pieces, crumble, disinte~

grate, disunite, divide, shatter, shiver, splinter, split, split up
▷ **Antonyms** ~*verb* bond, combine, compound, fuse, join together, link, marry, merge, synthesize, unify

fragmentary bitty, broken, disconnected, discrete, disjointed, incoherent, incomplete, partial, piecemeal, scattered, scrappy, sketchy, unsystematic

fragrance aroma, balm, bouquet, fragrancy, perfume, redolence, scent, smell, sweet odour
▷ **Antonyms** effluvium, miasma, niff (*Brit. slang*), offensive smell, pong (*Brit. informal*), reek, smell, stink, whiff (*Brit. slang*)

fragrant ambrosial, aromatic, balmy, odoriferous, odorous, perfumed, redolent, sweet-scented, sweet-smelling
▷ **Antonyms** fetid, foul-smelling, malodorous, niffy (*Brit. slang*), noisome, olid, pongy (*Brit. informal*), reeking, smelling, smelly, stinking

frail breakable, brittle, decrepit, delicate, feeble, flimsy, fragile, frangible, infirm, insubstantial, puny, slight, tender, unsound, vulnerable, weak, wispy
▷ **Antonyms** hale, healthy, robust, sound, stalwart, strong, sturdy, substantial, tough, vigorous

frailty **1.** fallibility, feebleness, frailness, infirmity, peccability, puniness, susceptibility, weakness **2.** blemish, chink in one's armour, defect, deficiency, failing, fault, flaw, foible, imperfection, peccadillo, shortcoming, vice, weak point
▷ **Antonyms** (*sense 1*) fortitude, might, robustness, strength (*sense 2*) asset, strong point, virtue

frame *verb* **1.** assemble, build, constitute, construct, fabricate, fashion, forge, form, institute, invent, make, manufacture, model, mould, put together, set up **2.** block out, compose, conceive, concoct, contrive, cook up, devise, draft, draw up, form, formulate, hatch, map out, plan, shape, sketch **3.** case, enclose, mount, surround ~*noun* **4.** casing, construction, fabric, form, framework, scheme, shell, structure, system **5.** anatomy, body, build, carcass, morphology, physique, skeleton **6.** mount, mounting, setting **7. frame of mind** attitude, disposition, fettle, humour, mood, outlook, spirit, state, temper

frame-up fabrication, fit-up (*slang*), put-up job, trumped-up charge

framework core, fabric, foundation, frame, frame of reference, groundwork, plan, schema, shell, skeleton, structure, the bare bones

franchise authorization, charter, exemption, freedom, immunity, prerogative, privilege, right, suffrage, vote

frank artless, blunt, candid, direct, downright, forthright, free, honest, ingenuous, open, outright, outspoken, plain, plain-spoken, round, sincere, straightforward, straight from the shoulder (*informal*), transparent, truthful, unconcealed, undisguised, unreserved, unrestricted, upfront (*informal*)
▷ **Antonyms** artful, crafty, cunning, evasive, indirect, inscrutable, reserved, reticent, secretive, shifty, shy, underhand

frankly **1.** candidly, honestly, in truth, to be honest **2.** bluntly, directly, freely, openly, overtly, plainly, straight, straight from the shoulder, without reserve

frankness absence of reserve, bluntness, candour, forthrightness, ingenuousness, laying it on the line, openness, outspokenness, plain speaking, truthfulness

frantic at one's wits' end, at the end of one's tether, berserk, beside oneself, desperate, distracted, distraught, fraught (*informal*), frenetic, frenzied, furious, hectic, mad, overwrought, raging, raving, uptight (*informal*), wild
▷ **Antonyms** calm, collected, composed, cool, laid-back, poised, self-possessed, together (*slang*), unfazed (*informal*), unruffled

fraternity association, brotherhood, camaraderie, circle, clan, club, companionship, company, comradeship, fellowship, guild, kinship, league, order, set, sodality, union

fraternize associate, concur, consort, cooperate, go around with, hang out (*informal*), hobnob, keep company, mingle, mix, socialize, sympathize, unite
▷ **Antonyms** avoid, eschew, keep away from, shun, steer clear of

fraud **1.** artifice, canard, cheat, chicane, chicanery, craft, deceit, deception, double-dealing, duplicity, guile, hoax, humbug, imposture, scam (*slang*), sharp practice, spuriousness, sting (*informal*), stratagems, swindling, treachery, trickery **2.** bluffer, charlatan, cheat, counterfeit, double-dealer, fake, forgery, fraudster, grifter (*slang, chiefly U.S. & Canad.*), hoax, hoaxer, impostor, mountebank, phoney *or* phony (*informal*), pretender, quack, sham, swindler
▷ **Antonyms** (*sense 1*) fairness, good faith, honesty, integrity, probity, rectitude, trustworthiness, virtue

fraudulent counterfeit, crafty, criminal, crooked (*informal*), deceitful, deceptive, dishonest, double-dealing, duplicitous, false, knavish, phoney *or* phony (*informal*), sham, spurious, swindling, treacherous
▷ **Antonyms** above board, genuine, honest, honourable, lawful, principled, reputable, true, trustworthy, upright

fraught **1.** (*with* **with**) abounding, accompanied, attended, bristling, charged, filled, full, heavy, laden, replete, stuffed

2. *informal* agitated, anxious, difficult, distracted, distressed, distressing, emotionally charged, emotive, hag-ridden, on tenterhooks, strung-up, tense, tricky, trying, uptight (*informal*), wired (*slang*)

fray[1] *noun* affray (*Law*), *bagarre,* battle, battle royal, brawl, broil, clash, combat, conflict, disturbance, donnybrook, fight, melee *or* mêlée, quarrel, riot, row, ruckus (*informal*), rumble (*U.S. & N.Z. slang*), rumpus, scrimmage, scuffle, set-to (*informal*), shindig (*informal*), shindy (*informal*), skirmish

fray[2] *verb* become threadbare, chafe, fret, rub, wear, wear away, wear thin

frayed frazzled, out at elbows, ragged, tattered, threadbare, worn

freak *noun* **1.** aberration, abnormality, abortion, anomaly, grotesque, malformation, monster, monstrosity, mutant, oddity, queer fish (*Brit. informal*), *rara avis,* sport (*Biology*), teratism, weirdo *or* weirdie (*informal*) **2.** caprice, crotchet, fad, fancy, folly, humour, irregularity, quirk, turn, twist, vagary, whim, whimsy **3.** *slang* addict, aficionado, buff (*informal*), devotee, enthusiast, fan, fanatic, fiend (*informal*), nut (*slang*) ~*adjective* **4.** aberrant, abnormal, atypical, bizarre, erratic, exceptional, fluky (*informal*), fortuitous, odd, queer, unaccountable, unexpected, unforeseen, unparalleled, unpredictable, unusual

freakish 1. arbitrary, capricious, changeable, erratic, fanciful, fitful, humorous, odd, unpredictable, vagarious (*rare*), wayward, whimsical **2.** aberrant, abnormal, fantastic, freaky (*slang*), grotesque, malformed, monstrous, odd, outlandish, *outré,* preternatural, strange, teratoid (*Biology*), unconventional, weird

freaky abnormal, bizarre, crazy, far-out (*slang*), freakish, odd, queer, rum (*Brit. slang*), strange, unconventional, weird, wild

free *adjective* **1.** buckshee (*Brit. slang*), complimentary, for free (*informal*), for nothing, free of charge, gratis, gratuitous, on the house, unpaid, without charge **2.** at large, at liberty, footloose, independent, liberated, loose, off the hook (*slang*), on the loose, uncommitted, unconstrained, unengaged, unfettered, unrestrained **3.** able, allowed, clear, disengaged, loose, open, permitted, unattached, unengaged, unhampered, unimpeded, unobstructed, unregulated, unrestricted, untrammelled **4.** (*with* **of**) above, beyond, deficient in, devoid of, exempt from, immune to, lacking (in), not liable to, safe from, sans (*archaic*), unaffected by, unencumbered by, untouched by, without **5.** autarchic, autonomous, democratic, emancipated, independent, self-governing, self-ruling, sovereign **6.** at leisure, available, empty, extra, idle, not tied down, spare, unemployed, uninhabited, unoccupied, unused, vacant **7.** casual, easy, familiar, forward, frank, free and easy, informal, laid-back (*informal*), lax, liberal, loose, natural, open, relaxed, spontaneous, unbidden, unceremonious, unconstrained, unforced, uninhibited **8.** big (*informal*), bounteous, bountiful, charitable, eager, generous, hospitable, lavish, liberal, munificent, open-handed, prodigal, unsparing, unstinting, willing **9. free and easy** casual, easy-going, informal, laid-back (*informal*), lax, lenient, liberal, relaxed, tolerant, unceremonious ~*adverb* **10.** at no cost, for love, gratis, without charge **11.** abundantly, copiously, freely, idly, loosely ~*verb* **12.** deliver, discharge, disenthrall, emancipate, let go, let out, liberate, loose, manumit, release, set at liberty, set free, turn loose, unbridle, uncage, unchain, unfetter, unleash, untie **13.** clear, cut loose, deliver, disengage, disentangle, exempt, extricate, ransom, redeem, relieve, rescue, rid, unburden, undo, unshackle

▷ **Antonyms** (*senses 2 & 3*) bound, captive, confined, dependent, fettered, immured, incarcerated, occupied, restrained, restricted, secured (*sense 7*) constrained, formal, official, stiff, unnatural (*sense 8*) close, mean, mingy (*informal*), stingy, tight, ungenerous (*senses 12 & 13*) confine, imprison, incarcerate, inhibit, limit, restrain, restrict, straiten

freebooter bandit, brigand, buccaneer, cateran (*Scot.*), highwayman, looter, marauder, pillager, pirate, plunderer, raider, reiver (*dialect*), robber, rover

freedom 1. autonomy, deliverance, emancipation, home rule, independence, liberty, manumission, release, self-government **2.** exemption, immunity, impunity, privilege **3.** ability, a free hand, blank cheque, carte blanche, discretion, elbowroom, facility, flexibility, free rein, latitude, leeway, licence, opportunity, play, power, range, scope **4.** abandon, candour, directness, ease, familiarity, frankness, informality, ingenuousness, lack of restraint *or* reserve, openness, unconstraint **5.** boldness, brazenness, disrespect, forwardness, impertinence, laxity, licence, overfamiliarity, presumption

▷ **Antonyms** (*sense 1*) bondage, captivity, dependence, imprisonment, servitude, slavery, thraldom (*sense 3*) limitation, restriction (*sense 4*) caution, restraint (*sense 5*) respectfulness

free-for-all affray (*Law*), *bagarre,* brawl, donnybrook, dust-up (*informal*), fight, fracas, melee *or* mêlée, riot, row, scrimmage, shindig (*informal*), shindy (*informal*)

free hand *noun* authority, blank cheque, carte blanche, discretion, freedom, latitude, liberty, scope

freely **1.** of one's own accord, of one's own free will, spontaneously, voluntarily, willingly, without prompting **2.** candidly, frankly, openly, plainly, unreservedly, without reserve **3.** as you please, unchallenged, without let or hindrance, without restraint **4.** abundantly, amply, bountifully, copiously, extravagantly, lavishly, liberally, like water, open-handedly, unstintingly, with a free hand **5.** cleanly, easily, loosely, readily, smoothly

freethinker agnostic, deist, doubter, infidel, sceptic, unbeliever

freewheel coast, drift, float, glide, relax one's efforts, rest on one's oars

freeze **1.** benumb, chill, congeal, glaciate, harden, ice over *or* up, stiffen **2.** fix, hold up, inhibit, peg, stop, suspend

freezing arctic, biting, bitter, chill, chilled, cold as ice, cutting, frost-bound, frosty, glacial, icy, numbing, parky (*Brit. informal*), penetrating, polar, raw, Siberian, wintry

freight *noun* **1.** carriage, conveyance, shipment, transportation **2.** bales, bulk, burden, cargo, consignment, contents, goods, haul, lading, load, merchandise, payload, tonnage

French Gallic

frenetic demented, distraught, excited, fanatical, frantic, frenzied, hyped up (*slang*), insane, mad, maniacal, obsessive, overwrought, unbalanced, wild

frenzied agitated, all het up (*informal*), berserk, convulsive, distracted, distraught, excited, feverish, frantic, frenetic, furious, hysterical, mad, maniacal, rabid, uncontrolled, wild

frenzy **1.** aberration, agitation, delirium, derangement, distraction, fury, hysteria, insanity, lunacy, madness, mania, paroxysm, passion, rage, seizure, transport, turmoil **2.** bout, burst, convulsion, fit, outburst, paroxysm, spasm
▷ **Antonyms** (*sense 1*) calm, collectedness, composure, coolness, sanity

frequency constancy, frequentness, periodicity, prevalence, recurrence, repetition

frequent[1] *adjective* common, constant, continual, customary, everyday, familiar, habitual, incessant, numerous, persistent, recurrent, recurring, reiterated, repeated, usual
▷ **Antonyms** few, few and far between, infrequent, occasional, rare, scanty, sporadic

frequent[2] *verb* attend, be a regular customer of, be found at, hang out at (*informal*), haunt, patronize, resort, visit
▷ **Antonyms** avoid, keep away, shun, spurn

frequenter client, fan, habitué, haunter, patron, regular, regular customer, regular visitor

frequently commonly, customarily, habitually, many a time, many times, much, not infrequently, oft (*archaic or poetic*), often, oftentimes (*archaic*), over and over again, repeatedly, thick and fast, very often
▷ **Antonyms** hardly ever, infrequently, occasionally, once in a blue moon (*informal*), rarely, seldom

fresh **1.** different, ground-breaking, latest, left-field (*informal*), modern, modernistic, new, new-fangled, novel, original, recent, this season's, unconventional, unusual, up-to-date **2.** added, additional, auxiliary, extra, further, more, other, renewed, supplementary **3.** bracing, bright, brisk, clean, clear, cool, crisp, invigorating, pure, refreshing, spanking, sparkling, stiff, sweet, unpolluted **4.** alert, bouncing, bright, bright-eyed and bushy-tailed (*informal*), chipper (*informal*), energetic, full of beans (*informal*), full of vim and vigour (*informal*), invigorated, keen, like a new man, lively, refreshed, rested, restored, revived, sprightly, spry, vigorous, vital **5.** blooming, clear, fair, florid, glowing, good, hardy, healthy, rosy, ruddy, wholesome **6.** dewy, undimmed, unfaded, unwearied, unwithered, verdant, vivid, young **7.** artless, callow, green, inexperienced, natural, new, raw, uncultivated, untrained, untried, youthful **8.** crude, green, natural, raw, uncured, undried, unprocessed, unsalted **9.** *informal* bold, brazen, cheeky, disrespectful, familiar, flip (*informal*), forward, impudent, insolent, pert, presumptuous, sassy (*U.S. informal*), saucy, smart-alecky (*informal*)
▷ **Antonyms** (*sense 1*) dull, old, ordinary, stereotyped, trite (*sense 3*) impure, musty, stale, warm (*sense 4*) exhausted, weary (*sense 5*) pallid, sickly (*sense 6*) old, weary (*sense 7*) experienced, old (*sense 8*) preserved, salted, tinned (*sense 9*) well-mannered

freshen **1.** enliven, freshen up, liven up, refresh, restore, revitalize, rouse, spruce up, titivate **2.** air, purify, ventilate

freshness **1.** innovativeness, inventiveness, newness, novelty, originality **2.** bloom, brightness, cleanness, clearness, dewiness, glow, shine, sparkle, vigour, wholesomeness

fret[1] *verb* **1.** affront, agonize, anguish, annoy, brood, chagrin, goad, grieve, harass, irritate, lose sleep over, provoke, ruffle, torment, upset *or* distress oneself, worry **2.** agitate, bother, distress, disturb, gall, irk, nag, nettle, peeve (*informal*), pique, rankle with, rile, trouble, vex

fret[2] *verb* abrade, chafe, erode, fray, gall, rub, wear, wear away

fretful captious, complaining, cross, crotchety (*informal*), edgy, fractious, irritable, out of sorts, peevish, petulant, querulous, ratty (*Brit. & N.Z. informal*), short-tempered, splenetic, testy, tetchy, touchy, uneasy

friable brittle, crisp, crumbly, powdery, pulverizable

friction 1. abrasion, attrition, chafing, erosion, fretting, grating, irritation, rasping, resistance, rubbing, scraping, wearing away **2.** animosity, antagonism, bad blood, bad feeling, bickering, conflict, disagreement, discontent, discord, disharmony, dispute, dissension, hostility, incompatibility, opposition, resentment, rivalry, wrangling

friend 1. Achates, alter ego, boon companion, bosom friend, buddy (*informal*), china (*Brit. slang*), chum (*informal*), cock (*Brit. informal*), companion, comrade, confidant, crony, familiar, homeboy (*slang, chiefly U.S.*), intimate, mate (*informal*), pal, partner, playmate, soul mate **2.** adherent, advocate, ally, associate, backer, benefactor, partisan, patron, protagonist, supporter, well-wisher
▷ **Antonyms** adversary, antagonist, competitor, enemy, foe, opponent, rival

friendless abandoned, alienated, all alone, alone, cut off, deserted, estranged, forlorn, forsaken, isolated, lonely, lonesome, ostracized, shunned, solitary, unattached, with no one to turn to, without a friend in the world, without ties

friendliness affability, amiability, companionability, congeniality, conviviality, geniality, kindliness, mateyness *or* matiness (*Brit. informal*), neighbourliness, open arms, sociability, warmth

friendly affable, affectionate, amiable, amicable, attached, attentive, auspicious, beneficial, benevolent, benign, buddy-buddy (*slang, chiefly U.S. & Canad.*), chummy (*informal*), close, clubby, companionable, comradely, conciliatory, confiding, convivial, cordial, familiar, favourable, fond, fraternal, genial, good, helpful, intimate, kind, kindly, matey *or* maty (*Brit. informal*), neighbourly, on good terms, on visiting terms, outgoing, pally (*informal*), palsy-walsy (*informal*), peaceable, propitious, receptive, sociable, sympathetic, thick (*informal*), welcoming, well-disposed
▷ **Antonyms** antagonistic, belligerent, cold, contentious, distant, inauspicious, sinister, uncongenial, unfriendly

friendship affection, affinity, alliance, amity, attachment, benevolence, closeness, concord, familiarity, fondness, friendliness, good-fellowship, goodwill, harmony, intimacy, love, rapport, regard
▷ **Antonyms** animosity, antagonism, antipathy, aversion, bad blood, conflict, enmity, hatred, hostility, resentment, strife, unfriendliness

fright 1. alarm, apprehension, (blue) funk (*informal*), cold sweat, consternation, dismay, dread, fear, fear and trembling, horror, panic, quaking, scare, shock, terror, the shivers, trepidation **2.** *informal* eyesore, frump, mess (*informal*), scarecrow, sight (*informal*)
▷ **Antonyms** boldness, bravery, courage, pluck, valor

frighten affright (*archaic*), alarm, appal, cow, daunt, dismay, freeze one's blood, intimidate, make one's blood run cold, make one's hair stand on end (*informal*), make (someone) jump out of his skin (*informal*), petrify, put the wind up (someone) (*informal*), scare, scare (someone) stiff, scare the living daylights out of (someone) (*informal*), shock, startle, terrify, terrorize, throw into a fright, throw into a panic, unman, unnerve
▷ **Antonyms** allay, assuage, calm, comfort, encourage, hearten, reassure, soothe

frightened abashed, affrighted (*archaic*), afraid, alarmed, cowed, dismayed, frozen, get the wind up, in a cold sweat, in a panic, in fear and trepidation, numb with fear, panicky, petrified, scared, scared shitless (*taboo slang*), scared stiff, shit-scared (*taboo slang*), startled, terrified, terrorized, terror-stricken, unnerved

frightening alarming, appalling, baleful, bloodcurdling, daunting, dismaying, dreadful, fearful, fearsome, hair-raising, horrifying, intimidating, menacing, scary (*informal*), shocking, spooky (*informal*), terrifying, unnerving

frightful 1. alarming, appalling, awful, dire, dread, dreadful, fearful, from hell (*informal*), ghastly, godawful (*slang*), grim, grisly, gruesome, harrowing, hellacious (*U.S. slang*), hideous, horrendous, horrible, horrid, lurid, macabre, petrifying, shocking, terrible, terrifying, traumatic, unnerving, unspeakable **2.** annoying, awful, disagreeable, dreadful, extreme, great, insufferable, terrible, terrific, unpleasant
▷ **Antonyms** attractive, beautiful, calming, lovely, moderate, nice, pleasant, slight, soothing

frigid 1. arctic, chill, cold, cool, frost-bound, frosty, frozen, gelid, glacial, hyperboreal, icy, Siberian, wintry **2.** aloof, austere, cold as ice, cold-hearted, forbidding, formal, icy, lifeless, passionless, passive, repellent, rigid, stiff, unapproachable, unbending, unfeeling, unloving, unresponsive
▷ **Antonyms** (*sense 1*) hot, stifling, swel~

tering, warm (*sense 2*) ardent, cordial, friendly, hospitable, hot, impassioned, passionate, responsive, sensual, warm

frigidity aloofness, austerity, chill, cold-heartedness, coldness, frostiness, iciness, impassivity, lack of response, lifelessness, passivity, touch-me-not attitude, unapproachability, unresponsiveness, wintriness

frill *noun* flounce, furbelow, gathering, purfle, ruche, ruching, ruff, ruffle, tuck

frills additions, affectation(s), bells and whistles, bits and pieces, decoration(s), dressing up, embellishment(s), extras, fanciness, fandangles, finery, frilliness, frippery, fuss, gewgaws, icing on the cake, jazz (*slang*), mannerisms, nonsense, ornamentation, ostentation, superfluities, tomfoolery, trimmings

frilly fancy, flouncy, frothy, lacy, ruched, ruffled

fringe *noun* **1.** binding, border, edging, hem, tassel, trimming **2.** borderline, edge, limits, march, marches, margin, outskirts, perimeter, periphery *~adjective* **3.** unconventional, unofficial, unorthodox *~verb* **4.** border, edge, enclose, skirt, surround, trim

fringed befringed, bordered, edged, margined, outlined, overhung

frippery **1.** fanciness, finery, flashiness, foppery, frilliness, frills, fussiness, gaudiness, glad rags (*informal*), meretriciousness, nonsense, ostentation, pretentiousness, showiness, tawdriness **2.** adornment, bauble, decoration, fandangle, gewgaw, icing on the cake, knick-knack, ornament, toy, trinket

frisk **1.** bounce, caper, cavort, curvet, dance, frolic, gambol, hop, jump, play, prance, rollick, romp, skip, sport, trip **2.** *informal* check, inspect, run over, search, shake down (*U.S. slang*)

frisky bouncy, coltish, frolicsome, full of beans (*informal*), full of joie de vivre, high-spirited, in high spirits, kittenish, lively, playful, rollicking, romping, spirited, sportive

▷ **Antonyms** demure, dull, lacklustre, pensive, sedate, stodgy, stolid, wooden

fritter (away) dally away, dissipate, fool away, idle (away), misspend, run through, spend like water, squander, waste

frivolity childishness, desipience, flightiness, flippancy, flummery, folly, frivolousness, fun, gaiety, giddiness, jest, levity, light-heartedness, lightness, nonsense, puerility, shallowness, silliness, superficiality, trifling, triviality

▷ **Antonyms** earnestness, gravity, humourlessness, importance, sedateness, seriousness, significance, soberness, sobriety

frivolous **1.** childish, ditsy (*U.S. informal*), dizzy, empty-headed, flighty, flip (*informal*), flippant, foolish, giddy, idle, ill-considered, juvenile, light-minded, nonserious, puerile, silly, superficial **2.** extravagant, footling (*informal*), impractical, light, minor, nickel-and-dime (*U.S. slang*), niggling, paltry, peripheral, petty, pointless, shallow, trifling, trivial, unimportant

▷ **Antonyms** earnest, important, mature, practical, responsible, sensible, serious, solemn, vital

frizzle crisp, fry, hiss, roast, scorch, sizzle, sputter

frizzy corrugated, crimped, crisp, frizzed, tight-curled, wiry

frolic *verb* **1.** caper, cavort, cut capers, frisk, gambol, lark, make merry, play, rollick, romp, sport *~noun* **2.** antic, blast (*U.S. slang*), escapade, gambado, gambol, game, lark, prank, revel, romp, spree **3.** amusement, drollery, fun, fun and games, gaiety, high jinks, merriment, skylarking (*informal*), sport

frolicsome coltish, frisky, full of beans (*informal*), gay, kittenish, lively, merry, playful, rollicking, sportive, sprightly, wanton (*archaic*)

front *noun* **1.** anterior, exterior, façade, face, facing, foreground, forepart, frontage, obverse **2.** beginning, fore, forefront, front line, head, lead, top, van, vanguard **3.** air, appearance, aspect, bearing, countenance, demeanour, expression, exterior, face, manner, mien, show **4.** blind, cover, cover-up, disguise, façade, mask, pretext, show **5. in front** ahead, before, first, in advance, in the lead, in the van, leading, preceding, to the fore *~adjective* **6.** first, foremost, head, headmost, lead, leading, topmost *~verb* **7.** face (onto), look over *or* onto, overlook

▷ **Antonyms** (*senses 1 & 2*) aft, back, back end, behind, hindmost, nethermost, rear

frontier borderland, borderline, bound, boundary, confines, edge, limit, marches, perimeter, verge

frost freeze, freeze-up, hoarfrost, Jack Frost, rime

frosty **1.** chilly, cold, frozen, hoar (*rare*), ice-capped, icicled, icy, parky (*Brit. informal*), rimy, wintry **2.** cold as ice, discouraging, frigid, off-putting (*Brit. informal*), standoffish, unenthusiastic, unfriendly, unwelcoming

froth **1.** *noun* bubbles, effervescence, foam, head, lather, scum, spume, suds **2.** *~verb* bubble over, come to a head, effervesce, fizz, foam, lather

frothy **1.** foaming, foamy, spumescent, spumous, spumy, sudsy **2.** *figurative* empty, frilly, frivolous, light, petty, slight, trifling, trivial, trumpery, unnecessary, unsubstantial, vain

frown 1. give a dirty look, glare, glower, knit one's brows, look daggers, lour *or* lower, scowl **2.** (*with* **on** *or* **upon**) disapprove of, discountenance, discourage, dislike, look askance at, not take kindly to, show disapproval *or* displeasure, take a dim view of, view with disfavour

frowsty close, fuggy, fusty, ill-smelling, musty, stale, stuffy

frowzy blowsy, dirty, draggletailed (*archaic*), frumpy, messy, slatternly, sloppy, slovenly, sluttish, ungroomed, unkempt, untidy, unwashed

frozen 1. arctic, chilled, chilled to the marrow, frigid, frosted, icebound, ice-cold, ice-covered, icy, numb **2.** fixed, pegged (*of prices*), petrified, rooted, stock-still, stopped, suspended, turned to stone

frugal abstemious, careful, cheeseparing, economical, meagre, niggardly, parsimonious, penny-wise, provident, prudent, saving, sparing, thrifty

▷ **Antonyms** excessive, extravagant, imprudent, lavish, luxurious, prodigal, profligate, spendthrift, wasteful

frugality carefulness, conservation, economizing, economy, good management, husbandry, moderation, providence, thrift, thriftiness

fruit 1. crop, harvest, produce, product, yield **2.** advantage, benefit, consequence, effect, end result, outcome, profit, result, return, reward

fruitful 1. fecund, fertile, fructiferous **2.** abundant, copious, flush, plenteous, plentiful, productive, profuse, prolific, rich, spawning **3.** advantageous, beneficial, effective, gainful, productive, profitable, rewarding, successful, useful, well-spent, worthwhile

▷ **Antonyms** barren, fruitless, futile, ineffectual, infertile, pointless, scarce, sterile, unfruitful, unproductive, useless, vain

fruition actualization, attainment, completion, consummation, enjoyment, fulfilment, materialization, maturation, maturity, perfection, realization, ripeness

fruitless abortive, barren, bootless, futile, idle, ineffectual, in vain, pointless, profitless, to no avail, to no effect, unavailing, unfruitful, unproductive, unprofitable, unprolific, unsuccessful, useless, vain

▷ **Antonyms** abundant, effective, fecund, fertile, fruitful, productive, profitable, prolific, useful

fruity 1. full, mellow, resonant, rich **2.** *informal* bawdy, blue, hot, indecent, indelicate, juicy, near the knuckle (*informal*), racy, ripe, risqué, salacious, sexy, smutty, spicy (*informal*), suggestive, titillating, vulgar

frumpy, frumpish badly-dressed, dated, dingy, dowdy, drab, dreary, frumpy, mumsy, out of date

frustrate 1. baffle, balk, block, check, circumvent, confront, counter, defeat, disappoint, foil, forestall, hobble, inhibit, neutralize, nullify, render null and void, stymie, thwart **2.** depress, discourage, dishearten

▷ **Antonyms** (*sense 1*) advance, encourage, endorse, forward, further, promote, satisfy, stimulate (*sense 2*) cheer, encourage, hearten

frustrated carrying a chip on one's shoulder (*informal*), choked, disappointed, discontented, discouraged, disheartened, embittered, foiled, irked, resentful, sick as a parrot (*informal*)

frustration 1. blocking, circumvention, contravention, curbing, failure, foiling, nonfulfilment, nonsuccess, obstruction, thwarting **2.** annoyance, disappointment, dissatisfaction, grievance, irritation, resentment, vexation

fuddled babalas (*S. African*), bevvied (*dialect*), bladdered (*slang*), blitzed (*slang*), blotto (*slang*), bombed (*slang*), Brahms and Liszt (*slang*), confused, drunk, flying (*slang*), inebriated, intoxicated, legless (*informal*), lit up (*slang*), muddled, muzzy, out of it (*slang*), out to it (*Austral. & N.Z. slang*), paralytic (*informal*), pissed (*taboo slang*), rat-arsed (*taboo slang*), smashed (*slang*), sozzled (*informal*), steamboats (*Scot. slang*), steaming (*slang*), stupefied, tipsy, wasted (*slang*), woozy (*informal*), wrecked (*slang*), zonked (*slang*)

fuddy-duddy *noun* back number (*informal*), conservative, dinosaur, dodo (*informal*), fossil, museum piece, (old) fogey, square (*informal*), stick-in-the-mud (*informal*), stuffed shirt (*informal*)

fudge *verb* avoid, cook (*slang*), dodge, equivocate, evade, fake, falsify, flannel (*Brit. informal*), hedge, misrepresent, patch up, shuffle, slant, stall

fuel 1. *noun figurative* ammunition, encouragement, fodder, food, incitement, material, means, nourishment, provocation **2.** *~verb* charge, fan, feed, fire, incite, inflame, nourish, stoke up, sustain

fug fetidity, fetor, frowst, frowstiness, fustiness, reek, stale air, staleness, stink

fuggy airless, fetid, foul, frowsty, noisome, noxious, stale, stuffy, suffocating, unventilated

fugitive 1. *noun* deserter, escapee, refugee, runagate (*archaic*), runaway **2.** *~adjective* brief, ephemeral, evanescent, fleeing, fleeting, flitting, flying, fugacious, momentary, passing, short, short-lived, temporary, transient, transitory, unstable

fulfil accomplish, achieve, answer, bring to completion, carry out, complete, comply with, conclude, conform to, discharge, effect, execute, fill, finish, keep, meet, obey, observe, perfect, perform, realise, satisfy

▷ **Antonyms** disappoint, dissatisfy, fail in, fail to meet, fall short of, neglect

fulfilment accomplishment, achievement, attainment, carrying out *or* through, completion, consummation, crowning, discharge, discharging, effecting, end, implementation, observance, perfection, realization

full 1. brimful, brimming, bursting at the seams, complete, entire, filled, gorged, intact, loaded, replete, sated, satiated, satisfied, saturated, stocked, sufficient **2.** abundant, adequate, all-inclusive, ample, broad, comprehensive, copious, detailed, exhaustive, extensive, generous, maximum, plenary, plenteous, plentiful, thorough, unabridged **3.** chock-a-block, chock-full, crammed, crowded, in use, jammed, occupied, packed, taken **4.** clear, deep, distinct, loud, resonant, rich, rounded **5.** baggy, balloonlike, buxom, capacious, curvaceous, large, loose, plump, puffy, rounded, voluminous, voluptuous **6. in full** completely, in its entirety, in total, *in toto,* without exception **7. to the full** completely, entirely, fully, thoroughly, to the utmost, without reservation

▷ **Antonyms** abridged, blank, devoid, empty, exhausted, faint, incomplete, limited, partial, restricted, thin, tight, vacant, void

full-blooded ballsy (*taboo slang*), gutsy (*slang*), hearty, lusty, mettlesome, red-blooded, vigorous, virile

full-bodied fruity, full-flavoured, heady, heavy, mellow, redolent, rich, strong, well-matured

full-grown adult, developed, full-fledged, grown-up, in one's prime, marriageable, mature, nubile, of age, ripe

▷ **Antonyms** adolescent, green, premature, undeveloped, unfledged, unformed, unripe, untimely, young

fullness 1. abundance, adequateness, ampleness, copiousness, fill, glut, plenty, profusion, repletion, satiety, saturation, sufficiency **2.** broadness, completeness, comprehensiveness, entirety, extensiveness, plenitude, totality, vastness, wealth, wholeness **3.** clearness, loudness, resonance, richness, strength **4.** curvaceousness, dilation, distension, enlargement, roundness, swelling, tumescence, voluptuousness

full-scale all-encompassing, all-out, comprehensive, exhaustive, extensive, full-dress, in-depth, major, proper, sweeping, thorough, thoroughgoing, wide-ranging

fully 1. absolutely, altogether, completely, entirely, every inch, from first to last, heart and soul, in all respects, intimately, lock, stock and barrel, one hundred per cent, perfectly, positively, thoroughly, totally, to the hilt, utterly, wholly **2.** abundantly, adequately, amply, comprehensively, enough, plentifully, satisfactorily, sufficiently **3.** at least, quite, without (any) exaggeration, without a word of a lie (*informal*)

fully-fledged experienced, mature, professional, proficient, qualified, senior, time-served, trained

fulminate animadvert upon, berate, blast, castigate, censure, criticize, curse, denounce, denunciate, excoriate, execrate, fume, inveigh against, lambast(e), protest against, put down, rage, rail against, reprobate, tear into (*informal*), thunder, upbraid, vilify, vituperate

fulmination condemnation, denunciation, diatribe, excoriation, invective, obloquy, philippic, reprobation, tirade

fulsome adulatory, cloying, excessive, extravagant, fawning, gross, icky (*informal*), immoderate, ingratiating, inordinate, insincere, nauseating, overdone, over the top, saccharine, sickening, smarmy (*Brit. informal*), sycophantic, unctuous

fumble 1. bumble, feel around, flounder, grope, paw (*informal*), scrabble **2.** bodge (*informal*), botch, bungle, cock up (*Brit. slang*), fuck up (*offensive taboo slang*), make a hash of (*informal*), make a nonsense of, mess up, misfield, mishandle, mismanage, muff, spoil

fume *figurative* **1.** *verb* blow a fuse (*slang, chiefly U.S.*), boil, chafe, champ at the bit (*informal*), crack up (*informal*), fly off the handle (*informal*), get hot under the collar (*informal*), get steamed up about (*slang*), go ballistic (*slang, chiefly U.S.*), go off the deep end (*informal*), go up the wall (*slang*), rage, rant, rave, see red (*informal*), seethe, smoulder, storm **2.** *~noun* agitation, dither (*chiefly Brit.*), fit, fret, fury, passion, rage, stew (*informal*), storm

fumes effluvium, exhalation, exhaust, gas, haze, miasma, pollution, reek, smog, smoke, stench, vapour

fumigate clean out *or* up, cleanse, disinfect, purify, sanitize, sterilize

fuming all steamed up (*slang*), angry, at boiling point (*informal*), choked, enraged, foaming at the mouth, in a rage, incensed, on the warpath (*informal*), raging, roused, seething, up in arms

fun *noun* **1.** amusement, beer and skittles (*informal*), cheer, distraction, diversion, enjoyment, entertainment, frolic, gaiety, good time, high jinks, jollification, jollity, joy, junketing, living it up, merriment, merrymaking, mirth, pleasure, recreation, romp, sport, treat, whoopee (*informal*) **2.** buffoonery, clowning, foolery, game, horseplay, jesting, jocularity, joking, nonsense, play, playfulness, skylarking (*informal*), sport, teasing, tomfoolery **3. in** *or* **for fun** facetiously, for a joke, for a laugh, in jest, jokingly, light-heartedly, mischievously, playfully, roguishly, teasingly, tongue in cheek, with a gleam *or* twinkle in one's eye, with a straight face **4. make fun of** deride, hold up to ridicule, lampoon, laugh at, make a fool of, make a monkey of, make game of, make sport of, make the butt of, mock, parody, poke fun at, rag, rib (*informal*), ridicule, satirize, scoff at, send up (*Brit. informal*), sneer at, take off, take the piss out of (*taboo slang*), taunt *~adjective* **5.** amusing, convivial, diverting, enjoyable, entertaining, lively, witty

▷ **Antonyms** (*sense 1*) depression, desolation, despair, distress, gloom, grief, melancholy, misery, sadness, sorrow, unhappiness, woe

function *noun* **1.** activity, business, capacity, charge, concern, duty, employment, exercise, job, mission, occupation, office, operation, part, post, province, purpose, raison d'être, responsibility, role, situation, task *~verb* **2.** act, act the part of, behave, be in business, be in commission, be in operation *or* action, be in running order, do duty, go, officiate, operate, perform, run, serve, serve one's turn, work *~noun* **3.** affair, do (*informal*), gathering, lig (*Brit. slang*), reception, social occasion

functional hard-wearing, operative, practical, serviceable, useful, utilitarian, utility, working

functionary dignitary, employee, office bearer, office holder, officer, official

fund *noun* **1.** capital, endowment, fall-back, foundation, kitty, pool, reserve, stock, store, supply **2.** hoard, mine, repository, reserve, reservoir, source, storehouse, treasury, vein *~verb* **3.** capitalize, endow, finance, float, pay for, promote, stake, subsidize, support

fundamental 1. *adjective* basic, cardinal, central, constitutional, crucial, elementary, essential, first, important, indispensable, integral, intrinsic, key, necessary, organic, primary, prime, principal, radical, rudimentary, underlying, vital **2.** *~noun* axiom, basic, cornerstone, essential, first principle, law, principle, rudiment, rule, *sine qua non*

▷ **Antonyms** advanced, back-up, extra, incidental, lesser, secondary, subsidiary, superfluous

fundamentally at bottom, at heart, basically, essentially, intrinsically, primarily, radically

funds 1. ackers (*slang*), brass (*Northern English dialect*), bread (*slang*), capital, cash, dibs (*slang*), dosh (*Brit. & Austral. slang*), dough (*slang*), finance, hard cash, money, necessary (*informal*), needful (*informal*), ready money, resources, rhino (*Brit. slang*), savings, shekels (*informal*), silver, spondulicks (*slang*), the ready (*informal*), the wherewithal, tin (*slang*) **2. in funds** flush (*informal*), in the black, solvent, well-off, well-supplied

funeral burial, cremation, inhumation, interment, obsequies

funereal dark, deathlike, depressing, dirgelike, dismal, dreary, gloomy, grave, lamenting, lugubrious, mournful, sad, sepulchral, solemn, sombre, woeful

funk 1. *verb* chicken out of (*informal*), dodge, duck out of (*informal*), flinch from, recoil from, take fright, turn tail **2. be in a (blue) funk** be in a cold sweat, be in a panic, be scared stiff, be sick with fear, cower, dread, fear, quail, quake, quiver, shake at the knees, shrink, tremble, tremble in one's boots

funnel *verb* channel, conduct, convey, direct, filter, move, pass, pour

funny *adjective* **1.** absurd, amusing, a card (*informal*), a caution (*informal*), a scream, comic, comical, diverting, droll, entertaining, facetious, farcical, hilarious, humorous, jocose, jocular, jolly, killing (*informal*), laughable, ludicrous, rich, ridiculous, riotous, risible, side-splitting, silly, slapstick, waggish, witty **2.** curious, dubious, mysterious, odd, peculiar, perplexing, puzzling, queer, remarkable, rum (*Brit. slang*), strange, suspicious, unusual, weird *~noun* **3.** *informal* crack (*slang*), jest, joke, play on words, pun, quip, wisecrack, witticism

▷ **Antonyms** (*sense 1*) grave, humourless, melancholy, serious, sober, solemn, stern, unfunny

furbish brighten, burnish, gussy up (*slang, chiefly U.S.*), polish, renovate, restore, rub, shine, smarten up, spruce up

furious 1. angry, beside oneself, boiling, choked, cross, enraged, foaming at the mouth, frantic, frenzied, fuming, incensed, infuriated, in high dudgeon, livid (*informal*), mad, maddened, on the warpath (*informal*), raging, up in arms, wrathful, wroth (*archaic*) **2.** agitated, boisterous, fierce, impetuous, intense, savage, stormy, tempestuous, tumultuous, turbulent, ungovernable, unrestrained, vehement, violent, wild

▷ **Antonyms** calm, dispassionate, impassive, imperturbable, mild, placated, pleased, serene, tranquil

furnish 1. appoint, decorate, equip, fit, fit out, fit up, outfit, provide, provision, purvey, rig, stock, store, supply **2.** afford, bestow, endow, give, grant, hand out, offer, present, provide, reveal, supply

furniture appliances, appointments, chattels, effects, equipment, fittings, furnishings, goods, household goods, movable property, movables, possessions, things (*informal*)

furore 1. brouhaha, commotion, disturbance, excitement, flap (*informal*), frenzy, fury, hullabaloo, outburst, outcry, stir, to-do, uproar **2.** craze, enthusiasm, mania, rage

furrow 1. *noun* channel, corrugation, crease, crow's-foot, fluting, groove, hollow, line, rut, seam, trench, wrinkle **2.** *~verb* corrugate, crease, draw together, flute, knit, seam, wrinkle

further 1. *adjective* additional, extra, fresh, more, new, other, supplementary **2.** *~adverb* additionally, also, as well as, besides, furthermore, in addition, into the bargain, moreover, on top of, over and above, to boot, what's more, yet **3.** *~verb* advance, aid, assist, champion, contribute to, encourage, expedite, facilitate, forward, foster, hasten, help, lend support to, patronize, pave the way for, plug (*informal*), promote, push, speed, succour, work for

▷ **Antonyms** *~verb* foil, frustrate, hinder, hobble, impede, obstruct, oppose, prevent, retard, stop, thwart

furtherance advancement, advocacy, backing, boosting, carrying-out, championship, promotion, prosecution, pursuit

furthermore additionally, as well, besides, further, in addition, into the bargain, moreover, not to mention, to boot, too, what's more

furthest extreme, farthest, furthermost, most distant, outermost, outmost, remotest, ultimate, uttermost

furtive behind someone's back, clandestine, cloaked, conspiratorial, covert, hidden, secret, secretive, skulking, slinking, sly, sneaking, sneaky, stealthy, surreptitious, underhand, under-the-table

▷ **Antonyms** above-board, candid, forthright, frank, open, public, straightforward, undisguised, unreserved

fury 1. anger, frenzy, impetuosity, ire, madness, passion, rage, red mist (*informal*), wrath **2.** ferocity, fierceness, force, intensity, power, savagery, severity, tempestuousness, turbulence, vehemence, violence **3.** bacchante, hag, hellcat, shrew, spitfire, termagant, virago, vixen

▷ **Antonyms** calm, calmness, composure, equanimity, hush, peace, peacefulness, serenity, stillness, tranquillity

fuse *verb* agglutinate, amalgamate, blend, coalesce, combine, commingle, dissolve, federate, integrate, intermingle, intermix, join, meld, melt, merge, run together, smelt, solder, unite, weld

▷ **Antonyms** diffuse, dispense, disseminate, dissipate, disunite, scatter, separate, spread, strew

fusillade barrage, broadside, burst, fire, hail, outburst, salvo, volley

fusion alloy, amalgam, amalgamation, blend, blending, coalescence, commingling, commixture, federation, integration, liquefaction, meld, merger, merging, mixture, smelting, synthesis, union, uniting, welding

fuss *noun* **1.** ado, agitation, bother, bustle, commotion, confusion, excitement, fidget, flap (*informal*), flurry, fluster, flutter, hue and cry, hurry, palaver, pother, stir, storm in a teacup (*Brit.*), to-do, upset, worry **2.** altercation, argument, bother, complaint, difficulty, display, furore, hassle (*informal*), objection, row, squabble, trouble, unrest, upset *~verb* **3.** bustle, chafe, fidget, flap (*informal*), fret, fume, get in a stew (*informal*), get worked up, labour over, make a meal of (*informal*), make a thing of (*informal*), niggle, take pains, worry

fusspot fidget, fussbudget (*U.S.*), nit-picker (*informal*), old woman, perfectionist, worrier

fussy 1. choosy (*informal*), dainty, difficult, discriminating, exacting, faddish, faddy, fastidious, finicky, hard to please, nit-picking (*informal*), old-maidish, old womanish, overparticular, particular, pernickety, picky (*informal*), squeamish **2.** busy, cluttered, overdecorated, overelaborate, overembellished, overworked, rococo

fustiness airlessness, dampness, frowstiness, fug, mouldiness, mustiness, smell of decay, staleness, stuffiness

fusty 1. airless, damp, frowsty, ill-smelling, malodorous, mildewed, mildewy, mouldering, mouldy, musty, rank, stale, stuffy **2.** antediluvian, antiquated, archaic, old-fashioned, old-fogeyish, outdated, out-of-date, out of the ark (*informal*), passé

futile 1. abortive, barren, bootless, empty, forlorn, fruitless, hollow, ineffectual, in vain, nugatory, otiose, profitless, sterile, to no avail, unavailing, unproductive, unprofitable, unsuccessful, useless, vain, valueless, without rhyme or reason, worthless **2.** idle, pointless, trifling, trivial, unimportant, wanky (*taboo slang*)

▷ **Antonyms** constructive, effective, fruitful, profitable, purposeful, significant, successful, useful, valuable, worthwhile

futility 1. bootlessness, emptiness, fruitlessness, hollowness, ineffectiveness, spitting in the wind, uselessness **2.** pointlessness, triviality, unimportance, vanity

future 1. *noun* expectation, hereafter, outlook, prospect, time to come **2.** *~adjective* approaching, coming, des~

tined, eventual, expected, fated, forth~coming, impending, in the offing, later, prospective, subsequent, to be, to come, ultimate, unborn

▷ **Antonyms** *~adjective* bygone, erst~while, ex-, former, late, past, preceding, previous, quondam

fuzz down, fibre, floss, fluff, hair, lint, nap, pile

fuzzy **1.** down-covered, downy, flossy, fluffy, frizzy, linty, napped, woolly **2.** bleary, blurred, distorted, faint, ill-defined, indistinct, muffled, out of focus, shadowy, unclear, unfocused, vague

▷ **Antonyms** (*sense 2*) clear, defined, de~tailed, distinct, in focus, precise

G, g

gab 1. *verb* babble, blabber, blather, buzz, chatter, chew the fat *or* rag (*slang*), gossip, jabber, jaw (*slang*), prattle, rabbit (*Brit. informal*), run off at the mouth (*slang*), spout, talk, waffle (*informal, chiefly Brit.*), yak (*slang*) **2.** *~noun* blab, blarney, blather, chat, chatter, chitchat, conversation, gossip, loquacity, palaver, small talk, talk, tête-à-tête, tittle-tattle, tongue-wagging, waffle (*informal, chiefly Brit.*), yackety-yak (*slang*), yak (*slang*)

gabble 1. *verb* babble, blab, blabber, cackle, chatter, gaggle, gibber, gush, jabber, prattle, rabbit (*Brit. informal*), rattle, run off at the mouth (*slang*), splutter, spout, sputter, waffle (*informal, chiefly Brit.*) **2.** *~noun* babble, blabber, cackling, chatter, drivel, gibberish, jargon, pap, prattle, twaddle, waffle (*informal, chiefly Brit.*)

gabby chatty, effusive, garrulous, glib, gossiping, gushing, long-winded, loquacious, mouthy, prattling, prolix, talkative, verbose, voluble, windy, wordy

gad (about *or* **around)** gallivant, ramble, range, roam, rove, run around, stravaig (*Scot. & northern English dialect*), stray, traipse (*informal*), wander

gadabout gallivanter, pleasure-seeker, rambler, rover, wanderer

gadget appliance, contraption (*informal*), contrivance, device, gimmick, gizmo (*slang, chiefly U.S.*), instrument, invention, novelty, thing, tool

gaffe bloomer (*informal*), blunder, boob (*Brit. slang*), boo-boo (*informal*), clanger (*informal*), faux pas, gaucherie, howler, indiscretion, lapse, mistake, slip, solecism

gaffer 1. granddad, greybeard, old boy (*informal*), old fellow, old man, old-timer (*U.S.*) **2.** *informal* boss (*informal*), foreman, ganger, manager, overseer, superintendent, supervisor

gag[1] *verb* **1.** curb, muffle, muzzle, quiet, silence, stifle, still, stop up, suppress, throttle **2.** *slang* barf (*slang*), disgorge, heave, puke (*slang*), retch, spew, throw up (*informal*), vomit **3.** *slang* choke, gasp, pant, struggle for breath

gag[2] *noun* crack (*slang*), funny (*informal*), hoax, jest, joke, wisecrack (*informal*), witticism

gage *noun* **1.** bond, deposit, earnest, guarantee, pawn, pledge, security, surety, token **2.** challenge, dare, defiance, gauntlet, glove

gaiety 1. animation, blitheness, blithesomeness (*literary*), cheerfulness, effervescence, elation, exhilaration, glee, good humour, high spirits, hilarity, *joie de vivre,* jollity, joviality, joyousness, light-heartedness, liveliness, merriment, mirth, sprightliness, vivacity **2.** celebration, conviviality, festivity, fun, jollification, merrymaking, revelry, revels **3.** brightness, brilliance, colour, colourfulness, gaudiness, glitter, show, showiness, sparkle

▷ **Antonyms** despondency, gloom, melancholy, misery, sadness

gaily 1. blithely, cheerfully, gleefully, happily, joyfully, light-heartedly, merrily **2.** brightly, brilliantly, colourfully, flamboyantly, flashily, gaudily, showily

gain *verb* **1.** achieve, acquire, advance, attain, bag, build up, capture, collect, enlist, gather, get, glean, harvest, improve, increase, land, net, obtain, pick up, procure, profit, realize, reap, score (*slang*), secure, win, win over **2.** acquire, bring in, clear, earn, get, make, net, obtain, produce, realize, win, yield **3.** (*usually with* **on:**) **a.** approach, catch up with, close with, get nearer, narrow the gap, overtake **b.** draw *or* pull away from, get farther away, leave behind, outdistance, recede, widen the gap **4.** arrive at, attain, come to, get to, reach **5.** **gain time** delay, procrastinate, stall, temporize, use delaying tactics *~noun* **6.** accretion, achievement, acquisition, advance, advancement, advantage, attainment, benefit, dividend, earnings, emolument, growth, headway, improvement, income, increase, increment, lucre, proceeds, produce, profit, progress, return, rise, winnings, yield

▷ **Antonyms** *~verb* fail, forfeit, lose, worsen *~noun* damage, forfeiture, injury, loss, privation

gainful advantageous, beneficial, expedient, fruitful, lucrative, moneymaking, paying, productive, profitable, remunerative, rewarding, useful, worthwhile

gains booty, earnings, gainings, pickings,

prize, proceeds, profits, revenue, takings, winnings

gainsay contradict, contravene, controvert, deny, disaffirm, disagree with, dispute, rebut, retract

▷ **Antonyms** agree with, back, confirm, support

gait bearing, carriage, pace, step, stride, tread, walk

gala **1.** *noun* beano (*Brit. slang*), carnival, celebration, festival, festivity, fête, hooley *or* hoolie (*chiefly Irish & N.Z.*), jamboree, pageant, party, rave (*Brit. slang*), rave-up (*Brit. slang*) **2.** *~adjective* celebratory, convivial, festal, festive, gay, jovial, joyful, merry

gale **1.** blast, cyclone, hurricane, squall, storm, tempest, tornado, typhoon **2.** *informal* burst, eruption, explosion, fit, howl, outbreak, outburst, peal, shout, shriek

gall[1] *noun* **1.** *informal* brass (*informal*), brass neck (*Brit. informal*), brazenness, cheek (*informal*), chutzpah (*U.S. & Canad. informal*), effrontery, face (*informal*), impertinence, impudence, insolence, neck (*informal*), nerve (*informal*), sassiness (*U.S. informal*), sauciness **2.** acrimony, animosity, animus, antipathy, bad blood, bile, bitterness, enmity, hostility, malevolence, malice, malignity, rancour, sourness, spite, spleen, venom

gall[2] *noun* **1.** abrasion, chafe, excoriation, raw spot, scrape, sore, sore spot, wound **2.** aggravation (*informal*), annoyance, bother, botheration (*informal*), exasperation, harassment, irritant, irritation, nuisance, pest, provocation, vexation *~verb* **3.** abrade, bark, chafe, excoriate, fret, graze, irritate, rub raw, scrape, skin **4.** aggravate (*informal*), annoy, be on one's back (*slang*), bother, exasperate, fret, get in one's hair (*informal*), get on one's nerves (*informal*), harass, hassle (*informal*), irk, irritate, nag, nark (*Brit., Austral., & N.Z. slang*), nettle, peeve (*informal*), pester, piss one off (*taboo slang*), plague, provoke, rankle, rile (*informal*), rub up the wrong way, ruffle, vex

gallant *adjective* **1.** bold, brave, courageous, daring, dashing, dauntless, doughty, fearless, game (*informal*), heroic, high-spirited, honourable, intrepid, lion-hearted, manful, manly, mettlesome, noble, plucky, valiant, valorous **2.** attentive, chivalrous, courteous, courtly, gentlemanly, gracious, magnanimous, noble, polite **3.** august, dignified, elegant, glorious, grand, imposing, lofty, magnificent, noble, splendid, stately *~noun* **4.** admirer, beau, boyfriend, escort, leman (*archaic*), lover, paramour, suitor, wooer **5.** beau, blade (*archaic*), buck (*informal*), dandy, fop, ladies' man, lady-killer (*informal*), man about town, man of fashion **6.** adventurer, cavalier, champion, daredevil, hero, knight, man of mettle, *preux chevalier*

▷ **Antonyms** (*sense 1*) cowardly, fearful, ignoble (*sense 2*) churlish, discourteous, ill-mannered, impolite, rude

gallantry **1.** audacity, boldness, bravery, courage, courageousness, daring, dauntlessness, derring-do (*archaic*), fearlessness, heroism, intrepidity, manliness, mettle, nerve, pluck, prowess, spirit, valiance, valour **2.** attentiveness, chivalry, courteousness, courtesy, courtliness, elegance, gentlemanliness, graciousness, nobility, politeness

▷ **Antonyms** (*sense 1*) cowardice, irresolution (*sense 2*) churlishness, discourtesy, rudeness, ungraciousness

galling aggravating (*informal*), annoying, bitter, bothersome, exasperating, harassing, humiliating, irksome, irritating, nettlesome, plaguing, provoking, rankling, vexatious, vexing

gallivant gad about, ramble, range, roam, rove, run around, stravaig (*Scot. & northern English dialect*), stray, traipse (*informal*), wander

gallop barrel (along) (*informal, chiefly U.S. & Canad.*), bolt, career, dart, dash, fly, hasten, hie (*archaic*), hurry, race, run, rush, scud, shoot, speed, sprint, tear along, zoom

galore à gogo (*informal*), all over the place, aplenty, everywhere, in abundance, in great quantity, in numbers, in profusion, to spare

galvanize arouse, awaken, electrify, excite, fire, inspire, invigorate, jolt, kick-start, move, prod, provoke, put a bomb under (*informal*), quicken, shock, spur, startle, stimulate, stir, thrill, vitalize, wake

gamble *verb* **1.** back, bet, game, have a flutter (*informal*), lay *or* make a bet, play, punt, put one's shirt on, stake, try one's luck, wager **2.** back, chance, hazard, put one's faith *or* trust in, risk, skate on thin ice, speculate, stake, stick one's neck out (*informal*), take a chance, take the plunge, venture *~noun* **3.** chance, leap in the dark, lottery, risk, speculation, uncertainty, venture **4.** bet, flutter (*informal*), punt, wager

▷ **Antonyms** (*sense 3*) certainty, foregone conclusion, safe bet, sure thing

gambol **1.** *verb* caper, cavort, curvet, cut a caper, frisk, frolic, hop, jump, prance, rollick, skip **2.** *~noun* antic, caper, frolic, gambado, hop, jump, prance, skip, spring

game[1] *noun* **1.** amusement, distraction, diversion, entertainment, frolic, fun, jest, joke, lark, merriment, pastime, play, recreation, romp, sport **2.** competition, contest, event, head-to-head, match, meeting, round, tournament **3.** adventure, business, enterprise, line, occupation, plan, proceeding, scheme, undertaking **4**. chase, prey, quarry, wild animals **5**. *informal* design, device, plan, plot, ploy, scheme, stratagem, strategy, tactic, trick **6. make (a) game of** deride, make a fool of, make a laughing stock, make a monkey of, make fun of, make sport of, mock, poke fun at, ridicule, send up (*Brit. informal*)

▷ **Antonyms** business, chore, duty, job, labour, toil, work

game[2] *adjective* **1**. ballsy (*taboo slang*), bold, brave, courageous, dauntless, dog~ged, fearless, feisty (*informal, chiefly U.S. & Canad.*), gallant, gritty, have-a-go (*informal*), heroic, intrepid, per~severing, persistent, plucky, resolute, spirited, unflinching, valiant, valorous **2**. desirous, disposed, eager, inclined, interested, keen, prepared, ready, up for it (*informal*), willing

▷ **Antonyms** cowardly, fearful, irresolute

game[3] *adjective* bad, crippled, deformed, disabled, gammy (*Brit. slang*), incapaci~tated, injured, lame, maimed

gamesome coltish, frisky, frolicsome, gay, lively, merry, playful, rollicking, sportive, vivacious

gamin guttersnipe, mudlark (*slang*), ragamuffin, street Arab (*offensive*), (street) urchin, waif

gammon 1. *verb* beguile, cheat, con, co~zen, deceive, dupe, gull (*archaic*), hoax, hoodwink, humbug, kid (*informal*), take for a ride (*informal*), trick **2**. *~noun* de~ceit, deception, humbug, imposition, nonsense, trick

gamut area, catalogue, compass, field, range, scale, scope, series, sweep

gang band, bevy, camp, circle, clique, club, company, coterie, crew (*informal*), crowd, group, herd, horde, lot, mob, pack, party, posse (*slang*), ring, set, shift, squad, team, troupe

gangling, gangly angular, awkward, lanky, loose-jointed, rangy, rawboned, skinny, spindly, tall

gangster bandit, brigand, crook (*infor~mal*), desperado, gang member, heavy (*slang*), hood (*U.S. slang*), hoodlum (*chiefly U.S.*), mobster (*U.S. slang*), racketeer, robber, ruffian, thug, tough, tsotsi (*S. African*)

gaol *see* JAIL

gap 1. blank, breach, break, breathing space, chink, cleft, crack, cranny, crev~ice, discontinuity, divide, entr'acte, hia~tus, hole, interlude, intermission, inter~ruption, interstice, interval, lacuna, lull, opening, pause, recess, rent, respite, rift, space, vacuity, void **2**. difference, disagreement, disparity, divergence, in~consistency

gape 1. gawk, gawp (*Brit. slang*), goggle, stare, wonder **2**. crack, open, split, yawn

gaping broad, cavernous, great, open, vast, wide, wide open, yawning

garb *noun* **1**. apparel, array, attire, clothes, clothing, costume, dress, gar~ment, gear (*slang*), habiliment, habit, outfit, raiment (*archaic*), robes, threads (*slang*), uniform, vestments, wear **2**. cut, fashion, look, mode, style **3**. appearance, aspect, attire, covering, guise, outward form *~verb* **4**. apparel, attire, clothe, cover, dress, rig out, robe

garbage 1. bits and pieces, debris, detri~tus, junk, litter, odds and ends, rubbish, scraps **2**. dreck (*slang, chiefly U.S.*), dross, filth, muck, offal, refuse, rubbish, scourings, slops, sweepings, swill, trash (*chiefly U.S.*), waste **3**. balderdash, balls (*taboo slang*), bilge (*informal*), bosh (*in~formal*), bull (*slang*), bullshit (*taboo slang*), bunkum *or* buncombe (*chiefly U.S.*), claptrap (*informal*), cobblers (*Brit. taboo slang*), codswallop (*Brit. slang*), crap (*slang*), drivel, eyewash (*informal*), flapdoodle (*slang*), gibberish, guff (*slang*), havers (*Scot.*), hogwash, hokum (*slang, chiefly U.S. & Canad.*), horsefeathers (*U.S. slang*), hot air (*in~formal*), kak (*S. African slang*), moon~shine, nonsense, pap, piffle (*informal*), poppycock (*informal*), rot, shit (*taboo slang*), stuff and nonsense, tommyrot, tosh (*informal*), trash, tripe (*informal*), twaddle

garble 1. confuse, jumble, mix up **2**. cor~rupt, distort, doctor, falsify, misinter~pret, misquote, misreport, misrepresent, misstate, mistranslate, mutilate, per~vert, slant, tamper with, twist

▷ **Antonyms** clarify, decipher, make in~telligible

gargantuan big, Brobdingnagian, colos~sal, elephantine, enormous, giant, gi~gantic, ginormous (*informal*), huge, hu~mongous *or* humungous (*U.S. slang*), immense, mammoth, massive, mon~strous, monumental, mountainous, pro~digious, stellar (*informal*), titanic, tow~ering, tremendous, vast

▷ **Antonyms** little, meagre, miniature, minute, paltry, petite, puny, pygmy *or* pigmy, small, tiny

garish brash, brassy, brummagem, cheap, flash (*informal*), flashy, flaunt~ing, gaudy, glaring, glittering, loud, meretricious, naff (*Brit. slang*), raffish, showy, tacky (*informal*), tasteless, taw~dry, vulgar

▷ **Antonyms** conservative, elegant, mod~est, plain, refined, sedate, sombre, un~obtrusive

garland 1. *noun* bays, chaplet, coronal, crown, festoon, honours, laurels, wreath **2**. *~verb* adorn, crown, deck, festoon, wreathe

garments apparel, array, articles of clothing, attire, clothes, clothing, cos~tume, dress, duds (*informal*), garb, gear (*slang*), habiliment, habit, outfit, raiment (*archaic*), robes, threads (*slang*), togs, uniform, vestments, wear

garner **1.** *verb* accumulate, amass, assemble, collect, deposit, gather, hoard, husband, lay in *or* up, put by, reserve, save, stockpile, store, stow away, treasure **2.** *~noun literary* depository, granary, store, storehouse, vault

garnish **1.** *verb* adorn, beautify, bedeck, deck, decorate, embellish, enhance, festoon, grace, ornament, set off, trim **2.** *~noun* adornment, decoration, embellishment, enhancement, festoon, garniture, ornament, ornamentation, trim, trimming

▷ **Antonyms** denude, spoil, strip

garniture accessories, adornment, appendages, appurtenances, decoration, embellishment, furniture, garnish, ornamentation, ornaments, trimmings

garrison *noun* **1.** armed force, command, detachment, troops, unit **2.** base, camp, encampment, fort, fortification, fortress, post, station, stronghold *~verb* **3.** assign, mount, position, post, put on duty, station **4.** defend, guard, man, occupy, protect, supply with troops

garrulity **1.** babble, babbling, chatter, chattering, chattiness, effusiveness, gabbiness (*informal*), garrulousness, gift of the gab (*informal*), glibness, loquacity, mouthiness, prating, prattle, talkativeness, verbosity, volubility **2.** diffuseness, long-windedness, prolixity, prosiness, verbosity, windiness, wordiness

garrulous **1.** babbling, chattering, chatty, effusive, gabby (*informal*), glib, gossiping, gushing, loquacious, mouthy, prating, prattling, talkative, verbose, voluble **2.** diffuse, gassy (*slang*), long-winded, prolix, prosy, verbose, windy, wordy

▷ **Antonyms** concise, reserved, reticent, succinct, taciturn, terse, tight-lipped, uncommunicative

gash **1.** *verb* cleave, cut, gouge, incise, lacerate, rend, slash, slit, split, tear, wound **2.** *~noun* cleft, cut, gouge, incision, laceration, rent, slash, slit, split, tear, wound

gasp **1.** *verb* blow, catch one's breath, choke, fight for breath, gulp, pant, puff **2.** *~noun* blow, ejaculation, exclamation, gulp, intake of breath, pant, puff, sharp intake of breath

gate access, barrier, door, doorway, egress, entrance, exit, gateway, opening, passage, port (*Scot.*), portal

gather **1.** accumulate, amass, assemble, bring *or* get together, collect, congregate, convene, flock, foregather, garner, group, heap, hoard, marshal, mass, muster, pile up, round up, stack up, stockpile **2.** assume, be led to believe, conclude, deduce, draw, hear, infer, learn, make, surmise, understand **3.** clasp, draw, embrace, enfold, hold, hug **4.** crop, cull, garner, glean, harvest, pick, pluck, reap, select **5.** build, deepen, enlarge, expand, grow, heighten, increase, intensify, rise, swell, thicken, wax **6.** fold, pleat, pucker, ruffle, shirr, tuck

▷ **Antonyms** (*sense 1*) diffuse, disperse, dissipate, scatter, separate

gathering **1.** assemblage, assembly, company, conclave, concourse, congregation, congress, convention, convocation, crowd, flock, get-together (*informal*), group, knot, meeting, muster, party, rally, throng, turnout **2.** accumulation, acquisition, aggregate, collecting, collection, concentration, gain, heap, hoard, mass, pile, procuring, roundup, stock, stockpile **3.** *informal* abscess, boil, carbuncle, pimple, pustule, sore, spot, tumour, ulcer

gauche awkward, clumsy, graceless, ignorant, ill-bred, ill-mannered, inelegant, inept, insensitive, lacking in social graces, maladroit, tactless, uncultured, unpolished, unsophisticated

▷ **Antonyms** elegant, gracious, polished, polite, refined, sophisticated, tasteful, urbane, well-mannered

gaucherie **1.** awkwardness, bad taste, clumsiness, gaucheness, gracelessness, ignorance, ill-breeding, inelegance, ineptness, insensitivity, lack of polish, maladroitness, tactlessness, unsophisticatedness **2.** bloomer (*informal*), blunder, boob (*slang*), breach of etiquette, clanger (*informal*), faux pas, gaffe, indiscretion, lapse, mistake, slip, solecism

gaudy brash, bright, brilliant, brummagem, flash (*informal*), flashy, florid, garish, gay, gimcrack, glaring, jazzy (*informal*), loud, meretricious, naff (*Brit. slang*), ostentatious, raffish, showy, tacky (*informal*), tasteless, tawdry, vulgar

▷ **Antonyms** colourless, conservative, dull, elegant, modest, quiet, refined, sedate, subtle, tasteful

gauge *verb* **1.** ascertain, calculate, check, compute, count, determine, measure, weigh **2.** adjudge, appraise, assess, estimate, evaluate, guess, judge, rate, reckon, value *~noun* **3.** basis, criterion, example, exemplar, guide, guideline, indicator, measure, meter, model, par, pattern, rule, sample, standard, test, touchstone, yardstick **4.** bore, capacity, degree, depth, extent, height, magnitude, measure, scope, size, span, thickness, width

gaunt **1.** angular, attenuated, bony, cadaverous, emaciated, haggard, lank, lean, macilent (*rare*), meagre, pinched, rawboned, scraggy, scrawny, skeletal, skin and bone, skinny, spare, thin, wasted **2.** bare, bleak, desolate, dismal,

dreary, forbidding, forlorn, grim, harsh, stark
▷ **Antonyms** (*sense 1*) chubby, corpulent, fat, lush, obese, plump, stout, well-fed (*sense 2*) inviting, lush, luxurious

gauzy delicate, diaphanous, filmy, flimsy, gossamer, insubstantial, light, see-through, sheer, thin, translucent, transparent

gawk 1. *noun* boor, churl, clod, clodhop~per (*informal*), dolt, dunderhead, galoot (*slang*), ignoramus, lout, lubber, lum~mox (*informal*), oaf **2.** *~verb* gape, gawp (*slang*), gaze open-mouthed, goggle, stare

gawky awkward, clownish, clumsy, gauche, loutish, lumbering, lumpish, maladroit, oafish, uncouth, ungainly
▷ **Antonyms** elegant, graceful, self-assured, well-coordinated

gay *adjective* **1.** bent (*offensive slang*), homosexual, lesbian, moffie (*S. African slang*), pink (*informal*), poofy (*offensive slang*), queer (*informal, derogatory*) **2.** animated, blithe, carefree, cheerful, debonair, full of beans (*informal*), glad, gleeful, happy, hilarious, insouciant, jolly, jovial, joyful, joyous, light-hearted, lively, merry, sparkling, sunny, viva~cious **3.** bright, brilliant, colourful, flam~boyant, flashy, fresh, garish, gaudy, rich, showy, vivid **4.** convivial, festive, frivolous, frolicsome, fun-loving, game~some, merry, playful, pleasure-seeking, rakish, rollicking, sportive, waggish *~noun* **5.** bull dyke (*offensive slang*), dyke (*offensive slang*), faggot (*U.S. offens. slang*), fairy (*offensive slang*), homosexual, invert, lesbian, poof (*offen~sive slang*), queer (*offensive slang*)
▷ **Antonyms** (*senses 1 & 5*) heterosexual, straight (*sense 2*) cheerless, colourless, conservative, down in the dumps (*infor~mal*), drab, dull, grave, grim, melan~choly, miserable, sad, sedate, serious, sober, solemn, sombre, unhappy

gaze 1. *verb* contemplate, eyeball (*U.S. slang*), gape, look, look fixedly, regard, stare, view, watch, wonder **2.** *~noun* fixed look, look, stare

gazette journal, newspaper, news-sheet, organ, paper, periodical

gear *noun* **1.** cog, cogwheel, gearwheel, toothed wheel **2.** cogs, gearing, machin~ery, mechanism, works **3.** accessories, accoutrements, apparatus, equipment, harness, instruments, outfit, parapher~nalia, rigging, supplies, tackle, tools, trappings **4.** baggage, belongings, ef~fects, kit, luggage, stuff, things **5.** *slang* apparel, array, attire, clothes, clothing, costume, dress, garb, garments, habit, outfit, rigout (*informal*), threads (*slang*), togs, wear *~verb* **6.** adapt, adjust, equip, fit, rig, suit, tailor

gelatinous gluey, glutinous, gummy, jelly-like, mucilaginous, sticky, viscid, viscous

gelid arctic, chilly, cold, freezing, frigid, frosty, frozen, glacial, ice-cold, icy, polar
▷ **Antonyms** hot, red-hot, scorching, sweltering, torrid

gem 1. jewel, precious stone, semi~precious stone, stone **2.** flower, jewel, masterpiece, pearl, pick, prize, treasure

genealogy ancestry, blood line, deriva~tion, descent, extraction, family tree, line, lineage, pedigree, progeniture, stemma, stirps, stock, strain

general 1. accepted, broad, common, ex~tensive, popular, prevailing, prevalent, public, universal, widespread **2.** accus~tomed, conventional, customary, every~day, habitual, normal, ordinary, regu~lar, typical, usual **3.** approximate, ill-defined, imprecise, inaccurate, indefi~nite, inexact, loose, undetailed, unspecific, vague **4.** across-the-board, all-inclusive, blanket, broad, catholic, collective, comprehensive, encyclopedic, generic, indiscriminate, miscellaneous, panoramic, sweeping, total, universal
▷ **Antonyms** definite, distinctive, exact, exceptional, extraordinary, individual, infrequent, particular, peculiar, precise, rare, special, specific, unusual

generality 1. abstract principle, generali~zation, loose statement, sweeping state~ment, vague notion **2.** acceptedness, commonness, extensiveness, popularity, prevalence, ubiquity, universality **3.** approximateness, impreciseness, indefi~niteness, inexactness, lack of detail, looseness, vagueness **4.** breadth, catho~licity, completeness, comprehensive~ness, miscellaneity, sweepingness, uni~versality

generally 1. almost always, as a rule, by and large, conventionally, customarily, for the most part, habitually, in most cases, largely, mainly, normally, on av~erage, on the whole, ordinarily, regular~ly, typically, usually **2.** commonly, ex~tensively, popularly, publicly, univer~sally, widely **3.** approximately, broadly, chiefly, for the most part, in the main, largely, mainly, mostly, on the whole, predominantly, principally
▷ **Antonyms** especially, individually, oc~casionally, particularly, rarely, unusu~ally

generate beget, breed, bring about, cause, create, engender, form, give rise to, ini~tiate, make, originate, procreate, prod~uce, propagate, spawn, whip up
▷ **Antonyms** annihilate, crush, destroy, end, extinguish, kill, terminate

generation 1. begetting, breeding, crea~tion, engenderment, formation, genesis, origination, procreation, production, propagation, reproduction **2.** age group, breed, crop **3.** age, day, days, epoch, era, period, time, times

generic all-encompassing, blanket, collective, common, comprehensive, general, inclusive, sweeping, universal, wide
▷ **Antonyms** individual, particular, precise, specific

generosity **1.** beneficence, benevolence, bounteousness, bounty, charity, kindness, largesse *or* largess, liberality, munificence, open-handedness **2.** disinterestedness, goodness, high-mindedness, magnanimity, nobleness, unselfishness

generous **1.** beneficent, benevolent, bounteous, bountiful, charitable, free, hospitable, kind, lavish, liberal, munificent, open-handed, princely, prodigal, ungrudging, unstinting **2.** big-hearted, disinterested, good, high-minded, lofty, magnanimous, noble, unselfish **3.** abundant, ample, copious, full, fulsome, lavish, liberal, overflowing, plentiful, rich, unstinting
▷ **Antonyms** (*senses 1 & 2*) avaricious, close-fisted, greedy, mean, miserly, parsimonious, selfish, stingy, tight (*sense 3*) cheap, minimal, scanty, small, tiny

genesis beginning, birth, commencement, creation, dawn, engendering, formation, generation, inception, origin, outset, propagation, root, source, start
▷ **Antonyms** completion, conclusion, end, finish, termination

genial affable, agreeable, amiable, cheerful, cheery, congenial, convivial, cordial, easygoing, enlivening, friendly, glad, good-natured, happy, hearty, jolly, jovial, joyous, kind, kindly, merry, pleasant, sunny, warm, warm-hearted
▷ **Antonyms** cheerless, cool, discourteous, frigid, morose, rude, sardonic, sullen, unfriendly, ungracious, unpleasant

geniality affability, agreeableness, amiability, cheerfulness, cheeriness, congenialness, conviviality, cordiality, friendliness, gladness, good cheer, good nature, happiness, heartiness, jollity, joviality, joy, joyousness, kindliness, kindness, mirth, pleasantness, sunniness, warm-heartedness, warmth

genitals genitalia, loins, private parts, pudenda, reproductive organs, sex organs

genius **1.** adept, brain (*informal*), brainbox, buff (*informal*), expert, hotshot (*informal*), intellect (*informal*), maestro, master, master-hand, mastermind, maven (*U.S.*), virtuoso, whiz (*informal*) **2.** ability, aptitude, bent, brilliance, capacity, creative power, endowment, faculty, flair, gift, inclination, knack, propensity, talent, turn
▷ **Antonyms** (*sense 1*) dolt, dunce, fool, half-wit, idiot, imbecile, nincompoop, simpleton

genre brand, category, character, class, fashion, genus, group, kind, school, sort, species, stamp, style, type

genteel aristocratic, civil, courteous, courtly, cultivated, cultured, elegant, fashionable, formal, gentlemanly, ladylike, mannerly, polished, polite, refined, respectable, sophisticated, stylish, urbane, well-bred, well-mannered
▷ **Antonyms** discourteous, ill-bred, impolite, inelegant, low-bred, natural, plebeian, rude, unaffected, uncultured, unmannerly, unpolished, unrefined

gentility **1.** breeding, civility, courtesy, courtliness, cultivation, culture, decorum, elegance, etiquette, formality, good breeding, good manners, mannerliness, polish, politeness, propriety, refinement, respectability, sophistication, urbanity **2.** blue blood, gentle birth, good family, high birth, nobility, rank **3.** aristocracy, elite, gentlefolk, gentry, nobility, nobles, ruling class, upper class

gentle **1.** amiable, benign, bland, compassionate, dove-like, humane, kind, kindly, lenient, meek, merciful, mild, pacific, peaceful, placid, quiet, soft, sweet-tempered, tender **2.** balmy, calm, clement, easy, light, low, mild, moderate, muted, placid, quiet, serene, slight, smooth, soft, soothing, temperate, tranquil, untroubled **3.** easy, gradual, imperceptible, light, mild, moderate, slight, slow **4.** biddable, broken, docile, manageable, placid, tame, tractable **5.** *archaic* aristocratic, civil, courteous, cultured, elegant, genteel, gentlemanlike, gentlemanly, high-born, ladylike, noble, polished, polite, refined, upper-class, well-born, well-bred
▷ **Antonyms** aggressive, cruel, fierce, hard, harsh, heartless, impolite, powerful, rough, savage, sharp, strong, sudden, unkind, unmanageable, violent, wild

gentlemanly civil, civilized, courteous, cultivated, debonair, gallant, genteel, gentlemanlike, honourable, mannerly, noble, obliging, polished, polite, refined, reputable, suave, urbane, well-bred, well-mannered

gentry aristocracy, elite, gentility, gentlefolk, nobility, nobles, ruling class, upper class, upper crust (*informal*)

genuine **1.** actual, authentic, bona fide, honest, legitimate, natural, on the level, original, pure, real, sound, sterling, the real McCoy, true, unadulterated, unalloyed, veritable **2.** artless, candid, earnest, frank, heartfelt, honest, sincere, unaffected, unfeigned
▷ **Antonyms** (*sense 1*) affected, artificial, bogus, counterfeit, fake, false, feigned, fraudulent, hypocritical, imitation, insincere, phoney, pseudo (*informal*), sham, simulated, spurious

genus breed, category, class, genre, group, kind, order, race, set, sort, type

germ **1.** bacterium, bug (*informal*), microbe, microorganism, virus **2.** beginning, bud, cause, embryo, origin, root, rudiment, seed, source, spark **3.** bud, egg, embryo, nucleus, ovule, ovum, seed, spore, sprout

germane akin, allied, apposite, appropriate, apropos, apt, cognate, connected, fitting, kindred, material, pertinent, proper, related, relevant, suitable, to the point *or* purpose

▷ **Antonyms** extraneous, foreign, immaterial, inappropriate, irrelevant, unrelated

germinate bud, develop, generate, grow, originate, pullulate, shoot, sprout, swell, vegetate

gestation development, evolution, incubation, maturation, pregnancy, ripening

gesticulate gesture, indicate, make a sign, motion, sign, signal, wave

gesture 1. *noun* action, gesticulation, indication, motion, sign, signal **2.** *~verb* gesticulate, indicate, motion, sign, signal, wave

get 1. achieve, acquire, attain, bag, bring, come by, come into possession of, earn, fall heir to, fetch, gain, glean, inherit, land, make, net, obtain, pick up, procure, realize, reap, receive, score (*slang*), secure, succeed to, win **2.** be afflicted with, become infected with, be smitten by, catch, come down with, contract, fall victim to, take **3.** arrest, capture, collar (*informal*), grab, lay hold of, nab (*informal*), nail (*informal*), seize, take, trap **4.** become, come to be, grow, turn, wax **5.** catch, comprehend, fathom, follow, get the picture, hear, notice, perceive, see, suss (out) (*slang*), take in, understand, work out **6.** arrive, come, make it (*informal*), reach **7.** arrange, contrive, fix, manage, succeed, wangle (*informal*) **8.** coax, convince, induce, influence, persuade, prevail upon, sway, talk into, wheedle, win over **9.** communicate with, contact, get in touch with, reach **10.** *informal* affect, arouse, excite, have an effect on, impact on, impress, move, stimulate, stir, touch, tug at (someone's) heartstrings (*often facetious*) **11.** *informal* annoy, bother, bug (*informal*), gall, get (someone's) goat (*slang*), irk, irritate, nark (*Brit., Austral., & N.Z. slang*), pique, rub (someone) up the wrong way, upset, vex **12.** baffle, confound, mystify, nonplus, perplex, puzzle, stump

get across 1. cross, ford, negotiate, pass over, traverse **2.** bring home to, communicate, convey, get (something) through to, impart, make clear *or* understood, put over, transmit

get ahead 1. advance, be successful, cut it (*informal*), do well, flourish, get on, make good, make one's mark, progress, prosper, succeed, thrive **2.** excel, leave behind, outdo, outmanoeuvre, overtake, surpass

get along 1. agree, be compatible, be friendly, get on, harmonize, hit it off (*informal*) **2.** cope, develop, fare, get by (*informal*), make out (*informal*), manage, progress, shift **3.** be off, depart, get on one's bike (*Brit. slang*), go, go away, go to hell (*informal*), leave, make tracks, move off, sling one's hook (*Brit. slang*), slope off

get at 1. acquire, attain, come to grips with, gain access to, get, get hold of, reach **2.** hint, imply, intend, lead up to, mean, suggest **3.** annoy, attack, be on one's back (*slang*), blame, carp, criticize, find fault with, hassle (*informal*), irritate, nag, nark (*Brit., Austral., & N.Z. slang*), pick on, put the boot into (*slang*), taunt **4.** bribe, buy off, corrupt, influence, suborn, tamper with

getaway break, break-out, decampment, escape, flight

get away abscond, break free, break out, decamp, depart, disappear, escape, flee, leave, make good one's escape, slope off

get back 1. recoup, recover, regain, repossess, retrieve **2.** arrive home, come back *or* home, return, revert, revisit **3.** (*with* **at**) be avenged, get even with, get one's own back, give tit for tat, hit back, retaliate, settle the score with, take vengeance on

get by 1. circumvent, get ahead of, go around, go past, overtake, pass, round **2.** *informal* contrive, cope, exist, fare, get along, keep one's head above water, make both ends meet, manage, subsist, survive

get down 1. alight, bring down, climb down, descend, disembark, dismount, get off, lower, step down **2.** bring down, depress, dishearten, dispirit

get in alight, appear, arrive, collect, come, embark, enter, include, infiltrate, insert, interpose, land, make inroads (into), mount, penetrate

get off 1. alight, depart, descend, disembark, dismount, escape, exit, leave **2.** detach, remove, shed, take off

get on 1. ascend, board, climb, embark, mount **2.** advance, cope, cut it (*informal*), fare, get along, make out (*informal*), manage, progress, prosper, succeed **3.** agree, be compatible, be friendly, concur, get along, harmonize, hit it off (*informal*)

get out alight, break out, clear out (*informal*), decamp, escape, evacuate, extricate oneself, free oneself, leave, vacate, withdraw

get out of avoid, body-swerve (*Scot.*), dodge, escape, evade, shirk

get over 1. cross, ford, get across, pass, pass over, surmount, traverse **2.** come round, get better, mend, pull through, rally, recover from, revive, survive **3.** defeat, get the better of, master, over~

come, shake off **4.** communicate, convey, get *or* put across, impart, make clear *or* understood

get round 1. bypass, circumvent, edge, evade, outmanoeuvre, skirt **2.** *informal* cajole, coax, convert, persuade, prevail upon, talk round, wheedle, win over

get together accumulate, assemble, col~ lect, congregate, convene, converge, gather, join, meet, muster, rally, unite

get up arise, ascend, climb, increase, mount, rise, scale, stand

gewgaw bagatelle, bauble, bijou, gaud, gimcrack, kickshaw, knick-knack, nov~ elty, plaything, toy, trifle, trinket

ghastly ashen, cadaverous, deathlike, deathly pale, dreadful, frightful, from hell (*informal*), godawful (*slang*), grim, grisly, gruesome, hideous, horrendous, horrible, horrid, like death warmed up (*informal*), livid, loathsome, pale, pallid, repellent, shocking, spectral, terrible, terrifying, wan

▷ **Antonyms** appealing, attractive, beau~ tiful, blooming, charming, healthy, lovely, pleasing

ghost 1. apparition, eidolon, manes, phantasm, phantom, revenant, shade (*literary*), soul, spectre, spirit, spook (*informal*), wraith **2.** glimmer, hint, pos~ sibility, semblance, shadow, suggestion, trace

ghostly eerie, ghostlike, illusory, insub~ stantial, phantasmal, phantom, spec~ tral, spooky (*informal*), supernatural, uncanny, unearthly, weird, wraithlike

ghoulish disgusting, grisly, gruesome, macabre, morbid, sick (*informal*), un~ wholesome

giant 1. *noun* behemoth, colossus, Hercu~ les, leviathan, monster, ogre, titan **2.** *~adjective* Brobdingnagian, colossal, el~ ephantine, enormous, gargantuan, gi~ gantic, ginormous (*informal*), huge, hu~ mongous *or* humungous (*U.S. slang*), immense, jumbo (*informal*), large, mammoth, monstrous, prodigious, stel~ lar (*informal*), titanic, vast

▷ **Antonyms** (*sense 2*) dwarf, Lilliputian, miniature, pygmy *or* pigmy, tiny

gibber babble, blab, blabber, blather, cackle, chatter, gabble, jabber, prattle, rabbit (*Brit. informal*), waffle (*informal, chiefly Brit.*)

gibberish all Greek (*informal*), babble, balderdash, balls (*taboo slang*), bilge (*informal*), blather, bosh (*informal*), bull (*slang*), bullshit (*taboo slang*), bunkum *or* buncombe (*chiefly U.S.*), cobblers (*Brit. taboo slang*), crap (*slang*), double talk, drivel, eyewash (*informal*), gabble, garbage (*informal*), gobbledegook (*in~ formal*), guff (*slang*), hogwash, hokum (*slang, chiefly U.S. & Canad.*), horsefeathers (*U.S. slang*), hot air (*in~ formal*), jabber, jargon, moonshine, mumbo jumbo, nonsense, pap, piffle (*in~ formal*), poppycock (*informal*), prattle, shit (*taboo slang*), tommyrot, tosh (*slang, chiefly Brit.*), tripe (*informal*), twaddle, yammer (*informal*)

gibbous bulging, convex, crookbacked, humpbacked, humped, hunchbacked, hunched, protuberant, rounded

gibe, jibe 1. *verb* deride, flout, jeer, make fun of, mock, poke fun at, ridicule, scoff, scorn, sneer, take the piss out of (*slang*), taunt, twit **2.** *~noun* barb, crack (*slang*), cutting remark, derision, dig, jeer, mockery, ridicule, sarcasm, scoffing, sneer, taunt

giddiness dizziness, faintness, light-headedness, vertigo

giddy 1. dizzy, dizzying, faint, light-headed, reeling, unsteady, vertiginous **2.** capricious, careless, changeable, changeful, ditsy (*U.S. informal*), dizzy, erratic, fickle, flighty, frivolous, heed~ less, impulsive, inconstant, irresolute, irresponsible, reckless, scatterbrained, silly, thoughtless, unbalanced, unstable, unsteady, vacillating, volatile, wild

▷ **Antonyms** calm, constant, determined, earnest, resolute, serious, steady

gift 1. benefaction, bequest, bonus, boon, bounty, contribution, donation, grant, gratuity, hand-out, largesse *or* largess, legacy, offering, present **2.** ability, apti~ tude, attribute, bent, capability, capac~ ity, endowment, faculty, flair, genius, knack, power, talent, turn

gifted able, accomplished, adroit, bril~ liant, capable, clever, expert, ingenious, intelligent, masterly, skilled, talented

▷ **Antonyms** amateur, backward, dull, incapable, inept, retarded, slow, talentless, unskilled

gigantic Brobdingnagian, colossal, Cyclo~ pean, elephantine, enormous, gargan~ tuan, giant, herculean, huge, humong~ ous *or* humungous (*U.S. slang*), im~ mense, mammoth, monstrous, prodi~ gious, stellar (*informal*), stupendous, ti~ tanic, tremendous, vast

▷ **Antonyms** diminutive, insignificant, little, miniature, puny, small, tiny, weak

giggle *verb/noun* cackle, chortle, chuckle, laugh, snigger, tee-hee, titter, twitter

gild adorn, beautify, bedeck, brighten, coat, deck, dress up, embellish, embroi~ der, enhance, enrich, garnish, grace, or~ nament

gimcrack 1. *adjective* cheap, rubbishy, shoddy, tawdry, trashy **2.** *~noun* bauble, gewgaw, kickshaw, plaything, toy, trin~ ket

gimmick contrivance, device, dodge, gadget, gambit, gizmo (*slang, chiefly U.S.*), ploy, scheme, stratagem, stunt, trick

gingerly 1. *adverb* carefully, cautiously, charily, circumspectly, daintily, delicately, fastidiously, hesitantly, reluctantly, squeamishly, suspiciously, timidly, warily 2. *~adjective* careful, cautious, chary, circumspect, dainty, delicate, fastidious, hesitant, reluctant, squeamish, suspicious, timid, wary
▷ **Antonyms** (*sense 1*) boldly, carelessly, confidently, rashly

gird[1] *verb* 1. belt, bind, girdle 2. blockade, encircle, enclose, encompass, enfold, engird, environ, hem in, pen, ring, surround 3. brace, fortify, make ready, prepare, ready, steel

gird[2] *verb* deride, gibe, jeer, make fun of, mock, poke fun at, ridicule, scoff, scorn, sneer, taunt

girdle 1. *noun* band, belt, cincture, cummerbund, fillet, sash, waistband 2. *~verb* bind, bound, encircle, enclose, encompass, engird, environ, enwreath, gird, hem, ring, surround

girl bird (*slang*), chick (*slang*), colleen (*Irish*), damsel (*archaic*), daughter, female child, lass, lassie (*informal*), maid (*archaic*), maiden (*archaic*), miss, wench

girth bulk, circumference, measure, size

gist core, drift, essence, force, idea, import, marrow, meaning, nub, pith, point, quintessence, sense, significance, substance

give 1. accord, administer, allow, award, bestow, commit, confer, consign, contribute, deliver, donate, entrust, furnish, grant, hand over *or* out, make over, permit, present, provide, purvey, supply, vouchsafe 2. announce, be a source of, communicate, emit, impart, issue, notify, pronounce, publish, render, transmit, utter 3. demonstrate, display, evidence, indicate, manifest, offer, proffer, provide, set forth, show 4. allow, cede, concede, devote, grant, hand over, lend, relinquish, surrender, yield 5. cause, do, engender, lead, make, occasion, perform, produce 6. bend, break, collapse, fall, recede, retire, sink
▷ **Antonyms** accept, get, hold, keep, receive, take, withdraw

give away betray, disclose, divulge, expose, grass (*Brit. slang*), grass up (*slang*), inform on, leak, let out, let slip, let the cat out of the bag (*informal*), put the finger on (*informal*), reveal, shop (*slang, chiefly Brit.*), uncover

give in admit defeat, capitulate, collapse, comply, concede, quit, submit, succumb, surrender, yield

given addicted, apt, disposed, inclined, liable, likely, prone

give off discharge, emit, exhale, exude, produce, release, send out, smell of, throw out, vent

give out 1. discharge, emit, exhale, exude, produce, release, send out, smell of, throw out, vent 2. announce, broadcast, communicate, disseminate, impart, make known, notify, publish, shout from the rooftops (*informal*), transmit, utter

give up abandon, call it a day *or* night, capitulate, cease, cede, cut out, desist, despair, fall by the wayside, forswear, hand over, kick (*informal*), kiss (something) goodbye, leave off, quit, relinquish, renounce, resign, say goodbye to, step down (*informal*), stop, surrender, throw in the sponge, throw in the towel, waive

glacial 1. arctic, biting, bitter, chill, chilly, cold, freezing, frigid, frosty, frozen, gelid, icy, piercing, polar, raw, wintry 2. antagonistic, cold, frigid, hostile, icy, inimical, unfriendly

glad 1. blithesome (*literary*), cheerful, chuffed (*slang*), contented, delighted, gay, gleeful, gratified, happy, jocund, jovial, joyful, overjoyed, pleased, willing 2. animated, cheerful, cheering, cheery, delightful, felicitous, gratifying, joyous, merry, pleasant, pleasing
▷ **Antonyms** depressed, discontented, displeased, melancholy, miserable, sad, sorrowful, unhappy

gladden cheer, delight, elate, enliven, exhilarate, gratify, hearten, please, rejoice

gladly cheerfully, freely, gaily, gleefully, happily, jovially, joyfully, joyously, lief (*rare*), merrily, readily, willingly, with (a) good grace, with pleasure
▷ **Antonyms** dolefully, grudgingly, reluctantly, sadly, unenthusiastically, unwillingly

gladness animation, blitheness, cheerfulness, delight, felicity, gaiety, glee, happiness, high spirits, hilarity, jollity, joy, joyousness, mirth, pleasure

glamorous alluring, attractive, beautiful, bewitching, captivating, charming, dazzling, elegant, enchanting, entrancing, exciting, fascinating, glittering, glitzy (*slang*), glossy, lovely, prestigious, smart
▷ **Antonyms** colourless, dull, unattractive, unexciting, unglamorous

glamour allure, appeal, attraction, beauty, bewitchment, charm, enchantment, fascination, magnetism, prestige, ravishment, witchery

glance *verb* 1. check, check out (*informal*), clock (*Brit. informal*), gaze, glimpse, look, peek, peep, scan, take a dekko at (*Brit. slang*), view 2. flash, gleam, glimmer, glint, glisten, glitter, reflect, shimmer, shine, twinkle 3. bounce, brush, graze, rebound, ricochet, skim 4. (*with* **over, through,** *etc.*) browse, dip into, flip through, leaf through, riffle through, run over *or* through, scan, skim through, thumb through *~noun* 5. brief look, butcher's (*Brit. slang*), dekko (*slang*), gander (*informal*), glimpse, look, peek, peep, quick look, shufti (*Brit. slang*), squint, view **6.** flash, gleam, glimmer, glint, reflection, sparkle, twinkle **7.** allusion, passing mention, reference

▷ **Antonyms** (*sense 1*) peruse, scrutinize, study (*sense 5*) examination, good look, inspection, perusal

glare *verb* **1.** frown, give a dirty look, glower, look daggers, lour *or* lower, scowl, stare angrily **2.** blaze, dazzle, flame, flare *~noun* **3.** angry stare, black look, dirty look, frown, glower, lour *or* lower, scowl **4.** blaze, brilliance, dazzle, flame, flare, glow **5.** flashiness, floridness, gaudiness, loudness, meretriciousness, showiness, tawdriness

glaring 1. audacious, blatant, conspicuous, egregious, flagrant, gross, manifest, obvious, open, outrageous, outstanding, overt, patent, rank, unconcealed, visible **2.** blazing, bright, dazzling, flashy, florid, garish, glowing, loud

▷ **Antonyms** (*sense 1*) concealed, hidden, inconspicuous, obscure (*sense 2*) soft, subdued, subtle

glassy 1. clear, glossy, icy, shiny, slick, slippery, smooth, transparent **2.** blank, cold, dazed, dull, empty, expressionless, fixed, glazed, lifeless, vacant

glaze 1. *verb* burnish, coat, enamel, furbish, gloss, lacquer, polish, varnish **2.** *~noun* coat, enamel, finish, gloss, lacquer, lustre, patina, polish, shine, varnish

gleam *noun* **1.** beam, flash, glimmer, glow, ray, sparkle **2.** brightness, brilliance, coruscation, flash, gloss, lustre, sheen, splendour **3.** flicker, glimmer, hint, inkling, ray, suggestion, trace *~verb* **4.** coruscate, flare, flash, glance, glimmer, glint, glisten, glitter, glow, scintillate, shimmer, shine, sparkle

glean accumulate, amass, collect, cull, garner, gather, harvest, learn, pick, pick up, reap, select

glee cheerfulness, delight, elation, exhilaration, exuberance, exultation, fun, gaiety, gladness, hilarity, jocularity, jollity, joviality, joy, joyfulness, joyousness, liveliness, merriment, mirth, sprightliness, triumph, verve

▷ **Antonyms** depression, gloom, melancholy, misery, sadness

gleeful cheerful, chirpy (*informal*), cock-a-hoop, delighted, elated, exuberant, exultant, gay, gratified, happy, jocund, jovial, joyful, joyous, jubilant, merry, mirthful, overjoyed, over the moon (*informal*), pleased, rapt, triumphant

glib artful, easy, fast-talking, fluent, garrulous, insincere, plausible, quick, ready, slick, slippery, smooth, smooth-tongued, suave, talkative, voluble

▷ **Antonyms** halting, hesitant, implausible, sincere, tongue-tied

glide coast, drift, float, flow, fly, roll, run, sail, skate, skim, slide, slip, soar

glimmer *verb* **1.** blink, flicker, gleam, glisten, glitter, glow, shimmer, shine, sparkle, twinkle *~noun* **2.** blink, flicker, gleam, glow, ray, shimmer, sparkle, twinkle **3.** flicker, gleam, grain, hint, inkling, ray, suggestion, trace

glimpse 1. *noun* brief view, butcher's (*Brit. slang*), gander (*informal*), glance, look, peek, peep, quick look, shufti (*Brit. slang*), sight, sighting, squint **2.** *~verb* catch sight of, clock (*Brit. informal*), descry, espy, sight, spot, spy, view

glint 1. *verb* flash, gleam, glimmer, glitter, shine, sparkle, twinkle **2.** *~noun* flash, gleam, glimmer, glitter, shine, sparkle, twinkle, twinkling

glisten coruscate, flash, glance, glare, gleam, glimmer, glint, glitter, scintillate, shimmer, shine, sparkle, twinkle

glitter *verb* **1.** coruscate, flare, flash, glare, gleam, glimmer, glint, glisten, scintillate, shimmer, shine, sparkle, twinkle *~noun* **2.** beam, brightness, brilliance, flash, glare, gleam, lustre, radiance, scintillation, sheen, shimmer, shine, sparkle **3.** display, gaudiness, gilt, glamour, pageantry, show, showiness, splendour, tinsel

gloaming dusk, eventide (*archaic*), half-light, nightfall, twilight

gloat crow, drool, exult, glory, relish, revel in, rub it in (*informal*), rub one's hands, rub someone's nose in it, triumph, vaunt

global 1. international, pandemic, planetary, universal, world, worldwide **2.** all-encompassing, all-inclusive, all-out, comprehensive, encyclopedic, exhaustive, general, thorough, total, unbounded, unlimited

▷ **Antonyms** (*sense 2*) limited, narrow, parochial, restricted, sectional

globe ball, earth, orb, planet, round, sphere, world

globular globate, globelike, globoid, globose, globous, globulous, orbicular, round, spherical, spheroid

globule bead, bubble, drop, droplet, particle, pearl, pellet

gloom 1. blackness, cloud, cloudiness, dark, darkness, dimness, dullness, dusk, duskiness, gloominess, murk, murkiness, obscurity, shade, shadow, twilight **2.** blues, dejection, depression, desolation, despair, despondency, downheartedness, low spirits, melancholy, misery, sadness, sorrow, the hump (*Brit. informal*), unhappiness, woe

▷ **Antonyms** brightness, cheerfulness, daylight, delight, happiness, high spirits, jollity, joy, light, mirth, radiance

gloomy 1. black, crepuscular, dark, dim, dismal, dreary, dull, dusky, grey, murky, obscure, overcast, shadowy, sombre, Stygian, tenebrous **2.** bad, black, cheerless, comfortless, depressing, disheartening, dismal, dispiriting, dreary, funereal, joyless, sad, saddening, sombre **3.** blue, chapfallen, cheerless, crestfallen, dejected, despondent, dismal, dispirited, down, downcast, downhearted, down in the dumps (*informal*), down in the mouth, glum, in low spirits, low, melancholy, miserable, moody, morose, pessimistic, sad, saturnine, sullen

▷ **Antonyms** blithe, bright, brilliant, cheerful, chirpy (*informal*), happy, high-spirited, jolly, jovial, light, merry, radiant, sunny, upbeat (*informal*)

glorify 1. add lustre to, adorn, aggrandize, augment, dignify, elevate, enhance, ennoble, illuminate, immortalize, lift up, magnify, raise **2.** adore, apotheosize, beatify, bless, canonize, deify, enshrine, exalt, honour, idolize, pay homage to, revere, sanctify, venerate, worship **3.** celebrate, crack up (*informal*), cry up (*informal*), eulogize, extol, hymn, laud, lionize, magnify, panegyrize, praise, sing *or* sound the praises of

▷ **Antonyms** condemn, debase, defile, degrade, desecrate, dishonour, humiliate, mock

glorious 1. celebrated, distinguished, elevated, eminent, excellent, famed, famous, grand, honoured, illustrious, magnificent, majestic, noble, noted, renowned, sublime, triumphant **2.** beautiful, bright, brilliant, dazzling, divine, effulgent, gorgeous, radiant, resplendent, shining, splendid, splendiferous (*facetious*), superb **3.** *informal* delightful, enjoyable, excellent, fine, gorgeous, great, heavenly (*informal*), marvellous, pleasurable, splendid, splendiferous (*facetious*), wonderful

▷ **Antonyms** awful, dreary, dull, gloomy, horrible, minor, ordinary, trivial, unimportant, unimpressive, unknown, unpleasant

glory *noun* **1.** celebrity, dignity, distinction, eminence, exaltation, fame, honour, illustriousness, immortality, kudos, praise, prestige, renown **2.** adoration, benediction, blessing, gratitude, homage, laudation, praise, thanksgiving, veneration, worship **3.** éclat, grandeur, greatness, magnificence, majesty, nobility, pageantry, pomp, splendour, sublimity, triumph **4.** beauty, brilliance, effulgence, gorgeousness, lustre, radiance, resplendence *~verb* **5.** boast, crow, drool, exult, gloat, pride oneself, relish, revel, take delight, triumph

▷ **Antonyms** blasphemy, condemnation, disgrace, dishonour, disrepute, infamy, shame, triviality, ugliness

gloss[1] *noun* **1.** brightness, brilliance, burnish, gleam, lustre, patina, polish, sheen, shine, varnish, veneer **2.** appearance, façade, front, mask, semblance, show, surface *~verb* **3.** burnish, finish, furbish, glaze, lacquer, polish, shine, varnish, veneer **4.** camouflage, conceal, cover up, disguise, hide, mask, smooth over, sweep under the carpet (*informal*), veil, whitewash (*informal*)

gloss[2] 1. *noun* annotation, comment, commentary, elucidation, explanation, footnote, interpretation, note, scholium, translation **2.** *~verb* annotate, comment, construe, elucidate, explain, interpret, translate

glossy bright, brilliant, burnished, glassy, glazed, lustrous, polished, sheeny, shining, shiny, silken, silky, sleek, smooth

▷ **Antonyms** drab, dull, mat *or* matt, subfusc

glow *noun* **1.** burning, gleam, glimmer, incandescence, lambency, light, luminosity, phosphorescence **2.** brightness, brilliance, effulgence, radiance, splendour, vividness **3.** ardour, earnestness, enthusiasm, excitement, fervour, gusto, impetuosity, intensity, passion, vehemence, warmth **4.** bloom, blush, flush, reddening, rosiness *~verb* **5.** brighten, burn, gleam, glimmer, redden, shine, smoulder **6.** be suffused, blush, colour, fill, flush, radiate, thrill, tingle

▷ **Antonyms** chill, coolness, dullness, greyness, half-heartedness, iciness, indifference, paleness, pallor, wanness

glower 1. *verb* frown, give a dirty look, glare, look daggers, lour *or* lower, scowl **2.** *~noun* angry stare, black look, dirty look, frown, glare, lour *or* lower, scowl

glowing 1. aglow, beaming, bright, flaming, florid, flushed, lambent, luminous, radiant, red, rich, ruddy, suffused, vibrant, vivid, warm **2.** adulatory, complimentary, ecstatic, enthusiastic, eulogistic, laudatory, panegyrical, rave (*informal*), rhapsodic

▷ **Antonyms** colourless, cool, cruel, dispassionate, dull, grey, pale, pallid, scathing, unenthusiastic, wan

glue 1. *noun* adhesive, cement, gum, mucilage, paste **2.** *~verb* affix, agglutinate, cement, fix, gum, paste, seal, stick

glum chapfallen, churlish, crabbed, crestfallen, crusty, dejected, doleful, down, gloomy, gruff, grumpy, huffy, ill-humoured, low, moody, morose, pessimistic, saturnine, sour, sulky, sullen, surly

▷ **Antonyms** cheerful, cheery, chirpy (*informal*), jolly, joyful, merry, upbeat (*informal*)

glut *noun* **1.** excess, overabundance, oversupply, plethora, saturation, superabundance, superfluity, surfeit, surplus *~verb* **2.** cram, fill, gorge, overfeed, satiate, stuff **3.** choke, clog, deluge, flood, inundate, overload, oversupply, saturate

▷ **Antonyms** dearth, lack, paucity, scarcity, shortage, want

glutinous adhesive, cohesive, gluey, gooey, gummy, mucilaginous, sticky, viscid, viscous

glutton gannet (*slang*), gobbler, gorger, gormandizer, gourmand, pig (*informal*)

gluttonous gormandizing, greedy, hoggish, insatiable, piggish, rapacious, ravenous, voracious

gluttony edacity, gormandizing, gourmandism, greed, greediness, piggishness, rapacity, voraciousness, voracity

gnarled contorted, knotted, knotty, knurled, leathery, rough, rugged, twisted, weather-beaten, wrinkled

gnaw 1. bite, chew, munch, nibble, worry **2.** consume, devour, eat away *or* into, erode, fret, wear away *or* down **3.** distress, fret, harry, haunt, nag, plague, prey on one's mind, trouble, worry

go *verb* **1.** advance, decamp, depart, fare (*archaic*), journey, leave, make for, make tracks, move, move out, pass, proceed, repair, set off, slope off, travel, withdraw **2.** function, move, operate, perform, run, work **3.** connect, extend, fit, give access, lead, reach, run, span, spread, stretch **4.** avail, concur, conduce, contribute, incline, lead to, serve, tend, work towards **5.** develop, eventuate, fall out, fare, happen, pan out (*informal*), proceed, result, turn out, work out **6.** accord, agree, blend, chime, complement, correspond, fit, harmonize, match, suit **7.** buy it (*U.S. slang*), check out (*U.S. slang*), croak (*slang*), die, expire, give up the ghost, go belly-up (*slang*), kick it (*slang*), kick the bucket (*slang*), pass away, peg it (*informal*), peg out (*informal*), perish, pop one's clogs (*informal*), snuff it (*informal*) **8.** elapse, expire, flow, lapse, pass, slip away *~noun* **9.** attempt, bid, crack (*informal*), effort, essay, shot (*informal*), stab (*informal*), try, turn, whack (*informal*), whirl (*informal*) **10.** *informal* activity, animation, brio, drive, energy, force, get-up-and-go (*informal*), life, oomph (*informal*), pep, spirit, verve, vigour, vitality, vivacity

▷ **Antonyms** (*sense 1*) arrive, halt, reach, remain, stay, stop (*sense 2*) break (down), fail, malfunction, stop

go about 1. circulate, move around, pass around, wander **2.** approach, begin, get the show on the road, set about, tackle, take the bit between one's teeth, undertake **3.** busy *or* occupy oneself with, devote oneself to

goad 1. *noun* impetus, incentive, incitement, irritation, motivation, pressure, spur, stimulation, stimulus, urge **2.** *~verb* annoy, arouse, be on one's back (*slang*), drive, egg on, exhort, harass, hassle (*informal*), hound, impel, incite, instigate, irritate, lash, nark (*Brit., Austral., & N.Z. slang*), prick, prod, prompt, propel, spur, stimulate, sting, urge, worry

go-ahead 1. *noun informal* assent, authorization, consent, green light, leave, O.K. *or* okay (*informal*), permission **2.** *~adjective* ambitious, enterprising, go-getting (*informal*), pioneering, progressive, up-and-coming

go ahead advance, begin, continue, go forward, go on, proceed, progress

goal aim, ambition, design, destination, end, Holy Grail (*informal*), intention, limit, mark, object, objective, purpose, target

go along 1. acquiesce, agree, assent, concur, cooperate, follow **2.** accompany, carry on, escort, join, keep up, move, pass, travel

go at argue, attack, blame, blast, criticize, go for the jugular, impugn, lambast(e), put down, set about, tear into (*informal*)

go away decamp, depart, exit, get on one's bike (*Brit. slang*), go to hell (*informal*), hook it (*slang*), leave, make tracks, move out, pack one's bags (*informal*), recede, sling one's hook (*Brit. slang*), slope off, withdraw

gob blob, chunk, clod, gobbet, hunk, lump, nugget, piece, wad, wodge (*Brit. informal*)

go back 1. retrocede, return, revert **2.** change one's mind, desert, forsake, renege, repudiate, retract

gobble bolt, cram, devour, gorge, gulp, guzzle, pig out on (*U.S. & Canad. slang*), stuff, swallow, wolf

gobbledegook babble, cant, double talk, gabble, gibberish, Greek (*informal*), hocus-pocus, jabber, jargon, mumbo jumbo, nonsense, officialese, rigmarole, twaddle

go-between agent, broker, dealer, factor, intermediary, liaison, mediator, medium, middleman

go by 1. elapse, exceed, flow on, move onward, pass, proceed **2.** adopt, be guided by, follow, heed, judge from, observe, take as guide

godforsaken abandoned, backward, bleak, deserted, desolate, dismal, dreary, forlorn, gloomy, lonely, neglected, remote, wretched

godless atheistic, depraved, evil, impious, irreligious, profane, ungodly, unprincipled, unrighteous, wicked

godlike celestial, deific, deiform, divine, heavenly, superhuman, transcendent

godly devout, god-fearing, good, holy, pious, religious, righteous, saintly

go down 1. be beaten, collapse, decline, decrease, drop, fall, founder, go under, lose, set, sink, submerge, submit, suffer defeat **2.** be commemorated, be recalled, be recorded, be remembered

godsend blessing, boon, manna, stroke of luck, windfall

go far advance, be successful, cut it (*informal*), do well, get ahead (*informal*), get on (*informal*), make a name for oneself, make one's mark, progress, succeed

go for 1. clutch at, fetch, obtain, reach, seek, stretch for **2.** admire, be attracted to, be fond of, choose, favour, hold with, like, prefer **3.** assail, assault, attack, launch oneself at, rush upon, set about *or* upon, spring upon

goggle gape, gawk, gawp (*slang*), peer, rubberneck (*slang*), stare

go in (for) adopt, embrace, engage in, enter, espouse, practise, pursue, take up, undertake

going-over 1. analysis, check, examination, inspection, investigation, perusal, recce (*slang*), review, scrutiny, study, survey **2.** beating, buffeting, doing (*informal*), drubbing, pasting (*slang*), thrashing, thumping, whipping **3.** castigation, chastisement, chiding, dressing-down (*informal*), lecture, rebuke, reprimand, row, scolding, talking-to (*informal*), tongue-lashing

go into 1. begin, develop, enter, participate in, undertake **2.** analyse, consider, delve into, discuss, examine, inquire into, investigate, look into, probe, pursue, research, review, scrutinize, study, work over

golden 1. blond *or* blonde, bright, brilliant, flaxen, resplendent, shining, yellow **2.** best, blissful, delightful, flourishing, glorious, halcyon, happy, joyful, joyous, precious, prosperous, rich, successful **3.** advantageous, auspicious, excellent, favourable, opportune, promising, propitious, rosy, valuable

▷ **Antonyms** (*sense 1*) black, brunette, dark, dull (*sense 2*) poorest, sad, unfavourable, worst (*sense 3*) black, dark, sad, unfavourable, untimely, wretched

gone 1. elapsed, ended, finished, over, past **2.** absent, astray, away, lacking, lost, missing, vanished **3.** dead, deceased, defunct, departed, extinct, no more **4.** consumed, done, finished, spent, used up

good *adjective* **1.** acceptable, admirable, agreeable, awesome (*slang*), bad (*slang*), bitchin' (*U.S. slang*), capital, choice, commendable, crucial (*slang*), divine, dope (*slang*), excellent, fine, first-class, first-rate, great, hunky-dory (*informal*), pleasant, pleasing, positive, precious, satisfactory, splendid, super (*informal*), superior, tiptop, valuable, wicked (*slang*), world-class, worthy **2.** admirable, estimable, ethical, exemplary, honest, honourable, moral, praiseworthy, right, righteous, trustworthy, upright, virtuous, worthy **3.** able, accomplished, adept, adroit, capable, clever, competent, dexterous, efficient, expert, first-rate, proficient, reliable, satisfactory, serviceable, skilled, sound, suitable, talented, thorough, useful **4.** adequate, advantageous, auspicious, beneficial, convenient, favourable, fit, fitting, healthy, helpful, opportune, profitable, propitious, salubrious, salutary, suitable, useful, wholesome **5.** eatable, fit to eat, sound, uncorrupted, untainted, whole **6.** altruistic, approving, beneficent, benevolent, charitable, friendly, gracious, humane, kind, kind-hearted, kindly, merciful, obliging, well-disposed **7.** authentic, bona fide, dependable, genuine, honest, legitimate, proper, real, reliable, sound, true, trustworthy, valid **8.** decorous, dutiful, mannerly, obedient, orderly, polite, proper, seemly, well-behaved, well-mannered **9.** agreeable, cheerful, congenial, convivial, enjoyable, gratifying, happy, pleasant, pleasing, pleasurable, satisfying **10.** adequate, ample, complete, considerable, entire, extensive, full, large, long, sizable *or* sizeable, solid, substantial, sufficient, whole **11.** best, fancy, finest, newest, nicest, precious, smartest, special, valuable **12.** *of weather* balmy, bright, calm, clear, clement, cloudless, fair, halcyon, mild, sunny, sunshiny, tranquil *~noun* **13.** advantage, avail, behalf, benefit, gain, interest, mileage (*informal*), profit, service, use, usefulness, welfare, wellbeing, worth **14.** excellence, goodness, merit, morality, probity, rectitude, right, righteousness, uprightness, virtue, worth **15. for good** finally, for ever, irrevocably, never to return, once and for all, permanently, *sine die*

▷ **Antonyms** *~adjective* (*sense 1*) awful, bad, boring, disagreeable, dull, inadequate, rotten, tedious, unpleasant (*sense 2*) bad, base, corrupt, dishonest, dishonourable, evil, immoral, improper, sinful (*sense 3*) bad, incompetent, inefficient, unsatisfactory, unskilled (*sense 4*) inappropriate, pathetic, unbecoming, unbefitting, unfavourable, unfitting, unsuitable, useless (*sense 5*) bad, decayed, mouldy, off, rotten, unsound (*sense 6*) cruel, evil, mean (*informal*), selfish, unkind, vicious, wicked (*sense 7*) counterfeit, false, fraudulent, invalid, phoney (*sense 8*) ill-mannered, mischievous, naughty, rude, unkind (*sense 10*) scant, short *~noun* (*sense 13*) detriment, disadvantage, failure, ill-fortune, loss (*sense 14*) badness, baseness, corruption, cruelty, dishonesty, evil, immorality, meanness, wickedness

goodbye adieu, farewell, leave-taking, parting

good-for-nothing 1. *noun* black sheep, idler, layabout, ne'er-do-well, profligate, rapscallion, scapegrace, skiver (*Brit. slang*), slacker (*informal*), waster, wast~

rel **2.** *~adjective* feckless, idle, irresponsible, useless, worthless

good-humoured affable, amiable, cheerful, congenial, genial, good-tempered, happy, pleasant

good-looking attractive, comely, fair, handsome, personable, pretty, well-favoured

goodly 1. ample, considerable, large, significant, sizable *or* sizeable, substantial, tidy (*informal*) **2.** agreeable, attractive, comely, desirable, elegant, fine, good-looking, graceful, handsome, personable, pleasant, pleasing, well-favoured

good-natured agreeable, amiable, benevolent, friendly, good-hearted, helpful, kind, kindly, tolerant, warm-hearted, well-disposed, willing to please

goodness 1. excellence, merit, quality, superiority, value, worth **2.** beneficence, benevolence, friendliness, generosity, goodwill, graciousness, humaneness, kind-heartedness, kindliness, kindness, mercy, obligingness **3.** honesty, honour, integrity, merit, morality, probity, rectitude, righteousness, uprightness, virtue **4.** advantage, benefit, nourishment, nutrition, salubriousness, wholesomeness

▷ **Antonyms** badness, corruption, detriment, disadvantage, dishonesty, evil, immorality, wickedness, worthlessness

goods 1. appurtenances, belongings, chattels, effects, furnishings, furniture, gear, movables, paraphernalia, possessions, property, things, trappings **2.** commodities, merchandise, stock, stuff, wares

goodwill amity, benevolence, favour, friendliness, friendship, heartiness, kindliness, zeal

gooey 1. gluey, glutinous, mucilaginous, soft, sticky, tacky, viscous **2.** maudlin, mawkish, sentimental, slushy (*informal*), syrupy (*informal*), tear-jerking (*informal*)

go off 1. blow up, detonate, explode, fire **2.** happen, occur, take place **3.** decamp, depart, go away, hook it (*slang*), leave, move out, pack one's bags (*informal*), part, quit, slope off **4.** *informal* go bad, go stale, rot

go on 1. continue, endure, happen, last, occur, persist, proceed, stay **2.** blether, carry on, chatter, prattle, rabbit (*Brit. informal*), ramble on, waffle (*informal, chiefly Brit.*), witter (on) (*informal*)

go out 1. depart, exit, leave **2.** be extinguished, die out, expire, fade out

go over 1. examine, inspect, rehearse, reiterate, review, revise, study, work over **2.** peruse, read, scan, skim

gore[1] *noun* blood, bloodshed, butchery, carnage, slaughter

gore[2] *verb* impale, pierce, spit, stab, transfix, wound

gorge[1] *noun* canyon, chasm, cleft, clough (*dialect*), defile, fissure, pass, ravine

gorge[2] *verb* bolt, cram, devour, feed, fill, glut, gobble, gormandize, gulp, guzzle, overeat, pig out (*U.S. & Canad. slang*), raven, sate, satiate, stuff, surfeit, swallow, wolf

gorgeous 1. beautiful, brilliant, dazzling, drop-dead (*slang*), elegant, glittering, grand, luxuriant, magnificent, opulent, ravishing, resplendent, showy, splendid, splendiferous (*facetious*), stunning (*informal*), sumptuous, superb **2.** *informal* attractive, bright, delightful, enjoyable, exquisite, fine, glorious, good, good-looking, lovely, pleasing

▷ **Antonyms** cheap, dismal, dreary, dull, gloomy, homely, plain, repulsive, shabby, shoddy, sombre, ugly, unattractive, unsightly

gory blood-soaked, bloodstained, bloodthirsty, bloody, ensanguined (*literary*), murderous, sanguinary

gospel 1. certainty, fact, the last word, truth, verity **2.** credo, creed, doctrine, message, news, revelation, tidings

gossamer *adjective* airy, delicate, diaphanous, fine, flimsy, gauzy, light, sheer, silky, thin, transparent

gossip *noun* **1.** blether, bush telegraph, buzz, chinwag (*Brit. informal*), chitchat, clishmaclaver (*Scot.*), dirt (*U.S. slang*), gen (*Brit. informal*), hearsay, idle talk, jaw (*Brit. slang*), latest (*informal*), newsmongering (*old-fashioned*), prattle, scandal, scuttlebutt (*U.S. slang*), small talk, tittle-tattle **2.** babbler, blatherskite, blether, busybody, chatterbox (*informal*), chatterer, flibbertigibbet, gossipmonger, newsmonger (*Brit. old-fashioned*), prattler, quidnunc, scandalmonger, tattler, telltale *~verb* **3.** blather, blether, chat, chew the fat *or* rag (*slang*), dish the dirt (*informal*), gabble, jaw (*slang*), prate, prattle, schmooze (*slang*), shoot the breeze (*slang, chiefly U.S.*), tattle

go through 1. bear, brave, endure, experience, suffer, tolerate, undergo, withstand **2.** consume, exhaust, squander, use **3.** check, examine, explore, forage, hunt, look, search, work over

go together 1. accord, agree, fit, harmonize, make a pair, match **2.** *informal* court, date (*informal, chiefly U.S.*), escort, go out with, go steady with (*informal*)

gouge 1. *verb* chisel, claw, cut, dig (out), gash, hollow (out), incise, scoop, score, scratch **2.** *~noun* cut, furrow, gash, groove, hollow, incision, notch, scoop, score, scratch, trench

go under default, die, drown, fail, fold (*informal*), founder, go down, sink, submerge, succumb

gourmet *bon vivant,* connoisseur, epicure, foodie (*informal*), gastronome

govern 1. administer, be in power, call the shots, call the tune, command, conduct, control, direct, guide, handle, hold sway, lead, manage, order, oversee, pilot, reign, rule, steer, superintend, supervise **2.** bridle, check, contain, control, curb, direct, discipline, get the better of, hold in check, inhibit, keep a tight rein on, master, regulate, restrain, subdue, tame **3.** decide, determine, guide, influence, rule, sway, underlie

government 1. administration, authority, dominion, execution, governance, law, polity, rule, sovereignty, state, statecraft **2.** administration, executive, ministry, powers-that-be, regime **3.** authority, command, control, direction, domination, guidance, management, regulation, restraint, superintendence, supervision, sway

governmental administrative, bureaucratic, executive, ministerial, official, political, sovereign, state

governor administrator, boss (*informal*), chief, commander, comptroller, controller, director, executive, head, leader, manager, overseer, ruler, superintendent, supervisor

go with accompany, agree, blend, complement, concur, correspond, fit, harmonize, match, suit

go without abstain, be denied, be deprived of, deny oneself, do without, go short, lack, want

gown costume, dress, frock, garb, garment, habit, robe

grab bag, capture, catch *or* take hold of, catch (up), clutch, grasp, grip, latch on to, nab (*informal*), nail (*informal*), pluck, seize, snap up, snatch

grace *noun* **1.** attractiveness, beauty, charm, comeliness, ease, elegance, finesse, gracefulness, loveliness, pleasantness, poise, polish, refinement, shapeliness, tastefulness **2.** benefaction, beneficence, benevolence, favour, generosity, goodness, goodwill, kindliness, kindness **3.** breeding, consideration, cultivation, decency, decorum, etiquette, mannerliness, manners, propriety, tact **4.** charity, clemency, compassion, forgiveness, indulgence, leniency, lenity, mercy, pardon, quarter, reprieve **5.** benediction, blessing, prayer, thanks, thanksgiving *~verb* **6.** adorn, beautify, bedeck, deck, decorate, dignify, distinguish, elevate, embellish, enhance, enrich, favour, garnish, glorify, honour, ornament, set off

▷ **Antonyms** *~noun* (*sense 1*) awkwardness, clumsiness, inelegance, stiffness, tastelessness, ugliness, ungainliness (*sense 2*) disfavour, ill will (*sense 3*) bad manners, tactlessness (*sense 4*) condemnation, harshness *~verb* desecrate, dishonour, insult, ruin, spoil

graceful agile, beautiful, becoming, charming, comely, easy, elegant, fine, flowing, gracile (*rare*), natural, pleasing, smooth, symmetrical, tasteful

▷ **Antonyms** awkward, clumsy, gawky, inelegant, plain, ponderous, stiff, ugly, ungainly, ungraceful

graceless 1. barbarous, boorish, coarse, crude, ill-mannered, improper, indecorous, loutish, rude, shameless, unmannerly, unsophisticated, vulgar **2.** awkward, clumsy, forced, gauche, gawky, inelegant, rough, uncouth, ungainly, untutored

Graces,the *Greek myth* Charities

gracious accommodating, affable, amiable, beneficent, benevolent, benign, benignant, charitable, chivalrous, civil, compassionate, considerate, cordial, courteous, courtly, friendly, hospitable, indulgent, kind, kindly, lenient, loving, merciful, mild, obliging, pleasing, polite, well-mannered

▷ **Antonyms** brusque, cold, discourteous, gruff, haughty, impolite, mean, remote, rude, surly, unfriendly, ungracious, unpleasant

gradation 1. array, progression, sequence, series, succession **2.** degree, grade, level, mark, measurement, notch, place, point, position, rank, stage, step **3.** arrangement, classification, grouping, ordering, sorting

grade *noun* **1.** brand, category, class, condition, degree, echelon, group, level, mark, notch, order, place, position, quality, rank, rung, size, stage, station, step **2. make the grade** *informal* come through with flying colours, come up to scratch (*informal*), measure up, measure up to expectations, pass muster, prove acceptable, succeed, win through **3.** acclivity, bank, declivity, gradient, hill, incline, rise, slope *~verb* **4.** arrange, brand, class, classify, evaluate, group, order, range, rank, rate, sequence, sort, value

gradient acclivity, bank, declivity, grade, hill, incline, rise, slope

gradual continuous, even, gentle, graduated, moderate, piecemeal, progressive, regular, slow, steady, successive, unhurried

▷ **Antonyms** abrupt, broken, instantaneous, overnight, sudden

gradually bit by bit, by degrees, drop by drop, evenly, gently, little by little, moderately, piece by piece, piecemeal, progressively, slowly, steadily, step by step, unhurriedly

graduate *verb* **1.** calibrate, grade, mark off, measure out, proportion, regulate **2.** arrange, classify, grade, group, order, range, rank, sequence, sort

graft **1.** *noun* bud, implant, scion, shoot, splice, sprout **2.** *~verb* affix, implant, ingraft, insert, join, splice, transplant

grain **1.** cereals, corn **2.** grist, kernel, seed **3.** atom, bit, crumb, fragment, granule, iota, jot, mite, modicum, molecule, morsel, mote, ounce, particle, piece, scintilla (*rare*), scrap, scruple, spark, speck, suspicion, trace, whit **4.** fibre, nap, pattern, surface, texture, weave **5.** character, disposition, humour, inclination, make-up, temper

grand **1.** ambitious, august, dignified, elevated, eminent, exalted, fine, glorious, gorgeous, grandiose, great, haughty, illustrious, imposing, impressive, large, lofty, lordly, luxurious, magnificent, majestic, monumental, noble, opulent, ostentatious, palatial, pompous, pretentious, princely, regal, splendid, splendiferous (*facetious*), stately, striking, sublime, sumptuous, superb **2.** admirable, awesome (*slang*), divine, excellent, fine, first-class, first-rate, great (*informal*), hunky-dory (*informal*), marvellous (*informal*), outstanding, smashing (*informal*), splendid, splendiferous (*facetious*), super (*informal*), superb, terrific (*informal*), very good, wonderful, world-class **3.** big-time (*informal*), chief, head, highest, lead, leading, main, major league (*informal*), pre-eminent, principal, supreme

▷ **Antonyms** (*sense 1*) undignified, unimportant, unimposing, worthless (*sense 2*) awful, bad, base, terrible (*sense 3*) chickenshit (*U.S. slang*), common, contemptible, crappy (*slang*), inferior, insignificant, little, mean, petty, poor, poxy (*slang*), secondary, small, trivial

grandeur augustness, dignity, greatness, importance, loftiness, magnificence, majesty, nobility, pomp, splendour, state, stateliness, sublimity

▷ **Antonyms** commonness, inferiority, insignificance, lowliness, pettiness, smallness, triviality, unimportance

grandiloquent bombastic, flowery, fustian, high-flown, high-sounding, inflated, magniloquent, orotund, pompous, pretentious, rhetorical

grandiose **1.** affected, ambitious, bombastic, extravagant, flamboyant, high-flown, ostentatious, pompous, pretentious, showy **2.** ambitious, grand, imposing, impressive, lofty, magnificent, majestic, monumental, stately

▷ **Antonyms** down-to-earth, humble, modest, small-scale, unpretentious

grant *verb* **1.** accede to, accord, acknowledge, admit, agree to, allocate, allot, allow, assign, award, bestow, cede, concede, confer, consent to, donate, give, hand out, impart, permit, present, vouchsafe, yield **2.** *Law* assign, convey, transfer, transmit *~noun* **3.** admission, allocation, allotment, allowance, award, benefaction, bequest, boon, bounty, concession, donation, endowment, gift, hand-out, present, stipend, subsidy

granular crumbly, grainy, granulated, gravelly, gritty, rough, sandy

granulate crumble, crush, crystallize, grind, levigate (*Chemistry*), pound, powder, pulverize, triturate

granule atom, crumb, fragment, grain, iota, jot, molecule, particle, scrap, speck

graphic **1.** clear, descriptive, detailed, explicit, expressive, forcible, illustrative, lively, lucid, picturesque, striking, telling, vivid, well-drawn **2.** delineated, diagrammatic, drawn, illustrative, pictorial, representational, seen, visible, visual

▷ **Antonyms** (*sense 1*) generalized, imprecise, impressionistic, unspecific, vague, woolly

grapple **1.** catch, clasp, clutch, come to grips, fasten, grab, grasp, grip, hold, hug, lay *or* take hold, make fast, seize, wrestle **2.** address oneself to, attack, battle, clash, combat, confront, contend, cope, deal with, do battle, encounter, engage, face, fight, get to grips with, struggle, tackle, take on, tussle, wrestle

grasp *verb* **1.** catch (up), clasp, clinch, clutch, grab, grapple, grip, hold, lay *or* take hold of, seize, snatch **2.** catch on, catch *or* get the drift of, comprehend, follow, get, get the hang of (*informal*), get the message, get the picture, realize, see, take in, understand *~noun* **3.** clasp, clutches, embrace, grip, hold, possession, tenure **4.** capacity, compass, control, extent, mastery, power, range, reach, scope, sway, sweep **5.** awareness, comprehension, grip, ken, knowledge, mastery, perception, realization, understanding

grasping acquisitive, avaricious, close-fisted, covetous, greedy, mean, miserly, niggardly, penny-pinching (*informal*), rapacious, selfish, snoep (*S. African informal*), stingy, tight-arsed (*taboo slang*), tight as a duck's arse (*taboo slang*), tight-assed (*U.S. taboo slang*), tightfisted, usurious, venal

▷ **Antonyms** altruistic, generous, unselfish

grate *verb* **1.** mince, pulverize, shred, triturate **2.** creak, grind, rasp, rub, scrape, scratch **3.** aggravate (*informal*), annoy, chafe, exasperate, fret, gall, get one down, get on one's nerves (*informal*), get on one's wick (*Brit. slang*), get under someone's skin (*informal*), get up someone's nose (*informal*), irk, irritate, jar, nark (*Brit., Austral., & N.Z. slang*), nettle, peeve, rankle, rub one up the wrong way, set one's teeth on edge, vex

grateful **1.** appreciative, beholden, indebted, obliged, thankful **2.** acceptable, agreeable, favourable, gratifying, nice, pleasing, refreshing, restful, satisfactory, satisfying, welcome

gratification delight, enjoyment, fruition, fulfilment, glee, indulgence, joy, kick *or* kicks (*informal*), pleasure, recompense, relish, reward, satisfaction, thrill
▷ **Antonyms** control, denial, disappointment, discipline, dissatisfaction, frustration, pain, restraint, sorrow

gratify cater to, delight, favour, fawn on, feed, fulfil, give pleasure, gladden, humour, indulge, pander to, please, recompense, requite, satisfy, thrill

grating[1] *adjective* annoying, disagreeable, discordant, displeasing, grinding, harsh, irksome, irritating, jarring, offensive, rasping, raucous, scraping, squeaky, strident, unpleasant, vexatious
▷ **Antonyms** agreeable, calming, mellifluous, musical, pleasing, soft, soothing

grating[2] *noun* grate, grid, gridiron, grille, lattice, trellis

gratis buckshee (*Brit. slang*), for nothing, free, freely, free of charge, gratuitously, on the house, unpaid

gratitude appreciation, gratefulness, indebtedness, obligation, recognition, sense of obligation, thankfulness, thanks
▷ **Antonyms** ingratitude, ungratefulness, unthankfulness

gratuitous 1. buckshee (*Brit. slang*), complimentary, free, gratis, spontaneous, unasked-for, unpaid, unrewarded, voluntary **2.** assumed, baseless, causeless, groundless, irrelevant, needless, superfluous, uncalled-for, unfounded, unjustified, unmerited, unnecessary, unprovoked, unwarranted, wanton
▷ **Antonyms** (*sense 1*) compulsory, involuntary, paid (*sense 2*) justifiable, provoked, relevant, well-founded

gratuity baksheesh, benefaction, bonsela (*S. African*), bonus, boon, bounty, donation, gift, largesse *or* largess, perquisite, *pourboire,* present, recompense, reward, tip

grave[1] *noun* burying place, crypt, last resting place, mausoleum, pit, sepulchre, tomb, vault

grave[2] *adjective* **1.** dignified, dour, dull, earnest, gloomy, grim-faced, heavy, leaden, long-faced, muted, quiet, sage (*obsolete*), sedate, serious, sober, solemn, sombre, staid, subdued, thoughtful, unsmiling **2.** acute, critical, crucial, dangerous, exigent, hazardous, important, life-and-death, momentous, of great consequence, perilous, pressing, serious, severe, significant, threatening, urgent, vital, weighty
▷ **Antonyms** carefree, exciting, flippant, happy, joyous, merry, undignified (*sense 2*) frivolous, insignificant, mild, trifling, unimportant

graveyard boneyard (*informal*), burial ground, cemetery, charnel house, churchyard, God's acre (*literary*), necropolis

gravitas gravity, seriousness, solemnity

gravitate 1. (*with* **to** *or* **towards**) be attracted, be drawn, be influenced, be pulled, incline, lean, move, tend **2.** be precipitated, descend, drop, fall, precipitate, settle, sink

gravity 1. acuteness, consequence, exigency, hazardousness, importance, moment, momentousness, perilousness, pressingness, seriousness, severity, significance, urgency, weightiness **2.** demureness, dignity, earnestness, gloom, gravitas, grimness, reserve, sedateness, seriousness, sobriety, solemnity, thoughtfulness
▷ **Antonyms** (*sense 1*) inconsequentiality, insignificance, triviality, unimportance (*sense 2*) flippancy, frivolity, gaiety, happiness, joy, levity, merriment, thoughtlessness

graze[1] *verb* browse, crop, feed, pasture

graze[2] *verb* **1.** brush, glance off, kiss, rub, scrape, shave, skim, touch **2.** abrade, bark, chafe, scrape, scratch, skin *~noun* **3.** abrasion, scrape, scratch

greasy 1. fatty, oily, oleaginous, slick, slimy, slippery **2.** fawning, glib, grovelling, ingratiating, oily, slick, smarmy (*Brit. informal*), smooth, sycophantic, toadying, unctuous

great 1. big, bulky, colossal, elephantine, enormous, extensive, gigantic, ginormous (*informal*), huge, humongous *or* humungous (*U.S. slang*), immense, large, mammoth, prodigious, stellar (*informal*), stupendous, tremendous, vast, voluminous **2.** extended, lengthy, long, prolonged, protracted **3.** big-time (*informal*), capital, chief, grand, head, lead, leading, main, major, major league (*informal*), paramount, primary, principal, prominent, superior **4.** considerable, decided, excessive, extravagant, extreme, grievous, high, inordinate, prodigious, pronounced, serious (*informal*), strong **5.** consequential, critical, crucial, grave, heavy, important, momentous, serious, significant, weighty **6.** celebrated, distinguished, eminent, exalted, excellent, famed, famous, glorious, illustrious, notable, noteworthy, outstanding, prominent, remarkable, renowned, superb, superlative, talented, world-class **7.** august, chivalrous, dignified, distinguished, exalted, fine, glorious, grand, heroic, high-minded, idealistic, impressive, lofty, magnanimous, noble, princely, sublime **8.** active, devoted, enthusiastic, keen, zealous **9.** able, adept, adroit, crack (*slang*), expert, good, masterly, proficient, skilful, skilled **10.** *informal* admirable, awesome (*slang*), bitchin', boffo (*slang*), brill (*informal*), chillin' (*U.S. slang*), cracking (*Brit. informal*), crucial (*slang*), def (*informal*), dope (*slang*), excellent, fantastic (*informal*), fine, first-rate, good, hunky-dory (*informal*), jim-dandy (*slang*), marvellous (*informal*), mean (*slang*), mega (*slang*), sovereign, superb, terrific (*informal*), the dog's bollocks (*taboo slang*), topping (*Brit. slang*), tremendous (*informal*), wonderful **11.** absolute, arrant, complete, consummate, downright, egregious, flagrant, out-and-out, perfect, positive, thoroughgoing, thundering (*informal*), total, unmitigated, unqualified, utter

▷ **Antonyms** (*sense 1*) diminutive, little, small (*sense 5*) inconsequential, inconsiderable, insignificant, petty, trivial, unimportant (*sense 6*) average, inferior, poor, secondary, second-rate, undistinguished, unnotable (*sense 7*) base, ignoble, inhumane, hateful, mean, unkind (*sense 9*) inexperienced, unskilled, untrained (*sense 10*) bad, terrible, weak

greatly abundantly, by leaps and bounds, by much, considerably, enormously, exceedingly, extremely, highly, hugely, immensely, markedly, mightily, much, notably, powerfully, remarkably, seriously (*informal*), to the nth degree, tremendously, vastly, very much

greatness 1. bulk, enormity, hugeness, immensity, largeness, length, magnitude, mass, prodigiousness, size, vastness **2.** amplitude, force, high degree, intensity, potency, power, strength **3.** gravity, heaviness, import, importance, moment, momentousness, seriousness, significance, urgency, weight **4.** celebrity, distinction, eminence, fame, glory, grandeur, illustriousness, lustre, note, renown **5.** chivalry, dignity, disinterestedness, generosity, grandeur, heroism, high-mindedness, idealism, loftiness, majesty, nobility, nobleness, stateliness, sublimity

greed, greediness 1. edacity, esurience, gluttony, gormandizing, hunger, insatiableness, ravenousness, voracity **2.** acquisitiveness, avarice, avidity, covetousness, craving, cupidity, desire, eagerness, graspingness, longing, rapacity, selfishness

▷ **Antonyms** altruism, benevolence, generosity, largesse *or* largess, munificence, self-restraint, unselfishness

greedy 1. edacious, esurient, gluttonous, gormandizing, hoggish, hungry, insatiable, piggish, ravenous, voracious **2.** acquisitive, avaricious, avid, covetous, craving, desirous, eager, grasping, hungry, impatient, rapacious, selfish

▷ **Antonyms** altruistic, apathetic, benevolent, full, generous, indifferent, munificent, self-restrained, unselfish

Greek 1. *noun* Hellene **2.** *~adjective* Hellenic

green *adjective* **1.** blooming, budding, flourishing, fresh, grassy, leafy, new, undecayed, verdant, verdurous **2.** fresh, immature, new, raw, recent, unripe **3.** conservationist, ecologically sound, environment-friendly, non-polluting, ozone-friendly **4.** callow, credulous, gullible, ignorant, immature, inexperienced, inexpert, ingenuous, innocent, naive, new, raw, unpolished, unpractised, unskilful, unsophisticated, untrained, unversed, wet behind the ears (*informal*) **5.** covetous, envious, grudging, jealous, resentful **6.** ill, nauseous, pale, sick, under the weather, unhealthy, wan **7.** immature, pliable, supple, tender, undried, unseasoned, young *~noun* **8.** common, grassplot, lawn, sward, turf

greenhorn apprentice, beginner, ignoramus, ingénue, learner, naïf, neophyte, newcomer, novice, raw recruit, simpleton, tyro

green light approval, authorization, blessing, clearance, confirmation, go-ahead (*informal*), imprimatur, O.K. *or* okay (*informal*), permission, sanction

greet accost, address, compliment, hail, meet, nod to, receive, salute, tip one's hat to, welcome

greeting 1. address, hail, reception, salutation, salute, welcome **2.** *plural* best wishes, compliments, devoirs, good wishes, regards, respects, salutations

gregarious affable, companionable, convivial, cordial, friendly, outgoing, sociable, social

▷ **Antonyms** antisocial, reserved, solitary, standoffish, unsociable, withdrawn

grey 1. ashen, bloodless, colourless, like death warmed up (*informal*), livid, pale, pallid, wan **2.** cheerless, cloudy, dark, depressing, dim, dismal, drab, dreary, dull, foggy, gloomy, misty, murky, overcast, sunless **3.** anonymous, characterless, colourless, dull, indistinct, neutral, unclear, unidentifiable **4.** aged, ancient, elderly, experienced, hoary, mature, old, venerable

grief 1. affliction, agony, anguish, bereavement, dejection, distress, grievance, hardship, heartache, heartbreak, misery, mournfulness, mourning, pain, regret, remorse, sadness, sorrow, suffering, trial, tribulation, trouble, woe **2. come to grief** *informal* come unstuck, fail, fall flat on one's face, meet with disaster, miscarry

▷ **Antonyms** (*sense 1*) cheer, comfort, consolation, delight, gladness, happiness, joy, rejoicing, solace

grief-stricken afflicted, agonized, broken, brokenhearted, crushed, desolate, despairing, devastated, heartbroken, inconsolable, overwhelmed, sorrowful, sorrowing, woebegone, wretched

grievance affliction, axe to grind, beef (*slang*), chip on one's shoulder (*informal*), complaint, damage, distress, grief, gripe (*informal*), hardship, injury, injustice, protest, resentment, sorrow, trial, tribulation, trouble, unhappiness, wrong

grieve 1. ache, bemoan, bewail, complain, deplore, lament, mourn, regret, rue, sorrow, suffer, wail, weep **2.** afflict, agonize, break the heart of, crush, distress, hurt, injure, make one's heart bleed, pain, sadden, wound

▷ **Antonyms** cheer, comfort, console, ease, gladden, please, rejoice, solace

grievous 1. afflicting, calamitous, damaging, distressing, dreadful, grave, harmful, heavy, hurtful, injurious, lamentable, oppressive, painful, severe, wounding **2.** appalling, atrocious, deplorable, dreadful, egregious, flagrant, glaring, heinous, intolerable, lamentable, monstrous, offensive, outrageous, shameful, shocking, unbearable **3.** agonized, grief-stricken, heart-rending, mournful, pitiful, sorrowful, tragic

▷ **Antonyms** delightful, glad, happy, insignificant, joyous, mild, pleasant, trivial, unimportant

grim cruel, ferocious, fierce, forbidding, formidable, frightful, ghastly, godawful (*slang*), grisly, gruesome, hard, harsh, hideous, horrible, horrid, implacable, merciless, morose, relentless, resolute, ruthless, severe, shocking, sinister, stern, sullen, surly, terrible, unrelenting, unyielding

▷ **Antonyms** amiable, attractive, benign, cheerful, easy, genial, gentle, happy, kind, pleasant, soft, sympathetic

grimace 1. *noun* face, frown, mouth, scowl, sneer, wry face **2.** *~verb* frown, lour *or* lower, make a face *or* faces, mouth, scowl, sneer

grime dirt, filth, grot (*slang*), smut, soot

grimy begrimed, besmeared, besmirched, dirty, filthy, foul, grubby, scuzzy (*slang*), smutty, soiled, sooty, unclean

grind *verb* **1.** abrade, comminute, crush, granulate, grate, kibble, mill, pound, powder, pulverize, triturate **2.** file, polish, sand, sharpen, smooth, whet **3.** gnash, grate, grit, scrape **4.** (*with* **down**) afflict, harass, hold down, hound, oppress, persecute, plague, trouble, tyrannize (over) *~noun* **5.** *informal* chore, drudgery, hard work, labour, sweat (*informal*), task, toil

grip *noun* **1.** clasp, handclasp (*U.S.*), purchase **2.** clutches, comprehension, control, domination, grasp, hold, influence, keeping, mastery, perception, possession, power, tenure, understanding **3.** **come** *or* **get to grips (with)** close with, confront, contend with, cope with, deal with, encounter, face up to, grapple with, grasp, handle, meet, tackle, take on, take the bit between one's teeth, undertake *~verb* **4.** clasp, clutch, grasp, hold, latch on to, seize, take hold of **5.** absorb, catch up, compel, engross, enthral, entrance, fascinate, hold, involve, mesmerize, rivet, spellbind

gripe *verb* **1.** *informal* beef (*slang*), bellyache (*slang*), bitch (*slang*), bleat, carp, complain, groan, grouch (*informal*), grouse, grumble, kvetch (*U.S. slang*), moan, nag, whine **2.** ache, compress, cramp, hurt, pain, pinch, press, squeeze *~noun* **3.** (*often plural*) ache, aching, affliction, colic, cramps, distress, griping, pain, pang, pinching, stomachache, twinge **4.** *informal* beef (*slang*), complaint, grievance, groan, grouch (*informal*), grouse, grumble, moan, objection, protest

gripping compelling, compulsive, engrossing, enthralling, entrancing, exciting, fascinating, riveting, spellbinding, thrilling, unputdownable (*informal*)

grisly abominable, appalling, awful, dreadful, frightful, ghastly, grim, gruesome, hellacious (*U.S. slang*), hideous, horrible, horrid, macabre, shocking, sickening, terrible, terrifying

▷ **Antonyms** agreeable, attractive, charming, innocuous, nice, pleasant

grit *noun* **1.** dust, gravel, pebbles, sand **2.** backbone, balls (*taboo slang*), courage, determination, doggedness, fortitude, gameness, guts (*informal*), hardihood, mettle, nerve, perseverance, pluck, resolution, spirit, tenacity, toughness *~verb* **3.** clench, gnash, grate, grind

gritty 1. abrasive, dusty, grainy, granular, gravelly, rasping, rough, sandy **2.** ballsy (*taboo slang*), brave, courageous, determined, dogged, feisty (*informal, chiefly U.S. & Canad.*), game, hardy, mettlesome, plucky, resolute, spirited, steadfast, tenacious, tough

grizzle fret, girn (*Scot.*), pule, snivel, whimper, whine, whinge (*informal*)

grizzled canescent, grey, grey-haired, grey-headed, greying, griseous, grizzly, hoary

groan *noun* **1.** cry, moan, sigh, whine **2.** *informal* beef (*slang*), complaint, gripe (*informal*), grouse, grumble, objection, protest *~verb* **3.** cry, moan, sigh, whine **4.** *informal* beef (*slang*), bemoan, bitch (*slang*), complain, gripe (*informal*), grouse, grumble, lament, object

groggy befuddled, confused, dazed, dizzy, faint, muzzy, punch-drunk, reeling, shaky, staggering, stunned, stupefied, unsteady, weak, wobbly, woozy (*informal*)

groom *noun* **1.** currier (*rare*), hostler *or* ostler (*archaic*), stableboy, stableman *~verb* **2.** clean, dress, get up (*informal*), gussy up (*slang, chiefly U.S.*), preen, primp, smarten up, spruce up, tidy, turn out **3.** brush, clean, curry, rub down, tend **4.** coach, drill, educate, make ready, nurture, prepare, prime, ready, train

groove channel, cut, cutting, flute, furrow, gutter, hollow, indentation, rebate, rut, score, trench, trough

grope cast about, feel, finger, fish, flounder, forage, fumble, grabble, scrabble, search

gross *adjective* **1.** big, bulky, corpulent, dense, fat, great, heavy, hulking, large, lumpish, massive, obese, overweight, thick **2.** aggregate, before deductions, before tax, entire, total, whole **3.** coarse, crude, improper, impure, indecent, indelicate, lewd, low, obscene, offensive, ribald, rude, sensual, smutty, unseemly, vulgar, X-rated (*informal*) **4.** apparent, arrant, blatant, downright, egregious, flagrant, glaring, grievous, heinous, manifest, obvious, outrageous, plain, rank, serious, shameful, sheer, shocking, unmitigated, unqualified, utter **5.** boorish, callous, coarse, crass, dull, ignorant, imperceptive, insensitive, tasteless, uncultured, undiscriminating, unfeeling, unrefined, unsophisticated *~verb* **6.** bring in, earn, make, rake in (*informal*), take

▷ **Antonyms** *~adjective* (*sense 1*) delicate, little, petite, slim, small, svelte, thin (*sense 2*) net (*sense 3*) decent, delicate, proper, pure (*sense 4*) partial, qualified (*sense 5*) cultivated, elegant *~verb* clear, net

grossness **1.** bigness, bulkiness, corpulence, fatness, greatness, heaviness, lumpishness, obesity, thickness **2.** bestiality, coarseness, crudity, impurity, indecency, indelicacy, licentiousness, obscenity, offensiveness, ribaldry, rudeness, sensuality, smut, smuttiness, unseemliness, vulgarity **3.** blatancy, egregiousness, flagrancy, grievousness, obviousness, rankness, seriousness, shamefulness **4.** coarseness, crassness, ignorance, insensitivity, lack of taste, pig-ignorance (*slang*), tastelessness

grotesque absurd, bizarre, deformed, distorted, extravagant, fanciful, fantastic, freakish, incongruous, ludicrous, malformed, misshapen, odd, outlandish, preposterous, ridiculous, strange, unnatural, weird, whimsical

▷ **Antonyms** average, classic, graceful, natural, normal, realistic

grouch *verb* **1.** beef (*slang*), bellyache (*slang*), bitch (*slang*), bleat, carp, complain, find fault, gripe (*informal*), grouse, grumble, kvetch (*U.S. slang*), moan, whine, whinge (*informal*) *~noun* **2.** beef (*slang*), complaint, grievance, gripe (*informal*), grouse, grumble, moan, objection, protest **3.** complainer, crab (*informal*), crosspatch (*informal*), curmudgeon, faultfinder, grouser, grumbler, malcontent, moaner, whiner

grouchy cantankerous, cross, discontented, grumbling, grumpy, huffy, ill-tempered, irascible, irritable, liverish, peevish, petulant, querulous, ratty (*Brit. & N.Z. informal*), sulky, surly, testy, tetchy

ground *noun* **1.** clod, dirt, dry land, dust, earth, field, land, loam, mould, sod, soil, terra firma, terrain, turf **2.** (*often plural*) area, country, district, domain, estate, fields, gardens, habitat, holding, land, property, realm, terrain, territory, tract **3.** (*usually plural*) account, argument, base, basis, call, cause, excuse, factor, foundation, inducement, justification, motive, occasion, premise, pretext, rationale, reason **4.** (*usually plural*) deposit, dregs, grouts, lees, sediment, settlings **5.** arena, field, park (*informal*), pitch, stadium *~verb* **6.** base, establish, fix, found, set, settle **7.** acquaint with, coach, familiarize with, inform, initiate, instruct, prepare, teach, train, tutor

groundless baseless, chimerical, empty, false, idle, illusory, imaginary, unauthorized, uncalled-for, unfounded, unjustified, unprovoked, unsupported, unwarranted

▷ **Antonyms** justified, logical, proven, real, reasonable, substantial, supported, true, well-founded

groundwork base, basis, cornerstone, footing, foundation, fundamentals, preliminaries, preparation, spadework, underpinnings

group *noun* **1.** aggregation, assemblage, association, band, batch, bevy, bunch, camp, category, circle, class, clique, clump, cluster, collection, company, congregation, coterie, crowd, faction, formation, gang, gathering, organization, pack, party, posse (*slang*), set, troop *~verb* **2.** arrange, assemble, associate, assort, bracket, class, classify, dispose, gather, marshal, order, organize, put together, range, sort **3.** associate, band together, cluster, congregate, consort, fraternize, gather, get together

grouse **1.** *verb* beef (*slang*), bellyache (*slang*), bitch (*slang*), bleat, carp, complain, find fault, gripe (*informal*), grouch (*informal*), grumble, kvetch (*U.S. slang*), moan, whine, whinge (*informal*) **2.** *~noun* beef (*slang*), complaint, grievance, gripe (*informal*), grouch (*informal*), grumble, moan, objection, protest

grove brake, coppice, copse, covert, hurst (*archaic*), plantation, spinney, thicket, wood, woodland

grovel abase oneself, bootlick (*informal*), bow and scrape, brown-nose (*taboo slang*), cower, crawl, creep, cringe, crouch, demean oneself, fawn, flatter, humble oneself, kiss ass (*taboo slang*), kowtow, lick someone's arse (*taboo *slang*), lick someone's boots, pander to, sneak, toady

▷ **Antonyms** be proud, domineer, face, hold one's head high, intimidate

grow **1.** develop, enlarge, expand, extend, fill out, get bigger, get taller, heighten, increase, multiply, spread, stretch, swell, thicken, widen **2.** develop, flourish, germinate, shoot, spring up, sprout, vegetate **3.** arise, issue, originate, spring, stem **4.** advance, expand, flourish, improve, progress, prosper, succeed, thrive **5.** become, come to be, develop (into), get, turn, wax **6.** breed, cultivate, farm, nurture, produce, propagate, raise

▷ **Antonyms** decline, decrease, die, diminish, dwindle, fail, lessen, shrink, subside, wane

grown-up **1.** *adjective* adult, fully-grown, mature, of age **2.** *~noun* adult, man, woman

growth **1.** aggrandizement, augmentation, development, enlargement, evolution, expansion, extension, growing, heightening, increase, multiplication, proliferation, stretching, thickening, widening **2.** crop, cultivation, development, germination, produce, production, shooting, sprouting, vegetation **3.** advance, advancement, expansion, improvement, progress, prosperity, rise, success **4.** *Medicine* excrescence, lump, tumour

▷ **Antonyms** (*sense 1*) decline, decrease, dwindling, failure, lessening, retreat, shrinkage, slackening, subsiding

grub *verb* **1.** burrow, dig up, probe, pull up, root (*informal*), rootle (*Brit.*), search for, uproot **2.** ferret, forage, hunt, rummage, scour, search, uncover, unearth **3.** drudge, grind (*informal*), labour, plod, slave, slog, sweat, toil *~noun* **4.** caterpillar, larva, maggot **5.** *slang* eats (*slang*), feed, food, nosebag (*slang*), nosh (*slang*), rations, sustenance, tack (*informal*), victuals, vittles (*obsolete or dialect*)

grubby besmeared, dirty, filthy, frowzy, grimy, grungy (*slang chiefly U.S. & Canad.*), manky (*Scot. dialect*), mean, messy, mucky, scruffy, scuzzy (*slang*), seedy, shabby, slovenly, smutty, soiled, sordid, squalid, unkempt, untidy, unwashed

grudge **1.** *noun* animosity, animus, antipathy, aversion, bitterness, chip on one's shoulder (*informal*), dislike, enmity, grievance, hard feelings, hate, ill will, malevolence, malice, pique, rancour, resentment, spite, venom **2.** *~verb* begrudge, be reluctant, complain, covet, envy, hold back, mind, resent, stint

▷ **Antonyms** *~noun* appreciation, goodwill, liking, thankfulness *~verb* be glad for, celebrate, welcome

gruelling arduous, backbreaking, brutal, crushing, demanding, difficult, exhausting, fatiguing, fierce, grinding, hard, harsh, laborious, punishing, severe, stiff, strenuous, taxing, tiring, trying

▷ **Antonyms** cushy (*informal*), easy, enjoyable, light, pleasant, undemanding

gruesome abominable, awful, fearful, from hell (*informal*), ghastly, grim, grisly, hellacious (*U.S. slang*), hideous, horrendous, horrible, horrid, horrific, horrifying, loathsome, macabre, obscene, repugnant, repulsive, shocking, spine-chilling, terrible

▷ **Antonyms** appealing, benign, cheerful, pleasant, sweet

gruff **1.** bad-tempered, bearish, blunt, brusque, churlish, crabbed, crusty, curt, discourteous, grouchy (*informal*), grumpy, ill-humoured, ill-natured, impolite, rough, rude, sour, sullen, surly, uncivil, ungracious, unmannerly **2.** croaking, guttural, harsh, hoarse, husky, low, rasping, rough, throaty

▷ **Antonyms** (*sense 1*) courteous, good-tempered, gracious, kind, pleasant, polite (*sense 2*) mellifluous, smooth, sweet

grumble *verb* **1.** beef (*slang*), bellyache (*slang*), bitch (*slang*), bleat, carp, complain, find fault, gripe (*informal*), grouch (*informal*), grouse, kvetch (*U.S. slang*), moan, repine, whine, whinge (*informal*) **2.** growl, gurgle, murmur, mutter, roar, rumble *~noun* **3.** beef (*slang*), complaint, grievance, gripe (*informal*), grouch (*informal*), grouse, moan, objection, protest **4.** growl, gurgle, murmur, muttering, roar, rumble

grumpy cantankerous, crabbed, cross, crotchety (*informal*), edgy, grouchy (*informal*), grumbling, huffy, ill-tempered, irritable, liverish, peevish, petulant, querulous, ratty (*Brit. & N.Z. informal*), sulky, sullen, surly, testy, tetchy

guarantee **1.** *noun* assurance, bond, certainty, collateral, covenant, earnest, guaranty, pledge, promise, security, surety, undertaking, warranty, word, word of honour **2.** *~verb* answer for, assure, certify, ensure, insure, maintain, make certain, pledge, promise, protect, secure, stand behind, swear, vouch for, warrant

guarantor backer, bailsman (*rare*), bondsman (*Law*), guarantee, sponsor, supporter, surety, underwriter, voucher, warrantor

guaranty **1.** agreement, assurance, bond, contract, covenant, guarantee, insurance, oath, pledge, promise, undertaking, warrant, warranty, word **2.** bail, bond, collateral, deposit, earnest, gage, pawn, pledge, security, token

guard *verb* **1.** cover, defend, escort, keep, mind, oversee, patrol, police, preserve, protect, safeguard, save, screen, secure, shelter, shield, supervise, tend, watch, watch over *~noun* **2.** custodian, defender, lookout, picket, protector, sentinel, sentry, warder, watch, watchman **3.** convoy, escort, patrol **4.** buffer, bulwark, bumper, defence, pad, protection, rampart, safeguard, screen, security, shield **5.** attention, care, caution, heed, vigilance, wariness, watchfulness **6. off (one's) guard** napping, unprepared, unready, unwary, with one's defences down **7. on (one's) guard** alert, cautious, circumspect, on the alert, on the lookout, on the qui vive, prepared, ready, vigilant, wary, watchful

guarded cagey (*informal*), careful, cautious, circumspect, discreet, leery (*slang*), noncommittal, prudent, reserved, restrained, reticent, suspicious, wary

guardian attendant, champion, curator, custodian, defender, escort, guard, keeper, preserver, protector, trustee, warden, warder

guerrilla freedom fighter, irregular, member of the underground *or* resistance, partisan, underground fighter

guess *verb* **1.** conjecture, estimate, fathom, hypothesize, penetrate, predict, solve, speculate, work out **2.** believe, conjecture, dare say, deem, divine, fancy, hazard, imagine, judge, reckon, suppose, surmise, suspect, think *~noun* **3.** ballpark figure (*informal*), conjecture, feeling, hypothesis, judgment, notion, prediction, reckoning, shot in the dark, speculation, supposition, surmise, suspicion, theory

▷ **Antonyms** *~verb* be certain, be sure, know, prove, show *~noun* certainty, fact

guesswork conjecture, estimation, presumption, speculation, supposition, surmise, suspicion, theory

guest boarder, caller, company, lodger, visitant, visitor

guff balderdash, balls (*taboo slang*), bilge (*informal*), bosh (*informal*), bull (*slang*), bullshit (*taboo slang*), bunkum *or* buncombe (*chiefly U.S.*), cobblers (*Brit. taboo slang*), crap (*slang*), drivel, empty talk, eyewash (*informal*), garbage (*informal*), guff (*slang*), hogwash, hokum (*slang, chiefly U.S. & Canad.*), horsefeathers (*U.S. slang*), hot air (*informal*), humbug, kak (*S. African slang*), moonshine, nonsense, pap, piffle (*informal*), poppycock (*informal*), rot, rubbish, shit (*taboo slang*), tommyrot, tosh (*slang, chiefly Brit.*), trash, tripe (*informal*)

guidance advice, auspices, conduct, control, counsel, counselling, direction, government, help, instruction, intelligence, leadership, management, teaching

guide *verb* **1.** accompany, attend, conduct, convoy, direct, escort, lead, pilot, shepherd, show the way, steer, usher **2.** command, control, direct, handle, manage, manoeuvre, steer **3.** advise, counsel, educate, govern, influence, instruct, oversee, regulate, rule, superintend, supervise, sway, teach, train *~noun* **4.** adviser, attendant, chaperon, cicerone, conductor, controller, counsellor, director, dragoman, escort, leader, mentor, monitor, pilot, steersman, teacher, torchbearer, usher **5.** criterion, example, exemplar, ideal, imago (*Psychoanalysis*), inspiration, lodestar, master, model, par, paradigm, standard **6.** beacon, clue, guiding light, key, landmark, lodestar, mark, marker, pointer, sign, signal, signpost **7.** Baedeker, catalogue, directory, guidebook, handbook, instructions, key, manual, vade mecum

guild association, brotherhood, club, company, corporation, fellowship, fraternity, league, lodge, order, organization, society, union

guile art, artfulness, artifice, cleverness, craft, craftiness, cunning, deceit, deception, duplicity, gamesmanship (*informal*), knavery, ruse, sharp practice, slyness, treachery, trickery, trickiness, wiliness

▷ **Antonyms** candour, frankness, honesty, sincerity, truthfulness

guileful artful, clever, crafty, cunning, deceitful, duplicitous, foxy, sly, sneaky, treacherous, tricky, underhand, wily

guileless above-board, artless, candid, frank, genuine, honest, ingenuous, innocent, naive, natural, open, simple, simple-minded, sincere, straightforward, truthful, undesigning, unsophisticated, upfront (*informal*)

guilt **1.** blame, blameworthiness, criminality, culpability, delinquency, guiltiness, iniquity, misconduct, responsibility, sinfulness, wickedness, wrong, wrongdoing **2.** bad conscience, contrition, disgrace, dishonour, guiltiness, guilty conscience, infamy, regret, remorse, self-condemnation, self-reproach, shame, stigma

▷ **Antonyms** blamelessness, honour, innocence, pride, righteousness, self-respect, sinlessness, virtue

guiltless blameless, clean (*slang*), clear, immaculate, impeccable, innocent, irreproachable, pure, sinless, spotless, squeaky-clean, unimpeachable, unsullied, untainted, untarnished

guilty **1.** at fault, blameworthy, convicted, criminal, culpable, delinquent, erring, evil, felonious, iniquitous, offending, reprehensible, responsible, sinful, to blame, wicked, wrong **2.** ashamed, conscience-stricken, contrite, hangdog, regretful, remorseful, rueful, shamefaced, sheepish, sorry

▷ **Antonyms** blameless, innocent, moral, proud, righteous, virtuous

guise air, appearance, aspect, behaviour, demeanour, disguise, dress, façade, face, fashion, form, front, mask, mode, pretence, semblance, shape, show

gulf 1. bay, bight, sea inlet 2. abyss, breach, chasm, cleft, gap, opening, rent, rift, separation, split, void, whirlpool

gull 1. *noun* babe in arms (*informal*), chump (*informal*), dupe, easy mark (*slang*), fool, gudgeon (*slang*), mug (*slang*), sap (*slang*), simpleton, sucker (*slang*) 2. *~verb* beguile, cheat, con (*slang*), cozen, deceive, defraud, dupe, hoax, pull a fast one on (*informal*), put one over on (*informal*), rook (*slang*), sell a pup to, skin (*slang*), stiff (*slang*), swindle, take for a ride (*informal*), take in (*informal*), trick

gullet craw, crop, maw, oesophagus, throat

gullibility credulity, innocence, naïveté, simplicity, trustingness

gullible as green as grass, born yesterday, credulous, easily taken in, foolish, green, innocent, naive, silly, simple, trusting, unsceptical, unsophisticated, unsuspecting, wet behind the ears (*informal*)

▷ **Antonyms** cynical, sophisticated, suspicious, untrusting, worldly

gully channel, ditch, gutter, watercourse

gulp *verb* 1. bolt, devour, gobble, guzzle, knock back (*informal*), quaff, swallow, swig (*informal*), swill, toss off, wolf 2. choke, gasp, stifle, swallow *~noun* 3. draught, mouthful, swallow, swig (*informal*)

gum 1. *noun* adhesive, cement, exudate, glue, mucilage, paste, resin 2. *~verb* affix, cement, clog, glue, paste, stick, stiffen

gummy adhesive, gluey, sticky, tacky, viscid

gumption ability, acumen, astuteness, cleverness, common sense, discernment, enterprise, get-up-and-go (*informal*), horse sense, initiative, mother wit, nous (*Brit. slang*), resourcefulness, sagacity, savvy (*slang*), shrewdness, spirit, wit(s)

gunman assassin, bandit, bravo, desperado, gangster, gunslinger (*U.S. slang*), heavy (*slang*), hit man (*slang*), killer, mobster (*U.S. slang*), murderer, terrorist, thug

gurgle 1. *verb* babble, bubble, burble, crow, lap, murmur, plash, purl, ripple, splash 2. *~noun* babble, murmur, purl, ripple

guru authority, guiding light, leader, maharishi, mahatma, master, mentor, sage, swami, teacher, torchbearer, tutor

gush *verb* 1. burst, cascade, flood, flow, issue, jet, pour, run, rush, spout, spurt, stream 2. babble, blather, chatter, effervesce, effuse, enthuse, jabber, overstate, spout *~noun* 3. burst, cascade, flood, flow, issue, jet, outburst, outflow, rush, spout, spurt, stream, torrent 4. babble, blather, chatter, effusion, exuberance

gushy cloying, effusive, emotional, excessive, fulsome, gushing, icky (*informal*), mawkish, overdone, overenthusiastic, over the top, sentimental

gust *noun* 1. blast, blow, breeze, flurry, gale, puff, rush, squall 2. burst, eruption, explosion, fit, gale, outburst, paroxysm, passion, storm, surge *~verb* 3. blast, blow, puff, squall

gusto appetite, appreciation, brio, delight, enjoyment, enthusiasm, exhilaration, fervour, liking, pleasure, relish, savour, verve, zeal, zest, zing (*informal*)

▷ **Antonyms** apathy, coolness, disinterest, distaste, inertia

gusty blowy, blustering, blustery, breezy, inclement, squally, stormy, tempestuous, windy

gut *noun* 1. (*often plural*) belly, bowels, entrails, innards (*informal*), insides (*informal*), intestines, inwards, paunch, stomach, viscera 2. *plural informal* audacity, backbone, boldness, bottle (*slang*), courage, daring, forcefulness, grit, hardihood, mettle, nerve, pluck, spirit, spunk (*informal*), willpower *~verb* 3. clean, disembowel, draw, dress, eviscerate 4. clean out, despoil, empty, pillage, plunder, ransack, ravage, rifle, sack, strip *~adjective* 5. *informal* basic, deep-seated, emotional, heartfelt, innate, instinctive, intuitive, involuntary, natural, spontaneous, unthinking, visceral

gutless abject, chicken (*slang*), chickenshit (*U.S. slang*), cowardly, craven, faint-hearted, feeble, irresolute, lily-livered, spineless, submissive, timid, weak

▷ **Antonyms** bold, brave, courageous, determined, resolute

gutsy ballsy (*taboo slang*), bold, brave, courageous, determined, feisty (*informal, chiefly U.S. & Canad.*), gallant, game (*informal*), gritty, have-a-go (*informal*), indomitable, mettlesome, plucky, resolute, spirited, staunch

gutter channel, conduit, ditch, drain, duct, pipe, sluice, trench, trough, tube

guttersnipe gamin, mudlark (*slang*), ragamuffin, street Arab (*offensive*), street urchin, waif

guttural deep, gravelly, gruff, hoarse, husky, low, rasping, rough, thick, throaty

guy 1. *noun informal* bloke (*Brit. informal*), cat (*slang*), chap, fellow, lad, man, person, youth 2. *~verb* caricature, make (a) game of, make fun of, mock, poke fun at, rib (*informal*), ridicule, send up (*Brit informal*), take off (*informal*), take the piss out of (*slang*)

guzzle bolt, carouse, cram, devour, drink, gobble, gorge, gormandize, knock back (*informal*), pig out (*U.S. & Canad. slang*), quaff, stuff (oneself), swill, tope, wolf

Gypsy, Gipsy Bohemian, nomad, rambler, roamer, Romany, rover, traveller, vaga~bond, vagrant, wanderer

gyrate circle, pirouette, revolve, rotate, spin, spiral, twirl, whirl

gyration convolution, pirouette, revolu~tion, rotation, spin, spinning, spiral, whirl, whirling

H, h

habiliment apparel, array, attire, clothes, clothing, costume, dress, garb, garment, habit, raiment (*archaic or poetic*), robes, uniform, vestments

habit *noun* **1.** bent, custom, disposition, manner, mannerism, practice, proclivity, propensity, quirk, tendency, way **2.** convention, custom, mode, practice, routine, rule, second nature, tradition, usage, wont **3.** constitution, disposition, frame of mind, make-up, nature **4.** addiction, dependence, fixation, obsession, weakness **5.** apparel, dress, garb, garment, habiliment, riding dress *~verb* **6.** array, attire, clothe, dress, equip

habitat abode, element, environment, home, home ground, locality, natural home, surroundings, terrain, territory

habitation **1.** abode, domicile, dwelling, dwelling house, home, house, living quarters, lodging, pad (*slang*), quarters, residence **2.** inhabitance, inhabitancy, occupancy, occupation, tenancy

habitual **1.** accustomed, common, customary, familiar, fixed, natural, normal, ordinary, regular, routine, standard, traditional, usual, wonted **2.** chronic, confirmed, constant, established, frequent, hardened, ingrained, inveterate, persistent, recurrent

▷ **Antonyms** abnormal, exceptional, extraordinary, infrequent, irregular, occasional, rare, strange, uncommon, unusual

habituate acclimatize, accustom, acquaint, break in, condition, discipline, familiarize, harden, inure, make used to, school, season, train

habituated acclimatized, accustomed, adapted, broken in, conditioned, disciplined, familiarized, hardened, inured, schooled, seasoned, trained, used (to)

▷ **Antonyms** unaccustomed, unfamiliar, unused (to)

habitué constant customer, frequenter, frequent visitor, regular (*informal*), regular patron

hack[1] *verb* **1.** chop, cut, gash, hew, kick, lacerate, mangle, mutilate, notch, slash *~noun* **2.** chop, cut, gash, notch, slash *~verb/noun* **3.** *informal* bark, cough, rasp

hack[2] *adjective* **1.** banal, mediocre, pedestrian, poor, stereotyped, tired, undistinguished, uninspired, unoriginal *~noun* **2.** Grub Street writer, literary hack, penny-a-liner, scribbler **3.** drudge, plodder, slave **4.** crock, hired horse, horse, jade, nag, poor old tired horse

hackles make one's hackles rise anger, annoy, bridle at, cause resentment, get one's dander up (*slang*), infuriate, make one see red (*informal*), rub one up the wrong way

hackneyed banal, clichéd, common, commonplace, overworked, pedestrian, played out (*informal*), run-of-the-mill, stale, stereotyped, stock, threadbare, timeworn, tired, trite, unoriginal, worn-out

▷ **Antonyms** fresh, imaginative, new, novel, original, striking, unusual

Hades hell, infernal regions, lower world, nether regions, realm of Pluto, (the) inferno, underworld

hag ballbreaker (*slang*), beldam (*archaic*), crone, fury, harridan, Jezebel, shrew, termagant, virago, vixen, witch

haggard careworn, drawn, emaciated, gaunt, ghastly, hollow-eyed, pinched, shrunken, thin, wan, wasted, wrinkled

▷ **Antonyms** bright-eyed, brisk, energetic, fresh, hale, robust, sleek, vigorous

haggle **1.** bargain, barter, beat down, chaffer, dicker (*chiefly U.S.*), drive a hard bargain, higgle, palter **2.** bicker, dispute, quarrel, squabble, wrangle

hail[1] *figurative* **1.** *noun* barrage, bombardment, downpour, pelting, rain, shower, storm, volley **2.** *~verb* barrage, batter, beat down upon, bombard, pelt, rain, rain down on, shower, storm, volley

hail[2] *verb* **1.** acclaim, acknowledge, applaud, cheer, exalt, glorify, greet, honour, salute, welcome **2.** accost, address, call, flag down, halloo, shout to, signal to, sing out, speak to, wave down **3.** (*with* **from**) be a native of, be born in, come from, originate in

▷ **Antonyms** (*sense 1*) boo, condemn, criticize, hiss, insult, jeer (*sense 2*) avoid, cut (*informal*), ignore, snub

hair **1.** head of hair, locks, mane, mop, shock, tresses **2. by a hair** by a fraction of an inch, by a hair's-breadth, by a narrow margin, by a split second, by a whisker, by the skin of one's teeth **3. get in one's hair** aggravate (*informal*), an~

noy, be on one's back (*slang*), exasperate, get on one's nerves (*informal*), get on one's wick (*Brit. slang*), get up one's nose (*informal*), harass, hassle (*informal*), irritate, nark (*Brit., Austral., & N.Z. slang*), pester, piss one off (*taboo slang*), plague **4. let one's hair down** chill out (*slang, chiefly U.S.*), let it all hang out (*informal*), let off steam (*informal*), let oneself go, mellow out (*informal*), relax, veg out (*slang, chiefly U.S.*) **5. not turn a hair** keep one's cool (*slang*), keep one's hair on (*Brit. informal*), not bat an eyelid, remain calm **6. split hairs** cavil, find fault, overrefine, pettifog, quibble

hairstyle coiffure, cut, haircut, hairdo, style

hairless bald, baldheaded, beardless, clean-shaven, depilated, glabrous *or* glabrate (*Biology*), shorn, tonsured

hair-raising alarming, bloodcurdling, breathtaking, creepy, exciting, frightening, horrifying, petrifying, scary, shocking, spine-chilling, startling, terrifying, thrilling

hair's-breadth 1. *noun* fraction, hair, jot, narrow margin, whisker **2.** *~adjective* close, hazardous, narrow

hairsplitting *adjective* captious, carping, cavilling, fault-finding, fine, finicky, nice, niggling, nit-picking (*informal*), overrefined, pettifogging, quibbling, subtle

hairy 1. bearded, bewhiskered, bushy, fleecy, furry, hirsute, pileous (*Biology*), pilose (*Biology*), shaggy, stubbly, unshaven, woolly **2.** *slang* dangerous, difficult, hazardous, perilous, risky, scaring

halcyon 1. calm, gentle, mild, pacific, peaceful, placid, quiet, serene, still, tranquil, undisturbed, unruffled **2.** *figurative* carefree, flourishing, golden, happy, palmy, prosperous

hale able-bodied, blooming, fit, flourishing, healthy, hearty, in fine fettle, in the pink, right as rain (*Brit. informal*), robust, sound, strong, vigorous, well

half 1. *noun* bisection, division, equal part, fifty per cent, fraction, hemisphere, portion, section **2.** *~adjective* divided, fractional, halved, incomplete, limited, moderate, partial **3.** *~adverb* after a fashion, all but, barely, inadequately, incompletely, in part, partially, partly, pretty nearly, slightly **4. by half** considerably, excessively, very much

half-baked 1. brainless, crackpot (*informal*), crazy, foolish, harebrained, inane, loopy (*informal*), senseless, silly, stupid **2.** ill-conceived, ill-judged, impractical, poorly planned, short-sighted, unformed, unthought out *or* through

half-hearted apathetic, cool, half-arsed (*Brit. slang*), half-assed (*U.S. & Canad. slang*), indifferent, lacklustre, listless, lukewarm, neutral, passive, perfunctory, spiritless, tame, unenthusiastic, uninterested

▷ **Antonyms** ambitious, animated, avid, concerned, determined, eager, emotional, energetic, enthusiastic, excited, spirited, warm, wholehearted, zealous

halfway *adverb* **1.** midway, to *or* in the middle, to the midpoint **2.** incompletely, moderately, nearly, partially, partly, rather **3. meet halfway** accommodate, come to terms, compromise, concede, give and take, strike a balance, trade off *~adjective* **4.** central, equidistant, intermediate, mid, middle, midway **5.** imperfect, incomplete, moderate, partial, part-way

halfwit airhead (*slang*), berk (*Brit. slang*), charlie (*Brit. informal*), coot, dickhead (*slang*), dimwit (*informal*), dipstick (*Brit. slang*), divvy (*Brit. slang*), dolt, dork (*slang*), dullard, dunce, dunderhead, dweeb (*U.S. slang*), fathead (*informal*), fool, fuckwit (*taboo slang*), geek (*slang*), gobshite (*Irish taboo slang*), gonzo (*slang*), idiot, imbecile (*informal*), jerk (*slang, chiefly U.S. & Canad.*), lamebrain (*informal*), mental defective, moron, nerd *or* nurd (*slang*), nitwit (*informal*), numbskull *or* numskull, numpty (*Scot. informal*), oaf, pillock (*Brit. slang*), plank (*Brit. slang*), plonker (*slang*), prat (*slang*), prick (*slang*), schmuck (*U.S. slang*), simpleton, twit (*informal, chiefly Brit.*), wally (*slang*)

half-witted addle-brained, barmy (*slang*), batty (*slang*), crazy, doltish, doolally (*slang*), dull, dull-witted, feeble-minded, flaky (*U.S. slang*), foolish, goofy (*informal*), idiotic, moronic, nerdish *or* nurdish (*slang*), obtuse, silly, simple, simple-minded, stupid

hall 1. corridor, entrance hall, entry, foyer, hallway, lobby, passage, passageway, vestibule **2.** assembly room, auditorium, chamber, concert hall, meeting place

hallmark 1. authentication, device, endorsement, mark, seal, sign, signet, stamp, symbol **2.** badge, emblem, indication, sure sign, telltale sign

halloo call, cry, hail, holla, shout

hallow bless, consecrate, dedicate, devote, enshrine, glorify, magnify (*archaic*), respect, revere, reverence, sanctify, venerate

hallowed beatified, blessed, consecrated, dedicated, holy, honoured, inviolable, revered, sacred, sacrosanct, sanctified

hallucinate daydream, envision, fantasize, freak out (*informal*), have hallucinations, imagine, trip (*informal*)

hallucination aberration, apparition, delusion, dream, fantasy, figment of the imagination, illusion, mirage, phantasmagoria, vision

halo aura, aureole *or* aureola, corona, halation (*Photography*), nimbus, radiance, ring of light

halt[1] *verb* **1.** break off, call it a day, cease, close down, come to an end, desist, draw up, pull up, rest, stand still, stop, wait **2.** arrest, block, bring to an end, check, curb, cut short, end, hold back, impede, nip in the bud, obstruct, staunch, stem, stem the flow, terminate *~noun* **3.** arrest, break, close, end, impasse, interruption, pause, stand, standstill, stop, stoppage, termination

▷ **Antonyms** *~verb* (*sense 1*) begin, commence, continue, go ahead, maintain, proceed, resume, start (*sense 2*) aid, boost, encourage, forward *~noun* beginning, commencement, continuation, resumption, start

halt[2] *verb* **1.** be defective, falter, hobble, limp, stumble **2.** be unsure, boggle, dither (*chiefly Brit.*), haver, hesitate, pause, stammer, swither (*Scot.*), think twice, waver *~adjective* **3.** *archaic* crippled, lame, limping

halting awkward, faltering, hesitant, imperfect, laboured, stammering, stumbling, stuttering

halve 1. *verb* bisect, cut in half, divide equally, reduce by fifty per cent, share equally, split in two **2.** *~noun plural* **by halves** imperfectly, incompletely, scrappily, skimpily

hammer *verb* **1.** bang, beat, drive, hit, knock, lambast(e), strike, tap **2.** beat out, fashion, forge, form, make, shape **3.** (*often with* **into**) din into, drive home, drub into, drum into, grind into, impress upon, instruct, repeat **4.** (*often with* **away (at)**) beaver away (*Brit. informal*), drudge, grind, keep on, peg away (*chiefly Brit.*), persevere, persist, plug away (*informal*), pound away, stick at, work **5.** *informal* beat, blow out of the water (*slang*), clobber (*slang*), defeat, drub, lick (*informal*), master, run rings around (*informal*), slate (*informal*), stuff (*slang*), tank (*slang*), thrash, trounce, undo, wipe the floor with (*informal*), worst

hammer out accomplish, bring about, come to a conclusion, complete, excogitate, finish, form a resolution, make a decision, negotiate, produce, settle, sort out, thrash out, work out

hamper *verb* bind, cramp, curb, embarrass, encumber, entangle, fetter, frustrate, hamstring, handicap, hinder, hobble, hold up, impede, interfere with, obstruct, prevent, restrain, restrict, slow down, thwart, trammel

▷ **Antonyms** aid, assist, boost, encourage, expedite, forward, further, help, promote, speed

hamstring 1. cripple, disable, hock, injure, lame **2.** balk, foil, frustrate, prevent, ruin, stop, thwart

hamstrung at a loss, crippled, disabled, helpless, *hors de combat*, incapacitated, paralysed

hand *noun* **1.** fist, hook, meathook (*slang*), mitt (*slang*), palm, paw (*informal*) **2.** agency, direction, influence, part, participation, share **3.** aid, assistance, help, support **4.** artificer, artisan, craftsman, employee, hired man, labourer, operative, worker, workman **5.** calligraphy, chirography, handwriting, longhand, penmanship, script **6.** clap, ovation, round of applause **7.** ability, art, artistry, skill **8. at** *or* **on hand** approaching, at one's fingertips, available, close, handy, imminent, just round the corner, near, nearby, on tap (*informal*), ready, within reach **9. from hand to mouth** by necessity, improvidently, in poverty, insecurely, on the breadline (*informal*), precariously, uncertainly **10. hand in glove** allied, in cahoots (*informal*), in league, in partnership **11. hand over fist** by leaps and bounds, easily, steadily, swiftly **12. in hand: a.** in order, receiving attention, under control **b.** available for use, in reserve, put by, ready *~verb* **13.** deliver, hand over, pass **14.** aid, assist, conduct, convey, give, guide, help, lead, present, transmit

handbook Baedeker, guide, guidebook, instruction book, manual, vade mecum

handcuff 1. *verb* fetter, manacle, shackle **2.** *~noun plural* bracelets (*slang*), cuffs (*informal*), fetters, manacles, shackles

hand down *or* **on** bequeath, give, grant, pass on *or* down, transfer, will

handful few, small number, small quantity, smattering, sprinkling

▷ **Antonyms** a lot, crowd, heaps, horde, large number, large quantity, loads (*informal*), masses (*informal*), mob, plenty, scores, stacks

handicap *noun* **1.** albatross, barrier, block, disadvantage, drawback, encumbrance, hazard, hindrance, impediment, limitation, millstone, obstacle, restriction, shortcoming, stumbling block **2.** advantage, edge, head start, odds, penalty, upper hand **3.** defect, disability, impairment *~verb* **4.** burden, encumber, hamper, hamstring, hinder, hobble, hold back, impede, limit, place at a disadvantage, restrict, retard

▷ **Antonyms** *~noun* (*sense 1*) advantage, asset, benefit, boost, edge *~verb* aid, assist, benefit, boost, forward, further, help, promote

handicraft art, artisanship, craft, craftsmanship, handiwork, skill, workmanship

handily 1. adroitly, capably, cleverly, deftly, dexterously, expertly, proficiently, skilfully **2.** accessibly, advantageously, conveniently, helpfully, readily, suitably

handiness 1. accessibility, availability, closeness, convenience, practicality, proximity, usefulness, workability **2.** adroitness, aptitude, cleverness, deftness, dexterity, efficiency, expertise, knack, proficiency, skill

handiwork 1. craft, handicraft, handwork **2.** achievement, artefact, creation, design, invention, product, production, result

handle *noun* **1.** grip, haft, handgrip, helve, hilt, knob, stock *~verb* **2.** feel, finger, fondle, grasp, hold, maul, paw (*informal*), pick up, poke, touch **3.** control, direct, guide, manage, manipulate, manoeuvre, operate, steer, use, wield **4.** administer, conduct, cope with, deal with, manage, supervise, take care of, treat **5.** discourse, discuss, treat **6.** carry, deal in, market, sell, stock, trade, traffic in

handling administration, approach, conduct, direction, management, manipulation, running, treatment

hand-me-down *adjective* cast-off, handed down, inherited, passed on, reach-me-down (*informal*), second-hand, used, worn

hand-out 1. alms, charity, dole **2.** bulletin, circular, free sample, leaflet, literature (*informal*), mailshot, press release

hand out deal out, disburse, dish out (*informal*), dispense, disseminate, distribute, give out, mete

hand over deliver, donate, fork out *or* up (*slang*), present, release, surrender, transfer, turn over, yield

hand-picked choice, chosen, elect, elite, recherché, select, selected

▷ **Antonyms** haphazard, indiscriminate, random, run-of-the-mill, wholesale

hands 1. authority, care, charge, command, control, custody, disposal, guardianship, keeping, possession, power, supervision **2. hands down** easily, effortlessly, with no contest, with no trouble

handsome 1. admirable, attractive, becoming, comely, dishy (*informal, chiefly Brit.*), elegant, fine, good-looking, gorgeous, graceful, majestic, personable, stately, well-proportioned **2.** abundant, ample, bountiful, considerable, generous, gracious, large, liberal, magnanimous, plentiful, sizable *or* sizeable

▷ **Antonyms** (*sense 1*) inelegant, meagre, tasteless, ugly, unattractive, unprepossessing, unsightly (*sense 2*) base, cheap, meagre, mean, miserly, selfish, small, stingy, ungenerous

handsomely abundantly, amply, bountifully, generously, liberally, magnanimously, munificently, plentifully, richly

handwriting calligraphy, chirography, fist, hand, longhand, penmanship, scrawl, script

handy 1. accessible, at *or* on hand, at one's fingertips, available, close, convenient, just round the corner, near, nearby, within reach **2.** convenient, easy to use, helpful, manageable, neat, practical, serviceable, useful, user-friendly **3.** adept, adroit, clever, deft, dexterous, expert, nimble, proficient, ready, skilful, skilled

▷ **Antonyms** (*sense 1*) awkward, inaccessible, inconvenient, out of the way, unavailable (*sense 2*) awkward, inconvenient, unwieldy, useless (*sense 3*) clumsy, ham-fisted, incompetent, inept, inexpert, maladroit, unaccomplished, unskilful, unskilled, useless

hang *verb* **1.** be pendent, dangle, depend, droop, incline, suspend **2.** execute, gibbet, lynch, send to the gallows, string up (*informal*) **3.** adhere, cling, hold, rest, stick **4.** attach, cover, deck, decorate, drape, fasten, fix, furnish **5.** be poised, drift, float, hover, remain, swing **6.** bend downward, bend forward, bow, dangle, drop, incline, lean over, let droop, loll, lower, sag, trail **7. hang fire** be slow, be suspended, delay, hang back, procrastinate, stall, stick, vacillate *~noun* **8. get the hang of** comprehend, get the knack *or* technique, grasp, understand

hang about *or* **around 1.** dally, linger, loiter, roam, tarry, waste time **2.** associate with, frequent, hang out (*informal*), haunt, resort

hang back be backward, be reluctant, demur, hesitate, hold back, recoil

hangdog *adjective* abject, browbeaten, cowed, cringing, defeated, downcast, furtive, guilty, shamefaced, sneaking, wretched

hanger-on cohort (*chiefly U.S.*), dependant, follower, freeloader (*slang*), lackey, leech, ligger (*slang*), minion, parasite, sponger (*informal*), sycophant

hanging *adjective* **1.** dangling, drooping, flapping, flopping, floppy, loose, pendent, suspended, swinging, unattached, unsupported **2.** undecided, unresolved, unsettled, up in the air (*informal*) **3.** beetle, beetling, jutting, overhanging, projecting, prominent

hang on 1. carry on, continue, endure, go on, hold on, hold out, persevere, persist, remain, stay the course **2.** cling, clutch, grasp, grip, hold fast **3.** be conditional upon, be contingent on, be dependent on, be determined by, depend on, hinge, rest, turn on **4.** *also* **hang onto, hang upon** be rapt, give ear, listen attentively **5.** *informal* hold on, hold the line, remain, stop, wait

hang-out den, dive (*slang*), haunt, home, joint (*slang*), resort

hangover aftereffects, crapulence, head (*informal*), morning after (*informal*)

hang over be imminent, impend, loom, menace, threaten

hang-up block, difficulty, inhibition, obsession, preoccupation, problem, thing (*informal*)

hank coil, length, loop, piece, roll, skein

hanker (*with* **for** *or* **after**) ache, covet, crave, desire, eat one's heart out over, hope, hunger, itch, long, lust, pine, set one's heart on, thirst, want, wish, yearn, yen (*informal*)

hankering ache, craving, desire, hope, hunger, itch, longing, pining, thirst, urge, wish, yearning, yen (*informal*)

hanky-panky chicanery, deception, devilry, funny business (*informal*), jiggery-pokery (*informal, chiefly Brit.*), knavery, machinations, mischief, monkey business (*informal*), shenanigans (*informal*), subterfuge, trickery

haphazard **1.** accidental, arbitrary, chance, fluky (*informal*), random **2.** aimless, careless, casual, disorderly, disorganized, hit or miss (*informal*), indiscriminate, slapdash, slipshod, unmethodical, unsystematic

▷ **Antonyms** (*sense 1*) arranged, deliberate, planned (*sense 2*) careful, considered, methodical, orderly, organized, systematic, thoughtful

hapless cursed, ill-fated, ill-starred, jinxed, luckless, miserable, unfortunate, unhappy, unlucky, wretched

happen **1.** appear, arise, come about, come off (*informal*), come to pass, crop up (*informal*), develop, ensue, eventuate, follow, materialize, occur, present itself, result, see the light of day, take place, transpire (*informal*) **2.** become of, befall, betide **3.** chance, fall out, have the fortune to be, pan out (*informal*), supervene, turn out

happening accident, adventure, affair, case, chance, episode, escapade, event, experience, incident, occasion, occurrence, phenomenon, proceeding, scene

happen on *or* **upon** chance upon, come upon, discover unexpectedly, find, hit upon, light upon, stumble on, turn up

happily **1.** agreeably, contentedly, delightedly, enthusiastically, freely, gladly, heartily, lief (*rare*), willingly, with pleasure **2.** blithely, cheerfully, gaily, gleefully, joyfully, joyously, merrily **3.** auspiciously, favourably, fortunately, luckily, opportunely, propitiously, providentially, seasonably **4.** appropriately, aptly, felicitously, gracefully, successfully

happiness beatitude, blessedness, bliss, cheer, cheerfulness, cheeriness, contentment, delight, ecstasy, elation, enjoyment, exuberance, felicity, gaiety, gladness, high spirits, joy, jubilation, light-heartedness, merriment, pleasure, prosperity, satisfaction, wellbeing

▷ **Antonyms** annoyance, bane, depression, despondency, distress, grief, low spirits, misery, misfortune, sadness, sorrow, unhappiness

happy **1.** blessed, blest, blissful, blithe, cheerful, cock-a-hoop, content, contented, delighted, ecstatic, elated, floating on air, glad, gratified, jolly, joyful, joyous, jubilant, merry, on cloud nine (*informal*), overjoyed, over the moon (*informal*), pleased, rapt, sunny, thrilled, walking on air (*informal*) **2.** advantageous, appropriate, apt, auspicious, befitting, convenient, enviable, favourable, felicitous, fortunate, lucky, opportune, promising, propitious, satisfactory, seasonable, successful, timely, well-timed

▷ **Antonyms** (*sense 1*) depressed, despondent, discontented, displeased, down in the dumps (*informal*), forlorn, gloomy, joyless, low, melancholy, miserable, mournful, sad, sombre, sorrowful, sorry, unhappy (*sense 2*) inapt, unfortunate, unhappy, unlucky

happy-go-lucky blithe, carefree, casual, devil-may-care, easy-going, heedless, improvident, insouciant, irresponsible, light-hearted, nonchalant, unconcerned, untroubled

▷ **Antonyms** careworn, cheerless, gloomy, melancholy, morose, sad, serious, unhappy

harangue **1.** *noun* address, declamation, diatribe, exhortation, lecture, oration, philippic, screed, speech, spiel (*informal*), tirade **2.** *~verb* address, declaim, exhort, hold forth, lecture, rant, spout (*informal*)

harass annoy, badger, bait, beleaguer, be on one's back (*slang*), bother, breathe down someone's neck, chivvy (*Brit.*), devil (*informal*), disturb, exasperate, exhaust, fatigue, harry, hassle (*informal*), hound, perplex, persecute, pester, plague, tease, tire, torment, trouble, vex, weary, worry

harassed careworn, distraught, harried, hassled (*informal*), plagued, strained, tormented, troubled, under pressure, under stress, vexed, worried

harassment aggravation (*informal*), annoyance, badgering, bedevilment, bother, grief (*informal*), hassle (*informal*), irritation, molestation, nuisance, persecution, pestering, torment, trouble, vexation

harbinger forerunner, foretoken, herald, indication, messenger, omen, portent, precursor, sign

harbour *noun* **1.** anchorage, destination, haven, port **2.** asylum, covert, haven, refuge, retreat, sanctuary, sanctum, security, shelter *~verb* **3.** conceal, hide, lodge, protect, provide refuge, relieve, secrete, shelter, shield **4.** believe, brood over, cherish, cling to, entertain, foster, hold, imagine, maintain, nurse, nurture, retain

hard *adjective* **1.** compact, dense, firm, impenetrable, inflexible, rigid, rocklike, solid, stiff, stony, strong, tough, unyielding **2.** arduous, backbreaking, burdensome, exacting, exhausting, fatiguing, formidable, Herculean, laborious, rigorous, strenuous, toilsome, tough, uphill, wearying **3.** baffling, complex, complicated, difficult, intricate, involved, knotty, perplexing, puzzling, tangled, thorny, unfathomable **4.** affectless, callous, cold, cruel, exacting, grim, hardhearted, harsh, implacable, obdurate, pitiless, ruthless, severe, stern, strict, stubborn, unfeeling, unjust, unkind, unrelenting, unsparing, unsympathetic **5.** calamitous, dark, disagreeable, disastrous, distressing, grievous, grim, intolerable, painful, unpleasant **6.** driving, fierce, forceful, heavy, powerful, strong, violent **7.** *of feelings or words* acrimonious, angry, antagonistic, bitter, hostile, rancorous, resentful **8.** *of truth or facts* actual, bare, cold, definite, indisputable, plain, undeniable, unvarnished, verified *~adverb* **9.** energetically, fiercely, forcefully, forcibly, heavily, intensely, powerfully, severely, sharply, strongly, vigorously, violently, with all one's might, with might and main **10.** assiduously, determinedly, diligently, doggedly, earnestly, industriously, intently, persistently, steadily, strenuously, untiringly **11.** agonizingly, badly, distressingly, harshly, laboriously, painfully, roughly, severely, with difficulty **12.** bitterly, hardly, keenly, rancorously, reluctantly, resentfully, slowly, sorely

▷ **Antonyms** *~adjective* (*sense 1*) flexible, malleable, pliable, soft, weak *~2* easy, easy-peasy (*slang*), lazy, light, soft (*sense 3*) clear, direct, easy, easy-peasy (*slang*), simple, straightforward, uncomplicated (*sense 4*) agreeable, amiable, careless, flexible, friendly, gentle, good, humane, kind, lenient, merciful, mild, permissive, pleasant *~adverb* (*senses 9 & 10*) lazily, lightly, loosely, softly, weakly (*sense 11*) easily, gently, softly (*sense 12*) calmly, mildly, serenely

hard and fast binding, immutable, incontrovertible, inflexible, invariable, rigid, set, strict, stringent, unalterable

hard-bitten *or* **hard-boiled** case-hardened, cynical, down-to-earth, hard-headed, hard-nosed (*informal*), matter-of-fact, practical, realistic, shrewd, tough, unsentimental

▷ **Antonyms** benign, compassionate, gentle, humane, idealistic, merciful, mild, romantic, sympathetic

hard-core **1.** dedicated, die-hard, dyed-in-the-wool, extreme, intransigent, obstinate, rigid, staunch, steadfast **2.** explicit, obscene, X-rated (*informal*)

harden **1.** anneal, bake, cake, freeze, set, solidify, stiffen **2.** brace, buttress, fortify, gird, indurate, nerve, reinforce, steel, strengthen, toughen **3.** accustom, brutalize, case-harden, habituate, inure, season, train

hardened **1.** chronic, fixed, habitual, incorrigible, inveterate, irredeemable, reprobate, set, shameless **2.** accustomed, habituated, inured, seasoned, toughened

▷ **Antonyms** infrequent, irregular, occasional, rare, unaccustomed

hard-favoured *or* **hard-featured** austere, coarse-featured, forbidding, grim visaged, ill-favoured, severe, ugly

hard-headed astute, cool, hard-boiled (*informal*), level-headed, practical, pragmatic, realistic, sensible, shrewd, tough, unsentimental

▷ **Antonyms** idealistic, impractical, sentimental, unrealistic

hardhearted afffectless, callous, cold, cruel, hard, hard as nails, heartless, indifferent, inhuman, insensitive, intolerant, merciless, pitiless, stony, uncaring, unfeeling, unkind, unsympathetic

▷ **Antonyms** compassionate, forgiving, gentle, humane, kind, loving, merciful, sensitive, soft-hearted, sympathetic, understanding, warm, warm-hearted

hard-hitting critical, no holds barred, pulling no punches, strongly worded, tough, uncompromising, unsparing, vigorous

hardihood **1.** backbone, boldness, bottle (*Brit. slang*), bravery, courage, daring, determination, firmness, grit, guts (*informal*), intrepidity, mettle, nerve, pluck, resolution, spirit, spunk (*informal*), strength **2.** assurance, audacity, effrontery, foolhardiness, impertinence, impetuousness, rashness, recklessness, temerity

hardiness boldness, courage, fortitude, intrepidity, resilience, resolution, robustness, ruggedness, sturdiness, toughness, valour

hardline definite, inflexible, intransigent, tough, uncompromising, undeviating, unyielding

hardly almost not, at a push, barely, by no means, faintly, infrequently, just, not at all, not quite, no way, only, only just, scarcely, with difficulty

▷ **Antonyms** abundantly, amply, by all means, certainly, completely, easily, fully, indubitably, more than, really, truly, undoubtedly, well over

hard-pressed harried, hotly pursued, in difficulties, pushed (*informal*), under attack, under pressure, up against it (*informal*), with one's back to the wall

hardship adversity, affliction, austerity, burden, calamity, destitution, difficulty, fatigue, grievance, labour, misery, misfortune, need, oppression, persecution, privation, suffering, toil, torment, trial, tribulation, trouble, want
▷ **Antonyms** aid, blessing, boon, comfort, ease, good fortune, happiness, help, prosperity, relief

hard up bankrupt, broke (*informal*), bust (*informal*), cleaned out (*slang*), dirt-poor (*informal*), down and out, flat broke (*informal*), impecunious, impoverished, in queer street, in the red (*informal*), on one's uppers (*informal*), on the breadline, out of pocket, penniless, poor, short, short of cash *or* funds, skint (*Brit. slang*), strapped for cash (*informal*), without two pennies to rub together (*informal*)
▷ **Antonyms** affluent, comfortable (*informal*), fortunate, loaded (*slang*), rich, wealthy, well-heeled (*informal*), well-off

hard-wearing durable, resilient, rugged, stout, strong, tough, well-made

hard-working assiduous, busy, conscientious, diligent, energetic, indefatigable, industrious, sedulous, zealous
▷ **Antonyms** careless, dilatory, good-for-nothing, inconstant, indifferent, lazy

hardy 1. firm, fit, hale, healthy, hearty, in fine fettle, lusty, robust, rugged, sound, stalwart, stout, strong, sturdy, tough, vigorous **2.** bold, brave, courageous, daring, feisty (*informal, chiefly U.S. & Canad.*), gritty, heroic, intrepid, manly, plucky, resolute, stouthearted, valiant, valorous **3.** audacious, brazen, foolhardy, headstrong, impudent, rash, reckless
▷ **Antonyms** (*sense 1*) delicate, feeble, fragile, frail, sickly, soft, weak, weedy (*sense 2*) faint-hearted, feeble, soft, weak, weedy (*informal*), wimpish *or* wimpy (*informal*)

harebrained asinine, careless, empty-headed, flighty, foolish, giddy, half-baked (*informal*), harum-scarum, heedless, inane, mindless, rash, reckless, scatterbrained, unstable, unsteady, wild

hark attend, give ear, give heed, hear, hearken (*archaic*), listen, mark, notice, pay attention

hark back look back, recall, recollect, regress, remember, revert, think back

harlot call girl, fallen woman, hussy, loose woman, pro (*slang*), prostitute, scrubber (*Brit. & Austral. slang*), slag (*Brit. slang*), slapper (*Brit. slang*), streetwalker, strumpet, tart (*informal*), tramp (*slang*), whore, working girl (*facetious slang*)

harm *noun* **1.** abuse, damage, detriment, disservice, hurt, ill, impairment, injury, loss, mischief, misfortune **2.** evil, immorality, iniquity, sin, sinfulness, vice, wickedness, wrong *~verb* **3.** abuse, blemish, damage, hurt, ill-treat, ill-use, impair, injure, lay a finger on, maltreat, mar, molest, ruin, spoil, wound
▷ **Antonyms** *~noun* (*sense 1*) aid, assistance, benefit, blessing, boon, gain, good, help, improvement, reparation (*sense 2*) good, goodness, righteousness *~verb* aid, alleviate, ameliorate, assist, benefit, better, cure, heal, help, improve, repair

harmful baleful, baneful, damaging, deleterious, destructive, detrimental, disadvantageous, evil, hurtful, injurious, maleficent, noxious, pernicious
▷ **Antonyms** beneficial, good, harmless, healthy, helpful, innocuous, safe, wholesome

harmless gentle, innocent, innocuous, innoxious, inoffensive, nontoxic, not dangerous, safe, unobjectionable
▷ **Antonyms** dangerous, destructive, harmful, unhealthy, unsafe, unwholesome

harmonious 1. agreeable, compatible, concordant, congruous, consonant, coordinated, correspondent, dulcet, euphonic, euphonious, harmonic, harmonizing, matching, mellifluous, melodious, musical, sweet-sounding, symphonious (*literary*), tuneful **2.** agreeable, amicable, compatible, concordant, congenial, cordial, *en rapport,* fraternal, friendly, in accord, in harmony, in unison, of one mind, sympathetic
▷ **Antonyms** (*sense 1*) cacophonous, discordant, grating, harsh, unmelodious (*sense 2*) contrasting, discordant, incompatible, inconsistent, unfriendly, unlike

harmonize accord, adapt, agree, arrange, attune, be in unison, be of one mind, blend, chime with, cohere, compose, coordinate, correspond, match, reconcile, suit, tally, tone in with

harmony 1. accord, agreement, amicability, amity, assent, compatibility, concord, conformity, consensus, cooperation, friendship, goodwill, like-mindedness, order, peace, rapport, sympathy, unanimity, understanding, unity **2.** balance, compatibility, concord, congruity, consistency, consonance, coordination, correspondence, fitness, parallelism, suitability, symmetry **3.** euphony, melodiousness, melody, tune, tunefulness, unison
▷ **Antonyms** (*sense 1*) antagonism, conflict, contention, disagreement, dissension, hostility, opposition (*sense 2*) conflict, disagreement, incongruity, inconsistency, unsuitability (*sense 3*) cacophony

harness *noun* **1.** equipment, gear, tack, tackle, trappings **2. in harness** active, at work, busy, in action, working *~verb* **3.** couple, hitch up, put in harness, saddle, yoke **4.** apply, channel, control, employ, exploit, make productive, mobilize, render useful, turn to account, utilize

harp (*with* **on** *or* **upon**) dwell on, go on, labour, press, reiterate, renew, repeat, rub it in

harping *noun* nagging, reiteration, repetition

harridan ballbreaker (*slang*), battle-axe (*informal*), nag, scold, shrew, tartar, termagant, virago, witch, Xanthippe

harried agitated, anxious, beset, bothered, distressed, hag-ridden, harassed, hard-pressed, hassled (*informal*), plagued, tormented, troubled, worried

harrow *verb figurative* agonize, distress, harass, lacerate, perturb, rack, rend, tear, torment, torture, vex, wound, wring

harrowing agonizing, alarming, chilling, distressing, disturbing, excruciating, frightening, heartbreaking, heart-rending, nerve-racking, painful, racking, scaring, terrifying, tormenting, traumatic

harry **1.** annoy, badger, bedevil, be on one's back (*slang*), bother, breathe down someone's neck, chivvy, disturb, fret, get in one's hair (*informal*), harass, hassle (*informal*), molest, persecute, pester, plague, tease, torment, trouble, vex, worry **2.** depredate (*rare*), despoil, devastate, pillage, plunder, raid, ravage, rob, sack

harsh **1.** coarse, croaking, crude, discordant, dissonant, glaring, grating, guttural, jarring, rasping, raucous, rough, strident, unmelodious **2.** abusive, austere, bitter, bleak, brutal, comfortless, cruel, dour, Draconian, drastic, grim, hard, pitiless, punitive, relentless, ruthless, severe, sharp, Spartan, stern, stringent, unfeeling, unkind, unpleasant, unrelenting

▷ **Antonyms** (*sense 1*) harmonious, mellifluous, smooth, soft, soothing, sweet (*sense 2*) agreeable, gentle, kind, loving, merciful, mild, pleasant, sweet

harshly brutally, cruelly, grimly, roughly, severely, sharply, sternly, strictly

harshness acerbity, acrimony, asperity, austerity, bitterness, brutality, churlishness, coarseness, crudity, hardness, ill-temper, rigour, roughness, severity, sourness, sternness

harum-scarum careless, erratic, giddy, haphazard, harebrained, hasty, ill-considered, impetuous, imprudent, inconstant, irresponsible, precipitate, rash, reckless, scatterbrained, scatty (*Brit. informal*), wild

harvest *noun* **1.** harvesting, harvest-time, ingathering, reaping **2.** crop, produce, yield **3.** *figurative* consequence, effect, fruition, product, result, return *~verb* **4.** gather, mow, pick, pluck, reap **5.** accumulate, acquire, amass, collect, garner

hash **1.** balls-up (*taboo slang*), cock-up (*Brit. slang*), confusion, fuck-up (*offensive taboo slang*), hodgepodge (*U.S.*), hotchpotch, jumble, mess, mishmash, mix-up, muddle, pig's breakfast (*informal*), pig's ear (*informal*), shambles, state **2. make a hash of** *informal* bodge (*informal*), botch, bungle, cock up (*Brit. slang*), flub (*U.S. slang*), fuck up (*offensive taboo slang*), jumble, make a nonsense of (*informal*), make a pig's ear of (*informal*), mess up, mishandle, mismanage, mix, muddle

hassle *noun* **1.** altercation, argument, bickering, disagreement, dispute, fight, quarrel, row, squabble, tussle, wrangle **2.** bother, difficulty, grief (*informal*), inconvenience, problem, struggle, trial, trouble, upset *~verb* **3.** annoy, badger, be on one's back (*slang*), bother, breath down someone's neck, bug (*informal*), get in one's hair (*informal*), get on one's nerves (*informal*), harass, harry, hound, pester

haste **1.** alacrity, briskness, celerity, dispatch, expedition, fleetness, nimbleness, promptitude, quickness, rapidity, rapidness, speed, swiftness, urgency, velocity **2.** bustle, hastiness, helter-skelter, hurry, hustle, impetuosity, precipitateness, rashness, recklessness, rush

▷ **Antonyms** calmness, care, delay, deliberation, leisureliness, slowness, sluggishness, sureness

hasten **1.** barrel (along) (*informal, chiefly U.S. & Canad.*), beetle, bolt, burn rubber (*informal*), dash, fly, get one's skates on (*informal*), haste, hurry (up), make haste, race, run, rush, scurry, scuttle, speed, sprint, step on it (*informal*), tear (along) **2.** accelerate, advance, dispatch, expedite, goad, hurry (up), precipitate, press, push forward, quicken, speed (up), step up (*informal*), urge

▷ **Antonyms** (*sense 1*) crawl, creep, dawdle, move slowly (*sense 2*) decelerate, delay, hinder, impede, retard, slow, slow down

hastily **1.** apace, double-quick, fast, hotfoot, pdq (*slang*), posthaste, promptly, pronto (*informal*), quickly, rapidly, speedily, straightaway **2.** heedlessly, hurriedly, impetuously, impulsively, on the spur of the moment, precipitately, rashly, recklessly, too quickly

hasty **1.** brisk, eager, expeditious, fast, fleet, hurried, prompt, rapid, speedy, swift, urgent **2.** brief, cursory, fleeting, passing, perfunctory, rushed, short, superficial **3.** foolhardy, headlong, heedless, impetuous, impulsive, indiscreet, precipitate, rash, reckless, thoughtless, unduly quick **4.** brusque, excited, fiery, hot-headed, hot-tempered, impatient, irascible, irritable, passionate, quick-tempered, snappy

▷ **Antonyms** careful, cautious, detailed,

dispassionate, leisurely, long, protracted, slow, thorough, thoughtful

hatch 1. breed, bring forth, brood, incubate **2.** *figurative* conceive, concoct, contrive, cook up (*informal*), design, devise, dream up (*informal*), manufacture, plan, plot, project, scheme, think up, trump up

hatchet man assassin, bravo, calumniator, cut-throat, debunker, defamer, destroyer, detractor, gunman, heavy (*slang*), hired assassin, hit man (*slang*), killer, murderer, smear campaigner, thug, traducer

hate *verb* **1.** abhor, abominate, be hostile to, be repelled by, be sick of, despise, detest, dislike, execrate, have an aversion to, loathe, recoil from **2.** be loath, be reluctant, be sorry, be unwilling, dislike, feel disinclined, have no stomach for, shrink from *~noun* **3.** abhorrence, abomination, animosity, animus, antagonism, antipathy, aversion, detestation, dislike, enmity, execration, hatred, hostility, loathing, odium

▷ **Antonyms** *~verb* be fond of, cherish, dote on, enjoy, esteem, fancy, like, love, relish, treasure, wish *~noun* affection, amity, devotion, fondness, goodwill, liking, love

hateful abhorrent, abominable, despicable, detestable, disgusting, execrable, forbidding, foul, heinous, horrible, loathsome, obnoxious, obscene, odious, offensive, repellent, repugnant, repulsive, revolting, vile

▷ **Antonyms** affectionate, attractive, beautiful, charming, desirable, devoted, friendly, good, kind, likable *or* likeable, lovable, loving, pleasant, wonderful

hatred abomination, animosity, animus, antagonism, antipathy, aversion, detestation, dislike, enmity, execration, hate, ill will, odium, repugnance, revulsion

▷ **Antonyms** affection, amity, attachment, devotion, fondness, friendliness, goodwill, liking, love

haughtiness airs, aloofness, arrogance, conceit, contempt, contemptuousness, disdain, hauteur, insolence, loftiness, pomposity, pride, snobbishness, superciliousness

haughty arrogant, assuming, conceited, contemptuous, disdainful, high, high and mighty (*informal*), hoity-toity (*informal*), imperious, lofty, on one's high horse (*informal*), overweening, proud, scornful, snobbish, snooty (*informal*), stuck-up (*informal*), supercilious, uppish (*Brit. informal*)

▷ **Antonyms** humble, meek, mild, modest, self-effacing, subservient, wimpish *or* wimpy (*informal*)

haul *verb* **1.** drag, draw, hale, heave, lug, pull, tow, trail, tug **2.** carry, cart, convey, hump (*Brit. slang*), move, transport *~noun* **3.** drag, heave, pull, tug **4.** booty, catch, find, gain, harvest, loot, spoils, takings, yield

haunt *verb* **1.** visit, walk **2.** beset, come back, obsess, plague, possess, prey on, recur, stay with, torment, trouble, weigh on **3.** frequent, hang around *or* about, repair, resort, visit *~noun* **4.** den, gathering place, hangout (*informal*), meeting place, rendezvous, resort, stamping ground

haunted 1. cursed, eerie, ghostly, jinxed, possessed, spooky (*informal*) **2.** obsessed, plagued, preoccupied, tormented, troubled, worried

haunting disturbing, eerie, evocative, indelible, nostalgic, persistent, poignant, recurrent, recurring, unforgettable

hauteur affectedness, airs, arrogance, contempt, dignity, disdain, haughtiness, loftiness, pride, snobbishness, stateliness, superciliousness

have 1. hold, keep, obtain, occupy, own, possess, retain **2.** accept, acquire, gain, get, obtain, procure, receive, secure, take **3.** comprehend, comprise, contain, embody, include, take in **4.** endure, enjoy, experience, feel, meet with, suffer, sustain, undergo **5.** *slang* cheat, deceive, dupe, fool, outwit, stiff (*slang*), swindle, take in (*informal*), trick **6.** (*usually* **have to**) be bound, be compelled, be forced, be obliged, have got to, must, ought, should **7.** allow, consider, entertain, permit, put up with (*informal*), think about, tolerate **8.** bear, beget, bring forth, bring into the world, deliver, give birth to **9. have had it** *informal* be defeated, be exhausted, be finished, be out, be past it (*informal*), be pooped (*U.S. slang*), be stonkered (*slang*)

haven 1. anchorage, harbour, port, roads (*Nautical*) **2.** *figurative* asylum, refuge, retreat, sanctuary, sanctum, shelter

have on 1. be clothed in, be dressed in, wear **2.** be committed to, be engaged to, have on the agenda, have planned **3.** *of a person* deceive, kid (*informal*), play a joke on, pull someone's leg, take the mickey, tease, trick, wind up (*Brit. slang*)

havoc 1. carnage, damage, desolation, despoliation, destruction, devastation, rack and ruin, ravages, ruin, slaughter, waste, wreck **2.** *informal* chaos, confusion, disorder, disruption, mayhem, shambles **3. play havoc (with)** bring into chaos, confuse, convulse, demolish, destroy, devastate, disorganize, disrupt, wreck

hawk *verb* **1.** bark (*informal*), cry, market, peddle, sell, tout (*informal*), vend **2.** (*often with* **about**) bandy about (*informal*), bruit about, buzz, noise abroad, put about, retail, rumour

hawker barrow boy (*Brit.*), cheap-jack (*informal*), colporteur, crier, huckster, pedlar, vendor

haywire 1. *of things* chaotic, confused, disarranged, disordered, disorganized, mixed up, on the blink (*slang*), out of commission, out of order, shambolic (*informal*), tangled, topsy-turvy **2.** *of people* crazy, erratic, gonzo (*slang*), mad, wild

hazard *noun* **1.** danger, endangerment, imperilment, jeopardy, peril, pitfall, risk, threat **2.** accident, chance, coincidence, fluke, luck, misfortune, mishap, stroke of luck *~verb* **3.** chance, dare, gamble, risk, skate on thin ice, stake **4.** advance, conjecture, offer, presume, proffer, speculate, submit, suppose, throw out, venture, volunteer **5.** endanger, expose, imperil, jeopardize, risk, threaten

hazardous 1. dangerous, dicey (*informal, chiefly Brit.*), difficult, fraught with danger, hairy (*slang*), insecure, parlous (*archaic or humorous*), perilous, precarious, risky, unsafe **2.** chancy (*informal*), haphazard, precarious, uncertain, unpredictable

▷ **Antonyms** reliable, safe, secure, sound, stable, sure

haze cloud, dimness, film, fog, mist, obscurity, smog, smokiness, steam, vapour

hazy 1. blurry, cloudy, dim, dull, faint, foggy, misty, nebulous, obscure, overcast, smoky, veiled **2.** *figurative* fuzzy, ill-defined, indefinite, indistinct, loose, muddled, muzzy, nebulous, uncertain, unclear, vague

▷ **Antonyms** (*sense 1*) bright, clear, light, sunny (*sense 2*) certain, clear, detailed, well-defined

head *noun* **1.** bean (*U.S. & Canad. slang*), conk (*slang*), cranium, crown, loaf (*slang*), noddle (*informal, chiefly Brit.*), noggin, nut (*slang*), pate, skull **2.** boss (*informal*), captain, chief, chieftain, commander, director, headmaster, headmistress, head teacher, leader, manager, master, principal, superintendent, supervisor **3.** apex, crest, crown, height, peak, pinnacle, pitch, summit, tip, top, vertex **4.** cutting edge, first place, fore, forefront, front, van, vanguard **5.** beginning, commencement, origin, rise, source, start **6.** ability, aptitude, brain, brains (*informal*), capacity, faculty, flair, intellect, intelligence, mentality, mind, talent, thought, understanding **7.** branch, category, class, department, division, heading, section, subject, topic **8.** climax, conclusion, crisis, culmination, end, turning point **9.** *Geography* cape, foreland, headland, point, promontory **10. go to one's head** dizzy, excite, intoxicate, make conceited, puff up **11. head over heels** completely, intensely, thoroughly, uncontrollably, utterly, wholeheartedly **12. put (our, their,** *etc.*) **heads together** *informal* confab (*informal*), confabulate, confer, consult, deliberate, discuss, palaver, powwow, talk over *~adjective* **13.** arch, chief, first, foremost, front, highest, leading, main, pre-eminent, premier, prime, principal, supreme, topmost *~verb* **14.** be *or* go first, cap, crown, lead, lead the way, precede, top **15.** be in charge of, command, control, direct, govern, guide, lead, manage, rule, run, supervise **16.** (*often with* **for**) aim, go to, make a beeline for, make for, point, set off for, set out, start towards, steer, turn

headache 1. cephalalgia (*Medical*), head (*informal*), migraine, neuralgia **2.** *informal* bane, bother, inconvenience, nuisance, problem, trouble, vexation, worry

headfirst 1. *adjective/adverb* diving, headlong, head-on **2.** *~adverb* carelessly, hastily, head over heels, precipitately, rashly, recklessly

heading 1. caption, headline, name, rubric, title **2.** category, class, division, section

headland bill, bluff, cape, cliff, foreland, head, mull (*Scot.*), point, promontory

headlong 1. *adjective/adverb* headfirst, headforemost, head-on **2.** *~adjective* breakneck, dangerous, hasty, impetuous, impulsive, inconsiderate, precipitate, reckless, thoughtless **3.** *~adverb* hastily, heedlessly, helter-skelter, hurriedly, pell-mell, precipitately, rashly, thoughtlessly, wildly

head off 1. block off, cut off, deflect, divert, intercept, interpose, intervene **2.** avert, fend off, forestall, parry, prevent, stop, ward off

headstrong contrary, foolhardy, froward (*archaic*), heedless, imprudent, impulsive, intractable, mulish, obstinate, perverse, pig-headed, rash, reckless, self-willed, stiff-necked, stubborn, ungovernable, unruly, wilful

▷ **Antonyms** cautious, impressionable, manageable, pliant, subservient, tractable

headway 1. advance, improvement, progress, progression, way **2. make headway** advance, come *or* get on, cover ground, develop, gain, gain ground, make inroads (into), make strides, progress

heady 1. inebriating, intoxicating, potent, spirituous, strong **2.** exciting, exhilarating, intoxicating, overwhelming, stimulating, thrilling **3.** hasty, impetuous, impulsive, inconsiderate, precipitate, rash, reckless, thoughtless

heal 1. cure, make well, mend, regenerate, remedy, restore, treat **2.** alleviate, ameliorate, compose, conciliate, harmonize, patch up, reconcile, settle, soothe

▷ **Antonyms** aggravate, exacerbate, harm, hurt, inflame, injure, make worse, reopen, wound

healing 1. analeptic, curative, medicinal, remedial, restorative, restoring, sanative, therapeutic **2.** assuaging, comforting, emollient, gentle, lenitive, mild, mitigative, palliative, soothing

health **1.** fitness, good condition, haleness, healthiness, robustness, salubrity, soundness, strength, vigour, wellbeing **2.** condition, constitution, fettle, form, shape, state, tone

▷ **Antonyms** (*sense 1*) debility, disease, frailty, illness, sickness, weakness

healthful beneficial, bracing, good for one, health-giving, healthy, invigorating, nourishing, nutritious, salubrious, salutary, wholesome

healthy **1.** active, alive and kicking, blooming, fighting fit, fit, fit as a fiddle (*informal*), flourishing, hale, hale and hearty, hardy, hearty, in fine feather, in fine fettle, in fine form, in good condition, in good shape (*informal*), in the pink, physically fit, right as rain (*Brit. informal*), robust, sound, strong, sturdy, vigorous, well **2.** beneficial, bracing, good for one, healthful, health-giving, hygienic, invigorating, nourishing, nutritious, salubrious, salutary, wholesome

▷ **Antonyms** (*sense 1*) ailing, at death's door, debilitated, delicate, diseased, feeble, fragile, frail, ill, infirm, poorly (*informal*), sick, sickly, unfit, unhealthy, unsound, unwell, weak, weedy (*informal*) (*sense 2*) unhealthy, unwholesome

heap *noun* **1.** accumulation, aggregation, collection, hoard, lot, mass, mound, mountain, pile, rick, stack, stockpile, store **2.** (*often plural*) *informal* abundance, a lot, great deal, lashings (*Brit. informal*), load(s) (*informal*), lots (*informal*), mass, mint, ocean(s), oodles (*informal*), plenty, pot(s) (*informal*), quantities, stack(s), tons *~verb* **3.** accumulate, amass, augment, bank, collect, gather, hoard, increase, mound, pile, stack, stockpile, store **4.** assign, bestow, burden, confer, load, shower upon

hear **1.** attend, be all ears (*informal*), catch, eavesdrop, give attention, hark, hearken (*archaic*), heed, listen in, listen to, overhear **2.** ascertain, be informed, be told of, discover, find out, gather, get wind of (*informal*), hear tell (*dialect*), learn, pick up, understand **3.** *Law* examine, investigate, judge, try

hearing **1.** audition, auditory, ear, perception **2.** audience, audition, chance to speak, interview **3.** auditory range, earshot, hearing distance, range, reach, sound **4.** industrial tribunal, inquiry, investigation, review, trial

hearsay buzz, dirt (*U.S. slang*), gossip, grapevine (*informal*), idle talk, mere talk, *on dit,* report, rumour, scuttlebutt (*slang, chiefly U.S.*), talk, talk of the town, tittle-tattle, word of mouth

heart **1.** character, disposition, emotion, feeling, inclination, nature, sentiment, soul, sympathy, temperament **2.** affection, benevolence, compassion, concern, humanity, love, pity, tenderness, understanding **3.** balls (*taboo slang*), boldness, bravery, courage, fortitude, guts (*informal*), mettle, mind, nerve, pluck, purpose, resolution, spirit, spunk (*informal*), will **4.** central part, centre, core, crux, essence, hub, kernel, marrow, middle, nucleus, pith, quintessence, root **5. at heart** *au fond,* basically, essentially, fundamentally, in essence, in reality, really, truly **6. by heart** by memory, by rote, off pat, parrot-fashion (*informal*), pat, word for word **7. eat one's heart out** agonize, brood, grieve, mope, mourn, pine, regret, repine, sorrow **8. from (the bottom of) one's heart** deeply, devoutly, fervently, heart and soul, heartily, sincerely, with all one's heart **9. heart and soul** absolutely, completely, devotedly, entirely, gladly, to the hilt, wholeheartedly **10. take heart** be comforted, be encouraged, be heartened, brighten up, buck up (*informal*), cheer up, perk up, revive

heartache affliction, agony, anguish, bitterness, despair, distress, grief, heartbreak, heartsickness, pain, remorse, sorrow, suffering, torment, torture

heartbreak anguish, desolation, despair, grief, misery, pain, sorrow, suffering

heartbreaking agonizing, bitter, desolating, disappointing, distressing, grievous, harrowing, heart-rending, pitiful, poignant, sad, tragic

▷ **Antonyms** cheerful, cheery, comic, glorious, happy, jolly, joyful, joyous, light-hearted

heartbroken brokenhearted, choked, crestfallen, crushed, dejected, desolate, despondent, disappointed, disconsolate, disheartened, dismal, dispirited, downcast, down in the dumps (*informal*), grieved, heartsick, miserable, sick as a parrot (*informal*)

▷ **Antonyms** cheerful, cock-a-hoop, elated, exuberant, happy, in seventh heaven, joyful, joyous, on cloud nine, over the moon (*informal*)

hearten animate, assure, buck up (*informal*), buoy up, cheer, comfort, console, embolden, encourage, incite, inspire, inspirit, raise someone's spirits, reassure, revivify, rouse, stimulate

heartfelt ardent, cordial, deep, devout, earnest, fervent, genuine, hearty, honest, profound, sincere, unfeigned, warm, wholehearted

▷ **Antonyms** false, feigned, flippant, fraudulent, frivolous, half-hearted, hypocritical, insincere, phoney *or* phony (*informal*), pretended, put on, reserved, unenthusiastic, unimpassioned

heartily **1.** cordially, deeply, feelingly, genuinely, profoundly, sincerely, unfeignedly, warmly **2.** eagerly, ear~

nestly, enthusiastically, resolutely, vigorously, zealously **3.** absolutely, completely, thoroughly, totally, very

heartless affectless, brutal, callous, cold, cold-blooded, cold-hearted, cruel, hard, hardhearted, harsh, inhuman, merciless, pitiless, uncaring, unfeeling, unkind

▷ **Antonyms** compassionate, generous, humane, kind, merciful, sensitive, sympathetic, warm-hearted

heart-rending affecting, distressing, harrowing, heartbreaking, moving, pathetic, piteous, pitiful, poignant, sad, tragic

heartsick dejected, despondent, dispirited, downcast, heartsore, heavy-hearted, sick at heart

heart-to-heart 1. *adjective* candid, intimate, open, personal, sincere, unreserved **2.** *~noun* cosy chat, tête-à-tête

heart-warming 1. gratifying, pleasing, rewarding, satisfying **2.** affecting, cheering, encouraging, heartening, moving, touching, warming

hearty 1. affable, ardent, back-slapping, cordial, eager, ebullient, effusive, enthusiastic, friendly, generous, genial, jovial, unreserved, warm **2.** earnest, genuine, heartfelt, honest, real, sincere, true, unfeigned, wholehearted **3.** active, alive and kicking, energetic, hale, hardy, healthy, right as rain (*Brit. informal*), robust, sound, strong, vigorous, well **4.** ample, filling, nourishing, sizable *or* sizeable, solid, square, substantial

▷ **Antonyms** (*sense 1*) cold, cool (*sense 2*) half-hearted, insincere, mild (*sense 3*) delicate, feeble, frail, sickly, unhealthy, weak

heat *noun* **1.** calefaction, fever, fieriness, high temperature, hotness, hot spell, sultriness, swelter, torridity, warmness, warmth **2.** *figurative* agitation, ardour, earnestness, excitement, fervour, fever, fury, impetuosity, intensity, passion, vehemence, violence, warmth, zeal *~verb* **3.** become warm, chafe, flush, glow, grow hot, make hot, reheat, warm up **4.** animate, excite, impassion, inflame, inspirit, rouse, stimulate, stir, warm

▷ **Antonyms** *~noun* (*sense 1*) cold, coldness, coolness (*sense 2*) calmness, coldness, composure, coolness *~verb* chill, cool, cool off, freeze

heated angry, bitter, excited, fierce, fiery, frenzied, furious, impassioned, intense, passionate, raging, stormy, tempestuous, vehement, violent

▷ **Antonyms** calm, civilized, dispassionate, friendly, half-hearted, mellow, mild, peaceful, quiet, rational, reasoned, serene, subdued, unemotional, unfazed (*informal*), unruffled

heathen *noun* **1.** idolater, idolatress, infidel, pagan, unbeliever **2.** barbarian, philistine, savage *~adjective* **3.** godless, heathenish, idolatrous, infidel, irreligious, pagan **4.** barbaric, philistine, savage, uncivilized, unenlightened

heave 1. drag (up), elevate, haul (up), heft (*informal*), hoist, lever, lift, pull (up), raise, tug **2.** cast, fling, hurl, pitch, send, sling, throw, toss **3.** breathe heavily, groan, puff, sigh, sob, suspire (*archaic*), utter wearily **4.** billow, breathe, dilate, exhale, expand, palpitate, pant, rise, surge, swell, throb **5.** barf (*U.S. slang*), be sick, chuck (up) (*slang, chiefly U.S.*), chunder (*slang, chiefly Austral.*), do a technicolour yawn (*slang*), gag, retch, spew, throw up (*informal*), toss one's cookies (*U.S. slang*), upchuck (*U.S. slang*), vomit

heaven 1. abode of God, bliss, Elysium *or* Elysian fields (*Greek myth*), happy hunting ground (*Amerind legend*), hereafter, life everlasting, life to come, next world, nirvana (*Buddhism, Hinduism*), paradise, Valhalla (*Norse myth*), Zion (*Christianity*) **2.** (*usually plural*) empyrean (*poetic*), ether, firmament, sky, welkin (*archaic*) **3.** *figurative* bliss, dreamland, ecstasy, enchantment, felicity, happiness, paradise, rapture, seventh heaven, sheer bliss, transport, utopia

heavenly 1. *informal* alluring, beautiful, blissful, delightful, divine (*informal*), entrancing, exquisite, glorious, lovely, rapturous, ravishing, sublime, wonderful **2.** angelic, beatific, blessed, blest, celestial, cherubic, divine, empyrean (*poetic*), extraterrestrial, godlike, holy, immortal, paradisaical, seraphic, superhuman, supernal (*literary*), supernatural

▷ **Antonyms** (*sense 1*) abominable, abysmal, appalling, awful, bad, depressing, dire, disagreeable, dreadful, dreary, dull, frightful, gloomy, grim, hellacious (*U.S. slang*), horrible, horrid, lousy (*slang*), miserable, rotten (*informal*), terrible, unpleasant, vile (*sense 2*) earthly, human, secular, worldly

heavily 1. awkwardly, clumsily, ponderously, weightily **2.** laboriously, painfully, with difficulty **3.** completely, decisively, roundly, thoroughly, utterly **4.** dejectedly, dully, gloomily, sluggishly, woodenly **5.** closely, compactly, densely, fast, hard, thick, thickly **6.** deep, deeply, profoundly, sound, soundly **7.** a great deal, considerably, copiously, excessively, frequently, to excess, very much

heaviness 1. gravity, heftiness, ponderousness, weight **2.** arduousness, burdensomeness, grievousness, onerousness, oppressiveness, severity, weightiness **3.** deadness, dullness, languor, lassitude, numbness, sluggishness, torpor **4.** dejection, depression, despondency, gloom, gloominess, glumness, melancholy, sadness, seriousness

heavy **1.** bulky, hefty, massive, ponderous, portly, weighty **2.** burdensome, difficult, grievous, hard, harsh, intolerable, laborious, onerous, oppressive, severe, tedious, vexatious, wearisome **3.** apathetic, drowsy, dull, inactive, indolent, inert, listless, slow, sluggish, stupid, torpid, wooden **4.** crestfallen, dejected, depressed, despondent, disconsolate, downcast, gloomy, grieving, melancholy, sad, sorrowful **5.** complex, deep, difficult, grave, profound, serious, solemn, weighty **6.** abundant, considerable, copious, excessive, large, profuse **7.** burdened, encumbered, laden, loaded, oppressed, weighted **8.** boisterous, rough, stormy, tempestuous, turbulent, violent, wild **9.** dull, gloomy, leaden, louring *or* lowering, overcast

▷ **Antonyms** (*sense 1*) agile, compact, handy, light, slight, small (*sense 2*) bearable, easy, light, mild, moderate (*sense 3*) agile, alert, brisk, quick (*sense 4*) calm, cheerful, happy, joyful (*sense 5*) exciting, inconsequential, trivial, unimportant (*sense 6*) light, moderate, slight, sparse (*sense 8*) gentle, mild, moderate, soft, weak

heavy-handed **1.** awkward, bungling, clumsy, graceless, ham-fisted (*informal*), ham-handed (*informal*), inept, inexpert, like a bull in a china shop (*informal*), maladroit, unhandy **2.** bungling, inconsiderate, insensitive, tactless, thoughtless **3.** autocratic, domineering, harsh, oppressive, overbearing

▷ **Antonyms** (*sense 1*) adept, adroit, competent, dexterous, effectual, efficient, gentle, graceful, skilful, smooth (*sense 2*) considered, diplomatic, intelligent, prudent, sensible, smart, suitable, tactful, well-advised, well-thought-out, wise (*sense 3*) considerate, submissive, subservient

heavy-hearted crushed, depressed, despondent, discouraged, disheartened, dismal, downcast, downhearted, down in the dumps (*informal*), forlorn, heartsick, melancholy, miserable, morose, mournful, sad, sick as a parrot (*informal*), sorrowful

heckle bait, barrack (*informal*), boo, disrupt, interrupt, jeer, pester, shout down, taunt

hectic animated, boisterous, chaotic, excited, fevered, feverish, flurrying, flustering, frantic, frenetic, frenzied, furious, heated, riotous, rumbustious, tumultuous, turbulent, wild

▷ **Antonyms** calm, peaceful, relaxing, tranquil

hector bluster, boast, browbeat, bully, bullyrag, harass, huff and puff, intimidate, menace, provoke, ride roughshod over, roister, threaten, worry

hedge *noun* **1.** hedgerow, quickset **2.** barrier, boundary, screen, windbreak **3.** compensation, counterbalance, guard, insurance cover, protection *~verb* **4.** border, edge, enclose, fence, surround **5.** block, confine, hem about, hem around, hem in, hinder, obstruct, restrict **6.** beg the question, be noncommittal, dodge, duck, equivocate, evade, flannel (*Brit. informal*), prevaricate, pussyfoot (*informal*), quibble, sidestep, temporize, waffle (*informal, chiefly Brit.*) **7.** cover, fortify, guard, insure, protect, safeguard, shield

hedonism **1.** epicureanism, epicurism, sybaritism **2.** dolce vita, gratification, luxuriousness, pleasure-seeking, pursuit of pleasure, self-indulgence, sensualism, sensuality

hedonist **1.** epicure, epicurean, sybarite **2.** *bon vivant,* pleasure seeker, sensualist, voluptuary

hedonistic **1.** bacchanalian, epicurean, sybaritic **2.** luxurious, pleasure-seeking, self-indulgent, voluptuous

heed **1.** *noun* attention, care, caution, consideration, ear, heedfulness, mind, note, notice, regard, respect, thought, watchfulness **2.** *~verb* attend, bear in mind, be guided by, consider, follow, give ear to, listen to, mark, mind, note, obey, observe, pay attention to, regard, take notice of, take to heart

▷ **Antonyms** *~noun* carelessness, disregard, inattention, laxity, laxness, neglect, thoughtlessness *~verb* be inattentive to, discount, disobey, disregard, flout, ignore, neglect, overlook, reject, shun, turn a deaf ear to

heedful attentive, careful, cautious, chary, circumspect, mindful, observant, prudent, vigilant, wary, watchful

heedless careless, foolhardy, imprudent, inattentive, incautious, neglectful, negligent, oblivious, precipitate, rash, reckless, thoughtless, unmindful, unobservant, unthinking

▷ **Antonyms** attentive, aware, careful, cautious, concerned, heedful, mindful, observant, thoughtful, vigilant, wary, watchful

heel[1] *noun* **1.** crust, end, remainder, rump, stub, stump **2.** *slang* blackguard, bounder (*old-fashioned Brit. slang*), cad (*Brit informal*), cocksucker (*taboo slang*), rotter (*slang, chiefly Brit.*), scally (*Northwest English dialect*), scoundrel, scumbag (*slang*), swine **3. down at heel** dowdy, impoverished, out at elbows, run-down, seedy, shabby, slipshod, slovenly, worn **4. take to one's heels** escape, flee, hook it (*slang*), run away *or* off, show a clean pair of heels, skedaddle (*informal*), take flight, turn tail, vamoose (*slang, chiefly U.S.*) **5. well-heeled** affluent, flush (*informal*), moneyed, prosperous, rich, wealthy, well-off, well-to-do

heel[2] *verb* cant, careen, incline, keel over, lean over, list, tilt

hefty 1. beefy (*informal*), big, brawny, burly, hulking, husky (*informal*), massive, muscular, robust, strapping, strong **2.** forceful, heavy, powerful, thumping (*slang*), vigorous **3.** ample, awkward, bulky, colossal, cumbersome, heavy, large, massive, ponderous, substantial, tremendous, unwieldy, weighty
▷ **Antonyms** agile, diminutive, feeble, frail, inconsequential, ineffectual, infinitesimal, insignificant, light, little, mild, minute, narrow, pocket-sized, scanty, short, slight, slim, small, soft, thin, tiny, weak, weedy (*informal*), wimpish *or* wimpy (*informal*)

height 1. altitude, elevation, highness, loftiness, stature, tallness **2.** apex, apogee, crest, crown, elevation, hill, mountain, peak, pinnacle, summit, top, vertex, zenith **3.** acme, dignity, eminence, exaltation, grandeur, loftiness, prominence **4.** climax, culmination, extremity, limit, maximum, *ne plus ultra,* ultimate, utmost degree, uttermost
▷ **Antonyms** (*sense 1*) depth, lowness, shortness, smallness (*sense 2*) abyss, base, bottom, canyon, chasm, depth, lowland, nadir, ravine, valley (*sense 3*) moderation, smallness, tininess, triviality (*sense 4*) low point, minimum, nadir

heighten 1. add to, aggravate, amplify, augment, enhance, improve, increase, intensify, magnify, sharpen, strengthen **2.** elevate, enhance, ennoble, exalt, magnify, raise, uplift

heinous abhorrent, abominable, atrocious, awful, evil, execrable, flagrant, grave, hateful, hideous, infamous, iniquitous, monstrous, nefarious, odious, outrageous, revolting, shocking, unspeakable, vicious, villainous

heir beneficiary, heiress (*fem.*), inheritor, inheritress *or* inheritrix (*fem.*), next in line, scion, successor

hell 1. Abaddon, abode of the damned, abyss, Acheron (*Greek myth*), bottomless pit, fire and brimstone, Gehenna (*New Testament, Judaism*), Hades (*Greek myth*), hellfire, infernal regions, inferno, lower world, nether world, Tartarus (*Greek myth*), underworld **2.** affliction, agony, anguish, martyrdom, misery, nightmare, ordeal, suffering, torment, trial, wretchedness **3. hell for leather** at a rate of knots, at the double, full-tilt, headlong, hotfoot, hurriedly, like a bat out of hell (*slang*), pell-mell, posthaste, quickly, speedily, swiftly

hellbent bent, determined, fixed, intent, resolved, set, settled

hellish 1. damnable, damned, demoniacal, devilish, diabolical, fiendish, infernal **2.** abominable, accursed, atrocious, barbarous, cruel, detestable, execrable, inhuman, monstrous, nefarious, vicious, wicked
▷ **Antonyms** admirable, agreeable, benevolent, delightful, fine, gentle, good, harmless, honourable, humane, innocuous, kind, merciful, noble, pleasant, virtuous, wonderful

helm 1. *Nautical* rudder, steering gear, tiller, wheel **2.** *figurative* command, control, direction, leadership, rule **3. at the helm** at the wheel, directing, in charge, in command, in control, in the driving seat, in the saddle

help *verb* **1.** abet, aid, assist, back, befriend, cooperate, encourage, give a leg up (*informal*), lend a hand, lend a helping hand, promote, relieve, save, second, serve, stand by, succour, support **2.** alleviate, ameliorate, cure, ease, facilitate, heal, improve, mitigate, relieve, remedy, restore **3.** abstain, avoid, control, eschew, forbear, hinder, keep from, prevent, refrain from, resist, shun, withstand *~noun* **4.** advice, aid, assistance, avail, benefit, cooperation, guidance, helping hand, promotion, service, support, use, utility **5.** assistant, employee, hand, helper, worker **6.** balm, corrective, cure, relief, remedy, restorative, salve, succour
▷ **Antonyms** *~verb* (*senses 1 & 2*) aggravate, bar, block, discourage, fight, foil, frustrate, harm, hinder, hobble, hurt, impede, injure, irritate, make worse, obstruct, oppose *~noun* (*senses 4 & 6*) aggravation, bane, block, discouragement, hindrance, irritant, obstruction, opposition

helper abettor, adjutant, aide, aider, ally, assistant, attendant, auxiliary, coadjutor, collaborator, colleague, deputy, helpmate, henchman, mate, partner, protagonist, right-hand man, second, subsidiary, supporter

helpful 1. advantageous, beneficial, constructive, favourable, fortunate, practical, productive, profitable, serviceable, timely, useful **2.** accommodating, beneficent, benevolent, caring, considerate, cooperative, friendly, kind, neighbourly, supportive, sympathetic

helping *noun* dollop (*informal*), piece, plateful, portion, ration, serving

helpless 1. abandoned, defenceless, dependent, destitute, exposed, forlorn, stranded, unprotected, vulnerable, wide open **2.** debilitated, disabled, feeble, impotent, incapable, incompetent, infirm, paralysed, powerless, unfit, weak
▷ **Antonyms** (*sense 1*) invulnerable, safe, secure, well-protected (*sense 2*) able, capable, competent, equipped, fit, hardy, healthy, hearty, mighty, powerful, robust, solid, strong, sturdy, thriving, tough

helpmate assistant, associate, companion, consort, helper, helpmeet, husband, partner, significant other (*U.S. informal*), spouse, support, wife

helter-skelter **1.** *adverb* carelessly, hastily, headlong, hurriedly, pell-mell, rashly, recklessly, wildly **2.** *~adjective* anyhow, confused, disordered, haphazard, higgledy-piggledy (*informal*), hit-or-miss, jumbled, muddled, random, topsy-turvy

hem **1.** *noun* border, edge, fringe, margin, trimming **2.** *~verb* (*usually with* **in**) beset, border, circumscribe, confine, edge, enclose, environ, hedge in, restrict, shut in, skirt, surround

hem and haw falter, fumble, hesitate, hum and haw, pause, stammer, stutter

hence ergo, for this reason, on that account, therefore, thus

henceforth from now on, from this day forward, hence, hereafter, hereinafter, in the future

henchman aide, associate, attendant, bodyguard, cohort (*chiefly U.S.*), crony, follower, heavy (*slang*), minder (*slang*), minion, myrmidon, right-hand man, satellite, sidekick (*slang*), subordinate, supporter

henpeck browbeat, bully, carp, cavil, chide, criticize, domineer, find fault, harass, hector, intimidate, nag, niggle, pester, pick at, scold, torment

henpecked browbeaten, bullied, cringing, dominated, led by the nose, meek, subject, subjugated, tied to someone's apron strings, timid, treated like dirt
▷ **Antonyms** aggressive, assertive, bossy (*informal*), dominating, domineering, forceful, macho, overbearing, self-assertive, spirited, wilful

herald *noun* **1.** bearer of tidings, crier, messenger **2.** forerunner, harbinger, indication, omen, precursor, sign, signal, token *~verb* **3.** advertise, announce, broadcast, proclaim, publicize, publish, trumpet **4.** foretoken, harbinger, indicate, pave the way, portend, precede, presage, promise, show, usher in

herculean **1.** arduous, demanding, difficult, exhausting, formidable, gruelling, hard, heavy, laborious, onerous, prodigious, strenuous, toilsome, tough **2.** athletic, brawny, husky (*informal*), mighty, muscular, powerful, rugged, sinewy, stalwart, strapping, strong, sturdy **3.** colossal, elephantine, enormous, gigantic, great, huge, humongous *or* humungous (*U.S. slang*), large, mammoth, massive, titanic

herd *noun* **1.** assemblage, collection, crowd, crush, drove, flock, horde, mass, mob, multitude, press, swarm, throng **2.** mob, populace, rabble, riffraff, the hoi polloi, the masses, the plebs *~verb* **3.** assemble, associate, collect, congregate, flock, gather, huddle, muster, rally **4.** drive, force, goad, guide, lead, shepherd, spur

herdsman cowherd, cowman, drover, grazier, stockman

hereafter **1.** *adverb* after this, from now on, hence, henceforth, henceforward, in future **2.** *~noun* afterlife, future life, life after death, next world, the beyond

hereditary **1.** family, genetic, inborn, inbred, inheritable, transmissible **2.** ancestral, bequeathed, handed down, inherited, patrimonial, traditional, transmitted, willed

heredity congenital traits, constitution, genetic make-up, genetics, inheritance

heresy apostasy, dissidence, error, heterodoxy, iconoclasm, impiety, revisionism, schism, unorthodoxy

heretic apostate, dissenter, dissident, nonconformist, renegade, revisionist, schismatic, sectarian, separatist

heretical freethinking, heterodox, iconoclastic, idolatrous, impious, revisionist, schismatic, unorthodox

heritage bequest, birthright, endowment, estate, inheritance, legacy, lot, patrimony, portion, share, tradition

hermetic, hermetical airtight, sealed, shut

hermit anchoret, anchorite, eremite, loner (*informal*), monk, recluse, solitary, stylite

hero **1.** celeb (*informal*), celebrity, champion, conqueror, exemplar, great man, heart-throb (*Brit.*), idol, man of the hour, megastar (*informal*), popular figure, star, superstar, victor **2.** lead actor, leading man, male lead, principal male character, protagonist

heroic **1.** bold, brave, courageous, daring, dauntless, doughty, fearless, gallant, intrepid, lion-hearted, stouthearted, undaunted, valiant, valorous **2.** classical, Homeric, legendary, mythological **3.** classic, elevated, epic, exaggerated, extravagant, grand, grandiose, high-flown, inflated
▷ **Antonyms** (*sense 1*) base, chicken (*slang*), cowardly, craven, faint-hearted, ignoble, irresolute, mean, timid (*sense 3*) lowbrow, simple, unadorned

heroine **1.** celeb (*informal*), celebrity, goddess, ideal, megastar (*informal*), woman of the hour **2.** diva, female lead, lead actress, leading lady, prima donna, principal female character, protagonist

heroism boldness, bravery, courage, courageousness, daring, fearlessness, fortitude, gallantry, intrepidity, prowess, spirit, valour

hero worship admiration, adoration, adulation, idealization, idolization, putting on a pedestal, veneration

hesitant diffident, doubtful, half-arsed, half-assed (*U.S. & Canad. slang*), half-hearted, halting, hanging back, hesitating, irresolute, lacking confidence, reluctant, sceptical, shy, timid, uncertain, unsure, vacillating, wavering

▷ **Antonyms** arrogant, avid, clear, confident, definite, determined, dogmatic, eager, enthusiastic, firm, forceful, keen, positive, resolute, self-assured, spirited, sure, unhesitating, unwavering

hesitate 1. be uncertain, delay, dither (*chiefly Brit.*), doubt, haver (*Brit.*), hum and haw, pause, shillyshally (*informal*), swither (*Scot.*), vacillate, wait, waver **2.** balk, be reluctant, be unwilling, boggle, demur, hang back, scruple, shrink from, think twice **3.** falter, fumble, hem and haw, stammer, stumble, stutter

▷ **Antonyms** (*sense 1*) be confident, be decisive, be firm, continue, decide (*sense 2*) be determined, resolve, welcome

hesitation 1. delay, doubt, dubiety, hesitancy, indecision, irresolution, uncertainty, vacillation **2.** demurral, misgiving(s), qualm(s), reluctance, scruple(s), unwillingness **3.** faltering, fumbling, hemming and hawing, stammering, stumbling, stuttering

heterodox dissident, heretical, iconoclastic, revisionist, schismatic, unorthodox, unsound

heterogeneous assorted, contrary, contrasted, different, discrepant, disparate, dissimilar, divergent, diverse, diversified, incongruous, manifold, miscellaneous, mixed, motley, opposed, unlike, unrelated, varied

hew 1. axe, chop, cut, hack, lop, split **2.** carve, fashion, form, make, model, sculpt, sculpture, shape, smooth

heyday bloom, flowering, pink, prime, prime of life, salad days

hiatus aperture, blank, breach, break, chasm, discontinuity, entr'acte, gap, interruption, interval, lacuna, lapse, opening, respite, rift, space

hibernate hole up, lie dormant, overwinter, remain torpid, sleep snug, vegetate, winter

hidden abstruse, clandestine, close, concealed, covered, covert, cryptic, dark, hermetic, hermetical, latent, masked, mysterious, mystic, mystical, obscure, occult, recondite, secret, shrouded, ulterior, under wraps, unrevealed, unseen, veiled

hide[1] *verb* **1.** cache, conceal, go into hiding, go to ground, go underground, hole up, lie low, secrete, stash (*informal*), take cover **2.** blot out, bury, camouflage, cloak, conceal, cover, disguise, eclipse, mask, obscure, screen, shelter, shroud, veil **3.** draw a veil over, hush up, keep dark, keep secret, keep under one's hat, suppress, withhold

▷ **Antonyms** admit, bare, confess, disclose, display, divulge, exhibit, expose, find, flaunt, reveal, show, uncover, unveil

hide[2] *noun* fell, pelt, skin

hideaway haven, hide-out, hiding place, nest, refuge, retreat, sanctuary, sequestered nook

hidebound brassbound, conventional, narrow, narrow-minded, puritan, rigid, set, set in one's ways, strait-laced, ultraconservative

▷ **Antonyms** broad-minded, flexible, liberal, open, receptive, tolerant, unconventional, unorthodox

hideous 1. ghastly, grim, grisly, grotesque, gruesome, monstrous, repulsive, revolting, ugly, unsightly **2.** abominable, appalling, awful, detestable, disgusting, dreadful, godawful (*slang*), horrendous, horrible, horrid, loathsome, macabre, obscene, odious, shocking, sickening, terrible, terrifying

▷ **Antonyms** appealing, beautiful, captivating, charming, entrancing, lovely, pleasant, pleasing

hide-out den, hideaway, hiding place, lair, secret place, shelter

hiding *noun* beating, caning, drubbing, flogging, larruping (*Brit. dialect*), lathering (*informal*), licking (*informal*), spanking, tanning (*slang*), thrashing, walloping (*informal*), whaling, whipping

hierarchy grading, pecking order, ranking

hieroglyphic *adjective* enigmatical, figurative, indecipherable, obscure, runic, symbolical

higgledy-piggledy 1. *adverb* all over the place, all over the shop (*informal*), anyhow, any old how, confusedly, disorderly, haphazard, helter-skelter, pell-mell, topsy-turvy **2.** *~adjective* haphazard, helter-skelter, indiscriminate, jumbled, muddled, pell-mell, topsy-turvy

high *adjective* **1.** elevated, lofty, soaring, steep, tall, towering **2.** excessive, extraordinary, extreme, great, intensified, sharp, strong **3.** arch, big-time (*informal*), chief, consequential, distinguished, eminent, exalted, important, influential, leading, major league (*informal*), notable, powerful, prominent, ruling, significant, superior **4.** arrogant, boastful, bragging, despotic, domineering, haughty, lofty, lordly, ostentatious, overbearing, proud, tyrannical, vainglorious **5.** capital, extreme, grave, important, serious **6.** boisterous, bouncy (*informal*), cheerful, elated, excited, exhilarated, exuberant, joyful, lighthearted, merry, strong, tumultuous, turbulent **7.** *informal* delirious, euphoric, freaked out (*informal*), hyped up (*slang*), inebriated, intoxicated, on a trip (*informal*), spaced out (*slang*), stoned (*slang*), tripping (*informal*), turned on (*slang*), zonked (*slang*) **8.** costly, dear, exorbitant, expensive, high-priced, steep (*informal*), stiff **9.** acute, high-pitched, penetrating, piercing, piping, sharp, shrill, soprano, strident, treble **10.** ex~

travagant, grand, lavish, luxurious, rich **11.** gamey, niffy (*Brit. slang*), pongy (*Brit. informal*), strong-flavoured, tainted, whiffy (*Brit. slang*) **12. high and dry** abandoned, bereft, destitute, helpless, stranded **13. high and low** all over, everywhere, exhaustively, far and wide, in every nook and cranny **14. high and mighty** *informal* arrogant, cavalier, conceited, disdainful, haughty, imperious, overbearing, self-important, snobbish, stuck-up (*informal*), superior *~adverb* **15.** aloft, at great height, far up, way up *~noun* **16.** apex, crest, height, peak, record level, summit, top **17.** *informal* delirium, ecstasy, euphoria, intoxication, trip (*informal*)

▷ **Antonyms** (*sense 1*) dwarfed, low, short, stunted (*sense 2*) average, low, mild, moderate, reduced, restrained, routine, suppressed (*sense 3*) average, common, degraded, ignoble, inconsequential, insignificant, low, lowly, low-ranking, menial, routine, secondary, undistinguished, unimportant (*sense 6*) angry, dejected, depressed, gloomy, low, melancholy, sad (*sense 9*) alto, bass, deep, gruff, low, low-pitched

highborn aristocratic, blue-blooded, gentle (*archaic*), noble, patrician, pedigreed, thoroughbred, well-born

highbrow 1. *noun* aesthete, Brahmin (*U.S.*), brain (*informal*), brainbox (*slang*), egghead (*informal*), intellectual, mastermind, savant, scholar **2.** *~adjective* bookish, brainy (*informal*), cultivated, cultured, deep, highbrowed, intellectual, sophisticated

▷ **Antonyms** *~noun* idiot, ignoramus, illiterate, imbecile (*informal*), lowbrow, moron, philistine *~adjective* ignorant, lowbrow, philistine, shallow, uncultivated, uninformed, unintellectual, unlearned, unsophisticated

high-class A1 *or* A-one (*informal*), choice, classy (*slang*), elite, exclusive, first-rate, high-quality, high-toned, posh (*informal, chiefly Brit.*), ritzy (*slang*), select, superior, swish (*informal, chiefly Brit.*), tip-top, top-drawer, top-flight, tops (*slang*), U (*Brit. informal*), up-market, upper-class

▷ **Antonyms** cheap, cheapo (*informal*), common, inferior, mediocre, ordinary, run-of-the-mill

highfalutin, highfaluting big, bombastic, florid, grandiose, high-flown, high-sounding, lofty, magniloquent, pompous, pretentious, supercilious, swanky (*informal*)

high-flown elaborate, exaggerated, extravagant, florid, grandiose, high-falutin (*informal*), inflated, lofty, magniloquent, overblown, pretentious

▷ **Antonyms** down-to-earth, moderate, modest, practical, pragmatic, realistic, reasonable, restrained, sensible, simple, straightforward, unpretentious

high-handed arbitrary, autocratic, bossy (*informal*), despotic, dictatorial, domineering, imperious, inconsiderate, oppressive, overbearing, peremptory, self-willed, tyrannical, wilful

high jinks fun and games, horseplay, jollity, junketing, merrymaking, revelry, skylarking (*informal*), sport, spree

highlands heights, hill country, hills, mesa, mountainous region, plateau, tableland, uplands

highlight 1. *noun* best part, climax, feature, focal point, focus, high point, high spot, main feature, memorable part, peak **2.** *~verb* accent, accentuate, bring to the fore, emphasize, feature, focus attention on, foreground, give prominence to, play up, set off, show up, spotlight, stress, underline

▷ **Antonyms** *~noun* disappointment, lowlight, low point *~verb* de-emphasize, gloss over, neglect, overlook, play down

highly 1. decidedly, eminently, exceptionally, extraordinarily, extremely, greatly, immensely, seriously (*informal*), supremely, tremendously, vastly, very, very much **2.** appreciatively, approvingly, enthusiastically, favourably, warmly, well

highly strung easily upset, edgy, excitable, irascible, irritable, nervous, nervy (*Brit. informal*), neurotic, on pins and needles, on tenterhooks, restless, sensitive, stressed, taut, temperamental, tense, tetchy, twitchy (*informal*), wired (*slang*)

▷ **Antonyms** calm, collected, easy-going, even-tempered, laid-back (*informal*), placid, relaxed, serene, unfazed (*informal*)

high-minded elevated, ethical, fair, good, honourable, idealistic, magnanimous, moral, noble, principled, pure, righteous, upright, virtuous, worthy

▷ **Antonyms** dishonest, dishonourable, unethical, unfair

high-powered aggressive, driving, dynamic, effective, energetic, enterprising, fast-track, forceful, go-ahead, go-getting (*informal*), highly capable, high-octane (*informal*), vigorous

high-pressure *of salesmanship* aggressive, bludgeoning, coercive, compelling, forceful, high-powered, importunate, insistent, intensive, in-your-face (*slang*), persistent, persuasive, pushy (*informal*)

high-priced costly, dear, excessive, exorbitant, expensive, extortionate, high, steep (*informal*), stiff, unreasonable

high-sounding affected, artificial, bombastic, extravagant, flamboyant, florid, grandiloquent, grandiose, high-flown, imposing, magniloquent, ostentatious, overblown, pompous, pretentious, stilted, strained

high-speed brisk, express, fast, hotted-up (*informal*), quick, rapid, souped-up (*informal*), streamlined, swift

high-spirited alive and kicking, animated, boisterous, bold, bouncy, daring, dashing, ebullient, effervescent, energetic, exuberant, frolicsome, full of beans (*informal*), full of life, fun-loving, gallant, lively, mettlesome, sparky, spirited, spunky (*informal*), vibrant, vital, vivacious

high spirits abandon, boisterousness, exhilaration, exuberance, good cheer, hilarity, *joie de vivre,* rare good humour

hijack commandeer, expropriate, seize, skyjack, take over

hike *verb* **1.** back-pack, hoof it (*slang*), leg it (*informal*), ramble, tramp, walk **2.** (*usually with* **up**) hitch up, jack up, lift, pull up, raise *~noun* **3.** journey on foot, march, ramble, tramp, trek, walk

hilarious amusing, comical, convivial, entertaining, exhilarated, funny, gay, happy, humorous, jolly, jovial, joyful, joyous, merry, mirthful, noisy, rollicking, side-splitting, uproarious

▷ **Antonyms** dull, gloomy, quiet, sad, sedate, serious

hilarity amusement, boisterousness, cheerfulness, conviviality, exhilaration, exuberance, gaiety, glee, high spirits, jollification, jollity, joviality, joyousness, laughter, levity, merriment, mirth

hill 1. brae (*Scot.*), down (*archaic*), elevation, eminence, fell, height, hillock, hilltop, knoll, mound, mount, prominence, tor **2.** drift, heap, hummock, mound, pile, rick, stack **3.** acclivity, brae (*Scot.*), climb, gradient, incline, rise, slope

hillock barrow, hummock, knap (*dialect*), knoll, monticule, mound, tump (*Western Brit. dialect*)

hilt 1. grip, haft, handgrip, handle, helve **2. to the hilt** completely, entirely, fully, totally, wholly

hind after, back, caudal (*Anatomy*), hinder, posterior, rear

hinder arrest, block, check, debar, delay, deter, encumber, frustrate, hamper, hamstring, handicap, hobble, hold up *or* back, impede, interrupt, obstruct, oppose, prevent, retard, slow down, stop, stymie, throw a spanner in the works, thwart, trammel

▷ **Antonyms** accelerate, advance, aid, benefit, encourage, expedite, facilitate, further, help, hurry, promote, quicken, speed, support

hindmost concluding, final, furthest, furthest behind, last, most remote, rearmost, terminal, trailing, ultimate

hindrance bar, barrier, block, check, deterrent, difficulty, drag, drawback, encumbrance, handicap, hazard, hitch, impediment, interruption, limitation, obstacle, obstruction, restraint, restriction, snag, stoppage, stumbling block, trammel

▷ **Antonyms** advancement, advantage, aid, asset, assistance, benefit, boon, boost, encouragement, furtherance, help, support

hinge *verb* be contingent, be subject to, depend, hang, pivot, rest, revolve around, turn

hint *noun* **1.** allusion, clue, implication, indication, inkling, innuendo, insinuation, intimation, mention, reminder, suggestion, tip-off, word to the wise **2.** advice, help, pointer, suggestion, tip, wrinkle (*informal*) **3.** breath, dash, *soupçon,* speck, suggestion, suspicion, taste, tinge, touch, trace, undertone, whiff, whisper *~verb* **4.** allude, cue, imply, indicate, insinuate, intimate, let it be known, mention, prompt, suggest, tip off, tip the wink (*informal*)

hip *adjective* aware, clued-up (*informal*), fashionable, in, informed, in on, knowledgeable, onto, trendy (*Brit. informal*), wise (*slang*), with it (*informal*)

hippy beatnik, bohemian, dropout, flower child

hire *verb* **1.** appoint, commission, employ, engage, sign up, take on **2.** charter, engage, lease, let, rent *~noun* **3.** charge, cost, fee, price, rent, rental

hirsute bearded, bewhiskered, bristly, hairy, hispid (*Biology*), shaggy, unshaven

hiss *noun* **1.** buzz, hissing, sibilance, sibilation **2.** boo, catcall, contempt, derision, jeer, raspberry *~verb* **3.** rasp, shrill, sibilate, wheeze, whirr, whistle, whiz **4.** blow a raspberry, boo, catcall, condemn, damn, decry, deride, hoot, jeer, mock, revile, ridicule

historian annalist, biographer, chronicler, historiographer, recorder

historic celebrated, consequential, epoch-making, extraordinary, famous, ground-breaking, momentous, notable, outstanding, red-letter, remarkable, significant

▷ **Antonyms** ordinary, uncelebrated, unimportant, unknown

historical actual, archival, attested, authentic, chronicled, documented, factual, real, verifiable

▷ **Antonyms** contemporary, current, fabulous, fictional, legendary, mythical, present-day

history 1. account, annals, autobiography, biography, chronicle, memoirs, narration, narrative, recapitulation, recital, record, relation, saga, story **2.** ancient history, antiquity, bygone times, days of old, days of yore, olden days, the good old days, the old days, the past, yesterday, yesteryear

histrionic actorly, actressy, affected, artificial, bogus, camp (*informal*), dramatic, forced, insincere, melodramatic, sensational, theatrical, unnatural

histrionics dramatics, performance, scene, staginess, tantrums, temperament, theatricality

hit *verb* **1.** bang, bash (*informal*), batter, beat, belt (*informal*), chin (*slang*), clip (*informal*), clobber (*slang*), clout (*informal*), cuff, deck (*slang*), flog, knock, lambast(e), lay one on (*slang*), lob, punch, slap, smack, smite (*archaic*), sock (*slang*), strike, swat, thump, tonk (*slang*), wallop (*informal*), whack **2.** bang into, bump, clash with, collide with, crash against, meet head-on, run into, smash into **3.** accomplish, achieve, arrive at, attain, gain, reach, secure, strike, touch **4.** affect, damage, devastate, impact on, impinge on, influence, leave a mark on, make an impact *or* impression on, move, overwhelm, touch *~noun* **5.** belt (*informal*), blow, bump, clash, clout (*informal*), collision, cuff, impact, knock, rap, shot, slap, smack, stroke, swipe (*informal*), wallop (*informal*) **6.** *informal* sellout, sensation, smash (*informal*), smasheroo (*informal*), success, triumph, winner

hitch *verb* **1.** attach, connect, couple, fasten, harness, join, make fast, tether, tie, unite, yoke **2.** (*often with* **up**) hoick, jerk, pull, tug, yank **3.** *informal* hitchhike, thumb a lift *~noun* **4.** catch, check, delay, difficulty, drawback, hassle (*informal*), hazard, hindrance, hold-up, impediment, mishap, obstacle, problem, snag, stoppage, trouble

hither close, closer, here, near, nearer, nigh (*archaic*), over here, to this place

hitherto heretofore, previously, so far, thus far, till now, until now, up to now

hit off 1. capture, catch, impersonate, mimic, represent, take off (*informal*) **2.** **hit it off** *informal* be on good terms, click (*slang*), get on like a house on fire (*informal*), get on (well) with, take to, warm to

hit on *or* **upon** arrive at, chance upon, come upon, discover, guess, invent, light upon, realize, strike upon, stumble on, think up

hit or miss aimless, casual, cursory, disorganized, haphazard, indiscriminate, perfunctory, random, undirected, uneven
▷ **Antonyms** arranged, deliberate, organized, planned, systematic

hit out (at) assail, attack, castigate, condemn, denounce, inveigh against, lash out, rail against, strike out at

hive 1. cluster, colony, swarm **2.** *figurative* centre, heart, hub, powerhouse (*slang*)

hoard 1. *noun* accumulation, cache, fallback, fund, heap, mass, pile, reserve, stockpile, store, supply, treasure-trove **2.** *~verb* accumulate, amass, buy up, cache, collect, deposit, garner, gather, hive, lay up, put away, put by, save, stash away (*informal*), stockpile, store, treasure

hoarder collector, magpie (*Brit.*), miser, niggard, saver, squirrel (*informal*), tight-arse (*taboo slang*), tight-ass (*U.S. taboo slang*)

hoarse croaky, discordant, grating, gravelly, growling, gruff, guttural, harsh, husky, rasping, raucous, rough, throaty
▷ **Antonyms** harmonious, mellifluous, mellow, melodious, smooth

hoary 1. frosty, grey, grey-haired, grizzled, hoar, silvery, white, white-haired **2.** aged, ancient, antiquated, antique, old, venerable

hoax 1. *noun* canard, cheat, con (*informal*), deception, fast one (*informal*), fraud, imposture, joke, practical joke, prank, ruse, spoof (*informal*), swindle, trick **2.** *~verb* bamboozle (*informal*), befool, bluff, con (*slang*), deceive, delude, dupe, fool, gammon (*Brit. informal*), gull (*archaic*), hoodwink, hornswoggle (*slang*), kid (*informal*), swindle, take in (*informal*), take (someone) for a ride (*informal*), trick, wind up (*Brit. slang*)

hoaxer bamboozler (*informal*), hoodwinker, humbug, joker, practical joker, prankster, spoofer (*informal*), trickster

hobble 1. dodder, falter, halt, limp, shamble, shuffle, stagger, stumble, totter **2.** clog, fasten, fetter, hamstring, restrict, shackle, tie

hobby diversion, favourite occupation, (leisure) activity, leisure pursuit, pastime, relaxation, sideline

hobgoblin apparition, bogey, goblin, hob, imp, spectre, spirit, sprite

hobnob associate, consort, fraternize, hang about, hang out (*informal*), keep company, mingle, mix, socialize

hocus-pocus 1. artifice, cheat, chicanery, deceit, deception, delusion, hoax, humbug, imposture, swindle, trickery **2.** abracadabra, cant, gibberish, gobbledegook (*informal*), Greek (*informal*), hokum (*slang, chiefly U.S. & Canad.*), jargon, mumbo jumbo, nonsense, rigmarole **3.** conjuring, jugglery, legerdemain, prestidigitation, sleight of hand

hoggish brutish, dirty, edacious, filthy, gluttonous, greedy, gross, mean, piggish, rapacious, ravenous, selfish, sordid, squalid, swinish, unclean

hogwash balderdash, balls (*taboo slang*), bilge (*informal*), bosh (*informal*), bull (*slang*), bullshit (*taboo slang*), bunk (*informal*), bunkum *or* buncombe (*chiefly*

U.S.), cobblers (*Brit. taboo slang*), crap (*slang*), drivel, eyewash (*informal*), garbage (*informal*), guff (*slang*), hokum (*slang, chiefly U.S. & Canad.*), hooey (*slang*), horsefeathers (*U.S. slang*), hot air (*informal*), kak (*S. African slang*), moonshine, nonsense, pap, piffle (*informal*), poppycock (*informal*), rot, rubbish, shit (*taboo slang*), tommyrot, tosh (*slang, chiefly Brit.*), trash, tripe (*informal*), twaddle

hoiden *see* HOYDEN

hoi polloi admass, *canaille,* commonalty, riffraff, the (common) herd, the common people, the great unwashed (*informal & derogatory*), the lower orders, the masses, the plebs, the populace, the proles (*derogatory slang, chiefly Brit.*), the proletariat, the rabble, the third estate, the underclass

hoist 1. *verb* elevate, erect, heave, lift, raise, rear, upraise **2.** *~noun* crane, elevator, lift, tackle, winch

hoity-toity arrogant, conceited, disdainful, haughty, high and mighty (*informal*), lofty, overweening, proud, scornful, snobbish, snooty (*informal*), stuck-up (*informal*), supercilious, toffee-nosed (*slang, chiefly Brit.*), uppish (*Brit. informal*)

hold *verb* **1.** have, keep, maintain, occupy, own, possess, retain **2.** adhere, clasp, cleave, clinch, cling, clutch, cradle, embrace, enfold, grasp, grip, stick **3.** arrest, bind, check, confine, curb, detain, impound, imprison, pound, restrain, stay, stop, suspend **4.** assume, believe, consider, deem, entertain, esteem, judge, maintain, presume, reckon, regard, think, view **5.** continue, endure, last, persevere, persist, remain, resist, stay, wear **6.** assemble, call, carry on, celebrate, conduct, convene, have, officiate at, preside over, run, solemnize **7.** bear, brace, carry, prop, shoulder, support, sustain, take **8.** accommodate, comprise, contain, have a capacity for, seat, take **9.** apply, be in force, be the case, exist, hold good, operate, remain true, remain valid, stand up **10. hold one's own** do well, hold fast, hold out, keep one's head above water, keep pace, keep up, maintain one's position, stand firm, stand one's ground, stay put, stick to one's guns (*informal*) *~noun* **11.** clasp, clutch, grasp, grip **12.** anchorage, foothold, footing, leverage, prop, purchase, stay, support, vantage **13.** ascendancy, authority, clout (*informal*), control, dominance, dominion, influence, mastery, pull (*informal*), sway

▷ **Antonyms** (*sense 1*) bestow, give, give up, hand over, offer, turn over (*sense 2*) come undone, let go, loosen (*sense 3*) free, let go, let loose, release (*sense 4*) deny, disavow, disclaim, put down, refute, reject (*sense 5*) give up, give way (*sense 6*) call off, cancel, postpone (*sense 7*) break, give way

hold back 1. check, control, curb, inhibit, rein, repress, restrain, stem the flow, suppress **2.** desist, forbear, keep back, refuse, withhold

holder 1. bearer, custodian, incumbent, keeper, occupant, owner, possessor, proprietor, purchaser **2.** case, container, cover, housing, receptacle, sheath

hold forth declaim, descant, discourse, go on, harangue, lecture, orate, preach, speak, speechify, spiel (*informal*), spout (*informal*)

holdings assets, estate, investments, land interests, possessions, property, resources, securities, stocks and shares

hold off 1. avoid, defer, delay, keep from, postpone, put off, refrain **2.** fend off, keep off, rebuff, repel, repulse, stave off

hold out 1. extend, give, offer, present, proffer **2.** carry on, continue, endure, hang on, last, persevere, persist, stand fast, stay the course, withstand

hold over adjourn, defer, delay, postpone, put off, suspend, take a rain check on (*U.S. & Canad. informal*), waive

hold-up 1. bottleneck, delay, difficulty, hitch, obstruction, setback, snag, stoppage, traffic jam, trouble, wait **2.** burglary, mugging (*informal*), robbery, steaming (*informal*), stick-up (*slang, chiefly U.S.*), theft

hold up 1. delay, detain, hinder, impede, retard, set back, slow down, stop **2.** bolster, brace, buttress, jack up, prop, shore up, support, sustain **3.** mug (*informal*), rob, stick up (*slang, chiefly U.S.*), waylay **4.** display, exhibit, flaunt, present, show **5.** bear up, endure, last, survive, wear

hold with agree to *or* with, approve of, be in favour of, countenance, subscribe to, support, take kindly to

▷ **Antonyms** be against, disagree with, disapprove of, hold out against, oppose

hole 1. aperture, breach, break, crack, fissure, gap, opening, orifice, outlet, perforation, puncture, rent, split, tear, vent **2.** cave, cavern, cavity, chamber, depression, excavation, hollow, pit, pocket, scoop, shaft **3.** burrow, covert, den, earth, lair, nest, retreat, shelter **4.** *informal* dive (*slang*), dump (*informal*), hovel, joint (*slang*), slum **5.** *informal* calaboose (*U.S. informal*), cell, dungeon, oubliette, prison **6.** defect, discrepancy, error, fallacy, fault, flaw, inconsistency, loophole **7.** *slang* dilemma, fix (*informal*), hot water (*informal*), imbroglio, jam (*informal*), mess, predicament, quandary, scrape (*informal*), spot (*informal*), tangle, tight spot **8. pick holes in** asperse, bad-mouth (*slang, chiefly U.S. & Canad.*), cavil, crab (*informal*), criticize, denigrate, disparage, disprove, find fault, knock (*informal*), niggle, pull to pieces, put down, rubbish (*informal*), run down, slag (off) (*slang*), slate (*informal*)

hole-and-corner backstairs, clandestine, furtive, secret, secretive, sneaky (*informal*), stealthy, surreptitious, underhand, under the counter (*informal*)
▷ **Antonyms** above-board, candid, frank, open, public

hole up go to earth, hibernate, hide, shelter, take cover, take refuge

holiday 1. break, leave, recess, time off, vacation **2.** anniversary, bank holiday, celebration, feast, festival, festivity, fête, gala, name day, public holiday, red-letter day, saint's day

holier-than-thou goody-goody (*informal*), pietistic, pietistical, priggish, religiose, sanctimonious, self-righteous, self-satisfied, smug, squeaky-clean, unctuous

holiness blessedness, devoutness, divinity, godliness, piety, purity, religiousness, righteousness, sacredness, saintliness, sanctity, spirituality, virtuousness

holler *verb/noun* bawl, bellow, call, cheer, clamour, cry, hail, halloo, hollo, hurrah, huzzah (*archaic*), roar, shout, whoop, yell

hollow *adjective* **1.** empty, not solid, unfilled, vacant, void **2.** cavernous, concave, deep-set, depressed, indented, sunken **3.** deep, dull, expressionless, flat, low, muffled, muted, reverberant, rumbling, sepulchral, toneless **4.** empty, fruitless, futile, meaningless, pointless, Pyrrhic, specious, unavailing, useless, vain, wanky (*taboo slang*), worthless **5.** empty, esurient, famished, hungry, ravenous, starved **6.** artificial, cynical, deceitful, faithless, false, flimsy, hollow-hearted, hypocritical, insincere, treacherous, unsound, weak **7. beat (someone) hollow** *informal* defeat, hammer (*informal*), outdo, overcome, rout, thrash, trounce, worst *~noun* **8.** basin, bowl, cave, cavern, cavity, concavity, crater, cup, den, dent, depression, dimple, excavation, hole, indentation, pit, trough **9.** bottom, dale, dell, dingle, glen, valley *~verb* **10.** channel, dig, dish, excavate, furrow, gouge, groove, pit, scoop
▷ **Antonyms** *~adjective* (*sense 1*) full, occupied, solid (*sense 2*) convex, rounded (*sense 3*) expressive, vibrant (*sense 4*) gratifying, meaningful, pleasing, satisfying, valuable, worthwhile (*sense 6*) genuine *~noun* (*sense 8*) bump, mound, projection (*sense 9*) bluff, height, hill, knoll, mountain, rise

holocaust annihilation, carnage, conflagration, destruction, devastation, fire, genocide, inferno, massacre, mass murder, pogrom

holy 1. devout, divine, faithful, god-fearing, godly, hallowed, pious, pure, religious, righteous, saintly, sublime, virtuous **2.** blessed, consecrated, dedicated, hallowed, sacred, sacrosanct, sanctified, venerable, venerated
▷ **Antonyms** (*sense 1*) blasphemous, corrupt, earthly, evil, human, immoral, impious, irreligious, sacrilegious, secular, sinful, unholy, wicked, worldly (*sense 2*) desecrated, unconsecrated, unhallowed, unholy, unsanctified

homage 1. admiration, adoration, adulation, awe, deference, devotion, duty, esteem, honour, respect, reverence, worship **2.** allegiance, devotion, faithfulness, fealty, fidelity, loyalty, obeisance, service, tribute, troth (*archaic*)
▷ **Antonyms** condemnation, contempt, disdain, disregard, disrespect, irreverence, scorn

home *noun* **1.** abode, domicile, dwelling, dwelling place, habitation, house, pad (*slang*), residence **2.** birthplace, family, fireside, hearth, homestead, home town, household **3.** abode, element, environment, habitat, habitation, haunt, home ground, range, stamping ground, territory **4. at home: a.** available, in, present **b.** at ease, comfortable, familiar, relaxed **c.** entertaining, giving a party, having guests, receiving **d.** (*as a noun*) party, reception, soirée **5. at home in, on,** *or* **with** conversant with, familiar with, knowledgeable, proficient, skilled, well-versed **6. bring home to** drive home, emphasize, impress upon, make clear, press home *~adjective* **7.** central, domestic, familiar, family, household, inland, internal, local, national, native

homeland country of origin, fatherland, mother country, motherland, native land

homeless 1. *adjective* abandoned, destitute, displaced, dispossessed, down-and-out, exiled, forlorn, forsaken, outcast, unsettled **2.** *~noun* **the homeless** dossers (*Brit. slang*), squatters, vagrants

homelike cheerful, comfortable, cosy, easy, familiar, homy, informal, intimate, relaxing, snug

homely comfortable, comfy (*informal*), cosy, domestic, downhome (*slang, chiefly U.S.*), down-to-earth, everyday, familiar, friendly, homelike, homespun, homy, informal, modest, natural, ordinary, plain, simple, unaffected, unassuming, unfussy, unpretentious, welcoming
▷ **Antonyms** affected, elaborate, elegant, grand, ostentatious, pretentious, refined, regal, sophisticated, splendid

Homeric epic, grand, heroic, imposing, impressive

homespun artless, coarse, homely, home-made, inelegant, plain, rough, rude, rustic, unpolished, unsophisticated

homicidal deadly, death-dealing, lethal, maniacal, mortal, murderous

homicide **1.** bloodshed, killing, manslaughter, murder, slaying **2.** killer, murderer, slayer

homily address, discourse, lecture, preaching, preachment, sermon

homogeneity analogousness, comparability, consistency, correspondence, identicalness, oneness, sameness, similarity, uniformity

homogeneous akin, alike, analogous, cognate, comparable, consistent, identical, kindred, similar, uniform, unvarying

▷ **Antonyms** different, disparate, dissimilar, divergent, diverse, heterogeneous, manifold, mixed, unlike, unrelated, varied, various, varying

homologous analogous, comparable, correspondent, corresponding, like, parallel, related, similar

homosexual *adjective* bent (*slang*), camp (*informal*), gay, homoerotic, lesbian, moffie (*S. African slang*), pink (*informal*), queer (*informal, derogatory*), sapphic

homy comfortable, comfy (*informal*), congenial, cosy, domestic, familiar, friendly, informal, intimate, pleasant, warm

hone *verb* edge, file, grind, point, polish, sharpen, strop, whet

honest **1.** conscientious, decent, ethical, high-minded, honourable, law-abiding, reliable, reputable, scrupulous, trustworthy, trusty, truthful, upright, veracious, virtuous **2.** above board, authentic, bona fide, genuine, honest to goodness, on the level (*informal*), on the up and up, proper, real, straight, true **3.** equitable, fair, fair and square, impartial, just **4.** candid, direct, forthright, frank, ingenuous, open, outright, plain, round, sincere, straightforward, undisguised, unfeigned, upfront (*informal*)

▷ **Antonyms** bad, corrupt, counterfeit, crooked, deceitful, disguised, dishonest, false, fraudulent, guilty, illegitimate, immoral, insincere, secretive, treacherous, unethical, unfair, unfaithful, unlawful, unprincipled, unreliable, unrighteous, unscrupulous, untrustworthy, untruthful

honestly **1.** by fair means, cleanly, ethically, honourably, in good faith, lawfully, legally, legitimately, on the level (*informal*), with clean hands **2.** candidly, frankly, in all sincerity, in plain English, plainly, straight (out), to one's face, truthfully

honesty **1.** faithfulness, fidelity, honour, incorruptibility, integrity, morality, probity, rectitude, reputability, scrupulousness, straightness, trustworthiness, truthfulness, uprightness, veracity, virtue **2.** bluntness, candour, equity, even-handedness, fairness, frankness, genuineness, openness, outspokenness, plainness, sincerity, straightforwardness

honeyed agreeable, alluring, cajoling, dulcet, enticing, flattering, mellow, melodious, seductive, soothing, sweet, sweetened, unctuous

honorary complimentary, ex officio, formal, *honoris causa,* in name *or* title only, nominal, titular, unofficial, unpaid

honour *noun* **1.** credit, dignity, distinction, elevation, eminence, esteem, fame, glory, high standing, prestige, rank, renown, reputation, repute **2.** acclaim, accolade, adoration, Brownie points, commendation, deference, homage, kudos, praise, recognition, regard, respect, reverence, tribute, veneration **3.** decency, fairness, goodness, honesty, integrity, morality, principles, probity, rectitude, righteousness, trustworthiness, uprightness **4.** compliment, credit, favour, pleasure, privilege, source of pride *or* satisfaction **5.** chastity, innocence, modesty, purity, virginity, virtue *~verb* **6.** admire, adore, appreciate, esteem, exalt, glorify, hallow, prize, respect, revere, reverence, value, venerate, worship **7.** be as good as (*informal*), be faithful to, be true to, carry out, discharge, fulfil, keep, live up to, observe **8.** acclaim, celebrate, commemorate, commend, compliment, crack up (*informal*), decorate, dignify, exalt, glorify, laud, lionize, praise **9.** accept, acknowledge, cash, clear, credit, pass, pay, take

▷ **Antonyms** *~noun* (*senses 1 & 2*) condemnation, contempt, disfavour, disgrace, dishonour, disrepute, disrespect, infamy, insult, scorn, shame, slight (*sense 3*) degradation, dishonesty, dishonour, insincerity, lowness, meanness, unscrupulousness *~verb* (*senses 6 & 8*) condemn, defame, degrade, dishonour, insult, offend, scorn, slight (*sense 7*) disobey, refuse (*sense 9*) refuse

honourable **1.** ethical, fair, high-minded, honest, just, moral, principled, true, trustworthy, trusty, upright, upstanding, virtuous **2.** distinguished, eminent, great, illustrious, noble, notable, noted, prestigious, renowned, venerable **3.** creditable, estimable, proper, reputable, respectable, respected, right, righteous, virtuous

honours adornments, awards, decorations, dignities, distinctions, laurels, titles

hoodwink bamboozle (*informal*), befool, cheat, con (*informal*), cozen, deceive, delude, dupe, fool, gull (*archaic*), hoax, impose, kid (*informal*), lead up the garden path (*informal*), mislead, pull a fast one on (*informal*), rook (*slang*), sell a pup, swindle, take (someone) for a ride (*informal*), trick

hook *noun* **1.** catch, clasp, fastener, hasp, holder, link, lock, peg **2.** noose, snare, springe, trap **3. by hook or by crook** by any means, by fair means or foul, somehow, somehow or other, someway **4. hook, line, and sinker** *informal* completely, entirely, lock, stock and barrel, thoroughly, through and through, totally, utterly, wholly **5. off the hook** *slang* acquitted, cleared, exonerated, in the clear, let off, under no obligation, vindicated *~verb* **6.** catch, clasp, fasten, fix, hasp, secure **7.** catch, enmesh, ensnare, entrap, snare, trap

hooked 1. aquiline, beaked, beaky, bent, curved, falcate (*Biology*), hamate (*rare*), hooklike, hook-shaped, unciform (*Anatomy, zoology, etc.*), uncinate (*Biology*) **2.** addicted to, devoted to, enamoured of, obsessed with, taken with, turned on (*slang*)

hooligan casual, delinquent, hoodlum (*chiefly U.S.*), lager lout, ned (*slang*), rowdy, ruffian, tough, vandal, yob *or* yobbo (*Brit. slang*)

hoop band, circlet, girdle, loop, ring, wheel

hoot *noun* **1.** call, cry, toot **2.** boo, catcall, hiss, jeer, yell **3.** *informal* card (*informal*), caution (*informal*), laugh (*informal*), scream (*informal*) *~verb* **4.** boo, catcall, condemn, decry, denounce, execrate, hiss, howl down, jeer, yell at **5.** cry, scream, shout, shriek, toot, whoop, yell

hop 1. *verb* bound, caper, dance, jump, leap, skip, spring, trip, vault **2.** *~noun* bounce, bound, jump, leap, skip, spring, step, vault

hope 1. *noun* ambition, anticipation, assumption, belief, confidence, desire, dream, expectancy, expectation, faith, light at the end of the tunnel, longing **2.** *~verb* anticipate, aspire, await, believe, contemplate, count on, cross one's fingers, desire, expect, foresee, keep one's fingers crossed, long, look forward to, rely, set one's heart on, trust

▷ **Antonyms** (*sense 1*) despair, distrust, doubt, dread, hopelessness

hopeful 1. anticipating, assured, buoyant, confident, expectant, looking forward to, optimistic, sanguine **2.** auspicious, bright, cheerful, encouraging, heartening, promising, propitious, reassuring, rosy

▷ **Antonyms** (*sense 1*) cheerless, dejected, despairing, hopeless, pessimistic (*sense 2*) depressing, discouraging, disheartening, unpromising

hopefully 1. confidently, expectantly, optimistically, sanguinely **2.** *informal* all being well, conceivably, expectedly, feasibly, probably

hopeless 1. abject, defeatist, dejected, demoralized, despairing, desperate, despondent, disconsolate, downhearted, forlorn, in despair, pessimistic, woebegone **2.** basket case, helpless, incurable, irremediable, irreparable, irreversible, lost, past remedy, remediless **3.** forlorn, futile, impossible, impracticable, not having a prayer, no-win, pointless, unachievable, unattainable, useless, vain **4.** *informal* inadequate, incompetent, ineffectual, inferior, no good, pathetic, poor, useless (*informal*)

▷ **Antonyms** (*sense 1*) assured, cheerful, confident, expectant, happy, heartened, hopeful, optimistic, uplifted (*sense 2*) curable, encouraging, favourable, heartening, promising, reassuring, remediable

horde band, crew, crowd, drove, gang, host, mob, multitude, pack, press, swarm, throng, troop

horizon 1. field of vision, skyline, vista **2.** ambit, compass, ken, perspective, prospect, purview, range, realm, scope, sphere, stretch

horrible 1. abhorrent, abominable, appalling, awful, dreadful, fearful, frightful, from hell (*informal*), ghastly, grim, grisly, gruesome, heinous, hellacious (*U.S. slang*), hideous, horrid, loathsome, obscene, repulsive, revolting, shameful, shocking, terrible, terrifying **2.** *informal* awful, beastly (*informal*), cruel, disagreeable, dreadful, ghastly (*informal*), horrid, mean, nasty, terrible, unkind, unpleasant

▷ **Antonyms** agreeable, appealing, attractive, charming, cute, delightful, enchanting, fetching, lovely, pleasant, wonderful

horrid 1. awful, disagreeable, disgusting, dreadful, horrible, nasty, obscene, offensive, terrible, unpleasant, yucky *or* yukky (*slang*) **2.** abominable, alarming, appalling, formidable, frightening, from hell (*informal*), hair-raising, harrowing, hideous, horrific, odious, repulsive, revolting, shocking, terrifying, terrorizing **3.** *informal* beastly (*informal*), cruel, mean, nasty, unkind

horrific appalling, awful, dreadful, frightening, frightful, from hell (*informal*), ghastly, grim, grisly, hellacious (*U.S. slang*), horrendous, horrifying, shocking, terrifying

horrify 1. affright, alarm, frighten, intimidate, petrify, put the wind up (*informal*), scare, terrify, terrorize **2.** appal, disgust, dismay, gross out (*U.S. slang*), make one's hair stand on end, outrage, shock, sicken

▷ **Antonyms** comfort, delight, enchant, encourage, gladden, hearten, please, reassure, soothe

horror 1. alarm, apprehension, awe, consternation, dismay, dread, fear, fright, panic, terror **2**. abhorrence, abomination, antipathy, aversion, detestation, disgust, hatred, loathing, odium, repugnance, revulsion

▷ **Antonyms** affinity, approval, attraction, delight, liking, love

horror-struck *or* **horror-stricken** aghast, appalled, awe-struck, frightened to death, horrified, petrified, scared out of one's wits, shocked

horse around *or* **about** clown, fool about *or* around, misbehave, play the fool, play the goat, roughhouse (*slang*)

horseman cavalier, cavalryman, dragoon, equestrian, horse-soldier, rider

horseplay buffoonery, clowning, fooling around, high jinks, pranks, romping, rough-and-tumble, roughhousing (*informal*), skylarking (*informal*)

horse sense common sense, gumption (*Brit. informal*), judgment, mother wit, nous (*Brit. slang*), practicality

hospitable 1. amicable, bountiful, cordial, friendly, generous, genial, gracious, kind, liberal, sociable, welcoming **2**. accessible, amenable, open-minded, receptive, responsive, tolerant

▷ **Antonyms** (*sense 1*) inhospitable, parsimonious (*sense 2*) inhospitable, intolerant, narrow-minded, unapproachable, unreceptive

hospitality cheer, conviviality, cordiality, friendliness, heartiness, hospitableness, neighbourliness, sociability, warmth, welcome

host[1] *noun* **1**. entertainer, innkeeper, landlord, master of ceremonies, proprietor **2**. anchor man, compere (*Brit.*), presenter ~*verb* **3**. compere (*Brit.*), front (*informal*), introduce, present

host[2] *noun* army, array, drove, horde, legion, multitude, myriad, swarm, throng

hostage captive, gage, pawn, pledge, prisoner, security, surety

hostile 1. antagonistic, anti (*informal*), bellicose, belligerent, contrary, ill-disposed, inimical, malevolent, opposed, opposite, rancorous, unkind, warlike **2**. adverse, alien, inhospitable, unfriendly, unpropitious, unsympathetic, unwelcoming

▷ **Antonyms** affable, agreeable, amiable, approving, congenial, cordial, friendly, kind, peaceful, sympathetic, warm

hostilities conflict, fighting, state of war, war, warfare

▷ **Antonyms** alliance, ceasefire, peace, treaty, truce

hostility abhorrence, animosity, animus, antagonism, antipathy, aversion, bad blood, detestation, enmity, hatred, ill will, malevolence, malice, opposition, resentment, unfriendliness

▷ **Antonyms** agreement, amity, approval, congeniality, cordiality, friendliness, goodwill, sympathy

hot 1. aboil, blistering, boiling, burning, fiery, flaming, heated, piping hot, roasting, scalding, scorching, searing, steaming, sultry, sweltering, torrid, warm **2**. acrid, biting, peppery, piquant, pungent, sharp, spicy **3**. *figurative* ablaze, animated, ardent, excited, fervent, fervid, fierce, fiery, flaming, impetuous, inflamed, intense, irascible, lustful, passionate, raging, stormy, touchy, vehement, violent **4**. fresh, just out, latest, new, recent, up to the minute **5**. approved, favoured, in demand, in vogue, popular, sought-after **6**. close, following closely, in hot pursuit, near

▷ **Antonyms** (*sense 1*) chilly, cold, cool, freezing, frigid, frosty, icy, parky (*Brit. informal*) (*sense 2*) mild (*sense 3*) apathetic, calm, dispassionate, half-hearted, indifferent, mild, moderate (*sense 4*) old, stale, trite (*sense 5*) out of favour, unpopular (*sense 6*) cold

hot air blather, blether, bombast, bosh (*informal*), bunkum *or* buncombe (*chiefly U.S.*), claptrap (*informal*), empty talk, gas (*informal*), guff (*slang*), rant, tall talk (*informal*), verbiage, wind

hotbed breeding ground, den, forcing house, nest, nursery, seedbed

hot-blooded ardent, excitable, fervent, fiery, heated, impulsive, passionate, rash, spirited, temperamental, wild

▷ **Antonyms** apathetic, calm, cold, cool, frigid, impassive, restrained, unenthusiastic

hotchpotch conglomeration, farrago, gallimaufry, hash, hodgepodge (*U.S.*), jumble, medley, *mélange,* mess, miscellany, mishmash, mixture, olio, olla podrida, potpourri

hotfoot hastily, helter-skelter, hurriedly, pell-mell, posthaste, quickly, speedily

hothead adrenalin junky (*slang*), daredevil, desperado, hotspur, madcap, tearaway

hot-headed fiery, foolhardy, hasty, hot-tempered, impetuous, precipitate, quick-tempered, rash, reckless, unruly, volatile

hothouse 1. *noun* conservatory, glasshouse, greenhouse **2**. ~*adjective* coddled, dainty, delicate, exotic, fragile, frail, overprotected, pampered, sensitive

hound *verb* **1**. chase, drive, give chase, hunt, hunt down, pursue **2**. badger, goad, harass, harry, impel, persecute, pester, prod, provoke

house *noun* **1**. abode, building, domicile, dwelling, edifice, habitation, home, homestead, pad (*slang*), residence **2**. family, household, ménage **3**. ancestry, clan, dynasty, family tree, kindred, line, lineage, race, tribe **4**. business, company, concern, establishment, firm, organization, outfit (*informal*), partnership **5**. assembly, Commons, legislative body, parliament **6**. hotel, inn, public house, tavern **7. on the house** for nothing, free, gratis, without expense *~verb* **8.** accommodate, billet, board, domicile, harbour, lodge, put up, quarter, take in **9.** contain, cover, keep, protect, sheathe, shelter, store

household 1. *noun* family, home, house, ménage **2.** *~adjective* domestic, domiciliary, family, ordinary, plain

householder homeowner, occupant, resident, tenant

housekeeping home economy, homemaking (*U.S.*), housecraft, household management, housewifery

housing 1. accommodation, dwellings, homes, houses **2.** case, casing, container, cover, covering, enclosure, sheath

hovel cabin, den, hole, hut, shack, shanty, shed

hover 1. be suspended, drift, float, flutter, fly, hang, poise **2.** hang about, linger, wait nearby **3.** alternate, dither (*chiefly Brit.*), falter, fluctuate, haver (*Brit.*), oscillate, pause, seesaw, swither (*Scot. dialect*), vacillate, waver

however after all, anyhow, be that as it may, but, even though, nevertheless, nonetheless, notwithstanding, on the other hand, still, though, yet

howl 1. *noun* bawl, bay, bell, bellow, clamour, cry, groan, hoot, outcry, roar, scream, shriek, ululation, wail, yelp, yowl **2.** *~verb* bawl, bell, bellow, cry, cry out, lament, quest (*used of hounds*), roar, scream, shout, shriek, ululate, wail, weep, yell, yelp

howler bloomer (*Brit. informal*), blunder, boner (*slang*), boob (*Brit. slang*), booboo (*informal*), bull (*slang*), clanger (*informal*), error, malapropism, mistake, schoolboy howler

hoyden, hoiden romp (*archaic*), tomboy

hoydenish, hoidenish boisterous, bold, ill-mannered, inelegant, rackety, uncouth, unfeminine, ungenteel, unladylike, unruly

hub centre, core, focal point, focus, heart, middle, nerve centre, pivot

hubbub babel, bedlam, brouhaha, clamour, confusion, din, disorder, disturbance, hue and cry, hullabaloo, hurly-burly, noise, pandemonium, racket, riot, ruckus (*informal*), ruction (*informal*), rumpus, tumult, uproar

huckster barker (*informal*), hawker, pedlar, pitchman (*U.S.*), salesman, vendor

huddle *noun* **1.** confusion, crowd, disorder, heap, jumble, mass, mess, muddle **2.** *informal* confab (*informal*), conference, discussion, meeting, powwow *~verb* **3.** cluster, converge, crowd, flock, gather, press, throng **4.** crouch, cuddle, curl up, hunch up, make oneself small, nestle, snuggle

hue 1. colour, dye, shade, tincture, tinge, tint, tone **2.** aspect, cast, complexion, light

hue and cry brouhaha, clamour, furore, hullabaloo, much ado, outcry, ruction (*informal*), rumpus, uproar

huff *noun* **1.** anger, bad mood, bate (*Brit. slang*), miff (*informal*), passion, pet, pique, rage, temper, wax (*informal, chiefly Brit.*) **2. in a huff** angered, annoyed, exasperated, hacked (off) (*U.S. slang*), hurt, in high dudgeon, irked, miffed (*informal*), nettled, peeved, piqued, pissed off (*taboo slang*), provoked, put out (*informal*), riled (*informal*), vexed *~verb* **3.** blow, exhale, puff

huffy, huffish angry, choked, crabbed, cross, crotchety (*informal*), crusty, curt, disgruntled, edgy, grumpy, irritable, moody, moping, offended, peevish, pettish, petulant, querulous, ratty (*Brit. & N.Z. informal*), resentful, shirty (*slang, chiefly Brit.*), short, snappy, sulky, sullen, surly, testy, tetchy, touchy, waspish
▷ **Antonyms** amiable, calm, cheerful, friendly, gay, good-humoured, happy, pleasant, sunny

hug *verb* **1.** clasp, cuddle, embrace, enfold, hold close, squeeze, take in one's arms **2.** cling to, follow closely, keep close, stay near **3.** cherish, cling, hold onto, nurse, retain *~noun* **4.** bear hug, clasp, clinch (*slang*), embrace, squeeze

huge Brobdingnagian, bulky, colossal, elephantine, enormous, extensive, gargantuan, giant, gigantic, ginormous (*informal*), great, humongous *or* humungous (*U.S. slang*), immense, jumbo (*informal*), large, mammoth, massive, mega (*slang*), monumental, mountainous, prodigious, stellar (*informal*), stupendous, titanic, tremendous, vast
▷ **Antonyms** insignificant, little, microscopic, minute, petty, puny, small, tiny

huggermugger confusion, disarray, disorder, disorganization, guddle (*Scot.*), hodgepodge (*U.S.*), hotchpotch, huddle, jumble, mess, muddle, pig's breakfast (*informal*), shambles, state

hulk 1. derelict, frame, hull, shell, shipwreck, wreck **2.** lout, lubber, lump (*informal*), oaf

hulking awkward, bulky, clumsy, clunky (*informal*), cumbersome, gross, lubberly, lumbering, lumpish, massive, oafish, overgrown, ponderous, ungainly, unwieldy

hull *noun* **1.** body, casing, covering, frame, framework, skeleton **2.** husk, peel, pod, rind, shell, shuck, skin *~verb* **3.** husk, peel, shell, shuck, skin, trim

hullabaloo babel, bedlam, brouhaha, clamour, commotion, confusion, din, disturbance, furore, hubbub, hue and cry, hurly-burly, noise, outcry, pandemonium, racket, ruckus (*informal*), ruction (*informal*), rumpus, to-do, tumult, turmoil, upheaval, uproar

hum 1. bombinate *or* bombilate (*literary*), buzz, croon, drone, mumble, murmur, purr, sing, throb, thrum, vibrate, whir **2.** be active, be busy, bustle, buzz, move, pulsate, pulse, stir, vibrate

human *adjective* **1.** anthropoid, fleshly, manlike, mortal **2.** approachable, compassionate, considerate, fallible, forgivable, humane, kind, kindly, natural, understandable, understanding, vulnerable *~noun* **3.** body, child, creature, human being, individual, man, mortal, person, soul, wight (*archaic*), woman

▷ **Antonyms** *~adjective* (*sense 1*) animal, nonhuman (*sense 2*) beastly, brutish, cruel, inhuman, unsympathetic *~noun* animal, god, nonhuman

humane benevolent, benign, charitable, clement, compassionate, forbearing, forgiving, gentle, good, good-natured, kind, kind-hearted, kindly, lenient, merciful, mild, sympathetic, tender, understanding

▷ **Antonyms** barbarous, brutal, cruel, inhuman, inhumane, ruthless, uncivilized, unkind, unmerciful, unsympathetic

humanitarian 1. *adjective* altruistic, beneficent, benevolent, charitable, compassionate, humane, philanthropic, public-spirited **2.** *~noun* altruist, benefactor, Good Samaritan, philanthropist

humanitarianism beneficence, benevolence, charity, generosity, goodwill, humanism, philanthropy

humanities classical studies, classics, liberal arts, literae humaniores

humanity 1. flesh, Homo sapiens, humankind, human race, man, mankind, men, mortality, people **2.** human nature, humanness, mortality **3.** benevolence, benignity, brotherly love, charity, compassion, fellow feeling, kind-heartedness, kindness, mercy, philanthropy, sympathy, tenderness, tolerance, understanding

humanize civilize, cultivate, educate, enlighten, improve, mellow, polish, reclaim, refine, soften, tame

humble *adjective* **1.** meek, modest, self-effacing, submissive, unassuming, unostentatious, unpretentious **2.** common, commonplace, insignificant, low, low-born, lowly, mean, modest, obscure, ordinary, plebeian, poor, simple, undistinguished, unimportant, unpretentious **3.** courteous, deferential, obliging, obsequious, polite, respectful, servile, subservient *~verb* **4.** abase, abash, break, bring down, chagrin, chasten, crush, debase, degrade, demean, disgrace, humiliate, lower, mortify, put down (*slang*), put (someone) in their place, reduce, shame, sink, subdue, take down a peg (*informal*) **5. humble oneself** abase oneself, eat crow (*U.S. informal*), eat humble pie, go on bended knee, grovel, swallow one's pride

▷ **Antonyms** *~adjective* (*senses 1 & 3*) arrogant, assuming, conceited, haughty, immodest, lordly, ostentatious, overbearing, pompous, presumptuous, pretentious, proud, snobbish, superior, vain (*sense 2*) aristocratic, distinguished, elegant, famous, glorious, high, important, rich, significant, superior, wealthy *~verb* elevate, exalt, magnify, raise

humbly cap in hand, deferentially, diffidently, meekly, modestly, obsequiously, on bended knee, respectfully, servilely, submissively, subserviently, unassumingly

humbug *noun* **1.** bluff, canard, cheat, deceit, deception, dodge, feint, fraud, hoax, imposition, imposture, ruse, sham, swindle, trick, trickery, wile **2.** charlatan, cheat, con man (*informal*), faker, fraud, fraudster, grifter (*slang, chiefly U.S. & Canad.*), impostor, phoney *or* phony (*informal*), quack, swindler, trickster **3.** baloney (*informal*), cant, charlatanry, claptrap (*informal*), eyewash (*informal*), gammon (*Brit. informal*), hypocrisy, nonsense, quackery, rubbish, trash *~verb* **4.** bamboozle (*informal*), befool, beguile, cheat, con (*informal*), cozen, deceive, delude, dupe, fool, gull (*archaic*), hoax, hoodwink, impose, mislead, swindle, take in (*informal*), trick

humdrum banal, boring, commonplace, dreary, dull, ho-hum (*informal*), mind-numbing, monotonous, mundane, ordinary, repetitious, routine, tedious, tiresome, uneventful, uninteresting, unvaried, wearisome

▷ **Antonyms** dramatic, entertaining, exciting, extraordinary, interesting, lively, sexy (*informal*), stimulating

humid clammy, damp, dank, moist, muggy, steamy, sticky, sultry, watery, wet

▷ **Antonyms** arid, dry, sunny, torrid

humidity clamminess, damp, dampness, dankness, dew, humidness, moistness, moisture, mugginess, sogginess, wetness

humiliate abase, abash, bring low, chagrin, chasten, crush, debase, degrade, discomfit, disgrace, embarrass, humble, make (someone) eat humble pie, mortify, put down, put (someone) in their place, shame, subdue, take down a peg (*informal*), take the wind out of someone's sails

▷ **Antonyms** elevate, honour, magnify, make proud

humiliating cringe-making (*Brit. informal*), cringeworthy (*Brit. informal*), crushing, degrading, disgracing, embarrassing, humbling, ignominious, mortifying, shaming

humiliation abasement, affront, chagrin, condescension, degradation, disgrace, dishonour, embarrassment, humbling, ignominy, indignity, loss of face, mortification, put-down, resignation, self-abasement, shame, submission, submissiveness

humility diffidence, humbleness, lack of pride, lowliness, meekness, modesty, self-abasement, servility, submissiveness, unpretentiousness

▷ **Antonyms** arrogance, conceit, disdain, haughtiness, pomposity, presumption, pretentiousness, pride, snobbishness, superciliousness, superiority, vanity

hummock hillock, hump, knoll, mound

humorist card (*informal*), comedian, comic, eccentric, funny man, jester, joker, wag, wit

humorous amusing, comic, comical, droll, entertaining, facetious, farcical, funny, hilarious, jocose, jocular, laughable, ludicrous, merry, playful, pleasant, side-splitting, waggish, whimsical, witty

▷ **Antonyms** earnest, grave, sad, serious, sober, solemn

humour *noun* **1.** amusement, comedy, drollery, facetiousness, fun, funniness, jocularity, ludicrousness, wit **2.** comedy, farce, gags (*informal*), jesting, jests, jokes, joking, pleasantry, wisecracks (*informal*), wit, witticisms, wittiness **3.** disposition, frame of mind, mood, spirits, temper **4.** bent, bias, fancy, freak, mood, propensity, quirk, vagary, whim *~verb* **5.** accommodate, cosset, favour, fawn on, feed, flatter, go along with, gratify, indulge, mollify, pamper, pander to, spoil

▷ **Antonyms** *~noun* (*senses 1 & 2*) gravity, grief, melancholy, sadness, seriousness, sobriety, solemnity, sorrow *~verb* aggravate, excite, oppose, rouse, stand up to

hump *noun* **1.** bulge, bump, hunch, knob, lump, mound, projection, protrusion, protuberance, swelling **2. the hump** *Brit. informal* megrims (*rare*), the blues, the doldrums, the dumps (*informal*), the grumps (*informal*), the mopes, the sulks *~verb* **3.** arch, curve, form a hump, hunch, lift, tense **4.** *slang* carry, heave, hoist, lug, shoulder

hunch 1. *noun* feeling, idea, impression, inkling, intuition, premonition, presentiment, suspicion **2.** *~verb* arch, bend, crouch, curve, draw in, huddle, hump, squat, stoop, tense

hunchback crookback (*rare*), crouch-back (*archaic*), humpback, kyphosis (*Pathology*), Quasimodo

hunchbacked deformed, gibbous, humpbacked, humped, malformed, misshapen, stooped

hunger *noun* **1.** appetite, emptiness, esurience, famine, hungriness, ravenousness, starvation, voracity **2.** ache, appetence, appetite, craving, desire, greediness, itch, lust, thirst, yearning, yen (*informal*) *~verb* **3.** ache, crave, desire, hanker, hope, itch, long, pine, starve, thirst, want, wish, yearn

hungry 1. empty, esurient, famished, famishing, hollow, peckish (*informal, chiefly Brit.*), ravenous, sharp-set, starved, starving, voracious **2.** athirst, avid, covetous, craving, desirous, eager, greedy, keen, yearning

hunk block, chunk, gobbet, lump, mass, nugget, piece, slab, wedge, wodge (*Brit. informal*)

hunt *verb* **1.** chase, gun for, hound, pursue, stalk, track, trail **2.** ferret about, forage, go in quest of, look, look high and low, rummage through, scour, search, seek, try to find *~noun* **3.** chase, hunting, investigation, pursuit, quest, search

hunted careworn, desperate, distraught, gaunt, haggard, harassed, harried, persecuted, stricken, terror-stricken, tormented, worn

hurdle *noun* **1.** barricade, barrier, block, fence, hedge, wall **2.** barrier, block, complication, difficulty, handicap, hazard, hindrance, impediment, obstacle, obstruction, snag, stumbling block

hurl cast, chuck (*informal*), fire, fling, heave, launch, let fly, pitch, project, propel, send, shy, sling, throw, toss

hurly-burly bedlam, brouhaha, chaos, commotion, confusion, disorder, furore, hubbub, pandemonium, tumult, turbulence, turmoil, upheaval, uproar

▷ **Antonyms** composure, order, organization, tidiness

hurricane cyclone, gale, storm, tempest, tornado, twister (*U.S. informal*), typhoon, willy-willy (*Austral.*), windstorm

hurried breakneck, brief, cursory, hasty, hectic, perfunctory, precipitate, quick, quickie (*informal*), rushed, short, slapdash, speedy, superficial, swift

hurry *verb* **1.** barrel (along) (*informal, chiefly U.S. & Canad.*), burn rubber (*informal*), dash, fly, get a move on (*informal*), get one's skates on (*informal*), lose no time, make haste, rush, scoot, scurry, step on it (*informal*) **2.** accelerate, expedite, goad, hasten, hustle, push on, quicken, speed (up), urge *~noun* **3.** bustle, celerity, commotion, dispatch, expedition, flurry, haste, precipitation, promptitude, quickness, rush, speed, urgency

▷ **Antonyms** *~verb* (*sense 1*) crawl, creep, dawdle, drag one's feet, move slowly (*sense 2*) delay, retard, slow, slow down *~noun* calmness, slowness

hurt *verb* **1.** bruise, damage, disable, harm, impair, injure, lay a finger on, mar, spoil, wound **2.** ache, be sore, be tender, burn, pain, smart, sting, throb **3.** afflict, aggrieve, annoy, cut to the quick, distress, grieve, pain, sadden, sting, upset, wound *~noun* **4.** discomfort, dis~

tress, pain, pang, soreness, suffering **5.** bruise, sore, wound **6.** damage, detriment, disadvantage, harm, injury, loss, mischief, wrong *~adjective* **7.** bruised, cut, damaged, grazed, harmed, injured, scarred, scraped, scratched, wounded **8.** aggrieved, crushed, injured, miffed (*informal*), offended, pained, piqued, rueful, sad, wounded

▷ **Antonyms** *~verb* (*senses 1 & 2*) alleviate, cure, heal, relieve, repair, restore, soothe (*sense 3*) aid, benefit, calm, compensate, compliment, console, forward, heighten, help, increase, please *~noun* (*sense 6*) delight, happiness, joy, pleasure, pride, satisfaction *~adjective* (*sense 7*) alleviated, assuaged, healed, relieved, repaired, restored, soothed (*sense 8*) calmed, consoled, placated

hurtful cruel, cutting, damaging, destructive, detrimental, disadvantageous, distressing, harmful, injurious, maleficent, malicious, mean, mischievous, nasty, pernicious, prejudicial, spiteful, unkind, upsetting, wounding

hurtle barrel (along) (*informal, chiefly U.S. & Canad.*), burn rubber (*informal*), charge, crash, fly, go hell for leather (*informal*), plunge, race, rush, rush headlong, scoot, scramble, shoot, speed, spurt, stampede, tear

husband *verb* budget, conserve, economize, hoard, manage thriftily, save, store, use sparingly

▷ **Antonyms** be extravagant, fritter away, spend, splash out (*informal, chiefly Brit.*), squander

husband

husbandry 1. agriculture, agronomy, cultivation, farming, land management, tillage **2.** careful management, economy, frugality, good housekeeping, thrift

hush *verb* **1.** mute, muzzle, quieten, shush, silence, still, suppress **2.** allay, appease, calm, compose, mollify, soothe *~noun* **3.** calm, peace, peacefulness, quiet, silence, still (*poetic*), stillness, tranquillity

hush-hush classified, confidential, restricted, secret, top-secret, under wraps

hush up conceal, cover up, draw a veil over, keep dark, keep secret, sit on (*informal*), smother, squash, suppress, sweep under the carpet (*informal*)

husk bark, chaff, covering, glume, hull, rind, shuck

huskiness dryness, harshness, hoarseness, raspingness, roughness

husky 1. croaking, croaky, gruff, guttural, harsh, hoarse, rasping, raucous, rough, throaty **2.** *informal* beefy (*informal*), brawny, burly, hefty, muscular, powerful, rugged, stocky, strapping, thickset

hussy baggage (*informal, old-fashioned*), floozy (*slang*), jade, minx, quean (*archaic*), scrubber (*Brit. & Austral. slang*), slapper (*Brit. slang*), slut, strumpet, tart (*informal*), tramp (*slang*), trollop, wanton, wench (*archaic*)

hustle bustle, crowd, elbow, force, haste, hasten, hurry, impel, jog, jostle, push, rush, shove, thrust

hut cabin, den, hovel, lean-to, refuge, shanty, shed, shelter

hybrid *noun* amalgam, composite, compound, cross, crossbreed, half-blood, half-breed, mixture, mongrel, mule

hygiene cleanliness, hygienics, sanitary measures, sanitation

hygienic aseptic, clean, disinfected, germ-free, healthy, pure, salutary, sanitary, sterile

▷ **Antonyms** dirty, filthy, germ-ridden, harmful, insanitary, polluted, unhealthy, unhygienic, unwholesome

hymn anthem, canticle, carol, chant, doxology, paean, psalm, song of praise

hype ballyhoo (*informal*), brouhaha, build-up, plugging (*informal*), promotion, publicity, puffing, racket, razzmatazz (*slang*)

hyperbole amplification, enlargement, exaggeration, magnification, overstatement

hypercritical captious, carping, cavilling, censorious, fault-finding, finicky, fussy, hairsplitting, niggling, overcritical, overexacting, overscrupulous, pernickety (*informal*), strict

hypnotic mesmeric, mesmerizing, narcotic, opiate, sleep-inducing, somniferous, soothing, soporific, spellbinding

hypnotize 1. mesmerize, put in a trance, put to sleep **2.** absorb, entrance, fascinate, magnetize, spellbind

hypochondria hypochondriasis, valetudinarianism

hypochondriac *adjective/noun* valetudinarian

hypocrisy cant, deceit, deceitfulness, deception, dissembling, duplicity, falsity, imposture, insincerity, pharisaism, phariseeism, phoneyness *or* phoniness (*informal*), pretence, sanctimoniousness, speciousness, two-facedness

▷ **Antonyms** honesty, sincerity, truthfulness

hypocrite charlatan, deceiver, dissembler, fraud, Holy Willie, impostor, Pecksniff, pharisee, phoney *or* phony (*informal*), pretender, Tartuffe, whited sepulchre

hypocritical canting, deceitful, deceptive, dissembling, duplicitous, false, fraudulent, hollow, insincere, Janus-faced, pharisaical, phoney *or* phony (*informal*), sanctimonious, specious, spurious, two-faced

hypothesis assumption, postulate, premise, premiss, proposition, supposition, theory, thesis

hypothetical academic, assumed, conjec~tural, imaginary, putative, speculative, supposed, theoretical
▷ **Antonyms** actual, confirmed, estab~lished, known, proven, real, true

hysteria agitation, delirium, frenzy, hys~terics, madness, panic, unreason

hysterical 1. berserk, beside oneself, con~vulsive, crazed, distracted, distraught, frantic, frenzied, mad, overwrought, raving, uncontrollable **2.** *informal* comical, farcical, hilarious, scream~ing, side-splitting, uproarious, wildly funny
▷ **Antonyms** (*sense 1*) calm, composed, poised, self-possessed, unfazed (*infor~mal*) (*sense 2*) grave, melancholy, sad, serious

I, i

ice **1. break the ice** begin, initiate the proceedings, kick off (*informal*), lead the way, make a start, start *or* set the ball rolling (*informal*), take the plunge (*informal*) **2. on thin ice** at risk, in jeopardy, open to attack, out on a limb, sticking one's neck out (*informal*), unsafe, vulnerable

ice-cold arctic, biting, bitter, chilled to the bone *or* marrow, freezing, frozen, glacial, icy, raw, refrigerated, shivering

iconoclast critic, dissident, heretic, radical, rebel

iconoclastic denunciatory, dissentient, impious, innovative, irreverent, questioning, radical, rebellious, subversive

icy **1.** arctic, biting, bitter, chill, chilling, chilly, cold, freezing, frost-bound, frosty, frozen over, ice-cold, parky (*Brit. informal*), raw **2.** glacial, glassy, like a sheet of glass, rimy, slippery, slippy (*informal or dialect*) **3.** *figurative* aloof, cold, distant, forbidding, frigid, frosty, glacial, hostile, indifferent, steely, stony, unfriendly, unwelcoming

▷ **Antonyms** (*sense 1*) blistering, boiling, hot, sizzling, warm (*sense 3*) cordial, friendly, gracious, warm

idea **1.** abstraction, concept, conception, conclusion, fancy, impression, judgment, perception, thought, understanding **2.** belief, conviction, doctrine, interpretation, notion, opinion, teaching, view, viewpoint **3.** approximation, ballpark figure, clue, estimate, guess, hint, impression, inkling, intimation, notion, suspicion **4.** aim, end, import, intention, meaning, object, objective, plan, purpose, *raison d'être,* reason, sense, significance **5.** design, hypothesis, plan, recommendation, scheme, solution, suggestion, theory **6.** archetype, essence, form, pattern

ideal *noun* **1.** archetype, criterion, epitome, example, exemplar, last word, model, nonpareil, paradigm, paragon, pattern, perfection, prototype, standard, standard of perfection **2.** (*often plural*) moral value, principle, standard ~*adjective* **3.** archetypal, classic, complete, consummate, model, optimal, perfect, quintessential, supreme **4.** abstract, conceptual, hypothetical, intellectual, mental, notional, theoretical, transcendental **5.** fanciful, imaginary, impractical, ivory-tower, unattainable, unreal, Utopian, visionary

▷ **Antonyms** ~*adjective* (*sense 3*) deficient, flawed, impaired, imperfect, unsuitable (*sense 5*) actual, factual, literal, mundane, ordinary, real

idealist *noun* dreamer, romantic, Utopian, visionary

idealistic impracticable, optimistic, perfectionist, quixotic, romantic, starry-eyed, Utopian, visionary

▷ **Antonyms** down-to-earth, practical, pragmatic, realistic, sensible

idealization ennoblement, exaltation, glorification, magnification, worship

idealize apotheosize, deify, ennoble, exalt, glorify, magnify, put on a pedestal, romanticize, worship

ideally all things being equal, if one had one's way, in a perfect world, under the best of circumstances

idée fixe bee in one's bonnet, fixation, fixed idea, hobbyhorse, monomania, obsession, one-track mind (*informal*), preoccupation, thing (*informal*)

identical a dead ringer (*slang*), alike, corresponding, duplicate, equal, equivalent, indistinguishable, interchangeable, like, like two peas in a pod, matching, selfsame, the dead spit (*informal*), the same, twin

▷ **Antonyms** different, disparate, distinct, diverse, separate, unlike

identifiable ascertainable, detectable, discernible, distinguishable, known, noticeable, recognizable, unmistakable

identification **1.** cataloguing, classifying, establishment of identity, labelling, naming, pinpointing, recognition **2.** association, connection, empathy, fellow feeling, involvement, rapport, relationship, sympathy **3.** credentials, ID, identity card, letters of introduction, papers

identify **1.** catalogue, classify, diagnose, flag, label, make out, name, pick out, pinpoint, place, put one's finger on (*informal*), recognize, single out, spot, tag **2.** (*often with* **with**) ally, associate, empathize, feel for, put in the same category, put oneself in the place *or* shoes of, relate to, respond to, see through another's eyes, think of in connection (with)

identity 1. distinctiveness, existence, individuality, oneness, particularity, personality, self, selfhood, singularity, uniqueness 2. accord, correspondence, empathy, rapport, sameness, unanimity, unity

ideology articles of faith, belief(s), creed, dogma, ideas, philosophy, principles, tenets, *Weltanschauung,* world view

idiocy abject stupidity, asininity, cretinism, fatuity, fatuousness, foolishness, imbecility, inanity, insanity, lunacy, senselessness, tomfoolery

▷ **Antonyms** acumen, sagacity, sanity, sense, soundness, wisdom

idiom 1. expression, locution, phrase, set phrase, turn of phrase 2. jargon, language, mode of expression, parlance, style, talk, usage, vernacular

idiomatic dialectal, native, vernacular

idiosyncrasy affectation, characteristic, eccentricity, habit, mannerism, oddity, peculiarity, personal trait, quirk, singularity, trick

idiosyncratic distinctive, individual, individualistic, peculiar

idiot airhead (*slang*), ass, berk (*Brit. slang*), blockhead, booby, charlie (*Brit. informal*), chump, coot, cretin, dickhead (*slang*), dimwit (*informal*), dipstick (*Brit. slang*), divvy (*Brit. slang*), dork (*slang*), dunderhead, dweeb (*U.S. slang*), fool, fuckwit (*taboo slang*), geek (*slang*), gobshite (*Irish taboo slang*), gonzo (*slang*), halfwit, imbecile, jerk (*slang, chiefly U.S. & Canad.*), lamebrain (*informal*), mooncalf, moron, nerd *or* nurd (*slang*), nincompoop, nitwit (*informal*), numbskull *or* numskull, numpty (*Scot. informal*), oaf, pillock (*Brit. slang*), plank (*Brit. slang*), plonker (*slang*), prat (*slang*), prick (*derogatory slang*), schmuck (*U.S. slang*), simpleton, twit (*informal, chiefly Brit.*), wally (*slang*)

idiotic asinine, braindead (*informal*), crackpot (*informal*), crazy, daft (*informal*), dumb (*informal*), fatuous, foolhardy, foolish, halfwitted, harebrained, imbecile, imbecilic, inane, insane, loopy (*informal*), lunatic, moronic, senseless, stupid, unintelligent

▷ **Antonyms** brilliant, commonsensical, intelligent, sensible, thoughtful, wise

idle *adjective* 1. dead, empty, gathering dust, inactive, jobless, mothballed, out of action *or* operation, out of work, redundant, stationary, ticking over, unemployed, unoccupied, unused, vacant 2. good-for-nothing, indolent, lackadaisical, lazy, shiftless, slothful, sluggish 3. frivolous, insignificant, irrelevant, nugatory, superficial, trivial, unhelpful, unnecessary 4. abortive, bootless, fruitless, futile, groundless, ineffective, of no avail, otiose, pointless, unavailing, unproductive, unsuccessful, useless, vain, worthless ~*verb* 5. (*often with* **away**) dally, dawdle, fool, fritter, hang out (*informal*), kill time, laze, loaf, loiter, lounge, potter, waste, while 6. bob off (*Brit. slang*), coast, drift, mark time, shirk, sit back and do nothing, skive (*Brit. slang*), slack, slow down, take it easy, vegetate, veg out (*slang*)

▷ **Antonyms** (*senses 1 & 2*) active, busy, employed, energetic, functional, industrious, occupied, operative, working (*sense 3*) important, meaningful (*sense 4*) advantageous, effective, fruitful, profitable, useful, worthwhile

idleness 1. inaction, inactivity, leisure, time on one's hands, unemployment 2. hibernation, inertia, laziness, shiftlessness, sloth, sluggishness, torpor, vegetating 3. dilly-dallying (*informal*), lazing, loafing, pottering, skiving (*Brit. slang*), time-wasting, trifling

idler clock-watcher, couch potato (*slang*), dawdler, deadbeat (*informal, chiefly U.S. & Canad.*), dodger, drone, laggard, layabout, lazybones, loafer, lounger, malingerer, shirker, skiver (*Brit. slang*), slacker, sloth, slouch (*informal*), slugabed, sluggard, time-waster, Weary Willie (*informal*)

idling *adjective* dawdling, drifting, loafing, pottering, resting, resting on one's oars, taking it easy, ticking over

idol 1. deity, god, graven image, image, pagan symbol 2. *figurative* beloved, darling, favourite, hero, pet, pin-up (*slang*), superstar

idolater 1. heathen, idol-worshipper, pagan 2. admirer, adorer, devotee, idolizer, votary, worshipper

idolatrous adoring, adulatory, reverential, uncritical, worshipful

idolatry adoration, adulation, apotheosis, deification, exaltation, glorification, hero worship, idolizing

idolize admire, adore, apotheosize, bow down before, deify, dote upon, exalt, glorify, hero-worship, look up to, love, revere, reverence, venerate, worship, worship to excess

idyllic arcadian, charming, halcyon, heavenly, ideal, idealized, out of this world, pastoral, peaceful, picturesque, rustic, unspoiled

if 1. *conjunction* admitting, allowing, assuming, granting, in case, on condition that, on the assumption that, provided, providing, supposing, though, whenever, wherever, whether 2. ~*noun* condition, doubt, hesitation, stipulation, uncertainty

iffy chancy (*informal*), conditional, doubtful, in the lap of the gods, problematical, uncertain, undecided, unpredictable, up in the air

ignis fatuus bubble, chimera, delusion, il~

lusion, mirage, phantasm, self-deception, will-o'-the-wisp

ignite burn, burst into flames, catch fire, fire, flare up, inflame, kindle, light, put a match to (*informal*), set alight, set fire to, take fire, torch, touch off

ignoble **1.** abject, base, contemptible, craven, dastardly, degenerate, degraded, despicable, disgraceful, dishonourable, heinous, infamous, low, mean, petty, shabby, shameless, unworthy, vile, wretched **2.** baseborn (*archaic*), common, humble, lowborn (*rare*), lowly, mean, of humble birth, peasant, plebeian, vulgar

ignominious abject, despicable, discreditable, disgraceful, dishonourable, disreputable, humiliating, indecorous, inglorious, mortifying, scandalous, shameful, sorry, undignified

▷ **Antonyms** creditable, honourable, reputable, worthy

ignominy bad odour, contempt, discredit, disgrace, dishonour, disrepute, humiliation, infamy, mortification, obloquy, odium, opprobrium, reproach, shame, stigma

▷ **Antonyms** credit, honour, repute

ignoramus ass, blockhead, bonehead (*slang*), dolt, donkey, duffer (*informal*), dullard, dunce, fathead (*informal*), fool, illiterate, lowbrow, numbskull *or* numskull, numpty (*Scot. informal*), simpleton

ignorance **1.** greenness, inexperience, innocence, nescience (*literary*), oblivion, unawareness, unconsciousness, unfamiliarity **2.** benightedness, blindness, illiteracy, lack of education, mental darkness, unenlightenment, unintelligence

▷ **Antonyms** (*sense 2*) comprehension, enlightenment, insight, intelligence, knowledge, understanding, wisdom

ignorant **1.** benighted, blind to, inexperienced, innocent, in the dark about, oblivious, unaware, unconscious, unenlightened, uninformed, uninitiated, unknowing, unschooled, unwitting **2.** as green as grass, green, illiterate, naive, unaware, uncultivated, uneducated, unknowledgeable, unlearned, unlettered, unread, untaught, untrained, untutored, wet behind the ears (*informal*) **3.** crass, crude, gross, half-baked (*informal*), insensitive, rude, shallow, superficial, uncomprehending, unscholarly

▷ **Antonyms** astute, aware, brilliant, conscious, cultured, educated, informed, knowledgeable, learned, literate, sagacious, sophisticated, wise

ignore be oblivious to, blank (*slang*), bury one's head in the sand, cold-shoulder, cut (*informal*), discount, disregard, give the cold shoulder to, neglect, overlook, pass over, pay no attention to, reject, send (someone) to Coventry, shut one's eyes to, take no notice of, turn a blind eye to, turn a deaf ear to, turn one's back on

▷ **Antonyms** acknowledge, heed, note, pay attention to, recognize, regard

ilk brand, breed, character, class, description, disposition, kidney, kind, sort, stamp, style, type, variety

ill *adjective* **1.** ailing, at death's door, dicky (*Brit. informal*), diseased, funny (*informal*), green about the gills, indisposed, infirm, laid up (*informal*), not up to snuff (*informal*), off-colour, on the sick list (*informal*), out of sorts (*informal*), poorly (*informal*), queasy, queer, seedy (*informal*), sick, under the weather (*informal*), unhealthy, unwell, valetudinarian **2.** bad, damaging, deleterious, detrimental, evil, foul, harmful, iniquitous, injurious, ruinous, unfortunate, unlucky, vile, wicked, wrong **3.** acrimonious, adverse, antagonistic, cantankerous, cross, harsh, hateful, hostile, hurtful, inimical, malevolent, malicious, sullen, surly, unfriendly, unkind **4.** disturbing, foreboding, inauspicious, ominous, sinister, threatening, unfavourable, unhealthy, unlucky, unpromising, unpropitious, unwholesome *~noun* **5.** affliction, hardship, harm, hurt, injury, misery, misfortune, pain, trial, tribulation, trouble, unpleasantness, woe **6.** ailment, complaint, disease, disorder, illness, indisposition, infirmity, malady, malaise, sickness **7.** abuse, badness, cruelty, damage, depravity, destruction, evil, ill usage, malice, mischief, suffering, wickedness *~adverb* **8.** badly, hard, inauspiciously, poorly, unfavourably, unfortunately, unluckily **9.** barely, by no means, hardly, insufficiently, scantily **10.** *as in* **ill-gotten** criminally, dishonestly, foully, fraudulently, illegally, illegitimately, illicitly, unlawfully, unscrupulously

▷ **Antonyms** *~adjective* (*sense 1*) hale, healthy, strong, well (*sense 2*) favourable, good (*sense 3*) generous, kind *~noun* good, honour, kindness *~adverb* easily, well

ill-advised foolhardy, foolish, ill-considered, ill-judged, impolitic, imprudent, inappropriate, incautious, indiscreet, injudicious, misguided, overhasty, rash, reckless, short-sighted, thoughtless, unseemly, unwise, wrong-headed

▷ **Antonyms** appropriate, cautious, discreet, judicious, politic, prudent, seemly, sensible, wise

ill-assorted incompatible, incongruous, inharmonious, mismatched, uncongenial, unsuited

ill at ease anxious, awkward, disquieted, disturbed, edgy, faltering, fidgety, hesitant, like a fish out of water, nervous, neurotic, on edge, on pins and needles (*informal*), on tenterhooks, out of place,

restless, self-conscious, strange, tense, twitchy (*informal*), uncomfortable, un~easy, unquiet, unrelaxed, unsettled, un~sure, wired (*slang*)
▷ **Antonyms** at ease, at home, comfort~able, easy, quiet, relaxed, settled, sure

ill-bred bad-mannered, boorish, churlish, coarse, crass, discourteous, ill-mannered, impolite, indelicate, rude, uncivil, uncivilized, uncouth, ungallant, ungentlemanly, unladylike, unmanner~ly, unrefined, vulgar
▷ **Antonyms** civil, courteous, delicate, mannerly, refined, urbane, well-bred

ill-considered careless, hasty, heedless, improvident, imprudent, injudicious, overhasty, precipitate, rash, unwise

ill-defined blurred, dim, fuzzy, indistinct, nebulous, shadowy, unclear, vague, woolly
▷ **Antonyms** apparent, bold, clear, con~spicuous, cut-and-dried, distinct, evi~dent, manifest, obvious, plain

ill-disposed against, antagonistic, anti (*informal*), antipathetic, averse, dis~obliging, down on (*informal*), hostile, inimical, opposed, uncooperative, un~friendly, unwelcoming
▷ **Antonyms** cooperative, friendly, oblig~ing, welcoming, well-disposed

illegal actionable (*Law*), banned, black-market, bootleg, criminal, felonious, forbidden, illicit, lawless, off limits, out~lawed, prohibited, proscribed, un~authorized, unconstitutional, under-the-counter, under-the-table, unlawful, unlicensed, unofficial, wrongful
▷ **Antonyms** lawful, legal, licit, permis~sible

illegality crime, criminality, felony, il~legitimacy, illicitness, lawlessness, un~lawfulness, wrong, wrongness

illegible crabbed, faint, hard to make out, hieroglyphic, indecipherable, obscure, scrawled, undecipherable, unreadable
▷ **Antonyms** clear, decipherable, legible, plain, readable

illegitimacy **1.** illegality, illicitness, ir~regularity, unconstitutionality, unlaw~fulness **2.** bastardism, bastardy

illegitimate **1.** illegal, illicit, improper, unauthorized, unconstitutional, under-the-table, unlawful, unsanctioned **2.** baseborn (*archaic*), bastard, born on the wrong side of the blanket, born out of wedlock, fatherless, misbegotten (*liter~ary*), natural, spurious (*rare*) **3.** illogical, incorrect, invalid, spurious, unsound
▷ **Antonyms** (*sense 1*) authorized, con~stitutional, lawful, legal, legitimate, proper, sanctioned

ill-fated blighted, doomed, hapless, ill-omened, ill-starred, luckless, star-crossed, unfortunate, unhappy, unlucky

ill-favoured hideous, no oil painting (*in~formal*), plain, repulsive, ugly, unat~tractive, unlovely, unprepossessing, un~sightly

ill feeling animosity, animus, antago~nism, bad blood, bitterness, chip on one's shoulder, disgruntlement, dissat~isfaction, dudgeon (*archaic*), enmity, frustration, hard feelings, hostility, ill will, indignation, offence, rancour, re~sentment
▷ **Antonyms** amity, benevolence, favour, friendship, goodwill, satisfaction

ill-founded baseless, empty, groundless, idle, unjustified, unproven, unreliable, unsubstantiated, unsupported

ill humour (bad) mood, (bad) temper, bate (*Brit. slang*), crabbiness, crossness, dis~agreeableness, grumpiness, irascibility, irritability, moodiness, moroseness, petulance, pique, sharpness, spleen, sulkiness, sulks, tartness, testiness

ill-humoured acrimonious, bad-tempered, crabbed, crabby, cross, disagreeable, grumpy, huffy, impatient, irascible, ir~ritable, like a bear with a sore head (*in~formal*), liverish, mardy (*dialect*), moody, morose, out of sorts, out of tem~per, petulant, ratty (*Brit. & N.Z. infor~mal*), sharp, snappish, snappy, sulky, sullen, tart, testy, tetchy, thin-skinned, touchy, waspish
▷ **Antonyms** affable, agreeable, amiable, charming, congenial, delightful, genial, good-humoured, good-natured, pleasant

illiberal **1.** bigoted, hidebound, intolerant, narrow-minded, prejudiced, reactionary, small-minded, uncharitable, ungener~ous **2.** close-fisted, mean, miserly, nig~gardly, parsimonious, selfish, sordid, stingy, tight, tight-arsed (*taboo slang*), tight as a duck's arse (*taboo slang*), tight-assed (*U.S. taboo slang*), tight~fisted, ungenerous
▷ **Antonyms** (*sense 1*) broad-minded, charitable, generous, liberal, open-minded, politically correct *or* PC, right-on (*informal*), tolerant

illicit **1.** black-market, bootleg, contra~band, criminal, felonious, illegal, il~legitimate, off limits, prohibited, un~authorized, unlawful, unlicensed **2.** clandestine, forbidden, furtive, guilty, immoral, improper, wrong
▷ **Antonyms** above-board, lawful, legal, legitimate, licit, permissible, proper

illimitable boundless, eternal, immeasur~able, immense, infinite, limitless, un~bounded, unending, unlimited, vast, without end

illiteracy benightedness, ignorance, illit~erateness, lack of education

illiterate benighted, ignorant, uncultured, uneducated, unlettered, untaught, un~tutored
▷ **Antonyms** cultured, educated, let~tered, literate, taught, tutored

ill-judged foolish, ill-advised, ill-considered, injudicious, misguided, overhasty, rash, short-sighted, unwise, wrong-headed

ill-mannered badly behaved, boorish, churlish, coarse, discourteous, ill-behaved, ill-bred, impolite, insolent, loutish, rude, uncivil, uncouth, unmannerly

▷ **Antonyms** civil, courteous, cultivated, mannerly, polished, polite, refined, well-mannered

ill-natured bad-tempered, catty (*informal*), churlish, crabbed, cross, cross-grained, disagreeable, disobliging, malevolent, malicious, mean, nasty, perverse, petulant, shrewish, spiteful, sulky, sullen, surly, unfriendly, unkind, unpleasant

▷ **Antonyms** agreeable, amiable, cheerful, congenial, friendly, good-natured, kind, obliging, pleasant

illness affliction, ailment, attack, complaint, disability, disease, disorder, ill health, indisposition, infirmity, lurgi (*informal*), malady, malaise, poor health, sickness

illogical absurd, fallacious, faulty, inconclusive, inconsistent, incorrect, invalid, irrational, meaningless, senseless, sophistical, specious, spurious, unreasonable, unscientific, unsound

▷ **Antonyms** coherent, consistent, correct, logical, rational, reasonable, scientific, sound, valid

ill-starred doomed, hapless, ill-fated, ill-omened, inauspicious, star-crossed, unfortunate, unhappy, unlucky

ill temper annoyance, bad temper, crossness, curtness, impatience, irascibility, irritability, petulance, sharpness, spitefulness, tetchiness

ill-tempered annoyed, bad-tempered, choleric, cross, curt, grumpy, ill-humoured, impatient, irascible, irritable, liverish, ratty (*Brit. & N.Z. informal*), sharp, spiteful, testy, tetchy, touchy

▷ **Antonyms** benign, cheerful, good-natured, mild-mannered, patient, pleasant, sweet-tempered

ill-timed awkward, inappropriate, inconvenient, inept, inopportune, unseasonable, untimely, unwelcome

▷ **Antonyms** appropriate, convenient, opportune, seasonable, timely, well-timed

ill-treat abuse, damage, dump on (*slang, chiefly U.S.*), handle roughly, harass, harm, harry, ill-use, injure, knock about *or* around, maltreat, mishandle, misuse, oppress, shit on (*taboo slang*), wrong

ill-treatment abuse, damage, harm, ill-use, injury, mistreatment, misuse, rough handling

illuminate 1. brighten, illumine (*literary*), irradiate, light, light up **2.** clarify, clear up, elucidate, enlighten, explain, explicate, give insight into, instruct, interpret, make clear, shed light on **3.** adorn, decorate, illustrate, ornament

▷ **Antonyms** (*sense 1*) black out, darken, dim, obscure, overshadow (*sense 2*) befog, cloud, dull, obfuscate, overcast, shade, veil

illuminating enlightening, explanatory, helpful, informative, instructive, revealing

▷ **Antonyms** confusing, obscuring, puzzling, unhelpful

illumination 1. beam, brightening, brightness, light, lighting, lighting up, lights, radiance, ray **2.** awareness, clarification, edification, enlightenment, insight, inspiration, instruction, perception, revelation, understanding

illuminations decorations, fairy lights, lights

illusion 1. chimera, daydream, fantasy, figment of the imagination, hallucination, ignis fatuus, mirage, mockery, phantasm, semblance, will-o'-the-wisp **2.** deception, delusion, error, fallacy, false impression, fancy, misapprehension, misconception

▷ **Antonyms** actuality, reality, truth

illusory *or* **illusive** apparent, Barmecide, beguiling, chimerical, deceitful, deceptive, delusive, fallacious, false, hallucinatory, misleading, mistaken, seeming, sham, unreal, untrue

▷ **Antonyms** authentic, down-to-earth, factual, genuine, real, reliable, solid, true

illustrate 1. bring home, clarify, demonstrate, elucidate, emphasize, exemplify, exhibit, explain, explicate, instance, interpret, make clear, make plain, point up, show **2.** adorn, decorate, depict, draw, ornament, picture, sketch

illustrated decorated, embellished, graphic, illuminated, pictorial, picture, pictured, with illustrations

illustration 1. analogy, case, case in point, clarification, demonstration, elucidation, example, exemplification, explanation, instance, interpretation, specimen **2.** adornment, decoration, figure, picture, plate, sketch

illustrative delineative, descriptive, diagrammatic, explanatory, explicatory, expository, graphic, illustrational, interpretive, pictorial, representative, sample, typical

illustrious brilliant, celebrated, distinguished, eminent, exalted, famed, famous, glorious, great, noble, notable, noted, prominent, remarkable, renowned, resplendent, signal, splendid

▷ **Antonyms** humble, ignoble, infamous, lowly, meek, notorious, obscure, unassuming

ill will acrimony, animosity, animus, antagonism, antipathy, aversion, bad

blood, dislike, enmity, envy, grudge, hard feelings, hatred, hostility, malevolence, malice, no love lost, rancour, resentment, spite, unfriendliness, venom
▷ **Antonyms** amiability, amity, charity, congeniality, cordiality, friendship, goodwill

image 1. appearance, effigy, figure, icon, idol, likeness, picture, portrait, reflection, representation, statue **2**. chip off the old block (*informal*), counterpart, (dead) ringer (*slang*), Doppelgänger, double, facsimile, replica, similitude, spit (*informal, chiefly Brit.*), spitting image *or* spit and image (*informal*) **3**. conceit, concept, conception, figure, idea, impression, mental picture, perception, trope

imaginable believable, comprehensible, conceivable, credible, likely, plausible, possible, supposable, thinkable, under the sun, within the bounds of possibility
▷ **Antonyms** impossible, incomprehensible, inconceivable, incredible, unbelievable, unimaginable, unlikely, unthinkable

imaginary assumed, chimerical, dreamlike, fancied, fanciful, fictional, fictitious, hallucinatory, hypothetical, ideal, illusive, illusory, imagined, invented, legendary, made-up, mythological, nonexistent, phantasmal, shadowy, supposed, suppositious, supposititious, unreal, unsubstantial, visionary
▷ **Antonyms** actual, factual, genuine, known, proven, real, substantial, tangible, true

imagination 1. creativity, enterprise, fancy, ingenuity, insight, inspiration, invention, inventiveness, originality, resourcefulness, vision, wit, wittiness **2**. chimera, conception, idea, ideality, illusion, image, invention, notion, supposition, unreality

imaginative clever, creative, dreamy, enterprising, fanciful, fantastic, ingenious, inspired, inventive, original, poetical, visionary, vivid, whimsical
▷ **Antonyms** literal, mundane, ordinary, uncreative, unimaginative, uninspired, unoriginal, unpoetical, unromantic

imagine 1. conceive, conceptualize, conjure up, create, devise, dream up (*informal*), envisage, fantasize, form a mental picture of, frame, invent, picture, plan, project, scheme, see in the mind's eye, think of, think up, visualize **2**. apprehend, assume, believe, conjecture, deduce, deem, fancy, gather, guess (*informal, chiefly U.S. & Canad.*), infer, realize, suppose, surmise, suspect, take for granted, take it, think

imbalance bias, disproportion, inequality, lack of proportion, lopsidedness, partiality, top-heaviness, unevenness, unfairness

imbecile 1. *noun* berk (*Brit. slang*), bungler, charlie (*Brit. informal*), chump, coot, cretin, dickhead (*slang*), dipstick (*Brit. slang*), divvy (*Brit. slang*), dolt, dork (*slang*), dotard, dweeb (*U.S. slang*), fool, fuckwit (*taboo slang*), geek (*slang*), gobshite (*Irish taboo slang*), gonzo (*slang*), halfwit, idiot, jerk (*slang, chiefly U.S. & Canad.*), moron, nerd *or* nurd (*slang*), numpty (*Scot. informal*), numbskull *or* numskull, pillock (*Brit. slang*), plank (*Brit. slang*), plonker (*slang*), prat (*slang*), prick (*derogatory slang*), schmuck (*U.S. slang*), thickhead, tosser (*Brit. slang*), twit (*informal, chiefly Brit.*), wally (*slang*) **2**. *~adjective* asinine, braindead (*informal*), dead from the neck up, fatuous, feeble-minded, foolish, idiotic, imbecilic, inane, ludicrous, moronic, simple, stupid, thick, witless

imbecility asininity, childishness, cretinism, fatuity, foolishness, idiocy, inanity, incompetency, stupidity
▷ **Antonyms** comprehension, intelligence, perspicacity, reasonableness, sagacity, sense, soundness, wisdom

imbibe 1. consume, drink, knock back (*informal*), quaff, sink (*informal*), suck, swallow, swig (*informal*) **2**. *literary* absorb, acquire, assimilate, gain, gather, ingest, receive, take in

imbroglio complexity, complication, embarrassment, entanglement, involvement, misunderstanding, quandary

imbue 1. *figurative* bathe, impregnate, inculcate, infuse, instil, permeate, pervade, saturate, steep **2**. colour, dye, ingrain, stain, suffuse, tinge, tint

imitate affect, ape, burlesque, caricature, copy, counterfeit, do (*informal*), do an impression of, duplicate, echo, emulate, follow, follow in the footsteps of, follow suit, impersonate, mimic, mirror, mock, parody, personate, repeat, send up (*Brit. informal*), simulate, spoof (*informal*), take a leaf out of (someone's) book, take off (*informal*), travesty

imitation *noun* **1**. aping, copy, counterfeit, counterfeiting, duplication, echoing, likeness, mimicry, resemblance, simulation **2**. carbon copy (*informal*), fake, forgery, impersonation, impression, mockery, parody, reflection, replica, reproduction, sham, substitution, takeoff (*informal*), travesty *~adjective* **3**. artificial, dummy, ersatz, man-made, mock, phoney *or* phony (*informal*), pseudo (*informal*), repro, reproduction, sham, simulated, synthetic
▷ **Antonyms** *~adjective* authentic, genuine, original, real, true, valid

imitative copied, copycat (*informal*), copying, derivative, echoic, mimetic, mimicking, mock, onomatopoeic, parrotlike, plagiarized, pseudo (*informal*), put-on, second-hand, simulated, unoriginal

imitator aper, carbon copy (*informal*), copier, copycat (*informal*), echo, epigone (*rare*), follower, impersonator, impressionist, mimic, parrot, shadow

immaculate 1. clean, impeccable, neat, neat as a new pin, spick-and-span, spruce, squeaky-clean, trim, unexceptionable **2.** above reproach, faultless, flawless, guiltless, impeccable, incorrupt, innocent, perfect, pure, sinless, spotless, squeaky-clean, stainless, unblemished, uncontaminated, undefiled, unpolluted, unsullied, untarnished, virtuous

▷ **Antonyms** contaminated, corrupt, dirty, filthy, impeachable, impure, polluted, stained, tainted, unclean

immanent congenital, inborn, indigenous, indwelling, inherent, innate, internal, intrinsic, mental, natural, subjective

immaterial 1. a matter of indifference, extraneous, impertinent, inapposite, inconsequential, inconsiderable, inessential, insignificant, irrelevant, of little account, of no consequence, of no importance, trifling, trivial, unimportant, unnecessary **2.** airy, disembodied, ethereal, ghostly, incorporeal, metaphysical, spiritual, unembodied, unsubstantial

▷ **Antonyms** (*sense 1*) crucial, essential, germane, important, material, relevant, significant, substantial (*sense 2*) earthly, physical, real, tangible

immature 1. adolescent, crude, green, imperfect, premature, raw, undeveloped, unfinished, unfledged, unformed, unripe, unseasonable, untimely, young **2.** babyish, callow, childish, inexperienced, infantile, jejune, juvenile, puerile, wet behind the ears (*informal*)

▷ **Antonyms** adult, developed, fully-fledged, mature, mellow, responsible, ripe

immaturity 1. crudeness, crudity, greenness, imperfection, rawness, unpreparedness, unripeness **2.** babyishness, callowness, childishness, inexperience, juvenility, puerility

immeasurable bottomless, boundless, endless, illimitable, immense, incalculable, inestimable, inexhaustible, infinite, limitless, measureless, unbounded, unfathomable, unlimited, vast

▷ **Antonyms** bounded, calculable, estimable, exhaustible, fathomable, finite, limited, measurable

immediate 1. instant, instantaneous **2.** adjacent, close, contiguous, direct, near, nearest, next, primary, proximate, recent **3.** actual, current, existing, extant, on hand, present, pressing, up to date, urgent

▷ **Antonyms** delayed, distant, far, late, later, leisurely, postponed, remote, slow, tardy

immediately 1. at once, before you could say Jack Robinson (*informal*), directly, forthwith, instantly, now, on the nail, posthaste, promptly, pronto (*informal*), right away, right now, straight away, this instant, this very minute, *tout de suite,* unhesitatingly, without delay, without hesitation **2.** at first hand, closely, directly, nearly

immemorial age-old, ancient, archaic, fixed, long-standing, of yore, olden (*archaic*), rooted, time-honoured, traditional

immense Brobdingnagian, colossal, elephantine, enormous, extensive, giant, gigantic, ginormous (*informal*), great, huge, humongous *or* humungous (*U.S. slang*), illimitable, immeasurable, infinite, interminable, jumbo (*informal*), large, mammoth, massive, mega (*slang*), monstrous, monumental, prodigious, stellar (*informal*), stupendous, titanic, tremendous, vast

▷ **Antonyms** infinitesimal, little, microscopic, minuscule, minute, puny, small, tiny

immensity bulk, enormity, expanse, extent, greatness, hugeness, infinity, magnitude, massiveness, scope, size, sweep, vastness

immerse 1. bathe, dip, douse, duck, dunk, plunge, sink, submerge, submerse **2.** *figurative* absorb, busy, engage, engross, involve, occupy, take up

immersed *figurative* absorbed, bound up, buried, busy, consumed, deep, engrossed, in a brown study, involved, mesmerized, occupied, rapt, spellbound, taken up, wrapped up

immersion 1. baptism, bathe, dip, dipping, dousing, ducking, dunking, plunging, submerging **2.** *figurative* absorption, concentration, involvement, preoccupation

immigrant incomer, newcomer, settler

imminent at hand, brewing, close, coming, fast-approaching, forthcoming, gathering, impending, in the air, in the offing, in the pipeline, just round the corner, looming, menacing, near, nigh (*archaic*), on the cards, on the horizon, on the way, threatening, upcoming

▷ **Antonyms** delayed, distant, far-off, remote

immobile at a standstill, at rest, fixed, frozen, immobilized, immotile, immovable, like a statue, motionless, rigid, riveted, rooted, stable, static, stationary, stiff, still, stock-still, stolid, unmoving

▷ **Antonyms** active, mobile, movable, on the move, pliant, portable, vigorous

immobility absence of movement, firmness, fixity, immovability, inertness, motionlessness, stability, steadiness, stillness

immobilize bring to a standstill, cripple, disable, freeze, halt, lay up (*informal*), paralyse, put out of action, render inop~erative, stop, transfix

immoderate egregious, enormous, exag~gerated, excessive, exorbitant, extrava~gant, extreme, inordinate, intemperate, O.T.T. (*slang*), over the odds (*informal*), over the top (*slang*), profligate, steep (*informal*), uncalled-for, unconscionable, uncontrolled, undue, unjustified, unrea~sonable, unrestrained, unwarranted, wanton

▷ **Antonyms** controlled, judicious, mild, moderate, reasonable, restrained, tem~perate

immoderation excess, exorbitance, ex~travagance, intemperance, lack of re~straint *or* balance, overindulgence, prodigality, unrestraint

immodest **1.** bawdy, coarse, depraved, flirtatious, gross, immoral, improper, impure, indecent, indecorous, indelicate, lewd, obscene, revealing, titillating, un~chaste **2.** bold, bold as brass, brass-necked (*Brit. informal*), brazen, for~ward, fresh (*informal*), impudent, pushy (*informal*), shameless, unblushing

immodesty **1.** bawdiness, coarseness, im~purity, indecorousness, indelicacy, lewdness, obscenity **2.** audacity, balls (*taboo slang*), boldness, brass neck (*Brit. informal*), forwardness, gall (*informal*), impudence, shamelessness, temerity

▷ **Antonyms** (*sense 1*) decency, decorous~ness, delicacy, modesty, restraint, so~briety

immolate kill, sacrifice

immolation offering up, sacrifice, slaugh~ter

immoral abandoned, bad, corrupt, de~bauched, degenerate, depraved, dishon~est, dissolute, evil, impure, indecent, iniquitous, lewd, licentious, nefarious, obscene, of easy virtue, pornographic, profligate, reprobate, sinful, sink, un~chaste, unethical, unprincipled, vicious, vile, wicked, wrong

▷ **Antonyms** conscientious, good, hon~ourable, inoffensive, law-abiding, moral, pure, upright, virtuous

immorality badness, corruption, de~bauchery, depravity, dissoluteness, evil, iniquity, licentiousness, profligacy, sin, turpitude, vice, wickedness, wrong

▷ **Antonyms** goodness, honesty, lawful~ness, morality, purity

immorally corruptly, degenerately, dis~honestly, dissolutely, evilly, sinfully, unethically, unrighteously, wickedly

immortal *adjective* **1.** abiding, constant, death-defying, deathless, endless, en~during, eternal, everlasting, imperish~able, incorruptible, indestructible, last~ing, perennial, perpetual, sempiternal (*literary*), timeless, undying, unfading *~noun* **2.** god, goddess, Olympian **3.** ge~nius, great (*usually plural*), hero, para~gon

▷ **Antonyms** *~adjective* ephemeral, fad~ing, fleeting, mortal, passing, perish~able, temporary, transitory

immortality **1.** deathlessness, endless~ness, eternity, everlasting life, incor~ruptibility, indestructibility, perpetuity, timelessness **2.** celebrity, fame, glorifi~cation, gloriousness, glory, greatness, renown

immortalize apotheosize, celebrate, com~memorate, enshrine, eternalize, eter~nize, exalt, glorify, memorialize, per~petuate, solemnize

immovable **1.** fast, firm, fixed, immutable, jammed, rooted, secure, set, stable, sta~tionary, stuck, unbudgeable **2.** adamant, constant, impassive, inflexible, obdu~rate, resolute, steadfast, stony-hearted, unchangeable, unimpressionable, un~shakable, unshaken, unwavering, un~yielding

▷ **Antonyms** (*sense 2*) changeable, flex~ible, impressionable, movable, shakable, wavering, yielding

immune clear, exempt, free, insuscep~tible, invulnerable, let off (*informal*), not affected, not liable, not subject, proof (against), protected, resistant, safe, un~affected

▷ **Antonyms** exposed, liable, prone, sus~ceptible, unprotected, vulnerable

immunity **1.** amnesty, charter, exemption, exoneration, franchise, freedom, indem~nity, invulnerability, liberty, licence, prerogative, privilege, release, right **2.** immunization, protection, resistance

▷ **Antonyms** (*sense 1*) exposure, liability, openness, proneness, susceptibility, vulnerability

immunize inoculate, protect, safeguard, vaccinate

immure cage, cloister, confine, enclose, imprison, incarcerate, jail, shut in *or* up, wall up *or* in

immutability agelessness, changeless~ness, constancy, durability, invariabil~ity, permanence, stability, unal~terableness, unchangeableness

immutable abiding, ageless, changeless, constant, enduring, fixed, fixed as the laws of the Medes and Persians, im~movable, inflexible, invariable, perma~nent, perpetual, sacrosanct, stable, steadfast, unalterable, unchangeable

imp brat, demon, devil, gamin, minx, pickle (*Brit. informal*), rascal, rogue, scamp, sprite, urchin

impact *noun* **1.** bang, blow, bump, colli~sion, concussion, contact, crash, force, jolt, knock, shock, smash, stroke, thump **2.** brunt, burden, consequences, effect, full force, impression, influence, mean~ing, power, repercussions, significance, thrust, weight *~verb* **3.** clash, collide, crash, crush, hit, strike

impair blunt, damage, debilitate, decrease, deteriorate, diminish, enervate, enfeeble, harm, hinder, injure, lessen, mar, reduce, spoil, undermine, vitiate, weaken, worsen
▷ **Antonyms** ameliorate, amend, better, enhance, facilitate, improve, strengthen

impaired damaged, defective, faulty, flawed, imperfect, unsound

impale lance, pierce, run through, skewer, spear, spike, spit, stick, transfix

impalpable airy, delicate, disembodied, fine, imperceptible, incorporeal, indistinct, insubstantial, intangible, shadowy, tenuous, thin, unsubstantial

impart **1.** communicate, convey, disclose, discover, divulge, make known, pass on, relate, reveal, tell **2.** accord, afford, bestow, confer, contribute, give, grant, lend, offer, yield

impartial detached, disinterested, equal, equitable, even-handed, fair, just, neutral, nondiscriminating, nonpartisan, objective, open-minded, unbiased, unprejudiced, without fear or favour
▷ **Antonyms** biased, bigoted, influenced, partial, prejudiced, swayed, unfair, unjust

impartiality detachment, disinterest, disinterestedness, dispassion, equality, equity, even-handedness, fairness, lack of bias, neutrality, nonpartisanship, objectivity, open-mindedness
▷ **Antonyms** bias, favouritism, partiality, partisanship, subjectivity, unfairness

impassable blocked, closed, impenetrable, obstructed, pathless, trackless, unnavigable

impasse blind alley (*informal*), dead end, deadlock, stalemate, standoff, standstill

impassioned ablaze, animated, ardent, blazing, excited, fervent, fervid, fiery, flaming, furious, glowing, heated, inflamed, inspired, intense, passionate, rousing, stirring, vehement, violent, vivid, warm, worked up
▷ **Antonyms** apathetic, cool, impassive, indifferent, objective, reasoned

impassive aloof, apathetic, callous, calm, composed, cool, dispassionate, emotionless, impassible (*rare*), imperturbable, indifferent, inscrutable, insensible, insusceptible, phlegmatic, poker-faced (*informal*), reserved, self-contained, serene, stoical, stolid, unconcerned, unemotional, unexcitable, unfazed (*informal*), unfeeling, unimpressible, unmoved, unruffled

impassivity aloofness, calmness, composure, dispassion, impassiveness, imperturbability, indifference, inscrutability, insensibility, nonchalance, phlegm, stoicism, stolidity

impatience **1.** haste, hastiness, heat, impetuosity, intolerance, irritability, irritableness, quick temper, rashness, shortness, snappiness, vehemence, violence **2.** agitation, anxiety, avidity, disquietude, eagerness, edginess, fretfulness, nervousness, restiveness, restlessness, uneasiness
▷ **Antonyms** (*sense 2*) calm, composure, control, forbearance, patience, restraint, serenity, tolerance

impatient **1.** abrupt, brusque, curt, demanding, edgy, hasty, hot-tempered, indignant, intolerant, irritable, quick-tempered, snappy, sudden, testy, vehement, violent **2.** agog, athirst, chafing, eager, fretful, headlong, impetuous, like a cat on hot bricks (*informal*), restless, straining at the leash
▷ **Antonyms** (*sense 1*) calm, composed, cool, easy-going, imperturbable, patient, quiet, serene, tolerant

impeach **1.** accuse, arraign, blame, censure, charge, criminate (*rare*), denounce, indict, tax **2.** call into question, cast aspersions on, cast doubt on, challenge, disparage, impugn, question

impeachment accusation, arraignment, indictment

impeccable above suspicion, blameless, exact, exquisite, faultless, flawless, immaculate, incorrupt, innocent, irreproachable, perfect, precise, pure, sinless, stainless, unblemished, unerring, unimpeachable
▷ **Antonyms** blameworthy, corrupt, cursory, defective, deficient, faulty, flawed, shallow, sinful, superficial

impecunious broke (*informal*), cleaned out (*slang*), destitute, dirt-poor (*informal*), down and out, flat broke (*informal*), indigent, in queer street, insolvent, penniless, poverty-stricken, short, skint (*Brit. slang*), stony (*Brit. slang*), strapped (*slang*), without two pennies to rub together (*informal*)
▷ **Antonyms** affluent, prosperous, rich, wealthy, well-off, well-to-do

impede bar, block, brake, check, clog, cumber, curb, delay, disrupt, encumber, hamper, hinder, hold up, obstruct, restrain, retard, slow (down), stop, throw a spanner in the works (*Brit. informal*), thwart
▷ **Antonyms** advance, aid, assist, further, help, promote

impediment bar, barrier, block, check, clog, curb, defect, difficulty, encumbrance, fly in the ointment, hazard, hindrance, millstone around one's neck, obstacle, obstruction, snag, stumbling block
▷ **Antonyms** advantage, aid, assistance, benefit, encouragement, relief, support

impedimenta accoutrements, baggage, belongings, effects, equipment, gear, junk (*informal*), luggage, movables, odds and ends, paraphernalia, possessions, stuff, things, trappings, traps

impel actuate, chivy, compel, constrain, drive, force, goad, incite, induce, influence, inspire, instigate, motivate, move, oblige, power, prod, prompt, propel, push, require, spur, stimulate, urge
▷ **Antonyms** check, discourage, dissuade, rebuff, repulse, restrain

impending approaching, brewing, coming, forthcoming, gathering, hovering, imminent, in the offing, in the pipeline, looming, menacing, near, nearing, on the horizon, threatening, upcoming

impenetrable 1. dense, hermetic, impassable, impermeable, impervious, inviolable, solid, thick, unpierceable **2.** arcane, baffling, cabbalistic, dark, enigmatic, enigmatical, hidden, incomprehensible, indiscernible, inexplicable, inscrutable, mysterious, obscure, unfathomable, unintelligible
▷ **Antonyms** (*sense 1*) accessible, enterable, passable, penetrable, pierceable, vulnerable (*sense 2*) clear, explicable, obvious, soluble, understandable

impenitence hardheartedness, impenitency, incorrigibility, obduracy, stubbornness

impenitent defiant, hardened, hardhearted, incorrigible, obdurate, recidivistic, relentless, remorseless, unabashed, unashamed, uncontrite, unreformed, unrepentant

imperative 1. compulsory, crucial, essential, exigent, indispensable, insistent, obligatory, pressing, urgent, vital **2.** authoritative, autocratic, commanding, dictatorial, domineering, high-handed, imperious, lordly, magisterial, peremptory
▷ **Antonyms** (*sense 1*) avoidable, discretional, nonessential, optional, unimportant, unnecessary

imperceptible faint, fine, gradual, impalpable, inappreciable, inaudible, indiscernible, indistinguishable, infinitesimal, insensible, invisible, microscopic, minute, shadowy, slight, small, subtle, teensy-weensy, teeny-weeny, tiny, undetectable, unnoticeable
▷ **Antonyms** audible, detectable, discernible, distinguishable, noticeable, perceptible, visible

imperceptibly by a hair's-breadth, inappreciably, indiscernibly, invisibly, little by little, slowly, subtly, unnoticeably, unobtrusively, unseen

imperceptive impercipient, insensitive, obtuse, superficial, unappreciative, unaware, undiscerning, unobservant, unseeing

imperfect broken, damaged, defective, deficient, faulty, flawed, immature, impaired, incomplete, inexact, limited, partial, patchy, rudimentary, sketchy, undeveloped, unfinished
▷ **Antonyms** complete, developed, exact, finished, flawless, perfect

imperfection blemish, defect, deficiency, failing, fallibility, fault, flaw, foible, frailty, inadequacy, incompleteness, infirmity, insufficiency, peccadillo, scar, shortcoming, stain, taint, weakness, weak point
▷ **Antonyms** adequacy, completeness, consummation, excellence, faultlessness, flawlessness, perfection, sufficiency

imperial 1. kingly, majestic, princely, queenly, regal, royal, sovereign **2.** august, exalted, grand, great, high, imperious, lofty, magnificent, noble, superior, supreme

imperil endanger, expose, hazard, jeopardize, risk
▷ **Antonyms** care for, guard, protect, safeguard, secure

imperious arrogant, authoritative, autocratic, bossy (*informal*), commanding, despotic, dictatorial, domineering, exacting, haughty, high-handed, imperative, lordly, magisterial, overbearing, overweening, tyrannical, tyrannous

imperishable abiding, enduring, eternal, everlasting, immortal, indestructible, perennial, permanent, perpetual, undying, unfading, unforgettable
▷ **Antonyms** destructible, dying, fading, forgettable, mortal, perishable

impermanent brief, elusive, ephemeral, evanescent, fleeting, fly-by-night (*informal*), flying, fugacious, fugitive, here today, gone tomorrow (*informal*), inconstant, momentary, mortal, passing, perishable, short-lived, temporary, transient, transitory

impermeable hermetic, impassable, impenetrable, impervious, nonporous, proof, resistant

impersonal aloof, bureaucratic, businesslike, cold, detached, dispassionate, formal, inhuman, neutral, remote
▷ **Antonyms** friendly, intimate, outgoing, personal, warm

impersonate act, ape, caricature, do (*informal*), do an impression of, enact, imitate, masquerade as, mimic, parody, pass oneself off as, personate, pose as (*informal*), take off (*informal*)

impersonation caricature, imitation, impression, mimicry, parody, takeoff (*informal*)

impertinence assurance, audacity, backchat (*informal*), boldness, brass neck (*Brit. informal*), brazenness, cheek (*informal*), chutzpah (*U.S. & Canad. informal*), disrespect, effrontery, face (*informal*), forwardness, front, impudence, incivility, insolence, neck (*informal*), nerve (*informal*), pertness, presumption, rudeness, sauce (*informal*)

impertinent 1. bold, brazen, cheeky (*informal*), discourteous, disrespectful, flip (*informal*), forward, fresh (*informal*),

impolite, impudent, insolent, interfering, lippy (*U.S. & Canad. slang*), pert, presumptuous, rude, sassy (*U.S. informal*), saucy (*informal*), uncivil, unmannerly **2.** inapplicable, inappropriate, incongruous, irrelevant
▷ **Antonyms** (*sense 1*) mannerly, polite, respectful (*sense 2*) appropriate, germane, important, pertinent, relevant, vital

imperturbable calm, collected, complacent, composed, cool, equanimous, nerveless, sedate, self-possessed, serene, stoic, stoical, tranquil, undisturbed, unexcitable, unfazed (*informal*), unflappable (*informal*), unmoved, unruffled
▷ **Antonyms** agitated, excitable, frantic, jittery (*informal*), nervous, panicky, ruffled, touchy, upset

impervious 1. hermetic, impassable, impenetrable, impermeable, imperviable, invulnerable, resistant, sealed **2.** closed to, immune, invulnerable, proof against, unaffected by, unmoved by, unreceptive, unswayable, untouched by

impetuosity haste, hastiness, impulsiveness, precipitancy, precipitateness, rashness, vehemence, violence

impetuous ardent, eager, fierce, furious, hasty, headlong, impassioned, impulsive, passionate, precipitate, rash, spontaneous, spur-of-the-moment, unbridled, unplanned, unpremeditated, unreflecting, unrestrained, unthinking, vehement, violent
▷ **Antonyms** cautious, leisurely, mild, slow, wary

impetuously helter-skelter, impulsively, in the heat of the moment, on the spur of the moment, passionately, rashly, recklessly, spontaneously, unthinkingly, vehemently, without thinking

impetus 1. catalyst, goad, impulse, impulsion, incentive, motivation, push, spur, stimulus **2.** energy, force, momentum, power

impiety godlessness, iniquity, irreligion, irreverence, profaneness, profanity, sacrilege, sinfulness, ungodliness, unholiness, unrighteousness, wickedness
▷ **Antonyms** devoutness, godliness, holiness, piety, respect, reverence, righteousness

impinge 1. encroach, invade, make inroads, obtrude, trespass, violate **2.** affect, bear upon, have a bearing on, impact, influence, infringe, relate to, touch, touch upon **3.** clash, collide, dash, strike

impious blasphemous, godless, iniquitous, irreligious, irreverent, profane, sacrilegious, sinful, ungodly, unholy, unrighteous, wicked
▷ **Antonyms** devout, godly, holy, pious, religious, reverent, righteous

impish devilish, elfin, mischievous, prankish, puckish, rascally, roguish, sportive, waggish

implacability implacableness, inexorability, inflexibility, intractability, mercilessness, pitilessness, relentlessness, ruthlessness, unforgivingness, vengefulness

implacable cruel, inexorable, inflexible, intractable, merciless, pitiless, rancorous, relentless, remorseless, ruthless, unappeasable, unbending, uncompromising, unforgiving, unrelenting, unyielding
▷ **Antonyms** appeasable, flexible, lenient, merciful, reconcilable, relenting, tolerant, yielding

implant 1. inculcate, infix, infuse, inseminate, instil, sow **2.** embed, fix, graft, ingraft, insert, place, plant, root, sow

implausible cock-and-bull (*informal*), dubious, far-fetched, flimsy, improbable, incredible, suspect, unbelievable, unconvincing, unlikely, unreasonable, weak

implement 1. *noun* agent, apparatus, appliance, device, gadget, instrument, tool, utensil **2.** *~verb* bring about, carry out, complete, effect, enforce, execute, fulfil, perform, put into action *or* effect, realize
▷ **Antonyms** *~verb* delay, hamper, hinder, impede, weaken

implementation accomplishment, carrying out, discharge, effecting, enforcement, execution, fulfilment, performance, performing, realization

implicate associate, compromise, concern, embroil, entangle, imply, include, incriminate, inculpate, involve, mire, stitch up (*slang*), tie up with
▷ **Antonyms** acquit, disentangle, dissociate, eliminate, exclude, exculpate, rule out

implicated incriminated, involved, suspected, under suspicion

implication 1. association, connection, entanglement, incrimination, involvement **2.** conclusion, inference, innuendo, meaning, overtone, presumption, ramification, significance, signification, suggestion

implicit 1. contained, implied, inferred, inherent, latent, tacit, taken for granted, undeclared, understood, unspoken **2.** absolute, constant, entire, firm, fixed, full, steadfast, total, unhesitating, unqualified, unreserved, unshakable, unshaken, wholehearted
▷ **Antonyms** (*sense 1*) declared, explicit, expressed, obvious, patent, spoken, stated

implicitly absolutely, completely, firmly, unconditionally, unhesitatingly, unreservedly, utterly, without reservation

implied hinted at, implicit, indirect, inherent, insinuated, suggested, tacit, un~

declared, unexpressed, unspoken, unstated

implore beg, beseech, conjure, crave, entreat, go on bended knee to, importune, plead with, pray, solicit, supplicate

imply **1.** connote, give (someone) to understand, hint, insinuate, intimate, signify, suggest **2.** betoken, denote, entail, evidence, import, include, indicate, involve, mean, point to, presuppose

impolite bad-mannered, boorish, churlish, discourteous, disrespectful, ill-bred, ill-mannered, indecorous, indelicate, insolent, loutish, rough, rude, uncivil, uncouth, ungallant, ungentlemanly, ungracious, unladylike, unmannerly, unrefined

▷ **Antonyms** courteous, decorous, gallant, gracious, mannerly, polite, refined, respectful, well-bred

impoliteness bad manners, boorishness, churlishness, discourtesy, disrespect, incivility, indelicacy, insolence, rudeness, unmannerliness

▷ **Antonyms** civility, courtesy, delicacy, mannerliness, politeness, respect

impolitic ill-advised, ill-judged, imprudent, indiscreet, inexpedient, injudicious, maladroit, misguided, undiplomatic, untimely, unwise

▷ **Antonyms** diplomatic, discreet, expedient, judicious, politic, prudent, timely, wise

import *noun* **1.** bearing, drift, gist, implication, intention, meaning, message, purport, sense, significance, thrust **2.** bottom, consequence, importance, magnitude, moment, significance, substance, weight *~verb* **3.** bring in, introduce, land

importance **1.** concern, consequence, import, interest, moment, momentousness, significance, substance, value, weight **2.** bottom, distinction, eminence, esteem, influence, mark, pre-eminence, prestige, prominence, standing, status, usefulness, worth

important **1.** far-reaching, grave, large, material, meaningful, momentous, of substance, primary, salient, serious, signal, significant, substantial, urgent, weighty **2.** big-time (*informal*), eminent, foremost, high-level, high-ranking, influential, leading, major league (*informal*), notable, noteworthy, of note, outstanding, powerful, pre-eminent, prominent, seminal **3.** (*usually with* **to**) basic, essential, of concern *or* interest, relevant, valuable, valued

▷ **Antonyms** inconsequential, insignificant, minor, needless, negligible, secondary, trivial, undistinctive, unimportant, unnecessary

importunate burning, clamant, clamorous, demanding, dogged, earnest, exigent, insistent, persistent, pertinacious, pressing, solicitous, troublesome, urgent

importune badger, beset, besiege, dun, entreat, harass, hound, lay siege to, pester, plague, press, solicit

importunity cajolery, dunning, entreaties, insistence, persistence, pressing, solicitations, urging

impose **1.** decree, establish, exact, fix, institute, introduce, lay, levy, ordain, place, promulgate, put, set **2.** appoint, charge with, dictate, enforce, enjoin, inflict, prescribe, saddle (someone) with **3.** (*with* **on** *or* **upon**) butt in, encroach, foist, force oneself, gate-crash (*informal*), horn in (*informal*), inflict, intrude, obtrude, presume, take liberties, trespass **4.** (*with* **on** *or* **upon:**) **a.** abuse, exploit, play on, take advantage of, use **b.** con (*informal*), deceive, dupe, hoodwink, pull the wool over (somebody's) eyes, trick

imposing august, commanding, dignified, effective, grand, impressive, majestic, stately, striking

▷ **Antonyms** insignificant, mean, modest, ordinary, petty, poor, unimposing

imposition **1.** application, decree, introduction, laying on, levying, promulgation **2.** cheek (*informal*), encroachment, intrusion, liberty, presumption **3.** artifice, cheating, con (*informal*), deception, dissimulation, fraud, hoax, imposture, stratagem, trickery **4.** burden, charge, constraint, duty, levy, tax

impossibility hopelessness, impracticability, inability, inconceivability

impossible **1.** beyond one, beyond the bounds of possibility, hopeless, impracticable, inconceivable, not to be thought of, out of the question, unachievable, unattainable, unobtainable, unthinkable **2.** absurd, inadmissible, insoluble, intolerable, ludicrous, outrageous, preposterous, unacceptable, unanswerable, ungovernable, unreasonable, unsuitable, unworkable

▷ **Antonyms** (*sense 1*) conceivable, imaginable, likely, plausible, possible, reasonable

impostor charlatan, cheat, deceiver, fake, fraud, hypocrite, impersonator, knave (*archaic*), phoney *or* phony (*informal*), pretender, quack, rogue, sham, trickster

imposture artifice, canard, cheat, con trick (*informal*), counterfeit, deception, fraud, hoax, impersonation, imposition, quackery, swindle, trick

impotence disability, enervation, feebleness, frailty, helplessness, inability, inadequacy, incapacity, incompetence, ineffectiveness, inefficacy, inefficiency, infirmity, paralysis, powerlessness, uselessness, weakness

▷ **Antonyms** ability, adequacy, competence, effectiveness, efficacy, efficiency, powerfulness, strength, usefulness

impotent disabled, emasculate, enervated, feeble, frail, helpless, incapable, in-

capacitated, incompetent, ineffective, infirm, nerveless, paralysed, powerless, unable, unmanned, weak
▷ **Antonyms** able, capable, competent, effective, manned, potent, powerful, strong

impoverish 1. bankrupt, beggar, break, ruin 2. deplete, diminish, drain, exhaust, pauperize, reduce, sap, use up, wear out

impoverished 1. bankrupt, destitute, distressed, impecunious, indigent, in reduced *or* straitened circumstances, necessitous, needy, on one's uppers, penurious, poverty-stricken, ruined, straitened 2. barren, denuded, depleted, drained, empty, exhausted, played out, reduced, spent, sterile, worn out
▷ **Antonyms** (*sense 1*) affluent, rich, wealthy, well-off (*sense 2*) fecund, fertile, productive

impracticability futility, hopelessness, impossibility, impracticality, unsuitableness, unworkability, uselessness

impracticable 1. impossible, out of the question, unachievable, unattainable, unfeasible, unworkable 2. awkward, impractical, inapplicable, inconvenient, unserviceable, unsuitable, useless
▷ **Antonyms** feasible, possible, practicable, practical, serviceable, suitable

impractical 1. impossible, impracticable, inoperable, nonviable, unrealistic, unserviceable, unworkable, visionary, wild 2. idealistic, romantic, starry-eyed, unbusinesslike, unrealistic, visionary
▷ **Antonyms** (*sense 1*) possible, practical, serviceable, viable, workable (*sense 2*) down-to-earth, realistic, sensible

impracticality hopelessness, impossibility, inapplicability, romanticism, unworkability

imprecation anathema, blasphemy, curse, denunciation, execration, malediction, profanity, vilification

imprecise ambiguous, blurred round the edges, careless, equivocal, estimated, fluctuating, hazy, ill-defined, inaccurate, indefinite, indeterminate, inexact, inexplicit, loose, rough, sloppy (*informal*), vague, wide of the mark, woolly
▷ **Antonyms** accurate, careful, definite, determinate, exact, explicit, precise

impregnable immovable, impenetrable, indestructible, invincible, invulnerable, secure, strong, unassailable, unbeatable, unconquerable, unshakable
▷ **Antonyms** destructible, exposed, insecure, movable, open, pregnable, shakable, vulnerable

impregnate 1. fill, imbrue (*rare*), imbue, infuse, percolate, permeate, pervade, saturate, seep, soak, steep, suffuse 2. fecundate, fertilize, fructify, get with child, inseminate, make pregnant

impress 1. affect, excite, grab (*informal*), influence, inspire, make an impression, move, stir, strike, sway, touch 2. (*often with* **on** *or* **upon**) bring home to, emphasize, fix, inculcate, instil into, stress 3. emboss, engrave, imprint, indent, mark, print, stamp

impression 1. effect, feeling, impact, influence, reaction, sway 2. **make an impression** arouse comment, be conspicuous, cause a stir, excite notice, find favour, make a hit (*informal*), make an impact, stand out 3. belief, concept, conviction, fancy, feeling, funny feeling (*informal*), hunch, idea, memory, notion, opinion, recollection, sense, suspicion 4. brand, dent, hollow, impress, imprint, indentation, mark, outline, stamp, stamping 5. edition, imprinting, issue, printing 6. imitation, impersonation, parody, send-up (*Brit. informal*), takeoff (*informal*)

impressionability ingenuousness, receptiveness, receptivity, sensitivity, suggestibility, susceptibility, vulnerability

impressionable feeling, gullible, ingenuous, open, receptive, responsive, sensitive, suggestible, susceptible, vulnerable
▷ **Antonyms** blasé, hardened, insensitive, jaded, unresponsive

impressive affecting, awesome, dramatic, exciting, forcible, grand, moving, powerful, stirring, striking, touching
▷ **Antonyms** ordinary, unimposing, unimpressive, uninspiring, unmemorable, weak

imprint 1. *noun* impression, indentation, mark, print, sign, stamp 2. *~verb* engrave, establish, etch, fix, impress, print, stamp

imprison confine, constrain, detain, immure, incarcerate, intern, jail, lock up, put away, put under lock and key, send down (*informal*), send to prison
▷ **Antonyms** discharge, emancipate, free, liberate, release

imprisoned behind bars, captive, confined, immured, incarcerated, in irons, in jail, inside (*slang*), interned, jailed, locked up, put away, under lock and key

imprisonment confinement, custody, detention, durance (*archaic*), duress, incarceration, internment, porridge (*slang*)

improbability doubt, doubtfulness, dubiety, uncertainty, unlikelihood

improbable cock-and-bull (*informal*), doubtful, dubious, fanciful, far-fetched, implausible, questionable, unbelievable, uncertain, unconvincing, unlikely, weak
▷ **Antonyms** certain, convincing, doubtless, likely, plausible, probable, reasonable

improbity chicanery, crookedness (*informal*), dishonesty, faithlessness, fraud, knavery, unfairness, unscrupulousness, villainy

impromptu 1. *adjective* ad-lib, extemporaneous, extempore, extemporized, improvised, offhand, off the cuff (*informal*), spontaneous, unpremeditated, unprepared, unrehearsed, unscripted, unstudied 2. *~adverb* ad lib, off the cuff (*informal*), off the top of one's head (*informal*), on the spur of the moment, spontaneously, without preparation

▷ **Antonyms** *~adjective* considered, planned, premeditated, prepared, rehearsed

improper 1. impolite, indecent, indecorous, indelicate, off-colour, risqué, smutty, suggestive, unbecoming, unfitting, unseemly, untoward, vulgar 2. ill-timed, inapplicable, inapposite, inappropriate, inapt, incongruous, infelicitous, inopportune, malapropos, out of place, uncalled-for, unfit, unseasonable, unsuitable, unsuited, unwarranted 3. abnormal, erroneous, false, inaccurate, incorrect, irregular, wrong

▷ **Antonyms** (*sense 1*) becoming, decent, decorous, delicate, fitting, proper, seemly (*sense 2*) apposite, appropriate, apt, felicitous, opportune, seasoned, suitable

impropriety 1. bad taste, immodesty, incongruity, indecency, indecorum, unsuitability, vulgarity 2. bloomer (*Brit. informal*), blunder, faux pas, gaffe, gaucherie, lapse, mistake, slip, solecism

▷ **Antonyms** (*sense 1*) decency, decorum, delicacy, modesty, propriety, suitability

improve 1. advance, ameliorate, amend, augment, better, correct, face-lift, help, mend, polish, rectify, touch up, upgrade 2. develop, enhance, gain strength, increase, look up (*informal*), make strides, perk up, pick up, progress, rally, reform, rise, take a turn for the better (*informal*), take on a new lease of life (*informal*) 3. be on the mend, convalesce, gain ground, gain strength, grow better, make progress, mend, recover, recuperate, turn the corner 4. clean up one's act (*informal*), get it together (*informal*), get one's act together (*informal*), pull one's socks up (*Brit. informal*), reform, shape up (*informal*), turn over a new leaf

▷ **Antonyms** (*sense 1*) damage, harm, impair, injure, mar, worsen

improvement 1. advancement, amelioration, amendment, augmentation, betterment, correction, face-lift, gain, rectification 2. advance, development, enhancement, furtherance, increase, progress, rally, recovery, reformation, rise, upswing

improvidence carelessness, extravagance, heedlessness, imprudence, lavishness, negligence, prodigality, profligacy, short-sightedness, thriftlessness, wastefulness

improvident careless, heedless, imprudent, inconsiderate, negligent, prodigal, profligate, reckless, shiftless, short-sighted, spendthrift, thoughtless, thriftless, uneconomical, unthrifty, wasteful

▷ **Antonyms** careful, considerate, economical, heedful, provident, prudent, thrifty

improvisation ad-lib, ad-libbing, expedient, extemporizing, impromptu, invention, makeshift, spontaneity

improvise 1. ad-lib, busk, coin, extemporize, invent, play it by ear (*informal*), speak off the cuff (*informal*), vamp, wing it (*informal*) 2. concoct, contrive, devise, make do, throw together

improvised ad-lib, extemporaneous, extempore, extemporized, makeshift, off the cuff (*informal*), spontaneous, spur-of-the-moment, unprepared, unrehearsed

imprudence carelessness, folly, foolhardiness, foolishness, heedlessness, improvidence, inadvisability, incaution, incautiousness, inconsideration, indiscretion, irresponsibility, rashness, recklessness, temerity

imprudent careless, foolhardy, foolish, heedless, ill-advised, ill-considered, ill-judged, impolitic, improvident, incautious, inconsiderate, indiscreet, injudicious, irresponsible, overhasty, rash, reckless, temerarious, unthinking, unwise

▷ **Antonyms** careful, cautious, considerate, discreet, judicious, politic, provident, prudent, responsible, wise

impudence assurance, audacity, backchat (*informal*), boldness, brass neck (*Brit. informal*), brazenness, bumptiousness, cheek (*informal*), chutzpah (*U.S. & Canad. informal*), effrontery, face (*informal*), front, impertinence, insolence, lip (*slang*), neck (*informal*), nerve (*informal*), pertness, presumption, rudeness, sassiness (*U.S. informal*), sauciness, shamelessness

impudent audacious, bold, bold-faced, brazen, bumptious, cheeky (*informal*), cocky (*informal*), forward, fresh (*informal*), immodest, impertinent, insolent, lippy (*U.S. & Canad. slang*), pert, presumptuous, rude, sassy (*U.S. informal*), saucy (*informal*), shameless

▷ **Antonyms** courteous, modest, polite, respectful, retiring, self-effacing, timid, well-behaved

impugn assail, attack, call into question, cast aspersions upon, cast doubt upon, challenge, criticize, dispute, gainsay (*archaic or literary*), oppose, question, resist, traduce

impulse 1. catalyst, force, impetus, momentum, movement, pressure, push, stimulus, surge, thrust 2. *figurative* caprice, drive, feeling, incitement, inclination, influence, instinct, motive, notion, passion, resolve, urge, whim, wish

impulsive devil-may-care, emotional, hasty, headlong, impetuous, instinctive, intuitive, passionate, precipitate, quick, rash, spontaneous, unconsidered, unpredictable, unpremeditated

▷ **Antonyms** arresting, calculating, cautious, considered, cool, deliberate, halting, planned, premeditated, rehearsed, restrained

impunity dispensation, exemption, freedom, immunity, liberty, licence, nonliability, permission, security

impure **1.** admixed, adulterated, alloyed, debased, mixed, unrefined **2.** contaminated, defiled, dirty, filthy, foul, infected, polluted, sullied, tainted, unclean, unwholesome, vitiated **3.** carnal, coarse, corrupt, gross, immodest, immoral, indecent, indelicate, lascivious, lewd, licentious, lustful, obscene, prurient, ribald, salacious, smutty, unchaste, unclean, X-rated (*informal*)

▷ **Antonyms** (*sense 2*) clean, immaculate, spotless, squeaky-clean, undefiled, unsullied (*sense 3*) chaste, decent, delicate, modest, moral, pure, wholesome

impurity **1.** admixture, adulteration, mixture **2.** befoulment, contamination, defilement, dirtiness, filth, foulness, infection, pollution, taint, uncleanness **3.** (*often plural*) bits, contaminant, dirt, dross, foreign body, foreign matter, grime, marks, pollutant, scum, spots, stains **4.** carnality, coarseness, corruption, grossness, immodesty, immorality, indecency, lasciviousness, lewdness, licentiousness, obscenity, prurience, salaciousness, smuttiness, unchastity, vulgarity

imputable accreditable, ascribable, attributable, chargeable, referable, traceable

imputation accusation, ascription, aspersion, attribution, blame, censure, charge, insinuation, reproach, slander, slur

impute accredit, ascribe, assign, attribute, credit, lay at the door of, refer, set down to

inability disability, disqualification, impotence, inadequacy, incapability, incapacity, incompetence, ineptitude, powerlessness

▷ **Antonyms** ability, adequacy, capability, capacity, competence, potential, power, talent

inaccessible impassable, out of reach, out of the way, remote, unapproachable, unattainable, un-get-at-able (*informal*), unreachable

▷ **Antonyms** accessible, approachable, attainable, reachable

inaccuracy **1.** erroneousness, imprecision, incorrectness, inexactness, unfaithfulness, unreliability **2.** blunder, boob (*Brit. slang*), corrigendum, defect, erratum, error, fault, howler (*informal*), lapse, literal (*Printing*), miscalculation, mistake, slip, typo (*informal, Printing*)

inaccurate careless, defective, discrepant, erroneous, faulty, imprecise, incorrect, in error, inexact, mistaken, off base (*U.S. & Canad. informal*), off beam (*informal*), out, unfaithful, unreliable, unsound, way off beam (*informal*), wide of the mark, wild, wrong

▷ **Antonyms** accurate, correct, exact, precise, reliable, sound

inaccurately carelessly, clumsily, imprecisely, inexactly, unfaithfully, unreliably

inaction dormancy, idleness, immobility, inactivity, inertia, rest, torpidity, torpor

inactive **1.** abeyant, dormant, idle, immobile, inert, inoperative, jobless, kicking one's heels, latent, mothballed, out of service, out of work, unemployed, unoccupied, unused **2.** dull, indolent, lazy, lethargic, low-key (*informal*), passive, quiet, sedentary, slothful, slow, sluggish, somnolent, torpid

▷ **Antonyms** (*sense 1*) employed, mobile, occupied, operative, running, used, working (*sense 2*) active, busy, diligent, energetic, industrious, vibrant

inactivity **1.** dormancy, hibernation, immobility, inaction, passivity, unemployment **2.** dilatoriness, *dolce far niente*, dullness, heaviness, indolence, inertia, inertness, lassitude, laziness, lethargy, quiescence, sloth, sluggishness, stagnation, torpor, vegetation

▷ **Antonyms** action, activeness, bustle, employment, exertion, mobility, movement

inadequacy **1.** dearth, deficiency, inadequateness, incompleteness, insufficiency, meagreness, paucity, poverty, scantiness, shortage, skimpiness **2.** defectiveness, faultiness, inability, inaptness, incapacity, incompetence, incompetency, ineffectiveness, inefficacy, unfitness, unsuitableness **3.** defect, failing, imperfection, lack, shortage, shortcoming, weakness

inadequate **1.** defective, deficient, faulty, imperfect, incommensurate, incomplete, insubstantial, insufficient, meagre, niggardly, pathetic, scant, scanty, short, sketchy, skimpy, sparse **2.** found wanting, inapt, incapable, incompetent, not up to scratch (*informal*), unequal, unfitted, unqualified

▷ **Antonyms** (*sense 1*) adequate, ample, complete, perfect, satisfactory, substantial, sufficient (*sense 2*) apt, capable, competent, equal, fit, qualified

inadequately imperfectly, insufficiently, meagrely, poorly, scantily, sketchily, skimpily, sparsely, thinly

inadmissible immaterial, improper, inappropriate, incompetent, irrelevant, unacceptable, unallowable, unqualified, unreasonable

inadvertence, inadvertency blunder, carelessness, error, heedlessness, inattention, inconsideration, inobservance, mistake, neglect, negligence, oversight, remissness, thoughtlessness

inadvertent accidental, careless, chance, heedless, negligent, thoughtless, unheeding, unintended, unintentional, unplanned, unpremeditated, unthinking, unwitting

inadvertently **1.** carelessly, heedlessly, in an unguarded moment, negligently, thoughtlessly, unguardedly, unthinkingly **2.** accidentally, by accident, by mistake, involuntarily, mistakenly, unintentionally, unwittingly

▷ **Antonyms** carefully, consciously, deliberately, heedfully, intentionally

inadvisable ill-advised, impolitic, imprudent, inexpedient, injudicious, unwise

inalienable absolute, entailed (*Law*), inherent, inviolable, non-negotiable, nontransferable, sacrosanct, unassailable, untransferable

inane asinine, daft (*informal*), devoid of intelligence, empty, fatuous, frivolous, futile, goofy (*informal*), idiotic, imbecilic, mindless, puerile, senseless, silly, stupid, trifling, unintelligent, vacuous, vain, vapid, worthless

▷ **Antonyms** meaningful, profound, sensible, serious, significant, weighty, worthwhile

inanimate cold, dead, defunct, extinct, inactive, inert, insensate, insentient, lifeless, quiescent, soulless, spiritless

▷ **Antonyms** active, alive, alive and kicking, animate, full of beans (*informal*), lively, living, moving

inanity asininity, bêtise (*rare*), daftness (*informal*), emptiness, fatuity, folly, frivolity, imbecility, puerility, senselessness, silliness, vacuity, vapidity, worthlessness

inapplicable inapposite, inappropriate, inapt, irrelevant, unsuitable, unsuited

▷ **Antonyms** applicable, apposite, appropriate, apt, fitting, pertinent, relevant, suitable

inapposite impertinent, inapplicable, inappropriate, infelicitous, irrelevant, out of place, unfit, unsuitable

inappreciable imperceptible, infinitesimal, insignificant, minuscule, negligible

inappropriate disproportionate, ill-fitted, ill-suited, ill-timed, improper, incongruous, malapropos, out of place, tasteless, unbecoming, unbefitting, unfit, unfitting, unseemly, unsuitable, untimely

▷ **Antonyms** appropriate, becoming, congruous, fitting, proper, seemly, suitable, timely

inapt **1.** ill-fitted, ill-suited, inapposite, inappropriate, infelicitous, unsuitable, unsuited **2.** awkward, clumsy, dull, gauche, incompetent, inept, inexpert, maladroit, slow, stupid

▷ **Antonyms** (*sense 1*) apposite, appropriate, apt, felicitous, fitting, suitable, suited

inaptitude awkwardness, clumsiness, incompetence, maladroitness, unfitness, unreadiness, unsuitableness

inarticulate **1.** blurred, incoherent, incomprehensible, indistinct, muffled, mumbled, unclear, unintelligible **2.** dumb, mute, silent, speechless, tongue-tied, unspoken, unuttered, unvoiced, voiceless, wordless **3.** faltering, halting, hesitant, poorly spoken

▷ **Antonyms** (*senses 1 & 3*) articulate, clear, coherent, comprehensible, intelligible, well-spoken

inattention absent-mindedness, carelessness, daydreaming, disregard, forgetfulness, heedlessness, inadvertence, inattentiveness, indifference, neglect, preoccupation, thoughtlessness, woolgathering

inattentive absent-minded, careless, distracted, distrait, dreamy, heedless, inadvertent, neglectful, negligent, preoccupied, regardless, remiss, slapdash, slipshod, thoughtless, unheeding, unmindful, unobservant, vague

▷ **Antonyms** attentive, aware, careful, considerate, heeding, mindful, observant, thoughtful

inaudible indistinct, low, mumbling, out of earshot, stifled, unheard

▷ **Antonyms** audible, clear, discernible, distinct, perceptible

inaugural dedicatory, first, initial, introductory, maiden, opening

inaugurate **1.** begin, commence, get under way, initiate, institute, introduce, kick off (*informal*), launch, originate, set in motion, set up, usher in **2.** induct, install, instate, invest **3.** commission, dedicate, open, ordain

inauguration **1.** initiation, institution, launch, launching, opening, setting up **2.** induction, installation, investiture

inauspicious bad, black, discouraging, ill-omened, ominous, unfavourable, unfortunate, unlucky, unpromising, unpropitious, untoward

▷ **Antonyms** auspicious, encouraging, favourable, fortunate, good, lucky, promising, propitious

inborn congenital, connate, hereditary, immanent, inbred, ingrained, inherent, inherited, innate, in one's blood, instinctive, intuitive, native, natural

inbred constitutional, deep-seated, immanent, ingrained, inherent, innate, native, natural

incalculable boundless, countless, enormous, immense, incomputable, inestimable, infinite, innumerable, limitless, measureless, numberless, uncountable, untold, vast, without number

incandescent brilliant, Day-Glo, glowing, luminous, phosphorescent, radiant, red-hot, shining, white-hot

incantation abracadabra, chant, charm, conjuration, formula, hex (*U.S. & Canad. informal*), invocation, spell

incapable 1. feeble, inadequate, incompetent, ineffective, inept, inexpert, insufficient, not equal to, not up to, unfit, unfitted, unqualified, weak **2.** helpless, impotent, powerless, unable, unfit **3.** (*with* **of**) impervious, not admitting of, not susceptible to, resistant

▷ **Antonyms** (*sense 1*) adequate, capable, competent, efficient, expert, fit, qualified, sufficient

incapacitate cripple, disable, disqualify, immobilize, lay up (*informal*), paralyse, prostrate, put out of action (*informal*), scupper (*Brit. slang*), unfit (*rare*)

incapacitated disqualified, *hors de combat,* immobilized, indisposed, laid up (*informal*), out of action (*informal*), unfit

incapacity disqualification, feebleness, impotence, inability, inadequacy, incapability, incompetency, ineffectiveness, powerlessness, unfitness, weakness

incapsulate *see* ENCAPSULATE

incarcerate commit, confine, coop up, detain, gaol, immure, impound, imprison, intern, jail, lock up, put under lock and key, restrain, restrict, send down (*Brit.*), throw in jail

incarceration bondage, captivity, confinement, detention, imprisonment, internment, porridge (*slang*), restraint

incarnate 1. in bodily form, in human form, in the flesh, made flesh **2.** embodied, personified, typified

incarnation avatar, bodily form, embodiment, epitome, exemplification, impersonation, manifestation, personification, type

incautious careless, hasty, heedless, ill-advised, ill-judged, improvident, imprudent, impulsive, inconsiderate, indiscreet, injudicious, negligent, precipitate, rash, reckless, thoughtless, unguarded, unthinking, unwary

▷ **Antonyms** careful, cautious, considerate, discreet, guarded, heedful, judicious, prudent, thoughtful, wary

incautiously imprudently, impulsively, indiscreetly, precipitately, rashly, recklessly, thoughtlessly, unthinkingly

incendiary *adjective* **1.** dissentious, inflammatory, provocative, rabble-rousing, seditious, subversive ~*noun* **2.** arsonist, firebug (*informal*), fire raiser, pyromaniac **3.** agitator, demagogue, firebrand, insurgent, rabble-rouser, revolutionary

incense[1] *verb* anger, enrage, exasperate, excite, gall, get one's hackles up, inflame, infuriate, irritate, madden, make one's blood boil (*informal*), make one see red (*informal*), make one's hackles rise, nark (*Brit., Austral., & N.Z. slang*), provoke, raise one's hackles, rile (*informal*), rub one up the wrong way

incense[2] *noun* aroma, balm, bouquet, fragrance, perfume, redolence, scent

incensed angry, choked, cross, enraged, exasperated, fuming, furious, hot under the collar (*informal*), indignant, infuriated, irate, ireful (*literary*), mad (*informal*), maddened, on the warpath (*informal*), steamed up (*slang*), up in arms, wrathful

incentive bait, carrot (*informal*), carrot and stick, encouragement, enticement, goad, impetus, impulse, inducement, lure, motivation, motive, spur, stimulant, stimulus

▷ **Antonyms** deterrent, discouragement, disincentive, dissuasion, warning

inception beginning, birth, commencement, dawn, inauguration, initiation, kickoff (*informal*), origin, outset, rise, start

▷ **Antonyms** completion, conclusion, end, ending, finish, termination

incessant ceaseless, constant, continual, continuous, endless, eternal, everlasting, interminable, never-ending, nonstop, perpetual, persistent, relentless, unbroken, unceasing, unending, unrelenting, unremitting

▷ **Antonyms** infrequent, intermittent, occasional, periodic, rare, sporadic

incessantly all the time, ceaselessly, constantly, continually, endlessly, eternally, everlastingly, interminably, nonstop, perpetually, persistently, without a break

inchoate 1. beginning, inceptive, incipient, nascent **2.** elementary, embryonic, formless, immature, imperfect, rudimentary, undeveloped, unformed

incidence amount, degree, extent, frequency, occurrence, prevalence, rate

incident 1. adventure, circumstance, episode, event, fact, happening, matter, occasion, occurrence **2.** brush, clash, commotion, confrontation, contretemps, disturbance, mishap, scene, skirmish

incidental 1. accidental, casual, chance, fortuitous, odd, random **2.** (*with* **to**) accompanying, attendant, by-the-way, concomitant, contingent, contributory, related **3.** ancillary, minor, nonessential, occasional, secondary, subordinate, subsidiary

▷ **Antonyms** (*sense 3*) crucial, essential, important, necessary, vital

incidentally 1. accidentally, by chance, casually, fortuitously **2.** by the bye, by the way, in passing, parenthetically

incidentals contingencies, extras, minutiae, odds and ends

incinerate burn up, carbonize, char, consume by fire, cremate, reduce to ashes

incipient beginning, commencing, developing, embryonic, inceptive, inchoate, nascent, originating, starting

incise carve, chisel, cut (into), engrave, etch, inscribe

incision cut, gash, notch, opening, slash, slit

incisive **1.** acute, keen, penetrating, perspicacious, piercing, trenchant **2.** acid, biting, caustic, cutting, mordacious, mordant, sarcastic, sardonic, satirical, severe, sharp, vitriolic
▷ **Antonyms** (*sense 1*) dense, dull, superficial, vague, woolly

incisiveness **1.** keenness, penetration, perspicacity, sharpness, trenchancy **2.** acidity, pungency, sarcasm

incite agitate for *or* against, animate, drive, egg on, encourage, excite, foment, goad, impel, inflame, instigate, prod, prompt, provoke, put up to, rouse, set on, spur, stimulate, stir up, urge, whip up
▷ **Antonyms** dampen, deter, discourage, dishearten, dissuade, restrain

incitement agitation, clarion call, encouragement, goad, impetus, impulse, inducement, instigation, motivation, motive, prompting, provocation, spur, stimulus

incivility bad manners, boorishness, discourteousness, discourtesy, disrespect, ill-breeding, impoliteness, rudeness, unmannerliness
▷ **Antonyms** civility, courteousness, courtesy, good manners, mannerliness, politeness, respect

inclemency **1.** bitterness, boisterousness, rawness, rigour, roughness, severity, storminess **2.** callousness, cruelty, harshness, mercilessness, severity, tyranny, unfeelingness

inclement **1.** bitter, boisterous, foul, harsh, intemperate, rigorous, rough, severe, stormy, tempestuous **2.** callous, cruel, draconian, harsh, intemperate, merciless, pitiless, rigorous, severe, tyrannical, unfeeling, unmerciful
▷ **Antonyms** (*sense 1*) balmy, calm, clement, fine, mild, pleasant, temperate (*sense 2*) compassionate, gentle, humane, kind, merciful, tender

inclination **1.** affection, aptitude, bent, bias, desire, disposition, fancy, fondness, leaning, liking, partiality, penchant, predilection, predisposition, prejudice, proclivity, proneness, propensity, stomach, taste, tendency, thirst, turn, turn of mind, wish **2.** bending, bow, bowing, nod **3.** angle, bend, bending, deviation, gradient, incline, leaning, pitch, slant, slope, tilt
▷ **Antonyms** (*sense 1*) antipathy, aversion, disinclination, dislike, revulsion

incline *verb* **1.** be disposed *or* predisposed, bias, influence, persuade, predispose, prejudice, sway, tend, turn **2.** bend, bow, lower, nod, nutate (*rare*), stoop **3.** bend, bevel, cant, deviate, diverge, heel, lean, slant, slope, tend, tilt, tip, veer ~*noun* **4.** acclivity, ascent, declivity, descent, dip, grade, gradient, ramp, rise, slope

inclined apt, disposed, given, liable, likely, minded, of a mind (*informal*), predisposed, prone, willing

inclose *see* ENCLOSE

include **1.** comprehend, comprise, contain, cover, embody, embrace, encompass, incorporate, involve, subsume, take in, take into account **2.** add, allow for, build in, count, enter, insert, introduce, number among
▷ **Antonyms** eliminate, exclude, leave out, omit, rule out

including as well as, containing, counting, inclusive of, plus, together with, with

inclusion addition, incorporation, insertion
▷ **Antonyms** exception, exclusion, omission, rejection

inclusive across-the-board, all-embracing, all in, all together, blanket, catch-all (*chiefly U.S.*), comprehensive, full, general, global, *in toto*, overall, sweeping, umbrella, without exception
▷ **Antonyms** confined, exclusive, limited, narrow, restricted, unique

incognito disguised, in disguise, under an assumed name, unknown, unrecognized

incoherence disconnectedness, disjointedness, inarticulateness, unintelligibility

incoherent confused, disconnected, disjointed, disordered, inarticulate, inconsistent, jumbled, loose, muddled, rambling, stammering, stuttering, unconnected, uncoordinated, unintelligible, wandering, wild
▷ **Antonyms** coherent, connected, intelligible, logical, rational

incombustible fireproof, flameproof, noncombustible, nonflammable, noninflammable

income earnings, gains, interest, means, pay, proceeds, profits, receipts, revenue, salary, takings, wages

incoming approaching, arriving, entering, homeward, landing, new, returning, succeeding
▷ **Antonyms** departing, exiting, leaving, outgoing

incommensurate disproportionate, inadequate, inequitable, insufficient, unequal

incommode annoy, be a trouble to, bother, disturb, embarrass, get in one's hair (*informal*), give (someone) bother *or* trouble, hassle (*informal*), hinder, im~

pede, inconvenience, irk, put out, put (someone) to trouble, trouble, upset, vex

incommodious awkward, confined, cramped, inconvenient, narrow, re~stricted, small, uncomfortable

incommunicable indescribable, ineffable, inexpressible, unspeakable, unutterable

incomparable beyond compare, inimi~table, matchless, paramount, peerless, superlative, supreme, transcendent, unequalled, unmatched, unparalleled, unrivalled

incomparably beyond compare, by far, easily, eminently, far and away, im~measurably

incompatibility antagonism, conflict, dis~crepancy, disparateness, incongruity, inconsistency, irreconcilability, uncon~geniality

incompatible antagonistic, antipathetic, conflicting, contradictory, discordant, discrepant, disparate, ill-assorted, in~congruous, inconsistent, inconsonant, irreconcilable, mismatched, uncongen~ial, unsuitable, unsuited
▷ **Antonyms** alike, appropriate, compat~ible, congenial, consistent, harmonious, reconcilable, suitable, suited

incompetence inability, inadequacy, in~capability, incapacity, incompetency, ineffectiveness, ineptitude, ineptness, insufficiency, skill-lessness, unfitness, uselessness

incompetent bungling, cowboy (*informal*), floundering, incapable, incapacitated, ineffectual, inept, inexpert, insufficient, skill-less, unable, unfit, unfitted, un~skilful, useless
▷ **Antonyms** able, capable, competent, expert, fit, proficient, skilful

incomplete broken, defective, deficient, fragmentary, imperfect, insufficient, lacking, partial, short, unaccomplished, undeveloped, undone, unexecuted, un~finished, wanting
▷ **Antonyms** accomplished, complete, developed, finished, perfect, unified, whole

incomprehensible above one's head, all Greek to one (*informal*), baffling, be~yond comprehension, beyond one's grasp, enigmatic, impenetrable, incon~ceivable, inscrutable, mysterious, ob~scure, opaque, perplexing, puzzling, un~fathomable, unimaginable, unintelli~gible, unthinkable
▷ **Antonyms** apparent, clear, compre~hensible, conceivable, evident, intelligi~ble, manifest, obvious, understandable

inconceivable beyond belief, impossible, incomprehensible, incredible, mind-boggling (*informal*), not to be thought of, out of the question, staggering (*in~formal*), unbelievable, unheard-of, un~imaginable, unknowable, unthinkable
▷ **Antonyms** believable, comprehensible, conceivable, credible, imaginable, likely, plausible, possible, reasonable

inconclusive ambiguous, indecisive, inde~terminate, open, uncertain, unconvinc~ing, undecided, unsettled, up in the air (*informal*), vague

incongruity conflict, discrepancy, dispar~ity, inappropriateness, inaptness, in~compatibility, inconsistency, inharmo~niousness, unsuitability

incongruous absurd, conflicting, contra~dictory, contrary, disconsonant, dis~cordant, extraneous, improper, inappro~priate, inapt, incoherent, incompatible, inconsistent, out of keeping, out of place, unbecoming, unsuitable, unsuited
▷ **Antonyms** appropriate, becoming, compatible, consistent, harmonious, suitable, suited

inconsequential immaterial, inconsider~able, insignificant, measly, minor, neg~ligible, nickel-and-dime (*U.S. slang*), of no significance, paltry, petty, trifling, trivial, unimportant, wanky (*taboo slang*)

inconsiderable exiguous, inconsequential, insignificant, light, minor, negligible, petty, slight, small, small-time (*infor~mal*), trifling, trivial, unimportant

inconsiderate careless, indelicate, insen~sitive, intolerant, rude, self-centred, selfish, tactless, thoughtless, unchari~table, ungracious, unkind, unthinking
▷ **Antonyms** attentive, careful, consider~ate, gracious, kind, sensitive, tactful, thoughtful, tolerant

inconsistency **1.** contrariety, disagree~ment, discrepancy, disparity, diver~gence, incompatibility, incongruity, in~consonance, paradox, variance **2.** fickle~ness, instability, unpredictability, unreliability, unsteadiness

inconsistent **1.** at odds, at variance, con~flicting, contradictory, contrary, dis~cordant, discrepant, incoherent, incom~patible, in conflict, incongruous, incon~stant, irreconcilable, out of step **2.** ca~pricious, changeable, erratic, fickle, in~constant, irregular, uneven, unpredict~able, unstable, unsteady, vagarious (*rare*), variable
▷ **Antonyms** (*sense 1*) coherent, compat~ible, homogenous, orderly, reconcilable, uniform (*sense 2*) consistent, constant, predictable, reliable, stable, steady, un~changing

inconsistently contradictorily, differently, eccentrically, erratically, inequably, randomly, unequally, unfairly, unpre~dictably, variably

inconsolable brokenhearted, desolate, despairing, heartbroken, heartsick, prostrate with grief, sick at heart

inconspicuous camouflaged, hidden, in~significant, modest, muted, ordinary, plain, quiet, retiring, unassuming, un~

noticeable, unobtrusive, unostentatious
▷ **Antonyms** bold, conspicuous, noticeable, obtrusive, obvious, salient, significant, visible

inconstant blowing hot and cold (*informal*), capricious, changeable, changeful, erratic, fickle, fluctuating, inconsistent, irresolute, mercurial, mutable, temperamental, uncertain, undependable, uneven, unreliable, unsettled, unstable, unsteady, vacillating, vagarious (*rare*), variable, volatile, wavering, wayward

incontestable beyond doubt, beyond question, certain, incontrovertible, indisputable, indubitable, irrefutable, self-evident, sure, undeniable, unquestionable

incontinent **1.** unbridled, unchecked, uncontrollable, uncontrolled, ungovernable, ungoverned, unrestrained **2.** debauched, lascivious, lecherous, lewd, loose, lustful, profligate, promiscuous, unchaste, wanton

incontrovertible beyond dispute, certain, established, incontestable, indisputable, indubitable, irrefutable, positive, sure, undeniable, unquestionable, unshakable

inconvenience *noun* **1.** annoyance, awkwardness, bother, difficulty, disadvantage, disruption, disturbance, downside, drawback, fuss, hassle (*informal*), hindrance, nuisance, trouble, uneasiness, upset, vexation **2.** awkwardness, cumbersomeness, unfitness, unhandiness, unsuitableness, untimeliness, unwieldiness *~verb* **3.** bother, discommode, disrupt, disturb, give (someone) bother *or* trouble, hassle (*informal*), irk, make (someone) go out of his way, put out, put to trouble, trouble, upset

inconvenient **1.** annoying, awkward, bothersome, disadvantageous, disturbing, embarrassing, inopportune, tiresome, troublesome, unseasonable, unsuitable, untimely, vexatious **2.** awkward, cumbersome, difficult, unhandy, unmanageable, unwieldy
▷ **Antonyms** (*sense 1*) convenient, handy, opportune, seasonable, suitable, timely

incorporate absorb, amalgamate, assimilate, blend, coalesce, combine, consolidate, embody, fuse, include, integrate, meld, merge, mix, subsume, unite

incorporation absorption, amalgamation, assimilation, blend, coalescence, federation, fusion, inclusion, integration, merger, unifying

incorrect erroneous, false, faulty, flawed, improper, inaccurate, inappropriate, inexact, mistaken, off base (*U.S. & Canad. informal*), off beam (*informal*), out, specious, unfitting, unsuitable, untrue, way off beam (*informal*), wide of the mark (*informal*), wrong
▷ **Antonyms** accurate, correct, exact, faultless, fitting, flawless, right, suitable, true

incorrectness erroneousness, error, fallacy, faultiness, impreciseness, imprecision, impropriety, inaccuracy, inexactness, speciousness, unsoundness, unsuitability, wrongness

incorrigible hardened, hopeless, incurable, intractable, inveterate, irredeemable, unreformed

incorruptibility honesty, honour, integrity, justness, uprightness

incorruptible **1.** above suspicion, honest, honourable, just, straight, trustworthy, unbribable, upright **2.** everlasting, imperishable, undecaying

increase *verb* **1.** add to, advance, aggrandize, amplify, augment, boost, build up, develop, dilate, enhance, enlarge, escalate, expand, extend, grow, heighten, inflate, intensify, magnify, mount, multiply, proliferate, prolong, raise, snowball, spread, step up (*informal*), strengthen, swell, wax *~noun* **2.** addition, augmentation, boost, development, enlargement, escalation, expansion, extension, gain, growth, increment, intensification, rise, upsurge, upturn **3.** **on the increase** developing, escalating, expanding, growing, increasing, multiplying, on the rise, proliferating, spreading
▷ **Antonyms** *~verb* abate, abbreviate, abridge, condense, curtail, decline, decrease, deflate, diminish, dwindle, lessen, reduce, shorten, shrink

increasingly more and more, progressively, to an increasing extent

incredible **1.** absurd, beyond belief, cock-and-bull (*informal*), far-fetched, implausible, impossible, improbable, inconceivable, not hold water, preposterous, unbelievable, unimaginable, unthinkable **2.** *informal* ace (*informal*), amazing, astonishing, astounding, awe-inspiring, brilliant, def (*slang*), extraordinary, far-out (*slang*), great, marvellous, mega (*slang*), prodigious, rad (*informal*), sensational (*informal*), superhuman, wonderful

incredulity disbelief, distrust, doubt, scepticism, unbelief

incredulous disbelieving, distrustful, doubtful, doubting, dubious, mistrustful, sceptical, suspicious, unbelieving, unconvinced, wet behind the ears (*informal*)
▷ **Antonyms** believing, credulous, gullible, naive, trusting, unsuspecting

increment accretion, accrual, accruement, addition, advancement, augmentation, enlargement, gain, increase, step (up), supplement

incriminate accuse, arraign, blacken the name of, blame, charge, impeach, implicate, inculpate, indict, involve, point the finger at (*informal*), stigmatize

inculcate drill, drum into, hammer into (*informal*), implant, impress, indoctri~nate, infuse, instil

inculpate accuse, blame, censure, charge, drag into (*informal*), impeach, impli~cate, incriminate, involve

incumbent binding, compulsory, manda~tory, necessary, obligatory

incur arouse, bring (upon oneself), con~tract, draw, earn, expose oneself to, gain, induce, lay oneself open to, meet with, provoke

incurable *adjective* **1.** dyed-in-the-wool, hopeless, incorrigible, inveterate **2.** fa~tal, inoperable, irrecoverable, irremedi~able, remediless, terminal

incurious apathetic, indifferent, pococu~rante, unconcerned, uninquiring, unin~terested

incursion foray, infiltration, inroad, inva~sion, irruption, penetration, raid

indebted beholden, grateful, in debt, ob~ligated, obliged, under an obligation

indecency bawdiness, coarseness, crud~ity, foulness, grossness, immodesty, im~propriety, impurity, indecorum, indeli~cacy, lewdness, licentiousness, obscen~ity, outrageousness, pornography, smut, smuttiness, unseemliness, vileness, vulgarity

▷ **Antonyms** decency, decorum, delicacy, modesty, propriety, purity, seemliness

indecent **1.** blue, coarse, crude, dirty, filthy, foul, gross, immodest, improper, impure, indelicate, lewd, licentious, pornographic, salacious, scatological, smutty, vile **2.** ill-bred, improper, in bad taste, indecorous, offensive, outrageous, tasteless, unbecoming, unseemly, vulgar

▷ **Antonyms** decent, decorous, delicate, modest, proper, pure, respectable, seemly, tasteful

indecipherable crabbed, illegible, indis~tinguishable, unintelligible, unreadable

indecision ambivalence, dithering (*chiefly Brit.*), doubt, hesitancy, hesitation, indecisiveness, irresolution, shilly-shallying (*informal*), uncertainty, vacil~lation, wavering

indecisive **1.** dithering (*chiefly Brit.*), doubtful, faltering, hesitating, in two minds (*informal*), irresolute, pussyfoot~ing (*informal*), tentative, uncertain, un~decided, undetermined, vacillating, wa~vering **2.** inconclusive, indefinite, inde~terminate, unclear, undecided

▷ **Antonyms** (*sense 1*) certain, decided, determined, positive, resolute, unhesi~tating (*sense 2*) clear, conclusive, deci~sive, definite, determinate, final

indecorous boorish, churlish, coarse, ill-bred, immodest, impolite, improper, in~decent, rude, tasteless, uncivil, uncouth, undignified, unmannerly, unseemly, untoward

indeed actually, certainly, doubtlessly, in point of fact, in truth, positively, really, strictly, to be sure, truly, undeniably, undoubtedly, verily (*archaic*), veritably

indefatigable assiduous, diligent, dogged, inexhaustible, patient, persevering, pertinacious, relentless, sedulous, tire~less, unflagging, unremitting, untiring, unwearied, unwearying

indefensible faulty, inexcusable, insup~portable, unforgivable, unjustifiable, unpardonable, untenable, unwarrant~able, wrong

▷ **Antonyms** defensible, excusable, for~givable, justifiable, legitimate, pardon~able, supportable, tenable, warrantable

indefinable dim, hazy, impalpable, inde~scribable, indistinct, inexpressible, nameless, obscure, unrealized, vague

indefinite ambiguous, confused, doubtful, equivocal, evasive, general, ill-defined, imprecise, indeterminate, indistinct, in~exact, loose, obscure, oracular, uncer~tain, unclear, undefined, undetermined, unfixed, unknown, unlimited, unsettled, vague

▷ **Antonyms** certain, clear, definite, de~terminate, distinct, exact, fixed, settled, specific

indefinitely ad infinitum, continually, endlessly, for ever, *sine die,* till the cows come home (*informal*)

indelible enduring, indestructible, inef~faceable, ineradicable, inexpungible, in~extirpable, ingrained, lasting, perma~nent

▷ **Antonyms** eradicable, erasable, im~permanent, removable, short-lived, temporary, washable

indelicacy bad taste, coarseness, crudity, grossness, immodesty, impropriety, in~decency, obscenity, offensiveness, rude~ness, smuttiness, suggestiveness, taste~lessness, vulgarity

indelicate blue, coarse, crude, embar~rassing, gross, immodest, improper, in~decent, indecorous, low, near the knuckle (*informal*), obscene, off-colour, offensive, risqué, rude, suggestive, tasteless, unbecoming, unseemly, unto~ward, vulgar, X-rated (*informal*)

▷ **Antonyms** becoming, decent, decorous, delicate, modest, proper, refined, seemly

indemnify **1.** endorse, guarantee, insure, protect, secure, underwrite **2.** compen~sate, pay, reimburse, remunerate, re~pair, repay, requite, satisfy

indemnity **1.** guarantee, insurance, pro~tection, security **2.** compensation, re~dress, reimbursement, remuneration, reparation, requital, restitution, satis~faction **3.** *Law* exemption, immunity, impunity, privilege

indent *verb* **1.** ask for, order, request, requisition **2.** cut, dint, mark, nick, notch, pink, scallop, score, serrate

indentation bash (*informal*), cut, dent, depression, dimple, dip, hollow, jag, nick, notch, pit

independence autarchy, autonomy, devolution, freedom, home rule, liberty, self-determination, self-government, self-reliance, self-rule, self-sufficiency, separation, sovereignty
▷ **Antonyms** bondage, dependence, subjection, subjugation, subordination, subservience

independent 1. absolute, free, liberated, separate, unconnected, unconstrained, uncontrolled, unrelated **2.** autarchic, autarchical, autonomous, decontrolled, nonaligned, self-determining, self-governing, separated, sovereign **3.** bold, individualistic, liberated, self-contained, self-reliant, self-sufficient, unaided, unconventional
▷ **Antonyms** (*sense 2*) aligned, controlled, dependent, restrained, subject, submissive, subordinate, subservient, subsidiary

independently alone, autonomously, by oneself, individually, on one's own, separately, solo, unaided, under one's own steam

indescribable beggaring description, beyond description, beyond words, incommunicable, indefinable, ineffable, inexpressible, unutterable

indestructible abiding, durable, enduring, everlasting, immortal, imperishable, incorruptible, indelible, indissoluble, lasting, nonperishable, permanent, unbreakable, unfading
▷ **Antonyms** breakable, corruptible, destructible, fading, impermanent, mortal, perishable

indeterminate imprecise, inconclusive, indefinite, inexact, uncertain, undefined, undetermined, unfixed, unspecified, unstipulated, vague
▷ **Antonyms** certain, clear, conclusive, definite, determinate, exact, fixed, precise, specified, stipulated

index 1. clue, guide, indication, mark, sign, symptom, token **2.** director, forefinger, hand, indicator, needle, pointer

indicate 1. add up to (*informal*), bespeak, be symptomatic of, betoken, denote, evince, imply, manifest, point to, reveal, show, signal, signify, suggest **2.** designate, point out, point to, specify **3.** display, express, mark, read, record, register, show

indicated advisable, called-for, desirable, necessary, needed, recommended, suggested

indication clue, evidence, explanation, forewarning, hint, index, inkling, intimation, manifestation, mark, note, omen, portent, sign, signal, suggestion, symptom, warning

indicative exhibitive, indicatory, indicial, pointing to, significant, suggestive, symptomatic

indicator display, gauge, guide, index, mark, marker, meter, pointer, sign, signal, signpost, symbol

indict accuse, arraign, charge, impeach, prosecute, serve with a summons, summon, summons, tax

indictment accusation, allegation, charge, impeachment, prosecution, summons

indifference 1. absence of feeling, aloofness, apathy, callousness, carelessness, coldness, coolness, detachment, disregard, heedlessness, inattention, lack of interest, negligence, nonchalance, stoicalness, unconcern **2.** disinterestedness, dispassion, equity, impartiality, neutrality, objectivity **3.** insignificance, irrelevance, triviality, unimportance
▷ **Antonyms** (*sense 1*) attention, care, commitment, concern, enthusiasm, heed, regard

indifferent 1. aloof, apathetic, callous, careless, cold, cool, detached, distant, heedless, impervious, inattentive, not give a monkey's (*slang*), regardless, uncaring, unconcerned, unimpressed, uninterested, unmoved, unresponsive, unsympathetic **2.** immaterial, insignificant, of no consequence, unimportant **3.** average, fair, mediocre, middling, moderate, no great shakes (*informal*), ordinary, passable, perfunctory, so-so (*informal*), undistinguished, uninspired **4.** disinterested, dispassionate, equitable, impartial, neutral, nonaligned, nonpartisan, objective, unbiased, uninvolved, unprejudiced
▷ **Antonyms** (*sense 1*) avid, compassionate, concerned, eager, enthusiastic, interested, keen, responsive, sensitive, susceptible, sympathetic (*sense 3*) excellent, exceptional, fine, first-class, notable, remarkable

indigence destitution, distress, necessity, need, penury, poverty, privation, want

indigenous 1. aboriginal, autochthonous, home-grown, native, original **2.** congenital, connate, immanent, inborn, inbred, inherent, innate

indigent destitute, dirt-poor, down and out, down at heel (*informal*), flat broke (*informal*), impecunious, impoverished, in want, necessitous, needy, on one's uppers (*informal*), on the breadline, penniless, penurious, poor, poverty-stricken, short, straitened, without two pennies to rub together (*informal*)
▷ **Antonyms** affluent, prosperous, rich, wealthy, well-off, well-to-do

indigestion dyspepsia, dyspepsy, heartburn, upset stomach

indignant angry, annoyed, choked, disgruntled, exasperated, fuming (*informal*), furious, hacked (off) (*U.S. slang*), heated, hot under the collar (*informal*), huffy (*informal*), in a huff, incensed, in high dudgeon, irate, livid (*informal*), mad (*informal*), miffed (*informal*), narked (*Brit., Austral., & N.Z. slang*), peeved (*informal*), pissed off (*taboo slang*), provoked, resentful, riled, scornful, seeing red (*informal*), sore (*informal*), up in arms (*informal*), wrathful

indignation anger, exasperation, fury, ire (*literary*), pique, rage, resentment, righteous anger, scorn, umbrage, wrath

indignity abuse, affront, contumely, dishonour, disrespect, humiliation, injury, insult, obloquy, opprobrium, outrage, reproach, slap in the face (*informal*), slight, snub

indirect **1.** backhanded, circuitous, circumlocutory, crooked, devious, long-drawn-out, meandering, oblique, periphrastic, rambling, roundabout, tortuous, wandering, winding, zigzag **2.** ancillary, collateral, contingent, incidental, secondary, subsidiary, unintended
▷ **Antonyms** (*sense 1*) clear-cut, direct, straight, straightforward, undeviating, uninterrupted (*sense 2*) direct, explicit, express, intended

indirectly by implication, circumlocutorily, in a roundabout way, obliquely, periphrastically, second-hand

indiscernible hidden, impalpable, imperceptible, indistinct, indistinguishable, invisible, unapparent, undiscernible
▷ **Antonyms** apparent, clear, discernible, distinct, distinguishable, perceptible, visible

indiscreet foolish, hasty, heedless, ill-advised, ill-considered, ill-judged, impolitic, imprudent, incautious, injudicious, naive, rash, reckless, tactless, undiplomatic, unthinking, unwise
▷ **Antonyms** cautious, diplomatic, discreet, judicious, politic, prudent, tactful, wise

indiscretion bloomer (*Brit. informal*), boob (*Brit. slang*), error, faux pas, folly, foolishness, gaffe, gaucherie, imprudence, lapse, mistake, rashness, recklessness, slip, slip of the tongue, tactlessness

indiscriminate **1.** aimless, careless, desultory, general, hit or miss (*informal*), random, sweeping, uncritical, undiscriminating, unmethodical, unselective, unsystematic, wholesale **2.** chaotic, confused, haphazard, higgledy-piggledy (*informal*), jumbled, mingled, miscellaneous, mixed, mongrel, motley, promiscuous, undistinguishable
▷ **Antonyms** (*sense 1*) deliberate, discriminating, exclusive, methodical, selective, systematic

indispensable crucial, essential, imperative, key, necessary, needed, needful, requisite, vital
▷ **Antonyms** dispensable, disposable, nonessential, superfluous, unimportant, unnecessary

indisposed **1.** ailing, confined to bed, ill, laid up (*informal*), on the sick list (*informal*), poorly (*informal*), sick, under the weather, unwell **2.** averse, disinclined, loath, reluctant, unwilling
▷ **Antonyms** (*sense 1*) fine, fit, hardy, healthy, sound, well

indisposition **1.** ailment, ill health, illness, sickness **2.** aversion, disinclination, dislike, distaste, hesitancy, reluctance, unwillingness

indisputable absolute, beyond doubt, certain, evident, incontestable, incontrovertible, indubitable, irrefutable, positive, sure, unassailable, undeniable, unquestionable
▷ **Antonyms** assailable, disputable, doubtful, indefinite, questionable, refutable, uncertain, vague

indissoluble abiding, binding, enduring, eternal, fixed, imperishable, incorruptible, indestructible, inseparable, lasting, permanent, solid, unbreakable

indistinct ambiguous, bleary, blurred, confused, dim, doubtful, faint, fuzzy, hazy, ill-defined, indefinite, indeterminate, indiscernible, indistinguishable, misty, muffled, obscure, out of focus, shadowy, unclear, undefined, unintelligible, vague, weak
▷ **Antonyms** clear, defined, determinate, discernible, distinct, distinguishable, evident, intelligible

indistinguishable **1.** alike, cut from the same cloth, identical, like as two peas in a pod (*informal*), (the) same, twin **2.** imperceptible, indiscernible, invisible, obscure

individual **1.** *adjective* characteristic, discrete, distinct, distinctive, exclusive, identical, idiosyncratic, own, particular, peculiar, personal, personalized, proper, respective, separate, several, single, singular, special, specific, unique **2.** *~noun* being, body (*informal*), character, creature, mortal, party, person, personage, soul, type, unit
▷ **Antonyms** *~adjective* collective, common, conventional, general, indistinct, ordinary, universal

individualism egocentricity, egoism, freethinking, independence, originality, self-direction, self-interest, self-reliance

individualist freethinker, independent, loner, lone wolf, maverick, nonconformist, original

individualistic **1.** characteristic, distinctive, idiosyncratic, individual, original, particular, special, typical, unique **2.** egocentric, egoistic, independent, self-reliant

individuality character, discreteness, distinction, distinctiveness, originality, pe~

culiarity, personality, separateness, singularity, uniqueness

individually apart, independently, one at a time, one by one, personally, separately, severally, singly

indoctrinate brainwash, drill, ground, imbue, initiate, instruct, school, teach, train

indoctrination brainwashing, drilling, grounding, inculcation, instruction, schooling, training

indolence faineance, faineancy, heaviness, idleness, inactivity, inertia, inertness, languidness, languor, laziness, lethargy, shirking, skiving (*Brit. slang*), slacking, sloth, sluggishness, torpidity, torpor

indolent fainéant, good-for-nothing, idle, inactive, inert, lackadaisical, languid, lazy, lethargic, listless, lumpish, slack, slothful, slow, sluggish, torpid, workshy

▷ **Antonyms** active, assiduous, busy, conscientious, diligent, energetic, industrious, vigorous

indomitable bold, invincible, resolute, set, staunch, steadfast, unbeatable, unconquerable, unflinching, untameable, unyielding

▷ **Antonyms** cowardly, faltering, feeble, shrinking, wavering, weak, yielding

indorse *see* ENDORSE

indorsement *see* ENDORSEMENT

indubitable certain, evident, incontestable, incontrovertible, indisputable, irrefutable, obvious, open-and-shut, sure, unarguable, undeniable, undoubted, unquestionable, veritable

induce **1.** actuate, convince, draw, encourage, get, impel, incite, influence, instigate, move, persuade, press, prevail upon, prompt, talk into **2.** bring about, cause, effect, engender, generate, give rise to, lead to, occasion, produce, set in motion, set off

▷ **Antonyms** curb, deter, discourage, dissuade, hinder, prevent, restrain, stop, suppress

inducement attraction, bait, carrot (*informal*), cause, clarion call, come-on (*informal*), consideration, encouragement, impulse, incentive, incitement, influence, lure, motive, reward, spur, stimulus, urge

induct inaugurate, initiate, install, introduce, invest, swear in

induction **1.** inauguration, initiation, installation, institution, introduction, investiture **2.** conclusion, generalization, inference

indulge **1.** cater to, feed, give way to, gratify, pander to, regale, satiate, satisfy, treat oneself to, yield to **2.** (*with* **in**) bask in, give free rein to, give oneself up to, luxuriate in, revel in, wallow in **3.** baby, coddle, cosset, favour, fawn on, foster, give in to, go along with, humour, mollycoddle, pamper, pet, spoil

indulgence **1.** excess, fondness, immoderation, intemperance, intemperateness, kindness, leniency, pampering, partiality, permissiveness, profligacy, profligateness, spoiling **2.** appeasement, fulfilment, gratification, satiation, satisfaction **3.** extravagance, favour, luxury, privilege, treat **4.** courtesy, forbearance, goodwill, patience, tolerance, understanding

▷ **Antonyms** (*sense 1*) moderation, strictness, temperance, temperateness

indulgent compliant, easy-going, favourable, fond, forbearing, gentle, gratifying, kind, kindly, lenient, liberal, mild, permissive, tender, tolerant, understanding

▷ **Antonyms** austere, demanding, harsh, intolerant, rigorous, stern, strict, stringent, unmerciful

industrialist baron, big businessman, boss, capitalist, captain of industry, financier, magnate, manufacturer, producer, tycoon

industrious active, assiduous, busy, conscientious, diligent, energetic, hard-working, laborious, persevering, persistent, productive, purposeful, sedulous, steady, tireless, zealous

▷ **Antonyms** good-for-nothing, idle, indolent, lackadaisical, lazy, shiftless, slothful

industriously assiduously, conscientiously, diligently, doggedly, hard, like a Trojan, nose to the grindstone (*informal*), perseveringly, sedulously, steadily, without slacking

industry **1.** business, commerce, commercial enterprise, manufacturing, production, trade **2.** activity, application, assiduity, determination, diligence, effort, labour, perseverance, persistence, tirelessness, toil, vigour, zeal

inebriate *verb* **1.** intoxicate, make drunk, stupefy **2.** animate, arouse, carry away, excite, exhilarate, fire, stimulate *~noun* **3.** alcoholic, boozer (*informal*), dipsomaniac, drunk, drunkard, heavy drinker, lush (*slang*), soak (*slang*), sot, toper

inebriated babalas (*S. African*), befuddled, bevvied (*dialect*), blind drunk, blitzed (*slang*), blotto (*slang*), bombed (*slang*), Brahms and Liszt (*slang*), drunk, drunk as a skunk, flying (*slang*), fou *or* fu' (*Scot.*), half-cut (*informal*), half seas over (*informal*), high (*informal*), high as a kite (*informal*), inebriate, in one's cups, intoxicated, legless (*informal*), lit up (*slang*), merry (*Brit. informal*), out of it (*slang*), out to it (*Austral. & N.Z. slang*), paralytic (*informal*), pie-eyed (*slang*), pissed (*taboo slang*), plastered (*slang*), rat-arsed (*taboo slang*), smashed (*slang*), sozzled (*informal*), steamboats (*Scot. slang*), steaming (*slang*), stoned (*slang*), the worse for drink, three sheets in the wind (*informal*), tight (*informal*), tipsy, under the influence (*informal*), under the weather (*informal*), wasted (*slang*), wrecked (*slang*), zonked (*slang*)

inebriation crapulence, drunkenness, in~ebriety, insobriety, intemperance, in~toxication, sottishness

ineffable beyond words, incommunicable, indefinable, indescribable, inexpress~ible, unspeakable, unutterable

ineffective barren, basket case, bootless, feeble, fruitless, futile, idle, impotent, inadequate, ineffectual, inefficacious, inefficient, pathetic, unavailing, unpro~ductive, useless, vain, weak, worthless
▷ **Antonyms** effective, efficacious, effi~cient, fruitful, potent, productive, useful, worthwhile

ineffectual abortive, basket case, bootless, emasculate, feeble, fruitless, futile, idle, impotent, inadequate, incompetent, in~effective, inefficacious, inefficient, inept, lame, pathetic, powerless, unavailing, useless, vain, weak

inefficacious abortive, futile, ineffective, ineffectual, unavailing, unproductive, unsuccessful

inefficacy futility, inadequacy, ineffec~tiveness, ineffectuality, nonsuccess, un~productiveness, uselessness

inefficiency carelessness, disorganization, incompetence, muddle, slackness, slop~piness

inefficient cowboy (*informal*), disorgan~ized, feeble, incapable, incompetent, in~effectual, inefficacious, inept, inexpert, slipshod, sloppy, wasteful, weak
▷ **Antonyms** able, capable, competent, effective, efficient, expert, organized, skilled

inelegant awkward, clumsy, coarse, crass, crude, gauche, graceless, indeli~cate, laboured, rough, uncouth, unculti~vated, ungainly, ungraceful, unpolished, unrefined

ineligible disqualified, incompetent (*Law*), objectionable, ruled out, unac~ceptable, undesirable, unequipped, unfit, unfitted, unqualified, unsuitable

inept **1.** awkward, bumbling, bungling, cack-handed (*informal*), clumsy, cowboy (*informal*), gauche, incompetent, inex~pert, maladroit, unhandy, unskilful, unworkmanlike **2.** absurd, improper, in~appropriate, inapt, infelicitous, malap~ropos, meaningless, out of place, point~less, ridiculous, unfit, unsuitable
▷ **Antonyms** (*sense 1*) able, adroit, com~petent, dexterous, efficient, qualified, skilful, talented (*sense 2*) appropriate, apt, effectual, germane, sensible, suit~able

ineptitude **1.** clumsiness, gaucheness, in~capacity, incompetence, inexpertness, unfitness, unhandiness **2.** absurdity, in~appropriateness, pointlessness, use~lessness

inequality bias, difference, disparity, dis~proportion, diversity, imparity, irregu~larity, lack of balance, preferentiality, prejudice, unevenness

inequitable biased, discriminatory, one-sided, partial, partisan, preferential, prejudiced, unfair, unjust
▷ **Antonyms** even-handed, fair, impar~tial, just, unbiased, unprejudiced

inequity bias, discrimination, injustice, one-sidedness, prejudice, unfairness, unjustness

inert dead, dormant, dull, idle, immobile, inactive, inanimate, indolent, lazy, leaden, lifeless, motionless, passive, quiescent, slack, slothful, sluggish, slumberous (*chiefly poetic*), static, still, torpid, unmoving, unreactive, unre~sponsive
▷ **Antonyms** active, alive, alive and kicking, animated, energetic, full of beans (*informal*), living, mobile, moving, reactive, responsive, vital

inertia apathy, deadness, disinclination to move, drowsiness, dullness, idleness, immobility, inactivity, indolence, lan~guor, lassitude, laziness, lethargy, list~lessness, passivity, sloth, sluggishness, stillness, stupor, torpor, unrespon~siveness
▷ **Antonyms** action, activity, animation, brio, energy, liveliness, vigour, vitality

inescapable certain, destined, fated, in~eluctable, ineludible (*rare*), inevitable, inexorable, sure, unavoidable

inessential **1.** *adjective* dispensable, extraneous, extrinsic, needless, option~al, redundant, spare, superfluous, sur~plus, uncalled-for, unnecessary **2.** *~noun* accessory, extra, extravagance, luxury, makeweight, superfluity, trimming

inestimable beyond price, immeasurable, incalculable, invaluable, precious, priceless, prodigious

inevitable assured, certain, decreed, des~tined, fixed, ineluctable, inescapable, inexorable, necessary, ordained, settled, sure, unavoidable, unpreventable
▷ **Antonyms** avoidable, escapable, evad~able, preventable, uncertain

inevitably as a necessary consequence, as a result, automatically, certainly, nec~essarily, of necessity, perforce, surely, unavoidably, willy-nilly

inexact imprecise, inaccurate, incorrect, indefinite, indeterminate, off

inexcusable indefensible, inexpiable, out~rageous, unforgivable, unjustifiable, unpardonable, unwarrantable
▷ **Antonyms** defensible, excusable, for~givable, justifiable, pardonable

inexhaustible **1.** bottomless, boundless, endless, illimitable, infinite, limitless, measureless, never-ending, unbounded

2. indefatigable, tireless, undaunted, unfailing, unflagging, untiring, unwearied, unwearying
▷ **Antonyms** (*sense 1*) bounded, exhaustible, finite, limitable, limited, measurable (*sense 2*) daunted, enervated, failing, flagging, tiring, wearied

inexorable adamant, cruel, hard, harsh, immovable, implacable, ineluctable, inescapable, inflexible, merciless, obdurate, pitiless, relentless, remorseless, severe, unappeasable, unbending, unrelenting, unyielding
▷ **Antonyms** bending, flexible, lenient, movable, relenting, yielding

inexorably implacably, inevitably, irresistibly, relentlessly, remorselessly, unrelentingly

inexpedient disadvantageous, ill-advised, ill-considered, ill-judged, impolitic, impractical, improper, imprudent, inadvisable, inappropriate, indiscreet, injudicious, misguided, unadvisable, undesirable, undiplomatic, unsuitable, unwise

inexpensive bargain, budget, cheap, economical, low-cost, low-priced, modest, reasonable
▷ **Antonyms** costly, dear, exorbitant, expensive, high-priced, pricey, uneconomical

inexperience callowness, greenness, ignorance, newness, rawness, unexpertness, unfamiliarity

inexperienced amateur, callow, fresh, green, immature, new, raw, unaccustomed, unacquainted, unfamiliar, unfledged, unpractised, unschooled, unseasoned, unskilled, untrained, untried, unused, unversed, wet behind the ears (*informal*)
▷ **Antonyms** experienced, familiar, knowledgeable, practised, seasoned, skilled, trained, versed

inexpert amateurish, awkward, bungling, cack-handed (*informal*), clumsy, inept, maladroit, skill-less, unhandy, unpractised, unprofessional, unskilful, unskilled, unworkmanlike

inexplicable baffling, beyond comprehension, enigmatic, incomprehensible, inscrutable, insoluble, mysterious, mystifying, strange, unaccountable, unfathomable, unintelligible
▷ **Antonyms** comprehensible, explainable, explicable, fathomable, intelligible, soluble, understandable

inexpressible incommunicable, indefinable, indescribable, ineffable, unspeakable, unutterable

inexpressive bland, blank, cold, dead, deadpan, emotionless, empty, expressionless, impassive, inanimate, inscrutable, lifeless, stony, vacant

inextinguishable enduring, eternal, immortal, imperishable, indestructible, irrepressible, undying, unquenchable, unsuppressible

inextricably indissolubly, indistinguishably, inseparably, intricately, irretrievably, totally

infallibility **1.** faultlessness, impeccability, irrefutability, omniscience, perfection, supremacy, unerringness **2.** dependability, reliability, safety, sureness, trustworthiness

infallible **1.** faultless, impeccable, omniscient, perfect, unerring, unimpeachable **2.** certain, dependable, foolproof, reliable, sure, sure-fire (*informal*), trustworthy, unbeatable, unfailing
▷ **Antonyms** (*sense 1*) errant, fallible, human, imperfect, mortal (*sense 2*) doubtful, dubious, uncertain, undependable, unreliable, unsure

infamous abominable, atrocious, base, detestable, disgraceful, dishonourable, disreputable, egregious, flagitious, hateful, heinous, ignominious, ill-famed, iniquitous, loathsome, monstrous, nefarious, notorious, odious, opprobrious, outrageous, scandalous, scurvy, shameful, shocking, vile, villainous, wicked
▷ **Antonyms** esteemed, glorious, honourable, noble, reputable, virtuous

infamy abomination, atrocity, discredit, disgrace, dishonour, disrepute, ignominy, notoriety, obloquy, odium, opprobrium, outrageousness, scandal, shame, stigma, villainy

infancy **1.** babyhood, early childhood **2.** beginnings, cradle, dawn, early stages, emergence, inception, origins, outset, start
▷ **Antonyms** (*sense 2*) close, conclusion, death, end, expiration, finish, termination

infant **1.** *noun* ankle-biter (*Austral. slang*), babe, babe in arms, baby, bairn (*Scot.*), child, little one, neonate, newborn child, rug rat (*slang*), sprog (*slang*), suckling, toddler, tot, wean (*Scot.*) **2.** *~adjective* baby, dawning, developing, early, emergent, growing, immature, initial, nascent, newborn, unfledged, young

infantile babyish, childish, immature, puerile, tender, weak, young
▷ **Antonyms** adult, developed, mature

infatuate befool, beguile, besot, bewitch, captivate, delude, enchant, enrapture, enravish, fascinate, make a fool of, mislead, obsess, stupefy, sweep one off one's feet, turn (someone's) head

infatuated beguiled, besotted, bewitched, captivated, carried away, crazy about (*informal*), enamoured, enraptured, fascinated, head over heels in love with, inflamed, intoxicated, obsessed, possessed, smitten (*informal*), spellbound, swept off one's feet, under the spell of

infatuation crush (*informal*), fixation, folly, foolishness, madness, obsession, passion, thing (*informal*)

infect affect, blight, contaminate, corrupt, defile, influence, poison, pollute, spread to *or* among, taint, touch, vitiate

infection contagion, contamination, corruption, defilement, poison, pollution, septicity, virus

infectious catching, communicable, contagious, contaminating, corrupting, defiling, infective, pestilential, poisoning, polluting, spreading, transmittable, virulent, vitiating

infelicity **1.** inappropriateness, inaptness, incongruity, unsuitability, wrongness **2.** bad luck, misery, misfortune, sadness, unhappiness, woe, wretchedness

infer conclude, conjecture, deduce, derive, gather, presume, put two and two together, read between the lines, surmise, understand

inference assumption, conclusion, conjecture, consequence, corollary, deduction, illation (*rare*), presumption, reading, surmise

inferior *adjective* **1.** junior, lesser, lower, menial, minor, secondary, subordinate, subsidiary, under, underneath **2.** bad, bush-league (*Austral. & N.Z. informal*), chickenshit (*U.S. slang*), crappy (*slang*), dime-a-dozen (*informal*), duff (*Brit. informal*), end-of-the-pier (*Brit. informal*), for the birds (*informal*), imperfect, indifferent, low-grade, low-rent (*informal, chiefly U.S.*), mean, mediocre, no great shakes (*informal*), not a patch on, not much cop (*Brit. slang*), of a sort *or* of sorts, piss-poor (*taboo slang*), poor, poorer, poxy (*slang*), second-class, second-rate, shoddy, strictly for the birds (*informal*), substandard, tinhorn (*U.S. slang*), two-bit (*U.S. & Canad. slang*), worse *~noun* **3.** junior, menial, subordinate, underling

▷ **Antonyms** (*sense 1*) greater, higher, senior, superior, top (*sense 2*) excellent, fine, first-class

inferiority **1.** badness, deficiency, imperfection, inadequacy, insignificance, meanness, mediocrity, shoddiness, unimportance, worthlessness **2.** abasement, inferior status *or* standing, lowliness, subordination, subservience

▷ **Antonyms** advantage, ascendancy, dominance, eminence, excellence, superiority

infernal **1.** chthonian, Hadean, hellish, lower, nether, Plutonian, Stygian, Tartarean (*literary*), underworld **2.** accursed, damnable, damned, demonic, devilish, diabolical, fiendish, hellish, malevolent, malicious, satanic

▷ **Antonyms** angelic, celestial, glorious, godlike, heavenly, seraphic

infertile barren, infecund, nonproductive, sterile, unfruitful, unproductive

▷ **Antonyms** fecund, fertile, fruitful, generative, productive

infertility barrenness, infecundity, sterility, unfruitfulness, unproductiveness

infest beset, flood, invade, overrun, penetrate, permeate, ravage, swarm, throng

infested alive, beset, crawling, lousy (*slang*), overrun, pervaded, plagued, ravaged, ridden, swarming, teeming

infidel atheist, freethinker, Gentile, giaour (*Turkish*), heathen, heretic, pagan, sceptic, unbeliever

infidelity **1.** adultery, bad faith, betrayal, cheating (*informal*), disloyalty, duplicity, faithlessness, false-heartedness, falseness, perfidy, unfaithfulness **2.** apostasy, disbelief, irreligion, scepticism, treachery, unbelief

infiltrate creep in, filter through, insinuate oneself, make inroads (into), penetrate, percolate, permeate, pervade, sneak in (*informal*), work *or* worm one's way into

infinite absolute, all-embracing, bottomless, boundless, enormous, eternal, everlasting, illimitable, immeasurable, immense, inestimable, inexhaustible, interminable, limitless, measureless, never-ending, numberless, perpetual, stupendous, total, unbounded, uncounted, untold, vast, wide, without end, without number

▷ **Antonyms** bounded, circumscribed, finite, limited, measurable, restricted

infinitesimal atomic, inappreciable, insignificant, microscopic, minuscule, minute, negligible, teensy-weensy, teeny, teeny-weeny, tiny, unnoticeable, wee

▷ **Antonyms** enormous, great, huge, infinite, large, vast

infinity boundlessness, endlessness, eternity, immensity, infinitude, perpetuity, vastness

infirm **1.** ailing, debilitated, decrepit, doddering, doddery, enfeebled, failing, feeble, frail, lame, weak **2.** faltering, indecisive, insecure, irresolute, shaky, unsound, unstable, vacillating, wavering, weak, wobbly

▷ **Antonyms** (*sense 1*) healthy, hearty, robust, sound, strong, sturdy, vigorous

infirmity **1.** debility, decrepitude, deficiency, feebleness, frailty, ill health, imperfection, sickliness, vulnerability **2.** ailment, defect, disorder, failing, fault, malady, sickness, weakness

▷ **Antonyms** health, soundness, stability, strength, vigour

infix **1.** engraft, fasten, implant, insert, inset, introduce, place, set **2.** drum into, entrench, impress, inculcate, ingrain, instil

inflame **1.** agitate, anger, arouse, embitter, enrage, exasperate, excite, fire, foment, heat, ignite, impassion, incense, infuriate, intoxicate, kindle, madden, make one's blood boil, provoke, rile, rouse, stimulate **2.** aggravate, exacerbate, exasperate, fan, increase, intensify, worsen

▷ **Antonyms** allay, calm, cool, discourage, extinguish, pacify, quench, quiet, soothe, suppress

inflamed angry, chafing, festering, fevered, heated, hot, infected, red, septic, sore, swollen

inflammable combustible, flammable, incendiary

inflammation burning, heat, painfulness, rash, redness, sore, soreness, tenderness

inflammatory anarchic, demagogic, explosive, fiery, incendiary, inflaming, instigative, insurgent, intemperate, provocative, rabble-rousing, rabid, red rag to a bull, riotous, seditious

inflate aerate, aggrandize, amplify, balloon, bloat, blow up, boost, dilate, distend, enlarge, escalate, exaggerate, expand, increase, puff up *or* out, pump up, swell

▷ **Antonyms** collapse, compress, contract, deflate, diminish, lessen, shrink

inflated bombastic, exaggerated, grandiloquent, ostentatious, overblown, swollen

inflation aggrandizement, blowing up, distension, enhancement, enlargement, escalation, expansion, extension, increase, intensification, puffiness, rise, spread, swelling, tumefaction

inflect 1. intonate, modulate **2.** *Grammar* conjugate, decline **3.** arch, bend, bow, crook, curve, flex, round

inflection 1. accentuation, bend, bow, crook, curvature, intonation, modulation **2.** *Grammar* conjugation, declension **3.** angle, arc, arch

inflexibility 1. hardness, immovability, inelasticity, rigidity, stiffness, stringency **2.** fixity, intransigence, obduracy, obstinacy, steeliness

inflexible 1. adamant, brassbound, dyed-in-the-wool, firm, fixed, hard and fast, immovable, immutable, implacable, inexorable, intractable, iron, obdurate, obstinate, relentless, resolute, rigorous, set, set in one's ways, steadfast, steely, stiff-necked, strict, stringent, stubborn, unadaptable, unbending, unchangeable, uncompromising, unyielding **2.** hard, hardened, inelastic, nonflexible, rigid, stiff, taut

▷ **Antonyms** elastic, flexible, irresolute, lissom(e), movable, pliable, pliant, supple, variable, yielding

inflict administer, apply, deliver, exact, impose, levy, mete *or* deal out, visit, wreak

infliction 1. administration, exaction, imposition, perpetration, wreaking **2.** affliction, penalty, punishment, trouble, visitation, worry

influence *noun* **1.** agency, ascendancy, authority, control, credit, direction, domination, effect, guidance, magnetism, mastery, power, pressure, rule, spell, sway, weight **2.** bottom, clout (*informal*), connections, good offices, hold, importance, leverage, power, prestige, pull (*informal*), weight *~verb* **3.** act *or* work upon, affect, arouse, bias, control, count, direct, dispose, guide, impact, impel, impress, incite, incline, induce, instigate, lead to believe, manipulate, modify, move, persuade, predispose, prompt, rouse, sway **4.** bring pressure to bear upon, carry weight with, make oneself felt, pull strings (*informal*)

influential authoritative, controlling, effective, efficacious, forcible, guiding, important, instrumental, leading, meaningful, momentous, moving, persuasive, potent, powerful, significant, telling, weighty

▷ **Antonyms** impotent, ineffective, ineffectual, powerless, unimportant, uninfluential, unpersuasive, weak

influx arrival, convergence, flow, incursion, inflow, inrush, inundation, invasion, rush

infold *see* ENFOLD

inform 1. acquaint, advise, apprise, clue in (*informal*), communicate, enlighten, give (someone) to understand, instruct, keep (someone) posted, leak to, let know, make conversant (with), notify, put (someone) in the picture (*informal*), send word to, teach, tell, tip off **2.** (*often with* **against** *or* **on**) betray, blab, blow the gaff (*Brit. slang*), blow the whistle on (*informal*), clype (*Scot.*), denounce, grass (*Brit. slang*), incriminate, inculpate, let the cat out of the bag, nark (*Brit., Austral., & N.Z. slang*), peach (*slang*), put the finger on (*informal*), rat (*informal*), shop (*slang, chiefly Brit.*), sing (*slang, chiefly U.S.*), snitch (*slang*), spill one's guts (*slang*), spill the beans (*informal*), squeal (*slang*), tell all, tell on (*informal*) **3.** animate, characterize, illuminate, imbue, inspire, permeate, suffuse, typify

informal casual, colloquial, cosy, easy, familiar, natural, relaxed, simple, unceremonious, unconstrained, unofficial

▷ **Antonyms** ceremonious, constrained, conventional, formal, official, stiff

informality casualness, ease, familiarity, lack of ceremony, naturalness, relaxation, simplicity

information advice, blurb, counsel, data, dope (*informal*), facts, gen (*Brit. informal*), info (*informal*), inside story, instruction, intelligence, knowledge, latest (*informal*), lowdown (*informal*), material, message, news, notice, report, tidings, word

informative chatty, communicative, edifying, educational, enlightening, forthcoming, gossipy, illuminating, instructive, newsy, revealing

informed abreast, acquainted, *au courant, au fait,* briefed, conversant, enlightened, erudite, expert, familiar, genned up (*Brit. informal*), in the know (*informal*), in the picture, keeping one's finger on the pulse, knowledgeable, learned, posted, primed, reliable, up, up to date, versed, well-read

informer accuser, betrayer, grass (*Brit. slang*), Judas, nark (*Brit., Austral., & N.Z. slang*), sneak, squealer (*slang*), stool pigeon

infraction breach, breaking, contravention, infringement, nonfulfilment, transgression, trespass, violation

infrequent few and far between, occasional, once in a blue moon, rare, sporadic, uncommon, unusual

▷ **Antonyms** common, customary, frequent, habitual, often, regular, usual

infringe 1. break, contravene, disobey, transgress, violate **2.** (*with* **on** *or* **upon**) encroach, intrude, trespass

infringement breach, contravention, infraction, noncompliance, nonobservance, transgression, trespass, violation

infuriate anger, be like a red rag to a bull, enrage, exasperate, gall, get one's back up, get one's goat (*slang*), incense, irritate, madden, make one's blood boil, make one see red (*informal*), make one's hackles rise, nark (*Brit., Austral., & N.Z. slang*), provoke, put one's back up, raise one's hackles, rile

▷ **Antonyms** appease, calm, mollify, pacify, placate, propitiate, soothe

infuriating aggravating (*informal*), annoying, exasperating, galling, irritating, maddening, mortifying, pestilential, provoking, vexatious

infuse 1. breathe into, engraft, impart to, implant, inculcate, inspire, instil, introduce **2.** brew, macerate, soak, steep

ingenious adroit, bright, brilliant, clever, crafty, creative, dexterous, fertile, inventive, masterly, original, ready, resourceful, shrewd, skilful, subtle

▷ **Antonyms** artless, clumsy, unimaginative, uninventive, unoriginal, unresourceful, unskilful

ingenuity adroitness, cleverness, faculty, flair, genius, gift, ingeniousness, inventiveness, knack, originality, resourcefulness, sharpness, shrewdness, skill, turn

▷ **Antonyms** clumsiness, dullness, incompetence, ineptitude, ineptness

ingenuous artless, candid, childlike, frank, guileless, honest, innocent, naive, open, plain, simple, sincere, trustful, trusting, unreserved, unsophisticated, unstudied

▷ **Antonyms** artful, crafty, devious, insincere, reserved, sly, sophisticated, subtle, wily

ingenuousness artlessness, candour, frankness, guilelessness, innocence, naivety, openness, trustingness, unsuspiciousness

▷ **Antonyms** artfulness, craftiness, insincerity, slyness, sophistication, subterfuge, subtlety

inglorious discreditable, disgraceful, dishonourable, disreputable, failed, humiliating, ignoble, ignominious, infamous, obscure, shameful, unheroic, unknown, unsuccessful, unsung

ingraft *see* ENGRAFT

ingrain embed, entrench, fix, imbue, implant, impress, imprint, instil, root, sow the seeds

ingrained brassbound, constitutional, deep-rooted, deep-seated, fixed, fundamental, hereditary, inborn, inbred, inbuilt, indelible, ineradicable, inherent, in the blood, intrinsic, inveterate, rooted

ingratiate be a yes man, blandish, brown-nose (*taboo slang*), crawl, curry favour, fawn, flatter, get in with, get on the right side of, grovel, insinuate oneself, keep (someone) sweet, kiss (someone's) ass (*U.S. & Canad. taboo slang*), lick someone's arse (*taboo slang*), lick (someone's) boots, pander to, play up to, rub (someone) up the right way (*informal*), seek the favour (of someone), suck up to (*informal*), toady, worm oneself into (someone's) favour

ingratiating bootlicking (*informal*), crawling, fawning, flattering, humble, obsequious, servile, sycophantic, timeserving, toadying, unctuous

ingratitude thanklessness, unappreciativeness, ungratefulness

▷ **Antonyms** appreciation, gratefulness, gratitude, thankfulness, thanks, thanksgiving

ingredient component, constituent, element, part

ingress access, admission, admittance, door, entrance, entrée, entry, right of entry, way in

ingulf *see* ENGULF

inhabit abide, dwell, live, lodge, make one's home, occupy, people, populate, possess, reside, take up residence in, tenant

inhabitant aborigine, citizen, denizen, dweller, indigene, indweller, inmate, native, occupant, occupier, resident, tenant

inhabited colonized, developed, held, occupied, peopled, populated, settled, tenanted

inhalation breath, breathing, inhaling, inspiration

inhale breathe in, draw in, gasp, respire, suck in
▷ **Antonyms** blow, breathe out, exhale, expire

inharmonious antipathetic, cacophonous, clashing, discordant, dissonant, grating, harsh, incompatible, inconsonant, jangling, jarring, strident, tuneless, unharmonious, unmelodious, unmusical

inherent basic, congenital, connate, essential, hereditary, immanent, inborn, inbred, inbuilt, ingrained, inherited, innate, in one's blood, instinctive, intrinsic, native, natural
▷ **Antonyms** alien, extraneous, extrinsic, imposed, superficial, supplementary

inherit accede to, be bequeathed, be left, come into, fall heir to, succeed to

inheritance bequest, birthright, heritage, legacy, patrimony

inheritor beneficiary, heir, legatee, recipient, successor

inhibit arrest, bar, bridle, check, constrain, cramp (someone's) style (*informal*), curb, debar, discourage, forbid, frustrate, hinder, hold back *or* in, impede, obstruct, prevent, prohibit, restrain, stem the flow, stop, throw a spanner in the works
▷ **Antonyms** abet, allow, enable, encourage, further, let, permit, support

inhibited constrained, frustrated, guarded, repressed, reserved, reticent, self-conscious, shy, subdued, uptight (*informal*), withdrawn
▷ **Antonyms** free, natural, outgoing, relaxed, spontaneous, uninhibited, unreserved

inhibition bar, block, check, embargo, hang-up (*informal*), hindrance, interdict, mental blockage, obstacle, prohibition, reserve, restraint, restriction, reticence, self-consciousness, shyness

inhospitable **1.** cool, uncongenial, unfriendly, ungenerous, unkind, unreceptive, unsociable, unwelcoming, xenophobic **2.** bare, barren, bleak, desolate, empty, forbidding, godforsaken, hostile, lonely, sterile, unfavourable, uninhabitable
▷ **Antonyms** (*sense 1*) amicable, friendly, generous, genial, gracious, hospitable, sociable, welcoming

inhuman animal, barbaric, barbarous, bestial, brutal, cold-blooded, cruel, diabolical, fiendish, heartless, merciless, pitiless, remorseless, ruthless, savage, unfeeling, vicious
▷ **Antonyms** charitable, compassionate, feeling, humane, merciful, sensitive, tender, warmhearted

inhumane brutal, cruel, heartless, pitiless, uncompassionate, unfeeling, unkind, unsympathetic

inhumanity atrocity, barbarism, brutality, brutishness, cold-bloodedness, cold-heartedness, cruelty, hardheartedness, heartlessness, pitilessness, ruthlessness, unkindness, viciousness

inhumation burial, entombment, interment, sepulture

inhume bury, entomb, inter, lay to rest, sepulchre

inimical adverse, antagonistic, antipathetic, contrary, destructive, disaffected, harmful, hostile, hurtful, ill-disposed, injurious, noxious, opposed, oppugnant (*rare*), pernicious, repugnant, unfavourable, unfriendly, unwelcoming
▷ **Antonyms** affable, amicable, congenial, favourable, friendly, good, helpful, kindly, sympathetic, welcoming

inimitable consummate, incomparable, matchless, nonpareil, peerless, supreme, unequalled, unexampled, unique, unmatched, unparalleled, unrivalled, unsurpassable

iniquitous abominable, accursed, atrocious, base, criminal, evil, heinous, immoral, infamous, nefarious, reprehensible, reprobate, sinful, unjust, unrighteous, vicious, wicked

iniquity abomination, baseness, crime, evil, evildoing, heinousness, infamy, injustice, misdeed, offence, sin, sinfulness, unrighteousness, wickedness, wrong, wrongdoing
▷ **Antonyms** fairness, goodness, honesty, integrity, justice, morality, righteousness, uprightness, virtue

initial *adjective* beginning, commencing, early, first, inaugural, inceptive, inchoate, incipient, introductory, opening, primary
▷ **Antonyms** closing, concluding, ending, final, last, terminal, ultimate

initially at first, at *or* in the beginning, at the outset, at the start, first, firstly, in the early stages, originally, primarily, to begin with

initiate *verb* **1.** begin, break the ice, commence, get under way, inaugurate, institute, kick off (*informal*), kick-start, launch, lay the foundations of, open, originate, pioneer, set going, set in motion, set the ball rolling, start **2.** acquaint with, coach, familiarize with, indoctrinate, induct, instate, instruct, introduce, invest, teach, train *~noun* **3.** beginner, convert, entrant, learner, member, novice, probationer, proselyte, tyro

initiation admission, baptism of fire, commencement, debut, enrolment, entrance, inauguration, inception, induction, installation, instatement, introduction, investiture

initiative **1.** advantage, beginning, commencement, first move, first step, lead **2.** ambition, drive, dynamism, enterprise, get-up-and-go (*informal*), inventiveness, leadership, originality, push (*informal*), resource, resourcefulness

inject 1. inoculate, jab (*informal*), shoot (*informal*), vaccinate 2. bring in, infuse, insert, instil, interject, introduce

injection 1. inoculation, jab (*informal*), shot (*informal*), vaccination, vaccine 2. dose, infusion, insertion, interjection, introduction

injudicious foolish, hasty, ill-advised, ill-judged, ill-timed, impolitic, imprudent, incautious, inconsiderate, indiscreet, inexpedient, rash, unthinking, unwise
▷ **Antonyms** cautious, considerate, discreet, expedient, judicious, polite, prudent, well-timed, wise

injunction admonition, command, dictate, exhortation, instruction, mandate, order, precept, ruling

injure abuse, blemish, blight, break, damage, deface, disable, harm, hurt, impair, maltreat, mar, ruin, spoil, tarnish, undermine, vitiate, weaken, wound, wrong

injured 1. broken, damaged, disabled, hurt, lamed, undermined, weakened, wounded 2. cut to the quick, disgruntled, displeased, hurt, long-suffering, put out, reproachful, stung, unhappy, upset, wounded 3. abused, blackened, blemished, defamed, ill-treated, maligned, maltreated, offended, tarnished, vilified, wronged

injurious adverse, bad, baneful (*archaic*), corrupting, damaging, deleterious, destructive, detrimental, disadvantageous, harmful, hurtful, iniquitous, maleficent, mischievous, noxious, pernicious, ruinous, slanderous, unconducive, unhealthy, unjust, wrongful

injury abuse, damage, detriment, disservice, evil, grievance, harm, hurt, ill, injustice, mischief, ruin, trauma (*Pathology*), wound, wrong

injustice bias, discrimination, favouritism, inequality, inequity, iniquity, one-sidedness, oppression, partiality, partisanship, prejudice, unfairness, unjustness, unlawfulness, wrong
▷ **Antonyms** equality, equity, fairness, impartiality, justice, lawfulness, rectitude, right

inkling clue, conception, faintest *or* foggiest idea, glimmering, hint, idea, indication, intimation, notion, suggestion, suspicion, whisper

inland *adjective* domestic, interior, internal, upcountry

inlet arm (of the sea), bay, bight, cove, creek, entrance, firth *or* frith (*Scot.*), fjord, ingress, passage, sea loch (*Scot.*)

inmost *or* **innermost** basic, buried, central, deep, deepest, essential, intimate, personal, private, secret

innards 1. entrails, guts, insides (*informal*), intestines, inwards, viscera, vitals 2. guts (*informal*), mechanism, works

innate congenital, connate, constitutional, essential, immanent, inborn, inbred, indigenous, ingrained, inherent, inherited, in one's blood, instinctive, intrinsic, intuitive, native, natural
▷ **Antonyms** accidental, acquired, affected, assumed, cultivated, fostered, incidental, learned, nurtured, unnatural

inner 1. central, essential, inside, interior, internal, intestinal, inward, middle 2. esoteric, hidden, intimate, personal, private, repressed, secret, unrevealed 3. emotional, mental, psychological, spiritual
▷ **Antonyms** (*sense 1*) exterior, external, outer, outside, outward (*sense 2*) exposed, obvious, overt, revealed, surface, unconcealed, unrepressed, visible

innkeeper host, hostess, hotelier, landlady, landlord, mine host, publican

innocence 1. blamelessness, chastity, clean hands, guiltlessness, incorruptibility, probity, purity, righteousness, sinlessness, stainlessness, uprightness, virginity, virtue 2. harmlessness, innocuousness, innoxiousness, inoffensiveness 3. artlessness, credulousness, freshness, guilelessness, gullibility, inexperience, ingenuousness, naïveté, simplicity, unsophistication, unworldliness 4. ignorance, lack of knowledge, nescience (*literary*), unawareness, unfamiliarity
▷ **Antonyms** (*sense 1*) corruption, guilt, impurity, offensiveness, sinfulness, wrongness (*sense 3*) artfulness, cunning, disingenuousness, guile, wiliness, worldliness

innocent *adjective* 1. blameless, clear, faultless, guiltless, honest, in the clear, not guilty, uninvolved, unoffending 2. chaste, immaculate, impeccable, incorrupt, pristine, pure, righteous, sinless, spotless, stainless, unblemished, unsullied, upright, virgin, virginal 3. (*with* **of**) clear of, empty of, free from, ignorant, lacking, nescient, unacquainted with, unaware, unfamiliar with, untouched by 4. harmless, innocuous, inoffensive, unmalicious, unobjectionable, well-intentioned, well-meant 5. artless, childlike, credulous, frank, guileless, gullible, ingenuous, naive, open, simple, unsuspicious, unworldly, wet behind the ears (*informal*) ~*noun* 6. babe (in arms) (*informal*), child, greenhorn (*informal*), ingénue *or (masc.)* ingénu
▷ **Antonyms** (*sense 1*) blameworthy, culpable, dishonest, guilty, responsible (*sense 2*) corrupt, immoral, impure, sinful, wrong (*sense 4*) evil, harmful, iniquitous, malicious, offensive, wicked (*sense 5*) artful, disingenuous, sophisticated, worldly

innocuous harmless, innocent, innoxious, inoffensive, safe, unobjectionable

innovation alteration, change, departure, introduction, modernism, modernization, newness, novelty, variation

innuendo aspersion, hint, implication, imputation, insinuation, intimation, overtone, suggestion, whisper

innumerable beyond number, countless, incalculable, infinite, many, multitudinous, myriad, numberless, numerous, unnumbered, untold
▷ **Antonyms** calculable, computable, finite, limited, measurable, numbered

inoffensive harmless, humble, innocent, innocuous, innoxious, mild, neutral, nonprovocative, peaceable, quiet, retiring, unobjectionable, unobtrusive, unoffending
▷ **Antonyms** abrasive, harmful, irksome, irritating, malicious, objectionable, offensive, provocative

inoperable impracticable, impractical, nonviable, unrealistic, unworkable

inoperative broken, broken-down, buggered (*slang, chiefly Brit.*), defective, *hors de combat,* ineffective, ineffectual, inefficacious, invalid, nonactive, null and void, on the fritz (*U.S. slang*), out of action, out of commission, out of order, out of service, unserviceable, unworkable, useless

inopportune ill-chosen, ill-timed, inappropriate, inauspicious, inconvenient, malapropos, mistimed, unfavourable, unfortunate, unpropitious, unseasonable, unsuitable, untimely
▷ **Antonyms** appropriate, auspicious, convenient, favourable, fortunate, opportune, seasonable, suitable, timely, well-timed

inordinate disproportionate, excessive, exorbitant, extravagant, immoderate, intemperate, preposterous, unconscionable, undue, unreasonable, unrestrained, unwarranted
▷ **Antonyms** inhibited, moderate, reasonable, restrained, rightful, sensible, temperate

inorganic artificial, chemical, man-made, mineral

inquest inquiry, inquisition, investigation, probe

inquietude anxiety, apprehension, disquiet, disquietude, jumpiness, nervousness, restlessness, the jitters (*informal*), trepidation, unease, uneasiness, worry

inquire 1. examine, explore, inspect, investigate, look into, make inquiries, probe, research, scrutinize, search **2.** *also* **enquire** ask, query, question, request information, seek information

inquiring analytical, curious, doubtful, inquisitive, interested, investigative, nosy (*informal*), outward-looking, probing, questioning, searching, wondering

inquiry 1. examination, exploration, inquest, interrogation, investigation, probe, research, scrutiny, search, study, survey **2.** *also* **enquiry** query, question

inquisition cross-examination, examination, grilling (*informal*), inquest, inquiry, investigation, question, quizzing, third degree (*informal*)

inquisitive curious, inquiring, intrusive, nosy (*informal*), nosy-parkering (*informal*), peering, probing, prying, questioning, scrutinizing, snooping (*informal*), snoopy (*informal*)
▷ **Antonyms** apathetic, incurious, indifferent, unconcerned, uninterested, unquestioning

inroad 1. advance, encroachment, foray, incursion, intrusion, invasion, irruption, onslaught, raid **2. make inroads upon** consume, eat away, eat up *or* into, encroach upon, use up

insalubrious injurious, insanitary, noxious, unhealthful, unhealthy, unwholesome

insane 1. as daft as a brush (*informal, chiefly Brit.*), barking (*slang*), barking mad (*slang*), crackpot (*informal*), crazed, crazy, demented, deranged, doolally (*slang*), gaga (*informal*), gonzo (*slang*), loopy (*informal*), mad, mentally disordered, mentally ill, *non compos mentis,* not the full shilling (*informal*), off one's trolley (*slang*), of unsound mind, out of one's mind, out to lunch (*informal*), unhinged, up the pole (*informal*), wacko *or* whacko (*informal*) **2.** barking (*slang*), barking mad (*slang*), barmy (*slang*), batty (*slang*), bonkers (*slang, chiefly Brit.*), cracked (*slang*), crackers (*Brit. slang*), cuckoo (*informal*), having a screw loose (*informal*), loony (*slang*), loopy (*informal*), mental (*slang*), not right in the head, nuts (*slang*), nutty (*slang*), off one's chump (*slang*), off one's head (*slang*), off one's nut (*slang*), off one's rocker (*slang*), off one's trolley (*slang*), round the bend (*informal*), round the twist (*informal*), screwy (*informal*) **3.** bizarre, daft (*informal*), fatuous, foolish, idiotic, impractical, inane, irrational, irresponsible, lunatic, preposterous, senseless, stupid
▷ **Antonyms** logical, lucid, normal, practical, rational, reasonable, reasoned, sane, sensible, sound

insanitary contaminated, dirtied, dirty, disease-ridden, feculent, filthy, impure, infected, infested, insalubrious, noxious, polluted, unclean, unhealthy, unhygienic
▷ **Antonyms** clean, healthy, hygienic, pure, salubrious, unpolluted

insanity 1. aberration, craziness, delirium, dementia, frenzy, madness, mental derangement, mental disorder, mental illness **2.** folly, irresponsibility, lunacy, preposterousness, senselessness, stu~

pidity
▷ **Antonyms** logic, lucidity, normality, rationality, reason, sanity, sense, soundness, wisdom

insatiable edacious, gluttonous, greedy, insatiate, intemperate, quenchless, rapacious, ravenous, unappeasable, unquenchable, voracious
▷ **Antonyms** appeasable, limited, quenchable, satiable, temperate

inscribe **1.** carve, cut, engrave, etch, impress, imprint **2.** engross, enlist, enrol, enter, record, register, write **3.** address, dedicate

inscription dedication, engraving, label, legend, lettering, saying, words

inscrutable **1.** blank, deadpan, enigmatic, impenetrable, poker-faced (*informal*), sphinxlike, unreadable **2.** hidden, incomprehensible, inexplicable, mysterious, undiscoverable, unexplainable, unfathomable, unintelligible
▷ **Antonyms** clear, comprehensible, evident, explainable, explicable, intelligible, lucid, manifest, obvious, open, palpable, patent, penetrable, plain, readable, revealing, transparent, understandable

insecure **1.** afraid, anxious, uncertain, unconfident, unsure **2.** dangerous, defenceless, exposed, hazardous, ill-protected, open to attack, perilous, unguarded, unprotected, unsafe, unshielded, vulnerable, wide-open **3.** built upon sand, flimsy, frail, insubstantial, loose, on thin ice, precarious, rickety, rocky, shaky, unreliable, unsound, unstable, unsteady, weak, wobbly
▷ **Antonyms** (*sense 1*) assured, certain, confident, decisive, secure (*senses 2 & 3*) firm, protected, reliable, safe, secure, sound, stable, steady, substantial, sure

insecurity **1.** anxiety, fear, uncertainty, unsureness, worry **2.** danger, defencelessness, hazard, peril, risk, uncertainty, vulnerability, weakness **3.** dubiety, frailness, instability, precariousness, shakiness, uncertainty, unreliability, unsteadiness, weakness
▷ **Antonyms** (*sense 1*) assurance, certainty, confidencc, security (*senses 2 & 3*) dependability, firmness, reliability, safety, security, stability, steadiness

insensate **1.** anaesthetized, dead, inanimate, inert, insensible, insentient, lifeless, numbed, out (*informal*), unconscious **2.** hardened, imperceptive, impercipient, indifferent, insensitive, inured, obtuse, stolid, thick-skinned, thoughtless, unfeeling, unperceiving **3.** brainless, fatuous, foolish, mindless, senseless, stupid, thoughtless, unreasonable, witless

insensibility **1.** apathy, callousness, dullness, indifference, inertia, insensitivity, lethargy, thoughtlessness, torpor **2.** inertness, numbness, unconsciousness

insensible **1.** anaesthetized, benumbed, dull, inert, insensate, numbed, senseless, stupid, torpid **2.** apathetic, callous, cold, deaf, hard-hearted, impassive, impervious, indifferent, oblivious, unaffected, unaware, unconscious, unfeeling, unmindful, unmoved, unresponsive, unsusceptible, untouched **3.** imperceivable, imperceptible, minuscule, negligible, unnoticeable
▷ **Antonyms** (*sense 2*) affected, aware, conscious, feeling, mindful, responsive, sensible

insensibly by degrees, gradually, imperceptibly, invisibly, little by little, slightly, unnoticeably

insensitive **1.** callous, crass, hardened, imperceptive, indifferent, obtuse, tactless, thick-skinned, tough, uncaring, unconcerned, unfeeling, unresponsive, unsusceptible **2.** (*with* **to**) dead to, immune to, impervious to, nonreactive, proof against, unaffected by, unmoved by
▷ **Antonyms** (*sense 1*) caring, concerned, perceptive, responsive, sensitive, sentient, susceptible, tactful, tender

inseparable **1.** conjoined, inalienable, indissoluble, indivisible, inseverable **2.** bosom, close, devoted, intimate

insert embed, enter, implant, infix, interject, interpolate, interpose, introduce, place, pop in (*informal*), put, set, stick in, tuck in, work in
▷ **Antonyms** delete, extract, pull out, remove, take out, withdraw

insertion addition, implant, inclusion, insert, inset, interpolation, introduction, supplement

inside *noun* **1.** contents, inner part, interior **2.** (*often plural*) *informal* belly, bowels, entrails, gut, guts, innards (*informal*), internal organs, stomach, viscera, vitals *~adverb* **3.** indoors, under cover, within *~adjective* **4.** inner, innermost, interior, internal, intramural, inward **5.** classified, confidential, esoteric, exclusive, internal, limited, private, restricted, secret
▷ **Antonyms** (*sense 4*) exterior, external, extramural, outer, outermost, outside, outward

insidious artful, crafty, crooked, cunning, deceitful, deceptive, designing, disingenuous, duplicitous, guileful, intriguing, Machiavellian, slick, sly, smooth, sneaking, stealthy, subtle, surreptitious, treacherous, tricky, wily
▷ **Antonyms** artless, conspicuous, forthright, harmless, honest, ingenuous, obvious, open, sincere, straightforward, upright

insight acumen, awareness, comprehension, discernment, intuition, intuitiveness, judgment, observation, penetration, perception, perspicacity, understanding, vision

insightful astute, discerning, knowledgeable, observant, penetrating, perceptive, perspicacious, sagacious, shrewd, understanding, wise

insignia badge, crest, decoration, distinguishing mark, earmark, emblem, ensign, symbol

insignificance immateriality, inconsequence, irrelevance, meaninglessness, negligibility, paltriness, pettiness, triviality, unimportance, worthlessness
▷ **Antonyms** consequence, importance, matter, meaningfulness, relevance, significance, weight, worth

insignificant flimsy, immaterial, inconsequential, inconsiderable, irrelevant, meagre, meaningless, measly, minor, negligible, nickel-and-dime (*U.S. slang*), nondescript, nonessential, not worth mentioning, nugatory, of no account, of no consequence, of no moment, paltry, petty, scanty, small potatoes, trifling, trivial, unimportant, unsubstantial, wanky (*taboo slang*)
▷ **Antonyms** consequential, considerable, essential, important, meaningful, momentous, relevant, significant, substantial, vital, weighty

insincere deceitful, deceptive, devious, dishonest, disingenuous, dissembling, dissimulating, double-dealing, duplicitous, evasive, faithless, false, hollow, hypocritical, Janus-faced, lying, mendacious, perfidious, pretended, two-faced, unfaithful, untrue, untruthful, with tongue in cheek
▷ **Antonyms** direct, earnest, faithful, genuine, honest, sincere, straightforward, true, truthful

insincerity deceitfulness, deviousness, dishonesty, disingenuousness, dissimulation, duplicity, faithlessness, hypocrisy, lip service, mendacity, perfidy, pretence, untruthfulness
▷ **Antonyms** directness, faithfulness, honesty, sincerity, truthfulness

insinuate 1. allude, hint, imply, indicate, intimate, suggest **2.** infiltrate, infuse, inject, instil, introduce **3.** curry favour, get in with, ingratiate, worm *or* work one's way in

insinuation 1. allusion, aspersion, hint, implication, innuendo, slur, suggestion **2.** infiltration, infusion, ingratiating, injection, instillation, introduction

insipid 1. anaemic, banal, bland, characterless, colourless, drab, dry, dull, flat, ho-hum (*informal*), jejune, lifeless, limp, pointless, prosaic, prosy, spiritless, stale, stupid, tame, tedious, tiresome, trite, unimaginative, uninteresting, vapid, weak, wearisome, wishy-washy (*informal*) **2.** bland, flavourless, savourless, tasteless, unappetizing, watered down, watery, wishy-washy (*informal*)
▷ **Antonyms** (*sense 1*) colourful, engaging, exciting, interesting, lively, provocative, spirited, stimulating (*sense 2*) appetizing, fiery, palatable, piquant, pungent, savoury, tasteful

insipidity, insipidness 1. banality, colourlessness, dullness, flatness, lack of imagination, pointlessness, staleness, tameness, tediousness, triteness, uninterestingness, vapidity **2.** blandness, flavourlessness, lack of flavour, tastelessness
▷ **Antonyms** (*sense 1*) animation, character, dynamism, gaiety, liveliness, spirit, vitality, vivacity

insist 1. be firm, brook no refusal, demand, lay down the law, not take no for an answer, persist, press (someone), put one's foot down (*informal*), require, stand firm, stand one's ground, take *or* make a stand, urge **2.** assert, asseverate, aver, claim, contend, hold, maintain, reiterate, repeat, swear, urge, vow

insistence assertion, contention, demands, emphasis, importunity, insistency, persistence, pressing, reiteration, stress, urging

insistent demanding, dogged, emphatic, exigent, forceful, importunate, incessant, peremptory, persevering, persistent, pressing, unrelenting, urgent

insobriety crapulence, drunkenness, inebriety, intemperance, intoxication

insolence abuse, audacity, backchat (*informal*), boldness, cheek (*informal*), chutzpah (*U.S. & Canad. informal*), contemptuousness, contumely, disrespect, effrontery, front, gall (*informal*), impertinence, impudence, incivility, insubordination, offensiveness, pertness, rudeness, sassiness (*U.S. informal*), sauce (*informal*), uncivility
▷ **Antonyms** civility, courtesy, deference, esteem, mannerliness, politeness, respect, submission

insolent abusive, bold, brazen-faced, contemptuous, fresh (*informal*), impertinent, impudent, insubordinate, insulting, pert, rude, saucy, uncivil
▷ **Antonyms** civil, courteous, deferential, mannerly, polite, respectful, submissive

insoluble baffling, impenetrable, indecipherable, inexplicable, mysterious, mystifying, obscure, unaccountable, unfathomable, unsolvable
▷ **Antonyms** accountable, comprehensible, explicable, fathomable, penetrable, soluble, solvable

insolvency bankruptcy, failure, liquidation, ruin

insolvent bankrupt, broke (*informal*), failed, gone bust (*informal*), gone to the wall, in queer street (*informal*), in receivership, in the hands of the receivers, on the rocks (*informal*), ruined

insomnia sleeplessness, wakefulness

insouciance airiness, breeziness, care~

freeness, jauntiness, light-heartedness, nonchalance

insouciant airy, breezy, buoyant, care~free, casual, free and easy, gay, happy-go-lucky, jaunty, light-hearted, noncha~lant, sunny, unconcerned, untroubled, unworried

inspect audit, check, check out (*infor~mal*), examine, eye, eyeball (*U.S. slang*), give (something *or* someone) the once-over (*informal*), go over *or* through, in~vestigate, look over, oversee, recce (*slang*), research, scan, scrutinize, search, superintend, supervise, survey, take a dekko at (*Brit. slang*), vet, work over

inspection check, checkup, examination, investigation, look-over, once-over (*in~formal*), recce (*slang*), review, scan, scrutiny, search, superintendence, supervision, surveillance, survey

inspector censor, checker, critic, examin~er, investigator, overseer, scrutineer, scrutinizer, superintendent, supervisor

inspiration **1.** arousal, awakening, en~couragement, influence, muse, spur, stimulus **2.** afflatus, creativity, eleva~tion, enthusiasm, exaltation, genius, il~lumination, insight, revelation, stimu~lation

▷ **Antonyms** depressant, deterrent, dis~couragement, disenchantment

inspire **1.** animate, be responsible for, en~courage, enliven, fire *or* touch the im~agination of, galvanize, hearten, imbue, influence, infuse, inspirit, instil, rouse, spark off, spur, stimulate **2.** arouse, en~kindle, excite, give rise to, produce, quicken, rouse, stir

▷ **Antonyms** daunt, deflate, depress, discourage, disenchant, dishearten, dis~pirit

inspired **1.** brilliant, dazzling, enthralling, exciting, impressive, memorable, of ge~nius, outstanding, superlative, thrilling, wonderful **2.** *of a guess* instinctive, in~stinctual, intuitive **3.** aroused, elated, enthused, exalted, exhilarated, galva~nized, possessed, stimulated, stirred up, uplifted

inspiring affecting, encouraging, exciting, exhilarating, heartening, moving, rous~ing, stimulating, stirring, uplifting

▷ **Antonyms** boring, depressing, dis~couraging, disheartening, dispiriting, dull, uninspiring

inspirit animate, cheer, embolden, en~courage, enliven, exhilarate, fire, galva~nize, give hope to, hearten, incite, in~spire, invigorate, move, nerve, put (new) heart into, rouse, stimulate

instability capriciousness, changeable~ness, disequilibrium, fickleness, fitful~ness, fluctuation, fluidity, frailty, im~balance, impermanence, inconstancy, insecurity, irresolution, mutability, os~cillation, precariousness, restlessness, shakiness, transience, unpredictability, unsteadiness, vacillation, variability, volatility, wavering, weakness

▷ **Antonyms** balance, constancy, equilib~rium, permanence, predictability, reso~lution, security, stability, steadiness, strength

install, instal **1.** fix, lay, lodge, place, posi~tion, put in, set up, station **2.** establish, inaugurate, induct, instate, institute, introduce, invest, set up **3.** ensconce, po~sition, settle

installation **1.** establishment, fitting, in~stalment, placing, positioning, setting up **2.** inauguration, induction, instate~ment, investiture **3.** equipment, ma~chinery, plant, system **4.** *Military* base, establishment, post, station

instalment chapter, division, episode, part, portion, repayment, section

instance *noun* **1.** case, case in point, ex~ample, illustration, occasion, occur~rence, precedent, situation, time **2.** ap~plication, behest, demand, entreaty, im~portunity, impulse, incitement, insist~ence, instigation, pressure, prompting, request, solicitation, urging *~verb* **3.** ad~duce, cite, mention, name, quote, specify

instant *noun* **1.** bat of an eye (*informal*), flash, jiffy (*informal*), moment, second, shake (*informal*), split second, tick (*Brit. informal*), trice, twinkling, twinkling of an eye (*informal*), two shakes of a lamb's tail (*informal*) **2. on the instant** forthwith, immediately, instantly, now, right away, without delay **3.** juncture, moment, occasion, point, time *~adjective* **4.** direct, immediate, instantaneous, on-the-spot, prompt, quick, quickie (*in~formal*), split-second, urgent **5.** conveni~ence, fast, precooked, ready-mixed **6.** burning, exigent, imperative, importu~nate, pressing, urgent

instantaneous direct, immediate, instant, on-the-spot, prompt

instantaneously at once, forthwith, im~mediately, in a fraction of a second, in~stantly, in the bat of an eye (*informal*), in the same breath, in the twinkling of an eye (*informal*), like a bat out of hell (*slang*), like greased lightning (*infor~mal*), on the instant, on the spot, post~haste, promptly, pronto (*informal*), quick as lightning, straight away, then and there

instantly at once, directly, forthwith, im~mediately, instantaneously, instanter (*Law*), now, on the spot, posthaste, pronto (*informal*), right away, right now, straight away, there and then, this minute, *tout de suite,* without delay

instate establish, inaugurate, induct, in~stall, invest, put in office

instead **1.** alternatively, in lieu, in pref~erence, on second thoughts, preferably, rather **2.** (*with* **of**) as an alternative *or* equivalent to, in lieu of, in place of, rather than

instigate actuate, bring about, encourage, foment, get going, impel, incite, influence, initiate, kick-start, kindle, move, persuade, prod, prompt, provoke, rouse, set off, set on, spur, start, stimulate, stir up, trigger, urge, whip up

▷ **Antonyms** discourage, repress, restrain, stop, suppress

instigation behest, bidding, encouragement, incentive, incitement, prompting, urging

instigator agitator, firebrand, fomenter, goad, incendiary, inciter, leader, mischief-maker, motivator, prime mover, ringleader, spur, stirrer (*informal*), troublemaker

instil, instill engender, engraft, imbue, implant, impress, inculcate, infix, infuse, insinuate, introduce, sow the seeds

instinct aptitude, faculty, feeling, gift, gut feeling (*informal*), gut reaction (*informal*), impulse, intuition, knack, natural inclination, predisposition, proclivity, sixth sense, talent, tendency, urge

instinctive automatic, inborn, inherent, innate, instinctual, intuitional, intuitive, involuntary, mechanical, native, natural, reflex, spontaneous, unlearned, unpremeditated, unthinking, visceral

▷ **Antonyms** acquired, calculated, considered, learned, mindful, premeditated, thinking, voluntary, willed

instinctively automatically, by instinct, in one's bones, intuitively, involuntarily, naturally, without thinking

institute[1] *verb* appoint, begin, bring into being, commence, constitute, enact, establish, fix, found, induct, initiate, install, introduce, invest, launch, ordain, organize, originate, pioneer, put into operation, set in motion, settle, set up, start

▷ **Antonyms** abandon, abolish, cancel, cease, discontinue, end, stop, suspend, terminate

institute[2] *noun* **1.** academy, association, college, conservatory, foundation, guild, institution, school, seat of learning, seminary, society **2.** custom, decree, doctrine, dogma, edict, law, maxim, precedent, precept, principle, regulation, rule, tenet

institution 1. constitution, creation, enactment, establishment, formation, foundation, initiation, introduction, investiture, investment, organization **2.** academy, college, establishment, foundation, hospital, institute, school, seminary, society, university **3.** convention, custom, fixture, law, practice, ritual, rule, tradition

institutional 1. accepted, bureaucratic, conventional, established, establishment (*informal*), formal, organized, orthodox, societal **2.** cheerless, clinical, cold, drab, dreary, dull, forbidding, formal, impersonal, monotonous, regimented, routine, uniform, unwelcoming

instruct 1. bid, canon, charge, command, direct, enjoin, order, tell **2.** coach, discipline, drill, educate, enlighten, ground, guide, inform, school, teach, train, tutor **3.** acquaint, advise, apprise, brief, counsel, inform, notify, tell

instruction 1. apprenticeship, coaching, discipline, drilling, education, enlightenment, grounding, guidance, information, lesson(s), preparation, schooling, teaching, training, tuition, tutelage **2.** briefing, command, demand, direction, directive, injunction, mandate, order, ruling

instructions advice, directions, guidance, information, key, orders, recommendations, rules

instructive cautionary, didactic, edifying, educational, enlightening, helpful, illuminating, informative, instructional, revealing, useful

instructor adviser, coach, demonstrator, exponent, guide, handler, master, mentor, mistress, pedagogue, preceptor (*rare*), schoolmaster, schoolmistress, teacher, trainer, tutor

instrument 1. apparatus, appliance, contraption (*informal*), contrivance, device, gadget, implement, mechanism, tool, utensil **2.** agency, agent, channel, factor, force, means, mechanism, medium, organ, vehicle **3.** *informal* cat's-paw, dupe, pawn, puppet, tool

instrumental active, assisting, auxiliary, conducive, contributory, helpful, helping, influential, involved, of help *or* service, subsidiary, useful

instrumentality agency, assistance, good offices, intercession, intervention, mediation, medium, vehicle

insubordinate contumacious, defiant, disobedient, disorderly, fractious, insurgent, mutinous, rebellious, recalcitrant, refractory, riotous, seditious, turbulent, undisciplined, ungovernable, unruly

▷ **Antonyms** compliant, deferential, disciplined, docile, obedient, orderly, submissive, subservient

insubordination defiance, disobedience, indiscipline, insurrection, mutinousness, mutiny, rebellion, recalcitrance, revolt, riotousness, sedition, ungovernability

▷ **Antonyms** acquiescence, compliance, deference, discipline, docility, obedience, submission, subordination

insubstantial 1. feeble, flimsy, frail, poor, slight, tenuous, thin, weak **2.** chimerical, ephemeral, false, fanciful, idle, illusory, imaginary, immaterial, incorporeal, unreal

▷ **Antonyms** (*sense 1*) firm, solid, strong, substantial, weighty

insufferable detestable, dreadful, enough to test the patience of a saint, enough to try the patience of Job, impossible, insupportable, intolerable, more than flesh and blood can stand, outrageous, past bearing, too much, unbearable, unendurable, unspeakable
▷ **Antonyms** appealing, attractive, bearable, charming, disarming, pleasant

insufficiency dearth, deficiency, inadequacy, inadequateness, lack, paucity, poverty, scantiness, scarcity, shortage, short supply, want

insufficient deficient, inadequate, incapable, incommensurate, incompetent, lacking, scant, short, unfitted, unqualified
▷ **Antonyms** adequate, ample, commensurate, competent, enough, plentiful, qualified, sufficient

insular *figurative* blinkered, circumscribed, closed, contracted, cut off, illiberal, inward-looking, isolated, limited, narrow, narrow-minded, parish-pump, parochial, petty, prejudiced, provincial
▷ **Antonyms** broad-minded, cosmopolitan, experienced, liberal, open-minded, tolerant, worldly

insulate *figurative* close off, cocoon, cushion, cut off, isolate, protect, sequester, shield, wrap up in cotton wool

insult 1. *noun* abuse, affront, aspersion, contumely, indignity, insolence, offence, outrage, put-down, rudeness, slap in the face (*informal*), slight, snub **2.** *~verb* abuse, affront, call names, give offence to, injure, miscall (*dialect*), offend, outrage, put down, revile, slag (off) (*slang*), slander, slight, snub
▷ **Antonyms** *~noun* compliment, flattery, honour *~verb* flatter, please, praise

insulting abusive, affronting, contemptuous, degrading, disparaging, insolent, offensive, rude, scurrilous, slighting
▷ **Antonyms** complimentary, deferential, flattering, laudatory, respectful

insuperable impassable, insurmountable, invincible, unconquerable
▷ **Antonyms** conquerable, possible, surmountable

insupportable 1. insufferable, intolerable, past bearing, unbearable, unendurable **2.** indefensible, unjustifiable, untenable

insurance assurance, cover, coverage, guarantee, indemnification, indemnity, protection, provision, safeguard, security, something to fall back on (*informal*), warranty

insure assure, cover, guarantee, indemnify, underwrite, warrant

insurgent 1. *noun* insurrectionist, mutineer, rebel, resister, revolter, revolutionary, revolutionist, rioter **2.** *~adjective* disobedient, insubordinate, insurrectionary, mutinous, rebellious, revolting, revolutionary, riotous, seditious

insurmountable hopeless, impassable, impossible, insuperable, invincible, overwhelming, unconquerable

insurrection coup, insurgency, mutiny, putsch, rebellion, revolt, revolution, riot, rising, sedition, uprising

insusceptible immovable, immune, indifferent, insensible, insensitive, proof against, unimpressible, unmoved, unresponsive

intact all in one piece, complete, entire, perfect, scatheless, sound, together, unbroken, undamaged, undefiled, unharmed, unhurt, unimpaired, uninjured, unscathed, untouched, unviolated, virgin, whole
▷ **Antonyms** broken, damaged, harmed, impaired, injured

intangible airy, dim, elusive, ethereal, evanescent, impalpable, imperceptible, incorporeal, indefinite, invisible, shadowy, unreal, unsubstantial, vague

integral 1. basic, component, constituent, elemental, essential, fundamental, indispensable, intrinsic, necessary, requisite **2.** complete, entire, full, intact, undivided, whole
▷ **Antonyms** fractional, inessential, unimportant, unnecessary

integrate accommodate, amalgamate, assimilate, blend, coalesce, combine, fuse, harmonize, incorporate, intermix, join, knit, meld, merge, mesh, unite
▷ **Antonyms** disperse, divide, segregate, separate

integration amalgamation, assimilation, blending, combining, commingling, fusing, harmony, incorporation, mixing, unification

integrity 1. candour, goodness, honesty, honour, incorruptibility, principle, probity, purity, rectitude, righteousness, uprightness, virtue **2.** coherence, cohesion, completeness, soundness, unity, wholeness
▷ **Antonyms** (*sense 1*) corruption, deceit, dishonesty, disrepute, duplicity, faultiness, flimsiness, fragility, immorality, uncertainty, unsoundness

intellect 1. brains (*informal*), intelligence, judgment, mind, reason, sense, understanding **2.** *informal* brain (*informal*), egghead (*informal*), genius, intellectual, intelligence, mind, thinker

intellectual 1. *adjective* bookish, cerebral, highbrow, intelligent, mental, rational, scholarly, studious, thoughtful **2.** *~noun* academic, bluestocking (*usually disparaging*), egghead (*informal*), highbrow, thinker
▷ **Antonyms** *~adjective* ignorant, illiterate, material, physical, stupid, unintellectual, unlearned *~noun* idiot, moron

intelligence **1.** acumen, alertness, apti~ tude, brain power, brains (*informal*), brightness, capacity, cleverness, com~ prehension, discernment, grey matter (*informal*), intellect, mind, nous (*Brit. slang*), penetration, perception, quick~ ness, reason, sense, smarts (*slang, chiefly U.S.*), understanding **2.** advice, data, disclosure, facts, findings, gen (*Brit. informal*), information, knowl~ edge, low-down (*informal*), news, notice, notification, report, rumour, tidings, tip-off, word

▷ **Antonyms** (*sense 1*) dullness, igno~ rance, stupidity (*sense 2*) concealment, misinformation

intelligent acute, alert, apt, brainy (*infor~ mal*), bright, clever, discerning, enlight~ ened, instructed, knowing, penetrating, perspicacious, quick, quick-witted, ra~ tional, sharp, smart, thinking, well-informed

▷ **Antonyms** dim-witted, dull, foolish, ignorant, obtuse, stupid, unintelligent

intelligentsia eggheads (*informal*), high~ brows, illuminati, intellectuals, literati, masterminds, the learned

intelligibility clarity, clearness, compre~ hensibility, distinctness, explicitness, lucidity, plainness, precision, simplicity

intelligible clear, comprehensible, dis~ tinct, lucid, open, plain, understandable

▷ **Antonyms** confused, garbled, incom~ prehensible, puzzling, unclear, unintel~ ligible

intemperance crapulence, excess, ex~ travagance, immoderation, inebriation, insobriety, intoxication, overindulgence, unrestraint

intemperate excessive, extravagant, ex~ treme, immoderate, incontinent, inordi~ nate, intoxicated, O.T.T. (*slang*), over the top (*slang*), passionate, prodigal, profligate, self-indulgent, severe, tem~ pestuous, unbridled, uncontrollable, ungovernable, unrestrained, violent, wild

▷ **Antonyms** continent, disciplined, moderate, restrained, self-controlled, temperate

intend **1.** aim, be resolved *or* determined, contemplate, determine, have in mind *or* view, mean, meditate, plan, propose, purpose, scheme **2.** (*often with* **for**) aim, consign, design, destine, earmark, mark out, mean, set apart

intended **1.** *adjective* betrothed, destined, future, planned, proposed **2.** *~noun in~ formal* betrothed, fiancé, fiancée, future wife *or* husband, husband- *or* wife-to-be

intense **1.** acute, agonizing, close, concen~ trated, deep, drastic, excessive, exquis~ ite, extreme, fierce, forceful, great, harsh, intensive, powerful, profound, protracted, serious (*informal*), severe, strained, unqualified **2.** ardent, burning, consuming, eager, earnest, energetic, fanatical, fervent, fervid, fierce, flaming, forcible, heightened, impassioned, keen, passionate, speaking, vehement

▷ **Antonyms** (*sense 1*) easy, gentle, mild, moderate, relaxed, slight (*sense 2*) cas~ ual, cool, indifferent, subdued, weak

intensely deeply, extremely, fiercely, passionately, profoundly, seriously (*in~ formal*), strongly

intensify add fuel to the flames (*infor~ mal*), add to, aggravate, augment, boost, concentrate, deepen, emphasize, en~ hance, escalate, exacerbate, fan the flames of, heighten, increase, magnify, quicken, redouble, reinforce, set off, sharpen, step up (*informal*), strengthen, whet

▷ **Antonyms** damp down, decrease, di~ lute, diminish, dull, lessen, minimize, weaken

intensity ardour, concentration, depth, earnestness, emotion, energy, excess, extremity, fanaticism, fervency, fervour, fierceness, fire, force, intenseness, keenness, passion, potency, power, se~ verity, strain, strength, tension, vehe~ mence, vigour

intensive all-out, comprehensive, concen~ trated, demanding, exhaustive, in-depth, thorough, thoroughgoing

▷ **Antonyms** apathetic, careless, feeble, hit-or-miss, superficial, weakened

intent *adjective* **1.** absorbed, alert, atten~ tive, committed, concentrated, deter~ mined, eager, earnest, engrossed, fixed, industrious, intense, occupied, piercing, preoccupied, rapt, resolute, resolved, steadfast, steady, watchful, wrapped up **2.** bent, hellbent (*informal*), set *~noun* **3.** aim, design, end, goal, intention, mean~ ing, object, objective, plan, purpose **4. to all intents and purposes** as good as, practically, virtually

▷ **Antonyms** *~adjective* (*sense 1*) casual, indifferent, irresolute, unsteady, wa~ vering *~noun* chance, fortune

intention aim, design, end, end in view, goal, idea, intent, meaning, object, ob~ jective, point, purpose, scope, target, view

intentional calculated, deliberate, de~ signed, done on purpose, intended, meant, planned, prearranged, precon~ certed, premeditated, purposed, studied, wilful

▷ **Antonyms** accidental, inadvertent, unintentional, unplanned

intentionally by design, deliberately, de~ signedly, on purpose, wilfully

intently attentively, closely, fixedly, hard, keenly, searchingly, steadily, watchfully

inter bury, entomb, inhume, inurn, lay to rest, sepulchre

intercede advocate, arbitrate, interpose, intervene, mediate, plead, speak

intercept arrest, block, catch, check, cut off, deflect, head off, interrupt, obstruct, seize, stop, take

intercession advocacy, entreaty, good offices, intervention, mediation, plea, pleading, prayer, solicitation, supplication

intercessor advocate, arbitrator, go-between, interceder, intermediary, mediator, middleman, negotiator, pleader

interchange 1. *verb* alternate, bandy, barter, exchange, reciprocate, swap (*informal*), switch, trade 2. *~noun* alternation, crossfire, exchange, give and take, intersection, junction, reciprocation

interchangeable commutable, equivalent, exchangeable, identical, reciprocal, synonymous, the same, transposable

intercourse 1. association, commerce, communication, communion, connection, contact, converse, correspondence, dealings, intercommunication, trade, traffic, truck 2. carnal knowledge, coition, coitus, congress, copulation, intimacy, legover (*slang*), nookie (*slang*), rumpy-pumpy (*slang*), sex (*informal*), sexual act, sexual intercourse, sexual relations, the other (*informal*)

interdict 1. *verb* ban, bar, debar, disallow, forbid, outlaw, prevent, prohibit, proscribe, veto 2. *~noun* ban, disallowance, disqualification, interdiction, prohibition, taboo, veto

interest *noun* 1. affection, attention, attentiveness, attraction, concern, curiosity, notice, regard, suspicion, sympathy 2. concern, consequence, importance, moment, note, relevance, significance, weight 3. activity, diversion, hobby, leisure activity, pastime, preoccupation, pursuit, relaxation 4. advantage, benefit, gain, good, profit 5. **in the interest of** for the sake of, on behalf of, on the part of, profitable to, to the advantage of 6. authority, claim, commitment, influence, investment, involvement, participation, portion, right, share, stake 7. (*often plural*) affair, business, care, concern, matter *~verb* 8. amuse, arouse one's curiosity, attract, catch one's eye, divert, engross, fascinate, hold the attention of, intrigue, move, touch 9. affect, concern, engage, involve

▷ **Antonyms** *~noun* (*sense 1*) boredom, coolness, disinterest, dispassion, disregard, unconcern (*sense 2*) inconsequence, insignificance, irrelevance, worthlessness *~verb* bore, burden, irk, repel, tire, weary

interested 1. affected, attentive, attracted, curious, drawn, excited, fascinated, intent, into (*informal*), keen, moved, responsive, stimulated 2. biased, concerned, implicated, involved, partial, partisan, predisposed, prejudiced

▷ **Antonyms** (*sense 1*) apathetic, bored, detached, inattentive, indifferent, unconcerned, uninterested, wearied

interesting absorbing, amusing, appealing, attractive, compelling, curious, engaging, engrossing, entertaining, gripping, intriguing, pleasing, provocative, stimulating, stirring, suspicious, thought-provoking, unusual

▷ **Antonyms** boring, dull, mind-numbing, tedious, tiresome, uninteresting

interfere 1. butt in, get involved, intermeddle, intervene, intrude, meddle, poke one's nose in (*informal*), put one's two cents in (*U.S. slang*), stick one's oar in (*informal*), tamper 2. (*often with* **with**) be a drag upon (*informal*), block, clash, collide, conflict, cramp, frustrate, get in the way of, hamper, handicap, hinder, impede, inhibit, obstruct, trammel

interference 1. intermeddling, intervention, intrusion, meddlesomeness, meddling, prying 2. clashing, collision, conflict, impedance, obstruction, opposition

interim 1. *adjective* acting, caretaker, improvised, intervening, makeshift, pro tem, provisional, stopgap, temporary 2. *~noun* entr'acte, interregnum, interval, meantime, meanwhile, respite

interior *adjective* 1. inner, inside, internal, inward 2. *Geography* central, inland, remote, upcountry 3. *Politics* domestic, home 4. hidden, inner, intimate, mental, personal, private, secret, spiritual *~noun* 5. bosom, centre, contents, core, heart, innards (*informal*), inside 6. *Geography* centre, heartland, upcountry

▷ **Antonyms** (*sense 1*) exposed, exterior, external, outer, outside, outward

interject interpolate, interpose, interrupt with, introduce, put in, throw in

interjection cry, ejaculation, exclamation, interpolation, interposition

interlace braid, cross, entwine, interlock, intersperse, intertwine, interweave, interwreathe, knit, plait, reticulate, twine

interlink interconnect, interlock, intertwine, interweave, knit, link, mesh

interloper gate-crasher (*informal*), intermeddler, intruder, meddler, trespasser, uninvited guest, unwanted visitor

interlude break, breathing space, delay, entr'acte, episode, halt, hiatus, intermission, interval, pause, respite, rest, spell, stop, stoppage, wait

intermediary *noun* agent, broker, entrepreneur, go-between, mediator, middleman

intermediate halfway, in-between (*informal*), intermediary, interposed, intervening, mean, mid, middle, midway, transitional

interment burial, burying, funeral, inhumation, sepulture

interminable boundless, ceaseless, dragging, endless, everlasting, immeasurable, infinite, limitless, long, long-drawn-out, long-winded, never-ending, perpetual, protracted, unbounded, unlimited, wearisome
▷ **Antonyms** bounded, finite, limited, measurable, restricted, temporary

intermingle amalgamate, blend, combine, commingle, commix, fuse, interlace, intermix, interweave, meld, merge, mix

intermission break, breathing space, cessation, entr'acte, interlude, interruption, interval, let-up (*informal*), lull, pause, recess, respite, rest, stop, stoppage, suspense, suspension

intermittent broken, discontinuous, fitful, irregular, occasional, periodic, punctuated, recurrent, recurring, spasmodic, sporadic, stop-go (*informal*)
▷ **Antonyms** continuous, steady, unceasing

intern confine, detain, hold, hold in custody

internal **1.** inner, inside, interior, intimate, private, subjective **2.** civic, domestic, home, in-house, intramural
▷ **Antonyms** (*sense 1*) exposed, exterior, external, outer, outermost, outside, revealed, unconcealed

international cosmopolitan, ecumenical (*rare*), global, intercontinental, universal, worldwide

internecine bloody, deadly, destructive, exterminating, exterminatory, fatal, mortal, ruinous

interplay give-and-take, interaction, meshing, reciprocation, reciprocity

interpolate add, insert, intercalate, introduce

interpolation addition, aside, insert, insertion, intercalation, interjection, introduction

interpose **1.** come *or* place between, intercede, interfere, intermediate, intervene, intrude, mediate, step in **2.** insert, interject, interrupt (with), introduce, put forth, put one's oar in

interpret adapt, clarify, construe, decipher, decode, define, elucidate, explain, explicate, expound, make sense of, paraphrase, read, render, solve, spell out, take, throw light on, translate, understand

interpretation analysis, clarification, construction, diagnosis, elucidation, exegesis, explanation, explication, exposition, meaning, performance, portrayal, reading, rendering, rendition, sense, signification, translation, understanding, version

interpreter annotator, commentator, exponent, scholiast, translator

interrogate ask, catechize, cross-examine, cross-question, enquire, examine, give (someone) the third degree (*informal*), grill (*informal*), inquire, investigate, pump, put the screws on (*informal*), question, quiz

interrogation cross-examination, cross-questioning, enquiry, examination, grilling (*informal*), inquiry, inquisition, probing, questioning, third degree (*informal*)

interrogative curious, inquiring, inquisitive, inquisitorial, questioning, quizzical

interrupt barge in (*informal*), break, break in, break off, break (someone's) train of thought, butt in, check, cut, cut off, cut short, delay, disconnect, discontinue, disjoin, disturb, disunite, divide, heckle, hinder, hold up, interfere (with), intrude, lay aside, obstruct, punctuate, separate, sever, stay, stop, suspend

interrupted broken, cut off, disconnected, discontinuous, disturbed, incomplete, intermittent, uneven

interruption break, cessation, disconnection, discontinuance, disruption, dissolution, disturbance, disuniting, division, halt, hiatus, hindrance, hitch, impediment, intrusion, obstacle, obstruction, pause, separation, severance, stop, stoppage, suspension

intersect bisect, crisscross, cross, cut, cut across, divide, meet

intersection crossing, crossroads, interchange, junction

intersperse bestrew, interlard, intermix, pepper, scatter, sprinkle

interstice aperture, chink, cleft, crack, cranny, crevice, fissure, gap, interval, opening, rift, slit, space, vent

intertwine braid, convolute, cross, entwine, interlace, interweave, interwreathe, inweave, link, reticulate, twist

interval break, delay, distance, entr'acte, gap, hiatus, interim, interlude, intermission, meantime, meanwhile, opening, pause, period, playtime, respite, rest, season, space, spell, term, time, wait

intervene **1.** arbitrate, intercede, interfere, interpose oneself, intrude, involve oneself, mediate, put one's oar in, put one's two cents in (*U.S. slang*), step in (*informal*), take a hand (*informal*) **2.** befall, come to pass, ensue, happen, occur, succeed, supervene, take place

intervention agency, intercession, interference, interposition, intrusion, mediation

interview **1.** *noun* audience, conference, consultation, dialogue, evaluation, meeting, oral (examination), press conference, talk **2.** *~verb* examine, interrogate, question, sound out, talk to

interviewer examiner, interlocutor, interrogator, investigator, questioner, reporter

interweave blend, braid, crisscross, cross,

interlace, intertwine, interwreathe, inweave, reticulate, splice

interwoven blended, connected, entwined, inmixed, interconnected, interlaced, interlocked, intermingled, knit

intestinal abdominal, coeliac, duodenal, gut (*informal*), inner, stomachic, visceral

intestines bowels, entrails, guts, innards (*informal*), insides (*informal*), internal organs, viscera, vitals

intimacy closeness, confidence, confidentiality, familiarity, fraternization, understanding
▷ **Antonyms** alienation, aloofness, coldness, detachment, distance, estrangement, remoteness, separation

intimate[1] *adjective* **1.** bosom, cherished, close, confidential, dear, friendly, near, nearest and dearest, thick (*informal*), warm **2.** confidential, personal, private, privy, secret **3.** deep, detailed, exhaustive, experienced, first-hand, immediate, in-depth, penetrating, personal, profound, thorough **4.** comfy (*informal*), cosy, friendly, informal, snug, tête-à-tête, warm *~noun* **5.** bosom friend, buddy (*informal*), china (*Brit. slang*), chum (*informal*), close friend, cock (*Brit. informal*), comrade, confidant, confidante, (constant) companion, crony, familiar, friend, gossip (*archaic*), homeboy (*slang, chiefly U.S.*), mate (*informal*), mucker (*Brit. slang*), pal
▷ **Antonyms** *~adjective* (*sense 1*) distant, remote, superficial (*sense 2*) known, open, public *~noun* enemy, foe, stranger

intimate[2] *verb* allude, announce, communicate, declare, drop a hint, give (someone) to understand, hint, impart, imply, indicate, insinuate, let it be known, make known, remind, state, suggest, tip (someone) the wink (*Brit. informal*), warn

intimately 1. affectionately, closely, confidentially, confidingly, familiarly, personally, tenderly, very well, warmly **2.** fully, in detail, inside out, thoroughly, through and through, to the core, very well

intimation 1. allusion, hint, indication, inkling, insinuation, reminder, suggestion, warning **2.** announcement, communication, declaration, notice

intimidate affright (*archaic*), alarm, appal, browbeat, bully, coerce, cow, daunt, dishearten, dismay, dispirit, frighten, lean on (*informal*), overawe, scare, scare off (*informal*), subdue, terrify, terrorize, threaten, twist someone's arm (*informal*)

intimidation arm-twisting (*informal*), browbeating, bullying, coercion, fear, menaces, pressure, terror, terrorization, threat(s)

intolerable beyond bearing, excruciating, impossible, insufferable, insupportable, more than flesh and blood can stand, not to be borne, painful, unbearable, unendurable
▷ **Antonyms** bearable, endurable, painless, possible, sufferable, supportable, tolerable

intolerance bigotry, chauvinism, discrimination, dogmatism, fanaticism, illiberality, impatience, jingoism, narrow-mindedness, narrowness, prejudice, racialism, racism, xenophobia
▷ **Antonyms** broad-mindedness, liberality, open-mindedness, patience, tolerance, understanding

intolerant bigoted, chauvinistic, dictatorial, dogmatic, fanatical, illiberal, impatient, narrow, narrow-minded, one-sided, prejudiced, racialist, racist, small-minded, uncharitable, xenophobic
▷ **Antonyms** broad-minded, charitable, lenient, liberal, open-minded, patient, tolerant, understanding

intonation 1. accentuation, cadence, inflection, modulation, tone **2.** chant, incantation

intone chant, croon, intonate, recite, sing

in toto as a whole, completely, entirely, in its entirety, totally, unabridged, uncut, wholly

intoxicate 1. addle, befuddle, fuddle, go to one's head, inebriate, put (someone) under the table (*informal*), stupefy **2.** *figurative* elate, excite, exhilarate, go to one's head, inflame, make one's head spin, stimulate

intoxicated 1. babalas (*S. African*), bevvied (*dialect*), blitzed (*slang*), blotto (*slang*), bombed (*slang*), Brahms and Liszt (*slang*), canned (*slang*), cut (*Brit. slang*), drunk, drunk as a skunk, drunken, flying (*slang*), fuddled, half seas over (*Brit. informal*), high (*informal*), inebriated, in one's cups (*informal*), legless (*informal*), lit up (*slang*), out of it (*slang*), out to it (*Austral. & N.Z. slang*), paralytic (*informal*), pissed (*taboo slang*), plastered (*slang*), rat-arsed (*taboo slang*), smashed (*slang*), sozzled (*informal*), steamboats (*Scot. slang*), steaming (*slang*), stewed (*slang*), stiff (*slang*), stoned (*slang*), the worse for drink, three sheets in the wind (*informal*), tight (*informal*), tipsy, under the influence, wasted (*slang*), wrecked (*slang*), zonked (*slang*) **2.** *figurative* dizzy, elated, enraptured, euphoric, excited, exhilarated, high (*informal*), infatuated, sent (*slang*), stimulated

intoxicating 1. alcoholic, inebriant, intoxicant, spirituous, strong **2.** *figurative* exciting, exhilarating, heady, sexy (*informal*), stimulating, thrilling

intoxication 1. drunkenness, inebriation, inebriety, insobriety, tipsiness **2.** *figurative* delirium, elation, euphoria, exalta~

tion, excitement, exhilaration, infatuation

intractability awkwardness, cantankerousness, contrariness, incorrigibility, indiscipline, indocility, mulishness, obduracy, obstinacy, perverseness, perversity, pig-headedness, stubbornness, uncooperativeness, ungovernability, waywardness

intractable awkward, bull-headed, cantankerous, contrary, difficult, fractious, headstrong, incurable, insoluble, intransigent, obdurate, obstinate, perverse, pig-headed, refractory, self-willed, stiff-necked, stubborn, unbending, uncooperative, undisciplined, ungovernable, unmanageable, unruly, unyielding, wayward, wild, wilful

intransigent hardline, immovable, intractable, obdurate, obstinate, stiff-necked, stubborn, tenacious, tough, unbending, unbudgeable, uncompromising, unyielding
▷ **Antonyms** acquiescent, compliant, compromising, flexible, open-minded

intrenched *see* ENTRENCHED

intrepid audacious, bold, brave, courageous, daring, dauntless, doughty, fearless, gallant, game (*informal*), have-a-go (*informal*), heroic, lion-hearted, nerveless, plucky, resolute, stalwart, stouthearted, unafraid, undaunted, unflinching, valiant, valorous
▷ **Antonyms** afraid, cautious, cowardly, craven, daunted, faint-hearted, fearful, flinching, irresolute, timid

intrepidity audacity, boldness, bravery, courage, daring, dauntlessness, doughtiness, fearlessness, fortitude, gallantry, grit, guts (*informal*), heroism, lion-heartedness, nerve, pluck, prowess, spirit, stoutheartedness, valour

intricacy complexity, complication, convolutions, elaborateness, entanglement, intricateness, involution, involvement, knottiness, obscurity

intricate baroque, Byzantine, complex, complicated, convoluted, daedal (*literary*), difficult, elaborate, fancy, involved, knotty, labyrinthine, obscure, perplexing, rococo, sophisticated, tangled, tortuous
▷ **Antonyms** clear, easy, obvious, plain, simple, straightforward

intrigue *verb* **1.** arouse the curiosity of, attract, charm, fascinate, interest, pique, rivet, tickle one's fancy, titillate **2.** connive, conspire, machinate, manoeuvre, plot, scheme ~*noun* **3.** cabal, chicanery, collusion, conspiracy, double-dealing, knavery, machination, manipulation, manoeuvre, plot, ruse, scheme, sharp practice, stratagem, trickery, wile **4.** affair, amour, intimacy, liaison, romance

intriguing beguiling, compelling, diverting, exciting, fascinating, interesting, tantalizing, titillating

intrinsic basic, built-in, central, congenital, constitutional, elemental, essential, fundamental, genuine, inborn, inbred, inherent, native, natural, radical, real, true, underlying
▷ **Antonyms** acquired, added, appended, artificial, extraneous, extrinsic, incidental

intrinsically as such, at heart, basically, by definition, constitutionally, essentially, fundamentally, in itself, per se

introduce 1. acquaint, do the honours, familiarize, make known, make the introduction, present **2.** begin, bring in, commence, establish, found, inaugurate, initiate, institute, launch, organize, pioneer, set up, start, usher in **3.** advance, air, bring up, broach, moot, offer, propose, put forward, recommend, set forth, submit, suggest, ventilate **4.** announce, lead into, lead off, open, preface **5.** add, inject, insert, interpolate, interpose, put in, throw in (*informal*)

introduction 1. baptism, debut, establishment, first acquaintance, inauguration, induction, initiation, institution, launch, pioneering, presentation **2.** commencement, exordium, foreword, intro (*informal*), lead-in, opening, opening passage, opening remarks, overture, preamble, preface, preliminaries, prelude, proem, prolegomena, prolegomenon, prologue **3.** addition, insertion, interpolation
▷ **Antonyms** (*sense 1*) completion, elimination, termination (*sense 2*) afterward, conclusion, end, epilogue (*sense 3*) extraction, removal, withdrawal

introductory early, elementary, first, inaugural, initial, initiatory, opening, precursory, prefatory, preliminary, preparatory, starting
▷ **Antonyms** closing, concluding, final, last, terminating

introspection brooding, heart-searching, introversion, navel-gazing (*slang*), self-analysis, self-examination

introspective brooding, contemplative, inner-directed, introverted, inward-looking, meditative, pensive, subjective

introverted indrawn, inner-directed, introspective, inward-looking, self-centred, self-contained, withdrawn

intrude butt in, encroach, infringe, interfere, interrupt, meddle, obtrude, push in, put one's two cents in (*U.S. slang*), thrust oneself in *or* forward, trespass, violate

intruder burglar, gate-crasher (*informal*), infiltrator, interloper, invader, prowler, raider, snooper (*informal*), squatter, thief, trespasser

intrusion encroachment, infringement, interference, interruption, invasion, trespass, violation

intrusive disturbing, forward, impertinent, importunate, interfering, invasive, meddlesome, nosy (*informal*), officious, presumptuous, pushy (*informal*), pushing, uncalled-for, unwanted

intrust *see* ENTRUST

intuition discernment, hunch, insight, instinct, perception, presentiment, sixth sense

intuitive innate, instinctive, instinctual, involuntary, spontaneous, unreflecting, untaught

intwine *see* ENTWINE

inundate deluge, drown, engulf, flood, glut, immerse, overflow, overrun, overwhelm, submerge, swamp

inundation deluge, flood, overflow, tidal wave, torrent

inure accustom, anneal, case-harden, desensitize, familiarize, habituate, harden, strengthen, temper, toughen, train

invade 1. assail, assault, attack, burst in, descend upon, encroach, infringe, make inroads, occupy, raid, violate **2.** infect, infest, overrun, overspread, penetrate, permeate, pervade, swarm over

invader aggressor, alien, attacker, looter, plunderer, raider, trespasser

invalid[1] **1.** *adjective* ailing, bedridden, disabled, feeble, frail, ill, infirm, poorly (*informal*), sick, sickly, valetudinarian, weak **2.** *~noun* convalescent, patient, valetudinarian

invalid[2] *adjective* baseless, fallacious, false, ill-founded, illogical, inoperative, irrational, not binding, nugatory, null, null and void, unfounded, unscientific, unsound, untrue, void, worthless

▷ **Antonyms** logical, operative, rational, solid, sound, true, valid, viable

invalidate abrogate, annul, cancel, nullify, overrule, overthrow, quash, render null and void, rescind, undermine, undo, weaken

▷ **Antonyms** authorize, empower, ratify, sanction, strengthen, validate

invalidism chronic illness, valetudinarianism

invalidity fallaciousness, fallacy, falsity, illogicality, inconsistency, irrationality, sophism, speciousness, unsoundness

invaluable beyond price, costly, inestimable, precious, priceless, valuable, worth one's *or* its weight in gold

▷ **Antonyms** cheap, rubbishy, valueless, worthless

invariable changeless, consistent, constant, fixed, immutable, inflexible, regular, rigid, set, unalterable, unchangeable, unchanging, unfailing, uniform, unvarying, unwavering

▷ **Antonyms** alterable, changeable, changing, differing, flexible, inconsistent, irregular, uneven, variable, varying

invariably always, consistently, customarily, day in, day out, ever, every time, habitually, inevitably, on every occasion, perpetually, regularly, unfailingly, without exception

invasion 1. aggression, assault, attack, campaign, foray, incursion, inroad, irruption, offensive, onslaught, raid **2.** breach, encroachment, infiltration, infraction, infringement, intrusion, overstepping, usurpation, violation

invective abuse, berating, billingsgate, castigation, censure, contumely, denunciation, diatribe, obloquy, philippic(s), reproach, revilement, sarcasm, tirade, tongue-lashing, vilification, vituperation

inveigh berate, blame, castigate, censure, condemn, denounce, excoriate, expostulate, lambast(e), rail, recriminate, reproach, sound off, tongue-lash, upbraid, vituperate

inveigle allure, bamboozle (*informal*), beguile, cajole, coax, con (*slang*), decoy, ensnare, entice, entrap, lead on, lure, manipulate, manoeuvre, persuade, seduce, sweet-talk (*informal*), wheedle

invent 1. coin, come up with (*informal*), conceive, contrive, create, design, devise, discover, dream up (*informal*), formulate, imagine, improvise, originate, think up **2.** concoct, cook up (*informal*), fabricate, feign, forge, make up, manufacture, trump up

invention 1. brainchild (*informal*), contraption, contrivance, creation, design, development, device, discovery, gadget, instrument **2.** coinage, creativeness, creativity, genius, imagination, ingenuity, inspiration, inventiveness, originality, resourcefulness **3.** deceit, fabrication, fake, falsehood, fantasy, fib (*informal*), fiction, figment *or* product of (someone's) imagination, forgery, lie, prevarication, sham, story, tall story (*informal*), untruth, yarn

inventive creative, fertile, gifted, ground-breaking, imaginative, ingenious, innovative, inspired, original, resourceful

▷ **Antonyms** imitative, pedestrian, trite, unimaginative, uninspired, uninventive

inventor architect, author, coiner, creator, designer, father, framer, maker, originator

inventory *noun* account, catalogue, file, list, record, register, roll, roster, schedule, stock book

inverse *adjective* contrary, converse, inverted, opposite, reverse, reversed, transposed

inversion antipode, antithesis, contraposition, contrariety, contrary, opposite, reversal, transposal, transposition

invert capsize, introvert, intussuscept (*Pathology*), invaginate (*Pathology*), overset, overturn, reverse, transpose, turn inside out, turn turtle, turn upside down, upset, upturn

invest 1. advance, devote, lay out, put in, sink, spend **2.** endow, endue, provide, supply **3.** authorize, charge, empower, license, sanction, vest **4.** adopt, consecrate, enthrone, establish, inaugurate, induct, install, ordain **5.** *Military* beleaguer, beset, besiege, enclose, lay siege to, surround **6.** *archaic* array, bedeck, bedizen (*archaic*), clothe, deck, drape, dress, robe

investigate consider, enquire into, examine, explore, go into, inquire into, inspect, look into, make enquiries, probe, put to the test, recce (*slang*), research, scrutinize, search, sift, study, work over

investigation analysis, enquiry, examination, exploration, fact finding, hearing, inquest, inquiry, inspection, probe, recce (*slang*), research, review, scrutiny, search, study, survey

investigative fact-finding, inspecting, investigating, research, researching

investigator dick (*slang, chiefly U.S.*), examiner, gumshoe (*U.S. slang*), inquirer, (private) detective, private eye (*informal*), researcher, reviewer, sleuth *or* sleuthhound (*informal*)

investiture admission, enthronement, inauguration, induction, installation, instatement, investing, investment, ordination

investment 1. asset, investing, speculation, transaction, venture **2.** ante (*informal*), contribution, stake **3.** *Military* beleaguering, besieging, blockading, siege, surrounding

inveterate chronic, confirmed, deep-dyed (*usually derogatory*), deep-rooted, deep-seated, dyed-in-the-wool, entrenched, established, habitual, hard-core, hardened, incorrigible, incurable, ineradicable, ingrained, long-standing, obstinate

invidious discriminatory, envious (*obsolete*), hateful, obnoxious, odious, offensive, repugnant, slighting, undesirable

▷ **Antonyms** benevolent, desirable, generous, gratifying, kind, pleasant, pleasing

invigorate animate, brace, buck up (*informal*), energize, enliven, exhilarate, fortify, freshen (up), galvanize, harden, liven up, nerve, pep up, perk up, put new heart into, quicken, refresh, rejuvenate, revitalize, stimulate, strengthen

invigorating bracing, energizing, exhilarating, fresh, healthful, refreshing, rejuvenating, rejuvenative, restorative, salubrious, stimulating, tonic, uplifting

invincible impregnable, indestructible, indomitable, inseparable, insuperable, invulnerable, unassailable, unbeatable, unconquerable, unsurmountable, unyielding

▷ **Antonyms** assailable, beatable, conquerable, defenceless, fallible, powerless, unprotected, vulnerable, weak, yielding

inviolability holiness, inalienability, inviolacy, invulnerability, sacredness, sanctity

inviolable hallowed, holy, inalienable, sacred, sacrosanct, unalterable

inviolate entire, intact, pure, sacred, stainless, unbroken, undefiled, undisturbed, unhurt, unpolluted, unstained, unsullied, untouched, virgin, whole

▷ **Antonyms** abused, broken, defiled, polluted, stained, sullied, touched, violated

invisible 1. imperceptible, indiscernible, out of sight, unperceivable, unseen **2.** concealed, disguised, hidden, inappreciable, inconspicuous, infinitesimal, microscopic

▷ **Antonyms** (*sense 1*) discernible, distinct, obvious, perceptible, seen, visible

invitation 1. asking, begging, bidding, call, invite (*informal*), request, solicitation, summons, supplication **2.** allurement, challenge, come-on (*informal*), coquetry, enticement, glad eye (*informal*), incitement, inducement, open door, overture, provocation, temptation

invite 1. ask, beg, bid, call, request, request the pleasure of (someone's) company, solicit, summon **2.** allure, ask for (*informal*), attract, bring on, court, draw, encourage, entice, lead, leave the door open to, provoke, solicit, tempt, welcome

inviting alluring, appealing, attractive, beguiling, captivating, delightful, engaging, enticing, fascinating, intriguing, magnetic, mouthwatering, pleasing, seductive, tempting, warm, welcoming, winning

▷ **Antonyms** disagreeable, offensive, off-putting (*Brit. informal*), repellent, unappealing, unattractive, undesirable, uninviting, unpleasant

invocation appeal, beseeching, entreaty, petition, prayer, supplication

invoke 1. adjure, appeal to, beg, beseech, call upon, conjure, entreat, implore, petition, pray, solicit, supplicate **2.** apply, call in, have recourse to, implement, initiate, put into effect, resort to, use

involuntary 1. compulsory, forced, obligatory, reluctant, unwilling **2.** automatic, blind, conditioned, instinctive, instinctual, reflex, spontaneous, unconscious, uncontrolled, unintentional, unthinking

▷ **Antonyms** (*sense 1*) optional, unconstrained, volitional, voluntary, willing (*sense 2*) calculated, deliberate, intentional, planned, purposed, wilful

involve 1. entail, imply, mean, necessitate, presuppose, require **2.** affect, associate, compromise, concern, connect, draw in, implicate, incriminate, inculpate, mix up (*informal*), stitch up (*slang*), touch **3**. comprehend, comprise, contain, cover, embrace, include, incorporate, number among, take in **4**. absorb, bind, commit, engage, engross, grip, hold, preoccupy, rivet, wrap up **5**. complicate, embroil, enmesh, entangle, link, mire, mix up, snarl up, tangle

involved 1. Byzantine, complex, complicated, confusing, convoluted, difficult, elaborate, intricate, knotty, labyrinthine, sophisticated, tangled, tortuous **2**. caught (up), concerned, implicated, in on (*informal*), mixed up in *or* with, occupied, participating, taking part, up to one's ears in

▷ **Antonyms** (*sense 1*) easy, easy-peasy (*slang*), elementary, simple, simplified, straightforward, uncomplicated, unsophisticated

involvement 1. association, commitment, concern, connection, dedication, interest, participation, responsibility **2**. complexity, complication, difficulty, embarrassment, entanglement, imbroglio, intricacy, problem, ramification

invulnerability impenetrability, inviolability, safety, security, strength, unassailability, untouchability

invulnerable impenetrable, indestructible, insusceptible, invincible, proof against, safe, secure, unassailable

▷ **Antonyms** assailable, defenceless, insecure, susceptible, unprotected, vulnerable, weak

inward *adjective* **1**. entering, inbound, incoming, inflowing, ingoing, inpouring, penetrating **2**. confidential, hidden, inmost, inner, innermost, inside, interior, internal, personal, private, privy, secret

▷ **Antonyms** (*sense 2*) exterior, external, open, outer, outermost, outside, outward, public

inwardly at heart, deep down, in one's head, in one's inmost heart, inside, privately, secretly, to oneself, within

iota atom, bit, grain, hint, jot, mite, particle, scintilla (*rare*), scrap, speck, tittle, trace, whit

irascibility asperity, bad temper, cantankerousness, choler, crossness, edginess, fieriness, ill temper, impatience, irritability, irritation, petulance, shortness, snappishness, testiness, touchiness, uncertain temper

irascible cantankerous, choleric, crabbed, cross, hasty, hot-tempered, irritable, narky (*Brit. slang*), peppery, petulant, quick-tempered, ratty (*Brit. & N.Z. informal*), short-tempered, testy, tetchy, touchy

irate angered, angry, annoyed, as black as thunder, choked, cross, enraged, exasperated, fuming (*informal*), furious, hacked (off) (*U.S. slang*), hot under the collar (*informal*), incensed, indignant, infuriated, irritated, livid, mad (*informal*), piqued, pissed off (*taboo slang*), provoked, riled, up in arms, worked up, wrathful, wroth (*archaic*)

ire anger, annoyance, choler, displeasure, exasperation, fury, indignation, passion, rage, wrath

iridescent nacreous, opalescent, opaline, pearly, polychromatic, prismatic, rainbow-coloured, shimmering, shot

Irish green, Hibernian

irk aggravate (*informal*), annoy, be on one's back (*slang*), bug (*informal*), gall, get in one's hair (*informal*), get one's back up, get on one's nerves (*informal*), irritate, miff (*informal*), nark (*Brit., Austral., & N.Z. slang*), nettle, peeve (*informal*), piss one off (*taboo slang*), provoke, put one's back up, put one's nose out of joint (*informal*), put out (*informal*), rile, rub one up the wrong way (*informal*), ruffle, vex

irksome aggravating, annoying, boring, bothersome, burdensome, disagreeable, exasperating, irritating, tedious, tiresome, troublesome, trying, uninteresting, unwelcome, vexatious, vexing, wearisome

▷ **Antonyms** agreeable, enjoyable, gratifying, interesting, pleasant, pleasing, welcome

iron *adjective* **1**. chalybeate, ferric, ferrous, irony **2**. *figurative* adamant, cruel, hard, heavy, immovable, implacable, indomitable, inflexible, obdurate, rigid, robust, steel, steely, strong, tough, unbending, unyielding

▷ **Antonyms** (*sense 2*) bending, easy, flexible, light, malleable, pliable, soft, weak, yielding

ironic, ironical 1. double-edged, mocking, mordacious, sarcastic, sardonic, satirical, scoffing, sneering, with tongue in cheek, wry **2**. incongruous, paradoxical

iron out clear up, eliminate, eradicate, erase, expedite, get rid of, harmonize, put right, reconcile, resolve, settle, simplify, smooth over, sort out, straighten out, unravel

irons bonds, chains, fetters, gyves (*archaic*), manacles, shackles

irony 1. mockery, sarcasm, satire **2**. contrariness, incongruity, paradox

irradiate brighten, cast light upon, enlighten, illume (*poetic*), illuminate, illumine, lighten, light up, shine upon

irrational 1. absurd, crackpot (*informal*), crazy, foolish, illogical, injudicious, loopy (*informal*), nonsensical, preposterous, silly, unreasonable, unreasoning, unsound, unthinking, unwise **2**. aberrant, brainless, crazy, demented, insane, mindless, muddle-headed, raving, senseless, unstable, wild

▷ **Antonyms** (*sense 1*) circumspect, judicious, logical, rational, reasonable, sensible, sound, wise

irrationality absurdity, brainlessness, illogicality, insanity, lack of judgment, lunacy, madness, preposterousness, senselessness, unreasonableness, unsoundness

irreconcilable 1. hardline, implacable, inexorable, inflexible, intransigent, unappeasable, uncompromising **2.** clashing, conflicting, diametrically opposed, incompatible, incongruous, inconsistent, opposed

irrecoverable gone for ever, irreclaimable, irredeemable, irremediable, irreparable, irretrievable, lost, unregainable, unsalvageable, unsavable

irrefutable apodeictic, apodictic, beyond question, certain, incontestable, incontrovertible, indisputable, indubitable, invincible, irrefragable, irresistible, sure, unanswerable, unassailable, undeniable, unquestionable

irregular *adjective* **1.** desultory, disconnected, eccentric, erratic, fitful, fluctuating, fragmentary, haphazard, inconstant, intermittent, nonuniform, occasional, out of order, patchy, random, shifting, spasmodic, sporadic, uncertain, uneven, unmethodical, unpunctual, unsteady, unsystematic, variable, wavering **2.** abnormal, anomalous, capricious, disorderly, eccentric, exceptional, extraordinary, immoderate, improper, inappropriate, inordinate, odd, peculiar, queer, quirky, rum (*Brit. slang*), unconventional, unofficial, unorthodox, unsuitable, unusual **3.** asymmetrical, broken, bumpy, craggy, crooked, elliptic, elliptical, holey, jagged, lopsided, lumpy, pitted, ragged, rough, serrated, unequal, uneven, unsymmetrical *~noun* **4.** guerrilla, partisan, volunteer

▷ **Antonyms** (*sense 1*) certain, invariable, methodical, punctual, reliable, steady, systematic (*sense 2*) appropriate, conventional, normal, orthodox, proper, regular, usual (*sense 3*) balanced, equal, even, regular, smooth, symmetrical

irregularity 1. asymmetry, bumpiness, crookedness, jaggedness, lack of symmetry, lopsidedness, lumpiness, patchiness, raggedness, roughness, spottiness, unevenness **2.** aberration, abnormality, anomaly, breach, deviation, eccentricity, freak, malfunction, malpractice, oddity, peculiarity, singularity, unconventionality, unorthodoxy **3.** confusion, desultoriness, disorderliness, disorganization, haphazardness, lack of method, randomness, uncertainty, unpunctuality, unsteadiness

irregularly anyhow, by fits and starts, disconnectedly, eccentrically, erratically, fitfully, haphazardly, in snatches, intermittently, jerkily, now and again, occasionally, off and on, out of sequence, spasmodically, unevenly, unmethodically, unpunctually

irrelevance, irrelevancy inappositeness, inappropriateness, inaptness, inconsequence, non sequitur

▷ **Antonyms** appositeness, appropriateness, aptness, consequence, pertinence, point, relevance, suitability

irrelevant beside the point, extraneous, immaterial, impertinent, inapplicable, inapposite, inappropriate, inapt, inconsequent, neither here nor there, unconnected, unrelated

▷ **Antonyms** applicable, apposite, appropriate, apt, connected, fitting, pertinent, related, relevant, suitable

irreligious 1. agnostic, atheistic, freethinking, godless, pagan, sceptical, unbelieving **2.** blasphemous, iconoclastic, impious, irreverent, profane, sacrilegious, sinful, undevout, ungodly, unholy, unrighteous, wicked

irremediable beyond redress, deadly, fatal, final, hopeless, incurable, irrecoverable, irredeemable, irreparable, irreversible, mortal, remediless, terminal

irreparable beyond repair, incurable, irrecoverable, irremediable, irreplaceable, irretrievable, irreversible

irreplaceable indispensable, invaluable, priceless, unique, vital

irrepressible boisterous, bubbling over, buoyant, ebullient, effervescent, insuppressible, uncontainable, uncontrollable, unmanageable, unquenchable, unrestrainable, unstoppable

irreproachable beyond reproach, blameless, faultless, guiltless, impeccable, inculpable, innocent, irreprehensible, irreprovable, perfect, pure, unblemished, unimpeachable

irresistible 1. compelling, compulsive, imperative, overmastering, overpowering, overwhelming, potent, urgent **2.** ineluctable, inescapable, inevitable, inexorable, unavoidable **3.** alluring, beckoning, enchanting, fascinating, ravishing, seductive, tempting

irresolute doubtful, fickle, half-arsed (*Brit. slang*), half-assed (*U.S. & Canad. slang*), half-hearted, hesitant, hesitating, indecisive, infirm, in two minds, tentative, undecided, undetermined, unsettled, unstable, unsteady, vacillating, wavering, weak

▷ **Antonyms** decisive, determined, firm, fixed, resolute, resolved, settled, stable, stalwart, steadfast, steady, strong

irresolution dithering (*chiefly Brit.*), faint-heartedness, half-heartedness, hesitancy, hesitation, indecisiveness, infirmity (of purpose), shillyshallying (*informal*), uncertainty, vacillation, wavering

irrespective of apart from, despite, discounting, in spite of, notwithstanding, regardless of, without reference to, without regard to

irresponsible careless, featherbrained, flighty, giddy, good-for-nothing, hare~brained, harum-scarum, ill-considered, immature, reckless, scatter-brained, shiftless, thoughtless, undependable, unreliable, untrustworthy, wild
▷ **Antonyms** careful, dependable, level-headed, mature, reliable, responsible, sensible, trustworthy

irreverence cheek (*informal*), cheekiness (*informal*), chutzpah (*U.S. & Canad. informal*), derision, disrespect, flippan~cy, impertinence, impudence, lack of re~spect, mockery, sauce (*informal*)

irreverent cheeky (*informal*), contemptu~ous, derisive, disrespectful, flip (*infor~mal*), flippant, fresh (*informal*), icono~clastic, impertinent, impious, impudent, mocking, sassy (*U.S. informal*), saucy, tongue-in-cheek
▷ **Antonyms** awed, deferential, meek, pious, respectful, reverent, submissive

irreversible final, incurable, irreparable, irrevocable, unalterable

irrevocable changeless, fated, fixed, im~mutable, invariable, irremediable, irre~trievable, irreversible, predestined, pre~determined, settled, unalterable, un~changeable, unreversible

irrigate flood, inundate, moisten, water, wet

irritability bad temper, ill humour, impa~tience, irascibility, peevishness, petu~lance, prickliness, testiness, tetchiness, touchiness
▷ **Antonyms** bonhomie, cheerfulness, complacence, good humour, patience

irritable bad-tempered, cantankerous, choleric, crabbed, crabby, cross, crotch~ety (*informal*), dyspeptic, edgy, exas~perated, fiery, fretful, hasty, hot, ill-humoured, ill-tempered, irascible, narky (*Brit. slang*), out of humour, oversensi~tive, peevish, petulant, prickly, ratty (*Brit. & N.Z. informal*), snappish, snap~py, snarling, tense, testy, tetchy, touchy
▷ **Antonyms** agreeable, calm, cheerful, complacent, composed, even-tempered, good-natured, imperturbable, patient, unexcitable

irritate 1. aggravate (*informal*), anger, annoy, bother, drive one up the wall (*slang*), enrage, exasperate, fret, gall, get in one's hair (*informal*), get one's back up, get one's dander up (*informal*), get one's goat (*slang*), get one's hackles up, get on one's nerves (*informal*), get on one's wick (*informal*), get under one's skin (*informal*), harass, incense, in~flame, infuriate, nark (*Brit., Austral., & N.Z. slang*), needle (*informal*), nettle, offend, pester, piss one off (*taboo slang*), provoke, put one's back up, raise one's hackles, rankle with, rub up the wrong way (*informal*), ruffle, try one's pa~tience, vex **2.** aggravate, chafe, fret, in~flame, intensify, pain, rub
▷ **Antonyms** (*sense 1*) calm, comfort, gratify, mollify, placate, please, soothe

irritated angry, annoyed, bothered, cross, displeased, exasperated, flustered, hacked (off) (*U.S. slang*), harassed, im~patient, irritable, nettled, out of hu~mour, peeved (*informal*), piqued, pissed off (*taboo slang*), put out, ruffled, vexed

irritating aggravating (*informal*), annoy~ing, displeasing, disquieting, disturbing, galling, infuriating, irksome, madden~ing, nagging, pestilential, provoking, thorny, troublesome, trying, upsetting, vexatious, worrisome
▷ **Antonyms** agreeable, assuaging, calming, comforting, mollifying, pleas~ant, pleasing, quieting, soothing

irritation 1. anger, annoyance, crossness, displeasure, exasperation, ill humour, ill temper, impatience, indignation, ir~ritability, resentment, shortness, snap~piness, testiness, vexation, wrath **2.** ag~gravation (*informal*), annoyance, drag (*informal*), gall, goad, irritant, nuisance, pain (*informal*), pain in the arse (*taboo informal*), pain in the neck (*informal*), pest, provocation, tease, thorn in one's flesh
▷ **Antonyms** (*sense 1*) calm, composure, ease, pleasure, quietude, satisfaction, serenity, tranquillity

irrupt break in, burst in, crash in (*infor~mal*), invade, rush in, storm in

irruption breaking in, foray, forcible en~try, incursion, inroad, intrusion, inva~sion, raid

isolate cut off, detach, disconnect, divor~ce, insulate, quarantine, segregate, separate, sequester, set apart

isolated 1. backwoods, hidden, incommu~nicado, in the middle of nowhere, lonely, off the beaten track, outlying, out-of-the-way, remote, retired, secluded, un~frequented **2.** abnormal, anomalous, ex~ceptional, freak, out on a limb, random, single, solitary, special, unique, unre~lated, untypical, unusual

isolation aloofness, detachment, discon~nection, exile, insularity, insulation, ivory tower, loneliness, quarantine, re~moteness, retirement, seclusion, segre~gation, self-sufficiency, separation, soli~tude, withdrawal

issue *noun* 1. affair, argument, bone of contention, can of worms (*informal*), concern, controversy, matter, matter of contention, point, point in question, problem, question, subject, topic **2. at is~sue** at variance, controversial, in dis~agreement, in dispute, to be decided, under discussion, unsettled **3. take issue** challenge, disagree, dispute, object, op~pose, raise an objection, take exception **4.** conclusion, consequence, culmination, effect, end, end result, finale, outcome, pay-off (*informal*), result, termination, upshot **5.** copy, edition, impression, in~

stalment, number, printing **6.** circulation, delivery, dispersal, dissemination, distribution, granting, issuance, issuing, publication, sending out, supply, supplying **7.** children, descendants, heirs, offspring, progeny, scions, seed (*chiefly biblical*) *~verb* **8.** announce, broadcast, circulate, deliver, distribute, emit, give out, promulgate, publish, put in circulation, put out, release **9.** arise, be a consequence of, come forth, emanate, emerge, flow, originate, proceed, rise, spring, stem

▷ **Antonyms** *~noun* (*sense 4*) beginning, cause, inception, start (*sense 6*) cancellation, recall (*sense 7*) parent, sire *~verb* cause, revoke, withdraw

itch *verb* **1.** crawl, irritate, prickle, tickle, tingle **2.** ache, burn, crave, hanker, hunger, long, lust, pant, pine, yearn *~noun* **3.** irritation, itchiness, prickling, tingling **4.** craving, desire, hankering, hunger, longing, lust, passion, restlessness, yearning, yen (*informal*)

itching agog, aquiver, atremble, avid, burning, consumed with curiosity, eager, impatient, inquisitive, longing, mad keen (*informal*), raring, spoiling for

itchy eager, edgy, fidgety, impatient, restive, restless, unsettled

item **1.** article, aspect, component, consideration, detail, entry, matter, particular, point, thing **2.** account, article, bulletin, dispatch, feature, note, notice, paragraph, piece, report

itemize count, detail, document, enumerate, instance, inventory, list, number, particularize, record, set out, specify

iterate go over, recap (*informal*), recapitulate, reiterate, repeat, restate

itinerant *adjective* ambulatory, Gypsy, journeying, migratory, nomadic, peripatetic, roaming, roving, travelling, unsettled, vagabond, vagrant, wandering, wayfaring

▷ **Antonyms** established, fixed, resident, rooted, settled, stable

itinerary **1.** circuit, journey, line, programme, route, schedule, timetable, tour **2.** Baedeker, guide, guidebook

ivory tower cloister, refuge, remoteness, retreat, sanctum, seclusion, splendid isolation, unreality, world of one's own

ivory-towered **1.** cloistered, far from the madding crowd, remote, retired, sequestered, sheltered, withdrawn **2.** academic, airy-fairy (*informal*), idealistic, quixotic, unrealizable, visionary

J, j

jab *verb/noun* dig, lunge, nudge, poke, prod, punch, stab, tap, thrust

jabber babble, blather, blether, chatter, drivel, gabble, mumble, prate, rabbit (on) (*Brit. informal*), ramble, run off at the mouth (*slang*), tattle, waffle (*informal, chiefly Brit.*), yap (*informal*)

jackass berk (*Brit. slang*), blockhead, charlie (*Brit. informal*), chump, coot, dickhead (*slang*), dimwit (*informal*), dipstick (*Brit. slang*), divvy (*Brit. slang*), dolt, dork (*slang*), dweeb (*U.S. slang*), fool, fuckwit (*taboo slang*), geek (*slang*), gobshite (*Irish taboo slang*), gonzo (*slang*), idiot, imbecile, jerk (*slang, chiefly U.S. & Canad.*), lamebrain (*informal*), nerd *or* nurd (*slang*), nincompoop, ninny, nitwit (*informal*), numbskull *or* numskull, numpty (*Scot. informal*), oaf, pillock (*Brit. slang*), plank (*Brit. slang*), plonker (*slang*), prat (*slang*), prick (*slang*), schmuck (*U.S. slang*), simpleton, twit (*informal, chiefly Brit.*), wally (*slang*)

jacket case, casing, coat, covering, envelope, folder, sheath, skin, wrapper, wrapping

jackpot award, bonanza, kitty, pool, pot, pot of gold at the end of the rainbow, prize, reward, winnings

jack up 1. elevate, heave, hoist, lift, lift up, raise, rear **2.** accelerate, augment, boost, escalate, increase, inflate, put up, raise

jade harridan, hussy, nag, shrew, slattern, slut, trollop, vixen, wench

jaded 1. clapped out (*Austral. & N.Z. informal*), exhausted, fagged (out) (*informal*), fatigued, spent, tired, tired-out, weary, zonked (*slang*) **2.** bored, cloyed, dulled, glutted, gorged, sated, satiated, surfeited, tired

▷ **Antonyms** bright-eyed and bushy-tailed (*informal*), eager, enthusiastic, fresh, keen, life-loving, naive, refreshed

jag[1] *noun* notch, point, projection, protuberance, snag, spur, tooth

jag[2] *noun* binge (*informal*), bout, carousal, carouse, fit, orgy, period, spell, spree

jagged barbed, broken, cleft, craggy, denticulate, indented, notched, pointed, ragged, ridged, rough, serrated, snaggy, spiked, toothed, uneven

▷ **Antonyms** glassy, level, regular, rounded, smooth

jail, gaol 1. *noun* borstal, brig (*chiefly U.S.*), calaboose (*U.S. informal*), can (*slang*), clink (*slang*), cooler (*slang*), inside (*slang*), jailhouse (*Southern U.S.*), jug (*slang*), lockup, nick (*Brit. slang*), penitentiary (*U.S.*), poky *or* pokey (*U.S. & Canad. slang*), prison, quod (*slang*), reformatory, slammer (*slang*), stir (*slang*) **2.** *~verb* confine, detain, immure, impound, imprison, incarcerate, lock up, send down

jailer, gaoler captor, guard, keeper, screw (*slang*), turnkey (*archaic*), warden, warder

jam *verb* **1.** cram, crowd, crush, force, pack, press, ram, squeeze, stuff, throng, wedge **2.** block, cease, clog, congest, halt, obstruct, stall, stick *~noun* **3.** crowd, crush, horde, mass, mob, multitude, pack, press, swarm, throng **4.** bind, deep water, dilemma, fix (*informal*), hole (*slang*), hot water, pickle (*informal*), plight, predicament, quandary, scrape (*informal*), spot (*informal*), strait, tight spot, trouble

jamboree beano (*Brit. slang*), blast (*U.S. slang*), carnival, carousal, carouse, celebration, festival, festivity, fête, frolic, hooley *or* hoolie (*chiefly Irish & N.Z.*), jubilee, merriment, party, rave (*Brit. slang*), rave-up (*Brit. slang*), revelry, spree

jangle 1. *verb* chime, clank, clash, clatter, jingle, rattle, vibrate **2.** *~noun* cacophony, clang, clangour, clash, din, dissonance, jar, racket, rattle, reverberation

▷ **Antonyms** (*sense 2*) harmoniousness, mellifluousness, quiet, silence

janitor caretaker, concierge, custodian, doorkeeper, porter

jar[1] *noun* amphora, carafe, container, crock, flagon, jug, pitcher, pot, receptacle, urn, vase, vessel

jar[2] *verb* **1.** bicker, clash, contend, disagree, interfere, oppose, quarrel, wrangle **2.** agitate, convulse, disturb, grate, irritate, jolt, offend, rasp, rattle (*informal*), rock, shake, vibrate **3.** annoy, clash, discompose, gall, get on one's nerves (*informal*), grate, grind, irk, irritate, nark (*Brit., Austral., & N.Z. slang*), nettle, piss one off (*taboo slang*)

~noun **4.** agitation, altercation, bickering, disagreement, discord, grating, irritation, jolt, quarrel, rasping, wrangling

jargon 1. argot, cant, dialect, idiom, lingo (*informal*), parlance, patois, patter, slang, tongue, usage **2.** balderdash, bunkum *or* buncombe (*chiefly U.S.*), drivel, gabble, gibberish, gobbledegook, Greek (*informal*), mumbo jumbo, nonsense, palaver, rigmarole, twaddle

jaundiced 1. cynical, preconceived, sceptical **2.** biased, bigoted, bitter, distorted, envious, hostile, jealous, partial, prejudiced, resentful, spiteful, suspicious

▷ **Antonyms** credulous, ingenuous, naive, open-minded, optimistic, trusting, unbiased

jaunt airing, excursion, expedition, outing, promenade, ramble, stroll, tour, trip

jaunty airy, breezy, buoyant, carefree, dapper, gay, high-spirited, lively, perky, self-confident, showy, smart, sparky, sprightly, spruce, trim

▷ **Antonyms** dignified, dull, lifeless, sedate, serious, staid

jaw *verb* **1.** babble, chat, chatter, chew the fat *or* rag (*slang*), gossip, lecture, run off at the mouth (*slang*), spout, talk **2.** abuse, censure, criticize, revile, scold *~noun* **3.** chat, chinwag (*Brit. informal*), conversation, gabfest (*informal, chiefly U.S. & Canad.*), gossip, natter, talk

jaws abyss, aperture, entrance, gates, ingress, maw, mouth, opening, orifice

jazz up animate, enhance, enliven, heighten, improve

jazzy animated, fancy, flashy, gaudy, lively, smart, snazzy (*informal*), spirited, vivacious, wild, zestful

jealous 1. covetous, desirous, emulous, envious, green, green-eyed, grudging, intolerant, invidious, resentful, rival **2.** anxious, apprehensive, attentive, guarded, mistrustful, protective, solicitous, suspicious, vigilant, wary, watchful, zealous

▷ **Antonyms** carefree, indifferent, satisfied, trusting

jealousy covetousness, distrust, envy, heart-burning, ill-will, mistrust, possessiveness, resentment, spite, suspicion

jeer 1. *verb* banter, barrack, cock a snook at (*Brit.*), contemn (*formal*), deride, flout, gibe, heckle, hector, knock (*informal*), mock, ridicule, scoff, sneer, taunt **2.** *~noun* abuse, aspersion, boo, catcall, derision, gibe, hiss, hoot, obloquy, ridicule, scoff, sneer, taunt

▷ **Antonyms** (*sense 1*) acclaim, applaud, cheer, clap, praise (*sense 2*) adulation, applause, cheers, encouragement, praise

jejune 1. childish, immature, juvenile, naive, pointless, puerile, senseless, silly, simple, unsophisticated **2.** banal, colourless, dry, dull, inane, insipid, prosaic, uninteresting, vapid, wishy-washy (*informal*)

jell 1. congeal, harden, set, solidify, thicken **2.** come together, crystallize, finalize, form, materialize, take shape

jeopardize chance, endanger, expose, gamble, hazard, imperil, risk, stake, venture

jeopardy danger, endangerment, exposure, hazard, insecurity, liability, peril, pitfall, precariousness, risk, venture, vulnerability

jeremiad complaint, groan, keen, lament, lamentation, moan, plaint, wail

jerk *verb/noun* jolt, lurch, pull, throw, thrust, tug, tweak, twitch, wrench, yank

jerky bouncy, bumpy, convulsive, fitful, jolting, jumpy, rough, shaky, spasmodic, tremulous, twitchy, uncontrolled

▷ **Antonyms** flowing, frictionless, gliding, smooth

jerry-built cheap, defective, faulty, flimsy, ramshackle, rickety, shabby, slipshod, thrown together, unsubstantial

▷ **Antonyms** sturdy, substantial, well-built, well-constructed

jest 1. *noun* banter, bon mot, crack (*slang*), fun, gag (*informal*), hoax, jape, joke, josh (*slang, chiefly U.S. & Canad.*), play, pleasantry, prank, quip, sally, sport, wisecrack (*informal*), witticism **2.** *~verb* banter, chaff, deride, gibe, jeer, joke, josh (*slang, chiefly U.S. & Canad.*), kid (*informal*), mock, quip, scoff, sneer, tease

jester 1. comedian, comic, humorist, joker, quipster, wag, wit **2.** buffoon, clown, fool, harlequin, madcap, mummer, pantaloon, prankster, zany

jet[1] *adjective* black, coal-black, ebony, inky, pitch-black, raven, sable

jet[2] *noun* **1.** flow, fountain, gush, spout, spray, spring, stream **2.** atomizer, nose, nozzle, rose, spout, sprayer, sprinkler *~verb* **3.** flow, gush, issue, rush, shoot, spew, spout, squirt, stream, surge **4.** fly, soar, zoom

jettison abandon, discard, dump, eject, expel, heave, scrap, throw overboard, unload

jetty breakwater, dock, groyne, mole, pier, quay, wharf

jewel 1. brilliant, gemstone, ornament, precious stone, rock (*slang*), sparkler (*informal*), trinket **2.** charm, collector's item, find, gem, humdinger (*slang*), masterpiece, paragon, pearl, prize, rarity, treasure, wonder

jewellery finery, gems, jewels, ornaments, precious stones, regalia, treasure, trinkets

Jezebel harlot, harridan, hussy, jade, virago, wanton, witch

jib balk, recoil, refuse, retreat, shrink, stop short

jibe *see* GIBE

jiffy bat of an eye (*informal*), flash, instant, moment, second, split second, trice, twinkling

jig *verb* bob, bounce, caper, jiggle, jounce, prance, shake, skip, twitch, wiggle, wobble

jiggle agitate, bounce, fidget, jerk, jig, jog, joggle, shake, shimmy, twitch, wiggle

jilt *verb* abandon, betray, break with, coquette, deceive, desert, disappoint, discard, ditch (*slang*), drop, forsake, leave (someone) in the lurch, reject, throw over

jingle *verb* **1.** chime, clatter, clink, jangle, rattle, ring, tinkle, tintinnabulate *~noun* **2.** clang, clangour, clink, rattle, reverberation, ringing, tinkle **3.** chorus, ditty, doggerel, limerick, melody, song, tune

jinx 1. *noun* black magic, curse, evil eye, hex (*U.S. & Canad. informal*), hoodoo (*informal*), nemesis, plague, voodoo **2.** *~verb* bewitch, curse, hex (*U.S. & Canad. informal*)

jitters anxiety, butterflies (in one's stomach) (*informal*), cold feet (*informal*), fidgets, heebie-jeebies (*slang*), nerves, nervousness, tenseness, the shakes (*informal*), the willies (*informal*)

jittery agitated, anxious, fidgety, hyper (*informal*), jumpy, nervous, neurotic, quivering, shaky, trembling, twitchy (*informal*), wired (*slang*)

▷ **Antonyms** calm, composed, laid-back (*informal*), relaxed, together (*slang*), unfazed (*informal*), unflustered

job 1. affair, assignment, charge, chore, concern, contribution, duty, enterprise, errand, function, pursuit, responsibility, role, stint, task, undertaking, venture, work **2.** activity, bread and butter (*informal*), business, calling, capacity, career, craft, employment, function, livelihood, métier, occupation, office, position, post, profession, situation, trade, vocation **3.** allotment, assignment, batch, commission, consignment, contract, lot, output, piece, portion, product, share

jobless idle, inactive, out of work, unemployed, unoccupied

jockey *verb* **1.** bamboozle, cheat, con (*informal*), deceive, dupe, fool, hoax, hoodwink, trick **2.** cajole, engineer, finagle (*informal*), ingratiate, insinuate, manage, manipulate, manoeuvre, negotiate, trim, wheedle

jocose blithe, comical, droll, facetious, funny, humorous, jesting, jocular, jovial, joyous, merry, mischievous, playful, pleasant, sportive, teasing, waggish, witty

jocular amusing, comical, droll, facetious, frolicsome, funny, humorous, jesting, jocose, jocund, joking, jolly, jovial, playful, roguish, sportive, teasing, waggish, whimsical, witty

▷ **Antonyms** earnest, humourless, serious, solemn

jog 1. activate, arouse, nudge, prod, prompt, push, remind, shake, stimulate, stir, suggest **2.** bounce, jar, jerk, jiggle, joggle, jolt, jostle, jounce, rock, shake **3.** canter, dogtrot, lope, run, trot **4.** lumber, plod, traipse (*informal*), tramp, trudge

joie de vivre ebullience, enjoyment, enthusiasm, gaiety, gusto, joy, joyfulness, pleasure, relish, zest

▷ **Antonyms** apathy, depression, distaste

join 1. accompany, add, adhere, annex, append, attach, cement, combine, connect, couple, fasten, knit, link, marry, splice, tie, unite, yoke **2.** affiliate with, associate with, enlist, enrol, enter, sign up **3.** adjoin, border, border on, butt, conjoin, extend, meet, reach, touch, verge on

▷ **Antonyms** (*sense 1*) detach, disconnect, disengage, disentangle, divide, separate, sever, unfasten (*sense 2*) leave, part, quit, resign

joint *noun* **1.** articulation, connection, hinge, intersection, junction, juncture, knot, nexus, node, seam, union *~adjective* **2.** collective, combined, communal, concerted, consolidated, cooperative, joined, mutual, shared, united *~verb* **3.** connect, couple, fasten, fit, join, unite **4.** carve, cut up, dismember, dissect, divide, segment, sever, sunder

jointly as one, collectively, in common, in conjunction, in league, in partnership, mutually, together, unitedly

▷ **Antonyms** individually, separately, singly

joke *noun* **1.** frolic, fun, gag (*informal*), jape, jest, josh (*slang, chiefly U.S. & Canad.*), lark, play, prank, pun, quip, quirk, sally, sport, whimsy, wisecrack (*informal*), witticism, yarn **2.** buffoon, butt, clown, laughing stock, simpleton, target *~verb* **3.** banter, chaff, deride, frolic, gambol, jest, josh (*slang, chiefly U.S. & Canad.*), kid (*informal*), mock, play the fool, quip, ridicule, taunt, tease, wind up (*Brit. slang*)

joker buffoon, clown, comedian, comic, humorist, jester, kidder (*informal*), prankster, trickster, wag, wit

jolly blithesome, carefree, cheerful, chirpy (*informal*), convivial, festive, frolicsome, funny, gay, genial, gladsome (*archaic*), hilarious, jocund, jovial, joyful, joyous, jubilant, merry, mirthful, playful, sportive, sprightly, upbeat (*informal*)

▷ **Antonyms** doleful, down in the dumps (*informal*), gaunt, grave, lugubrious, miserable, morose, saturnine, serious, solemn

jolt *verb* **1.** jar, jerk, jog, jostle, knock, push, shake, shove **2.** astonish, discompose, disturb, perturb, stagger, startle, stun, surprise, upset *~noun* **3.** bump, jar, jerk, jog, jump, lurch, quiver, shake, start **4.** blow, bolt from the blue, bomb~shell, reversal, setback, shock, surprise, thunderbolt, whammy (*informal, chiefly U.S.*)

jostle bump, butt, crowd, elbow, hustle, jog, joggle, jolt, press, push, scramble, shake, shove, squeeze, throng, thrust

jot 1. *noun* ace, atom, bit, detail, fraction, grain, iota, mite, morsel, particle, scin~tilla, scrap, smidgen *or* smidgin (*infor~mal, chiefly U.S. & Canad.*), speck, tit~tle, trifle, whit **2.** *~verb* list, note, note down, record, register, scribble, tad (*in~formal, chiefly U.S.*), tally

journal 1. chronicle, daily, gazette, maga~zine, monthly, newspaper, paper, peri~odical, record, register, review, tabloid, weekly **2.** chronicle, commonplace book, daybook, diary, log, record

journalist broadcaster, columnist, com~mentator, contributor, correspondent, hack, journo (*slang*), newsman, news~paperman, pressman, reporter, scribe (*informal*), stringer

journey 1. *noun* excursion, expedition, jaunt, odyssey, outing, passage, per~egrination, pilgrimage, progress, ram~ble, tour, travel, trek, trip, voyage **2.** *~verb* fare, fly, go, peregrinate, proceed, ramble, range, roam, rove, tour, travel, traverse, trek, voyage, wander, wend

joust 1. *noun* combat, duel, encounter, engagement, lists, match, passage of arms, set-to, tilt, tournament, tourney **2.** *~verb* break a lance, cross swords, enga~ge, enter the lists, fight, tilt, trade blows

jovial airy, animated, blithe, buoyant, cheery, convivial, cordial, gay, glad, happy, hilarious, jocose, jocund, jolly, jubilant, merry, mirthful
▷ **Antonyms** antisocial, doleful, grumpy, morose, solemn, unfriendly

joviality fun, gaiety, glee, hilarity, jollity, merriment, mirth

joy 1. bliss, delight, ecstasy, elation, ex~altation, exultation, felicity, festivity, gaiety, gladness, glee, hilarity, pleasure, rapture, ravishment, satisfaction, transport **2.** charm, delight, gem, jewel, pride, prize, treasure, treat, wonder
▷ **Antonyms** bane, despair, grief, misery, sorrow, tribulation, unhappiness

joyful blithesome, cock-a-hoop, delighted, elated, enraptured, floating on air, glad, gladsome (*archaic*), gratified, happy, jocund, jolly, jovial, jubilant, light-hearted, merry, on cloud nine (*infor~mal*), over the moon (*informal*), pleased, rapt, satisfied

joyless cheerless, dejected, depressed, dismal, dispirited, downcast, down in the dumps (*informal*), dreary, gloomy, miserable, sad, unhappy

joyous blithe, cheerful, festive, hearten~ing, joyful, merry, rapturous

jubilant cock-a-hoop, elated, enraptured, euphoric, excited, exuberant, exultant, glad, joyous, overjoyed, over the moon (*informal*), rejoicing, rhapsodic, thrilled, triumphal, triumphant
▷ **Antonyms** despondent, doleful, down~cast, melancholy, sad, sorrowful

jubilation celebration, ecstasy, elation, excitement, exultation, festivity, jambo~ree, joy, jubilee, triumph

jubilee carnival, celebration, festival, fes~tivity, fête, gala, holiday

Judas betrayer, deceiver, renegade, trai~tor, turncoat

judge *noun* **1.** adjudicator, arbiter, arbi~trator, moderator, referee, umpire **2.** appraiser, arbiter, assessor, authority, connoisseur, critic, evaluator, expert **3.** beak (*Brit. slang*), justice, magistrate *~verb* **4.** adjudge, adjudicate, arbitrate, ascertain, conclude, decide, determine, discern, distinguish, mediate, referee, umpire **5.** appraise, appreciate, assess, consider, criticize, esteem, estimate, evaluate, examine, rate, review, value **6.** adjudge, condemn, decree, doom, find, pass sentence, pronounce sentence, rule, sentence, sit, try

judgment 1. acumen, common sense, dis~cernment, discrimination, intelligence, penetration, percipience, perspicacity, prudence, sagacity, sense, shrewdness, smarts (*slang, chiefly U.S.*), taste, understanding, wisdom **2.** arbitration, award, conclusion, decision, decree, de~termination, finding, order, result, rul~ing, sentence, verdict **3.** appraisal, as~sessment, belief, conviction, deduction, diagnosis, estimate, finding, opinion, valuation, view **4.** damnation, doom, fate, misfortune, punishment, retribu~tion

judicial 1. judiciary, juridical, legal, offi~cial **2.** discriminating, distinguished, impartial, judgelike, magisterial, mag~istral

judicious acute, astute, careful, cautious, circumspect, considered, diplomatic, discerning, discreet, discriminating, en~lightened, expedient, informed, politic, prudent, rational, reasonable, saga~cious, sage, sane, sapient, sensible, shrewd, skilful, sober, sound, thought~ful, well-advised, well-judged, wise
▷ **Antonyms** imprudent, indiscreet, in~judicious, tactless, thoughtless

jug carafe, container, crock, ewer, jar, pitcher, urn, vessel

juggle alter, change, disguise, doctor (*in~formal*), falsify, fix (*informal*), manipu~late, manoeuvre, misrepresent, modify, tamper with

juice extract, fluid, liquid, liquor, nectar, sap, secretion, serum

juicy **1**. lush, moist, sappy, succulent, watery **2**. colourful, interesting, provocative, racy, risqué, sensational, spicy (*informal*), suggestive, vivid

jumble **1**. *verb* confound, confuse, disarrange, dishevel, disorder, disorganize, entangle, mistake, mix, muddle, ravel, shuffle, tangle **2**. *~noun* chaos, clutter, confusion, disarrangement, disarray, disorder, farrago, gallimaufry, hodgepodge, hotchpotch (*U.S.*), litter, medley, *mélange,* mess, miscellany, mishmash, mixture, muddle, pig's breakfast (*informal*)

jumbo elephantine, giant, gigantic, ginormous (*informal*), huge, humongous *or* humungous (*U.S. slang*), immense, large, mega (*informal*), oversized
▷ **Antonyms** baby, dwarf, micro, mini, pocket, tiny, wee

jump *verb* **1**. bounce, bound, caper, clear, gambol, hop, hurdle, leap, skip, spring, vault **2**. flinch, jerk, recoil, start, wince **3**. avoid, digress, evade, miss, omit, overshoot, skip, switch **4**. advance, ascend, boost, escalate, gain, hike, increase, mount, rise, surge *~noun* **5**. bound, buck, caper, hop, leap, skip, spring, vault **6**. barricade, barrier, fence, hurdle, impediment, obstacle, rail **7**. breach, break, gap, hiatus, interruption, lacuna, space **8**. advance, augmentation, boost, increase, increment, rise, upsurge, upturn **9**. jar, jerk, jolt, lurch, shock, start, swerve, twitch, wrench

jumper jersey, pullover, sweater, woolly

jumpy agitated, anxious, apprehensive, fidgety, hyper (*informal*), jittery (*informal*), nervous, neurotic, on edge, restless, shaky, tense, timorous, twitchy (*informal*), wired (*slang*)
▷ **Antonyms** calm, composed, laid-back (*informal*), nerveless, together (*slang*), unfazed (*informal*), unflustered

junction alliance, combination, connection, coupling, joint, juncture, linking, seam, union

juncture **1**. conjuncture, contingency, crisis, crux, emergency, exigency, moment, occasion, point, predicament, strait, time **2**. bond, connection, convergence, edge, intersection, junction, link, seam, weld

junior inferior, lesser, lower, minor, secondary, subordinate, younger
▷ **Antonyms** elder, higher-ranking, older, senior, superior

junk clutter, debris, dreck (*slang, chiefly U.S.*), leavings, litter, oddments, odds and ends, refuse, rubbish, rummage, scrap, trash, waste

junta assembly, cabal, camp, clique, combination, confederacy, convocation, coterie, council, crew, faction, gang, league, party, ring, schism, set

jurisdiction **1**. authority, command, control, dominion, influence, power, prerogative, rule, say, sway **2**. area, bounds, circuit, compass, district, dominion, field, orbit, province, range, scope, sphere, zone

just *adjective* **1**. blameless, conscientious, decent, equitable, fair, fairminded, good, honest, honourable, impartial, lawful, pure, right, righteous, unbiased, upright, virtuous **2**. accurate, correct, exact, faithful, normal, precise, proper, regular, sound, true **3**. appropriate, apt, condign, deserved, due, fitting, justified, legitimate, merited, proper, reasonable, rightful, sensible, suitable, well-deserved *~adverb* **4**. absolutely, completely, entirely, exactly, perfectly, precisely **5**. hardly, lately, only now, recently, scarcely **6**. at a push, at most, but, by the skin of one's teeth, merely, no more than, nothing but, only, simply, solely
▷ **Antonyms** *~adjective* corrupt, devious, dishonest, inappropriate, inequitable, prejudiced, undeserved, unfair, unfit, unjust, unlawful, unreasonable, untrue

just about all but, almost, around, close to, nearly, not quite, practically, well-nigh

justice **1**. equity, fairness, honesty, impartiality, integrity, justness, law, legality, legitimacy, reasonableness, rectitude, right **2**. amends, compensation, correction, penalty, recompense, redress, reparation **3**. judge, magistrate
▷ **Antonyms** dishonesty, favouritism, inequity, injustice, partiality, unfairness, unlawfulness, unreasonableness, untruth, wrong

justifiable acceptable, defensible, excusable, fit, lawful, legitimate, proper, reasonable, right, sensible, sound, tenable, understandable, valid, vindicable, warrantable, well-founded
▷ **Antonyms** arbitrary, capricious, indefensible, inexcusable, unreasonable, unwarranted

justification **1**. absolution, apology, approval, defence, exculpation, excuse, exoneration, explanation, extenuation, plea, rationalization, vindication **2**. basis, defence, grounds, plea, reason, warrant

justify absolve, acquit, approve, confirm, defend, establish, exculpate, excuse, exonerate, explain, legalize, legitimize, maintain, substantiate, support, sustain, uphold, validate, vindicate, warrant

justly accurately, correctly, equally, equitably, fairly, honestly, impartially, lawfully, properly

jut bulge, extend, impend, overhang, poke, project, protrude, stick out

juvenile **1.** *noun* adolescent, boy, child, girl, infant, minor, youth **2.** *~adjective* babyish, boyish, callow, childish, girlish, immature, inexperienced, infantile, jejune, puerile, undeve~loped, unsophisticated, young, youth~ful

▷ **Antonyms** *~noun* adult, grown-up *~adjective* adult, grown-up, mature, re~sponsible

juxtaposition adjacency, closeness, con~tact, contiguity, nearness, propinquity, proximity, vicinity

K, k

kaleidoscopic **1.** changeable, fluctuating, fluid, many-coloured, mobile, motley, mutable, unstable, variegated **2.** complex, complicated, confused, convoluted, disordered, intricate, jumbled, varied

kamikaze *adjective* foolhardy, self-destructive, suicidal

kaput broken, dead, defunct, destroyed, extinct, finished, ruined, undone, wrecked

keel over black out (*informal*), capsize, collapse, faint, founder, overturn, pass out, swoon (*literary*), topple over, upset

keen[1] *adjective* **1.** ardent, avid, bright-eyed and bushy-tailed (*informal*), devoted to, eager, earnest, ebullient, enthusiastic, fervid, fierce, fond of, impassioned, intense, into (*informal*), zealous **2.** acid, acute, biting, caustic, cutting, edged, finely honed, incisive, penetrating, piercing, pointed, razorlike, sardonic, satirical, sharp, tart, trenchant, vitriolic **3.** astute, brilliant, canny, clever, discerning, discriminating, perceptive, perspicacious, quick, sagacious, sapient, sensitive, shrewd, wise
▷ **Antonyms** (*sense 1*) apathetic, half-hearted, indifferent, laodicean, lukewarm, unenthusiastic, uninterested (*sense 2*) blunt, dull (*sense 3*) dull, obtuse, unperceptive

keen[2] **1.** *verb* bewail, grieve, lament, mourn, wail, weep **2.** *~noun* coronach (*Scot. & Irish*), dirge, lament, lamentation, mourning, wailing, weeping

keenness **1.** ardour, avidity, avidness, diligence, eagerness, earnestness, ebullience, enthusiasm, fervour, impatience, intensity, passion, zeal, zest **2.** acerbity, harshness, incisiveness, mordancy, penetration, pungency, rigour, severity, sharpness, sternness, trenchancy, unkindness, virulence **3.** astuteness, canniness, cleverness, discernment, insight, sagacity, sapience, sensitivity, shrewdness, wisdom

keep *verb* **1.** conserve, control, hold, maintain, possess, preserve, retain **2.** accumulate, amass, carry, deal in, deposit, furnish, garner, heap, hold, pile, place, stack, stock, store, trade in **3.** care for, defend, guard, look after, maintain, manage, mind, operate, protect, safeguard, shelter, shield, tend, watch over **4.** board, feed, foster, maintain, nourish, nurture, provide for, provision, subsidize, support, sustain, victual **5.** accompany, associate with, consort with, fraternize with **6.** arrest, block, check, constrain, control, curb, delay, detain, deter, hamper, hamstring, hinder, hold, hold back, impede, inhibit, keep back, limit, obstruct, prevent, restrain, retard, shackle, stall, withhold **7.** adhere to, celebrate, commemorate, comply with, fulfil, hold, honour, obey, observe, perform, respect, ritualize, solemnize *~noun* **8.** board, food, livelihood, living, maintenance, means, nourishment, subsistence, support **9.** castle, citadel, donjon, dungeon, fastness, stronghold, tower
▷ **Antonyms** *~verb* abandon, discard, disregard, expedite, free, give up, ignore, liberate, lose, release, speed

keep at be steadfast, carry on, complete, continue, drudge, endure, finish, grind, labour, last, maintain, persevere, persist, remain, slave, stay, stick, toil

keep back **1.** check, constrain, control, curb, delay, hold back, keep a tight rein on, limit, prohibit, restrain, restrict, retard, withhold **2.** censor, conceal, hide, keep dark, keep under one's hat, reserve, suppress, withhold

keeper attendant, caretaker, curator, custodian, defender, gaoler, governor, guard, guardian, jailer, overseer, preserver, steward, superintendent, warden, warder

keeping **1.** aegis, auspices, care, charge, custody, guardianship, keep, maintenance, patronage, possession, protection, safekeeping, trust **2.** accord, agreement, balance, compliance, conformity, congruity, consistency, correspondence, harmony, observance, proportion

keep on carry on, continue, endure, last, persevere, persist, prolong, remain

keepsake emblem, favour, memento, relic, remembrance, reminder, souvenir, symbol, token

keep up balance, compete, contend, continue, emulate, keep pace, maintain, match, persevere, preserve, rival, sustain, vie

keg barrel, cask, drum, firkin, hogshead, tun, vat

ken 1. compass, field, range, scope, sight, view, vision **2.** acquaintance, awareness, cognizance, comprehension, knowledge, notice, understanding

kerchief babushka, headscarf, head~square, scarf, square

kernel core, essence, germ, gist, grain, marrow, nub, pith, seed, substance

key *noun* **1.** latchkey, opener **2.** *figurative* answer, clue, cue, explanation, guide, indicator, interpretation, lead, means, pointer, sign, solution, translation *~adjective* **3.** basic, chief, crucial, deci~sive, essential, fundamental, important, leading, main, major, pivotal, principal

▷ **Antonyms** (*sense 3*) minor, secondary, subsidiary, superficial

key in enter, input, keyboard, type

keynote centre, core, essence, gist, heart, kernel, marrow, pith, substance, theme

keystone basis, core, cornerstone, crux, fundament, ground, lynchpin, main~spring, motive, principle, quoin, root, source, spring

kick *verb* **1.** boot, punt, put the boot in(to) (*slang*) **2.** *figurative* complain, gripe (*in~formal*), grumble, object, oppose, pro~test, rebel, resist, spurn **3.** *informal* abandon, desist from, give up, leave off, quit, stop *~noun* **4.** force, intensity, pep, power, punch, pungency, snap (*infor~mal*), sparkle, strength, tang, verve, vi~tality, zest **5.** buzz (*slang*), enjoyment, excitement, fun, gratification, jollies (*slang*), pleasure, stimulation, thrill

kickback bribe, cut (*informal*), gift, graft (*informal*), payment, payoff, recom~pense, reward, share, sop, sweetener (*slang*)

kickoff *noun* beginning, commencement, opening, outset, start

kick off *verb* begin, commence, get the show on the road, get under way, initi~ate, kick-start, open, start

kick out discharge, dismiss, eject, evict, expel, get rid of, give (someone) their marching orders, give the boot (*slang*), give the bum's rush (*slang*), give the push, kiss off (*slang, chiefly U.S. & Canad.*), oust, reject, remove, sack (*in~formal*), show one the door, throw out on one's ear (*informal*), toss out

kid 1. *noun* ankle-biter (*Austral. slang*), baby, bairn, boy, child, girl, infant, lad, lass, little one, rug rat (*U.S. & Canad. informal*), sprog (*slang*), stripling, teen~ager, tot, youngster, youth **2.** *~verb* bamboozle, beguile, cozen, delude, fool, gull (*archaic*), hoax, hoodwink, jest, joke, mock, plague, pretend, rag (*Brit.*), ridicule, tease, trick, wind up (*Brit. slang*)

kidnap abduct, capture, hijack, hold to ransom, remove, seize, steal

kill 1. annihilate, assassinate, blow away (*slang, chiefly U.S.*), bump off (*slang*), butcher, destroy, dispatch, do away with, do in (*slang*), eradicate, execute, exterminate, extirpate, knock off (*slang*), liquidate, massacre, murder, neutralize, obliterate, slaughter, slay, take out (*slang*), take (someone's) life, waste (*informal*), wipe from the face of the earth (*informal*) **2.** *figurative* cancel, cease, deaden, defeat, extinguish, halt, quash, quell, ruin, scotch, smother, sti~fle, still, stop, suppress, veto

killer assassin, butcher, cut-throat, de~stroyer, executioner, exterminator, gunman, hit man (*slang*), liquidator, murderer, slaughterer, slayer

killing *noun* **1.** bloodshed, carnage, ex~ecution, extermination, fatality, homi~cide, manslaughter, massacre, murder, slaughter, slaying **2.** *informal* bomb (*slang*), bonanza, cleanup (*informal*), coup, gain, profit, success, windfall *~adjective* **3.** deadly, death-dealing, deathly, fatal, lethal, mortal, murderous **4.** *informal* debilitating, enervating, ex~hausting, fatiguing, punishing, tiring **5.** *informal* absurd, amusing, comical, hi~larious, ludicrous, uproarious

kill-joy dampener, damper, spoilsport, wet blanket (*informal*)

kin *noun* **1.** affinity, blood, connection, consanguinity, extraction, kinship, line~age, relationship, stock **2.** connections, family, kindred, kinsfolk, kinsmen, kith, people, relations, relatives *~adjective* **3.** akin, allied, close, cognate, consanguine, consanguineous, kindred, near, related

kind[1] *noun* **1.** brand, breed, class, family, genus, ilk, race, set, sort, species, stamp, variety **2.** character, description, essence, habit, manner, mould, nature, persuasion, sort, style, temperament, type

kind[2] *adjective* affectionate, amiable, amicable, beneficent, benevolent, be~nign, bounteous, charitable, clement, compassionate, congenial, considerate, cordial, courteous, friendly, generous, gentle, good, gracious, humane, indul~gent, kind-hearted, kindly, lenient, lov~ing, mild, neighbourly, obliging, phil~anthropic, propitious, sympathetic, tender-hearted, thoughtful, under~standing

▷ **Antonyms** cruel, hard-hearted, harsh, heartless, merciless, severe, unkind, unsympathetic, vicious

kind-hearted altruistic, amicable, com~passionate, considerate, generous, good-natured, gracious, helpful, hu~mane, kind, sympathetic, tender, tender-hearted

▷ **Antonyms** cold, cold-hearted, cruel, hard-hearted, harsh, heartless, selfish, severe, unkind, unsympathetic

kindle 1. fire, ignite, inflame, light, set fire to **2.** *figurative* agitate, animate, arouse, awaken, bestir, enkindle, exas~

perate, excite, foment, incite, induce, inflame, inspire, provoke, rouse, sharpen, stimulate, stir, thrill
▷ **Antonyms** douse, extinguish, quell, quench

kindliness amiability, beneficence, benevolence, benignity, charity, compassion, friendliness, gentleness, humanity, kind-heartedness, kindness, sympathy

kindly **1.** *adjective* affable, beneficial, benevolent, benign, compassionate, cordial, favourable, genial, gentle, good-natured, hearty, helpful, kind, mild, pleasant, polite, sympathetic, warm **2.** *~adverb* agreeably, cordially, graciously, politely, tenderly, thoughtfully
▷ **Antonyms** *~adjective* cruel, harsh, malevolent, malicious, mean, severe, spiteful, unkindly, unsympathetic *~adverb* cruelly, harshly, malevolently, maliciously, meanly, spitefully, unkindly, unsympathetically

kindness **1.** affection, amiability, beneficence, benevolence, charity, clemency, compassion, decency, fellow-feeling, generosity, gentleness, goodness, goodwill, grace, hospitality, humanity, indulgence, kindliness, magnanimity, patience, philanthropy, tenderness, tolerance, understanding **2.** aid, assistance, benefaction, bounty, favour, generosity, good deed, help, service
▷ **Antonyms** (*sense 1*) animosity, callousness, cold-heartedness, cruelty, hard-heartedness, heartlessness, ill will, inhumanity, malevolence, malice, misanthropy, viciousness

kindred *noun* **1.** affinity, consanguinity, relationship **2.** connections, family, flesh, kin, kinsfolk, kinsmen, lineage, relations, relatives *~adjective* **3.** affiliated, akin, allied, cognate, congenial, corresponding, kin, like, matching, related, similar

king crowned head, emperor, majesty, monarch, overlord, prince, ruler, sovereign

kingdom **1.** dominion, dynasty, empire, monarchy, realm, reign, sovereignty **2.** commonwealth, county, division, nation, province, state, territory, tract **3.** area, domain, field, province, sphere, territory

kingly **1.** imperial, monarchical, regal, royal, sovereign **2.** august, glorious, grand, grandiose, imposing, majestic, noble, splendid, stately

kink **1.** bend, coil, corkscrew, crimp, entanglement, frizz, knot, tangle, twist, wrinkle **2.** cramp, crick, pang, pinch, spasm, stab, tweak, twinge **3.** complication, defect, difficulty, flaw, hitch, imperfection, knot, tangle **4.** crotchet, eccentricity, fetish, foible, idiosyncrasy, quirk, singularity, vagary, whim

kinky **1.** bizarre, eccentric, odd, oddball (*informal*), off-the-wall (*slang*), outlandish, outré, peculiar, queer, quirky, strange, unconventional, wacko (*slang*), weird **2.** degenerated, depraved, deviant, licentious, perverted, pervy (*slang*), unnatural, warped **3.** coiled, crimped, curled, curly, frizzled, frizzy, tangled, twisted

kinsfolk connections, family, kin, kindred, kinsmen, relations, relatives

kinship **1.** blood relationship, consanguinity, kin, relation, ties of blood **2.** affinity, alliance, association, bearing, connection, correspondence, relationship, similarity

kinsman blood relative, fellow clansman, fellow tribesman, relation, relative

kiosk bookstall, booth, counter, newsstand, stall, stand

kismet destiny, fate, fortune, karma, lot, portion, preordination, Providence

kiss *verb* **1.** buss (*archaic*), canoodle (*slang*), greet, neck (*informal*), osculate, peck (*informal*), salute, smooch (*informal*) **2.** brush, caress, glance, graze, scrape, touch *~noun* **3.** buss (*archaic*), osculation, peck (*informal*), smacker (*slang*)

kit accoutrements, apparatus, effects, equipment, gear, impedimenta, implements, instruments, outfit, paraphernalia, provisions, rig, supplies, tackle, tools, trappings, utensils

kitchen cookhouse, galley, kitchenette

kit out *or* **up** accoutre, arm, deck out, equip, fit out, fix up, furnish, outfit, provide with, supply

kittenish coquettish, coy, flirtatious, frisky, frolicsome, funloving (*literary*), playful, sportive

knack ability, adroitness, aptitude, bent, capacity, dexterity, expertise, expertness, facility, flair, forte, genius, gift, handiness, ingenuity, propensity, quickness, skilfulness, skill, talent, trick
▷ **Antonyms** awkwardness, clumsiness, disability, ineptitude

knave blackguard, bounder (*old-fashioned Brit. slang*), cheat, cocksucker (*taboo slang*), rapscallion, rascal, reprobate, rogue, rotter (*slang, chiefly Brit.*), scally (*Northwest English dialect*), scallywag (*informal*), scamp, scapegrace, scoundrel, scumbag (*slang*), swindler, varlet (*archaic*), villain

knavery chicanery, corruption, deceit, deception, dishonesty, double-dealing, duplicity, fraud, imposture, rascality, roguery, trickery, villainy

knavish deceitful, deceptive, dishonest, dishonourable, fraudulent, lying, rascally, roguish, scoundrelly, tricky, unprincipled, unscrupulous, villainous
▷ **Antonyms** honest, honourable, noble, principled, trustworthy

knead blend, form, manipulate, massage, mould, press, rub, shape, squeeze, stroke, work

kneel bow, bow down, curtsey, curtsy, genuflect, get down on one's knees, kowtow, make obeisance, stoop

knell 1. *verb* announce, chime, herald, peal, resound, ring, sound, toll 2. *~noun* chime, peal, ringing, sound, toll

knickers bloomers, briefs, drawers, panties, smalls, underwear

knick-knack bagatelle, bauble, bibelot, bric-a-brac, gewgaw, gimcrack, kick~shaw, plaything, trifle, trinket

knife 1. *noun* blade, cutter, cutting tool 2. *~verb* cut, impale, lacerate, pierce, slash, stab, wound

knightly chivalrous, courageous, courtly, gallant, gracious, heroic, noble, val~iant

knit 1. affix, ally, bind, connect, contract, fasten, heal, interlace, intertwine, join, link, loop, mend, secure, tie, unite, weave 2. crease, furrow, knot, pucker, wrinkle

knob boss, bulk, bump, bunch, hump, knot, knurl, lump, nub, projection, pro~trusion, protuberance, snag, stud, swell, swelling, tumour

knock *verb* 1. belt (*informal*), buffet, chin (*slang*), clap, cuff, deck (*slang*), hit, lay one on (*slang*), punch, rap, slap, smack, smite (*archaic*), strike, thump, thwack *~noun* 2. belt (*informal*), blow, box, clip, clout (*informal*), cuff, hammering, rap, slap, smack, thump *~verb* 3. *informal* abuse, asperse, belittle, carp, cavil, cen~sure, condemn, criticize, denigrate, dep~recate, disparage, find fault, have a go (at) (*informal*), lambast(e), run down, slag (off) (*slang*), slam (*slang*) *~noun* 4. blame, censure, condemnation, criti~cism, defeat, failure, heat (*slang, chiefly U.S. & Canad.*), rebuff, rejection, rever~sal, setback, slagging (off) (*slang*), stick (*slang*), stricture

knock about *or* **around** 1. ramble, range, roam, rove, traipse, travel, wander 2. abuse, batter, beat up (*informal*), bruise, buffet, clobber (*slang*), damage, hit, hurt, lambast(e), maltreat, man~handle, maul, mistreat, strike, work over (*slang*), wound

knock down batter, clout (*informal*), deck (*slang*), demolish, destroy, fell, floor, level, pound, raze, smash, wallop (*infor~mal*), wreck

knock off 1. clock off, clock out, complete, conclude, finish, stop work, terminate 2. blag (*slang*), cabbage (*Brit. slang*), filch, nick (*slang, chiefly Brit.*), pilfer, pinch, purloin, rob, steal, thieve 3. assassinate, blow away (*slang, chiefly U.S.*), bump off (*slang*), do away with, do in (*slang*), kill, liquidate, murder, slay, take out (*slang*), waste (*informal*)

knockout 1. *coup de grâce,* kayo (*slang*), KO *or* K.O. (*slang*) 2. hit, sensation, smash, smasheroo (*informal*), smash-hit, stunner (*informal*), success, tri~umph, winner

▷ **Antonyms** (*sense 2*) failure, flop (*infor~mal*), turkey (*informal*)

knoll barrow, hill, hillock, hummock, mound, swell

knot *verb* 1. bind, complicate, entangle, knit, loop, secure, tether, tie, weave *~noun* 2. bond, bow, braid, connection, joint, ligature, loop, rosette, tie 3. ag~gregation, bunch, clump, cluster, collec~tion, heap, mass, pile, tuft 4. assem~blage, band, circle, clique, company, crew (*informal*), crowd, gang, group, mob, pack, set, squad

knotty 1. bumpy, gnarled, knobby, knot~ted, nodular, rough, rugged 2. baffling, complex, complicated, difficult, hard, intricate, mystifying, perplexing, prob~lematical, puzzling, thorny, tricky, troublesome

know 1. apprehend, comprehend, experi~ence, fathom, feel certain, ken (*Scot.*), learn, notice, perceive, realize, recog~nize, see, undergo, understand 2. asso~ciate with, be acquainted with, be fa~miliar with, fraternize with, have deal~ings with, have knowledge of, recognize 3. differentiate, discern, distinguish, identify, make out, perceive, recognize, see, tell

▷ **Antonyms** (*sense 1*) be ignorant, be unfamiliar with, misunderstand

know-how ability, adroitness, aptitude, capability, craft, dexterity, experience, expertise, faculty, flair, ingenuity, knack, knowledge, proficiency, savoir-faire, skill, talent

knowing 1. astute, clever, clued-up (*in~formal*), competent, discerning, experi~enced, expert, intelligent, qualified, skilful, well-informed 2. acute, cunning, eloquent, expressive, meaningful, per~ceptive, sagacious, shrewd, significant 3. aware, conscious, deliberate, intended, intentional

▷ **Antonyms** accidental, ignorant, in~genuous, naive, obtuse, unintentional, wet behind the ears (*informal*)

knowingly consciously, deliberately, in~tentionally, on purpose, purposely, wil~fully, wittingly

knowledge 1. education, enlightenment, erudition, instruction, intelligence, learning, scholarship, schooling, science, tuition, wisdom 2. ability, apprehension, cognition, comprehension, conscious~ness, discernment, grasp, judgment, recognition, understanding 3. acquaint~ance, cognizance, familiarity, informa~tion, intimacy, notice

▷ **Antonyms** ignorance, illiteracy, mis~understanding, unawareness, unfamili~arity

knowledgeable 1. acquainted, *au courant, au fait,* aware, clued-up (*informal*), cog~

nizant, conscious, conversant, experienced, familiar, in the know (*informal*), understanding, well-informed **2.** educated, erudite, intelligent, learned, lettered, scholarly

known acknowledged, admitted, avowed, celebrated, common, confessed, familiar, famous, manifest, noted, obvious, patent, plain, popular, published, recognized, well-known

▷ **Antonyms** closet (*informal*), concealed, hidden, secret, unfamiliar, unknown, unrecognized, unrevealed

knuckle under *verb* accede, acquiesce, capitulate, give in, give way, submit, succumb, surrender, yield

▷ **Antonyms** be defiant, dig one's heels in (*informal*), hold out (against), kick up (a fuss *or* stink), rebel, resist

knurl bulb, bulge, burl, gnarl, knot, lump, node, protuberance, ridge

kowtow **1.** bow, genuflect, kneel **2.** brown-nose (*taboo slang*), court, cringe, fawn, flatter, grovel, kiss (someone's) ass (*U.S. & Canad. taboo slang*), lick someone's arse (*taboo slang*), lick someone's boots, pander to, suck up to (*slang*), toady, truckle

kudos acclaim, applause, distinction, esteem, fame, glory, honour, laudation, notability, plaudits, praise, prestige, regard, renown, repute

L, l

label *noun* **1.** docket (*chiefly Brit.*), flag, marker, sticker, tag, tally, ticket **2.** characterization, classification, description, epithet **3.** brand, company, mark, trademark *~verb* **4.** docket (*chiefly Brit.*), flag, mark, stamp, sticker, tag, tally **5.** brand, call, characterize, class, classify, define, describe, designate, identify, name

laborious 1. arduous, backbreaking, burdensome, difficult, exhausting, fatiguing, hard, herculean, onerous, strenuous, tiresome, tiring, toilsome, tough, uphill, wearing, wearisome **2.** assiduous, diligent, hard-working, indefatigable, industrious, painstaking, persevering, sedulous, tireless, unflagging **3.** *of literary style, etc.* forced, laboured, not fluent, ponderous, strained

▷ **Antonyms** (*sense 1*) easy, easy-peasy (*slang*), effortless, light (*sense 3*) natural, simple

labour *noun* **1.** industry, toil, work **2.** employees, hands, labourers, workers, workforce, workmen **3.** donkey-work, drudgery, effort, exertion, grind (*informal*), industry, pains, painstaking, sweat (*informal*), toil, travail **4.** chore, job, task, undertaking **5.** childbirth, contractions, delivery, labour pains, pains, parturition, throes, travail *~verb* **6.** drudge, endeavour, grind (*informal*), peg along *or* away (*chiefly Brit.*), plod, plug along *or* away (*informal*), slave, strive, struggle, sweat (*informal*), toil, travail, work **7.** (*usually with* **under**) be a victim of, be burdened by, be disadvantaged, suffer **8.** dwell on, elaborate, make a federal case of (*U.S. informal*), make a production (out) of (*informal*), overdo, overemphasize, strain **9.** *of a ship* heave, pitch, roll, toss

▷ **Antonyms** *~noun* ease, idleness, leisure, relaxation, repose, respite, rest *~verb* relax, rest

laboured 1. awkward, difficult, forced, heavy, stiff, strained **2.** affected, contrived, overdone, overwrought, ponderous, studied, unnatural

labourer blue-collar worker, drudge, hand, labouring man, manual worker, navvy (*Brit. informal*), unskilled worker, worker, working man, workman

labyrinth coil, complexity, complication, convolution, entanglement, intricacy, jungle, knotty problem, maze, perplexity, puzzle, riddle, snarl, tangle, windings

labyrinthine Byzantine, complex, confused, convoluted, Daedalian, Gordian, intricate, involved, knotty, mazelike, mazy, perplexing, puzzling, tangled, tortuous, winding

lace *noun* **1.** filigree, netting, openwork, tatting **2.** bootlace, cord, shoelace, string, thong, tie *~verb* **3.** attach, bind, close, do up, fasten, intertwine, interweave, thread, tie, twine **4.** add to, fortify, mix in, spike

lace into assail, attack, belabour, berate, castigate, flay, lay into (*informal*), light into (*informal*), set about, vituperate

lacerate 1. claw, cut, gash, jag, maim, mangle, rend, rip, slash, tear, wound **2.** *figurative* afflict, distress, harrow, rend, torment, torture, wound

laceration cut, gash, injury, mutilation, rent, rip, slash, tear, trauma (*Pathology*), wound

lachrymose crying, dolorous, lugubrious, mournful, sad, tearful, weeping, weepy (*informal*), woeful

lack 1. *noun* absence, dearth, deficiency, deprivation, destitution, insufficiency, need, privation, scantiness, scarcity, shortage, shortcoming, shortness, want **2.** *~verb* be deficient in, be short of, be without, miss, need, require, want

▷ **Antonyms** *~noun* abundance, adequacy, excess, plentifulness, sufficiency, surplus *~verb* enjoy, have, own, possess

lackadaisical 1. apathetic, dull, enervated, half-arsed (*Brit. slang*), half-assed (*U.S. & Canad. slang*), half-hearted, indifferent, languid, languorous, lethargic, limp, listless, spiritless **2.** abstracted, dreamy, idle, indolent, inert, lazy

▷ **Antonyms** ambitious, diligent, excited, inspired, spirited

lackey 1. ass-kisser (*U.S. & Canad. taboo slang*), brown-noser (*taboo slang*), creature, fawner, flatterer, flunky, hanger-on, instrument, menial, minion, parasite, pawn, sycophant, toady, tool, yes man **2.** attendant, cohort (*chiefly U.S.*), flunky, footman, manservant, valet, varlet (*archaic*)

lacking defective, deficient, flawed, impaired, inadequate, minus (*informal*), missing, needing, sans (*archaic*), wanting, without

lacklustre boring, dim, drab, dry, dull, flat, leaden, lifeless, lustreless, muted, prosaic, sombre, unimaginative, uninspired, vapid

laconic brief, clipped, compact, concise, crisp, curt, monosyllabic, pithy, sententious, short, succinct, terse, to the point
▷ **Antonyms** long-winded, loquacious, rambling, verbose, voluble, wordy

lacuna blank, break, gap, hiatus, omission, space, void

lacy delicate, filigree, fine, frilly, gauzy, gossamer, lacelike, meshy, netlike, open, sheer

lad boy, chap (*informal*), fellow, guy (*informal*), juvenile, kid (*informal*), laddie (*Scot.*), schoolboy, shaver (*informal*), stripling, youngster, youth

laden burdened, charged, encumbered, fraught, full, hampered, loaded, oppressed, taxed, weighed down, weighted

la-di-da affected, conceited, highfalutin (*informal*), mannered, mincing, overrefined, posh (*informal, chiefly Brit.*), precious, pretentious, snobbish, snooty (*informal*), stuck-up (*informal*), toffee-nosed (*slang, chiefly Brit.*), too-too

lady-killer Casanova, Don Juan, heartbreaker, ladies' man, libertine, Lothario, philanderer, rake, roué, wolf (*informal*), womanizer

ladylike courtly, cultured, decorous, elegant, genteel, modest, polite, proper, refined, respectable, sophisticated, well-bred
▷ **Antonyms** discourteous, ill-bred, ill-mannered, impolite, rude, uncultured, unladylike, unmannerly, unrefined

lag 1. be behind, dawdle, delay, drag (behind), drag one's feet (*informal*), hang back, idle, linger, loiter, saunter, straggle, tarry, trail 2. decrease, diminish, ebb, fail, fall off, flag, lose strength, slacken, wane

laggard dawdler, idler, lingerer, loafer, loiterer, lounger, saunterer, skiver (*Brit. slang*), slowcoach (*Brit. informal*), slowpoke (*U.S. & Canad. informal*), sluggard, snail, straggler

laid-back at ease, casual, easy-going, easy-oasy (*slang*), free and easy, relaxed, together (*slang*), unflappable (*informal*), unhurried
▷ **Antonyms** edgy, jittery (*informal*), jumpy, keyed-up, nervous, on edge, tense, twitchy (*informal*), uptight (*informal*), wound-up (*informal*)

laid up bedridden, disabled, housebound, ill, immobilized, incapacitated, injured, on the sick list, out of action (*informal*), sick

lair 1. burrow, den, earth, form, hole, nest, resting place 2. *informal* den, hide-out, refuge, retreat, sanctuary

laissez faire *or* **laisser faire** *noun* free enterprise, free trade, individualism, live and let live, nonintervention

lam batter, beat, hit, knock, lambast(e), pelt, pound, strike, thrash

lambast(e) 1. beat, bludgeon, cosh (*Brit.*), cudgel, drub, flog, strike, thrash, whip 2. bawl out (*informal*), berate, carpet (*informal*), castigate, censure, chew out (*U.S. & Canad. informal*), excoriate, flay, give a rocket (*Brit. & N.Z. informal*), rap over the knuckles, read the riot act, rebuke, reprimand, scold, slap on the wrist, tear into (*informal*), tear (someone) off a strip (*Brit. informal*), upbraid

lambent 1. dancing, flickering, fluttering, licking, touching, twinkling 2. gleaming, glistening, glowing, luminous, lustrous, radiant, refulgent, shimmering 3. *of wit or humour* brilliant, light, sparkling

lamblike 1. gentle, meek, mild, passive, peaceable, submissive 2. artless, childlike, guileless, innocent, naive, simple, trusting

lame 1. crippled, defective, disabled, game, halt (*archaic*), handicapped, hobbling, limping 2. *figurative* feeble, flimsy, inadequate, insufficient, pathetic, poor, thin, unconvincing, unsatisfactory, weak

lament *verb* 1. bemoan, bewail, complain, deplore, grieve, mourn, regret, sorrow, wail, weep ~*noun* 2. complaint, keening, lamentation, moan, moaning, plaint, ululation, wail, wailing 3. coronach (*Scot. & Irish*), dirge, elegy, monody, requiem, threnody

lamentable 1. deplorable, distressing, grievous, harrowing, mournful, regrettable, sorrowful, tragic, unfortunate, woeful 2. low, meagre, mean, miserable, not much cop (*Brit. slang*), pitiful, poor, unsatisfactory, wretched

lamentation dirge, grief, grieving, keening, lament, moan, mourning, plaint, sobbing, sorrow, ululation, wailing, weeping

laminate 1. coat, cover, face, foliate, layer, stratify, veneer 2. exfoliate, flake, separate, split

lampoon 1. *noun* burlesque, caricature, parody, pasquinade, satire, send-up (*Brit. informal*), skit, squib, takeoff (*informal*) 2. ~*verb* burlesque, caricature, make fun of, mock, parody, pasquinade, ridicule, satirize, send up (*Brit. informal*), squib, take off (*informal*)

land *noun* 1. dry land, earth, ground, terra firma 2. dirt, ground, loam, soil 3. countryside, farming, farmland, rural districts 4. acres, estate, grounds, property, real property, realty 5. country, district, fatherland, motherland, nation, province, region, territory, tract *~verb* **6.** alight, arrive, berth, come to rest, debark, disembark, dock, touch down **7.** (*sometimes with* **up**) arrive, bring, carry, cause, end up, lead, turn up, wind up **8.** *informal* acquire, gain, get, obtain, score (*slang*), secure, win

landlord 1. host, hotelier, hotel-keeper, innkeeper **2.** freeholder, lessor, owner, proprietor

landmark 1. feature, monument **2.** crisis, milestone, turning point, watershed **3.** benchmark, boundary, cairn, milepost, signpost

landscape countryside, outlook, panorama, prospect, scene, scenery, view, vista

landslide 1. *noun* avalanche, landslip, rockfall **2.** *~adjective* decisive, overwhelming, runaway

language 1. communication, conversation, discourse, expression, interchange, parlance, speech, talk, utterance, verbalization, vocalization **2.** argot, cant, dialect, idiom, jargon, lingo (*informal*), lingua franca, patois, patter, speech, terminology, tongue, vernacular, vocabulary **3.** diction, expression, phraseology, phrasing, style, wording

languid 1. drooping, faint, feeble, languorous, limp, pining, sickly, weak, weary **2.** indifferent, lackadaisical, languorous, lazy, listless, spiritless, unenthusiastic, uninterested **3.** dull, heavy, inactive, inert, lethargic, sluggish, torpid

▷ **Antonyms** active, alive and kicking, energetic, strong, tireless, vigorous

languish 1. decline, droop, fade, fail, faint, flag, sicken, waste, weaken, wilt, wither **2.** (*often with* **for**) desire, eat one's heart out over, hanker, hunger, long, pine, sigh, suspire, want, yearn **3.** be abandoned, be disregarded, be neglected, rot, suffer, waste away **4.** brood, despond, grieve, repine, sorrow

▷ **Antonyms** bloom, flourish, prosper, thrive

languishing 1. declining, deteriorating, drooping, droopy, fading, failing, flagging, sickening, sinking, wasting away, weak, weakening, wilting, withering **2.** dreamy, longing, lovelorn, lovesick, melancholic, nostalgic, pensive, pining, soulful, tender, wistful, woebegone, yearning

languor 1. apathy, debility, enervation, ennui, faintness, fatigue, feebleness, frailty, heaviness, inertia, lassitude, lethargy, listlessness, torpor, weakness, weariness **2.** dreaminess, drowsiness, indolence, laziness, lotus-eating, relaxation, sleepiness, sloth **3.** calm, hush, lull, oppressiveness, silence, stillness

lank 1. dull, lifeless, limp, long, lustreless, straggling **2.** attenuated, emaciated, gaunt, lanky, lean, rawboned, scraggy, scrawny, skinny, slender, slim, spare, thin

lanky angular, bony, gangling, gaunt, loose-jointed, rangy, rawboned, scraggy, scrawny, spare, tall, thin, weedy (*informal*)

▷ **Antonyms** brawny, burly, chubby, fat, muscular, plump, portly, rotund, rounded, short, sinewy, stocky, stout

lap[1] 1. *noun* circle, circuit, course, distance, loop, orbit, round, tour **2.** *~verb* cover, enfold, envelop, fold, swaddle, swathe, turn, twist, wrap

lap[2] *verb* **1.** gurgle, plash, purl, ripple, slap, splash, swish, wash **2.** drink, lick, sip, sup

lapse *noun* **1.** error, failing, fault, indiscretion, mistake, negligence, omission, oversight, slip **2.** break, breathing space, gap, intermission, interruption, interval, lull, passage, pause **3.** backsliding, decline, descent, deterioration, drop, fall, relapse *~verb* **4.** decline, degenerate, deteriorate, drop, fail, fall, sink, slide, slip **5.** become obsolete, become void, end, expire, run out, stop, terminate

lapsed 1. discontinued, ended, expired, finished, invalid, out of date, run out, unrenewed **2.** backsliding, lacking faith, nonpractising

larceny burglary, misappropriation, pilfering, purloining, robbery, stealing, theft

large 1. big, bulky, colossal, considerable, elephantine, enormous, giant, gigantic, ginormous (*informal*), goodly, great, huge, humongous *or* humungous (*U.S. slang*), immense, jumbo (*informal*), king-size, man-size, massive, mega (*slang*), monumental, sizable *or* sizeable, stellar (*informal*), substantial, tidy (*informal*), vast **2.** abundant, ample, broad, capacious, comprehensive, copious, extensive, full, generous, grand, grandiose, liberal, plentiful, roomy, spacious, sweeping, wide **3. at large: a.** at liberty, free, on the loose, on the run, roaming, unconfined **b.** as a whole, chiefly, generally, in general, in the main, mainly **c.** at length, considerably, exhaustively, greatly, in full detail

▷ **Antonyms** (*senses 1 & 2*) brief, inconsiderable, infinitesimal, little, minute, narrow, petty, scanty, scarce, short, slender, slight, slim, small, sparse, thin, tiny, trivial

large-hearted big-hearted, compassionate, good, good-hearted, kind, kind-hearted, large-souled, magnanimous, sympathetic, understanding

largely as a rule, by and large, chiefly, considerably, extensively, generally, mainly, mostly, predominantly, primarily, principally, to a great extent, widely

large-scale broad, extensive, far-reaching,

global, sweeping, vast, wholesale, wide, wide-ranging

largesse, largess **1.** alms-giving, benefaction, bounty, charity, generosity, liberality, munificence, open-handedness, philanthropy **2.** bequest, bounty, donation, endowment, gift, grant, present

lark **1.** *noun* antic, caper, escapade, fling, frolic, fun, gambol, game, jape, mischief, prank, revel, rollick, romp, skylark, spree **2.** *~verb* caper, cavort, cut capers, frolic, gambol, have fun, make mischief, play, rollick, romp, sport

lascivious **1.** horny (*slang*), lecherous, lewd, libidinous, licentious, lustful, prurient, randy (*informal, chiefly Brit.*), salacious, sensual, unchaste, voluptuous, wanton **2.** bawdy, blue, coarse, crude, dirty, indecent, obscene, offensive, pornographic, ribald, scurrilous, smutty, suggestive, vulgar, X-rated (*informal*)

lash[1] *noun* **1.** blow, hit, stripe, stroke, swipe (*informal*) *~verb* **2.** beat, birch, chastise, flagellate, flog, horsewhip, lam (*slang*), lambast(e), scourge, thrash, whip **3.** beat, buffet, dash, drum, hammer, hit, knock, lambast(e), larrup (*dialect*), pound, punch, smack, strike **4.** attack, belabour, berate, blast, castigate, censure, criticize, flay, lambast(e), lampoon, put down, ridicule, satirize, scold, slate (*informal, chiefly Brit.*), tear into (*informal*), upbraid

lash[2] *verb* bind, fasten, join, make fast, rope, secure, strap, tie

lass bird (*slang*), chick (*slang*), colleen (*Irish*), damsel, girl, lassie (*informal*), maid, maiden, miss, schoolgirl, wench (*facetious*), young woman

lassitude apathy, drowsiness, dullness, enervation, ennui, exhaustion, fatigue, heaviness, inertia, languor, lethargy, listlessness, prostration, sluggardliness, sluggishness, tiredness, torpor, weariness

last[1] *adjective* **1.** aftermost, at the end, hindmost, rearmost **2.** latest, most recent **3.** closing, concluding, extreme, final, furthest, remotest, terminal, ultimate, utmost *~adverb* **4.** after, behind, bringing up the rear, in *or* at the end, in the rear *~noun* **5.** close, completion, conclusion, end, ending, finale, finish, termination **6. at last** at length, at the end of the day, eventually, finally, in conclusion, in the end, in the fullness of time, ultimately

▷ **Antonyms** (*sense 1*) first, foremost, leading (*sense 3*) earliest, first, initial, introductory, opening

last[2] *verb* abide, carry on, continue, endure, hold on, hold out, keep, keep on, persist, remain, stand up, survive, wear

▷ **Antonyms** cease, depart, die, end, expire, fade, fail, stop, terminate

last-ditch all-out (*informal*), desperate, final, frantic, heroic, straining, struggling

lasting abiding, continuing, deep-rooted, durable, enduring, eternal, indelible, lifelong, long-standing, long-term, perennial, permanent, perpetual, unceasing, undying, unending

▷ **Antonyms** ephemeral, fleeting, momentary, passing, short-lived, transient, transitory

lastly after all, all in all, at last, finally, in conclusion, in the end, to conclude, to sum up, ultimately

last word, the **1.** final say, finis, mother (of all), summation, ultimatum **2.** best, cream, *crème de la crème,* crown, epitome, *ne plus ultra,* perfection, quintessence, ultimate **3.** *dernier cri,* fashion, latest, newest, rage, vogue

latch **1.** *noun* bar, bolt, catch, clamp, fastening, hasp, hook, lock, sneck (*dialect*) **2.** *~verb* bar, bolt, fasten, lock, make fast, secure, sneck (*dialect*)

late *adjective* **1.** behind, behindhand, belated, delayed, last-minute, overdue, slow, tardy, unpunctual **2.** advanced, fresh, modern, new, recent **3.** dead, deceased, defunct, departed, ex-, former, old, past, preceding, previous *~adverb* **4.** at the last minute, behindhand, behind time, belatedly, dilatorily, slowly, tardily, unpunctually

▷ **Antonyms** *~adjective* (*sense 1*) beforehand, early, prompt, punctual, seasoned, timely (*sense 2*) old (*sense 3*) alive, existing *~adverb* beforehand, early, in advance

lately in recent times, just now, latterly, not long ago, of late, recently

lateness advanced hour, belatedness, delay, late date, retardation, tardiness, unpunctuality

latent concealed, dormant, hidden, immanent, inherent, invisible, lurking, potential, quiescent, secret, undeveloped, unexpressed, unrealized, unseen, veiled

▷ **Antonyms** apparent, conspicuous, developed, evident, expressed, manifest, obvious, realized

later *adverb* after, afterwards, by and by, in a while, in time, later on, next, subsequently, thereafter

lateral edgeways, flanking, side, sideward, sideways

latest *adjective* current, fashionable, happening (*informal*), in, modern, most recent, newest, now, up-to-date, up-to-the-minute, with it (*informal*)

lather *noun* **1.** bubbles, foam, froth, soap, soapsuds, suds **2.** *informal* dither (*chiefly Brit.*), fever, flap (*informal*), fluster, fuss, pother, state (*informal*), stew (*informal*), sweat, tizzy (*informal*), twitter (*informal*) *~verb* **3.** foam, froth, soap **4.** *informal* beat, cane, drub, flog, lambast(e), strike, thrash, whip

lathery bubbly, foamy, frothy, soapy, sudsy

latitude 1. breadth, compass, extent, range, reach, room, scope, space, span, spread, sweep, width **2.** a free hand, elbowroom, freedom, indulgence, laxity, leeway, liberty, licence, play, unrestrictedness

latter closing, concluding, last, last-mentioned, later, latest, modern, recent, second

▷ **Antonyms** antecedent, earlier, foregoing, former, preceding, previous, prior

latterly hitherto, lately, of late, recently

lattice fretwork, grating, grid, grille, latticework, mesh, network, openwork, reticulation, tracery, trellis, web

laud acclaim, approve, celebrate, crack up (*informal*), extol, glorify, honour, magnify (*archaic*), praise, sing *or* sound the praises of

laudable admirable, commendable, creditable, estimable, excellent, meritorious, of note, praiseworthy, worthy

▷ **Antonyms** base, blameworthy, contemptible, ignoble, lowly, unworthy

laudatory acclamatory, adulatory, approbatory, approving, commendatory, complimentary, eulogistic, panegyrical

laugh *verb* **1.** be convulsed (*informal*), be in stitches, be rolling in the aisles (*informal*), bust a gut (*informal*), chortle, chuckle, crack up (*informal*), crease up (*informal*), giggle, guffaw, roar with laughter, snigger, split one's sides, titter **2. laugh at** belittle, deride, jeer, lampoon, make a mock of, make fun of, mock, ridicule, scoff at, take the mickey (out of) (*informal*), taunt *~noun* **3.** belly laugh (*informal*), chortle, chuckle, giggle, guffaw, roar *or* shriek of laughter, snigger, titter **4.** *informal* card (*informal*), caution (*informal*), clown, comedian, comic, entertainer, hoot (*informal*), humorist, joke, lark, scream (*informal*), wag, wit

laughable 1. absurd, derisive, derisory, ludicrous, nonsensical, preposterous, ridiculous, worthy of scorn **2.** amusing, comical, diverting, droll, farcical, funny, hilarious, humorous, mirthful, risible

laughing stock Aunt Sally (*Brit.*), butt, everybody's fool, fair game, figure of fun, target, victim

laugh off brush aside, dismiss, disregard, ignore, minimize, pooh-pooh, shrug off

laughter 1. cachinnation, chortling, chuckling, giggling, guffawing, laughing, tittering **2.** amusement, glee, hilarity, merriment, mirth

launch 1. cast, discharge, dispatch, fire, project, propel, send off, set afloat, set in motion, throw **2.** begin, commence, embark upon, inaugurate, initiate, instigate, introduce, open, start

laurels acclaim, awards, bays, Brownie points, commendation, credit, distinction, fame, glory, honour, kudos, praise, prestige, recognition, renown, reward

lavatory bathroom, bog (*slang*), can (*U.S. & Canad. slang*), cloakroom (*Brit.*), crapper (*taboo slang*), Gents, head(s) (*Nautical slang*), john (*slang, chiefly U.S. & Canad.*), khazi (*slang*), Ladies, latrine, little boy's room (*informal*), little girl's room (*informal*), loo (*Brit. informal*), *pissoir*, powder room, (public) convenience, toilet, washroom, water closet, W.C.

lavish *adjective* **1.** abundant, copious, exuberant, lush, luxuriant, opulent, plentiful, profuse, prolific, sumptuous **2.** bountiful, effusive, free, generous, liberal, munificent, open-handed, unstinting **3.** exaggerated, excessive, extravagant, immoderate, improvident, intemperate, prodigal, thriftless, unreasonable, unrestrained, wasteful, wild *~verb* **4.** deluge, dissipate, expend, heap, pour, shower, spend, squander, waste

▷ **Antonyms** *~adjective* cheap, frugal, meagre, miserly, parsimonious, scanty, sparing, stingy, thrifty, tight-fisted *~verb* begrudge, economize, stint, withhold

law 1. charter, code, constitution, jurisprudence **2.** act, canon, code, command, commandment, covenant, decree, demand, edict, enactment, order, ordinance, rule, statute **3.** axiom, canon, criterion, formula, precept, principle, regulation, standard **4. lay down the law** dictate, dogmatize, emphasize, pontificate

law-abiding compliant, dutiful, good, honest, honourable, lawful, obedient, orderly, peaceable, peaceful

lawbreaker convict, criminal, crook (*informal*), culprit, delinquent, felon (*formerly criminal law*), miscreant, offender, sinner, skelm (*S. African*), transgressor, trespasser, villain, violater, wrongdoer

lawful allowable, authorized, constitutional, just, legal, legalized, legitimate, licit, permissible, proper, rightful, valid, warranted

▷ **Antonyms** banned, forbidden, illegal, illegitimate, illicit, prohibited, unauthorized, unlawful

lawless anarchic, chaotic, disorderly, insubordinate, insurgent, mutinous, rebellious, reckless, riotous, seditious, ungoverned, unrestrained, unruly, wild

▷ **Antonyms** civilized, compliant, disciplined, law-abiding, lawful, legitimate, licit, obedient, orderly, regimented, restrained, well-governed

lawlessness anarchy, chaos, disorder,

mobocracy, mob rule, ochlocracy, reign of terror

lawsuit action, argument, case, cause, contest, dispute, industrial tribunal, litigation, proceedings, prosecution, suit, trial

lawyer advocate, attorney, barrister, counsel, counsellor, legal adviser, solicitor

lax 1. careless, casual, easy-going, easy-oasy (*slang*), lenient, neglectful, negligent, overindulgent, remiss, slack, slapdash, slipshod **2.** broad, general, imprecise, inaccurate, indefinite, inexact, nonspecific, shapeless, vague **3.** flabby, flaccid, loose, slack, soft, yielding

▷ **Antonyms** (*sense 1*) conscientious, disciplined, firm, heedful, moral, rigid, scrupulous, severe, stern, strict, stringent (*sense 3*) firm, rigid

laxative aperient, cathartic, physic (*rare*), purgative, purge, salts

lay[1] *verb* **1.** deposit, establish, leave, place, plant, posit, put, set, set down, settle, spread **2.** arrange, dispose, locate, organize, position, set out **3.** bear, deposit, produce **4.** advance, bring forward, lodge, offer, present, put forward, submit **5.** allocate, allot, ascribe, assign, attribute, charge, impute **6.** concoct, contrive, design, devise, hatch, plan, plot, prepare, work out **7.** apply, assess, burden, charge, encumber, impose, saddle, tax **8.** bet, gamble, give odds, hazard, risk, stake, wager **9.** allay, alleviate, appease, assuage, calm, quiet, relieve, soothe, still, suppress **10. lay bare** disclose, divulge, explain, expose, reveal, show, unveil **11. lay hands on: a.** acquire, get, get hold of, grab, grasp, seize **b.** assault, attack, beat up, lay into (*informal*), set on, work over (*slang*) **c.** discover, find, unearth **d.** *Christianity* bless, confirm, consecrate, ordain **12. lay hold of** get, get hold of, grab, grasp, grip, seize, snatch

lay[2] *adjective* **1.** laic, laical, nonclerical, secular **2.** amateur, inexpert, nonprofessional, nonspecialist

lay[3] *noun* ballad, lyric, ode, poem, song

layabout beachcomber, couch potato (*slang*), good-for-nothing, idler, laggard, loafer, lounger, ne'er-do-well, shirker, skiver (*Brit. slang*), slubberdegullion (*archaic*), vagrant, wastrel

lay aside abandon, cast aside, dismiss, postpone, put aside, put off, reject, shelve

lay away accumulate, collect, hoard, keep, lay aside, lay in, salt away, save, stash (*informal*), stockpile, store

lay down 1. discard, drop, give, give up, relinquish, surrender, yield **2.** affirm, assume, establish, formulate, ordain, postulate, prescribe, stipulate

layer 1. bed, ply, row, seam, stratum, thickness, tier **2.** blanket, coat, coating, cover, covering, film, mantle, sheet

lay in accumulate, amass, build up, collect, hoard, stockpile, stock up, store (up)

lay into assail, attack, belabour, go for the jugular, hit out at, lambast(e), let fly at, pitch into (*informal*), set about

layman amateur, lay person, nonprofessional, outsider

lay-off discharge, dismissal, unemployment

lay off 1. discharge, dismiss, drop, give the boot to (*slang*), let go, make redundant, oust, pay off **2.** *informal* cease, desist, get off someone's back (*informal*), give it a rest (*informal*), give over (*informal*), give up, leave alone, leave off, let up, quit, stop

lay on 1. cater (for), furnish, give, provide, purvey, supply **2. lay it on** *slang* butter up, exaggerate, flatter, overdo it, overpraise, soft-soap (*informal*)

layout arrangement, design, draft, formation, geography, outline, plan

lay out 1. arrange, design, display, exhibit, plan, spread out **2.** *informal* disburse, expend, fork out (*slang*), invest, pay, shell out (*informal*), spend **3.** *informal* kayo (*slang*), knock for six (*informal*), knock out, knock unconscious, KO *or* K.O. (*slang*)

lay up 1. accumulate, amass, garner, hoard, keep, preserve, put away, save, store up, treasure **2.** *informal* confine (to bed), hospitalize, incapacitate

laze 1. hang around, idle, loaf, loll, lounge, stand around **2.** (*often with* **away**) fool away, fritter away, kill time, pass time, veg out (*slang, chiefly U.S.*), waste time, while away the hours

laziness dilatoriness, do-nothingness, faineance, faineancy, idleness, inactivity, indolence, lackadaisicalness, slackness, sloth, slothfulness, slowness, sluggishness, tardiness

lazy 1. good-for-nothing, idle, inactive, indolent, inert, remiss, shiftless, slack, slothful, slow, workshy **2.** drowsy, languid, languorous, lethargic, sleepy, slow-moving, sluggish, somnolent, torpid

▷ **Antonyms** active, assiduous, diligent, energetic, industrious, quick, stimulated

lazybones couch potato (*slang*), loafer, lounger, shirker, skiver (*Brit. slang*), sleepyhead, slugabed, sluggard

leach drain, extract, filter, filtrate, lixiviate (*Chemistry*), percolate, seep, strain

lead *verb* **1.** conduct, escort, guide, pilot, precede, show the way, steer, usher **2.** cause, dispose, draw, incline, induce, influence, persuade, prevail, prompt **3.** command, direct, govern, head, manage, preside over, supervise **4.** be ahead (of), blaze a trail, come first, exceed, excel, outdo, outstrip, surpass, transcend **5.** experience, have, live, pass, spend, undergo **6.** bring on, cause, conduce, contribute, produce, result in, serve, tend *~noun* **7.** advance, advantage, cutting edge, edge, first place, margin, precedence, primacy, priority, start, supremacy, van, vanguard **8.** direction, example, guidance, leadership, model **9.** clue, guide, hint, indication, suggestion, tip, trace **10.** leading role, principal, protagonist, star part, title role *~adjective* **11.** chief, first, foremost, head, leading, main, most important, premier, primary, prime, principal

leaden 1. burdensome, crushing, cumbersome, heavy, inert, lead, onerous, oppressive **2.** humdrum, laboured, plodding, sluggish, stiff, stilted, wooden **3.** dismal, dreary, dull, gloomy, languid, lifeless, listless, spiritless **4.** dingy, grey, greyish, lacklustre, louring *or* lowering, lustreless, overcast, sombre

leader bellwether, boss (*informal*), captain, chief, chieftain, commander, conductor, counsellor, director, guide, head, number one, principal, ringleader, ruler, superior, torchbearer

▷ **Antonyms** adherent, disciple, follower, hanger-on, henchman, sidekick (*slang*), supporter

leadership 1. administration, direction, directorship, domination, guidance, management, running, superintendency **2.** authority, command, control, influence, initiative, pre-eminence, supremacy, sway

leading chief, dominant, first, foremost, governing, greatest, highest, main, number one, outstanding, pre-eminent, primary, principal, ruling, superior

▷ **Antonyms** following, hindmost, incidental, inferior, lesser, minor, secondary, subordinate, superficial

lead off begin, commence, get going, get under way, inaugurate, initiate, kick off (*informal*), open, set out, start, start the ball rolling (*informal*)

lead on beguile, deceive, draw on, entice, inveigle, lure, seduce, string along (*informal*), tempt

lead up to approach, intimate, introduce, make advances, make overtures, pave the way, prepare for, prepare the way, work round to

leaf *noun* **1.** blade, bract, flag, foliole, frond, needle, pad **2.** folio, page, sheet **3. turn over a new leaf** amend, begin anew, change, change one's ways, improve, reform *~verb* **4.** bud, green, put out leaves, turn green **5.** browse, flip, glance, riffle, skim, thumb (through)

leaflet advert (*Brit. informal*), bill, booklet, brochure, circular, handbill, mailshot, pamphlet

leafy bosky (*literary*), green, in foliage, leafed, leaved, shaded, shady, springlike, summery, verdant, wooded

league *noun* **1.** alliance, association, band, coalition, combination, combine, compact, confederacy, confederation, consortium, federation, fellowship, fraternity, group, guild, order, partnership, union **2.** ability group, category, class, level **3. in league (with)** allied, collaborating, hand in glove, in cahoots (*informal*), leagued *~verb* **4.** ally, amalgamate, associate, band, collaborate, combine, confederate, join forces, unite

leak *noun* **1.** aperture, chink, crack, crevice, fissure, hole, opening, puncture **2.** drip, leakage, leaking, oozing, percolation, seepage **3.** disclosure, divulgence *~verb* **4.** discharge, drip, escape, exude, ooze, pass, percolate, seep, spill, trickle **5.** blow wide open (*slang*), disclose, divulge, give away, let slip, let the cat out of the bag, make known, make public, pass on, reveal, spill the beans (*informal*), tell

leaky cracked, holey, leaking, not watertight, perforated, porous, punctured, split, waterlogged

lean[1] *verb* **1.** be supported, prop, recline, repose, rest **2.** bend, heel, incline, slant, slope, tilt, tip **3.** be disposed to, be prone to, favour, gravitate towards, have a propensity, prefer, tend **4.** confide, count on, depend, have faith in, rely, trust

lean[2] *adjective* **1.** angular, bony, emaciated, gaunt, lank, macilent (*rare*), rangy, scraggy, scrawny, skinny, slender, slim, spare, thin, unfatty, wiry **2.** bare, barren, inadequate, infertile, meagre, pathetic, pitiful, poor, scanty, sparse, unfruitful, unproductive

▷ **Antonyms** (*sense 1*) ample, brawny, burly, fat, full, obese, plump, portly (*sense 2*) abundant, fertile, plentiful, profuse, rich

leaning aptitude, bent, bias, disposition, inclination, liking, partiality, penchant, predilection, proclivity, proneness, propensity, taste, tendency

leap *verb* **1.** bounce, bound, caper, cavort, frisk, gambol, hop, jump, skip, spring **2.** *figurative* arrive at, come to, form hastily, hasten, hurry, jump, reach, rush **3.** clear, jump (over), vault **4.** advance, become prominent, escalate, gain attention, increase, rocket, soar, surge *~noun* **5.** bound, caper, frisk, hop, jump, skip, spring, vault **6.** escalation, increase, rise, surge, upsurge, upswing

learn 1. acquire, attain, become able, grasp, imbibe, master, pick up **2.** commit to memory, con (*archaic*), get off pat, get (something) word-perfect, learn by heart, memorize **3.** ascertain, detect, determine, discern, discover, find out, gain, gather, hear, suss (out) (*slang*), understand

learned academic, cultured, erudite, experienced, expert, highbrow, intellectual, lettered, literate, scholarly, skilled, versed, well-informed, well-read
▷ **Antonyms** ignorant, illiterate, uneducated, unlearned

learner 1. apprentice, beginner, neophyte, novice, tyro **2.** disciple, pupil, scholar, student, trainee
▷ **Antonyms** (*sense 1*) adept, expert, grandmaster, master, maven, past-master, virtuoso, wizard (*sense 2*) coach, instructor, mentor, teacher, tutor

learning acquirements, attainments, culture, education, erudition, information, knowledge, letters, literature, lore, research, scholarship, schooling, study, tuition, wisdom

lease *verb* charter, hire, let, loan, rent

leash *noun* **1.** lead, rein, tether **2.** check, control, curb, hold, restraint *~verb* **3.** fasten, secure, tether, tie up **4.** check, control, curb, hold back, restrain, suppress

least feeblest, fewest, last, lowest, meanest, minimum, minutest, poorest, slightest, smallest, tiniest

leathery coriaceous, durable, hard, hardened, leatherlike, leathern (*archaic*), rough, rugged, tough, wrinkled

leave¹ *verb* **1.** abandon, abscond, decamp, depart, desert, disappear, do a bunk (*Brit. slang*), exit, flit (*informal*), forsake, go, go away, hook it (*slang*), make tracks, move, pack one's bags (*informal*), pull out, quit, relinquish, retire, set out, sling one's hook (*Brit. slang*), slope off, take off (*informal*), withdraw **2.** forget, lay down, leave behind, mislay **3.** cause, deposit, generate, produce, result in **4.** abandon, cease, desert, desist, drop, evacuate, forbear, give up, refrain, relinquish, renounce, stop, surrender **5.** allot, assign, cede, commit, consign, entrust, give over, refer **6.** bequeath, demise, devise (*Law*), hand down, transmit, will
▷ **Antonyms** appear, arrive, assume, come, continue, emerge, hold, persist, remove, retain, stay

leave² *noun* **1.** allowance, authorization, concession, consent, dispensation, freedom, liberty, permission, sanction **2.** furlough, holiday, leave of absence, sabbatical, time off, vacation **3.** adieu, departure, farewell, goodbye, leave-taking, parting, retirement, withdrawal
▷ **Antonyms** (*sense 1*) denial, prohibition, refusal, rejection (*sense 2*) duty (*sense 3*) arrival, stay

leaven *noun* **1.** barm, ferment, leavening, yeast **2.** *figurative* catalyst, influence, inspiration *~verb* **3.** ferment, lighten, raise, work **4.** *figurative* elevate, imbue, inspire, permeate, pervade, quicken, stimulate, suffuse

leave off abstain, break off, cease, desist, discontinue, end, give over (*informal*), give up, halt, kick (*informal*), knock off (*informal*), refrain, stop

leave out bar, cast aside, count out, disregard, except, exclude, ignore, neglect, omit, overlook, reject

leave-taking departure, farewell, going, goodbye, leaving, parting, sendoff (*informal*), valediction

leavings bits, dregs, fragments, leftovers, orts (*archaic or dialect*), pieces, refuse, remains, remnants, residue, scraps, spoil, sweepings, waste

lecher adulterer, Casanova, debauchee, dirty old man (*slang*), Don Juan, fornicator, goat (*informal*), lech *or* letch (*informal*), libertine, profligate, rake, roué, satyr, seducer, sensualist, wanton, wolf (*informal*), womanizer

lecherous carnal, concupiscent, goatish (*archaic or literary*), lascivious, lewd, libidinous, licentious, lubricious (*U.S. slang*), lubricous, lustful, prurient, randy (*informal, chiefly Brit.*), raunchy (*slang*), ruttish, salacious, unchaste, wanton
▷ **Antonyms** prim, proper, prudish, puritanical, strait-laced, virginal, virtuous

lechery carnality, concupiscence, debauchery, lasciviousness, lecherousness, leching (*informal*), lewdness, libertinism, libidinousness, licentiousness, lubricity, lust, lustfulness, profligacy, prurience, rakishness, randiness (*informal, chiefly Brit.*), salaciousness, sensuality, wantonness, womanizing

lecture *noun* **1.** address, discourse, disquisition, harangue, instruction, lesson, speech, talk *~verb* **2.** address, discourse, expound, give a talk, harangue, hold forth, speak, spout, talk, teach *~noun* **3.** castigation, censure, chiding, dressing-down (*informal*), going-over (*informal*), heat (*slang, chiefly U.S. & Canad.*), rebuke, reprimand, reproof, scolding, talking-to (*informal*), telling off (*informal*), wigging (*Brit. slang*) *~verb* **4.** admonish, bawl out (*informal*), berate, carpet (*informal*), castigate, censure, chew out (*U.S. & Canad. informal*), chide, give a rocket (*Brit. & N.Z. informal*), rate, read the riot act, reprimand, reprove, scold, tear into (*informal*), tear (someone) off a strip (*Brit. informal*), tell off (*informal*)

ledge mantle, projection, ridge, shelf, sill, step

lee cover, protection, refuge, screen, shade, shadow, shelter, shield

leech *figurative* bloodsucker (*informal*), freeloader (*slang*), hanger-on, ligger (*slang*), parasite, sponger (*informal*), sycophant

leer *noun/verb* drool, eye, gloat, goggle, grin, ogle, smirk, squint, stare, wink

leery careful, cautious, chary, distrustful, doubting, dubious, on one's guard, sceptical, shy, suspicious, uncertain, unsure, wary

lees deposit, dregs, grounds, precipitate, refuse, sediment, settlings

leeway elbowroom, latitude, margin, play, room, scope, space

left *adjective* **1.** larboard (*Nautical*), left-hand, port, sinistral **2.** *of politics* leftist, left-wing, liberal, progressive, radical, socialist

left-handed **1.** *archaic* awkward, cack-handed (*informal*), careless, clumsy, fumbling, gauche, maladroit **2.** ambiguous, backhanded, double-edged, enigmatic, equivocal, indirect, ironic, sardonic

leftover *noun* **1.** legacy, remainder, residue, surplus, survivor **2.** *plural* leavings, oddments, odds and ends, remains, remnants, scraps *~adjective* **3.** excess, extra, remaining, surplus, uneaten, unused, unwanted

leg *noun* **1.** limb, lower limb, member, pin (*informal*), stump (*informal*) **2.** brace, prop, support, upright **3.** lap, part, portion, section, segment, stage, stretch **4. a leg up** assistance, boost, help, helping hand, push, support **5. not have a leg to stand on** *informal* be defenceless, be full of holes, be illogical, be invalid, be undermined, be vulnerable, lack support **6. on one's (its) last legs** about to break down, about to collapse, at death's door, dying, exhausted, failing, giving up the ghost, worn out **7. pull someone's leg** *informal* chaff, deceive, fool, kid (*informal*), make fun of, tease, trick, wind up (*Brit. slang*) **8. shake a leg** *slang* **a.** get a move on (*informal*), get cracking (*informal*), hasten, hurry, look lively (*informal*), rush, stir one's stumps **b.** boogie (*slang*), dance, get down (*informal, chiefly U.S.*), hoof it (*slang*), trip the light fantastic **9. stretch one's legs** exercise, go for a walk, move about, promenade, stroll, take a walk, take the air *~verb* **10. leg it** *informal* go on foot, hotfoot, hurry, run, skedaddle (*informal*), walk

legacy **1.** bequest, devise (*Law*), estate, gift, heirloom, inheritance **2.** birthright, endowment, heritage, inheritance, patrimony, throwback, tradition

legal **1.** allowable, allowed, authorized, constitutional, lawful, legalized, legitimate, licit, permissible, proper, rightful, sanctioned, valid **2.** forensic, judicial, juridical

legalistic contentious, disputatious, hairsplitting, literal, litigious, narrow, narrow-minded, polemical, strict

legality accordance with the law, admissibleness, lawfulness, legitimacy, permissibility, rightfulness, validity

legalize allow, approve, authorize, decriminalize, legitimate, legitimize, license, permit, sanction, validate

legate ambassador, delegate, depute (*Scot.*), deputy, emissary, envoy, messenger, nuncio

legatee beneficiary, heir, inheritor, recipient

legation consulate, delegation, diplomatic mission, embassy, envoys, ministry, representation

legend **1.** fable, fiction, folk tale, myth, narrative, saga, story, tale, urban legend **2.** big name, celeb (*informal*), celebrity, luminary, marvel, megastar (*informal*), phenomenon, prodigy, spectacle, wonder **3.** caption, device, inscription, motto **4.** cipher, code, key, table of symbols

legendary **1.** apocryphal, fabled, fabulous, fanciful, fictitious, mythical, romantic, storied, traditional **2.** celebrated, famed, famous, illustrious, immortal, renowned, well-known

▷ **Antonyms** (*sense 1*) factual, genuine, historical (*sense 2*) unknown

legerdemain **1.** prestidigitation, sleight of hand **2.** artfulness, artifice, chicanery, contrivance, craftiness, cunning, deception, feint, hocus-pocus, manipulation, manoeuvring, subterfuge, trickery

legibility clarity, decipherability, ease of reading, legibleness, neatness, plainness, readability, readableness

legible bold, clear, decipherable, distinct, easily read, easy to read, neat, plain, readable

legion *noun* **1.** army, brigade, company, division, force, troop **2.** drove, horde, host, mass, multitude, myriad, number, throng *~adjective* **3.** countless, multitudinous, myriad, numberless, numerous, very many

legislate codify, constitute, enact, establish, make laws, ordain, pass laws, prescribe, put in force

legislation **1.** codification, enactment, lawmaking, prescription, regulation **2.** act, bill, charter, law, measure, regulation, ruling, statute

legislative *adjective* congressional, judicial, juridical, jurisdictive, lawgiving, lawmaking, ordaining, parliamentary

legislator lawgiver, lawmaker, parliamentarian

legislature assembly, chamber, congress, diet, house, lawmaking body, parliament, senate

legitimate *adjective* **1.** acknowledged, authentic, authorized, genuine, kosher (*informal*), lawful, legal, legit (*slang*), licit, proper, real, rightful, sanctioned, statutory, true **2.** admissible, correct, just, justifiable, logical, reasonable, sensible, valid, warranted, well-founded *~verb* **3.** authorize, give the green light

for, legalize, legitimatize, legitimize, permit, pronounce lawful, sanction
▷ **Antonyms** ~*adjective* false, fraudulent, illegal, illegitimate, unfair, unfounded, unjustified, unlawful, unreasonable, unsound

legitimize, legitimise authorize, give the green light for, legalize, legitimate, permit, pronounce lawful, sanction

leisure 1. breathing space, ease, freedom, free time, holiday, liberty, opportunity, pause, quiet, recreation, relaxation, respite, rest, retirement, spare moments, spare time, time off, vacation **2. at leisure: a.** available, free, not booked up, on holiday, unengaged, unoccupied **b.** *also* **at one's leisure** at an unhurried pace, at one's convenience, deliberately, in one's own (good) time, unhurriedly, when it suits one, when one gets round to it (*informal*), without hurry
▷ **Antonyms** business, duty, employment, labour, obligation, occupation, work

leisurely 1. *adjective* comfortable, easy, gentle, laid-back (*informal*), lazy, relaxed, restful, slow, unhurried **2.** ~*adverb* at one's convenience, at one's leisure, comfortably, deliberately, easily, indolently, lazily, lingeringly, slowly, unhurriedly, without haste
▷ **Antonyms** ~*adjective* brisk, fast, hasty, hectic, hurried, quick, rapid, rushed ~*adverb* briskly, hastily, hurriedly, quickly, rapidly

leitmotif (*all with* **recurrent** *or* **recurring**) air, convention, device, idea, melody, motif, phrase, strain, theme

lend 1. accommodate one with, advance, loan **2.** add, afford, bestow, confer, contribute, furnish, give, grant, hand out, impart, present, provide, supply **3. lend an ear** give ear, hearken (*archaic*), heed, listen, take notice **4. lend a hand** aid, assist, give a (helping) hand, help, help out **5. lend itself to** be adaptable, be appropriate, be serviceable, fit, present opportunities of, suit **6. lend oneself to** agree, consent, cooperate, countenance, espouse, support

length 1. *of linear extent* distance, extent, longitude, measure, reach, span **2.** *of time* duration, period, space, span, stretch, term **3.** measure, piece, portion, section, segment **4.** elongation, extensiveness, lengthiness, protractedness **5. at length: a.** completely, fully, in depth, in detail, thoroughly, to the full **b.** for ages, for a long time, for hours, interminably **c.** at last, at long last, eventually, finally, in the end

lengthen continue, draw out, elongate, expand, extend, increase, make longer, prolong, protract, spin out, stretch
▷ **Antonyms** abbreviate, abridge, curtail, cut, cut down, diminish, shorten, trim

lengthy diffuse, drawn-out, extended, interminable, lengthened, long, long-drawn-out, long-winded, overlong, prolix, prolonged, protracted, tedious, verbose, very long
▷ **Antonyms** brief, concise, condensed, limited, short, succinct, terse, to the point

leniency, lenience clemency, compassion, forbearance, gentleness, indulgence, lenity, mercy, mildness, moderation, pity, quarter, tenderness, tolerance

lenient clement, compassionate, forbearing, forgiving, gentle, indulgent, kind, merciful, mild, sparing, tender, tolerant
▷ **Antonyms** harsh, merciless, rigid, rigorous, severe, stern, strict, stringent

lenitive alleviative, assuaging, calming, easing, mitigative, mollifying, palliative, relieving, soothing

leper lazar (*archaic*), outcast, pariah, untouchable

lesbian 1. *noun* butch (*slang*), dyke (*slang*), sapphist, tribade **2.** ~*adjective* butch (*slang*), gay, homosexual, sapphic, tribadic

lesion abrasion, bruise, contusion, hurt, impairment, injury, sore, trauma (*Pathology*), wound

less *adjective* **1.** shorter, slighter, smaller **2.** inferior, minor, secondary, subordinate ~*adverb* **3.** barely, little, meagrely, to a smaller extent ~*preposition* **4.** excepting, lacking, minus, subtracting, without

lessen abate, abridge, contract, curtail, decrease, de-escalate, degrade, die down, diminish, downsize, dwindle, ease, erode, grow less, impair, lighten, lower, minimize, moderate, narrow, reduce, relax, shrink, slacken, slow down, weaken, wind down
▷ **Antonyms** add to, augment, boost, enhance, enlarge, expand, increase, magnify, multiply, raise

lessening abatement, contraction, curtailment, decline, decrease, de-escalation, diminution, dwindling, ebbing, erosion, let-up (*informal*), meltdown (*informal*), minimization, moderation, petering out, reduction, shrinkage, slackening, slowing down, waning, weakening

lesser inferior, less important, lower, minor, secondary, slighter, subordinate, under-
▷ **Antonyms** greater, higher, major, primary, superior

lesson 1. class, coaching, instruction, period, schooling, teaching, tutoring **2.** assignment, drill, exercise, homework, lecture, practice, reading, recitation, task **3.** deterrent, example, exemplar, message, model, moral, precept **4.** admonition, censure, chiding, punishment, rebuke, reprimand, reproof, scolding, warning

let[1] *verb* **1.** allow, authorize, entitle, give leave, give permission, give the go-ahead, give the green light, give the O.K. *or* okay (*informal*), grant, permit, sanction, suffer (*archaic*), tolerate, warrant **2.** hire, lease, rent **3.** allow, cause, enable, grant, make, permit

let[2] *noun* constraint, hindrance, impediment, interference, obstacle, obstruction, prohibition, restriction

letdown anticlimax, bitter pill, blow, comedown (*informal*), disappointment, disgruntlement, disillusionment, frustration, setback, washout (*informal*), whammy (*informal, chiefly U.S.*)

let down disappoint, disenchant, disillusion, dissatisfy, fail, fall short, leave in the lurch, leave stranded

lethal baneful, dangerous, deadly, deathly, destructive, devastating, fatal, mortal, murderous, noxious, pernicious, poisonous, virulent
▷ **Antonyms** harmless, healthy, innocuous, safe, wholesome

lethargic apathetic, comatose, debilitated, drowsy, dull, enervated, heavy, inactive, indifferent, inert, languid, lazy, listless, sleepy, slothful, slow, sluggish, somnolent, stupefied, torpid
▷ **Antonyms** active, alert, animated, energetic, responsive, spirited, stimulated, vigorous

lethargy apathy, drowsiness, dullness, hebetude (*rare*), inaction, indifference, inertia, languor, lassitude, listlessness, sleepiness, sloth, slowness, sluggishness, stupor, torpidity, torpor
▷ **Antonyms** animation, brio, energy, life, liveliness, spirit, verve, vigour, vim, vitality, vivacity, zeal, zest

let in admit, allow to enter, give access to, greet, include, incorporate, receive, take in, welcome

let off 1. detonate, discharge, emit, explode, exude, fire, give off, leak, release **2.** absolve, discharge, dispense, excuse, exempt, exonerate, forgive, pardon, release, spare

let on 1. admit, disclose, divulge, give away, let the cat out of the bag (*informal*), make known, reveal, say **2.** act, counterfeit, dissemble, dissimulate, feign, make believe, make out, pretend, profess, simulate

let out 1. emit, give vent to, produce **2.** discharge, free, let go, liberate, release **3.** betray, blow wide open (*slang*), disclose, leak, let fall, let slip, make known, reveal, take the wraps off

letter 1. character, sign, symbol **2.** acknowledgment, answer, billet (*archaic*), communication, dispatch, epistle, line, message, missive, note, reply **3. to the letter** accurately, exactly, literally, precisely, strictly, word for word

lettered accomplished, cultivated, cultured, educated, erudite, informed, knowledgeable, learned, literate, scholarly, versed, well-educated, well-read

letters belles-lettres, culture, erudition, humanities, learning, literature, scholarship

let-up abatement, break, breathing space, cessation, interval, lessening, lull, pause, recess, remission, respite, slackening

let up abate, decrease, diminish, ease (up), moderate, relax, slacken, stop, subside

levee ceremony, entertainment, gathering, party, reception

level *adjective* **1.** as flat as a pancake, consistent, even, flat, horizontal, plain, plane, smooth, uniform **2.** aligned, balanced, commensurate, comparable, equal, equivalent, even, flush, in line, neck and neck, on a line, on a par, proportionate **3.** calm, equable, even, even-tempered, stable, steady *~verb* **4.** even off *or* out, flatten, make flat, plane, smooth **5.** bulldoze, demolish, destroy, devastate, equalize, flatten, knock down, lay low, pull down, raze, smooth, tear down, wreck **6.** aim, beam, direct, focus, point, train **7.** *informal* be above board, be frank, be honest, be open, be straightforward, be up front (*slang*), come clean (*informal*), keep nothing back *~noun* **8.** altitude, elevation, height, vertical position **9.** achievement, degree, grade, position, rank, stage, standard, standing, status **10.** bed, floor, layer, storey, stratum, zone **11.** flat surface, horizontal, plain, plane **12. on the level** *informal* above board, fair, genuine, honest, open, sincere, square, straight, straightforward, up front (*slang*)
▷ **Antonyms** *~adjective* (*sense 1*) bumpy, hilly, slanted, tilted, uneven, vertical, warped (*sense 2*) above, below *~verb* (*sense 5*) build, erect, raise, roughen

level-headed balanced, calm, collected, composed, cool, dependable, even-tempered, reasonable, sane, self-possessed, sensible, steady, together (*slang*), unflappable (*informal*)

lever 1. *noun* bar, crowbar, handle, handspike, jemmy **2.** *~verb* force, jemmy, move, prise, pry (*U.S.*), purchase, raise

leverage ascendancy, authority, clout (*informal*), influence, pull (*informal*), purchasing power, rank, weight

leviathan behemoth, colossus, hulk, mammoth, monster, Titan, whale

levity buoyancy, facetiousness, fickleness, flightiness, flippancy, frivolity, giddiness, light-heartedness, light-mindedness, silliness, skittishness, triviality

▷ **Antonyms** earnestness, gravity, seriousness, solemnity

levy *verb* **1.** charge, collect, demand, exact, gather, impose, tax **2.** call, call up, conscript, mobilize, muster, press, raise, summon *~noun* **3.** assessment, collection, exaction, gathering, imposition **4.** assessment, duty, excise, fee, imposition, impost, tariff, tax, toll

lewd bawdy, blue, dirty, impure, indecent, lascivious, libidinous, licentious, loose, lustful, obscene, pornographic, profligate, salacious, smutty, unchaste, vile, vulgar, wanton, wicked, X-rated (*informal*)

lewdness bawdiness, carnality, crudity, debauchery, depravity, impurity, indecency, lasciviousness, lechery, licentiousness, lubricity, obscenity, pornography, profligacy, salaciousness, smut, smuttiness, unchastity, vulgarity, wantonness

lexicon dictionary, glossary, vocabulary, wordbook, word list

liabilities accounts payable, debts, expenditure, obligations

liability **1.** accountability, answerability, culpability, duty, obligation, onus, responsibility **2.** arrear, debit, debt, indebtedness, obligation **3.** albatross, burden, disadvantage, drag, drawback, encumbrance, handicap, hindrance, impediment, inconvenience, millstone, minus (*informal*), nuisance **4.** likelihood, probability, proneness, susceptibility, tendency

liable **1.** accountable, amenable, answerable, bound, chargeable, obligated, responsible **2.** exposed, open, subject, susceptible, vulnerable **3.** apt, disposed, inclined, likely, prone, tending **4.** **render oneself liable to** expose oneself to, incur, lay oneself open to, run the risk of

liaison **1.** communication, connection, contact, go-between, hook-up, interchange, intermediary **2.** affair, amour, entanglement, illicit romance, intrigue, love affair, romance

liar fabricator, falsifier, fibber, perjurer, prevaricator, storyteller (*informal*)

libel **1.** *noun* aspersion, calumny, defamation, denigration, obloquy, slander, smear, vituperation **2.** *~verb* blacken, calumniate, defame, derogate, drag (someone's) name through the mud, malign, revile, slander, slur, smear, traduce, vilify

libellous aspersive, calumniatory, calumnious, defamatory, derogatory, false, injurious, malicious, maligning, scurrilous, slanderous, traducing, untrue, vilifying, vituperative

liberal **1.** advanced, humanistic, latitudinarian, libertarian, politically correct *or* PC, progressive, radical, reformist, right-on (*informal*) **2.** altruistic, beneficent, bounteous, bountiful, charitable, free-handed, generous, good, kind, open-handed, open-hearted, prodigal, unstinting **3.** advanced, broad-minded, catholic, enlightened, high-minded, humanitarian, indulgent, magnanimous, permissive, politically correct *or* PC, right-on (*informal*), tolerant, unbiased, unbigoted, unprejudiced **4.** abundant, ample, bountiful, copious, handsome, lavish, munificent, plentiful, profuse, rich **5.** broad, flexible, free, general, inexact, lenient, loose, not close, not literal, not strict

▷ **Antonyms** (*sense 1*) conservative, reactionary, right-wing (*sense 3*) biased, bigoted, intolerant, prejudiced (*sense 4*) cheap, inadequate, limited, skimpy, small, stingy (*sense 5*) fixed, inflexible, literal, strict

liberalism freethinking, humanitarianism, latitudinarianism, libertarianism, progressivism, radicalism

liberality **1.** altruism, beneficence, benevolence, bounty, charity, free-handedness, generosity, kindness, largesse *or* largess, munificence, open-handedness, philanthropy **2.** breadth, broad-mindedness, candour, catholicity, impartiality, latitude, liberalism, libertarianism, magnanimity, permissiveness, progressivism, toleration

liberalize ameliorate, broaden, ease, expand, extend, loosen, mitigate, moderate, modify, relax, slacken, soften, stretch

liberate deliver, discharge, disenthral, emancipate, free, let loose, let out, manumit, redeem, release, rescue, set free

▷ **Antonyms** confine, detain, immure, imprison, incarcerate, intern, jail, lock up, put away

liberation deliverance, emancipation, enfranchisement, freedom, freeing, liberating, liberty, manumission, redemption, release, unfettering, unshackling

liberator deliverer, emancipator, freer, manumitter, redeemer, rescuer, saviour

libertine **1.** *noun* debauchee, lech *or* letch (*informal*), lecher, loose liver, profligate, rake, reprobate, roué, seducer, sensualist, voluptuary, womanizer **2.** *~adjective* abandoned, corrupt, debauched, decadent, degenerate, depraved, dissolute, immoral, licentious, profligate, rakish, reprobate, voluptuous, wanton

liberty **1.** autonomy, emancipation, freedom, immunity, independence, liberation, release, self-determination, sovereignty **2.** authorization, blank cheque, carte blanche, dispensation, exemption, franchise, freedom, leave, licence, permission, prerogative, privilege, right, sanction **3.** (*often plural*) disrespect, familiarity, forwardness, impertinence, impropriety, impudence, insolence, overfamiliarity, presumption, presumptuousness **4. at liberty** free, not confined, on the loose, unlimited, unoccupied, unrestricted

▷ **Antonyms** (*sense 1*) captivity, compulsion, constraint, duress, enslavement, imprisonment, restraint, restriction, slavery, tyranny

libidinous carnal, concupiscent, debauched, impure, incontinent, lascivious, lecherous, lickerish (*archaic*), loose, lustful, prurient, randy (*informal, chiefly Brit.*), ruttish, salacious, sensual, unchaste, wanton, wicked

libretto book, lines, lyrics, script, words

licence *noun* **1.** authority, authorization, blank cheque, carte blanche, certificate, charter, dispensation, entitlement, exemption, immunity, leave, liberty, permission, permit, privilege, right, warrant **2.** a free hand, freedom, independence, latitude, leeway, liberty, self-determination **3.** abandon, anarchy, disorder, excess, immoderation, impropriety, indulgence, irresponsibility, lawlessness, laxity, profligacy, unruliness

▷ **Antonyms** constraint, denial, moderation, prohibition, restraint, restriction, strictness

license *verb* accredit, allow, authorize, certify, commission, empower, enable, entitle, give a blank cheque to, permit, sanction, warrant

▷ **Antonyms** ban, debar, disallow, forbid, outlaw, prohibit, proscribe, rule out, veto

licentious abandoned, debauched, disorderly, dissolute, immoral, impure, lascivious, lax, lewd, libertine, libidinous, lubricious, lubricous, lustful, profligate, promiscuous, sensual, uncontrollable, uncontrolled, uncurbed, unruly, wanton

▷ **Antonyms** chaste, law-abiding, lawful, moral, principled, proper, scrupulous, virtuous

licentiousness abandon, debauchery, dissipation, dissoluteness, lechery, lewdness, libertinism, libidinousness, lubricity, lust, lustfulness, profligacy, promiscuity, prurience, salaciousness, salacity, wantonness

lick *verb* **1.** brush, lap, taste, tongue, touch, wash **2.** *of flames* dart, flick, flicker, ignite, kindle, play over, ripple, touch **3.** *informal* **a.** blow out of the water (*slang*), clobber (*slang*), defeat, master, overcome, rout, run rings around (*informal*), stuff (*slang*), tank (*slang*), trounce, undo, vanquish, wipe the floor with (*informal*) **b.** beat, clobber (*slang*), flog, lambast(e), slap, spank, strike, thrash, wallop (*informal*) **c.** beat, best, blow out of the water (*slang*), clobber (*slang*), excel, outdo, outstrip, run rings around (*informal*), surpass, tank (*slang*), top, wipe the floor with (*informal*) ~*noun* **4.** bit, brush, dab, little, sample, speck, stroke, taste, touch **5.** *informal* clip (*informal*), pace, rate, speed

licking **1.** beating, drubbing, flogging, hiding (*informal*), spanking, tanning (*slang*), thrashing, whipping **2.** beating, defeat, drubbing, pasting (*slang*), trouncing

lie[1] **1.** *verb* dissimulate, equivocate, fabricate, falsify, fib, forswear oneself, invent, misrepresent, perjure, prevaricate, tell a lie, tell untruths **2.** ~*noun* deceit, fabrication, falsehood, falsification, falsity, fib, fiction, invention, mendacity, pork pie (*Brit. slang*), porky (*Brit. slang*), prevarication, untruth, white lie

lie[2] *verb* **1.** be prone, be prostrate, be recumbent, be supine, couch, loll, lounge, recline, repose, rest, sprawl, stretch out **2.** be, be buried, be found, be interred, be located, belong, be placed, be situated, exist, extend, remain **3.** (*usually with* **on** *or* **upon**) burden, oppress, press, rest, weigh **4.** (*usually with* **in**) be present, consist, dwell, exist, inhere, pertain **5. lie low** conceal oneself, go to earth, go underground, hide, hide away, hide out, hole up, keep a low profile, keep out of sight, lurk, skulk, take cover

liege chieftain, feudal lord, master, overlord, seigneur, sovereign, superior, suzerain

lieu place, room, stead

life **1.** animation, being, breath, entity, growth, sentience, viability, vitality **2.** being, career, continuance, course, duration, existence, lifetime, span, time **3.** human, human being, individual, mortal, person, soul **4.** autobiography, biography, career, confessions, history, life story, memoirs, story **5.** behaviour, conduct, life style, way of life **6.** the human condition, the school of hard knocks, the times, the world, this mortal coil, trials and tribulations, vicissitudes **7.** activity, animation, brio, energy, get-up-and-go (*informal*), go (*informal*), high spirits, liveliness, oomph (*informal*), pep, sparkle, spirit, verve, vigour, vitality, vivacity, zest **8.** animating spirit, *élan vital,* essence, heart, lifeblood, soul, spirit, vital spark **9.** creatures, living beings, living things, organisms, wildlife **10. come to life** awaken, become animate, revive, rouse, show signs of life **11. for dear life** *informal* desperately, for all one is worth, intensely, quickly, urgently, vigorously

lifeblood animating force, driving force, essence, guts (*informal*), heart, inspiration, life, stimulus, vital spark

lifeless **1.** cold, dead, deceased, defunct, extinct, inanimate, inert **2.** bare, barren, desert, empty, sterile, uninhabited, unproductive, waste **3.** cold, colourless, dull, flat, heavy, hollow, lacklustre, lethargic, listless, passive, pointless, slow, sluggish, spent, spiritless, static, stiff,

torpid, wooden **4.** comatose, dead to the world (*informal*), in a faint, inert, insensate, insensible, out cold, out for six, unconscious
▷ **Antonyms** active, alive, alive and kicking, animate, animated, live, lively, living, spirited, vital

lifelike authentic, exact, faithful, graphic, natural, photographic, real, realistic, true-to-life, undistorted, vivid

lifelong constant, deep-rooted, enduring, for all one's life, for life, lasting, lifetime, long-lasting, long-standing, perennial, permanent, persistent

lifetime all one's born days, career, course, day(s), existence, life span, one's natural life, period, span, time

life work business, calling, career, interest, mission, occupation, profession, purpose, pursuit, vocation, work

lift *verb* **1.** bear aloft, buoy up, draw up, elevate, heft (*informal*), hoist, pick up, raise, raise high, rear, upheave, uplift, upraise **2.** advance, ameliorate, boost, dignify, elevate, enhance, exalt, improve, promote, raise, upgrade **3.** annul, cancel, countermand, end, relax, remove, rescind, revoke, stop, terminate **4.** ascend, be dispelled, climb, disappear, disperse, dissipate, mount, rise, vanish **5.** *informal* appropriate, blag (*slang*), cabbage (*Brit. slang*), copy, crib (*informal*), half-inch (*old-fashioned slang*), nick (*slang, chiefly Brit.*), pilfer, pinch (*informal*), pirate, plagiarize, pocket, purloin, steal, take, thieve *~noun* **6.** car ride, drive, ride, run, transport **7.** boost, encouragement, fillip, pick-me-up, reassurance, shot in the arm (*informal*), uplift **8.** elevator (*chiefly U.S.*)
▷ **Antonyms** *~verb* (*sense 1*) dash, depress, drop, hang, lower (*sense 3*) establish, impose (*sense 4*) descend, drop, fall, lower *~noun* (*sense 7*) blow, letdown

ligature band, bandage, binding, bond, connection, ligament, link, tie

light[1] *noun* **1.** blaze, brightness, brilliance, effulgence, flash, glare, gleam, glint, glow, illumination, incandescence, lambency, luminescence, luminosity, lustre, phosphorescence, radiance, ray, refulgence, scintillation, shine, sparkle **2.** beacon, bulb, candle, flare, lamp, lantern, lighthouse, star, taper, torch, windowpane **3.** broad day, cockcrow, dawn, daybreak, daylight, daytime, morn (*poetic*), morning, sun, sunbeam, sunrise, sunshine **4.** *figurative* angle, approach, aspect, attitude, context, interpretation, point of view, slant, vantage point, viewpoint **5.** awareness, comprehension, elucidation, explanation, illustration, information, insight, knowledge, understanding **6.** example, exemplar, guiding light, model, paragon, shining example **7.** flame, lighter, match **8. bring to light** disclose, discover, expose, reveal, show, uncover, unearth, unveil **9. come to light** appear, be disclosed, be discovered, be revealed, come out, transpire, turn up **10. in (the) light of** bearing in mind, because of, considering, in view of, taking into account, with knowledge of **11. shed** *or* **throw light on** clarify, clear up, elucidate, explain, simplify *~adjective* **12.** aglow, bright, brilliant, glowing, illuminated, luminous, lustrous, shining, sunny, well-lighted, well-lit **13.** bleached, blond, faded, fair, light-hued, light-toned, pale, pastel *~verb* **14.** fire, ignite, inflame, kindle, set a match to, torch **15.** brighten, clarify, floodlight, flood with light, illuminate, illumine, irradiate, lighten, light up, put on, switch on, turn on **16.** animate, brighten, cheer, irradiate, lighten
▷ **Antonyms** *~noun* cloud, dark, darkness, dusk, mystery, obscurity, shade, shadow *~adjective* dark, deep, dim, dusky, gloomy *~verb* cloud, darken, douse, dull, extinguish, put out, quench

light[2] *adjective* **1.** airy, buoyant, delicate, easy, flimsy, imponderous, insubstantial, lightsome, lightweight, portable, slight, underweight **2.** faint, gentle, indistinct, mild, moderate, slight, soft, weak **3.** inconsequential, inconsiderable, insignificant, minute, scanty, slight, small, thin, tiny, trifling, trivial, unsubstantial, wee **4.** cushy (*informal*), easy, effortless, manageable, moderate, simple, undemanding, unexacting, untaxing **5.** agile, airy, graceful, light-footed, lithe, nimble, sprightly, sylphlike **6.** amusing, diverting, entertaining, frivolous, funny, gay, humorous, light-hearted, pleasing, superficial, trifling, trivial, witty **7.** airy, animated, blithe, carefree, cheerful, cheery, fickle, frivolous, gay, lively, merry, sunny **8.** dizzy, giddy, light-headed, reeling, unsteady, volatile **9.** digestible, frugal, modest, not heavy, not rich, restricted, small **10.** crumbly, friable, loose, porous, sandy, spongy *~verb* **11.** alight, land, perch, settle **12.** (*with* **on** *or* **upon**) chance, come across, discover, encounter, find, happen upon, hit upon, stumble on
▷ **Antonyms** *~adjective* (*sense 1*) heavy (*sense 2*) forceful, strong (*sense 3*) deep, profound, serious, weighty (*sense 4*) burdensome, strenuous (*sense 5*) clumsy (*senses 6 & 7*) serious, sombre (*sense 9*) intense, rich, substantial (*sense 10*) hard, strong

lighten[1] *verb* become light, brighten, flash, gleam, illuminate, irradiate, light up, make bright, shine

lighten[2] *verb* **1.** disburden, ease, make lighter, reduce in weight, unload **2.** allay, alleviate, ameliorate, assuage, ease, facilitate, lessen, mitigate, reduce, relieve **3.** brighten, buoy up, cheer, elate,

encourage, gladden, hearten, inspire, lift, perk up, revive
▷ **Antonyms** (*sense 1*) burden, encumber, handicap (*sense 2*) aggravate, heighten, increase, intensify, make worse, worsen (*sense 3*) depress, oppress, sadden, weigh down

light-fingered crafty, crooked (*informal*), dishonest, furtive, pilfering, pinching (*informal*), shifty, sly, stealing, thieving, underhand

light-footed agile, buoyant, graceful, lithe, nimble, sprightly, spry, swift, tripping, winged

light-headed **1.** bird-brained (*informal*), featherbrained, fickle, flighty, flippant, foolish, frivolous, giddy, inane, rattlebrained (*slang*), shallow, silly, superficial, trifling **2.** delirious, dizzy, faint, giddy, hazy, vertiginous, woozy (*informal*)

light-hearted blithe, blithesome (*literary*), bright, carefree, cheerful, chirpy (*informal*), effervescent, frolicsome, gay, genial, glad, gleeful, happy-go-lucky, insouciant, jocund, jolly, jovial, joyful, joyous, merry, playful, sunny, untroubled, upbeat (*informal*)
▷ **Antonyms** cheerless, dejected, depressed, despondent, gloomy, heavy-hearted, low, melancholy, morose, sad

light into assail, attack, belabour, clobber (*slang*), flail, flay, go at hammer and tongs, lambast(e), lay into (*informal*), let fly at, pitch into (*informal*), sail into (*informal*), set about, tear into (*informal*)

lightless caliginous (*archaic*), dark, dim, dusky, gloomy, inky, jet black, murky, pitch-black, pitch-dark, pitchy, Stygian, sunless, tenebrous, unilluminated, unlighted, unlit

lightly **1.** airily, delicately, faintly, gently, gingerly, slightly, softly, timidly **2.** moderately, sparingly, sparsely, thinly **3.** easily, effortlessly, readily, simply **4.** breezily, carelessly, flippantly, frivolously, heedlessly, indifferently, slightingly, thoughtlessly
▷ **Antonyms** abundantly, arduously, awkwardly, carefully, earnestly, firmly, forcefully, heavily, ponderously, seriously, slowly, thickly, with difficulty

light out abscond, depart, do a bunk (*Brit. slang*), do a runner (*slang*), escape, fly the coop (*U.S. & Canad. informal*), make off, quit, run away, scarper (*Brit. slang*), skedaddle (*informal*), take a powder (*U.S. & Canad. slang*), take it on the lam (*U.S. & Canad. slang*)

lightweight *adjective* inconsequential, insignificant, nickel-and-dime (*U.S. informal*), of no account, paltry, petty, slight, trifling, trivial, unimportant, wanky (*taboo slang*), worthless
▷ **Antonyms** important, momentous, serious, significant, substantial, weighty

likable, likeable agreeable, amiable, appealing, attractive, charming, engaging, friendly, genial, nice, pleasant, pleasing, sympathetic, winning, winsome

like[1] **1.** *adjective* akin, alike, allied, analogous, approximating, cognate, corresponding, equivalent, identical, parallel, relating, resembling, same, similar **2.** *~noun* counterpart, equal, fellow, match, parallel, twin
▷ **Antonyms** *~adjective* contrasted, different, dissimilar, divergent, diverse, opposite, unlike *~noun* opposite

like[2] *verb* **1.** adore (*informal*), be fond of, be keen on, be partial to, delight in, dig (*slang*), enjoy, go for, love, relish, revel in **2.** admire, appreciate, approve, cherish, esteem, hold dear, prize, take a shine to (*informal*), take to **3.** care to, choose, choose to, desire, fancy, feel inclined, prefer, select, want, wish *~noun* **4.** (*usually plural*) cup of tea (*informal*), favourite, liking, partiality, predilection, preference
▷ **Antonyms** *~verb* abominate, despise, detest, dislike, hate, loathe

likelihood chance, good chance, liability, likeliness, possibility, probability, prospect, reasonableness, strong possibility

likely *adjective* **1.** anticipated, apt, disposed, expected, in a fair way, inclined, liable, on the cards, possible, probable, prone, tending, to be expected **2. be** *or* **seem likely** be in the running for, bid fair, incline towards, promise, stand a good chance, suggest, tend **3.** believable, credible, feasible, plausible, reasonable, verisimilar **4.** acceptable, agreeable, appropriate, befitting, fit, pleasing, proper, qualified, suitable **5.** fair, favourite, hopeful, odds-on, promising, up-and-coming *~adverb* **6.** doubtlessly, in all probability, like as not (*informal*), like enough (*informal*), no doubt, presumably, probably

like-minded agreeing, compatible, *en rapport,* harmonious, in accord, in harmony, of one mind, of the same mind, unanimous

liken compare, equate, juxtapose, match, mention in the same breath, parallel, relate, set beside

likeness **1.** affinity, correspondence, resemblance, similarity, similitude **2.** copy, counterpart, delineation, depiction, effigy, facsimile, image, model, photograph, picture, portrait, replica, representation, reproduction, study **3.** appearance, form, guise, semblance

likewise **1.** also, besides, further, furthermore, in addition, moreover, too **2.** in like manner, in the same way, similarly

liking affection, affinity, appreciation, attraction, bent, bias, desire, fondness, inclination, love, partiality, penchant, predilection, preference, proneness, propensity, soft spot, stomach, taste, tendency, thirst, weakness

▷ **Antonyms** abhorrence, aversion, dislike, hatred, loathing, repugnance

Lilliputian **1.** *noun* dwarf, homunculus, hop-o'-my-thumb, manikin, midget, munchkin (*informal, chiefly U.S.*), pygmy *or* pigmy, Tom Thumb **2.** *~adjective* baby, bantam, diminutive, dwarf, little, mini, miniature, minuscule, petite, pocket-sized, pygmy *or* pigmy, small, teensy-weensy, teeny, teeny-weeny, tiny, wee

lilt beat, cadence, rhythm, sway, swing

lily-livered abject, base, chicken (*slang*), chicken-hearted, chickenshit (*U.S. slang*), cowardly, craven, faint-hearted, fearful, gutless (*informal*), pusillanimous, scared, spineless, timid, timorous, yellow (*informal*), yellow-bellied (*slang*)

lily-white **1.** milk-white, pure white, white, white as snow, white-skinned **2.** *informal* chaste, impeccable, innocent, irreproachable, pure, spotless, unsullied, untainted, untarnished, virgin, virtuous

limb **1.** appendage, arm, extension, extremity, leg, member, part, wing **2.** bough, branch, offshoot, projection, spur

limber *adjective* **1.** elastic, flexible, plastic, pliable, pliant, supple **2.** agile, graceful, lissom(e), lithe, loose-jointed, loose-limbed, supple *~verb* **3.** (*with* **up**) exercise, get ready, loosen up, prepare, warm up

limelight attention, celebrity, fame, glare of publicity, prominence, public eye, publicity, public notice, recognition, stardom, the spotlight

limit *noun* **1.** bound, breaking point, cutoff point, deadline, end, end point, furthest bound, greatest extent, termination, the bitter end, ultimate, utmost **2.** (*often plural*) border, boundary, confines, edge, end, extent, frontier, pale, perimeter, periphery, precinct **3.** ceiling, check, curb, limitation, maximum, obstruction, restraint, restriction **4.** **the limit** *informal* enough, it (*informal*), the end, the last straw *~verb* **5.** bound, check, circumscribe, confine, curb, delimit, demarcate, fix, hem in, hinder, ration, restrain, restrict, specify, straiten

limitation block, check, condition, constraint, control, curb, disadvantage, drawback, impediment, obstruction, qualification, reservation, restraint, restriction, snag

limited **1.** bounded, checked, circumscribed, confined, constrained, controlled, curbed, defined, finite, fixed, hampered, hemmed in, restricted **2.** cramped, diminished, inadequate, insufficient, minimal, narrow, reduced, restricted, scant, short, unsatisfactory

▷ **Antonyms** boundless, limitless, unlimited, unrestricted

limitless boundless, countless, endless, illimitable, immeasurable, immense, inexhaustible, infinite, measureless, never-ending, numberless, unbounded, uncalculable, undefined, unending, unlimited, untold, vast

limp[1] **1.** *verb* falter, halt (*archaic*), hobble, hop, shamble, shuffle **2.** *~noun* hobble, lameness

limp[2] *adjective* **1.** drooping, flabby, flaccid, flexible, floppy, lax, limber, loose, pliable, relaxed, slack, soft **2.** debilitated, enervated, exhausted, lethargic, spent, tired, weak, worn out

▷ **Antonyms** (*sense 1*) firm, hard, rigid, solid, stiff, taut, tense, unyielding (*sense 2*) hardy, powerful, robust, strong, sturdy, tough

limpid **1.** bright, clear, crystal-clear, crystalline, pellucid, pure, translucent, transparent **2.** clear, comprehensible, intelligible, lucid, perspicuous, unambiguous **3.** calm, peaceful, placid, quiet, serene, still, tranquil, unruffled, untroubled

line[1] *noun* **1.** band, bar, channel, dash, groove, mark, rule, score, scratch, streak, stripe, stroke, underline **2.** crease, crow's foot, furrow, mark, wrinkle **3.** border, borderline, boundary, demarcation, edge, frontier, limit, mark **4.** configuration, contour, features, figure, outline, profile, silhouette **5.** cable, cord, filament, rope, strand, string, thread, wire, wisp **6.** axis, course, direction, path, route, track, trajectory **7.** approach, avenue, belief, course, course of action, ideology, method, policy, position, practice, procedure, scheme, system **8.** activity, area, bag (*slang*), business, calling, department, employment, field, forte, interest, job, occupation, profession, province, pursuit, specialization, trade, vocation **9.** column, crocodile (*Brit.*), file, procession, queue, rank, row, sequence, series **10.** ancestry, breed, family, lineage, race, stock, strain, succession **11.** card, letter, message, note, postcard, report, word **12.** clue, hint, indication, information, lead **13.** *Military* disposition, firing line, formation, front, front line, position, trenches **14.** **draw the line** lay down the law, object, prohibit, put one's foot down, restrict, set a limit **15.** **in line: a.** in alignment, in a row, plumb, straight, true **b.** in accord, in agreement, in conformity, in harmony, in step **16.** **in line for** a candidate for, being considered for, due for, in the running for, next in succession to, on the short list for *~verb* **17.** crease, cut, draw, furrow, inscribe, mark, rule, score, trace, underline **18.** border, bound, edge, fringe, rank, rim, skirt, verge

line[2] *verb* ceil, cover, face, fill, interline

lineage ancestry, birth, breed, descendants, descent, extraction, family, forebears, forefathers, genealogy, heredity, house, line, offspring, pedigree, progeny, stirps, stock, succession

lineaments configuration, countenance, face, features, line, outline, phiz *or* phizog (*slang, chiefly Brit.*), physiognomy, trait, visage

lined **1.** feint, ruled **2.** furrowed, wizened, worn, wrinkled

lines **1.** appearance, configuration, contour, cut, outline, shape, style **2.** convention, example, model, pattern, plan, principle, procedure **3.** part, script, words

line-up arrangement, array, row, selection, team

line up **1.** fall in, form ranks, queue up **2.** assemble, come up with, lay on, obtain, organize, prepare, procure, produce, secure **3.** align, arrange, array, marshal, order, range, regiment, sequence, straighten

linger **1.** hang around, hang in the air, loiter, remain, stay, stop, tarry, wait **2.** dally, dawdle, delay, drag one's feet *or* heels, idle, lag, procrastinate, take one's time **3.** cling to life, die slowly, hang on, last, survive **4.** abide, continue, endure, persist, remain, stay

lingering dragging, long-drawn-out, persistent, protracted, remaining, slow

lingo argot, cant, dialect, idiom, jargon, language, patois, patter, speech, talk, tongue, vernacular

liniment balm, balsam, cream, embrocation, emollient, lotion, ointment, salve, unguent

link *noun* **1.** component, constituent, division, element, member, part, piece **2.** affiliation, affinity, association, attachment, bond, connection, joint, knot, liaison, relationship, tie, tie-up, vinculum *~verb* **3.** attach, bind, connect, couple, fasten, join, tie, unite, yoke **4.** associate, bracket, connect, identify, relate

▷ **Antonyms** *~verb* detach, disconnect, divide, separate, sever, split, sunder

lion *figurative* **1.** brave man, champion, conqueror, fighter, hero, warrior **2.** big name, celeb (*informal*), celebrity, idol, luminary, megastar (*informal*), notable, prodigy, star, superstar, V.I.P., wonder **3. beard the lion in his den** brave, confront, court destruction, defy danger, face, stand up to, tempt providence

lion-hearted bold, brave, courageous, daring, dauntless, heroic, intrepid, resolute, stalwart, valiant, valorous

▷ **Antonyms** abject, chicken-hearted, chickenshit (*U.S. slang*), cowardly, craven, faint-hearted, gutless (*informal*), lily-livered, pusillanimous, spineless, timorous, wimpish *or* wimpy (*informal*), yellow (*informal*)

lionize acclaim, adulate, aggrandize, celebrate, crack up (*informal*), eulogize, exalt, fête, glorify, hero-worship, honour, idolize, make much of, mob, sing *or* sound the praises of

lip **1.** brim, brink, edge, flange, margin, rim **2.** *slang* backchat (*informal*), cheek (*informal*), effrontery, impertinence, insolence, rudeness, sauce (*informal*) **3.** *Music* control, embouchure **4. smack** *or* **lick one's lips** anticipate, delight in, drool over, enjoy, gloat over, relish, savour, slaver over

liquefaction deliquescence, dissolution, dissolving, fusion, melting, thawing

liquefy deliquesce, dissolve, flux, fuse, liquesce, liquidize, melt, run, thaw

liquid *noun* **1.** fluid, juice, liquor, solution *~adjective* **2.** aqueous, flowing, fluid, liquefied, melted, molten, running, runny, thawed, wet **3.** bright, brilliant, clear, limpid, shining, translucent, transparent **4.** dulcet, fluent, mellifluent, mellifluous, melting, smooth, soft, sweet **5.** *of assets* convertible, negotiable

liquidate **1.** clear, discharge, honour, pay, pay off, settle, square **2.** abolish, annul, cancel, dissolve, terminate **3.** cash, convert to cash, realize, sell off, sell up **4.** annihilate, blow away (*slang, chiefly U.S.*), bump off (*slang*), destroy, dispatch, do away with, do in (*slang*), eliminate, exterminate, finish off, get rid of, kill, murder, remove, rub out (*U.S. slang*), silence, take out (*slang*), wipe out (*informal*)

liquor **1.** alcohol, booze (*informal*), drink, Dutch courage (*informal*), grog, hard stuff (*informal*), hooch *or* hootch (*informal, chiefly U.S. & Canad.*), intoxicant, juice (*informal*), spirits, strong drink **2.** broth, extract, gravy, infusion, juice, liquid, stock

lissom(e) agile, flexible, graceful, light, limber, lithe, loose-jointed, loose-limbed, nimble, pliable, pliant, supple, willowy

list[1] **1.** *noun* catalogue, directory, file, index, inventory, invoice, leet (*Scot.*), listing, record, register, roll, schedule, series, syllabus, tabulation, tally **2.** *~verb* bill, book, catalogue, enrol, enter, enumerate, file, index, itemize, note, record, register, schedule, set down, tabulate, write down

list[2] **1.** *verb* cant, careen, heel, heel over, incline, lean, tilt, tip **2.** *~noun* cant, leaning, slant, tilt

listen **1.** attend, be all ears, be attentive, give ear, hang on (someone's) words, hark, hear, hearken (*archaic*), keep one's ears open, lend an ear, pin back one's ears (*informal*), prick up one's ears **2.** concentrate, do as one is told, give heed to, heed, mind, obey, observe, pay attention, take notice

listless apathetic, enervated, heavy, im~passive, inattentive, indifferent, indo~lent, inert, languid, languishing, lethar~gic, lifeless, limp, lymphatic, mopish, sluggish, spiritless, supine, torpid, va~cant

▷ **Antonyms** active, alert, alive and kicking, attentive, energetic, full of beans (*informal*), lively, sparky, spirit~ed, wide-awake

listlessness apathy, enervation, ennui, inattention, indifference, indolence, in~ertia, languidness, languor, lethargy, lifelessness, sluggishness, spiritless~ness, supineness, torpidity

litany 1. invocation, petition, prayer, sup~plication **2**. account, catalogue, enu~meration, list, recital, recitation, re~frain, repetition, tale

literacy ability, articulacy, articulateness, cultivation, education, knowledge, learning, proficiency, scholarship

literal 1. accurate, close, exact, faithful, strict, verbatim, word for word **2**. boring, colourless, down-to-earth, dull, factual, matter-of-fact, prosaic, prosy, unimagi~native, uninspired **3**. actual, bona fide, genuine, gospel, plain, real, simple, true, unexaggerated, unvarnished

literally actually, exactly, faithfully, plainly, precisely, really, simply, strict~ly, to the letter, truly, verbatim, word for word

literary bookish, erudite, formal, learned, lettered, literate, scholarly, well-read

literate cultivated, cultured, educated, erudite, informed, knowledgeable, learned, lettered, scholarly, well-informed, well-read

literature 1. belles-lettres, letters, lore, writings, written works **2**. brochure, in~formation, leaflet, mailshot, pamphlet

lithe flexible, limber, lissom(e), loose-jointed, loose-limbed, pliable, pliant, supple

litigant claimant, contestant, disputant, litigator, party, plaintiff

litigate contest at law, file a suit, go to court, go to law, institute legal proceed~ings, press charges, prosecute, sue

litigation action, case, contending, dis~puting, lawsuit, process, prosecution

litigious argumentative, belligerent, con~tentious, disputatious, quarrelsome

litter *noun* **1**. debris, detritus, fragments, garbage (*chiefly U.S.*), grot (*slang*), muck, refuse, rubbish, shreds, trash **2**. clutter, confusion, disarray, disorder, jumble, mess, scatter, untidiness **3**. brood, family, offspring, progeny, young **4**. bedding, couch, floor cover, mulch, straw-bed **5**. palanquin, stretcher ~*verb* **6**. clutter, derange, disarrange, disorder, mess up, scatter, strew

little *adjective* **1**. diminutive, dwarf, elfin, infinitesimal, Lilliputian, mini, minia~ture, minute, munchkin (*informal, chiefly U.S.*), petite, pygmy *or* pigmy, short, slender, small, teensy-weensy, teeny-weeny, tiny, wee **2**. babyish, im~mature, infant, junior, undeveloped, young **3**. hardly any, insufficient, mea~gre, measly, scant, skimpy, small, sparse **4**. brief, fleeting, hasty, passing, short, short-lived **5**. inconsiderable, in~significant, minor, negligible, paltry, trifling, trivial, unimportant **6**. base, cheap, illiberal, mean, narrow-minded, petty, small-minded ~*adverb* **7**. barely, hardly, not much, not quite, only just **8**. hardly ever, not often, rarely, scarcely, seldom **9**. **little by little** bit by bit, by de~grees, gradually, imperceptibly, piece~meal, progressively, slowly, step by step ~*noun* **10**. bit, dab, dash, fragment, hint, modicum, particle, pinch, small amount, snippet, speck, spot, tad (*informal, chiefly U.S.*), taste, touch, trace, trifle

▷ **Antonyms** ~*adjective* abundant, ample, big, colossal, considerable, enormous, giant, ginormous (*informal*), grave, great, huge, immense, important, large, long, major, mega (*slang*), momentous, much, plentiful, serious, significant ~*adverb* always, certainly, much, surely ~*noun* lot, many, much

liturgical ceremonial, eucharistic, formal, ritual, sacramental, solemn

liturgy celebration, ceremony, form of worship, formula, rite, ritual, sacra~ment, service, services, worship

livable 1. adequate, comfortable, fit (for human habitation), habitable, inhabit~able, satisfactory **2**. acceptable, bear~able, endurable, passable, sufferable, supportable, tolerable, worth living, worthwhile **3**. (*with* **with**) companion~able, compatible, congenial, easy, easy to live with, harmonious, sociable

live[1] *verb* **1**. be, be alive, breathe, draw breath, exist, have life **2**. be permanent, be remembered, last, persist, prevail, remain alive **3**. (*sometimes with* **in**) abide, dwell, hang out (*informal*), in~habit, lodge, occupy, reside, settle, stay (*chiefly Scot.*) **4**. abide, continue, earn a living, endure, fare, feed, get along, lead, make ends meet, pass, remain, subsist, support oneself, survive **5**. be happy, enjoy life, flourish, luxuriate, make the most of life, prosper, thrive **6**. **live it up** *informal* celebrate, enjoy one~self, have a ball (*informal*), have fun, make whoopee (*informal*), paint the town red, push the boat out (*Brit. infor~mal*), revel

live[2] *adjective* **1**. alive, animate, breath~ing, existent, living, quick (*archaic*), vi~tal **2**. active, burning, controversial, current, hot, pertinent, pressing, preva~lent, topical, unsettled, vital **3**. *informal* active, alert, brisk, dynamic, earnest, energetic, lively, sparky, vigorous, vivid, wide-awake **4.** active, alight, blazing, burning, connected, glowing, hot, ignited, smouldering, switched on

livelihood bread and butter (*informal*), employment, job, living, maintenance, means, (means of) support, occupation, (source of) income, subsistence, sustenance, work

liveliness activity, animation, boisterousness, brio, briskness, dynamism, energy, gaiety, quickness, smartness, spirit, sprightliness, vitality, vivacity

livelong complete, dragged out, entire, everlasting, full, long-drawn-out, unbroken, whole

lively 1. active, agile, alert, alive and kicking, bright-eyed and bushy-tailed, brisk, chipper (*informal*), chirpy (*informal*), energetic, full of beans (*informal*), full of pep (*informal*), keen, nimble, perky, quick, sprightly, spry, vigorous **2.** animated, blithe, blithesome, cheerful, chirpy (*informal*), frisky, frolicsome, gay, merry, sparkling, sparky, spirited, upbeat (*informal*), vivacious **3.** astir, bustling, busy, buzzing, crowded, eventful, moving, stirring **4.** bright, colourful, exciting, forceful, invigorating, racy, refreshing, stimulating, vivid

▷ **Antonyms** apathetic, debilitated, disabled, dull, inactive, lifeless, listless, slow, sluggish, torpid

liven (up) animate, brighten, buck up (*informal*), enliven, hot up (*informal*), pep up, perk up, put life into, rouse, stir, vitalize, vivify

liverish 1. bilious, queasy, sick **2.** crotchety (*informal*), crusty, disagreeable, fratchy (*informal*), grumpy, ill-humoured, irascible, irritable, like a bear with a sore head, peevish, ratty (*Brit. & N.Z. informal*), snappy, splenetic, tetchy

livery attire, clothing, costume, dress, garb, raiment (*archaic or poetic*), regalia, suit, uniform, vestments

live wire ball of fire (*informal*), dynamo, go-getter (*informal*), hustler (*U.S. & Canad. slang*), life and soul of the party, self-starter

livid 1. angry, black-and-blue, bruised, contused, discoloured, purple **2.** ashen, blanched, bloodless, doughy, greyish, leaden, pale, pallid, pasty, wan, waxen **3.** *informal* angry, as black as thunder, beside oneself, boiling, choked, cross, enraged, exasperated, fuming, furious, hot under the collar (*informal*), incensed, indignant, infuriated, mad (*informal*), outraged

▷ **Antonyms** (*sense 3*) assuaged, blissful, content, delighted, enchanted, forgiving, happy, mollified, overjoyed, pleased

living *adjective* **1.** active, alive, alive and kicking, animated, breathing, existing, in the land of the living (*informal*), lively, quick (*archaic*), strong, vigorous, vital **2.** active, contemporary, continuing, current, developing, extant, in use, ongoing, operative, persisting *~noun* **3.** animation, being, existence, existing, life, subsistence **4.** life style, mode of living, way of life **5.** bread and butter (*informal*), job, livelihood, maintenance, (means of) support, occupation, (source of) income, subsistence, sustenance, work **6.** *Church of England* benefice, incumbency, stipend **7. the living** flesh and blood, the quick (*archaic*)

▷ **Antonyms** *~adjective* (*sense 1*) dead, deceased, defunct, departed, expired, late, lifeless, perished (*sense 2*) obsolescent, obsolete, out-of-date, vanishing

load *noun* **1.** bale, cargo, consignment, freight, lading, shipment **2.** affliction, albatross, burden, encumbrance, incubus, millstone, onus, oppression, pressure, trouble, weight, worry *~verb* **3.** cram, fill, freight, heap, lade, pack, pile, stack, stuff **4.** burden, encumber, hamper, oppress, saddle with, trouble, weigh down, worry **5.** *of firearms* charge, make ready, prepare to fire, prime **6. load the dice** fix, rig, set up

loaded 1. burdened, charged, freighted, full, laden, weighted **2.** biased, distorted, weighted **3.** artful, insidious, manipulative, prejudicial, tricky **4.** at the ready, charged, primed, ready to shoot *or* fire **5.** *slang* affluent, flush (*informal*), moneyed, rich, rolling (*slang*), wealthy, well-heeled (*informal*), well off, well-to-do

loaf[1] *noun* **1.** block, cake, cube, lump, slab **2.** *slang* block (*informal*), chump (*Brit. slang*), gumption (*Brit. informal*), head, noddle (*informal, chiefly Brit.*), nous (*Brit. slang*), sense

loaf[2] *verb* **1.** be indolent, idle, laze, lie around, loiter, loll, lounge around, take it easy **2.** (*with* **away**) fritter away, kill time, pass time, veg out (*slang, chiefly U.S.*), waste time, while away the hours

loafer bum (*informal*), couch potato (*slang*), drone (*Brit.*), idler, layabout, lazybones (*informal*), lounger, ne'er-do-well, shirker, skiver (*Brit. slang*), time-waster, wastrel

loan 1. *noun* accommodation, advance, allowance, credit, mortgage, touch (*slang*) **2.** *~verb* accommodate, advance, allow, credit, lend, let out

loath, loth against, averse, backward, counter, disinclined, indisposed, opposed, reluctant, resisting, unwilling

▷ **Antonyms** anxious, avid, desirous, eager, enthusiastic, keen, willing

loathe abhor, abominate, despise, detest, dislike, execrate, feel repugnance towards, find disgusting, hate, have a strong aversion to, not be able to bear *or* abide

loathing abhorrence, abomination, antipathy, aversion, detestation, disgust, execration, hatred, horror, odium, repugnance, repulsion, revulsion

loathsome abhorrent, abominable, detestable, disgusting, execrable, hateful, horrible, nasty, nauseating, obnoxious, obscene, odious, offensive, repugnant, repulsive, revolting, vile, yucky *or* yukky (*slang*)

▷ **Antonyms** adorable, amiable, attractive, charming, delightful, enchanting, engaging, fetching, likable *or* likeable, lovable, lovely

lob *verb* fling, launch, lift, loft, pitch, shy (*informal*), throw, toss

lobby *noun* **1.** corridor, entrance hall, foyer, hall, hallway, passage, passageway, porch, vestibule **2.** pressure group *~verb* **3.** bring pressure to bear, campaign for, exert influence, influence, persuade, press for, pressure, promote, pull strings (*Brit. informal*), push for, solicit votes, urge

local *adjective* **1.** community, district, neighbourhood, parish, provincial, regional **2.** confined, limited, narrow, parish pump, parochial, provincial, restricted, small-town *~noun* **3.** character (*informal*), inhabitant, local yokel (*disparaging*), native, resident

locale locality, location, locus, place, position, scene, setting, site, spot, venue

locality 1. area, district, neck of the woods (*informal*), neighbourhood, region, vicinity **2.** locale, location, place, position, scene, setting, site, spot

localize 1. circumscribe, concentrate, confine, contain, delimit, delimitate, limit, restrain, restrict **2.** ascribe, assign, narrow down, pinpoint, specify

locate 1. come across, detect, discover, find, lay one's hands on, pin down, pinpoint, run to earth *or* ground, track down, unearth **2.** establish, fix, place, put, seat, set, settle, situate

location bearings, locale, locus, place, point, position, site, situation, spot, venue, whereabouts

lock[1] *noun* **1.** bolt, clasp, fastening, padlock *~verb* **2.** bolt, close, fasten, latch, seal, secure, shut, sneck (*dialect*) **3.** clench, engage, entangle, entwine, join, link, mesh, unite **4.** clasp, clutch, embrace, encircle, enclose, grapple, grasp, hug, press

lock[2] *noun* curl, ringlet, strand, tress, tuft

lock out ban, bar, debar, exclude, keep out, refuse admittance to, shut out

lockup can (*slang*), cell, cooler (*slang*), gaol, jail, jug (*slang*), police cell

lock up cage, confine, detain, imprison, incarcerate, jail, put behind bars, shut up

locomotion action, headway, motion, movement, moving, progress, progression, travel, travelling

locution 1. collocation, expression, idiom, phrase, term, turn of speech, wording **2.** accent, articulation, diction, inflection, intonation, manner of speech, phrasing, style

lodestar beacon, guide, model, par, pattern, signal, standard

lodestone beacon, focal point, focus, lodestar, magnet

lodge *noun* **1.** cabin, chalet, cottage, gatehouse, house, hunting lodge, hut, shelter **2.** assemblage, association, branch, chapter, club, group, society **3.** den, haunt, lair, retreat *~verb* **4.** accommodate, billet, board, entertain, harbour, put up, quarter, room, shelter, sojourn, stay, stop **5.** become fixed, catch, come to rest, imbed, implant, stick **6.** deposit, file, lay, place, put, put on record, register, set, submit

lodger boarder, guest, paying guest, P.G., resident, roomer, tenant

lodging (*often plural*) abode, accommodation, apartments, boarding, digs (*Brit. informal*), dwelling, habitation, quarters, residence, rooms, shelter

lofty 1. elevated, high, raised, sky-high, soaring, tall, towering **2.** dignified, distinguished, elevated, exalted, grand, illustrious, imposing, majestic, noble, renowned, stately, sublime, superior **3.** arrogant, condescending, disdainful, haughty, high and mighty (*informal*), lordly, patronizing, proud, snooty (*informal*), supercilious, toffee-nosed (*slang, chiefly Brit.*)

▷ **Antonyms** (*sense 1*) dwarfed, low, short, stunted (*sense 2*) debased, degraded, humble, low, lowly, mean (*sense 3*) friendly, modest, unassuming, warm

log *noun* **1.** block, bole, chunk, piece of timber, stump, trunk *~verb* **2.** chop, cut, fell, hew *~noun* **3.** account, chart, daybook, journal, listing, logbook, record, tally *~verb* **4.** book, chart, make a note of, note, record, register, report, set down, tally

loggerhead at loggerheads at daggers drawn, at each other's throats, at enmity, at odds, estranged, feuding, in dispute, opposed, quarrelling

logic 1. argumentation, deduction, dialectics, ratiocination, science of reasoning, syllogistic reasoning **2.** good reason, good sense, reason, sense, sound judgment **3.** chain of thought, coherence, connection, link, rationale, relationship

logical 1. clear, cogent, coherent, consistent, deducible, pertinent, rational, reasonable, relevant, sound, valid, well-organized **2.** judicious, most likely, necessary, obvious, plausible, reasonable, sensible, wise

▷ **Antonyms** illogical, implausible, in~ stinctive, irrational, unlikely, unorgan~ ized, unreasonable

logistics coordination, engineering, man~ agement, masterminding, orchestration, organization, plans, strategy

loiter dally, dawdle, delay, dilly-dally (*informal*), hang about *or* around, idle, lag, linger, loaf, loll, saunter, skulk, stroll

loll 1. flop, lean, loaf, lounge, recline, re~ lax, slouch, slump, sprawl **2.** dangle, droop, drop, flap, flop, hang, hang loose~ ly, sag

lone by oneself, deserted, isolated, lone~ some, one, only, separate, separated, single, sole, solitary, unaccompanied

loneliness aloneness, desertedness, deso~ lation, dreariness, forlornness, isolation, lonesomeness, seclusion, solitariness, solitude

lonely 1. abandoned, destitute, estranged, forlorn, forsaken, friendless, lonesome, outcast **2.** alone, apart, by oneself, com~ panionless, isolated, lone, single, soli~ tary, withdrawn **3.** deserted, desolate, godforsaken, isolated, off the beaten track (*informal*), out-of-the-way, remote, secluded, sequestered, solitary, unfre~ quented, uninhabited

▷ **Antonyms** (*sense 1*) accompanied, be~ friended, popular, together (*sense 3*) bustling, crowded, frequented, populous, teeming

loner hermit, individualist, lone wolf, maverick, misanthrope, outsider, re~ cluse, solitary

lonesome cheerless, companionless, de~ serted, desolate, dreary, forlorn, friend~ less, gloomy, isolated, lone, lonely

long[1] *adjective* **1.** elongated, expanded, extended, extensive, far-reaching, lengthy, spread out, stretched **2.** drag~ ging, interminable, late, lengthy, lin~ gering, long-drawn-out, prolonged, pro~ tracted, slow, sustained, tardy

▷ **Antonyms** abbreviated, abridged, brief, compressed, contracted, little, momentary, quick, short, short-lived, small

long[2] *verb* ache, covet, crave, desire, dream of, eat one's heart out over, hanker, hunger, itch, lust, pine, set one's heart on, want, wish, would give one's eyeteeth for, yearn

long-drawn-out dragged out, intermi~ nable, lengthy, marathon, overextended, overlong, prolonged, protracted, spun out

long-headed acute, astute, discerning, far-sighted, penetrating, perceptive, sa~ gacious, shrewd, wise

longing 1. *noun* ache, ambition, aspira~ tion, coveting, craving, desire, hanker~ ing, hope, hungering, itch, thirst, urge, wish, yearning, yen (*informal*) **2.** *~adjective* anxious, ardent, avid, crav~ ing, desirous, eager, hungry, languish~ ing, pining, wishful, wistful, yearning

▷ **Antonyms** *~noun* abhorrence, antipa~ thy, apathy, disgust, disregard, indif~ ference, loathing, revulsion, unconcern *~adjective* apathetic, cold, disgusted, hateful, indifferent, loathing, uncon~ cerned, uninterested

long-lived enduring, full of years, lon~ gevous, long-lasting, old as Methuselah

long-standing abiding, enduring, estab~ lished, fixed, hallowed by time, long-established, long-lasting, long-lived, time-honoured

long-suffering easygoing, forbearing, for~ giving, patient, resigned, stoical, toler~ ant, uncomplaining

long-winded diffuse, discursive, garru~ lous, lengthy, long-drawn-out, overlong, prolix, prolonged, rambling, repetitious, tedious, tiresome, verbose, wordy

▷ **Antonyms** brief, concise, crisp, curt, laconic, pithy, sententious, short, suc~ cinct, terse, to the point

look *verb* **1.** behold (*archaic*), check, check out (*informal*), clock (*Brit. slang*), consider, contemplate, examine, eye, eyeball (*U.S. slang*), feast one's eyes upon, gaze, get a load of (*informal*), glance, inspect, observe, peep, recce (*slang*), regard, scan, scrutinize, see, study, survey, take a dekko at (*Brit. slang*), take a gander at (*informal*), view, watch **2.** appear, display, evidence, exhibit, look like, make clear, manifest, present, seem, seem to be, show, strike one as **3.** face, front, front on, give onto, overlook **4.** anticipate, await, expect, hope, reckon on **5.** forage, hunt, search, seek **6.** gape, gawk, gawp (*Brit. slang*), glower, goggle, ogle, rubberneck (*slang*), stare **7. look like** be the image of, fa~ vour, make one think of, put one in mind of, remind one of, resemble, take after *~noun* **8.** butcher's (*Brit. slang*), examination, eyeful (*informal*), gander (*informal*), gaze, glance, glimpse, in~ spection, look-see (*slang*), observation, once-over (*informal*), peek, recce (*slang*), review, shufti (*Brit. slang*), sight, squint (*informal*), survey, view **9.** air, appear~ ance, aspect, bearing, cast, complexion, countenance, demeanour, effect, ex~ pression, face, fashion, guise, manner, mien (*literary*), semblance

look after attend to, care for, guard, keep an eye on, mind, nurse, protect, sit with, supervise, take care of, take charge of, tend, watch

lookalike clone, dead ringer (*slang*), dou~ ble, exact match, living image, replica, ringer (*slang*), spit (*informal, chiefly Brit.*), spit and image (*informal*), spit~ ting image (*informal*), twin

look down on *or* **upon** contemn, despise, disdain, hold in contempt, look down one's nose at (*informal*), misprize, scorn, sneer, spurn, treat with contempt, turn one's nose up (at) (*informal*)

look forward to anticipate, await, count on, count the days until, expect, hope for, long for, look for, set one's heart on, wait for

look into check out, delve into, examine, explore, follow up, go into, inquire about, inspect, investigate, look over, make enquiries, make inquiries, probe, research, scrutinize, study

lookout 1. guard, qui vive, readiness, vigil, watch **2**. guard, sentinel, sentry, vedette (*Military*), watchman **3**. beacon, citadel, observation post, observatory, post, tower, watchtower **4**. *informal* business, concern, funeral (*informal*), pigeon (*Brit. informal*), worry **5**. chances, future, likelihood, outlook, prospect, view

look out be alert, be careful, be on guard, be on the qui vive, be vigilant, beware, keep an eye out, keep one's eyes open, keep one's eyes peeled, keep one's eyes skinned, pay attention, watch out

look over cast an eye over, check, check out (*informal*), examine, eyeball (*U.S. slang*), flick through, inspect, look through, monitor, peruse, scan, take a dekko at (*Brit. slang*), view, work over

look up 1. find, hunt for, research, search for, seek out, track down **2**. ameliorate, come along, get better, improve, perk up, pick up, progress, shape up (*informal*), show improvement **3**. (*with* **to**) admire, defer to, esteem, have a high opinion of, honour, regard highly, respect, revere **4**. call (on), drop in on (*informal*), go to see, look in on, pay a visit to, visit

loom 1. appear, become visible, be imminent, bulk, emerge, hover, impend, menace, take shape, threaten **2**. dominate, hang over, mount, overhang, overshadow, overtop, rise, soar, tower

loop 1. *noun* bend, circle, coil, convolution, curl, curve, eyelet, hoop, kink, loophole, noose, ring, spiral, twirl, twist, whorl **2**. *~verb* bend, braid, circle, coil, connect, curl, curve round, encircle, fold, join, knot, roll, spiral, turn, twist, wind round

loophole 1. aperture, knothole, opening, slot **2**. *figurative* avoidance, escape, evasion, excuse, let-out, means of escape, plea, pretence, pretext, subterfuge

loose *adjective* **1**. floating, free, insecure, movable, released, unattached, unbound, unconfined, unfastened, unfettered, unrestricted, unsecured, untied, wobbly **2**. baggy, easy, hanging, loosened, not fitting, not tight, relaxed, slack, slackened, sloppy **3**. diffuse, disconnected, disordered, ill-defined, imprecise, inaccurate, indefinite, indistinct, inexact, rambling, random, vague **4**. abandoned, debauched, disreputable, dissipated, dissolute, fast, immoral, lewd, libertine, licentious, profligate, promiscuous, unchaste, wanton **5**. careless, heedless, imprudent, lax, negligent, rash, thoughtless, unmindful *~verb* **6**. detach, disconnect, disengage, ease, free, let go, liberate, loosen, release, set free, slacken, unbind, unbridle, undo, unfasten, unleash, unloose, untie

▷ **Antonyms** *~adjective* (*sense 1*) bound, curbed, fastened, fettered, restrained, secured, tethered, tied (*sense 2*) tight (*sense 3*) accurate, clear, concise, exact, precise (*sense 4*) chaste, disciplined, moral, virtuous *~verb* bind, cage, capture, fasten, fetter, imprison, tether

loose-jointed *or* **loose-limbed** agile, elastic, flexible, limber, lissom(e), lithe, pliable, pliant, supple

loosen 1. detach, let out, separate, slacken, unbind, undo, unloose, unstick, untie, work free, work loose **2**. deliver, free, let go, liberate, release, set free **3**. (*often with* **up**) ease up *or* off, go easy (*informal*), lessen, let up, lighten up (*slang*), mitigate, moderate, relax, soften, weaken

loot 1. *noun* booty, goods, haul, plunder, prize, spoils, swag (*slang*) **2**. *~verb* despoil, pillage, plunder, raid, ransack, ravage, rifle, rob, sack

lop chop, clip, crop, curtail, cut, detach, dock, hack, prune, sever, shorten, trim, truncate

lope bound, canter, gallop, lollop, spring, stride

lopsided askew, asymmetrical, awry, cockeyed, crooked, disproportionate, off balance, one-sided, out of shape, out of true, skewwhiff (*Brit. informal*), squint, tilting, unbalanced, unequal, uneven, warped

loquacious babbling, blathering, chattering, chatty, gabby (*informal*), garrulous, gassy (*informal*), gossipy, talkative, voluble, wordy

loquacity babbling, chattering, chattiness, effusiveness, gabbling, garrulity, gassiness (*informal*), talkativeness, volubility

lord 1. commander, governor, king, leader, liege, master, monarch, overlord, potentate, prince, ruler, seigneur, sovereign, superior **2**. earl, noble, nobleman, peer, viscount **3**. **lord it over** act big (*slang*), be overbearing, boss around (*informal*), domineer, order around, play the lord, pull rank, put on airs, swagger

Lord, Our *or* **The** the Almighty, Christ, the Galilean, God, the Good Shepherd, Jehovah, Jesus Christ, the Nazarene

lordly 1. arrogant, condescending, despotic, dictatorial, disdainful, domineering, haughty, high and mighty (*informal*), high-handed, hoity-toity (*infor-*

mal), imperious, lofty, overbearing, patronizing, proud, stuck-up (*informal*), supercilious, toffee-nosed (*slang, chiefly Brit.*), tyrannical **2.** aristocratic, dignified, exalted, gracious, grand, imperial, lofty, majestic, noble, princely, regal, stately

lore 1. beliefs, doctrine, experience, folk-wisdom, mythos, saws, sayings, teaching, traditional wisdom, traditions, wisdom **2.** erudition, knowhow (*informal*), knowledge, learning, letters, scholarship

lose 1. be deprived of, displace, drop, fail to keep, forget, mislay, misplace, miss, suffer loss **2.** capitulate, default, fail, fall short, forfeit, lose out on (*informal*), miss, pass up (*informal*), yield **3.** be defeated, be the loser, be worsted, come a cropper (*informal*), come to grief, get the worst of, lose out, suffer defeat, take a licking (*informal*) **4.** consume, deplete, dissipate, drain, exhaust, expend, lavish, misspend, squander, use up, waste **5.** confuse, miss, stray from, wander from **6.** lap, leave behind, outdistance, outrun, outstrip, overtake, pass **7.** dodge, duck, elude, escape, evade, give someone the slip, shake off, slip away, throw off

loser also-ran, clinker (*slang, chiefly U.S.*), dud (*informal*), failure, flop (*informal*), lemon (*slang*), no-hoper (*Austral. slang*), underdog, washout (*informal*)

loss 1. bereavement, deprivation, disappearance, drain, failure, forfeiture, losing, misfortune, mislaying, privation, squandering, waste **2.** cost, damage, defeat, destruction, detriment, disadvantage, harm, hurt, impairment, injury, ruin **3.** *plural* casualties, dead, death toll, fatalities, number captured, number injured, number killed, number missing, number wounded **4.** (*sometimes plural*) debit, debt, deficiency, deficit, depletion, losings, shrinkage **5. at a loss** at one's wits' end, baffled, bewildered, confused, helpless, nonplussed, perplexed, puzzled, stuck (*informal*), stumped

▷ **Antonyms** (*sense 1*) acquisition, advantage, finding, gain, preservation, recovery, reimbursement, restoration, saving, winning

lost 1. disappeared, forfeited, mislaid, misplaced, missed, missing, strayed, vanished, wayward **2.** adrift, astray, at sea, disoriented, off-course, off-track **3.** baffled, bewildered, clueless (*slang*), confused, helpless, ignorant, mystified, perplexed, puzzled **4.** abolished, annihilated, demolished, destroyed, devastated, eradicated, exterminated, obliterated, perished, ruined, wasted, wiped out, wrecked **5.** absent, absorbed, abstracted, distracted, dreamy, engrossed, entranced, preoccupied, rapt, spellbound, taken up **6.** consumed, dissipated, frittered away, misapplied, misdirected, misspent, misused, squandered, wasted **7.** bygone, dead, extinct, forgotten, gone, lapsed, obsolete, out-of-date, past, unremembered **8.** abandoned, corrupt, damned, depraved, dissolute, fallen, irreclaimable, licentious, profligate, unchaste, wanton

lot 1. assortment, batch, bunch (*informal*), collection, consignment, crowd, group, quantity, set **2.** accident, chance, destiny, doom, fate, fortune, hazard, plight, portion **3.** allowance, cut (*informal*), parcel, part, percentage, piece, portion, quota, ration, share **4. a lot** *or* **lots** abundance, a great deal, an arm and a leg (*informal*), heap(s), large amount, load(s) (*informal*), masses (*informal*), numbers, ocean(s), oodles (*informal*), piles (*informal*), plenty, quantities, reams (*informal*), scores, stack(s) **5. draw lots** choose, cut for aces, cut straws (*informal*), decide, pick, select, spin a coin, toss up **6. throw in one's lot with** ally *or* align oneself with, join, join forces with, join fortunes with, make common cause with, support

loth *see* LOATH

lotion balm, cream, embrocation, liniment, salve, solution

lottery 1. draw, raffle, sweepstake **2.** chance, gamble, hazard, risk, toss-up (*informal*), venture

loud 1. blaring, blatant, boisterous, booming, clamorous, deafening, ear-piercing, ear-splitting, forte (*Music*), high-sounding, noisy, obstreperous, piercing, resounding, rowdy, sonorous, stentorian, strident, strong, thundering, tumultuous, turbulent, vehement, vociferous **2.** *figurative* brash, brassy, flamboyant, flashy, garish, gaudy, glaring, lurid, naff (*Brit. slang*), ostentatious, showy, tacky (*informal*), tasteless, tawdry, vulgar **3.** brash, brazen, coarse, crass, crude, loud-mouthed (*informal*), offensive, raucous, vulgar

▷ **Antonyms** (*sense 1*) gentle, inaudible, low, low-pitched, quiet, silent, soft, soundless, subdued (*sense 2*) conservative, dull, sober, sombre (*sense 3*) quiet, reserved, retiring, shy, unassuming

loudly at full volume, at the top of one's voice, clamorously, deafeningly, fortissimo (*Music*), lustily, noisily, shrilly, uproariously, vehemently, vigorously, vociferously

loudmouth bigmouth (*slang*), blowhard (*informal*), blusterer, brag, braggadocio, braggart, bullshit artist (*taboo slang*), bullshitter (*taboo slang*), gasbag (*informal*), swaggerer, windbag (*slang*)

lounge *verb* **1.** laze, lie about, loaf, loiter, loll, make oneself at home, recline, relax, saunter, sprawl, take it easy **2.**

dawdle, fritter time away, hang out (*informal*), idle, kill time, pass time idly, potter, veg out (*slang, chiefly U.S.*), waste time

lour, lower 1. be brewing, blacken, cloud up *or* over, darken, loom, menace, threaten **2.** frown, give a dirty look, glare, glower, look daggers, look sullen, scowl

louring, lowering 1. black, clouded, cloudy, dark, darkening, forbidding, foreboding, gloomy, grey, heavy, menacing, ominous, overcast, threatening **2.** brooding, forbidding, frowning, glowering, grim, scowling, sullen, surly

lousy 1. *slang* base, contemptible, despicable, dirty, hateful, low, mean, rotten (*informal*), shitty (*taboo slang*), vicious, vile **2.** *slang* awful, bad, bush-league (*Austral. & N.Z. informal*), chickenshit (*U.S. slang*), dime-a-dozen (*informal*), duff, for the birds (*informal*), inferior, low-rent (*informal, chiefly U.S.*), miserable, no good, not much cop (*Brit. slang*), of a sort *or* of sorts, piss-poor (*taboo slang*), poor, poxy (*slang*), rotten (*informal*), second-rate, shitty (*taboo slang*), shoddy, slovenly, strictly for the birds (*informal*), terrible, tinhorn (*U.S. slang*), two-bit (*U.S. & Canad. slang*) **3.** lice-infected, lice-infested, lice-ridden, pedicular, pediculous **4. lousy with** *slang* **a.** amply supplied with, not short of, rolling in (*slang*), well-supplied with **b.** alive with, overrun by, swarming with, teeming with

lout bear, boor, bumpkin, churl, clod, clumsy idiot, dolt, gawk, lubber, lummox (*informal*), ned (*slang*), oaf, yahoo, yob *or* yobbo (*Brit. slang*)

loutish boorish, bungling, churlish, clodhopping (*informal*), coarse, doltish, gawky, gross, ill-bred, ill-mannered, lubberly, lumpen (*informal*), lumpish, oafish, rough, stolid, swinish, uncouth, unmannerly

lovable adorable, amiable, attractive, captivating, charming, cuddly, cute, delightful, enchanting, endearing, engaging, fetching (*informal*), likable *or* likeable, lovely, pleasing, sweet, winning, winsome

▷ **Antonyms** abhorrent, abominable, detestable, hateful, loathsome, obnoxious, odious, offensive, revolting

love *verb* **1.** adore, adulate, be attached to, be in love with, cherish, dote on, have affection for, hold dear, idolize, prize, think the world of, treasure, worship **2.** appreciate, delight in, desire, enjoy, fancy, have a weakness for, like, relish, savour, take pleasure in **3.** canoodle (*slang*), caress, cuddle, embrace, fondle, kiss, neck (*informal*), pet *~noun* **4.** adoration, adulation, affection, amity, ardour, attachment, devotion, fondness, friendship, infatuation, liking, passion, rapture, regard, tenderness, warmth **5.** delight, devotion, enjoyment, fondness, inclination, liking, partiality, relish, soft spot, taste, weakness **6.** angel, beloved, darling, dear, dearest, dear one, inamorata, inamorato, leman (*archaic*), loved one, lover, sweet, sweetheart, truelove **7. for love** for nothing, freely, free of charge, gratis, pleasurably, without payment **8. for love or money** by any means, ever, under any conditions **9. in love** besotted, charmed, enamoured, enraptured, infatuated, smitten **10. fall in love (with)** bestow one's affections on, be taken with, fall for, lose one's heart (to), take a shine to (*informal*)

▷ **Antonyms** *~verb* (*senses 1 & 2*) abhor, abominate, detest, dislike, hate, scorn *~noun* (*senses 4 & 5*) abhorrence, abomination, animosity, antagonism, antipathy, aversion, bad blood, bitterness, detestation, disgust, dislike, hate, hatred, hostility, ill will, incompatibility, loathing, malice, repugnance, resentment, scorn (*sense 6*) enemy, foe

love affair 1. affair, *affaire de coeur,* amour, intrigue, liaison, relationship, romance **2.** appreciation, devotion, enthusiasm, love, mania, passion

loveless 1. disliked, forsaken, friendless, lovelorn, unappreciated, uncherished, unloved, unvalued **2.** cold, cold-hearted, frigid, hard, heartless, icy, insensitive, unfeeling, unfriendly, unloving, unresponsive

lovelorn crossed in love, jilted, languishing, lovesick, mooning, moping, pining, slighted, spurned, unrequited, yearning

lovely 1. admirable, adorable, amiable, attractive, beautiful, charming, comely, exquisite, graceful, handsome, pretty, sweet, winning **2.** agreeable, captivating, delightful, enchanting, engaging, enjoyable, gratifying, nice, pleasant, pleasing

▷ **Antonyms** abhorrent, detestable, hateful, hideous, loathsome, odious, repellent, repugnant, revolting, ugly, unattractive

lovemaking act of love, carnal knowledge, coition, coitus, copulation, intercourse, intimacy, mating, nookie (*slang*), rumpy-pumpy (*slang*), sexual intercourse, sexual relations, sexual union *or* congress, the other (*informal*)

lover admirer, beau, beloved, boyfriend, fancy bit (*slang*), fancy man (*slang*), fancy woman (*slang*), fiancé, fiancée, flame (*informal*), girlfriend, inamorata, inamorato, leman (*archaic*), mistress, paramour, suitor, swain (*archaic*), sweetheart, toy boy

lovesick desiring, languishing, longing, lovelorn, pining, yearning

loving affectionate, amorous, ardent, cordial, dear, demonstrative, devoted, doting, fond, friendly, kind, solicitous, tender, warm, warm-hearted

▷ **Antonyms** aloof, cold, contemptuous, cruel, detached, distasteful, hateful, hostile, indifferent, mean, scornful, unconcerned, unloving

low[1] *adjective* **1.** fubsy (*archaic or dialect*), little, short, small, squat, stunted **2.** deep, depressed, ground-level, low-lying, shallow, subsided, sunken **3.** depleted, insignificant, little, meagre, measly, paltry, reduced, scant, small, sparse, trifling **4.** deficient, inadequate, inferior, low-grade, low-rent (*informal, chiefly U.S.*), mediocre, pathetic, poor, puny, second-rate, shoddy, substandard, worthless **5.** coarse, common, crude, disgraceful, dishonourable, disreputable, gross, ill-bred, obscene, rough, rude, unbecoming, undignified, unrefined, vulgar **6.** humble, lowborn, lowly, meek, obscure, plain, plebeian, poor, simple, unpretentious **7.** blue, brassed off (*Brit. slang*), dejected, depressed, despondent, disheartened, dismal, down, downcast, down in the dumps (*informal*), fed up, forlorn, gloomy, glum, miserable, morose, sad, sick as a parrot (*informal*), unhappy **8.** debilitated, dying, exhausted, feeble, frail, ill, prostrate, reduced, sinking, stricken, weak **9.** gentle, hushed, muffled, muted, quiet, soft, subdued, whispered **10.** cheap, economical, inexpensive, moderate, modest, reasonable **11.** abject, base, contemptible, cowardly, dastardly, degraded, depraved, despicable, ignoble, mean, menial, nasty, scurvy, servile, sordid, unworthy, vile, vulgar

▷ **Antonyms** (*sense 1*) tall, towering (*sense 2*) elevated (*sense 3*) important, significant (*senses 4,6, & 11*) brave, eminent, exalted, fine, grand, high-ranking, honourable, laudable, lofty, praiseworthy, superior, worthy (*sense 7*) cheerful, elated, happy, high (*sense 8*) alert, energetic, enthusiastic, strong (*sense 9*) loud, noisy

low[2] **1.** *verb* bellow, moo **2.** *~noun* bellow, bellowing, lowing, moo, mooing

lowdown *informal* dope (*informal*), gen (*Brit. informal*), info (*informal*), information, inside story, intelligence

low-down base, cheap (*informal*), contemptible, despicable, low, mean, nasty, reprehensible, scurvy, ugly, underhand

lower[1] *adjective* **1.** inferior, junior, lesser, low-level, minor, secondary, second-class, smaller, subordinate, under **2.** curtailed, decreased, diminished, lessened, pared down, reduced *~verb* **3.** depress, drop, fall, let down, make lower, sink, submerge, take down **4.** abase, belittle, condescend, debase, degrade, deign, demean, devalue, disgrace, downgrade, humble, humiliate, stoop **5.** abate, curtail, cut, decrease, diminish, lessen, minimize, moderate, prune, reduce, slash **6.** soften, tone down

▷ **Antonyms** *~adjective* enlarged, higher, increased *~verb* amplify, augment, boost, elevate, enlarge, extend, hoist, increase, inflate, lift, magnify, raise

lower[2] *see* LOUR

lowering *see* LOURING

low-grade bad, bush-league (*Austral. & N.Z. informal*), chickenshit (*U.S. slang*), dime-a-dozen (*informal*), duff (*informal*), inferior, low-rent (*informal, chiefly U.S.*), not good enough, not up to snuff (*informal*), of a sort *or* of sorts, piss-poor (*taboo slang*), poor, poxy (*slang*), second-rate, substandard, tinhorn (*U.S. slang*), two-bit (*U.S. & Canad. slang*)

low-key keeping a low profile, low-pitched, muffled, muted, played down, quiet, restrained, subdued, toned down, understated

lowly 1. ignoble, inferior, lowborn, mean, obscure, plebeian, proletarian, subordinate **2.** docile, dutiful, gentle, humble, meek, mild, modest, submissive, unassuming **3.** average, common, homespun, modest, ordinary, plain, poor, simple, unpretentious

low-minded coarse, crude, dirty, disgusting, filthy, foul, gross, indecent, obscene, rude, smutty, uncouth, vulgar

low-spirited apathetic, blue, brassed off (*Brit. slang*), dejected, depressed, despondent, dismal, down, down-hearted, down in the dumps (*informal*), down in the mouth, fed up, gloomy, heavy-hearted, low, miserable, moody, sad, unhappy

loyal attached, constant, dependable, devoted, dutiful, faithful, immovable, patriotic, staunch, steadfast, tried and true, true, true-blue, true-hearted, trustworthy, trusty, unswerving, unwavering

▷ **Antonyms** disloyal, false, perfidious, traitorous, treacherous, unfaithful, untrustworthy

loyalty allegiance, constancy, dependability, devotion, faithfulness, fealty, fidelity, patriotism, reliability, staunchness, steadfastness, troth (*archaic*), true-heartedness, trueness, trustiness, trustworthiness

lozenge cough drop, jujube, pastille, tablet, troche

lubberly *adjective* awkward, blundering, bungling, churlish, clodhopping (*informal*), clownish, clumsy, coarse, crude, doltish, gawky, heavy-handed, loutish, lumbering, lumpen (*informal*), lumpish, oafish, uncouth, ungainly

lubricate grease, make slippery, make smooth, oil, oil the wheels, smear, smooth the way

lucid 1. clear, clear-cut, comprehensible, crystal clear, distinct, evident, explicit, intelligible, limpid, obvious, pellucid, plain, transparent **2.** beaming, bright, brilliant, effulgent, gleaming, luminous, radiant, resplendent, shining **3.** clear, crystalline, diaphanous, glassy, limpid, pellucid, pure, translucent, transparent **4.** all there, clear-headed, *compos mentis,* in one's right mind, rational, reasonable, sane, sensible, sober, sound

▷ **Antonyms** (*sense 1*) ambiguous, clear as mud (*informal*), confused, equivocal, incomprehensible, indistinct, muddled, unclear, unintelligible, vague (*sense 2*) dull (*sense 3*) unclear (*sense 4*) confused, irrational, muddled, unclear, unperceptive, vague

luck 1. accident, chance, destiny, fate, fortuity, fortune, hap (*archaic*), hazard **2.** advantage, blessing, break (*informal*), fluke, godsend, good fortune, good luck, prosperity, serendipity, stroke, success, windfall

luckily 1. favourably, fortunately, happily, opportunely, propitiously, providentially **2.** as it chanced, as luck would have it, by chance, fortuitously

luckless calamitous, cursed, disastrous, doomed, hapless, hopeless, ill-fated, ill-starred, jinxed, star-crossed, unfortunate, unhappy, unlucky, unpropitious, unsuccessful

lucky 1. advantageous, blessed, charmed, favoured, fortunate, jammy (*Brit. slang*), on a roll (*informal*), prosperous, serendipitous, successful **2.** adventitious, auspicious, fortuitous, opportune, propitious, providential, timely

▷ **Antonyms** bad, detrimental, ominous, unfavourable, unfortunate, unhappy, unlucky, unpromising, untimely

lucrative advantageous, fat, fruitful, gainful, high-income, money-making, paying, productive, profitable, remunerative, well-paid

lucre gain, mammon, money, pelf, profit, riches, spoils, wealth

lucubration 1. brainwork, grind (*informal*), meditation, study **2.** dissertation, opus, production, treatise

ludicrous absurd, burlesque, comic, comical, crazy, droll, farcical, funny, incongruous, laughable, nonsensical, odd, outlandish, preposterous, ridiculous, silly, zany

▷ **Antonyms** grave, logical, sad, sensible, serious, solemn

lug carry, drag, haul, heave, hump (*Brit. slang*), pull, tow, yank

luggage baggage, bags, cases, gear, impedimenta, paraphernalia, suitcases, things, trunks

lugubrious dirgelike, dismal, doleful, dreary, funereal, gloomy, melancholy, morose, mournful, sad, serious, sombre, sorrowful, woebegone, woeful

lukewarm 1. blood-warm, tepid, warm **2.** *figurative* apathetic, cold, cool, half-arsed (*Brit. slang*), half-assed (*U.S. & Canad. slang*), half-hearted, indifferent, laodicean, phlegmatic, unconcerned, unenthusiastic, uninterested, unresponsive

lull *verb* **1.** allay, calm, compose, hush, lullaby, pacify, quell, quiet, rock to sleep, soothe, still, subdue, tranquillize **2.** abate, cease, decrease, diminish, dwindle, ease off, let up, moderate, quieten down, slacken, subside, wane ~*noun* **3.** calm, calmness, hush, let-up (*informal*), pause, quiet, respite, silence, stillness, tranquillity

lullaby berceuse, cradlesong

lumber[1] 1. *noun* castoffs, clutter, discards, jumble, junk, refuse, rubbish, trash, trumpery, white elephants **2.** ~*verb Brit. slang* burden, encumber, impose upon, land, load, saddle

lumber[2] *verb* clump, lump along, plod, shamble, shuffle, stump, trudge, trundle, waddle

lumbering awkward, blundering, bovine, bumbling, clumsy, elephantine, heavy, heavy-footed, hulking, lubberly, overgrown, ponderous, ungainly, unwieldy

luminary big name, celeb (*informal*), celebrity, dignitary, leading light, lion, megastar (*informal*), notable, personage, somebody, star, V.I.P., worthy

luminescent Day-Glo, effulgent, fluorescent, glowing, luminous, phosphorescent, radiant, shining

luminous 1. bright, brilliant, glowing, illuminated, lighted, lit, luminescent, lustrous, radiant, resplendent, shining, vivid **2.** clear, evident, intelligible, lucid, obvious, perspicuous, plain, transparent

lump[1] *noun* **1.** ball, bunch, cake, chunk, clod, cluster, dab, gob, gobbet, group, hunk, mass, nugget, piece, spot, wedge **2.** bulge, bump, growth, hump, protrusion, protuberance, swelling, tumescence, tumour ~*verb* **3.** agglutinate, aggregate, batch, bunch, coalesce, collect, combine, conglomerate, consolidate, group, mass, pool, unite

lump[2] *verb* bear, brook, endure, hack (*slang*), put up with, stand, suffer, take, thole (*Northern English dialect*), tolerate

lumpish awkward, bungling, clumsy, doltish, elephantine, gawky, heavy, lethargic, lumbering, oafish, obtuse, puddingy, stolid, stupid, ungainly

lumpy bumpy, clotted, curdled, full of lumps, grainy, granular, knobbly, uneven

lunacy 1. dementia, derangement, idiocy, insanity, madness, mania, psychosis **2.** aberration, absurdity, craziness, folly, foolhardiness, foolishness, idiocy, imbecility, madness, senselessness, stupidity, tomfoolery

▷ **Antonyms** prudence, reason, sanity, sense

lunatic 1. *adjective* as daft as a brush (*informal, chiefly Brit.*), barking (*slang*), barking mad (*slang*), barmy (*slang*), bonkers (*slang, chiefly Brit.*), crack-brained, crackpot (*informal*), crazy, daft, demented, deranged, gonzo (*slang*), insane, irrational, loopy (*informal*), mad, maniacal, not the full shilling (*informal*), nuts (*slang*), off one's trolley (*slang*), out to lunch (*informal*), psychotic, unhinged, up the pole (*informal*), wacko *or* whacko (*informal*) 2. *~noun* headbanger (*informal*), headcase (*informal*), loony (*slang*), madman, maniac, nut (*slang*), nutcase (*slang*), nutter (*Brit. slang*), psychopath

lunge 1. *noun* charge, cut, jab, pass, pounce, spring, stab, swing, swipe (*informal*), thrust 2. *~verb* bound, charge, cut, dash, dive, fall upon, hit at, jab, leap, pitch into (*informal*), plunge, poke, pounce, set upon, stab, strike at, thrust

lurch 1. heave, heel, lean, list, pitch, rock, roll, tilt, wallow 2. reel, stagger, stumble, sway, totter, weave

lure 1. *verb* allure, attract, beckon, decoy, draw, ensnare, entice, inveigle, invite, lead on, seduce, tempt 2. *~noun* allurement, attraction, bait, carrot (*informal*), come-on (*informal*), decoy, enticement, incentive, inducement, magnet, siren song, temptation

lurid 1. exaggerated, graphic, melodramatic, sensational, shock-horror (*facetious*), shocking, startling, unrestrained, vivid, yellow (*of journalism*) 2. disgusting, ghastly, gory, grim, grisly, gruesome, macabre, revolting, savage, violent 3. ashen, ghastly, pale, pallid, sallow, wan 4. bloody, fiery, flaming, glaring, glowering, intense, livid, overbright, sanguine

▷ **Antonyms** (*senses 1 & 2*) breezy, bright, carefree, controlled, factual, jaunty, light-hearted, mild (*sense 4*) pale, pastel, watery

lurk conceal oneself, crouch, go furtively, hide, lie in wait, move with stealth, prowl, skulk, slink, sneak, snoop

luscious appetizing, delectable, delicious, honeyed, juicy, mouth-watering, palatable, rich, savoury, scrumptious (*informal*), succulent, sweet, toothsome, yummy (*slang*)

lush 1. abundant, dense, flourishing, green, lavish, overgrown, prolific, rank, teeming, verdant 2. fresh, juicy, ripe, succulent, tender 3. elaborate, extravagant, grand, lavish, luxurious, opulent, ornate, palatial, plush (*informal*), ritzy (*slang*), sumptuous

lust *noun* 1. carnality, concupiscence, lasciviousness, lechery, lewdness, libido, licentiousness, pruriency, randiness (*informal, chiefly Brit.*), salaciousness, sensuality, the hots (*slang*), wantonness 2. appetence, appetite, avidity, covetousness, craving, cupidity, desire, greed, longing, passion, thirst *~verb* 3. be consumed with desire for, covet, crave, desire, hunger for *or* after, lech after (*informal*), need, slaver over, want, yearn

lustful carnal, concupiscent, craving, hankering, horny (*slang*), hot-blooded, lascivious, lecherous, lewd, libidinous, licentious, passionate, prurient, randy (*informal, chiefly Brit.*), raunchy (*slang*), sensual, sexy (*informal*), unchaste, wanton

lustily forcefully, hard, loudly, powerfully, strongly, vigorously, with all one's might, with might and main

lustre 1. burnish, gleam, glint, glitter, gloss, glow, sheen, shimmer, shine, sparkle 2. brightness, brilliance, dazzle, lambency, luminousness, radiance, resplendence 3. distinction, fame, glory, honour, illustriousness, prestige, renown

lustreless colourless, dingy, drab, dull, faded, flat, lacklustre, lifeless, matt, pale, tarnished, unpolished, washed out

lustrous bright, burnished, dazzling, gleaming, glistening, glossy, glowing, luminous, radiant, shimmering, shining, shiny, sparkling

lusty brawny, energetic, hale, healthy, hearty, in fine fettle, powerful, red-blooded (*informal*), robust, rugged, stalwart, stout, strapping, strong, sturdy, vigorous, virile

luxuriant 1. abundant, ample, copious, excessive, lavish, plenteous, plentiful, prodigal, profuse, superabundant 2. baroque, corinthian, decorated, elaborate, extravagant, fancy, festooned, flamboyant, florid, flowery, ornate, rococo, sumptuous 3. dense, exuberant, fecund, fertile, flourishing, fruitful, lush, overflowing, productive, prolific, rank, rich, riotous, teeming, thriving

▷ **Antonyms** barren, meagre, plain, scanty, simple, sparse, thin, unadorned

luxuriate 1. bask, delight, enjoy, flourish, indulge, relish, revel, wallow 2. abound, bloom, burgeon, flourish, grow, prosper, thrive 3. be in clover, have the time of one's life, live in luxury, live the life of Riley, take it easy, wanton

luxurious 1. comfortable, costly, de luxe, expensive, lavish, magnificent, opulent, plush (*informal*), rich, ritzy (*slang*), splendid, sumptuous, well-appointed 2. epicurean, pampered, pleasure-loving, self-indulgent, sensual, sybaritic, voluptuous

▷ **Antonyms** ascetic, austere, deprived, economical, plain, poor, sparing, Spartan, squalid, thrifty

luxury 1. affluence, hedonism, opulence, richness, splendour, sumptuousness, voluptuousness **2.** bliss, comfort, delight, enjoyment, gratification, indulgence, pleasure, satisfaction, wellbeing **3.** ex~ tra, extravagance, frill, indulgence, nonessential, treat

▷ **Antonyms** austerity, burden, depriva~ tion, destitution, difficulty, discomfort, hardship, infliction, misery, necessity, need, poverty, privation, want

lying 1. *noun* deceit, dishonesty, dissimu~ lation, double-dealing, duplicity, fabri~ cation, falsity, fibbing, guile, mendacity, perjury, prevarication, untruthfulness **2.** *~adjective* deceitful, dishonest, dissem~ bling, double-dealing, false, guileful, mendacious, perfidious, treacherous, two-faced, untruthful

▷ **Antonyms** *~adjective* candid, forth~ right, frank, honest, reliable, sincere, straight, straightforward, truthful, ve~ racious

lyric *adjective* **1.** *of poetry* expressive, lyrical, melodic, musical, songlike **2.** *of a voice* clear, dulcet, flowing, graceful, light, silvery *~noun* **3.** *plural* book, libretto, text, the words, words of a song

lyrical carried away, ecstatic, effusive, emotional, enthusiastic, expressive, im~ passioned, inspired, poetic, rapturous, rhapsodic

M, m

macabre cadaverous, deathlike, deathly, dreadful, eerie, frightening, frightful, ghastly, ghostly, ghoulish, grim, grisly, gruesome, hideous, horrid, morbid, unearthly, weird
▷ **Antonyms** appealing, beautiful, charming, delightful, lovely, pleasant

macerate mash, pulp, soak, soften, steep

machiavellian amoral, artful, astute, crafty, cunning, cynical, deceitful, designing, double-dealing, foxy, intriguing, opportunist, perfidious, scheming, shrewd, sly, underhand, unscrupulous, wily

machinate conspire, contrive, design, devise, engineer, hatch, intrigue, invent, manoeuvre, plan, plot, scheme

machination artifice, cabal, conspiracy, design, device, dodge, intrigue, manoeuvre, plot, ploy, ruse, scheme, stratagem, trick

machine 1. apparatus, appliance, contraption, contrivance, device, engine, instrument, mechanism, tool **2.** agency, machinery, organization, party, setup (*informal*), structure, system **3.** *figurative* agent, automaton, mechanical man, puppet, robot, zombie

machinery 1. apparatus, equipment, gear, instruments, mechanism, tackle, tools, works **2.** agency, channels, machine, organization, procedure, structure, system

mad 1. aberrant, as daft as a brush (*informal, chiefly Brit.*), bananas (*slang*), barking (*slang*), barking mad (*slang*), barmy (*slang*), batty (*slang*), bonkers (*slang, chiefly Brit.*), crackers (*Brit. slang*), crackpot (*informal*), crazed, crazy (*informal*), cuckoo (*informal*), delirious, demented, deranged, distracted, doolally (*slang*), flaky (*U.S. slang*), frantic, frenzied, gonzo (*slang*), insane, loony (*slang*), loopy (*informal*), lost one's marbles (*informal*), lunatic, mental (*slang*), *non compos mentis,* not right in the head, not the full shilling (*informal*), nuts (*slang*), nutty (*slang*), off one's chump (*slang*), off one's head (*slang*), off one's nut (*slang*), off one's rocker (*slang*), off one's trolley (*slang*), of unsound mind, out of one's mind, out to lunch (*informal*), psychotic, rabid, raving, round the bend (*Brit. slang*), round the twist (*Brit. slang*), screwy (*informal*), unbalanced, unhinged, unstable, up the pole (*informal*), wacko *or* whacko (*informal*) **2.** absurd, as daft as a brush (*informal, chiefly Brit.*), asinine, daft (*informal*), foolhardy, foolish, imprudent, inane, irrational, ludicrous, nonsensical, preposterous, senseless, unreasonable, unsafe, unsound, wild **3.** *informal* angry, ape (*slang*), apeshit (*slang*), berserk, choked, cross, enraged, exasperated, fuming, furious, in a wax (*informal, chiefly Brit.*), incensed, infuriated, irate, irritated, livid (*informal*), raging, resentful, seeing red (*informal*), wild, wrathful **4.** ardent, avid, crazy, daft (*informal*), devoted, dotty (*slang, chiefly Brit.*), enamoured, enthusiastic, fanatical, fond, hooked, impassioned, infatuated, in love with, keen, nuts (*slang*), wild, zealous **5.** abandoned, agitated, boisterous, ebullient, energetic, excited, frenetic, frenzied, full-on (*informal*), gay, riotous, uncontrolled, unrestrained, wild **6. like mad** *informal* energetically, enthusiastically, excitedly, furiously, hell for leather, like greased lightning (*informal*), like lightning, like nobody's business (*informal*), like the clappers (*Brit. informal*), madly, quickly, rapidly, speedily, unrestrainedly, violently, wildly, with might and main
▷ **Antonyms** appeased, calm, composed, cool, mollified, nonchalant, rational, sane, sensible, sound, uncaring

madcap 1. *adjective* crackpot (*informal*), crazy, foolhardy, hare-brained, heedless, hot-headed, ill-advised, imprudent, impulsive, lively, rash, reckless, thoughtless, wild **2.** *~noun* daredevil, hothead, tearaway, wild man

madden aggravate (*informal*), annoy, craze, dement, derange, drive one crazy, drive one off one's head (*slang*), drive one out of one's mind, drive one round the bend (*Brit. slang*), drive one round the twist (*Brit. slang*), drive one to distraction (*informal*), enrage, exasperate, gall, get one's back up, get one's dander up (*informal*), get one's goat (*slang*), get one's hackles up, incense, inflame, infuriate, irritate, make one's blood boil, make one see red (*informal*), make one's hackles rise, nark (*Brit., Austral., &*

N.Z. slang), piss one off (*taboo slang*), provoke, put one's back up, raise one's hackles, unhinge, upset, vex
▷ **Antonyms** appease, calm, mollify, pacify, soothe

made-up fabricated, false, fictional, imaginary, invented, make-believe, mythical, specious, trumped-up, unreal, untrue

madhouse 1. funny farm (*facetious*), insane asylum, laughing academy (*U.S. slang*), loony bin (*slang*), lunatic asylum, mental hospital, mental institution, nuthouse (*slang*), psychiatric hospital, rubber room (*U.S. slang*) **2.** Babel, bedlam, chaos, pandemonium, turmoil, uproar

madly 1. crazily, deliriously, dementedly, distractedly, frantically, frenziedly, hysterically, insanely, rabidly **2.** absurdly, foolishly, irrationally, ludicrously, nonsensically, senselessly, unreasonably, wildly **3.** energetically, excitedly, furiously, hastily, hell for leather, hotfoot, hurriedly, like greased lightning (*informal*), like lightning, like mad (*informal*), like nobody's business (*informal*), like the clappers (*Brit. informal*), quickly, rapidly, recklessly, speedily, violently, wildly **4.** *informal* desperately, devotedly, exceedingly, excessively, extremely, intensely, passionately, to distraction

madman *or* **madwoman** headbanger (*informal*), headcase (*informal*), loony (*slang*), lunatic, maniac, mental case (*slang*), nut (*slang*), nutcase (*slang*), nutter (*Brit. slang*), psycho (*slang*), psychopath, psychotic

madness 1. aberration, craziness, delusion, dementia, derangement, distraction, insanity, lunacy, mania, mental illness, psychopathy, psychosis **2.** absurdity, daftness (*informal*), folly, foolhardiness, foolishness, idiocy, nonsense, preposterousness, wildness **3.** anger, exasperation, frenzy, fury, ire, rage, raving, wildness, wrath **4.** ardour, craze, enthusiasm, fanaticism, fondness, infatuation, keenness, passion, rage, zeal **5.** abandon, agitation, excitement, frenzy, furore, intoxication, riot, unrestraint, uproar

maelstrom 1. vortex, whirlpool **2.** bedlam, chaos, confusion, disorder, pandemonium, tumult, turmoil, upheaval, uproar

maestro expert, genius, master, virtuoso

magazine 1. journal, pamphlet, paper, periodical **2.** ammunition dump, arsenal, depot, powder room (*obsolete*), store, storehouse, warehouse

magic *noun* **1.** black art, enchantment, necromancy, occultism, sorcery, sortilege, spell, theurgy, witchcraft, wizardry **2.** conjuring, hocus-pocus, illusion, jiggery-pokery (*informal, chiefly Brit.*), jugglery, legerdemain, prestidigitation, sleight of hand, trickery **3.** allurement, charm, enchantment, fascination, glamour, magnetism, power *~adjective* **4.** *also* **magical** bewitching, charismatic, charming, enchanting, entrancing, fascinating, magnetic, marvellous, miraculous, sorcerous, spellbinding

magician 1. archimage (*rare*), conjuror *or* conjuror, enchanter, enchantress, illusionist, necromancer, sorcerer, thaumaturge (*rare*), theurgist, warlock, witch, wizard **2.** genius, marvel, miracle-worker, spellbinder, virtuoso, wizard, wonder-worker

magisterial arrogant, assertive, authoritative, bossy (*informal*), commanding, dictatorial, domineering, high-handed, imperious, lordly, masterful, overbearing, peremptory
▷ **Antonyms** deferential, diffident, humble, servile, shy, submissive, subservient, wimpish *or* wimpy (*informal*)

magistrate bailie (*Scot.*), J.P., judge, justice, justice of the peace, provost (*Scot.*)

magnanimity beneficence, benevolence, big-heartedness, bountifulness, charitableness, generosity, high-mindedness, largesse *or* largess, munificence, nobility, open-handedness, selflessness, unselfishness

magnanimous beneficent, big, big-hearted, bountiful, charitable, free, generous, great-hearted, handsome, high-minded, kind, kindly, munificent, noble, open-handed, selfless, ungrudging, unselfish, unstinting
▷ **Antonyms** miserly, petty, resentful, selfish, small, unforgiving, vindictive

magnate 1. baron, big cheese (*slang, old-fashioned*), big noise (*informal*), big shot (*informal*), big wheel (*slang*), bigwig (*informal*), captain of industry, chief, fat cat (*slang, chiefly U.S.*), leader, Mister Big (*slang, chiefly U.S.*), mogul, nabob (*informal*), notable, plutocrat, tycoon, V.I.P. **2.** aristo (*informal*), aristocrat, baron, bashaw, grandee, magnifico, merchant, nob (*slang, chiefly Brit.*), noble, notable, personage, prince

magnetic alluring, attractive, captivating, charismatic, charming, enchanting, entrancing, fascinating, hypnotic, irresistible, mesmerizing, seductive
▷ **Antonyms** disagreeable, offensive, repellent, repulsive, unappealing, unattractive, unlikable *or* unlikeable, unpleasant

magnetism allure, appeal, attraction, attractiveness, captivatingness, charisma, charm, draw, drawing power, enchantment, fascination, hypnotism, magic, mesmerism, power, pull, seductiveness, spell

magnification aggrandizement, amplification, augmentation, blow-up (*informal*), boost, build-up, deepening, dilation, enhancement, enlargement, exaggeration, expansion, heightening, increase, inflation, intensification

magnificence brilliance, éclat, glory, gorgeousness, grandeur, luxuriousness, luxury, majesty, nobility, opulence, pomp, resplendence, splendour, stateliness, sublimity, sumptuousness

magnificent august, brilliant, divine (*informal*), elegant, elevated, exalted, excellent, fine, glorious, gorgeous, grand, grandiose, imposing, impressive, lavish, luxurious, majestic, noble, opulent, outstanding, princely, regal, resplendent, rich, splendid, splendiferous (*facetious*), stately, striking, sublime, sumptuous, superb, superior, transcendent
▷ **Antonyms** bad, humble, ignoble, lowly, mean, modest, ordinary, petty, poor, trivial, undistinguished, unimposing

magnifico **1.** aristo (*informal*), aristocrat, grandee, lord, magnate, nob (*slang, chiefly Brit.*), noble, patrician, seigneur **2.** bashaw, big cheese (*slang, old-fashioned*), big noise (*informal*), big shot (*informal*), big wheel (*slang*), bigwig (*informal*), mogul, nabob (*informal*), notable, personage, V.I.P.

magnify **1.** aggrandize, amplify, augment, blow up (*informal*), boost, build up, deepen, dilate, enlarge, expand, heighten, increase, intensify **2.** aggravate, blow up, blow up out of all proportion, dramatize, enhance, exaggerate, inflate, make a federal case of (*U.S. informal*), make a mountain out of a molehill, make a production (out) of (*informal*), overdo, overemphasize, overestimate, overplay, overrate, overstate
▷ **Antonyms** belittle, decrease, deflate, denigrate, deprecate, diminish, disparage, lessen, lower, minimize, reduce, shrink, understate

magniloquence bombast, fustian, grandiloquence, loftiness, pomposity, pretentiousness, turgidity

magniloquent bombastic, declamatory, elevated, exalted, grandiloquent, high-flown, high-sounding, lofty, orotund, overblown, pompous, pretentious, rhetorical, sonorous, stilted, turgid

magnitude **1.** consequence, eminence, grandeur, greatness, importance, mark, moment, note, significance, weight **2.** amount, amplitude, bigness, bulk, capacity, dimensions, enormity, expanse, extent, hugeness, immensity, intensity, largeness, mass, measure, proportions, quantity, size, space, strength, vastness, volume
▷ **Antonyms** insignificance, meanness, smallness, triviality, unimportance

maid **1.** damsel, girl, lass, lassie (*informal*), maiden, miss, nymph (*poetic*), wench **2.** abigail (*archaic*), handmaiden (*archaic*), housemaid, maidservant, servant, serving-maid

maiden *noun* **1.** damsel, girl, lass, lassie (*informal*), maid, miss, nymph (*poetic*), virgin, wench *~adjective* **2.** chaste, intact, pure, undefiled, unmarried, unwed, virgin, virginal **3.** first, inaugural, initial, initiatory, introductory **4.** fresh, new, unbroached, untapped, untried, unused

maidenly chaste, decent, decorous, demure, gentle, girlish, modest, pure, reserved, undefiled, unsullied, vestal, virginal, virtuous
▷ **Antonyms** brazen, corrupt, defiled, depraved, dirty, immodest, immoral, impure, indecent, loose, promiscuous, shameless, sinful, unchaste, wanton, wicked

mail *noun* **1.** correspondence, letters, packages, parcels, post **2.** post, postal service, postal system *~verb* **3.** dispatch, forward, post, send, send by mail *or* post

maim cripple, disable, hamstring, hurt, impair, incapacitate, injure, lame, mangle, mar, mutilate, put out of action, wound

main *adjective* **1.** capital, cardinal, central, chief, critical, crucial, essential, foremost, head, leading, necessary, outstanding, paramount, particular, predominant, pre-eminent, premier, primary, prime, principal, special, supreme, vital **2.** absolute, brute, direct, downright, entire, mere, pure, sheer, undisguised, utmost, utter *~noun* **3.** cable, channel, conduit, duct, line, pipe **4.** effort, force, might, potency, power, puissance, strength **5. in** *or* **for the main** for the most part, generally, in general, mainly, mostly, on the whole
▷ **Antonyms** *~adjective* auxiliary, dependent, insignificant, least, lesser, minor, secondary, subordinate, trivial, unimportant

mainly above all, chiefly, first and foremost, for the most part, generally, in general, in the main, largely, mostly, most of all, on the whole, overall, predominantly, primarily, principally, substantially, to the greatest extent, usually

mainspring cause, driving force, generator, impulse, incentive, inspiration, motivation, motive, origin, prime mover, source

mainstay anchor, backbone, bulwark, buttress, chief support, lynchpin, pillar, prop

maintain **1.** care for, carry on, conserve, continue, finance, keep, keep up, look after, nurture, perpetuate, preserve, prolong, provide, retain, supply, support, sustain, take care of, uphold **2.** affirm, allege, assert, asseverate, aver, avow, claim, contend, declare, hold, insist, profess, state **3.** advocate, argue for, back, champion, defend, fight for, justify, plead for, stand by, take up the

cudgels for, uphold, vindicate
▷ **Antonyms** (*sense 1*) abolish, break off, conclude, discontinue, drop, end, finish, give up, relinquish, suspend, terminate (*sense 2*) disavow (*sense 3*) abandon, desert

maintenance 1. care, carrying-on, conservation, continuance, continuation, keeping, nurture, perpetuation, preservation, prolongation, provision, repairs, retainment, supply, support, sustainment, sustention, upkeep **2.** aliment, alimony, allowance, food, keep, livelihood, living, subsistence, support, sustenance, upkeep

majestic august, awesome, dignified, elevated, exalted, grand, grandiose, imperial, imposing, impressive, kingly, lofty, magnificent, monumental, noble, pompous, princely, regal, royal, splendid, splendiferous (*facetious*), stately, sublime, superb
▷ **Antonyms** humble, ignoble, lowly, mean, modest, ordinary, unassuming, undistinguished, unimposing

majesty augustness, awesomeness, dignity, exaltedness, glory, grandeur, imposingness, impressiveness, kingliness, loftiness, magnificence, nobility, pomp, queenliness, royalty, splendour, state, stateliness, sublimity
▷ **Antonyms** disgrace, meanness, shame, triviality

major 1. better, bigger, chief, elder, greater, head, higher, larger, lead, leading, main, most, senior, superior, supreme, uppermost **2.** critical, crucial, grave, great, important, mega (*slang*), notable, outstanding, pre-eminent, radical, serious, significant, vital, weighty
▷ **Antonyms** auxiliary, inconsequential, insignificant, lesser, minor, secondary, smaller, subordinate, trivial, unimportant

majority 1. best part, bulk, greater number, mass, more, most, plurality, preponderance, superiority **2.** adulthood, manhood, maturity, seniority, womanhood

make *verb* **1.** assemble, build, compose, constitute, construct, create, fabricate, fashion, forge, form, frame, manufacture, mould, originate, produce, put together, shape, synthesize **2.** accomplish, beget, bring about, cause, create, effect, engender, generate, give rise to, lead to, occasion, produce **3.** cause, coerce, compel, constrain, dragoon, drive, force, impel, induce, oblige, press, pressurize, prevail upon, railroad (*informal*), require **4.** appoint, assign, create, designate, elect, install, invest, nominate, ordain **5.** draw up, enact, establish, fix, form, frame, pass **6.** add up to, amount to, compose, constitute, embody, form, represent **7.** act, carry out, do, effect, engage in, execute, perform, practise, prosecute **8.** calculate, estimate, gauge, judge, reckon, suppose, think **9.** acquire, clear, earn, gain, get, net, obtain, realize, secure, take in, win **10.** arrive at, arrive in time for, attain, catch, get to, meet, reach **11. make it** *informal* arrive (*informal*), be successful, come through, crack it (*informal*), cut it (*informal*), get on, get somewhere, prosper, pull through, succeed, survive ~*noun* **12.** brand, build, character, composition, constitution, construction, cut, designation, form, kind, make-up, mark, model, shape, sort, structure, style, type, variety **13.** cast of mind, character, disposition, frame of mind, humour, kidney, make-up, nature, stamp, temper, temperament

make as if *or* **though** act as if *or* though, affect, feign, feint, give the impression that, make a show of, pretend

make away 1. abscond, beat a hasty retreat, clear out (*informal*), cut and run (*informal*), decamp, depart, do a runner (*slang*), flee, fly, fly the coop (*U.S. & Canad. informal*), hook it (*slang*), make off, run away *or* off, run for it (*informal*), scoot, skedaddle (*informal*), slope off, take a powder (*U.S. & Canad. slang*), take it on the lam (*U.S. & Canad. slang*), take to one's heels **2.** (*with* **with**) abduct, cabbage (*Brit. slang*), carry off, cart off (*slang*), filch, kidnap, knock off (*slang*), make off with, nab (*informal*), nick (*slang, chiefly Brit.*), pilfer, pinch (*informal*), purloin, steal, swipe (*slang*) **3.** (*with* **with**) blow away (*slang, chiefly U.S.*), bump off (*slang*), destroy, dispose of, do away with, do in (*slang*), eliminate, get rid of, kill, murder, rub out (*U.S. slang*)

make-believe 1. *noun* charade, dream, fantasy, imagination, play-acting, pretence, unreality **2.** ~*adjective* dream, fantasized, fantasy, imaginary, imagined, made-up, mock, pretend, pretended, sham, unreal
▷ **Antonyms** ~*noun* actuality, fact, reality, truthfulness ~*adjective* authentic, genuine, real, unfeigned

make believe act as if *or* though, dream, enact, fantasize, imagine, play, play-act, pretend

make do cope, get along *or* by, improvise, manage, muddle through, scrape along *or* by

make for 1. aim for, be bound for, head for *or* towards, proceed towards, steer (a course) for **2.** assail, assault, attack, fall on, fly at, go for, have a go at (*informal*), lunge at, set upon **3.** be conducive to, conduce to, contribute to, facilitate, favour, promote

make off 1. abscond, beat a hasty retreat, bolt, clear out (*informal*), cut and run (*informal*), decamp, do a runner (*slang*), flee, fly, fly the coop (*U.S. & Canad. informal*), hook it (*slang*), make away, run away *or* off, run for it (*informal*), skedaddle (*informal*), slope off, take a powder (*U.S. & Canad. slang*), take it on the lam (*U.S. & Canad. slang*), take to one's heels **2.** (*with* **with**) abduct, cabbage (*Brit. slang*), carry off, cart off (*slang*), filch, kidnap, knock off (*slang*), make away with, nab (*informal*), nick (*slang, chiefly Brit.*), pilfer, pinch (*informal*), purloin, run away *or* off with, steal, swipe (*slang*)

make out 1. descry, detect, discern, discover, distinguish, espy, perceive, recognize, see **2.** comprehend, decipher, fathom, follow, grasp, perceive, realize, see, suss (out) (*slang*), understand, work out **3.** complete, draw up, fill in *or* out, inscribe, write (out) **4.** demonstrate, describe, prove, represent, show **5.** assert, claim, let on, make as if *or* though, pretend **6.** fare, get on, manage, prosper, succeed, thrive

maker author, builder, constructor, director, fabricator, framer, manufacturer, producer

Maker Creator, God

makeshift 1. *adjective* expedient, jury (*chiefly Nautical*), make-do, provisional, rough and ready, stopgap, substitute, temporary **2.** *~noun* expedient, shift, stopgap, substitute

make-up 1. cosmetics, face (*informal*), greasepaint (*Theatre*), *maquillage*, paint (*informal*), powder, war paint (*informal, humorous*) **2.** arrangement, assembly, composition, configuration, constitution, construction, form, format, formation, organization, structure **3.** build, cast of mind, character, constitution, disposition, figure, frame of mind, make, nature, stamp, temper, temperament

make up 1. compose, comprise, constitute, form **2.** coin, compose, concoct, construct, cook up (*informal*), create, devise, dream up, fabricate, formulate, frame, hatch, invent, manufacture, originate, trump up, write **3.** complete, fill, meet, supply **4.** (*with* **for**) atone, balance, compensate, make amends, offset, recompense, redeem, redress, requite **5.** bury the hatchet, call it quits, come to terms, compose, forgive and forget, make peace, mend, reconcile, settle, shake hands **6. make up one's mind** choose, come to a decision, decide, determine, make a decision, reach a decision, resolve, settle **7. make up to** *informal* chat up (*informal*), court, curry favour with, flirt with, make overtures to, woo

making 1. assembly, building, composition, construction, creation, fabrication, forging, manufacture, production **2. in the making** budding, coming, emergent, growing, nascent, potential

makings 1. beginnings, capability, capacity, ingredients, materials, potentiality, potential(s), qualities **2.** earnings, income, proceeds, profits, returns, revenue, takings

maladjusted alienated, disturbed, estranged, hung-up (*slang*), neurotic, unstable

maladministration blundering, bungling, corruption, dishonesty, incompetence, inefficiency, malfeasance (*Law*), malpractice, misgovernment, mismanagement, misrule

maladroit 1. awkward, bungling, cack-handed (*informal*), clumsy, hamfisted *or* -handed (*informal*), inept, inexpert, unhandy, unskilful **2.** gauche, inconsiderate, inelegant, insensitive, tactless, thoughtless, undiplomatic, untoward

malady affliction, ailment, complaint, disease, disorder, ill, illness, indisposition, infirmity, lurgi (*informal*), sickness

malaise angst, anxiety, depression, discomfort, disquiet, doldrums, enervation, illness, lassitude, melancholy, sickness, unease, weakness

malapropos 1. *adjective* ill-timed, impertinent, inapposite, inappropriate, inapt, inopportune, misapplied, out of place, unseemly, unsuitable **2.** *~adverb* impertinently, inappositely, inappropriately, inaptly, inopportunely, out of turn, unseasonably, unsuitably, untimely **3.** *~noun* blunder, faux pas, gaffe, malapropism, solecism

malcontent 1. *adjective* disaffected, discontented, disgruntled, disgusted, dissatisfied, dissentious, factious, ill-disposed, rebellious, resentful, restive, unhappy, unsatisfied **2.** *~noun* agitator, complainer, fault-finder, grouch (*informal*), grouser, grumbler, mischief-maker, rebel, stirrer (*informal*), troublemaker

male manful, manlike, manly, masculine, virile

▷ **Antonyms** camp (*informal*), effeminate, female, feminine, unmanly, wimpish *or* wimpy (*informal*), womanish, womanly

malediction anathema, curse, damnation, damning, denunciation, execration, imprecation, malison (*archaic*)

malefactor convict, criminal, crook (*informal*), culprit, delinquent, evildoer, felon, lawbreaker, miscreant, offender, outlaw, transgressor, villain, wrongdoer

maleficent baleful, deleterious, destructive, detrimental, evil, harmful, hurtful, injurious, malign, malignant, noxious, pernicious

malevolence hate, hatred, ill will, malice, maliciousness, malignity, rancour, spite, spitefulness, vengefulness, vindictiveness

malevolent baleful, evil-minded, hateful (*archaic*), hostile, ill-natured, maleficent, malicious, malign, malignant, pernicious, rancorous, spiteful, vengeful, vicious, vindictive
▷ **Antonyms** amiable, benevolent, benign, friendly, gracious, kind, warm-hearted

malformation crookedness, deformity, distortion, misshape, misshapenness

malformed abnormal, contorted, crooked, deformed, distorted, irregular, misshapen, twisted

malfunction 1. *verb* break down, develop a fault, fail, go wrong **2.** *~noun* breakdown, defect, failure, fault, flaw, glitch, impairment

malice animosity, animus, bad blood, bitterness, enmity, evil intent, hate, hatred, ill will, malevolence, maliciousness, malignity, rancour, spite, spitefulness, spleen, vengefulness, venom, vindictiveness

malicious baleful, bitchy (*informal*), bitter, catty (*informal*), evil-minded, hateful, ill-disposed, ill-natured, injurious, malevolent, malignant, mischievous, pernicious, rancorous, resentful, shrewish, spiteful, vengeful, vicious
▷ **Antonyms** amiable, big, benevolent, friendly, kind, warm-hearted

malign 1. *adjective* bad, baleful, baneful, deleterious, destructive, evil, harmful, hostile, hurtful, injurious, maleficent, malevolent, malignant, pernicious, vicious, wicked **2.** *~verb* abuse, asperse, bad-mouth (*slang, chiefly U.S. & Canad.*), blacken (someone's name), calumniate, defame, denigrate, derogate, disparage, do a hatchet job on (*informal*), harm, injure, knock (*informal*), libel, revile, rubbish (*informal*), run down, slag (off) (*slang*), slander, smear, speak ill of, traduce, vilify
▷ **Antonyms** *~adjective* agreeable, amiable, beneficial, benevolent, benign, friendly, good, harmless, honourable, innocuous, kind, moral, virtuous, warm-hearted, wholesome *~verb* commend, compliment, extol, praise

malignant 1. baleful, bitter, destructive, harmful, hostile, hurtful, inimical, injurious, maleficent, malevolent, malicious, malign, of evil intent, pernicious, spiteful, vicious **2.** *Medical* cancerous, dangerous, deadly, evil, fatal, irremediable, metastatic, uncontrollable, virulent
▷ **Antonyms** (*sense 1*) amicable, benign, friendly, kind, warm-hearted (*sense 2*) benign

malignity 1. animosity, animus, bad blood, bitterness, evil, hate, hatred, hostility, ill will, malevolence, malice, maliciousness, rancour, spite, vengefulness, venom, viciousness, vindictiveness, wickedness **2.** balefulness, deadliness, destructiveness, harmfulness, hurtfulness, perniciousness, virulence

malleable 1. ductile, plastic, soft, tensile, workable **2.** adaptable, biddable, compliant, governable, impressionable, like putty in one's hands, manageable, pliable, tractable

malodorous evil-smelling, fetid, foul-smelling, mephitic, nauseating, niffy (*Brit. slang*), noisome, offensive, olid, putrid, rank, reeking, smelly, stinking

malpractice 1. abuse, dereliction, misbehaviour, misconduct, mismanagement, negligence **2.** abuse, misdeed, offence, transgression

maltreat abuse, bully, damage, handle roughly, harm, hurt, ill-treat, injure, mistreat

maltreatment abuse, bullying, harm, ill-treatment, ill-usage, injury, mistreatment, rough handling

mammoth Brobdingnagian, colossal, elephantine, enormous, gargantuan, giant, gigantic, ginormous (*informal*), huge, humongous *or* humungous (*U.S. slang*), immense, jumbo (*informal*), massive, mega (*slang*), mighty, monumental, mountainous, prodigious, stellar (*informal*), stupendous, titanic, vast
▷ **Antonyms** diminutive, insignificant, little, miniature, minute, puny, small, tiny, trivial

man *noun* **1.** bloke (*Brit. informal*), chap (*informal*), gentleman, guy (*informal*), male **2.** adult, being, body, human, human being, individual, one, person, personage, somebody, soul **3.** Homo sapiens, humanity, humankind, human race, mankind, mortals, people **4.** attendant, employee, follower, hand, hireling, liegeman, manservant, retainer, servant, soldier, subject, subordinate, valet, vassal, worker, workman **5.** beau, boyfriend, husband, lover, partner, significant other (*U.S. informal*), spouse **6. to a man** bar none, every one, one and all, unanimously, without exception *~verb* **7.** crew, fill, furnish with men, garrison, occupy, people, staff

manacle 1. *noun* bond, chain, fetter, gyve (*archaic*), handcuff, iron, shackle, tie **2.** *~verb* bind, chain, check, clap *or* put in irons, confine, constrain, curb, fetter, hamper, handcuff, inhibit, put in chains, restrain, shackle, tie one's hands

manage 1. administer, be in charge (of), call the shots, call the tune, command, concert, conduct, direct, govern, handle, manipulate, oversee, preside over, rule, run, superintend, supervise **2.** accomplish, arrange, bring about *or* off, contrive, cope with, crack it (*informal*), cut it (*informal*), deal with, effect, engineer, succeed **3.** control, dominate, govern, guide, handle, influence, manipulate, operate, pilot, ply, steer, train, use, wield **4.** carry on, cope, fare, get along,

get by (*informal*), get on, make do, make out, muddle through, shift, survive
▷ **Antonyms** (*sense 2*) bodge (*informal*), botch, fail, follow, make a mess of, make a nonsense of, mismanage, muff, spoil, starve

manageable amenable, compliant, controllable, convenient, docile, easy, governable, handy, submissive, tamable, tractable, user-friendly, wieldy
▷ **Antonyms** demanding, difficult, disobedient, hard, headstrong, obstinate, refractory, stubborn, ungovernable, unruly, unyielding, wild

management **1.** administration, board, bosses (*informal*), directorate, directors, employers, executive(s) **2.** administration, care, charge, command, conduct, control, direction, governance, government, guidance, handling, manipulation, operation, rule, running, superintendence, supervision

manager administrator, boss (*informal*), comptroller, conductor, controller, director, executive, gaffer (*informal, chiefly Brit.*), governor, head, organizer, overseer, proprietor, superintendent, supervisor

mandate authority, authorization, bidding, canon, charge, command, commission, decree, directive, edict, fiat, injunction, instruction, order, precept, sanction, warrant

mandatory binding, compulsory, obligatory, required, requisite
▷ **Antonyms** discretionary, nonbinding, noncompulsory, nonobligatory, optional, unnecessary, voluntary

manful bold, brave, courageous, daring, determined, gallant, hardy, heroic, indomitable, intrepid, manly, noble, powerful, resolute, stalwart, stout, stout-hearted, strong, valiant, vigorous

manfully boldly, bravely, courageously, desperately, determinedly, gallantly, hard, heroically, intrepidly, like a Trojan, like one possessed, like the devil, nobly, powerfully, resolutely, stalwartly, stoutly, strongly, to the best of one's ability, valiantly, vigorously, with might and main

mangle butcher, cripple, crush, cut, deform, destroy, disfigure, distort, hack, lacerate, maim, mar, maul, mutilate, rend, ruin, spoil, tear, total (*slang*), trash (*slang*), wreck

mangy dirty, grungy (*slang, chiefly U.S.*), mean, moth-eaten, scabby (*informal*), scruffy, scuzzy (*slang, chiefly U.S.*), seedy, shabby, shoddy, squalid
▷ **Antonyms** attractive, choice, clean, de luxe, fine, splendid, spotless, superb, tidy, well-dressed, well-kempt, well-kept

manhandle **1.** handle roughly, knock about *or* around, maul, paw (*informal*), pull, push, rough up **2.** carry, haul, heave, hump (*Brit. slang*), lift, manoeuvre, pull, push, shove, tug

manhood bravery, courage, determination, firmness, fortitude, hardihood, manfulness, manliness, masculinity, maturity, mettle, resolution, spirit, strength, valour, virility

mania **1.** aberration, craziness, delirium, dementia, derangement, disorder, frenzy, insanity, lunacy, madness **2.** cacoethes, craving, craze, desire, enthusiasm, fad (*informal*), fetish, fixation, obsession, partiality, passion, preoccupation, rage, thing (*informal*)

maniac **1.** headbanger (*informal*), headcase (*informal*), loony (*slang*), lunatic, madman, madwoman, nutcase (*slang*), nutter (*Brit. slang*), psycho (*slang*), psychopath **2.** energumen, enthusiast, fan, fanatic, fiend (*informal*), freak (*informal*)

maniacal *or* **manic** berserk, crazed, crazy, demented, deranged, frenzied, gonzo (*slang*), insane, lunatic, mad, neurotic, nutty (*slang*), psychotic, raving, unbalanced, wild

manifest **1.** *adjective* apparent, blatant, bold, clear, conspicuous, distinct, evident, glaring, noticeable, obvious, open, palpable, patent, plain, salient, unmistakable, visible **2.** *~verb* declare, demonstrate, display, establish, evince, exhibit, expose, express, make plain, prove, reveal, set forth, show
▷ **Antonyms** *~adjective* concealed, disguised, hidden, inconspicuous, indistinct, masked, suppressed, unapparent, vague, veiled *~verb* conceal, cover, cover up, deny, hide, mask, obscure, refute

manifestation appearance, demonstration, disclosure, display, exhibition, exposure, expression, indication, instance, mark, materialization, revelation, show, sign, symptom, token

manifold abundant, assorted, copious, diverse, diversified, many, multifarious, multifold, multiple, multiplied, multitudinous, numerous, varied, various

manipulate **1.** employ, handle, operate, ply, use, wield, work **2.** conduct, control, direct, do a number on (*chiefly U.S.*), engineer, guide, influence, manoeuvre, negotiate, steer, twist around one's little finger

mankind Homo sapiens, humanity, humankind, human race, man, people

manliness boldness, bravery, courage, fearlessness, firmness, hardihood, heroism, independence, intrepidity, machismo, manfulness, manhood, masculinity, mettle, resolution, stoutheartedness, valour, vigour, virility

manly bold, brave, butch (*slang*), courageous, daring, dauntless, fearless, gallant, hardy, heroic, macho, male, manful, masculine, muscular, noble, power~

ful, red-blooded (*informal*), resolute, robust, stout-hearted, strapping, strong, valiant, valorous, vigorous, virile, well-built
▷ **Antonyms** camp (*informal*), cowardly, craven, delicate, effeminate, faint-hearted, feeble, feminine, frail, ignoble, irresolute, sickly, soft, timid, unmanly, weak, wimpish *or* wimpy (*informal*), womanish

man-made artificial, ersatz, manufactured, mock, plastic (*slang*), synthetic

manner 1. air, appearance, aspect, bearing, behaviour, comportment, conduct, demeanour, deportment, look, mien (*literary*), presence, tone **2.** approach, custom, fashion, form, genre, habit, line, means, method, mode, practice, procedure, process, routine, style, tack, tenor, usage, way, wont **3.** brand, breed, category, form, kind, nature, sort, type, variety

mannered affected, artificial, posed, pretentious, pseudo (*informal*), put-on, stilted
▷ **Antonyms** genuine, honest, natural, real, sincere, unaffected, unpretentious

mannerism characteristic, foible, habit, idiosyncrasy, peculiarity, quirk, trait, trick

mannerly civil, civilized, courteous, decorous, genteel, gentlemanly, gracious, ladylike, polished, polite, refined, respectful, well-behaved, well-bred, well-mannered
▷ **Antonyms** boorish, discourteous, disrespectful, ill-mannered, impertinent, impolite, impudent, insolent, rude, unmannerly

manners 1. bearing, behaviour, breeding, carriage, comportment, conduct, demeanour, deportment **2.** ceremony, courtesy, decorum, etiquette, formalities, good form, polish, politeness, politesse, proprieties, protocol, p's and q's, refinement, social graces, the done thing

manoeuvrable fast-moving, handleable, manipulatable, mobile, responsive, versatile

manoeuvre *noun* **1.** action, artifice, dodge, intrigue, machination, move, movement, plan, plot, ploy, ruse, scheme, stratagem, subterfuge, tactic, trick **2.** deployment, evolution, exercise, movement, operation *~verb* **3.** contrive, devise, engineer, intrigue, machinate, manage, manipulate, plan, plot, pull strings, scheme, wangle (*informal*) **4.** deploy, exercise, move **5.** direct, drive, guide, handle, navigate, negotiate, pilot, steer

mansion abode, dwelling, habitation, hall, manor, residence, seat, villa

mantle *noun* **1.** *archaic* cape, cloak, hood, shawl, wrap **2.** blanket, canopy, cloud, cover, covering, curtain, envelope, pall, screen, shroud, veil *~verb* **3.** blanket, cloak, cloud, cover, disguise, envelop, hide, mask, overspread, screen, shroud, veil, wrap

manual 1. *adjective* done by hand, hand-operated, human, physical **2.** *~noun* bible, enchiridion (*rare*), guide, guidebook, handbook, instructions, workbook

manufacture *verb* **1.** assemble, build, compose, construct, create, fabricate, forge, form, make, mass-produce, mould, process, produce, put together, shape, turn out **2.** concoct, cook up (*informal*), devise, fabricate, hatch, invent, make up, think up, trump up *~noun* **3.** assembly, construction, creation, fabrication, making, mass-production, produce, production

manufacturer builder, constructor, creator, fabricator, factory-owner, industrialist, maker, producer

manumission deliverance, emancipation, enfranchisement, freeing, liberation, release, unchaining

manumit deliver, emancipate, enfranchise, free, liberate, release, set free, unchain

manure compost, droppings, dung, excrement, fertilizer, muck, ordure

many *adjective* **1.** abundant, copious, countless, divers (*archaic*), frequent, innumerable, manifold, multifarious, multifold, multitudinous, myriad, numerous, profuse, sundry, umpteen (*informal*), varied, various *~noun* **2.** a horde, a lot, a mass, a multitude, a thousand and one, heaps (*informal*), large numbers, lots (*informal*), piles (*informal*), plenty, scores, tons (*informal*), umpteen (*informal*) **3. the many** crowd, hoi polloi, majority, masses, multitude, people, rank and file

mar blemish, blight, blot, damage, deface, detract from, disfigure, harm, hurt, impair, injure, maim, mangle, mutilate, put a damper on, ruin, scar, spoil, stain, sully, taint, tarnish, vitiate
▷ **Antonyms** adorn, ameliorate, better, embellish, improve, ornament

maraud despoil, forage, foray, harry, loot, pillage, plunder, raid, ransack, ravage, reive (*dialect*), sack

marauder bandit, brigand, buccaneer, cateran (*Scot.*), corsair, freebooter, mosstrooper, outlaw, pillager, pirate, plunderer, raider, ravager, reiver (*dialect*), robber

march *verb* **1.** file, footslog, pace, parade, stalk, stride, strut, tramp, tread, walk *~noun* **2.** hike, routemarch, tramp, trek, walk **3.** demo (*informal*), demonstration, parade, procession **4.** gait, pace, step, stride **5.** advance, development, evolution, progress, progression **6. on the march** advancing, afoot, astir, en route, marching, on one's way, on the way, proceeding, progressing, under way

marches borderland, borders, boundaries, confines, frontiers, limits, marchlands

margin 1. border, bound, boundary, brim, brink, confine, edge, limit, perimeter, periphery, rim, side, verge **2.** allowance, compass, elbowroom, extra, latitude, leeway, play, room, scope, space, surplus

marginal 1. bordering, borderline, on the edge, peripheral **2.** insignificant, low, minimal, minor, negligible, slight, small

marijuana bhang, blow (*slang*), cannabis, charas, chronic (*U.S. slang*), dope (*slang*), gage (*U.S. old-fashioned slang*), ganja, grass (*slang*), hash (*slang*), hashish, hemp, kif, leaf (*slang*), mary jane (*U.S. slang*), pot (*slang*), sinsemilla, smoke (*informal*), stuff (*slang*), tea (*U.S. slang*), wacky baccy (*slang*), weed (*slang*)

marine maritime, nautical, naval, ocean-going, oceanic, pelagic, saltwater, sea, seafaring, seagoing, thalassic

mariner bluejacket, gob (*U.S. slang*), hand, Jack Tar, matelot (*slang, chiefly Brit.*), navigator, sailor, salt, sea dog, seafarer, seafaring man, seaman, tar

marital conjugal, connubial, married, matrimonial, nuptial, spousal, wedded

maritime 1. marine, nautical, naval, oceanic, sea, seafaring **2.** coastal, littoral, seaside

mark *noun* **1.** blemish, blot, blotch, bruise, dent, impression, line, nick, pock, scar, scratch, smirch, smudge, splotch, spot, stain, streak **2.** badge, blaze, brand, characteristic, device, earmark, emblem, evidence, feature, flag, hallmark, impression, incision, index, indication, label, note, print, proof, seal, sign, signet, stamp, symbol, symptom, token **3.** criterion, level, measure, norm, par, standard, yardstick **4.** aim, end, goal, object, objective, purpose, target **5.** consequence, dignity, distinction, eminence, fame, importance, influence, notability, note, notice, prestige, quality, regard, standing **6.** footmark, footprint, sign, trace, track, trail, vestige **7. make one's mark** achieve recognition, be a success, find a place in the sun, get on in the world, make a success of oneself, make good, make it (*informal*), make something of oneself, prosper, succeed ~*verb* **8.** blemish, blot, blotch, brand, bruise, dent, impress, imprint, nick, scar, scratch, smirch, smudge, splotch, stain, streak **9.** brand, characterize, flag, identify, label, stamp **10.** betoken, denote, distinguish, evince, exemplify, illustrate, show **11.** attend, hearken (*archaic*), mind, note, notice, observe, pay attention, pay heed, regard, remark, watch **12.** appraise, assess, correct, evaluate, grade

marked apparent, blatant, clear, considerable, conspicuous, decided, distinct, dramatic, evident, manifest, notable, noted, noticeable, obvious, outstanding, patent, prominent, pronounced, remarkable, salient, signal, striking
▷ **Antonyms** concealed, doubtful, dubious, hidden, imperceptible, inconspicuous, indistinct, insignificant, obscure, unclear, unnoticeable, vague

markedly clearly, considerably, conspicuously, decidedly, distinctly, evidently, greatly, manifestly, notably, noticeably, obviously, outstandingly, patently, remarkably, seriously (*informal*), signally, strikingly, to a great extent

market 1. *noun* bazaar, fair, mart **2.** ~*verb* offer for sale, retail, sell, vend

marketable in demand, merchantable, saleable, sought after, vendible, wanted

marksman, -woman crack shot (*informal*), deadeye (*informal, chiefly U.S.*), dead shot (*informal*), good shot, sharpshooter

maroon abandon, cast ashore, cast away, desert, leave, leave high and dry (*informal*), strand

marriage 1. espousal, match, matrimony, nuptial rites, nuptials, wedding, wedding ceremony, wedlock **2.** alliance, amalgamation, association, confederation, coupling, link, merger, union

married 1. hitched (*slang*), joined, one, spliced (*informal*), united, wed, wedded **2.** conjugal, connubial, husbandly, marital, matrimonial, nuptial, spousal, wifely

marrow core, cream, essence, gist, heart, kernel, pith, quick, quintessence, soul, spirit, substance

marry 1. become man and wife, espouse, get hitched (*slang*), get spliced (*informal*), plight one's troth (*old-fashioned*), take the plunge (*informal*), take to wife, tie the knot (*informal*), walk down the aisle (*informal*), wed, wive (*archaic*) **2.** ally, bond, join, knit, link, match, merge, splice, tie, unify, unite, yoke

marsh bog, fen, morass, moss (*Scot. & northern English dialect*), quagmire, slough, swamp

marshal 1. align, arrange, array, assemble, collect, deploy, dispose, draw up, gather, group, line up, muster, order, organize, rank, sequence **2.** conduct, escort, guide, lead, shepherd, usher

marshy boggy, fenny, miry, quaggy, spongy, swampy, waterlogged, wet

martial bellicose, belligerent, brave, heroic, military, soldierly, warlike

martinet disciplinarian, drillmaster, stickler

martyrdom agony, anguish, ordeal, persecution, suffering, torment, torture
▷ **Antonyms** bliss, ecstasy, happiness, joy

marvel 1. *verb* be amazed, be awed, be filled with surprise, gape, gaze, goggle, wonder **2.** *~noun* genius, miracle, phenomenon, portent, prodigy, whizz (*informal*), wonder

marvellous **1.** amazing, astonishing, astounding, breathtaking, brilliant, extraordinary, miraculous, phenomenal, prodigious, remarkable, sensational (*informal*), singular, spectacular, stupendous, wondrous (*archaic or literary*) **2.** difficult *or* hard to believe, fabulous, fantastic, implausible, improbable, incredible, surprising, unbelievable, unlikely **3.** *informal* awesome (*slang*), bad (*slang*), bodacious (*slang, chiefly U.S.*), boffo (*slang*), brill (*informal*), chillin' (*U.S. slang*), colossal, cracking (*Brit. informal*), crucial (*slang*), def (*slang*), divine (*informal*), excellent, fabulous (*informal*), fantastic (*informal*), glorious, great (*informal*), jim-dandy (*slang*), magnificent, mean (*slang*), mega (*slang*), sensational (*informal*), smashing (*informal*), sovereign, splendid, stupendous, super (*informal*), superb, terrific (*informal*), topping (*Brit. slang*), wicked (*informal*), wonderful

▷ **Antonyms** awful, bad, believable, commonplace, credible, everyday, ordinary, terrible

masculine **1.** male, manful, manlike, manly, mannish, virile **2.** bold, brave, butch (*slang*), gallant, hardy, macho, muscular, powerful, red-blooded (*informal*), resolute, robust, stout-hearted, strapping, strong, vigorous, well-built

mask *noun* **1.** domino, false face, visor, vizard (*archaic*) **2.** blind, camouflage, cloak, concealment, cover, cover-up, disguise, façade, front, guise, screen, semblance, show, veil, veneer *~verb* **3.** camouflage, cloak, conceal, cover, disguise, hide, obscure, screen, veil

masquerade *noun* **1.** costume ball, fancy dress party, mask, masked ball, masked party, mummery, revel **2.** costume, disguise, domino **3.** cloak, cover, cover-up, deception, disguise, dissimulation, front (*informal*), guise, imposture, mask, pose, pretence, put-on (*slang*), screen, subterfuge *~verb* **4.** disguise, dissemble, dissimulate, impersonate, mask, pass oneself off, pose, pretend (to be)

mass *noun* **1.** block, chunk, concretion, hunk, lump, piece **2.** aggregate, body, collection, entirety, sum, sum total, totality, whole **3.** accumulation, aggregation, assemblage, batch, bunch, collection, combination, conglomeration, heap, load, lot, pile, quantity, rick, stack **4.** assemblage, band, body, bunch (*informal*), crowd, group, horde, host, lot, mob, number, throng, troop **5.** body, bulk, greater part, lion's share, majority, preponderance **6.** bulk, dimension, greatness, magnitude, size **7. the masses** commonalty, common people, crowd, hoi polloi, multitude *~adjective* **8.** extensive, general, indiscriminate, large-scale, pandemic, popular, wholesale, widespread *~verb* **9.** accumulate, amass, assemble, collect, congregate, foregather, gather, mob, muster, rally, swarm, throng

massacre **1.** *noun* annihilation, blood bath, butchery, carnage, extermination, holocaust, killing, mass slaughter, murder, slaughter **2.** *~verb* annihilate, blow away (*slang, chiefly U.S.*), butcher, cut to pieces, exterminate, kill, mow down, murder, slaughter, slay, take out (*slang*), wipe out

massage **1.** *noun* acupressure, kneading, manipulation, reflexology, rubbing, rubdown, shiatsu **2.** *~verb* knead, manipulate, rub, rub down

massive big, bulky, colossal, elephantine, enormous, extensive, gargantuan, gigantic, ginormous (*informal*), great, heavy, hefty, huge, hulking, humongous *or* humungous (*U.S. slang*), immense, imposing, impressive, mammoth, mega (*slang*), monster, monumental, ponderous, solid, stellar (*informal*), substantial, titanic, vast, weighty, whacking (*informal*), whopping (*informal*)

▷ **Antonyms** frail, light, little, minute, petty, slight, small, thin, tiny, trivial

master *noun* **1.** boss (*informal*), captain, chief, commander, controller, director, employer, governor, head, lord, manager, overlord, overseer, owner, principal, ruler, skipper (*informal*), superintendent **2.** ace (*informal*), adept, dab hand (*Brit. informal*), doyen, expert, genius, grandmaster, maestro, maven (*U.S.*), past master, pro (*informal*), virtuoso, wizard **3.** guide, guru, instructor, pedagogue, preceptor, schoolmaster, spiritual leader, swami, teacher, torchbearer, tutor *~adjective* **4.** adept, crack (*informal*), expert, masterly, proficient, skilful, skilled **5.** chief, controlling, foremost, grand, great, leading, main, predominant, prime, principal *~verb* **6.** acquire, become proficient in, get the hang of (*informal*), grasp, learn **7.** bridle, check, conquer, curb, defeat, lick (*informal*), overcome, overpower, quash, quell, subdue, subjugate, suppress, tame, triumph over, vanquish **8.** command, control, direct, dominate, govern, manage, regulate, rule

▷ **Antonyms** *~noun* (*sense 1*) crew, servant, slave, subject (*sense 2*) amateur, novice (*sense 3*) student *~adjective* (*sense 4*) amateurish, clumsy, incompetent, inept, novice, unaccomplished, unskilled, untalented (*sense 5*) lesser, minor *~verb* (*sense 7*) give in, surrender, yield

masterful **1.** adept, adroit, clever, consummate, crack (*informal*), deft, dexterous, excellent, expert, exquisite, fine, finished, first-rate, masterly, skilful, skilled, superior, superlative, supreme,

world-class **2.** arrogant, authoritative, bossy (*informal*), despotic, dictatorial, domineering, high-handed, imperious, magisterial, overbearing, overweening, peremptory, self-willed, tyrannical
▷ **Antonyms** (*sense 1*) amateurish, clumsy, incompetent, inept, unaccomplished, unskilled, untalented (*sense 2*) irresolute, meek, spineless, weak, wimpish *or* wimpy (*informal*)

masterly adept, adroit, clever, consummate, crack (*informal*), dexterous, excellent, expert, exquisite, fine, finished, first-rate, masterful, skilful, skilled, superior, superlative, supreme, world-class

mastermind 1. *verb* be the brains behind (*informal*), conceive, devise, direct, manage, organize, plan **2.** *~noun* architect, authority, brain(s) (*informal*), brainbox, director, engineer, genius, intellect, manager, organizer, planner, virtuoso

masterpiece *chef d'oeuvre,* classic, jewel, magnum opus, master work, *pièce de résistance, tour de force*

mastery 1. command, comprehension, familiarity, grasp, grip, knowledge, understanding **2.** ability, acquirement, attainment, cleverness, deftness, dexterity, expertise, finesse, know-how (*informal*), proficiency, prowess, skill, virtuosity **3.** ascendancy, authority, command, conquest, control, domination, dominion, pre-eminence, rule, superiority, supremacy, sway, triumph, upper hand, victory, whip hand

masticate champ, chew, crunch, eat, munch

masturbation autoeroticism, onanism, playing with oneself (*slang*), self-abuse

match *noun* **1.** bout, competition, contest, game, head-to-head, test, trial **2.** competitor, counterpart, equal, equivalent, peer, rival **3.** companion, complement, counterpart, equal, equivalent, fellow, mate, tally **4.** copy, dead ringer (*slang*), double, duplicate, equal, lookalike, replica, ringer (*slang*), spit (*informal, chiefly Brit.*), spit and image (*informal*), spitting image (*informal*), twin **5.** affiliation, alliance, combination, couple, duet, item (*informal*), marriage, pair, pairing, partnership, union *~verb* **6.** ally, combine, couple, join, link, marry, mate, pair, unite, yoke **7.** accompany, accord, adapt, agree, blend, coordinate, correspond, fit, go with, harmonize, suit, tally, tone with **8.** compare, compete, contend, emulate, equal, measure up to, oppose, pit against, rival, vie

matching analogous, comparable, coordinating, corresponding, double, duplicate, equal, equivalent, identical, like, paired, parallel, same, toning, twin
▷ **Antonyms** different, disparate, dissimilar, distinct, divergent, diverse, nonparallel, other, unequal, unlike

matchless consummate, exquisite, incomparable, inimitable, peerless, perfect, superlative, supreme, unequalled, unique, unmatched, unparalleled, unrivalled, unsurpassed
▷ **Antonyms** average, cheaper, common, commonplace, comparable, equalled, everyday, excelled, inferior, lesser, mediocre, no great shakes (*informal*), ordinary, second-class, surpassed

mate *noun* **1.** better half (*humorous*), husband, partner, significant other (*U.S. informal*), spouse, wife **2.** *informal* buddy (*informal*), china (*Brit. slang*), chum (*informal*), cock (*Brit. informal*), comrade, crony, friend, homeboy (*slang, chiefly U.S.*), pal (*informal*) **3.** associate, colleague, companion, compeer, co-worker, fellow-worker **4.** assistant, helper, subordinate **5.** companion, double, fellow, match, twin *~verb* **6.** breed, copulate, couple, pair **7.** marry, match, wed **8.** couple, join, match, pair, yoke

material *noun* **1.** body, constituents, element, matter, stuff, substance **2.** data, evidence, facts, information, notes, work **3.** cloth, fabric, stuff *~adjective* **4.** bodily, concrete, corporeal, fleshly, nonspiritual, palpable, physical, substantial, tangible, worldly **5.** consequential, essential, grave, important, indispensable, key, meaningful, momentous, serious, significant, vital, weighty **6.** applicable, apposite, apropos, germane, pertinent, relevant

materialize appear, come about, come into being, come to pass, happen, occur, take place, take shape, turn up

materially considerably, essentially, gravely, greatly, much, seriously, significantly, substantially
▷ **Antonyms** barely, hardly, insignificantly, little, scarcely, superficially, unsubstantially

materiel accoutrements, apparatus, equipment, gear, hardware, machinery, materials, stores, supplies, tackle, tools

maternal motherly

maternity motherhood, motherliness

matrimonial conjugal, connubial, hymeneal, marital, married, nuptial, spousal, wedded, wedding

matrimony marital rites, marriage, nuptials, wedding ceremony, wedlock

matrix forge, mould, origin, source, womb

matted knotted, tangled, tousled, uncombed

matter *noun* **1.** body, material, stuff, substance **2.** affair, business, concern, episode, event, incident, issue, occurrence, proceeding, question, situation, subject, thing, topic, transaction **3.** amount, quantity, sum **4.** argument, context, purport, sense, subject, substance, text, thesis **5**. consequence, import, importance, moment, note, significance, weight **6**. complication, difficulty, distress, problem, trouble, upset, worry **7**. *Medical* discharge, purulence, pus, secretion *~verb* **8**. be important, be of consequence, carry weight, count, have influence, make a difference, mean something, signify

matter-of-fact deadpan, down-to-earth, dry, dull, emotionless, flat, lifeless, mundane, plain, prosaic, sober, unembellished, unimaginative, unsentimental, unvarnished

mature 1. *adjective* adult, complete, fit, full-blown, full-grown, fully fledged, grown, grown-up, matured, mellow, of age, perfect, prepared, ready, ripe, ripened, seasoned **2**. *~verb* age, become adult, bloom, blossom, come of age, develop, grow up, maturate, mellow, perfect, reach adulthood, ripen, season

▷ **Antonyms** *~adjective* adolescent, childish, green, immature, incomplete, juvenile, puerile, undeveloped, unfinished, unperfected, unripe, young, youthful

maturity adulthood, completion, experience, full bloom, full growth, fullness, majority, manhood, maturation, matureness, perfection, ripeness, wisdom, womanhood

▷ **Antonyms** childishness, excitability, immaturity, imperfection, incompletion, irresponsibility, juvenility, puerility, youthfulness

maudlin lachrymose, mawkish, mushy (*informal*), overemotional, sentimental, slushy (*informal*), soppy (*Brit. informal*), tearful, weepy (*informal*)

maul 1. abuse, handle roughly, ill-treat, manhandle, molest, paw **2**. batter, beat, beat up (*informal*), claw, knock about *or* around, lacerate, lambast(e), mangle, pummel, rough up, thrash, work over (*slang*)

maunder 1. dawdle, dilly-dally (*informal*), drift, idle, loaf, meander, mooch (*slang*), potter, ramble, straggle, stray, traipse (*informal*) **2**. babble, blather, blether, chatter, gabble, prattle, rabbit (on) (*Brit. informal*), ramble, rattle on, waffle (*informal, chiefly Brit.*), witter (*informal*)

maverick 1. *noun* dissenter, dissentient, eccentric, heretic, iconoclast, individualist, nonconformist, protester, radical, rebel **2**. *~adj* dissenting, eccentric, heretical, iconoclastic, individualistic, nonconformist, radical, rebel

▷ **Antonyms** Babbitt (*U.S.*), conventionalist, stick-in-the-mud (*informal*), traditionalist, yes man

maw craw, crop, gullet, jaws, mouth, stomach, throat

mawkish 1. emotional, feeble, gushy (*informal*), maudlin, mushy (*informal*), schmaltzy (*slang*), sentimental, slushy (*informal*), soppy (*Brit. informal*) **2**. disgusting, flat, foul, insipid, jejune, loathsome, nauseous, offensive, stale, vapid

maxim adage, aphorism, apophthegm, axiom, byword, dictum, gnome, motto, proverb, rule, saw, saying

maximum 1. *noun* apogee, ceiling, crest, extremity, height, most, peak, pinnacle, summit, top, upper limit, utmost, uttermost, zenith **2**. *~adjective* greatest, highest, maximal, most, paramount, supreme, topmost, utmost

▷ **Antonyms** (*sense 1*) bottom, minimum (*sense 2*) least, lowest, minimal

maybe it could be, mayhap (*archaic*), peradventure (*archaic*), perchance (*archaic*), perhaps, possibly

mayhem chaos, commotion, confusion, destruction, disorder, fracas, havoc, trouble, violence

maze 1. convolutions, intricacy, labyrinth, meander **2**. *figurative* bewilderment, confusion, imbroglio, mesh, perplexity, puzzle, snarl, tangle, uncertainty, web

mazy baffling, bewildering, confused, confusing, intricate, labyrinthine, perplexing, puzzling, serpentine, twisting, twisting and turning, winding

meadow field, grassland, lea (*poetic*), ley, pasture

meagre 1. deficient, exiguous, inadequate, insubstantial, little, measly, paltry, pathetic, poor, puny, scant, scanty, scrimpy, short, skimpy, slender, slight, small, spare, sparse **2**. bony, emaciated, gaunt, hungry, lank, lean, scraggy, scrawny, skinny, starved, thin, underfed **3**. barren, infertile, poor, unfruitful, unproductive, weak

mealy-mouthed afraid, doubtful, equivocal, euphemistic, hesitant, indirect, mincing, overdelicate, prim, reticent

mean[1] *verb* **1**. betoken, connote, convey, denote, drive at, express, hint at, imply, indicate, purport, represent, say, signify, spell, stand for, suggest, symbolize **2**. aim, aspire, contemplate, design, desire, have in mind, intend, plan, propose, purpose, set out, want, wish **3**. design, destine, fate, fit, make, match, predestine, preordain, suit **4**. bring about, cause, engender, entail, give rise to, involve, lead to, necessitate, produce, result in **5**. adumbrate, augur, betoken, foreshadow, foretell, herald, portend, presage, promise

mean[2] *adjective* **1**. beggarly, close (*informal*), mercenary, mingy (*Brit. informal*), miserly, near (*informal*), niggardly, parsimonious, penny-pinching, penurious, selfish, skimpy, snoep (*S. African informal*), stingy, tight, tight-arsed (*taboo slang*), tight as a duck's arse (*taboo slang*), tight-assed (*U.S. taboo slang*),

tight-fisted, ungenerous **2.** bad-tempered, cantankerous, churlish, disagreeable, hostile, ill-tempered, malicious, nasty, rude, sour, unfriendly, unpleasant **3.** abject, base, callous, contemptible, degenerate, degraded, despicable, disgraceful, dishonourable, hard-hearted, ignoble, low-minded, narrow-minded, petty, scurvy, shabby, shameful, sordid, vile, wretched **4.** beggarly, contemptible, down-at-heel, grungy (*slang, chiefly U.S.*), insignificant, low-rent (*informal, chiefly U.S.*), miserable, paltry, poor, run-down, scruffy, scuzzy (*slang, chiefly U.S.*), seedy, shabby, sordid, squalid, tawdry, wretched **5.** base, baseborn (*archaic*), common, humble, ignoble, inferior, low, lowborn, lowly, menial, modest, obscure, ordinary, plebeian, proletarian, servile, undistinguished, vulgar
▷ **Antonyms** (*sense 1*) altruistic, big, bountiful, generous, munificent, prodigal, unselfish (*sense 2*) agreeable (*sense 3*) compassionate, gentle, good, honourable, humane, kind, liberal, praiseworthy, sympathetic, warm-hearted (*sense 4*) attractive, choice, de luxe, excellent, first-rate, pleasing, superb, superior (*sense 5*) consequential, high, important, noble, princely, significant

mean[3] **1.** *noun* average, balance, compromise, happy medium, median, middle, middle course *or* way, mid-point, norm **2.** *~adjective* average, intermediate, medial, median, medium, middle, middling, normal, standard

meander **1.** *verb* ramble, snake, stravaig (*Scot. & northern English dialect*), stray, stroll, turn, wander, wind, zigzag **2.** *~noun* bend, coil, curve, loop, turn, twist, zigzag

meandering anfractuous, circuitous, convoluted, indirect, roundabout, serpentine, snaking, tortuous, wandering, winding
▷ **Antonyms** direct, straight, straightforward, undeviating

meaning *noun* **1.** connotation, denotation, drift, explanation, gist, implication, import, interpretation, message, purport, sense, significance, signification, substance, upshot, value **2.** aim, design, end, goal, idea, intention, object, plan, point, purpose, trend **3.** effect, efficacy, force, point, thrust, use, usefulness, validity, value, worth *~adjective* **4.** eloquent, expressive, meaningful, pointed, pregnant, speaking, suggestive

meaningful **1.** important, material, purposeful, relevant, serious, significant, useful, valid, worthwhile **2.** eloquent, expressive, meaning, pointed, pregnant, speaking, suggestive
▷ **Antonyms** inconsequential, insignificant, meaningless, senseless, superficial, trivial, unimportant, useless, worthless

meaningless aimless, empty, futile, hollow, inane, inconsequential, insignificant, insubstantial, nonsensical, nugatory, pointless, purposeless, senseless, trifling, trivial, useless, vain, valueless, wanky (*taboo slang*), worthless
▷ **Antonyms** clear, coherent, comprehensible, consequential, decipherable, deep, evident, important, intelligible, legible, meaningful, obvious, purposeful, sensible, significant, understandable, useful, valuable, worthwhile

meanness **1.** minginess (*Brit. informal*), miserliness, niggardliness, parsimony, penuriousness, selfishness, stinginess, tight-fistedness **2.** bad temper, cantankerousness, churlishness, disagreeableness, hostility, ill temper, malice, maliciousness, nastiness, rudeness, sourness, unfriendliness, unpleasantness **3.** abjectness, baseness, degeneracy, degradation, despicableness, disgracefulness, dishonourableness, ignobility, low-mindedness, narrow-mindedness, pettiness, scurviness, shabbiness, shamefulness, sordidness, vileness, wretchedness **4.** beggarliness, contemptibleness, insignificance, paltriness, pettiness, poorness, scruffiness, seediness, shabbiness, sordidness, squalor, tawdriness, wretchedness **5.** baseness, humbleness, lowliness, obscurity, servility

means **1.** agency, avenue, channel, course, expedient, instrument, measure, medium, method, mode, process, way **2.** affluence, capital, estate, fortune, funds, income, money, property, resources, riches, substance, wealth, wherewithal **3.** **by all means** absolutely, certainly, definitely, doubtlessly, of course, positively, surely **4.** **by means of** by dint of, by way of, through, using, utilizing, via, with the aid of **5.** **by no means** absolutely not, definitely not, in no way, not at all, not in the least, not in the slightest, not the least bit, no way, on no account

meantime, meanwhile at the same time, concurrently, for now, for the duration, for the moment, for then, in the interim, in the interval, in the intervening time, in the meantime, in the meanwhile, simultaneously

measly beggarly, contemptible, meagre, mean, mingy (*Brit. informal*), miserable, miserly, niggardly, paltry, pathetic, petty, pitiful, poor, puny, scanty, skimpy, snoep (*S. African informal*), stingy, ungenerous

measurable assessable, computable, determinable, gaugeable, material, mensurable, perceptible, quantifiable, quantitative, significant

measure *noun* **1.** allotment, allowance, amount, amplitude, capacity, degree, extent, magnitude, portion, proportion, quantity, quota, range, ration, reach, scope, share, size **2.** gauge, metre, rule, scale, yardstick **3.** method, standard, system **4.** criterion, example, model, norm, par, standard, test, touchstone, yardstick **5.** bounds, control, limit, limi~tation, moderation, restraint **6.** act, ac~tion, course, deed, expedient, manoeu~vre, means, procedure, proceeding, step **7.** act, bill, enactment, law, resolution, statute **8.** beat, cadence, foot, metre, rhythm, verse **9. for good measure** as a bonus, besides, in addition, into the bargain, to boot *~verb* **10.** appraise, as~sess, calculate, calibrate, compute, de~termine, estimate, evaluate, gauge, judge, mark out, quantify, rate, size, sound, survey, value, weigh **11.** adapt, adjust, calculate, choose, fit, judge, tai~lor

measured 1. exact, gauged, modulated, precise, predetermined, quantified, regulated, standard, verified **2.** digni~fied, even, leisurely, regular, sedate, slow, solemn, stately, steady, unhurried **3.** calculated, considered, deliberate, grave, planned, premeditated, reasoned, sober, studied, well-thought-out

measureless beyond measure, boundless, endless, immeasurable, immense, incal~culable, inestimable, infinite, limitless, unbounded, vast

measurement 1. appraisal, assessment, calculation, calibration, computation, estimation, evaluation, judgment, men~suration, metage, survey, valuation **2.** amount, amplitude, area, capacity, depth, dimension, extent, height, length, magnitude, size, volume, weight, width

measure off circumscribe, delimit, de~marcate, determine, fix, lay down, limit, mark out, pace out

measure out allot, apportion, assign, deal out, dispense, distribute, divide, divvy up (*informal*), dole out, issue, mete out, parcel out, pour out, share out

measure up (to) be adequate, be capable, be equal to, be fit, be suitable, be suited, come up to scratch (*informal*), come up to standard, compare, cut the mustard (*U.S. slang*), equal, fit *or* fill the bill, fulfil the expectations, make the grade (*informal*), match, meet, rival

meat 1. aliment, cheer, chow (*informal*), comestibles, eats (*slang*), fare, flesh, food, grub (*slang*), nosh (*slang*), nour~ishment, nutriment, provender, provi~sions, rations, subsistence, sustenance, viands, victuals **2.** core, essence, gist, heart, kernel, marrow, nub, nucleus, pith, point, substance

meaty 1. hearty, nourishing, rich, sub~stantial **2.** beefy (*informal*), brawny, burly, fleshy, heavily built, heavy, husky (*informal*), muscular, solid, strapping, sturdy **3.** interesting, mean~ingful, pithy, profound, rich, significant, substantial

mechanical 1. automated, automatic, machine-driven **2.** automatic, cold, cur~sory, dead, emotionless, habitual, im~personal, instinctive, involuntary, lack~lustre, lifeless, machine-like, matter-of-fact, perfunctory, routine, spiritless, unconscious, unfeeling, unthinking

▷ **Antonyms** (*sense 1*) manual (*sense 2*) conscious, genuine, sincere, thinking, voluntary, warm, wholehearted

mechanism 1. apparatus, appliance, con~trivance, device, instrument, machine, structure, system, tool **2.** action, compo~nents, gears, innards (*informal*), ma~chinery, motor, workings, works **3.** agency, execution, functioning, means, medium, method, operation, perfor~mance, procedure, process, system, technique, workings

meddle butt in, interfere, intermeddle, interpose, intervene, intrude, pry, put one's oar in, put one's two cents in (*U.S. slang*), stick one's nose in (*informal*), tamper

meddlesome interfering, intermeddling, intruding, intrusive, meddling, mischie~vous, officious, prying

mediate act as middleman, arbitrate, bring to an agreement, bring to terms, conciliate, intercede, interpose, inter~vene, make peace between, moderate, reconcile, referee, resolve, restore har~mony, settle, step in (*informal*), umpire

mediation arbitration, conciliation, good offices, intercession, interposition, intervention, reconciliation

mediator advocate, arbiter, arbitrator, go-between, honest broker, interceder, intermediary, judge, middleman, mod~erator, negotiator, peacemaker, referee, umpire

medicable curable, healable, remediable, treatable

medicinal analeptic, curative, healing, medical, remedial, restorative, roborant, sanatory, therapeutic

medicine cure, drug, medicament, medi~cation, nostrum, physic, remedy

medieval 1. Gothic **2.** *informal* antedilu~vian, antiquated, antique, archaic, old-fashioned, primitive, unenlightened

mediocre average, banal, bog-standard (*Brit. & Irish slang*), commonplace, fair to middling (*informal*), indifferent, infe~rior, insignificant, mean, medium, mid~dling, no great shakes (*informal*), ordi~nary, passable, pedestrian, run-of-the-mill, second-rate, so-so (*informal*), tol~erable, undistinguished, uninspired, vanilla (*slang*)

▷ **Antonyms** distinctive, distinguished, excellent, extraordinary, fine, incompa~

rable, superb, superior, unexcelled, unique, unrivalled, unsurpassed

mediocrity **1.** commonplaceness, indifference, inferiority, insignificance, meanness, ordinariness, poorness, unimportance **2.** cipher, lightweight (*informal*), nobody, nonentity, second-rater

meditate **1.** be in a brown study, cogitate, consider, contemplate, deliberate, muse, ponder, reflect, ruminate, study, think **2.** consider, contemplate, design, devise, have in mind, intend, mull over, plan, purpose, scheme, think over

meditation brown study, cerebration, cogitation, concentration, contemplation, musing, pondering, reflection, reverie, ruminating, rumination, study, thought

meditative cogitative, contemplative, deliberative, pensive, reflective, ruminative, studious, thoughtful

medium *adjective* **1.** average, fair, intermediate, mean, medial, median, mediocre, middle, middling, midway *~noun* **2.** average, centre, compromise, mean, middle, middle course, middle ground, middle path, middle way, midpoint **3.** agency, avenue, channel, form, instrument, instrumentality, means, mode, organ, vehicle, way **4.** atmosphere, conditions, element, environment, habitat, influences, milieu, setting, surroundings **5.** channeller, spiritist, spiritualist

▷ **Antonyms** *~adjective* curious, distinctive, extraordinary, extreme, uncommon, unique, unusual, utmost

medley assortment, confusion, farrago, gallimaufry, hodgepodge, hotchpotch, jumble, *mélange,* miscellany, mishmash, mixed bag (*informal*), mixture, olio, omnium-gatherum, pastiche, patchwork, potpourri, salmagundi

meek **1.** deferential, docile, forbearing, gentle, humble, long-suffering, mild, modest, patient, peaceful, soft, submissive, unassuming, unpretentious, yielding **2.** acquiescent, compliant, resigned, spineless, spiritless, tame, timid, unresisting, weak, weak-kneed (*informal*), wimpish *or* wimpy (*informal*)

▷ **Antonyms** arrogant, bold, bossy, domineering, feisty (*informal, chiefly U.S. & Canad.*), forward, immodest, overbearing, presumptuous, pretentious, proud, self-assertive, spirited, wilful

meekness **1.** deference, docility, forbearance, gentleness, humbleness, humility, long-suffering, lowliness, mildness, modesty, patience, peacefulness, resignation, softness, submission, submissiveness **2.** acquiescence, compliance, resignation, spinelessness, spiritlessness, tameness, timidity, weakness

meet **1.** bump into, chance on, come across, confront, contact, encounter, find, happen on, run across, run into **2.** abut, adjoin, come together, connect, converge, cross, intersect, join, link up, touch, unite **3.** answer, carry out, come up to, comply, cope with, discharge, equal, fulfil, gratify, handle, match, measure up, perform, satisfy **4.** assemble, collect, come together, congregate, convene, foregather, gather, muster, rally **5.** bear, encounter, endure, experience, face, go through, suffer, undergo

▷ **Antonyms** (*sense 1*) avoid, elude, escape, miss (*sense 2*) diverge (*sense 3*) fail, fall short, renege (*sense 4*) adjourn, disperse, scatter

meeting **1.** assignation, confrontation, encounter, engagement, introduction, rendezvous, tryst (*archaic*) **2.** assembly, audience, company, conclave, conference, congregation, congress, convention, convocation, gathering, get-together (*informal*), meet, powwow, rally, reunion, session **3.** concourse, confluence, conjunction, convergence, crossing, intersection, junction, union

melancholy **1.** *noun* blues, dejection, depression, despondency, gloom, gloominess, low spirits, misery, pensiveness, sadness, sorrow, the hump (*Brit. informal*), unhappiness, woe **2.** *~adjective* blue, dejected, depressed, despondent, disconsolate, dismal, dispirited, doleful, down, downcast, downhearted, down in the dumps (*informal*), down in the mouth, gloomy, glum, heavy-hearted, joyless, low, low-spirited, lugubrious, melancholic, miserable, moody, mournful, pensive, sad, sombre, sorrowful, unhappy, woebegone, woeful

▷ **Antonyms** *~noun* delight, gladness, happiness, joy, pleasure *~adjective* blithe, bright, cheerful, gay, glad, happy, jolly, joyful, joyous, light-hearted, lively, merry, sunny

mélange assortment, confusion, farrago, gallimaufry, hodge-podge, hotch-potch, jumble, medley, miscellany, mishmash, mix, mixed bag (*informal*), mixture, olio, omnium-gatherum, pastiche, potpourri, salmagundi

melee, mêlée affray (*Law*), *bagarre,* battle royal, brawl, broil, donnybrook, fight, fracas, fray, free-for-all (*informal*), ruckus (*informal*), ruction (*informal*), rumpus, scrimmage, scuffle, set-to (*informal*), shindig (*informal*), shindy (*informal*), skirmish, stramash (*Scot.*), tussle

mellifluous, mellifluent dulcet, euphonious, honeyed, mellow, silvery, smooth, soft, soothing, sweet, sweet-sounding

mellow *adjective* **1.** delicate, full-flavoured, juicy, mature, perfect, rich, ripe, soft, sweet, well-matured **2.** dulcet, euphonic, full, mellifluous, melodious, rich, rounded, smooth, sweet, tuneful, well-tuned **3.** cheerful, cordial, elevated, expansive, genial, half-tipsy, happy, jol~

ly, jovial, merry (*Brit. informal*), relaxed *~verb* **4**. develop, improve, mature, perfect, ripen, season, soften, sweeten
▷ **Antonyms** *~adjective* (*sense 1*) green, immature, raw, sour, unripe *~verb* brutalize, harden

melodious concordant, dulcet, euphonic, euphonious, harmonious, melodic, musical, silvery, sweet-sounding, sweet-toned, tuneful
▷ **Antonyms** cacophonous, discordant, grating, harsh, unharmonious, unmelodic, unmelodious, unmusical, untuneful

melodramatic actorly, actressy, blood-and-thunder, extravagant, hammy (*informal*), histrionic, overdramatic, overemotional, sensational, theatrical

melody 1. air, descant, music, refrain, song, strain, theme, tune **2**. euphony, harmony, melodiousness, music, musicality, tunefulness

melt 1. deliquesce, diffuse, dissolve, flux, fuse, liquefy, soften, thaw **2**. (*often with* **away**) disappear, disperse, dissolve, evanesce, evaporate, fade, vanish **3**. disarm, mollify, relax, soften, touch

member 1. associate, fellow, representative **2**. appendage, arm, component, constituent, element, extremity, leg, limb, organ, part, portion

membership 1. associates, body, fellows, members **2**. belonging, enrolment, fellowship, participation

memento keepsake, memorial, relic, remembrance, reminder, souvenir, token, trophy

memoir account, biography, essay, journal, life, monograph, narrative, record, register

memoirs 1. autobiography, diary, experiences, journals, life, life story, memories, recollections, reminiscences **2**. annals, chronicles, records, transactions

memorable catchy, celebrated, distinguished, extraordinary, famous, historic, illustrious, important, impressive, momentous, notable, noteworthy, remarkable, signal, significant, striking, unforgettable
▷ **Antonyms** commonplace, forgettable, insignificant, ordinary, trivial, undistinguished, unimportant, unimpressive, unmemorable

memorial *adjective* **1**. commemorative, monumental *~noun* **2**. cairn, memento, monument, plaque, record, remembrance, souvenir **3**. address, memorandum, petition, statement

memorize commit to memory, con (*archaic*), get by heart, learn, learn by heart, learn by rote, remember

memory 1. recall, recollection, remembrance, reminiscence, retention **2**. commemoration, honour, remembrance **3**. celebrity, fame, glory, name, renown, reputation, repute

menace *verb* **1**. alarm, bode ill, browbeat, bully, frighten, impend, intimidate, loom, lour *or* lower, terrorize, threaten, utter threats to *~noun* **2**. commination, intimidation, scare, threat, warning **3**. danger, hazard, jeopardy, peril **4**. *informal* annoyance, nuisance, pest, plague, troublemaker

menacing alarming, baleful, dangerous, forbidding, frightening, intimidating, intimidatory, looming, louring *or* lowering, minacious, minatory, ominous, threatening
▷ **Antonyms** auspicious, encouraging, favourable, promising

mend *verb* **1**. cure, darn, fix, heal, patch, rectify, refit, reform, remedy, renew, renovate, repair, restore, retouch **2**. ameliorate, amend, better, correct, emend, improve, rectify, reform, revise **3**. convalesce, get better, heal, recover, recuperate *~noun* **4**. darn, patch, repair, stitch **5**. **on the mend** convalescent, convalescing, getting better, improving, recovering, recuperating

mendacious deceitful, deceptive, dishonest, duplicitous, fallacious, false, fraudulent, insincere, lying, perfidious, perjured, untrue, untruthful
▷ **Antonyms** genuine, honest, true, truthful

mendacity deceit, deceitfulness, dishonesty, distortion, duplicity, falsehood, falsification, fraudulence, insincerity, inveracity, lie, lying, mendaciousness, misrepresentation, perfidy, perjury, untruth, untruthfulness

mendicant 1. *adjective* begging **2**. *~noun* beggar, pauper

menial *adjective* **1**. boring, dull, humdrum, low-status, routine, unskilled **2**. abject, base, degrading, demeaning, fawning, grovelling, humble, ignoble, ignominious, low, lowly, mean, obsequious, servile, slavish, sorry, subservient, sycophantic, vile *~noun* **3**. attendant, dogsbody (*informal*), domestic, drudge, flunky, labourer, lackey, serf, servant, skivvy (*chiefly Brit.*), slave, underling, varlet (*archaic*), vassal
▷ **Antonyms** *~adjective* (*sense 2*) aristocratic, autocratic, bossy, dignified, domineering, elevated, haughty, high, noble, overbearing, proud *~noun* boss, chief, commander, lord, master, superior

menstruation catamenia (*Physiology*), courses (*Physiology*), flow (*informal*), menses, menstrual cycle, monthly (*informal*), period, the curse (*informal*)

mensuration assessment, calculation, calibration, computation, estimation, measurement, measuring, metage, survey, surveying

mental 1. cerebral, intellectual **2.** as daft as a brush (*informal, chiefly Brit.*), deranged, disturbed, insane, lunatic, mad, mentally ill, not right in the head, psychiatric, psychotic, round the bend (*Brit. slang*), unbalanced, unstable

mentality 1. brainpower, brains, comprehension, grey matter (*informal*), intellect, intelligence quotient, I.Q., mental age, mind, rationality, understanding, wit **2.** attitude, cast of mind, character, disposition, frame of mind, make-up, outlook, personality, psychology, turn of mind, way of thinking

mentally in one's head, intellectually, in the mind, inwardly, psychologically, rationally, subjectively

mention *verb* **1.** acknowledge, adduce, allude to, bring up, broach, call attention to, cite, communicate, declare, disclose, divulge, hint at, impart, intimate, make known, name, point out, recount, refer to, report, reveal, speak about *or* of, state, tell, touch upon **2. not to mention** as well as, besides, not counting, to say nothing of *~noun* **3.** acknowledgment, citation, recognition, tribute **4.** allusion, announcement, indication, notification, observation, reference, remark

mentor adviser, coach, counsellor, guide, guru, instructor, teacher, tutor

menu bill of fare, carte du jour, tariff (*chiefly Brit.*)

mephitic baleful, baneful, evil- *or* ill-smelling, fetid, foul, foul-smelling, malodorous, miasmal, miasmatic, miasmic, noisome, noxious, olid, pestilential, poisonous, putrid, stinking

mercantile commercial, marketable, trade, trading

mercenary *adjective* **1.** acquisitive, avaricious, bribable, covetous, grasping, greedy, money-grubbing (*informal*), sordid, venal **2.** bought, hired, paid, venal *~noun* **3.** condottiere (*History*), free companion (*History*), freelance (*History*), hireling, soldier of fortune

▷ **Antonyms** *~adjective* (*sense 1*) altruistic, benevolent, generous, idealistic, liberal, munificent, philanthropic, unselfish

merchandise 1. *noun* commodities, goods, produce, products, staples, stock, stock in trade, truck, vendibles, wares **2.** *~verb* buy and sell, deal in, distribute, do business in, market, retail, sell, trade, traffic in, vend

merchant broker, dealer, purveyor, retailer, salesman, seller, shopkeeper, supplier, trader, tradesman, trafficker, vendor, wholesaler

merchantable marketable, saleable, tradable, vendible

merciful beneficent, benignant, clement, compassionate, forbearing, forgiving, generous, gracious, humane, kind, lenient, liberal, mild, pitying, soft, sparing, sympathetic, tender-hearted

▷ **Antonyms** cruel, hard-hearted, inhumane, merciless, pitiless, uncompassionate, unfeeling

merciless barbarous, callous, cruel, fell (*archaic*), hard, hard-hearted, harsh, heartless, implacable, inexorable, inhumane, pitiless, relentless, ruthless, severe, unappeasable, unfeeling, unforgiving, unmerciful, unpitying, unsparing, unsympathetic

mercurial active, capricious, changeable, erratic, fickle, flighty, gay, impulsive, inconstant, irrepressible, light-hearted, lively, mobile, quicksilver, spirited, sprightly, temperamental, unpredictable, unstable, variable, volatile

▷ **Antonyms** consistent, constant, dependable, reliable, stable, steady, unchanging

mercy 1. benevolence, charity, clemency, compassion, favour, forbearance, forgiveness, grace, kindness, leniency, pity, quarter **2.** benison (*archaic*), blessing, boon, godsend, piece of luck, relief **3. at the mercy of** defenceless against, exposed to, in the clutches of, in the power of, naked before, open to, prey to, subject to, threatened by, unprotected against, vulnerable to

▷ **Antonyms** (*sense 1*) brutality, cruelty, harshness, inhumanity, pitilessness, severity

mere *adjective* absolute, bare, common, complete, entire, nothing more than, plain, pure, pure and simple, sheer, simple, stark, unadulterated, unmitigated, unmixed, utter

meretricious 1. flashy, garish, gaudy, gimcrack, plastic (*slang*), showy, tawdry, tinsel, trashy **2.** bogus, counterfeit, deceitful, false, hollow, insincere, mock, phoney *or* phony (*informal*), pseudo (*informal*), put-on, sham, specious, spurious

merge amalgamate, become lost in, be swallowed up by, blend, coalesce, combine, consolidate, converge, fuse, incorporate, intermix, join, meet, meld, melt into, mingle, mix, tone with, unite

▷ **Antonyms** detach, diverge, divide, part, separate, sever

merger amalgamation, coalition, combination, consolidation, fusion, incorporation, union

meridian acme, apex, apogee, climax, crest, culmination, high noon, high-water mark, peak, pinnacle, summit, zenith

merit *noun* **1.** advantage, asset, excellence, good, goodness, integrity, quality, strong point, talent, value, virtue, worth, worthiness **2.** claim, credit, desert, due, right *~verb* **3.** be entitled to, be worthy of, deserve, earn, have a claim to, have a right to, have coming to one, incur, rate, warrant

merited appropriate, condign, deserved, earned, entitled, just, justified, rightful, rightly due, warranted

meritorious admirable, commendable, creditable, deserving, excellent, exemplary, good, honourable, laudable, praiseworthy, right, righteous, virtuous, worthy

▷ **Antonyms** discreditable, dishonourable, ignoble, unchivalrous, undeserving, unexceptional, ungenerous, unpraiseworthy

merriment amusement, conviviality, festivity, frolic, fun, gaiety, glee, hilarity, jocularity, jollity, joviality, laughter, levity, liveliness, merrymaking, mirth, revelry, sport

merry **1.** blithe, blithesome, carefree, cheerful, chirpy (*informal*), convivial, festive, frolicsome, fun-loving, gay, genial, glad, gleeful, happy, jocund, jolly, joyful, joyous, light-hearted, mirthful, rollicking, sportive, upbeat (*informal*), vivacious **2.** amusing, comic, comical, facetious, funny, hilarious, humorous, jocular, mirthful **3.** *Brit. informal* elevated (*informal*), happy, mellow, squiffy (*Brit. informal*), tiddly (*slang, chiefly Brit.*), tipsy **4. make merry** carouse, celebrate, enjoy oneself, feast, frolic, have a good time, have fun, make whoopee (*informal*), revel

▷ **Antonyms** (*sense 1*) dejected, dismal, down in the dumps (*informal*), gloomy, miserable, sad, unhappy

merrymaking beano (*Brit. slang*), carousal, carouse, celebration, conviviality, festivity, fun, gaiety, hooley *or* hoolie (*chiefly Irish & N.Z.*), jollification, merriment, party, rave (*Brit. slang*), rave-up (*Brit. slang*), revelry

mesh *noun* **1.** net, netting, network, plexus, reticulation, tracery, web **2.** entanglement, snare, tangle, toils, trap, web *~verb* **3.** catch, enmesh, ensnare, entangle, net, snare, tangle, trap **4.** combine, come together, connect, coordinate, dovetail, engage, fit together, harmonize, interlock, knit

mesmerize absorb, captivate, enthral, entrance, fascinate, grip, hold spellbound, hypnotize, magnetize, spellbind

mess *noun* **1.** balls-up (*taboo slang*), bodge (*informal*), botch, chaos, clutter, cock-up (*Brit. slang*), confusion, dirtiness, disarray, disorder, disorganization, fuck-up (*offensive taboo slang*), grot (*slang*), hash, hodgepodge (*U.S.*), hotchpotch, jumble, litter, mishmash, pig's breakfast (*informal*), shambles, state, turmoil, untidiness **2.** deep water, difficulty, dilemma, fine kettle of fish (*informal*), fix (*informal*), hot water (*informal*), imbroglio, jam (*informal*), mix-up, muddle, perplexity, pickle (*informal*), plight, predicament, spot (*informal*), stew (*informal*), tight spot *~verb* **3.** (*often with* **up**) befoul, besmirch, botch, bungle, clutter, cock up (*Brit. slang*), dirty, disarrange, dishevel, foul, fuck up (*offensive taboo slang*), litter, make a hash of (*informal*), make a nonsense of, make a pig's ear of (*informal*), muck up (*Brit. slang*), muddle, pollute, scramble **4.** (*often with* **with**) fiddle (*informal*), interfere, meddle, play, tamper, tinker

mess about *or* **around** **1.** amuse oneself, dabble, fool (about *or* around), footle (*informal*), muck about (*informal*), piss about *or* around (*taboo slang*), play about *or* around, potter, trifle **2.** fiddle (*informal*), fool (about *or* around), interfere, meddle, piss about *or* around (*taboo slang*), play, tamper, tinker, toy

message **1.** bulletin, communication, communiqué, dispatch, intimation, letter, memorandum, missive, note, notice, tidings, word **2.** idea, import, meaning, moral, point, purport, theme **3.** commission, errand, job, mission, task **4. get the message** catch on (*informal*), comprehend, get it, get the point, see, take the hint, twig (*Brit. informal*), understand

messenger agent, bearer, carrier, courier, delivery boy, emissary, envoy, errand-boy, go-between, harbinger, herald, runner

messy chaotic, cluttered, confused, dirty, dishevelled, disordered, disorganized, grubby, littered, muddled, scuzzy (*slang, chiefly U.S.*), shambolic (*informal*), sloppy (*informal*), slovenly, unkempt, untidy

▷ **Antonyms** clean, meticulous, neat, ordered, orderly, shipshape, smart, squeaky-clean, tidy

metamorphose alter, be reborn, change, convert, mutate, remake, remodel, reshape, transfigure, transform, translate, transmogrify (*jocular*), transmute, transubstantiate

metamorphosis alteration, change, changeover, conversion, mutation, rebirth, transfiguration, transformation, translation, transmogrification (*jocular*), transmutation, transubstantiation

metaphor allegory, analogy, emblem, figure of speech, image, symbol, trope

metaphorical allegorical, emblematic, emblematical, figurative, symbolic, tropical (*rhetoric*)

metaphysical **1.** basic, esoteric, essential, eternal, fundamental, general, ideal, intellectual, philosophical, profound, speculative, spiritual, subjective, universal **2.** abstract, abstruse, deep, high-flown, oversubtle, recondite, theoretical, transcendental **3.** immaterial, impalpable, incorporeal, intangible, spiritual, supernatural, unreal, unsubstantial

mete *verb* administer, allot, apportion, assign, deal, dispense, distribute, divide, dole, measure, parcel, portion, ration, share

meteoric brief, brilliant, dazzling, ephemeral, fast, flashing, fleeting, momentary, overnight, rapid, spectacular, speedy, sudden, swift, transient
▷ **Antonyms** gradual, lengthy, long, prolonged, slow, steady, unhurried

method **1.** approach, arrangement, course, fashion, form, manner, mode, modus operandi, plan, practice, procedure, process, programme, routine, rule, scheme, style, system, technique, way **2.** design, form, order, orderliness, organization, pattern, planning, purpose, regularity, structure, system

methodical businesslike, deliberate, disciplined, efficient, meticulous, neat, ordered, orderly, organized, painstaking, planned, precise, regular, structured, systematic, tidy, well-regulated
▷ **Antonyms** casual, chaotic, confused, disordered, disorderly, haphazard, irregular, random, unmethodical

meticulous detailed, exact, fastidious, fussy, microscopic, painstaking, particular, perfectionist, precise, punctilious, scrupulous, strict, thorough
▷ **Antonyms** careless, haphazard, imprecise, inexact, loose, negligent, slapdash, sloppy

métier **1.** calling, craft, line, occupation, profession, pursuit, trade, vocation **2.** forte, long suit (*informal*), speciality, specialty, strong point, strong suit

metropolis capital, city

mettle **1.** ardour, balls (*taboo slang*), boldness, bottle (*Brit. slang*), bravery, courage, daring, fire, fortitude, gallantry, gameness, grit, guts (*informal*), hardihood, heart, indomitability, life, nerve, pluck, resolution, resolve, spirit, spunk (*informal*), valour, vigour **2.** calibre, character, disposition, kidney, make-up, nature, quality, stamp, temper, temperament

mettlesome ardent, bold, brisk, courageous, daring, dashing, feisty (*informal, chiefly U.S. & Canad.*), fiery, frisky, game (*informal*), have-a-go (*informal*), high-spirited, lively, mettled, plucky, sprightly, valiant, vigorous

mewl blubber, cry, grizzle (*informal, chiefly Brit.*), pule, snivel, whimper, whine, whinge (*informal*)

miasma effluvium, fetor, mephitis, niff (*Brit. slang*), odour, pollution, reek, smell, stench

miasmal fetid, foul, insalubrious, malodorous, mephitic, niffy (*Brit. slang*), noisome, noxious, olid, polluted, putrid, reeking, smelly, stinking, unwholesome

microbe bacillus, bacterium, bug (*informal*), germ, microorganism, virus

microscopic imperceptible, infinitesimal, invisible, minuscule, minute, negligible, teensy-weensy, teeny-weeny, tiny
▷ **Antonyms** enormous, gigantic, ginormous (*informal*), great, huge, immense, large, vast

midday noon, noonday, noontide, noontime, twelve noon, twelve o'clock

middle *adjective* **1.** central, halfway, inner, inside, intermediate, intervening, mean, medial, median, medium, mid ~*noun* **2.** centre, focus, halfway point, heart, inside, mean, midpoint, midsection, midst, thick **3.** midriff, midsection, waist

middleman broker, distributor, entrepreneur, go-between, intermediary

middling adequate, all right, average, bog-standard (*Brit. & Irish slang*), fair, indifferent, mediocre, medium, moderate, modest, O.K. *or* okay (*informal*), ordinary, passable, run-of-the-mill, so-so (*informal*), tolerable, unexceptional, unremarkable

midget **1.** *noun* dwarf, gnome, homuncule, homunculus, manikin, munchkin (*informal, chiefly U.S.*), pygmy *or* pigmy, shrimp (*informal*), Tom Thumb **2.** ~*adjective* baby, dwarf, Lilliputian, little, miniature, pocket, pygmy *or* pigmy, small, teensy-weensy, teeny-weeny, tiny

midnight dead of night, middle of the night, the witching hour, twelve o'clock (at night)

midst **1.** bosom, centre, core, depths, heart, hub, interior, middle, thick **2. in the midst of** amidst, among, during, enveloped by, in the middle of, in the thick of, surrounded by

midway betwixt and between, halfway, in the middle

mien air, appearance, aspect, aura, bearing, carriage, countenance, demeanour, deportment, look, manner, presence

miffed aggrieved, annoyed, displeased, hacked (off) (*U.S. slang*), hurt, in a huff, irked, irritated, narked (*Brit., Austral., & N.Z. slang*), nettled, offended, piqued, pissed off (*taboo slang*), put out, resentful, upset, vexed

might **1.** ability, capability, capacity, clout (*informal*), efficacy, efficiency, energy, force, potency, power, prowess, puissance, strength, sway, valour, vigour **2. (with) might and main** as hard as one can, as hard as possible, forcefully, full blast, full force, lustily, manfully, mightily, vigorously, with all one's might *or* strength

mightily **1.** decidedly, exceedingly, extremely, greatly, highly, hugely, intensely, much, seriously (*informal*), very, very much **2.** energetically, forcefully, lustily, manfully, powerfully, strongly, vigorously, with all one's might and main, with all one's strength

mighty 1. doughty, forceful, hardy, indomitable, lusty, manful, potent, powerful, puissant, robust, stalwart, stout, strapping, strong, sturdy, vigorous **2**. bulky, colossal, elephantine, enormous, gigantic, ginormous (*informal*), grand, great, huge, humongous *or* humungous (*U.S. slang*), immense, large, massive, mega (*slang*), monumental, prodigious, stellar (*informal*), stupendous, titanic, towering, tremendous, vast

▷ **Antonyms** (*sense 1*) feeble, impotent, weak, weedy (*informal*), wimpish *or* wimpy (*informal*) (*sense 2*) small, tiny, unimposing, unimpressive

migrant 1. *noun* drifter, emigrant, gypsy, immigrant, itinerant, nomad, rover, tinker, transient, traveller, vagrant, wanderer **2**. *~adjective* drifting, gypsy, immigrant, itinerant, migratory, nomadic, roving, shifting, transient, travelling, vagrant, wandering

migrate drift, emigrate, journey, move, roam, rove, shift, travel, trek, voyage, wander

migration emigration, journey, movement, roving, shift, travel, trek, voyage, wandering

migratory gypsy, itinerant, migrant, nomadic, peripatetic, roving, shifting, transient, travelling, unsettled, vagrant, wandering

mild 1. amiable, balmy, bland, calm, clement, compassionate, docile, easy, easy-going, easy-oasy (*slang*), equable, forbearing, forgiving, gentle, indulgent, kind, meek, mellow, merciful, moderate, pacific, peaceable, placid, pleasant, serene, smooth, soft, temperate, tender, tranquil, warm **2**. demulcent, emollient, lenitive, mollifying, soothing

▷ **Antonyms** (*sense 1*) bitter, cold, fierce, harsh, rough, stormy, unkind, unpleasant, violent, wild (*sense 2*) harsh, powerful, severe, sharp, strong

mildness blandness, calmness, clemency, docility, forbearance, gentleness, indulgence, kindness, leniency, lenity, meekness, mellowness, moderation, placidity, smoothness, softness, temperateness, tenderness, tranquillity, warmth

milieu background, element, environment, locale, location, *mise en scène*, scene, setting, sphere, surroundings

militant *adjective* **1**. active, aggressive, assertive, combative, vigorous **2**. belligerent, combating, contending, embattled, fighting, in arms, warring *~noun* **3**. activist, partisan **4**. belligerent, combatant, fighter, gladiator, warrior

▷ **Antonyms** concessive, pacific, pacifist, peaceful

military 1. *adjective* armed, martial, soldierlike, soldierly, warlike **2**. *~noun* armed forces, army, forces, services

militate 1. (*with* **against**) be detrimental to, conflict with, contend, count, counter, counteract, oppose, resist, tell, weigh **2**. (*with* **for**) advance, aid, further, help, promote

militia fencibles (*History*), National Guard (*U.S.*), reserve(s), Territorial Army (*Brit.*), trainband (*History*), yeomanry (*History*)

milk *verb* **1**. drain, draw off, express, extract, let out, press, siphon, tap **2**. bleed, drain, exploit, extract, impose on, pump, take advantage of, use, wring

milk-and-water feeble, innocuous, insipid, jejune, nerdy *or* nurdy (*slang*), vapid, weak, weedy (*informal*), wimpish *or* wimpy (*informal*), wishy-washy (*informal*)

▷ **Antonyms** effective, energetic, forceful, healthy, strong

milksop chinless wonder (*Brit. informal*), coward, dastard (*archaic*), jessie (*Scot. slang*), namby-pamby, sissy, weakling, wimp (*informal*), wuss (*U.S. slang*)

milky alabaster, clouded, cloudy, milk-white, opaque, white, whitish

mill *noun* **1**. factory, foundry, plant, shop, works **2**. crusher, grinder **3**. **run of the mill** average, bog-standard (*Brit. & Irish slang*), commonplace, everyday, fair, middling, ordinary, routine, unexceptional, unremarkable *~verb* **4**. comminute, crush, granulate, grate, grind, pound, powder, press, pulverize **5**. crowd, seethe, swarm, throng

millstone 1. grindstone, quernstone **2**. affliction, albatross, burden, dead weight, drag, encumbrance, load, weight

mime 1. *noun* dumb show, gesture, mummery, pantomime **2**. *~verb* act out, gesture, pantomime, represent, simulate

mimic *verb* **1**. ape, caricature, do (*informal*), imitate, impersonate, parody, take off (*informal*) **2**. echo, look like, mirror, resemble, simulate, take on the appearance of *~noun* **3**. caricaturist, copycat (*informal*), imitator, impersonator, impressionist, parodist, parrot *~adjective* **4**. echoic, imitation, imitative, make-believe, mimetic, mock, sham, simulated

mimicry apery, burlesque, caricature, copying, imitating, imitation, impersonation, impression, mimicking, mockery, parody, take-off (*informal*)

minatory baleful, dangerous, menacing, minacious, minatorial, threatening

mince 1. chop, crumble, cut, grind, hash **2**. diminish, euphemize, extenuate, hold back, moderate, palliate, soften, spare, tone down, weaken **3**. attitudinize, give oneself airs, ponce (*slang*), pose, posture

mincing affected, camp (*informal*), dainty, effeminate, foppish, lah-di-dah (*informal*), nice, niminy-piminy, poncy (*slang*), precious, pretentious, sissy

mind *noun* **1.** brain(s) (*informal*), grey matter (*informal*), intellect, intelligence, mentality, ratiocination, reason, sense, spirit, understanding, wits **2.** memory, recollection, remembrance **3.** brain, head, imagination, psyche **4.** brain (*informal*), brainbox, genius, intellect, intellectual, thinker **5.** attitude, belief, feeling, judgment, opinion, outlook, point of view, sentiment, thoughts, view, way of thinking **6.** bent, desire, disposition, fancy, inclination, intention, leaning, notion, purpose, tendency, urge, will, wish **7.** attention, concentration, thinking, thoughts **8.** judgment, marbles (*informal*), mental balance, rationality, reason, sanity, senses, wits **9. in** *or* **of two minds** dithering (*chiefly Brit.*), hesitant, shillyshallying (*informal*), swithering (*Scot.*), uncertain, undecided, unsure, vacillating, wavering **10. make up one's mind** choose, come to a decision, decide, determine, reach a decision, resolve **11. bear** *or* **keep in mind** be cognizant of, be mindful of, remember, take note of *~verb* **12.** be affronted, be bothered, care, disapprove, dislike, look askance at, object, resent, take offence **13.** adhere to, attend, comply with, follow, heed, listen to, mark, note, notice, obey, observe, pay attention, pay heed to, regard, respect, take heed, watch **14.** be sure, ensure, make certain **15.** attend to, guard, have charge of, keep an eye on, look after, take care of, tend, watch **16.** be careful, be cautious, be on (one's) guard, be wary, take care, watch **17. never mind** disregard, do not concern yourself, don't bother, don't give (it) a second thought, forget (it), it does not matter, it's none of your business, it's nothing to do with you, pay no attention

mindful alert, alive to, attentive, aware, careful, chary, cognizant, conscious, heedful, regardful, respectful, sensible, thoughtful, wary, watchful

▷ **Antonyms** heedless, inattentive, incautious, mindless, oblivious, thoughtless, unaware

mindless 1. asinine, braindead (*informal*), brutish, careless, dead from the neck up (*informal*), foolish, forgetful, gratuitous, heedless, idiotic, imbecilic, inane, inattentive, moronic, neglectful, negligent, oblivious, obtuse, stupid, thoughtless, unintelligent, unmindful, unthinking, witless **2.** automatic, brainless, mechanical

▷ **Antonyms** attentive, aware, considerate, intelligent, mindful, reasonable, reasoning, sane, sensitive, thinking

mind out be careful, be on one's guard, beware, keep one's eyes open, look out, pay attention, take care, watch

mind's eye head, imagination, memory, mind, recollection, remembrance

mine *noun* **1.** coalfield, colliery, deposit, excavation, lode, pit, shaft, vein **2.** abundance, fund, hoard, reserve, source, stock, store, supply, treasury, wealth **3.** sap, trench, tunnel *~verb* **4.** delve, dig for, dig up, excavate, extract, hew, quarry, unearth **5.** lay mines in *or* under, sow with mines **6.** sap, subvert, tunnel, undermine, weaken

miner coalminer, collier (*Brit.*), pitman (*Brit.*)

mingle 1. admix, alloy, blend, coalesce, combine, commingle, compound, intermingle, intermix, interweave, join, marry, meld, merge, mix, unite **2.** associate, circulate, consort, fraternize, hang about *or* around, hang out (*informal*), hobnob, rub shoulders (*informal*), socialize

▷ **Antonyms** avoid, detach, dissociate, dissolve, divide, estrange, part, separate

miniature *adjective* baby, diminutive, dwarf, Lilliputian, little, midget, mini, minuscule, minute, pocket, pygmy *or* pigmy, reduced, scaled-down, small, teensy-weensy, teeny-weeny, tiny, toy, wee

▷ **Antonyms** big, enlarged, enormous, giant, gigantic, ginormous (*informal*), great, huge, immense, large, mega (*slang*), oversize

minimal least, least possible, littlest, minimum, nominal, slightest, smallest, token

minimize 1. abbreviate, attenuate, curtail, decrease, diminish, downsize, miniaturize, prune, reduce, shrink **2.** belittle, decry, deprecate, depreciate, discount, disparage, make light *or* little of, play down, underestimate, underrate

▷ **Antonyms** augment, boast about, elevate, enhance, enlarge, exalt, expand, extend, heighten, increase, magnify, praise, vaunt

minimum 1. *noun* bottom, depth, least, lowest, nadir, slightest **2.** *~adjective* least, least possible, littlest, lowest, minimal, slightest, smallest

▷ **Antonyms** greatest, highest, largest, maximum, most

minion bootlicker (*informal*), cohort (*chiefly U.S.*), creature, darling, dependant, favourite, flatterer, flunky, follower, hanger-on, henchman, hireling, lackey, lickspittle, myrmidon, parasite, pet, sycophant, toady, underling, yes man

minister *noun* **1.** chaplain, churchman, clergyman, cleric, divine, ecclesiastic, padre (*informal*), parson, pastor, preacher, priest, rector, vicar **2.** administrator, ambassador, cabinet member, delegate, diplomat, envoy, executive, office-holder, official, plenipotentiary **3.** agent, aide, assistant, lieutenant, servant, subordinate, underling *~verb* **4.** accommodate, administer, answer, attend, be solicitous of, cater to, pander to, serve, take care of, tend

ministration aid, assistance, favour, help, patronage, relief, service, succour, support

ministry 1. administration, bureau, cabinet, council, department, government, office, quango **2.** holy orders, the church, the priesthood, the pulpit

minor inconsequential, inconsiderable, inferior, insignificant, junior, lesser, light, negligible, nickel-and-dime (*U.S. slang*), paltry, petty, secondary, slight, small, smaller, subordinate, trifling, trivial, unimportant, younger

▷ **Antonyms** appreciable, consequential, considerable, essential, grand, great, heavy, important, major, profound, serious, significant, substantial, superior, vital, weighty

minstrel bard, harper, jongleur, musician, singer, songstress, troubadour

mint *noun* **1.** bomb (*Brit. slang*), bundle (*slang*), fortune, heap (*informal*), King's ransom, million, packet (*slang*), pile (*informal*) *~adjective* **2.** brand-new, excellent, first-class, fresh, perfect, unblemished, undamaged, untarnished *~verb* **3.** cast, coin, make, produce, punch, stamp, strike **4.** coin, construct, devise, fabricate, fashion, forge, invent, make up, produce, think up

minuscule diminutive, fine, infinitesimal, Lilliputian, little, microscopic, miniature, minute, teensy-weensy, teeny-weeny, tiny, very small

minute[1] *noun* **1.** sixtieth of an hour, sixty seconds **2.** flash, instant, jiffy (*informal*), moment, second, shake (*informal*), tick (*Brit. informal*), trice **3. any minute** any moment, any second, any time, at any time, before long, very soon **4. up to the minute** all the rage, in, latest, modish, (most) fashionable, newest, now (*informal*), smart, stylish, trendiest, trendy (*Brit. informal*), up to date, vogue, with it (*informal*)

minute[2] *adjective* **1.** diminutive, fine, infinitesimal, Lilliputian, little, microscopic, miniature, minuscule, slender, small, teensy-weensy, teeny-weeny, tiny **2.** inconsiderable, negligible, paltry, petty, picayune (*U.S.*), piddling (*informal*), puny, slight, trifling, trivial, unimportant **3.** close, critical, detailed, exact, exhaustive, meticulous, painstaking, precise, punctilious

▷ **Antonyms** (*senses 1 & 2*) enormous, generous, gigantic, ginormous (*informal*), grand, great, huge, immense, important, major, mega (*slang*), monstrous, significant, vital (*sense 3*) careless, haphazard, imprecise, inexact, loose, quick, rough, superficial

minutely closely, critically, exactly, exhaustively, in detail, meticulously, painstakingly, precisely, with a fine-tooth comb

minutes memorandum, notes, proceedings, record(s), transactions, transcript

minutiae details, finer points, ins and outs, niceties, particulars, subtleties, trifles, trivia

minx baggage (*informal, old-fashioned*), coquette, flirt, hoyden, hussy, jade, tomboy, wanton

miracle marvel, phenomenon, prodigy, thaumaturgy, wonder

miraculous amazing, astonishing, astounding, extraordinary, incredible, inexplicable, magical, marvellous, phenomenal, preternatural, prodigious, superhuman, supernatural, thaumaturgic, unaccountable, unbelievable, wonderful, wondrous (*archaic or literary*)

▷ **Antonyms** awful, bad, banal, common, commonplace, everyday, normal, ordinary, run-of-the-mill, terrible, unexceptional, unremarkable, usual

mirage hallucination, illusion, optical illusion, phantasm

mire *noun* **1.** bog, marsh, morass, quagmire, swamp **2.** dirt, gloop (*informal*), grot (*slang*), muck, mud, ooze, slime, slob (*Irish*) **3. in the mire** encumbered, entangled, in difficulties, in trouble *~verb* **4.** bog down, flounder, sink, stick in the mud **5.** begrime, besmirch, bespatter, cake, dirty, muddy, soil **6.** catch up, enmesh, entangle, involve

mirror *noun* **1.** glass, looking-glass, reflector, speculum **2.** copy, double, image, likeness, reflection, replica, representation, twin *~verb* **3.** copy, depict, echo, emulate, follow, reflect, represent, show

mirth amusement, cheerfulness, festivity, frolic, fun, gaiety, gladness, glee, hilarity, jocularity, jollity, joviality, joyousness, laughter, levity, merriment, merrymaking, pleasure, rejoicing, revelry, sport

mirthful amused, amusing, blithe, cheerful, cheery, festive, frolicsome, funny, gay, glad, gladsome (*archaic*), happy, hilarious, jocund, jolly, jovial, laughable, light-hearted, merry, playful, sportive, uproarious, vivacious

▷ **Antonyms** dejected, depressed, despondent, dismal, down in the dumps (*informal*), gloomy, grave, lugubrious, melancholy, miserable, morose, sad, saturnine, sedate, serious, solemn, sombre, sorrowful, unhappy

misadventure accident, bad break (*informal*), bad luck, bummer (*slang*), calamity, catastrophe, debacle, disaster, failure, ill fortune, ill luck, mischance, misfortune, mishap, reverse, setback

misanthrope cynic, egoist, egotist, mankind-hater, misanthropist

misanthropic antisocial, cynical, egoistic,

inhumane, malevolent, unfriendly, unsociable

misanthropy cynicism, egoism, hatred of mankind, inhumanity, malevolence

misapply abuse, misappropriate, misemploy, misuse, pervert

misapprehend get hold of the wrong end of the stick, get one's lines crossed, get the wrong idea *or* impression, misconceive, misconstrue, misinterpret, misread, mistake, misunderstand

misapprehension delusion, error, fallacy, false belief, false impression, misconception, misconstruction, misinterpretation, misreading, mistake, misunderstanding, wrong idea *or* impression

misappropriate cabbage (*Brit. slang*), defalcate (*Law*), embezzle, misapply, misspend, misuse, peculate, pocket, steal, swindle

misbegotten **1.** dishonest, disreputable, ill-gotten, illicit, purloined, shady (*informal*), stolen, unlawful, unrespectable **2.** abortive, hare-brained, ill-advised, ill-conceived, poorly thought-out **3.** *literary* bastard, born out of wedlock, illegitimate, natural, spurious (*rare*)

misbehave act up (*informal*), be bad, be insubordinate, be naughty, carry on (*informal*), get up to mischief (*informal*), muck about (*Brit. slang*)

▷ **Antonyms** act correctly, be good, behave, conduct oneself properly, mind one's manners, mind one's p's and q's, toe the line

misbehaviour acting up (*informal*), bad behaviour, impropriety, incivility, indiscipline, insubordination, mischief, misconduct, misdeeds, misdemeanour, monkey business (*informal*), naughtiness, rudeness, shenanigans (*informal*)

misbelief delusion, error, fallacy, false belief, heresy, unorthodoxy

miscalculate blunder, calculate wrongly, err, get (it) wrong, go wrong, make a mistake, misjudge, overestimate, overrate, slip up, underestimate, underrate

miscarriage **1.** miss (*informal*), spontaneous abortion **2.** botch (*informal*), breakdown, error, failure, misadventure, mischance, misfire, mishap, mismanagement, nonsuccess, perversion, thwarting, undoing

miscarry **1.** abort **2.** come to grief, come to nothing, fail, fall through, gang agley (*Scot.*), go amiss, go astray, go awry, go wrong, misfire

miscellaneous assorted, confused, diverse, diversified, farraginous, heterogeneous, indiscriminate, jumbled, manifold, many, mingled, mixed, motley, multifarious, multiform, promiscuous, sundry, varied, various

miscellany anthology, assortment, collection, diversity, farrago, gallimaufry, hotchpotch, jumble, medley, *mélange*, mixed bag, mixture, omnium-gatherum, potpourri, salmagundi, variety

mischance accident, bad break (*informal*), bad luck, bummer (*slang*), calamity, contretemps, disaster, ill chance, ill fortune, ill luck, infelicity, misadventure, misfortune, mishap

mischief **1.** devilment, impishness, misbehaviour, monkey business (*informal*), naughtiness, pranks, roguery, roguishness, shenanigans (*informal*), trouble, waywardness **2.** damage, detriment, disadvantage, disruption, evil, harm, hurt, injury, misfortune, trouble **3.** devil, imp, monkey, nuisance, pest, rascal, rogue, scallywag (*informal*), scamp, tyke (*informal*), villain

mischievous **1.** arch, bad, badly behaved, exasperating, frolicsome, impish, naughty, playful, puckish, rascally, roguish, sportive, teasing, troublesome, vexatious, wayward **2.** bad, damaging, deleterious, destructive, detrimental, evil, harmful, hurtful, injurious, malicious, malignant, pernicious, sinful, spiteful, troublesome, vicious, wicked

misconceive fail to understand, get one's lines crossed, get the wrong idea (about), misapprehend, misconstrue, misjudge, mistake, misunderstand

misconception delusion, error, fallacy, misapprehension, misconstruction, mistaken belief, misunderstanding, wrong end of the stick, wrong idea

misconduct **1.** *noun* delinquency, dereliction, immorality, impropriety, malfeasance (*Law*), malpractice, malversation (*rare*), misbehaviour, misdemeanour, mismanagement, naughtiness, rudeness, transgression, unethical behaviour, wrongdoing **2.** ~*verb* behave badly, botch (up), bungle, err, make a mess of, misdirect, mismanage, sin

misconstruction false interpretation, misapprehension, misinterpretation, misreading, mistake, mistaken *or* false impression, misunderstanding, wrong idea

misconstrue get a false impression, get one's lines crossed, make a wrong interpretation, misapprehend, misconceive, misinterpret, misjudge, misread, mistake, mistranslate, misunderstand, take the wrong way (*informal*)

miscreant **1.** *noun* blackguard, caitiff (*archaic*), criminal, evildoer, knave (*archaic*), malefactor, rascal, reprobate, rogue, scally (*Northwest English dialect*), scoundrel, sinner, skelm (*S. African*), vagabond, villain, wrongdoer **2.** ~*adjective* corrupt, criminal, depraved, evil, iniquitous, nefarious, rascally, reprehensible, reprobate, scoundrelly, unprincipled, vicious, villainous, wicked

misdeed crime, fault, misconduct, misdemeanour, offence, sin, transgression, trespass, villainy, wrong

misdemeanour fault, infringement, misbehaviour, misconduct, misdeed, offence, peccadillo, transgression, trespass

miser cheapskate (*informal*), churl (*archaic*), curmudgeon, hunks (*rare*), niggard, penny-pincher (*informal*), screw (*slang*), Scrooge, skinflint, tight-arse (*taboo slang*), tight-ass (*U.S. taboo slang*), tightwad (*U.S. & Canad. slang*)

miserable 1. afflicted, broken-hearted, crestfallen, dejected, depressed, desolate, despondent, disconsolate, dismal, distressed, doleful, down, downcast, down in the dumps (*informal*), down in the mouth (*informal*), forlorn, gloomy, heartbroken, low, melancholy, mournful, sorrowful, unhappy, woebegone, wretched **2.** destitute, dirt-poor (*informal*), down and out, flat broke (*informal*), impoverished, indigent, meagre, needy, penniless, poor, poverty-stricken, scanty, short, without two pennies to rub together (*informal*) **3.** abject, bad, contemptible, deplorable, despicable, detestable, disgraceful, lamentable, low, mean, pathetic, piteous, pitiable, scurvy, shabby, shameful, sordid, sorry, squalid, vile, worthless, wretched
▷ **Antonyms** (*sense 1*) cheerful, happy (*sense 2*) comfortable, rich (*sense 3*) admirable, good, respectable

miserliness avarice, cheeseparing, churlishness, close- *or* tightfistedness, covetousness, graspingness, meanness, minginess (*Brit. informal*), nearness, niggardliness, parsimony, penny-pinching (*informal*), penuriousness, stinginess

miserly avaricious, beggarly, close, close-fisted, covetous, grasping, illiberal, mean, mingy (*Brit. informal*), near, niggardly, parsimonious, penny-pinching (*informal*), penurious, snoep (*S. African informal*), sordid, stingy, tight-arsed (*taboo slang*), tight as a duck's arse (*taboo slang*), tight-assed (*U.S. taboo slang*), tightfisted, ungenerous
▷ **Antonyms** charitable, extravagant, generous, prodigal, unselfish

misery 1. agony, anguish, depression, desolation, despair, discomfort, distress, gloom, grief, hardship, melancholy, sadness, sorrow, suffering, torment, torture, unhappiness, woe, wretchedness **2.** affliction, bitter pill (*informal*), burden, calamity, catastrophe, curse, disaster, hardship, load, misfortune, ordeal, sorrow, trial, tribulation, trouble, woe **3.** destitution, indigence, need, penury, poverty, privation, sordidness, squalor, want, wretchedness **4.** *Brit. informal* grouch (*informal*), killjoy, moaner, pessimist, prophet of doom, sourpuss (*informal*), spoilsport, wet blanket (*informal*)
▷ **Antonyms** comfort, contentment, ease, enjoyment, happiness, joy, luxury, pleasure

misfire fail, fail to go off, fall through, go phut (*informal*), go wrong, miscarry

misfit eccentric, fish out of water (*informal*), nonconformist, oddball (*informal*), square peg (in a round hole) (*informal*)

misfortune 1. bad luck, evil fortune, hard luck, ill luck, infelicity **2.** accident, adversity, affliction, blow, bummer (*slang*), calamity, disaster, evil chance, failure, hardship, harm, loss, misadventure, mischance, misery, mishap, reverse, setback, stroke of bad luck, tragedy, trial, tribulation, trouble, whammy (*informal, chiefly U.S.*)
▷ **Antonyms** fortune, good luck, relief

misgiving anxiety, apprehension, distrust, doubt, dubiety, hesitation, qualm, reservation, scruple, suspicion, trepidation, uncertainty, unease, worry

misguided deluded, erroneous, foolish, ill-advised, imprudent, injudicious, labouring under a delusion *or* misapprehension, misled, misplaced, mistaken, uncalled-for, unreasonable, unwarranted, unwise

mishandle bodge (*informal*), botch, bungle, flub (*U.S. slang*), make a hash of (*informal*), make a mess of, make a nonsense of, mess up (*informal*), mismanage, muff, screw (up) (*informal*)

mishap accident, adversity, bad luck, calamity, contretemps, disaster, evil chance, evil fortune, hard luck, ill fortune, ill luck, infelicity, misadventure, mischance, misfortune

mishmash farrago, gallimaufry, hash, hotchpotch, jumble, medley, potpourri, salmagundi

misinform deceive, give (someone) a bum steer (*informal, chiefly U.S.*), give (someone) duff gen (*Brit. informal*), misdirect, misguide, mislead

misinterpret distort, falsify, get wrong, misapprehend, misconceive, misconstrue, misjudge, misread, misrepresent, mistake, misunderstand, pervert

misjudge be wrong about, get the wrong idea about, miscalculate, overestimate, overrate, underestimate, underrate

mislay be unable to find, be unable to put *or* lay one's hand on, forget the whereabouts of, lose, lose track of, misplace, miss

mislead beguile, bluff, deceive, delude, fool, give (someone) a bum steer (*informal, chiefly U.S.*), hoodwink, lead astray, misdirect, misguide, misinform, pull the wool over (someone's) eyes (*informal*), take for a ride (*informal*), take in (*informal*)

misleading ambiguous, casuistical, confusing, deceitful, deceptive, delusive, delusory, disingenuous, evasive, false, sophistical, specious, spurious, tricky

(*informal*), unstraightforward
▷ **Antonyms** candid, clear, correct, direct, explicit, frank, genuine, honest, obvious, open, plain, simple, sincere, straightforward, true, truthful

mismanage be incompetent, be inefficient, bodge (*informal*), botch, bungle, make a hash of (*informal*), make a mess of, make a nonsense of, maladminister, mess up, misconduct, misdirect, misgovern, mishandle

mismatched clashing, discordant, disparate, ill-assorted, incompatible, incongruous, irregular, misallied, unreconcilable, unsuited

misplace 1. be unable to find, be unable to put *or* lay one's hand on, forget the whereabouts of, lose, lose track of, misfile, mislay, miss, put in the wrong place **2.** place unwisely, place wrongly

misprint corrigendum, erratum, literal, mistake, printing error, typo (*informal*), typographical error

misprize disparage, fail to appreciate, hold cheap, look down on, set no store by, slight, underestimate, underrate, undervalue

misquote distort, falsify, garble, mangle, misreport, misrepresent, misstate, muddle, pervert, quote *or* take out of context, twist

misrepresent belie, disguise, distort, falsify, garble, misinterpret, misstate, pervert, twist

misrule 1. bad government, maladministration, misgovernment, mismanagement **2.** anarchy, chaos, confusion, disorder, lawlessness, tumult, turmoil

miss[1] *verb* **1.** avoid, be late for, blunder, err, escape, evade, fail, fail to grasp, fail to notice, forego, lack, leave out, let go, let slip, lose, miscarry, mistake, omit, overlook, pass over, pass up, skip, slip, trip **2.** feel the loss of, hunger for, long for, need, pine for, want, wish, yearn for *~noun* **3.** blunder, error, failure, fault, loss, mistake, omission, oversight, want

miss[2] *noun* damsel, girl, lass, lassie (*informal*), maid, maiden, schoolgirl, spinster, young lady

misshapen contorted, crippled, crooked, deformed, distorted, grotesque, ill-made, ill-proportioned, malformed, twisted, ugly, ungainly, unshapely, unsightly, warped, wry

missile projectile, rocket, weapon

missing absent, astray, gone, lacking, left behind, left out, lost, mislaid, misplaced, not present, nowhere to be found, unaccounted-for, wanting
▷ **Antonyms** accounted for, at hand, available, here, in attendance, on hand, present, there, to hand

mission 1. aim, assignment, business, calling, charge, commission, duty, errand, goal, job, office, operation, purpose, pursuit, quest, task, trust, undertaking, vocation, work **2.** commission, delegation, deputation, embassy, legation, ministry, task force

missionary apostle, converter, evangelist, preacher, propagandist, proselytizer

missive communication, dispatch, epistle, letter, memorandum, message, note, report

misspent dissipated, idle, imprudent, misapplied, prodigal, profitless, squandered, thrown away, wasted
▷ **Antonyms** active, fruitful, industrious, meaningful, profitable, useful, worthwhile

misstate distort, falsify, garble, give a false impression, misquote, misreport, misrepresent, pervert, twist

misstep bad move, blunder, error, false step, faux pas, gaffe, indiscretion, lapse, mistake, slip, slip-up (*informal*), stumble, trip, wrong move

mist 1. *noun* cloud, condensation, dew, drizzle, film, fog, haar (*Eastern Brit.*), haze, smog, smur *or* smir (*Scot.*), spray, steam, vapour **2.** *~verb* becloud, befog, blear, blur, cloud, film, fog, obscure, steam (up)

mistake *noun* **1.** bloomer (*Brit. informal*), blunder, boob (*Brit. slang*), boo-boo (*informal*), clanger (*informal*), erratum, error, error of judgment, false move, fault, faux pas, gaffe, goof (*informal*), howler (*informal*), inaccuracy, miscalculation, misconception, misstep, misunderstanding, oversight, slip, slip-up (*informal*), solecism *~verb* **2.** get wrong, misapprehend, misconceive, misconstrue, misinterpret, misjudge, misread, misunderstand **3.** accept as, confound, confuse with, misinterpret as, mix up with, take for **4.** be wide of *or* be off the mark, be wrong, blunder, boob (*Brit. slang*), drop a clanger (*informal*), err, goof (*informal*), miscalculate, misjudge, put one's foot in it (*informal*), slip up (*informal*)

mistaken barking up the wrong tree (*informal*), erroneous, fallacious, false, faulty, getting the wrong end of the stick (*informal*), inaccurate, inappropriate, incorrect, in the wrong, labouring under a misapprehension, misguided, misinformed, misled, off base (*U.S. & Canad. informal*), off beam (*informal*), off target, off the mark, unfounded, unsound, way off beam (*informal*), wide of the mark, wrong
▷ **Antonyms** accurate, correct, logical, right, sound, true

mistakenly by mistake, erroneously, fallaciously, falsely, inaccurately, inappropriately, incorrectly, in error, misguidedly, wrongly

mistimed badly timed, ill-timed, inconvenient, inopportune, unseasonable, unsynchronized, untimely

mistreat abuse, brutalize, handle roughly, harm, ill-treat, ill-use, injure, knock about *or* around, maltreat, manhandle, maul, misuse, molest, rough up, wrong

mistreatment abuse, brutalization, harm, ill-treatment, ill-usage, injury, maltreatment, manhandling, mauling, misuse, molestation, rough handling, roughing up, unkindness

mistress concubine, doxy (*archaic*), fancy bit (*slang*), fancy woman (*slang*), floozy (*slang*), girlfriend, inamorata, kept woman, ladylove (*rare*), lover, paramour

mistrust 1. *verb* apprehend, beware, be wary of, distrust, doubt, fear, have doubts about, suspect **2.** *~noun* apprehension, distrust, doubt, dubiety, fear, misgiving, scepticism, suspicion, uncertainty, wariness

mistrustful apprehensive, cautious, chary, cynical, distrustful, doubtful, dubious, fearful, hesitant, leery (*slang*), nervous, sceptical, suspicious, uncertain, wary

▷ **Antonyms** certain, definite, positive, sure, unafraid

misty bleary, blurred, cloudy, dark, dim, foggy, fuzzy, hazy, indistinct, murky, nebulous, obscure, opaque, overcast, unclear, vague

▷ **Antonyms** bright, clear, distinct, lucid, obvious, plain, sunny, well-defined

misunderstand be at cross-purposes, get (it) wrong, get one's lines crossed, get one's wires crossed, get the wrong end of the stick, get the wrong idea (about), misapprehend, misconceive, misconstrue, mishear, misinterpret, misjudge, misread, miss the point (of), mistake

misunderstanding 1. error, false impression, misapprehension, misconception, misconstruction, misinterpretation, misjudgment, misreading, mistake, mix-up, wrong idea **2.** argument, breach, conflict, difference, difficulty, disagreement, discord, dissension, falling-out (*informal*), quarrel, rift, rupture, squabble, variance

misunderstood misconstrued, misheard, misinterpreted, misjudged, misread, unappreciated, unrecognized

misuse *noun* **1.** abuse, barbarism, catachresis, corruption, desecration, dissipation, malapropism, misapplication, misemployment, misusage, perversion, profanation, solecism, squandering, waste **2.** abuse, cruel treatment, exploitation, harm, ill-treatment, ill-usage, inhumane treatment, injury, maltreatment, manhandling, mistreatment, rough handling *~verb* **3.** abuse, corrupt, desecrate, dissipate, misapply, misemploy, pervert, profane, prostitute, squander, waste **4.** abuse, brutalize, exploit, handle roughly, harm, ill-treat, ill-use, injure, maltreat, manhandle, maul, mistreat, molest, wrong

▷ **Antonyms** *~verb* appreciate, cherish, honour, prize, respect, treasure, use

mitigate abate, allay, appease, assuage, blunt, calm, check, diminish, dull, ease, extenuate, lessen, lighten, moderate, modify, mollify, pacify, palliate, placate, quiet, reduce the force of, remit, soften, soothe, subdue, take the edge off, temper, tone down, tranquillize, weaken

▷ **Antonyms** aggravate, augment, enhance, heighten, increase, intensify, strengthen

mitigation abatement, allaying, alleviation, assuagement, diminution, easement, extenuation, moderation, mollification, palliation, relief, remission

mix *verb* **1.** alloy, amalgamate, associate, blend, coalesce, combine, commingle, commix, compound, cross, fuse, incorporate, intermingle, interweave, join, jumble, meld, merge, mingle, put together, unite **2.** associate, come together, consort, fraternize, hang out (*informal*), hobnob, join, mingle, socialize *~noun* **3.** alloy, amalgam, assortment, blend, combination, compound, fusion, medley, meld, mixed bag (*informal*), mixture

mixed 1. alloyed, amalgamated, blended, combined, composite, compound, fused, incorporated, joint, mingled, united **2.** assorted, cosmopolitan, diverse, diversified, heterogeneous, manifold, miscellaneous, motley, varied **3.** crossbred, hybrid, interbred, interdenominational, mongrel **4.** ambivalent, equivocal, indecisive, uncertain

▷ **Antonyms** homogeneous, isolated, pure, straight, unmixed

mixed-up at sea, bewildered, confused, distraught, disturbed, maladjusted, muddled, perplexed, puzzled, upset

mixture admixture, alloy, amalgam, amalgamation, association, assortment, blend, brew, combine, composite, compound, concoction, conglomeration, cross, fusion, hotchpotch, jumble, medley, *mélange,* meld, miscellany, mix, mixed bag (*informal*), potpourri, salmagundi, union, variety

mix-up confusion, disorder, fankle (*Scot.*), jumble, mess, mistake, misunderstanding, muddle, snarl-up (*informal, chiefly Brit.*), tangle

mix up 1. blend, combine, commix, mix **2.** confound, confuse, muddle **3.** bewilder, confuse, disturb, fluster, muddle, perplex, puzzle, throw into confusion, unnerve, upset **4.** embroil, entangle, implicate, involve, rope in

moan *noun* **1.** groan, lament, lamentation, sigh, sob, sough, wail, whine **2.** *informal* beef (*slang*), bitch (*slang*), complaint, gripe (*informal*), grouch (*informal*), grouse, grumble, kvetch (*U.S. slang*), protest, whine *~verb* **3.** bemoan, bewail, deplore, grieve, groan, keen, la~

ment, mourn, sigh, sob, sough, whine **4.** *informal* beef (*slang*), bitch (*slang*), bleat, carp, complain, gripe (*informal*), groan, grouch (*informal*), grouse, grumble, moan and groan, whine, whinge (*informal*)

mob *noun* **1.** assemblage, body, collection, crowd, drove, flock, gang, gathering, herd, horde, host, mass, multitude, pack, press, swarm, throng **2.** class, company, crew (*informal*), gang, group, lot, set, troop **3.** *canaille*, commonalty, great unwashed (*informal & derogatory*), hoi polloi, masses, rabble, riffraff, scum *~verb* **4.** crowd around, jostle, overrun, set upon, surround, swarm around **5.** cram into, crowd, crowd into, fill, fill to overflowing, jam, pack

mobile 1. ambulatory, itinerant, locomotive, migrant, motile, movable, moving, peripatetic, portable, travelling, wandering **2.** animated, changeable, ever-changing, expressive

mobilize activate, animate, call to arms, call up, get *or* make ready, marshal, muster, organize, prepare, put in motion, rally, ready

mock *verb* **1.** chaff, deride, flout, insult, jeer, laugh at, laugh to scorn, make a monkey out of, make fun of, poke fun at, ridicule, scoff, scorn, show contempt for, sneer, take the mickey (out of) (*informal*), take the piss (out of) (*taboo slang*), taunt, tease, wind up (*Brit. slang*) **2.** ape, burlesque, caricature, counterfeit, do (*informal*), imitate, lampoon, mimic, parody, satirize, send up (*Brit. informal*), take off (*informal*), travesty **3.** belie, cheat, deceive, delude, disappoint, dupe, elude, fool, let down, mislead **4.** defeat, defy, disappoint, foil, frustrate, thwart *~noun* **5.** banter, derision, gibe, jeering, mockery, ridicule, scorn, sneer, sneering **6.** Aunt Sally (*Brit.*), butt, dupe, fool, jest, laughing stock, sport, travesty **7.** counterfeit, fake, forgery, fraud, imitation, phoney *or* phony (*informal*), sham *~adjective* **8.** artificial, bogus, counterfeit, dummy, ersatz, fake, faked, false, feigned, forged, fraudulent, imitation, phoney *or* phony (*informal*), pretended, pseudo (*informal*), sham, spurious

▷ **Antonyms** *~verb* encourage, praise, respect, revere *~adjective* authentic, genuine, natural, real, sincere, true, unfeigned

mockery 1. contempt, contumely, derision, disdain, disrespect, gibes, insults, jeering, ridicule, scoffing, scorn **2.** burlesque, caricature, deception, farce, imitation, lampoon, laughing stock, mimicry, parody, pretence, send-up (*Brit. informal*), sham, spoof (*informal*), take-off (*informal*), travesty **3.** apology, disappointment, farce, joke, letdown

mocking contemptuous, contumelious, derisive, derisory, disdainful, disrespectful, insulting, irreverent, sarcastic, sardonic, satiric, satirical, scoffing, scornful, taunting

mode 1. approach, condition, course, custom, fashion, form, manner, method, plan, practice, procedure, process, quality, rule, state, style, system, technique, vein, way **2.** craze, fashion, look, rage, style, trend, vogue

model *noun* **1.** copy, dummy, facsimile, image, imitation, miniature, mock-up, replica, representation **2.** archetype, design, epitome, example, exemplar, gauge, ideal, lodestar, mould, norm, original, par, paradigm, paragon, pattern, prototype, standard, type **3.** poser, sitter, subject **4.** mannequin **5.** configuration, design, form, kind, mark, mode, stamp, style, type, variety, version *~verb* **6.** base, carve, cast, design, fashion, form, mould, pattern, plan, sculpt, shape, stamp **7.** display, show off, sport (*informal*), wear *~adjective* **8.** copy, dummy, facsimile, imitation, miniature **9.** archetypal, exemplary, ideal, illustrative, paradigmatic, perfect, standard, typical

▷ **Antonyms** *~adjective* (*sense 9*) deficient, flawed, impaired, imperfect

moderate *adjective* **1.** calm, controlled, cool, deliberate, equable, gentle, judicious, limited, middle-of-the-road, mild, modest, peaceable, reasonable, restrained, sober, steady, temperate **2.** average, fair, fairish, fair to middling (*informal*), indifferent, mediocre, medium, middling, ordinary, passable, so-so (*informal*), unexceptional *~verb* **3.** abate, allay, appease, assuage, calm, clear the air, control, curb, decrease, diminish, ease, lessen, mitigate, modulate, pacify, play down, quiet, regulate, relax, repress, restrain, soften, soft-pedal (*informal*), subdue, tame, temper, tone down **4.** arbitrate, chair, judge, mediate, preside, referee, take the chair

▷ **Antonyms** *~adjective* (*sense 1*) extreme, intemperate, ruffled, unreasonable, wild (*sense 2*) excessive, expensive, extreme, immoderate, inordinate, unusual *~verb* (*sense 3*) heighten, increase, intensify

moderately fairly, gently, in moderation, passably, quite, rather, reasonably, slightly, somewhat, to a degree, tolerably, to some extent, within limits, within reason

moderation 1. calmness, composure, coolness, equanimity, fairness, judiciousness, justice, justness, mildness, moderateness, reasonableness, restraint, sedateness, temperance **2. in moderation** moderately, within limits, within reason

modern contemporary, current, fresh, late, latest, neoteric (*rare*), new, newfangled, novel, present, present-day, re~

cent, twentieth-century, up-to-date, up-to-the-minute, with it (*informal*)

▷ **Antonyms** ancient, antiquated, archaic, former, obsolete, old, old-fashioned, old hat, outmoded, passé, past, square (*informal*), uncool (*slang*)

modernity contemporaneity, currency, freshness, innovation, newness, novelty, recentness

modernize bring into the twentieth century, bring up to date, face-lift, make over, rejuvenate, remake, remodel, renew, renovate, revamp, update

modest **1.** bashful, blushing, coy, demure, diffident, discreet, humble, meek, quiet, reserved, reticent, retiring, self-conscious, self-effacing, shy, simple, unassuming, unpretentious **2.** fair, limited, middling, moderate, ordinary, small, unexceptional

modesty bashfulness, coyness, decency, demureness, diffidence, discreetness, humbleness, humility, lack of pretension, meekness, propriety, quietness, reserve, reticence, self-effacement, shyness, simplicity, timidity, unobtrusiveness, unpretentiousness

▷ **Antonyms** arrogance, assurance, boastfulness, boldness, conceit, confidence, egotism, extravagance, forwardness, haughtiness, immodesty, indecency, ostentation, presumption, pretentiousness, pride, showiness, vanity

modicum atom, bit, crumb, dash, drop, fragment, grain, inch, iota, little, mite, ounce, particle, pinch, scrap, shred, small amount, speck, tad (*informal, chiefly U.S.*), tinge, touch

modification adjustment, alteration, change, modulation, mutation, qualification, refinement, reformation, restriction, revision, variation

modify **1.** adapt, adjust, alter, change, convert, recast, redo, refashion, reform, remodel, reorganize, reshape, revise, rework, transform, tweak (*informal*), vary **2.** abate, ease, lessen, limit, lower, moderate, qualify, reduce, relax, restrain, restrict, soften, temper, tone down

modish à la mode, all the rage, chic, contemporary, current, fashionable, hip (*slang*), in, now (*informal*), smart, stylish, trendy (*Brit. informal*), up-to-the-minute, vogue, voguish, with it (*informal*)

modulate adjust, attune, balance, harmonize, inflect, regulate, tone, tune, vary

modus operandi method, operation, practice, praxis, procedure, process, system, technique, way

mogul baron, bashaw, big cheese (*slang, old-fashioned*), big gun (*informal*), big noise (*informal*), big shot (*informal*), big wheel (*slang*), lord, magnate, nabob (*informal*), nob (*slang, chiefly Brit.*), notable, personage, potentate, tycoon, V.I.P.

moiety fifty percent, half, part, piece, portion, share

moist clammy, damp, dampish, dank, dewy, dripping, drizzly, humid, not dry, rainy, soggy, wet, wettish

moisten bedew, damp, dampen, humidify, lick, moisturize, soak, water, wet

moisture damp, dampness, dankness, dew, humidity, liquid, perspiration, sweat, water, wateriness, wetness

mole breakwater, dike, dyke, embankment, groyne, jetty, pier, sea wall

molecule atom, iota, jot, mite, mote, particle, speck

molest **1.** abuse, afflict, annoy, badger, beset, bother, bug (*informal*), disturb, harass, harry, hector, irritate, persecute, pester, plague, tease, torment, upset, vex, worry **2.** abuse, accost, assail, attack, harm, hurt, ill-treat, injure, interfere with, maltreat, manhandle

mollify **1.** appease, calm, compose, conciliate, pacify, placate, pour oil on troubled waters, propitiate, quell, quiet, soothe, sweeten **2.** abate, allay, assuage, blunt, curb, cushion, ease, lessen, lull, mitigate, moderate, modify, relieve, soften, temper, tone down, tranquillize

mollycoddle **1.** *verb* baby, coddle, cosset, indulge, pamper, pet, ruin, spoil **2.** *~noun* baby, chinless wonder (*Brit. informal*), crybaby, milksop, milquetoast (*U.S.*), namby-pamby, sissy, weakling

moment **1.** bat of an eye (*informal*), flash, instant, jiffy (*informal*), minute, no time, second, shake (*informal*), split second, tick (*Brit. informal*), trice, twinkling, two shakes (*informal*), two shakes of a lamb's tail (*informal*) **2.** hour, instant, juncture, point, point in time, stage, time **3.** concern, consequence, gravity, import, importance, seriousness, significance, substance, value, weight, weightiness, worth

momentarily briefly, for a little while, for a minute, for a moment, for an instant, for a second, for a short time, for a short while, for the nonce, temporarily

momentary brief, ephemeral, evanescent, fleeting, flying, fugitive, hasty, passing, quick, short, short-lived, temporary, transitory

▷ **Antonyms** lasting, lengthy, long-lived, permanent

momentous consequential, critical, crucial, decisive, earth-shaking (*informal*), fateful, grave, historic, important, of moment, pivotal, serious, significant, vital, weighty

▷ **Antonyms** inconsequential, insignificant, trifling, trivial, unimportant

momentum drive, energy, force, impetus,

power, propulsion, push, strength, thrust

monarch crowned head, emperor, empress, king, potentate, prince, princess, queen, ruler, sovereign

monarchy **1.** absolutism, autocracy, despotism, kingship, monocracy, royalism, sovereignty **2.** empire, kingdom, principality, realm

monastery abbey, cloister, convent, friary, house, nunnery, priory, religious community

monastic ascetic, austere, celibate, cenobitic, cloistered, cloistral, coenobitic, contemplative, conventual, eremitic, hermit-like, monachal, monkish, recluse, reclusive, secluded, sequestered, withdrawn

monetary budgetary, capital, cash, financial, fiscal, pecuniary

money **1.** ackers (*slang*), banknotes, brass (*Northern English dialect*), bread (*slang*), capital, cash, coin, currency, dibs (*slang*), dosh (*Brit. & Austral. slang*), dough (*slang*), filthy lucre (*facetious*), funds, gelt (*slang, chiefly U.S.*), green (*slang*), hard cash, legal tender, lolly (*Brit. slang*), loot (*informal*), mazuma (*slang, chiefly U.S.*), megabucks (*U.S. & Canad. slang*), moolah (*slang*), necessary (*informal*), needful (*informal*), pelf (*contemptuous*), readies (*informal*), rhino (*Brit. slang*), riches, shekels (*informal*), silver, specie, spondulicks (*slang*), the ready (*informal*), the wherewithal, tin (*slang*), wealth **2.** **in the money** affluent, flush (*informal*), in clover (*informal*), loaded (*slang*), on Easy Street (*informal*), prosperous, rich, rolling (*slang*), wealthy, well-heeled (*informal*), well-off, well-to-do

moneyed, monied affluent, flush (*informal*), loaded (*slang*), prosperous, rich, wealthy, well-heeled (*informal*), well-off, well-to-do

moneymaking *adjective* gainful, going, lucrative, paying, profitable, remunerative, successful, thriving

mongrel **1.** *noun* bigener (*Biology*), cross, crossbreed, half-breed, hybrid, mixed breed **2.** *~adjective* bastard, crossbred, half-breed, hybrid, of mixed breed

monitor **1.** *noun* guide, invigilator, overseer, prefect (*Brit.*), supervisor, watchdog **2.** *~verb* check, follow, keep an eye on, keep tabs on, keep track of, observe, oversee, record, scan, supervise, survey, watch

monitory admonishing, admonitory, cautionary, cautioning, reproving, warning

monk brother, friar (*loosely*), monastic, religious

monkey *noun* **1.** jackanapes (*archaic*), primate, simian **2.** devil, imp, mischief maker, pickle (*Brit. informal*), rascal, rogue, scamp **3.** *slang* ass, butt, dupe, fool, laughing stock **4.** **make a monkey of** make a fool of, make (someone) a laughing stock, make fun of, make (someone) look foolish, make (someone) look ridiculous, make (someone) look silly, play a trick on, ridicule *~verb* **5.** fiddle (*informal*), fool, interfere, meddle, mess, play, tamper, tinker, trifle

monkey business **1.** carry-on (*informal, chiefly Brit.*), clowning, horseplay, mischief, monkey tricks, pranks, shenanigans (*informal*), skylarking (*informal*), tomfoolery **2.** chicanery, dishonesty, funny business, hanky-panky (*informal*), skulduggery (*informal*), trickery

monolithic colossal, giant, gigantic, huge, immovable, impenetrable, imposing, intractable, massive, monumental, solid, substantial, undifferentiated, undivided, unitary

monologue harangue, lecture, sermon, soliloquy, speech

monomania bee in one's bonnet (*informal*), fanaticism, fixation, hobbyhorse, *idée fixe,* obsession, one-track mind (*informal*)

monopolize control, corner, corner the market in, dominate, engross, exercise *or* have a monopoly of, hog (*slang*), keep to oneself, take over, take up

monotonous all the same, boring, colourless, droning, dull, flat, ho-hum (*informal*), humdrum, mind-numbing, plodding, repetitious, repetitive, samey (*informal*), soporific, tedious, tiresome, toneless, unchanging, uniform, uninflected, unvaried, wearisome

▷ **Antonyms** animated, enjoyable, entertaining, enthralling, exciting, exhilarating, interesting, lively, sexy (*informal*), stimulating

monotony boredom, colourlessness, dullness, flatness, humdrumness, monotonousness, repetitiousness, repetitiveness, routine, sameness, tediousness, tedium, tiresomeness, uniformity, wearisomeness

monster *noun* **1.** barbarian, beast, bogeyman, brute, demon, devil, fiend, ghoul, ogre, savage, villain **2.** abortion, freak, lusus naturae, miscreation, monstrosity, mutant, teratism **3.** behemoth, Brobdingnagian, colossus, giant, leviathan, mammoth, titan *~adjective* **4.** Brobdingnagian, colossal, elephantine, enormous, gargantuan, giant, gigantic, ginormous (*informal*), huge, humongous *or* humungous (*U.S. slang*), immense, jumbo (*informal*), mammoth, massive, mega (*slang*), monstrous, stellar (*informal*), stupendous, titanic, tremendous

monstrosity **1.** abortion, eyesore, freak, horror, lusus naturae, miscreation, monster, mutant, ogre, teratism **2.** abnormality, atrocity, dreadfulness, evil, frightfulness, heinousness, hellishness, hideousness, horror, loathsomeness, obscenity

monstrous 1. abnormal, dreadful, enormous, fiendish, freakish, frightful, grotesque, gruesome, hellish, hideous, horrendous, horrible, miscreated, obscene, teratoid, terrible, unnatural **2.** atrocious, cruel, devilish, diabolical, disgraceful, egregious, evil, fiendish, foul, heinous, horrifying, infamous, inhuman, intolerable, loathsome, odious, outrageous, satanic, scandalous, shocking, vicious, villainous **3.** colossal, elephantine, enormous, gargantuan, giant, gigantic, ginormous (*informal*), great, huge, humongous *or* humungous (*U.S. slang*), immense, mammoth, massive, mega (*slang*), prodigious, stellar (*informal*), stupendous, titanic, towering, tremendous, vast

▷ **Antonyms** (*sense 1*) appealing, attractive, beautiful, delightful, lovely, natural, normal, ordinary, pleasant (*sense 2*) admirable, decent, fine, good, honourable, humane, kind, merciful, mild (*sense 3*) diminutive, insignificant, little, meagre, miniature, minute, puny, slight, small, tiny

month four weeks, moon, thirty days

monument 1. cairn, cenotaph, commemoration, gravestone, headstone, marker, mausoleum, memorial, obelisk, pillar, shrine, statue, tombstone **2.** memento, record, remembrance, reminder, testament, token, witness

monumental 1. awe-inspiring, awesome, classic, enduring, enormous, epoch-making, historic, immortal, important, lasting, majestic, memorable, outstanding, prodigious, significant, stupendous, unforgettable **2.** commemorative, cyclopean, funerary, memorial, monolithic, statuary **3.** *informal* catastrophic, colossal, egregious, gigantic, great, horrible, immense, indefensible, massive, staggering, terrible, tremendous, unforgivable, whopping (*informal*)

▷ **Antonyms** (*sense 1*) ephemeral, inconsequential, insignificant, modest, negligible, ordinary, trivial, undistinguished, unimportant, unimpressive, unremarkable (*sense 3*) average, insignificant, mild, petty, slight, small, tiny, trivial

mood 1. disposition, frame of mind, humour, spirit, state of mind, temper, tenor, vein **2.** bad temper, bate (*Brit. slang*), blues, depression, doldrums, dumps (*informal*), fit of pique, grumps (*informal*), low spirits, melancholy, sulk, the hump (*Brit. informal*), the sulks, wax (*informal, chiefly Brit.*) **3. in the mood** disposed (towards), eager, favourable, inclined, interested, in the (right) frame of mind, keen, minded, willing

moody 1. angry, broody, cantankerous, crabbed, crabby, crestfallen, cross, crotchety (*informal*), crusty, curt, dismal, doleful, dour, downcast, down in the dumps (*informal*), down in the mouth (*informal*), frowning, gloomy, glum, huffish, huffy, ill-humoured, ill-tempered, in a huff, in the doldrums, introspective, irascible, irritable, lugubrious, melancholy, miserable, mopish, mopy, morose, offended, out of sorts (*informal*), pensive, petulant, piqued, sad, saturnine, short-tempered, splenetic, sulky, sullen, temperamental, testy, tetchy, touchy, waspish, wounded **2.** capricious, changeable, erratic, faddish, fickle, fitful, flighty, impulsive, inconstant, mercurial, temperamental, unpredictable, unstable, unsteady, volatile

▷ **Antonyms** (*sense 1*) amiable, cheerful, compatible, gay, happy, optimistic (*sense 2*) constant, stable, steady

moon *noun* **1.** satellite **2. once in a blue moon** almost never, hardly ever, rarely, very seldom *~verb* **3.** daydream, idle, languish, mooch (*slang*), mope, waste time

moonshine 1. moonbeams, moonlight **2.** *U.S.* bootleg, hooch *or* hootch (*informal, chiefly U.S. & Canad.*), poteen **3.** blather, blether, bosh (*informal*), bunk (*informal*), bunkum *or* buncombe (*chiefly U.S.*), claptrap (*informal*), foolish talk, gas (*informal*), guff (*slang*), havers (*Scot.*), hogwash, hot air (*informal*), nonsense, piffle (*informal*), rubbish, stuff and nonsense, tarradiddle, tosh (*slang, chiefly Brit.*), trash, tripe (*informal*), twaddle

moor[1] *noun* fell (*Brit.*), heath, moorland, muir (*Scot.*)

moor[2] *verb* anchor, berth, dock, fasten, fix, lash, make fast, secure, tie up

moot 1. *adjective* arguable, at issue, contestable, controversial, debatable, disputable, doubtful, open, open to debate, undecided, unresolved, unsettled **2.** *~verb* bring up, broach, introduce, propose, put forward, suggest, ventilate

mop *noun* **1.** sponge, squeegee, swab **2.** mane, shock, tangle, thatch *~verb* **3.** clean, soak up, sponge, swab, wash, wipe

mope be apathetic, be dejected, be down in the mouth (*informal*), be gloomy, brood, eat one's heart out, fret, go about like a half-shut knife (*informal*), hang around, have a long face, idle, languish, moon, pine, pout, sulk, waste time, wear a long face

mop up 1. clean up, mop, soak up, sponge, swab, wash, wipe **2.** *Military* account for, clean out, clear, eliminate, finish off, neutralize, pacify, round up, secure

moral *adjective* **1.** ethical **2.** blameless, chaste, decent, ethical, good, high-minded, honest, honourable, incorruptible, innocent, just, meritorious, noble, principled, proper, pure, right, right~

eous, upright, upstanding, virtuous *~noun* **3.** lesson, meaning, message, point, significance **4.** adage, aphorism, apophthegm, epigram, gnome, maxim, motto, proverb, saw, saying

▷ **Antonyms** *~adjective* amoral, dishonest, dishonourable, immoral, improper, sinful, unethical, unfair, unjust, wrong

morale confidence, esprit de corps, heart, mettle, self-esteem, spirit, temper

morality 1. chastity, decency, ethicality, ethicalness, goodness, honesty, integrity, justice, principle, rectitude, righteousness, rightness, uprightness, virtue **2.** conduct, ethics, habits, ideals, manners, moral code, morals, mores, philosophy, principles, standards

morals behaviour, conduct, ethics, habits, integrity, manners, morality, mores, principles, scruples, standards

morass 1. bog, fen, marsh, marshland, moss (*Scot. & northern English dialect*), quagmire, slough, swamp **2.** chaos, confusion, jam (*informal*), mess, mix-up, muddle, quagmire, tangle

moratorium freeze, halt, postponement, respite, standstill, stay, suspension

morbid 1. brooding, funereal, ghoulish, gloomy, grim, melancholy, pessimistic, sick, sombre, unhealthy, unwholesome **2.** dreadful, ghastly, grisly, gruesome, hideous, horrid, macabre **3.** ailing, deadly, diseased, infected, malignant, pathological, sick, sickly, unhealthy, unsound

▷ **Antonyms** bright, cheerful, happy, healthy, salubrious, wholesome

mordant 1. acerbic, acid, acrimonious, astringent, biting, caustic, cutting, edged, harsh, incisive, mordacious, pungent, sarcastic, scathing, sharp, stinging, trenchant, venomous, vitriolic, waspish **2.** acid, acidic, caustic, corrosive, pungent, vitriolic

more 1. *adjective* added, additional, extra, fresh, further, new, other, spare, supplementary **2.** *~adverb* better, further, longer, to a greater extent

moreover additionally, also, as well, besides, further, furthermore, in addition, into the bargain, likewise, to boot, too, what is more, withal (*literary*)

morgue mortuary

moribund 1. at death's door, breathing one's last, doomed, dying, fading fast, failing, (having) one foot in the grave, *in extremis,* near death, near the end, on one's deathbed, on one's last legs **2.** at a standstill, declining, forceless, obsolescent, on its last legs, on the way out, stagnant, stagnating, standing still, waning, weak

morning a.m., break of day, dawn, daybreak, forenoon, morn (*poetic*), morrow (*archaic*), sunrise

moron airhead (*slang*), ass, berk (*Brit. slang*), blockhead, bonehead (*slang*), charlie (*Brit. informal*), chump, coot, cretin, dickhead (*slang*), dimwit (*informal*), dipstick (*Brit. slang*), divvy (*Brit. slang*), dolt, dope (*informal*), dork (*slang*), dummy (*slang*), dunce, dunderhead, dweeb (*U.S. slang*), fathead (*informal*), fool, fuckwit (*taboo slang*), geek (*slang*), gobshite (*Irish taboo slang*), gonzo (*slang*), halfwit, idiot, imbecile, jerk (*slang, chiefly U.S. & Canad.*), lamebrain (*informal*), mental defective, muttonhead (*slang*), nerd *or* nurd (*slang*), nitwit (*informal*), numbskull *or* numskull, numpty (*Scot. informal*), oaf, pillock (*Brit. slang*), plank (*Brit. slang*), plonker (*slang*), prat (*slang*), prick (*derogatory slang*), schmuck (*U.S. slang*), simpleton, thickhead, tosser (*Brit. slang*), twit (*informal, chiefly Brit.*), wally (*slang*)

moronic asinine, Boeotian, braindead (*informal*), brainless, cretinous, daft (*informal*), dead from the neck up (*informal*), dimwitted (*informal*), doltish, foolish, gormless (*Brit. informal*), half-witted, idiotic, imbecilic, mentally defective, mindless, muttonheaded (*slang*), retarded, simple, stupid, thick, unintelligent

morose blue, churlish, crabbed, crabby, cross, crusty, depressed, dour, down, down in the dumps (*informal*), gloomy, glum, grouchy (*informal*), gruff, ill-humoured, ill-natured, ill-tempered, in a bad mood, low, melancholy, miserable, moody, mournful, perverse, pessimistic, saturnine, sour, sulky, sullen, surly, taciturn

▷ **Antonyms** amiable, blithe, cheerful, chirpy (*informal*), friendly, gay, genial, good-humoured, good-natured, happy, pleasant, sweet

morsel bit, bite, crumb, fraction, fragment, grain, mouthful, nibble, part, piece, scrap, segment, slice, snack, soupçon, tad (*informal, chiefly U.S.*), taste, titbit

mortal *adjective* **1.** corporeal, earthly, ephemeral, human, impermanent, passing, sublunary, temporal, transient, worldly **2.** deadly, death-dealing, destructive, fatal, killing, lethal, murderous, terminal **3.** bitter, deadly, implacable, irreconcilable, out-and-out, remorseless, sworn, to the death, unrelenting **4.** agonizing, awful, dire, enormous, extreme, grave, great, intense, serious, severe, terrible *~noun* **5.** being, body, earthling, human, human being, individual, man, person, woman

mortality 1. ephemerality, humanity, impermanence, temporality, transience **2.** bloodshed, carnage, death, destruction, fatality, killing, loss of life

mortification **1**. abasement, annoyance, chagrin, discomfiture, dissatisfaction, embarrassment, humiliation, loss of face, shame, vexation **2**. abasement, chastening, control, denial, discipline, subjugation **3**. *Medical* corruption, festering, gangrene, necrosis, putrescence

mortified **1**. abashed, affronted, annoyed, ashamed, chagrined, chastened, confounded, crushed, deflated, discomfited, displeased, embarrassed, given a showing-up (*informal*), humbled, humiliated, made to eat humble pie (*informal*), put down, put out (*informal*), put to shame, rendered speechless, shamed, vexed **2**. abased, chastened, conquered, controlled, crushed, disciplined, subdued **3**. *of flesh* decayed, gangrenous, necrotic, rotted

mortify **1**. abase, abash, affront, annoy, chagrin, chasten, confound, crush, deflate, disappoint, discomfit, displease, embarrass, humble, humiliate, make (someone) eat humble pie (*informal*), put down, put to shame, shame, take (someone) down a peg (*informal*), vex **2**. abase, chasten, control, deny, discipline, subdue **3**. *of flesh* become gangrenous, corrupt, deaden, die, fester, gangrene, necrose, putrefy

mortuary funeral home (*U.S.*), funeral parlour, morgue

mostly above all, almost entirely, as a rule, chiefly, customarily, for the most part, generally, largely, mainly, most often, on the whole, particularly, predominantly, primarily, principally, usually

mote atom, grain, mite, particle, speck, spot

moth-eaten antiquated, decayed, decrepit, dilapidated, grungy (*slang, chiefly U.S.*), obsolete, outdated, outworn, ragged, scuzzy (*slang, chiefly U.S.*), seedy, shabby, stale, tattered, threadbare, worn-out

mother *noun* **1**. dam, ma (*informal*), mater, mom (*U.S. informal*), mum (*Brit. informal*), mummy (*Brit. informal*), old lady (*informal*), old woman (*informal*) *~adjective* **2**. connate, inborn, innate, native, natural *~verb* **3**. bear, bring forth, drop, give birth to, produce **4**. care for, cherish, nurse, nurture, protect, raise, rear, tend **5**. baby, fuss over, indulge, pamper, spoil

motherly affectionate, caring, comforting, fond, gentle, kind, loving, maternal, protective, sheltering, tender, warm

mother wit brains, common sense, gumption (*Brit. informal*), horse sense, judgment, native intelligence, nous (*Brit. slang*), savvy (*slang*), smarts (*slang, chiefly U.S.*)

motif **1**. concept, idea, leitmotif, subject, theme **2**. decoration, design, form, ornament, shape

motion *noun* **1**. action, change, flow, kinesics, locomotion, mobility, motility, move, movement, passage, passing, progress, travel **2**. gesticulation, gesture, sign, signal, wave **3**. proposal, proposition, recommendation, submission, suggestion **4**. **in motion** afoot, functioning, going, in progress, moving, on the go (*informal*), on the move (*informal*), operational, travelling, under way, working *~verb* **5**. beckon, direct, gesticulate, gesture, nod, signal, wave

motionless at a standstill, at rest, calm, fixed, frozen, halted, immobile, inanimate, inert, lifeless, paralysed, standing, static, stationary, still, stock-still, transfixed, unmoved, unmoving

▷ **Antonyms** active, agitated, animated, frantic, lively, mobile, moving, restless, travelling

motivate actuate, arouse, bring, cause, draw, drive, get going, give incentive to, impel, induce, inspire, inspirit, instigate, lead, move, persuade, prod, prompt, provoke, set off, set on, stimulate, stir, trigger

motivation **1**. ambition, desire, drive, hunger, inspiration, interest, wish **2**. carrot and stick, impulse, incentive, incitement, inducement, inspiration, instigation, motive, persuasion, reason, spur, stimulus

motive **1**. *noun* cause, design, ground(s), incentive, incitement, inducement, influence, inspiration, intention, mainspring, motivation, object, occasion, purpose, rationale, reason, spur, stimulus, the why and wherefore, thinking **2**. *~adjective* activating, driving, impelling, motivating, moving, operative, prompting

motley **1**. assorted, disparate, dissimilar, diversified, heterogeneous, mingled, miscellaneous, mixed, unlike, varied **2**. chequered, multicoloured, particoloured, polychromatic, polychrome, polychromous, rainbow, variegated

▷ **Antonyms** (*sense 1*) homogeneous, similar, uniform (*sense 2*) monochromatic, plain, self-coloured, solid

mottled blotchy, brindled, chequered, dappled, flecked, freckled, marbled, piebald, pied, speckled, spotted, stippled, streaked, tabby, variegated

motto adage, byword, cry, dictum, formula, gnome, maxim, precept, proverb, rule, saw, saying, slogan, watchword

mould[1] *noun* **1**. cast, die, form, matrix, pattern, shape, stamp **2**. brand, build, configuration, construction, cut, design, fashion, form, format, frame, kind, line, make, pattern, shape, stamp, structure, style **3**. calibre, character, ilk, kidney, kind, nature, quality, sort, stamp, type *~verb* **4**. carve, cast, construct, create, fashion, forge, form, make, model, sculpt, shape, stamp, work **5**. affect, control, direct, form, influence, make, shape

mould[2] *noun* blight, fungus, mildew, mouldiness, mustiness

mould[3] *noun* dirt, earth, humus, loam, soil

moulder break down, crumble, decay, decompose, disintegrate, perish, rot, waste

mouldy bad, blighted, decaying, fusty, mildewed, musty, rotten, rotting, spoiled, stale

mound 1. bing (*Scot.*), drift, heap, pile, rick, stack **2.** bank, dune, embankment, hill, hillock, knoll, rise **3.** *Archaeology* barrow, tumulus **4.** bulwark, earthwork, motte (*History*), rampart

mount *verb* **1.** ascend, clamber up, climb, escalade, go up, make one's way up, scale **2.** bestride, climb onto, climb up on, get astride, get (up) on, jump on **3.** arise, ascend, rise, soar, tower **4.** accumulate, build, escalate, grow, increase, intensify, multiply, pile up, swell **5.** display, frame, set, set off **6.** exhibit, get up (*informal*), prepare, produce, put on, stage **7.** *Military* deliver, launch, prepare, ready, set in motion, stage **8.** emplace, fit, install, place, position, put in place, set up ~*noun* **9.** backing, base, fixture, foil, frame, mounting, setting, stand, support **10.** horse, steed (*literary*)

▷ **Antonyms** (*sense 1*) descend, drop, go down, make one's way down (*sense 2*) climb down from, climb off, dismount, get down from, get off, jump off (*sense 4*) contract, decline, decrease, diminish, dwindle, fall, lessen, lower, reduce, shrink, wane

mountain 1. alp, ben (*Scot.*), berg (*S. Afr.*), elevation, eminence, fell (*Brit.*), height, mount, Munro, peak **2.** abundance, heap, mass, mound, pile, stack, ton

mountainous 1. alpine, high, highland, rocky, soaring, steep, towering, upland **2.** daunting, enormous, gigantic, great, huge, hulking, immense, mammoth, mighty, monumental, ponderous, prodigious

▷ **Antonyms** (*sense 2*) diminutive, insignificant, little, minute, petty, puny, small, tiny, trivial, weak

mountebank charlatan, cheat, chiseller (*informal*), confidence trickster, con man (*informal*), fake, fraud, fraudster, grifter (*slang, chiefly U.S. & Canad.*), hustler (*U.S. informal*), impostor, phoney *or* phony (*informal*), pretender, quack, rogue, swindler

mourn bemoan, bewail, deplore, grieve, keen, lament, miss, rue, sorrow, wail, wear black, weep

mournful 1. afflicting, calamitous, deplorable, distressing, grievous, harrowing, lamentable, melancholy, painful, piteous, plaintive, sad, sorrowful, tragic, unhappy, woeful **2.** brokenhearted, cheerless, desolate, disconsolate, dismal, downcast, down in the dumps (*informal*), funereal, gloomy, grief-stricken, grieving, heartbroken, heavy, heavy-hearted, joyless, lugubrious, melancholy, miserable, rueful, sad, sombre, unhappy, woeful

▷ **Antonyms** (*sense 1*) agreeable, cheerful, fortunate, happy, lucky, pleasant, satisfying (*sense 2*) bright, cheerful, chirpy (*informal*), genial, happy, jolly, joyful, light-hearted, sunny, upbeat (*informal*)

mourning 1. bereavement, grief, grieving, keening, lamentation, weeping, woe **2.** black, sackcloth and ashes, weeds, widow's weeds

mousy, mousey 1. brownish, colourless, drab, dull, indeterminate, plain **2.** diffident, ineffectual, quiet, self-effacing, shy, timid, timorous, unassertive

mouth *noun* **1.** chops (*slang*), gob (*slang, especially Brit.*), jaws, lips, maw, trap (*slang*), yap (*slang*) **2.** *informal* boasting, braggadocio, bragging, empty talk, gas (*informal*), hot air (*slang*), idle talk **3.** *informal* backchat (*informal*), cheek (*informal*), impudence, insolence, lip (*slang*), rudeness, sauce (*informal*) **4.** aperture, cavity, crevice, door, entrance, gateway, inlet, lips, opening, orifice, rim **5.** face, grimace, *moue,* pout, wry face **6. down in** *or* **at the mouth** blue, crestfallen, dejected, depressed, disheartened, dispirited, down, downcast, down in the dumps (*informal*), in low spirits, melancholy, miserable, sad, sick as a parrot (*informal*), unhappy

mouthful bit, bite, drop, forkful, little, morsel, sample, sip, spoonful, sup, swallow, taste

mouthpiece 1. agent, delegate, representative, spokesman, spokeswoman **2.** journal, organ, periodical, publication

movable detachable, mobile, not fixed, portable, portative, transferable, transportable

movables belongings, chattels, effects, furniture, gear, goods, possessions, property, stuff (*informal*), things (*informal*)

move *verb* **1.** advance, budge, change position, drift, go, march, proceed, progress, shift, stir, walk **2.** carry, change, shift, switch, transfer, transport, transpose **3.** change residence, flit (*Scot. & northern English dialect*), go away, leave, migrate, move house, pack one's bags (*informal*), quit, relocate, remove **4.** activate, drive, impel, motivate, operate, prod, propel, push, set going, shift, shove, start, turn **5.** actuate, affect, agitate, cause, excite, give rise to, impel, impress, incite, induce, influence, inspire, instigate, lead, make an impression on, motivate, persuade, prompt, rouse, stimulate, touch, tug at (someone's) heartstrings (*often facetious*), urge **6.** advocate, propose, put forward, recommend, suggest, urge *~noun* **7.** act, action, deed, manoeuvre, measure, motion, movement, ploy, shift, step, stratagem, stroke, turn **8.** change of address, flit (*Scot. & northern English dialect*), flitting (*Scot. & northern English dialect*), migration, relocation, removal, shift, transfer **9. get a move on** get cracking (*informal*), get going, hurry (up), make haste, shake a leg (*informal*), speed up, step on it (*informal*), stir oneself **10. on the move** *informal* **a.** in transit, journeying, moving, on the road (*informal*), on the run, on the wing, travelling, under way, voyaging **b.** active, advancing, astir, going forward, moving, progressing, stirring, succeeding

▷ **Antonyms** (*sense 5*) deter, discourage, dissuade, prevent, stop

movement 1. act, action, activity, advance, agitation, change, development, displacement, exercise, flow, gesture, manoeuvre, motion, move, moving, operation, progress, progression, shift, steps, stir, stirring, transfer **2.** camp, campaign, crusade, drive, faction, front, group, grouping, organization, party **3.** current, drift, flow, swing, tendency, trend **4.** action, innards (*informal*), machinery, mechanism, workings, works **5.** *Music* division, part, passage, section **6.** beat, cadence, measure (*Prosody*), metre, pace, rhythm, swing, tempo

movie 1. feature, film, flick (*slang*), motion picture, moving picture (*U.S.*), picture **2.** *plural* cinema, film, films, flicks (*slang*), pictures (*informal*), silver screen (*informal*)

moving 1. affecting, arousing, emotional, emotive, exciting, impelling, impressive, inspiring, pathetic, persuasive, poignant, stirring, touching **2.** mobile, motile, movable, portable, running, unfixed **3.** dynamic, impelling, inspirational, motivating, propelling, stimulating, stimulative

▷ **Antonyms** (*sense 1*) unemotional, unexciting, unimpressive, uninspiring (*sense 2*) fixed, immobile, immovable, stationary, still, unmoving

mow crop, cut, scythe, shear, trim

mow down blow away (*slang, chiefly U.S.*), butcher, cut down, cut to pieces, massacre, shoot down, slaughter

much 1. *adjective* abundant, a lot of, ample, considerable, copious, great, plenteous, plenty of, sizeable, substantial **2.** *~adverb* a great deal, a lot, considerably, decidedly, exceedingly, frequently, greatly, indeed, often, regularly **3.** *~noun* a good deal, a great deal, a lot, an appreciable amount, heaps (*informal*), loads (*informal*), lots (*informal*), plenty

▷ **Antonyms** *~adjective* inadequate, insufficient, little, scant *~adverb* barely, hardly, infrequently, irregularly, not a lot, not much, occasionally, only just, rarely, scarcely, seldom, slightly *~noun* hardly anything, little, next to nothing, not a lot, not much, practically nothing, very little

muck 1. crap (*taboo slang*), dung, manure, ordure, shit (*taboo slang*) **2.** crap (*slang*), crud (*slang*), dirt, filth, grot (*slang*), gunge (*informal*), gunk (*informal*), kak (*S. African informal*), mire, mud, ooze, scum, sewage, shit (*taboo slang*), slime, slob (*Irish*), sludge **3. make a muck of** *slang* blow (*slang*), botch, bungle, cock up (*Brit. slang*), flub (*U.S. slang*), fuck up (*offensive taboo slang*), make a mess of, make a nonsense of, make a pig's ear of (*informal*), mar, mess up, muff, ruin, screw up (*informal*), spoil

muck up blow (*slang*), bodge (*informal*), botch, bungle, cock up (*Brit. slang*), flub (*U.S. slang*), fuck up (*offensive taboo slang*), make a mess of, make a muck of (*slang*), make a nonsense of, make a pig's ear of (*informal*), mar, mess up, muff, ruin, screw up (*informal*), spoil

mucky begrimed, bespattered, dirty, filthy, grimy, messy, mud-caked, muddy, soiled, sticky

mucous glutinous, gummy, mucilaginous, slimy, viscid, viscous

mud clay, dirt, gloop (*informal*), mire, ooze, silt, slime, slob (*Irish*), sludge

muddle *verb* **1.** confuse, disarrange, disorder, disorganize, jumble, make a mess of, mess, muddle, ravel, scramble, spoil, tangle **2.** befuddle, bewilder, confound, confuse, daze, disorient, perplex, stupefy *~noun* **3.** chaos, clutter, confusion, daze, disarray, disorder, disorganization, fankle (*Scot.*), hodgepodge (*U.S.*), hotchpotch, jumble, mess, mix-up, perplexity, pig's breakfast (*informal*), plight, predicament, ravel, tangle

muddle along *or* **through** cope, get along, get by (*informal*), make it, manage, manage somehow, scrape by

muddled 1. chaotic, confused, disarrayed, disordered, disorganized, higgledy-piggledy (*informal*), jumbled, messy, mixed-up, scrambled, tangled **2.** at sea, befuddled, bewildered, confused, dazed, disoriented, perplexed, stupefied, vague **3.** confused, incoherent, loose, muddleheaded, unclear, woolly

▷ **Antonyms** clear, cut-and-dried (*informal*), exact, orderly, organized, precise

muddy *adjective* **1.** bespattered, boggy, clarty (*Scot., & northern English dialect*), dirty, grimy, marshy, miry, mucky, mud-caked, quaggy, soiled, swampy **2.** blurred, dingy, dull, flat, lustreless, smoky, unclear, washed-out **3.** cloudy, dirty, foul, impure, opaque, turbid **4.** confused, fuzzy, hazy, indistinct, mud~

dled, unclear, vague, woolly *~verb* **5.** begrime, bespatter, cloud, dirty, smear, smirch, soil

muff *verb* bodge (*informal*), botch, bungle, cock up (*Brit. slang*), flub (*U.S. slang*), fluff (*informal*), fuck up (*offensive taboo slang*), make a mess of, make a muck of (*informal*), make a nonsense of, make a pig's ear of (*informal*), mess up, mismanage, screw up (*informal*), spoil

muffle 1. cloak, conceal, cover, disguise, envelop, hood, mask, shroud, swaddle, swathe, wrap up **2.** deaden, dull, gag, hush, muzzle, quieten, silence, soften, stifle, suppress

muffled dim, dull, faint, indistinct, muted, stifled, strangled, subdued, suppressed

mug[1] *noun* beaker, cup, flagon, jug, pot, stein, tankard, toby jug

mug[2] *noun* clock (*Brit. slang*), countenance, dial (*slang*), face, features, kisser (*slang*), mush (*Brit. slang*), phiz *or* phizog (*Brit. slang*), puss (*slang*), visage

mug[3] 1. *noun* charlie (*Brit. informal*), chump (*informal*), easy *or* soft touch (*slang*), fool, gull (*archaic*), innocent, mark (*slang*), muggins (*Brit. slang*), simpleton, sucker (*slang*) **2.** *~verb* assail, assault, attack, beat up, do over (*Brit., Austral., & N.Z. slang*), duff up (*Brit. slang*), hold up, lay into (*informal*), put the boot in (*slang*), rob, set about *or* upon, steam (*informal*), work over (*slang*)

muggy clammy, close, damp, humid, moist, oppressive, sticky, stuffy, sultry

mug up bone up on (*informal*), burn the midnight oil (*informal*), cram (*informal*), get up (*informal*), study, swot (*Brit. informal*)

mulish bull-headed, cross-grained, difficult, headstrong, inflexible, intractable, intransigent, obstinate, perverse, pig-headed, recalcitrant, refractory, rigid, self-willed, stiff-necked, stubborn, unreasonable, wilful

mull consider, contemplate, deliberate, examine, meditate, muse on, ponder, reflect on, review, ruminate, study, think about, think over, turn over in one's mind, weigh

multifarious different, diverse, diversified, legion, manifold, many, miscellaneous, multiform, multiple, multitudinous, numerous, sundry, varied, variegated

multiple collective, manifold, many, multitudinous, numerous, several, sundry, various

multiplicity abundance, array, diversity, heaps (*informal*), host, loads (*informal*), lot, lots (*informal*), mass, myriad, number, oodles (*informal*), piles (*informal*), profusion, scores, stacks, tons, variety

multiply accumulate, augment, breed, build up, expand, extend, increase, proliferate, propagate, reproduce, spread

▷ **Antonyms** abate, decline, decrease, diminish, lessen, reduce

multitude 1. army, assemblage, assembly, collection, concourse, congregation, crowd, great number, horde, host, legion, lot, lots (*informal*), mass, mob, myriad, sea, swarm, throng **2.** commonalty, common people, herd, hoi polloi, mob, populace, proletariat, public, rabble

multitudinous abounding, abundant, considerable, copious, countless, great, infinite, innumerable, legion, manifold, many, myriad, numerous, profuse, teeming, very numerous

mum 1. closemouthed, dumb, mute, quiet, secretive, silent, tight-lipped, uncommunicative, unforthcoming **2. mum's the word** don't let on, don't tell a soul, keep quiet, keep silent, keep (something) secret, keep (something) to oneself, keep (something) under one's hat, play dumb, say nothing, tell no-one

mumbo jumbo 1. abracadabra, chant, charm, conjuration, hocus-pocus, incantation, magic, rite, ritual, spell, superstition **2.** cant, claptrap (*informal*), double talk, gibberish, gobbledegook (*informal*), Greek (*informal*), humbug, jargon, nonsense, rigmarole

mumsy dowdy, drab, fogeyish, frumpy *or* frumpish, homely, old-fashioned, plain, square (*informal*), unfashionable, unglamorous, unsophisticated

▷ **Antonyms** attractive, beautiful, chic, elegant, fashionable, glamorous, modern, modish, smart, sophisticated, well-dressed

munch champ, chew, chomp, crunch, masticate, scrunch

mundane 1. banal, commonplace, day-to-day, everyday, humdrum, ordinary, prosaic, routine, vanilla (*slang*), workaday **2.** earthly, fleshly, human, material, mortal, secular, sublunary, temporal, terrestrial, worldly

▷ **Antonyms** (*sense 1*) dramatic, exciting, extraordinary, ground-breaking, imaginative, interesting, left-field (*informal*), novel, original, special, uncommon, unusual (*sense 2*) ethereal, heavenly, spiritual, unworldly

municipal borough, city, civic, community, public, town, urban

municipality borough, burgh (*Scot.*), city, district, town, township, urban community

munificence beneficence, benevolence, big-heartedness, bounteousness, bounty, generosity, generousness, largesse *or* largess, liberality, magnanimousness, open-handedness, philanthropy

munificent beneficent, benevolent, big-hearted, bounteous, bountiful, free-handed, generous, lavish, liberal, magnanimous, open-handed, philanthropical, princely, rich, unstinting
▷ **Antonyms** cheap, mean, miserly, parsimonious, small, stingy

murder *noun* **1.** assassination, bloodshed, butchery, carnage, homicide, killing, manslaughter, massacre, slaying **2.** *informal* agony, an ordeal, a trial, danger, difficulty, hell (*informal*), misery, trouble *~verb* **3.** assassinate, blow away (*slang, chiefly U.S.*), bump off (*slang*), butcher, destroy, dispatch, do in (*informal*), do to death, eliminate (*slang*), hit (*slang*), kill, massacre, rub out (*U.S. slang*), slaughter, slay, take out (*slang*), take the life of, waste (*informal*) **4.** abuse, butcher, destroy, mangle, mar, misuse, ruin, spoil **5.** *informal* beat decisively, blow out of the water (*slang*), cream (*slang, chiefly U.S.*), defeat utterly, drub, hammer (*informal*), lick (*informal*), make mincemeat of (*informal*), slaughter, stuff (*slang*), tank (*slang*), thrash, wipe the floor with (*informal*)

murderer assassin, butcher, cut-throat, hit man (*slang*), homicide, killer, slaughterer, slayer

murderous **1.** barbarous, bloodthirsty, bloody, brutal, cruel, cut-throat, deadly, death-dealing, destructive, devastating, fatal, fell (*archaic*), ferocious, internecine, lethal, sanguinary, savage, slaughterous, withering **2.** *informal* arduous, dangerous, difficult, exhausting, harrowing, hellish (*informal*), killing (*informal*), sapping, strenuous, unpleasant

murky cheerless, cloudy, dark, dim, dismal, dreary, dull, dusky, foggy, gloomy, grey, impenetrable, misty, nebulous, obscure, overcast
▷ **Antonyms** bright, cheerful, clear, distinct, sunny

murmur **1.** *noun* babble, buzzing, drone, humming, mumble, muttering, purr, rumble, susurrus (*literary*), undertone, whisper, whispering **2.** *~verb* babble, buzz, drone, hum, mumble, mutter, purr, rumble, speak in an undertone, whisper **3.** *~noun* beef (*slang*), complaint, gripe (*informal*), grouse, grumble, moan (*informal*), word **4.** *~verb* beef (*slang*), carp, cavil, complain, gripe (*informal*), grouse, grumble, moan (*informal*)

muscle *noun* **1.** muscle tissue, sinew, tendon, thew **2.** brawn, clout (*informal*), force, forcefulness, might, potency, power, stamina, strength, sturdiness, weight *~verb* **3.** **muscle in** *informal* butt in, elbow one's way in, force one's way in, impose oneself

muscular athletic, beefy (*informal*), brawny, husky (*informal*), lusty, powerful, powerfully built, robust, sinewy, stalwart, strapping, strong, sturdy, thickset, vigorous, well-knit

muse be in a brown study, be lost in thought, brood, cogitate, consider, contemplate, deliberate, dream, meditate, mull over, ponder, reflect, ruminate, speculate, think, think over, weigh

Muses, the *Greek myth* Camenae (*Roman myth*), Pierides (*Greek myth*)

mush **1.** dough, mash, pap, paste, pulp **2.** *informal* corn (*informal*), mawkishness, schmaltz (*slang*), sentimentality, slush (*informal*)

mushroom *verb* boom, burgeon, expand, flourish, grow rapidly, increase, luxuriate, proliferate, shoot up, spread, spring up, sprout

mushy **1.** doughy, pappy, paste-like, pulpy, semi-liquid, semi-solid, slushy, soft, squashy, squelchy, squidgy (*informal*) **2.** *informal* corny (*slang*), maudlin, mawkish, saccharine, schmaltzy (*slang*), sentimental, sloppy (*informal*), slushy (*informal*), sugary, syrupy, weepy, wet (*Brit. informal*)

musical dulcet, euphonic, euphonious, harmonious, lilting, lyrical, melodic, melodious, sweet-sounding, tuneful
▷ **Antonyms** discordant, grating, harsh, unmelodious, unmusical

musing *noun* absent-mindedness, abstraction, brooding, brown study, cerebration, cogitation, contemplation, day-dreaming, introspection, meditation, reflection, reverie, rumination, thinking, woolgathering

must[1] *noun* duty, essential, fundamental, imperative, necessary thing, necessity, obligation, prerequisite, requirement, requisite, *sine qua non*

must[2] *noun* decay, fetor, fustiness, mildew, mould, mouldiness, mustiness, rot

muster *verb* **1.** assemble, call together, call up, collect, come together, congregate, convene, convoke, enrol, gather, group, marshal, meet, mobilize, rally, round up, summon *~noun* **2.** assemblage, assembly, collection, concourse, congregation, convention, convocation, gathering, meeting, mobilization, rally, round-up **3.** **pass muster** be acceptable, be *or* come up to scratch, fill the bill (*informal*), make the grade, measure up, qualify

musty **1.** airless, dank, decayed, frowsty, fusty, mildewed, mildewy, mouldy, old, smelly, stale, stuffy **2.** ancient, antediluvian, antiquated, banal, clichéd, dull, hackneyed, hoary, moth-eaten, obsolete, old-fashioned, stale, threadbare, trite, worn-out
▷ **Antonyms** (*sense 2*) current, exciting, fashionable, fresh, imaginative, inter~

esting, lively, modern, modish, new, novel, original, unusual, up-to-date, with it (*informal*)

mutability alteration, change, evolution, metamorphosis, transition, variation, vicissitude

mutable adaptable, alterable, change~ able, changing, fickle, flexible, immu~ table, inconsistent, inconstant, irreso~ lute, uncertain, undependable, unreli~ able, unsettled, unstable, unsteady, vacillating, variable, volatile, wavering

mutation 1. alteration, change, deviation, evolution, metamorphosis, modification, transfiguration, transformation, vari~ ation **2.** anomaly, deviant, mutant

mute 1. *adjective* aphasiac, aphasic, aphonic, dumb, mum, silent, speechless, unexpressed, unspeaking, unspoken, voiceless, wordless **2.** *~verb* dampen, deaden, lower, moderate, muffle, soften, soft-pedal, subdue, tone down, turn down

mutilate 1. amputate, butcher, cripple, cut to pieces, cut up, damage, disable, disfigure, dismember, hack, injure, lac~ erate, lame, maim, mangle **2.** adulter~ ate, bowdlerize, butcher, censor, cut, damage, distort, expurgate, hack, mar, spoil

mutinous bolshie (*Brit. informal*), contu~ macious, disobedient, insubordinate, in~ surgent, rebellious, refractory, revolu~ tionary, riotous, seditious, subversive, turbulent, ungovernable, unmanage~ able, unruly

mutiny 1. *noun* defiance, disobedience, insubordination, insurrection, rebellion, refusal to obey orders, resistance, revolt, revolution, riot, rising, strike, uprising **2.** *~verb* be insubordinate, defy author~ ity, disobey, rebel, refuse to obey orders, resist, revolt, rise up, strike

mutt 1. berk (*Brit. slang*), charlie (*Brit. informal*), coot, dickhead (*slang*), dip~ stick (*Brit. slang*), divvy (*Brit. slang*), dolt, dork (*slang*), dunderhead, dweeb (*U.S. slang*), fool, fuckwit (*taboo slang*), geek (*slang*), gobshite (*Irish taboo slang*), gonzo (*slang*), idiot, ignoramus, imbecile (*informal*), jerk (*slang, chiefly U.S. & Canad.*), moron, nerd *or* nurd (*slang*), numbskull *or* numskull, numpty (*Scot. informal*), pillock (*Brit. slang*), plank (*Brit. slang*), plonker (*slang*), prat (*slang*), prick (*derogatory slang*), schmuck (*U.S. slang*), thickhead, twit (*informal, chiefly Brit.*), wally (*slang*) **2.** cur, dog, mongrel

mutter complain, grouch (*informal*), grouse, grumble, mumble, murmur, rumble

mutual common, communal, correlative, interactive, interchangeable, inter~ changed, joint, reciprocal, reciprocated, requited, returned, shared

muzzle *noun* **1.** jaws, mouth, nose, snout **2.** gag, guard *~verb* **3.** censor, choke, curb, gag, restrain, silence, stifle, sup~ press

myopic near-sighted, short-sighted

myriad 1. *adjective* a thousand and one, countless, immeasurable, incalculable, innumerable, multitudinous, untold **2.** *~noun* a million, army, a thousand, flood, horde, host, millions, mountain, multitude, scores, sea, swarm, thou~ sands

mysterious abstruse, arcane, baffling, cloak-and-dagger, concealed, covert, cryptic, curious, dark, Delphic, enig~ matic, furtive, hidden, impenetrable, incomprehensible, inexplicable, inscru~ table, insoluble, mystical, mystifying, obscure, perplexing, puzzling, recondite, secret, secretive, sphinxlike, strange, uncanny, unfathomable, unknown, veiled, weird

▷ **Antonyms** apparent, clear, intelligible, manifest, open, plain

mystery cloak and dagger, closed book, conundrum, enigma, problem, puzzle, question, riddle, secrecy, secret, teaser

mystic, mystical abstruse, arcane, caba~ listic, cryptic, enigmatical, esoteric, hid~ den, inscrutable, metaphysical, mys~ terious, nonrational, occult, other~ worldly, paranormal, preternatural, supernatural, transcendental

mystify baffle, bamboozle (*informal*), be all Greek to (*informal*), beat (*slang*), be~ fog, bewilder, confound, confuse, elude, escape, flummox, nonplus, perplex, puz~ zle, stump

mystique awe, charisma, charm, fascina~ tion, glamour, magic, spell

myth 1. allegory, fable, fairy story, fic~ tion, folk tale, legend, parable, saga, story, tradition, urban legend **2.** delu~ sion, fancy, fantasy, figment, illusion, imagination, superstition, tall story

mythical 1. allegorical, chimerical, fabled, fabulous, fairy-tale, legendary, mytho~ logical, storied **2.** fabricated, fanciful, fantasy, fictitious, imaginary, invented, made-up, make-believe, nonexistent, pretended, unreal, untrue

mythological fabulous, folkloric, heroic, legendary, mythic, mythical, traditional

mythology folklore, folk tales, legend, lore, mythos, myths, stories, tradition

N, n

nab apprehend, arrest, capture, catch, catch in the act, collar (*informal*), feel one's collar (*slang*), grab, lift (*slang*), nail (*informal*), nick (*slang, chiefly Brit.*), seize, snatch

nabob billionaire, Croesus, fat cat (*informal*), millionaire, moneybags (*informal*), multimillionaire

nadir bottom, depths, lowest point, minimum, rock bottom, zero

▷ **Antonyms** acme, apex, climax, crest, height, high point, peak, pinnacle, summit, top, vertex, zenith

nag[1] **1.** *verb* annoy, badger, bend someone's ear (*informal*), be on one's back (*slang*), berate, breathe down someone's neck, chivvy, goad, harass, harry, hassle (*informal*), henpeck, irritate, nark (*Brit., Austral., & N.Z. slang*), pester, plague, provoke, scold, torment, upbraid, vex, worry **2.** *~noun* harpy, scold, shrew, tartar, termagant, virago

nag[2] *noun* hack, horse, jade, plug (*U.S.*)

nagging continuous, critical, distressing, irritating, on someone's back (*informal*), painful, persistent, scolding, shrewish, worrying

naiad nymph, Oceanid (*Greek myth*), sprite, undine, water nymph

nail *verb* attach, beat, fasten, fix, hammer, join, pin, secure, tack

naive 1. artless, candid, childlike, confiding, frank, guileless, ingenuous, innocent, jejune, natural, open, simple, trusting, unaffected, unpretentious, unsophisticated, unworldly **2.** as green as grass, callow, credulous, green, gullible, unsuspicious, wet behind the ears (*informal*)

▷ **Antonyms** artful, disingenuous, experienced, sly, sophisticated, urbane, worldly, worldly-wise

naïveté, naivety 1. artlessness, candour, frankness, guilelessness, inexperience, ingenuousness, innocence, naturalness, openness, simplicity **2.** callowness, credulity, gullibility

naked 1. bare, buck naked (*slang*), denuded, disrobed, divested, exposed, in one's birthday suit (*informal*), in the altogether (*informal*), in the bare scud (*slang*), in the buff (*informal*), in the raw (*informal*), naked as the day one was born (*informal*), nude, scuddy (*slang*), starkers (*informal*), stripped, unclothed, unconcealed, uncovered, undraped, undressed, without a stitch on (*informal*) **2.** blatant, evident, manifest, open, overt, patent, plain, simple, stark, unadorned, undisguised, unexaggerated, unmistakable, unqualified, unvarnished **3.** defenceless, helpless, insecure, unarmed, unguarded, unprotected, vulnerable, wide open

▷ **Antonyms** (*sense 1*) clothed, concealed, covered, dressed, wrapped up (*sense 2*) concealed

nakedness 1. baldness, bareness, nudity, undress **2.** openness, plainness, simplicity, starkness

namby-pamby anaemic, colourless, feeble, insipid, mawkish, niminy-piminy, prim, prissy (*informal*), sentimental, spineless, vapid, weak, weedy (*informal*), wimpish *or* wimpy (*informal*), wishy-washy (*informal*)

name *noun* **1.** appellation, cognomen, denomination, designation, epithet, handle (*slang*), moniker *or* monicker (*slang*), nickname, sobriquet, term, title **2.** distinction, eminence, esteem, fame, honour, note, praise, renown, repute **3.** character, credit, reputation *~verb* **4.** baptize, call, christen, denominate, dub, entitle, label, style, term **5.** appoint, choose, cite, classify, commission, designate, flag, identify, mention, nominate, select, specify

named 1. baptized, called, christened, denominated, dubbed, entitled, known as, labelled, styled, termed **2.** appointed, chosen, cited, classified, commissioned, designated, identified, mentioned, nominated, picked, selected, singled out, specified

nameless 1. anonymous, innominate, undesignated, unnamed, untitled **2.** incognito, obscure, undistinguished, unheard-of, unknown, unsung **3.** abominable, horrible, indescribable, ineffable, inexpressible, unmentionable, unspeakable, unutterable

namely i.e., specifically, that is to say, to wit, viz.

nap[1] **1.** *verb* catnap, doze, drop off (*informal*), drowse, kip (*Brit. slang*), nod, nod off (*informal*), rest, sleep, snooze (*infor-*

mal), zizz (*Brit. informal*) **2.** *~noun* catnap, forty winks (*informal*), kip (*Brit. slang*), rest, shuteye (*slang*), siesta, sleep, zizz (*Brit. informal*)

nap[2] *noun* down, fibre, grain, pile, shag, weave

narcissism egotism, self-admiration, self-love, vanity

narcotic 1. *noun* anaesthetic, analgesic, anodyne, drug, opiate, painkiller, sedative, tranquillizer **2.** *~adjective* analgesic, calming, dulling, hypnotic, Lethean, numbing, painkilling, sedative, somnolent, soporific, stupefacient, stupefactive, stupefying

nark aggravate (*informal*), annoy, bother, bug, exasperate, gall, get on one's nerves (*informal*), irk, irritate, miff (*informal*), nettle, peeve, pique, piss one off (*taboo slang*), provoke, rile

narrate chronicle, describe, detail, recite, recount, rehearse, relate, repeat, report, set forth, tell, unfold

narration description, explanation, reading, recital, rehearsal, relation, storytelling, telling, voice-over (*in film*)

narrative account, chronicle, detail, history, report, statement, story, tale

narrator annalist, author, bard, chronicler, commentator, raconteur, reciter, relater, reporter, storyteller, writer

narrow *adjective* **1.** circumscribed, close, confined, constricted, contracted, cramped, incapacious, limited, meagre, near, pinched, restricted, scanty, straitened, tight **2.** biased, bigoted, dogmatic, illiberal, insular, intolerant, narrow-minded, partial, prejudiced, puritan, reactionary, small-minded **3.** attenuated, fine, slender, slim, spare, tapering, thin **4.** exclusive, select **5.** *informal* avaricious, close (*informal*), mean, mercenary, niggardly, ungenerous *~verb* **6.** circumscribe, constrict, diminish, limit, reduce, simplify, straiten, tighten

▷ **Antonyms** (*sense 1*) ample, big, broad, generous, open, spacious, wide (*sense 2*) broad-minded, generous, liberal, receptive, tolerant (*sense 3*) broad, wide (*sense 5*) generous, liberal

narrowly 1. barely, by a whisker *or* hair's-breadth, by the skin of one's teeth, just, only just, scarcely **2.** carefully, closely, painstakingly, scrutinizingly

narrow-minded biased, bigoted, conservative, hidebound, illiberal, insular, intolerant, opinionated, parochial, petty, prejudiced, provincial, reactionary, short-sighted, small-minded, strait-laced

▷ **Antonyms** broad-minded, catholic, cosmopolitan, freethinking, indulgent, open-minded, permissive, tolerant, unprejudiced

narrows channel, gulf, passage, sound, straits

nascent beginning, budding, dawning, developing, evolving, incipient

nastiness 1. defilement, dirtiness, filth, filthiness, foulness, impurity, pollution, squalor, uncleanliness **2.** indecency, licentiousness, obscenity, pollution, porn (*informal*), pornography, ribaldry, smuttiness **3.** disagreeableness, malice, meanness, offensiveness, spitefulness, unpleasantness

nasty 1. dirty, disagreeable, disgusting, filthy, foul, grotty (*slang*), horrible, loathsome, malodorous, mephitic, nauseating, noisome, objectionable, obnoxious, odious, offensive, polluted, repellent, repugnant, sickening, unappetizing, unpleasant, vile, yucky *or* yukky (*slang*) **2.** blue, foul, gross, impure, indecent, lascivious, lewd, licentious, obscene, pornographic, ribald, smutty **3.** abusive, annoying, bad-tempered, despicable, disagreeable, distasteful, malicious, mean, spiteful, unpleasant, vicious, vile **4.** bad, critical, dangerous, painful, serious, severe

▷ **Antonyms** (*sense 1*) admirable, agreeable, enjoyable, nice, pleasant, sweet (*sense 2*) clean, decent (*sense 3*) decent, kind, nice, pleasant, sweet

nation commonwealth, community, country, people, population, race, realm, society, state, tribe

national *adjective* **1.** civil, countrywide, governmental, nationwide, public, state, widespread **2.** domestic, internal, social *~noun* **3.** citizen, inhabitant, native, resident, subject

nationalism allegiance, chauvinism, fealty, jingoism, loyalty, nationality, patriotism

nationalistic chauvinistic, jingoistic, loyal, patriotic, xenophobic

nationality birth, ethnic group, nation, race

nationwide countrywide, general, national, overall, widespread

native *adjective* **1.** built-in, congenital, endemic, hereditary, immanent, inborn, inbred, indigenous, ingrained, inherent, inherited, innate, instinctive, intrinsic, inveterate, natal, natural **2.** genuine, original, real **3.** domestic, home, home-grown, home-made, indigenous, local, mother, vernacular **4.** aboriginal, autochthonous *~noun* **5.** aborigine, autochthon, citizen, countryman, dweller, inhabitant, national, resident

nativity 1. birth, delivery, parturition **2.** crèche, manger scene

▷ **Antonyms** (*sense 1*) death, demise, dying, expiration

natter 1. *verb* blather, blether, chatter, chew the fat *or* rag (*slang*), gabble, gossip, jabber, jaw (*slang*), palaver, prate, prattle, rabbit (on) (*Brit. informal*), run off at the mouth (*slang*), shoot the breeze (*informal*), talk, talk idly, witter (*informal*) **2.** *~noun* blather, blether, chat, chinwag (*Brit. informal*), chitchat, confabulation, conversation, gab (*informal*), gabble, gabfest (*informal, chiefly U.S. & Canad.*), gossip, jabber, jaw (*slang*), palaver, prattle, talk

natty chic, crucial (*slang*), dapper, elegant, fashionable, neat, smart, snazzy (*informal*), spruce, stylish, trendy (*Brit. informal*), trim, well-dressed, well-turned-out

natural 1. common, everyday, legitimate, logical, normal, ordinary, regular, typical, usual **2.** characteristic, congenital, essential, immanent, inborn, indigenous, inherent, innate, in one's blood, instinctive, intuitive, natal, native **3.** artless, candid, frank, genuine, ingenuous, open, real, simple, spontaneous, unaffected, unpretentious, unsophisticated, unstudied **4.** organic, plain, pure, unbleached, unmixed, unpolished, unrefined, whole

▷ **Antonyms** (*sense 1*) abnormal, irregular, out of the ordinary, strange, untypical (*sense 3*) affected, artificial, assumed, counterfeit, feigned, phoney *or* phony (*informal*), unnatural (*sense 4*) manufactured, processed, synthetic, unnatural

naturalism factualism, realism, verisimilitude

naturalist 1. biologist, botanist, ecologist, zoologist **2.** factualist, realist

naturalistic factualistic, kitchen sink, lifelike, photographic, realistic, real-life, representational, true-to-life, vérité, warts and all (*informal*)

naturalize acclimate, acclimatize, acculturate, accustom, adapt, adopt, domesticate, enfranchise, familiarize, grant citizenship, habituate

naturally 1. *adverb* as anticipated, customarily, genuinely, informally, normally, simply, spontaneously, typically, unaffectedly, unpretentiously **2.** *~interjection* absolutely, as a matter of course, certainly, of course

naturalness 1. artlessness, candidness, frankness, genuineness, ingenuousness, openness, realism, simpleness, simplicity, spontaneousness, unaffectedness, unpretentiousness, unsophisticatedness, unstudiedness **2.** plainness, pureness, purity, wholeness

nature 1. attributes, character, complexion, constitution, essence, features, make-up, quality, traits **2.** category, description, kind, sort, species, style, type, variety **3.** cosmos, creation, earth, environment, universe, world **4.** disposition, humour, mood, outlook, temper, temperament **5.** country, countryside, landscape, natural history, scenery

naturist nudist

naught nil, nothing, nothingness, nought, zero

naughty 1. annoying, bad, disobedient, exasperating, fractious, impish, misbehaved, mischievous, perverse, playful, refractory, roguish, sinful, teasing, wayward, wicked, worthless **2.** bawdy, blue, improper, lewd, obscene, off-colour, ribald, risqué, smutty, vulgar, X-rated (*informal*)

▷ **Antonyms** (*sense 1*) good, obedient, polite, proper, seemly, well-behaved, well-mannered (*sense 2*) polite, proper

nausea 1. biliousness, qualm(s), queasiness, retching, sickness, squeamishness, vomiting **2.** abhorrence, aversion, disgust, loathing, odium, repugnance, revulsion

nauseate disgust, gross out (*U.S. slang*), horrify, offend, repel, repulse, revolt, sicken, turn one's stomach

nauseous abhorrent, detestable, disgusting, distasteful, loathsome, nauseating, offensive, repugnant, repulsive, revolting, sickening, yucky *or* yukky (*slang*)

nautical marine, maritime, naval, oceanic, seafaring, seagoing, yachting

naval marine, maritime, nautical, oceanic

navel 1. bellybutton (*informal*), omphalos (*literary*), umbilicus **2.** central point, centre, hub, middle

navigable 1. clear, negotiable, passable, traversable, unobstructed **2.** controllable, dirigible, sailable, steerable

navigate con (*Nautical*), cross, cruise, direct, drive, guide, handle, journey, manoeuvre, pilot, plan, plot, sail, skipper, steer, voyage

navigation cruising, helmsmanship, pilotage, sailing, seamanship, steering, voyaging

navigator mariner, pilot, seaman

navvy ganger, labourer, worker, workman

navy argosy (*archaic*), armada, fleet, flotilla, warships

near *adjective* **1.** adjacent, adjoining, a hop, skip and a jump away (*informal*), alongside, at close quarters, beside, bordering, close, close by, contiguous, just round the corner, nearby, neighbouring, nigh, proximate, touching, within sniffing distance (*informal*) **2.** approaching, forthcoming, imminent, impending, in the offing, looming, near-at-hand, next, on the cards (*informal*), upcoming **3.** akin, allied, attached, connected, dear, familiar, intimate, related **4.** *informal* close-fisted, mean, miserly, niggardly, parsimonious, stingy, tightfisted, ungenerous

▷ **Antonyms** (*senses 1, 2 & 3*) distant, far, faraway, far-flung, far-off, far-removed, long, outlying, out-of-the-way, remote, removed

nearby 1. *adjective* adjacent, adjoining, convenient, handy, neighbouring 2. *~adverb* at close quarters, close at hand, just round the corner, not far away, proximate, within reach, within sniffing distance (*informal*)

nearing advancing, approaching, approximating, coming, imminent, impending, upcoming

nearly *adverb* about, all but, almost, approaching, approximately, as good as, closely, just about, not quite, practically, roughly, virtually, well-nigh

nearness 1. accessibility, availability, closeness, contiguity, handiness, juxtaposition, propinquity, proximity, vicinity 2. immediacy, imminence 3. dearness, familiarity, intimacy 4. *informal* meanness, niggardliness, parsimony, stinginess

near-sighted myopic, short-sighted

near thing close shave (*informal*), narrow escape, near miss

neat 1. accurate, dainty, fastidious, methodical, nice, orderly, shipshape, smart, spick-and-span, spruce, straight, systematic, tidy, trim, uncluttered 2. adept, adroit, agile, apt, clever, deft, dexterous, efficient, effortless, elegant, expert, graceful, handy, nimble, practised, precise, skilful, stylish, well-judged 3. *of alcoholic drinks* pure, straight, undiluted, unmixed

▷ **Antonyms** (*sense 1*) awful, bad, clumsy, cluttered, disarrayed, disorderly, disorganized, inelegant, messy, slobby (*informal*), sloppy (*informal*), terrible, untidy (*sense 2*) awful, bad, clumsy, incompetent, inefficient, terrible

neaten arrange, clean up, groom, put to rights, straighten out *or* up, tidy, tidy up, trig (*archaic or dialect*), trim

neatly 1. accurately, daintily, fastidiously, methodically, nicely, smartly, sprucely, systematically, tidily 2. adeptly, adroitly, agilely, aptly, cleverly, deftly, dexterously, efficiently, effortlessly, elegantly, expertly, gracefully, handily, nimbly, precisely, skilfully, stylishly

neatness 1. accuracy, daintiness, fastidiousness, methodicalness, niceness, nicety, orderliness, smartness, spruceness, straightness, tidiness, trimness 2. adeptness, adroitness, agility, aptness, cleverness, deftness, dexterity, efficiency, effortlessness, elegance, expertness, grace, gracefulness, handiness, nimbleness, preciseness, precision, skilfulness, skill, style, stylishness

nebulous ambiguous, amorphous, cloudy, confused, dim, hazy, imprecise, indefinite, indeterminate, indistinct, misty, murky, obscure, shadowy, shapeless, uncertain, unclear, unformed, vague

necessarily accordingly, automatically, axiomatically, by definition, certainly, compulsorily, consequently, incontrovertibly, ineluctably, inevitably, inexorably, irresistibly, naturally, *nolens volens,* of course, of necessity, perforce, undoubtedly, willy-nilly

necessary 1. compulsory, *de rigueur,* essential, imperative, indispensable, mandatory, needed, needful, obligatory, required, requisite, vital 2. certain, fated, inescapable, inevitable, inexorable, unavoidable

▷ **Antonyms** (*sense 1*) dispensable, expendable, inessential, nonessential, superfluous, unnecessary (*sense 2*) unnecessary

necessitate call for, coerce, compel, constrain, demand, entail, force, impel, make necessary, oblige, require

necessities essentials, exigencies, fundamentals, indispensables, needs, requirements

necessitous destitute, distressed, impecunious, impoverished, indigent, needy, penniless, penurious, poor, poverty-stricken

necessity 1. demand, exigency, indispensability, need, needfulness, requirement 2. desideratum, essential, fundamental, necessary, need, prerequisite, requirement, requisite, *sine qua non,* want 3. destitution, extremity, indigence, need, penury, poverty, privation 4. compulsion, destiny, fate, inevitability, inexorableness, obligation

necromancer black magician, diviner, enchanter, enchantress, magician, sorcerer, sorceress, warlock, witch, wizard

necromancy black art, black magic, demonology, divination, enchantment, magic, sorcery, thaumaturgy (*rare*), voodoo, witchcraft, witchery, wizardry

necropolis burial ground, cemetery, churchyard, God's acre, graveyard

need *verb* 1. call for, demand, entail, have occasion to *or* for, lack, miss, necessitate, require, want *~noun* 2. longing, requisite, want, wish 3. deprivation, destitution, distress, extremity, impecuniousness, inadequacy, indigence, insufficiency, lack, neediness, paucity, penury, poverty, privation, shortage 4. emergency, exigency, necessity, obligation, urgency, want 5. demand, desideratum, essential, requirement, requisite

needed called for, desired, lacked, necessary, required, wanted

needful essential, indispensable, necessary, needed, required, requisite, stipulated, vital

needle *verb* aggravate (*informal*), annoy, bait, be on one's back (*slang*), gall, get in one's hair (*informal*), get on one's nerves (*informal*), get under one's skin (*informal*), goad, harass, hassle (*informal*), irk, irritate, nag, nark (*Brit., Austral., &*

N.Z. slang), nettle, pester, piss one off (*taboo slang*), prick, prod, provoke, rile, ruffle, spur, sting, taunt

needless causeless, dispensable, excessive, expendable, gratuitous, groundless, nonessential, pointless, redundant, superfluous, uncalled-for, undesired, unnecessary, unwanted, useless

▷ **Antonyms** beneficial, essential, obligatory, required, useful

needlework embroidery, fancywork, needlecraft, sewing, stitching, tailoring

needy deprived, destitute, dirt-poor, disadvantaged, down at heel (*informal*), impecunious, impoverished, indigent, on the breadline (*informal*), penniless, poor, poverty-stricken, underprivileged

▷ **Antonyms** affluent, comfortable, moneyed, prosperous, rich, wealthy, well-off, well-to-do

ne'er-do-well black sheep, good-for-nothing, idler, layabout, loafer, loser, skiver (*Brit. slang*), wastrel

nefarious abominable, atrocious, base, criminal, depraved, detestable, dreadful, evil, execrable, foul, heinous, horrible, infamous, infernal, iniquitous, monstrous, odious, opprobrious, shameful, sinful, vicious, vile, villainous, wicked

▷ **Antonyms** admirable, good, honest, honourable, just, noble, praiseworthy, upright, virtuous

negate **1.** abrogate, annul, cancel, countermand, invalidate, neutralize, nullify, obviate, repeal, rescind, retract, reverse, revoke, void, wipe out **2.** contradict, deny, disallow, disprove, gainsay (*archaic or literary*), oppose, rebut, refute

▷ **Antonyms** affirm, assert, attest, avouch, avow, certify, confirm, declare, maintain, pronounce, ratify, state, swear, testify

negation **1.** antithesis, antonym, contradiction, contrary, converse, counterpart, denial, disavowal, disclaimer, inverse, opposite, rejection, renunciation, reverse **2.** opposition, proscription, refusal, repudiation, veto **3.** cancellation, neutralization, nullification **4.** blank, nonexistence, nothingness, nullity, vacuity, void

negative *adjective* **1.** contradictory, contrary, denying, dissenting, opposing, recusant, refusing, rejecting, resisting **2.** annulling, counteractive, invalidating, neutralizing, nullifying **3.** antagonistic, colourless, contrary, cynical, gloomy, jaundiced, neutral, pessimistic, uncooperative, unenthusiastic, uninterested, unwilling, weak *~noun* **4.** contradiction, denial, refusal

▷ **Antonyms** *~adjective* (*sense 1*) affirmative, approving, assenting, concurring (*sense 3*) cheerful, enthusiastic, optimistic, positive

negativeness, negativity **1.** contradiction, contradictoriness, contrariness, denial, dissent, opposition, recusancy, refusal, rejection, resistance **2.** antagonism, colourlessness, contrariness, cynicism, gloom, neutrality, pessimism, uncooperativeness, uninterestedness, unwillingness, weakness

neglect *verb* **1.** contemn, discount, disdain, disregard, ignore, leave alone, overlook, pass by, rebuff, scorn, slight, spurn, turn one's back on **2.** be remiss, evade, forget, let slide, omit, pass over, procrastinate, shirk, skimp *~noun* **3.** disdain, disregard, disrespect, heedlessness, inattention, indifference, slight, unconcern **4.** carelessness, default, dereliction, failure, forgetfulness, laxity, laxness, neglectfulness, negligence, oversight, remissness, slackness, slovenliness

▷ **Antonyms** *~verb* appreciate, attend to, notice, observe, regard, remember, value *~noun* attention, care, consideration, notice, regard, respect

neglected **1.** abandoned, derelict, overgrown **2.** disregarded, unappreciated, underestimated, undervalued

neglectful careless, disregardful, heedless, inattentive, indifferent, lax, negligent, remiss, thoughtless, uncaring, unmindful

negligence carelessness, default, dereliction, disregard, failure, forgetfulness, heedlessness, inadvertence, inattention, inattentiveness, indifference, laxity, laxness, neglect, omission, oversight, remissness, shortcoming, slackness, thoughtlessness

negligent careless, cursory, disregardful, forgetful, heedless, inadvertent, inattentive, indifferent, neglectful, nonchalant, offhand, regardless, remiss, slack, slapdash, slipshod, thoughtless, unmindful, unthinking

▷ **Antonyms** attentive, careful, considerate, mindful, painstaking, rigorous, thorough, thoughtful

negligible imperceptible, inconsequential, insignificant, minor, minute, nickel-and-dime (*U.S. slang*), petty, small, trifling, trivial, unimportant

▷ **Antonyms** important, noteworthy, significant, vital

negotiable debatable, discussable *or* discussible, transactional, transferable, variable

negotiate **1.** adjudicate, arbitrate, arrange, bargain, conciliate, confer, consult, contract, deal, debate, discuss, handle, manage, mediate, parley, settle, transact, work out **2.** clear, cross, get over, get past, get round, pass, pass through, surmount

negotiation arbitration, bargaining, debate, diplomacy, discussion, mediation, transaction, wheeling and dealing (*informal*)

negotiator adjudicator, ambassador, arbitrator, delegate, diplomat, honest broker, intermediary, mediator, moderator

neighbourhood community, confines, district, environs, locale, locality, precincts, proximity, purlieus, quarter, region, surroundings, vicinity

neighbouring abutting, adjacent, adjoining, bordering, connecting, contiguous, near, nearby, nearest, next, surrounding
▷ **Antonyms** distant, far, far-off, remote

neighbourly amiable, civil, companionable, considerate, friendly, genial, harmonious, helpful, hospitable, kind, obliging, sociable, social, well-disposed

nemesis destiny, destruction, fate, retribution, vengeance

neologism buzz word (*informal*), coinage, new phrase, new word, nonce word, vogue word

neophyte amateur, apprentice, beginner, catechumen, disciple, learner, novice, novitiate, probationer, proselyte, pupil, recruit, student, trainee, tyro

ne plus ultra acme, culmination, extreme, perfection, the last word, ultimate, uttermost point

nerve *noun* **1.** balls (*taboo slang*), ballsiness (*taboo slang*), bottle (*Brit. slang*), bravery, coolness, courage, daring, determination, endurance, energy, face (*informal*), fearlessness, firmness, force, fortitude, gameness, grit, guts (*informal*), hardihood, intrepidity, mettle, might, pluck, resolution, spirit, spunk (*informal*), steadfastness, vigour, will **2.** *informal* audacity, boldness, brass (*informal*), brass neck (*Brit. informal*), brazenness, cheek (*informal*), chutzpah (*U.S. & Canad. informal*), effrontery, front, gall, impertinence, impudence, insolence, neck (*informal*), sassiness (*U.S. slang*), sauce (*informal*), temerity *~verb* **3.** brace, embolden, encourage, fortify, hearten, invigorate, steel, strengthen

nerveless 1. calm, collected, composed, controlled, cool, impassive, imperturbable, self-possessed, unemotional **2.** afraid, cowardly, debilitated, enervated, feeble, nervous, spineless, timid, weak

nerve-racking annoying, difficult, distressing, frightening, harassing, harrowing, maddening, stressful, tense, trying, worrying

nerves anxiety, butterflies (in one's stomach) (*informal*), cold feet (*informal*), fretfulness, heebie-jeebies (*slang*), imbalance, nervousness, strain, stress, tension, worry

nervous agitated, anxious, apprehensive, edgy, excitable, fearful, fidgety, flustered, hesitant, highly strung, hyper (*informal*), hysterical, jittery (*informal*), jumpy, nervy (*Brit. informal*), neurotic, on edge, ruffled, shaky, tense, timid, timorous, twitchy (*informal*), uneasy, uptight (*informal*), weak, wired (*slang*), worried
▷ **Antonyms** bold, calm, confident, constant, cool, equable, even, laid-back (*informal*), peaceful, relaxed, steady, together (*slang*), unfazed (*informal*)

nervous breakdown breakdown, collapse, crack-up (*informal*), nervous disorder, neurasthenia (*obsolete*)

nervousness agitation, anxiety, disquiet, excitability, fluster, perturbation, tension, timidity, touchiness, tremulousness, worry

nervy agitated, anxious, excitable, fidgety, jittery (*informal*), jumpy, nervous, on edge, restless, tense, twitchy (*informal*), wired (*slang*)

nescience 1. ignorance, lack of knowledge, obliviousness, unawareness, unconsciousness, unenlightenment **2.** agnosticism, doubt, irreligion, unbelief

nescient 1. ignorant, oblivious, unaware, unconscious, unenlightened, unknowing, unknowledgeable **2.** agnostic, doubting, irreligious, unbelieving

nest 1. den, haunt, hideaway, refuge, resort, retreat, snuggery **2.** breeding-ground, den, hotbed

nest egg cache, deposit, fall-back, fund(s), reserve, savings, store

nestle cuddle, curl up, huddle, nuzzle, snuggle

nestling 1. chick, fledgling **2.** babe, babe in arms, baby, infant, suckling

net[1] 1. *noun* lacework, lattice, mesh, netting, network, openwork, reticulum, tracery, web **2.** *~verb* bag, capture, catch, enmesh, ensnare, entangle, nab (*informal*), trap

net[2], nett *adjective* **1.** after taxes, clear, final, take-home **2.** closing, conclusive, final *~verb* **3.** accumulate, bring in, clear, earn, gain, make, realize, reap

nether basal, below, beneath, bottom, inferior, lower, Stygian, under, underground

nether world Avernus, Hades, hell, infernal regions, nether regions, underworld

nettle aggravate (*informal*), annoy, chafe, exasperate, fret, gall, get on one's nerves (*informal*), goad, harass, hassle (*informal*), incense, irritate, nark (*Brit., Austral., & N.Z. slang*), pique, piss one off (*taboo slang*), provoke, ruffle, sting, tease, vex

nettled aggrieved, angry, annoyed, chafed, choked, cross, exasperated, galled, goaded, hacked (off) (*U.S. slang*), harassed, huffy, incensed, irritable, irritated, peeved, peevish, piqued, pissed off (*taboo slang*), provoked, put out, rat~

ty (*Brit. & N.Z. informal*), riled, ruffled, stung, teased, tetchy, touchy, vexed

network arrangement, channels, circuitry, complex, convolution, grid, grill, interconnections, labyrinth, lattice, maze, mesh, net, nexus, organization, plexus, structure, system, tracks, web

neurosis abnormality, affliction, derangement, deviation, instability, maladjustment, mental disturbance, mental illness, obsession, phobia, psychological *or* emotional disorder

neurotic abnormal, anxious, compulsive, deviant, disordered, distraught, disturbed, hyper (*informal*), maladjusted, manic, nervous, obsessive, overwrought, twitchy (*informal*), unhealthy, unstable
▷ **Antonyms** calm, laid-back (*informal*), level-headed, normal, rational, sane, stable, together (*slang*), well-adjusted, well-balanced

neuter *verb* castrate, doctor (*informal*), dress, emasculate, fix (*informal*), geld, spay

neutral 1. disinterested, dispassionate, even-handed, impartial, indifferent, nonaligned, nonbelligerent, noncombatant, noncommittal, nonpartisan, sitting on the fence, unaligned, unbiased, uncommitted, undecided, uninvolved, unprejudiced **2.** achromatic, colourless, dull, expressionless, indeterminate, indistinct, indistinguishable, intermediate, toneless, undefined
▷ **Antonyms** (*sense 1*) active, belligerent, biased, decided, interested, interfering, partial, participating, positive, prejudiced

neutrality detachment, disinterestedness, impartiality, nonalignment, noninterference, noninterventionism, noninvolvement, nonpartisanship

neutralize cancel, compensate for, counteract, counterbalance, frustrate, invalidate, negate, nullify, offset, undo

never at no time, not at all, not for love nor money (*informal*), not on your life (*informal*), not on your nelly (*Brit. slang*), no way, on no account, under no circumstances
▷ **Antonyms** always, aye (*Scot.*), constantly, continually, every time, forever, perpetually, without exception

never-ending boundless, ceaseless, constant, continual, continuous, eternal, everlasting, incessant, interminable, nonstop, perpetual, persistent, relentless, unbroken, unceasing, unchanging, uninterrupted, unremitting

never-never hire-purchase (*Brit.*), H.P. (*Brit.*)

nevertheless but, even so, (even) though, however, nonetheless, notwithstanding, regardless, still, yet

new 1. advanced, all-singing all-dancing, contemporary, current, different, fresh, ground-breaking, happening (*informal*), latest, modern, modernistic, modish, newfangled, novel, original, recent, state-of-the-art, topical, ultramodern, unfamiliar, unknown, unused, unusual, up-to-date, virgin **2.** added, extra, more, supplementary **3.** altered, changed, improved, modernized, redesigned, renewed, restored
▷ **Antonyms** (*sense 1*) aged, ancient, antiquated, antique, hackneyed, old, old-fashioned, outmoded, passé, stale, trite

newcomer alien, arrival, beginner, foreigner, immigrant, incomer, Johnny-come-lately (*informal*), novice, outsider, parvenu, settler, stranger

newfangled all-singing all-dancing, contemporary, fashionable, gimmicky, modern, new, new-fashioned, novel, recent, state-of-the-art
▷ **Antonyms** antiquated, dated, obsolete, old-fashioned, outmoded, out-of-date, passé

newly anew, freshly, just, lately, latterly, recently

newness freshness, innovation, novelty, oddity, originality, strangeness, unfamiliarity, uniqueness

news account, advice, bulletin, buzz, communiqué, dirt (*U.S. slang*), disclosure, dispatch, exposé, gen (*Brit. informal*), gossip, hearsay, information, intelligence, latest (*informal*), leak, news flash, release, report, revelation, rumour, scandal, scuttlebutt (*U.S. slang*), statement, story, tidings, word

newsworthy arresting, important, interesting, notable, noteworthy, remarkable, significant, stimulating

next *adjective* **1.** consequent, ensuing, following, later, subsequent, succeeding **2.** adjacent, adjoining, closest, nearest, neighbouring *~adverb* **3.** afterwards, closely, following, later, subsequently, thereafter

next world afterlife, afterworld, heaven, hereafter, nirvana, paradise

nexus bond, connection, joining, junction, link, tie

nibble 1. *noun* bite, crumb, morsel, peck, snack, *soupçon,* taste, titbit **2.** *~verb* bite, eat, gnaw, munch, nip, peck, pick at

nice 1. agreeable, amiable, attractive, charming, commendable, courteous, delightful, friendly, good, kind, likable *or* likeable, pleasant, pleasurable, polite, prepossessing, refined, well-mannered **2.** dainty, fine, neat, tidy, trim **3.** accurate, careful, critical, delicate, discriminating, exact, exacting, fastidious, fine, meticulous, precise, rigorous, scrupulous, strict, subtle **4.** cultured, genteel, refined, respectable, virtuous, well-bred
▷ **Antonyms** (*sense 1*) awful, disagreeable, dreadful, mean, miserable, un~

friendly, unkind, unpleasant, vulgar (*sense 2*) coarse, crude, rough, shabby, sloppy (*informal*) (*sense 3*) careless, rough, sloppy (*informal*), vague (*sense 4*) coarse, crude, ill-bred, vulgar

nicely **1.** acceptably, agreeably, amiably, attractively, charmingly, commendably, courteously, delightfully, kindly, likably, pleasantly, pleasingly, pleasurably, politely, prepossessingly, well **2.** daintily, finely, neatly, tidily, trimly **3.** accurately, carefully, critically, delicately, exactingly, exactly, fastidiously, finely, meticulously, precisely, rigorously, scrupulously, strictly, subtly **4.** genteelly, respectably, virtuously

▷ **Antonyms** (*sense 1*) unattractively, unpleasantly (*sense 2*) sloppily (*informal*) (*sense 3*) carelessly, sloppily (*informal*)

niceness **1.** agreeableness, amiability, attractiveness, charm, courtesy, delightfulness, friendliness, good manners, goodness, kindness, likableness *or* likeableness, pleasantness, pleasurableness, politeness, refinement **2.** daintiness, fineness, neatness, tidiness, trimness **3.** accuracy, care, carefulness, criticalness, delicacy, discrimination, exactingness, exactitude, exactness, fastidiousness, fineness, meticulosity, meticulousness, preciseness, precision, rigorousness, rigour, scrupulosity, scrupulousness, strictness, subtleness, subtlety **4.** gentility, good breeding, refinement, respectability, virtue

nicety **1.** accuracy, exactness, fastidiousness, finesse, meticulousness, minuteness, precision **2.** daintiness, delicacy, discrimination, distinction, nuance, refinement, subtlety

niche **1.** alcove, corner, hollow, nook, opening, recess **2.** calling, pigeonhole (*informal*), place, position, slot (*informal*), vocation

nick[1] *noun/verb* chip, cut, damage, dent, mark, notch, scar, score, scratch, snick

nick[2] *verb* finger (*slang*), knock off (*slang*), pilfer, pinch (*informal*), snitch (*slang*), steal, swipe (*slang*)

nickname diminutive, epithet, familiar name, handle (*slang*), label, moniker *or* monicker (*slang*), pet name, sobriquet

nifty agile, apt, attractive, chic, clever, deft, enjoyable, excellent, neat, pleasing, quick, sharp, smart, spruce, stylish

niggard cheapskate (*Brit. informal*), cheeseparer, churl (*archaic*), meanie *or* meany (*informal, chiefly Brit.*), miser, penny-pincher (*informal*), screw (*slang*), Scrooge, skinflint, tight-arse (*taboo slang*), tight-ass (*U.S. taboo slang*)

niggardliness **1.** avarice, avariciousness, closeness, covetousness, frugality, grudgingness, meanness, mercenariness, miserliness, nearness (*informal*), parsimony, penuriousness, sordidness, sparingness, stinginess, thrift, tightfistedness, ungenerousness **2.** beggarliness, inadequacy, insufficiency, meagreness, meanness, miserableness, paltriness, scantiness, skimpiness, smallness, wretchedness

niggardly **1.** avaricious, close, covetous, frugal, grudging, mean, mercenary, miserly, near (*informal*), parsimonious, penurious, Scroogelike, snoep (*S. African informal*), sordid, sparing, stinging, stingy, tight-arse (*taboo slang*), tight-arsed (*taboo slang*), tight as a duck's arse (*taboo slang*), tight-ass (*U.S. taboo slang*), tight-assed (*U.S. taboo slang*), tightfisted, ungenerous **2.** beggarly, inadequate, insufficient, meagre, mean, measly, miserable, paltry, pathetic, scant, scanty, skimpy, small, wretched

▷ **Antonyms** abundant, ample, bountiful, copious, generous, handsome, lavish, liberal, munificent, plentiful, prodigal, profuse

niggle **1.** carp, cavil, criticize, find fault, fuss **2.** annoy, irritate, rankle, worry

niggler carper, caviller, fault-finder, fusspot (*Brit. informal*), nag, nit-picker (*informal*), pettifogger, quibbler

niggling **1.** cavilling, finicky, fussy, insignificant, minor, nit-picking (*informal*), pettifogging, petty, picky (*informal*), piddling (*informal*), quibbling, trifling, unimportant **2.** gnawing, irritating, persistent, troubling, worrying

nigh **1.** *adjective* adjacent, adjoining, approximate, at hand, bordering, close, contiguous, imminent, impending, near, next, upcoming **2.** *~adverb* about, almost, approximately, close, near, practically

night dark, darkness, dead of night, hours of darkness, night-time, night watches

night and day all the time, ceaselessly, constantly, continually, continuously, day in, day out, endlessly, incessantly, interminably, unremittingly

nightfall crepuscule, dusk, eve (*archaic*), evening, eventide, gloaming (*Scot. or poetic*), sundown, sunset, twilight, vespers

▷ **Antonyms** aurora (*poetic*), cockcrow, dawn, dawning, daybreak, daylight, morning, sunrise

nightly **1.** *adverb/adjective* each night, every night, night after night, nights (*informal*) **2.** *~adverb* after dark, at night, by night, in the night, nights (*informal*), nocturnally **3.** *~adjective* night-time, nocturnal

nightmare **1.** bad dream, hallucination, incubus, night terror, succubus **2.** hell on earth, horror, ordeal, torment, trial, tribulation

nightmarish agonizing, alarming, creepy (*informal*), disturbing, frightening, har~

rowing, horrible, Kafkaesque, scaring, terrifying, unreal

nihilism 1. abnegation, agnosticism, atheism, denial, disbelief, nonbelief, rejection, renunciation, repudiation, scepticism **2.** blank, emptiness, negation, nonexistence, nothingness, nullity, oblivion **3.** anarchy, disorder, lawlessness, terrorism

nihilist 1. agnostic, atheist, cynic, disbeliever, nonbeliever, pessimist, sceptic **2.** agitator, anarchist, extremist, revolutionary, terrorist

nil duck, love, naught, *nihil,* none, nothing, zero, zilch (*slang*)

nimble active, agile, alert, bright (*informal*), brisk, deft, dexterous, lively, nippy (*Brit. informal*), pdq (*slang*), proficient, prompt, quick, quick-witted, ready, smart, sprightly, spry, swift

▷ **Antonyms** awkward, clumsy, dull, heavy, inactive, indolent, lethargic, slow

nimbleness adroitness, agility, alacrity, alertness, dexterity, finesse, grace, lightness, nippiness (*Brit. informal*), skill, smartness, sprightliness, spryness

nimbly actively, acutely, agilely, alertly, briskly, deftly, dexterously, easily, fast, fleetly, hotfoot, pdq (*slang*), posthaste, proficiently, promptly, pronto (*informal*), quickly, quick-wittedly, readily, sharply, smartly, speedily, spryly, swiftly

nimbus ambience, atmosphere, aura, aureole, cloud, corona, glow, halo, irradiation

nincompoop berk (*Brit. slang*), blockhead, charlie (*Brit. informal*), chump, coot, dickhead (*slang*), dimwit (*informal*), dipstick (*Brit. slang*), divvy (*slang*), dolt, dork (*slang*), dunce, dweeb (*U.S. slang*), fathead (*informal*), fool, fuckwit (*taboo slang*), geek (*slang*), gobshite (*Irish taboo slang*), gonzo (*slang*), idiot, jerk (*slang, chiefly U.S. & Canad.*), lamebrain (*informal*), nerd *or* nurd (*slang*), ninny, nitwit (*informal*), noodle, numbskull *or* numskull, numpty (*Scot. informal*), oaf, pillock (*Brit. slang*), plank (*Brit. slang*), plonker (*slang*), prat (*slang*), prick (*slang*), schmuck (*U.S. slang*), simpleton, twit (*informal, chiefly Brit.*), wally (*slang*)

nip[1] *verb* **1.** bite, catch, clip, compress, grip, nibble, pinch, snag, snap, snip, squeeze, tweak, twitch **2.** check, frustrate, thwart

nip[2] *noun* dram, draught, drop, finger, mouthful, peg (*Brit.*), portion, shot (*informal*), sip, snifter (*informal*), *soupçon,* sup, swallow, taste

nipper 1. claw, pincer **2.** *informal* ankle-biter (*Austral. slang*), baby, boy, child, girl, infant, kid (*informal*), little one, rug rat (*slang*), sprog (*slang*), tot

nipple boob (*slang*), breast, dug, mamilla, pap, papilla, teat, tit, udder

nippy 1. biting, chilly, nipping, sharp, stinging **2.** *Brit. informal* active, agile, fast, nimble, pdq (*slang*), quick, spry

nirvana bliss, joy, paradise, peace, serenity, tranquillity

nit-picking captious, carping, cavilling, finicky, fussy, hairsplitting, pedantic, pettifogging, quibbling

nitty-gritty basics, bottom line, brass tacks (*informal*), core, crux, essence, essentials, facts, fundamentals, gist, heart of the matter, ins and outs, nuts and bolts, reality, substance

nitwit *informal* dickhead (*slang*), dimwit (*informal*), dipstick (*Brit. slang*), divvy (*slang*), dork (*slang*), dummy (*slang*), fool, fuckwit (*taboo slang*), geek (*slang*), gobshite (*Irish taboo slang*), halfwit, lamebrain (*informal*), nincompoop, ninny, numpty (*Scot. informal*), oaf, plank (*Brit. slang*), simpleton

nob aristo (*informal*), aristocrat, big shot (*informal*), bigwig (*informal*), celeb (*informal*), fat cat (*slang, chiefly U.S.*), nabob (*informal*), toff (*Brit. slang*), V.I.P.

nobble 1. disable, handicap, incapacitate, weaken **2.** bribe, get at, influence, intimidate, outwit, win over **3.** filch, knock off (*slang*), nick (*slang, chiefly Brit.*), pilfer, pinch (*informal*), purloin, snitch (*slang*), steal, swipe (*slang*) **4.** get hold of, grab, take

nobbly nubby, projecting, protruding, protuberant, ridged, rough

nobility 1. aristocracy, elite, high society, lords, nobles, patricians, peerage, ruling class, upper class **2.** dignity, eminence, excellence, grandeur, greatness, illustriousness, loftiness, magnificence, majesty, nobleness, stateliness, sublimity, superiority, worthiness **3.** honour, incorruptibility, integrity, uprightness, virtue

noble *noun* **1.** aristo (*informal*), aristocrat, lord, nobleman, peer *~adjective* **2.** aristocratic, blue-blooded, gentle (*archaic*), highborn, lordly, patrician, titled **3.** august, dignified, distinguished, elevated, eminent, excellent, grand, great, imposing, impressive, lofty, splendid, stately, superb **4.** generous, honourable, magnanimous, upright, virtuous, worthy

▷ **Antonyms** *~noun* commoner, peasant, serf *~adjective* (*sense 2*) base, humble, ignoble, lowborn, lowly, peasant, plebeian, vulgar (*sense 3*) base, humble, ignoble, insignificant, lowly, mean, modest, plain (*sense 4*) contemptible, despicable, dishonest, selfish

nobody 1. no-one **2.** cipher, lightweight (*informal*), menial, nonentity, nothing (*informal*)

▷ **Antonyms** (*sense 2*) big name, big

noise (*informal*), big shot (*slang*), celeb (*informal*), celebrity, megastar (*informal*), personage, star, superstar, V.I.P.

nocturnal night, nightly, night-time, of the night

nod *verb* **1.** acknowledge, bob, bow, dip, duck, gesture, indicate, nutate (*rare*), salute, signal **2.** agree, assent, concur, show agreement **3.** be sleepy, doze, droop, drowse, kip (*Brit. slang*), nap, sleep, slump, zizz (*Brit. informal*) *~noun* **4.** acknowledgment, beck, gesture, greeting, indication, salute, sign, signal

node bud, bump, burl, growth, knob, knot, lump, nodule, protuberance, swelling

noggin 1. gill, quarter-pint **2.** cup, dram, mug, nip, tot **3.** *informal* bean (*U.S. & Canad. slang*), block (*informal*), bonce (*Brit. slang*), conk (*slang*), dome (*slang*), head, napper (*slang*), noddle (*informal, chiefly Brit.*), nut (*slang*)

no go futile, hopeless, impossible, not on (*informal*), vain

noise 1. *noun* babble, blare, clamour, clatter, commotion, cry, din, fracas, hubbub, outcry, pandemonium, racket, row, rumpus, sound, talk, tumult, uproar **2.** *~verb* advertise, bruit, circulate, gossip, publicize, repeat, report, rumour

noiseless hushed, inaudible, mute, muted, quiet, silent, soundless, still

noisome 1. bad, baneful (*archaic*), deleterious, harmful, hurtful, injurious, mischievous, pernicious, pestiferous, pestilential, poisonous, unhealthy, unwholesome **2.** disgusting, fetid, foul, malodorous, mephitic, niffy (*Brit. slang*), noxious, offensive, olid, putrid, reeking, smelly, stinking

noisy boisterous, cacophonous, chattering, clamorous, deafening, ear-splitting, loud, obstreperous, piercing, riotous, strident, tumultuous, turbulent, uproarious, vociferous

▷ **Antonyms** hushed, quiet, silent, still, subdued, tranquil, tuneful

nomad drifter, itinerant, migrant, rambler, rover, vagabond, wanderer

nomadic itinerant, migrant, migratory, pastoral, peripatetic, roaming, roving, travelling, vagrant, wandering

nom de plume alias, assumed name, nom de guerre, pen name, pseudonym

nomenclature classification, codification, locution, phraseology, taxonomy, terminology, vocabulary

nominal 1. formal, ostensible, pretended, professed, puppet, purported, self-styled, so-called, *soi-disant,* supposed, theoretical, titular **2.** inconsiderable, insignificant, minimal, small, symbolic, token, trifling, trivial

nominate appoint, assign, choose, commission, designate, elect, elevate, empower, name, present, propose, recommend, select, submit, suggest, term

nomination appointment, choice, designation, election, proposal, recommendation, selection, suggestion

nominee aspirant, candidate, contestant, entrant, favourite, protégé, runner

nonaligned impartial, neutral, uncommitted, undecided

nonchalance calm, composure, cool (*slang*), equanimity, imperturbability, indifference, sang-froid, self-possession, unconcern

nonchalant airy, apathetic, blasé, calm, careless, casual, collected, cool, detached, dispassionate, indifferent, insouciant, laid-back (*informal*), offhand, unconcerned, unemotional, unfazed (*informal*), unperturbed

▷ **Antonyms** anxious, caring, concerned, involved, worried

noncombatant civilian, neutral, nonbelligerent

noncommittal ambiguous, careful, cautious, circumspect, discreet, equivocal, evasive, guarded, indefinite, neutral, politic, reserved, tactful, temporizing, tentative, unrevealing, vague, wary

non compos mentis crazy, deranged, insane, mentally ill, of unsound mind, unbalanced, unhinged

▷ **Antonyms** all there (*informal*), *compos mentis,* in one's right mind, lucid, mentally sound, rational, sane

nonconformist dissenter, dissentient, eccentric, heretic, iconoclast, individualist, maverick, protester, radical, rebel

▷ **Antonyms** Babbitt (*U.S.*), conventionalist, stick-in-the-mud (*informal*), traditionalist, yes man

nonconformity dissent, eccentricity, heresy, heterodoxy, unconventionality

nondescript bog-standard (*Brit. & Irish slang*), characterless, common or garden (*informal*), commonplace, dull, featureless, indeterminate, mousy, nothing to write home about, ordinary, run-of-the-mill, unclassifiable, unclassified, undistinguished, unexceptional, uninspiring, uninteresting, unmemorable, unremarkable, vague, vanilla (*informal*)

▷ **Antonyms** distinctive, extraordinary, memorable, remarkable, unique, unusual

none bugger all (*slang*), f.a. (*Brit. slang*), fuck all (*Brit. taboo slang*), nil, nobody, no-one, no part, not a bit, not any, nothing, not one, sweet F.A. (*Brit. slang*), sweet Fanny Adams (*Brit. slang*), zero, zilch (*slang, chiefly U.S. & Canad.*)

nonentity cipher, lightweight (*informal*), mediocrity, nobody, small fry, unimportant person

nonessential dispensable, excessive, expendable, extraneous, inessential, peripheral, superfluous, unimportant, un-

necessary
▷ **Antonyms** appropriate, essential, important, indispensable, significant, vital

nonetheless despite that, even so, however, in spite of that, nevertheless, yet

nonexistent chimerical, fancied, fictional, hallucinatory, hypothetical, illusory, imaginary, imagined, insubstantial, legendary, missing, mythical, unreal
▷ **Antonyms** actual, existent, existing, genuine, real, true, veritable

nonpareil 1. *noun* ideal, nonesuch (*archaic*), paragon, perfection **2.** *~adjective* incomparable, matchless, peerless, supreme, unequalled, unique, unmatched, unparalleled, unrivalled, unsurpassed

nonpartisan detached, impartial, independent, neutral, nonpolitical, objective, unaffiliated, unbiased, unprejudiced

nonplus astonish, astound, baffle, be all Greek to (*informal*), bewilder, confound, confuse, discomfit, disconcert, discountenance, dismay, dumbfound, embarrass, faze, flummox, mystify, perplex, puzzle, stump, stun, take aback

nonsense absurdity, balderdash, balls (*taboo slang*), bilge (*informal*), blather, bollocks (*Brit. taboo slang*), bombast, bosh (*informal*), bull (*slang*), bullshit (*taboo slang*), bunk (*informal*), bunkum *or* buncombe (*chiefly U.S.*), claptrap (*informal*), cobblers (*Brit. taboo slang*), crap (*slang*), double Dutch (*Brit. informal*), drivel, eyewash (*informal*), fatuity, folly, foolishness, garbage (*informal*), gibberish, guff (*slang*), hogwash, hokum (*slang, chiefly U.S. & Canad.*), horsefeathers (*U.S. slang*), hot air (*informal*), idiocy, inanity, jest, ludicrousness, moonshine, pap, piffle (*informal*), poppycock (*informal*), rhubarb, ridiculousness, rot, rubbish, senselessness, shit (*taboo slang*), silliness, stuff, stupidity, tommyrot, tosh (*slang, chiefly Brit.*), trash, tripe (*informal*), twaddle, waffle (*informal, chiefly Brit.*)
▷ **Antonyms** fact, reality, reason, sense, seriousness, truth, wisdom

nonsensical absurd, asinine, crazy, foolish, inane, incomprehensible, irrational, ludicrous, meaningless, ridiculous, senseless, silly

nonstop 1. *adjective* ceaseless, constant, continuous, direct, endless, incessant, interminable, relentless, steady, unbroken, unending, unfaltering, uninterrupted, unremitting **2.** *~adverb* ceaselessly, constantly, continuously, directly, endlessly, incessantly, interminably, perpetually, relentlessly, steadily, unbrokenly, unendingly, unfalteringly, uninterruptedly, unremittingly, without stopping
▷ **Antonyms** *~adjective* broken, discontinuous, fitful, intermittent, irregular, occasional, periodic, punctuated, recurrent, spasmodic, sporadic, stop-go (*informal*)

nonviolent nonbelligerent, pacifist, peaceable, peaceful

nook alcove, cavity, corner, cranny, crevice, cubbyhole, hide-out, inglenook (*Brit.*), niche, opening, recess, retreat

noon high noon, midday, noonday, noontide, noontime, twelve noon

norm average, benchmark, criterion, mean, measure, model, par, pattern, rule, standard, type, yardstick

normal 1. accustomed, acknowledged, average, bog-standard (*Brit. & Irish slang*), common, conventional, habitual, natural, ordinary, popular, regular, routine, run-of-the-mill, standard, typical, usual **2.** rational, reasonable, sane, well-adjusted
▷ **Antonyms** (*sense 1*) abnormal, exceptional, irregular, peculiar, rare, remarkable, singular, uncommon, unnatural, unusual

normality 1. accustomedness, averageness, commonness, commonplaceness, conventionality, habitualness, naturalness, ordinariness, popularity, regularity, routineness, typicality, usualness **2.** adjustment, balance, rationality, reason, sanity

normally as a rule, commonly, generally, habitually, ordinarily, regularly, typically, usually

normative controlling, normalizing, prescriptive, regularizing, regulating, standardizing

north 1. *adjective* Arctic, boreal, northerly, northern, polar **2.** *~adverb* northerly, northward(s)

North Star lodestar, Polaris, Pole Star

nose *noun* **1.** beak, bill, conk (*slang*), hooter (*slang*), neb (*archaic or dialect*), proboscis, schnozzle (*slang, chiefly U.S.*), snitch (*slang*), snout (*slang*) *~verb* **2.** detect, scent, search (for), smell, sniff **3.** ease forward, nudge, nuzzle, push, shove **4.** meddle, pry, snoop (*informal*)

nose dive dive, drop, plummet, plunge

nosegay bouquet, posy

nosh 1. *noun* aliment, chow (*informal*), comestibles, eats (*slang*), fare, feed, food, grub (*slang*), meal, nosebag (*slang*), repast, scoff (*slang*), sustenance, tack (*informal*), viands, victuals, vittles (*obsolete or dialect*) **2.** *~verb* consume, eat, scoff (*slang*)

nostalgia homesickness, longing, pining, regret, regretfulness, remembrance, reminiscence, wistfulness, yearning

nostalgic emotional, homesick, longing, maudlin, regretful, sentimental, wistful

nostrum cure, cure-all, drug, elixir, medicine, panacea, patent medicine, potion, quack medicine, remedy, sovereign cure, specific, treatment

nosy, nosey curious, eavesdropping, inquisitive, interfering, intrusive, meddlesome, prying, snooping (*informal*)

notability **1.** celebrity, distinction, eminence, esteem, fame, renown **2.** big name, celeb (*informal*), celebrity, dignitary, megastar (*informal*), notable, personage, V.I.P., worthy

notable **1.** *adjective* celebrated, conspicuous, distinguished, eminent, evident, extraordinary, famous, manifest, marked, memorable, noteworthy, noticeable, notorious, outstanding, preeminent, pronounced, rare, remarkable, renowned, salient, striking, uncommon, unusual, well-known **2.** *~noun* big name, celeb (*informal*), celebrity, dignitary, megastar (*informal*), notability, personage, V.I.P., worthy

▷ **Antonyms** *~adjective* anonymous, concealed, hidden, imperceptible, obscure, unknown, vague

notably conspicuously, distinctly, especially, markedly, noticeably, outstandingly, particularly, remarkably, seriously (*informal*), signally, strikingly, uncommonly

notation **1.** characters, code, script, signs, symbols, system **2.** jotting, notating, note, noting, record

notch *noun* **1.** cleft, cut, incision, indentation, mark, nick, score **2.** *informal* cut (*informal*), degree, grade, level, step *~verb* **3.** cut, indent, mark, nick, score, scratch

notch up achieve, gain, make, register, score

note *noun* **1.** annotation, comment, communication, epistle, gloss, jotting, letter, memo, memorandum, message, minute, record, remark, reminder **2.** indication, mark, sign, symbol, token **3.** heed, notice, observation, regard **4.** celebrity, character, consequence, distinction, eminence, fame, prestige, renown, reputation *~verb* **5.** denote, designate, indicate, mark, mention, notice, observe, perceive, record, register, remark, see

notebook commonplace book, diary, exercise book, Filofax (*Trademark*), jotter, journal, memorandum book, notepad, record book

noted acclaimed, celebrated, conspicuous, distinguished, eminent, famous, illustrious, notable, notorious, prominent, recognized, renowned, well-known

▷ **Antonyms** infamous, obscure, undistinguished, unknown

notes impressions, jottings, outline, record, report, sketch

noteworthy exceptional, extraordinary, important, notable, outstanding, remarkable, significant, unusual

▷ **Antonyms** commonplace, insignificant, normal, ordinary, pedestrian, run-of-the-mill, unexceptional, unremarkable

nothing bagatelle, cipher, emptiness, naught, nil, nobody, nonentity, nonexistence, nothingness, nought, nullity, trifle, void, zero

nothingness **1.** nihility, nonbeing, nonexistence, nullity, oblivion **2.** insignificance, unimportance, worthlessness

notice *verb* **1.** behold (*archaic or literary*), detect, discern, distinguish, heed, mark, mind, note, observe, perceive, remark, see, spot *~noun* **2.** cognizance, consideration, heed, interest, note, observation, regard **3.** advice, announcement, communication, instruction, intelligence, intimation, news, notification, order, warning **4.** advertisement, comment, criticism, poster, review, sign **5.** attention, civility, respect

▷ **Antonyms** *~verb* disregard, ignore, neglect, overlook *~noun* (*sense 2*) disregard, ignorance, neglect, omission, oversight

noticeable appreciable, blatant, bold, clear, conspicuous, distinct, evident, manifest, observable, obvious, perceptible, plain, salient, striking, unmistakable

notification advice, alert, announcement, declaration, information, intelligence, message, notice, notifying, publication, statement, telling, warning

notify acquaint, advise, alert, announce, apprise, declare, inform, make known, publish, tell, warn

notion **1.** apprehension, belief, concept, conception, idea, impression, inkling, judgment, knowledge, opinion, sentiment, understanding, view **2.** caprice, desire, fancy, impulse, inclination, whim, wish

notional abstract, conceptual, fanciful, hypothetical, ideal, imaginary, speculative, theoretical, unreal, visionary

▷ **Antonyms** actual, factual, genuine, real

notoriety dishonour, disrepute, infamy, obloquy, opprobrium, scandal

notorious **1.** dishonourable, disreputable, infamous, opprobrious, scandalous **2.** blatant, flagrant, glaring, obvious, open, overt, patent, undisputed

notoriously **1.** dishonourably, disreputably, infamously, opprobriously, scandalously **2.** blatantly, flagrantly, glaringly, notably, obviously, openly, overtly, particularly, patently, spectacularly, undisputedly

notwithstanding although, despite, (even) though, however, nevertheless, nonetheless, though, yet

nought naught, nil, nothing, nothingness, zero

nourish **1.** attend, feed, furnish, nurse, nurture, supply, sustain, tend **2.** com~

fort, cultivate, encourage, foster, main~ tain, promote, support

nourishing alimentative, beneficial, healthful, health-giving, nutritious, nu~ tritive, wholesome

nourishment aliment, diet, food, nutri~ ment, nutrition, sustenance, tack (*in~ formal*), viands, victuals, vittles (*obso~ lete or dialect*)

nouveau riche arriviste, new-rich, par~ venu, upstart

novel **1.** *adjective* different, fresh, ground-breaking, innovative, left-field (*informal*), new, original, rare, singular, strange, uncommon, unfamiliar, un~ usual **2.** *~noun* fiction, narrative, ro~ mance, story, tale

▷ **Antonyms** *~adjective* ancient, common, customary, familiar, habitual, old-fashioned, ordinary, run-of-the-mill, traditional, usual

novelty **1.** freshness, innovation, new~ ness, oddity, originality, strangeness, surprise, unfamiliarity, uniqueness **2.** bagatelle, bauble, curiosity, gadget, gewgaw, gimcrack, gimmick, knick-knack, memento, souvenir, trifle, trin~ ket

novice amateur, apprentice, beginner, convert, learner, neophyte, newcomer, novitiate, probationer, proselyte, pupil, trainee, tyro

▷ **Antonyms** ace, doyen, expert, grand~ master, master, maven, old hand, pro~ fessional, teacher

novitiate **1.** apprenticeship, probation, training **2.** novice

now **1.** at once, immediately, instanter (*Law*), instantly, presently (*Scot. & U.S.*), promptly, straightaway **2.** any more, at the moment, nowadays, these days **3. now and then** *or* **again** at times, from time to time, infrequently, inter~ mittently, occasionally, on and off, once in a while, on occasion, sometimes, spo~ radically

nowadays any more, at the moment, in this day and age, now, these days, today

noxious baneful (*archaic*), corrupting, deadly, deleterious, destructive, detri~ mental, foul, harmful, hurtful, injuri~ ous, insalubrious, noisome, pernicious, pestilential, poisonous, unhealthy, un~ wholesome

▷ **Antonyms** innocuous, innoxious, inof~ fensive, nontoxic, not dangerous, safe, unobjectionable

nuance degree, distinction, gradation, graduation, hint, nicety, refinement, shade, shadow, subtlety, suggestion, suspicion, tinge, touch, trace

nub **1.** core, crux, essence, gist, heart, kernel, nucleus, pith, point **2.** bulge, bump, knob, knot, lump, node, protu~ berance, swelling

nubile marriageable, ripe (*informal*)

nucleus basis, centre, core, focus, heart, kernel, nub, pivot

nude *au naturel,* bare, buck naked (*slang*), disrobed, exposed, in one's birthday suit (*informal*), in the alto~ gether (*informal*), in the bare scud (*slang*), in the buff (*informal*), in the raw (*informal*), naked, naked as the day one was born (*informal*), scuddy (*slang*), starkers (*informal*), stark-naked, stripped, unclad, unclothed, uncovered, undraped, undressed, without a stitch on (*informal*)

▷ **Antonyms** attired, clothed, covered, dressed

nudge *verb* bump, dig, elbow, jog, poke, prod, push, shove, touch

nudity bareness, deshabille, nakedness, nudism, undress

nugatory **1.** insignificant, trifling, trivial, valueless, worthless **2.** bootless, futile, ineffectual, inoperative, invalid, null and void, unavailing, useless, vain

nugget chunk, clump, hunk, lump, mass, piece

nuisance annoyance, bore, bother, drag (*informal*), gall, hassle (*informal*), in~ convenience, infliction, irritation, of~ fence, pain in the arse (*taboo informal*), pain in the backside, pain in the butt (*informal*), pain in the neck, pest, plague, problem, trouble, vexation

▷ **Antonyms** benefit, blessing, delight, happiness, joy, pleasure, satisfaction

null characterless, ineffectual, inopera~ tive, invalid, nonexistent, null and void, powerless, useless, vain, valueless, void, worthless

nullify abolish, abrogate, annul, bring to naught, cancel, counteract, countervail, invalidate, negate, neutralize, obviate, quash, rebut, render null and void, re~ peal, rescind, revoke, veto, void

▷ **Antonyms** authorize, confirm, endorse, ratify, validate

nullity characterlessness, ineffectualness, invalidity, nonexistence, powerlessness, uselessness, valuelessness, voidness, worthlessness

numb **1.** *adjective* benumbed, dead, dead~ ened, frozen, immobilized, insensible, insensitive, paralysed, stupefied, torpid, unfeeling **2.** *~verb* benumb, deaden, dull, freeze, immobilize, paralyse, stun, stu~ pefy

▷ **Antonyms** *~adjective* feeling, respon~ sive, sensitive, sentient

number *noun* **1.** character, count, digit, figure, integer, numeral, sum, total, unit **2.** aggregate, amount, collection, company, crowd, horde, many, multi~ tude, quantity, throng **3.** copy, edition, imprint, issue, printing *~verb* **4.** account, add, calculate, compute, count, enumer~ ate, include, reckon, tell, total

▷ **Antonyms** *~noun* (*sense 2*) insufficien~

cy, lack, scantiness, scarcity, shortage, want *~verb* conjecture, guess, theorize

numbered categorized, contained, counted, designated, fixed, included, limited, limited in number, specified, totalled

numberless countless, endless, infinite, innumerable, multitudinous, myriad, unnumbered, untold

numbness deadness, dullness, insensibility, insensitivity, paralysis, stupefaction, torpor, unfeelingness

numeral character, cipher, digit, figure, integer, number, symbol

numerous abundant, copious, many, plentiful, profuse, several, thick on the ground

▷ **Antonyms** few, not many, scarcely any

numinous awe-inspiring, divine, heavenly, holy, mysterious, religious, spiritual, supernatural

numbskull, numskull berk (*Brit. slang*), blockhead, bonehead (*slang*), buffoon, charlie (*Brit. informal*), clot (*Brit. informal*), coot, dickhead (*slang*), dimwit (*informal*), dipstick (*Brit. slang*), divvy (*slang*), dolt, dope (*informal*), dork (*slang*), dullard, dummy (*slang*), dunce, dunderhead, dweeb (*U.S. slang*), fathead (*informal*), fool, fuckwit (*taboo slang*), geek (*slang*), gobshite (*Irish taboo slang*), gonzo (*slang*), jerk (*slang, chiefly U.S. & Canad.*), lamebrain (*informal*), nerd *or* nurd (*slang*), nitwit (*informal*), numpty (*Scot. informal*), oaf, pillock (*Brit. slang*), plank (*Brit. slang*), plonker (*slang*), prat (*slang*), prick (*slang*), schmuck (*U.S. slang*), simpleton, thickhead, twit (*informal*), wally (*slang*)

nuncio ambassador, envoy, legate, messenger

nunnery abbey, cloister, convent, house, monastery

nuptial *adjective* bridal, conjugal, connubial, epithalamial (*poetic*), hymeneal (*poetic*), marital, matrimonial, wedded, wedding

nuptials espousal (*archaic*), marriage, matrimony, wedding

nurse *verb* **1.** care for, look after, minister to, tend, treat **2.** breast-feed, feed, nourish, nurture, suckle, wet-nurse **3.** *figurative* cherish, cultivate, encourage, foster, harbour, keep alive, preserve, promote, succour, support

nurture *noun* **1.** diet, food, nourishment **2.** development, discipline, education, instruction, rearing, training, upbringing *~verb* **3.** feed, nourish, nurse, support, sustain, tend **4.** bring up, cultivate, develop, discipline, educate, instruct, rear, school, train

▷ **Antonyms** *~verb* deprive, disregard, ignore, neglect, overlook

nut 1. kernel, pip, seed, stone **2.** *slang* brain, head, mind, reason, senses **3.** *slang* crackpot (*informal*), crank (*informal*), eccentric, headbanger (*informal*), headcase (*informal*), loony (*slang*), lunatic, madman, maniac, nutcase (*slang*), nutter (*Brit. slang*), oddball (*informal*), psycho (*slang*), wacko (*slang*)

nutriment aliment, diet, food, foodstuff, nourishment, nutrition, subsistence, support, sustenance

nutrition food, nourishment, nutriment, sustenance

nutritious alimental, alimentative, beneficial, healthful, health-giving, invigorating, nourishing, nutritive, strengthening, wholesome

nuts as daft as a brush (*informal, chiefly Brit.*), bananas (*slang*), barking (*slang*), barking mad (*slang*), batty (*slang*), crazy (*informal*), demented, deranged, doolally (*slang*), eccentric, gonzo (*slang*), insane, irrational, loony (*slang*), loopy (*informal*), mad, not the full shilling (*informal*), nutty (*slang*), off one's trolley (*slang*), out to lunch (*informal*), psycho (*slang*), psychopathic, up the pole (*informal*), wacko *or* whacko (*informal*)

nuts and bolts basics, details, essentials, fundamentals, ins and outs, nitty-gritty (*informal*), practicalities

nuzzle burrow, cuddle, fondle, nestle, nudge, pet, snuggle

nymph damsel, dryad, girl, hamadryad, lass, maid, maiden, naiad, Oceanid (*Greek myth*), oread, sylph

O, o

oaf airhead (*slang*), berk (*Brit. slang*), blockhead, bonehead (*slang*), booby, brute, charlie (*Brit. informal*), clod, coot, dickhead (*slang*), dipstick (*Brit. slang*), divvy (*Brit. slang*), dolt, dork (*slang*), dullard, dummy (*slang*), dunce, dweeb (*U.S. slang*), fathead (*informal*), fool, fuckwit (*taboo slang*), galoot (*slang, chiefly U.S.*), gawk, geek (*slang*), gob~shite (*Irish taboo slang*), gonzo (*slang*), goon, gorilla (*informal*), halfwit, idiot, imbecile, jerk (*slang, chiefly U.S. & Canad.*), lout, lummox (*informal*), mor~on, nerd *or* nurd (*slang*), nincompoop, nitwit (*informal*), numbskull *or* num~skull, numpty (*Scot. informal*), pillock (*Brit. slang*), plank (*Brit. slang*), plonker (*slang*), prat (*slang*), sap (*slang*), schmuck (*U.S. slang*), simpleton, twit (*informal, chiefly Brit.*), wally (*slang*)
▷ **Antonyms** brain (*informal*), egghead (*informal*), genius, intellect, smart aleck (*informal*), wiseacre

oafish blockish, Boeotian, boneheaded (*slang*), bovine, brutish, dense, dim, dim-witted (*informal*), doltish, dozy (*Brit. informal*), dull, dumb (*informal*), heavy, loutish, lubberly, lumbering, moronic, obtuse, slow on the uptake (*in~formal*), stupid, thick
▷ **Antonyms** acute, brainy (*informal*), bright, clever, intelligent, quick-witted, sharp, smart

oasis *figurative* haven, island, refuge, resting place, retreat, sanctuary, sanc~tum

oath 1. affirmation, avowal, bond, pledge, promise, sworn statement, vow, word **2.** blasphemy, curse, cuss (*informal*), ex~pletive, imprecation, malediction, pro~fanity, strong language, swearword

obdurate adamant, callous, dogged, firm, fixed, hard, hard-hearted, harsh, im~movable, implacable, indurate (*rare*), inexorable, inflexible, iron, mulish, ob~stinate, perverse, pig-headed, proof against persuasion, relentless, stiff-necked, stubborn, unbending, unfeeling, unimpressible, unrelenting, unshak~able, unyielding
▷ **Antonyms** amenable, biddable, com~pliant, flexible, malleable, pliant, soft-hearted, submissive, tender, tractable, yielding

obedience accordance, acquiescence, agreement, assent, compliance, con~formability, deference, docility, dutiful~ness, duty, observance, respect, rever~ence, submission, submissiveness, sub~servience, tractability
▷ **Antonyms** defiance, disobedience, in~subordination, obstinacy, recalcitrance, stubbornness, wilfulness

obedient acquiescent, amenable, bid~dable, compliant, deferential, docile, duteous, dutiful, law-abiding, obser~vant, regardful, respectful, submissive, subservient, tractable, under control, well-trained, yielding
▷ **Antonyms** arrogant, contrary, dis~obedient, disrespectful, intractable, ob~durate, obstinate, rebellious, stubborn, undutiful, ungovernable, unmanage~able, unruly, wayward

obeisance bending of the knee, bow, curtsy *or* curtsey, deference, genuflec~tion, homage, kowtow, respect, rever~ence, salaam, salutation

obelisk column, monolith, monument, needle, pillar, shaft

obese corpulent, Falstaffian, fat, fleshy, gross, heavy, outsize, overweight, paunchy, plump, podgy, portly, roly-poly, rotund, stout, tubby, well-upholstered (*informal*)
▷ **Antonyms** emaciated, gaunt, lean, scraggy, skeletal, skinny, slender, thin

obesity beef (*informal*), bulk, corpulence, *embonpoint,* fatness, fleshiness, gross~ness, overweight, portliness, stoutness, tubbiness, weight problem
▷ **Antonyms** emaciation, gauntness, leanness, skinniness, slenderness, thin~ness

obey 1. abide by, act upon, adhere to, be ruled by, carry out, comply, conform, discharge, do what is expected, em~brace, execute, follow, fulfil, heed, keep, mind, observe, perform, respond, serve **2.** bow to, come to heel, do what one is told, get into line, give in, give way, knuckle under (*informal*), submit, suc~cumb, surrender (to), take orders from, toe the line, yield
▷ **Antonyms** contravene, defy, disobey, disregard, ignore, rebel, transgress, vio~late

obfuscate befog, bewilder, cloud, confuse, darken, muddy the waters, obscure, perplex

object[1] *noun* **1.** article, body, entity, fact, item, phenomenon, reality, thing **2.** aim, butt, focus, recipient, target, victim **3.** design, end, end in view, end purpose, goal, idea, intent, intention, motive, objective, point, purpose, reason, the why and wherefore

object[2] *verb* argue against, demur, draw the line (at something), expostulate, oppose, protest, raise objections, take exception

▷ **Antonyms** accept, acquiesce, admire, agree, approve, assent, compliment, comply, concur, consent, like, relish, take on board, welcome

objection cavil, censure, counter-argument, demur, doubt, exception, niggle (*informal*), opposition, protest, remonstrance, scruple

▷ **Antonyms** acceptance, affirmation, agreement, approbation, assent, concession, endorsement, support

objectionable abhorrent, beyond the pale, deplorable, disagreeable, dislikable *or* dislikeable, displeasing, distasteful, exceptionable, indecorous, insufferable, intolerable, noxious, obnoxious, offensive, regrettable, repugnant, unacceptable, undesirable, unpleasant, unseemly, unsociable

▷ **Antonyms** acceptable, agreeable, desirable, likable *or* likeable, pleasant, pleasing, welcome

objective **1.** *adjective* detached, disinterested, dispassionate, equitable, even-handed, fair, impartial, impersonal, judicial, just, open-minded, unbiased, uncoloured, unemotional, uninvolved, unprejudiced **2.** *~noun* aim, ambition, aspiration, design, end, end in view, goal, Holy Grail (*informal*), intention, mark, object, purpose, target

▷ **Antonyms** (*sense 1*) abstract, biased, personal, prejudiced, subjective, theoretical, unfair, unjust

objectively disinterestedly, dispassionately, even-handedly, impartially, with an open mind, with objectivity *or* impartiality, without fear or favour

objectivity detachment, disinterest, disinterestedness, dispassion, equitableness, impartiality, impersonality

▷ **Antonyms** bent, bias, partiality, predisposition, prejudice, subjectivity

obligation **1.** accountability, accountableness, burden, charge, compulsion, culpability, duty, liability, onus, pigeon (*informal*), requirement, responsibility, trust **2.** agreement, bond, commitment, contract, debt, engagement, promise, understanding **3. under an obligation** beholden, duty-bound, grateful, honour-bound, indebted, in (someone's) debt, obligated, obliged, owing a favour, thankful

obligatory binding, coercive, compulsory, *de rigueur,* enforced, essential, imperative, mandatory, necessary, required, requisite, unavoidable

▷ **Antonyms** discretionary, elective, noncompulsory, optional, voluntary

oblige **1.** bind, coerce, compel, constrain, dragoon, force, impel, make, necessitate, obligate, railroad (*informal*), require **2.** accommodate, benefit, do (someone) a favour *or* a kindness, favour, gratify, indulge, please, put oneself out for, serve

▷ **Antonyms** (*sense 2*) bother, discommode, disoblige, disrupt, inconvenience, put out, trouble

obliged **1.** appreciative, beholden, grateful, gratified, indebted, in (someone's) debt, thankful **2.** bound, compelled, forced, required, under an obligation, under compulsion, without any option

obliging accommodating, agreeable, amiable, civil, complaisant, considerate, co-operative, courteous, eager to please, friendly, good-natured, helpful, kind, polite, willing

▷ **Antonyms** discourteous, disobliging, inconsiderate, rude, sullen, surly, unaccommodating, uncooperative, unhelpful, unobliging

oblique **1.** angled, aslant, at an angle, atilt, inclined, slanted, slanting, sloped, sloping, tilted **2.** backhanded, circuitous, circumlocutory, evasive, implied, indirect, roundabout, sidelong

▷ **Antonyms** (*sense 2*) blunt, candid, direct, downright, forthright, frank, open, straightforward

obliquely **1.** aslant, aslope, at an angle, diagonally, slantwise **2.** circuitously, evasively, in a roundabout manner *or* way, indirectly, not in so many words

obliterate annihilate, blot out, blow sky-high, cancel, delete, destroy, destroy root and branch, efface, eradicate, erase, expunge, extirpate, root out, wipe from the face of the earth, wipe off the face of the earth, wipe out

▷ **Antonyms** build, construct, create, establish, form, formulate, generate, make

obliteration annihilation, blotting out, deletion, effacement, elimination, eradication, erasure, expunction, extirpation, rooting out, sponging out, wiping out

▷ **Antonyms** building, construction, creation, establishment, formation, generation, making

oblivion **1.** abeyance, disregard, forgetfulness, insensibility, neglect, obliviousness, unawareness, unconsciousness, (waters of) Lethe **2.** blackness, darkness, eclipse, extinction, limbo, nothingness, obscurity, void

▷ **Antonyms** (*sense 1*) awareness, con~

sciousness, perception, realization, recognition, sensibility

oblivious blind, careless, deaf, disregardful, forgetful, heedless, ignorant, inattentive, insensible, neglectful, negligent, regardless, unaware, unconcerned, unconscious, unmindful, unobservant

▷ **Antonyms** alert, attentive, aware, conscious, heedful, mindful, observant, watchful

obloquy **1.** abuse, animadversion, aspersion, attack, bad press, blame, calumny, censure, character assassination, contumely, criticism, defamation, detraction, invective, opprobrium, reproach, slander, stick (*slang*), vilification **2.** discredit, disfavour, disgrace, dishonour, humiliation, ignominy, ill fame, ill repute, infamy, odium, shame, stigma

obnoxious abhorrent, abominable, detestable, disagreeable, disgusting, dislikable *or* dislikeable, foul, hateable, hateful, horrid, insufferable, loathsome, nasty, nauseating, objectionable, obscene, odious, offensive, repellent, reprehensible, repugnant, repulsive, revolting, sickening, unpleasant

▷ **Antonyms** agreeable, amiable, charming, congenial, delightful, likable *or* likeable, pleasant, pleasing

obscene **1.** bawdy, blue, coarse, dirty, disgusting, Fescennine (*rare*), filthy, foul, gross, immodest, immoral, improper, impure, indecent, lewd, licentious, loose, offensive, pornographic, prurient, ribald, salacious, scabrous, shameless, smutty, suggestive, unchaste, unwholesome, X-rated (*informal*) **2.** *figurative* atrocious, evil, heinous, loathsome, outrageous, shocking, sickening, vile, wicked

▷ **Antonyms** (*sense 1*) chaste, decent, decorous, inoffensive, modest, proper, pure, refined, respectable, seemly

obscenity **1.** bawdiness, blueness, coarseness, dirtiness, filthiness, foulness, grossness, immodesty, impurity, lewdness, licentiousness, pornography, prurience, salacity, smuttiness, suggestiveness, vileness **2.** four-letter word, impropriety, indecency, indelicacy, profanity, smut, swearword, vulgarism **3.** abomination, affront, atrocity, blight, evil, offence, outrage, vileness, wrong

▷ **Antonyms** (*sense 1*) chastity, decency, decorum, delicacy, innocence, modesty, propriety, purity

obscure *adjective* **1.** abstruse, ambiguous, arcane, clear as mud (*informal*), concealed, confusing, cryptic, deep, Delphic, doubtful, enigmatic, esoteric, hazy, hidden, incomprehensible, indefinite, intricate, involved, mysterious, occult, opaque, recondite, unclear, vague **2.** blurred, clouded, cloudy, dim, dusky, faint, gloomy, indistinct, murky, obfuscated, shadowy, shady, sombre, tenebrous, unlit, veiled **3.** humble, inconspicuous, inglorious, little-known, lowly, minor, nameless, out-of-the-way, remote, undistinguished, unheard-of, unhonoured, unimportant, unknown, unnoted, unseen, unsung *~verb* **4.** conceal, cover, disguise, hide, muddy, obfuscate, screen, throw a veil over, veil **5.** adumbrate, bedim, befog, block, block out, blur, cloak, cloud, darken, dim, dull, eclipse, mask, overshadow, shade, shroud

▷ **Antonyms** *~adjective* (*sense 1*) apparent, clear, conspicuous, definite, distinct, evident, explicit, intelligible, lucid, manifest, obvious, plain, prominent, straightforward, transparent, unmistakable (*sense 2*) apparent, bright, clear, conspicuous, definite, distinct, evident, manifest, obvious, plain, prominent, sharp, transparent, unmistakable, well-defined (*sense 3*) celebrated, distinguished, eminent, familiar, famous, illustrious, important, major, prominent, renowned, significant, well-known, widely-known *~verb* brighten, clarify, disclose, explain, explicate, expose, interpret, reveal, show, uncover, unmask, unveil

obscurity **1.** abstruseness, ambiguity, complexity, impenetrableness, incomprehensibility, intricacy, reconditeness, vagueness **2.** darkness, dimness, dusk, duskiness, gloom, haze, haziness, indistinctness, murkiness, shadowiness, shadows **3.** inconspicuousness, ingloriousness, insignificance, lowliness, namelessness, nonrecognition, unimportance

▷ **Antonyms** (*sense 1*) clarity, clearness, comprehensibility, explicitness, lucidity, obviousness, transparency

obsequies burial, burial service, exequies, funeral, funeral rites, last offices

obsequious abject, cringing, deferential, fawning, flattering, grovelling, ingratiating, mealy-mouthed, menial, servile, slavish, smarmy (*Brit. informal*), submissive, sycophantic, toadying, unctuous

obsequiously abjectly, cringingly, deferentially, fawningly, ingratiatingly, on one's knees, servilely, slavishly, smarmily (*Brit. informal*), sycophantically, unctuously

observable apparent, appreciable, blatant, clear, detectable, discernible, evident, noticeable, obvious, open, patent, perceivable, perceptible, recognizable, visible

observance **1.** adherence to, attention, carrying out, celebration, compliance, discharge, fulfilment, heeding, honouring, notice, observation, performance **2.** ceremonial, ceremony, custom, fashion, form, formality, practice, rite, ritual, service, tradition

▷ **Antonyms** (*sense 1*) disdain, disregard, evasion, heedlessness, inattention, neglect, nonobservance, omission, oversight

observant alert, attentive, eagle-eyed, heedful, mindful, obedient, perceptive, quick, sharp-eyed, submissive, vigilant, watchful, wide-awake

▷ **Antonyms** distracted, dreamy, heedless, inattentive, indifferent, negligent, preoccupied, unobservant, vague

observation 1. attention, cognition, consideration, examination, experience, information, inspection, knowledge, monitoring, notice, review, scrutiny, study, surveillance, watching **2.** annotation, comment, finding, note, obiter dictum, opinion, pronouncement, reflection, remark, thought, utterance

observe 1. detect, discern, discover, espy, note, notice, perceive, see, spot, witness **2.** behold (*archaic or literary*), check, check out (*informal*), clock (*Brit. slang*), contemplate, eye, eyeball (*U.S. slang*), get a load of (*informal*), keep an eye on (*informal*), keep tabs on (*informal*), keep track of, keep under observation, look at, monitor, pay attention to, recce (*slang*), regard, scrutinize, study, survey, take a dekko at (*Brit. slang*), view, watch, watch like a hawk **3.** animadvert, comment, declare, mention, note, opine, remark, say, state **4.** abide by, adhere to, comply, conform to, follow, fulfil, heed, honour, keep, mind, obey, perform, respect **5.** celebrate, commemorate, keep, remember, solemnize

▷ **Antonyms** (*sense 4*) disregard, ignore, miss, neglect, omit, overlook, violate

observer beholder, bystander, commentator, eyewitness, fly on the wall, looker-on, onlooker, spectator, spotter, viewer, watcher, witness

obsess bedevil, be on one's mind, be uppermost in one's thoughts, consume, dominate, engross, grip, haunt, monopolize, plague, possess, preoccupy, prey on one's mind, rule, torment

obsessed beset, dominated, gripped, hag-ridden, haunted, having a one-track mind, hung up on (*slang*), immersed in, infatuated, in the grip of, preoccupied, troubled

▷ **Antonyms** aloof, apathetic, detached, disinterested, impassive, indifferent, uncaring, unconcerned

obsession addiction, bee in one's bonnet (*informal*), complex, enthusiasm, fetish, fixation, hang-up (*informal*), *idée fixe*, infatuation, mania, phobia, preoccupation, ruling passion, thing (*informal*)

obsessive besetting, compulsive, consuming, fixed, gripping, haunting, tormenting, unforgettable

obsolescent ageing, declining, dying out, not with it (*informal*), on the decline, on the wane, on the way out, past its prime, waning

obsolete anachronistic, ancient, antediluvian, antiquated, antique, archaic, bygone, dated, *démodé*, discarded, disused, extinct, musty, old, old-fashioned, old hat, out, outmoded, out of date, out of fashion, out of the ark (*informal*), outworn, passé, past it, superannuated, *vieux jeu*

▷ **Antonyms** à la mode, contemporary, current, fashionable, in, in vogue, modern, new, present day, trendy (*Brit. informal*), up-to-date

obstacle bar, barrier, block, check, difficulty, hindrance, hitch, hurdle, impediment, interference, interruption, obstruction, snag, stumbling block

▷ **Antonyms** advantage, aid, asset, assistance, benefit, crutch, help, support

obstinacy doggedness, firmness, inflexibility, intransigence, mulishness, obduracy, perseverance, persistence, pertinacity, pig-headedness, resoluteness, stubbornness, tenacity, wilfulness

▷ **Antonyms** compliance, cooperativeness, docility, flexibility, meekness, submissiveness, tractability

obstinate contumacious, cussed, determined, dogged, firm, headstrong, immovable, inflexible, intractable, intransigent, mulish, opinionated, persistent, pertinacious, perverse, pig-headed, recalcitrant, refractory, self-willed, steadfast, stiff-necked, strong-minded, stubborn, tenacious, unyielding, wilful

▷ **Antonyms** amenable, biddable, complaisant, compliant, docile, flexible, irresolute, manageable, obedient, submissive, tractable, undecided, wavering

obstreperous boisterous, clamorous, disorderly, loud, noisy, out of control, out of hand, rackety, rambunctious (*informal*), rampaging, raucous, restive, riotous, rip-roaring (*informal*), roistering, roisterous, rough, rowdy, stroppy (*Brit. slang*), tempestuous, tumultuous, turbulent, uncontrolled, undisciplined, unmanageable, unruly, uproarious, vociferous, wild

▷ **Antonyms** calm, controlled, disciplined, docile, gentle, orderly, peaceful, placid, quiet

obstruct arrest, bar, barricade, block, bring to a standstill, bung, check, choke, clog, cumber, curb, cut off, frustrate, get in the way of, hamper, hamstring, hide, hinder, hold up, impede, inhibit, interfere with, interrupt, mask, obscure, prevent, restrict, retard, shield, shut off, slow down, stop, thwart, trammel

▷ **Antonyms** abet, advance, aid, assist, encourage, favour, further, help, promote, support

obstruction bar, barricade, barrier, block, blockage, check, difficulty, hazard, hindrance, impediment, obstacle, occlusion,

snag, stop, stoppage, trammel
▷ **Antonyms** aid, assistance, cooperation, encouragement, favour, furtherance, help, support

obstructive awkward, blocking, delaying, hindering, inhibiting, preventative, restrictive, stalling, uncooperative, unhelpful
▷ **Antonyms** cooperative, encouraging, favourable, helpful, obliging, supportive

obtain 1. achieve, acquire, attain, come by, earn, gain, get, get hold of, get one's hands on, land, procure, score (*slang*), secure **2.** be in force, be prevalent, be the case, exist, hold, prevail, stand
▷ **Antonyms** (*sense 1*) forfeit, forgo, give up, hand over, lose, relinquish, renounce, surrender

obtainable achievable, at hand, attainable, available, on tap (*informal*), procurable, ready, realizable, to be had

obtrusive 1. forward, importunate, interfering, intrusive, meddling, nosy, officious, prying, pushy (*informal*) **2.** blatant, noticeable, obvious, prominent, protruding, protuberant, sticking out
▷ **Antonyms** (*sense 1*) bashful, decorous, diffident, modest, reserved, reticent, retiring, shy, unassuming (*sense 2*) concealed, covert, hidden, inconspicuous, low-key, muted, unnoticeable, unobtrusive

obtrusively blatantly, bluntly, boldly, crassly, importunately, obviously, officiously, pushily

obtuse 1. boneheaded (*slang*), dead from the neck up (*informal*), dense, dopey (*informal*), dull, dull-witted, dumb (*informal*), heavy, imperceptive, insensitive, muttonheaded (*slang*), retarded, slow, slow on the uptake (*informal*), stolid, stupid, thick, thick-skinned, uncomprehending, unintelligent **2.** blunt, rounded
▷ **Antonyms** (*sense 1*) astute, bright, clever, keen, quick, sensitive, sharp, shrewd, smart

obviate anticipate, avert, counter, counteract, do away with, preclude, prevent, remove, render unnecessary

obvious apparent, blatant, bold, clear, clear as a bell, conspicuous, cut-and-dried (*informal*), distinct, evident, indisputable, manifest, much in evidence, noticeable, open, open-and-shut, overt, palpable, patent, perceptible, plain, plain as the nose on your face (*informal*), pronounced, recognizable, right under one's nose (*informal*), salient, self-evident, self-explanatory, staring one in the face (*informal*), sticking out a mile (*informal*), straightforward, transparent, unconcealed, undeniable, undisguised, unmistakable, unsubtle, visible
▷ **Antonyms** ambiguous, clear as mud (*informal*), concealed, dark, hidden, imperceptible, inconspicuous, indistinct, invisible, obscure, unapparent, unclear, vague

obviously certainly, clearly, distinctly, manifestly, needless to say, of course, palpably, patently, plainly, undeniably, unmistakably, unquestionably, without doubt

occasion *noun* **1.** chance, convenience, incident, moment, occurrence, opening, opportunity, time, window **2.** affair, celebration, event, experience, happening, occurrence **3.** call, cause, excuse, ground(s), inducement, influence, justification, motive, prompting, provocation, reason *~verb* **4.** bring about, cause, create, effect, elicit, engender, evoke, generate, give rise to, induce, influence, inspire, lead to, move, originate, persuade, produce, prompt, provoke

occasional casual, desultory, incidental, infrequent, intermittent, irregular, odd, rare, sporadic, uncommon
▷ **Antonyms** constant, continual, customary, frequent, habitual, incessant, regular, routine, usual

occasionally at intervals, at times, (every) now and then, every so often, from time to time, irregularly, now and again, off and on, on and off, once in a while, on occasion, periodically, sometimes
▷ **Antonyms** constantly, continually, continuously, frequently, habitually, often, regularly, routinely

occlude block, bung, choke, clog, close, fill, hinder, obstruct, plug, seal, shut, stop up

occult abstruse, arcane, cabbalistic, concealed, esoteric, hidden, invisible, magical, mysterious, mystic, mystical, obscure, preternatural, recondite, secret, supernatural, unknown, unrevealed, veiled
▷ **Antonyms** apparent, blatant, evident, exposed, manifest, obvious, open, overt, plain, revealed, visible

occultism black magic, diabolism, magic, sorcery, supernaturalism, the black arts, witchcraft

occupancy habitation, holding, inhabitancy, occupation, possession, residence, tenancy, tenure, term, use

occupant addressee, denizen, holder, incumbent, indweller, inhabitant, inmate, lessee, occupier, resident, tenant, user

occupation 1. activity, business, calling, craft, employment, job, line (of work), post, profession, pursuit, trade, vocation, walk of life, work **2.** control, holding, occupancy, possession, residence, tenancy, tenure, use **3.** conquest, foreign rule, invasion, seizure, subjugation

occupied 1. busy, employed, engaged, hard at it (*informal*), tied up (*informal*), working **2.** engaged, full, in use, taken,

unavailable **3.** full, inhabited, lived-in, peopled, settled, tenanted
▷ **Antonyms** (*sense 3*) deserted, empty, tenantless, uninhabited, unoccupied, untenanted, vacant, void

occupy 1. (*often passive*) absorb, amuse, busy, divert, employ, engage, engross, entertain, hold the attention of, im~ merse, interest, involve, keep busy *or* occupied, monopolize, preoccupy, take up, tie up **2.** be established in, be in residence in, dwell in, ensconce oneself in, establish oneself in, inhabit, live in, own, possess, reside in, stay in (*Scot.*), tenant **3.** cover, fill, hold, permeate, per~ vade, take up, use, utilize **4.** capture, garrison, hold, invade, keep, overrun, seize, take over, take possession of
▷ **Antonyms** (*senses 2 & 4*) abandon, de~ part, desert, evacuate, quit, retreat, va~ cate, withdraw

occur 1. arise, befall, betide, chance, come about, come off (*informal*), come to pass (*archaic*), crop up (*informal*), eventuate, happen, materialize, result, take place, turn up (*informal*) **2.** appear, be found, be met with, be present, develop, exist, manifest itself, obtain, show itself **3.** (*with* **to**) come to mind, come to one, cross one's mind, dawn on, enter one's head, offer itself, present itself, spring to mind, strike one, suggest itself

occurrence 1. adventure, affair, circum~ stance, episode, event, happening, inci~ dent, instance, proceeding, transaction **2.** appearance, development, existence, manifestation, materialization

odd 1. abnormal, atypical, bizarre, curi~ ous, deviant, different, eccentric, excep~ tional, extraordinary, fantastic, freak, freakish, freaky (*slang*), funny, irregu~ lar, kinky (*informal*), left-field (*infor~ mal*), oddball (*informal*), off-the-wall (*slang*), outlandish, out of the ordinary, outré, peculiar, quaint, queer, rare, re~ markable, rum (*Brit. slang*), singular, strange, uncanny, uncommon, uncon~ ventional, unusual, wacko (*slang*), weird, whimsical **2.** casual, fragmentary, incidental, irregular, miscellaneous, oc~ casional, periodic, random, seasonal, sundry, varied, various **3.** leftover, lone, remaining, single, solitary, spare, sur~ plus, unconsumed, uneven, unmatched, unpaired
▷ **Antonyms** (*sense 1*) common, custom~ ary, familiar, natural, normal, ordinary, regular, typical, unexceptional, unre~ markable, usual (*sense 2*) habitual, per~ manent, regular, steady (*sense 3*) even, matched, paired

oddity 1. abnormality, anomaly, eccentri~ city, freak, idiosyncrasy, irregularity, kink, peculiarity, phenomenon, quirk, rarity **2.** card (*informal*), crank (*infor~ mal*), fish out of water, loose cannon, maverick, misfit, nut (*slang*), oddball (*informal*), odd bird (*informal*), odd fish (*Brit. informal*), rara avis, screwball (*slang, chiefly U.S. & Canad.*), wacko (*slang*), weirdo *or* weirdie (*informal*) **3.** abnormality, bizarreness, eccentricity, extraordinariness, freakishness, incon~ gruity, oddness, outlandishness, peculi~ arity, queerness, singularity, strange~ ness, unconventionality, unnaturalness

odd man out exception, freak, maverick, misfit, nonconformist, outsider, square peg in a round hole (*informal*)

oddment bit, butt, end, end of a line, fag end, fragment, leftover, off cut, rem~ nant, scrap, shred, sliver, snippet, stub, tail end

odds 1. advantage, allowance, edge, lead, superiority **2.** balance, chances, likeli~ hood, probability **3.** *Brit.* difference, dis~ parity, dissimilarity, distinction **4. at odds** at daggers drawn, at loggerheads, at sixes and sevens, at variance, in con~ flict, in disagreement, in opposition to, not in keeping, on bad terms, out of line

odds and ends bits, bits and pieces, de~ bris, leavings, litter, oddments, rem~ nants, rubbish, scraps, sundry *or* mis~ cellaneous items

odious abhorrent, abominable, detest~ able, disgusting, execrable, foul, hateful, horrible, horrid, loathsome, obnoxious, obscene, offensive, repellent, repugnant, repulsive, revolting, unpleasant, vile, yucky *or* yukky (*slang*)
▷ **Antonyms** agreeable, charming, con~ genial, delightful, enchanting, enjoy~ able, pleasant, pleasing, winsome

odium abhorrence, antipathy, censure, condemnation, detestation, disapproba~ tion, disapproval, discredit, disfavour, disgrace, dishonour, dislike, disrepute, execration, hatred, infamy, obloquy, op~ probrium, reprobation, shame

odorous aromatic, balmy, fragrant, odor~ iferous, perfumed, redolent, scented, sweet-smelling

odour 1. aroma, bouquet, essence, fra~ grance, niff (*Brit. slang*), perfume, redo~ lence, scent, smell, stench, stink **2.** air, atmosphere, aura, emanation, flavour, quality, spirit

odyssey crusade, journey, peregrination, pilgrimage, quest, trek, voyage

off *adjective* **1.** absent, cancelled, fin~ ished, gone, inoperative, postponed, un~ available **2.** bad, below par, disappoint~ ing, disheartening, displeasing, low-quality, mortifying, poor, quiet, slack, substandard, unrewarding, unsatisfac~ tory **3.** bad, decomposed, high, mouldy, rancid, rotten, sour, turned *~adverb* **4.** apart, aside, away, elsewhere, out

off and on (every) now and again, every once in a while, from time to time, intermittently, now and then, occasion~ ally, on and off, sometimes, sporadically

offbeat bizarre, Bohemian, eccentric, far-out (*slang*), freaky (*slang*), idiosyncratic, kinky (*informal*), left-field (*informal*), novel, oddball (*informal*), off-the-wall (*slang*), *outré,* rum (*Brit. slang*), strange, uncommon, unconventional, unorthodox, unusual, wacko (*slang*), way-out (*informal*), weird

▷ **Antonyms** common, conventional, normal, ordinary, orthodox, run-of-the-mill, stereotyped, traditional, unoriginal, usual

off colour green about the gills, ill, not up to par, off form, out of sorts, peaky, peely-wally (*Scot.*), poorly (*informal*), queasy, run down, sick, under par, under the weather (*informal*), unwell, washed out

offence 1. breach of conduct, crime, delinquency, fault, lapse, misdeed, misdemeanour, peccadillo, sin, transgression, trespass, wrong, wrongdoing **2.** affront, displeasure, harm, hurt, indignity, injury, injustice, insult, outrage, put-down (*slang*), slight, snub **3.** anger, annoyance, displeasure, hard feelings, huff, indignation, ire (*literary*), needle (*informal*), pique, resentment, umbrage, wounded feelings, wrath **4. take offence** be disgruntled, be offended, get riled, go into a huff, resent, take the huff, take the needle (*informal*), take umbrage

offend 1. affront, aggravate (*informal*), annoy, cut to the quick, disgruntle, displease, fret, gall, get (someone's) goat (*slang*), give offence, hurt (someone's) feelings, insult, irritate, miff (*informal*), nark (*Brit., Austral., & N.Z. slang*), outrage, pain, pique, piss one off (*taboo slang*), provoke, put down, put (someone's) back up, put (someone's) nose out of joint, rile, slight, snub, tread on (someone's) toes (*informal*), upset, vex, wound **2.** be disagreeable to, disgust, gross out (*U.S. slang*), make (someone) sick, nauseate, repel, repulse, sicken, turn (someone) off (*informal*)

▷ **Antonyms** (*sense 1*) appease, assuage, conciliate, delight, mollify, placate, please, soothe

offended affronted, disgruntled, displeased, huffy, in a huff, miffed (*informal*), outraged, pained, piqued, put out (*informal*), resentful, smarting, stung, upset

offender criminal, crook, culprit, delinquent, lawbreaker, malefactor, miscreant, sinner, transgressor, villain, wrongdoer

offensive *adjective* **1.** abusive, annoying, detestable, discourteous, displeasing, disrespectful, embarrassing, impertinent, insolent, insulting, irritating, objectionable, rude, uncivil, unmannerly **2.** abominable, detestable, disagreeable, disgusting, grisly, loathsome, nasty, nauseating, noisome, obnoxious, odious, repellent, revolting, sickening, unpalatable, unpleasant, unsavoury, vile, yucky *or* yukky (*slang*) **3.** aggressive, attacking, invading *~noun* **4.** attack, campaign, drive, onslaught, push (*informal*) **5. on the offensive** advancing, aggressive, attacking, invading, invasive, on the warpath (*informal*)

▷ **Antonyms** *~adjective* agreeable, attractive, captivating, charming, civil, conciliatory, courteous, defensive, deferential, delightful, pleasant, polite, respectful *~noun* defensive

offer *verb* **1.** bid, extend, give, hold out, proffer, put on the market, put under the hammer, put up for sale, tender **2.** afford, furnish, make available, place at (someone's) disposal, present, provide, purvey, show **3.** advance, extend, move, propose, put forth, put forward, submit, suggest **4.** be at (someone's) service, come forward, offer one's services, volunteer *~noun* **5.** attempt, bid, endeavour, essay, overture, proposal, proposition, submission, suggestion, tender

▷ **Antonyms** (*senses 1 & 3*) recant, refuse, retract, revoke, take back, withdraw, withhold

offering contribution, donation, gift, hand-out, oblation (*in religious contexts*), present, sacrifice, subscription, widow's mite

off form below par, having lost one's touch, not at one's best, not up to scratch (*informal*), on a bad day, out of practice, out of training, unpractised

offhand 1. *adjective* abrupt, aloof, brusque, careless, casual, cavalier, couldn't-care-less, curt, glib, informal, offhanded, perfunctory, take-it-or-leave-it (*informal*), unceremonious, unconcerned, uninterested **2.** *~adverb* ad lib, extempore, impromptu, just like that (*informal*), off the cuff (*informal*), off the top of one's head (*informal*), without preparation

▷ **Antonyms** *~adjective* attentive, careful, grave, intent, planned, premeditated, prepared, responsible, serious, thoughtful

office 1. appointment, business, capacity, charge, commission, duty, employment, function, obligation, occupation, place, post, responsibility, role, service, situation, station, trust, work **2.** *plural* advocacy, aegis, aid, auspices, backing, favour, help, intercession, intervention, mediation, patronage, recommendation, referral, support, word

officer agent, appointee, bureaucrat, dignitary, executive, functionary, office-holder, official, public servant, representative

official 1. *adjective* accredited, authentic, authoritative, authorized, bona fide, certified, endorsed, ex cathedra, ex officio, formal, legitimate, licensed, proper, sanctioned, signed and sealed, straight from the horse's mouth (*informal*) **2.** *~noun* agent, bureaucrat, executive, functionary, office bearer, officer, representative

▷ **Antonyms** *~adjective* casual, doubtful, dubious, informal, unauthorized, unofficial, unreliable

officiate chair, conduct, emcee (*informal*), manage, oversee, preside, serve, superintend

officious bustling, dictatorial, forward, impertinent, inquisitive, interfering, intrusive, meddlesome, meddling, mischievous, obtrusive, opinionated, overbusy, overzealous, pragmatical (*rare*), pushy (*informal*), self-important

▷ **Antonyms** aloof, detached, indifferent, reserved, reticent, retiring, shy, taciturn, unforthcoming, withdrawn

offing in the offing close at hand, coming up, hovering, imminent, in prospect, in the immediate future, in the wings, on the horizon, on the way, upcoming

off key discordant, dissonant, inharmonious, jarring, out of keeping, out of tune

off-load disburden, discharge, dump, get rid of, jettison, lighten, shift, take off, transfer, unburden, unload, unship

off-putting daunting, discomfiting, disconcerting, discouraging, dismaying, dispiriting, disturbing, formidable, frustrating, intimidating, unnerving, unsettling, upsetting

offset 1. *verb* balance out, cancel out, compensate for, counteract, counterbalance, counterpoise, countervail, make up for, neutralize **2.** *~noun* balance, compensation, counterbalance, counterweight, equipoise

offshoot adjunct, appendage, branch, by-product, development, limb, outgrowth, scion, spin-off, sprout

offspring brood, child, children, descendant, descendants, family, fry, heir, heirs, issue, kids (*informal*), progeny, scion, seed (*chiefly biblical*), spawn, successor, successors, young

▷ **Antonyms** ancestor, begetter, forebear, forefather, forerunner, parent, predecessor, procreator, progenitor

often again and again, frequently, generally, many a time, much, oft (*archaic or poetic*), oftentimes (*archaic*), ofttimes (*archaic*), over and over again, repeatedly, time after time, time and again

▷ **Antonyms** hardly ever, infrequently, irregularly, never, now and then, occasionally, rarely, scarcely, seldom

ogle eye up (*informal*), gawp at (*Brit. slang*), give the glad eye (*informal*), give the once-over (*informal*), lech *or* letch after (*informal*), leer, make sheep's eyes at (*informal*)

ogre bogey, bogeyman, bugbear, demon, devil, giant, monster, spectre

oil *verb* grease, lubricate

oily 1. fatty, greasy, oiled, oleaginous, smeary, swimming **2.** flattering, fulsome, glib, hypocritical, obsequious, plausible, servile, smarmy (*Brit. informal*), smooth, unctuous

ointment balm, cerate, cream, embrocation, emollient, liniment, lotion, salve, unguent

O.K., okay 1. *adjective* acceptable, accurate, adequate, all right, approved, convenient, correct, fair, fine, good, in order, middling, not bad (*informal*), passable, permitted, satisfactory, so-so (*informal*), tolerable, up to scratch (*informal*) **2.** *~noun* agreement, approbation, approval, assent, authorization, consent, endorsement, go-ahead (*informal*), green light, permission, sanction, say-so (*informal*), seal of approval **3.** *~verb* agree to, approve, authorize, consent to, endorse, entitle, give one's consent to, give the go-ahead, give the green light, give the thumbs up (*informal*), pass, rubber-stamp (*informal*), sanction, say yes to **4.** *~interjection* agreed, all right, right, roger, very good, very well, yes

▷ **Antonyms** *~adjective* displeasing, inaccurate, inadequate, incorrect, not up to scratch (*informal*), poor, unacceptable, unsatisfactory, unsuitable

old 1. advanced in years, aged, ancient, decrepit, elderly, full of years, getting on, grey, grey-haired, grizzled, hoary, mature, over the hill (*informal*), past it, past one's prime, patriarchal, senescent, senile, venerable **2.** antediluvian, antiquated, antique, cast-off, crumbling, dated, decayed, done, hackneyed, obsolete, old-fashioned, outdated, outmoded, out of date, out of the ark (*informal*), passé, stale, superannuated, timeworn, unfashionable, unoriginal, worn-out **3.** aboriginal, antique, archaic, bygone, early, immemorial, of old, of yore, olden (*archaic*), original, primeval, primitive, primordial, pristine, remote **4.** age-old, experienced, familiar, hardened, long-established, of long standing, practised, skilled, time-honoured, traditional, versed, veteran, vintage **5.** earlier, erstwhile, ex-, former, one-time, previous, quondam

▷ **Antonyms** (*sense 1*) immature, juvenile, young, youthful (*sense 2*) current, fashionable, modern, modish, new, novel, recent, up-to-date

old age advancing years, age, agedness, Anno Domini (*informal*), autumn *or* evening of one's life, declining years, dotage, eld (*archaic*), senescence, senility, Third Age

▷ **Antonyms** adolescence, childhood, early life, immaturity, juvenescence, young days, youth

old-fashioned ancient, antiquated, ar~ chaic, behind the times, corny (*slang*), dated, dead, *démodé,* fusty, musty, not with it (*informal*), obsolescent, obsolete, oldfangled, (old-)fogeyish, old hat, old-time, outdated, outmoded, out of date, out of style, out of the ark (*informal*), passé, past, square (*informal*), superan~ nuated, unfashionable
▷ **Antonyms** chic, contemporary, cur~ rent, fashionable, happening (*informal*), modern, modish, trendy (*Brit. informal*), up-to-date, voguish, with it (*informal*)

old hand expert, old soldier, old-timer, one of the old school, past master, vet~ eran

old man coffin-dodger (*slang*), elder, elder statesman, father, gaffer, grandfather, greybeard, O.A.P. (*Brit.*), old codger (*in~ formal*), old stager, oldster (*informal*), old-timer (*U.S.*), papa (*old-fashioned informal*), patriarch, senior citizen, slang

old-time ancient, antique, bygone, for~ mer, old-fashioned, past, vintage

old womanish finicky, fussy, niggly, niminy-piminy, old-maidish (*informal*), overcautious, overparticular, pernickety (*informal*), prim, prudish, strait-laced, timid, timorous

old-world archaic, ceremonious, chival~ rous, courtly, gallant, old-fashioned, picturesque, quaint, traditional

oleaginous adipose, fat, fatty, greasy, oily, sebaceous, unguinous (*obsolete*)

Olympian elevated, exalted, glorious, godlike, lofty, majestic, rarefied, splen~ did, sublime

omen augury, foreboding, foretoken, in~ dication, portent, premonition, presage, prognostic, prognostication, sign, straw in the wind, warning, writing on the wall

ominous baleful, dark, fateful, forbid~ ding, foreboding, inauspicious, menac~ ing, minatory, portentous, premonitory, sinister, threatening, unpromising, un~ propitious
▷ **Antonyms** auspicious, encouraging, favourable, promising, propitious

omission default, exclusion, failure, for~ getfulness, gap, lack, leaving out, ne~ glect, noninclusion, oversight
▷ **Antonyms** addition, inclusion, incor~ poration, insertion

omit disregard, drop, eliminate, exclude, fail, forget, give (something) a miss (*in~ formal*), leave out, leave (something) undone, let (something) slide, miss (out), neglect, overlook, pass over, skip
▷ **Antonyms** add, enter, include, incor~ porate, insert, put in

omnipotence divine right, invincibility, mastery, sovereignty, supremacy, su~ preme power, undisputed sway
▷ **Antonyms** frailty, impotence, inability, inferiority, powerlessness, vulnerability, weakness

omnipotent all-powerful, almighty, su~ preme
▷ **Antonyms** feeble, frail, impotent, in~ capable, inferior, powerless, vulnerable, weak

omniscient all-knowing, all-seeing, all-wise

on and off by fits and starts, discontinu~ ously, (every) now and again, fitfully, from time to time, intermittently, now and then, off and on, on occasion, some~ times, spasmodically

once 1. at one time, formerly, in the old days, in the past, in times gone by, in times past, long ago, once upon a time, previously **2. at once: a.** directly, forth~ with, immediately, instantly, now, right away, straight away, straightway (*ar~ chaic*), this (very) minute, without de~ lay, without hesitation **b.** at *or* in one go (*informal*), at the same time, simul~ taneously, together **3. once and for all** conclusively, decisively, finally, for all time, for good, for the last time, perma~ nently, positively, with finality **4. once in a while** at intervals, at times, every now and then, from time to time, now and again, occasionally, once in a blue moon (*informal*), on occasion, sometimes

oncoming advancing, approaching, forthcoming, imminent, impending, looming, onrushing, upcoming

one-horse backwoods, inferior, minor, obscure, petty, quiet, sleepy, slow, small, small-time (*informal*), tinpot (*Brit. informal*), unimportant

onerous backbreaking, burdensome, crushing, demanding, difficult, exacting, exhausting, exigent, formidable, grave, hard, heavy, laborious, oppressive, re~ sponsible, taxing, weighty
▷ **Antonyms** cushy (*informal*), easy, ef~ fortless, facile, light, painless, simple, trifling, undemanding, unexacting, untaxing

one-sided biased, coloured, discrimina~ tory, inequitable, lopsided, partial, par~ tisan, prejudiced, unequal, unfair, un~ just
▷ **Antonyms** equal, equitable, fair, im~ partial, just, unbiased, uncoloured, un~ prejudiced

one-time erstwhile, ex-, former, late, previous, quondam, sometime

ongoing advancing, continuous, current, developing, evolving, extant, growing, in progress, progressing, successful, unfin~ ished, unfolding

onlooker bystander, eyewitness, looker-on, observer, spectator, viewer, watcher, witness

only 1. *adverb* at most, barely, exclusive~ ly, just, merely, purely, simply **2.** *~adjective* exclusive, individual, lone,

one and only, single, sole, solitary, unique

onomatopoeic echoic, imitative, onomatopoetic

onrush charge, flood, flow, onset, onslaught, push, rush, stampede, stream, surge

onset **1.** assault, attack, charge, onrush, onslaught **2.** beginning, inception, kick-off (*informal*), outbreak, start
▷ **Antonyms** (*sense 2*) conclusion, culmination, end, ending, finish, outcome, termination, wind-up

onslaught assault, attack, blitz, charge, offensive, onrush, onset
▷ **Antonyms** defensive, escape, flight, recession, retreat, rout, stampede, withdrawal

onus burden, liability, load, obligation, responsibility, task
▷ **Antonyms** easement, exemption, exoneration, liberation, pardon, release, relief, remission

onward, onwards *adverb* ahead, beyond, forth, forward, in front, on

ooze **1.** *verb* bleed, discharge, drain, dribble, drip, drop, emit, escape, exude, filter, leach, leak, overflow with, percolate, seep, strain, sweat, weep **2.** *~noun* alluvium, gloop (*informal*), mire, muck, mud, silt, slime, slob (*Irish*), sludge

oozy dewy, dripping, miry, moist, mucky, slimy, sloppy, sludgy, sweaty, weeping

opacity cloudiness, density, dullness, filminess, impermeability, milkiness, murkiness, obscurity, opaqueness

opalescent iridescent, lustrous, nacreous, opaline, pearly, prismatic, rainbow-hued, shot

opaque **1.** clouded, cloudy, dim, dull, filmy, hazy, impenetrable, lustreless, muddied, muddy, murky, obfuscated, turbid **2.** abstruse, baffling, cryptic, difficult, enigmatic, incomprehensible, obscure, unclear, unfathomable, unintelligible
▷ **Antonyms** (*sense 1*) bright, clear, crystal clear, limpid, lucid, pellucid, transparent, transpicuous (*sense 2*) clear, crystal clear, lucid

open *adjective* **1.** agape, ajar, expanded, extended, gaping, revealed, spread out, unbarred, unclosed, uncovered, unfastened, unfolded, unfurled, unlocked, unobstructed, unsealed, yawning **2.** airy, bare, clear, exposed, extensive, free, navigable, not built-up, passable, rolling, spacious, sweeping, uncluttered, uncrowded, unenclosed, unfenced, unsheltered, wide, wide-open **3.** accessible, available, free, free to all, general, nondiscriminatory, public, unconditional, unengaged, unoccupied, unqualified, unrestricted, up for grabs (*informal*), vacant **4.** apparent, avowed, barefaced, blatant, bold, clear, conspicuous, downright, evident, flagrant, frank, manifest, noticeable, obvious, overt, plain, unconcealed, undisguised, visible **5.** arguable, debatable, moot, undecided, unresolved, unsettled, up in the air, yet to be decided **6.** disinterested, free, impartial, objective, receptive, unbiased, uncommitted, unprejudiced **7.** (*with* **to**) an easy target for, at the mercy of, defenceless against, disposed, exposed, liable, susceptible, vulnerable **8.** above board, artless, candid, fair, frank, guileless, honest, ingenuous, innocent, natural, sincere, transparent, unreserved **9.** filigree, fretted, holey, honeycombed, lacy, loose, openwork, porous, spongy **10.** bounteous, bountiful, generous, liberal, munificent, prodigal **11.** exposed, undefended, unfortified, unprotected *~verb* **12.** begin, begin business, commence, get *or* start the ball rolling, inaugurate, initiate, kick off (*informal*), launch, put up one's plate, set in motion, set up shop, start **13.** clear, crack, throw wide, unbar, unblock, unclose, uncork, uncover, undo, unfasten, unlock, unseal, untie, unwrap **14.** expand, spread (out), unfold, unfurl, unroll **15.** come apart, crack, rupture, separate, split **16.** disclose, divulge, exhibit, explain, lay bare, pour out, show, uncover
▷ **Antonyms** *~adjective* (*senses 1 & 2*) bounded, closed, concealed, confined, covered, crowded, enclosed, fastened, limited, locked, obstructed, restricted, sealed, shut (*senses 3 & 4*) covert, disguised, hidden, inaccessible, private, protected, restricted, secret, veiled (*sense 6*) biased, partial, prejudiced (*senses 7 & 11*) defended, protected (*sense 8*) artful, cunning, introverted, reserved, secretive, sly, withdrawn *~verb* (*sense 12*) close, conclude, end, finish, terminate (*sense 13*) block, close, fasten, lock, obstruct, seal, shut (*sense 14*) fold

open-air alfresco, outdoor

open-and-shut foregone, noncontroversial, obvious, simple, straightforward

open-handed bountiful, free, generous, lavish, liberal, munificent, prodigal, unstinting
▷ **Antonyms** avaricious, close-fisted, grasping, grudging, mean, miserly, parsimonious, penny-pinching (*informal*), stingy, tight-fisted

opening *noun* **1.** aperture, breach, break, chink, cleft, crack, fissure, gap, hole, interstice, orifice, perforation, rent, rupture, slot, space, split, vent **2.** break (*informal*), chance, look-in (*informal*), occasion, opportunity, place, vacancy, window **3.** beginning, birth, commencement, dawn, inauguration, inception, initiation, kickoff (*informal*), launch, launching, onset, opening move, outset, overture, start *~adjective* **4.** beginning, commencing, early, first, inaugural, initial, initiatory, introductory, maiden, primary

▷ **Antonyms** (*sense 1*) blockage, cessation, closing, closure, obstruction, occlusion, plug, seal, stoppage (*sense 3*) close, completion, conclusion, culmination, ending, finale, finish, termination, winding up (*informal*)

openly 1. candidly, face to face, forthrightly, frankly, overtly, plainly, straight from the shoulder (*informal*), unhesitatingly, unreservedly **2.** blatantly, brazenly, flagrantly, in full view, in public, publicly, shamelessly, unabashedly, unashamedly, wantonly, without pretence

▷ **Antonyms** covertly, furtively, in camera, privately, quietly, secretly, slyly, surreptitiously

open-minded broad, broad-minded, catholic, dispassionate, enlightened, free, impartial, liberal, reasonable, receptive, tolerant, unbiased, undogmatic, unprejudiced

▷ **Antonyms** assertive, biased, bigoted, dogmatic, intolerant, narrow-minded, opinionated, pig-headed, prejudiced, uncompromising

operate 1. act, be in action, be in business, function, go, perform, run, work **2.** be in charge of, handle, manage, manoeuvre, use, work **3.** perform surgery

▷ **Antonyms** (*sense 1*) break down, conk out (*informal*), cut out (*informal*), fail, falter, halt, seize up, stall, stop

operation 1. action, affair, course, exercise, motion, movement, performance, procedure, process, use, working **2. in operation** effective, functioning, going, in action, in business, in force, operative **3.** activity, agency, effect, effort, force, influence, instrumentality, manipulation **4.** affair, business, deal, enterprise, proceeding, transaction, undertaking **5.** assault, campaign, exercise, manoeuvre **6.** surgery

operational functional, going, in working order, operative, prepared, ready, up and running, usable, viable, workable, working

▷ **Antonyms** broken, ineffective, inoperative, kaput (*informal*), nonfunctional, on the blink (*slang*), out of order

operative *adjective* **1.** active, current, effective, efficient, functional, functioning, in business, in force, in operation, operational, serviceable, standing, workable **2.** crucial, important, indicative, influential, key, relevant, significant ~*noun* **3.** artisan, employee, hand, labourer, machinist, mechanic, worker

▷ **Antonyms** (*sense 1*) ineffective, inefficient, inoperative, nonfunctional, powerless, unusable, unworkable

operator 1. conductor, driver, handler, mechanic, operative, practitioner, skilled employee, technician, worker **2.** administrator, contractor, dealer, director, manager, speculator, trader **3.** *informal* Machiavellian, machinator, manipulator, mover, shyster (*slang, chiefly U.S.*), smart aleck (*informal*), wheeler-dealer (*informal*), wirepuller, worker

opiate anodyne, bromide, downer (*slang*), drug, narcotic, nepenthe, pacifier, sedative, soporific, tranquillizer

opine believe, conceive, conclude, conjecture, declare, give as one's opinion, judge, presume, say, suggest, suppose, surmise, think, venture, volunteer, ween (*poetic*)

opinion 1. assessment, belief, conception, conjecture, estimation, feeling, idea, impression, judgment, mind, notion, persuasion, point of view, sentiment, theory, view **2. be of the opinion** be convinced, believe, be under the impression, conclude, consider, hold, judge, reckon, suppose, surmise, think **3. matter of opinion** debatable point, matter of judgment, moot point, open question, open to debate, up to the individual

opinionated adamant, biased, bigoted, bull-headed, cocksure, dictatorial, doctrinaire, dogmatic, inflexible, obdurate, obstinate, overbearing, pig-headed, prejudiced, self-assertive, single-minded, stubborn, uncompromising

▷ **Antonyms** broad-minded, compliant, compromising, dispassionate, flexible, open-minded, receptive, tolerant, unbiased, unbigoted, unprejudiced

opponent adversary, antagonist, challenger, competitor, contestant, disputant, dissentient, enemy, foe, opposer, rival, the opposition

▷ **Antonyms** accomplice, ally, associate, colleague, friend, helper, mate, supporter

opportune advantageous, appropriate, apt, auspicious, convenient, falling into one's lap, favourable, felicitous, fit, fitting, fortunate, happy, lucky, proper, propitious, seasonable, suitable, timely, well-timed

▷ **Antonyms** inappropriate, inconvenient, inopportune, unfavourable, unfortunate, unsuitable, untimely

opportunism expediency, exploitation, Machiavellianism, making hay while the sun shines (*informal*), pragmatism, realism, *Realpolitik,* striking while the iron is hot (*informal*), trimming, unscrupulousness

opportunity break (*informal*), chance, convenience, hour, look-in (*informal*), moment, occasion, opening, scope, time, window

oppose 1. bar, block, check, combat, confront, contradict, counter, counterattack, defy, face, fight, fly in the face of, hinder, obstruct, prevent, resist, set

one's face against, speak against, stand up to, take a stand against, take issue with, take on, thwart, withstand **2.** compare, contrast, counterbalance, match, pit *or* set against, play off
▷ **Antonyms** (*sense 1*) advance, advocate, aid, back, defend, espouse, help, promote, support

opposed against, antagonistic, anti (*informal*), antipathetic, antithetical, at daggers drawn, averse, clashing, conflicting, contra (*informal*), contrary, dissentient, hostile, incompatible, inimical, in opposition, opposing, opposite

opposing antagonistic, antipathetic, clashing, combatant, conflicting, contrary, enemy, hostile, incompatible, irreconcilable, opposed, opposite, rival, warring

opposite *adjective* **1.** corresponding, facing, fronting **2.** adverse, antagonistic, antithetical, conflicting, contradictory, contrary, contrasted, diametrically opposed, different, differing, diverse, hostile, inconsistent, inimical, irreconcilable, opposed, poles apart, reverse, unlike *~noun* **3.** antithesis, contradiction, contrary, converse, inverse, reverse, the other extreme, the other side of the coin (*informal*)
▷ **Antonyms** (*sense 2*) alike, consistent, corresponding, identical, like, matching, same, similar, uniform

opposition 1. antagonism, competition, contrariety, counteraction, disapproval, hostility, obstruction, obstructiveness, prevention, resistance, unfriendliness **2.** antagonist, competition, foe, opponent, other side, rival
▷ **Antonyms** (*sense 1*) agreement, approval, assent, collaboration, concurrence, cooperation, correspondence, friendliness, responsiveness

oppress 1. afflict, burden, depress, dispirit, harass, lie *or* weigh heavy upon, sadden, take the heart out of, torment, vex **2.** abuse, crush, harry, maltreat, overpower, overwhelm, persecute, rule with an iron hand, subdue, subjugate, suppress, trample underfoot, tyrannize over, wrong
▷ **Antonyms** deliver, emancipate, free, liberate, loose, release, set free, unburden

oppressed abused, browbeaten, burdened, disadvantaged, downtrodden, enslaved, harassed, henpecked, maltreated, misused, prostrate, slave, subject, troubled, tyrannized, underprivileged
▷ **Antonyms** advantaged, exalted, favoured, honoured, liberated, privileged

oppression abuse, brutality, calamity, cruelty, hardship, harshness, injury, injustice, iron hand, maltreatment, misery, persecution, severity, subjection, suffering, tyranny
▷ **Antonyms** benevolence, clemency, compassion, goodness, humaneness, justice, kindness, mercy, sympathy, tenderness

oppressive 1. brutal, burdensome, cruel, despotic, grinding, harsh, heavy, inhuman, onerous, overbearing, overwhelming, repressive, severe, tyrannical, unjust **2.** airless, close, heavy, muggy, overpowering, stifling, stuffy, suffocating, sultry, torrid
▷ **Antonyms** (*sense 1*) encouraging, gentle, humane, just, lenient, merciful, propitious, soft

oppressor autocrat, bully, despot, harrier, intimidator, iron hand, persecutor, scourge, slave-driver, taskmaster, tormentor, tyrant

opprobrious 1. abusive, calumniatory, contemptuous, contumelious, damaging, defamatory, hateful, insolent, insulting, invective, offensive, scandalous, scurrilous, vitriolic, vituperative **2.** abominable, contemptible, despicable, dishonourable, disreputable, hateful, ignominious, infamous, notorious, reprehensible, shameful

opprobrium calumny, censure, contumely, discredit, disfavour, disgrace, dishonour, disrepute, ignominy, ill repute, infamy, obloquy, odium, reproach, scurrility, shame, slur, stigma

oppugn argue, assail, attack, call into question, cast doubt on, combat, dispute, oppose, resist, withstand

opt (for) choose, decide (on), elect, exercise one's discretion (in favour of), go for, make a selection, plump for, prefer
▷ **Antonyms** decide against, dismiss, eliminate, exclude, preclude, reject, rule out, turn down

optimistic 1. disposed to take a favourable view, idealistic, seen through rose-coloured spectacles, Utopian **2.** assured, bright, buoyant, buoyed up, cheerful, confident, encouraged, expectant, hopeful, looking on the bright side, positive, sanguine
▷ **Antonyms** bleak, cynical, despairing, despondent, downhearted, fatalistic, gloomy, glum, hopeless, pessimistic, resigned

optimum *adjective* A1 *or* A-one (*informal*), best, choicest, flawless, highest, ideal, most favourable *or* advantageous, optimal, peak, perfect, superlative
▷ **Antonyms** inferior, least, lowest, minimal, poorest, worst

option alternative, choice, election, preference, selection

optional discretionary, elective, extra, noncompulsory, open, possible, up to the individual, voluntary
▷ **Antonyms** compulsory, de rigeur, mandatory, obligatory, required

opulence **1.** affluence, big bucks (*informal, chiefly U.S.*), big money, easy circumstances, Easy Street (*informal*), fortune, lavishness, luxuriance, luxury, megabucks (*U.S. & Canad. slang*), plenty, pretty penny (*informal*), prosperity, riches, richness, sumptuousness, tidy sum (*informal*), wad (*U.S. & Canad. slang*), wealth **2.** abundance, copiousness, cornucopia, fullness, profusion, richness, superabundance

▷ **Antonyms** (*sense 1*) impecuniousness, indigence, lack, penury, poverty, privation, want (*sense 2*) dearth, lack, paucity, scantiness, scarcity, want

opulent **1.** affluent, lavish, luxurious, moneyed, prosperous, rich, sumptuous, wealthy, well-heeled (*informal*), well-off, well-to-do **2.** abundant, copious, lavish, luxuriant, plentiful, profuse, prolific

▷ **Antonyms** (*sense 1*) broke (*informal*), destitute, down and out, indigent, moneyless, needy, on the rocks, penurious, poor, poverty-stricken

opus brainchild, composition, creation, *oeuvre,* piece, production, work

oracle **1.** augur, Cassandra, prophet, seer, sibyl, soothsayer **2.** answer, augury, divination, divine utterance, prediction, prognostication, prophecy, revelation, vision **3.** adviser, authority, guru, high priest, horse's mouth, mastermind, mentor, pundit, source, wizard

oracular **1.** auspicious, foreboding, haruspical, mantic, ominous, portentous, prescient, prophetic, pythonic, sibylline, vatic (*rare*) **2.** authoritative, dictatorial, dogmatic, grave, positive, sage, significant, venerable, wise **3.** ambiguous, arcane, cryptic, Delphic, equivocal, mysterious, obscure, two-edged

oral spoken, verbal, viva voce, vocal

orate declaim, discourse, hold forth, make a speech, pontificate, speak, speechify, talk

oration address, declamation, discourse, harangue, homily, lecture, speech, spiel (*informal*)

orator Cicero, declaimer, lecturer, public speaker, rhetorician, speaker, spellbinder, spieler (*informal*)

oratorical bombastic, Ciceronian, declamatory, eloquent, grandiloquent, high-flown, magniloquent, rhetorical, silver-tongued, sonorous

oratory declamation, elocution, eloquence, grandiloquence, public speaking, rhetoric, speechifying, speech-making, spieling (*informal*)

orb ball, circle, globe, ring, round, sphere

orbit *noun* **1.** circle, circumgyration, course, cycle, ellipse, path, revolution, rotation, track, trajectory **2.** *figurative* ambit, compass, course, domain, influence, range, reach, scope, sphere, sphere of influence, sweep ~*verb* **3.** circle, circumnavigate, encircle, revolve around

orchestrate **1.** arrange, score **2.** arrange, concert, coordinate, integrate, organize, present, put together, set up, stage-manage

ordain **1.** anoint, appoint, call, consecrate, destine, elect, frock, invest, nominate **2.** fate, foreordain, intend, predestine, predetermine **3.** decree, demand, dictate, enact, enjoin, establish, fix, lay down, legislate, order, prescribe, pronounce, rule, set, will

ordeal affliction, agony, anguish, baptism of fire, hardship, nightmare, suffering, test, torture, trial, tribulation(s), trouble(s)

▷ **Antonyms** bliss, delight, elation, enjoyment, gladness, happiness, joy, pleasure

order *noun* **1.** arrangement, harmony, method, neatness, orderliness, organization, pattern, plan, propriety, regularity, symmetry, system, tidiness **2.** arrangement, array, categorization, classification, codification, disposal, disposition, grouping, layout, line, line-up, ordering, placement, progression, sequence, series, setup (*informal*), structure, succession **3. in order: a.** arranged, in sequence, neat, orderly, shipshape, tidy **b.** acceptable, appropriate, called for, correct, fitting, O.K. *or* okay (*informal*), right, suitable **4. out of order: a.** broken, broken-down, buggered (*slang, chiefly Brit.*), bust (*informal*), gone haywire (*informal*), gone phut (*informal*), in disrepair, inoperative, kaput (*informal*), nonfunctional, not working, on the blink (*slang*), on the fritz (*U.S. slang*), out of commission, U.S. (*informal*), wonky (*Brit. slang*) **b.** improper, indecorous, not cricket (*informal*), not done, not on (*informal*), out of place, out of turn, uncalled-for, wrong **5.** calm, control, discipline, law, law and order, peace, quiet, tranquillity **6.** caste, class, degree, grade, hierarchy, pecking order (*informal*), position, rank, status **7.** breed, cast, class, family, genre, genus, ilk, kind, sort, species, subclass, taxonomic group, tribe, type **8.** behest, canon, command, decree, dictate, direction, directive, injunction, instruction, law, mandate, ordinance, precept, regulation, rule, say-so (*informal*), stipulation **9.** application, booking, commission, request, requisition, reservation **10.** association, brotherhood, community, company, fraternity, guild, league, lodge, organization, sect, sisterhood, society, sodality, union ~*verb* **11.** adjure, bid, charge, command, decree, demand, direct, enact, enjoin, instruct, ordain, prescribe, require **12.** apply for, authorize, book, call for, contract for, demand, engage, prescribe, request, reserve, send away for **13.** adjust, align, arrange, catalogue, class, classify, conduct, control, dispose, group, lay out, manage, marshal, neaten, organize, put to rights, regulate, sequence, set in order, sort out, systematize, tabulate, tidy

▷ **Antonyms** ~*noun* (*senses 1 & 2*) chaos, clutter, confusion, disarray, disorder, jumble, mess, muddle, pandemonium, shambles ~*verb* (*sense 13*) clutter, confuse, disarrange, disorder, disturb, jumble up, mess up, mix up, muddle, scramble

orderly *adjective* **1.** businesslike, in apple-pie order (*informal*), in order, methodical, neat, regular, scientific, shipshape, systematic, systematized, tidy, trim, well-organized, well-regulated **2.** controlled, decorous, disciplined, law-abiding, nonviolent, peaceable, quiet, restrained, well-behaved

▷ **Antonyms** (*sense 1*) chaotic, disorderly, disorganized, higgledy-piggledy (*informal*), messy, sloppy, unsystematic (*sense 2*) disorderly, riotous, uncontrolled, undisciplined

ordinance **1.** canon, command, decree, dictum, edict, enactment, fiat, law, order, precept, regulation, rule, ruling, statute **2.** ceremony, institution, observance, practice, rite, ritual, sacrament, usage

ordinarily as a rule, commonly, customarily, generally, habitually, in general, in the general run (of things), in the usual way, normally, usually

▷ **Antonyms** hardly ever, infrequently, occasionally, rarely, scarcely, seldom, uncommonly

ordinary **1.** accustomed, banal, common, customary, established, everyday, habitual, humdrum, mundane, normal, prevailing, quotidian, regular, routine, settled, standard, stock, typical, usual, wonted **2.** common or garden (*informal*), conventional, down-to-earth, familiar, homespun, household, humble, modest, plain, prosaic, run-of-the-mill, simple, unmemorable, unpretentious, unremarkable, workaday **3.** average, commonplace, dime-a-dozen (*informal*), fair, indifferent, inferior, mean, mediocre, no great shakes (*informal*), pedestrian, second-rate, stereotyped, undistinguished, unexceptional, uninspired, unremarkable **4. out of the ordinary** atypical, distinguished, exceptional, exciting, extraordinary, high-calibre, imaginative, important, impressive, inspired, noteworthy, outstanding, rare, remarkable, significant, special, striking, superior, uncommon, unusual

▷ **Antonyms** (*senses 1, 2 & 3*) distinguished, exceptional, extraordinary, important, impressive, inspired, notable, novel, outstanding, rare, significant, superior, uncommon, unconventional, unique, unusual

ordnance arms, artillery, big guns, cannon, guns, materiel, munitions, weapons

organ **1.** device, implement, instrument, tool **2.** element, member, part, process, structure, unit **3.** agency, channel, forum, journal, means, medium, mouthpiece, newspaper, paper, periodical, publication, vehicle, voice

organic **1.** animate, biological, biotic, live, living, natural **2.** integrated, methodical, ordered, organized, structured, systematic **3.** anatomical, constitutional, fundamental, immanent, inherent, innate, integral, structural

organism animal, being, body, creature, entity, living thing, structure

organization **1.** assembling, assembly, construction, coordination, direction, disposal, formation, forming, formulation, making, management, methodology, organizing, planning, regulation, running, standardization, structuring **2.** arrangement, chemistry, composition, configuration, conformation, constitution, design, format, framework, grouping, make-up, method, organism, pattern, plan, structure, system, unity, whole **3.** association, body, combine, company, concern, confederation, consortium, corporation, federation, group, institution, league, outfit (*informal*), syndicate

organize arrange, be responsible for, catalogue, classify, codify, constitute, construct, coordinate, dispose, establish, form, frame, get going, get together, group, lay the foundations of, lick into shape, look after, marshal, pigeonhole, put in order, put together, run, see to (*informal*), set up, shape, straighten out, systematize, tabulate, take care of

▷ **Antonyms** confuse, derange, disorganize, disrupt, jumble, mix up, muddle, scramble, upset

orgiastic abandoned, bacchanalian, bacchic, debauched, depraved, Dionysian, dissolute, frenetic, riotous, Saturnalian, wanton, wild

orgy **1.** bacchanal, bacchanalia, carousal, carouse, debauch, revel, revelry, Saturnalia **2.** binge (*informal*), bout, excess, indulgence, overindulgence, splurge, spree, surfeit

orient *verb* acclimatize, adapt, adjust, align, familiarize, find one's feet (*informal*), get one's bearings, get the lie of the land, orientate

orientation **1.** bearings, coordination, direction, location, position, sense of direction **2.** acclimatization, adaptation, adjustment, assimilation, breaking in, familiarization, introduction, settling in

orifice aperture, cleft, hole, mouth, opening, perforation, pore, rent, vent

origin **1.** base, basis, cause, derivation, *fons et origo,* font (*poetic*), fount, fountain, fountainhead, occasion, provenance, root, roots, source, spring, wellspring **2.** beginning, birth, commencement, creation, dawning, early stages, emergence, foundation, genesis, inauguration, inception, launch, origination, outset, start **3.** ancestry, beginnings, birth, descent, extraction, family, heritage, lineage, parentage, pedigree, stirps, stock

▷ **Antonyms** conclusion, culmination, death, end, expiry, finale, finish, outcome, termination

original *adjective* **1.** aboriginal, autochthonous, commencing, earliest, early, embryonic, first, infant, initial, introductory, opening, primary, primitive, primordial, pristine, rudimentary, starting **2.** creative, fertile, fresh, ground-breaking, imaginative, ingenious, innovative, innovatory, inventive, new, novel, resourceful, seminal, unconventional, unprecedented, untried, unusual **3.** archetypal, authentic, first, first-hand, genuine, master, primary, prototypical *~noun* **4.** archetype, master, model, paradigm, pattern, precedent, prototype, standard, type **5.** anomaly, card (*informal*), case (*informal*), character, eccentric, nonconformist, nut (*slang*), oddball (*informal*), oddity, queer fish (*Brit. informal*), wacko (*slang*), weirdo *or* weirdie (*informal*)

▷ **Antonyms** *~adjective* (*sense 1*) final, last, latest (*sense 2*) antiquated, banal, commonplace, conventional, familiar, normal, old, old-fashioned, ordinary, stale, standard, stock, traditional, typical, unimaginative, unoriginal, usual (*sense 3*) borrowed, copied, secondary, unoriginal *~noun* (*sense 4*) copy, imitation, replica, reproduction

originality boldness, break with tradition, cleverness, creativeness, creative spirit, creativity, daring, freshness, imagination, imaginativeness, individuality, ingenuity, innovation, innovativeness, inventiveness, new ideas, newness, novelty, resourcefulness, unconventionality, unorthodoxy

▷ **Antonyms** conformity, conventionality, imitativeness, normality, orthodoxy, regularity, staleness, traditionalism

originally at first, at the outset, at the start, by birth, by derivation, by origin, first, initially, in the beginning, in the first place, to begin with

originate **1.** arise, be born, begin, come, derive, emanate, emerge, flow, issue, proceed, result, rise, spring, start, stem **2.** bring about, conceive, create, develop, discover, evolve, form, formulate, generate, give birth to, inaugurate, initiate, institute, introduce, invent, launch, pioneer, produce, set in motion, set up

▷ **Antonyms** cease, conclude, culminate, end, expire, finish, terminate, wind up

originator architect, author, creator, father, founder, generator, innovator, inventor, maker, mother, pioneer, prime mover

ornament *noun* **1.** accessory, adornment, bauble, decoration, embellishment, festoon, frill, furbelow, garnish, gewgaw, knick-knack, trimming, trinket **2.** flower, honour, jewel, leading light, pride, treasure *~verb* **3.** adorn, beautify, bedizen (*archaic*), brighten, deck, decorate, dress up, embellish, festoon, garnish, gild, grace, prettify, prink, trim

ornamental attractive, beautifying, decorative, embellishing, for show, showy

ornamentation adornment, decoration, elaboration, embellishment, embroidery, frills, ornateness

ornate aureate, baroque, beautiful, bedecked, busy, convoluted, decorated, elaborate, elegant, fancy, florid, flowery, fussy, high-wrought, ornamented, overelaborate, rococo

▷ **Antonyms** austere, bare, basic, ordinary, plain, severe, simple, spartan, stark, subdued, unadorned, unfussy

orthodox accepted, approved, conformist, conventional, correct, customary, doctrinal, established, kosher (*informal*), official, received, sound, traditional, true, well-established

▷ **Antonyms** eccentric, heretical, left-field (*informal*), liberal, nonconformist, novel, off-the-wall (*slang*), original, radical, unconventional, unorthodox, unusual

orthodoxy authenticity, authoritativeness, authority, conformism, conformity, conventionality, devotion, devoutness, faithfulness, inflexibility, received wisdom, soundness, traditionalism

▷ **Antonyms** flexibility, heresy, heterodoxy, impiety, nonconformism, nonconformity, unconventionality

oscillate fluctuate, seesaw, sway, swing, vacillate, vary, vibrate, waver

▷ **Antonyms** commit oneself, decide, determine, purpose, resolve, settle

oscillation fluctuation, instability, seesawing, swing, vacillation, variation, wavering

ossified bony, fixed, fossilized, frozen, hardened, indurated (*rare*), inflexible, petrified, rigid, rigidified, solid

ossify fossilize, freeze, harden, indurate (*rare*), petrify, solidify, stiffen

ostensible alleged, apparent, avowed, exhibited, manifest, outward, plausible, pretended, professed, purported, seeming, so-called, specious, superficial, supposed

ostensibly apparently, for the ostensible purpose of, on the face of it, on the surface, professedly, seemingly, supposedly, to all intents and purposes

ostentation affectation, boasting, display, exhibitionism, flamboyance, flashiness, flaunting, flourish, pageantry, parade, pomp, pretension, pretentiousness, show, showiness, showing off (*informal*), swank (*informal*), vaunting, window-dressing
▷ **Antonyms** humility, inconspicuousness, modesty, plainness, reserve, simplicity, unpretentiousness

ostentatious boastful, brash, conspicuous, crass, dashing, extravagant, flamboyant, flash (*informal*), flashy, flaunted, gaudy, loud, obtrusive, pompous, pretentious, showy, swanky (*informal*), vain, vulgar
▷ **Antonyms** conservative, inconspicuous, low-key, modest, plain, reserved, simple, sombre

ostracism avoidance, banishment, boycott, cold-shouldering, exclusion, exile, expulsion, isolation, rejection
▷ **Antonyms** acceptance, admission, approval, inclusion, invitation, reception, welcome

ostracize avoid, banish, blackball, blacklist, boycott, cast out, cold-shoulder, exclude, excommunicate, exile, expatriate, expel, give (someone) the cold shoulder, reject, send to Coventry, shun, snub
▷ **Antonyms** accept, admit, approve, embrace, greet, include, invite, receive, welcome

other *adjective* **1.** added, additional, alternative, auxiliary, extra, further, more, spare, supplementary **2.** contrasting, different, dissimilar, distinct, diverse, remaining, separate, unrelated, variant

otherwise *adverb* **1.** if not, or else, or then **2.** any other way, contrarily, differently

ounce atom, crumb, drop, grain, iota, particle, scrap, shred, speck, trace, whit

oust depose, disinherit, dislodge, displace, dispossess, eject, evict, expel, relegate, throw out, topple, turn out, unseat

out *adjective* **1.** impossible, not allowed, not on (*informal*), ruled out, unacceptable **2.** abroad, absent, away, elsewhere, gone, not at home, outside **3.** antiquated, behind the times, dated, dead, *démodé,* old-fashioned, old hat, passé, square (*informal*), unfashionable **4.** at an end, cold, dead, doused, ended, exhausted, expired, extinguished, finished, used up
▷ **Antonyms** (*sense 3*) à la mode, fashionable, in, in fashion, latest, modern, trendy (*Brit. informal*), up-to-date, with it (*informal*)

out-and-out absolute, arrant, complete, consummate, deep-dyed (*usually derogatory*), downright, dyed-in-the-wool, outright, perfect, thoroughgoing, total, unmitigated, unqualified, utter

outbreak burst, epidemic, eruption, explosion, flare-up, flash, outburst, rash, spasm, upsurge

outburst access, attack, discharge, eruption, explosion, fit of temper, flare-up, gush, outbreak, outpouring, paroxysm, spasm, storm, surge

outcast *noun* castaway, derelict, displaced person, exile, leper, pariah, *persona non grata,* refugee, reprobate, untouchable, vagabond, wretch

outclass be a cut above (*informal*), beat, eclipse, exceed, excel, leave *or* put in the shade, leave standing (*informal*), outdistance, outdo, outrank, outshine, outstrip, overshadow, run rings around (*informal*), surpass

outcome aftereffect, aftermath, conclusion, consequence, end, end result, issue, payoff (*informal*), result, sequel, upshot

outcry clamour, commotion, complaint, cry, exclamation, howl, hue and cry, hullaballoo, noise, outburst, protest, scream, screech, uproar, yell

outdated antiquated, antique, archaic, behind the times, *démodé,* obsolete, old-fashioned, outmoded, out of date, out of style, out of the ark (*informal*), passé, unfashionable
▷ **Antonyms** à la mode, all the rage, contemporary, current, fashionable, in vogue, modern, modish, stylish, trendy (*Brit. informal*), up-to-date, with it (*informal*)

outdistance leave behind, leave standing (*informal*), lose, outrun, outstrip, shake off

outdo beat, be one up on, best, eclipse, exceed, excel, get the better of, go one better than (*informal*), outclass, outdistance, outfox, outjockey, outmanoeuvre, outshine, outsmart (*informal*), overcome, run rings around (*informal*), score points off, surpass, top, transcend

outdoor alfresco, open-air, out-of-door(s), outside
▷ **Antonyms** indoor, inside, interior, within

outer exposed, exterior, external, outlying, outside, outward, peripheral, remote, superficial, surface
▷ **Antonyms** central, closer, inner, inside, interior, internal, inward, nearer

outface beard, brave, confront, defy, look straight in the eye, outstare, square up to, stare down, stare out (of countenance)

outfit *noun* **1.** accoutrements, clothes, costume, ensemble, garb, gear (*informal*), get-up (*informal*), kit, rigout (*informal*), suit, threads (*slang*), togs (*informal*), trappings **2.** *informal* clique, company, corps, coterie, crew, firm, *galère,* group, organization, set, setup (*informal*), squad, team, unit *~verb* **3.** accoutre, appoint, equip, fit out, furnish, kit out, provision, stock, supply, turn out

outfitter clothier, costumier, couturier, dressmaker, haberdasher (*U.S.*), modiste, tailor

outflow discharge, drainage, ebb, effluence, efflux, effusion, emanation, emergence, gush, issue, jet, outfall, outpouring, rush, spout

outgoing 1. departing, ex-, former, last, leaving, past, retiring, withdrawing **2.** approachable, communicative, cordial, demonstrative, easy, expansive, extrovert, friendly, genial, gregarious, informal, open, sociable, sympathetic, unreserved, warm

▷ **Antonyms** (*sense 1*) arriving, entering, incoming (*sense 2*) austere, cold, indifferent, reserved, retiring, withdrawn

outgoings costs, expenditure, expenses, outlay, overheads

outgrowth 1. bulge, excrescence, node, offshoot, outcrop, process, projection, protuberance, scion, shoot, sprout **2.** by-product, consequence, derivative, development, emergence, issue, product, result, spin-off, yield

outing excursion, expedition, jaunt, pleasure trip, spin (*informal*), trip

outlandish alien, barbarous, bizarre, eccentric, exotic, fantastic, far-out (*slang*), foreign, freakish, grotesque, left-field (*informal*), *outré,* preposterous, queer, strange, unheard-of, weird

▷ **Antonyms** banal, commonplace, everyday, familiar, humdrum, mundane, normal, ordinary, usual, well-known

outlast endure beyond, outlive, outstay, outwear, survive

outlaw 1. *noun* bandit, brigand, desperado, footpad (*archaic*), fugitive, highwayman, marauder, outcast, pariah, robber **2.** *~verb* ban, banish, bar, condemn, disallow, embargo, exclude, forbid, interdict, make illegal, prohibit, proscribe, put a price on (someone's) head

▷ **Antonyms** *~verb* allow, approve, authorize, consent, endorse, legalise, permit, sanction, support

outlay *noun* cost, disbursement, expenditure, expenses, investment, outgoings, spending

outlet 1. avenue, channel, duct, egress, exit, means of expression, opening, orifice, release, safety valve, vent, way out **2.** market, shop, store

outline *noun* **1.** draft, drawing, frame, framework, layout, lineament(s), plan, rough, skeleton, sketch, tracing **2.** bare facts, main features, recapitulation, résumé, rough idea, rundown, summary, synopsis, thumbnail sketch **3.** configuration, contour, delineation, figure, form, profile, shape, silhouette *~verb* **4.** adumbrate, delineate, draft, plan, rough out, sketch (in), summarize, trace

outlive come through, endure beyond, live through, outlast, survive

outlook 1. angle, attitude, frame of mind, perspective, point of view, slant, standpoint, viewpoint, views **2.** expectations, forecast, future, prospect **3.** aspect, panorama, prospect, scene, view, vista

outlying backwoods, distant, far-flung, in the middle of nowhere, outer, out-of-the-way, peripheral, provincial, remote

outmanoeuvre circumvent, get the better of, outdo, outflank, outfox, outgeneral, outjockey, outsmart (*informal*), outwit, run rings round (*informal*), steal a march on (*informal*)

outmoded anachronistic, antediluvian, antiquated, antique, archaic, behind the times, bygone, dated, *démodé,* fossilized, obsolescent, obsolete, olden (*archaic*), oldfangled, old-fashioned, old-time, out, out of date, out of style, out of the ark (*informal*), outworn, passé, square (*informal*), superannuated, superseded, unfashionable, unusable

▷ **Antonyms** all the rage, fashionable, fresh, in vogue, latest, modern, modish, new, recent, usable

out of date antiquated, archaic, dated, discarded, elapsed, expired, extinct, invalid, lapsed, obsolete, old-fashioned, outmoded, out of the ark (*informal*), outworn, passé, stale, superannuated, superseded, unfashionable

▷ **Antonyms** contemporary, current, fashionable, in, new, now (*informal*), trendy (*Brit. informal*), up to date, valid

out-of-the-way 1. distant, far-flung, inaccessible, isolated, lonely, obscure, off the beaten track, outlying, remote, secluded, unfrequented **2.** abnormal, curious, exceptional, extraordinary, odd, outlandish, out of the ordinary, peculiar, strange, uncommon, unusual

▷ **Antonyms** (*sense 1*) accessible, close, convenient, frequented, handy, near, nearby, proximate, reachable, within sniffing distance (*informal*)

out of work idle, jobless, laid off, on the dole (*Brit.*), out of a job, redundant, unemployed

outpouring cascade, debouchment, deluge, effluence, efflux, effusion, emanation, flow, flux, issue, outflow, spate, spurt, stream, torrent

output achievement, manufacture, outturn (*rare*), product, production, productivity, yield

outrage *noun* **1.** atrocity, barbarism, enormity, evil, inhumanity **2.** abuse, affront, desecration, indignity, injury, insult, offence, profanation, rape, ravishing, sacrilege, shock, violation, violence **3.** anger, fury, hurt, indignation, resentment, shock, wrath *~verb* **4.** affront, incense, infuriate, madden, make one's blood boil, offend, scandalize, shock **5.** abuse, defile, desecrate, injure, insult, maltreat, rape, ravage, ravish, violate

outrageous **1.** abominable, atrocious, barbaric, beastly, egregious, flagrant, heinous, horrible, infamous, inhuman, iniquitous, nefarious, scandalous, shocking, unspeakable, villainous, violent, wicked **2.** disgraceful, excessive, exorbitant, extravagant, immoderate, offensive, O.T.T. (*slang*), over the top (*slang*), preposterous, scandalous, shocking, steep (*informal*), unreasonable

▷ **Antonyms** equitable, fair, just, mild, minor, moderate, reasonable, tolerable, trivial

outré bizarre, eccentric, extravagant, fantastic, freakish, freaky (*slang*), grotesque, indecorous, kinky (*informal*), left-field (*informal*), odd, off-the-wall (*slang*), outlandish, rum (*Brit. slang*), unconventional, way-out (*informal*), weird

outrider advance guard, advance man, attendant, bodyguard, escort, guard, harbinger, herald, precursor, scout, squire

outright *adjective* **1.** absolute, arrant, complete, consummate, deep-dyed (*usually derogatory*), downright, out-and-out, perfect, pure, thorough, thoroughgoing, total, unconditional, undeniable, unmitigated, unqualified, utter, wholesale **2.** definite, direct, flat, straightforward, unequivocal, unqualified *~adverb* **3.** absolutely, completely, explicitly, openly, overtly, straightforwardly, thoroughly, to the full, without hesitation, without restraint **4.** at once, cleanly, immediately, instantaneously, instantly, on the spot, straight away, there and then, without more ado

outrun beat, escape, exceed, excel, get away from, leave behind, lose, outdistance, outdo, outpace, outstrip, shake off, surpass

outset beginning, commencement, early days, inauguration, inception, kickoff (*informal*), onset, opening, start, starting point

▷ **Antonyms** closing, completion, conclusion, consummation, end, finale, finish, termination

outshine be head and shoulders above, be superior to, eclipse, leave *or* put in the shade, outclass, outdo, outstrip, overshadow, surpass, top, transcend, upstage

outside *adjective* **1.** exterior, external, extramural, extraneous, extreme, out, outdoor, outer, outermost, outward, surface **2.** distant, faint, marginal, negligible, remote, slight, slim, small, unlikely *~noun* **3.** exterior, façade, face, front, skin, surface, topside

▷ **Antonyms** (*sense 1*) in, indoor, inner, innermost, inside, interior, internal, intramural, inward

outsider alien, foreigner, incomer, interloper, intruder, newcomer, nonmember, odd man out, outlander, stranger

outskirts borders, boundary, edge, environs, faubourgs, periphery, purlieus, suburbia, suburbs, vicinity

outsmart deceive, dupe, get the better of, go one better than (*informal*), make a fool of (*informal*), outfox, outjockey, outmanoeuvre, outperform, outthink, outwit, pull a fast one on (*informal*), put one over on (*informal*), run rings round (*informal*), trick

outspoken abrupt, blunt, candid, direct, downright, explicit, forthright, frank, free, free-spoken, open, plain-spoken, round, unceremonious, undissembling, unequivocal, unreserved

▷ **Antonyms** diplomatic, gracious, judicious, reserved, reticent, tactful

outspread **1.** *adjective* expanded, extended, fanlike, fanned out, flared, open, opened up, outstretched, unfolded, unfurled, wide-open **2.** *~verb* expand, extend, fan out, open, open wide, outstretch, spread out, unfold, unfurl

outstanding **1.** celebrated, distinguished, eminent, excellent, exceptional, great, important, impressive, meritorious, pre-eminent, special, stellar (*informal*), superior, superlative, well-known **2.** arresting, conspicuous, eye-catching, marked, memorable, notable, noteworthy, prominent, salient, signal, striking **3.** due, ongoing, open, owing, payable, pending, remaining, uncollected, unpaid, unresolved, unsettled

▷ **Antonyms** (*senses 1 & 2*) dull, inferior, insignificant, mediocre, no great shakes (*informal*), ordinary, pedestrian, run-of-the-mill, unexceptional, unimpressive

outstrip beat, better, eclipse, exceed, excel, get ahead of, knock spots off (*informal*), leave behind, leave standing (*informal*), lose, outclass, outdistance, outdo, outpace, outperform, outrun, outshine, overtake, run rings around (*informal*), shake off, surpass, top, transcend

outward *adjective* apparent, evident, exterior, external, noticeable, observable, obvious, ostensible, outer, outside, perceptible, superficial, surface, visible

▷ **Antonyms** inner, inside, interior, internal, invisible, inward, obscure, unnoticeable

outwardly apparently, as far as one can see, externally, officially, on the face of it, on the surface, ostensibly, professedly, seemingly, superficially, to all ap~

pearances, to all intents and purposes, to the eye

outweigh cancel (out), compensate for, eclipse, make up for, outbalance, overcome, override, predominate, preponderate, prevail over, take precedence over, tip the scales

outwit cheat, circumvent, deceive, defraud, dupe, get the better of, gull (*archaic*), make a fool *or* monkey of, outfox, outjockey, outmanoeuvre, outsmart (*informal*), outthink, put one over on (*informal*), run rings round (*informal*), swindle, take in (*informal*)

outworn abandoned, antiquated, behind the times, defunct, discredited, disused, exhausted, hackneyed, obsolete, outdated, outmoded, out of date, overused, rejected, stale, superannuated, threadbare, tired, worn-out

▷ **Antonyms** credited, fresh, modish, new, recent, up to date, used

oval *adjective* egg-shaped, ellipsoidal, elliptical, ovate, oviform, ovoid

ovation acclaim, acclamation, applause, big hand, cheering, cheers, clapping, laudation, plaudits, tribute

▷ **Antonyms** abuse, booing, catcalls, derision, heckling, jeers, jibes, mockery, ridicule

over *adjective* **1.** accomplished, ancient history (*informal*), at an end, by, bygone, closed, completed, concluded, done (with), ended, finished, gone, past, settled, up (*informal*) *~adjective/adverb* **2.** beyond, extra, in addition, in excess, left over, remaining, superfluous, surplus, unused *~preposition* **3.** above, on, on top of, superior to, upon **4.** above, exceeding, in excess of, more than *~adverb* **5.** above, aloft, on high, overhead **6. over and above** added to, as well as, besides, in addition to, let alone, not to mention, on top of, plus **7. over and over (again)** ad nauseam, again and again, frequently, often, repeatedly, time and again

overabundance embarrassment of riches, excess, glut, oversupply, plethora, profusion, superabundance, superfluity, surfeit, surplus, too much of a good thing

overact exaggerate, ham *or* ham up (*informal*), overdo, overplay

overall 1. *adjective* all-embracing, blanket, complete, comprehensive, general, global, inclusive, long-range, long-term, total, umbrella **2.** *~adverb* generally speaking, in general, in (the) large, in the long term, on the whole

overawe abash, alarm, browbeat, cow, daunt, frighten, intimidate, scare, terrify

▷ **Antonyms** bolster, buoy up, cheer up, comfort, console, hearten, reassure

overbalance capsize, keel over, lose one's balance, lose one's footing, overset, overturn, slip, take a tumble, tip over, topple over, tumble, turn turtle, upset

overbearing arrogant, autocratic, bossy (*informal*), cavalier, despotic, dictatorial, dogmatic, domineering, haughty, high-handed, imperious, lordly, magisterial, officious, oppressive, overweening, peremptory, supercilious, superior, tyrannical

▷ **Antonyms** deferential, humble, modest, self-effacing, submissive, unassertive, unassuming

overblown 1. disproportionate, excessive, fulsome, immoderate, inflated, overdone, over the top, undue **2.** aureate, bombastic, euphuistic, florid, flowery, fustian, grandiloquent, magniloquent, pompous, turgid, windy

overcast clouded, clouded over, cloudy, darkened, dismal, dreary, dull, grey, hazy, leaden, louring *or* lowering, murky, sombre, sunless, threatening

▷ **Antonyms** bright, brilliant, clear, cloudless, fine, sunny, unclouded

overcharge 1. cheat, clip (*slang*), diddle (*informal*), do (*slang*), fleece, rip off (*slang*), rook (*slang*), short-change, skin (*slang*), sting (*informal*), surcharge **2.** burden, oppress, overburden, overload, overtask, overtax, strain, surfeit **3.** *literary* embellish, embroider, exaggerate, hyperbolize, lay it on thick (*informal*), overstate

overcome 1. *verb* beat, best, be victorious, blow out of the water (*slang*), bring (someone) to their knees (*informal*), clobber (*slang*), come out on top (*informal*), conquer, crush, defeat, get the better of, lick (*informal*), make mincemeat of (*informal*), master, overpower, overthrow, overwhelm, prevail, render helpless, render incapable, render powerless, rise above, stuff (*slang*), subdue, subjugate, surmount, survive, tank (*slang*), triumph over, undo, vanquish, weather, wipe the floor with (*informal*), worst **2.** *~adjective* affected, at a loss for words, bowled over (*informal*), overwhelmed, speechless, swept off one's feet, unable to continue, visibly moved

overconfident brash, cocksure, foolhardy, hubristic, overweening, presumptuous, riding for a fall (*informal*), uppish (*Brit. informal*)

▷ **Antonyms** cautious, diffident, doubtful, hesitant, insecure, timid, timorous, uncertain, unsure

overcritical captious, carping, cavilling, fault-finding, hairsplitting, hard to please, hypercritical, nit-picking (*informal*), overparticular, pedantic, pernickety (*informal*), picky (*informal*)

▷ **Antonyms** easily pleased, easy-going, laid-back (*informal*), lenient, tolerant, uncritical, undemanding, unfussy

overcrowded bursting at the seams, choked, congested, crammed full,

hoatching (*Scot.*), jam-packed, like the Black Hole of Calcutta, overloaded, overpopulated, packed (out), swarming
▷ **Antonyms** abandoned, deserted, desolate, empty, forsaken, unoccupied, vacant

overdo **1.** be intemperate, belabour, carry too far, do to death (*informal*), exaggerate, gild the lily, go overboard (*informal*), go to extremes, lay it on thick (*informal*), not know when to stop, overindulge, overplay, overreach, overstate, overuse, overwork, run riot **2. overdo it** bite off more than one can chew, burn the candle at both ends (*informal*), drive oneself, fatigue, go too far, have too many irons in the fire, overburden, overload, overtax one's strength, overtire, overwork, strain *or* overstrain oneself, wear oneself out
▷ **Antonyms** (*sense 1*) belittle, disparage, minimize, play down, underplay, underrate, understate, underuse, undervalue

overdone **1.** beyond all bounds, exaggerated, excessive, fulsome, hyped, immoderate, inordinate, overelaborate, preposterous, too much, undue, unnecessary **2.** burnt, burnt to a cinder, charred, dried up, overcooked, spoiled
▷ **Antonyms** (*sense 1*) belittled, minimized, moderated, played down, underdone, underplayed, understated

overdue behindhand, behind schedule, behind time, belated, late, late in the day, long delayed, not before time (*informal*), owing, tardy, unpunctual
▷ **Antonyms** ahead of time, beforehand, early, in advance, in good time, punctual

overeat binge (*informal*), eat like a horse (*informal*), gorge, gormandize, guzzle, make a pig of oneself (*informal*), overindulge, pack away (*slang*), pig away (*slang*), pig out (*slang*), stuff, stuff oneself

overemphasize belabour, blow up out of all proportion, lay too much stress on, make a big thing of (*informal*), make a federal case of (*U.S. informal*), make a mountain out of a molehill (*informal*), make a production (out) of (*informal*), make something out of nothing, make too much of, overdramatize, overstress
▷ **Antonyms** belittle, downplay, make light of, minimize, play down, underplay, underrate, understate

overexert burn the candle at both ends (*informal*), do too much, drive (oneself), fatigue, knock (oneself) out, overstrain, overtax, overtire, overwork, push (oneself) too hard, strain, wear out, work to death

overflow *verb* **1.** brim over, bubble over, discharge, fall over, pour out, pour over, run over, run with, shower, slop over, spill, spray, surge, teem, well over **2.** cover, deluge, drown, flood, inundate, soak, submerge, swamp *~noun* **3.** discharge, flash flood, flood, flooding, inundation, overabundance, spill, spilling over, surplus

overflowing abounding, bountiful, brimful, copious, plentiful, profuse, rife, superabundant, swarming, teeming, thronged
▷ **Antonyms** deficient, inadequate, insufficient, lacking, missing, scarce, wanting

overhang *verb* beetle, bulge, cast a shadow, extend, impend, jut, loom, project, protrude, stick out, threaten

overhaul **1.** *verb* check, do up (*informal*), examine, inspect, recondition, re-examine, repair, restore, service, survey **2.** *~noun* check, checkup, examination, going-over (*informal*), inspection, reconditioning, service **3.** *~verb* catch up with, draw level with, get ahead of, overtake, pass

overhead **1.** *adverb* above, aloft, atop, in the sky, on high, skyward, up above, upward **2.** *~adjective* aerial, overhanging, roof, upper
▷ **Antonyms** *~adverb* below, beneath, downward, underfoot, underneath

overheads burden, oncosts, operating cost(s), running cost(s)

overheated agitated, fiery, flaming, impassioned, inflamed, overexcited, roused
▷ **Antonyms** calm, collected, composed, cool, dispassionate, unemotional, unexcited, unfazed (*informal*), unruffled

overindulge be immoderate *or* intemperate, drink *or* eat too much, have a binge (*informal*), live it up (*informal*), make a pig of oneself (*informal*), overdo it, pig out (*slang*)

overindulgence excess, immoderation, intemperance, overeating, surfeit

overjoyed cock-a-hoop, delighted, deliriously happy, elated, euphoric, floating on air, happy as a lark, in raptures, joyful, jubilant, on cloud nine (*informal*), only too happy, over the moon (*informal*), rapt, rapturous, thrilled, tickled pink (*informal*), transported
▷ **Antonyms** crestfallen, dejected, disappointed, downcast, down in the dumps (*informal*), heartbroken, miserable, sad, unhappy, woebegone

overlay **1.** *verb* adorn, blanket, cover, inlay, laminate, ornament, overspread, superimpose, veneer **2.** *~noun* adornment, appliqué, covering, decoration, ornamentation, veneer

overload burden, encumber, oppress, overburden, overcharge, overtax, saddle (with), strain, weigh down

overlook **1.** disregard, fail to notice, forget, ignore, leave out of consideration, leave undone, miss, neglect, omit, pass, slight, slip up on **2.** blink at, condone,

disregard, excuse, forgive, let bygones be bygones, let one off with, let pass, let ride, make allowances for, pardon, turn a blind eye to, wink at **3.** afford a view of, command a view of, front on to, give upon, have a view of, look over *or* out on
▷ **Antonyms** (*sense 1*) discern, heed, mark, note, notice, observe, perceive, regard, spot

overly exceedingly, excessively, immoderately, inordinately, over, too, unduly, very much

overpower beat, clobber (*slang*), conquer, crush, defeat, get the upper hand over, immobilize, knock out, lick (*informal*), make mincemeat of (*informal*), master, overcome, overthrow, overwhelm, quell, subdue, subjugate, vanquish

overpowering compelling, compulsive, extreme, forceful, invincible, irrefutable, irresistible, nauseating, overwhelming, powerful, sickening, strong, suffocating, telling, unbearable, uncontrollable

overrate assess too highly, exaggerate, make too much of, overestimate, overpraise, overprize, oversell, overvalue, rate too highly, think *or* expect too much of, think too highly of

overreach 1. overreach oneself be hoist with one's own petard, bite off more than one can chew, defeat one's own ends, go too far, have one's schemes backfire on one, have one's schemes boomerang on one, have one's schemes rebound on one, try to be too clever **2.** cheat, circumvent, deceive, defraud, dupe, gull (*archaic*), outsmart (*informal*), outwit, swindle, trick, victimize

override annul, cancel, countermand, discount, disregard, ignore, nullify, outweigh, overrule, quash, reverse, ride roughshod over, set aside, supersede, take no account of, trample underfoot, upset, vanquish

overriding cardinal, compelling, determining, dominant, final, major, mother (of all) (*informal*), number one, overruling, paramount, pivotal, predominant, prevailing, primary, prime, ruling, supreme, ultimate
▷ **Antonyms** immaterial, inconsequential, insignificant, irrelevant, minor, negligible, paltry, petty, trifling, trivial, unimportant

overrule 1. alter, annul, cancel, countermand, disallow, invalidate, make null and void, outvote, override, overturn, recall, repeal, rescind, reverse, revoke, rule against, set aside, veto **2.** bend to one's will, control, direct, dominate, govern, influence, prevail over, sway
▷ **Antonyms** (*sense 1*) allow, approve, consent to, endorse, pass, permit, sanction

overrun 1. cut to pieces, invade, massacre, occupy, overwhelm, put to flight, rout, swamp **2.** choke, infest, inundate, overflow, overgrow, permeate, ravage, spread like wildfire, spread over, surge over, swarm over **3.** exceed, go beyond, overshoot, run over *or* on

overseer boss (*informal*), chief, foreman, gaffer (*informal, chiefly Brit.*), manager, master, super (*informal*), superintendent, superior, supervisor

overshadow 1. dominate, dwarf, eclipse, excel, leave *or* put in the shade, outshine, outweigh, render insignificant by comparison, rise above, steal the limelight from, surpass, take precedence over, throw into the shade, tower above **2.** adumbrate, becloud, bedim, cloud, darken, dim, obfuscate, obscure, veil **3.** blight, cast a gloom upon, mar, put a damper on, ruin, spoil, take the edge off, take the pleasure *or* enjoyment out of, temper

oversight 1. blunder, carelessness, delinquency, error, fault, inattention, lapse, laxity, mistake, neglect, omission, slip **2.** administration, care, charge, control, custody, direction, handling, inspection, keeping, management, superintendence, supervision, surveillance

overt apparent, blatant, bold, manifest, observable, obvious, open, patent, plain, public, unconcealed, undisguised, visible
▷ **Antonyms** concealed, covert, disguised, hidden, hush-hush (*informal*), invisible, secret, surreptitious, underhand

overtake 1. catch up with, do better than, draw level with, get past, leave behind, outdistance, outdo, outstrip, overhaul, pass **2.** befall, catch unprepared, come upon, engulf, happen, hit, overwhelm, strike, take by surprise

overthrow *verb* **1.** abolish, beat, bring down, conquer, crush, defeat, depose, dethrone, do away with, master, oust, overcome, overpower, overwhelm, subdue, subjugate, topple, unseat, vanquish **2.** bring to ruin, demolish, destroy, knock down, level, overturn, put an end to, put paid to, raze, ruin, subvert, upend, upset *~noun* **3.** defeat, deposition, destruction, dethronement, discomfiture, disestablishment, displacement, dispossession, downfall, end, fall, ousting, prostration, rout, ruin, subjugation, subversion, suppression, undoing, unseating
▷ **Antonyms** *~verb* defend, guard, keep, maintain, preserve, protect, restore, support, uphold *~noun* defence, preservation, protection

overtone association, connotation, flavour, hint, implication, innuendo, intimation, nuance, sense, suggestion, undercurrent

overture 1. (*often plural*) advance, approach, conciliatory move, invitation, offer, opening move, proposal, proposition, signal, tender **2.** *Music* introduction, opening, prelude

▷ **Antonyms** (*sense 1*) close, rebuke, rejection, withdrawal (*sense 2*) coda, finale

overturn 1. capsize, keel over, knock over *or* down, overbalance, reverse, spill, tip over, topple, tumble, upend, upset, upturn **2.** abolish, annul, bring down, countermand, depose, destroy, invalidate, obviate, overthrow, repeal, rescind, reverse, set aside, unseat

overused cliché'd, hackneyed, platitudinous, played out, stale, stereotyped, threadbare, tired, unoriginal, worn (out)

overweening 1. arrogant, cavalier, cocksure, cocky, conceited, egotistical, haughty, high and mighty (*informal*), high-handed, insolent, lordly, opinionated, pompous, presumptuous, proud, self-confident, supercilious, uppish (*Brit. informal*), vain, vainglorious **2.** blown up out of all proportion, excessive, extravagant, immoderate

▷ **Antonyms** (*sense 1*) deferential, diffident, hesitant, modest, self-conscious, self-effacing, timid, unassuming, unobtrusive

overweight *adjective* ample, bulky, buxom, chubby, chunky, corpulent, fat, fleshy, gross, heavy, hefty, huge, massive, obese, on the plump side, outsize, plump, podgy, portly, stout, tubby (*informal*), well-padded (*informal*), well-upholstered (*informal*)

▷ **Antonyms** emaciated, gaunt, lean, pinched, scraggy, scrawny, skinny, thin, underweight

overwhelm 1. bury, crush, deluge, engulf, flood, inundate, snow under, submerge, swamp **2.** bowl over (*informal*), confuse, devastate, knock (someone) for six (*informal*), make mincemeat of (*informal*), overcome, overpower, prostrate, render speechless, stagger, sweep (someone) off his *or* her feet, take (someone's) breath away **3.** crush, cut to pieces, destroy, massacre, overpower, overrun, rout

overwhelming breathtaking, crushing, devastating, invincible, irresistible, overpowering, shattering, stunning, towering, uncontrollable, vast, vastly superior

▷ **Antonyms** commonplace, incidental, insignificant, negligible, paltry, resistible, trivial, unimportant

overwork be a slave-driver *or* hard taskmaster to, burden, burn the candle at both ends, burn the midnight oil, drive into the ground, exhaust, exploit, fatigue, oppress, overstrain, overtax, overuse, prostrate, strain, sweat (*informal*), wear out, weary, work one's fingers to the bone

overwrought 1. agitated, beside oneself, distracted, excited, frantic, in a state, in a tizzy (*informal*), in a twitter (*informal*), keyed up, on edge, overexcited, overworked, stirred, strung up (*informal*), tense, uptight (*informal*), wired (*slang*), worked up (*informal*), wound up (*informal*) **2.** baroque, busy, contrived, florid, flowery, fussy, overdone, overelaborate, overembellished, overornate, rococo

▷ **Antonyms** (*sense 1*) calm, collected, controlled, cool, dispassionate, emotionless, impassive, self-contained, unfazed (*informal*), unmoved

owe be beholden to, be in arrears, be in debt, be obligated *or* indebted, be under an obligation to

owing *adjective* due, outstanding, overdue, owed, payable, unpaid, unsettled

owing to *preposition* as a result of, because of, on account of

own *adjective* **1.** individual, particular, personal, private *~pronoun* **2. on one's own** alone, by oneself, by one's own efforts, independently, isolated, left to one's own devices, off one's own bat, on one's tod (*Brit. slang*), singly, (standing) on one's own two feet, unaided, unassisted, under one's own steam **3. hold one's own** compete, keep going, keep one's end up, keep one's head above water, maintain one's position *~verb* **4.** be in possession of, be responsible for, enjoy, have, hold, keep, possess, retain **5. own up (to)** admit, come clean (about), come out of the closet (*informal*), confess, cough (*slang*), make a clean breast of, tell the truth (about) **6.** acknowledge, admit, allow, allow to be valid, avow, concede, confess, disclose, go along with, grant, recognize

owner holder, landlord, lord, master, mistress, possessor, proprietor, proprietress, proprietrix

ownership dominion, possession, proprietary rights, proprietorship, right of possession, title

P, p

pace *noun* **1.** gait, measure, step, stride, tread, walk **2.** clip (*informal*), lick (*informal*), momentum, motion, movement, progress, rate, speed, tempo, time, velocity *~verb* **3.** march, patrol, pound, stride, walk back and forth, walk up and down **4.** count, determine, mark out, measure, step

pacific 1. appeasing, conciliatory, diplomatic, irenic, pacificatory, peacemaking, placatory, propitiatory **2.** dovelike, dovish, friendly, gentle, mild, nonbelligerent, nonviolent, pacifist, peaceable, peace-loving **3.** at peace, calm, halcyon, peaceful, placid, quiet, serene, smooth, still, tranquil, unruffled
▷ **Antonyms** aggressive, antagonistic, belligerent, hostile, nonconciliatory, pugnacious, unforgiving, unfriendly, violent, warlike

pacifist conchie (*informal*), conscientious objector, dove, passive resister, peace lover, peacemonger, peacenik (*informal*), satyagrahi

pacify 1. allay, ameliorate, appease, assuage, calm, clear the air, compose, conciliate, make peace, moderate, mollify, placate, pour oil on troubled waters, propitiate, quiet, restore harmony, smooth down *or* over, smooth one's ruffled feathers, soften, soothe, still, tranquillize **2.** chasten, crush, impose peace, put down, quell, repress, silence, subdue, tame

pack *noun* **1.** back pack, bale, bundle, burden, fardel (*archaic*), kit, kitbag, knapsack, load, package, packet, parcel, rucksack, truss **2.** assemblage, band, bunch, collection, company, crew, crowd, deck, drove, flock, gang, group, herd, lot, mob, set, troop *~verb* **3.** batch, bundle, burden, load, package, packet, store, stow **4.** charge, compact, compress, cram, crowd, fill, jam, mob, press, ram, stuff, tamp, throng, wedge **5.** (*with* **off**) bundle out, dismiss, hustle out, send away, send packing (*informal*), send someone about his business

package *noun* **1.** box, carton, container, packet, parcel **2.** amalgamation, combination, entity, unit, whole *~verb* **3.** batch, box, pack, packet, parcel (up), wrap, wrap up

packed brimful, bursting at the seams, chock-a-block, chock-full, congested, cram-full, crammed, crowded, filled, full, hoatching (*Scot.*), jammed, jam-packed, loaded *or* full to the gunwales, overflowing, overloaded, packed like sardines, seething, swarming
▷ **Antonyms** deserted, empty, uncongested, uncrowded

packet 1. bag, carton, container, package, parcel, poke (*dialect*), wrapper, wrapping **2.** *slang* a bob or two (*Brit. informal*), an arm and a leg (*informal*), big bucks (*informal, chiefly U.S.*), big money, bomb (*Brit. slang*), bundle (*slang*), fortune, king's ransom (*informal*), lot(s), megabucks (*U.S. & Canad. slang*), mint, pile (*informal*), pot(s) (*informal*), pretty penny (*informal*), tidy sum (*informal*), wad (*U.S. & Canad. slang*)

pack in 1. attract, cram, draw, fill to capacity, squeeze in **2.** *Brit. informal* cease, chuck (*informal*), desist, give up *or* over, jack in, kick (*informal*), leave off, stop

pack up 1. put away, store, tidy up **2.** *informal* call it a day (*informal*), call it a night (*informal*), finish, give up, pack in (*Brit. informal*) **3.** break down, conk out (*informal*), fail, give out, stall, stop

pact agreement, alliance, arrangement, bargain, bond, compact, concord, concordat, contract, convention, covenant, deal, league, protocol, treaty, understanding

pad[1] *noun* **1.** buffer, cushion, protection, stiffening, stuffing, wad **2.** block, jotter, notepad, tablet, writing pad **3.** foot, paw, sole **4.** *slang* apartment, flat, hang-out (*informal*), home, place, quarters, room *~verb* **5.** cushion, fill, line, pack, protect, shape, stuff **6.** (*often with* **out**) amplify, augment, eke, elaborate, fill out, flesh out, inflate, lengthen, protract, spin out, stretch

pad[2] *verb* **1.** creep, go barefoot, pussyfoot (*informal*), sneak, steal **2.** hike, march, plod, traipse (*informal*), tramp, trek, trudge, walk

padding 1. filling, packing, stuffing, wadding **2.** hot air (*informal*), prolixity, verbiage, verbosity, waffle (*informal, chiefly Brit.*), wordiness

paddle[1] **1.** *noun* oar, scull, sweep **2.** *~verb* oar, propel, pull, row, scull

paddle[2] *verb* dabble, plash, slop, splash (about), stir, wade

paddy bate (*Brit. slang*), fit of temper, paddywhack (*Brit. informal*), passion, rage, tantrum, temper, tiff, wax (*informal, chiefly Brit.*)

paean 1. anthem, hymn, psalm, thanksgiving **2.** encomium, eulogy, hymn of praise, ovation, panegyric, rave review (*informal*)

pagan 1. *noun* Gentile, heathen, idolater, infidel, polytheist, unbeliever **2.** *~adjective* Gentile, heathen, heathenish, idolatrous, infidel, irreligious, polytheistic

page[1] *noun* **1.** folio, leaf, sheet, side **2.** chapter, episode, epoch, era, event, incident, period, phase, point, stage, time *~verb* **3.** foliate, number, paginate

page[2] **1.** *noun* attendant, bellboy (*U.S.*), footboy, pageboy, servant, squire **2.** *~verb* announce, call, call out, preconize, seek, send for, summon

pageant display, extravaganza, parade, procession, ritual, show, spectacle, tableau

pageantry display, drama, extravagance, glamour, glitter, grandeur, magnificence, parade, pomp, show, showiness, spectacle, splash (*informal*), splendour, state, theatricality

pain *noun* **1.** ache, cramp, discomfort, hurt, irritation, pang, smarting, soreness, spasm, suffering, tenderness, throb, throe (*rare*), trouble, twinge **2.** affliction, agony, anguish, bitterness, distress, grief, hardship, heartache, misery, suffering, torment, torture, tribulation, woe, wretchedness **3.** *informal* aggravation, annoyance, bore, bother, drag (*informal*), gall, headache (*informal*), irritation, nuisance, pain in the arse (*taboo informal*), pain in the neck (*informal*), pest, vexation *~verb* **4.** ail, chafe, discomfort, harm, hurt, inflame, injure, smart, sting, throb **5.** afflict, aggrieve, agonize, cut to the quick, disquiet, distress, grieve, hurt, sadden, torment, torture, vex, worry, wound **6.** *informal* annoy, exasperate, gall, harass, irritate, nark (*Brit., Austral., & N.Z. slang*), rile, vex

pained aggrieved, anguished, distressed, hurt, injured, miffed (*informal*), offended, reproachful, stung, unhappy, upset, worried, wounded

painful 1. afflictive, disagreeable, distasteful, distressing, grievous, saddening, unpleasant **2.** aching, agonizing, excruciating, harrowing, hurting, inflamed, raw, smarting, sore, tender, throbbing **3.** arduous, difficult, hard, laborious, severe, tedious, troublesome, trying, vexatious **4.** *informal* abysmal, awful, dire, dreadful, excruciating, extremely bad, godawful, terrible

▷ **Antonyms** (*sense 1*) agreeable, enjoyable, pleasant, satisfying (*sense 2*) comforting, painless, relieving, soothing (*sense 3*) a piece of cake (*informal*), easy, effortless, interesting, short, simple, straightforward, undemanding

painfully alarmingly, clearly, deplorably, distressingly, dreadfully, excessively, markedly, sadly, unfortunately, woefully

painkiller anaesthetic, analgesic, anodyne, drug, palliative, remedy, sedative

painless easy, effortless, fast, no trouble, pain-free, quick, simple, trouble-free

pains 1. assiduousness, bother, care, diligence, effort, industry, labour, special attention, trouble **2.** birth-pangs, childbirth, contractions, labour

painstaking assiduous, careful, conscientious, diligent, earnest, exacting, hard-working, industrious, meticulous, persevering, punctilious, scrupulous, sedulous, strenuous, thorough, thoroughgoing

▷ **Antonyms** careless, half-hearted, haphazard, heedless, lazy, negligent, slapdash, slipshod, thoughtless

paint *noun* **1.** colour, colouring, dye, emulsion, pigment, stain, tint **2.** *informal* cosmetics, face (*informal*), greasepaint, make-up, *maquillage,* war paint (*informal*) *~verb* **3.** catch a likeness, delineate, depict, draw, figure, picture, portray, represent, sketch **4.** apply, coat, colour, cover, daub, decorate, slap on (*informal*) **5.** bring to life, capture, conjure up a vision, depict, describe, evoke, make one see, portray, put graphically, recount, tell vividly **6. paint the town red** *informal* carouse, celebrate, go on a binge (*informal*), go on a spree, go on the town, live it up (*informal*), make merry, make whoopee (*informal*), revel

pair 1. *noun* brace, combination, couple, doublet, duo, match, matched set, span, twins, two of a kind, twosome, yoke **2.** *~verb* bracket, couple, join, marry, match, match up, mate, pair off, put together, team, twin, wed, yoke

pal boon companion, buddy (*informal*), chum (*informal*), cock (*Brit. informal*), companion, comrade, crony, friend, homeboy (*slang, chiefly U.S.*), mate (*informal*)

palatable 1. appetizing, delectable, delicious, luscious, mouthwatering, savoury, tasty, toothsome **2.** acceptable, agreeable, attractive, enjoyable, fair, pleasant, satisfactory

▷ **Antonyms** (*sense 1*) bland, flat, insipid, stale, tasteless, unappetizing, unpalatable

palate 1. appetite, heart, stomach, taste **2.** appreciation, enjoyment, gusto, liking, relish, zest

palatial de luxe, gorgeous, grand, grandiose, illustrious, imposing, luxurious, magnificent, majestic, opulent, plush (*informal*), regal, spacious, splendid, splendiferous (*facetious*), stately, sumptuous

palaver *noun* **1.** business (*informal*), carry-on (*informal, chiefly Brit.*), pantomime (*informal, chiefly Brit.*), performance (*informal*), procedure, rigmarole, song and dance (*Brit. informal*), to-do **2.** babble, blather, blether, chatter, hubbub, natter (*Brit.*), prattle, tongue-wagging, yak (*slang*) **3.** colloquy, confab (*informal*), conference, discussion, get-together (*informal*), parley, powwow, session *~verb* **4.** confab (*informal*), confer, discuss, go into a huddle (*informal*), parley, powwow, put heads together **5.** blather, blether, chatter, gabble, jabber, jaw (*slang*), natter (*Brit.*), prattle, yak (*slang*)

pale[1] *adjective* **1.** anaemic, ashen, ashy, bleached, bloodless, colourless, faded, light, like death warmed up (*informal*), pallid, pasty, sallow, wan, washed-out, white, whitish **2.** dim, faint, feeble, inadequate, pathetic, poor, thin, weak *~verb* **3.** become pale, blanch, go white, lose colour, whiten **4.** decrease, dim, diminish, dull, fade, grow dull, lessen, lose lustre

▷ **Antonyms** (*sense 1*) blooming, florid, flushed, glowing, rosy-cheeked, rubicund, ruddy, sanguine

pale[2] *noun* **1.** paling, palisade, picket, post, slat, stake, upright **2.** barricade, barrier, fence, palisade, railing **3.** border, boundary, bounds, confines, district, limits, region, territory **4. beyond the pale** barbaric, forbidden, improper, inadmissible, indecent, irregular, not done, out of line, unacceptable, unseemly, unspeakable, unsuitable

palisade bulwark, defence, enclosure, fence, paling, stockade

pall[1] *noun* **1.** cloud, mantle, shadow, shroud, veil **2.** check, damp, damper, dismay, gloom, melancholy

pall[2] *verb* become dull *or* tedious, bore, cloy, glut, jade, satiate, sicken, surfeit, tire, weary

palliate 1. abate, allay, alleviate, assuage, diminish, ease, mitigate, moderate, mollify, relax, relieve, soften, soothe, temper **2.** cloak, conceal, cover, excuse, extenuate, gloss over, hide, lessen, minimize, paper over the cracks (*informal*), varnish, whitewash (*informal*)

palliative 1. *adjective* alleviative, anodyne, assuasive, calmative, calming, demulcent, lenitive, mitigative, mitigatory, mollifying, soothing **2.** *~noun* analgesic, anodyne, calmative, demulcent, drug, lenitive, painkiller, sedative, tranquillizer

pallid 1. anaemic, ashen, ashy, cadaverous, colourless, like death warmed up (*informal*), pale, pasty, sallow, wan, waxen, wheyfaced, whitish **2.** anaemic, bloodless, colourless, insipid, lifeless, spiritless, sterile, tame, tired, uninspired, vapid

pallor ashen hue, bloodlessness, lack of colour, paleness, pallidness, wanness, whiteness

pally affectionate, buddy-buddy (*slang, chiefly U.S. & Canad.*), chummy (*informal*), close, familiar, friendly, intimate, palsy-walsy (*informal*), thick as thieves (*informal*)

palm[1] *noun* **1.** hand, hook, meathook (*slang*), mitt (*slang*), paw (*informal*) **2. in the palm of one's hand** at one's mercy, in one's clutches, in one's control, in one's power **3. grease someone's palm** *slang* bribe, buy, corrupt, fix (*informal*), give a backhander (*slang*), induce, influence, pay off (*informal*), square, suborn

palm[2] *noun figurative* bays, crown, fame, glory, honour, laurels, merit, prize, success, triumph, trophy, victory

palm off 1. (*with* **on** *or* **with**) fob off, foist off, pass off **2.** (*with* **on**) foist on, force upon, impose upon, take advantage of, thrust upon, unload upon

palmy flourishing, fortunate, glorious, golden, halcyon, happy, joyous, luxurious, prosperous, thriving, triumphant

palpable 1. apparent, blatant, clear, conspicuous, evident, manifest, obvious, open, patent, plain, salient, unmistakable, visible **2.** concrete, material, real, solid, substantial, tangible, touchable

palpitate beat, flutter, pitapat, pitter-patter, pound, pulsate, pulse, quiver, shiver, throb, tremble, vibrate

palsied arthritic, atonic (*Pathology*), crippled, debilitated, disabled, helpless, paralysed, paralytic, rheumatic, sclerotic, shaking, shaky, spastic, trembling

palter 1. be evasive, deceive, double-talk, equivocate, flannel (*Brit. informal*), fudge, hedge, mislead, prevaricate, shuffle, tergiversate, trifle **2.** bargain, barter, chaffer, dicker (*chiefly U.S.*), haggle, higgle

paltry base, beggarly, chickenshit (*U.S. slang*), contemptible, crappy (*slang*), derisory, despicable, inconsiderable, insignificant, low, meagre, mean, measly, Mickey Mouse (*slang*), minor, miserable, nickel-and-dime (*U.S. slang*), petty, picayune (*U.S.*), piddling (*informal*), pitiful, poor, poxy (*slang*), puny, slight, small, sorry, trifling, trivial, twopenny-halfpenny (*Brit. informal*), unimportant, worthless, wretched

▷ **Antonyms** consequential, considerable, essential, grand, important, major, mega (*slang*), significant, valuable

pamper baby, cater to one's every whim, coddle, cosset, fondle, gratify, humour, indulge, mollycoddle, pander to, pet, spoil, wait on (someone) hand and foot

pamphlet booklet, brochure, circular, folder, leaflet, tract

pan[1] *noun* **1.** container, pot, saucepan, vessel *~verb* **2.** look for, search for, separate, sift out, wash **3.** *informal* blast, censure, criticize, flay, hammer (*Brit. informal*), knock (*informal*), lambast(e), put down, roast (*informal*), rubbish (*informal*), slag (off) (*slang*), slam (*slang*), slate (*informal*), tear into (*informal*), throw brickbats at (*informal*)

pan[2] *verb* follow, move, scan, sweep, swing, track, traverse

panacea catholicon, cure-all, elixir, nostrum, sovereign remedy, universal cure

panache a flourish, brio, dash, élan, flair, flamboyance, spirit, style, swagger, verve

pandemonium babel, bedlam, chaos, clamour, commotion, confusion, din, hubbub, hue and cry, hullabaloo, racket, ruckus (*informal*), ruction (*informal*), rumpus, tumult, turmoil, uproar
▷ **Antonyms** arrangement, calm, hush, order, peace, peacefulness, quietude, repose, stillness, tranquillity

pander 1. *verb* (*with* **to**) cater to, fawn on, gratify, indulge, play up to (*informal*), please, satisfy **2.** *~noun* go-between, mack (*slang*), pimp, ponce (*slang*), procurer, white-slaver, whoremaster (*archaic*)

panegyric accolade, commendation, encomium, eulogy, homage, paean, praise, tribute

panegyrical commendatory, complimentary, encomiastic, eulogistic, favourable, flattering, glowing, laudatory

pang ache, agony, anguish, discomfort, distress, gripe, pain, prick, spasm, stab, sting, stitch, throe (*rare*), twinge, wrench

panic *noun* **1.** agitation, alarm, consternation, dismay, fear, fright, horror, hysteria, scare, terror *~verb* **2.** become hysterical, be terror-stricken, go to pieces, have kittens (*informal*), lose one's bottle (*Brit. slang*), lose one's nerve, overreact **3.** alarm, put the wind up (someone) (*informal*), scare, startle, terrify, unnerve

panicky afraid, agitated, distressed, fearful, frantic, frenzied, frightened, hysterical, in a flap (*informal*), in a tizzy (*informal*), jittery (*informal*), nervous, windy (*slang*), worked up, worried
▷ **Antonyms** calm, collected, composed, confident, cool, imperturbable, self-controlled, together (*slang*), unexcitable, unfazed (*informal*), unflappable, unruffled

panic-stricken *or* **panic-struck** aghast, agitated, alarmed, appalled, fearful, frenzied, frightened, frightened out of one's wits, frightened to death, horrified, horror-stricken, hysterical, in a cold sweat (*informal*), panicky, petrified, scared, scared shitless (*taboo slang*), scared stiff, shit-scared (*taboo slang*), startled, terrified, terror-stricken, unnerved

panoply array, attire, dress, garb, get-up (*informal*), insignia, raiment (*archaic or poetic*), regalia, show, trappings, turnout

panorama 1. bird's-eye view, prospect, scenery, scenic view, view, vista **2.** overall picture, overview, perspective, survey

panoramic all-embracing, bird's-eye, comprehensive, extensive, far-reaching, general, inclusive, overall, scenic, sweeping, wide

pan out come out, come to pass (*archaic*), culminate, eventuate, happen, result, turn out, work out

pant *verb* **1.** blow, breathe, gasp, heave, huff, palpitate, puff, throb, wheeze **2.** *figurative* ache, covet, crave, desire, eat one's heart out over, hanker after, hunger, long, pine, set one's heart on, sigh, suspire (*archaic or poetic*), thirst, want, yearn *~noun* **3.** gasp, huff, puff, wheeze

panting *adjective* **1.** breathless, gasping, out of breath, out of puff, out of whack (*informal*), puffed, puffed out, puffing, short of breath, winded **2.** agog, all agog, anxious, champing at the bit (*informal*), eager, impatient, raring to go

pants 1. *Brit.* boxer shorts, briefs, broekies (*S. African*), drawers, knickers, panties, underpants, Y-fronts (*Trademark*) **2.** *U.S.* slacks, trousers

pap 1. baby food, mash, mush, pulp **2.** drivel, rubbish, trash, trivia

paper *noun* **1.** (*often plural*) certificate, deed, documents, instrument, record **2.** (*plural*) archive, diaries, documents, dossier, file, letters, records **3.** blat, daily, gazette, journal, news, newspaper, organ, rag (*informal*) **4.** analysis, article, assignment, composition, critique, dissertation, essay, examination, monograph, report, script, study, thesis, treatise **5. on paper** ideally, in the abstract, in theory, theoretically *~adjective* **6.** cardboard, disposable, flimsy, insubstantial, paper-thin, papery, thin *~verb* **7.** cover with paper, hang, line, paste up, wallpaper

papery flimsy, fragile, frail, insubstantial, light, lightweight, paperlike, paper-thin, thin

par *noun* **1.** average, level, mean, median, norm, standard, usual **2.** balance, equal footing, equality, equilibrium, equivalence, parity **3. above par** excellent, ex~

ceptional, first-rate (*informal*), outstanding, superior **4. below par: a.** below average, bush-league (*Austral. & N.Z. informal*), dime-a-dozen (*informal*), inferior, lacking, not up to scratch (*informal*), poor, second-rate, substandard, tinhorn (*U.S. slang*), two-bit (*U.S. & Canad. slang*), wanting **b.** not oneself, off colour (*chiefly Brit.*), off form, poorly (*informal*), sick, under the weather (*informal*), unfit, unhealthy **5. par for the course** average, expected, ordinary, predictable, standard, typical, usual **6. on a par** equal, much the same, the same, well-matched **7. up to par** acceptable, adequate, good enough, passable, satisfactory, up to scratch (*informal*), up to the mark

parable allegory, exemplum, fable, lesson, moral tale, story

parabolic allegorical, figurative, metaphoric, symbolic

parade *noun* **1.** array, cavalcade, ceremony, column, march, pageant, procession, review, spectacle, train **2.** array, display, exhibition, flaunting, ostentation, pomp, show, spectacle, vaunting *~verb* **3.** defile, march, process **4.** air, brandish, display, exhibit, flaunt, make a show of, show, show off (*informal*), strut, swagger, vaunt

paradigm archetype, example, exemplar, ideal, model, norm, original, pattern, prototype

paradise 1. City of God, divine abode, Elysian fields, garden of delights (*Islam*), heaven, heavenly kingdom, Olympus (*poetic*), Promised Land, Zion (*Christianity*) **2.** Eden, Garden of Eden **3.** bliss, delight, felicity, heaven, seventh heaven, utopia

paradisiacal blessed, blissful, celestial, divine, Elysian, glorious, golden, heavenly, out of this world (*informal*), utopian

paradox absurdity, ambiguity, anomaly, contradiction, enigma, inconsistency, mystery, oddity, puzzle

paradoxical absurd, ambiguous, baffling, confounding, contradictory, enigmatic, equivocal, illogical, impossible, improbable, inconsistent, oracular, puzzling, riddling

paragon apotheosis, archetype, best thing since sliced bread (*informal*), criterion, cynosure, epitome, exemplar, greatest thing since sliced bread (*informal*), ideal, jewel, masterpiece, model, nonesuch (*archaic*), nonpareil, norm, paradigm, pattern, prototype, quintessence, standard

paragraph clause, item, notice, part, passage, portion, section, subdivision

parallel *adjective* **1.** aligned, alongside, coextensive, equidistant, side by side **2.** akin, analogous, complementary, correspondent, corresponding, like, matching, resembling, similar, uniform *~noun* **3.** analogue, complement, corollary, counterpart, duplicate, equal, equivalent, likeness, match, twin **4.** analogy, comparison, correlation, correspondence, likeness, parallelism, resemblance, similarity *~verb* **5.** agree, be alike, chime with, compare, complement, conform, correlate, correspond, equal, keep pace (with), match

▷ **Antonyms** *~adjective* different, dissimilar, divergent, non-parallel, unlike *~noun* difference, dissimilarity, divergence, opposite, reverse *~verb* be unlike, differ, diverge

paralyse 1. cripple, debilitate, disable, incapacitate, lame **2.** anaesthetize, arrest, benumb, freeze, halt, immobilize, numb, petrify, stop dead, stun, stupefy, transfix

paralysis 1. immobility, palsy, paresis (*Pathology*) **2.** arrest, breakdown, halt, shutdown, stagnation, standstill, stoppage

paralytic *adjective* **1.** crippled, disabled, immobile, immobilized, incapacitated, lame, numb, palsied, paralysed **2.** *informal* bevvied (*dialect*), blitzed (*slang*), blotto (*slang*), bombed (*slang*), Brahms and Liszt (*slang*), canned (*slang*), drunk, flying (*slang*), inebriated, intoxicated, legless (*informal*), lit up (*slang*), out of it (*slang*), out to it (*Austral. & N.Z. slang*), pie-eyed (*slang*), pissed (*taboo slang*), plastered (*slang*), rat-arsed (*taboo slang*), sloshed (*slang*), smashed (*slang*), steamboats (*Scot. slang*), steaming (*slang*), stewed (*slang*), stoned (*slang*), tired and emotional (*euphemistic*), wasted (*slang*), wrecked (*slang*), zonked (*slang*)

parameter constant, criterion, framework, guideline, limit, limitation, restriction, specification

paramount capital, cardinal, chief, dominant, eminent, first, foremost, main, outstanding, predominant, pre-eminent, primary, prime, principal, superior, supreme

▷ **Antonyms** inferior, insignificant, least, minor, negligible, secondary, slight, subordinate, trifling, unimportant

paramour beau, concubine, courtesan, fancy bit (*slang*), fancy man (*slang*), fancy woman (*slang*), inamorata, inamorato, kept woman, lover, mistress

paraphernalia accoutrements, apparatus, appurtenances, baggage, belongings, clobber (*Brit. slang*), effects, equipage, equipment, gear, impedimenta, material, stuff, tackle, things, trappings

paraphrase 1. *noun* interpretation, rehash, rendering, rendition, rephrasing, restatement, rewording, translation, version **2.** *~verb* express in other words *or* one's own words, interpret, rehash, render, rephrase, restate, reword

parasite bloodsucker (*informal*), cadger, drone (*Brit.*), hanger-on, leech, scrounger (*informal*), sponge (*informal*), sponger (*informal*)

parasitic, parasitical bloodsucking (*informal*), cadging, leechlike, scrounging (*informal*), sponging (*informal*)

parcel *noun* **1.** bundle, carton, pack, package, packet **2.** band, batch, bunch, collection, company, crew, crowd, gang, group, lot, pack **3.** piece of land, plot, property, tract ~*verb* **4.** (*often with* **up**) do up, pack, package, tie up, wrap **5.** (*often with* **out**) allocate, allot, apportion, carve up, deal out, dispense, distribute, divide, dole out, mete out, portion, share out, split up

parch blister, burn, dehydrate, desiccate, dry up, evaporate, make thirsty, scorch, sear, shrivel, wither

parched arid, dehydrated, dried out *or* up, drouthy (*Scot.*), dry, scorched, shrivelled, thirsty, torrid, waterless, withered

parching *adjective* baking, blistering, burning, dry, drying, hot, roasting (*informal*), scorching, searing, sweltering, withering

pardon 1. *verb* absolve, acquit, amnesty, condone, exculpate, excuse, exonerate, forgive, free, let off (*informal*), liberate, overlook, release, remit, reprieve **2.** ~*noun* absolution, acquittal, allowance, amnesty, condonation, discharge, excuse, exoneration, forgiveness, grace, indulgence, mercy, release, remission, reprieve

▷ **Antonyms** ~*verb* admonish, blame, castigate, censure, chasten, chastise, condemn, discipline, excoriate, fine, penalize, punish, rebuke ~*noun* condemnation, guilt, penalty, punishment, redress, retaliation, retribution, revenge, vengeance

pardonable allowable, condonable, excusable, forgivable, minor, not serious, permissible, understandable, venial

pare 1. clip, cut, peel, shave, skin, trim **2.** crop, cut, cut back, decrease, dock, lop, prune, reduce, retrench, shear

parent 1. begetter, father, guardian, mother, procreator, progenitor, sire **2.** architect, author, cause, creator, forerunner, origin, originator, prototype, root, source, wellspring

parentage ancestry, birth, derivation, descent, extraction, family, line, lineage, origin, paternity, pedigree, race, stirps, stock

parenthetic, parenthetical bracketed, by-the-way, explanatory, extraneous, extrinsic, incidental, in parenthesis, inserted, interposed, qualifying

parenthetically by the bye, by the way, by way of explanation, incidentally, in parenthesis, in passing

pariah exile, leper, outcast, outlaw, undesirable, unperson, untouchable

paring *noun* clipping, flake, fragment, peel, peeling, rind, shaving, shred, skin, slice, sliver, snippet

parish church, churchgoers, community, congregation, flock, fold, parishioners

parity 1. consistency, equality, equal terms, equivalence, par, parallelism, quits (*informal*), uniformity, unity **2.** affinity, agreement, analogy, conformity, congruity, correspondence, likeness, resemblance, sameness, similarity, similitude

park 1. *noun* estate, garden, grounds, parkland, pleasure garden, recreation ground, woodland **2.** ~*verb* leave, manoeuvre, position, station

parlance idiom, jargon, language, lingo (*informal*), manner of speaking, phraseology, -speak, speech, talk, tongue

parley 1. *noun* colloquy, confab (*informal*), conference, congress, council, dialogue, discussion, meeting, palaver, powwow, seminar, talk(s) **2.** ~*verb* confabulate, confer, deliberate, discuss, negotiate, palaver, powwow, speak, talk

parliament 1. assembly, congress, convention, convocation, council, diet, legislature, senate, talking shop (*informal*) **2. Parliament** Houses of Parliament, Mother of Parliaments, the House, the House of Commons and the House of Lords, Westminster

parliamentary congressional, deliberative, governmental, lawgiving, lawmaking, legislative

parlour best room, drawing room, front room, lounge, reception room, sitting room

parlous chancy (*informal*), dangerous, desperate, difficult, dire, hairy (*slang*), hazardous, perilous, risky

parochial insular, inward-looking, limited, narrow, narrow-minded, parish-pump, petty, provincial, restricted, small-minded

▷ **Antonyms** all-embracing, broad, broad-minded, cosmopolitan, international, liberal, national, universal, world-wide

parodist burlesquer, caricaturist, humorist, impressionist, ironist, lampooner, mimic, mocker, pasquinader, satirist

parody *noun* **1.** burlesque, caricature, imitation, lampoon, satire, send-up (*Brit. informal*), skit, spoof (*informal*), takeoff (*informal*) **2.** apology, caricature, farce, mockery, travesty ~*verb* **3.** burlesque, caricature, do a takeoff of (*informal*), lampoon, mimic, poke fun at, satirize, send up (*Brit. informal*), spoof (*in~

formal), take off (*informal*), take the piss out of (*taboo slang*), travesty

paroxysm attack, convulsion, eruption, fit, flare-up (*informal*), outburst, sei~zure, spasm

parrot 1. *noun figurative* copycat (*infor~mal*), imitator, (little) echo, mimic **2.** *~adverb* **parrot-fashion** *informal* by rote, mechanically, mindlessly **3.** *~verb* copy, echo, imitate, mimic, reiterate, re~peat

parry 1. block, deflect, fend off, hold at bay, rebuff, repel, repulse, stave off, ward off **2.** avoid, circumvent, dodge, duck (*informal*), evade, fence, fight shy of, shun, sidestep

parsimonious cheeseparing, close, close-fisted, frugal, grasping, mean, mingy (*Brit. informal*), miserable, miserly, near (*informal*), niggardly, penny-pinching (*informal*), penurious, saving, scrimpy, skinflinty, snoep (*S. African informal*), sparing, stingy, stinting, tight-arse (*taboo slang*), tight-arsed (*ta~boo slang*), tight as a duck's arse (*taboo slang*), tight-ass (*U.S. taboo slang*), tight-assed (*U.S. taboo slang*), tight~fisted

▷ **Antonyms** extravagant, generous, lav~ish, munificent, open-handed, spend~thrift, wasteful

parsimony frugality, meanness, mingi~ness (*Brit. informal*), miserliness, near~ness (*informal*), niggardliness, penny-pinching (*informal*), stinginess, tight~ness

parson churchman, clergyman, cleric, di~vine, ecclesiastic, incumbent, man of God, man of the cloth, minister, pastor, preacher, priest, rector, reverend (*infor~mal*), vicar

part *noun* **1.** bit, fraction, fragment, lot, particle, piece, portion, scrap, section, sector, segment, share, slice **2.** branch, component, constituent, department, division, element, ingredient, limb, member, module, organ, piece, unit **3.** behalf, cause, concern, faction, interest, party, side **4.** bit, business, capacity, charge, duty, function, involvement, of~fice, place, responsibility, role, say, share, task, work **5.** *Theatre* character, lines, role **6.** (*often plural*) airt (*Scot.*), area, district, neck of the woods (*infor~mal*), neighbourhood, quarter, region, territory, vicinity **7. for the most part** chiefly, generally, in the main, largely, mainly, mostly, on the whole, principal~ly **8. in good part** cheerfully, cordially, good-naturedly, well, without offence **9. in part** a little, in some measure, par~tially, partly, slightly, somewhat, to a certain extent, to some degree **10. on the part of** for the sake of, in support of, in the name of, on behalf of **11. take part in** associate oneself with, be instrumental in, be involved in, have a hand in, join in, partake in, participate in, play a part in, put one's twopence-worth in, take a hand in *~verb* **12.** break, cleave, come apart, detach, disconnect, disjoin, dis~mantle, disunite, divide, rend, separate, sever, split, tear **13.** break up, depart, go, go away, go (their) separate ways, leave, part company, quit, say goodbye, separate, split up, take one's leave, withdraw **14. part with** abandon, dis~card, forgo, give up, let go of, relinquish, renounce, sacrifice, surrender, yield

▷ **Antonyms** *~noun* (*senses 1 & 2*) bulk, entirety, mass, totality, whole *~verb* (*sense 12*) adhere, close, combine, hold, join, stick, unite (*sense 13*) appear, ar~rive, come, gather, remain, show up (*in~formal*), stay, turn up

partake 1. (*with* **in**) engage, enter into, participate, share, take part **2.** (*with* **of**) consume, eat, receive, share, take **3.** (*with* **of**) evince, evoke, have the quality of, show, suggest

partial 1. fragmentary, imperfect, incom~plete, limited, uncompleted, unfinished **2.** biased, discriminatory, influenced, interested, one-sided, partisan, predis~posed, prejudiced, tendentious, unfair, unjust **3. be partial to** be fond of, be keen on, be taken with, care for, have a liking for, have a soft spot for, have a weakness for

▷ **Antonyms** (*sense 1*) complete, entire, finished, full, total, whole (*sense 2*) im~partial, objective, unbiased, unpreju~diced

partiality 1. bias, favouritism, partisan~ship, predisposition, preference, preju~dice **2.** affinity, bag (*slang*), cup of tea (*informal*), fondness, inclination, liking, love, penchant, predilection, predisposi~tion, preference, proclivity, taste, weak~ness

▷ **Antonyms** (*sense 1*) disinterest, equity, fairness, impartiality, objectivity (*sense 2*) abhorrence, antipathy, aversion, dis~gust, disinclination, dislike, distaste, loathing, revulsion

partially fractionally, halfway, incom~pletely, in part, moderately, not wholly, partly, piecemeal, somewhat, to a cer~tain extent *or* degree

participant associate, contributor, mem~ber, partaker, participator, party, play~er, shareholder

participate be a participant, be a party to, engage in, enter into, get in on the act, have a hand in, join in, partake, per~form, share, take part

▷ **Antonyms** abstain, boycott, forgo, for~sake, forswear, opt out, pass up, refrain from, take no part of

participation assistance, contribution, in~volvement, joining in, partaking, part~nership, sharing in, taking part

particle atom, bit, crumb, grain, iota, jot,

mite, molecule, mote, piece, scrap, shred, speck, tittle, whit

particular *adjective* **1.** distinct, exact, express, peculiar, precise, special, specific **2.** especial, exceptional, marked, notable, noteworthy, remarkable, singular, uncommon, unusual **3.** blow-by-blow, circumstantial, detailed, itemized, minute, painstaking, precise, selective, thorough **4.** choosy (*informal*), critical, dainty, demanding, discriminating, exacting, fastidious, finicky, fussy, meticulous, nice (*rare*), overnice, pernickety (*informal*), picky (*informal*) *~noun* **5.** (*usually plural*) circumstance, detail, fact, feature, item, specification **6. in particular** distinctly, especially, exactly, expressly, particularly, specifically

▷ **Antonyms** (*sense 1*) general, imprecise, indefinite, indistinct, inexact, unspecified, vague (*sense 4*) casual, easy, easy to please, indiscriminate, negligent, slack, sloppy, uncritical

particularity **1.** (*often plural*) circumstance, detail, fact, instance, item, point **2.** carefulness, choosiness (*informal*), fastidiousness, fussiness, meticulousness **3.** accuracy, detail, precision, thoroughness **4.** characteristic, distinctiveness, feature, idiosyncrasy, individuality, peculiarity, property, singularity, trait

particularize detail, enumerate, itemize, specify, spell out, stipulate

particularly **1.** decidedly, especially, exceptionally, markedly, notably, outstandingly, peculiarly, singularly, surprisingly, uncommonly, unusually **2.** distinctly, especially, explicitly, expressly, in particular, specifically

parting *noun* **1.** adieu, departure, farewell, going, goodbye, leave-taking, valediction **2.** breaking, detachment, divergence, division, partition, rift, rupture, separation, split *~adjective* **3.** departing, farewell, final, last, valedictory

partisan *noun* **1.** adherent, backer, champion, devotee, disciple, follower, stalwart, supporter, upholder, votary *~adjective* **2.** biased, factional, interested, one-sided, partial, prejudiced, sectarian, tendentious *~noun* **3.** guerrilla, irregular, resistance fighter, underground fighter *~adjective* **4.** guerrilla, irregular, resistance, underground

▷ **Antonyms** *~noun* adversary, contender, critic, detractor, foe, knocker (*informal*), leader, opponent, rival *~adjective* bipartisan, broad-minded, disinterested, impartial, non-partisan, unbiased, unprejudiced

partition *noun* **1.** dividing, division, segregation, separation, severance, splitting **2.** barrier, divider, room divider, screen, wall **3.** allotment, apportionment, distribution, portion, rationing out, share *~verb* **4.** apportion, cut up, divide, parcel out, portion, section, segment, separate, share, split up, subdivide **5.** divide, fence off, screen, separate, wall off

partly halfway, incompletely, in part, in some measure, not fully, partially, relatively, slightly, somewhat, to a certain degree *or* extent, up to a certain point

▷ **Antonyms** completely, entirely, fully, in full, totally, wholly

partner **1.** accomplice, ally, associate, bedfellow, collaborator, colleague, companion, comrade, confederate, copartner, helper, mate, participant, teammate **2.** bedfellow, consort, helpmate, her indoors (*Brit. slang*), husband, mate, significant other (*U.S. informal*), spouse, wife

partnership **1.** companionship, connection, cooperation, copartnership, fellowship, interest, participation, sharing **2.** alliance, association, combine, company, conglomerate, cooperative, corporation, firm, house, society, union

parts **1.** ability, accomplishments, attributes, calibre, capabilities, endowments, faculties, genius, gifts, intellect, intelligence, talents **2.** bits and pieces, components, spare parts, spares

party **1.** at-home, bash (*informal*), beano (*Brit. slang*), celebration, do (*informal*), festivity, function, gathering, get-together (*informal*), hooley *or* hoolie (*chiefly Irish & N.Z.*), knees-up (*Brit. informal*), rave (*Brit. slang*), rave-up (*Brit. slang*), reception, shindig (*informal*), social, social gathering, soirée **2.** band, body, bunch (*informal*), company, crew, detachment (*Military*), gang, gathering, group, squad, team, unit **3.** alliance, association, cabal, camp, clique, coalition, combination, confederacy, coterie, faction, grouping, league, schism, set, side **4.** individual, person, somebody, someone **5.** *Law* contractor (*Law*), defendant, litigant, participant, plaintiff

parvenu **1.** *noun* arriviste, *nouveau riche,* social climber, upstart **2.** *~adjective nouveau riche,* upstart

pass[1] *verb* **1.** depart, elapse, flow, go, go by *or* past, lapse, leave, move, move onwards, proceed, roll, run **2.** beat, exceed, excel, go beyond, outdistance, outdo, outstrip, surmount, surpass, transcend **3.** answer, come up to scratch (*informal*), do, get through, graduate, pass muster, qualify, succeed, suffice, suit **4.** beguile, devote, employ, experience, fill, occupy, spend, suffer, undergo, while away **5.** befall, come up, develop, fall out, happen, occur, take place **6.** convey, deliver, exchange, give, hand, kick, let have, reach, send, throw, transfer, transmit **7.** accept, adopt, approve, authorize, decree, enact, establish, legislate, ordain, ratify, sanction, validate

8. declare, deliver, express, pronounce, utter **9.** disregard, ignore, miss, neglect, not heed, omit, overlook, skip (*informal*) **10.** crap (*taboo slang*), defecate, discharge, eliminate, empty, evacuate, excrete, expel, shit (*taboo slang*), void **11.** blow over, cease, die, disappear, dissolve, dwindle, ebb, end, evaporate, expire, fade, go, melt away, terminate, vanish, wane **12.** (*with* **for** *or* **as**) be accepted as, be mistaken for, be regarded as, be taken for, impersonate, serve as

▷ **Antonyms** (*sense 1*) bring *or* come to a standstill, cease, halt, pause, stop (*senses 2 & 3*) be inadequate, be inferior to, be unsuccessful, come a cropper (*informal*), fail, lose, suffer defeat (*sense 7*) ban, disallow, invalidate, overrule, prohibit, refuse, reject, veto (*sense 9*) acknowledge, heed, note, notice, observe, pay attention to

pass[2] *noun* **1.** canyon, col, defile, gap, gorge, ravine **2.** authorization, identification, identity card, licence, passport, permission, permit, safe-conduct, ticket, warrant **3.** *informal* advances, approach, overture, play (*informal*), proposition, suggestion **4.** condition, juncture, pinch, plight, predicament, situation, stage, state, state of affairs, straits **5.** feint, jab, lunge, push, swing, thrust

passable 1. acceptable, adequate, admissible, allowable, all right, average, fair, fair enough, mediocre, middling, moderate, not too bad, ordinary, presentable, so-so (*informal*), tolerable, unexceptional **2.** clear, crossable, navigable, open, traversable, unobstructed

▷ **Antonyms** (*sense 1*) A1 *or* A-one (*informal*), exceptional, extraordinary, first-class, inadequate, inadmissible, marvellous, outstanding, superb, tops (*slang*), unacceptable, unsatisfactory (*sense 2*) blocked, closed, impassable, obstructed, sealed off, unnavigable

passably after a fashion, fairly, moderately, pretty much, rather, relatively, somewhat, tolerably, well enough

passage 1. alley, avenue, channel, course, lane, opening, path, road, route, thoroughfare, way **2.** aisle, corridor, doorway, entrance, entrance hall, exit, hall, hallway, lobby, passageway, vestibule **3.** clause, excerpt, extract, paragraph, piece, quotation, reading, section, sentence, text, verse **4.** crossing, journey, tour, trek, trip, voyage **5.** advance, change, conversion, flow, motion, movement, passing, progress, progression, transit, transition **6.** allowance, authorization, freedom, permission, right, safe-conduct, visa, warrant **7.** acceptance, enactment, establishment, legalization, legislation, passing, ratification

passageway aisle, alley, corridor, cut, entrance, exit, hall, hallway, lane, lobby, passage, wynd (*Scot.*)

pass away buy it (*U.S. slang*), buy the farm (*U.S. slang*), check out (*U.S. slang*), croak (*slang*), decease, depart (this life), die, expire, go belly-up (*slang*), kick it (*slang*), kick the bucket (*slang*), pass on, pass over, peg it (*informal*), peg out (*informal*), pop one's clogs (*informal*), shuffle off this mortal coil, snuff it (*informal*)

pass by 1. go past, leave, move past, pass **2.** disregard, miss, neglect, not choose, overlook, pass over

passé antiquated, dated, *démodé,* obsolete, old-fashioned, old hat, outdated, outmoded, out-of-date, outworn, unfashionable

passenger fare, hitchhiker, pillion rider, rider, traveller

passer-by bystander, onlooker, witness

passing *adjective* **1.** brief, ephemeral, fleeting, momentary, short, short-lived, temporary, transient, transitory **2.** casual, cursory, glancing, hasty, quick, shallow, short, slight, superficial *~noun* **3.** death, decease, demise, end, finish, loss, termination **4. in passing** accidentally, by the bye, by the way, en passant, incidentally, on the way

passion 1. animation, ardour, eagerness, emotion, excitement, feeling, fervour, fire, heat, intensity, joy, rapture, spirit, transport, warmth, zeal, zest **2.** adoration, affection, ardour, attachment, concupiscence, desire, fondness, infatuation, itch, keenness, love, lust, the hots (*slang*) **3.** bug (*informal*), craving, craze, enthusiasm, fancy, fascination, idol, infatuation, mania, obsession **4.** anger, fit, flare-up (*informal*), frenzy, fury, indignation, ire, outburst, paroxysm, rage, resentment, storm, vehemence, wrath

▷ **Antonyms** apathy, calmness, coldness, coolness, frigidity, hate, indifference, unconcern

passionate 1. amorous, ardent, aroused, desirous, erotic, hot, loving, lustful, sensual, sexy (*informal*), steamy (*informal*), wanton **2.** ablaze, animated, ardent, eager, emotional, enthusiastic, excited, fervent, fervid, fierce, flaming, frenzied, heartfelt, impassioned, impetuous, impulsive, intense, strong, vehement, warm, wild, zealous **3.** choleric, excitable, fiery, hot-headed, hot-tempered, irascible, irritable, peppery, quick-tempered, stormy, tempestuous, violent

▷ **Antonyms** (*sense 1*) cold, frigid, passionless, unloving, unresponsive (*sense 2*) apathetic, calm, cold, half-hearted, indifferent, languorous, nonchalant, subdued, unemotional, unenthusiastic (*sense 3*) agreeable, calm, easy-going, even-tempered, nonviolent, placid, unexcitable

passionless 1. apathetic, cold, cold-blooded, cold-hearted, emotionless, frigid, icy, indifferent, uncaring, unfeeling, unloving, unresponsive 2. calm, detached, dispassionate, impartial, impassive, neutral, restrained, unemotional, uninvolved

passive acquiescent, compliant, docile, enduring, inactive, inert, lifeless, long-suffering, nonviolent, patient, quiescent, receptive, resigned, submissive, unassertive, uninvolved, unresisting
▷ **Antonyms** active, alive, assertive, bossy (*informal*), defiant, domineering, energetic, feisty (*informal, chiefly U.S. & Canad.*), impatient, involved, lively, rebellious, spirited, violent, zippy (*informal*)

pass off 1. counterfeit, fake, feign, make a pretence of, palm off 2. come to an end, die away, disappear, fade out, vanish 3. emit, evaporate, give off, send forth, vaporize 4. be completed, go off, happen, occur, take place, turn out 5. dismiss, disregard, ignore, pass by, wink at

pass out 1. *informal* become unconscious, black out (*informal*), drop, faint, flake out (*informal*), keel over (*informal*), lose consciousness, swoon (*literary*) 2. deal out, distribute, dole out, hand out

pass over discount, disregard, forget, ignore, not dwell on, omit, overlook, pass by, take no notice of

pass up abstain, decline, forgo, give (something) a miss (*informal*), ignore, let go, let slip, miss, neglect, refuse, reject

password countersign, key word, open sesame, signal, watchword

past *adjective* 1. accomplished, completed, done, elapsed, ended, extinct, finished, forgotten, gone, over, over and done with, spent 2. ancient, bygone, early, erstwhile, foregoing, former, late, long-ago, olden, preceding, previous, prior, quondam, recent ~*noun* 3. **the past** antiquity, days gone by, days of yore, former times, good old days, history, long ago, olden days, old times, times past, yesteryear (*literary*) 4. background, experience, history, life, past life ~*adverb* 5. across, beyond, by, on, over ~*preposition* 6. after, beyond, farther than, later than, outside, over, subsequent to
▷ **Antonyms** ~*adjective* arrived, begun, coming, future, now, present ~*noun* future, now, present, time to come, today, tomorrow

paste 1. *noun* adhesive, cement, glue, gum, mucilage 2. ~*verb* cement, fasten, fix, glue, gum, stick

pastel *adjective* delicate, light, muted, pale, soft, soft-hued
▷ **Antonyms** bright, deep, rich, strong, vibrant, vivid

pastiche blend, farrago, gallimaufry, hotchpotch, medley, *mélange,* miscellany, mixture, motley

pastille cough drop, jujube, lozenge, tablet, troche (*Medical*)

pastime activity, amusement, distraction, diversion, entertainment, game, hobby, leisure, play, recreation, relaxation, sport

past master ace (*informal*), artist, dab hand (*Brit. informal*), expert, old hand, virtuoso, wizard

pastor churchman, clergyman, divine, ecclesiastic, minister, parson, priest, rector, vicar

pastoral *adjective* 1. agrestic, Arcadian, bucolic, country, georgic (*literary*), idyllic, rural, rustic, simple 2. clerical, ecclesiastical, ministerial, priestly

pasture grass, grassland, grazing, grazing land, lea (*poetic*), meadow, pasturage, shieling (*Scot.*)

pasty *adjective* 1. doughy, glutinous, mucilaginous, starchy, sticky 2. anaemic, like death warmed up (*informal*), pale, pallid, sallow, sickly, unhealthy, wan, wheyfaced

pat[1] *verb* 1. caress, dab, fondle, pet, slap, stroke, tap, touch ~*noun* 2. clap, dab, light blow, slap, stroke, tap 3. cake, dab, lump, portion, small piece

pat[2] *adverb* 1. exactly, faultlessly, flawlessly, off pat, perfectly, precisely 2. aptly, bang, dead on, fittingly, just right, opportunely, plumb (*informal*), relevantly, seasonably ~*adjective* 3. apposite, apropos, apt, felicitous, fitting, happy, neat, pertinent, relevant, spot-on (*Brit. informal*), suitable, to the point 4. automatic, easy, facile, glib, ready, simplistic, slick, smooth

patch *noun* 1. piece of material, reinforcement 2. bit, scrap, shred, small piece, spot, stretch 3. area, ground, land, plot, tract ~*verb* 4. cover, fix, mend, reinforce, repair, sew up 5. (*with* **up**) bury the hatchet, conciliate, make friends, placate, restore, settle, settle differences, smooth

patchwork confusion, hash, hotchpotch, jumble, medley, mishmash, mixture, pastiche

patchy bitty, erratic, fitful, inconstant, irregular, random, sketchy, spotty, uneven, variable, varying
▷ **Antonyms** constant, even, regular, unbroken, unvarying

patent 1. *adjective* apparent, blatant, clear, conspicuous, downright, evident, flagrant, glaring, indisputable, manifest, obvious, open, palpable, transparent, unconcealed, unequivocal, unmistakable 2. ~*noun* copyright, invention, licence

paternal 1. benevolent, concerned,

fatherlike, fatherly, protective, solicitous, vigilant **2.** patrilineal, patrimonial

paternity 1. fatherhood, fathership **2.** descent, extraction, family, lineage, parentage **3.** authorship, derivation, origin, source

path 1. footpath, footway, pathway, towpath, track, trail, walkway (*chiefly U.S.*) **2.** avenue, course, direction, passage, procedure, road, route, track, walk, way

pathetic 1. affecting, distressing, harrowing, heartbreaking, heart-rending, melting, moving, pitiable, plaintive, poignant, sad, tender, touching **2.** deplorable, feeble, inadequate, lamentable, meagre, measly, miserable, not much cop (*Brit. slang*), paltry, petty, pitiful, poor, puny, sorry, wet (*Brit. informal*), woeful **3.** *slang* chickenshit (*U.S. slang*), crappy (*slang*), crummy (*slang*), poxy (*slang*), rubbishy, trashy, uninteresting, useless, wanky (*taboo slang*), worthless

▷ **Antonyms** (*sense 1*) amusing, comical, droll, entertaining, funny, laughable, ludicrous, ridiculous

pathfinder discoverer, explorer, guide, pioneer, scout, trailblazer

pathless impassable, impenetrable, trackless, uncharted, unexplored, untrodden, waste, wild

pathos pitiableness, pitifulness, plaintiveness, poignancy, sadness

patience 1. calmness, composure, cool (*slang*), equanimity, even temper, forbearance, imperturbability, restraint, serenity, sufferance, tolerance, toleration **2.** constancy, diligence, endurance, fortitude, long-suffering, perseverance, persistence, resignation, stoicism, submission

▷ **Antonyms** (*sense 1*) agitation, exasperation, excitement, impatience, irritation, nervousness, passion, restlessness (*sense 2*) irresolution, vacillation

patient *adjective* **1.** calm, composed, enduring, long-suffering, persevering, persistent, philosophical, quiet, resigned, self-possessed, serene, stoical, submissive, uncomplaining, untiring **2.** accommodating, even-tempered, forbearing, forgiving, indulgent, lenient, mild, tolerant, understanding *~noun* **3.** case, invalid, sick person, sufferer

patois 1. dialect **2.** argot, cant, jargon, lingo (*informal*), patter, slang, vernacular

patriarch 1. father, paterfamilias, sire **2.** elder, grandfather, greybeard, old man

patrician 1. *noun* aristo (*informal*), aristocrat, noble, nobleman, peer **2.** *~adjective* aristocratic, blue-blooded, gentle (*archaic*), highborn, high-class, lordly, noble

patrimony bequest, birthright, heritage, inheritance, legacy, portion, share

patriot chauvinist, flag-waver (*informal*), jingo, lover of one's country, loyalist, nationalist

patriotic chauvinistic, flag-waving (*informal*), jingoistic, loyal, nationalistic

patriotism flag-waving (*informal*), jingoism, love of one's country, loyalty, nationalism

patrol *noun* **1.** guarding, policing, protecting, rounds, safeguarding, vigilance, watching **2.** garrison, guard, patrolman, sentinel, watch, watchman *~verb* **3.** cruise, guard, inspect, keep guard, keep watch, make the rounds, police, pound, range, safeguard, walk the beat

patron 1. advocate, angel (*informal*), backer, benefactor, champion, defender, friend, guardian, helper, philanthropist, protagonist, protector, sponsor, supporter **2.** buyer, client, customer, frequenter, habitué, shopper

patronage 1. aid, assistance, backing, benefaction, championship, encouragement, espousal, help, promotion, sponsorship, support **2.** business, clientele, commerce, custom, trade, trading, traffic **3.** condescension, deigning, disdain, patronizing, stooping

patronize 1. be lofty with, look down on, talk down to, treat as inferior, treat condescendingly, treat like a child **2.** assist, back, befriend, foster, fund, help, maintain, promote, sponsor, subscribe to, support **3.** be a customer *or* client of, buy from, deal with, do business with, frequent, shop at, trade with

patronizing condescending, contemptuous, disdainful, gracious, haughty, lofty, snobbish, stooping, supercilious, superior, toffee-nosed (*slang, chiefly Brit.*)

▷ **Antonyms** deferential, humble, obsequious, respectful, servile

patter[1] *verb* **1.** scurry, scuttle, skip, tiptoe, trip, walk lightly **2.** beat, pat, pelt, pitapat, pitter-patter, rat-a-tat, spatter, tap *~noun* **3.** pattering, pitapat, pitter-patter, tapping

patter[2] *noun* **1.** line, monologue, pitch, spiel (*informal*) **2.** chatter, gabble, jabber, nattering, prattle, yak (*slang*) **3.** argot, cant, jargon, lingo (*informal*), patois, slang, vernacular *~verb* **4.** babble, blab, chatter, hold forth, jabber, prate, rattle off, rattle on, spiel (*informal*), spout (*informal*), tattle

pattern *noun* **1.** arrangement, decoration, decorative design, design, device, figure, motif, ornament **2.** arrangement, method, order, orderliness, plan, sequence, system **3.** kind, shape, sort, style, type, variety **4.** design, diagram, guide, instructions, original, plan, stencil, template **5.** archetype, criterion, cynosure, example, exemplar, guide, model, norm, original, par, paradigm, paragon, prototype, sample, specimen, standard *~verb* **6.** copy, emulate, follow, form, imitate, model, mould, order, shape, style **7.** decorate, design, trim

paucity dearth, deficiency, fewness, insufficiency, lack, meagreness, paltriness, poverty, rarity, scantiness, scarcity, shortage, slenderness, slightness, smallness, sparseness, sparsity

paunch abdomen, beer-belly (*informal*), belly, corporation (*informal*), middle-age spread (*informal*), pot, potbelly, spare tyre (*Brit. slang*), spread (*informal*)

pauper bankrupt, beggar, down-and-out, have-not, indigent, insolvent, mendicant, poor person

pauperism beggary, destitution, impecuniousness, indigence, mendicancy, need, neediness, pennilessness, penury, poverty, privation, want

pauperize bankrupt, beggar, break, bust (*informal*), cripple financially, impoverish, reduce to beggary, ruin

pause 1. *verb* break, cease, delay, deliberate, desist, discontinue, halt, have a breather (*informal*), hesitate, interrupt, rest, stop briefly, take a break, wait, waver **2.** *~noun* break, breather (*informal*), breathing space, caesura, cessation, delay, discontinuance, entr'acte, gap, halt, hesitation, interlude, intermission, interruption, interval, let-up (*informal*), lull, respite, rest, stay, stoppage, wait

▷ **Antonyms** *~verb* advance, continue, proceed, progress *~noun* advancement, continuance, progression

pave asphalt, concrete, cover, flag, floor, macadamize, surface, tar, tile

paw *verb* grab, handle roughly, manhandle, maul, molest

pawn[1] 1. *verb* deposit, gage (*archaic*), hazard, hock (*informal, chiefly U.S.*), mortgage, pledge, pop (*informal*), stake, wager **2.** *~noun* assurance, bond, collateral, gage, guarantee, guaranty, pledge, security

pawn[2] *noun* cat's-paw, creature, dupe, instrument, plaything, puppet, stooge (*slang*), tool, toy

pay *verb* **1.** clear, compensate, cough up (*informal*), discharge, foot, give, honour, liquidate, meet, offer, recompense, reimburse, remit, remunerate, render, requite, reward, settle, square up **2.** be advantageous, benefit, be worthwhile, repay, serve **3.** bestow, extend, give, grant, hand out, present, proffer, render **4.** (*often with* **for**) answer for, atone, be punished, compensate, get one's deserts, make amends, suffer, suffer the consequences **5.** bring in, produce, profit, return, yield **6.** be profitable, be remunerative, make a return, make money, provide a living **7.** avenge oneself for, get even with (*informal*), get revenge on, pay back, punish, reciprocate, repay, requite, settle a score *~noun* **8.** allowance, compensation, earnings, emoluments, fee, hand-out, hire, income, meed (*archaic*), payment, recompense, reimbursement, remuneration, reward, salary, stipend, takings, wages

payable due, mature, obligatory, outstanding, owed, owing, receivable, to be paid

pay back 1. get even with (*informal*), get one's own back, hit back, reciprocate, recompense, retaliate, settle a score **2.** refund, reimburse, repay, return, settle up, square

payment 1. defrayal, discharge, outlay, paying, remittance, settlement **2.** advance, deposit, instalment, portion, premium, remittance **3.** fee, hire, remuneration, reward, wage

payoff *noun* **1.** conclusion, day of reckoning, final reckoning, judgment, retribution, reward, settlement **2.** *informal* climax, clincher (*informal*), consequence, culmination, finale, moment of truth, outcome, punch line, result, the crunch (*informal*), upshot

pay off 1. discharge, dismiss, fire, lay off, let go, sack (*informal*) **2.** clear, discharge, liquidate, pay in full, settle, square **3.** be effective, be profitable, be successful, succeed, work **4.** get even with (*informal*), pay back, retaliate, settle a score **5.** *informal* bribe, buy off, corrupt, get at, grease the palm of (*slang*), oil (*informal*), suborn

pay out 1. cough up (*informal*), disburse, expend, fork out *or* over *or* up (*slang*), lay out (*informal*), shell out (*informal*), spend **2.** get even with (*informal*), pay back, retaliate, settle a score

peace 1. accord, agreement, amity, concord, harmony **2.** armistice, cessation of hostilities, conciliation, pacification, treaty, truce **3.** calm, composure, contentment, placidity, relaxation, repose, serenity **4.** calm, calmness, hush, peacefulness, quiet, quietude, repose, rest, silence, stillness, tranquillity

peaceable 1. amiable, amicable, conciliatory, dovish, friendly, gentle, inoffensive, mild, nonbelligerent, pacific, peaceful, peace-loving, placid, unwarlike **2.** balmy, calm, peaceful, quiet, restful, serene, still, tranquil, undisturbed

peaceful 1. amicable, at peace, free from strife, friendly, harmonious, nonviolent, on friendly *or* good terms, without hostility **2.** calm, gentle, placid, quiet, restful, serene, still, tranquil, undisturbed, unruffled, untroubled **3.** conciliatory, irenic, pacific, peaceable, peace-loving, placatory, unwarlike

▷ **Antonyms** agitated, antagonistic, belligerent, bitter, disquieted, disturbed, hostile, loud, nervous, noisy, raucous, restless, unfriendly, upset, violent, warlike, warring, wartime

peacemaker appeaser, arbitrator, conciliator, mediator, pacifier, peacemonger

peak *noun* **1.** aiguille, apex, brow, crest, pinnacle, point, summit, tip, top **2.** acme, apogee, climax, crown, culmination, high point, maximum point, *ne plus ultra,* zenith *~verb* **3.** be at its height, climax, come to a head, culminate, reach its highest point, reach the zenith

peaky emaciated, green about the gills, ill, in poor shape, like death warmed up (*informal*), off colour, pale, peelie-wally (*Scot.*), pinched, poorly (*informal*), sick, sickly, under the weather (*informal*), unwell, wan

peal 1. *noun* blast, carillon, chime, clamour, clang, clap, crash, resounding, reverberation, ring, ringing, roar, rumble, sound, tintinnabulation **2.** *~verb* chime, crack, crash, resonate, resound, reverberate, ring, roar, roll, rumble, sound, tintinnabulate, toll

peasant 1. churl (*archaic*), countryman, hind (*obsolete*), rustic, son of the soil, swain (*archaic*) **2.** *informal* boor, churl, country bumpkin, hayseed (*U.S. & Canad. informal*), hick (*informal, chiefly U.S. & Canad.*), lout, provincial, yokel

peccadillo error, indiscretion, infraction, lapse, misdeed, misdemeanour, petty offence, slip, trifling fault

peck *verb/noun* bite, dig, hit, jab, kiss, nibble, pick, poke, prick, strike, tap

peculate appropriate, defalcate (*Law*), defraud, embezzle, misapply, misappropriate, pilfer, purloin, rob, steal

peculiar 1. abnormal, bizarre, curious, eccentric, exceptional, extraordinary, far-out (*slang*), freakish, funny, odd, offbeat, off-the-wall (*slang*), outlandish, out-of-the-way, outré, quaint, queer, singular, strange, uncommon, unconventional, unusual, wacko (*slang*), weird **2.** appropriate, characteristic, distinct, distinctive, distinguishing, endemic, idiosyncratic, individual, local, particular, personal, private, restricted, special, specific, unique

▷ **Antonyms** (*sense 1*) commonplace, conventional, expected, familiar, ordinary, usual (*sense 2*) common, general, indistinctive, unspecific

peculiarity 1. abnormality, bizarreness, eccentricity, foible, freakishness, idiosyncrasy, mannerism, oddity, odd trait, queerness, quirk **2.** attribute, characteristic, distinctiveness, feature, mark, particularity, property, quality, singularity, speciality, trait

pecuniary commercial, financial, fiscal, monetary

pedagogue dogmatist, dominie (*Scot.*), educator, instructor, master, mistress, pedant, schoolmaster, schoolmistress, teacher

pedant casuist, doctrinaire, dogmatist, hairsplitter, literalist, nit-picker (*informal*), pedagogue, pettifogger, precisian, quibbler, scholastic, sophist

pedantic abstruse, academic, bookish, didactic, donnish, erudite, formal, fussy, hairsplitting, nit-picking (*informal*), overnice, particular, pedagogic, picky (*informal*), pompous, precise, priggish, punctilious, scholastic, schoolmasterly, sententious, stilted

pedantry bookishness, finicality, hairsplitting, overnicety, pedagogism, pettifoggery, pomposity, punctiliousness, quibbling, sophistry, stuffiness

peddle flog (*slang*), hawk, huckster, market, push (*informal*), sell, sell door to door, trade, vend

pedestal 1. base, dado (*Architecture*), foot, foundation, mounting, pier, plinth, socle, stand, support **2. put on a pedestal** apotheosize, deify, dignify, ennoble, exalt, glorify, idealize, worship

pedestrian 1. *noun* footslogger, foot-traveller, walker **2.** *~adjective* banal, boring, commonplace, dull, flat, ho-hum (*informal*), humdrum, mediocre, mundane, no great shakes (*informal*), ordinary, plodding, prosaic, run-of-the-mill, unimaginative, uninspired, uninteresting

▷ **Antonyms** *~noun* driver *~adjective* exciting, fascinating, imaginative, important, interesting, noteworthy, outstanding, remarkable, significant

pedigree 1. *noun* ancestry, blood, breed, derivation, descent, extraction, family, family tree, genealogy, heritage, line, lineage, race, stemma, stirps, stock **2.** *~adjective* full-blooded, purebred, thoroughbred

pedlar cheap-jack (*informal*), colporteur, door-to-door salesman, duffer (*dialect*), hawker, huckster, seller, vendor

peek 1. *verb* glance, keek (*Scot.*), look, peep, peer, snatch a glimpse, sneak a look, spy, squinny, take *or* have a gander (*informal*), take a look **2.** *~noun* blink, butcher's (*Brit. slang*), gander (*informal*), glance, glim (*Scot.*), glimpse, keek (*Scot.*), look, look-see (*slang*), peep, shufti (*Brit. slang*)

peel 1. *verb* decorticate, desquamate, flake off, pare, scale, skin, strip off **2.** *~noun* epicarp, exocarp, peeling, rind, skin

peep[1] *verb* **1.** keek (*Scot.*), look from hiding, look surreptitiously, peek, peer, sneak a look, spy, steal a look **2.** appear briefly, emerge, peer out, show partially *~noun* **3.** butcher's (*Brit. slang*), gander (*informal*), glim (*Scot.*), glimpse, keek (*Scot.*), look, look-see (*slang*), peek, shufti (*Brit. slang*)

peep[2] *verb/noun* cheep, chirp, chirrup, pipe, squeak, tweet, twitter

peephole aperture, chink, crack, crevice, fissure, hole, keyhole, opening, pinhole, slit, spyhole

peer[1] *noun* **1.** aristo (*informal*), aristocrat, baron, count, duke, earl, lord, marquess, marquis, noble, nobleman, viscount **2.** coequal, compeer, equal, fellow, like, match

peer[2] *verb* **1.** gaze, inspect, peep, scan, scrutinize, snoop, spy, squinny, squint **2.** appear, become visible, emerge, peep out

peerage aristocracy, lords and ladies, nobility, peers, titled classes

peerless beyond compare, excellent, incomparable, matchless, nonpareil, outstanding, second to none, superlative, unequalled, unique, unmatched, unparalleled, unrivalled, unsurpassed

▷ **Antonyms** commonplace, inferior, mediocre, no great shakes (*informal*), ordinary, poor, second-rate

peeve 1. *verb* annoy, bother, bug (*informal*), exasperate, gall, get (*informal*), get one's goat (*slang*), get on one's nerves (*informal*), irk, irritate, nark (*Brit., Austral., & N.Z. slang*), nettle, pique, piss one off (*taboo slang*), provoke, rile, rub (up) the wrong way, vex **2.** *~noun* annoyance, bother, gripe (*informal*), nuisance, pest, sore point, vexation

peeved annoyed, exasperated, galled, hacked (off) (*U.S. slang*), irked, irritated, nettled, piqued, pissed off (*taboo slang*), put out, riled, sore, upset, vexed

peevish acrimonious, cantankerous, captious, childish, churlish, crabbed, cross, crotchety (*informal*), crusty, fractious, fretful, grumpy, huffy, ill-natured, ill-tempered, irritable, liverish, pettish, petulant, querulous, ratty (*Brit. & N.Z. informal*), short-tempered, shrewish, snappy, splenetic, sulky, sullen, surly, testy, tetchy, touchy, waspish, whingeing (*informal*)

▷ **Antonyms** affable, agreeable, cheerful, cheery, easy-going, even-tempered, genial, good-natured, happy, merry, pleasant, sweet

peg *verb* **1.** attach, fasten, fix, join, make fast, secure **2.** (*with* **along** *or* **away**) apply oneself to, beaver away (*Brit. informal*), keep at it, keep going, keep on, persist, plod along, plug away at (*informal*), stick to it, work at, work away **3.** *of prices, etc.* control, fix, freeze, limit, set

pejorative belittling, debasing, deprecatory, depreciatory, derogatory, detractive, detractory, disparaging, negative, slighting, uncomplimentary, unpleasant

pell-mell 1. *adverb* full tilt, hastily, heedlessly, helter-skelter, hurriedly, impetuously, posthaste, precipitously, rashly, recklessly **2.** *~adjective* chaotic, confused, disordered, disorganized, haphazard, tumultuous **3.** *~noun* anarchy, chaos, confusion, disarray, disorder, ferment, helter-skelter, pandemonium, tumult, turmoil, upheaval

pellucid 1. bright, clear, crystalline, glassy, limpid, translucent, transparent **2.** clear, comprehensible, limpid, lucid, perspicuous, plain, straightforward, unambiguous

pelt[1] *verb* **1.** assail, batter, beat, belabour, bombard, cast, hurl, pepper, pummel, shower, sling, strike, thrash, throw, wallop (*informal*) **2.** barrel (along) (*informal, chiefly U.S. & Canad.*), belt (*slang*), burn rubber (*informal*), career, charge, dash, hurry, run fast, rush, shoot, speed, stampede, tear, whizz (*informal*) **3.** bucket down (*informal*), pour, rain cats and dogs (*informal*), rain hard, teem

pelt[2] *noun* coat, fell, hide, skin

pen[1] *verb* commit to paper, compose, draft, draw up, jot down, write

pen[2] **1.** *noun* cage, coop, corral (*chiefly U.S. & Canad.*), enclosure, fold, hutch, pound, sty **2.** *~verb* cage, confine, coop up, enclose, fence in, hedge, hem in, hurdle, impound, mew (up), pound, shut up *or* in

penal corrective, disciplinary, penalizing, punitive, retributive

penalize award a penalty against (*Sport*), correct, discipline, handicap, impose a penalty on, inflict a handicap on, punish, put at a disadvantage

penalty disadvantage, fine, forfeit, forfeiture, handicap, mulct, price, punishment, retribution

penance 1. atonement, mortification, penalty, punishment, reparation, sackcloth and ashes **2. do penance** accept punishment, atone, make amends, make reparation, mortify oneself, show contrition, suffer

penchant affinity, bent, bias, disposition, fondness, inclination, leaning, liking, partiality, predilection, predisposition, proclivity, proneness, propensity, taste, tendency, turn

pendent *adjective* dangling, drooping, hanging, pendulous, suspended, swinging

pending awaiting, forthcoming, hanging fire, imminent, impending, in the balance, in the offing, undecided, undetermined, unsettled, up in the air

pendulous dangling, drooping, hanging, pendent, sagging, swaying, swinging

penetrable accessible, clear, comprehensible, fathomable, intelligible, open, passable, permeable, pervious, porous

penetrate 1. bore, enter, go through, impale, perforate, pierce, prick, probe, stab **2.** diffuse, enter, get in, infiltrate, make inroads (into), permeate, pervade, seep, suffuse **3.** *figurative* affect, become clear, be understood, come across, get through to, impress, touch **4.** *figurative* comprehend, decipher, discern, fathom, figure out (*informal*), get to the bottom of, grasp, suss (out) (*slang*), understand, unravel, work out

penetrating 1. biting, carrying, harsh, intrusive, pervasive, piercing, pungent, sharp, shrill, stinging, strong **2.** *figurative* acute, astute, critical, discerning, discriminating, incisive, intelligent, keen, perceptive, perspicacious, profound, quick, sagacious, searching, sharp, sharp-witted, shrewd

▷ **Antonyms** (*sense 1*) blunt, dull, mild, sweet (*sense 2*) apathetic, dull, indifferent, obtuse, shallow, stupid, uncomprehending, unperceptive

penetration 1. entrance, entry, incision, inroad, invasion, perforation, piercing, puncturing **2.** acuteness, astuteness, discernment, insight, keenness, perception, perspicacity, sharpness, shrewdness, wit

penis chopper (*Brit. slang*), cock (*taboo slang*), dick (*taboo slang*), dong (*slang*), John Thomas (*taboo slang*), joystick (*slang*), knob (*Brit. taboo slang*), member, organ, pecker (*U.S. & Canad. taboo slang*), phallus, pizzle (*archaic & dialect*), plonker (*slang*), prick (*taboo slang*), schlong (*U.S. slang*), tadger (*Brit. slang*), tool (*taboo slang*), wang (*U.S. slang*), weenie (*U.S. slang*), whang (*U.S. slang*), willie *or* willy (*Brit. informal*), winkle (*Brit. slang*)

penitence compunction, contrition, regret, remorse, repentance, ruefulness, self-reproach, shame, sorrow

penitent *adjective* abject, apologetic, atoning, conscience-stricken, contrite, regretful, remorseful, repentant, rueful, sorrowful, sorry

▷ **Antonyms** callous, impenitent, remorseless, unrepentant

penmanship calligraphy, chirography, fist (*informal*), hand, handwriting, longhand, script, writing

pen name allonym, nom de plume, pseudonym

pennant banderole, banner, burgee (*Nautical*), ensign, flag, jack, pennon, streamer

penniless bankrupt, broke (*informal*), cleaned out (*slang*), destitute, dirt-poor (*informal*), down and out, down at heel, flat broke (*informal*), impecunious, impoverished, indigent, in queer street, moneyless, necessitous, needy, on one's uppers, on the breadline, penurious, poor, poverty-stricken, ruined, short, skint (*Brit. slang*), stony-broke (*Brit. slang*), strapped (*slang*), without a penny to one's name, without two pennies to rub together (*informal*)

▷ **Antonyms** affluent, filthy rich, loaded (*slang*), rich, rolling (*slang*), wealthy, well-heeled (*informal*)

penny-pincher meany (*informal*), miser, niggard, pinchpenny, screw (*slang*), Scrooge, skinflint, tight-arse (*taboo slang*), tight-ass (*U.S. taboo slang*)

penny-pinching *adjective* cheeseparing, close, frugal, mean, mingy (*Brit. informal*), miserly, near (*informal*), niggardly, scrimping, Scroogelike, snoep (*S. African informal*), stingy, tight-arse (*taboo slang*), tight-arsed (*taboo slang*), tight as a duck's arse (*taboo slang*), tight-ass (*U.S. taboo slang*), tight-assed (*U.S. taboo slang*), tightfisted

▷ **Antonyms** generous, kind, liberal, munificent, prodigal, unstinting

pennyworth bit, crumb, jot, little, mite, modicum, particle, scrap, small amount, tittle

pension allowance, annuity, benefit, superannuation

pensioner O.A.P., retired person, senior citizen

pensive blue (*informal*), cogitative, contemplative, dreamy, grave, in a brown study (*informal*), meditative, melancholy, mournful, musing, preoccupied, reflective, ruminative, sad, serious, sober, solemn, sorrowful, thoughtful, wistful

▷ **Antonyms** active, carefree, cheerful, frivolous, gay, happy, joyous, lighthearted

pent-up bottled up, bridled, checked, constrained, curbed, held back, inhibited, repressed, smothered, stifled, suppressed

penurious 1. cheeseparing, close, close-fisted, frugal, grudging, mean, miserly, near (*informal*), niggardly, parsimonious, skimping, stingy, tight-arse (*taboo slang*), tight-arsed (*taboo slang*), tight as a duck's arse (*taboo slang*), tight-ass (*U.S. taboo slang*), tight-assed (*U.S. taboo slang*), tightfisted, ungenerous **2.** destitute, down and out, down at heel, impecunious, impoverished, indigent, needy, on the breadline, penniless, poor, poverty-stricken **3.** beggarly, deficient, inadequate, meagre, miserable, miserly, paltry, pathetic, poor, scanty

penury 1. beggary, destitution, indigence, need, pauperism, poverty, privation, straitened circumstances, want **2.** dearth, deficiency, lack, paucity, scantiness, scarcity, shortage, sparseness

people *noun* **1.** human beings, humanity, humans, mankind, men and women, mortals, persons **2.** citizens, clan, community, family, folk, inhabitants, nation, population, public, race, tribe **3.** commonalty, crowd, general public, grass roots, hoi polloi, masses, mob, multitude, plebs, populace, proles (*derogatory slang, chiefly Brit.*), proletariat, rabble, rank and file, the herd ~*verb* **4.**

colonize, inhabit, occupy, populate, settle

pep **1.** *noun* animation, brio, energy, get-up-and-go (*informal*), gusto, high spirits, life, liveliness, spirit, verve, vigour, vim (*slang*), vitality, vivacity, zip (*informal*) **2.** *~verb* (*with* **up**) animate, enliven, exhilarate, inspire, invigorate, jazz up (*informal*), quicken, stimulate, vitalize, vivify

pepper *verb* **1.** flavour, season, spice **2.** bespeckle, dot, fleck, spatter, speck, sprinkle, stipple, stud **3.** bombard, pelt, riddle, scatter, shower

peppery **1.** fiery, highly seasoned, hot, piquant, pungent, spicy **2.** choleric, hot-tempered, irascible, irritable, quick-tempered, snappish, testy, touchy, vitriolic, waspish **3.** astringent, biting, caustic, incisive, sarcastic, sharp, stinging, trenchant, vitriolic

▷ **Antonyms** (*sense 1*) bland, insipid, mild, tasteless, vapid

perceive **1.** be aware of, behold, descry, discern, discover, distinguish, espy, make out, note, notice, observe, recognize, remark, see, spot **2.** appreciate, apprehend, comprehend, conclude, deduce, feel, gather, get (*informal*), get the message, get the picture, grasp, know, learn, realize, see, sense, suss (out) (*slang*), understand

perceptible apparent, appreciable, blatant, clear, conspicuous, detectable, discernible, distinct, evident, noticeable, observable, obvious, palpable, perceivable, recognizable, tangible, visible

▷ **Antonyms** concealed, hidden, imperceptible, inconspicuous, indiscernible, invisible, unapparent, undetectable, unnoticeable

perception apprehension, awareness, conception, consciousness, discernment, feeling, grasp, idea, impression, insight, notion, observation, recognition, sensation, sense, taste, understanding

perceptive acute, alert, astute, aware, discerning, insightful, intuitive, observant, penetrating, percipient, perspicacious, quick, responsive, sensitive, sharp

▷ **Antonyms** dull, indifferent, insensitive, obtuse, slow-witted, stupid, thick

perch **1.** *noun* branch, pole, post, resting place, roost **2.** *~verb* alight, balance, land, rest, roost, settle, sit on

perchance by chance, for all one knows, haply (*archaic*), maybe, mayhap (*archaic*), peradventure (*archaic*), perhaps, possibly, probably

percipience acuity, alertness, astuteness, awareness, discernment, insight, intuition, penetration, perception, perspicacity, sagacity, sensitivity, understanding

percipient alert, alive, astute, aware, bright (*informal*), discerning, discriminating, intelligent, penetrating, perceptive, perspicacious, quick-witted, sharp, wide-awake

percolate drain, drip, exude, filter, filtrate, leach, ooze, penetrate, perk (*of coffee, informal*), permeate, pervade, seep, strain, transfuse

percussion blow, brunt, bump, clash, collision, concussion, crash, impact, jolt, knock, shock, smash, thump

perdition condemnation, damnation, destruction, doom, downfall, everlasting punishment, hell, hellfire, ruin

peregrination **1.** expedition, exploration, journey, odyssey, tour, trek, trip, voyage **2.** globetrotting, roaming, roving, travelling, trekking, wandering, wayfaring

peremptory **1.** absolute, binding, categorical, commanding, compelling, decisive, final, imperative, incontrovertible, irrefutable, obligatory, undeniable **2.** arbitrary, assertive, authoritative, autocratic, bossy (*informal*), dictatorial, dogmatic, domineering, high-handed, imperious, intolerant, overbearing

perennial **1.** abiding, chronic, constant, continual, continuing, enduring, incessant, inveterate, lasting, lifelong, persistent, recurrent, unchanging **2.** ceaseless, deathless, eternal, everlasting, immortal, imperishable, never-ending, permanent, perpetual, unceasing, undying, unfailing, uninterrupted

perfect *adjective* **1.** absolute, complete, completed, consummate, entire, finished, full, out-and-out, sheer, unadulterated, unalloyed, unmitigated, utter, whole **2.** blameless, clean, excellent, faultless, flawless, ideal, immaculate, impeccable, pure, splendid, spotless, sublime, superb, superlative, supreme, unblemished, unmarred, untarnished **3.** accurate, close, correct, exact, faithful, precise, right, spot-on (*Brit. informal*), strict, true, unerring **4.** accomplished, adept, experienced, expert, finished, masterly, polished, practised, skilful, skilled *~verb* **5.** accomplish, achieve, carry out, complete, consummate, effect, finish, fulfil, perform, realize **6.** ameliorate, cultivate, develop, elaborate, hone, improve, polish, refine

▷ **Antonyms** *~adjective* bad, damaged, defective, deficient, faulty, flawed, impaired, imperfect, impure, incomplete, inferior, partial, poor, ruined, spoiled, unfinished, unskilled, worthless *~verb* mar

perfection **1.** accomplishment, achievement, achieving, completion, consummation, evolution, fulfilment, realization **2.** completeness, exactness, excellence, exquisiteness, faultlessness, integrity, maturity, perfectness, precision, purity, sublimity, superiority, wholeness **3.** acme, crown, ideal, paragon

perfectionist formalist, precisian, precisionist, purist, stickler

perfectly **1.** absolutely, altogether, completely, consummately, entirely, every inch, fully, quite, thoroughly, totally, utterly, wholly **2.** admirably, exquisitely, faultlessly, flawlessly, ideally, impeccably, like a dream, superbly, superlatively, supremely, to perfection, wonderfully

▷ **Antonyms** (*sense 1*) inaccurately, incompletely, mistakenly, partially (*sense 2*) badly, defectively, faultily, imperfectly, poorly

perfidious corrupt, deceitful, dishonest, disloyal, double-dealing, double-faced, faithless, false, recreant (*archaic*), traitorous, treacherous, treasonous, two-faced, unfaithful, untrustworthy

perfidy betrayal, deceit, disloyalty, double-dealing, duplicity, faithlessness, falsity, infidelity, perfidiousness, treachery, treason

perforate bore, drill, hole, honeycomb, penetrate, pierce, punch, puncture

perforce by force of circumstances, by necessity, inevitably, necessarily, needs must, of necessity, unavoidably, willy-nilly, without choice

perform **1.** accomplish, achieve, act, bring about, carry out, complete, comply with, discharge, do, effect, execute, fulfil, function, observe, pull off, satisfy, transact, work **2.** act, appear as, depict, enact, play, present, produce, put on, render, represent, stage

performance **1.** accomplishment, achievement, act, carrying out, completion, conduct, consummation, discharge, execution, exploit, feat, fulfilment, work **2.** acting, appearance, exhibition, gig (*informal*), interpretation, play, portrayal, presentation, production, representation, show **3.** action, conduct, efficiency, functioning, operation, practice, running, working **4.** *informal* act, behaviour, bother, business, carry-on (*informal, chiefly Brit.*), fuss, pantomime (*informal, chiefly Brit.*), pother, rigmarole, to-do

performer actor, actress, artiste, play-actor, player, Thespian, trouper

perfume aroma, attar, balminess, bouquet, cologne, essence, fragrance, incense, niff (*Brit. slang*), odour, redolence, scent, smell, sweetness

perfunctory automatic, careless, cursory, heedless, inattentive, indifferent, mechanical, negligent, offhand, routine, sketchy, slipshod, slovenly, stereotyped, superficial, unconcerned, unthinking, wooden

▷ **Antonyms** ardent, assiduous, attentive, careful, diligent, keen, spirited, thorough, thoughtful, zealous

perhaps as the case may be, conceivably, feasibly, for all one knows, it may be, maybe, perchance (*archaic*), possibly

peril danger, exposure, hazard, insecurity, jeopardy, menace, pitfall, risk, uncertainty, vulnerability

▷ **Antonyms** certainty, impregnability, invulnerability, safety, security, surety

perilous chancy (*informal*), dangerous, exposed, fraught with danger, hairy (*slang*), hazardous, parlous (*archaic*), precarious, risky, threatening, unsafe, unsure, vulnerable

perimeter ambit, border, borderline, boundary, bounds, circumference, confines, edge, limit, margin, periphery

▷ **Antonyms** central part, centre, core, heart, hub, middle, nucleus

period **1.** interval, season, space, span, spell, stretch, term, time, while **2.** aeon, age, course, cycle, date, days, epoch, era, generation, season, stage, term, time, years

periodic at fixed intervals, cyclic, cyclical, every once in a while, every so often, infrequent, intermittent, occasional, periodical, recurrent, regular, repeated, seasonal, spasmodic, sporadic

periodical *noun* journal, magazine, monthly, organ, paper, publication, quarterly, review, serial, weekly

peripatetic ambulant, itinerant, migrant, mobile, nomadic, roaming, roving, travelling, vagabond, vagrant, wandering

peripheral **1.** beside the point, borderline, incidental, inessential, irrelevant, marginal, minor, secondary, superficial, tangential, unimportant **2.** exterior, external, outer, outermost, outside, perimetric, surface

periphery ambit, border, boundary, brim, brink, circumference, edge, fringe, hem, outer edge, outskirts, perimeter, rim, skirt, verge

periphrastic circuitous, circumlocutory, pleonastic, prolix, roundabout, tautological, verbose, wordy

perish **1.** be killed, be lost, decease, die, expire, lose one's life, pass away **2.** be destroyed, collapse, decline, disappear, fall, go under, vanish **3.** break down, decay, decompose, disintegrate, moulder, rot, waste, wither

perishable decaying, decomposable, destructible, easily spoilt, liable to rot, short-lived, unstable

▷ **Antonyms** durable, lasting, long-life, long-lived, non-perishable

perjure (oneself) bear false witness, commit perjury, forswear, give false testimony, lie under oath, swear falsely

perjured deceitful, false, forsworn, lying, mendacious, perfidious, traitorous, treacherous, untrue, untruthful

perjury bearing false witness, false oath, false statement, false swearing, forswearing, giving false testimony, lying under oath, oath breaking, violation of an oath, wilful falsehood

perk benefit, bonus, dividend, extra, fringe benefit, icing on the cake, perquisite, plus

perk up brighten, buck up (*informal*), cheer up, liven up, look up, pep up, rally, recover, recuperate, revive, take heart

perky animated, bouncy, bright, bright-eyed and bushy-tailed (*informal*), bubbly, buoyant, cheerful, cheery, chirpy (*informal*), full of beans (*informal*), gay, genial, in fine fettle, jaunty, lively, spirited, sprightly, sunny, upbeat (*informal*), vivacious

permanence constancy, continuance, continuity, dependability, durability, duration, endurance, finality, fixedness, fixity, immortality, indestructibility, lastingness, perdurability (*rare*), permanency, perpetuity, stability, survival

permanent abiding, constant, durable, enduring, eternal, everlasting, fixed, immovable, immutable, imperishable, indestructible, invariable, lasting, long-lasting, perennial, perpetual, persistent, stable, steadfast, unchanging, unfading

▷ **Antonyms** brief, changing, ephemeral, finite, fleeting, impermanent, inconstant, momentary, mortal, passing, short-lived, temporary, transitory, variable

permeable absorbent, absorptive, penetrable, pervious, porous, spongy

permeate charge, diffuse throughout, fill, filter through, imbue, impregnate, infiltrate, pass through, penetrate, percolate, pervade, saturate, seep through, soak through, spread throughout

permissible acceptable, admissible, allowable, all right, authorized, kosher (*informal*), lawful, legal, legit (*slang*), legitimate, licit, O.K. *or* okay (*informal*), permitted, proper, sanctioned

▷ **Antonyms** banned, forbidden, illegal, illicit, prohibited, unauthorized, unlawful

permission allowance, approval, assent, authorization, blank cheque, consent, dispensation, freedom, go-ahead (*informal*), green light, leave, liberty, licence, permit, sanction, sufferance, tolerance

permissive acquiescent, easy-going, easy-oasy (*slang*), forbearing, free, indulgent, latitudinarian, lax, lenient, liberal, open-minded, tolerant

▷ **Antonyms** authoritarian, denying, domineering, forbidding, grudging, rigid, strict

permit 1. *verb* admit, agree, allow, authorize, consent, empower, enable, endorse, endure, entitle, give leave *or* permission, give the green light to, grant, let, license, own, sanction, suffer, tolerate, warrant **2.** *~noun* authorization, liberty, licence, pass, passport, permission, sanction, warrant

permutation alteration, change, shift, transformation, transmutation, transposition

pernicious bad, baleful, baneful (*archaic*), damaging, dangerous, deadly, deleterious, destructive, detrimental, evil, fatal, harmful, hurtful, injurious, maleficent, malevolent, malicious, malign, malignant, noisome, noxious, offensive, pestilent, poisonous, ruinous, venomous, wicked

pernickety 1. careful, carping, difficult to please, exacting, fastidious, finicky, fussy, hairsplitting, nice, nit-picking (*informal*), overprecise, painstaking, particular, picky (*informal*), punctilious **2.** detailed, exacting, fiddly, fine, tricky

▷ **Antonyms** (*sense 1*) careless, easy to please, haphazard, heedless, inattentive, lax, slack, slapdash, slipshod, sloppy, uncritical (*sense 2*) easy, simple

peroration closing remarks, conclusion, recapitulation, recapping (*informal*), reiteration, summing-up

perpendicular at right angles to, on end, plumb, straight, upright, vertical

perpetrate be responsible for, bring about, carry out, commit, do, effect, enact, execute, inflict, perform, wreak

perpetual 1. abiding, endless, enduring, eternal, everlasting, immortal, infinite, lasting, never-ending, perennial, permanent, sempiternal (*literary*), unchanging, undying, unending **2.** ceaseless, constant, continual, continuous, endless, incessant, interminable, never-ending, perennial, persistent, recurrent, repeated, unceasing, unfailing, uninterrupted, unremitting

▷ **Antonyms** brief, ephemeral, fleeting, impermanent, momentary, passing, short-lived, temporary, transitory

perpetuate continue, eternalize, immortalize, keep alive, keep going, keep up, maintain, preserve, sustain

▷ **Antonyms** abolish, destroy, end, forget, ignore, put an end to, stamp out, suppress

perplex 1. baffle, befuddle, bemuse, beset, bewilder, confound, confuse, dumbfound, faze, flummox, mix up, muddle, mystify, nonplus, puzzle, stump **2.** complicate, encumber, entangle, involve, jumble, mix up, snarl up, tangle, thicken

perplexing baffling, bewildering, complex, complicated, confusing, difficult, enigmatic, hard, inexplicable, intricate, involved, knotty, labyrinthine, mysterious, mystifying, paradoxical, puzzling, strange, taxing, thorny, unaccountable, weird

perplexity 1. bafflement, bewilderment, confusion, incomprehension, mystification, puzzlement, stupefaction **2.** complexity, difficulty, inextricability, intricacy, involvement, obscurity **3.** can of worms (*informal*), difficulty, dilemma, enigma, fix (*informal*), how-do-you-do (*informal*), knotty problem, mystery, paradox, puzzle, snarl

perquisite benefit, bonus, dividend, extra, fringe benefit, icing on the cake, perk (*Brit. informal*), plus

per se as such, by definition, by itself, by its very nature, essentially, in essence, in itself, intrinsically, of itself

persecute 1. afflict, be on one's back (*slang*), distress, dragoon, harass, hassle (*informal*), hound, hunt, ill-treat, injure, maltreat, martyr, molest, oppress, pur~ sue, torment, torture, victimize **2.** an~ noy, badger, bait, bother, pester, tease, vex, worry

▷ **Antonyms** accommodate, back, calm, coddle, comfort, console, cosset, humour, indulge, leave alone, let alone, molly~ coddle, pamper, pet, spoil, support

perseverance constancy, dedication, de~ termination, diligence, doggedness, en~ durance, indefatigability, persistence, pertinacity, purposefulness, resolution, sedulity, stamina, steadfastness, tenac~ ity

persevere be determined *or* resolved, carry on, continue, endure, go on, hang on, hold fast, hold on (*informal*), keep going, keep on *or* at, keep one's hand in, maintain, persist, plug away (*informal*), pursue, remain, stand firm, stay the course, stick at *or* to

▷ **Antonyms** be irresolute, dither (*chiefly Brit.*), end, falter, give in, give up, hesi~ tate, quit, shillyshally (*informal*), swither (*Scot.*), throw in the towel, vac~ illate, waver

persiflage badinage, banter, chaff, frivol~ ity, pleasantry, raillery, repartee, teas~ ing, wit, wittiness, wordplay

persist 1. be resolute, continue, hold on (*informal*), insist, persevere, stand firm, stay the course **2.** abide, carry on, con~ tinue, endure, hang in the air, keep up, last, linger, remain

persistence constancy, determination, diligence, doggedness, endurance, grit, indefatigability, perseverance, perti~ nacity, pluck, resolution, stamina, steadfastness, tenacity, tirelessness

persistent 1. assiduous, determined, dog~ ged, enduring, fixed, immovable, inde~ fatigable, obdurate, obstinate, persever~ ing, pertinacious, resolute, steadfast, steady, stiff-necked, stubborn, tena~ cious, tireless, unflagging **2.** constant, continual, continuous, endless, inces~ sant, interminable, lasting, never-ending, perpetual, relentless, repeated, unrelenting, unremitting

▷ **Antonyms** (*sense 1*) changeable, flex~ ible, irresolute, tractable, yielding (*sense 2*) inconstant, intermittent, irregular, occasional, off-and-on, periodic

person 1. being, body, human, human being, individual, living soul, soul **2. in person** bodily, in the flesh, oneself, per~ sonally

persona assumed role, character, façade, face, front, mask, part, personality, public face, role

personable affable, agreeable, amiable, attractive, charming, good-looking, handsome, likable *or* likeable, nice, pleasant, pleasing, presentable, winning

▷ **Antonyms** disagreeable, sullen, surly, ugly, unattractive, unpleasant, un~ sightly

personage big name, big noise (*informal*), big shot (*informal*), celeb (*informal*), ce~ lebrity, dignitary, luminary, megastar (*informal*), notable, personality, public figure, somebody, V.I.P., well-known person, worthy

personal 1. exclusive, individual, inti~ mate, own, particular, peculiar, private, privy, special **2.** bodily, corporal, corpo~ real, exterior, material, physical **3.** de~ rogatory, disparaging, insulting, nasty, offensive, pejorative, slighting

personality 1. character, disposition, identity, individuality, make-up, nature, psyche, temper, temperament, traits **2.** attraction, attractiveness, character, charisma, charm, dynamism, likable~ ness *or* likeableness, magnetism, pleas~ antness **3.** big name, celeb (*informal*), celebrity, famous name, household name, megastar (*informal*), notable, personage, star, well-known face, well-known person

personally 1. alone, by oneself, indepen~ dently, in person, in the flesh, on one's own, solely **2.** for oneself, for one's part, from one's own viewpoint, in one's books, in one's own view **3.** individualis~ tically, individually, privately, specially, subjectively

personate act, depict, do (*informal*), en~ act, feign, imitate, impersonate, play-act, portray, represent

personification embodiment, epitome, image, incarnation, likeness, portrayal, recreation, representation, semblance

personify body forth, embody, epitomize, exemplify, express, image (*rare*), incar~ nate, mirror, represent, symbolize, typi~ fy

personnel employees, helpers, human re~ sources, liveware, members, men and women, people, staff, workers, work~ force

perspective 1. angle, attitude, broad view, context, frame of reference, objectivity, outlook, overview, proportion, relation, relative importance, relativity, way of looking **2.** outlook, panorama, prospect, scene, view, vista

perspicacious acute, alert, astute, aware, clear-sighted, clever, discerning, keen, observant, penetrating, perceptive, percipient, sagacious, sharp, sharp-witted, shrewd

perspicacity acumen, acuteness, discernment, discrimination, insight, keenness, penetration, perceptiveness, percipience, perspicaciousness, perspicuity, sagaciousness, sagacity, sharpness, shrewdness, smarts (*slang, chiefly U.S.*), suss (*slang*), wit

perspicuity clarity, clearness, comprehensibility, distinctness, explicitness, intelligibility, limpidity, limpidness, lucidity, plainness, precision, straightforwardness, transparency

perspicuous clear, comprehensible, crystal-clear, distinct, easily understood, explicit, intelligible, limpid, lucid, obvious, plain, self-evident, straightforward, transparent, unambiguous, understandable

perspiration exudation, moisture, sweat, wetness

perspire be damp, be wet, drip, exude, glow, pour with sweat, secrete, sweat, swelter

persuade 1. actuate, advise, allure, bring round (*informal*), coax, counsel, entice, impel, incite, induce, influence, inveigle, prevail upon, prompt, sway, talk into, twist (someone's) arm, urge, win over **2.** cause to believe, convert, convince, satisfy

▷ **Antonyms** deter, discourage, dissuade, forbid, prohibit

persuasion 1. blandishment, cajolery, conversion, enticement, exhortation, inducement, influencing, inveiglement, wheedling **2.** cogency, force, persuasiveness, potency, power, pull (*informal*) **3.** belief, certitude, conviction, credo, creed, faith, firm belief, fixed opinion, opinion, tenet, views **4.** camp, cult, denomination, faction, party, school, school of thought, sect, side

persuasive cogent, compelling, convincing, credible, effective, eloquent, forceful, impelling, impressive, inducing, influential, logical, moving, plausible, sound, telling, touching, valid, weighty, winning

▷ **Antonyms** feeble, flimsy, illogical, implausible, incredible, ineffective, invalid, unconvincing, unimpressive, weak

pert 1. bold, brash, cheeky, flip (*informal*), flippant, forward, fresh (*informal*), impertinent, impudent, insolent, lippy (*U.S. & Canad. slang*), presumptuous, pushy (*informal*), sassy (*U.S. informal*), saucy, smart **2.** brisk, dapper, daring, dashing, gay, jaunty, lively, nimble, perky, smart, spirited, sprightly

pertain appertain, apply, be appropriate, bear on, befit, belong, be part of, be relevant, concern, refer, regard, relate

pertinacious bull-headed, determined, dogged, headstrong, inflexible, intractable, mulish, obdurate, obstinate, persevering, persistent, perverse, pig-headed, relentless, resolute, self-willed, stiff-necked, strong-willed, stubborn, tenacious, unyielding, wilful

pertinent admissible, *ad rem,* applicable, apposite, appropriate, apropos, apt, fit, fitting, germane, material, pat, proper, relevant, suitable, to the point, to the purpose

▷ **Antonyms** discordant, foreign, immaterial, inappropriate, incongruous, irrelevant, unfitting, unrelated, unsuitable

pertness audacity, brashness, brass (*informal*), bumptiousness, cheek (*informal*), cheekiness, chutzpah (*U.S. & Canad. informal*), cockiness, effrontery, forwardness, front, impertinence, impudence, insolence, presumption, rudeness, sauciness

perturb 1. agitate, alarm, bother, discompose, disconcert, discountenance, disquiet, disturb, faze, fluster, ruffle, trouble, unnerve, unsettle, upset, vex, worry **2.** confuse, disarrange, disorder, muddle, unsettle

perturbed agitated, alarmed, anxious, disconcerted, disquieted, disturbed, fearful, flurried, flustered, ill at ease, nervous, restless, shaken, troubled, uncomfortable, uneasy, upset, worried

▷ **Antonyms** assured, at ease, comfortable, composed, cool, impassive, relaxed, unperturbed, unruffled

perusal browse, check, examination, inspection, look through, read, scrutiny, study

peruse browse, check, examine, inspect, look through, read, run one's eye over, scan, scrutinize, study, work over

pervade affect, charge, diffuse, extend, fill, imbue, infuse, overspread, penetrate, percolate, permeate, spread through, suffuse

pervasive common, extensive, general, inescapable, omnipresent, permeating, pervading, prevalent, rife, ubiquitous, universal, widespread

perverse 1. abnormal, contradictory, contrary, delinquent, depraved, deviant, disobedient, improper, incorrect, miscreant, rebellious, refractory, troublesome, unhealthy, unmanageable, unreasonable **2.** contrary, contumacious, cross-grained, dogged, headstrong, intractable, intransigent, obdurate, wilful, wrong-headed **3.** contrary, cussed (*informal*), mulish, obstinate, pig-headed, stiff-necked, stubborn, unyielding, wayward **4.** cantankerous, churlish, crabbed, cross, fractious, ill-natured, ill-tempered, peevish, petulant, shrewish, spiteful, stroppy (*Brit. slang*), surly

▷ **Antonyms** accommodating, agreeable,

amiable, complaisant, cooperative, flexible, good-natured, malleable, obedient, obliging

perversion **1.** aberration, abnormality, debauchery, depravity, deviation, immorality, kink (*Brit. informal*), kinkiness (*slang*), unnaturalness, vice, vitiation, wickedness **2.** corruption, distortion, falsification, misinterpretation, misrepresentation, misuse, twisting

perversity contradictiveness, contradictoriness, contrariness, contumacy, frowardness (*archaic*), intransigence, obduracy, refractoriness, waywardness, wrong-headedness

pervert *verb* **1.** abuse, distort, falsify, garble, misconstrue, misinterpret, misrepresent, misuse, twist, warp **2.** corrupt, debase, debauch, degrade, deprave, desecrate, initiate, lead astray, subvert *~noun* **3.** debauchee, degenerate, deviant, sicko (*informal*), sleazeball (*slang*), weirdo *or* weirdie (*informal*)

perverted aberrant, abnormal, corrupt, debased, debauched, depraved, deviant, distorted, evil, immoral, impaired, kinky (*slang*), misguided, pervy (*slang*), sick, sicko (*slang*), twisted, unhealthy, unnatural, vicious, vitiated, warped, wicked

pessimism cynicism, dejection, depression, despair, despondency, distrust, gloom, gloominess, gloomy outlook, glumness, hopelessness, melancholy, the hump (*Brit. informal*)

pessimist cynic, defeatist, doomster, gloom merchant (*informal*), kill-joy, melancholic, misanthrope, prophet of doom, wet blanket (*informal*), worrier

pessimistic bleak, cynical, dark, dejected, depressed, despairing, despondent, distrustful, downhearted, fatalistic, foreboding, gloomy, glum, hopeless, melancholy, misanthropic, morose, resigned, sad

▷ **Antonyms** assured, bright, buoyant, cheerful, cheery, encouraged, exhilarated, hopeful, in good heart, optimistic, sanguine

pest **1.** annoyance, bane, bore, bother, drag (*informal*), gall, irritation, nuisance, pain (*informal*), pain in the arse (*taboo informal*), pain in the neck (*informal*), thorn in one's flesh, trial, vexation **2.** bane, blight, bug, curse, epidemic, infection, pestilence, plague, scourge

pester aggravate (*informal*), annoy, badger, bedevil, bend someone's ear (*informal*), be on one's back (*slang*), bother, bug (*informal*), chivvy, disturb, drive one up the wall (*slang*), fret, get at, get in one's hair (*informal*), get on one's nerves (*informal*), harass, harry, hassle (*informal*), irk, nag, pick on, plague, ride (*informal*), torment, worry

pestilence **1.** Black Death, epidemic, pandemic, plague, visitation **2.** affliction, bane, blight, cancer, canker, curse, scourge

pestilent **1.** annoying, bothersome, galling, irksome, irritating, plaguy (*informal*), tiresome, vexing **2.** corrupting, deleterious, destructive, detrimental, evil, harmful, injurious, pernicious, ruinous, vicious **3.** catching, contagious, contaminated, diseased, disease-ridden, infected, infectious, plague-ridden, tainted

pestilential **1.** annoying, dangerous, deleterious, destructive, detrimental, evil, foul, harmful, hazardous, injurious, pernicious, ruinous, troublesome **2.** catching, contagious, contaminated, deadly, disease-ridden, infectious, malignant, noxious, pestiferous, poisonous, venomous

pet[1] *noun* **1.** apple of one's eye, blue-eyed boy (*informal*), darling, favourite, idol, jewel, treasure *~adjective* **2.** cherished, dearest, dear to one's heart, favoured, favourite, particular, preferred, special **3.** domesticated, house, house-broken, house-trained (*Brit.*), tame, trained *~verb* **4.** baby, coddle, cosset, mollycoddle, pamper, spoil **5.** caress, fondle, pat, stroke **6.** *informal* canoodle (*slang*), cuddle, kiss, neck (*informal*), smooch (*informal*), snog (*Brit. slang*)

pet[2] *noun* bad mood, bate (*Brit. slang*), huff, ill temper, miff (*informal*), paddy (*Brit. informal*), paddywhack (*Brit. informal*), pique, pout, sulk, sulks, tantrum, temper

peter out come to nothing, die out, dwindle, ebb, evaporate, fade, fail, give out, run dry, run out, stop, taper off, wane

petite dainty, delicate, dinky (*Brit. informal*), elfin, little, slight, small

petition **1.** *noun* address, appeal, application, entreaty, invocation, memorial, plea, prayer, request, round robin, solicitation, suit, supplication **2.** *~verb* adjure, appeal, ask, beg, beseech, call upon, crave, entreat, plead, pray, press, solicit, sue, supplicate, urge

petrified **1.** fossilized, ossified, rocklike **2.** aghast, appalled, dazed, dumbfounded, frozen, horrified, numb, scared shitless (*taboo slang*), scared stiff, shit-scared (*taboo slang*), shocked, speechless, stunned, stupefied, terrified, terror-stricken

petrify **1.** calcify, fossilize, harden, set, solidify, turn to stone **2.** amaze, appal, astonish, astound, confound, dumbfound, horrify, immobilize, paralyse, stun, stupefy, terrify, transfix

pettifoggery cheating, corruption, deceit, deception, dishonesty, double-dealing, duplicity, fraud, gerrymandering, jobbery, swindling

pettifogging captious, casuistic, cavilling, equivocating, hairsplitting, insignifi~

cant, mean, niggling, nit-picking (*informal*), paltry, petty, piddling (*informal*), quibbling, sophistical, sophisticated, subtle

pettish cross, fractious, fretful, grumpy, huffy, ill-humoured, irritable, liverish, peevish, petulant, querulous, ratty (*Brit. & N.Z. informal*), sulky, tetchy, thin-skinned, touchy, waspish

petty 1. contemptible, inconsiderable, inessential, inferior, insignificant, little, measly (*informal*), negligible, nickel-and-dime (*U.S. slang*), paltry, piddling (*informal*), slight, small, trifling, trivial, unimportant **2.** cheap, grudging, mean, mean-minded, shabby, small-minded, spiteful, stingy, ungenerous **3.** inferior, junior, lesser, lower, minor, secondary, subordinate
▷ **Antonyms** (*sense 1*) consequential, considerable, essential, important, major, momentous, significant (*sense 2*) broad-minded, generous, liberal, magnanimous, open-minded, tolerant

petulance bad temper, crabbiness, ill humour, irritability, peevishness, pettishness, pique, pouts, querulousness, spleen, sulkiness, sullenness, waspishness

petulant bad-tempered, captious, cavilling, crabbed, cross, crusty, fault-finding, fretful, huffy, ill-humoured, impatient, irritable, moody, peevish, perverse, pouting, querulous, ratty (*Brit. & N.Z. informal*), snappish, sour, sulky, sullen, ungracious, waspish
▷ **Antonyms** affable, cheerful, congenial, easy-going, even-tempered, good-humoured, good-natured, happy, patient, smiling

phantasm 1. apparition, eidolon, ghost, phantom, revenant, shade (*literary*), spectre, spirit, spook (*informal*), wraith **2.** chimera, figment, figment of the imagination, hallucination, illusion, vision

phantasmagoric, phantasmagorical chimerical, dreamlike, hallucinatory, illusory, Kafkaesque, kaleidoscopic, nightmarish, phantasmal, psychedelic, surreal, unreal

phantasmal chimerical, delusory, fancied, fanciful, ghostlike, ghostly, illusory, imaginary, imagined, phantasmagoric, phantasmagorical, phantomlike, shadowy, spectral, unreal, wraithlike

phantasy *see* FANTASY

phantom 1. apparition, eidolon, ghost, phantasm, revenant, shade (*literary*), spectre, spirit, spook (*informal*), wraith **2.** chimera, figment, figment of the imagination, hallucination, illusion, vision

pharisaic, pharisaical canting, formal, goody-goody, holier-than-thou, hypocritical, insincere, Pecksniffian, pietistic, sanctimonious, self-righteous

pharisaism cant, false piety, hypocrisy, insincerity, lip service, pietism, religiosity, sanctimoniousness, self-righteousness

pharisee canter, dissembler, dissimulator, fraud, humbug, hypocrite, phoney *or* phony (*informal*), pietist, whited sepulchre

phase aspect, chapter, condition, development, juncture, period, point, position, stage, state, step, time

phase out axe (*informal*), close, deactivate, dispose of gradually, ease off, eliminate, pull, pull out, remove, replace, run down, taper off, terminate, wind down, wind up, withdraw
▷ **Antonyms** activate, begin, create, establish, form, initiate, open, set up, start

phenomenal exceptional, extraordinary, fantastic, marvellous, miraculous, notable, outstanding, prodigious, remarkable, sensational, singular, stellar (*informal*), uncommon, unique, unparalleled, unusual, wondrous (*archaic or literary*)
▷ **Antonyms** average, common, mediocre, no great shakes (*informal*), ordinary, poor, run-of-the-mill, second-rate, unexceptional, unremarkable, usual

phenomenon 1. circumstance, episode, event, fact, happening, incident, occurrence **2.** exception, marvel, miracle, nonpareil, prodigy, rarity, sensation, sight, spectacle, wonder

philander coquet, court, dally, flirt, fool around (*informal*), toy, trifle, womanize (*informal*)

philanderer Casanova, dallier, Don Juan, flirt, gallant, gay dog, ladies' man, lady-killer (*informal*), Lothario, playboy, stud (*slang*), trifler, wolf (*informal*), womanizer (*informal*)

philanthropic alms-giving, altruistic, beneficent, benevolent, benignant, charitable, eleemosynary, gracious, humane, humanitarian, kind, kind-hearted, munificent, public-spirited
▷ **Antonyms** egoistic, mean, miserly, niggardly, penurious, selfish, self-seeking, stingy

philanthropist alms-giver, altruist, benefactor, contributor, donor, giver, humanitarian, patron

philanthropy alms-giving, altruism, beneficence, benevolence, benignity, bounty, brotherly love, charitableness, charity, generosity, generousness, humanitarianism, kind-heartedness, largesse *or* largess, liberality, munificence, open-handedness, patronage, public-spiritedness

philippic condemnation, denunciation, diatribe, fulmination, harangue, invective, obloquy, stream of abuse, tirade, vituperation

philistine 1. *noun* barbarian, boor, bourgeois, Goth, ignoramus, lout, lowbrow, vulgarian, yahoo **2.** *~adjective* anti-intellectual, boorish, bourgeois, crass, ignorant, inartistic, lowbrow, tasteless, uncultivated, uncultured, uneducated, unrefined

philosopher dialectician, logician, mahatma, metaphysician, sage, seeker after truth, theorist, thinker, wise man

philosophical, philosophic 1. abstract, erudite, learned, logical, rational, sagacious, theoretical, thoughtful, wise **2.** calm, collected, composed, cool, impassive, imperturbable, patient, resigned, sedate, serene, stoical, tranquil, unruffled

▷ **Antonyms** (*sense 1*) factual, illogical, irrational, practical, pragmatic, scientific (*sense 2*) emotional, hot-headed, impulsive, perturbed, rash, restless, upset

philosophy 1. aesthetics, knowledge, logic, metaphysics, rationalism, reason, reasoning, thinking, thought, wisdom **2.** attitude to life, basic idea, beliefs, convictions, doctrine, ideology, principle, tenets, thinking, values, viewpoint, *Weltanschauung,* world-view **3.** composure, coolness, dispassion, equanimity, resignation, restraint, self-possession, serenity, stoicism

phlegmatic apathetic, bovine, cold, dull, frigid, heavy, impassive, indifferent, lethargic, listless, lymphatic, matter-of-fact, placid, sluggish, stoical, stolid, undemonstrative, unemotional, unfeeling

▷ **Antonyms** active, alert, animated, emotional, energetic, excited, hyper (*informal*), lively, passionate

phobia aversion, detestation, dislike, distaste, dread, fear, hatred, horror, irrational fear, loathing, obsession, overwhelming anxiety, repulsion, revulsion, terror, thing (*informal*)

▷ **Antonyms** bent, fancy, fondness, inclination, liking, love, partiality, passion, penchant, soft spot

phone *noun* **1.** blower (*informal*), telephone **2.** bell (*Brit. slang*), buzz (*informal*), call, ring (*informal, chiefly Brit.*), tinkle (*Brit. informal*) *~verb* **3.** buzz (*informal*), call, get on the blower (*informal*), give someone a bell (*Brit. slang*), give someone a buzz (*informal*), give someone a call, give someone a ring (*informal, chiefly Brit.*), give someone a tinkle (*Brit. informal*), make a call, ring (up) (*informal, chiefly Brit.*), telephone

phoney 1. *adjective* affected, assumed, bogus, counterfeit, ersatz, fake, false, forged, imitation, pseudo (*informal*), put-on, sham, spurious, trick **2.** *~noun* counterfeit, fake, faker, forgery, fraud, humbug, impostor, pretender, pseud (*informal*), sham

▷ **Antonyms** *~adjective* authentic, bona fide, genuine, original, real, sincere, unaffected, unassumed, unfeigned

photograph 1. *noun* image, likeness, photo (*informal*), picture, print, shot, slide, snap (*informal*), snapshot, transparency **2.** *~verb* capture on film, film, get a shot of, record, shoot, snap (*informal*), take, take a picture of, take (someone's) picture

photographic accurate, cinematic, detailed, exact, faithful, filmic, graphic, lifelike, minute, natural, pictorial, precise, realistic, retentive, visual, vivid

phrase 1. *noun* expression, group of words, idiom, locution, motto, remark, saying, tag, utterance, way of speaking **2.** *~verb* couch, express, formulate, frame, present, put, put into words, say, term, utter, voice, word

phraseology choice of words, diction, expression, idiom, language, parlance, phrase, phrasing, speech, style, syntax, wording

physical 1. bodily, carnal, corporal, corporeal, earthly, fleshly, incarnate, mortal, somatic, unspiritual **2.** material, natural, palpable, real, sensible, solid, substantial, tangible, visible

physician doc (*informal*), doctor, doctor of medicine, general practitioner, G.P., healer, M.D., medic (*informal*), medical practitioner, medico (*informal*), sawbones (*slang*), specialist

physiognomy clock (*Brit. slang*), countenance, dial (*Brit. slang*), face, features, look, phiz (*slang*), phizog (*slang*), visage

physique body, build, constitution, figure, form, frame, make-up, shape, structure

pick *verb* **1.** cherry-pick, choose, decide upon, elect, fix upon, hand-pick, mark out, opt for, select, settle upon, sift out, single out, sort out **2.** collect, cull, cut, gather, harvest, pluck, pull **3.** have no appetite, nibble, peck at, play *or* toy with, push the food round the plate **4.** foment, incite, instigate, provoke, start **5.** break into, break open, crack, force, jemmy, open, prise open **6. pick one's way** be tentative, find *or* make one's way, move cautiously, tread carefully, work through *~noun* **7.** choice, choosing, decision, option, preference, selection **8.** choicest, *crème de la crème,* elect, elite, flower, pride, prize, the best, the cream, the tops (*slang*)

▷ **Antonyms** (*sense 1*) cast aside, decline, discard, dismiss, reject, spurn, turn down

pick at carp, cavil, criticize, find fault, get at, nag, pick holes, pick to pieces, quibble

picket *noun* **1.** pale, paling, palisade, peg, post, stake, stanchion, upright **2.** demonstrator, flying picket, picketer, protester **3.** guard, lookout, patrol, scout, sentinel, sentry, spotter, vedette (*Mili-*

tary), watch *~verb* **4.** blockade, boycott, demonstrate **5.** corral (*U.S.*), enclose, fence, hedge in, palisade, pen in, rail in, shut in, wall in

pickings booty, earnings, gravy (*slang*), ill-gotten gains, loot, plunder, proceeds, profits, returns, rewards, spoils, yield

pickle *noun* **1.** *informal* bind (*informal*), difficulty, dilemma, fix (*informal*), hot water (*informal*), jam (*informal*), pre~dicament, quandary, scrape (*informal*), spot (*informal*), tight spot **2.** *Brit. infor~mal* little horror, mischief, mischief maker, monkey, naughty child, rascal *~verb* **3.** cure, keep, marinade, preserve, steep

pick-me-up bracer (*informal*), drink, pick-up (*slang*), refreshment, restora~tive, roborant, shot in the arm (*infor~mal*), stimulant, tonic

pick on badger, bait, blame, bully, goad, hector, tease, torment

pick out 1. choose, cull, hand-pick, select, separate the sheep from the goats, sin~gle out, sort out **2.** discriminate, distin~guish, identify, make distinct, make out, notice, perceive, recognize, tell apart

pick-up *noun* **1.** acceleration, response, revving (*informal*), speed-up **2.** change for the better, gain, improvement, rally, recovery, revival, rise, strengthening, upswing, upturn

pick up *verb* **1.** gather, grasp, hoist, lift, raise, take up, uplift **2.** buy, come across, find, garner, happen upon, obtain, pur~chase, score (*slang*) **3.** be on the mend, gain, gain ground, get better, improve, make a comeback (*informal*), mend, perk up, rally, recover, take a turn for the better, turn the corner **4.** call for, collect, get, give someone a lift, go to get, uplift (*Scot.*) **5.** acquire, get the hang of (*informal*), learn, master **6.** *slang* apprehend, arrest, bust (*infor~mal*), collar (*informal*), do (*slang*), feel one's collar (*slang*), lift (*slang*), nab (*in~formal*), nail (*informal*), nick (*slang, chiefly Brit.*), pinch (*informal*), pull in (*Brit. slang*), run in (*slang*), take into custody

picky captious, carping, cavilling, choosy, critical, dainty, fastidious, fault-finding, finicky, fussy, nice, particular, pernick~ety (*informal*)

picnic 1. excursion, *fête champêtre,* out~door meal, outing **2.** *informal* breeze (*U.S. & Canad. informal*), cakewalk (*informal*), child's play (*informal*), cinch (*slang*), duck soup (*U.S. slang*), piece of cake (*Brit. informal*), pushover (*slang*), snap (*informal*), walkover (*informal*)

pictorial expressive, graphic, illustrated, picturesque, representational, scenic, striking, vivid

picture *noun* **1.** delineation, drawing, ef~figy, engraving, illustration, image, likeness, painting, photograph, portrait, portrayal, print, representation, simili~tude, sketch **2.** account, depiction, de~scription, image, impression, re-creation, report **3.** carbon copy, copy, dead ringer (*slang*), double, duplicate, image, likeness, living image, lookalike, replica, ringer (*slang*), spit (*informal, chiefly Brit.*), spit and image (*informal*), spitting image (*informal*), twin **4.** arche~type, embodiment, epitome, essence, living example, perfect example, per~sonification **5.** film, flick (*slang*), motion picture, movie (*U.S. informal*) *~verb* **6.** conceive of, envision, image, see, see in the mind's eye, visualize **7.** delineate, depict, describe, draw, illustrate, paint, photograph, portray, render, represent, show, sketch

picturesque attractive, beautiful, charm~ing, colourful, graphic, pretty, quaint, scenic, striking, vivid

▷ **Antonyms** commonplace, drab, dull, everyday, inartistic, unattractive, unin~teresting

piddling chickenshit (*U.S. slang*), crappy (*slang*), derisory, fiddling, insignificant, little, measly (*informal*), Mickey Mouse (*slang*), nickel-and-dime (*U.S. slang*), paltry, petty, piffling, poxy (*slang*), puny, trifling, trivial, unimportant, useless, wanky (*taboo slang*), worthless

▷ **Antonyms** considerable, important, major, significant, sizable *or* sizeable, substantial, tidy (*informal*), useful, valuable

piebald black and white, brindled, dap~pled, flecked, mottled, pied, speckled, spotted

piece *noun* **1.** allotment, bit, chunk, divi~sion, fraction, fragment, length, morsel, mouthful, part, portion, quantity, scrap, section, segment, share, shred, slice **2.** case, example, instance, occurrence, sample, specimen, stroke **3.** article, bit (*informal*), composition, creation, item, production, study, work, work of art **4. go to pieces** break down, crack up (*in~formal*), crumple, disintegrate, fall apart, lose control, lose one's head **5. in pieces** broken, bust (*informal*), dam~aged, disintegrated, in bits, in smither~eens, ruined, shattered, smashed **6. of a piece** alike, analogous, consistent, iden~tical, of the same kind, similar, the same, uniform *~verb* **7.** (*often with* **to~gether**) assemble, compose, fix, join, mend, patch, repair, restore, unite

pièce de résistance *chef-d'oeuvre,* jewel, masterpiece, masterwork, showpiece

piecemeal 1. *adverb* at intervals, bit by bit, by degrees, by fits and starts, fitful~ly, intermittently, little by little, par~tially, slowly **2.** *~adjective* fragmentary, intermittent, interrupted, partial, patchy, spotty, unsystematic

pied dappled, flecked, irregular, motley, mottled, multicoloured, parti-coloured, piebald, spotted, streaked, varicoloured, variegated

pier *noun* **1.** jetty, landing place, promenade, quay, wharf **2.** buttress, column, pile, piling, pillar, post, support, upright

pierce 1. bore, drill, enter, impale, lance, penetrate, perforate, prick, probe, puncture, run through, spike, stab, stick into, transfix **2.** comprehend, discern, discover, fathom, grasp, realize, see, understand **3.** *figurative* affect, cut, cut to the quick, excite, hurt, move, pain, rouse, sting, stir, strike, thrill, touch, wound

piercing 1. *usually of sound* ear-splitting, high-pitched, loud, penetrating, sharp, shattering, shrill **2.** alert, aware, bright (*informal*), keen, penetrating, perceptive, perspicacious, probing, quick-witted, searching, sharp, shrewd **3.** *usually of weather* arctic, biting, bitter, cold, freezing, frosty, keen, nipping, nippy, numbing, raw, wintry **4.** acute, agonizing, excruciating, exquisite, fierce, intense, painful, powerful, racking, severe, sharp, shooting, stabbing
▷ **Antonyms** (*sense 1*) inaudible, low, low-pitched, mellifluous, quiet, soundless (*sense 2*) obtuse, slow, slow-witted, thick, unperceptive

piety devotion, devoutness, dutifulness, duty, faith, godliness, grace, holiness, piousness, religion, reverence, sanctity, veneration

piffle balderdash, balls (*taboo slang*), bilge (*informal*), bollocks (*Brit. taboo slang*), bosh (*informal*), bull (*slang*), bullshit (*taboo slang*), bunk (*informal*), bunkum *or* buncombe (*chiefly U.S.*), cobblers (*Brit. taboo slang*), codswallop (*Brit. slang*), crap (*slang*), drivel, eyewash (*informal*), garbage (*informal*), guff (*slang*), hogwash, hokum (*slang, chiefly U.S. & Canad.*), hooey (*slang*), horsefeathers (*U.S. slang*), hot air (*informal*), moonshine, nonsense, pap, poppycock (*informal*), rot, rubbish, shit (*taboo slang*), tarradiddle, tommyrot, tosh (*slang, chiefly Brit.*), trash, tripe (*informal*), twaddle

piffling chickenshit (*U.S. slang*), crappy (*slang*), derisory, fiddling, insignificant, little, measly (*informal*), Mickey Mouse (*slang*), nickel-and-dime (*U.S. slang*), paltry, petty, piddling (*informal*), poxy (*slang*), puny, trifling, trivial, unimportant, useless, wanky (*taboo slang*), worthless

pig 1. boar, grunter, hog, piggy, piglet, porker, shoat, sow, swine **2.** *informal* animal, beast, boor, brute, glutton, greedy guts (*slang*), guzzler, hog (*informal*), slob (*slang*), sloven, swine

pigeon 1. bird, culver (*archaic*), cushat, dove, squab **2.** *slang* dupe, fall guy (*informal*), gull (*archaic*), mug (*Brit. slang*), sitting duck, sitting target, sucker (*slang*), victim **3.** *Brit. informal* baby (*slang*), business, concern, lookout (*informal*), responsibility, worry

pigeonhole *noun* **1.** compartment, cubbyhole, cubicle, locker, niche, place, section **2.** *informal* category, class, classification, slot (*informal*) ~*verb* **3.** defer, file, postpone, put off, shelve **4.** catalogue, characterize, classify, codify, compartmentalize, ghettoize, label, slot (*informal*), sort

piggish 1. boorish, crude, gluttonous, greedy, hoggish, piggy, rude, swinish, voracious **2.** *informal* hoggish, mean, obstinate, pig-headed, possessive, selfish, stubborn

pig-headed bull-headed, contrary, cross-grained, dense, froward (*archaic*), inflexible, mulish, obstinate, perverse, self-willed, stiff-necked, stubborn, stupid, unyielding, wilful, wrong-headed
▷ **Antonyms** agreeable, amiable, complaisant, cooperative, flexible, obliging, open-minded, tractable

pigment colorant, colour, colouring, colouring matter, dye, dyestuff, paint, stain, tincture, tint

pile[1] *noun* **1.** accumulation, assemblage, assortment, collection, heap, hoard, mass, mound, mountain, rick, stack, stockpile **2.** *informal* big bucks (*informal, chiefly U.S.*), big money, bomb (*Brit. slang*), fortune, megabucks (*U.S. & Canad. slang*), mint, money, packet (*slang*), pot, pretty penny (*informal*), tidy sum (*informal*), wad (*U.S. & Canad. slang*), wealth **3.** (*often plural*) *informal* a lot, great deal, ocean, oodles (*informal*), quantity, stacks **4.** building, edifice, erection, structure ~*verb* **5.** accumulate, amass, assemble, collect, gather, heap, hoard, load up, mass, stack, store **6.** charge, crowd, crush, flock, flood, jam, pack, rush, stream

pile[2] *noun* beam, column, foundation, pier, piling, pillar, post, support, upright

pile[3] *noun* down, fibre, filament, fur, hair, nap, plush, shag, surface

piles haemorrhoids

pile-up accident, collision, crash, multiple collision, smash, smash-up (*informal*)

pilfer appropriate, blag (*slang*), cabbage (*Brit. slang*), embezzle, filch, knock off (*slang*), lift (*informal*), nick (*slang, chiefly Brit.*), pinch (*informal*), purloin, rifle, rob, snaffle (*Brit. informal*), snitch (*slang*), steal, swipe (*slang*), take, thieve, walk off with

pilgrim crusader, hajji, palmer, traveller, wanderer, wayfarer

pilgrimage crusade, excursion, expedition, hajj, journey, mission, tour, trip

pill 1. bolus, capsule, pellet, pilule, tablet **2. the pill** oral contraceptive **3.** *slang* bore, drag (*informal*), nuisance, pain (*informal*), pain in the neck (*informal*), pest, trial

pillage *verb* **1.** depredate (*rare*), despoil, freeboot, loot, maraud, plunder, raid, ransack, ravage, reive (*dialect*), rifle, rob, sack, spoil (*archaic*), spoliate, strip *~noun* **2.** depredation, devastation, marauding, plunder, rapine, robbery, sack, spoliation **3.** booty, loot, plunder, spoils

pillar 1. column, obelisk, pier, pilaster, piling, post, prop, shaft, stanchion, support, upright **2.** leader, leading light (*informal*), mainstay, rock, supporter, torchbearer, tower of strength, upholder, worthy

pillory *verb* brand, cast a slur on, denounce, expose to ridicule, heap *or* pour scorn on, hold up to shame, lash, show up, stigmatize

pilot 1. *noun* airman, aviator, captain, conductor, coxswain, director, flyer, guide, helmsman, leader, navigator, steersman **2.** *~verb* conduct, control, direct, drive, fly, guide, handle, lead, manage, navigate, operate, shepherd, steer **3.** *~adjective* experimental, model, test, trial

pimp 1. *noun* bawd (*archaic*), go-between, pander, panderer, procurer, white-slaver, whoremaster (*archaic*) **2.** *~verb* live off immoral earnings, procure, sell, solicit, tout

pimple boil, papule (*Pathology*), plook (*Scot.*), pustule, spot, swelling, zit (*slang*)

pin *verb* **1.** affix, attach, fasten, fix, join, secure **2.** fix, hold down, hold fast, immobilize, pinion, press, restrain

pinch *verb* **1.** compress, grasp, nip, press, squeeze, tweak **2.** chafe, confine, cramp, crush, hurt, pain **3.** afflict, be stingy, distress, economize, oppress, pinch pennies, press, scrimp, skimp, spare, stint, tighten one's belt **4.** *informal* blag (*slang*), cabbage (*Brit. slang*), filch, knock off (*slang*), lift (*informal*), nick (*slang, chiefly Brit.*), pilfer, purloin, rob, snaffle (*Brit. informal*), snatch, snitch (*slang*), steal, swipe (*slang*) **5.** *informal* apprehend, arrest, bust (*informal*), collar (*informal*), do (*slang*), feel one's collar (*slang*), lift (*slang*), nab (*informal*), nail (*informal*), nick (*slang, chiefly Brit.*), pick up (*slang*), pull in (*Brit. slang*), run in (*slang*), take into custody *~noun* **6.** nip, squeeze, tweak **7.** bit, dash, jot, mite, small quantity, *soupçon*, speck, taste **8.** crisis, difficulty, emergency, exigency, hardship, necessity, oppression, pass, plight, predicament, pressure, strait, stress

▷ **Antonyms** (*sense 3*) be extravagant, blow (*slang*), fritter away, spend like water, squander, waste (*sense 5*) free, let go, let out, release, set free

pinchbeck 1. *noun* counterfeit, fake, imitation, paste, phoney *or* phony (*informal*), sham **2.** *~adjective* artificial, bogus, counterfeit, ersatz, fake, imitation, pseudo (*informal*), spurious

pinched careworn, drawn, gaunt, haggard, peaky, starved, thin, worn

▷ **Antonyms** blooming, chubby, fat, glowing, hale and hearty, healthy, plump, radiant, ruddy, well-fed

pin down 1. compel, constrain, force, make, press, pressurize **2.** designate, determine, home in on, identify, locate, name, pinpoint, specify **3.** bind, confine, constrain, fix, hold, hold down, immobilize, nail down, tie down

pine 1. (*often with* **for**) ache, carry a torch for, covet, crave, desire, eat one's heart out over, hanker, hunger for, long, lust after, sigh, suspire (*archaic or poetic*), thirst for, wish, yearn **2.** decay, decline, droop, dwindle, fade, flag, languish, peak, sicken, sink, waste, weaken, wilt, wither

pinion *verb* bind, chain, confine, fasten, fetter, immobilize, manacle, pin down, shackle, tie

pink[1] 1. *noun* acme, best, height, peak, perfection, summit **2.** *~adjective* flesh, flushed, reddish, rose, roseate, rosy, salmon

pink[2] *verb* incise, notch, perforate, prick, punch, scallop, score

pinnacle 1. acme, apex, apogee, crest, crown, eminence, height, meridian, peak, summit, top, vertex, zenith **2.** belfry, cone, needle, obelisk, pyramid, spire, steeple

pinpoint define, distinguish, get a fix on, home in on, identify, locate, spot

pint ale, beer, jar (*Brit. informal*), jug (*Brit. informal*)

pint-size diminutive, little, midget, miniature, pocket, pygmy *or* pigmy, small, teensy-weensy, teeny-weeny, tiny, wee

pioneer *noun* **1.** colonist, colonizer, explorer, frontiersman, settler **2.** developer, founder, founding father, innovator, leader, trailblazer *~verb* **3.** create, develop, discover, establish, initiate, instigate, institute, invent, launch, lay the groundwork, map out, open up, originate, prepare, show the way, start, take the lead

pious 1. dedicated, devoted, devout, God-fearing, godly, holy, religious, reverent, righteous, saintly, spiritual **2.** goody-goody, holier-than-thou, hypocritical, pietistic, religiose, sanctimonious, self-righteous, unctuous

▷ **Antonyms** (*sense 1*) impious, irreligious, irreverent, ungodly, unholy (*sense 2*) humble, meek, sincere

pipe *noun* **1.** conduit, conveyor, duct, hose, line, main, passage, pipeline, tube **2.** briar, clay, meerschaum **3.** fife, horn, tooter, whistle, wind instrument *~verb* **4.** cheep, peep, play, sing, sound, tootle, trill, tweet, twitter, warble, whistle **5.** bring in, channel, conduct, convey, siphon, supply, transmit

pipe down belt up (*slang*), be quiet, button it (*slang*), button one's lip (*slang*), hold one's tongue, hush, put a sock in it (*Brit. slang*), quieten down, shush, shut one's mouth, shut up (*informal*), silence

pipe dream castle in the air, chimera, daydream, delusion, dream, fantasy, notion, reverie, vagary

pipeline 1. conduit, conveyor, duct, line, passage, pipe, tube **2. in the pipeline** brewing, coming, getting ready, in process, in production, on the way, under way

pipe up have one's say, make oneself heard, put one's oar in, raise one's voice, speak, speak up, volunteer

pipsqueak creep (*slang*), nobody, nonentity, nothing (*informal*), squirt (*informal*), upstart, whippersnapper

piquancy 1. bite (*informal*), edge, flavour, kick (*informal*), pungency, relish, sharpness, spice, spiciness, tang, zest **2.** colour, excitement, interest, pep, pizzazz *or* pizazz (*informal*), raciness, spirit, vigour, vitality, zing (*informal*), zip (*informal*)

piquant 1. acerb, biting, highly-seasoned, peppery, pungent, savoury, sharp, spicy, stinging, tangy, tart, with a kick (*informal*), zesty **2.** interesting, lively, provocative, racy, salty, scintillating, sparkling, spirited, stimulating

▷ **Antonyms** banal, bland, boring, dull, insipid, mild, tame, uninteresting

pique *noun* **1.** annoyance, displeasure, huff, hurt feelings, irritation, miff (*informal*), offence, resentment, umbrage, vexation, wounded pride *~verb* **2.** affront, annoy, displease, gall, get (*informal*), incense, irk, irritate, miff (*informal*), mortify, nark (*Brit., Austral., & N.Z. slang*), nettle, offend, peeve (*informal*), provoke, put out, put someone's nose out of joint (*informal*), rile, sting, vex, wound **3.** arouse, excite, galvanize, goad, kindle, provoke, rouse, spur, stimulate, stir, whet **4.** (*with* **on** *or* **upon**) *of oneself* congratulate, flatter, plume, preen, pride

piracy buccaneering, freebooting, hijacking, infringement, plagiarism, rapine, robbery at sea, stealing, theft

pirate *noun* **1.** buccaneer, corsair, filibuster, freebooter, marauder, raider, rover, sea robber, sea rover, sea wolf **2.** cribber (*informal*), infringer, plagiarist, plagiarizer *~verb* **3.** appropriate, borrow, copy, crib (*informal*), lift (*informal*), plagiarize, poach, reproduce, steal

piratical buccaneering, criminal, dishonest, felonious, fraudulent, lawless, pillaging, plundering, rapacious, thieving, unprincipled, wolfish

pirouette *noun/verb* pivot, spin, turn, twirl, whirl

pit *noun* **1.** abyss, cavity, chasm, coal mine, crater, dent, depression, dimple, excavation, gulf, hole, hollow, indentation, mine, pockmark, pothole, trench *~verb* **2.** (*often with* **against**) match, oppose, put in opposition, set against **3.** dent, dint, gouge, hole, indent, mark, nick, notch, pockmark, scar

pitch *verb* **1.** bung (*Brit. slang*), cast, chuck (*informal*), fling, heave, hurl, launch, lob (*informal*), sling, throw, toss **2.** erect, fix, locate, place, plant, put up, raise, settle, set up, station **3.** flounder, lurch, make heavy weather, plunge, roll, toss, wallow, welter **4.** dive, drop, fall headlong, stagger, topple, tumble *~noun* **5.** angle, cant, dip, gradient, incline, slope, steepness, tilt **6.** degree, height, highest point, level, point, summit **7.** harmonic, modulation, sound, timbre, tone **8.** line, patter, sales talk, spiel (*informal*) **9.** field of play, ground, park (*U.S. & Canad.*), sports field

pitch-black dark, ebony, inky, jet, jet-black, pitch-dark, raven, sable, unlit

pitch-dark black, dark, pitch-black, pitchy, Stygian, unilluminated, unlit

pitch in 1. chip in (*informal*), contribute, cooperate, do one's bit, help, join in, lend a hand, lend a helping hand, participate **2.** begin, fall to, get busy, get cracking (*informal*), plunge into, set about, set to, tackle

pitch into assail, assault, attack, get stuck into (*informal*), lace into, light into (*informal*), sail into (*informal*), tear into (*informal*)

pitch on *or* **upon** choose, decide on, determine, elect, light on, opt for, pick, plump for, select, single out

pitchy black, coal-black, dark, ebony, inky, jet, jetty, moonless, pitch-black, raven, sable, unilluminated, unlighted

piteous affecting, deplorable, dismal, distressing, doleful, grievous, harrowing, heartbreaking, heart-rending, lamentable, miserable, mournful, moving, pathetic, pitiable, pitiful, plaintive, poignant, sad, sorrowful, woeful, wretched

pitfall 1. banana skin (*informal*), catch, danger, difficulty, drawback, hazard, peril, snag, trap **2.** deadfall, downfall, pit, snare, trap

pith 1. core, crux, essence, gist, heart, heart of the matter, kernel, marrow, meat, nub, point, quintessence, salient point, the long and the short of it **2.** consequence, depth, force, import, importance, matter, moment, power, signifi~

cance, strength, substance, value, weight

pithy brief, cogent, compact, concise, epigrammatic, expressive, finely honed, forceful, laconic, meaningful, pointed, short, succinct, terse, to the point, trenchant
▷ **Antonyms** diffuse, garrulous, long, long-winded, loquacious, prolix, verbose, wordy

pitiable deplorable, dismal, distressing, doleful, grievous, harrowing, lamentable, miserable, mournful, pathetic, piteous, poor, sad, sorry, woeful, wretched

pitiful 1. deplorable, distressing, grievous, harrowing, heartbreaking, heart-rending, lamentable, miserable, pathetic, piteous, pitiable, sad, woeful, wretched **2.** abject, base, beggarly, contemptible, despicable, dismal, inadequate, insignificant, low, mean, measly, miserable, paltry, scurvy, shabby, sorry, vile, worthless
▷ **Antonyms** (*sense 1*) amusing, cheerful, cheering, comical, funny, happy, heartening, laughable, merry (*sense 2*) adequate, admirable, honourable, laudable, praiseworthy, significant, valuable

pitiless brutal, callous, cold-blooded, cold-hearted, cruel, hardhearted, harsh, heartless, implacable, inexorable, inhuman, merciless, relentless, ruthless, uncaring, unfeeling, unmerciful, unsympathetic
▷ **Antonyms** caring, compassionate, kind, merciful, relenting, responsive, soft-hearted, sparing

pittance allowance, chicken feed (*slang*), drop, mite, modicum, peanuts (*slang*), portion, ration, slave wages, trifle

pitted blemished, dented, eaten away, holey, indented, marked, pockmarked, pocky, potholed, riddled, rough, rutty, scarred, scratched

pity *noun* **1.** charity, clemency, commiseration, compassion, condolence, fellow feeling, forbearance, kindness, mercy, quarter, sympathy, tenderness, understanding **2.** bummer (*slang*), crime (*informal*), crying shame, misfortune, regret, sad thing, shame, sin **3. take pity on** feel compassion for, forgive, have mercy on, melt, pardon, put out of one's misery, relent, reprieve, show mercy, spare *~verb* **4.** bleed for, commiserate with, condole with, feel for, feel sorry for, grieve for, have compassion for, sympathize with, weep for
▷ **Antonyms** (*sense 1*) anger, apathy, brutality, cruelty, disdain, fury, hard-heartedness, indifference, inhumanity, mercilessness, pitilessness, ruthlessness, scorn, severity, unconcern, wrath

pivot *noun* **1.** axis, axle, fulcrum, spindle, swivel **2.** centre, focal point, heart, hinge, hub, kingpin *~verb* **3.** revolve, rotate, spin, swivel, turn, twirl **4.** be contingent, depend, hang, hinge, rely, revolve round, turn

pivotal central, climactic, critical, crucial, decisive, determining, focal, vital

pixie brownie, elf, fairy, peri, sprite

placard advertisement, *affiche,* bill, poster, public notice, sticker

placate appease, assuage, calm, conciliate, humour, mollify, pacify, propitiate, satisfy, soothe, win over

placatory appeasing, conciliatory, designed to please, pacificatory, peacemaking, propitiative

place *noun* **1.** area, location, locus, point, position, site, situation, spot, station, venue, whereabouts **2.** city, district, hamlet, locale, locality, neighbourhood, quarter, region, town, vicinity, village **3.** grade, position, rank, station, status **4.** appointment, berth (*informal*), billet (*informal*), employment, job, position, post **5.** abode, apartment, domicile, dwelling, flat, home, house, manor, mansion, pad (*slang*), property, residence, seat **6.** accommodation, room, space, stead **7.** affair, charge, concern, duty, function, prerogative, responsibility, right, role **8. in place of** as an alternative to, as a substitute for, in exchange for, in lieu of, instead of, taking the place of **9. put (someone) in his place** bring down, cut down to size, humble, humiliate, make (someone) eat humble pie, make (someone) swallow his pride, mortify, take down a peg (*informal*) **10. take place** befall, betide, come about, come to pass (*archaic*), go on, happen, occur, transpire (*informal*) *~verb* **11.** bung (*Brit. slang*), deposit, dispose, establish, fix, install, lay, locate, plant, position, put, rest, set, settle, situate, stand, station, stick (*informal*) **12.** arrange, class, classify, grade, group, order, rank, sort **13.** associate, identify, know, put one's finger on, recognize, remember, set in context **14.** allocate, appoint, assign, charge, commission, entrust, give

placement 1. arrangement, deployment, disposition, distribution, emplacement, installation, locating, location, ordering, positioning, stationing **2.** appointment, assignment, employment, engagement

placid calm, collected, composed, cool, equable, even, even-tempered, gentle, halcyon, imperturbable, mild, peaceful, quiet, self-possessed, serene, still, tranquil, undisturbed, unexcitable, unfazed (*informal*), unmoved, unruffled, untroubled
▷ **Antonyms** agitated, disturbed, emotional, excitable, impulsive, passionate, rough, temperamental, tempestuous

plagiarism appropriation, borrowing, copying, cribbing (*informal*), infringement, lifting (*informal*), piracy, theft

plagiarize appropriate, borrow, crib (*informal*), infringe, lift (*informal*), pirate, steal, thieve

plague *noun* **1.** contagion, disease, epidemic, infection, lurgi (*informal*), pandemic, pestilence **2.** *figurative* affliction, bane, blight, calamity, cancer, curse, evil, scourge, torment, trial **3.** *informal* aggravation (*informal*), annoyance, bother, hassle (*informal*), irritant, nuisance, pain (*informal*), pest, problem, thorn in one's flesh, vexation *~verb* **4.** afflict, annoy, badger, bedevil, be on one's back (*slang*), bother, disturb, fret, get in one's hair (*informal*), get on one's nerves (*informal*), harass, harry, hassle (*informal*), haunt, molest, pain, persecute, pester, tease, torment, torture, trouble, vex

plaguy annoying, disagreeable, harassing, impossible, irksome, irritating, provoking, troublesome, trying, vexing, wretched

plain *adjective* **1.** apparent, bold, clear, comprehensible, distinct, evident, legible, lucid, manifest, obvious, overt, patent, transparent, unambiguous, understandable, unmistakable, visible **2.** artless, blunt, candid, direct, downright, forthright, frank, guileless, honest, ingenuous, open, outspoken, round, sincere, straightforward, upfront (*informal*) **3.** common, commonplace, everyday, frugal, homely, lowly, modest, ordinary, simple, unaffected, unpretentious, workaday **4.** austere, bare, basic, discreet, modest, muted, pure, restrained, severe, simple, Spartan, stark, unadorned, unembellished, unfussy, unornamented, unpatterned, unvarnished **5.** ill-favoured, no oil painting (*informal*), not beautiful, not striking, ordinary, ugly, unalluring, unattractive, unlovely, unprepossessing **6.** even, flat, level, plane, smooth *~noun* **7.** flatland, grassland, llano, lowland, mesa, open country, pampas, plateau, prairie, steppe, tableland, veld

▷ **Antonyms** (*sense 1*) ambiguous, complex, concealed, deceptive, difficult, disguised, hidden, illegible, incomprehensible, inconspicuous, indiscernible, indistinct, obscure, vague, veiled (*sense 2*) circuitous, indirect, meandering, rambling, roundabout (*sense 3*) affected, distinguished, egotistic, ostentatious, pretentious, sophisticated, worldly (*sense 4*) adorned, decorated, fancy, ornate (*sense 5*) attractive, beautiful, comely, good-looking, gorgeous, handsome (*sense 6*) bumpy, not level, uneven

plain-spoken blunt, candid, direct, downright, explicit, forthright, frank, open, outright, outspoken, straightforward, unequivocal, upfront (*informal*)

▷ **Antonyms** diplomatic, discreet, evasive, guarded, indirect, reticent, subtle, tactful, thoughtful

plaintive disconsolate, doleful, grief-stricken, grievous, heart-rending, melancholy, mournful, pathetic, piteous, pitiful, rueful, sad, sorrowful, wistful, woebegone, woeful

plan *noun* **1.** contrivance, design, device, idea, method, plot, procedure, programme, project, proposal, proposition, scenario, scheme, strategy, suggestion, system **2.** blueprint, chart, delineation, diagram, drawing, illustration, layout, map, representation, scale drawing, sketch *~verb* **3.** arrange, concoct, contrive, design, devise, draft, formulate, frame, invent, organize, outline, plot, prepare, represent, scheme, think out **4.** aim, contemplate, envisage, foresee, intend, mean, propose, purpose

plane *noun* **1.** flat surface, level surface **2.** condition, degree, footing, level, position, stratum **3.** aeroplane, aircraft, jet *~adjective* **4.** even, flat, flush, horizontal, level, plain, regular, smooth, uniform *~verb* **5.** glide, sail, skate, skim, volplane

planetary **1.** earthly, mundane, sublunary, tellurian, terrene, terrestrial **2.** aberrant, erratic, journeying, moving, travelling, vacillating, variable, wandering

plangent clangorous, deep-toned, loud, mournful, plaintive, resonant, resounding, reverberating, ringing, sonorous

plant *noun* **1.** bush, flower, herb, shrub, vegetable, weed **2.** factory, foundry, mill, shop, works, yard **3.** apparatus, equipment, gear, machinery *~verb* **4.** implant, put in the ground, scatter, seed, set out, sow, transplant **5.** establish, fix, found, imbed, insert, institute, lodge, root, set, settle, sow the seeds

plaque badge, brooch, cartouch(e), medal, medallion, panel, plate, slab, tablet

plaster *noun* **1.** gesso, gypsum, mortar, plaster of Paris, stucco **2.** adhesive plaster, bandage, dressing, Elastoplast (*Trademark*), sticking plaster *~verb* **3.** bedaub, besmear, coat, cover, daub, overlay, smear, spread

plastic *adjective* **1.** compliant, docile, easily influenced, impressionable, malleable, manageable, pliable, receptive, responsive, tractable **2.** ductile, fictile, flexible, mouldable, pliable, pliant, soft, supple, tensile **3.** *slang* artificial, false, meretricious, mock, phoney *or* phony (*informal*), pseudo (*informal*), sham, specious, spurious, superficial, synthetic

▷ **Antonyms** (*sense 1*) intractable, rebellious, recalcitrant, refractory, unmanageable, unreceptive (*sense 2*) brittle, hard, inflexible, rigid, stiff, unbending, unyielding (*sense 3*) authentic, genuine, natural, real, sincere, true

plasticity flexibility, malleability, pliability, pliableness, suppleness, tractability

plate *noun* **1.** dish, platter, trencher (*archaic*) **2.** course, dish, helping, portion, serving **3.** layer, panel, sheet, slab **4.** illustration, lithograph, print *~verb* **5.** anodize, coat, cover, electroplate, face, gild, laminate, nickel, overlay, platinize, silver

plateau 1. highland, mesa, table, tableland, upland **2.** level, levelling off, stability, stage

platform 1. dais, podium, rostrum, stage, stand **2.** manifesto, objective(s), party line, policy, principle, programme, tenet(s)

platitude 1. banality, bromide, cliché, commonplace, hackneyed saying, inanity, stereotype, trite remark, truism **2.** banality, dullness, inanity, insipidity, triteness, triviality, vapidity, verbiage

platitudinous banal, clichéd, commonplace, corny (*slang*), hack, hackneyed, overworked, set, stale, stereotyped, stock, tired, trite, truistic, vapid, well-worn

platonic *all of love* ideal, idealistic, intellectual, nonphysical, spiritual, transcendent

platoon company, group, outfit (*informal*), patrol, squad, squadron, team

platter charger, dish, plate, salver, tray, trencher (*archaic*)

plaudit (*usually plural*) acclaim, acclamation, applause, approbation, approval, clapping, commendation, congratulation, hand, kudos, ovation, praise, round of applause

plausible believable, colourable, conceivable, credible, fair-spoken, glib, likely, persuasive, possible, probable, reasonable, smooth, smooth-talking, smooth-tongued, specious, tenable, verisimilar
▷ **Antonyms** genuine, illogical, implausible, impossible, improbable, inconceivable, incredible, real, unbelievable, unlikely

play *verb* **1.** amuse oneself, caper, engage in games, entertain oneself, fool, frisk, frolic, gambol, have fun, revel, romp, sport, trifle **2.** be in a team, challenge, compete, contend against, participate, rival, take on, take part, vie with **3.** act, act the part of, execute, impersonate, perform, personate, portray, represent, take the part of **4.** bet, chance, gamble, hazard, punt (*chiefly Brit.*), risk, speculate, take, wager **5. play ball** *informal* collaborate, cooperate, go along, play along, reciprocate, respond, show willing **6. play by ear** ad lib, extemporize, improvise, rise to the occasion, take it as it comes **7. play for time** delay, drag one's feet (*informal*), filibuster, hang fire, procrastinate, stall, temporize **8. play the fool** act the goat (*informal*), clown, clown around, horse around (*informal*), lark (about) (*informal*), mess about, monkey around, skylark (*informal*) **9. play the game** *informal* conform, follow the rules, go along with, keep in step, play by the rules, play fair, toe the line *~noun* **10.** comedy, drama, dramatic piece, entertainment, farce, masque, pantomime, performance, piece, radio play, show, soap opera, stage show, television drama, tragedy **11.** amusement, caper, diversion, entertainment, frolic, fun, gambol, game, jest, pastime, prank, recreation, romp, sport **12.** gambling, gaming **13.** action, activity, elbowroom, exercise, give (*informal*), latitude, leeway, margin, motion, movement, operation, range, room, scope, space, sweep, swing **14.** action, activity, employment, function, operation, transaction, working **15.** foolery, fun, humour, jest, joking, lark (*informal*), prank, sport, teasing

play around dally, fool around, mess around, philander, take lightly, trifle, womanize

playboy gay dog, ladies' man, lady-killer (*informal*), lover boy (*slang*), man about town, philanderer, pleasure seeker, rake, roué, socialite, womanizer

play down gloss over, make light of, make little of, minimize, set no store by, soft-pedal (*informal*), underplay, underrate

player 1. competitor, contestant, participant, sportsman, sportswoman, team member **2.** actor, actress, entertainer, performer, Thespian, trouper **3.** artist, instrumentalist, musician, music maker, performer, virtuoso

playful 1. cheerful, coltish, frisky, frolicsome, gay, impish, joyous, kittenish, larkish (*informal*), lively, merry, mischievous, puckish, rollicking, spirited, sportive, sprightly, vivacious **2.** arch, coy, flirtatious, good-natured, humorous, jesting, jokey, joking, roguish, teasing, tongue-in-cheek, waggish
▷ **Antonyms** despondent, gloomy, grave, morose, sedate, serious

playmate chum (*informal*), companion, comrade, friend, neighbour, pal (*informal*), playfellow

play on *or* **upon** abuse, capitalize on, exploit, impose on, milk, profit by, take advantage of, trade on, turn to account, utilize

plaything amusement, bauble, game, gewgaw, gimcrack, pastime, toy, trifle, trinket

play up 1. accentuate, bring to the fore, call attention to, emphasize, highlight, magnify, point up, stress, turn the spotlight on, underline **2.** *Brit. informal* be painful, be sore, bother, give one gyp (*Brit. & N.Z. slang*), give one trouble, hurt, pain, trouble **3.** *Brit. informal* be awkward, be bolshie (*Brit. informal*), be cussed (*informal*), be disobedient, be stroppy (*Brit. slang*), give trouble, mis~

behave **4.** *Brit. informal* be on the blink (*slang*), be wonky (*Brit. slang*), malfunction, not work properly **5. play up to** *informal* bootlick (*informal*), brown-nose (*taboo slang*), butter up, curry favour, fawn, flatter, get in with, ingratiate oneself, keep (someone) sweet, kiss (someone's) ass (*U.S. & Canad. taboo slang*), pander to, suck up to (*informal*), toady

play with 1. amuse oneself with, flirt with, string along, toy with, trifle with **2.** fiddle with (*informal*), fidget with, fool around, interfere with, jiggle, mess about, waggle, wiggle

playwright bard, dramatist, dramaturge, dramaturgist

plea 1. appeal, begging, entreaty, intercession, overture, petition, prayer, request, suit, supplication **2.** *Law* action, allegation, cause, suit **3.** apology, claim, defence, excuse, explanation, extenuation, justification, pretext, vindication

plead 1. appeal (to), ask, beg, beseech, crave, entreat, implore, importune, petition, request, solicit, supplicate **2.** adduce, allege, argue, assert, maintain, put forward, use as an excuse

pleasant 1. acceptable, agreeable, amusing, delectable, delightful, enjoyable, fine, gratifying, lovely, nice, pleasing, pleasurable, refreshing, satisfying, welcome **2.** affable, agreeable, amiable, charming, cheerful, cheery, congenial, engaging, friendly, genial, good-humoured, likable *or* likeable, nice

▷ **Antonyms** awful, cold, disagreeable, distasteful, horrible, horrid, impolite, miserable, offensive, repulsive, rude, unfriendly, unlikable *or* unlikeable, unpleasant

pleasantry badinage, banter, bon mot, good-natured remark, jest, joke, josh (*slang, chiefly U.S. & Canad.*), quip, sally, witticism

please 1. amuse, charm, cheer, content, delight, entertain, give pleasure to, gladden, gratify, humour, indulge, rejoice, satisfy, suit, tickle, tickle pink (*informal*) **2.** be inclined, choose, desire, like, opt, prefer, see fit, want, will, wish

▷ **Antonyms** (*sense 1*) anger, annoy, depress, disgust, displease, dissatisfy, grieve, incense, offend, provoke, sadden, vex

pleased chuffed (*Brit. slang*), contented, delighted, euphoric, glad, gratified, happy, in high spirits, over the moon (*informal*), pleased as punch (*informal*), rapt, satisfied, thrilled, tickled, tickled pink (*informal*)

pleasing agreeable, amiable, amusing, attractive, charming, delightful, engaging, enjoyable, entertaining, gratifying, likable *or* likeable, pleasurable, polite, satisfying, winning

▷ **Antonyms** boring, disagreeable, dull, monotonous, rude, unattractive, unlikable *or* unlikeable, unpleasant

pleasurable agreeable, congenial, delightful, diverting, enjoyable, entertaining, fun, good, gratifying, lovely, nice, pleasant, welcome

pleasure 1. amusement, beer and skittles (*informal*), bliss, comfort, contentment, delectation, delight, diversion, ease, enjoyment, gladness, gratification, happiness, jollies (*slang*), joy, recreation, satisfaction, solace **2.** choice, command, desire, inclination, mind, option, preference, purpose, will, wish

▷ **Antonyms** abstinence, anger, disinclination, displeasure, duty, labour, misery, necessity, obligation, pain, sadness, sorrow, suffering, unhappiness

plebeian 1. *adjective* base, coarse, common, ignoble, low, lowborn, lower-class, mean, non-U (*Brit. informal*), proletarian, uncultivated, unrefined, vulgar, working-class **2.** *~noun* commoner, common man, man in the street, peasant, pleb, prole (*derogatory slang, chiefly Brit.*), proletarian

▷ **Antonyms** *~adjective* aristocratic, cultivated, highborn, high-class, patrician, polished, refined, upper-class, well-bred

plebiscite ballot, poll, referendum, vote

pledge *noun* **1.** assurance, covenant, oath, promise, undertaking, vow, warrant, word, word of honour **2.** bail, bond, collateral, deposit, earnest, gage, guarantee, pawn, security, surety **3.** health, toast *~verb* **4.** contract, engage, give one's oath, give one's word, give one's word of honour, promise, swear, undertake, vouch, vow **5.** bind, engage, gage (*archaic*), guarantee, mortgage, plight **6.** drink the health of, drink to, toast

plenary 1. absolute, complete, full, sweeping, thorough, unconditional, unlimited, unqualified, unrestricted **2.** *of assemblies, councils, etc.* complete, entire, full, general, open, whole

plenipotentiary ambassador, emissary, envoy, legate, minister

plenitude 1. abundance, bounty, copiousness, cornucopia, excess, plenteousness, plenty, plethora, profusion, wealth **2.** amplitude, completeness, fullness, repletion

plenteous 1. abundant, ample, bounteous (*literary*), bountiful, copious, generous, inexhaustible, infinite, lavish, liberal, overflowing, plentiful, profuse, thick on the ground **2.** bumper, fertile, fruitful, luxuriant, plentiful, productive, prolific

plentiful 1. abundant, ample, bounteous (*literary*), bountiful, complete, copious, generous, inexhaustible, infinite, lavish, liberal, overflowing, plenteous, profuse, thick on the ground **2.** bumper, fertile, fruitful, luxuriant, plenteous, productive, prolific

▷ **Antonyms** deficient, inadequate, in~

sufficient, scant, scarce, skimpy, small, sparing, sparse, thin on the ground

plenty **1**. abundance, enough, fund, good deal, great deal, heap(s) (*informal*), lots (*informal*), mass, masses, mine, mountain(s), oodles (*informal*), pile(s) (*informal*), plethora, quantities, quantity, stack(s), store, sufficiency, volume **2**. abundance, affluence, copiousness, fertility, fruitfulness, luxury, opulence, plenitude, plenteousness, plentifulness, profusion, prosperity, wealth

pleonasm circuitousness, circumlocution, convolution, periphrasis, redundancy, repetition, tautology, verbiage, verbosity, wordiness

pleonastic circuitous, circumlocutory, convoluted, iterative, periphrastic, prolix, redundant, repetitious, superfluous, tautological, verbose, wordy

plethora excess, glut, overabundance, profusion, superabundance, superfluity, surfeit, surplus
▷ **Antonyms** dearth, deficiency, lack, scarcity, shortage, want

pliability **1**. bendability, ductility, elasticity, flexibility, malleability, mobility, plasticity, pliancy **2**. adaptability, amenability, compliance, docility, impressionableness, susceptibility, tractableness

pliable **1**. bendable, bendy, ductile, flexible, limber, lithe, malleable, plastic, pliant, supple, tensile **2**. adaptable, compliant, docile, easily led, impressionable, influenceable, like putty in one's hands, manageable, persuadable, pliant, receptive, responsive, susceptible, tractable, yielding
▷ **Antonyms** (*sense 1*) rigid, stiff (*sense 2*) headstrong, inflexible, intractable, obdurate, obstinate, stubborn, unadaptable, unbending, unyielding, wilful

pliant **1**. bendable, bendy, ductile, flexible, lithe, plastic, pliable, supple, tensile **2**. adaptable, biddable, compliant, easily led, impressionable, influenceable, manageable, persuadable, pliable, susceptible, tractable, yielding

plight[1] *noun* case, circumstances, condition, difficulty, dilemma, extremity, hole (*slang*), hot water (*informal*), jam (*informal*), perplexity, pickle (*informal*), predicament, scrape (*informal*), situation, spot (*informal*), state, straits, tight spot, trouble

plight[2] *verb* contract, covenant, engage, guarantee, pledge, promise, propose, swear, vouch, vow

plod **1**. clump, drag, lumber, slog, stomp (*informal*), tramp, tread, trudge **2**. drudge, grind (*informal*), grub, labour, peg away, persevere, plough through, plug away (*informal*), slog, soldier on, toil

plot[1] *noun* **1**. cabal, conspiracy, covin (*Law*), intrigue, machination, plan, scheme, stratagem **2**. action, narrative, outline, scenario, story, story line, subject, theme, thread *~verb* **3**. cabal, collude, conspire, contrive, hatch, intrigue, machinate, manoeuvre, plan, scheme **4**. calculate, chart, compute, draft, draw, locate, map, mark, outline **5**. brew, conceive, concoct, contrive, cook up (*informal*), design, devise, frame, hatch, imagine, lay, project

plot[2] *noun* allotment, area, ground, lot, parcel, patch, tract

plough *verb* **1**. break ground, cultivate, dig, furrow, ridge, till, turn over **2**. (*usually with* **through**) cut, drive, flounder, forge, plod, plunge, press, push, stagger, surge, wade **3**. (*with* **into**) bulldoze, career, crash, hurtle, plunge, shove, smash

ploy contrivance, device, dodge, gambit, game, manoeuvre, move, ruse, scheme, stratagem, subterfuge, tactic, trick, wile

pluck[1] *noun* backbone, balls (*taboo slang*), ballsiness (*taboo slang*), boldness, bottle (*Brit. slang*), bravery, courage, determination, grit, guts (*informal*), hardihood, heart, intrepidity, mettle, nerve, resolution, spirit, spunk (*informal*)

pluck[2] *verb* **1**. collect, draw, gather, harvest, pick, pull out *or* off **2**. catch, clutch, jerk, pull at, snatch, tug, tweak, yank **3**. finger, pick, plunk, strum, thrum, twang

plucky ballsy (*taboo slang*), bold, brave, courageous, daring, doughty, feisty (*informal, chiefly U.S. & Canad.*), game, gritty, gutsy (*slang*), hardy, have-a-go (*informal*), heroic, intrepid, mettlesome, spirited, spunky (*informal*), undaunted, unflinching, valiant
▷ **Antonyms** afraid, chicken (*slang*), cowardly, dastardly, dispirited, lifeless, scared, spineless, spiritless, timid, weary, yellow (*informal*)

plug *noun* **1**. bung, cork, spigot, stopper, stopple **2**. cake, chew, pigtail, quid, twist, wad **3**. *informal* advert (*Brit. informal*), advertisement, good word, hype, mention, publicity, puff, push *~verb* **4**. block, bung, choke, close, cork, cover, fill, pack, seal, stop, stopper, stopple, stop up, stuff **5**. *informal* advertise, build up, hype, mention, promote, publicize, puff, push, write up **6**. *slang* blow away (*slang, chiefly U.S.*), gun down, pick off, pop, pot, put a bullet in, shoot **7**. (*with* **along** *or* **away**) *informal* drudge, grind (*informal*), labour, peg away, plod, slog, toil

plum *figurative* **1**. *noun* bonus, cream, find, pick, prize, treasure **2**. *~adjective* best, choice, first-class, prize

plumb *noun* **1**. lead, plumb bob, plummet, weight *~adverb* **2**. perpendicularly, up and down, vertically **3**. bang, exactly, precisely, slap, spot-on (*Brit. informal*) *~verb* **4**. delve, explore, fathom, gauge, go into, measure, penetrate, probe, search, sound, unravel

plume 1. *noun* aigrette, crest, feather, pinion, quill **2**. *~verb* (*with* **on** *or* **upon**) congratulate oneself, pat oneself on the back, pique oneself, preen oneself, pride oneself

plummet crash, descend, dive, drop down, fall, nose-dive, plunge, stoop, swoop, tumble

plump[1] *adjective* beefy (*informal*), burly, buxom, chubby, corpulent, dumpy, fat, fleshy, full, obese, podgy, portly, roly-poly, rotund, round, stout, tubby, well-covered, well-upholstered (*informal*)
▷ **Antonyms** anorexic, bony, emaciated, lanky, lean, scrawny, skinny, slender, slim, sylphlike, thin

plump[2] *verb* **1**. drop, dump, fall, flop, sink, slump **2**. (*with* **for**) back, choose, come down in favour of, favour, opt for, side with, support *~adjective* **3**. abrupt, direct, downright, forthright, plain, unqualified, unreserved

plunder 1. *verb* despoil, devastate, loot, pillage, raid, ransack, ravage, rifle, rob, sack, spoil, steal, strip **2**. *~noun* booty, ill-gotten gains, loot, pillage, prey, prize, rapine, spoils, swag (*slang*)

plunge *verb* **1**. cast, descend, dip, dive, douse, drop, fall, go down, immerse, jump, nose-dive, pitch, plummet, sink, submerge, swoop, throw, tumble **2**. career, charge, dash, hurtle, lurch, rush, tear *~noun* **3**. descent, dive, drop, fall, immersion, jump, submersion, swoop

plurality 1. diversity, multiplicity, numerousness, profusion, variety **2**. bulk, majority, mass, most, nearly all, overwhelming number, preponderance

plus 1. *preposition* added to, and, coupled with, with, with the addition of **2**. *~adjective* added, additional, add-on, extra, positive, supplementary **3**. *~noun informal* advantage, asset, benefit, bonus, extra, gain, good point, icing on the cake, perk (*Brit. informal*), surplus

plush costly, de luxe, lavish, luxurious, luxury, opulent, palatial, rich, ritzy (*slang*), sumptuous
▷ **Antonyms** cheap, cheap and nasty, inexpensive, ordinary, plain, spartan

plutocrat capitalist, Croesus, Dives, fat cat (*slang, chiefly U.S.*), magnate, millionaire, moneybags (*slang*), rich man, tycoon

ply[1] *verb* **1**. carry on, exercise, follow, practise, pursue, work at **2**. employ, handle, manipulate, swing, utilize, wield **3**. assail, beset, besiege, bombard, harass, importune, press, urge

ply[2] *noun* fold, layer, leaf, sheet, strand, thickness

poach appropriate, encroach, hunt *or* fish illegally, infringe, intrude, plunder, rob, steal, steal game, trespass

pock blemish, flaw, mark, pimple, pockmark, pustule, scar, spot

pocket *noun* **1**. bag, compartment, hollow, pouch, receptacle, sack *~adjective* **2**. abridged, compact, concise, little, miniature, pint-size(d) (*informal*), portable, potted (*informal*), small *~verb* **3**. appropriate, cabbage (*Brit. slang*), filch, help oneself to, lift (*informal*), pilfer, purloin, snaffle (*Brit. informal*), steal, take **4**. accept, bear, brook, endure, put up with (*informal*), stomach, swallow, take, tolerate

pockmark blemish, pit, pock, scar

pod *noun/verb* hull, husk, shell, shuck

podgy chubby, chunky, dumpy, fat, fleshy, fubsy (*archaic or dialect*), plump, roly-poly, rotund, short and fat, squat, stout, stubby, stumpy, tubby

podium dais, platform, rostrum, stage

poem lyric, ode, rhyme, song, sonnet, verse

poet bard, lyricist, maker (*archaic*), rhymer, versifier

poetic elegiac, lyric, lyrical, metrical, rhythmic, rhythmical, songlike

poetry metrical composition, poems, poesy (*archaic*), rhyme, rhyming, verse

po-faced disapproving, humourless, narrow-minded, prim, prudish, puritanical, solemn, stolid, strait-laced

poignancy 1. emotion, emotionalism, evocativeness, feeling, pathos, piteousness, plaintiveness, sadness, sentiment, tenderness **2**. bitterness, intensity, keenness, piquancy, pungency, sharpness

poignant 1. affecting, agonizing, bitter, distressing, harrowing, heartbreaking, heart-rending, intense, moving, painful, pathetic, sad, touching, upsetting **2**. acute, biting, caustic, keen, penetrating, piercing, pointed, sarcastic, severe **3**. acrid, piquant, pungent, sharp, stinging, tangy

point *noun* **1**. dot, full stop, mark, period, speck, stop **2**. location, place, position, site, spot, stage, station **3**. apex, end, nib, prong, sharp end, spike, spur, summit, tine, tip, top **4**. bill, cape, foreland, head, headland, ness (*archaic*), promontory **5**. circumstance, condition, degree, extent, position, stage **6**. instant, juncture, moment, time, very minute **7**. aim, design, end, goal, intent, intention, motive, object, objective, purpose, reason, use, usefulness, utility **8**. burden, core, crux, drift, essence, gist, heart, import, main idea, marrow, matter, meaning, nub, pith, proposition, question, subject, text, theme, thrust **9**. aspect, detail, facet, feature, instance, item, nicety, particular **10**. aspect, at~

tribute, characteristic, peculiarity, property, quality, respect, side, trait **11.** score, tally, unit **12. beside the point** immaterial, incidental, inconsequential, irrelevant, not to the purpose, off the subject, out of the way, pointless, unimportant, without connection **13. to the point** applicable, apposite, appropriate, apropos, apt, brief, fitting, germane, pertinent, pithy, pointed, relevant, short, suitable, terse *~verb* **14.** bespeak, call attention to, denote, designate, direct, indicate, show, signify **15.** aim, bring to bear, direct, level, train **16.** barb, edge, sharpen, taper, whet

point-blank 1. *adjective* abrupt, blunt, categorical, direct, downright, explicit, express, plain, rude, straight-from-the-shoulder, unreserved **2.** *~adverb* bluntly, brusquely, candidly, directly, explicitly, forthrightly, frankly, openly, overtly, plainly, straight, straightforwardly

pointed 1. acicular, acuminate, acute, barbed, cuspidate, edged, mucronate, sharp **2.** accurate, acute, biting, cutting, incisive, keen, penetrating, pertinent, sharp, telling, trenchant

pointer 1. guide, hand, indicator, needle **2.** advice, caution, hint, information, recommendation, suggestion, tip, warning

pointless absurd, aimless, fruitless, futile, inane, ineffectual, irrelevant, meaningless, nonsensical, senseless, silly, stupid, unavailing, unproductive, unprofitable, useless, vague, vain, without rhyme or reason, worthless

▷ **Antonyms** appropriate, beneficial, desirable, fitting, fruitful, logical, meaningful, productive, profitable, proper, sensible, to the point, useful, worthwhile

point of view 1. angle, orientation, outlook, perspective, position, standpoint **2.** approach, attitude, belief, judgment, opinion, slant, view, viewpoint, way of looking at it

point out allude to, bring up, call attention to, identify, indicate, mention, remind, reveal, show, specify

point up accent, accentuate, emphasize, make clear, stress, underline

poise 1. *noun* aplomb, assurance, calmness, composure, cool (*slang*), coolness, dignity, elegance, equanimity, equilibrium, grace, presence, presence of mind, sang-froid, savoir-faire, self-possession, serenity **2.** *~verb* balance, float, hang, hang in midair, hang suspended, hold, hover, position, support, suspend

poised 1. calm, collected, composed, debonair, dignified, graceful, nonchalant, self-confident, self-possessed, serene, suave, together (*informal*), unfazed (*informal*), unruffled, urbane **2.** all set, in the wings, on the brink, prepared, ready, standing by, waiting

▷ **Antonyms** (*sense 1*) agitated, annoyed, discomposed, disturbed, excited, irritated, ruffled, worked up

poison *noun* **1.** bane, toxin, venom **2.** bane, blight, cancer, canker, contagion, contamination, corruption, malignancy, miasma, virus *~verb* **3.** adulterate, contaminate, envenom, give (someone) poison, infect, kill, murder, pollute **4.** corrupt, defile, deprave, pervert, subvert, taint, undermine, vitiate, warp *~adjective* **5.** deadly, lethal, poisonous, toxic, venomous

poisonous 1. baneful (*archaic*), deadly, fatal, lethal, mephitic, mortal, noxious, toxic, venomous, virulent **2.** baleful, baneful (*archaic*), corruptive, evil, malicious, noxious, pernicious, pestiferous, pestilential, vicious

poke *verb* **1.** butt, dig, elbow, hit, jab, nudge, prod, punch, push, shove, stab, stick, thrust **2.** butt in, interfere, intrude, meddle, nose, peek, poke one's nose into (*informal*), pry, put one's two cents in (*U.S. slang*), snoop (*informal*), tamper **3. poke fun at** chaff, jeer, make a mock of, make fun of, mock, rib (*informal*), ridicule, send up (*Brit. informal*), take the mickey (*informal*), take the piss (out of) (*taboo slang*), tease *~noun* **4.** butt, dig, hit, jab, nudge, prod, punch, thrust

poky confined, cramped, incommodious, narrow, small, tiny

▷ **Antonyms** capacious, commodious, large, open, roomy, spacious, wide

polar 1. Antarctic, Arctic, cold, extreme, freezing, frozen, furthest, glacial, icy, terminal **2.** beacon-like, cardinal, guiding, leading, pivotal **3.** antagonistic, antipodal, antithetical, contradictory, contrary, diametric, opposed, opposite

polarity ambivalence, contradiction, contrariety, dichotomy, duality, opposition, paradox

pole¹ *noun* bar, mast, post, rod, shaft, spar, staff, standard, stick

pole² *noun* **1.** antipode, extremity, limit, terminus **2. poles apart** at opposite ends of the earth, at opposite extremes, incompatible, irreconcilable, miles apart, widely separated, worlds apart

polemic 1. *noun* argument, controversy, debate, dispute **2.** *~adjective* argumentative, contentious, controversial, disputatious, polemical

polemics argument, argumentation, contention, controversy, debate, disputation, dispute

police *noun* **1.** boys in blue (*informal*), constabulary, fuzz (*slang*), law enforcement agency, police force, the law (*informal*), the Old Bill (*slang*) *~verb* **2.** control, guard, keep in order, keep the peace, patrol, protect, regulate, watch **3.**

figurative check, monitor, observe, oversee, supervise

policeman bobby (*informal*), bogey (*slang*), constable, cop (*slang*), copper (*slang*), flatfoot (*slang*), fuzz (*slang*), gendarme (*slang*), officer, peeler (*obsolete Brit. slang*), pig (*slang*), rozzer (*slang*), woodentop (*slang*)

policy **1.** action, approach, code, course, custom, guideline, line, plan, practice, procedure, programme, protocol, rule, scheme, stratagem, theory **2.** discretion, good sense, prudence, sagacity, shrewdness, wisdom

polish *verb* **1.** brighten, buff, burnish, clean, furbish, rub, shine, smooth, wax **2.** brush up, correct, cultivate, emend, enhance, finish, improve, perfect, refine, touch up *~noun* **3.** brightness, brilliance, finish, glaze, gloss, lustre, sheen, smoothness, sparkle, veneer **4.** varnish, wax **5.** *figurative* breeding, class (*informal*), elegance, finesse, finish, grace, politesse, refinement, style, suavity, urbanity

polished **1.** bright, burnished, furbished, glassy, gleaming, glossy, shining, slippery, smooth **2.** *figurative* civilized, courtly, cultivated, elegant, finished, genteel, polite, refined, sophisticated, urbane, well-bred **3.** accomplished, adept, expert, faultless, fine, flawless, impeccable, masterly, outstanding, professional, skilful, superlative
▷ **Antonyms** (*sense 1*) dark, dull, matt, rough (*sense 2*) inelegant, uncivilized, uncultivated, unrefined, unsophisticated (*sense 3*) amateurish, inept, inexpert, unaccomplished, unskilled

polish off **1.** consume, down, eat up, finish, put away, shift (*informal*), swill, wolf **2.** blow away (*slang, chiefly U.S.*), bump off (*informal*), dispose of, do away with, do in (*slang*), eliminate, get rid of, kill, liquidate, murder, take out (*slang*)

polite **1.** affable, civil, complaisant, courteous, deferential, gracious, mannerly, obliging, respectful, well-behaved, well-mannered **2.** civilized, courtly, cultured, elegant, genteel, polished, refined, sophisticated, urbane, well-bred
▷ **Antonyms** crude, discourteous, ill-mannered, impertinent, impolite, impudent, insulting, rude, uncultured, unrefined

politic **1.** artful, astute, canny, crafty, cunning, designing, ingenious, intriguing, Machiavellian, scheming, shrewd, sly, subtle, unscrupulous **2.** advisable, diplomatic, discreet, expedient, in one's best interests, judicious, prudent, sagacious, sensible, tactful, wise

politician legislator, Member of Parliament, M.P., office bearer, politico (*informal, chiefly U.S.*), public servant, statesman

politics **1.** affairs of state, civics, government, government policy, political science, polity, statecraft, statesmanship **2.** Machiavellianism, machination, power struggle, *Realpolitik*

poll *noun* **1.** figures, returns, tally, vote, voting **2.** ballot, canvass, census, count, Gallup Poll, (public) opinion poll, sampling, survey *~verb* **3.** register, tally **4.** ballot, canvass, fly a kite, interview, question, sample, survey

pollute **1.** adulterate, befoul, contaminate, dirty, foul, infect, make filthy, mar, poison, smirch, soil, spoil, stain, taint **2.** besmirch, corrupt, debase, debauch, defile, deprave, desecrate, dishonour, profane, sully, violate
▷ **Antonyms** (*sense 1*) clean, cleanse, decontaminate, disinfect, purge, sanitize, sterilize (*sense 2*) esteem, honour

pollution adulteration, contamination, corruption, defilement, dirtying, foulness, impurity, taint, uncleanness, vitiation

poltroon caitiff (*archaic*), chicken (*slang*), coward, craven, cur, dastard (*archaic*), recreant (*archaic*), skunk (*informal*), yellow-belly (*slang*)

polychromatic many-coloured, many-hued, multicoloured, of all the colours of the rainbow, polychrome, rainbow, varicoloured, variegated

pomp **1.** ceremony, éclat, flourish, grandeur, magnificence, pageant, pageantry, parade, solemnity, splendour, state **2.** display, grandiosity, ostentation, pomposity, show, vainglory

pomposity **1.** affectation, airs, arrogance, flaunting, grandiosity, haughtiness, pompousness, portentousness, presumption, pretension, pretentiousness, self-importance, vainglory, vanity **2.** bombast, fustian, grandiloquence, hot air (*informal*), loftiness, magniloquence, rant, turgidity

pompous **1.** affected, arrogant, bloated, grandiose, imperious, magisterial, ostentatious, overbearing, pontifical, portentous, pretentious, puffed up, self-important, showy, supercilious, vainglorious **2.** boastful, bombastic, flatulent, fustian, grandiloquent, high-flown, inflated, magniloquent, orotund, overblown, turgid, windy
▷ **Antonyms** direct, humble, modest, natural, plain-spoken, self-effacing, simple, succinct, unaffected, unpretentious

pond dew pond, duck pond, fish pond, lochan (*Scot.*), millpond, pool, small lake, tarn

ponder brood, cerebrate, cogitate, consider, contemplate, deliberate, examine, excogitate, give thought to, meditate, mull over, muse, puzzle over, rack one's brains, reflect, ruminate, study, think, weigh

ponderous **1.** bulky, clunky (*informal*), cumbersome, cumbrous, heavy, hefty, huge, massive, unwieldy, weighty **2.** awkward, clumsy, elephantine, graceless, heavy-footed, laborious, lumbering **3.** dreary, dull, heavy, laboured, lifeless, long-winded, pedantic, pedestrian, plodding, prolix, stilted, stodgy, tedious, tiresome, verbose
▷ **Antonyms** (*senses 1 & 2*) graceful, handy, light, light-footed, little, small, tiny, weightless

poniard bodkin (*archaic*), dagger, dirk, misericord (*archaic*), stiletto

pontifical **1.** apostolic, ecclesiastical, papal, prelatic **2.** bloated, condescending, dogmatic, imperious, magisterial, overbearing, pompous, portentous, pretentious, self-important

pontificate declaim, dogmatize, expound, hold forth, lay down the law, pontify, preach, pronounce, sound off

pooh-pooh belittle, brush aside, deride, disdain, dismiss, disregard, make little of, play down, scoff, scorn, slight, sneer, sniff at, spurn, turn up one's nose at (*informal*)
▷ **Antonyms** exalt, extol, glorify, praise

pool[1] *noun* **1.** lake, mere, pond, puddle, splash, tarn **2.** swimming bath, swimming pool

pool[2] *noun* **1.** collective, combine, consortium, group, syndicate, team, trust **2.** bank, funds, jackpot, kitty, pot, stakes *~verb* **3.** amalgamate, combine, join forces, league, merge, put together, share

poor **1.** badly off, broke (*informal*), destitute, dirt-poor (*informal*), down and out, down at heel, flat broke (*informal*), hard up (*informal*), impecunious, impoverished, indigent, in need, in queer street, in want, necessitous, needy, not have two beans to rub together, on one's beam-ends, on one's uppers, on the breadline, on the rocks, penniless, penurious, poverty-stricken, short, skint (*Brit. slang*), stony-broke (*Brit. slang*), without two pennies to rub together (*informal*) **2.** deficient, exiguous, inadequate, incomplete, insufficient, lacking, meagre, measly, miserable, niggardly, pathetic, pitiable, reduced, scant, scanty, skimpy, slight, sparse, straitened **3.** below par, chickenshit (*U.S. slang*), crappy (*slang*), faulty, feeble, for the birds (*informal*), inferior, low-grade, low-rent (*informal chiefly U.S.*), mediocre, no great shakes (*informal*), not much cop (*Brit. slang*), piss-poor (*taboo slang*), poxy (*slang*), rotten (*informal*), rubbishy, second-rate, shabby, shoddy, sorry, strictly for the birds (*informal*), substandard, unsatisfactory, valueless, weak, worthless **4.** bad, bare, barren, depleted, exhausted, fruitless, impoverished, infertile, sterile, unfruitful, unproductive **5.** hapless, ill-fated, luckless, miserable, pathetic, pitiable, unfortunate, unhappy, unlucky, wretched **6.** humble, insignificant, lowly, mean, modest, paltry, plain, trivial
▷ **Antonyms** (*sense 1*) affluent, comfortable (*informal*), prosperous, rich, wealthy, well-heeled (*informal*), well-off (*sense 2*) abundant, adequate, ample, complete, dense, plentiful, satisfactory, sufficient, thick (*sense 3*) excellent, exceptional, first-class, first-rate, satisfactory, superior, valuable (*sense 4*) fertile, fruitful, productive, teeming, yielding (*sense 5*) fortunate, happy, lucky, successful

poorly **1.** *adverb* badly, crudely, inadequately, incompetently, inexpertly, inferiorly, insufficiently, meanly, shabbily, unsatisfactorily, unsuccessfully **2.** *~adjective informal* ailing, below par, ill, indisposed, off colour, out of sorts, rotten (*informal*), seedy (*informal*), sick, under the weather (*informal*), unwell
▷ **Antonyms** (*sense 1*) acceptably, adequately, competently, expertly, satisfactorily, sufficiently, well (*sense 2*) fit, hale and hearty, healthy, in good health, in the pink, well

pop *verb* **1.** bang, burst, crack, explode, go off, report, snap **2.** (*often with* **in, out,** *etc.*) *informal* appear, call, come *or* go suddenly, drop in (*informal*), leave quickly, nip in (*Brit. informal*), nip out (*Brit. informal*), visit **3.** *especially of eyes* bulge, protrude, stick out **4.** insert, push, put, shove, slip, stick, thrust, tuck *~noun* **5.** bang, burst, crack, explosion, noise, report **6.** *informal* fizzy drink, ginger (*Scot.*), lemonade, soda water, soft drink

pope Bishop of Rome, Holy Father, pontiff, Vicar of Christ

popinjay buck (*archaic*), coxcomb (*archaic*), dandy, fop, jackanapes, peacock, swell (*informal*)

poppycock babble, balderdash, balls (*taboo slang*), baloney (*informal*), bilge (*informal*), bollocks (*Brit. taboo slang*), bosh (*informal*), bull (*slang*), bullshit (*taboo slang*), bunk (*informal*), bunkum *or* buncombe (*chiefly U.S.*), cobblers (*Brit. taboo slang*), crap (*slang*), drivel, eyewash (*informal*), garbage (*informal*), gibberish, gobbledegook (*informal*), guff (*slang*), hogwash, hokum (*slang, chiefly U.S. & Canad.*), hooey (*slang*), horsefeathers (*U.S. slang*), hot air (*informal*), moonshine, nonsense, pap, piffle (*informal*), rot, rubbish, shit (*taboo slang*), tommyrot, tosh (*slang, chiefly Brit.*), trash, tripe (*informal*), twaddle

populace commonalty, crowd, general public, hoi polloi, inhabitants, Joe (and Eileen) Public (*slang*), Joe Six-Pack (*U.S. slang*), masses, mob, multitude, people, rabble, throng

popular 1. accepted, approved, celebrated, famous, fashionable, favoured, favourite, in, in demand, in favour, liked, sought-after, well-liked **2.** common, conventional, current, general, prevailing, prevalent, public, standard, stock, ubiquitous, universal, widespread
▷ **Antonyms** (*sense 1*) despised, detested, disliked, hated, loathed, unaccepted, unpopular (*sense 2*) infrequent, rare, uncommon, unusual

popularity acceptance, acclaim, adoration, approval, celebrity, currency, esteem, fame, favour, idolization, lionization, recognition, regard, renown, reputation, repute, vogue

popularize disseminate, familiarize, give currency to, give mass appeal, make available to all, simplify, spread, universalize

popularly commonly, conventionally, customarily, generally, ordinarily, regularly, traditionally, universally, usually, widely

populate colonize, inhabit, live in, occupy, people, settle

population citizenry, community, denizens, folk, inhabitants, natives, people, populace, residents, society

populous crowded, heavily populated, overpopulated, packed, populated, swarming, teeming, thronged

pore[1] *verb* brood, contemplate, dwell on, examine, go over, peruse, ponder, read, scrutinize, study, work over

pore[2] *noun* hole, opening, orifice, outlet, stoma

pornographic blue, dirty, filthy, indecent, lewd, obscene, offensive, prurient, salacious, smutty, X-rated (*informal*)

pornography dirt, erotica, filth, indecency, obscenity, porn (*informal*), porno (*informal*), smut

porous absorbent, absorptive, penetrable, permeable, pervious, spongy
▷ **Antonyms** impenetrable, impermeable, impervious, nonporous

port *Nautical* anchorage, harbour, haven, roads, roadstead, seaport

portable compact, convenient, easily carried, handy, light, lightweight, manageable, movable, portative

portal door, doorway, entrance, entrance way, entry, gateway, way in

portend adumbrate, augur, bespeak, betoken, bode, foreshadow, foretell, foretoken, forewarn, harbinger, herald, indicate, omen, point to, predict, presage, prognosticate, promise, threaten, vaticinate (*rare*), warn of

portent augury, foreboding, foreshadowing, forewarning, harbinger, indication, omen, premonition, presage, presentiment, prognostic, prognostication, sign, threat, warning

portentous 1. alarming, crucial, fateful, forbidding, important, menacing, minatory, momentous, ominous, significant, sinister, threatening **2.** amazing, astounding, awe-inspiring, extraordinary, miraculous, phenomenal, prodigious, remarkable, wondrous (*archaic or literary*) **3.** bloated, elephantine, heavy, pompous, ponderous, pontifical, self-important, solemn

porter[1] *noun* baggage attendant, bearer, carrier

porter[2] *noun* caretaker, concierge, doorman, gatekeeper, janitor

portion *noun* **1.** bit, fraction, fragment, morsel, part, piece, scrap, section, segment **2.** allocation, allotment, allowance, division, lot, measure, parcel, quantity, quota, ration, share **3.** helping, piece, serving **4.** cup, destiny, fate, fortune, lot, luck *~verb* **5.** allocate, allot, apportion, assign, deal, distribute, divide, divvy up (*informal*), dole out, parcel out, partition, share out

portly ample, beefy (*informal*), bulky, burly, corpulent, fat, fleshy, heavy, large, obese, overweight, plump, rotund, stout, tubby (*informal*)

portrait 1. image, likeness, painting, photograph, picture, portraiture, representation, sketch **2.** account, characterization, depiction, description, portrayal, profile, thumbnail sketch, vignette

portray 1. delineate, depict, draw, figure, illustrate, limn, paint, picture, render, represent, sketch **2.** characterize, depict, describe, paint a mental picture of, put in words **3.** act the part of, play, represent

portrayal characterization, delineation, depiction, description, impersonation, interpretation, performance, picture, rendering, representation, take (*informal, chiefly U.S.*)

pose *verb* **1.** arrange, model, position, sit, sit for **2.** (*often with* **as**) feign, impersonate, masquerade as, pass oneself off as, pretend to be, profess to be, sham **3.** affect, attitudinize, posture, put on airs, show off (*informal*), strike an attitude **4.** advance, posit, present, propound, put, put forward, set, state, submit *~noun* **5.** attitude, bearing, mien (*literary*), position, posture, stance **6.** act, affectation, air, attitudinizing, façade, front, mannerism, masquerade, posturing, pretence, role

poser brain-teaser (*informal*), conundrum, enigma, knotty point, problem, puzzle, question, riddle, teaser, tough one, vexed question

poseur attitudinizer, exhibitionist, hot dog (*chiefly U.S.*), impostor, mannerist, masquerader, poser, posturer, self-publicist, show-off (*informal*)

posh classy (*slang*), elegant, exclusive, fashionable, grand, high-class, high-toned, la-di-da (*informal*), luxurious, luxury, ritzy (*slang*), smart, stylish, swanky (*informal*), swish (*informal, chiefly Brit.*), top-drawer, up-market, upper-class

posit advance, assert, assume, postulate, predicate, presume, propound, put forward, state, submit

position *noun* **1.** area, bearings, locale, locality, location, place, point, post, reference, site, situation, spot, station, whereabouts **2.** arrangement, attitude, disposition, pose, posture, stance **3.** angle, attitude, belief, opinion, outlook, point of view, slant, stance, stand, standpoint, view, viewpoint **4.** circumstances, condition, lie of the land, pass, plight, predicament, situation, state, strait(s) **5.** caste, class, consequence, eminence, importance, place, prestige, rank, reputation, standing, station, stature, status **6.** berth (*informal*), billet (*informal*), capacity, duty, employment, function, job, occupation, office, place, post, role, situation *~verb* **7.** arrange, array, dispose, fix, lay out, locate, place, put, sequence, set, settle, stand, stick (*informal*)

positive **1.** absolute, actual, affirmative, categorical, certain, clear, clear-cut, conclusive, concrete, decisive, definite, direct, explicit, express, firm, incontrovertible, indisputable, real, unequivocal, unmistakable **2.** assured, certain, confident, convinced, sure **3.** assertive, cocksure, decided, dogmatic, emphatic, firm, forceful, opinionated, peremptory, resolute, stubborn **4.** beneficial, constructive, effective, efficacious, forward-looking, helpful, practical, productive, progressive, useful **5.** *informal* absolute, complete, consummate, out-and-out, perfect, rank, thorough, thoroughgoing, unmitigated, utter
▷ **Antonyms** (*sense 1*) contestable, disputable, doubtful, inconclusive, indecisive, indefinite, uncertain (*sense 2*) not confident, unassured, uncertain, unconvinced, unsure (*sense 3*) diffident, open-minded, receptive, retiring, timid, unassertive, unobtrusive (*sense 4*) conservative, detrimental, harmful, impractical, reactionary, unhelpful, useless

positively absolutely, assuredly, categorically, certainly, definitely, emphatically, firmly, surely, undeniably, unequivocally, unmistakably, unquestionably, with certainty, without qualification

possess **1.** be blessed with, be born with, be endowed with, enjoy, have, have to one's name, hold, own **2.** acquire, control, dominate, hold, occupy, seize, take over, take possession of **3.** bewitch, consume, control, dominate, enchant, fixate, influence, mesmerize, obsess, put under a spell

possessed bedevilled, berserk, bewitched, consumed, crazed, cursed, demented, enchanted, frenetic, frenzied, hagridden, haunted, maddened, obsessed, raving, under a spell

possession **1.** control, custody, hold, occupancy, occupation, ownership, proprietorship, tenure, title **2.** (*plural*) assets, belongings, chattels, effects, estate, goods and chattels, property, things, wealth **3.** colony, dominion, protectorate, province, territory

possessive acquisitive, controlling, covetous, dominating, domineering, grasping, jealous, overprotective, selfish

possibility **1.** feasibility, likelihood, plausibility, potentiality, practicability, workableness **2.** chance, hazard, hope, liability, likelihood, odds, probability, prospect, risk **3.** (*often plural*) capabilities, potential, potentiality, promise, prospects, talent

possible **1.** conceivable, credible, hypothetical, imaginable, likely, potential **2.** attainable, doable, feasible, on (*informal*), practicable, realizable, viable, within reach, workable **3.** hopeful, likely, potential, probable, promising
▷ **Antonyms** impossible, impracticable, improbable, inconceivable, incredible, unfeasible, unimaginable, unlikely, unobtainable, unreasonable, unthinkable

possibly **1.** God willing, haply (*archaic*), maybe, mayhap (*archaic*), peradventure (*archaic*), perchance (*archaic*), perhaps **2.** at all, by any chance, by any means, in any way

post¹ **1.** *noun* column, newel, pale, palisade, picket, pillar, pole, shaft, stake, standard, stock, support, upright **2.** *~verb* advertise, affix, announce, display, make known, pin up, proclaim, promulgate, publicize, publish, put up, stick up

post² *noun* **1.** appointment, assignment, berth (*informal*), billet (*informal*), employment, job, office, place, position, situation **2.** beat, place, position, station *~verb* **3.** assign, establish, locate, place, position, put, situate, station

post³ *noun* **1.** collection, delivery, mail, postal service *~verb* **2.** dispatch, mail, send, transmit **3.** advise, brief, fill in on (*informal*), inform, notify, report to

poster advertisement, *affiche,* announcement, bill, notice, placard, public notice, sticker

posterior *adjective* **1.** after, back, behind, hind, hinder, rear **2.** ensuing, following, later, latter, subsequent

posterity **1.** children, descendants, family, heirs, issue, offspring, progeny, scions, seed (*chiefly biblical*) **2.** future, future generations, succeeding generations

posthaste at once, before one can say Jack Robinson, directly, double-quick, full tilt, hastily, hotfoot, pdq (*slang*), promptly, pronto (*informal*), quickly, speedily, straightaway, swiftly

postmortem *noun* analysis, autopsy, dis~section, examination, necropsy

postpone adjourn, defer, delay, hold over, put back, put off, put on ice (*informal*), put on the back burner (*informal*), shelve, suspend, table, take a rain check on (*U.S. & Canad. informal*)
▷ **Antonyms** advance, bring forward, call to order, carry out, go ahead with

postponement adjournment, deferment, deferral, delay, moratorium, respite, stay, suspension

postscript addition, afterthought, after~word, appendix, P.S., supplement

postulate advance, assume, hypothesize, posit, predicate, presuppose, propose, put forward, suppose, take for granted, theorize

posture *noun* **1.** attitude, bearing, car~riage, disposition, mien (*literary*), pose, position, set, stance **2.** circumstance, condition, mode, phase, position, situa~tion, state **3.** attitude, disposition, feel~ing, frame of mind, inclination, mood, outlook, point of view, stance, stand~point *~verb* **4.** affect, attitudinize, do for effect, hot-dog (*chiefly U.S.*), make a show, pose, put on airs, show off (*infor~mal*), try to attract attention

posy bouquet, boutonniere, buttonhole, corsage, nosegay, spray

potbellied bloated, corpulent, distended, fat, obese, overweight, paunchy

potbelly beer belly (*informal*), corpora~tion (*informal*), gut, middle-age spread (*informal*), paunch, pot, spare tyre (*Brit. slang*), spread (*informal*)

potency authority, capacity, control, ef~fectiveness, efficacy, energy, force, in~fluence, might, muscle, potential, power, puissance, strength, sway, vigour

potent **1.** efficacious, forceful, mighty, powerful, puissant, strong, vigorous **2.** cogent, compelling, convincing, effective, forceful, impressive, persuasive, telling **3.** authoritative, commanding, domi~nant, dynamic, influential, powerful
▷ **Antonyms** impotent, ineffective, un~convincing, weak

potentate emperor, king, mogul, mon~arch, overlord, prince, ruler, sovereign

potential **1.** *adjective* budding, dormant, embryonic, future, hidden, inherent, la~tent, likely, possible, promising, unde~veloped, unrealized **2.** *~noun* ability, ap~titude, capability, capacity, possibility, potentiality, power, the makings, what it takes (*informal*), wherewithal

potentiality ability, aptitude, capability, capacity, likelihood, potential, promise, prospect, the makings

pother bother, carry-on (*informal, chiefly Brit.*), commotion, disturbance, flap (*in~formal*), fuss, hoo-ha, lather (*informal*), ruction (*informal*), stew (*informal*), tizzy (*informal*), to-do

potion brew, concoction, cup, dose, draught, elixir, mixture, philtre, tonic

potpourri collection, combination, galli~maufry, hotchpotch, medley, *mélange,* miscellany, mixed bag (*informal*), mix~ture, motley, pastiche, patchwork, sal~magundi

potter dabble, fiddle (*informal*), footle (*informal*), fribble, fritter, mess about, poke along, tinker

pottery ceramics, earthenware, stone~ware, terracotta

potty **1.** barmy (*slang*), crackers (*Brit. slang*), crackpot (*informal*), crazy, daft (*informal*), dippy (*slang*), doolally (*slang*), dotty (*slang, chiefly Brit.*), ec~centric, foolish, gonzo (*slang*), loopy (*in~formal*), oddball (*informal*), off one's chump (*slang*), off one's trolley (*slang*), off the rails, off-the-wall (*slang*), out to lunch (*informal*), silly, soft (*informal*), touched, up the pole (*informal*), wacko *or* whacko (*informal*) **2.** footling (*infor~mal*), insignificant, petty, piddling (*in~formal*), trifling, trivial

pouch bag, container, pocket, poke (*dia~lect*), purse, sack

pounce **1.** *verb* ambush, attack, bound onto, dash at, drop, fall upon, jump, leap at, snatch, spring, strike, swoop, take by surprise, take unawares **2.** *~noun* as~sault, attack, bound, jump, leap, spring, swoop

pound[1] *verb* **1.** batter, beat, beat the liv~ing daylights out of, belabour, clobber (*slang*), hammer, pelt, pummel, strike, thrash, thump **2.** bray (*dialect*), bruise, comminute, crush, powder, pulverize, triturate **3.** din into, drub into, drum into, hammer into **4.** (*with* **out**) bang, beat, hammer, thump **5.** clomp, march, stomp (*informal*), thunder, tramp **6.** beat, palpitate, pitapat, pulsate, pulse, throb

pound[2] *noun* compound, corral (*chiefly U.S. & Canad.*), enclosure, pen, yard

pour **1.** decant, let flow, spill, splash **2.** course, emit, flow, gush, run, rush, spew, spout, stream **3.** bucket down (*in~formal*), come down in torrents, pelt (down), rain, rain cats and dogs (*infor~mal*), rain hard *or* heavily, sheet, teem **4.** crowd, stream, swarm, teem, throng

pout **1.** *verb* glower, look petulant, look sullen, lour *or* lower, make a *moue,* mope, pull a long face, purse one's lips, sulk, turn down the corners of one's mouth **2.** *~noun* glower, long face, *moue,* sullen look

pouting bad-tempered, cross, huffy, ill-humoured, long-faced, moody, moping, morose, peevish, petulant, sulky, sullen

poverty 1. beggary, destitution, distress, hand-to-mouth existence, hardship, indigence, insolvency, necessitousness, necessity, need, pauperism, pennilessness, penury, privation, want **2.** dearth, deficiency, insufficiency, lack, paucity, scarcity, shortage **3.** aridity, bareness, barrenness, deficiency, infertility, meagreness, poorness, sterility, unfruitfulness

▷ **Antonyms** (*sense 1*) affluence, comfort, luxury, opulence, richness, wealth (*sense 2*) abundance, plethora, sufficiency (*sense 3*) fecundity, fertility, fruitfulness, productiveness

poverty-stricken bankrupt, beggared, broke (*informal*), destitute, dirt-poor (*informal*), distressed, down and out, down at heel, flat broke (*informal*), impecunious, impoverished, indigent, in queer street, needy, on one's beam-ends, on one's uppers, on the breadline, penniless, penurious, poor, short, skint (*Brit. slang*), stony-broke (*Brit. slang*), without two pennies to rub together (*informal*)

powder *noun* **1.** dust, fine grains, loose particles, pounce, talc *~verb* **2.** crush, granulate, grind, pestle, pound, pulverize **3.** cover, dredge, dust, scatter, sprinkle, strew

powdery chalky, crumbling, crumbly, dry, dusty, fine, friable, grainy, granular, loose, pulverized, sandy

power 1. ability, capability, capacity, competence, competency, faculty, potential **2.** brawn, energy, force, forcefulness, intensity, might, muscle, potency, strength, vigour, weight **3.** ascendancy, authority, bottom, command, control, dominance, domination, dominion, influence, mastery, rule, sovereignty, supremacy, sway **4.** authority, authorization, licence, prerogative, privilege, right, warrant

▷ **Antonyms** (*sense 1*) inability, incapability, incapacity, incompetence (*sense 2*) enervation, feebleness, impotence, listlessness, weakness

powerful 1. energetic, mighty, potent, robust, stalwart, strapping, strong, sturdy, vigorous **2.** authoritative, commanding, controlling, dominant, influential, prevailing, puissant, sovereign, supreme **3.** cogent, compelling, convincing, effective, effectual, forceful, forcible, impressive, persuasive, striking, telling, weighty

powerfully forcefully, forcibly, hard, mightily, strongly, vigorously, with might and main

powerless 1. debilitated, disabled, etiolated, feeble, frail, helpless, impotent, incapable, incapacitated, ineffectual, infirm, paralysed, prostrate, weak **2.** defenceless, dependent, disenfranchised, disfranchised, ineffective, over a barrel (*informal*), subject, tied, unarmed, vulnerable

▷ **Antonyms** (*sense 1*) able-bodied, fit, healthy, lusty, powerful, robust, strong, sturdy

powwow 1. *noun* chinwag (*Brit. informal*), confab (*informal*), confabulation, conference, congress, consultation, council, discussion, get-together (*informal*), huddle (*informal*), meeting, palaver, parley, seminar, talk **2.** *~verb* confab (*informal*), confer, discuss, get together, go into a huddle (*informal*), meet, palaver, parley, talk

practicability advantage, feasibility, operability, possibility, practicality, use, usefulness, value, viability, workability

practicable achievable, attainable, doable, feasible, performable, possible, viable, within the realm of possibility, workable

▷ **Antonyms** beyond the bounds of possibility, impossible, out of the question, unachievable, unattainable, unfeasible, unworkable

practical 1. applied, efficient, empirical, experimental, factual, functional, pragmatic, realistic, utilitarian **2.** businesslike, down-to-earth, everyday, hard-headed, matter-of-fact, mundane, ordinary, realistic, sensible, workaday **3.** doable, feasible, practicable, serviceable, sound, useful, workable **4.** accomplished, efficient, experienced, proficient, qualified, seasoned, skilled, trained, veteran, working

▷ **Antonyms** (*senses 1, 2, & 3*) impossible, impracticable, impractical, inefficient, speculative, theoretical, unpractical, unrealistic, unsound, unworkable, useless (*sense 4*) inefficient, inexperienced, unaccomplished, unqualified, unskilled, untrained

practically 1. all but, almost, basically, close to, essentially, fundamentally, in effect, just about, nearly, to all intents and purposes, very nearly, virtually, well-nigh **2.** clearly, matter-of-factly, rationally, realistically, reasonably, sensibly, unsentimentally, with common sense

practice 1. custom, habit, method, mode, praxis, routine, rule, system, tradition, usage, use, usual procedure, way, wont **2.** discipline, drill, exercise, preparation, rehearsal, repetition, study, training, work-out **3.** action, application, effect, exercise, experience, operation, use **4.** business, career, profession, vocation, work

practise 1. discipline, drill, exercise, go over, go through, keep one's hand in, polish, prepare, rehearse, repeat, study, train, warm up, work out 2. apply, carry out, do, follow, live up to, observe, perform, put into practice 3. carry on, engage in, ply, pursue, specialize in, undertake, work at

practised able, accomplished, experienced, expert, proficient, qualified, seasoned, skilled, trained, versed
▷ **Antonyms** amateurish, bungling, incompetent, inexperienced, inexpert, unqualified, unskilled, untrained

pragmatic businesslike, down-to-earth, efficient, hard-headed, matter-of-fact, practical, realistic, sensible, utilitarian
▷ **Antonyms** airy-fairy, idealistic, impractical, inefficient, starry-eyed, stupid, theoretical, unprofessional, unrealistic

praise *noun* 1. acclaim, acclamation, accolade, applause, approbation, approval, cheering, commendation, compliment, congratulation, encomium, eulogy, good word, kudos, laudation, ovation, panegyric, plaudit, tribute 2. adoration, devotion, glory, homage, thanks, worship ~*verb* 3. acclaim, admire, applaud, approve, cheer, compliment, congratulate, crack up (*informal*), cry up, eulogize, extol, honour, laud, pat on the back, pay tribute to, sing the praises of, take one's hat off to 4. adore, bless, exalt, give thanks to, glorify, magnify (*archaic*), pay homage to, worship

praiseworthy admirable, commendable, creditable, estimable, excellent, exemplary, fine, honourable, laudable, meritorious, worthy
▷ **Antonyms** condemnable, deplorable, despicable, discreditable, disgraceful, dishonourable, ignoble, reprehensible

prance 1. bound, caper, cavort, cut a rug (*informal*), dance, frisk, gambol, jump, leap, romp, skip, spring, trip 2. parade, show off (*informal*), stalk, strut, swagger, swank (*informal*)

prank antic, caper, escapade, frolic, jape, lark (*informal*), practical joke, skylarking (*informal*), trick

prate babble, blather, boast, brag, chatter, drivel, gab (*informal*), gas (*informal*), go on and on, jaw (*slang*), rabbit (on) (*Brit. informal*), shoot off one's mouth (*slang*), waffle (*informal, chiefly Brit.*), witter on (*informal*), yak (*slang*)

prattle babble, blather, blether, chatter, clack, drivel, gabble, jabber, patter, rabbit (on) (*Brit. informal*), rattle on, run off at the mouth (*slang*), run on, twitter, waffle (*informal, chiefly Brit.*), witter (*informal*)

pray 1. offer a prayer, recite the rosary, say one's prayers 2. adjure, ask, beg, beseech, call upon, crave, cry for, entreat, implore, importune, invoke, petition, plead, request, solicit, sue, supplicate, urge

prayer 1. communion, devotion, invocation, litany, orison, supplication 2. appeal, entreaty, petition, plea, request, suit, supplication

preach 1. address, deliver a sermon, evangelize, exhort, orate 2. admonish, advocate, exhort, harangue, lecture, moralize, sermonize, urge

preacher clergyman, evangelist, minister, missionary, parson, revivalist

preachify drone on, go on and on, harangue, hold forth, lecture, moralize, prose, sermonize

preachy canting, didactic, edifying, holier-than-thou, homiletic, moralizing, pharisaic, pietistic, pontifical, religiose, sanctimonious, self-righteous

preamble exordium, foreword, introduction, opening move, opening statement *or* remarks, overture, preface, prelude, proem, prolegomenon

precarious built on sand, chancy (*informal*), dangerous, dicey (*informal, chiefly Brit.*), dodgy (*Brit., Austral., & N.Z. informal*), doubtful, dubious, hairy (*slang*), hazardous, insecure, perilous, risky, shaky, slippery, touch and go, tricky, uncertain, unreliable, unsafe, unsettled, unstable, unsteady, unsure
▷ **Antonyms** certain, dependable, reliable, safe, secure, stable, steady

precaution 1. belt and braces (*informal*), insurance, preventative measure, protection, provision, safeguard, safety measure 2. anticipation, care, caution, circumspection, foresight, forethought, providence, prudence, wariness

precede antecede, antedate, come first, forerun, go ahead of, go before, head, herald, introduce, lead, pave the way, preface, take precedence, usher

precedence antecedence, lead, preeminence, preference, primacy, priority, rank, seniority, superiority, supremacy

precedent *noun* antecedent, authority, criterion, example, exemplar, instance, model, paradigm, pattern, previous example, prototype, standard

preceding above, aforementioned, aforesaid, anterior, earlier, foregoing, former, past, previous, prior

precept 1. behest, canon, command, commandment, decree, dictum, direction, instruction, law, mandate, order, ordinance, principle, regulation, rule, statute 2. axiom, byword, dictum, guideline, maxim, motto, principle, rule, saying

precinct 1. bound, boundary, confine, enclosure, limit 2. area, district, quarter, section, sector, zone

precincts borders, bounds, confines, district, environs, limits, milieu, neighbourhood, purlieus, region, surrounding area

precious 1. adored, beloved, cherished, darling, dear, dearest, favourite, idolized, loved, prized, treasured, valued, worth one's *or* its weight in gold **2.** choice, costly, dear, expensive, exquisite, fine, high-priced, inestimable, invaluable, priceless, prized, rare, recherché, valuable **3.** affected, alembicated, artificial, chichi, fastidious, overnice, overrefined, twee (*Brit. informal*)

precipice bluff, brink, cliff, cliff face, crag, height, rock face, sheer drop, steep

precipitate *verb* **1.** accelerate, advance, bring on, dispatch, expedite, further, hasten, hurry, press, push forward, quicken, speed up, trigger **2.** cast, discharge, fling, hurl, launch, let fly, send forth, throw *~adjective* **3.** breakneck, headlong, plunging, rapid, rushing, swift, violent **4.** frantic, harum-scarum, hasty, heedless, hurried, ill-advised, impetuous, impulsive, indiscreet, madcap, precipitous, rash, reckless **5.** abrupt, brief, quick, sudden, unexpected, without warning

precipitous 1. abrupt, dizzy, falling sharply, high, perpendicular, sheer, steep **2.** abrupt, careless, harum-scarum, hasty, heedless, hurried, ill-advised, precipitate, rash, reckless, sudden

précis 1. *noun* abridgment, abstract, *aperçu,* compendium, condensation, digest, outline, résumé, rundown, sketch, summary, synopsis **2.** *~verb* abridge, abstract, compress, condense, outline, shorten, summarize, sum up

precise 1. absolute, accurate, actual, clear-cut, correct, definite, exact, explicit, express, fixed, literal, particular, specific, strict, unequivocal **2.** careful, ceremonious, exact, fastidious, finicky, formal, inflexible, meticulous, nice, particular, prim, punctilious, puritanical, rigid, scrupulous, stiff, strict

▷ **Antonyms** (*sense 1*) ambiguous, careless, equivocal, incorrect, indefinite, indistinct, inexact, loose, vague (*sense 2*) flexible, haphazard, inexact, informal, relaxed, unceremonious

precisely absolutely, accurately, bang, correctly, exactly, just, just so, literally, neither more nor less, on the button (*informal*), plumb (*informal*), slap (*informal*), smack (*informal*), square, squarely, strictly, to the letter

precision accuracy, care, correctness, definiteness, dotting the i's and crossing the t's, exactitude, exactness, fidelity, meticulousness, nicety, particularity, preciseness, rigour

preclude check, debar, exclude, forestall, hinder, inhibit, make impossible, make impracticable, obviate, prevent, prohibit, put a stop to, restrain, rule out, stop

precocious advanced, ahead, bright, developed, forward, quick, smart

▷ **Antonyms** backward, dense, dull, retarded, slow, underdeveloped, unresponsive

preconception bias, notion, preconceived idea *or* notion, predisposition, prejudice, prepossession, presumption, presupposition

precondition essential, must, necessity, prerequisite, requirement, *sine qua non*

precursor 1. forerunner, harbinger, herald, messenger, usher, vanguard **2.** antecedent, forebear, forerunner, originator, pioneer, predecessor

precursory antecedent, introductory, preceding, prefatory, preliminary, preparatory, previous, prior

predatory 1. carnivorous, hunting, predacious, rapacious, raptorial, ravening **2.** despoiling, greedy, marauding, pillaging, plundering, rapacious, ravaging, thieving, voracious, vulturine, vulturous

predecessor 1. antecedent, forerunner, former job holder, precursor, previous job holder, prior job holder **2.** ancestor, antecedent, forebear, forefather

predestination destiny, doom, election (*Theology*), fate, foreordainment, foreordination, lot, necessity, predetermination

predestine doom, fate, foreordain, mean, predestinate, predetermine, pre-elect, preordain

predetermined agreed, arranged in advance, cut and dried (*informal*), decided beforehand, fixed, prearranged, preplanned, set, settled, set up

predicament corner, dilemma, emergency, fix (*informal*), hole (*slang*), hot water (*informal*), how-do-you-do (*informal*), jam (*informal*), mess, pickle (*informal*), pinch, plight, quandary, scrape (*informal*), situation, spot (*informal*), state, tight spot

predicate 1. affirm, assert, aver, avouch, avow, contend, declare, maintain, proclaim, state **2.** connote, imply, indicate, intimate, signify, suggest **3.** (*with* **on** *or* **upon**) base, build, establish, found, ground, postulate, rest

predict augur, divine, forebode, forecast, foresee, foretell, portend, presage, prognosticate, prophesy, soothsay, vaticinate (*rare*)

predictable anticipated, calculable, certain, expected, foreseeable, foreseen, likely, on the cards, reliable, sure, sure-fire (*informal*)

▷ **Antonyms** out of the blue, surprising, unexpected, unforeseen, unlikely, unpredictable

prediction augury, divination, forecast, prognosis, prognostication, prophecy, soothsaying, sortilege

predilection bag (*slang*), bias, cup of tea (*informal*), fancy, fondness, inclination, leaning, liking, love, partiality, pen~

chant, predisposition, preference, proclivity, proneness, propensity, taste, tendency, weakness

predispose affect, bias, dispose, incline, induce, influence, lead, make (one) of a mind to, prejudice, prepare, prime, prompt, sway

predisposed agreeable, amenable, given to, inclined, liable, minded, prone, ready, subject, susceptible, willing

predisposition bent, bias, disposition, inclination, likelihood, penchant, potentiality, predilection, proclivity, proneness, propensity, susceptibility, tendency, willingness

predominance ascendancy, control, dominance, dominion, edge, greater number, hold, leadership, mastery, paramountcy, preponderance, supremacy, sway, upper hand, weight

predominant ascendant, capital, chief, controlling, dominant, important, leading, main, notable, paramount, preponderant, prevailing, prevalent, primary, prime, principal, prominent, ruling, sovereign, superior, supreme, top-priority

▷ **Antonyms** inferior, minor, secondary, subordinate, unimportant, uninfluential

predominate be most noticeable, carry weight, get the upper hand, hold sway, outweigh, overrule, overshadow, preponderate, prevail, reign, rule, tell

pre-eminence distinction, excellence, paramountcy, predominance, prestige, prominence, renown, superiority, supremacy, transcendence

pre-eminent chief, consummate, distinguished, excellent, foremost, incomparable, matchless, outstanding, paramount, peerless, predominant, renowned, superior, supreme, transcendent, unequalled, unrivalled, unsurpassed

pre-eminently above all, by far, conspicuously, eminently, emphatically, exceptionally, far and away, incomparably, inimitably, matchlessly, notably, *par excellence,* particularly, second to none, signally, singularly, strikingly, superlatively, supremely

pre-empt acquire, anticipate, appropriate, arrogate, assume, seize, take over, usurp

preen 1. *of birds* clean, plume **2.** array, deck out, doll up (*slang*), dress up, prettify, primp, prink, spruce up, titivate, trig (*archaic or dialect*), trim **3. preen oneself (on)** congratulate oneself, pique oneself, plume oneself, pride oneself

preface 1. *noun* exordium, foreword, introduction, preamble, preliminary, prelude, proem, prolegomenon, prologue **2.** *~verb* begin, introduce, launch, lead up to, open, precede, prefix

prefatory antecedent, introductory, opening, precursory, prefatorial, preliminary, prelusive, prelusory, preparatory, proemial, prolegomenal

prefer 1. adopt, be partial to, choose, desire, elect, fancy, favour, go for, incline towards, like better, opt for, pick, plump for, select, single out, wish, would rather, would sooner **2.** file, lodge, place, present, press, put forward **3.** advance, aggrandize, elevate, move up, promote, raise, upgrade

preferable best, better, choice, chosen, favoured, more desirable, more eligible, superior, worthier

▷ **Antonyms** average, fair, ineligible, inferior, mediocre, poor, second-rate, undesirable

preferably as a matter of choice, by choice, first, in *or* for preference, much rather, much sooner, rather, sooner, willingly

preference 1. bag (*slang*), choice, cup of tea (*informal*), desire, election, favourite, first choice, option, partiality, pick, predilection, selection, top of the list **2.** advantage, favoured treatment, favouritism, first place, precedence, pride of place, priority

preferential advantageous, better, favoured, partial, partisan, privileged, special, superior

preferment advancement, dignity, elevation, exaltation, promotion, rise, upgrading

prefigure 1. adumbrate, foreshadow, foretoken, indicate, intimate, portend, presage, shadow forth, suggest **2.** consider, fancy, imagine, picture, presuppose

pregnancy gestation, gravidity

pregnant 1. big *or* heavy with child, enceinte, expectant, expecting (*informal*), gravid, in the club (*Brit. slang*), in the family way (*informal*), in the pudding club (*slang*), preggers (*Brit. informal*), with child **2.** charged, eloquent, expressive, loaded, meaningful, pointed, significant, suggestive, telling, weighty **3.** creative, imaginative, inventive, original, seminal **4.** abounding in, abundant, fecund, fertile, fraught, fruitful, full, productive, prolific, replete, rich in, teeming

prehistoric 1. earliest, early, primeval, primitive, primordial **2.** ancient, antediluvian, antiquated, archaic, out of date, out of the ark (*informal*)

prejudge anticipate, forejudge, jump to conclusions, make a hasty assessment, presume, presuppose

prejudice *noun* **1.** bias, jaundiced eye, partiality, preconceived notion, preconception, prejudgment, warp **2.** bigotry, chauvinism, discrimination, injustice, intolerance, narrow-mindedness, rac~

ism, sexism, unfairness **3.** damage, detriment, disadvantage, harm, hurt, impairment, loss, mischief *~verb* **4.** bias, colour, distort, influence, jaundice, poison, predispose, prepossess, slant, sway, warp **5.** damage, harm, hinder, hurt, impair, injure, mar, spoil, undermine

prejudiced biased, bigoted, conditioned, discriminatory, influenced, intolerant, jaundiced, narrow-minded, one-sided, opinionated, partial, partisan, prepossessed, unfair
▷ **Antonyms** fair, impartial, just, neutral, not bigoted, not prejudiced, open-minded, unbiased

prejudicial counterproductive, damaging, deleterious, detrimental, disadvantageous, harmful, hurtful, inimical, injurious, undermining, unfavourable

preliminary 1. *adjective* exploratory, first, initial, initiatory, introductory, opening, pilot, precursory, prefatory, preparatory, prior, qualifying, test, trial **2.** *~noun* beginning, first round, foundation, groundwork, initiation, introduction, opening, overture, preamble, preface, prelims, prelude, preparation, start

prelude beginning, commencement, curtain-raiser, exordium, foreword, intro (*informal*), introduction, overture, preamble, preface, preliminary, preparation, proem, prolegomenon, prologue, start

premature 1. abortive, early, embryonic, forward, green, immature, incomplete, predeveloped, raw, undeveloped, unfledged, unripe, unseasonable, untimely **2.** *figurative* hasty, ill-considered, ill-timed, impulsive, inopportune, jumping the gun, overhasty, precipitate, previous (*informal*), rash, too soon, untimely

prematurely 1. before one's time, too early, too soon, untimely **2.** at half-cock, half-cocked, overhastily, precipitately, rashly, too hastily, too soon

premeditated aforethought, calculated, conscious, considered, contrived, deliberate, intended, intentional, planned, prepense, studied, wilful
▷ **Antonyms** accidental, inadvertent, unintentional, unplanned, unpremeditated, unwitting

premeditation deliberation, design, determination, forethought, intention, malice aforethought, planning, plotting, prearrangement, predetermination, purpose

premier *noun* **1.** chancellor, chief minister, head of government, P.M., prime minister *~adjective* **2.** arch, chief, first, foremost, head, highest, leading, main, primary, prime, principal, top **3.** earliest, first, inaugural, initial, original

premiere debut, first night, first performance, first showing, opening

premise *verb* assume, hypothesize, posit, postulate, predicate, presuppose, state

premises building, establishment, place, property, site

premiss, premise argument, assertion, assumption, ground, hypothesis, postulate, postulation, presupposition, proposition, supposition, thesis

premium 1. bonus, boon, bounty, fee, percentage (*informal*), perk (*Brit. informal*), perquisite, prize, recompense, remuneration, reward **2.** appreciation, regard, stock, store, value **3. at a premium** beyond one's means, costly, expensive, hard to come by, in great demand, in short supply, like gold dust, not to be had for love or money, rare, scarce, valuable

premonition apprehension, feeling, feeling in one's bones, foreboding, forewarning, funny feeling (*informal*), hunch, idea, intuition, misgiving, omen, portent, presage, presentiment, sign, suspicion, warning

preoccupation 1. absence of mind, absent-mindedness, absorption, abstraction, brown study, daydreaming, engrossment, immersion, inattentiveness, musing, oblivion, pensiveness, prepossession, reverie, woolgathering **2.** bee in one's bonnet, concern, fixation, hang-up (*informal*), hobbyhorse, *idée fixe,* obsession, pet subject

preoccupied absent-minded, absorbed, abstracted, caught up in, distracted, distrait, engrossed, faraway, heedless, immersed, in a brown study, intent, lost in, lost in thought, oblivious, rapt, taken up, unaware, wrapped up

preordain destine, doom, fate, map out in advance, predestine, predetermine

preparation 1. development, getting ready, groundwork, preparing, putting in order **2.** alertness, anticipation, expectation, foresight, precaution, preparedness, provision, readiness, safeguard **3.** (*often plural*) arrangement, measure, plan, provision **4.** composition, compound, concoction, medicine, mixture, tincture **5.** homework, prep (*informal*), revision, schoolwork, study, swotting (*Brit. informal*)

preparatory 1. basic, elementary, introductory, opening, prefatory, preliminary, preparative, primary **2. preparatory to** before, in advance of, in anticipation of, in preparation for, prior to

prepare 1. adapt, adjust, anticipate, arrange, coach, dispose, form, groom, make provision, make ready, plan, practise, prime, put in order, train, warm up **2.** brace, fortify, gird, ready, steel, strengthen **3.** assemble, concoct, construct, contrive, draw up, fashion, fix up, get up (*informal*), make, produce, put together, turn out **4.** accoutre, equip, fit, fit out, furnish, outfit, provide, supply

prepared 1. all set, all systems go (*informal*), arranged, fit, in order, in readiness, planned, primed, ready, set **2**. able, disposed, inclined, minded, of a mind, predisposed, willing

preparedness alertness, fitness, order, preparation, readiness

preponderance ascendancy, bulk, dominance, domination, dominion, extensiveness, greater numbers, greater part, lion's share, mass, power, predominance, prevalence, superiority, supremacy, sway, weight

preponderant ascendant, dominant, extensive, foremost, greater, important, larger, paramount, predominant, prevailing, prevalent, significant

preponderate dominate, hold sway, outnumber, predominate, prevail, reign supreme, rule

prepossessed biased, inclined, partial, partisan, predisposed, prejudiced

prepossessing alluring, amiable, appealing, attractive, beautiful, bewitching, captivating, charming, engaging, fair, fascinating, fetching, glamorous, good-looking, handsome, inviting, likable *or* likeable, lovable, magnetic, pleasing, striking, taking, winning

▷ **Antonyms** disagreeable, displeasing, objectionable, offensive, repulsive, ugly, unattractive, uninviting, unlikable *or* unlikeable

prepossession 1. absorption, engrossment, preoccupation **2**. bias, inclination, liking, partiality, predilection, predisposition, prejudice

preposterous absurd, asinine, bizarre, crazy, excessive, exorbitant, extravagant, extreme, foolish, impossible, incredible, insane, irrational, laughable, ludicrous, monstrous, nonsensical, out of the question, outrageous, ridiculous, risible, senseless, shocking, unreasonable, unthinkable

prerequisite 1. *adjective* called for, essential, imperative, indispensable, mandatory, necessary, needful, obligatory, of the essence, required, requisite, vital **2**. *~noun* condition, essential, imperative, must, necessity, precondition, qualification, requirement, requisite, *sine qua non*

prerogative advantage, authority, birthright, choice, claim, droit, due, exemption, immunity, liberty, perquisite, privilege, right, sanction, title

presage *noun* **1**. augury, auspice, forecast, forewarning, harbinger, intimation, omen, portent, prediction, prognostic, prognostication, prophecy, sign, warning **2**. apprehension, boding, feeling, foreboding, intuition, misgiving, premonition, presentiment *~verb* **3**. divine, feel, foresee, have a feeling, intuit, sense **4**. adumbrate, augur, betoken, bode, forebode, foreshadow, foretoken, omen, point to, portend, signify, warn **5**. forecast, foretell, forewarn, predict, prognosticate, prophesy, soothsay, vaticinate (*rare*)

prescience clairvoyance, foreknowledge, foresight, precognition, prevision (*rare*), second sight

prescient clairvoyant, discerning, divinatory, divining, far-sighted, foresighted, mantic, perceptive, prophetic, psychic

prescribe appoint, assign, command, decree, define, dictate, direct, enjoin, establish, fix, impose, lay down, ordain, order, require, rule, set, specify, stipulate

prescript canon, command, dictate, dictum, direction, directive, edict, instruction, law, mandate, order, ordinance, precept, regulation, requirement, rule

prescription 1. direction, formula, instruction, recipe **2**. drug, medicine, mixture, preparation, remedy

prescriptive authoritarian, dictatorial, didactic, dogmatic, legislating, preceptive, rigid

presence 1. attendance, being, companionship, company, existence, habitation, inhabitance, occupancy, residence **2**. closeness, immediate circle, nearness, neighbourhood, propinquity, proximity, vicinity **3**. air, appearance, aspect, aura, bearing, carriage, comportment, demeanour, ease, mien (*literary*), personality, poise, self-assurance **4**. apparition, eidolon, ghost, manifestation, revenant, shade (*literary*), spectre, spirit, supernatural being, wraith

presence of mind alertness, aplomb, calmness, composure, cool (*slang*), coolness, dignity, imperturbability, level-headedness, phlegm, quickness, sangfroid, self-assurance, self-command, self-possession, wits

present[1] *adjective* **1**. contemporary, current, existent, existing, extant, immediate, instant, present-day **2**. accounted for, at hand, available, here, in attendance, near, nearby, ready, there, to hand *~noun* **3**. here and now, now, present moment, the time being, this day and age, today **4**. **at present** at the moment, just now, now, nowadays, right now **5**. **for the present** for a while, for the moment, for the nonce, for the time being, in the meantime, not for long, provisionally, temporarily

present[2] *verb* **1**. acquaint with, introduce, make known **2**. demonstrate, display, exhibit, give, mount, put before the public, put on, show, stage **3**. adduce, advance, declare, expound, extend, hold out, introduce, offer, pose, produce, proffer, put forward, raise, recount, relate, state, submit, suggest, tender **4**.

award, bestow, confer, donate, entrust, furnish, give, grant, hand out, hand over, offer, proffer, put at (someone's) disposal *~noun* **5.** benefaction, bonsela (*S. African*), boon, bounty, donation, endowment, favour, gift, grant, gratuity, hand-out, largesse *or* largess, offering, prezzie (*informal*)

presentable acceptable, becoming, decent, fit to be seen, good enough, not bad (*informal*), O.K. *or* okay (*informal*), passable, proper, respectable, satisfactory, suitable, tolerable

▷ **Antonyms** below par, not good enough, not up to scratch, poor, rubbishy, unacceptable, unpresentable, unsatisfactory

presentation 1. award, bestowal, conferral, donation, giving, investiture, offering **2.** appearance, arrangement, delivery, exposition, production, rendition, staging, submission **3.** demonstration, display, exhibition, performance, production, representation, show **4.** coming out, debut, introduction, launch, launching, reception

presentiment anticipation, apprehension, expectation, fear, feeling, foreboding, forecast, forethought, hunch, intuition, misgiving, premonition, presage

presently anon (*archaic*), before long, by and by, erelong (*archaic or poetic*), in a minute, in a moment, in a short while, pretty soon (*informal*), shortly, soon

preservation conservation, defence, keeping, maintenance, perpetuation, protection, safeguarding, safekeeping, safety, salvation, security, storage, support, upholding

preserve *verb* **1.** care for, conserve, defend, guard, keep, protect, safeguard, save, secure, shelter, shield **2.** continue, keep, keep up, maintain, perpetuate, retain, sustain, uphold **3.** conserve, keep, put up, save, store *~noun* **4.** area, domain, field, realm, specialism, sphere **5.** (*often plural*) confection, confiture, conserve, jam, jelly, marmalade, sweetmeat **6.** game reserve, reservation, reserve, sanctuary

▷ **Antonyms** (*sense 1*) assail, assault, attack, leave unprotected, turn out (*sense 2*) abandon, discontinue, drop, end, give up (*sense 3*) blow (*slang*), consume, fritter away, spend, squander, waste

preside administer, be at the head of, be in authority, chair, conduct, control, direct, govern, head, lead, manage, officiate, run, supervise

press *verb* **1.** bear down on, compress, condense, crush, depress, force down, jam, mash, push, reduce, squeeze, stuff **2.** calender, finish, flatten, iron, mangle, put the creases in, smooth, steam **3.** clasp, crush, embrace, encircle, enfold, fold in one's arms, hold close, hug, squeeze **4.** compel, constrain, demand, enforce, enjoin, force, insist on **5.** beg, entreat, exhort, implore, importune, petition, plead, pressurize, sue, supplicate, urge **6.** afflict, assail, beset, besiege, disquiet, harass, plague, torment, trouble, vex, worry **7. be pressed** be hard put, be hurried, be pushed, be rushed (*informal*), be short of **8.** cluster, crowd, flock, gather, hasten, herd, hurry, mill, push, rush, seethe, surge, swarm, throng *~noun* **9. the press: a.** Fleet Street, fourth estate, journalism, news media, newspapers, the papers **b.** columnists, correspondents, gentlemen of the press, journalists, journos (*slang*), newsmen, photographers, pressmen, reporters **10.** bunch, crowd, crush, flock, herd, horde, host, mob, multitude, pack, push (*informal*), swarm, throng **11.** bustle, demand, hassle (*informal*), hurry, pressure, strain, stress, urgency

pressing burning, constraining, crucial, exigent, high-priority, imperative, important, importunate, now or never, serious, urgent, vital

▷ **Antonyms** dispensable, regular, routine, unimportant, unnecessary

pressure 1. compressing, compression, crushing, force, heaviness, squeezing, weight **2.** coercion, compulsion, constraint, force, influence, obligation, power, sway **3.** adversity, affliction, burden, demands, difficulty, distress, exigency, hassle (*informal*), heat, hurry, load, press, strain, stress, urgency

prestige authority, bottom, Brownie points, cachet, celebrity, credit, distinction, eminence, esteem, fame, honour, importance, influence, kudos, regard, renown, reputation, standing, stature, status, weight

prestigious celebrated, eminent, esteemed, exalted, great, illustrious, important, imposing, impressive, influential, notable, prominent, renowned, reputable, respected

▷ **Antonyms** humble, lowly, minor, obscure, unimportant, unimpressive, unknown

presumably apparently, doubtless, doubtlessly, in all likelihood, in all probability, it would seem, likely, most likely, on the face of it, probably, seemingly

presume 1. assume, believe, conjecture, guess (*informal, chiefly U.S. & Canad.*), infer, posit, postulate, presuppose, suppose, surmise, take for granted, take it, think **2.** dare, go so far, have the audacity, make bold, make so bold, take the liberty, undertake, venture **3.** bank on, count on, depend, rely, trust

presumption 1. assurance, audacity, boldness, brass (*informal*), brass neck (*Brit. informal*), cheek (*informal*), chutzpah (*U.S. & Canad. informal*), effrontery, forwardness, front, gall (*informal*), impudence, insolence, neck (*infor-

mal), nerve (*informal*), presumptuousness, sassiness (*U.S. informal*), temerity **2**. anticipation, assumption, belief, conjecture, guess, hypothesis, opinion, premiss, presupposition, supposition, surmise **3**. basis, chance, grounds, likelihood, plausibility, probability, reason

presumptive 1. assumed, believed, expected, hypothetical, inferred, supposed, understood **2**. believable, conceivable, credible, likely, plausible, possible, probable, reasonable, verisimilar

presumptuous arrogant, audacious, bigheaded (*informal*), bold, conceited, foolhardy, forward, insolent, overconfident, overfamiliar, overweening, presuming, pushy (*informal*), rash, too big for one's boots, uppish (*Brit. informal*)
▷ **Antonyms** bashful, humble, modest, retiring, shy, timid, unassuming

presuppose accept, assume, consider, imply, posit, postulate, presume, suppose, take as read, take for granted, take it

presupposition assumption, belief, hypothesis, preconceived idea, preconception, premiss, presumption, supposition, theory

pretence 1. acting, charade, deceit, deception, fabrication, fakery, faking, falsehood, feigning, invention, make-believe, sham, simulation, subterfuge, trickery **2**. affectation, appearance, artifice, display, façade, hokum (*slang, chiefly U.S. & Canad.*), posing, posturing, pretentiousness, show, veneer **3**. claim, cloak, colour, cover, excuse, façade, garb, guise, mask, masquerade, pretext, ruse, semblance, show, veil, wile
▷ **Antonyms** (*sense 1*) actuality, fact, reality (*sense 2*) candour, frankness, honesty, ingenuousness, openness

pretend 1. affect, allege, assume, counterfeit, dissemble, dissimulate, fake, falsify, feign, impersonate, make out, pass oneself off as, profess, put on, sham, simulate **2**. act, imagine, make believe, make up, play, play the part of, suppose **3**. allege, aspire, claim, lay claim, profess, purport

pretended alleged, avowed, bogus, counterfeit, fake, false, feigned, fictitious, imaginary, ostensible, phoney *or* phony (*informal*), pretend (*informal*), professed, pseudo (*informal*), purported, sham, so-called, spurious

pretender aspirant, claimant, claimer

pretension 1. aspiration, assertion, assumption, claim, demand, pretence, profession **2**. affectation, airs, conceit, hypocrisy, ostentation, pomposity, pretentiousness, self-importance, show, showiness, snobbery, snobbishness, vainglory, vanity

pretentious affected, assuming, bombastic, conceited, exaggerated, extravagant, flaunting, grandiloquent, grandiose, highfalutin (*informal*), high-flown, high-sounding, hollow, inflated, magniloquent, mannered, ostentatious, overambitious, pompous, puffed up, showy, snobbish, specious, vainglorious
▷ **Antonyms** modest, natural, plain, simple, unaffected, unassuming, unpretentious

preternatural abnormal, anomalous, extraordinary, inexplicable, irregular, marvellous, miraculous, mysterious, odd, peculiar, strange, supernatural, unaccountable, unearthly, unnatural, unusual

pretext affectation, alleged reason, appearance, cloak, cover, device, excuse, guise, mask, ploy, pretence, red herring, ruse, semblance, show, simulation, veil

prettify adorn, deck out, decorate, doll up (*slang*), do up, embellish, garnish, gild, ornament, pretty up, tart up (*Brit. slang*), titivate, trick out, trim

pretty *adjective* **1**. appealing, attractive, beautiful, bonny, charming, comely, cute, fair, good-looking, graceful, lovely, personable **2**. bijou, dainty, delicate, elegant, fine, neat, nice, pleasing, tasteful, trim *~adverb* **3**. *informal* fairly, kind of (*informal*), moderately, quite, rather, reasonably, somewhat
▷ **Antonyms** (*sense 1*) plain, ugly, unattractive, unshapely, unsightly

prevail 1. be victorious, carry the day, gain mastery, overcome, overrule, prove superior, succeed, triumph, win **2**. abound, be current, be prevalent, be widespread, exist generally, obtain, predominate, preponderate **3**. (*often with* **on** *or* **upon**) bring round, convince, dispose, incline, induce, influence, persuade, prompt, sway, talk into, win over

prevailing 1. common, current, customary, established, fashionable, general, in style, in vogue, ordinary, popular, prevalent, set, usual, widespread **2**. dominant, influential, main, operative, predominating, preponderating, principal, ruling

prevalence 1. acceptance, commonness, common occurrence, currency, frequency, pervasiveness, popularity, profusion, regularity, ubiquity, universality **2**. ascendancy, hold, mastery, predominance, preponderance, primacy, rule, sway

prevalent 1. accepted, common, commonplace, current, customary, established, everyday, extensive, frequent, general, habitual, popular, rampant, rife, ubiquitous, universal, usual, widespread **2**. ascendant, compelling, dominant, governing, powerful, predominant, prevailing, successful, superior
▷ **Antonyms** (*sense 1*) confined, infrequent, limited, localized, rare, restricted, uncommon, unusual

prevaricate beat about the bush, beg the question, cavil, deceive, dodge, equivocate, evade, flannel (*Brit. informal*), give a false colour to, hedge, lie, palter, quibble, shift, shuffle, stretch the truth, tergiversate
▷ **Antonyms** be blunt, be direct, be frank, be straightforward, come straight to the point, not beat about the bush

prevarication cavilling, deceit, deception, equivocation, evasion, falsehood, falsification, lie, misrepresentation, pretence, quibbling, tergiversation, untruth

prevaricator Ananias, deceiver, dissembler, dodger, equivocator, evader, fibber, hypocrite, liar, pettifogger, quibbler, sophist

prevent anticipate, avert, avoid, balk, bar, block, check, counteract, defend against, foil, forestall, frustrate, hamper, head off, hinder, impede, inhibit, intercept, nip in the bud, obstruct, obviate, preclude, restrain, stave off, stop, thwart, ward off
▷ **Antonyms** allow, encourage, help, incite, permit, support, urge

prevention **1.** anticipation, avoidance, deterrence, elimination, forestalling, obviation, precaution, preclusion, prophylaxis, safeguard, thwarting **2.** bar, check, deterrence, frustration, hindrance, impediment, interruption, obstacle, obstruction, stoppage

preventive, preventative *adjective* **1.** hampering, hindering, impeding, obstructive **2.** counteractive, deterrent, inhibitory, precautionary, prophylactic, protective, shielding *~noun* **3.** block, hindrance, impediment, obstacle, obstruction **4.** deterrent, neutralizer, prevention, prophylactic, protection, protective, remedy, safeguard, shield

previous **1.** antecedent, anterior, earlier, erstwhile, ex-, foregoing, former, one-time, past, preceding, prior, quondam, sometime **2.** *informal* ahead of oneself, precipitate, premature, too early, too soon, untimely
▷ **Antonyms** (*sense 1*) consequent, following, later, subsequent, succeeding

previously at one time, a while ago, before, beforehand, earlier, formerly, heretofore, hitherto, in advance, in anticipation, in days *or* years gone by, in the past, once, then, until now

prey *noun* **1.** game, kill, quarry **2.** dupe, fall guy (*informal*), mark, mug (*Brit. slang*), target, victim *~verb* **3.** devour, eat, feed upon, hunt, live off, seize **4.** blackmail, bleed (*informal*), bully, exploit, intimidate, take advantage of, terrorize, victimize **5.** burden, distress, hang over, haunt, oppress, trouble, weigh down, weigh heavily, worry

price *noun* **1.** amount, asking price, assessment, bill, charge, cost, damage (*informal*), estimate, expenditure, expense, face value, fee, figure, outlay, payment, rate, valuation, value, worth **2.** consequences, cost, penalty, sacrifice, toll **3.** bounty, compensation, premium, recompense, reward **4. at any price** anyhow, cost what it may, expense no object, no matter what the cost, regardless, whatever the cost **5. beyond price** inestimable, invaluable, of incalculable value, precious, priceless, treasured, without price *~verb* **6.** assess, cost, estimate, evaluate, put a price on, rate, value

priceless **1.** beyond price, cherished, costly, dear, expensive, incalculable, incomparable, inestimable, invaluable, irreplaceable, precious, prized, rare, rich, treasured, worth a king's ransom, worth one's *or* its weight in gold **2.** *informal* absurd, amusing, comic, droll, funny, hilarious, killing (*informal*), rib-tickling, ridiculous, riotous, side-splitting
▷ **Antonyms** cheap, cheapo (*informal*), common, inexpensive, worthless

pricey, pricy costly, dear, exorbitant, expensive, extortionate, high-priced, over the odds (*Brit. informal*), steep (*informal*)

prick *verb* **1.** bore, impale, jab, lance, perforate, pierce, pink, punch, puncture, stab **2.** bite, itch, prickle, smart, sting, tingle **3.** cut, distress, grieve, move, pain, stab, touch, trouble, wound **4.** (*usually with* **up**) point, raise, rise, stand erect *~noun* **5.** cut, gash, hole, perforation, pinhole, puncture, wound **6.** gnawing, pang, prickle, smart, spasm, sting, twinge

prickle *noun* **1.** barb, needle, point, spike, spine, spur, thorn **2.** chill, formication, goose flesh, paraesthesia (*Medical*), pins and needles (*informal*), smart, tickle, tingle, tingling *~verb* **3.** itch, smart, sting, tingle, twitch **4.** jab, nick, prick, stick

prickly **1.** barbed, brambly, briery, bristly, spiny, thorny **2.** crawling, itchy, pricking, prickling, scratchy, sharp, smarting, stinging, tingling **3.** bad-tempered, cantankerous, edgy, fractious, grumpy, irritable, liverish, peevish, pettish, petulant, ratty (*Brit. & N.Z. informal*), shirty (*slang, chiefly Brit.*), snappish, stroppy (*Brit. slang*), tetchy, touchy, waspish **4.** complicated, difficult, intricate, involved, knotty, thorny, ticklish, tricky, troublesome, trying

pride *noun* **1.** *amour-propre,* dignity, honour, self-esteem, self-respect, self-worth **2.** arrogance, bigheadedness (*informal*), conceit, egotism, haughtiness, hauteur, hubris, loftiness, *morgue,* presumption, pretension, pretentiousness, self-importance, self-love, smugness, snobbery, superciliousness, vainglory, vanity **3.** boast, gem, jewel, pride and joy, prize, treasure **4.** delight, gratifica-

tion, joy, pleasure, satisfaction **5.** best, choice, cream, elite, flower, glory, pick *~verb* **6.** be proud of, boast, brag, congratulate oneself, crow, exult, flatter oneself, glory in, pique, plume, preen, revel in, take pride, vaunt
▷ **Antonyms** (*sense 1*) humility, meekness, modesty

priest churchman, clergyman, cleric, curate, divine, ecclesiastic, father, father confessor, holy man, man of God, man of the cloth, minister, padre (*informal*), pastor, vicar

priestly canonical, clerical, ecclesiastic, hieratic, pastoral, priestlike, sacerdotal

prig goody-goody (*informal*), Holy Joe (*informal*), Holy Willie (*informal*), Mrs Grundy, old maid (*informal*), pedant, prude, puritan, stuffed shirt (*informal*)

priggish goody-goody (*informal*), holier-than-thou, narrow-minded, pedantic, prim, prudish, puritanical, self-righteous, self-satisfied, smug, starchy (*informal*), stiff, stuffy

prim demure, fastidious, formal, fussy, niminy-piminy, old-maidish (*informal*), particular, precise, priggish, prissy (*informal*), proper, prudish, puritanical, schoolmarmish (*Brit. informal*), starchy (*informal*), stiff, strait-laced
▷ **Antonyms** carefree, casual, easy-going, informal, laid-back, relaxed

primacy ascendancy, command, dominance, dominion, leadership, pre-eminence, superiority, supremacy

prima donna diva, leading lady, star

primal 1. earliest, first, initial, original, primary, prime, primitive, primordial, pristine **2.** central, chief, first, greatest, highest, main, major, most important, paramount, prime, principal

primarily 1. above all, basically, chiefly, especially, essentially, for the most part, fundamentally, generally, largely, mainly, mostly, on the whole, principally **2.** at first, at *or* from the start, first and foremost, initially, in the beginning, in the first place, originally

primary 1. best, capital, cardinal, chief, dominant, first, greatest, highest, leading, main, paramount, prime, principal, top **2.** aboriginal, earliest, initial, original, primal, primeval, primitive, primordial, pristine **3.** basic, beginning, bog-standard (*informal*), elemental, essential, fundamental, radical, ultimate, underlying **4.** elementary, introductory, rudimentary, simple
▷ **Antonyms** (*sense 1*) inferior, lesser, lowest, subordinate, supplementary, unimportant (*sense 4*) ensuing, following, later, secondary, subsequent, succeeding

prime *adjective* **1.** best, capital, choice, excellent, first-class, first-rate, grade A, highest, quality, select, selected, superior, top **2.** basic, bog-standard (*informal*), earliest, fundamental, original, primary, underlying **3.** chief, leading, main, predominant, pre-eminent, primary, principal, ruling, senior *~noun* **4.** best days, bloom, flower, full flowering, height, heyday, maturity, peak, perfection, zenith **5.** beginning, morning, opening, spring, start *~verb* **6.** break in, coach, fit, get ready, groom, make ready, prepare, train **7.** brief, clue in (*informal*), clue up (*informal*), fill in (*informal*), gen up (*Brit. informal*), give someone the lowdown (*informal*), inform, notify, tell

primeval, primaeval ancient, earliest, early, first, old, original, prehistoric, primal, primitive, primordial, pristine

primitive 1. earliest, early, elementary, first, original, primary, primeval, primordial, pristine **2.** barbarian, barbaric, crude, rough, rude, rudimentary, savage, simple, uncivilized, uncultivated, undeveloped, unrefined **3.** childlike, naive, simple, undeveloped, unsophisticated, untrained, untutored
▷ **Antonyms** (*sense 1*) advanced, later, modern (*sense 2*) civilized, comfortable, developed, elaborate, refined (*sense 3*) adult, developed, mature, sophisticated, trained, tutored

primordial 1. earliest, first, prehistoric, primal, primeval, primitive, pristine **2.** basic, elemental, fundamental, original, radical

primp be in full fig (*slang*), deck out, doll up (*slang*), dress up, fig up (*slang*), gussy up (*slang*), prank, preen, prink, put on one's best bib and tucker (*informal*), put on one's gladrags (*slang*)

prince lord, monarch, potentate, ruler, sovereign

princely 1. bounteous, bountiful, generous, gracious, lavish, liberal, magnanimous, munificent, open-handed, rich **2.** august, dignified, grand, high-born, imperial, imposing, lofty, magnificent, majestic, noble, regal, royal, sovereign, stately

principal *adjective* **1.** arch, capital, cardinal, chief, controlling, dominant, essential, first, foremost, highest, key, leading, main, most important, paramount, pre-eminent, primary, prime, strongest *~noun* **2.** boss (*informal*), chief, director, head, leader, master, ruler, superintendent **3.** dean, director, head (*informal*), headmaster, headmistress, head teacher, master, rector **4.** assets, capital, capital funds, money **5.** first violin, lead, leader, star
▷ **Antonyms** auxiliary, inferior, minor, subordinate, subsidiary, supplementary, weakest

principally above all, chiefly, especially, first and foremost, for the most part, in the main, largely, mainly, mostly, particularly, predominantly, primarily

principle 1. assumption, axiom, canon, criterion, dictum, doctrine, dogma, ethic, formula, fundamental, golden rule, law, maxim, moral law, precept, proposition, rule, standard, truth, verity 2. attitude, belief, code, credo, ethic, morality, opinion, tenet 3. conscience, integrity, morals, probity, rectitude, scruples, sense of duty, sense of honour, uprightness 4. **in principle** ideally, in essence, in theory, theoretically

principled conscientious, correct, decent, ethical, high-minded, honourable, just, moral, righteous, right-minded, scrupulous, upright, virtuous

prink adorn, deck, doll up (*slang*), dress to kill (*informal*), dress up, dress (up) to the nines (*informal*), fig up (*slang*), groom, gussy up (*slang*), prank, preen, primp, titivate, trick out

print *verb* 1. engrave, go to press, impress, imprint, issue, mark, publish, put to bed (*informal*), run off, stamp *~noun* 2. book, magazine, newspaper, newsprint, periodical, printed matter, publication, typescript 3. **in print: a.** in black and white, on paper, on the streets, out, printed, published **b.** available, current, in the shops, obtainable, on the market, on the shelves 4. **out of print** no longer published, o.p., unavailable, unobtainable 5. copy, engraving, photo (*informal*), photograph, picture, reproduction 6. characters, face, font (*chiefly U.S.*), fount, lettering, letters, type, typeface

prior 1. aforementioned, antecedent, anterior, earlier, foregoing, former, preceding, pre-existent, pre-existing, previous 2. **prior to** before, earlier than, preceding, previous to

priority first concern, greater importance, precedence, pre-eminence, preference, prerogative, rank, right of way, seniority, superiority, supremacy, the lead

priory abbey, cloister, convent, monastery, nunnery, religious house

prison calaboose (*U.S. informal*), can (*slang*), choky (*slang*), clink (*slang*), confinement, cooler (*slang*), dungeon, gaol, glasshouse (*Military informal*), jail, jug (*slang*), lockup, nick (*Brit. slang*), penal institution, penitentiary (*U.S.*), poky *or* pokey (*U.S. & Canad. slang*), pound, quod (*slang*), slammer (*slang*), stir (*slang*)

prisoner 1. con (*slang*), convict, jailbird, lag (*slang*) 2. captive, detainee, hostage, internee

prissy fastidious, finicky, fussy, niminy-piminy, old-maidish (*informal*), overnice, precious, prim, prim and proper, prudish, schoolmarmish (*Brit. informal*), squeamish, strait-laced

pristine 1. earliest, first, former, initial, original, primal, primary, primeval, primitive, primordial 2. immaculate, new, pure, uncorrupted, undefiled, unspoiled, unsullied, untouched, virgin, virginal

privacy 1. isolation, privateness, retirement, retreat, seclusion, separateness, sequestration, solitude 2. clandestineness, concealment, confidentiality, secrecy

private *adjective* 1. clandestine, closet, confidential, covert, hush-hush (*informal*), in camera, inside, off the record, privy (*archaic*), secret, unofficial 2. exclusive, individual, intimate, own, particular, personal, reserved, special 3. independent, nonpublic 4. concealed, isolated, not overlooked, retired, secluded, secret, separate, sequestered, solitary, withdrawn 5. **in private** behind closed doors, confidentially, in camera, in secret, personally, privately *~noun* 6. enlisted man (*U.S.*), private soldier, squaddie *or* squaddy (*Brit. slang*), tommy (*Brit. informal*), Tommy Atkins (*Brit. informal*)

▷ **Antonyms** (*sense 1*) disclosed, known, official, open, public, revealed (*sense 2*) common, general, open, public, unlimited, unrestricted (*sense 3*) bustling, busy, frequented, outgoing, sociable, unsecluded

privation destitution, distress, hardship, indigence, lack, loss, misery, necessity, need, neediness, penury, poverty, suffering, want

privilege advantage, benefit, birthright, claim, concession, due, entitlement, franchise, freedom, immunity, liberty, prerogative, right, sanction

privileged 1. advantaged, elite, entitled, favoured, honoured, indulged, powerful, ruling, special 2. allowed, empowered, exempt, free, granted, licensed, sanctioned, vested 3. *of information* confidential, exceptional, inside, not for publication, off the record, privy, special

privy *adjective* 1. (*with* **to**) apprised of, aware of, cognizant of, hip to (*slang*), informed, in on, in the know (*informal*), wise to (*slang*) 2. *archaic* confidential, hidden, hush-hush (*informal*), off the record, personal, private, secret *~noun* 3. bog (*slang*), closet, earth closet, latrine, lavatory, outside toilet, *pissoir*

prize[1] *noun* 1. accolade, award, honour, premium, reward, trophy 2. haul, jackpot, purse, stakes, windfall, winnings 3. aim, ambition, conquest, desire, gain, goal, Holy Grail (*informal*), hope 4. booty, capture, loot, pickings, pillage, plunder, spoil(s), trophy *~adjective* 5. award-winning, best, champion, first-rate, outstanding, top, top-notch (*informal*), winning

prize[2] *verb* appreciate, cherish, esteem, hold dear, regard highly, set store by, treasure, value

prizefighter boxer, bruiser (*informal*), fighter, pug (*slang*), pugilist

prizefighting boxing, fighting, pugilism, the noble art *or* science, the prize ring, the ring

probability chance(s), expectation, liabil~ ity, likelihood, likeliness, odds, pre~ sumption, prospect

probable apparent, credible, feasible, likely, most likely, odds-on, on the cards, ostensible, plausible, possible, presumable, presumed, reasonable, seeming, verisimilar

▷ **Antonyms** doubtful, improbable, not likely, unlikely

probably as likely as not, doubtless, in all likelihood, in all probability, likely, maybe, most likely, perchance (*archaic*), perhaps, possibly, presumably

probation apprenticeship, examination, initiation, novitiate, test, trial, trial pe~ riod

probe *verb* **1.** examine, explore, go into, investigate, look into, query, research, scrutinize, search, sift, sound, test, verify, work over **2.** explore, feel around, poke, prod *~noun* **3.** detection, examina~ tion, exploration, inquest, inquiry, in~ vestigation, research, scrutiny, study

probity equity, fairness, fidelity, good~ ness, honesty, honour, integrity, justice, morality, rectitude, righteousness, sin~ cerity, trustworthiness, truthfulness, uprightness, virtue, worth

problem *noun* **1.** can of worms (*informal*), complication, difficulty, dilemma, dis~ agreement, dispute, disputed point, doubt, Gordian knot, hard nut to crack (*informal*), how-do-you-do (*informal*), point at issue, predicament, quandary, trouble **2.** brain-teaser (*informal*), co~ nundrum, enigma, poser, puzzle, ques~ tion, riddle, teaser *~adjective* **3.** delin~ quent, difficult, intractable, uncontrol~ lable, unmanageable, unruly

problematic chancy (*informal*), debatable, doubtful, dubious, enigmatic, moot, open to doubt, problematical, puzzling, questionable, tricky, uncertain, unset~ tled

▷ **Antonyms** beyond question, certain, clear, definite, indisputable, settled, un~ debatable, unquestionable

procedure action, conduct, course, cus~ tom, form, formula, method, modus op~ erandi, operation, performance, plan of action, policy, practice, process, routine, scheme, step, strategy, system, transac~ tion

proceed **1.** advance, carry on, continue, get going, get on with, get under way with, go ahead, go on, make a start, move on, press on, progress, set in mo~ tion **2.** arise, come, derive, emanate, en~ sue, flow, follow, issue, originate, result, spring, stem

▷ **Antonyms** (*sense 1*) break off, cease, discontinue, end, get behind, halt, leave off, pack in (*Brit. informal*), retreat, stop

proceeding **1.** act, action, course of action, deed, measure, move, occurrence, pro~ cedure, process, step, undertaking, ven~ ture **2.** (*plural*) account, affairs, annals, archives, business, dealings, doings, matters, minutes, records, report, transactions

proceeds earnings, gain, income, prod~ uce, products, profit, receipts, returns, revenue, takings, yield

process *noun* **1.** action, course, course of action, manner, means, measure, meth~ od, mode, operation, performance, prac~ tice, procedure, proceeding, system, transaction **2.** advance, course, develop~ ment, evolution, formation, growth, movement, progress, progression, stage, step, unfolding **3.** *Law* action, case, suit, trial *~verb* **4.** deal with, dispose of, fulfil, handle, take care of **5.** alter, convert, prepare, refine, transform, treat

procession **1.** cavalcade, column, cortege, file, march, motorcade, parade, train **2.** course, cycle, run, sequence, series, string, succession, train

proclaim advertise, affirm, announce, blaze (abroad), blazon (abroad), circu~ late, declare, enunciate, give out, her~ ald, indicate, make known, profess, promulgate, publish, shout from the housetops (*informal*), show, trumpet

▷ **Antonyms** conceal, hush up, keep back, keep secret, suppress, withhold

proclamation announcement, declaration, decree, edict, manifesto, notice, notifi~ cation, promulgation, pronouncement, pronunciamento, publication

proclivity bent, bias, disposition, facility, inclination, leaning, liableness, pen~ chant, predilection, predisposition, proneness, propensity, tendency, weak~ ness

procrastinate adjourn, be dilatory, dally, defer, delay, drag one's feet (*informal*), gain time, play a waiting game, play for time, postpone, prolong, protract, put off, retard, stall, temporize

▷ **Antonyms** advance, expedite, get on with, hasten, hurry (up), proceed, speed up

procreate beget, breed, bring into being, engender, father, generate, mother, produce, propagate, reproduce, sire

procure acquire, appropriate, buy, come by, earn, effect, find, gain, get, get hold of, land, lay hands on, manage to get, obtain, pick up, purchase, score (*slang*), secure, win

procurer bawd (*archaic*), madam, pander,

panderer, pimp, procuress, white-slaver, whoremaster (*archaic*)

prod *verb* **1.** dig, drive, elbow, jab, nudge, poke, prick, propel, push, shove **2.** egg on, goad, impel, incite, motivate, move, prompt, put a bomb under (*informal*), rouse, spur, stimulate, stir up, urge *~noun* **3.** boost, dig, elbow, jab, nudge, poke, push, shove **4.** goad, poker, spur, stick **5.** boost, cue, prompt, reminder, signal, stimulus

prodigal *adjective* **1.** excessive, extravagant, immoderate, improvident, intemperate, profligate, reckless, spendthrift, squandering, wanton, wasteful **2.** bounteous, bountiful, copious, exuberant, lavish, luxuriant, profuse, sumptuous, superabundant, teeming *~noun* **3.** big spender, profligate, spendthrift, squanderer, wastrel
▷ **Antonyms** (*sense 1*) economical, frugal, miserly, parsimonious, sparing, stingy, thrifty, tight (*sense 2*) deficient, lacking, meagre, scanty, scarce, short, sparse

prodigality 1. abandon, dissipation, excess, extravagance, immoderation, intemperance, profligacy, recklessness, squandering, wantonness, waste, wastefulness **2.** abundance, amplitude, bounteousness, bounty, copiousness, cornucopia, exuberance, horn of plenty, lavishness, luxuriance, plenteousness, plenty, profusion, richness, sumptuousness

prodigious 1. colossal, enormous, giant, gigantic, huge, immeasurable, immense, inordinate, mammoth, massive, monstrous, monumental, stellar (*informal*), stupendous, tremendous, vast **2.** abnormal, amazing, astounding, dramatic, exceptional, extraordinary, fabulous, fantastic (*informal*), flabbergasting (*informal*), impressive, marvellous, miraculous, phenomenal, remarkable, staggering, startling, striking, stupendous, unusual, wonderful
▷ **Antonyms** (*sense 1*) negligible, small, tiny (*sense 2*) normal, ordinary, unexceptional, unimpressive, unremarkable, usual

prodigy 1. brainbox, child genius, genius, mastermind, talent, whizz (*informal*), whizz kid (*informal*), wizard, wonder child, wunderkind **2.** marvel, miracle, one in a million, phenomenon, rare bird (*informal*), sensation, wonder **3.** abnormality, curiosity, freak, grotesque, monster, monstrosity, mutation, spectacle

produce *verb* **1.** compose, construct, create, develop, fabricate, invent, make, manufacture, originate, put together, turn out **2.** afford, bear, beget, breed, bring forth, deliver, engender, furnish, give, render, supply, yield **3.** bring about, cause, effect, generate, give rise to, make for, occasion, provoke, set off **4.** advance, bring forward, bring to light, demonstrate, exhibit, offer, present, put forward, set forth, show **5.** direct, do, exhibit, mount, present, put before the public, put on, show, stage **6.** *Geometry* extend, lengthen, prolong, protract *~noun* **7.** crop, fruit and vegetables, greengrocery, harvest, product, yield

producer 1. director, impresario, *régisseur* **2.** farmer, grower, maker, manufacturer

product 1. artefact, commodity, concoction, creation, goods, invention, merchandise, produce, production, work **2.** consequence, effect, end result, fruit, issue, legacy, offshoot, outcome, result, returns, spin-off, upshot, yield

production 1. assembly, construction, creation, fabrication, formation, making, manufacture, manufacturing, origination, preparation, producing **2.** direction, management, presentation, staging

productive 1. creative, dynamic, energetic, fecund, fertile, fruitful, generative, inventive, plentiful, producing, prolific, rich, teeming, vigorous **2.** advantageous, beneficial, constructive, effective, fruitful, gainful, gratifying, profitable, rewarding, useful, valuable, worthwhile
▷ **Antonyms** barren, poor, sterile, unfertile, unfruitful, unproductive, unprofitable, useless

productivity abundance, mass production, output, production, productive capacity, productiveness, work rate, yield

profane *adjective* **1.** disrespectful, godless, heathen, idolatrous, impious, impure, irreligious, irreverent, pagan, sacrilegious, sinful, ungodly, wicked **2.** lay, secular, temporal, unconsecrated, unhallowed, unholy, unsanctified, worldly **3.** abusive, blasphemous, coarse, crude, filthy, foul, obscene, vulgar *~verb* **4.** abuse, commit sacrilege, contaminate, debase, defile, desecrate, misuse, pervert, pollute, prostitute, violate, vitiate
▷ **Antonyms** *~adjective* clean, decorous, holy, proper, religious, respectful, reverent, sacred, spiritual

profanity abuse, blasphemy, curse, cursing, execration, foul language, four-letter word, impiety, imprecation, irreverence, malediction, obscenity, profaneness, sacrilege, swearing, swearword

profess 1. acknowledge, admit, affirm, announce, assert, asseverate, aver, avow, certify, confess, confirm, declare, maintain, own, proclaim, state, vouch **2.** act as if, allege, call oneself, claim, dissemble, fake, feign, let on, make out, pretend, purport, sham

professed 1. avowed, certified, confessed, confirmed, declared, proclaimed, self-acknowledged, self-confessed **2.** alleged, apparent, ostensible, pretended, purported, self-styled, so-called, *soi-disant,* supposed, would-be

professedly **1.** allegedly, apparently, by one's own account, falsely, ostensibly, purportedly, supposedly, under the pre~ text of **2.** admittedly, avowedly, by open declaration, confessedly

profession **1.** business, calling, career, employment, line, line of work, métier, occupation, office, position, sphere, vo~ cation, walk of life **2.** acknowledgment, affirmation, assertion, attestation, avowal, claim, confession, declaration, statement, testimony, vow

professional **1.** *adjective* ace (*informal*), adept, competent, crack (*slang*), effi~ cient, experienced, expert, finished, masterly, polished, practised, proficient, qualified, skilled, slick, trained **2.** *~noun* adept, authority, buff (*informal*), dab hand (*Brit. informal*), expert, hotshot (*informal*), maestro, master, maven (*U.S.*), past master, pro (*informal*), spe~ cialist, virtuoso, whizz (*informal*), wiz~ ard

▷ **Antonyms** amateurish, incapable, in~ competent, inefficient, inept, inexperi~ enced, unpolished, unqualified, un~ skilled, untrained

professor don (*Brit.*), fellow (*Brit.*), head of faculty, prof (*informal*)

proffer extend, hand, hold out, offer, pre~ sent, propose, propound, submit, sug~ gest, tender, volunteer

proficiency ability, accomplishment, ap~ titude, competence, craft, dexterity, ex~ pertise, expertness, facility, knack, know-how (*informal*), mastery, skilful~ ness, skill, talent

proficient able, accomplished, adept, apt, capable, clever, competent, conversant, efficient, experienced, expert, gifted, masterly, qualified, skilful, skilled, tal~ ented, trained, versed

▷ **Antonyms** bad, incapable, incompe~ tent, inept, unaccomplished, unskilled

profile *noun* **1.** contour, drawing, figure, form, outline, portrait, shape, side view, silhouette, sketch **2.** biography, charac~ terization, character sketch, sketch, thumbnail sketch, vignette **3.** analysis, chart, diagram, examination, graph, re~ view, study, survey, table

profit *noun* **1.** (*often plural*) bottom line, earnings, emoluments, gain, percentage (*informal*), proceeds, receipts, return, revenue, surplus, takings, winnings, yield **2.** advancement, advantage, avail, benefit, gain, good, interest, mileage (*informal*), use, value *~verb* **3.** aid, avail, benefit, be of advantage to, better, con~ tribute, gain, help, improve, promote, serve, stand in good stead **4.** capitalize on, cash in on (*informal*), exploit, learn from, make capital of, make good use of, make the most of, put to good use, rake in (*informal*), reap the benefit of, take advantage of, turn to advantage *or* ac~ count, use, utilize **5.** clean up (*informal*), clear, earn, gain, make a good thing of (*informal*), make a killing (*informal*), make money

profitable **1.** commercial, cost-effective, fruitful, gainful, lucrative, money-making, paying, remunerative, reward~ ing, worthwhile **2.** advantageous, ben~ eficial, economic, expedient, fruitful, productive, rewarding, serviceable, useful, valuable, worthwhile

▷ **Antonyms** disadvantageous, fruitless, unremunerative, unrewarding, useless, vain, worthless

profiteer **1.** *noun* exploiter, racketeer **2.** *~verb* exploit, fleece, make a quick buck (*slang*), make someone pay through the nose, overcharge, racketeer, skin (*slang*), sting (*informal*)

profitless basket case, bootless, fruitless, futile, idle, ineffective, ineffectual, pointless, thankless, to no purpose, un~ availing, unproductive, unprofitable, unremunerative, useless, vain, worth~ less

profligacy **1.** abandon, corruption, de~ bauchery, degeneracy, depravity, dissi~ pation, dissoluteness, dolce vita, immo~ rality, laxity, libertinism, licentious~ ness, promiscuity, unrestraint, wanton~ ness **2.** excess, extravagance, improvi~ dence, lavishness, prodigality, reckless~ ness, squandering, waste, wastefulness

profligate *adjective* **1.** abandoned, cor~ rupt, debauched, degenerate, depraved, dissipated, dissolute, immoral, iniqui~ tous, libertine, licentious, loose, promis~ cuous, shameless, sink, unprincipled, vicious, vitiated, wanton, wicked, wild **2.** extravagant, immoderate, improvident, prodigal, reckless, spendthrift, squan~ dering, wasteful *~noun* **3.** debauchee, degenerate, dissipater, libertine, rake, reprobate, roué **4.** prodigal, spendthrift, squanderer, waster, wastrel

▷ **Antonyms** (*sense 1*) chaste, decent, moral, principled, pure, upright, virgin~ al, virtuous

profound **1.** abstruse, deep, discerning, erudite, learned, penetrating, philo~ sophical, recondite, sagacious, sage, serious, skilled, subtle, thoughtful, weighty, wise **2.** abysmal, bottomless, cavernous, deep, fathomless, yawning **3.** abject, acute, deeply felt, extreme, great, heartfelt, heartrending, hearty, intense, keen, sincere **4.** absolute, com~ plete, consummate, exhaustive, exten~ sive, extreme, far-reaching, intense, out-and-out, pronounced, serious (*infor~ mal*), thoroughgoing, total, unqualified, utter

▷ **Antonyms** (*sense 1*) imprudent, stupid, thoughtless, uneducated, uninformed, unknowledgeable, unwise (*sense 3*) in~ sincere, shallow (*sense 4*) slight, super~ ficial

profoundly abjectly, acutely, deeply, extremely, from the bottom of one's heart, greatly, heartily, intensely, keenly, seriously, sincerely, thoroughly, to the core, to the nth degree, very

profundity 1. acuity, acumen, depth, erudition, insight, intelligence, learning, penetration, perceptiveness, perspicacity, perspicuity, sagacity, wisdom 2. depth, extremity, intensity, seriousness, severity, strength

profuse 1. abundant, ample, bountiful, copious, luxuriant, overflowing, plentiful, prolific, teeming 2. excessive, extravagant, exuberant, fulsome, generous, immoderate, lavish, liberal, open-handed, prodigal, unstinting
▷ **Antonyms** (*sense 1*) deficient, inadequate, meagre, scanty, scarce, skimpy, sparse (*sense 2*) frugal, illiberal, moderate, provident, thrifty

profusion abundance, bounty, copiousness, cornucopia, excess, extravagance, exuberance, glut, lavishness, luxuriance, multitude, oversupply, plenitude, plethora, prodigality, quantity, riot, superabundance, superfluity, surplus, wealth

progenitor 1. ancestor, begetter, forebear, forefather, parent, primogenitor, procreator 2. antecedent, forerunner, instigator, originator, precursor, predecessor, source

progeny breed, children, descendants, family, issue, lineage, offspring, posterity, race, scions, seed (*chiefly biblical*), stock, young

prognosis diagnosis, expectation, forecast, prediction, prognostication, projection, speculation, surmise

prognostic 1. *adjective* diagnostic, foretelling, indicating, predicting, predictive, prophetic 2. *~noun* forecast, indication, omen, portent, preindication, sign, symptom, warning

prognosticate 1. divine, forecast, foretell, predict, presage, prophesy, soothsay, vaticinate (*rare*) 2. augur, betoken, forebode, foreshadow, harbinger, herald, point to, portend, presage

prognostication expectation, forecast, prediction, prognosis, projection, prophecy, speculation, surmise

programme *noun* 1. agenda, curriculum, line-up, list, listing, list of players, order of events, order of the day, plan, schedule, syllabus, timetable 2. broadcast, performance, presentation, production, show 3. design, order of the day, plan, plan of action, procedure, project, scheme *~verb* 4. arrange, bill, book, design, engage, formulate, itemize, lay on, line up, list, map out, plan, prearrange, schedule, work out

progress *noun* 1. advance, course, movement, onward course, passage, progression, way 2. advance, advancement, amelioration, betterment, breakthrough, development, gain, gaining ground, growth, headway, improvement, increase, progression, promotion, step forward 3. **in progress** being done, going on, happening, occurring, proceeding, taking place, under way *~verb* 4. advance, come on, continue, cover ground, forge ahead, gain ground, gather way, get on, go forward, make headway, make inroads (into), make one's way, make strides, move on, proceed, travel 5. advance, ameliorate, better, blossom, develop, gain, grow, improve, increase, mature
▷ **Antonyms** *~noun* decline, failure, recession, regression, relapse, retrogression *~verb* decrease, get behind, lose, lose ground, recede, regress, retrogress

progression 1. advance, advancement, furtherance, gain, headway, movement forward, progress 2. chain, course, cycle, order, sequence, series, string, succession

progressive 1. accelerating, advancing, continuing, continuous, developing, escalating, growing, increasing, intensifying, ongoing 2. advanced, avant-garde, dynamic, enlightened, enterprising, forward-looking, go-ahead, liberal, modern, radical, reformist, revolutionary, up-and-coming

prohibit 1. ban, debar, disallow, forbid, interdict, outlaw, proscribe, veto 2. constrain, hamper, hinder, impede, make impossible, obstruct, preclude, prevent, restrict, rule out, stop
▷ **Antonyms** allow, authorize, command, consent to, endure, further, give leave, let, license, order, permit, suffer, tolerate

prohibited banned, barred, forbidden, not allowed, off limits, proscribed, taboo, *verboten,* vetoed

prohibition 1. constraint, disqualification, exclusion, forbiddance, interdiction, negation, obstruction, prevention, restriction 2. ban, bar, boycott, disallowance, embargo, injunction, interdict, proscription, veto

prohibitive 1. forbidding, prohibiting, proscriptive, repressive, restraining, restrictive, suppressive 2. *especially of prices* beyond one's means, excessive, exorbitant, extortionate, high-priced, preposterous, sky-high, steep (*informal*)

project *noun* 1. activity, assignment, design, enterprise, job, occupation, plan, programme, proposal, scheme, task, undertaking, venture, work *~verb* 2. contemplate, contrive, design, devise, draft, frame, map out, outline, plan, propose, purpose, scheme 3. cast, discharge, fling, hurl, launch, make carry, propel, shoot, throw, transmit 4. beetle, bulge, extend, jut, overhang, protrude, stand out, stick out **5.** calculate, estimate, extrapolate, forecast, gauge, predetermine, predict, reckon

projectile bullet, missile, rocket, shell

projection **1.** bulge, eaves, jut, ledge, overhang, protrusion, protuberance, ridge, shelf, sill **2.** blueprint, diagram, map, outline, plan, representation **3.** calculation, computation, estimate, estimation, extrapolation, forecast, prediction, reckoning

proletarian **1.** *adjective* cloth-cap (*informal*), common, plebeian, working-class **2.** *~noun* commoner, Joe Bloggs (*Brit. informal*), man of the people, pleb, plebeian, prole (*derogatory slang, chiefly Brit.*), worker

proletariat commonalty, commoners, hoi polloi, labouring classes, lower classes, lower orders, plebs, proles (*derogatory slang, chiefly Brit.*), the common people, the great unwashed (*informal & derogatory*), the herd, the masses, the rabble, wage-earners, working class

▷ **Antonyms** aristo (*informal*), aristocracy, gentry, nobility, peerage, ruling class, upper class, upper crust (*informal*)

proliferate breed, burgeon, escalate, expand, grow rapidly, increase, multiply, mushroom, run riot, snowball

proliferation build-up, concentration, escalation, expansion, extension, increase, intensification, multiplication, spread, step-up (*informal*)

prolific abundant, bountiful, copious, fecund, fertile, fruitful, generative, luxuriant, productive, profuse, rank, rich, teeming

▷ **Antonyms** barren, fruitless, infertile, sterile, unfruitful, unproductive, unprolific

prolix boring, diffuse, digressive, discursive, dragged out, full of verbiage, lengthy, long, long-drawn-out, long-winded, prolonged, protracted, rambling, spun out, tedious, tiresome, verbose, wordy

prolixity boringness, circuity, diffuseness, discursiveness, long-windedness, maundering, pleonasm, rambling, redundancy, tautology, tediousness, verbiage, verboseness, verbosity, wandering, wordiness

prologue exordium, foreword, introduction, preamble, preface, preliminary, prelude, proem

prolong carry on, continue, delay, drag out, draw out, extend, lengthen, make longer, perpetuate, protract, spin out, stretch

▷ **Antonyms** abbreviate, abridge, curtail, cut, cut down, shorten, summarize

promenade *noun* **1.** boulevard, esplanade, parade, prom, public walk, walkway **2.** airing, constitutional, saunter, stroll, turn, walk *~verb* **3.** perambulate, saunter, stretch one's legs, stroll, take a walk, walk **4.** flaunt, parade, strut, swagger

prominence **1.** cliff, crag, crest, elevation, headland, height, high point, hummock, mound, pinnacle, projection, promontory, rise, rising ground, spur **2.** bulge, jutting, projection, protrusion, protuberance, swelling **3.** conspicuousness, markedness, outstandingness, precedence, salience, specialness, top billing, weight **4.** celebrity, distinction, eminence, fame, greatness, importance, name, notability, pre-eminence, prestige, rank, reputation, standing

prominent **1.** bulging, hanging over, jutting, projecting, protruding, protrusive, protuberant, standing out **2.** blatant, conspicuous, easily seen, eye-catching, in the foreground, noticeable, obtrusive, obvious, outstanding, pronounced, remarkable, salient, striking, to the fore, unmistakable **3.** big-time (*informal*), celebrated, chief, distinguished, eminent, famous, foremost, important, leading, main, major league (*informal*), notable, noted, outstanding, popular, pre-eminent, renowned, respected, top, well-known, well-thought-of

▷ **Antonyms** (*sense 1*) concave, indented, receding (*sense 2*) inconspicuous, indistinct, insignificant, unnoticeable (*sense 3*) insignificant, minor, secondary, undistinguished, unimportant, unknown, unnotable

promiscuity abandon, amorality, debauchery, depravity, dissipation, immorality, incontinence, laxity, laxness, lechery, libertinism, licentiousness, looseness, permissiveness, profligacy, promiscuousness, sleeping around (*informal*), wantonness

promiscuous **1.** abandoned, debauched, dissipated, dissolute, fast, immoral, lax, libertine, licentious, loose, of easy virtue, profligate, unbridled, unchaste, wanton, wild **2.** chaotic, confused, disordered, diverse, heterogeneous, ill-assorted, indiscriminate, intermingled, intermixed, jumbled, mingled, miscellaneous, mixed, motley **3.** careless, casual, haphazard, heedless, indifferent, indiscriminate, irregular, irresponsible, random, slovenly, uncontrolled, uncritical, undiscriminating, unfastidious, unselective

▷ **Antonyms** (*sense 1*) chaste, decent, innocent, modest, moral, pure, undefiled, unsullied, vestal, virginal, virtuous (*sense 2*) homogeneous, identical, neat, ordered, orderly, organized, shipshape, uniform, unmixed (*sense 3*) careful, critical, discriminating, fastidious, responsible, selective

promise *verb* **1.** assure, contract, cross one's heart, engage, give an undertaking, give one's word, guarantee, pledge, plight, stipulate, swear, take an oath, undertake, vouch, vow, warrant **2.** augur, bespeak, betoken, bid fair, denote, give hope of, hint at, hold a probability, hold out hopes of, indicate, lead one to expect, look like, seem likely to, show signs of, suggest *~noun* **3.** assurance, bond, commitment, compact, covenant, engagement, guarantee, oath, pledge, undertaking, vow, word, word of honour **4.** ability, aptitude, capability, capacity, flair, potential, talent

promising 1. auspicious, bright, encouraging, favourable, full of promise, hopeful, likely, propitious, reassuring, rosy **2.** able, gifted, likely, rising, talented, up-and-coming

▷ **Antonyms** (*sense 1*) discouraging, unauspicious, unfavourable, unpromising

promontory cape, foreland, head, headland, ness (*archaic*), point, spur

promote 1. advance, aid, assist, back, boost, contribute to, develop, encourage, forward, foster, further, help, nurture, stimulate, support **2.** aggrandize, dignify, elevate, exalt, honour, kick upstairs (*informal*), prefer, raise, upgrade **3.** advocate, call attention to, champion, endorse, espouse, popularize, prescribe, push for, recommend, speak for, sponsor, support, urge, work for **4.** advertise, beat the drum for (*informal*), hype, plug (*informal*), publicize, puff, push, sell

▷ **Antonyms** (*sense 1*) discourage, hinder, hold back, impede, obstruct, oppose, prevent (*sense 2*) demote, downgrade, lower *or* reduce in rank

promotion 1. advancement, aggrandizement, elevation, ennoblement, exaltation, honour, move up, preferment, rise, upgrading **2.** advancement, advocacy, backing, boosting, cultivation, development, encouragement, espousal, furtherance, progress, support **3.** advertising, advertising campaign, ballyhoo (*informal*), hard sell, hype, media hype, plugging (*informal*), propaganda, publicity, puffery (*informal*), pushing

prompt *adjective* **1.** early, immediate, instant, instantaneous, on time, pdq (*slang*), punctual, quick, rapid, speedy, swift, timely, unhesitating **2.** alert, brisk, eager, efficient, expeditious, quick, ready, responsive, smart, willing *~adverb* **3.** *informal* exactly, on the dot, promptly, punctually, sharp *~verb* **4.** cause, impel, incite, induce, inspire, instigate, motivate, move, provoke, spur, stimulate, urge **5.** assist, cue, help out, jog the memory, prod, refresh the memory, remind **6.** call forth, cause, elicit, evoke, give rise to, occasion, provoke *~noun* **7.** cue, help, hint, jog, jolt, prod, reminder, spur, stimulus

▷ **Antonyms** *~adjective* hesitating, inactive, inattentive, inefficient, late, remiss, slack, slow, tardy, unresponsive *~verb* deter, discourage, prevent, restrain, talk out of

prompter 1. autocue, idiot board (*slang*), Teleprompter (*Trademark*) **2.** agitator, catalyst, gadfly, inspirer, instigator, moving spirit, prime mover

prompting assistance, clarion call, encouragement, hint, incitement, influence, jogging, persuasion, pressing, pressure, prodding, pushing, reminder, reminding, suggestion, urging

promptly at once, by return, directly, hotfoot, immediately, instantly, on the dot, on time, pdq (*slang*), posthaste, pronto (*informal*), punctually, quickly, speedily, swiftly, unhesitatingly

promptness alacrity, alertness, briskness, dispatch, eagerness, haste, promptitude, punctuality, quickness, readiness, speed, swiftness, willingness

promulgate advertise, announce, broadcast, circulate, communicate, declare, decree, disseminate, issue, make known, make public, notify, proclaim, promote, publish, spread

prone 1. face down, flat, horizontal, lying down, procumbent, prostrate, recumbent, supine **2.** apt, bent, disposed, given, inclined, liable, likely, predisposed, subject, susceptible, tending

▷ **Antonyms** (*sense 1*) erect, face up, perpendicular, supine, upright, vertical (*sense 2*) averse, disinclined, indisposed, not likely, unlikely

proneness bent, bias, disposition, inclination, leaning, liability, partiality, proclivity, propensity, susceptibility, tendency, weakness

prong point, projection, spike, tine, tip

pronounce 1. accent, articulate, enunciate, say, sound, speak, stress, utter, vocalize, voice **2.** affirm, announce, assert, declare, decree, deliver, judge, proclaim

pronounced broad, clear, conspicuous, decided, definite, distinct, evident, marked, noticeable, obvious, salient, striking, strong, unmistakable

▷ **Antonyms** concealed, hidden, imperceptible, inconspicuous, unapparent, unnoticeable, vague

pronouncement announcement, declaration, decree, dictum, edict, judgment, manifesto, notification, proclamation, promulgation, pronunciamento, statement

pronunciation accent, accentuation, articulation, diction, elocution, enunciation, inflection, intonation, speech, stress

proof *noun* **1.** attestation, authentication, certification, confirmation, corroboration, demonstration, evidence, substantiation, testimony, verification **2.** *as in* **put to the proof** assay, examination, experiment, ordeal, scrutiny, test, trial

3. *Printing* galley, galley proof, page proof, pull, slip, trial impression, trial print *~adjective* **4.** impenetrable, impervious, repellent, resistant, strong, tight, treated **5. be proof against** hold out against, resist, stand firm against, stand up to, withstand

prop *verb* **1.** bolster, brace, buttress, hold up, maintain, shore, stay, support, sustain, truss, uphold **2.** lean, rest, set, stand *~noun* **3.** brace, buttress, mainstay, stanchion, stay, support, truss

propaganda advertising, agitprop, ballyhoo (*informal*), brainwashing, disinformation, hype, information, newspeak, promotion, publicity

propagandist advocate, evangelist, indoctrinator, pamphleteer, promoter, proponent, proselytizer, publicist

propagandize brainwash, convince, indoctrinate, instil, persuade, proselytize

propagate 1. beget, breed, engender, generate, increase, multiply, procreate, produce, proliferate, reproduce **2.** broadcast, circulate, diffuse, disseminate, make known, proclaim, promote, promulgate, publicize, publish, spread, transmit

▷ **Antonyms** (*sense 2*) cover up, hide, hush up, keep under wraps, stifle, suppress, withhold

propagation 1. breeding, generation, increase, multiplication, procreation, proliferation, reproduction **2.** circulation, communication, diffusion, dissemination, distribution, promotion, promulgation, spread, spreading, transmission

propel drive, force, impel, launch, push, send, set in motion, shoot, shove, start, thrust

▷ **Antonyms** check, delay, hold back, pull, slow, stop

propensity aptness, bent, bias, disposition, inclination, leaning, liability, penchant, predisposition, proclivity, proneness, susceptibility, tendency, weakness

proper 1. appropriate, apt, becoming, befitting, fit, fitting, legitimate, meet (*archaic*), right, suitable, suited **2.** *comme il faut,* decent, decorous, *de rigueur,* genteel, gentlemanly, ladylike, mannerly, polite, punctilious, refined, respectable, seemly **3.** accepted, accurate, conventional, correct, established, exact, formal, kosher (*informal*), orthodox, precise, right **4.** characteristic, individual, own, particular, peculiar, personal, respective, special, specific

▷ **Antonyms** (*senses 1, 2, & 3*) coarse, common, crude, discourteous, impolite, improper, inappropriate, indecent, rude, unbecoming, unconventional, ungentlemanly, unladylike, unorthodox, unrefined, unseemly, unsuitable, wrong

property 1. assets, belongings, building(s), capital, chattels, effects, estate, goods, holdings, house(s), means, possessions, resources, riches, wealth **2.** acres, estate, freehold, holding, land, real estate, real property, realty, title **3.** ability, attribute, characteristic, feature, hallmark, idiosyncrasy, mark, peculiarity, quality, trait, virtue

prophecy augury, divination, forecast, foretelling, prediction, prognosis, prognostication, revelation, second sight, soothsaying, sortilege, vaticination (*rare*)

prophesy augur, divine, forecast, foresee, foretell, forewarn, predict, presage, prognosticate, soothsay, vaticinate (*rare*)

prophet augur, Cassandra, clairvoyant, diviner, forecaster, oracle, prognosticator, prophesier, seer, sibyl, soothsayer

prophetic augural, divinatory, fatidic (*rare*), foreshadowing, mantic, oracular, predictive, presaging, prescient, prognostic, sibylline, vatic (*rare*)

propinquity 1. adjacency, closeness, contiguity, nearness, neighbourhood, proximity, vicinity **2.** affiliation, affinity, blood, connection, consanguinity, kindred, kinship, relation, relationship, tie, ties of blood

propitiate appease, conciliate, make peace, mollify, pacify, placate, reconcile, satisfy

propitiation appeasement, conciliation, mollification, peacemaking, placation, reconciliation

propitiatory appeasing, assuaging, conciliatory, pacificatory, pacifying, peacemaking, placative, placatory, propitiative, reconciliatory

propitious 1. advantageous, auspicious, bright, encouraging, favourable, fortunate, full of promise, happy, lucky, opportune, promising, prosperous, rosy, timely **2.** benevolent, benign, favourably inclined, friendly, gracious, kind, well-disposed

proponent advocate, apologist, backer, champion, defender, enthusiast, exponent, friend, partisan, patron, spokesman, spokeswoman, subscriber, supporter, upholder, vindicator

proportion 1. distribution, ratio, relationship, relative amount **2.** agreement, balance, congruity, correspondence, harmony, symmetry **3.** amount, cut (*informal*), division, fraction, measure, part, percentage, quota, segment, share **4.** (*plural*) amplitude, breadth, bulk, capacity, dimensions, expanse, extent, magnitude, measurements, range, scope, size, volume

proportional, proportionate balanced, commensurate, comparable, compatible, consistent, correspondent, corresponding, equitable, equivalent, even, in proportion, just

▷ **Antonyms** different, discordant, disproportionate, dissimilar, incommensurable, incompatible, inconsistent, unequal

proposal bid, design, motion, offer, overture, plan, presentation, proffer, programme, project, proposition, recommendation, scheme, suggestion, tender, terms

propose 1. advance, come up with, present, proffer, propound, put forward, submit, suggest, tender **2.** introduce, invite, name, nominate, present, put up, recommend **3.** aim, design, have every intention, have in mind, intend, mean, plan, purpose, scheme **4.** ask for someone's hand (in marriage), offer marriage, pay suit, pop the question (*informal*)

proposition 1. *noun* motion, plan, programme, project, proposal, recommendation, scheme, suggestion **2.** *~verb* accost, make an improper suggestion, make an indecent proposal, make a pass at, solicit

propound advance, advocate, contend, lay down, postulate, present, propose, put forward, set forth, submit, suggest

proprietor, proprietress deed holder, freeholder, landlady, landlord, landowner, owner, possessor, titleholder

propriety 1. appropriateness, aptness, becomingness, correctness, fitness, rightness, seemliness, suitableness **2.** breeding, courtesy, decency, decorum, delicacy, etiquette, good form, good manners, manners, modesty, politeness, protocol, punctilio, rectitude, refinement, respectability, seemliness **3. the proprieties** accepted conduct, amenities, civilities, etiquette, niceties, rules of conduct, social code, social conventions, social graces, the done thing

▷ **Antonyms** (*sense 2*) bad form, bad manners, immodesty, impoliteness, indecency, indecorum, indelicacy, vulgarity

propulsion drive, impetus, impulse, impulsion, momentum, motive power, power, pressure, propelling force, push, thrust

prosaic banal, boring, commonplace, dry, dull, everyday, flat, hackneyed, humdrum, matter-of-fact, mundane, ordinary, pedestrian, routine, stale, tame, trite, unimaginative, uninspiring, vapid, workaday

▷ **Antonyms** entertaining, exciting, extraordinary, fascinating, imaginative, interesting, poetical, unusual

proscribe 1. ban, boycott, censure, condemn, damn, denounce, doom, embargo, forbid, interdict, prohibit, reject **2.** attaint (*archaic*), banish, blackball, deport, exclude, excommunicate, exile, expatriate, expel, ostracize, outlaw

▷ **Antonyms** (*sense 1*) allow, authorize, endorse, give leave, give permission, license, permit, sanction, warrant

proscription 1. ban, boycott, censure, condemnation, damning, denunciation, dooming, embargo, interdict, prohibition, rejection **2.** attainder (*archaic*), banishment, deportation, ejection, eviction, exclusion, excommunication, exile, expatriation, expulsion, ostracism, outlawry

prosecute 1. *Law* arraign, bring action against, bring suit against, bring to trial, do (*slang*), indict, litigate, prefer charges, put in the dock, put on trial, seek redress, sue, summon, take to court, try **2.** carry on, conduct, direct, discharge, engage in, manage, perform, practise, work at **3.** carry through, continue, follow through, persevere, persist, pursue, see through

proselyte catechumen, convert, initiate, neophyte, new believer, novice, tyro

proselytize bring into the fold, bring to God, convert, evangelize, make converts, propagandize, spread the gospel, win over

prospect *noun* **1.** anticipation, calculation, contemplation, expectation, future, hope, odds, opening, outlook, plan, presumption, probability, promise, proposal, thought **2.** landscape, outlook, panorama, perspective, scene, sight, spectacle, view, vision, vista **3. in prospect** in sight, in store, in the offing, in the wind, in view, on the cards, on the horizon, planned, projected **4.** (*sometimes plural*) chance, likelihood, possibility *~verb* **5.** explore, go after, look for, search, seek, survey

prospective about to be, anticipated, approaching, awaited, coming, destined, eventual, expected, forthcoming, future, hoped-for, imminent, intended, likely, looked-for, on the cards, possible, potential, soon-to-be, -to-be, to come, upcoming

prospectus announcement, catalogue, conspectus, list, outline, plan, programme, scheme, syllabus, synopsis

prosper advance, be fortunate, bloom, do well, fare well, flourish, flower, get on, grow rich, make good, make it (*informal*), progress, succeed, thrive

prosperity affluence, boom, ease, fortune, good fortune, good times, life of luxury, life of Riley (*informal*), luxury, plenty, prosperousness, riches, success, the good life, wealth, well-being

▷ **Antonyms** adversity, depression, destitution, failure, indigence, misfortune, poverty, shortage, want

prosperous 1. blooming, booming, doing well, flourishing, fortunate, lucky, on a roll, on the up and up (*Brit.*), palmy, prospering, successful, thriving **2.** affluent, in clover (*informal*), in the money (*informal*), moneyed, opulent, rich, wealthy, well-heeled (*informal*), well-off, well-to-do **3.** advantageous, auspicious, bright, favourable, good, profitable, promising, propitious, timely

▷ **Antonyms** defeated, failing, impoverished, inauspicious, poor, unfavourable, unfortunate, unlucky, unpromising, unsuccessful, untimely

prostitute 1. *noun* bawd (*archaic*), brass (*slang*), call girl, camp follower, cocotte, courtesan, fallen woman, *fille de joie,* harlot, hooker (*U.S. slang*), hustler (*U.S. & Canad. slang*), loose woman, moll (*slang*), pro (*slang*), scrubber (*Brit. & Austral. slang*), streetwalker, strumpet, tart (*informal*), trollop, white slave, whore, working girl (*facetious slang*) **2.** *~verb* cheapen, debase, degrade, demean, devalue, misapply, pervert, profane

prostitution harlotry, harlot's trade, Mrs. Warren's profession, streetwalking, the game (*slang*), the oldest profession, vice, whoredom

prostrate *adjective* **1.** abject, bowed low, flat, horizontal, kowtowing, procumbent, prone **2.** at a low ebb, dejected, depressed, desolate, drained, exhausted, fagged out (*informal*), fallen, inconsolable, overcome, spent, worn out **3.** brought to one's knees, defenceless, disarmed, helpless, impotent, overwhelmed, paralysed, powerless, reduced *~verb* **4.** *of oneself* abase, bend the knee to, bow before, bow down to, cast oneself before, cringe, fall at (someone's) feet, fall on one's knees before, grovel, kneel, kowtow, submit **5.** bring low, crush, depress, disarm, lay low, overcome, overthrow, overturn, overwhelm, paralyse, reduce, ruin **6.** drain, exhaust, fag out (*informal*), fatigue, sap, tire, wear out, weary

prostration 1. abasement, bow, genuflection, kneeling, kowtow, obeisance, submission **2.** collapse, dejection, depression, depth of misery, desolation, despair, despondency, exhaustion, grief, helplessness, paralysis, weakness, weariness

prosy boring, commonplace, dull, flat, humdrum, long, long-drawn-out, long-winded, monotonous, overlong, pedestrian, prosaic, prosing, stale, tedious, tiresome, unimaginative, uninteresting, wordy

protagonist 1. central character, hero, heroine, lead, leading character, principal **2.** advocate, champion, exponent, leader, mainstay, moving spirit, prime mover, standard-bearer, supporter, torchbearer

protean changeable, ever-changing, many-sided, mercurial, multiform, mutable, polymorphous, temperamental, variable, versatile, volatile

protect care for, chaperon, cover, cover up for, defend, foster, give sanctuary, guard, harbour, keep, keep safe, look after, mount *or* stand guard over, preserve, safeguard, save, screen, secure, shelter, shield, stick up for (*informal*), support, take under one's wing, watch over

▷ **Antonyms** assail, assault, attack, betray, endanger, expose, expose to danger, threaten

protection 1. aegis, care, charge, custody, defence, guardianship, guarding, preservation, protecting, safeguard, safekeeping, safety, security **2.** armour, barrier, buffer, bulwark, cover, guard, refuge, safeguard, screen, shelter, shield

protective careful, covering, defensive, fatherly, insulating, jealous, maternal, motherly, paternal, possessive, protecting, safeguarding, sheltering, shielding, vigilant, warm, watchful

protector advocate, benefactor, bodyguard, champion, counsel, defender, guard, guardian, guardian angel, knight in shining armour, patron, safeguard, tower of strength

protégé, protégée charge, dependant, discovery, pupil, student, ward

protest *noun* **1.** complaint, declaration, demur, demurral, disapproval, dissent, formal complaint, objection, outcry, protestation, remonstrance *~verb* **2.** complain, cry out, demonstrate, demur, disagree, disapprove, expostulate, express disapproval, kick (against) (*informal*), object, oppose, remonstrate, say no to, take exception, take up the cudgels **3.** affirm, argue, assert, asseverate, attest, avow, contend, declare, insist, maintain, profess, testify, vow

protestation 1. complaint, disagreement, dissent, expostulation, objection, outcry, protest, remonstrance, remonstration **2.** affirmation, asseveration, avowal, declaration, oath, pledge, profession, vow

protester agitator, demonstrator, dissenter, dissident, protest marcher, rebel

protocol 1. code of behaviour, conventions, courtesies, customs, decorum, etiquette, formalities, good form, manners, politesse, propriety, p's and q's, rules of conduct **2.** agreement, compact, concordat, contract, convention, covenant, pact, treaty

prototype archetype, example, first, mock-up, model, norm, original, paradigm, pattern, precedent, standard, type

protract continue, drag on *or* out, draw out, extend, keep going, lengthen, prolong, spin out, stretch out

▷ **Antonyms** abbreviate, abridge, compress, curtail, reduce, shorten, summarize

protracted dragged out, drawn-out, extended, interminable, lengthy, long,

long-drawn-out, never-ending, overlong, prolonged, spun out, time-consuming

protrude bulge, come through, extend, jut, obtrude, point, pop (*of eyes*), project, shoot out, stand out, start (from), stick out, stick out like a sore thumb

protrusion bulge, bump, hump, jut, lump, outgrowth, projection, protuberance, swelling

protuberance bulge, bump, excrescence, hump, knob, lump, outgrowth, process, projection, prominence, protrusion, swelling, tumour

protuberant beetling, bulbous, bulging, gibbous, hanging over, jutting, popping (*of eyes*), prominent, protruding, protrusive, proud (*dialect*), swelling, swollen

▷ **Antonyms** concave, flat, indented, receding, sunken

proud 1. appreciative, content, contented, glad, gratified, honoured, pleased, satisfied, self-respecting, well-pleased **2.** arrogant, boastful, conceited, disdainful, egotistical, haughty, high and mighty (*informal*), imperious, lordly, narcissistic, orgulous (*archaic*), overbearing, presumptuous, self-important, self-satisfied, snobbish, snooty (*informal*), stuck-up (*informal*), supercilious, toffee-nosed (*slang, chiefly Brit.*), too big for one's boots *or* breeches, vain **3.** exalted, glorious, gratifying, illustrious, memorable, pleasing, red-letter, rewarding, satisfying **4.** august, distinguished, eminent, grand, great, illustrious, imposing, magnificent, majestic, noble, splendid, stately

▷ **Antonyms** (*sense 1*) discontented, displeased, dissatisfied (*sense 2*) abject, ashamed, deferential, meek, modest, submissive, unobtrusive (*sense 4*) base, humble, ignoble, ignominious, lowly, unassuming, undignified

provable attestable, demonstrable, evincible, testable, verifiable

prove 1. ascertain, attest, authenticate, bear out, confirm, corroborate, demonstrate, determine, establish, evidence, evince, justify, show, show clearly, substantiate, verify **2.** analyse, assay, check, examine, experiment, put to the test, put to trial, test, try **3.** be found to be, come out, end up, result, turn out

▷ **Antonyms** (*sense 1*) discredit, disprove, give the lie to, refute, rule out

proven *adjective* accepted, attested, authentic, certified, checked, confirmed, definite, dependable, established, proved, reliable, tested, tried, trustworthy, undoubted, valid, verified

provenance birthplace, derivation, origin, source

provender 1. feed, fodder, forage **2.** comestibles, eatables, eats (*slang*), edibles, fare, feed, food, foodstuffs, groceries, grub (*slang*), nosebag (*slang*), nosh (*slang*), provisions, rations, supplies, sustenance, tack (*informal*), victuals, vittles (*obsolete or dialect*)

proverb adage, aphorism, apophthegm, byword, dictum, gnome, maxim, saw, saying

proverbial accepted, acknowledged, archetypal, axiomatic, conventional, current, customary, famed, famous, legendary, notorious, self-evident, time-honoured, traditional, typical, unquestioned, well-known

provide 1. accommodate, cater, contribute, equip, furnish, outfit, provision, purvey, stock up, supply **2.** add, afford, bring, give, impart, lend, present, produce, render, serve, yield **3.** (*with* **for** *or* **against**) anticipate, arrange for, forearm, get ready, make arrangements, make plans, plan ahead, plan for, prepare for, take measures, take precautions **4.** (*with* **for**) care for, keep, look after, maintain, support, sustain, take care of **5.** determine, lay down, require, specify, state, stipulate

▷ **Antonyms** (*sense 1*) deprive, keep back, refuse, withhold (*sense 3*) disregard, fail to notice, miss, neglect, overlook (*sense 4*) neglect

providence 1. destiny, divine intervention, fate, fortune, God's will, predestination **2.** care, caution, discretion, far-sightedness, foresight, forethought, perspicacity, presence of mind, prudence

provident canny, careful, cautious, discreet, economical, equipped, far-seeing, far-sighted, forearmed, foresighted, frugal, prudent, sagacious, shrewd, thrifty, vigilant, well-prepared, wise

▷ **Antonyms** careless, heedless, improvident, imprudent, negligent, prodigal, profligate, reckless, short-sighted, spendthrift, thoughtless, thriftless, uneconomical, unthrifty, wasteful

providential fortuitous, fortunate, happy, heaven-sent, lucky, opportune, timely, welcome

provider 1. benefactor, donor, giver, source, supplier **2.** breadwinner, earner, mainstay, supporter, wage earner

providing, provided *conjunction* as long as, contingent upon, given, if and only if, in case, in the event, on condition, on the assumption, subject to, upon these terms, with the proviso, with the understanding

province 1. colony, county, department, dependency, district, division, domain, patch, region, section, territory, tract, turf (*U.S. slang*), zone **2.** *figurative* area, business, capacity, charge, concern, duty, employment, field, function, line, orbit, part, pigeon (*Brit. informal*), post, responsibility, role, sphere, turf (*U.S. slang*)

provincial *adjective* **1.** country, hick (*informal, chiefly U.S. & Canad.*), home-grown, homespun, local, rural, rustic **2.** insular, inward-looking, limited, narrow, narrow-minded, parish-pump, parochial, small-minded, small-town (*U.S.*), uninformed, unsophisticated, upcountry ~*noun* **3.** country cousin, hayseed (*U.S. & Canad. informal*), hick (*informal, chiefly U.S. & Canad.*), rustic, yokel

▷ **Antonyms** cosmopolitan, fashionable, polished, refined, sophisticated, urban, urbane

provincialism 1. insularity, lack of sophistication, narrow-mindedness, parochialism, sectionalism **2.** dialect, idiom, localism, patois, regionalism, vernacularism

provision 1. accoutrement, catering, equipping, fitting out, furnishing, providing, supplying, victualling **2.** arrangement, plan, prearrangement, precaution, preparation **3.** *figurative* agreement, clause, condition, demand, proviso, requirement, rider, specification, stipulation, term

provisional conditional, contingent, interim, limited, pro tem, provisory, qualified, stopgap, temporary, tentative, transitional

▷ **Antonyms** definite, fixed, permanent

provisions comestibles, eatables, eats (*slang*), edibles, fare, feed, food, foodstuff, groceries, grub (*slang*), nosebag (*slang*), provender, rations, stores, supplies, sustenance, tack (*informal*), viands, victuals, vittles (*obsolete or dialect*)

proviso clause, condition, limitation, provision, qualification, requirement, reservation, restriction, rider, stipulation, strings

provocation 1. *casus belli,* cause, grounds, incitement, inducement, instigation, justification, motivation, reason, stimulus **2.** affront, annoyance, challenge, dare, grievance, indignity, injury, insult, offence, red rag, taunt, vexation

provocative 1. aggravating (*informal*), annoying, challenging, disturbing, galling, goading, incensing, insulting, offensive, outrageous, provoking, stimulating **2.** alluring, arousing, erotic, exciting, inviting, seductive, sexy (*informal*), stimulating, suggestive, tantalizing, tempting

provoke 1. affront, aggravate (*informal*), anger, annoy, chafe, enrage, exasperate, gall, get in one's hair (*informal*), get one's back up, get on one's nerves (*informal*), hassle (*informal*), incense, infuriate, insult, irk, irritate, madden, make one's blood boil, nark (*Brit., Austral., & N.Z. slang*), offend, pique, piss one off (*taboo slang*), put one's back up, put out, rile, rub (someone) up the wrong way (*informal*), take a rise out of, try one's patience, vex **2.** bring about, bring on *or* down, call forth, cause, draw forth, elicit, evoke, excite, fire, foment, generate, give rise to, incite, induce, inflame, inspire, instigate, kindle, lead to, motivate, move, occasion, precipitate, produce, promote, prompt, rouse, stimulate, stir

▷ **Antonyms** (*sense 1*) appease, calm, conciliate, mollify, pacify, placate, propitiate, quiet, soothe, sweeten (*sense 2*) abate, allay, assuage, blunt, curb, ease, lessen, lull, mitigate, moderate, modify, relieve, temper

provoking aggravating (*informal*), annoying, exasperating, galling, irking, irksome, irritating, maddening, obstructive, offensive, tiresome, vexatious, vexing

prow bow(s), fore, forepart, front, head, nose, sharp end (*jocular*), stem

prowess 1. ability, accomplishment, adeptness, adroitness, aptitude, attainment, command, dexterity, excellence, expertise, expertness, facility, genius, mastery, skill, talent **2.** boldness, bravery, courage, daring, dauntlessness, doughtiness, fearlessness, gallantry, hardihood, heroism, intrepidity, mettle, valiance, valour

▷ **Antonyms** (*sense 1*) clumsiness, inability, incapability, incompetence, ineptitude, ineptness, inexpertise (*sense 2*) cowardice, faint-heartedness, fear, gutlessness, timidity

prowl cruise, hunt, lurk, move stealthily, nose around, patrol, range, roam, rove, scavenge, skulk, slink, sneak, stalk, steal

proximity adjacency, closeness, contiguity, juxtaposition, nearness, neighbourhood, propinquity, vicinity

proxy agent, attorney, delegate, deputy, factor, representative, substitute, surrogate

prude Grundy, old maid (*informal*), prig, puritan, schoolmarm (*Brit. informal*)

prudence 1. canniness, care, caution, circumspection, common sense, discretion, good sense, heedfulness, judgment, judiciousness, sagacity, vigilance, wariness, wisdom **2.** careful budgeting, economizing, economy, far-sightedness, foresight, forethought, frugality, good management, husbandry, planning, precaution, preparedness, providence, saving, thrift

prudent 1. canny, careful, cautious, circumspect, discerning, discreet, judicious, politic, sagacious, sage, sensible, shrewd, vigilant, wary, wise **2.** canny, careful, economical, far-sighted, frugal, provident, sparing, thrifty

▷ **Antonyms** careless, extravagant, heedless, improvident, imprudent, inconsiderate, indiscreet, irrational, rash, thoughtless, unwise, wasteful

prudery Grundyism, old-maidishness (*informal*), overmodesty, priggishness, primness, prudishness, puritanicalness, squeamishness, starchiness (*informal*), strictness, stuffiness

prudish demure, formal, narrow-minded, niminy-piminy, old-maidish (*informal*), overmodest, overnice, priggish, prim, prissy (*informal*), proper, puritanical, schoolmarmish (*informal, chiefly Brit.*), squeamish, starchy (*informal*), strait-laced, stuffy, Victorian
▷ **Antonyms** broad-minded, liberal, open-minded, permissive

prune clip, cut, cut back, dock, lop, pare down, reduce, shape, shorten, snip, trim

prurient **1.** concupiscent, desirous, hankering, itching, lascivious, lecherous, libidinous, longing, lustful, salacious **2.** dirty, erotic, indecent, lewd, obscene, pornographic, salacious, smutty, steamy (*informal*), voyeuristic, X-rated (*informal*)

pry be a busybody, be inquisitive, be nosy (*informal*), ferret about, interfere, intrude, meddle, nose into, peep, peer, poke, poke one's nose in *or* into (*informal*), snoop (*informal*)

prying curious, eavesdropping, impertinent, inquisitive, interfering, intrusive, meddlesome, meddling, nosy (*informal*), snooping (*informal*), snoopy (*informal*), spying

psalm carol, chant, hymn, paean, song of praise

pseud *noun* fraud, humbug, phoney *or* phony (*informal*), poser (*informal*), trendy (*Brit. informal*)

pseudo *adjective* artificial, bogus, counterfeit, ersatz, fake, false, imitation, mock, not genuine, phoney *or* phony (*informal*), pretended, quasi-, sham, spurious
▷ **Antonyms** actual, authentic, bona fide, genuine, heartfelt, honest, real, sincere, true, unfeigned

pseudonym alias, assumed name, false name, incognito, nom de guerre, nom de plume, pen name, professional name, stage name

psyche anima, essential nature, individuality, inner man, innermost self, mind, personality, pneuma (*Philosophy*), self, soul, spirit, subconscious, true being

psychedelic **1.** consciousness-expanding, hallucinatory, hallucinogenic, mind-bending (*informal*), mind-blowing (*informal*), mind-expanding, psychoactive, psychotomimetic, psychotropic **2.** *informal* crazy, freaky (*slang*), kaleidoscopic, multicoloured, wild

psychiatrist analyst, headshrinker (*slang*), psychoanalyser, psychoanalyst, psychologist, psychotherapist, shrink (*slang*), therapist

psychic **1.** clairvoyant, extrasensory, mystic, occult, preternatural, supernatural, telekinetic, telepathic **2.** mental, psychogenic, psychological, spiritual

psychological **1.** cerebral, cognitive, intellectual, mental **2.** all in the mind, emotional, imaginary, irrational, psychosomatic, subconscious, subjective, unconscious, unreal

psychology **1.** behaviourism, science of mind, study of personality **2.** *informal* attitude, mental make-up, mental processes, thought processes, way of thinking, what makes one tick

psychopath headbanger (*Brit. informal*), headcase (*informal*), insane person, lunatic, madman, maniac, mental case (*slang*), nutcase (*slang*), nutter (*Brit. slang*), psychotic, sociopath

psychotic *adjective* certifiable, demented, deranged, insane, lunatic, mad, mental (*slang*), *non compos mentis,* not right in the head, off one's chump, off one's head (*slang*), off one's rocker (*slang*), off one's trolley (*slang*), psychopathic, round the bend (*Brit. slang*), unbalanced

pub *or* **public house** alehouse (*archaic*), bar, boozer (*Brit., Austral., & N.Z. informal*), hostelry (*archaic or facetious*), inn, local (*Brit. informal*), roadhouse, taproom, tavern, watering hole (*facetious slang*)

puberty adolescence, awkward age, juvenescence, pubescence, teenage, teens, young adulthood

public *adjective* **1.** civic, civil, common, general, national, popular, social, state, universal, widespread **2.** accessible, communal, community, free to all, not private, open, open to the public, unrestricted **3.** acknowledged, exposed, in circulation, known, notorious, obvious, open, overt, patent, plain, published, recognized **4.** important, prominent, respected, well-known *~noun* **5.** citizens, commonalty, community, country, electorate, everyone, hoi polloi, Joe (and Eileen) Public (*slang*), Joe Six-Pack (*U.S. slang*), masses, multitude, nation, people, populace, population, society, voters **6.** audience, buyers, clientele, followers, following, patrons, supporters, those interested, trade **7.** **in public** *coram populo,* for all to see, in full view, openly, overtly, publicly
▷ **Antonyms** (*sense 2*) barred, closed, exclusive, inaccessible, personal, private, restricted, unavailable (*sense 3*) hidden, secluded, secret, unknown, unrevealed

publication **1.** advertisement, airing, announcement, appearance, broadcasting, declaration, disclosure, dissemination, notification, proclamation, promulgation, publishing, reporting **2.** book, booklet, brochure, handbill, hardback, issue, leaflet, magazine, newspaper, pamphlet, paperback, periodical, title

publicity advertising, attention, ballyhoo (*informal*), boost, build-up, hype, plug (*informal*), press, promotion, public notice, puff, puffery (*informal*)

publicize advertise, beat the drum for (*informal*), bring to public notice, broadcast, give publicity to, hype, make known, play up, plug (*informal*), promote, puff, push, spotlight, spread about, write up
▷ **Antonyms** conceal, contain, cover up, keep dark, keep secret, smother, stifle, suppress, withhold

public-spirited altruistic, charitable, community-minded, generous, humanitarian, philanthropic, unselfish

publish 1. bring out, issue, print, produce, put out **2.** advertise, announce, blow wide open (*slang*), broadcast, circulate, communicate, declare, disclose, distribute, divulge, impart, leak, proclaim, promulgate, publicize, reveal, shout from the rooftops (*informal*), spread

pucker 1. *verb* compress, contract, crease, crinkle, crumple, draw together, furrow, gather, knit, pout, purse, ruckle, ruck up, ruffle, screw up, tighten, wrinkle **2.** *~noun* crease, crinkle, crumple, fold, ruck, ruckle, wrinkle

puckish frolicsome, impish, mischievous, naughty, playful, roguish, sly, sportive, teasing, waggish, whimsical

pudding afters (*Brit. informal*), dessert, last course, pud (*informal*), second course, sweet

puerile babyish, childish, foolish, immature, inane, infantile, irresponsible, jejune, juvenile, naive, petty, ridiculous, silly, trivial, weak
▷ **Antonyms** adult, grown-up, mature, responsible, sensible

puff *noun* **1.** blast, breath, draught, emanation, flurry, gust, whiff **2.** drag (*slang*), pull, smoke **3.** bulge, bunching, swelling **4.** advertisement, commendation, favourable mention, good word, plug (*informal*), sales talk *~verb* **5.** blow, breathe, exhale, gasp, gulp, pant, wheeze **6.** drag (*slang*), draw, inhale, pull at *or* on, smoke, suck **7.** (*usually with* **up**) bloat, dilate, distend, expand, inflate, swell **8.** crack up (*informal*), hype, overpraise, plug (*informal*), praise, promote, publicize, push

puffed 1. breathless, done in (*informal*), exhausted, gasping, out of breath, out of whack (*informal*), panting, shagged out (*Brit. slang*), short of breath, spent, winded, wiped out (*informal*) **2. puffed up** bigheaded (*informal*), full of oneself, high and mighty (*informal*), proud, swollen-headed, too big for one's boots
▷ **Antonyms** (*sense 2*) humble, modest, self-effacing

puffy bloated, distended, enlarged, inflamed, inflated, puffed up, swollen

pugilism boxing, fighting, prizefighting, the noble art *or* science, the prize ring, the ring

pugilist boxer, bruiser (*informal*), fighter, prizefighter, pug (*slang*)

pugnacious aggressive, antagonistic, argumentative, bellicose, belligerent, choleric, combative, contentious, disputatious, hot-tempered, irascible, irritable, petulant, quarrelsome
▷ **Antonyms** calm, conciliatory, gentle, irenic, pacific, peaceable, peaceful, peace-loving, placatory, placid, quiet

puke barf (*U.S. slang*), be nauseated, be sick, chuck (up) (*slang, chiefly U.S.*), chunder (*slang, chiefly Austral.*), disgorge, do a technicolour yawn (*slang*), heave, regurgitate, retch, spew, throw up (*informal*), toss one's cookies (*U.S. slang*), upchuck (*U.S. slang*), vomit

pukka authentic, bona fide, genuine, official, on the level (*informal*), proper, real, the real McCoy

pull *verb* **1.** drag, draw, haul, jerk, tow, trail, tug, yank **2.** cull, draw out, extract, gather, pick, pluck, remove, take out, uproot, weed **3.** dislocate, rend, rip, sprain, strain, stretch, tear, wrench **4.** *informal* attract, draw, entice, lure, magnetize **5. pull apart** *or* **to pieces** attack, blast, criticize, find fault, flay, lambast(e), lay into (*informal*), pan (*informal*), pick holes in, put down, run down, slam (*slang*), slate (*informal*), tear into (*informal*) **6. pull oneself together** *informal* buck up (*informal*), get a grip on oneself, get over it, regain composure, snap out of it (*informal*) **7. pull strings** *Brit. informal* influence, pull wires (*U.S.*), use one's influence **8. pull someone's leg** *informal* chaff, have (someone) on, joke, make fun of, poke fun at, rag, rib (*informal*), tease, twit, wind up (*Brit. slang*) *~noun* **9.** jerk, tug, twitch, yank **10.** attraction, drawing power, effort, exertion, force, forcefulness, influence, lure, magnetism, power **11.** *informal* advantage, bottom, clout (*informal*), influence, leverage, muscle, weight **12.** drag (*slang*), inhalation, puff
▷ **Antonyms** *~verb* (*sense 1*) drive, nudge, push, ram, shove, thrust (*sense 2*) implant, insert, plant (*sense 4*) deter, discourage, put one off, repel *~noun* (*sense 9*) nudge, push, shove, thrust

pull down bulldoze, demolish, destroy, raze, remove
▷ **Antonyms** build, construct, erect, put up, raise, set up

pull in 1. arrive, come in, draw in, draw up, reach, stop **2.** attract, bring in, draw **3.** *Brit. slang* arrest, bust (*informal*), collar (*informal*), feel one's collar (*slang*), lift (*slang*), nab (*informal*), nail (*informal*), pinch (*informal*), run in (*slang*), take into custody **4.** clear, earn, gain, gross, make, net, pocket, take home

pull off **1.** detach, doff, remove, rip off, tear off, wrench off **2.** accomplish, bring off, carry out, crack it (*informal*), cut it (*informal*), do the trick, manage, score a success, secure one's object, succeed

pull out abandon, back off, depart, evacuate, leave, quit, rat on, retreat, stop participating, withdraw

pull through come through, get better, get over, pull round, rally, recover, survive, turn the corner, weather

pull up **1.** dig out, lift, raise, uproot **2.** brake, come to a halt, halt, reach a standstill, stop **3.** admonish, bawl out (*informal*), carpet (*informal*), castigate, chew out (*U.S. & Canad. informal*), dress down (*informal*), give a rocket (*Brit. & N.Z. informal*), rap over the knuckles, read the riot act, rebuke, reprimand, reprove, slap on the wrist, take to task, tear into (*informal*), tear (someone) off a strip (*Brit. informal*), tell off (*informal*), tick off (*informal*)

pulp *noun* **1.** flesh, marrow, soft part **2.** mash, mush, pap, paste, pomace, semiliquid, semisolid, triturate *~verb* **3.** crush, mash, pulverize, squash, triturate *~adjective* **4.** cheap, lurid, mushy (*informal*), rubbishy, sensational, trashy

pulpy fleshy, mushy, pappy, soft, squashy, succulent

pulsate beat, hammer, oscillate, palpitate, pound, pulse, quiver, throb, thud, thump, tick, vibrate

pulse **1.** *noun* beat, beating, oscillation, pulsation, rhythm, stroke, throb, throbbing, vibration **2.** *~verb* beat, pulsate, throb, tick, vibrate

pulverize **1.** bray, comminute, crush, granulate, grind, levigate (*Chemistry*), mill, pestle, pound, triturate **2.** *figurative* annihilate, blow out of the water (*slang*), crush, defeat, demolish, destroy, flatten, lick (*informal*), smash, stuff (*slang*), tank (*slang*), vanquish, wipe the floor with (*informal*), wreck

pummel bang, batter, beat, beat the living daylights out of, belt (*informal*), clobber (*slang*), hammer, knock, lambast(e), pound, punch, rain blows upon, strike, thump

pump *verb* **1.** (*with* **out**) bail out, drain, draw off, drive out, empty, force out, siphon **2.** (*with* **up**) blow up, dilate, inflate **3.** drive, force, inject, pour, push, send, supply **4.** cross-examine, give (someone) the third degree, grill (*informal*), interrogate, probe, question closely, quiz, worm out of

pun double entendre, equivoque, paronomasia (*Rhetoric*), play on words, quip, witticism

punch¹ *verb* **1.** bash (*informal*), belt (*informal*), biff (*slang*), bop (*informal*), box, clout (*informal*), hit, plug (*slang*), pummel, slam, slug, smash, sock (*slang*), strike, wallop (*informal*) *~noun* **2.** bash (*informal*), biff (*slang*), blow, bop (*informal*), clout (*informal*), hit, jab, knock, plug (*slang*), sock (*slang*), thump, wallop (*informal*) **3.** *informal* bite, drive, effectiveness, force, forcefulness, impact, point, verve, vigour

punch² *verb* bore, cut, drill, perforate, pierce, pink, prick, puncture, stamp

punch-drunk befuddled, confused, dazed, groggy (*informal*), in a daze, knocked silly, punchy (*informal*), reeling, slap-happy (*informal*), staggering, stupefied, unsteady, woozy (*informal*)

punch-up argument, *bagarre,* battle royal, brawl, dingdong, dust-up (*informal*), fight, free-for-all (*informal*), row, scrap (*informal*), set-to (*informal*), shindig (*informal*), shindy (*informal*), stand-up fight (*informal*)

punchy aggressive, dynamic, effective, forceful, incisive, in-your-face (*slang*), lively, spirited, vigorous

punctilio **1.** exactitude, finickiness, meticulousness, particularity, precision, punctiliousness, scrupulousness, strictness **2.** convention, delicacy, distinction, fine point, formality, nicety, particular, refinement

punctilious careful, ceremonious, conscientious, exact, finicky, formal, fussy, meticulous, nice, particular, precise, proper, scrupulous, strict

punctual early, exact, in good time, on the dot, on time, precise, prompt, punctilious, seasonable, strict, timely

▷ **Antonyms** behind, behindhand, belated, delayed, late, overdue, tardy, unpunctual

punctuality promptitude, promptness, readiness, regularity

punctuate **1.** break, interject, interrupt, intersperse, pepper, sprinkle **2.** accentuate, emphasize, lay stress on, mark, point up, stress, underline

puncture *noun* **1.** break, cut, damage, hole, leak, nick, opening, perforation, rupture, slit **2.** flat, flat tyre *~verb* **3.** bore, cut, impale, nick, penetrate, perforate, pierce, prick, rupture **4.** deflate, go down, go flat **5.** deflate, discourage, disillusion, flatten, humble, take down a peg (*informal*)

pundit buff (*informal*), maestro, one of the cognoscenti, (self-appointed) expert *or* authority

pungent **1.** acerb, acid, acrid, aromatic, bitter, highly flavoured, hot, peppery, piquant, seasoned, sharp, sour, spicy, stinging, strong, tangy, tart **2.** acrimonious, acute, barbed, biting, caustic, cutting, incisive, keen, mordacious, mordant, penetrating, piercing, poignant, pointed, sarcastic, scathing, sharp,

stinging, stringent, telling, trenchant, vitriolic
▷ **Antonyms** bland, dull, inane, mild, moderate, tasteless, unsavoury, un~ stimulating, weak

punish 1. beat, bring to book, cane, casti~ gate, chasten, chastise, correct, disci~ pline, flog, give a lesson to, give (some~ one) the works (*slang*), lash, penalize, rap someone's knuckles, scourge, sen~ tence, slap someone's wrist, throw the book at, whip **2.** abuse, batter, give (someone) a going-over (*informal*), harm, hurt, injure, knock about, mal~ treat, manhandle, misuse, oppress, rough up

punishable blameworthy, chargeable, convictable, criminal, culpable, indict~ able

punishing arduous, backbreaking, bur~ densome, demanding, exhausting, grinding, gruelling, hard, strenuous, taxing, tiring, uphill, wearing
▷ **Antonyms** cushy (*informal*), easy, ef~ fortless, light, simple, undemanding, unexacting, untaxing

punishment 1. chastening, chastisement, comeuppance (*slang*), correction, disci~ pline, just deserts, penalty, penance, punitive measures, retribution, sanc~ tion, what for (*informal*) **2.** *informal* abuse, beating, hard work, maltreat~ ment, manhandling, pain, rough treat~ ment, slave labour, torture, victimiza~ tion

punitive in reprisal, in retaliation, puni~ tory, retaliative, retaliatory, revengeful, vindictive

punt *verb* **1.** back, bet, gamble, lay, stake, wager *~noun* **2.** bet, gamble, stake, wa~ ger **3.** backer, better, gambler, punter

punter *noun* **1.** backer, better, gambler, punt (*chiefly Brit.*) **2.** *informal* bloke (*Brit. informal*), fellow, guy (*informal*), man in the street, person **3.** *informal* client, customer

puny 1. diminutive, dwarfish, feeble, frail, little, pint-sized (*informal*), pygmy *or* pigmy, sickly, stunted, tiny, under~ fed, undersized, undeveloped, weak, weakly **2.** inconsequential, inferior, in~ significant, minor, paltry, petty, pid~ dling (*informal*), trifling, trivial, worth~ less
▷ **Antonyms** (*sense 1*) brawny, burly, healthy, hefty (*informal*), husky (*infor~ mal*), powerful, robust, strong, sturdy, well-built, well-developed

pup *or* **puppy** *figurative* braggart, cub, jackanapes, popinjay, whelp, whipper~ snapper, young dog

pupil beginner, catechumen, disciple, learner, neophyte, novice, scholar, schoolboy, schoolgirl, student, trainee, tyro
▷ **Antonyms** coach, instructor, master, mistress, schoolmaster, schoolmistress, schoolteacher, teacher, trainer, tutor

puppet 1. doll, marionette **2.** *figurative* cat's-paw, creature, dupe, figurehead, gull (*archaic*), instrument, mouthpiece, pawn, stooge, tool

purchasable 1. bribable, corrupt, corrup~ tible, dishonest, having one's price, un~ scrupulous, venal **2.** available, for sale, in stock, obtainable, on sale, on the market, to be had

purchase *verb* **1.** acquire, buy, come by, gain, get, get hold of, invest in, make a purchase, obtain, pay for, pick up, pro~ cure, score (*slang*), secure, shop for **2.** achieve, attain, earn, gain, realize, win *~noun* **3.** acquisition, asset, buy, gain, investment, possession, property **4.** ad~ vantage, edge, foothold, footing, grasp, grip, hold, influence, lever, leverage, support, toehold
▷ **Antonyms** *~verb* (*sense 1*) hawk, mar~ ket, merchandise, peddle, retail, sell, trade in, vend *~noun* (*sense 3*) market~ ing, sale, selling, vending

purchaser buyer, consumer, customer, vendee (*Law*)
▷ **Antonyms** dealer, merchant, retailer, salesman, salesperson, saleswoman, seller, shopkeeper, tradesman, vendor

pure 1. authentic, clear, flawless, genu~ ine, natural, neat, perfect, real, simple, straight, true, unalloyed, unmixed **2.** clean, disinfected, germ-free, immacu~ late, pasteurized, sanitary, spotless, squeaky-clean, sterile, sterilized, un~ adulterated, unblemished, uncontami~ nated, unpolluted, untainted, whole~ some **3.** blameless, chaste, guileless, honest, immaculate, impeccable, inno~ cent, maidenly, modest, true, uncor~ rupted, undefiled, unspotted, unstained, unsullied, upright, virgin, virginal, vir~ tuous **4.** absolute, complete, mere, out~ right, sheer, thorough, unmitigated, unqualified, utter **5.** abstract, academic, philosophical, speculative, theoretical
▷ **Antonyms** (*senses 1 & 2*) adulterated, contaminated, dirty, filthy, flawed, im~ perfect, impure, infected, insincere, mixed, polluted, tainted (*sense 3*) con~ taminated, corrupt, defiled, guilty, im~ modest, immoral, impure, indecent, ob~ scene, sinful, spoiled, unchaste, un~ clean, untrue (*sense 4*) qualified (*sense 5*) applied, practical

purebred blood, full-blooded, pedigree, thoroughbred

purely absolutely, completely, entirely, exclusively, just, merely, only, plainly, simply, solely, totally, wholly

purgative 1. *noun* aperient (*Medical*), ca~ thartic, depurative, emetic, enema, evacuant, laxative, physic (*rare*), purge **2.** *~adjective* aperient (*Medical*), cleans~ ing, depurative, evacuant, laxative, purging

purgatory *as used informally* agony, hell (*informal*), hell on earth, misery, murder (*informal*), the rack, torment, torture

purge *verb* **1.** axe (*informal*), clean out, dismiss, do away with, eject, eradicate, expel, exterminate, get rid of, kill, liquidate, oust, remove, rid of, rout out, sweep out, wipe from the face of the earth, wipe out **2.** absolve, cleanse, clear, exonerate, expiate, forgive, pardon, purify, wash *~noun* **3.** cleanup, crushing, ejection, elimination, eradication, expulsion, liquidation, reign of terror, removal, suppression, witch hunt **4.** aperient (*Medical*), cathartic, dose of salts, emetic, enema, laxative, physic (*rare*), purgative (*Medical*)

purify 1. clarify, clean, cleanse, decontaminate, disinfect, filter, fumigate, refine, sanitize, wash **2.** absolve, cleanse, exculpate, exonerate, lustrate, redeem, sanctify, shrive

▷ **Antonyms** adulterate, befoul, contaminate, corrupt, defile, foul, infect, pollute, soil, stain, sully, taint, tarnish, vitiate

purist classicist, formalist, pedant, precisian, stickler

puritan 1. *noun* fanatic, moralist, pietist, prude, rigorist, zealot **2.** *~adjective* ascetic, austere, hidebound, intolerant, moralistic, narrow, narrow-minded, prudish, puritanical, severe, strait-laced, strict

puritanical ascetic, austere, bigoted, disapproving, fanatical, forbidding, narrow, narrow-minded, prim, proper, prudish, puritan, rigid, severe, stiff, strait-laced, strict, stuffy

▷ **Antonyms** broad-minded, hedonistic, indulgent, latitudinarian, liberal, permissive, tolerant

purity 1. brilliance, clarity, cleanliness, cleanness, clearness, faultlessness, fineness, genuineness, immaculateness, pureness, untaintedness, wholesomeness **2.** blamelessness, chasteness, chastity, decency, guilelessness, honesty, innocence, integrity, piety, rectitude, sincerity, virginity, virtue, virtuousness

▷ **Antonyms** (*sense 1*) cloudiness, contamination, impurity (*sense 2*) immodesty, immorality, impurity, unchasteness, vice, wickedness

purlieus 1. borders, confines, environs, fringes, limits, neighbourhood, outskirts, periphery, precincts, suburbs, vicinity **2.** (*sometimes singular*) hang-out (*informal*), haunt, patch, resort, stamping ground, territory

purloin appropriate, blag (*slang*), cabbage (*Brit. slang*), filch, knock off (*slang*), lift (*informal*), nick (*slang, chiefly Brit.*), nobble (*Brit. slang*), pilfer, pinch (*informal*), prig (*Brit. slang*), rob, snaffle (*Brit. informal*), snitch (*slang*), steal, swipe (*slang*), thieve, walk off with

purport *verb* **1.** allege, assert, claim, declare, maintain, pose as, pretend, proclaim, profess **2.** betoken, convey, denote, express, imply, import, indicate, intend, mean, point to, signify, suggest *~noun* **3.** bearing, drift, gist, idea, implication, import, meaning, sense, significance, spirit, tendency, tenor **4.** aim, design, intent, intention, object, objective, plan, purpose

purpose *noun* **1.** aim, design, function, idea, intention, object, point, principle, reason, the why and wherefore **2.** aim, ambition, aspiration, design, desire, end, goal, Holy Grail (*informal*), hope, intention, object, objective, plan, project, scheme, target, view, wish **3.** constancy, determination, firmness, persistence, resolution, resolve, single-mindedness, steadfastness, tenacity, will **4.** advantage, avail, benefit, effect, gain, good, mileage (*informal*), outcome, profit, result, return, use, utility **5. on purpose** by design, deliberately, designedly, intentionally, knowingly, purposely, wilfully, wittingly *~verb* **6.** aim, aspire, commit oneself, contemplate, decide, design, determine, have a mind to, intend, make up one's mind, mean, meditate, plan, propose, resolve, set one's sights on, think to, work towards

purposeful decided, deliberate, determined, firm, fixed, immovable, positive, resolute, resolved, settled, single-minded, steadfast, strong-willed, tenacious, unfaltering

▷ **Antonyms** aimless, faltering, irresolute, otiose, purposeless, undecided, undetermined, vacillating, wavering

purposeless aimless, empty, goalless, motiveless, needless, otiose, pointless, senseless, uncalled-for, unnecessary, useless, vacuous, wanky (*taboo slang*), wanton, without rhyme or reason

purposely by design, calculatedly, consciously, deliberately, designedly, expressly, intentionally, knowingly, on purpose, wilfully, with intent

▷ **Antonyms** accidentally, by accident, by chance, by mistake, inadvertently, unconsciously, unintentionally, unknowingly, unwittingly

purse *noun* **1.** money-bag, pouch, wallet **2.** coffers, exchequer, funds, means, money, resources, treasury, wealth, wherewithal **3.** award, gift, present, prize, reward *~verb* **4.** close, contract, knit, pout, press together, pucker, tighten, wrinkle

pursuance bringing about, carrying out, discharge, doing, effecting, execution, following, performance, prosecution, pursuing

pursue 1. accompany, attend, chase, dog, follow, give chase to, go after, harass, harry, haunt, hound, hunt, hunt down, plague, run after, shadow, stalk, tail (*informal*), track **2**. aim for, aspire to, desire, have as one's goal, purpose, seek, strive for, try for, work towards **3**. adhere to, carry on, continue, cultivate, hold to, keep on, maintain, persevere in, persist in, proceed, see through **4**. apply oneself, carry on, conduct, engage in, perform, ply, practise, prosecute, tackle, wage, work at **5**. chase after, court, make up to (*informal*), pay attention to, pay court to, set one's cap at, woo

▷ **Antonyms** avoid, eschew, fight shy of, flee, give (someone *or* something) a wide berth, keep away from, run away from, shun, steer clear of

pursuit 1. chase, hunt, hunting, inquiry, quest, search, seeking, tracking, trail, trailing **2**. activity, hobby, interest, line, occupation, pastime, pleasure, vocation

purvey 1. cater, deal in, furnish, provide, provision, retail, sell, supply, trade in, victual **2**. communicate, make available, pass on, publish, retail, spread, transmit

purview 1. ambit, compass, confine(s), extent, field, limit, orbit, province, range, reach, scope, sphere **2**. comprehension, ken, overview, perspective, range of view, understanding

push *verb* **1**. depress, drive, poke, press, propel, ram, shove, thrust **2**. elbow, jostle, make *or* force one's way, move, shoulder, shove, squeeze, thrust **3**. egg on, encourage, expedite, hurry, impel, incite, persuade, press, prod, speed (up), spur, urge **4**. advertise, boost, cry up, hype, make known, plug (*informal*), promote, propagandize, publicize, puff **5**. browbeat, coerce, constrain, dragoon, encourage, exert influence on, influence, oblige *~noun* **6**. butt, jolt, nudge, poke, prod, shove, thrust **7**. *informal* ambition, determination, drive, dynamism, energy, enterprise, get-up-and-go (*informal*), go (*informal*), gumption (*informal*), initiative, pep, vigour, vitality **8**. *informal* advance, assault, attack, campaign, charge, effort, offensive, onset, thrust **9**. **the push** *slang* discharge, dismissal, kiss-off (*slang, chiefly U.S. & Canad.*), marching orders (*informal*), one's books (*informal*), one's cards, the boot (*slang*), the (old) heave-ho (*informal*), the order of the boot (*slang*), the sack (*informal*)

▷ **Antonyms** *~verb* (*sense 1*) drag, draw, haul, jerk, pull, tow, trail, tug, yank (*sense 3*) deter, discourage, dissuade, put off *~noun* (*sense 6*) jerk, pull, tug, yank

pushed (*often with* **for**) hurried, in difficulty, pressed, rushed, short of, tight, under pressure, up against it (*informal*)

pushing 1. ambitious, determined, driving, dynamic, enterprising, go-ahead, on the go, purposeful, resourceful **2**. assertive, bold, brash, bumptious, forward, impertinent, intrusive, presumptuous, pushy (*informal*), self-assertive

push off beat it (*slang*), depart, get lost (*informal*), go away, hit the road (*slang*), hook it (*slang*), launch, leave, light out (*informal*), make oneself scarce (*informal*), make tracks, pack one's bags (*informal*), shove off (*informal*), slope off, take off (*informal*)

pushover 1. breeze (*U.S. & Canad. informal*), cakewalk (*informal*), child's play (*informal*), cinch (*slang*), doddle (*Brit. slang*), duck soup (*U.S. slang*), picnic (*informal*), piece of cake (*Brit. informal*), piece of piss (*taboo slang*), plain sailing, walkover (*informal*) **2**. chump (*informal*), easy game (*informal*), easy *or* soft mark (*informal*), mug (*Brit. slang*), soft touch (*slang*), stooge (*slang*), sucker (*slang*), walkover (*informal*)

▷ **Antonyms** (*sense 1*) challenge, hassle (*informal*), ordeal, test, trial, undertaking

pushy aggressive, ambitious, bold, brash, bumptious, forceful, loud, obnoxious, obtrusive, offensive, officious, presumptuous, pushing, self-assertive

▷ **Antonyms** diffident, inoffensive, meek, mousy, quiet, reserved, retiring, self-effacing, shy, timid, unassertive, unassuming, unobtrusive

pusillanimous abject, chicken-hearted, cowardly, craven, faint-hearted, fearful, feeble, gutless (*informal*), lily-livered, recreant (*archaic*), spineless, timid, timorous, weak, yellow (*informal*)

▷ **Antonyms** bold, brave, courageous, daring, dauntless, fearless, gallant, heroic, intrepid, plucky, valiant, valorous

pussyfoot 1. creep, prowl, slink, steal, tiptoe, tread warily **2**. beat about the bush, be noncommittal, equivocate, flannel (*Brit. informal*), hedge, hum and haw, prevaricate, sit on the fence, tergiversate

pustule abscess, blister, boil, fester, gathering, pimple, ulcer, zit (*slang*)

put 1. bring, deposit, establish, fix, lay, place, position, rest, set, settle, situate **2**. commit, condemn, consign, doom, enjoin, impose, inflict, levy, subject **3**. assign, constrain, employ, force, induce, make, oblige, require, set, subject to **4**. express, phrase, pose, set, state, utter, word **5**. advance, bring forward, forward, offer, posit, present, propose, set before, submit, tender **6**. cast, fling, heave, hurl, lob, pitch, throw, toss

put across *or* **over** communicate, convey, explain, get across, get through, make clear, make oneself understood, spell out

put aside *or* **by 1**. cache, deposit, keep in reserve, lay by, salt away, save, squirrel away, stockpile, store, stow away **2**. bury, discount, disregard, forget, ignore

putative alleged, assumed, commonly believed, imputed, presumed, presumptive, reported, reputed, supposed

put away 1. put back, replace, return to (its) place, tidy away **2.** deposit, keep, lay in, put by, save, set aside, store away **3.** certify, commit, confine, institutionalize, lock up **4.** consume, devour, eat up, gobble, gulp down, wolf down **5.** destroy, do away with, put down, put out of its misery, put to sleep

put-down barb, dig, disparagement, gibe, humiliation, kick in the teeth (*slang*), knock (*informal*), one in the eye (*informal*), rebuff, sarcasm, slight, sneer, snub

put down 1. enter, inscribe, log, record, set down, take down, transcribe, write down **2.** crush, quash, quell, repress, silence, stamp out, suppress **3.** (*with* **to**) ascribe, attribute, impute, set down **4.** destroy, do away with, put away, put out of its misery, put to sleep **5.** *slang* condemn, crush, deflate, dismiss, disparage, humiliate, mortify, reject, shame, slight, snub

put forward advance, introduce, move, nominate, prescribe, present, press, proffer, propose, recommend, submit, suggest, tender

put off 1. defer, delay, hold over, postpone, put back, put on ice, put on the back burner (*informal*), reschedule, take a rain check on (*U.S. & Canad. informal*) **2.** abash, confuse, discomfit, disconcert, dismay, distress, faze, nonplus, perturb, rattle (*informal*), take the wind out of someone's sails, throw (*informal*), unsettle **3.** discourage, dishearten, dissuade

▷ **Antonyms** (*sense 3*) egg on, encourage, incite, persuade, prompt, push, spur, urge

put on 1. change into, don, dress, get dressed in, slip into **2.** affect, assume, fake, feign, make believe, play-act, pretend, sham, simulate **3.** do, mount, present, produce, show, stage **4.** add, gain, increase by **5.** back, bet, lay, place, wager

▷ **Antonyms** (*sense 1*) cast off, doff, remove, shed, slip off, slip out of, take off, throw off, undress

put out 1. anger, annoy, confound, disturb, exasperate, harass, irk, irritate, nettle, perturb, provoke, vex **2.** blow out, douse, extinguish, quench, smother, snuff out, stamp out **3.** bother, discomfit, discommode, discompose, disconcert, discountenance, disturb, embarrass, impose upon, incommode, inconvenience, put on the spot, take the wind out of someone's sails, trouble, upset **4.** bring out, broadcast, circulate, issue, make known, make public, publish, release

putrefy break down, corrupt, decay, decompose, deteriorate, go bad, rot, spoil, stink, taint

putrescent decaying, decomposing, going bad, rotting, stinking

putrid bad, contaminated, corrupt, decayed, decomposed, fetid, foul, off, olid, putrefied, rancid, rank, reeking, rotten, rotting, spoiled, stinking, tainted

▷ **Antonyms** clean, fresh, pure, sweet, uncontaminated, untainted, wholesome

put through accomplish, achieve, bring off, carry through, conclude, do, effect, execute, manage, pull off, realize

put up 1. build, construct, erect, fabricate, raise **2.** accommodate, board, entertain, give one lodging, house, lodge, take in **3.** float, nominate, offer, present, propose, put forward, recommend, submit **4.** advance, give, invest, pay, pledge, provide, supply **5. put up to** egg on, encourage, goad, incite, instigate, prompt, put the idea into one's head, urge **6. put up with** *informal* abide, bear, brook, endure, hack (*slang*), lump (*informal*), pocket, stand, stand for, stomach, suffer, swallow, take, tolerate

▷ **Antonyms** (*sense 1*) demolish, destroy, flatten, knock down, level, pull down, raze, tear down (*sense 6*) not stand for, object to, oppose, protest against, reject, take exception to

put-upon abused, beset, exploited, harried, imposed upon, inconvenienced, overworked, put-out, saddled, taken advantage of, taken for a fool, taken for granted, troubled

puzzle *verb* **1.** baffle, beat (*slang*), bewilder, confound, confuse, flummox, mystify, nonplus, perplex, stump **2.** ask oneself, brood, cudgel *or* rack one's brains, mull over, muse, ponder, study, think about, think hard, wonder **3.** (*usually with* **out**) clear up, crack, crack the code, decipher, figure out, find the key, get it, get the answer, resolve, see, solve, sort out, suss (out) (*slang*), think through, unravel, work out *~noun* **4.** brain-teaser (*informal*), conundrum, enigma, labyrinth, maze, mystery, paradox, poser, problem, question, question mark, riddle, teaser **5.** bafflement, bewilderment, confusion, difficulty, dilemma, perplexity, quandary, uncertainty

puzzled at a loss, at sea, baffled, beaten, bewildered, clueless, confused, doubtful, flummoxed, in a fog, lost, mixed up, mystified, nonplussed, perplexed, stuck, stumped, without a clue

puzzlement bafflement, bewilderment, confusion, disorientation, doubt, doubtfulness, mystification, perplexity, questioning, surprise, uncertainty, wonder

puzzling abstruse, ambiguous, baffling, bewildering, beyond one, enigmatic, full of surprises, hard, incomprehensible, inexplicable, involved, knotty, labyrinthine, misleading, mystifying, oracular, perplexing, unaccountable, unclear, unfathomable

▷ **Antonyms** clear, comprehensible, easy, evident, intelligible, lucid, manifest, obvious, patent, plain, simple, unambiguous, unequivocal, unmistakable

pygmy, pigmy *noun* **1.** dwarf, homunculus, Lilliputian, manikin, midget, munchkin (*informal, chiefly U.S.*), shrimp (*informal*), Tom Thumb **2.** cipher, lightweight (*informal*), mediocrity, nobody, nonentity, pipsqueak (*informal*), small fry *~adjective* **3.** baby, diminutive, dwarf, dwarfish, elfin, Lilliputian, midget, miniature, minuscule, pocket, pygmean, small, stunted, teensy-weensy, teeny-weeny, tiny, undersized, wee

pyromaniac arsonist, firebug (*informal*), fire raiser, incendiary

Q, q

quack 1. *noun* charlatan, fake, fraud, humbug, impostor, mountebank, phoney *or* phony (*informal*), pretender, quacksalver (*archaic*) **2.** *~adjective* counterfeit, fake, fraudulent, phoney *or* phony (*informal*), pretended, sham

quaff bend the elbow (*informal*), bevvy (*dialect*), carouse, down, drink, gulp, guzzle, imbibe, swallow, swig (*informal*), tope

quaggy boggy, fenny, marshy, miry, muddy, mushy, paludal, soft, soggy, squelchy, swampy, yielding

quagmire 1. bog, fen, marsh, mire, morass, quicksand, slough, swamp **2.** difficulty, dilemma, entanglement, fix (*informal*), imbroglio, impasse, jam (*informal*), muddle, pass, pickle (*informal*), pinch, plight, predicament, quandary, scrape (*informal*)

quail blanch, blench, cower, cringe, droop, faint, falter, flinch, have cold feet (*informal*), quake, recoil, shake, shrink, shudder, tremble

quaint 1. bizarre, curious, droll, eccentric, fanciful, fantastic, odd, old-fashioned, original, peculiar, queer, rum (*Brit. slang*), singular, strange, unusual, whimsical **2.** antiquated, antique, artful, charming, gothic, ingenious, old-fashioned, old-world, picturesque

▷ **Antonyms** fashionable, modern, new, normal, ordinary, up-to-date

quake convulse, move, pulsate, quail, quiver, rock, shake, shiver, shudder, throb, totter, tremble, vibrate, waver, wobble

qualification 1. ability, accomplishment, aptitude, attribute, capability, capacity, eligibility, endowment(s), fitness, quality, skill, suitability, suitableness **2.** allowance, caveat, condition, criterion, exception, exemption, limitation, modification, objection, prerequisite, proviso, requirement, reservation, restriction, rider, stipulation

qualified 1. able, accomplished, adept, capable, certificated, competent, efficient, eligible, equipped, experienced, expert, fit, knowledgeable, licensed, practised, proficient, skilful, talented, trained **2.** bounded, circumscribed, conditional, confined, contingent, equivocal, guarded, limited, modified, provisional, reserved, restricted

▷ **Antonyms** (*sense 1*) amateur, apprentice, self-styled, self-taught, trainee, uncertificated, unqualified, untrained (*sense 2*) categorical, outright, unconditional, unequivocal, whole-hearted

qualify 1. capacitate, certify, commission, condition, empower, endow, equip, fit, ground, permit, prepare, ready, sanction, train **2.** abate, adapt, assuage, circumscribe, diminish, ease, lessen, limit, mitigate, moderate, modify, modulate, reduce, regulate, restrain, restrict, soften, temper, vary **3.** characterize, describe, designate, distinguish, modify, name

▷ **Antonyms** (*sense 1*) ban, debar, disqualify, forbid, preclude, prevent

quality 1. aspect, attribute, characteristic, condition, feature, mark, peculiarity, property, trait **2.** character, constitution, description, essence, kind, make, nature, sort **3.** calibre, distinction, excellence, grade, merit, position, pre-eminence, rank, standing, status, superiority, value, worth **4.** *obsolete* aristocracy, gentry, nobility, ruling class, upper class

qualm 1. anxiety, apprehension, compunction, disquiet, doubt, hesitation, misgiving, regret, reluctance, remorse, scruple, twinge *or* pang of conscience, uncertainty, uneasiness **2.** agony, attack, nausea, pang, queasiness, sickness, spasm, throe (*rare*), twinge

quandary bewilderment, cleft stick, delicate situation, difficulty, dilemma, doubt, embarrassment, impasse, perplexity, plight, predicament, puzzle, strait, uncertainty

quantity 1. aggregate, allotment, amount, lot, number, part, portion, quota, sum, total **2.** bulk, capacity, expanse, extent, greatness, length, magnitude, mass, measure, size, volume

quarrel *noun* **1.** affray, altercation, argument, *bagarre,* brawl, breach, broil, commotion, contention, controversy, difference (of opinion), disagreement, discord, disputation, dispute, dissension, dissidence, disturbance, feud, fight, fracas, fray, misunderstanding, row, scrap (*informal*), shindig (*informal*), shindy (*informal*), skirmish, spat, squabble, strife, tiff, tumult, vendetta, wrangle *~verb* **2.** altercate, argue, bicker, brawl, clash, differ, disagree, dispute, fall out (*informal*), fight, fight like cat and dog, go at it hammer and tongs, row, spar, squabble, wrangle **3.** carp, cavil, complain, decry, disapprove, find fault, object to, take exception to

▷ **Antonyms** (*sense 1*) accord, agreement, concord (*sense 2*) agree, get on *or* along (with)

quarrelsome argumentative, belligerent, cantankerous, cat-and-dog (*informal*), choleric, combative, contentious, cross, disputatious, fractious, ill-tempered, irascible, irritable, litigious, peevish, petulant, pugnacious, querulous

▷ **Antonyms** easy-going, equable, even-tempered, placid

quarry aim, game, goal, objective, prey, prize, victim

quarter *noun* **1.** area, direction, district, locality, location, neighbourhood, part, place, point, position, province, region, side, spot, station, territory, zone **2.** clemency, compassion, favour, forgiveness, leniency, mercy, pity *~verb* **3.** accommodate, billet, board, house, install, lodge, place, post, put up, station

quarters abode, accommodation, barracks, billet, cantonment (*Military*), chambers, digs (*Brit. informal*), domicile, dwelling, habitation, lodging, lodgings, post, residence, rooms, shelter, station

quash 1. beat, crush, destroy, extinguish, extirpate, overthrow, put down, quell, quench, repress, squash, subdue, suppress **2.** annul, cancel, declare null and void, invalidate, nullify, overrule, overthrow, rescind, reverse, revoke, set aside, void

quasi- 1. almost, apparently, partly, seemingly, supposedly **2.** apparent, fake, mock, near, nominal, pretended, pseudo-, seeming, semi-, sham, so-called, synthetic, virtual, would-be

quaver 1. *verb* flicker, flutter, oscillate, pulsate, quake, quiver, shake, shudder, thrill, tremble, trill, twitter, vibrate, waver **2.** *~noun* break, quiver, shake, sob, throb, tremble, trembling, tremor, trill, vibration, warble

queasy 1. bilious, giddy, green around the gills (*informal*), groggy (*informal*), ill, indisposed, nauseated, off colour, queer, sick, sickish, squeamish, uncomfortable, unwell, upset **2.** anxious, concerned, fidgety, ill at ease, restless, troubled, uncertain, uneasy, worried

queen 1. consort, monarch, ruler, sovereign **2.** diva, doyenne, ideal, idol, mistress, model, perfection, prima donna, star

queenly grand, imperial, majestic, noble, regal, royal, stately

queer *adjective* **1.** abnormal, anomalous, atypical, curious, disquieting, droll, eerie, erratic, extraordinary, funny, left-field (*informal*), odd, outlandish, *outré,* peculiar, remarkable, rum (*Brit. slang*), singular, strange, uncanny, uncommon, unconventional, unnatural, unorthodox, unusual, weird **2.** doubtful, dubious, fishy (*informal*), irregular, mysterious, puzzling, questionable, shady (*informal*), suspicious **3.** dizzy, faint, giddy, light-headed, queasy, reeling, uneasy **4.** crazy, demented, eccentric, idiosyncratic, irrational, mad, odd, touched, unbalanced, unhinged *~verb* **5.** bodge (*informal*), botch, endanger, harm, impair, imperil, injure, jeopardize, mar, ruin, spoil, thwart, wreck

▷ **Antonyms** *~adjective* believable, common, conventional, customary, natural, normal, ordinary, orthodox, rational, regular, straight, unexceptional, unoriginal *~verb* aid, boost, enhance, help

quell 1. conquer, crush, defeat, extinguish, overcome, overpower, put down, quash, squelch, stamp out, stifle, subdue, suppress, vanquish **2.** allay, alleviate, appease, assuage, calm, compose, deaden, dull, mitigate, moderate, mollify, pacify, quiet, silence, soothe

quench 1. check, crush, destroy, douse, end, extinguish, put out, smother, snuff out, squelch, stifle, suppress **2.** allay, appease, cool, sate, satiate, satisfy, slake

querulous cantankerous, captious, carping, censorious, complaining, critical, cross, discontented, dissatisfied, fault-finding, fretful, grouchy (*informal*), grumbling, hard to please, irascible, irritable, murmuring, peevish, petulant, plaintive, ratty (*Brit. & N.Z. informal*), sour, testy, tetchy, touchy, waspish, whining

▷ **Antonyms** contented, easy to please, equable, placid, uncomplaining, uncritical, undemanding

query *verb* **1.** ask, enquire, question **2.** challenge, disbelieve, dispute, distrust, doubt, mistrust, suspect *~noun* **3.** demand, doubt, hesitation, inquiry, objection, problem, question, reservation, scepticism, suspicion

quest *noun* adventure, crusade, enterprise, expedition, exploration, hunt, journey, mission, pilgrimage, pursuit, search, voyage

question *verb* **1.** ask, catechize, cross-examine, enquire, examine, grill (*informal*), interrogate, interview, investigate, probe, pump (*informal*), quiz, sound out **2.** call into question, cast doubt upon, challenge, controvert, disbelieve, dispute, distrust, doubt, impugn, mistrust, oppose, query, suspect *~noun* **3.** examination, inquiry, interrogation, investigation **4.** argument, can of worms (*informal*), confusion, contention, controversy, debate, difficulty, dispute, doubt, dubiety, misgiving, problem, query, uncertainty **5.** bone of contention, issue, motion, point, point at issue, proposal, proposition, subject, theme, topic **6. in question** at issue, in doubt, open to debate, under discussion **7. out of the question** impossible, inconceivable, not to be thought of, unthinkable

▷ **Antonyms** (*senses 1 & 3*) answer, reply (*sense 2*) accept, believe, buy (*slang*), swallow (*informal*), take on board, take on trust

questionable arguable, controversial, controvertible, debatable, disputable, dodgy (*Brit., Austral., & N.Z. informal*), doubtful, dubious, dubitable, equivocal, fishy (*informal*), iffy (*informal*), moot, paradoxical, problematical, shady (*informal*), suspect, suspicious, uncertain, unproven, unreliable

▷ **Antonyms** authoritative, certain, incontrovertible, indisputable, straightforward, unequivocal

queue chain, concatenation, file, line, order, progression, sequence, series, string, succession, train

quibble 1. *verb* carp, cavil, equivocate, evade, pretend, prevaricate, shift, split hairs **2.** *~noun* artifice, cavil, complaint, criticism, duplicity, equivocation, evasion, nicety, niggle, objection, pretence, prevarication, protest, quiddity, quirk, shift, sophism, subterfuge, subtlety

quibbling ambiguous, carping, caviling, critical, equivocal, evasive, hair-splitting, jesuitical, niggling, nit-picking (*informal*), overnice, sophistical

quick 1. active, brief, brisk, cursory, expeditious, express, fast, fleet, hasty, headlong, hurried, pdq (*slang*), perfunctory, prompt, quickie (*informal*), rapid, speedy, sudden, swift **2.** agile, alert, animated, energetic, flying, keen, lively, nimble, spirited, sprightly, spry, vivacious, winged **3.** able, acute, adept, adroit, all there (*informal*), apt, astute, bright (*informal*), clever, deft, dexterous, discerning, intelligent, nimble-witted, perceptive, quick on the uptake (*informal*), quick-witted, receptive, sharp, shrewd, skilful, smart **4.** abrupt, curt, excitable, hasty, impatient, irascible, irritable, passionate, petulant, testy, touchy **5.** *archaic* alive, animate, existing, live, living, viable

▷ **Antonyms** (*sense 1*) gradual, long (*sense 2*) dull, heavy, inactive, lazy, lethargic, slow, sluggish, unresponsive (*sense 3*) inexpert, maladroit, stupid, unintelligent, unskilful (*sense 4*) calm, deliberate, patient, restrained

quicken 1. accelerate, dispatch, expedite, hasten, hurry, impel, precipitate, speed **2.** activate, animate, arouse, energize, excite, galvanize, incite, inspire, invigorate, kindle, refresh, reinvigorate, resuscitate, revitalize, revive, rouse, stimulate, strengthen, vitalize, vivify

quickly abruptly, apace, at a rate of knots (*informal*), at *or* on the double, at speed, briskly, expeditiously, fast, hastily, hell for leather (*informal*), hotfoot, hurriedly, immediately, instantly, like greased lightning (*informal*), like lightning, like nobody's business (*informal*), like the clappers (*Brit. informal*), pdq (*slang*), posthaste, promptly, pronto (*informal*), quick, rapidly, soon, speedily, swiftly, with all speed

▷ **Antonyms** carefully, eventually, slowly, sluggishly, unhurriedly

quick-tempered cantankerous, choleric, excitable, fiery, hot-tempered, impatient, impulsive, irascible, irritable, petulant, quarrelsome, ratty (*Brit. & N.Z. informal*), shrewish, splenetic, testy, tetchy, waspish

▷ **Antonyms** cool, dispassionate, phlegmatic, placid, slow to anger, tolerant

quick-witted alert, astute, bright (*informal*), clever, keen, perceptive, sharp, shrewd, smart

▷ **Antonyms** dull, obtuse, slow, slow-witted, stupid, thick (*informal*), unperceptive

quid pro quo compensation, equivalent, exchange, interchange, reprisal, retaliation, substitution, tit for tat

quiescent calm, dormant, in abeyance, inactive, latent, motionless, peaceful, placid, quiet, resting, serene, silent, smooth, still, tranquil, unagitated, undisturbed, unmoving, unruffled

quiet *adjective* **1.** dumb, hushed, inaudible, low, low-pitched, noiseless, peaceful, silent, soft, soundless **2.** calm, contented, gentle, mild, motionless, pacific, peaceful, placid, restful, serene, smooth, tranquil, untroubled **3.** isolated, private, retired, secluded, secret, sequestered, undisturbed, unfrequented **4.** conservative, modest, plain, restrained, simple, sober, subdued, unassuming, unobtrusive, unpretentious **5.** collected, docile, even-tempered, gentle, imperturbable, meek, mild, phlegmatic, reserved, retiring, sedate, shy, unexcitable *~noun* **6.** calmness, ease, peace, quietness, repose, rest, serenity, silence, stillness, tranquillity

▷ **Antonyms** *~adjective* (*sense 1*) deafening, ear-splitting, high-decibel, high-volume, loud, noisy, stentorian (*sense 2*) agitated, alert, excitable, exciting, frenetic, troubled, turbulent, violent (*sense 3*) bustling, busy, crowded, exciting, fashionable, lively, popular, vibrant (*sense 4*) blatant, brash, bright, conspicuous, glaring, loud, obtrusive, ostentatious, pretentious, showy (*sense 5*) excitable, excited, high-spirited, impatient, loquacious, passionate, restless, talkative, verbose, violent *~noun* (*sense 6*) activity, bustle, commotion, din, disturbance, noise, racket

quieten *verb* allay, alleviate, appease, assuage, blunt, calm, compose, deaden, dull, hush, lull, mitigate, mollify, muffle, mute, palliate, quell, quiet, shush (*informal*), silence, soothe, stifle, still, stop, subdue, tranquillize

▷ **Antonyms** aggravate, exacerbate, intensify, provoke, upset, worsen

quietly 1. confidentially, dumbly, in a low voice *or* whisper, in an undertone, inaudibly, in hushed tones, in silence, mutely, noiselessly, privately, secretly, silently, softly, without talking **2.** calmly, contentedly, dispassionately, meekly, mildly, patiently, placidly, serenely, undemonstratively **3.** coyly, demurely, diffidently, humbly, modestly, unassumingly, unobtrusively, unostentatiously, unpretentiously

quietness calm, calmness, hush, peace, placidity, quiescence, quiet, quietude, repose, rest, serenity, silence, still, stillness, tranquillity

quietus clincher (*informal*), *coup de grâce,* death, deathblow, demise, end, final blow, finish

quilt bedspread, comforter (*U.S.*), continental quilt, counterpane, coverlet, doona (*Austral.*), downie (*informal*), duvet, eiderdown

quintessence core, distillation, essence, extract, gist, heart, kernel, lifeblood, marrow, pith, soul, spirit

quip *noun* badinage, *bon mot,* counterattack, gibe, jest, joke, pleasantry, repartee, retort, riposte, sally, wisecrack (*informal*), witticism

quirk aberration, bee in one's bonnet, caprice, characteristic, eccentricity, fancy, fetish, foible, habit, *idée fixe,* idiosyncrasy, kink, mannerism, oddity, peculiarity, singularity, trait, vagary, whim

quirky capricious, curious, eccentric, fanciful, idiosyncratic, odd, offbeat, peculiar, rum (*Brit. slang*), singular, unpredictable, unusual, whimsical

quisling betrayer, collaborator, fifth columnist, Judas, renegade, traitor, turncoat

quit *verb* **1.** abandon, abdicate, decamp, depart, desert, exit, forsake, go, leave, pack one's bags (*informal*), pull out, relinquish, renounce, resign, retire, step down (*informal*), surrender, take off (*informal*), withdraw **2.** abandon, cease, conclude, discontinue, drop, end, give up, halt, stop, suspend, throw in the towel *~adjective* **3.** absolved, acquitted, clear, discharged, exculpated, exempt, exonerated, free, released, rid of

▷ **Antonyms** (*sense 2*) complete, continue, finish, go on with, see through

quite 1. absolutely, completely, considerably, entirely, fully, in all respects, largely, perfectly, precisely, totally, wholly, without reservation **2.** fairly, moderately, rather, reasonably, relatively, somewhat, to a certain extent, to some degree **3.** in fact, in reality, in truth, really, truly

quiver 1. *verb* agitate, convulse, oscillate, palpitate, pulsate, quake, quaver, shake, shiver, shudder, tremble, vibrate **2.** *~noun* convulsion, oscillation, palpitation, pulsation, shake, shiver, shudder, spasm, throb, tic, tremble, tremor, vibration

quixotic absurd, chimerical, chivalrous, dreamy, fanciful, fantastical, idealistic, imaginary, impracticable, impractical, impulsive, mad, romantic, unrealistic, unworldly, Utopian, visionary, wild

quiz 1. *noun* examination, investigation, questioning, test **2.** *~verb* ask, catechize, examine, grill (*informal*), interrogate, investigate, pump (*informal*), question

quizzical arch, bantering, curious, derisive, inquiring, mocking, questioning, sardonic, supercilious, teasing

quondam bygone, earlier, ex-, foregoing, former, late, one-time, past, previous, retired, sometime

quota allocation, allowance, assignment, cut (*informal*), part, portion, proportion, ration, share, slice, whack (*informal*)

quotation 1. citation, cutting, excerpt, extract, passage, quote (*informal*), reference, selection **2.** *Commerce* bid price, charge, cost, estimate, figure, price, quote (*informal*), rate, tender

quote adduce, attest, cite, detail, extract, instance, name, paraphrase, proclaim, recall, recite, recollect, refer to, repeat, retell

quotidian 1. daily, diurnal **2.** common, commonplace, customary, everyday, habitual, ordinary, regular, routine

R, r

rabble **1.** canaille, crowd, herd, horde, mob, swarm, throng **2.** *derogatory* canaille, commonalty, commoners, common people, crowd, dregs, hoi polloi, lower classes, lumpenproletariat, masses, peasantry, populace, proletariat, riffraff, scum, the great unwashed (*informal & derogatory*), trash (*chiefly U.S. & Canad.*)

▷ **Antonyms** (*sense 2*) aristocracy, bourgeoisie, elite, gentry, high society, nobility, upper classes

rabble-rouser agitator, demagogue, firebrand, incendiary, stirrer (*informal*), troublemaker

Rabelaisian bawdy, broad, coarse, earthy, extravagant, exuberant, gross, lusty, raunchy (*slang*), robust, satirical, uninhibited, unrestrained

rabid **1.** hydrophobic, mad **2.** berserk, crazed, frantic, frenzied, furious, infuriated, mad, maniacal, raging, violent, wild **3.** bigoted, extreme, fanatical, fervent, intemperate, intolerant, irrational, narrow-minded, zealous

▷ **Antonyms** (*sense 3*) half-hearted, moderate, wishy-washy (*informal*)

race[1] **1.** *noun* chase, competition, contention, contest, dash, pursuit, rivalry **2.** *~verb* barrel (along) (*informal, chiefly U.S. & Canad.*), burn rubber (*informal*), career, compete, contest, dart, dash, fly, gallop, go like a bomb (*Brit. & N.Z. informal*), hare (*Brit. informal*), hasten, hurry, run, run like mad (*informal*), speed, tear, zoom

race[2] *noun* blood, breed, clan, ethnic group, family, folk, house, issue, kin, kindred, line, lineage, nation, offspring, people, progeny, seed (*chiefly biblical*), stock, tribe, type

racial ethnic, ethnological, folk, genealogical, genetic, national, tribal

rack *noun* **1.** frame, framework, stand, structure **2.** affliction, agony, anguish, misery, pain, pang, persecution, suffering, torment, torture *~verb* **3.** afflict, agonize, crucify, distress, excruciate, harass, harrow, oppress, pain, torment, torture **4.** force, pull, shake, strain, stress, stretch, tear, wrench

racket **1.** babel, ballyhoo (*informal*), clamour, commotion, din, disturbance, fuss, hubbub, hullabaloo, noise, outcry, pandemonium, row, rumpus, shouting, tumult, uproar **2.** criminal activity, fraud, illegal enterprise, scheme **3.** *slang* business, game (*informal*), line, occupation

rackety blaring, boisterous, clamorous, disorderly, noisy, rowdy, uproarious

racy **1.** animated, buoyant, dramatic, energetic, entertaining, exciting, exhilarating, heady, lively, sexy (*informal*), sparkling, spirited, stimulating, vigorous, zestful **2.** distinctive, piquant, pungent, rich, sharp, spicy, strong, tangy, tart, tasty **3.** bawdy, blue, broad, immodest, indecent, indelicate, naughty, near the knuckle (*informal*), off colour, risqué, smutty, spicy (*informal*), suggestive

raddled broken-down, coarsened, dilapidated, dishevelled, haggard, run-down, tattered, the worse for wear, unkempt

radiance **1.** brightness, brilliance, effulgence, glare, gleam, glitter, glow, incandescence, light, luminosity, lustre, resplendence, shine **2.** delight, gaiety, happiness, joy, pleasure, rapture, warmth

radiant **1.** beaming, bright, brilliant, effulgent, gleaming, glittering, glorious, glowing, incandescent, luminous, lustrous, resplendent, shining, sparkling, sunny **2.** beaming, beatific, blissed out, blissful, delighted, ecstatic, floating on air, gay, glowing, happy, joyful, joyous, on cloud nine (*informal*), rapt, rapturous, sent

▷ **Antonyms** (*sense 1*) black, dark, dull, gloomy, sombre (*sense 2*) disconsolate, down in the dumps (*informal*), gloomy, joyless, low, miserable, sad, sombre, sorrowful

radiate **1.** diffuse, disseminate, emanate, emit, give off *or* out, gleam, glitter, pour, scatter, send out, shed, shine, spread **2.** branch out, diverge, issue, spread out

radiation emanation, emission, rays

radical *adjective* **1.** basic, constitutional, deep-seated, essential, fundamental, innate, native, natural, organic, profound, thoroughgoing **2.** complete, drastic, entire, excessive, extreme, extremist, fanatical, revolutionary, severe, sweeping,

thorough, violent ~*noun* **3.** extremist, fanatic, militant, revolutionary
▷ **Antonyms** ~*adjective* insignificant, minor, superficial, token, trivial ~*noun* conservative, moderate, reactionary

raffish 1. bohemian, careless, casual, dashing, devil-may-care, disreputable, jaunty, rakish, sporty, unconventional **2.** coarse, flash (*informal*), garish, gaudy, gross, loud, meretricious, showy, tasteless, tawdry, trashy, uncouth, vulgar

raffle draw, lottery, sweep, sweepstake

ragamuffin gamin, guttersnipe, scarecrow (*informal*), street arab, tatterdemalion (*rare*), urchin

ragbag 1. confusion, hotchpotch, jumble, medley, miscellany, mixed bag (*informal*), mixture, omnium-gatherum, potpourri **2.** *informal* frump, scarecrow (*informal*), scruff (*informal*), slattern, sloven, slut, trollop

rage *noun* **1.** agitation, anger, frenzy, fury, high dudgeon, ire, madness, mania, obsession, passion, rampage, raving, vehemence, violence, wrath **2.** craze, enthusiasm, fad (*informal*), fashion, latest thing, mode, style, vogue ~*verb* **3.** be beside oneself, be furious, blow a fuse (*slang, chiefly U.S.*), blow one's top, blow up (*informal*), chafe, crack up (*informal*), flip one's lid (*slang*), fly off the handle (*informal*), foam at the mouth, fret, fume, go ballistic (*slang, chiefly U.S.*), go off the deep end (*informal*), go up the wall (*slang*), rant and rave, rave, see red (*informal*), seethe, storm, throw a fit (*informal*) **4.** be at its height, be uncontrollable, rampage, storm, surge
▷ **Antonyms** ~*noun* (*sense 1*) acceptance, calmness, equanimity, gladness, good humour, joy, pleasure, resignation ~*verb* (*sense 3*) accept, keep one's cool, remain unruffled, resign oneself to, stay calm

ragged 1. contemptible, down at heel, frayed, in holes, in rags, in tatters, mean, poor, rent, scraggy, shabby, shaggy, tattered, tatty, threadbare, torn, unkempt, worn-out **2.** crude, jagged, notched, poor, rough, rugged, serrated, uneven, unfinished **3.** broken, desultory, disorganized, fragmented, irregular, uneven
▷ **Antonyms** (*sense 1*) fashionable, smart, well-dressed

raging beside oneself, boiling mad (*informal*), doing one's nut (*Brit. slang*), enraged, fit to be tied (*slang*), fizzing (*Scot.*), foaming at the mouth, frenzied, fuming, furious, incensed, infuriated, mad, raving, seething

rags 1. castoffs, old clothes, tattered clothing, tatters **2. in rags** down at heel, out at elbow, ragged, seedy, shabby, tattered
▷ **Antonyms** (*sense 1*) finery, gladrags, Sunday best

raid 1. *noun* attack, break-in, descent, foray, hit-and-run attack, incursion, inroad, invasion, irruption, onset, sally, seizure, sortie, surprise attack **2.** ~*verb* assault, attack, break into, descend on, fall upon, forage (*Military*), foray, invade, pillage, plunder, reive (*dialect*), rifle, sack, sally forth, swoop down upon

raider attacker, forager (*Military*), invader, marauder, plunderer, reiver (*dialect*), robber, thief

rail *verb* abuse, attack, blast, castigate, censure, complain, criticize, fulminate, inveigh, lambast(e), put down, revile, scold, tear into (*informal*), upbraid, vituperate, vociferate

railing balustrade, barrier, fence, paling, rails

raillery badinage, banter, chaff, irony, jesting, joke, joking, josh (*slang, chiefly U.S. & Canad.*), kidding (*informal*), mockery, persiflage, pleasantry, repartee, ridicule, satire, sport, teasing

rain *noun* **1.** cloudburst, deluge, downpour, drizzle, fall, precipitation, raindrops, rainfall, showers **2.** deluge, flood, hail, shower, spate, stream, torrent, volley ~*verb* **3.** bucket down (*informal*), come down in buckets (*informal*), drizzle, fall, pelt (down), pour, rain cats and dogs (*informal*), shower, teem **4.** deposit, drop, fall, shower, sprinkle **5.** bestow, lavish, pour, shower

rainy damp, drizzly, showery, wet
▷ **Antonyms** arid, dry, fine, sunny

raise 1. build, construct, elevate, erect, exalt, heave, hoist, lift, move up, promote, put up, rear, set upright, uplift **2.** advance, aggravate, amplify, augment, boost, enhance, enlarge, escalate, exaggerate, heighten, hike (up) (*informal*), increase, inflate, intensify, jack up, magnify, put up, reinforce, strengthen **3.** advance, aggrandize, elevate, exalt, prefer, promote, upgrade **4.** activate, arouse, awaken, cause, evoke, excite, foment, foster, incite, instigate, kindle, motivate, provoke, rouse, set on foot, stir up, summon up, whip up **5.** bring about, cause, create, engender, give rise to, occasion, originate, produce, provoke, start **6.** advance, bring up, broach, introduce, moot, put forward, suggest **7.** assemble, collect, form, gather, get, levy, mass, mobilize, muster, obtain, rally, recruit **8.** breed, bring up, cultivate, develop, grow, nurture, produce, propagate, rear **9.** abandon, end, give up, lift, relieve, relinquish, remove, terminate
▷ **Antonyms** (*sense 1*) demolish, destroy, level, ruin, wreck (*sense 2*) cut, decrease, diminish, drop, lessen, lower, reduce, sink (*sense 3*) demote, downgrade, reduce (*sense 4*) calm, depress, lessen, lower, quash, quell, reduce, sink, soothe, suppress (*sense 9*) begin, establish, start

rake[1] *verb* **1.** collect, gather, remove, scrape up **2.** break up, harrow, hoe, scour, scrape, scratch **3.** (*with* **up** *or* **together**) assemble, collect, dig up, dredge up, gather, scrape together **4.** comb, examine, forage, hunt, ransack, scan, scour, scrutinize, search **5.** graze, scrape, scratch **6.** enfilade, pepper, sweep

rake[2] *noun* debauchee, dissolute man, lech *or* letch (*informal*), lecher, libertine, playboy, profligate, rakehell (*archaic*), roué, sensualist, voluptuary

▷ **Antonyms** ascetic, celibate, monk, puritan

rakish[1] *adjective* abandoned, debauched, depraved, dissipated, dissolute, immoral, lecherous, licentious, loose, prodigal, profligate, sinful, wanton

rakish[2] *adjective* breezy, dapper, dashing, debonair, devil-may-care, flashy, jaunty, natty (*informal*), raffish, smart, snazzy (*informal*), sporty

rally[1] **1.** *verb* bring *or* come to order, reassemble, re-form, regroup, reorganize, unite **2.** *~noun* regrouping, reorganization, reunion, stand **3.** *~verb* assemble, bond together, bring *or* come together, collect, convene, gather, get together, marshal, mobilize, muster, organize, round up, summon, unite **4.** *~noun* assembly, conference, congregation, congress, convention, convocation, gathering, mass meeting, meeting, muster **5.** *~verb* be on the mend, come round, get better, get one's second wind, improve, perk up, pick up, pull through, recover, recuperate, regain one's strength, revive, take a turn for the better, turn the corner **6.** *~noun* comeback (*informal*), improvement, recovery, recuperation, renewal, resurgence, revival, turn for the better

▷ **Antonyms** *~verb* (*sense 3*) disband, disperse, separate, split up (*sense 5*) deteriorate, fail, get worse, relapse, take a turn for the worse, worsen *~noun* (*sense 6*) collapse, deterioration, relapse, turn for the worse

rally[2] *verb* chaff, make fun of, mock, poke fun at, ridicule, send up (*Brit. informal*), take the mickey out of (*informal*), taunt, tease, twit

ram *verb* **1.** butt, collide with, crash, dash, drive, force, hit, impact, run into, slam, smash, strike **2.** beat, cram, crowd, drum, force, hammer, jam, pack, pound, stuff, tamp, thrust

ramble *verb* **1.** amble, drift, perambulate, peregrinate, range, roam, rove, saunter, straggle, stravaig (*Scot. & northern English dialect*), stray, stroll, traipse (*informal*), walk, wander **2.** meander, snake, twist and turn, wind, zigzag **3.** babble, chatter, digress, expatiate, maunder, rabbit (on) (*Brit. informal*), rattle on, run off at the mouth (*slang*), waffle (*informal, chiefly Brit.*), wander, witter on (*informal*) *~noun* **4.** excursion, hike, perambulation, peregrination, roaming, roving, saunter, stroll, tour, traipse (*informal*), trip, walk

rambler drifter, hiker, roamer, rover, stroller, walker, wanderer, wayfarer

rambling 1. circuitous, desultory, diffuse, digressive, disconnected, discursive, disjointed, incoherent, irregular, long-winded, periphrastic, prolix, wordy **2.** irregular, sprawling, spreading, straggling, trailing

▷ **Antonyms** (*sense 1*) coherent, concise, direct, to the point

ramification 1. branch, development, divarication, division, excrescence, extension, forking, offshoot, outgrowth, subdivision **2.** complication, consequence, development, result, sequel, upshot

ramify 1. branch, divaricate, divide, fork, separate, split up **2.** become complicated, multiply, thicken

ramp grade, gradient, incline, inclined plane, rise, slope

rampage *verb* **1.** go ape (*slang*), go apeshit (*slang*), go ballistic (*slang, chiefly U.S.*), go berserk, rage, run amuck, run riot, run wild, storm, tear *~noun* **2.** destruction, frenzy, fury, rage, storm, tempest, tumult, uproar, violence **3. on the rampage** amuck, berserk, destructive, out of control, raging, rampant, riotous, violent, wild

rampant 1. aggressive, dominant, excessive, flagrant, on the rampage, out of control, out of hand, outrageous, raging, rampaging, riotous, unbridled, uncontrollable, ungovernable, unrestrained, vehement, violent, wanton, wild **2.** epidemic, exuberant, luxuriant, prevalent, profuse, rank, rife, spreading like wildfire, unchecked, uncontrolled, unrestrained, widespread **3.** *Heraldry* erect, rearing, standing, upright

rampart barricade, bastion, breastwork, bulwark, defence, earthwork, embankment, fence, fort, fortification, guard, parapet, security, stronghold, wall

ramshackle broken-down, crumbling, decrepit, derelict, dilapidated, flimsy, jerry-built, rickety, shaky, tottering, tumbledown, unsafe, unsteady

▷ **Antonyms** solid, stable, steady, well-built

rancid bad, fetid, foul, frowsty, fusty, musty, off, putrid, rank, rotten, sour, stale, strong-smelling, tainted

▷ **Antonyms** fresh, pure, undecayed

rancorous acrimonious, bitter, hostile, implacable, malevolent, malicious, malign, malignant, resentful, spiteful, splenetic, venomous, vindictive, virulent

rancour animosity, animus, antipathy, bad blood, bitterness, chip on one's shoulder (*informal*), enmity, grudge, hate, hatred, hostility, ill feeling, ill will, malevolence, malice, malignity, resentfulness, resentment, spite, spleen, venom

random **1.** accidental, adventitious, aimless, arbitrary, casual, chance, desultory, fortuitous, haphazard, hit or miss, incidental, indiscriminate, purposeless, spot, stray, unplanned, unpremeditated **2. at random** accidentally, adventitiously, aimlessly, arbitrarily, by chance, casually, haphazardly, indiscriminately, irregularly, purposelessly, randomly, unsystematically, willy-nilly
▷ **Antonyms** (*sense 1*) definite, deliberate, intended, planned, premeditated, specific

randy amorous, aroused, concupiscent, horny (*slang*), hot, lascivious, lecherous, lustful, raunchy (*slang*), satyric, sexually excited, sexy (*informal*), turned-on (*slang*)

range *noun* **1.** ambit, amplitude, area, bounds, compass, confines, distance, domain, extent, field, latitude, limits, orbit, pale, parameters (*informal*), province, purview, radius, reach, scope, span, sphere, sweep **2.** chain, file, line, rank, row, sequence, series, string, tier **3.** assortment, class, collection, gamut, kind, lot, order, selection, series, sort, variety *~verb* **4.** align, arrange, array, dispose, draw up, line up, order, sequence **5.** arrange, bracket, catalogue, categorize, class, classify, file, grade, group, pigeonhole, rank **6.** aim, align, direct, level, point, train **7.** cruise, explore, ramble, roam, rove, straggle, stray, stroll, sweep, traverse, wander **8.** extend, fluctuate, go, reach, run, stretch, vary between

rangy gangling, lanky, leggy, long-legged, long-limbed

rank[1] *noun* **1.** caste, class, classification, degree, dignity, division, echelon, grade, level, nobility, order, position, quality, sort, standing, station, status, stratum, type **2.** column, file, formation, group, line, range, row, series, tier *~verb* **3.** align, arrange, array, class, classify, dispose, grade, line up, locate, marshal, order, position, range, sequence, sort

rank[2] *adjective* **1.** abundant, dense, exuberant, flourishing, lush, luxuriant, productive, profuse, strong-growing, vigorous **2.** bad, disagreeable, disgusting, fetid, foul, fusty, gamey, mephitic, musty, noisome, noxious, off, offensive, olid, pungent, putrid, rancid, revolting, stale, stinking, strong-smelling, yucky *or* yukky (*slang*) **3.** absolute, arrant, blatant, complete, downright, egregious, excessive, extravagant, flagrant, glaring, gross, rampant, sheer, thorough, total, undisguised, unmitigated, utter **4.** abusive, atrocious, coarse, crass, filthy, foul, gross, indecent, nasty, obscene, outrageous, scurrilous, shocking, vulgar

rank and file **1.** lower ranks, men, other ranks, private soldiers, soldiers, troops **2.** body, general public, Joe (and Eileen) Public (*slang*), Joe Six-Pack (*U.S. slang*), majority, mass, masses

rankle anger, annoy, chafe, embitter, fester, gall, get one's goat (*slang*), get on one's nerves (*informal*), irk, irritate, piss one off (*taboo slang*), rile

ransack **1.** comb, explore, forage, go through, rake, rummage, scour, search, turn inside out **2.** despoil, gut, loot, pillage, plunder, raid, ravage, rifle, sack, strip

ransom *noun* **1.** deliverance, liberation, redemption, release, rescue **2.** money, payment, payoff, price *~verb* **3.** buy (someone) out (*informal*), buy the freedom of, deliver, liberate, obtain *or* pay for the release of, redeem, release, rescue, set free

rant **1.** *verb* bellow, bluster, cry, declaim, rave, roar, shout, spout (*informal*), vociferate, yell **2.** *~noun* bluster, bombast, diatribe, fanfaronade (*rare*), harangue, philippic, rhetoric, tirade, vociferation

rap *verb* **1.** crack, hit, knock, strike, tap **2.** bark, speak abruptly, spit **3.** *slang, chiefly U.S.* chat, confabulate, converse, discourse, shoot the breeze (*slang, chiefly U.S.*), talk **4.** blast, carpet (*informal*), castigate, censure, chew out (*U.S. & Canad. informal*), criticize, give a rocket (*Brit. & N.Z. informal*), knock (*informal*), lambast(e), pan (*informal*), read the riot act, reprimand, scold, tick off (*informal*) *~noun* **5.** blow, clout (*informal*), crack, knock, tap **6.** *slang, chiefly U.S.* chat, colloquy, confabulation, conversation, dialogue, discourse, discussion, talk **7.** *slang* blame, censure, chiding, punishment, rebuke, responsibility, sentence

rapacious avaricious, extortionate, grasping, greedy, insatiable, marauding, plundering, predatory, preying, ravenous, usurious, voracious, wolfish

rapacity avarice, avidity, cupidity, graspingness, greed, greediness, insatiableness, predatoriness, rapaciousness, ravenousness, usury, voraciousness, voracity, wolfishness

rape *noun* **1.** outrage, ravishment, sexual assault, violation **2.** depredation, despoilment, despoliation, pillage, plundering, rapine, sack, spoliation **3.** abuse, defilement, desecration, maltreatment, perversion, violation *~verb* **4.** abuse, force, outrage, ravish, sexually assault, violate **5.** despoil, loot, pillage, plunder, ransack, sack, spoliate

rapid brisk, expeditious, express, fast, fleet, flying, hasty, hurried, pdq (*slang*), precipitate, prompt, quick, quickie (*informal*), speedy, swift

▷ **Antonyms** deliberate, gradual, leisurely, slow, tardy, unhurried

rapidity alacrity, briskness, celerity, dispatch, expedition, fleetness, haste, hurry, precipitateness, promptitude, promptness, quickness, rush, speed, speediness, swiftness, velocity

rapidly apace, at speed, briskly, expeditiously, fast, hastily, hell for leather, hotfoot, hurriedly, in a hurry, in a rush, in haste, like a shot, like greased lightning (*informal*), like lightning, like nobody's business (*informal*), like the clappers (*Brit. informal*), pdq (*slang*), posthaste, precipitately, promptly, pronto (*informal*), quickly, speedily, swiftly, with dispatch

rapine depredation, despoilment, despoliation, looting, marauding, pillage, plunder, ransacking, rape, robbery, sack, seizure, spoliation, theft

rapport affinity, bond, empathy, harmony, interrelationship, link, relationship, sympathy, tie, understanding

rapprochement détente, reconcilement, reconciliation, restoration of harmony, reunion, softening

▷ **Antonyms** antagonism, dissension, exacerbation, falling-out, quarrel, resumption of hostilities, schism

rapscallion bad egg (*old-fashioned informal*), blackguard, black sheep, cad, disgrace, good-for-nothing, knave (*archaic*), ne'er-do-well, rascal, rogue, scally (*Northwest English dialect*), scallywag (*informal*), scamp, scoundrel, wastrel

rapt **1.** absorbed, carried away, engrossed, enthralled, entranced, fascinated, gripped, held, intent, preoccupied, spellbound **2.** bewitched, blissed out, blissful, captivated, charmed, delighted, ecstatic, enchanted, enraptured, rapturous, ravished, sent, transported

▷ **Antonyms** bored, detached, left cold, unaffected, uninterested, uninvolved, unmoved

rapture beatitude, bliss, cloud nine (*informal*), delectation, delight, ecstasy, enthusiasm, euphoria, exaltation, felicity, happiness, joy, ravishment, rhapsody, seventh heaven, spell, transport

rapturous blissed out, blissful, delighted, ecstatic, enthusiastic, euphoric, exalted, floating on air, happy, in seventh heaven, joyful, joyous, on cloud nine (*informal*), overjoyed, over the moon (*informal*), rapt, ravished, rhapsodic, sent, transported

rare[1] *adjective* **1.** exceptional, few, infrequent, out of the ordinary, recherché, scarce, singular, sparse, sporadic, strange, thin on the ground, uncommon, unusual **2.** admirable, choice, excellent, exquisite, extreme, fine, great, incomparable, peerless, superb, superlative **3.** invaluable, precious, priceless, rich

▷ **Antonyms** (*sense 1*) abundant, bountiful, common, frequent, habitual, manifold, many, plentiful, profuse, regular

rare[2] *adjective* bloody, half-cooked, half-raw, undercooked, underdone

rarefied **1.** elevated, exalted, high, lofty, noble, spiritual, sublime **2.** clannish, cliquish, esoteric, exclusive, occult, private, select

rarefy attenuate, clarify, purify, refine, sublimate, subtilize, thin out

rarely **1.** almost never, hardly, hardly ever, infrequently, little, once in a blue moon, once in a while, only now and then, on rare occasions, scarcely ever, seldom **2.** exceptionally, extraordinarily, finely, notably, remarkably, singularly, uncommonly, unusually

▷ **Antonyms** commonly, frequently, often, regularly, usually

raring athirst, avid, champing at the bit (*informal*), desperate, eager, enthusiastic, impatient, keen, keen as mustard, longing, ready, willing, yearning

rarity **1.** collector's item, curio, curiosity, find, gem, one-off, pearl, treasure **2.** infrequency, scarcity, shortage, singularity, sparseness, strangeness, uncommonness, unusualness **3.** choiceness, excellence, exquisiteness, fineness, incomparability, incomparableness, peerlessness, quality, superbness **4.** invaluableness, preciousness, pricelessness, richness, value, worth

rascal bad egg (*old-fashioned informal*), blackguard, caitiff (*archaic*), devil, disgrace, good-for-nothing, imp, knave (*archaic*), miscreant, ne'er-do-well, pickle (*Brit. informal*), rake, rapscallion, reprobate, rogue, scally (*Northwest English dialect*), scallywag (*informal*), scamp, scoundrel, varmint (*informal*), villain, wastrel, wretch

rascally bad, base, crooked, dishonest, disreputable, evil, good-for-nothing, low, mean, reprobate, scoundrelly, unscrupulous, vicious, villainous, wicked

rash[1] *adjective* adventurous, audacious, brash, careless, foolhardy, harebrained, harum-scarum, hasty, headlong, headstrong, heedless, helter-skelter, hot-headed, ill-advised, ill-considered, impetuous, imprudent, impulsive, incautious, indiscreet, injudicious, madcap, precipitate, premature, reckless, thoughtless, unguarded, unthinking, unwary, venturesome

▷ **Antonyms** canny, careful, cautious, considered, premeditated, prudent, well-thought-out

rash[2] *noun* **1.** eruption, outbreak **2.** epidemic, flood, outbreak, plague, series, spate, succession, wave

rashness adventurousness, audacity, brashness, carelessness, foolhardiness, hastiness, heedlessness, indiscretion, precipitation, recklessness, temerity, thoughtlessness

rasp *noun* **1**. grating, grinding, scrape, scratch *~verb* **2**. abrade, excoriate, file, grind, rub, sand, scour, scrape **3**. grate (upon), irk, irritate, jar (upon), rub (someone) up the wrong way, set one's teeth on edge, wear upon

rasping *or* **raspy** creaking, croaking, croaky, grating, gravelly, gruff, harsh, hoarse, husky, jarring, rough, scratchy

rate[1] *noun* **1**. degree, percentage, proportion, ratio, relation, scale, standard **2**. charge, cost, dues, duty, fee, figure, hire, price, tariff, tax, toll **3**. gait, measure, pace, speed, tempo, time, velocity **4**. class, classification, degree, grade, position, quality, rank, rating, status, value, worth **5**. **at any rate** anyhow, anyway, at all events, in any case, nevertheless *~verb* **6**. adjudge, appraise, assess, class, classify, consider, count, esteem, estimate, evaluate, grade, measure, rank, reckon, regard, value, weigh **7**. be entitled to, be worthy of, deserve, merit **8**. *slang* admire, esteem, respect, think highly of, value

rate[2] *verb* bawl out (*informal*), berate, blame, carpet (*informal*), castigate, censure, chew out (*U.S. & Canad. informal*), chide, criticize severely, give a rocket (*Brit. & N.Z. informal*), haul over the coals (*informal*), read the riot act, rebuke, reprimand, reprove, roast (*informal*), scold, take to task, tear into (*informal*), tear (someone) off a strip (*informal*), tell off (*informal*), tongue-lash, upbraid

rather **1**. a bit, a little, fairly, kind of (*informal*), moderately, pretty (*informal*), quite, relatively, slightly, somewhat, sort of (*informal*), to some degree, to some extent **2**. a good bit, noticeably, significantly, very **3**. instead, more readily, more willingly, preferably, sooner

ratify affirm, approve, authenticate, authorize, bear out, bind, certify, confirm, consent to, corroborate, endorse, establish, sanction, sign, uphold, validate

▷ **Antonyms** abrogate, annul, cancel, reject, repeal, repudiate, revoke

rating[1] *noun* class, classification, degree, designation, estimate, evaluation, grade, order, placing, position, rank, rate, standing, status

rating[2] *noun* chiding, dressing down (*informal*), lecture, piece of one's mind, rebuke, reprimand, reproof, roasting (*informal*), row (*informal*), scolding, telling-off (*informal*), ticking-off (*informal*), tongue-lashing, wigging (*Brit. slang*)

ratio arrangement, correlation, correspondence, equation, fraction, percentage, proportion, rate, relation, relationship

ration *noun* **1**. allotment, allowance, dole, helping, measure, part, portion, provision, quota, share **2**. (*plural*) commons (*Brit.*), food, provender, provisions, stores, supplies *~verb* **3**. (*with* **out**) allocate, allot, apportion, deal, distribute, dole, give out, issue, measure out, mete, parcel out **4**. budget, conserve, control, limit, restrict, save

rational **1**. enlightened, intelligent, judicious, logical, lucid, realistic, reasonable, sagacious, sane, sensible, sound, wise **2**. cerebral, cognitive, ratiocinative, reasoning, thinking **3**. all there (*informal*), balanced, *compos mentis,* in one's right mind, lucid, normal, of sound mind, sane

▷ **Antonyms** insane, irrational, unreasonable, unsound

rationale exposition, grounds, logic, motivation, philosophy, principle, *raison d'être,* reasons, theory

rationalize **1**. account for, excuse, explain away, extenuate, justify, make allowance for, make excuses for, vindicate **2**. apply logic to, elucidate, reason out, resolve, think through **3**. make cuts, make more efficient, streamline, trim

rattle *verb* **1**. bang, clatter, jangle **2**. bounce, jar, jiggle, jolt, jounce, shake, vibrate **3**. (*with* **on**) blether, cackle, chatter, gabble, gibber, jabber, prate, prattle, rabbit (on) (*Brit. informal*), run on, witter (*informal*), yak (away) (*slang*) **4**. *informal* discomfit, discompose, disconcert, discountenance, disturb, faze, frighten, perturb, put (someone) off his stride, put (someone) out of countenance, scare, shake, upset **5**. (*with* **off**) list, recite, reel off, rehearse, run through, spiel off (*informal*)

ratty angry, annoyed, crabbed, cross, impatient, irritable, short-tempered, snappy, testy, tetchy, touchy

raucous grating, harsh, hoarse, husky, loud, noisy, rasping, rough, strident

▷ **Antonyms** dulcet, mellifluous, quiet, smooth, sweet

ravage **1**. *verb* demolish, desolate, despoil, destroy, devastate, gut, lay waste, leave in ruins, loot, pillage, plunder, ransack, raze, ruin, sack, shatter, spoil, wreak havoc on, wreck **2**. *~noun* (*often plural*) damage, demolition, depredation, desolation, destruction, devastation, havoc, pillage, plunder, rapine, ruin, ruination, spoliation, waste

rave *verb* **1**. babble, be delirious, fume, go mad (*informal*), rage, rant, roar, run amuck, splutter, storm, talk wildly, thunder **2**. (*with* **about**) *informal* be delighted by, be mad about (*informal*), be wild about (*informal*), cry up, enthuse, gush, praise, rhapsodize *~noun* **3**. *informal* acclaim, applause, encomium, praise **4.** *also* **rave-up** *Brit. slang* affair, bash (*informal*), beano (*Brit. slang*), blow-out (*slang*), celebration, do (*informal*), hooley *or* hoolie (*chiefly Irish & N.Z.*), party **5.** *Brit. slang* craze, fad, fashion, vogue *~adjective* **6.** *informal* ecstatic, enthusiastic, excellent, favourable, laudatory

ravenous 1. esurient, famished, starved, starving, very hungry **2.** avaricious, covetous, devouring, edacious, ferocious, gluttonous, grasping, greedy, insatiable, insatiate, predatory, rapacious, ravening, voracious, wolfish

▷ **Antonyms** full, glutted, sated, satiated

ravine canyon, clough (*dialect*), defile, flume, gap (*U.S.*), gorge, gulch (*U.S.*), gully, linn (*Scot.*), pass

raving berserk, crazed, crazy, delirious, frantic, frenzied, furious, gonzo (*slang*), hysterical, insane, irrational, mad, out of one's mind, rabid, raging, wild

ravish 1. captivate, charm, delight, enchant, enrapture, entrance, fascinate, overjoy, spellbind, transport **2.** abuse, force, outrage, rape, sexually assault, violate

ravishing beautiful, bewitching, charming, dazzling, delightful, drop-dead (*slang*), enchanting, entrancing, gorgeous, lovely, radiant, stunning (*informal*)

raw 1. bloody (*of meat*), fresh, natural, uncooked, undressed, unprepared **2.** basic, coarse, crude, green, natural, organic, rough, unfinished, unprocessed, unrefined, unripe, untreated **3.** abraded, chafed, grazed, open, scratched, sensitive, skinned, sore, tender **4.** callow, green, ignorant, immature, inexperienced, new, undisciplined, unpractised, unseasoned, unskilled, untrained, untried **5.** bare, blunt, brutal, candid, frank, naked, plain, realistic, unembellished, unvarnished **6.** biting, bitter, bleak, chill, chilly, cold, damp, freezing, harsh, parky (*Brit. informal*), piercing, unpleasant, wet

▷ **Antonyms** (*sense 1*) baked, cooked, done (*sense 2*) finished, prepared, refined (*sense 4*) experienced, practised, professional, skilled, trained (*sense 5*) embellished, gilded

ray 1. bar, beam, flash, gleam, shaft **2.** flicker, glimmer, hint, indication, scintilla, spark, trace

raze 1. bulldoze, demolish, destroy, flatten, knock down, level, pull down, remove, ruin, tear down, throw down **2.** delete, efface, erase, excise, expunge, extinguish, extirpate, obliterate, rub out, scratch out, strike out, wipe from the face of the earth, wipe out

re about, anent (*Scot.*), apropos, concerning, in respect of, on the subject of, regarding, respecting, with reference to, with regard to

reach *verb* **1.** arrive at, attain, get as far as, get to, land at, make **2.** contact, extend to, get (a) hold of, go as far as, grasp, stretch to, touch **3.** amount to, arrive at, attain, climb to, come to, drop, fall, move, rise, sink **4.** *informal* hand, hold out, pass, stretch **5.** communicate with, contact, establish contact with, find, get, get hold of, get in touch with, get through to, make contact with *~noun* **6.** ambit, capacity, command, compass, distance, extension, extent, grasp, influence, jurisdiction, mastery, power, range, scope, spread, stretch, sweep

react 1. acknowledge, answer, reply, respond, rise to the bait, take the bait **2.** act, behave, conduct oneself, function, operate, proceed, work

reaction 1. acknowledgment, answer, feedback, reply, response **2.** compensation, counteraction, counterbalance, counterpoise, recoil **3.** conservatism, counter-revolution, obscurantism, the right

reactionary 1. *adjective* blimpish, conservative, counter-revolutionary, obscurantist, rightist **2.** *~noun* Colonel Blimp, conservative, counter-revolutionary, die-hard, obscurantist, rightist, right-winger

▷ **Antonyms** *~adjective/noun* leftist, progressive, radical, reformist, revolutionary, socialist

read 1. glance at, look at, peruse, pore over, refer to, run one's eye over, scan, study **2.** announce, declaim, deliver, recite, speak, utter **3.** comprehend, construe, decipher, discover, interpret, perceive the meaning of, see, understand **4.** display, indicate, record, register, show

readable 1. clear, comprehensible, decipherable, intelligible, legible, plain, understandable **2.** easy to read, enjoyable, entertaining, enthralling, gripping, interesting, pleasant, worth reading

▷ **Antonyms** (*sense 1*) illegible, incomprehensible, indecipherable, unintelligible, unreadable (*sense 2*) as dry as dust, badly-written, boring, dull, heavy, heavy going, pretentious, turgid, unreadable

readily 1. cheerfully, eagerly, freely, gladly, lief (*rare*), promptly, quickly, voluntarily, willingly, with good grace, with pleasure **2.** at once, easily, effortlessly, hotfoot, in no time, pdq (*slang*), quickly, right away, smoothly, speedily, straight away, unhesitatingly, without delay, without demur, without difficulty, without hesitation

▷ **Antonyms** hesitatingly, reluctantly, slowly, unwillingly, with difficulty

readiness 1. fitness, maturity, preparation, preparedness, ripeness **2.** aptness, eagerness, gameness (*informal*), inclination, keenness, willingness **3.** adroitness, dexterity, ease, facility, handiness, promptitude, promptness, quickness, rapidity, skill **4. in readiness** all set, at *or* on hand, at the ready, fit, prepared, primed, ready, set, waiting, waiting in the wings

reading 1. examination, inspection, perusal, review, scrutiny, study **2.** homily, lecture, lesson, performance, recital, rendering, rendition, sermon **3.** conception, construction, grasp, impression, interpretation, take (*informal, chiefly U.S.*), treatment, understanding, version **4.** book-learning, edification, education, erudition, knowledge, learning, scholarship

ready *adjective* **1.** all set, arranged, completed, fit, in readiness, organized, prepared, primed, ripe, set **2.** agreeable, apt, disposed, eager, game (*informal*), glad, happy, have-a-go (*informal*), inclined, keen, minded, predisposed, prone, willing **3.** acute, adroit, alert, apt, astute, bright, clever, deft, dexterous, expert, handy, intelligent, keen, perceptive, prompt, quick, quick-witted, rapid, resourceful, sharp, skilful, smart **4.** about, close, in danger of, liable, likely, on the brink of, on the point of, on the verge of **5.** accessible, at *or* on hand, at one's fingertips, at the ready, available, close to hand, convenient, handy, near, on call, on tap (*informal*), present *~noun* **6. at the ready** all systems go, in readiness, poised, prepared, ready for action, waiting *~verb* **7.** arrange, equip, fit out, get ready, make ready, order, organize, prepare, set

▷ **Antonyms** *~adjective* (*sense 1*) immature, unequipped, unfit, unprepared (*sense 2*) disinclined, hesitant, loath, reluctant, unprepared, unwilling (*sense 3*) inexpert, slow, unequipped, unfit, unhandy (*sense 5*) distant, inaccessible, late, unavailable

real absolute, actual, authentic, bona fide, certain, essential, existent, factual, genuine, heartfelt, honest, intrinsic, legitimate, positive, right, rightful, sincere, true, unaffected, unfeigned, valid, veritable

▷ **Antonyms** affected, counterfeit, fake, faked, false, feigned, imaginary, imitation, insincere

realistic 1. businesslike, common-sense, down-to-earth, hard-headed, level-headed, matter-of-fact, practical, pragmatic, rational, real, sensible, sober, unromantic, unsentimental **2.** authentic, faithful, genuine, graphic, lifelike, natural, naturalistic, representational, true, true to life, truthful, vérité

▷ **Antonyms** fanciful, idealistic, impractical, unrealistic

reality 1. actuality, authenticity, certainty, corporeality, fact, genuineness, materiality, realism, truth, validity, verisimilitude, verity **2. in reality** actually, as a matter of fact, in actuality, in fact, in point of fact, in truth, really

realization 1. appreciation, apprehension, awareness, cognizance, comprehension, conception, consciousness, grasp, imagination, perception, recognition, the penny drops (*informal*), understanding **2.** accomplishment, achievement, carrying-out, completion, consummation, effectuation, fulfilment

realize 1. appreciate, apprehend, be cognizant of, become aware of, become conscious of, catch on (*informal*), comprehend, conceive, get the message, grasp, imagine, recognize, take in, twig (*Brit. informal*), understand **2.** accomplish, actualize, bring about, bring off, bring to fruition, carry out *or* through, complete, consummate, do, effect, effectuate, fulfil, incarnate, make concrete, make happen, perform, reify **3.** acquire, bring *or* take in, clear, earn, gain, get, go for, make, net, obtain, produce, sell for

really absolutely, actually, assuredly, categorically, certainly, genuinely, in actuality, indeed, in fact, in reality, positively, surely, truly, undoubtedly, verily, without a doubt

realm 1. country, domain, dominion, empire, kingdom, land, monarchy, principality, province, state **2.** area, branch, department, field, orbit, patch, province, region, sphere, territory, turf (*U.S. slang*), world, zone

reap acquire, bring in, collect, cut, derive, gain, garner, gather, get, harvest, obtain, win

rear[1] 1. *noun* back, back end, end, rearguard, stern, tail, tail end **2.** *~adjective* aft, after (*Nautical*), back, following, hind, hindmost, last, trailing

▷ **Antonyms** *~noun* bow, forward end, front, nose, stem, vanguard *~adjective* foremost, forward, front, leading

rear[2] *verb* **1.** breed, bring up, care for, cultivate, educate, foster, grow, nurse, nurture, raise, train **2.** elevate, hoist, hold up, lift, raise, set upright **3.** build, construct, erect, fabricate, put up **4.** loom, rise, soar, tower

reason *noun* **1.** apprehension, brains, comprehension, intellect, judgment, logic, mentality, mind, ratiocination, rationality, reasoning, sanity, sense(s), sound mind, soundness, understanding **2.** aim, basis, cause, design, end, goal, grounds, impetus, incentive, inducement, intention, motive, object, occasion, purpose, target, warrant, why and wherefore (*informal*) **3.** apologia, apology, argument, case, defence, excuse, explanation, exposition, ground, justification, rationale, vindication **4.** bounds, limits, moderation, propriety, reasonableness, sense, sensibleness, wisdom **5. in** *or* **within reason** in moderation, proper, reasonable, sensible, warrantable, within bounds, within limits *~verb* **6.** conclude, deduce, draw conclusions, infer, make out, ratiocinate, resolve, solve, syllogize, think, work out **7.** (*with* **with**) argue, bring round (*informal*), debate, dispute, dissuade, expostulate, move, persuade, prevail upon, remonstrate, show (someone) the error of his ways, talk into *or* out of, urge, win over

▷ **Antonyms** (*sense 1*) emotion, feeling, instinct, sentiment

reasonable 1. advisable, arguable, believable, credible, intelligent, judicious, justifiable, logical, plausible, practical, rational, reasoned, sane, sensible, sober, sound, tenable, well-advised, well-thought-out, wise **2.** acceptable, average, equitable, fair, fit, honest, inexpensive, just, moderate, modest, O.K. *or* okay (*informal*), proper, right, tolerable, within reason

▷ **Antonyms** (*sense 1*) impossible, irrational, unintelligent, unreasonable, unsound (*sense 2*) unfair, unreasonable

reasoned clear, judicious, logical, sensible, systematic, well expressed, well presented, well-thought-out

reasoning 1. analysis, cogitation, deduction, logic, ratiocination, reason, thinking, thought **2.** argument, case, exposition, hypothesis, interpretation, proof, train of thought

reassure bolster, buoy up, cheer up, comfort, encourage, hearten, inspirit, put *or* set one's mind at rest, relieve (someone) of anxiety, restore confidence to

rebate allowance, bonus, deduction, discount, reduction, refund

rebel *verb* **1.** man the barricades, mutiny, resist, revolt, rise up, take to the streets, take up arms **2.** come out against, defy, dig one's heels in (*informal*), disobey, dissent, refuse to obey **3.** flinch, recoil, show repugnance, shrink, shy away *~noun* **4.** insurgent, insurrectionary, mutineer, resistance fighter, revolutionary, revolutionist, secessionist **5.** apostate, dissenter, heretic, nonconformist, schismatic *~adjective* **6.** insubordinate, insurgent, insurrectionary, mutinous, rebellious, revolutionary

rebellion 1. insurgence, insurgency, insurrection, mutiny, resistance, revolt, revolution, rising, uprising **2.** apostasy, defiance, disobedience, dissent, heresy, insubordination, nonconformity, schism

rebellious 1. contumacious, defiant, disaffected, disloyal, disobedient, disorderly, insubordinate, insurgent, insurrectionary, intractable, mutinous, rebel, recalcitrant, revolutionary, seditious, turbulent, ungovernable, unruly **2.** difficult, incorrigible, obstinate, recalcitrant, refractory, resistant, unmanageable

▷ **Antonyms** (*sense 1*) dutiful, loyal, obedient, patriotic, subordinate, subservient (*sense 2*) dutiful, obedient, subservient

rebirth new beginning, regeneration, reincarnation, renaissance, renascence, renewal, restoration, resurgence, resurrection, revitalization, revival

rebound *verb* **1.** bounce, recoil, resound, return, ricochet, spring back **2.** backfire, boomerang, misfire, recoil *~noun* **3.** bounce, comeback, kickback, repercussion, return, ricochet

rebuff 1. *verb* brush off (*slang*), check, cold-shoulder, cut, decline, deny, discourage, put off, refuse, reject, repulse, resist, slight, snub, spurn, turn down **2.** *~noun* brush-off (*slang*), bum's rush (*slang*), check, cold shoulder, defeat, denial, discouragement, kick in the teeth (*slang*), knock-back (*slang*), opposition, refusal, rejection, repulse, slap in the face (*informal*), slight, snub, the (old) heave-ho (*informal*), thumbs down

▷ **Antonyms** *~verb* encourage, lead on (*informal*), submit to, welcome *~noun* come-on (*informal*), encouragement, thumbs up, welcome

rebuke 1. *verb* admonish, bawl out (*informal*), berate, blame, carpet (*informal*), castigate, censure, chew out (*U.S. & Canad. informal*), chew (someone's) ass (*U.S. & Canad. taboo slang*), chide, dress down (*informal*), give a rocket (*Brit. & N.Z. informal*), haul (someone) over the coals (*informal*), lecture, read the riot act, reprehend, reprimand, reproach, reprove, scold, take to task, tear into (*informal*), tear (someone) off a strip (*informal*), tell off (*informal*), tick off (*informal*), upbraid **2.** *~noun* admonition, blame, castigation, censure, dressing down (*informal*), lecture, reprimand, reproach, reproof, reproval, row, telling-off (*informal*), ticking-off (*informal*), tongue-lashing, wigging (*Brit. slang*)

▷ **Antonyms** *~verb* applaud, approve, commend, compliment, congratulate, laud, praise *~noun* commendation, compliment, laudation, praise

rebut confute, defeat, disprove, invalidate, negate, overturn, prove wrong, quash, refute

rebuttal confutation, defeat, disproof, invalidation, negation, refutation

recalcitrant contrary, contumacious, defiant, disobedient, insubordinate, intractable, obstinate, refractory, stubborn, uncontrollable, ungovernable, unmanageable, unruly, unwilling, wayward, wilful

▷ **Antonyms** amenable, compliant, docile, obedient, submissive

recall *verb* **1.** bring *or* call to mind, call *or* summon up, evoke, look *or* think back to, mind (*dialect*), recollect, remember, reminisce about **2.** abjure, annul, call back, call in, cancel, countermand, nul~

lify, repeal, rescind, retract, revoke, take back, withdraw *~noun* **3.** annulment, cancellation, nullification, recision, repeal, rescindment, rescission, retraction, revocation, withdrawal **4.** memory, recollection, remembrance

recant abjure, apostatize, deny, disavow, disclaim, disown, forswear, recall, renege, renounce, repudiate, retract, revoke, take back, unsay, withdraw

▷ **Antonyms** insist, maintain, profess, reaffirm, reiterate, repeat, restate, uphold

recapitulate epitomize, go over again, outline, recap (*informal*), recount, reiterate, repeat, restate, review, run over, run through again, summarize, sum up

recede 1. abate, back off, draw back, ebb, fall back, go back, regress, retire, retreat, retrocede, retrogress, return, subside, withdraw **2.** decline, diminish, dwindle, fade, lessen, shrink, sink, wane

receipt 1. acknowledgment, counterfoil, proof of purchase, sales slip, stub, voucher **2.** acceptance, delivery, receiving, reception, recipience **3.** (*plural*) gains, gate, income, proceeds, profits, return, takings

receive 1. accept, accept delivery of, acquire, be given, be in receipt of, collect, derive, get, obtain, pick up, take **2.** apprehend, be informed of, be told, gather, hear, perceive **3.** bear, be subjected to, encounter, experience, go through, meet with, suffer, sustain, undergo **4.** accommodate, admit, be at home to, entertain, greet, meet, take in, welcome

recent contemporary, current, fresh, happening (*informal*), late, latter, latter-day, modern, new, novel, present-day, up-to-date, young

▷ **Antonyms** ancient, antique, earlier, early, former, historical, old

recently currently, freshly, lately, latterly, newly, not long ago, of late

receptacle container, holder, repository

reception 1. acceptance, admission, receipt, receiving, recipience **2.** acknowledgment, greeting, reaction, recognition, response, treatment, welcome **3.** do (*informal*), entertainment, function, levee, party, soirée

receptive 1. alert, bright, perceptive, quick on the uptake (*informal*), responsive, sensitive **2.** accessible, amenable, approachable, favourable, friendly, hospitable, interested, open, open-minded, open to suggestions, susceptible, sympathetic, welcoming

▷ **Antonyms** (*sense 1*) unreceptive, unresponsive biased, narrow-minded, prejudiced, unreceptive, unresponsive

recess 1. alcove, bay, cavity, corner, depression, hollow, indentation, niche, nook, oriel **2.** (*plural*) bowels, depths, heart, innards (*informal*), innermost parts, penetralia, reaches, retreats, secret places **3.** break, cessation of business, closure, holiday, intermission, interval, respite, rest, vacation

recession decline, depression, downturn, drop, slump

▷ **Antonyms** boom, upturn

recherché arcane, choice, esoteric, exotic, far-fetched, rare, refined

recipe 1. directions, ingredients, instructions, receipt (*obsolete*) **2.** formula, method, modus operandi, prescription, procedure, process, programme, technique

reciprocal alternate, complementary, correlative, corresponding, equivalent, exchanged, give-and-take, interchangeable, interdependent, mutual, reciprocative, reciprocatory

▷ **Antonyms** one-way, unilateral, unreciprocated

reciprocate 1. barter, exchange, feel in return, interchange, reply, requite, respond, return, return the compliment, swap, trade **2.** be equivalent, correspond, equal, match

recital account, description, detailing, enumeration, narration, narrative, performance, reading, recapitulation, recitation, rehearsal, relation, rendering, repetition, statement, story, tale, telling

recitation lecture, narration, passage, performance, piece, reading, recital, rendering, telling

recite declaim, deliver, describe, detail, do one's party piece (*informal*), enumerate, itemize, narrate, perform, recapitulate, recount, rehearse, relate, repeat, speak, tell

reckless careless, daredevil, devil-may-care, foolhardy, harebrained, harum-scarum, hasty, headlong, heedless, ill-advised, imprudent, inattentive, incautious, indiscreet, irresponsible, madcap, mindless, negligent, overventuresome, precipitate, rash, regardless, thoughtless, wild

▷ **Antonyms** careful, cautious, heedful, mindful, observant, responsible, thoughtful, wary

reckon 1. add up, calculate, compute, count, enumerate, figure, number, tally, total **2.** account, appraise, consider, count, deem, esteem, estimate, evaluate, gauge, hold, judge, look upon, rate, regard, think of **3.** assume, believe, be of the opinion, conjecture, expect, fancy, guess (*informal, chiefly U.S. & Canad.*), imagine, suppose, surmise, think **4.** (*with* **with**) cope, deal, face, handle, settle accounts, treat **5.** (*with* **with**) anticipate, bargain for, bear in mind, be prepared for, expect, foresee, plan for, take cognizance of, take into account **6.** (*with* **on** *or* **upon**) bank, calculate, count, depend, hope for, rely, take for granted, trust in **7. to be reckoned with** conse~

quential, considerable, important, influential, powerful, significant, strong, weighty

reckoning **1.** adding, addition, calculation, computation, count, counting, estimate, summation, working **2.** account, bill, charge, due, score, settlement **3.** doom, judgment, last judgment, retribution

reclaim get *or* take back, recapture, recover, redeem, reform, regain, regenerate, reinstate, rescue, restore, retrieve, salvage

recline be recumbent, lay (something) down, lean, lie (down), loll, lounge, repose, rest, sprawl, stretch out
▷ **Antonyms** get up, rise, sit up, stand, stand up, stand upright

recluse anchoress, anchorite, ascetic, eremite, hermit, monk, solitary

reclusive ascetic, cloistered, eremitic, hermitic, hermit-like, isolated, monastic, recluse, retiring, secluded, sequestered, solitary, withdrawn
▷ **Antonyms** gregarious, sociable

recognition **1.** detection, discovery, identification, recall, recollection, remembrance **2.** acceptance, acknowledgment, admission, allowance, appreciation, avowal, awareness, cognizance, concession, confession, notice, perception, realization, respect, understanding **3.** acknowledgment, appreciation, approval, gratitude, greeting, honour, salute

recognize **1.** identify, know, know again, make out, notice, place, put one's finger on, recall, recollect, remember, spot **2.** accept, acknowledge, admit, allow, appreciate, avow, be aware of, concede, confess, grant, own, perceive, realize, respect, see, take on board, understand **3.** acknowledge, appreciate, approve, greet, honour, salute
▷ **Antonyms** (*sense 2*) be unaware of, forget, ignore, overlook

recoil *verb* **1.** jerk back, kick, react, rebound, resile, spring back **2.** balk at, draw back, falter, flinch, quail, shrink, shy away **3.** backfire, boomerang, go wrong, misfire, rebound *~noun* **4.** backlash, kick, reaction, rebound, repercussion

recollect call to mind, mind (*dialect*), place, recall, remember, reminisce, summon up

recollection impression, memory, mental image, recall, remembrance, reminiscence

recommend **1.** advance, advise, advocate, counsel, enjoin, exhort, prescribe, propose, put forward, suggest, urge **2.** approve, commend, endorse, praise, put in a good word for, speak well of, vouch for **3.** make acceptable, make appealing, make attractive, make interesting
▷ **Antonyms** argue against, disapprove of, reject, veto

recommendation **1.** advice, counsel, proposal, suggestion, urging **2.** advocacy, approbation, approval, blessing, commendation, endorsement, favourable mention, good word, plug (*informal*), praise, reference, sanction, testimonial

recompense *verb* **1.** pay, remunerate, reward **2.** compensate, indemnify, make amends for, make good, make restitution for, make up for, pay for, redress, reimburse, repay, requite, satisfy *~noun* **3.** amends, compensation, damages, emolument, indemnification, indemnity, meed (*archaic*), pay, payment, remuneration, reparation, repayment, requital, restitution, return, reward, satisfaction, wages

reconcilable **1.** compatible, congruous, consistent **2.** appeasable, conciliatory, forgiving, peaceable, placable

reconcile **1.** accept, accommodate, get used, make the best of, put up with (*informal*), resign, submit, yield **2.** appease, bring to terms, conciliate, make peace between, pacify, placate, propitiate, re-establish friendly relations between, restore harmony between, reunite **3.** adjust, compose, harmonize, patch up, put to rights, rectify, resolve, settle, square

reconciliation **1.** appeasement, conciliation, détente, pacification, propitiation, *rapprochement,* reconcilement, reunion, understanding **2.** accommodation, adjustment, compromise, harmony, rectification, settlement
▷ **Antonyms** alienation, antagonism, break-up, estrangement, falling-out, separation

recondite abstruse, arcane, cabbalistic, concealed, dark, deep, difficult, esoteric, hidden, involved, mysterious, mystical, obscure, occult, profound, secret
▷ **Antonyms** exoteric, simple, straightforward

recondition do up (*informal*), fix up (*informal, chiefly U.S. & Canad.*), overhaul, remodel, renew, renovate, repair, restore, revamp

reconnaissance exploration, inspection, investigation, observation, patrol, recce (*slang*), reconnoitring, scan, scouting, scrutiny, survey

reconnoitre case (*slang*), explore, get the lie of the land, inspect, investigate, make a reconnaissance (of), observe, patrol, recce (*slang*), scan, scout, scrutinize, see how the land lies, spy out, survey

reconsider change one's mind, have second thoughts, reassess, re-evaluate, re-examine, rethink, review, revise, take another look at, think again, think better of, think over, think twice

reconstruct **1.** reassemble, rebuild, recreate, re-establish, reform, regenerate, remake, remodel, renovate, reorganize, restore **2**. build up, build up a picture of, deduce, piece together

record *noun* **1**. account, annals, archives, chronicle, diary, document, entry, file, journal, log, memoir, memorandum, memorial, minute, register, report **2**. documentation, evidence, memorial, re~membrance, testimony, trace, witness **3**. background, career, curriculum vitae, history, performance, track record (*in~formal*) **4**. album, black disc, disc, EP, forty-five, gramophone record, LP, plat~ter (*U.S. slang*), recording, release, seventy-eight, single, vinyl, waxing (*in~formal*) **5. off the record** confidential, confidentially, in confidence, in private, not for publication, private, sub rosa, under the rose, unofficial, unofficially *~verb* **6**. chalk up (*informal*), chronicle, document, enrol, enter, inscribe, log, minute, note, preserve, put down, put on file, put on record, register, report, set down, take down, transcribe, write down **7**. contain, give evidence of, indi~cate, read, register, say, show **8**. cut, lay down (*slang*), make a recording of, put on wax (*informal*), tape, tape-record, video, video-tape, wax (*informal*)

recorder annalist, archivist, chronicler, clerk, diarist, historian, registrar, scorekeeper, scorer, scribe

recording cut (*informal*), disc, gramo~phone record, record, tape, video

recount delineate, depict, describe, detail, enumerate, give an account of, narrate, portray, recite, rehearse, relate, repeat, report, tell, tell the story of

recoup 1. make good, recover, redeem, regain, retrieve, win back **2**. compen~sate, make redress for, make up for, re~fund, reimburse, remunerate, repay, re~quite, satisfy

recourse alternative, appeal, choice, ex~pedient, option, refuge, remedy, resort, resource, way out

recover 1. find again, get back, make good, recapture, reclaim, recoup, re~deem, regain, repair, repossess, restore, retake, retrieve, take back, win back **2**. be on the mend, bounce back, come round, convalesce, feel oneself again, get back on one's feet, get better, get well, heal, improve, mend, pick up, pull through, rally, recuperate, regain one's health *or* strength, revive, take a turn for the better, turn the corner

▷ **Antonyms** (*sense 1*) abandon, forfeit, lose (*sense 2*) deteriorate, go downhill, relapse, take a turn for the worse, weaken, worsen

recovery 1. convalescence, healing, im~provement, mending, rally, recupera~tion, return to health, revival, turn for the better **2**. amelioration, betterment, improvement, rally, rehabilitation, res~toration, revival, upturn **3**. recapture, reclamation, redemption, repair, repos~session, restoration, retrieval

recreation amusement, beer and skittles (*informal*), distraction, diversion, enjoy~ment, entertainment, exercise, fun, hobby, leisure activity, pastime, play, pleasure, refreshment, relaxation, relief, sport

recrimination bickering, counterattack, countercharge, mutual accusation, name-calling, quarrel, retaliation, re~tort, squabbling

recruit *verb* **1**. draft, enlist, enrol, im~press, levy, mobilize, muster, raise, strengthen **2**. engage, enrol, gather, ob~tain, procure, proselytize, round up, take on, win (over) **3**. augment, build up, refresh, reinforce, renew, replenish, re~store, strengthen, supply *~noun* **4**. ap~prentice, beginner, convert, greenhorn (*informal*), helper, initiate, learner, neophyte, novice, proselyte, rookie (*in~formal*), trainee, tyro

▷ **Antonyms** (*sense 1*) dismiss, fire, lay off, make redundant, sack (*informal*)

rectify 1. adjust, amend, correct, emend, fix, improve, make good, mend, put right, redress, reform, remedy, repair, right, set the record straight, square **2**. *Chemistry* distil, purify, refine, separate

rectitude 1. correctness, decency, equity, goodness, honesty, honour, incorrupt~ibility, integrity, justice, morality, prin~ciple, probity, righteousness, scrupu~lousness, uprightness, virtue **2**. accura~cy, correctness, exactness, justice, pre~cision, rightness, soundness, verity

▷ **Antonyms** (*sense 1*) baseness, corrup~tion, dishonesty, dishonour, immorality, scandalousness

recumbent flat, flat on one's back, hori~zontal, leaning, lying, lying down, prone, prostrate, reclining, resting, stretched out, supine

recuperate be on the mend, convalesce, get back on one's feet, get better, im~prove, mend, pick up, recover, regain one's health, turn the corner

recur 1. come again, come and go, come back, happen again, persist, reappear, repeat, return, revert **2**. be remembered, come back, haunt one's thoughts, return to mind, run through one's mind

recurrent continued, cyclical, frequent, habitual, periodic, recurring, regular, repeated, repetitive

▷ **Antonyms** isolated, one-off

recycle reclaim, reprocess, reuse, salvage, save

red *adjective* **1**. cardinal, carmine, cherry, claret, coral, crimson, gules (*Heraldry*), maroon, pink, rose, ruby, scarlet, ver~meil, vermilion, wine **2**. bay, carroty, chestnut, flame-coloured, flaming, foxy, reddish, sandy, titian **3**. blushing, em~barrassed, florid, flushed, rubicund, shamefaced, suffused **4.** blooming, glowing, healthy, roseate, rosy, ruddy **5.** bloodshot, inflamed, red-rimmed **6.** bloodstained, bloody, ensanguined (*literary*), gory, sanguine *~noun* **7.** colour, redness **8. in the red** *informal* bankrupt, in arrears, in debit, in debt, in deficit, insolvent, on the rocks, overdrawn, owing money, showing a loss **9. see red** *informal* be beside oneself with rage (*informal*), become enraged, be *or* get very angry, blow a fuse (*slang, chiefly U.S.*), blow one's top, boil, crack up (*informal*), fly off the handle (*informal*), go ballistic (*slang, chiefly U.S.*), go mad (*informal*), go off one's head (*slang*), go off the deep end (*informal*), go up the wall (*slang*), lose one's rag (*slang*), lose one's temper, seethe

red-blooded hearty, lusty, manly, robust, strong, vigorous, virile, vital

redden blush, colour (up), crimson, flush, go red, suffuse

redeem 1. buy back, reclaim, recover, recover possession of, regain, repossess, repurchase, retrieve, win back **2.** cash (in), change, exchange, trade in **3.** abide by, acquit, adhere to, be faithful to, carry out, discharge, fulfil, hold to, keep, keep faith with, make good, meet, perform, satisfy **4.** absolve, rehabilitate, reinstate, restore to favour **5.** atone for, compensate for, defray, make amends for, make good, make up for, offset, outweigh, redress, save **6.** buy the freedom of, deliver, emancipate, extricate, free, liberate, pay the ransom of, ransom, rescue, save, set free

redemption 1. reclamation, recovery, repossession, repurchase, retrieval **2.** discharge, exchange, fulfilment, performance, quid pro quo, trade-in **3.** amends, atonement, compensation, expiation, reparation **4.** deliverance, emancipation, liberation, ransom, release, rescue, salvation

red-handed bang to rights (*slang*), (in) flagrante delicto, in the act, with one's fingers *or* hand in the till (*informal*), with one's pants down (*U.S. slang*)

redolent 1. aromatic, fragrant, odorous, perfumed, scented, sweet-smelling **2.** evocative, remindful, reminiscent, suggestive

redoubtable awful, doughty, dreadful, fearful, fearsome, formidable, mighty, powerful, resolute, strong, terrible, valiant

redound 1. conduce, contribute, effect, lead to, militate for, tend **2.** accrue, come back, ensue, rebound, recoil, reflect, result

redress *verb* **1.** compensate for, make amends for, make reparation for, make restitution for, make up for, pay for, put right, recompense for **2.** adjust, amend, balance, correct, ease, even up, mend, put right, rectify, reform, regulate, relieve, remedy, repair, restore the balance, square *~noun* **3.** aid, assistance, correction, cure, ease, help, justice, rectification, relief, remedy, satisfaction **4.** amends, atonement, compensation, payment, quittance, recompense, reparation, requital, restitution

reduce 1. abate, abridge, contract, curtail, cut down, debase, decrease, depress, dilute, diminish, downsize, impair, lessen, lower, moderate, shorten, slow down, tone down, truncate, turn down, weaken, wind down **2.** bankrupt, break, impoverish, pauperize, ruin **3.** bring, bring to the point of, conquer, drive, force, master, overpower, subdue, vanquish **4.** be *or* go on a diet, diet, lose weight, shed weight, slenderize (*chiefly U.S.*), slim, trim **5.** bring down the price of, cheapen, cut, discount, lower, mark down, slash **6.** break, bring low, degrade, demote, downgrade, humble, humiliate, lower in rank, lower the status of, take down a peg (*informal*)

▷ **Antonyms** (*sense 1*) augment, enhance, enlarge, extend, heighten, increase (*sense 6*) elevate, enhance, exalt, promote

redundant 1. *de trop,* excessive, extra, inessential, inordinate, supererogatory, superfluous, supernumerary, surplus, unnecessary, unwanted **2.** diffuse, iterative, padded, periphrastic, pleonastic, prolix, repetitious, tautological, verbose, wordy

▷ **Antonyms** (*sense 1*) essential, necessary, needed, vital

reek *verb* **1.** hum (*slang*), pong (*Brit. informal*), smell, smell to high heaven, stink **2.** be characterized by, be permeated by, be redolent of **3.** *dialect* fume, give off smoke *or* fumes, smoke, steam *~noun* **4.** effluvium, fetor, malodour, mephitis, niff (*Brit. slang*), odour, pong (*Brit. informal*), smell, stench, stink **5.** *dialect* exhalation, fumes, smoke, steam, vapour

reel 1. falter, lurch, pitch, rock, roll, stagger, stumble, sway, totter, waver, wobble **2.** go round and round, revolve, spin, swim, swirl, twirl, whirl

refer 1. advert, allude, bring up, cite, hint, invoke, make mention of, make reference, mention, speak of, touch on **2.** direct, guide, point, recommend, send **3.** apply, consult, go, have recourse to, look up, seek information from, turn to **4.** apply, be directed to, belong, be relevant to, concern, pertain, relate **5.** accredit, ascribe, assign, attribute, credit, impute, put down to **6.** commit, consign, deliver, hand over, pass on, submit, transfer, turn over

referee 1. *noun* adjudicator, arbiter, arbitrator, judge, ref (*informal*), umpire **2.**

~*verb* adjudicate, arbitrate, judge, mediate, umpire

reference **1.** allusion, citation, mention, note, quotation, remark **2.** applicability, bearing, concern, connection, consideration, regard, relation, respect **3.** certification, character, credentials, endorsement, good word, recommendation, testimonial

referendum plebiscite, popular vote, public vote

refine **1.** clarify, cleanse, distil, filter, process, purify, rarefy **2.** civilize, cultivate, elevate, hone, improve, perfect, polish, temper

refined **1.** civil, civilized, courtly, cultivated, cultured, elegant, genteel, gentlemanly, gracious, ladylike, polished, polite, sophisticated, urbane, well-bred, well-mannered **2.** cultured, delicate, discerning, discriminating, exact, fastidious, fine, nice, precise, punctilious, sensitive, sublime, subtle **3.** clarified, clean, distilled, filtered, processed, pure, purified

▷ **Antonyms** (*senses 1 & 2*) boorish, coarse, common, ill-bred, inelegant, uncultured, ungentlemanly, unladylike, unmannerly, unrefined (*sense 3*) coarse, impure, unrefined

refinement **1.** clarification, cleansing, distillation, filtering, processing, purification, rarefaction, rectification **2.** fine point, fine tuning, nicety, nuance, subtlety **3.** breeding, civility, civilization, courtesy, courtliness, cultivation, culture, delicacy, discrimination, elegance, fastidiousness, fineness, finesse, finish, gentility, good breeding, good manners, grace, graciousness, polish, politeness, politesse, precision, sophistication, style, taste, urbanity

reflect **1.** echo, give back, imitate, mirror, reproduce, return, throw back **2.** bear out, bespeak, communicate, demonstrate, display, evince, exhibit, express, indicate, manifest, reveal, show **3.** cogitate, consider, contemplate, deliberate, meditate, mull over, muse, ponder, ruminate, think, wonder

reflection **1.** counterpart, echo, image, mirror image **2.** cerebration, cogitation, consideration, contemplation, deliberation, idea, impression, meditation, musing, observation, opinion, perusal, pondering, rumination, study, thinking, thought, view **3.** aspersion, censure, criticism, derogation, imputation, reproach, slur

reflective cogitating, contemplative, deliberative, meditative, pensive, pondering, reasoning, ruminative, thoughtful

reform *verb* **1.** ameliorate, amend, better, correct, emend, improve, mend, rebuild, reclaim, reconstitute, reconstruct, rectify, regenerate, rehabilitate, remodel, renovate, reorganize, repair, restore, revolutionize **2.** clean up one's act (*informal*), get back on the straight and narrow (*informal*), get it together (*informal*), get one's act together (*informal*), go straight (*informal*), mend one's ways, pull one's socks up (*Brit. informal*), shape up (*informal*), turn over a new leaf ~*noun* **3.** amelioration, amendment, betterment, correction, improvement, rectification, rehabilitation, renovation

refractory cantankerous, contentious, contumacious, difficult, disobedient, disputatious, headstrong, intractable, mulish, obstinate, perverse, recalcitrant, stiff-necked, stubborn, uncontrollable, uncooperative, unmanageable, unruly, wilful

refrain[1] *verb* abstain, avoid, cease, desist, do without, eschew, forbear, give up, kick (*informal*), leave off, renounce, stop

refrain[2] *noun* burden, chorus, melody, song, tune

refresh **1.** brace, breathe new life into, cheer, cool, enliven, freshen, inspirit, kick-start (*informal*), reanimate, reinvigorate, rejuvenate, revitalize, revive, revivify, stimulate **2.** brush up (*informal*), jog, prod, prompt, renew, stimulate **3.** renew, renovate, repair, replenish, restore, top up

refreshing bracing, cooling, different, fresh, inspiriting, invigorating, new, novel, original, revivifying, stimulating, thirst-quenching

▷ **Antonyms** enervating, exhausting, soporific, tiring, wearisome

refreshment **1.** enlivenment, freshening, reanimation, renewal, renovation, repair, restoration, revival, stimulation **2.** (*plural*) drinks, food and drink, snacks, titbits

refrigerate chill, cool, freeze, keep cold

refuge asylum, bolt hole, harbour, haven, hide-out, protection, resort, retreat, sanctuary, security, shelter

refugee displaced person, émigré, escapee, exile, fugitive, runaway

refulgent bright, brilliant, gleaming, irradiant, lambent, lustrous, radiant, resplendent, shining

refund **1.** *verb* give back, make good, pay back, reimburse, repay, restore, return **2.** ~*noun* reimbursement, repayment, return

refurbish clean up, do up (*informal*), fix up (*informal, chiefly U.S. & Canad.*), mend, overhaul, re-equip, refit, remodel, renovate, repair, restore, revamp, set to rights, spruce up

refusal **1.** defiance, denial, kick in the teeth (*slang*), knockback (*slang*), negation, no, rebuff, rejection, repudiation, thumbs down **2.** choice, consideration, opportunity, option

refuse[1] *verb* abstain, decline, deny, reject, repel, repudiate, say no, spurn, turn down, withhold
▷ **Antonyms** accept, agree, allow, ap~ prove, consent, give, permit
refuse[2] *noun* dreck (*slang, chiefly U.S.*), dregs, dross, garbage, junk (*informal*), leavings, lees, litter, offscourings, rub~ bish, scum, sediment, sweepings, trash, waste
refute blow out of the water (*slang*), con~ fute, counter, discredit, disprove, give the lie to, negate, overthrow, prove false, rebut, silence
▷ **Antonyms** confirm, prove, substantiate
regain 1. get back, recapture, recoup, re~ cover, redeem, repossess, retake, re~ trieve, take back, win back **2.** get back to, reach again, reattain, return to
regal fit for a king *or* queen, kingly, mag~ nificent, majestic, noble, princely, proud, queenly, royal, sovereign
regale amuse, delight, divert, entertain, feast, gratify, ply, refresh, serve
regard *verb* **1.** behold, check, check out (*informal*), clock (*Brit. slang*), eye, eye~ ball (*U.S. slang*), gaze at, get a load of (*informal*), look closely at, mark, notice, observe, remark, scrutinize, take a dek~ ko at (*Brit. slang*), view, watch **2.** ac~ count, adjudge, believe, consider, deem, esteem, estimate, hold, imagine, judge, look upon, rate, see, suppose, think, treat, value, view **3.** apply to, be rel~ evant to, concern, have a bearing on, have to do with, interest, pertain to, re~ late to **4.** attend, heed, listen to, mind, note, pay attention to, respect, take into consideration, take notice of *~noun* **5.** attention, heed, interest, mind, notice **6.** account, affection, attachment, care, concern, consideration, deference, es~ teem, honour, love, note, reputation, re~ pute, respect, store, sympathy, thought **7.** aspect, detail, feature, item, matter, particular, point, respect **8.** gaze, glance, look, scrutiny, stare **9.** bearing, concern, connection, reference, relation, rel~ evance **10.** (*plural*) best wishes, compli~ ments, devoirs, good wishes, greetings, respects, salutations
regardful attentive, aware, careful, con~ siderate, dutiful, heedful, mindful, ob~ servant, respectful, thoughtful, watchful
regarding about, apropos, as regards, as to, concerning, in *or* with regard to, in re, in respect of, in the matter of, on the subject of, re, respecting, with reference to
regardless 1. *adjective* disregarding, heedless, inattentive, inconsiderate, in~ different, neglectful, negligent, rash, reckless, remiss, unconcerned, unmind~ ful **2.** *~adverb* anyway, come what may, despite everything, for all that, in any case, in spite of everything, neverthe~ less, no matter what, nonetheless, rain or shine
▷ **Antonyms** *~adjective* heedful, mindful, regardful
regenerate breathe new life into, change, give a shot in the arm, inspirit, invigor~ ate, kick-start (*informal*), reawaken, re~ construct, re-establish, reinvigorate, re~ juvenate, renew, renovate, reproduce, restore, revive, revivify, uplift
▷ **Antonyms** become moribund, decline, degenerate, stagnate, stultify
regime administration, establishment, government, leadership, management, reign, rule, system
regiment *verb* bully, control, discipline, order, organize, regulate, systematize
region 1. area, country, district, division, expanse, land, locality, part, patch, place, province, quarter, section, sector, territory, tract, turf (*U.S. slang*), zone **2.** domain, field, province, realm, sphere, world **3.** area, locality, neighbourhood, range, scope, vicinity
regional district, local, parochial, provin~ cial, sectional, zonal
register *noun* **1.** annals, archives, cata~ logue, chronicle, diary, file, ledger, list, log, memorandum, record, roll, roster, schedule *~verb* **2.** catalogue, check in, chronicle, enlist, enrol, enter, inscribe, list, note, record, set down, sign on *or* up, take down **3.** be shown, bespeak, be~ tray, display, exhibit, express, indicate, manifest, mark, read, record, reflect, reveal, say, show **4.** *informal* come home, dawn on, get through, have an effect, impress, make an impression, sink in, tell
regress backslide, degenerate, deterio~ rate, ebb, fall away *or* off, fall back, go back, lapse, lose ground, recede, relapse, retreat, retrocede, retrogress, return, revert, turn the clock back, wane
▷ **Antonyms** advance, improve, progress, wax
regret 1. *verb* bemoan, be upset, bewail, cry over spilt milk, deplore, feel remorse for, feel sorry for, grieve, lament, miss, mourn, repent, rue, weep over **2.** *~noun* bitterness, compunction, contrition, dis~ appointment, grief, lamentation, pang of conscience, penitence, remorse, repent~ ance, ruefulness, self-reproach, sorrow
▷ **Antonyms** *~verb* be happy, be satisfied, feel satisfaction, have not looked back, rejoice *~noun* callousness, contentment, impenitence, lack of compassion, pleas~ ure, satisfaction
regretful apologetic, ashamed, contrite, disappointed, mournful, penitent, re~ morseful, repentant, rueful, sad, sor~ rowful, sorry
regrettable deplorable, disappointing, distressing, ill-advised, lamentable, pitiable, sad, shameful, unfortunate, unhappy, woeful, wrong

regular **1.** common, commonplace, customary, daily, everyday, habitual, normal, ordinary, routine, typical, unvarying, usual **2.** consistent, constant, established, even, fixed, ordered, periodic, rhythmic, set, stated, steady, systematic, uniform **3.** dependable, efficient, formal, methodical, orderly, standardized, steady, systematic **4.** balanced, even, flat, level, smooth, straight, symmetrical, uniform **5.** approved, bona fide, classic, correct, established, formal, official, orthodox, prevailing, proper, sanctioned, standard, time-honoured, traditional

▷ **Antonyms** (*sense 1*) abnormal, exceptional, infrequent, irregular, occasional, rare, uncommon, unconventional, unusual (*sense 2*) erratic, inconsistent, inconstant, irregular, varied (*sense 3*) disorderly, unmethodical (*sense 4*) erratic, irregular, uneven

regulate adjust, administer, arrange, balance, conduct, control, direct, fit, govern, guide, handle, manage, moderate, modulate, monitor, order, organize, oversee, rule, run, settle, superintend, supervise, systematize, tune

regulation *noun* **1.** adjustment, administration, arrangement, control, direction, governance, government, management, modulation, supervision, tuning **2.** canon, commandment, decree, dictate, direction, edict, law, order, ordinance, precept, procedure, requirement, rule, standing order, statute *~adjective* **3.** customary, mandatory, normal, official, prescribed, required, standard, usual

regurgitate barf (*U.S. slang*), chuck (up) (*slang, chiefly U.S.*), chunder (*slang, chiefly Austral.*), disgorge, puke (*slang*), sick up (*informal*), spew (out *or* up), throw up (*informal*), vomit

rehabilitate **1.** adjust, redeem, reform, reintegrate, save **2.** clear, convert, fix up (*informal, chiefly U.S. & Canad.*), make good, mend, rebuild, recondition, reconstitute, reconstruct, re-establish, reinstate, reinvigorate, renew, renovate, restore

rehash **1.** *verb* alter, change, make over, rearrange, refashion, rejig (*informal*), reshuffle, reuse, rework, rewrite **2.** *~noun* new version, rearrangement, reworking, rewrite

rehearsal **1.** drill, going-over (*informal*), practice, practice session, preparation, reading, rehearsing, run-through **2.** account, catalogue, description, enumeration, list, narration, recital, recounting, relation, telling

rehearse **1.** act, drill, go over, practise, prepare, ready, recite, repeat, run through, study, train, try out **2.** delineate, depict, describe, detail, enumerate, go over, list, narrate, recite, recount, relate, review, run through, spell out, tell, trot out (*informal*)

reign *noun* **1.** ascendancy, command, control, dominion, empire, hegemony, influence, monarchy, power, rule, sovereignty, supremacy, sway *~verb* **2.** administer, be in power, command, govern, hold sway, influence, occupy *or* sit on the throne, rule, wear the crown, wield the sceptre **3.** be rampant, be rife, be supreme, hold sway, obtain, predominate, prevail

reimburse compensate, indemnify, pay back, recompense, refund, remunerate, repay, restore, return, square up

rein *noun* **1.** brake, bridle, check, control, curb, harness, hold, restraint, restriction **2. give (a) free rein (to)** free, give a blank cheque (to), give a free hand, give carte blanche, give (someone) his *or* her head, give way to, indulge, let go, remove restraints *~verb* **3.** bridle, check, control, curb, halt, hold, hold back, limit, restrain, restrict, slow down

reincarnation metempsychosis, rebirth, transmigration of souls

reinforce augment, bolster, buttress, emphasize, fortify, harden, increase, prop, shore up, stiffen, strengthen, stress, supplement, support, toughen, underline

▷ **Antonyms** contradict, undermine, weaken

reinforcement **1.** addition, amplification, augmentation, enlargement, fortification, increase, strengthening, supplement **2.** brace, buttress, prop, shore, stay, support **3.** (*plural*) additional *or* fresh troops, auxiliaries, reserves, support

reinstate bring back, recall, re-establish, rehabilitate, replace, restore, return

reiterate do again, iterate, recapitulate, repeat, restate, retell, say again

reject **1.** *verb* bin, cast aside, decline, deny, despise, disallow, discard, eliminate, exclude, jettison, jilt, rebuff, refuse, renounce, repel, repudiate, repulse, say no to, scrap, spurn, throw away *or* out, turn down, veto **2.** *~noun* castoff, discard, failure, flotsam, second

▷ **Antonyms** *~verb* accept, agree, allow, approve, permit, receive, select *~noun* prize, treasure

rejection brushoff (*slang*), bum's rush (*slang*), denial, dismissal, elimination, exclusion, kick in the teeth (*slang*), knock-back (*slang*), rebuff, refusal, renunciation, repudiation, the (old) heave-ho (*informal*), thumbs down, veto

▷ **Antonyms** acceptance, affirmation, approval, selection

rejoice be glad, be happy, be overjoyed, celebrate, delight, exult, glory, joy, jump for joy, make merry, revel, triumph

▷ **Antonyms** be sad, be unhappy, be upset, grieve, lament, mourn

rejoicing celebration, cheer, delight, elation, exultation, festivity, gaiety, gladness, happiness, joy, jubilation, merrymaking, revelry, triumph

rejoin answer, come back with, reply, respond, retort, return, riposte

rejoinder answer, comeback (*informal*), counter, counterattack, reply, response, retort, riposte

rejuvenate breathe new life into, give new life to, make young again, reanimate, refresh, regenerate, reinvigorate, renew, restore, restore vitality to, revitalize, revivify

relapse *verb* **1.** backslide, degenerate, fail, fall back, lapse, regress, retrogress, revert, slip back, weaken **2.** deteriorate, fade, fail, sicken, sink, weaken, worsen *~noun* **3.** backsliding, fall from grace, lapse, recidivism, regression, retrogression, reversion **4.** deterioration, recurrence, setback, turn for the worse, weakening, worsening

▷ **Antonyms** *~verb* (*sense 2*) get better, improve, rally, recover *~noun* (*sense 4*) improvement, rally, recovery, turn for the better

relate 1. chronicle, describe, detail, give an account of, impart, narrate, present, recite, recount, rehearse, report, set forth, tell **2.** ally, associate, connect, coordinate, correlate, couple, join, link **3.** appertain, apply, bear upon, be relevant to, concern, have reference to, have to do with, pertain, refer

▷ **Antonyms** (*sense 2*) detach, disconnect, dissociate, divorce (*sense 3*) be irrelevant to, be unconnected, have nothing to do with

related 1. accompanying, affiliated, agnate, akin, allied, associated, cognate, concomitant, connected, correlated, interconnected, joint, linked **2.** agnate, akin, cognate, consanguineous, kin, kindred

▷ **Antonyms** separate, unconnected, unrelated

relation 1. affiliation, affinity, consanguinity, kindred, kinship, propinquity, relationship **2.** kin, kinsman, kinswoman, relative **3.** application, bearing, bond, comparison, connection, correlation, interdependence, link, pertinence, reference, regard, similarity, tie-in **4.** account, description, narration, narrative, recital, recountal, report, story, tale

relations 1. affairs, associations, communications, connections, contact, dealings, interaction, intercourse, liaison, meetings, rapport, relationship, terms **2.** clan, family, kin, kindred, kinsfolk, kinsmen, relatives, tribe

relationship affair, affinity, association, bond, communications, conjunction, connection, correlation, exchange, kinship, liaison, link, parallel, proportion, rapport, ratio, similarity, tie-up

relative *adjective* **1.** allied, associated, comparative, connected, contingent, corresponding, dependent, proportionate, reciprocal, related, respective **2.** applicable, apposite, appropriate, appurtenant, apropos, germane, pertinent, relevant **3.** (*with* **to**) corresponding to, in proportion to, proportional to *~noun* **4.** connection, kinsman, kinswoman, member of one's *or* the family, relation

relatively comparatively, in *or* by comparison, rather, somewhat, to some extent

relax 1. abate, diminish, ease, ebb, lessen, let up, loosen, lower, mitigate, moderate, reduce, relieve, slacken, weaken **2.** be *or* feel at ease, calm, chill out (*slang, chiefly U.S.*), hang loose (*slang*), laze, let oneself go (*informal*), let one's hair down (*informal*), lighten up (*slang*), loosen up, make oneself at home, mellow out (*informal*), put one's feet up, rest, soften, take it easy, take one's ease, tranquillize, unbend, unwind

▷ **Antonyms** (*sense 1*) heighten, increase, intensify, tense, tighten, work (*sense 2*) alarm, alert

relaxation 1. amusement, beer and skittles (*informal*), enjoyment, entertainment, fun, leisure, pleasure, recreation, refreshment, rest **2.** abatement, diminution, easing, lessening, let-up (*informal*), moderation, reduction, slackening, weakening

relay *noun* **1.** relief, shift, turn **2.** communication, dispatch, message, transmission *~verb* **3.** broadcast, carry, communicate, hand on, pass on, send, spread, transmit

release *verb* **1.** deliver, discharge, disengage, drop, emancipate, extricate, free, let go, let out, liberate, loose, manumit, set free, turn loose, unbridle, unchain, undo, unfasten, unfetter, unloose, unshackle, untie **2.** absolve, acquit, dispense, excuse, exempt, exonerate, let go, let off **3.** break, circulate, disseminate, distribute, issue, launch, make known, make public, present, publish, put out, unveil *~noun* **4.** acquittal, deliverance, delivery, discharge, emancipation, freedom, liberation, liberty, manumission, relief **5.** absolution, acquittance, dispensation, exemption, exoneration, let-off (*informal*) **6.** announcement, issue, offering, proclamation, publication

▷ **Antonyms** *~verb* (*senses 1 & 2*) detain, engage, fasten, hold, imprison, incarcerate, keep (*sense 3*) suppress, withhold *~noun* (*senses 4 & 5*) detention, imprisonment, incarceration, internment

relegate 1. demote, downgrade **2.** assign, consign, delegate, entrust, pass on, re~

fer, transfer **3.** banish, deport, eject, exile, expatriate, expel, oust, throw out

relent 1. acquiesce, be merciful, capitulate, change one's mind, come round, forbear, give in, give quarter, give way, have pity, melt, show mercy, soften, unbend, yield **2.** die down, drop, ease, fall, let up, relax, slacken, slow, weaken

▷ **Antonyms** (*sense 1*) be unyielding, give no quarter, remain firm, show no mercy (*sense 2*) increase, intensify, strengthen

relentless 1. cruel, fierce, grim, hard, harsh, implacable, inexorable, inflexible, merciless, pitiless, remorseless, ruthless, uncompromising, undeviating, unforgiving, unrelenting, unstoppable, unyielding **2.** incessant, nonstop, persistent, punishing, sustained, unabated, unbroken, unfaltering, unflagging, unrelenting, unrelieved, unremitting, unstoppable

▷ **Antonyms** (*sense 1*) compassionate, forgiving, merciful, submissive, yielding

relevant admissible, *ad rem,* applicable, apposite, appropriate, appurtenant, apt, fitting, germane, material, pertinent, proper, related, relative, significant, suited, to the point, to the purpose

▷ **Antonyms** beside the point, extraneous, extrinsic, immaterial, inapplicable, inappropriate, irrelevant, unconnected, unrelated

reliable certain, dependable, faithful, honest, predictable, regular, reputable, responsible, safe, sound, stable, staunch, sure, tried and true, true, trustworthy, trusty, unfailing, upright

▷ **Antonyms** irresponsible, undependable, unreliable, untrustworthy

reliance assurance, belief, confidence, credence, credit, dependence, faith, trust

relic fragment, keepsake, memento, remembrance, remnant, scrap, souvenir, survival, token, trace, vestige

relief 1. abatement, alleviation, assuagement, balm, comfort, cure, deliverance, ease, easement, mitigation, palliation, release, remedy, solace **2.** aid, assistance, help, succour, support, sustenance **3.** break, breather (*informal*), diversion, let-up (*informal*), refreshment, relaxation, remission, respite, rest

relieve 1. abate, allay, alleviate, appease, assuage, calm, comfort, console, cure, diminish, dull, ease, mitigate, mollify, palliate, relax, salve, soften, solace, soothe **2.** aid, assist, bring aid to, help, succour, support, sustain **3.** give (someone) a break *or* rest, stand in for, substitute for, take over from, take the place of **4.** deliver, discharge, disembarrass, disencumber, exempt, free, release, unburden **5.** break, brighten, interrupt, let up on (*informal*), lighten, slacken, vary

▷ **Antonyms** (*sense 1*) aggravate, exacerbate, heighten, intensify, worsen

religious 1. churchgoing, devotional, devout, divine, doctrinal, faithful, god-fearing, godly, holy, pious, pure, reverent, righteous, sacred, scriptural, sectarian, spiritual, theological **2.** conscientious, exact, faithful, fastidious, meticulous, punctilious, rigid, rigorous, scrupulous, unerring, unswerving

▷ **Antonyms** (*sense 1*) godless, infidel, irreligious, rational, secular, unbelieving

relinquish abandon, abdicate, cast off, cede, desert, drop, forgo, forsake, give up, hand over, kiss (something) goodbye, lay aside, leave, let go, quit, release, renounce, repudiate, resign, retire from, say goodbye to, surrender, vacate, waive, withdraw from, yield

relish *verb* **1.** appreciate, delight in, enjoy, fancy, lick one's lips, like, look forward to, luxuriate in, prefer, revel in, savour, taste *~noun* **2.** appetite, appreciation, enjoyment, fancy, fondness, gusto, liking, love, partiality, penchant, predilection, stomach, taste, zest, zing (*informal*) **3.** appetizer, condiment, sauce, seasoning **4.** flavour, piquancy, savour, smack, spice, tang, taste, trace

▷ **Antonyms** *~verb* be unenthusiastic about, dislike, loathe *~noun* (*sense 2*) dislike, distaste, loathing

reluctance aversion, backwardness, disinclination, dislike, disrelish, distaste, hesitancy, indisposition, loathing, repugnance, unwillingness

reluctant averse, backward, disinclined, grudging, hesitant, indisposed, loath, recalcitrant, slow, unenthusiastic, unwilling

▷ **Antonyms** eager, enthusiastic, inclined, keen, willing

rely bank, be confident of, be sure of, bet, count, depend, have confidence in, lean, reckon, repose trust in, swear by, trust

remain abide, be left, bide, cling, continue, delay, dwell, endure, go on, hang in the air, last, linger, persist, prevail, rest, stand, stay, stay behind, stay put (*informal*), survive, tarry, wait

▷ **Antonyms** depart, go, leave

remainder balance, butt, dregs, excess, leavings, oddment, relic, remains, remnant, residue, residuum, rest, stub, surplus, tail end, trace, vestige(s)

remaining abiding, extant, lasting, left, lingering, outstanding, persisting, residual, surviving, unfinished

remains 1. balance, crumbs, debris, detritus, dregs, fragments, leavings, leftovers, oddments, odds and ends, pieces, relics, remainder, remnants, residue, rest, scraps, traces, vestiges **2.** body, cadaver, carcass, corpse

remark *verb* **1.** animadvert, comment, declare, mention, observe, pass comment, reflect, say, state **2**. espy, heed, make out, mark, note, notice, observe, perceive, regard, see, take note *or* notice of *~noun* **3**. assertion, comment, declaration, observation, opinion, reflection, statement, thought, utterance, word **4**. acknowledgment, attention, comment, consideration, heed, mention, notice, observation, recognition, regard, thought

remarkable conspicuous, distinguished, extraordinary, famous, impressive, miraculous, notable, noteworthy, odd, outstanding, phenomenal, pre-eminent, prominent, rare, signal, singular, strange, striking, surprising, uncommon, unusual, wonderful

▷ **Antonyms** banal, common, commonplace, everyday, insignificant, mundane, ordinary, unexceptional, unimpressive, unsurprising, usual

remediable corrigible, curable, medicable, repairable, soluble, solvable, treatable

remedy *noun* **1**. antidote, counteractive, cure, medicament, medicine, nostrum, panacea, physic (*rare*), relief, restorative, specific, therapy, treatment **2**. antidote, corrective, countermeasure, panacea, redress, relief, solution *~verb* **3**. alleviate, assuage, control, cure, ease, heal, help, mitigate, palliate, relieve, restore, soothe, treat **4**. ameliorate, correct, fix, put right, rectify, redress, reform, relieve, repair, set to rights, solve

remember bear in mind, call to mind, call up, commemorate, keep in mind, look back (on), put one's finger on, recall, recognize, recollect, reminisce, retain, summon up, think back

▷ **Antonyms** disregard, forget, ignore, neglect, overlook

remembrance **1**. anamnesis, memory, mind, recall, recognition, recollection, regard, reminiscence, retrospect, thought **2**. commemoration, keepsake, memento, memorial, monument, relic, remembrancer (*archaic*), reminder, souvenir, testimonial, token

remind awaken memories of, bring back to, bring to mind, call to mind, call up, jog one's memory, make (someone) remember, prompt, put in mind, refresh one's memory

reminisce go over in the memory, hark back, live in the past, look back, recall, recollect, remember, review, think back

reminiscence anecdote, memoir, memory, recall, recollection, reflection, remembrance, retrospection, review

reminiscent evocative, redolent, remindful, similar, suggestive

remiss careless, culpable, delinquent, derelict, dilatory, forgetful, heedless, inattentive, indifferent, lackadaisical, lax, neglectful, negligent, regardless, slack, slapdash, slipshod, sloppy (*informal*), slothful, slow, tardy, thoughtless, unmindful

▷ **Antonyms** attentive, careful, diligent, painstaking, scrupulous

remission **1**. absolution, acquittal, amnesty, discharge, excuse, exemption, exoneration, forgiveness, indulgence, pardon, release, reprieve **2**. abatement, abeyance, alleviation, amelioration, decrease, diminution, ebb, lessening, let-up (*informal*), lull, moderation, reduction, relaxation, respite, suspension

remit *verb* **1**. dispatch, forward, mail, post, send, transmit **2**. cancel, desist, forbear, halt, repeal, rescind, stop **3**. abate, alleviate, decrease, diminish, dwindle, ease up, fall away, mitigate, moderate, reduce, relax, sink, slacken, soften, wane, weaken **4**. defer, delay, postpone, put off, put on the back burner (*informal*), shelve, suspend, take a rain check on (*U.S. & Canad. informal*) *~noun* **5**. authorization, brief, guidelines, instructions, orders, terms of reference

remittance allowance, consideration, fee, payment

remnant balance, bit, butt, end, fragment, hangover, leftovers, oddment, piece, remainder, remains, residue, residuum, rest, rump, scrap, shred, stub, survival, tail end, trace, vestige

remonstrance complaint, expostulation, grievance, objection, petition, protest, protestation, reprimand, reproof

remonstrate argue, challenge, complain, dispute, dissent, expostulate, object, protest, take exception, take issue

remorse anguish, bad *or* guilty conscience, compassion, compunction, contrition, grief, guilt, pangs of conscience, penitence, pity, regret, repentance, ruefulness, self-reproach, shame, sorrow

remorseful apologetic, ashamed, chastened, conscience-stricken, contrite, guilt-ridden, guilty, penitent, regretful, repentant, rueful, sad, self-reproachful, sorrowful, sorry

remorseless **1**. inexorable, relentless, unrelenting, unremitting, unstoppable **2**. callous, cruel, hard, hardhearted, harsh, implacable, inhumane, merciless, pitiless, ruthless, savage, uncompassionate, unforgiving, unmerciful

remote **1**. backwoods, distant, far, faraway, far-off, godforsaken, inaccessible, in the middle of nowhere, isolated, lonely, off the beaten track, outlying, out-of-the-way, secluded **2**. alien, extraneous, extrinsic, foreign, immaterial, irrelevant, outside, removed, unconnected, unrelated **3**. doubtful, dubious, faint, implausible, inconsiderable, meagre, negligible, outside, poor, slender, slight, slim, small, unlikely **4**. abstracted, aloof, cold, detached, distant, faraway, indifferent, introspective, introverted, removed, reserved, standoffish, unap~

proachable, uncommunicative, uninterested, uninvolved, withdrawn
▷ **Antonyms** (*sense 1*) adjacent, central, close, just round the corner, near, nearby, neighbouring (*sense 2*) intrinsic, related, relevant (*sense 3*) considerable, good, likely, strong (*sense 4*) alert, attentive, aware, gregarious, interested, involved, outgoing, sociable

removal 1. abstraction, dislodgment, dismissal, displacement, dispossession, ejection, elimination, eradication, erasure, expulsion, expunction, extraction, purging, stripping, subtraction, taking off, uprooting, withdrawal **2.** departure, flitting (*Scot. & northern English dialect*), move, relocation, transfer

remove 1. abolish, abstract, amputate, carry off *or* away, cart off (*slang*), delete, depose, detach, dethrone, discharge, dislodge, dismiss, displace, do away with, doff, efface, eject, eliminate, erase, excise, expel, expunge, extract, get rid of, give the bum's rush (*slang*), move, oust, pull, purge, relegate, see the back of, shed, show one the door, strike out, take away, take off, take out, throw out, throw out on one's ear (*informal*), transfer, transport, unseat, wipe from the face of the earth, wipe out, withdraw **2.** depart, flit (*Scot. & northern English dialect*), move, move away, quit, relocate, shift, transfer, transport, vacate **3.** *figurative* assassinate, bump off (*slang*), dispose of, do away with, do in (*slang*), eliminate, execute, get rid of, kill, liquidate, murder, take out (*slang*), wipe from the face of the earth
▷ **Antonyms** (*sense 1*) appoint, don, insert, install, join, link, place, put, put back, put in, put on, replace, set

remunerate compensate, indemnify, pay, recompense, redress, reimburse, repay, requite, reward

remuneration compensation, earnings, emolument, fee, income, indemnity, meed (*archaic*), pay, payment, profit, recompense, reimbursement, reparation, repayment, retainer, return, reward, salary, stipend, wages

remunerative economic, gainful, lucrative, moneymaking, paying, profitable, recompensing, rewarding, rich, worthwhile

renaissance, renascence awakening, new birth, new dawn, reappearance, reawakening, rebirth, re-emergence, regeneration, renewal, restoration, resurgence, resurrection, revival

renascent reanimated, reawakening, reborn, redivivus (*rare*), re-emerging, renewed, resurgent, resurrected, reviving

rend 1. break, burst, cleave, crack, dissever, disturb, divide, fracture, lacerate, pierce, pull, rip, rive, rupture, separate, sever, shatter, smash, splinter, split, sunder (*literary*), tear, tear to pieces, wrench **2.** afflict, anguish, break, distress, hurt, lacerate, pain, pierce, stab, torment, wound, wring

render 1. contribute, deliver, furnish, give, hand out, make available, pay, present, provide, show, submit, supply, tender, turn over, yield **2.** display, evince, exhibit, manifest, show **3.** exchange, give, return, swap, trade **4.** cause to become, leave, make **5.** act, depict, do, give, interpret, perform, play, portray, present, represent **6.** construe, explain, interpret, put, reproduce, restate, transcribe, translate **7.** cede, deliver, give, give up, hand over, relinquish, surrender, turn over, yield **8.** give back, make restitution, pay back, repay, restore, return

rendezvous *noun* **1.** appointment, assignation, date, engagement, meeting, tryst (*archaic*) **2.** gathering point, meeting place, place of assignation, trysting-place (*archaic*), venue *~verb* **3.** assemble, be reunited, collect, come together, converge, gather, get together, join up, meet, muster, rally

rendition 1. arrangement, delivery, depiction, execution, interpretation, performance, portrayal, presentation, reading, rendering, take (*informal, chiefly U.S.*), version **2.** construction, explanation, interpretation, reading, transcription, translation, version

renegade 1. *noun* apostate, backslider, betrayer, defector, deserter, dissident, mutineer, outlaw, rebel, recreant (*archaic*), runaway, traitor, turncoat **2.** *~adjective* apostate, backsliding, disloyal, dissident, mutinous, outlaw, rebel, rebellious, recreant (*archaic*), runaway, traitorous, unfaithful

renege, renegue back out, break a promise, break one's word, default, go back, repudiate, welsh (*slang*)

renew begin again, breathe new life into, bring up to date, continue, extend, fix up (*informal, chiefly U.S. & Canad.*), mend, modernize, overhaul, prolong, reaffirm, recommence, recreate, re-establish, refit, refresh, refurbish, regenerate, rejuvenate, renovate, reopen, repair, repeat, replace, replenish, restate, restock, restore, resume, revitalize, transform

renounce abandon, abdicate, abjure, abnegate, abstain from, cast off, decline, deny, discard, disclaim, disown, eschew, forgo, forsake, forswear, give up, leave off, quit, recant, reject, relinquish, renege, repudiate, resign, retract, spurn, swear off, throw off, waive, wash one's hands of
▷ **Antonyms** assert, avow, claim, maintain, reassert

renovate do up (*informal*), fix up (*informal, chiefly U.S. & Canad.*), modernize, overhaul, recondition, reconstitute, recreate, refit, reform, refurbish, rehabilitate, remodel, renew, repair, restore, revamp

renown acclaim, celebrity, distinction, eminence, fame, glory, honour, illustriousness, lustre, mark, note, reputation, repute, stardom

renowned acclaimed, celebrated, distinguished, eminent, esteemed, famed, famous, illustrious, notable, noted, well-known

▷ **Antonyms** forgotten, little-known, neglected, obscure, unknown

rent[1] **1.** *noun* fee, hire, lease, payment, rental, tariff **2.** *~verb* charter, hire, lease, let

rent[2] *noun* **1.** breach, break, chink, crack, flaw, gash, hole, opening, perforation, rip, slash, slit, split, tear **2.** breach, break, cleavage, discord, dissension, disunity, division, faction, rift, rupture, schism, split

renunciation abandonment, abdication, abjuration, abnegation, abstention, denial, disavowal, disclaimer, eschewal, forswearing, giving up, rejection, relinquishment, repudiation, resignation, spurning, surrender, waiver

repair[1] *verb* **1.** compensate for, fix, heal, make good, make up for, mend, patch, patch up, put back together, put right, recover, rectify, redress, renew, renovate, restore, restore to working order, retrieve, square *~noun* **2.** adjustment, darn, mend, overhaul, patch, restoration **3.** condition, fettle, form, nick (*informal*), shape (*informal*), state

▷ **Antonyms** *~verb* damage, destroy, harm, ruin, wreck

repair[2] *verb* **1.** betake oneself, go, head for, leave for, move, remove, retire, set off for, withdraw **2.** have recourse, resort, turn

reparable corrigible, curable, recoverable, rectifiable, remediable, restorable, retrievable, salvageable

reparation amends, atonement, compensation, damages, indemnity, propitiation, recompense, redress, renewal, repair, requital, restitution, satisfaction

repartee badinage, banter, bon mot, persiflage, pleasantry, raillery, riposte, sally, wit, witticism, wittiness, wordplay

repast collation, food, meal, nourishment, refection, spread (*informal*), victuals

repay **1.** compensate, make restitution, pay back, recompense, refund, reimburse, remunerate, requite, restore, return, reward, settle up with, square **2.** avenge, even *or* settle the score with, get back at, get even with (*informal*), get one's own back on (*informal*), hit back, make reprisal, pay (someone) back in his *or* her own coin, reciprocate, retaliate, return the compliment, revenge

repeal **1.** *verb* abolish, abrogate, annul, cancel, countermand, declare null and void, invalidate, nullify, obviate, recall, rescind, reverse, revoke, set aside, withdraw **2.** *~noun* abolition, abrogation, annulment, cancellation, invalidation, nullification, rescinding, rescindment, rescission, revocation, withdrawal

▷ **Antonyms** *~verb* confirm, enact, introduce, pass, ratify, reaffirm, validate *~noun* confirmation, enactment, introduction, passing, ratification, reaffirmation, validation

repeat **1.** *verb* duplicate, echo, iterate, quote, recapitulate, recite, redo, rehearse, reiterate, relate, renew, replay, reproduce, rerun, reshow, restate, retell **2.** *~noun* duplicate, echo, recapitulation, reiteration, repetition, replay, reproduction, rerun, reshowing

repeatedly again and again, frequently, many a time and oft (*archaic or poetic*), many times, often, over and over, time after time, time and (time) again

repel **1.** beat off, check, confront, decline, drive off, fight, hold off, keep at arm's length, oppose, parry, put to flight, rebuff, refuse, reject, repulse, resist, ward off **2.** disgust, give one the creeps (*informal*), gross out (*U.S. slang*), make one shudder, make one sick, nauseate, offend, put one off, revolt, sicken, turn one off (*informal*), turn one's stomach

▷ **Antonyms** attract, delight, draw, entrance, fascinate, invite, please, submit

repellent **1.** abhorrent, abominable, cringe-making (*Brit. informal*), discouraging, disgusting, distasteful, hateful, horrid, loathsome, nauseating, noxious, obnoxious, obscene, odious, offensive, off-putting (*Brit. informal*), repugnant, repulsive, revolting, sickening, yucky *or* yukky (*slang*) **2.** impermeable, proof, repelling, resistant

repent atone, be ashamed, be contrite, be sorry, deplore, feel remorse, lament, regret, relent, reproach oneself, rue, see the error of one's ways, show penitence, sorrow

repentance compunction, contrition, grief, guilt, penitence, regret, remorse, sackcloth and ashes, self-reproach, sorriness, sorrow

repentant apologetic, ashamed, chastened, contrite, penitent, regretful, remorseful, rueful, self-reproachful, sorry

repercussion backlash, consequence, echo, rebound, recoil, result, reverberation, sequel, side effect

repertory collection, list, range, repertoire, repository, stock, store, supply

repetition duplication, echo, iteration, reappearance, recapitulation, recital, recurrence, redundancy, rehearsal, reiteration, relation, renewal, repeat, repetitiousness, replication, restatement, return, tautology

repetitious iterative, long-winded, pleonastic, prolix, redundant, tautological, tedious, verbose, windy, wordy

repetitive boring, dull, mechanical, monotonous, recurrent, samey (*informal*), tedious, unchanging, unvaried

rephrase paraphrase, put differently, recast, reword, say in other words

repine brood, complain, eat one's heart out, fret, grieve, grumble, lament, languish, moan, mope, murmur, sulk

replace fill (someone's) shoes *or* boots, follow, oust, put back, re-establish, reinstate, restore, stand in lieu of, step into (someone's) shoes *or* boots, substitute, succeed, supersede, supplant, supply, take over from, take the place of

replacement double, fill-in, proxy, stand-in, substitute, successor, surrogate, understudy

replenish fill, furnish, make up, provide, refill, reload, renew, replace, restock, restore, stock, supply, top up
▷ **Antonyms** consume, drain, empty, exhaust, use up

replete abounding, brimful, brimming, charged, chock-full, crammed, filled, full, full to bursting, full up, glutted, gorged, jammed, jam-packed, sated, satiated, stuffed, teeming, well-provided, well-stocked
▷ **Antonyms** bare, barren, empty, esurient, famished, hungry, lacking, starving, wanting

repletion completeness, fullness, glut, overfullness, plethora, satiation, satiety, superfluity, surfeit

replica carbon copy (*informal*), copy, duplicate, facsimile, imitation, model, reproduction
▷ **Antonyms** original

replicate ape, copy, duplicate, follow, mimic, recreate, reduplicate, repeat, reproduce

reply 1. *verb* acknowledge, answer, come back, counter, echo, make answer, react, reciprocate, rejoin, respond, retaliate, retort, return, riposte, write back **2.** *~noun* acknowledgment, answer, comeback (*informal*), counter, counterattack, echo, reaction, reciprocation, rejoinder, response, retaliation, retort, return, riposte

report *noun* **1.** account, announcement, article, communication, communiqué, declaration, description, detail, dispatch, information, message, narrative, news, note, paper, piece, recital, record, relation, statement, story, summary, tale, tidings, version, word, write-up **2.** buzz, gossip, hearsay, rumour, scuttlebutt (*U.S. slang*), talk **3.** character, eminence, esteem, fame, regard, reputation, repute **4.** bang, blast, boom, crack, crash, detonation, discharge, explosion, noise, reverberation, sound *~verb* **5.** air, announce, bring word, broadcast, circulate, communicate, cover, declare, describe, detail, document, give an account of, inform of, mention, narrate, note, notify, pass on, proclaim, publish, recite, record, recount, relate, relay, state, tell, write up **6.** appear, arrive, be present, clock in *or* on, come, present oneself, show up (*informal*), turn up

reporter announcer, correspondent, hack (*derogatory*), journalist, journo (*slang*), leader writer, newscaster, newshound (*informal*), newspaperman, newspaperwoman, pressman, writer

repose[1] *noun* **1.** ease, inactivity, peace, quiet, quietness, quietude, relaxation, respite, rest, restfulness, sleep, slumber, stillness, tranquillity **2.** aplomb, calmness, composure, dignity, equanimity, peace of mind, poise, self-possession, serenity, tranquillity *~verb* **3.** drowse, lay down, lie, lie down, lie upon, recline, relax, rest, rest upon, sleep, slumber, take it easy, take one's ease

repose[2] *verb* confide, deposit, entrust, invest, lodge, place, put, store

repository archive, charnel house, depository, depot, emporium, magazine, receptacle, store, storehouse, treasury, vault, warehouse

reprehensible bad, blameworthy, censurable, condemnable, culpable, delinquent, discreditable, disgraceful, errant, erring, ignoble, objectionable, opprobrious, remiss, shameful, unworthy
▷ **Antonyms** acceptable, admirable, forgivable, laudable, pardonable, praiseworthy, unobjectionable

represent 1. act for, be, betoken, correspond to, equal, equate with, express, mean, serve as, speak for, stand for, substitute for, symbolize **2.** embody, epitomize, exemplify, personify, symbolize, typify **3.** delineate, denote, depict, describe, designate, evoke, express, illustrate, outline, picture, portray, render, reproduce, show, sketch **4.** describe as, make out to be, pass off as, pose as, pretend to be **5.** act, appear as, assume the role of, enact, exhibit, perform, play the part of, produce, put on, show, stage

representation 1. account, delineation, depiction, description, illustration, image, likeness, model, narration, narrative, picture, portrait, portrayal, relation, resemblance, sketch **2.** body of representatives, committee, delegates, delegation, embassy **3.** exhibition, performance, play, production, show, sight, spectacle **4.** (*often plural*) account, argument, explanation, exposition, expostulation, remonstrance, statement

representative *noun* **1.** agent, commercial traveller, rep, salesman, traveller **2.** archetype, embodiment, epitome, exemplar, personification, type, typical example **3.** agent, commissioner, council~

lor, delegate, depute (*Scot.*), deputy, member, member of parliament, M.P., proxy, spokesman, spokeswoman *~adjective* **4.** archetypal, characteristic, emblematic, evocative, exemplary, illustrative, symbolic, typical **5.** chosen, delegated, elected, elective

▷ **Antonyms** (*sense 4*) atypical, extraordinary, uncharacteristic

repress bottle up, chasten, check, control, crush, curb, hold back, hold in, inhibit, keep in check, master, muffle, overcome, overpower, quash, quell, restrain, silence, smother, stifle, subdue, subjugate, suppress, swallow

▷ **Antonyms** encourage, express, free, give free rein to, let out, liberate, release, support

repression authoritarianism, censorship, coercion, constraint, control, despotism, domination, inhibition, restraint, subjugation, suppression, tyranny

repressive absolute, authoritarian, coercive, despotic, dictatorial, harsh, oppressive, severe, tough, tyrannical

▷ **Antonyms** democratic, liberal, libertarian

reprieve *verb* **1.** grant a stay of execution to, let off the hook (*slang*), pardon, postpone *or* remit the punishment of **2.** abate, allay, alleviate, mitigate, palliate, relieve, respite *~noun* **3.** abeyance, amnesty, deferment, pardon, postponement, remission, stay of execution, suspension **4.** abatement, alleviation, let-up (*informal*), mitigation, palliation, relief, respite

reprimand 1. *noun* admonition, blame, castigation, censure, dressing-down (*informal*), flea in one's ear (*informal*), lecture, rebuke, reprehension, reproach, reproof, row, talking-to (*informal*), telling-off (*informal*), ticking-off (*informal*), tongue-lashing, wigging (*Brit. slang*) **2.** *~verb* admonish, bawl out (*informal*), blame, carpet (*informal*), castigate, censure, check, chew out (*U.S. & Canad. informal*), chew someone's ass (*U.S. & Canad. taboo slang*), chide, dress down (*informal*), give a rocket (*Brit. & N.Z. informal*), give (someone) a row (*informal*), haul over the coals (*informal*), lecture, rap over the knuckles, read the riot act, rebuke, reprehend, reproach, reprove, scold, send one away with a flea in one's ear (*informal*), slap on the wrist (*informal*), take to task, tear into (*informal*), tear (someone) off a strip (*Brit. informal*), tell off (*informal*), tick off (*informal*), tongue-lash, upbraid

▷ **Antonyms** *~noun* commendation, compliment, congratulations, praise *~verb* applaud, commend, compliment, congratulate, praise

reprisal an eye for an eye, counterstroke, requital, retaliation, retribution, revenge, vengeance

reproach 1. *verb* abuse, bawl out (*informal*), blame, blast, carpet (*informal*), censure, chew out (*U.S. & Canad. informal*), chide, condemn, criticize, defame, discredit, disparage, find fault with, give a rocket (*Brit. & N.Z. informal*), have a go at (*informal*), lambast(e), read the riot act, rebuke, reprehend, reprimand, reprove, scold, take to task, tear into (*informal*), tear (someone) off a strip (*Brit. informal*), upbraid **2.** *~noun* abuse, blame, blemish, censure, condemnation, contempt, disapproval, discredit, disgrace, dishonour, disrepute, ignominy, indignity, obloquy, odium, opprobrium, scorn, shame, slight, slur, stain, stigma

reproachful abusive, admonitory, castigatory, censorious, condemnatory, contemptuous, critical, disappointed, disapproving, fault-finding, reproving, scolding, upbraiding

reprobate 1. *adjective* abandoned, bad, base, corrupt, damned, degenerate, depraved, dissolute, hardened, immoral, incorrigible, profligate, shameless, sinful, sink, unprincipled, vile, wicked **2.** *~noun* asshole (*U.S. & Canad. taboo slang*), asswipe (*U.S. & Canad. taboo slang*), bad egg (*old-fashioned informal*), bastard (*offensive*), blackguard, bugger (*taboo slang*), cocksucker (*taboo slang*), degenerate, evildoer, miscreant, mother (*taboo slang, chiefly U.S.*), motherfucker (*taboo slang, chiefly U.S.*), ne'er-do-well, outcast, pariah, profligate, rake, rakehell (*archaic*), rascal, roué, scoundrel, scumbag (*slang*), shit (*taboo slang*), sinner, skelm (*S. African*), son-of-a-bitch (*slang, chiefly U.S. & Canad.*), turd (*taboo slang*), villain, wastrel, wretch, wrongdoer **3.** *~verb* condemn, damn, denounce, disapprove of, frown upon, reprehend, vilify

reproduce 1. copy, duplicate, echo, emulate, imitate, match, mirror, parallel, print, recreate, repeat, replicate, represent, transcribe **2.** breed, generate, multiply, procreate, produce young, proliferate, propagate, spawn

reproduction 1. breeding, generation, increase, multiplication, procreation, proliferation, propagation **2.** copy, duplicate, facsimile, imitation, picture, print, replica

▷ **Antonyms** (*sense 2*) original

reproof admonition, blame, castigation, censure, chiding, condemnation, criticism, dressing-down (*informal*), rebuke, reprehension, reprimand, reproach, reproval, scolding, ticking-off (*informal*), tongue-lashing, upbraiding

▷ **Antonyms** commendation, compliment, encouragement, praise

reprove abuse, admonish, bawl out (*informal*), berate, blame, carpet (*informal*), censure, check, chew out (*U.S. &

Canad. informal), chide, condemn, give a rocket (*Brit. & N.Z. informal*), read the riot act, rebuke, reprehend, reprimand, scold, take to task, tear into (*informal*), tear (someone) off a strip (*Brit. informal*), tell off (*informal*), tick off (*informal*), upbraid
▷ **Antonyms** applaud, commend, compliment, encourage, praise

repudiate abandon, abjure, cast off, cut off, deny, desert, disavow, discard, disclaim, disown, forsake, reject, renounce, rescind, retract, reverse, revoke, turn one's back on, wash one's hands of
▷ **Antonyms** accept, acknowledge, admit, assert, avow, defend, own, proclaim, ratify

repugnance abhorrence, antipathy, aversion, disgust, dislike, disrelish, distaste, hatred, loathing, odium, reluctance, repulsion, revulsion

repugnant **1.** abhorrent, abominable, disgusting, distasteful, foul, hateful, horrid, loathsome, nauseating, objectionable, obnoxious, odious, offensive, repellent, revolting, sickening, vile, yucky *or* yukky (*slang*) **2.** adverse, antagonistic, antipathetic, averse, contradictory, hostile, incompatible, inconsistent, inimical, opposed
▷ **Antonyms** (*sense 1*) agreeable, attractive, pleasant, unobjectionable (*sense 2*) compatible

repulse *verb* **1.** beat off, check, defeat, drive back, fight off, rebuff, repel, throw back, ward off **2.** disdain, disregard, give the cold shoulder to, rebuff, refuse, reject, snub, spurn, turn down *~noun* **3.** check, defeat, disappointment, failure, reverse **4.** cold shoulder, kick in the teeth (*slang*), knock-back (*slang*), rebuff, refusal, rejection, snub, spurning, the (old) heave-ho (*informal*)

repulsion abhorrence, aversion, detestation, disgust, disrelish, distaste, hatred, loathing, odium, repugnance, revulsion

repulsive abhorrent, abominable, disagreeable, disgusting, distasteful, forbidding, foul, hateful, hideous, horrid, loathsome, nauseating, objectionable, obnoxious, obscene, odious, offensive, repellent, revolting, sickening, ugly, unpleasant, vile
▷ **Antonyms** appealing, attractive, delightful, enticing, lovely, pleasant

reputable creditable, estimable, excellent, good, honourable, honoured, legitimate, of good repute, reliable, respectable, trustworthy, upright, well-thought-of, worthy
▷ **Antonyms** cowboy (*informal*), disreputable, fly-by-night, shady (*informal*), unreliable, untrustworthy

reputation character, credit, distinction, eminence, esteem, estimation, fame, honour, name, opinion, renown, repute, standing, stature

repute celebrity, distinction, eminence, esteem, estimation, fame, name, renown, reputation, standing, stature

reputed accounted, alleged, believed, considered, deemed, estimated, held, ostensible, putative, reckoned, regarded, rumoured, said, seeming, supposed, thought

reputedly allegedly, apparently, ostensibly, seemingly, supposedly

request **1.** *verb* appeal for, apply for, ask (for), beg, beseech, call for, demand, desire, entreat, invite, petition, pray, put in for, requisition, seek, solicit, sue for, supplicate **2.** *~noun* appeal, application, asking, begging, call, demand, desire, entreaty, petition, prayer, requisition, solicitation, suit, supplication
▷ **Antonyms** *~verb/noun* command, order

require **1.** crave, depend upon, desire, have need of, lack, miss, need, stand in need of, want, wish **2.** ask, beg, beseech, bid, call upon, command, compel, constrain, demand, direct, enjoin, exact, insist upon, instruct, oblige, order, request **3.** call for, demand, entail, involve, necessitate, take

required called for, compulsory, demanded, essential, mandatory, necessary, needed, obligatory, prescribed, recommended, requisite, set, unavoidable, vital
▷ **Antonyms** elective, noncompulsory, not necessary, not vital, optional, unimportant, voluntary

requirement demand, desideratum, essential, lack, must, necessity, need, precondition, prerequisite, qualification, requisite, *sine qua non,* specification, stipulation, want

requisite **1.** *adjective* called for, essential, indispensable, mandatory, necessary, needed, needful, obligatory, prerequisite, required, vital **2.** *~noun* condition, desideratum, essential, must, necessity, need, precondition, prerequisite, requirement, *sine qua non*

requisition *noun* **1.** application, call, demand, request, summons **2.** appropriation, commandeering, occupation, seizure, takeover *~verb* **3.** apply for, call for, demand, put in for, request **4.** appropriate, commandeer, occupy, seize, take over, take possession of

requital amends, compensation, payment, recompense, redress, reimbursement, remuneration, repayment, restitution, return, reward

requite compensate, get even, give in return, give tit for tat, make amends, make good, make restitution, pay, pay (someone) back in his *or* her own coin, reciprocate, recompense, redress, reimburse, remunerate, repay, respond, retaliate, return, return like for like, reward, satisfy

rescind abrogate, annul, cancel, countermand, declare null and void, invalidate, obviate, overturn, quash, recall, repeal, retract, reverse, revoke, set aside, void
▷ **Antonyms** confirm, enact, implement, reaffirm, support, uphold, validate

rescission abrogation, annulment, cancellation, invalidation, recall, repeal, rescindment, retraction, reversal, revocation, setting aside, voidance

rescue **1.** *verb* deliver, extricate, free, get out, liberate, recover, redeem, release, salvage, save, save (someone's) bacon (*Brit. informal*), save the life of, set free **2.** *~noun* deliverance, extrication, liberation, recovery, redemption, release, relief, salvage, salvation, saving
▷ **Antonyms** *~verb* abandon, desert, leave, leave behind, lose, strand

research **1.** *noun* analysis, delving, examination, experimentation, exploration, fact-finding, groundwork, inquiry, investigation, probe, scrutiny, study **2.** *~verb* analyse, consult the archives, do tests, examine, experiment, explore, investigate, look into, make inquiries, probe, scrutinize, study, work over

resemblance affinity, analogy, closeness, comparability, comparison, conformity, correspondence, counterpart, facsimile, image, kinship, likeness, parallel, parity, sameness, semblance, similarity, similitude
▷ **Antonyms** difference, disparity, dissimilarity, heterogeneity, unlikeness, variation

resemble bear a resemblance to, be like, be similar to, duplicate, echo, favour (*informal*), look like, mirror, parallel, put one in mind of, remind one of, take after

resent be angry about, bear a grudge about, begrudge, be in a huff about, be offended by, dislike, feel bitter about, grudge, harbour a grudge against, have hard feelings about, object to, take amiss, take as an insult, take exception to, take offence at, take umbrage at
▷ **Antonyms** accept, approve, be content with, be pleased by, feel flattered by, like, welcome

resentful aggrieved, angry, bitter, choked, embittered, exasperated, grudging, huffish, huffy, hurt, in a huff, incensed, indignant, in high dudgeon, irate, jealous, miffed (*informal*), offended, peeved (*informal*), piqued, put out, revengeful, unforgiving, wounded
▷ **Antonyms** content, flattered, gratified, pleased, satisfied

resentment anger, animosity, bad blood, bitterness, chip on one's shoulder (*informal*), displeasure, fury, grudge, huff, hurt, ill feeling, ill will, indignation, ire, irritation, malice, pique, rage, rancour, umbrage, vexation, wrath

reservation **1.** condition, demur, doubt, hesitancy, proviso, qualification, rider, scepticism, scruple, stipulation **2.** enclave, homeland, preserve, reserve, sanctuary, territory, tract

reserve *verb* **1.** conserve, hang on to, hoard, hold, husband, keep, keep back, lay up, preserve, put by, retain, save, set aside, stockpile, store, withhold **2.** bespeak, book, engage, prearrange, pre-engage, retain, secure **3.** defer, delay, keep back, postpone, put off, withhold *~noun* **4.** backlog, cache, capital, fall-back, fund, hoard, reservoir, savings, stock, stockpile, store, supply **5.** park, preserve, reservation, sanctuary, tract **6.** aloofness, constraint, coolness, formality, modesty, reluctance, reservation, restraint, reticence, secretiveness, shyness, silence, taciturnity *~adjective* **7.** alternate, auxiliary, extra, fall-back, secondary, spare, substitute

reserved **1.** booked, engaged, held, kept, restricted, retained, set aside, spoken for, taken **2.** aloof, cautious, close-mouthed, cold, cool, demure, formal, modest, prim, restrained, reticent, retiring, secretive, shy, silent, standoffish, taciturn, unapproachable, uncommunicative, undemonstrative, unforthcoming, unresponsive, unsociable **3.** bound, destined, fated, intended, meant, predestined
▷ **Antonyms** (*sense 2*) ardent, demonstrative, forward, open, sociable, uninhibited, unreserved, warm

reservoir **1.** basin, lake, pond, tank **2.** container, holder, receptacle, repository, store, tank **3.** accumulation, fund, pool, reserves, source, stock, stockpile, store, supply

reshuffle **1.** *noun* change, interchange, realignment, rearrangement, redistribution, regrouping, reorganization, restructuring, revision, shake-up (*informal*) **2.** *~verb* change around, change the line-up of, interchange, realign, rearrange, redistribute, regroup, reorganize, restructure, revise, shake up (*informal*)

reside **1.** abide, dwell, hang out (*informal*), have one's home, inhabit, live, lodge, remain, settle, sojourn, stay **2.** abide, be intrinsic to, be vested, consist, dwell, exist, inhere, lie, rest with
▷ **Antonyms** (*sense 1*) holiday in, visit

residence **1.** abode, domicile, dwelling, flat, habitation, home, house, household, lodging, pad (*slang*), place, quarters **2.** hall, manor, mansion, palace, seat, villa **3.** occupancy, occupation, sojourn, stay, tenancy

resident **1.** *noun* citizen, denizen, indweller, inhabitant, local, lodger, occupant, tenant **2.** *~adjective* dwelling, inhabiting, living, local, neighbourhood, settled

▷ **Antonyms** *~noun* nonresident, visitor *~adjective* nonresident, visiting

residual leftover, net, nett, remaining, unconsumed, unused, vestigial

residue balance, dregs, excess, extra, leftovers, remainder, remains, remnant, residuum, rest, surplus

resign 1. abandon, abdicate, call it a day *or* night, cede, forgo, forsake, give in one's notice, give up, hand over, leave, quit, relinquish, renounce, step down (*informal*), surrender, turn over, vacate, yield **2. resign oneself** accept, acquiesce, bow, give in, give up, reconcile, submit, succumb, yield

resignation 1. abandonment, abdication, departure, leaving, notice, relinquishment, renunciation, retirement, surrender **2.** acceptance, acquiescence, compliance, endurance, forbearing, fortitude, nonresistance, passivity, patience, submission, sufferance

▷ **Antonyms** (*sense 2*) defiance, dissent, kicking up a fuss, protest, resistance

resigned acquiescent, compliant, long-suffering, patient, stoical, subdued, submissive, unprotesting, unresisting

resilient 1. bouncy, elastic, flexible, plastic, pliable, rubbery, springy, supple, whippy **2.** bouncy, buoyant, feisty (*informal, chiefly U.S. & Canad.*), hardy, irrepressible, quick to recover, strong, tough

▷ **Antonyms** (*sense 1*) flaccid, inflexible, limp, rigid, stiff (*sense 2*) delicate, effete, sensitive, sickly, weak

resist 1. battle, be proof against, check, combat, confront, contend with, counteract, countervail, curb, defy, dispute, fight back, hinder, hold out against, oppose, put up a fight (against), refuse, repel, stand up to, struggle against, thwart, weather, withstand **2.** abstain from, avoid, forbear, forgo, keep from, leave alone, prevent oneself from, refrain from, refuse, turn down

▷ **Antonyms** (*sense 1*) accept, acquiesce, give in, submit, succumb, surrender, welcome, yield (*sense 2*) enjoy, give in to, indulge in, surrender to

resistance battle, combat, contention, counteraction, defiance, fight, fighting, hindrance, impediment, intransigence, obstruction, opposition, refusal, struggle

Resistance freedom fighters, guerrillas, irregulars, maquis, partisans, underground

resistant 1. hard, impervious, insusceptible, proof against, strong, tough, unaffected by, unyielding **2.** antagonistic, combative, defiant, dissident, hostile, intractable, intransigent, opposed, recalcitrant, unwilling

resolute bold, constant, determined, dogged, firm, fixed, immovable, inflexible, obstinate, persevering, purposeful, relentless, set, stalwart, staunch, steadfast, strong-willed, stubborn, tenacious, unbending, undaunted, unflinching, unshakable, unshaken, unwavering

▷ **Antonyms** doubtful, irresolute, undecided, undetermined, unresolved, unsteady, weak

resolution 1. boldness, constancy, courage, dedication, determination, doggedness, earnestness, energy, firmness, fortitude, obstinacy, perseverance, purpose, relentlessness, resoluteness, resolve, sincerity, staunchness, staying power, steadfastness, stubbornness, tenacity, willpower **2.** aim, decision, declaration, determination, intent, intention, judgment, motion, purpose, resolve, verdict **3.** answer, end, finding, outcome, settlement, solution, solving, sorting out, unravelling, upshot, working out

resolve *verb* **1.** agree, conclude, decide, design, determine, fix, intend, make up one's mind, purpose, settle, undertake **2.** answer, clear up, crack, elucidate, fathom, find the solution to, suss (out) (*slang*), work out **3.** banish, clear up, dispel, explain, remove **4.** analyse, anatomize, break down, clear, disentangle, disintegrate, dissect, dissolve, liquefy, melt, reduce, separate, solve, split up, unravel **5.** alter, change, convert, metamorphose, transform, transmute *~noun* **6.** conclusion, decision, design, intention, objective, project, purpose, resolution, undertaking **7.** boldness, courage, determination, earnestness, firmness, resoluteness, resolution, steadfastness, willpower

▷ **Antonyms** (*sense 7*) cowardice, half-heartedness, indecision, vacillation, wavering

resonant booming, echoing, full, resounding, reverberant, reverberating, rich, ringing, sonorous, vibrant

resort *verb* **1.** avail oneself of, bring into play, employ, exercise, fall back on, have recourse to, look to, make use of, turn to, use, utilize **2.** frequent, go, haunt, head for, repair, visit *~noun* **3.** haunt, holiday centre, refuge, retreat, spot, tourist centre, watering place (*Brit.*) **4.** alternative, chance, course, expedient, hope, possibility, recourse, reference

resound echo, fill the air, re-echo, resonate, reverberate, ring

resounding booming, echoing, full, powerful, resonant, reverberating, rich, ringing, sonorous, sounding, vibrant

resource 1. ability, capability, cleverness, ingenuity, initiative, inventiveness, quick-wittedness, resourcefulness, talent **2.** hoard, reserve, source, stockpile, supply **3.** appliance, contrivance, course, device, expedient, means, resort

resourceful able, bright, capable, clever, creative, imaginative, ingenious, inventive, quick-witted, sharp, talented
▷ **Antonyms** fushionless (*Scot.*), gormless (*Brit. informal*), unimaginative, uninventive

resources assets, capital, funds, holdings, materials, means, money, property, reserves, riches, supplies, wealth, wherewithal

respect *noun* **1.** admiration, appreciation, approbation, consideration, deference, esteem, estimation, honour, recognition, regard, reverence, veneration **2.** aspect, characteristic, detail, facet, feature, matter, particular, point, sense, way **3.** bearing, connection, reference, regard, relation **4.** (*plural*) compliments, devoirs, good wishes, greetings, regards, salutations *~verb* **5.** admire, adore, appreciate, defer to, esteem, have a good *or* high opinion of, honour, look up to, recognize, regard, revere, reverence, set store by, show consideration for, think highly of, value, venerate **6.** abide by, adhere to, attend, comply with, follow, heed, honour, notice, obey, observe, pay attention to, regard, show consideration for
▷ **Antonyms** *~noun* (*sense 1*) contempt, disdain, disregard, disrespect, irreverence, scorn *~verb* abuse, disregard, disrespect, ignore, neglect, scorn

respectable **1.** admirable, decent, decorous, dignified, estimable, good, honest, honourable, proper, reputable, respected, upright, venerable, worthy **2.** ample, appreciable, considerable, decent, fair, fairly good, goodly, presentable, reasonable, sizable *or* sizeable, substantial, tidy (*informal*), tolerable
▷ **Antonyms** (*sense 1*) dishonourable, disreputable, ignoble, impolite, improper, indecent, unrefined, unworthy (*sense 2*) paltry, poor, small

respectful civil, courteous, courtly, deferential, dutiful, gracious, humble, mannerly, obedient, polite, regardful, reverent, reverential, self-effacing, solicitous, submissive, well-mannered

respective corresponding, individual, own, particular, personal, relevant, separate, several, specific, various

respite **1.** break, breather (*informal*), breathing space, cessation, halt, hiatus, intermission, interruption, interval, let-up (*informal*), lull, pause, recess, relaxation, relief, rest **2.** adjournment, delay, moratorium, postponement, reprieve, stay, suspension

resplendent beaming, bright, brilliant, dazzling, effulgent, gleaming, glittering, glorious, irradiant, luminous, lustrous, radiant, refulgent (*literary*), shining, splendid

respond acknowledge, act in response, answer, come back, counter, react, reciprocate, rejoin, reply, retort, return, rise to the bait, take the bait
▷ **Antonyms** ignore, remain silent, turn a blind eye

response acknowledgment, answer, comeback (*informal*), counterattack, counterblast, feedback, reaction, rejoinder, reply, retort, return, riposte

responsibility **1.** accountability, amenability, answerability, care, charge, duty, liability, obligation, onus, pigeon (*informal*), trust **2.** authority, importance, power **3.** blame, burden, culpability, fault, guilt **4.** conscientiousness, dependability, level-headedness, maturity, rationality, reliability, sensibleness, soberness, stability, trustworthiness

responsible **1.** at the helm, carrying the can (*informal*), in authority, in charge, in control **2.** accountable, amenable, answerable, bound, chargeable, duty-bound, liable, subject, under obligation **3.** authoritative, decision-making, executive, high, important **4.** at fault, culpable, guilty, to blame **5.** adult, conscientious, dependable, level-headed, mature, rational, reliable, sensible, sober, sound, stable, trustworthy
▷ **Antonyms** (*sense 2*) unaccountable (*sense 4*) irresponsible, unconscientious, undependable, unreliable, untrustworthy

responsive alive, awake, aware, forthcoming, impressionable, open, perceptive, quick to react, reactive, receptive, sensitive, sharp, susceptible, sympathetic
▷ **Antonyms** apathetic, impassive, insensitive, silent, unresponsive, unsympathetic

rest[1] *noun* **1.** calm, doze, forty winks (*informal*), idleness, inactivity, kip (*Brit. slang*), leisure, lie-down, motionlessness, nap, refreshment, relaxation, relief, repose, siesta, sleep, slumber, snooze (*informal*), somnolence, standstill, stillness, tranquillity, zizz (*Brit. informal*) **2. at rest** asleep, at a standstill, at peace, calm, dead, motionless, peaceful, resting, sleeping, still, stopped, tranquil, unmoving **3.** break, breather (*informal*), breathing space, cessation, halt, holiday, interlude, intermission, interval, lull, pause, respite, stop, time off, vacation **4.** haven, lodging, refuge, retreat, shelter **5.** base, holder, prop, shelf, stand, support, trestle *~verb* **6.** be at ease, be calm, doze, drowse, have a snooze (*informal*), have forty winks (*informal*), idle, kip (*Brit. slang*), laze, lie down, lie still, mellow out (*informal*), nap, put one's feet up, refresh oneself, relax, sit down, sleep, slumber, snooze (*informal*), take a nap, take it easy, take one's ease, zizz (*Brit. informal*) **7.** be supported, lay, lean, lie, prop, recline, repose, sit, stand, stretch

out **8.** break off, cease, come to a standstill, desist, discontinue, halt, have a break, knock off (*informal*), stay, stop, take a breather (*informal*) **9.** base, be based, be founded, depend, found, hang, hinge, lie, rely, reside, turn
▷ **Antonyms** *~noun* (*senses 1 & 3*) activity, bustle, work *~verb* (*senses 6 & 8*) keep going, slog away (*informal*), work

rest[2] **1.** *noun* balance, excess, leftovers, others, remainder, remains, remnants, residue, residuum, rump, surplus **2.** *~verb* be left, continue being, go on being, keep, remain, stay

restful calm, calming, comfortable, languid, pacific, peaceful, placid, quiet, relaxed, relaxing, serene, sleepy, soothing, tranquil, tranquillizing, undisturbed, unhurried
▷ **Antonyms** agitated, busy, disturbing, restless, uncomfortable, unrelaxed

restitution amends, compensation, indemnification, indemnity, recompense, redress, refund, reimbursement, remuneration, reparation, repayment, requital, restoration, return, satisfaction

restive agitated, edgy, fidgety, fractious, fretful, ill at ease, impatient, jittery (*informal*), jumpy, nervous, on edge, recalcitrant, refractory, restless, uneasy, unquiet, unruly
▷ **Antonyms** at ease, calm, content, peaceful, relaxed, satisfied, serene, tranquil

restless **1.** active, bustling, changeable, footloose, hurried, inconstant, irresolute, moving, nomadic, roving, transient, turbulent, unsettled, unstable, unsteady, wandering **2.** agitated, anxious, disturbed, edgy, fidgeting, fidgety, fitful, fretful, having itchy feet, ill at ease, jumpy, nervous, on edge, restive, sleepless, tossing and turning, troubled, uneasy, unquiet, unruly, unsettled, worried
▷ **Antonyms** (*sense 1*) settled, stable, steady (*sense 2*) comfortable, composed, easy, quiet, relaxed, restful, undisturbed

restlessness **1.** activity, bustle, hurry, hurry-scurry, inconstancy, instability, movement, transience, turbulence, turmoil, unrest, unsettledness **2.** agitation, ants in one's pants (*slang*), anxiety, disquiet, disturbance, edginess, fitfulness, fretfulness, heebie-jeebies (*slang*), inquietude, insomnia, jitters (*informal*), jumpiness, nervousness, restiveness, uneasiness, worriedness

restoration **1.** reconstruction, recovery, refreshment, refurbishing, rehabilitation, rejuvenation, renewal, renovation, repair, revitalization, revival **2.** recovery, re-establishment, reinstallation, reinstatement, replacement, restitution, return
▷ **Antonyms** (*sense 1*) demolition, scrapping, wrecking (*sense 2*) abolition, overthrow

restore **1.** fix, mend, rebuild, recondition, reconstruct, recover, refurbish, rehabilitate, renew, renovate, repair, retouch, set to rights, touch up **2.** bring back to health, build up, reanimate, refresh, rejuvenate, revitalize, revive, revivify, strengthen **3.** bring back, give back, hand back, recover, re-establish, reinstate, replace, retrocede, return, send back **4.** reconstitute, re-enforce, reimpose, reinstate, reintroduce
▷ **Antonyms** (*sense 1*) demolish, scrap, wreck (*sense 2*) make worse, sicken, weaken (*sense 4*) abolish, abrogate, repeal, rescind

restrain **1.** bridle, check, confine, constrain, contain, control, curb, curtail, debar, govern, hamper, handicap, harness, have on a tight leash, hinder, hold, hold back, inhibit, keep, keep under control, limit, muzzle, prevent, rein, repress, restrict, straiten, subdue, suppress **2.** arrest, bind, chain, confine, detain, fetter, hold, imprison, jail, lock up, manacle, pinion, tie up
▷ **Antonyms** (*sense 1*) assist, encourage, help, incite, urge on (*sense 2*) free, liberate, release

restrained **1.** calm, controlled, mild, moderate, muted, reasonable, reticent, self-controlled, soft, steady, temperate, undemonstrative **2.** discreet, quiet, subdued, tasteful, unobtrusive
▷ **Antonyms** (*sense 1*) fiery, hot-headed, intemperate, unrestrained, wild (*sense 2*) garish, loud, over-the-top, self-indulgent, tasteless

restraint **1.** coercion, command, compulsion, confines, constraint, control, curtailment, grip, hindrance, hold, inhibition, limitation, moderation, prevention, pulling one's punches, restriction, self-control, self-discipline, self-possession, self-restraint, suppression **2.** arrest, bondage, bonds, captivity, chains, confinement, detention, fetters, imprisonment, manacles, pinions, straitjacket **3.** ban, boycott, bridle, check, curb, disqualification, embargo, interdict, limit, limitation, rein, taboo
▷ **Antonyms** (*sense 1*) excess, immoderation, intemperance, licence, self-indulgence (*senses 2 & 3*) freedom, liberty

restrict bound, circumscribe, clip someone's wings, confine, contain, cramp, demarcate, hamper, handicap, hem in, impede, inhibit, keep within bounds *or* limits, limit, regulate, restrain, straiten
▷ **Antonyms** broaden, encourage, foster, free, promote, widen

restriction check, condition, confinement, constraint, containment, control, curb, demarcation, handicap, inhibition, limi~

tation, regulation, restraint, rule, stipulation

result *noun* **1.** conclusion, consequence, decision, development, effect, end, end result, event, fruit, issue, outcome, product, reaction, sequel, termination, upshot *~verb* **2.** appear, arise, derive, develop, emanate, ensue, eventuate, flow, follow, happen, issue, spring, stem, turn out **3.** (*with* **in**) culminate, end, finish, pan out (*informal*), terminate, wind up

▷ **Antonyms** *~noun* beginning, cause, germ, origin, outset, root, source

resume 1. begin again, carry on, continue, go on, proceed, recommence, reinstitute, reopen, restart, take up *or* pick up where one left off **2.** assume again, occupy again, reoccupy, take back, take up again

▷ **Antonyms** (*sense 1*) cease, discontinue, stop

résumé abstract, digest, epitome, précis, recapitulation, review, rundown, summary, synopsis

resumption carrying on, continuation, fresh outbreak, new beginning, re-establishment, renewal, reopening, restart, resurgence

resurgence rebirth, recrudescence, re-emergence, renaissance, renascence, resumption, resurrection, return, revival

resurrect breathe new life into, bring back, kick-start (*informal*), raise from the dead, reintroduce, renew, restore to life, revive

resurrection comeback (*informal*), raising *or* rising from the dead, reappearance, rebirth, renaissance, renascence, renewal, restoration, resurgence, resuscitation, return, return from the dead, revival

▷ **Antonyms** burial, demise, killing off

resuscitate breathe new life into, bring round, bring to life, give artificial respiration to, give the kiss of life, quicken, reanimate, renew, rescue, restore, resurrect, revitalize, revive, revivify, save

retain 1. absorb, contain, detain, grasp, grip, hang *or* hold onto, hold, hold back, hold fast, keep, keep possession of, maintain, preserve, reserve, restrain, save **2.** bear in mind, impress on the memory, keep in mind, memorize, recall, recollect, remember **3.** commission, employ, engage, hire, pay, reserve

▷ **Antonyms** (*sense 1*) let go, lose, release, use up (*sense 2*) forget

retainer 1. attendant, dependant, domestic, flunky, footman, henchman, lackey, servant, supporter, valet, vassal **2.** advance, deposit, fee

retaliate even the score, exact retribution, get back at, get even with (*informal*), get one's own back (*informal*), give as good as one gets (*informal*), give (someone) a taste of his *or* her own medicine, give tit for tat, hit back, make reprisal, pay (someone) back in his *or* her own coin, reciprocate, return like for like, strike back, take an eye for an eye, take revenge, wreak vengeance

▷ **Antonyms** accept, submit, turn the other cheek

retaliation an eye for an eye, a taste of one's own medicine, counterblow, counterstroke, reciprocation, repayment, reprisal, requital, retribution, revenge, tit for tat, vengeance

retard arrest, brake, check, clog, decelerate, defer, delay, detain, encumber, handicap, hinder, hold back *or* up, impede, obstruct, set back, slow down, stall

▷ **Antonyms** accelerate, advance, expedite, hasten, speed, speed up, stimulate

retch barf (*U.S. slang*), be sick, chuck (up) (*slang, chiefly U.S.*), chunder (*slang, chiefly Austral.*), disgorge, do a technicolour yawn (*slang*), gag, heave, puke (*slang*), regurgitate, spew, throw up (*informal*), toss one's cookies (*U.S. slang*), upchuck (*U.S. slang*), vomit

reticence quietness, reserve, restraint, secretiveness, silence, taciturnity, uncommunicativeness, unforthcomingness

reticent close-mouthed, mum, quiet, reserved, restrained, secretive, silent, taciturn, tight-lipped, uncommunicative, unforthcoming, unspeaking

▷ **Antonyms** candid, communicative, expansive, frank, open, talkative, voluble

retinue aides, attendants, cortege, entourage, escort, followers, following, servants, suite, train

retire 1. be pensioned off, (be) put out to grass (*informal*), give up work, stop working **2.** absent oneself, betake oneself, depart, exit, go away, leave, remove, withdraw **3.** go to bed, go to one's room, go to sleep, hit the hay (*slang*), hit the sack (*slang*), kip down (*Brit. slang*), turn in (*informal*) **4.** back off, decamp, ebb, fall back, give ground, give way, pull back, pull out, recede, retreat, withdraw

retirement loneliness, obscurity, privacy, retreat, seclusion, solitude, withdrawal

retiring bashful, coy, demure, diffident, humble, meek, modest, quiet, reclusive, reserved, reticent, self-effacing, shrinking, shy, timid, timorous, unassertive, unassuming

▷ **Antonyms** audacious, bold, brassy, forward, gregarious, outgoing, sociable

retort 1. *verb* answer, answer back, come back with, counter, rejoin, reply, respond, retaliate, return, riposte **2.** *~noun* answer, comeback (*informal*), rejoinder, reply, response, riposte

retouch brush up, correct, finish, improve, recondition, renovate, restore, touch up

retract **1.** draw in, pull back, pull in, reel in, sheathe **2.** abjure, cancel, deny, disavow, disclaim, disown, eat one's words, recall, recant, renege, renounce, repeal, repudiate, rescind, reverse, revoke, take back, unsay, withdraw **3.** back out of, go back on, renege on

retreat *verb* **1.** back away, back off, depart, draw back, ebb, fall back, give ground, go back, leave, pull back, recede, recoil, retire, shrink, turn tail, withdraw *~noun* **2.** departure, ebb, evacuation, flight, retirement, withdrawal **3.** asylum, den, haunt, haven, hideaway, privacy, refuge, resort, retirement, sanctuary, seclusion, shelter

▷ **Antonyms** *~verb* advance, engage, move forward *~noun* (*sense 2*) advance, charge, entrance

retrench curtail, cut, cut back, decrease, diminish, economize, husband, lessen, limit, make economies, pare, prune, reduce, save, tighten one's belt, trim

retrenchment contraction, cost-cutting, curtailment, cut, cutback, economy, pruning, reduction, rundown, tightening one's belt

▷ **Antonyms** expansion, investment

retribution an eye for an eye, compensation, justice, Nemesis, punishment, reckoning, recompense, redress, repayment, reprisal, requital, retaliation, revenge, reward, satisfaction, vengeance

retrieve fetch back, get back, recall, recapture, recoup, recover, redeem, regain, repair, repossess, rescue, restore, salvage, save, win back

retrograde **1.** *adjective* backward, declining, degenerative, deteriorating, downward, inverse, negative, regressive, relapsing, retreating, retrogressive, reverse, waning, worsening **2.** *~verb* backslide, decline, degenerate, deteriorate, go downhill (*informal*), regress, relapse, retreat, retrogress, revert, wane, worsen

retrogress **1.** backslide, decline, deteriorate, go back, go downhill (*informal*), regress, relapse, retrocede, retrograde, return, revert, worsen **2.** drop, ebb, fall, go back, lose ground, recede, retire, retreat, sink, wane, withdraw

retrospect afterthought, hindsight, recollection, re-examination, remembrance, reminiscence, review, survey

▷ **Antonyms** anticipation, foresight

return *verb* **1.** come back, come round again, go back, reappear, rebound, recoil, recur, repair, retreat, revert, turn back **2.** carry back, convey, give back, put back, re-establish, reinstate, remit, render, replace, restore, retrocede, send, send back, take back, transmit **3.** give back, pay back, reciprocate, recompense, refund, reimburse, repay, requite **4.** bring in, earn, make, net, repay, yield **5.** answer, come back (with), communicate, rejoin, reply, respond, retort **6.** choose, elect, pick, vote in **7.** announce, arrive at, bring in, come to, deliver, render, report, submit *~noun* **8.** homecoming, reappearance, rebound, recoil, recrudescence, recurrence, retreat, reversion **9.** re-establishment, reinstatement, replacement, restoration **10.** advantage, benefit, gain, income, interest, proceeds, profit, revenue, takings, yield **11.** compensation, meed (*archaic*), reciprocation, recompense, reimbursement, reparation, repayment, requital, retaliation, reward **12.** account, form, list, report, statement, summary **13.** answer, comeback (*informal*), rejoinder, reply, response, retort, riposte

▷ **Antonyms** *~verb* (*sense 1*) depart, disappear, go away, leave (*senses 2 & 3*) hold, keep, leave, remove, retain (*sense 4*) lose *~noun* (*sense 8*) departure, leaving (*sense 9*) removal

revamp do up (*informal*), fix up (*informal, chiefly U.S. & Canad.*), give a face-lift to, overhaul, patch up, recondition, refit, refurbish, rehabilitate, renovate, repair, restore

reveal **1.** announce, betray, blow wide open (*slang*), broadcast, communicate, disclose, divulge, get off one's chest (*informal*), give away, give out, impart, leak, let on, let out, let slip, make known, make public, proclaim, publish, take the wraps off (*informal*), tell **2.** bare, bring to light, display, exhibit, expose to view, lay bare, manifest, open, show, uncover, unearth, unmask, unveil

▷ **Antonyms** conceal, cover up, hide, keep quiet about, sweep under the carpet (*informal*)

revel *verb* **1.** (*with* **in**) bask, crow, delight, drool, gloat, indulge, joy, lap up, luxuriate, rejoice, relish, rub one's hands, savour, take pleasure, thrive on, wallow **2.** carouse, celebrate, go on a spree, live it up (*informal*), make merry, paint the town red (*informal*), push the boat out (*Brit. informal*), rave (*Brit. slang*), roister, whoop it up (*informal*) *~noun* **3.** (*often plural*) bacchanal, beano (*Brit. slang*), carousal, carouse, celebration, debauch, festivity, gala, hooley *or* hoolie (*chiefly Irish & N.Z.*), jollification, merrymaking, party, rave (*Brit. slang*), rave-up (*Brit. slang*), saturnalia, spree

▷ **Antonyms** (*sense 1*) abhor, be uninterested in, dislike, hate, have no taste for

revelation announcement, betrayal, broadcasting, communication, disclosure, discovery, display, exhibition, exposé, exposition, exposure, giveaway, leak, manifestation, news, proclamation, publication, telling, uncovering, unearthing, unveiling

reveller carouser, celebrator, merrymaker, partygoer, pleasure-seeker, roisterer

revelry beano (*Brit. slang*), carousal, carouse, celebration, debauch, debauchery, festivity, fun, hooley *or* hoolie (*chiefly Irish & N.Z.*), jollification, jollity, merrymaking, party, rave (*Brit. slang*), rave-up (*Brit. slang*), roistering, saturnalia, spree

revenge 1. *noun* an eye for an eye, reprisal, requital, retaliation, retribution, satisfaction, vengeance, vindictiveness **2.** *~verb* avenge, even the score for, get even, get one's own back for (*informal*), hit back, make reprisal for, pay (someone) back in his *or* her own coin, repay, requite, retaliate, take an eye for an eye for, take revenge for, vindicate

revengeful bitter, implacable, malevolent, malicious, malignant, merciless, pitiless, resentful, spiteful, unforgiving, unmerciful, vengeful, vindictive

revenue gain, income, interest, proceeds, profits, receipts, returns, rewards, takings, yield
▷ **Antonyms** expenditure, expenses, outgoings

reverberate echo, rebound, recoil, re-echo, resound, ring, vibrate

reverberation 1. echo, rebound, recoil, re-echoing, reflection, resonance, resounding, ringing, vibration **2.** *figurative* (*usually plural*) consequences, effects, repercussions, results

revere adore, be in awe of, defer to, exalt, have a high opinion of, honour, look up to, put on a pedestal, respect, reverence, think highly of, venerate, worship
▷ **Antonyms** deride, despise, hold in contempt, scorn, sneer at

reverence 1. *noun* admiration, adoration, awe, deference, devotion, high esteem, homage, honour, respect, veneration, worship **2.** *~verb* admire, adore, be in awe of, hold in awe, honour, pay homage to, respect, revere, venerate, worship
▷ **Antonyms** *~noun* contempt, contumely, derision, disdain, scorn

reverent adoring, awed, decorous, deferential, devout, humble, loving, meek, pious, respectful, reverential, solemn, submissive
▷ **Antonyms** cheeky, disrespectful, flippant, impious, irreverent, mocking, sacrilegious

reverie absent-mindedness, abstraction, brown study, castles in the air *or* Spain, daydream, daydreaming, inattention, musing, preoccupation, trance, woolgathering

reverse *verb* **1.** invert, transpose, turn back, turn over, turn round, turn upside down, upend **2.** alter, annul, cancel, change, countermand, declare null and void, invalidate, negate, obviate, overrule, overset, overthrow, overturn, quash, repeal, rescind, retract, revoke, set aside, undo, upset **3.** back, backtrack, back up, go backwards, move backwards, retreat *~noun* **4.** antithesis, contradiction, contrary, converse, inverse, opposite **5.** back, flip side, other side, rear, underside, verso, wrong side **6.** adversity, affliction, blow, check, defeat, disappointment, failure, hardship, misadventure, misfortune, mishap, repulse, reversal, setback, trial, vicissitude *~adjective* **7.** back to front, backward, contrary, converse, inverse, inverted, opposite
▷ **Antonyms** *~verb* (*sense 2*) carry out, enforce, implement, validate (*sense 3*) advance, go forward, move forward *~noun* (*sense 5*) forward side, front, obverse, recto, right side

revert backslide, come back, go back, hark back, lapse, recur, regress, relapse, resume, return, take up where one left off

review *verb* **1.** go over again, look at again, reassess, recapitulate, reconsider, re-evaluate, re-examine, rethink, revise, run over, take another look at, think over **2.** call to mind, look back on, recall, recollect, reflect on, remember, summon up **3.** assess, criticize, discuss, evaluate, examine, give one's opinion of, inspect, judge, read through, scrutinize, study, weigh, write a critique of *~noun* **4.** analysis, examination, perusal, report, scrutiny, study, survey **5.** commentary, critical assessment, criticism, critique, evaluation, judgment, notice, study **6.** journal, magazine, periodical **7.** another look, fresh look, reassessment, recapitulation, reconsideration, re-evaluation, re-examination, rethink, retrospect, revision, second look **8.** *Military* display, inspection, march past, parade, procession

reviewer arbiter, commentator, connoisseur, critic, essayist, judge

revile abuse, asperse, bad-mouth (*slang, chiefly U.S. & Canad.*), calumniate, defame, denigrate, knock (*informal*), libel, malign, reproach, rubbish (*informal*), run down, scorn, slag (off) (*slang*), slander, smear, traduce, vilify, vituperate

revise 1. alter, amend, change, correct, edit, emend, modify, reconsider, redo, re-examine, revamp, review, rework, rewrite, update **2.** go over, memorize, reread, run through, study, swot up (*Brit. informal*)

revision 1. alteration, amendment, change, correction, editing, emendation, modification, re-examination, review, rewriting, updating **2.** homework, memorizing, rereading, studying, swotting (*Brit. informal*)

revitalize breathe new life into, bring back to life, reanimate, refresh, rejuvenate, renew, restore, resurrect, revivify

revival awakening, quickening, reanimation, reawakening, rebirth, recrudescence, refreshment, renaissance, renascence, renewal, restoration, resurgence, resurrection, resuscitation, revitalization, revivification
▷ **Antonyms** disappearance, extinction, falling off, suppression

revive animate, awaken, breathe new life into, bring back to life, bring round, cheer, come round, comfort, invigorate, kick-start (*informal*), quicken, rally, reanimate, recover, refresh, rekindle, renew, renovate, restore, resuscitate, revitalize, rouse, spring up again
▷ **Antonyms** die out, disappear, enervate, exhaust, tire out, weary

revivify breathe new life into, give new life to, inspirit, invigorate, kick-start (*informal*), reanimate, refresh, renew, restore, resuscitate, revive

revoke abolish, abrogate, annul, call back, cancel, countermand, declare null and void, disclaim, invalidate, negate, nullify, obviate, quash, recall, recant, renege, renounce, repeal, repudiate, rescind, retract, reverse, set aside, take back, withdraw
▷ **Antonyms** confirm, endorse, implement, maintain, put into effect, uphold

revolt *noun* **1.** defection, insurgency, insurrection, mutiny, putsch, rebellion, revolution, rising, sedition, uprising ~*verb* **2.** defect, mutiny, rebel, resist, rise, take to the streets, take up arms (against) **3.** disgust, give one the creeps (*informal*), gross out (*U.S. slang*), make one's flesh creep, nauseate, offend, repel, repulse, shock, sicken, turn off (*informal*), turn one's stomach

revolting abhorrent, abominable, appalling, cringe-making (*Brit. informal*), disgusting, distasteful, foul, horrible, horrid, loathsome, nasty, nauseating, nauseous, noisome, obnoxious, obscene, offensive, repellent, repugnant, repulsive, shocking, sickening, yucky *or* yukky (*slang*)
▷ **Antonyms** agreeable, attractive, delightful, fragrant, palatable, pleasant

revolution *noun* **1.** coup, coup d'état, insurgency, mutiny, putsch, rebellion, revolt, rising, uprising **2.** drastic *or* radical change, innovation, metamorphosis, reformation, sea change, shift, transformation, upheaval **3.** circle, circuit, cycle, gyration, lap, orbit, rotation, round, spin, turn, wheel, whirl

revolutionary *noun* **1.** insurgent, insurrectionary, insurrectionist, mutineer, rebel, revolutionist ~*adjective* **2.** extremist, insurgent, insurrectionary, mutinous, radical, rebel, seditious, subversive **3.** avant-garde, different, drastic, experimental, fundamental, ground-breaking, innovative, new, novel, progressive, radical, thoroughgoing
▷ **Antonyms** (*senses 1 & 2*) counter-revolutionary, loyalist, reactionary (*sense 3*) conservative, conventional, mainstream, minor, traditional, trivial

revolve 1. circle, go round, gyrate, orbit, rotate, spin, turn, twist, wheel, whirl **2.** consider, deliberate, meditate, mull over, ponder, reflect, ruminate, study, think about, think over, turn over (in one's mind)

revulsion abhorrence, abomination, aversion, detestation, disgust, distaste, loathing, odium, recoil, repugnance, repulsion
▷ **Antonyms** attraction, desire, fascination, liking, pleasure

reward *noun* **1.** benefit, bonus, bounty, compensation, gain, honour, meed (*archaic*), merit, payment, premium, prize, profit, recompense, remuneration, repayment, requital, return, wages **2.** comeuppance (*slang*), desert, just deserts, punishment, requital, retribution ~*verb* **3.** compensate, honour, make it worth one's while, pay, recompense, remunerate, repay, requite
▷ **Antonyms** ~*noun* (*sense 1*) fine, penalty, punishment ~*verb* fine, penalize, punish

rewarding advantageous, beneficial, economic, edifying, enriching, fruitful, fulfilling, gainful, gratifying, pleasing, productive, profitable, remunerative, satisfying, valuable, worthwhile
▷ **Antonyms** barren, boring, fruitless, unproductive, unprofitable, unrewarding, vain

reword express differently, paraphrase, put another way, put in other words, recast, rephrase

rewrite correct, edit, emend, recast, redraft, revise, touch up

rhetoric 1. eloquence, oratory **2.** bombast, fustian, grandiloquence, hot air (*informal*), hyperbole, magniloquence, pomposity, rant, verbosity, wordiness

rhetorical 1. bombastic, declamatory, flamboyant, flashy, florid, flowery, grandiloquent, high-flown, high-sounding, hyperbolic, magniloquent, oratorical, pompous, pretentious, showy, silver-tongued, verbose, windy **2.** linguistic, oratorical, stylistic, verbal

rhyme *noun* **1.** ode, poem, poetry, song, verse **2. rhyme or reason** logic, meaning, method, plan, sense ~*verb* **3.** chime, harmonize, sound like

rhythm accent, beat, cadence, flow, lilt, measure (*Prosody*), metre, movement, pattern, periodicity, pulse, swing, tempo, time

rhythmic, rhythmical cadenced, flowing, harmonious, lilting, melodious, metrical, musical, periodic, pulsating, throbbing

ribald bawdy, blue, broad, coarse, earthy, filthy, gross, indecent, licentious, naughty, near the knuckle (*informal*), obscene, off colour, Rabelaisian, racy, raunchy (*slang*), risqué, rude, scurrilous, smutty, vulgar, X-rated (*informal*)
▷ **Antonyms** chaste, decent, decorous, genteel, inoffensive, polite, proper, refined, tasteful

ribaldry bawdiness, billingsgate, coarseness, earthiness, filth, grossness, indecency, licentiousness, naughtiness, obscenity, raciness, rudeness, scurrility, smut, smuttiness, vulgarity

rich 1. affluent, filthy rich, flush (*informal*), loaded (*slang*), made of money (*informal*), moneyed, opulent, propertied, prosperous, rolling (*slang*), stinking rich (*informal*), wealthy, well-heeled (*informal*), well-off, well-to-do **2.** abounding, full, productive, well-endowed, well-provided, well-stocked, well-supplied **3.** abounding, abundant, ample, copious, exuberant, fecund, fertile, fruitful, full, lush, luxurious, plenteous, plentiful, productive, prolific **4.** beyond price, costly, elaborate, elegant, expensive, exquisite, fine, gorgeous, lavish, palatial, precious, priceless, splendid, sumptuous, superb, valuable **5.** creamy, delicious, fatty, flavoursome, full-bodied, heavy, highly-flavoured, juicy, luscious, savoury, spicy, succulent, sweet, tasty **6.** bright, deep, gay, intense, strong, vibrant, vivid, warm **7.** deep, dulcet, full, mellifluous, mellow, resonant **8.** amusing, comical, funny, hilarious, humorous, laughable, ludicrous, ridiculous, risible, side-splitting
▷ **Antonyms** (*sense 1*) destitute, impoverished, needy, penniless, poor (*sense 2*) lacking, poor, scarce, wanting (*sense 3*) barren, poor, unfertile, unfruitful, unproductive (*sense 4*) cheap, cheapo (*informal*), inexpensive, valueless, worthless (*sense 5*) bland, dull (*sense 6*) dull, insipid, weak (*sense 7*) high-pitched

riches abundance, affluence, assets, fortune, gold, money, opulence, plenty, property, resources, richness, substance, treasure, wealth
▷ **Antonyms** dearth, indigence, lack, need, paucity, poverty, scantiness, scarcity, want

richly 1. elaborately, elegantly, expensively, exquisitely, gorgeously, lavishly, luxuriously, opulently, palatially, splendidly, sumptuously **2.** amply, appropriately, fully, in full measure, properly, suitably, thoroughly, well

rickety broken, broken-down, decrepit, derelict, dilapidated, feeble, flimsy, frail, imperfect, infirm, insecure, jerry-built, precarious, ramshackle, shaky, tottering, unsound, unsteady, weak, wobbly

rid 1. clear, deliver, disabuse, disburden, disembarrass, disencumber, free, lighten, make free, purge, relieve, unburden **2. get rid of** dispense with, dispose of, do away with, dump, eject, eliminate, expel, give the bum's rush (*slang*), jettison, remove, see the back of, shake off, throw away *or* out, unload, weed out, wipe from the face of the earth

riddance clearance, clearing out, deliverance, disposal, ejection, elimination, expulsion, freedom, release, relief, removal

riddle¹ *noun* brain-teaser (*informal*), Chinese puzzle, conundrum, enigma, mystery, poser, problem, puzzle, rebus, teaser

riddle² *verb* **1.** honeycomb, pepper, perforate, pierce, puncture **2.** corrupt, damage, fill, impair, infest, mar, permeate, pervade, spoil **3.** bolt, filter, screen, sieve, sift, strain, winnow *~noun* **4.** filter, screen, sieve, strainer

ride *verb* **1.** control, handle, manage, sit on **2.** be borne, be carried, be supported, float, go, journey, move, progress, sit, travel **3.** dominate, enslave, grip, haunt, oppress, tyrannize over *~noun* **4.** drive, jaunt, journey, lift, outing, spin (*informal*), trip, whirl (*informal*)

ridicule 1. *noun* banter, chaff, derision, gibe, guy, irony, jeer, laughter, mockery, raillery, rib, sarcasm, satire, scorn, sneer, taunting **2.** *~verb* banter, caricature, chaff, deride, humiliate, jeer, lampoon, laugh at, laugh out of court, laugh to scorn, make a fool of, make a monkey out of, make fun of, make one a laughing stock, mock, parody, poke fun at, pooh-pooh, satirize, scoff, send up (*Brit. informal*), sneer, take the mickey out of (*informal*), take the piss (out of) (*taboo slang*), taunt

ridiculous absurd, comical, contemptible, derisory, farcical, foolish, funny, hilarious, inane, incredible, laughable, ludicrous, nonsensical, outrageous, preposterous, risible, silly, stupid, unbelievable, zany
▷ **Antonyms** bright, clever, intelligent, logical, prudent, rational, reasonable, sagacious, sane, sensible, serious, smart, solemn, well-thought-out, wise

rife abundant, common, current, epidemic, frequent, general, plentiful, prevailing, prevalent, raging, rampant, teeming, ubiquitous, universal, widespread

riffraff *canaille,* dregs of society, hoi polloi, rabble, ragtag and bobtail, scum, undesirables

rifle *verb* burgle, despoil, go through, gut, loot, pillage, plunder, ransack, rob, rummage, sack, strip

rift **1.** breach, break, chink, cleavage, cleft, crack, cranny, crevice, fault, fissure, flaw, fracture, gap, opening, space, split **2.** alienation, breach, difference, disagreement, division, estrangement, falling out (*informal*), quarrel, schism, separation, split

rig *verb* **1.** accoutre, equip, fit out, furnish, kit out, outfit, provision, supply, turn out **2.** arrange, doctor, engineer, fake, falsify, fiddle with (*informal*), fix (*informal*), gerrymander, juggle, manipulate, tamper with, trump up *~noun* **3.** accoutrements, apparatus, equipage, equipment, fitments, fittings, fixtures, gear, machinery, outfit, tackle

right *adjective* **1.** equitable, ethical, fair, good, honest, honourable, just, lawful, moral, proper, righteous, true, upright, virtuous **2.** accurate, admissible, authentic, correct, exact, factual, genuine, precise, satisfactory, sound, spot-on (*Brit. informal*), true, unerring, valid, veracious **3.** advantageous, appropriate, becoming, *comme il faut,* convenient, deserved, desirable, done, due, favourable, fit, fitting, ideal, opportune, proper, propitious, rightful, seemly, suitable **4.** all there (*informal*), balanced, *compos mentis,* fine, fit, healthy, in good health, in the pink, lucid, normal, rational, reasonable, sane, sound, unimpaired, up to par, well **5.** conservative, reactionary, Tory **6.** absolute, complete, out-and-out, outright, pure, real, thorough, thoroughgoing, utter *~adverb* **7.** accurately, aright, correctly, exactly, factually, genuinely, precisely, truly **8.** appropriately, aptly, befittingly, fittingly, properly, satisfactorily, suitably **9.** directly, immediately, instantly, promptly, quickly, straight, straightaway, without delay **10.** bang, exactly, precisely, slap-bang (*informal*), squarely **11.** absolutely, all the way, altogether, completely, entirely, perfectly, quite, thoroughly, totally, utterly, wholly **12.** ethically, fairly, honestly, honourably, justly, morally, properly, righteously, virtuously **13.** advantageously, beneficially, favourably, for the better, fortunately, to advantage, well *~noun* **14.** authority, business, claim, due, freedom, interest, liberty, licence, permission, power, prerogative, privilege, title **15.** equity, good, goodness, honour, integrity, justice, lawfulness, legality, morality, propriety, reason, rectitude, righteousness, truth, uprightness, virtue **16. by rights** equitably, in fairness, justly, properly **17. to rights** arranged, in order, straight, tidy *~verb* **18.** compensate for, correct, fix, put right, rectify, redress, repair, settle, set upright, sort out, straighten, vindicate

▷ **Antonyms** *~adjective* (*sense 1*) bad, dishonest, immoral, improper, indecent, unethical, unfair, unjust, wrong (*sense 2*) counterfeit, erroneous, fake, false, fraudulent, illegal, illicit, inaccurate, incorrect, inexact, invalid, mistaken, questionable, uncertain, unlawful, untruthful, wrong (*sense 3*) disadvantageous, inappropriate, inconvenient, undesirable, unfitting, unseemly, unsuitable, wrong (*sense 4*) abnormal, unsound (*sense 5*) left, leftist, left-wing, liberal, radical, right-on (*informal*), socialist *~adverb* (*sense 7*) inaccurately, incorrectly (*sense 8*) improperly (*sense 9*) incompletely, indirectly, slowly (*sense 13*) badly, poorly, unfavourably *~noun* (*sense 15*) badness, dishonour, evil, immorality, impropriety *~verb* (*sense 18*) make crooked, topple

right away at once, directly, forthwith, immediately, instantly, now, posthaste, promptly, pronto (*informal*), right off, straightaway, straight off (*informal*), this instant, without delay, without hesitation

righteous blameless, equitable, ethical, fair, good, honest, honourable, just, law-abiding, moral, pure, squeaky-clean, upright, virtuous

▷ **Antonyms** bad, corrupt, dishonest, dishonourable, evil, false, guilty, immoral, improper, indecent, insincere, sinful, unethical, unfair, unjust, unprincipled, unrighteous, unscrupulous, unseemly, wicked

righteousness blamelessness, equity, ethicalness, faithfulness, goodness, honesty, honour, integrity, justice, morality, probity, purity, rectitude, uprightness, virtue

rightful authorized, bona fide, de jure, due, just, lawful, legal, legitimate, proper, real, suitable, true, valid

rigid adamant, austere, exact, fixed, harsh, inelastic, inflexible, intransigent, invariable, rigorous, set, severe, stern, stiff, strict, stringent, unalterable, unbending, uncompromising, undeviating, unrelenting, unyielding

▷ **Antonyms** bending, elastic, flexible, indulgent, lax, lenient, limber, lissom(e), merciful, mobile, pliable, pliant, soft, supple, tolerant, yielding

rigmarole balderdash, bother, carry-on (*informal, chiefly Brit.*), gibberish, hassle (*informal*), jargon, nonsense, palaver, pantomime (*informal*), performance (*informal*), red tape, to-do, trash, twaddle

rigorous **1.** austere, challenging, demanding, exacting, firm, hard, harsh, inflexible, rigid, severe, stern, strict, stringent, tough **2.** accurate, conscientious, exact, meticulous, nice, painstaking, precise, punctilious, scrupulous, thorough **3.** bad, bleak, extreme, harsh, inclement, inhospitable, severe

▷ **Antonyms** (*sense 1*) easy, flexible,

friendly, genial, gentle, humane, indulgent, kind, lax, lenient, loose, merciful, mild, permissive, relaxed, soft, sympathetic, tolerant, weak (*sense 2*) careless, half-hearted, haphazard, imperfect, inaccurate, incorrect, inexact, loose, negligent, slapdash, sloppy, slovenly, unscrupulous (*sense 3*) agreeable, mild, pleasant

rigour **1.** asperity, austerity, firmness, hardness, hardship, harshness, inflexibility, ordeal, privation, rigidity, sternness, strictness, stringency, suffering, trial **2.** accuracy, conscientiousness, exactitude, exactness, meticulousness, preciseness, precision, punctiliousness, thoroughness

rig-out apparel, clobber (*Brit. slang*), clothing, costume, dress, garb, gear (*informal*), get-up (*informal*), habit, outfit, raiment (*archaic or poetic*), togs

rig out **1.** accoutre, equip, fit, furnish, kit out, outfit, set up **2.** array, attire, clothe, costume, dress, kit out

rig up arrange, assemble, build, cobble together, construct, erect, fix up, improvise, put together, put up, set up, throw together

rile aggravate (*informal*), anger, annoy, bug (*informal*), gall, get one's back up, get one's goat (*slang*), get on one's nerves (*informal*), get under one's skin (*informal*), irk, irritate, nark (*Brit., Austral., & N.Z. slang*), nettle, peeve (*informal*), pique, piss one off (*taboo slang*), provoke, put one's back up, rub one up the wrong way, try one's patience, upset, vex

rim border, brim, brink, circumference, edge, flange, lip, margin, verge

rind crust, epicarp, husk, integument, outer layer, peel, skin

ring[1] *noun* **1.** band, circle, circuit, halo, hoop, loop, round **2.** arena, circus, enclosure, rink **3.** association, band, cabal, cartel, cell, circle, clique, combine, coterie, crew (*informal*), gang, group, junta, knot, mob, organization, syndicate *~verb* **4.** circumscribe, encircle, enclose, encompass, gird, girdle, hem in, seal off, surround

ring[2] *verb* **1.** chime, clang, peal, resonate, resound, reverberate, sound, toll **2.** buzz (*informal*), call, phone, telephone *~noun* **3.** chime, knell, peal **4.** buzz (*informal*), call, phone call

rinse **1.** *verb* bathe, clean, cleanse, dip, splash, wash, wash out, wet **2.** *~noun* bath, dip, splash, wash, wetting

riot *noun* **1.** anarchy, commotion, confusion, disorder, disturbance, donnybrook, fray, lawlessness, mob violence, quarrel, row, street fighting, strife, tumult, turbulence, turmoil, upheaval, uproar **2.** blast (*U.S. slang*), boisterousness, carousal, excess, festivity, frolic, high jinks, jollification, merrymaking, revelry, romp **3.** display, extravaganza, flourish, show, splash **4. run riot: a.** be out of control, break *or* cut loose, go wild, let oneself go, raise hell, rampage, throw off all restraint **b.** grow like weeds, grow profusely, luxuriate, spread like wildfire *~verb* **5.** fight in the streets, go on the rampage, raise an uproar, rampage, run riot, take to the streets **6.** carouse, cut loose, frolic, go on a binge (*informal*), go on a spree, make merry, paint the town red (*informal*), revel, roister, romp

riotous **1.** anarchic, disorderly, insubordinate, lawless, mutinous, rampageous, rebellious, refractory, rowdy, tumultuous, ungovernable, unruly, uproarious, violent **2.** boisterous, loud, luxurious, noisy, orgiastic, rambunctious (*informal*), roisterous, rollicking, saturnalian, side-splitting, unrestrained, uproarious, wanton, wild

▷ **Antonyms** calm, civilized, disciplined, gentle, lawful, mild, obedient, orderly, peaceful, quiet, restrained, well-behaved

rip **1.** *verb* be rent, burst, claw, cut, gash, hack, lacerate, rend, score, slash, slit, split, tear **2.** *~noun* cleavage, cut, gash, hole, laceration, rent, slash, slit, split, tear

ripe **1.** fully developed, fully grown, mature, mellow, ready, ripened, seasoned **2.** accomplished, complete, finished, in readiness, perfect, prepared, ready **3.** auspicious, favourable, ideal, opportune, right, suitable, timely

▷ **Antonyms** (*sense 1*) green, immature, undeveloped, unripe (*sense 2*) imperfect, incomplete, unaccomplished, unfinished, unfit, unprepared (*sense 3*) disadvantageous, inappropriate, inconvenient, inopportune, unfavourable, unfitting, unseemly, unsuitable, untimely

ripen burgeon, come of age, come to fruition, develop, get ready, grow ripe, make ripe, mature, prepare, season

rip-off cheat, con (*informal*), con trick (*informal*), daylight robbery (*informal*), exploitation, fraud, robbery, scam (*slang*), sting (*informal*), swindle, theft

rip off cabbage (*Brit. slang*), cheat, con (*informal*), cozen, defraud, diddle (*informal*), do the dirty on (*Brit. informal*), dupe, filch, fleece, gyp (*slang*), knock off (*slang*), lift (*informal*), pilfer, pinch (*informal*), rob, skin (*slang*), steal from, stiff (*slang*), swindle, swipe (*slang*), thieve, trick

riposte **1.** *noun* answer, comeback (*informal*), counterattack, rejoinder, repartee, reply, response, retort, return, sally **2.** *~verb* answer, come back, reciprocate, rejoin, reply, respond, retort, return

rise *verb* **1.** arise, get out of bed, get to one's feet, get up, rise and shine, stand up, surface **2.** arise, ascend, climb, en~

large, go up, grow, improve, increase, intensify, levitate, lift, mount, move up, soar, swell, wax **3**. advance, be promoted, climb the ladder, get on, get somewhere, go places (*informal*), progress, prosper, work one's way up **4**. appear, become apparent, crop up, emanate, emerge, eventuate, flow, happen, issue, occur, originate, spring, turn up **5**. mount the barricades, mutiny, rebel, resist, revolt, take up arms **6**. ascend, climb, get steeper, go uphill, mount, slope upwards *~noun* **7**. advance, ascent, climb, improvement, increase, upsurge, upswing, upturn, upward turn **8**. advancement, aggrandizement, climb, progress, promotion **9**. acclivity, ascent, elevation, hillock, incline, rising ground, upward slope **10**. increment, pay increase, raise (*U.S.*) **11**. **give rise to** bring about, bring on, cause, effect, produce, provoke, result in

▷ **Antonyms** *~verb* (*sense 2*) abate, abbreviate, abridge, condense, curtail, decline, decrease, descend, diminish, drop, dwindle, fall, lessen, plunge, reduce, shrink, sink, wane (*sense 6*) descend, drop, fall, plunge, sink *~noun* (*sense 7*) blip, decline, decrease, downswing, downturn, drop, fall

risible absurd, amusing, comical, droll, farcical, funny, hilarious, humorous, laughable, ludicrous, rib-tickling (*informal*), ridiculous, side-splitting

risk 1. *noun* chance, danger, gamble, hazard, jeopardy, peril, pitfall, possibility, speculation, uncertainty, venture **2**. *~verb* chance, dare, endanger, expose to danger, gamble, hazard, imperil, jeopardize, put in jeopardy, skate on thin ice, take a chance on, take the plunge, venture

risky chancy (*informal*), dangerous, dicey (*informal, chiefly Brit.*), dodgy (*Brit., Austral., & N.Z. informal*), fraught with danger, hazardous, perilous, precarious, touch-and-go, tricky, uncertain, unsafe

▷ **Antonyms** certain, reliable, safe, secure, stable, sure

risqué bawdy, blue, daring, immodest, improper, indelicate, naughty, near the knuckle (*informal*), off colour, Rabelaisian, racy, ribald, suggestive

rite act, ceremonial, ceremony, communion, custom, form, formality, liturgy, mystery, observance, ordinance, practice, procedure, ritual, sacrament, service, solemnity, usage

ritual *noun* **1**. ceremonial, ceremony, communion, liturgy, mystery, observance, rite, sacrament, service, solemnity **2**. convention, custom, form, formality, habit, ordinance, practice, prescription, procedure, protocol, red tape, routine, stereotype, tradition, usage *~adjective* **3**. ceremonial, ceremonious, conventional, customary, formal, habitual, prescribed, procedural, routine, stereotyped

rival *noun* **1**. adversary, antagonist, challenger, competitor, contender, contestant, emulator, opponent **2**. compeer, equal, equivalent, fellow, match, peer *~adjective* **3**. competing, competitive, conflicting, emulating, opposed, opposing *~verb* **4**. be a match for, bear comparison with, come up to, compare with, compete, contend, emulate, equal, match, measure up to, oppose, seek to displace, vie with

▷ **Antonyms** *~noun* (*sense 1*) ally, friend, helper, supporter *~verb* aid, back, help, support

rivalry antagonism, competition, competitiveness, conflict, contention, contest, duel, emulation, opposition, struggle, vying

riveting absorbing, arresting, captivating, engrossing, enthralling, fascinating, gripping, hypnotic, spellbinding

road 1. avenue, course, direction, highway, lane, motorway, path, pathway, roadway, route, street, thoroughfare, track, way **2**. *Nautical* anchorage, roadstead

roam drift, meander, peregrinate, prowl, ramble, range, rove, stravaig (*Scot. & northern English dialect*), stray, stroll, travel, walk, wander

roar *verb* **1**. bawl, bay, bell, bellow, clamour, crash, cry, howl, rumble, shout, thunder, vociferate, yell **2**. bust a gut (*informal*), crack up (*informal*), guffaw, hoot, laugh heartily, split one's sides (*informal*) *~noun* **3**. bellow, clamour, crash, cry, howl, outcry, rumble, shout, thunder, yell **4**. belly laugh (*informal*), guffaw, hoot

rob bereave, burgle, cheat, con (*informal*), defraud, deprive, despoil, dispossess, do out of (*informal*), gyp (*slang*), hold up, loot, mug (*informal*), pillage, plunder, raid, ransack, rifle, rip off (*slang*), sack, skin (*slang*), steam (*informal*), stiff (*slang*), strip, swindle

robber bandit, brigand, burglar, cheat, con man (*informal*), footpad (*archaic*), fraud, fraudster, grifter (*slang, chiefly U.S. & Canad.*), highwayman, looter, mugger (*informal*), pirate, plunderer, raider, stealer, swindler, thief

robbery burglary, depredation, embezzlement, filching, fraud, hold-up, larceny, mugging (*informal*), pillage, plunder, raid, rapine, rip-off (*slang*), spoliation, stealing, steaming (*informal*), stick-up (*slang, chiefly U.S.*), swindle, theft, thievery

robe *noun* **1**. costume, gown, habit, vestment **2**. bathrobe, dressing gown, housecoat, negligee, peignoir, wrapper *~verb* **3**. apparel (*archaic*), attire, clothe, drape, dress, garb

robot android, automaton, machine, mechanical man

robust 1. able-bodied, alive and kicking, athletic, brawny, fighting fit, fit, fit as a fiddle (*informal*), hale, hardy, healthy, hearty, husky (*informal*), in fine fettle, in good health, lusty, muscular, powerful, rude, rugged, sinewy, sound, staunch, stout, strapping, strong, sturdy, thickset, tough, vigorous, well **2.** boisterous, coarse, earthy, indecorous, raunchy (*slang*), raw, roisterous, rollicking, rough, rude, unsubtle **3.** common-sensical, down-to-earth, hard-headed, practical, pragmatic, realistic, sensible, straightforward

▷ **Antonyms** (*sense 1*) delicate, feeble, frail, hothouse (*informal, often disparaging*), infirm, sickly, slender, unfit, unhealthy, unsound, weak, weedy (*informal*), wimpish *or* wimpy (*informal*) (*sense 2*) refined

rock[1] *noun* **1.** boulder, stone **2.** anchor, bulwark, cornerstone, foundation, mainstay, protection, support, tower of strength

rock[2] *verb* **1.** lurch, pitch, reel, roll, sway, swing, toss, wobble **2.** astonish, astound, daze, dumbfound, jar, set one back on one's heels (*informal*), shake, shock, stagger, stun, surprise

rocky[1] *adjective* **1.** boulder-strewn, craggy, pebbly, rough, rugged, stony **2.** adamant, firm, flinty, hard, rocklike, rugged, solid, steady, tough, unyielding

rocky[2] *adjective* **1.** doubtful, rickety, shaky, uncertain, undependable, unreliable, unstable, unsteady, weak, wobbly **2.** *informal* dizzy, ill, sick, sickly, staggering, tottering, unsteady, unwell, weak, wobbly

rod bar, baton, birch, cane, crook, dowel, mace, pole, sceptre, shaft, staff, stick, switch, wand

rogue blackguard, charlatan, cheat, con man (*informal*), crook (*informal*), deceiver, devil, fraud, fraudster, grifter (*slang, chiefly U.S. & Canad.*), knave (*archaic*), mountebank, ne'er-do-well, rapscallion, rascal, reprobate, scally (*Northwest English dialect*), scamp, scoundrel, scumbag (*slang*), sharper, skelm (*S. African*), swindler, villain

roguish 1. criminal, crooked, deceitful, deceiving, dishonest, fraudulent, knavish, raffish, rascally, shady (*informal*), swindling, unprincipled, unscrupulous, villainous **2.** arch, cheeky, coquettish, frolicsome, impish, mischievous, playful, puckish, sportive, waggish

roister 1. carouse, celebrate, frolic, go on a spree, live it up (*informal*), make merry, paint the town red (*informal*), push the boat out (*Brit. informal*), rave (*Brit. slang*), revel, rollick, romp, whoop it up (*informal*) **2.** bluster, boast, brag, show off (*informal*), strut, swagger

role 1. character, impersonation, part, portrayal, representation **2.** capacity, duty, function, job, part, position, post, task

roll *verb* **1.** elapse, flow, go past, go round, gyrate, pass, pivot, reel, revolve, rock, rotate, run, spin, swivel, trundle, turn, twirl, undulate, wheel, whirl **2.** bind, coil, curl, enfold, entwine, envelop, furl, swathe, twist, wind, wrap **3.** even, flatten, level, press, smooth, spread **4.** boom, drum, echo, grumble, resound, reverberate, roar, rumble, thunder **5.** billow, lurch, reel, rock, sway, swing, toss, tumble, wallow, welter **6.** lumber, lurch, reel, stagger, swagger, sway, waddle *~noun* **7.** cycle, gyration, reel, revolution, rotation, run, spin, turn, twirl, undulation, wheel, whirl **8.** ball, bobbin, cylinder, reel, scroll, spool **9.** annals, catalogue, census, chronicle, directory, index, inventory, list, record, register, roster, schedule, scroll, table **10.** billowing, lurching, pitching, rocking, rolling, swell, tossing, undulation, wallowing, waves **11.** boom, drumming, growl, grumble, resonance, reverberation, roar, rumble, thunder

rollick caper, cavort, frisk, galumph (*informal*), gambol, make merry, revel, romp

rollicking[1] *adjective* boisterous, carefree, cavorting, devil-may-care, exuberant, frisky, frolicsome, full of beans (*informal*), hearty, jaunty, jovial, joyous, lively, merry, playful, rip-roaring (*informal*), romping, spirited, sportive, sprightly, swashbuckling

▷ **Antonyms** cheerless, despondent, dull, gloomy, lifeless, melancholy, morose, sad, sedate, serious, unhappy

rollicking[2] *noun* dressing-down (*informal*), lecture, reprimand, roasting (*informal*), scolding, telling-off (*informal*), ticking off (*informal*), tongue-lashing, wigging (*Brit. slang*)

roly-poly buxom, chubby, fat, overweight, plump, podgy, pudgy, rotund, rounded, tubby

romance *noun* **1.** affair, *affaire (du coeur)*, affair of the heart, amour, attachment, intrigue, liaison, love affair, passion, relationship **2.** adventure, charm, colour, excitement, exoticness, fascination, glamour, mystery, nostalgia, sentiment **3.** fairy tale, fantasy, fiction, idyll, legend, love story, melodrama, novel, story, tale, tear-jerker (*informal*) **4.** absurdity, exaggeration, fabrication, fairy tale, falsehood, fiction, flight of fancy, invention, lie, tall story (*informal*), trumped-up story *~verb* **5.** be economical with the truth, exaggerate, fantasize, let one's imagination run away with one, lie, make up stories, stretch the truth, tell stories

romantic *adjective* **1.** amorous, fond, lovey-dovey, loving, mushy (*informal*), passionate, sentimental, sloppy (*informal*), soppy (*Brit. informal*), tender **2.** charming, colourful, exciting, exotic, fascinating, glamorous, mysterious, nostalgic, picturesque **3.** dreamy, high-flown, idealistic, impractical, quixotic, starry-eyed, unrealistic, utopian, visionary, whimsical **4.** chimerical, exaggerated, extravagant, fabulous, fairy-tale, fanciful, fantastic, fictitious, idyllic, imaginary, imaginative, improbable, legendary, made-up, unrealistic, wild *~noun* **5.** Don Quixote, dreamer, idealist, romancer, sentimentalist, utopian, visionary

▷ **Antonyms** *~adjective* (*sense 1*) cold-hearted, insensitive, unaffectionate, unimpassioned, unloving, unromantic, unsentimental (*sense 2*) uninspiring (*sense 3*) practical, realistic (*sense 4*) realistic

romp *verb* **1.** caper, cavort, cut capers, frisk, frolic, gambol, have fun, make merry, revel, roister, rollick, skip, sport **2. romp home** *or* **in** run away with it, walk it (*informal*), win by a mile (*informal*), win easily, win hands down *~noun* **3.** caper, frolic, lark (*informal*)

rook *verb* bilk, cheat, clip (*slang*), cozen, defraud, diddle (*informal*), do (*slang*), fleece, gyp (*slang*), mulct, overcharge, rip off (*slang*), skin (*slang*), stiff (*slang*), sting (*informal*), swindle

room 1. allowance, area, capacity, compass, elbowroom, expanse, extent, latitude, leeway, margin, play, range, scope, space, territory, volume **2.** apartment, chamber, office **3.** chance, occasion, opportunity, scope

roomy ample, broad, capacious, commodious, extensive, generous, large, sizable *or* sizeable, spacious, wide

▷ **Antonyms** bounded, confined, cramped, narrow, small, tiny, uncomfortable

root[1] *noun* **1.** radicle, radix, rhizome, stem, tuber **2.** base, beginnings, bottom, cause, core, crux, derivation, essence, foundation, fountainhead, fundamental, germ, heart, mainspring, nub, nucleus, occasion, origin, seat, seed, source, starting point **3.** (*plural*) birthplace, cradle, family, heritage, home, origins, sense of belonging **4. root and branch** completely, entirely, finally, radically, thoroughly, totally, to the last man, utterly, wholly, without exception *~verb* **5.** anchor, become established, become settled, embed, entrench, establish, fasten, fix, ground, implant, moor, set, stick, take root

root[2] *verb* burrow, delve, dig, ferret, forage, hunt, nose, poke, pry, rootle, rummage

rooted confirmed, deep, deeply felt, deep-seated, entrenched, established, firm, fixed, ingrained, radical, rigid

root out 1. *also* **root up** abolish, cut out, destroy, dig up by the roots, do away with, efface, eliminate, eradicate, erase, exterminate, extirpate, get rid of, remove, tear out by the roots, uproot, weed out, wipe from the face of the earth **2.** bring to light, dig out, discover, dredge up, produce, turn up, unearth

rope *noun* **1.** cable, cord, hawser, line, strand **2. the rope** capital punishment, halter, hanging, lynching, noose **3. know the ropes** be an old hand, be experienced, be knowledgeable, know all the ins and outs, know one's way around, know the score (*informal*), know what's what, know where it's at (*slang*) *~verb* **4.** bind, fasten, hitch, lash, lasso, moor, pinion, tether, tie

rope in drag in, engage, enlist, inveigle, involve, persuade, talk into

ropey, ropy 1. deficient, inadequate, indifferent, inferior, mediocre, no great shakes (*informal*), of poor quality, poor, sketchy, substandard **2.** *informal* below par, off colour, poorly (*informal*), rough (*informal*), sickish, under the weather (*informal*), unwell

roseate 1. blooming, blushing, pink, pinkish, red, rose-coloured, rosy, rubicund, ruddy **2.** idealistic, overoptimistic, rose-coloured, unrealistic, utopian

roster agenda, catalogue, inventory, list, listing, register, roll, rota, schedule, scroll, table

rostrum dais, platform, podium, stage, stand

rosy 1. pink, red, roseate, rose-coloured **2.** blooming, blushing, flushed, fresh, glowing, healthy-looking, radiant, reddish, roseate, rubicund, ruddy **3.** auspicious, bright, cheerful, encouraging, favourable, hopeful, optimistic, promising, reassuring, roseate, rose-coloured, sunny

▷ **Antonyms** (*sense 2*) ashen, colourless, grey, pale, pallid, sickly, wan, white (*sense 3*) cheerless, depressing, discouraging, dismal, down in the dumps (*informal*), dull, gloomy, hopeless, miserable, pessimistic, unhappy, unpromising

rot *verb* **1.** break down, corrode, corrupt, crumble, decay, decompose, degenerate, deteriorate, disintegrate, fester, go bad, moulder, perish, putrefy, spoil, taint **2.** decline, degenerate, deteriorate, languish, waste away, wither away *~noun* **3.** blight, canker, corrosion, corruption, decay, decomposition, deterioration, disintegration, mould, putrefaction, putrescence **4.** balderdash, balls (*taboo slang*), bilge (*informal*), bosh (*informal*), bull (*slang*), bullshit (*taboo slang*), bunk (*informal*), bunkum *or* buncombe (*chiefly U.S.*), claptrap (*informal*), cobblers (*Brit. taboo slang*), codswallop (*Brit. slang*), crap (*slang*), drivel, eyewash (*informal*), flapdoodle (*slang*), garbage (*chiefly U.S.*), guff (*slang*), hogwash, hokum (*slang, chiefly U.S. & Canad.*), horsefeathers (*U.S. slang*), hot air (*informal*), moonshine, nonsense, pap, piffle (*informal*), poppycock (*informal*), rubbish, shit (*taboo slang*), stuff and nonsense, tommyrot, tosh (*slang, chiefly Brit.*), trash, tripe (*informal*), twaddle

rotary gyratory, revolving, rotating, rotational, rotatory, spinning, turning

rotate 1. go round, gyrate, pirouette, pivot, reel, revolve, spin, swivel, turn, wheel **2.** alternate, follow in sequence, interchange, switch, take turns

rotation 1. gyration, orbit, pirouette, reel, revolution, spin, spinning, turn, turning, wheel **2.** alternation, cycle, interchanging, sequence, succession, switching

rotten 1. bad, corroded, corrupt, crumbling, decayed, decaying, decomposed, decomposing, disintegrating, festering, fetid, foul, mouldering, mouldy, perished, putrescent, putrid, rank, sour, stinking, tainted, unsound **2.** bent (*slang*), corrupt, crooked (*informal*), deceitful, degenerate, dishonest, dishonourable, disloyal, faithless, immoral, mercenary, perfidious, sink, treacherous, untrustworthy, venal, vicious **3.** *informal* base, contemptible, despicable, dirty, disagreeable, filthy, mean, nasty, scurrilous, shitty (*taboo slang*), unpleasant, vile, wicked **4.** *informal* bad, deplorable, disappointing, regrettable, unfortunate, unlucky **5.** *informal* chickenshit (*U.S. slang*), crummy (*slang*), duff (*Brit. informal*), ill-considered, ill-thought-out, inadequate, inferior, lousy (*slang*), low-grade, of a sort *or* of sorts, poor, poxy (*slang*), punk, ropey *or* ropy (*Brit. informal*), sorry, substandard, unacceptable, unsatisfactory **6.** *informal* bad, below par, ill, off colour, poorly (*informal*), ropey *or* ropy (*Brit. informal*), rough (*informal*), sick, under the weather (*informal*), unwell

▷ **Antonyms** (*sense 1*) fresh, good, pure, sweet, wholesome (*sense 2*) decent, honest, honourable, moral, scrupulous, trustworthy

rotter bad lot, blackguard, blighter (*Brit. informal*), bounder (*old-fashioned Brit. slang*), cad (*Brit. informal*), cocksucker (*taboo slang*), cur, louse (*slang*), rat (*informal*), scumbag (*slang*), stinker (*slang*), swine

rotund 1. bulbous, globular, orbicular, round, rounded, spherical **2.** chubby, corpulent, fat, fleshy, heavy, obese, plump, podgy, portly, roly-poly, rounded, stout, tubby **3.** full, grandiloquent, magniloquent, orotund, resonant, rich, round, sonorous

▷ **Antonyms** (*sense 2*) angular, gaunt, lank, lanky, lean, scrawny, skinny, slender, slight, slim, thin

roué debauchee, dirty old man (*slang*), lech *or* letch (*informal*), lecher, libertine, profligate, rake, sensualist, wanton

rough *adjective* **1.** broken, bumpy, craggy, irregular, jagged, rocky, rugged, stony, uneven **2.** bristly, bushy, coarse, dishevelled, disordered, fuzzy, hairy, shaggy, tangled, tousled, uncut, unshaven, unshorn **3.** agitated, boisterous, choppy, inclement, squally, stormy, tempestuous, turbulent, wild **4.** bearish, bluff, blunt, brusque, churlish, coarse, curt, discourteous, ill-bred, ill-mannered, impolite, inconsiderate, indelicate, loutish, rude, unceremonious, uncivil, uncouth, uncultured, ungracious, unmannerly, unpolished, unrefined, untutored **5.** boisterous, cruel, curt, drastic, extreme, hard, harsh, nasty, rowdy, severe, sharp, tough, unfeeling, unjust, unpleasant, violent **6.** *informal* below par, ill, not a hundred per cent (*informal*), off colour, poorly (*informal*), ropey *or* ropy (*Brit. informal*), rotten (*informal*), sick, under the weather (*informal*), unwell, upset **7.** cacophonous, discordant, grating, gruff, harsh, husky, inharmonious, jarring, rasping, raucous, unmusical **8.** arduous, austere, hard, rugged, spartan, tough, uncomfortable, unpleasant, unrefined **9.** basic, crude, cursory, formless, hasty, imperfect, incomplete, quick, raw, rough-and-ready, rough-hewn, rudimentary, shapeless, sketchy, unfinished, unpolished, unrefined, untutored **10.** crude, raw, rough-hewn, uncut, undressed, unhewn, unpolished, unprocessed, unwrought **11.** amorphous, approximate, estimated, foggy, general, hazy, imprecise, inexact, sketchy, vague *~noun* **12.** draft, mock-up, outline, preliminary sketch, suggestion **13.** *informal* bruiser, bully boy, casual, lager lout, ned (*slang*), roughneck (*slang*), rowdy, ruffian, thug, tough *~verb* **14. rough out** adumbrate, block out, delineate, draft, outline, plan, sketch, suggest **15. rough up** bash up (*informal*), batter, beat the living daylights out of (*informal*), beat up, do over (*Brit., Austral., & N.Z. slang*), knock about *or* around, maltreat, manhandle, mistreat, thrash, work over (*slang*)

▷ **Antonyms** (*sense 1*) even, level, regular, smooth, unbroken (*sense 2*) smooth, soft (*sense 3*) calm, gentle, quiet, smooth, tranquil (*sense 4*) civil, considerate, courteous, courtly, delicate, elegant, graceful, gracious, pleasant, polite, refined, smooth, sophisticated, urbane, well-bred, well-mannered (*sense 5*) gentle, just, kind, mild, pleasant, quiet, soft (*sense 7*) harmonious, smooth (*sense 8*) comfortable, cushy (*informal*), easy, pleasant, soft (*sense 9*) complete, detailed, finished, perfected, polished, refined, specific (*sense 10*) smooth (*sense 11*) exact, perfected, specific

rough-and-ready adequate, cobbled to~ gether, crude, improvised, makeshift, provisional, sketchy, stopgap, thrown together, unpolished, unrefined

rough-and-tumble 1. *noun* affray (*Law*), brawl, donnybrook, dust-up (*informal*), fight, fracas, melee *or* mêlée, punch-up (*Brit. informal*), roughhouse (*slang*), scrap (*informal*), scrimmage, scuffle, shindig (*informal*), shindy (*informal*), struggle **2.** *~adjective* boisterous, disor~ derly, haphazard, indisciplined, irregu~ lar, rough, rowdy, scrambled, scram~ bling

roughhouse 1. *noun* boisterousness, brawl, brawling, disorderliness, dis~ turbance, horseplay, rough behaviour, row, rowdiness, rowdyism, skylarking (*informal*) **2.** *~verb* brawl, handle rough~ ly, ill-treat, kick up a row (*informal*), knock about *or* around, maltreat, man~ handle, mistreat, paw, skylark (*infor~ mal*)

roughneck bruiser (*informal*), bully boy, heavy (*slang*), rough (*informal*), rowdy, ruffian, thug, tough

round *adjective* **1.** annular, ball-shaped, bowed, bulbous, circular, curved, curvi~ linear, cylindrical, discoid, disc-shaped, globular, orbicular, ring-shaped, rotund, rounded, spherical **2.** complete, entire, full, solid, unbroken, undivided, whole **3.** ample, bounteous, bountiful, consider~ able, generous, great, large, liberal, substantial **4.** ample, fleshy, full, full-fleshed, plump, roly-poly, rotund, rounded **5.** full, mellifluous, orotund, resonant, rich, rotund, sonorous **6.** blunt, candid, direct, downright, frank, outspoken, plain, straightforward, un~ modified *~noun* **7.** ball, band, circle, disc, globe, orb, ring, sphere **8.** bout, cycle, sequence, series, session, succession **9.** division, lap, level, period, session, stage, turn **10.** ambit, beat, circuit, com~ pass, course, routine, schedule, series, tour, turn **11.** bullet, cartridge, dis~ charge, shell, shot *~verb* **12.** bypass, cir~ cle, circumnavigate, encircle, flank, go round, skirt, turn

roundabout *adjective* circuitous, circum~ locutory, devious, discursive, evasive, indirect, meandering, oblique, peri~ phrastic, tortuous

▷ **Antonyms** direct, straight, straight~ forward

roundly bitterly, bluntly, fiercely, frank~ ly, intensely, outspokenly, rigorously, severely, sharply, thoroughly, vehe~ mently, violently

round off bring to a close, cap, close, complete, conclude, crown, finish off, put the finishing touch to, settle

▷ **Antonyms** begin, commence, initiate, open, start

round on abuse, attack, bite (someone's) head off (*informal*), have a go at (*Brit. slang*), lose one's temper with, retaliate, snap at, turn on, wade into

roundup **1.** assembly, collection, gather~ ing, herding, marshalling, muster, rally **2.** *informal* collation, summary, survey

round up assemble, bring together, col~ lect, drive, gather, group, herd, mar~ shal, muster, rally

rouse **1.** arouse, awaken, call, get up, rise, wake, wake up **2.** agitate, anger, animate, arouse, bestir, disturb, excite, exhilarate, galvanize, get going, incite, inflame, instigate, move, prod, provoke, startle, stimulate, stir, whip up

rousing brisk, electrifying, exciting, ex~ hilarating, inflammatory, inspiring, lively, moving, spirited, stimulating, stirring, vigorous

▷ **Antonyms** boring, dreary, dull, lifeless, sluggish, spiritless, unenergetic, weari~ some, wishy-washy (*informal*)

rout **1.** *noun* beating, debacle, defeat, dis~ orderly retreat, drubbing, headlong flight, hiding (*informal*), licking (*infor~ mal*), overthrow, overwhelming defeat, pasting (*slang*), ruin, shambles, thrash~ ing **2.** *~verb* beat, chase, clobber (*slang*), conquer, crush, cut to pieces, defeat, de~ stroy, dispel, drive off, drub, lick (*infor~ mal*), overpower, overthrow, put to flight, put to rout, scatter, stuff (*slang*), tank (*slang*), thrash, throw back in con~ fusion, wipe the floor with (*informal*), worst

route **1.** *noun* avenue, beat, circuit, course, direction, itinerary, journey, passage, path, road, round, run, way **2.** *~verb* convey, direct, dispatch, forward, send, steer

routine *noun* **1.** custom, formula, grind (*informal*), groove, method, order, pat~ tern, practice, procedure, programme, usage, way, wont **2.** *informal* act, bit (*informal*), line, performance, piece, spiel (*informal*) *~adjective* **3.** conven~ tional, customary, everyday, familiar, habitual, normal, ordinary, standard, typical, usual, wonted, workaday **4.** bor~ ing, clichéd, dull, hackneyed, humdrum, mind-numbing, predictable, run-of-the-mill, shtick (*slang*), tedious, tire~ some, unimaginative, uninspired, un~ original

▷ **Antonyms** *~adjective* abnormal, differ~ ent, exceptional, irregular, special, un~ usual

rove cruise, drift, gad about, gallivant, meander, ramble, range, roam, stravaig (*Scot. & northern English dialect*), stray, stroll, traipse (*informal*), wander

rover bird of passage, drifter, gadabout (*informal*), gypsy, itinerant, nomad, rambler, ranger, rolling stone, stroller, transient, traveller, vagrant, wanderer

row[1] *noun* bank, column, file, line, queue, range, rank, sequence, series, string, tier

row[2] *noun* **1.** altercation, *bagarre,* brawl, commotion, controversy, dispute, disturbance, falling-out (*informal*), fracas, fray, fuss, noise, quarrel, racket, ruckus (*informal*), ruction (*informal*), rumpus, scrap (*informal*), shindig (*informal*), shindy (*informal*), shouting match (*informal*), slanging match (*Brit.*), squabble, tiff, trouble, tumult, uproar **2.** castigation, dressing-down (*informal*), flea in one's ear (*informal*), lecture, reprimand, reproof, rollicking (*Brit. informal*), talking-to (*informal*), telling-off (*informal*), ticking-off (*informal*), tongue-lashing *~verb* **3.** argue, brawl, dispute, fight, go at it hammer and tongs, scrap (*informal*), spar, squabble, wrangle

rowdy 1. *adjective* boisterous, disorderly, loud, loutish, noisy, obstreperous, rough, unruly, uproarious, wild **2.** *~noun* brawler, casual, hooligan, lager lout, lout, ned (*slang*), rough (*informal*), ruffian, tearaway (*Brit.*), tough, troublemaker, yahoo, yob *or* yobbo (*Brit. slang*)

▷ **Antonyms** *~adjective* decorous, gentle, law-abiding, mannerly, orderly, peaceful, refined

royal 1. imperial, kinglike, kingly, monarchical, princely, queenly, regal, sovereign **2.** august, grand, impressive, magnificent, majestic, splendid, stately, superb, superior

rub *verb* **1.** abrade, caress, chafe, clean, fray, grate, knead, massage, polish, scour, scrape, shine, smooth, stroke, wipe **2.** apply, put, smear, spread **3. rub up the wrong way** aggravate (*informal*), anger, annoy, bug (*informal*), get in one's hair (*informal*), get one's goat (*slang*), get on one's nerves (*informal*), get under one's skin (*informal*), irk, irritate, nark (*Brit., Austral., & N.Z. slang*), peeve (*informal*), piss one off (*taboo slang*), vex *~noun* **4.** caress, kneading, massage, polish, shine, stroke, wipe **5.** catch, difficulty, drawback, hazard, hindrance, hitch, impediment, obstacle, problem, snag, trouble

rubbish 1. crap (*slang*), debris, dreck (*slang, chiefly U.S.*), dregs, dross, flotsam and jetsam, garbage (*chiefly U.S.*), grot (*slang*), junk (*informal*), litter, lumber, offal, offscourings, refuse, scrap, trash, waste **2.** balderdash, balls (*taboo slang*), bilge (*informal*), bollocks (*Brit. taboo slang*), bosh (*informal*), bull (*slang*), bullshit (*taboo slang*), bunkum *or* buncombe (*chiefly U.S.*), claptrap (*informal*), cobblers (*Brit. taboo slang*), codswallop (*Brit. slang*), crap (*slang*), drivel, eyewash (*informal*), flapdoodle (*slang*), garbage (*chiefly U.S.*), gibberish, guff (*slang*), havers (*Scot.*), hogwash, hokum (*slang, chiefly U.S. & Canad.*), horsefeathers (*U.S. slang*), hot air (*informal*), moonshine, nonsense, pap, piffle (*informal*), poppycock (*informal*), rot, shit (*taboo slang*), stuff and nonsense, tommyrot, tosh (*slang, chiefly Brit.*), trash, tripe (*informal*), twaddle

rubbishy brummagem, cheap, gimcrack, paltry, shoddy, tatty, tawdry, throwaway, trashy, twopenny, twopenny-halfpenny, valueless, worthless

rubicund blushing, florid, flushed, pink, reddish, roseate, rosy, ruddy

rub out 1. cancel, delete, efface, erase, excise, expunge, obliterate, remove, wipe out **2.** *U.S. slang* assassinate, blow away (*slang, chiefly U.S.*), bump off (*slang*), butcher, dispatch, do in (*informal*), eliminate (*slang*), hit (*slang*), kill, knock off (*slang*), murder, slaughter, slay, take out (*slang*), waste (*informal*)

ruction altercation, brawl, commotion, dispute, disturbance, fracas, fuss, hue and cry, quarrel, racket, row, rumpus, scrap (*informal*), scrimmage, shindig (*informal*), shindy (*informal*), storm, to-do, trouble, uproar

ruddy 1. blooming, blushing, florid, flushed, fresh, glowing, healthy, radiant, red, reddish, rosy, rosy-cheeked, rubicund, sanguine, sunburnt **2.** crimson, pink, red, reddish, roseate, ruby, scarlet

▷ **Antonyms** (*sense 1*) anaemic, ashen, colourless, grey, pale, pallid, sickly, wan, white

rude 1. abrupt, abusive, blunt, brusque, cheeky, churlish, curt, discourteous, disrespectful, ill-mannered, impertinent, impolite, impudent, inconsiderate, insolent, insulting, offhand, peremptory, short, uncivil, unmannerly **2.** barbarous, boorish, brutish, coarse, crude, graceless, gross, ignorant, illiterate, loutish, low, oafish, obscene, rough, savage, scurrilous, uncivilized, uncouth, uncultured, uneducated, ungracious, unpolished, unrefined, untutored, vulgar **3.** artless, crude, inartistic, inelegant, makeshift, primitive, raw, rough, rough-hewn, roughly-made, simple **4.** abrupt, harsh, sharp, startling, sudden, unpleasant, violent

▷ **Antonyms** (*sense 1*) civil, considerate, cordial, courteous, courtly, decent, gentlemanly, gracious, ladylike, mannerly, polite, respectful, sociable, urbane, well-bred (*sense 2*) civilized, cultured, educated, elegant, learned, polished, refined, sophisticated, urbane (*sense 3*) artful, even, finished, shapely, smooth, well-made

rudimentary basic, early, elementary, embryonic, fundamental, immature, initial, introductory, primary, primitive, undeveloped, vestigial

▷ **Antonyms** advanced, complete, developed, higher, later, mature, refined, secondary, sophisticated, supplementary

rudiments basics, beginnings, elements, essentials, first principles, foundation, fundamentals, nuts and bolts

rue bemoan, be sorry for, bewail, deplore, grieve, kick oneself for, lament, mourn, regret, repent, reproach oneself for, sorrow for, weep over

rueful conscience-stricken, contrite, dismal, doleful, grievous, lugubrious, melancholy, mournful, penitent, pitiable, pitiful, plaintive, regretful, remorseful, repentant, sad, self-reproachful, sorrowful, sorry, woebegone, woeful

▷ **Antonyms** cheerful, delighted, glad, happy, joyful, pleased, unrepentant

ruffian bruiser (*informal*), brute, bully, bully boy, casual, heavy (*slang*), hoodlum, hooligan, lager lout, miscreant, ned (*slang*), rascal, rogue, rough (*informal*), roughneck (*slang*), rowdy, scoundrel, thug, tough, tsotsi (*S. African*), villain, wretch, yardie

ruffle 1. derange, disarrange, discompose, dishevel, disorder, mess up, rumple, tousle, wrinkle **2.** agitate, annoy, confuse, disconcert, disquiet, disturb, faze, fluster, harass, hassle (*informal*), irritate, nettle, peeve (*informal*), perturb, put out, rattle (*informal*), shake up (*informal*), stir, torment, trouble, unnerve, unsettle, upset, vex, worry

▷ **Antonyms** (*sense 2*) appease, calm, comfort, compose, console, ease, mollify, solace, soothe

rugged 1. broken, bumpy, craggy, difficult, irregular, jagged, ragged, rocky, rough, stark, uneven **2.** furrowed, leathery, lined, rough-hewn, strong-featured, weather-beaten, weathered, worn, wrinkled **3.** austere, crabbed, dour, gruff, hard, harsh, rough, rude, severe, sour, stern, surly **4.** barbarous, blunt, churlish, crude, graceless, rude, uncouth, uncultured, unpolished, unrefined **5.** arduous, demanding, difficult, exacting, hard, harsh, laborious, rigorous, stern, strenuous, taxing, tough, trying, uncompromising **6.** beefy (*informal*), brawny, burly, hale, hardy, husky (*informal*), muscular, robust, strong, sturdy, tough, vigorous, well-built

▷ **Antonyms** (*sense 1*) even, gentle, level, regular, smooth, unbroken (*sense 2*) delicate, pretty, refined, smooth, unmarked, youthful (*sense 4*) civil, courteous, cultivated, cultured, elegant, polished, polite, refined, sophisticated, subtle, urbane, well-bred (*sense 5*) agreeable, easy, gentle, mild, pleasant, simple, soft, tender, uncomplicated, unexacting (*sense 6*) delicate, feeble, fragile, frail, infirm, sickly, skinny, soft, weak

ruin *noun* **1.** bankruptcy, breakdown, collapse, crackup (*informal*), crash, damage, decay, defeat, destitution, destruction, devastation, disintegration, disrepair, dissolution, downfall, failure, fall, havoc, insolvency, nemesis, overthrow, ruination, subversion, the end, undoing, Waterloo, wreck, wreckage *~verb* **2.** bankrupt, break, bring down, bring to nothing, bring to ruin, crush, defeat, demolish, destroy, devastate, impoverish, lay in ruins, lay waste, overthrow, overturn, overwhelm, pauperize, raze, shatter, smash, total (*slang*), trash (*slang*), wreak havoc upon, wreck **3.** blow (*slang*), bodge (*informal*), botch, cock up (*Brit. slang*), damage, disfigure, fuck up (*offensive taboo slang*), injure, make a mess of, mangle, mar, mess up, screw up (*informal*), spoil, undo

▷ **Antonyms** *~noun* creation, preservation, success, triumph, victory *~verb* build, construct, create, enhance, enrich, improve, keep, mend, preserve, repair, restore, save, start, strengthen, submit to, succumb to, support, surrender to, yield to

ruinous 1. baleful, baneful (*archaic*), calamitous, catastrophic, crippling, deadly, deleterious, destructive, devastating, dire, disastrous, extravagant, fatal, immoderate, injurious, murderous, noxious, pernicious, shattering, wasteful, withering **2.** broken-down, decrepit, derelict, dilapidated, in ruins, ramshackle, ruined

rule *noun* **1.** axiom, canon, criterion, decree, dictum, direction, guide, guideline, law, maxim, order, ordinance, precept, principle, regulation, ruling, standard, tenet **2.** administration, ascendancy, authority, command, control, direction, domination, dominion, empire, government, influence, jurisdiction, leadership, mastery, power, regime, reign, supremacy, sway **3.** condition, convention, custom, form, habit, order *or* way of things, practice, procedure, routine, tradition, wont **4.** course, formula, method, policy, procedure, way **5. as a rule** customarily, for the most part, generally, mainly, normally, on the whole, ordinarily, usually *~verb* **6.** administer, be in authority, be in power, be number one (*informal*), command, control, direct, dominate, govern, guide, hold sway, lead, manage, preside over, regulate, reign, wear the crown **7.** adjudge, adjudicate, decide, decree, determine, establish, find, judge, lay down, pronounce, resolve, settle **8.** be customary, be pre-eminent, be prevalent, be superior, hold sway, obtain, predominate, preponderate, prevail

rule out ban, debar, dismiss, disqualify, eliminate, exclude, forbid, leave out, obviate, preclude, prevent, prohibit, pro~

scribe, reject
▷ **Antonyms** allow, approve, authorize, let, license, order, permit, sanction

ruler 1. commander, controller, crowned head, emperor, empress, governor, head of state, king, leader, lord, monarch, potentate, prince, princess, queen, sovereign **2.** measure, rule, straight edge, yardstick

ruling *noun* **1.** adjudication, decision, decree, finding, judgment, pronouncement, resolution, verdict *~adjective* **2.** commanding, controlling, dominant, governing, leading, regnant, reigning, upper **3.** chief, current, dominant, main, predominant, pre-eminent, preponderant, prevailing, prevalent, principal, regnant, supreme
▷ **Antonyms** (*sense 3*) auxiliary, inferior, least, minor, secondary, subordinate, subsidiary, unimportant

rum curious, dodgy (*Brit., Austral., & N.Z. informal*), funny, odd, peculiar, queer, singular, strange, suspect, suspicious, unusual, weird

rumbustious boisterous, clamorous, disorderly, exuberant, loud, noisy, obstreperous, refractory, robust, rough, rowdy, unmanageable, unruly, uproarious, wayward, wild, wilful

ruminate brood, chew over, cogitate, consider, contemplate, deliberate, meditate, mull over, muse, ponder, rack one's brains, reflect, revolve, think, turn over in one's mind, weigh

rummage delve, examine, explore, forage, hunt, ransack, root, rootle, search

rumour 1. *noun* bruit (*archaic*), bush telegraph, buzz, canard, dirt (*U.S. slang*), gossip, hearsay, news, report, scuttlebutt (*U.S. slang*), story, talk, tidings, whisper, word **2.** *~verb* bruit, circulate, gossip, noise abroad, pass around, publish, put about, report, say, tell, whisper

rump arse (*taboo slang*), ass (*U.S. & Canad. taboo slang*), backside (*informal*), bottom, bum (*Brit. slang*), buns (*U.S. slang*), butt (*U.S. & Canad. informal*), buttocks, croup, derrière (*euphemistic*), haunch, hindquarters, jacksy (*Brit. slang*), posterior, rear, rear end, seat, tail (*informal*)

rumple crease, crinkle, crumple, crush, derange, dishevel, disorder, mess up, pucker, ruffle, screw up, scrunch, tousle, wrinkle

rumpus brouhaha, commotion, confusion, disruption, disturbance, furore, fuss, hue and cry, kerfuffle (*informal*), noise, row, shindig (*informal*), shindy (*informal*), tumult, uproar

run *verb* **1.** barrel (along) (*informal, chiefly U.S. & Canad.*), bolt, career, dart, dash, gallop, hare (*Brit. informal*), hasten, hie, hotfoot, hurry, jog, leg it (*informal*), lope, race, rush, scamper, scramble, scud, scurry, speed, sprint, stampede **2.** abscond, beat a retreat, beat it (*slang*), bolt, clear out, cut and run (*informal*), decamp, depart, do a runner (*slang*), escape, flee, fly the coop (*U.S. & Canad. informal*), leg it (*informal*), make a run for it, make off, scarper (*Brit. slang*), show a clean pair of heels, skedaddle (*informal*), slope off, take a powder (*U.S. & Canad. slang*), take flight, take it on the lam (*U.S. & Canad. slang*), take off (*informal*), take to one's heels **3.** course, glide, go, move, pass, roll, skim, slide **4.** bear, carry, convey, drive, give a lift to, manoeuvre, operate, propel, transport **5.** go, operate, ply **6.** function, go, operate, perform, tick, work **7.** administer, be in charge of, boss (*informal*), carry on, conduct, control, coordinate, direct, handle, head, lead, look after, manage, mastermind, operate, oversee, own, regulate, superintend, supervise, take care of **8.** continue, extend, go, last, lie, proceed, range, reach, stretch **9.** cascade, discharge, flow, go, gush, issue, leak, move, pour, proceed, spill, spout, stream **10.** dissolve, fuse, go soft, liquefy, melt, turn to liquid **11.** be diffused, bleed, lose colour, mix, spread **12.** come apart, come undone, ladder, tear, unravel **13.** be current, circulate, climb, creep, go round, spread, trail **14.** display, feature, print, publish **15.** be a candidate, challenge, compete, contend, put oneself up for, stand, take part **16.** bootleg, deal in, ship, smuggle, sneak, traffic in **17. run for it** abscond, bolt, cut and run (*informal*), decamp, do a bunk (*Brit. slang*), do a runner (*slang*), escape, flee, fly, fly the coop (*U.S. & Canad. informal*), make a break for it, make off, scarper (*Brit. slang*), scram (*informal*), show a clean pair of heels, skedaddle (*informal*), take a powder (*U.S. & Canad. slang*), take flight, take it on the lam (*U.S. & Canad. slang*), take off *~noun* **18.** dash, gallop, jog, race, rush, sprint, spurt **19.** drive, excursion, jaunt, journey, joy ride (*informal*), lift, outing, ride, round, spin (*informal*), trip **20.** chain, course, cycle, passage, period, round, season, sequence, series, spell, streak, stretch, string **21.** category, class, kind, order, sort, type, variety **22.** application, demand, pressure, rush **23.** ladder, rip, snag, tear **24.** course, current, direction, drift, flow, motion, movement, passage, path, progress, stream, tendency, tenor, tide, trend, way **25.** coop, enclosure, pen **26. in the long run** at the end of the day, eventually, in the end, in the final analysis, in the fullness of time, in time, ultimately, when all is said and done **27. on the run: a.** at liberty, escaping, fugitive, in flight, on the lam (*U.S. slang*), on the loose **b.** defeated, falling back, fleeing, in flight, in retreat, retreating, running away **c.** at speed, hastily, hurriedly, hurrying, in a hurry, in a rush, in haste

▷ **Antonyms** (*sense 1*) crawl, creep, dawdle, walk (*sense 2*) remain, stay (*sense 8*) cease, stop

run across bump into, chance upon, come across, come upon, encounter, meet, meet with, run into

run after chase, follow, give chase, pursue

runaway *noun* **1.** absconder, deserter, escapee, escaper, fugitive, refugee, truant ~*adjective* **2.** escaped, fleeing, fugitive, loose, out of control, uncontrolled, wild **3.** easily won, easy, effortless

run away 1. abscond, beat it (*slang*), bolt, clear out, cut and run (*informal*), decamp, do a bunk (*Brit. slang*), do a runner (*slang*), escape, flee, fly the coop (*U.S. & Canad. informal*), hook it (*slang*), make a run for it, run off, scarper (*Brit. slang*), scram (*informal*), show a clean pair of heels, skedaddle (*informal*), take a powder (*U.S. & Canad. slang*), take flight, take it on the lam (*U.S. & Canad. slang*), take off, take to one's heels, turn tail **2.** (*with* **with**) **a.** abduct, abscond, elope **b.** abscond, make off, pinch (*informal*), run off, snatch, steal **c.** romp home, walk it (*informal*), win by a mile (*informal*), win easily, win hands down

rundown briefing, outline, précis, recap (*informal*), résumé, review, run-through, sketch, summary, synopsis

run-down 1. below par, debilitated, drained, enervated, exhausted, fatigued, out of condition, peaky, tired, under the weather (*informal*), unhealthy, weak, weary, worn-out **2.** broken-down, decrepit, dilapidated, dingy, ramshackle, seedy, shabby, tumble-down, worn-out

▷ **Antonyms** (*sense 1*) fighting fit, fine, fit, fit as a fiddle, full of beans (*informal*), healthy, well

run down 1. curtail, cut, cut back, decrease, downsize, drop, pare down, reduce, trim **2.** debilitate, exhaust, sap the strength of, tire, undermine the health of, weaken **3.** asperse, bad-mouth (*slang, chiefly U.S. & Canad.*), belittle, criticize adversely, decry, defame, denigrate, disparage, knock (*informal*), put down, revile, rubbish (*informal*), slag (off) (*slang*), speak ill of, vilify **4.** hit, knock down, knock over, run into, run over, strike

run-in altercation, argument, brush, confrontation, contretemps, dispute, dust-up (*informal*), encounter, face-off (*slang*), fight, quarrel, row, set-to (*informal*), skirmish, tussle

run in 1. break in gently, run gently **2.** *slang* apprehend, arrest, bust (*informal*), collar (*informal*), feel one's collar (*slang*), jail, lift (*slang*), nab (*informal*), nail (*informal*), pick up, pinch (*informal*), pull in (*Brit. slang*), take into custody, take to jail, throw in jail

run into 1. bump into, collide with, crash into, dash against, hit, ram, strike **2.** be beset by, be confronted by, bump into, chance upon, come across, come upon, encounter, meet, meet with, run across

runner 1. athlete, harrier, jogger, miler, sprinter **2.** courier, dispatch bearer, errand boy, messenger **3.** offshoot, shoot, sprig, sprout, stem, stolon (*Botany*), tendril

running *adjective* **1.** constant, continuous, incessant, in succession, on the trot (*informal*), perpetual, together, unbroken, unceasing, uninterrupted **2.** flowing, moving, streaming ~*noun* **3.** administration, charge, conduct, control, coordination, direction, leadership, management, organization, regulation, superintendency, supervision **4.** functioning, maintenance, operation, performance, working **5.** competition, contention, contest

runny diluted, flowing, fluid, liquefied, liquid, melted, streaming, watery

run off 1. bolt, clear out, cut and run (*informal*), decamp, do a runner (*slang*), escape, flee, fly the coop (*U.S. & Canad. informal*), hook it (*slang*), make off, run away, scarper (*Brit. slang*), show a clean pair of heels, skedaddle (*informal*), take a powder (*U.S. & Canad. slang*), take flight, take it on the lam (*U.S. & Canad. slang*), take to one's heels, turn tail **2.** churn out (*informal*), duplicate, print, produce **3.** bleed, drain, flow away, siphon, tap **4.** (*with* **with**) **a.** lift (*informal*), make off, pinch (*informal*), purloin, run away, steal, swipe (*slang*) **b.** abscond, elope, run away

run-of-the-mill average, banal, bog-standard (*Brit. & Irish slang*), common, commonplace, dime-a-dozen (*informal*), fair, mediocre, middling, modest, no great shakes (*informal*), ordinary, passable, tolerable, undistinguished, unexceptional, unexciting, unimpressive, vanilla (*informal*)

▷ **Antonyms** excellent, exceptional, extraordinary, marvellous, out of the ordinary, splendid, unusual

run out 1. be exhausted, cease, close, come to a close, dry up, end, expire, fail, finish, give out, peter out, terminate **2.** (*with* **of**) be cleaned out, be out of, exhaust one's supply of, have no more of, have none left, have no remaining **3.** (*with* **on**) *informal* abandon, desert, forsake, leave high and dry, leave holding the baby, leave in the lurch, rat (*informal*), run away from, strand

run over 1. hit, knock down, knock over, run down, strike **2.** brim over, overflow, spill, spill over **3.** check, examine, go over, go through, rehearse, reiterate, review, run through, survey

run through **1.** impale, pierce, spit, stab, stick, transfix **2.** blow (*slang*), dissipate, exhaust, fritter away, spend like water, squander, throw away, waste **3.** go over, practise, read, rehearse, run over **4.** check, examine, go through, look over, review, run over, survey

rupture *noun* **1.** breach, break, burst, cleavage, cleft, crack, fissure, fracture, rent, split, tear **2.** altercation, breach, break, bust-up (*informal*), contention, disagreement, disruption, dissolution, estrangement, falling-out (*informal*), feud, hostility, quarrel, rift, schism, split **3.** *Medical* hernia *~verb* **4.** break, burst, cleave, crack, fracture, puncture, rend, separate, sever, split, tear **5.** break off, cause a breach, come between, disrupt, dissever, divide, split

rural agrarian, agrestic, agricultural, Arcadian, bucolic, countrified, country, hick (*informal, chiefly U.S. & Canad.*), pastoral, rustic, sylvan, upcountry

▷ **Antonyms** city, cosmopolitan, town, urban

ruse artifice, blind, deception, device, dodge, hoax, imposture, manoeuvre, ploy, sham, stratagem, subterfuge, trick, wile

rush *verb* **1.** accelerate, barrel (along) (*informal, chiefly U.S. & Canad.*), bolt, burn rubber (*informal*), career, dart, dash, dispatch, expedite, fly, hasten, hotfoot, hurry, hustle, lose no time, make haste, make short work of, press, push, quicken, race, run, scramble, scurry, shoot, speed, speed up, sprint, stampede, tear *~noun* **2.** charge, dash, dispatch, expedition, haste, hurry, race, scramble, speed, stampede, surge, swiftness, urgency *~verb* **3.** attack, capture, charge, overcome, storm, take by storm *~noun* **4.** assault, charge, onslaught, push, storm, surge *~adjective* **5.** brisk, cursory, emergency, expeditious, fast, hasty, hurried, prompt, quick, rapid, swift, urgent

▷ **Antonyms** (*sense 1*) dally, dawdle, delay, procrastinate, slow down, tarry, wait (*sense 5*) careful, detailed, leisurely, not urgent, slow, thorough, unhurried

rust *noun* **1.** corrosion, oxidation *~verb* **2.** corrode, oxidize *~noun* **3.** blight, mildew, mould, must, rot *~verb* **4.** atrophy, decay, decline, deteriorate, go stale, stagnate, tarnish

rustic *adjective* **1.** agrestic, Arcadian, bucolic, countrified, country, pastoral, rural, sylvan, upcountry **2.** artless, homely, homespun, plain, simple, unaffected, unpolished, unrefined, unsophisticated **3.** awkward, boorish, churlish, cloddish, clodhopping (*informal*), clownish, coarse, crude, graceless, hick (*informal, chiefly U.S. & Canad.*), loutish, lumpish, maladroit, rough, uncouth, uncultured, unmannerly *~noun* **4.** boor, bumpkin, clod, clodhopper (*informal*), clown, country boy, country cousin, countryman, countrywoman, hayseed (*U.S. & Canad. informal*), hick (*informal, chiefly U.S. & Canad.*), hillbilly, Hodge, peasant, son of the soil, swain (*archaic*), yokel

▷ **Antonyms** *~adjective* (*sense 1*) cosmopolitan, urban (*sense 2*) elegant, grand, polished, refined, sophisticated (*sense 3*) courtly, polished, refined, sophisticated, urbane *~noun* city slicker, cosmopolitan, courtier, sophisticate, townee, townsman

rustle **1.** *verb* crackle, crepitate, crinkle, susurrate (*literary*), swish, whish, whisper, whoosh **2.** *~noun* crackle, crepitation, crinkling, rustling, susurration *or* susurrus (*literary*), whisper

rusty **1.** corroded, oxidized, rust-covered, rusted **2.** chestnut, coppery, reddish, reddish-brown, russet, rust-coloured **3.** cracked, creaking, croaking, croaky, hoarse **4.** ancient, antiquated, antique, dated, old-fashioned, outmoded, out of date, passé **5.** deficient, impaired, not what it was, out of practice, sluggish, stale, unpractised, weak

rut *noun* **1.** furrow, gouge, groove, indentation, pothole, score, track, trough, wheelmark **2.** dead end, groove, habit, humdrum existence, pattern, routine, system *~verb* **3.** cut, furrow, gouge, groove, hole, indent, mark, score

ruthless adamant, barbarous, brutal, callous, cruel, ferocious, fierce, hard, hard-hearted, harsh, heartless, inexorable, inhuman, merciless, pitiless, relentless, remorseless, savage, severe, stern, unfeeling, unmerciful, unpitying, unrelenting, without pity

▷ **Antonyms** compassionate, forgiving, gentle, humane, kind, lenient, merciful, pitying, sparing

ruttish **1.** in heat, in rut, in season, sexually excited **2.** aroused, horny (*slang*), lascivious, lecherous, lewd, libidinous, lustful, randy (*informal, chiefly Brit.*), salacious

S, s

sable *adjective* black, dark, dusty, ebon (*poetic*), ebony, jet, jetty, raven, sombre

sabotage 1. *verb* cripple, damage, destroy, disable, disrupt, incapacitate, sap the foundations of, subvert, throw a spanner in the works (*Brit. informal*), undermine, vandalize, wreck **2.** *~noun* damage, destruction, disruption, subversion, treachery, treason, wrecking

sac bag, bladder, bursa, cyst, pocket, pod, pouch, vesicle

saccharine cloying, honeyed, icky (*informal*), maudlin, mawkish, nauseating, oversweet, sentimental, sickly, soppy (*Brit. informal*), sugary, syrupy (*informal*), treacly

sack[1] 1. *verb* axe (*informal*), discharge, dismiss, fire (*informal*), give (someone) his books (*informal*), give (someone) his cards, give (someone) his marching orders, give (someone) the boot (*slang*), give (someone) the bullet (*Brit. slang*), give (someone) the elbow, give (someone) the push (*informal*), kick out (*informal*), kiss off (*slang, chiefly U.S. & Canad.*) **2.** *~noun* **the sack** discharge, dismissal, termination of employment, the axe (*informal*), the boot (*slang*), the chop (*Brit. slang*), the (old) heave-ho (*informal*), the order of the boot (*slang*), the push (*slang*)

sack[2] 1. *verb* demolish, depredate (*rare*), despoil, destroy, devastate, lay waste, loot, maraud, pillage, plunder, raid, ravage, rifle, rob, ruin, spoil, strip **2.** *~noun* depredation, despoliation, destruction, devastation, looting, pillage, plunder, plundering, rape, rapine, ravage, ruin, waste

sack[3] *noun* **hit the sack** bed down, go to bed, hit the hay (*slang*), retire, turn in (*informal*)

sackcloth and ashes compunction, contrition, grief, hair shirt, mortification, mourning, penance, penitence, remorse, repentance

sacred 1. blessed, consecrated, divine, hallowed, holy, revered, sanctified, venerable **2.** inviolable, inviolate, invulnerable, protected, sacrosanct, secure **3.** ecclesiastical, holy, religious, solemn

▷ **Antonyms** lay, nonspiritual, profane, secular, temporal, unconsecrated, worldly

sacrifice 1. *verb* forego, forfeit, give up, immolate, let go, lose, offer, offer up, say goodbye to, surrender **2.** *~noun* burnt offering, destruction, hecatomb, holocaust (*rare*), immolation, loss, oblation, renunciation, surrender, votive offering

sacrificial atoning, expiatory, oblatory, propitiatory, reparative

sacrilege blasphemy, desecration, heresy, impiety, irreverence, mockery, profanation, profaneness, profanity, violation

▷ **Antonyms** piety, respect, reverence

sacrilegious blasphemous, desecrating, godless, impious, irreligious, irreverent, profane, ungodly, unholy

sacrosanct hallowed, inviolable, inviolate, sacred, sanctified, set apart, untouchable

sad 1. blue, cheerless, dejected, depressed, disconsolate, dismal, doleful, down, downcast, down in the dumps (*informal*), down in the mouth (*informal*), gloomy, glum, grief-stricken, grieved, heavy-hearted, low, low-spirited, lugubrious, melancholy, mournful, pensive, sick at heart, sombre, triste (*archaic*), unhappy, wistful, woebegone **2.** calamitous, dark, depressing, disastrous, dismal, grievous, harrowing, heart-rending, lachrymose, moving, pathetic, pitiable, pitiful, poignant, sorry, tearful, tragic, upsetting **3.** bad, deplorable, dismal, distressing, grave, lamentable, miserable, regrettable, serious, shabby, sorry, to be deplored, unfortunate, unhappy, unsatisfactory, wretched

▷ **Antonyms** blithe, cheerful, cheery, chirpy (*informal*), fortunate, glad, good, happy, in good spirits, jolly, joyful, joyous, light-hearted, merry, pleased

sadden aggrieve, bring tears to one's eyes, cast a gloom upon, cast down, dash, deject, depress, desolate, dispirit, distress, grieve, make blue, make one's heart bleed, upset

saddle *verb* burden, charge, encumber, load, lumber (*Brit. informal*), task, tax

sadistic barbarous, beastly, brutal, cruel, fiendish, inhuman, perverse, perverted, ruthless, savage, vicious

sadness bleakness, cheerlessness, dejection, depression, despondency, dolefulness, dolour (*poetic*), gloominess, grief, heavy heart, melancholy, misery, mournfulness, poignancy, sorrow, sorrowfulness, the blues, the dumps (*informal*), the hump (*Brit. informal*), tragedy, unhappiness, wretchedness

safe *adjective* **1.** all right, free from harm, impregnable, in safe hands, in safety, intact, O.K. *or* okay (*informal*), out of danger, out of harm's way, out of the woods, protected, safe and sound, secure, undamaged, unharmed, unhurt, unscathed **2.** harmless, innocuous, nonpoisonous, nontoxic, pure, tame, unpolluted, wholesome **3.** cautious, circumspect, conservative, dependable, discreet, on the safe side, prudent, realistic, reliable, sure, tried and true, trustworthy, unadventurous **4.** certain, impregnable, risk-free, riskless, secure, sound *~noun* **5.** coffer, deposit box, repository, safe-deposit box, strongbox, vault

▷ **Antonyms** (*sense 1*) at risk, damaged, endangered, imperilled, insecure, jeopardized, put at risk, put in danger, threatened (*sense 2*) baneful, dangerous, harmful, hazardous, hurtful, injurious, noxious, pernicious, unsafe (*sense 3*) imprudent, incautious, reckless, risky, unsafe

safe-conduct authorization, licence, pass, passport, permit, safeguard, warrant

safeguard 1. *verb* defend, guard, look after, preserve, protect, screen, shield, watch over **2.** *~noun* aegis, armour, bulwark, convoy, defence, escort, guard, protection, security, shield, surety

safekeeping care, charge, custody, guardianship, keeping, protection, supervision, surveillance, trust, tutelage, ward

safely in one piece, in safety, safe and sound, securely, with impunity, without risk, with safety

safety assurance, cover, immunity, impregnability, protection, refuge, sanctuary, security, shelter

sag *verb* **1.** bag, bulge, cave in, dip, droop, drop, fall, fall unevenly, give way, hang loosely, seat (*of skirts, etc.*), settle, sink, slump, swag **2.** decline, droop, fall, flag, slide, slip, slump, wane, weaken, wilt *~noun* **3.** decline, depression, dip, downturn, drop, fall, lapse, slip, slump

saga adventure, chronicle, epic, narrative, *roman-fleuve,* soap opera, story, tale, yarn

sagacious able, acute, apt, astute, canny, clear-sighted, discerning, downy (*Brit. slang*), far-sighted, fly (*slang*), insightful, intelligent, judicious, knowing, long-headed, perceptive, perspicacious, sage, sharp, sharp-witted, shrewd, smart, wise

sagacity acuteness, astuteness, canniness, discernment, foresight, insight, judiciousness, knowingness, penetration, perspicacity, prudence, sapience, sense, sharpness, shrewdness, understanding, wisdom

sage 1. *adjective* acute, canny, discerning, intelligent, judicious, learned, perspicacious, politic, prudent, sagacious, sapient, sensible, wise **2.** *~noun* authority, elder, expert, guru, mahatma, man of learning, master, Nestor, philosopher, pundit, savant, Solomon, Solon, wise man

sail *verb* **1.** cast *or* weigh anchor, embark, get under way, hoist the blue peter, put to sea, set sail **2.** captain, cruise, go by water, navigate, pilot, ride the waves, skipper, steer, voyage **3.** drift, float, fly, glide, scud, shoot, skim, skirr, soar, sweep, wing **4.** *informal* (*with* **in** *or* **into**) assault, attack, begin, belabour, fall upon, get going, get to work on, lambast(e), set about, tear into (*informal*)

sailor hearty (*informal*), Jack Tar, lascar, leatherneck (*slang*), marine, mariner, matelot (*slang, chiefly Brit.*), navigator, salt, sea dog, seafarer, seafaring man, seaman, tar (*informal*)

saintly angelic, beatific, blameless, blessed, devout, full of good works, god-fearing, godly, holy, pious, religious, righteous, sainted, saintlike, sinless, virtuous, worthy

sake 1. account, advantage, behalf, benefit, consideration, gain, good, interest, profit, regard, respect, welfare, wellbeing **2.** aim, cause, end, motive, objective, principle, purpose, reason

salacious bawdy, blue, carnal, concupiscent, erotic, indecent, lascivious, lecherous, lewd, libidinous, lickerish (*archaic*), lustful, obscene, pornographic, prurient, ribald, ruttish, smutty, steamy (*informal*), wanton, X-rated (*informal*)

salary earnings, emolument, income, pay, remuneration, stipend, wage, wages

sale 1. auction, deal, disposal, marketing, selling, transaction, vending **2.** buyers, consumers, customers, demand, market, outlet, purchasers **3. for sale** available, in stock, obtainable, on offer, on sale, on the market

salient arresting, conspicuous, important, jutting, marked, noticeable, outstanding, projecting, prominent, pronounced, protruding, remarkable, signal, striking

sallow anaemic, bilious, jaundiced-looking, pale, pallid, pasty, peely-wally (*Scot.*), sickly, unhealthy, wan, yellowish

▷ **Antonyms** glowing, healthy-looking, radiant, rosy, ruddy

sally *verb* **1.** erupt, go forth, issue, rush, set out, surge *~noun* **2.** *Military* campaign, foray, incursion, offensive, raid, sortie, thrust **3.** *figurative* bon mot, crack (*informal*), jest, joke, quip, retort, riposte, smart remark, wisecrack (*infor~*

mal), witticism **4**. escapade, excursion, frolic, jaunt, trip

salt *noun* **1**. flavour, relish, savour, seasoning, taste **2. with a grain** *or* **pinch of salt** cynically, disbelievingly, doubtfully, sceptically, suspiciously, with reservations **3**. *figurative* Attic wit, bite, dry humour, liveliness, piquancy, punch, pungency, sarcasm, sharpness, wit, zest, zip (*informal*) **4**. mariner, sailor, sea dog, seaman, tar (*informal*) *~adjective* **5**. brackish, briny, saline, salted, salty

salt away accumulate, amass, bank, cache, hide, hoard up, lay by, lay in, lay up, put by, save, save for a rainy day, stash away (*informal*), stockpile

salty 1. brackish, brak (*S. African*), briny, over-salted, saline, salt, salted **2**. colourful, humorous, lively, piquant, pungent, racy, sharp, snappy (*informal*), spicy, tangy, tart, witty, zestful

salubrious beneficial, good for one, healthful, health-giving, healthy, invigorating, salutary, wholesome

salutary 1. advantageous, beneficial, good, good for one, helpful, practical, profitable, timely, useful, valuable **2**. healthful, healthy, salubrious

salutation address, greeting, obeisance, salute, welcome

salute *verb* **1**. accost, acknowledge, address, doff one's cap to, greet, hail, kiss, pay one's respects to, salaam, welcome **2**. acknowledge, honour, pay tribute *or* homage to, present arms, recognize, take one's hat off to (*informal*) *~noun* **3**. address, greeting, kiss, obeisance, recognition, salaam, salutation, tribute

salvage *verb* glean, recover, redeem, rescue, restore, retrieve, save

salvation deliverance, escape, lifeline, preservation, redemption, rescue, restoration, saving

▷ **Antonyms** condemnation, damnation, doom, downfall, hell, loss, perdition, ruin

salve *noun* balm, cream, dressing, emollient, liniment, lotion, lubricant, medication, ointment, unguent

same *adjective* **1**. aforementioned, aforesaid, selfsame, very **2**. alike, corresponding, duplicate, equal, equivalent, identical, indistinguishable, interchangeable, synonymous, twin **3**. changeless, consistent, constant, invariable, unaltered, unchanged, unfailing, uniform, unvarying **4. all the same: a.** after all, anyhow, be that as it may, in any event, just the same, nevertheless, nonetheless, still **b.** immaterial, not worth mentioning, of no consequence, unimportant

▷ **Antonyms** altered, different, dissimilar, diverse, inconsistent, miscellaneous, other, variable

sameness consistency, identicalness, identity, indistinguishability, lack of variety, likeness, monotony, oneness, predictability, repetition, resemblance, similarity, standardization, tedium, uniformity

sample 1. *noun* cross section, example, exemplification, illustration, indication, instance, model, pattern, representative, sign, specimen **2**. *~verb* experience, inspect, partake of, taste, test, try **3**. *~adjective* illustrative, pilot, representative, specimen, test, trial

sanctify absolve, anoint, bless, cleanse, consecrate, hallow, purify, set apart

sanctimonious canting, false, goody-goody (*informal*), holier-than-thou, hypocritical, pharisaical, pi (*Brit. slang*), pietistic, pious, priggish, self-righteous, self-satisfied, smug, Tartuffian *or* Tartufian, too good to be true, unctuous

sanction *noun* **1**. allowance, approbation, approval, authority, authorization, backing, confirmation, countenance, endorsement, O.K. *or* okay (*informal*), ratification, stamp *or* seal of approval, support **2**. (*often plural*) ban, boycott, coercive measures, embargo, penalty *~verb* **3**. allow, approve, authorize, back, countenance, endorse, entitle, lend one's name to, permit, support, vouch for **4**. confirm, ratify, warrant

▷ **Antonyms** *~noun* (*sense 1*) ban, disapproval, embargo, prohibition, proscription, refusal, veto (*sense 2*) approbation, approval, authority, authorization, dispensation, licence, permission *~verb* ban, boycott, disallow, forbid, refuse, reject, veto

sanctity 1. devotion, godliness, goodness, grace, holiness, piety, purity, religiousness, righteousness, sanctitude, spirituality **2**. inviolability, sacredness, solemnity

sanctuary 1. altar, church, Holy of Holies, sanctum, shrine, temple **2**. asylum, haven, protection, refuge, retreat, shelter **3**. conservation area, national park, nature reserve, reserve

sanctum 1. Holy of Holies, sanctuary, shrine **2**. den, private room, refuge, retreat, study

sane 1. all there (*informal*), *compos mentis,* in one's right mind, in possession of all one's faculties, lucid, mentally sound, normal, of sound mind, rational **2**. balanced, judicious, level-headed, moderate, reasonable, sensible, sober, sound

▷ **Antonyms** bonkers (*slang, chiefly Brit.*), crackpot (*informal*), crazy, daft (*informal*), doolally (*slang*), foolish, insane, loony (*slang*), loopy (*informal*), mad, mentally ill, *non compos mentis,* nuts (*slang*), off one's head (*slang*), off one's trolley (*slang*), out to lunch (*informal*), round the bend *or* twist (*slang*), stupid, unreasonable, unsound, up the pole (*informal*), wacko *or* whacko (*informal*)

sang-froid aplomb, calmness, composure, cool (*slang*), cool-headedness, coolness, equanimity, imperturbability, indifference, nonchalance, phlegm, poise, self-possession, unflappability (*informal*)

sanguinary bloodied, bloodthirsty, bloody, cruel, fell (*archaic*), flowing with blood, gory, grim, merciless, murderous, pitiless, ruthless, savage

sanguine 1. animated, assured, buoyant, cheerful, confident, hopeful, in good heart, lively, optimistic, spirited **2.** florid, red, rubicund, ruddy

▷ **Antonyms** (*sense 1*) despondent, dispirited, down, gloomy, heavy-hearted, melancholy, pessimistic (*sense 2*) anaemic, ashen, pale, pallid, peely-wally (*Scot.*)

sanitary clean, germ-free, healthy, hygienic, salubrious, unpolluted, wholesome

sanity 1. mental health, normality, rationality, reason, right mind (*informal*), saneness, stability **2.** common sense, good sense, judiciousness, level-headedness, rationality, sense, soundness of judgment

▷ **Antonyms** craziness, dementia, folly, insanity, lunacy, madness, mental derangement, mental illness, senselessness, stupidity

sap[1] *noun* **1.** animating force, essence, lifeblood, vital fluid **2.** *informal* charlie (*Brit. informal*), chump (*informal*), drip (*informal*), dweeb (*U.S. slang*), fool, gobshite (*Irish taboo slang*), gull (*archaic*), idiot, jerk (*slang, chiefly U.S. & Canad.*), muggins (*Brit. slang*), nerd *or* nurd (*slang*), nincompoop, ninny, nitwit (*informal*), noddy, noodle, numpty (*Scot. informal*), numskull *or* numbskull, oaf, plonker (*slang*), prat (*slang*), Simple Simon, simpleton, twit (*informal*), wally (*slang*), weakling, wet (*Brit. informal*)

sap[2] *verb* bleed, deplete, devitalize, drain, enervate, erode, exhaust, rob, undermine, weaken, wear down

sapience acuity, acuteness, discernment, insight, mother wit, nous (*Brit. slang*), perspicacity, sagacity, sense, shrewdness, suss (*slang*), understanding, wisdom

sapient acute, canny, discerning, discriminating, intelligent, judicious, knowing, long-headed, perspicacious, sagacious, sage, shrewd, wise, would-be-wise

sarcasm bitterness, causticness, contempt, cynicism, derision, irony, mockery, mordancy, satire, scorn, sneering, venom, vitriol

sarcastic acerb, acerbic, acid, acrimonious, backhanded, bitchy (*informal*), biting, caustic, contemptuous, cutting, cynical, derisive, disparaging, ironical, mocking, mordacious, mordant, sardonic, sarky (*Brit. informal*), satirical, sharp, sneering, taunting, vitriolic

sardonic bitter, cynical, derisive, dry, ironical, jeering, malevolent, malicious, malignant, mocking, mordacious, mordant, sarcastic, sneering, wry

Satan Apollyon, Beelzebub, Lord of the Flies, Lucifer, Mephistopheles, Old Nick (*informal*), Old Scratch (*informal*), Prince of Darkness, The Devil, The Evil One

satanic accursed, black, demoniac, demoniacal, demonic, devilish, diabolic, evil, fiendish, hellish, infernal, inhuman, iniquitous, malevolent, malignant, wicked

▷ **Antonyms** benevolent, benign, divine, godly, holy

sate 1. indulge to the full, satiate, satisfy, slake **2.** cloy, glut, gorge, overfill, saturate, sicken, surfeit, weary

satellite *noun* **1.** communications satellite, moon, sputnik **2.** *figurative* attendant, cohort (*chiefly U.S.*), dependant, follower, hanger-on, lackey, minion, parasite, retainer, sidekick (*slang*), sycophant, vassal *~adjective* **3.** *figurative* client, dependent, puppet, subordinate, tributary, vassal

satiate 1. cloy, glut, gorge, jade, nauseate, overfill, stuff **2.** sate, satisfy, slake, surfeit

satiety 1. overindulgence, saturation, surfeit **2.** fullness, gratification, repletion, satiation, satisfaction

satire burlesque, caricature, irony, lampoon, parody, pasquinade, raillery, ridicule, sarcasm, send-up (*Brit. informal*), skit, spoof (*informal*), takeoff (*informal*), travesty, wit

satirical, satiric biting, bitter, burlesque, caustic, censorious, cutting, cynical, incisive, ironical, mocking, mordacious, mordant, pungent, Rabelaisian, sarcastic, sardonic, taunting, vitriolic

satirize abuse, burlesque, censure, criticize, deride, hold up to ridicule, lampoon, lash, parody, pillory, ridicule, send up (*Brit. informal*), take off (*informal*), travesty

satisfaction 1. comfort, complacency, content, contentedness, contentment, ease, enjoyment, gratification, happiness, peace of mind, pleasure, pride, repletion, satiety, well-being **2.** achievement, appeasing, assuaging, fulfilment, gratification, resolution, settlement **3.** amends, atonement, compensation, damages, indemnification, justice, recompense, redress, reimbursement, remuneration, reparation, requital, restitution, settlement, vindication

▷ **Antonyms** (*senses 1 & 2*) annoyance, discontent, displeasure, dissatisfaction, frustration, grief, injury, misgivings, pain, shame, unhappiness

satisfactory acceptable, adequate, all right, average, competent, fair, good enough, passable, sufficient, suitable, up to scratch, up to standard, up to the mark

▷ **Antonyms** bad, below par, inadequate, insufficient, leaving a lot to be desired, mediocre, no great shakes (*informal*), not up to scratch (*informal*), poor, substandard, unacceptable, unsatisfactory, unsuitable

satisfied at ease, complacent, content, contented, convinced, easy in one's mind, happy, like the cat that swallowed the canary (*informal*), pacified, positive, smug, sure

satisfy 1. appease, assuage, content, feed, fill, gratify, indulge, mollify, pacify, pander to, please, quench, sate, satiate, slake, surfeit **2.** answer, be adequate, be enough, be sufficient, come up to expectations, cut the mustard, do, fill the bill (*informal*), fulfil, meet, qualify, serve, serve the purpose, suffice **3.** assure, convince, dispel (someone's) doubts, persuade, put (someone's) mind at rest, quiet, reassure **4.** answer, comply with, discharge, fulfil, meet, pay (off), settle, square up **5.** atone, compensate, indemnify, make good, make reparation for, recompense, remunerate, requite, reward

▷ **Antonyms** (*senses 1, 2, 3 & 4*) annoy, displease, dissatisfy, dissuade, exasperate, fail to meet, fail to persuade, frustrate, give cause for complaint

satisfying cheering, convincing, filling, gratifying, pleasing, pleasurable, satisfactory

saturate douse, drench, drouk (*Scot.*), imbue, impregnate, ret (*used of flax, etc.*), seep, soak, souse, steep, suffuse, waterlog, wet through

saturated drenched, dripping, droukit *or* drookit (*Scot.*), soaked, soaked to the skin, soaking (wet), sodden, sopping (wet), waterlogged, wet through, wringing wet

saturnine dour, dull, gloomy, glum, grave, heavy, morose, phlegmatic, sedate, sluggish, sombre, taciturn, uncommunicative

sauce *noun* audacity, backchat (*informal*), brass (*informal*), brass neck (*Brit. informal*), cheek (*informal*), cheekiness, disrespectfulness, face (*informal*), front, impertinence, impudence, insolence, lip (*slang*), neck (*informal*), nerve (*informal*), rudeness

sauciness backchat (*informal*), brass (*informal*), brazenness, cheek (*informal*), flippancy, impertinence, impudence, insolence, lip (*slang*), pertness, rudeness, sauce (*informal*)

saucy 1. cheeky (*informal*), disrespectful, flip (*informal*), flippant, forward, fresh (*informal*), impertinent, impudent, insolent, lippy (*U.S. & Canad. slang*), pert, presumptuous, rude, sassy (*U.S. informal*), smart-alecky (*informal*) **2.** dashing, gay, jaunty, natty (*informal*), perky, rakish, sporty

saunter 1. *verb* amble, dally, linger, loiter, meander, mosey (*informal*), ramble, roam, rove, stravaig (*Scot. & northern English dialect*), stroll, take a stroll, tarry, wander **2.** *~noun* airing, amble, breather, constitutional, perambulation, promenade, ramble, stroll, turn, walk

savage *adjective* **1.** feral, rough, rugged, uncivilized, uncultivated, undomesticated, untamed, wild **2.** barbarous, beastly, bestial, bloodthirsty, bloody, brutal, brutish, cruel, devilish, diabolical, ferocious, fierce, harsh, inhuman, merciless, murderous, pitiless, ravening, ruthless, sadistic, vicious **3.** in a state of nature, nonliterate, primitive, rude, unspoilt *~noun* **4.** autochthon, barbarian, heathen, indigene, native, primitive **5.** barbarian, bear, boor, lout, roughneck (*slang*), yahoo, yob (*Brit. slang*), yobbo (*Brit. slang*) **6.** beast, brute, fiend, monster *~verb* **7.** attack, lacerate, mangle, maul, tear into (*informal*)

▷ **Antonyms** *~adjective* balmy, civilized, cultivated, domesticated, gentle, humane, kind, merciful, mild, refined, restrained, tame *~verb* acclaim, celebrate, praise, rave about (*informal*)

savagery barbarity, bestiality, bloodthirstiness, brutality, cruelty, ferocity, fierceness, inhumanity, ruthlessness, sadism, viciousness

savant authority, intellectual, mahatma, master, mastermind, philosopher, sage, scholar

save 1. bail (someone) out, come to (someone's) rescue, deliver, free, liberate, recover, redeem, rescue, salvage, save (someone's) bacon (*British informal*), set free **2.** be frugal, be thrifty, collect, economize, gather, hide away, hoard, hold, husband, keep, keep up one's sleeve (*informal*), lay by, put aside for a rainy day, put by, reserve, retrench, salt away, set aside, store, tighten one's belt (*informal*), treasure up **3.** conserve, guard, keep safe, look after, preserve, protect, safeguard, screen, shield, take care of **4.** hinder, obviate, prevent, rule out, spare

▷ **Antonyms** (*senses 1 & 3*) abandon, condemn, discard, endanger, expose, imperil, risk, threaten (*sense 2*) be extravagant, blow (*slang*), consume, fritter away, spend, splurge, squander, use, use up, waste

saving 1. *adjective* compensatory, extenuating, qualifying, redeeming **2.**

~noun bargain, discount, economy, reduction

savings fall-back, fund, nest egg, provision for a rainy day, reserves, resources, store

saviour defender, deliverer, friend in need, Good Samaritan, guardian, knight in shining armour, liberator, preserver, protector, redeemer, rescuer, salvation

Saviour, Our *or* The Christ, Jesus, Messiah, Redeemer

savoir-faire accomplishment, address, diplomacy, discretion, finesse, poise, social graces, social know-how (*informal*), tact, urbanity

savour *noun* **1.** flavour, piquancy, relish, smack, smell, tang, taste, zest, zing (*informal*) **2.** distinctive quality, excitement, flavour, interest, salt, spice, zest *~verb* **3.** (*often with* **of**) bear the hallmarks, be indicative, be suggestive, partake, show signs, smack, suggest, verge on **4.** appreciate, delight in, drool, enjoy, enjoy to the full, gloat over, like, luxuriate in, partake, relish, revel in, smack one's lips over

savoury 1. agreeable, appetizing, dainty, delectable, delicious, full-flavoured, good, luscious, mouthwatering, palatable, piquant, rich, scrumptious (*informal*), spicy, tangy, tasty, toothsome **2.** apple-pie (*informal*), decent, edifying, honest, reputable, respectable, wholesome

▷ **Antonyms** disreputable, distasteful, insipid, nasty, tasteless, unappetizing, unpalatable, unpleasant, unsavoury, wersh (*Scots.*)

saw adage, aphorism, apophthegm, axiom, byword, dictum, gnome, maxim, proverb, saying

saw-toothed crenate (*Botany, Zoology*), dentate, denticulate (*Biology*), notched, serrate, serrated

say *verb* **1.** add, affirm, announce, assert, asseverate, come out with (*informal*), declare, give voice *or* utterance to, maintain, mention, pronounce, put into words, remark, speak, state, utter, voice **2.** answer, disclose, divulge, give as one's opinion, make known, reply, respond, reveal, tell **3.** allege, bruit, claim, noise abroad, put about, report, rumour, suggest **4.** deliver, do, orate, perform, read, recite, rehearse, render, repeat **5.** assume, conjecture, dare say, estimate, guess, hazard a guess, imagine, judge, presume, suppose, surmise **6.** communicate, convey, express, give the impression that, imply **7. go without saying** be accepted, be a matter of course, be obvious, be self-evident, be taken as read, be taken for granted, be understood **8. to say the least** at the very least, to put it mildly, without any exaggeration *~noun* **9.** chance to speak, crack (*informal*), opportunity to speak, turn to speak, voice, vote **10.** authority, clout (*informal*), influence, power, sway, weight

saying adage, aphorism, apophthegm, axiom, byword, dictum, gnome, maxim, proverb, saw, slogan

say-so 1. assertion, asseveration, assurance, dictum, guarantee, word **2.** agreement, assent, authority, authorization, consent, O.K. *or* okay (*informal*), permission, sanction

scalding blistering, boiling, burning, piping hot, searing

scale[1] *noun* **1.** calibration, degrees, gamut, gradation, graduated system, graduation, hierarchy, ladder, pecking order (*informal*), progression, ranking, register, seniority system, sequence, series, spectrum, spread, steps **2.** proportion, ratio **3.** degree, extent, range, reach, scope, way *~verb* **4.** ascend, clamber, climb, escalade, mount, surmount **5.** adjust, proportion, prorate (*chiefly U.S.*), regulate

scale[2] *noun* flake, lamina, layer, plate, squama (*Biology*)

scaly flaky, furfuraceous (*Medical*), scabrous, scurfy, squamous *or* squamose (*Biology*), squamulose

scamp devil, imp, knave (*archaic*), mischief-maker, monkey, pickle (*Brit. informal*), prankster, rascal, rogue, scallywag (*informal*), scapegrace, toerag (*slang*), tyke (*informal*), whippersnapper, wretch

scamper beetle, dart, dash, fly, hasten, hie (*archaic*), hurry, romp, run, scoot, scurry, scuttle, sprint

scan check, check out (*informal*), clock (*Brit. slang*), con (*archaic*), examine, eye, eyeball (*U.S. slang*), get a load of (*informal*), glance over, investigate, look one up and down, look through, recce (*slang*), run one's eye over, run over, scour, scrutinize, search, size up (*informal*), skim, survey, sweep, take a dekko at (*Brit. slang*), take stock of

scandal 1. crime, crying shame (*informal*), disgrace, embarrassment, offence, sin, wrongdoing **2.** calumny, defamation, detraction, discredit, disgrace, dishonour, ignominy, infamy, obloquy, offence, opprobrium, reproach, shame, stigma **3.** abuse, aspersion, backbiting, dirt, dirty linen (*informal*), gossip, rumours, skeleton in the cupboard, slander, talk, tattle

scandalize affront, appal, cause a few raised eyebrows (*informal*), disgust, horrify, offend, outrage, raise eyebrows, shock

scandalmonger calumniator, defamer, destroyer of reputations, gossip, muckraker, tattle, tattler, traducer

scandalous 1. atrocious, disgraceful, disreputable, highly improper, infamous, monstrous, odious, opprobrious, outra-

geous, shameful, shocking, unseemly **2.** defamatory, gossiping, libellous, scurrilous, slanderous, untrue
▷ **Antonyms** decent, kind, laudatory, proper, reputable, respectable, seemly, unimpeachable, upright

scant bare, barely sufficient, deficient, inadequate, insufficient, limited, little, minimal, sparse
▷ **Antonyms** abundant, adequate, ample, full, generous, plentiful, satisfactory, sufficient

scanty bare, deficient, exiguous, inadequate, insufficient, meagre, narrow, pathetic, poor, restricted, scant, short, skimpy, slender, sparing, sparse, thin

scapegoat fall guy (*informal*), whipping boy

scapegrace bad lot (*informal*), good-for-nothing, limb of Satan, ne'er-do-well, rascal, rogue, scallywag (*informal*), scamp, the despair of

scar 1. *noun* blemish, cicatrix, injury, mark, trauma (*Pathology*), wound **2.** *~verb* brand, damage, disfigure, mark, traumatize

scarce at a premium, deficient, few, few and far between, infrequent, in short supply, insufficient, rare, seldom met with, thin on the ground, uncommon, unusual, wanting
▷ **Antonyms** abundant, ample, common, commonplace, frequent, numerous, plenteous, plentiful, sufficient

scarcely 1. barely, hardly, only just, scarce (*archaic*) **2.** by no means, definitely not, hardly, not at all, on no account, under no circumstances

scarcity dearth, deficiency, infrequency, insufficiency, lack, paucity, poverty, rareness, shortage, undersupply, want
▷ **Antonyms** abundance, excess, glut, superfluity, surfeit, surplus

scare 1. *verb* affright (*archaic*), alarm, daunt, dismay, frighten, give (someone) a fright, give (someone) a turn (*informal*), intimidate, panic, put the wind up (someone) (*informal*), shock, startle, terrify, terrorize **2.** *~noun* alarm, alert, fright, panic, shock, start, terror

scared fearful, frightened, panicky, panic-stricken, petrified, scared shitless (*taboo slang*), shaken, shit-scared (*taboo slang*), startled, terrified

scaremonger alarmist, Calamity Jane, doom merchant (*informal*), prophet of doom, spreader of despair and despondency

scarper abscond, beat a hasty retreat, beat it (*slang*), clear off (*informal*), cut and run (*informal*), decamp, depart, disappear, do a bunk (*Brit. slang*), flee, go, hook it (*slang*), make off, make oneself scarce (*informal*), run away, run for it, scram (*informal*), skedaddle (*informal*), slope off, take flight, take oneself off, take to one's heels, vamoose (*slang, chiefly U.S.*)

scary alarming, bloodcurdling, chilling, creepy (*informal*), frightening, hair-raising, hairy (*slang*), horrendous, horrifying, intimidating, shocking, spine-chilling, spooky (*informal*), terrifying, unnerving

scathing belittling, biting, brutal, caustic, critical, cutting, harsh, mordacious, mordant, sarcastic, savage, scornful, searing, trenchant, vitriolic, withering

scatter 1. broadcast, diffuse, disseminate, fling, litter, shower, sow, spread, sprinkle, strew **2.** disband, dispel, disperse, dissipate, disunite, put to flight, separate
▷ **Antonyms** assemble, cluster, collect, congregate, converge, rally, unite

scatterbrain bird-brain (*informal*), butterfly, featherbrain, flibbertigibbet, grasshopper mind, madcap

scatterbrained bird-brained (*informal*), careless, empty-headed, featherbrained, forgetful, frivolous, giddy, goofy (*informal*), inattentive, irresponsible, madcap, scatty (*Brit. informal*), silly, slaphappy (*informal*), thoughtless

scattering few, handful, scatter, smatter, smattering, sprinkling

scenario master plan, outline, résumé, rundown, scheme, sequence of events, sketch, story line, summary, synopsis

scene 1. display, drama, exhibition, pageant, picture, representation, show, sight, spectacle, tableau **2.** area, locality, place, position, setting, site, situation, spot, whereabouts **3.** backdrop, background, location, *mise en scène,* set, setting **4.** act, division, episode, incident, part, stage **5.** carry-on (*informal, chiefly Brit.*), commotion, confrontation, display of emotion, drama, exhibition, fuss, hue and cry, performance, row, tantrum, to-do, upset **6.** landscape, panorama, prospect, view, vista **7.** *informal* arena, business, environment, field of interest, milieu, world

scenery 1. landscape, surroundings, terrain, view, vista **2.** *Theatre* backdrop, décor, flats, *mise en scène,* set, setting, stage set

scenic beautiful, breathtaking, grand, impressive, panoramic, picturesque, spectacular, striking

scent *noun* **1.** aroma, bouquet, fragrance, niff (*Brit. slang*), odour, perfume, redolence, smell **2.** spoor, track, trail *~verb* **3.** be on the track *or* trail of, detect, discern, get wind of (*informal*), nose out, recognize, sense, smell, sniff, sniff out

scented aromatic, fragrant, odoriferous, perfumed, redolent, sweet-smelling

sceptic agnostic, cynic, disbeliever, doubter, doubting Thomas, Pyrrhonist, scoffer, unbeliever

sceptical cynical, disbelieving, doubtful, doubting, dubious, hesitating, incredulous, mistrustful, questioning, quizzical, scoffing, take with a pinch of salt, unbelieving, unconvinced
▷ **Antonyms** believing, certain, convinced, credulous, dogmatic, free from doubt, of fixed mind, sure, trusting, undoubting, unquestioning

scepticism agnosticism, cynicism, disbelief, doubt, incredulity, Pyrrhonism, suspicion, unbelief

schedule 1. *noun* agenda, calendar, catalogue, inventory, itinerary, list, list of appointments, plan, programme, timetable **2.** *~verb* appoint, arrange, be due, book, organize, plan, programme, slot (*informal*), time

schematic diagrammatic, diagrammatical, graphic, illustrative, representational

schematize arrange, catalogue, categorize, classify, file, grade, methodize, order, pigeonhole, put into order, regulate, sort, standardize, systematize, systemize, tabulate

scheme *noun* **1.** contrivance, course of action, design, device, plan, programme, project, proposal, strategy, system, tactics, theory **2.** arrangement, blueprint, chart, codification, diagram, disposition, draft, layout, outline, pattern, schedule, schema, system **3.** conspiracy, dodge, game (*informal*), intrigue, machinations, manoeuvre, plot, ploy, ruse, shift, stratagem, subterfuge *~verb* **4.** contrive, design, devise, frame, imagine, lay plans, plan, project, work out **5.** collude, conspire, intrigue, machinate, manoeuvre, plot, wheel and deal (*informal*)

schemer conniver, deceiver, intriguer, Machiavelli, plotter, slyboots (*informal*), wangler (*informal*), wheeler-dealer (*informal*)

scheming artful, calculating, conniving, cunning, deceitful, designing, duplicitous, foxy, Machiavellian, slippery, sly, tricky, underhand, wily
▷ **Antonyms** above-board, artless, guileless, honest, ingenuous, naive, straightforward, trustworthy, undesigning

schism breach, break, discord, disunion, division, rift, rupture, separation, splintering, split

schismatic, schismatical *adjective* discordant, dissentient, dissenting, dissident, heretical, heterodox, seceding, separatist, splinter

scholar 1. academic, bluestocking (*usually disparaging*), bookworm, egghead (*informal*), intellectual, man of letters, savant **2.** disciple, learner, pupil, schoolboy, schoolgirl, student

scholarly academic, bookish, erudite, intellectual, learned, lettered, scholastic, studious, well-read
▷ **Antonyms** lowbrow, middlebrow, philistine, unacademic, uneducated, unintellectual, unlettered

scholarship 1. accomplishments, attainments, book-learning, education, erudition, knowledge, learning, lore **2.** bursary, exhibition, fellowship

scholastic 1. academic, bookish, learned, lettered, literary, scholarly **2.** pedagogic, pedantic, precise

school *noun* **1.** academy, alma mater, college, department, discipline, faculty, institute, institution, seminary **2.** adherents, circle, class, clique, denomination, devotees, disciples, faction, followers, following, group, pupils, schism, sect, set **3.** creed, faith, outlook, persuasion, school of thought, stamp, way of life *~verb* **4.** coach, discipline, drill, educate, indoctrinate, instruct, prepare, prime, train, tutor, verse

schooling 1. book-learning, education, formal education, teaching, tuition **2.** coaching, drill, grounding, guidance, instruction, preparation, training

schoolteacher dominie (*Scot.*), instructor, pedagogue, schoolmarm (*informal*), schoolmaster, schoolmistress

science 1. body of knowledge, branch of knowledge, discipline **2.** art, skill, technique

scientific accurate, controlled, exact, mathematical, precise, systematic

scintillate blaze, coruscate, flash, give off sparks, gleam, glint, glisten, glitter, sparkle, twinkle

scintillating animated, bright, brilliant, dazzling, ebullient, exciting, glittering, lively, sparkling, stimulating, witty

scion 1. child, descendant, heir, offspring, successor **2.** branch, graft, offshoot, shoot, slip, sprout, twig

scoff[1] *verb* belittle, deride, despise, flout, gibe, jeer, knock (*informal*), laugh at, make light of, make sport of, mock, poke fun at, pooh-pooh, revile, ridicule, scorn, scout (*archaic*), slag (off) (*slang*), sneer, take the piss (out of) (*taboo slang*), taunt, twit

scoff[2] **1.** *verb* bolt, cram, cram oneself on, devour, gobble (up), gollop, gorge oneself on, gulp down, guzzle, make a pig of oneself on (*informal*), put away, stuff oneself on, wolf **2.** *~noun* chow (*informal*), eats (*slang*), fare, feed, food, grub (*slang*), meal, nosh (*slang*), nosh-up (*Brit. slang*), rations

scold 1. *verb* bawl out (*informal*), berate, blame, bring (someone) to book, carpet (*informal*), castigate, censure, chew out (*U.S. & Canad. informal*), chide, find fault with, give a rocket (*Brit. & N.Z. informal*), give (someone) a dressing-down, give (someone) a row, give (someone) a talking-to (*informal*), go on at, haul (someone) over the coals (*infor-

mal), have (someone) on the carpet (*informal*), lecture, nag, rate, read the riot act, rebuke, remonstrate with, reprimand, reproach, reprove, slate (*informal, chiefly Brit.*), take (someone) to task, tear into (*informal*), tear (someone) off a strip (*Brit. informal*), tell off (*informal*), tick off (*informal*), upbraid, vituperate **2.** *~noun* nag, shrew, termagant (*rare*), Xanthippe

▷ **Antonyms** *~verb* acclaim, applaud, approve, commend, compliment, extol, laud, praise

scolding dressing-down (*informal*), (good) talking-to (*informal*), lecture, piece of one's mind, rebuke, row, telling-off (*informal*), ticking-off (*informal*), tongue-lashing, wigging (*Brit. slang*)

scoop *noun* **1.** dipper, ladle, spoon **2.** coup, exclusive, exposé, inside story, revelation, sensation *~verb* **3.** (*often with* **up**) clear away, gather up, lift, pick up, remove, sweep up *or* away, take up **4.** bail, dig, dip, empty, excavate, gouge, hollow, ladle, scrape, shovel

scoot bolt, dart, dash, run, scamper, scurry, scuttle, skedaddle (*informal*), skirr, skitter, sprint, zip

scope ambit, area, capacity, compass, confines, elbowroom, extent, field of reference, freedom, latitude, liberty, opportunity, orbit, outlook, purview, range, reach, room, space, span, sphere

scorch blacken, blister, burn, char, parch, roast, sear, shrivel, singe, wither

scorching baking, boiling, broiling, burning, fiery, flaming, red-hot, roasting, searing, sizzling, sweltering, torrid, tropical, unbearably hot

score *noun* **1.** grade, mark, outcome, points, record, result, total **2. the score** *informal* the facts, the lie of the land, the reality, the setup (*informal*), the situation, the truth **3.** *plural* a flock, a great number, an army, a throng, crowds, droves, hosts, hundreds, legions, lots, masses, millions, multitudes, myriads, swarms, very many **4.** account, basis, cause, ground, grounds, reason **5.** a bone to pick, grievance, grudge, injury, injustice, wrong **6. pay off old scores** avenge, get even with (*informal*), get one's own back (*informal*), give an eye for an eye, give like for like *or* tit for tat, give (someone) a taste of his own medicine, hit back, pay (someone) back (in his own coin), repay, requite, retaliate **7.** account, amount due, bill, charge, debt, obligation, reckoning, tab (*U.S. informal*), tally, total *~verb* **8.** achieve, amass, chalk up (*informal*), gain, make, notch up (*informal*), win **9.** count, keep a tally of, keep count, record, register, tally **10.** crosshatch, cut, deface, gouge, graze, indent, mar, mark, nick, notch, scrape, scratch, slash **11.** (*with* **out** *or* **through**) cancel, cross out, delete, obliterate, put a line through, strike out **12.** *Music* adapt, arrange, orchestrate, set **13.** gain an advantage, go down well with (someone), impress, make a hit (*informal*), make an impact *or* impression, make a point, put oneself across, triumph

score off be one up on (*informal*), get the better of, have the laugh on, humiliate, make a fool of, make (someone) look silly, worst

scorn **1.** *noun* contempt, contemptuousness, contumely, derision, despite, disdain, disparagement, mockery, sarcasm, scornfulness, slight, sneer **2.** *~verb* be above, consider beneath one, contemn, curl one's lip at, deride, disdain, flout, hold in contempt, look down on, make fun of, reject, scoff at, scout (*archaic*), slight, sneer at, spurn, turn up one's nose at (*informal*)

▷ **Antonyms** *~noun* acceptance, admiration, affection, esteem, high regard, respect, tolerance, toleration, veneration, worship *~verb* accept, admire, esteem, look favourably on, respect, revere, tolerate, venerate, worship

scornful contemptuous, contumelious, defiant, derisive, disdainful, haughty, insolent, insulting, jeering, mocking, sarcastic, sardonic, scathing, scoffing, slighting, sneering, supercilious, withering

scornfully contemptuously, disdainfully, dismissively, scathingly, slightingly, with a sneer, with contempt, with disdain, witheringly, with lip curled

scot-free clear, safe, scatheless (*archaic*), undamaged, unharmed, unhurt, uninjured, unpunished, unscathed, without a scratch

Scots Caledonian, Scottish

scoundrel asshole (*U.S. & Canad. taboo slang*), asswipe (*U.S. & Canad. taboo slang*), bad egg (*old-fashioned informal*), bastard (*offensive*), blackguard, bugger (*taboo slang*), caitiff (*archaic*), cheat, cocksucker (*taboo slang*), dastard (*archaic*), good-for-nothing, heel (*slang*), incorrigible, knave (*archaic*), miscreant, mother, motherfucker (*taboo slang, chiefly U.S.*), ne'er-do-well, rascal, reprobate, rogue, rotter (*slang, chiefly Brit.*), scally (*Northwest English dialect*), scamp, scapegrace, scumbag (*slang*), shit (*taboo slang*), skelm (*S. African*), son-of-a-bitch (*slang, chiefly U.S. & Canad.*), swine, turd (*taboo slang*), vagabond, villain, wretch

scour[1] *verb* abrade, buff, burnish, clean, cleanse, flush, furbish, polish, purge, rub, scrub, wash, whiten

scour[2] *verb* beat, comb, forage, go over with a fine-tooth comb, hunt, look high and low, rake, ransack, search

scourge *noun* **1.** affliction, bane, curse, infliction, misfortune, penalty, pest, plague, punishment, terror, torment, visitation **2.** cat, cat-o'-nine-tails, lash, strap, switch, thong, whip *~verb* **3.** beat, belt (*informal*), cane, castigate, chastise, discipline, flog, horsewhip, lash, lather (*informal*), leather, punish, take a strap to, tan (someone's) hide (*slang*), thrash, trounce, wallop (*informal*), whale, whip **4.** afflict, curse, excoriate, harass, plague, terrorize, torment

▷ **Antonyms** *~noun* (*sense 1*) benefit, blessing, boon, favour, gift, godsend

scout *verb* **1.** case (*slang*), check out, in~ vestigate, make a reconnaissance, nark (*Brit., Austral., & N.Z. slang*), observe, probe, recce (*slang*), reconnoitre, see how the land lies, spy, spy out, survey, watch **2.** (*often with* **out, up,** *or* **around**) cast around for, ferret out, hunt for, look for, rustle up, search for, search out, seek, track down *~noun* **3.** advance guard, escort, lookout, outrider, precur~ sor, reconnoitrer, vanguard **4.** recruiter, talent scout

scowl 1. *verb* frown, glower, grimace, look daggers at, lour *or* lower **2.** *~noun* black look, dirty look, frown, glower, grimace

scrabble clamber, claw, dig, grope, paw, scramble, scrape, scratch

scraggy 1. angular, bony, emaciated, gangling, gaunt, lanky, lean, rawboned, scrawny, skinny, undernourished **2.** draggletailed (*archaic*), grotty (*slang*), lank, meagre, rough, scanty, scruffy, tousled, unkempt

scram abscond, beat it (*slang*), bugger off (*taboo slang*), clear off (*informal*), de~ part, disappear, fuck off (*offensive taboo slang*), get lost (*informal*), get on one's bike (*Brit. slang*), go away, go to hell (*informal*), hook it (*slang*), leave, make oneself scarce (*informal*), make tracks, pack one's bags (*informal*), quit, scarper (*Brit. slang*), scoot, skedaddle (*infor~ mal*), sling one's hook (*Brit. slang*), slope off, take oneself off, vamoose (*slang, chiefly U.S.*)

scramble *verb* **1.** clamber, climb, crawl, move with difficulty, push, scrabble, struggle, swarm **2.** contend, hasten, jockey for position, jostle, look lively *or* snappy (*informal*), make haste, push, run, rush, strive, vie *~noun* **3.** climb, trek **4.** commotion, competition, confu~ sion, free-for-all (*informal*), hassle (*in~ formal*), hustle, melee *or* mêlée, muddle, race, rat race, rush, struggle, tussle

scrap[1] *noun* **1.** atom, bit, bite, crumb, fragment, grain, iota, mite, modicum, morsel, mouthful, part, particle, piece, portion, remnant, sliver, snatch, snip~ pet, trace **2.** junk, off cuts, waste **3. on the scrap heap** discarded, ditched (*slang*), jettisoned, put out to grass (*in~ formal*), redundant, written off **4.** *plural* bits, leavings, leftovers, remains, scrap~ ings *~verb* **5.** abandon, break up, chuck (*informal*), demolish, discard, dispense with, ditch (*slang*), drop, get rid of, jet~ tison, junk (*informal*), shed, throw away *or* out, throw on the scrapheap, toss out, trash (*slang*), write off

▷ **Antonyms** *~verb* bring back, recall, re-establish, reinstall, reinstate, restore, return

scrap[2] **1.** *noun* argument, *bagarre,* battle, brawl, disagreement, dispute, dust-up (*informal*), fight, quarrel, row, scrim~ mage, scuffle, set-to (*informal*), shindig (*informal*), shindy (*informal*), squabble, tiff, wrangle **2.** *~verb* argue, barney (*in~ formal*), bicker, come to blows, fall out (*informal*), fight, have a shouting match (*informal*), have words, row, spar, squabble, wrangle

scrape *verb* **1.** abrade, bark, graze, rub, scratch, scuff, skin **2.** grate, grind, rasp, scratch, screech, set one's teeth on edge, squeak **3.** clean, erase, file, remove, rub, scour **4.** live from hand to mouth, pinch, save, scrimp, skimp, stint, tighten one's belt **5. scrape by, in,** *or* **through** barely make it, cut it fine (*informal*), get by (*informal*), have a close shave (*infor~ mal*), struggle *~noun* **6.** *informal* awk~ ward *or* embarrassing situation, diffi~ culty, dilemma, distress, fix (*informal*), mess, plight, predicament, pretty pickle (*informal*), spot (*informal*), tight spot, trouble

scrape together amass, dredge up, get hold of, glean, hoard, muster, rake up *or* together, save

scrappy bitty, disjointed, fragmentary, incomplete, perfunctory, piecemeal, sketchy, thrown together

scraps bits, leavings, leftovers, remains, scrapings

scratch *verb* **1.** claw, cut, damage, etch, grate, graze, incise, lacerate, make a mark on, mark, rub, score, scrape **2.** an~ nul, cancel, delete, eliminate, erase, pull out, stand down, strike off, withdraw *~noun* **3.** blemish, claw mark, gash, graze, laceration, mark, scrape **4. up to scratch** acceptable, adequate, capable, competent, satisfactory, sufficient, up to snuff (*informal*), up to standard *~adjective* **5.** haphazard, hastily pre~ pared, impromptu, improvised, rough, rough-and-ready

scrawl doodle, scrabble, scratch, scribble, squiggle, writing

scrawny angular, bony, gaunt, lanky, lean, macilent (*rare*), rawboned, scrag~ gy, skeletal, skin-and-bones (*informal*), skinny, thin, undernourished

scream *verb* **1.** bawl, cry, holler (*infor~ mal*), screech, shriek, shrill, sing out, squeal, yell **2.** *figurative* be conspicuous, clash, jar, shriek *~noun* **3.** howl, outcry, screech, shriek, wail, yell, yelp **4.** *infor~ mal* card (*informal*), caution (*informal*), character (*informal*), comedian, comic, entertainer, hoot (*informal*), joker, laugh, riot (*slang*), sensation, wag, wit

screech cry, scream, shriek, squawk, squeal, yelp

screen *verb* **1.** cloak, conceal, cover, hide, mask, shade, shroud, shut out, veil **2.** defend, guard, protect, safeguard, shelter, shield **3.** cull, evaluate, examine, filter, gauge, grade, process, riddle, scan, sieve, sift, sort, vet **4.** broadcast, present, put on, show *~noun* **5.** awning, canopy, cloak, concealment, cover, guard, hedge, mantle, shade, shelter, shield, shroud **6.** mesh, net, partition, room divider

screw *verb* **1.** tighten, turn, twist, work in **2.** contort, contract, crumple, distort, pucker, wrinkle **3.** *informal* bring pressure to bear on, coerce, constrain, force, hold a knife to (someone's) throat, oppress, pressurize, put the screws on (*informal*), squeeze **4.** *informal, (often with* **out of**) bleed, extort, extract, wrest, wring

screwed up anxious, apprehensive, confused, edgy, in a mess, keyed up, mixed up, nervous, neurotic, on edge, strung up (*informal*), tense, uptight (*informal*), wired (*slang*), worked up, worried

screw up 1. contort, contract, crumple, distort, knit, knot, pucker, wrinkle **2.** *informal* bitch (up) (*slang*), bodge (*informal*), botch, bungle, cock up (*Brit. slang*), flub (*U.S. slang*), fuck up (*offensive taboo slang*), louse up (*slang*), make a hash of (*informal*), make a mess *or* muck-up of (*slang*), make a nonsense of, mess up, mishandle, mismanage, queer (*informal*), spoil

screwy batty (*slang*), cracked (*slang*), crackers (*Brit. slang*), crackpot (*informal*), crazy, doolally (*slang*), dotty (*slang, chiefly Brit.*), eccentric, gonzo (*slang*), loopy (*informal*), nutty (*slang*), odd, oddball (*informal*), off one's trolley (*slang*), off-the-wall (*slang*), outré, out to lunch (*informal*), queer (*informal*), round the bend (*Brit. slang*), rum (*Brit. slang*), up the pole (*informal*), wacko *or* whacko (*informal*), weird

scribble *verb* dash off, doodle, jot, pen, scratch, scrawl, write

scribe amanuensis, clerk, copyist, notary (*archaic*), penman (*rare*), scrivener (*archaic*), secretary, writer

scrimmage affray (*Law*), *bagarre,* bovver (*Brit. slang*), brawl, disturbance, dust-up (*informal*), fight, fray, free-for-all (*informal*), melee *or* mêlée, riot, row, scrap (*informal*), scuffle, set-to (*informal*), shindig (*informal*), shindy (*informal*), skirmish, squabble, struggle

scrimp be frugal, curtail, economize, limit, pinch, pinch pennies, reduce, save, scrape, shorten, skimp, stint, straiten, tighten one's belt

script 1. calligraphy, hand, handwriting, letters, longhand, penmanship, writing **2.** book, copy, dialogue, libretto, lines, manuscript, text, words

Scripture Holy Bible, Holy Scripture, Holy Writ, The Bible, The Book of Books, The Good Book, The Gospels, The Scriptures, The Word, The Word of God

scroll inventory, list, parchment, roll

Scrooge cheapskate (*informal*), meanie *or* meany (*informal, chiefly Brit.*), miser, money-grubber (*informal*), niggard, penny-pincher (*informal*), skinflint, tight-arse (*taboo slang*), tight-ass (*U.S. taboo slang*), tightwad (*U.S. & Canad. slang*)

scrounge beg, blag (*slang*), bum (*informal*), cadge, forage for, freeload (*slang*), hunt around (for), mooch (*slang*), sorn (*Scot.*), sponge (*informal*), touch (someone) for (*slang*), wheedle

scrounger bum (*informal*), cadger, freeloader (*slang*), parasite, sorner (*Scot.*), sponger (*informal*)

scrub *verb* **1.** clean, cleanse, rub, scour **2.** *informal* abandon, abolish, call off, cancel, delete, discontinue, do away with, drop, forget about, give up

scrubby insignificant, meagre, paltry, scrawny, spindly, stunted, underdeveloped, undersized

scruff 1. nape, scrag (*informal*) **2.** *informal* ragamuffin, ragbag (*informal*), scarecrow, sloven, tatterdemalion (*rare*), tramp

scruffy disreputable, draggletailed (*archaic*), frowzy, grungy, ill-groomed, mangy, messy, ragged, run-down, scrubby (*Brit. informal*), seedy, shabby, slatternly, sloppy (*informal*), slovenly, sluttish, squalid, tattered, tatty, ungroomed, unkempt, untidy

▷ **Antonyms** chic, dapper, natty, neat, soigné *or* soignée, spruce, tidy, well-dressed, well-groomed, well-turned-out

scrumptious appetizing, delectable, delicious, exquisite, inviting, luscious, magnificent, moreish (*informal*), mouthwatering, succulent, yummy (*slang*)

scrunch champ, chew, crumple, crunch, crush, mash, ruck up, squash

scruple 1. *verb* balk at, be loath, be reluctant, demur, doubt, falter, have misgivings about, have qualms about, hesitate, stick at, think twice about, vacillate, waver **2.** *~noun* caution, compunction, difficulty, doubt, hesitation, misgiving, perplexity, qualm, reluctance, second thoughts, squeamishness, twinge of conscience, uneasiness

scrupulous careful, conscientious, exact, fastidious, honourable, meticulous, minute, moral, nice, painstaking, precise, principled, punctilious, rigorous, strict, upright

▷ **Antonyms** amoral, careless, dishonest, inexact, reckless, slapdash, superficial, uncaring, unconscientious, unprincipled, unscrupulous, without scruples

scrutinize analyse, dissect, examine, explore, go over with a fine-tooth comb, inquire into, inspect, investigate, peruse, pore over, probe, research, scan, search, sift, study, work over

scrutiny analysis, close study, examination, exploration, inquiry, inspection, investigation, once-over (*informal*), perusal, search, sifting, study

scud blow, fly, haste, hasten, race, sail, shoot, skim, speed

scuffle 1. *verb* clash, come to blows, contend, exchange blows, fight, grapple, jostle, struggle, tussle 2. *~noun* affray (*Law*), *bagarre,* barney (*informal*), brawl, commotion, disturbance, fight, fray, ruck (*slang*), ruckus (*informal*), ruction (*informal*), rumpus, scrap (*informal*), scrimmage, set-to (*informal*), shindig (*informal*), shindy (*informal*), skirmish, tussle

sculpture *verb* carve, chisel, cut, fashion, form, hew, model, mould, sculp, sculpt, shape

scum 1. algae, crust, dross, film, froth, impurities, offscourings, scruff 2. *figurative canaille,* dregs of society, dross, lowest of the low, rabble, ragtag and bobtail, riffraff, rubbish, trash (*chiefly U.S. & Canad.*)

scupper defeat, demolish, destroy, disable, discomfit, overthrow, overwhelm, put paid to, ruin, torpedo, undo, wreck

scurrility abusiveness, billingsgate, coarseness, grossness, indecency, infamousness, invective, obloquy, obscenity, offensiveness, scurrilousness, vituperation

scurrilous abusive, coarse, defamatory, foul, foul-mouthed, gross, indecent, infamous, insulting, low, obscene, offensive, Rabelaisian, ribald, salacious, scabrous, scandalous, slanderous, vituperative, vulgar

▷ **Antonyms** civilized, decent, polite, proper, refined, respectful

scurry 1. *verb* beetle, dart, dash, fly, hurry, race, scamper, scoot, scud, scuttle, skim, sprint, whisk 2. *~noun* bustle, flurry, scampering, whirl

▷ **Antonyms** *~verb* amble, mooch (*slang*), mosey (*informal*), saunter, stroll, toddle, wander

scurvy *adjective* abject, bad, base, contemptible, despicable, dishonourable, ignoble, low, low-down (*informal*), mean, pitiful, rotten, scabby (*informal*), shabby, sorry, vile, worthless

scuttle beetle, bustle, hare (*Brit. informal*), hasten, hurry, run, rush, scamper, scoot, scramble, scud, scurry, scutter (*Brit. informal*)

sea *noun* 1. main, ocean, the briny (*informal*), the deep, the drink (*informal*), the waves 2. *figurative* abundance, expanse, mass, multitude, plethora, profusion, sheet, vast number 3. **at sea** adrift, astray, at a loss, at sixes and sevens, baffled, bewildered, confused, disoriented, lost, mystified, puzzled, upset *~adjective* 4. aquatic, briny, marine, maritime, ocean, ocean-going, oceanic, pelagic, salt, saltwater, seagoing

seafaring marine, maritime, nautical, naval, oceanic

seal *verb* 1. bung, close, cork, enclose, fasten, make airtight, plug, secure, shut, stop, stopper, stop up, waterproof 2. assure, attest, authenticate, confirm, establish, ratify, stamp, validate 3. clinch, conclude, consummate, finalize, settle, shake hands on (*informal*) 4. (*with* **off**) board up, fence off, isolate, put out of bounds, quarantine, segregate *~noun* 5. assurance, attestation, authentication, confirmation, imprimatur, insignia, notification, ratification, stamp

seam *noun* 1. closure, joint, suture (*Surgery*) 2. layer, lode, stratum, vein 3. furrow, line, ridge, scar, wrinkle

seamy corrupt, dark, degraded, disagreeable, disreputable, low, nasty, rough, sordid, squalid, unpleasant, unwholesome

sear blight, brand, burn, cauterize, desiccate, dry up *or* out, scorch, seal, shrivel, sizzle, wilt, wither

search *verb* 1. cast around, check, comb, examine, explore, ferret, forage, frisk (*informal*), go over with a fine-tooth comb, inquire, inspect, investigate, leave no stone unturned, look, look high and low, probe, pry, ransack, rifle through, rummage through, scour, scrutinize, seek, sift, turn inside out, turn upside down *~noun* 2. examination, exploration, going-over (*informal*), hunt, inquiry, inspection, investigation, pursuit, quest, researches, rummage, scrutiny 3. **in search of** hunting for, in need of, in pursuit of, looking for, making enquiries concerning, on the lookout for, on the track of, seeking

searching *adjective* close, intent, keen, minute, penetrating, piercing, probing, quizzical, severe, sharp, thorough

▷ **Antonyms** cursory, perfunctory, peripheral, sketchy, superficial

seasickness *mal de mer*

season *noun* 1. division, interval, juncture, occasion, opportunity, period, spell, term, time, time of year *~verb* 2. colour, enliven, flavour, lace, leaven, pep up, salt, salt and pepper, spice 3. acclimatize, accustom, anneal, discipline, habituate, harden, inure, mature, pre~

pare, toughen, train **4.** mitigate, moderate, qualify, temper

seasonable appropriate, convenient, fit, opportune, providential, suitable, timely, welcome, well-timed

seasoned battle-scarred, experienced, hardened, long-serving, mature, old, practised, time-served, veteran, weathered, well-versed

▷ **Antonyms** callow, green, inexperienced, new, novice, unpractised, unseasoned, unskilled

seasoning condiment, dressing, flavouring, relish, salt and pepper, sauce, spice

seat *noun* **1.** bench, chair, pew, settle, stall, stool, throne **2.** axis, capital, centre, cradle, headquarters, heart, hub, location, place, site, situation, source, station **3.** base, bed, bottom, cause, footing, foundation, ground, groundwork **4.** abode, ancestral hall, house, mansion, residence **5.** chair, constituency, incumbency, membership, place *~verb* **6.** accommodate, cater for, contain, have room *or* capacity for, hold, sit, take **7.** deposit, fix, install, locate, place, set, settle, sit

seating accommodation, chairs, places, room, seats

secede apostatize, break with, disaffiliate, leave, pull out, quit, resign, retire, separate, split from, withdraw

secession apostasy, break, defection, disaffiliation, seceding, split, withdrawal

secluded cloistered, cut off, isolated, lonely, off the beaten track, out-of-the-way, private, reclusive, remote, retired, sequestered, sheltered, solitary, tucked away, unfrequented

▷ **Antonyms** accessible, busy, frequented, open, public, sociable

seclusion concealment, hiding, isolation, ivory tower, privacy, purdah, remoteness, retirement, retreat, shelter, solitude

second[1] *adjective* **1.** following, next, subsequent, succeeding **2.** additional, alternative, extra, further, other, repeated **3.** inferior, lesser, lower, secondary, subordinate, supporting **4.** double, duplicate, reproduction, twin *~noun* **5.** assistant, backer, helper, supporter *~verb* **6.** advance, aid, approve, assist, back, commend, encourage, endorse, forward, further, give moral support to, go along with, help, promote, support

second[2] *noun* bat of an eye (*informal*), flash, instant, jiffy (*informal*), minute, moment, sec (*informal*), split second, tick (*Brit. informal*), trice, twinkling, twinkling of an eye, two shakes of a lamb's tail (*informal*)

secondary 1. derivative, derived, indirect, resultant, resulting, second-hand **2.** consequential, contingent, inferior, lesser, lower, minor, second-rate, subordinate, unimportant **3.** alternate, auxiliary, backup, extra, fall-back, relief, reserve, second, subsidiary, supporting

▷ **Antonyms** cardinal, chief, head, larger, main, major, more important, only, original, preceding, primary, prime, principal, superior

second childhood Alzheimer's disease, caducity, dotage, senility

second class *adjective* déclassé, indifferent, inferior, mediocre, no great shakes (*informal*), outclassed, second-best, second-rate, undistinguished, uninspiring

second-hand 1. *adjective* handed down, hand-me-down (*informal*), nearly new, reach-me-down (*informal*), used **2.** *~adverb* at second-hand, indirectly, on the grapevine (*informal*)

second in command depute (*Scot.*), deputy, number two, right-hand man, successor designate

secondly in the second place, next, second

second-rate bush-league (*Austral. & N.Z. informal*), cheap, cheap and nasty (*informal*), commonplace, dime-a-dozen (*informal*), end-of-the-pier (*Brit. informal*), for the birds (*informal*), inferior, low-grade, low-quality, low-rent (*informal, chiefly U.S.*), mediocre, no great shakes (*informal*), not much cop (*Brit. slang*), piss-poor (*taboo slang*), poor, rubbishy, shoddy, strictly for the birds (*informal*), substandard, tacky (*informal*), tawdry, tinhorn (*U.S. slang*), two-bit (*U.S. & Canad. slang*)

▷ **Antonyms** a cut above (*informal*), choice, de luxe, excellent, fine, first-class, first-rate, good quality, high-class, quality, superior

secrecy 1. cloak and dagger, concealment, confidentiality, huggermugger (*rare*), mystery, privacy, retirement, seclusion, silence, solitude, surreptitiousness **2.** clandestineness, covertness, furtiveness, secretiveness, stealth

secret *adjective* **1.** backstairs, behind someone's back, camouflaged, cloak-and-dagger, close, closet (*informal*), concealed, conspiratorial, covered, covert, disguised, furtive, hidden, hole-and-corner (*informal*), hush-hush (*informal*), reticent, shrouded, undercover, underground, under wraps, undisclosed, unknown, unpublished, unrevealed, unseen **2.** abstruse, arcane, cabbalistic, clandestine, classified, cryptic, esoteric, mysterious, occult, recondite **3.** hidden, out-of-the-way, private, retired, secluded, unfrequented, unknown **4.** close, deep, discreet, reticent, secretive, sly, stealthy, underhand *~noun* **5.** code, confidence, enigma, formula, key, mystery, recipe, skeleton in the cupboard **6. in secret** behind closed doors, by stealth, huggermugger (*archaic*), in camera, in~

cognito, secretly, slyly, surreptitiously
▷ **Antonyms** ~*adjective* apparent, candid, disclosed, exoteric, frank, manifest, obvious, open, overt, public, straightforward, unconcealed, visible, well-known

secret agent cloak-and-dagger man, nark (*Brit., Austral., & N.Z. slang*), spook (*U.S. & Canad. informal*), spy, undercover agent

secrete[1] *verb* bury, cache, conceal, cover, disguise, harbour, hide, screen, secure, shroud, stash (*informal*), stash away (*informal*), stow, veil
▷ **Antonyms** bare, display, exhibit, expose to view, leave in the open, reveal, show, uncover, unmask, unveil

secrete[2] *verb* emanate, emit, extravasate (*Medical*), extrude, exude, give off

secretion discharge, emission, excretion, extravasation (*Medical*), exudation

secretive cagey (*informal*), clamlike, close, cryptic, deep, enigmatic, playing one's cards close to one's chest, reserved, reticent, tight-lipped, uncommunicative, unforthcoming, withdrawn
▷ **Antonyms** candid, communicative, expansive, forthcoming, frank, open, unreserved

secretly behind closed doors, behind (someone's) back, clandestinely, confidentially, covertly, furtively, in camera, in confidence, in one's heart, in one's heart of hearts, in one's innermost thoughts, in secret, on the fly (*slang, chiefly Brit.*), on the q.t. (*informal*), on the sly, privately, quietly, stealthily, surreptitiously, under the counter, unobserved

sect camp, denomination, division, faction, group, party, schism, school, school of thought, splinter group, wing

sectarian **1.** *adjective* bigoted, clannish, cliquish, doctrinaire, dogmatic, exclusive, factional, fanatic, fanatical, hidebound, insular, limited, narrow-minded, parochial, partisan, rigid **2.** ~*noun* adherent, bigot, disciple, dogmatist, extremist, fanatic, partisan, true believer, zealot
▷ **Antonyms** ~*adjective* broad-minded, catholic, free-thinking, liberal, non-sectarian, open-minded, tolerant, unbigoted, unprejudiced

section *noun* **1.** component, cross section, division, fraction, fragment, instalment, part, passage, piece, portion, sample, segment, slice, subdivision **2.** *chiefly U.S.* area, department, district, region, sector, zone

sectional divided, exclusive, factional, local, localized, partial, regional, separate, separatist

sector area, category, district, division, part, quarter, region, stratum, subdivision, zone

secular civil, earthly, laic, laical, lay, nonspiritual, profane, state, temporal, worldly
▷ **Antonyms** divine, holy, religious, sacred, spiritual, theological

secure *adjective* **1.** immune, impregnable, in safe hands, out of harm's way, protected, safe, sheltered, shielded, unassailable, undamaged, unharmed **2.** dependable, fast, fastened, firm, fixed, fortified, immovable, stable, steady, tight **3.** assured, certain, confident, easy, reassured, sure **4.** absolute, conclusive, definite, in the bag (*informal*), reliable, solid, steadfast, tried and true, well-founded ~*verb* **5.** acquire, come by, gain, get, get hold of, land (*informal*), make sure of, obtain, pick up, procure, score (*slang*), win possession of **6.** attach, batten down, bolt, chain, fasten, fix, lash, lock, lock up, make fast, moor, padlock, rivet, tie up **7.** assure, ensure, guarantee, insure
▷ **Antonyms** ~*adjective* endangered, ill-at-ease, insecure, loose, not fastened, precarious, unassured, uncertain, uneasy, unfixed, unprotected, unsafe, unsound, unsure ~*verb* endanger, give up, imperil, leave unguaranteed, let (something) slip through (one's) fingers, loose, lose, unloose, untie

security **1.** asylum, care, cover, custody, immunity, preservation, protection, refuge, retreat, safekeeping, safety, sanctuary **2.** defence, guards, precautions, protection, safeguards, safety measures, surveillance **3.** assurance, certainty, confidence, conviction, ease of mind, freedom from doubt, positiveness, reliance, sureness **4.** collateral, gage, guarantee, hostage, insurance, pawn, pledge, surety
▷ **Antonyms** (*senses 1, 2 & 3*) exposure, insecurity, jeopardy, uncertainty, vulnerability

sedate calm, collected, composed, cool, decorous, deliberate, demure, dignified, earnest, grave, imperturbable, middle-aged, placid, proper, quiet, seemly, serene, serious, slow-moving, sober, solemn, staid, tranquil, unflappable (*informal*), unruffled
▷ **Antonyms** agitated, excitable, excited, flighty, impassioned, jumpy, nervous, undignified, uninhibited, unsteady, wild

sedative **1.** *adjective* allaying, anodyne, calmative, calming, lenitive, relaxing, sleep-inducing, soothing, soporific, tranquillizing **2.** ~*noun* anodyne, calmative, downer *or* down (*slang*), narcotic, opiate, sleeping pill, tranquillizer

sedentary desk, desk-bound, inactive, motionless, seated, sitting, torpid
▷ **Antonyms** active, mobile, motile, moving, on the go (*informal*)

sediment deposit, dregs, grounds, lees, precipitate, residuum, settlings

sedition agitation, disloyalty, incitement to riot, rabble-rousing, subversion, treason

seditious disloyal, dissident, insubordinate, mutinous, rebellious, refractory, revolutionary, subversive, treasonable

seduce 1. betray, corrupt, debauch, deflower, deprave, dishonour, ruin (*archaic*) **2.** allure, attract, beguile, deceive, decoy, ensnare, entice, inveigle, lead astray, lure, mislead, tempt

seduction 1. corruption, defloration, ruin (*archaic*) **2.** allure, enticement, lure, snare, temptation

seductive alluring, attractive, beguiling, bewitching, captivating, come-hither (*informal*), come-to-bed (*informal*), enticing, flirtatious, inviting, irresistible, provocative, ravishing, sexy (*informal*), siren, specious, tempting

seductress Circe, enchantress, *femme fatale,* Lorelei, siren, temptress, vamp (*informal*)

sedulous assiduous, busy, conscientious, constant, diligent, industrious, laborious, painstaking, persevering, persistent, tireless, unflagging, unremitting

see[1] *verb* **1.** behold, catch a glimpse of, catch sight of, check, check out (*informal*), clock (*Brit. slang*), descry, discern, distinguish, espy, eye, eyeball (*U.S. slang*), get a load of (*slang*), glimpse, heed, identify, lay *or* clap eyes on (*informal*), look, make out, mark, note, notice, observe, perceive, recognize, regard, sight, spot, take a dekko at (*Brit. slang*), view, witness **2.** appreciate, catch on (*informal*), comprehend, fathom, feel, follow, get, get the drift of, get the hang of (*informal*), grasp, know, make out, realize, take in, understand **3.** ascertain, determine, discover, find out, investigate, learn, make enquiries, refer to **4.** ensure, guarantee, make certain, make sure, mind, see to it, take care **5.** consider, decide, deliberate, give some thought to, judge, make up one's mind, mull over, reflect, think over **6.** confer with, consult, encounter, interview, meet, receive, run into, speak to, visit **7.** accompany, attend, escort, lead, show, usher, walk **8.** consort *or* associate with, court, date (*informal, chiefly U.S.*), go out with, go steady with (*informal*), keep company with, walk out with (*obsolete*) **9.** anticipate, divine, envisage, foresee, foretell, imagine, picture, visualize

see[2] *noun* bishopric, diocese

see about 1. attend to, consider, deal with, give some thought to, look after, see to, take care of **2.** investigate, look into, make enquiries, research

seed 1. egg, egg cell, embryo, germ, grain, kernel, ovule, ovum, pip, spore **2.** beginning, germ, inkling, nucleus, source, start, suspicion **3.** *figurative* children, descendants, heirs, issue, offspring, progeny, race, scions, spawn, successors **4. go *or* run to seed** decay, decline, degenerate, deteriorate, go downhill (*informal*), go to pieces, go to pot, go to rack and ruin, go to waste, let oneself go, retrogress

seedy 1. crummy (*slang*), decaying, dilapidated, down at heel, faded, grotty (*slang*), grubby, mangy, manky (*Scot. dialect*), old, run-down, scruffy, shabby, sleazy, slovenly, squalid, tatty, unkempt, worn **2.** *informal* ailing, ill, off colour, out of sorts, peely-wally (*Scot.*), poorly (*informal*), sickly, under the weather (*informal*), unwell

▷ **Antonyms** (*sense 1*) classy, elegant, fashionable, high-toned, posh (*informal, chiefly Brit.*), ritzy (*slang*), smart, swanky (*informal*), swish (*informal, chiefly Brit.*), top-drawer, up-market

see eye to eye accord, agree, click, coincide, concur, correspond, fit, get along, get on like a house on fire (*informal*), get on (together), harmonize, speak the same language

seeing *conjunction* as, inasmuch as, in view of the fact that, since

seek 1. be after, follow, go gunning for, go in pursuit of, go in quest of, go in search of, hunt, inquire, look for, pursue, search for **2.** aim, aspire to, attempt, endeavour, essay, have a go (*informal*), strive, try **3.** ask, beg, entreat, inquire, invite, petition, request, solicit

seem appear, assume, give the impression, have the *or* every appearance of, look, look as if, look like, look to be, pretend, sound like, strike one as being

seeming *adjective* apparent, appearing, illusory, ostensible, outward, quasi-, specious, surface

seemingly apparently, as far as anyone could tell, on the face of it, on the surface, ostensibly, outwardly, to all appearances, to all intents and purposes

seemly appropriate, becoming, befitting, *comme il faut,* decent, decorous, fit, fitting, in good taste, meet (*archaic*), nice, proper, suitable, suited, the done thing

▷ **Antonyms** improper, inappropriate, indecorous, in poor taste, out of keeping, out of place, unbecoming, unbefitting, unseemly, unsuitable

see over inspect, look round, see round, tour

seep bleed, exude, leach, leak, ooze, percolate, permeate, soak, trickle, weep, well

seepage exudation, leak, leakage, oozing, percolation

seer augur, predictor, prophet, sibyl, soothsayer

seesaw *verb* alternate, fluctuate, go from one extreme to the other, oscillate, pitch, swing, teeter

seethe 1. boil, bubble, churn, ferment, fizz, foam, froth 2. be in a state (*informal*), be furious, be incensed, be livid, breathe fire and slaughter, foam at the mouth, fume, get hot under the collar (*informal*), go ballistic (*slang, chiefly U.S.*), rage, see red (*informal*), simmer, storm 3. be alive with, swarm, teem

see-through diaphanous, filmy, fine, flimsy, gauzy, gossamer, sheer, thin, translucent, transparent

see through *verb* 1. be undeceived by, be wise to (*informal*), fathom, get to the bottom of, have (someone's) number (*informal*), not fall for, penetrate, read (someone) like a book 2. **see (something** *or* **someone) through** help out, keep at, persevere (with), persist, see out, stay to the bitter end, stick by, stick out (*informal*), support

see to arrange, attend to, be responsible for, do, look after, manage, organize, sort out, take care of, take charge of

segment bit, compartment, division, part, piece, portion, section, slice, wedge

segregate discriminate against, dissociate, isolate, separate, set apart, single out

▷ **Antonyms** amalgamate, desegregate, join together, mix, unify, unite

segregation apartheid (*in South Africa*), discrimination, isolation, separation

seize 1. catch up, clutch, collar (*informal*), fasten, grab, grasp, grip, lay hands on, snatch, take 2. apprehend, catch, get, grasp, nab (*informal*), nail (*informal*) 3. abduct, annex, appropriate, arrest, capture, commandeer, confiscate, hijack, impound, take by storm, take captive, take possession of

▷ **Antonyms** free, hand back, let go, let pass, loose, release, relinquish, set free, turn loose

seizure 1. abduction, annexation, apprehension, arrest, capture, commandeering, confiscation, grabbing, taking 2. attack, convulsion, fit, paroxysm, spasm

seldom hardly ever, infrequently, not often, occasionally, once in a blue moon (*informal*), rarely, scarcely ever

▷ **Antonyms** again and again, frequently, many a time, much, often, over and over again, time after time, time and again

select *verb* 1. cherry-pick, choose, opt for, pick, prefer, single out, sort out ~*adjective* 2. choice, excellent, first-class, first-rate, hand-picked, picked, posh (*informal, chiefly Brit.*), preferable, prime, rare, recherché, selected, special, superior, top-notch (*informal*) 3. cliquish, elite, exclusive, limited, privileged

▷ **Antonyms** ~*verb* eliminate, reject, turn down ~*adjective* cheap, indifferent, indiscriminate, inferior, ordinary, random, run-of-the-mill, second-rate, shoddy, substandard, unremarkable

selection 1. choice, choosing, option, pick, preference 2. anthology, assortment, choice, collection, line-up, medley, miscellany, mixed bag (*informal*), pick 'n' mix, potpourri, range, variety

selective careful, discerning, discriminating, discriminatory, eclectic, particular

▷ **Antonyms** all-embracing, careless, desultory, indiscriminate, unselective

self-assurance assertiveness, confidence, nerve, poise, positiveness, self-confidence, self-possession

self-centred egotistic, inward looking, narcissistic, self-absorbed, selfish, self-seeking, wrapped up in oneself

self-confidence aplomb, confidence, high morale, nerve, poise, self-assurance, self-reliance, self-respect

self-confident assured, confident, fearless, poised, secure, self-assured, self-reliant, sure of oneself

self-conscious affected, awkward, bashful, diffident, embarrassed, ill at ease, insecure, like a fish out of water, nervous, out of countenance, shamefaced, sheepish, uncomfortable

self-control calmness, cool, coolness, restraint, self-discipline, self-mastery, self-restraint, strength of mind *or* will, willpower

self-denial abstemiousness, asceticism, renunciation, self-abnegation, selflessness, self-sacrifice, unselfishness

self-esteem *amour-propre,* confidence, faith in oneself, pride, self-assurance, self-regard, self-respect, vanity

self-evident axiomatic, clear, cut-and-dried (*informal*), incontrovertible, inescapable, manifestly *or* patently true, obvious, undeniable, written all over (something)

self-government autonomy, democracy, devolution, home rule, independence, self-determination, self-rule, sovereignty

self-important arrogant, big-headed, bumptious, cocky, conceited, full of oneself, overbearing, pompous, presumptuous, pushy (*informal*), strutting, swaggering, swollen-headed

self-indulgence dissipation, excess, extravagance, incontinence, intemperance, self-gratification, sensualism

selfish egoistic, egoistical, egotistic, egotistical, greedy, looking out for number one (*informal*), mean, mercenary, narrow, self-centred, self-interested, self-seeking, ungenerous

▷ **Antonyms** altruistic, benevolent, considerate, generous, magnanimous, philanthropic, self-denying, selfless, self-sacrificing, ungrudging, unselfish

selfless altruistic, generous, magnanimous, self-denying, self-sacrificing, ungrudging, unselfish

self-possessed collected, confident, cool, cool as a cucumber (*informal*), poised, self-assured, sure of oneself, together (*slang*), unruffled

self-possession aplomb, composure, confidence, cool (*slang*), poise, sang-froid, self-command, unflappability (*informal*)

self-reliant able to stand on one's own two feet (*informal*), capable, independent, self-sufficient, self-supporting
▷ **Antonyms** dependent, helpless, reliant, relying on

self-respect *amour-propre,* dignity, faith in oneself, morale, one's own image, pride, self-esteem

self-restraint abstemiousness, forbearance, patience, self-command, self-control, self-discipline, willpower

self-righteous complacent, goody-goody (*informal*), holier-than-thou, hypocritical, pharisaic, pi (*Brit. slang*), pietistic, pious, priggish, sanctimonious, self-satisfied, smug, superior, too good to be true

self-sacrifice altruism, generosity, self-abnegation, self-denial, selflessness

self-satisfaction complacency, contentment, ease of mind, flush of success, glow of achievement, pride, self-approbation, self-approval, smugness

self-satisfied complacent, flushed with success, like a cat that has swallowed the cream *or* the canary, pleased with oneself, proud of oneself, puffed up, self-congratulatory, smug, too big for one's boots *or* breeches, well-pleased

self-seeking *adjective* acquisitive, calculating, careerist, fortune-hunting, gold-digging, looking out for number one (*informal*), mercenary, on the make (*slang*), opportunistic, out for what one can get, self-interested, selfish, self-serving

self-styled professed, quasi-, self-appointed, so-called, *soi-disant,* would-be

self-willed cussed (*informal*), headstrong, intractable, obstinate, opinionated, pig-headed, refractory, stiff-necked, stubborn, stubborn as a mule, ungovernable, wilful

sell **1**. barter, dispose of, exchange, put up for sale, trade **2**. be in the business of, deal in, handle, hawk, market, merchandise, peddle, retail, stock, trade in, traffic in, vend **3**. gain acceptance for, promote, put across **4**. *informal* (*with* **on**) convert to, convince of, get (someone) hooked on, persuade of, talk (someone) into, win (someone) over to **5**. betray, deliver up, give up, sell down the river (*informal*), sell out (*informal*), surrender
▷ **Antonyms** (*senses 1 & 2*) acquire, get, invest in, obtain, pay for, procure, purchase, shop for

seller agent, dealer, merchant, purveyor, rep, representative, retailer, salesman, saleswoman, shopkeeper, supplier, tradesman, traveller, vendor

selling **1**. business, commercial transactions, dealing, trading, traffic **2**. marketing, merchandising, promotion, salesmanship

sell out **1**. be out of stock of, dispose of, get rid of, run out of, sell up **2**. *informal* betray, break faith with, double-cross (*informal*), fail, give away, play false, rat on (*informal*), sell down the river (*informal*), stab in the back

semblance air, appearance, aspect, bearing, façade, figure, form, front, guise, image, likeness, mask, mien, pretence, resemblance, show, similarity, veneer

semidarkness dusk, gloaming (*Scot. or poetic*), gloom, half-light, murk, twilight, waning light

seminal *figurative* creative, formative, ground-breaking, imaginative, important, influential, innovative, original, productive

seminary academy, college, high school, institute, institution, school

send **1**. communicate, consign, convey, direct, dispatch, forward, remit, transmit **2**. cast, deliver, fire, fling, hurl, let fly, propel, shoot **3**. (*with* **off, out,** *etc.*) broadcast, discharge, emit, exude, give off, radiate **4**. *slang* charm, delight, electrify, enrapture, enthrall, excite, intoxicate, move, please, ravish, stir, thrill, titillate, turn (someone) on (*slang*) **5**. **send (someone) packing** discharge, dismiss, give (someone) the bird (*informal*), give (someone) the brushoff (*slang*), send away, send (someone) about his *or* her business, send (someone) away with a flea in his *or* her ear (*informal*)

send for call for, demand, order, request, summon

sendoff departure, farewell, going-away party, leave-taking, start, valediction

send-up imitation, mickey-take (*informal*), mockery, parody, satire, skit, spoof (*informal*), take-off (*informal*)

send up burlesque, imitate, lampoon, make fun of, mimic, mock, parody, satirize, spoof (*informal*), take off (*informal*), take the mickey out of (*informal*), take the piss out of (*taboo slang*)

senile decrepit, doddering, doting, failing, gaga (*informal*), imbecile, in one's dotage, in one's second childhood

senility Alzheimer's disease, caducity, decrepitude, dotage, infirmity, loss of one's faculties, second childhood, senescence, senile dementia

senior *adjective* elder, higher ranking, major (*Brit.*), older, superior
▷ **Antonyms** inferior, junior, lesser, lower, minor, subordinate, younger

senior citizen elder, O.A.P., old age pensioner, old *or* elderly person, pensioner, retired person

seniority eldership, longer service, precedence, priority, rank, superiority

sensation **1.** awareness, consciousness, feeling, impression, perception, sense, tingle **2.** agitation, commotion, crowd puller (*informal*), excitement, furore, hit (*informal*), scandal, stir, surprise, thrill, vibes (*slang*), wow (*slang, chiefly U.S.*)

sensational **1.** amazing, astounding, breathtaking, dramatic, electrifying, exciting, hair-raising, horrifying, lurid, melodramatic, revealing, scandalous, sensationalistic, shock-horror (*facetious*), shocking, spectacular, staggering, startling, thrilling, yellow (*of the press*) **2.** *informal* awesome (*slang*), bodacious (*slang, chiefly U.S.*), boffo (*slang*), brill (*informal*), brilliant, chillin' (*U.S. slang*), cracking (*Brit. informal*), crucial (*slang*), def (*slang*), excellent, exceptional, fabulous (*informal*), first class, impressive, jim-dandy (*slang*), marvellous, mean (*slang*), mega (*slang*), mind-blowing (*informal*), out of this world (*informal*), smashing (*informal*), sovereign, superb, topping (*Brit. slang*)
▷ **Antonyms** boring, commonplace, dull, humdrum, in good taste, mediocre, no great shakes (*informal*), ordinary, prosaic, run-of-the-mill, understated, undramatic, unexaggerated, unexciting, vanilla (*informal*)

sense *noun* **1.** faculty, feeling, sensation, sensibility **2.** appreciation, atmosphere, aura, awareness, consciousness, feel, impression, intuition, perception, premonition, presentiment, sentiment **3.** definition, denotation, drift, gist, implication, import, interpretation, meaning, message, nuance, purport, significance, signification, substance **4.** (*sometimes plural*) brains (*informal*), clear-headedness, cleverness, common sense, discernment, discrimination, gumption (*Brit. informal*), intelligence, judgment, mother wit, nous (*Brit. slang*), quickness, reason, sagacity, sanity, sharpness, smarts (*slang, chiefly U.S.*), tact, understanding, wisdom, wit(s) **5.** advantage, good, logic, point, purpose, reason, use, value, worth *~verb* **6.** appreciate, apprehend, be aware of, discern, divine, feel, get the impression, grasp, have a feeling in one's bones (*informal*), have a funny feeling (*informal*), have a hunch, just know, notice, observe, perceive, pick up, realize, suspect, understand
▷ **Antonyms** *~noun* (*sense 4*) bêtise (*rare*), folly, foolishness, idiocy, nonsense, silliness, stupidity *~verb* be unaware of, fail to grasp *or* notice, miss, misunderstand, overlook

senseless **1.** absurd, asinine, crazy, daft (*informal*), fatuous, foolish, goofy (*informal*), halfwitted, idiotic, illogical, imbecilic, inane, incongruous, inconsistent, irrational, ludicrous, mad, meaningless, mindless, moronic, nonsensical, pointless, ridiculous, silly, simple, stupid, unintelligent, unreasonable, unwise, without rhyme or reason **2.** anaesthetized, cold, deadened, insensate, insensible, numb, numbed, out, out cold, stunned, unconscious, unfeeling
▷ **Antonyms** conscious, intelligent, meaningful, rational, reasonable, sensible, sensitive, useful, valid, wise, worthwhile

sensibility **1.** responsiveness, sensitiveness, sensitivity, susceptibility **2.** (*often plural*) emotions, feelings, moral sense, sentiments, susceptibilities **3.** appreciation, awareness, delicacy, discernment, insight, intuition, perceptiveness, taste
▷ **Antonyms** deadness, insensibility, insensitivity, lack of awareness, numbness, unconsciousness, unperceptiveness, unresponsiveness

sensible **1.** canny, discreet, discriminating, down-to-earth, far-sighted, intelligent, judicious, matter-of-fact, practical, prudent, rational, realistic, reasonable, sagacious, sage, sane, shrewd, sober, sound, well-reasoned, well-thought-out, wise **2.** (*usually with* **of**) acquainted with, alive to, aware, conscious, convinced, mindful, observant, sensitive to, understanding **3.** appreciable, considerable, discernable, noticeable, palpable, perceptible, significant, tangible, visible
▷ **Antonyms** (*senses 1 & 2*) blind, daft (*informal*), foolish, idiotic, ignorant, injudicious, insensible, insensitive, irrational, senseless, silly, stupid, unaware, unmindful, unreasonable, unwise

sensitive **1.** delicate, easily affected, impressionable, reactive, responsive, sentient, susceptible, touchy-feely (*informal*) **2.** delicate, easily hurt, easily offended, easily upset, irritable, temperamental, tender, thin-skinned, touchy, umbrageous (*rare*) **3.** acute, fine, keen, perceptive, precise
▷ **Antonyms** approximate, callous, hard, hardened, imprecise, inexact, insensitive, obtuse, thick-skinned, tough, uncaring, unfeeling, unperceptive

sensitivity delicacy, reactiveness, reactivity, receptiveness, responsiveness, sensitiveness, susceptibility

sensual **1.** animal, bodily, carnal, epicurean, fleshly, luxurious, physical, unspiritual, voluptuous **2.** erotic, lascivious, lecherous, lewd, libidinous, licentious, lustful, randy (*informal, chiefly*

Brit.), raunchy (*slang*), sexual, sexy (*informal*), steamy (*informal*), unchaste

sensualist *bon vivant,* bon viveur, epicure, epicurean, hedonist, pleasure-lover, sybarite, voluptuary

sensuality animalism, carnality, eroticism, lasciviousness, lecherousness, lewdness, libidinousness, licentiousness, prurience, salaciousness, sexiness (*informal*), voluptuousness

sensuous bacchanalian, epicurean, gratifying, hedonistic, lush, pleasurable, rich, sensory, sumptuous, sybaritic
▷ **Antonyms** abstemious, ascetic, celibate, plain, self-denying, Spartan

sentence 1. *noun* condemnation, decision, decree, doom, judgment, order, pronouncement, ruling, verdict **2.** *~verb* condemn, doom, mete out justice to, pass judgment on, penalize

sententious 1. aphoristic, axiomatic, brief, compact, concise, epigrammatic, gnomic, laconic, pithy, pointed, short, succinct, terse **2.** canting, judgmental, moralistic, pompous, ponderous, preachifying (*informal*), sanctimonious

sentient conscious, feeling, live, living, reactive, sensitive

sentiment 1. emotion, sensibility, soft-heartedness, tender feeling, tenderness **2.** (*often plural*) attitude, belief, feeling, idea, judgment, opinion, persuasion, saying, thought, view, way of thinking **3.** emotionalism, mawkishness, overemotionalism, romanticism, sentimentality, slush (*informal*)

sentimental corny (*slang*), dewy-eyed, drippy (*informal*), emotional, gushy (*informal*), impressionable, maudlin, mawkish, mushy (*informal*), nostalgic, overemotional, pathetic, romantic, schmaltzy (*slang*), simpering, sloppy (*informal*), slushy (*informal*), soft-hearted, tearful, tear-jerking (*informal*), tender, touching, weepy (*informal*)
▷ **Antonyms** commonsensical, dispassionate, down-to-earth, earthy, hard-headed, practical, realistic, undemonstrative, unemotional, unfeeling, unromantic, unsentimental

sentimentality bathos, corniness (*slang*), emotionalism, gush (*informal*), mawkishness, mush (*informal*), nostalgia, pathos, play on the emotions, romanticism, schmaltz (*slang*), sloppiness (*informal*), slush (*informal*), sob stuff (*informal*), tenderness

sentinel *or* **sentry** guard, lookout, picket, watch, watchman

separable detachable, distinguishable, divisible, scissile, severable

separate *verb* **1.** break off, cleave, come apart, come away, come between, detach, disconnect, disentangle, disjoin, divide, keep apart, remove, sever, split, sunder, uncouple **2.** discriminate between, isolate, put on one side, segregate, single out, sort out **3.** bifurcate, break up, disunite, diverge, divorce, estrange, go different ways, part, part company, set at variance *or* at odds, split up *~adjective* **4.** detached, disconnected, discrete, disjointed, divided, divorced, isolated, unattached, unconnected **5.** alone, apart, autonomous, distinct, independent, individual, particular, single, solitary
▷ **Antonyms** *~verb* amalgamate, combine, connect, join, link, merge, mix, unite *~adjective* affiliated, alike, connected, interdependent, joined, similar, unified, united

separated apart, broken up, disassociated, disconnected, disunited, divided, living apart, parted, put asunder, separate, split up, sundered

separately alone, apart, independently, individually, one at a time, one by one, personally, severally, singly
▷ **Antonyms** as a group, as one, collectively, in a body, in concert, in unison, jointly, together

separation 1. break, detachment, disconnection, disengagement, disjunction, dissociation, disunion, division, gap, segregation, severance **2.** break-up, divorce, estrangement, farewell, leave-taking, parting, rift, split, split-up

septic festering, infected, poisoned, pussy, putrefactive, putrefying, putrid, suppurating, toxic

sepulchral 1. cheerless, dismal, funereal, gloomy, grave, lugubrious, melancholy, morbid, mournful, sad, sombre, Stygian, woeful **2.** deep, hollow, lugubrious, reverberating, sonorous

sepulchre burial place, grave, mausoleum, sarcophagus, tomb, vault

sequel conclusion, consequence, continuation, development, end, follow-up, issue, outcome, payoff (*informal*), result, upshot

sequence arrangement, chain, course, cycle, order, procession, progression, series, succession

sequestered cloistered, isolated, lonely, out-of-the-way, private, quiet, remote, retired, secluded, unfrequented

seraphic angelic, beatific, blissful, celestial, divine, heavenly, holy, pure, sublime

serene 1. calm, composed, imperturbable, peaceful, placid, sedate, tranquil, undisturbed, unruffled, untroubled **2.** bright, clear, cloudless, fair, halcyon, unclouded
▷ **Antonyms** (*sense 1*) agitated, anxious, disturbed, excitable, flustered, perturbed, troubled, uptight (*informal*)

serenity 1. calm, calmness, composure, peace, peacefulness, peace of mind, placidity, quietness, quietude, stillness, tranquillity **2.** brightness, clearness, fairness

serf bondsman, helot, liegeman, servant, slave, thrall, varlet (*archaic*), vassal, villein

series arrangement, chain, course, line, order, progression, run, sequence, set, string, succession, train

serious 1. grave, humourless, long-faced, pensive, sedate, sober, solemn, stern, thoughtful, unsmiling **2.** deliberate, determined, earnest, genuine, honest, in earnest, resolute, resolved, sincere **3.** crucial, deep, difficult, far-reaching, fateful, grim, important, momentous, no laughing matter, of moment *or* consequence, pressing, significant, urgent, weighty, worrying **4.** acute, alarming, critical, dangerous, grave, severe

▷ **Antonyms** capricious, carefree, flighty, flippant, frivolous, insignificant, insincere, jolly, joyful, light-hearted, minor, slight, smiling, trivial, uncommitted, undecided, unimportant

seriously 1. all joking aside, earnestly, gravely, in all conscience, in earnest, no joking (*informal*), sincerely, solemnly, thoughtfully, with a straight face **2.** acutely, badly, critically, dangerously, distressingly, gravely, grievously, severely, sorely

seriousness 1. earnestness, gravitas, gravity, humourlessness, sedateness, sobriety, solemnity, staidness, sternness **2.** danger, gravity, importance, moment, significance, urgency, weight

sermon 1. address, exhortation, homily **2.** dressing-down (*informal*), harangue, lecture, talking-to (*informal*)

serpentine coiling, crooked, meandering, sinuous, snaking, snaky, tortuous, twisting, twisty, winding

serrated notched, sawlike, sawtoothed, serrate, serriform (*Biology*), serrulate, toothed

serried assembled, close, compact, dense, massed, phalanxed

servant attendant, domestic, drudge, help, helper, lackey, liegeman, maid, menial, retainer, servitor (*archaic*), skivvy (*chiefly Brit.*), slave, varlet (*archaic*), vassal

serve 1. aid, assist, attend to, be in the service of, be of assistance, be of use, help, minister to, oblige, succour, wait on, work for **2.** act, attend, complete, discharge, do, fulfil, go through, observe, officiate, pass, perform **3.** answer, answer the purpose, be acceptable, be adequate, be good enough, content, do, do duty as, do the work of, fill the bill (*informal*), function as, satisfy, suffice, suit **4.** arrange, deal, deliver, dish up, distribute, handle, present, provide, purvey, set out, supply

service *noun* **1.** advantage, assistance, avail, benefit, help, ministrations, supply, use, usefulness, utility **2.** check, maintenance, overhaul, servicing **3.** business, duty, employ, employment, labour, office, work **4.** ceremony, function, observance, rite, worship *~verb* **5.** check, fine tune, go over, maintain, overhaul, recondition, repair, tune (up)

serviceable advantageous, beneficial, convenient, dependable, durable, efficient, functional, hard-wearing, helpful, operative, practical, profitable, usable, useful, utilitarian

▷ **Antonyms** impractical, inefficient, unserviceable, unusable, useless, worn-out

servile abject, base, bootlicking (*informal*), craven, cringing, fawning, grovelling, humble, low, mean, menial, obsequious, slavish, submissive, subservient, sycophantic, toadying, toadyish, unctuous

servility abjection, baseness, bootlicking (*informal*), fawning, grovelling, meanness, obsequiousness, self-abasement, slavishness, submissiveness, subservience, sycophancy, toadyism, unctuousness

serving *noun* helping, plateful, portion

servitude bondage, bonds, chains, enslavement, obedience, serfdom, slavery, subjugation, thraldom, thrall, vassalage

session assembly, conference, congress, discussion, get-together (*informal*), hearing, meeting, period, seminar, sitting, term

set[1] *verb* **1.** aim, apply, deposit, direct, embed, fasten, fix, install, lay, locate, lodge, mount, park (*informal*), place, plant, plonk, plump, position, put, rest, seat, situate, station, stick, turn **2.** agree upon, allocate, appoint, arrange, assign, conclude, decide (upon), designate, determine, establish, fix, fix up, name, ordain, regulate, resolve, schedule, settle, specify **3.** arrange, lay, make ready, prepare, spread **4.** adjust, coordinate, rectify, regulate, synchronize **5.** cake, condense, congeal, crystallize, gelatinize, harden, jell, solidify, stiffen, thicken **6.** allot, decree, impose, lay down, ordain, prescribe, specify **7.** decline, dip, disappear, go down, sink, subside, vanish *~noun* **8.** attitude, bearing, carriage, fit, hang, position, posture, turn **9.** *mise-en-scène,* scene, scenery, setting, stage set, stage setting *~adjective* **10.** agreed, appointed, arranged, customary, decided, definite, established, firm, fixed, prearranged, predetermined, prescribed, regular, scheduled, settled, usual **11.** artificial, conventional, formal, hackneyed, rehearsed, routine, standard, stereotyped, stock, traditional, unspontaneous **12.** entrenched, firm, hard and fast, hardened, hidebound, immovable, inflexible, rigid, strict,

stubborn **13.** (*with* **on** *or* **upon**) bent, determined, intent, resolute
▷ **Antonyms** (*sense 12*) flexible, free, open, open-minded, undecided

set[2] *noun* **1.** band, circle, class, clique, company, coterie, crew (*informal*), crowd, faction, gang, group, outfit, posse (*informal*), schism, sect **2.** assemblage, assortment, batch, collection, compendium, coordinated group, kit, outfit, series

set about 1. address oneself to, attack, begin, get cracking (*informal*), get down to, get to work, get weaving (*informal*), make a start on, put one's shoulder to the wheel (*informal*), roll up one's sleeves, sail into (*informal*), set to, start, tackle, take the first step, wade into **2.** assail, assault, attack, belabour, lambast(e), mug (*informal*), sail into (*informal*)

set against 1. balance, compare, contrast, juxtapose, weigh **2.** alienate, disunite, divide, drive a wedge between, estrange, make bad blood, make mischief, oppose, set at cross purposes, set at odds, set by the ears (*informal*), sow dissension

set aside 1. earmark, keep, keep back, put on one side, reserve, save, select, separate, set apart, single out **2.** abrogate, annul, cancel, discard, dismiss, nullify, overrule, overturn, quash, reject, render null and void, repudiate, reverse

setback bit of trouble, blow, bummer (*slang*), check, defeat, disappointment, hitch, hold-up, misfortune, rebuff, reverse, upset, whammy (*informal, chiefly U.S.*)

set back delay, hinder, hold up, impede, retard, slow

set off 1. depart, embark, leave, sally forth, set out, start out **2.** detonate, explode, ignite, kick-start, light, set in motion, touch off, trigger (off) **3.** bring out the highlights in, enhance, show off, throw into relief

set on assail, assault, attack, fall upon, fly at, go for, incite, instigate, let fly at, pitch into (*informal*), pounce on, sail into (*informal*), set about, sic, spur on, urge

set out 1. arrange, array, describe, detail, display, dispose, elaborate, elucidate, exhibit, explain, expose to view, lay out, present, set forth **2.** begin, embark, get under way, hit the road (*slang*), sally forth, set off, start out, take to the road

setting backdrop, background, back story, context, frame, locale, location, *mise en scène,* mounting, perspective, scene, scenery, set, site, surround, surroundings

settle 1. adjust, dispose, order, put into order, regulate, set to rights, straighten out, work out **2.** choose, clear up, complete, conclude, decide, dispose of, put an end to, reconcile, resolve **3.** (*often with* **on** *or* **upon**) agree, appoint, arrange, choose, come to an agreement, confirm, decide, determine, establish, fix **4.** allay, calm, compose, lull, pacify, quell, quiet, quieten, reassure, relax, relieve, sedate, soothe, tranquillize **5.** alight, bed down, come to rest, descend, land, light, make oneself comfortable **6.** dwell, inhabit, live, make one's home, move to, put down roots, reside, set up home, take up residence **7.** colonize, found, people, pioneer, plant, populate **8.** acquit oneself of, clear, discharge, liquidate, pay, quit, square (up) **9.** decline, fall, sink, subside
▷ **Antonyms** (*sense 4*) agitate, bother, discompose, disquieten, disturb, rattle, trouble, unsettle, upset

settlement 1. adjustment, agreement, arrangement, completion, conclusion, confirmation, disposition, establishment, resolution, termination, working out **2.** clearance, clearing, defrayal, discharge, liquidation, payment, satisfaction **3.** colonization, colony, community, encampment, hamlet, outpost, peopling

settler colonist, colonizer, frontiersman, immigrant, pioneer, planter

set-to argument, argy-bargy (*Brit. informal*), barney (*informal*), brush, disagreement, dust-up (*informal*), fight, fracas, quarrel, row, scrap (*informal*), slanging match (*Brit.*), spat, squabble, wrangle

setup arrangement, circumstances, conditions, organization, regime, structure, system

set up 1. arrange, begin, compose, establish, found, initiate, install, institute, make provision for, organize, prearrange, prepare **2.** back, build up, establish, finance, promote, put some beef into (*informal*), strengthen, subsidize **3.** assemble, build, construct, elevate, erect, put together, put up, raise

set upon ambush, assail, assault, attack, beat up, fall upon, go for, lay into (*informal*), mug (*informal*), put the boot in (*slang*), set about, turn on, work over (*slang*)

sever 1. bisect, cleave, cut, cut in two, detach, disconnect, disjoin, disunite, divide, part, rend, separate, split, sunder **2.** abandon, break off, dissociate, dissolve, put an end to, terminate
▷ **Antonyms** (*sense 1*) attach, connect, fix together, join, link, unite (*sense 2*) continue, maintain, uphold

several *adjective* assorted, different, disparate, distinct, divers (*archaic*), diverse, indefinite, individual, manifold, many, particular, respective, single, some, sundry, various

severe 1. austere, cruel, Draconian, drastic, hard, harsh, inexorable, iron-handed, oppressive, pitiless, relentless, rigid, strict, unbending, unrelenting **2.** cold, disapproving, dour, flinty, forbidding, grave, grim, serious, sober, stern, strait-laced, tight-lipped, unsmiling **3.** acute, bitter, critical, dangerous, distressing, extreme, fierce, grinding, inclement, intense, violent **4.** ascetic, austere, chaste, classic, forbidding, functional, plain, restrained, severe, simple, Spartan, unadorned, unembellished, unfussy **5.** arduous, demanding, difficult, exacting, fierce, hard, punishing, rigorous, stringent, taxing, tough, unrelenting **6.** astringent, biting, caustic, cutting, harsh, mordacious, mordant, satirical, scathing, unsparing, vitriolic

▷ **Antonyms** (*senses 1, 2, 3, 5 & 6*) affable, clement, compassionate, easy, genial, gentle, kind, lax, lenient, manageable, mild, minor, moderate, relaxed, temperate, tractable (*sense 4*) embellished, fancy, ornamental, ornate

severely 1. harshly, like a ton of bricks (*informal*), rigorously, sharply, sternly, strictly, with an iron hand, with a rod of iron **2.** acutely, badly, critically, dangerously, extremely, gravely, hard, seriously, sorely

severity austerity, gravity, hardness, harshness, plainness, rigour, seriousness, severeness, sternness, strictness, stringency, toughness

sex 1. gender **2.** *informal* coition, coitus, copulation, fornication, going to bed (with someone), intimacy, legover (*slang*), lovemaking, nookie (*slang*), rumpy-pumpy (*slang*), (sexual) intercourse, sexual relations, the other (*informal*) **3.** desire, facts of life, libido, reproduction, sexuality, the birds and the bees (*informal*)

sex appeal allure, desirability, glamour, it (*informal*), magnetism, oomph (*informal*), seductiveness, sensuality, sexiness (*informal*), voluptuousness

sexless androgynous, asexual, epicene, hermaphrodite, neuter, nonsexual, parthenogenetic

sexual 1. carnal, coital, erotic, intimate, of the flesh, sensual, sexy **2.** genital, procreative, reproductive, sex, venereal

sexual intercourse bonking (*informal*), carnal knowledge, coition, coitus, commerce (*archaic*), congress, consummation, copulation, coupling, fucking (*taboo*), intimacy, legover (*slang*), mating, nookie (*slang*), penetration, rumpy-pumpy (*slang*), screwing (*taboo*), shagging (*taboo*), the other (*informal*), union

sexuality bodily appetites, carnality, desire, eroticism, lust, sensuality, sexiness (*informal*), virility, voluptuousness

sexy arousing, beddable, bedroom, come-hither (*informal*), cuddly, erotic, flirtatious, inviting, kissable, naughty, provocative, provoking, seductive, sensual, sensuous, slinky, suggestive, titillating, voluptuous

shabby 1. dilapidated, down at heel, faded, frayed, having seen better days, mean, neglected, poor, ragged, run-down, scruffy, seedy, tattered, tatty, the worse for wear, threadbare, worn, worn-out **2.** cheap, contemptible, despicable, dirty, dishonourable, ignoble, low, low-down (*informal*), mean, rotten (*informal*), scurvy, shameful, shoddy, ungentlemanly, unworthy

▷ **Antonyms** (*sense 1*) handsome, in mint condition, neat, new, smart, well-dressed, well-kempt, well-kept, well-to-do (*sense 2*) fair, generous, honourable, praiseworthy, worthy

shack cabin, dump (*informal*), hovel, hut, lean-to, shanty, shiel (*Scot.*), shieling (*Scot.*)

shackle *noun* **1.** (*often plural*) bond, chain, fetter, gyve (*archaic*), handcuff, hobble, iron, leg-iron, manacle, rope, tether *~verb* **2.** bind, chain, fetter, handcuff, hobble, manacle, pinion, put in irons, secure, tether, tie, trammel **3.** constrain, embarrass, encumber, hamper, hamstring, impede, inhibit, limit, obstruct, restrain, restrict, tie (someone's) hands

shade *noun* **1.** coolness, dimness, dusk, gloom, gloominess, obscurity, screen, semidarkness, shadiness, shadow, shadows **2. put into the shade** eclipse, make pale by comparison, outclass, outshine, overshadow **3.** blind, canopy, cover, covering, curtain, screen, shield, veil **4.** colour, hue, stain, tinge, tint, tone **5.** amount, dash, degree, difference, gradation, graduation, hint, nuance, semblance, suggestion, suspicion, trace, variety **6.** apparition, eidolon, ghost, manes, phantom, shadow, spectre, spirit *~verb* **7.** cast a shadow over, cloud, conceal, cover, darken, dim, hide, mute, obscure, protect, screen, shadow, shield, shut out the light, veil

shadow *noun* **1.** cover, darkness, dimness, dusk, gathering darkness, gloaming (*Scot. or poetic*), gloom, obscurity, protection, shade, shelter **2.** hint, suggestion, suspicion, trace **3.** eidolon, ghost, image, phantom, remnant, representation, spectre, vestige **4.** blight, cloud, gloom, sadness *~verb* **5.** cast a shadow over, darken, overhang, screen, shade, shield **6.** dog, follow, spy on, stalk, tail (*informal*), trail

shadowy 1. crepuscular, dark, dim, dusky, funereal, gloomy, indistinct, murky, obscure, shaded, shady, tenebrious, tenebrous **2.** dim, dreamlike, faint, ghostly, illusory, imaginary, impalpable, intangible, nebulous, obscure, phantom, spectral, undefined, unreal, unsubstantial, vague, wraithlike

shady **1.** bosky (*literary*), bowery, cool, dim, leafy, shaded, shadowy, umbrageous **2.** *informal* crooked, disreputable, dodgy (*Brit., Austral., & N.Z. informal*), dubious, fishy (*informal*), questionable, shifty, slippery, suspect, suspicious, unethical, unscrupulous, untrustworthy

▷ **Antonyms** (*sense 1*) bright, exposed, open, out in the open, sunlit, sunny, unshaded (*sense 2*) above-board, ethical, honest, honourable, reputable, respectable, straight, trustworthy, upright

shaft **1.** handle, pole, rod, shank, stem, upright **2.** beam, gleam, ray, streak **3.** barb, cut, dart, gibe, sting, thrust

shaggy hairy, hirsute, long-haired, rough, tousled, unkempt, unshorn

▷ **Antonyms** close-cropped, crew-cut, cropped, flat-woven, neatly-trimmed, shorn, short-haired, short-piled, smooth

shake *verb* **1.** bump, fluctuate, jar, joggle, jolt, jounce, oscillate, quake, quiver, rock, shiver, shudder, sway, totter, tremble, vibrate, waver, wobble **2.** brandish, flourish, wave **3.** (*often with* **up**) agitate, churn, convulse, rouse, stir **4.** discompose, distress, disturb, frighten, intimidate, move, rattle (*informal*), shock, unnerve, upset **5.** impair, pull the rug out from under (*informal*), undermine, weaken *~noun* **6.** agitation, convulsion, disturbance, jar, jerk, jolt, jounce, pulsation, quaking, shiver, shock, shudder, trembling, tremor, vibration **7.** *informal* instant, jiffy (*informal*), moment, second, tick (*Brit. informal*), trice

shake off dislodge, elude, get away from, get rid of, get shot of (*slang*), give the slip, leave behind, lose, rid oneself of, throw off

shake up agitate, churn (up), disturb, mix, overturn, reorganize, shock, stir (up), turn upside down, unsettle, upset

shaky **1.** all of a quiver (*informal*), faltering, insecure, precarious, quivery, rickety, tottering, trembling, tremulous, unstable, unsteady, weak, wobbly **2.** dubious, iffy (*informal*), questionable, suspect, uncertain, undependable, unreliable, unsound, unsupported

▷ **Antonyms** dependable, firm, secure, stable, steady, strong

shallow **1.** *adjective figurative* empty, flimsy, foolish, frivolous, idle, ignorant, meaningless, puerile, simple, skin-deep, slight, superficial, surface, trivial, unintelligent **2.** *~noun* (*often plural*) bank, flat, sandbank, sand bar, shelf, shoal

▷ **Antonyms** *~adjective* analytical, comprehensive, deep, in-depth, meaningful, penetrating, perceptive, profound, searching, serious, thoughtful, weighty *~noun* abyss, chasm, deep, depth, gorge, gulf, pit, void

sham **1.** *noun* counterfeit, feint, forgery, fraud, hoax, humbug, imitation, impostor, imposture, phoney *or* phony (*informal*), pretence, pretender, pseud (*informal*), wolf in sheep's clothing **2.** *~adjective* artificial, bogus, counterfeit, ersatz, false, feigned, imitation, mock, phoney *or* phony (*informal*), pretended, pseud (*informal*), pseudo (*informal*), simulated, spurious, synthetic **3.** *~verb* affect, assume, counterfeit, fake, feign, imitate, play possum, pretend, put on, simulate

▷ **Antonyms** *~noun* master, original, the genuine article, the real McCoy (*or* McKay), the real thing *~adjective* authentic, bona fide, genuine, legitimate, natural, real, sound, true, unfeigned, veritable

shambles anarchy, chaos, confusion, disarray, disorder, disorganization, havoc, madhouse, mess, muddle

shambling awkward, clumsy, lumbering, lurching, shuffling, ungainly, unsteady

shambolic anarchic, at sixes and sevens, chaotic, confused, disordered, disorganized, inefficient, in total disarray, muddled, topsy-turvy, unsystematic

shame *noun* **1.** blot, contempt, degradation, derision, discredit, disgrace, dishonour, disrepute, ill repute, infamy, obloquy, odium, opprobrium, reproach, scandal, skeleton in the cupboard, smear **2.** abashment, chagrin, compunction, embarrassment, humiliation, ignominy, loss of face, mortification, shamefacedness **3. put to shame** disgrace, eclipse, outclass, outdo, outstrip, show up, surpass *~verb* **4.** abash, confound, disconcert, disgrace, embarrass, humble, humiliate, mortify, reproach, ridicule, take (someone) down a peg (*informal*) **5.** blot, debase, defile, degrade, discredit, dishonour, smear, stain

▷ **Antonyms** *~noun* (*sense 1*) credit, distinction, esteem, glory, honour, pride, renown, self-respect (*sense 2*) brass neck (*Brit. informal*), brazenness, cheek, shamelessness, unabashedness *~verb* acclaim, credit, do credit to, enhance the reputation of, honour, make proud

shamefaced **1.** bashful, blushing, diffident, hesitant, modest, shrinking, shy, timid **2.** abashed, ashamed, chagrined, conscience-stricken, contrite, discomfited, embarrassed, humiliated, mortified, red-faced, remorseful, sheepish

shameful **1.** atrocious, base, dastardly, degrading, disgraceful, dishonourable, ignominious, indecent, infamous, low, mean, outrageous, reprehensible, scandalous, unbecoming, unworthy, vile, wicked **2.** blush-making (*informal*), cringe-making (*Brit. informal*), degrading, embarrassing, humiliating, mortifying, shaming

▷ **Antonyms** admirable, creditable, estimable, exemplary, honourable, laudable, right, worthy

shameless abandoned, audacious, barefaced, brash, brazen, corrupt, depraved, dissolute, flagrant, hardened, immodest, improper, impudent, incorrigible, indecent, insolent, profligate, reprobate, unabashed, unashamed, unblushing, unprincipled, wanton

shanty bothy (*Scot.*), cabin, hovel, hut, lean-to, shack, shed, shiel (*Scot.*), shieling (*Scot.*)

shape *noun* **1.** build, configuration, contours, cut, figure, form, lines, make, outline, profile, silhouette **2.** frame, model, mould, pattern **3.** appearance, aspect, form, guise, likeness, semblance **4.** condition, fettle, health, kilter, state, trim *~verb* **5.** create, fashion, form, make, model, mould, produce **6.** accommodate, adapt, convert, define, develop, devise, frame, guide, modify, plan, prepare, regulate, remodel

shapeless amorphous, asymmetrical, battered, embryonic, formless, indeterminate, irregular, misshapen, nebulous, undeveloped, unstructured
▷ **Antonyms** comely, curvaceous, elegant, graceful, neat, trim, well-formed, well-proportioned, well-turned

shapely comely, curvaceous, elegant, graceful, neat, sightly, trim, well-formed, well-proportioned, well-turned

shape up be promising, come on, develop, look good, proceed, progress, turn out

share **1.** *verb* apportion, assign, distribute, divide, divvy up (*informal*), go Dutch (*informal*), go fifty-fifty (*informal*), go halves, parcel out, partake, participate, receive, split, use in common **2.** *~noun* allotment, allowance, contribution, cut (*informal*), division, due, lot, part, portion, proportion, quota, ration, whack (*informal*)

sharp *adjective* **1.** acute, cutting, honed, jagged, keen, knife-edged, knifelike, pointed, razor-sharp, serrated, sharpened, spiky **2.** abrupt, distinct, extreme, marked, sudden **3.** alert, apt, astute, bright, clever, discerning, knowing, long-headed, observant, on the ball (*informal*), penetrating, perceptive, quick, quick-witted, ready, subtle **4.** artful, crafty, cunning, dishonest, fly (*slang*), shrewd, sly, smart, unscrupulous, wily **5.** acute, distressing, excruciating, fierce, intense, painful, piercing, severe, shooting, sore, stabbing, stinging, violent **6.** clear, clear-cut, crisp, distinct, well-defined **7.** *informal* chic, classy (*slang*), dressy, fashionable, natty (*informal*), smart, snappy, stylish, trendy (*informal*) **8.** acerb, acrimonious, barbed, biting, bitter, caustic, cutting, harsh, hurtful, mordacious, mordant, sarcastic, sardonic, scathing, severe, trenchant, vitriolic **9.** acerb, acerbic, acetic, acid, acrid, burning, hot, piquant, pungent, sour, tart, vinegary *~adverb* **10.** exactly, on the dot, on time, precisely, promptly, punctually **11.** abruptly, suddenly, unexpectedly, without warning
▷ **Antonyms** *~adjective* (*sense 1*) blunt, dull, edgeless, pointed, rounded, unsharpened (*sense 2*) even, gentle, gradual, moderate, progressive (*sense 3*) dim, dull-witted, dumb (*informal*), slow, slow-on-the-uptake, stupid (*sense 4*) artless, guileless, ingenuous, innocent, naive, simple, undesigning (*sense 6*) blurred, fuzzy, ill-defined, indistinct, unclear (*sense 8*) amicable, courteous, friendly, gentle, kindly, mild (*sense 9*) bland, mild, tasteless *~adverb* (*sense 10*) approximately, more or less, roughly, round about, vaguely (*sense 11*) bit by bit, gently, gradually, slowly

sharpen edge, grind, hone, put an edge on, strop, whet

shatter **1.** break, burst, crack, crush, crush to smithereens, demolish, explode, implode, pulverize, shiver, smash, split **2.** blast, blight, bring to nought, demolish, destroy, disable, exhaust, impair, overturn, ruin, torpedo, wreck **3.** break (someone's) heart, crush, devastate, dumbfound, knock the stuffing out of (someone) (*informal*), upset

shattered all in (*slang*), clapped out (*Austral. & N.Z. informal*), crushed, dead beat (*informal*), dead tired (*informal*), devastated, dog-tired (*informal*), done in (*informal*), drained, exhausted, jiggered (*informal*), knackered (*slang*), ready to drop, shagged out (*Brit. slang*), spent, tired out, weary, wiped out (*informal*), worn out, zonked (*slang*)

shattering crushing, devastating, overwhelming, paralysing, severe, stunning

shave *verb* **1.** crop, pare, plane, shear, trim **2.** brush, graze, touch

shed *verb* **1.** afford, cast, diffuse, drop, emit, give, give forth, pour forth, radiate, scatter, shower, spill, throw **2.** cast off, discard, exuviate, moult, slough

sheen brightness, burnish, gleam, gloss, lustre, patina, polish, shine, shininess

sheepish abashed, ashamed, chagrined, embarrassed, foolish, mortified, self-conscious, shamefaced, silly, uncomfortable
▷ **Antonyms** assertive, audacious, bold, brash, brass-necked (*Brit. informal*), brazen, confident, intractable, obdurate, unabashed, unapologetic, unblushing, unembarrassed

sheer **1.** abrupt, headlong (*archaic*), perpendicular, precipitous, steep **2.** absolute, arrant, complete, downright, out-and-out, pure, rank, thoroughgoing, total, unadulterated, unalloyed, unmitigated, unqualified, utter **3.** *of fabrics* diaphanous, fine, gauzy, gossamer, see-through, thin, transparent
▷ **Antonyms** (*sense 1*) gentle, gradual,

horizontal, moderate, slanting, sloping (*sense 3*) coarse, heavy, impenetrable, opaque, thick

sheet 1. coat, film, folio, lamina, layer, leaf, membrane, overlay, pane, panel, piece, plate, slab, stratum, surface, veneer **2.** area, blanket, covering, expanse, stretch, sweep

shell *noun* **1.** carapace, case, husk, pod *~verb* **2.** husk, shuck **3.** attack, barrage, blitz, bomb, bombard, strafe, strike *~noun* **4.** chassis, frame, framework, hull, skeleton, structure

shell out ante up (*informal, chiefly U.S.*), disburse, expend, fork out (*slang*), give, hand over, lay out (*informal*), pay out

shelter 1. *verb* cover, defend, guard, harbour, hide, protect, safeguard, seek refuge, shield, take in, take shelter **2.** *~noun* asylum, awning, cover, covert, defence, guard, haven, protection, refuge, retreat, roof over one's head, safety, sanctuary, screen, security, shiel (*Scot.*), umbrella

▷ **Antonyms** *~verb* endanger, expose, hazard, imperil, lay open, leave open, make vulnerable, risk, subject

sheltered cloistered, conventual, ensconced, hermitic, isolated, protected, quiet, reclusive, retired, screened, secluded, shaded, shielded, withdrawn

▷ **Antonyms** exposed, laid bare, made public, open, public, unconcealed, unprotected, unsheltered

shelve defer, dismiss, freeze, hold in abeyance, hold over, lay aside, mothball, pigeonhole, postpone, put aside, put off, put on ice, put on the back burner (*informal*), suspend, table (*U.S.*), take a rain check on (*U.S. & Canad. informal*)

shepherd *verb* conduct, convoy, guide, herd, marshal, steer, usher

shield *noun* **1.** buckler, escutcheon (*Heraldry*), targe (*archaic*) **2.** aegis, bulwark, cover, defence, guard, protection, rampart, safeguard, screen, shelter, ward (*archaic*) *~verb* **3.** cover, defend, guard, protect, safeguard, screen, shelter, ward off

shift *verb* **1.** alter, budge, change, displace, fluctuate, move, move around, rearrange, relocate, remove, reposition, swerve, switch, transfer, transpose, vary, veer **2.** *as in* **shift for oneself** assume responsibility, contrive, devise, fend, get along, look after, make do, manage, plan, scheme, take care of *~noun* **3.** about-turn, alteration, change, displacement, fluctuation, modification, move, permutation, rearrangement, removal, shifting, switch, transfer, veering **4.** artifice, contrivance, craft, device, dodge, equivocation, evasion, expedient, move, resource, ruse, stratagem, subterfuge, trick, wile

shiftless aimless, good-for-nothing, idle, incompetent, indolent, inefficient, inept, irresponsible, lackadaisical, lazy, slothful, unambitious, unenterprising

shifty contriving, crafty, deceitful, devious, duplicitous, evasive, fly-by-night (*informal*), furtive, scheming, slippery, sly, tricky, underhand, unprincipled, untrustworthy, wily

▷ **Antonyms** dependable, guileless, honest, honourable, open, reliable, trustworthy, upright

shillyshally *verb* be irresolute *or* indecisive, dilly-dally (*informal*), dither (*chiefly Brit.*), falter, fluctuate, haver (*Brit.*), hem and haw, hesitate, hum and haw, seesaw, swither (*Scot.*), vacillate, waver, yo-yo (*informal*)

shimmer 1. *verb* dance, gleam, glisten, phosphoresce, scintillate, twinkle **2.** *~noun* diffused light, gleam, glimmer, glow, incandescence, iridescence, lustre, phosphorescence, unsteady light

shin *verb* ascend, clamber, climb, scale, scramble, swarm

shine *verb* **1.** beam, emit light, flash, give off light, glare, gleam, glimmer, glisten, glitter, glow, radiate, scintillate, shimmer, sparkle, twinkle **2.** be conspicuous, be distinguished, be outstanding, be pre-eminent, excel, stand out, stand out in a crowd, star, steal the show **3.** brush, buff, burnish, polish, rub up *~noun* **4.** brightness, glare, gleam, lambency, light, luminosity, radiance, shimmer, sparkle **5.** glaze, gloss, lustre, patina, polish, sheen

shining 1. aglow, beaming, bright, brilliant, effulgent, gleaming, glistening, glittering, luminous, radiant, resplendent, shimmering, sparkling **2.** *figurative* brilliant, celebrated, conspicuous, distinguished, eminent, glorious, illustrious, leading, outstanding, splendid

shiny agleam, bright, burnished, gleaming, glistening, glossy, lustrous, nitid (*poetic*), polished, satiny, sheeny

shipshape Bristol fashion, businesslike, neat, orderly, spick-and-span, tidy, trig (*archaic or dialect*), trim, uncluttered, well-ordered, well-organized, well-regulated

shirk avoid, bob off (*Brit. slang*), bodyswerve (*Scot.*), dodge, duck (out of) (*informal*), evade, get out of, scrimshank (*Brit. military slang*), shun, sidestep, skive (*Brit. slang*), slack

shirker clock-watcher, dodger, gold brick (*U.S. slang*), idler, malingerer, quitter, scrimshanker (*Brit. military slang*), shirk, skiver (*Brit. slang*), slacker

shiver[1] *verb* **1.** palpitate, quake, quiver, shake, shudder, tremble *~noun* **2.** flutter, *frisson,* quiver, shudder, thrill, tremble, trembling, tremor **3. the shivers** chattering teeth, chill, goose flesh, goose pimples, the shakes (*informal*)

shiver[2] *verb* break, crack, fragment, shatter, smash, smash to smithereens, splinter

shivery chilled, chilly, cold, quaking, quivery, shaking, shuddery, trembly

shoal sandbank, sand bar, shallow, shelf

shock *verb* **1.** agitate, appal, astound, disgust, disquiet, give (someone) a turn (*informal*), gross out (*U.S. slang*), horrify, jar, jolt, nauseate, numb, offend, outrage, paralyse, raise eyebrows, revolt, scandalize, shake, shake out of one's complacency, shake up (*informal*), sicken, stagger, stun, stupefy, traumatize, unsettle *~noun* **2.** blow, bolt from the blue, bombshell, breakdown, collapse, consternation, distress, disturbance, prostration, rude awakening, state of shock, stupefaction, stupor, trauma, turn (*informal*), upset, whammy (*informal, chiefly U.S.*) **3.** blow, clash, collision, encounter, impact, jarring, jolt

shocking abominable, appalling, atrocious, detestable, disgraceful, disgusting, disquieting, distressing, dreadful, foul, frightful, from hell (*informal*), ghastly, hellacious (*U.S. slang*), hideous, horrible, horrifying, loathsome, monstrous, nauseating, obscene, odious, offensive, outrageous, repulsive, revolting, scandalous, sickening, stupefying, unspeakable, X-rated (*informal*)
▷ **Antonyms** admirable, decent, delightful, excellent, expected, fine, first-rate, gratifying, honourable, laudable, marvellous, pleasant, praiseworthy, satisfying, unsurprising, wonderful

shoddy cheap-jack (*informal*), cheapo (*informal*), inferior, junky (*informal*), low-rent (*informal, chiefly U.S.*), poor, rubbishy, second-rate, slipshod, tacky (*informal*), tatty, tawdry, trashy
▷ **Antonyms** accurate, careful, considerate, craftsman-like, excellent, fastidious, fine, first-rate, meticulous, noble, quality, superlative, well-made

shoemaker bootmaker, cobbler, souter (*Scot.*)

shoot[1] *verb* **1.** bag, blast (*slang*), blow away (*slang, chiefly U.S.*), bring down, hit, kill, open fire, pick off, plug (*slang*), pump full of lead (*slang*), zap (*slang*) **2.** discharge, emit, fire, fling, hurl, launch, let fly, project, propel **3.** barrel (along) (*informal, chiefly U.S. & Canad.*), bolt, burn rubber (*informal*), charge, dart, dash, flash, fly, hurtle, race, rush, scoot, speed, spring, streak, tear, whisk, whizz (*informal*)

shoot[2] **1.** *noun* branch, bud, offshoot, scion, slip, sprig, sprout, twig **2.** *~verb* bud, burgeon, germinate, put forth new growth, sprout

shop boutique, emporium, hypermarket, market, mart, store, supermarket

shore *noun* beach, coast, foreshore, lakeside, sands, seaboard (*chiefly U.S.*), seashore, strand (*poetic*), waterside

shore (up) augment, brace, buttress, hold, prop, reinforce, strengthen, support, underpin

short *adjective* **1.** abridged, brief, clipped, compendious, compressed, concise, curtailed, laconic, pithy, sententious, succinct, summary, terse **2.** diminutive, dumpy, fubsy (*archaic or dialect*), knee high to a gnat, knee high to a grasshopper, little, low, petite, small, squat, wee **3.** brief, fleeting, momentary, short-lived, short-term **4.** (*often with* **of**) deficient, inadequate, insufficient, lacking, limited, low (on), meagre, poor, scant, scanty, scarce, short-handed, slender, slim, sparse, strapped (for) (*slang*), tight, wanting **5.** abrupt, blunt, brusque, crusty, curt, discourteous, gruff, impolite, offhand, sharp, terse, testy, uncivil **6.** direct, straight **7.** *of pastry* brittle, crisp, crumbly, friable *~adverb* **8.** abruptly, by surprise, suddenly, unaware, without warning **9. cut short** abbreviate, arrest, butt in, curtail, cut in on, dock, halt, interrupt, nip (something) in the bud, reduce, stop, terminate **10. fall short** be inadequate, disappoint, fail, fall down on (*informal*), not come up to expectations *or* scratch (*informal*) **11. in short** briefly, in a nutshell, in a word, in essence, to come to the point, to cut a long story short, to put it briefly **12. short of: a.** apart from, except, other than, unless **b.** deficient in, in need of, lacking, low (on), missing, wanting
▷ **Antonyms** *~adjective* (*sense 1*) diffuse, lengthy, long, long-drawn-out, long-winded, prolonged, rambling, unabridged, verbose, wordy (*sense 2*) big, high, lanky, lofty, tall (*sense 3*) extended, long, long-term (*sense 4*) abundant, adequate, ample, bountiful, copious, inexhaustible, plentiful, sufficient, well-stocked (*sense 5*) civil, courteous, polite *~adverb* (*sense 8*) bit by bit, gently, gradually, little by little, slowly

shortage dearth, deficiency, deficit, failure, inadequacy, insufficiency, lack, leanness, paucity, poverty, scarcity, shortfall, want
▷ **Antonyms** abundance, adequate amount, excess, overabundance, plethora, profusion, sufficiency, surfeit, surplus

shortcoming defect, drawback, failing, fault, flaw, foible, frailty, imperfection, weakness, weak point

shorten abbreviate, abridge, curtail, cut, cut back, cut down, decrease, diminish, dock, downsize, lessen, prune, reduce, trim, truncate, turn up
▷ **Antonyms** draw out, elongate, expand, extend, increase, lengthen, make longer, prolong, protract, spin out, stretch

short-lived brief, ephemeral, fleeting, impermanent, passing, short, temporary, transient, transitory

shortly 1. anon (*archaic*), any minute now, before long, erelong (*archaic or poetic*), in a little while, presently, soon **2.** abruptly, curtly, sharply, tartly, tersely **3.** briefly, concisely, in a few words, succinctly

short-sighted 1. blind as a bat, myopic, near-sighted **2.** careless, ill-advised, ill-considered, impolitic, impractical, improvident, imprudent, injudicious, seeing no further than (the end of) one's nose, unthinking

short-staffed below strength, short-handed, undermanned, understaffed

short-tempered choleric, fiery, hot-tempered, impatient, irascible, peppery, quick-tempered, ratty (*Brit. & N.Z. informal*), testy, touchy

shot[1] *noun* **1.** discharge, lob, pot shot, throw **2.** ball, bullet, lead, pellet, projectile, slug **3.** marksman, shooter **4.** *informal* attempt, chance, conjecture, crack (*informal*), effort, endeavour, essay, go (*informal*), guess, opportunity, stab (*informal*), surmise, try, turn **5. by a long shot: a.** by far, easily, far and away, indubitably, undoubtedly, without doubt **b.** by any means, in any circumstances, on any account **6.** attempt, have a bash (*informal*), have a crack (*informal*), have a go **have a shot** *informal* have a stab (*informal*), tackle, try, try one's luck **7. like a shot** at once, eagerly, immediately, like a bat out of hell (*slang*), like a flash, quickly, unhesitatingly **8. shot in the arm** *informal* boost, encouragement, fillip, impetus, lift, stimulus

shot[2] *adjective* iridescent, moiré, opalescent, watered

shoulder *noun* **1. give (someone) the cold shoulder** blank (*slang*), cut (*informal*), ignore, kick in the teeth (*slang*), ostracize, put down, rebuff, send (someone) to Coventry, shun, snub **2. put one's shoulder to the wheel** *informal* apply oneself, buckle down to (*informal*), exert oneself, get down to, make every effort, set to work, strive **3. rub shoulders with** *informal* associate with, consort with, fraternize with, hobnob with, mix with, socialize with **4. shoulder to shoulder** as one, in cooperation, in partnership, in unity, jointly, side by side, together, united **5. straight from the shoulder** candidly, directly, frankly, man to man, outright, plainly, pulling no punches (*informal*), straight, unequivocally, with no holds barred *~verb* **6.** accept, assume, bear, be responsible for, carry, take on, take upon oneself **7.** elbow, jostle, press, push, shove, thrust

shoulder blade scapula

shout 1. *noun* bellow, call, cry, roar, scream, yell **2.** *~verb* bawl, bay, bellow, call (out), cry (out), holler (*informal*), hollo, raise one's voice, roar, scream, yell

shout down drown, drown out, overwhelm, silence

shove *verb* crowd, drive, elbow, impel, jostle, press, propel, push, shoulder, thrust

shovel *verb* convey, dredge, heap, ladle, load, move, scoop, shift, spoon, toss

shove off bugger off (*taboo slang*), clear off (*informal*), depart, fuck off (*offensive taboo slang*), get on one's bike (*Brit. slang*), go away, go to hell (*informal*), leave, pack one's bags (*informal*), push off (*informal*), scram (*informal*), sling one's hook (*Brit. slang*), slope off, take oneself off, vamoose (*slang, chiefly U.S.*)

show *verb* **1.** appear, be visible, blow wide open (*slang*), disclose, display, divulge, evidence, evince, exhibit, indicate, make known, manifest, present, register, reveal, testify to **2.** assert, clarify, demonstrate, elucidate, evince, explain, instruct, point out, present, prove, teach **3.** accompany, attend, conduct, escort, guide, lead **4.** accord, act with, bestow, confer, grant *~noun* **5.** array, demonstration, display, exhibition, expo (*informal*), exposition, fair, manifestation, pageant, pageantry, parade, representation, sight, spectacle, view **6.** affectation, air, appearance, display, illusion, likeness, ostentation, parade, pose, pretence, pretext, profession, semblance **7.** entertainment, presentation, production

▷ **Antonyms** (*senses 1 & 2*) be invisible, conceal, deny, disprove, gainsay (*archaic or literary*), hide, keep secret, mask, obscure, refute, suppress, veil, withhold

showdown breaking point, clash, climax, confrontation, crisis, culmination, *dénouement,* exposé, face-off (*slang*), moment of truth

shower *noun* **1.** *figurative* barrage, deluge, downpour, fusillade, plethora, rain, stream, torrent, volley **2.** *Brit. slang* bunch of layabouts, crew, rabble *~verb* **3.** deluge, heap, inundate, lavish, load, pour, rain, spray, sprinkle

showing *noun* **1.** demonstration, display, exhibition, presentation, staging **2.** account of oneself, appearance, demonstration, impression, performance, show, track record **3.** evidence, representation, statement

showman entertainer, impresario, performer, publicist, stage manager

show-off boaster, braggadocio, braggart, egotist, exhibitionist, hot dog (*chiefly U.S.*), peacock, poseur, swaggerer

show off 1. advertise, demonstrate, display, exhibit, flaunt, parade, spread out **2.** blow one's own trumpet, boast, brag, hot-dog (*chiefly U.S.*), make a spectacle of oneself, shoot a line (*informal*), strut one's stuff (*chiefly U.S.*), swagger

show up 1. expose, highlight, lay bare, pinpoint, put the spotlight on, reveal, unmask **2.** appear, be conspicuous, be visible, catch the eye, leap to the eye, stand out **3.** *informal* embarrass, let down, mortify, put to shame, shame, show in a bad light **4.** *informal* appear, arrive, come, make an appearance, put in an appearance, show one's face, turn up

showy brash, flamboyant, flash (*informal*), flashy, garish, gaudy, loud, ostentatious, over the top (*informal*), pompous, pretentious, splashy (*informal*), tawdry, tinselly
▷ **Antonyms** discreet, low-key, muted, quiet, restrained, subdued, tasteful, unobtrusive

shred *noun* **1.** bit, fragment, piece, rag, ribbon, scrap, sliver, snippet, tatter **2.** *figurative* atom, grain, iota, jot, particle, scrap, trace, whit

shrew ballbreaker (*slang*), dragon (*informal*), fury, harpy, harridan, nag, scold, spitfire, termagant (*rare*), virago, vixen, Xanthippe

shrewd acute, artful, astute, calculated, calculating, canny, clever, crafty, cunning, discerning, discriminating, far-seeing, far-sighted, fly (*slang*), intelligent, keen, knowing, long-headed, perceptive, perspicacious, sagacious, sharp, sly, smart, wily
▷ **Antonyms** artless, dull, gullible, imprudent, ingenuous, innocent, naive, obtuse, slow-witted, stupid, trusting, undiscerning, unsophisticated, unworldly

shrewdly artfully, astutely, cannily, cleverly, far-sightedly, knowingly, perceptively, perspicaciously, sagaciously, with all one's wits about one, with consummate skill

shrewdness acumen, acuteness, astuteness, canniness, discernment, grasp, judgment, penetration, perspicacity, quick wits, sagacity, sharpness, smartness, suss (*slang*)

shrewish bad-tempered, cantankerous, complaining, discontented, fault-finding, ill-humoured, ill-natured, ill-tempered, litigious, nagging, peevish, petulant, quarrelsome, scolding, sharp-tongued, vixenish

shriek *verb/noun* cry, holler, howl, scream, screech, squeal, wail, whoop, yell

shrill acute, ear-piercing, ear-splitting, high, high-pitched, penetrating, piercing, piping, screeching, sharp
▷ **Antonyms** deep, dulcet, mellifluous, silver-toned, soft, soothing, sweet-sounding, velvety, well-modulated

shrink 1. contract, decrease, deflate, diminish, downsize, drop off, dwindle, fall off, grow smaller, lessen, narrow, shorten, shrivel, wither, wrinkle **2.** cower, cringe, draw back, flinch, hang back, quail, recoil, retire, shy away, wince, withdraw
▷ **Antonyms** (*sense 1*) balloon, dilate, distend, enlarge, expand, increase, inflate, mushroom, stretch, swell (*sense 2*) attack, challenge, confront, embrace, face, receive, welcome

shrivel 1. burn, dry (up), parch, scorch, sear **2.** dehydrate, desiccate, dwindle, shrink, wilt, wither, wizen, wrinkle

shrivelled desiccated, dried up, dry, sere (*archaic*), shrunken, withered, wizened, wrinkled

shroud *verb* **1.** blanket, cloak, conceal, cover, envelop, hide, screen, swathe, veil *~noun* **2.** cerecloth, cerement, covering, grave clothes, winding sheet **3.** cloud, mantle, pall, screen, veil

shudder 1. *verb* convulse, quake, quiver, shake, shiver, tremble **2.** *~noun* convulsion, quiver, spasm, trembling, tremor

shuffle 1. drag, scrape, scuff, scuffle, shamble **2.** confuse, disarrange, disorder, intermix, jumble, mix, rearrange, shift **3.** (*usually with* **off** *or* **out of**) beat about the bush, beg the question, cavil, dodge, equivocate, evade, flannel (*Brit. informal*), gloss over, hedge, prevaricate, pussyfoot (*informal*), quibble

shun avoid, body-swerve (*Scot.*), cold-shoulder, elude, eschew, evade, fight shy of, give (someone *or* something) a wide berth, have no part in, keep away from, shy away from, steer clear of

shut 1. bar, close, draw to, fasten, push to, seal, secure, slam **2.** (*with* **in, out,** *etc.*) cage, confine, enclose, exclude, impound, imprison, pound, wall off *or* up
▷ **Antonyms** (*sense 1*) open, throw wide, unbar, unclose, undo, unfasten, unlock

shut down cease, cease operating, close, discontinue, halt, shut up, stop, switch off

shut out 1. bar, black, blackball, debar, exclude, keep out, lock out, ostracize **2.** block out, conceal, cover, hide, mask, screen, veil

shuttle *verb* alternate, commute, go back and forth, go to and fro, ply, seesaw, shunt

shut up 1. bottle up, box in, cage, confine, coop up, immure, imprison, incarcerate, intern, keep in **2.** *informal* be quiet, button it (*slang*), button one's lip (*slang*), cut the cackle (*informal*), fall silent, gag, hold one's tongue, hush, keep one's trap shut (*slang*), muzzle, pipe down (*slang*), put a sock in it (*Brit. slang*), silence

shy[1] **1.** *adjective* backward, bashful, cautious, chary, coy, diffident, distrustful, hesitant, modest, mousy, nervous, reserved, reticent, retiring, self-conscious, self-effacing, shrinking, suspicious, timid, wary **2.** *~verb (sometimes with* **off** *or* **away**) balk, buck, draw back, flinch, quail, rear, recoil, start, swerve, take fright, wince

▷ **Antonyms** *~adjective* assured, bold, brash, cheeky, confident, fearless, forward, pushy (*informal*), rash, reckless, self-assured, self-confident, unsuspecting, unwary

shy[2] *verb* cast, chuck (*informal*), fling, hurl, lob (*informal*), pitch, propel, send, sling, throw, toss

shyness bashfulness, diffidence, lack of confidence, modesty, mousiness, nervousness, reticence, self-consciousness, timidity, timidness, timorousness

sibyl Cassandra, oracle, prophetess, Pythia, pythoness, seer

sick 1. green about the gills (*informal*), green around the gills (*informal*), ill, nauseated, nauseous, puking (*slang*), qualmish, queasy **2.** ailing, diseased, feeble, indisposed, laid up (*informal*), on the sick list (*informal*), poorly (*informal*), under par (*informal*), under the weather, unwell, weak **3.** *informal* black, ghoulish, macabre, morbid, sadistic **4.** *informal (often with* **of**) blasé, bored, disgusted, displeased, fed up, jaded, revolted, satiated, tired, weary

▷ **Antonyms** (*senses 1 & 2*) able-bodied, fine, fit, fit and well, fit as a fiddle, hale and hearty, healthy, robust, tranquil, untroubled, unworried, up to par, well

sicken 1. disgust, gross out (*U.S. slang*), make one's gorge rise, nauseate, repel, revolt, turn one's stomach **2.** ail, be stricken by, contract, fall ill, go down with, show symptoms of, take sick

sickening cringe-making (*Brit. informal*), disgusting, distasteful, foul, loathsome, nauseating, nauseous, noisome, offensive, putrid, repulsive, revolting, stomach-turning (*informal*), vile, yucky *or* yukky (*slang*)

▷ **Antonyms** beneficial, curative, delightful, health-giving, heartening, inviting, marvellous, mouth-watering, pleasant, salutary, tempting, therapeutic, wholesome, wonderful

sickly 1. ailing, bilious, bloodless, delicate, faint, feeble, indisposed, infirm, in poor health, lacklustre, languid, pallid, peaky, pining, unhealthy, wan, weak **2.** bilious (*informal*), cloying, icky (*informal*), mawkish, nauseating, revolting (*informal*), syrupy (*informal*)

sickness 1. barfing (*U.S. slang*), (the) collywobbles (*slang*), nausea, queasiness, puking (*slang*), vomiting **2.** affliction, ailment, bug (*informal*), complaint, disease, disorder, illness, indisposition, infirmity, lurgi (*informal*), malady

side *noun* **1.** border, boundary, division, edge, limit, margin, part, perimeter, periphery, rim, sector, verge **2.** aspect, face, facet, flank, hand, part, surface, view **3.** angle, light, opinion, point of view, position, slant, stand, standpoint, viewpoint **4.** camp, cause, faction, party, sect, team **5.** *Brit. slang* airs, arrogance, insolence, pretentiousness *~adjective* **6.** flanking, lateral **7.** ancillary, incidental, indirect, lesser, marginal, minor, oblique, roundabout, secondary, subordinate, subsidiary *~verb* **8.** *(usually with* **with**) ally with, associate oneself with, befriend, favour, go along with, join with, second, support, take the part of, team up with (*informal*)

▷ **Antonyms** *~noun (sense 1)* centre, core, heart, middle *~adjective* central, essential, focal, fundamental, key, main, middle, primary, principal *~verb* counter, oppose, stand against, withstand

sidelong *adjective* covert, indirect, oblique, sideways

side-splitting farcical, hilarious, hysterical, rollicking, uproarious

sidestep avoid, body-swerve (*Scot.*), bypass, circumvent, dodge, duck (*informal*), elude, evade, find a way round, skip, skirt

sidetrack deflect, distract, divert, lead off the subject

sideways 1. *adverb* crabwise, edgeways, laterally, obliquely, sidelong, sidewards, to the side **2.** *~adjective* oblique, side, sidelong, slanted

sidle creep, edge, inch, slink, sneak, steal

siesta catnap, doze, forty winks (*informal*), kip (*Brit. slang*), nap, rest, sleep, snooze (*informal*), zizz (*Brit. informal*)

sieve 1. *noun* colander, riddle, screen, sifter, strainer, tammy cloth **2.** *~verb* bolt, remove, riddle, separate, sift, strain

sift 1. bolt, filter, pan, part, riddle, separate, sieve **2.** analyse, examine, fathom, go through, investigate, pore over, probe, research, screen, scrutinize, work over

sigh *verb* **1.** breathe, complain, grieve, lament, moan, sorrow, sough, suspire (*archaic*) **2.** *(often with* **for**) eat one's heart out over, languish, long, mourn, pine, yearn

sight *noun* **1.** eye, eyes, eyesight, seeing, vision **2.** appearance, apprehension, eyeshot, field of vision, ken, perception, range of vision, view, viewing, visibility **3.** display, exhibition, pageant, scene, show, spectacle, vista **4.** *informal* blot on the landscape (*informal*), eyesore, fright (*informal*), mess, monstrosity, spectacle **5. catch sight of** descry, espy, glimpse, recognize, spot, view *~verb* **6.** behold, discern, distinguish, make out, observe, perceive, see, spot

sign *noun* **1.** clue, evidence, gesture, giveaway, hint, indication, manifestation, mark, note, proof, signal, spoor, suggestion, symptom, token, trace, vestige **2.** board, notice, placard, warning **3.** badge, character, cipher, device, emblem, ensign, figure, logo, mark, representation, symbol **4.** augury, auspice, foreboding, forewarning, omen, portent, presage, warning, writing on the wall *~verb* **5.** autograph, endorse, initial, inscribe, set one's hand to, subscribe **6.** beckon, gesticulate, gesture, indicate, signal, use sign language, wave

signal 1. *noun* beacon, cue, flare, gesture, go-ahead (*informal*), green light, indication, indicator, mark, sign, token **2.** *~adjective* conspicuous, distinguished, eminent, exceptional, extraordinary, famous, memorable, momentous, notable, noteworthy, outstanding, remarkable, serious (*informal*), significant, striking **3.** *~verb* beckon, communicate, gesticulate, gesture, give a sign to, indicate, motion, nod, sign, wave

sign away abandon, dispose of, forgo, give up all claim to, lose, relinquish, renounce, surrender, transfer, waive

significance 1. force, implication(s), import, meaning, message, point, purport, sense, signification **2.** consequence, consideration, importance, impressiveness, matter, moment, relevance, weight

significant 1. denoting, eloquent, expressing, expressive, indicative, knowing, meaning, meaningful, pregnant, suggestive **2.** critical, important, material, momentous, noteworthy, serious, vital, weighty

▷ **Antonyms** immaterial, inconsequential, insignificant, irrelevant, meaningless, nit-picking, nugatory, of no consequence, paltry, petty, trivial, unimportant, worthless

signify 1. announce, be a sign of, betoken, communicate, connote, convey, denote, evidence, exhibit, express, imply, indicate, intimate, matter, mean, portend, proclaim, represent, show, stand for, suggest, symbolize **2.** *informal* be of importance *or* significance, carry weight, count, matter

sign on *or* **up 1.** contract with, enlist, enrol, join, join up, register, volunteer **2.** employ, engage, hire, put on the payroll, recruit, take into service, take on, take on board (*informal*)

silence *noun* **1.** calm, hush, lull, noiselessness, peace, quiescence, quiet, stillness **2.** dumbness, muteness, reticence, speechlessness, taciturnity, uncommunicativeness *~verb* **3.** cut off, cut short, deaden, extinguish, gag, muffle, quell, quiet, quieten, stifle, still, strike dumb, subdue, suppress

▷ **Antonyms** *~noun* babble, bawling, cacophony, chatter, clamour, din, garrulousness, hubbub, loquaciousness, murmuring, noise, prattle, racket, shouting, sound, speech, talk, talking, tumult, uproar, verbosity, whispering, yelling *~verb* amplify, broadcast, champion, disseminate, encourage, foster, make louder, promote, promulgate, publicize, rouse, spread, support, ungag

silent 1. hushed, muted, noiseless, quiet, soundless, still, stilly (*poetic*) **2.** dumb, mum, mute, nonvocal, not talkative, speechless, struck dumb, taciturn, tongue-tied, uncommunicative, unspeaking, voiceless, wordless **3.** aphonic (*Phonetics*), implicit, implied, tacit, undeclared, understood, unexpressed, unpronounced, unspoken

silently as quietly as a mouse (*informal*), dumbly, inaudibly, in silence, mutely, noiselessly, quietly, soundlessly, speechlessly, without a sound, wordlessly

silhouette 1. *noun* delineation, form, outline, profile, shape **2.** *~verb* delineate, etch, outline, stand out

silky silken, sleek, smooth, velvety

silly *adjective* **1.** absurd, asinine, brainless, childish, dopy (*slang*), dozy (*Brit. informal*), fatuous, foolhardy, foolish, frivolous, giddy, goofy (*informal*), idiotic, immature, imprudent, inane, inappropriate, irresponsible, meaningless, pointless, preposterous, puerile, ridiculous, senseless, stupid, unwise, witless **2.** *informal* benumbed, dazed, groggy (*informal*), in a daze, muzzy, stunned, stupefied *~noun* **3.** *informal* clot (*Brit. informal*), duffer (*informal*), dweeb (*U.S. slang*), goose (*informal*), ignoramus, nerd *or* nurd (*slang*), ninny, nitwit (*informal*), plonker (*slang*), prat (*slang*), silly-billy (*informal*), simpleton, twit (*informal*), wally (*slang*)

▷ **Antonyms** *~adjective* acute, aware, bright, clever, intelligent, mature, perceptive, profound, prudent, reasonable, sane, sensible, serious, smart, thoughtful, well-thought-out, wise

silt 1. *noun* alluvium, deposit, ooze, residue, sediment, sludge **2.** *~verb* (*usually with* **up**) choke, clog, congest, dam

silver 1. *adjective* argent (*poetic*), pearly, silvered, silvery **2.** *~noun* silver plate, silverware

similar alike, analogous, close, comparable, congruous, corresponding, cut from the same cloth, homogeneous, homogenous, in agreement, like, much the same, of a piece, resembling, uniform

▷ **Antonyms** antithetical, clashing, contradictory, contrary, different, disparate, dissimilar, diverse, heterogeneous, irreconcilable, opposite, unalike, unrelated, various, varying

similarity affinity, agreement, analogy, closeness, comparability, concordance, congruence, correspondence, likeness,

point of comparison, relation, resemblance, sameness, similitude
▷ **Antonyms** antithesis, contradictoriness, difference, disagreement, discordance, discrepancy, disparity, dissimilarity, diversity, heterogeneity, incomparability, irreconcilability, unalikeness, variation, variety

similarly by the same token, correspondingly, in like manner, likewise

simmer *verb figurative* be agitated, be angry, be tense, be uptight (*informal*), boil, burn, fume, rage, see red (*informal*), seethe, smart, smoulder

simmer down calm down, collect oneself, contain oneself, control oneself, cool off *or* down, get down off one's high horse (*informal*), grow quieter, unwind (*informal*)

simper grimace, smile affectedly, smile coyly, smile self-consciously, smirk, titter

simpering *adjective* affected, coy, self-conscious

simple 1. clear, easy, easy-peasy (*slang*), elementary, intelligible, lucid, manageable, plain, straightforward, uncomplicated, understandable, uninvolved **2.** classic, clean, natural, plain, severe, Spartan, unadorned, uncluttered, unembellished, unfussy **3.** elementary, pure, single, unalloyed, unblended, uncombined, undivided, unmixed **4.** artless, childlike, frank, green, guileless, ingenuous, innocent, naive, natural, simplistic, sincere, unaffected, unpretentious, unsophisticated **5.** bald, basic, direct, frank, honest, naked, plain, sincere, stark, undeniable, unvarnished **6.** homely, humble, lowly, modest, rustic, unpretentious **7.** brainless, credulous, dense, dumb (*informal*), feeble, feeble-minded, foolish, half-witted, moronic, obtuse, shallow, silly, slow, stupid, thick
▷ **Antonyms** (*sense 1*) advanced, complex, complicated, convoluted, difficult, elaborate, highly developed, intricate, involved, refined, sophisticated (*sense 2*) contrived, elaborate, fussy, intricate, ornate (*sense 4*) artful, smart, sophisticated, worldly, worldly-wise (*sense 6*) extravagant, fancy, flashy (*sense 7*) astute, bright, clever, intelligent, knowing, on the ball, quick, quick on the uptake, quick-witted, sharp, smart, wise

simple-minded 1. a bit lacking (*informal*), addle-brained, backward, brainless, dead from the neck up (*informal*), dim-witted, feeble-minded, foolish, idiot, idiotic, moronic, retarded, simple, stupid **2.** artless, natural, unsophisticated

simpleton berk (*Brit. slang*), blockhead, booby, charlie (*Brit. informal*), chump, coot, dickhead (*slang*), dipstick (*Brit. slang*), divvy (*Brit. slang*), dolt, dope (*informal*), dork (*slang*), dullard, dunce, dweeb (*U.S. slang*), fathead (*informal*), fool, fuckwit (*taboo slang*), geek (*slang*), gobshite (*Irish taboo slang*), gonzo (*slang*), goose (*informal*), greenhorn (*informal*), idiot, imbecile (*informal*), jackass, jerk (*slang, chiefly U.S. & Canad.*), moron, nerd *or* nurd (*slang*), nincompoop, ninny, nitwit (*informal*), numpty (*Scot. informal*), numskull *or* numbskull, oaf, plank (*Brit. slang*), schmuck (*U.S. slang*), Simple Simon, stupid (*informal*), twerp *or* twirp (*informal*), twit (*informal, chiefly Brit.*), wally (*slang*)

simplicity 1. absence of complications, clarity, clearness, ease, easiness, elementariness, obviousness, straightforwardness **2.** clean lines, lack of adornment, modesty, naturalness, plainness, purity, restraint **3.** artlessness, candour, directness, guilelessness, innocence, lack of sophistication, naivety, openness
▷ **Antonyms** (*sense 1*) complexity, complicatedness, difficulty, intricacy, lack of clarity (*sense 2*) decoration, elaborateness, embellishment, fanciness, fussiness, ornateness, ostentation (*sense 3*) brains, craftiness, cunning, deviousness, guile, insincerity, knowingness, sharpness, slyness, smartness, sophistication, wariness, wisdom, worldliness

simplify abridge, decipher, disentangle, facilitate, make intelligible, reduce to essentials, streamline

simplistic naive, oversimplified

simply 1. clearly, directly, easily, intelligibly, modestly, naturally, plainly, straightforwardly, unaffectedly, unpretentiously, without any elaboration **2.** just, merely, only, purely, solely **3.** absolutely, altogether, completely, really, totally, unreservedly, utterly, wholly

simulate act, affect, assume, counterfeit, fabricate, feign, imitate, make believe, pretend, put on, reproduce, sham

simulated 1. artificial, fake, imitation, man-made, mock, pseudo (*informal*), sham, substitute, synthetic **2.** artificial, assumed, feigned, insincere, make-believe, phoney *or* phony (*informal*), pretended, put-on

simultaneous at the same time, coincident, coinciding, concurrent, contemporaneous, synchronous

simultaneously all together, at the same time, concurrently, in chorus, in concert, in the same breath, in unison, together

sin 1. *noun* crime, damnation, error, evil, guilt, iniquity, misdeed, offence, sinfulness, transgression, trespass, ungodliness, unrighteousness, wickedness, wrong, wrongdoing **2.** *~verb* err, fall, fall from grace, go astray, lapse, offend, transgress, trespass (*archaic*)

sincere artless, bona fide, candid, earnest, frank, genuine, guileless, heartfelt, honest, natural, no-nonsense, open, real, serious, straightforward, true, un~

affected, unfeigned, upfront (*informal*), wholehearted
▷ **Antonyms** affected, artful, artificial, deceitful, deceptive, dishonest, false, feigned, hollow, insincere, phoney *or* phony (*informal*), pretended, put on, synthetic, token, two-faced

sincerely earnestly, from the bottom of one's heart, genuinely, honestly, in all sincerity, in earnest, in good faith, really, seriously, truly, wholeheartedly

sincerity artlessness, bona fides, candour, frankness, genuineness, good faith, guilelessness, honesty, probity, seriousness, straightforwardness, truth, wholeheartedness

sinecure cushy number (*informal*), gravy train (*slang*), money for jam *or* old rope (*informal*), soft job (*informal*), soft option

sinewy athletic, brawny, lusty, muscular, powerful, robust, strong, sturdy, vigorous, wiry

sinful bad, corrupt, criminal, depraved, erring, guilty, immoral, iniquitous, irreligious, morally wrong, ungodly, unholy, unrighteous, wicked
▷ **Antonyms** beatified, blessed, chaste, decent, free from sin, godly, holy, honest, honourable, immaculate, moral, pure, righteous, sinless, spotless, unblemished, upright, virtuous, without sin

sing 1. carol, chant, chirp, croon, make melody, pipe, trill, vocalize, warble, yodel **2.** *slang, chiefly U.S.* betray, blow the whistle (on) (*informal*), fink (on) (*slang, chiefly U.S.*), grass (*Brit. slang*), inform (on), peach (*slang*), rat (on) (*informal*), shop (*slang, chiefly Brit.*), spill one's guts (*slang*), spill the beans (*informal*), squeal (*slang*), tell all, turn in (*informal*) **3.** buzz, hum, purr, whine, whistle

singe burn, char, scorch, sear

singer balladeer, cantor, chanteuse (*fem.*), chorister, crooner, minstrel, soloist, songster, songstress, troubadour, vocalist

single *adjective* **1.** distinct, individual, lone, one, only, particular, separate, singular, sole, solitary, unique **2.** free, unattached, unmarried, unwed **3.** exclusive, individual, separate, simple, unblended, uncompounded, undivided, unmixed, unshared *~verb* **4.** (*usually with* **out**) choose, cull, distinguish, fix on, pick, pick on *or* out, put on one side, select, separate, set apart, winnow

single-handed alone, by oneself, independently, on one's own, solo, unaided, unassisted, under one's own steam, without help

single-minded dedicated, determined, dogged, fixed, hellbent (*informal*), monomaniacal, steadfast, stubborn, tireless, undeviating, unswerving, unwavering

singly individually, one at a time, one by one, separately

sing out call (out), cooee, cry (out), halloo, holler (*informal*), make oneself heard, shout, shout ahoy, yell

singsong *adjective* droning, monotone, monotonous, repetitious, toneless

singular 1. conspicuous, eminent, exceptional, notable, noteworthy, outstanding, prodigious, rare, remarkable, uncommon, unique, unparalleled **2.** atypical, curious, eccentric, extraordinary, odd, oddball (*informal*), out-of-the-way, outré, peculiar, puzzling, queer, strange, unusual, wacko (*slang*) **3.** individual, separate, single, sole
▷ **Antonyms** common, common or garden, commonplace, conventional, everyday, familiar, normal, routine, run-of-the-mill, unexceptional, unremarkable, usual

singularity 1. abnormality, curiousness, extraordinariness, irregularity, oddness, peculiarity, queerness, strangeness **2.** eccentricity, idiosyncrasy, oddity, particularity, peculiarity, quirk, twist

singularly conspicuously, especially, exceptionally, extraordinarily, notably, outstandingly, particularly, prodigiously, remarkably, seriously (*informal*), surprisingly, uncommonly, unusually

sinister baleful, dire, disquieting, evil, forbidding, injurious, malevolent, malign, malignant, menacing, ominous, threatening
▷ **Antonyms** auspicious, benevolent, benign, calming, encouraging, good, heartening, heroic, honourable, just, noble, promising, propitious, reassuring, righteous, upright, worthy

sink *verb* **1.** cave in, decline, descend, dip, disappear, droop, drop, drown, ebb, engulf, fall, founder, go down, go under, lower, merge, plummet, plunge, sag, slope, submerge, subside **2.** abate, collapse, drop, fall, lapse, relapse, retrogress, slip, slump, subside **3.** decay, decline, decrease, degenerate, depreciate, deteriorate, die, diminish, dwindle, fade, fail, flag, go downhill (*informal*), lessen, weaken, worsen **4.** bore, dig, drill, drive, excavate, lay, put down **5.** be the ruin of, defeat, destroy, finish, overwhelm, ruin, scupper (*Brit. slang*), seal the doom of **6.** be reduced to, debase oneself, lower oneself, stoop, succumb
▷ **Antonyms** (*senses 1, 2 & 3*) arise, ascend, climb, enlarge, go up, grow, improve, increase, intensify, move up, rise, rise up, swell, wax

sink in be understood, get through to, make an impression, penetrate, register (*informal*), take hold of

sinless faultless, guiltless, immaculate, innocent, pure, unblemished, uncor~

rupted, undefiled, unsullied, virtuous, without fault, without sin

sinner evildoer, malefactor, miscreant, offender, reprobate, transgressor, trespasser (*archaic*), wrongdoer

sinuous coiling, crooked, curved, curvy, lithe, mazy, meandering, serpentine, supple, tortuous, twisty, undulating, winding

sip 1. *verb* sample, sup, taste **2.** *~noun* drop, swallow, taste, thimbleful

siren charmer, Circe, *femme fatale,* Lorelei, seductress, temptress, vamp (*informal*), witch

sissy 1. *noun* baby, coward, jessie (*Scot. slang*), milksop, milquetoast (*U.S.*), mollycoddle, mummy's boy, namby-pamby, pansy, sisspot (*informal*), softie (*informal*), weakling, wet (*Brit. informal*), wimp (*informal*) **2.** *~adjective* cowardly, effeminate, feeble, namby-pamby, sissified (*informal*), soft (*informal*), unmanly, weak, wet (*Brit. informal*), wimpish *or* wimpy (*informal*)

sit 1. be seated, perch, rest, settle, take a seat, take the weight off one's feet **2.** assemble, be in session, convene, deliberate, meet, officiate, preside **3.** accommodate, contain, have space for, hold, seat

site 1. *noun* ground, location, place, plot, position, setting, spot **2.** *~verb* install, locate, place, position, set, situate

sitting *noun* congress, consultation, get-together (*informal*), hearing, meeting, period, session

situation 1. locale, locality, location, place, position, seat, setting, site, spot **2.** ball game (*informal*), case, circumstances, condition, kettle of fish (*informal*), lie of the land, plight, scenario, state, state of affairs, status quo, the picture (*informal*) **3.** rank, sphere, station, status **4.** berth (*informal*), employment, job, office, place, position, post

sixth sense clairvoyance, feyness, intuition, second sight

sizable *or* **sizeable** considerable, decent, decent-sized, goodly, large, largish, respectable, substantial, tidy (*informal*)

size amount, bigness, bulk, dimensions, extent, greatness, hugeness, immensity, largeness, magnitude, mass, measurement(s), proportions, range, vastness, volume

size up appraise, assess, evaluate, eye up, get (something) taped (*Brit. informal*), get the measure of, take stock of

sizzle crackle, frizzle, fry, hiss, spit, sputter

skedaddle abscond, beat a hasty retreat, bolt, decamp, disappear, do a bunk (*Brit. slang*), flee, hook it (*slang*), hop it (*Brit. slang*), run away, scarper (*Brit. slang*), scoot, scram (*informal*), scurry away, scuttle away, vamoose (*slang, chiefly U.S.*)

skeletal cadaverous, emaciated, fleshless, gaunt, hollow-cheeked, lantern-jawed, skin-and-bone (*informal*), wasted, worn to a shadow

skeleton *figurative* bare bones, bones, draft, frame, framework, outline, sketch, structure

sketch 1. *verb* block out, delineate, depict, draft, draw, outline, paint, plot, portray, represent, rough out **2.** *~noun* delineation, design, draft, drawing, outline, plan, skeleton

sketchily cursorily, hastily, imperfectly, incompletely, patchily, perfunctorily, roughly

sketchy bitty, cobbled together, crude, cursory, inadequate, incomplete, outline, perfunctory, rough, scrappy, skimpy, slight, superficial, unfinished, vague

▷ **Antonyms** complete, detailed, full, thorough

skewwhiff askew, aslant, cockeyed (*informal*), crooked, out of true, squint (*informal*), tilted

skilful able, accomplished, adept, adroit, apt, clever, competent, dexterous, experienced, expert, handy, masterly, practised, professional, proficient, quick, ready, skilled, trained

▷ **Antonyms** amateurish, awkward, bungling, cack-handed, clumsy, cowboy (*informal*), ham-fisted, incompetent, inept, inexperienced, inexpert, maladroit, slapdash, unaccomplished, unqualified, unskilful, unskilled

skill ability, accomplishment, adroitness, aptitude, art, cleverness, competence, craft, dexterity, experience, expertise, expertness, facility, finesse, handiness, ingenuity, intelligence, knack, proficiency, quickness, readiness, skilfulness, talent, technique

▷ **Antonyms** awkwardness, brute force, cack-handedness, clumsiness, gaucheness, ham-fistedness, inability, incompetence, ineptitude, inexperience, lack of finesse, maladroitness, unhandiness

skilled able, accomplished, a dab hand at (*Brit. informal*), experienced, expert, masterly, practised, professional, proficient, skilful, trained

▷ **Antonyms** amateurish, cowboy (*informal*), inexperienced, inexpert, uneducated, unprofessional, unqualified, unskilled, untalented, untrained

skim 1. cream, separate **2.** brush, coast, dart, float, fly, glide, sail, soar **3.** (*usually with* **through**) glance, run one's eye over, scan, skip (*informal*), thumb *or* leaf through

skimp be mean with, be niggardly, be sparing with, cut corners, pinch, scamp, scant, scrimp, stint, tighten one's belt, withhold

▷ **Antonyms** act as if one had money to burn, be extravagant, be generous with, be prodigal, blow (*slang*), fritter away, lavish, overspend, pour on, splurge, squander, throw money away

skimpy exiguous, inadequate, insufficient, meagre, miserly, niggardly, scant, scanty, short, sparse, thin, tight

skin *noun* **1.** fell, hide, integument, pelt, tegument **2.** casing, coating, crust, film, husk, membrane, outside, peel, rind **3. by the skin of one's teeth** by a hair's-breadth, by a narrow margin, by a whisker (*informal*), narrowly, only just **4. get under one's skin** aggravate (*informal*), annoy, get in one's hair (*informal*), get on one's nerves (*informal*), grate on, irk, irritate, needle (*informal*), nettle, piss one off (*taboo slang*), rub up the wrong way *~verb* **5.** abrade, bark, excoriate, flay, graze, peel, scrape

skin-deep artificial, external, meaningless, on the surface, shallow, superficial, surface

skinflint meanie *or* meany (*informal, chiefly Brit.*), miser, niggard, penny-pincher (*informal*), Scrooge, tight-arse (*taboo slang*), tight-ass (*U.S. taboo slang*), tightwad (*U.S. & Canad. slang*)

skinny emaciated, lean, macilent (*rare*), scraggy, scrawny, skeletal, skin-and-bone (*informal*), thin, twiggy, undernourished

▷ **Antonyms** beefy (*informal*), broad in the beam (*informal*), fat, fleshy, heavy, obese, plump, podgy, portly, stout, tubby

skip *verb* **1.** bob, bounce, caper, cavort, dance, flit, frisk, gambol, hop, prance, trip **2.** eschew, give (something) a miss, leave out, miss out, omit, pass over, skim over **3.** *informal* bunk off (*slang*), cut (*informal*), dog it *or* dog off (*dialect*), miss, play truant from, wag (*dialect*)

skirmish 1. *noun* affair, affray (*Law*), battle, brush, clash, combat, conflict, contest, dust-up (*informal*), encounter, engagement, fracas, incident, scrap (*informal*), scrimmage, set-to (*informal*), spat, tussle **2.** *~verb* clash, collide, come to blows, scrap (*informal*), tussle

skirt *verb* **1.** border, edge, flank, lie alongside **2.** (*often with* **around** *or* **round**) avoid, body-swerve (*Scot.*), bypass, circumvent, detour, evade, steer clear of *~noun* **3.** (*often plural*) border, edge, fringe, hem, margin, outskirts, periphery, purlieus, rim

skit burlesque, parody, sketch, spoof (*informal*), takeoff (*informal*), travesty, turn

skittish excitable, fickle, fidgety, frivolous, highly strung, jumpy, lively, nervous, playful, restive

▷ **Antonyms** calm, composed, demure, laid-back, placid, relaxed, sober, staid, steady, unexcitable, unfazed (*informal*), unflappable, unruffled

skive *verb* bob off (*Brit. slang*), dodge, gold-brick (*U.S. slang*), idle, malinger, scrimshank (*Brit. military slang*), shirk, skulk, slack, swing the lead

skiver dodger, do-nothing, gold brick (*U.S. slang*), idler, loafer, scrimshanker (*Brit. military slang*), shirker, slacker

skulduggery double-dealing, duplicity, fraudulence, machinations, shenanigan(s) (*informal*), swindling, trickery, underhandedness, unscrupulousness

skulk creep, lie in wait, loiter, lurk, pad, prowl, slink, sneak

sky *noun* **1.** azure (*poetic*), empyrean (*poetic*), firmament, heavens, upper atmosphere, vault of heaven, welkin (*archaic*) **2. to the skies** excessively, extravagantly, fulsomely, highly, immoderately, inordinately, profusely

slab chunk, hunk, lump, nugget, piece, portion, slice, wedge, wodge (*Brit. informal*)

slack *adjective* **1.** baggy, easy, flaccid, flexible, lax, limp, loose, not taut, relaxed **2.** asleep on the job (*informal*), easy-going, idle, inactive, inattentive, lax, lazy, neglectful, negligent, permissive, remiss, slapdash, slipshod, tardy **3.** dull, inactive, quiet, slow, slow-moving, sluggish *~noun* **4.** excess, give (*informal*), leeway, looseness, play, room *~verb* **5.** bob off (*Brit. slang*), dodge, flag, idle, neglect, relax, shirk, skive (*Brit. slang*), slacken

▷ **Antonyms** *~adjective* (*sense 1*) inflexible, rigid, stiff, strained, stretched, taut, tight (*senses 2 & 3*) active, bustling, busy, concerned, diligent, exacting, fast-moving, hard, hard-working, hectic, meticulous, stern, strict

slacken (off) abate, decrease, diminish, drop off, ease (off), lessen, let up, loosen, moderate, reduce, relax, release, slack off, slow down, tire

slacker dodger, do-nothing, gold brick (*U.S. slang*), good-for-nothing, idler, layabout, loafer, passenger, scrimshanker (*Brit. military slang*), shirker, skiver (*Brit. slang*)

slag (off) *verb* abuse, berate, criticise, deride, insult, lambast(e), malign, mock, slam, slander, slang, slate

slake assuage, gratify, quench, sate, satiate, satisfy

slam 1. bang, crash, dash, fling, hurl, smash, throw, thump **2.** *slang* attack, blast, castigate, criticize, damn, excoriate, lambast(e), pan (*informal*), pillory, shoot down (*informal*), slate (*informal*), tear into (*informal*), vilify

slander 1. *noun* aspersion, backbiting, calumny, defamation, detraction, libel, misrepresentation, muckraking, obloquy, scandal, smear **2.** *~verb* backbite, blacken (someone's) name, calumniate, decry, defame, detract, disparage, libel, malign, muckrake, slur, smear, traduce, vilify

▷ **Antonyms** *~noun* acclaim, acclamation, approval, laudation, praise, tribute *~verb* acclaim, applaud, approve, compliment, eulogize, laud, praise, sing the praises of

slanderous abusive, calumnious, damaging, defamatory, libellous, malicious

slang *verb* abuse, berate, call names, hurl insults at, insult, inveigh against, malign, rail against, revile, vilify, vituperate

slanging match altercation, argument, argy-bargy (*Brit. informal*), barney (*informal*), battle of words, ding-dong, quarrel, row, set-to (*informal*), spat

slant *verb* **1.** angle off, bend, bevel, cant, heel, incline, lean, list, shelve, skew, slope, tilt *~noun* **2.** camber, declination, diagonal, gradient, incline, pitch, rake, ramp, slope, tilt *~verb* **3.** angle, bias, colour, distort, twist, weight *~noun* **4.** angle, attitude, bias, emphasis, leaning, one-sidedness, point of view, prejudice, viewpoint

slanting angled, aslant, asymmetrical, at an angle, atilt, bent, canted, cater-cornered (*U.S. informal*), diagonal, inclined, oblique, on the bias, sideways, slanted, slantwise, sloping, tilted, tilting

slap *noun* **1.** bang, blow, chin (*slang*), clout (*informal*), cuff, deck (*slang*), lay one on (*slang*), smack, spank, wallop (*informal*), whack **2. a slap in the face** affront, blow, humiliation, insult, put-down, rebuff, rebuke, rejection, repulse, snub *~verb* **3.** bang, clap, clout (*informal*), cuff, hit, spank, strike, whack **4.** *informal* daub, plaster, plonk, spread *~adverb* **5.** *informal* bang, directly, exactly, plumb (*informal*), precisely, slap-bang (*informal*), smack (*informal*)

slapdash careless, clumsy, disorderly, haphazard, hasty, hurried, last-minute, messy, negligent, perfunctory, slipshod, sloppy (*informal*), slovenly, thoughtless, thrown-together, untidy

▷ **Antonyms** careful, conscientious, fastidious, meticulous, ordered, orderly, painstaking, precise, punctilious, thoughtful, tidy

slap down bring to heel, put (someone) in his place, rebuke, reprimand, restrain, squash

slaphappy 1. casual, haphazard, happy-go-lucky, hit-or-miss (*informal*), irresponsible, nonchalant **2.** dazed, giddy, punch-drunk, reeling, woozy (*informal*)

slapstick *noun* buffoonery, farce, horseplay, knockabout comedy

slap-up elaborate, excellent, first-rate, fit for a king, lavish, luxurious, magnificent, no-expense-spared, princely, splendid, sumptuous, superb

slash 1. *verb* cut, gash, hack, lacerate, rend, rip, score, slit **2.** *~noun* cut, gash, incision, laceration, rent, rip, slit **3.** *~verb* cut, drop, lower, reduce

slashing aggressive, biting, brutal, ferocious, harsh, savage, searing, vicious

slate *verb* berate, blame, blast, castigate, censure, criticize, excoriate, haul over the coals (*informal*), lambas(t)e, lay into (*informal*), pan (*informal*), pitch into (*informal*), rail against, rap (someone's) knuckles, rebuke, roast (*informal*), scold, slam (*slang*), slang, take to task, tear into (*informal*), tear (someone) off a strip (*informal*)

slattern drab (*archaic*), sloven, slut, trollop

slatternly bedraggled, dirty, draggletailed (*archaic*), frowzy, slipshod, sloppy (*informal*), slovenly, sluttish, unclean, unkempt, untidy

slaughter *noun* **1.** blood bath, bloodshed, butchery, carnage, extermination, holocaust, killing, liquidation, massacre, murder, slaying *~verb* **2.** butcher, destroy, do to death, exterminate, kill, liquidate, massacre, murder, put to the sword, slay, take out (*slang*) **3.** *informal* blow out of the water (*slang*), crush, defeat, hammer (*informal*), lick (*informal*), overwhelm, rout, stuff (*slang*), tank (*slang*), thrash, trounce, undo, vanquish, wipe the floor with (*informal*)

slaughterhouse abattoir, butchery, shambles

slave 1. *noun* bondservant, bondsman, drudge, scullion (*archaic*), serf, servant, skivvy (*chiefly Brit.*), slavey (*Brit. informal*), varlet (*archaic*), vassal, villein **2.** *~verb* drudge, grind (*informal*), skivvy (*Brit.*), slog, sweat, toil, work one's fingers to the bone

slaver dribble, drool, salivate, slobber

slavery bondage, captivity, enslavement, serfdom, servitude, subjugation, thraldom, thrall, vassalage

▷ **Antonyms** emancipation, freedom, liberty, manumission, release

slavish 1. abject, base, cringing, despicable, fawning, grovelling, low, mean, menial, obsequious, servile, submissive, sycophantic **2.** conventional, imitative, second-hand, unimaginative, uninspired, unoriginal

▷ **Antonyms** (*sense 1*) assertive, domineering, masterful, rebellious, self-willed, wilful (*sense 2*) creative, imaginative, independent, inventive, original, radical, revolutionary

slay 1. annihilate, assassinate, butcher, destroy, dispatch, do away with, do in (*slang*), eliminate, exterminate, kill, massacre, mow down, murder, rub out (*U.S. slang*), slaughter **2.** *informal* amuse, be the death of (*informal*), im~

press, make a hit with (*informal*), wow (*slang, chiefly U.S.*)

sleazy crummy, disreputable, low, run-down, seedy, sordid, squalid, tacky (*informal*)

sleek glossy, lustrous, shiny, smooth, well-fed, well-groomed

▷ **Antonyms** badly groomed, bedraggled, dishevelled, frowzy, ill-nourished, in poor condition, ratty (*informal*), rough, shaggy, sloppy, slovenly, unkempt

sleep 1. *verb* be in the land of Nod, catnap, doze, drop off (*informal*), drowse, go out like a light, hibernate, kip (*Brit. slang*), nod off (*informal*), rest in the arms of Morpheus, slumber, snooze (*informal*), snore, take a nap, take forty winks (*informal*), zizz (*Brit. informal*) **2.** ~*noun* beauty sleep (*informal*), dormancy, doze, forty winks (*informal*), hibernation, kip (*Brit. slang*), nap, repose, rest, shuteye (*slang*), siesta, slumber(s), snooze (*informal*), zizz (*Brit. informal*)

sleepiness doziness, drowsiness, heaviness, lethargy, somnolence, torpor

sleepless 1. disturbed, insomniac, restless, unsleeping, wakeful **2.** alert, unsleeping, vigilant, watchful, wide awake

sleeplessness insomnia, wakefulness

sleepwalker noctambulist, somnambulist

sleepwalking noctambulation, noctambulism, somnambulation, somnambulism

sleepy 1. drowsy, dull, heavy, inactive, lethargic, sluggish, slumbersome, somnolent, torpid **2.** dull, hypnotic, inactive, quiet, sleep-inducing, slow, slumberous, somnolent, soporific

▷ **Antonyms** active, alert, alive and kicking, animated, attentive, awake, boisterous, bustling, busy, energetic, full of beans (*informal*), lively, restless, thriving, wakeful, wide-awake

sleight of hand adroitness, artifice, dexterity, legerdemain, manipulation, prestidigitation, skill

slender 1. lean, narrow, slight, slim, svelte, sylphlike, willowy **2.** inadequate, inconsiderable, insufficient, little, meagre, scant, scanty, small, spare **3.** faint, feeble, flimsy, fragile, poor, remote, slight, slim, tenuous, thin, weak

▷ **Antonyms** (*sense 1*) bulky, chubby, fat, heavy, large, podgy, stout, tubby, well-built (*sense 2*) ample, appreciable, considerable, generous, large, substantial (*sense 3*) good, solid, strong

sleuth detective, dick (*slang, chiefly U.S.*), gumshoe (*U.S. slang*), private eye (*informal*), (private) investigator, sleuthhound (*informal*), tail (*informal*)

slice 1. *noun* cut, helping, piece, portion, segment, share, sliver, wedge **2.** ~*verb* carve, cut, divide, sever

slick *adjective* **1.** glib, meretricious, plausible, polished, smooth, sophistical, specious **2.** adroit, deft, dexterous, dextrous, polished, professional, sharp, skilful ~*verb* **3.** make glossy, plaster down, sleek, smarm down (*Brit. informal*), smooth

▷ **Antonyms** ~*adjective* amateur, amateurish, clumsy, crude, inexpert, unaccomplished, unpolished, unprofessional, unskilful

slide *verb* **1.** coast, glide, glissade, skim, slip, slither, toboggan, veer **2. let slide** forget, gloss over, ignore, let ride, neglect, pass over, push to the back of one's mind, turn a blind eye to

slight *adjective* **1.** feeble, inconsiderable, insignificant, insubstantial, meagre, measly, minor, modest, negligible, paltry, scanty, small, superficial, trifling, trivial, unimportant, weak **2.** delicate, feeble, fragile, lightly-built, slim, small, spare ~*verb* **3.** affront, cold-shoulder, despise, disdain, disparage, give offence *or* umbrage to, ignore, insult, neglect, put down, scorn, show disrespect for, snub, treat with contempt ~*noun* **4.** affront, contempt, discourtesy, disdain, disregard, disrespect, inattention, indifference, insult, neglect, rebuff, slap in the face (*informal*), snub, (the) cold shoulder

▷ **Antonyms** ~*adjective* appreciable, considerable, great, heavy, important, large, muscular, noticeable, obvious, significant, solid, strong, sturdy, substantial, well-built ~*verb* compliment, flatter, praise, speak well of, treat considerately ~*noun* compliment, flattery, praise

slighting belittling, derogatory, disdainful, disparaging, disrespectful, insulting, offensive, scornful, supercilious, uncomplimentary

slightly a little, marginally, on a small scale, somewhat, to some extent *or* degree

slim *adjective* **1.** lean, narrow, slender, slight, svelte, sylphlike, thin, trim **2.** faint, poor, remote, slender, slight ~*verb* **3.** diet, lose weight, reduce, slenderize (*chiefly U.S.*)

▷ **Antonyms** ~*adjective* (*sense 1*) broad, bulky, chubby, fat, heavy, muscular, obese, overweight, sturdy, tubby, well-built, wide (*sense 2*) good, strong ~*verb* build oneself up, put on weight

slimy 1. clammy, gloopy (*informal*), glutinous, miry, mucous, muddy, oozy, viscous **2.** creeping, grovelling, obsequious, oily, servile, smarmy (*Brit. informal*), soapy (*slang*), sycophantic, toadying, unctuous

sling *verb* **1.** cast, chuck (*informal*), fling, heave, hurl, lob (*informal*), shy, throw, toss **2.** dangle, hang, suspend, swing

slink creep, prowl, pussyfoot (*informal*), skulk, slip, sneak, steal

slinky clinging, close-fitting, feline, figure-hugging, sinuous, skintight, sleek

slip[1] *verb* **1.** glide, skate, slide, slither **2.** fall, lose one's balance, miss *or* lose one's footing, skid, trip (over) **3.** conceal, creep, hide, insinuate oneself, sneak, steal **4.** (*sometimes with* **up**) blunder, boob (*Brit. slang*), drop a brick *or* clanger (*informal*), err, go wrong, make a mistake, miscalculate, misjudge, mistake **5.** break away from, break free from, disappear, escape, get away, get clear of, take French leave **6. let slip** blurt out, come out with (*informal*), disclose, divulge, give away, leak, let out (*informal*), let the cat out of the bag, reveal *~noun* **7.** bloomer (*Brit. informal*), blunder, boob (*Brit. slang*), error, failure, fault, faux pas, imprudence, indiscretion, lapse, mistake, omission, oversight, slip of the tongue, slip-up (*informal*) **8. give (someone) the slip** dodge, elude, escape from, evade, get away from, lose (someone), outwit, shake (someone) off

slip[2] *noun* **1.** piece, sliver, strip **2.** cutting, offshoot, runner, scion, shoot, sprig, sprout

slippery 1. glassy, greasy, icy, lubricious (*rare*), perilous, skiddy (*informal*), slippy (*informal or dialect*), smooth, unsafe, unstable, unsteady **2.** crafty, cunning, devious, dishonest, duplicitous, evasive, false, foxy, shifty, sneaky, treacherous, tricky, two-faced, unpredictable, unreliable, untrustworthy

slipshod careless, casual, loose, slapdash, sloppy (*informal*), slovenly, unsystematic, untidy

slit 1. *verb* cut (open), gash, impale, knife, lance, pierce, rip, slash, split open **2.** *~noun* cut, fissure, gash, incision, opening, rent, split, tear

slither *verb* glide, skitter, slide, slink, slip, snake, undulate

sliver *noun* flake, fragment, paring, shaving, shred, slip, splinter

slob boor, churl, couch potato (*slang*), lout, oaf, yahoo, yob (*Brit. slang*)

slobber *verb* dribble, drivel, drool, salivate, slabber (*dialect*), slaver, water at the mouth

slobbish messy, slatternly, sloppy (*informal*), slovenly, unclean, unkempt, untidy

slog *verb* **1.** hit, hit for six, punch, slosh (*Brit. slang*), slug, sock (*slang*), strike, thump, wallop (*informal*) **2.** apply oneself to, keep one's nose to the grindstone, labour, peg away at, persevere, plod, plough through, slave, sweat blood (*informal*), toil, tramp, trek, trudge, work, work one's fingers to the bone *~noun* **3.** blood, sweat, and tears (*informal*), effort, exertion, hike, labour, struggle, tramp, trek, trudge

slogan catch-phrase, catchword, jingle, motto, rallying cry

slop *verb* overflow, slosh (*informal*), spatter, spill, splash, splatter

slop around *or* **about** flop, loaf, lollop, lounge, shamble, shuffle, slouch, slump, sprawl, veg out (*slang, chiefly U.S.*)

slope *verb* **1.** drop away, fall, incline, lean, pitch, rise, slant, tilt *~noun* **2.** brae (*Scot.*), declination, declivity, descent, downgrade (*chiefly U.S.*), gradient, inclination, incline, ramp, rise, scarp, slant, tilt *~verb* **3.** (*with* **off, away,** *etc.*) creep, make oneself scarce, skulk, slink, slip, steal

sloping atilt, bevelled, cant, inclined, inclining, leaning, oblique, slanting

sloppy 1. sludgy, slushy, splashy, watery, wet **2.** *informal* amateurish, careless, clumsy, hit-or-miss (*informal*), inattentive, messy, slipshod, slovenly, unkempt, untidy, weak **3.** banal, gushing, mawkish, mushy (*informal*), overemotional, sentimental, slushy (*informal*), soppy (*Brit. informal*), trite, wet (*Brit. informal*)

slosh *verb* **1.** flounder, plash, pour, shower, slap, slop, splash, spray, swash, wade **2.** *Brit. slang* bash (*informal*), belt (*informal*), biff (*slang*), hit, punch, slog, slug, sock (*slang*), strike, swipe (*informal*), thwack, wallop (*informal*)

slot *noun* **1.** aperture, channel, groove, hole, slit, vent **2.** *informal* niche, opening, place, position, space, time, vacancy *~verb* **3.** adjust, assign, fit, fit in, insert, pigeonhole

sloth faineance, idleness, inactivity, indolence, inertia, laziness, slackness, slothfulness, sluggishness, torpor

slothful do-nothing (*informal*), fainéant, good-for-nothing, idle, inactive, indolent, inert, lazy, skiving (*Brit. slang*), slack, sluggish, torpid, workshy

slouch *verb* droop, loll, slump, stoop

slouching awkward, loutish, lumbering, shambling, uncouth, ungainly

slovenly careless, disorderly, heedless, loose, negligent, slack, slapdash, slatternly, slipshod, sloppy (*informal*), unkempt, untidy

▷ **Antonyms** careful, clean, conscientious, disciplined, methodical, meticulous, neat, orderly, shipshape, smart, soigné *or* soignée, tidy, trim, well-groomed, well-ordered

slow *adjective* **1.** creeping, dawdling, deliberate, easy, lackadaisical, laggard, lagging, lazy, leaden, leisurely, loitering, measured, plodding, ponderous, slow-moving, sluggardly, sluggish, tortoise-like, unhurried **2.** backward, behind, behindhand, delayed, dilatory, late, long-delayed, tardy, unpunctual **3.** gradual, lingering, long-drawn-out, prolonged, protracted, time-consuming **4.**

behind the times, boring, conservative, dead, dead-and-alive (*Brit.*), dull, inactive, one-horse (*informal*), quiet, slack, sleepy, sluggish, stagnant, tame, tedious, uneventful, uninteresting, unproductive, unprogressive, wearisome **5.** blockish, bovine, braindead (*informal*), dense, dim, dozy (*Brit. informal*), dull, dull-witted, dumb (*informal*), obtuse, retarded, slow on the uptake (*informal*), slow-witted, stupid, thick, unresponsive **6.** (*with* **to**) averse, disinclined, hesitant, indisposed, loath, reluctant, unwilling *~verb* **7.** (*often with* **up** *or* **down**) brake, check, curb, decelerate, delay, detain, handicap, hold up, lag, reduce speed, rein in, relax, restrict, retard, slacken (off), spin out

▷ **Antonyms** *~adjective* (*senses 1, 2, 3 & 4*) action-packed, animated, brisk, eager, exciting, fast, hectic, hurried, interesting, lively, precipitate, prompt, quick, quickie (*informal*), quick-moving, sharp, speedy, stimulating, swift (*sense 5*) bright, clever, intelligent, perceptive, quick, quick-witted, sharp, smart *~verb* accelerate, advance, aid, boost, help, pick up speed, quicken, speed up

slowly at a snail's pace, at one's leisure, by degrees, gradually, inchmeal, in one's own (good) time, leisurely, ploddingly, steadily, taking one's time, unhurriedly, with leaden steps

sludge dregs, gloop (*informal*), mire, muck, mud, ooze, residue, sediment, silt, slime, slob (*Irish*), slop, slush

sluggish dull, heavy, inactive, indolent, inert, lethargic, lifeless, listless, phlegmatic, slothful, slow, slow-moving, torpid, unresponsive

▷ **Antonyms** alive and kicking, animated, brisk, dynamic, energetic, enthusiastic, fast, free-flowing, full of beans (*informal*), full of life, industrious, lively, swift, vigorous

sluggishness apathy, drowsiness, dullness, heaviness, indolence, inertia, languor, lassitude, lethargy, listlessness, slothfulness, somnolence, stagnation, torpor

sluice *verb* cleanse, drain, drench, flush, irrigate, wash down, wash out

slumber *verb* be inactive, doze, drowse, kip (*Brit. slang*), lie dormant, nap, repose, sleep, snooze (*informal*), zizz (*Brit. informal*)

slummy decayed, overcrowded, run-down, seedy, sleazy, sordid, squalid, wretched

slump *verb* **1.** collapse, crash, decline, deteriorate, fall, fall off, go downhill (*informal*), plummet, plunge, reach a new low, sink, slip *~noun* **2.** collapse, crash, decline, depreciation, depression, downturn, drop, failure, fall, falling-off, lapse, low, meltdown (*informal*), recession, reverse, stagnation, trough *~verb* **3.** bend, droop, hunch, loll, sag, slouch

▷ **Antonyms** *~verb* (*sense 1*) advance, boom, develop, expand, flourish, grow, increase, prosper, thrive *~noun* advance, boom, boost, development, expansion, gain, growth, improvement, increase, upsurge, upswing, upturn

slur *noun* affront, aspersion, blot, blot on one's escutcheon, brand, calumny, discredit, disgrace, innuendo, insinuation, insult, reproach, smear, stain, stigma

slut drab (*archaic*), scrubber (*Brit. & Austral. slang*), slattern, sloven, tart, trollop

sly *adjective* **1.** artful, astute, clever, conniving, covert, crafty, cunning, devious, foxy, furtive, guileful, insidious, scheming, secret, shifty, stealthy, subtle, underhand, wily **2.** arch, impish, knowing, mischievous, roguish *~noun* **3. on the sly** behind (someone's) back, covertly, like a thief in the night, on the q.t. (*informal*), on the quiet, privately, secretly, surreptitiously, underhandedly, under the counter (*informal*)

▷ **Antonyms** *~adjective* above-board, artless, direct, frank, guileless, honest, ingenuous, open, straightforward, trustworthy *~noun* above-board, candidly, forthrightly, on the level, openly, overtly, publicly

smack *verb* **1.** box, clap, cuff, hit, pat, slap, sock (*slang*), spank, strike, tap *~noun* **2.** blow, crack, slap **3. smack in the eye** blow, rebuff, repulse, setback, slap in the face, snub *~adverb* **4.** *informal* directly, exactly, plumb, point-blank, precisely, right, slap (*informal*), squarely, straight

smack of bear the stamp of, be redolent of, be suggestive *or* indicative of, betoken, have all the hallmarks of, reek of, smell of, suggest, testify to

small 1. diminutive, immature, Lilliputian, little, mini, miniature, minute, petite, pint-sized (*informal*), pocket-sized, puny, pygmy *or* pigmy, slight, teensy-weensy, teeny, teeny-weeny, tiny, undersized, wee, young **2.** insignificant, lesser, minor, negligible, paltry, petty, trifling, trivial, unimportant **3.** inadequate, inconsiderable, insufficient, limited, meagre, measly, scant, scanty **4.** humble, modest, small-scale, unpretentious **5.** base, grudging, illiberal, mean, narrow, petty, selfish **6. make (someone) feel small** chagrin, disconcert, humble, humiliate, make (someone) look foolish, mortify, put down (*slang*), show up (*informal*), take down a peg or two (*informal*)

▷ **Antonyms** (*sense 1*) ample, big, colossal, enormous, great, huge, immense, massive, mega (*slang*), sizable *or* sizeable, stellar (*informal*), vast (*sense 2*) appreciable, important, major, powerful, serious, significant, urgent, vital, weighty (*sense 3*) considerable, generous, substantial (*sense 4*) grand, large-scale

small-minded bigoted, envious, grudging, hidebound, intolerant, mean, narrow-minded, petty, rigid, ungenerous

▷ **Antonyms** broad-minded, far-sighted, generous, liberal, open, open-minded, tolerant, unbigoted

small-time insignificant, minor, no-account (*U.S. informal*), of no account, of no consequence, petty, piddling (*informal*), unimportant

smarmy bootlicking (*informal*), bowing and scraping, crawling, fawning, fulsome, greasy, ingratiating, obsequious, oily, servile, slimy, smooth, soapy (*slang*), suave, sycophantic, toadying, unctuous

smart[1] *adjective* **1.** acute, adept, agile, apt, astute, bright, brisk, canny, clever, ingenious, intelligent, keen, nimble, quick, quick-witted, ready, sharp, shrewd **2.** as fresh as a daisy, chic, elegant, fashionable, fine, modish, natty (*informal*), neat, smart, snappy, spruce, stylish, trendy (*Brit. informal*), trim, well turned-out **3.** effective, impertinent, nimble-witted, pointed, ready, saucy, smart-alecky (*informal*), witty **4.** brisk, cracking (*informal*), jaunty, lively, quick, spanking, spirited, vigorous

▷ **Antonyms** (*sense 1*) daft (*informal*), dense, dim-witted (*informal*), dull, dumb (*informal*), foolish, idiotic, moronic, slow, stupid, thick, unintelligent (*sense 2*) dowdy, dull, fogeyish, naff (*Brit. slang*), old-fashioned, outmoded, out-of-date, passé, scruffy, sloppy, uncool, unfashionable, untrendy (*Brit. informal*) (*sense 3*) modest, polite, respectful, restrained, unobtrusive

smart[2] **1.** *verb* burn, hurt, pain, sting, throb, tingle **2.** *~adjective* hard, keen, painful, piercing, resounding, sharp, stinging **3.** *~noun* burning sensation, pain, pang, smarting, soreness, sting

smart aleck clever-clogs (*informal*), clever Dick (*informal*), know-all (*informal*), smartarse (*slang*), smarty boots (*informal*), smarty pants (*informal*), wise guy (*informal*)

smarten beautify, groom, gussy up (*slang, chiefly U.S.*), put in order, put to rights, spruce up, tidy

smash *verb* **1.** break, collide, crash, crush, demolish, disintegrate, pulverize, shatter, shiver *~noun* **2.** accident, collision, crash, pile-up (*informal*), smash-up (*informal*) *~verb* **3.** defeat, destroy, lay waste, overthrow, ruin, total (*slang*), trash (*slang*), wreck *~noun* **4.** collapse, defeat, destruction, disaster, downfall, failure, ruin, shattering

smashing awesome (*slang*), bodacious (*slang, chiefly U.S.*), boffo (*slang*), brill (*informal*), brilliant (*informal*), chillin' (*U.S. slang*), cracking (*Brit. informal*), crucial (*slang*), def (*slang*), excellent, exhilarating, fab (*informal, chiefly Brit.*), fabulous (*informal*), fantastic (*informal*), first-class, first-rate, great (*informal*), jim-dandy (*slang*), magnificent, marvellous, mean (*slang*), mega (*slang*), out of this world (*informal*), sensational (*informal*), sovereign, stupendous, super (*informal*), superb, superlative, terrific (*informal*), topping (*Brit. slang*), wonderful, world-class

▷ **Antonyms** abysmal, appalling, average, awful, bad, boring, crap (*slang*), disappointing, disgraceful, disgusting, dreadful, dreary, dull, hideous, horrible, mediocre, no great shakes (*informal*), ordinary, rotten, run-of-the-mill, sickening, terrible, unexciting, uninspired, vile

smattering bit, dash, elements, modicum, nodding acquaintance, passing acquaintance, rudiments, smatter, sprinkling

smear *verb* **1.** bedaub, bedim, besmirch, blur, coat, cover, daub, dirty, patch, plaster, rub on, smirch, smudge, soil, spread over, stain, sully *~noun* **2.** blot, blotch, daub, smirch, smudge, splotch, streak *~verb* **3.** asperse, besmirch, blacken, calumniate, drag (someone's) name through the mud, malign, sully, tarnish, traduce, vilify *~noun* **4.** calumny, defamation, libel, mudslinging, slander, vilification, whispering campaign

smell *noun* **1.** aroma, bouquet, fragrance, niff (*Brit. slang*), odour, perfume, redolence, scent, whiff *~verb* **2.** get a whiff of, nose, scent, sniff *~noun* **3.** fetor, malodour, niff (*Brit. slang*), pong (*Brit. informal*), stench, stink *~verb* **4.** be malodorous, hum (*slang*), niff (*Brit. slang*), pong (*Brit. informal*), reek, stink, stink to high heaven (*informal*), whiff (*Brit. slang*)

smelly evil-smelling, fetid, foul, foul-smelling, high, malodorous, mephitic, niffy (*Brit. slang*), noisome, olid, pongy (*Brit. informal*), putrid, reeking, stinking, stinky (*informal*), strong, strong-smelling, whiffy (*Brit. slang*)

smirk *noun* grin, leer, simper, smug look, sneer

smitten **1.** afflicted, beset, laid low, plagued, struck **2.** beguiled, bewitched, bowled over (*informal*), captivated, charmed, enamoured, infatuated, swept off one's feet

smoky begrimed, black, caliginous (*archaic*), grey, grimy, hazy, murky, reeky, smoke-darkened, sooty, thick

smooth *adjective* **1.** even, flat, flush, horizontal, level, plain, plane, unwrinkled **2.** glossy, polished, shiny, silky, sleek, soft, velvety **3.** calm, equable, glassy, mirror-like, peaceful, se~

rene, tranquil, undisturbed, unruffled **4.** agreeable, bland, mellow, mild, pleasant, soothing **5.** debonair, facile, glib, ingratiating, persuasive, silky, slick, smarmy (*Brit. informal*), suave, unctuous, urbane **6.** easy, effortless, flowing, fluent, frictionless, regular, rhythmic, steady, unbroken, uneventful, uniform, uninterrupted, untroubled, well-ordered *~verb* **7.** flatten, iron, level, plane, polish, press **8.** allay, alleviate, appease, assuage, calm, ease, extenuate, facilitate, iron out the difficulties of, mitigate, mollify, palliate, pave the way, soften

▷ **Antonyms** *~adjective* (*senses 1 & 2*) abrasive, bumpy, coarse, irregular, jagged, lumpy, rough, sharp, uneven (*sense 3*) agitated, disturbed, edgy, excitable, nervous, ruffled, troubled, troublesome, turbulent, uneasy *~verb* (*sense 8*) aggravate, exacerbate, hamper, hinder, intensify, make worse, roughen

smoothness 1. evenness, flushness, levelness, regularity, unbrokenness **2.** silkiness, sleekness, smooth texture, softness, velvetiness **3.** calmness, glassiness, placidity, serenity, stillness, unruffled surface **4.** glibness, oiliness, smarminess (*Brit. informal*), suavity, urbanity **5.** ease, efficiency, effortlessness, felicity, finish, flow, fluency, polish, rhythm, slickness, smooth running

smother *verb* **1.** choke, extinguish, snuff, stifle, strangle, suffocate **2.** conceal, hide, keep back, muffle, repress, stifle, suppress **3.** be swimming in, cocoon, cover, envelop, heap, inundate, overwhelm, shower, shroud, surround *~noun* **4.** fug (*chiefly Brit.*), smog

smoulder *figurative* be resentful, boil, burn, fester, fume, rage, seethe, simmer, smart under

smudge 1. *verb* blacken, blur, daub, dirty, mark, smear, smirch, soil **2.** *~noun* blemish, blot, blur, smear, smut, smutch

smug complacent, conceited, holier-than-thou, priggish, self-opinionated, self-righteous, self-satisfied, superior

smuggler bootlegger, contrabandist, gentleman, moonshiner (*U.S.*), rum-runner, runner, trafficker, wrecker

smutty bawdy, blue, coarse, crude, dirty, filthy, improper, indecent, indelicate, lewd, obscene, off colour, pornographic, prurient, racy, raunchy (*U.S. slang*), risqué, salacious, suggestive, vulgar, X-rated (*informal*)

snack bite, bite to eat, break, elevenses (*Brit. informal*), light meal, nibble, refreshment(s), titbit

snag 1. *noun* catch, complication, difficulty, disadvantage, downside, drawback, hazard, hitch, inconvenience, obstacle, problem, stumbling block, the rub **2.** *~verb* catch, hole, rip, tear

snaky 1. convoluted, serpentine, sinuous, tortuous, twisting, twisty, writhing **2.** crafty, insidious, perfidious, sly, treacherous, venomous

snap *verb* **1.** break, come apart, crack, give way, separate **2.** bite, bite at, catch, grip, nip, seize, snatch **3.** bark, flare out, flash, fly off the handle at (*informal*), growl, jump down (someone's) throat (*informal*), lash out at, retort, snarl, speak sharply **4.** click, crackle, pop **5.** **snap one's fingers at** cock a snook at (*Brit.*), defy, flout, pay no attention to, scorn, set at naught, wave two fingers at (*slang*) **6.** **snap out of it** cheer up, get a grip on oneself, get over, liven up, perk up, pull oneself together (*informal*), recover *~noun* **7.** crackle, fillip, flick, pop **8.** bite, grab, nip **9.** *informal* energy, get-up-and-go (*informal*), go (*informal*), liveliness, pep, pizzazz *or* pizazz (*informal*), vigour, zip (*informal*) *~adjective* **10.** abrupt, immediate, instant, on-the-spot, sudden, unpremeditated

snappy 1. apt to fly off the handle (*informal*), cross, edgy, hasty, impatient, irritable, like a bear with a sore head (*informal*), quick-tempered, ratty (*Brit. & N.Z. informal*), snappish, tart, testy, tetchy, touchy, waspish **2.** chic, dapper, fashionable, modish, natty (*informal*), smart, stylish, trendy (*Brit. informal*), up-to-the-minute, voguish **3.** **look snappy** be quick, buck up (*informal*), get a move on (*informal*), get one's skates on, hurry (up), look lively, make haste

snap up avail oneself of, grab, grasp, nab (*informal*), pounce upon, seize, swoop down on, take advantage of

snare 1. *verb* catch, entrap, net, seize, springe, trap, trepan (*archaic*), wire **2.** *~noun* catch, gin, net, noose, pitfall, springe, trap, wire

snarl[1] *verb* complain, growl, grumble, mumble, murmur, show its teeth (*of an animal*)

snarl[2] *verb* (*often with* **up**) complicate, confuse, embroil, enmesh, entangle, entwine, muddle, ravel, tangle

snarl-up confusion, entanglement, muddle, tangle, (traffic) jam

snatch 1. *verb* catch up, clutch, gain, grab, grasp, grip, make off with, pluck, pull, rescue, seize, take, win, wrench, wrest **2.** *~noun* bit, fragment, part, piece, smattering, snippet, spell

snazzy attractive, dashing, flamboyant, flashy, jazzy (*informal*), raffish, ritzy (*slang*), showy, smart, sophisticated, sporty, stylish, swinging (*slang*), with it (*informal*)

sneak *verb* **1.** cower, lurk, pad, sidle, skulk, slink, slip, smuggle, spirit, steal **2.** *informal* grass on (*Brit. slang*), inform on, peach (*slang*), shop (*slang, chiefly Brit.*), sing (*slang, chiefly U.S.*), spill one's guts (*slang*), tell on (*informal*), tell tales *~noun* **3.** informer, snake in the grass, telltale *~adjective* **4.** clandestine, furtive, quick, secret, stealthy, surprise

sneaking 1. hidden, private, secret, suppressed, unavowed, unconfessed, undivulged, unexpressed, unvoiced **2.** intuitive, nagging, niggling, persistent, uncomfortable, worrying **3.** contemptible, furtive, mean, sly, sneaky, surreptitious, two-faced, underhand

sneaky base, contemptible, cowardly, deceitful, devious, dishonest, disingenuous, double-dealing, furtive, low, malicious, mean, nasty, shifty, slippery, sly, snide, unreliable, unscrupulous, untrustworthy

sneer 1. *verb* curl one's lip, deride, disdain, gibe, hold in contempt, hold up to ridicule, jeer, laugh, look down on, mock, ridicule, scoff, scorn, sniff at, snigger, turn up one's nose (*informal*) **2.** *~noun* derision, disdain, gibe, jeer, mockery, ridicule, scorn, snidery, snigger

snide cynical, disparaging, hurtful, ill-natured, insinuating, malicious, mean, nasty, sarcastic, scornful, shrewish, sneering, spiteful, unkind

sniff *verb* breathe, inhale, smell, snuff, snuffle

sniffy condescending, contemptuous, disdainful, haughty, supercilious, superior

snigger giggle, laugh, smirk, sneer, snicker, titter

snip *verb* **1.** clip, crop, cut, dock, nick, nip off, notch, shave, trim *~noun* **2.** bit, clipping, fragment, piece, scrap, shred, snippet **3.** *informal* bargain, giveaway, good buy, steal (*informal*)

snippet fragment, part, particle, piece, scrap, shred, snatch

snivel blubber, cry, girn (*Scot. & northern English dialect*), gripe (*informal*), grizzle (*informal, chiefly Brit.*), mewl, moan, sniffle, snuffle, weep, whimper, whine, whinge (*informal*)

snobbery airs, arrogance, condescension, pretension, pride, side (*Brit. slang*), snobbishness, snootiness (*informal*), uppishness (*Brit. informal*)

snobbish arrogant, condescending, high and mighty (*informal*), high-hat (*informal, chiefly U.S.*), hoity-toity (*informal*), patronizing, pretentious, snooty (*informal*), stuck-up (*informal*), superior, toffee-nosed (*slang, chiefly Brit.*), uppish (*Brit. informal*), uppity

▷ **Antonyms** down to earth, humble, modest, natural, unassuming, unostentatious, unpretentious, without airs

snoop interfere, poke one's nose in (*informal*), pry, spy

snooper busybody, meddler, nosy parker (*informal*), Paul Pry, pry, snoop (*informal*), stickybeak (*Austral. informal*)

snooze 1. *verb* catnap, doze, drop off (*informal*), drowse, kip (*Brit. slang*), nap, nod off (*informal*), take forty winks (*informal*) **2.** *~noun* catnap, doze, forty winks (*informal*), kip (*Brit. slang*), nap, siesta

snub 1. *verb* cold-shoulder, cut (*informal*), cut dead (*informal*), give (someone) the brush-off (*slang*), give (someone) the cold shoulder, humble, humiliate, kick in the teeth (*slang*), mortify, put down, rebuff, shame, slight **2.** *~noun* affront, brush-off (*slang*), bum's rush (*slang*), humiliation, insult, put-down, slap in the face

snug 1. comfortable, comfy (*informal*), cosy, homely, intimate, sheltered, warm **2.** close, compact, neat, trim

snuggle cuddle, nestle, nuzzle

soak *verb* **1.** bathe, damp, drench, immerse, infuse, marinate (*Cookery*), moisten, penetrate, permeate, saturate, seep, steep, wet **2.** (*with* **up**) absorb, assimilate, drink in, take up *or* in

soaking drenched, dripping, droukit *or* drookit (*Scot.*), like a drowned rat, saturated, soaked, soaked to the skin, sodden, sopping, streaming, waterlogged, wet through, wringing wet

soar 1. ascend, fly, mount, rise, tower, wing **2.** climb, escalate, rise, rocket, shoot up

▷ **Antonyms** descend, dive, drop down, fall, nose-dive, plummet, plunge, swoop

sob *verb* bawl, blubber, boohoo, cry, greet (*Scot. or archaic*), howl, shed tears, snivel, weep

sober *adjective* **1.** abstemious, abstinent, moderate, on the wagon (*informal*), temperate **2.** calm, clear-headed, cold, composed, cool, dispassionate, grave, level-headed, lucid, peaceful, practical, rational, realistic, reasonable, sedate, serene, serious, solemn, sound, staid, steady, unexcited, unruffled **3.** dark, drab, plain, quiet, severe, sombre, subdued *~verb* **4.** (*usually with* **up**) bring (someone) back to earth, calm down, clear one's head, come *or* bring to one's senses, give (someone) pause for thought, make (someone) stop and think

▷ **Antonyms** *~adjective* (*sense 1*) bevvied (*dialect*), blitzed (*slang*), blotto (*slang*), bombed (*slang*), Brahms and Liszt (*slang*), drunk, flying (*slang*), fu' (*Scot.*), guttered (*slang*), had one too many, inebriated, intoxicated, merry (*Brit. informal*), paralytic (*informal*), pie-eyed (*slang*), pissed (*taboo slang*), plastered, rat-arsed (*taboo slang*), sloshed (*slang*), smashed (*slang*), steamboats (*Scot. slang*), steaming (*slang*), tiddly (*slang, chiefly Brit.*), tight (*informal*), tipsy, tired and emotional (*euphemistic*), wasted (*slang*), wrecked (*slang*), zonked (*slang*) (*sense 2*) excessive, flamboyant, frivolous, giddy, happy, immoderate, imprudent, injudicious, irrational, lighthearted, lively, sensational, unre~

alistic (*sense 3*) bright, flashy, garish, gaudy, light *~verb* become intoxicated, get drunk

sobriety **1.** abstemiousness, abstinence, moderation, nonindulgence, self-restraint, soberness, temperance **2.** calmness, composure, coolness, gravity, level-headedness, reasonableness, restraint, sedateness, seriousness, solemnity, staidness, steadiness

so-called alleged, ostensible, pretended, professed, self-styled, *soi-disant,* supposed

sociability affability, companionability, congeniality, conviviality, cordiality, friendliness, gregariousness, neighbourliness

sociable accessible, affable, approachable, companionable, conversable, convivial, cordial, familiar, friendly, genial, gregarious, neighbourly, outgoing, social, warm

▷ **Antonyms** antisocial, boorish, cold, distant, formal, introverted, reclusive, standoffish, stiff, tense, uncommunicative, unfriendly, unsociable, uptight (*informal*) withdrawn

social *adjective* **1.** collective, common, communal, community, general, group, organized, public, societal **2.** companionable, friendly, gregarious, neighbourly, sociable *~noun* **3.** do (*informal*), gathering, get-together (*informal*), party

socialism

socialize be a good mixer, break the ice, entertain, fraternize, get about *or* around, get together, go out, mix

society **1.** civilization, culture, humanity, mankind, people, population, social order, the community, the general public, the public, the world at large **2.** camaraderie, companionship, company, fellowship, friendship **3.** association, brotherhood, circle, club, corporation, fellowship, fraternity, group, guild, institute, league, order, organization, sisterhood, union **4.** beau monde, elite, gentry, *haut monde,* high society, polite society, the country set, the nobs (*slang*), the smart set, the swells (*informal*), the toffs (*Brit. slang*), the top drawer, upper classes, upper crust (*informal*)

sodden boggy, drenched, droukit *or* drookit (*Scot.*), marshy, miry, saturated, soaked, soggy, sopping, waterlogged

soft **1.** creamy, cushioned, cushiony, doughy, elastic, gelatinous, pulpy, quaggy, spongy, squashy, swampy, yielding **2.** bendable, ductile (*of metals*), elastic, flexible, impressible, malleable, mouldable, plastic, pliable, supple, tensile **3.** downy, feathery, fleecy, flowing, fluid, furry, like a baby's bottom (*informal*), rounded, silky, smooth, velvety **4.** balmy, bland, caressing, delicate, diffuse, dim, dimmed, dulcet, faint, gentle, light, low, mellifluous, mellow, melodious, mild, murmured, muted, pale, pastel, pleasing, quiet, restful, shaded, soft-toned, soothing, subdued, sweet, temperate, twilight, understated, whispered **5.** compassionate, gentle, kind, pitying, sensitive, sentimental, sympathetic, tender, tenderhearted, touchy-feely (*informal*) **6.** easy-going, indulgent, lax, lenient, liberal, overindulgent, permissive, spineless, weak **7.** *informal* comfortable, cushy (*informal*), easy, easy-peasy (*slang*), undemanding **8.** effeminate, flabby, flaccid, limp, namby-pamby, out of condition, out of training, overindulged, pampered, podgy, weak **9.** *informal* a bit lacking (*informal*), daft (*informal*), feeble-minded, foolish, silly, simple, soft in the head (*informal*), soppy (*Brit. informal*)

▷ **Antonyms** (*senses 1 & 2*) firm, hard, inflexible, rigid, solid, stiff, tough, unyielding (*sense 3*) abrasive, coarse, grating, hard, rough (*sense 4*) bright, garish, gaudy, glaring, hard, harsh, loud, noisy, strident, unpleasant (*sense 6*) austere, harsh, no-nonsense, stern, strict

soften abate, allay, alleviate, appease, assuage, calm, cushion, diminish, ease, lessen, lighten, lower, melt, mitigate, moderate, modify, mollify, muffle, palliate, quell, relax, soothe, still, subdue, temper, tone down, turn down

soften up conciliate, disarm, melt, soft-soap (*informal*), weaken, win over, work on

softhearted charitable, compassionate, generous, indulgent, kind, sentimental, sympathetic, tender, tenderhearted, warm-hearted

▷ **Antonyms** callous, cold, cruel, hard, hard-hearted, heartless, insensitive, uncaring, unkind, unsympathetic

soft pedal de-emphasize, go easy (*informal*), moderate, play down, tone down

soft spot fondness, liking, partiality, weakness

soggy dripping, heavy, moist, mushy, pulpy, saturated, soaked, sodden, sopping, spongy, waterlogged

soil[1] *noun* **1.** clay, dirt, dust, earth, ground, loam **2.** country, land, region, terra firma

soil[2] *verb* bedraggle, befoul, begrime, besmirch, defile, dirty, foul, maculate (*literary*), muddy, pollute, smear, smirch, spatter, spot, stain, sully, tarnish

sojourn **1.** *noun* rest, stay, stop, stopover, visit **2.** *~verb* abide, dwell, lodge, reside, rest, stay, stop, tarry

solace **1.** *noun* alleviation, assuagement, comfort, consolation, relief **2.** *~verb* allay, alleviate, comfort, console, mitigate, soften, soothe

soldier enlisted man (*U.S.*), fighter, GI (*U.S. informal*), man-at-arms, military man, redcoat, serviceman, squaddie *or* squaddy (*Brit. slang*), Tommy (*Brit. informal*), trooper, warrior

sole alone, exclusive, individual, one, one and only, only, single, singular, solitary

solecism bloomer (*Brit. informal*), blunder, boo-boo (*informal*), breach of etiquette, cacology, faux pas, gaffe, gaucherie, impropriety, incongruity, indecorum, lapse, mistake

solely alone, completely, entirely, exclusively, merely, only, single-handedly, singly

solemn 1. earnest, glum, grave, portentous, sedate, serious, sober, staid, thoughtful **2.** august, awe-inspiring, ceremonial, ceremonious, dignified, formal, grand, grave, imposing, impressive, majestic, momentous, stately **3.** devotional, hallowed, holy, religious, reverential, ritual, sacred, sanctified, venerable

▷ **Antonyms** (*senses 1 & 2*) bright, cheerful, chirpy (*informal*), comical, frivolous, genial, happy, informal, jovial, light-hearted, merry, relaxed, unceremonious (*sense 3*) irreligious, irreverent, unholy

solemnity 1. earnestness, grandeur, gravitas, gravity, impressiveness, momentousness, portentousness, sacredness, sanctity, seriousness **2.** (*often plural*) celebration, ceremonial, ceremony, formalities, observance, proceedings, rite, ritual

solemnize celebrate, commemorate, honour, keep, observe

solicit ask, beg, beseech, canvass, crave, entreat, implore, importune, petition, plead for, pray, seek, supplicate

solicitous anxious, apprehensive, attentive, careful, caring, concerned, eager, earnest, troubled, uneasy, worried, zealous

solicitude anxiety, attentiveness, care, concern, considerateness, consideration, regard, worry

solid *adjective* **1.** compact, concrete, dense, firm, hard, massed, stable, strong, sturdy, substantial, unshakable **2.** genuine, good, pure, real, reliable, sound **3.** agreed, complete, continuous, unalloyed, unanimous, unbroken, undivided, uninterrupted, united, unmixed **4.** constant, decent, dependable, estimable, law-abiding, level-headed, reliable, sensible, serious, sober, trusty, upright, upstanding, worthy

▷ **Antonyms** (*sense 1*) broken, crumbling, decaying, flimsy, gaseous, hollow, liquid, permeable, precarious, shaky, unstable, unsteady, unsubstantial (*sense 2*) impure, unreliable, unsound (*sense 3*) at odds, divided, mixed, split, undecided (*sense 4*) flighty, irresponsible, unreliable, unsound, unstable, unsteady

solidarity accord, camaraderie, cohesion, community of interest, concordance, esprit de corps, harmony, like-mindedness, singleness of purpose, soundness, stability, team spirit, unanimity, unification, unity

solidify cake, coagulate, cohere, congeal, harden, jell, set

solitary *adjective* **1.** desolate, hidden, isolated, lonely, out-of-the-way, remote, retired, secluded, sequestered, unfrequented, unvisited **2.** alone, lone, single, sole **3.** cloistered, companionless, friendless, hermitical, lonely, lonesome, reclusive, unsociable, unsocial *~noun* **4.** hermit, introvert, loner (*informal*), lone wolf, recluse

▷ **Antonyms** *~adjective* (*sense 1*) bustling, busy, frequented, public, well-frequented (*sense 3*) companionable, convivial, cordial, gregarious, outgoing, sociable, social *~noun* extrovert, mixer, socialite

solitude 1. isolation, ivory tower, loneliness, privacy, reclusiveness, retirement, seclusion **2.** *poetic* desert, emptiness, waste, wasteland, wilderness

solution 1. answer, clarification, elucidation, explanation, explication, key, resolution, result, solving, unfolding, unravelling **2.** blend, compound, emulsion, mix, mixture, solvent, suspension (*Chemistry*) **3.** disconnection, dissolution, liquefaction, melting

solve answer, clarify, clear up, crack, decipher, disentangle, elucidate, explain, expound, get to the bottom of, interpret, resolve, suss (out) (*slang*), unfold, unravel, work out

sombre dark, dim, dismal, doleful, drab, dull, dusky, funereal, gloomy, grave, joyless, lugubrious, melancholy, mournful, obscure, sad, sepulchral, shadowy, shady, sober

▷ **Antonyms** bright, cheerful, chirpy (*informal*), colourful, dazzling, effusive, full of beans, garish, gaudy, genial, happy, lively, sunny, upbeat (*informal*)

somebody *noun* big name, big noise (*informal*), big shot (*informal*), big wheel (*slang*), bigwig (*informal*), celeb (*informal*), celebrity, dignitary, heavyweight (*informal*), household name, luminary, megastar (*informal*), name, notable, personage, person of note, public figure, star, superstar, V.I.P.

▷ **Antonyms** also-ran, cipher, lightweight (*informal*), menial, nobody, nonentity, nothing (*informal*)

someday eventually, in the fullness of time, one day, one of these (fine) days, sooner or later, ultimately

somehow by fair means or foul, by hook or (by) crook, by some means or other, come hell or high water (*informal*), come what may, one way or another

sometimes at times, every now and then, every so often, from time to time, now and again, now and then, occasionally, off and on, once in a while, on occasion

▷ **Antonyms** always, consistently, constantly, continually, eternally, ever, everlastingly, evermore, forever, invariably, perpetually, unceasingly, without exception

somnolent comatose, dozy, drowsy, half-awake, heavy-eyed, nodding off (*informal*), sleepy, soporific, torpid

song air, anthem, ballad, canticle, canzonet, carol, chant, chorus, ditty, hymn, lay, lyric, melody, number, pop song, psalm, shanty, strain, tune

song and dance ado, commotion, flap (*informal*), fuss, hoo-ha, kerfuffle (*informal*), pantomime (*informal*), performance (*informal*), pother, shindig (*informal*), shindy (*informal*), stir, to-do

sonorous full, grandiloquent, high-flown, high-sounding, loud, orotund, plangent, resonant, resounding, rich, ringing, rounded, sounding

soon anon (*archaic*), any minute now, before long, betimes (*archaic*), erelong (*archaic or poetic*), in a couple of shakes, in a little while, in a minute, in a short time, in the near future, in two shakes of a lamb's tail, shortly

soothe allay, alleviate, appease, assuage, calm, calm down, compose, ease, hush, lull, mitigate, mollify, pacify, quiet, relieve, settle, smooth down, soften, still, tranquillize

▷ **Antonyms** aggravate (*informal*), agitate, annoy, disquiet, disturb, exacerbate, excite, get on one's nerves (*informal*), hassle (*informal*), increase, inflame, irritate, rouse, stimulate, upset, vex, worry

soothing balsamic, calming, demulcent, easeful, emollient, lenitive, palliative, relaxing, restful

soothsayer augur, diviner, foreteller, prophet, seer, sibyl

sophisticated 1. blasé, citified, cosmopolitan, cultivated, cultured, jet-set, refined, seasoned, urbane, worldly, worldly-wise, world-weary **2.** advanced, complex, complicated, delicate, elaborate, highly-developed, intricate, multifaceted, refined, subtle

▷ **Antonyms** basic, naive, old-fashioned, plain, primitive, simple, uncomplicated, unrefined, unsophisticated, unsubtle, unworldly, wet behind the ears (*informal*)

sophistication finesse, poise, savoir-faire, *savoir-vivre,* urbanity, worldliness, worldly wisdom

sophistry casuistry, fallacy, quibble, sophism

soporific 1. *adjective* hypnotic, sedative, sleep-inducing, sleepy, somniferous (*rare*), somnolent, tranquillizing **2.** *~noun* anaesthetic, hypnotic, narcotic, opiate, sedative, tranquillizer

soppy corny (*slang*), daft (*informal*), drippy (*informal*), gushy (*informal*), lovey-dovey, mawkish, overemotional, schmaltzy (*slang*), sentimental, silly, slushy (*informal*), soft (*informal*), weepy (*informal*)

sorcerer enchanter, mage (*archaic*), magician, magus, necromancer, sorceress, warlock, witch, wizard

sorcery black art, black magic, charm, divination, enchantment, incantation, magic, necromancy, spell, witchcraft, witchery, wizardry

sordid 1. dirty, filthy, foul, mean, seamy, seedy, sleazy, slovenly, slummy, squalid, unclean, wretched **2.** base, debauched, degenerate, degraded, despicable, disreputable, low, shabby, shameful, vicious, vile **3.** avaricious, corrupt, covetous, grasping, mercenary, miserly, niggardly, selfish, self-seeking, ungenerous, venal

▷ **Antonyms** blameless, clean, decent, fresh, honourable, noble, pure, spotless, squeaky-clean, unblemished, undefiled, unsullied, upright

sore *adjective* **1.** angry, burning, chafed, choked, inflamed, irritated, painful, raw, reddened, sensitive, smarting, tender **2.** annoying, distressing, grievous, harrowing, severe, sharp, troublesome **3.** acute, critical, desperate, dire, extreme, pressing, urgent **4.** afflicted, aggrieved, angry, annoyed, cross, grieved, hurt, irked, irritated, pained, peeved (*informal*), resentful, stung, upset, vexed *~noun* **5.** abscess, boil, chafe, gathering, inflammation, ulcer

sorrow *noun* **1.** affliction, anguish, distress, grief, heartache, heartbreak, misery, mourning, regret, sadness, unhappiness, woe **2.** affliction, blow, bummer (*slang*), hardship, misfortune, trial, tribulation, trouble, woe, worry *~verb* **3.** agonize, bemoan, be sad, bewail, eat one's heart out, grieve, lament, moan, mourn, weep

▷ **Antonyms** *~noun* bliss, delight, elation, exaltation, exultation, gladness, good fortune, happiness, joy, lucky break, pleasure *~verb* celebrate, delight, exult, jump for joy, rejoice, revel

sorrowful affecting, afflicted, dejected, depressed, disconsolate, dismal, distressing, doleful, down in the dumps (*informal*), grievous, harrowing, heartbroken, heart-rending, heavy-hearted, lamentable, lugubrious, melancholy, miserable, mournful, painful, piteous, rueful, sad, sick at heart, sorry, tearful, unhappy, woebegone, woeful, wretched

sorry 1. apologetic, conscience-stricken, contrite, guilt-ridden, in sackcloth and ashes, penitent, regretful, remorseful, repentant, self-reproachful, shamefaced **2.** disconsolate, distressed, grieved, melancholy, mournful, sad, sorrowful, unhappy **3.** commiserative, compassionate, full of pity, moved, pitying, sympathetic **4.** abject, base, deplorable, dismal, distressing, mean, miserable, paltry, pathetic, piteous, pitiable, pitiful, poor, sad, shabby, vile, wretched

▷ **Antonyms** (*sense 1*) impenitent, not contrite, shameless, unapologetic, unashamed, unremorseful, unrepentant (*sense 2*) cheerful, delighted, elated, happy, joyful (*sense 3*) compassionless (*rare*), heartless, indifferent, uncompassionate, unconcerned, unmoved, unpitying, unsympathetic

sort *noun* **1.** brand, breed, category, character, class, denomination, description, family, genus, group, ilk, kind, make, nature, order, quality, race, species, stamp, style, type, variety **2. out of sorts** crotchety, down in the dumps (*informal*), down in the mouth (*informal*), grouchy (*informal*), in low spirits, mopy, not up to par, not up to snuff (*informal*), off colour, poorly (*informal*), under the weather (*informal*) **3. sort of** as it were, in part, moderately, rather, reasonably, slightly, somewhat, to some extent *~verb* **4.** arrange, assort, catalogue, categorize, choose, class, classify, distribute, divide, file, grade, group, order, put in order, rank, select, separate, sequence, systematize, tabulate

sort out 1. clarify, clear up, organize, put *or* get straight, resolve, tidy up **2.** pick out, put on one side, segregate, select, separate, sift

so-so *adjective* adequate, average, fair, fair to middling (*informal*), indifferent, middling, moderate, not bad (*informal*), O.K. *or* okay (*informal*), ordinary, passable, respectable, run-of-the-mill, tolerable, undistinguished

sought-after coveted, desirable, enviable, in demand, like gold dust, longed-for, to-die-for, wanted

soul 1. animating principle, essence, intellect, life, mind, psyche, reason, spirit, vital force **2.** being, body, creature, individual, man, mortal, person, woman **3.** embodiment, epitome, essence, incarnation, personification, quintessence, type **4.** animation, ardour, courage, energy, feeling, fervour, force, inspiration, nobility, vitality, vivacity

soulful eloquent, expressive, heartfelt, meaningful, mournful, moving, profound, sensitive

soulless 1. callous, cold, cruel, harsh, inhuman, unfeeling, unkind, unsympathetic **2.** dead, lifeless, mechanical, soul-destroying, spiritless, uninteresting

sound[1] *noun* **1.** din, noise, report, resonance, reverberation, tone, voice **2.** drift, idea, implication(s), impression, look, tenor **3.** earshot, hearing, range *~verb* **4.** echo, resonate, resound, reverberate **5.** appear, give the impression of, look, seem, strike one as being **6.** announce, articulate, declare, enunciate, express, pronounce, signal, utter

sound[2] *adjective* **1.** complete, entire, firm, fit, hale, hale and hearty, healthy, intact, perfect, robust, solid, sturdy, substantial, undamaged, unhurt, unimpaired, uninjured, vigorous, well-constructed, whole **2.** correct, fair, just, level-headed, logical, orthodox, proper, prudent, rational, reasonable, reliable, responsible, right, right-thinking, sensible, true, trustworthy, valid, well-founded, well-grounded, wise **3.** established, orthodox, proven, recognized, reliable, reputable, safe, secure, solid, solvent, stable, tried-and-true **4.** deep, peaceful, unbroken, undisturbed, untroubled

▷ **Antonyms** (*sense 1*) ailing, damaged, flimsy, frail, light, shaky, sketchy, superficial, unbalanced, unstable, weak (*senses 2 & 3*) fallacious, faulty, flawed, incompetent, irrational, irresponsible, specious, unreliable, unsound, unstable (*sense 4*) broken, fitful, shallow, troubled

sound[3] *verb* **1.** fathom, plumb, probe **2.** examine, inspect, investigate, test

sound[4] *noun* **1.** channel, passage, strait **2.** arm of the sea, fjord, inlet, voe

sound out canvass, examine, probe, pump, put out feelers to, question, see how the land lies, test the water

sour *adjective* **1.** acerb, acetic, acid, acidulated, bitter, pungent, sharp, tart, unpleasant **2.** bad, curdled, fermented, gone off, rancid, turned, unsavoury, unwholesome **3.** acrid, acrimonious, churlish, crabbed, cynical, disagreeable, discontented, embittered, grouchy (*informal*), grudging, ill-natured, ill-tempered, jaundiced, peevish, tart, ungenerous, waspish *~verb* **4.** alienate, disenchant, embitter, envenom, exacerbate, exasperate, turn off (*informal*)

▷ **Antonyms** *~adjective* (*sense 1*) agreeable, bland, mild, pleasant, savoury, sugary, sweet (*sense 2*) fresh, unimpaired, unspoiled (*sense 3*) affable, amiable, congenial, friendly, genial, good-humoured, good-natured, pleasant, warm-hearted *~verb* enhance, improve, strengthen

source 1. author, begetter, beginning, cause, commencement, derivation, fount, fountainhead, origin, originator, rise, spring, wellspring **2.** authority, informant

sourpuss crosspatch (*informal*), grouser, grump (*informal*), killjoy, misery (*Brit. informal*), prophet of doom, shrew

souse drench, dunk, immerse, marinate (*Cookery*), pickle, soak, steep

souvenir keepsake, memento, relic, remembrancer (*archaic*), reminder, token

sovereign *noun* **1.** chief, emperor, empress, king, monarch, potentate, prince, queen, ruler, shah, supreme ruler, tsar *~adjective* **2.** absolute, chief, dominant, imperial, kingly, monarchal, paramount, predominant, principal, queenly, regal, royal, ruling, supreme, unlimited **3.** effectual, efficacious, efficient, excellent

sovereignty ascendancy, domination, kingship, primacy, supremacy, supreme power, suzerainty, sway

sow broadcast, disseminate, implant, inseminate, lodge, plant, scatter, seed

space 1. amplitude, capacity, elbowroom, expanse, extension, extent, leeway, margin, play, room, scope, spaciousness, volume **2.** blank, distance, gap, interval, lacuna, omission **3.** duration, interval, period, span, time, while **4.** accommodation, berth, place, seat

spaceman *or* **spacewoman** astronaut, cosmonaut

spacious ample, broad, capacious, comfortable, commodious, expansive, extensive, huge, large, roomy, sizable *or* sizeable, uncrowded, vast

▷ **Antonyms** close, confined, cramped, crowded, limited, narrow, poky, restricted, small

spadework donkey-work, groundwork, labour, preparation

span *noun* **1.** amount, distance, extent, length, reach, spread, stretch **2.** duration, period, spell, term *~verb* **3.** arch across, bridge, cover, cross, extend across, link, range over, traverse, vault

spank *verb* belt (*informal*), cuff, give (someone) a hiding (*informal*), put (someone) over one's knee, slap, slipper (*informal*), smack, tan (*slang*), wallop (*informal*), whack

spanking *adjective* **1.** brisk, energetic, fast, invigorating, lively, quick, smart, snappy, vigorous **2.** *informal* brand-new, fine, gleaming, smart

spar *verb* argue, bicker, dispute, exchange blows, fall out (*informal*), have a tiff, lead a cat-and-dog life, row, scrap (*informal*), skirmish, spat (*U.S.*), squabble, wrangle, wrestle

spare *adjective* **1.** additional, emergency, extra, free, going begging, in excess, in reserve, leftover, odd, over, superfluous, supernumerary, surplus, unoccupied, unused, unwanted **2.** gaunt, lank, lean, macilent (*rare*), meagre, slender, slight, slim, wiry **3.** economical, frugal, meagre, modest, scanty, sparing **4. go spare** *Brit. slang* become angry, become distracted, become distraught, become enraged, become mad (*informal*), become upset, blow one's top (*informal*), do one's nut (*Brit. slang*), go mental (*slang*), go up the wall (*slang*), have *or* throw a fit (*informal*) *~verb* **5.** afford, allow, bestow, dispense with, do without, give, grant, let (someone) have, manage without, part with, relinquish **6.** be merciful to, deal leniently with, go easy on (*informal*), have mercy on, leave, let off (*informal*), pardon, refrain from, release, relieve from, save from

▷ **Antonyms** *~adjective* (*sense 1*) allocated, designated, earmarked, in use, necessary, needed, set aside, spoken for (*sense 2*) corpulent, fat, flabby, fleshy, generous, heavy, large, plump *~verb* (*sense 6*) afflict, condemn, damn, destroy, hurt, punish, show no mercy to

spare time free time, leisure, odd moments, time on one's hands, time to kill

sparing careful, chary, cost-conscious, economical, frugal, money-conscious, prudent, saving, thrifty

▷ **Antonyms** extravagant, lavish, liberal, open-handed, prodigal, spendthrift

spark *noun* **1.** flare, flash, flicker, gleam, glint, scintillation, spit **2.** atom, hint, jot, scintilla, scrap, trace, vestige *~verb* **3.** (*often with* **off**) animate, excite, inspire, kick-start, kindle, precipitate, prod, provoke, rouse, set in motion, set off, start, stimulate, stir, touch off, trigger (off)

sparkle *verb* **1.** beam, coruscate, dance, flash, gleam, glint, glisten, glister (*archaic*), glitter, glow, scintillate, shimmer, shine, spark, twinkle, wink **2.** bubble, effervesce, fizz, fizzle *~noun* **3.** brilliance, coruscation, dazzle, flash, flicker, gleam, glint, radiance, spark, twinkle **4.** animation, brio, dash, élan, gaiety, life, panache, spirit, vim (*slang*), vitality, vivacity, zip (*informal*)

sparse few and far between, meagre, scanty, scarce, scattered, sporadic

▷ **Antonyms** crowded, dense, lavish, lush, luxuriant, numerous, plentiful, thick

spartan 1. abstemious, ascetic, austere, bleak, disciplined, extreme, frugal, plain, rigorous, self-denying, severe, stern, strict, stringent **2.** bold, brave, courageous, daring, dauntless, doughty, fearless, hardy, heroic, intrepid, resolute, unflinching, valorous

spasm 1. contraction, convulsion, paroxysm, throe (*rare*), twitch **2.** access, burst, eruption, fit, frenzy, outburst, seizure

spasmodic convulsive, erratic, fitful, intermittent, irregular, jerky, sporadic

spate deluge, flood, flow, outpouring, rush, torrent

spatter bespatter, bestrew, daub, dirty, scatter, soil, speckle, splash, splodge, spray, sprinkle

speak 1. articulate, communicate, converse, discourse, enunciate, express, make known, pronounce, say, state, talk, tell, utter, voice **2.** address, argue, declaim, deliver an address, descant, discourse, harangue, hold forth, lecture, plead, speechify, spiel (*informal*), spout **3.** (*with* **of**) advert to, allude to, comment on, deal with, discuss, make reference to, mention, refer to

speaker lecturer, mouthpiece, orator, public speaker, spieler (*informal*), spokesman, spokesperson, spokeswoman, word-spinner

speak for act for *or* on behalf of, appear for, hold a brief for, hold a mandate for, represent

speaking *adjective* eloquent, expressive, moving, noticeable, striking

speak out *or* **up 1.** make oneself heard, say it loud and clear, speak loudly **2.** have one's say, make one's position plain, sound off, speak one's mind, stand up and be counted

speak to 1. accost, address, apostrophize, direct one's words at, talk to **2.** admonish, bring to book, dress down (*informal*), lecture, rebuke, reprimand, scold, tell off (*informal*), tick off (*informal*), warn

spearhead *verb* be in the van, blaze the trail, head, initiate, launch, lay the first stone, lead, lead the way, pioneer, set in motion, set off

special 1. distinguished, especial, exceptional, extraordinary, festive, gala, important, memorable, momentous, one in a million, out of the ordinary, red-letter, significant, uncommon, unique, unusual **2.** appropriate, certain, characteristic, distinctive, especial, individual, particular, peculiar, precise, specialized, specific **3.** chief, main, major, particular, primary

▷ **Antonyms** common, everyday, general, humdrum, mediocre, multi-purpose, no great shakes (*informal*), normal, ordinary, routine, run-of-the-mill, undistinctive, undistinguished, unexceptional, unspecialized, usual

specialist *noun* authority, buff (*informal*), connoisseur, consultant, expert, hotshot (*informal*), master, maven (*U.S.*), professional, whizz (*informal*)

speciality bag (*slang*), claim to fame, distinctive *or* distinguishing feature, forte, métier, *pièce de résistance,* special, specialty

species breed, category, class, collection, description, genus, group, kind, sort, type, variety

specific *adjective* **1.** clear-cut, definite, exact, explicit, express, limited, particular, precise, unambiguous, unequivocal **2.** characteristic, distinguishing, especial, peculiar, special

▷ **Antonyms** (*sense 1*) approximate, general, hazy, imprecise, non-specific, uncertain, unclear, vague, woolly (*sense 2*) common, general

specification condition, detail, item, particular, qualification, requirement, stipulation

specify be specific about, cite, define, designate, detail, enumerate, indicate, individualize, itemize, mention, name, particularize, spell out, stipulate

specimen copy, embodiment, example, exemplar, exemplification, exhibit, individual, instance, model, pattern, proof, representative, sample, type

specious casuistic, deceptive, fallacious, misleading, plausible, sophistic, sophistical, unsound

speck 1. blemish, blot, defect, dot, fault, flaw, fleck, mark, mote, speckle, spot, stain **2.** atom, bit, dot, grain, iota, jot, mite, modicum, particle, shred, tittle, whit

speckled brindled, dappled, dotted, flecked, freckled, mottled, speckledy, spotted, spotty, sprinkled, stippled

spectacle 1. display, event, exhibition, extravaganza, pageant, parade, performance, show, sight **2.** curiosity, laughing stock, marvel, phenomenon, scene, sight, wonder

spectacular 1. *adjective* breathtaking, daring, dazzling, dramatic, eye-catching, fantastic (*informal*), grand, impressive, magnificent, marked, remarkable, sensational, splendid, staggering, striking, stunning (*informal*) **2.** *~noun* display, extravaganza, show, spectacle

▷ **Antonyms** *~adjective* easy, everyday, modest, ordinary, plain, run-of-the-mill, simple, unimpressive, unostentatious, unspectacular

spectator beholder, bystander, eyewitness, looker-on, observer, onlooker, viewer, watcher, witness

▷ **Antonyms** contestant, contributor, partaker, participant, participator, party, player

spectral eerie, ghostly, incorporeal, insubstantial, phantom, shadowy, spooky (*informal*), supernatural, uncanny, unearthly, weird, wraithlike

spectre apparition, eidolon, ghost, phantom, presence, shade (*literary*), shadow, spirit, vision, wraith

speculate 1. cogitate, conjecture, consider, contemplate, deliberate, hypothesize, meditate, muse, scheme, suppose, surmise, theorize, wonder **2.** gamble, have a flutter (*informal*), hazard, play the market, risk, take a chance with, venture

speculation 1. conjecture, consideration, contemplation, deliberation, guess, guesswork, hypothesis, opinion, supposition, surmise, theory **2.** gamble, gambling, hazard, risk

speculative 1. abstract, academic, conjectural, hypothetical, notional, suppositional, tentative, theoretical 2. chancy (*informal*), dicey (*informal, chiefly Brit.*), hazardous, risky, uncertain, unpredictable

speech 1. communication, conversation, dialogue, discussion, intercourse, talk 2. address, discourse, disquisition, harangue, homily, lecture, oration, spiel (*informal*) 3. articulation, dialect, diction, enunciation, idiom, jargon, language, lingo (*informal*), parlance, tongue, utterance, voice

speechless 1. dumb, inarticulate, lost for words, mum, mute, silent, tongue-tied, unable to get a word out (*informal*), wordless 2. *figurative* aghast, amazed, astounded, dazed, dumbfounded, dumbstruck, shocked, thunderstruck

speed *noun* 1. acceleration, celerity, expedition, fleetness, haste, hurry, momentum, pace, precipitation, quickness, rapidity, rush, swiftness, velocity *~verb* 2. barrel (along) (*informal, chiefly U.S. & Canad.*), belt (along) (*slang*), bomb (along), bowl along, burn rubber (*informal*), career, dispatch, exceed the speed limit, expedite, flash, gallop, get a move on (*informal*), go hell for leather (*informal*), go like a bat out of hell, go like a bomb (*Brit. & N.Z. informal*), go like the wind, hasten, hurry, lose no time, make haste, press on, put one's foot down (*informal*), quicken, race, rush, sprint, step on it (*informal*), tear, urge, zoom 3. advance, aid, assist, boost, expedite, facilitate, further, help, impel, promote

▷ **Antonyms** *~noun* delay, slowness, sluggishness, tardiness *~verb* (*sense 2*) crawl, creep, dawdle, delay, take one's time, tarry (*sense 3*) delay, hamper, hinder, hold up, retard, slow

speed up accelerate, gather momentum, get moving, get under way, increase, increase the tempo, open up the throttle, put one's foot down (*informal*), put on speed

▷ **Antonyms** brake, decelerate, reduce speed, rein in, slacken (off), slow down

speedy expeditious, express, fast, fleet, fleet of foot, hasty, headlong, hurried, immediate, nimble, pdq (*slang*), precipitate, prompt, quick, quickie (*informal*), rapid, summary, swift, winged

▷ **Antonyms** dead slow and stop, delayed, dilatory, late, leisurely, lingering, long-drawn-out, plodding, slow, sluggish, tardy, unhurried, unrushed

spell[1] *noun* bout, course, interval, patch, period, season, stint, stretch, term, time, tour of duty, turn

spell[2] *noun* 1. abracadabra, charm, conjuration, exorcism, incantation, sorcery, witchery 2. allure, bewitchment, enchantment, fascination, glamour, magic, trance

spell[3] *verb* amount to, augur, herald, imply, indicate, mean, point to, portend, presage, promise, signify, suggest

spellbound bemused, bewitched, captivated, charmed, enthralled, entranced, fascinated, gripped, hooked, mesmerized, possessed, rapt, transfixed, transported, under a spell

spelling orthography

spell out 1. clarify, elucidate, explicate, make clear *or* plain, make explicit, specify 2. discern, make out, puzzle out

spend 1. disburse, expend, fork out (*slang*), lay out, pay out, shell out (*informal*), splash out (*Brit. informal*) 2. blow (*slang*), consume, deplete, dispense, dissipate, drain, empty, exhaust, fritter away, run through, squander, use up, waste 3. apply, bestow, concentrate, devote, employ, exert, invest, lavish, put in, use 4. fill, occupy, pass, while away

▷ **Antonyms** (*senses 1 & 2*) hoard, invest, keep, put aside, put by, save, store

spendthrift 1. *noun* big spender, prodigal, profligate, spender, squanderer, waster, wastrel 2. *~adjective* extravagant, improvident, prodigal, profligate, wasteful

▷ **Antonyms** *~noun* meanie *or* meany (*informal, chiefly Brit.*), miser, penny-pincher (*informal*), Scrooge, skinflint, tight-arse (*taboo slang*), tight-ass (*U.S. taboo slang*), tightwad (*U.S. & Canad. slang*) *~adjective* careful, economical, frugal, parsimonious, provident, prudent, sparing, thrifty

spent *adjective* 1. all in (*slang*), burnt out, bushed (*informal*), clapped out (*Austral. & N.Z. informal*), dead beat (*informal*), debilitated, dog-tired (*informal*), done in *or* up (*informal*), drained, effete, exhausted, fagged (out) (*informal*), knackered (*slang*), played out (*informal*), prostrate, ready to drop (*informal*), shagged out (*Brit. slang*), shattered (*informal*), tired out, weakened, wearied, weary, whacked (*Brit. informal*), wiped out (*informal*), worn out, zonked (*informal*) 2. consumed, expended, finished, gone, used up

spew barf (*U.S. slang*), belch forth, chuck (up) (*slang, chiefly U.S.*), chunder (*slang, chiefly Austral.*), disgorge, do a technicolour yawn (*slang*), puke (*slang*), regurgitate, spit out, throw up (*informal*), toss one's cookies (*U.S. slang*), upchuck (*U.S. slang*), vomit

sphere 1. ball, circle, globe, globule, orb 2. capacity, compass, department, domain, employment, field, function, pale, patch, province, range, rank, realm, scope, station, stratum, territory, turf (*U.S. slang*), walk of life

spherical globe-shaped, globular, orbicular, rotund, round

spice *noun* 1. relish, savour, seasoning 2. colour, excitement, gusto, kick (*infor~*

mal), pep, piquancy, tang, zap (*slang*), zest, zing (*informal*), zip (*informal*)

spick-and-span clean, fresh as paint, immaculate, impeccable, in apple-pie order (*informal*), neat as a new pin, shipshape, spotless, spruce, tidy, trim

spicy 1. aromatic, flavoursome, hot, piquant, pungent, savoury, seasoned, tangy **2.** *informal* broad, hot (*informal*), improper, indecorous, indelicate, off-colour, racy, ribald, risqué, scandalous, sensational, suggestive, titillating, unseemly

spiel 1. *verb* expatiate on, hold forth, lecture, recite, speechify, spout (*informal*) **2.** *~noun* harangue, patter, pitch, recital, sales patter, sales talk, speech

spike *noun* **1.** barb, point, prong, spine *~verb* **2.** impale, spear, spit, stick **3.** block, foil, frustrate, render ineffective, thwart

spill *verb* **1.** discharge, disgorge, overflow, overturn, scatter, shed, slop over, spill *or* run over, teem, throw off, upset **2. spill the beans** *informal* betray a secret, blab, blow the gaff (*Brit. slang*), give the game away, grass (*Brit. slang*), inform, let the cat out of the bag, shop (*slang, chiefly Brit.*), sing (*slang, chiefly U.S.*), spill one's guts (*slang*), split (*slang*), squeal (*slang*), talk out of turn, tattle, tell all *~noun* **3.** *informal* accident, cropper (*informal*), fall, tumble

spin *verb* **1.** birl (*Scot.*), gyrate, pirouette, reel, revolve, rotate, turn, twirl, twist, wheel, whirl **2.** concoct, develop, invent, narrate, recount, relate, tell, unfold **3.** be giddy, be in a whirl, grow dizzy, reel, swim, whirl *~noun* **4.** gyration, revolution, roll, twist, whirl **5. (flat) spin** *informal* agitation, commotion, flap (*informal*), panic, state (*informal*), tiz-woz (*informal*), tizzy (*informal*) **6.** *informal* drive, hurl (*Scot.*), joy ride (*informal*), ride, turn, whirl

spindly attenuated, gangling, gangly, lanky, leggy, spidery, spindle-shanked, twiggy

spine 1. backbone, spinal column, vertebrae, vertebral column **2.** barb, needle, quill, rachis, ray, spike, spur

spine-chilling bloodcurdling, eerie, frightening, hair-raising, horrifying, scary (*informal*), spooky (*informal*), terrifying

spineless chickenshit (*U.S. slang*), cowardly, faint-hearted, feeble, gutless (*informal*), inadequate, ineffective, irresolute, lily-livered, pathetic, soft, spiritless, squeamish, submissive, vacillating, weak, weak-kneed (*informal*), weak-willed, without a will of one's own, yellow (*informal*)

▷ **Antonyms** ballsy (*taboo slang*), bold, brave, courageous, gritty, strong, strong-willed

spin out amplify, delay, drag out, draw out, extend, lengthen, pad out, prolong, prolongate, protract

spiral 1. *adjective* circular, cochlear, cochleate (*Biology*), coiled, corkscrew, helical, scrolled, voluted, whorled, winding **2.** *~noun* coil, corkscrew, curlicue, gyre (*literary*), helix, screw, volute, whorl

spirit *noun* **1.** air, breath, life, life force, psyche, soul, vital spark **2.** attitude, character, complexion, disposition, essence, humour, outlook, quality, temper, temperament **3.** animation, ardour, backbone, balls (*taboo slang*), ballsiness (*taboo slang*), brio, courage, dauntlessness, earnestness, energy, enterprise, enthusiasm, fire, force, gameness, grit, guts (*informal*), life, liveliness, mettle, resolution, sparkle, spunk (*informal*), stoutheartedness, vigour, warmth, zest **4.** motivation, resolution, resolve, will, willpower **5.** atmosphere, feeling, gist, humour, tenor, tone **6.** essence, intent, intention, meaning, purport, purpose, sense, substance **7.** *plural* feelings, frame of mind, humour, mood, morale **8.** apparition, eidolon, ghost, phantom, shade (*literary*), shadow, spectre, spook (*informal*), sprite, vision *~verb* **9.** (*with* **away** *or* **off**) abduct, abstract, carry, convey, make away with, purloin, remove, seize, snaffle (*Brit. informal*), steal, whisk

spirited active, animated, ardent, bold, courageous, energetic, feisty (*informal, chiefly U.S. & Canad.*), game, have-a-go (*informal*), high-spirited, lively, mettlesome, plucky, sparkling, sprightly, spunky (*informal*), vigorous, vivacious

▷ **Antonyms** apathetic, bland, calm, dispirited, dull, feeble, half-hearted, lacklustre, lifeless, low-key, spiritless, timid, token, unenthusiastic, weary

spiritless apathetic, dejected, depressed, despondent, dispirited, droopy, dull, lacklustre, languid, lifeless, listless, low (*informal*), melancholic, melancholy, mopy, torpid, unenthusiastic, unmoved

spirits alcohol, firewater, liquor, strong liquor, the hard stuff (*informal*)

spiritual devotional, divine, ethereal, ghostly, holy, immaterial, incorporeal, nonmaterial, otherworldly, pure, religious, sacred

▷ **Antonyms** concrete, corporeal, material, nonspiritual, palpable, physical, substantial, tangible

spit 1. *verb* discharge, eject, expectorate, hiss, spew, splutter, sputter, throw out **2.** *~noun* dribble, drool, saliva, slaver, spittle, sputum

spite *noun* **1.** animosity, bitchiness (*slang*), gall, grudge, hate, hatred, ill will, malevolence, malice, malignity, pique, rancour, spitefulness, spleen, venom **2. in spite of** despite, (even) though, in defiance of, notwithstanding, regardless of *~verb* **3.** annoy, discomfit, gall, harm, hurt, injure, needle (*informal*), nettle, offend, pique, provoke, put out, put (someone's) nose out of joint (*informal*), vex

▷ **Antonyms** *~noun* benevolence, big-heartedness, charity, compassion, generosity of spirit, goodwill, kindliness, kindness, love, warm-heartedness *~verb* aid, benefit, encourage, go along with, help, please, serve, support

spiteful barbed, bitchy (*informal*), catty (*informal*), cruel, ill-disposed, ill-natured, malevolent, malicious, malignant, nasty, rancorous, shrewish, snide, splenetic, venomous, vindictive

spitting image clone, (dead) ringer (*slang*), double, likeness, living image, lookalike, picture, replica, spit (*informal, chiefly Brit.*), spit and image (*informal*)

splash *verb* **1.** bespatter, shower, slop, slosh (*informal*), spatter, splodge, spray, spread, sprinkle, squirt, strew, wet **2.** bathe, dabble, paddle, plunge, wade, wallow **3.** batter, break, buffet, dash, plash, plop, smack, strike, surge, wash **4.** blazon, broadcast, flaunt, headline, plaster, publicize, tout, trumpet *~noun* **5.** burst, dash, patch, spattering, splodge, touch **6.** *informal* display, effect, impact, sensation, splurge, stir **7.** **make a splash** be ostentatious, cause a stir, cut a dash, go overboard (*informal*), go to town, splurge

splash out be extravagant, lash out (*informal*), push the boat out (*Brit. informal*), spare no expense, spend, splurge

spleen acrimony, anger, animosity, animus, bad temper, bile, bitterness, gall, hatred, hostility, ill humour, ill will, malevolence, malice, malignity, peevishness, pique, rancour, resentment, spite, spitefulness, venom, vindictiveness, wrath

splendid **1.** admirable, brilliant, exceptional, glorious, grand, heroic, illustrious, magnificent, outstanding, rare, remarkable, renowned, sterling, sublime, superb, supreme **2.** costly, dazzling, gorgeous, imposing, impressive, lavish, luxurious, magnificent, ornate, resplendent, rich, splendiferous (*facetious*), sumptuous, superb **3.** awesome (*slang*), bodacious (*slang, chiefly U.S.*), boffo (*slang*), brill (*informal*), chillin' (*U.S. slang*), cracking (*Brit. informal*), crucial (*slang*), def (*slang*), excellent, fantastic (*informal*), fine, first-class, glorious, great (*informal*), marvellous, mean (*slang*), mega (*slang*), sovereign, topping (*Brit. slang*), wonderful **4.** beaming, bright, brilliant, glittering, glowing, lustrous, radiant, refulgent

▷ **Antonyms** beggarly, depressing, disgusting, distressed, drab, dull, ignoble, ignominious, lacklustre, low, mean, mediocre, miserable, no great shakes (*informal*), ordinary, pathetic, plain, poor, poverty-stricken, rotten, run-of-the-mill, sombre, sordid, squalid, tarnished, tawdry, undistinguished, unexceptional

splendour brightness, brilliance, ceremony, dazzle, display, éclat, effulgence, glory, gorgeousness, grandeur, lustre, magnificence, majesty, pomp, radiance, refulgence, renown, resplendence, richness, show, solemnity, spectacle, stateliness, sumptuousness

▷ **Antonyms** dullness, ignominy, lacklustreness, meanness, ordinariness, plainness, poverty, simplicity, sobriety, squalor, tawdriness

splenetic acid, bitchy (*informal*), choleric, churlish, crabbed, crabby, cross, envenomed, fretful, irascible, irritable, morose, peevish, petulant, rancorous, ratty (*Brit. & N.Z. informal*), sour, spiteful, sullen, testy, tetchy, touchy

splice *verb* braid, entwine, graft, interlace, intertwine, intertwist, interweave, join, knit, marry, mesh, plait, unite, wed, yoke

splinter **1.** *noun* chip, flake, fragment, needle, paring, shaving, sliver **2.** *~verb* break into smithereens, disintegrate, fracture, shatter, shiver, split

split *verb* **1.** bifurcate, branch, break, break up, burst, cleave, come apart, come undone, crack, disband, disunite, diverge, fork, gape, give way, go separate ways, open, part, pull apart, rend, rip, separate, slash, slit, snap, splinter **2.** allocate, allot, apportion, carve up, distribute, divide, divvy up (*informal*), dole out, halve, parcel out, partition, share out, slice up **3.** (*with* **on**) *slang* betray, give away, grass (*Brit. slang*), inform on, peach (*slang*), shop (*slang, chiefly Brit.*), sing (*slang, chiefly U.S.*), spill one's guts (*slang*), squeal (*slang*) *~noun* **4.** breach, crack, damage, division, fissure, gap, rent, rip, separation, slash, slit, tear **5.** breach, break, break-up, difference, discord, disruption, dissension, disunion, divergence, division, estrangement, partition, rift, rupture, schism *~adjective* **6.** ambivalent, bisected, broken, cleft, cracked, divided, dual, fractured, ruptured, twofold

split up break up, disband, divorce, go separate ways, part, part company, separate

spoil *verb* **1.** blemish, blow (*slang*), damage, debase, deface, destroy, disfigure, harm, impair, injure, mar, mess up, put a damper on, ruin, scar, total (*slang*), trash (*slang*), undo, upset, wreck **2.** baby, cocker (*rare*), coddle, cosset, indulge, kill with kindness, mollycoddle, overindulge, pamper, spoon-feed **3.** addle, become tainted, curdle, decay, decompose, go bad, go off (*Brit. informal*), mildew, putrefy, rot, turn **4.** **spoiling for**

bent upon, desirous of, eager for, enthusiastic about, keen to, looking for, out to get (*informal*), raring to
▷ **Antonyms** (*sense 1*) augment, conserve, enhance, improve, keep, preserve, save (*sense 2*) be strict with, deprive, ignore, pay no attention to, treat harshly

spoils boodle (*slang, chiefly U.S.*), booty, gain, loot, pickings, pillage, plunder, prey, prizes, rapine, swag (*slang*)

spoilsport damper, dog in the manger, kill-joy, misery (*Brit. informal*), party-pooper (*U.S. slang*), wet blanket (*informal*)

spoken by word of mouth, expressed, oral, phonetic, put into words, said, told, unwritten, uttered, verbal, viva voce, voiced

sponger bloodsucker (*informal*), cadge (*Brit.*), cadger, freeloader (*slang*), hanger-on, leech, parasite, scrounger (*informal*)

spongy absorbent, cushioned, cushiony, elastic, light, porous, springy

sponsor **1.** *noun* angel (*informal*), backer, godparent, guarantor, patron, promoter **2.** *~verb* back, finance, fund, guarantee, lend one's name to, patronize, promote, put up the money for, subsidize

spontaneous extempore, free, impromptu, impulsive, instinctive, natural, unbidden, uncompelled, unconstrained, unforced, unpremeditated, unprompted, voluntary, willing
▷ **Antonyms** arranged, calculated, contrived, deliberate, forced, mannered, orchestrated, planned, prearranged, premeditated, preplanned, stage-managed, studied

spontaneously extempore, freely, impromptu, impulsively, instinctively, in the heat of the moment, off one's own bat, off the cuff (*informal*), of one's own accord, on impulse, quite unprompted, voluntarily

spoof *noun* **1.** burlesque, caricature, lampoon, mockery, parody, satire, send-up (*Brit. informal*), take-off (*informal*), travesty **2.** bluff, canard, deception, game, hoax, joke, leg-pull (*Brit. informal*), prank, trick

spooky chilling, creepy (*informal*), eerie, frightening, ghostly, mysterious, scary (*informal*), spine-chilling, supernatural, uncanny, unearthly, weird

spoon-feed baby, cosset, featherbed, mollycoddle, overindulge, overprotect, spoil, wrap up in cotton wool (*informal*)

sporadic infrequent, intermittent, irregular, isolated, occasional, on and off, random, scattered, spasmodic
▷ **Antonyms** consistent, frequent, recurrent, regular, set, steady, systematic

sport *noun* **1.** amusement, diversion, entertainment, exercise, game, pastime, physical activity, play, recreation **2.** badinage, banter, frolic, fun, jest, joking, josh (*slang, chiefly U.S. & Canad.*), kidding (*informal*), merriment, mirth, raillery, teasing **3.** buffoon, butt, derision, fair game, game, laughing stock, mockery, plaything, ridicule *~verb* **4.** (*with* **with**) amuse oneself, dally, flirt, fool, play, take advantage of, toy, treat lightly *or* cavalierly, trifle **5.** *informal* display, exhibit, show off, wear **6.** caper, disport, frolic, gambol, play, romp

sporting fair, game (*informal*), gentlemanly, sportsman-like
▷ **Antonyms** unfair, unsporting, unsportsmanlike

sportive coltish, frisky, frolicsome, full of beans (*informal*), full of fun, gamesome, gay, joyous, kittenish, lively, merry, playful, prankish, rollicking, skittish, sprightly

sporty **1.** casual, flashy, gay, informal, jaunty, jazzy (*informal*), loud, raffish, rakish, showy, snazzy (*informal*), stylish, trendy (*Brit. informal*) **2.** athletic, energetic, hearty, outdoor

spot *noun* **1.** blemish, blot, blotch, daub, discoloration, flaw, mark, pimple, plook (*Scot.*), pustule, scar, smudge, speck, speckle, stain, taint, zit (*slang*) **2.** locality, location, place, point, position, scene, site, situation **3.** *informal* bit, little, morsel, splash **4.** *informal* difficulty, hot water (*informal*), mess, plight, predicament, quandary, tight spot, trouble *~verb* **5.** behold (*archaic or literary*), catch sight of, descry, detect, discern, espy, identify, make out, observe, pick out, recognize, see, sight **6.** besmirch, blot, dirty, dot, fleck, mark, mottle, scar, smirch, soil, spatter, speckle, splodge, splotch, stain, sully, taint, tarnish

spotless above reproach, blameless, chaste, clean, faultless, flawless, gleaming, immaculate, impeccable, innocent, irreproachable, pure, shining, snowy, unblemished, unimpeachable, unstained, unsullied, untarnished, virgin, virginal, white
▷ **Antonyms** besmirched, bespattered, blemished, defiled, dirty, filthy, flawed, impure, messy, notorious, reprehensible, soiled, spotted, stained, sullied, tainted, tarnished, unchaste, untidy

spotlight *figurative* **1.** *verb* accentuate, draw attention to, feature, focus attention on, give prominence to, highlight, illuminate, point up, throw into relief **2.** *~noun* attention, fame, interest, limelight, notoriety, public attention, public eye

spot-on accurate, correct, exact, hitting the nail on the head (*informal*), on the bull's-eye (*informal*), precise, punctual (to the minute), right, unerring

spotted dappled, dotted, flecked, mottled, pied, polka-dot, specked, speckled

spotty 1. blotchy, pimpled, pimply, plooky-faced (*Scot.*), poor-complexioned 2. erratic, fluctuating, irregular, patchy, sporadic, uneven

spouse better half (*humorous*), compan~ion, consort, helpmate, her indoors (*Brit. slang*), husband, mate, partner, significant other (*U.S. informal*), wife

spout *verb* 1. discharge, emit, erupt, gush, jet, shoot, spray, spurt, squirt, stream, surge 2. *informal* declaim, ex~patiate, go on (*informal*), hold forth, orate, pontificate, rabbit (on) (*Brit. in~formal*), ramble (on), rant, speechify, spiel (*informal*), talk

sprawl *verb* flop, loll, lounge, ramble, slouch, slump, spread, straggle, trail

spray[1] *verb* 1. atomize, diffuse, scatter, shower, sprinkle *~noun* 2. drizzle, drop~lets, fine mist, moisture, spindrift, spoondrift 3. aerosol, atomizer, sprinkler

spray[2] *noun* bough, branch, corsage, flo~ral arrangement, shoot, sprig

spread *verb* 1. be displayed, bloat, broad~en, dilate, expand, extend, fan out, open, open out, sprawl, stretch, swell, unfold, unfurl, unroll, widen 2. escalate, multiply, mushroom, proliferate 3. ad~vertise, blazon, broadcast, bruit, cast, circulate, cover, diffuse, disseminate, distribute, make known, make public, proclaim, promulgate, propagate, publi~cize, publish, radiate, scatter, shed, strew, transmit 4. arrange, array, cover, furnish, lay, prepare, set *~noun* 5. ad~vance, advancement, development, dif~fusion, dispersal, dissemination, escala~tion, expansion, increase, proliferation, spreading, suffusion, transmission 6. compass, extent, period, reach, span, stretch, sweep, term 7. *informal* array, banquet, blowout (*slang*), feast, repast

▷ **Antonyms** *~verb* (*sense 3*) contain, con~trol, curb, hold back, hold in, repress, restrain, stifle

spree bacchanalia, beano (*Brit. slang*), bender (*informal*), binge (*informal*), ca~rousal, carouse, debauch, fling, jag (*slang*), junketing, orgy, revel, splurge

sprightly active, agile, airy, alert, ani~mated, blithe, bright-eyed and bushy-tailed, brisk, cheerful, energetic, frolic~some, gay, jaunty, joyous, lively, nimble, perky, playful, spirited, sportive, spry, vivacious

▷ **Antonyms** dull, inactive, lethargic, sedentary, sluggish, torpid, unenergetic

spring *verb* 1. bounce, bound, hop, jump, leap, rebound, recoil, vault 2. (*often with* **from**) arise, be derived, be descended, come, derive, descend, emanate, emerge, grow, issue, originate, proceed, start, stem 3. (*with* **up**) appear, burgeon, come into existence *or* being, develop, mushroom, shoot up *~noun* 4. bound, buck, hop, jump, leap, saltation, vault 5. bounce, bounciness, buoyancy, elastici~ty, flexibility, give (*informal*), recoil, re~silience, springiness 6. beginning, cause, fount, fountainhead, origin, root, source, well, wellspring *~adjective* 7. *of the sea~son* springlike, vernal

springy bouncy, buoyant, elastic, flexible, resilient, rubbery, spongy

sprinkle *verb* dredge, dust, pepper, pow~der, scatter, shower, spray, strew

sprinkling admixture, dash, dusting, few, handful, scatter, scattering, smattering, sprinkle

sprint *verb* barrel (along) (*informal, chiefly U.S. & Canad.*), dart, dash, go at top speed, go like a bomb (*Brit. & N.Z. informal*), hare (*Brit. informal*), hotfoot, put on a burst of speed, race, scamper, shoot, tear, whizz (*informal*)

sprite apparition, brownie, dryad, elf, fairy, goblin, imp, leprechaun, naiad, nymph, Oceanid (*Greek myth*), peri, pixie, spirit, sylph

sprout *verb* bud, develop, germinate, grow, push, shoot, spring, vegetate

spruce as if one had just stepped out of a bandbox, dainty, dapper, elegant, natty (*informal*), neat, smart, soigné *or* soi~gnée, trig (*archaic or dialect*), trim, well-groomed, well turned out

▷ **Antonyms** bedraggled, disarrayed, di~shevelled, frowsy, messy, rumpled, un~combed, unkempt, untidy

spruce up groom, gussy up (*slang, chiefly U.S.*), have a wash and brush-up (*Brit.*), smarten up, tidy, titivate

spry active, agile, alert, brisk, nimble, nippy (*Brit. informal*), quick, ready, sprightly, supple

▷ **Antonyms** awkward, decrepit, dodder~ing, inactive, lethargic, slow, sluggish, stiff

spunk backbone, balls (*taboo slang*), ballsiness (*taboo slang*), bottle (*Brit. slang*), courage, gameness, grit, gump~tion (*informal*), guts (*informal*), mettle, nerve, pluck, resolution, spirit, tough~ness

spur *verb* 1. animate, drive, goad, impel, incite, press, prick, prod, prompt, put a bomb under (*informal*), stimulate, urge *~noun* 2. goad, prick, rowel 3. impetus, impulse, incentive, incitement, induce~ment, kick up the backside (*informal*), motive, stimulus 4. **on the spur of the moment** impetuously, impromptu, im~pulsively, on impulse, on the spot, un~premeditatedly, unthinkingly, without planning, without thinking

spurious artificial, bogus, contrived, counterfeit, deceitful, ersatz, fake, false, feigned, forged, imitation, mock, phoney *or* phony (*informal*), pretended, pseudo (*informal*), sham, simulated, specious, unauthentic

▷ **Antonyms** authentic, bona fide, genu~

ine, honest, kosher (*informal*), legitimate, real, sound, unfeigned, valid

spurn cold-shoulder, contemn, despise, disdain, disregard, kick in the teeth (*slang*), put down, rebuff, reject, repulse, scorn, slight, snub, turn one's nose up at (*informal*)

▷ **Antonyms** embrace, grasp, seize, take up, welcome

spurt **1.** *verb* burst, erupt, gush, jet, shoot, spew, squirt, surge **2.** *~noun* access, burst, fit, rush, spate, surge

spy *noun* **1.** double agent, fifth columnist, foreign agent, mole, nark (*Brit., Austral., & N.Z. slang*), secret agent, secret service agent, undercover agent *~verb* **2.** (*usually with* **on**) follow, keep under surveillance, keep watch on, shadow, tail (*informal*), trail, watch **3.** behold (*archaic or literary*), catch sight of, descry, espy, glimpse, notice, observe, set eyes on, spot

spying *noun* espionage, secret service

squabble **1.** *verb* argue, bicker, brawl, clash, dispute, fall out (*informal*), fight, fight like cat and dog, go at it hammer and tongs, have words, quarrel, row, scrap (*informal*), spar, wrangle **2.** *~noun* argument, *bagarre,* barney (*informal*), difference of opinion, disagreement, dispute, fight, row, scrap (*informal*), set-to (*informal*), spat, tiff

squad band, company, crew, force, gang, group, team, troop

squalid broken-down, decayed, dirty, disgusting, fetid, filthy, foul, low, nasty, poverty-stricken, repulsive, run-down, seedy, sleazy, slovenly, slummy, sordid, unclean, yucky *or* yukky (*slang*)

▷ **Antonyms** attractive, clean, genial, hygienic, in good condition, pleasant, salubrious, spick-and-span, spotless, tidy, well-kempt, well looked-after

squally blustery, gusty, inclement, rough, stormy, tempestuous, turbulent, wild, windy

squalor decay, filth, foulness, meanness, sleaziness, slumminess, squalidness, wretchedness

▷ **Antonyms** beauty, cleanliness, fine condition, luxury, neatness, order, pleasantness, splendour

squander be prodigal with, blow (*slang*), consume, dissipate, expend, fritter away, frivol away, lavish, misspend, misuse, run through, scatter, spend, spend like water, throw away, waste

▷ **Antonyms** be frugal, be thrifty, economize, keep, put aside for a rainy day, save, store

square *figurative verb* **1.** (*often with* **with**) accord, agree, conform, correspond, fit, harmonize, match, reconcile, tally **2.** (*sometimes with* **up**) balance, clear (up), discharge, liquidate, make even, pay off, quit, satisfy, settle **3.** accommodate, adapt, adjust, align, even up, level, regulate, suit, tailor, true (up) **4.** *slang* bribe, buy off, corrupt, fix (*informal*), rig, suborn *~adjective* **5.** aboveboard, decent, equitable, ethical, fair, fair and square, genuine, honest, just, kosher (*informal*), on the level (*informal*), on the up and up, straight, straightforward, upfront (*informal*), upright **6.** *informal* behind the times, bourgeois, conservative, conventional, dated, old-fashioned, out of date, out of the ark (*informal*), Pooterish, straight (*slang*), strait-laced, stuffy *~noun* **7.** *informal* antediluvian, back number (*informal*), conservative, die-hard, dinosaur, fuddy-duddy (*informal*), old buffer (*Brit. informal*), (old) fogey, stick-in-the-mud (*informal*), traditionalist

▷ **Antonyms** *~adjective* (*sense 6*) fashionable, in vogue, modern, modish, stylish, trendy (*Brit. informal*), voguish

squash *verb* **1.** compress, crush, distort, flatten, mash, pound, press, pulp, smash, stamp on, trample down **2.** annihilate, crush, humiliate, put down (*slang*), put (someone) in his (*or* her) place, quash, quell, silence, sit on (*informal*), suppress

squashy mushy, pappy, pulpy, soft, spongy, yielding

squawk *verb* **1.** cackle, crow, cry, hoot, screech, yelp **2.** *informal* complain, kick up a fuss (*informal*), protest, raise Cain (*slang*), squeal (*informal, chiefly Brit.*)

squeak *verb* peep, pipe, shrill, squeal, whine, yelp

squeal *noun* **1.** scream, screech, shriek, wail, yell, yelp, yowl *~verb* **2.** scream, screech, shout, shriek, shrill, wail, yelp **3.** *slang* betray, blab, blow the gaff (*Brit. slang*), grass (*Brit. slang*), inform on, peach (*slang*), rat on (*informal*), sell (someone) down the river (*informal*), shop (*slang, chiefly Brit.*), sing (*slang, chiefly U.S.*), snitch (*slang*), spill one's guts (*slang*), spill the beans (*informal*), tell all **4.** *informal* complain, kick up a fuss (*informal*), moan, protest, squawk (*informal*)

squeamish **1.** delicate, fastidious, finicky, nice (*rare*), particular, prissy (*informal*), prudish, punctilious, scrupulous, strait-laced **2.** nauseous, qualmish, queasy, queer, sick, sickish

▷ **Antonyms** (*sense 1*) bold, brassy, brazen, coarse, earthy, immodest, indifferent, tough, wanton (*sense 2*) strong-stomached

squeeze *verb* **1.** clutch, compress, crush, grip, nip, pinch, press, squash, wring **2.** cram, crowd, force, jam, jostle, pack, press, ram, stuff, thrust, wedge **3.** clasp, cuddle, embrace, enfold, hold tight, hug **4.** bleed (*informal*), bring pressure to bear on, extort, lean on (*informal*), milk, oppress, pressurize, put the screws on (*informal*), put the squeeze on (*informal*), wrest *~noun* **5.** clasp, embrace, handclasp, hold, hug **6.** congestion, crowd, crush, jam, press, squash

squint askew, aslant, awry, cockeyed, crooked, oblique, off-centre, skew-whiff (*informal*)
▷ **Antonyms** aligned, even, horizontal, in line, level, perpendicular, plum, square, straight, true, vertical

squire *verb* accompany, attend, companion, escort

squirm agonize, fidget, flounder, shift, twist, wiggle, wriggle, writhe

stab *verb* **1.** bayonet, cut, gore, impale, injure, jab, knife, pierce, puncture, run through, spear, spill blood, stick, thrust, transfix, wound **2. stab in the back** betray, break faith with, deceive, do the dirty on (*Brit. slang*), double-cross (*informal*), give the Judas kiss to, inform on, let down, play false, sell, sell out (*informal*), slander *~noun* **3.** gash, incision, jab, puncture, rent, thrust, wound **4.** ache, pang, prick, twinge **5. make a stab at** attempt, endeavour, essay, give it one's best shot (*informal*), have a crack (*informal*), have a go, have a shot (*informal*), have a stab (*informal*), try, try one's hand at, venture

stability constancy, durability, firmness, permanence, solidity, soundness, steadfastness, steadiness, strength
▷ **Antonyms** changeableness, fickleness, fragility, frailty, inconstancy, instability, unpredictability, unreliability, unsteadiness

stable abiding, constant, deep-rooted, durable, enduring, established, fast, firm, fixed, immovable, immutable, invariable, lasting, permanent, reliable, secure, sound, staunch, steadfast, steady, strong, sturdy, sure, unalterable, unchangeable, unwavering, well-founded
▷ **Antonyms** changeable, deteriorating, erratic, excitable, fickle, frail, inconstant, insecure, irresolute, mercurial, mutable, over-emotional, shaky, shifting, temperamental, uncertain, unpredictable, unreliable, unstable, unsteady, variable, volatile, wavering

stack 1. *noun* clamp (*Brit. agriculture*), cock, heap, hoard, load, mass, mound, mountain, pile, rick **2.** *~verb* accumulate, amass, assemble, bank up, heap up, load, pile, stockpile

staff *noun* **1.** employees, lecturers, officers, organization, personnel, teachers, team, workers, workforce **2.** cane, crook, pole, prop, rod, sceptre, stave, wand

stage 1. *noun* division, juncture, lap, leg, length, level, period, phase, point, step **2.** *~verb* arrange, do, engineer, give, lay on, mount, orchestrate, organize, perform, play, present, produce, put on

stagger *verb* **1.** falter, hesitate, lurch, reel, sway, teeter, totter, vacillate, waver, wobble **2.** amaze, astonish, astound, bowl over (*informal*), confound, dumbfound, flabbergast, give (someone) a shock, nonplus, overwhelm, shake, shock, strike (someone) dumb, stun, stupefy, surprise, take (someone) aback, take (someone's) breath away, throw off balance **3.** alternate, overlap, step, zigzag

stagnant brackish, motionless, quiet, sluggish, stale, standing, still
▷ **Antonyms** active, clear, flowing, fresh, lively, moving, pure, running, thriving, unpolluted

stagnate decay, decline, deteriorate, fester, go to seed, idle, languish, lie fallow, rot, rust, stand still, vegetate

staid calm, composed, decorous, demure, grave, quiet, sedate, self-restrained, serious, set in one's ways, sober, solemn, steady
▷ **Antonyms** adventurous, capricious, demonstrative, exuberant, flighty, giddy, indecorous, lively, rowdy, sportive, wild

stain *verb* **1.** blemish, blot, colour, dirty, discolour, dye, mark, smirch, soil, spot, tarnish, tinge **2.** besmirch, blacken, contaminate, corrupt, defile, deprave, disgrace, drag through the mud, sully, taint *~noun* **3.** blemish, blot, discoloration, dye, smirch, spot, tint **4.** blemish, blot on the escutcheon, disgrace, dishonour, infamy, reproach, shame, slur, stigma

stake[1] *noun* **1.** pale, paling, palisade, picket, pole, post, spike, stave, stick *~verb* **2.** brace, prop, secure, support, tether, tie up **3.** (*often with* **out**) define, delimit, demarcate, lay claim to, mark out, outline, reserve

stake[2] *noun* **1.** ante, bet, chance, hazard, peril, pledge, risk, venture, wager **2.** claim, concern, interest, investment, involvement, share *~verb* **3.** bet, chance, gamble, hazard, imperil, jeopardize, pledge, put on, risk, venture, wager

stale 1. decayed, dry, faded, fetid, flat, fusty, hard, insipid, musty, old, sour, stagnant, tasteless **2.** antiquated, banal, cliché-ridden, common, commonplace, drab, effete, flat, hackneyed, insipid, old hat, overused, platitudinous, repetitious, stereotyped, threadbare, trite, unoriginal, worn-out
▷ **Antonyms** crisp, different, fresh, imaginative, innovative, lively, new, novel, original, refreshing

stalemate deadlock, draw, impasse, standstill, tie

stalk *verb* **1.** creep up on, follow, haunt, hunt, pursue, shadow, tail (*informal*), track **2.** flounce, march, pace, stride, strut

stall *verb* beat about the bush (*informal*), hedge, play for time, stonewall, temporize

stalwart athletic, beefy (*informal*), brawny, daring, dependable, hefty (*informal*), husky (*informal*), indomitable, intrepid, lusty, manly, muscular, redoubtable, robust, rugged, sinewy, staunch, stout, strapping, strong, sturdy, valiant, vigorous

▷ **Antonyms** faint-hearted, feeble, frail, infirm, namby-pamby, puny, shilpit (*Scot.*), sickly, timid, weak

stamina endurance, energy, force, grit, indefatigability, lustiness, power, power of endurance, resilience, resistance, staying power, strength, tenacity, vigour

stammer *verb* falter, hem and haw, hesitate, pause, splutter, stumble, stutter

stamp *verb* **1.** beat, crush, trample **2.** engrave, fix, impress, imprint, inscribe, mark, mould, print **3.** betray, brand, categorize, exhibit, identify, label, mark, pronounce, reveal, show to be, typecast *~noun* **4.** brand, cast, earmark, hallmark, imprint, mark, mould, signature **5.** breed, cast, character, cut, description, fashion, form, kind, sort, type

stamp collecting philately

stampede *noun* charge, flight, rout, rush, scattering

stamp out crush, destroy, eliminate, eradicate, extinguish, extirpate, put down, put out, quell, quench, scotch, suppress

stance **1.** bearing, carriage, deportment, posture **2.** attitude, position, stand, standpoint, viewpoint

stanch, staunch arrest, check, dam, halt, plug, stay, stem, stop

stand *verb* **1.** be erect, be upright, be vertical, rise **2.** mount, place, position, put, rank, set **3.** be in force, belong, be situated *or* located, be valid, continue, exist, halt, hold, obtain, pause, prevail, remain, rest, stay, stop **4.** abide, allow, bear, brook, cope with, countenance, endure, experience, hack (*slang*), handle, put up with (*informal*), stomach, submit to, suffer, support, sustain, take, thole (*dialect*), tolerate, undergo, wear (*Brit. slang*), weather, withstand *~noun* **5.** halt, rest, standstill, stay, stop, stopover **6.** attitude, determination, firm stand, opinion, position, stance, standpoint **7.** base, booth, bracket, dais, frame, grandstand, place, platform, rack, rank, stage, staging, stall, stance (*chiefly Scot.*), support, table, tripod, trivet

standard[1] *noun* **1.** average, benchmark, canon, criterion, example, gauge, grade, guide, guideline, measure, model, norm, par, pattern, principle, requirement, rule, sample, specification, touchstone, type, yardstick **2.** (*often plural*) code of honour, ethics, ideals, moral principles, morals, principles *~adjective* **3.** accepted, average, basic, customary, normal, orthodox, popular, prevailing, regular, set, staple, stock, typical, usual **4.** approved, authoritative, classic, definitive, established, official, recognized

▷ **Antonyms** *~adjective* abnormal, atypical, exceptional, extraordinary, irregular, singular, strange, unauthorised, uncommon, unconventional, unofficial, unusual

standard[2] *noun* banner, colours, ensign, flag, pennant, pennon, streamer

standardize assimilate, bring into line, institutionalize, mass-produce, regiment, stereotype

stand by **1.** back, befriend, be loyal to, champion, defend, stick up for (*informal*), support, take (someone's) part, uphold **2.** be prepared, wait, wait in the wings

stand for **1.** betoken, denote, exemplify, indicate, mean, represent, signify, symbolize **2.** *informal* bear, brook, endure, lie down under (*informal*), put up with, suffer, tolerate, wear (*Brit. informal*)

stand in for cover for, deputize for, do duty for, hold the fort for, replace, represent, substitute for, take the place of, understudy

standing *noun* **1.** condition, credit, eminence, estimation, footing, position, rank, reputation, repute, station, status **2.** continuance, duration, existence, experience *~adjective* **3.** fixed, lasting, permanent, perpetual, regular, repeated **4.** erect, perpendicular, rampant (*Heraldry*), upended, upright, vertical

standoffish aloof, cold, distant, haughty, remote, reserved, unapproachable, unsociable

▷ **Antonyms** affable, approachable, congenial, cordial, friendly, open, sociable, warm

stand out attract attention, be conspicuous, be distinct, be highlighted, be obvious, be prominent, be striking, be thrown into relief, bulk large, catch the eye, leap to the eye, project, stare one in the face (*informal*), stick out a mile (*informal*), stick out like a sore thumb (*informal*)

standpoint angle, point of view, position, post, stance, station, vantage point, viewpoint

stand up for champion, come to the defence of, defend, side with, stick up for (*informal*), support, uphold

stand up to brave, confront, defy, endure, oppose, resist, tackle, withstand

staple *adjective* basic, chief, essential, fundamental, key, main, predominant, primary, principal

star *noun* **1.** heavenly body **2.** big name, celeb (*informal*), celebrity, draw, idol, lead, leading man *or* lady, luminary, main attraction, megastar (*informal*), name *~adjective* **3.** brilliant, celebrated, illustrious, leading, major, paramount, principal, prominent, talented, well-known

starchy ceremonious, conventional, formal, precise, prim, punctilious, stiff, stuffy

stare *verb* gape, gawk, gawp (*Brit. slang*), gaze, goggle, look, ogle, rubberneck (*slang*), watch

stark *adjective* **1.** absolute, arrant, bald, bare, blunt, consummate, downright, entire, flagrant, out-and-out, palpable, patent, pure, sheer, simple, unalloyed, unmitigated, utter **2.** austere, bare, barren, bleak, cold, depressing, desolate, drear (*literary*), dreary, forsaken, godforsaken, grim, hard, harsh, plain, severe, solitary, unadorned *~adverb* **3.** absolutely, altogether, clean, completely, entirely, quite, utterly, wholly

stark-naked buck naked (*slang*), in a state of nature, in one's birthday suit (*informal*), in the altogether (*informal*), in the bare scud (*slang*), in the buff (*informal*), in the raw (*informal*), naked, naked as the day one was born (*informal*), nude, scuddy (*slang*), stark, starkers (*informal*), stripped, unclad, undressed, without a stitch on (*informal*)

start *verb* **1.** appear, arise, begin, come into being, come into existence, commence, depart, first see the light of day, get on the road, get under way, go ahead, hit the road (*informal*), issue, leave, originate, pitch in (*informal*), sally forth, set off, set out **2.** activate, embark upon, engender, enter upon, get going, get (something) off the ground (*informal*), get the ball rolling, initiate, instigate, kick off (*informal*), kick-start, make a beginning, open, originate, put one's hand to the plough (*informal*), set about, set in motion, set the ball rolling, start the ball rolling, take the first step, take the plunge (*informal*), trigger, turn on **3.** begin, create, establish, father, found, inaugurate, initiate, institute, introduce, launch, lay the foundations of, pioneer, set up **4.** blench, flinch, jerk, jump, recoil, shy, twitch *~noun* **5.** beginning, birth, commencement, dawn, first step(s), foundation, inauguration, inception, initiation, kickoff (*informal*), onset, opening, opening move, outset **6.** advantage, edge, head start, lead **7.** backing, break (*informal*), chance, helping hand, introduction, opening, opportunity, sponsorship **8.** convulsion, jar, jump, spasm, twitch

▷ **Antonyms** *~verb* (*senses 1, 2 & 3*) abandon, bring to an end, call it a day (*informal*), cease, conclude, delay, desist, end, finish, give up, put aside, put off, quit, stop, switch off, terminate, turn off, wind up *~noun* (*sense 5*) cessation, conclusion, dénouement, end, finale, finish, outcome, result, stop, termination, turning off, wind-up

startle agitate, alarm, amaze, astonish, astound, frighten, give (someone) a turn (*informal*), make (someone) jump, scare, shock, surprise, take (someone) aback

startling alarming, astonishing, astounding, extraordinary, shocking, staggering, sudden, surprising, unexpected, unforeseen

starving esurient, faint from lack of food, famished, hungering, hungry, ravenous, ready to eat a horse (*informal*), sharp-set, starved

stash *verb* cache, hide, hoard, lay up, put aside for a rainy day, salt away, save up, secrete, stockpile, stow

state[1] *verb* **1.** affirm, articulate, assert, asseverate, aver, declare, enumerate, explain, expound, express, present, propound, put, report, say, specify, utter, voice *~noun* **2.** case, category, circumstances, condition, mode, pass, plight, position, predicament, shape, situation, state of affairs **3.** attitude, frame of mind, humour, mood, spirits **4.** ceremony, dignity, display, glory, grandeur, majesty, pomp, splendour, style **5.** *informal* bother, flap (*informal*), panic, pother, tiz-woz (*informal*), tizzy (*informal*) **6. in a state** *informal* agitated, all steamed up (*slang*), anxious, distressed, disturbed, flustered, het up, panic-stricken, ruffled, upset, uptight (*informal*)

state[2] *noun* body politic, commonwealth, country, federation, government, kingdom, land, nation, republic, territory

stately august, ceremonious, deliberate, dignified, elegant, grand, imperial, imposing, impressive, lofty, majestic, measured, noble, pompous, regal, royal, solemn

▷ **Antonyms** common, humble, lowly, modest, simple, undignified, undistinguished, unimpressive

statement account, announcement, communication, communiqué, declaration, explanation, proclamation, recital, relation, report, testimony, utterance

static changeless, constant, fixed, immobile, inert, motionless, stagnant, stationary, still, stock-still, unmoving, unvarying

▷ **Antonyms** active, dynamic, kinetic, lively, mobile, moving, travelling, varied

station *noun* **1.** base, depot, headquarters, location, place, position, post, seat, situation **2.** appointment, business, calling, employment, grade, occupation, position, post, rank, situation, sphere, standing, status *~verb* **3.** assign, estab~

lish, fix, garrison, install, locate, post, set

stationary at a standstill, fixed, inert, moored, motionless, parked, standing, static, stock-still, unmoving
▷ **Antonyms** changeable, changing, inconstant, mobile, moving, shifting, travelling, unstable, variable, varying, volatile

statuesque dignified, imposing, Junoesque, majestic, regal, stately

stature consequence, eminence, high station, importance, prestige, prominence, rank, size, standing

status condition, consequence, degree, distinction, eminence, grade, position, prestige, rank, standing

statute act, decree, edict, enactment, ordinance, regulation, rule

staunch constant, dependable, faithful, firm, immovable, loyal, reliable, resolute, sound, stalwart, steadfast, stout, strong, sure, tried and true, true, true-blue, trustworthy, trusty

stave off avert, evade, fend off, foil, hold off, keep at arm's length, keep at bay, parry, ward off

stay[1] *verb* **1.** abide, bide, continue, delay, establish oneself, halt, hang around (*informal*), hang in the air, hover, linger, loiter, pause, put down roots, remain, reside, settle, sojourn, stand, stay put, stop, tarry, wait **2.** (*often with* **at**) be accommodated at, lodge, put up at, sojourn, visit **3.** adjourn, defer, discontinue, hold in abeyance, hold over, prorogue, put off, suspend **4.** *archaic* arrest, check, curb, delay, detain, hinder, hold, impede, obstruct, prevent *~noun* **5.** holiday, sojourn, stop, stopover, visit **6.** deferment, delay, halt, pause, postponement, remission, reprieve, stopping, suspension
▷ **Antonyms** *~verb* (*sense 1*) abandon, depart, exit, go, leave, move on, pack one's bags (*informal*), pass through, quit, withdraw

stay[2] *noun* brace, buttress, prop, reinforcement, shoring, stanchion, support

staying power endurance, stamina, strength, toughness

steadfast constant, dedicated, dependable, established, faithful, fast, firm, fixed, immovable, intent, loyal, persevering, reliable, resolute, single-minded, stable, stalwart, staunch, steady, unfaltering, unflinching, unswerving, unwavering
▷ **Antonyms** capricious, faint-hearted, faltering, fickle, flagging, half-hearted, inconstant, irresolute, uncommitted, undependable, unreliable, unstable, vacillating, wavering

steady *adjective* **1.** firm, fixed, immovable, on an even keel, safe, stable, substantial, unchangeable, uniform **2.** balanced, calm, dependable, equable, having both feet on the ground, imperturbable, level-headed, reliable, sedate, sensible, serene, serious-minded, settled, sober, staid, staunch, steadfast **3.** ceaseless, confirmed, consistent, constant, continuous, even, faithful, habitual, incessant, nonstop, persistent, regular, rhythmic, unbroken, unfaltering, unfluctuating, uninterrupted, unremitting, unvarying, unwavering *~verb* **4.** balance, brace, secure, stabilize, support **5.** compose *or* calm oneself, cool down, get a grip on oneself, sober (up)
▷ **Antonyms** *~adjective* careless, changeable, faltering, fickle, fluctuating, half-hearted, inconsistent, infrequent, insecure, intermittent, in two minds, irregular, occasional, sporadic, uncommitted, unconscientious, undependable, unpredictable, unreliable, unsettled, unstable, unsteady, vacillating, wavering *~verb* agitate, shake, tilt, upset, worry

steal **1.** appropriate, be light-fingered, blag (*slang*), cabbage (*Brit. slang*), embezzle, filch, half-inch (*old-fashioned slang*), heist (*U.S. slang*), lift (*informal*), misappropriate, nick (*slang, chiefly Brit.*), peculate, pilfer, pinch (*informal*), pirate, plagiarize, poach, prig (*Brit. slang*), purloin, shoplift, snitch (*slang*), swipe (*slang*), take, thieve, walk *or* make off with **2.** creep, flit, insinuate oneself, slink, slip, sneak, tiptoe

stealing embezzlement, larceny, misappropriation, pilferage, pilfering, plagiarism, robbery, shoplifting, theft, thievery, thieving

stealth furtiveness, secrecy, slyness, sneakiness, stealthiness, surreptitiousness, unobtrusiveness

stealthy clandestine, covert, furtive, secret, secretive, skulking, sly, sneaking, sneaky, surreptitious, underhand

steel *verb* brace, fortify, grit one's teeth, harden, make up one's mind

steep[1] *adjective* **1.** abrupt, headlong, precipitous, sheer **2.** *informal* excessive, exorbitant, extortionate, extreme, high, overpriced, stiff, uncalled-for, unreasonable
▷ **Antonyms** (*sense 1*) easy, gentle, gradual, moderate, slight (*sense 2*) fair, moderate, reasonable

steep[2] *verb* **1.** damp, drench, imbrue (*rare*), immerse, macerate, marinate (*Cookery*), moisten, soak, souse, submerge **2.** fill, imbue, infuse, permeate, pervade, saturate, suffuse

steer **1.** administer, be in the driver's seat, conduct, control, direct, govern, guide, handle, pilot **2.** **steer clear of** avoid, body-swerve (*Scot.*), circumvent, eschew, evade, give a wide berth to, sheer off, shun

steersman cox, coxswain, helmsman, pilot, wheelman (*U.S.*)

stem[1] **1.** *noun* axis, branch, peduncle, shoot, stalk, stock, trunk **2.** *~verb* (*usually with* **from**) arise, be bred by, be brought about by, be caused by, be generated by, derive, develop, emanate, flow, issue, originate

stem[2] *verb* bring to a standstill, check, contain, curb, dam, hold back, oppose, resist, restrain, stanch, staunch, stay (*archaic*), stop, withstand

stench foul odour, malodour, mephitis, niff (*Brit. slang*), noisomeness, pong (*Brit. informal*), reek, stink, whiff (*Brit. slang*)

step *noun* **1.** footfall, footprint, footstep, gait, impression, pace, print, stride, trace, track, walk **2.** act, action, deed, expedient, manoeuvre, means, measure, move, procedure, proceeding **3. take steps** act, intervene, move in, prepare, take action, take measures, take the initiative **4.** advance, advancement, move, phase, point, process, progression, stage **5.** degree, level, rank, remove **6.** doorstep, round, rung, stair, tread **7. in step** coinciding, conforming, in agreement, in conformity, in harmony, in line, in unison **8. out of step** erratic, incongruous, in disagreement, out of harmony, out of line, out of phase, pulling different ways **9. watch one's step** be canny, be careful, be cautious, be discreet, be on one's guard, have one's wits about one, look out, mind how one goes, mind one's p's and q's, take care, take heed, tread carefully *~verb* **10.** move, pace, tread, walk

step down abdicate, bow out, give up, hand over, leave, pull out, quit, resign, retire

step in become involved, chip in (*informal*), intercede, intervene, take action, take a hand

step up accelerate, augment, boost, escalate, increase, intensify, raise, speed up, up

stereotype 1. *noun* formula, mould, pattern, received idea **2.** *~verb* categorize, conventionalize, dub, ghettoize, pigeonhole, standardize, take to be, typecast

stereotyped banal, cliché-ridden, conventional, corny (*slang*), hackneyed, mass-produced, overused, platitudinous, played out, stale, standard, standardized, stock, threadbare, tired, trite, unoriginal

sterile 1. abortive, bare, barren, dry, empty, fruitless, infecund, unfruitful, unproductive, unprofitable, unprolific **2.** antiseptic, aseptic, disinfected, germ-free, sterilized

▷ **Antonyms** (*sense 1*) fecund, fertile, fruitful, productive, prolific (*sense 2*) contaminated, dirty, germ-ridden, infected, insanitary, unhygienic, unsterile

sterilize autoclave, disinfect, fumigate, purify

sterling authentic, excellent, fine, first-class, genuine, pure, real, sound, standard, substantial, superlative, true

stern austere, authoritarian, bitter, cruel, drastic, flinty, forbidding, frowning, grim, hard, harsh, inflexible, relentless, rigid, rigorous, serious, severe, steely, strict, unrelenting, unsparing, unyielding

▷ **Antonyms** amused, approachable, compassionate, flexible, friendly, gentle, kind, lenient, liberal, permissive, soft, sympathetic, tolerant, warm

stick[1] *verb* **1.** adhere, affix, attach, bind, bond, cement, cleave, cling, fasten, fix, fuse, glue, hold, hold on, join, paste, weld **2.** dig, gore, insert, jab, penetrate, pierce, pin, poke, prod, puncture, spear, stab, thrust, transfix **3.** (*with* **out, up,** *etc.*) bulge, extend, jut, obtrude, poke, project, protrude, show **4.** *informal* deposit, drop, fix, install, lay, place, plant, plonk, position, put, set, store, stuff **5.** be bogged down, become immobilized, be embedded, catch, clog, come to a standstill, jam, lodge, snag, stop **6.** linger, persist, remain, stay **7.** *slang* abide, bear up under, endure, get on with, hack (*slang*), stand, stomach, take, tolerate **8. stick it out** *informal* bear, endure, grin and bear it (*informal*), last out, put up with (*informal*), see it through, see through to the bitter end, soldier on, take it (*informal*), weather **9. stick up for** *informal* champion, defend, stand up for, support, take the part *or* side of, uphold

stick[2] *noun* **1.** baton, birch, cane, crook, pole, rod, sceptre, staff, stake, switch, twig, wand **2.** *informal* dinosaur, fuddy-duddy (*informal*), (old) fogey, pain (*informal*), prig, stick-in-the-mud (*informal*) **3.** *Brit. slang* abuse, blame, criticism, flak (*informal*), hostility, punishment

stick at 1. continue, keep at, persevere in, persist, plug away at (*informal*), see (something) through **2.** balk, be conscience-stricken, be deterred by, demur, doubt, hesitate, pause, recoil, scruple, shrink from, stop at

stick-in-the-mud Colonel Blimp, conservative, die-hard, dinosaur, fuddy-duddy (*informal*), (old) fogey, reactionary, sobersides, stick (*informal*)

stickler fanatic, fusspot (*Brit. informal*), hard taskmaster, maniac (*informal*), martinet, nut (*slang*), pedant, perfectionist, purist

stick to adhere to, cleave to, continue in, honour, keep, persevere in, remain faithful, remain loyal, remain true, stick at

sticky 1. adhesive, claggy (*dialect*), clinging, gluey, glutinous, gooey (*informal*), gummy, syrupy, tacky, tenacious, viscid, viscous **2.** *informal* awkward, delicate, difficult, discomforting, embarrassing, hairy (*slang*), nasty, painful, thorny, tricky, unpleasant **3.** clammy, close, humid, muggy, oppressive, sultry, sweltering

stiff 1. brittle, firm, hard, hardened, inelastic, inflexible, rigid, solid, solidified, taut, tense, tight, unbending, unyielding **2.** artificial, austere, ceremonious, chilly, cold, constrained, forced, formal, laboured, mannered, pompous, priggish, prim, punctilious, standoffish, starchy (*informal*), stilted, uneasy, unnatural, unrelaxed, wooden **3.** arthritic, awkward, clumsy, creaky (*informal*), crude, graceless, inelegant, jerky, rheumaticky (*informal*), ungainly, ungraceful, unsupple **4.** arduous, difficult, exacting, fatiguing, formidable, hard, laborious, tough, trying, uphill **5.** austere, cruel, drastic, extreme, great, hard, harsh, heavy, inexorable, oppressive, pitiless, rigorous, severe, sharp, strict, stringent **6.** brisk, fresh, powerful, strong, vigorous

▷ **Antonyms** (*senses 1 & 3*) bendable, ductile, elastic, flexible, limber, lissom(e), lithe, pliable, pliant, supple, yielding (*sense 2*) casual, easy, informal, laid-back, natural, relaxed, spontaneous, unceremonious, unofficial

stiffen brace, coagulate, congeal, crystallize, harden, jell, reinforce, set, solidify, starch, tauten, tense, thicken

stiff-necked boneheaded (*slang*), contumacious, haughty, obstinate, opinionated, stubborn, uncompromising, unreceptive

stifle 1. asphyxiate, choke, smother, strangle, suffocate **2.** check, choke back, cover up, curb, extinguish, gag, hush, muffle, prevent, repress, restrain, silence, smother, stop, suppress

stigma blot, brand, disgrace, dishonour, imputation, mark, reproach, shame, slur, smirch, spot, stain

stigmatize brand, cast a slur upon, defame, denounce, discredit, label, mark, pillory

still 1. *adjective* at rest, calm, hushed, inert, lifeless, motionless, noiseless, pacific, peaceful, placid, quiet, restful, serene, silent, smooth, stationary, stilly (*poetic*), tranquil, undisturbed, unruffled, unstirring **2.** *~verb* allay, alleviate, appease, calm, hush, lull, pacify, quiet, quieten, settle, silence, smooth, smooth over, soothe, subdue, tranquillize **3.** *~conjunction* but, for all that, however, nevertheless, notwithstanding, yet **4.** *~noun poetic* hush, peace, quiet, silence, stillness, tranquillity

▷ **Antonyms** *~adjective* active, agitated, astir, bustling, busy, humming, lively, moving, noisy, restless, turbulent *~verb* aggravate, agitate, exacerbate, increase, inflame, rouse, stir up *~noun* bustle, clamour, hubbub, noise, uproar

stilted artificial, bombastic, constrained, forced, fustian, grandiloquent, high-flown, high-sounding, inflated, laboured, pedantic, pompous, pretentious, stiff, unnatural, wooden

▷ **Antonyms** flowing, fluid, free, natural, spontaneous, unaffected, unpretentious

stimulant analeptic, bracer (*informal*), energizer, excitant, pep pill (*informal*), pick-me-up (*informal*), restorative, reviver, tonic, upper (*slang*)

▷ **Antonyms** calmant, depressant, downer (*slang*), sedative, tranquilliser

stimulate animate, arouse, encourage, fan, fire, foment, goad, impel, incite, inflame, instigate, prod, prompt, provoke, quicken, rouse, spur, turn on (*slang*), urge, whet

stimulating exciting, exhilarating, galvanic, inspiring, intriguing, provocative, provoking, rousing, stirring, thought-provoking

▷ **Antonyms** as dry as dust, boring, dull, mind-numbing, unexciting, unimaginative, uninspiring, uninteresting, unstimulating

stimulus clarion call, encouragement, fillip, goad, impetus, incentive, incitement, inducement, provocation, shot in the arm (*informal*), spur

sting *verb* **1.** burn, hurt, pain, smart, tingle, wound **2.** anger, gall, incense, inflame, infuriate, nettle, pique, provoke, rile **3.** *informal* cheat, defraud, do (*slang*), fleece, overcharge, rip off (*slang*), skin (*slang*), stiff (*slang*), swindle, take for a ride (*informal*)

stingy 1. avaricious, cheeseparing, close-fisted, covetous, illiberal, mean, mingy (*Brit. informal*), miserly, near, niggardly, parsimonious, penny-pinching (*informal*), penurious, scrimping, snoep (*S. African informal*), tight-arse (*taboo slang*), tight-arsed (*taboo slang*), tight as a duck's arse (*taboo slang*), tight-ass (*U.S. taboo slang*), tight-assed (*U.S. taboo slang*), tightfisted, ungenerous **2.** inadequate, insufficient, meagre, measly (*informal*), mouldy (*informal*), on the small side, pathetic, scant, scanty, skimpy, small

stink *verb* **1.** offend the nostrils, pong (*Brit. informal*), reek, stink to high heaven (*informal*), whiff (*Brit. slang*) **2.** *slang* be abhorrent, be bad, be detestable, be held in disrepute, be no good, be offensive, be rotten, have a bad name *~noun* **3.** fetor, foulness, foul odour, malodour, noisomeness, pong (*Brit. informal*), stench **4.** *slang* brouhaha, commotion, deal of trouble (*informal*), disturbance, fuss, hubbub, row, rumpus, scandal, stir, to-do, uproar, upset

stinker **1.** bounder (*old-fashioned Brit. slang*), cad (*Brit. informal*), cocksucker (*taboo slang*), cur, dastard (*archaic*), heel, nasty piece of work (*informal*), rotter (*slang, chiefly Brit.*), scab, scoundrel, sod (*slang*), swine **2.** affliction, beast, difficulty, fine how-do-you-do (*informal*), horror, impediment, plight, poser, predicament, problem, shocker

stinking **1.** fetid, foul-smelling, ill-smelling, malodorous, mephitic, niffy (*Brit. slang*), noisome, olid, pongy (*Brit. informal*), reeking, smelly, whiffy (*Brit. slang*) **2.** *informal* contemptible, disgusting, low, low-down (*informal*), mean, rotten, shitty (*taboo slang*), unpleasant, vile, wretched **3.** *slang* bevvied (*dialect*), blitzed (*slang*), blotto (*slang*), bombed (*slang*), boozed, Brahms and Liszt (*slang*), canned (*slang*), drunk, drunk as a lord, flying (*slang*), intoxicated, legless (*informal*), lit up (*slang*), out of it (*slang*), out to it (*Austral. & N.Z. slang*), paralytic (*informal*), pissed (*taboo slang*), plastered (*slang*), rat-arsed (*taboo slang*), smashed (*slang*), sozzled (*informal*), steamboats (*Scot. slang*), steaming (*slang*), stewed (*slang*), stoned (*slang*), wasted (*slang*), wrecked (*slang*), zonked (*slang*)

stint **1.** *noun* assignment, bit, period, quota, share, shift, spell, stretch, term, time, tour, turn **2.** *~verb* be frugal, begrudge, be mean, be mingy (*Brit. informal*), be parsimonious, be sparing, economize, hold back, save, scrimp, skimp on, spoil the ship for a ha'porth of tar, withhold

stipulate agree, contract, covenant, engage, guarantee, insist upon, lay down, lay down *or* impose conditions, make a point of, pledge, postulate, promise, require, settle, specify

stipulation agreement, clause, condition, contract, engagement, precondition, prerequisite, provision, proviso, qualification, requirement, restriction, rider, settlement, *sine qua non,* specification, term

stir *verb* **1.** agitate, beat, disturb, flutter, mix, move, quiver, rustle, shake, tremble **2.** (*often with* **up**) animate, arouse, awaken, excite, incite, inflame, instigate, kindle, prod, prompt, provoke, quicken, raise, rouse, spur, stimulate, urge **3.** affect, electrify, excite, fire, inspire, move, thrill, touch **4.** bestir, be up and about (*informal*), budge, exert oneself, get a move on (*informal*), get moving, hasten, look lively (*informal*), make an effort, mill about, move, shake a leg (*informal*) *~noun* **5.** activity, ado, agitation, bustle, commotion, disorder, disturbance, excitement, ferment, flurry, fuss, movement, to-do, tumult, uproar

▷ **Antonyms** *~verb* (*senses 2 & 3*) check, curb, dampen, inhibit, restrain, stifle, suppress, throw cold water on (*informal*)

stirring animating, dramatic, emotive, exciting, exhilarating, heady, impassioned, inspiring, intoxicating, lively, moving, rousing, spirited, stimulating, thrilling

stock *noun* **1.** array, assets, assortment, cache, choice, commodities, fund, goods, hoard, inventory, merchandise, range, reserve, reservoir, selection, stockpile, store, supply, variety, wares **2.** *animals* beasts, cattle, domestic animals, flocks, herds, horses, livestock, sheep **3.** ancestry, background, breed, descent, extraction, family, forebears, house, line, lineage, line of descent, parentage, pedigree, race, strain, type, variety **4.** *Money* capital, funds, investment, property **5.** **take stock** appraise, estimate, review the situation, see how the land lies, size up (*informal*), weigh up *~adjective* **6.** banal, basic, commonplace, conventional, customary, formal, hackneyed, ordinary, overused, regular, routine, run-of-the-mill, set, standard, staple, stereotyped, traditional, trite, usual, worn-out *~verb* **7.** deal in, handle, keep, sell, supply, trade in **8.** (*with* **up**) accumulate, amass, buy up, gather, hoard, lay in, put away, replenish, save, store (up), supply **9.** equip, fill, fit out, furnish, kit out, provide with, provision, supply

stocky chunky, dumpy, mesomorphic, solid, stubby, stumpy, sturdy, thickset

stodgy **1.** filling, heavy, leaden, starchy, substantial **2.** boring, dull, dull as ditchwater, formal, fuddy-duddy (*informal*), heavy going, ho-hum, laboured, staid, stuffy, tedious, tiresome, turgid, unexciting, unimaginative, uninspired

▷ **Antonyms** (*sense 1*) appetizing, fluffy, insubstantial, light (*sense 2*) animated, exciting, fashionable, fresh, interesting, light, lively, readable, stimulating, trendy (*Brit. informal*), up-to-date

stoical calm, cool, dispassionate, impassive, imperturbable, indifferent, long-suffering, philosophic, phlegmatic, resigned, stoic, stolid

stoicism acceptance, calmness, dispassion, fatalism, forbearance, fortitude, impassivity, imperturbability, indifference, long-suffering, patience, resignation, stolidity

stolid apathetic, bovine, doltish, dozy (*Brit. informal*), dull, heavy, lumpish, obtuse, slow, stupid, unemotional, wooden

▷ **Antonyms** acute, animated, bright, emotional, energetic, excitable, intelligent, interested, lively, passionate, sharp, smart

stomach *noun* **1.** abdomen, belly, breadbasket (*slang*), gut (*informal*), inside(s) (*informal*), paunch, pot, potbelly, spare tyre (*informal*), tummy (*informal*) **2.** ap~

petite, desire, inclination, mind, relish, taste *~verb* **3.** abide, bear, endure, hack (*slang*), put up with (*informal*), reconcile *or* resign oneself to, submit to, suffer, swallow, take, tolerate

stony *figurative* adamant, blank, callous, chilly, cold as ice, expressionless, frigid, hard, harsh, heartless, hostile, icy, indifferent, inexorable, merciless, obdurate, pitiless, unfeeling, unforgiving, unresponsive

stooge 1. *noun* butt, dupe, fall guy (*informal*), foil, henchman, lackey, patsy (*slang, chiefly U.S. & Canad.*), pawn, puppet **2.** *~verb informal* flit, fly, hang about (*informal*), meander, mooch (*slang*), mosey (*informal*), move, wander

stoop *verb* **1.** be bowed *or* round-shouldered, bend, bow, crouch, descend, duck, hunch, incline, kneel, lean, squat **2.** (*often with* **to**) condescend, deign, demean oneself, descend, lower oneself, resort, sink, vouchsafe *~noun* **3.** bad posture, droop, round-shoulderedness, sag, slouch, slump

stop *verb* **1.** axe (*informal*), be over, break off, bring *or* come to a halt, bring *or* come to a standstill, call it a day (*informal*), cease, come to an end, conclude, cut out (*informal*), cut short, desist, discontinue, draw up, end, finish, halt, leave off, pack in (*Brit. informal*), pause, peter out, pull up, put an end to, quit, refrain, run down, run its course, shut down, stall, terminate **2.** arrest, bar, block, break, bung, check, close, forestall, frustrate, hinder, hold back, impede, intercept, interrupt, nip (something) in the bud, obstruct, plug, prevent, rein in, repress, restrain, seal, silence, staunch, stem, suspend **3.** break one's journey, lodge, put up, rest, sojourn, stay, tarry *~noun* **4.** cessation, conclusion, discontinuation, end, finish, halt, standstill **5.** break, rest, sojourn, stay, stopover, visit **6.** bar, block, break, check, control, hindrance, impediment, plug, stoppage **7.** depot, destination, halt, stage, station, termination, terminus

▷ **Antonyms** *~verb* (*senses 1 & 3*) advance, begin, commence, continue, get going, get under way, give the go ahead, go, institute, keep going, keep on, kick off (*informal*), proceed, set in motion, set off, start (*sense 2*) assist, boost, encourage, expedite, facilitate, further, hasten, promote, push *~noun* (*sense 4*) beginning, commencement, kick-off (*informal*), start (*sense 6*) boost, encouragement, incitement

stopgap 1. *noun* improvisation, makeshift, resort, shift, substitute, temporary expedient **2.** *~adjective* emergency, impromptu, improvised, makeshift, provisional, rough-and-ready, temporary

stoppage 1. abeyance, arrest, close, closure, cutoff, deduction, discontinuance, halt, hindrance, lay-off, shutdown, standstill, stopping **2.** blockage, check, curtailment, interruption, obstruction, occlusion, stopping up

store *verb* **1.** accumulate, deposit, garner, hoard, husband, keep, keep in reserve, lay by *or* in, lock away, put aside, put aside for a rainy day, put by, put in storage, reserve, salt away, save, stash (*informal*), stock, stockpile *~noun* **2.** abundance, accumulation, cache, fund, hoard, lot, mine, plenty, plethora, provision, quantity, reserve, reservoir, stock, stockpile, supply, wealth **3.** chain store, department store, emporium, hypermarket, market, mart, outlet, shop, supermarket **4.** depository, depot, repository, storehouse, storeroom, warehouse **5. set store by** appreciate, esteem, hold in high regard, prize, think highly of, value

storm *noun* **1.** blast, blizzard, cyclone, gale, gust, hurricane, squall, tempest, tornado, whirlwind **2.** *figurative* agitation, anger, clamour, commotion, disturbance, furore, hubbub, outbreak, outburst, outcry, passion, roar, row, rumpus, stir, strife, tumult, turmoil, violence *~verb* **3.** assail, assault, beset, charge, rush, take by storm *~noun* **4.** assault, attack, blitz, blitzkrieg, offensive, onset, onslaught, rush *~verb* **5.** bluster, complain, fly off the handle (*informal*), fume, go ballistic (*slang, chiefly U.S.*), rage, rant, rave, scold, thunder **6.** flounce, fly, rush, stalk, stamp, stomp (*informal*)

stormy blustering, blustery, boisterous, dirty, foul, gusty, inclement, raging, rough, squally, tempestuous, turbulent, wild, windy

story 1. account, anecdote, chronicle, fictional account, history, legend, narration, narrative, novel, recital, record, relation, romance, tale, urban legend, version, yarn **2.** *informal* falsehood, fib, fiction, lie, pork pie (*Brit. slang*), porky (*Brit. slang*), untruth, white lie **3.** article, feature, news, news item, report, scoop

storyteller anecdotist, author, bard, chronicler, fabulist, narrator, novelist, raconteur, romancer, spinner of yarns

stout 1. big, bulky, burly, corpulent, fat, fleshy, heavy, obese, on the large *or* heavy side, overweight, plump, portly, rotund, substantial, tubby **2.** able-bodied, athletic, beefy (*informal*), brawny, hardy, hulking, husky (*informal*), lusty, muscular, robust, stalwart, strapping, strong, sturdy, substantial, thickset, tough, vigorous **3.** bold, brave, courageous, dauntless, doughty, fearless, gallant, indomitable, intrepid, lion-hearted, manly, plucky, resolute,

valiant, valorous
▷ **Antonyms** (*senses 1 & 2*) feeble, flimsy, frail, insubstantial, lanky, lean, puny, skin-and-bones (*informal*), skinny, slender, slight, slim (*sense 3*) cowardly, faint-hearted, fearful, irresolute, shrinking, soft, spineless, timid, weak

stouthearted ballsy (*taboo slang*), bold, brave, courageous, dauntless, doughty, fearless, great-hearted, gutsy (*slang*), heroic, indomitable, intrepid, lion-hearted, plucky, spirited, stalwart, valiant, valorous

stow bundle, cram, deposit, jam, load, pack, put away, secrete, stash (*informal*), store, stuff, tuck

straggle drift, lag, loiter, ramble, range, roam, rove, spread, stray, string out, trail, wander

straggly aimless, disorganized, drifting, irregular, loose, rambling, random, spreading, spread out, straggling, straying, untidy

straight *adjective* **1.** direct, near, short, undeviating, unswerving **2.** aligned, erect, even, horizontal, in line, level, perpendicular, plumb, right, smooth, square, true, upright, vertical **3.** blunt, bold, candid, downright, forthright, frank, honest, outright, plain, point-blank, straightforward, unqualified, upfront (*informal*) **4.** above board, accurate, authentic, decent, equitable, fair, fair and square, honest, honourable, just, law-abiding, reliable, respectable, trustworthy, upright **5.** arranged, in order, neat, orderly, organized, put to rights, shipshape, sorted out, tidy **6.** consecutive, continuous, nonstop, running, solid, successive, sustained, through, uninterrupted, unrelieved **7.** *slang* bourgeois, conservative, conventional, orthodox, Pooterish, square (*informal*), traditional **8.** neat, pure, unadulterated, undiluted, unmixed *~adverb* **9.** as the crow flies, at once, directly, immediately, instantly **10.** candidly, frankly, honestly, in plain English, point-blank, pulling no punches (*informal*), with no holds barred
▷ **Antonyms** *~adjective* (*sense 1*) circuitous, indirect, roundabout, winding, zigzag (*sense 2*) askew, bent, crooked, curved, skewwhiff (*Brit. informal*), twisted, uneven (*sense 3*) ambiguous, cryptic, equivocal, evasive, indirect, vague (*sense 4*) bent (*slang*), crooked (*informal*), dishonest, dishonourable, shady (*informal*), unlawful (*sense 5*) confused, disorderly, disorganized, in disarray, messy, untidy (*sense 6*) broken, discontinuous, interrupted, non-consecutive (*sense 7*) *slang* cool, fashionable, trendy (*Brit. informal*), voguish

straightaway at once, directly, immediately, instantly, now, on the spot, right away, straightway (*archaic*), there and then, this minute, without any delay, without more ado

straighten arrange, neaten, order, put in order, set *or* put to rights, smarten up, spruce up, tidy (up)

straighten out become clear, clear up, correct, disentangle, put right, rectify, regularize, resolve, settle, sort out, unsnarl, work out

straightforward **1.** above board, candid, direct, forthright, genuine, guileless, honest, open, sincere, truthful, upfront (*informal*) **2.** clear-cut, easy, easy-peasy (*slang*), elementary, routine, simple, uncomplicated, undemanding
▷ **Antonyms** complex, complicated, confused, convoluted, devious, disingenuous, roundabout, shady, sharp, unclear, unscrupulous

strain[1] *verb* **1.** distend, draw tight, extend, stretch, tauten, tighten **2.** drive, exert, fatigue, injure, overexert, overtax, overwork, pull, push to the limit, sprain, tax, tear, test, tire, twist, weaken, wrench **3.** bend over backwards (*informal*), break one's back, break one's neck (*informal*), bust a gut (*informal*), do one's damnedest (*informal*), endeavour, give it one's all (*informal*), give it one's best shot (*informal*), go all out for (*informal*), go for broke (*slang*), go for it (*informal*), knock oneself out (*informal*), labour, make an all-out effort (*informal*), make a supreme effort, rupture oneself (*informal*), strive, struggle **4.** filter, percolate, purify, riddle, screen, seep, separate, sieve, sift *~noun* **5.** effort, exertion, force, injury, pull, sprain, struggle, tautness, tension, tensity (*rare*), wrench **6.** anxiety, burden, pressure, stress, tension **7.** (*often plural*) air, lay, measure (*poetic*), melody, song, theme, tune
▷ **Antonyms** *~verb* (*senses 2 & 3*) idle, loose, pamper, relax, rest, slacken, take it easy, yield *~noun* (*senses 5 & 6*) ease, effortlessness, lack of tension, relaxation

strain[2] *noun* **1.** ancestry, blood, descent, extraction, family, lineage, pedigree, race, stock **2.** streak, suggestion, suspicion, tendency, trace, trait **3.** humour, manner, spirit, style, temper, tone, vein, way

strained artificial, awkward, constrained, difficult, embarrassed, false, forced, laboured, put on, self-conscious, stiff, tense, uncomfortable, uneasy, unnatural, unrelaxed
▷ **Antonyms** comfortable, natural, relaxed

straitened difficult, distressed, embarrassed, limited, reduced, restricted

strait-laced moralistic, narrow, narrow-minded, niminy-piminy, of the old school, old-maidish (*informal*), over-

scrupulous, prim, proper, prudish, puritanical, strict, Victorian
▷ **Antonyms** broad-minded, earthy, immoral, loose, relaxed, uninhibited, unreserved

straits *noun* (*sometimes singular*) **1.** crisis, difficulty, dilemma, distress, embarrassment, emergency, extremity, hardship, hole (*slang*), mess, panic stations (*informal*), pass, perplexity, plight, predicament, pretty *or* fine kettle of fish (*informal*) **2.** channel, narrows, sound

strand *noun* fibre, filament, length, lock, rope, string, thread, tress, twist, wisp

stranded 1. aground, ashore, beached, cast away, grounded, marooned, shipwrecked **2.** *figurative* abandoned, helpless, high and dry, homeless, left in the lurch, penniless

strange 1. abnormal, astonishing, bizarre, curious, curiouser and curiouser, eccentric, exceptional, extraordinary, fantastic, funny, irregular, left-field (*informal*), marvellous, mystifying, odd, oddball (*informal*), off-the-wall (*slang*), out-of-the-way, outré, peculiar, perplexing, queer, rare, remarkable, rum (*Brit. slang*), singular, unaccountable, uncanny, uncommon, unheard of, weird, wonderful **2.** alien, exotic, foreign, new, novel, outside one's experience, remote, unexplored, unfamiliar, unknown, untried **3.** (*often with* **to**) a stranger to, ignorant of, inexperienced, new to, unaccustomed, unpractised, unseasoned, unused, unversed in **4.** awkward, bewildered, disoriented, ill at ease, like a fish out of water, lost, out of place, uncomfortable
▷ **Antonyms** (*senses 1 & 2*) accustomed, bog-standard (*Brit. & Irish slang*), common, commonplace, conventional, familiar, habitual, ordinary, regular, routine, run-of-the-mill, standard, typical, unexceptional, usual, well-known (*sense 3*) accustomed, familiar, habitual (*sense 4*) at ease, at home, comfortable, relaxed

stranger alien, foreigner, guest, incomer, new arrival, newcomer, outlander, unknown, visitor

strangle 1. asphyxiate, choke, garrotte, smother, strangulate, suffocate, throttle **2.** gag, inhibit, repress, stifle, suppress

strap *noun* **1.** belt, leash, thong, tie *~verb* **2.** bind, buckle, fasten, lash, secure, tie, truss **3.** beat, belt (*informal*), flog, lash, scourge, whip

strapping beefy (*informal*), big, brawny, burly, hefty (*informal*), hulking, husky (*informal*), powerful, robust, stalwart, sturdy, well-built, well set-up

stratagem artifice, device, dodge, feint, intrigue, manoeuvre, plan, plot, ploy, ruse, scheme, subterfuge, trick, wile

strategic 1. cardinal, critical, crucial, decisive, important, key, vital **2.** calculated, deliberate, diplomatic, planned, politic, tactical

strategy approach, grand design, manoeuvring, plan, planning, policy, procedure, programme, scheme

stratum 1. bed, layer, level, lode, seam, stratification, table, tier, vein **2.** bracket, caste, category, class, estate, grade, group, level, rank, station

stray *verb* **1.** deviate, digress, diverge, get off the point, get sidetracked, go off at a tangent, ramble **2.** be abandoned *or* lost, drift, err, go astray, lose one's way, meander, range, roam, rove, straggle, wander *~adjective* **3.** abandoned, homeless, lost, roaming, vagrant **4.** accidental, chance, erratic, freak, odd, random, scattered

streak *noun* **1.** band, layer, line, slash, smear, strip, stripe, stroke, vein **2.** dash, element, strain, touch, trace, vein *~verb* **3.** band, daub, fleck, slash, smear, striate, stripe **4.** barrel (along) (*informal, chiefly U.S. & Canad.*), burn rubber (*informal*), dart, flash, fly, hurtle, move like greased lightning (*informal*), speed, sprint, sweep, tear, whistle, whizz (*informal*), zoom

stream 1. *noun* bayou, beck, brook, burn, course, creek (*U.S.*), current, drift, flow, freshet, outpouring, rill, river, rivulet, run, rush, surge, tide, tideway, torrent, tributary, undertow **2.** *~verb* cascade, course, emit, flood, flow, glide, gush, issue, pour, run, shed, spill, spout

streamer banner, colours, ensign, flag, gonfalon, pennant, pennon, ribbon, standard

streamlined efficient, modernized, organized, rationalized, sleek, slick, smooth, smooth-running, time-saving, well-run

street 1. avenue, boulevard, lane, road, roadway, row, terrace, thoroughfare **2. (right) up one's street** acceptable, compatible, congenial, familiar, one's cup of tea (*informal*), pleasing, suitable, to one's liking, to one's taste

strength 1. backbone, brawn, brawniness, courage, firmness, fortitude, health, lustiness, might, muscle, robustness, sinew, stamina, stoutness, sturdiness, toughness **2.** cogency, concentration, effectiveness, efficacy, energy, force, intensity, potency, power, resolution, spirit, vehemence, vigour, virtue (*archaic*) **3.** advantage, anchor, asset, mainstay, security, strong point, succour, tower of strength
▷ **Antonyms** (*senses 1 & 2*) debility, feebleness, frailty, impotence, infirmity, powerlessness, weakness (*sense 3*) Achilles heel, chink in one's armour, defect, failing, flaw, shortcoming, weakness

strengthen 1. animate, brace up, consolidate, encourage, fortify, give new energy to, harden, hearten, invigorate, nerve,

nourish, rejuvenate, restore, stiffen, toughen **2.** augment, bolster, brace, build up, buttress, confirm, corroborate, enhance, establish, give a boost to, harden, heighten, increase, intensify, justify, reinforce, steel, substantiate, support
▷ **Antonyms** crush, debilitate, destroy, dilute, enervate, render impotent, sap, subvert, undermine, weaken

strenuous 1. arduous, demanding, exhausting, hard, Herculean, laborious, taxing, toilsome, tough, tough going, unrelaxing, uphill **2.** active, bold, determined, eager, earnest, energetic, persistent, resolute, spirited, strong, tireless, vigorous, zealous
▷ **Antonyms** (*sense 1*) easy, effortless, relaxing, undemanding, untaxing (*sense 2*) relaxed, unenergetic

stress *noun* **1.** emphasis, force, importance, significance, urgency, weight **2.** anxiety, burden, hassle (*informal*), nervous tension, oppression, pressure, strain, tautness, tension, trauma, worry **3.** accent, accentuation, beat, emphasis, ictus *~verb* **4.** accentuate, belabour, dwell on, emphasize, harp on, lay emphasis upon, point up, repeat, rub in, underline, underscore

stretch *verb* **1.** cover, extend, put forth, reach, spread, unfold, unroll **2.** distend, draw out, elongate, expand, inflate, lengthen, pull, pull out of shape, rack, strain, swell, tighten *~noun* **3.** area, distance, expanse, extent, spread, sweep, tract **4.** bit, period, run, space, spell, stint, term, time

strew bestrew, disperse, litter, scatter, spread, sprinkle, toss

stricken affected, afflicted, hit, injured, laid low, smitten, struck, struck down

strict 1. austere, authoritarian, firm, harsh, no-nonsense, rigid, rigorous, severe, stern, stringent **2.** accurate, close, exact, faithful, meticulous, particular, precise, religious, scrupulous, true **3.** absolute, complete, perfect, total, utter
▷ **Antonyms** (*sense 1*) easy-going, easy-oasy (*slang*), flexible, laid-back (*informal*), lax, mild, moderate, soft, tolerant

stricture animadversion, bad press, blame, censure, criticism, flak (*informal*), rebuke, stick (*slang*)

strident clamorous, clashing, discordant, grating, harsh, jangling, jarring, rasping, raucous, screeching, shrill, stridulant, stridulous, unmusical, vociferous
▷ **Antonyms** calm, dulcet, gentle, harmonious, mellifluous, mellow, quiet, soft, soothing, sweet

strife animosity, battle, bickering, clash, clashes, combat, conflict, contention, contest, controversy, discord, dissension, friction, quarrel, rivalry, row, squabbling, struggle, warfare, wrangling

strike *verb* **1.** bang, beat, box, buffet, chastise, chin (*slang*), clobber (*slang*), clout (*informal*), clump (*slang*), cuff, deck (*slang*), hammer, hit, knock, lambast(e), lay a finger on (*informal*), lay one on (*slang*), pound, punch, punish, slap, smack, smite, sock (*slang*), thump, wallop (*informal*) **2.** be in collision with, bump into, clash, collide with, come into contact with, dash, hit, knock into, run into, smash into, touch **3.** drive, force, hit, impel, thrust **4.** affect, come to, come to the mind of, dawn on *or* upon, hit, impress, make an impact on, occur to, reach, register (*informal*), seem **5.** (*sometimes with* **upon**) come upon *or* across, discover, encounter, find, happen *or* chance upon, hit upon, light upon, reach, stumble upon *or* across, turn up, uncover, unearth **6.** affect, assail, assault, attack, deal a blow to, devastate, fall upon, hit, invade, set upon, smite **7.** achieve, arrange, arrive at, attain, effect, reach **8.** down tools, mutiny, revolt, walk out

strike down afflict, bring low, deal a deathblow to, destroy, kill, ruin, slay, smite

strike out 1. *also* **strike off, strike through** cancel, cross out, delete, efface, erase, excise, expunge, remove, score out **2.** begin, get under way, set out, start out

striking astonishing, conspicuous, dazzling, dramatic, drop-dead (*slang*), extraordinary, forcible, impressive, memorable, noticeable, out of the ordinary, outstanding, stunning (*informal*), wonderful
▷ **Antonyms** average, dull, indifferent, undistinguished, unexceptional, unextraordinary, unimpressive, uninteresting, vanilla (*informal*)

string *noun* **1.** cord, fibre, twine **2.** chain, file, line, procession, queue, row, sequence, series, strand, succession *~verb* **3.** festoon, hang, link, loop, sling, stretch, suspend, thread **4.** (*with* **out**) disperse, extend, fan out, lengthen, protract, space out, spread out, straggle

string along 1. (*often with* **with**) agree, assent, collaborate, go along with **2.** *also* **string on** bluff, deceive, dupe, fool, hoax, kid (*informal*), play fast and loose with (someone) (*informal*), play (someone) false, put one over on (someone) (*informal*), take (someone) for a ride (*informal*)

stringent binding, demanding, exacting, inflexible, rigid, rigorous, severe, strict, tight, tough
▷ **Antonyms** equivocal, flexible, inconclusive, lax, loose, relaxed, slack, unrigorous, vague

strings *figurative* catches (*informal*), complications, conditions, obligations, prerequisites, provisos, qualifications, requirements, riders, stipulations

stringy chewy, fibrous, gristly, sinewy, tough, wiry

strip[1] *verb* **1.** bare, denude, deprive, despoil, dismantle, divest, empty, gut, lay bare, loot, peel, pillage, plunder, ransack, rob, sack, skin, spoil **2.** disrobe, unclothe, uncover, undress

strip[2] *noun* band, belt, bit, fillet, piece, ribbon, shred, slip, swathe, tongue

striped banded, barred, striated, stripy

stripling adolescent, boy, fledgling, hobbledehoy (*archaic*), lad, shaver (*informal*), young fellow, youngster, youth

strive attempt, bend over backwards (*informal*), break one's neck (*informal*), bust a gut (*informal*), compete, contend, do all one can, do one's best, do one's damnedest (*informal*), do one's utmost, endeavour, exert oneself, fight, give it one's all (*informal*), give it one's best shot (*informal*), go all out (*informal*), go for broke (*slang*), go for it (*informal*), jump through hoops (*informal*), knock oneself out (*informal*), labour, leave no stone unturned, make an all-out effort (*informal*), make every effort, rupture oneself (*informal*), strain, struggle, toil, try, try hard

stroke *noun* **1.** accomplishment, achievement, blow, feat, flourish, hit, knock, move, movement, pat, rap, thump **2.** apoplexy, attack, collapse, fit, seizure, shock *~verb* **3.** caress, fondle, pat, pet, rub

stroll 1. *verb* amble, make one's way, mooch (*slang*), mosey (*informal*), promenade, ramble, saunter, stooge (*slang*), stretch one's legs, take a turn, toddle, wander **2.** *~noun* airing, breath of air, constitutional, excursion, promenade, ramble, turn, walk

strong 1. athletic, beefy (*informal*), brawny, burly, capable, fighting fit, fit, fit as a fiddle, hale, hardy, healthy, Herculean, lusty, muscular, powerful, robust, sinewy, sound, stalwart, stout, strapping, sturdy, tough, virile **2.** aggressive, brave, courageous, determined, feisty (*informal, chiefly U.S. & Canad.*), firm in spirit, forceful, hard as nails, hard-nosed (*informal*), high-powered, plucky, resilient, resolute, resourceful, self-assertive, steadfast, stouthearted, tenacious, tough, unyielding **3.** acute, dedicated, deep, deep-rooted, eager, fervent, fervid, fierce, firm, intense, keen, severe, staunch, vehement, violent, zealous **4.** clear, clear-cut, cogent, compelling, convincing, distinct, effective, formidable, great, marked, overpowering, persuasive, potent, redoubtable, sound, telling, trenchant, unmistakable, urgent, weighty, well-established, well-founded **5.** Draconian, drastic, extreme, forceful, severe **6.** durable, hard-wearing, heavy-duty, on a firm foundation, reinforced, sturdy, substantial, well-armed, well-built, well-protected **7.** bold, bright, brilliant, dazzling, glaring, loud, stark **8.** biting, concentrated, heady, highly-flavoured, highly-seasoned, hot, intoxicating, piquant, pungent, pure, sharp, spicy, undiluted

▷ **Antonyms** (*senses 1, 2, 3, 4, 5 & 6*) characterless, delicate, faint-hearted, feeble, frail, ineffectual, lacking drive, namby-pamby, puny, slight, spineless, timid, unassertive, uncommitted, unimpassioned, weak (*sense 7*) dull, insipid, pale, pastel, washed-out (*sense 8*) bland, mild, tasteless, vapid, weak

strong-arm *adjective* aggressive, bullying, coercive, forceful, high-pressure, terror, terrorizing, threatening, thuggish, violent

stronghold bastion, bulwark, castle, citadel, fastness, fort, fortress, keep, refuge

strong-minded determined, firm, independent, iron-willed, resolute, strong-willed, unbending, uncompromising

strong point advantage, asset, forte, long suit (*informal*), métier, speciality, strength, strong suit

stroppy awkward, bloody-minded (*Brit. informal*), cantankerous, destructive, difficult, litigious, obstreperous, perverse, quarrelsome, uncooperative, unhelpful

structure *noun* **1.** arrangement, configuration, conformation, construction, design, fabric, form, formation, interrelation of parts, make, make-up, organization **2.** building, construction, edifice, erection, pile *~verb* **3.** arrange, assemble, build up, design, organize, put together, shape

struggle *verb* **1.** bend over backwards (*informal*), break one's neck (*informal*), bust a gut (*informal*), do one's damnedest (*informal*), exert oneself, give it one's all (*informal*), give it one's best shot (*informal*), go all out (*informal*), go for broke (*slang*), go for it (*informal*), knock oneself out (*informal*), labour, make an all-out effort (*informal*), make every effort, rupture oneself (*informal*), strain, strive, toil, work, work like a Trojan *~noun* **2.** effort, exertion, grind (*informal*), labour, long haul, pains, scramble, toil, work *~verb* **3.** battle, compete, contend, fight, grapple, lock horns, scuffle, wrestle *~noun* **4.** battle, brush, clash, combat, conflict, contest, encounter, hostilities, skirmish, strife, tussle

strung up a bundle of nerves (*informal*), edgy, jittery (*informal*), keyed up, nervous, on edge, on tenterhooks, tense, twitchy (*informal*), under a strain, uptight (*informal*), wired (*slang*)

strut *verb* parade, peacock, prance, stalk, swagger

stub *noun* butt, counterfoil, dog-end (*in~*

formal), end, fag end (*informal*), remnant, stump, tail, tail end

stubborn bull-headed, contumacious, cross-grained, dogged, dour, fixed, headstrong, inflexible, intractable, mulish, obdurate, obstinate, opinionated, persistent, pig-headed, recalcitrant, refractory, self-willed, stiff-necked, tenacious, unbending, unmanageable, unshakable, unyielding, wilful

▷ **Antonyms** biddable, compliant, docile, flexible, half-hearted, irresolute, malleable, manageable, pliable, pliant, tractable, vacillating, wavering, yielding

stubby **1**. chunky, dumpy, fubsy (*archaic or dialect*), short, squat, stocky, stumpy, thickset **2**. bristling, bristly, prickly, rough, stubbly

stuck **1**. cemented, fast, fastened, firm, fixed, glued, joined **2**. *informal* at a loss, at a standstill, at one's wits' end, baffled, beaten, bereft of ideas, nonplussed, stumped, up against a brick wall (*informal*) **3**. *slang* (*with* **on**) crazy about, for, *or* over (*informal*), enthusiastic about, hung up on (*slang*), infatuated, keen, mad, obsessed with, wild about (*informal*) **4**. **get stuck into** *informal* get down to, make a start on, set about, tackle, take the bit between one's teeth

stuck-up arrogant, big-headed (*informal*), conceited, condescending, haughty, high and mighty (*informal*), hoity-toity (*informal*), patronizing, proud, snobbish, snooty (*informal*), swollen-headed, toffee-nosed (*slang, chiefly Brit.*), uppish (*Brit. informal*), uppity (*informal*)

stud *verb* bejewel, bespangle, dot, fleck, ornament, spangle, speckle, spot, sprinkle

student apprentice, disciple, learner, observer, pupil, scholar, trainee, undergraduate

studied calculated, conscious, deliberate, intentional, planned, premeditated, purposeful, well-considered, wilful

▷ **Antonyms** impulsive, natural, spontaneous, spur-of-the-moment, unplanned, unpremeditated

studio atelier, workshop

studious academic, assiduous, attentive, bookish, careful, diligent, eager, earnest, hard-working, intellectual, meditative, reflective, scholarly, sedulous, serious, thoughtful

▷ **Antonyms** careless, frivolous, idle, inattentive, indifferent, lazy, loafing, negligent, unacademic, unintellectual, unscholarly

study *verb* **1**. apply oneself (to), bone up on (*informal*), burn the midnight oil, cogitate, con (*archaic*), consider, contemplate, cram (*informal*), examine, go into, hammer away at, learn, lucubrate (*rare*), meditate, mug up (*Brit. slang*), ponder, pore over, read, read up, swot (up) (*Brit. informal*) **2**. analyse, deliberate, examine, investigate, look into, peruse, research, scrutinize, survey, work over *~noun* **3**. academic work, application, book work, cramming (*informal*), learning, lessons, reading, research, school work, swotting (*Brit. informal*), thought **4**. analysis, attention, cogitation, consideration, contemplation, examination, inquiry, inspection, investigation, perusal, review, scrutiny, survey

stuff *verb* **1**. compress, cram, crowd, fill, force, jam, load, pack, pad, push, ram, shove, squeeze, stow, wedge **2**. gobble, gorge, gormandize, guzzle, make a pig of oneself (*informal*), overindulge, pig out (*slang*), sate, satiate *~noun* **3**. belongings, bits and pieces, clobber (*Brit. slang*), effects, equipment, gear, goods and chattels, impedimenta, junk, kit, luggage, materials, objects, paraphernalia, possessions, tackle, things, trappings **4**. cloth, fabric, material, raw material, textile **5**. essence, matter, pith, quintessence, staple, substance **6**. balderdash, baloney (*informal*), bosh (*informal*), bunk (*informal*), bunkum, claptrap (*informal*), foolishness, humbug, nonsense, poppycock (*informal*), rot, rubbish, stuff and nonsense, tommyrot, trash, tripe (*informal*), twaddle, verbiage

stuffing **1**. filler, kapok, packing, quilting, wadding **2**. farce, farcemeat, forcemeat

stuffy **1**. airless, close, fetid, frowsty, fuggy, heavy, muggy, oppressive, stale, stifling, suffocating, sultry, unventilated **2**. as dry as dust, conventional, deadly, dreary, dull, fusty, humourless, musty, niminy-piminy, old-fashioned, old-fogeyish, pompous, priggish, prim, prim and proper, staid, stilted, stodgy, strait-laced, uninteresting

▷ **Antonyms** (*sense 1*) airy, breezy, cool, draughty, fresh, gusty, pleasant, well-ventilated

stumble **1**. blunder about, come a cropper (*informal*), fall, falter, flounder, hesitate, lose one's balance, lurch, reel, slip, stagger, trip **2**. (*with* **on** *or* **upon**) blunder upon, chance upon, come across, discover, encounter, find, happen upon, light upon, run across, turn up **3**. falter, fluff (*informal*), stammer, stutter

stumbling block bar, barrier, difficulty, hazard, hindrance, hurdle, impediment, obstacle, obstruction, snag

stump *verb* **1**. baffle, bewilder, bring (someone) up short, confound, confuse, dumbfound, flummox, foil, mystify, nonplus, outwit, perplex, puzzle, snooker, stop, stymie **2**. clomp, clump, lumber, plod, stamp, stomp (*informal*), trudge

stumped at a loss, at one's wits' end, at sea, baffled, brought to a standstill, floored (*informal*), flummoxed, in despair, nonplussed, perplexed, stymied, uncertain which way to turn

stump up chip in (*informal*), come across with (*informal*), contribute, cough up (*informal*), donate, fork out (*slang*), hand over, pay, shell out (*informal*)

stumpy chunky, dumpy, fubsy (*archaic or dialect*), heavy, short, squat, stocky, stubby, thick, thickset

stun *figurative* amaze, astonish, astound, bewilder, confound, confuse, daze, dumbfound, flabbergast (*informal*), hit (someone) like a ton of bricks (*informal*), knock out, knock (someone) for six (*informal*), overcome, overpower, shock, stagger, strike (someone) dumb, stupefy, take (someone's) breath away

stung angered, exasperated, goaded, hurt, incensed, nettled, piqued, resentful, roused, wounded

stunned *figurative* astounded, at a loss for words, bowled over (*informal*), dazed, devastated, dumbfounded, flabbergasted (*informal*), gobsmacked (*Brit. slang*), numb, shocked, staggered, struck dumb

stunner beauty, charmer, dazzler, dish (*informal*), dolly (*slang*), eyeful (*informal*), glamour puss, good-looker, heart-throb, honey (*informal*), humdinger (*slang*), knockout (*informal*), looker (*informal, chiefly U.S.*), lovely (*slang*), peach (*informal*), sensation, smasher (*informal*), wow (*slang, chiefly U.S.*)

stunning beautiful, brilliant, dazzling, devastating (*informal*), dramatic, drop-dead (*slang*), gorgeous, great (*informal*), heavenly, impressive, lovely, marvellous, out of this world (*informal*), ravishing, remarkable, sensational (*informal*), smashing (*informal*), spectacular, striking, wonderful

▷ **Antonyms** average, dreadful, horrible, mediocre, no great shakes (*informal*), ordinary, plain, poor, rotten, run-of-the-mill, ugly, unattractive, unimpressive, uninspiring, unremarkable

stunt *noun* act, deed, exploit, feat, feature, gest (*archaic*), *tour de force*, trick

stunted diminutive, dwarfed, dwarfish, little, small, tiny, undersized

stupefaction amazement, astonishment, awe, wonder, wonderment

stupefy amaze, astound, bewilder, confound, daze, dumbfound, knock senseless, numb, shock, stagger, stun

stupendous amazing, astounding, breathtaking, brilliant, colossal, enormous, fabulous (*informal*), fantastic (*informal*), gigantic, huge, marvellous, mega (*slang*), mind-blowing (*informal*), mind-boggling (*informal*), out of this world (*informal*), overwhelming, phenomenal, prodigious, sensational (*informal*), staggering, stunning (*informal*), superb, surpassing belief, surprising, tremendous (*informal*), vast, wonderful, wondrous (*archaic or literary*)

▷ **Antonyms** average, diminutive, mediocre, modest, no great shakes (*informal*), ordinary, petty, puny, tiny, unexciting, unimpressive, unremarkable, unsurprising

stupid 1. Boeotian, braindead (*informal*), brainless, crass, cretinous, dead from the neck up, deficient, dense, dim, doltish, dopey (*informal*), dozy (*Brit. informal*), dull, dumb (*informal*), foolish, gullible, half-witted, moronic, naive, obtuse, simple, simple-minded, slow, slow on the uptake (*informal*), slow-witted, sluggish, stolid, thick, thick as mince (*Scot. informal*), thickheaded, unintelligent, witless, woodenheaded (*informal*) **2.** asinine, crackbrained, crackpot (*informal*), daft (*informal*), futile, half-baked (*informal*), idiotic, ill-advised, imbecilic, inane, indiscreet, irrelevant, irresponsible, laughable, ludicrous, meaningless, mindless, nonsensical, pointless, puerile, rash, senseless, short-sighted, trivial, unintelligent, unthinking **3.** dazed, groggy, in a daze, insensate, punch-drunk, semiconscious, senseless, stunned, stupefied

▷ **Antonyms** astute, brainy, bright, brilliant, clear-headed, clever, intelligent, lucid, on the ball (*informal*), prudent, quick, quick on the uptake, quick-witted, realistic, reasonable, sensible, sharp, shrewd, smart, thoughtful, well-thought-out, wise

stupidity 1. asininity, brainlessness, craziness, denseness, dimness, dopiness (*slang*), doziness (*Brit. informal*), dullness, dumbness (*informal*), feeble-mindedness, imbecility, lack of brain, lack of intelligence, naivety, obtuseness, puerility, simplicity, slowness, thickheadedness, thickness **2.** absurdity, bêtise (*rare*), fatuity, fatuousness, folly, foolhardiness, foolishness, futility, idiocy, impracticality, inanity, indiscretion, ineptitude, irresponsibility, ludicrousness, lunacy, madness, pointlessness, rashness, senselessness, silliness

stupor coma, daze, inertia, insensibility, lethargy, numbness, stupefaction, torpor, trance, unconsciousness

sturdy athletic, brawny, built to last, determined, durable, firm, flourishing, hardy, hearty, lusty, muscular, powerful, resolute, robust, secure, solid, stalwart, staunch, steadfast, stouthearted, substantial, thickset, vigorous, well-built, well-made

▷ **Antonyms** feeble, flimsy, frail, infirm, irresolute, puny, rickety, skinny, uncertain, unsubstantial, weak, weakly

stutter *verb* falter, hesitate, speak haltingly, splutter, stammer, stumble

Stygian black, caliginous (*archaic*), dark, dreary, gloomy, Hadean, hellish, infernal, sombre, Tartarean, tenebrous

style *noun* **1.** cut, design, form, hand, manner, technique **2.** fashion, mode, rage, trend, vogue **3.** approach, custom, manner, method, mode, way **4.** *bon ton,* chic, cosmopolitanism, dash, dressiness (*informal*), élan, elegance, fashionable~ness, flair, grace, panache, polish, re~finement, savoir-faire, smartness, so~phistication, stylishness, taste, urbanity **5.** affluence, comfort, ease, elegance, gracious living, grandeur, luxury **6.** ap~pearance, category, characteristic, gen~re, kind, pattern, sort, spirit, strain, tenor, tone, type, variety **7.** diction, ex~pression, mode of expression, phraseol~ogy, phrasing, treatment, turn of phrase, vein, wording *~verb* **8.** adapt, arrange, cut, design, dress, fashion, shape, tailor **9.** address, call, christen, denominate, designate, dub, entitle, la~bel, name, term

stylish à la mode, chic, classy (*slang*), dapper, dressy (*informal*), fashionable, in fashion, in vogue, modish, natty (*in~formal*), polished, smart, snappy, snazzy (*informal*), trendy (*Brit. informal*), urbane, voguish, well turned-out

▷ **Antonyms** badly-tailored, naff (*Brit. slang*), old-fashioned, outmoded, out-of-date, passé, scruffy, shabby, slovenly, tacky, tawdry, unfashionable, unstylish, untrendy (*Brit. informal*)

stymie balk, confound, defeat, flummox, foil, frustrate, hinder, mystify, nonplus, puzzle, snooker, spike (someone's) guns, stump, throw a spanner in the works (*Brit. informal*), thwart

suave affable, agreeable, bland, charm~ing, civilized, cool (*informal*), courteous, debonair, diplomatic, gracious, obliging, pleasing, polite, smooth, smooth-tongued, sophisticated, svelte, urbane, worldly

subconscious *adjective* hidden, inner, innermost, intuitive, latent, repressed, subliminal, suppressed

▷ **Antonyms** aware, conscious, knowing, sensible, sentient

subdue 1. beat down, break, conquer, control, crush, defeat, discipline, gain ascendancy over, get the better of, get the upper hand over, get under control, humble, master, overcome, overpower, overrun, put down, quell, tame, tram~ple, triumph over, vanquish **2.** check, control, mellow, moderate, quieten down, repress, soften, suppress, tone down

▷ **Antonyms** (*sense 2*) agitate, arouse, awaken, incite, provoke, stir up, waken, whip up

subdued 1. chastened, crestfallen, deject~ed, downcast, down in the mouth, grave, out of spirits, quiet, repentant, re~pressed, restrained, sad, sadder and wiser, serious, sobered, solemn **2.** dim, hushed, low-key, muted, quiet, shaded, sober, soft, subtle, toned down, unob~trusive

▷ **Antonyms** (*sense 1*) cheerful, enthusi~astic, full of beans (*informal*), happy, lively, vivacious (*sense 2*) bright, loud, strident

subject *noun* **1.** affair, business, field of enquiry *or* reference, issue, matter, ob~ject, point, question, subject matter, substance, theme, topic **2.** case, client, guinea pig (*informal*), participant, pa~tient, victim **3.** citizen, dependant, liegeman, national, subordinate, vassal *~adjective* **4.** at the mercy of, disposed, exposed, in danger of, liable, open, prone, susceptible, vulnerable **5.** condi~tional, contingent, dependent **6.** an~swerable, bound by, captive, dependent, enslaved, inferior, obedient, satellite, subjugated, submissive, subordinate, subservient *~verb* **7.** expose, lay open, make liable, put through, submit, treat

subjective biased, emotional, idiosyn~cratic, instinctive, intuitive, nonobjec~tive, personal, prejudiced

▷ **Antonyms** concrete, detached, disin~terested, dispassionate, impartial, im~personal, objective, open-minded, unbi~ased

subjugate bring (someone) to his knees, bring to heel, bring under the yoke, conquer, crush, defeat, enslave, hold sway over, lick (*informal*), master, over~come, overpower, overthrow, put down, quell, reduce, rule over, subdue, sup~press, tame, vanquish

sublimate 1. channel, divert, redirect, transfer, turn **2.** elevate, exalt, heighten, refine

sublime elevated, eminent, exalted, glo~rious, grand, great, high, imposing, lofty, magnificent, majestic, noble, transcendent

▷ **Antonyms** bad, commonplace, lowly, mundane, ordinary, poor, ridiculous, worldly

submerge deluge, dip, drown, duck, dunk, engulf, flood, immerse, inundate, overflow, overwhelm, plunge, sink, swamp

submerged drowned, immersed, sub~aquatic, subaqueous, submarine, sub~mersed, sunk, sunken, undersea, underwater

submission 1. acquiescence, assent, ca~pitulation, giving in, surrender, yielding **2.** compliance, deference, docility, meekness, obedience, passivity, resig~nation, submissiveness, tractability, unassertiveness **3.** argument, conten~tion, proposal **4.** entry, handing in, presentation, submitting, tendering

submissive abject, accommodating, ac~quiescent, amenable, biddable, bootlick~ing (*informal*), compliant, deferential, docile, dutiful, humble, ingratiating, lowly, malleable, meek, obedient, obei~

sant, obsequious, passive, patient, pliant, resigned, subdued, tractable, uncomplaining, unresisting, yielding
▷ **Antonyms** awkward, difficult, disobedient, headstrong, intractable, obstinate, stubborn, uncooperative, unyielding

submit 1. accede, acquiesce, agree, bend, bow, capitulate, comply, defer, endure, give in, hoist the white flag, knuckle under, lay down arms, put up with (*informal*), resign oneself, stoop, succumb, surrender, throw in the sponge, toe the line, tolerate, yield **2.** commit, hand in, present, proffer, put forward, refer, table, tender **3.** advance, argue, assert, claim, contend, move, propose, propound, put, state, suggest, volunteer

subnormal cretinous, E.S.N., feeble-minded, imbecilic, mentally defective, moronic, retarded, simple, slow

subordinate *adjective* **1.** dependent, inferior, junior, lesser, lower, minor, secondary, subject, subservient **2.** ancillary, auxiliary, subsidiary, supplementary ~*noun* **3.** aide, assistant, attendant, dependant, inferior, junior, second, subaltern, underling
▷ **Antonyms** ~*adjective* central, essential, greater, higher, key, main, necessary, predominant, senior, superior, vital ~*noun* boss (*informal*), captain, chief, commander, head, leader, master, principal, senior, superior

subordination inferiority, inferior *or* secondary status, servitude, subjection, submission

sub rosa behind closed doors, in camera, in secret, in strict confidence, secretly

subscribe 1. chip in (*informal*), contribute, donate, give, offer, pledge, promise **2.** acquiesce, advocate, agree, consent, countenance, endorse, support

subscription annual payment, contribution, donation, dues, gift, membership fee, offering

subsequent after, consequent, consequential, ensuing, following, later, succeeding, successive
▷ **Antonyms** antecedent, earlier, erstwhile, former, on-time, past, preceding, previous, prior

subsequently afterwards, at a later date, consequently, in the aftermath (of), in the end, later

subservient 1. abject, bootlicking (*informal*), deferential, inferior, obsequious, servile, slavish, subject, submissive, sycophantic, truckling **2.** accessory, ancillary, auxiliary, conducive, helpful, instrumental, serviceable, subordinate, subsidiary, useful
▷ **Antonyms** (*sense 1*) bolshie, bossy, disobedient, domineering, overbearing, overriding, rebellious, superior, wilful

subside 1. abate, decrease, de-escalate, diminish, dwindle, ease, ebb, lessen, let up, level off, melt away, moderate, peter out, quieten, recede, slacken, wane **2.** cave in, collapse, decline, descend, drop, ebb, lower, settle, sink
▷ **Antonyms** escalate, grow, heighten, increase, inflate, intensify, mount, rise, soar, swell, tumefy, wax

subsidence 1. decline, descent, ebb, settlement, settling, sinking **2.** abatement, decrease, de-escalation, diminution, easing off, lessening, slackening

subsidiary aiding, ancillary, assistant, auxiliary, contributory, cooperative, helpful, lesser, minor, secondary, serviceable, subordinate, subservient, supplemental, supplementary, useful
▷ **Antonyms** central, chief, head, key, leading, main, major, primary, principal, vital

subsidize finance, fund, promote, put up the money for, sponsor, support, underwrite

subsidy aid, allowance, assistance, contribution, financial aid, grant, help, stipend, subvention, support

subsist be, continue, eke out an existence, endure, exist, keep going, keep one's head above water, last, live, make ends meet, remain, stay alive, survive, sustain oneself

subsistence aliment, existence, food, keep, livelihood, living, maintenance, provision, rations, support, survival, sustenance, upkeep, victuals

substance 1. body, element, fabric, material, stuff, texture **2.** burden, essence, gist, gravamen (*Law*), import, main point, matter, meaning, pith, significance, subject, sum and substance, theme **3.** actuality, concreteness, entity, force, reality **4.** affluence, assets, estate, means, property, resources, wealth

substandard damaged, imperfect, inadequate, inferior, second-rate, shoddy, unacceptable

substantial 1. ample, big, considerable, generous, goodly, important, large, significant, sizable *or* sizeable, tidy (*informal*), worthwhile **2.** bulky, durable, firm, hefty, massive, solid, sound, stout, strong, sturdy, well-built **3.** actual, existent, material, positive, real, true, valid, weighty
▷ **Antonyms** (*senses 1 & 2*) feeble, frail, inadequate, inconsiderable, infirm, insignificant, insubstantial, jerry-built, light-weight, meagre, niggardly, pathetic, poor, rickety, skimpy, small, weak (*sense 3*) fictitious, imaginary, imagined, insubstantial, nonexistent, unreal

substantially essentially, in essence, in essentials, in substance, in the main, largely, materially, to a large extent

substantiate affirm, attest to, authenticate, bear out, confirm, corroborate, establish, prove, support, validate, verify
▷ **Antonyms** confute, contradict, controvert, disprove, expose, invalidate, make a nonsense of, negate, prove false, rebut, refute

substitute *verb* **1.** change, commute, exchange, interchange, replace, swap (*informal*), switch **2.** (*with* **for**) act for, be in place of, cover for, deputize, double for, fill in for, hold the fort for, relieve, stand in for, take over *~noun* **3.** agent, depute (*Scot.*), deputy, equivalent, expedient, locum, locum tenens, makeshift, proxy, relief, replacement, representative, reserve, stand-by, stopgap, sub, supply, surrogate, temp (*informal*), temporary *~adjective* **4.** acting, additional, alternative, fall-back, proxy, replacement, reserve, second, surrogate, temporary

substitution change, exchange, interchange, replacement, swap (*informal*), switch

subterfuge artifice, deception, deviousness, dodge, duplicity, evasion, excuse, machination, manoeuvre, ploy, pretence, pretext, quibble, ruse, shift, stall, stratagem, trick

subtle 1. deep, delicate, discriminating, ingenious, nice, penetrating, profound, refined, sophisticated **2.** delicate, faint, implied, indirect, insinuated, slight, understated **3.** artful, astute, crafty, cunning, designing, devious, intriguing, keen, Machiavellian, scheming, shrewd, sly, wily
▷ **Antonyms** artless, blunt, crass, direct, downright, guileless, heavy-handed, lacking finesse, obvious, overwhelming, simple, straightforward, strong, tactless, unsophisticated, unsubtle

subtlety 1. acumen, acuteness, cleverness, delicacy, discernment, fine point, intricacy, nicety, refinement, sagacity, skill, sophistication **2.** discernment, discrimination, finesse, penetration **3.** artfulness, astuteness, craftiness, cunning, deviousness, guile, slyness, wiliness

subtract deduct, detract, diminish, remove, take away, take from, take off, withdraw
▷ **Antonyms** add, add to, append, increase by, supplement

suburbs dormitory area (*Brit.*), environs, faubourgs, neighbourhood, outskirts, precincts, purlieus, residential areas, suburbia

subversive 1. *adjective* destructive, incendiary, inflammatory, insurrectionary, overthrowing, perversive, riotous, seditious, treasonous, underground, undermining **2.** *~noun* deviationist, dissident, fifth columnist, insurrectionary, quisling, saboteur, seditionary, seditionist, terrorist, traitor

subvert 1. demolish, destroy, invalidate, overturn, raze, ruin, sabotage, undermine, upset, wreck **2.** confound, contaminate, corrupt, debase, demoralize, deprave, pervert, poison, vitiate

succeed 1. arrive (*informal*), be successful, bring home the bacon (*informal*), carry all before one, come off (*informal*), crack it (*informal*), cut it (*informal*), do all right for oneself (*informal*), do the trick (*informal*), flourish, gain one's end, get to the top, go down a bomb (*informal, chiefly Brit.*), go like a bomb (*Brit. & N.Z. informal*), hit the jackpot (*informal*), make good, make it (*informal*), make one's mark (*informal*), make the grade (*informal*), prosper, thrive, triumph, turn out well, work **2.** be subsequent, come next, ensue, follow, result, supervene **3.** (*usually with* **to**) accede, assume the office of, come into, come into possession of, enter upon, fill (someone's) boots, inherit, replace, step into (someone's) boots, take over
▷ **Antonyms** (*sense 1*) be unsuccessful, collapse, come a cropper (*informal*), fail, fall by the wayside, fall flat, fall short, flop (*informal*), go belly up (*informal*), go by the board, not make the grade, not manage to (*sense 2*) be a precursor of, come before, go ahead of, go before, pave the way, precede

succeeding ensuing, following, next, subsequent, successive
▷ **Antonyms** antecedent, earlier, former, preceding, previous, prior

success 1. ascendancy, eminence, fame, favourable outcome, fortune, happiness, hit (*informal*), luck, prosperity, triumph **2.** best seller, big name, celebrity, hit (*informal*), market leader, megastar (*informal*), sensation, smash (*informal*), smash hit (*informal*), somebody, star, V.I.P., winner, wow (*slang*)
▷ **Antonyms** (*sense 1*) collapse, dead duck (*slang*), disaster, downfall, failure, fiasco, flop (*informal*), loser, misfortune, washout (*sense 2*) loser, nobody, no-hoper

successful acknowledged, at the top of the tree, best-selling, booming, efficacious, favourable, flourishing, fortunate, fruitful, going places, home and dry (*Brit. informal*), lucky, lucrative, moneymaking, on a roll, out in front (*informal*), paying, profitable, prosperous, rewarding, thriving, top, unbeaten, victorious, wealthy
▷ **Antonyms** defeated, failed, ineffective, losing, luckless, uneconomic, unprofitable, unsuccessful, useless

successfully famously (*informal*), favourably, in triumph, swimmingly, victoriously, well, with flying colours

succession 1. chain, continuation, course, cycle, flow, order, procession, progression, run, sequence, series, train **2. in**

succession consecutively, one after the other, one behind the other, on the trot (*informal*), running, successively **3.** accession, assumption, elevation, entering upon, inheritance, taking over **4.** descendants, descent, line, lineage, race

successive consecutive, following, in a row, in succession, sequent, succeeding

succinct brief, compact, compendious, concise, condensed, gnomic, in a few well-chosen words, laconic, pithy, summary, terse, to the point
▷ **Antonyms** circuitous, circumlocutory, diffuse, discursive, long-winded, prolix, rambling, verbose, wordy

succour 1. *verb* aid, assist, befriend, comfort, encourage, foster, give aid and encouragement to, help, minister to, nurse, relieve, render assistance to, support **2.** *~noun* aid, assistance, comfort, help, relief, support

succulent juicy, luscious, lush, mellow, moist, mouthwatering, rich

succumb capitulate, die, fall, fall victim to, give in, give way, go under, knuckle under, submit, surrender, yield
▷ **Antonyms** beat, conquer, get the better of, master, overcome, rise above, surmount, triumph over

sucker butt, cat's paw, dupe, easy game *or* mark (*informal*), fool, mug (*Brit. slang*), nerd *or* nurd (*slang*), pushover (*slang*), sap (*slang*), sitting duck (*informal*), sitting target, victim

suck up to brown-nose (*taboo slang*), butter up, curry favour with, dance attendance on, fawn on, flatter, get on the right side of, ingratiate oneself with, keep in with (*informal*), kiss (someone's) ass (*U.S. & Canad. taboo slang*), lick (someone's) boots, pander to, play up to (*informal*), toady, truckle, worm oneself into (someone's) favour

sudden abrupt, hasty, hurried, impulsive, quick, rapid, rash, swift, unexpected, unforeseen, unusual
▷ **Antonyms** anticipated, deliberate, expected, foreseen, gentle, gradual, slow, unhasty

suddenly abruptly, all at once, all of a sudden, on the spur of the moment, out of the blue (*informal*), unexpectedly, without warning

sue 1. *Law* bring an action against (someone), charge, have the law on (someone) (*informal*), indict, institute legal proceedings against (someone), prefer charges against (someone), prosecute, summon, take (someone) to court **2.** appeal for, beg, beseech, entreat, petition, plead, solicit, supplicate

suffer 1. ache, agonize, be affected, be in pain, be racked, feel wretched, go through a lot (*informal*), go through the mill (*informal*), grieve, have a thin *or* bad time, hurt **2.** bear, endure, experience, feel, go through, put up with (*informal*), support, sustain, tolerate, undergo **3.** appear in a poor light, be handicapped, be impaired, deteriorate, fall off, show to disadvantage **4.** *archaic* allow, let, permit

suffering *noun* affliction, agony, anguish, discomfort, distress, hardship, martyrdom, misery, ordeal, pain, torment, torture

suffice answer, be adequate, be enough, be sufficient, content, do, fill the bill (*informal*), meet requirements, satisfy, serve

sufficient adequate, competent, enough, enow (*archaic*), satisfactory
▷ **Antonyms** deficient, inadequate, insufficient, meagre, not enough, poor, scant, short, sparse

suffocate asphyxiate, choke, smother, stifle, strangle

suffrage ballot, consent, franchise, right to vote, voice (*figurative*), vote

suffuse bathe, cover, flood, imbue, infuse, mantle, overspread, permeate, pervade, spread over, steep, transfuse

suggest 1. advise, advocate, move, offer a suggestion, prescribe, propose, put forward, recommend **2.** bring to mind, connote, evoke, put one in mind of **3.** hint, imply, indicate, insinuate, intimate, lead one to believe

suggestion 1. motion, plan, proposal, proposition, recommendation **2.** breath, hint, indication, insinuation, intimation, suspicion, trace, whisper

suggestive 1. (*with* **of**) evocative, expressive, indicative, redolent, reminiscent **2.** bawdy, blue, immodest, improper, indecent, indelicate, off colour, provocative, prurient, racy, ribald, risqué, rude, smutty, spicy (*informal*), titillating, unseemly

suit *verb* **1.** agree, agree with, answer, be acceptable to, become, befit, be seemly, conform to, correspond, do, go with, gratify, harmonize, match, please, satisfy, tally **2.** accommodate, adapt, adjust, customize, fashion, fit, modify, proportion, tailor *~noun* **3.** addresses, appeal, attentions, courtship, entreaty, invocation, petition, prayer, request **4.** *Law* action, case, cause, industrial tribunal, lawsuit, proceeding, prosecution, trial **5.** clothing, costume, dress, ensemble, habit, outfit **6. follow suit** accord with, copy, emulate, run with the herd, take one's cue from

suitability appropriateness, aptness, fitness, opportuneness, rightness, timeliness

suitable acceptable, applicable, apposite, appropriate, apt, becoming, befitting, convenient, cut out for, due, fit, fitting, in character, in keeping, opportune, pertinent, proper, relevant, right, satis~

factory, seemly, suited
▷ **Antonyms** discordant, inapposite, inappropriate, incorrect, inopportune, jarring, out of character, out of keeping, unbecoming, unfitting, unseemly, unsuitable, unsuited

suite 1. apartment, collection, furniture, rooms, series, set **2**. attendants, entourage, escort, followers, retainers, retinue, train

suitor admirer, beau, follower (*obsolete*), swain (*archaic*), wooer, young man

sulk be in a huff, be put out, brood, have the hump (*Brit. informal*), look sullen, pout

sulky aloof, churlish, cross, disgruntled, huffy, ill-humoured, in the sulks, moody, morose, perverse, petulant, put out, querulous, resentful, sullen, vexed

sullen brooding, cheerless, cross, dismal, dour, dull, gloomy, glowering, heavy, moody, morose, obstinate, out of humour, perverse, silent, sombre, sour, stubborn, surly, unsociable
▷ **Antonyms** amiable, bright, cheerful, cheery, chirpy (*informal*), genial, good-humoured, good-natured, pleasant, sociable, sunny, warm, warm-hearted

sullenness glumness, heaviness, ill humour, moodiness, moroseness, sourness, sulkiness, sulks

sully befoul, besmirch, blemish, contaminate, darken, defile, dirty, disgrace, dishonour, pollute, smirch, spoil, spot, stain, taint, tarnish

sultry 1. close, hot, humid, muggy, oppressive, sticky, stifling, stuffy, sweltering **2**. amorous, come-hither (*informal*), erotic, passionate, provocative, seductive, sensual, sexy (*informal*), voluptuous
▷ **Antonyms** (*sense 1*) cool, fresh, invigorating, refreshing

sum aggregate, amount, entirety, quantity, reckoning, score, sum total, tally, total, totality, whole

summarily arbitrarily, at short notice, expeditiously, forthwith, immediately, on the spot, peremptorily, promptly, speedily, swiftly, without delay, without wasting words

summarize abridge, condense, encapsulate, epitomize, give a rundown of, give the main points of, outline, précis, put in a nutshell, recap, recapitulate, review, sum up

summary 1. *noun* abridgment, abstract, compendium, digest, epitome, essence, extract, outline, précis, recapitulation, résumé, review, rundown, summing-up, synopsis **2**. *~adjective* arbitrary, brief, compact, compendious, concise, condensed, cursory, hasty, laconic, perfunctory, pithy, succinct

summit acme, apex, crest, crown, crowning point, culmination, head, height, peak, pinnacle, top, zenith
▷ **Antonyms** base, bottom, depths, foot, lowest point, nadir

summon 1. arouse, assemble, bid, call, call together, cite, convene, convoke, invite, rally, rouse, send for **2**. (*often with* **up**) call into action, draw on, gather, invoke, mobilize, muster

sumptuous costly, dear, de luxe, expensive, extravagant, gorgeous, grand, lavish, luxurious, magnificent, opulent, palatial, plush (*informal*), posh (*informal, chiefly Brit.*), rich, ritzy (*slang*), splendid, splendiferous (*facetious*), superb
▷ **Antonyms** austere, basic, cheap, frugal, inexpensive, meagre, mean, miserly, plain, shabby, wretched

sum up 1. close, conclude, put in a nutshell, recapitulate, review, summarize **2**. estimate, form an opinion of, get the measure of, size up (*informal*)

sun 1. *noun* daystar (*poetic*), eye of heaven, Helios (*Greek myth*), Phoebus (*Greek myth*), Phoebus Apollo (*Greek myth*), Sol (*Roman myth*) **2**. *~verb* bake, bask, sunbathe, tan

sunburnt bronzed, brown, brown as a berry, burnt, burnt to a crisp, like a lobster, peeling, red, ruddy, scarlet, tanned

sundry assorted, different, divers (*archaic*), miscellaneous, several, some, varied, various

sunk all washed up (*informal*), done for (*informal*), finished, lost, on the rocks, ruined, up the creek without a paddle (*informal*)

sunken 1. concave, drawn, haggard, hollow, hollowed **2**. at a lower level, below ground, buried, depressed, immersed, lower, recessed, submerged

sunless bleak, cheerless, cloudy, dark, depressing, gloomy, grey, hazy, overcast, sombre

sunny 1. bright, brilliant, clear, fine, luminous, radiant, summery, sunlit, sunshiny, unclouded, without a cloud in the sky **2**. *figurative* beaming, blithe, buoyant, cheerful, cheery, chirpy (*informal*), genial, happy, joyful, light-hearted, optimistic, pleasant, smiling
▷ **Antonyms** (*sense 1*) cloudy, depressing, dreary, dreich (*Scot.*), dull, gloomy, murky, overcast, rainy, shaded, shadowy, sunless, wet, wintry (*sense 2*) doleful, down in the dumps (*informal*), gloomy, miserable, morbid, unsmiling

sunrise aurora (*poetic*), break of day, cockcrow, dawn, daybreak, daylight, dayspring (*poetic*), sunup

sunset close of (the) day, dusk, eventide, gloaming (*Scot. or poetic*), nightfall, sundown

super awesome (*slang*), boffo (*slang*), brill (*informal*), chillin' (*U.S. slang*), cracking (*Brit. informal*), crucial (*slang*), def (*slang*), excellent, glorious, incompa~

rable, jim-dandy (*slang*), magnificent, marvellous, matchless, mean (*slang*), mega (*slang*), out of this world (*informal*), outstanding, peerless, sensational (*informal*), smashing (*informal*), sovereign, superb, terrific (*informal*), top-notch (*informal*), topping (*Brit. slang*), wonderful

superannuated aged, antiquated, decrepit, discharged, obsolete, old, past it (*informal*), pensioned off, put out to grass (*informal*), retired, senile, unfit

superb admirable, awesome (*slang*), bodacious (*slang, chiefly U.S.*), boffo (*slang*), breathtaking, brill (*informal*), chillin' (*U.S. slang*), choice, divine, excellent, exquisite, fine, first-rate, gorgeous, grand, magnificent, marvellous, mega (*slang*), of the first water, splendid, splendiferous (*facetious*), superior, superlative, topping (*Brit. slang*), unrivalled, world-class
▷ **Antonyms** abysmal, awful, bad, disappointing, dreadful, inferior, mediocre, no great shakes (*informal*), pathetic, poor quality, run-of-the-mill, terrible, third-rate, uninspired, woeful

supercilious arrogant, condescending, contemptuous, disdainful, haughty, high and mighty (*informal*), hoity-toity (*informal*), imperious, insolent, lofty, lordly, overbearing, patronizing, proud, scornful, snooty (*informal*), stuck-up (*informal*), toffee-nosed (*slang, chiefly Brit.*), uppish (*Brit. informal*), vainglorious
▷ **Antonyms** deferential, generous, humble, meek, modest, obsequious, self-effacing, submissive, unassuming, unpretentious, warm-hearted

superficial **1.** exterior, external, on the surface, peripheral, shallow, skin-deep, slight, surface **2.** casual, cosmetic, cursory, desultory, facile, hasty, hurried, inattentive, nodding, passing, perfunctory, sketchy, slapdash **3.** empty, empty-headed, frivolous, lightweight, shallow, silly, trivial **4.** apparent, evident, ostensible, outward, seeming
▷ **Antonyms** complete, comprehensive, deep, detailed, earnest, exhaustive, in depth, major, penetrating, probing, profound, serious, substantial, thorough

superficiality emptiness, lack of depth, lack of substance, shallowness, triviality

superficially apparently, at face value, at first glance, externally, on the surface, ostensibly, to the casual eye

superfluity excess, exuberance, glut, plethora, redundancy, superabundance, surfeit, surplus

superfluous excess, excessive, extra, in excess, left over, needless, on one's hands, pleonastic (*Rhetoric*), redundant, remaining, residuary, spare, superabundant, supererogatory, supernumerary, surplus, surplus to requirements, uncalled-for, unnecessary, unneeded, unrequired
▷ **Antonyms** called for, essential, imperative, indispensable, necessary, needed, requisite, vital, wanted

superhuman **1.** herculean, heroic, phenomenal, prodigious, stupendous, valiant **2.** divine, paranormal, preternatural, supernatural

superintend administer, control, direct, handle, inspect, look after, manage, overlook, oversee, run, supervise

superintendence care, charge, control, direction, government, guidance, inspection, management, supervision, surveillance

superintendent administrator, chief, conductor, controller, director, governor, inspector, manager, overseer, supervisor

superior *adjective* **1.** better, grander, greater, higher, more advanced, more expert, more extensive, more skilful, paramount, predominant, preferred, prevailing, surpassing, unrivalled **2.** a cut above (*informal*), admirable, choice, de luxe, distinguished, excellent, exceptional, exclusive, fine, first-class, first-rate, good, good quality, high calibre, high-class, of the first order, running rings around (*informal*), streets ahead (*informal*), world-class **3.** airy, condescending, disdainful, haughty, lofty, lordly, on one's high horse (*informal*), patronizing, pretentious, snobbish, stuck-up (*informal*), supercilious *~noun* **4.** boss (*informal*), chief, director, manager, principal, senior, supervisor
▷ **Antonyms** *~adjective* (*senses 1 & 2*) average, inferior, less, lesser, lower, mediocre, no great shakes (*informal*), not as good, ordinary, poorer, second-class, second-rate, substandard, unremarkable, worse *~noun* assistant, cohort (*chiefly U.S.*), dogsbody, inferior, junior, lackey, minion, subordinate, underling

superiority advantage, ascendancy, excellence, lead, predominance, pre-eminence, preponderance, prevalence, supremacy

superlative *adjective* consummate, crack (*slang*), excellent, greatest, highest, magnificent, matchless, of the first water, of the highest order, outstanding, peerless, stellar (*informal*), supreme, surpassing, transcendent, unparalleled, unrivalled, unsurpassed
▷ **Antonyms** abysmal, appalling, average, dreadful, easily outclassed, inferior, ordinary, poor, rotten, run-of-the-mill, undistinguished, unexceptional, uninspired, unspectacular

supernatural abnormal, dark, ghostly, hidden, miraculous, mysterious, mystic, occult, paranormal, phantom, preternatural, psychic, spectral, supranatural, uncanny, unearthly, unnatural

supernumerary excess, excessive, extra, in excess, odd, redundant, spare, superfluous, surplus, unrequired

supersede annul, displace, fill (someone's) boots, oust, overrule, remove, replace, set aside, step into (someone's) boots, supplant, supplement, suspend, take over, take the place of, usurp

supervise administer, be on duty at, be responsible for, conduct, control, direct, handle, have *or* be in charge of, inspect, keep an eye on, look after, manage, oversee, preside over, run, superintend

supervision administration, auspices, care, charge, control, direction, guidance, instruction, management, oversight, stewardship, superintendence, surveillance

supervisor administrator, boss (*informal*), chief, foreman, gaffer (*informal, chiefly Brit.*), inspector, manager, overseer, steward, superintendent

supervisory administrative, executive, managerial, overseeing, superintendent

supine 1. flat, flat on one's back, horizontal, recumbent **2.** apathetic, careless, heedless, idle, incurious, indifferent, indolent, inert, languid, lazy, lethargic, listless, lymphatic, negligent, passive, slothful, sluggish, spineless, spiritless, torpid, uninterested
▷ **Antonyms** (*sense 1*) lying on one's face, prone, prostrate

supplant displace, oust, overthrow, remove, replace, supersede, take over, take the place of, undermine, unseat

supple bending, elastic, flexible, limber, lissom(e), lithe, loose-limbed, plastic, pliable, pliant
▷ **Antonyms** awkward, creaky (*informal*), firm, graceless, inflexible, rigid, stiff, taut, unbending, unsupple, unyielding

supplement 1. *noun* added feature, addendum, addition, add-on, appendix, codicil, complement, extra, insert, postscript, pull-out, sequel **2.** *~verb* add, augment, complement, extend, fill out, reinforce, supply, top up

supplementary accompanying, additional, add-on, ancillary, auxiliary, complementary, extra, secondary, supplemental

suppliant 1. *adjective* begging, beseeching, craving, entreating, imploring, importunate, on bended knee **2.** *~noun* applicant, petitioner, suitor, supplicant

supplication appeal, entreaty, invocation, petition, plea, pleading, prayer, request, solicitation, suit

supply *verb* **1.** afford, cater to *or* for, come up with, contribute, endow, equip, fill, furnish, give, grant, minister, outfit, produce, provide, purvey, replenish, satisfy, stock, store, victual, yield *~noun* **2.** cache, fund, hoard, quantity, reserve, reservoir, source, stock, stockpile, store **3.** (*usually plural*) equipment, food, foodstuff, items, materials, necessities, provender, provisions, rations, stores

support *verb* **1.** bear, bolster, brace, buttress, carry, hold, hold up, prop, reinforce, shore up, sustain, underpin, uphold **2.** be a source of strength to, buoy up, cherish, encourage, finance, foster, fund, hold (someone's) hand, keep, look after, maintain, nourish, provide for, strengthen, subsidize, succour, sustain, take care of, underwrite **3.** advocate, aid, assist, back, boost (someone's) morale, champion, defend, espouse, forward, go along with, help, promote, second, side with, stand behind, stand up for, stick up for (*informal*), take (someone's) part, take up the cudgels for, uphold **4.** attest to, authenticate, bear out, confirm, corroborate, document, endorse, lend credence to, substantiate, verify **5.** bear, brook, countenance, endure, put up with (*informal*), stand (for), stomach, submit, suffer, thole (*dialect*), tolerate, undergo *~noun* **6.** abutment, back, brace, foundation, lining, pillar, post, prop, shore, stanchion, stay, stiffener, underpinning **7.** aid, approval, assistance, backing, blessing, championship, comfort, encouragement, espousal, friendship, furtherance, help, loyalty, moral support, patronage, promotion, protection, relief, succour, sustenance **8.** keep, livelihood, maintenance, subsistence, sustenance, upkeep **9.** backbone, backer, comforter, mainstay, prop, second, stay, supporter, tower of strength
▷ **Antonyms** *~verb* (*sense 2*) live off, sponge off (*senses 3, 4 & 5*) challenge, contradict, deny, go against, hinder, hold out against, oppose, refute, reject, stab in the back, turn one's back on, undermine, walk away from *~noun* (*senses 7 & 9*) antagonist, burden, denial, encumbrance, hindrance, impediment, opposition, refutation, rejection, undermining

supporter adherent, advocate, ally, apologist, champion, co-worker, defender, fan, follower, friend, helper, henchman, patron, protagonist, sponsor, upholder, well-wisher
▷ **Antonyms** adversary, antagonist, challenger, competitor, foe, opponent, rival

supportive caring, encouraging, helpful, reassuring, sympathetic, understanding

suppose 1. assume, calculate (*U.S. dialect*), conjecture, dare say, expect, guess (*informal, chiefly U.S. & Canad.*), imagine, infer, judge, opine, presume, presuppose, surmise, take as read, take for granted, think **2.** believe, conceive, con~

clude, conjecture, consider, fancy, hypothesize, imagine, postulate, pretend

supposed **1.** accepted, alleged, assumed, hypothetical, presumed, presupposed, professed, putative, reputed, rumoured **2.** (*with* **to**) expected, meant, obliged, ought, required

supposedly allegedly, at a guess, avowedly, by all accounts, hypothetically, ostensibly, presumably, professedly, purportedly, theoretically

▷ **Antonyms** absolutely, actually, certainly, in actuality, in fact, really, surely, truly, undoubtedly, without a doubt

supposition conjecture, doubt, guess, guesswork, hypothesis, idea, notion, postulate, presumption, speculation, surmise, theory

suppress **1.** beat down, check, clamp down on, conquer, crack down on, crush, drive underground, extinguish, overpower, overthrow, put an end to, quash, quell, quench, snuff out, stamp out, stop, subdue, trample on **2.** censor, conceal, contain, cover up, curb, hold in *or* back, hold in check, keep secret, muffle, muzzle, repress, restrain, silence, smother, stifle, sweep under the carpet (*informal*), withhold

▷ **Antonyms** encourage, foster, further, incite, inflame, promote, rouse, spread, stimulate, stir up, whip up

suppression check, clampdown, crackdown, crushing, dissolution, elimination, extinction, inhibition, prohibition, quashing, smothering, termination

suppurate discharge, fester, gather, maturate, ooze, weep

supremacy absolute rule, ascendancy, dominance, domination, dominion, lordship, mastery, paramountcy, predominance, pre-eminence, primacy, sovereignty, supreme authority, sway

supreme cardinal, chief, crowning, culminating, extreme, final, first, foremost, greatest, head, highest, incomparable, leading, matchless, mother (of all), paramount, peerless, predominant, pre-eminent, prevailing, prime, principal, sovereign, superlative, surpassing, top, ultimate, unsurpassed, utmost

▷ **Antonyms** least, least successful, lowest, most inferior, most minor, most subordinate, most trivial, poorest, worst

sure **1.** assured, certain, clear, confident, convinced, decided, definite, free from doubt, persuaded, positive, satisfied **2.** accurate, dependable, effective, foolproof, honest, indisputable, infallible, never-failing, precise, reliable, sure-fire (*informal*), tried and true, trustworthy, trusty, undeniable, undoubted, unerring, unfailing, unmistakable, well-proven **3.** assured, bound, guaranteed, ineluctable, inescapable, inevitable, in the bag (*slang*), irrevocable **4.** fast, firm, fixed, safe, secure, solid, stable, staunch, steady, tight

▷ **Antonyms** distrustful, dodgy (*Brit., Austral., & N.Z. informal*), doubtful, dubious, fallible, iffy (*informal*), insecure, sceptical, touch-and-go, unassured, uncertain, unconvinced, undependable, uneasy, unreliable, unsure, untrustworthy, vague

surely assuredly, beyond the shadow of a doubt, certainly, come what may, definitely, doubtlessly, for certain, indubitably, inevitably, inexorably, undoubtedly, unquestionably, without doubt, without fail

surety **1.** bail, bond, deposit, guarantee, indemnity, insurance, pledge, safety, security, warranty **2.** bondsman, guarantor, hostage, mortgagor, sponsor

surface *noun* **1.** covering, exterior, façade, face, facet, outside, plane, side, skin, superficies (*rare*), top, veneer **2. on the surface** apparently, at first glance, ostensibly, outwardly, seemingly, superficially, to all appearances, to the eye *~adjective* **3.** apparent, exterior, external, outward, superficial *~verb* **4.** appear, come to light, come up, crop up (*informal*), emerge, materialize, rise, transpire

surfeit **1.** *noun* excess, glut, overindulgence, plethora, satiety, superabundance, superfluity **2.** *~verb* cram, fill, glut, gorge, overfeed, overfill, satiate, stuff

▷ **Antonyms** *~noun* dearth, deficiency, insufficiency, lack, scarcity, shortage, shortness, want

surge **1.** *verb* billow, eddy, gush, heave, rise, roll, rush, swell, swirl, tower, undulate, well forth **2.** *~noun* billow, breaker, efflux, flood, flow, gush, intensification, outpouring, roller, rush, swell, uprush, upsurge, wave

surly bearish, brusque, churlish, crabbed, cross, crusty, curmudgeonly, grouchy (*informal*), gruff, ill-natured, morose, perverse, shrewish, sulky, sullen, testy, uncivil, ungracious

▷ **Antonyms** agreeable, cheerful, cheery, genial, good-natured, happy, pleasant, sunny

surmise **1.** *verb* come to the conclusion, conclude, conjecture, consider, deduce, fancy, guess, hazard a guess, imagine, infer, opine, presume, speculate, suppose, suspect **2.** *~noun* assumption, conclusion, conjecture, deduction, guess, hypothesis, idea, inference, notion, possibility, presumption, speculation, supposition, suspicion, thought

surmount conquer, exceed, master, overcome, overpower, overtop, pass, prevail over, surpass, triumph over, vanquish

surpass beat, best, cap (*informal*), eclipse, exceed, excel, go one better than (*informal*), outdo, outshine, outstrip, override, overshadow, put in the shade, top, tower above, transcend

surpassing exceptional, extraordinary, incomparable, matchless, outstanding, phenomenal, rare, stellar (*informal*), supreme, transcendent, unrivalled

surplus 1. *noun* balance, excess, remainder, residue, superabundance, superfluity, surfeit **2.** *~adjective* excess, extra, in excess, left over, odd, remaining, spare, superfluous, unused

▷ **Antonyms** *~noun* dearth, deficiency, deficit, insufficiency, lack, paucity, shortage, shortfall *~adjective* deficient, falling short, inadequate, insufficient, lacking, limited, scant, scanty, scarce

surprise *verb* **1.** amaze, astonish, astound, bewilder, bowl over (*informal*), confuse, disconcert, flabbergast (*informal*), leave open-mouthed, nonplus, stagger, stun, take aback, take (someone's) breath away **2.** burst in on, catch in the act *or* red-handed, catch napping, catch on the hop (*informal*), catch unawares *or* off-guard, come down on like a bolt from the blue, discover, spring upon, startle *~noun* **3.** amazement, astonishment, bewilderment, incredulity, stupefaction, wonder **4.** bolt from the blue, bombshell, eye-opener (*informal*), jolt, revelation, shock, start (*informal*), turn-up for the books (*informal*)

surprised amazed, astonished, at a loss, caught on the hop (*Brit. informal*), caught on the wrong foot (*informal*), disconcerted, incredulous, nonplussed, open-mouthed, speechless, startled, taken aback, taken by surprise, thunderstruck, unable to believe one's eyes

surprising amazing, astonishing, bewildering, extraordinary, incredible, marvellous, remarkable, staggering, startling, unexpected, unlooked-for, unusual, wonderful

surrender *verb* **1.** abandon, cede, concede, deliver up, forego, give up, part with, relinquish, renounce, resign, waive, yield **2.** capitulate, give in, give oneself up, give way, lay down arms, quit, show the white flag, submit, succumb, throw in the towel, yield *~noun* **3.** capitulation, delivery, relinquishment, renunciation, resignation, submission, yielding

▷ **Antonyms** *~verb* defy, fight (on), make a stand against, oppose, resist, stand up to, withstand

surreptitious clandestine, covert, fraudulent, furtive, secret, sly, sneaking, stealthy, unauthorized, underhand, veiled

▷ **Antonyms** blatant, conspicuous, frank, honest, manifest, obvious, open, overt, unconcealed, undisguised

surrogate *noun* deputy, proxy, representative, stand-in, substitute

surround 1. close in on, encircle, enclose, encompass, envelop, environ, enwreath, fence in, girdle, hem in, ring **2.** *Military* beset, besiege, invest (*rare*), lay siege to

surrounding nearby, neighbouring

surroundings background, environment, environs, location, milieu, neighbourhood, setting

surveillance care, control, direction, inspection, observation, scrutiny, superintendence, supervision, vigilance, watch

survey *verb* **1.** contemplate, examine, eye up, inspect, look over, observe, recce (*slang*), reconnoitre, research, review, scan, scrutinize, study, supervise, view **2.** appraise, assess, estimate, eye up, measure, plan, plot, prospect, size up, take stock of, triangulate *~noun* **3.** examination, inquiry, inspection, once-over (*informal*), overview, perusal, random sample, review, scrutiny, study

survive be extant, endure, exist, fight for one's life, hold out, keep body and soul together (*informal*), keep one's head above water, last, live, live on, outlast, outlive, pull through, remain alive, subsist

susceptibility liability, predisposition, proneness, propensity, responsiveness, sensitivity, suggestibility, vulnerability, weakness

susceptible 1. (*usually with* **to**) disposed, given, inclined, liable, open, predisposed, prone, subject, vulnerable **2.** alive to, easily moved, impressionable, receptive, responsive, sensitive, suggestible, tender

▷ **Antonyms** immune, incapable, insensible, insusceptible, invulnerable, resistant, unaffected by, unmoved by, unresponsive

suspect *verb* **1.** distrust, doubt, harbour suspicions about, have one's doubts about, mistrust, smell a rat (*informal*) **2.** believe, conclude, conjecture, consider, fancy, feel, guess, have a sneaking suspicion, hazard a guess, speculate, suppose, surmise, think probable *~adjective* **3.** dodgy (*Brit., Austral., & N.Z. informal*), doubtful, dubious, fishy (*informal*), iffy (*informal*), open to suspicion, questionable

▷ **Antonyms** *~verb* accept, be certain, be confident of, believe, buy (*slang*), have faith in, know, swallow (*informal*), think innocent, trust *~adjective* above suspicion, innocent, reliable, straightforward, trustworthy, trusty

suspend 1. append, attach, dangle, hang, swing **2.** adjourn, arrest, cease, cut short, debar, defer, delay, discontinue, hold off, interrupt, lay aside, pigeonhole, postpone, put in cold storage, put off, shelve, stay, withhold

▷ **Antonyms** (*sense 2*) carry on, continue,

reestablish, reinstate, restore, resume, return

suspense 1. anticipation, anxiety, apprehension, doubt, expectancy, expectation, indecision, insecurity, irresolution, tension, uncertainty, wavering **2. in suspense** anxious, in an agony of doubt, keyed up, on edge, on tenterhooks, with bated breath

suspenseful cliffhanging, exciting, gripping, hair-raising, spine-chilling, thrilling

suspension abeyance, adjournment, break, breaking off, deferment, delay, disbarment, discontinuation, interruption, moratorium, postponement, remission, respite, stay

suspicion 1. bad vibes (*slang*), chariness, distrust, doubt, dubiety, funny feeling (*informal*), jealousy, lack of confidence, misgiving, mistrust, qualm, scepticism, wariness **2. above suspicion** above reproach, blameless, honourable, like Caesar's wife, pure, sinless, unimpeachable, virtuous **3.** conjecture, guess, gut feeling (*informal*), hunch, idea, impression, notion, supposition, surmise **4.** glimmer, hint, shade, shadow, *soupçon,* strain, streak, suggestion, tinge, touch, trace

suspicious 1. apprehensive, distrustful, doubtful, jealous, leery (*slang*), mistrustful, sceptical, suspecting, unbelieving, wary **2.** dodgy (*Brit., Austral., & N.Z. informal*), doubtful, dubious, fishy (*informal*), funny, irregular, of doubtful honesty, open to doubt *or* misconstruction, queer, questionable, shady (*informal*), suspect

▷ **Antonyms** (*sense 1*) believing, credulous, gullible, open, trustful, trusting, unsuspecting, unsuspicious (*sense 2*) above board, beyond suspicion, not open to question, open, straight, straightforward, unquestionable, upright

sustain 1. bear, carry, keep from falling, keep up, support, uphold **2.** bear, bear up under, endure, experience, feel, suffer, undergo, withstand **3.** aid, assist, comfort, foster, help, keep alive, nourish, nurture, provide for, relieve **4.** approve, confirm, continue, keep alive, keep going, keep up, maintain, prolong, protract, ratify **5.** endorse, uphold, validate, verify

sustained constant, continuous, nonstop, perpetual, prolonged, steady, unremitting

▷ **Antonyms** broken, discontinuous, intermittent, irregular, periodic, spasmodic, sporadic

sustenance 1. aliment, comestibles, daily bread, eatables, edibles, food, nourishment, provender, provisions, rations, refection, refreshments, victuals **2.** livelihood, maintenance, subsistence, support

svelte 1. graceful, lissom(e), lithe, slender, slinky, sylphlike, willowy **2.** polished, smooth, sophisticated, urbane

swagger 1. *verb* bluster, boast, brag, bully, gasconade (*rare*), hector, hot-dog (*chiefly U.S.*), parade, prance, show off (*informal*), strut, swank (*informal*) **2.** *~noun* arrogance, bluster, braggadocio, display, gasconade (*rare*), ostentation, pomposity, show, showing off (*informal*), swank (*informal*), swashbuckling

swallow *verb* **1.** absorb, consume, devour, down (*informal*), drink, eat, gulp, ingest, swig (*informal*), swill, wash down **2.** (*often with* **up**) absorb, assimilate, consume, engulf, envelop, overrun, overwhelm, use up, waste **3.** choke back, hold in, repress **4.** *informal* accept, believe, buy (*slang*), fall for, take (something) as gospel

swamp *noun* **1.** bog, everglade(s) (*U.S.*), fen, marsh, mire, morass, moss (*Scot. & northern English dialect*), quagmire, slough *~verb* **2.** capsize, drench, engulf, flood, inundate, overwhelm, sink, submerge, swallow up, upset, wash over, waterlog **3.** beset, besiege, deluge, flood, inundate, overload, overwhelm, snow under

swampy boggy, fenny, marish (*obsolete*), marshy, miry, quaggy, waterlogged, wet

swank *verb* **1.** give oneself airs, hot-dog (*chiefly U.S.*), posture, put on side (*Brit. slang*), show off (*informal*), swagger *~noun* **2.** attitudinizer, braggadocio, hot dog (*chiefly U.S.*), poser, poseur, show-off (*informal*), swankpot (*informal*), swashbuckler **3.** boastfulness, display, ostentation, show, swagger, vainglory

swanky de luxe, exclusive, expensive, fancy, fashionable, flash, flashy, glamorous, glitzy (*slang*), gorgeous, grand, lavish, luxurious, ostentatious, plush (*informal*), plushy (*informal*), posh (*informal, chiefly Brit.*), rich, ritzy (*slang*), showy, smart, stylish, sumptuous, swank (*informal*), swish (*informal, chiefly Brit.*)

▷ **Antonyms** discreet, humble, inconspicuous, low-key, low-profile, modest, subdued, unassuming, unostentatious, unpretentious

swap, swop *verb* bandy, barter, exchange, interchange, switch, trade, traffic

swarm *noun* **1.** army, bevy, concourse, crowd, drove, flock, herd, horde, host, mass, multitude, myriad, shoal, throng *~verb* **2.** congregate, crowd, flock, mass, stream, throng **3.** (*with* **with**) abound, be alive, be infested, be overrun, bristle, crawl, teem

swarthy black, brown, dark, dark-complexioned, dark-skinned, dusky, swart (*archaic*), tawny

swashbuckling bold, daredevil, dashing,

flamboyant, gallant, mettlesome, roisterous, spirited, swaggering

swastika crooked cross, fylfot

swathe bandage, bind, bundle up, cloak, drape, envelop, enwrap, fold, furl, lap, muffle up, sheathe, shroud, swaddle, wrap

sway *verb* **1.** bend, fluctuate, incline, lean, lurch, oscillate, rock, roll, swing, wave **2.** affect, control, direct, dominate, govern, guide, induce, influence, persuade, prevail on, win over *~noun* **3.** ascendency, authority, clout (*informal*), command, control, dominion, government, influence, jurisdiction, power, predominance, rule, sovereignty **4. hold sway** predominate, prevail, reign, rule, run

swear 1. affirm, assert, asseverate, attest, avow, declare, depose, give one's word, pledge oneself, promise, state under oath, swear blind, take an oath, testify, vow, warrant **2.** be foul-mouthed, blaspheme, curse, cuss (*informal*), imprecate, take the Lord's name in vain, turn the air blue (*informal*), utter profanities **3.** (*with* **by**) depend on, have confidence in, rely on, trust

swearing bad language, blasphemy, cursing, cussing (*informal*), foul language, imprecations, malediction, profanity

swearword curse, cuss (*informal*), expletive, four-letter word, oath, obscenity, profanity

sweat *noun* **1.** diaphoresis (*Medical*), exudation, perspiration, sudor (*Medical*) **2.** *informal* agitation, anxiety, distress, flap (*informal*), panic, strain, worry **3.** *informal* backbreaking task, chore, drudgery, effort, labour, toil *~verb* **4.** break out in a sweat, exude moisture, glow, perspire **5.** *informal* agonize, be on pins and needles (*informal*), be on tenterhooks, chafe, fret, lose sleep over, suffer, torture oneself, worry **6. sweat it out** *informal* endure, see (something) through, stay the course, stick it out (*informal*)

sweaty bathed in perspiration, clammy, drenched in perspiration, glowing, perspiring, soaked in perspiration, sticky, sweating

sweep *verb* **1.** brush, clean, clear, remove **2.** career, flounce, fly, glance, glide, hurtle, pass, sail, scud, skim, tear, zoom *~noun* **3.** arc, bend, curve, gesture, move, movement, stroke, swing **4.** compass, extent, range, scope, span, stretch, vista **5.** draw, lottery, raffle, sweepstake

sweeping 1. all-embracing, all-inclusive, bird's-eye, broad, comprehensive, extensive, global, radical, thoroughgoing, wide, wide-ranging **2.** across-the-board, blanket, exaggerated, indiscriminate, overdrawn, overstated, unqualified, wholesale

▷ **Antonyms** constrained, limited, minor, modest, narrow, qualified, restricted, token, trifling, unimportant

sweet *adjective* **1.** cloying, honeyed, icky (*informal*), luscious, melting, saccharine, sugary, sweetened, syrupy, toothsome, treacly **2.** affectionate, agreeable, amiable, appealing, attractive, beautiful, charming, cute, delightful, engaging, fair, gentle, kind, likable *or* likeable, lovable, sweet-tempered, taking, tender, unselfish, winning, winsome **3.** beloved, cherished, darling, dear, dearest, pet, precious, treasured **4.** aromatic, balmy, clean, fragrant, fresh, new, perfumed, pure, redolent, sweet-smelling, wholesome **5.** dulcet, euphonic, euphonious, harmonious, mellow, melodious, musical, silver-toned, silvery, soft, sweet-sounding, tuneful **6. sweet on** enamoured of, gone on (*slang*), head over heels in love with, infatuated by, in love with, keen on, obsessed *or* bewitched by, taken with, wild *or* mad about (*informal*) *~noun* **7.** afters (*Brit. informal*), dessert, pudding, sweet course **8.** (*usually plural*) bonbon, candy (*U.S.*), confectionery, sweetie, sweetmeats

▷ **Antonyms** *~adjective* (*sense 1*) acerbic, acetic, acid, bitter, savoury, sharp, sour, tart, vinegary (*senses 2, 3 & 4*) bad-tempered, disagreeable, fetid, foul, grouchy (*informal*), grumpy, hated, ill-tempered, loathsome, nasty, noisome, objectionable, obnoxious, rank, stinking, unappealing, unattractive, unlovable, unpleasant, unwanted (*sense 5*) cacophonous, discordant, grating, harsh, shrill, strident, unharmonious, unmusical, unpleasant

sweeten 1. honey, sugar, sugar-coat **2.** alleviate, appease, mollify, pacify, soften up, soothe, sugar the pill

sweetheart admirer, beau, beloved, boyfriend, darling, dear, flame (*informal*), follower (*obsolete*), girlfriend, inamorata, inamorato, leman (*archaic*), love, lover, steady (*informal*), suitor, swain (*archaic*), sweetie (*informal*), truelove, valentine

sweet-scented ambrosial, aromatic, fragrant, perfumed, sweet-smelling

▷ **Antonyms** fetid, foul-smelling, malodorous, niffy (*Brit. slang*), noisome, olid, pongy (*Brit. informal*), smelly, stinking, stinky (*informal*), whiffy (*Brit. slang*)

swell *verb* **1.** balloon, become bloated *or* distended, become larger, be inflated, belly, billow, bloat, bulge, dilate, distend, enlarge, expand, extend, fatten, grow, increase, protrude, puff up, rise, round out, tumefy, well up **2.** add to, aggravate, augment, enhance, heighten, intensify, mount, surge *~noun* **3.** billow, rise, surge, undulation, wave **4.** *informal* beau, blade (*archaic*), cockscomb (*infor-*

mal), dandy, fashion plate, fop, nob (*slang*), toff (*Brit. slang*) ~*adjective* **5.** *informal* de luxe, exclusive, fashionable, grand, plush *or* plushy (*informal*), posh (*informal, chiefly Brit.*), ritzy (*slang*), smart, stylish

▷ **Antonyms** ~*verb* become smaller, contract, decrease, deflate, diminish, ebb, fall, go down, lessen, reduce, shrink, wane ~*adjective* common, grotty (*slang*), ordinary, plebeian, poor, run down, seedy, shabby, sordid, tatty, unimpressive, vulgar

swelling *noun* blister, bruise, bulge, bump, dilation, distension, enlargement, inflammation, lump, protuberance, puffiness, tumescence

sweltering airless, baking, boiling, burning, hot, humid, oppressive, roasting, scorching, steaming, stifling, sultry, torrid

swerve *verb* bend, deflect, depart from, deviate, diverge, incline, sheer off, shift, skew, stray, swing, turn, turn aside, veer, wander, wind

swift abrupt, expeditious, express, fast, fleet, fleet-footed, flying, hurried, nimble, nippy (*Brit. informal*), pdq (*slang*), prompt, quick, quickie (*informal*), rapid, ready, short, short-lived, spanking, speedy, sudden, winged

▷ **Antonyms** lead-footed, lingering, plodding, ponderous, slow, sluggish, tardy, tortoise-like, unhurried

swiftly apace, as fast as one's legs can carry one, (at) full tilt, double-quick, fast, hell for leather, hotfoot, hurriedly, in less than no time, like greased lightning (*informal*), like lightning, like the clappers (*Brit. informal*), nippily (*Brit. informal*), posthaste, promptly, pronto (*informal*), rapidly, speedily, without losing time

swiftness alacrity, celerity, dispatch, expedition, fleetness, promptness, quickness, rapidity, speed, speediness, velocity

swill *verb* **1.** bend the elbow (*informal*), bevvy (*dialect*), consume, drain, drink (down), gulp, guzzle, imbibe, pour down one's gullet, quaff, swallow, swig (*informal*), toss off **2.** (*often with* **out**) drench, flush, rinse, sluice, wash down, wash out ~*noun* **3.** hogwash, mash, mush, pigswill, scourings, slops, waste

swimmingly as planned, cosily, effortlessly, like a dream, like clockwork, smoothly, successfully, very well, with no trouble, without a hitch

swindle 1. *verb* bamboozle (*informal*), bilk (of), cheat, con, cozen, deceive, defraud, diddle (*informal*), do (*slang*), dupe, fleece, hornswoggle (*slang*), overcharge, pull a fast one (on someone) (*informal*), put one over on (someone) (*informal*), rip (someone) off (*slang*), rook (*slang*), sell a pup (to) (*slang*), skin (*slang*), stiff (*slang*), sting (*informal*), take (someone) for a ride (*informal*), take to the cleaners (*informal*), trick **2.** ~*noun* con trick (*informal*), deceit, deception, double-dealing, fiddle (*Brit. informal*), fraud, imposition, knavery, racket, rip-off (*slang*), roguery, scam (*slang*), sharp practice, sting (*informal*), swizz (*Brit. informal*), swizzle (*Brit. informal*), trickery

swindler charlatan, cheat, chiseller (*informal*), confidence man, con man (*informal*), fraud, fraudster, grifter (*slang, chiefly U.S. & Canad.*), hustler (*U.S. informal*), impostor, knave (*archaic*), mountebank, rascal, rogue, rook (*slang*), shark, sharper, trickster

swing *verb* **1.** be pendent, be suspended, dangle, hang, move back and forth, suspend **2.** fluctuate, oscillate, rock, sway, vary, veer, vibrate, wave **3.** (*usually with* **round**) curve, pivot, rotate, swivel, turn, turn on one's heel, wheel ~*noun* **4.** fluctuation, oscillation, stroke, sway, swaying, vibration **5. in full swing** animated, at its height, lively, on the go (*informal*), under way

swingeing daunting, Draconian, drastic, excessive, exorbitant, harsh, heavy, huge, oppressive, punishing, severe, stringent

swinging dynamic, fashionable, full of go *or* pep (*informal*), groovy (*dated slang*), happening (*informal*), hip (*slang*), in the swim (*informal*), lively, trendy (*Brit. informal*), up-to-date, up to the minute, with it (*informal*)

swipe *verb* **1.** chin (*slang*), clip (*informal*), deck (*slang*), fetch (someone) a blow, hit, lash out at, lay one on (*slang*), slap, slosh (*Brit. slang*), sock (*slang*), strike, wallop (*informal*) ~*noun* **2.** blow, clip (*informal*), clout (*informal*), clump (*slang*), cuff, slap, smack, wallop (*informal*) ~*verb* **3.** *slang* appropriate, cabbage (*Brit. slang*), filch, lift (*informal*), make off with, nick (*slang, chiefly Brit.*), pilfer, pinch (*informal*), purloin, snaffle (*Brit. informal*), steal

swirl *verb* agitate, boil, churn, eddy, spin, surge, twirl, twist, whirl

swish *adjective* de luxe, elegant, exclusive, fashionable, grand, plush *or* plushy (*informal*), posh (*informal, chiefly Brit.*), ritzy (*slang*), smart, sumptuous, swell (*informal*)

switch *verb* **1.** change, change course, deflect, deviate, divert, exchange, interchange, rearrange, replace by, shift, substitute, swap (*informal*), trade, turn aside ~*noun* **2.** about-turn, alteration, change, change of direction, exchange, reversal, shift, substitution, swap (*informal*) ~*verb* **3.** lash, swish, twitch, wave, whip

swivel *verb* pirouette, pivot, revolve, rotate, spin, swing round, turn

swollen bloated, distended, dropsical, edematous, enlarged, inflamed, oedematous, puffed up, puffy, tumescent, tumid

swollen-headed bigheaded (*informal*), bumptious, cocky, full of oneself, proud, puffed up, self-important, too big for one's boots, too big for one's breeches, vain, vainglorious

swoop **1.** *verb* descend, dive, pounce, rush, stoop, sweep **2.** *~noun* descent, drop, lunge, plunge, pounce, rush, stoop, sweep

swop *see* SWAP

sword **1.** blade, brand (*archaic*), trusty steel **2.** **cross swords** argue, come to blows, dispute, fight, spar, wrangle **3.** **the sword** aggression, arms, butchery, death, massacre, military might, murder, slaying, violence, war

swot *verb* apply oneself to, bone up on (*informal*), burn the midnight oil, cram (*informal*), get up (*informal*), lucubrate (*rare*), mug up (*Brit. slang*), pore over, revise, study, toil over, work

sybarite epicure, epicurean, hedonist, playboy, sensualist, voluptuary

sybaritic bacchanalian, epicurean, hedonistic, Lucullan, luxurious, luxury-loving, pleasure-loving, self-indulgent, sensual, voluptuous

sycophancy adulation, bootlicking (*informal*), cringing, fawning, flattery, grovelling, kowtowing, obsequiousness, servility, slavishness, toadyism, truckling

sycophant apple polisher (*U.S. slang*), ass-kisser (*U.S. & Canad. taboo slang*), bootlicker (*informal*), brown-noser (*taboo slang*), cringer, fawner, flatterer, hanger-on, lickspittle, parasite, slave, sponger, toadeater (*rare*), toady, truckler, yes man

sycophantic all over (someone) (*informal*), arse-licking (*taboo slang*), bootlicking (*informal*), cringing, fawning, flattering, grovelling, ingratiating, obsequious, parasitical, servile, slavish, slimy, smarmy (*Brit. informal*), time-serving, toadying, unctuous

syllabus course of study, curriculum

sylphlike graceful, lithe, slender, svelte, willowy

symbol badge, emblem, figure, image, logo, mark, representation, sign, token, type

symbolic, symbolical allegorical, emblematic, figurative, representative, significant, token, typical

symbolize betoken, body forth, connote, denote, exemplify, mean, personify, represent, signify, stand for, typify

symmetrical balanced, in proportion, proportional, regular, well-proportioned
▷ **Antonyms** asymmetrical, disorderly, irregular, lopsided, unbalanced, unequal, unsymmetrical

symmetry agreement, balance, correspondence, evenness, form, harmony, order, proportion, regularity

sympathetic **1.** affectionate, caring, commiserating, compassionate, concerned, condoling, feeling, interested, kind, kindly, pitying, responsive, supportive, tender, understanding, warm, warm-hearted **2.** (*often with* **to**) agreeable, approving, encouraging, favourably disposed, friendly, in sympathy with, pro, well-disposed **3.** agreeable, appreciative, companionable, compatible, congenial, friendly, like-minded, responsive, well-intentioned
▷ **Antonyms** apathetic, callous, cold, cold-hearted, disdainful, disinterested, indifferent, inhumane, insensitive, scornful, steely, uncaring, uncompassionate, uncongenial, unfeeling, uninterested, unmoved, unresponsive, unsympathetic

sympathetically appreciatively, feelingly, kindly, perceptively, responsively, sensitively, understandingly, warm-heartedly, warmly, with compassion, with feeling, with interest

sympathize **1.** bleed for, commiserate, condole, empathize, feel for, feel one's heart go out to, grieve with, have compassion, offer consolation, pity, share another's sorrow **2.** agree, be in accord, be in sympathy, go along with, identify with, side with, understand
▷ **Antonyms** disagree, disregard, fail to understand, have no feelings for, misunderstand, mock, oppose, reject, scorn

sympathizer condoler, fellow traveller, partisan, protagonist, supporter, well-wisher

sympathy **1.** commiseration, compassion, condolence(s), empathy, pity, tenderness, thoughtfulness, understanding **2.** affinity, agreement, congeniality, correspondence, fellow feeling, harmony, rapport, union, warmth
▷ **Antonyms** (*sense 1*) callousness, coldness, disdain, hard-heartedness, indifference, insensitivity, lack of feeling *or* understanding *or* sympathy, pitilessness, scorn (*sense 2*) antagonism, disapproval, hostility, opposition, resistance, unfriendliness

symptom expression, indication, mark, note, sign, syndrome, token, warning

symptomatic characteristic, indicative, suggestive

synonymous equal, equivalent, identical, identified, interchangeable, one and the same, similar, tantamount, the same

synopsis abridgment, abstract, *aperçu*, compendium, condensation, conspectus, digest, epitome, outline, outline sketch, précis, résumé, review, rundown, summary

synthesis **1.** amalgamation, coalescence, combination, integration, unification, welding **2.** amalgam, blend, combination, composite, compound, fusion, meld, union

synthetic artificial, ersatz, fake, man-made, manufactured, mock, pseudo (*informal*), sham, simulated

▷ **Antonyms** authentic, genuine, kosher (*informal*), natural, real

system 1. arrangement, classification, combination, coordination, organization, scheme, setup (*informal*), structure **2.** fixed order, frame of reference, method, methodology, modus operandi, practice, procedure, routine, technique, theory, usage **3.** definite plan, logical process, method, methodicalness, orderliness, regularity, systematization

systematic businesslike, efficient, methodical, orderly, organized, precise, standardized, systematized, well-ordered

▷ **Antonyms** arbitrary, cursory, disorderly, disorganized, haphazard, indiscriminate, random, slapdash, unbusinesslike, unmethodical, unpremeditated, unsystematic

systematize arrange, classify, dispose, make uniform, methodize, organize, put in order, rationalize, regulate, schematize, sequence, standardize, tabulate

T, t

tab flag, flap, label, marker, sticker, tag, ticket

tabby banded, brindled, streaked, striped, stripy, wavy

table *noun* **1.** bench, board, counter, slab, stand **2.** board, diet, fare, food, spread (*informal*), victuals **3.** flat, flatland, mesa, plain, plateau, tableland **4.** agenda, catalogue, chart, diagram, digest, graph, index, inventory, list, plan, record, register, roll, schedule, synopsis, tabulation *~verb* **5.** enter, move, propose, put forward, submit, suggest

tableau picture, representation, scene, spectacle

tableland flat, flatland, mesa, plain, plateau, table

taboo 1. *adjective* anathema, banned, beyond the pale, disapproved of, forbidden, frowned on, not allowed, not permitted, off limits, outlawed, prohibited, proscribed, ruled out, unacceptable, unmentionable, unthinkable **2.** *~noun* anathema, ban, disapproval, interdict, prohibition, proscription, restriction
▷ **Antonyms** *~adjective* acceptable, allowed, permitted, sanctioned

tabulate arrange, catalogue, categorize, chart, classify, codify, index, list, order, range, systematize, tabularize

tacit implicit, implied, inferred, silent, taken for granted, undeclared, understood, unexpressed, unspoken, unstated, wordless
▷ **Antonyms** explicit, express, spelled-out, spoken, stated

taciturn aloof, antisocial, close-lipped, cold, distant, dumb, mute, quiet, reserved, reticent, silent, tight-lipped, uncommunicative, unforthcoming, withdrawn
▷ **Antonyms** blethering, chatty, communicative, forthcoming, garrulous, loquacious, open, outgoing, prattling, sociable, talkative, unreserved, verbose, voluble, wordy

tack *noun* **1.** drawing pin, nail, pin, staple, thumbtack (*U.S.*), tintack **2.** approach, bearing, course, direction, heading, line, method, path, plan, procedure, tactic, tenor, way *~verb* **3.** affix, attach, fasten, fix, nail, pin, staple **4.** baste, stitch **5.** add, annex, append, attach, tag

tackle *noun* **1.** accoutrements, apparatus, equipment, gear, implements, outfit, paraphernalia, rig, rigging, tools, trappings **2.** block, challenge, stop *~verb* **3.** apply oneself to, attempt, begin, come or get to grips with, deal with, embark upon, engage in, essay, get stuck into (*informal*), have a go at (*informal*), have a stab at (*informal*), set about, sink one's teeth into, take on, take the bit between one's teeth, try, turn one's hand to, undertake, wade into **4.** block, bring down, challenge, clutch, confront, grab, grasp, halt, intercept, seize, stop, take hold of, throw

tacky 1. adhesive, gluey, gummy, sticky, wet **2.** *informal* cheap, messy, naff (*Brit. slang*), nasty, seedy, shabby, shoddy, sleazy, tasteless, tatty, vulgar

tact address, adroitness, consideration, delicacy, diplomacy, discretion, finesse, judgment, perception, savoir-faire, sensitivity, skill, thoughtfulness, understanding
▷ **Antonyms** awkwardness, clumsiness, gaucherie, heavy-handedness, indiscretion, insensitivity, lack of consideration, lack of discretion, tactlessness

tactful careful, considerate, delicate, diplomatic, discreet, judicious, perceptive, polished, polite, politic, prudent, sensitive, subtle, thoughtful, treating with kid gloves, understanding
▷ **Antonyms** awkward, clumsy, gauche, inconsiderate, indiscreet, insensitive, tactless, tasteless, thoughtless, undiplomatic, unsubtle, untoward

tactic 1. approach, course, device, line, manoeuvre, means, method, move, ploy, policy, scheme, stratagem, tack, trick, way **2.** *plural* campaign, generalship, manoeuvres, plans, strategy

tactical adroit, artful, clever, cunning, diplomatic, foxy, politic, shrewd, skilful, smart, strategic
▷ **Antonyms** blundering, clumsy, gauche, impolitic, inept

tactician brain (*informal*), campaigner, coordinator, director, general, mastermind, planner, strategist

tactless blundering, boorish, careless, clumsy, discourteous, gauche, harsh, impolite, impolitic, imprudent, inconsiderate, indelicate, indiscreet, inept, injudicious, insensitive, maladroit, rough, rude, sharp, thoughtless, uncivil, undiplomatic, unfeeling, unkind, unsubtle

▷ **Antonyms** considerate, diplomatic, discreet, polite, subtle, tactful

tag *noun* **1.** docket, flag, flap, identification, label, mark, marker, note, slip, sticker, tab, ticket *~verb* **2.** earmark, flag, identify, label, mark, ticket **3.** add, adjoin, affix, annex, append, fasten, tack **4.** (*with* **on** *or* **along**) accompany, attend, dog, follow, shadow, tail (*informal*), trail **5.** call, christen, dub, label, name, nickname, style, term

tail *noun* **1.** appendage, conclusion, empennage, end, extremity, rear end, tailpiece, train **2.** file, line, queue, tailback, train **3.** *of hair* braid, pigtail, plait, ponytail, tress **4.** *informal* arse (*taboo slang*), ass (*U.S. & Canad. taboo slang*), backside (*informal*), behind (*informal*), bottom, bum (*Brit. slang*), buns (*U.S. slang*), butt (*U.S. & Canad. informal*), buttocks, croup, derrière (*euphemistic*), jacksy (*Brit. slang*), posterior, rear (*informal*), rear end, rump **5. turn tail** cut and run, escape, flee, hook it (*slang*), make off, retreat, run away, run for it (*informal*), run off, scarper (*Brit. slang*), show a clean pair of heels, skedaddle (*informal*), take off (*informal*), take to one's heels *~verb* **6.** *informal* dog the footsteps of, follow, keep an eye on, shadow, stalk, track, trail

tail off *or* **away** decrease, die out, drop, dwindle, fade, fall away, peter out, wane

▷ **Antonyms** grow, increase, intensify, wax

tailor 1. *noun* clothier, costumier, couturier, dressmaker, garment maker, outfitter, seamstress **2.** *~verb* accommodate, adapt, adjust, alter, convert, customize, cut, fashion, fit, modify, mould, shape, style, suit

tailor-made 1. cut to fit, fitted, made-to-measure, made to order **2.** custom-made, ideal, just right, perfect, right, right up one's street (*informal*), suitable, up one's alley

taint *verb* **1.** adulterate, blight, contaminate, corrupt, dirty, foul, infect, poison, pollute, soil, spoil **2.** besmirch, blacken, blemish, blot, brand, damage, defile, disgrace, dishonour, muddy, ruin, shame, smear, smirch, stain, stigmatize, sully, tarnish, vitiate *~noun* **3.** black mark, blemish, blot, blot on one's escutcheon, defect, demerit, disgrace, dishonour, fault, flaw, shame, smear, smirch, spot, stain, stigma **4.** contagion, contamination, infection, pollution

▷ **Antonyms** *~verb* (*sense 1*) clean, cleanse, decontaminate, disinfect, purify

take *verb* **1.** abduct, acquire, arrest, capture, carry off, cart off (*slang*), catch, clutch, ensnare, entrap, gain possession of, get, get hold of, grasp, grip, have, help oneself to, lay hold of, obtain, receive, secure, seize, win **2.** abstract, appropriate, blag (*slang*), cabbage (*Brit. slang*), carry off, filch, misappropriate, nick (*slang, chiefly Brit.*), pinch (*informal*), pocket, purloin, run off with, steal, swipe (*slang*), walk off with **3.** book, buy, engage, hire, lease, pay for, pick, purchase, rent, reserve, select **4.** abide, bear, brave, brook, endure, go through, hack (*slang*), pocket, put up with (*informal*), stand, stomach, submit to, suffer, swallow, thole (*Scot.*), tolerate, undergo, weather, withstand **5.** consume, drink, eat, imbibe, ingest, inhale, swallow **6.** accept, adopt, assume, enter upon, undertake **7.** do, effect, execute, have, make, perform **8.** assume, believe, consider, deem, hold, interpret as, perceive, presume, receive, regard, see as, think of as, understand **9.** be efficacious, do the trick (*informal*), have effect, operate, succeed, work **10.** bear, bring, carry, cart, convey, ferry, fetch, haul, tote (*informal*), transport **11.** accompany, bring, conduct, convoy, escort, guide, hold (someone's) hand, lead, usher **12.** attract, become popular, captivate, charm, delight, enchant, fascinate, please, win favour **13.** call for, demand, necessitate, need, require **14.** deduct, eliminate, remove, subtract **15.** accept, accommodate, contain, have room for, hold **16.** *slang* bilk, cheat, con (*informal*), deceive, defraud, do (*slang*), dupe, fiddle (*informal*), gull (*archaic*), pull a fast one on (*informal*), stiff (*slang*), swindle *~noun* **17.** catch, gate, haul, proceeds, profits, receipts, return, revenue, takings, yield

▷ **Antonyms** (*sense 1*) free, let go, release (*sense 2*) give, give back, hand over, restore, return, surrender, yield (*sense 4*) avoid, dodge, give in, give way (*sense 6*) decline, dismiss, eschew, ignore, refuse, reject, scorn, spurn (*sense 9*) fail, flop (*informal*) (*sense 10*) send (*sense 14*) add, put

take aback astonish, astound, bewilder, disconcert, flabbergast (*informal*), floor (*informal*), nonplus, stagger, startle, stun, surprise

take back 1. disavow, disclaim, recant, renege, renounce, retract, unsay, withdraw **2.** get back, recapture, reclaim, reconquer, regain, repossess, retake **3.** accept back, exchange, give one a refund for

take down 1. make a note of, minute, note, put on record, record, set down, transcribe, write down **2.** depress, drop, haul down, let down, lower, pull down, remove, take off **3.** demolish, disassemble, dismantle, level, raze, take apart, take to pieces, tear down **4.** deflate, humble, humiliate, mortify, put down (*slang*)

take in 1. absorb, assimilate, comprehend, digest, get the hang of (*informal*), grasp, understand **2.** comprise, contain, cover, embrace, encompass, include **3.** accommodate, admit, let in, receive **4.** *informal* bilk, cheat, con (*informal*), cozen, deceive, do (*slang*), dupe, fool, gull (*archaic*), hoodwink, mislead, pull the wool over (someone's) eyes (*informal*), stiff (*slang*), swindle, trick

takeoff 1. departure, launch, liftoff **2.** *informal* caricature, imitation, lampoon, mocking, parody, satire, send-up (*Brit. informal*), spoof (*informal*), travesty

take off 1. discard, divest oneself of, doff, drop, peel off, remove, strip off **2.** become airborne, leave the ground, lift off, take to the air **3.** *informal* abscond, beat it (*slang*), decamp, depart, disappear, go, hit the road (*slang*), hook it (*slang*), leave, pack one's bags (*informal*), set out, slope off, split (*slang*), strike out **4.** *informal* caricature, hit off, imitate, lampoon, mimic, mock, parody, satirize, send up (*Brit. informal*), spoof (*informal*), take the piss (out of) (*taboo slang*), travesty

take on 1. employ, engage, enlist, enrol, hire, retain **2.** acquire, assume, come to have **3.** accept, address oneself to, agree to do, have a go at (*informal*), tackle, undertake **4.** compete against, contend with, enter the lists against, face, fight, match oneself against, oppose, pit oneself against, vie with **5.** *informal* break down, get excited, get upset, give way, make a fuss

takeover change of leadership, coup, incorporation, merger

take over assume control of, become leader of, come to power, gain control of, succeed to, take command of

take to 1. flee to, head for, make for, man, run for **2.** become friendly, be pleased by, be taken with, conceive an affection for, get on with, like, warm to **3.** have recourse to, make a habit of, resort to

take up 1. adopt, assume, become involved in, engage in, start **2.** begin again, carry on, continue, follow on, go on, pick up, proceed, recommence, restart, resume **3.** absorb, consume, cover, extend over, fill, occupy, use up

taking *adjective* **1.** attractive, beguiling, captivating, charming, compelling, cute, delightful, enchanting, engaging, fascinating, fetching (*informal*), intriguing, likable *or* likeable, pleasing, prepossessing, winning **2.** *informal* catching, contagious, infectious *~noun* **3.** *plural* earnings, gain, gate, income, pickings, proceeds, profits, receipts, returns, revenue, take, yield

▷ **Antonyms** (*sense 1*) abhorrent, loathsome, offensive, repulsive, unattractive, unpleasant

tale 1. account, anecdote, *conte,* fable, fiction, legend, narration, narrative, novel, relation, report, romance, saga, short story, spiel (*informal*), story, urban legend, yarn (*informal*) **2.** cock-and-bull story (*informal*), fabrication, falsehood, fib, lie, rigmarole, rumour, spiel (*informal*), tall story (*informal*), untruth

talent ability, aptitude, bent, capacity, endowment, faculty, flair, forte, genius, gift, knack, parts, power

talented able, artistic, brilliant, gifted, well-endowed

talisman amulet, charm, fetish, juju, lucky charm, mascot, periapt (*rare*)

talk *verb* **1.** articulate, chat, chatter, communicate, converse, crack (*Scot. & Irish*), express oneself, gab (*informal*), give voice to, gossip, natter, prate, prattle, rap (*slang*), run off at the mouth (*slang*), say, shoot the breeze (*U.S. slang*), speak, spout, utter, verbalize, witter (*informal*) **2.** chew the rag *or* fat (*slang*), confabulate, confer, have a confab (*informal*), hold discussions, negotiate, palaver, parley **3.** blab, crack, give the game away, grass (*Brit. slang*), inform, let the cat out of the bag, reveal information, shop (*slang, chiefly Brit.*), sing (*slang, chiefly U.S.*), spill one's guts (*slang*), spill the beans (*informal*), squeak (*informal*), squeal (*slang*), tell all *~noun* **4.** address, discourse, disquisition, dissertation, harangue, lecture, oration, sermon, speech **5.** blather, blether, chat, chatter, chitchat, conversation, crack (*Scot. & Irish*), gab (*informal*), gossip, hearsay, jaw (*slang*), natter, rap (*slang*), rumour, tittle-tattle **6.** colloquy, conclave, confab (*informal*), confabulation, conference, congress, consultation, dialogue, discussion, meeting, negotiation, palaver, parley, seminar, symposium **7.** argot, dialect, jargon, language, lingo (*informal*), patois, slang, speech, words

talkative big-mouthed (*slang*), chatty, effusive, gabby (*informal*), garrulous, gossipy, long-winded, loquacious, mouthy, prolix, verbose, voluble, wordy

▷ **Antonyms** quiet, reserved, reticent, silent, taciturn, tight-lipped, uncommunicative, unforthcoming

talk big blow one's own trumpet, bluster, boast, brag, crow, exaggerate, vaunt

talker chatterbox, conversationalist, lecturer, orator, speaker, speechmaker

talking-to criticism, dressing-down (*informal*), lecture, rap on the knuckles, rebuke, reprimand, reproach, reproof, row, scolding, slating (*informal*), telling-off (*informal*), ticking-off (*informal*), wigging (*Brit. slang*)

▷ **Antonyms** acclaim, approbation, commendation, encouragement, praise

talk into bring round (*informal*), convince, persuade, prevail on *or* upon, sway, win over

tall 1. big, elevated, giant, high, lanky, lofty, soaring, towering **2.** *informal* absurd, cock-and-bull (*informal*), embellished, exaggerated, far-fetched, implausible, incredible, overblown, preposterous, steep (*Brit. informal*), unbelievable **3.** *informal* demanding, difficult, exorbitant, hard, unreasonable, well-nigh impossible

▷ **Antonyms** (*sense 1*) fubsy (*archaic or dialect*), short, small, squat, stumpy, tiny, wee (*sense 2*) accurate, believable, easy, plausible, realistic, reasonable, true, unexaggerated

tally *verb* **1.** accord, agree, coincide, concur, conform, correspond, fit, harmonize, jibe (*informal*), match, parallel, square, suit **2.** compute, count up, keep score, mark, reckon, record, register, total *~noun* **3.** count, mark, reckoning, record, running total, score, total **4.** counterfoil, counterpart, duplicate, match, mate, stub

▷ **Antonyms** (*sense 1*) clash, conflict, contradict, differ, disagree

tame *adjective* **1.** amenable, broken, cultivated, disciplined, docile, domesticated, gentle, obedient, tractable **2.** fearless, unafraid, used to human contact **3.** compliant, docile, manageable, meek, obedient, spiritless, subdued, submissive, unresisting **4.** bland, boring, dull, flat, humdrum, insipid, lifeless, prosaic, tedious, tiresome, unexciting, uninspiring, uninteresting, vapid, wearisome *~verb* **5.** break in, domesticate, gentle, house-train, make tame, pacify, train **6.** break the spirit of, bridle, bring to heel, conquer, curb, discipline, enslave, humble, master, repress, subdue, subjugate, suppress **7.** mitigate, mute, soften, soft-pedal (*informal*), subdue, temper, tone down, water down

▷ **Antonyms** *~adjective* (*senses 1 & 2*) aggressive, feral, ferocious, savage, undomesticated, untamed, wild (*sense 3*) aggressive, argumentative, obdurate, strong-willed, stubborn, unmanageable (*sense 4*) exciting, frenzied, hot, interesting, lively, stimulating *~verb* (*senses 5 & 6*) make fiercer (*sense 7*) arouse, incite, intensify

tamper 1. alter, damage, fiddle (*informal*), fool about (*informal*), interfere, intrude, meddle, mess about, monkey around, muck about (*Brit. slang*), poke one's nose into (*informal*), tinker **2.** bribe, corrupt, fix (*informal*), get at, influence, manipulate, rig

tang 1. aroma, bite, flavour, odour, piquancy, reek, savour, scent, smack, smell, taste **2.** hint, suggestion, tinge, touch, trace, whiff

tangible actual, concrete, corporeal, definite, discernible, evident, manifest, material, objective, palpable, perceptible, physical, positive, real, solid, substantial, tactile, touchable

▷ **Antonyms** abstract, disembodied, ethereal, immaterial, impalpable, imperceptible, indiscernible, insubstantial, intangible, theoretical, unreal

tangle *noun* **1.** coil, confusion, entanglement, jam, jungle, knot, mass, mat, mesh, ravel, snarl, twist, web **2.** complication, entanglement, fix (*informal*), imbroglio, labyrinth, maze, mess, mix-up *~verb* **3.** coil, confuse, entangle, interlace, interlock, intertwist, interweave, jam, kink, knot, mat, mesh, ravel, snarl, twist **4.** (*often with* **with**) come into conflict, come up against, contend, contest, cross swords, dispute, lock horns **5.** catch, drag into, embroil, enmesh, ensnare, entangle, entrap, implicate, involve

▷ **Antonyms** (*sense 3*) disentangle, extricate, free, straighten out, unravel, untangle

tangled 1. entangled, jumbled, knotted, knotty, matted, messy, scrambled, snarled, tousled, twisted **2.** complex, complicated, confused, convoluted, involved, knotty, messy, mixed-up

tangy acerb, biting, briny, fresh, piquant, pungent, sharp, spicy, tart

tantalize baffle, balk, disappoint, entice, frustrate, keep (someone) hanging on, lead on, make (someone's) mouth water, provoke, taunt, tease, thwart, titillate, torment, torture

tantamount as good as, commensurate, equal, equivalent, synonymous, the same as

tantrum bate (*Brit. slang*), fit, flare-up, hysterics, ill humour, outburst, paddy (*Brit. informal*), paroxysm, storm, temper, wax (*informal, chiefly Brit.*)

tap[1] 1. *verb* beat, drum, knock, pat, rap, strike, touch **2.** *~noun* beat, knock, light blow, pat, rap, touch

tap[2] *noun* **1.** faucet (*U.S.*), spigot, spout, stopcock, valve **2.** bung, plug, spile, stopper **3.** bug (*informal*), listening device **4. on tap: a.** *informal* at hand, available, in reserve, on hand, ready **b.** on draught *~verb* **5.** bleed, broach, drain, draw off, open, pierce, siphon off, unplug **6.** draw on, exploit, make use of, milk, mine, put to use, turn to account, use, utilize **7.** bug (*informal*), eavesdrop on, listen in on

tape *noun* **1.** band, ribbon, strip *~verb* **2.** bind, seal, secure, stick, wrap **3.** record, tape-record, video

taper 1. come to a point, narrow, thin **2.** (*with* **off**) decrease, die away, die out, dwindle, fade, lessen, reduce, subside, thin out, wane, weaken, wind down

▷ **Antonyms** (*sense 2*) grow, increase, intensify, step up, strengthen, swell, widen

tardiness belatedness, delay, dilatoriness, lateness, procrastination, slowness, unpunctuality

tardy backward, behindhand, belated, dawdling, dilatory, late, loitering, overdue, procrastinating, retarded, slack, slow, sluggish, unpunctual

target 1. aim, ambition, bull's-eye, end, goal, Holy Grail (*informal*), intention, mark, object, objective **2.** butt, quarry, scapegoat, victim

tariff 1. assessment, duty, excise, impost, levy, rate, tax, toll **2.** bill of fare, charges, menu, price list, schedule

tarnish 1. *verb* befoul, blacken, blemish, blot, darken, dim, discolour, drag through the mud, dull, lose lustre *or* shine, rust, smirch, soil, spot, stain, sully, taint **2.** *~noun* blackening, black mark, blemish, blot, discoloration, rust, smirch, spot, stain, taint

▷ **Antonyms** *~verb* brighten, enhance, gleam, polish up, shine

tarry abide, bide, dally, dawdle, delay, drag one's feet *or* heels, dwell, hang around (*informal*), linger, lodge, loiter, lose time, pause, remain, rest, sojourn, stay, take one's time, wait

▷ **Antonyms** hasten, hurry, move on, rush, scoot, step on it (*informal*)

tart[1] *noun* **1.** pastry, pie, tartlet **2.** call girl, fallen woman, *fille de joie,* floozy (*slang*), harlot, hooker (*U.S. slang*), loose woman, prostitute, scrubber (*Brit. & Austral. slang*), slag (*Brit. slang*), slut, streetwalker, strumpet, trollop, whore, woman of easy virtue, working girl (*facetious slang*)

tart[2] *adjective* **1.** acerb, acid, acidulous, astringent, bitter, piquant, pungent, sharp, sour, tangy, vinegary **2.** acrimonious, astringent, barbed, biting, caustic, crusty, cutting, harsh, mordacious, mordant, nasty, scathing, sharp, short, snappish, testy, trenchant, vitriolic, wounding

▷ **Antonyms** (*sense 1*) honeyed, sugary, sweet, syrupy, toothsome (*sense 2*) agreeable, delightful, gentle, kind, pleasant

task *noun* **1.** assignment, business, charge, chore, duty, employment, enterprise, exercise, job, labour, mission, occupation, toil, undertaking, work **2. take to task** bawl out (*informal*), blame, blast, carpet (*informal*), censure, chew out (*U.S. & Canad. informal*), criticize, give a rocket (*Brit. & N.Z. informal*), lambast(e), lecture, read the riot act, reprimand, reproach, reprove, scold, tear into (*informal*), tear (someone) off a strip (*Brit. informal*), tell off (*informal*), upbraid *~verb* **3.** assign to, charge, entrust **4.** burden, exhaust, load, lumber (*Brit. informal*), oppress, overload, push, saddle, strain, tax, test, weary

taste *noun* **1.** flavour, relish, savour, smack, tang **2.** bit, bite, dash, drop, morsel, mouthful, nip, sample, sip, *soupçon,* spoonful, swallow, titbit, touch **3.** appetite, bent, desire, fancy, fondness, inclination, leaning, liking, palate, partiality, penchant, predilection, preference, relish **4.** appreciation, cultivation, culture, discernment, discrimination, elegance, grace, judgment, perception, polish, refinement, sophistication, style **5.** correctness, decorum, delicacy, discretion, nicety, politeness, propriety, restraint, tact, tactfulness *~verb* **6.** differentiate, discern, distinguish, perceive **7.** assay, nibble, relish, sample, savour, sip, test, try **8.** have a flavour of, savour of, smack **9.** come up against, encounter, experience, feel, have knowledge of, know, meet with, partake of, undergo

▷ **Antonyms** *~noun* (*sense 1*) blandness, insipidity, tastelessness (*sense 3*) disinclination, dislike, distaste, hatred, loathing (*sense 4*) lack of discernment, lack of judgment, mawkishness, tackiness, tastelessness (*sense 5*) bawdiness, blueness, coarseness, crudeness, impropriety, indelicacy, obscenity (*informal*), tactlessness, unsubtlety *~verb* (*sense 6*) fail to discern (*sense 9*) fail to achieve, miss, remain ignorant of

tasteful aesthetically pleasing, artistic, beautiful, charming, cultivated, cultured, delicate, discriminating, elegant, exquisite, fastidious, graceful, handsome, harmonious, in good taste, polished, refined, restrained, smart, stylish, urbane

▷ **Antonyms** brash, flashy, garish, gaudy, inelegant, loud, objectionable, offensive, showy, sick, tacky (*informal*), tasteless, tawdry, twee, uncultured, unrefined, vulgar

tasteless 1. bland, boring, dull, flat, flavourless, insipid, mild, stale, tame, thin, uninspired, uninteresting, vapid, watered-down, weak **2.** cheap, coarse, crass, crude, flashy, garish, gaudy, graceless, gross, impolite, improper, indecorous, indelicate, indiscreet, inelegant, low, naff (*Brit. slang*), rude, tacky (*informal*), tactless, tawdry, uncouth, unseemly, vulgar

▷ **Antonyms** (*sense 1*) appetizing, delectable, delicious, flavoursome, savoury, scrumptious (*informal*), tasty (*sense 2*) elegant, graceful, refined, tasteful

tasty appetizing, delectable, delicious, flavourful, flavoursome, full-flavoured, good-tasting, luscious, palatable, sapid, savoury, scrumptious (*informal*), toothsome, yummy (*slang*)

▷ **Antonyms** bland, flavourless, insipid, tasteless, unappetizing, unsavoury

tatter 1. bit, piece, rag, scrap, shred **2. in tatters** down at heel, in rags, in shreds, ragged, ripped, tattered, threadbare, torn

tattle **1.** *verb* babble, blab, blather, blether, chat, chatter, gossip, jabber, natter, prate, prattle, run off at the mouth (*slang*), spread rumours, talk idly, tell tales, tittle-tattle, yak (*slang*) **2.** *~noun* babble, blather, blether, chat, chatter, chitchat, gossip, hearsay, idle talk, jabber, prattle, small talk, tittle-tattle, yak (*slang*), yap (*slang*)

tattler bigmouth (*slang*), gossip, quidnunc, rumourmonger, scandalmonger, talebearer, taleteller, telltale

taunt **1.** *verb* deride, flout, gibe, guy (*informal*), insult, jeer, mock, provoke, reproach, revile, ridicule, sneer, take the piss (out of) (*taboo slang*), tease, torment, twit, upbraid **2.** *~noun* barb, censure, cut, derision, dig, gibe, insult, jeer, provocation, reproach, ridicule, sarcasm, teasing

taut **1.** flexed, rigid, strained, stressed, stretched, tense, tight **2.** *Nautical* in good order, neat, orderly, shipshape, spruce, tidy, tight, trim, well-ordered, well-regulated

▷ **Antonyms** (*sense 1*) loose, relaxed, slack

tautological iterative, pleonastic, prolix, redundant, repetitious, repetitive, verbose

tautology iteration, pleonasm, prolixity, redundancy, repetition, repetitiousness, repetitiveness, verbiage, verbosity

tavern alehouse (*archaic*), bar, boozer (*Brit., Austral. & N.Z. informal*), hostelry, inn, pub (*informal, chiefly Brit.*), public house, taproom, watering hole (*facetious slang*)

tawdry brummagem, cheap, cheap-jack (*informal*), flashy, gaudy, gimcrack, glittering, meretricious, naff (*Brit. slang*), plastic (*slang*), raffish, showy, tacky (*informal*), tasteless, tatty, tinsel, tinselly, vulgar

▷ **Antonyms** elegant, graceful, plain, refined, simple, stylish, tasteful, unflashy, unostentatious, well-tailored

tax *noun* **1.** assessment, charge, contribution, customs, duty, excise, imposition, impost, levy, rate, tariff, tithe, toll, tribute **2.** burden, demand, drain, load, pressure, strain, weight *~verb* **3.** assess, charge, demand, exact, extract, impose, levy a tax on, rate, tithe **4.** burden, drain, enervate, exhaust, load, make heavy demands on, overburden, push, put pressure on, sap, strain, stretch, task, test, try, weaken, wear out, weary, weigh heavily on **5.** accuse, arraign, blame, charge, impeach, impugn, incriminate, lay at one's door

▷ **Antonyms** (*sense 5*) acquit, clear, exculpate, exonerate, vindicate

taxing burdensome, demanding, enervating, exacting, heavy, onerous, punishing, sapping, stressful, tiring, tough, trying, wearing, wearisome

▷ **Antonyms** easy, easy-peasy (*slang*), effortless, light, unburdensome, undemanding

teach advise, coach, demonstrate, direct, discipline, drill, edify, educate, enlighten, give lessons in, guide, impart, implant, inculcate, inform, instil, instruct, school, show, train, tutor

teacher coach, dominie (*Scot.*), don, educator, guide, guru, handler, instructor, lecturer, master, mentor, mistress, pedagogue, professor, schoolmaster, schoolmistress, schoolteacher, trainer, tutor

team *noun* **1.** band, body, bunch, company, crew, gang, group, line-up, posse (*informal*), set, side, squad, troupe **2.** pair, span, yoke *~verb* **3.** (*often with* **up**) band together, cooperate, couple, get together, join, link, unite, work together, yoke

teamwork collaboration, concert, cooperation, coordination, esprit de corps, fellowship, harmony, joint action, unity

tear *verb* **1.** claw, divide, lacerate, mangle, mutilate, pull apart, rend, rip, rive, run, rupture, scratch, sever, shred, split, sunder **2.** barrel (along) (*informal, chiefly U.S. & Canad.*), belt (*slang*), bolt, burn rubber (*informal*), career, charge, dart, dash, fly, gallop, hurry, race, run, rush, shoot, speed, sprint, zoom **3.** grab, pluck, pull, rip, seize, snatch, wrench, wrest, yank *~noun* **4.** hole, laceration, mutilation, rent, rip, run, rupture, scratch, split

tearaway daredevil, delinquent, good-for-nothing, hooligan, madcap, rough (*informal*), roughneck (*slang*), rowdy, ruffian, tough

tearful **1.** blubbering, crying, in tears, lachrymose, sobbing, weeping, weepy (*informal*), whimpering **2.** distressing, dolorous, harrowing, lamentable, mournful, pathetic, pitiable, pitiful, poignant, sad, sorrowful, upsetting, woeful

tears **1.** blubbering, crying, distress, lamentation, mourning, pain, regret, sadness, sobbing, sorrow, wailing, weeping, whimpering, woe **2.** **in tears** blubbering, crying, distressed, sobbing, visibly moved, weeping, whimpering

tease aggravate (*informal*), annoy, badger, bait, bedevil, bother, chaff, gibe, goad, guy (*informal*), lead on, mock, needle (*informal*), pester, plague (*informal*), provoke, pull someone's leg (*informal*), rag, rib (*informal*), ridicule, take the mickey (*informal*), take the piss (out of) (*taboo slang*), tantalize, taunt, torment, twit, vex, wind up (*Brit. slang*), worry

technique **1.** approach, course, fashion, manner, means, method, mode, modus operandi, procedure, style, system, way **2.** address, adroitness, art, artistry, craft, craftsmanship, delivery, execution, facility, knack, know-how (*informal*), performance, proficiency, skill, touch

tedious annoying, banal, boring, deadly dull, drab, dreary, dreich (*Scot.*), dull, fatiguing, ho-hum (*informal*), humdrum, irksome, laborious, lifeless, long-drawn-out, mind-numbing, monotonous, prosaic, prosy, soporific, tiresome, tiring, unexciting, uninteresting, vapid, wearisome

▷ **Antonyms** enjoyable, enthralling, exciting, exhilarating, imaginative, inspiring, interesting, quickly finished, short, stimulating

tedium banality, boredom, deadness, drabness, dreariness, dullness, ennui, lifelessness, monotony, routine, sameness, tediousness, the doldrums

▷ **Antonyms** challenge, excitement, exhilaration, fascination, interest, liveliness, stimulation

teem[1] *verb* abound, be abundant, bear, be crawling with, be full of, be prolific, brim, bristle, burst at the seams, overflow, produce, pullulate, swarm

teem[2] *verb* belt (*slang*), bucket down (*informal*), lash, pelt (down), pour, rain cats and dogs (*informal*), sheet, stream

teeming[1] *adjective* abundant, alive, brimful, brimming, bristling, bursting, chock-a-block, chock-full, crawling, fruitful, full, numerous, overflowing, packed, replete, swarming, thick

▷ **Antonyms** deficient, lacking, short, wanting

teeming[2] *adjective* belting (*slang*), bucketing down (*informal*), lashing, pelting, pouring, sheeting, streaming

teenage adolescent, immature, juvenile, youthful

teenager adolescent, boy, girl, juvenile, minor, youth

teeny diminutive, microscopic, miniature, minuscule, minute, teensy-weensy, teeny-weeny, tiny, wee

teeter balance, pivot, rock, seesaw, stagger, sway, totter, tremble, waver, wobble

teetotaller abstainer, nondrinker, Rechabite

telegram cable, radiogram, telegraph, telex, wire (*informal*)

telegraph *noun* **1.** tape machine (*Stock Exchange*), teleprinter, telex **2.** cable, radiogram, telegram, telex, wire (*informal*) ~*verb* **3.** cable, send, telex, transmit, wire (*informal*)

telepathy mind-reading, sixth sense, thought transference

telephone **1.** *noun* blower (*informal*), handset, line, phone **2.** ~*verb* buzz (*informal*), call, call up, dial, get on the blower (*informal*), give (someone) a bell (*Brit. slang*), give (someone) a buzz (*informal*), give (someone) a call, give (someone) a ring (*informal, chiefly Brit.*), give someone a tinkle (*Brit. informal*), phone, put a call through to, ring (*informal, chiefly Brit.*)

telescope *noun* **1.** glass, spyglass ~*verb* **2.** concertina, crush, squash **3.** abbreviate, abridge, capsulize, compress, condense, consolidate, contract, curtail, cut, shorten, shrink, tighten, trim, truncate

▷ **Antonyms** ~*verb* (*sense 3*) amplify, draw out, elongate, extend, flesh out, lengthen, protract, spread out

television gogglebox (*Brit. slang*), idiot box (*slang*), receiver, small screen (*informal*), telly (*Brit. informal*), the box (*Brit. informal*), the tube (*slang*), TV, TV set

tell *verb* **1.** acquaint, announce, apprise, communicate, confess, disclose, divulge, express, get off one's chest (*informal*), impart, inform, let know, make known, mention, notify, proclaim, reveal, say, speak, state, utter **2.** authorize, bid, call upon, command, direct, enjoin, instruct, order, require, summon **3.** chronicle, depict, describe, give an account of, narrate, portray, recount, rehearse, relate, report **4.** comprehend, discern, discover, make out, see, understand **5.** differentiate, discern, discriminate, distinguish, identify **6.** carry weight, count, have *or* take effect, have force, make its presence felt, register, take its toll, weigh **7.** calculate, compute, count, enumerate, number, reckon, tally

telling considerable, decisive, effective, effectual, forceful, forcible, impressive, influential, marked, potent, powerful, significant, solid, striking, trenchant, weighty

▷ **Antonyms** easily ignored, inconsequential, indecisive, ineffectual, insignificant, light-weight, minor, negligible, slight, trivial, unimportant

tell off bawl out (*informal*), berate, carpet (*informal*), censure, chew out (*U.S. & Canad. informal*), chide, give (someone) a piece of one's mind, give (someone) a rocket (*Brit. & N.Z. informal*), haul over the coals (*informal*), lecture, read the riot act, rebuke, reprimand, reproach, reprove, scold, take to task, tear into (*informal*), tear (someone) off a strip (*Brit. informal*), tick off (*informal*), upbraid

temerity assurance, audacity, boldness, brass neck (*Brit. informal*), chutzpah (*U.S. & Canad. informal*), effrontery, foolhardiness, forwardness, front, gall (*informal*), heedlessness, impudence, impulsiveness, intrepidity, nerve (*informal*), pluck, rashness, recklessness, sassiness (*U.S. informal*)

temper *noun* **1.** attitude, character, constitution, disposition, frame of mind, humour, mind, mood, nature, temperament, tenor, vein **2.** bad mood, bate (*Brit. slang*), fit of pique, fury, gall, paddy (*Brit. informal*), passion, rage, tantrum, wax (*informal, chiefly Brit.*) **3.** anger, annoyance, heat, hot-headedness, ill humour, irascibility, irritability, irritation, passion, peevishness, petulance, resentment, surliness **4.** calm, calmness, composure, cool (*slang*), coolness, equanimity, good humour, moderation, self-control, tranquillity *~verb* **5.** abate, admix, allay, assuage, calm, lessen, mitigate, moderate, mollify, palliate, restrain, soften, soft-pedal (*informal*), soothe, tone down **6.** anneal, harden, strengthen, toughen

▷ **Antonyms** *~noun* (*sense 3*) contentment, goodwill, pleasant mood (*sense 4*) agitation, anger, bad mood, excitability, foul humour, fury, grumpiness, indignation, irascibility, irritation, pique, vexation, wrath *~verb* (*sense 5*) aggravate, arouse, excite, heighten, intensify, provoke, stir (*sense 6*) soften

temperament **1.** bent, cast of mind, character, complexion, constitution, disposition, frame of mind, humour, make-up, mettle, nature, outlook, personality, quality, soul, spirit, stamp, temper, tendencies, tendency **2.** anger, excitability, explosiveness, hot-headedness, impatience, mercurialness, moodiness, moods, petulance, volatility

temperamental **1.** capricious, easily upset, emotional, erratic, excitable, explosive, fiery, highly strung, hot-headed, hypersensitive, impatient, irritable, mercurial, moody, neurotic, passionate, petulant, sensitive, touchy, volatile **2.** congenital, constitutional, inborn, ingrained, inherent, innate, natural **3.** erratic, inconsistent, inconstant, undependable, unpredictable, unreliable

▷ **Antonyms** (*sense 1*) calm, cool-headed, easy-going, even-tempered, level-headed, phlegmatic, unexcitable, unflappable, unperturbable (*sense 3*) constant, dependable, reliable, stable, steady

temperance **1.** continence, discretion, forbearance, moderation, restraint, self-control, self-discipline, self-restraint **2.** abstemiousness, abstinence, prohibition, sobriety, teetotalism

▷ **Antonyms** crapulence, excess, immoderation, intemperance, overindulgence, prodigality

temperate **1.** agreeable, balmy, calm, clement, cool, fair, gentle, mild, moderate, pleasant, soft **2.** calm, composed, dispassionate, equable, even-tempered, mild, moderate, reasonable, self-controlled, self-restrained, sensible, stable **3.** abstemious, abstinent, continent, moderate, sober

▷ **Antonyms** (*sense 1*) extreme, harsh, inclement, intemperate, severe, torrid (*sense 2*) intemperate, uncontrolled, undisciplined, unreasonable, unrestrained, wild (*sense 3*) excessive, extreme, immoderate, inordinate, intemperate, prodigal

tempest **1.** cyclone, gale, hurricane, squall, storm, tornado, typhoon **2.** commotion, disturbance, ferment, furore, storm, tumult, upheaval, uproar

▷ **Antonyms** (*sense 2*) calm, peace, quiet, serenity, stillness, tranquillity

tempestuous **1.** agitated, blustery, boisterous, breezy, gusty, inclement, raging, squally, stormy, turbulent, windy **2.** ablaze, agitated, boisterous, emotional, excited, feverish, flaming, furious, heated, hysterical, impassioned, intense, passionate, stormy, turbulent, uncontrolled, violent, wild

▷ **Antonyms** (*sense 2*) calm, peaceful, quiet, serene, still, tranquil, undisturbed, unruffled

temple church, holy place, place of worship, sanctuary, shrine

tempo beat, cadence, measure (*Prosody*), metre, pace, pulse, rate, rhythm, speed, time

temporal **1.** carnal, civil, earthly, fleshly, lay, material, mortal, mundane, profane, secular, sublunary, terrestrial, worldly **2.** evanescent, fleeting, fugacious, fugitive, impermanent, momentary, passing, short-lived, temporary, transient, transitory

temporarily briefly, fleetingly, for a little while, for a moment, for a short time, for a short while, for the moment, for the nonce, for the time being, momentarily, pro tem

temporary brief, ephemeral, evanescent, fleeting, fugacious, fugitive, here today and gone tomorrow, impermanent, interim, momentary, passing, pro tem, *pro tempore,* provisional, short-lived, transient, transitory

▷ **Antonyms** durable, enduring, eternal, everlasting, long-lasting, long-term, permanent

temporize beat about the bush, be evasive, delay, equivocate, gain time, hum and haw, play a waiting game, play for time, procrastinate, stall, tergiversate

tempt **1.** allure, appeal to, attract, coax, decoy, draw, entice, inveigle, invite, lead on, lure, make one's mouth water, seduce, tantalize, whet the appetite of, woo **2.** bait, dare, fly in the face of, provoke, risk, test, try

▷ **Antonyms** (*sense 1*) deter, discourage, dissuade, hinder, inhibit, put off

temptation allurement, appeal, attraction, attractiveness, bait, blandishments, coaxing, come-on (*informal*), decoy, draw, enticement, inducement, in~

vitation, lure, pull, seduction, snare, tantalization

tempting alluring, appetizing, attractive, enticing, inviting, mouthwatering, seductive, tantalizing
▷ **Antonyms** off-putting (*Brit. informal*), unappetizing, unattractive, undesirable, uninviting, untempting

tenable arguable, believable, defendable, defensible, justifiable, maintainable, plausible, rational, reasonable, sound, viable
▷ **Antonyms** indefensible, insupportable, unjustifiable, untenable

tenacious 1. clinging, fast, firm, forceful, immovable, iron, strong, tight, unshakable **2.** retentive, unforgetful **3.** adamant, determined, dogged, firm, immovable, inflexible, intransigent, obdurate, obstinate, persistent, pertinacious, resolute, staunch, steadfast, stiff-necked, strong-willed, stubborn, sure, unswerving, unyielding **4.** coherent, cohesive, solid, strong, tough **5.** adhesive, clinging, gluey, glutinous, mucilaginous, sticky
▷ **Antonyms** (*sense 3*) changeable, flexible, irresolute, vacillating, wavering, yielding

tenacity 1. fastness, firmness, force, forcefulness, power, strength **2.** firm grasp, retention, retentiveness **3.** application, determination, diligence, doggedness, firmness, inflexibility, intransigence, obduracy, obstinacy, perseverance, persistence, pertinacity, resoluteness, resolution, resolve, staunchness, steadfastness, strength of purpose, strength of will, stubbornness **4.** coherence, cohesiveness, solidity, solidness, strength, toughness **5.** adhesiveness, clingingness, stickiness
▷ **Antonyms** (*sense 1*) looseness, powerlessness, slackness, weakness

tenancy 1. holding, lease, occupancy, occupation, possession, renting, residence **2.** incumbency, period of office, tenure, time in office

tenant holder, inhabitant, leaseholder, lessee, occupant, occupier, renter, resident

tend[1] *verb* **1.** be apt, be biased, be disposed, be inclined, be liable, be likely, gravitate, have a leaning, have an inclination, have a tendency, incline, lean, trend **2.** aim, bear, be conducive, conduce, contribute, go, head, influence, lead, make for, move, point

tend[2] *verb* attend, care for, cater to, control, cultivate, feed, guard, handle, keep, keep an eye on, look after, maintain, manage, minister to, nurse, nurture, protect, see to, serve, take care of, wait on, watch, watch over
▷ **Antonyms** disregard, ignore, neglect, overlook, shirk

tendency 1. bent, disposition, inclination, leaning, liability, partiality, penchant, predilection, predisposition, proclivity, proneness, propensity, readiness, susceptibility **2.** bearing, bias, course, direction, drift, drive, heading, movement, purport, tenor, trend, turning

tender[1] *adjective* **1.** breakable, delicate, feeble, fragile, frail, soft, weak **2.** callow, green, immature, impressionable, inexperienced, new, raw, sensitive, unripe, vulnerable, wet behind the ears (*informal*), young, youthful **3.** affectionate, amorous, benevolent, caring, compassionate, considerate, fond, gentle, humane, kind, loving, merciful, pitiful, sentimental, softhearted, sympathetic, tenderhearted, touchy-feely (*informal*), warm, warm-hearted **4.** emotional, evocative, moving, poignant, romantic, touching **5.** complicated, dangerous, difficult, risky, sensitive, ticklish, touchy, tricky **6.** aching, acute, bruised, inflamed, irritated, painful, raw, sensitive, smarting, sore
▷ **Antonyms** (*sense 1*) hard, leathery, strong, tough (*sense 2*) advanced, elderly, experienced, grown-up, mature, seasoned, sophisticated, worldly, worldly-wise (*sense 3*) brutal, cold-hearted, cruel, hard, hard-hearted, inhuman, insensitive, pitiless, tough, uncaring, unkind, unsympathetic

tender[2] *verb* **1.** extend, give, hand in, offer, present, proffer, propose, put forward, submit, suggest, volunteer *~noun* **2.** bid, estimate, offer, proffer, proposal, submission, suggestion **3.** currency, medium, money, payment, specie

tenderhearted affectionate, benevolent, benign, caring, compassionate, considerate, fond, gentle, humane, kind, kind-hearted, kindly, loving, merciful, mild, responsive, sensitive, sentimental, softhearted, sympathetic, touchy-feely (*informal*), warm, warm-hearted

tenderness 1. delicateness, feebleness, fragility, frailness, sensitiveness, sensitivity, softness, vulnerability, weakness **2.** callowness, greenness, immaturity, impressionableness, inexperience, newness, rawness, sensitivity, vulnerability, youth, youthfulness **3.** affection, amorousness, attachment, benevolence, care, compassion, consideration, devotion, fondness, gentleness, humaneness, humanity, kindness, liking, love, mercy, pity, sentimentality, softheartedness, sympathy, tenderheartedness, warm-heartedness, warmth **4.** ache, aching, bruising, inflammation, irritation, pain, painfulness, rawness, sensitiveness, sensitivity, smart, soreness
▷ **Antonyms** (*sense 3*) cruelty, hardness, harshness, indifference, insensitivity, unkindness

tenebrous dark, dim, dingy, dusky, gloomy, murky, obscure, shadowy, shady, sombre, Stygian, sunless, unlit

tenet article of faith, belief, canon, conviction, creed, doctrine, dogma, maxim, opinion, precept, principle, rule, teaching, thesis, view

tenor aim, burden, course, direction, drift, evolution, intent, meaning, path, purport, purpose, sense, substance, tendency, theme, trend, way

tense *adjective* **1.** rigid, strained, stretched, taut, tight **2.** anxious, apprehensive, edgy, fidgety, jittery (*informal*), jumpy, keyed up, nervous, on edge, on tenterhooks, overwrought, restless, strained, strung up (*informal*), twitchy (*informal*), under pressure, uptight (*informal*), wired (*slang*), wound up (*informal*), wrought up **3.** exciting, moving, nerve-racking, stressful, worrying *~verb* **4.** brace, flex, strain, stretch, tauten, tighten

▷ **Antonyms** *~adjective* (*sense 1*) flaccid, flexible, limp, loose, pliant, relaxed (*sense 2*) calm, collected, cool-headed, easy-going, self-possessed, serene, unconcerned, unruffled, unworried (*sense 3*) boring, dull, uninteresting *~verb* loosen, relax, slacken

tension 1. pressure, rigidity, stiffness, straining, stress, stretching, tautness, tightness **2.** anxiety, apprehension, edginess, hostility, ill feeling, nervousness, pressure, restlessness, strain, stress, suspense, the jitters (*informal*), unease

▷ **Antonyms** (*sense 2*) calmness, peacefulness, relaxation, restfulness, serenity, tranquillity

tentative 1. conjectural, experimental, indefinite, provisional, speculative, unconfirmed, unsettled **2.** backward, cautious, diffident, doubtful, faltering, hesitant, timid, uncertain, undecided, unsure

▷ **Antonyms** (*sense 1*) conclusive, decisive, definite, final, fixed, resolved, settled (*sense 2*) assured, bold, certain, confident, unhesitating

tenuous 1. doubtful, dubious, flimsy, insignificant, insubstantial, nebulous, questionable, shaky, sketchy, slight, weak **2.** attenuated, delicate, fine, gossamer, slim

▷ **Antonyms** (*sense 1*) significant, solid, sound, strong, substantial

tenure holding, incumbency, occupancy, occupation, possession, proprietorship, residence, tenancy, term, time

tepid 1. lukewarm, slightly warm, warmish **2.** apathetic, cool, half-arsed (*Brit. slang*), half-assed (*U.S. & Canad. slang*), half-hearted, indifferent, lukewarm, unenthusiastic

▷ **Antonyms** (*sense 2*) animated, eager, enthusiastic, excited, keen, passionate, vibrant, zealous

tergiversate 1. apostatize, change sides, defect, desert, go over to the other side, renege, turn traitor **2.** beat about the bush, blow hot and cold (*informal*), dodge, equivocate, fence, hedge, prevaricate, pussyfoot (*informal*), vacillate

term *noun* **1.** appellation, denomination, designation, expression, locution, name, phrase, title, word **2.** duration, interval, period, season, space, span, spell, time, while **3.** course, session **4.** bound, boundary, close, conclusion, confine, culmination, end, finish, fruition, limit, terminus *~verb* **5.** call, denominate, designate, dub, entitle, label, name, style

terminal *adjective* **1.** bounding, concluding, extreme, final, last, limiting, ultimate, utmost **2.** deadly, fatal, incurable, killing, lethal, mortal *~noun* **3.** boundary, end, extremity, limit, termination, terminus **4.** depot, end of the line, station, terminus

▷ **Antonyms** (*sense 1*) beginning, commencing, first, initial, introductory, opening

terminate abort, axe (*informal*), bring *or* come to an end, cease, close, complete, conclude, cut off, discontinue, end, expire, finish, issue, lapse, pull the plug on (*informal*), put an end to, result, run out, stop, wind up

▷ **Antonyms** begin, commence, inaugurate, initiate, instigate, introduce, open, start

termination abortion, cessation, close, completion, conclusion, consequence, cut-off point, discontinuation, effect, end, ending, expiry, finale, finis, finish, issue, result, wind-up

▷ **Antonyms** beginning, commencement, inauguration, initiation, opening, start

terminology argot, cant, jargon, language, lingo (*informal*), nomenclature, patois, phraseology, terms, vocabulary

terminus 1. boundary, close, end, extremity, final point, goal, limit, target, termination **2.** depot, end of the line, garage, last stop, station

terms 1. language, manner of speaking, phraseology, terminology **2.** conditions, particulars, premises (*Law*), provisions, provisos, qualifications, specifications, stipulations **3.** charges, fee, payment, price, rates **4.** footing, position, relations, relationship, standing, status **5. come to terms** be reconciled, come to an agreement, come to an understanding, conclude agreement, learn to live with, reach acceptance, reach agreement

terrain country, going, ground, land, landscape, topography

terrestrial 1. *adjective* earthly, global, mundane, sublunary, tellurian, terrene, worldly **2.** *~noun* earthling, earthman, earthwoman, human

terrible 1. bad, dangerous, desperate, extreme, serious, severe **2.** *informal* abhorrent, abysmal, awful, bad, beastly (*informal*), dire, dreadful, duff (*Brit. informal*), foul, frightful, from hell (*informal*), godawful (*slang*), hateful, hideous, loathsome, obnoxious, obscene, odious, offensive, poor, repulsive, revolting, rotten (*informal*), shitty (*taboo slang*), unpleasant, vile **3.** appalling, awful, dread, dreaded, dreadful, fearful, frightful, gruesome, harrowing, hellacious (*U.S. slang*), horrendous, horrible, horrid, horrifying, monstrous, shocking, terrifying, unspeakable

▷ **Antonyms** (*sense 1*) harmless, insignificant, mild, moderate, paltry, small (*sense 2*) admirable, brilliant, delightful, excellent, fine, great, magic, noteworthy, pleasant, remarkable, super, superb, terrific, very good, wonderful (*sense 3*) calming, comforting, encouraging, reassuring, settling, soothing

terribly awfully (*informal*), decidedly, desperately, exceedingly, extremely, gravely, greatly, much, seriously, thoroughly, very

terrific 1. awesome, awful, dreadful, enormous, excessive, extreme, fearful, fierce, gigantic, great, harsh, horrific, huge, intense, monstrous, severe, terrible, tremendous **2.** *informal* ace (*informal*), amazing, awesome (*slang*), bodacious (*slang, chiefly U.S.*), boffo (*slang*), breathtaking, brill (*informal*), brilliant, chillin' (*U.S. slang*), cracking (*Brit. informal*), excellent, fabulous (*informal*), fantastic (*informal*), fine, great (*informal*), jim-dandy (*slang*), magnificent, marvellous, mean (*slang*), outstanding, sensational (*informal*), smashing (*informal*), sovereign, stupendous, super (*informal*), superb, topping (*Brit. slang*), very good, wonderful

▷ **Antonyms** appalling, awful, bad, calming, comforting, dreadful, encouraging, harmless, hideous, insignificant, lousy (*slang*), mediocre, mild, moderate, no great shakes (*informal*), paltry, reassuring, rotten, settling (*informal*), shocking, soothing, terrible, uninspired, unpleasant

terrified alarmed, appalled, awed, dismayed, frightened, frightened out of one's wits, horrified, horror-struck, intimidated, panic-stricken, petrified, scared, scared shitless (*taboo slang*), scared stiff, scared to death, shit-scared (*taboo slang*), shocked, terror-stricken

terrify alarm, appal, awe, dismay, fill with terror, frighten, frighten out of one's wits, horrify, intimidate, make one's blood run cold, make one's flesh creep, make one's hair stand on end, petrify, put the fear of God into, scare, scare to death, shock, terrorize

territory area, bailiwick, country, district, domain, land, patch, province, region, sector, state, terrain, tract, turf (*U.S. slang*), zone

terror 1. alarm, anxiety, awe, consternation, dismay, dread, fear, fear and trembling, fright, horror, intimidation, panic, shock **2.** bogeyman, bugbear, devil, fiend, monster, scourge

terrorize 1. browbeat, bully, coerce, intimidate, menace, oppress, strong-arm (*informal*), threaten **2.** alarm, appal, awe, dismay, fill with terror, frighten, frighten out of one's wits, horrify, inspire panic in, intimidate, make one's blood run cold, make one's flesh creep, make one's hair stand on end, petrify, put the fear of God into, scare, scare to death, shock, strike terror into, terrify

terse 1. aphoristic, brief, clipped, compact, concise, condensed, crisp, elliptical, epigrammatic, gnomic, incisive, laconic, monosyllabic, neat, pithy, sententious, short, succinct, summary, to the point **2.** abrupt, brusque, curt, short, snappy

▷ **Antonyms** ambiguous, chatty, circumlocutory, confused, discursive, lengthy, long-winded, polite, rambling, roundabout, vague, verbose, wordy

test 1. *verb* analyse, assay, assess, check, examine, experiment, investigate, prove, put through their paces, put to the proof, put to the test, research, try, try out, verify, work over **2.** *~noun* acid test, analysis, assessment, attempt, catechism, check, evaluation, examination, investigation, ordeal, probation, proof, research, trial

testament 1. last wishes, will **2.** attestation, demonstration, earnest, evidence, exemplification, proof, testimony, tribute, witness

testicles balls (*taboo slang*), bollocks *or* ballocks (*taboo slang*), *cojones* (*U.S. taboo slang*), family jewels (*slang*), nuts (*taboo slang*), rocks (*U.S. taboo slang*)

testify affirm, assert, asseverate, attest, bear witness, certify, corroborate, declare, depone (*Scots Law*), depose (*Law*), evince, give testimony, show, state, swear, vouch, witness

▷ **Antonyms** belie, contradict, controvert, disprove, dispute, gainsay (*archaic or literary*), oppose

testimonial certificate, character, commendation, credential, endorsement, recommendation, reference, tribute

testimony 1. affidavit, affirmation, attestation, avowal, confirmation, corroboration, declaration, deposition, evidence, information, profession, statement, submission, witness **2.** corroboration, demonstration, evidence, indication, manifestation, proof, support, verification

testy bad-tempered, cantankerous, captious, crabbed, cross, fretful, grumpy, impatient, irascible, irritable, liverish, peevish, peppery, petulant, quarrelsome, quick-tempered, ratty (*Brit. & N.Z. informal*), short-tempered, snappish, snappy, splenetic, sullen, tetchy, touchy, waspish

tetchy bad-tempered, cantankerous, captious, crabbed, cross, fretful, grumpy, impatient, irascible, irritable, liverish, peevish, peppery, petulant, quarrelsome, quick-tempered, ratty (*Brit. & N.Z. informal*), short-tempered, snappish, snappy, splenetic, sullen, testy, touchy, waspish

tête-à-tête **1.** *noun* chat, confab (*informal*), cosy chat, parley, private conversation, private word, talk **2.** ~*adverb* in private, intimately, privately

tether *noun* **1.** bond, chain, fastening, fetter, halter, lead, leash, restraint, rope, shackle **2. at the end of one's tether** at one's wits' end, at the limit of one's endurance, exasperated, exhausted, finished, out of patience ~*verb* **3.** bind, chain, fasten, fetter, leash, manacle, picket, restrain, rope, secure, shackle, tie

text **1.** body, contents, main body, matter **2.** wording, words **3.** *Bible* paragraph, passage, sentence, verse **4.** argument, matter, motif, subject, theme, topic **5.** reader, reference book, source, textbook

texture character, composition, consistency, constitution, fabric, feel, grain, make, quality, structure, surface, tissue, weave

thank express gratitude, say thank you, show gratitude, show one's appreciation

thankful appreciative, beholden, grateful, indebted, obliged, pleased, relieved
▷ **Antonyms** thankless, unappreciative, ungrateful

thankless **1.** fruitless, unappreciated, unprofitable, unrequited, unrewarding, useless **2.** inconsiderate, unappreciative, ungracious, ungrateful, unmindful, unthankful
▷ **Antonyms** (*sense 1*) fruitful, productive, profitable, rewarding, useful, worthwhile (*sense 2*) appreciative, grateful, thankful

thanks **1.** acknowledgment, appreciation, Brownie points, credit, gratefulness, gratitude, recognition, thanksgiving **2. thanks to** as a result of, because of, by reason of, due to, owing to, through

thaw defrost, dissolve, liquefy, melt, soften, unfreeze, warm
▷ **Antonyms** chill, congeal, freeze, harden, solidify, stiffen

theatrical **1.** dramatic, dramaturgic, melodramatic, scenic, Thespian **2.** actorly, actressy, affected, artificial, camp (*informal*), ceremonious, dramatic, exaggerated, hammy (*informal*), histrionic, mannered, ostentatious, overdone, pompous, showy, stagy, stilted, unreal
▷ **Antonyms** (*sense 2*) natural, plain, simple, straightforward, unaffected, unassuming, unexaggerated, unpretentious, unsophisticated

theft embezzlement, fraud, larceny, pilfering, purloining, rip-off (*slang*), robbery, stealing, swindling, thievery, thieving

theme **1.** argument, burden, idea, keynote, matter, subject, subject matter, text, thesis, topic **2.** leitmotif, motif, recurrent image, unifying idea **3.** composition, dissertation, essay, exercise, paper

theological divine, doctrinal, ecclesiastical, religious

theorem deduction, dictum, formula, hypothesis, principle, proposition, rule, statement

theoretical abstract, academic, conjectural, hypothetical, ideal, impractical, notional, pure, speculative
▷ **Antonyms** applied, experiential, factual, practical, realistic

theorize conjecture, formulate, guess, hypothesize, project, propound, speculate, suppose

theory **1.** assumption, conjecture, guess, hypothesis, presumption, speculation, supposition, surmise, thesis **2.** philosophy, plan, proposal, scheme, system
▷ **Antonyms** (*sense 1*) certainty, experience, fact, practice, reality

therapeutic ameliorative, analeptic, beneficial, corrective, curative, good, healing, remedial, restorative, salubrious, salutary, sanative
▷ **Antonyms** adverse, damaging, destructive, detrimental, harmful

therapy cure, healing, remedial treatment, remedy, treatment

therefore accordingly, as a result, consequently, ergo, for that reason, hence, so, then, thence, thus, whence

thesaurus dictionary, encyclopedia, repository, storehouse, treasury, wordbook

thesis **1.** composition, disquisition, dissertation, essay, monograph, paper, treatise **2.** contention, hypothesis, idea, line of argument, opinion, proposal, proposition, theory, view **3.** area, subject, theme, topic **4.** assumption, postulate, premise, proposition, statement, supposition, surmise

thick *adjective* **1.** broad, bulky, deep, fat, solid, substantial, wide **2.** close, clotted, coagulated, compact, concentrated, condensed, crowded, deep, dense, heavy, impenetrable, opaque **3.** abundant, brimming, bristling, bursting, chock-a-block, chock-full, covered, crawling, fre~

quent, full, numerous, packed, replete, swarming, teeming **4.** blockheaded, braindead (*informal*), brainless, dense, dim-witted (*informal*), dopey (*informal*), dozy (*Brit. informal*), dull, insensitive, moronic, obtuse, slow, slow-witted, stupid, thickheaded **5.** dense, heavy, impenetrable, soupy **6.** distorted, guttural, hoarse, husky, inarticulate, indistinct, throaty **7.** broad, decided, distinct, marked, pronounced, rich, strong **8.** *informal* buddy-buddy (*slang, chiefly U.S. & Canad.*), chummy (*informal*), close, confidential, devoted, familiar, friendly, hand in glove, inseparable, intimate, matey *or* maty (*Brit. informal*), on good terms, pally (*informal*), palsy-walsy (*informal*), well in (*informal*) **9. a bit thick** excessive, over the score (*informal*), too much, unfair, unjust, unreasonable *~noun* **10.** centre, heart, middle, midst

▷ **Antonyms** (*sense 1*) narrow, slight, slim, thin (*sense 2*) clear, diluted, runny, thin, watery, weak (*sense 3*) bare, clear, devoid of, empty, free from, sparse, thin (*sense 4*) articulate, brainy, bright, clever, intellectual, intelligent, quick-witted, sharp, smart (*sense 5*) clear, thin (*sense 6*) articulate, clear, distinct, sharp, shrill, thin (*sense 7*) faint, slight, vague, weak (*sense 8*) antagonistic, distant, hostile, unfriendly

thicken cake, clot, coagulate, condense, congeal, deepen, gel, inspissate (*archaic*), jell, set

▷ **Antonyms** dilute, thin, water down, weaken

thicket brake, clump, coppice, copse, covert, grove, hurst (*archaic*), spinney (*Brit.*), wood, woodland

thickhead berk (*Brit. slang*), blockhead, bonehead (*slang*), charlie (*Brit. informal*), chump, clot (*Brit. informal*), dickhead (*slang*), dimwit (*informal*), dipstick (*Brit. slang*), divvy (*Brit. slang*), dolt, dope (*informal*), dork (*slang*), dummy (*slang*), dunce, dunderhead, dweeb (*U.S. slang*), fathead (*informal*), fool, fuckwit (*taboo slang*), geek (*slang*), gobshite (*Irish taboo slang*), gonzo (*slang*), idiot, imbecile, lamebrain (*informal*), moron, nerd *or* nurd (*slang*), numbskull *or* numskull, numpty (*Scot. informal*), pillock (*Brit. slang*), pinhead (*slang*), plank (*Brit. slang*), plonker (*slang*), prat (*slang*), prick (*slang*), twit (*informal, chiefly Brit.*), wally (*slang*)

thickheaded blockheaded, braindead (*informal*), brainless, dense, dim-witted (*informal*), doltish, dopey (*informal*), dozy (*Brit. informal*), idiotic, moronic, obtuse, slow, slow-witted, stupid, thick

thickset 1. beefy (*informal*), brawny, bulky, burly, heavy, muscular, powerfully built, stocky, strong, stubby, sturdy, well-built **2.** closely packed, dense, densely planted, solid, thick

▷ **Antonyms** (*sense 1*) angular, bony, gangling, gaunt, lanky, rawboned, scraggy, scrawny, weedy (*informal*)

thick-skinned callous, case-hardened, hard-boiled (*informal*), hardened, impervious, insensitive, stolid, tough, unfeeling, unsusceptible

▷ **Antonyms** concerned, feeling, sensitive, tender, thin-skinned, touchy

thief bandit, burglar, cheat, cracksman (*slang*), crook (*informal*), embezzler, footpad (*archaic*), housebreaker, larcenist, mugger (*informal*), pickpocket, pilferer, plunderer, purloiner, robber, shoplifter, stealer, swindler

thieve blag (*slang*), cabbage (*Brit. slang*), cheat, embezzle, filch, half-inch (*old-fashioned slang*), have sticky fingers (*informal*), knock off (*slang*), lift (*informal*), misappropriate, nick (*slang, chiefly Brit.*), peculate, pilfer, pinch (*informal*), plunder, poach, purloin, rip off (*slang*), rob, run off with, snitch (*slang*), steal, swindle, swipe (*slang*)

thievery banditry, burglary, crookedness (*informal*), embezzlement, larceny, mugging (*informal*), pilfering, plundering, robbery, shoplifting, stealing, theft, thieving

thievish crooked (*informal*), dishonest, fraudulent, larcenous, light-fingered, predatory, rapacious, sticky-fingered (*informal*), thieving

thimbleful capful, dab, dash, dram, drop, jot, modicum, nip, pinch, sip, *soupçon,* spoonful, spot, taste, toothful

thin *adjective* **1.** attenuate, attenuated, fine, narrow, threadlike **2.** delicate, diaphanous, filmy, fine, flimsy, gossamer, see-through, sheer, translucent, transparent, unsubstantial **3.** bony, emaciated, lank, lanky, lean, light, macilent (*rare*), meagre, scraggy, scrawny, skeletal, skin and bone, skinny, slender, slight, slim, spare, spindly, thin as a rake, undernourished, underweight **4.** deficient, meagre, scanty, scarce, scattered, skimpy, sparse, wispy **5.** dilute, diluted, rarefied, runny, watery, weak, wishy-washy (*informal*) **6.** feeble, flimsy, inadequate, insufficient, lame, poor, scant, scanty, shallow, slight, superficial, unconvincing, unsubstantial, weak *~verb* **7.** attenuate, cut back, dilute, diminish, emaciate, prune, rarefy, reduce, refine, trim, water down, weaken, weed out

▷ **Antonyms** (*sense 1*) heavy, thick (*sense 2*) bulky, dense, heavy, strong, substantial, thick (*sense 3*) bulky, corpulent, fat, heavy, obese, stout (*sense 4*) abundant, adequate, plentiful, profuse (*sense 5*) concentrated, dense, strong, thick, viscous (*sense 6*) adequate, convincing, strong, substantial

thing 1. affair, article, being, body, circumstance, concept, entity, fact, matter, object, part, portion, something, substance **2**. act, deed, event, eventuality, feat, happening, incident, occurrence, phenomenon, proceeding **3**. apparatus, contrivance, device, gadget, implement, instrument, machine, means, mechanism, tool **4**. aspect, detail, facet, factor, feature, item, particular, point, statement, thought **5**. *plural* baggage, belongings, bits and pieces, clobber (*Brit. slang*), clothes, effects, equipment, gear, goods, impedimenta, luggage, odds and ends, paraphernalia, possessions, stuff **6**. *informal* attitude, bee in one's bonnet, fetish, fixation, hang-up (*informal*), *idée fixe,* mania, obsession, phobia, preoccupation, quirk

think *verb* **1**. believe, conceive, conclude, consider, deem, determine, esteem, estimate, guess (*informal, chiefly U.S. & Canad.*), hold, imagine, judge, reckon, regard, suppose, surmise **2**. brood, cerebrate, chew over (*informal*), cogitate, consider, contemplate, deliberate, have in mind, meditate, mull over, muse, ponder, rack one's brains, reason, reflect, revolve, ruminate, turn over in one's mind, weigh up **3**. call to mind, recall, recollect, remember **4**. anticipate, envisage, expect, foresee, imagine, plan for, presume, suppose **5**. **think better of** change one's mind about, decide against, go back on, have second thoughts about, reconsider, repent, think again, think twice about **6**. **think much of** admire, attach importance to, esteem, have a high opinion of, hold in high regard, rate (*slang*), respect, set store by, think highly of, value **7**. **think nothing of** consider unimportant, have no compunction about, have no hesitation about, regard as routine, set no store by, take in one's stride *~noun* **8**. assessment, consideration, contemplation, deliberation, look, reflection

thinkable conceivable, feasible, imaginable, likely, possible, reasonable, within the bounds of possibility

▷ **Antonyms** absurd, impossible, inconceivable, not on (*informal*), out of the question, unlikely, unreasonable, unthinkable

thinker brain (*informal*), intellect (*informal*), mahatma, mastermind, philosopher, sage, theorist, wise man

thinking 1. *noun* assessment, conclusions, conjecture, idea, judgment, opinion, outlook, philosophy, position, reasoning, theory, thoughts, view **2**. *~adjective* contemplative, cultured, intelligent, meditative, philosophical, ratiocinative, rational, reasoning, reflective, sophisticated, thoughtful

think over chew over (*informal*), consider, consider the pros and cons of, contemplate, give thought to, mull over, ponder, rack one's brains, reflect upon, turn over in one's mind, weigh up

think up come up with, concoct, contrive, create, devise, dream up, imagine, improvise, invent, manufacture, trump up, visualize

thin-skinned easily hurt, hypersensitive, quick to take offence, sensitive, soft, susceptible, tender, touchy, vulnerable

▷ **Antonyms** callous, hard, heartless, insensitive, obdurate, stolid, thick-skinned, tough, unfeeling

third-rate bad, cheap-jack, chickenshit (*U.S. slang*), duff (*Brit. informal*), indifferent, inferior, low-grade, mediocre, no great shakes (*informal*), not much cop (*informal*), of a sort *or* of sorts, poor, poor-quality, ropey *or* ropy (*Brit. informal*), shoddy

thirst *noun* **1**. craving to drink, drought, dryness, thirstiness **2**. ache, appetite, craving, desire, eagerness, hankering, hunger, keenness, longing, lust, passion, yearning, yen (*informal*)

▷ **Antonyms** (*sense 2*) apathy, aversion, disinclination, dislike, distaste, loathing, revulsion

thirsty 1. arid, dehydrated, dry, parched **2**. athirst, avid, burning, craving, desirous, dying, eager, greedy, hankering, hungry, itching, longing, lusting, thirsting, yearning

thorn 1. barb, prickle, spike, spine **2**. affliction, annoyance, bane, bother, curse, hassle (*informal*), irritant, irritation, nuisance, pest, plague, scourge, torment, torture, trouble

▷ **Antonyms** (*sense 2*) balm, benefaction, blessing, comfort, manna, solace, succour

thorny 1. barbed, bristling with thorns, bristly, pointed, prickly, sharp, spiky, spinous, spiny **2**. awkward, difficult, harassing, hard, irksome, problematic(al), sticky (*informal*), ticklish, tough, troublesome, trying, unpleasant, upsetting, vexatious, worrying

thorough *or* **thoroughgoing 1**. all-embracing, all-inclusive, assiduous, careful, complete, comprehensive, conscientious, efficient, exhaustive, full, in-depth, intensive, leaving no stone unturned, meticulous, painstaking, scrupulous, sweeping **2**. absolute, arrant, complete, deep-dyed (*usually derogatory*), downright, entire, out-and-out, outright, perfect, pure, sheer, total, unmitigated, unqualified, utter

▷ **Antonyms** careless, cursory, half-hearted, haphazard, imperfect, incomplete, lackadaisical, partial, sloppy, superficial

thoroughbred *adjective* blood, full-blooded, of unmixed stock, pedigree, pure-blooded, purebred

▷ **Antonyms** crossbred, crossed, half-breed, hybrid, mongrel, of mixed breed

thoroughfare access, avenue, highway, passage, passageway, road, roadway, street, way

thoroughly 1. assiduously, carefully, completely, comprehensively, conscientiously, efficiently, exhaustively, from top to bottom, fully, inside out, intensively, leaving no stone unturned, meticulously, painstakingly, scrupulously, sweepingly, through and through, throughout 2. absolutely, completely, downright, entirely, perfectly, quite, totally, to the full, to the hilt, utterly, without reservation
▷ **Antonyms** carelessly, cursorily, halfheartedly, haphazardly, imperfectly, incompletely, in part, lackadaisically, partly, sloppily, somewhat, superficially

though 1. *conjunction* albeit, allowing, although, despite the fact that, even if, even supposing, even though, granted, notwithstanding, tho' (*U.S. or poetic*), while 2. *~adverb* all the same, for all that, however, nevertheless, nonetheless, notwithstanding, still, yet

thought 1. brainwork, cerebration, cogitation, consideration, contemplation, deliberation, introspection, meditation, musing, navel-gazing (*slang*), reflection, regard, rumination, thinking 2. assessment, belief, concept, conception, conclusion, conjecture, conviction, estimation, idea, judgment, notion, opinion, thinking, view 3. attention, consideration, heed, regard, scrutiny, study 4. aim, design, idea, intention, notion, object, plan, purpose 5. anticipation, aspiration, dream, expectation, hope, prospect 6. dash, jot, little, small amount, *soupçon,* touch, trifle, whisker (*informal*) 7. anxiety, attentiveness, care, compassion, concern, kindness, regard, solicitude, sympathy, thoughtfulness

thoughtful 1. attentive, caring, considerate, helpful, kind, kindly, solicitous, unselfish 2. astute, canny, careful, cautious, circumspect, deliberate, discreet, heedful, mindful, prudent, wary, well-thought-out 3. contemplative, deliberative, in a brown study, introspective, lost in thought, meditative, musing, pensive, rapt, reflective, ruminative, serious, studious, thinking, wistful
▷ **Antonyms** (*sense 1*) cold-hearted, impolite, inconsiderate, insensitive, neglectful, selfish, uncaring (*sense 2*) flippant, heedless, irresponsible, rash, thoughtless, unthinking (*sense 3*) extrovert, shallow, superficial

thoughtless 1. impolite, inconsiderate, indiscreet, insensitive, rude, selfish, tactless, uncaring, undiplomatic, unkind 2. absent-minded, careless, foolish, heedless, ill-considered, imprudent, inadvertent, inattentive, injudicious, mindless, neglectful, negligent, rash, reckless, regardless, remiss, silly, slapdash, slipshod, stupid, unmindful, unobservant, unthinking
▷ **Antonyms** (*sense 1*) attentive, considerate, diplomatic, tactful, thoughtful, unselfish (*sense 2*) considered, intelligent, prudent, smart, well-advised, well-thought-out, wise

thraldom bondage, enslavement, serfdom, servitude, slavery, subjection, subjugation, thrall, vassalage

thrall 1. bondage, enslavement, serfdom, servitude, slavery, subjection, subjugation, thraldom, vassalage 2. bondservant, bondsman, serf, slave, subject, varlet (*archaic*), vassal

thrash 1. beat, belt (*informal*), birch, cane, chastise, clobber (*slang*), drub, flagellate, flog, give (someone) a (good) hiding (*informal*), hide (*informal*), horsewhip, lambast(e), leather, lick (*informal*), paste (*slang*), punish, scourge, spank, take a stick to, tan (*slang*), whip 2. beat, beat (someone) hollow (*Brit. informal*), blow out of the water (*slang*), clobber (*slang*), crush, defeat, drub, hammer (*informal*), lick (*informal*), make mincemeat of (*informal*), maul, overwhelm, paste (*slang*), rout, run rings around (*informal*), slaughter (*informal*), stuff (*slang*), tank (*slang*), trounce, wipe the floor with (*informal*) 3. flail, heave, jerk, plunge, squirm, thresh, toss, toss and turn, writhe

thrashing 1. beating, belting (*informal*), caning, chastisement, drubbing, flogging, hiding (*informal*), lashing, pasting (*slang*), punishment, tanning (*slang*), whipping 2. beating, defeat, drubbing, hammering (*informal*), hiding (*informal*), mauling, pasting (*slang*), rout, trouncing

thrash out argue out, debate, discuss, have out, resolve, settle, solve, talk over

thread *noun* 1. cotton, fibre, filament, line, strand, string, yarn 2. course, direction, drift, motif, plot, story line, strain, tenor, theme, train of thought *~verb* 3. ease, inch, loop, meander, pass, pick (one's way), squeeze through, string, wind

threadbare 1. down at heel, frayed, old, ragged, scruffy, shabby, tattered, tatty, used, worn, worn-out 2. clichéd, cliché-ridden, common, commonplace, conventional, corny (*slang*), familiar, hackneyed, overused, stale, stereotyped, stock, tired, trite, well-worn
▷ **Antonyms** (*sense 1*) brand-new, good, new, smart, unused, well-preserved (*sense 2*) different, fresh, new, novel, original, unconventional, unfamiliar, unusual

threat 1. commination, intimidatory remark, menace, threatening remark, warning 2. foreboding, foreshadowing, omen, portent, presage, warning, writ~

ing on the wall **3.** danger, hazard, menace, peril, risk

threaten 1. endanger, imperil, jeopardize, put at risk, put in jeopardy, put on the line **2.** be imminent, be in the air, be in the offing, forebode, foreshadow, hang over, hang over (someone's) head, impend, loom over, portend, presage, warn **3.** browbeat, bully, cow, intimidate, lean on (*slang*), make threats to, menace, pressurize, terrorize, warn

▷ **Antonyms** (*senses 1 & 3*) defend, guard, protect, safeguard, shelter, shield

threatening 1. bullying, cautionary, comminatory, intimidatory, menacing, minatory, terrorizing, warning **2.** baleful, forbidding, grim, inauspicious, ominous, sinister

▷ **Antonyms** (*sense 2*) auspicious, bright, comforting, encouraging, favourable, promising, propitious, reassuring

threesome triad, trilogy, trine, trinity, trio, triple, triplet, triplex, triptych, triumvirate, triune, troika

threnody coronach (*Scot. & Irish*), dirge, elegy, funeral ode, keen, lament, monody, requiem

threshold 1. door, doorsill, doorstep, doorway, entrance, sill **2.** beginning, brink, dawn, inception, opening, outset, start, starting point, verge **3.** lower limit, minimum

▷ **Antonyms** (*sense 2*) close, decline, end, finish, twilight

thrift carefulness, economy, frugality, good husbandry, parsimony, prudence, saving, thriftiness

▷ **Antonyms** carelessness, extravagance, prodigality, profligacy, recklessness, squandering, waste

thriftless extravagant, improvident, imprudent, lavish, prodigal, profligate, spendthrift, unthrifty, wasteful

▷ **Antonyms** careful, economical, frugal, provident, prudent, sparing, thrifty

thrifty careful, economical, frugal, parsimonious, provident, prudent, saving, sparing

▷ **Antonyms** extravagant, free-spending, generous, improvident, prodigal, spendthrift, wasteful

thrill *noun* **1.** adventure, buzz (*slang*), charge (*slang*), flush of excitement, glow, kick (*informal*), pleasure, sensation, stimulation, tingle, titillation **2.** flutter, fluttering, quiver, shudder, throb, tremble, tremor, vibration *~verb* **3.** arouse, electrify, excite, flush, get a charge (*slang*), get a kick (*informal*), glow, move, send (*slang*), stimulate, stir, tingle, titillate **4.** flutter, quake, quiver, shake, shudder, throb, tremble, vibrate

▷ **Antonyms** (*sense 1*) boredom, dreariness, dullness, ennui, monotony, tedium

thrilling 1. electrifying, exciting, gripping, hair-raising, rip-roaring (*informal*), riveting, rousing, sensational, sexy (*informal*), stimulating, stirring **2.** quaking, shaking, shivering, shuddering, trembling, vibrating

▷ **Antonyms** (*sense 1*) boring, dreary, dull, monotonous, quiet, staid, tedious, tiresome, uninteresting, unmoving

thrive advance, bloom, boom, burgeon, develop, do well, flourish, get on, grow, grow rich, increase, prosper, succeed, wax

▷ **Antonyms** decline, droop, fail, languish, perish, shrivel, stagnate, wane, wilt, wither

thriving blooming, booming, burgeoning, developing, doing well, flourishing, going strong, growing, healthy, prosperous, successful, wealthy, well

▷ **Antonyms** ailing, bankrupt, failing, impoverished, languishing, on the rocks, poverty-stricken, unsuccessful, withering

throaty deep, gruff, guttural, hoarse, husky, low, thick

throb 1. *verb* beat, palpitate, pound, pulsate, pulse, thump, vibrate **2.** *~noun* beat, palpitation, pounding, pulsating, pulse, thump, thumping, vibration

throe 1. convulsion, fit, pain, pang, paroxysm, spasm, stab **2.** *plural* agony, anguish, pain, suffering, torture, travail **3. in the throes of** agonized by, anguished by, in the midst of, in the pangs of, in the process of, struggling with, suffering from, toiling with, wrestling with

throng 1. *noun* assemblage, concourse, congregation, crowd, crush, horde, host, jam, mass, mob, multitude, pack, press, swarm **2.** *~verb* bunch, congregate, converge, cram, crowd, fill, flock, hem in, herd, jam, mill around, pack, press, swarm around, troop

▷ **Antonyms** *~verb* break up, disband, dispel, disperse, scatter, separate, spread out

throttle *verb* **1.** choke, garrotte, strangle, strangulate **2.** control, gag, inhibit, silence, stifle, suppress

through *preposition* **1.** between, by, from end to end of, from one side to the other of, in and out of, past **2.** as a consequence *or* result of, because of, by means of, by virtue of, by way of, using, via, with the help of **3.** during, in, in the middle of, throughout **4.** (*with* **with**) at the end of, done, finished, having completed, having had enough of *~adjective* **5.** completed, done, ended, finished, terminated, washed up (*informal*) *~adverb* **6. through and through** altogether, completely, entirely, fully, thoroughly, totally, to the core, unreservedly, utterly, wholly

▷ **Antonyms** *~adverb* moderately, more or less, partially, partly, somewhat, to some extent

throughout all over, all the time, all through, during the whole of, everywhere, for the duration of, from beginning to end, from end to end, from start to finish, from the start, in every nook and cranny, over the length and breadth of, right through, the whole time, through the whole of

throw *verb* **1.** cast, chuck (*informal*), fling, heave, hurl, launch, lob (*informal*), pitch, project, propel, put, send, shy, sling, toss **2.** *informal* astonish, baffle, confound, confuse, disconcert, dumbfound, faze, put one off one's stroke, throw off, throw one off one's stride, throw out **3.** bring down, dislodge, fell, floor, hurl to the ground, overturn, unseat, upset *~noun* **4.** cast, fling, heave, lob (*informal*), pitch, projection, put, shy, sling, toss **5.** *informal* attempt, chance, essay, gamble, hazard, try, venture, wager

throwaway *adjective* careless, casual, offhand, passing, understated

throw away 1. axe (*informal*), bin (*informal*), cast off, chuck (*informal*), discard, dispense with, dispose of, ditch (*slang*), dump (*informal*), get rid of, jettison, junk (*informal*), reject, scrap, throw out **2.** blow (*slang*), fail to exploit, fritter away, lose, make poor use of, squander, waste

▷ **Antonyms** (*sense 1*) conserve, keep, preserve, rescue, retain, retrieve, salvage, save

throw off 1. abandon, cast off, discard, drop, free oneself of, rid oneself of, shake off **2.** elude, escape from, evade, get away from, give (someone) the slip, leave behind, lose, outdistance, outrun, shake off, show a clean pair of heels to **3.** confuse, disconcert, disturb, faze, put one off one's stroke, throw (*informal*), throw one off one's stride, unsettle, upset

throw out 1. bin (*informal*), cast off, chuck (*informal*), discard, dismiss, dispense with, ditch (*slang*), dump (*informal*), eject, evict, expel, get rid of, give the bum's rush (*slang*), jettison, junk (*informal*), kick out (*informal*), kiss off (*slang, chiefly U.S. & Canad.*), oust, reject, relegate, scrap, show one the door, throw away, turf out (*Brit. informal*), turn down **2.** confuse, disconcert, disturb, put one off one's stroke, throw (*informal*), throw one off one's stride, unsettle, upset **3.** diffuse, disseminate, emit, give off, put forth, radiate

throw over abandon, break with, chuck (*informal*), desert, discard, drop (*informal*), finish with, forsake, jilt, leave, quit, split up with, walk out on (*informal*)

throw up 1. abandon, chuck (*informal*), give up, jack in, leave, quit, relinquish, renounce, resign from, step down from (*informal*) **2.** bring forward, bring to light, bring to notice, bring to the surface, produce, reveal **3.** *informal* barf (*U.S. slang*), be sick, bring up, chuck (up) (*slang, chiefly U.S.*), chunder (*slang, chiefly Austral.*), disgorge, do a technicolour yawn (*slang*), heave, puke (*slang*), regurgitate, retch, spew, toss one's cookies (*U.S. slang*), upchuck (*U.S. slang*), vomit **4.** jerry-build, run up, slap together, throw together

thrust *verb* **1.** butt, drive, elbow *or* shoulder one's way, force, impel, jam, plunge, poke, press, prod, propel, push, ram, shove, urge **2.** jab, lunge, pierce, stab, stick *~noun* **3.** drive, lunge, poke, prod, push, shove, stab **4.** impetus, momentum, motive force, motive power, propulsive force

thud *noun/verb* clonk, clump, clunk, crash, knock, smack, thump, wallop (*informal*)

thug assassin, bandit, bruiser (*informal*), bully boy, cut-throat, gangster, heavy (*slang*), hooligan, killer, mugger (*informal*), murderer, robber, ruffian, tough, tsotsi (*S. African*)

thumb *noun* **1.** pollex **2. all thumbs** butterfingered (*informal*), cack-handed (*informal*), clumsy, ham-fisted (*informal*), inept, maladroit **3. thumbs down** disapproval, negation, no, rebuff, refusal, rejection **4. thumbs up** acceptance, affirmation, approval, encouragement, go-ahead (*informal*), green light, O.K. *or* okay (*informal*), yes *~verb* **5.** hitch (*informal*), hitchhike **6.** (*often with* **through**) browse through, flick through, flip through, glance at, leaf through, riffle through, run one's eye over, scan the pages of, skim through, turn over **7.** dog-ear, finger, handle, mark **8. thumb one's nose at** be contemptuous of, cock a snook at, deride, flout, jeer at, laugh at, laugh in the face of, mock, ridicule, show contempt for, show disrespect to

thumbnail *adjective* brief, compact, concise, pithy, quick, short, succinct

thump 1. *noun* bang, blow, clout (*informal*), clunk, crash, knock, punch, rap, smack, thud, thwack, wallop (*informal*), whack **2.** *~verb* bang, batter, beat, belabour, chin (*slang*), clobber (*slang*), clout (*informal*), crash, deck (*slang*), hit, knock, lambast(e), lay one on (*slang*), pound, punch, rap, smack, strike, thrash, throb, thud, thwack, wallop (*informal*), whack

thumping colossal, elephantine, enormous, excessive, exorbitant, gargantuan, gigantic, great, huge, humongous *or* humungous (*U.S. slang*), impressive, mammoth, massive, monumental, stellar (*informal*), terrific, thundering (*slang*), titanic, tremendous, whopping (*informal*)

▷ **Antonyms** inconsequential, insignifi~

cant, meagre, measly (*informal*), negligible, paltry, petty, piddling (*informal*), trifling, trivial

thunder *noun* **1.** boom, booming, cracking, crash, crashing, detonation, explosion, pealing, rumble, rumbling *~verb* **2.** blast, boom, clap, crack, crash, detonate, explode, peal, resound, reverberate, roar, rumble **3.** bark, bellow, declaim, roar, shout, yell **4.** curse, denounce, fulminate, rail, threaten, utter threats

thundering decided, enormous, excessive, great, monumental, remarkable, unmitigated, utter

thunderous booming, deafening, ear-splitting, loud, noisy, resounding, roaring, tumultuous

thunderstruck aghast, amazed, astonished, astounded, bowled over (*informal*), dazed, dumbfounded, flabbergasted (*informal*), floored (*informal*), flummoxed, gobsmacked (*Brit. slang*), knocked for six (*informal*), left speechless, nonplussed, open-mouthed, paralysed, petrified, rooted to the spot, shocked, staggered, struck dumb, stunned, taken aback

thus **1.** as follows, in this fashion, in this manner, in this way, like so, like this, so, to such a degree **2.** accordingly, consequently, ergo, for this reason, hence, on that account, so, then, therefore

thwack **1.** *verb* bash (*informal*), beat, chin (*slang*), clout (*informal*), deck (*slang*), flog, hit, lambast(e), lay one on (*slang*), smack, thump, wallop (*informal*), whack **2.** *~noun* bash (*informal*), blow, clout (*informal*), smack, thump, wallop (*informal*), whack

thwart baffle, balk, check, cook (someone's) goose (*informal*), defeat, foil, frustrate, hinder, impede, obstruct, oppose, outwit, prevent, put a spoke in someone's wheel (*informal*), snooker, stop, stymie

▷ **Antonyms** aggravate, aid, assist, encourage, exacerbate, facilitate, hasten, help, intensify, support

tic jerk, spasm, twitch

tick[1] *noun* **1.** clack, click, clicking, tap, tapping, ticktock **2.** *Brit. informal* bat of an eye (*informal*), flash, half a mo (*Brit. informal*), instant, jiffy (*informal*), minute, moment, sec (*informal*), second, shake (*informal*), split second, trice, twinkling, two shakes of a lamb's tail (*informal*) **3.** dash, mark, stroke *~verb* **4.** clack, click, tap, ticktock **5.** check off, choose, indicate, mark, mark off, select **6. what makes someone tick** drive, motivation, motive, *raison d'être*

tick[2] *noun* account, credit, deferred payment, the slate (*Brit. informal*)

ticket **1.** card, certificate, coupon, pass, slip, token, voucher **2.** card, docket, label, marker, slip, sticker, tab, tag

tickle *figurative* amuse, delight, divert, entertain, excite, gratify, please, thrill, titillate

▷ **Antonyms** annoy, bore, bother, irritate, pester, trouble, vex, weary

ticklish awkward, critical, delicate, difficult, nice, risky, sensitive, thorny, touchy, tricky, uncertain, unstable, unsteady

tick off **1.** check off, mark off, put a tick at **2.** *informal* bawl out (*informal*), berate, carpet (*informal*), censure, chew out (*U.S. & Canad. informal*), chide, give a rocket (*Brit. & N.Z. informal*), haul over the coals (*informal*), lecture, read the riot act, rebuke, reprimand, reproach, reprove, scold, take to task, tear into (*informal*), tear (someone) off a strip (*Brit. informal*), tell off (*informal*), upbraid

tide **1.** course, current, ebb, flow, stream, tideway, undertow **2.** course, current, direction, drift, movement, tendency, trend

tide over aid, assist, bridge the gap, help, keep one going, keep one's head above water, keep the wolf from the door, see one through

tidings advice, bulletin, communication, gen (*Brit. informal*), greetings, information, intelligence, latest (*informal*), message, news, report, word

tidy *adjective* **1.** businesslike, clean, cleanly, in apple-pie order (*informal*), methodical, neat, ordered, orderly, shipshape, spick-and-span, spruce, systematic, trig (*archaic or dialect*), trim, well-groomed, well-kept, well-ordered **2.** *informal* ample, considerable, fair, generous, good, goodly, handsome, healthy, large, largish, respectable, sizable *or* sizeable, substantial *~verb* **3.** clean, groom, neaten, order, put in order, put in trim, put to rights, spruce up, straighten

▷ **Antonyms** *~adjective* (*sense 1*) careless, dirty, dishevelled, disordered, disorderly, filthy, in disarray, messy, scruffy, sloppy, slovenly, unbusinesslike, unkempt, unmethodical, unsystematic, untidy (*sense 2*) inconsiderable, insignificant, little, small, tiny *~verb* (*sense 3*) dirty, dishevel, disorder, mess, mess up

tie *verb* **1.** attach, bind, connect, fasten, interlace, join, knot, lash, link, make fast, moor, rope, secure, tether, truss, unite **2.** bind, confine, hamper, hinder, hold, limit, restrain, restrict **3.** be even, be neck and neck, draw, equal, match *~noun* **4.** band, bond, connection, cord, fastening, fetter, joint, knot, ligature, link, rope, string **5.** affiliation, affinity, allegiance, bond, commitment, connection, duty, kinship, liaison, obligation, relationship **6.** encumbrance, hindrance, limitation, restraint, restriction **7.** dead heat, deadlock, draw, stalemate **8.** *Brit.*

contest, fixture, game, match
▷ **Antonyms** *~verb* (*senses 1 & 2*) free, loose, release, separate, undo, unfasten, unhitch, unknot, untie

tie-in association, connection, coordination, hook-up, liaison, link, relation, relationship, tie-up

tie in be relevant, come in, connect, coordinate, fit in, have bearing, link, relate

tier bank, echelon, file, layer, level, line, order, rank, row, series, storey, stratum

tie-up association, connection, coordination, hook-up, liaison, link, linkup, relation, relationship, tie-in

tie up **1**. attach, bind, pinion, restrain, tether, truss **2**. lash, make fast, moor, rope, secure **3**. engage, engross, keep busy, occupy **4**. bring to a close, conclude, end, finish off, settle, terminate, wind up, wrap up (*informal*)

tiff **1**. difference, disagreement, dispute, falling-out (*informal*), petty quarrel, quarrel, row, scrap (*informal*), squabble, words **2**. bad mood, fit of ill humour, fit of pique, huff, ill humour, pet, sulk, tantrum, temper, wax (*informal, chiefly Brit.*)

tight **1**. close, close-fitting, compact, constricted, cramped, fast, firm, fixed, narrow, rigid, secure, snug, stiff, stretched, taut, tense **2**. hermetic, impervious, proof, sealed, sound, watertight **3**. harsh, inflexible, rigid, rigorous, severe, stern, strict, stringent, tough, uncompromising, unyielding **4**. close, grasping, mean, miserly, niggardly, parsimonious, penurious, sparing, stingy, tight-arse (*taboo slang*), tight-arsed (*taboo slang*), tight as a duck's arse (*taboo slang*), tight-ass (*U.S. taboo slang*), tight-assed (*U.S. taboo slang*), tightfisted **5**. dangerous, difficult, hazardous, perilous, precarious, problematic, sticky (*informal*), ticklish, tough, tricky, troublesome, worrisome **6**. close, even, evenly-balanced, near, well-matched **7**. *informal* bevvied (*dialect*), blitzed (*slang*), blotto (*slang*), bombed (*slang*), Brahms and Liszt (*slang*), drunk, flying (*slang*), half cut (*Brit. slang*), half seas over (*Brit. informal*), inebriated, in one's cups, intoxicated, legless (*informal*), lit up (*slang*), out of it (*slang*), out to it (*Austral. & N.Z. slang*), paralytic (*informal*), pickled (*informal*), pie-eyed (*slang*), pissed (*taboo slang*), plastered (*slang*), rat-arsed (*taboo slang*), smashed (*slang*), sozzled (*informal*), steamboats (*Scot. slang*), steaming (*slang*), stewed (*slang*), stoned (*slang*), three sheets in the wind (*slang*), tiddly (*slang, chiefly Brit.*), tipsy, under the influence (*informal*), wasted (*slang*), wrecked (*slang*), zonked (*slang*)
▷ **Antonyms** (*sense 1*) lax, loose, relaxed, slack, spacious (*sense 2*) loose, open, porous (*sense 3*) easy, easy-going, generous, lax, lenient, liberal, relaxed, soft, undemanding (*sense 4*) abundant, extravagant, generous, lavish, munificent, open, prodigal, profuse, spendthrift (*sense 5*) easy (*sense 6*) easy, landslide, overwhelming, runaway, uneven (*sense 7*) sober

tighten close, constrict, cramp, fasten, fix, narrow, rigidify, screw, secure, squeeze, stiffen, stretch, tauten, tense
▷ **Antonyms** ease off, let out, loosen, relax, slacken, unbind, weaken

tightfisted close, close-fisted, grasping, mean, mingy (*Brit. informal*), miserly, niggardly, parsimonious, penurious, snoep (*S. African informal*), sparing, stingy, tight, tight-arse (*taboo slang*), tight-arsed (*taboo slang*), tight as a duck's arse (*taboo slang*), tight-ass (*U.S. taboo slang*), tight-assed (*U.S. taboo slang*)

tight-lipped close-lipped, close-mouthed, mum, mute, quiet, reserved, reticent, secretive, silent, taciturn, uncommunicative, unforthcoming

till[1] *verb* cultivate, dig, plough, turn over, work

till[2] *noun* cash box, cash drawer, cash register

tilt *verb* **1**. cant, heel, incline, lean, list, slant, slope, tip **2**. attack, break a lance, clash, contend, cross swords, duel, encounter, fight, joust, lock horns, overthrow, spar *~noun* **3**. angle, cant, inclination, incline, list, pitch, slant, slope **4**. *Medieval history* clash, combat, duel, encounter, fight, joust, lists, set-to (*informal*), tournament, tourney **5**. **(at) full tilt** for dear life, full force, full speed, headlong, like a bat out of hell (*slang*), like the clappers (*Brit. informal*)

timber beams, boards, forest, logs, planks, trees, wood

timbre colour, quality of sound, resonance, ring, tonality, tone, tone colour

time *noun* **1**. age, chronology, date, duration, epoch, era, generation, hour, interval, period, season, space, span, spell, stretch, term, while **2**. instance, juncture, occasion, point, stage **3**. allotted span, day, duration, life, life span, lifetime, season **4**. heyday, hour, peak **5**. *Music* beat, measure, metre, rhythm, tempo **6**. **all the time** always, at all times, constantly, continually, continuously, ever, for the duration, perpetually, throughout **7**. **at one time: a.** for a while, formerly, hitherto, once, once upon a time, previously **b.** all at once, at the same time, simultaneously, together **8**. **at times** every now and then, every so often, from time to time, now and then, occasionally, once in a while, on occasion, sometimes **9**. **behind the times** antiquated, dated, obsolete, old-fashioned, old hat, outdated, outmoded, out of date, out of fashion, out of style, passé, square (*informal*) **10. for the time being** for now, for the moment, for the nonce, for the present, in the meantime, meantime, meanwhile, pro tem, temporarily **11. from time to time** at times, every now and then, every so often, now and then, occasionally, once in a while, on occasion, sometimes **12. in good time: a.** early, on time, with time to spare **b.** quickly, rapidly, speedily, swiftly, with dispatch **13. in no time** apace, before one knows it, before you can say Jack Robinson, in a flash, in a jiffy (*informal*), in a moment, in an instant, in a trice, in two shakes of a lamb's tail (*informal*), quickly, rapidly, speedily, swiftly **14. in time: a.** at the appointed time, early, in good time, on schedule, on time, with time to spare **b.** by and by, eventually, in the fullness of time, one day, someday, sooner or later, ultimately **15. on time** in good time, on the dot, punctually **16. time and again** frequently, many times, often, on many occasions, over and over again, repeatedly, time after time *~verb* **17.** clock, control, count, judge, measure, regulate, schedule, set

time-honoured age-old, ancient, conventional, customary, established, fixed, long-established, old, traditional, usual, venerable

timeless abiding, ageless, ceaseless, changeless, deathless, endless, enduring, eternal, everlasting, immortal, immutable, imperishable, indestructible, lasting, permanent, persistent, undying
▷ **Antonyms** ephemeral, evanescent, momentary, mortal, passing, temporal, temporary, transitory

timely appropriate, at the right time, convenient, judicious, opportune, prompt, propitious, punctual, seasonable, suitable, well-timed
▷ **Antonyms** ill-timed, inconvenient, inopportune, late, tardy, unseasonable, untimely

timeserver hypocrite, opportunist, self-seeker, trimmer, Vicar of Bray, weathercock

timetable agenda, calendar, curriculum, diary, list, order of the day, programme, schedule

timeworn 1. aged, ancient, broken-down, decrepit, dog-eared, lined, ragged, run-down, shabby, the worse for wear, weathered, worn, wrinkled **2.** ancient, clichéd, dated, hackneyed, hoary, old hat, out of date, outworn, passé, stale, stock, threadbare, tired, trite, well-worn

timid afraid, apprehensive, bashful, cowardly, coy, diffident, faint-hearted, fearful, irresolute, modest, mousy, nervous, pusillanimous, retiring, shrinking, shy, timorous
▷ **Antonyms** aggressive, arrogant, ballsy (*taboo slang*), bold, brave, confident, daring, fearless, fierce, forceful, forward, presumptuous, self-assured, self-confident, shameless, unabashed

timorous afraid, apprehensive, bashful, cowardly, coy, diffident, faint-hearted, fearful, frightened, irresolute, mousy, nervous, pusillanimous, retiring, shrinking, shy, timid, trembling
▷ **Antonyms** assertive, assured, audacious, bold, confident, courageous, daring, fearless

tincture 1. *noun* aroma, colour, dash, flavour, hint, hue, seasoning, shade, smack, *soupçon,* stain, suggestion, tinge, tint, touch, trace **2.** *~verb* colour, dye, flavour, scent, season, stain, tinge, tint

tinge *noun* **1.** cast, colour, dye, shade, stain, tincture, tint, wash **2.** bit, dash, drop, pinch, smack, smattering, *soupçon,* sprinkling, suggestion, touch, trace *~verb* **3.** colour, dye, imbue, shade, stain, suffuse, tinge, tint

tingle 1. *verb* have goose pimples, itch, prickle, sting, tickle **2.** *~noun* goose pimples, itch, itching, pins and needles (*informal*), prickling, quiver, shiver, stinging, thrill, tickle, tickling

tinker *verb* dabble, fiddle (*informal*), meddle, mess about, monkey, muck about (*Brit. slang*), play, potter, toy

tinsel *adjective* brummagem, cheap, flashy, gaudy, gimcrack, meretricious, ostentatious, pinchbeck, plastic (*slang*), sham, showy, specious, superficial, tawdry, trashy

tint *noun* **1.** cast, colour, hue, shade, tone **2.** dye, rinse, stain, tincture, tinge, wash **3.** hint, shade, suggestion, tinge, touch, trace *~verb* **4.** colour, dye, rinse, stain, tincture, tinge **5.** affect, colour, influence, taint, tinge

tiny diminutive, dwarfish, infinitesimal, insignificant, Lilliputian, little, microscopic, mini, miniature, minute, negligible, petite, pint-sized (*informal*), puny, pygmy *or* pigmy, slight, small, teensy-weensy, teeny-weeny, trifling, wee
▷ **Antonyms** colossal, enormous, extra-large, gargantuan, giant, gigantic, great, huge, immense, mammoth, massive, monstrous, titanic, vast

tip[1] **1.** *noun* apex, cap, crown, end, extremity, head, peak, pinnacle, point, summit, top **2.** *~verb* cap, crown, finish, surmount, top

tip[2] *verb* **1.** cant, capsize, incline, lean, list, overturn, slant, spill, tilt, topple over, upend, upset **2.** *Brit.* ditch (*slang*), dump, empty, pour out, unload *~noun* **3.** *Brit.* dump, midden (*dialect*), refuse heap, rubbish heap

tip[3] *noun* **1.** baksheesh, gift, gratuity, perquisite, *pourboire* **2.** *also* **tip-off** clue, forecast, gen (*Brit. informal*), hint, information, inside information, pointer, suggestion, warning, word, word of advice *~verb* **3.** remunerate, reward **4.** *also* **tip off** advise, caution, forewarn, give a clue, give a hint, suggest, tip (someone) the wink (*Brit. informal*), warn

tipple 1. *verb* bend the elbow (*informal*), bevvy (*dialect*), drink, imbibe, indulge (*informal*), quaff, swig, take a drink, tope **2.** *~noun* alcohol, booze (*informal*), drink, John Barleycorn, liquor, poison (*informal*)

tippler bibber, boozer (*informal*), drinker, drunk, drunkard, inebriate, soak (*slang*), sot, sponge (*informal*), toper

tipsy babalas (*S. African*), elevated (*informal*), fuddled, happy (*informal*), mellow, merry (*Brit. informal*), slightly drunk, tiddly (*slang, chiefly Brit.*), woozy (*informal*)

tirade abuse, denunciation, diatribe, fulmination, harangue, invective, lecture, outburst, philippic

tire 1. drain, droop, enervate, exhaust, fag (*informal*), fail, fatigue, flag, jade, knacker (*slang*), sink, take it out of (*informal*), wear down, wear out, weary, whack (*Brit. informal*) **2.** aggravate (*informal*), annoy, bore, exasperate, get on one's nerves (*informal*), harass, hassle (*informal*), irk, irritate, piss one off (*taboo slang*), weary

▷ **Antonyms** (*sense 1*) energize, enliven, exhilarate, invigorate, liven up, pep up, refresh, restore, revive

tired 1. all in (*slang*), asleep *or* dead on one's feet (*informal*), clapped out (*Austral. & N.Z. informal*), dead beat (*informal*), dog-tired (*informal*), done in (*informal*), drained, drooping, drowsy, enervated, exhausted, fagged (*informal*), fatigued, flagging, jaded, knackered (*slang*), ready to drop, sleepy, spent, weary, whacked (*Brit. informal*), worn out, zonked (*slang*) **2.** (*with* **of**) annoyed with, bored with, exasperated by, fed up with, irked by, irritated by, pissed off with (*taboo slang*), sick of, weary of **3.** clichéd, conventional, corny (*slang*), familiar, hackneyed, old, outworn, stale, stock, threadbare, trite, well-worn

▷ **Antonyms** (*sense 1*) alive and kicking, energetic, fresh, full of beans (*informal*), lively, refreshed, rested, wide-awake (*sense 2*) enthusiastic about, fond of, keen on (*sense 3*) innovative, original

tireless determined, energetic, indefatigable, industrious, resolute, unflagging, untiring, unwearied, vigorous

▷ **Antonyms** drained, exhausted, fatigued, flagging, tired, weak, weary, worn out

tiresome annoying, boring, dull, exasperating, flat, irksome, irritating, laborious, monotonous, tedious, trying, uninteresting, vexatious, wearing, wearisome

▷ **Antonyms** exhilarating, inspiring, interesting, refreshing, rousing, stimulating

tiring arduous, demanding, enervative, exacting, exhausting, fatiguing, laborious, strenuous, tough, wearing, wearying

tiro *see* TYRO

tissue 1. fabric, gauze, mesh, structure, stuff, texture, web **2.** paper, paper handkerchief, wrapping paper **3.** accumulation, chain, collection, combination, concatenation, conglomeration, fabrication, mass, network, pack, series, web

titan colossus, giant, leviathan, ogre, superman

titanic Brobdingnagian, colossal, elephantine, enormous, giant, gigantic, herculean, huge, humongous *or* humungous (*U.S. slang*), immense, jumbo (*informal*), mammoth, massive, mighty, monstrous, mountainous, prodigious, stellar (*informal*), stupendous, towering, vast

titbit *bonne bouche,* choice item, dainty, delicacy, goody, juicy bit, morsel, scrap, snack, treat

tit for tat an eye for an eye, as good as one gets, a tooth for a tooth, blow for blow, like for like, measure for measure, retaliation

tithe *noun* **1.** assessment, duty, impost, levy, tariff, tax, tenth, toll, tribute *~verb* **2.** assess, charge, levy, rate, tax **3.** give up, pay, pay a tithe on, render, surrender, turn over

titillate arouse, excite, interest, provoke, stimulate, tantalize, tease, thrill, tickle, turn on (*slang*)

titillating arousing, exciting, interesting, lewd, lurid, provocative, sensational, stimulating, suggestive, teasing, thrilling

titivate doll up (*slang*), do up (*informal*), gussy up (*slang, chiefly U.S.*), make up, prank, preen, primp, prink, refurbish, smarten up, tart up (*Brit. slang*), touch up

title *noun* **1.** caption, heading, inscription, label, legend, name, style **2.** appellation, denomination, designation, epithet, handle (*slang*), moniker *or* monicker (*slang*), name, nickname, nom de plume, pseudonym, sobriquet, term **3.** championship, crown, laurels **4.** claim, entitlement, ownership, prerogative, privilege, right *~verb* **5.** call, designate, label, name, style, term

titter chortle (*informal*), chuckle, giggle, laugh, snigger, tee-hee, te-hee

tittle atom, bit, dash, drop, grain, iota, jot, mite, particle, scrap, shred, speck, whit

tittle-tattle 1. *noun* babble, blather, blether, cackle, chatter, chitchat, clishmaclaver (*Scot.*), dirt (*U.S. slang*), gossip, hearsay, idle chat, jaw (*slang*), nat~

ter, prattle, rumour, twaddle, yackety-yak (*slang*), yatter (*informal*) **2.** *~verb* babble, blather, blether, cackle, chat, chatter, chitchat, gossip, jaw (*slang*), natter, prattle, run off at the mouth (*slang*), witter (*informal*), yak (*slang*), yatter (*informal*)

titular honorary, in name only, nominal, puppet, putative, so-called, theoretical, token

▷ **Antonyms** actual, effective, functioning, real, true

toady 1. *noun* apple polisher (*U.S. slang*), ass-kisser (*U.S. & Canad. taboo slang*), bootlicker (*informal*), brown-noser (*taboo slang*), crawler (*slang*), creep (*slang*), fawner, flatterer, flunkey, groveller, hanger-on, jackal, lackey, lickspittle, minion, parasite, spaniel, sycophant, truckler, yes man **2.** *~verb* be obsequious to, bow and scrape, brown-nose (*taboo slang*), butter up, crawl, creep, cringe, curry favour with, fawn on, flatter, grovel, kiss (someone's) ass (*U.S. & Canad. taboo slang*), kiss the feet of, kowtow to, lick (someone's) arse (*taboo slang*), lick (someone's) boots, pander to, suck up to (*informal*)

▷ **Antonyms** *~verb* confront, defy, oppose, rebel, resist, stand against, withstand

toast[1] *verb* brown, grill, heat, roast, warm

toast[2] *noun* **1.** compliment, drink, health, pledge, salutation, salute, tribute **2.** darling, favourite, heroine *~verb* **3.** drink to, drink (to) the health of, pledge, salute

to-do agitation, bother, brouhaha, bustle, commotion, disturbance, excitement, flap (*informal*), furore, fuss, hoo-ha, hue and cry, performance (*informal*), quarrel, ruction (*informal*), rumpus, stir, tumult, turmoil, unrest, upheaval, uproar

together *adverb* **1.** as a group, as one, cheek by jowl, closely, collectively, hand in glove, hand in hand, in a body, in concert, in cooperation, in unison, jointly, mutually, shoulder to shoulder, side by side **2.** all at once, as one, at one fell swoop, at the same time, concurrently, contemporaneously, en masse, in unison, simultaneously, with one accord **3.** consecutively, continuously, in a row, in succession, one after the other, on end, successively, without a break, without interruption **4.** *informal* arranged, fixed, ordered, organized, settled, sorted out, straight, to rights *~adjective* **5.** *slang* calm, composed, cool, stable, well-adjusted, well-balanced, well-organized

▷ **Antonyms** (*sense 1*) alone, apart, independently, individually, one at a time, one by one, separately, singly

toil 1. *noun* application, blood, sweat, and tears (*informal*), donkey-work, drudgery, effort, elbow grease (*informal*), exertion, graft (*informal*), hard work, industry, labour, pains, slog, sweat, travail **2.** *~verb* bend over backwards (*informal*), break one's neck (*informal*), bust a gut (*informal*), do one's damnedest (*informal*), drag oneself, drudge, give it one's all (*informal*), give it one's best shot (*informal*), go for broke (*slang*), go for it (*informal*), graft (*informal*), grind (*informal*), grub, knock oneself out (*informal*), labour, make an all-out effort (*informal*), push oneself, rupture oneself (*informal*), slave, slog, strive, struggle, sweat (*informal*), work, work like a dog, work like a Trojan, work one's fingers to the bone

▷ **Antonyms** *~noun* idleness, inactivity, indolence, inertia, laziness, sloth, torpor

toilet 1. ablutions (*Military informal*), bathroom, bog (*slang*), can (*U.S. & Canad. slang*), closet, convenience, crapper (*taboo slang*), gents (*Brit. informal*), john (*slang, chiefly U.S. & Canad.*), khazi (*slang*), ladies' room, latrine, lavatory, little boy's room (*informal*), little girl's room (*informal*), loo (*Brit. informal*), outhouse, *pissoir*, powder room, privy, throne (*informal*), urinal, washroom, water closet, W.C. **2.** ablutions, bathing, dressing, grooming, toilette

toilsome arduous, backbreaking, difficult, fatiguing, hard, herculean, laborious, painful, severe, strenuous, taxing, tedious, tiresome, tough, wearisome

token *noun* **1.** badge, clue, demonstration, earnest, evidence, expression, index, indication, manifestation, mark, note, proof, representation, sign, symbol, warning **2.** keepsake, memento, memorial, remembrance, reminder, souvenir *~adjective* **3.** hollow, minimal, nominal, perfunctory, superficial, symbolic

tolerable 1. acceptable, allowable, bearable, endurable, sufferable, supportable **2.** acceptable, adequate, all right, average, fair, fairly good, fair to middling, good enough, indifferent, mediocre, middling, not bad (*informal*), O.K. *or* okay (*informal*), ordinary, passable, run-of-the-mill, so-so (*informal*), unexceptional

▷ **Antonyms** (*sense 1*) insufferable, intolerable, unacceptable, unbearable, unendurable (*sense 2*) awful, bad, dreadful, rotten

tolerance 1. broad-mindedness, charity, forbearance, indulgence, lenity, magnanimity, open-mindedness, patience, permissiveness, sufferance, sympathy **2.** endurance, fortitude, hardiness, hardness, resilience, resistance, stamina, staying power, toughness **3.** fluctuation, play, swing, variation

▷ **Antonyms** (*sense 1*) bigotry, discrimination, intolerance, narrow-mindedness, prejudice, sectarianism

tolerant 1. broad-minded, catholic, charitable, fair, forbearing, latitudinarian, liberal, long-suffering, magnanimous, open-minded, patient, sympathetic, unbigoted, understanding, unprejudiced **2.** complaisant, easy-going, easy-oasy (*slang*), free and easy, indulgent, kind-hearted, lax, lenient, permissive, soft
▷ **Antonyms** authoritarian, biased, bigoted, despotic, dictatorial, dogmatic, illiberal, intolerant, narrow-minded, prejudiced, repressive, rigid, sectarian, stern, strict, tyrannical, uncharitable

tolerate abide, accept, admit, allow, bear, brook, condone, countenance, endure, hack (*slang*), indulge, permit, pocket, put up with (*informal*), receive, sanction, stand, stomach, submit to, suffer, swallow, take, thole (*Scot.*), turn a blind eye to, undergo, wink at
▷ **Antonyms** ban, disallow, disapprove, forbid, outlaw, preclude, prohibit, veto

toleration 1. acceptance, allowance, condonation, endurance, indulgence, permissiveness, sanction, sufferance **2.** freedom of conscience, freedom of worship, religious freedom

toll[1] *verb* **1.** chime, clang, knell, peal, ring, sound, strike **2.** announce, call, signal, summon, warn *~noun* **3.** chime, clang, knell, peal, ring, ringing, tolling

toll[2] *noun* **1.** assessment, charge, customs, demand, duty, fee, impost, levy, payment, rate, tariff, tax, tribute **2.** cost, damage, inroad, loss, penalty

tomb burial chamber, catacomb, crypt, grave, mausoleum, sarcophagus, sepulchre, vault

tombstone gravestone, headstone, marker, memorial, monument

tome book, title, volume, work

tomfool 1. *noun* ass, berk (*Brit. slang*), blockhead, charlie (*Brit. informal*), chump (*informal*), clown, dickhead (*slang*), dipstick (*Brit. slang*), divvy (*Brit. slang*), dolt, dork (*slang*), dweeb (*U.S. slang*), fool, fuckwit (*taboo slang*), geek (*slang*), gonzo (*slang*), idiot, nerd *or* nurd (*slang*), nincompoop, ninny, nitwit (*informal*), numbskull *or* numskull, oaf, pillock (*Brit. slang*), plank (*Brit. slang*), plonker (*slang*), prat (*slang*), prick (*slang*), simpleton, twit (*informal, chiefly Brit.*), wally (*slang*) **2.** *~adjective* asinine, crackbrained, crazy, daft (*informal*), foolish, halfwitted, harebrained, idiotic, inane, rash, senseless, silly, stupid

tomfoolery 1. buffoonery, childishness, clowning, fooling around (*informal*), foolishness, horseplay, idiocy, larks (*informal*), messing around (*informal*), shenanigans (*informal*), silliness, skylarking (*informal*), stupidity **2.** balderdash, baloney (*informal*), bilge (*informal*), bosh (*informal*), bunk (*informal*), bunkum *or* buncombe (*chiefly U.S.*), claptrap (*informal*), hogwash, hooey (*slang*), inanity, nonsense, poppycock (*informal*), rot, rubbish, stuff and nonsense, tommyrot, tosh (*slang, chiefly Brit.*), trash, twaddle
▷ **Antonyms** (*sense 1*) demureness, gravity, heaviness, reserve, sedateness, seriousness, sobriety, solemnity, sternness

tone *noun* **1.** accent, emphasis, force, inflection, intonation, modulation, pitch, strength, stress, timbre, tonality, volume **2.** air, approach, aspect, attitude, character, drift, effect, feel, frame, grain, manner, mood, note, quality, spirit, style, temper, tenor, vein **3.** cast, colour, hue, shade, tinge, tint *~verb* **4.** blend, go well with, harmonize, match, suit

tone down dampen, dim, mitigate, moderate, modulate, play down, reduce, restrain, soften, soft-pedal (*informal*), subdue, temper

tone up freshen, get in shape, get into condition, invigorate, limber up, shape up, sharpen up, trim, tune up

tongue 1. argot, dialect, idiom, language, lingo (*informal*), parlance, patois, speech, talk, vernacular **2.** articulation, speech, utterance, verbal expression, voice

tongue-lashing dressing-down (*informal*), lecture, rebuke, reprimand, reproach, reproof, scolding, slating (*informal*), talking-to (*informal*), telling-off (*informal*), ticking-off (*informal*), wigging (*Brit. slang*)

tongue-tied at a loss for words, dumb, dumbstruck, inarticulate, mute, speechless, struck dumb
▷ **Antonyms** articulate, chatty, effusive, garrulous, loquacious, talkative, verbose, voluble, wordy

tonic analeptic, boost, bracer (*informal*), cordial, fillip, livener, pick-me-up (*informal*), refresher, restorative, roborant, shot in the arm (*informal*), stimulant

too 1. also, as well, besides, further, in addition, into the bargain, likewise, moreover, to boot **2.** excessively, exorbitantly, extremely, immoderately, inordinately, over-, overly, unduly, unreasonably, very

tool *noun* **1.** apparatus, appliance, contraption, contrivance, device, gadget, implement, instrument, machine, utensil **2.** agency, agent, intermediary, means, medium, vehicle, wherewithal **3.** cat's-paw, creature, dupe, flunkey, hireling, jackal, lackey, minion, pawn, puppet, stooge (*slang*) *~verb* **4.** chase, cut, decorate, ornament, shape, work

toothsome agreeable, appetizing, dainty, delectable, delicious, luscious, mouthwatering, nice, palatable, savoury, scrumptious (*informal*), sweet, tasty, tempting, yummy (*slang*)

top *noun* **1.** acme, apex, apogee, crest, crown, culmination, head, height, high point, meridian, peak, pinnacle, summit, vertex, zenith **2.** cap, cork, cover, lid, stopper **3.** first place, head, highest rank, lead **4. blow one's top** *informal* blow up (*informal*), do one's nut (*Brit. slang*), explode, fly into a temper, fly off the handle (*informal*), go spare (*Brit. slang*), have a fit (*informal*), lose one's temper, see red (*informal*), throw a tantrum **5. over the top** a bit much (*informal*), excessive, going too far, immoderate, inordinate, over the limit, too much, uncalled-for *~adjective* **6.** best, chief, crack (*informal*), crowning, culminating, dominant, elite, finest, first, foremost, greatest, head, highest, lead, leading, pre-eminent, prime, principal, ruling, sovereign, superior, topmost, upper, uppermost *~verb* **7.** cap, cover, crown, finish, garnish, roof, tip **8.** ascend, climb, crest, reach the top of, scale, surmount **9.** be first, be in charge of, command, head, lead, rule **10.** beat, best, better, eclipse, exceed, excel, go beyond, outdo, outshine, outstrip, surpass, transcend

▷ **Antonyms** *~noun* (*sense 1*) base, bottom, foot, nadir, underneath, underside *~adjective* amateurish, bottom, incompetent, inept, inferior, least, lower, lowest, second-rate, unknown, unranked, worst *~verb* (*sense 10*) fail to equal, fall short of, not be as good as

topic issue, matter, point, question, subject, subject matter, text, theme, thesis

topical 1. contemporary, current, newsworthy, popular, up-to-date, up-to-the-minute **2.** local, parochial, regional, restricted

topmost dominant, foremost, highest, leading, loftiest, paramount, principal, supreme, top, upper, uppermost

▷ **Antonyms** base, basic, bottom, bottommost, last, lowest, undermost

topple 1. capsize, collapse, fall, fall headlong, fall over, keel over, knock down, knock over, overbalance, overturn, tip over, totter, tumble, upset **2.** bring down, bring low, oust, overthrow, overturn, unseat

▷ **Antonyms** (*sense 1*) ascend, build, mount, rise, tower

topsy-turvy chaotic, confused, disarranged, disorderly, disorganized, inside-out, jumbled, messy, mixed-up, untidy, upside-down

▷ **Antonyms** neat, ordered, orderly, organized, shipshape, systematic, tidy

torment *verb* **1.** afflict, agonize, crucify, distress, excruciate, harrow, pain, rack, torture **2.** aggravate (*informal*), annoy, bedevil, bother, chivvy, devil (*informal*), harass, harry, hassle (*informal*), hound, irritate, lead (someone) a merry dance (*Brit. informal*), nag, persecute, pester, plague, provoke, tease, trouble, vex, worry *~noun* **3.** agony, anguish, distress, hell, misery, pain, suffering, torture **4.** affliction, annoyance, bane, bother, harassment, hassle (*informal*), irritation, nag, nagging, nuisance, pain in the neck (*informal*), persecution, pest, plague, provocation, scourge, thorn in one's flesh, trouble, vexation, worry

▷ **Antonyms** *~verb* comfort, delight, ease, encourage, make happy, put at ease, reassure, soothe *~noun* bliss, comfort, ease, ecstasy, encouragement, happiness, joy, reassurance, rest

torn *adjective* **1.** cut, lacerated, ragged, rent, ripped, slit, split **2.** divided, in two minds (*informal*), irresolute, split, uncertain, undecided, unsure, vacillating, wavering

tornado cyclone, gale, hurricane, squall, storm, tempest, twister (*U.S. informal*), typhoon, whirlwind, windstorm

torpid apathetic, benumbed, dormant, drowsy, dull, fainéant, inactive, indolent, inert, lackadaisical, languid, languorous, lazy, lethargic, listless, lymphatic, motionless, numb, passive, slothful, slow, slow-moving, sluggish, somnolent, stagnant

torpor accidie, acedia, apathy, dormancy, drowsiness, dullness, inactivity, inanition, indolence, inertia, inertness, languor, laziness, lethargy, listlessness, numbness, passivity, sloth, sluggishness, somnolence, stagnancy, stupor, torpidity

▷ **Antonyms** animation, energy, get-up-and-go (*informal*), go, liveliness, pep, vigour

torrent cascade, deluge, downpour, effusion, flood, flow, gush, outburst, rush, spate, stream, tide

torrid 1. arid, blistering, boiling, broiling, burning, dried, dry, fiery, flaming, hot, parched, parching, scorched, scorching, sizzling, stifling, sultry, sweltering, tropical **2.** ardent, erotic, fervent, flaming, hot, intense, passionate, sexy (*informal*), steamy (*informal*)

tortuous 1. bent, circuitous, convoluted, crooked, curved, indirect, mazy, meandering, serpentine, sinuous, twisted, twisting, twisty, winding, zigzag **2.** ambiguous, complicated, convoluted, cunning, deceptive, devious, indirect, involved, mazy, misleading, roundabout, tricky

▷ **Antonyms** (*sense 2*) candid, direct, honest, ingenuous, open, reliable, straightforward, upright

torture 1. *verb* afflict, agonize, crucify, distress, excruciate, harrow, lacerate, martyr, pain, persecute, put on the rack, rack, torment **2.** *~noun* affliction, agony, anguish, distress, hell, laceration, martyrdom, misery, pain, pang(s), persecution, rack, suffering, torment

▷ **Antonyms** *~verb* alleviate, comfort,

console, ease, mollify, relieve, salve, solace, soothe ~*noun* amusement, bliss, delight, enjoyment, happiness, joy, pleasure, well-being

toss *verb* **1.** cast, chuck (*informal*), fling, flip, hurl, launch, lob (*informal*), pitch, project, propel, shy, sling, throw **2.** agitate, disturb, jiggle, joggle, jolt, rock, roll, shake, thrash, tumble, wriggle, writhe **3.** heave, labour, lurch, pitch, roll, wallow ~*noun* **4.** cast, fling, lob (*informal*), pitch, shy, throw

tot[1] *noun* **1.** ankle-biter (*Austral. slang*), baby, child, infant, little one, mite, rug rat (*slang*), sprog (*slang*), toddler, wean (*Scot.*) **2.** dram, finger, measure, nip, shot (*informal*), slug, snifter (*informal*), toothful

tot[2] *verb* add up, calculate, count up, reckon, sum (up), tally, total

total 1. *noun* aggregate, all, amount, entirety, full amount, mass, sum, totality, whole **2.** ~*adjective* absolute, all-out, arrant, complete, comprehensive, consummate, deep-dyed (*usually derogatory*), downright, entire, full, gross, integral, out-and-out, outright, perfect, sheer, sweeping, thorough, thoroughgoing, unconditional, undisputed, undivided, unmitigated, unqualified, utter, whole **3.** ~*verb* add up, amount to, come to, mount up to, reach, reckon, sum up, tot up

▷ **Antonyms** ~*noun* individual amount, part, subtotal ~*adjective* conditional, fragmentary, incomplete, limited, mixed, part, partial, qualified, restricted, uncombined ~*verb* deduct, subtract

totalitarian authoritarian, despotic, dictatorial, monolithic, one-party, oppressive, tyrannous, undemocratic

▷ **Antonyms** autonomous, democratic, egalitarian, popular, self-governing

totality 1. aggregate, all, entirety, everything, sum, total, whole **2.** completeness, entireness, fullness, wholeness

totally absolutely, completely, comprehensively, consummately, entirely, fully, one hundred per cent, perfectly, quite, thoroughly, to the hilt, unconditionally, unmitigatedly, utterly, wholeheartedly, wholly

▷ **Antonyms** incompletely, in part, partially, partly, somewhat, to a certain extent

totter falter, lurch, quiver, reel, rock, shake, stagger, stumble, sway, teeter, tremble, walk unsteadily, waver

touch *noun* **1.** feel, feeling, handling, palpation, physical contact, tactility **2.** blow, brush, caress, contact, fondling, hit, pat, push, stroke, tap **3.** bit, dash, detail, drop, hint, intimation, jot, pinch, smack, small amount, smattering, *soupçon,* speck, spot, suggestion, suspicion, taste, tincture, tinge, trace, whiff **4.** direction, effect, hand, influence **5.** approach, characteristic, handiwork, manner, method, style, technique, trademark, way **6.** ability, adroitness, art, artistry, command, craft, deftness, facility, flair, knack, mastery, skill, virtuosity **7.** acquaintance, awareness, communication, contact, correspondence, familiarity, understanding ~*verb* **8.** brush, caress, contact, feel, finger, fondle, graze, handle, hit, lay a finger on, palpate, pat, push, strike, stroke, tap **9.** abut, adjoin, be in contact, border, brush, come together, contact, converge, graze, impinge upon, meet **10.** affect, disturb, get through to, get to (*informal*), have an effect on, impress, influence, inspire, make an impression on, mark, melt, move, soften, stir, strike, tug at (someone's) heartstrings (*often facetious*), upset **11.** be a party to, concern oneself with, consume, deal with, drink, eat, get involved in, handle, have to do with, partake of, use, utilize **12.** (*with* **on**) allude to, bring in, cover, deal with, mention, refer to, speak of **13.** bear upon, concern, have to do with, interest, pertain to, regard **14.** be a match for, be in the same league as, be on a par with, come near, come up to, compare with, equal, hold a candle to (*informal*), match, parallel, rival **15.** arrive at, attain, come to, reach

touch-and-go close, critical, dangerous, hairy (*slang*), hazardous, near, nerve-racking, parlous, perilous, precarious, risky, sticky (*informal*), tricky

touched 1. affected, disturbed, impressed, melted, moved, softened, stirred, swayed, upset **2.** barmy (*slang*), batty (*slang*), bonkers (*slang, chiefly Brit.*), crackpot (*informal*), crazy, cuckoo (*informal*), daft (*informal*), doolally (*slang*), gonzo (*slang*), loopy (*informal*), not all there, not right in the head, nuts (*slang*), nutty (*slang*), nutty as a fruitcake (*slang*), off one's rocker (*slang*), off one's trolley (*slang*), out to lunch (*informal*), soft in the head (*informal*), up the pole (*informal*), wacko *or* whacko (*informal*)

touchiness bad temper, crabbedness, fretfulness, grouchiness (*informal*), irascibility, irritability, peevishness, pettishness, petulance, surliness, testiness, tetchiness, ticklishness

touching affecting, emotive, heartbreaking, melting, moving, pathetic, piteous, pitiable, pitiful, poignant, sad, stirring, tender

touch off 1. fire, ignite, light, put a match to, set off **2.** arouse, begin, cause, foment, give rise to, initiate, provoke, set in motion, spark off, trigger (off)

touchstone criterion, gauge, measure, norm, par, standard, yardstick

touch up 1. finish off, perfect, put the finishing touches to, round off **2.** brush up, enhance, fake (up), falsify, give a face-lift to, gloss over, improve, patch up, polish up, renovate, retouch, revamp, titivate, whitewash (*informal*)

touchy bad-tempered, captious, crabbed, cross, easily offended, grouchy (*informal*), grumpy, irascible, irritable, oversensitive, peevish, pettish, petulant, querulous, quick-tempered, ratty (*Brit. & N.Z. informal*), splenetic, surly, testy, tetchy, thin-skinned, ticklish
▷ **Antonyms** affable, cheerful, easy-going, genial, good-humoured, imperious, indifferent, insensitive, light-hearted, pleasant, sunny, sweet, thick-skinned, unconcerned

tough *adjective* **1.** cohesive, durable, firm, hard, inflexible, leathery, resilient, resistant, rigid, rugged, solid, stiff, strong, sturdy, tenacious **2.** brawny, fit, hard as nails, hardened, hardy, resilient, seasoned, stalwart, stout, strapping, strong, sturdy, vigorous **3.** hard-bitten, pugnacious, rough, ruffianly, ruthless, vicious, violent **4.** adamant, callous, exacting, firm, hard, hard-boiled (*informal*), hard-nosed (*informal*), inflexible, intractable, merciless, obdurate, obstinate, refractory, resolute, severe, stern, strict, stubborn, unbending, unforgiving, unyielding **5.** arduous, baffling, difficult, exacting, exhausting, hard, intractable, irksome, knotty, laborious, perplexing, puzzling, strenuous, thorny, troublesome, uphill **6.** *informal* bad, hard cheese (*Brit. slang*), hard lines (*Brit. informal*), hard luck, lamentable, regrettable, too bad (*informal*), unfortunate, unlucky *~noun* **7.** bravo, bruiser (*informal*), brute, bully, bully boy, heavy (*slang*), hooligan, rough (*informal*), roughneck (*slang*), rowdy, ruffian, thug, tsotsi (*S. African*)
▷ **Antonyms** (*sense 1*) delicate, flexible, flimsy, fragile, soft, tender, weak (*sense 2*) delicate, soft, weak (*sense 3*) civilized, gentle, humane, soft, tender (*sense 4*) accommodating, benign, compassionate, considerate, easy, flexible, gentle, humane, indulgent, kind, lenient, merciful, mild, soft, sympathetic, tender, unexacting (*sense 5*) easy, easy-peasy (*slang*), unexacting

tour *noun* **1.** excursion, expedition, jaunt, journey, outing, peregrination, progress, trip **2.** circuit, course, round *~verb* **3.** explore, go on the road, go round, holiday in, journey, sightsee, travel round, travel through, visit

tourist excursionist, globetrotter, holiday-maker, journeyer, sightseer, traveller, tripper, voyager

tournament **1.** competition, contest, event, match, meeting, series **2.** *Medieval* joust, the lists, tourney

tousle disarrange, disarray, dishevel, disorder, mess up, ruffle, rumple, tangle

tow *verb* drag, draw, haul, lug, pull, trail, trawl, tug

towards **1.** en route for, for, in the direction of, in the vicinity of, on the road to, on the way to, to **2.** about, concerning, for, regarding, with regard to, with respect to **3.** almost, close to, coming up to, getting on for, just before, nearing, nearly, not quite, shortly before

tower *noun* **1.** belfry, column, obelisk, pillar, skyscraper, steeple, turret **2.** castle, citadel, fort, fortification, fortress, keep, refuge, stronghold *~verb* **3.** ascend, be head and shoulders above, dominate, exceed, loom, mount, overlook, overtop, rear, rise, soar, surpass, top, transcend

towering **1.** colossal, elevated, extraordinary, gigantic, great, high, imposing, impressive, lofty, magnificent, outstanding, paramount, prodigious, soaring, stellar (*informal*), striking, sublime, superior, supreme, surpassing, tall, transcendent **2.** burning, excessive, extreme, fiery, immoderate, inordinate, intemperate, intense, mighty, passionate, vehement, violent

toxic baneful (*archaic*), deadly, harmful, lethal, noxious, pernicious, pestilential, poisonous, septic
▷ **Antonyms** harmless, invigorating, non-poisonous, nontoxic, safe, salubrious

toy *noun* **1.** doll, game, plaything **2.** bauble, gewgaw, knick-knack, trifle, trinket *~verb* **3.** amuse oneself, dally, fiddle (*informal*), flirt, fool (about *or* around), play, play fast and loose (*informal*), sport, trifle, wanton

trace *noun* **1.** evidence, indication, mark, record, relic, remains, remnant, sign, survival, token, vestige **2.** bit, dash, drop, hint, iota, jot, shadow, *soupçon*, suggestion, suspicion, tincture, tinge, touch, trifle, whiff **3.** footmark, footprint, footstep, path, slot, spoor, track, trail *~verb* **4.** ascertain, detect, determine, discover, ferret out, find, follow, hunt down, pursue, search for, seek, shadow, stalk, track, trail, unearth **5.** chart, copy, delineate, depict, draw, map, mark out, outline, record, show, sketch

track *noun* **1.** footmark, footprint, footstep, mark, path, scent, slipstream, slot, spoor, trace, trail, wake **2.** course, flight path, line, orbit, path, pathway, road, track, trajectory, way **3.** line, permanent way, rail, rails **4. keep track of** follow, keep an eye on, keep in sight, keep in touch with, keep up to date with, keep up with, monitor, oversee, watch **5. lose track of** lose, lose sight of, misplace *~verb* **6.** chase, dog, follow, follow the trail of, hunt down, pursue, shadow, stalk, tail (*informal*), trace, trail

track down apprehend, bring to light, capture, catch, dig up, discover, expose, ferret out, find, hunt down, run to earth *or* ground, sniff out, trace, unearth

trackless empty, pathless, solitary, un~charted, unexplored, unfrequented, un~trodden, unused, virgin

tracks 1. footprints, impressions, im~prints, trail, tyremarks, tyreprints, wheelmarks 2. **make tracks** beat it (*slang*), depart, disappear, get going, get moving, go, head off, hit the road (*slang*), leave, pack one's bags (*infor~mal*), set out, split (*slang*), take off (*in~formal*) 3. **stop in one's tracks** bring to a standstill, freeze, immobilize, petrify, rivet to the spot, stop dead, transfix

tract[1] *noun* area, district, estate, ex~panse, extent, lot, plot, quarter, region, stretch, territory, zone

tract[2] *noun* booklet, brochure, disquisi~tion, dissertation, essay, homily, leaflet, monograph, pamphlet, tractate, treatise

tractable 1. amenable, biddable, compli~ant, controllable, docile, governable, manageable, obedient, persuadable, submissive, tame, willing, yielding 2. ductile, fictile, malleable, plastic, pli~able, pliant, tensile, tractile, workable

▷ **Antonyms** (*sense 1*) defiant, head~strong, obstinate, refractory, stiff-necked, stubborn, unruly, wilful

traction adhesion, drag, draught, draw~ing, friction, grip, haulage, pull, pulling, purchase, resistance

trade *noun* 1. barter, business, buying and selling, commerce, dealing, ex~change, traffic, transactions, truck 2. avocation, business, calling, craft, em~ployment, job, line, line of work, métier, occupation, profession, pursuit, skill 3. deal, exchange, interchange, swap 4. clientele, custom, customers, market, patrons, public *~verb* 5. bargain, barter, buy and sell, deal, do business, ex~change, have dealings, peddle, traffic, transact, truck 6. barter, exchange, swap, switch

trader broker, buyer, dealer, marketer, merchandiser, merchant, purveyor, seller, supplier

tradesman 1. dealer, merchant, purveyor, retailer, seller, shopkeeper, supplier, vendor 2. artisan, craftsman, journey~man, skilled worker, workman

tradition convention, custom, customs, established practice, folklore, habit, in~stitution, lore, praxis, ritual, unwritten law, usage

traditional accustomed, ancestral, con~ventional, customary, established, fixed, folk, historic, long-established, old, oral, time-honoured, transmitted, unwritten, usual

▷ **Antonyms** avant-garde, contemporary, ground-breaking, innovative, modern, new, novel, off-the-wall (*slang*), original, revolutionary, unconventional, unusual

traduce abuse, asperse, bad-mouth (*slang, chiefly U.S. & Canad.*), blacken, calumniate, decry, defame, denigrate, deprecate, depreciate, detract, dispar~age, drag through the mud, dump on (*slang, chiefly U.S.*), knock (*informal*), malign, misrepresent, revile, rubbish (*informal*), run down, slag (off) (*slang*), slander, smear, speak ill of, vilify

traducer abuser, asperser, calumniator, defamer, denigrator, deprecator, de~tractor, disparager, slanderer, smearer, vilifier

traffic *noun* 1. coming and going, freight, movement, passengers, transport, transportation, vehicles 2. barter, busi~ness, buying and selling, commerce, communication, dealing, dealings, do~ings, exchange, intercourse, peddling, relations, trade, truck *~verb* 3. bargain, barter, buy and sell, deal, do business, exchange, have dealings, have transac~tions, market, peddle, trade, truck

tragedy adversity, affliction, bummer (*slang*), calamity, catastrophe, disaster, grievous blow, misfortune, whammy (*informal, chiefly U.S.*)

▷ **Antonyms** fortune, happiness, joy, prosperity, success

tragic anguished, appalling, awful, ca~lamitous, catastrophic, deadly, dire, disastrous, dismal, doleful, dreadful, fa~tal, grievous, heartbreaking, heart-rending, ill-fated, ill-starred, lamen~table, miserable, mournful, pathetic, pitiable, ruinous, sad, shocking, sorrow~ful, unfortunate, woeful, wretched

▷ **Antonyms** agreeable, beneficial, cheerful, comic, fortunate, glorious, happy, joyful, lucky, satisfying, worth~while

trail *verb* 1. dangle, drag, draw, hang down, haul, pull, stream, tow 2. chase, follow, hunt, pursue, shadow, stalk, tail (*informal*), trace, track 3. bring up the rear, dawdle, drag oneself, fall behind, follow, hang back, lag, linger, loiter, straggle, traipse (*informal*) 4. dangle, droop, extend, hang, straggle *~noun* 5. footprints, footsteps, mark, marks, path, scent, slipstream, spoor, trace, track, wake 6. beaten track, footpath, path, road, route, track, way 7. appendage, stream, tail, train

trail away *or* **off** decrease, die away, di~minish, dwindle, fade away *or* out, fall away, grow faint, grow weak, lessen, peter out, shrink, sink, subside, tail off, taper off, weaken

train *verb* 1. coach, discipline, drill, edu~cate, guide, improve, instruct, prepare, rear, rehearse, school, teach, tutor 2. exercise, improve, prepare, work out 3. aim, bring to bear, direct, focus, level, line up, point *~noun* 4. chain, concat~enation, course, order, progression, se~quence, series, set, string, succession 5.

caravan, column, convoy, file, procession **6.** appendage, tail, trail **7.** attendants, cortege, court, entourage, followers, following, household, retinue, staff, suite

trainer coach, handler

training 1. coaching, discipline, education, grounding, guidance, instruction, schooling, teaching, tuition, tutelage, upbringing **2.** body building, exercise, practice, preparation, working-out

traipse 1. *verb* drag oneself, footslog, slouch, trail, tramp, trudge **2.** *~noun* long walk, slog, tramp, trek, trudge

trait attribute, characteristic, feature, idiosyncrasy, lineament, mannerism, peculiarity, quality, quirk

traitor apostate, back-stabber, betrayer, deceiver, defector, deserter, double-crosser (*informal*), fifth columnist, informer, Judas, miscreant, quisling, rebel, renegade, snake in the grass (*informal*), turncoat

▷ **Antonyms** defender, loyalist, patriot, supporter

traitorous apostate, disloyal, double-crossing (*informal*), double-dealing, faithless, false, perfidious, renegade, seditious, treacherous, treasonable, unfaithful, untrue

▷ **Antonyms** constant, faithful, loyal, patriotic, staunch, steadfast, true, trusty

trajectory course, flight, flight path, line, path, route, track

trammel 1. *noun* bar, block, bond, chain, check, clog, curb, fetter, handicap, hazard, hindrance, impediment, obstacle, rein, shackle, stumbling block **2.** *~verb* bar, block, capture, catch, check, clog, curb, enmesh, ensnare, entrap, fetter, hamper, handicap, hinder, impede, net, restrain, restrict, snag, tie

▷ **Antonyms** *~verb* advance, assist, expedite, facilitate, foster, further, promote, support

tramp *verb* **1.** footslog, hike, march, ramble, range, roam, rove, slog, trek, walk, yomp **2.** march, plod, stamp, stump, toil, traipse (*informal*), trudge, walk heavily **3.** crush, stamp, stomp (*informal*), trample, tread, walk over *~noun* **4.** bag lady (*chiefly U.S.*), bum (*informal*), derelict, dosser (*Brit. slang*), down-and-out, drifter, hobo (*chiefly U.S.*), vagabond, vagrant **5.** hike, march, ramble, slog, trek **6.** footfall, footstep, stamp, tread

trample 1. crush, flatten, run over, squash, stamp, tread, walk over **2.** do violence to, encroach upon, hurt, infringe, ride roughshod over, show no consideration for, violate

trance abstraction, daze, dream, ecstasy, hypnotic state, muse, rapture, reverie, spell, stupor, unconsciousness

tranquil at peace, calm, composed, cool, pacific, peaceful, placid, quiet, restful, sedate, serene, still, undisturbed, unexcited, unperturbed, unruffled, untroubled

▷ **Antonyms** agitated, busy, confused, disturbed, excited, hectic, restless, troubled

tranquillity ataraxia, calm, calmness, composure, coolness, equanimity, hush, imperturbability, peace, peacefulness, placidity, quiet, quietness, quietude, repose, rest, restfulness, sedateness, serenity, stillness

▷ **Antonyms** agitation, commotion, confusion, disturbance, excitement, noise, restlessness, turmoil, upset

tranquillize calm, compose, lull, pacify, quell, quiet, relax, sedate, settle one's nerves, soothe

▷ **Antonyms** agitate, confuse, distress, disturb, harass, perturb, ruffle, trouble, upset

tranquillizer barbiturate, bromide, downer (*slang*), opiate, red (*slang*), sedative

transact accomplish, carry on, carry out, conclude, conduct, discharge, do, enact, execute, handle, manage, negotiate, perform, prosecute, see to, settle, take care of

transaction 1. action, affair, bargain, business, coup, deal, deed, enterprise, event, matter, negotiation, occurrence, proceeding, undertaking **2.** *plural* affairs, annals, doings, goings-on (*informal*), minutes, proceedings, record

transcend eclipse, exceed, excel, go above, go beyond, leave behind, leave in the shade (*informal*), outdo, outrival, outshine, outstrip, outvie, overstep, rise above, surpass

transcendence, transcendency ascendancy, excellence, greatness, incomparability, matchlessness, paramountcy, pre-eminence, sublimity, superiority, supremacy

transcendent consummate, exceeding, extraordinary, incomparable, matchless, peerless, pre-eminent, second to none, sublime, superior, transcendental, unequalled, unique, unparalleled, unrivalled

transcribe 1. copy out, engross, note, reproduce, rewrite, set out, take down, transfer, write out **2.** interpret, render, translate, transliterate **3.** record, tape, tape-record

transcript carbon, carbon copy, copy, duplicate, manuscript, note, notes, record, reproduction, transcription, translation, transliteration, version

transfer 1. *verb* carry, change, consign, convey, displace, hand over, make over, move, pass on, relocate, remove, shift, translate, transmit, transplant, transport, transpose, turn over **2.** *~noun* change, displacement, handover, move, relocation, removal, shift, transference, translation, transmission, transposition

transfigure alter, apotheosize, change, convert, exalt, glorify, idealize, metamorphose, transform, transmute

transfix 1. engross, fascinate, halt *or* stop in one's tracks, hold, hypnotize, mesmerize, paralyse, petrify, rivet the attention of, root to the spot, spellbind, stop dead, stun **2.** fix, impale, pierce, puncture, run through, skewer, spear, spit, transpierce

▷ **Antonyms** (*sense 1*) bore, fatigue, tire, weary

transform alter, change, convert, make over, metamorphose, reconstruct, remodel, renew, revolutionize, transfigure, translate, transmogrify (*jocular*), transmute

transformation alteration, change, conversion, metamorphosis, radical change, renewal, revolution, revolutionary change, sea change, transfiguration, transmogrification (*jocular*), transmutation

transfuse permeate, pervade, spread over, suffuse

transgress be out of order, break, break the law, contravene, defy, disobey, do *or* go wrong, encroach, err, exceed, fall from grace, go astray, go beyond, infringe, lapse, misbehave, offend, overstep, sin, trespass, violate

transgression breach, contravention, crime, encroachment, error, fault, infraction, infringement, iniquity, lapse, misbehaviour, misdeed, misdemeanour, offence, peccadillo, sin, trespass, violation, wrong, wrongdoing

transgressor criminal, culprit, delinquent, evildoer, felon, lawbreaker, malefactor, miscreant, offender, sinner, trespasser, villain, wrongdoer

transience brevity, briefness, ephemerality, evanescence, fleetingness, fugacity, fugitiveness, impermanence, momentariness, shortness, transitoriness

transient brief, ephemeral, evanescent, fleeting, flying, fugacious, fugitive, here today and gone tomorrow, impermanent, momentary, passing, short, short-lived, short-term, temporary, transitory

▷ **Antonyms** abiding, constant, durable, enduring, eternal, imperishable, long-lasting, long-term, permanent, perpetual, persistent, undying

transit *noun* **1.** carriage, conveyance, crossing, motion, movement, passage, portage, shipment, transfer, transport, transportation, travel, traverse **2.** alteration, change, changeover, conversion, shift, transition **3. in transit** during passage, en route, on the journey, on the move, on the road, on the way, while travelling *~verb* **4.** cross, journey, move, pass, travel, traverse

transition alteration, change, changeover, conversion, development, evolution, flux, metamorphosis, metastasis, passage, passing, progression, shift, transit, transmutation, upheaval

transitional changing, developmental, fluid, intermediate, passing, provisional, temporary, transitionary, unsettled

transitory brief, ephemeral, evanescent, fleeting, flying, fugacious, here today and gone tomorrow, impermanent, momentary, passing, short, short-lived, short-term, temporary, transient

▷ **Antonyms** abiding, enduring, eternal, everlasting, lasting, long-lived, long-term, permanent, perpetual, persistent, undying

translate 1. construe, convert, decipher, decode, interpret, paraphrase, render, transcribe, transliterate **2.** elucidate, explain, make clear, paraphrase, put in plain English, simplify, spell out, state in layman's language **3.** alter, change, convert, metamorphose, transfigure, transform, transmute, turn **4.** carry, convey, move, remove, send, transfer, transplant, transport, transpose

translation 1. construction, decoding, gloss, interpretation, paraphrase, rendering, rendition, transcription, transliteration, version **2.** elucidation, explanation, paraphrase, rephrasing, rewording, simplification **3.** alteration, change, conversion, metamorphosis, transfiguration, transformation, transmutation **4.** conveyance, move, removal, transference, transposition

translator interpreter, linguist, metaphrast, paraphrast

translucent clear, diaphanous, limpid, lucent, pellucid, semitransparent

transmigration journey, metempsychosis, migration, movement, passage, rebirth, reincarnation, travel

transmission 1. carriage, communication, conveyance, diffusion, dispatch, dissemination, remission, sending, shipment, spread, transfer, transference, transport **2.** broadcasting, dissemination, putting out, relaying, sending, showing **3.** broadcast, programme, show

transmit 1. bear, carry, communicate, convey, diffuse, dispatch, disseminate, forward, hand down, hand on, impart, pass on, remit, send, spread, take, transfer, transport **2.** broadcast, disseminate, put on the air, radio, relay, send, send out

transmute alchemize, alter, change, convert, metamorphose, remake, transfigure, transform

transparency 1. clarity, clearness, diaphaneity, diaphanousness, filminess, gauziness, limpidity, limpidness, pellu~

cidity, pellucidness, sheerness, translucence, translucency, transparence **2**. apparentness, distinctness, explicitness, obviousness, patentness, perspicuousness, plainness, unambiguousness, visibility **3**. candour, directness, forthrightness, frankness, openness, straightforwardness **4**. photograph, slide
▷ **Antonyms** (*sense 1*) cloudiness, murkiness, opacity, unclearness (*sense 2*) obscurity, unclearness, vagueness (*sense 3*) ambiguity, vagueness

transparent 1. clear, crystal clear, crystalline, diaphanous, filmy, gauzy, limpid, lucent, lucid, pellucid, see-through, sheer, translucent, transpicuous **2**. apparent, as plain as the nose on one's face (*informal*), bold, distinct, easy, evident, explicit, manifest, obvious, patent, perspicuous, plain, recognizable, unambiguous, understandable, undisguised, visible **3**. candid, direct, forthright, frank, open, plain-spoken, straight, straightforward, unambiguous, unequivocal
▷ **Antonyms** (*sense 1*) cloudy, muddy, opaque, thick, turbid, unclear (*sense 2*) hidden, mysterious, opaque, uncertain, unclear, vague (*sense 3*) ambiguous, deceptive, disingenuous, mysterious, unclear, vague

transpire 1. *informal* arise, befall, chance, come about, come to pass (*archaic*), happen, occur, take place, turn up **2**. become known, be disclosed, be discovered, be made public, come out, come to light, emerge

transplant displace, relocate, remove, resettle, shift, transfer, uproot

transport *verb* **1**. bear, bring, carry, convey, fetch, haul, move, remove, run, ship, take, transfer **2**. banish, deport, exile, sentence to transportation **3**. captivate, carry away, delight, electrify, enchant, enrapture, entrance, move, ravish, spellbind *~noun* **4**. conveyance, transportation, vehicle, wheels (*informal*) **5**. carriage, conveyance, removal, shipment, shipping, transference, transportation **6**. cloud nine (*informal*), enchantment, euphoria, heaven, rapture, seventh heaven **7**. bliss, delight, ecstasy, happiness, ravishment
▷ **Antonyms** *~noun* (*sense 6*) blues (*informal*), depression, despondency, doldrums, dumps (*informal*), melancholy

transpose alter, change, exchange, interchange, move, rearrange, relocate, reorder, shift, substitute, swap (*informal*), switch, transfer

transverse athwart, crossways, crosswise, diagonal, oblique

trap *noun* **1**. ambush, gin, net, noose, pitfall, snare, springe, toils **2**. ambush, artifice, deception, device, ruse, stratagem, subterfuge, trick, wile *~verb* **3**. catch, corner, enmesh, ensnare, entrap, snare, take **4**. ambush, beguile, deceive, dupe, ensnare, inveigle, trick

trapped ambushed, at bay, beguiled, caught, cornered, cut off, deceived, duped, ensnared, in a tight corner, in a tight spot, inveigled, netted, snared, stuck (*informal*), surrounded, tricked, with one's back to the wall

trappings accoutrements, adornments, bells and whistles, decorations, dress, equipment, finery, fittings, fixtures, fripperies, furnishings, gear, livery, ornaments, panoply, paraphernalia, raiment (*archaic or poetic*), things, trimmings

trash 1. balderdash, balls (*taboo slang*), bilge (*informal*), bosh (*informal*), bull (*slang*), bullshit (*taboo slang*), bunkum *or* buncombe (*chiefly U.S.*), cobblers (*Brit. taboo slang*), crap (*slang*), drivel, eyewash (*informal*), foolish talk, garbage (*informal*), guff (*slang*), hogwash, hokum (*slang, chiefly U.S. & Canad.*), horsefeathers (*U.S. slang*), hot air (*informal*), inanity, kak (*S. African slang*), moonshine, nonsense, pap, piffle (*informal*), poppycock (*informal*), rot, rubbish, shit (*taboo slang*), tommyrot, tosh (*slang, chiefly Brit.*), tripe (*informal*), trumpery, twaddle **2**. dreck (*slang, chiefly U.S.*), dregs, dross, garbage, junk (*informal*), litter, offscourings, refuse, rubbish, sweepings, waste
▷ **Antonyms** (*sense 1*) logic, reason, sense, significance

trashy brummagem, catchpenny, cheap, cheap-jack (*informal*), chickenshit (*U.S. slang*), crappy (*slang*), flimsy, inferior, meretricious, of a sort *or* of sorts, poxy (*slang*), rubbishy, shabby, shoddy, tawdry, thrown together, tinsel, worthless
▷ **Antonyms** A1 *or* A-one (*informal*), excellent, exceptional, first-class, first-rate, outstanding, superlative

trauma agony, anguish, damage, disturbance, hurt, injury, jolt, ordeal, pain, shock, strain, suffering, torture, upheaval, upset, wound

traumatic agonizing, damaging, disturbing, hurtful, injurious, painful, scarring, shocking, upsetting, wounding
▷ **Antonyms** calming, healing, helpful, relaxing, therapeutic, wholesome

travail *noun* **1**. distress, drudgery, effort, exertion, grind (*informal*), hardship, hard work, labour, pain, slavery, slog, strain, stress, suffering, sweat, tears, toil **2**. birth pangs, childbirth, labour, labour pains *~verb* **3**. drudge, grind (*informal*), labour, slave, slog, suffer, sweat, toil

travel *verb* **1**. cross, go, journey, make a journey, make one's way, move, proceed, progress, ramble, roam, rove, take a trip, tour, traverse, trek, voyage, walk, wander, wend **2**. be transmitted, carry, get through, move *~noun* **3**. (*usually* *plural*) excursion, expedition, globe~trotting, journey, movement, passage, peregrination, ramble, tour, touring, trip, voyage, walk, wandering

traveller **1.** excursionist, explorer, globe~trotter, gypsy, hiker, holiday-maker, journeyer, migrant, nomad, passenger, tourist, tripper, voyager, wanderer, wayfarer **2.** agent, commercial traveller, rep, representative, salesman, travel~ling salesman

travelling *adjective* itinerant, migrant, migratory, mobile, moving, nomadic, peripatetic, restless, roaming, roving, touring, unsettled, wandering, way~faring

traverse **1.** bridge, cover, cross, cut across, go across, go over, make one's way across, negotiate, pass over, ply, range, roam, span, travel over, wander **2.** balk, contravene, counter, counteract, deny, frustrate, go against, hinder, impede, obstruct, oppose, thwart **3.** check, con~sider, examine, eye, inspect, investigate, look into, look over, pore over, range over, review, scan, scrutinize, study

travesty **1.** *noun* burlesque, caricature, distortion, lampoon, mockery, parody, perversion, send-up (*Brit. informal*), sham, spoof (*informal*), takeoff (*infor~mal*) **2.** *~verb* burlesque, caricature, de~ride, distort, lampoon, make a mockery of, make fun of, mock, parody, pervert, ridicule, send up (*Brit. informal*), sham, spoof (*informal*), take off (*informal*)

treacherous **1.** deceitful, disloyal, double-crossing (*informal*), double-dealing, duplicitous, faithless, false, perfidious, recreant (*archaic*), traitor~ous, treasonable, unfaithful, unreliable, untrue, untrustworthy **2.** dangerous, deceptive, hazardous, icy, perilous, pre~carious, risky, slippery, slippy (*informal or dialect*), tricky, unreliable, unsafe, unstable

▷ **Antonyms** (*sense 1*) dependable, faith~ful, loyal, reliable, true, trustworthy (*sense 2*) reliable, safe

treachery betrayal, disloyalty, double-cross (*informal*), double-dealing, duplic~ity, faithlessness, infidelity, perfidious~ness, perfidy, stab in the back, treason

▷ **Antonyms** allegiance, dependability, faithfulness, fealty, fidelity, loyalty, re~liability

tread *verb* **1.** hike, march, pace, plod, stamp, step, stride, tramp, trudge, walk **2.** crush underfoot, squash, trample **3.** bear down, crush, oppress, quell, re~press, ride roughshod over, subdue, subjugate, suppress **4. tread on someone's toes** affront, annoy, bruise, disgruntle, get someone's back up, hurt, hurt someone's feelings, infringe, injure, irk, offend, vex *~noun* **5.** footfall, foot~step, gait, pace, step, stride, walk

treason disaffection, disloyalty, duplicity, lese-majesty, mutiny, perfidy, sedition, subversion, traitorousness, treachery

▷ **Antonyms** allegiance, faithfulness, fe~alty, fidelity, loyalty, patriotism

treasonable disloyal, false, mutinous, perfidious, seditious, subversive, trai~torous, treacherous, treasonous

▷ **Antonyms** dependable, faithful, loyal, patriotic, reliable, trustworthy

treasure *noun* **1.** cash, fortune, funds, gold, jewels, money, riches, valuables, wealth **2.** apple of one's eye, best thing since sliced bread (*informal*), darling, gem, greatest thing since sliced bread (*informal*), jewel, nonpareil, paragon, pearl, precious, pride and joy, prize *~verb* **3.** adore, cherish, dote upon, es~teem, hold dear, idolize, love, prize, re~vere, value, venerate, worship **4.** accu~mulate, cache, collect, garner, hoard, husband, lay up, salt away, save, stash (away) (*informal*), store up

treasury **1.** bank, cache, hoard, repository, store, storehouse, vault **2.** assets, capi~tal, coffers, exchequer, finances, funds, money, resources, revenues

treat *noun* **1.** banquet, celebration, enter~tainment, feast, gift, party, refreshment **2.** delight, enjoyment, fun, gratification, joy, pleasure, satisfaction, surprise, thrill *~verb* **3.** act towards, behave to~wards, consider, deal with, handle, look upon, manage, regard, use **4.** apply treatment to, attend to, care for, doctor, medicate, nurse **5.** buy for, entertain, feast, foot *or* pay the bill, give, lay on, pay for, provide, regale, stand (*infor~mal*), take out, wine and dine **6.** be con~cerned with, contain, deal with, dis~course upon, discuss, go into, touch upon **7.** bargain, come to terms, confer, have talks, make terms, negotiate, par~ley

treatise disquisition, dissertation, essay, exposition, monograph, pamphlet, pa~per, study, thesis, tract, work, writing

treatment **1.** care, cure, healing, medica~tion, medicine, remedy, surgery, thera~py **2.** action towards, behaviour towards, conduct, dealing, handling, manage~ment, manipulation, reception, usage

treaty agreement, alliance, bargain, bond, compact, concordat, contract, con~vention, covenant, entente, pact

trek **1.** *noun* expedition, footslog, hike, journey, long haul, march, odyssey, sa~fari, slog, tramp **2.** *~verb* footslog, hike, journey, march, plod, range, roam, rove, slog, traipse (*informal*), tramp, trudge, yomp

tremble **1.** *verb* oscillate, quake, quake in one's boots, quiver, rock, shake, shake in one's boots, shake in one's shoes, shiver, shudder, teeter, totter, vibrate, wobble **2.** *~noun* oscillation, quake, quiver, shake, shiver, shudder, tremor, vibration, wobble

tremendous **1.** appalling, awesome, awful, colossal, deafening, dreadful, enormous, fearful, formidable, frightful, gargantuan, gigantic, great, huge, immense, mammoth, monstrous, prodigious, stellar (*informal*), stupendous, terrible, terrific, titanic, towering, vast, whopping (*informal*) **2.** *informal* ace (*informal*), amazing, awesome (*slang*), bodacious (*slang, chiefly U.S.*), boffo (*slang*), brill (*informal*), brilliant, chillin' (*U.S. slang*), cracking (*Brit. informal*), excellent, exceptional, extraordinary, fabulous (*informal*), fantastic (*informal*), great, incredible, jim-dandy (*slang*), marvellous, mean (*slang*), sensational (*informal*), sovereign, super (*informal*), terrific (*informal*), topping (*Brit. slang*), wonderful

▷ **Antonyms** (*sense 1*) diminutive, little, minuscule, minute, small, tiny (*sense 2*) abysmal, appalling, average, awful, dreadful, mediocre, no great shakes (*informal*), ordinary, rotten, run-of-the-mill, so-so, terrible

tremor **1.** agitation, quaking, quaver, quiver, quivering, shake, shaking, shiver, tremble, trembling, trepidation, vibration, wobble **2.** earthquake, quake (*informal*), shock

tremulous aflutter, afraid, agitated, agog, anxious, aquiver, excited, fearful, frightened, jittery (*informal*), jumpy, nervous, quavering, quivering, quivery, scared, shaking, shivering, timid, trembling, vibrating, wavering

trench channel, cut, ditch, drain, earthwork, entrenchment, excavation, fosse, furrow, gutter, pit, trough, waterway

trenchant **1.** acerbic, acid, acidulous, acute, astringent, biting, caustic, cutting, hurtful, incisive, keen, mordacious, mordant, penetrating, piquant, pointed, pungent, sarcastic, scathing, severe, sharp, tart, vitriolic **2.** driving, effective, effectual, emphatic, energetic, forceful, potent, powerful, strong, vigorous **3.** clear, clear-cut, crisp, distinct, distinctly defined, explicit, salient, unequivocal, well-defined

▷ **Antonyms** (*sense 1*) appeasing, kind, mollifying, soothing (*sense 3*) ill-defined, indistinct, nebulous, obscure, unclear, vague, woolly

trend *noun* **1.** bias, course, current, direction, drift, flow, inclination, leaning, tendency **2.** craze, fad (*informal*), fashion, look, mode, rage, style, thing, vogue *~verb* **3.** bend, flow, head, incline, lean, run, stretch, swing, tend, turn, veer

trendsetter arbiter of taste, avant-gardist, leader of fashion, pacemaker, pacesetter

trendy **1.** *adjective* fashionable, flash (*informal*), in (*slang*), in fashion, in vogue, latest, modish, now (*informal*), stylish, up to the minute, voguish, with it (*informal*) **2.** *~noun* poser (*informal*), pseud (*informal*)

trepidation agitation, alarm, anxiety, apprehension, blue funk (*informal*), butterflies (*informal*), cold feet (*informal*), cold sweat (*informal*), consternation, dismay, disquiet, disturbance, dread, emotion, excitement, fear, fright, jitters (*informal*), nervousness, palpitation, perturbation, quivering, shaking, the heebie-jeebies (*slang*), trembling, tremor, uneasiness, worry

▷ **Antonyms** aplomb, calm, composure, confidence, coolness, equanimity, self-assurance

trespass *verb* **1.** encroach, infringe, intrude, invade, obtrude, poach **2.** *archaic* offend, sin, transgress, violate, wrong *~noun* **3.** encroachment, infringement, intrusion, invasion, poaching, unlawful entry, wrongful entry **4.** breach, crime, delinquency, error, evildoing, fault, infraction, iniquity, injury, misbehaviour, misconduct, misdeed, misdemeanour, offence, sin, transgression, wrongdoing

trespasser **1.** infringer, interloper, intruder, invader, poacher, unwelcome visitor **2.** *archaic* criminal, delinquent, evildoer, malefactor, offender, sinner, transgressor, wrongdoer

tress braid, curl, lock, pigtail, plait, ringlet

triad threesome, trilogy, trine, trinity, trio, triple, triplet, triptych, triumvirate, triune

trial *noun* **1.** assay, audition, check, dry run (*informal*), examination, experience, experiment, probation, proof, test, testing, test-run **2.** contest, hearing, industrial tribunal, judicial examination, litigation, tribunal **3.** attempt, crack (*informal*), effort, endeavour, go (*informal*), shot (*informal*), stab (*informal*), try, venture, whack (*informal*) **4.** adversity, affliction, burden, cross to bear, distress, grief, hardship, hard times, load, misery, ordeal, pain, suffering, tribulation, trouble, unhappiness, vexation, woe, wretchedness **5.** bane, bother, drag (*informal*), hassle (*informal*), irritation, nuisance, pain in the arse (*taboo informal*), pain in the neck (*informal*), pest, plague (*informal*), thorn in one's flesh, vexation *~adjective* **6.** experimental, exploratory, pilot, probationary, provisional, testing

tribe blood, caste, clan, class, division, dynasty, ethnic group, family, gens, house, people, race, seed (*chiefly biblical*), sept, stock

tribulation adversity, affliction, bad luck, blow, bummer (*slang*), burden, care, cross to bear, curse, distress, grief, hardship, hassle (*informal*), heartache, ill fortune, misery, misfortune, ordeal,

pain, reverse, sorrow, suffering, trial, trouble, unhappiness, vexation, woe, worry, wretchedness
▷ **Antonyms** blessing, bliss, ease, good fortune, happiness, joy, pleasure, rest

tribunal bar, bench, court, hearing, industrial tribunal, judgment seat, judicial examination, trial

tribute 1. accolade, acknowledgment, applause, commendation, compliment, encomium, esteem, eulogy, gift, gratitude, honour, laudation, panegyric, praise, recognition, respect, testimonial **2.** charge, contribution, customs, duty, excise, homage, impost, offering, payment, ransom, subsidy, tax, toll
▷ **Antonyms** (*sense 1*) blame, complaint, condemnation, criticism, disapproval, reproach, reproof

trice bat of an eye (*informal*), flash, instant, jiffy (*informal*), minute, moment, second, shake (*informal*), split second, tick (*Brit. informal*), twinkling, twinkling of an eye, two shakes of a lamb's tail (*informal*)

trick *noun* **1.** artifice, canard, con (*slang*), deceit, deception, device, dodge, feint, fraud, gimmick, hoax, imposition, imposture, manoeuvre, ploy, ruse, scam (*slang*), sting (*informal*), stratagem, subterfuge, swindle, trap, wile **2.** antic, cantrip (*Scot.*), caper, device, feat, frolic, gag (*informal*), gambol, jape, joke, juggle, legerdemain, leg-pull (*Brit. informal*), practical joke, prank, put-on (*slang*), sleight of hand, stunt **3.** art, command, craft, device, expertise, gift, hang (*informal*), knack, know-how (*informal*), secret, skill, technique **4.** characteristic, crotchet, foible, habit, idiosyncrasy, mannerism, peculiarity, practice, quirk, trait **5. do the trick** *informal* be effective *or* effectual, have effect, produce the desired result, work *~verb* **6.** bamboozle (*informal*), cheat, con (*informal*), deceive, defraud, delude, dupe, fool, gull (*archaic*), have (someone) on, hoax, hoodwink, impose upon, kid (*informal*), mislead, pull a fast one on (*informal*), pull the wool over (someone's) eyes, put one over on (someone) (*informal*), stiff (*slang*), sting (*informal*), swindle, take in (*informal*), trap

trickery cheating, chicanery, con (*informal*), deceit, deception, dishonesty, double-dealing, fraud, funny business, guile, hanky-panky (*informal*), hoax, hokum (*slang, chiefly U.S. & Canad.*), imposture, jiggery-pokery (*informal, chiefly Brit.*), monkey business (*informal*), pretence, skulduggery (*informal*), swindling
▷ **Antonyms** artlessness, candour, directness, frankness, honesty, openness, straightforwardness, uprightness

trickle 1. *verb* crawl, creep, dribble, drip, drop, exude, ooze, percolate, run, seep, stream **2.** *~noun* dribble, drip, seepage

trick out *or* **up** adorn, array, attire, bedeck, deck out, doll up (*slang*), do up (*informal*), dress up, get up (*informal*), ornament, prank, prink

trickster cheat, chiseller (*informal*), con man (*informal*), deceiver, fraud, fraudster, grifter (*slang, chiefly U.S. & Canad.*), hoaxer, hustler (*U.S. informal*), impostor, joker, practical joker, pretender, swindler

tricky 1. complicated, delicate, difficult, knotty, problematic, risky, sticky (*informal*), thorny, ticklish, touch-and-go **2.** artful, crafty, cunning, deceitful, deceptive, devious, foxy, scheming, slippery, sly, subtle, wily
▷ **Antonyms** (*sense 1*) clear, easy, obvious, simple, straightforward, uncomplicated (*sense 2*) above board, artless, direct, genuine, honest, ingenuous, open, sincere, truthful

trifle *noun* **1.** bagatelle, bauble, child's play (*informal*), gewgaw, knick-knack, nothing, plaything, toy, triviality **2.** bit, dash, drop, jot, little, pinch, spot, touch, trace *~verb* **3.** amuse oneself, coquet, dally, dawdle, flirt, fritter, idle, mess about, palter, play, play fast and loose (*informal*), toy, wanton, waste, waste time

trifler dilettante, good-for-nothing, idler, layabout, loafer, ne'er-do-well, skiver (*Brit. slang*), waster

trifling empty, footling (*informal*), frivolous, idle, inconsiderable, insignificant, measly, minuscule, negligible, nickel-and-dime (*U.S. slang*), paltry, petty, piddling (*informal*), puny, shallow, silly, slight, small, tiny, trivial, unimportant, valueless, worthless
▷ **Antonyms** considerable, crucial, important, large, major, serious, significant, vital, weighty

trigger *verb* activate, bring about, cause, elicit, generate, give rise to, produce, prompt, provoke, set in motion, set off, spark off, start
▷ **Antonyms** bar, block, hinder, impede, inhibit, obstruct, prevent, repress, stop

trim *adjective* **1.** compact, dapper, natty (*informal*), neat, nice, orderly, shipshape, smart, soigné *or* soignée, spick-and-span, spruce, tidy, trig (*archaic or dialect*), well-groomed, well-ordered, well turned-out **2.** fit, shapely, sleek, slender, slim, streamlined, svelte, willowy *~verb* **3.** barber, clip, crop, curtail, cut, cut back, dock, even up, lop, pare, prune, shave, shear, tidy **4.** adorn, array, beautify, bedeck, deck out, decorate, dress, embellish, embroider, garnish, ornament, trick out **5.** adjust, arrange, balance, distribute, order, prepare, settle *~noun* **6.** adornment, border, decoration, edging, embellishment, frill,

fringe, garnish, ornamentation, piping, trimming **7**. condition, fettle, fitness, form, health, order, repair, shape (*informal*), situation, state **8**. clipping, crop, cut, pruning, shave, shearing, tidying up, trimming **9**. array, attire, dress, equipment, gear, trappings
▷ **Antonyms** *~adjective* (*sense 1*) disarrayed, disorderly, messy, scruffy, shabby, sloppy, ungroomed, unkempt, untidy

trimming 1. adornment, border, braid, decoration, edging, embellishment, festoon, frill, fringe, garnish, ornamentation, piping **2**. *plural* accessories, accompaniments, appurtenances, extras, frills, garnish, ornaments, paraphernalia, trappings **3**. *plural* brash, clippings, cuttings, ends, parings, shavings

trinity threesome, triad, trilogy, trine, trio, triple, triplet, triptych, triumvirate, triune

trinket bagatelle, bauble, bibelot, gewgaw, gimcrack, kickshaw, knick-knack, nothing, ornament, piece of bric-a-brac, toy, trifle

trio threesome, triad, trilogy, trine, trinity, triple, triplet, triptych, triumvirate, triune

trip *noun* **1**. errand, excursion, expedition, foray, jaunt, journey, outing, ramble, run, tour, travel, voyage **2**. bloomer (*Brit. informal*), blunder, boob (*Brit. slang*), error, fall, false move, false step, faux pas, indiscretion, lapse, misstep, slip, stumble *~verb* **3**. blunder, boob (*Brit. slang*), err, fall, go wrong, lapse, lose one's balance, lose one's footing, make a false move, make a faux pas, miscalculate, misstep, slip, slip up (*informal*), stumble, tumble **4**. catch out, confuse, disconcert, put off one's stride, throw off, trap, unsettle **5**. go, ramble, tour, travel, voyage **6**. caper, dance, flit, frisk, gambol, hop, skip, spring, tread lightly **7**. *informal* get high (*informal*), get stoned (*slang*), take drugs, turn on (*slang*) **8**. activate, engage, flip, pull, release, set off, switch on, throw, turn on

tripe balderdash, balls (*taboo slang*), bilge (*informal*), bollocks (*Brit. taboo slang*), bosh (*informal*), bull (*slang*), bullshit (*taboo slang*), bunkum *or* buncombe (*chiefly U.S.*), claptrap (*informal*), cobblers (*Brit. taboo slang*), crap (*slang*), drivel, eyewash (*informal*), foolish talk, garbage (*informal*), guff (*slang*), hogwash, hokum (*slang, chiefly U.S. & Canad.*), horsefeathers (*U.S. slang*), hot air (*informal*), inanity, moonshine, nonsense, pap, piffle (*informal*), poppycock (*informal*), rot, rubbish, shit (*taboo slang*), tommyrot, tosh (*slang, chiefly Brit.*), trash, trumpery, twaddle

triple 1. *adjective* threefold, three times as much, three-way, tripartite **2**. *~noun* threesome, triad, trilogy, trine, trinity, trio, triplet, triumvirate, triune **3**. *~verb* increase threefold, treble, triplicate

triplet threesome, triad, trilogy, trine, trinity, trio, triple, triumvirate, triune

tripper excursionist, holiday-maker, journeyer, sightseer, tourist, voyager

trite banal, bromidic, clichéd, common, commonplace, corny (*slang*), dull, hack, hackneyed, ordinary, pedestrian, routine, run-of-the-mill, stale, stereotyped, stock, threadbare, tired, uninspired, unoriginal, worn
▷ **Antonyms** exciting, fresh, interesting, new, novel, original, out-of-the-ordinary, uncommon, unexpected, unfamiliar

triturate beat, bray, bruise, comminute, crush, grind, masticate, pound, powder, pulverize

triumph *noun* **1**. elation, exultation, happiness, joy, jubilation, pride, rejoicing **2**. accomplishment, achievement, ascendancy, attainment, conquest, coup, feat, feather in one's cap, hit (*informal*), mastery, sensation, smash (*informal*), smasheroo (*slang*), smash-hit (*informal*), success, *tour de force,* victory, walkover (*informal*) *~verb* **3**. (*often with* **over**) best, carry the day, come out on top (*informal*), dominate, flourish, get the better of, overcome, overwhelm, prevail, prosper, subdue, succeed, take the honours, thrive, vanquish, win **4**. celebrate, crow, drool, exult, gloat, glory, jubilate, rejoice, revel, swagger
▷ **Antonyms** *~noun* (*sense 2*) catastrophe, defeat, disaster, failure, fiasco, flop (*informal*), washout (*informal*) *~verb* (*sense 3*) come a cropper (*informal*), fail, fall, flop (*informal*), lose

triumphant boastful, celebratory, cock-a-hoop, conquering, dominant, elated, exultant, glorious, jubilant, proud, rejoicing, successful, swaggering, triumphal, undefeated, victorious, winning
▷ **Antonyms** beaten, defeated, embarrassed, humbled, humiliated, shamed, unsuccessful

trivia details, minutiae, petty details, trifles, trivialities
▷ **Antonyms** basics, brass tacks (*informal*), core, essentials, fundamentals, nitty-gritty (*informal*), rudiments

trivial chickenshit (*U.S. slang*), commonplace, everyday, frivolous, incidental, inconsequential, inconsiderable, insignificant, little, meaningless, minor, negligible, nickel-and-dime (*U.S. slang*), paltry, petty, puny, slight, small, trifling, trite, unimportant, valueless, wanky (*taboo slang*), worthless
▷ **Antonyms** considerable, crucial, essential, important, profound, serious, significant, uncommon, unusual, vital, weighty, worthwhile

triviality 1. frivolity, inconsequentiality, insignificance, littleness, meaninglessness, much ado about nothing, negligibility, paltriness, pettiness, slightness, smallness, triteness, unimportance, valuelessness, worthlessness **2.** detail, no big thing, no great matter, nothing, petty detail, technicality, trifle

▷ **Antonyms** (*sense 1*) consequence, essential, importance, rudiment, significance, value, worth

trivialize belittle, laugh off, make light of, minimize, play down, scoff at, underestimate, underplay, undervalue

trollop fallen woman, floozy (*slang*), harlot, hussy, loose woman, prostitute, scrubber (*Brit. & Austral. slang*), slag (*Brit. slang*), slattern, slut, streetwalker, strumpet, tart (*informal*), wanton, whore, working girl (*facetious slang*)

troop *noun* **1.** assemblage, band, bevy, body, bunch (*informal*), company, contingent, crew (*informal*), crowd, drove, flock, gang, gathering, group, herd, horde, multitude, pack, posse (*informal*), squad, swarm, team, throng, unit **2.** *plural* armed forces, army, fighting men, men, military, servicemen, soldiers, soldiery *~verb* **3.** crowd, flock, march, parade, stream, swarm, throng, traipse (*informal*)

trophy award, bays, booty, cup, laurels, memento, prize, souvenir, spoils

tropical hot, humid, lush, steamy, stifling, sultry, sweltering, torrid

▷ **Antonyms** arctic, chilly, cold, cool, freezing, frosty, frozen, parky (*Brit. informal*)

trot *verb* **1.** canter, go briskly, jog, lope, run, scamper *~noun* **2.** brisk pace, canter, jog, lope, run **3. on the trot** *informal* consecutively, in a row, in succession, one after the other, without break, without interruption

trot out bring forward, bring up, come out with, drag up, exhibit, recite, rehearse, reiterate, relate, repeat

troubadour balladeer, jongleur, lyric poet, minstrel, poet, singer

trouble *noun* **1.** agitation, annoyance, anxiety, bummer (*slang*), disquiet, distress, grief, hardship, hassle (*informal*), heartache, irritation, misfortune, pain, sorrow, suffering, torment, tribulation, vexation, woe, worry **2.** agitation, bother (*informal*), commotion, discontent, discord, disorder, dissatisfaction, disturbance, hassle (*informal*), Pandora's box, row, strife, tumult, unrest **3.** ailment, complaint, defect, disability, disease, disorder, failure, illness, malfunction, upset **4.** bother, concern, danger, deep water (*informal*), difficulty, dilemma, dire straits, hassle (*informal*), hot water (*informal*), mess, nuisance, pest, pickle (*informal*), predicament, problem, scrape (*informal*), spot (*informal*), tight spot **5.** attention, bother, care, effort, exertion, inconvenience, labour, pains, struggle, thought, work *~verb* **6.** afflict, agitate, annoy, bother, discompose, disconcert, disquiet, distress, disturb, faze, fret, grieve, harass, hassle (*informal*), inconvenience, pain, perplex, perturb, pester, plague, put *or* get someone's back up, sadden, torment, upset, vex, worry **7.** be concerned, bother, burden, discomfort, discommode, disturb, impose upon, incommode, inconvenience, put out **8.** exert oneself, go to the effort of, make an effort, take pains, take the time

▷ **Antonyms** *~noun* (*sense 1*) comfort, contentment, good fortune, happiness, pleasure, tranquillity (*sense 2*) agreement, contentment, harmony, peace, tranquillity, unity (*sense 5*) convenience, ease, facility *~verb* (*sense 6*) appease, calm, mollify, please, relieve, soothe (*sense 7*) be unharassed, relieve (*sense 8*) avoid, dodge

troublemaker *agent provocateur,* agitator, bad apple (*U.S. informal*), firebrand, incendiary, instigator, meddler, mischief-maker, rabble-rouser, rotten apple (*Brit. informal*), stirrer (*informal*), stormy petrel

▷ **Antonyms** appeaser, arbitrator, conciliator, pacifier, peace-maker

troublesome 1. annoying, arduous, bothersome, burdensome, demanding, difficult, harassing, hard, importunate, inconvenient, irksome, irritating, laborious, oppressive, pestilential, plaguy (*informal*), taxing, tiresome, tricky, trying, upsetting, vexatious, wearisome, worrisome, worrying **2.** disorderly, insubordinate, rebellious, recalcitrant, refractory, rowdy, turbulent, uncooperative, undisciplined, unruly, violent

▷ **Antonyms** (*sense 1*) agreeable, calming, congenial, easy, pleasant, simple, soothing, undemanding (*sense 2*) disciplined, eager-to-please, obedient, well-behaved

trough 1. crib, manger, water trough **2.** canal, channel, depression, ditch, duct, flume, furrow, gully, gutter, trench, watercourse

trounce beat, beat (someone) hollow (*Brit. informal*), blow out of the water (*slang*), clobber (*slang*), crush, defeat heavily *or* utterly, drub, give a hiding (*informal*), give a pasting (*slang*), hammer (*informal*), lick (*informal*), make mincemeat of, overwhelm, paste (*slang*), rout, run rings around (*informal*), slaughter (*informal*), stuff (*slang*), tank (*slang*), thrash, walk over (*informal*), wipe the floor with (*informal*)

troupe band, cast, company

trouper actor, artiste, entertainer, performer, player, theatrical, thespian

truancy absence, absence without leave, malingering, shirking, skiving (*Brit. slang*)

truant *noun* **1.** absentee, delinquent, de~ serter, dodger, malingerer, runaway, shirker, skiver (*Brit. slang*), straggler **2.** *~adjective* absent, absent without leave, A.W.O.L., missing, skiving (*Brit. slang*) *~verb* **3.** absent oneself, bob off (*Brit. slang*), bunk off (*slang*), desert, dodge, go missing, malinger, play truant, run away, shirk, skive (*Brit. slang*), wag (*dialect*)

truce armistice, break, ceasefire, cessa~ tion, cessation of hostilities, intermis~ sion, interval, let-up (*informal*), lull, moratorium, peace, respite, rest, stay, treaty

truck *noun* **1.** commercial goods, com~ modities, goods, merchandise, stock, stuff, wares **2.** barter, business, buying and selling, commerce, communication, connection, contact, dealings, exchange, relations, trade, traffic *~verb* **3.** bargain, barter, buy and sell, deal, do business, exchange, have dealings, negotiate, swap, trade, traffic, transact business

truckle bend the knee, bow and scrape, concede, cringe, crouch, defer, fawn, give in, give way, knuckle under, kow~ tow, lick (someone's) boots, pander to, stoop, submit, toady, yield

truculent aggressive, antagonistic, bad-tempered, bellicose, belligerent, com~ bative, contentious, cross, defiant, fierce, hostile, ill-tempered, itching *or* spoiling for a fight (*informal*), obstrep~ erous, pugnacious, scrappy (*informal*), sullen, violent

▷ **Antonyms** agreeable, amiable, civil, co-operative, gentle, good-natured, peaceable, placid

trudge 1. *verb* clump, drag oneself, foot~ slog, hike, lumber, march, plod, slog, stump, traipse (*informal*), tramp, trek, walk heavily, yomp **2.** *~noun* footslog, haul, hike, march, slog, traipse (*infor~ mal*), tramp, trek, yomp

true *adjective* **1.** accurate, actual, authentic, bona fide, correct, exact, fac~ tual, genuine, legitimate, natural, pre~ cise, pure, real, right, truthful, valid, veracious, veritable **2.** confirmed, con~ stant, dedicated, devoted, dutiful, faith~ ful, fast, firm, honest, honourable, loyal, pure, reliable, sincere, staunch, steady, true-blue, trustworthy, trusty, un~ swerving, upright **3.** accurate, correct, exact, on target, perfect, precise, proper, spot-on (*Brit. informal*), unerring *~adverb* **4.** honestly, rightly, truthfully, veraciously, veritably **5.** accurately, cor~ rectly, on target, perfectly, precisely, properly, unerringly **6. come true** be~ come reality, be granted, be realized, come to pass, happen, occur

▷ **Antonyms** (*sense 1*) abnormal, artifi~ cial, atypical, bogus, counterfeit, erro~ neous, fake, false, fictional, fictitious, il~ legitimate, imaginary, inaccurate, in~ correct, made-up, make-believe, phoney *or* phony (*informal*), pretended, self-styled, spurious, unofficial, untrue, un~ truthful (*sense 2*) deceitful, disloyal, faithless, false, treacherous, unreliable, untrue, untrustworthy (*sense 3*) askew, awry, erroneous, inaccurate, incorrect, untrue

true-blue confirmed, constant, dedicated, devoted, dyed-in-the-wool, faithful, loy~ al, orthodox, staunch, trusty, uncom~ promising, unwavering

truism axiom, bromide, cliché, common~ place, platitude, stock phrase, trite say~ ing

truly 1. accurately, authentically, beyond doubt, beyond question, correctly, ex~ actly, factually, genuinely, in actuality, in fact, in reality, in truth, legitimately, precisely, really, rightly, truthfully, ve~ raciously, veritably, without a doubt **2.** confirmedly, constantly, devotedly, du~ tifully, faithfully, firmly, honestly, hon~ ourably, loyally, sincerely, staunchly, steadily, with all one's heart, with dedi~ cation, with devotion **3.** exceptionally, extremely, greatly, indeed, of course, really, seriously (*informal*), to be sure, verily, very

▷ **Antonyms** (*sense 1*) doubtfully, falsely, fraudulently, inaccurately, incorrectly, mistakenly

trumped-up concocted, contrived, cooked-up (*informal*), fabricated, fake, false, falsified, invented, made-up, manufactured, phoney *or* phony (*infor~ mal*), untrue

▷ **Antonyms** actual, authentic, bona fide, genuine, real, sound, true, veritable

trumpery *noun* **1.** balderdash, balls (*taboo slang*), bilge (*informal*), bosh (*informal*), bull (*slang*), bullshit (*taboo slang*), bun~ kum *or* buncombe (*chiefly U.S.*), clap~ trap (*informal*), cobblers (*Brit. taboo slang*), crap (*slang*), drivel, eyewash (*informal*), foolishness, foolish talk, garbage (*informal*), guff (*slang*), hog~ wash, hokum (*slang, chiefly U.S. & Canad.*), horsefeathers (*U.S. slang*), hot air (*informal*), idiocy, inanity, moon~ shine, nonsense, pap, piffle (*informal*), poppycock (*informal*), rot, rubbish, shit (*taboo slang*), stuff, tommyrot, tosh (*slang, chiefly Brit.*), trash, tripe (*infor~ mal*), twaddle **2.** bagatelle, bauble, gew~ gaw, kickshaw, knick-knack, toy, trifle, trinket *~adjective* **3.** brummagem, cheap, flashy, meretricious, nasty, rubbishy, shabby, shoddy, tawdry, trashy, trifling, useless, valueless, worthless

trumpet *noun* **1.** bugle, clarion, horn **2.** bay, bellow, call, cry, roar **3. blow one's own trumpet** boast, brag, crow, sing one's own praises, vaunt *~verb* **4.** adver~ tise, announce, broadcast, crack up (*in~ formal*), extol, noise abroad, proclaim,

publish, shout from the rooftops, sound loudly, tout (*informal*)
▷ **Antonyms** *~verb* conceal, hide, hush up, keep secret, make light of, play down, soft pedal (*informal*)

trump up concoct, contrive, cook up (*informal*), create, fabricate, fake, invent, make up, manufacture

truncate abbreviate, clip, crop, curtail, cut, cut short, dock, lop, pare, prune, shorten, trim
▷ **Antonyms** drag out, draw out, extend, lengthen, prolong, protract, spin out, stretch

truncheon baton, club, cudgel, staff

trunk 1. bole, stalk, stem, stock **2.** body, torso **3.** proboscis, snout **4.** bin, box, case, casket, chest, coffer, crate, kist (*Scot. & northern English dialect*), locker, portmanteau

truss *verb* **1.** bind, bundle, fasten, make fast, pack, pinion, secure, strap, tether, tie *~noun* **2.** beam, brace, buttress, joist, prop, shore, stanchion, stay, strut, support **3.** *Medical* bandage, support **4.** bale, bundle, package, packet

trust *noun* **1.** assurance, belief, certainty, certitude, confidence, conviction, credence, credit, expectation, faith, hope, reliance **2.** duty, obligation, responsibility **3.** care, charge, custody, guard, guardianship, protection, safekeeping, trusteeship *~verb* **4.** assume, believe, expect, hope, presume, suppose, surmise, think likely **5.** bank on, believe, count on, depend on, have faith in, lean on, pin one's faith on, place confidence in, place one's trust in, place reliance on, rely upon, swear by, take as gospel, take at face value **6.** assign, command, commit, confide, consign, delegate, entrust, give, put into the hands of, sign over, turn over
▷ **Antonyms** *~noun* (*sense 1*) distrust, doubt, fear, incredulity, lack of faith, mistrust, scepticism, suspicion, uncertainty, wariness *~verb* (*senses 4 & 5*) be sceptical of, beware, disbelieve, discredit, distrust, doubt, lack confidence in, lack faith in, mistrust, suspect

trustful, trusting confiding, credulous, gullible, innocent, naive, optimistic, simple, unguarded, unsuspecting, unsuspicious, unwary
▷ **Antonyms** cagey (*informal*), cautious, chary, distrustful, guarded, on one's guard, suspicious, wary

trustworthy dependable, ethical, honest, honourable, level-headed, mature, principled, reliable, reputable, responsible, righteous, sensible, staunch, steadfast, to be trusted, true, trusty, truthful, upright
▷ **Antonyms** deceitful, dishonest, disloyal, irresponsible, treacherous, undependable, unethical, unprincipled, unreliable, untrustworthy

trusty dependable, faithful, firm, honest, reliable, responsible, solid, staunch, steady, straightforward, strong, true, trustworthy, upright
▷ **Antonyms** dishonest, irresolute, irresponsible, undependable, unfaithful, unreliable

truth 1. accuracy, actuality, exactness, fact, factuality, factualness, genuineness, legitimacy, precision, reality, truthfulness, validity, veracity, verity **2.** candour, constancy, dedication, devotion, dutifulness, faith, faithfulness, fidelity, frankness, honesty, integrity, loyalty, naturalism, realism, uprightness **3.** axiom, certainty, fact, law, maxim, proven principle, reality, truism, verity
▷ **Antonyms** (*sense 1*) error, falsity, inaccuracy (*sense 2*) deceit, deception, dishonesty (*sense 3*) delusion, fabrication, falsehood, fiction, invention, legend, lie, make-believe, myth, old wives' tale, untruth

truthful accurate, candid, correct, exact, faithful, forthright, frank, honest, literal, naturalistic, plain-spoken, precise, realistic, reliable, sincere, straight, straightforward, true, trustworthy, upfront (*informal*), veracious, veritable
▷ **Antonyms** deceptive, dishonest, fabricated, false, fictional, fictitious, inaccurate, incorrect, insincere, lying, made-up, untrue, untruthful

truthless deceitful, deceptive, dishonest, faithless, false, fraudulent, insincere, lying, mendacious, perjured, treacherous, untrue, untrustworthy

try *verb* **1.** aim, attempt, bend over backwards (*informal*), break one's neck (*informal*), bust a gut (*informal*), do one's best, do one's damnedest (*informal*), endeavour, essay, exert oneself, give it one's all (*informal*), give it one's best shot (*informal*), go for broke (*slang*), go for it (*informal*), have a crack (*informal*), have a go, have a shot (*informal*), have a stab (*informal*), have a whack (*informal*), knock oneself out (*informal*), make an all-out effort (*informal*), make an attempt, make an effort, move heaven and earth, rupture oneself (*informal*), seek, strive, struggle, undertake **2.** appraise, check out, evaluate, examine, experiment, inspect, investigate, prove, put to the test, sample, taste, test **3.** afflict, annoy, inconvenience, irk, irritate, pain, plague, strain, stress, tax, tire, trouble, upset, vex, weary **4.** adjudge, adjudicate, examine, hear *~noun* **5.** attempt, crack (*informal*), effort, endeavour, essay, go (*informal*), shot (*informal*), stab (*informal*), whack (*informal*) **6.** appraisal, evaluation, experiment, inspection, sample, taste, test, trial

trying aggravating (*informal*), annoying, arduous, bothersome, difficult, exasperating, fatiguing, hard, irksome, irritating, stressful, taxing, tiresome, tough, troublesome, upsetting, vexing, wearisome

▷ **Antonyms** calming, easy, no bother, no trouble, painless, simple, straightforward, undemanding

try out appraise, check out, evaluate, experiment with, inspect, put into practice, put to the test, sample, taste, test

tsar, czar autocrat, despot, emperor, head, leader, overlord, ruler, sovereign, tyrant

tubby chubby, corpulent, fat, obese, overweight, paunchy, plump, podgy, portly, roly-poly, stout

tuck *verb* **1.** fold, gather, insert, push ~*noun* **2.** fold, gather, pinch, pleat **3.** *informal* comestibles, eats (*slang*), food, grub (*slang*), nosebag (*slang*), nosh (*slang*), scoff (*slang*), tack (*informal*), victuals, vittles (*obsolete or dialect*)

tuck in 1. bed down, enfold, fold under, make snug, put to bed, swaddle, wrap up **2.** chow down (*slang*), eat heartily, eat up, fall to, get stuck in (*informal*)

tuft bunch, clump, cluster, collection, knot, shock, topknot, tussock

tug 1. *verb* drag, draw, haul, heave, jerk, lug, pull, tow, wrench, yank **2.** ~*noun* drag, haul, heave, jerk, pull, tow, traction, wrench, yank

tuition education, instruction, lessons, schooling, teaching, training, tutelage, tutoring

tumble 1. *verb* drop, fall, fall end over end, fall headlong, fall head over heels, flop, lose one's footing, pitch, plummet, roll, stumble, topple, toss, trip up **2.** ~*noun* collapse, drop, fall, flop, headlong fall, plunge, roll, spill, stumble, toss, trip

tumble-down crumbling, decrepit, dilapidated, disintegrating, falling to pieces, ramshackle, rickety, ruined, shaky, tottering

▷ **Antonyms** durable, firm, solid, sound, stable, sturdy, substantial, well-kept

tumid 1. bloated, bulging, distended, enlarged, inflated, protuberant, puffed up, puffy, swollen, tumescent **2.** bombastic, flowery, fulsome, fustian, grandiloquent, grandiose, high-flown, inflated, magniloquent, orotund, overblown, pompous, pretentious, sesquipedalian, stilted, turgid

tumour cancer, carcinoma (*Pathology*), growth, lump, neoplasm (*Medical*), sarcoma (*Medical*), swelling

tumult ado, affray (*Law*), agitation, altercation, bedlam, brawl, brouhaha, clamour, commotion, din, disorder, disturbance, excitement, fracas, hubbub, hullabaloo, outbreak, pandemonium, quarrel, racket, riot, row, ruction (*informal*), stir, stramash (*Scot.*), strife, turmoil, unrest, upheaval, uproar

▷ **Antonyms** calm, hush, peace, quiet, repose, serenity, silence, stillness

tumultuous agitated, boisterous, clamorous, confused, disorderly, disturbed, excited, fierce, full-on (*informal*), hectic, irregular, lawless, noisy, obstreperous, passionate, raging, restless, riotous, rowdy, rumbustious, stormy, turbulent, unrestrained, unruly, uproarious, violent, vociferous, wild

▷ **Antonyms** calm, hushed, peaceful, quiet, restful, serene, still, tranquil

tune *noun* **1.** air, melody, melody line, motif, song, strain, theme **2.** agreement, concert, concord, consonance, euphony, harmony, pitch, sympathy, unison **3.** attitude, demeanour, disposition, frame of mind, mood **4. call the tune** be in charge, be in command, be in control, call the shots (*slang*), command, dictate, govern, lead, rule, rule the roost **5. change one's tune** change one's mind, do an about-face, have a change of heart, reconsider, take a different tack, think again ~*verb* **6.** adapt, adjust, attune, bring into harmony, harmonize, pitch, regulate

▷ **Antonyms** ~*noun* (*sense 2*) clashing, conflict, contention, disagreement, discord, discordance, disharmony, disunity, friction

tuneful catchy, consonant (*Music*), easy on the ear (*informal*), euphonic, euphonious, harmonious, mellifluous, melodic, melodious, musical, pleasant, symphonic

▷ **Antonyms** cacophonous, clashing, discordant, dissonant, harsh, jangly, tuneless, unmelodious

tuneless atonal, cacophonous, clashing, discordant, dissonant, harsh, unmelodic, unmelodious, unmusical

▷ **Antonyms** harmonious, melodious, musical, pleasing, sonorous, symphonic, tuneful

tunnel 1. *noun* burrow, channel, hole, passage, passageway, shaft, subway, underpass **2.** ~*verb* burrow, dig, dig one's way, excavate, mine, penetrate, scoop out, undermine

turbid clouded, cloudy, confused, dense, dim, dreggy, foggy, foul, fuzzy, hazy, impure, incoherent, muddled, muddy, murky, opaque, roiled, thick, unclear, unsettled

turbulence agitation, boiling, commotion, confusion, disorder, instability, pandemonium, roughness, storm, tumult, turmoil, unrest, upheaval

▷ **Antonyms** calm, peace, quiet, repose, rest, stillness

turbulent 1. agitated, blustery, boiling, choppy, confused, disordered, foaming, furious, raging, rough, tempestuous, tumultuous, unsettled, unstable **2.** agitated, anarchic, boisterous, disorderly, insubordinate, lawless, mutinous, ob~

streperous, rebellious, refractory, riotous, rowdy, seditious, tumultuous, unbridled, undisciplined, ungovernable, unruly, uproarious, violent, wild
▷ **Antonyms** (*sense 1*) calm, glassy, peaceful, quiet, smooth, still, unruffled

turf 1. clod, divot, grass, green, sod, sward **2. the turf** horse-racing, racecourse, racetrack, racing, the flat

turf out banish, bounce (*slang*), cast out, chuck out (*informal*), discharge, dismiss, dispossess, eject, evict, expel, fire (*informal*), fling out, give one the bum's rush (*slang*), give one the sack (*informal*), kick out (*informal*), kiss off (*slang, chiefly U.S. & Canad.*), oust, relegate, sack (*informal*), show one the door, throw out

turgid 1. bloated, bulging, congested, distended, inflated, protuberant, puffed up, puffy, swollen, tumescent, tumid **2.** bombastic, flowery, fulsome, fustian, grandiloquent, grandiose, high-flown, inflated, magniloquent, orotund, ostentatious, overblown, pompous, pretentious, sesquipedalian, stilted, tumid, windy

turmoil agitation, bedlam, brouhaha, bustle, chaos, commotion, confusion, disarray, disorder, disturbance, ferment, flurry, hubbub, noise, pandemonium, row, stir, strife, trouble, tumult, turbulence, upheaval, uproar, violence
▷ **Antonyms** calm, peace, quiet, repose, rest, serenity, stillness, tranquillity

turn *verb* **1.** circle, go round, gyrate, move in a circle, pivot, revolve, roll, rotate, spin, swivel, twirl, twist, wheel, whirl **2.** change course, change position, go back, move, return, reverse, shift, swerve, switch, veer, wheel **3.** arc, come round, corner, go round, negotiate, pass, pass around, take a bend **4.** adapt, alter, become, change, convert, divert, fashion, fit, form, metamorphose, mould, mutate, remodel, shape, transfigure, transform, transmute **5.** become rancid, curdle, go bad, go off (*Brit. informal*), go sour, make rancid, sour, spoil, taint **6.** appeal, apply, approach, go, have recourse, look, resort **7.** nauseate, sicken, upset **8.** apostatize, bring round (*informal*), change one's mind, change sides, defect, desert, go over, influence, persuade, prejudice, prevail upon, renege, retract, talk into **9.** construct, deliver, execute, fashion, frame, make, mould, perform, shape, write **10. turn tail** beat a hasty retreat, bolt, cut and run (*informal*), flee, hook it (*slang*), run away, run off, show a clean pair of heels, take off (*informal*), take to one's heels ~*noun* **11.** bend, change, circle, curve, cycle, gyration, pivot, reversal, revolution, rotation, spin, swing, turning, twist, whirl **12.** bias, direction, drift, heading, tendency, trend **13.** bend, change of course, change of direction, curve, departure, deviation, shift **14.** chance, crack (*informal*), fling, go, opportunity, period, round, shift, shot (*informal*), spell, stint, succession, time, try, whack (*informal*) **15.** airing, circuit, constitutional, drive, excursion, jaunt, outing, promenade, ride, saunter, spin (*informal*), stroll, walk **16.** affinity, aptitude, bent, bias, flair, gift, inclination, knack, leaning, propensity, talent **17.** cast, fashion, form, format, guise, make-up, manner, mode, mould, shape, style, way **18.** act, action, deed, favour, gesture, service **19.** bend, distortion, twist, warp **20.** *informal* fright, scare, shock, start, surprise **21. by turns** alternately, in succession, one after another, reciprocally, turn and turn about **22. to a turn** correctly, exactly, just right, perfectly, precisely

turncoat apostate, backslider, defector, deserter, rat (*informal*), recreant (*archaic*), renegade, seceder, tergiversator, traitor

turn down 1. diminish, lessen, lower, muffle, mute, quieten, reduce the volume of, soften **2.** abstain from, decline, rebuff, refuse, reject, repudiate, say no to, spurn, throw out
▷ **Antonyms** (*sense 1*) amplify, augment, boost, increase, raise, strengthen, swell, turn up (*sense 2*) accede, accept, acquiesce, agree, receive, take

turn in 1. go to bed, go to sleep, hit the hay (*slang*), hit the sack (*slang*), retire for the night **2.** deliver, give back, give up, hand in, hand over, return, submit, surrender, tender

turning bend, crossroads, curve, junction, side road, turn, turn-off

turning point change, climacteric, crisis, critical moment, crossroads, crux, decisive moment, moment of decision, moment of truth

turn-off branch, exit, side road, turn, turning

turn off 1. branch off, change direction, depart from, deviate, leave, quit, take another road, take a side road **2.** cut out, kill, put out, shut down, stop, switch off, turn out, unplug **3.** *informal* alienate, bore, disenchant, disgust, displease, gross out (*U.S. slang*), irritate, lose one's interest, nauseate, offend, put off, repel, sicken

turn on 1. activate, energize, ignite, kick-start, put on, set in motion, start, start up, switch on **2.** balance, be contingent on, be decided by, depend, hang, hinge, pivot, rest **3.** assail, assault, attack, fall on, lose one's temper with, round on **4.** *slang* arouse, arouse one's desire, attract, excite, please, press one's buttons (*slang*), ring (someone's) bell (*U.S. slang*), stimulate, thrill, titillate, work up **5.** *slang* get high (*informal*), get stoned (*slang*), take drugs, trip (*informal*) **6.** *slang* expose, get one started with, inform, initiate, introduce, show

▷ **Antonyms** (*sense 1*) cut out, put out, shut off, stop, switch off, turn off

turnout 1. assemblage, assembly, attendance, audience, congregation, crowd, gate, number, throng **2.** amount produced, output, outturn (*rare*), production, production quota, productivity, turnover, volume, yield **3.** array, attire, costume, dress, equipage, equipment, gear (*informal*), get-up (*informal*), outfit, rigout (*informal*)

turn out 1. put out, switch off, turn off, unplug **2.** bring out, fabricate, finish, make, manufacture, process, produce, put out **3.** axe (*informal*), banish, cashier, cast out, deport, discharge, dismiss, dispossess, drive out, drum out, evict, expel, fire (*informal*), give one the sack (*informal*), give the bum's rush (*slang*), kick out (*informal*), kiss off (*slang, chiefly U.S. & Canad.*), oust, put out, relegate, sack (*informal*), show one the door, throw out, turf out (*Brit. informal*), unseat **4.** clean out, clear, discharge, empty, take out the contents of **5.** become, come about, come to be, come to light, crop up (*informal*), develop, emerge, end up, eventuate, evolve, happen, prove to be, result, transpire (*informal*), work out **6.** accoutre, apparel (*archaic*), attire, clothe, dress, fit, outfit, rig out **7.** appear, assemble, attend, be present, come, gather, go, put in an appearance, show up (*informal*), turn up

turnover 1. business, flow, output, outturn (*rare*), production, productivity, volume, yield **2.** change, coming and going, movement, replacement

turn over 1. capsize, flip over, keel over, overturn, reverse, tip over, upend, upset **2.** activate, crank, press the starter button, set going, set in motion, start up, switch on, switch on the ignition, warm up **3.** assign, commend, commit, deliver, give over, give up, hand over, pass on, render, surrender, transfer, yield **4.** consider, contemplate, deliberate, give thought to, mull over, ponder, reflect on, revolve, ruminate about, think about, think over, wonder about **5.** break up, dig, plough

turn up 1. appear, arrive, attend, come, put in an appearance, show (*informal*), show one's face, show up (*informal*) **2.** appear, become known, be found, bring to light, come to light, come to pass, come up with, crop up (*informal*), dig up, disclose, discover, expose, find, pop up, reveal, transpire, unearth **3.** amplify, boost, enhance, increase, increase the volume of, intensify, make louder, raise

▷ **Antonyms** (*sense 2*) disappear, evaporate, fade, hide, vanish (*sense 3*) diminish, lessen, lower, reduce, soften, turn down

turpitude badness, baseness, corruption, criminality, degeneracy, depravity, evil, foulness, immorality, iniquity, nefariousness, sinfulness, viciousness, vileness, villainy, wickedness

tussle 1. *verb* battle, brawl, contend, fight, grapple, scrap (*informal*), scuffle, struggle, vie, wrestle **2.** ~*noun bagarre,* battle, bout, brawl, competition, conflict, contention, contest, fight, fracas, fray, punch-up (*Brit. informal*), scrap (*informal*), scrimmage, scuffle, set-to (*informal*), shindig (*informal*), shindy (*informal*), struggle

tutelage care, charge, custody, dependence, education, guardianship, guidance, instruction, patronage, preparation, protection, schooling, teaching, tuition, wardship

tutor 1. *noun* coach, educator, governor, guardian, guide, guru, instructor, lecturer, master, mentor, preceptor, schoolmaster, teacher **2.** ~*verb* coach, direct, discipline, drill, edify, educate, guide, instruct, lecture, school, teach, train

tutorial 1. *noun* individual instruction, lesson, seminar **2.** ~*adjective* coaching, guiding, instructional, teaching

TV gogglebox (*Brit. slang*), idiot box (*slang*), receiver, small screen (*informal*), television, television set, telly (*Brit. informal*), the box (*Brit. informal*), the tube (*slang*), TV set

twaddle 1. *noun* balderdash, balls (*taboo slang*), bilge (*informal*), blather, bosh (*informal*), bull (*slang*), bullshit (*taboo slang*), bunkum *or* buncombe (*chiefly U.S.*), chatter, claptrap (*informal*), cobblers (*Brit. taboo slang*), crap (*slang*), drivel, eyewash (*informal*), foolish talk, gabble, garbage (*informal*), gobbledegook (*informal*), gossip, guff (*slang*), hogwash, hokum (*slang, chiefly U.S. & Canad.*), horsefeathers (*U.S. slang*), hot air (*informal*), inanity, moonshine, nonsense, pap, piffle (*informal*), poppycock (*informal*), rigmarole, rot, rubbish, shit (*taboo slang*), tattle, tommyrot, tosh (*slang, chiefly Brit.*), trash, tripe (*informal*), trumpery, verbiage, waffle (*informal, chiefly Brit.*) **2.** ~*verb* blather, chatter, gabble, gossip, prattle, rattle on, talk nonsense, talk through one's hat, tattle, waffle (*informal, chiefly Brit.*)

tweak *verb/noun* jerk, nip, pinch, pull, squeeze, twist, twitch

twee bijou, cute, dainty, precious, pretty, quaint, sentimental, sweet

twiddle 1. adjust, fiddle (*informal*), finger, jiggle, juggle, monkey with (*informal*), play with, twirl, wiggle **2. twiddle one's thumbs** be idle, be unoccupied, do nothing, have nothing to do, malinger, mark time, sit around

twig[1] *noun* branch, offshoot, shoot, spray, sprig, stick, withe

twig[2] *verb* catch on (*informal*), comprehend, fathom, find out, get, grasp, make out, rumble (*Brit. informal*), see, tumble to (*informal*), understand

twilight *noun* **1.** dimness, dusk, evening, gloaming (*Scot. or poetic*), gloom, half-light, sundown, sunset **2.** decline, ebb, last phase *~adjective* **3.** crepuscular, darkening, dim, evening **4.** declining, dying, ebbing, final, last

▷ **Antonyms** *~noun* (*sense 1*) dawn, daybreak, morning, sunrise, sunup (*sense 2*) climax, crowning moment, height, peak

twin 1. *noun* clone, corollary, counterpart, double, duplicate, fellow, likeness, lookalike, match, mate, ringer (*slang*) **2.** *~adjective* corresponding, double, dual, duplicate, geminate, identical, matched, matching, paired, parallel, twofold **3.** *~verb* couple, join, link, match, pair, yoke

twine *noun* **1.** cord, string, yarn **2.** coil, convolution, interlacing, twist, whorl **3.** knot, snarl, tangle *~verb* **4.** braid, entwine, interlace, interweave, knit, plait, splice, twist, twist together, weave **5.** bend, coil, curl, encircle, loop, meander, spiral, surround, twist, wind, wrap, wreathe

twinge bite, gripe, pain, pang, pinch, prick, sharp pain, spasm, stab, stitch, throb, throe (*rare*), tic, tweak, twist, twitch

twinkle *verb* **1.** blink, coruscate, flash, flicker, gleam, glint, glisten, glitter, scintillate, shimmer, shine, sparkle, wink *~noun* **2.** blink, coruscation, flash, flicker, gleam, glimmer, glistening, glittering, light, scintillation, shimmer, shine, spark, sparkle, wink **3.** flash, instant, jiffy (*informal*), moment, second, shake (*informal*), split second, tick (*Brit. informal*), trice, twinkling, two shakes of a lamb's tail (*informal*)

twinkling 1. blink, coruscation, flash, flashing, flicker, gleam, glimmer, glistening, glittering, scintillation, shimmer, shining, sparkle, twinkle, wink **2.** bat of an eye (*informal*), flash, instant, jiffy (*informal*), moment, second, shake (*informal*), split second, tick (*Brit. informal*), trice, twinkle, two shakes of a lamb's tail (*informal*)

twirl *verb* **1.** gyrate, pirouette, pivot, revolve, rotate, spin, turn, turn on one's heel, twiddle, twist, wheel, whirl, wind *~noun* **2.** gyration, pirouette, revolution, rotation, spin, turn, twist, wheel, whirl **3.** coil, spiral, twist

twist *verb* **1.** coil, corkscrew, curl, encircle, entwine, intertwine, screw, spin, swivel, twine, weave, wind, wrap, wreathe, wring **2.** contort, distort, screw up **3.** rick, sprain, turn, wrench **4.** alter, change, distort, falsify, garble, misquote, misrepresent, pervert, warp **5.** squirm, wriggle, writhe **6. twist someone's arm** bully, coerce, force, persuade, pressurize, talk into *~noun* **7.** coil, curl, spin, swivel, twine, wind **8.** braid, coil, curl, hank, plug, quid, roll **9.** change, development, revelation, slant, surprise, turn, variation **10.** arc, bend, convolution, curve, meander, turn, undulation, zigzag **11.** defect, deformation, distortion, flaw, imperfection, kink, warp **12.** jerk, pull, sprain, turn, wrench **13.** aberration, bent, characteristic, crotchet, eccentricity, fault, foible, idiosyncrasy, oddity, peculiarity, proclivity, quirk, trait **14.** confusion, entanglement, kink, knot, mess, mix-up, ravel, snarl, tangle **15. round the twist** *Brit. slang* barmy (*slang*), batty (*slang*), bonkers (*slang, chiefly Brit.*), crazy, cuckoo (*informal*), daft (*informal*), gonzo (*slang*), insane, loopy (*informal*), mad, not all there, not right in the head, nuts (*slang*), nutty (*slang*), nutty as a fruitcake (*slang*), off one's rocker (*slang*), off one's trolley (*slang*), out to lunch (*informal*), up the pole (*informal*), wacko *or* whacko (*informal*)

▷ **Antonyms** (*sense 1*) straighten, uncoil, unravel, unroll, untwist, unwind (*sense 2*) straighten, untwist (*sense 5*) hold stationary, hold steady, hold still

twister cheat, chiseller (*informal*), con man (*informal*), crook (*informal*), deceiver, fraud, fraudster, grifter (*slang, chiefly U.S. & Canad.*), hustler (*U.S. informal*), rogue, swindler, trickster

twit[1] *verb* banter, berate, blame, censure, deride, jeer, make fun of, scorn, taunt, tease, upbraid

twit[2] *noun* airhead (*slang*), ass, berk (*Brit. slang*), blockhead, charlie (*Brit. informal*), chump (*informal*), clown, dickhead (*slang*), dipstick (*Brit. slang*), divvy (*Brit. slang*), dope (*informal*), dork (*slang*), dweeb (*U.S. slang*), fool, fuckwit (*taboo slang*), geek (*slang*), gobshite (*Irish taboo slang*), gonzo (*slang*), halfwit, idiot, jerk (*slang, chiefly U.S. & Canad.*), juggins (*Brit. informal*), nerd *or* nurd (*slang*), nincompoop, ninny, nitwit (*informal*), numbskull *or* numskull, numpty (*Scot. informal*), oaf, pillock (*Brit. slang*), plank (*Brit. slang*), plonker (*slang*), prat (*slang*), prick (*slang*), schmuck (*U.S. slang*), silly-billy (*informal*), simpleton, twerp *or* twirp (*informal*), wally (*slang*)

twitch 1. *verb* blink, flutter, jerk, jump, pluck, pull, snatch, squirm, tug, yank **2.** *~noun* blink, flutter, jerk, jump, pull, spasm, tic, tremor, twinge

twitter *verb* **1.** chatter, cheep, chirp, chirrup, trill, tweet, warble, whistle **2.** chatter, giggle, prattle, simper, snigger, titter *~noun* **3.** call, chatter, cheep, chirp, chirrup, cry, song, trill, tweet, warble, whistle **4**. agitation, anxiety, bustle, dither (*chiefly Brit.*), excitement, flurry, fluster, flutter, nervousness, tizzy (*informal*), whirl

two-edged ambiguous, ambivalent, backhanded, double-edged, equivocal

two-faced deceitful, deceiving, dissembling, double-dealing, duplicitous, false, hypocritical, insincere, Janus-faced, perfidious, treacherous, untrustworthy
▷ **Antonyms** artless, candid, frank, genuine, honest, ingenuous, sincere, trustworthy

tycoon baron, big cheese (*slang, old-fashioned*), big noise (*informal*), capitalist, captain of industry, fat cat (*slang, chiefly U.S.*), financier, industrialist, magnate, merchant prince, mogul, plutocrat, potentate, wealthy businessman

type 1. breed, category, class, classification, form, genre, group, ilk, kidney, kind, order, sort, species, stamp, strain, style, subdivision, variety **2**. case, characters, face, fount, print, printing **3**. archetype, epitome, essence, example, exemplar, model, norm, original, paradigm, pattern, personification, prototype, quintessence, specimen, standard

typhoon cyclone, squall, storm, tempest, tornado, tropical storm

typical archetypal, average, bog-standard (*Brit. & Irish slang*), characteristic, classic, conventional, essential, illustrative, in character, indicative, in keeping, model, normal, orthodox, representative, standard, stock, true to type, usual
▷ **Antonyms** atypical, exceptional, out of keeping, out of the ordinary, singular, uncharacteristic, unconventional, unexpected, unique, unrepresentative, unusual

typify characterize, embody, epitomize, exemplify, illustrate, incarnate, personify, represent, sum up, symbolize

tyrannical absolute, arbitrary, authoritarian, autocratic, coercive, cruel, despotic, dictatorial, domineering, high-handed, imperious, inhuman, magisterial, oppressive, overbearing, overweening, peremptory, severe, tyrannous, unjust, unreasonable
▷ **Antonyms** democratic, easy-going, lax, lenient, liberal, reasonable, tolerant, understanding

tyrannize browbeat, bully, coerce, dictate, domineer, enslave, have (someone) under one's thumb, intimidate, oppress, ride roughshod over, rule with an iron hand, subjugate, terrorize

tyranny absolutism, authoritarianism, autocracy, coercion, cruelty, despotism, dictatorship, harsh discipline, high-handedness, imperiousness, oppression, peremptoriness, reign of terror, unreasonableness
▷ **Antonyms** democracy, ease, laxity, leniency, liberality, mercy, relaxation, tolerance, understanding

tyrant absolutist, authoritarian, autocrat, bully, despot, dictator, Hitler, martinet, oppressor, slave-driver

tyro apprentice, beginner, catechumen, greenhorn (*informal*), initiate, learner, neophyte, novice, novitiate, pupil, student, trainee

U, u

ubiquitous all-over, ever-present, every~ where, omnipresent, pervasive, univer~ sal

ugly **1.** hard-favoured, hard-featured, homely (*chiefly U.S.*), ill-favoured, mis~ shapen, no oil painting (*informal*), not much to look at, plain, unattractive, unlovely, unprepossessing, unsightly **2.** disagreeable, disgusting, distasteful, frightful, hideous, horrid, monstrous, objectionable, obscene, offensive, repug~ nant, repulsive, revolting, shocking, terrible, unpleasant, vile **3.** baleful, dangerous, forbidding, menacing, omi~ nous, sinister, threatening **4.** angry, bad-tempered, dark, evil, malevolent, nasty, spiteful, sullen, surly

▷ **Antonyms** (*sense 1*) attractive, beauti~ ful, cute, good-looking, gorgeous, hand~ some, lovely, pretty (*sense 2*) agreeable, pleasant (*sense 3*) auspicious, promising (*sense 4*) friendly, good-humoured, good-natured, likable *or* likeable, peace~ ful

ulcer abscess, boil, fester, gathering, gumboil, peptic ulcer, pustule, sore

ulcerous cankered, cankerous, festering, furunculous (*Pathology*), suppurative, ulcerative

ulterior concealed, covert, hidden, per~ sonal, secondary, secret, selfish, undis~ closed, unexpressed

▷ **Antonyms** apparent, declared, mani~ fest, obvious, overt, plain

ultimate *adjective* **1.** conclusive, decisive, end, eventual, extreme, final, furthest, last, terminal **2.** extreme, greatest, highest, maximum, most significant, paramount, superlative, supreme, top~ most, utmost **3.** basic, elemental, funda~ mental, primary, radical *~noun* **4.** cul~ mination, epitome, extreme, greatest, height, mother (of all), peak, perfection, summit, the last word

ultimately after all, at last, at the end of the day, basically, eventually, finally, fundamentally, in due time, in the end, in the fullness of time, sooner or later

ultra *adjective* excessive, extreme, fa~ natical, immoderate, rabid, radical, revolutionary

ultramodern advanced, ahead of its time, avant-garde, futuristic, modernistic, neoteric (*rare*), progressive, way-out (*informal*)

ululate bawl, cry, howl, keen, lament, moan, mourn, sob, wail, weep

umbrage anger, chagrin, displeasure, grudge, high dudgeon, huff, indignation, offence, pique, resentment, sense of in~ jury

▷ **Antonyms** amity, cordiality, goodwill, harmony, pleasure, understanding

umbrella **1.** brolly (*Brit. informal*), gamp (*Brit. informal*) **2.** aegis, agency, cover, patronage, protection

umpire **1.** *noun* adjudicator, arbiter, arbi~ trator, judge, moderator, ref (*informal*), referee **2.** *~verb* adjudicate, arbitrate, call (*Sport*), judge, mediate, moderate, referee

umpteen a good many, a thousand and one, considerable, countless, ever so many, millions, n, numerous, very many

unabashed blatant, bold, brazen, confi~ dent, unawed, unblushing, uncon~ cerned, undaunted, undismayed, unem~ barrassed

▷ **Antonyms** abashed, embarrassed, humbled, mortified, shame-faced, sheepish

unable impotent, inadequate, incapable, ineffectual, no good, not able, not equal to, not up to, powerless, unfit, unfitted, unqualified

▷ **Antonyms** able, adept, adequate, ca~ pable, competent, effective, potent, powerful

unabridged complete, full-length, uncon~ densed, uncut, unexpurgated, un~ shortened, whole

unacceptable beyond the pale, disagree~ able, displeasing, distasteful, improper, inadmissible, insupportable, objection~ able, offensive, undesirable, unpleasant, unsatisfactory, unwelcome

▷ **Antonyms** acceptable, agreeable, de~ lightful, desirable, pleasant, pleasing, welcome

unaccompanied a cappella (*Music*), alone, by oneself, lone, on one's own, solo, un~ escorted

unaccomplished **1.** incomplete, un~ achieved, uncompleted, undone, unfin~ ished, unperformed **2.** inexpert, lacking finesse, uncultivated, unskilful, unskilled

unaccountable **1.** baffling, incomprehensible, inexplicable, inscrutable, mysterious, odd, peculiar, puzzling, strange, unexplainable, unfathomable, unintelligible **2.** astonishing, extraordinary, uncommon, unheard-of, unusual, unwonted **3.** clear, exempt, free, not answerable, not responsible, unliable
▷ **Antonyms** (*sense 1*) accountable, comprehensible, explicable, intelligible, understandable

unaccounted-for lost, missing, not explained, not taken into consideration, not understood, unexplained

unaccustomed **1.** (*with* **to**) a newcomer to, a novice at, green, inexperienced, not given to, not used to, unfamiliar with, unpractised, unused to, unversed in **2.** new, out of the ordinary, remarkable, special, strange, surprising, uncommon, unexpected, unfamiliar, unprecedented, unusual, unwonted
▷ **Antonyms** (*sense 1*) experienced, given to, habituated, practised, seasoned, used to, well-versed (*sense 2*) accustomed, familiar, ordinary, regular, usual

unadorned plain, restrained, severe, simple, stark, straightforward, unembellished, unfussy, unornamented, unvarnished

unadvised **1.** careless, hasty, heedless, ill-advised, imprudent, inadvisable, indiscreet, injudicious, rash, reckless, unwary, unwise **2.** ignorant, in the dark, unaware, uninformed, unknowing, unsuspecting, unwarned

unaffected[1] *adjective* artless, genuine, honest, ingenuous, naive, natural, plain, simple, sincere, straightforward, unassuming, unpretentious, unsophisticated, unspoilt, unstudied, without airs
▷ **Antonyms** affected, assumed, designing, devious, insincere, mannered, pretentious, put-on, snobbish, sophisticated

unaffected[2] *adjective* aloof, impervious, not influenced, proof, unaltered, unchanged, unimpressed, unmoved, unresponsive, unstirred, untouched
▷ **Antonyms** affected, changed, concerned, disrupted, hard-hit, influenced, interested, responsive, sympathetic, touched

unafraid confident, daring, dauntless, fearless, intrepid, unfearing, unshakable
▷ **Antonyms** afraid, alarmed, anxious, fearful, frightened, scared

unalterable fixed, fixed as the laws of the Medes and the Persians, immovable, immutable, invariable, permanent, steadfast, unchangeable, unchanging
▷ **Antonyms** alterable, changeable, changing, flexible, mutable, variable

unanimity accord, agreement, assent, chorus, concert, concord, concurrence, consensus, harmony, like-mindedness, one mind, unison, unity
▷ **Antonyms** difference, disagreement, discord, disunity, division, variance

unanimous agreed, agreeing, at one, common, concerted, concordant, harmonious, in agreement, in complete accord, like-minded, of one mind, united
▷ **Antonyms** differing, discordant, dissident, disunited, divided, schismatic, split

unanimously by common consent, nem. con., unitedly, unopposed, with one accord, without exception, without opposition

unanswerable **1.** absolute, conclusive, incontestable, incontrovertible, indisputable, irrefutable, unarguable, undeniable **2.** insoluble, insolvable, unascertainable, unexplainable, unresolvable

unanswered disputed, ignored, in doubt, open, undecided, undenied, unnoticed, unrefuted, unresolved, unsettled, up in the air, vexed

unappetizing distasteful, insipid, off-putting (*Brit. informal*), tasteless, unappealing, unattractive, uninteresting, uninviting, unpalatable, unpleasant, unsavoury, vapid
▷ **Antonyms** agreeable, appealing, appetizing, attractive, interesting, palatable, savoury, tasty, toothsome

unapproachable **1.** aloof, chilly, cool, distant, frigid, offish (*informal*), remote, reserved, standoffish, unfriendly, unsociable, withdrawn **2.** inaccessible, out of reach, out-of-the-way, remote, un-get-at-able (*informal*), unreachable
▷ **Antonyms** (*sense 1*) affable, approachable, congenial, cordial, friendly, sociable

unapt **1.** inapplicable, inapposite, inappropriate, inapt, out of character, out of keeping, out of place, unfit, unfitted, unsuitable **2.** backward, dim, dim-witted (*informal*), dull, incompetent, slow, stupid, thick **3.** averse, disinclined, loath, not prone, reluctant, undisposed, unlikely, unwilling

unarmed assailable, defenceless, exposed, helpless, open, open to attack, unarmoured, unprotected, weak, weaponless, without arms
▷ **Antonyms** armed, equipped, fortified, protected, ready, strengthened

unasked **1.** gratuitous, spontaneous, unbidden, undemanded, undesired, uninvited, unprompted, unrequested, unsought, unwanted **2.** off one's own bat, of one's own accord, voluntarily, without prompting

unassailable **1.** impregnable, invincible, invulnerable, secure, well-defended **2.** absolute, conclusive, incontestable, incontrovertible, indisputable, irrefutable,

positive, proven, sound, undeniable
▷ **Antonyms** (*sense 2*) debatable, doubtful, dubious, inconclusive, uncertain, unfounded, unproven, unsound

unassertive backward, bashful, diffident, meek, mousy, retiring, self-effacing, timid, timorous, unassuming
▷ **Antonyms** aggressive, assertive, confident, feisty (*informal, chiefly U.S. & Canad.*), forceful, overbearing, pushy (*informal*)

unassuming diffident, humble, meek, modest, quiet, reserved, retiring, self-effacing, simple, unassertive, unobtrusive, unostentatious, unpretentious
▷ **Antonyms** assuming, audacious, conceited, ostentatious, overconfident, presumptuous, pretentious

unattached **1.** autonomous, free, independent, nonaligned, unaffiliated, uncommitted **2.** a free agent, available, by oneself, footloose and fancy-free, left on the shelf, not spoken for, on one's own, single, unengaged, unmarried
▷ **Antonyms** (*sense 1*) affiliated, aligned, attached, committed, dependent, implicated, involved

unattended **1.** abandoned, disregarded, ignored, left alone, not cared for, unguarded, unwatched **2.** alone, on one's own, unaccompanied, unescorted

unauthorized illegal, off the record, unapproved, unconstitutional, under-the-table, unlawful, unofficial, unsanctioned, unwarranted
▷ **Antonyms** authorized, constitutional, lawful, legal, official, sanctioned, warranted

unavailing abortive, bootless, fruitless, futile, idle, ineffective, ineffectual, of no avail, pointless, to no purpose, unproductive, unsuccessful, useless, vain
▷ **Antonyms** effective, fruitful, productive, rewarding, successful, useful, worthwhile

unavoidable bound to happen, certain, compulsory, fated, ineluctable, inescapable, inevitable, inexorable, necessary, obligatory, sure

unaware heedless, ignorant, incognizant, oblivious, unconscious, unenlightened, uninformed, unknowing, unmindful, unsuspecting
▷ **Antonyms** attentive, aware, conscious, informed, knowing, mindful

unawares **1.** aback, abruptly, by surprise, caught napping, off guard, on the hop (*Brit. informal*), suddenly, unexpectedly, unprepared, without warning **2.** accidentally, by accident, by mistake, inadvertently, mistakenly, unconsciously, unintentionally, unknowingly, unwittingly
▷ **Antonyms** deliberately, forewarned, knowingly, on purpose, on the lookout, prepared, wittingly

unbalanced **1.** asymmetrical, irregular, lopsided, not balanced, shaky, unequal, uneven, unstable, unsymmetrical, wobbly **2.** barking (*slang*), barking mad (*slang*), crazy, demented, deranged, disturbed, doolally (*slang*), eccentric, erratic, gonzo (*slang*), insane, irrational, loopy (*informal*), lunatic, mad, *non compos mentis,* not all there, not the full shilling (*informal*), off one's trolley (*slang*), out to lunch (*informal*), touched, unhinged, unsound, unstable, up the pole (*informal*), wacko *or* whacko (*informal*) **3.** biased, inequitable, one-sided, partial, partisan, prejudiced, unfair, unjust
▷ **Antonyms** (*sense 1*) balanced, equal, even, stable, symmetrical

unbearable insufferable, insupportable, intolerable, oppressive, too much (*informal*), unacceptable, unendurable
▷ **Antonyms** acceptable, bearable, endurable, supportable, tolerable

unbeatable indomitable, invincible, more than a match for, unconquerable, unstoppable, unsurpassable

unbeaten **1.** triumphant, unbowed, undefeated, unsubdued, unsurpassed, unvanquished, victorious, winning **2.** new, untouched, untried, untrodden, virgin

unbecoming **1.** ill-suited, inappropriate, incongruous, unattractive, unbefitting, unfit, unflattering, unsightly, unsuitable, unsuited **2.** discreditable, improper, indecorous, indelicate, offensive, tasteless, unseemly
▷ **Antonyms** (*sense 2*) becoming, decent, decorous, delicate, proper, seemly

unbelief atheism, disbelief, distrust, doubt, incredulity, scepticism
▷ **Antonyms** belief, credence, credulity, faith, trust

unbelievable astonishing, beyond belief, cock-and-bull (*informal*), far-fetched, implausible, impossible, improbable, inconceivable, incredible, outlandish, preposterous, questionable, staggering, unconvincing, unimaginable, unthinkable
▷ **Antonyms** authentic, believable, credible, likely, plausible, possible, probable, trustworthy

unbeliever agnostic, atheist, disbeliever, doubting Thomas, infidel, sceptic

unbelieving disbelieving, distrustful, doubtful, doubting, dubious, incredulous, sceptical, suspicious, unconvinced
▷ **Antonyms** believing, convinced, credulous, trustful, undoubting, unsuspicious

unbend **1.** be informal, calm down, chill out (*slang, chiefly U.S.*), cool it (*slang*), ease up, let it all hang out (*slang*), let oneself go, let up, lighten up (*slang*), loosen up, relax, slacken, slow down, take it easy, unbutton (*informal*), unwind **2.** put straight, straighten, uncoil, uncurl

unbending **1.** aloof, distant, formal, inflexible, reserved, rigid, stiff, uptight (*informal*) **2.** firm, hardline, intractable, resolute, severe, strict, stubborn, tough, uncompromising, unyielding

▷ **Antonyms** (*sense 1*) approachable, at ease, flexible, friendly, outgoing, relaxed, sociable

unbiased disinterested, dispassionate, equitable, even-handed, fair, impartial, just, neutral, objective, open-minded, unprejudiced

▷ **Antonyms** biased, bigoted, partial, prejudiced, slanted, swayed, unfair, unjust

unbidden **1.** free, spontaneous, unforced, unprompted, voluntary, willing **2.** unasked, uninvited, unwanted, unwelcome

unbind free, loosen, release, set free, unbridle, unchain, unclasp, undo, unfasten, unfetter, unloose, unshackle, unstrap, untie, unyoke

▷ **Antonyms** bind, chain, fasten, fetter, restrain, shackle, tie, yoke

unblemished flawless, immaculate, impeccable, perfect, pure, spotless, unflawed, unspotted, unstained, unsullied, untarnished

▷ **Antonyms** blemished, flawed, imperfect, impure, stained, sullied, tarnished

unblinking **1.** calm, cool, emotionless, impassive, unemotional, unfaltering, unwavering **2.** fearless, steady, unafraid, unflinching, unshrinking

unblushing amoral, bold, brazen, forward, immodest, shameless, unabashed, unashamed, unembarrassed

unborn **1.** awaited, embryonic, expected, *in utero* **2.** coming, future, hereafter, latter, subsequent, to come

unbosom admit, confess, confide, disburden, disclose, divulge, get (something) off one's chest (*informal*), get (something) out of one's system, lay bare, let out, reveal, spill one's guts about (*slang*), tell, unburden

▷ **Antonyms** conceal, cover up, guard, hold back, suppress, withhold

unbounded absolute, boundless, endless, immeasurable, infinite, lavish, limitless, unbridled, unchecked, unconstrained, uncontrolled, unlimited, unrestrained, vast

▷ **Antonyms** bounded, confined, constrained, curbed, limited, restricted

unbreakable armoured, durable, indestructible, infrangible, lasting, nonbreakable, resistant, rugged, shatterproof, solid, strong, toughened

▷ **Antonyms** breakable, brittle, delicate, flimsy, fragile, frangible

unbridled excessive, full-on (*informal*), intemperate, licentious, rampant, riotous, unchecked, unconstrained, uncontrolled, uncurbed, ungovernable, ungoverned, unrestrained, unruly, violent, wanton

unbroken **1.** complete, entire, intact, solid, total, unimpaired, whole **2.** ceaseless, constant, continuous, endless, incessant, progressive, serried, successive, uninterrupted, unremitting **3.** deep, fast, profound, sound, undisturbed, unruffled, untroubled **4.** unbowed, unsubdued, untamed

▷ **Antonyms** (*sense 1*) broken, cracked, damaged, fragmented, in pieces, shattered (*sense 2*) erratic, fitful, intermittent, interrupted, irregular, occasional, off-and-on, uneven

unburden **1.** disburden, discharge, disencumber, ease the load, empty, lighten, relieve, unload **2.** come clean (*informal*), confess, confide, disclose, get (something) off one's chest (*informal*), lay bare, make a clean breast of, reveal, spill one's guts about (*slang*), tell all, unbosom

uncalled-for gratuitous, inappropriate, needless, undeserved, unjust, unjustified, unnecessary, unprovoked, unwarranted, unwelcome

▷ **Antonyms** appropriate, deserved, just, justified, necessary, needed, provoked, warranted

uncanny **1.** creepy (*informal*), eerie, eldritch (*poetic*), mysterious, preternatural, queer, spooky (*informal*), strange, supernatural, unearthly, unnatural, weird **2.** astonishing, astounding, exceptional, extraordinary, fantastic, incredible, inspired, miraculous, prodigious, remarkable, singular, unheard-of, unusual

uncaring indifferent, negligent, unconcerned, unfeeling, uninterested, unmoved, unresponsive, unsympathetic

unceasing ceaseless, constant, continual, continuing, continuous, endless, incessant, never-ending, nonstop, perpetual, persistent, unending, unfailing, unremitting

▷ **Antonyms** fitful, intermittent, irregular, occasional, periodic, spasmodic, sporadic

uncertain **1.** ambiguous, chancy, conjectural, doubtful, iffy (*informal*), incalculable, indefinite, indeterminate, indistinct, questionable, risky, speculative, undetermined, unforeseeable, unpredictable **2.** ambivalent, at a loss, doubtful, dubious, hazy, in the balance, in two minds, irresolute, unclear, unconfirmed, undecided, undetermined, unfixed, unresolved, unsettled, unsure, up in the air, vacillating, vague **3.** changeable, erratic, fitful, hesitant, iffy (*informal*), inconstant, insecure, irregular, precarious, unpredictable, unreliable, vacillating, variable, wavering

▷ **Antonyms** certain, clear, clear-cut, decided, definite, firm, fixed, known, positive, predictable, resolute, settled, sure, unambiguous, unhesitating, unvarying, unwavering

uncertainty ambiguity, bewilderment, confusion, dilemma, doubt, dubiety, hesitancy, hesitation, inconclusiveness, indecision, irresolution, lack of confidence, misgiving, mystification, perplexity, puzzlement, qualm, quandary, scepticism, state of suspense, unpredictability, vagueness

▷ **Antonyms** assurance, certainty, confidence, decision, predictability, resolution, sureness, trust

unchangeable changeless, constant, fixed, immovable, immutable, inevitable, invariable, irreversible, permanent, stable, steadfast, strong, unalterable

▷ **Antonyms** changeable, inconstant, irregular, mutable, shifting, unstable, variable, wavering

unchanging abiding, changeless, constant, continuing, enduring, eternal, immutable, imperishable, lasting, permanent, perpetual, unchanged, unfading, unvarying

uncharitable cruel, hardhearted, insensitive, mean, merciless, stingy, unchristian, unfeeling, unforgiving, unfriendly, ungenerous, unkind, unsympathetic

▷ **Antonyms** charitable, feeling, friendly, generous, kind, merciful, sensitive, sympathetic

uncharted not mapped, strange, undiscovered, unexplored, unfamiliar, unknown, unplumbed, virgin

unchaste depraved, dissolute, fallen, immodest, immoral, impure, lewd, loose, promiscuous, unvirtuous, wanton

▷ **Antonyms** chaste, decent, innocent, modest, moral, pure, virtuous

uncivil bad-mannered, bearish, boorish, brusque, churlish, discourteous, disrespectful, gruff, ill-bred, ill-mannered, impolite, rude, surly, uncouth, unmannerly

▷ **Antonyms** civil, courteous, mannerly, polished, polite, refined, respectful, well-bred, well-mannered

uncivilized **1**. barbarian, barbaric, barbarous, illiterate, primitive, savage, wild **2**. beyond the pale, boorish, brutish, churlish, coarse, gross, philistine, uncouth, uncultivated, uncultured, uneducated, unmannered, unpolished, unsophisticated, vulgar

unclad bare, buck naked (*slang*), in one's birthday suit (*informal*), in the altogether (*informal*), in the bare scud (*slang*), in the buff (*informal*), in the raw (*informal*), naked, naked as the day one was born (*informal*), nude, scuddy (*slang*), starkers (*informal*), stripped, unclothed, undressed, with nothing on, without a stitch on (*informal*)

unclean contaminated, corrupt, defiled, dirty, evil, filthy, foul, impure, nasty, polluted, scuzzy (*slang, chiefly U.S.*), soiled, spotted, stained, sullied, tainted

▷ **Antonyms** clean, faultless, flawless, pure, spotless, unblemished, unstained, unsullied

unclear ambiguous, bleary, blurred, confused, dim, doubtful, faint, fuzzy, hazy, ill-defined, indefinite, indeterminate, indiscernible, indistinct, indistinguishable, misty, muffled, obscure, out of focus, shadowy, undefined, unintelligible, vague, weak

▷ **Antonyms** clear, defined, determinate, discernible, distinct, distinguishable, evident, intelligible

uncomfortable **1**. awkward, causing discomfort, cramped, disagreeable, hard, ill-fitting, incommodious, irritating, painful, rough, troublesome **2**. awkward, confused, discomfited, disquieted, distressed, disturbed, embarrassed, ill at ease, like a fish out of water, out of place, self-conscious, troubled, uneasy

▷ **Antonyms** (*sense 2*) at ease, at home, comfortable, easy, relaxed, serene, untroubled

uncommitted floating, free, free-floating, neutral, nonaligned, nonpartisan, not involved, (sitting) on the fence, unattached, uninvolved

uncommon **1**. bizarre, curious, few and far between, infrequent, novel, odd, out of the ordinary, peculiar, queer, rare, scarce, singular, strange, thin on the ground, unfamiliar, unusual **2**. distinctive, exceptional, extraordinary, incomparable, inimitable, notable, noteworthy, outstanding, rare, remarkable, singular, special, superior, unparalleled, unprecedented

▷ **Antonyms** (*sense 1*) common, familiar, frequent, regular, routine, usual (*sense 2*) average, banal, commonplace, everyday, humdrum, mundane, ordinary, run-of-the-mill

uncommonly **1**. hardly ever, infrequently, not often, occasionally, only now and then, rarely, scarcely ever, seldom **2**. exceptionally, extremely, particularly, peculiarly, remarkably, seriously (*informal*), strangely, to the nth degree, unusually, very

uncommunicative close, curt, guarded, reserved, reticent, retiring, secretive, short, shy, silent, taciturn, tight-lipped, unforthcoming, unresponsive, unsociable, withdrawn

▷ **Antonyms** chatty, communicative, forthcoming, garrulous, loquacious, responsive, talkative, voluble

uncompromising decided, die-hard, firm, hardline, inexorable, inflexible, intransigent, obdurate, obstinate, rigid, steadfast, stiff-necked, strict, stubborn, tough, unbending, unyielding

unconcern aloofness, apathy, detachment, indifference, insouciance, lack of interest, nonchalance, remoteness, uninterestedness

unconcerned 1. aloof, apathetic, cool, detached, dispassionate, distant, incurious, indifferent, oblivious, uninterested, uninvolved, unmoved, unsympathetic **2.** blithe, callous, carefree, careless, easy, insouciant, nonchalant, not bothered, not giving a toss (*informal*), relaxed, serene, unperturbed, unruffled, untroubled, unworried

▷ **Antonyms** (*sense 1*) avid, curious, eager, interested, involved (*sense 2*) agitated, anxious, concerned, distressed, perturbed, uneasy, worried

unconditional absolute, arrant, categorical, complete, downright, entire, explicit, full, out-and-out, outright, plenary, positive, thoroughgoing, total, unlimited, unqualified, unreserved, unrestricted, utter

▷ **Antonyms** conditional, limited, partial, qualified, reserved, restricted

uncongenial antagonistic, antipathetic, disagreeable, discordant, displeasing, distasteful, incompatible, not one's cup of tea (*informal*), unharmonious, uninviting, unpleasant, unsuited, unsympathetic

▷ **Antonyms** affable, agreeable, compatible, congenial, genial, harmonious, pleasant, pleasing, sympathetic

unconnected 1. detached, disconnected, divided, independent, separate **2.** disconnected, disjointed, illogical, incoherent, irrelevant, meaningless, nonsensical, not related, unrelated

▷ **Antonyms** (*sense 2*) coherent, connected, intelligible, logical, meaningful, related, relevant

unconquerable 1. indomitable, invincible, unbeatable, undefeatable, unyielding **2.** enduring, ingrained, innate, insurmountable, inveterate, irrepressible, irresistible, overpowering

unconscionable 1. amoral, criminal, unethical, unfair, unjust, unprincipled, unscrupulous **2.** excessive, exorbitant, extravagant, extreme, immoderate, inordinate, outrageous, preposterous, unreasonable

unconscious 1. blacked out (*informal*), comatose, dead to the world (*informal*), insensible, knocked out, numb, out, out cold, out for the count (*Boxing*), senseless, stunned **2.** blind to, deaf to, heedless, ignorant, in ignorance, lost to, oblivious, unaware, unknowing, unmindful, unsuspecting **3.** accidental, inadvertent, unintended, unintentional, unpremeditated, unwitting **4.** automatic, gut (*informal*), inherent, innate, instinctive, involuntary, latent, reflex, repressed, subconscious, subliminal, suppressed, unrealized

▷ **Antonyms** (*sense 1*) alert, awake, aware, conscious, responsive, sensible (*sense 3*) calculated, conscious, deliberate, intentional, planned, studied, wilful

uncontrollable beside oneself, carried away, frantic, furious, irrepressible, irresistible, like one possessed, mad, strong, ungovernable, unmanageable, unruly, violent, wild

uncontrolled boisterous, full-on (*informal*), furious, lacking self-control, out of control, out of hand, rampant, riotous, running wild, unbridled, unchecked, uncurbed, undisciplined, ungoverned, unrestrained, unruly, unsubmissive, untrammelled, violent

▷ **Antonyms** contained, controlled, disciplined, restrained, subdued, submissive

unconventional atypical, bizarre, bohemian, different, eccentric, far-out (*slang*), freakish, idiosyncratic, individual, individualistic, informal, irregular, left-field (*informal*), nonconformist, odd, oddball (*informal*), offbeat, off-the-wall (*slang*), original, out of the ordinary, outré, uncustomary, unorthodox, unusual, wacko (*slang*), way-out (*informal*)

▷ **Antonyms** conventional, normal, ordinary, orthodox, proper, regular, typical, usual

unconvincing cock-and-bull (*informal*), dubious, feeble, fishy (*informal*), flimsy, hard to believe, implausible, improbable, inconclusive, lame, questionable, specious, suspect, thin, unlikely, unpersuasive, weak

▷ **Antonyms** believable, conclusive, convincing, credible, likely, persuasive, plausible, probable

uncoordinated all thumbs, awkward, bumbling, bungling, butterfingered (*informal*), clodhopping (*informal*), clumsy, graceless, heavy-footed, inept, lumbering, maladroit, ungainly, ungraceful

uncounted countless, infinite, innumerable, legion, multitudinous, myriad, numberless, unnumbered, untold

uncouth awkward, barbaric, boorish, clownish, clumsy, coarse, crude, gawky, graceless, gross, ill-mannered, loutish, lubberly, oafish, rough, rude, rustic, uncivilized, uncultivated, ungainly, unrefined, unseemly, vulgar

▷ **Antonyms** civilized, courteous, cultivated, elegant, graceful, refined, seemly, well-mannered

uncover 1. bare, lay open, lift the lid, open, show, strip, take the wraps off, unwrap **2.** blow wide open (*slang*), bring to light, disclose, discover, divulge, expose, lay bare, make known, reveal, unearth, unmask

▷ **Antonyms** clothe, conceal, cover, cover up, drape, dress, hide, keep under wraps, suppress

uncritical easily pleased, indiscriminate, undiscerning, undiscriminating, unexacting, unfussy, unperceptive, unselective, unthinking

▷ **Antonyms** critical, discerning, discriminating, fastidious, fussy, perceptive, selective

unctuous **1.** fawning, glib, gushing, ingratiating, insincere, obsequious, oily, plausible, slick, smarmy (*Brit. informal*), smooth, suave, sycophantic **2.** greasy, oily, oleaginous, slippery, slithery

undaunted bold, brave, courageous, dauntless, fearless, gallant, gritty, indomitable, intrepid, not discouraged, nothing daunted, not put off, resolute, steadfast, undeterred, undiscouraged, undismayed, unfaltering, unflinching, unshrinking

undeceive be honest with, correct, disabuse, disillusion, enlighten, open (someone's) eyes (to), put (someone) right, set (someone) straight, shatter (someone's) illusions

undecided **1.** ambivalent, dithering (*chiefly Brit.*), doubtful, dubious, hesitant, in two minds, irresolute, swithering (*Scot.*), torn, uncertain, uncommitted, unsure, wavering **2.** debatable, iffy (*informal*), indefinite, in the balance, moot, open, pending, tentative, unconcluded, undetermined, unsettled, up in the air, vague

▷ **Antonyms** certain, committed, decided, definite, determined, resolute, resolved, settled, sure

undecipherable crabbed, cryptic, hieroglyphic, illegible, impenetrable, incomprehensible, indecipherable, indistinct, undistinguishable, unreadable, unrecognizable

undefended defenceless, exposed, naked, open to attack, unarmed, unfortified, unguarded, unprotected, vulnerable, wide open

▷ **Antonyms** armed, defended, fortified, guarded, protected

undefiled chaste, clean, clear, flawless, immaculate, impeccable, pure, sinless, spotless, squeaky-clean, unblemished, unsoiled, unspotted, unstained, unsullied, virginal

▷ **Antonyms** blemished, defiled, flawed, impure, sinful, soiled, spotted, stained, sullied

undefined **1.** formless, hazy, indefinite, indistinct, shadowy, tenuous, vague **2.** imprecise, indeterminate, inexact, unclear, unexplained, unspecified

▷ **Antonyms** (*sense 2*) clear, defined, definite, determinate, exact, explicit, precise, specified

undemonstrative aloof, cold, contained, distant, formal, impassive, reserved, restrained, reticent, stiff, stolid, unaffectionate, uncommunicative, unemotional, unresponsive, withdrawn

▷ **Antonyms** affectionate, demonstrative, emotional, expressive, friendly, outgoing, overemotional, unreserved, warm

undeniable beyond (a) doubt, beyond question, certain, clear, evident, incontestable, incontrovertible, indisputable, indubitable, irrefutable, manifest, obvious, patent, proven, sound, sure, unassailable, undoubted, unquestionable

▷ **Antonyms** debatable, deniable, doubtful, dubious, questionable, uncertain, unproven

undependable capricious, changeable, erratic, fickle, inconsistent, inconstant, irresponsible, treacherous, uncertain, unpredictable, unreliable, unstable, untrustworthy, variable

under *preposition* **1.** below, beneath, on the bottom of, underneath **2.** directed by, governed by, inferior to, junior to, reporting to, secondary to, subject to, subordinate to, subservient to **3.** belonging to, comprised in, included in, subsumed under *~adverb* **4.** below, beneath, down, downward, lower, to the bottom

▷ **Antonyms** (*senses 1 & 4*) above, over, up, upper, upward

underclothes lingerie, smalls (*informal*), underclothing, undergarments, underlinen, underthings, underwear, undies (*informal*), unmentionables (*humorous*)

undercover clandestine, concealed, confidential, covert, hidden, hush-hush (*informal*), intelligence, private, secret, spy, surreptitious, underground

▷ **Antonyms** manifest, open, overt, plain, unconcealed, visible

undercurrent **1.** crosscurrent, rip, rip current, riptide, tideway, underflow, undertow **2.** atmosphere, aura, drift, feeling, flavour, hidden feeling, hint, murmur, overtone, sense, suggestion, tendency, tenor, tinge, trend, undertone, vibes (*slang*), vibrations

undercut **1.** sacrifice, sell at a loss, sell cheaply, undercharge, underprice, undersell **2.** cut away, cut out, excavate, gouge out, hollow out, mine, undermine

underdog fall guy (*informal*), little fellow (*informal*), loser, victim, weaker party

underestimate belittle, hold cheap, minimize, miscalculate, misprize, not do justice to, rate too low, sell short (*informal*), set no store by, think too little of, underrate, undervalue

▷ **Antonyms** exaggerate, inflate, overdo, overestimate, overrate, overstate

undergo bear, be subjected to, endure, experience, go through, stand, submit to, suffer, sustain, weather, withstand

underground *adjective* **1.** below ground, below the surface, buried, covered, subterranean **2.** clandestine, concealed, covert, hidden, secret, surreptitious, undercover **3.** alternative, avant-garde, experimental, radical, revolutionary, subversive *~noun* **the underground 4.** the metro, the subway, the tube (*Brit.*) **5.** partisans, the Maquis, the Resistance

undergrowth bracken, brambles, briars, brush, brushwood, scrub, underbrush, underbush, underwood

underhand below the belt (*informal*), clandestine, crafty, crooked (*informal*), deceitful, deceptive, devious, dishonest, dishonourable, fraudulent, furtive, secret, secretive, sly, sneaky, stealthy, surreptitious, treacherous, underhanded, unethical, unscrupulous

▷ **Antonyms** above board, frank, honest, honourable, legal, open, outright, principled, scrupulous

underline 1. italicize, mark, rule a line under, underscore **2.** accentuate, bring home, call *or* draw attention to, emphasize, give emphasis to, highlight, point up, stress

▷ **Antonyms** (*sense 2*) gloss over, make light of, minimize, play down, soft-pedal (*informal*), underrate

underling cohort (*chiefly U.S.*), flunky, hireling, inferior, lackey, menial, minion, nonentity, retainer, servant, slave, subordinate, understrapper

underlying 1. concealed, hidden, latent, lurking, veiled **2.** basal, basic, elementary, essential, fundamental, intrinsic, primary, prime, radical, root

undermine 1. dig out, eat away at, erode, excavate, mine, tunnel, undercut, wear away **2.** debilitate, disable, impair, sabotage, sap, subvert, threaten, weaken

▷ **Antonyms** (*sense 2*) buttress, fortify, promote, reinforce, strengthen, sustain

underpinning 1. base, footing, foundation, groundwork, substructure, support **2.** *plural* backbone, basis, foundation, ground, support

underprivileged badly off, deprived, destitute, disadvantaged, impoverished, in need, in want, needy, on the breadline, poor

underrate belittle, discount, disparage, fail to appreciate, misprize, not do justice to, set (too) little store by, underestimate, undervalue

▷ **Antonyms** exaggerate, overestimate, overprize, overrate, overvalue

undersell 1. cut, mark down, reduce, slash, undercharge, undercut **2.** play down, understate

undersized atrophied, dwarfish, miniature, pygmy *or* pigmy, runtish, runty, small, squat, stunted, teensy-weensy, teeny-weeny, tiny, underdeveloped, underweight

▷ **Antonyms** big, colossal, giant, huge, massive, oversized, overweight

understand 1. appreciate, apprehend, be aware, catch on (*informal*), comprehend, conceive, cotton on (*informal*), discern, fathom, follow, get, get one's head round, get the hang of (*informal*), get to the bottom of, grasp, know, make head or tail of (*informal*), make out, penetrate, perceive, realize, recognize, savvy (*slang*), see, see the light, take in, tumble to (*informal*), twig (*Brit. informal*) **2.** assume, be informed, believe, conclude, gather, hear, learn, presume, suppose, take it, think **3.** accept, appreciate, be able to see, commiserate, show compassion for, sympathize with, tolerate

understanding *noun* **1.** appreciation, awareness, comprehension, discernment, grasp, insight, intelligence, judgment, knowledge, penetration, perception, sense **2.** belief, conclusion, estimation, idea, interpretation, judgment, notion, opinion, perception, view, viewpoint **3.** accord, agreement, common view, gentlemen's agreement, meeting of minds, pact *~adjective* **4.** accepting, compassionate, considerate, discerning, forbearing, forgiving, kind, kindly, patient, perceptive, responsive, sensitive, sympathetic, tolerant

▷ **Antonyms** *~noun* (*sense 1*) ignorance, incomprehension, insensitivity, misapprehension, misunderstanding, obtuseness (*sense 3*) aloofness, coldness, disagreement, dispute *~adjective* inconsiderate, insensitive, intolerant, obtuse, rigid, strict, unfeeling, unsympathetic

understood 1. implicit, implied, inferred, tacit, unspoken, unstated **2.** accepted, assumed, axiomatic, presumed, taken for granted

understudy *noun* double, fill-in, replacement, reserve, stand-in, sub, substitute

undertake 1. agree, bargain, commit oneself, contract, covenant, engage, guarantee, pledge, promise, stipulate, take upon oneself **2.** attempt, begin, commence, embark on, endeavour, enter upon, set about, tackle, take on, try

undertaker funeral director, mortician (*U.S.*)

undertaking 1. affair, attempt, business, effort, endeavour, enterprise, game, operation, project, task, venture **2.** assurance, commitment, pledge, promise, solemn word, vow, word, word of honour

undertone 1. low tone, murmur, subdued voice, whisper **2.** atmosphere, feeling, flavour, hint, suggestion, tinge, touch, trace, undercurrent, vibes (*slang*)

undervalue depreciate, hold cheap, look down on, make light of, minimize, misjudge, misprize, set no store by, underestimate, underrate

▷ **Antonyms** exaggerate, overestimate, overrate, overvalue

underwater submarine, submerged, sunken, undersea

under way afoot, begun, going on, in business, in motion, in operation, in progress, started

underwear lingerie, smalls (*informal*), underclothes, underclothing, undergarments, underlinen, underthings, undies (*informal*), unmentionables (*humorous*)

underweight emaciated, half-starved, puny, skin and bone (*informal*), skinny, undernourished, undersized

underworld 1. criminal element, criminals, gangland (*informal*), gangsters, organized crime 2. abode of the dead, Hades, hell, infernal region, nether regions, nether world, the inferno

underwrite 1. back, finance, fund, guarantee, insure, provide security, sponsor, subsidize 2. countersign, endorse, initial, sign, subscribe 3. agree to, approve, consent, O.K. *or* okay (*informal*), sanction

undesigned accidental, fortuitous, inadvertent, not meant, unintended, unintentional, unpremeditated

undesirable disagreeable, disliked, distasteful, dreaded, for the birds (*informal*), objectionable, obnoxious, offensive, out of place, repugnant, strictly for the birds (*informal*), (to be) avoided, unacceptable, unattractive, unpleasing, unpopular, unsavoury, unsuitable, unwanted, unwelcome, unwished-for

▷ **Antonyms** acceptable, agreeable, appealing, attractive, desirable, inviting, pleasing, popular, welcome

undeveloped embryonic, immature, inchoate, in embryo, latent, potential, primordial (*Biology*)

undignified beneath one, beneath one's dignity, improper, inappropriate, indecorous, inelegant, infra dig (*informal*), lacking dignity, unbecoming, ungentlemanly, unladylike, unrefined, unseemly, unsuitable

▷ **Antonyms** appropriate, becoming, decorous, dignified, elegant, proper, refined, seemly, suitable

undisciplined disobedient, erratic, fitful, obstreperous, uncontrolled, unpredictable, unreliable, unrestrained, unruly, unschooled, unsteady, unsystematic, untrained, wayward, wild, wilful

▷ **Antonyms** controlled, disciplined, obedient, predictable, reliable, restrained, steady, trained

undisguised blatant, complete, evident, explicit, genuine, manifest, obvious, open, out-and-out, overt, patent, thoroughgoing, transparent, unconcealed, unfeigned, unmistakable, utter, wholehearted

▷ **Antonyms** concealed, covert, disguised, feigned, hidden, secret

undisputed accepted, acknowledged, beyond question, certain, conclusive, freely admitted, incontestable, incontrovertible, indisputable, irrefutable, not disputed, recognized, sure, unchallenged, uncontested, undeniable, undoubted, unquestioned

▷ **Antonyms** deniable, disputed, doubtful, dubious, inconclusive, questioned, uncertain

undistinguished commonplace, everyday, indifferent, mediocre, no great shakes (*informal*), nothing to write home about (*informal*), ordinary, pedestrian, prosaic, run-of-the-mill, so-so (*informal*), unexceptional, unexciting, unimpressive, unremarkable, vanilla (*informal*)

▷ **Antonyms** distinguished, exceptional, exciting, extraordinary, impressive, notable, outstanding, remarkable, striking

undisturbed 1. not moved, quiet, uninterrupted, untouched, without interruption 2. calm, collected, composed, equable, even, motionless, placid, sedate, serene, tranquil, unagitated, unbothered, unfazed (*informal*), unperturbed, unruffled, untroubled

▷ **Antonyms** (*sense 1*) confused, disordered, interfered with, interrupted, moved, muddled (*sense 2*) agitated, bothered, busy, disturbed, excited, flustered, nervous, perturbed, troubled, upset

undivided combined, complete, concentrated, concerted, entire, exclusive, full, solid, thorough, unanimous, undistracted, united, whole, wholehearted

undo 1. disengage, disentangle, loose, loosen, open, unbutton, unclasp, unfasten, unlock, unstrap, untie, unwrap 2. annul, cancel, invalidate, neutralize, nullify, offset, reverse, wipe out 3. bring to naught, defeat, destroy, impoverish, invalidate, mar, overturn, quash, ruin, shatter, subvert, undermine, upset, wreck

undoing 1. collapse, defeat, destruction, disgrace, downfall, humiliation, overthrow, overturn, reversal, ruin, ruination, shame 2. affliction, blight, curse, fatal flaw, misfortune, the last straw, trial, trouble, weakness

undone[1] *adjective* incomplete, left, neglected, not completed, not done, omitted, outstanding, passed over, unattended to, unfinished, unfulfilled, unperformed

▷ **Antonyms** accomplished, attended to, complete, done, finished, fulfilled, performed

undone[2] *adjective* betrayed, destroyed, forlorn, hapless, overcome, prostrate, ruined, wretched

undoubted acknowledged, certain, definite, evident, incontrovertible, indisputable, indubitable, obvious, sure, undisputed, unquestionable, unquestioned

undoubtedly assuredly, beyond a shadow of (a) doubt, beyond question, certainly, come hell or high water (*informal*), definitely, doubtless, of course, surely, undeniably, unmistakably, unquestionably, without doubt

undreamed of astonishing, inconceivable, incredible, miraculous, undreamt, un~expected, unforeseen, unheard-of, un~imagined, unsuspected, unthought-of

undress 1. *verb* disrobe, divest oneself of, peel off (*slang*), shed, strip, take off one's clothes **2.** *~noun* deshabille, disar~ray, nakedness, nudity

undue disproportionate, excessive, ex~travagant, extreme, immoderate, im~proper, inordinate, intemperate, need~less, overmuch, too great, too much, uncalled-for, undeserved, unnecessary, unseemly, unwarranted

▷ **Antonyms** appropriate, due, fitting, justified, necessary, proper, suitable, well-considered

undulate billow, heave, ripple, rise and fall, roll, surge, swell, wave

unduly disproportionately, excessively, extravagantly, immoderately, improp~erly, inordinately, out of all proportion, overly, overmuch, unjustifiably, unnec~essarily, unreasonably

▷ **Antonyms** duly, justifiably, moderate~ly, ordinately, properly, proportionately, reasonably

undying constant, continuing, deathless, eternal, everlasting, immortal, imper~ishable, indestructible, inextinguish~able, infinite, perennial, permanent, perpetual, sempiternal (*literary*), undi~minished, unending, unfading

▷ **Antonyms** ephemeral, finite, fleeting, impermanent, inconstant, momentary, mortal, perishable, short-lived

unearth 1. dig up, disinter, dredge up, excavate, exhume **2.** bring to light, dis~cover, expose, ferret out, find, reveal, root up, turn up, uncover

unearthly 1. eerie, eldritch (*poetic*), ghostly, haunted, nightmarish, phan~tom, spectral, spooky (*informal*), strange, uncanny, weird **2.** ethereal, heavenly, not of this world, preternatu~ral, sublime, supernatural **3.** abnormal, absurd, extraordinary, ridiculous, strange, ungodly (*informal*), unholy (*in~formal*), unreasonable

uneasiness agitation, alarm, anxiety, ap~prehension, apprehensiveness, disquiet, doubt, dubiety, misgiving, nervousness, perturbation, qualms, suspicion, trepi~dation, worry

▷ **Antonyms** calm, composure, cool, ease, peace, quiet, serenity

uneasy 1. agitated, anxious, apprehen~sive, discomposed, disturbed, edgy, ill at ease, impatient, jittery (*informal*), like a fish out of water, nervous, on edge, per~turbed, restive, restless, troubled, twitchy (*informal*), uncomfortable, un~settled, upset, wired (*slang*), worried **2.** awkward, constrained, insecure, pre~carious, shaky, strained, tense, uncom~fortable, unstable **3.** bothering, dismay~ing, disquieting, disturbing, troubling, upsetting, worrying

▷ **Antonyms** (*sense 1*) at ease, calm, comfortable, relaxed, tranquil, unfazed (*informal*), unflustered, unperturbed, unruffled

uneconomic loss-making, nonpaying, non-profit-making, nonviable, unprof~itable

▷ **Antonyms** economic, money-making, productive, profitable, remunerative, viable

uneducated 1. ignorant, illiterate, unlet~tered, unread, unschooled, untaught **2.** benighted, lowbrow, uncultivated, un~cultured

▷ **Antonyms** (*sense 1*) educated, in~formed, instructed, literate, schooled, taught, tutored

unembellished austere, bald, bare, func~tional, modest, plain, severe, simple, spartan, stark, unadorned, unfussy, un~ornamented, unvarnished

unemotional apathetic, cold, cool, impas~sive, indifferent, listless, passionless, phlegmatic, reserved, undemonstrative, unexcitable, unfeeling, unimpression~able, unresponsive

▷ **Antonyms** demonstrative, emotional, excitable, feeling, passionate, respon~sive, sensitive

unemployed idle, jobless, laid off, on the dole (*Brit. informal*), out of a job, out of work, redundant, resting (*of an actor*), workless

unending ceaseless, constant, continual, endless, eternal, everlasting, incessant, interminable, never-ending, perpetual, unceasing, unremitting

unendurable insufferable, insupportable, intolerable, more than flesh and blood can stand, unbearable

▷ **Antonyms** bearable, endurable, suf~ferable, supportable, tolerable

unenthusiastic apathetic, blasé, bored, half-arsed (*Brit. slang*), half-assed (*U.S. & Canad. slang*), half-hearted, indiffer~ent, lukewarm, neutral, nonchalant, unimpressed, uninterested, unmoved, unresponsive

▷ **Antonyms** ardent, eager, enthusiastic, excited, interested, keen, passionate

unenviable disagreeable, painful, thank~less, uncomfortable, undesirable, un~pleasant

▷ **Antonyms** agreeable, attractive, desir~able, enviable, pleasant

unequal 1. different, differing, disparate, dissimilar, not uniform, unlike, un~matched, variable, varying **2.** (*with* **to**) found wanting, inadequate, insufficient, not up to **3.** asymmetrical, dispropor~tionate, ill-matched, irregular, unbal~anced, uneven

▷ **Antonyms** (*sense 1*) equal, equivalent, identical, like, matched, similar, uni~form

unequalled beyond compare, incomparable, inimitable, matchless, nonpareil, paramount, peerless, pre-eminent, second to none, supreme, transcendent, unmatched, unparalleled, unrivalled, unsurpassed, without equal

unequivocal absolute, black-and-white, certain, clear, clear-cut, cut-and-dried (*informal*), decisive, definite, direct, evident, explicit, incontrovertible, indubitable, manifest, plain, positive, straight, unambiguous, uncontestable, unmistakable
▷ **Antonyms** ambiguous, doubtful, equivocal, evasive, indecisive, noncommittal, vague

unerring accurate, certain, exact, faultless, impeccable, infallible, perfect, sure, unfailing

unethical dirty, dishonest, dishonourable, disreputable, illegal, immoral, improper, not cricket (*informal*), shady (*informal*), underhand, under-the-table, unfair, unprincipled, unprofessional, unscrupulous, wrong
▷ **Antonyms** ethical, honest, honourable, legal, moral, proper, scrupulous, upright

uneven 1. bumpy, not flat, not level, not smooth, rough **2.** broken, changeable, fitful, fluctuating, intermittent, irregular, jerky, patchy, spasmodic, unsteady, variable **3.** asymmetrical, lopsided, not parallel, odd, out of true, unbalanced **4.** disparate, ill-matched, one-sided, unequal, unfair
▷ **Antonyms** (*sense 1*) even, flat, level, plane, smooth

uneventful boring, commonplace, dull, ho-hum (*informal*), humdrum, monotonous, ordinary, quiet, routine, tedious, unexceptional, unexciting, uninteresting, unmemorable, unremarkable, unvaried
▷ **Antonyms** eventful, exceptional, exciting, interesting, memorable, momentous, remarkable

unexampled unequalled, unheard-of, unique, unmatched, unparalleled, unprecedented

unexceptional bog-standard (*Brit. & Irish slang*), common or garden (*informal*), commonplace, conventional, insignificant, mediocre, no great shakes (*informal*), normal, nothing to write home about (*informal*), ordinary, pedestrian, run-of-the-mill, undistinguished, unimpressive, unremarkable, usual
▷ **Antonyms** distinguished, exceptional, impressive, notable, noteworthy, outstanding, remarkable, significant, unusual

unexpected abrupt, accidental, astonishing, chance, fortuitous, not bargained for, out of the blue, startling, sudden, surprising, unanticipated, unforeseen, unlooked-for, unpredictable
▷ **Antonyms** anticipated, awaited, expected, foreseen, normal, planned, predictable

unexpressive blank, emotionless, expressionless, impassive, inexpressive, inscrutable, vacant

unfailing 1. bottomless, boundless, ceaseless, continual, continuous, endless, inexhaustible, never-failing, persistent, unflagging, unlimited **2.** certain, constant, dependable, faithful, infallible, loyal, reliable, staunch, steadfast, sure, tried and true, true
▷ **Antonyms** (*sense 2*) disloyal, fallible, inconstant, uncertain, unfaithful, unreliable, unsure, untrustworthy

unfair 1. arbitrary, biased, bigoted, discriminatory, inequitable, one-sided, partial, partisan, prejudiced, unjust **2.** crooked (*informal*), dishonest, dishonourable, uncalled-for, unethical, unprincipled, unscrupulous, unsporting, unwarranted, wrongful
▷ **Antonyms** (*sense 2*) ethical, fair, honest, just, principled, scrupulous

unfaithful 1. deceitful, disloyal, faithless, false, false-hearted, perfidious, recreant (*archaic*), traitorous, treacherous, treasonable, unreliable, untrustworthy **2.** adulterous, faithless, fickle, inconstant, two-timing (*informal*), unchaste, untrue **3.** distorted, erroneous, imperfect, imprecise, inaccurate, inexact, unreliable, untrustworthy
▷ **Antonyms** (*sense 1*) constant, faithful, loyal, steadfast, true, trustworthy (*sense 3*) accurate, exact, perfect, precise, reliable

unfaltering firm, indefatigable, persevering, resolute, steadfast, steady, tireless, unfailing, unflagging, unflinching, unswerving, untiring, unwavering

unfamiliar 1. alien, beyond one's ken, curious, different, little known, new, novel, out-of-the-way, strange, unaccustomed, uncommon, unknown, unusual **2.** (*with* **with**) a stranger to, inexperienced in, unaccustomed to, unacquainted, unconversant, uninformed about, uninitiated in, unpractised in, unskilled at, unversed in
▷ **Antonyms** accustomed, acquainted, average, common, commonplace, conversant, everyday, experienced, familiar, knowledgeable, normal, unexceptional, well-known, well-versed

unfashionable antiquated, behind the times, dated, obsolete, old-fashioned, old hat, out, outmoded, out of date, out of fashion, out of the ark (*informal*), passé, square (*informal*), unpopular
▷ **Antonyms** à la mode, fashionable, modern, popular, stylish, trendy (*Brit. informal*)

unfasten detach, disconnect, let go, loosen, open, separate, unclasp, uncouple, undo, unlace, unlock, unstrap, untie

unfathomable 1. bottomless, immeasurable, unmeasured, unplumbed, unsounded **2.** abstruse, baffling, deep, esoteric, impenetrable, incomprehensible, indecipherable, inexplicable, profound, unknowable

unfavourable 1. adverse, bad, contrary, disadvantageous, hostile, ill-suited, infelicitous, inimical, low, negative, poor, unfortunate, unfriendly, unsuited **2.** inauspicious, inopportune, ominous, threatening, unlucky, unpromising, unpropitious, unseasonable, untimely, untoward

▷ **Antonyms** (*sense 1*) amicable, approving, favourable, friendly, positive, warm, well-disposed

unfeeling 1. apathetic, callous, cold, cruel, hardened, hardhearted, heartless, inhuman, insensitive, pitiless, stony, uncaring, unsympathetic **2.** insensate, insensible, numb, sensationless

▷ **Antonyms** (*sense 1*) benevolent, caring, concerned, feeling, gentle, humane, kind, sensitive, sympathetic

unfeigned genuine, heartfelt, natural, pure, real, sincere, unaffected, unforced, wholehearted

unfettered free, unbridled, unchecked, unconfined, unconstrained, unrestrained, unshackled, untrammelled

unfinished 1. deficient, half-done, imperfect, incomplete, in the making, lacking, unaccomplished, uncompleted, undone, unfulfilled, wanting **2.** bare, crude, natural, raw, rough, sketchy, unpolished, unrefined, unvarnished

▷ **Antonyms** (*sense 2*) finished, flawless, perfected, polished, refined, smooth, varnished

unfit 1. ill-equipped, inadequate, incapable, incompetent, ineligible, no good, not cut out for, not equal to, not up to, unprepared, unqualified, untrained, useless **2.** ill-adapted, inadequate, inappropriate, ineffective, not designed, not fit, unsuitable, unsuited, useless **3.** debilitated, decrepit, feeble, flabby, in poor condition, out of kelter, out of shape, out of trim, unhealthy

▷ **Antonyms** (*senses 1 & 2*) able, acceptable, capable, competent, equipped, qualified, ready, suitable (*sense 3*) fit, healthy, in good condition, strong, sturdy, well

unflagging constant, fixed, indefatigable, persevering, persistent, staunch, steady, tireless, unceasing, undeviating, unfailing, unfaltering, unremitting, untiring, unwearied

unflappable calm, collected, composed, cool, impassive, imperturbable, level-headed, not given to worry, self-possessed, unfazed (*informal*), unruffled

▷ **Antonyms** excitable, flappable, hot-headed, nervous, temperamental, twitchy (*informal*), volatile

unflattering 1. blunt, candid, critical, honest, uncomplimentary, warts and all **2.** not shown in the best light, not shown to advantage, plain, unattractive, unbecoming, unprepossessing

unfledged callow, green, immature, inexperienced, raw, undeveloped, untried, young

unflinching bold, constant, determined, firm, immovable, resolute, stalwart, staunch, steadfast, steady, unfaltering, unshaken, unshrinking, unswerving, unwavering

▷ **Antonyms** cowed, faltering, scared, shaken, shrinking, wavering

unfold 1. disentangle, expand, flatten, open, spread out, straighten, stretch out, undo, unfurl, unravel, unroll, unwrap **2.** *figurative* clarify, describe, disclose, divulge, explain, illustrate, make known, present, reveal, show, uncover **3.** bear fruit, blossom, develop, evolve, expand, grow, mature

unforeseen abrupt, accidental, out of the blue, startling, sudden, surprise, surprising, unanticipated, unexpected, unlooked-for, unpredicted

▷ **Antonyms** anticipated, envisaged, expected, foreseen, intended, predicted

unforgettable exceptional, extraordinary, fixed in the mind, impressive, memorable, never to be forgotten, notable, striking

unforgivable deplorable, disgraceful, indefensible, inexcusable, shameful, unjustifiable, unpardonable, unwarrantable

▷ **Antonyms** allowable, excusable, forgivable, justifiable, pardonable, venial

unfortunate 1. adverse, calamitous, disastrous, ill-fated, ill-starred, inopportune, ruinous, unfavourable, untoward **2.** cursed, doomed, hapless, hopeless, luckless, out of luck, poor, star-crossed, unhappy, unlucky, unprosperous, unsuccessful, wretched **3.** deplorable, ill-advised, inappropriate, infelicitous, lamentable, regrettable, unbecoming, unsuitable

▷ **Antonyms** (*senses 1 & 3*) appropriate, opportune, suitable, tactful, timely (*sense 2*) auspicious, felicitous, fortuitous, fortunate, happy, lucky, successful

unfounded baseless, fabricated, false, groundless, idle, spurious, trumped up, unjustified, unproven, unsubstantiated, vain, without basis, without foundation

▷ **Antonyms** attested, confirmed, factual, justified, proven, substantiated, verified

unfrequented deserted, godforsaken, isolated, lone, lonely, off the beaten track, remote, sequestered, solitary, uninhabited, unvisited

unfriendly 1. aloof, antagonistic, chilly, cold, disagreeable, distant, hostile, ill-disposed, inhospitable, not on speaking terms, quarrelsome, sour, surly, uncon~

genial, unneighbourly, unsociable **2.** alien, hostile, inauspicious, inhospitable, inimical, unfavourable, unpropitious

▷ **Antonyms** affable, amiable, auspicious, congenial, convivial, friendly, hospitable, propitious, sociable, warm

unfruitful barren, fruitless, infecund, infertile, sterile, unproductive, unprofitable, unprolific, unrewarding

▷ **Antonyms** abundant, fecund, fertile, fruitful, productive, profuse, prolific, rewarding

ungainly awkward, clumsy, gangling, gawky, inelegant, loutish, lubberly, lumbering, slouching, uncoordinated, uncouth, ungraceful

▷ **Antonyms** attractive, comely, elegant, graceful, pleasing

ungodly 1. blasphemous, corrupt, depraved, godless, immoral, impious, irreligious, profane, sinful, vile, wicked **2.** *informal* dreadful, horrendous, intolerable, outrageous, unearthly, unholy (*informal*), unreasonable, unseemly

ungovernable rebellious, refractory, uncontrollable, unmanageable, unrestrainable, unruly, wild

ungracious bad-mannered, churlish, discourteous, ill-bred, impolite, offhand, rude, uncivil, unmannerly

▷ **Antonyms** affable, civil, courteous, gracious, mannerly, polite, well-mannered

ungrateful heedless, ingrate (*archaic*), selfish, thankless, unappreciative, unmindful, unthankful

▷ **Antonyms** appreciative, aware, grateful, mindful, thankful

unguarded 1. careless, foolhardy, heedless, ill-considered, impolitic, imprudent, incautious, indiscreet, rash, thoughtless, uncircumspect, undiplomatic, unthinking, unwary **2.** defenceless, open to attack, undefended, unpatrolled, unprotected, vulnerable **3.** artless, candid, direct, frank, guileless, open, straightforward

▷ **Antonyms** (*sense 1*) cagey (*informal*), careful, cautious, diplomatic, discreet, guarded, prudent, wary

unhallowed 1. not sacred, unblessed, unconsecrated, unholy, unsanctified **2.** damnable, evil, godless, irreverent, profane, sinful, wicked

unhandy 1. awkward, bumbling, bungling, clumsy, fumbling, heavy-handed, incompetent, inept, inexpert, maladroit, unskilful **2.** awkward, cumbersome, hampering, ill-arranged, ill-contrived, inconvenient, unwieldy

unhappy 1. blue, crestfallen, dejected, depressed, despondent, disconsolate, dispirited, down, downcast, down in the dumps (*informal*), gloomy, long-faced, low, melancholy, miserable, mournful, sad, sorrowful **2.** cursed, hapless, ill-fated, ill-omened, luckless, unfortunate, unlucky, wretched **3.** awkward, clumsy, gauche, ill-advised, ill-timed, inappropriate, inept, infelicitous, injudicious, malapropos, tactless, unsuitable, untactful

▷ **Antonyms** (*sense 1*) cheerful, chirpy (*informal*), content, exuberant, genial, good-humoured, happy, joyful, light-hearted, overjoyed, over the moon (*informal*), satisfied (*senses 2 & 3*) apt, becoming, fortunate, lucky, prudent, suitable, tactful

unharmed in one piece (*informal*), intact, safe, safe and sound, sound, undamaged, unhurt, uninjured, unscarred, unscathed, untouched, whole, without a scratch

▷ **Antonyms** damaged, harmed, hurt, impaired, injured, scarred, scathed

unhealthy 1. ailing, delicate, feeble, frail, infirm, in poor health, invalid, poorly (*informal*), sick, sickly, unsound, unwell, weak **2.** deleterious, detrimental, harmful, insalubrious, insanitary, noisome, noxious, unwholesome **3.** bad, baneful (*archaic*), corrupt, corrupting, degrading, demoralizing, morbid, negative, undesirable

▷ **Antonyms** (*senses 1 & 2*) beneficial, fit, good, healthy, robust, salubrious, salutary, well, wholesome (*sense 3*) desirable, moral, positive

unheard-of 1. little known, obscure, undiscovered, unfamiliar, unknown, unregarded, unremarked, unsung **2.** ground-breaking, inconceivable, never before encountered, new, novel, singular, unbelievable, undreamed of, unexampled, unique, unprecedented, unusual **3.** disgraceful, extreme, offensive, outlandish, outrageous, preposterous, shocking, unacceptable, unthinkable

unheeded disobeyed, disregarded, forgotten, ignored, neglected, overlooked, unfollowed, unnoticed, unobserved, untaken

▷ **Antonyms** heeded, noted, noticed, obeyed, observed, regarded, remembered

unheralded out of the blue, surprise, unacclaimed, unannounced, unexpected, unforeseen, unnoticed, unproclaimed, unpublicized, unrecognized, unsung

unhesitating 1. implicit, resolute, steadfast, unfaltering, unquestioning, unreserved, unswerving, unwavering, wholehearted **2.** immediate, instant, instantaneous, prompt, ready, without delay

▷ **Antonyms** (*sense 1*) diffident, hesitant, irresolute, questioning, tentative, uncertain, unsure, wavering

unhinge 1. confound, confuse, craze, dement, derange, disorder, distemper (*archaic*), drive out of one's mind, madden, unbalance, unsettle **2.** detach, disconnect, disjoint, dislodge, remove

unholy **1.** base, corrupt, depraved, dishonest, evil, heinous, immoral, iniquitous, irreligious, profane, sinful, ungodly, vile, wicked **2.** *informal* appalling, awful, dreadful, horrendous, outrageous, shocking, unearthly, ungodly (*informal*), unnatural, unreasonable
▷ **Antonyms** (*sense 1*) devout, faithful, godly, holy, pious, religious, saintly, virtuous

unhoped-for beyond one's wildest dreams, incredible, like a dream come true, out of the blue, surprising, unanticipated, unbelievable, undreamed of, unexpected, unimaginable, unlooked-for

unhurried calm, deliberate, easy, easy-going, leisurely, sedate, slow, slow and steady, slow-paced
▷ **Antonyms** brief, cursory, hasty, hectic, hurried, quick, rushed, speedy, swift

unidentified anonymous, mysterious, nameless, unclassified, unfamiliar, unknown, unmarked, unnamed, unrecognized, unrevealed
▷ **Antonyms** classified, familiar, identified, known, marked, named, recognized

unification alliance, amalgamation, coalescence, coalition, combination, confederation, federation, fusion, merger, union, uniting

uniform *noun* **1.** costume, dress, garb, habit, livery, outfit, regalia, regimentals, suit *~adjective* **2.** consistent, constant, equable, even, regular, smooth, unbroken, unchanging, undeviating, unvarying **3.** alike, equal, identical, like, same, selfsame, similar
▷ **Antonyms** *~adjective* (*sense 2*) changeable, changing, deviating, inconsistent, irregular, uneven, variable

uniformity **1.** constancy, evenness, homogeneity, invariability, regularity, sameness, similarity **2.** drabness, dullness, flatness, lack of diversity, monotony, sameness, tedium

unify amalgamate, bind, bring together, combine, confederate, consolidate, federate, fuse, join, merge, unite
▷ **Antonyms** alienate, disconnect, disjoin, disunite, divide, separate, sever, split

unimaginable beyond one's wildest dreams, fantastic, impossible, inconceivable, incredible, indescribable, ineffable, mind-boggling (*informal*), unbelievable, unheard-of, unthinkable

unimaginative banal, barren, commonplace, derivative, dry, dull, hackneyed, lifeless, matter-of-fact, ordinary, pedestrian, predictable, prosaic, routine, tame, uncreative, uninspired, unoriginal, unromantic, usual, vanilla (*informal*)
▷ **Antonyms** creative, different, exciting, fresh, ground-breaking, imaginative, innovative, inventive, original, unhackneyed, unusual

unimpassioned calm, collected, composed, controlled, cool, dispassionate, impassive, moderate, rational, sedate, temperate, tranquil, undemonstrative, unemotional, unmoved

unimpeachable above reproach, beyond criticism, beyond question, blameless, faultless, impeccable, irreproachable, perfect, unassailable, unblemished, unchallengeable, unexceptionable, unquestionable
▷ **Antonyms** blameworthy, faulty, imperfect, reprehensible, reproachable, shameful

unimpeded free, open, unblocked, unchecked, unconstrained, unhampered, unhindered, unrestrained, untrammelled
▷ **Antonyms** blocked, checked, constrained, hampered, hindered, impeded, restrained

unimportant immaterial, inconsequential, insignificant, irrelevant, low-ranking, minor, nickel-and-dime (*U.S. slang*), not worth mentioning, nugatory, of no account, of no consequence, of no moment, paltry, petty, slight, trifling, trivial, worthless
▷ **Antonyms** essential, grave, important, major, significant, urgent, vital, weighty

uninhabited abandoned, barren, desert, deserted, desolate, empty, lonely, unoccupied, unpopulated, unsettled, untenanted, vacant, waste

uninhibited **1.** candid, frank, free, free and easy, informal, instinctive, liberated, natural, open, relaxed, spontaneous, unrepressed, unreserved, unselfconscious **2.** free, unbridled, unchecked, unconstrained, uncontrolled, uncurbed, unrestrained, unrestricted
▷ **Antonyms** bashful, careful, checked, constrained, controlled, curbed, demure, hampered, inhibited, modest, restrained, self-conscious, shy, uptight (*informal*)

uninspired banal, commonplace, dull, humdrum, indifferent, ordinary, prosaic, stale, stock, unexciting, unimaginative, uninspiring, uninteresting, unoriginal, vanilla (*informal*)
▷ **Antonyms** brilliant, different, exciting, imaginative, inspired, interesting, original, outstanding

unintelligent braindead (*informal*), brainless, dense, dozy (*Brit. informal*), dull, empty-headed, foolish, gormless (*Brit. informal*), obtuse, slow, stupid, thick, unreasoning, unthinking
▷ **Antonyms** bright, clever, intelligent, sharp, smart, thinking

unintelligible double Dutch (*Brit. informal*), Greek (*informal*), illegible, inarticulate, incoherent, incomprehensible, indecipherable, indistinct, jumbled, meaningless, muddled, unfathomable
▷ **Antonyms** clear, coherent, compre~

hensible, intelligible, legible, lucid, understandable

unintentional accidental, casual, fortuitous, inadvertent, involuntary, unconscious, undesigned, unintended, unpremeditated, unthinking, unwitting
▷ **Antonyms** conscious, deliberate, designed, intended, intentional, premeditated, voluntary, wilful

uninterested apathetic, blasé, bored, distant, impassive, incurious, indifferent, listless, unconcerned, uninvolved, unresponsive
▷ **Antonyms** alert, concerned, curious, enthusiastic, interested, involved, keen, responsive

uninteresting as dry as dust, boring, commonplace, drab, dreary, dry, dull, flat, ho-hum (*informal*), humdrum, mind-numbing, monotonous, tedious, tiresome, unenjoyable, uneventful, unexciting, uninspiring, wearisome
▷ **Antonyms** absorbing, compelling, enjoyable, exciting, gripping, inspiring, interesting, intriguing, stimulating

uninterrupted constant, continual, continuous, nonstop, peaceful, steady, sustained, unbroken, undisturbed, unending

uninvited not asked, not invited, unasked, unbidden, unwanted, unwelcome

uninviting disagreeable, offensive, off-putting (*Brit. informal*), repellent, repulsive, unappealing, unappetizing, unattractive, undesirable, unpleasant, untempting, unwelcoming
▷ **Antonyms** agreeable, appealing, appetizing, attractive, desirable, inviting, pleasant, tempting, welcoming

union 1. amalgam, amalgamation, blend, combination, conjunction, fusion, junction, mixture, synthesis, uniting **2.** alliance, association, Bund, coalition, confederacy, confederation, federation, league **3.** accord, agreement, concord, concurrence, harmony, unanimity, unison, unity **4.** coition, coitus, copulation, coupling, intercourse, marriage, matrimony, nookie (*slang*), rumpy-pumpy (*slang*), the other (*informal*), wedlock

unique 1. lone, one and only, only, single, solitary, sui generis **2.** incomparable, inimitable, matchless, nonpareil, peerless, unequalled, unexampled, unmatched, unparalleled, unrivalled, without equal

unison accord, accordance, agreement, concert, concord, cooperation, harmony, unanimity, unity
▷ **Antonyms** disagreement, discord, disharmony, dissension, dissidence, dissonance

unit 1. assembly, detachment, entity, group, section, system, whole **2.** component, constituent, element, item, member, module, part, piece, portion, section, segment **3.** measure, measurement, module, quantity

unite 1. amalgamate, blend, coalesce, combine, confederate, consolidate, couple, fuse, incorporate, join, link, marry, meld, merge, unify, wed **2.** ally, associate, band, close ranks, club together, cooperate, join forces, join together, league, pool, pull together
▷ **Antonyms** break, detach, disunite, divide, divorce, part, separate, sever, split

united 1. affiliated, allied, banded together, collective, combined, concerted, in partnership, leagued, pooled, unified **2.** agreed, in accord, in agreement, like-minded, of like mind, of one mind, of the same opinion, one, unanimous

unity 1. entity, integrity, oneness, singleness, undividedness, unification, union, wholeness **2.** accord, agreement, assent, concord, concurrence, consensus, harmony, peace, solidarity, unanimity, unison
▷ **Antonyms** disagreement, discord, disunity, division, factionalism, heterogeneity, ill will, independence, individuality, in-fighting, multiplicity, separation, strife

universal all-embracing, catholic, common, ecumenical, entire, general, omnipresent, total, unlimited, whole, widespread, worldwide

universality all-inclusiveness, completeness, comprehensiveness, entirety, generality, generalization, totality, ubiquity

universally across the board, always, everywhere, in all cases, in every instance, invariably, uniformly, without exception

universe cosmos, creation, everything, macrocosm, nature, the natural world

unjust biased, inequitable, one-sided, partial, partisan, prejudiced, undeserved, unfair, unjustified, unmerited, wrong, wrongful
▷ **Antonyms** equitable, ethical, fair, impartial, just, justified, right, unbiased

unjustifiable indefensible, inexcusable, outrageous, unacceptable, unforgivable, unjust, unpardonable, unwarrantable, wrong

unkempt bedraggled, blowsy, disarranged, disarrayed, dishevelled, disordered, frowzy, messy, rumpled, scruffy, shabby, shaggy, slatternly, sloppy (*informal*), slovenly, sluttish, tousled, uncombed, ungroomed, untidy
▷ **Antonyms** neat, presentable, soigné *or* soignée, spruce, tidy, trim, well-groomed

unkind cruel, hardhearted, harsh, inconsiderate, inhuman, insensitive, malicious, mean, nasty, spiteful, thoughtless, uncaring, uncharitable, unchristian, unfeeling, unfriendly, unsympathetic
▷ **Antonyms** benevolent, caring, chari-

table, considerate, generous, kind, soft-hearted, sympathetic, thoughtful

unknown 1. alien, concealed, dark, hidden, mysterious, new, secret, strange, unrecognized, unrevealed, untold **2.** anonymous, beyond one's ken, nameless, uncharted, undiscovered, unexplored, unidentified, unnamed **3.** humble, little known, obscure, undistinguished, unfamiliar, unheard-of, unrenowned, unsung

▷ **Antonyms** (*sense 3*) celebrated, distinguished, familiar, known, recognized, renowned, well-known

unladylike coarse, ill-bred, impolite, indelicate, rude, uncivil, ungracious, unmannerly, unrefined

▷ **Antonyms** civil, delicate, gracious, ladylike, mannerly, polite, refined, seemly

unlamented unbemoaned, unbewailed, undeplored, unmissed, unmourned, unregretted, unwept

unlawful actionable, against the law, banned, criminal, forbidden, illegal, illegitimate, illicit, outlawed, prohibited, unauthorized, under-the-table, unlicensed

unleash free, let go, let loose, release, unbridle, unloose, untie

unlettered ignorant, illiterate, uneducated, unlearned, unschooled, untaught, untutored

▷ **Antonyms** educated, learned, literate, schooled, taught, tutored

unlike as different as chalk and cheese (*informal*), contrasted, different, dissimilar, distinct, divergent, diverse, ill-matched, incompatible, not alike, opposite, unequal, unrelated

▷ **Antonyms** compatible, equal, like, matched, related, similar

unlikely 1. doubtful, faint, improbable, not likely, remote, slight, unimaginable **2.** cock-and-bull (*informal*), implausible, incredible, questionable, unbelievable, unconvincing

unlimited 1. boundless, countless, endless, extensive, great, illimitable, immeasurable, immense, incalculable, infinite, limitless, stellar (*informal*), unbounded, vast **2.** absolute, all-encompassing, complete, full, total, unconditional, unconstrained, unfettered, unqualified, unrestricted

▷ **Antonyms** (*sense 1*) bounded, circumscribed, confined, constrained, finite, limited, restricted

unload disburden, discharge, dump, empty, lighten, off-load, relieve, unburden, unlade, unpack

unlock free, let loose, open, release, unbar, unbolt, undo, unfasten, unlatch

unlooked-for chance, fortuitous, out of the blue, surprise, surprising, unanticipated, undreamed of, unexpected, unforeseen, unhoped-for, unpredicted, unthought-of

unloved disliked, forsaken, loveless, neglected, rejected, spurned, uncared-for, uncherished, unpopular, unwanted

▷ **Antonyms** adored, beloved, cherished, liked, loved, popular, precious, wanted

unlucky 1. cursed, disastrous, hapless, luckless, miserable, unfortunate, unhappy, unsuccessful, wretched **2.** doomed, ill-fated, ill-omened, ill-starred, inauspicious, ominous, unfavourable, untimely

▷ **Antonyms** (*sense 1*) blessed, favoured, fortunate, happy, lucky, prosperous

unman daunt, demoralize, discourage, dispirit, emasculate, enervate, enfeeble, intimidate, psych out (*informal*), unnerve, weaken

unmanageable 1. awkward, bulky, clunky (*informal*), cumbersome, difficult to handle, inconvenient, unhandy, unwieldy **2.** difficult, fractious, intractable, obstreperous, out of hand, refractory, stroppy (*Brit. slang*), uncontrollable, unruly, wild

▷ **Antonyms** (*sense 2*) amenable, compliant, docile, easy, manageable, submissive, tractable, wieldy

unmanly 1. camp (*informal*), effeminate, feeble, sissy, soft (*informal*), weak, womanish **2.** abject, chicken-hearted, cowardly, craven, dishonourable, ignoble, weak-kneed (*informal*), yellow (*informal*)

unmannerly badly behaved, bad-mannered, discourteous, disrespectful, ill-bred, ill-mannered, impolite, misbehaved, rude, uncivil, uncouth

▷ **Antonyms** civil, courteous, mannerly, polite, respectful, well-behaved, well-bred, well-mannered

unmarried bachelor, celibate, maiden, on the shelf, single, unattached, unwed, unwedded, virgin

unmask bare, bring to light, disclose, discover, expose, lay bare, reveal, show up, uncloak, uncover, unveil

unmatched beyond compare, consummate, incomparable, matchless, paramount, peerless, second to none, supreme, unequalled, unparalleled, unrivalled, unsurpassed

unmentionable disgraceful, disreputable, forbidden, frowned on, immodest, indecent, obscene, scandalous, shameful, shocking, taboo, unspeakable, unutterable, X-rated (*informal*)

unmerciful brutal, cruel, hard, heartless, implacable, merciless, pitiless, relentless, remorseless, ruthless, uncaring, unfeeling, unsparing

▷ **Antonyms** beneficent, caring, feeling, humane, merciful, pitying, sparing, tender-hearted

unmethodical confused, desultory, disorderly, haphazard, irregular, muddled, orderless, random, systemless, unorganized, unsystematic

unmindful careless, forgetful, heedless, inattentive, indifferent, lax, neglectful, negligent, oblivious, remiss, slack, unheeding
▷ **Antonyms** alert, attentive, aware, careful, heedful, mindful, regardful, watchful

unmistakable blatant, certain, clear, conspicuous, decided, distinct, evident, glaring, indisputable, manifest, obvious, palpable, patent, plain, positive, pronounced, sure, unambiguous, unequivocal
▷ **Antonyms** ambiguous, dim, doubtful, equivocal, hidden, mistakable, obscure, uncertain, unclear, unsure

unmitigated 1. grim, harsh, intense, oppressive, persistent, relentless, unabated, unalleviated, unbroken, undiminished, unmodified, unqualified, unredeemed, unrelieved **2.** absolute, arrant, complete, consummate, deep-dyed (*usually derogatory*), downright, out-and-out, outright, perfect, rank, sheer, thorough, thoroughgoing, utter

unmoved 1. fast, firm, in place, in position, steady, unchanged, untouched **2.** cold, dry-eyed, impassive, indifferent, unaffected, unfeeling, unimpressed, unresponsive, unstirred, untouched **3.** determined, firm, inflexible, resolute, resolved, steadfast, undeviating, unshaken, unwavering
▷ **Antonyms** (*sense 1*) shifted, touched, transferred (*sense 2*) affected, concerned, impressed, moved, persuaded, stirred, swayed, touched (*sense 3*) adaptable, flexible, shaken, wavering

unnatural 1. aberrant, abnormal, anomalous, irregular, odd, perverse, perverted, unusual **2.** bizarre, extraordinary, freakish, outlandish, queer, strange, supernatural, unaccountable, uncanny **3.** affected, artificial, assumed, contrived, factitious, false, feigned, forced, insincere, laboured, mannered, phoney *or* phony (*informal*), self-conscious, stagy, stiff, stilted, strained, studied, theatrical **4.** brutal, callous, cold-blooded, evil, fiendish, heartless, inhuman, monstrous, ruthless, savage, unfeeling, wicked
▷ **Antonyms** (*senses 1 & 2*) normal, ordinary, typical (*sense 3*) genuine, honest, natural, sincere, unaffected, unfeigned, unpretentious (*sense 4*) caring, humane, loving, warm

unnecessary dispensable, expendable, inessential, needless, nonessential, redundant, supererogatory, superfluous, surplus to requirements, uncalled-for, unneeded, unrequired, useless
▷ **Antonyms** essential, indispensable, necessary, needed, required, vital

unnerve confound, daunt, demoralize, disarm, disconcert, discourage, dishearten, dismay, dispirit, faze, fluster, frighten, intimidate, psych out (*informal*), rattle (*informal*), shake, throw off balance, unhinge, unman, upset
▷ **Antonyms** arm, brace, encourage, hearten, nerve, steel, strengthen, support

unnoticed disregarded, ignored, neglected, overlooked, undiscovered, unheeded, unobserved, unperceived, unrecognized, unremarked, unseen
▷ **Antonyms** discovered, heeded, noted, noticed, observed, perceived, recognized, remarked

unobtrusive humble, inconspicuous, keeping a low profile, low-key, meek, modest, quiet, restrained, retiring, self-effacing, subdued, unassuming, unnoticeable, unostentatious, unpretentious
▷ **Antonyms** assertive, blatant, bold, conspicuous, eccentric, eye-catching, getting in the way, high-profile, noticeable, obtrusive, outgoing, prominent

unoccupied 1. empty, tenantless, uninhabited, untenanted, vacant **2.** at a loose end, at leisure, disengaged, idle, inactive, unemployed

unofficial informal, off the record, personal, private, unauthorized, unconfirmed, wildcat

unorthodox abnormal, heterodox, irregular, off-the-wall (*slang*), unconventional, uncustomary, unusual, unwonted
▷ **Antonyms** conventional, customary, established, orthodox, sound, traditional, usual

unpaid 1. due, not discharged, outstanding, overdue, owing, payable, unsettled **2.** honorary, unsalaried, voluntary

unpalatable bitter, disagreeable, displeasing, distasteful, horrid, offensive, repugnant, unappetizing, unattractive, uneatable, unpleasant, unsavoury
▷ **Antonyms** agreeable, appetizing, attractive, eatable, palatable, pleasant, pleasing, savoury, tasteful

unparalleled beyond compare, consummate, exceptional, incomparable, matchless, peerless, rare, singular, superlative, unequalled, unique, unmatched, unprecedented, unrivalled, unsurpassed, without equal

unpardonable deplorable, disgraceful, indefensible, inexcusable, outrageous, scandalous, shameful, unforgivable, unjustifiable

unperturbed as cool as a cucumber, calm, collected, composed, cool, placid, poised, self-possessed, tranquil, undismayed, unfazed (*informal*), unflustered, unruffled, untroubled, unworried

▷ **Antonyms** anxious, dismayed, flustered, perturbed, ruffled, troubled, worried

unpleasant abhorrent, bad, disagreeable, displeasing, distasteful, horrid, ill-natured, irksome, nasty, objectionable, obnoxious, repulsive, troublesome, unattractive, unlikable *or* unlikeable, unlovely, unpalatable

▷ **Antonyms** agreeable, congenial, delicious, good-natured, likable *or* likeable, lovely, nice, pleasant

unpolished 1. crude, rough, rough and ready, rude, sketchy, unfashioned, unfinished, unworked **2.** uncivilized, uncouth, uncultivated, uncultured, unrefined, unsophisticated, vulgar

unpopular avoided, detested, disliked, not sought out, out in the cold, out of favour, rejected, shunned, unattractive, undesirable, unloved, unwanted, unwelcome

▷ **Antonyms** desirable, favoured, liked, loved, popular, wanted, welcome

unprecedented abnormal, exceptional, extraordinary, freakish, ground-breaking, new, novel, original, remarkable, singular, unexampled, unheard-of, unparalleled, unrivalled, unusual

unpredictable chance, changeable, doubtful, erratic, fickle, fluky (*informal*), hit-and-miss (*informal*), hit-or-miss (*informal*), iffy (*informal*), inconstant, random, unforeseeable, unreliable, unstable, variable

▷ **Antonyms** certain, constant, dependable, foreseeable, predictable, reliable, stable, steady, unchanging

unprejudiced balanced, even-handed, fair, fair-minded, impartial, just, nonpartisan, objective, open-minded, unbiased, uninfluenced

▷ **Antonyms** biased, bigoted, influenced, narrow-minded, partial, prejudiced, unfair, unjust

unpremeditated extempore, impromptu, impulsive, offhand, off the cuff (*informal*), spontaneous, spur-of-the-moment, unplanned, unprepared

unprepared 1. half-baked (*informal*), ill-considered, incomplete, not thought out, unfinished, unplanned **2.** caught napping, caught on the hop (*Brit. informal*), surprised, taken aback, taken off guard, unaware, unready, unsuspecting **3.** ad-lib, extemporaneous, improvised, off the cuff (*informal*), spontaneous

unpretentious homely, honest, humble, modest, plain, simple, straightforward, unaffected, unassuming, unimposing, unobtrusive, unostentatious, unspoiled

▷ **Antonyms** affected, assuming, brash, conceited, flaunting, inflated, obtrusive, ostentatious, pretentious, showy

unprincipled amoral, corrupt, crooked, deceitful, devious, dishonest, immoral, sink, tricky, unconscionable, underhand, unethical, unprofessional, unscrupulous

▷ **Antonyms** decent, ethical, honest, honourable, moral, righteous, scrupulous, upright, virtuous

unproductive 1. basket case, bootless, fruitless, futile, idle, ineffective, inefficacious, otiose, unavailing, unprofitable, unremunerative, unrewarding, useless, vain, valueless, worthless **2.** barren, dry, fruitless, sterile, unprolific

▷ **Antonyms** (*sense 1*) effective, fruitful, profitable, remunerative, rewarding, useful, worthwhile (*sense 2*) abundant, fertile, fruitful, productive, prolific

unprofessional 1. improper, lax, negligent, unethical, unfitting, unprincipled, unseemly, unworthy **2.** amateur, amateurish, cowboy (*informal*), incompetent, inefficient, inexperienced, inexpert, slapdash, slipshod, untrained

▷ **Antonyms** (*sense 2*) adept, competent, efficient, experienced, expert, professional, skilful

unpromising adverse, discouraging, doubtful, gloomy, inauspicious, infelicitous, ominous, unfavourable, unpropitious

unprotected defenceless, exposed, helpless, naked, open, open to attack, pregnable, unarmed, undefended, unguarded, unsheltered, unshielded, vulnerable

▷ **Antonyms** defended, guarded, immune, protected, safe, secure, shielded

unqualified 1. ill-equipped, incapable, incompetent, ineligible, not equal to, not up to, unfit, unprepared **2.** categorical, downright, outright, unconditional, unmitigated, unreserved, unrestricted, without reservation **3.** absolute, arrant, complete, consummate, deep-dyed (*usually derogatory*), downright, out-and-out, outright, thorough, thoroughgoing, total, utter

unquestionable absolute, beyond a shadow of doubt, certain, clear, conclusive, definite, faultless, flawless, incontestable, incontrovertible, indisputable, indubitable, irrefutable, manifest, patent, perfect, self-evident, sure, undeniable, unequivocal, unmistakable

▷ **Antonyms** ambiguous, doubtful, dubious, inconclusive, questionable, uncertain, unclear

unravel 1. disentangle, extricate, free, separate, straighten out, undo, unknot, untangle, unwind **2.** clear up, explain, figure out (*informal*), get straight, get to the bottom of, interpret, make out, puzzle out, resolve, solve, suss (out) (*slang*), work out

unreadable 1. crabbed, illegible, undecipherable **2.** badly written, dry as dust, heavy going, turgid

unreal 1. chimerical, dreamlike, fabulous, fanciful, fictitious, illusory, imaginary, make-believe, phantasmagoric, story~

book, visionary **2**. hypothetical, imma~ terial, impalpable, insubstantial, intan~ gible, mythical, nebulous **3**. artificial, fake, false, insincere, mock, ostensible, pretended, seeming, sham

▷ **Antonyms** authentic, bona fide, genu~ ine, real, realistic, sincere, true, veri~ table

unrealistic 1. half-baked (*informal*), im~ practicable, impractical, improbable, quixotic, romantic, starry-eyed, theo~ retical, unworkable **2**. non-naturalistic, unauthentic, unlifelike, unreal

▷ **Antonyms** (*sense 1*) practical, prag~ matic, probable, realistic, sensible, un~ romantic, workable

unreasonable 1. excessive, exorbitant, ex~ tortionate, extravagant, immoderate, steep (*informal*), too great, uncalled-for, undue, unfair, unjust, unwarranted **2**. arbitrary, biased, blinkered, capricious, erratic, headstrong, inconsistent, opin~ ionated, quirky **3**. absurd, far-fetched, foolish, illogical, irrational, mad, non~ sensical, preposterous, senseless, silly, stupid

▷ **Antonyms** (*sense 1*) fair, just, justified, moderate, reasonable, temperate, war~ ranted (*sense 2*) fair-minded, flexible, open-minded (*sense 3*) logical, rational, sensible, wise

unrefined 1. crude, raw, unfinished, un~ polished, unpurified, untreated **2**. boor~ ish, coarse, inelegant, rude, uncultured, unsophisticated, vulgar

unregenerate 1. godless, impious, pro~ fane, sinful, unconverted, unreformed, unrepentant, wicked **2**. hardened, in~ tractable, obdurate, obstinate, recalci~ trant, refractory, self-willed, stubborn

▷ **Antonyms** (*sense 1*) converted, godly, pious, reformed, regenerate, repentant, virtuous

unrelated 1. different, dissimilar, not kin, not kindred, not related, unconnected, unlike **2**. beside the point, extraneous, inapplicable, inappropriate, irrelevant, not germane, unassociated, unconnected

unrelenting 1. cruel, implacable, inexo~ rable, intransigent, merciless, pitiless, relentless, remorseless, ruthless, stern, tough, unsparing **2**. ceaseless, constant, continual, continuous, endless, inces~ sant, perpetual, steady, unabated, un~ broken, unremitting, unwavering

unreliable 1. disreputable, irresponsible, not conscientious, treacherous, unde~ pendable, unstable, untrustworthy **2**. deceptive, delusive, erroneous, fake, fallible, false, implausible, inaccurate, mistaken, specious, uncertain, uncon~ vincing, unsound

▷ **Antonyms** (*sense 1*) conscientious, de~ pendable, regular, reliable, responsible, stable, trustworthy (*sense 2*) accurate, infallible

unremitting assiduous, constant, contin~ ual, continuous, diligent, incessant, in~ defatigable, perpetual, relentless, re~ morseless, sedulous, unabated, unbro~ ken, unceasing, unwavering, unwearied

unrepentant abandoned, callous, hard~ ened, impenitent, incorrigible, not con~ trite, obdurate, shameless, unregener~ ate, unremorseful, unrepenting

▷ **Antonyms** ashamed, contrite, peni~ tent, remorseful, repentant, rueful, sor~ ry

unreserved 1. demonstrative, extrovert, forthright, frank, free, open, open-hearted, outgoing, outspoken, uninhib~ ited, unrestrained, unreticent **2**. abso~ lute, complete, entire, full, total, uncon~ ditional, unlimited, unqualified, whole~ hearted, without reservation

▷ **Antonyms** (*sense 1*) demure, inhibited, modest, reserved, restrained, reticent, shy, undemonstrative

unresolved doubtful, moot, open to ques~ tion, pending, problematical, unan~ swered, undecided, undetermined, un~ settled, unsolved, up in the air, vague, yet to be decided

unrest 1. agitation, disaffection, discon~ tent, discord, dissatisfaction, dissension, protest, rebellion, sedition, strife, tu~ mult, turmoil, upheaval **2**. agitation, anxiety, disquiet, distress, perturbation, restlessness, trepidation, uneasiness, worry

▷ **Antonyms** calm, contentment, peace, relaxation, repose, rest, stillness, tran~ quillity

unrestrained abandoned, boisterous, free, immoderate, inordinate, intemperate, natural, unbounded, unbridled, un~ checked, unconstrained, uncontrolled, unhindered, uninhibited, unrepressed

▷ **Antonyms** checked, constrained, frus~ trated, hindered, inhibited, repressed, restrained

unrestricted 1. absolute, free, free-for-all (*informal*), freewheeling (*informal*), open, unbounded, uncircumscribed, un~ hindered, unlimited, unregulated **2**. clear, open, public, unobstructed, unop~ posed

unrivalled beyond compare, incompa~ rable, matchless, nonpareil, peerless, supreme, unequalled, unexcelled, un~ matched, unparalleled, unsurpassed, without equal

unruffled 1. calm, collected, composed, cool, peaceful, placid, sedate, serene, tranquil, undisturbed, unfazed (*infor~ mal*), unflustered, unmoved, unper~ turbed **2**. even, flat, level, smooth, un~ broken

unruly disobedient, disorderly, fractious, headstrong, insubordinate, intractable, lawless, mutinous, obstreperous, rebel~ lious, refractory, riotous, rowdy, turbu~ lent, uncontrollable, ungovernable, un~

manageable, wayward, wild, wilful
▷ **Antonyms** amenable, biddable, docile, governable, manageable, obedient, orderly, tractable

unsafe dangerous, hazardous, insecure, perilous, precarious, risky, threatening, treacherous, uncertain, unreliable, unsound, unstable
▷ **Antonyms** certain, harmless, reliable, safe, secure, sound, stable, sure

unsaid left to the imagination, tacit, undeclared, unexpressed, unspoken, unstated, unuttered, unvoiced

unsanitary dirty, filthy, germ-ridden, infected, insalubrious, insanitary, sordid, squalid, unclean, unhealthy, unhygienic

unsatisfactory deficient, disappointing, displeasing, inadequate, insufficient, mediocre, no great shakes (*informal*), not good enough, not much cop (*Brit. slang*), not up to par, not up to scratch (*informal*), pathetic, poor, unacceptable, unsuitable, unworthy, weak
▷ **Antonyms** acceptable, adequate, passable, pleasing, satisfactory, sufficient, suitable

unsavoury **1.** distasteful, nasty, objectionable, obnoxious, offensive, repellent, repugnant, repulsive, revolting, unpleasant **2.** disagreeable, distasteful, nauseating, sickening, unappetizing, unpalatable
▷ **Antonyms** appetizing, palatable, pleasant, savoury, tasteful, tasty, toothsome

unscathed in one piece, safe, sound, unharmed, unhurt, uninjured, unmarked, unscarred, unscratched, untouched, whole

unscrupulous conscienceless, corrupt, crooked (*informal*), dishonest, dishonourable, exploitative, immoral, improper, knavish, roguish, ruthless, sink, unconscientious, unconscionable, unethical, unprincipled
▷ **Antonyms** ethical, honest, honourable, moral, principled, proper, scrupulous, upright

unseasonable ill-timed, inappropriate, inopportune, mistimed, out of keeping, unsuitable, untimely

unseat **1.** throw, unhorse, unsaddle **2.** depose, dethrone, discharge, dismiss, displace, oust, overthrow, remove

unseemly discreditable, disreputable, improper, inappropriate, indecorous, indelicate, in poor taste, out of keeping, out of place, unbecoming, unbefitting, undignified, unrefined, unsuitable
▷ **Antonyms** acceptable, appropriate, becoming, decorous, fitting, proper, refined, seemly, suitable

unseen concealed, hidden, invisible, lurking, obscure, undetected, unnoticed, unobserved, unobtrusive, unperceived, veiled

unselfish altruistic, charitable, devoted, disinterested, generous, humanitarian, kind, liberal, magnanimous, noble, self-denying, selfless, self-sacrificing

unsettle agitate, bother, confuse, discompose, disconcert, disorder, disturb, faze, fluster, perturb, rattle (*informal*), ruffle, throw (*informal*), throw into confusion, throw into disorder, throw into uproar, throw off balance, trouble, unbalance, unnerve, upset

unsettled **1.** disorderly, insecure, shaky, unstable, unsteady **2.** changeable, changing, inconstant, uncertain, unpredictable, variable **3.** agitated, anxious, confused, disturbed, flustered, on edge, perturbed, restive, restless, shaken, tense, troubled, uneasy, unnerved, wired (*slang*) **4.** debatable, doubtful, moot, open, undecided, undetermined, unresolved, up in the air **5.** due, in arrears, outstanding, owing, payable, pending **6.** uninhabited, unoccupied, unpeopled, unpopulated

unshakable absolute, constant, firm, fixed, immovable, resolute, staunch, steadfast, sure, unassailable, unswerving, unwavering, well-founded
▷ **Antonyms** insecure, shaky, uncertain, unsure, wavering, wobbly

unshaken calm, collected, composed, impassive, unaffected, unalarmed, undaunted, undismayed, undisturbed, unfazed (*informal*), unmoved, unperturbed, unruffled

unsheltered exposed, open, out in the open, unprotected, unscreened, unshielded

unsightly disagreeable, hideous, horrid, repulsive, revolting (*informal*), ugly, unattractive, unpleasant, unprepossessing
▷ **Antonyms** agreeable, attractive, beautiful, comely, cute, handsome, pleasing, prepossessing, pretty

unskilful awkward, bungling, clumsy, cowboy (*informal*), fumbling, incompetent, inept, inexpert, maladroit, unhandy, unpractised, unworkmanlike

unskilled amateurish, cowboy (*informal*), inexperienced, uneducated, unprofessional, unqualified, untalented, untrained
▷ **Antonyms** adept, expert, masterly, professional, qualified, skilled, talented

unsociable chilly, cold, distant, hostile, inhospitable, introverted, reclusive, retiring, standoffish, uncongenial, unforthcoming, unfriendly, unneighbourly, unsocial, withdrawn
▷ **Antonyms** congenial, convivial, friendly, gregarious, hospitable, neighbourly, outgoing, sociable

unsolicited free-will, gratuitous, spontaneous, unasked for, uncalled-for, unforced, uninvited, unrequested, unsought, unwelcome, voluntary, volunteered

unsophisticated 1. artless, childlike, guileless, inexperienced, ingenuous, innocent, naive, natural, unaffected, untutored, unworldly 2. plain, simple, straightforward, uncomplex, uncomplicated, uninvolved, unrefined, unspecialized 3. genuine, not artificial, pure, unadulterated
▷ **Antonyms** (*sense 2*) advanced, complex, complicated, elegant, esoteric, intricate, sophisticated

unsound 1. ailing, defective, delicate, deranged, diseased, frail, ill, in poor health, unbalanced, unhealthy, unhinged, unstable, unwell, weak 2. defective, erroneous, fallacious, false, faulty, flawed, ill-founded, illogical, invalid, shaky, specious, unreliable, weak 3. flimsy, insecure, not solid, rickety, shaky, tottering, unreliable, unsafe, unstable, unsteady, wobbly
▷ **Antonyms** (*sense 3*) reliable, safe, solid, sound, stable, steady, strong, sturdy, substantial

unsparing 1. abundant, bountiful, generous, lavish, liberal, munificent, open-handed, plenteous, prodigal, profuse, ungrudging, unstinting 2. cold-blooded, hard, harsh, implacable, inexorable, relentless, rigorous, ruthless, severe, stern, stringent, uncompromising, unforgiving, unmerciful

unspeakable 1. beyond description, beyond words, inconceivable, indescribable, ineffable, inexpressible, overwhelming, unbelievable, unimaginable, unutterable, wonderful 2. abominable, abysmal, appalling, awful, bad, dreadful, evil, execrable, frightful, from hell (*informal*), heinous, hellacious (*U.S. slang*), horrible, loathsome, monstrous, odious, repellent, shocking, too horrible for words

unspoiled, unspoilt 1. intact, perfect, preserved, unaffected, unblemished, unchanged, undamaged, unharmed, unimpaired, untouched 2. artless, innocent, natural, unaffected, unassuming, unstudied, wholesome
▷ **Antonyms** (*sense 1*) affected, blemished, changed, damaged, harmed, impaired, imperfect, spoilt, touched

unspoken 1. assumed, implicit, implied, inferred, left to the imagination, not put into words, not spelt out, tacit, taken for granted, undeclared, understood, unexpressed, unstated 2. mute, silent, unsaid, unuttered, voiceless, wordless
▷ **Antonyms** (*sense 1*) clear, declared, explicit, expressed, spoken, stated

unstable 1. insecure, not fixed, precarious, rickety, risky, shaky, tottering, unsettled, unsteady, wobbly 2. capricious, changeable, erratic, fitful, fluctuating, inconsistent, inconstant, irrational, temperamental, unpredictable, unsteady, untrustworthy, vacillating, variable, volatile
▷ **Antonyms** (*sense 2*) consistent, constant, level-headed, predictable, rational, reliable, stable, steady, trustworthy

unsteady 1. infirm, insecure, precarious, reeling, rickety, shaky, tottering, treacherous, unsafe, unstable, wobbly 2. changeable, erratic, flickering, flighty, fluctuating, inconstant, irregular, temperamental, unreliable, unsettled, vacillating, variable, volatile, wavering

unstinted abundant, ample, bountiful, full, generous, large, lavish, liberal, plentiful, prodigal, profuse

unsubstantial 1. airy, flimsy, fragile, frail, inadequate, light, slight, thin 2. erroneous, full of holes, ill-founded, superficial, tenuous, unsound, unsupported, weak 3. dreamlike, fanciful, illusory, imaginary, immaterial, impalpable, visionary

unsubstantiated open to question, unattested, unconfirmed, uncorroborated, unestablished, unproven, unsupported
▷ **Antonyms** attested, confirmed, corroborated, established, proven, substantiated, supported

unsuccessful 1. abortive, bootless, failed, fruitless, futile, ineffective, unavailing, unproductive, useless, vain 2. at a low ebb, balked, defeated, foiled, frustrated, hapless, ill-starred, losing, luckless, unfortunate, unlucky
▷ **Antonyms** (*sense 1*) flourishing, fruitful, productive, prosperous, remunerative, successful, thriving, useful, worthwhile (*sense 2*) fortunate, lucky, triumphant, victorious, winning

unsuitable improper, inapposite, inappropriate, inapt, incompatible, incongruous, ineligible, infelicitous, out of character, out of keeping, out of place, unacceptable, unbecoming, unbefitting, unfit, unfitting, unseasonable, unseemly, unsuited
▷ **Antonyms** acceptable, apposite, appropriate, apt, compatible, eligible, fitting, proper, suitable

unsullied clean, immaculate, impeccable, pristine, pure, spotless, squeaky-clean, stainless, unblackened, unblemished, uncorrupted, undefiled, unsoiled, untainted, untarnished, untouched

unsung anonymous, disregarded, neglected, unacclaimed, unacknowledged, uncelebrated, unhailed, unhonoured, unknown, unnamed, unrecognized

unsure 1. insecure, lacking in confidence, unassured, unconfident 2. distrustful, doubtful, dubious, hesitant, in a quandary, irresolute, mistrustful, sceptical, suspicious, unconvinced, undecided
▷ **Antonyms** assured, certain, confident,

convinced, decided, persuaded, resolute, sure

unsurpassed consummate, exceptional, incomparable, matchless, nonpareil, paramount, peerless, second to none, superlative, supreme, transcendent, unequalled, unexcelled, unparalleled, unrivalled, without an equal

unsuspecting confiding, credulous, gullible, inexperienced, ingenuous, innocent, naive, off guard, trustful, trusting, unconscious, unsuspicious, unwarned, unwary

unswerving constant, dedicated, devoted, direct, firm, resolute, single-minded, staunch, steadfast, steady, true, undeviating, unfaltering, unflagging, untiring, unwavering

unsympathetic apathetic, callous, cold, compassionless (*rare*), cruel, hard, harsh, heartless, indifferent, insensitive, soulless, stony-hearted, tough, uncompassionate, unconcerned, unfeeling, unkind, unmoved, unpitying, unresponsive

▷ **Antonyms** caring, compassionate, concerned, kind, pitying, sensitive, supportive, sympathetic, understanding

unsystematic chaotic, confused, disorderly, disorganized, haphazard, irregular, jumbled, muddled, random, slapdash, unmethodical, unorganized, unplanned, unsystematized

untamed barbarous, feral, fierce, not broken in, savage, unbroken, uncontrollable, undomesticated, untameable, wild

untangle clear up, disentangle, explain, extricate, solve, straighten out, unravel, unsnarl

▷ **Antonyms** complicate, confuse, enmesh, entangle, jumble, muddle, puzzle, snarl, tangle

untarnished bright, burnished, clean, glowing, immaculate, impeccable, polished, pure, shining, spotless, squeaky-clean, unblemished, unimpeachable, unsoiled, unspotted, unstained, unsullied

untenable fallacious, flawed, groundless, illogical, indefensible, insupportable, shaky, unreasonable, unsound, unsustainable, weak

▷ **Antonyms** justified, logical, rational, reasonable, sensible, supported, unarguable, uncontestable, valid, verifiable, well-grounded

unthinkable **1.** absurd, illogical, impossible, improbable, not on (*informal*), out of the question, preposterous, unlikely, unreasonable **2.** beyond belief, beyond the bounds of possibility, implausible, inconceivable, incredible, insupportable, unbelievable, unimaginable

unthinking **1.** blundering, inconsiderate, insensitive, rude, selfish, tactless, thoughtless, undiplomatic **2.** careless, heedless, impulsive, inadvertent, instinctive, mechanical, negligent, oblivious, rash, senseless, unconscious, unmindful, vacant, witless

▷ **Antonyms** (*sense 2*) careful, conscious, deliberate, heedful, mindful, sensible, witting

untidy bedraggled, chaotic, cluttered, disarrayed, disorderly, higgledy-piggledy (*informal*), jumbled, littered, messy, muddled, muddly, mussy (*U.S. informal*), rumpled, shambolic, slatternly, slipshod, sloppy (*informal*), slovenly, topsy-turvy, unkempt

▷ **Antonyms** methodical, neat, orderly, presentable, ship-shape, spruce, systematic, tidy, well-kept

untie free, loosen, release, unbind, unbridle, unclasp, undo, unfasten, unknot, unlace, unstrap

untimely awkward, badly timed, early, ill-timed, inappropriate, inauspicious, inconvenient, inopportune, mistimed, premature, unfortunate, unseasonable, unsuitable

▷ **Antonyms** appropriate, auspicious, convenient, fortunate, opportune, seasonable, suitable, timely, welcome, well-timed

untiring constant, dedicated, determined, devoted, dogged, incessant, indefatigable, patient, persevering, persistent, staunch, steady, tireless, unfaltering, unflagging, unremitting, unwearied

untold **1.** indescribable, inexpressible, undreamed of, unimaginable, unspeakable, unthinkable, unutterable **2.** countless, incalculable, innumerable, measureless, myriad, numberless, uncountable, uncounted, unnumbered **3.** hidden, private, secret, undisclosed, unknown, unpublished, unrecounted, unrelated, unrevealed

untouched **1.** intact, safe and sound, undamaged, unharmed, unhurt, uninjured, unscathed, without a scratch **2.** dry-eyed, indifferent, unaffected, unconcerned, unimpressed, unmoved, unstirred

▷ **Antonyms** (*sense 2*) affected, concerned, impressed, moved, softened, stirred, touched

untoward **1.** annoying, awkward, disastrous, ill-timed, inconvenient, inimical, irritating, troublesome, unfortunate, vexatious **2.** adverse, contrary, inauspicious, inopportune, unfavourable, unlucky, untimely **3.** improper, inappropriate, indecorous, out of place, unbecoming, unfitting, unseemly, unsuitable

untrained amateur, green, inexperienced, raw, uneducated, unpractised, unqualified, unschooled, unskilled, untaught, untutored

▷ **Antonyms** educated, experienced, expert, qualified, schooled, skilled, taught, trained

untried in the experimental stage, new, novel, unattempted, unessayed, unproved, untested

untroubled calm, composed, cool, peaceful, placid, sedate, serene, steady, tranquil, unagitated, unconcerned, undisturbed, unfazed (*informal*), unflappable (*informal*), unflustered, unperturbed, unruffled, unstirred, unworried

▷ **Antonyms** agitated, anxious, concerned, disturbed, flustered, perturbed, ruffled, troubled, worried

untrue 1. deceptive, dishonest, erroneous, fallacious, false, inaccurate, incorrect, lying, misleading, mistaken, sham, spurious, untruthful, wrong **2.** deceitful, disloyal, faithless, false, forsworn, inconstant, perfidious, traitorous, treacherous, two-faced, unfaithful, untrustworthy **3.** deviant, distorted, inaccurate, off, out of line, out of true, wide

▷ **Antonyms** (*sense 1*) accurate, correct, factual, right, true (*sense 2*) constant, dependable, faithful, honest, honourable, loyal, truthful, virtuous

untrustworthy capricious, deceitful, devious, dishonest, disloyal, fair-weather, faithless, false, fickle, fly-by-night (*informal*), not to be depended on, slippery, treacherous, tricky, two-faced, undependable, unfaithful, unreliable, untrue, untrusty

▷ **Antonyms** dependable, faithful, honest, loyal, reliable, reputable, steadfast, true, trustworthy, trusty

untruth 1. deceitfulness, duplicity, falsity, inveracity (*rare*), lying, mendacity, perjury, truthlessness, untruthfulness **2.** deceit, fabrication, falsehood, falsification, fib, fiction, lie, pork pie (*Brit. slang*), porky (*Brit. slang*), prevarication, story, tale, trick, whopper (*informal*)

untruthful crooked (*informal*), deceitful, deceptive, dishonest, dissembling, false, fibbing, hypocritical, lying, mendacious

▷ **Antonyms** candid, honest, sincere, true, truthful, veracious

untutored 1. ignorant, illiterate, uneducated, unlearned, unschooled, untrained, unversed **2.** artless, inexperienced, simple, unpractised, unrefined, unsophisticated

unused 1. fresh, intact, new, pristine, untouched **2.** (*with* **to**) a stranger to, inexperienced in, new to, not ready for, not up to, unaccustomed to, unfamiliar with, unhabituated to **3.** available, extra, left, leftover, remaining, unconsumed, unexhausted, unutilized

unusual abnormal, atypical, bizarre, curious, different, exceptional, extraordinary, left-field (*informal*), notable, odd, out of the ordinary, phenomenal, queer, rare, remarkable, singular, strange, surprising, uncommon, unconventional, unexpected, unfamiliar, unwonted

▷ **Antonyms** average, banal, commonplace, conventional, everyday, familiar, normal, routine, traditional, typical, unremarkable, usual

unutterable beyond words, extreme, indescribable, ineffable, overwhelming, unimaginable, unspeakable

unvarnished bare, candid, frank, honest, naked, plain, pure, pure and simple, simple, sincere, stark, straightforward, unadorned, unembellished

unveil bare, bring to light, disclose, divulge, expose, lay bare, lay open, make known, make public, reveal, uncover

▷ **Antonyms** cloak, conceal, cover, disguise, hide, mask, obscure, veil

unwanted *de trop,* going begging, outcast, rejected, superfluous, surplus to requirements, unasked, undesired, uninvited, unneeded, unsolicited, unwelcome, useless

▷ **Antonyms** desired, necessary, needed, useful, wanted, welcome

unwarranted gratuitous, groundless, indefensible, inexcusable, uncalled-for, unjust, unjustified, unprovoked, unreasonable, wrong

unwary careless, hasty, heedless, imprudent, incautious, indiscreet, rash, reckless, thoughtless, uncircumspect, unguarded, unwatchful

▷ **Antonyms** cautious, chary, circumspect, discreet, guarded, prudent, wary, watchful

unwavering consistent, dedicated, determined, immovable, resolute, single-minded, staunch, steadfast, steady, undeviating, unfaltering, unflagging, unshakable, unshaken, unswerving, untiring

unwelcome 1. excluded, rejected, unacceptable, undesirable, uninvited, unpopular, unwanted, unwished for **2.** disagreeable, displeasing, distasteful, thankless, undesirable, unpleasant

▷ **Antonyms** acceptable, agreeable, desirable, pleasant, pleasing, popular, wanted, welcome

unwell ailing, at death's door, green about the gills, ill, indisposed, in poor health, off colour, out of sorts, poorly (*informal*), sick, sickly, under the weather (*informal*), unhealthy

▷ **Antonyms** fine, healthy, robust, sound, well

unwholesome 1. deleterious, harmful, insalubrious, junk (*informal*), noxious, poisonous, tainted, unhealthy, unnourishing **2.** bad, corrupting, degrading, demoralizing, depraving, evil, immoral, maleficent, perverting, wicked **3.** anaemic, pale, pallid, pasty, sickly, wan

▷ **Antonyms** (*sense 1*) beneficial, germ-free, healthy, hygienic, salubrious, sanitary, wholesome (*sense 2*) edifying, moral

unwieldy **1.** awkward, burdensome, cum~bersome, inconvenient, unhandy, un~manageable **2.** bulky, clumsy, clunky (*informal*), hefty, massive, ponderous, ungainly, weighty

unwilling averse, demurring, disinclined, grudging, indisposed, laggard (*rare*), loath, not in the mood, opposed, reluc~tant, resistant, unenthusiastic

▷ **Antonyms** amenable, compliant, dis~posed, eager, enthusiastic, inclined, vol~untary, willing

unwind **1.** disentangle, slacken, uncoil, undo, unravel, unreel, unroll, untwine, untwist **2.** calm down, let oneself go, loosen up, make oneself at home, mel~low out (*informal*), quieten down, relax, sit back, slow down, take a break, take it easy, wind down

unwise asinine, foolhardy, foolish, ill-advised, ill-considered, ill-judged, im~politic, improvident, imprudent, inad~visable, inane, indiscreet, injudicious, irresponsible, rash, reckless, senseless, short-sighted, silly, stupid

▷ **Antonyms** discreet, judicious, politic, prudent, responsible, sensible, shrewd, wise

unwitting **1.** ignorant, innocent, unaware, unconscious, unknowing, unsuspecting **2.** accidental, chance, inadvertent, in~voluntary, undesigned, unintended, un~intentional, unmeant, unplanned

▷ **Antonyms** (*sense 2*) conscious, deliber~ate, designed, intended, intentional, knowing, meant, planned, witting

unwonted atypical, extraordinary, infre~quent, out of the ordinary, peculiar, rare, seldom seen, singular, unaccus~tomed, uncommon, uncustomary, unex~pected, unfamiliar, unheard-of, unusual

unworldly **1.** abstract, celestial, meta~physical, nonmaterialistic, religious, spiritual, transcendental **2.** as green as grass, green, idealistic, inexperienced, innocent, naive, raw, trusting, unso~phisticated, wet behind the ears (*infor~mal*) **3.** ethereal, extraterrestrial, other~worldly, unearthly

unworthy **1.** (*with* **of**) beneath the dignity of, improper, inappropriate, out of char~acter, out of place, unbecoming, unbe~fitting, unfitting, unseemly, unsuitable **2.** base, contemptible, degrading, dis~creditable, disgraceful, dishonourable, disreputable, ignoble, shameful **3.** ineli~gible, not deserving of, not fit for, not good enough, not worth, undeserving

▷ **Antonyms** (*sense 3*) commendable, creditable, deserving, eligible, fit, hon~ourable, meritorious, worthy

unwritten **1.** oral, unrecorded, vocal, word-of-mouth **2.** accepted, convention~al, customary, tacit, traditional, under~stood, unformulated

unyielding adamant, determined, firm, hardline, immovable, inexorable, inflex~ible, intractable, obdurate, obstinate, relentless, resolute, rigid, staunch, steadfast, stiff-necked, stubborn, tough, unbending, uncompromising, unwaver~ing

▷ **Antonyms** adaptable, compliant, com~promising, cooperative, flexible, mov~able, tractable, yielding

up-and-coming ambitious, eager, go-getting (*informal*), on the make (*slang*), promising, pushing

upbeat *adjective* buoyant, cheerful, cheery, encouraging, favourable, forward-looking, heartening, hopeful, looking up, optimistic, positive, promis~ing, rosy

upbraid admonish, bawl out (*informal*), berate, blame, carpet (*informal*), casti~gate, censure, chew out (*U.S. & Canad. informal*), chide, condemn, dress down (*informal*), excoriate, give (someone) a rocket (*Brit. & N.Z. informal*), lecture, rap (someone) over the knuckles, read the riot act, rebuke, reprimand, re~proach, reprove, scold, slap on the wrist, take to task, tear into (*informal*), tear (someone) off a strip (*Brit. informal*), tell off (*informal*), tick off (*informal*)

upbringing breeding, bringing-up, care, cultivation, education, nurture, raising, rearing, tending, training

update amend, bring up to date, modern~ize, renew, revise

upgrade advance, ameliorate, better, el~evate, enhance, improve, promote, raise

▷ **Antonyms** decry, degrade, demote, denigrate, downgrade, lower

upheaval cataclysm, disorder, disruption, disturbance, eruption, overthrow, revo~lution, turmoil, violent change

uphill *adjective* **1.** ascending, climbing, mounting, rising **2.** arduous, difficult, exhausting, gruelling, hard, laborious, punishing, Sisyphean, strenuous, tax~ing, tough, wearisome

▷ **Antonyms** (*sense 1*) descending, down~hill, lowering

uphold advocate, aid, back, champion, defend, encourage, endorse, hold to, justify, maintain, promote, stand by, stick up for (*informal*), support, sustain, vindicate

upkeep **1.** conservation, keep, mainte~nance, preservation, repair, running, subsistence, support, sustenance **2.** ex~penditure, expenses, oncosts (*Brit.*), op~erating costs, outlay, overheads, run~ning costs

uplift *verb* **1.** elevate, heave, hoist, lift up, raise **2.** advance, ameliorate, better, civilize, cultivate, edify, improve, in~spire, raise, refine, upgrade *~noun* **3.** advancement, betterment, cultivation, edification, enhancement, enlighten~ment, enrichment, improvement, re~finement

upper 1. high, higher, loftier, top, topmost **2.** elevated, eminent, greater, important, superior
▷ **Antonyms** bottom, inferior, junior, low, lower

upper-class aristocratic, blue-blooded, highborn, high-class, noble, patrician, top-drawer, well-bred

upper hand advantage, ascendancy, control, dominion, edge, mastery, superiority, supremacy, sway, whip hand

uppermost 1. highest, loftiest, most elevated, top, topmost, upmost **2.** chief, dominant, foremost, greatest, leading, main, paramount, predominant, pre-eminent, primary, principal, supreme
▷ **Antonyms** bottom, bottommost, humblest, least, lowermost, lowest, lowliest, slightest

uppish affected, arrogant, cocky, conceited, high and mighty (*informal*), hoity-toity (*informal*), overweening, presumptuous, putting on airs, self-important, snobbish, stuck-up (*informal*), supercilious, toffee-nosed (*slang, chiefly Brit.*), uppity (*informal*)
▷ **Antonyms** diffident, humble, lowly, meek, obsequious, servile, unaffected, unassertive

uppity bigheaded (*informal*), bumptious, cocky, conceited, full of oneself, impertinent, on one's high horse (*informal*), overweening, self-important, swanky (*informal*), too big for one's boots *or* breeches (*informal*), uppish (*Brit. informal*)

upright 1. erect, on end, perpendicular, straight, vertical **2.** *figurative* above board, conscientious, ethical, faithful, good, high-minded, honest, honourable, incorruptible, just, principled, righteous, straightforward, true, trustworthy, unimpeachable, virtuous
▷ **Antonyms** (*sense 1*) flat, horizontal, lying, prone, prostrate, supine (*sense 2*) corrupt, devious, dishonest, dishonourable, unethical, unjust, untrustworthy, wicked

uprightness fairness, faithfulness, goodness, high-mindedness, honesty, incorruptibility, integrity, justice, probity, rectitude, righteousness, straightforwardness, trustworthiness, virtue

uprising disturbance, insurgence, insurrection, mutiny, outbreak, putsch, rebellion, revolt, revolution, rising, upheaval

uproar *bagarre,* brawl, brouhaha, clamour, commotion, confusion, din, furore, hubbub, hullabaloo, hurly-burly, mayhem, noise, outcry, pandemonium, racket, riot, ruckus (*informal*), ruction (*informal*), rumpus, turbulence, turmoil

uproarious 1. clamorous, confused, disorderly, loud, noisy, riotous, rowdy, tempestuous, tumultuous, turbulent, wild **2.** convulsive (*informal*), hilarious, hysterical, killing (*informal*), rib-tickling, rip-roaring (*informal*), screamingly funny, side-splitting, very funny **3.** boisterous, gleeful, loud, rollicking, unrestrained
▷ **Antonyms** (*sense 1*) inaudible, low-key, orderly, peaceful, quiet, still (*sense 2*) morose, mournful, sad, serious, sorrowful, tragic

uproot 1. deracinate, dig up, extirpate, grub up, pull out by the roots, pull up, rip up, root out, weed out **2.** deracinate, disorient, displace, exile **3.** destroy, do away with, eliminate, eradicate, extirpate, remove, wipe out

ups and downs changes, ebb and flow, fluctuations, moods, vicissitudes, wheel of fortune

upset *verb* **1.** capsize, knock over, overturn, spill, tip over, topple over **2.** change, disorder, disorganize, disturb, mess up, mix up, put out of order, spoil, turn topsy-turvy **3.** agitate, bother, discompose, disconcert, dismay, disquiet, distress, disturb, faze, fluster, grieve, hassle (*informal*), perturb, ruffle, throw (someone) off balance, trouble, unnerve **4.** be victorious over, conquer, defeat, get the better of, overcome, overthrow, triumph over, win against the odds ~*noun* **5.** defeat, reverse, shake-up (*informal*), sudden change, surprise **6.** bug (*informal*), complaint, disorder, disturbance, illness, indisposition, malady, queasiness, sickness **7.** agitation, bother, discomposure, disquiet, distress, disturbance, hassle (*informal*), shock, trouble, worry ~*adjective* **8.** capsized, overturned, spilled, tipped over, toppled, tumbled, upside down **9.** disordered, disturbed, gippy (*slang*), ill, poorly (*informal*), queasy, sick **10.** agitated, bothered, confused, disconcerted, dismayed, disquieted, distressed, disturbed, frantic, grieved, hassled (*informal*), hurt, overwrought, put out, ruffled, troubled, worried **11.** at sixes and sevens, chaotic, confused, disarrayed, disordered, in disarray *or* disorder, messed up, muddled, topsy-turvy **12.** beaten, conquered, defeated, overcome, overthrown, vanquished

upshot conclusion, consequence, culmination, end, end result, event, finale, issue, outcome, payoff (*informal*), result, sequel

upside down 1. bottom up, inverted, on its head, overturned, upturned, wrong side up **2.** *informal* chaotic, confused, disordered, higgledy-piggledy (*informal*), in chaos, in confusion, in disarray, in disorder, jumbled, muddled, topsy-turvy

upstanding 1. ethical, good, honest, honourable, incorruptible, moral, principled, true, trustworthy, upright **2.** firm, hale and hearty, hardy, healthy, robust, stalwart, strong, sturdy, upright, vigorous

▷ **Antonyms** (*sense 1*) bad, corrupt, dishonest, false, immoral, unethical, unprincipled, untrustworthy (*sense 2*) delicate, feeble, frail, infirm, puny, unhealthy, weak

upstart arriviste, nobody, *nouveau riche,* parvenu, social climber, status seeker

uptight anxious, edgy, nervy (*Brit. informal*), neurotic, on edge, on the defensive, prickly, tense, uneasy, wired (*slang*), withdrawn

up-to-date all the rage, current, fashionable, happening (*informal*), having one's finger on the pulse, in, in vogue, modern, newest, now (*informal*), stylish, trendy (*Brit. informal*), up-to-the-minute, with it (*informal*)

▷ **Antonyms** antiquated, dated, *démodé,* obsolete, old fashioned, outmoded, out of date, out of the ark (*informal*), passé

upturn *noun* advancement, boost, improvement, increase, recovery, revival, rise, upsurge, upswing

urban city, civic, inner-city, metropolitan, municipal, oppidan (*rare*), town

urbane civil, civilized, cosmopolitan, courteous, cultivated, cultured, debonair, elegant, mannerly, polished, refined, smooth, sophisticated, suave, well-bred, well-mannered

▷ **Antonyms** boorish, clownish, discourteous, gauche, impolite, rude, uncivilized, uncouth, uncultured

urbanity charm, civility, courtesy, culture, elegance, grace, mannerliness, polish, refinement, sophistication, suavity, worldliness

urchin brat, gamin, guttersnipe, mudlark (*slang*), ragamuffin, street Arab (*offensive*), waif, young rogue

urge *verb* **1.** appeal to, beg, beseech, entreat, exhort, implore, plead, press, solicit **2.** advise, advocate, champion, counsel, insist on, push for, recommend, support **3.** compel, constrain, drive, egg on, encourage, force, goad, hasten, impel, incite, induce, instigate, press, prompt, propel, push, spur, stimulate *~noun* **4.** compulsion, desire, drive, fancy, impulse, itch, longing, thirst, wish, yearning, yen (*informal*)

▷ **Antonyms** *~verb* (*senses 1 & 2*) caution, deter, discourage, dissuade, remonstrate, warn *~noun* aversion, disinclination, distaste, indisposition, reluctance, repugnance

urgency exigency, extremity, gravity, hurry, imperativeness, importance, importunity, necessity, need, pressure, seriousness, stress

urgent **1.** compelling, critical, crucial, exigent, immediate, imperative, important, instant, not to be delayed, now or never, pressing, top-priority **2.** clamorous, earnest, importunate, insistent, intense, persistent, persuasive

▷ **Antonyms** apathetic, casual, feeble, half-hearted, lackadaisical, low-priority, minor, perfunctory, trivial, unimportant, weak

urinate leak (*slang*), make water, micturate, pass water, pee (*slang*), piddle (*informal*), piss (*taboo slang*), spend a penny (*Brit. informal*), tinkle (*Brit. informal*), wee (*informal*), wee-wee (*informal*)

usable at one's disposal, available, current, fit for use, functional, in running order, practical, ready for use, serviceable, utilizable, valid, working

usage **1.** control, employment, handling, management, operation, regulation, running, treatment, use **2.** convention, custom, form, habit, matter of course, method, mode, practice, procedure, regime, routine, rule, tradition, wont

use *verb* **1.** apply, avail oneself of, bring into play, employ, exercise, exert, find a use for, make use of, operate, ply, practise, profit by, put to use, turn to account, utilize, wield, work **2.** act towards, behave towards, deal with, exploit, handle, manipulate, misuse, take advantage of, treat **3.** consume, exhaust, expend, run through, spend, waste *~noun* **4.** application, employment, exercise, handling, operation, practice, service, treatment, usage, wear and tear **5.** advantage, application, avail, benefit, good, help, mileage (*informal*), point, profit, service, usefulness, utility, value, worth **6.** custom, habit, practice, usage, way, wont **7.** call, cause, end, necessity, need, object, occasion, point, purpose, reason

used cast-off, hand-me-down (*informal*), nearly new, not new, reach-me-down (*informal*), second-hand, shopsoiled, worn

▷ **Antonyms** brand-new, fresh, intact, new, pristine, unused

used to accustomed to, at home in, attuned to, familiar with, given to, habituated to, hardened to, in the habit of, inured to, tolerant of, wont to

useful advantageous, all-purpose, beneficial, effective, fruitful, general-purpose, helpful, of help, of service, of use, practical, profitable, salutary, serviceable, valuable, worthwhile

▷ **Antonyms** inadequate, ineffective, unbeneficial, unhelpful, unproductive, useless, vain, worthless

useless **1.** basket case, bootless, disadvantageous, fruitless, futile, hopeless, idle, impractical, ineffective, ineffectual, of no use, pointless, profitless, unavailing, unproductive, unworkable, vain, valueless, wanky (*taboo slang*), worthless **2.** *informal* a dead loss, hopeless, incompetent, ineffectual, inept, no good, stupid, weak

▷ **Antonyms** (*sense 1*) advantageous, effective, fruitful, practical, productive, profitable, useful, valuable, workable, worthwhile

use up absorb, burn up, consume, deplete, devour, drain, exhaust, finish, fritter away, run through, squander, swallow up, waste

usher *noun* **1.** attendant, doorkeeper, doorman, escort, guide, usherette *~verb* **2.** conduct, direct, escort, guide, lead, pilot, show in *or* out, steer **3.** (*usually with* **in**) bring in, herald, inaugurate, initiate, introduce, launch, open the door to, pave the way for, precede, ring in

usual accustomed, bog-standard (*Brit. & Irish slang*), common, constant, customary, everyday, expected, familiar, fixed, general, habitual, normal, ordinary, regular, routine, standard, stock, typical, wonted

▷ **Antonyms** exceptional, extraordinary, new, novel, off-beat, out of the ordinary, peculiar, rare, singular, strange, uncommon, unexpected, unhackneyed, unique, unorthodox, unusual

usually as a rule, as is the custom, as is usual, by and large, commonly, for the most part, generally, habitually, in the main, mainly, mostly, most often, normally, on the whole, ordinarily, regularly, routinely

usurp appropriate, arrogate, assume, commandeer, infringe upon, lay hold of, seize, take, take over, wrest

utility advantageousness, avail, benefit, convenience, efficacy, fitness, mileage (*informal*), point, practicality, profit, service, serviceableness, use, usefulness

utilize appropriate, avail oneself of, employ, have recourse to, make the most of, make use of, profit by, put to use, resort to, take advantage of, turn to account, use

utmost *adjective* **1.** chief, extreme, greatest, highest, maximum, paramount, pre-eminent, supreme **2.** extreme, farthest, final, last, most distant, outermost, remotest, uttermost *~noun* **3.** best, greatest, hardest, highest, most

Utopia bliss, Eden, Erewhon, Garden of Eden, heaven, ideal life, paradise, perfect place, seventh heaven, Shangri-la

Utopian 1. *adjective* airy, chimerical, dream, fanciful, fantasy, ideal, idealistic, illusory, imaginary, impractical, perfect, romantic, visionary **2.** *~noun* Don Quixote, dreamer, idealist, romanticist, visionary

utter[1] *verb* **1.** articulate, enunciate, express, pronounce, put into words, say, speak, verbalize, vocalize, voice **2.** declare, divulge, give expression to, make known, proclaim, promulgate, publish, reveal, state

utter[2] *adjective* absolute, arrant, complete, consummate, deep-dyed (*usually derogatory*), downright, entire, out-and-out, outright, perfect, sheer, stark, thorough, thoroughgoing, total, unmitigated, unqualified

utterance 1. announcement, declaration, expression, opinion, remark, speech, statement, words **2.** articulation, delivery, ejaculation, expression, verbalization, vocalization, vociferation

utterly absolutely, completely, entirely, extremely, fully, one hundred per cent, perfectly, thoroughly, totally, to the core, to the nth degree, wholly

uttermost extreme, farthest, final, last, outermost, remotest, utmost

V, v

vacancy **1.** job, opening, opportunity, position, post, room, situation **2.** absent-mindedness, abstraction, blankness, inanity, inattentiveness, incomprehension, incuriousness, lack of interest, vacuousness **3.** emptiness, gap, space, vacuum, void

vacant **1.** available, disengaged, empty, free, idle, not in use, to let, unemployed, unengaged, unfilled, unoccupied, untenanted, void **2.** absent-minded, abstracted, blank, dreaming, dreamy, expressionless, idle, inane, incurious, thoughtless, unthinking, vacuous, vague

▷ **Antonyms** (*sense 1*) busy, engaged, full, inhabited, in use, occupied, taken (*sense 2*) animated, engrossed, expressive, lively, reflective, thoughtful

vacate depart, evacuate, give up, go away, leave, leave empty, move out of, quit, relinquish possession of, withdraw

vacillate be irresolute *or* indecisive, blow hot and cold (*informal*), chop and change, dither (*chiefly Brit.*), fluctuate, haver, hesitate, keep changing one's mind, oscillate, reel, rock, shillyshally (*informal*), sway, swither (*Scot.*), waver

vacillating hesitant, in two minds (*informal*), irresolute, oscillating, shillyshallying (*informal*), uncertain, unresolved, wavering

vacillation dithering (*chiefly Brit.*), fluctuation, hesitation, inconstancy, indecisiveness, irresoluteness, irresolution, shillyshallying (*informal*), unsteadiness, wavering

vacuity **1.** blankness, emptiness, inanity, incognizance, incomprehension, vacuousness **2.** emptiness, nothingness, space, vacuum, void

vacuous **1.** blank, inane, stupid, uncomprehending, unintelligent, vacant **2.** empty, unfilled, vacant, void

vacuum emptiness, free space, gap, nothingness, space, vacuity, void

vagabond **1.** *noun* bag lady (*chiefly U.S.*), beggar, bum (*informal*), down-and-out, hobo (*U.S.*), itinerant, knight of the road, migrant, nomad, outcast, rascal, rover, tramp, vagrant, wanderer, wayfarer **2.** *~adjective* destitute, down and out, drifting, fly-by-night (*informal*), footloose, homeless, idle, itinerant, journeying, nomadic, rootless, roving, shiftless, vagrant, wandering

vagary caprice, crotchet, fancy, humour, megrim (*archaic*), notion, whim, whimsy

vagrant **1.** *noun* bag lady (*chiefly U.S.*), beggar, bird of passage, bum (*informal*), drifter, hobo (*U.S.*), itinerant, person of no fixed address, rolling stone, tramp, wanderer **2.** *~adjective* itinerant, nomadic, roaming, rootless, roving, unsettled, vagabond

▷ **Antonyms** *~adjective* established, fixed, purposeful, rooted, settled

vague amorphous, blurred, dim, doubtful, fuzzy, generalized, hazy, ill-defined, imprecise, indefinite, indeterminate, indistinct, lax, loose, nebulous, obscure, shadowy, uncertain, unclear, unknown, unspecified, woolly

▷ **Antonyms** clear, clear-cut, definite, distinct, exact, explicit, lucid, precise, specific, well-defined

vaguely absent-mindedly, dimly, evasively, imprecisely, in a general way, obscurely, slightly, through a glass darkly, vacantly

vagueness ambiguity, impreciseness, inexactitude, lack of preciseness, looseness, obscurity, undecidedness, woolliness

▷ **Antonyms** clarity, clearness, definition, exactness, obviousness, preciseness, precision

vain **1.** arrogant, bigheaded (*informal*), cocky, conceited, egotistical, inflated, narcissistic, ostentatious, overweening, peacockish, pleased with oneself, proud, self-important, stuck-up (*informal*), swaggering, swanky (*Brit. informal*), swollen-headed (*informal*), vainglorious **2.** abortive, empty, fruitless, futile, hollow, idle, nugatory, pointless, senseless, time-wasting, trifling, trivial, unavailing, unimportant, unproductive, unprofitable, useless, wanky (*taboo slang*), worthless **3. be vain** have a high opinion of oneself, have a swelled head (*informal*), have one's head turned, think a lot of oneself, think oneself it (*informal*), think oneself the cat's whiskers *or* pyjamas (*slang*) **4. in vain** bootless, fruitless(ly), ineffectual(ly), to no avail, to no purpose, unsuccessful(ly), useless(ly), vain(ly), wasted, without success

▷ **Antonyms** (*sense 1*) bashful, humble, meek, modest, self-deprecating (*sense 2*) fruitful, profitable, serious, successful, useful, valid, worthwhile, worthy

valediction adieu, farewell, goodbye, leave-taking, sendoff (*informal*), *vale*

valedictory *adjective* farewell, final, parting

valetudinarian *adjective* delicate, feeble, frail, hypochondriac, infirm, in poor health, invalid, sickly, weakly

valiant bold, brave, courageous, dauntless, doughty, fearless, gallant, heroic, indomitable, intrepid, lion-hearted, plucky, redoubtable, stouthearted, valorous, worthy

▷ **Antonyms** cowardly, craven, fearful, shrinking, spineless, timid, weak

valid 1. acceptable, binding, cogent, conclusive, convincing, efficacious, efficient, good, just, logical, powerful, sensible, sound, substantial, telling, weighty, well-founded, well-grounded **2.** authentic, bona fide, genuine, in force, lawful, legal, legally binding, legitimate, official, signed and sealed

▷ **Antonyms** (*sense 1*) baseless, bogus, fallacious, false, illogical, sham, spurious, unacceptable, unfounded, unrealistic, unrecognized, untrue, weak (*sense 2*) illegal, inoperative, invalid, unlawful, unofficial

validate authenticate, authorize, certify, confirm, corroborate, endorse, legalize, make legally binding, ratify, set one's seal on *or* to, substantiate

validity 1. cogency, force, foundation, grounds, point, power, soundness, strength, substance, weight **2.** authority, lawfulness, legality, legitimacy, right

valley coomb, cwm (*Welsh*), dale, dell, depression, dingle, glen, hollow, strath (*Scot.*), vale

valorous bold, brave, courageous, dauntless, doughty, fearless, gallant, heroic, intrepid, lion-hearted, plucky, valiant

valour boldness, bravery, courage, derring-do (*archaic*), doughtiness, fearlessness, gallantry, heroism, intrepidity, lion-heartedness, spirit

▷ **Antonyms** cowardice, dread, fear, timidity, trepidation, weakness

valuable *adjective* **1.** costly, dear, expensive, high-priced, precious **2.** beneficial, cherished, esteemed, estimable, held dear, helpful, important, prized, profitable, serviceable, treasured, useful, valued, worth one's *or* its weight in gold, worthwhile, worthy *~noun* **3.** (*usually plural*) heirloom, treasure(s)

▷ **Antonyms** *~adjective* (*sense 1*) cheap, cheapo (*informal*), chickenshit (*U.S. slang*), crappy (*slang*), inexpensive, worthless (*sense 2*) insignificant, pointless, silly, trifling, trivial, unimportant, useless, worthless

value *noun* **1.** cost, equivalent, market price, monetary worth, rate **2.** advantage, benefit, desirability, help, importance, merit, mileage (*informal*), profit, serviceableness, significance, use, usefulness, utility, worth **3.** *plural* code of behaviour, ethics, (moral) standards, principles *~verb* **4.** account, appraise, assess, compute, estimate, evaluate, price, put a price on, rate, set at, survey **5.** appreciate, cherish, esteem, hold dear, hold in high regard *or* esteem, prize, regard highly, respect, set store by, treasure

▷ **Antonyms** *~noun* (*sense 2*) insignificance, unimportance, uselessness, worthlessness *~verb* disregard, have no time for, hold a low opinion of, underestimate, undervalue

valued cherished, dear, esteemed, highly regarded, loved, prized, treasured

valueless miserable, no good, of no earthly use, of no value, unsaleable, useless, worthless

vamoose bugger off (*taboo slang*), clear off (*informal*), decamp, do a bunk (*Brit. slang*), fuck off (*offensive taboo slang*), get on one's bike (*Brit. slang*), go away, go to hell (*informal*), hook it (*slang*), make off, make oneself scarce (*informal*), run away, scarper (*Brit. slang*), scram (*informal*), skedaddle (*informal*), sling one's hook (*Brit. slang*), take flight, take oneself off

vanguard advance guard, cutting edge, forefront, forerunners, front, front line, front rank, leaders, spearhead, trailblazers, trendsetters, van

▷ **Antonyms** back, rear, rearguard, stern, tail, tail end

vanish become invisible, be lost to sight, die out, disappear, disappear from sight *or* from the face of the earth, dissolve, evanesce, evaporate, exit, fade (away), melt (away), vanish off the face of the earth

▷ **Antonyms** appear, arrive, become visible, come into view, materialize, pop up

vanity 1. affected ways, airs, arrogance, bigheadedness (*informal*), conceit, conceitedness, egotism, narcissism, ostentation, pretension, pride, self-admiration, self-love, showing off (*informal*), swollen-headedness (*informal*), vainglory **2.** emptiness, frivolity, fruitlessness, futility, hollowness, inanity, pointlessness, profitlessness, triviality, unproductiveness, unreality, unsubstantiality, uselessness, worthlessness

▷ **Antonyms** (*sense 1*) humility, meekness, modesty, self-abasement, self-deprecation (*sense 2*) importance, value, worth

vanquish beat, blow out of the water (*slang*), clobber (*slang*), conquer, crush, defeat, get the upper hand over, lick (*informal*), master, overcome, overpower, overwhelm, put down, put to flight, put to rout, quell, reduce, repress, rout, run rings around (*informal*), stuff (*slang*), subdue, subjugate, tank (*slang*), triumph over, undo, wipe the floor with (*informal*)

vapid 1. bland, dead, flat, flavourless, insipid, lifeless, milk-and-water, stale, tasteless, unpalatable, watery, weak, wishy-washy (*informal*) **2.** boring, colourless, dull, flat, limp, tame, tedious, tiresome, uninspiring, uninteresting

vapour breath, dampness, exhalation, fog, fumes, haze, miasma, mist, smoke, steam

variable capricious, chameleonic, changeable, fickle, fitful, flexible, fluctuating, inconstant, mercurial, mutable, protean, shifting, temperamental, uneven, unstable, unsteady, vacillating, wavering

▷ **Antonyms** constant, firm, fixed, settled, stable, steady, unalterable, unchanging

variance 1. difference, difference of opinion, disagreement, discord, discrepancy, dissension, dissent, divergence, inconsistency, lack of harmony, strife, variation **2. at variance** at loggerheads, at odds, at sixes and sevens (*informal*), conflicting, in disagreement, in opposition, out of harmony, out of line

▷ **Antonyms** (*sense 1*) accord, agreement, congruity, correspondence, harmony, similarity, unison

variant 1. *adjective* alternative, derived, different, divergent, exceptional, modified **2.** *~noun* alternative, derived form, development, modification, sport (*Biology*), variation

variation alteration, break in routine, change, departure, departure from the norm, deviation, difference, discrepancy, diversification, diversity, innovation, modification, novelty, variety

▷ **Antonyms** dullness, monotony, sameness, tedium, uniformity

varied assorted, different, diverse, heterogeneous, manifold, miscellaneous, mixed, motley, sundry, various

▷ **Antonyms** homogeneous, repetitive, similar, standardized, uniform, unvarying

variegated diversified, many-coloured, motley, mottled, parti-coloured, pied, streaked, varicoloured

variety 1. change, difference, discrepancy, diversification, diversity, many-sidedness, multifariousness, variation **2.** array, assortment, collection, cross section, intermixture, medley, miscellany, mixed bag (*informal*), mixture, multiplicity, range **3.** brand, breed, category, class, kind, make, order, sort, species, strain, type

▷ **Antonyms** (*sense 1*) homogeneity, invariability, monotony, similarity, similitude, uniformity

various assorted, different, differing, disparate, distinct, divers (*archaic*), diverse, diversified, heterogeneous, manifold, many, many-sided, miscellaneous, several, sundry, varied, variegated

▷ **Antonyms** alike, equivalent, matching, same, similar, uniform

varnish *verb* adorn, decorate, embellish, gild, glaze, gloss, japan, lacquer, polish, shellac

vary alter, alternate, be unlike, change, depart, differ, disagree, diverge, diversify, fluctuate, intermix, modify, permutate, reorder, transform

varying changing, different, distinct, distinguishable, diverse, fluctuating, inconsistent

▷ **Antonyms** consistent, fixed, monotonous, regular, settled, unchanging, unvarying

vassal bondman, bondservant, bondsman, liegeman, retainer, serf, slave, subject, thrall, varlet (*archaic*)

vassalage bondage, dependence, serfdom, servitude, slavery, subjection, thraldom

vast astronomical, boundless, colossal, elephantine, enormous, extensive, gigantic, ginormous (*informal*), great, huge, humongous *or* humungous (*U.S. slang*), illimitable, immeasurable, immense, limitless, mammoth, massive, measureless, mega (*slang*), monstrous, monumental, never-ending, prodigious, sweeping, tremendous, unbounded, unlimited, vasty (*archaic*), voluminous, wide

▷ **Antonyms** bounded, limited, microscopic, narrow, negligible, paltry, puny, small, tiny, trifling

vault[1] *verb* bound, clear, hurdle, jump, leap, spring

vault[2] *noun* **1.** arch, ceiling, roof, span **2.** catacomb, cellar, charnel house, crypt, mausoleum, tomb, undercroft **3.** depository, repository, strongroom *~verb* **4.** arch, bend, bow, curve, overarch, span

vaulted arched, cavernous, domed, hemispheric

vaunt boast about, brag about, crow about, exult in, flaunt, give oneself airs about, make a display of, make much of, parade, prate about, show off, talk big about (*informal*)

veer be deflected, change, change course, change direction, sheer, shift, swerve, tack, turn

vegetate 1. be inert, deteriorate, exist, go to seed, idle, languish, loaf, moulder, stagnate, veg out (*slang, chiefly U.S.*) **2.** burgeon, germinate, grow, shoot, spring, sprout, swell

▷ **Antonyms** (*sense 1*) accomplish, devel~

op, grow, participate, perform, react, respond

vehemence ardour, eagerness, earnestness, emphasis, energy, enthusiasm, fervency, fervour, fire, force, forcefulness, heat, impetuosity, intensity, keenness, passion, verve, vigour, violence, warmth, zeal
▷ **Antonyms** apathy, coolness, indifference, inertia, lethargy, listlessness, passivity, stoicism, torpor

vehement ablaze, ardent, eager, earnest, emphatic, enthusiastic, fervent, fervid, fierce, flaming, forceful, forcible, impassioned, impetuous, intense, passionate, powerful, strong, violent, zealous
▷ **Antonyms** apathetic, calm, cool, dispassionate, half-hearted, impassive, lukewarm, moderate

vehicle *noun figurative* apparatus, channel, means, means of expression, mechanism, medium, organ

veil **1.** *verb* cloak, conceal, cover, dim, disguise, hide, mantle, mask, obscure, screen, shield **2.** *~noun* blind, cloak, cover, curtain, disguise, film, mask, screen, shade, shroud
▷ **Antonyms** *~verb* disclose, display, divulge, expose, lay bare, reveal, uncover, unveil

veiled concealed, covert, disguised, hinted at, implied, masked, suppressed

vein **1.** blood vessel, course, current, lode, seam, stratum, streak, stripe **2.** dash, hint, strain, streak, thread, trait **3.** attitude, bent, character, faculty, humour, mode, mood, note, style, temper, tenor, tone, turn

velocity celerity, fleetness, impetus, pace, quickness, rapidity, speed, swiftness

velvety delicate, downy, mossy, smooth, soft, velutinous, velvet-like

venal bent (*slang*), corrupt, corruptible, crooked (*informal*), dishonourable, grafting (*informal*), mercenary, prostituted, purchasable, rapacious, simoniacal, sordid, unprincipled
▷ **Antonyms** honest, honourable, incorruptible, law-abiding, principled, upright

vendetta bad blood, blood feud, feud, quarrel

veneer *noun figurative* appearance, façade, false front, finish, front, gloss, guise, mask, pretence, semblance, show

venerable august, esteemed, grave, honoured, respected, revered, reverenced, sage, sedate, wise, worshipped
▷ **Antonyms** callow, discredited, disdained, disgraced, dishonourable, disreputable, green, ignominious, immature, inexperienced, inglorious, scorned, young, youthful

venerate adore, esteem, hold in awe, honour, look up to, respect, revere, reverence, worship
▷ **Antonyms** deride, dishonour, disregard, execrate, mock, scorn, spurn

veneration adoration, awe, deference, esteem, respect, reverence, worship

vengeance **1.** an eye for an eye, avenging, lex talionis, reprisal, requital, retaliation, retribution, revenge, settling of scores **2. with a vengeance: a.** forcefully, furiously, vehemently, violently **b.** and no mistake, extremely, greatly, to the full, to the nth degree, to the utmost, with no holds barred
▷ **Antonyms** (*sense 1*) absolution, acquittal, exoneration, forbearance, forgiveness, mercy, pardon, remission

vengeful avenging, implacable, punitive, rancorous, relentless, retaliatory, revengeful, spiteful, thirsting for revenge, unforgiving, vindictive

venial allowable, excusable, forgivable, insignificant, minor, pardonable, slight, trivial

venom **1.** bane, poison, toxin **2.** acidity, acrimony, bitterness, gall, grudge, hate, ill will, malevolence, malice, maliciousness, malignity, pungency, rancour, spite, spitefulness, spleen, virulence
▷ **Antonyms** (*sense 2*) benevolence, charity, compassion, favour, goodwill, kindness, love, mercy

venomous **1.** baneful (*archaic*), envenomed, mephitic, noxious, poison, poisonous, toxic, virulent **2.** baleful, hostile, malicious, malignant, rancorous, savage, spiteful, vicious, vindictive, virulent
▷ **Antonyms** (*sense 1*) harmless, nonpoisonous, nontoxic, nonvenomous (*sense 2*) affectionate, benevolent, compassionate, forgiving, harmless, loving, magnanimous

vent **1.** *noun* aperture, duct, hole, opening, orifice, outlet, split **2.** *~verb* air, come out with, discharge, emit, empty, express, give expression to, give vent to, pour out, release, utter, voice
▷ **Antonyms** *~verb* bottle up, curb, hold back, inhibit, quash, quell, repress, stifle, subdue

ventilate *figurative* air, bring out into the open, broadcast, debate, discuss, examine, make known, scrutinize, sift, talk about

venture *verb* **1.** chance, endanger, hazard, imperil, jeopardize, put in jeopardy, risk, speculate, stake, wager **2.** advance, dare, dare say, hazard, make bold, presume, stick one's neck out (*informal*), take the liberty, volunteer **3.** (*with* **out, forth,** *etc.*) embark on, go, plunge into, set out *~noun* **4.** adventure, chance, endeavour, enterprise, fling, gamble, hazard, jeopardy, project, risk, speculation, undertaking

venturesome adventurous, bold, courageous, daredevil, daring, doughty, en~

terprising, fearless, intrepid, plucky, spirited

veracious accurate, credible, dependable, ethical, factual, faithful, frank, genu~ine, high-principled, honest, reliable, straightforward, true, trustworthy, truthful, veridical

veracity accuracy, candour, credibility, exactitude, frankness, honesty, integ~rity, precision, probity, rectitude, trust~worthiness, truth, truthfulness, up~rightness

verbal literal, oral, spoken, unwritten, verbatim, word-of-mouth

verbally by word of mouth, orally

verbatim exactly, precisely, to the letter, word for word

verbiage circumlocution, periphrasis, pleonasm, prolixity, redundancy, rep~etition, tautology, verbosity

verbose circumlocutory, diffuse, garru~lous, long-winded, periphrastic, pleo~nastic, prolix, tautological, windy, wordy

▷ **Antonyms** brief, brusque, concise, curt, quiet, reticent, short, succinct, terse, untalkative

verbosely at great length, at undue length, long-windedly, wordily

verbosity garrulity, logorrhoea, long-windedness, loquaciousness, prolixity, rambling, verbiage, verboseness, windi~ness, wordiness

verdant flourishing, fresh, grassy, green, leafy, lush

verdict adjudication, conclusion, decision, finding, judgment, opinion, sentence

verge 1. *noun* border, boundary, brim, brink, edge, extreme, limit, lip, margin, roadside, threshold **2.** *~verb* approach, border, come near

verification authentication, confirmation, corroboration, proof, substantiation, validation

verify attest, attest to, authenticate, bear out, check, confirm, corroborate, prove, substantiate, support, validate

▷ **Antonyms** deny, discount, discredit, dispute, invalidate, nullify, undermine, weaken

verisimilitude authenticity, colour, cred~ibility, likeliness, likeness, plausibility, realism, resemblance, semblance, show of

verminous alive, crawling, flea-ridden, lousy, rat-infested

vernacular 1. *adjective* colloquial, com~mon, indigenous, informal, local, moth~er, native, popular, vulgar **2.** *~noun* ar~got, cant, dialect, idiom, jargon, native language, parlance, patois, speech, vul~gar tongue

versatile adaptable, adjustable, all-purpose, all-round, all-singing, all-dancing, flexible, functional, handy, many-sided, multifaceted, protean, re~sourceful, variable

▷ **Antonyms** fixed, inflexible, invariable, limited, one-sided, unadaptable

versed accomplished, acquainted, com~petent, conversant, experienced, famili~ar, knowledgeable, practised, proficient, qualified, seasoned, skilled, well in~formed, well up in (*informal*)

▷ **Antonyms** callow, green, ignorant, in~experienced, new, raw, unacquainted, unfledged, unpractised, unschooled, un~skilled, unversed

version 1. account, adaptation, exercise, interpretation, portrayal, reading, ren~dering, side, take (*informal, chiefly U.S.*), translation **2.** design, form, kind, model, style, type, variant

vertex acme, apex, apogee, crest, crown, culmination, extremity, height, pinna~cle, summit, top, zenith

vertical erect, on end, perpendicular, upright

▷ **Antonyms** flat, horizontal, level, plane, prone

vertigo dizziness, giddiness, light-headedness, loss of equilibrium, swim~ming of the head

verve animation, brio, dash, élan, energy, enthusiasm, force, get-up-and-go (*infor~mal*), gusto, life, liveliness, pep, punch (*informal*), sparkle, spirit, vigour, vim (*slang*), vitality, vivacity, zeal, zip (*in~formal*)

▷ **Antonyms** apathy, disdain, half-heartedness, indifference, inertia, lack of enthusiasm, languor, lethargy, life~lessness, reluctance, torpor

very *adverb* **1.** absolutely, acutely, awful~ly (*informal*), decidedly, deeply, emi~nently, exceedingly, excessively, ex~tremely, greatly, highly, jolly (*Brit.*), noticeably, particularly, profoundly, re~ally, remarkably, seriously (*informal*), superlatively, surpassingly, terribly, truly, uncommonly, unusually, wonder~fully *~adjective* **2.** actual, appropriate, exact, express, identical, perfect, pre~cise, real, same, selfsame, unqualified **3.** bare, mere, plain, pure, sheer, simple

vessel 1. barque (*poetic*), boat, craft, ship **2.** container, pot, receptacle, utensil

vest *verb* **1.** (*with* **in** *or* **with**) authorize, be devolved upon, bestow, confer, con~sign, empower, endow, entrust, furnish, invest, lodge, place, put in the hands of, settle **2.** apparel, bedeck, clothe, cover, dress, envelop, garb, robe

vestibule anteroom, entrance hall, foyer, hall, lobby, porch, portico

vestige evidence, glimmer, hint, indica~tion, relic, remainder, remains, rem~nant, residue, scrap, sign, suspicion, to~ken, trace, track

vestigial imperfect, incomplete, nonfunc~tional, rudimentary, surviving, unde~veloped

▷ **Antonyms** complete, developed, functional, perfect, practical, useful

vet *verb* appraise, check, check out, examine, give (someone *or* something) the once-over (*informal*), investigate, look over, pass under review, review, scan, scrutinize, size up (*informal*)

veteran **1.** *noun* master, old hand, old stager, old-timer, past master, past mistress, pro (*informal*), trouper, warhorse (*informal*) **2.** *~adjective* adept, battle-scarred, expert, long-serving, old, proficient, seasoned

▷ **Antonyms** *~noun* apprentice, beginner, freshman, initiate, neophyte, novice, recruit, tyro

veto **1.** *verb* ban, boycott, disallow, forbid, give the thumbs down to, interdict, kill (*informal*), negative, prohibit, put the kibosh on (*slang*), refuse permission, reject, rule out, turn down **2.** *~noun* ban, boycott, embargo, interdict, nonconsent, prohibition

▷ **Antonyms** *~verb* approve, endorse, O.K. *or* okay (*informal*), pass, ratify *~noun* approval, endorsement, go-ahead (*informal*), ratification

vex afflict, aggravate (*informal*), agitate, annoy, bother, bug (*informal*), displease, distress, disturb, exasperate, fret, gall, get one's back up, get on one's nerves (*informal*), grate on, harass, hassle (*informal*), irritate, molest, nark (*Brit., Austral., & N.Z. slang*), needle (*informal*), nettle, offend, peeve (*informal*), perplex, pester, pique, plague, provoke, put one's back up, put out, rile, tease, torment, trouble, upset, worry

▷ **Antonyms** allay, appease, comfort, console, gratify, hush, mollify, please, quiet, soothe

vexation **1.** aggravation (*informal*), annoyance, chagrin, displeasure, dissatisfaction, exasperation, frustration, irritation, pique **2.** bother, difficulty, hassle (*informal*), headache (*informal*), irritant, misfortune, nuisance, problem, thorn in one's flesh, trouble, upset, worry

vexatious afflicting, aggravating (*informal*), annoying, bothersome, burdensome, disagreeable, disappointing, distressing, exasperating, harassing, irksome, irritating, nagging, plaguy (*archaic*), provoking, teasing, tormenting, troublesome, trying, unpleasant, upsetting, worrisome, worrying

▷ **Antonyms** agreeable, balmy, calming, comforting, pleasant, reassuring, relaxing, soothing

vexed **1.** afflicted, aggravated (*informal*), agitated, annoyed, bothered, confused, displeased, distressed, disturbed, exasperated, fed up, hacked (off) (*U.S. slang*), harassed, irritated, miffed (*informal*), nettled, out of countenance, peeved (*informal*), perplexed, pissed off (*taboo slang*), provoked, put out, riled, ruffled, tormented, troubled, upset, worried **2.** contested, controversial, disputed, moot, much debated

viable applicable, feasible, operable, practicable, usable, within the bounds of possibility, workable

▷ **Antonyms** hopeless, impossible, impracticable, inconceivable, out of the question, unthinkable, unworkable

vibes atmosphere, aura, emanation, emotions, feelings, reaction, response, vibrations

vibrant **1.** aquiver, oscillating, palpitating, pulsating, quivering, trembling **2.** alive, animated, colourful, dynamic, electrifying, full of pep (*informal*), responsive, sensitive, sparkling, spirited, vivacious, vivid

vibrate fluctuate, judder (*informal*), oscillate, pulsate, pulse, quiver, resonate, reverberate, shake, shiver, sway, swing, throb, tremble, undulate

vibration juddering (*informal*), oscillation, pulsation, pulse, quiver, resonance, reverberation, shaking, throb, throbbing, trembling, tremor

vicarious acting, at one remove, commissioned, delegated, deputed, empathetic, indirect, substituted, surrogate

vice **1.** corruption, degeneracy, depravity, evil, evildoing, immorality, iniquity, profligacy, sin, turpitude, venality, wickedness **2.** blemish, defect, failing, fault, imperfection, shortcoming, weakness

▷ **Antonyms** (*sense 1*) honour, morality, virtue (*sense 2*) attainment, gift, good point, strong point, talent

vice versa contrariwise, conversely, in reverse, the other way round

vicinity area, district, environs, locality, neck of the woods (*informal*), neighbourhood, precincts, propinquity, proximity, purlieus

vicious **1.** abandoned, abhorrent, atrocious, bad, barbarous, corrupt, cruel, dangerous, debased, degenerate, degraded, depraved, diabolical, ferocious, fiendish, foul, heinous, immoral, infamous, monstrous, profligate, savage, sinful, unprincipled, vile, violent, wicked, worthless, wrong **2.** backbiting, bitchy (*informal*), cruel, defamatory, malicious, mean, rancorous, slanderous, spiteful, venomous, vindictive

▷ **Antonyms** (*sense 1*) docile, friendly, gentle, good, honourable, kind, playful, tame, upright, virtuous (*sense 2*) appreciative, complimentary, congratulatory

viciousness **1.** badness, corruption, cruelty, depravity, ferocity, immorality, profligacy, savagery, wickedness **2.** bitchiness (*slang*), malice, rancour, spite, spitefulness, venom

▷ **Antonyms** (*sense 2*) gentleness, good~

ness, goodwill, graciousness, kindness, mercy, virtue

vicissitude alteration, alternation, change, fluctuation of fortune, mutation, one of life's ups and downs (*informal*), revolution, shift, variation

victim 1. casualty, fatality, injured party, martyr, sacrifice, scapegoat, sufferer **2.** dupe, easy prey, fall guy (*informal*), gull (*archaic*), innocent, patsy (*slang, chiefly U.S. & Canad.*), sitting duck (*informal*), sitting target, sucker (*slang*)
▷ **Antonyms** (*sense 1*) survivor (*sense 2*) assailant, attacker, culprit, guilty party, offender

victimize 1. demonize, discriminate against, have a down on (someone) (*informal*), have it in for (someone) (*informal*), have one's knife into (someone), persecute, pick on **2.** cheat, deceive, defraud, dupe, exploit, fool, gull (*archaic*), hoodwink, prey on, swindle, take advantage of, use

victor champ (*informal*), champion, conquering hero, conqueror, first, prizewinner, top dog (*informal*), vanquisher, winner
▷ **Antonyms** also-ran, dud (*informal*), failure, flop (*informal*), loser, vanquished

victorious champion, conquering, first, prizewinning, successful, triumphant, vanquishing, winning
▷ **Antonyms** beaten, conquered, defeated, failed, losing, overcome, unsuccessful, vanquished

victory conquest, laurels, mastery, success, superiority, the palm, the prize, triumph, win
▷ **Antonyms** defeat, failure, loss

victuals bread, comestibles, eatables, eats (*slang*), edibles, food, grub (*slang*), meat, nosebag (*slang*), nosh (*slang*), provisions, rations, stores, supplies, tack (*informal*), viands, vittles (*obsolete*)

vie be rivals, compete, contend, contest, match oneself against, strive, struggle

view *noun* **1.** aspect, landscape, outlook, panorama, perspective, picture, prospect, scene, spectacle, vista **2.** range *or* field of vision, sight, vision **3.** (*sometimes plural*) attitude, belief, conviction, feeling, impression, judgment, notion, opinion, point of view, sentiment, thought, way of thinking **4.** contemplation, display, examination, inspection, look, recce (*slang*), scan, scrutiny, sight, survey, viewing **5. with a view to** in order to, in the hope of, so as to, with the aim *or* intention of *~verb* **6.** behold, check, check out (*informal*), clock (*Brit. slang*), contemplate, examine, explore, eye, eyeball (*U.S. slang*), gaze at, get a load of (*informal*), inspect, look at, observe, recce (*slang*), regard, scan, spectate, stare at, survey, take a dekko at (*Brit. slang*), watch, witness **7.** consider, deem, judge, look on, regard, think about

viewer observer, one of an audience, onlooker, spectator, TV watcher, watcher

viewpoint angle, frame of reference, perspective, point of view, position, slant, stance, standpoint, vantage point, way of thinking

vigilance alertness, attentiveness, carefulness, caution, circumspection, observance, watchfulness

vigilant alert, Argus-eyed, attentive, careful, cautious, circumspect, keeping one's eyes peeled *or* skinned (*informal*), on one's guard, on one's toes, on the alert, on the lookout, on the qui vive, on the watch, sleepless, unsleeping, wakeful, watchful, wide awake
▷ **Antonyms** careless, inattentive, lax, neglectful, negligent, remiss, slack

vigorous active, alive and kicking, brisk, dynamic, effective, efficient, energetic, enterprising, fighting fit, fit as a fiddle (*informal*), flourishing, forceful, forcible, full of beans (*informal*), full of energy, hale, hale and hearty, hardy, healthy, intense, lively, lusty, powerful, red-blooded, robust, sound, spanking, spirited, strenuous, strong, virile, vital, zippy (*informal*)
▷ **Antonyms** apathetic, effete, enervated, feeble, frail, inactive, indolent, lethargic, lifeless, spiritless, torpid, weak, weedy (*informal*), wimpish *or* wimpy (*informal*), wishy-washy

vigorously all out, eagerly, energetically, forcefully, hammer and tongs, hard, like mad (*slang*), lustily, strenuously, strongly, with a vengeance, with might and main

vigour activity, animation, balls (*taboo slang*), brio, dash, dynamism, energy, force, forcefulness, gusto, health, liveliness, might, oomph (*informal*), pep, power, punch (*informal*), robustness, snap (*informal*), soundness, spirit, strength, verve, vim (*slang*), virility, vitality, zip (*informal*)
▷ **Antonyms** apathy, feebleness, fragility, frailty, impotence, inactivity, inertia, infirmity, lethargy, sluggishness, weakness

vile 1. abandoned, abject, appalling, bad, base, coarse, contemptible, corrupt, debased, degenerate, degrading, depraved, despicable, disgraceful, evil, humiliating, ignoble, impure, loathsome, low, mean, miserable, nefarious, perverted, shocking, sinful, ugly, vicious, vulgar, wicked, worthless, wretched **2.** disgusting, foul, horrid, loathsome, nasty, nauseating, noxious, obscene, offensive, repellent, repugnant, repulsive, revolting, sickening, yucky *or* yukky (*slang*)
▷ **Antonyms** agreeable, chaste, cultured, delicate, genteel, honourable, lovely, marvellous, noble, pleasant, polite,

pure, refined, righteous, splendid, sublime, upright, worthy

vileness coarseness, corruption, degeneracy, depravity, dreadfulness, enormity, evil, foulness, heinousness, noxiousness, offensiveness, outrage, profanity, turpitude, ugliness, wickedness

vilification abuse, aspersion, calumniation, calumny, contumely, defamation, denigration, disparagement, invective, mudslinging, scurrility, vituperation

vilify abuse, asperse, bad-mouth (*slang, chiefly U.S. & Canad.*), berate, calumniate, debase, decry, defame, denigrate, disparage, dump on (*slang, chiefly U.S.*), knock (*informal*), malign, pull to pieces (*informal*), revile, rubbish (*informal*), run down, slag (off) (*slang*), slander, smear, speak ill of, traduce, vilipend (*rare*), vituperate

▷ **Antonyms** adore, commend, esteem, exalt, glorify, honour, praise, revere, venerate

villain 1. blackguard, caitiff (*archaic*), criminal, evildoer, knave (*archaic*), libertine, malefactor, miscreant, profligate, rapscallion, reprobate, rogue, scoundrel, wretch 2. antihero, baddy (*informal*) 3. devil, monkey, rascal, rogue, scallywag (*informal*), scamp

▷ **Antonyms** (*senses 2 & 3*) angel, goody, hero, heroine, idol

villainous atrocious, bad, base, blackguardly, criminal, cruel, debased, degenerate, depraved, detestable, diabolical, evil, fiendish, hateful, heinous, ignoble, infamous, inhuman, mean, nefarious, outrageous, ruffianly, scoundrelly, sinful, terrible, thievish, vicious, vile, wicked

▷ **Antonyms** angelic, good, heroic, humane, moral, noble, righteous, saintly, virtuous

villainy atrocity, baseness, crime, criminality, delinquency, depravity, devilry, iniquity, knavery, rascality, sin, turpitude, vice, wickedness

vindicate 1. absolve, acquit, clear, defend, do justice to, exculpate, excuse, exonerate, free from blame, justify, rehabilitate 2. advocate, assert, establish, maintain, support, uphold

▷ **Antonyms** (*sense 1*) accuse, blame, condemn, convict, incriminate, punish, reproach

vindication apology, assertion, defence, exculpating, exculpation, excuse, exoneration, justification, maintenance, plea, rehabilitation, substantiation, support

vindictive full of spleen, implacable, malicious, malignant, rancorous, relentless, resentful, revengeful, spiteful, unforgiving, unrelenting, vengeful, venomous

▷ **Antonyms** forgiving, generous, magnanimous, merciful, relenting, unvindictive

vintage 1. *noun* collection, crop, epoch, era, generation, harvest, origin, year 2. *~adjective* best, choice, classic, mature, prime, rare, ripe, select, superior, venerable

violate 1. break, contravene, disobey, disregard, encroach upon, infract, infringe, transgress 2. abuse, assault, befoul, debauch, defile, desecrate, dishonour, invade, outrage, pollute, profane, rape, ravish

▷ **Antonyms** (*sense 1*) honour, obey, respect, uphold (*sense 2*) defend, honour, protect, respect, revere, set on a pedestal

violation 1. abuse, breach, contravention, encroachment, infraction, infringement, transgression, trespass 2. defilement, desecration, profanation, sacrilege, spoliation

violence 1. bestiality, bloodshed, bloodthirstiness, brutality, brute force, cruelty, destructiveness, ferocity, fierceness, fighting, force, frenzy, fury, murderousness, passion, rough handling, savagery, strong-arm tactics (*informal*), terrorism, thuggery, vehemence, wildness 2. boisterousness, power, raging, roughness, storminess, tumult, turbulence, wildness 3. abandon, acuteness, fervour, force, harshness, intensity, severity, sharpness, vehemence

violent 1. berserk, bloodthirsty, brutal, cruel, destructive, fiery, flaming, forcible, furious, headstrong, homicidal, hot-headed, impetuous, intemperate, maddened, maniacal, murderous, passionate, powerful, raging, riotous, rough, savage, strong, tempestuous, uncontrollable, ungovernable, unrestrained, vehement, vicious, wild 2. blustery, boisterous, devastating, full of force, gale force, powerful, raging, ruinous, strong, tempestuous, tumultuous, turbulent, wild 3. acute, agonizing, biting, excruciating, extreme, harsh, inordinate, intense, outrageous, painful, severe, sharp

▷ **Antonyms** (*sense 1*) calm, composed, gentle, mild, peaceful, placid, quiet, rational, sane, serene, unruffled, well-behaved (*sense 2*) calm, gentle, mild, placid, serene

V.I.P. big name, big noise (*informal*), big shot (*informal*), bigwig (*informal*), celebrity, leading light (*informal*), lion, luminary, man *or* woman of the hour, notable, personage, public figure, somebody, star

virago ballbreaker (*slang*), battle-axe (*informal*), fury, harridan, scold, shrew, termagant (*rare*), vixen, Xanthippe

virgin 1. *noun* damsel (*archaic*), girl, maid (*archaic*), maiden (*archaic*), vestal, virgo intacta 2. *~adjective* chaste, fresh, im-

maculate, maidenly, modest, new, pristine, pure, snowy, uncorrupted, undefiled, unsullied, untouched, unused, vestal, virginal
▷ **Antonyms** *~adjective* contaminated, corrupted, defiled, dirty, impure, polluted, spoiled, used

virginal celibate, chaste, fresh, immaculate, maidenly, pristine, pure, snowy, spotless, uncorrupted, undefiled, undisturbed, untouched, virgin, white

virginity chastity, maidenhead, maidenhood

virile forceful, lusty, macho, male, manlike, manly, masculine, potent, red-blooded, robust, strong, vigorous
▷ **Antonyms** camp (*informal*), effeminate, emasculate, feminine, impotent, unmanly, weak, weedy (*informal*), wimpish *or* wimpy (*informal*)

virility machismo, manhood, masculinity, potency, vigour
▷ **Antonyms** effeminacy, femininity, impotence, softness, unmanliness, weakness

virtual essential, implicit, implied, in all but name, indirect, potential, practical, tacit, unacknowledged

virtually as good as, effectually, for all practical purposes, in all but name, in effect, in essence, nearly, practically, to all intents and purposes

virtue 1. ethicalness, excellence, goodness, high-mindedness, incorruptibility, integrity, justice, morality, probity, quality, rectitude, righteousness, uprightness, worth, worthiness **2.** advantage, asset, attribute, credit, good point, good quality, merit, plus (*informal*), strength **3.** chastity, honour, innocence, morality, purity, virginity **4. by virtue of** as a result of, by dint of, by reason of, in view of, on account of, owing to, thanks to
▷ **Antonyms** (*sense 1*) corruption, debauchery, depravity, dishonesty, dishonour, evil, immorality, sin, sinfulness, turpitude, vice (*sense 2*) drawback, failing, frailty, shortcoming, weak point (*sense 3*) promiscuity, unchastity

virtuosity brilliance, craft, éclat, expertise, finish, flair, mastery, panache, polish, skill

virtuoso 1. *noun* artist, genius, grandmaster, maestro, magician, master, master hand, maven (*U.S.*) **2.** *~adjective* bravura (*Music*), brilliant, dazzling, masterly

virtuous 1. blameless, ethical, excellent, exemplary, good, high-principled, honest, honourable, incorruptible, just, moral, praiseworthy, pure, righteous, squeaky-clean, upright, worthy **2.** celibate, chaste, clean-living, innocent, pure, spotless, virginal
▷ **Antonyms** (*sense 1*) corrupt, debauched, depraved, dishonest, evil, immoral, sinful, unrighteous, vicious, wicked (*sense 2*) impure, loose, promiscuous, unchaste

virulence 1. deadliness, harmfulness, hurtfulness, infectiousness, injuriousness, malignancy, noxiousness, poisonousness, toxicity, virulency **2.** acrimony, antagonism, bitterness, hatred, hostility, ill will, malevolence, malice, poison, pungency, rancour, resentment, spite, spleen, venom, viciousness, vindictiveness

virulent 1. baneful (*archaic*), deadly, infective, injurious, lethal, malignant, pernicious, poisonous, septic, toxic, venomous **2.** acrimonious, bitter, envenomed, hostile, malevolent, malicious, rancorous, resentful, spiteful, splenetic, venomous, vicious, vindictive
▷ **Antonyms** (*sense 1*) harmless, innocuous, nonpoisonous, nontoxic (*sense 2*) amiable, benign, compassionate, kind, magnanimous, sympathetic, warm

viscous adhesive, clammy, gelatinous, gluey, glutinous, gooey (*informal*), gummy, mucilaginous, sticky, syrupy, tenacious, thick, treacly, viscid

visible anywhere to be seen, apparent, bold, clear, conspicuous, detectable, discernible, discoverable, distinguishable, evident, in sight, in view, manifest, not hidden, noticeable, observable, obvious, palpable, patent, perceivable, perceptible, plain, salient, to be seen, unconcealed, unmistakable
▷ **Antonyms** concealed, hidden, imperceptible, invisible, obscured, unnoticeable, unseen

vision 1. eyes, eyesight, perception, seeing, sight, view **2.** breadth of view, discernment, farsightedness, foresight, imagination, insight, intuition, penetration, prescience **3.** castle in the air, concept, conception, daydream, dream, fantasy, idea, ideal, image, imago (*Psychoanal.*), mental picture, pipe dream **4.** apparition, chimera, delusion, eidolon, ghost, hallucination, illusion, mirage, phantasm, phantom, revelation, spectre, wraith **5.** dream, feast for the eyes, perfect picture, picture, sight, sight for sore eyes, spectacle

visionary *adjective* **1.** dreaming, dreamy, idealistic, quixotic, romantic, starry-eyed, with one's head in the clouds **2.** chimerical, delusory, fanciful, fantastic, ideal, idealized, illusory, imaginary, impractical, prophetic, speculative, unreal, unrealistic, unworkable, utopian *~noun* **3.** daydreamer, Don Quixote, dreamer, enthusiast (*archaic*), idealist, mystic, prophet, romantic, seer, theorist, utopian, zealot
▷ **Antonyms** *~adjective* actual, mundane, pragmatic, real, realistic, unimaginary *~noun* cynic, pessimist, pragmatist, realist

visit *verb* **1.** be the guest of, call in, call on, drop in on (*informal*), go to see, inspect, look (someone) up, pay a call on, pop in (*informal*), stay at, stay with, stop by, take in (*informal*) **2.** afflict, assail, attack, befall, descend upon, haunt, smite, trouble **3.** (*with* **on** *or* **upon**) bring down upon, execute, impose, inflict, wreak *~noun* **4.** call, sojourn, stay, stop

visitation 1. examination, inspection, visit **2.** bane, blight, calamity, cataclysm, catastrophe, disaster, infliction, ordeal, punishment, scourge, trial

visitor caller, company, guest, visitant

vista panorama, perspective, prospect, view

visual 1. ocular, optic, optical **2.** discernible, observable, perceptible, visible

▷ **Antonyms** (*sense 2*) imperceptible, indiscernible, invisible, out of sight, unnoticeable, unperceivable

visualize conceive of, conjure up a mental picture of, envisage, imagine, picture, see in the mind's eye

vital 1. basic, cardinal, essential, fundamental, imperative, indispensable, necessary, radical, requisite **2.** critical, crucial, decisive, important, key, life-or-death, significant, urgent **3.** animated, dynamic, energetic, forceful, full of beans (*informal*), full of the joy of living, lively, sparky, spirited, vibrant, vigorous, vivacious, zestful **4.** alive, alive and kicking, animate, generative, invigorative, life-giving, live, living, quickening

▷ **Antonyms** (*sense 1*) dispensable, inessential, nonessential, unnecessary (*sense 2*) minor, trivial, unimportant (*sense 3*) apathetic, lethargic, listless, uninvolved (*sense 4*) dead, dying, inanimate, moribund

vitality animation, brio, energy, exuberance, go (*informal*), life, liveliness, lustiness, pep, robustness, sparkle, stamina, strength, vigour, vim (*slang*), vivaciousness, vivacity

▷ **Antonyms** apathy, inertia, lethargy, listlessness, sluggishness, weakness

vitiate 1. blemish, devalue, harm, impair, injure, invalidate, mar, spoil, undermine, water down **2.** blight, contaminate, corrupt, debase, defile, deprave, deteriorate, pervert, pollute, sully, taint

vitiation 1. deterioration, devaluation, dilution, impairment, marring, reduction, spoiling, undermining **2.** adulteration, contamination, corruption, debasement, degradation, perversion, pollution, sullying

vitriolic *figurative* acerbic, acid, bitchy (*informal*), bitter, caustic, destructive, dripping with malice, envenomed, sardonic, scathing, venomous, virulent, withering

vituperate abuse, asperse, berate, blame, castigate, censure, cry down, denounce, excoriate, find fault with, rail against, rate, reproach, revile, run down, slang, slate (*informal*), tear into (*informal*), upbraid, vilify

vituperation abuse, billingsgate, blame, castigation, censure, fault-finding, flak (*informal*), invective, obloquy, rebuke, reprimand, reproach, scurrility, tongue-lashing, vilification

▷ **Antonyms** acclaim, approval, commendation, eulogy, flattery, praise, tribute

vituperative abusive, belittling, calumniatory, censorious, defamatory, denunciatory, derogatory, harsh, insulting, malign, opprobrious, sardonic, scurrilous, withering

vivacious animated, bubbling, cheerful, chirpy (*informal*), ebullient, effervescent, frolicsome, full of beans (*informal*), full of life, gay, high-spirited, jolly, light-hearted, lively, merry, scintillating, sparkling, sparky, spirited, sportive, sprightly, upbeat (*informal*), vital

▷ **Antonyms** boring, dull, languid, lifeless, listless, melancholy, spiritless, unenthusiastic

vivacity animation, brio, ebullience, effervescence, energy, gaiety, high spirits, life, liveliness, pep, quickness, sparkle, spirit, sprightliness

▷ **Antonyms** apathy, ennui, fatigue, heaviness, inertia, languor, lethargy, listlessness, weariness

vivid 1. bright, brilliant, clear, colourful, glowing, intense, rich **2.** distinct, dramatic, graphic, highly-coloured, lifelike, memorable, powerful, realistic, sharp, sharply-etched, stirring, strong, telling, true to life **3.** active, animated, dynamic, energetic, expressive, flamboyant, lively, quick, spirited, striking, strong, vigorous

▷ **Antonyms** colourless, cool, drab, dull, lifeless, nondescript, ordinary, pale, pastel, quiet, routine, run-of-the-mill, sombre, unclear, unmemorable, unremarkable, vague

vividness 1. brightness, brilliancy, glow, life, radiance, resplendence, sprightliness **2.** clarity, distinctness, graphicness, immediacy, intensity, realism, sharpness, strength

vixen *figurative* ballbreaker (*slang*), fury, harpy, harridan, hellcat, scold, shrew, spitfire, termagant (*rare*), virago, Xanthippe

viz. namely, that is to say, to wit, videlicet

vocabulary dictionary, glossary, language, lexicon, wordbook, word hoard, words, word stock

vocal *adjective* **1.** articulate, articulated, oral, put into words, said, spoken, uttered, voiced **2.** articulate, blunt, clamorous, eloquent, expressive, forthright, frank, free-spoken, noisy, outspo-

ken, plain-spoken, strident, vociferous
▷ **Antonyms** (*sense 2*) inarticulate, quiet, reserved, reticent, retiring, shy, silent, uncommunicative

vocation business, calling, career, employment, job, life's work, life work, métier, mission, office, post, profession, pursuit, role, trade

vociferous clamant, clamorous, loud, loudmouthed (*informal*), noisy, obstreperous, outspoken, ranting, shouting, strident, uproarious, vehement, vocal
▷ **Antonyms** hushed, muted, noiseless, quiet, silent, still

vogue *noun* **1.** craze, custom, *dernier cri,* fashion, last word, mode, style, the latest, the rage, the thing (*informal*), trend, way **2.** acceptance, currency, fashionableness, favour, popularity, prevalence, usage, use *~adjective* **3.** fashionable, in, modish, now (*informal*), popular, prevalent, trendy (*Brit. informal*), up-to-the-minute, voguish, with it (*informal*)

voice *noun* **1.** articulation, language, power of speech, sound, tone, utterance, words **2.** decision, expression, part, say, view, vote, will, wish **3.** agency, instrument, medium, mouthpiece, organ, spokesman, spokesperson, spokeswoman, vehicle *~verb* **4.** air, articulate, assert, come out with (*informal*), declare, divulge, enunciate, express, give expression *or* utterance to, put into words, say, utter, ventilate

void *adjective* **1.** bare, clear, drained, emptied, empty, free, tenantless, unfilled, unoccupied, vacant **2.** (*with* **of**) destitute, devoid, lacking, without **3.** dead, ineffective, ineffectual, inoperative, invalid, nonviable, nugatory, null and void, unenforceable, useless, vain, worthless *~noun* **4.** blank, blankness, emptiness, gap, lack, opening, space, vacuity, vacuum, want *~verb* **5.** discharge, drain, eject, eliminate (*Physiology*), emit, empty, evacuate **6.** abnegate, cancel, invalidate, nullify, rescind
▷ **Antonyms** *~adjective* (*sense 1*) abounding, complete, filled, full, occupied, replete, tenanted

volatile airy, changeable, erratic, explosive, fickle, flighty, gay, giddy, inconstant, lively, mercurial, sprightly, temperamental, unsettled, unstable, unsteady, up and down (*informal*), variable, whimsical
▷ **Antonyms** calm, consistent, constant, cool-headed, dependable, inert, reliable, self-controlled, settled, sober, stable, steady

volition choice, choosing, determination, discretion, election, free will, option, preference, purpose, resolution, will

volley *noun* barrage, blast, bombardment, burst, cannonade, discharge, explosion, fusillade, hail, salvo, shower

volubility fluency, garrulity, gift of the gab, glibness, loquaciousness, loquacity

voluble articulate, blessed with the gift of the gab, fluent, forthcoming, glib, loquacious, talkative
▷ **Antonyms** hesitant, inarticulate, reticent, succinct, taciturn, terse, tongue-tied, unforthcoming

volume 1. aggregate, amount, body, bulk, capacity, compass, cubic content, dimensions, mass, quantity, total **2.** book, publication, title, tome, treatise

voluminous ample, big, billowing, bulky, capacious, cavernous, copious, full, large, massive, prolific, roomy, vast
▷ **Antonyms** inadequate, insufficient, scanty, skimpy, slight, small, tiny

voluntarily by choice, freely, lief (*rare*), off one's own bat, of one's own accord, of one's own free will, on one's own initiative, willingly, without being asked, without prompting

voluntary discretional, discretionary, free, gratuitous, honorary, intended, intentional, optional, spontaneous, uncompelled, unconstrained, unforced, unpaid, volunteer, willing
▷ **Antonyms** automatic, conscripted, forced, instinctive, involuntary, obligatory, unintentional

volunteer *verb* advance, let oneself in for (*informal*), need no invitation, offer, offer one's services, present, proffer, propose, put forward, put oneself at (someone's) disposal, step forward, suggest, tender
▷ **Antonyms** begrudge, deny, keep, refuse, retain, withdraw, withhold

voluptuary *bon vivant,* epicurean, hedonist, luxury-lover, playboy, pleasure seeker, profligate, sensualist, sybarite

voluptuous 1. bacchanalian, epicurean, hedonistic, licentious, luxurious, pleasure-loving, self-indulgent, sensual, sybaritic **2.** ample, buxom, curvaceous (*informal*), enticing, erotic, full-bosomed, provocative, seductive, shapely, well-stacked (*Brit. slang*)
▷ **Antonyms** (*sense 1*) abstemious, ascetic, celibate, rigorous, self-denying, Spartan

voluptuousness animalism, carnality, curvaceousness (*informal*), licentiousness, opulence, seductiveness, sensuality, shapeliness

vomit *verb* barf (*U.S. slang*), belch forth, be sick, bring up, chuck (up) (*slang, chiefly U.S.*), chunder (*slang, chiefly Austral.*), disgorge, do a technicolour yawn (*slang*), eject, emit, heave, puke (*slang*), regurgitate, retch, sick up (*informal*), spew out *or* up, throw up (*informal*), toss one's cookies (*U.S. slang*), upchuck (*U.S. slang*)

voracious avid, devouring, edacious, esurient, gluttonous, greedy, hungry, insa~

tiable, omnivorous, prodigious, rapacious, ravening, ravenous, uncontrolled, unquenchable
▷ **Antonyms** moderate, sated, satisfied, self-controlled, temperate

voracity avidity, eagerness, edacity, greed, hunger, rapacity, ravenousness

vortex eddy, maelstrom, whirlpool

votary adherent, aficionado, believer, devotee, disciple, follower

vote *noun* **1.** ballot, franchise, plebiscite, poll, referendum, right to vote, show of hands, suffrage *~verb* **2.** ballot, cast one's vote, elect, go to the polls, opt, return **3.** *informal* declare, judge, pronounce, propose, recommend, suggest

vouch (*usually with* **for**) affirm, answer for, assert, asseverate, attest to, back, certify, confirm, give assurance of, go bail for, guarantee, stand witness, support, swear to, uphold

vouchsafe accord, cede, condescend to give, confer, deign, favour (someone) with, grant, yield

vow 1. *verb* affirm, consecrate, dedicate, devote, pledge, promise, swear, undertake solemnly **2.** *~noun* oath, pledge, promise, troth (*archaic*)

voyage *noun* crossing, cruise, journey, passage, travels, trip

vulgar 1. blue, boorish, cheap and nasty, coarse, common, common as muck, crude, dirty, flashy, gaudy, gross, ill-bred, impolite, improper, indecent, indecorous, indelicate, low, nasty, naughty, off colour, ribald, risqué, rude, suggestive, tasteless, tawdry, uncouth, unmannerly, unrefined **2.** general, native, ordinary, unrefined, vernacular
▷ **Antonyms** aristocratic, classical, decorous, elegant, genteel, high-brow, polite, refined, sophisticated, tasteful, upper-class, urbane, well-mannered

vulgarian arriviste, boor, churl, *nouveau riche,* parvenu, philistine, upstart

vulgarity bad taste, coarseness, crudeness, crudity, gaudiness, grossness, indecorum, indelicacy, lack of refinement, ribaldry, rudeness, suggestiveness, tastelessness, tawdriness
▷ **Antonyms** decorum, gentility, good breeding, good manners, good taste, refinement, sensitivity, sophistication, tastefulness

vulnerable accessible, assailable, defenceless, exposed, open to attack, sensitive, susceptible, tender, thin-skinned, unprotected, weak, wide open
▷ **Antonyms** guarded, immune, impervious, insensitive, invulnerable, thick-skinned, unassailable, well-protected

W, w

wacky crazy, daft (*informal*), eccentric, erratic, gonzo (*slang*), goofy (*informal*), irrational, loony (*slang*), nutty (*slang*), odd, oddball (*informal*), off-the-wall (*slang*), outré, screwy (*informal*), silly, unpredictable, wacko *or* whacko (*informal*), wild, zany

wad ball, block, bundle, chunk, hunk, lump, mass, plug, roll

wadding filler, lining, packing, padding, stuffing

waddle rock, shuffle, sway, toddle, totter, wobble

wade 1. ford, paddle, splash, walk through **2.** (*with* **through**) drudge, labour, peg away, plough through, toil, work one's way **3.** (*with* **in** *or* **into**) assail, attack, get stuck in (*informal*), go for, launch oneself at, light into (*informal*), set about, tackle, tear into (*informal*)

waffle 1. *verb* blather, jabber, prate, prattle, rabbit (on) (*Brit. informal*), verbalize, witter on (*informal*) **2.** *~noun* blather, jabber, padding, prating, prattle, prolixity, verbiage, verbosity, wordiness

waft 1. *verb* bear, be carried, carry, convey, drift, float, ride, transmit, transport **2.** *~noun* breath, breeze, current, draught, puff, whiff

wag¹ 1. *verb* bob, flutter, nod, oscillate, quiver, rock, shake, stir, vibrate, waggle, wave, wiggle **2.** *~noun* bob, flutter, nod, oscillation, quiver, shake, toss, vibration, waggle, wave, wiggle

wag² *noun* card (*informal*), clown, comedian, comic, humorist, jester, joker, wit

wage 1. *noun also* **wages** allowance, compensation, earnings, emolument, fee, hire, pay, payment, recompense, remuneration, reward, stipend **2.** *~verb* carry on, conduct, engage in, practise, proceed with, prosecute, pursue, undertake

wager 1. *noun* bet, flutter (*Brit. informal*), gamble, pledge, punt (*chiefly Brit.*), stake, venture **2.** *~verb* bet, chance, gamble, hazard, lay, pledge, punt (*chiefly Brit.*), put on, risk, speculate, stake, venture

waggish amusing, comical, droll, facetious, funny, humorous, impish, jesting, jocose, jocular, merry, mischievous, playful, puckish, risible, sportive, witty

waggle 1. *verb* flutter, oscillate, shake, wag, wave, wiggle, wobble **2.** *~noun* flutter, oscillation, shake, wag, wave, wiggle, wobble

waif foundling, orphan, stray

wail 1. *verb* bawl, bemoan, bewail, cry, deplore, grieve, howl, keen, lament, ululate, weep, yowl **2.** *~noun* complaint, cry, grief, howl, keen, lament, lamentation, moan, ululation, weeping, yowl

wait 1. *verb* abide, bide one's time, cool one's heels, dally, delay, hang fire, hold back, hold on (*informal*), kick one's heels, linger, mark time, pause, remain, rest, stand by, stay, tarry **2.** *~noun* delay, entr'acte, halt, hold-up, interval, pause, rest, stay

▷ **Antonyms** (*sense 1*) depart, go, go away, leave, move off, quit, set off, take off (*informal*)

waiter, waitress attendant, server, steward, stewardess

wait on *or* **upon** attend, minister to, serve, tend

waive abandon, defer, dispense with, forgo, give up, postpone, put off, refrain from, relinquish, remit, renounce, resign, set aside, surrender

▷ **Antonyms** claim, demand, insist, maintain, press, profess, pursue, uphold

waiver abandonment, abdication, disclaimer, giving up, relinquishment, remission, renunciation, resignation, setting aside, surrender

wake¹ *verb* **1.** arise, awake, awaken, bestir, come to, get up, rouse, rouse from sleep, stir **2.** activate, animate, arouse, awaken, enliven, excite, fire, galvanize, kindle, provoke, quicken, rouse, stimulate, stir up *~noun* **3.** deathwatch, funeral, vigil, watch

▷ **Antonyms** (*sense 1*) catnap, doze, drop off (*informal*), hibernate, nod off (*informal*), sleep, snooze (*informal*), take a nap

wake² *noun* aftermath, backwash, path, slipstream, track, trail, train, wash, waves

wakeful 1. insomniac, restless, sleepless, unsleeping **2.** alert, alive, attentive, heedful, observant, on guard, on the

alert, on the lookout, on the qui vive, unsleeping, vigilant, wary, watchful
▷ **Antonyms** (*sense 2*) asleep, dormant, dozing, dreamy, drowsy, heedless, inattentive, off guard, sleepy

waken activate, animate, arouse, awake, awaken, be roused, come awake, come to, enliven, fire, galvanize, get up, kindle, quicken, rouse, stimulate, stir
▷ **Antonyms** be inactive, doze, lie dormant, nap, repose, sleep, slumber, snooze (*informal*)

wale contusion, mark, scar, streak, stripe, weal, welt, wheal

walk *verb* **1.** advance, amble, foot it, go, go by shanks's pony (*informal*), go on foot, hike, hoof it (*slang*), march, move, pace, perambulate, promenade, saunter, step, stride, stroll, traipse (*informal*), tramp, travel on foot, tread, trek, trudge **2.** accompany, convoy, escort, take *~noun* **3.** constitutional, hike, march, perambulation, promenade, ramble, saunter, stroll, traipse (*informal*), tramp, trek, trudge, turn **4.** carriage, gait, manner of walking, pace, step, stride **5.** aisle, alley, avenue, esplanade, footpath, lane, path, pathway, pavement, promenade, sidewalk, trail **6.** area, arena, calling, career, course, field, line, métier, profession, sphere, trade, vocation

walker footslogger, hiker, pedestrian, rambler, wayfarer

walkout industrial action, protest, stoppage, strike

walk out 1. flounce out, get up and go, leave suddenly, storm out, take off (*informal*), vote with one's feet **2.** down tools, go on strike, stop work, strike, take industrial action, withdraw one's labour **3.** (*with* **on**) abandon, chuck (*informal*), desert, forsake, jilt, leave, leave in the lurch, pack in (*informal*), run away from, strand, throw over
▷ **Antonyms** (*sense 3*) be loyal to, defend, remain, stand by, stay, stick with, support, uphold

walkover breeze (*U.S. & Canad. informal*), cakewalk (*informal*), child's play (*informal*), cinch (*slang*), doddle (*Brit. slang*), duck soup (*U.S. slang*), easy victory, picnic (*informal*), piece of cake (*informal*), pushover (*slang*), snap (*informal*)
▷ **Antonyms** drudgery, effort, grind (*informal*), labour, ordeal, strain, struggle, trial

wall 1. divider, enclosure, panel, partition, screen **2.** barricade, breastwork, bulwark, embankment, fortification, palisade, parapet, rampart, stockade **3.** barrier, block, fence, hedge, impediment, obstacle, obstruction **4. go to the wall** *informal* be ruined, collapse, fail, fall, go bust (*informal*), go under **5. drive up the wall** *slang* aggravate (*informal*), annoy, dement, derange, drive crazy (*informal*), drive insane, exasperate, get on one's nerves (*informal*), infuriate, irritate, madden, piss one off (*taboo slang*), send off one's head (*slang*), try

wallet case, holder, notecase, pocketbook, pouch, purse

wallop *verb* **1.** batter, beat, belt (*informal*), buffet, chin (*slang*), clobber (*slang*), deck (*slang*), hit, lambast(e), lay one on (*slang*), paste (*slang*), pound, pummel, punch, slug, smack, strike, thrash, thump, whack **2.** beat, best, blow out of the water (*slang*), clobber (*slang*), crush, defeat, drub, hammer (*informal*), lick (*informal*), rout, run rings around (*informal*), stuff (*slang*), thrash, trounce, vanquish, wipe the floor with (*informal*), worst *~noun* **3.** bash, belt (*informal*), blow, haymaker (*slang*), kick, punch, slug, smack, thump, thwack, whack

wallow 1. lie, roll about, splash around, tumble, welter **2.** flounder, lurch, stagger, stumble, wade **3.** bask, delight, glory, indulge oneself, luxuriate, relish, revel, take pleasure
▷ **Antonyms** (*sense 3*) abstain, avoid, do without, eschew, forgo, give up, refrain

wan 1. anaemic, ashen, bloodless, cadaverous, colourless, discoloured, ghastly, like death warmed up (*informal*), livid, pale, pallid, pasty, sickly, washed out, waxen, wheyfaced, white **2.** dim, faint, feeble, pale, weak
▷ **Antonyms** (*sense 1*) blooming, bright, flourishing, glowing, healthy, roseate, rosy, rubicund, ruddy, vibrant

wand baton, rod, sprig, stick, twig, withe, withy

wander *verb* **1.** cruise, drift, knock about *or* around, meander, mooch around (*slang*), peregrinate, ramble, range, roam, rove, straggle, stravaig (*Scot. & northern English dialect*), stray, stroll, traipse (*informal*) **2.** depart, deviate, digress, divagate (*rare*), diverge, err, get lost, go astray, go off at a tangent, go off course, lapse, lose concentration, lose one's train of thought, lose one's way, swerve, veer **3.** babble, be delirious, be incoherent, ramble, rave, speak incoherently, talk nonsense *~noun* **4.** cruise, excursion, meander, peregrination, ramble, traipse (*informal*)
▷ **Antonyms** (*sense 2*) comply, conform, fall in with, follow, run with the pack, toe the line

wanderer bird of passage, drifter, gypsy, itinerant, nomad, rambler, ranger, rolling stone, rover, stroller, traveller, vagabond, vagrant, voyager

wandering drifting, homeless, itinerant, migratory, nomadic, peripatetic, rambling, rootless, roving, strolling, travelling, vagabond, vagrant, voyaging, wayfaring

wanderlust itchy feet (*informal*), restlessness, urge to travel

wane *verb* **1.** abate, atrophy, decline, decrease, die out, dim, diminish, draw to a close, drop, dwindle, ebb, fade, fade away, fail, lessen, sink, subside, taper off, weaken, wind down, wither *~noun* **2.** abatement, atrophy, decay, declension, decrease, diminution, drop, dwindling, ebb, fading, failure, fall, falling off, lessening, sinking, subsidence, tapering off, withering **3. on the wane** at its lowest ebb, declining, dropping, dwindling, dying out, ebbing, fading, lessening, obsolescent, on its last legs, on the decline, on the way out, subsiding, tapering off, weakening, withering

▷ **Antonyms** *~verb* blossom, brighten, develop, expand, grow, improve, increase, rise, strengthen, wax *~noun* advancement, development, expansion, growth, increase, rise, strengthening, waxing

wangle arrange, bring off, contrive, engineer, fiddle (*informal*), finagle (*informal*), fix (*informal*), manipulate, manoeuvre, pull off, scheme, work (*informal*)

want *verb* **1.** covet, crave, desire, eat one's heart out over, feel a need for, hanker after, have a fancy for, have a yen for (*informal*), hope for, hunger for, long for, need, pine for, require, set one's heart on, thirst for, wish, would give one's eyeteeth for, yearn for **2.** be able to do with, be deficient in, be short of, be without, call for, demand, fall short in, have need of, lack, miss, need, require, stand in need of *~noun* **3.** appetite, craving, demand, desire, fancy, hankering, hunger, longing, necessity, need, requirement, thirst, wish, yearning, yen (*informal*) **4.** absence, dearth, default, deficiency, famine, insufficiency, lack, paucity, scantiness, scarcity, shortage **5.** destitution, indigence, need, neediness, pauperism, penury, poverty, privation

▷ **Antonyms** *~verb* be sated, detest, dislike, enjoy, hate, have, loathe, own, possess, reject, spurn, surfeit *~noun* abundance, adequacy, comfort, ease, excess, luxury, plenty, sufficiency, surplus, wealth

wanting 1. absent, incomplete, lacking, less, missing, short, shy **2.** defective, deficient, disappointing, faulty, imperfect, inadequate, inferior, leaving much to be desired, not good enough, not much cop (*Brit. slang*), not up to expectations, not up to par, patchy, pathetic, poor, sketchy, substandard, unsound

▷ **Antonyms** adequate, complete, enough, full, replete, satisfactory, saturated, sufficient

wanton *adjective* **1.** abandoned, dissipated, dissolute, fast, immoral, lecherous, lewd, libertine, libidinous, licentious, loose, lustful, of easy virtue, promiscuous, rakish, shameless, unchaste **2.** arbitrary, cruel, evil, gratuitous, groundless, malevolent, malicious, motiveless, needless, senseless, spiteful, uncalled-for, unjustifiable, unjustified, unprovoked, vicious, wicked, wilful **3.** careless, devil-may-care, extravagant, heedless, immoderate, intemperate, lavish, outrageous, rash, reckless, unrestrained, wild *~noun* **4.** Casanova, debauchee, Don Juan, gigolo, harlot, lech *or* letch (*informal*), lecher, libertine, loose woman, profligate, prostitute, rake, roué, scrubber (*Brit. & Austral. slang*), slag (*Brit. slang*), slut, strumpet, tart (*informal*), trollop, voluptuary, whore, woman of easy virtue *~verb* **5.** debauch, dissipate, revel, riot, sleep around (*informal*), wench (*archaic*), whore **6.** fritter away, misspend, squander, throw away, waste

▷ **Antonyms** (*sense 1*) overmodest, priggish, prim, prudish, puritanical, rigid, strait-laced, stuffy, Victorian (*sense 2*) called-for, excusable, justified, legitimate, motivated, provoked, warranted (*sense 3*) cautious, circumspect, guarded, inhibited, moderate, prudent, reserved, restrained, temperate

war 1. *noun* armed conflict, battle, bloodshed, combat, conflict, contention, contest, enmity, fighting, hostilities, hostility, strife, struggle, warfare **2.** *~verb* battle, campaign against, carry on hostilities, clash, combat, conduct a war, contend, contest, fight, make war, strive, struggle, take up arms, wage war

▷ **Antonyms** *~noun* accord, armistice, cease-fire, co-existence, compliance, co-operation, harmony, peace, peace-time, treaty, truce *~verb* call a ceasefire, co-exist, co-operate, make peace

warble 1. *verb* chirp, chirrup, quaver, sing, trill, twitter **2.** *~noun* call, chirp, chirrup, cry, quaver, song, trill, twitter

war cry battle cry, rallying cry, slogan, war whoop

ward 1. area, district, division, precinct, quarter, zone **2.** apartment, cubicle, room **3.** charge, dependant, minor, protégé, pupil **4.** care, charge, custody, guardianship, keeping, protection, safekeeping

warden administrator, caretaker, curator, custodian, guardian, janitor, keeper, ranger, steward, superintendent, warder, watchman

warder, wardress custodian, gaoler, guard, jailer, keeper, prison officer, screw (*slang*), turnkey (*archaic*)

ward off avert, avoid, beat off, block, deflect, fend off, forestall, keep at arm's length, keep at bay, parry, repel, stave off, thwart, turn aside, turn away

▷ **Antonyms** accept, admit, allow, embrace, permit, receive, take in, welcome

wardrobe 1. closet, clothes cupboard, clothes-press 2. apparel, attire, clothes, collection of clothes, outfit

warehouse depository, depot, stockroom, store, storehouse

wares commodities, goods, lines, manufactures, merchandise, produce, products, stock, stuff

warfare armed conflict, armed struggle, arms, battle, blows, campaigning, clash of arms, combat, conflict, contest, discord, fighting, hostilities, passage of arms, strategy, strife, struggle, war

▷ **Antonyms** accord, amity, armistice, ceasefire, cessation of hostilities, conciliation, harmony, peace, treaty, truce

warily cagily (*informal*), carefully, cautiously, charily, circumspectly, distrustfully, gingerly, guardedly, suspiciously, vigilantly, watchfully, with care

▷ **Antonyms** carelessly, hastily, heedlessly, irresponsibly, rashly, recklessly, thoughtlessly, unwarily

wariness alertness, attention, caginess (*informal*), care, carefulness, caution, circumspection, discretion, distrust, foresight, heedfulness, mindfulness, prudence, suspicion, vigilance, watchfulness

▷ **Antonyms** carelessness, heedlessness, inattention, mindlessness, negligence, oblivion, recklessness, thoughtlessness

warlike aggressive, bellicose, belligerent, bloodthirsty, combative, hawkish, hostile, inimical, jingoistic, martial, militaristic, military, pugnacious, sabre-rattling, unfriendly, warmongering

▷ **Antonyms** amicable, conciliatory, friendly, nonbelligerent, pacific, peaceable, peaceful, placid, unwarlike

warlock conjuror, enchanter, magician, necromancer, sorcerer, witch, wizard

warm *adjective* 1. balmy, heated, lukewarm, moderately hot, pleasant, sunny, tepid, thermal 2. affable, affectionate, amiable, amorous, cheerful, congenial, cordial, friendly, genial, happy, hearty, hospitable, kindly, likable *or* likeable, loving, pleasant, tender 3. ablaze, animated, ardent, cordial, earnest, effusive, emotional, enthusiastic, excited, fervent, glowing, heated, intense, keen, lively, passionate, spirited, stormy, vehement, vigorous, violent, zealous 4. irascible, irritable, passionate, quick, sensitive, short, touchy 5. *informal* dangerous, disagreeable, hazardous, perilous, tricky, uncomfortable, unpleasant *~verb* 6. heat, heat up, melt, thaw, warm up 7. animate, awaken, excite, get going, interest, make enthusiastic, put some life into, rouse, stimulate, stir, turn on (*slang*)

▷ **Antonyms** *~adjective* aloof, apathetic, chilly, cold, cool, distant, freezing, half-hearted, hostile, icy, phlegmatic, remote, stand-offish, uncaring, unenthusiastic, unfriendly, unwelcoming *~verb* alienate, chill, cool, cool down, depress, freeze, sadden

warm-blooded ardent, earnest, emotional, enthusiastic, excitable, fervent, impetuous, lively, passionate, rash, spirited, vivacious

warm-hearted affectionate, compassionate, cordial, generous, kind-hearted, kindly, loving, sympathetic, tender, tender-hearted

▷ **Antonyms** callous, cold, cold-hearted, hard, hard-hearted, harsh, heartless, insensitive, mean, merciless, unfeeling, unsympathetic

warmonger belligerent, hawk, jingo, militarist, sabre-rattler

warmth 1. heat, hotness, warmness 2. animation, ardour, eagerness, earnestness, effusiveness, enthusiasm, excitement, fervency, fervour, fire, heat, intensity, passion, spirit, transport, vehemence, vigour, violence, zeal, zest 3. affability, affection, amorousness, cheerfulness, cordiality, happiness, heartiness, hospitableness, kindliness, love, tenderness

▷ **Antonyms** aloofness, apathy, austerity, chill, chilliness, cold, cold-heartedness, coldness, coolness, hard-heartedness, hostility, iciness, indifference, insincerity, lack of enthusiasm, remoteness, sternness

warn admonish, advise, alert, apprise, caution, forewarn, give fair warning, give notice, inform, make (someone) aware, notify, put one on one's guard, summon, tip off

warning 1. *noun* admonition, advice, alarm, alert, augury, caution, caveat, foretoken, hint, notice, notification, omen, premonition, presage, sign, signal, threat, tip, tip-off, token, word, word to the wise 2. *~adjective* admonitory, cautionary, monitory, ominous, premonitory, threatening

warp 1. *verb* bend, contort, deform, deviate, distort, misshape, pervert, swerve, turn, twist 2. *~noun* bend, bent, bias, contortion, deformation, deviation, distortion, kink, perversion, quirk, turn, twist

warrant *noun* 1. assurance, authority, authorization, carte blanche, commission, guarantee, licence, permission, permit, pledge, sanction, security, warranty *~verb* 2. affirm, answer for, assure, attest, avouch, certify, declare, guarantee, pledge, secure, stand behind, underwrite, uphold, vouch for 3. approve, authorize, call for, commission, demand, deserve, empower, entail, entitle, excuse, give ground for, justify, license, necessitate, permit, require, sanction

warrantable accountable, allowable, defensible, justifiable, lawful, necessary,

unreasonable, permissible, proper, reasonable, right
▷ **Antonyms** indefensible, uncalled-for, undue, unjustifiable, unnecessary, unreasonable, unwarrantable, wrong

warranty assurance, bond, certificate, contract, covenant, guarantee, pledge

warring at daggers drawn, at war, belligerent, combatant, conflicting, contending, embattled, fighting, hostile, opposed

warrior champion, combatant, fighter, fighting man, gladiator, man-at-arms, soldier

wary alert, attentive, cagey (*informal*), careful, cautious, chary, circumspect, distrustful, guarded, heedful, leery (*slang*), on one's guard, on the lookout, on the qui vive, prudent, suspicious, vigilant, watchful, wide-awake
▷ **Antonyms** careless, foolhardy, imprudent, negligent, rash, reckless, remiss, unguarded, unsuspecting, unwary

wash *verb* **1.** bath, bathe, clean, cleanse, launder, moisten, rinse, scrub, shampoo, shower, wet **2.** (*with* **away**) bear away, carry off, erode, move, sweep away, wash off **3.** *informal* bear scrutiny, be convincing, be plausible, carry weight, hold up, hold water, stand up, stick **4.** **wash one's hands of** abandon, accept no responsibility for, give up on, have nothing to do with, leave to one's own devices *~noun* **5.** ablution, bath, bathe, cleaning, cleansing, laundering, rinse, scrub, shampoo, shower, washing **6.** ebb and flow, flow, roll, surge, sweep, swell, wave **7.** coat, coating, film, layer, overlay, screen, stain, suffusion

washed out **1.** blanched, bleached, colourless, etiolated, faded, flat, lacklustre, mat, pale **2.** all in (*slang*), clapped out (*Austral. & N.Z. informal*), dead on one's feet (*informal*), dog-tired (*informal*), done in (*informal*), drained, drawn, exhausted, fatigued, haggard, knackered (*slang*), pale, spent, tired-out, wan, weary, wiped out (*informal*), worn-out, zonked (*slang*)
▷ **Antonyms** (*sense 2*) alert, chirpy, energetic, full of beans (*informal*), full of pep (*informal*), lively, perky, refreshed, sprightly, zippy (*informal*)

washout **1.** clinker (*slang, chiefly U.S.*), disappointment, disaster, dud (*informal*), failure, fiasco, flop (*informal*), mess **2.** failure, incompetent, loser
▷ **Antonyms** (*sense 1*) conquest, feat, success, triumph, victory, winner

washy attenuated, diluted, feeble, insipid, overdiluted, thin, watered-down, watery, weak, wishy-washy (*informal*)

waspish bad-tempered, cantankerous, captious, crabbed, crabby, cross, crotchety (*informal*), fretful, grumpy, ill-tempered, irascible, irritable, liverish, peevish, peppery, pettish, petulant, ratty (*Brit. & N.Z. informal*), snappish, splenetic, testy, tetchy, touchy, waxy (*informal, chiefly Brit.*)
▷ **Antonyms** affable, agreeable, cheerful, easy-going, genial, good-humoured, good-natured, jovial, pleasant

waste *verb* **1.** blow (*slang*), dissipate, fritter away, frivol away (*informal*), lavish, misuse, run through, squander, throw away **2.** atrophy, consume, corrode, crumble, debilitate, decay, decline, deplete, disable, drain, dwindle, eat away, ebb, emaciate, enfeeble, exhaust, fade, gnaw, perish, sap the strength of, sink, undermine, wane, wear out, wither **3.** despoil, destroy, devastate, lay waste, pillage, rape, ravage, raze, ruin, sack, spoil, total (*slang*), trash (*slang*), undo, wreak havoc upon *~noun* **4.** dissipation, expenditure, extravagance, frittering away, loss, lost opportunity, misapplication, misuse, prodigality, squandering, unthriftiness, wastefulness **5.** desolation, destruction, devastation, havoc, ravage, ruin **6.** debris, dregs, dross, garbage, leavings, leftovers, litter, offal, offscourings, refuse, rubbish, scrap, sweepings, trash **7.** desert, solitude, void, wasteland, wild, wilderness *~adjective* **8.** leftover, superfluous, supernumerary, unused, unwanted, useless, worthless **9.** bare, barren, desolate, devastated, dismal, dreary, empty, uncultivated, uninhabited, unproductive, wild **10.** **lay waste** depredate (*rare*), despoil, destroy, devastate, pillage, rape, ravage, raze, ruin, sack, spoil, wreak havoc upon
▷ **Antonyms** *~verb* build, conserve, defend, develop, economize, husband, increase, preserve, protect, rally, restore, save, strengthen *~noun* economy, frugality, good housekeeping, saving, thrift *~adjective* arable, developed, fruitful, habitable, in use, necessary, needed, productive, utilized, verdant

wasteful extravagant, improvident, lavish, prodigal, profligate, ruinous, spendthrift, thriftless, uneconomical, unthrifty
▷ **Antonyms** economical, frugal, money-saving, parsimonious, penny-wise, provident, sparing, thrifty

wasteland desert, void, waste, wild, wilderness

waster drone, good-for-nothing, idler, layabout, loafer, loser, malingerer, ne'er-do-well, shirker, skiver (*Brit. slang*), wastrel

wastrel **1.** prodigal, profligate, spendthrift, squanderer **2.** drone, good-for-nothing, idler, layabout, loafer, loser, malingerer, ne'er-do-well, shirker, skiver (*Brit. slang*), waster

watch *verb* **1.** check, check out (*informal*), clock (*Brit. slang*), contemplate, eye, eyeball (*U.S. slang*), feast one's eyes on, gaze at, get a load of (*informal*), look, look at, look on, mark, note, observe, pay attention, peer at, regard, see, stare at, take a dekko at (*Brit. slang*), view **2.** attend, be on the alert, be on the look~out, be vigilant, be wary, be watchful, keep an eye open (*informal*), look out, take heed, wait **3.** guard, keep, look af~ter, mind, protect, superintend, take care of, tend *~noun* **4.** chronometer, clock, pocket watch, timepiece, wrist~watch **5.** alertness, attention, eye, heed, inspection, lookout, notice, observation, supervision, surveillance, vigil, vigi~lance, watchfulness

watchdog 1. guard dog **2.** custodian, guardian, inspector, monitor, protector, scrutineer

watcher fly on the wall, looker-on, look~out, observer, onlooker, spectator, spy, viewer, witness

watchful alert, attentive, circumspect, guarded, heedful, observant, on one's guard, on the lookout, on the qui vive, on the watch, suspicious, vigilant, wary, wide awake

▷ **Antonyms** careless, inattentive, reck~less, thoughtless, unaware, unguarded, unmindful, unobservant, unwary

watchfulness alertness, attention, atten~tiveness, caution, cautiousness, circum~spection, heedfulness, vigilance, wari~ness

▷ **Antonyms** carelessness, heedlessness, inattention, indiscretion, irresponsibil~ity, neglect, recklessness, thoughtless~ness

watchman caretaker, custodian, guard, security guard, security man

watch out be alert, be careful, be on one's guard, be on the alert, be on (the) watch, be vigilant, be watchful, have a care, keep a sharp lookout, keep a weather eye open, keep one's eyes open, keep one's eyes peeled *or* skinned (*in~formal*), look out, mind out, watch one~self

watch over defend, guard, keep safe, look after, preserve, protect, shelter, shield, stand guard over

watchword 1. countersign, magic word, password, shibboleth **2.** battle cry, by~word, catch phrase, catchword, maxim, motto, rallying cry, slogan

water *noun* **1.** Adam's ale *or* wine, aqua, H_2O **2. hold water** bear examination *or* scrutiny, be credible, be logical, be sound, make sense, pass the test, ring true, work **3. of the first water** excellent, of the best, of the best quality, of the finest quality, of the highest degree, of the highest grade *~verb* **4.** damp, damp~en, douse, drench, flood, hose, irrigate, moisten, soak, souse, spray, sprinkle **5.** add water to, adulterate, dilute, put water in, thin, water down, weaken

water down 1. add water to, adulterate, dilute, put water in, thin, water, weak~en **2.** adulterate, mitigate, qualify, sof~ten, tone down, weaken

▷ **Antonyms** (*sense 1*) fortify, purify, strengthen, thicken

waterfall cascade, cataract, chute, fall, force (*Northern English dialect*), linn (*Scot.*)

watertight 1. sound, waterproof **2.** air~tight, firm, flawless, foolproof, impreg~nable, incontrovertible, sound, unas~sailable

▷ **Antonyms** defective, flawed, leaky, questionable, shaky, tenuous, uncer~tain, unsound, weak

watery 1. aqueous, damp, fluid, humid, liquid, marshy, moist, soggy, squelchy, wet **2.** rheumy, tear-filled, tearful, weepy **3.** adulterated, dilute, diluted, flavourless, insipid, runny, tasteless, thin, washy, watered-down, waterish, weak, wishy-washy (*informal*)

▷ **Antonyms** concentrated, condensed, dense, fortified, solid, strong, thick

wave *verb* **1.** brandish, flap, flourish, flutter, move to and fro, oscillate, quiv~er, ripple, shake, stir, sway, swing, un~dulate, wag, waver, wield **2.** beckon, di~rect, gesticulate, gesture, indicate, sign, signal *~noun* **3.** billow, breaker, comber, ridge, ripple, roller, sea surf, swell, un~dulation, unevenness **4.** current, drift, flood, ground swell, movement, out~break, rash, rush, stream, surge, sweep, tendency, trend, upsurge

waver 1. be indecisive, be irresolute, be unable to decide, be unable to make up one's mind, blow hot and cold (*infor~mal*), dither (*chiefly Brit.*), falter, fluctu~ate, hesitate, hum and haw, seesaw, shillyshally (*informal*), swither (*Scot.*), vacillate **2.** flicker, fluctuate, quiver, reel, shake, sway, totter, tremble, un~dulate, vary, wave, weave, wobble

▷ **Antonyms** be decisive, be determined, be of fixed opinion, be resolute, deter~mine, resolve, stand firm

wax *verb* become fuller, become larger, develop, dilate, enlarge, expand, fill out, get bigger, grow, increase, magnify, mount, rise, swell

▷ **Antonyms** contract, decline, decrease, diminish, dwindle, fade, lessen, narrow, shrink, wane

waxen anaemic, ashen, bloodless, colour~less, ghastly, pale, pallid, wan, white, whitish

way 1. approach, course of action, fash~ion, manner, means, method, mode, plan, practice, procedure, process, scheme, system, technique **2.** access, av~enue, channel, course, direction, high~way, lane, path, pathway, road, route, street, thoroughfare, track, trail **3.** elbowroom, opening, room, space **4.** dis~tance, journey, length, stretch, trail **5.**

advance, approach, journey, march, passage, progress **6.** characteristic, conduct, custom, habit, idiosyncrasy, manner, nature, personality, practice, style, trait, usage, wont **7.** aspect, detail, feature, particular, point, respect, sense **8.** aim, ambition, choice, demand, desire, goal, pleasure, will, wish **9.** *informal* circumstance, condition, fettle, shape (*informal*), situation, state, status **10.** forward motion, headway, movement, passage, progress **11. by the way** by the bye, en passant, incidentally, in parenthesis, in passing **12. give way: a.** break down, cave in, collapse, crack, crumple, fall, fall to pieces, give, go to pieces, subside **b.** accede, acknowledge defeat, acquiesce, back down, concede, make concessions, withdraw, yield **13. under way** afoot, begun, going, in motion, in progress, moving, on the go (*informal*), on the move, started

wayfarer bird of passage, globetrotter, Gypsy, itinerant, journeyer, nomad, rover, traveller, trekker, voyager, walker, wanderer

wayfaring *adjective* drifting, itinerant, journeying, nomadic, peripatetic, rambling, roving, travelling, voyaging, walking, wandering

waylay accost, ambush, attack, catch, hold up, intercept, lie in wait for, pounce on, set upon, surprise, swoop down on

way-out 1. advanced, avant-garde, bizarre, crazy, eccentric, experimental, far-out (*slang*), freaky (*slang*), oddball (*informal*), offbeat, off-the-wall (*slang*), outlandish, outré, progressive, unconventional, unorthodox, wacko *or* whacko (*informal*), weird, wild **2.** amazing, awesome (*informal*), brilliant, excellent, fantastic (*informal*), great (*informal*), marvellous, sensational (*informal*), tremendous (*informal*), wonderful

ways and means ability, capability, capacity, course, funds, methods, procedure, reserves, resources, tools, way, wherewithal

wayward capricious, changeable, contrary, contumacious, cross-grained, disobedient, erratic, fickle, flighty, froward (*archaic*), headstrong, inconstant, incorrigible, insubordinate, intractable, mulish, obdurate, obstinate, perverse, rebellious, refractory, self-willed, stubborn, undependable, ungovernable, unmanageable, unpredictable, unruly, wilful

▷ **Antonyms** complaisant, compliant, dependable, good-natured, malleable, manageable, obedient, obliging, predictable, reliable, submissive, tractable

weak 1. anaemic, debilitated, decrepit, delicate, effete, enervated, exhausted, faint, feeble, fragile, frail, infirm, languid, puny, shaky, sickly, spent, tender, unsound, unsteady, wasted, weakly **2.** cowardly, impotent, indecisive, ineffectual, infirm, irresolute, namby-pamby, pathetic, powerless, soft, spineless, timorous, weak-kneed (*informal*) **3.** distant, dull, faint, imperceptible, low, muffled, poor, quiet, slight, small, soft **4.** deficient, faulty, inadequate, lacking, pathetic, poor, substandard, under-strength, wanting **5.** feeble, flimsy, hollow, inconclusive, invalid, lame, pathetic, shallow, slight, unconvincing, unsatisfactory **6.** defenceless, exposed, helpless, unguarded, unprotected, unsafe, untenable, vulnerable, wide open **7.** diluted, insipid, milk-and-water, runny, tasteless, thin, under-strength, waterish, watery, wishy-washy (*informal*)

▷ **Antonyms** (*senses 1, 2, & 4*) able, capable, effective, energetic, firm, hardy, healthy, hefty, mighty, resolute, solid, strong, substantial, tough (*sense 5*) conclusive, convincing, forceful, incontrovertible, obvious, powerful, solid, trustworthy, valid (*sense 6*) invulnerable, safe, secure, well-defended (*sense 7*) flavoursome, intoxicating, potent, tasty

weaken 1. abate, debilitate, depress, diminish, droop, dwindle, ease up, enervate, fade, fail, flag, give way, impair, invalidate, lessen, lower, mitigate, moderate, reduce, sap, sap the strength of, soften up, take the edge off, temper, tire, undermine, wane **2.** adulterate, cut, debase, dilute, thin, thin out, water down

▷ **Antonyms** boost, enhance, grow, improve, increase, invigorate, revitalize, strengthen

weakling coward, doormat (*slang*), drip (*informal*), jellyfish (*informal*), jessie (*Scot. slang*), milksop, mouse, sissy, wet (*Brit. informal*), wimp (*informal*), wuss (*U.S. slang*)

weakness 1. debility, decrepitude, enervation, faintness, feebleness, fragility, frailty, impotence, infirmity, irresolution, powerlessness, vulnerability **2.** Achilles heel, blemish, chink in one's armour, defect, deficiency, failing, fault, flaw, imperfection, lack, shortcoming **3.** fondness, inclination, liking, partiality, passion, penchant, predilection, proclivity, proneness, soft spot

▷ **Antonyms** (*sense 1*) hardiness, health, impregnability, potency, power, stamina, sturdiness, validity, vigour, virtue, vitality (*sense 2*) advantage, forte, strength, strong point (*sense 3*) aversion, dislike, hatred, loathing

weal contusion, mark, ridge, scar, streak, stripe, wale, welt, wheal

wealth 1. affluence, assets, big bucks (*informal, chiefly U.S.*), big money, capital, cash, estate, fortune, funds, goods, lucre, means, megabucks (*U.S. & Canad.*

slang), money, opulence, pelf, possessions, pretty penny (*informal*), property, prosperity, resources, riches, substance, tidy sum (*informal*), wad (*U.S. & Canad. slang*) **2.** abundance, bounty, copiousness, cornucopia, fullness, plenitude, plenty, profusion, richness, store

▷ **Antonyms** dearth, deprivation, destitution, indigence, lack, need, paucity, penury, poverty, scarcity, shortage, want, wretchedness

wealthy affluent, comfortable, filthy rich, flush (*informal*), in the money (*informal*), loaded (*slang*), made of money (*informal*), moneyed, on Easy Street (*informal*), opulent, prosperous, quids in (*slang*), rich, rolling in it (*slang*), stinking rich (*slang*), well-heeled (*informal*), well-off, well-to-do

▷ **Antonyms** broke (*informal*), deprived, destitute, dirt-poor (*informal*), down and out, down at heel, flat broke (*informal*), impoverished, indigent, needy, on the breadline, penniless, poor, poverty-stricken, short, skint (*Brit. slang*), without two pennies to rub together (*informal*)

wear *verb* **1.** bear, be clothed in, be dressed in, carry, clothe oneself, don, dress in, have on, put on, sport (*informal*) **2.** display, exhibit, fly, show **3.** abrade, consume, corrode, deteriorate, erode, fray, grind, impair, rub, use, wash away, waste **4.** bear up, be durable, endure, hold up, last, stand up **5.** annoy, drain, enervate, exasperate, fatigue, get on one's nerves (*informal*), harass, irk, pester, tax, undermine, vex, weaken, weary **6.** *Brit. slang* accept, allow, brook, countenance, fall for, permit, put up with (*informal*), stand for, stomach, swallow (*informal*), take ~*noun* **7.** employment, mileage (*informal*), service, use, usefulness, utility **8.** apparel, attire, clothes, costume, dress, garb, garments, gear (*informal*), habit, outfit, things, threads (*slang*) **9.** abrasion, attrition, corrosion, damage, depreciation, deterioration, erosion, friction, use, wear and tear

▷ **Antonyms** (*sense 9*) conservation, maintenance, preservation, repair, upkeep

wear down 1. abrade, be consumed, consume, corrode, erode, grind down, rub away **2.** chip away at (*informal*), fight a war of attrition against, overcome gradually, reduce, undermine

weariness drowsiness, enervation, exhaustion, fatigue, languor, lassitude, lethargy, listlessness, prostration, tiredness

▷ **Antonyms** drive, energy, freshness, get-up-and-go (*informal*), liveliness, stamina, vigour, vitality, zeal, zest

wearing exasperating, exhausting, fatiguing, irksome, oppressive, taxing, tiresome, tiring, trying, wearisome

▷ **Antonyms** easy, effortless, light, no bother, painless, refreshing, stimulating, undemanding

wearisome annoying, boring, bothersome, burdensome, dull, exasperating, exhausting, fatiguing, humdrum, irksome, mind-numbing, monotonous, oppressive, pestilential, prosaic, tedious, tiresome, troublesome, trying, uninteresting, vexatious, wearing

▷ **Antonyms** agreeable, delightful, enjoyable, exhilarating, interesting, invigorating, pleasurable, refreshing, stimulating

wear off 1. abate, decrease, diminish, disappear, dwindle, ebb, fade, lose effect, lose strength, peter out, subside, wane, weaken **2.** abrade, disappear, efface, fade, rub away

▷ **Antonyms** grow, increase, intensify, magnify, persist, reinforce, step up, strengthen, wax

wear out 1. become useless, become worn, consume, deteriorate, erode, fray, impair, use up, wear through **2.** enervate, exhaust, fag out (*informal*), fatigue, frazzle (*informal*), knacker (*slang*), prostrate, sap, tire, weary

▷ **Antonyms** (*sense 2*) buck up (*informal*), energize, invigorate, pep up, perk up, refresh, revitalize, stimulate, strengthen

weary *adjective* **1.** all in (*slang*), asleep *or* dead on one's feet (*informal*), clapped out (*Austral. & N.Z. informal*), dead beat (*informal*), dog-tired (*informal*), done in (*informal*), drained, drooping, drowsy, enervated, exhausted, fagged (*informal*), fatigued, flagging, jaded, knackered (*slang*), ready to drop, sleepy, spent, tired, wearied, whacked (*Brit. informal*), worn out, zonked (*slang*) **2.** arduous, enervative, irksome, laborious, taxing, tiresome, tiring, wearing, wearisome **3.** bored, browned-off (*informal*), discontented, fed up, impatient, indifferent, jaded, sick (*informal*), sick and tired (*informal*) ~*verb* **4.** burden, debilitate, drain, droop, enervate, fade, fag (*informal*), fail, fatigue, grow tired, sap, take it out of (*informal*), tax, tire, tire out, wear out **5.** annoy, become bored, bore, exasperate, have had enough, irk, jade, make discontented, plague, sicken, try the patience of, vex

▷ **Antonyms** ~*adjective* amused, energetic, excited, exciting, forebearing, fresh, full of beans (*informal*), full of get-up-and-go (*informal*), invigorated, invigorating, lively, original, patient, refreshed, refreshing, stimulated ~*verb* amuse, enliven, excite, interest, invigorate, refresh, revive, stimulate

weather *noun* **1.** climate, conditions **2.** **under the weather: a.** ailing, below par, ill, indisposed, nauseous, not well, off-colour, out of sorts, poorly (*informal*), seedy (*informal*), sick **b.** crapulent, crapulous, drunk, flying (*slang*), groggy (*informal*), hung over (*informal*), inebriated, intoxicated, one over the eight (*slang*), the worse for drink, three sheets in the wind (*informal*), under the influence (*informal*) *~verb* **3.** expose, harden, season, toughen **4.** bear up against, brave, come through, endure, get through, live through, make it (*informal*), overcome, pull through, resist, ride out, rise above, stand, stick it out (*informal*), suffer, surmount, survive, withstand

▷ **Antonyms** (*sense 4*) cave in, collapse, fail, fall, give in, go under, succumb, surrender, yield

weave 1. blend, braid, entwine, fuse, incorporate, interlace, intermingle, intertwine, introduce, knit, mat, merge, plait, twist, unite **2.** build, construct, contrive, create, fabricate, make, make up, put together, spin **3.** crisscross, move in and out, weave one's way, wind, zigzag **4. get weaving** *informal* get a move on, get going, get one's finger out (*Brit. informal*), get under way, hurry, make a start, shake a leg (*slang*), start

web 1. cobweb, spider's web **2.** interlacing, lattice, mesh, net, netting, network, screen, tangle, toils, weave, webbing

wed 1. become man and wife, be married to, espouse, get hitched (*slang*), get married, join, make one, marry, plight one's troth (*old-fashioned*), splice (*informal*), take as one's husband, take as one's wife, take the plunge (*informal*), take to wife, tie the knot (*informal*), unite **2.** ally, blend, coalesce, combine, commingle, dedicate, fuse, interweave, join, link, marry, merge, unify, unite, yoke

▷ **Antonyms** (*sense 2*) break up, disunite, divide, divorce, part, separate, sever, split

wedding espousals, marriage, marriage ceremony, nuptial rite, nuptials, wedlock

wedge 1. *noun* block, chock, chunk, lump, wodge (*Brit. informal*) **2.** *~verb* block, cram, crowd, force, jam, lodge, pack, ram, split, squeeze, stuff, thrust

wedlock marriage, matrimony

wee diminutive, insignificant, itsy-bitsy (*informal*), Lilliputian, little, microscopic, miniature, minuscule, minute, negligible, pygmy *or* pigmy, small, teensy-weensy, teeny, teeny-weeny, tiny

weed out dispense with, eliminate, eradicate, extirpate, get rid of, remove, root out, separate out, shed, uproot

weedy feeble, frail, ineffectual, namby-pamby, nerdy *or* nurdy (*slang*), puny, skinny, thin, undersized, weak, weak-kneed (*informal*)

weekly by the week, every week, hebdomadal, hebdomadally, hebdomadary, once a week

weep bemoan, bewail, blub (*slang*), blubber, boohoo, complain, cry, greet (*Scot. or archaic*), keen, lament, moan, mourn, shed tears, snivel, sob, ululate, whimper, whinge (*informal*)

▷ **Antonyms** be glad, celebrate, delight, exult, joy, rejoice, revel, triumph

weepy 1. *adjective* blubbering, close to tears, crying, lachrymose, on the verge of tears, sobbing, tearful, weeping, whimpering **2.** *~noun* tear-jerker (*informal*)

weigh 1. have a weight of, measure the weight of, put on the scales, tip the scales at (*informal*) **2.** apportion, deal out, dole out, measure **3.** consider, contemplate, deliberate upon, evaluate, examine, eye up, give thought to, meditate upon, mull over, ponder, reflect upon, study, think over **4.** be influential, carry weight, count, cut any ice (*informal*), have influence, impress, matter, tell **5.** bear down, burden, oppress, prey

weigh down bear down, burden, depress, get down, oppress, overburden, overload, press down, trouble, weigh upon, worry

▷ **Antonyms** alleviate, ease, hearten, help, lift, lighten, refresh, relieve, unburden

weight *noun* **1.** avoirdupois, burden, gravity, heaviness, heft (*informal*), load, mass, poundage, pressure, tonnage **2.** ballast, heavy object, load, mass **3.** albatross, burden, load, millstone, oppression, pressure, strain **4.** greatest force, main force, onus, preponderance **5.** authority, bottom, clout (*informal*), consequence, consideration, efficacy, emphasis, impact, import, importance, influence, moment, persuasiveness, power, significance, substance, value *~verb* **6.** add weight to, ballast, charge, freight, increase the load on, increase the weight of, load, make heavier **7.** burden, encumber, handicap, impede, oppress, overburden, weigh down **8.** bias, load, unbalance

weighty 1. burdensome, cumbersome, dense, heavy, hefty (*informal*), massive, ponderous **2.** consequential, considerable, critical, crucial, forcible, grave, important, momentous, portentous, serious, significant, solemn, substantial **3.** backbreaking, burdensome, crushing, demanding, difficult, exacting, onerous, oppressive, taxing, worrisome, worrying

▷ **Antonyms** (*sense 2*) frivolous, immaterial, incidental, inconsequential, insignificant, minor, petty, trivial, unimportant

weird bizarre, creepy (*informal*), eerie, eldritch (*poetic*), far-out (*slang*), freakish, ghostly, grotesque, mysterious, odd, outlandish, queer, spooky (*informal*), strange, supernatural, uncanny, unearthly, unnatural

▷ **Antonyms** common, mundane, natural, normal, ordinary, regular, typical, usual

weirdo, weirdie crackpot (*informal*), crank (*informal*), eccentric, freak (*informal*), headbanger (*informal*), headcase (*informal*), loony (*slang*), nut (*slang*), nutcase (*slang*), nutter (*Brit. slang*), oddball (*informal*), queer fish (*Brit. informal*)

welcome *adjective* **1.** acceptable, accepted, agreeable, appreciated, delightful, desirable, gladly received, gratifying, pleasant, pleasing, pleasurable, refreshing, wanted **2.** at home, free, invited, under no obligation *~noun* **3.** acceptance, entertainment, greeting, hospitality, reception, salutation *~verb* **4.** accept gladly, bid welcome, embrace, greet, hail, meet, offer hospitality to, receive, receive with open arms, roll out the red carpet for, usher in

▷ **Antonyms** (*sense 1*) disagreeable, excluded, rebuffed, rejected, unacceptable, undesirable, unpleasant, unwanted, unwelcome (*sense 3*) cold shoulder, exclusion, ostracism, rebuff, rejection, slight, snub (*sense 4*) exclude, rebuff, refuse, reject, slight, snub, spurn, turn away

weld 1. *verb* bind, bond, braze, cement, connect, fuse, join, link, solder, unite **2.** *~noun* bond, joint, juncture, seam

welfare advantage, benefit, good, happiness, health, interest, profit, prosperity, success, wellbeing

well[1] *adverb* **1.** agreeably, capitally, famously (*informal*), happily, in a satisfactory manner, like nobody's business (*informal*), nicely, pleasantly, satisfactorily, smoothly, splendidly, successfully **2.** ably, adeptly, adequately, admirably, conscientiously, correctly, effectively, efficiently, expertly, proficiently, properly, skilfully, with skill **3.** accurately, attentively, carefully, closely **4.** comfortably, flourishingly, prosperously **5.** correctly, easily, fairly, fittingly, in all fairness, justly, properly, readily, rightly, suitably **6.** closely, completely, deeply, fully, intimately, personally, profoundly, thoroughly **7.** approvingly, favourably, glowingly, graciously, highly, kindly, warmly **8.** abundantly, amply, completely, considerably, fully, greatly, heartily, highly, substantially, sufficiently, thoroughly, very much **9. as well** also, besides, in addition, into the bargain, to boot, too **10. as well as** along with, at the same time as, in addition to, including, over and above *~adjective* **11.** able-bodied, alive and kicking, fighting fit (*informal*), fit, fit as a fiddle, hale, healthy, hearty, in fine fettle, in good health, robust, sound, strong, up to par **12.** advisable, agreeable, bright, fine, fitting, flourishing, fortunate, good, happy, lucky, pleasing, profitable, proper, prudent, right, satisfactory, thriving, useful

▷ **Antonyms** *~adverb* badly, coldly, disapprovingly, gracelessly, ham-fistedly, inadequately, incompetently, incorrectly, ineptly, inexpertly, poorly, slightly, sloppily, somewhat, unfairly, unjustly, unkindly, unskilfully, unsuitably, unsympathetically, vaguely, wrongly *~adjective* ailing, at death's door, below par, feeble, frail, going badly, green about the gills, ill, improper, infirm, poorly, run-down, sick, sickly, under-the-weather, unfitting, unsatisfactory, unsuccessful, unwell, weak, wrong

well[2] *noun* **1.** fount, fountain, pool, source, spring, waterhole **2.** bore, hole, pit, shaft **3.** fount, mine, repository, source, wellspring *~verb* **4.** exude, flow, gush, jet, ooze, pour, rise, run, seep, spout, spring, spurt, stream, surge, trickle

well-balanced 1. graceful, harmonious, proportional, symmetrical, well-proportioned **2.** judicious, level-headed, rational, reasonable, sane, sensible, sober, sound, together (*slang*), well-adjusted

▷ **Antonyms** (*sense 2*) erratic, insane, irrational, neurotic, unbalanced, unreasonable, unsound, unstable, volatile

well-bred 1. aristocratic, blue-blooded, gentle, highborn, noble, patrician, well-born **2.** civil, courteous, courtly, cultivated, cultured, gallant, genteel, gentlemanly, ladylike, mannerly, polished, polite, refined, sophisticated, urbane, well-brought-up, well-mannered

▷ **Antonyms** (*sense 2*) bad-mannered, base, coarse, discourteous, ill-bred, rude, uncivilized, uncouth, uncultured, vulgar

well-favoured attractive, beautiful, bonny, comely, fair, good-looking, handsome, lovely, nice-looking, pretty

well-fed 1. healthy, in good condition, well-nourished **2.** chubby, fat, fleshy, plump, podgy, portly, rotund, rounded, stout

well-groomed dapper, neat, smart, soigné *or* soignée, spruce, tidy, trim, well-dressed, well turned out

well-known celebrated, familiar, famous, illustrious, notable, noted, on the map, popular, renowned, widely known

well-nigh all but, almost, just about, more or less, nearly, next to, practically, virtually

well-off 1. comfortable, flourishing, fortunate, lucky, successful, thriving **2.** affluent, comfortable, flush (*informal*), loaded (*slang*), moneyed, prosperous, rich,

wealthy, well-heeled (*informal*), well-to-do
▷ **Antonyms** (*sense 2*) badly off, broke (*informal*), destitute, dirt-poor (*informal*), down and out, down at heel, flat broke (*informal*), hard up (*informal*), impoverished, indigent, needy, on the breadline, on the rocks (*informal*), penniless, poor, poverty-stricken, short, without two pennies to rub together (*informal*)

wellspring 1. fount, fountainhead, origin, source, wellhead **2.** fount, fund, mine, repository, reserve, reservoir, source, supply, well

well-thought-of admired, esteemed, highly regarded, of good repute, reputable, respected, revered, venerated
▷ **Antonyms** abhorred, derided, despised, disdained, reviled, scorned, spurned

well-to-do affluent, comfortable, flush (*informal*), loaded (*slang*), moneyed, prosperous, rich, wealthy, well-heeled (*informal*), well-off
▷ **Antonyms** bankrupt, broke (*informal*), destitute, down at heel, hard up (*informal*), indigent, insolvent, needy, on the breadline, poor, ruined

well-worn banal, commonplace, hackneyed, overused, stale, stereotyped, threadbare, timeworn, tired, trite

welt contusion, mark, ridge, scar, streak, stripe, wale, weal, wheal

welter *verb* **1.** flounder, lie, roll, splash, tumble, wade, wallow, writhe **2.** billow, heave, pitch, roll, surge, swell, toss *~noun* **3.** confusion, hotchpotch, jumble, mess, muddle, tangle, web

wend direct one's course, go, make for, move, proceed, progress, travel

wet *adjective* **1.** aqueous, damp, dank, drenched, dripping, humid, moist, moistened, saturated, soaked, soaking, sodden, soggy, sopping, waterlogged, watery, wringing wet **2.** clammy, dank, drizzling, humid, misty, pouring, raining, rainy, showery, teeming **3.** *Brit. informal* effete, feeble, foolish, ineffectual, irresolute, namby-pamby, nerdy *or* nurdy (*slang*), silly, soft, spineless, timorous, weak, weedy (*informal*) **4. wet behind the ears** *informal* as green as grass, born yesterday, callow, green, immature, inexperienced, innocent, naive, new, raw *~noun* **5.** clamminess, condensation, damp, dampness, humidity, liquid, moisture, water, wetness **6.** damp weather, drizzle, rain, rains, rainy season, rainy weather **7.** *Brit. informal* drip (*informal*), milksop, weakling, weed (*informal*), wimp (*informal*), wuss (*U.S. slang*) *~verb* **8.** damp, dampen, dip, douse, drench, humidify, irrigate, moisten, saturate, soak, splash, spray, sprinkle, steep, water
▷ **Antonyms** *~adjective* arid, bone-dry, dried, dry, fine, hardened, parched, set, sunny *~noun* dryness, dry weather, fine weather *~verb* dehydrate, desiccate, dry, parch

wetness clamminess, condensation, damp, dampness, humidity, liquid, moisture, sogginess, water, wet

whack *verb* **1.** bang, bash (*informal*), beat, belabour, belt (*informal*), box, buffet, chin (*slang*), clobber (*slang*), clout (*informal*), cuff, deck (*slang*), hit, lambast(e), lay one on (*slang*), rap, slap, slug, smack, sock (*slang*), strike, thrash, thump, thwack, wallop (*informal*) *~noun* **2.** bang, bash (*informal*), belt (*informal*), blow, box, buffet, clout (*informal*), cuff, hit, rap, slap, slug, smack, sock (*slang*), stroke, thump, thwack, wallop (*informal*), wham **3.** *informal* allotment, bit, cut (*informal*), part, portion, quota, share **4.** *informal* attempt, bash (*informal*), crack (*informal*), go (*informal*), shot (*informal*), stab (*informal*), try, turn

whacking big, elephantine, enormous, extraordinary, giant, gigantic, great, huge, humongous *or* humungous (*U.S. slang*), large, mammoth, monstrous, prodigious, tremendous, whopping (*informal*)

wham bang, bash (*informal*), blow, concussion, impact, slam, smack, thump, thwack, wallop (*informal*), whack, whang

wharf dock, jetty, landing stage, pier, quay

wheal contusion, mark, ridge, scar, streak, stripe, wale, weal

wheedle butter up, cajole, charm, coax, court, draw, entice, flatter, inveigle, persuade, talk into, worm

wheel *noun* **1.** circle, gyration, pivot, revolution, roll, rotation, spin, turn, twirl, whirl **2. at the wheel** at the helm, driving, in charge, in command, in control, in the driving seat, steering *~verb* **3.** circle, gyrate, orbit, pirouette, revolve, roll, rotate, spin, swing, swivel, turn, twirl, whirl

wheeze *verb* **1.** breathe roughly, catch one's breath, cough, gasp, hiss, rasp, whistle *~noun* **2.** cough, gasp, hiss, rasp, whistle **3.** *Brit. slang* expedient, idea, plan, ploy, ruse, scheme, stunt, trick, wrinkle (*informal*) **4.** *informal* anecdote, chestnut (*informal*), crack (*slang*), gag (*informal*), joke, old joke, one-liner (*slang*), story

whereabouts location, position, site, situation

wherewithal capital, equipment, essentials, funds, means, money, ready (*informal*), ready money, resources, supplies

whet 1. edge, file, grind, hone, sharpen, strop **2.** animate, arouse, awaken, en~

hance, excite, incite, increase, kindle, pique, provoke, quicken, rouse, stimu~ late, stir

▷ **Antonyms** (*sense 2*) blunt, dampen, deaden, depress, dull, numb, smother, stifle, subdue, suppress

whiff *noun* **1.** aroma, blast, breath, draught, gust, hint, niff (*Brit. slang*), odour, puff, scent, smell, sniff *~verb* **2.** breathe, inhale, puff, smell, smoke, sniff, waft **3.** *Brit. slang* hum (*slang*), malodour, niff (*Brit. slang*), pong (*Brit. informal*), reek, stink

whim caprice, conceit, craze, crotchet, fad (*informal*), fancy, freak, humour, im~ pulse, notion, passing thought, quirk, sport, sudden notion, urge, vagary, whimsy

whimper 1. *verb* blub (*slang*), blubber, cry, grizzle (*informal, chiefly Brit.*), mewl, moan, pule, snivel, sob, weep, whine, whinge (*informal*) **2.** *~noun* moan, snivel, sob, whine

whimsical capricious, chimerical, crotch~ ety, curious, droll, eccentric, fanciful, fantastic, fantastical, freakish, funny, mischievous, odd, peculiar, playful, quaint, queer, singular, unusual, wag~ gish, weird

whine *noun* **1.** cry, moan, plaintive cry, sob, wail, whimper **2.** beef (*slang*), com~ plaint, gripe (*informal*), grouch (*infor~ mal*), grouse, grumble, moan *~verb* **3.** beef (*slang*), bellyache (*slang*), bleat, carp, complain, cry, gripe (*informal*), grizzle (*informal, chiefly Brit.*), grouch (*informal*), grouse, grumble, kvetch (*U.S. slang*), moan, sob, wail, whimper, whinge (*informal*)

whiner complainer, fault-finder, grouch (*informal*), grouser, grumbler, malcon~ tent, moaner, whinger (*informal*)

whip *verb* **1.** beat, birch, cane, castigate, flagellate, flog, give a hiding (*informal*), lambast(e), lash, leather, lick (*informal*), punish, scourge, spank, strap, switch, tan (*slang*), thrash **2.** exhibit, flash, jerk, produce, pull, remove, seize, show, snatch, whisk **3.** *informal* dart, dash, dive, flit, flounce, fly, rush, shoot, tear, whisk **4.** *informal* beat, best, blow out of the water (*slang*), clobber (*slang*), con~ quer, defeat, drub, hammer (*informal*), lick (*informal*), make mincemeat out of (*informal*), outdo, overcome, overpower, overwhelm, rout, run rings around (*in~ formal*), stuff (*slang*), take apart (*slang*), thrash, trounce, wipe the floor with (*in~ formal*), worst **5.** agitate, compel, drive, foment, goad, hound, incite, instigate, prick, prod, provoke, push, spur, stir, urge, work up **6.** beat, whisk *~noun* **7.** birch, bullwhip, cane, cat-o'-nine-tails, crop, horsewhip, knout, lash, rawhide, riding crop, scourge, switch, thong

whipping beating, birching, caning, cas~ tigation, flagellation, flogging, hiding (*informal*), lashing, leathering, punish~ ment, spanking, tanning (*slang*), the strap, thrashing

whip up agitate, arouse, excite, foment, incite, inflame, instigate, kindle, pro~ voke, rouse, stir up, work up

whirl *verb* **1.** circle, gyrate, pirouette, piv~ ot, reel, revolve, roll, rotate, spin, swirl, turn, twirl, twist, wheel **2.** feel dizzy, reel, spin *~noun* **3.** birl (*Scot.*), circle, gy~ ration, pirouette, reel, revolution, roll, rotation, spin, swirl, turn, twirl, twist, wheel **4.** confusion, daze, dither (*chiefly Brit.*), flurry, giddiness, spin **5.** flurry, merry-go-round, round, series, succes~ sion **6.** agitation, bustle, commotion, confusion, flurry, hurly-burly, stir, tu~ mult, uproar **7. give (something) a whirl** *informal* attempt, have a bash, have a crack (*informal*), have a go (*informal*), have a shot (*informal*), have a stab (*in~ formal*), have a whack (*informal*), try

whirlwind 1. *noun* dust devil, tornado, waterspout **2.** *~adjective* hasty, head~ long, impetuous, impulsive, lightning, quick, quickie (*informal*), rapid, rash, short, speedy, swift

▷ **Antonyms** (*sense 2*) calculated, cau~ tious, considered, deliberate, measured, prudent, slow, unhurried

whisk *verb* **1.** brush, flick, sweep, whip, wipe **2.** barrel (along) (*informal, chiefly U.S. & Canad.*), burn rubber (*informal*), dart, dash, fly, hasten, hurry, race, rush, shoot, speed, sweep, tear **3.** beat, fluff up, whip *~noun* **4.** brush, flick, sweep, whip, wipe **5.** beater

whisky barley-bree (*Scot.*), bourbon, fire~ water, John Barleycorn, malt, rye, Scotch, usquebaugh

whisper *verb* **1.** breathe, murmur, say softly, speak in hushed tones, utter un~ der the breath **2.** gossip, hint, insinuate, intimate, murmur, spread rumours **3.** hiss, murmur, rustle, sigh, sough, su~ surrate (*literary*), swish *~noun* **4.** hushed tone, low voice, murmur, soft voice, undertone **5.** hiss, murmur, rustle, sigh, sighing, soughing, susurration *or* su~ surrus (*literary*), swish **6.** breath, frac~ tion, hint, shadow, suggestion, suspi~ cion, tinge, trace, whiff **7.** *informal* buzz, dirt (*U.S. slang*), gossip, innuendo, in~ sinuation, report, rumour, scuttlebutt (*U.S. slang*), word

▷ **Antonyms** (*sense 1*) bawl, bellow, clamour, roar, shout, thunder, yell

whit atom, bit, crumb, dash, drop, frag~ ment, grain, iota, jot, least bit, little, mite, modicum, particle, piece, pinch, scrap, shred, speck, trace

white 1. ashen, bloodless, ghastly, grey, like death warmed up (*informal*), pale, pallid, pasty, wan, waxen, wheyfaced **2.** grey, grizzled, hoary, silver, snowy **3.** clean, immaculate, impeccable, inno~

cent, pure, spotless, squeaky-clean, stainless, unblemished, unsullied
▷ **Antonyms** (*senses 2 & 3*) black, blackish, blemished, dark, dirty, impure, soiled, stained, tarnished

white-collar clerical, executive, nonmanual, office, professional, salaried

whiten blanch, bleach, blench, etiolate, fade, go white, pale, turn pale
▷ **Antonyms** blacken, colour, darken

whitewash 1. *noun* camouflage, concealment, cover-up, deception, extenuation **2.** *~verb* camouflage, conceal, cover up, extenuate, gloss over, make light of, suppress
▷ **Antonyms** *~verb* disclose, expose, lay bare, reveal, uncover, unmask, unveil

whittle 1. carve, cut, hew, pare, shape, shave, trim **2.** consume, destroy, eat away, erode, reduce, undermine, wear away

whole *adjective* **1.** complete, entire, full, in one piece, integral, total, unabridged, uncut, undivided **2.** faultless, flawless, good, in one piece, intact, inviolate, mint, perfect, sound, unbroken, undamaged, unharmed, unhurt, unimpaired, uninjured, unmutilated, unscathed, untouched **3.** able-bodied, better, cured, fit, hale, healed, healthy, in fine fettle, in good health, recovered, robust, sound, strong, well *~adverb* **4.** in one, in one piece *~noun* **5.** aggregate, all, everything, lot, sum total, the entire amount, total **6.** ensemble, entirety, entity, fullness, piece, totality, unit, unity **7. on the whole: a.** all in all, all things considered, by and large, taking everything into consideration **b.** as a rule, for the most part, generally, in general, in the main, mostly, predominantly
▷ **Antonyms** *~adjective* ailing, broken, cut, damaged, diseased, divided, fragmented, ill, incomplete, in pieces, partial, sick, sickly, under-the-weather, unwell *~noun* bit, component, constituent, division, element, fragment, part, piece, portion

wholehearted committed, complete, dedicated, determined, devoted, earnest, emphatic, enthusiastic, genuine, heartfelt, hearty, real, sincere, true, unfeigned, unqualified, unreserved, unstinting, warm, zealous
▷ **Antonyms** cool, grudging, half-hearted, insincere, qualified, reserved, unreal

wholesale 1. *adjective* all-inclusive, broad, comprehensive, extensive, far-reaching, indiscriminate, mass, sweeping, wide-ranging **2.** *~adverb* all at once, comprehensively, extensively, indiscriminately, on a large scale, without exception
▷ **Antonyms** *~adjective* confined, discriminate, limited, partial, restricted, selective

wholesome 1. beneficial, good, healthful, health-giving, healthy, helpful, hygienic, invigorating, nourishing, nutritious, salubrious, salutary, sanitary, strengthening **2.** apple-pie (*informal*), clean, decent, edifying, ethical, exemplary, honourable, improving, innocent, moral, nice, pure, respectable, righteous, squeaky-clean, uplifting, virtuous, worthy
▷ **Antonyms** (*sense 1*) putrid, rotten, unhealthy, unhygienic, unwholesome (*sense 2*) blue, corrupt, degrading, dirty, dishonest, evil, filthy, immoral, lewd, obscene, pernicious, pornographic, tasteless, trashy, unprincipled, unwholesome, X-rated (*informal*)

wholly 1. all, altogether, completely, comprehensively, entirely, fully, heart and soul, in every respect, one hundred per cent (*informal*), perfectly, thoroughly, totally, utterly **2.** exclusively, only, solely, without exception
▷ **Antonyms** (*sense 1*) incompletely, in part, moderately, partially, partly, relatively, slightly, somewhat

whoop cheer, cry, halloo, holler (*informal*), hoot, hurrah, scream, shout, shriek, yell

whopper 1. colossus, crackerjack (*informal*), giant, jumbo (*informal*), leviathan, mammoth, monster **2.** big lie, fable, fabrication, falsehood, tall story (*informal*), untruth

whopping big, elephantine, enormous, extraordinary, giant, gigantic, great, huge, humongous *or* humungous (*U.S. slang*), large, mammoth, massive, monstrous, prodigious, tremendous, whacking (*informal*)

whore *noun* **1.** brass (*slang*), call girl, cocotte, courtesan, demimondaine, demirep (*rare*), fallen woman, *fille de joie*, harlot, hooker (*U.S. slang*), hustler (*U.S. & Canad. slang*), lady of the night, loose woman, prostitute, scrubber (*Brit. & Austral. slang*), slag (*Brit. slang*), streetwalker, strumpet, tart (*informal*), trollop, woman of easy virtue, woman of ill repute, working girl (*facetious slang*) *~verb* **2.** be on the game (*slang*), hustle (*U.S. & Canad. slang*), prostitute oneself, sell one's body, sell oneself, solicit, walk the streets **3.** fornicate, lech *or* letch (*informal*), sleep around (*informal*), wanton, wench (*archaic*), womanize

whorehouse bagnio, bordello, brothel, cathouse (*U.S. slang*), disorderly house, house of ill fame *or* repute, house of prostitution, knocking-shop (*Brit. slang*)

whorl coil, corkscrew, helix, spiral, swirl, twist, vortex

wicked 1. abandoned, abominable, amoral, atrocious, bad, black-hearted, corrupt, debased, depraved, devilish, dissolute, egregious, evil, fiendish, flagi~

tious, foul, guilty, heinous, immoral, impious, iniquitous, irreligious, maleficent, nefarious, scandalous, shameful, sinful, sink, unprincipled, unrighteous, vicious, vile, villainous, worthless **2.** arch, impish, incorrigible, mischievous, naughty, rascally, roguish **3.** acute, agonizing, awful, crashing, destructive, dreadful, fearful, fierce, harmful, injurious, intense, mighty, painful, severe, terrible **4.** bothersome, difficult, distressing, galling, offensive, troublesome, trying, unpleasant **5.** *slang* adept, adroit, deft, expert, masterly, mighty, outstanding, powerful, skilful, strong

▷ **Antonyms** benevolent, ethical, good, harmless, honourable, innocuous, mannerly, mild, moral, noble, obedient, pleasant, principled, virtuous, well-behaved, wholesome

wide *adjective* **1.** ample, broad, catholic, comprehensive, distended, encyclopedic, expanded, expansive, extensive, far-reaching, general, immense, inclusive, large, sweeping, vast **2.** away, distant, off, off course, off target, remote **3.** dilated, distended, expanded, fully open, outspread, outstretched **4.** ample, baggy, capacious, commodious, full, loose, roomy, spacious *~adverb* **5.** as far as possible, completely, fully, right out, to the furthest extent **6.** astray, nowhere near, off course, off target, off the mark, out

▷ **Antonyms** *~adjective* closed, confined, constricted, cramped, limited, narrow, restricted, shut, strict, tight *~adverb* barely, narrowly, partially, partly

wide-awake **1.** conscious, fully awake, roused, wakened **2.** alert, aware, heedful, keen, observant, on one's toes, on the alert, on the ball (*informal*), on the qui vive, vigilant, wary, watchful

▷ **Antonyms** (*sense 2*) distracted, dreamy, heedless, inattentive, negligent, oblivious, preoccupied, unaware, unobservant

wide-eyed as green as grass, credulous, green, impressionable, ingenuous, innocent, naive, simple, trusting, unsophisticated, unsuspicious, wet behind the ears (*informal*)

widen broaden, dilate, enlarge, expand, extend, open out *or* up, open wide, spread, stretch

▷ **Antonyms** compress, constrict, contract, cramp, diminish, narrow, reduce, shrink, tighten

wide-open **1.** fully extended, fully open, gaping, outspread, outstretched, splayed, spread **2.** at risk, defenceless, exposed, in danger, in peril, open, susceptible, unprotected, vulnerable **3.** anybody's guess (*informal*), indeterminate, uncertain, unpredictable, unsettled, up for grabs (*informal*)

widespread broad, common, epidemic, extensive, far-flung, far-reaching, general, pervasive, popular, prevalent, rife, sweeping, universal, wholesale

▷ **Antonyms** confined, exclusive, limited, local, narrow, rare, sporadic, uncommon

width breadth, compass, diameter, extent, girth, measure, range, reach, scope, span, thickness, wideness

wield **1.** brandish, employ, flourish, handle, manage, manipulate, ply, swing, use **2.** apply, be possessed of, command, control, exercise, exert, have, have at one's disposal, hold, maintain, make use of, manage, possess, put to use, utilize

wife better half (*humorous*), bride, helpmate, helpmeet, her indoors (*Brit. slang*), little woman (*informal*), mate, old lady (*informal*), old woman (*informal*), partner, significant other (*U.S. informal*), spouse, (the) missis *or* missus (*informal*), vrou (*S. African*), woman (*informal*)

wiggle *verb/noun* jerk, jiggle, shake, shimmy, squirm, twitch, wag, waggle, writhe

wild *adjective* **1.** feral, ferocious, fierce, savage, unbroken, undomesticated, untamed **2.** free, indigenous, native, natural, uncultivated **3.** desert, deserted, desolate, empty, godforsaken, lonely, trackless, uncivilized, uncultivated, uninhabited, unpopulated, virgin **4.** barbaric, barbarous, brutish, ferocious, fierce, primitive, rude, savage, uncivilized **5.** boisterous, chaotic, disorderly, impetuous, lawless, noisy, riotous, rough, rowdy, self-willed, turbulent, unbridled, uncontrolled, undisciplined, unfettered, ungovernable, unmanageable, unrestrained, unruly, uproarious, violent, wayward **6.** blustery, choppy, furious, howling, intense, raging, rough, tempestuous, violent **7.** dishevelled, disordered, straggly, tousled, unkempt, untidy, windblown **8.** at one's wits' end, berserk, beside oneself, crazed, crazy, delirious, demented, excited, frantic, frenzied, hysterical, irrational, mad, maniacal, rabid, raving **9.** extravagant, fantastic, flighty, foolhardy, foolish, giddy, ill-considered, impracticable, imprudent, madcap, outrageous, preposterous, rash, reckless **10.** *informal* agog, avid, crazy (*informal*), daft (*informal*), eager, enthusiastic, excited, gonzo (*slang*), mad (*informal*), nuts (*slang*), potty (*Brit. informal*) *~adverb* **11. run wild: a.** grow unchecked, ramble, spread, straggle **b.** abandon all restraint, cut loose, go on the rampage, kick over the traces, rampage, run free, run riot, stray *~noun* **12.** (*often plural*) back of beyond (*informal*), desert, middle of nowhere (*informal*), uninhabited area, wasteland, wilderness

▷ **Antonyms** *~adjective* (*sense 1*) broken,

domesticated, tame (*senses 2 & 3*) civilized, cultivated, farmed, inhabited, planted, populated, urban (*sense 4*) advanced, civilized (*sense 5*) calm, careful, controlled, disciplined, domesticated, friendly, genteel, gentle, lawful, mild, ordered, orderly, peaceful, polite, quiet, restrained, self controlled, thoughtful, well-behaved (*sense 9*) logical, practical, realistic, well-thought-out (*sense 10*) unenthusiastic, uninterested

wilderness 1. desert, jungle, waste, wasteland, wild **2.** clutter, confused mass, confusion, congeries, jumble, maze, muddle, tangle, welter

wildlife flora and fauna

wile 1. artfulness, artifice, cheating, chicanery, craft, craftiness, cunning, fraud, guile, slyness, trickery **2.** (*usually plural*) artifice, contrivance, device, dodge, imposition, lure, manoeuvre, ploy, ruse, stratagem, subterfuge, trick

wilful 1. adamant, bull-headed, determined, dogged, froward (*archaic*), headstrong, inflexible, intractable, intransigent, mulish, obdurate, obstinate, persistent, perverse, pig-headed, refractory, self-willed, stiff-necked, stubborn, uncompromising, unyielding **2.** conscious, deliberate, intended, intentional, purposeful, volitional, voluntary, willed

▷ **Antonyms** (*sense 1*) biddable, complaisant, compromising, docile, flexible, good-natured, obedient, pliant, tractable, yielding (*sense 2*) accidental, involuntary, uncalculated, unconscious, unintentional, unplanned, unwitting

will *noun* **1.** choice, decision, determination, discretion, option, prerogative, volition **2.** declaration, last wishes, testament **3.** choice, decision, decree, desire, fancy, inclination, mind, pleasure, preference, wish **4.** aim, determination, intention, purpose, resolution, resolve, willpower **5.** attitude, disposition, feeling **6. at will** as one pleases, as one thinks fit, as one wishes, at one's desire, at one's discretion, at one's inclination, at one's pleasure, at one's whim, at one's wish *~verb* **7.** bid, bring about, cause, command, decree, determine, direct, effect, ordain, order, resolve **8.** choose, desire, elect, opt, prefer, see fit, want, wish **9.** bequeath, confer, give, leave, pass on, transfer

willing agreeable, amenable, compliant, consenting, content, desirous, disposed, eager, enthusiastic, favourable, game (*informal*), happy, inclined, in favour, in the mood, nothing loath, pleased, prepared, ready, so-minded

▷ **Antonyms** averse, disinclined, grudging, indisposed, loath, not keen, reluctant, unenthusiastic, unwilling

willingly by choice, cheerfully, eagerly, freely, gladly, happily, lief (*rare*), of one's own accord, of one's own free will, readily, voluntarily, with all one's heart, without hesitation, with pleasure

▷ **Antonyms** grudgingly, hesitantly, involuntarily, reluctantly, unwillingly

willingness agreeableness, agreement, consent, desire, disposition, enthusiasm, favour, goodwill, inclination, volition, will, wish

▷ **Antonyms** aversion, disagreement, disinclination, hesitation, loathing, reluctance, unwillingness

willowy graceful, limber, lissom(e), lithe, slender, slim, supple, svelte, sylphlike

willpower determination, drive, firmness of purpose *or* will, fixity of purpose, force *or* strength of will, grit, resolution, resolve, self-control, self-discipline, single-mindedness

▷ **Antonyms** apathy, hesitancy, indecision, irresolution, languor, lethargy, shilly-shallying (*informal*), torpor, uncertainty, weakness

willy-nilly 1. *adverb* necessarily, *nolens volens,* of necessity, perforce, whether desired or not, whether one likes it or not, whether or no **2.** *~adjective* inevitable, irrespective of one's wishes, necessary, unavoidable

wilt 1. become limp *or* flaccid, droop, sag, shrivel, wither **2.** diminish, dwindle, ebb, fade, fail, flag, languish, lose courage, melt away, sag, sink, wane, weaken, wither

wily arch, artful, astute, cagey (*informal*), crafty, crooked, cunning, deceitful, deceptive, designing, fly (*slang*), foxy, guileful, intriguing, scheming, sharp, shifty, shrewd, sly, tricky, underhand

▷ **Antonyms** above-board, artless, candid, dull, guileless, honest, ingenuous, naive, simple, straightforward

win *verb* **1.** achieve first place, achieve mastery, be victorious, carry all before one, carry the day, come first, conquer, finish first, gain victory, overcome, prevail, succeed, sweep the board, take the prize, triumph **2.** accomplish, achieve, acquire, attain, bag (*informal*), catch, collect, come away with, earn, gain, get, land, net, obtain, pick up, procure, receive, secure **3.** (*often with* **over**) allure, attract, bring *or* talk round, carry, charm, convert, convince, disarm, induce, influence, persuade, prevail upon, sway *~noun* **4.** *informal* conquest, success, triumph, victory

▷ **Antonyms** *~verb* fail, fall, forfeit, lose, miss, suffer defeat, suffer loss *~noun* beating, defeat, downfall, failure, loss, washout (*informal*)

wince 1. *verb* blench, cower, cringe, draw back, flinch, quail, recoil, shrink, start **2.** *~noun* cringe, flinch, start

wind[1] 1. *noun* air, air-current, blast, breath, breeze, current of air, draught, gust, zephyr **2.** *informal* clue, hint, inkling, intimation, notice, report, rumour, suggestion, tidings, warning, whisper **3.** babble, blather, bluster, boasting, empty talk, gab (*informal*), hot air, humbug, idle talk, talk, verbalizing **4.** breath, puff, respiration **5.** *informal* flatulence, flatus, gas **6. get** *or* **have the wind up** *informal* be afraid, be alarmed, be frightened, be scared, fear, take fright **7. in the wind** about to happen, approaching, close at hand, coming, imminent, impending, in the offing, near, on the cards (*informal*), on the way **8. put the wind up** *informal* alarm, discourage, frighten, frighten off, scare, scare off

wind[2] *verb* **1.** coil, curl, encircle, furl, loop, reel, roll, spiral, turn around, twine, twist, wreathe **2.** bend, curve, deviate, meander, ramble, snake, turn, twist, zigzag *~noun* **3.** bend, curve, meander, turn, twist, zigzag

windbag bigmouth (*slang*), blether (*Scot.*), blowhard (*informal*), boaster, bore, braggart, bullshit artist (*taboo slang*), bullshitter (*taboo slang*), gasbag (*informal*), gossip, loudmouth (*informal*), prattler

wind down cool off, decline, diminish, dwindle, lessen, reduce, relax, slacken, subside, taper off, unwind

▷ **Antonyms** accelerate, amplify, escalate, expand, heat up, increase, intensify, magnify, step up

winded breathless, gasping for breath, out of breath, out of puff, out of whack (*informal*), panting, puffed, puffed out

windfall bonanza, find, godsend, jackpot, manna from heaven, pot of gold at the end of the rainbow, stroke of luck

▷ **Antonyms** bad luck, disaster, infelicity, misadventure, mischance, misfortune, mishap

winding 1. *noun* bend, convolution, curve, meander, turn, twist, undulation **2.** *~adjective* anfractuous, bending, circuitous, convoluted, crooked, curving, flexuous, indirect, meandering, roundabout, serpentine, sinuous, spiral, tortuous, turning, twisting, twisty

▷ **Antonyms** *~adjective* direct, even, level, plumb, smooth, straight, undeviating, unswerving

wind-up close, conclusion, culmination, dénouement, end, finale, finish, termination

wind up 1. bring to a close, close, close down, conclude, end, finalize, finish, liquidate, settle, terminate, tie up the loose ends (*informal*), wrap up **2.** *informal* excite, make nervous, make tense, put on edge, work up **3.** *informal* be left, end one's days, end up, find oneself, finish up

▷ **Antonyms** (*sense 1*) begin, commence, embark on, initiate, instigate, institute, open, start

windy 1. blowy, blustering, blustery, boisterous, breezy, gusty, inclement, squally, stormy, tempestuous, wild, windswept **2.** boastful, bombastic, diffuse, empty, garrulous, long-winded, loquacious, meandering, pompous, prolix, rambling, turgid, verbose, wordy **3.** *slang* afraid, chicken (*slang*), chickenshit (*U.S. slang*), cowardly, fearful, frightened, nervous, nervy (*informal*), scared, timid

▷ **Antonyms** (*sense 1*) becalmed, calm, motionless, smooth, still, windless (*sense 2*) modest, quiet, reserved, restrained, reticent, shy, taciturn, unforthcoming (*sense 3*) bold, brave, courageous, daring, fearless, gallant, unafraid, undaunted

wing *noun* **1.** organ of flight, pennon (*poetic*), pinion (*poetic*) **2.** arm, branch, cabal, circle, clique, coterie, faction, group, grouping, schism, section, segment, set, side **3.** adjunct, annexe, ell, extension *~verb* **4.** fly, glide, soar **5.** fleet, fly, hasten, hurry, race, speed, zoom **6.** clip, hit, nick, wound

wink *verb* **1.** bat, blink, flutter, nictate, nictitate **2.** flash, gleam, glimmer, sparkle, twinkle *~noun* **3.** blink, flutter, nictation **4.** flash, gleam, glimmering, sparkle, twinkle **5.** instant, jiffy (*informal*), moment, second, split second, twinkling

wink at allow, blink at, condone, connive at, disregard, ignore, overlook, pretend not to notice, put up with (*informal*), shut one's eyes to, tolerate, turn a blind eye to

winkle out dig out, dislodge, draw out, extract, extricate, force out, prise out, smoke out, worm out

winner champ (*informal*), champion, conquering hero, conqueror, first, master, vanquisher, victor

winning 1. alluring, amiable, attractive, bewitching, captivating, charming, cute, delectable, delightful, disarming, enchanting, endearing, engaging, fascinating, fetching, likable *or* likeable, lovely, pleasing, prepossessing, sweet, taking, winsome **2.** conquering, successful, triumphant, victorious

▷ **Antonyms** (*sense 1*) disagreeable, irksome, offensive, repellent, tiresome, unappealing, unattractive, uninteresting, unpleasant

winnings booty, gains, prize(s), proceeds, profits, spoils, takings

winnow comb, cull, divide, fan, part, screen, select, separate, separate the wheat from the chaff, sift, sort out

winsome agreeable, alluring, amiable, attractive, bewitching, captivating, charming, comely, cute, delectable, disarming, enchanting, endearing, engaging, fair, fascinating, fetching, likable *or* likeable, pleasant, pleasing, pretty, sweet, taking, winning

wintry **1.** brumal, chilly, cold, freezing, frosty, frozen, harsh, hibernal, hiemal, icy, snowy **2.** bleak, cheerless, cold, desolate, dismal

▷ **Antonyms** balmy, bright, mild, pleasant, summery, sunny, tepid, warm

wipe *verb* **1.** brush, clean, dry, dust, mop, rub, sponge, swab **2.** clean off, erase, get rid of, remove, rub off, take away, take off *~noun* **3.** brush, lick, rub, swab

wipe out annihilate, blot out, blow away (*slang, chiefly U.S.*), destroy, efface, eradicate, erase, expunge, exterminate, extirpate, kill to the last man, massacre, obliterate, take out (*slang*), wipe from the face of the earth

wiry **1.** lean, sinewy, strong, tough **2.** bristly, kinky, stiff

▷ **Antonyms** (*sense 1*) fat, feeble, flabby, fleshy, frail, podgy, puny, spineless, weak

wisdom astuteness, circumspection, comprehension, discernment, enlightenment, erudition, foresight, insight, intelligence, judgment, judiciousness, knowledge, learning, penetration, prudence, reason, sagacity, sapience, sense, smarts (*slang, chiefly U.S.*), sound judgment, understanding

▷ **Antonyms** absurdity, bêtise (*rare*), daftness (*informal*), folly, foolishness, idiocy, injudiciousness, nonsense, senselessness, silliness, stupidity

wise **1.** aware, clever, clued-up (*informal*), discerning, enlightened, erudite, informed, intelligent, judicious, knowing, perceptive, politic, prudent, rational, reasonable, sagacious, sage, sapient, sensible, shrewd, sound, understanding, well-advised, well-informed **2. put wise** *slang* alert, apprise, clue in *or* up (*informal*), inform, let (someone) into the secret, notify, tell, tip off, warn

▷ **Antonyms** (*sense 1*) daft (*informal*), foolish, injudicious, rash, silly, stupid, unintelligent, unwise

wisecrack **1.** *noun* barb, funny (*informal*), gag (*informal*), jest, jibe, joke, pithy remark, quip, sally, sardonic remark, smart remark, witticism **2.** *~verb* be facetious, jest, jibe, joke, quip, tell jokes

wish *verb* **1.** aspire, covet, crave, desiderate, desire, hanker, hope, hunger, long, need, set one's heart on, sigh for, thirst, want, yearn **2.** bid, greet with **3.** ask, bid, command, desire, direct, instruct, order, require *~noun* **4.** aspiration, desire, hankering, hope, hunger, inclination, intention, liking, longing, thirst, urge, want, whim, will, yearning **5.** bidding, command, desire, order, request, will

▷ **Antonyms** (*sense 4*) aversion, disinclination, dislike, distaste, loathing, reluctance, repulsion, revulsion

wishy-washy bland, feeble, flat, ineffective, ineffectual, insipid, jejune, tasteless, thin, vapid, watered-down, watery, weak

wisp piece, shred, snippet, strand, thread, twist

wispy attenuate, attenuated, delicate, diaphanous, ethereal, faint, fine, flimsy, fragile, frail, gossamer, insubstantial, light, thin, wisplike

wistful contemplative, disconsolate, dreaming, dreamy, forlorn, longing, meditative, melancholy, mournful, musing, pensive, reflective, sad, thoughtful, yearning

wit **1.** badinage, banter, drollery, facetiousness, fun, humour, jocularity, levity, pleasantry, raillery, repartee, wordplay **2.** card (*informal*), comedian, epigrammatist, *farceur,* humorist, joker, punster, wag **3.** acumen, brains, cleverness, common sense, comprehension, discernment, ingenuity, insight, intellect, judgment, mind, nous (*Brit. slang*), perception, practical intelligence, reason, sense, smarts (*slang, chiefly U.S.*), understanding, wisdom

▷ **Antonyms** (*sense 1*) dullness, gravity, humourlessness, seriousness, sobriety, solemnity (*sense 3*) folly, foolishness, ignorance, lack of perception, obtuseness, silliness, stupidity

witch crone, enchantress, hag, magician, necromancer, occultist, sorceress

witchcraft enchantment, incantation, magic, necromancy, occultism, sorcery, sortilege, spell, the black art, the occult, voodoo, witchery, witching, wizardry

withdraw **1.** draw back, draw out, extract, pull, pull out, remove, take away, take off **2.** abjure, disavow, disclaim, recall, recant, rescind, retract, revoke, take back, unsay **3.** absent oneself, back off, back out, cop out (*slang*), depart, detach oneself, disengage, drop out, fall back, go, leave, make oneself scarce (*informal*), pull back, pull out, retire, retreat, secede

▷ **Antonyms** (*senses 1 & 3*) advance, forge ahead, go on, move forward, persist, press on, proceed, progress

withdrawal **1.** extraction, removal **2.** abjuration, disavowal, disclaimer, recall, recantation, repudiation, rescission, retraction, revocation **3.** departure, disengagement, exit, exodus, retirement, retreat, secession

withdrawn **1.** aloof, detached, distant, introverted, quiet, reserved, retiring, shrinking, shy, silent, taciturn, timorous, uncommunicative, unforthcoming **2.** hidden, isolated, out-of-the-way, private, remote, secluded, solitary

▷ **Antonyms** (*sense 1*) extrovert, forward, friendly, gregarious, open, outgoing, sociable (*sense 2*) boisterous, bustling, busy, easily accessible

wither **1.** atrophy, blast, blight, decay, decline, desiccate, disintegrate, droop, dry, fade, languish, perish, shrink, shrivel, wane, waste, wilt **2.** abash, blast, humiliate, mortify, put down, shame, snub

▷ **Antonyms** (*sense 1*) bloom, blossom, develop, flourish, increase, prosper, succeed, thrive, wax

withering 1. blasting, blighting, devas~tating, humiliating, hurtful, mortifying, scornful, snubbing **2.** deadly, death-dealing, destructive, devastating, kill~ing, murderous, slaughterous

withhold 1. check, conceal, deduct, hide, hold back, keep, keep back, keep secret, refuse, repress, reserve, resist, restrain, retain, sit on (*informal*), suppress **2.** (*with* **from**) forbear, keep oneself, re~frain, stop oneself

▷ **Antonyms** (*sense 1*) accord, expose, get off one's chest (*informal*), give, grant, hand over, let go, release, relinquish, reveal

with it fashionable, happening (*infor~mal*), in (*informal*), latest (*informal*), modern, modish, progressive, stylish, swinging (*slang*), trendy (*Brit. infor~mal*), up-to-date, up-to-the-minute, vogue

withstand 1. bear, brave, combat, con~front, cope with, defy, endure, face, grapple with, hold off, hold out against, oppose, put up with (*informal*), resist, stand up to, suffer, take, take on, thwart, tolerate, weather **2.** endure, hold *or* stand one's ground, hold out, re~main firm, stand, stand fast, stand firm

▷ **Antonyms** capitulate, falter, give in, give way, relent, succumb, surrender, weaken, yield

witless asinine, braindead (*informal*), crackpot (*informal*), crazy, daft (*infor~mal*), dozy (*Brit. informal*), dull, empty-headed, foolish, goofy (*informal*), halfwitted, idiotic, imbecilic, inane, loopy (*informal*), moronic, obtuse, rattlebrained (*slang*), senseless, silly, stupid, unintelligent

witness *noun* **1.** beholder, bystander, eyewitness, looker-on, observer, on~looker, spectator, viewer, watcher **2.** at~testant, corroborator, deponent, testifier **3. bear witness: a.** depone, depose, give evidence, give testimony, testify **b.** at~test to, bear out, be evidence of, be proof of, betoken, confirm, constitute proof of, corroborate, demonstrate, evince, prove, show, testify to, vouch for *~verb* **4.** at~tend, behold (*archaic or literary*), be present at, look on, mark, note, notice, observe, perceive, see, view, watch **5.** attest, authenticate, bear out, bear wit~ness, confirm, corroborate, depone, de~pose, give evidence, give testimony, tes~tify **6.** countersign, endorse, sign

wits 1. acumen, astuteness, brains (*in~formal*), cleverness, comprehension, faculties, ingenuity, intelligence, judg~ment, nous (*Brit. slang*), reason, sense, smarts (*slang, chiefly U.S.*), under~standing **2. at one's wits' end** at a loss, at the end of one's tether, baffled, be~wildered, in despair, lost, stuck (*infor~mal*), stumped

witticism bon mot, clever remark, epi~gram, one-liner (*slang*), play on words, pleasantry, pun, quip, repartee, riposte, sally, witty remark

witty amusing, brilliant, clever, droll, epigrammatic, facetious, fanciful, funny, gay, humorous, ingenious, jocular, live~ly, original, piquant, sparkling, wag~gish, whimsical

▷ **Antonyms** boring, dull, humourless, stupid, tedious, tiresome, unamusing, uninteresting, witless

wizard 1. conjuror, enchanter, mage (*ar~chaic*), magician, magus, necromancer, occultist, shaman, sorcerer, thauma~turge (*rare*), warlock, witch **2.** ace (*in~formal*), adept, buff (*informal*), expert, genius, hotshot (*informal*), maestro, master, maven (*U.S.*), prodigy, star, virtuoso, whizz (*informal*), whizz kid (*informal*), wiz (*informal*)

wizardry conjuration, enchantment, magic, necromancy, occultism, sorcery, sortilege, the black art, voodoo, witch~craft, witchery, witching

wizened dried up, gnarled, lined, sere (*archaic*), shrivelled, shrunken, with~ered, worn, wrinkled

▷ **Antonyms** bloated, plump, rounded, smooth, swollen, turgid

wobble *verb* **1.** quake, rock, seesaw, shake, sway, teeter, totter, tremble, vi~brate, waver **2.** be unable to make up one's mind, be undecided, dither (*chiefly Brit.*), fluctuate, hesitate, shillyshally (*informal*), swither (*Scot.*), vacillate, waver *~noun* **3.** quaking, shake, tremble, tremor, unsteadiness, vibration

wobbly rickety, shaky, teetering, totter~ing, unbalanced, uneven, unsafe, unsta~ble, unsteady, wonky (*Brit. slang*)

woe adversity, affliction, agony, anguish, burden, curse, dejection, depression, disaster, distress, gloom, grief, hard~ship, heartache, heartbreak, melan~choly, misery, misfortune, pain, sad~ness, sorrow, suffering, trial, tribula~tion, trouble, unhappiness, wretched~ness

▷ **Antonyms** bliss, elation, felicity, for~tune, happiness, joy, jubilation, pleas~ure, prosperity, rapture

woebegone blue, chapfallen, cheerless, crestfallen, dejected, disconsolate, dole~ful, downcast, downhearted, down in the dumps (*informal*), down in the mouth (*informal*), forlorn, funereal, gloomy, grief-stricken, hangdog, long-faced, low, lugubrious, miserable, mournful, sad, sorrowful, troubled, wretched

woeful **1.** afflicted, agonized, anguished, calamitous, catastrophic, cruel, deplorable, disastrous, disconsolate, dismal, distressing, doleful, dreadful, gloomy, grieving, grievous, harrowing, heartbreaking, heart-rending, lamentable, miserable, mournful, pathetic, piteous, pitiable, pitiful, plaintive, sad, sorrowful, tragic, unhappy, wretched **2.** abysmal, appalling, awful, bad, deplorable, disappointing, disgraceful, dreadful, duff (*Brit. informal*), feeble, godawful (*slang*), hopeless, inadequate, lousy (*slang*), mean, miserable, not much cop (*Brit. slang*), paltry, pathetic, pitiable, pitiful, poor, rotten (*informal*), shitty (*taboo slang*), shocking, sorry, terrible, wretched

▷ **Antonyms** (*sense 1*) carefree, cheerful, chirpy (*informal*), contented, delighted, glad, happy, jolly, joyful, jubilant, light-hearted (*sense 2*) abundant, ample, bountiful, enviable, extensive, generous, lavish, luxurious, profuse, prosperous

wolf *noun* **1.** *figurative* devil, fiend, killer, mercenary, pirate, predator, robber, savage, shark **2.** *informal* Casanova, Don Juan, lady-killer, lech *or* letch (*informal*), lecher, Lothario, philanderer, seducer, womanizer ~*verb* **3.** (*with* **down**) bolt, cram, devour, eat like a horse, gobble, gollop, gorge, gulp, pack away (*informal*), pig out (*slang*), scoff (*slang*), stuff

▷ **Antonyms** ~*verb* bite, nibble, nip, peck, pick at

wolfish avaricious, edacious, fierce, gluttonous, greedy, insatiable, predatory, rapacious, ravenous, savage, voracious

woman **1.** bird (*slang*), chick (*slang*), dame (*slang*), female, gal (*slang*), girl, lady, lass, lassie (*informal*), maid (*archaic*), maiden (*archaic*), miss, she, wench (*facetious*) **2.** chambermaid, char (*informal*), charwoman, domestic, female servant, handmaiden, housekeeper, lady-in-waiting, maid, maidservant **3.** *informal* bride, girl, girlfriend, ladylove, mate, mistress, old lady (*informal*), partner, significant other (*U.S. informal*), spouse, sweetheart, wife

▷ **Antonyms** (*sense 1*) bloke (*Brit. informal*), boy, chap (*informal*), gentleman, guy (*informal*), lad, laddie, male, man

womanizer Casanova, Don Juan, lady-killer, lech *or* letch (*informal*), lecher, Lothario, philanderer, seducer, wolf (*informal*)

womanly female, feminine, ladylike, matronly, motherly, tender, warm

wonder *noun* **1.** admiration, amazement, astonishment, awe, bewilderment, curiosity, fascination, stupefaction, surprise, wonderment **2.** curiosity, marvel, miracle, nonpareil, phenomenon, portent, prodigy, rarity, sight, spectacle, wonderment ~*verb* **3.** ask oneself, be curious, be inquisitive, conjecture, cudgel one's brains (*informal*), doubt, inquire, meditate, ponder, puzzle, query, question, speculate, think **4.** be amazed, be astonished, be awed, be dumbstruck, be flabbergasted (*informal*), boggle, gape, gawk, marvel, stand amazed, stare

wonderful **1.** amazing, astonishing, astounding, awe-inspiring, awesome, extraordinary, fantastic, incredible, marvellous, miraculous, odd, peculiar, phenomenal, remarkable, staggering, startling, strange, surprising, unheard-of, wondrous (*archaic or literary*) **2.** ace (*informal*), admirable, awesome (*slang*), bodacious (*slang, chiefly U.S.*), boffo (*slang*), brill (*informal*), brilliant, chillin' (*U.S. slang*), cracking (*Brit. informal*), excellent, fabulous (*informal*), fantastic (*informal*), great (*informal*), jim-dandy (*slang*), like a dream come true, magnificent, marvellous, mean (*slang*), out of this world (*informal*), outstanding, sensational (*informal*), smashing (*informal*), sovereign, stupendous, super (*informal*), superb, terrific, tiptop, topping (*Brit. slang*), tremendous

▷ **Antonyms** abominable, abysmal, appalling, average, awful, bad, common, commonplace, depressing, dire, dreadful, frightful, grim, hellacious (*U.S. slang*), indifferent, lousy (*slang*), mediocre, miserable, modest, no great shakes (*informal*), ordinary, paltry, rotten, run-of-the-mill, terrible, uninteresting, unpleasant, unremarkable, usual, vile

wonky **1.** groggy (*informal*), infirm, shaky, unsteady, weak, wobbly, woozy (*informal*) **2.** askew, awry, out of alignment, skewwhiff (*Brit. informal*), squint (*informal*)

wont **1.** *adjective* accustomed, given, in the habit of, used **2.** ~*noun* custom, habit, practice, rule, use, way

wonted **1.** accustomed, given, habituated, in the habit of, used **2.** accustomed, common, conventional, customary, familiar, frequent, habitual, normal, regular, usual

woo chase, court, cultivate, importune, pay court to, pay one's addresses to, pay suit to, press one's suit with, pursue, seek after, seek the hand of, seek to win, solicit the goodwill of, spark (*rare*)

wood **1.** *also* **woods** coppice, copse, forest, grove, hurst (*archaic*), thicket, trees, woodland **2.** **out of the wood(s)** clear, home and dry (*Brit. slang*), in the clear, out of danger, safe, safe and sound, secure **3.** planks, timber

wooded forested, sylvan (*poetic*), timbered, tree-clad, tree-covered, woody

wooden **1.** ligneous, made of wood, of wood, timber, woody **2.** awkward, clumsy, gauche, gawky, graceless, inelegant, maladroit, rigid, stiff, ungainly **3.** blank, colourless, deadpan, dull, emotionless, empty, expressionless, glassy, lifeless, spiritless, unemotional, unresponsive, vacant **4.** inflexible, obstinate, rigid, stiff, unbending, unyielding **5.** dense, dim, dim-witted (*informal*), dozy (*Brit. informal*), dull, dull-witted, obtuse, slow, stupid, thick, witless, wooden~headed (*informal*) **6.** dull, muffled

▷ **Antonyms** (*senses 2 & 4*) agile, comely, elegant, flexible, flowing, graceful, lis~som(e), nimble, supple

wool 1. fleece, hair, yarn **2. dyed in the wool** confirmed, diehard, fixed, hard~ened, inflexible, inveterate, settled, un~changeable, uncompromising, unshak~able **3. pull the wool over someone's eyes** bamboozle (*informal*), con (*slang*), deceive, delude, dupe, fool, hoodwink, kid (*informal*), lead (someone) up the garden path (*informal*), pull a fast one (on someone) (*informal*), put one over on (*slang*), take in (*informal*), trick

woolgathering absent-mindedness, ab~straction, building castles in the air, daydreaming, dreaming, inattention, musing, preoccupation, reverie

▷ **Antonyms** alertness, attention, awareness, concentration, heed, obser~vation, thoughtfulness, vigilance, watchfulness

woolly *adjective* **1.** fleecy, flocculent, hairy, made of wool, shaggy, woollen **2.** blurred, clouded, confused, foggy, fuzzy, hazy, ill-defined, indefinite, indistinct, muddled, nebulous, unclear, vague

▷ **Antonyms** (*sense 2*) clear, clear-cut, definite, distinct, exact, obvious, precise, sharp, well-defined

woozy befuddled, bemused, confused, dazed, dizzy, nauseated, rocky (*infor~mal*), tipsy, unsteady, wobbly

word *noun* **1.** brief conversation, chat, chitchat, colloquy, confab (*informal*), confabulation, consultation, discussion, talk, tête-à-tête **2.** brief statement, com~ment, declaration, expression, remark, utterance **3.** expression, locution, name, term, vocable **4.** account, advice, bul~letin, communication, communiqué, dispatch, gen (*Brit. informal*), informa~tion, intelligence, intimation, latest (*in~formal*), message, news, notice, report, tidings **5.** command, go-ahead (*infor~mal*), green light, order, signal **6.** affir~mation, assertion, assurance, guaran~tee, oath, parole, pledge, promise, sol~emn oath, solemn word, undertaking, vow, word of honour **7.** bidding, com~mand, commandment, decree, edict, mandate, order, ukase (*rare*), will **8.** countersign, password, slogan, watch~word **9. in a word** briefly, concisely, in a nutshell, in short, succinctly, to put it briefly, to sum up *~verb* **10.** couch, ex~press, phrase, put, say, state, utter

wording choice of words, language, mode of expression, phraseology, phrasing, terminology, words

wordplay punning, puns, repartee, wit, witticisms

words 1. lyrics, text **2.** altercation, angry exchange, angry speech, argument, bar~ney (*informal*), bickering, disagreement, dispute, falling-out (*informal*), quarrel, row, run-in (*informal*), set-to (*informal*), squabble

wordy diffuse, discursive, garrulous, long-winded, loquacious, pleonastic, prolix, rambling, verbose, windy

▷ **Antonyms** brief, concise, laconic, pithy, short, succinct, terse, to the point

work *noun* **1.** drudgery, effort, elbow grease (*facetious*), exertion, grind (*in~formal*), industry, labour, slog, sweat, toil, travail (*literary*) **2.** bread and butter (*informal*), business, calling, craft, duty, employment, job, line, livelihood, méti~er, occupation, office, profession, pur~suit, trade **3.** assignment, chore, com~mission, duty, job, stint, task, under~taking **4.** achievement, composition, creation, handiwork, *oeuvre*, opus, per~formance, piece, production **5.** art, craft, skill, workmanship **6. out of work** idle, jobless, on the dole (*Brit. informal*), on the street, out of a job, unemployed *~verb* **7.** break one's back, drudge, exert oneself, labour, peg away, slave, slog (away), sweat, toil **8.** be employed, be in work, do business, earn a living, have a job **9.** act, control, direct, drive, handle, manage, manipulate, move, operate, ply, use, wield **10.** function, go, operate, perform, run **11.** cultivate, dig, farm, till **12.** fashion, form, handle, knead, make, manipulate, mould, process, shape **13.** be agitated, convulse, move, twitch, writhe **14.** (*often with* **up**) arouse, excite, move, prompt, provoke, rouse, stir **15.** accomplish, achieve, bring about, carry out, cause, contrive, create, effect, en~compass, execute, implement **16.** force, make one's way, manoeuvre, move, pro~gress **17.** *informal* arrange, bring off, contrive, exploit, fiddle (*informal*), fix (*informal*), handle, manipulate, pull off, swing (*informal*)

▷ **Antonyms** *~noun* (*sense 1*) ease, lei~sure, relaxation, rest (*sense 2*) enter~tainment, hobby, holiday, play, recrea~tion, retirement, spare time, unemploy~ment (*sense 3*) child's play (*informal*) *~verb* (*sense 7*) have fun, mark time, play, relax, skive (*Brit. slang*), take it easy (*sense 10*) be broken, be out of or~der (*sense 15*) counteract, nullify, pre~vent, reverse (*sense 16*) remain

workable doable, feasible, possible, prac~ticable, practical, viable

▷ **Antonyms** hopeless, impossible, im~practical, inconceivable, unattainable, unthinkable, unworkable, useless

workaday bog-standard (*Brit. & Irish slang*), common, commonplace, everyday, familiar, humdrum, mundane, ordinary, practical, prosaic, routine, run-of-the-mill
▷ **Antonyms** atypical, different, exciting, extraordinary, rare, special, uncommon, unfamiliar, unusual

worker artisan, craftsman, employee, hand, labourer, proletarian, tradesman, wage earner, working man, working woman, workman

working *noun* **1.** action, functioning, manner, method, mode of operation, operation, running **2.** *plural* diggings, excavations, mine, pit, quarry, shaft ~*adjective* **3.** active, employed, in a job, in work, labouring **4.** functioning, going, operative, running **5.** effective, practical, useful, viable

workman artificer, artisan, craftsman, employee, hand, journeyman, labourer, mechanic, operative, tradesman, worker

workmanlike, workmanly adept, careful, efficient, expert, masterly, painstaking, professional, proficient, satisfactory, skilful, skilled, thorough
▷ **Antonyms** amateurish, botchy, careless, clumsy, cowboy (*informal*), incompetent, slap-dash, slipshod, unprofessional, unskilful

workmanship art, artistry, craft, craftsmanship, execution, expertise, handicraft, handiwork, manufacture, skill, technique, work

work-out drill, exercise, exercise session, practice session, training, training session, warm-up

work out 1. accomplish, achieve, attain, win **2.** calculate, clear up, figure out, find out, puzzle out, resolve, solve, suss (out) (*slang*) **3.** arrange, construct, contrive, develop, devise, elaborate, evolve, form, formulate, plan, put together **4.** be effective, flourish, go as planned, go well, prosper, prove satisfactory, succeed **5.** come out, develop, evolve, go, happen, pan out (*informal*), result, turn out **6.** do exercises, drill, exercise, practise, train, warm up **7.** add up to, amount to, come to, reach, reach a total of

works 1. factory, mill, plant, shop, workshop **2.** canon, *oeuvre*, output, productions, writings **3.** actions, acts, deeds, doings **4.** action, guts (*informal*), innards (*informal*), insides (*informal*), machinery, mechanism, movement, moving parts, parts, workings

workshop 1. atelier, factory, mill, plant, shop, studio, workroom, works **2.** class, discussion group, seminar, study group

work up agitate, animate, arouse, enkindle, excite, foment, generate, get (someone) all steamed up (*slang*), incite, inflame, instigate, move, rouse, spur, stir up, wind up (*informal*)

world 1. earth, earthly sphere, globe **2.** everybody, *Homo sapiens*, humanity, humankind, human race, man, mankind, men, the public, the race of man **3.** cosmos, creation, existence, life, nature, universe **4.** heavenly body, planet, star **5.** area, domain, environment, field, kingdom, province, realm, sphere, system **6.** age, days, epoch, era, period, times **7. for all the world** exactly, in every respect, in every way, just as if, just like, precisely, to all intents and purposes **8. on top of the world** *informal* beside oneself with joy, cock-a-hoop, ecstatic, elated, exultant, happy, in raptures, on cloud nine (*informal*), overjoyed, over the moon (*informal*) **9. out of this world** *informal* awesome (*slang*), bodacious (*slang, chiefly U.S.*), excellent, fabulous (*informal*), fantastic (*informal*), great (*informal*), incredible, indescribable, marvellous, superb, unbelievable, wonderful

worldly 1. carnal, earthly, fleshly, lay, mundane, physical, profane, secular, sublunary, temporal, terrestrial **2.** avaricious, covetous, grasping, greedy, materialistic, selfish, worldly-minded **3.** blasé, cosmopolitan, experienced, knowing, politic, sophisticated, urbane, well versed in the ways of the world, worldly-wise
▷ **Antonyms** (*sense 1*) divine, ethereal, heavenly, immaterial, noncorporeal, spiritual, transcendental, unworldly (*sense 2*) moral, nonmaterialistic, unworldly (*sense 3*) ingenuous, innocent, naive, unsophisticated, unworldly

worldwide general, global, international, omnipresent, pandemic, ubiquitous, universal
▷ **Antonyms** confined, insular, limited, local, narrow, national, parochial, provincial, restricted

worn 1. frayed, ragged, shabby, shiny, tattered, tatty, the worse for wear, threadbare **2.** careworn, drawn, haggard, lined, pinched, wizened **3.** exhausted, fatigued, jaded, played-out (*informal*), spent, tired, tired out, wearied, weary, worn-out

worn-out 1. broken-down, clapped out (*Brit., Austral., & N.Z. informal*), decrepit, done, frayed, moth-eaten, on its last legs, ragged, run-down, shabby, tattered, tatty, threadbare, used, used-up, useless, worn **2.** all in (*slang*), clapped out (*Austral. & N.Z. informal*), dead *or* out on one's feet (*informal*), dog-tired (*informal*), done in (*informal*), exhausted, fatigued, fit to drop, jiggered (*dialect*), knackered (*slang*), played-out, prostrate, shagged out (*Brit. slang*), spent, tired, tired out, weary, wiped out (*informal*), zonked (*slang*)
▷ **Antonyms** (*sense 2*) fresh, refreshed,

relaxed, renewed, rested, restored, revived, strengthened

worried afraid, anxious, apprehensive, bothered, concerned, distracted, distraught, distressed, disturbed, fearful, fretful, frightened, hot and bothered, ill at ease, nervous, on edge, overwrought, perturbed, tense, tormented, troubled, uneasy, unquiet, upset, wired (*slang*)
▷ **Antonyms** calm, fearless, peaceful, quiet, tranquil, unafraid, unconcerned, unfazed (*informal*), unworried

worrisome **1.** bothersome, disquieting, distressing, disturbing, irksome, perturbing, troublesome, upsetting, vexing, worrying **2.** anxious, apprehensive, fretful, insecure, jittery (*informal*), nervous, neurotic, uneasy

worry *verb* **1.** agonize, annoy, badger, be anxious, bother, brood, disquiet, distress, disturb, feel uneasy, fret, harass, harry, hassle (*informal*), hector, importune, irritate, make anxious, perturb, pester, plague, tantalize, tease, torment, trouble, unsettle, upset, vex **2.** attack, bite, gnaw at, go for, harass, harry, kill, lacerate, savage, tear *~noun* **3.** annoyance, bother, care, hassle (*informal*), irritation, pest, plague, problem, torment, trial, trouble, vexation **4.** annoyance, anxiety, apprehension, care, concern, disturbance, fear, irritation, misery, misgiving, perplexity, torment, trepidation, trouble, unease, vexation, woe
▷ **Antonyms** *~verb* be apathetic, be unconcerned, be unperturbed, calm, comfort, console, solace, soothe *~noun* calm, comfort, consolation, peace of mind, reassurance, serenity, solace, tranquillity

worsen aggravate, damage, decay, decline, degenerate, deteriorate, exacerbate, get worse, go downhill (*informal*), go from bad to worse, retrogress, sink, take a turn for the worse
▷ **Antonyms** ameliorate, be on the mend, better, enhance, improve, mend, recover, rectify, upgrade

worship **1.** *verb* adore, adulate, deify, exalt, glorify, honour, idolize, laud, love, praise, pray to, put on a pedestal, respect, revere, reverence, venerate **2.** *~noun* adoration, adulation, deification, devotion, exaltation, glorification, glory, homage, honour, laudation, love, praise, prayer(s), regard, respect, reverence
▷ **Antonyms** *~verb* blaspheme, deride, despise, disdain, dishonour, flout, mock, revile, ridicule, scoff at, spurn

worst *verb* beat, best, blow out of the water (*slang*), clobber (*slang*), conquer, crush, defeat, gain the advantage over, get the better of, lick (*informal*), master, overcome, overpower, overthrow, run rings around (*informal*), subdue, subjugate, undo, vanquish, wipe the floor with (*informal*)

worth **1.** aid, assistance, avail, benefit, credit, desert(s), estimation, excellence, goodness, help, importance, merit, quality, usefulness, utility, value, virtue, worthiness **2.** cost, price, rate, valuation, value
▷ **Antonyms** (*sense 1*) futility, insignificance, paltriness, triviality, unworthiness, uselessness, worthlessness, wretchedness

worthless **1.** a dime a dozen, chickenshit (*U.S. slang*), futile, ineffectual, insignificant, inutile, meaningless, measly, miserable, nickel-and-dime (*U.S. slang*), not much cop (*Brit.slang*), not worth a hill of beans (*chiefly U.S.*), no use, nugatory, paltry, pointless, poor, poxy (*slang*), rubbishy, trashy, trifling, trivial, two a penny (*informal*), unavailing, unimportant, unusable, useless, valueless, wanky (*taboo slang*), wretched **2.** abandoned, abject, base, contemptible, depraved, despicable, good-for-nothing, ignoble, useless, vile
▷ **Antonyms** consequential, decent, effective, fruitful, honourable, important, noble, precious, productive, profitable, significant, upright, useful, valuable, worthwhile, worthy

worthwhile beneficial, constructive, expedient, gainful, good, helpful, justifiable, productive, profitable, useful, valuable, worthy
▷ **Antonyms** inconsequential, pointless, trivial, unimportant, unworthy, useless, vain, valueless, wasteful, worthless

worthy **1.** *adjective* admirable, commendable, creditable, decent, dependable, deserving, estimable, excellent, good, honest, honourable, laudable, meritorious, praiseworthy, reliable, reputable, respectable, righteous, upright, valuable, virtuous, worthwhile **2.** *~noun* big shot (*informal*), bigwig (*informal*), dignitary, luminary, notable, personage
▷ **Antonyms** *~adjective* demeaning, disreputable, dubious, ignoble, undeserving, unproductive, untrustworthy, unworthy, useless *~noun* member of the rank and file, nobody, pleb, punter (*informal*)

wound *noun* **1.** cut, damage, gash, harm, hurt, injury, laceration, lesion, slash, trauma (*Pathology*) **2.** anguish, distress, grief, heartbreak, injury, insult, offence, pain, pang, sense of loss, shock, slight, torment, torture, trauma *~verb* **3.** cut, damage, gash, harm, hit, hurt, injure, irritate, lacerate, pierce, slash, wing **4.** annoy, cut (someone) to the quick, distress, grieve, hurt, hurt the feelings of, mortify, offend, pain, shock, sting, traumatize

wraith apparition, eidolon, ghost, phantom, revenant, shade (*literary*), spectre, spirit, spook (*informal*)

wrangle 1. *verb* altercate, argue, bicker, brawl, contend, disagree, dispute, fall out (*informal*), fight, have words, quarrel, row, scrap, spar, squabble **2.** *~noun* altercation, angry exchange, argy-bargy (*Brit. informal*), *bagarre,* barney (*informal*), bickering, brawl, clash, contest, controversy, dispute, falling-out (*informal*), quarrel, row, set-to (*informal*), slanging match (*Brit.*), squabble, tiff

wrap 1. *verb* absorb, bind, bundle up, cloak, cover, encase, enclose, enfold, envelop, fold, immerse, muffle, pack, package, roll up, sheathe, shroud, surround, swathe, wind **2.** *~noun* cape, cloak, mantle, shawl, stole

▷ **Antonyms** *~verb* disclose, open, strip, uncover, unfold, unpack, unwind, unwrap

wrapper case, cover, envelope, jacket, packaging, paper, sheath, sleeve, wrapping

wrap up 1. bundle up, enclose, enwrap, giftwrap, pack, package **2.** dress warmly, muffle up, put warm clothes on, wear something warm **3.** *slang* be quiet, be silent, button it (*slang*), button one's lip (*slang*), hold one's tongue, put a sock in it (*Brit. slang*), shut one's face (*Brit. slang*), shut one's mouth (*slang*), shut one's trap (*slang*), shut up **4.** *informal* bring to a close, conclude, end, finish off, polish off, round off, terminate, tidy up, wind up

wrath anger, choler, displeasure, exasperation, fury, indignation, ire, irritation, passion, rage, resentment, temper

▷ **Antonyms** amusement, contentment, delight, enjoyment, gladness, gratification, happiness, joy, pleasure, satisfaction

wrathful angry, beside oneself with rage, choked, displeased, enraged, furious, incensed, indignant, infuriated, irate, on the warpath (*informal*), raging, wroth (*archaic*)

▷ **Antonyms** amused, calm, contented, delighted, glad, gratified, happy, joyful, pleased, satisfied

wreak 1. bring about, carry out, cause, create, effect, execute, exercise, inflict, visit, work **2.** express, give free rein to, give vent to, gratify, indulge, unleash, vent

wreath band, chaplet, coronet, crown, festoon, garland, loop, ring

wreathe adorn, coil, crown, encircle, enfold, entwine, envelop, enwrap, festoon, intertwine, interweave, surround, twine, twist, wind, wrap, writhe

wreck *verb* **1.** blow (*slang*), break, cock up (*Brit. slang*), dash to pieces, demolish, destroy, devastate, fuck up (*offensive taboo slang*), mar, play havoc with, ravage, ruin, screw up (*informal*), shatter, smash, spoil, total (*slang*), trash (*slang*), undo **2.** founder, go *or* run aground, run onto the rocks, shipwreck, strand *~noun* **3.** derelict, hulk, shipwreck, sunken vessel **4.** desolation, destruction, devastation, disruption, mess, overthrow, ruin, undoing

▷ **Antonyms** *~verb* build, conserve, create, fulfil, make possible, preserve, reconstruct, salvage, save *~noun* conservation, creation, formation, fulfilment, preservation, restoration, salvage, saving

wreckage debris, fragments, hulk, pieces, remains, rubble, ruin, wrack

wrench *verb* **1.** force, jerk, pull, rip, tear, tug, twist, wrest, wring, yank **2.** distort, rick, sprain, strain *~noun* **3.** jerk, pull, rip, tug, twist, yank **4.** sprain, strain, twist **5.** ache, blow, pain, pang, shock, upheaval, uprooting **6.** adjustable spanner, shifting spanner, spanner

wrest extract, force, pull, seize, strain, take, twist, win, wrench, wring

wrestle battle, combat, contend, fight, grapple, scuffle, strive, struggle, tussle

wretch 1. asshole (*U.S. & Canad. taboo slang*), asswipe (*U.S. & Canad. taboo slang*), bad egg (*old-fashioned informal*), bastard (*offensive*), blackguard, bugger (*taboo slang*), cocksucker (*taboo slang*), cur, good-for-nothing, miscreant, mother (*taboo slang, chiefly U.S.*), motherfucker (*taboo slang, chiefly U.S.*), outcast, profligate, rascal, rat (*informal*), rogue, rotter (*slang, chiefly Brit.*), ruffian, scoundrel, scumbag (*slang*), shit (*taboo slang*), son-of-a-bitch (*slang, chiefly U.S. & Canad.*), swine, turd (*taboo slang*), vagabond, villain, worm **2.** poor thing, unfortunate

wretched 1. abject, brokenhearted, cheerless, comfortless, crestfallen, dejected, deplorable, depressed, disconsolate, dismal, distressed, doleful, downcast, down in the dumps (*informal*), forlorn, funereal, gloomy, hapless, hopeless, melancholy, miserable, pathetic, pitiable, pitiful, poor, sorry, unfortunate, unhappy, woebegone, woeful, worthless **2.** calamitous, deplorable, inferior, miserable, paltry, pathetic, poor, sorry, worthless **3.** base, contemptible, crappy (*slang*), despicable, low, low-down (*informal*), mean, paltry, poxy (*slang*), scurvy, shabby, shameful, vile

▷ **Antonyms** admirable, carefree, cheerful, contented, decent, enviable, excellent, flourishing, fortunate, great, happy, jovial, light-hearted, noble, prosperous, splendid, successful, thriving, untroubled, wonderful, worthy

wriggle *verb* **1.** jerk, jiggle, squirm, turn, twist, wag, waggle, wiggle, writhe **2.** crawl, slink, snake, twist and turn, worm, zigzag **3.** crawl, dodge, extricate oneself, manoeuvre, sneak, talk one's way out, worm *~noun* **4.** jerk, jiggle, squirm, turn, twist, wag, waggle, wiggle

wring **1.** coerce, extort, extract, force, screw, squeeze, twist, wrench, wrest **2.** distress, hurt, lacerate, pain, pierce, rack, rend, stab, tear at, wound

wrinkle[1] **1.** *noun* corrugation, crease, crinkle, crow's-foot, crumple, fold, furrow, gather, line, pucker, rumple **2.** *~verb* corrugate, crease, crinkle, crumple, fold, furrow, gather, line, pucker, ruck, rumple

▷ **Antonyms** *~verb* even out, flatten, iron, level, press, smooth, straighten, unfold

wrinkle[2] *noun* device, dodge, gimmick, idea, plan, ploy, ruse, scheme, stunt, tip, trick, wheeze (*Brit. slang*)

writ court order, decree, document, summons

write author (*nonstandard*), commit to paper, compose, copy, correspond, create, draft, draw up, indite, inscribe, jot down, pen, put down in black and white, put in writing, record, scribble, set down, take down, tell, transcribe

write off **1.** cancel, cross out, disregard, forget about, give up for lost, score out, shelve **2.** *informal* crash, damage beyond repair, destroy, smash up, total (*slang*), trash (*slang*), wreck

writer author, columnist, essayist, hack, littérateur, man of letters, novelist, penman, penny-a-liner (*rare*), pen-pusher, scribbler, scribe, wordsmith

writhe contort, distort, jerk, squirm, struggle, thrash, thresh, toss, twist, wiggle, wriggle

writing **1.** calligraphy, chirography, hand, handwriting, penmanship, print, scrawl, scribble, script **2.** book, composition, document, letter, opus, publication, title, work **3.** belles-lettres, letters, literature

wrong *adjective* **1.** erroneous, fallacious, false, faulty, inaccurate, incorrect, in error, mistaken, off base (*U.S. & Canad. informal*), off beam (*informal*), off target, out, unsound, untrue, way off beam (*informal*), wide of the mark **2.** bad, blameworthy, criminal, crooked, dishonest, dishonourable, evil, felonious, illegal, illicit, immoral, iniquitous, not cricket (*informal*), reprehensible, sinful, under-the-table, unethical, unfair, unjust, unlawful, wicked, wrongful **3.** funny, improper, inappropriate, inapt, incongruous, incorrect, indecorous, infelicitous, malapropos, not done, unacceptable, unbecoming, unconventional, undesirable, unfitting, unhappy, unseemly, unsuitable **4.** amiss, askew, awry, defective, faulty, not working, out of commission, out of order **5.** inside, inverse, opposite, reverse *~adverb* **6.** amiss, askew, astray, awry, badly, erroneously, inaccurately, incorrectly, mistakenly, wrongly **7. go wrong: a.** come to grief (*informal*), come to nothing, fail, fall through, flop (*informal*), miscarry, misfire **b.** boob (*Brit. slang*), err, go astray, make a mistake, slip up (*informal*) **c.** break down, cease to function, conk out (*informal*), fail, go kaput (*informal*), go on the blink (*slang*), go phut (*informal*), malfunction, misfire **d.** err, fall from grace, go astray, go off the straight and narrow (*informal*), go to the bad, lapse, sin *~noun* **8.** abuse, bad *or* evil deed, crime, error, grievance, immorality, inequity, infraction, infringement, iniquity, injury, injustice, misdeed, offence, sin, sinfulness, transgression, trespass, unfairness, wickedness **9. in the wrong** at fault, blameworthy, guilty, in error, mistaken, off beam (*informal*), off course, off target, to be blamed *~verb* **10.** abuse, cheat, discredit, dishonour, dump on (*slang, chiefly U.S.*), harm, hurt, ill-treat, ill-use, impose upon, injure, malign, maltreat, misrepresent, mistreat, oppress, shit on (*taboo slang*), take advantage of

▷ **Antonyms** *~adjective* (*sense 1*) accurate, precise (*sense 2*) ethical, fair, fitting, godly, honest, honourable, just, lawful, legal, moral, righteous, rightful, square, true, upright, virtuous (*sense 3*) appropriate, apt, becoming, commendable, correct, fitting, laudable, praiseworthy, proper, seemly, sensible, suitable *~adverb* accurately, correctly, exactly, precisely, properly, squarely, truly *~noun* decency, fairness, favour, good, good deed, goodness, good turn, high-mindedness, honesty, lawfulness, legality, morality, propriety, virtue *~verb* aid, do a favour, help, support, treat well

wrongdoer criminal, culprit, delinquent, evildoer, lawbreaker, malefactor, miscreant, offender, sinner, transgressor, trespasser (*archaic*), villain

wrongful blameworthy, criminal, dishonest, dishonourable, evil, felonious, illegal, illegitimate, illicit, immoral, improper, reprehensible, under-the-table, unethical, unfair, unjust, unlawful, wicked

▷ **Antonyms** ethical, fair, honest, honourable, just, lawful, legal, legitimate, moral, proper, rightful

wrong-headed **1.** bull-headed, contrary, cross-grained, dogged, froward (*archaic*), inflexible, intransigent, mulish, obdurate, obstinate, perverse, pig-headed, refractory, self-willed, stubborn, wilful **2.** erroneous, fallacious, false, faulty, incorrect, in error, misguided, mistaken, off target, unsound, wrong

wrought-up agitated, animated, aroused, at fever pitch, beside oneself, excited, inflamed, keyed up, moved, overwrought, roused, stirred, strung up (*informal*), worked-up, wound up (*informal*)

wry **1**. askew, aslant, awry, contorted, crooked, deformed, distorted, off the level, skewwhiff (*Brit. informal*), twisted, uneven, warped **2**. droll, dry, ironic, mocking, mordacious, pawky (*Scot.*), sarcastic, sardonic

▷ **Antonyms** (*sense 1*) aligned, even, level, smooth, straight, unbent

X, x

Xmas Christmas, Christmastide, festive season, Noel, Yule (*archaic*), Yuletide (*archaic*)

X-rays Röntgen rays (*old name*)

Y, y

yahoo barbarian, beast, boor, brute, churl, lout, philistine, roughneck (*slang*), rowdy, savage, yob *or* yobbo (*Brit. slang*)

yak 1. *verb* blather, chatter, chew the fat *or* rag (*slang*), gab (*informal*), gossip, jabber, jaw (*slang*), rabbit (on) (*Brit. informal*), run off at the mouth (*sang*), run on, spout, tattle, waffle (*informal, chiefly Brit.*), witter on (*informal*), yap (*informal*) **2.** *~noun* blather, chat, chinwag (*Brit. informal*), confab (*informal*), gossip, hot air (*informal*), jaw (*slang*), waffle (*informal, chiefly Brit.*), yackety-yak (*slang*), yammer (*informal*)

yank *verb/noun* hitch, jerk, pull, snatch, tug, wrench

yap *verb* **1.** yammer (*informal*), yelp, yip (*chiefly U.S.*) **2.** *informal* babble, blather, chatter, chew the fat *or* rag, go on, gossip, jabber, jaw (*slang*), prattle, rabbit (on) (*Brit. informal*), run off at the mouth (*slang*), spout, talk, tattle, waffle (*informal, chiefly Brit.*)

yardstick benchmark, criterion, gauge, measure, par, standard, touchstone

yarn *noun* **1.** fibre, thread **2.** *informal* anecdote, cock-and-bull story (*informal*), fable, story, tale, tall story

yawning cavernous, chasmal, gaping, vast, wide, wide-open

yearly annual, annually, every year, once a year, per annum

yearn ache, covet, crave, desire, eat one's heart out over, hanker, have a yen for (*informal*), hunger, itch, languish, long, lust, pant, pine, set one's heart upon, suspire (*archaic or poetic*), would give one's eyeteeth for

years 1. age, dotage, eld (*archaic*), old age, second childhood, senescence, senility **2.** days, generation(s), lifetime, span, time

yell 1. *verb* bawl, holler (*informal*), howl, scream, screech, shout, shriek, squeal **2.** *~noun* cry, howl, scream, screech, shriek, whoop

▷ **Antonyms** *~verb* mumble, murmur, mutter, say softly, whisper

yelp cry, yammer (*informal*), yap, yip (*chiefly U.S.*), yowl

yen *noun* ache, craving, desire, hankering, hunger, itch, longing, passion, thirst, yearning

yes man ass-kisser (*U.S. & Canad. taboo slang*), bootlicker (*informal*), bosses' lackey, company man, crawler (*slang*), creature, minion, sycophant, time-server, toady

yet 1. as yet, so far, thus far, until now, up to now **2.** however, nevertheless, notwithstanding, still **3.** additionally, as well, besides, further, in addition, into the bargain, moreover, over and above, still, to boot **4.** already, just now, now, right now, so soon

yield *verb* **1.** afford, bear, bring forth, bring in, earn, furnish, generate, give, net, pay, produce, provide, return, supply *~noun* **2.** crop, earnings, harvest, income, output, produce, profit, return, revenue, takings *~verb* **3.** abandon, abdicate, admit defeat, bow, capitulate, cave in (*informal*), cede, cry quits, give in, give up the struggle, give way, knuckle under, lay down one's arms, lose, part with, raise the white flag, relinquish, resign, resign oneself, submit, succumb, surrender, throw in the towel **4.** accede, agree, allow, bow, comply, concede, consent, go along with, grant, permit

▷ **Antonyms** *~verb* (*sense 1*) appropriate, commandeer, consume, grab, seize, use, use up (*sense 3*) attack, combat, counterattack, defy, hold on to, hold out, keep, maintain, oppose, reserve, resist, retain, struggle *~noun* consumption, input, loss

yielding 1. accommodating, acquiescent, biddable, compliant, docile, easy, flexible, obedient, pliant, submissive, tractable **2.** elastic, pliable, quaggy, resilient, soft, spongy, springy, supple, unresisting

▷ **Antonyms** (*sense 1*) dogged, headstrong, mulish, obstinate, opinionated, perverse, stiff-necked, stubborn, tenacious, wilful

yob, yobbo heavy (*slang*), hoodlum, hooligan, lout, rough (*informal*), roughneck (*slang*), rowdy, ruffian, thug, tough, tsotsi (*S. African*), yahoo

yoke *noun* **1.** bond, chain, coupling, ligament, link, tie **2.** bondage, burden, enslavement, helotry, oppression, serfdom, service, servility, servitude, slavery, thraldom, vassalage *~verb* **3.** bracket, connect, couple, harness, hitch, join, link, tie, unite

yokel boor, bucolic, clodhopper (*informal*), (country) bumpkin, country cousin, countryman, hayseed (*U.S. & Canad. informal*), hick (*informal, chiefly U.S. & Canad.*), hillbilly, hind (*obsolete*), peasant (*informal*), rustic

young *adjective* **1.** adolescent, callow, green, growing, immature, infant, in the springtime of life, junior, juvenile, little, unfledged, youthful **2.** at an early stage, early, fledgling, new, newish, not far advanced, recent, undeveloped *~noun* **3.** babies, brood, family, issue, litter, little ones, offspring, progeny

▷ **Antonyms** *~adjective* adult, advanced, aged, developed, elderly, experienced, full-grown, grown-up, mature, old, ripe, senior, venerable *~noun* adult, grown-up, parent

youngster boy, cub, girl, juvenile, kid (*informal*), lad, lass, pup (*informal, chiefly Brit.*), teenager, teenybopper (*slang*), urchin, young adult, young hopeful, young person, young shaver (*informal*), young 'un (*informal*), youth

youth 1. adolescence, boyhood, early life, girlhood, immaturity, juvenescence, salad days, young days **2.** adolescent, boy, kid (*informal*), lad, shaveling (*archaic*), stripling, teenager, young man, young shaver (*informal*), youngster **3.** teenagers, the rising generation, the young, younger generation, young people

▷ **Antonyms** (*sense 1*) adulthood, age, later life, manhood, maturity, old age, womanhood (*sense 2*) adult, grown-up, OAP, pensioner, senior citizen (*sense 3*) the aged, the elderly, the old

youthful 1. boyish, childish, girlish, immature, inexperienced, juvenile, pubescent, puerile, young **2.** active, fresh, spry, vigorous, young at heart, young looking

▷ **Antonyms** adult, aged, ageing, ancient, careworn, decaying, decrepit, elderly, grown-up, hoary, mature, old, over the hill, senile, senior, tired, waning, weary

yowl *verb* bawl, bay, caterwaul, cry, give tongue, howl, screech, squall, ululate, wail, yell

yucky, yukky beastly, dirty, disgusting, foul, grotty (*slang*), horrible, messy, mucky, revolting (*informal*), unpleasant

Z, z

zany 1. *adjective* clownish, comical, crazy, eccentric, funny, goofy (*informal*), kooky (*U.S. informal*), loony (*slang*), madcap, nutty (*slang*), oddball (*informal*), wacko *or* whacko (*informal*), wacky (*slang*) **2.** ~*noun* buffoon, clown, comedian, jester, joker, merry-andrew, nut (*slang*), screwball (*slang, chiefly U.S. & Canad.*), wag

zeal ardour, devotion, eagerness, earnestness, enthusiasm, fanaticism, fervency, fervour, fire, gusto, keenness, militancy, passion, spirit, verve, warmth, zest

▷ **Antonyms** apathy, coolness, indifference, passivity, stoicism, torpor, unresponsiveness

zealot bigot, energumen, enthusiast, extremist, fanatic, fiend (*informal*), maniac, militant

zealous ablaze, afire, ardent, burning, devoted, eager, earnest, enthusiastic, fanatical, fervent, fervid, impassioned, keen, militant, passionate, rabid, spirited

▷ **Antonyms** apathetic, cold, cool, half-hearted, indifferent, lackadaisical, lacklustre, languorous, listless, low-key, sceptical, torpid, unenthusiastic, unimpassioned

zenith acme, apex, apogee, climax, crest, height, high noon, high point, meridian, peak, pinnacle, summit, top, vertex

▷ **Antonyms** base, bottom, depths, lowest point, nadir, rock bottom

zero 1. cipher, naught, nil, nothing, nought **2.** bottom, lowest point *or* ebb, nadir, nothing, rock bottom

zero hour appointed hour, crisis, moment of decision, moment of truth, turning point, vital moment

zero in (on) aim, bring to bear, concentrate, converge, direct, focus, home in, level, pinpoint, train

zest 1. appetite, delectation, enjoyment, gusto, keenness, relish, zeal, zing (*informal*) **2.** charm, flavour, interest, kick (*informal*), piquancy, pungency, relish, savour, smack, spice, tang, taste

▷ **Antonyms** (*sense 1*) abhorrence, apathy, aversion, disinclination, distaste, indifference, lack of enthusiasm, loathing, repugnance, weariness

zing animation, brio, dash, energy, go (*informal*), life, liveliness, oomph (*informal*), pep, pizzazz *or* pizazz (*informal*), spirit, vigour, vitality, zest, zip (*informal*)

zip 1. *noun figurative* brio, drive, energy, get-up-and-go (*informal*), go (*informal*), gusto, life, liveliness, oomph (*informal*), pep, pizzazz *or* pizazz (*informal*), punch (*informal*), sparkle, spirit, verve, vigour, vim (*slang*), vitality, zest, zing (*informal*) **2.** ~*verb* barrel (along) (*informal, chiefly U.S. & Canad.*), burn rubber (*informal*), dash, flash, fly, hurry, rush, shoot, speed, tear, whizz (*informal*), zoom

▷ **Antonyms** (*sense 1*) apathy, indifference, inertia, laziness, lethargy, listlessness, sloth, sluggishness

zone area, belt, district, region, section, sector, sphere

zoom *verb* barrel (along) (*informal, chiefly U.S. & Canad.*), burn rubber (*informal*), buzz, dash, dive, flash, fly, hare (*Brit. informal*), hum (*slang*), hurtle, pelt, rip (*informal*), rush, shoot, speed, streak, tear, whirl, whizz (*informal*), zip (*informal*)